The National Hockey League

Official Guide & Record Book 1995-96

Published by the National Hockey League.
Compiled by the NHL Public Relations Department
and the 26 NHL Club Public Relations Directors.
Copyright © 1995 by the National Hockey League

THE NATIONAL HOCKEY LEAGUE
Official Guide & Record Book/1995-96

Staff

For the NHL: Charlie Schmitt, Michael Berger; Supervising Editor: Greg Inglis; Statistician: Benny Ercolani; Editorial Staff: David Keon, Sherry McKeown, Justin Sanft

Managing Editors: Ralph Dinger, James Duplacey

Contributing Editor: Igor Kuperman,

Contributors:
David Allessi, Francois Beauchemin, Blue Line Publishing (Minneapolis), Ray Bolen, Rocky Bonanno, Chris Charles, Ernie Fitzsimmons, Mel Foster, Herb Morell (OHL), NHL Broadcasters' Association, NHL Central Registry, NHL Players' Association, Jim Price (CHL), Valentina Riazanova, Kevin Reynolds, David Rosenbaum (Hockey International newsletter), Michael Stofjakovic, Christian Tobin, Michel Vigneault, Jeff Weiss (CCHA),

Consulting Publisher: Dan Diamond

Photo Credits

Historical and special event photos: Bruce Bennett, David Bier, Michael Burns, Graphic Artists Collection, NHL Images/Sylvia Pecota, New York Rangers, Rice Studio, Robert Shaver, Imperial Oil Turofsky Collection, Hockey Hall of Fame.

Current photos: Graig Abel, Toronto; Joe Angeles, St. Louis; Steve Babineau, Boston; Sol Benjamin, Chicago; Bruce Bennett, NY Islanders; Tony Biegun, Winnipeg; Bob Binder, Anaheim; Denis Brodeur, Montreal; Mark Buckner, St. Louis; J. Cassidy, Philadelphia; Denny Cavanaugh, Pittsburgh; Steve Crandall, New Jersey; Edmonton Northlands; Bob Fisher, Montreal; Ray Grabowski, Chicago; Bill Gutweiler, St. Louis; John Hartman, Detroit; Jonathan Hayt, Tampa Bay; J. Henson Photographics, Washington; Glenn James, Dallas; Walter Kaiser, Winnipeg; George Kalinsky, NY Rangers; Deborah King, Washington; David Klutho, St. Louis; V.J. Lovero, Anaheim; Jim Mackey, Detroit; Doug MacLellan; McElligott-Teckles Sports Focus Imaging, Ottawa; Al Messerschmidt, Florida; Jack Murray, Vancouver; Tim Parker, St. Louis; Photography Ink, Los Angeles; Andre Pichette, Montreal and Quebec; Richard Pilling, New Jersey; Len Redkoles, Philadelphia; Wen Roberts, Los Angeles; Al Ruelle, Boston; Harry Scull, Jr., Buffalo; Don Smith, San Jose; Diane Sobolewski, Hartford; Gerry Thomas, Edmonton; Jim Turner, New Jersey; Brad Watson, Calgary; Rocky Widner, San Jose; Bill Wippert, Buffalo.

Distribution

Canadian representatives:
North 49 Books, 193 Bartley Drive, Toronto, Ontario M4A 1E6
416/750-7777; FAX 416/750-2049
NHL Publishing, 194 Dovercourt Road, Toronto, Ontario M6J 3C8
416/531-6535; FAX 416/531-3939

U.S. representatives: Triumph Books,
644 South Clark Street, Chicago, Illinois 60605   312/939-3330; FAX 312/663-3557

International representatives: Barkers Worldwide Publications,
155 Maybury Road, Woking, Surrey, England GU21 5JR
Tel. and FAX: 011/44/483/776-141

Data Management and Typesetting: Caledon Data Management, Caledon, Ontario
Additional Typesetting: Moveable Type, Toronto, Ontario
Film Output and Process Camera: Stafford Graphics, Toronto, Ontario
Printing: Moore Data Management Services, Scarborough, Ontario
Production Management: Dan Diamond and Associates, Inc., Toronto, Ontario

The National Hockey League
1251 Avenue of the Americas, 47th Floor, New York, New York 10020-1198
1800 McGill College Ave., Suite 2600, Montreal, Quebec H3A 3J6
75 International Boulevard, Suite 300, Toronto, Ontario M9W 6L9

Table of Contents

13 CLUBS   records, rosters, management

117 FINAL STATISTICS 1994-95

Table of Contents *continued*

(1995-96 NHL Schedule begins inside front cover)

Introduction

WELCOME TO *THE* **NHL** *OFFICIAL* **GUIDE & RECORD BOOK FOR 1995-96.** This 64th edition of the *Guide* brought with it a particular challenge: how do we deal with the statistical results of the shortened 1994-95 season? Labor strife postponed the start of the season until January 20, 1995 and resulted in each club playing just 48 games, all of which were within its own conference. This past season wasn't the NHL's first experience with a 48-game schedule; the League played a 48-game format for 11 seasons beginning in 1931-32. (Interestingly, no scoring champion in those years matched the 70-point efforts of Jaromir Jagr and Eric Lindros in 1995.) As well, In the fall of 1994, dozens of NHLers went to Europe to play for one-or-more teams under short-term contracts. We have tracked this activity and have included it in each player's data panel. Of particular note is the result of one game Jaromir Jagr played for Shalke in the German Second Division: one goal, ten assists, 11 points. The Player Register begins on page 251. The Goaltender Register begins on page 423. Late Additions to the registers are found on page 250.

Club records for fewest points, wins, ties, losses, goals and goals-against are restricted to seasons of 70-or-more games. This exempts results from 1994-95. Because the League has played 70-or-more games every season since 1950-51, this limit has long been in place, though until this year, it only affected the League's six oldest franchises. Other than Boston, Chicago, Detroit, Montreal, NY Rangers, and Toronto, no existing NHL club had ever played a schedule with fewer than 74 games. All other statistics generated during 1994-95 stand. We have not extrapolated or "grossed-up" any 48-game numbers for comparison with full-season statistics.

This year's *Guide & Record Book* contains a very special feature that traces the history of six of the League's single-season and career scoring marks. Beginning with "Phantom" Joe Malone's 44 goals for the Canadiens in 1917-18, these marks have inched steadily upward. The records for goals, assists and points have passed through the hands of a veritable *Who's Who* of hockey talent including Howie Morenz, Bill Cowley, Nels Stewart, Rocket Richard, Gordie Howe, Bobby Hull and Phil Esposito. It is worth noting that all six benchmarks are currently held by Wayne Gretzky.

For 1995-96, the NHL welcomes the Colorado Avalanche who will play in the Pacific Division. With the addition of Colorado to the Western Conference, each of the NHL's two conferences now has 13 teams. The Avalanche will play their home games in McNichols Sports Arena.

The opening of new and revamped arenas will be a prominent feature throughout the 1995-96 season. The Boston Bruins will open the new FleetCenter (17,565 capacity) on October 7 vs. the Islanders. The Vancouver Canucks will play their first regular-season game in the new 19,056-seat General Motors Place on October 9 vs. Detroit. The Calgary Flames open the remodeled 20,000-seat Saddledome on October 25 vs. Colorado. The Ottawa Senators make their debut in the 18,500-seat Palladium on January 17 vs. Montreal while the Canadiens open the new Forum (21,401 capacity) on March 16 vs. the Rangers.

THE **1995-96 NHL S**CHEDULE will see each of the League's 26 member clubs play 82 games, 41 at home and 41 on the road. Each club will play either five or six games against its divisional opponents, four games against teams in the other division of its own conference and two games against each of the 13 teams in the League's other conference.

As always, our thanks to readers, correspondents and members of the media who take the time to comment on the *Guide & Record Book*. Thanks as well to the people working in the communications departments of the NHL's member clubs and to their counterparts in the AHL, IHL, ECHL, Central, Colonial and junior leagues as well as in college athletic conferences and European hockey federations.

Best wishes for an enjoyable 1995-96 NHL season.

ACCURACY REMAINS THE *GUIDE & RECORD BOOK*'S TOP PRIORITY.
We appreciate comments and clarification from our readers. Please direct these to:

Greg Inglis   47th floor, 1251 Avenue of the Americas, New York, New York 10020-1198 . . . or . . .

David Keon   75 International Blvd., suite 300, Rexdale, Ontario M9W 6L9.

Your involvement makes a better book.

NATIONAL HOCKEY LEAGUE

Established November 22, 1917

Board of Governors

Chairman of the Board – Harley N. Hotchkiss

Mighty Ducks of Anaheim
Disney Sports Enterprises, Inc.

Michael D. Eisner ....Governor
Tony Tavares ....Alternate Governor

Boston Bruins
Boston Professional Hockey Association, Inc.

Jeremy M. Jacobs ....Governor
Louis Jacobs ....Alternate Governor
Harry J. Sinden ....Alternate Governor

Buffalo Sabres
Niagara Frontier Hockey, L.P.

Seymour H. Knox III ....Governor
Seymour H. Knox IV ....Alternate Governor
Douglas G. Moss ....Alternate Governor
John J. Rigas ....Alternate Governor
Robert O. Swados ....Alternate Governor

Calgary Flames
Calgary Flames Limited Partnership

Harley N. Hotchkiss ....Governor
Byron J. Seaman ....Alternate Governor

Chicago Blackhawks
Chicago Blackhawks Hockey Team, Inc.

William W. Wirtz ....Governor
Gene Gozdecki ....Alternate Governor
Thomas N. Ivan ....Alternate Governor
Robert J. Pulford ....Alternate Governor
Arthur M. Wirtz, Jr. ....Alternate Governor
W. Rockwell Wirtz ....Alternate Governor

Colorado Avalanche
Colorado Avalanche, LLC

Charlie Lyons ....Governor
Bruce Crockett ....Alternate Governor
Pierre Lacroix ....Alternate Governor

Dallas Stars
Dallas Hockey Club, Inc.

Norman Green ....Governor
John W. G. Donahue ....Alternate Governor
James R. Lites ....Alternate Governor

Detroit Red Wings
Detroit Red Wings, Inc.

Michael Ilitch ....Governor
Jay A. Bielfield ....Alternate Governor
Jim Devellano ....Alternate Governor
Atanas Ilitch ....Alternate Governor
Christopher Ilitch ....Alternate Governor

Edmonton Oilers
Edmonton Oilers Hockey Corp.

Peter Pocklington ....Governor
Lorne J. Ruzicka ....Alternate Governor
Glen Sather ....Alternate Governor

Florida Panthers
Florida Panthers Hockey Club, Ltd.

William A. Torrey ....Governor
Dean Jordan ....Alternate Governor

Hartford Whalers
KTR Hockey Limited Partnership

Peter Karmanos, Jr. ....Governor
Jim Rutherford ....Alternate Governor

Los Angeles Kings
LAK Acquisition Corp.

Joe Cohen ....Governor
Sam McMaster ....Alternate Governor
Rogie Vachon ....Alternate Governor

Montréal Canadiens
Le Club de Hockey Canadien, Inc.

Ronald L. Corey ....Governor
A. Barry Joslin ....Alternate Governor
Serge Savard ....Alternate Governor

New Jersey Devils
Meadowlanders, Inc.

Dr. John J. McMullen ....Governor
Louis A. Lamoriello ....Alternate Governor
Peter McMullen ....Alternate Governor

New York Islanders
New York Islanders Hockey Club, L.P.

Robert Rosenthal ....Governor
Steve Walsh ....Alternate Governor
John H. Krumpe ....Alternate Governor
Don Maloney ....Alternate Governor
Ralph F. Palleschi ....Alternate Governor

New York Rangers
The New York Rangers Hockey Club
A Division of Madison Square Garden Center, Inc.

Charles F. Dolan ....Governor
Rand V. Araskog ....Alternate Governor
David Checketts ....Alternate Governor
James L. Dolan ....Alternate Governor
Ken Munoz ....Alternate Governor
Neil Smith ....Alternate Governor

Ottawa Senators
Ottawa Senators Hockey Club Limited Partnership

Roderick M. Bryden ....Governor
Bernard J. Ashe ....Alternate Governor
Cyril Leeder ....Alternate Governor
Randy J. Sexton ....Alternate Governor

Philadelphia Flyers
Philadelphia Flyers Limited Partnership

Edward M. Snider ....Governor
Bob Clarke ....Alternate Governor
Ronald K. Ryan ....Alternate Governor
Jay T. Snider ....Alternate Governor

Pittsburgh Penguins
Pittsburgh Hockey Associates

Howard L. Baldwin ....Governor
Morris Belzberg ....Alternate Governor
Robert L. Caporale ....Alternate Governor
John H. Kelley ....Alternate Governor
Craig Patrick ....Alternate Governor
Thomas V. Ruta ....Alternate Governor

St. Louis Blues
Kiel Center Partners, L.P.

Jack Quinn..............................Governor
Ron Caron ....Alternate Governor
Thomas J. Guilfoil ....Alternate Governor
Mike Keenan ....Alternate Governor

San Jose Sharks
San Jose Sharks Corp.

George Gund III ....Governor
Gordon Gund ....Alternate Governor
Irvin A. Leonard ....Alternate Governor
Dean Lombardi ....Alternate Governor
Arthur L. Savage ....Alternate Governor

Tampa Bay Lightning
Lightning Partners, Inc.

David E. LeFevre ....Governor
Phil Esposito ....Alternate Governor
Mel Lowell ....Alternate Governor
Steve Oto ....Alternate Governor
Chris Phillips ....Alternate Governor

Toronto Maple Leafs
Maple Leaf Gardens Ltd.

Steve A. Stavro..............................Governor
Brian P. Bellmore ....Alternate Governor
Cliff Fletcher ....Alternate Governor

Vancouver Canucks
Orca Bay Sports & Entertainment

Arthur R. Griffiths ....Governor
John E. McCaw, Jr. ....Alternate Governor
Michael Korenberg ....Alternate Governor
J.B. Patrick Quinn ....Alternate Governor

Washington Capitals
Washington Hockey Limited Partnership

Richard M. Patrick ....Governor
Abe Pollin ....Alternate Governor
Peter O'Malley ....Alternate Governor
David Osnos ....Alternate Governor
David R. Poile ....Alternate Governor

Winnipeg Jets
Jets Hockey Ventures
(A Limited Partnership)

Barry L. Shenkarow ....Governor
Bill Davis ....Alternate Governor
John Paddock ....Alternate Governor

League Offices

New York – 1251 Avenue of the Americas, 47th Floor, New York, NY 10020-1198, (212)789-2000, Fax: (212)789-2020
Montreal – 1800 McGill College Avenue, Suite 2600, Montreal, Quebec H3A 3J6, (514)288-9220, Fax: (514)284-0300
Toronto – 75 International Blvd., Suite 300, Rexdale, Ontario M9W 6L9, (416)798-0809, Fax: (416)798-0819
NHL Enterprises – 1251 Avenue of the Americas, 47th Floor, New York, NY 10020-1198, (212)789-2000, Fax: (212)789-2020
NHL Enterprises Canada – 75 International Blvd., Suite 301, Rexdale, Ontario M9W 6L9, 416/798-9388, Fax: 416/798-9395
NHL Productions – 183 Oak Tree Road, Tappan, NY 10983-2809, (914)365-6701, Fax: (914)365-6010
NHL Europe – Signaustrasse 1, 8008 Zurich – Switzerland

National Hockey League Staff Directory

Commissioner .... Gary B. Bettman
Senior VP and Chief Operating Officer .... Stephen J. Solomon
Senior VP and General Counsel .... Jeffrey Pash
Senior VP and Director of Hockey Operations .... Brian P. Burke
Executive Assistant to the Commissioner .... Debbie Walsh

Administration
Director ....Janet A. Meyers

Broadcasting / NHL Productions
VP Broadcasting .... Glenn Adamo
Coordinating Producer, NHL Productions .... Ken Rosen
Manager, Broadcasting .... Adam Acone
Manager, Broadcast Operations .... Patti Fallick
Manager, Video Services, NHL Productions .... Mott Linn

Corporate Communications
VP Corporate Communications .... Bernadette Mansur
Director, Corporate Communications ....Mary Pat Clarke
Director, Creative Services ....David F. Haney

Finance
VP and Chief Financial Officer .... John Huston
Controller and Office Manager (Montreal) ....Joseph DeSousa
Controller ....Phil Litwinoff
Assistant Controller (Montreal) ....Olivia Pietrantonio
Assistant Controller .... Patricia Cooper
Accounting Supervisor (Montreal) ....Donna Gillman

Hockey Operations
VP Hockey Operations (Toronto) ....Jim Gregory
Director, Central Registry (Montreal) ....Garry Lovegrove
Assistant Director, Central Registry (Montreal) ....Madeleine Supino
Director of Central Scouting (Toronto) .... Frank Bonello
Director of Officiating (Toronto) .... Bryan Lewis
Assistant Director of Officiating (Toronto) .... Wally Harris
Hockey Operations Manager .... David Nonis
Consultant (Montreal) .... Brian F. O'Neill
Video Director, Hockey Operations .... Taran Singleton

Information Systems
Director (Montreal) .... Mario Carangi
Assistant Director (Montreal) .... Luc Coulombe

Legal
VP and Associate General Counsel .... David Zimmerman
Associate Counsel .... Katherine Jones

Pension
Director (Montreal) ....Yvon Chamberland
Controller, Pension (Montreal) .... Mary Skiadopoulos
Manager, Pension (Montreal) .... Lise DeJocas

Public Relations
VP Public Relations ....Arthur Pincus
Director, Public Relations (Toronto) ....Gary Meagher
Chief Statistician (Toronto) .... Benny Ercolani
Manager, Media Relations .... Susan Aglietti
Manager, News Services .... Greg Inglis
Manager, Public Relations and News Services ....Andrew McGowan
Public Relations Assistant .... David Keon

Security
VP Security ....Dennis Cunningham

Special Events / Event Marketing
VP Special Events .... Frank Supovitz
Director, Special Events .... Lori Boesch
Director, Event Marketing .... Karen Hovsepian
Manager, Event Marketing .... Patricia L. Conrad
Manager, Special Events .... Ann Devney Marciano
Manager, Special Events .... Anne I. Grotefeld
Manager, Special Events .... Michael Santos
Manager, Special Events .... Maria Sutherland

Television and Business Affairs
VP Television and Business Affairs ....Ellis T. "Skip" Prince III
Director, New Business Development ....Bryant S. McBride
Assistant Director, Business Affairs (Montreal) .... Steve Hatze Petros
Manager, Broadcast Business Affairs .... Samuel Esposito, Jr.
Manager, New Business Development .... John Knebel

NHL Europe
Managing Director, Europe ....Guido Tognoni

NHL Enterprises, Inc. Directory
Senior VP and Chief Operating Officer .... Rick Dudley

Corporate Marketing
VP Corporate Marketing .... Ed Horne
Director, Corporate Marketing ....Dina Gilbertie
Director, Corporate Marketing ....Todd Parker
Director, Club Marketing .... Scott Carmichael
Manager, Corporate Marketing ....Jim Haskins
Manager, Corporate Marketing .... Gord Lang

Fan Development
Director, Fan Development Programs .... Ken Yaffe
Director, Off-Ice Programs .... Brian Mullen
Manager, Fan Development Programs .... Alysse Soll
Manager, Street Hockey Division .... Kamini Sharma

Publishing
Director ....Charlie Schmitt
Director, Editorial Services ....Michael Berger

Finance
Controller, Retail Licensing .... Mary C. McCarthy
Assistant Controller, Marketing .... Donna MacPhee
Assistant Controller, Corporate ....Pamela Wakoff
Manager, Accounts Payable .... Evelyn Torres
Manager, Information Systems ....John Ho

Legal
Senior VP and General Counsel .... Richard Zahnd
Associate General Counsel – Intellectual Property ....Mary Sotis
Staff Attorney .... Leslie Gittess
Director, Licensing and Trademark Compliance ....Ruth Gruhin
Manager of Contract Administration .... Heather Bell

Retail Licensing
VP Licensing ....Fred Scalera
Group Director, Licensing ....Tina Ellis
Director, Apparel Licensing .... Brian Jennings
Director, Non-Apparel Licensing ....Judith Salsberg
Director, Collectibles and Trading Card Licensing ....Ilene Kent
Director, Special Programs Licensing .... Brendan McQuillan
Manager, Children's Licensing .... Ann Kiely
National Sales Manager .... Bill Tighe
Sales Manager, Mid-Western Region ....Christopher Agnew
Sales Manager, Western Region .... Mark Cordon
Sales Manager, Eastern Region ....Brian Way

International
Director, European Licensing ....Brad Kwong
Director, Pacific Rim Licensing ....Frank Nakano

NHL Enterprises Canada, Inc.
Managing Director ....Bob McLaughlin
Director, Corporate Sponsorship .... Paul MacLaren
Licensing Manager, Apparel .... Karen Hanson
Licensing Manager, Collectibles ....Fiona Hastie
Retail Merchandising Manager ....Barry Monaghan

Commissioner and League Presidents

Gary B. Bettman

Gary B. Bettman took office as the NHL's first Commissioner on February 1, 1993. Since the League was formed in 1917, there have been five League Presidents.

NHL President	Years in Office
Frank Calder	1917-1943
Mervyn "Red" Dutton	1943-1946
Clarence Campbell	1946-1977
John A. Ziegler, Jr.	1977-1992
Gil Stein	1992-1993

NHL Enterprises B.V.
Polakweg 14
2288 GG Rijswijk
Nederland
Phone: 31-(0)70-390-7797
Fax: 31-(0)70-390-7625

Stephen J. Solomon – Director
Richard Zahnd – Director
Cyril Speijer – Director

Hockey Hall of Fame
BCE Place
30 Yonge Street
Toronto, Ontario M5E 1X8
Phone: 416/360-7735
Fax: 416/360-1501

Ian "Scotty" Morrison – Chairman
David Taylor – President
Bryan Black – Vice President, Marketing
Jeff Denomme – Vice President, Finance/Treasurer
Ray Paquet – Manager, Facility Systems and
    Exhibit Development
Phil Pritchard – Manager, Resource Center and
    Acquisitions
Sue Bolender – Manager, Facility Sales
Scott North – Manager, Operations and Services
Christine Simpson – Marketing Manager
Bryan McDermott – Retail and Merchandise Manager

National Hockey League Players' Association
One Dundas Street West, Suite 2300
Toronto, Ontario M5G 1Z3
Phone: 416/408-4040
Fax: 416/408-3685
E-mail: smcall@nhlpa.com
Internet: http://www.nhlpa.com

Robert W. Goodenow – Executive Director and
    General Counsel
Ian Pulver – Associate Counsel
Jeffrey Citron – Associate Counsel
JP Barry – Associate Counsel
Ted Saskin – Senior Director, Business Affairs
    and Licensing
Michael Merhab – Collectibles and Media Projects
Jon Ram – Retail and Promotional Licensing
Barbara Larcina – Director of Business Administration
Doug Wilson – Coordinator of Player Relations and
    Business Development
Steve McAllister – Manager, Media Relations
Dominic Dodds – Manager, Information Systems
Kim Murdoch – Manager, Pensions and Benefits

NHL On-Ice Officials

Total NHL Games and 94-95 Games columns include regular-season games only.

Referees

#	Name	Birthplace	Birthdate	First NHL Game	Total NHL Games	94-95 Games
9	Blaine Angus	Shawville, Que	9/25/61	10/17/92	19	4
30	Bernard Degrace	Lameque, N.B.	5/1/67	*10/15/91	*157	0
10	Paul Devorski	Guelph, Ont.	8/18/58	10/14/89	255	45
11	Mark Faucette	Springfield, MA	6/9/58	12/23/87	370	35
2	Kerry Fraser	Sarnia, Ont.	5/30/52	4/6/75	920	34
4	Terry Gregson	Erin, Ont.	11/7/53	12/19/81	796	43
8	Dave Jackson	Montreal, Que.	11/28/64	12/23/90	123	40
18	Greg Kimmerly	Toronto, Ont.	12/8/64		0	0
12	Don Koharski	Halifax, N.S.	12/2/55	10/14/77	928	47
14	Dennis LaRue	Savannah, GA	7/14/59	3/26/91	39	2
6	Dan Marouelli	Edmonton, Alta.	7/16/55	11/2/84	646	42
26	Rob Martell	Winnipeg, Man.	10/21/63	3/14/84	1	0
7	Bill McCreary	Guelph, Ont.	11/17/55	11/3/84	666	42
19	Mick McGeough	Regina, Sask.	6/20/57	1/19/89	251	40
15	Dan O'Halloran	Leamington, Ont.	3/25/64		0	0
20	Lance Roberts	Edmonton, Alta.	5/28/57	11/3/89	147	37
31	Lyle Seitz	Brooks, Alta.	1/22/69	*10/6/92	*102	0
16	Rob Shick	Port Alberni, B.C.	12/4/57	4/6/86	464	23
22	Paul Stewart	Boston, MA	3/21/55	3/27/87	496	42
17	Richard Trottier	Laval, Que.	2/28/57	12/13/89	160	38
25	Andy Van Hellemond	Winnipeg, Man.	2/16/48	11/22/72	1412	39
21	Don Van Massenhoven	London, Ont.	7/17/60	11/11/93	51	38
24	Stephen Walkom	North Bay, Ont.	8/8/63	10/18/92	53	33
23	Brad Watson	Regina, Sask.	10/4/61	2/5/94	1	1
29	Scott Zelkin	Wilmette, IL	9/12/68		0	0

* Games worked as a Linesman.

Linesmen

#	Name	Birthplace	Birthdate	First NHL Game	Total NHL Games	94-95 Games
38	Ron Asselstine	Toronto, Ont.	11/6/46	10/10/79	1220	45
94	Wayne Bonney	Ottawa, Ont.	5/27/53	10/10/79	1104	31
55	Gord Broseker	Baltimore, MD	7/8/50	1/14/75	1446	39
35	Pierre Champoux	Ville St-Pierre, Que.	4/18/63	10/8/88	426	41
50	Kevin Collins	Springfield, MA	12/15/50	10/13/77	1389	44
88	Mike Cvik	Calgary, Alta.	7/6/62	10/8/87	509	44
98	Pat Dapuzzo	Hoboken, NJ	12/29/58	12/5/84	855	37
44	Greg Devorski	Guelph, Ont.	8/3/69	10/9/93	94	40
68	Scott Driscoll	Seaforth, Ont.	5/2/68	10/10/92	156	38
77	Ron Finn	Toronto, Ont.	12/1/40	10/11/69	1932	39
36	Gerard Gauthier	Montreal, Que.	9/5/48	10/16/71	1788	45
95	Conrad Hache	Sudbury, Ont.	5/15/72	2/27/95	4	4
91	Don Henderson	Calgary, Alta.	9/23/68	3/10/95	1	1
64	Shane Heyer	Summerland, B.C.	2/7/64	10/5/88	475	40
37	Bob Hodges	Hespeler, Ont.	8/16/44	10/14/72	1566	31
48	Swede Knox	Edmonton, Alta.	3/2/48	10/14/72	1730	35
86	Brad Lazarowich	Vancouver, B.C.	8/4/62	10/9/86	613	39
46	Dan McCourt	Falconbridge, Ont.	8/14/54	12/27/80	996	46
90	Andy McElman	Chicago Heights, IL	8/4/61	10/7/93	103	43
39	Randy Mitton	Fredericton, N.B.	9/22/50	2/2/74	1537	40
41	Jean Morin	Sorel, Que.	8/10/63	10/5/91	209	41
93	Brian Murphy	Dover, NH	12/13/64	10/7/88	432	38
40	Thor Nelson	Westminister, CA	1/6/68	2/16/95	4	4
43	Tim Nowak	Buffalo, NY	9/6/67	10/8/93	87	39
79	Mark Pare	Windsor, Ont.	7/26/57	10/11/79	1186	40
51	Baron Parker	Vancouver, B.C.	3/5/67	1/25/95	38	38
72	Stephane Provost	Montreal, Que.	5/5/67	1/25/95	45	45
34	Pierre Racicot	Verdun, Que.	2/15/67	10/12/93	95	41
32	Ray Scapinello	Guelph, Ont.	11/5/46	10/17/71	1871	40
47	Dan Schachte	Madison, WI	7/13/58	10/6/82	915	39
57	Jay Sharrers	Jamaica, West Indies	7/3/67	10/6/90	285	41
33	Leon Stickle	Toronto, Ont.	4/20/48	10/17/70	1825	39
56	Mark Wheler	North Battleford, Sask.	9/20/65	10/10/92	173	39

NHL History

1917 — National Hockey League organized November 22 in Montreal following suspension of operations by the National Hockey Association of Canada Limited (NHA). Montreal Canadiens, Montreal Wanderers, Ottawa Senators and Quebec Bulldogs attended founding meeting. Delegates decided to use NHA rules.

Toronto Arenas were later admitted as fifth team; Quebec decided not to operate during the first season. Quebec players allocated to remaining four teams.

Frank Calder elected president and secretary-treasurer.

First NHL games played December 19, with Toronto only arena with artificial ice. Clubs played 22-game split schedule.

1918 — Emergency meeting held January 3 due to destruction by fire of Montreal Arena which was home ice for both Canadiens and Wanderers.

Wanderers withdrew, reducing the NHL to three teams; Canadiens played remaining home games at 3,250-seat Jubilee rink.

Quebec franchise sold to P.J. Quinn of Toronto on October 18 on the condition that the team operate in Quebec City for 1918-19 season. Quinn did not attend the November League meeting and Quebec did not play in 1918-19.

1919-20 — NHL reactivated Quebec Bulldogs franchise. Former Quebec players returned to the club. New Mount Royal Arena became home of Canadiens. Toronto Arenas changed name to St. Patricks. Clubs played 24-game split schedule.

1920-21 — H.P. Thompson of Hamilton, Ontario made application for the purchase of an NHL franchise. Quebec franchise shifted to Hamilton with other NHL teams providing players to strengthen the club.

1921-22 — Split schedule abandoned. First and second place teams at the end of full schedule to play for championship.

1922-23 — Clubs agreed that players could not be sold or traded to clubs in any other league without first being offered to all other clubs in the NHL. In March, Foster Hewitt broadcasts radio's first hockey game.

1923-24 — Ottawa's new 10,000-seat arena opened. First U.S. franchise granted to Boston for following season.

Dr. Cecil Hart Trophy donated to NHL to be awarded to the player judged most useful to his team.

1924-25 — Canadian Arena Company of Montreal granted a franchise to operate Montreal Maroons. NHL now six team league with two clubs in Montreal. Inaugural game in new Montreal Forum played November 29, 1924 as Canadiens defeated Toronto 7-1. Forum was home rink for the Maroons, but no ice was available in the Canadiens arena November 29, resulting in shift to Forum.

Hamilton finished first in the standings, receiving a bye into the finals. But Hamilton players, demanding $200 each for additional games in the playoffs, went on strike. The NHL suspended all players, fining them $200 each. Stanley Cup finalist to be the winner of NHL semi-final between Toronto and Canadiens.

Prince of Wales and Lady Byng trophies donated to NHL.

Clubs played 30-game schedule.

1925-26 — Hamilton club dropped from NHL. Players signed by new New York Americans franchise. Franchise granted to Pittsburgh.

Clubs played 36-game schedule.

1926-27 — New York Rangers granted franchise May 15, 1926. Chicago Black Hawks and Detroit Cougars granted franchises September 25, 1926. NHL now ten-team league with an American and a Canadian Division.

Stanley Cup came under the control of NHL. In previous seasons, winners of the now-defunct Western or Pacific Coast leagues would play NHL champion in Cup finals.

Toronto franchise sold to a new company controlled by Hugh Aird and Conn Smythe. Name changed from St. Patricks to Maple Leafs.

Clubs played 44-game schedule.

The Montreal Canadiens donated the Vezina Trophy to be awarded to the team allowing the fewest goals-against in regular season play. The winning team would, in turn, present the trophy to the goaltender playing in the greatest number of games during the season.

1929-30 — Detroit franchise changed name from Cougars to Falcons.

1930-31 — Pittsburgh transferred to Philadelphia for one season. Pirates changed name to Philadelphia Quakers. Trading deadline for teams set at February 15 of each year. NHL approved operation of farm teams by Rangers, Americans, Falcons and Bruins. Four-sided electric arena clock first demonstrated.

1931-32 — Philadelphia dropped out. Ottawa withdrew for one season. New Maple Leaf Gardens completed.

Clubs played 48-game schedule

1932-33 — Detroit franchise changed name from Falcons to Red Wings. Franchise application received from St. Louis but refused because of additional travel costs. Ottawa team resumed play.

1933-34 — First All-Star Game played as a benefit for injured player Ace Bailey. Leafs defeated All-Stars 7-3 in Toronto.

1934-35 — Ottawa franchise transferred to St. Louis. Team called St. Louis Eagles and consisted largely of Ottawa's players.

1935-36 — Ottawa-St. Louis franchise terminated. Montreal Canadiens finished season with very poor record. To strengthen the club, NHL gave Canadiens first call on the services of all French-Canadian players for three seasons.

1937-38 — Second benefit all-star game staged November 2 in Montreal in aid of the family of the late Canadiens star Howie Morenz.

Montreal Maroons withdrew from the NHL on June 22, 1938, leaving seven clubs in the League.

1938-39 — Expenses for each club regulated at $5 per man per day for meals and $2.50 per man per day for accommodation.

1939-40 — Benefit All-Star Game played October 29, 1939 in Montreal for the children of the late Albert (Babe) Siebert.

1940-41 — Ross-Tyer puck adopted as the official puck of the NHL. Early in the season it was apparent that this puck was too soft. The Spalding puck was adopted in its place.

After the playoffs, Arthur Ross, NHL governor from Boston, donated a perpetual trophy to be awarded annually to the player voted outstanding in the league.

1941-42 — New York Americans changed name to Brooklyn Americans.

1942-43 — Brooklyn Americans withdrew from NHL, leaving six teams: Boston, Chicago, Detroit, Montreal, New York and Toronto. Playoff format saw first-place team play third-place team and second play fourth.

Clubs played 50-game schedule.

Frank Calder, president of the NHL since its inception, died in Montreal. Meryn "Red" Dutton, former manager of the New York Americans, became president. The NHL commissioned the Calder Memorial Trophy to be awarded to the League's outstanding rookie each year.

1945-46 — Philadelphia, Los Angeles and San Francisco applied for NHL franchises.

The Philadelphia Arena Company of the American Hockey League applied for an injunction to prevent the possible operation of an NHL franchise in that city.

1946-47 — Mervyn Dutton retired as president of the NHL prior to the start of the season. He was succeeded by Clarence S. Campbell.

Individual trophy winners and all-star team members to receive $1,000 awards.

Playoff guarantees for players introduced.

Clubs played 60-game schedule.

1947-48 — The first annual All-Star Game for the benefit of the players' pension fund was played when the All-Stars defeated the Stanley Cup Champion Toronto Maple Leafs 4-3 in Toronto on October 13, 1947.

Ross Trophy, awarded to the NHL's outstanding player since 1941, to be awarded annually to the League's scoring leader.

Philadelphia and Los Angeles franchise applications refused.

National Hockey League Pension Society formed.

1949-50 — Clubs played 70-game schedule.

First intra-league draft held April 30, 1950. Clubs allowed to protect 30 players. Remaining players available for $25,000 each.

1951-52 — Referees included in the League's pension plan.

1952-53 — In May of 1952, City of Cleveland applied for NHL franchise. Application denied. In March of 1953, the Cleveland Barons of the AHL challenged the NHL champions for the Stanley Cup. The NHL governors did not accept this challenge.

1953-54 — The James Norris Memorial Trophy presented to the NHL for annual presentation to the League's best defenseman.

Intra-league draft rules amended to allow teams to protect 18 skaters and two goaltenders, claiming price reduced to $15,000.

1954-55 — Each arena to operate an "out-of-town" scoreboard. Referees and linesmen to wear shirts of black and white vertical stripes. Teams agree to wear colored uniforms at home and white uniforms on the road.

1956-57 — Standardized signals for referees and linesmen introduced.

1960-61 — Canadian National Exhibition, City of Toronto and NHL reach agreement for the construction of a Hockey Hall of Fame on the CNE grounds. Hall opens on August 26, 1961.

1963-64 — Player development league established with clubs operated by NHL franchises located in Minneapolis, St. Paul, Indianapolis, Omaha and, beginning in 1964-65, Tulsa. First universal amateur draft took place. All players of qualifying age (17) unaffected by sponsorship of junior teams available to be drafted.

1964-65 — Conn Smythe Trophy presented to the NHL to be awarded annually to the outstanding player in the Stanley Cup playoffs.

Minimum age of players subject to amateur draft changed to 18.

1965-66 — NHL announced expansion plans for a second six-team division to begin play in 1967-68.

1966-67 — Fourteen applications for NHL franchises received.

Lester Patrick Trophy presented to the NHL to be awarded annually for outstanding service to hockey in the United States.

NHL sponsorship of junior teams ceased, making all players of qualifying age not already on NHL-sponsored lists eligible for the amateur draft.

1967-68 — Six new teams added: California Seals, Los Angeles Kings, Minnesota North Stars, Philadelphia Flyers, Pittsburgh Penguins, St. Louis Blues. New teams to play in West Division. Remaining six teams to play in East Division.

Minimum age of players subject to amateur draft changed to 20.

Clubs played 74-game schedule.

Clarence S. Campbell Trophy awarded to team finishing the regular season in first place in West Division.

California Seals changed name to Oakland Seals on December 8, 1967.

1968-69 — Clubs played 76-game schedule.

Amateur draft expanded to cover any amateur player of qualifying age throughout the world.

1970-71 — Two new teams added: Buffalo Sabres and Vancouver Canucks. These teams joined East Division: Chicago switched to West Division.

Clubs played 78-game schedule.

1971-72 — Playoff format amended. In each division, first to play fourth; second to play third.

1972-73 — Soviet Nationals and Canadian NHL stars play eight-game pre-season series. Canadians win 4-3-1.

Two new teams added: Atlanta Flames join West Division; New York Islanders join East Division.

1974-75 — Two new teams added: Kansas City Scouts and Washington Capitals. Teams realigned into two nine-team conferences, the Prince of Wales made up of the Norris and Adams Divisions, and the Clarence Campbell made up of the Smythe and Patrick Divisions.

Clubs played 80-game schedule.

NHL History — *continued*

1976-77 — California franchise transferred to Cleveland. Team named Cleveland Barons. Kansas City franchise transferred to Denver. Team named Colorado Rockies.

1977-78 — Clarence S. Campbell retires as NHL president. Succeeded by John A. Ziegler, Jr.

1978-79 — Cleveland and Minnesota franchises merge, leaving NHL with 17 teams. Merged team placed in Adams Division, playing home games in Minnesota.
  Minimum age of players subject to amateur draft changed to 19.

1979-80 — Four new teams added: Edmonton Oilers, Hartford Whalers, Quebec Nordiques and Winnipeg Jets.
  Minimum age of players subject to entry draft changed to 18.

1980-81 — Atlanta franchise.shifted to Calgary, retaining "Flames" name.

1981-82 — Teams realigned within existing divisions. New groupings based on geographical areas. Unbalanced schedule adopted.

1982-83 — Colorado Rockies franchise shifted to East Rutherford, New Jersey. Team named New Jersey Devils. Franchise moved to Patrick Division from Smythe; Winnipeg moved to Smythe Division from Norris.

1991-92 — San Jose Sharks added, making the NHL a 22-team league. NHL celebrates 75th Anniversary Season. The 1991-92 regular season suspended due to a strike by members of the NHL Players' Association on April 1, 1992. Play resumed April 12, 1992.

1992-93 — Gil Stein named NHL president (October, 1992). Gary Bettman named first NHL Commissioner (February, 1993). Ottawa Senators and Tampa Bay Lightning added, making the NHL a 24-team league. NHL celebrates Stanley Cup Centennial. Clubs played 84-game schedule.

1993-94 — Mighty Ducks of Anaheim and Florida Panthers added, making the NHL a 26-team league. Minnesota franchise shifted to Dallas, team named Dallas Stars. Prince of Wales and Clarence Campbell Conferences renamed Eastern and Western. Adams, Patrick, Norris and Smythe Divisions renamed Northeast, Atlantic, Central and Pacific. Winnipeg moved to Central Division from Pacific; Tampa Bay moved to Atlantic Division from Central; Pittsburgh moved to Northeast Division from Atlantic.

1994-95 — A labor disruption forced the cancellation of 468 games from October 1, 1994 to January 19, 1995. Clubs played a 48-game schedule that began January 20, 1995 and ended May 3, 1995. No inter-conference games were played.

1995-96 — Quebec franchise transferred to Denver. Team named Colorado Avalanche and placed in Pacific Division of Western Conference. Clubs to play 82-game schedule.

NHL Attendance

Season	Regular Season Games	Regular Season Attendance	Playoffs Games	Playoffs Attendance	Total Attendance
1960-61	210	2,317,142	17	242,000	2,559,142
1961-62	210	2,435,424	18	277,000	2,712,424
1962-63	210	2,590,574	16	220,906	2,811,480
1963-64	210	2,732,642	21	309,149	3,041,791
1964-65	210	2,822,635	20	303,859	3,126,494
1965-66	210	2,941,164	16	249,000	3,190,184
1966-67	210	3,084,759	16	248,336	3,333,095
1967-68[1]	444	4,938,043	40	495,089	5,433,132
1968-69	456	5,550,613	33	431,739	5,982,352
1969-70	456	5,992,065	34	461,694	6,453,759
1970-71[2]	546	7,257,677	43	707,633	7,965,310
1971-72	546	7,609,368	36	582,666	8,192,034
1972-73[3]	624	8,575,651	38	624,637	9,200,288
1973-74	624	8,640,978	38	600,442	9,241,420
1974-75[4]	720	9,521,536	51	784,181	10,305,717
1975-76	720	9,103,761	48	726,279	9,830,040
1976-77	720	8,563,890	44	646,279	9,210,169
1977-78	720	8,526,564	45	686,634	9,213,198
1978-79	680	7,758,053	45	694,521	8,452,574
1979-80[5]	840	10,533,623	63	976,699	11,510,322
1980-81	840	10,726,198	68	966,390	11,692,588
1981-82	840	10,710,894	71	1,058,948	11,769,842
1982-83	840	11,020,610	66	1,088,222	12,028,832
1983-84	840	11,359,386	70	1,107,400	12,466,786
1984-85	840	11,633,730	70	1,107,500	12,741,230
1985-86	840	11,621,000	72	1,152,503	12,773,503
1986-87	840	11,855,880	87	1,383,967	13,239,847
1987-88	840	12,117,512	83	1,336,901	13,454,413
1988-89	840	12,417,969	83	1,327,214	13,745,183
1989-90	840	12,579,651	85	1,355,593	13,935,244
1990-91	840	12,343,897	92	1,442,203	13,786,100
1991-92[6]	880	12,769,676	86	1,327,920	14,097,596
1992-93[7]	1,008	14,158,177 [8]	83	1,346,034	15,504,211
1993-94[9]	1,092	16,105,604 [10]	90	1,440,095	17,545,699
1994-95	624	9,233,884	81	1,329,130	10,563,014

[1] First expansion: Los Angeles, Pittsburgh, California (Cleveland),Philadelphia, St. Louis and Minnesota (Dallas)
[2] Second expansion: Buffalo and Vancouver
[3] Third expansion: Atlanta (Calgary) and New York Islanders
[4] Fourth expansion: Kansas City (Colorado, New Jersey) and Washington
[5] Fifth expansion: Edmonton, Hartford, Quebec (Colorado) and Winnipeg
[6] Sixth expansion: San Jose
[7] Seventh expansion: Ottawa and Tampa Bay
[8] Includes 24 neutral site games
[9] Eighth expansion: Anaheim and Florida
[10] Includes 26 neutral site games

Major Rule Changes

1910-11 — Game changed from two 30-minute periods to three 20-minute periods.

1911-12 — National Hockey Association (forerunner of the NHL) originated six-man hockey, replacing seven-man game.

1917-18 — Goalies permitted to fall to the ice to make saves. Previously a goaltender was penalized for dropping to the ice.

1918-19 — Penalty rules amended. For minor fouls, substitutes not allowed until penalized player had served three minutes. For major fouls, no substitutes for five minutes. For match fouls, no substitutes allowed for the remainder of the game.
  With the addition of two lines painted on the ice twenty feet from center, three playing zones were created, producing a forty-foot neutral center ice area in which forward passing was permitted. Kicking the puck was permitted in this neutral zone.
  Tabulation of assists began.

1921-22 — Goaltenders allowed to pass the puck forward up to their own blue line.
  Overtime limited to twenty minutes.
  Minor penalties changed from three minutes to two minutes.

1923-24 — Match foul defined as actions deliberately injuring or disabling an opponent. For such actions, a player was fined not less than $50 and ruled off the ice for the balance of the game. A player assessed a match penalty may be replaced by a substitute at the end of 20 minutes. Match penalty recipients must meet with the League president who can assess additional punishment.

1925-26 — Delayed penalty rules introduced. Each team must have a minimum of four players on the ice at all times.
  Two rules were amended to encourage offense: No more than two defensemen permitted to remain inside a team's own blue line when the puck has left the defensive zone. A faceoff to be called for ragging the puck unless short-handed.
  Team captains only players allowed to talk to referees.
  Goaltender's leg pads limited to 12-inch width.
  Timekeeper's gong to mark end of periods rather than referee's whistle. Teams to dress a maximum of 12 players for each game from a roster of no more than 14 players.

1926-27 — Blue lines repositioned to sixty feet from each goal-line, thereby enlarging the neutral zone and standardizing distance from blueline to goal.
  Uniform goal nets adopted throughout NHL with goal posts securely fastened to the ice.

1927-28 — To further encourage offense, forward passes allowed in defending and neutral zones and goaltender's pads reduced in width from 12 to 10 inches.
  Game standardized at three twenty-minute periods of stop-time separated by ten-minute intermissions.
  Teams to change ends after each period.
  Ten minutes of sudden-death overtime to be played if the score is tied after regulation time.
  Minor penalty to be assessed to any player other than a goaltender for deliberately picking up the puck while it is in play. Minor penalty to be assessed for deliberately shooting the puck out of play.
  The Art Ross goal net adopted as the official net of the NHL.
  Maximum length of hockey sticks limited to 53 inches measured from heel of blade to end of handle. No minimum length stipulated.
  Home teams given choice of goals to defend at start of game.

1928-29 — Forward passing permitted in defensive and neutral zones and into attacking zone if pass receiver is in neutral zone when pass is made. No forward passing allowed inside attacking zone.
  Minor penalty to be assessed to any player who delays the game by passing the puck back into his defensive zone.
  Ten-minute overtime without sudden-death provision to be played in games tied after regulation time. Games tied after this overtime period declared a draw.
  Exclusive of goaltenders, team to dress at least 8 and no more than 12 skaters.

1929-30 — Forward passing permitted inside all three zones but not permitted across either blue line.

Kicking the puck allowed, but a goal cannot be scored by kicking the puck in.

No more than three players including the goaltender may remain in their defensive zone when the puck has gone up ice. Minor penalties to be assessed for the first two violations of this rule in a game; major penalties thereafter.

Goaltenders forbidden to hold the puck. Pucks caught must be cleared immediately. For infringement of this rule, a faceoff to be taken ten feet in front of the goal with no player except the goaltender standing between the faceoff spot and the goal-line.

Highsticking penalties introduced.

Maximum number of players in uniform increased from 12 to 15.

December 21, 1929 — Forward passing rules instituted at the beginning of the 1929-30 season more than doubled number of goals scored. Partway through the season, these rules were further amended to read, ''No attacking player allowed to precede the play when entering the opposing defensive zone.'' This is similar to modern offside rule.

1930-31 — A player without a complete stick ruled out of play and forbidden from taking part in further action until a new stick is obtained. A player who has broken his stick must obtain a replacement at his bench.

A further refinement of the offside rule stated that the puck must first be propelled into the attacking zone before any player of the attacking side can enter that zone; for infringement of this rule a faceoff to take place at the spot where the infraction took place.

1931-32 — Though there is no record of a team attempting to play with two goaltenders on the ice, a rule was instituted which stated that each team was allowed only one goaltender on the ice at one time.

Attacking players forbidden to impede the movement or obstruct the vision of opposing goaltenders.

Defending players with the exception of the goaltender forbidden from falling on the puck within 10 feet of the net.

1932-33 — Each team to have captain on the ice at all times.

If the goaltender is removed from the ice to serve a penalty, the manager of the club to appoint a substitute.

Match penalty with substitution after five minutes instituted for kicking another player.

1933-34 — Number of players permitted to stand in defensive zone restricted to three including goaltender.

Visible time clocks required in each rink.

Two referees replace one referee and one linesman.

1934-35 — Penalty shot awarded when a player is tripped and thus prevented from having a clear shot on goal, having no player to pass to other than the offending player. Shot taken from inside a 10-foot circle located 38 feet from the goal. The goaltender must not advance more than one foot from his goal-line when the shot is taken.

1937-38 — Rules introduced governing icing the puck.

Penalty shot awarded when a player other than a goaltender falls on the puck within 10 feet of the goal.

1938-39 — Penalty shot modified to allow puck carrier to skate in before shooting.

One referee and one linesman replace two referee system.

Blue line widened to 12 inches.

Maximum number of players in uniform increased from 14 to 15.

1939-40 — A substitute replacing a goaltender removed from ice to serve a penalty may use a goaltender's stick and gloves but no other goaltending equipment.

1940-41 — Flooding ice surface between periods made obligatory.

1941-42 — Penalty shots classified as minor and major. Minor shot to be taken from a line 28 feet from the goal. Major shot, awarded when a player is tripped with only the goaltender to beat, permits the player taking the penalty shot to skate right into the goalkeeper and shoot from point-blank range.

One referee and two linesmen employed to officiate games.

For playoffs, standby minor league goaltenders employed by NHL as emergency substitutes.

1942-43 — Because of wartime restrictions on train scheduling, regular-season overtime was discontinued on November 21, 1942.

Player limit reduced from 15 to 14. Minimum of 12 men in uniform abolished.

1943-44 — Red line at center ice introduced to speed up the game and reduce offside calls. This rule is considered to mark the beginning of the modern era in the NHL.

Delayed penalty rules introduced.

1945-46 — Goal indicator lights synchronized with official time clock required at all rinks.

1946-47 — System of signals by officials to indicate infractions introduced.

Linesmen from neutral cities employed for all games.

1947-48 — Goal awarded when a player with the puck has an open net to shoot at and a thrown stick prevents the shot on goal. Major penalty to any player who throws his stick in any zone other than defending zone. If a stick is thrown by a player in his defending zone but the thrown stick is not considered to have prevented a goal, a penalty shot is awarded.

All playoff games played until a winner determined, with 20-minute sudden-death overtime periods separated by 10-minute intermissions.

1949-50 — Ice surface painted white.

Clubs allowed to dress 17 players exclusive of goaltenders.

Major penalties incurred by goaltenders served by a member of the goaltender's team instead of resulting in a penalty shot.

1950-51 — Each team required to provide an emergency goaltender in attendance with full equipment at each game for use by either team in the event of illness or injury to a regular goaltender.

1951-52 — Home teams to wear basic white uniforms; visiting teams basic colored uniforms.

Goal crease enlarged from 3 × 7 feet to 4 × 8 feet.

Number of players in uniform reduced to 15 plus goaltenders.

Faceoff circles enlarged from 10-foot to 15-foot radius.

1952-53 — Teams permitted to dress 15 skaters on the road and 16 at home.

1953-54 — Number of players in uniform set at 16 plus goaltenders.

1954-55 — Number of players in uniform set at 18 plus goaltenders up to December 1 and 16 plus goaltenders thereafter.

1956-57 — Player serving a minor penalty allowed to return to ice when a goal is scored by opposing team.

1959-60 — Players prevented from leaving their benches to enter into an altercation. Substitutions permitted providing substitutes do not enter into altercation.

1960-61 — Number of players in uniform set at 16 plus goaltenders.

1961-62 — Penalty shots to be taken by the player against whom the foul was committed. In the event of a penalty shot called in a situation where a particular player hasn't been fouled, the penalty shot to be taken by any player on the ice when the foul was committed.

1964-65 — No bodily contact on faceoffs.

In playoff games, each team to have its substitute goaltender dressed in his regular uniform except for leg pads and body protector. All previous rules governing standby goaltenders terminated.

1965-66 — Teams required to dress two goaltenders for each regular-season game.

1966-67 — Substitution allowed on coincidental major penalties.

Between-periods intermissions fixed at 15 minutes.

1967-68 — If a penalty incurred by a goaltender is a co-incident major, the penalty to be served by a player of the goaltender's team on the ice at the time the penalty was called. Limit of curvature of hockey stick blade set at 1-$\frac{1}{2}$ inches.

1969-70 — Limit of curvature of hockey stick blade set at 1 inch.

1970-71 — Home teams to wear basic white uniforms; visiting teams basic colored uniforms.

Limit of curvature of hockey stick blade set at $\frac{1}{2}$ inch.

Minor penalty for deliberately shooting the puck out of the playing area.

1971-72 — Number of players in uniform set at 17 plus 2 goaltenders.

Third man to enter an altercation assessed an automatic game misconduct penalty.

1972-73 — Minimum width of stick blade reduced to 2 inches from 2-$\frac{1}{2}$ inches.

1974-75 — Bench minor penalty imposed if a penalized player does not proceed directly and immediately to the penalty box.

1976-77 — Rule dealing with fighting amended to provide a major and game misconduct penalty for any player who is clearly the instigator of a fight.

1977-78 — Teams requesting a stick measurement to be assessed a minor penalty in the event that the measured stick does not violate the rules.

1981-82 — If both of a team's listed goaltenders are incapacitated, the team can dress and play any eligible goaltender who is available.

1982-83 — Number of players in uniform set at 18 plus 2 goaltenders.

1983-84 — Five-minute sudden-death overtime to be played in regular-season games that are tied at the end of regulation time.

1985-86 — Substitutions allowed in the event of co-incidental minor penalties.

1986-87 — Delayed off-side is no longer in effect once the players of the offending team have cleared the opponents' defensive zone.

1991-92 — Video replays employed to assist referees in goal/no goal situations. Size of goal crease increased. Crease changed to semi-circular configuration. Time clock to record tenths of a second in last minute of each period and overtime. Major and game misconduct penalty for checking from behind into boards. Penalties added for crease infringement and unnecessary contact with goaltender. Goal disallowed if puck enters net while a player of the attacking team is standing on the goal crease line, is in the goal crease or places his stick in the goal crease.

1992-93 — No substitutions allowed in the event of coincidental minor penalties called when both teams are at full strength. Wearing of helmets made optional for forwards and defensemen. Minor penalty for attempting to draw a penalty (''diving''). Major and game misconduct penalty for checking from behind into goal frame. Game misconduct penalty for instigating a fight. Highsticking redefined to include any use of the stick above waist-height. Previous rule stipulated shoulder-height.

1993-94 — High sticking redefined to allow goals scored with a high stick below the height of the crossbar of the goal frame.

Milt Schmidt (15) is robbed by New York Ranger netminder ''Sugar'' Jim Henry during Boston's 2-1 victory over the Blues on November 15, 1941. Prior to the 1945-46 season, the NHL ruled that all exposed equipment, such as the elbow pads sported here by Schmidt, were to be worn inside the uniform.

Notes

Rebounding from an injury-plagued 1993-94 season, Teemu Selanne notched 22 goals in 1994-95, including eight powerplay and two shorthanded markers.

Mighty Ducks of Anaheim

1994-95 Results: 16w-27L-5T 37PTS. Sixth, Pacific Division

Schedule

Oct.	Mon.	9	at Winnipeg		
	Wed.	11	at Hartford		
	Fri.	13	at Buffalo		
	Sat.	14	at Pittsburgh		
	Wed.	18	Vancouver		
	Fri.	20	Philadelphia		
	Sun.	22	Winnipeg		
	Mon.	23	at Colorado		
	Thur.	26	at Dallas		
	Fri.	27	at St. Louis		
	Sun.	29	Calgary		
Nov.	Wed.	1	St. Louis		
	Fri.	3	NY Rangers		
	Sun.	5	New Jersey		
	Tues.	7	at Toronto		
	Wed.	8	at Montreal		
	Sat.	11	at Ottawa*		
	Mon.	13	Los Angeles		
	Wed.	15	Colorado		
	Fri.	17	NY Islanders		
	Sun.	19	Florida		
	Tues.	21	at Calgary		
	Wed.	22	at Edmonton		
	Fri.	24	Chicago*		
	Wed.	29	Washington		
Dec.	Fri.	1	at Detroit		
	Sat.	2	at Toronto		
	Mon.	4	at NY Rangers		
	Wed.	6	at Tampa Bay		
	Thur.	7	at Florida		
	Sun.	10	Edmonton		
	Wed.	13	Pittsburgh		
	Fri.	15	Ottawa		
	Sun.	17	Toronto		
	Tues.	19	San Jose		
	Wed.	20	Detroit		
	Fri.	22	Vancouver		
	Wed.	27	at Los Angeles		
	Fri.	29	San Jose		
	Sun.	31	Los Angeles*		
Jan.	Fri.	5	at Calgary		
	Sun.	7	at Edmonton		
	Tues.	9	at Philadelphia		
	Thur.	11	at Boston		
	Fri.	12	at Chicago		
	Sun.	14	at Winnipeg		
	Wed.	17	Calgary		
	Wed.	24	at Vancouver		
	Sat.	27	at Los Angeles*		
	Wed.	31	Colorado		
Feb.	Fri.	2	Hartford		
	Sun.	4	Chicago		
	Wed.	7	Toronto		
	Sat.	10	at NY Islanders*		
	Sun.	11	at New Jersey		
	Wed.	14	at Edmonton		
	Thur.	15	at Vancouver		
	Sat.	17	at Los Angeles		
	Wed.	21	Boston		
	Fri.	23	at Calgary		
	Sun.	25	San Jose*		
	Mon.	26	at Colorado		
	Wed.	28	Montreal		
Mar.	Sun.	3	Tampa Bay		
	Tues.	5	Dallas		
	Fri.	8	Buffalo		
	Sun.	10	Los Angeles		
	Wed.	13	Colorado		
	Sun.	17	St. Louis		
	Tues.	19	at Washington		
	Fri.	22	at St. Louis		
	Sun.	24	at Chicago*		
	Mon.	25	at Detroit		
	Thur.	28	at Dallas		
	Sun.	31	at San Jose*		
Apr.	Wed.	3	Edmonton		
	Fri.	5	Detroit		
	Sun.	7	at San Jose*		
	Mon.	8	Vancouver		
	Wed.	10	at Colorado		
	Fri.	12	Dallas		
	Sun.	14	Winnipeg		

* Denotes afternoon game.

Home Starting Times:

Weeknights	7:35 p.m.
Sundays	5:05 p.m.
Matinees	1:05 p.m.
Except Mon. Oct. 9	5:05 p.m.
Sun. Dec. 10	7:05 p.m.

Franchise date: June 15, 1993

**3rd
NHL
Season**

**PACIFIC
DIVISION**

Year-by-Year Record

Season	GP	Home W	L	T	Road W	L	T	Overall W	L	T	GF	GA	Pts.	Finished		Playoff Result
1994-95	48	11	9	4	5	18	1	16	27	5	125	164	37	6th,	Pacific Div.	Out of Playoffs
1993-94	84	14	26	2	19	20	3	33	46	5	229	251	71	4th,	Pacific Div.	Out of Playoffs

Paul Kariya led all NHL rookies in goals (18) and shots (134) during the 1994-95 season and was selected to the NHL/Upper Deck All-Rookie Team.

1995-96 Player Personnel

FORWARDS	HT	WT	S	Place of Birth	Date	1994-95 Club
BETS, Maxim	6-1	185	L	Chelyabinsk, USSR	1/31/74	San Diego-Worcester
CARNBACK, Patrik	6-0	187	L	Goteborg, Sweden	2/1/68	V. Frolunda-Anaheim
CORKUM, Bob	6-2	185	R	Salisbury, MA	12/18/67	Anaheim
DOURIS, Peter	6-1	195	R	Toronto, Ont.	2/19/66	Anaheim
EWEN, Todd	6-2	220	R	Saskatoon, Sask.	3/22/66	Anaheim
JOMPHE, Jean-Francois	6-1	195	L	Harve' St. Pierre, Que.	12/28/72	Cdn. National
KARIYA, Paul	5-11	175	L	Vancouver, B.C.	10/16/74	Anaheim
KARPOV, Valeri	5-10	176	L	Chelyabinsk, USSR	8/5/71	Chelyabinsk-Anaheim-San Diego
KILGER, Chad	6-3	204	L	Cornwall, Ont.	11/27/76	Kingston
KING, Steven	6-0	195	R	Greenwich, RI	7/22/69	DID NOT PLAY
KRYGIER, Todd	6-0	185	L	Chicago Heights, MI	10/12/65	Anaheim
LAMBERT, Denny	5-11	200	L	Wawa, Ont.	1/7/70	San Diego-Anaheim
LILLEY, John	5-9	170	R	Wakefield, MA	8/3/72	San Diego-Anaheim
MANELUK, Mike	5-11	188	R	Winnipeg, Man.	10/1/73	Cdn. National-San Diego
NIKULIN, Igor	6-1	190	L	Cherepovets, USSR	8/26/72	Cherepovets
PRONGER, Sean	6-2	205	L	Dryden, Ont.	11/30/72	Knoxville-Greensboro-San Diego
REICHERT, Craig	6-1	196	R	Winnipeg, Man.	5/11/74	San Diego
RUCCHIN, Steve	6-3	210	L	London, Ont.	7/4/71	San Diego-Anaheim
SACCO, David	6-0	180	R	Malden, MA	7/31/70	San Diego-Anaheim
SACCO, Joe	6-1	195	R	Medford, MA	2/4/69	Anaheim
SILLINGER, Mike	5-10	190	R	Regina, Sask.	6/29/71	Detroit-Wien-Anaheim
SKALDE, Jarrod	6-0	175	L	Niagara Falls, Ont.	2/26/71	Las Vegas
STEVENSON, Jeremy	6-2	215	L	San Bernadino, CA	7/28/74	Greensboro
VALK, Garry	6-1	205	L	Edmonton, Alta.	11/27/67	Anaheim
VAN ALLEN, Shaun	6-1	200	L	Shaunavon, Sask.	8/29/67	Anaheim
WESENBERG, Brian	6-3	173	R	Peterborough, Ont.	5/9/77	Guelph

DEFENSEMEN						
BRISKE, Byron	6-2	194	R	Humboldt, Sask.	1/23/76	Red Deer-Tri-City
CHARTIER, Scott	6-1	200	R	St. Lazare, Man.	1/19/72	Greensboro-San Diego
CORCORAN, Brian	6-2	247	L	Baldwinsville, NY	4/23/72	U. Mass.
DESANTIS, Mark	6-0	205	R	Brampton, Ont.	1/12/72	San Diego-Greensboro
DEEKS, Alain	6-5	230	R	Hawkesbury, Ont.	4/15/69	Knoxville-Las Vegas
DIRK, Robert	6-4	210	L	Regina, Sask.	8/20/66	Anaheim
DOLLAS, Bobby	6-2	212	L	Montreal, Que.	1/31/65	Anaheim
HICKS, Alex	6-1	195	L	Calgary, Alta.	9/4/69	Las Vegas
HOLAN, Milos	5-11	191	L	Bilovec, Czech.	4/22/71	Hershey-Anaheim
KARPA, Dave	6-1	202	R	Regina, Sask.	5/7/71	Quebec-Cornwall-Anaheim
LADOUCEUR, Randy	6-2	220	L	Brockville, Ont.	6/30/60	Anaheim
MARSHALL, Jason	6-2	195	R	Cranbrook, B.C.	2/22/71	San Diego-Anaheim
McSWEEN, Don	5-11	197	L	Detroit, MI	6/9/64	Anaheim
MIKULCHIK, Oleg	6-2	200	R	Minsk, USSR	6/27/64	Springfield-Winnipeg
TRNKA, Pavel	6-3	190	L	Plzen, Czech.	7/27/76	Kladno-Interconex Plzen
TSULYGIN, Nikolai	6-4	205	R	Ufa, USSR	6/29/75	CSKA-Ufa Salavat
TVERDOVSKY, Oleg	6-0	185	L	Donetsk, USSR	5/18/76	Brandon-Anaheim
VAN IMPE, Darren	6-0	195	L	Saskatoon, Sask.	5/18/73	San Diego-Anaheim
YORK, Jason	6-2	195	R	Ottawa, Ont.	5/20/70	Detroit-Adirondack-Anaheim

GOALTENDERS	HT	WT	C	Place of Birth	Date	1994-95 Club
HEBERT, Guy	5-11	185	L	Troy, NY	1/7/67	Anaheim
O'NEILL, Mike	5-7	160	L	LaSalle, Que.	11/3/67	Ft. Wayne-Phoenix
PENSTOCK, Byron	5-9	180	L	Regina, Sask.	9/9/74	Brandon
SHTALENKOV, Mikhail	6-2	180	L	Moscow, USSR	10/20/65	Anaheim
TANNER, John	6-3	182	L	Cambridge, Ont.	3/17/71	Greensboro-San Diego

After being obtained by Anaheim from Washington in February, 1995, Todd Krygier collected 11 goals and 11 assists in 35 games.

Coaching History

Ron Wilson, 1993-94 to date.

Captains' History

Troy Loney, 1993-94; Randy Ladouceur, 1994-95.

1994-95 Scoring

* – rookie

Regular Season

Pos	#	Player	Team	GP	G	A	Pts	+/–	PIM	PP	SH	GW	GT	S	%
L	9	* Paul Kariya	ANA	47	18	21	39	–17	4	7	1	3	1	134	13.4
C	22	Shaun Van Allen	ANA	45	8	21	29	–4	32	1	1	1	0	68	11.8
C	47	Stephan Lebeau	ANA	38	8	16	24	6	12	1	0	2	0	70	11.4
C	25	Todd Krygier	ANA	35	11	11	22	1	10	1	0	1	0	90	12.2
R	16	Peter Douris	ANA	46	10	11	21	4	12	0	0	4	0	69	14.5
R	21	Patrik Carnback	ANA	41	6	15	21	–8	32	0	0	1	0	58	10.3
D	2	Bobby Dollas	ANA	45	7	13	20	–3	12	3	1	1	0	70	10.0
C	19	Bob Corkum	ANA	44	10	9	19	–7	25	0	0	1	1	100	10.0
R	14	Joe Sacco	ANA	41	10	8	18	–8	23	2	0	0	0	77	13.0
C	20	* Steve Rucchin	ANA	43	6	11	17	7	23	0	0	1	0	59	10.2
R	26	Mike Sillinger	DET	13	2	6	8	3	2	0	0	0	0	11	18.2
			ANA	15	2	5	7	1	6	2	0	0	0	28	7.1
			TOTAL	28	4	11	15	4	8	2	0	0	0	39	10.3
D	10	* Oleg Tverdovsky	ANA	36	3	9	12	–6	14	1	1	0	0	26	11.5
L	11	* Valeri Karpov	ANA	30	4	7	11	–4	6	0	0	0	0	48	8.3
D	3	* Jason York	DET	10	1	2	3	0	2	0	0	0	0	6	16.7
			ANA	15	0	8	8	4	12	0	0	0	0	22	0.0
			TOTAL	25	1	10	11	4	14	0	0	0	0	28	3.6
D	7	* Milos Holan	ANA	25	2	8	10	4	14	1	0	1	0	93	2.2
L	18	Garry Valk	ANA	36	3	6	9	–4	34	0	0	1	0	53	5.7
D	24	Tom Kurvers	ANA	22	4	3	7	–13	6	1	0	1	0	44	9.1
D	29	Randy Ladouceur	ANA	44	2	4	6	2	36	0	0	0	0	42	4.8
D	15	Dave Karpa	QUE	2	0	0	0	–1	0	0	0	0	0	1	0.0
			ANA	26	1	5	6	0	91	0	0	0	0	32	3.1
			TOTAL	28	1	5	6	–1	91	0	0	0	0	33	3.0
C	27	John Lilley	ANA	9	2	3	5	0	2	5	1	0	0	10	20.0
D	4	David Williams	ANA	21	2	2	4	–5	26	0	0	1	0	30	6.7
L	42	* Denny Lambert	ANA	13	1	3	4	3	4	0	0	0	0	14	7.1
D	5	Robert Dirk	ANA	38	1	3	4	–3	56	0	0	0	0	15	6.7
L	8	Tim Sweeney	ANA	13	1	1	2	–3	2	0	0	0	0	11	9.1
L	12	* David Sacco	ANA	8	0	2	2	–3	0	0	0	0	0	5	0.0
D	48	* Darren Van Impe	ANA	1	0	1	1	0	0	0	0	0	0	1	0.0
D	23	* Jason Marshall	ANA	1	0	0	0	–2	0	0	0	0	0	1	0.0
D	6	Don McSween	ANA	1	0	0	0	0	0	0	0	0	0	1	0.0
G	35	M. Shtalenkov	ANA	18	0	0	0	0	0	0	0	0	0	0	0.0
R	36	Todd Ewen	ANA	24	0	0	0	–2	90	0	0	0	0	14	0.0
G	31	Guy Hebert	ANA	39	0	0	0	0	2	0	0	0	0	0	0.0

Goaltending

No.	Goaltender	GPI	Mins	Avg	W	L	T	EN	SO	GA	SA	S%
31	Guy Hebert	39	2092	3.13	12	20	4	4	2	109	1132	.904
35	Mikhail Shtalenkov	18	810	3.63	4	7	1	2	0	49	448	.891
	Totals	48	2913	3.38	16	27	5	6	2	164	1586	.897

General Manager

FERREIRA, JACK
Vice-President/General Manager, The Mighty Ducks of Anaheim.
Born in Providence, RI, June 9, 1944.

Jack Ferreira was named as the first vice president/general manager of the Mighty Ducks on March 23, 1993. A veteran of over 21 years in professional hockey, Ferreira's expertise lies in evaluating talent. He is responsible for the overall hockey operations of the club.

Experienced in building an NHL team from the ground-up, Ferreira assembled a nucleus in Anaheim that tied a record for most wins by an NHL first-year club (33), as the Mighty Ducks stayed in contention for a Western Conference playoff berth for most of the season in 1993-94. He received several votes in the Hockey News' 1993-94 NHL Executive of the Year balloting.

Ferreira came to the Mighty Ducks from the Montreal Canadiens, where he served as director of pro scouting during the 1992-93 season for the eventual Stanley Cup champions.

A Providence, RI, native, Ferreira's professional career began in 1972 with the New England Whalers of the World Hockey Association, where he served in many capacities, including head scout, assistant coach and assistant general manager through 1977.

From 1977-80, Ferreira served as a New England scout for the NHL's Central Scouting Bureau before moving to the Calgary Flames as a U.S. and college scout from 1980-86.

Ferreira took a post as director of player development for the New York Rangers in 1986, serving in that capacity until 19888. He then joined the Minnesota North Stars, where he served as vice president and general manager from 1988-90.

Ferreira helped start the San Jose Sharks franchise, serving as the team's executive vice president and general manager from 1990-92. Ferreira made acquisitions during the Sharks' first season that would be part of the foundation in San Jose's recent success over the past two campaigns.

A former All-American goaltender at Boston University, Ferreira was an assistant coach on the collegiate level at Princeton in 1969. He also served as an assistant coach with Brown University from 1970-72.

Ferreira earned a bachelor's degree in history from Boston University. Ferreira and his wife Kathy have two daughters, Jennifer and Julie, and two sons, Eric and Kent.

General Managers' History

Jack Ferreira, 1993-94 to date.

Club Records

Team

(Figures in brackets for season records are games played; records for fewest points, wins, ties, losses, goals, goals against are for 70 or more games)

Most Points	71	1993-94 (84)
Most Wins	33	1993-94 (84)
Most Ties	5	1993-94 (84)
		1994-95 (48)
Most Losses	46	1993-94 (84)
Most Goals	229	1993-94 (84)
Most Goals Against	251	1993-94 (84)
Fewest Points	71	1993-94 (84)
Fewest Wins	33	1993-94 (84)
Fewest Ties	5	1993-94 (84)
Fewest Losses	46	1993-94 (84)
Fewest Goals	229	1993-94 (84)
Fewest Goals Against	251	1993-94 (84)

Longest Winning Streak
Over-all . . . . 4 Nov. 19-24/93
Home . . . . 3 Mar. 30-Apr. 5/95
Away . . . . 4 Nov. 19-24/93

Longest Undefeated Streak
Over-all . . . . 4 Oct. 13-19/93 (2 wins, 2 ties); Nov. 19-24/93 (4 wins)
Home . . . . 4 Mar. 21-Apr. 5/95 (3 wins, 1 tie)
Away . . . . 5 Jan. 2-19/94 (3 wins, 2 ties)

Longest Losing Streak
Over-all . . . . 6 Oct. 20-31/93
Home . . . . 6 Dec. 22/93-Jan. 12/94
Away . . . . 6 Three times

Longest Winless Streak
Over-all . . . . 6 Oct. 20-31/93 (6 losses)
Home . . . . 4 Three times
Away . . . . 8 Mar. 26-Apr. 30/95 (7 losses, 1 tie)

Most Shutouts, Season 2 1993-94 (84) 1994-95 (48)
Most PIM, Season 1,507 1993-94 (84)
Most Goals, Game . . . . 7 Dec. 20/93 (Ana. 7 at Wpg. 5)

Individual

Most Seasons . . . . 2 Numerous
Most Games . . . . 125 Joe Sacco, Randy Ladouceur, Shaun Van Allen

Most Goals, Career . . . . 33 Bob Corkum
Most Assists, Career . . . . 46 Shaun Van Allen
Most Points, Career . . . . 70 Bob Corkum (33 goals, 37 assists)

Most PIM, Career . . . . 365 Todd Ewen
Most Shutouts, Career . . . . 4 Guy Hebert

Longest Consecutive Games Streak . . . . 84 Joe Sacco
Most Goals, Season . . . . 23 Bob Corkum (1993-94)
Most Assists, Season . . . . 31 Terry Yake (1993-94)
Most Points, Season . . . . 52 Terry Yake (1993-94) (21 goals, 31 assists)
Most PIM, Season . . . . 272 Todd Ewen (1993-94)

Most Points, Defenseman
Season . . . . 39 Bill Houlder (1993-94) (14 goals, 25 assists)

Most Points, Center
Season . . . . 51 Bob Corkum (1993-94) (23 goals, 28 assists)

Most Points, Right Wing
Season . . . . 52 Terry Yake (1993-94) (21 goals, 31 assists)

Most Points, Left Wing
Season . . . . 45 Garry Valk (1993-94) (18 goals, 27 assists)

Most Points, Rookie
Season . . . . 39 Paul Kariya (1994-95) (18 goals, 21 assists)

Most Shutouts, Season . . . . 2 Guy Hebert (1993-94, 1994-95)
Most Goals, Game . . . . 3 Terry Yake (Oct. 19/93)
Most Assists, Game . . . . 4 Shaun Van Allen (Mar. 9/95)
Most Points, Game . . . . 4 5 times, most recent Shaun Van Allen (Mar. 9/95)

* NHL Record.

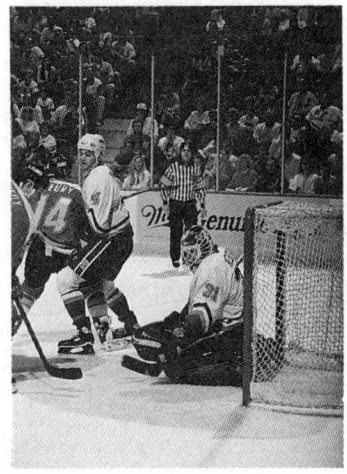

Guy Hebert appeared in 39 games for the Mighty Ducks in 1994-95, recording two shutouts and an impressive 3.13 goals-against average.

A graduate of the University of Western Ontario, Steve Rucchin collected 17 points in 43 games for the Ducks in 1994-95.

All-time Record vs. Other Clubs

Regular Season

			At Home						On Road						Total					
	GP	W	L	T	GF	GA	PTS	GP	W	L	T	GF	GA	PTS	GP	W	L	T	GF	GA	PTS
Boston	1	0	0	1	1	1	1	1	1	0	1	0	3	5	0	2	0	1	1	4	6	1
Buffalo	1	0	1	0	0	3	0	1	1	0	0	2	4	0	2	0	2	0	2	7	0
Calgary	6	2	3	1	13	17	5	5	5	2	3	0	14	15	4	11	4	6	1	27	32	9
Chicago	4	1	3	0	7	10	2	5	2	5	1	4	0	8	15	2	9	2	7	0	15	25	4
Dallas	5	2	3	0	12	15	4	4	4	1	3	0	8	19	2	9	3	6	0	20	34	6
Detroit	4	0	3	1	12	22	1	4	0	3	1	15	21	1	8	0	6	2	27	43	2
Edmonton	5	4	1	0	19	14	8	5	5	3	2	0	14	10	6	10	7	3	0	33	24	14
Florida	1	0	1	0	2	3	0	1	1	0	1	0	2	4	0	2	0	4	0	4	7	0
Hartford	1	1	0	0	6	3	2	1	1	0	0	3	2	2	2	2	0	0	9	5	4
Los Angeles	5	2	2	1	18	14	5	6	6	2	3	1	14	16	5	11	4	5	2	32	30	10
Montreal	1	0	1	0	2	5	0	1	1	0	1	0	1	4	0	2	0	2	0	3	9	0
New Jersey	1	0	1	0	3	6	0	1	1	0	1	0	1	4	0	2	0	2	0	3	10	0
NY Islanders	1	0	1	0	3	4	0	1	1	1	0	0	3	2	2	1	1	0	6	4	2
NY Rangers	1	1	0	0	3	2	2	1	1	0	4	2	2	2	2	0	0	7	4	4
Ottawa	1	1	0	0	5	1	2	1	1	0	1	0	1	4	0	2	1	0	6	5	4
Philadelphia	1	1	0	0	6	3	2	1	1	0	0	3	2	2	2	0	0	9	5	4
Pittsburgh	1	0	1	0	4	5	0	1	0	0	1	2	2	1	2	0	1	6	7	1
Quebec	1	0	1	0	0	1	0	1	1	0	0	6	3	2	2	1	1	0	6	4	2
St. Louis	4	1	3	0	9	13	2	4	1	3	0	11	20	2	8	2	6	0	20	33	4
San Jose	6	2	4	0	16	20	4	5	5	2	3	0	15	17	4	11	4	7	0	31	37	8
Tampa Bay	1	0	1	0	2	4	0	1	1	0	0	4	1	2	2	1	1	0	6	5	2
Toronto	4	2	1	1	15	9	5	4	1	2	1	7	9	3	8	3	3	2	22	18	8
Vancouver	5	1	3	1	10	11	3	6	2	4	0	15	23	4	11	3	7	1	25	34	7
Washington	1	0	1	0	2	5	0	1	0	0	3	0	2	0	0	2	0	2	8	0
Winnipeg	4	4	0	0	14	6	8	4	3	1	0	15	13	6	8	7	1	0	29	19	14
Totals	**66**	**25**	**35**	**6**	**184**	**197**	**56**	**66**	**24**	**38**	**4**	**170**	**218**	**52**	**132**	**49**	**73**	**10**	**354**	**415**	**108**

1994-95 Results

Jan.	20	at	Edmonton	1-2	17	Toronto	3-3
	21	at	Winnipeg	4-3	19	St. Louis	2-4
	23		Edmonton	5-4	21	Los Angeles	3-3
	25		Dallas	1-4	23 at	San Jose	6-3
	27		Winnipeg	3-2	26 at	Chicago	2-5
	31	at	St. Louis	2-7	28 at	Detroit	4-6
Feb.	1	at	Dallas	2-9	30	Winnipeg	3-1
	3		Detroit	2-5	31 at	Vancouver	1-6
	5	at	Los Angeles	3-2	Apr. 2	San Jose	5-4
	7		Chicago	0-3	5	Edmonton	4-3
	9	at	Calgary	1-5	7	Dallas	0-2
	12	at	Edmonton	0-2	9	Los Angeles	5-1
	17		Vancouver	2-2	11 at	Vancouver	0-5
	18	at	San Jose	6-3	13	Calgary	4-2
	23	at	Toronto	1-3	15	Vancouver	1-3
	24	at	Winnipeg	2-4	17	San Jose	3-0
	26		Calgary	3-5	19 at	Toronto	2-3
Mar.	1		Chicago	3-1	21 at	Detroit	5-6
	3	at	Dallas	0-4	23 at	Los Angeles	2-2
	5	at	Chicago	0-3	24	Calgary	2-1
	7	at	St. Louis	3-6	26	San Jose	2-5
	9		Detroit	4-4	30 at	Los Angeles	1-2
	11	at	Vancouver	3-5	May 1	St. Louis	3-5
	15	at	Calgary	5-0	3	Toronto	6-1

Entry Draft
Selections 1995-93

1995 Pick		1994 Pick		1993 Pick	
4	Chad Kilger	2	Oleg Tverdovsky	4	Paul Kariya
29	Brian Wesenberg	28	Johan Davidsson	30	Nikolai Tsulygin
55	Mike Leclerc	67	Craig Reichert	56	Valeri Karpov
107	Igor Nikulin	80	Byron Briske	82	Joel Gagnon
133	Peter Leboutillier	106	Pavel Trnka	108	Mikhail Shtalenkov
159	Mike Laplante	132	Jon Battaglia	134	Antti Aalto
185	Igor Karpenko	158	Mark (Rocky) Welsing	160	Matt Peterson
		184	John Brad Englehart	186	Tom Askey
		236	Tommi Miettinen	212	Vitaly Kozel
		262	Jeremy Stevenson	238	Anatoli Fedotov
				264	David Penney

© Mighty Ducks

Coach

WILSON, RON
Head Coach, The Mighty Ducks of Anaheim.
Born in Windsor, Ont., May 28, 1955.

On June 30, 1993 Disney Sports Enterprises, Inc., introduced Ron Wilson as the first head coach in Mighty Ducks history. In his first year as a head coach in the NHL, Wilson led Anaheim to a 33-46-5 record and 71 points as the Mighty Ducks made a substantial run at a playoff berth in the Western Conference. Wilson received 12 points in the voting for the Jack Adams NHL coach of the year Award, including one first-place vote.

With several new players and an overall younger roster, Wilson's Ducks squad finished their second NHL season strongly, going 8-9-1 in their last 18 games and 10-13-4 in their last 27. The team stayed in the hunt for a playoff spot for most of the season, finally being eliminated with only two games remaining.

Wilson, 40, came to the Mighty Ducks after serving the previous three seasons as an assistant coach to Pat Quinn for the Vancouver Canucks. During Wilson's three seasons in Vancouver, the Canucks posted a 116-98-30 record (.537) and qualified for the Stanley Cup playoffs all three years.

Prior to becoming an assistant coach with Vancouver, Wilson was an assistant coach for the Milwaukee Admirals (IHL) under Ron LaPointe.

Wilson has significant playing experience in professional, amateur and international hockey. He played four years at Providence College where he was a two-time All-American and four-time All-Hockey East. Wilson was Hockey East Player of the Year in 1975 when he led the nation in scoring with 26-61-87 points in 26 games. He remains Providence's all-time leading scorer and ranks as the all-time NCAA leading scorer among defensemen with 250 points. Wilson received a Bachelor of Arts Degree in economics from Providence College.

Drafted by the Toronto Maple Leafs (132nd overall) in 1975, Wilson began his professional hockey career in 1976-77 with the Dallas Blackhawks in the old Central Hockey League. He joined the Toronto Maple Leafs in 1977-78, playing in 64 NHL contests over three seasons. Wilson then moved to Switzerland in 1980 and competed for the Swiss teams Klöten and Davos for six seasons. The former defenseman/winger signed with the Minnesota North Stars as a free agent in 1985 where he played through 1988, closing out his pro career.

Though he was born in Canada, Wilson was raised in the United States. He is a four-time player for U.S. National Teams (1975, 1981, 1983, 1987) and coached the 1994 squad at the World Championships in Italy, leading Team USA to a 4-4-0 record with a fourth-place finish – its highest ranking since 1991. Wilson led the U.S. team to its first victory over Russia in international competition since the 1980 "miracle on ice" game during the 1980 Winter Olympics at Lake Placid, NY. Wilson was assisted by Mighty Ducks Assistant Coach Tim Army on the 1994 U.S. squad that included six players from the Mighty Ducks' inaugural season.

The Windsor, Ontario native also has some family ties to the NHL. His father, Larry, played six NHL seasons with the Detroit Red Wings and Chicago Blackhawks and coached pro hockey for 11 seasons, including one with Detroit. Ron Wilson's uncle, Johnny, played 13 years in the NHL and also coached for Detroit, Los Angeles, Colorado and Pittsburgh. Johnny Wilson once played 580 consecutive games in the NHL, a record at that time. Ron Wilson's brothers, Brad and Randy, played at Providence.

Wilson is active in all Disney GOALS charity events and is part of the Mighty Ducks' Speakers Bureau. He is known for his keen sense of humor and is an avid golfer. Wilson and his wife Maureen reside in Orange, CA. They have two daughters, Kristen, 18, and Lauren, 15.

Coaching Record

Season	Team	Games	Regular Season W	L	T	%	Playoffs Games	W	L	%
1993-94	Anaheim (NHL)	84	33	46	5	.423	....	....	....	....
1994-95	Anaheim (NHL)	48	16	27	5	.385	....	....	....	....
	NHL Totals	132	49	73	10	.409	....	....	....	....

Club Directory

Disney Sports Enterprises, Inc.
Arrowhead Pond of Anaheim
2695 Katella Ave.
P.O. Box 61077
Anaheim, CA 92803-6177
Phone **714/704-2700**
FAX 714/704-2753
Capacity: 17,174

Executive Management
Governor . . . . Michael Eisner
President and Alternate Governor. . . . . Tony Tavares
   Administrative Assistant to the President . . . . Janet Conley
Vice President/General Manager. . . . . Jack Ferreira
   Administrative Assistant to the General Manager . Debbie Blanchard
Vice President of Finance/Administration . . . . Andy Roundtree
   Administrative Assistant. . . . . Barbara Potts
Assistant General Manager. . . . . Pierre Gauthier
Vice President of Hockey Operations . . . . Kevin Gilmore

Coaching Staff
Head Coach . . . . Ron Wilson
Assistant Coaches. . . . . Al Sims, Tim Army

Hockey Club Operations
Director of Player Personnel . . . . David McNab
Coordinator of Computer Scouting and Video . . . . . Angela Gorgone
Pro Scout . . . . Paul Fenton
Amateur Scouts . . . . Thommie Bergman, Alain Chainey, Al Godfrey, Richard Green
Scouting Staff. . . . . Pavel Beranek, Matti Peltonen, Mike McGraw, Mark Odnokon, Ed Wright
Head Athletic Trainer/Physical Therapist . . . . Paddy Jarit
Equipment Manager. . . . . Mark O'Neill
Assistant Equipment Manager. . . . . John Allaway
Supervisor of Off-Ice Officials . . . . Tony Guanci
Team Physicians . . . . Dr. Ronald Glousman, Dr. Craig Milhouse
Oral Surgeon . . . . Dr. Jeff Pulver
Strength and Conditioning Coach . . . . Jamie Yanchar

Communications Department
Director of Public Relations. . . . . Bill Robertson
Media Services Coordinator . . . . Rob Scichili
Public Relations Intern. Barbara Oldani

Finance and Administration Department
Controller . . . . Martin Greenspun
Manager of Administration/Community Relations . . Jenny Price
Community Relations/Game Operations
   Coordinator. . . . . Tory Whittingham
Senior Accountant . . . . Melody Martin
Junior Accountant . . . . Shelly Baker

Marketing Department
Director of Sales and Marketing . . . . Bill Holford
Director of Advertising Sales & Servicing. . . . . Bob Wagner
Manager of Promotions and Sponsorship Services . . Michelle Amiro
Merchandise Manager . . . . Shelley Gartner
Sponsorship Services Coordinator . . . . Matthew Stys
Advertising Sales Managers . . . . John Covarrubias, Dave Severson
Sales and Marketing Administrative Assistant. . . . . . Cindy Williams
Advertising Sales Administrative Assistant . . . . Kelly Lockman

Television and Radio Broadcasting Department
Director of Broadcasting. Lisa Seltzer
Associate Producers . . . . Mark Vittorio, Tim Davis
Television, KCAL (Ch. 9) & Prime Sports (Cable) . . . . Chris Madsen and Brian Hayward
Radio, KEZY (95.9 FM) . . . . Matt McConnell and Charlie Simmer

Ticketing Department
Season Ticket Manager. . . . . Don Boudreau
Manager of Premium Ticket Services . . . . Anne McNiff
Ticketing Assistant . . . . Kevin Gidden, Andrea Morales
Account Executives. . . . . Lisa Manning, Jennifer Sampson, Jennifer Flaa
Ticket Sales Administrative Assistant. . . . . Debbie Nielander
Receptionist . . . . Anne Mason
Public Address Announcer . . . . Mike Carlucci

Miscellaneous
Team Colors . . . . Purple (PMS 518C), Jade (PMS 329C), Silver (PMS 429C) and White
Practice Facilities . . . . Disney ICE (300 W. Lincoln Ave.) and the Arrowhead Pond (2695 Katella Ave.)
Developmental Affiliate . . . . Baltimore Bandits (AHL)
Press Box Phone 714/704-2623
Press Room . . . . 714/704-2514 or 2517

Boston Bruins

1994-95 Results: 27w-18l-3t 57pts. Third, Northeast Division

Once again Cam Neely's dedication and perseverance paid off for Boston, as the Bruins' sharpshooter led the NHL with 16 powerplay goals.

Schedule

Oct.	Sat.	7	NY Islanders
	Mon.	9	Buffalo*
	Wed.	11	at Colorado
	Thur.	12	at San Jose
	Sat.	14	at Dallas
	Tues.	17	at St. Louis
	Sat.	21	at Detroit*
	Thur.	26	Washington
	Sat.	28	Hartford
	Tues.	31	Montreal
Nov.	Thur.	2	Detroit
	Sat.	4	at Montreal
	Tues.	7	at Washington
	Thur.	9	Ottawa
	Sat.	11	Toronto
	Tues.	14	at Tampa Bay
	Thur.	16	New Jersey
	Sat.	18	St. Louis
	Tues.	21	Winnipeg
	Fri.	24	Los Angeles*
	Sat.	25	at Ottawa
	Thur.	30	Pittsburgh
Dec.	Sat.	2	Buffalo
	Sun.	3	at Philadelphia
	Tues.	5	Dallas
	Fri.	8	at Tampa Bay
	Sat.	9	at Florida
	Wed.	13	at NY Rangers
	Thur.	14	Florida
	Sat.	16	Calgary
	Fri.	22	at Buffalo
	Sat.	23	Tampa Bay
	Tues.	26	at NY Islanders
	Sun.	31	at Winnipeg*
Jan.	Tues.	2	Chicago
	Wed.	3	at Toronto
	Sat.	6	Hartford
	Mon.	8	Colorado
	Thur.	11	Anaheim
	Sat.	13	New Jersey*
	Mon.	15	Vancouver*
	Tue.	16	at New Jersey
	Mon.	22	at Pittsburgh
	Thur.	25	Tampa Bay
	Sat.	27	NY Rangers*
	Sun.	28	at Montreal*
	Wed.	31	at Ottawa
Feb.	Thur.	1	Florida
	Sat.	3	Buffalo*
	Tues.	6	at Pittsburgh
	Wed.	7	at Buffalo
	Sat.	10	Philadelphia*
	Wed.	14	at Hartford
	Thur.	15	at Chicago
	Sat.	17	at Vancouver
	Mon.	19	at Los Angeles*
	Wed.	21	at Anaheim
	Fri.	23	at Edmonton
	Sat.	24	at Calgary
	Tues.	27	Edmonton
	Wed.	28	at NY Rangers
Mar.	Sat.	2	Washington*
	Tues.	5	at NY Islanders
	Thur.	7	NY Islanders
	Sat.	9	Philadelphia*
	Sun.	10	at Florida
	Thur.	14	Pittsburgh
	Fri.	15	at Washington
	Mon.	18	San Jose
	Wed.	20	at New Jersey
	Thur.	21	Ottawa
	Sat.	23	NY Rangers*
	Wed.	27	at Hartford
	Thur.	28	Montreal
	Sun.	31	at Buffalo*
Apr.	Mon.	1	at Ottawa
	Wed.	3	at Montreal
	Thur.	4	Montreal
	Sun.	7	at Philadelphia*
	Thur.	11	Hartford
	Sat.	13	at Hartford*
	Sun.	14	Pittsburgh*

* Denotes afternoon game.

Home Starting Times:
Weeknights . . . . 7:30 p.m.
Saturdays and Sundays . . . . 7:00 p.m.
Matinees . . . . 1:30 p.m.
Except   Sat. Nov. 11 . . . . 7:30 p.m.
             Fri. Nov. 24 . . . . 1:00 p.m.
             Sat. Jan. 27 . . . . 3:00 p.m.
             Sat. Feb. 2 . . . . 3:00 p.m.
             Sat. Feb. 10 . . . . 3:00 p.m.
             Sun. Apr. 14 . . . . 3:00 p.m.

Franchise date: November 1, 1924

NORTHEAST DIVISION

72nd NHL Season

Year-by-Year Record

		Home			Road			Overall							
Season	GP	W	L	T	W	L	T	W	L	T	GF	GA	Pts.	Finished	Playoff Result
1994-95	48	15	7	2	12	11	1	27	18	3	150	127	57	3rd, Northeast Div.	Lost Conf. Quarter-Final
1993-94	84	20	14	8	22	15	5	42	29	13	289	252	97	2nd, Northeast Div.	Lost Conf. Semi-Final
1992-93	84	29	10	3	22	16	4	51	26	7	332	268	109	1st, Adams Div.	Lost Div. Semi-Final
1991-92	80	23	11	6	13	21	6	36	32	12	270	275	84	2nd, Adams Div.	Lost Conf. Championship
1990-91	80	26	9	5	18	15	7	44	24	12	299	264	100	1st, Adams Div.	Lost Conf. Championship
1989-90	80	23	13	4	23	12	5	46	25	9	289	232	101	1st, Adams Div.	Lost Final
1988-89	80	17	15	8	20	14	6	37	29	14	289	256	88	2nd, Adams Div.	Lost Div. Final
1987-88	80	24	13	3	20	17	3	44	30	6	300	251	94	2nd, Adams Div.	Lost Final
1986-87	80	25	11	4	14	23	3	39	34	7	301	276	85	3rd, Adams Div.	Lost Div. Semi-Final
1985-86	80	24	9	7	13	22	5	37	31	12	311	288	86	3rd, Adams Div.	Lost Div. Semi-Final
1984-85	80	21	15	4	15	19	6	36	34	10	303	287	82	4th, Adams Div.	Lost Div. Semi-Final
1983-84	80	25	12	3	24	13	3	49	25	6	336	261	104	1st, Adams Div.	Lost Div. Semi-Final
1982-83	80	28	6	6	22	14	4	50	20	10	327	228	110	1st, Adams Div.	Lost Conf. Championship
1981-82	80	24	12	4	19	15	6	43	27	10	323	285	96	2nd, Adams Div.	Lost Div. Final
1980-81	80	26	10	4	11	20	9	37	30	13	316	272	87	2nd, Adams Div.	Lost Prelim. Round
1979-80	80	27	9	4	19	12	9	46	21	13	310	234	105	2nd, Adams Div.	Lost Quarter-Final
1978-79	80	25	10	5	18	13	9	43	23	14	316	270	100	1st, Adams Div.	Lost Semi-Final
1977-78	80	29	6	5	22	12	6	51	18	11	333	218	113	1st, Adams Div.	Lost Final
1976-77	80	27	7	6	22	16	2	49	23	8	312	240	106	1st, Adams Div.	Lost Final
1975-76	80	27	5	8	21	10	9	48	15	17	313	237	113	1st, Adams Div.	Lost Semi-Final
1974-75	80	29	5	6	11	21	8	40	26	14	345	245	94	2nd, Adams Div.	Lost Prelim. Round
1973-74	78	33	4	2	19	13	7	52	17	9	349	221	113	1st, East Div.	Lost Final
1972-73	78	27	10	2	24	12	3	51	22	5	330	235	107	2nd, East Div.	Lost Quarter-Final
1971-72	**78**	**28**	**4**	**7**	**26**	**9**	**4**	**54**	**13**	**11**	**330**	**204**	**119**	**1st, East Div.**	**Won Stanley Cup**
1970-71	78	33	4	2	24	10	5	57	14	7	399	207	121	1st, East Div.	Lost Quarter-Final
1969-70	**76**	**27**	**3**	**8**	**13**	**14**	**11**	**40**	**17**	**19**	**277**	**216**	**99**	**2nd, East Div.**	**Won Stanley Cup**
1968-69	76	29	3	6	13	15	10	42	18	16	303	221	100	2nd, East Div.	Lost Semi-Final
1967-68	74	22	9	6	15	18	4	37	27	10	259	216	84	3rd, East Div.	Lost Quarter-Final
1966-67	70	10	21	4	7	22	6	17	43	10	182	253	44	6th,	Out of Playoffs
1965-66	70	15	17	3	6	26	3	21	43	6	174	275	48	5th,	Out of Playoffs
1964-65	70	12	17	6	9	26	0	21	43	6	166	253	48	6th,	Out of Playoffs
1963-64	70	13	15	7	5	25	5	18	40	12	170	212	48	6th,	Out of Playoffs
1962-63	70	7	18	10	7	21	7	14	39	17	198	281	45	6th,	Out of Playoffs
1961-62	70	9	22	4	6	25	4	15	47	8	177	306	38	6th,	Out of Playoffs
1960-61	70	13	17	5	2	25	8	15	42	13	176	254	43	6th,	Out of Playoffs
1959-60	70	21	11	3	7	23	5	28	34	8	220	241	64	5th,	Out of Playoffs
1958-59	70	21	13	1	11	18	6	32	29	9	205	215	73	2nd,	Lost Semi-Final
1957-58	70	15	14	6	12	14	9	27	28	15	199	194	69	4th,	Lost Final
1956-57	70	20	9	6	14	15	6	34	24	12	195	174	80	3rd,	Lost Final
1955-56	70	14	14	7	9	20	6	23	34	13	147	185	59	5th,	Out of Playoffs
1954-55	70	16	10	9	7	16	12	23	26	21	169	188	67	4th,	Lost Semi-Final
1953-54	70	22	8	5	10	20	5	32	28	10	177	181	74	4th,	Lost Semi-Final
1952-53	70	19	10	6	9	19	7	28	29	13	152	172	69	3rd,	Lost Final
1951-52	70	15	12	8	10	17	8	25	29	16	162	176	66	4th,	Lost Semi-Final
1950-51	70	13	12	10	9	18	8	22	30	18	178	197	62	4th,	Lost Semi-Final
1949-50	70	15	12	8	7	20	8	22	32	16	198	228	60	5th,	Out of Playoffs
1948-49	60	18	10	2	11	13	6	29	23	8	178	163	66	2nd,	Lost Semi-Final
1947-48	60	12	8	10	11	16	3	23	24	13	167	168	59	3rd,	Lost Semi-Final
1946-47	60	18	7	5	8	16	6	26	23	11	190	175	63	3rd,	Lost Semi-Final
1945-46	50	11	5	4	13	13	4	24	18	8	167	156	56		Lost Final
1944-45	50	11	12	2	5	18	2	16	30	4	179	219	36	4th,	Lost Semi-Final
1943-44	50	15	8	2	4	18	3	19	26	5	223	268	43	5th,	Out of Playoffs
1942-43	50	17	3	5	7	14	4	24	17	9	195	176	57	2nd,	Lost Final
1941-42	48	17	4	3	8	13	3	25	17	6	160	118	56	3rd,	Lost Semi-Final
1940-41	**48**	**15**	**4**	**5**	**12**	**4**	**8**	**27**	**8**	**13**	**168**	**102**	**67**	**1st,**	**Won Stanley Cup**
1939-40	48	20	3	1	11	9	4	31	12	5	170	98	67	1st,	Lost Semi-Final
1938-39	**48**	**20**	**2**	**2**	**16**	**8**	**0**	**36**	**10**	**2**	**156**	**76**	**74**	**1st,**	**Won Stanley Cup**
1937-38	48	18	3	3	12	8	4	30	11	7	142	89	67	1st, Amn. Div.	Lost Semi-Final
1936-37	48	9	11	4	14	7	3	23	18	7	120	110	53	2nd, Amn. Div.	Lost Quarter-Final
1935-36	48	15	8	1	7	12	5	22	20	6	92	83	50	2nd, Amn. Div.	Lost Quarter-Final
1934-35	48	17	7	0	9	9	6	26	16	6	129	112	58	1st, Amn. Div.	Lost Semi-Final
1933-34	48	11	11	2	7	14	3	18	25	5	111	130	41	4th, Amn. Div.	Out of Playoffs
1932-33	48	20	2	3	5	13	5	25	15	8	124	88	58	1st, Amn. Div.	Lost Semi-Final
1931-32	48	11	10	3	4	11	9	15	21	12	122	117	42	4th, Amn. Div.	Out of Playoffs
1930-31	44	17	1	5	11	9	1	28	10	6	143	90	62	1st, Amn. Div.	Lost Semi-Final
1929-30	44	23	1	0	15	4	1	38	5	1	179	98	77	1st, Amn. Div.	Lost Final
1928-29	**44**	**16**	**6**	**1**	**10**	**7**	**4**	**26**	**13**	**5**	**89**	**52**	**57**	**1st, Amn. Div.**	**Won Stanley Cup**
1927-28	44	13	4	5	7	9	6	20	13	11	77	70	51	1st, Amn. Div.	Lost Semi-Final
1926-27	44	15	7	0	6	13	3	21	20	3	97	89	45	2nd, Amn. Div.	Lost Final
1925-26	36	10	7	1	7	8	3	17	15	4	92	85	38	4th,	Out of Playoffs
1924-25	30	3	12	0	3	12	0	6	24	0	49	119	12	6th,	Out of Playoffs

1995-96 Player Personnel

FORWARDS	HT	WT	S	Place of Birth	Date	1994-95 Club
BEDDOES, Clayton	5-11	190	L	Bentley, Alta.	11/10/70	Providence (AHL)
CZERKAWSKI, Mariusz	6-0	195	R	Radomsko, Poland	4/13/72	Kiekko-Espoo-Boston
DONATO, Ted	5-10	181	L	Dedham, MA	4/28/69	TuTo-Boston
ELIK, Todd	6-2	195	L	Brampton, Ont.	4/15/66	San Jose-St. Louis
GONEAU, Daniel	6-1	196	L	Montreal, Que.	1/16/76	Laval
HEINZE, Stephen	5-11	193	R	Lawrence, MA	1/30/70	Boston
HUGHES, Brent	5-11	195	L	New Westminster, B.C.	4/5/66	Boston
KNIPSCHEER, Fred	5-11	185	L	Ft. Wayne, IN	9/3/69	Providence (AHL)-Boston
LEACH, Stephen	5-11	197	R	Cambridge, MA	1/16/66	Boston
MANN, Cameron	6-0	190	R	Thompson, Man.	4/20/77	Peterborough
McCAULEY, Bill	6-1	191	L	Detroit, MI	4/20/75	Detroit (OHL)
McEACHERN, Shawn	5-11	195	L	Waltham, MA	2/28/69	Kiekko-Espoo-Pittsburgh
MOGER, Sandy	6-3	215	R	100 Mile House, B.C.	3/21/69	Providence (AHL)-Boston
NEELY, Cam	6-1	218	R	Comox, B.C.	6/6/65	Boston
OATES, Adam	5-11	185	R	Weston, Ont.	8/27/62	Boston
POTVIN, Marc	6-1	200	R	Ottawa, Ont.	1/29/67	Boston-Providence (AHL)
REID, David	6-1	217	L	Toronto, Ont.	5/15/64	Boston-Providence (AHL)
ROY, Andre	6-3	178	L	Port Chester, NY	2/8/75	Chicoutimi-Drummondville
SCHAEFER, Jeremy	6-3	195	L	Carston, Alta.	2/27/76	Medicine Hat
STEVENS, Kevin	6-3	217	L	Brockton, MA	4/15/65	Pittsburgh
STEWART, Cameron	5-11	196	L	Kitchener, Ont.	9/18/71	Boston-Providence (AHL)
STUMPEL, Jozef	6-1	208	R	Nitra, Czech.	6/20/72	Koln-Boston
SWEENEY, Tim	5-11	185	L	Boston, MA	4/12/67	Anaheim-Providence (AHL)

DEFENSEMEN	HT	WT	S	Place of Birth	Date	1994-95 Club
BOURQUE, Ray	5-11	215	L	Montreal, Que.	12/28/60	Boston
BROWN, Sean	6-3	196	L	Oshawa, Ont.	11/5/76	Belleville
CROWLEY, Ted	6-2	188	R	Concord, MA	5/3/70	Chicago (IHL)-Houston
GRUDEN, John	6-0	189	L	Hastings, MN	4/6/70	Boston-Providence (AHL)
HODGE, Dan	6-3	205	R	Melrose, MA	9/18/71	Merrimack
HUSCROFT, Jamie	6-2	200	R	Creston, B.C.	1/9/67	Boston
IAFRATE, Al	6-3	235	L	Dearborn, MI	3/21/66	DID NOT PLAY
KASATONOV, Alexei	6-1	215	L	Leningrad, USSR	10/14/59	CSKA-Boston
MASTAD, Milt	6-3	205	L	Regina, Sask.	3/5/75	Moose Jaw
McLAREN, Kyle	6-4	210	L	Humbolt, Sask.	6/18/77	Tacoma
PAQUETTE, Charles	6-1	193	L	Lachute, Que.	6/17/75	Sherbrooke
ROHLOFF, Jon	5-11	220	R	Mankato, MN	10/3/69	Boston-Providence (AHL)
SWEENEY, Don	5-10	188	L	St. Stephen, N.B.	8/17/66	Boston
TAGLIANETTI, Peter	6-2	195	L	Framingham, MA	8/15/63	Pittsburgh-Cleveland
VON STEFENELLI, Phil	6-1	200	L	Vancouver, B.C.	4/10/69	Providence (AHL)
WRIGHT, Darren	6-1	182	L	Duncan, B.C.	5/22/76	Detroit (ColHL)-Prince Albert

GOALTENDERS	HT	WT	C	Place of Birth	Date	1994-95 Club
BAILEY, Scott	6-0	195	L	Calgary, Alta.	5/2/72	Providence (AHL)
BILLINGTON, Craig	5-10	170	L	London, Ont.	9/11/66	Ottawa-Boston
GRAHAME, John	6-2	195	L	Denver, CO	8/31/75	Lake Superior
LACHER, Blaine	6-1	205	L	Medicine Hat, Alta.	9/5/70	Boston-Providence (AHL)
RYABCHIKOV, Evgeny	5-11	167	L	Yaroslavl, Soviet Union	1/16/74	Providence (AHL)-Magnitogorsk
SAVARY, Neil	6-0	170	L	Halifax, N.S.	4/3/76	Hull
SCHAFER, Paxton	5-9	152	L	Medicine Hat, Alta.	2/26/76	Medicine Hat

General Managers' History

Arthur Ross, 1924-25 to 1953-54; Lynn Patrick, 1954-55 to 1964-65; Leighton "Hap" Emms, 1965-66 to 1966-67; Milt Schmidt, 1967-68 to 1971-72; Harry Sinden, 1972-73 to date.

Captains' History

No Captain, 1924-25 to 1926-27; Lionel Hitchman, 1927-28 to 1930-31; George Owen, 1931-32; "Dit" Clapper, 1932-33 to 1937-38; "Cooney" Weiland, 1938-39; "Dit" Clapper, 1939-40 to 1945-46; "Dit" Clapper and John Crawford, 1946-47; John Crawford 1947-48 to 1949-50; Milt Schmidt, 1950-51 to 1953-54; Milt Schmidt, Ed Sanford, 1954-55; Fern Flaman, 1955-56 to 1960-61; Don McKenney, 1961-62, 1962-63; Leo Boivin, 1963-64 to 1965-66; John Bucyk, 1966-67; no captain, 1967-68 to 1972-73; John Bucyk, 1973-74 to 1976-77; Wayne Cashman, 1977-78 to 1982-83; Terry O'Reilly, 1983-84, 1984-85; Ray Bourque, Rick Middleton (co-captains) 1985-86 to 1987-88; Ray Bourque, 1988-89 to date.

Coaching History

Arthur Ross, 1924-25 to 1927-28; Cy Denneny, 1928-29; Arthur Ross, 1929-30 to 1933-34; Frank Patrick, 1934-35 to 1935-36; Arthur Ross, 1936-37 to 1938-39; "Cooney" Weiland, 1939-40 to 1940-41; Arthur Ross, 1941-42 to 1944-45; "Dit" Clapper, 1945-46 to 1948-49; George Boucher, 1949-50; Lynn Patrick, 1950-51 to 1953-54; Lynn Patrick and Milt Schmidt, 1954-55; Milt Schmidt, 1955-56 to 1960-61; Phil Watson, 1961-62; Phil Watson and Milt Schmidt, 1962-63; Milt Schmidt, 1963-64 to 1965-66; Harry Sinden, 1966-67 to 1969-70; Tom Johnson, 1970-71 to 1971-72; Tom Johnson and "Bep" Guidolin, 1972-73; "Bep" Guidolin, 1973-74; Don Cherry, 1974-75 to 1978-79; Fred Creighton and Harry Sinden, 1979-80; Gerry Cheevers, 1980-81 to 1983-84; Gerry Cheevers and Harry Sinden, 1984-85; "Butch" Goring, 1985-86; "Butch" Goring and Terry O'Reilly, 1986-87; Terry O'Reilly, 1987-88 to 1988-89; Mike Milbury, 1989-90 to 1990-91; Rick Bowness, 1991-92; Brian Sutter, 1992-93 to 1994-95; Steve Kasper, 1995-96.

1994-95 Scoring
– rookie

Regular Season

Pos	#	Player	Team	GP	G	A	Pts	+/-	PIM	PP	SH	GW	GT	S	%
C	12	Adam Oates	BOS	48	12	41	53	-11	8	4	1	2	0	109	11.0
D	77	Ray Bourque	BOS	46	12	31	43	3	20	9	0	2	0	210	5.7
R	8	Cam Neely	BOS	42	27	14	41	7	72	16	0	5	1	178	15.2
C	20	Bryan Smolinski	BOS	44	18	13	31	-3	31	6	0	5	0	121	14.9
R	19	* Mariusz Czerkawski	BOS	47	12	14	26	4	31	1	0	2	0	126	9.5
L	26	Mats Naslund	BOS	34	8	14	22	-4	4	2	0	1	0	48	16.7
C	32	Don Sweeney	BOS	47	3	19	22	6	24	1	0	2	0	102	2.9
C	21	Ted Donato	BOS	47	10	10	20	3	10	1	0	1	0	71	14.1
R	22	Jozef Stumpel	BOS	44	5	13	18	4	8	1	0	2	0	46	10.9
R	23	Steve Heinze	BOS	36	7	9	16	0	23	0	1	0	0	70	10.0
D	6	Alexei Kasatonov	BOS	44	2	14	16	-2	33	0	1	0	0	50	4.0
L	18	Brent Hughes	BOS	44	6	6	12	6	139	0	0	1	0	75	8.0
R	27	Stephen Leach	BOS	35	5	6	11	-3	68	1	0	1	0	82	6.1
D	38	* Jon Rohloff	BOS	34	3	8	11	1	39	0	0	1	1	51	5.9
L	17	Dave Reid	BOS	38	5	5	10	8	10	0	0	1	0	47	10.6
R	45	* Sandy Moger	BOS	18	2	6	8	-1	6	2	0	0	0	32	6.3
R	44	Glen Murray	BOS	35	5	2	7	-11	46	0	0	2	0	64	7.8
D	34	David Shaw	BOS	44	3	4	7	-9	36	1	0	0	0	58	5.2
D	28	Jamie Huscroft	BOS	34	0	6	6	-3	103	0	0	0	0	30	0.0
D	36	* John Gruden	BOS	38	0	6	6	3	22	0	0	0	0	30	0.0
L	48	* Fred Knipscheer	BOS	16	3	1	4	1	2	0	0	1	0	20	15.0
R	42	Mikko Makela	BOS	11	1	2	3	0	0	1	0	0	0	10	10.0
C	40	* Brett Harkins	BOS	1	0	1	1	0	0	0	0	0	0	1	0.0
R	29	Marc Potvin	BOS	6	0	1	1	1	4	0	0	0	0	4	0.0
G	31	* Blaine Lacher	BOS	35	0	1	1	0	0	0	0	0	0	0	0.0
D	49	Jeff Serowik	BOS	1	0	0	0	1	0	0	0	0	0	1	0.0
L	13	Grigori Panteleev	BOS	1	0	0	0	0	0	0	0	0	0	0	0.0
C	16	Cameron Stewart	BOS	5	0	0	0	1	0	0	0	0	0	2	0.0
G	37	Vincent Riendeau	BOS	11	0	0	0	0	0	0	0	0	0	0	0.0
G	1	Craig Billington	OTT	9	0	0	0	0	4	0	0	0	0	0	0.0
			BOS	8	0	0	0	0	0	0	0	0	0	0	0.0
			TOTAL	17	0	0	0	0	4	0	0	0	0	0	0.0

Goaltending

No.	Goaltender	GPI	Mins	Avg	W	L	T	EN	SO	GA	SA	S%
31	* Blaine Lacher	35	1965	2.41	19	11	2	0	4	79	805	.902
37	Vincent Riendeau	11	565	2.87	3	6	1	2	0	27	221	.878
1	Craig Billington	8	373	3.06	5	1	0	0	0	19	140	.864
	Totals	**48**	**2911**	**2.62**	**27**	**18**	**3**	**2**	**4**	**127**	**1168**	**.891**

Playoffs

Pos	#	Player	Team	GP	G	A	Pts	+/-	PIM	PP	SH	GW	OT	S	%
D	77	Ray Bourque	BOS	5	0	3	3	-5	0	0	0	0	0	15	0.0
R	8	Cam Neely	BOS	5	2	0	2	-4	2	1	0	1	0	13	15.4
L	26	Mats Naslund	BOS	5	1	0	1	-3	0	0	0	0	0	7	14.3
C	12	Adam Oates	BOS	5	1	0	1	-6	2	1	0	0	0	7	14.3
R	19	* Mariusz Czerkawski	BOS	5	1	0	1	0	0	0	0	0	0	11	9.1
D	34	David Shaw	BOS	5	0	1	1	-2	4	0	0	0	0	9	0.0
D	20	Bryan Smolinski	BOS	5	0	1	1	-2	4	0	0	0	0	12	0.0
G	1	Craig Billington	BOS	1	0	0	0	0	0	0	0	0	0	0	0.0
R	44	Glen Murray	BOS	2	0	0	0	-1	2	0	0	0	0	2	0.0
C	41	Guy Larose	BOS	4	0	0	0	0	0	0	0	0	0	0	0.0
L	48	* Fred Knipscheer	BOS	4	0	0	0	0	0	0	0	0	0	2	0.0
L	18	Brent Hughes	BOS	5	0	0	0	-2	4	0	0	0	0	7	0.0
D	28	Jamie Huscroft	BOS	5	0	0	0	0	11	0	0	0	0	4	0.0
D	6	Alexei Kasatonov	BOS	5	0	0	0	0	2	0	0	0	0	4	0.0
L	17	Dave Reid	BOS	5	0	0	0	1	0	0	0	0	0	2	0.0
C	32	Don Sweeney	BOS	5	0	0	0	-4	4	0	0	0	0	8	0.0
C	21	Ted Donato	BOS	5	0	0	0	0	0	0	0	0	0	5	0.0
R	23	Steve Heinze	BOS	5	0	0	0	0	0	0	0	0	0	10	0.0
D	38	* Jon Rohloff	BOS	5	0	0	0	-1	6	0	0	0	0	4	0.0
R	22	Jozef Stumpel	BOS	5	0	0	0	-1	0	0	0	0	0	8	0.0
G	31	* Blaine Lacher	BOS	5	0	0	0	0	0	0	0	0	0	0	0.0

Goaltending

No.	Goaltender	GPI	Mins	Avg	W	L	EN	SO	GA	SA	S%
1	Craig Billington	1	25	2.40	0	0	0	0	1	10	.900
31	* Blaine Lacher	5	283	2.54	1	4	1	0	12	125	.904
	Totals	**5**	**309**	**2.72**	**1**	**4**	**1**	**0**	**14**	**136**	**.897**

Retired Numbers

2	Eddie Shore	1926-1940
3	Lionel Hitchman	1925-1934
4	Bobby Orr	1966-1976
5	Dit Clapper	1927-1947
7	Phil Esposito	1967-1975
9	John Bucyk	1957-1978
15	Milt Schmidt	1936-1955

Club Records

Team

(Figures in brackets for season records are games played; records for fewest points, wins, ties, losses, goals, goals against are for 70 or more games)

Most Points	121	1970-71 (78)
Most Wins	57	1970-71 (78)
Most Ties	21	1954-55 (70)
Most Losses	47	1961-62 (70)
Most Goals	399	1970-71 (78)
Most Goals Against	306	1961-62 (70)
Fewest Points	38	1961-62 (70)
Fewest Wins	14	1962-63 (70)
Fewest Ties	5	1972-73 (78)
Fewest Losses	13	1971-72 (78)
Fewest Goals	147	1955-56 (70)
Fewest Goals Against	172	1952-53 (70)

Longest Winning Streak

Over-all	14	Dec. 3/29-Jan. 9/30
Home	*20	Dec. 3/29-Mar. 18/30
Away	8	Feb. 17-Mar. 8/72; Mar. 15-Apr. 14/93

Longest Undefeated Streak

Over-all	23	Dec. 22/40-Feb. 23/41 (15 wins, 8 ties)
Home	27	Nov. 22/70-Mar. 20/71 (26 wins, 1 tie)
Away	15	Dec. 22/40-Mar. 16/41 (9 wins, 6 ties)

Longest Losing Streak

Over-all	11	Dec. 3/24-Jan. 5/25
Home	*11	Dec. 8/24-Feb. 17/25
Away	14	Dec. 27/64-Feb. 21/65

Longest Winless Streak

Over-all	20	Jan. 28-Mar. 11/62 (16 losses, 4 ties)
Home	11	Dec. 8/24-Feb. 17/25 (11 losses)
Away	14	Three times
Most Shutouts, Season	15	1927-28 (44)
Most PIM, Season	2,443	1987-88 (80)
Most Goals, Game	14	Jan. 21/45 (NYR 3 at Bos. 14)

Individual

Most Seasons	21	John Bucyk
Most Games	1,436	John Bucyk
Most Goals, Career	545	John Bucyk
Most Assists, Career	908	Ray Bourque
Most Points, Career	1,339	John Bucyk (545 goals, 794 assists)
Most PIM, Career	2,095	Terry O'Reilly
Most Shutouts, Career	74	Tiny Thompson

Longest Consecutive

Games Streak	418	John Bucyk (Jan. 23/69-Mar. 2/75)
Most Goals, Season	76	Phil Esposito (1970-71)
Most Assists, Season	102	Bobby Orr (1970-71)
Most Points, Season	152	Phil Esposito (1970-71) (76 goals, 76 assists)
Most PIM, Season	304	Jay Miller (1987-88)

Most Points, Defenseman

Season	*139	Bobby Orr (1970-71) (37 goals, 102 assists)

Most Points, Center

Season	152	Phil Esposito (1970-71) (76 goals, 76 assists)

Most Points, Right Wing

Season	105	Ken Hodge (1970-71) (43 goals, 62 assists) Ken Hodge (1973-74) (50 goals, 55 assists) Rick Middleton (1983-84) (47 goals, 58 assists)

Most Points, Left Wing

Season	116	John Bucyk (1970-71) (51 goals, 65 assists)

Most Points, Rookie

Season	102	Joe Juneau (1992-93) (32 goals, 70 assists)
Most Shutouts, Season	15	Hal Winkler (1927-28)
Most Goals, Game	4	Several players
Most Assists, Game	6	Ken Hodge (Feb. 9/71) Bobby Orr (Jan. 1/73)
Most Points, Game	7	Bobby Orr (Nov. 15/73) Phil Esposito (Dec. 19/74) Barry Pederson (Apr. 4/82) Cam Neely (Oct. 16/88)

* NHL Record.

All-time Record vs. Other Clubs

Regular Season

			At Home							On Road							Total				
	GP	W	L	T	GF	GA	PTS	GP	W	L	T	GF	GA	PTS	GP	W	L	T	GF	GA	PTS
Anaheim	1	1	0	0	5	3	2	1	0	0	1	1	1	1	2	1	0	1	6	4	3
Buffalo	83	48	24	11	341	253	107	84	29	41	14	263	316	72	167	77	65	25	604	569	179
Calgary	39	24	10	5	138	107	53	38	20	15	3	140	144	43	77	44	25	8	278	251	96
Chicago	276	159	85	32	1003	778	350	278	93	141	44	745	896	230	554	252	226	76	1748	1674	580
Dallas	53	38	6	9	239	125	85	53	33	13	11	198	145	69	106	67	19	20	437	270	154
Detroit	279	151	85	43	986	739	345	278	76	150	52	699	930	204	557	227	235	95	1685	1669	549
Edmonton	23	17	4	2	107	63	36	22	11	8	3	76	76	25	45	28	12	5	183	139	61
Florida	4	1	2	1	6	8	3	3	2	1	0	7	8	4	7	3	3	1	13	16	7
Hartford	57	40	12	5	232	150	85	55	24	24	7	199	193	55	112	64	36	12	431	343	140
Los Angeles	54	41	10	3	261	149	85	53	30	18	5	203	185	65	107	71	28	8	464	334	150
Montreal	311	144	114	53	924	840	341	310	86	179	45	720	1056	217	621	230	293	98	1644	1896	558
New Jersey	38	25	10	3	170	120	53	35	20	7	8	130	96	48	73	45	17	11	300	216	101
NY Islanders	41	23	9	9	161	115	55	43	23	16	4	148	136	50	84	46	25	13	309	251	105
NY Rangers	280	151	89	40	1016	781	342	284	107	123	54	797	863	268	564	258	212	94	1813	1644	610
Ottawa	9	9	0	0	48	25	18	7	7	0	0	32	13	14	16	16	0	0	80	38	32
Philadelphia	58	38	13	7	242	167	83	55	25	24	6	167	183	56	113	63	37	13	409	350	139
Pittsburgh	58	41	11	6	267	167	88	60	26	23	11	226	207	63	118	67	34	17	493	374	151
Quebec	55	29	18	8	223	174	66	57	33	18	6	252	208	72	112	62	36	14	475	382	138
St. Louis	51	33	11	7	225	138	73	52	22	21	9	181	163	53	103	55	32	16	406	301	126
San Jose	3	3	0	0	14	10	6	3	2	0	1	13	4	5	6	5	0	1	27	14	11
Tampa Bay	4	2	1	1	11	8	5	5	2	1	2	15	14	6	9	4	2	3	26	22	11
Toronto	280	151	82	47	924	749	349	280	86	147	47	728	953	219	560	237	229	94	1652	1702	568
Vancouver	43	35	4	4	194	96	74	44	22	14	8	187	149	52	87	57	18	12	381	245	126
Washington	38	23	10	5	158	107	51	37	19	10	8	141	112	46	75	42	20	13	299	219	97
Winnipeg	22	16	3	3	105	70	35	23	12	9	2	86	83	26	45	28	12	5	191	153	61
Defunct Clubs	164	112	39	13	525	306	237	164	79	67	18	496	440	176	328	191	106	31	1021	746	413
Totals	**2324**	**1355**	**652**	**317**	**8525**	**6248**	**3027**	**2324**	**885**	**1070**	**369**	**6850**	**7574**	**2139**	**4648**	**2240**	**1722**	**686**	**15375**	**13822**	**5166**

Calgary totals include Atlanta, 1972-73 to 1979-80. Dallas totals include Minnesota, 1967-68 to 1992-93.
New Jersey totals include Kansas City, 1974-75 to 1975-76, and Colorado, 1976-77 to 1981-82.

Playoffs

	Series	W	L	GP	W	L	T	GF	GA	Last Mtg.	Round	Result
Buffalo	6	5	1	33	19	14	0	132	113	1993	DSF	L 0-4
Chicago	6	5	1	22	16	5	1	97	63	1978	QF	W 4-0
Dallas	1	0	1	3	0	3	0	13	20	1981	PR	L 0-3
Detroit	7	4	3	33	19	14	0	96	98	1957	SF	W 4-1
Edmonton	2	0	2	9	1	8	0	20	41	1990	F	L 1-4
Hartford	2	2	0	13	8	5	0	24	17	1991	DSF	W 4-2
Los Angeles	2	2	0	13	8	5	0	56	38	1977	QF	W 4-2
Montreal	28	7	21	139	52	87	0	339	430	1994	CQF	W 4-3
New Jersey	3	1	2	18	7	11	0	52	55	1995	CQF	L 1-4
NY Islanders	2	0	2	11	3	8	0	35	49	1983	CF	L 2-4
NY Rangers	9	6	3	42	22	18	2	114	104	1973	QF	L 1-4
Philadelphia	4	2	2	20	11	9	0	60	57	1978	SF	W 4-1
Pittsburgh	4	2	2	19	9	10	0	62	67	1992	CF	L 0-4
Quebec	2	1	1	11	6	5	0	37	36	1983	DSF	W 3-1
St. Louis	2	2	0	8	4	4	0	48	15	1972	SF	W 4-0
Toronto	13	5	8	62	30	31	1	153	150	1974	QF	W 4-0
Washington	1	1	0	4	4	0	0	15	6	1990	CF	W 4-0
Defunct Clubs	3	1	2	11	4	5	2	20	20			
Totals	**97**	**46**	**51**	**471**	**227**	**238**	**6**	**1389**	**1400**			

Playoff Results 1995-91

Year	Round	Opponent	Result	GF	GA
1995	CQF	New Jersey	L 1-4	5	14
1994	CSF	New Jersey	L 2-4	17	22
	CQF	Montreal	W 4-3	22	20
1993	DSF	Buffalo	L 0-4	12	19
1992	CF	Pittsburgh	L 0-4	7	19
	DF	Montreal	W 4-0	14	8
	DSF	Buffalo	W 4-3	19	24
1991	CF	Pittsburgh	L 2-4	18	27
	DF	Montreal	W 4-3	18	18
	DSF	Hartford	W 4-2	24	17

Abbreviations: Round: F – Final;
CF – conference final; **CQF** – conference quarter-final;
CSF – conference semi-final; **DF** – division final;
DSF – division semi-final; **SF** – semi-final;
QF – quarter-final; **PR** – preliminary round.

1994-95 Results

Jan.	22		Philadelphia	4-1	16	Montreal	6-0
	23	at	NY Rangers	2-1	18	NY Islanders	4-3
	26		New Jersey	1-0	19	at New Jersey	3-4
	28	at	Philadelphia	1-2	22	at Quebec	2-6
	30		Florida	1-2	24	at Tampa Bay	4-3
Feb.	2		Ottawa	6-4	28	Philadelphia	5-1
	4		Hartford	5-4	30	at NY Islanders	3-2
	7		Montreal	7-4	Apr. 1	NY Rangers	2-3
	9		Quebec	3-4	2	at Washington	1-2
	11		Washington	1-1	6	Buffalo	1-1
	12	at	Buffalo	2-1	8	Tampa Bay	5-1
	14	at	Pittsburgh	3-5	9	at Buffalo	6-5
	17		Florida	5-4	12	Quebec	0-4
	18	at	Tampa Bay	1-3	14	at NY Rangers	3-5
	22	at	Hartford	1-2	15	at Montreal	3-5
	23	at	New Jersey	3-2	19	Buffalo	4-1
	25	at	Quebec	1-1	20	at Ottawa	6-5
	27	at	Ottawa	2-0	23	NY Rangers	5-4
Mar.	2		New Jersey	7-2	24	at NY Islanders	3-5
	4		Pittsburgh	3-4	26	Hartford	1-0
	5	at	Hartford	5-2	28	at Pittsburgh	1-4
	7		Washington	1-3	30	Pittsburgh	5-2
	9	at	Philadelphia	2-3	May 1	Ottawa	5-4
	11		Florida	0-2	3	at Montreal	4-2

Entry Draft
Selections 1995-81

1995
Pick
- 9 Kyle McLaren
- 21 Sean Brown
- 47 Paxton Schafer
- 73 Bill McCauley
- 99 Cameron Mann
- 151 Yevgeny Shaldybin
- 177 Per Johan Axelsson
- 203 Sergei Zhukov
- 229 Jonathan Murphy

1994
Pick
- 21 Evgeni Ryabchikov
- 47 Daniel Goneau
- 99 Eric Nickulas
- 125 Darren Wright
- 151 Andre Roy
- 177 Jeremy Schaefer
- 229 John Grahame
- 255 Neil Savary
- 281 Andrei Yakhanov

1993
Pick
- 25 Kevyn Adams
- 51 Matt Alvey
- 88 Charles Paquette
- 103 Shawn Bates
- 129 Andrei Sapozhnikov
- 155 Milt Mastad
- 181 Ryan Golden
- 207 Hal Gill
- 233 Joel Prpic
- 259 Joakim Persson

1992
Pick
- 16 Dmitri Kvartalnov
- 55 Sergei Zholtok
- 112 Scott Bailey
- 133 Jiri Dopita
- 136 Grigori Panteleev
- 184 Kurt Seher
- 208 Mattias Timander
- 232 Chris Crombie
- 256 Denis Chervyakov
- 257 Evgeny Pavlov

1991
Pick
- 18 Glen Murray
- 40 Jozef Stumpel
- 62 Marcel Cousineau
- 84 Brad Tiley
- 106 Mariusz Czerkawski
- 150 Gary Golczewski
- 172 John Moser
- 194 Daniel Hodge
- 216 Steve Norton
- 238 Stephen Lombardi
- 260 Torsten Kienass

1990
Pick
- 21 Bryan Smolinski
- 63 Cameron Stewart
- 84 Jerome Buckley
- 105 Mike Bales
- 126 Mark Woolf
- 147 Jim Mackey
- 168 John Gruden
- 189 Darren Wetherill
- 210 Dean Capuano
- 231 Andy Bezeau
- 252 Ted Miskolczi

1989
Pick
- 17 Shayne Stevenson
- 38 Mike Parson
- 57 Wes Walz
- 80 Jackson Penney
- 101 Mark Montanari
- 122 Stephen Foster
- 143 Otto Hascak
- 164 Rick Allain
- 185 James Lavish
- 206 Geoff Simpson
- 227 David Franzosa

1988
Pick
- 18 Robert Cimetta
- 60 Stephen Heinze
- 81 Joe Juneau
- 102 Daniel Murphy
- 123 Derek Geary
- 165 Mark Krys
- 186 Jon Rohloff
- 228 Eric Reisman
- 249 Doug Jones

1987
Pick
- 3 Glen Wesley
- 14 Stephane Quintal
- 56 Todd Lalonde
- 67 Darwin McPherson
- 77 Matt Delguidice
- 98 Ted Donato
- 119 Matt Glennon
- 140 Rob Cheevers
- 161 Chris Winnes
- 182 Paul Ohman
- 203 Casey Jones
- 224 Eric Lemarque
- 245 Sean Gorman

1986
Pick
- 13 Craig Janney
- 34 Pekka Tirkkonen
- 76 Dean Hall
- 97 Matt Pesklewis
- 118 Garth Premak
- 139 Paul Beraldo
- 160 Brian Ferreira
- 181 Jeff Flaherty
- 202 Greg Hawgood
- 223 Staffan Malmqvist
- 244 Joel Gardner

1985
Pick
- 31 Alain Cote
- 52 Bill Ranford
- 73 Jaime Kelly
- 94 Steve Moore
- 115 Gord Hynes
- 136 Per Martinelle
- 157 Randy Burridge
- 178 Gord Cruickshank
- 199 Dave Buda
- 210 Bob Beers
- 220 John Byce
- 241 Marc West

1984
Pick
- 19 Dave Pasin
- 40 Ray Podloski
- 61 Jeff Cornelius
- 82 Robert Joyce
- 103 Mike Bishop
- 124 Randy Oswald
- 145 Mark Thietke
- 166 Don Sweeney
- 186 Kevin Heffernan
- 207 J.D. Urbanic
- 227 Bill Kopecky
- 248 Jim Newhouse

1983
Pick
- 21 Nevin Markwart
- 42 Greg Johnston
- 62 Greg Puhalski
- 82 Alain Larochelle
- 102 Allen Pederson
- 122 Terry Taillefer
- 142 Ian Armstrong
- 162 Francois Olivier
- 182 Harri Laurilla
- 202 Paul Fitzsimmons
- 222 Norm Foster
- 242 Greg Murphy

1982
Pick
- 1 Gord Kluzak
- 22 Brian Curran
- 39 Lyndon Byers
- 60 Dave Reid
- 102 Bob Nicholson
- 123 Bob Sweeney
- 144 John Meulenbroeks
- 165 Tony Fiore
- 186 Doug Kostynski
- 207 Tony Gilliard
- 228 Tommy Lehmann
- 249 Bruno Campese

1981
Pick
- 14 Normand Leveille
- 35 Luc Dufour
- 77 Scott McLellan
- 98 Joe Mantione
- 119 Bruce Milton
- 140 Mats Thelin
- 161 Armel Parisee
- 182 Don Sylvestri
- 203 Richard Bourque

Club Directory

FleetCenter
Boston, Massachusetts 02114
Phone **617/624-1050**
FAX 617/523-7184
Capacity: 17,565

Executive
Owner and Governor	Jeremy M. Jacobs
Alternative Governor	Louis Jacobs
President, General Manager and Alternative Governor	Harry Sinden
Vice President	Tom Johnson
Assistant General Manager	Mike O'Connell
Sr. Assistant to the President	Nate Greenberg
General Counsel	Michael F. Wall
Director of Administration	Dale Hamilton
Assistant to the President	Joe Curnane
Administrative Assistant	Carol Gould
Receptionist	Karen Leonard

Coaching Staff
Coach	Steve Kasper
Assistant Coaches	Cap Raeder, Tim Watters
Coach, Providence Bruins	Bobby Francis
Coach, Charlotte Checkers	John Marks

Scouting Staff
Chief of Scouting	Gordie Clark
Director of Player Evaluation	Bart Bradley
Director of Development	Bob Tindall
Assistant Director of Scouting	Jim Morrison
Coordinator of Scouting Information	Jeff Gorton
Scouting Staff	Don Saatzer, Jean Ratelle, Scott Bradley, Scott McLellan, Svenake Svensson (Europe), Yuri Karmanov (CIS), Gerry Cheevers (Pro)

Communications Staff
Director of Media Relations	Heidi Holland
Media Relations Assistant	Rusty Ingram
Director of Community Relations, Marketing Services	Sue Byrne
Community Relations & Marketing Services Assistant	Brian Oates
Director of Alumni Community Relations	John Bucyk
Administrative Assistant, Alumni Office	Mal Viola

Medical and Training Staff
Athletic Trainer	Don Del Negro
Physical Therapist	Tim Trahant
Rehabilitation Consultant	Jim Kausek, AdvantageHEALTH Corp.
Equipment Manager	Ken Fleger
Assistant Equipment Manager	Keith Robinson
Team Physicians	Dr. Bertram Zarins, Dr. Ashby Moncure, Dr. John J. Boyle
Team Dentists	Dr. John Kelly and Dr. Bruce Donoff
Team Psychologist	Dr. Fred Neff

Ticketing and Finance Staff
Director of Ticket Operations	Matt Brennan
Assistant Director of Ticket Operations	Jim Foley
Ticket Office Assistants	Linda Bartlett, Justin Brennan
Controller	Bob Vogel
Accounting Manager	Richard McGlinchey
Accounts Payable	Barbara Johnson

Television and Radio
Broadcasters (UPN 38 WSBK-TV)	Fred Cusick and Derek Sanderson
Broadcasters (NESN)	Dale Arnold and Gord Kluzak
Broadcasters (Radio)	Bob Neumeier and Barry Pederson
TV Channels	New England Sports Network (NESN) and UPN38 WSBK-TV
Radio Station	WBZ (1030 AM) and Bruins Radio Network

General Manager

SINDEN, HARRY JAMES
President and General Manager, Boston Bruins.
Born in Collins Bay, Ont., September 14, 1932.

Harry Sinden never played a game in the NHL but stepped into the Bruins' organization with an impressive coaching background in minor professional hockey and his continued excellence has earned him a place in the Hockey Hall of Fame as one of the true builders in hockey history. In 1965-66 as playing-coach of Oklahoma City Blazers in the CPHL, Sinden led the club to second place in the regular standings and then to eight straight playoff victories for the Jack Adams Trophy. After five years in OHA Senior hockey — including 1958 with the IIHF World Amateur Champion Whitby Dunlops — Sinden became a playing-coach in the old Eastern Professional League and its successor, the Central Professional League.

Under his guidance, the Bruins of 1967-68 made the playoffs for the first time in nine seasons, finishing third in the East Division, and were nosed out of first place in 1968-69 by Montreal. In 1969-70, Sinden led the Bruins to their first Stanley Cup win since 1940-41.

The following season he went into private business but returned to the hockey scene in the summer of 1972 when he was appointed coach of Team Canada. He molded that group of NHL stars into a powerful unit and led them into an exciting eight-game series against the Soviet national team in September of 1972. Team Canada emerged the winner by a narrow margin with a record of four wins, three losses and one tie.

Sinden then returned to the Bruins organization early in the 1972-73 season. Sinden last took over as the Bruins' coach in February 1985, after replacing Gerry Cheevers. Boston finished 11-10-3 with Sinden behind the bench before being defeated by Montreal in five games in the Adams Division semi-finals.

NHL Coaching Record

Season	Team		Regular Season					Playoffs			
		Games	W	L	T	%	Games	W	L	%
1966-67	Boston	70	17	43	10	.314				
1967-68	Boston	74	37	27	10	.568	4	0	4	.000
1968-69	Boston	76	42	18	16	.658	10	6	4	.600
1969-70	Boston	76	40	17	19	.651	14	12	2	.857*
1979-80	Boston	10	4	6	0	.400	9	4	5	.444
1984-85	Boston	24	11	10	3	.521	5	2	3	.400
	NHL Totals	**330**	**151**	**121**	**58**	**.545**	**42**	**24**	**18**	**.571**

* Stanley Cup win.

Coach

KASPER, STEVE
Coach, Boston Bruins. Born in Montreal, Que., September 28, 1961.

Steve Kasper was named as the Bruins head coach on May 25, 1995. He became the Bruins' 21st head coach and enters this season as the NHL's youngest head coach.

Kasper, 34, began his coaching career as an assistant coach with the Bruins during the 1993-94 season. On July 22, 1994, he was named as head coach of Boston's American Hockey League affiliate in Providence and in 1994-95 he led the AHL Bruins to fifth place overall in the AHL standings, with a 39-30-11 record. His club set team records for fewest losses, fewest goals against and longest win streak during the regular season and also set a club record for most playoff victories.

A native of Montreal, Kasper joined the coaching ranks following a 13-year playing career during which he earned a reputation as one of the top defensive forwards in the league. He was drafted by the Bruins as their third pick, 81st overall, in the 1980 NHL Entry Draft following a junior career in the Quebec Major Junior Hockey League. He played eight-plus seasons in a Bruins uniform, winning the Selke Trophy as the league's top defensive forward in 1981-82, and enjoyed his best offensive NHL season with 26 goals and 70 points in 1987-88 as the Bruins advanced to the Stanley Cup finals. He went to Los Angeles in a January, 1989 trade for Bobby Carpenter and played his final four-plus NHL seasons with Los Angeles, Philadelphia and Tampa Bay before retiring as a player at the conclusion of the 1992-93 season. Kasper and his wife, Kathy, reside in North Andover with their two sons, Jordan and Michael.

Coaching Record

Season	Team		Regular Season					Playoffs			
		Games	W	L	T	%	Games	W	L	%
1994-95	Providence (AHL)	80	39	30	11	.550	13	6	7	.460

Buffalo Sabres

1994-95 Results: 22W-19L-7T 51PTS. Fourth, Northeast Division

Schedule

Oct.	Sat.	7	at Ottawa	Fri.	12	at Calgary
	Mon.	9	at Boston*	Sat.	13	at Edmonton
	Fri.	13	Anaheim	Wed.	17	Pittsburgh
	Sun.	15	New Jersey	Wed.	24	Hartford
	Wed.	18	Edmonton	Fri.	26	at Washington
	Fri.	20	NY Rangers	Sat.	27	at Florida
	Sun.	22	St. Louis	Tues.	30	at NY Islanders
	Tues.	24	at Dallas	Wed.	31	Florida
	Fri.	27	at Colorado	**Feb.** Sat.	3	at Boston*
	Sun.	29	at Chicago	Sun.	4	Tampa Bay*
Nov.	Wed.	1	Detroit	Wed.	7	Boston
	Fri.	3	Pittsburgh	Thur.	8	at Philadelphia
	Sun.	5	Winnipeg	Sat.	10	at Toronto
	Wed.	8	San Jose	Wed.	14	Los Angeles
	Sat.	11	at Florida	Fri.	16	New Jersey
	Sun.	12	at Tampa Bay	Sat.	17	at Hartford
	Wed.	15	Dallas	Wed.	21	Pittsburgh
	Sat.	18	at New Jersey*	Fri.	23	Philadelphia
	Sun.	19	Ottawa	Sun.	25	Florida
	Fri.	24	NY Islanders	Wed.	28	at Ottawa
	Sat.	25	at Pittsburgh	**Mar.** Fri.	1	at NY Rangers
	Mon.	27	at St. Louis	Sun.	3	Vancouver*
	Wed.	29	at NY Rangers	Wed.	6	at Vancouver
Dec.	Fri.	1	Hartford	Fri.	8	at Anaheim
	Sat.	2	at Boston	Sun.	10	at San Jose*
	Thur.	7	at Philadelphia	Wed.	13	at Los Angeles
	Fri.	8	Washington	Fri.	15	Calgary
	Sun.	10	Tampa Bay	Sat.	16	at Hartford
	Wed.	13	Colorado	Mon.	18	at Montreal
	Fri.	15	NY Rangers	Fri.	22	Montreal
	Sat.	16	at New Jersey	Sat.	23	at Pittsburgh
	Wed.	20	Montreal	Wed.	27	at Detroit
	Fri.	22	Boston	Fri.	29	Philadelphia
	Sat.	23	at Ottawa	Sun.	31	Boston*
	Tues.	26	at Pittsburgh	**Apr.** Mon.	1	at Montreal
	Wed.	27	Ottawa	Wed.	3	Washington
	Fri.	29	Chicago	Fri.	5	at Tampa Bay
	Sun.	31	NY Islanders	Sat.	6	at NY Islanders
Jan.	Fri.	5	Toronto	Wed.	10	Ottawa
	Sat.	6	at Montreal	Sat.	13	at Washington
	Wed.	10	at Winnipeg	Sun.	14	Hartford

* Denotes afternoon game.

Home Starting Times:
Wednesdays and Fridays . . . . 7:35 p.m.
Sundays. 7:05 p.m.
Matinees . . . . 3:05 p.m.
Except Sun. Apr. 14. . . . . 6:05 p.m.

Franchise date: May 22, 1970

EASTERN NHL CONFERENCE

NORTHEAST DIVISION

26th NHL Season

An 11-year NHL veteran, Doug Bodger finished second among Buffalo defensemen in scoring in 1994-95, collecting 20 points in 44 games.

Year-by-Year Record

		Home			Road			Overall							
Season	GP	W	L	T	W	L	T	W	L	T	GF	GA	Pts.	Finished		Playoff Result
1994-95	48	15	8	1	7	11	6	22	19	7	130	119	51	4th,	Northeast Div.	Lost Conf. Quarter-Final
1993-94	84	22	17	3	21	15	6	43	32	9	282	218	95	4th,	Northeast Div.	Lost Conf. Quarter-Final
1992-93	84	25	15	2	13	21	8	38	36	10	335	297	86	4th,	Adams Div.	Lost Div. Final
1991-92	80	22	13	5	9	24	7	31	37	12	289	299	74	3rd,	Adams Div.	Lost Div. Semi-Final
1990-91	80	15	13	12	16	17	7	31	30	19	292	278	81	3rd,	Adams Div.	Lost Div. Semi-Final
1989-90	80	27	11	2	18	16	6	45	27	8	286	248	98	2nd,	Adams Div.	Lost Div. Semi-Final
1988-89	80	25	12	3	13	23	4	38	35	7	291	299	83	3rd,	Adams Div.	Lost Div. Semi-Final
1987-88	80	19	14	7	18	18	4	37	32	11	283	305	85	3rd,	Adams Div.	Lost Div. Semi-Final
1986-87	80	18	18	4	10	26	4	28	44	8	280	308	64	5th,	Adams Div.	Out of Playoffs
1985-86	80	23	16	1	14	21	5	37	37	6	296	291	80	5th,	Adams Div.	Out of Playoffs
1984-85	80	23	10	7	15	18	7	38	28	14	290	237	90	3rd,	Adams Div.	Lost Div. Semi-Final
1983-84	80	25	9	6	23	16	1	48	25	7	315	257	103	2nd,	Adams Div.	Lost Div. Semi-Final
1982-83	80	25	7	8	13	22	5	38	29	13	318	285	89	3rd,	Adams Div.	Lost Div. Final
1981-82	80	23	8	9	16	18	6	39	26	15	307	273	93	3rd,	Adams Div.	Lost Div. Semi-Final
1980-81	80	21	7	12	18	13	9	39	20	21	327	250	99	1st,	Adams Div.	Lost Quarter-Final
1979-80	80	27	5	8	20	12	8	47	17	16	318	201	110	1st,	Adams Div.	Lost Semi-Final
1978-79	80	19	13	8	17	15	8	36	28	16	280	263	88	2nd,	Adams Div.	Lost Prelim. Round
1977-78	80	25	7	8	19	12	9	44	19	17	288	215	105	2nd,	Adams Div.	Lost Quarter-Final
1976-77	80	27	8	5	21	16	3	48	24	8	301	220	104	2nd,	Adams Div.	Lost Quarter-Final
1975-76	80	28	7	5	18	14	8	46	21	13	339	240	105	2nd,	Adams Div.	Lost Quarter-Final
1974-75	80	28	6	6	21	10	9	49	16	15	354	240	113	1st,	Adams Div.	Lost Final
1973-74	78	23	10	6	9	24	6	32	34	12	242	250	76	5th,	East Div.	Out of Playoffs
1972-73	78	30	6	3	7	21	11	37	27	14	257	219	88	4th,	East Div.	Lost Quarter-Final
1971-72	78	11	19	9	5	24	10	16	43	19	203	289	51	6th,	East Div.	Out of Playoffs

1995-96 Player Personnel

FORWARDS	HT	WT	S	Place of Birth	Date	1994-95 Club
AMBROZIAK, Peter	6-0	206	L	Toronto, Ont.	9/15/71	Rochester-Buffalo
AUDETTE, Donald	5-8	175	R	Laval, Que.	9/23/69	Buffalo
BARNABY, Matthew	6-0	170	L	Ottawa, Ont.	5/4/73	Rochester-Buffalo
BARRIE, Mike	6-1	170	R	Kelowna, B.C.	3/16/74	Rochester-South Carolina
BIENVENUE, Daniel	6-0	195	L	Val d'Or, Que.	6/10/77	Val d'Or
BROWN, Curtis	6-0	182	L	Unity, Sask.	2/12/76	Moose Jaw-Buffalo
DAVIDSON, Matt	6-2	190	R	Flin Flon, Man.	8/9/77	Portland (WHL)
DAWE, Jason	5-10	195	L	North York, Ont.	5/29/73	Rochester-Buffalo
DUTIAUME, Mark	6-0	200	L	Winnipeg, Man.	1/31/77	Brandon
HANNAN, Dave	5-10	180	L	Sudbury, Ont.	11/26/61	Buffalo
HOLZINGER, Brian	5-11	180	R	Parma, OH	10/10/72	Bowling Green-Buffalo
KHMYLEV, Yuri	6-1	189	R	Moscow, USSR	8/9/64	Soviet Wings-Buffalo
LaFONTAINE, Pat	5-10	180	R	St. Louis, MO	2/22/65	Buffalo
MAY, Brad	6-1	210	L	Toronto, Ont.	11/29/71	Buffalo
MOORE, Barrie	5-11	175	L	London, Ont.	5/22/75	Sudbury
NICHOL, Scott	5-8	160	R	Edmonton, Alta.	12/31/74	Rochester
PEARSON, Scott	6-1	205	L	Cornwall, Ont.	12/19/69	Edmonton-Buffalo
PECA, Mike	5-11	180	R	Toronto, Ont.	3/26/74	Syracuse-Vancouver
PHILPOTT, Ethan	6-4	230	R	Rochester, MN	2/11/75	Des Moines
PLANTE, Derek	5-11	180	L	Cloquet, MN	1/17/71	Buffalo
POLAK, Mark	6-0	188	R	Edmonton, Alta.	5/16/76	Medicine Hat
PRIMEAU, Wayne	6-3	193	L	Scarborough, Ont.	6/4/76	Owen Sound-Buffalo
RAY, Rob	6-0	203	L	Belleville, Ont.	6/8/68	Buffalo
RUSHFORTH, Paul	6-0	189	R	Prince George, B.C.	4/22/74	South Carolina-Rochester
SUNDERLAND, Mathieu	6-4	192	R	Quebec City, Que.	11/30/76	Drummondville
SWEENEY, Bob	6-3	200	R	Concord, MA	1/25/64	Buffalo
VOLKOV, Mikhail	5-10	174	R	Voronezh, USSR	3/9/72	Rochester
WARD, Dixon	6-0	200	R	Leduc, Alta.	9/23/68	Tor-St.J.-Det (IHL)
WEBB, Steve	5-11	205	R	Peterborough, Ont.	4/30/75	Peterborough
WESTERBY, Bob	6-1	195	L	Kelowna, B.C.	10/29/75	Kamloops
DEFENSEMEN						
ASTLEY, Mark	5-11	185	L	Calgary, Alta.	3/30/69	Rochester-Buffalo
BENAZIC, Cal	6-3	187	L	Mackenzie, B.C.	9/29/75	Medicine Hat-Rochester
BODGER, Doug	6-2	213	L	Chemainus, B.C.	6/18/66	Buffalo
COOPER, David	6-2	204	L	Ottawa, Ont.	11/2/73	Rochester-South Carolina
GALLEY, Garry	6-0	204	L	Montreal, Que.	4/16/63	Philadelphia-Buffalo
HNIDY, Shane	6-1	200	R	Neepawa, Man.	11/8/75	Prince Albert
HOUDA, Doug	6-2	190	R	Blairmore, Alta.	6/3/66	Buffalo
HUDDY, Charlie	6-0	210	L	Oshawa, Ont.	6/2/59	Los Angeles-Buffalo
JENNINGS, Grant	6-3	210	L	Hudson Bay, Sask.	5/5/65	Pittsburgh-Toronto
KLIMENTJEV, Sergei	5-11	200	L	Kiev, USSR	4/5/75	Medicine Hat-Rochester
McKEE, Jay	6-2	175	L	Kingston, Ont.	9/8/77	Niagara Falls
MELANSON, Dean	5-11	211	R	Antigonish, N.S.	11/19/73	Rochester-Buffalo
MENHART, Marian	6-3	220	L	Most, Czech.	2/14/77	Litvinov
MILLAR, Craig	6-2	200	L	Winnipeg, Man.	7/12/76	Swift Current
MUNI, Craig	6-3	208	L	Toronto, Ont.	7/19/62	Buffalo
NDUR, Rumun	6-2	200	L	Zaria, Nigeria	7/7/75	Guelph
POPP, Kevin	6-1	198	L	Surrey, B.C.	2/26/76	Seattle
SMEHLIK, Richard	6-3	208	L	Ostrava, Czech.	1/23/70	Vitkovice-Buffalo
WILSON, Mike	6-4	195	L	Brampton, Ont.	2/26/75	Sudbury
WRIGHT, Shayne	6-0	189	L	Welland, Ont.	6/30/75	Owen Sound
ZHITNIK, Alexei	5-11	190	L	Kiev, USSR	10/10/72	Los Angeles-Buffalo

GOALTENDERS	HT	WT	C	Place of Birth	Date	1994-95 Club
BIRON, Martin	6-1	154	L	Lac St. Charles, Que.	8/15/77	Beauport
DAVIS, Chris	6-3	177	L	Calgary, Alta.	12/1/74	Alaska-Anch.
HASEK, Dominik	5-11	168	L	Pardubice, Czech.	1/29/65	Pardubice-Buffalo
SHIELDS, Steve	6-3	210	L	Toronto, Ont.	7/19/72	Rochester-South Carolina
STAUBER, Robb	5-11	180	L	Duluth, MN	11/25/67	Los Angeles-Buffalo
TREFILOV, Andrei	6-0	180	L	Kirovo-Chepetsk, USSR	8/31/69	Calgary-Saint John

Coach

NOLAN, TED
Coach, Buffalo Sabres. Born in Sault Ste. Marie, Ont., April 7, 1958.

Fans looking at the Buffalo bench this season have a new face to look at in Ted Nolan. Only, he'll be standing behind the bench, not sitting on it. Nolan was named the 14th person in team history to coach the Sabres when general manager John Muckler made the July 18 announcement. The move for Nolan came just 13 months after having been named as an assistant coach with the Hartford Whalers.

It comes as no surprise that just over a year after Nolan got his first position on an NHL coaching staff he already secures his first head coaching job. The 37-year old built a successful resume in junior hockey, guiding the 1992-93 Sault Ste. Marie Greyhounds of the Ontario Hockey League to the Memorial Cup championship, after having taken that team to the OHL title the two years prior.

An Ojibway Indian, he is no stranger to the NHL however, or the Sabres' organization for that matter. Nolan played 78 NHL games over the course of five seasons with Detroit and Pittsburgh from 1981-82 to 1985-86 after the Red Wings had made him their seventh draft choice (78th overall) in 1978. In between these two cities, Theodore John (Ted) Nolan had ties to Buffalo when he was signed as a free agent on March 7, 1985 by the Sabres, who sold his rights to the Penguins just over six months later. He also spent the entire 1984-85 season as a player with Rochester, being named team captain at the halfway mark of the season. His AHL days also included a Calder Cup championship while playing for Adirondack. In the final year of his NHL playing career ('85-'86), he played in Pittsburgh with current Sabres Doug Bodger and Dave Hannan, as well as Penguin star Mario Lemieux.

One of 12 children (he has six brothers and five sisters), Ted is married to Sandra. They have two children, sons Brandon and Jordan.

Coaching Record

		Regular Season					Playoffs			
Season	Team	Games	W	L	T	%	Games	W	L	%
1988-89	S.S. Marie (OHL)	38	12	25	1	.329	....	....	....	....
1989-90	S.S. Marie (OHL)	66	18	42	6	.318	....	....	....	....
1990-91	S.S. Marie (OHL)	66	42	21	3	.659	14	12	2	.857
1991-92	S.S. Marie (OHL)	66	41	19	6	.667	19	12	7	.632
1992-93	S.S. Marie (OHL)	66	38	23	5	.614	18	13	5	.722
1993-94	S.S. Marie (OHL)	66	35	24	7	.583	14	10	4	.714

1994-95 Scoring

* – rookie

Regular Season

Pos	#	Player	Team	GP	G	A	Pts	+/–	PIM	PP	SH	GW	GT	S	%
R	89	Alexander Mogilny	BUF	44	19	28	47	0	36	12	0	2	1	148	12.8
R	28	Donald Audette	BUF	46	24	13	37	–3	27	13	0	7	0	124	19.4
D	3	Garry Galley	PHI	33	2	20	22	0	20	1	0	0	0	66	3.0
			BUF	14	1	9	10	4	10	1	0	0	0	31	3.2
			TOTAL	47	3	29	32	4	30	2	0	0	0	97	3.1
C	16	Pat LaFontaine	BUF	22	12	15	27	2	4	6	1	3	1	54	22.2
L	13	Yuri Khmylev	BUF	48	8	17	25	8	14	2	1	1	0	71	11.3
C	26	Derek Plante	BUF	47	3	19	22	–4	12	2	0	0	0	94	3.2
D	8	Doug Bodger	BUF	44	3	17	20	–3	47	2	0	0	0	87	3.4
R	18	Wayne Presley	BUF	46	14	5	19	5	41	0	5	2	0	90	15.6
C	10	Dale Hawerchuk	BUF	23	5	11	16	–2	2	2	0	2	0	56	8.9
C	14	Dave Hannan	BUF	42	4	12	16	3	32	0	2	0	0	36	11.1
D	44	Alexei Zhitnik	L.A.	11	2	5	7	–3	27	2	0	0	0	33	6.1
			BUF	21	2	5	7	–3	34	1	0	0	0	33	6.1
			TOTAL	32	4	10	14	–6	61	3	0	0	0	66	6.1
L	43	Jason Dawe	BUF	42	7	4	11	–6	19	0	1	2	0	51	13.7
L	17	Craig Simpson	BUF	24	4	7	11	–5	26	1	0	0	1	20	20.0
D	42	Richard Smehlik	BUF	39	4	7	11	5	46	0	1	1	0	49	8.2
C	20	Bob Sweeney	BUF	45	5	4	9	–6	18	1	2	0	0	47	10.6
L	29	Scott Pearson	EDM	28	1	4	5	–11	54	0	0	0	0	21	4.8
			BUF	14	2	1	3	–3	20	0	0	0	0	19	10.5
			TOTAL	42	3	5	8	–14	74	0	0	0	0	40	7.5
D	22	Charlie Huddy	L.A.	9	0	1	1	–6	6	0	0	0	0	11	0.0
			BUF	32	2	4	6	–1	36	1	0	0	0	40	5.0
			TOTAL	41	2	5	7	–7	42	1	0	0	0	51	3.9
L	27	Brad May	BUF	33	3	3	6	5	87	1	0	0	0	42	7.1
D	5	Craig Muni	BUF	40	0	6	6	–4	36	0	0	0	0	32	0.0
D	33 *	Mark Astley	BUF	14	2	1	3	–2	12	0	0	0	0	21	9.5
D	6	Doug Houda	BUF	28	1	2	3	1	68	0	0	0	0	21	4.8
C	19 *	Brian Holzinger	BUF	4	0	3	3	2	0	0	0	0	0	3	0.0
L	32	Rob Ray	BUF	47	0	3	3	–4	173	0	0	0	0	7	0.0
C	37 *	Curtis Brown	BUF	1	1	1	2	2	2	0	0	0	0	4	25.0
L	36	Matthew Barnaby	BUF	23	1	1	2	–2	116	0	0	0	0	27	3.7
R	9 *	Viktor Gordiouk	BUF	10	0	2	2	–3	0	0	0	0	0	10	0.0
C	76 *	Wayne Primeau	BUF	1	1	0	1	–2	0	0	0	1	0	2	50.0
L	12 *	Peter Ambroziak	BUF	12	0	1	1	–1	0	0	0	0	0	3	0.0
L	44 *	Doug MacDonald	BUF	2	0	0	0	–1	0	0	0	0	0	0	0.0
D	3 *	Dean Melanson	BUF	5	0	0	0	–1	4	0	0	0	0	1	0.0
G	35	Robb Stauber	L.A.	1	0	0	0	0	0	0	0	0	0	0	0.0
			BUF	6	0	0	0	0	0	0	0	0	0	0	0.0

Playoffs

Pos	#	Player	Team	GP	G	A	Pts	+/–	PIM	PP	SH	GW	OT	S	%
R	89	Alexander Mogilny	BUF	5	3	2	5	–6	2	0	0	0	0	18	16.7
R	18	Wayne Presley	BUF	5	3	1	4	3	8	0	1	1	0	14	21.4
C	16	Pat Lafontaine	BUF	5	2	2	4	–2	2	1	0	0	0	11	18.2
D	8	Doug Bodger	BUF	5	0	4	4	1	0	0	0	0	0	12	0.0
C	19 *	Brian Holzinger	BUF	4	2	1	3	–3	2	1	0	0	0	6	33.3
L	43	Jason Dawe	BUF	5	2	1	3	–2	6	0	0	0	0	10	20.0
D	3	Garry Galley	BUF	5	0	3	3	–3	4	0	0	0	0	12	0.0
R	28	Donald Audette	BUF	5	1	1	2	–2	4	1	0	0	0	12	8.3
C	14	Dave Hannan	BUF	5	0	2	2	2	2	0	0	0	0	1	0.0
D	5	Craig Muni	BUF	5	0	1	1	0	2	0	0	0	0	3	0.0
D	44	Alexei Zhitnik	BUF	5	0	1	1	–7	14	0	0	0	0	12	0.0
L	13	Yuri Khmylev	BUF	5	0	1	1	–1	8	0	0	0	0	7	0.0
C	10	Dale Hawerchuk	BUF	2	0	0	0	–1	0	0	0	0	0	3	0.0
D	33 *	Mark Astley	BUF	2	0	0	0	–2	0	0	0	0	0	0	0.0
D	22	Charlie Huddy	BUF	3	0	0	0	1	0	0	0	0	0	5	0.0
L	27	Brad May	BUF	4	0	0	0	0	2	0	0	0	0	4	0.0
G	39	Dominik Hasek	BUF	5	0	0	0	0	0	0	0	0	0	0	0.0
L	29	Scott Pearson	BUF	5	0	0	0	–1	4	0	0	0	0	9	0.0
L	32	Rob Ray	BUF	5	0	0	0	0	14	0	0	0	0	0	0.0
C	20	Bob Sweeney	BUF	5	0	0	0	–1	4	0	0	0	0	5	0.0
D	42	Richard Smehlik	BUF	5	0	0	0	–1	2	0	0	0	0	3	0.0

Goaltending

No.	Goaltender	GPI	Mins	Avg	W	L	EN	SO	GA	SA	S%
39	Dominik Hasek	5	309	3.50	1	4	0	0	18	131	.863
	Totals	**5**	**310**	**3.48**	**1**	**4**	**0**	**0**	**18**	**131**	**.863**

General Manager

MUCKLER, JOHN
General Manager, Buffalo Sabres. Born in Midland, Ont., April 3, 1934.

In 1995-96, Muckler enters his fifth season with the Sabres. He was hired as the director of hockey operations in the summer of 1991 and also took over as coach in December of that season. His first full season behind the Buffalo bench came in 1992-93 when he helped lead Buffalo to its first appearance in the second round of the playoffs since 1983. John added g.m.'s duties to his job in the summer of 1993.

In two seasons as head coach in Edmonton prior to joining the Sabres, Muckler led the Oilers to the Stanley Cup in 1989-90, and to the Conference Finals in 1990-91.

NHL Coaching Record

		Regular Season					Playoffs			
Season	Team	Games	W	L	T	%	Games	W	L	%
1968-69	Minnesota	35	6	23	6	.257	....	....	....	....
1989-90	Edmonton	80	38	28	14	.563	22	16	6	.727*
1990-91	Edmonton	80	37	37	6	.500	18	9	9	.500
1991-92	Buffalo	52	22	22	8	.500	7	3	4	.429
1992-93	Buffalo	84	38	36	10	.512	8	4	4	.500
1993-94	Buffalo	84	43	32	9	.565	7	3	4	.429
1994-95	Buffalo	48	22	19	7	.531	5	1	4	.200
	NHL Totals	**463**	**206**	**197**	**60**	**.510**	**67**	**36**	**31**	**.537**

* Won Stanley Cup.

Club Records

Team

(Figures in brackets for season records are games played; records for fewest points, wins, ties, losses, goals, goals against are for 70 or more games)

Most Points	**113**	1974-75 (80)
Most Wins	**49**	1974-75 (80)
Most Ties	**21**	1980-81 (80)
Most Losses	**44**	1986-87 (80)
Most Goals	**354**	1974-75 (80)
Most Goals Against	**308**	1986-87 (80)
Fewest Points	**51**	1971-72 (78)
Fewest Wins	**16**	1971-72 (78)
Fewest Ties	**6**	1985-86 (80)
Fewest Losses	**16**	1974-75 (80)
Fewest Goals	**203**	1971-72 (78)
Fewest Goals Against	**201**	1979-80 (80)
Longest Winning Streak		
Over-all	**10**	Jan. 4-23/84
Home	**12**	Nov. 12/72-Jan. 7/73; Oct. 13-Dec. 10/89
Away	***10**	Dec. 10/83-Jan. 23/84
Longest Undefeated Streak		
Over-all	**14**	March 6-April 6/80 (8 wins, 6 ties)
Home	**21**	Oct. 8/72-Jan. 7/73 (18 wins, 3 ties)
Away	***10**	Dec. 10/83-Jan. 23/84 (10 wins)
Longest Losing Streak		
Over-all	**7**	Oct. 25-Nov. 8/70; Apr. 3-15/93; Oct. 9-22/93
Home	**6**	Oct. 10-Nov. 10/93
Away	**7**	Oct. 14-Nov. 7/70; Feb. 6-27/71
Longest Winless Streak		
Over-all	**12**	Nov. 23-Dec. 20/91 (8 losses, 4 ties)
Home	**12**	Jan. 27-Mar. 10/91 (7 losses, 5 ties)
Away	**23**	Oct. 30/71-Feb. 19/72 (15 losses, 8 ties)
Most Shutouts, Season	**9**	1993-94 (84)
Most PIM, Season	**2,712**	1991-92 (80)
Most Goals, Game	**14**	Jan. 21/75 (Wsh. 2 at Buf. 14) Mar. 19/81 (Tor. 4 at Buf. 14)

Individual

Most Seasons	**17**	Gilbert Perreault
Most Games	**1,191**	Gilbert Perreault
Most Goals, Career	**512**	Gilbert Perreault
Most Assists, Career	**814**	Gilbert Perreault
Most Points, Career	**1,326**	Gilbert Perreault
Most PIM, Career	**1,459**	Rob Ray
Most Shutouts, Career	**14**	Don Edwards
Longest Consecutive Games Streak	**776**	Craig Ramsay (Mar. 27/73-Feb. 10/83)
Most Goals, Season	**76**	Alexander Mogilny (1992-93)
Most Assists, Season	**95**	Pat LaFontaine (1992-93)
Most Points, Season	**148**	Pat LaFontaine (1992-93) (53 goals, 95 assists)
Most PIM, Season	**354**	Rob Ray (1991-92)
Most Points, Defenseman Season	**81**	Phil Housley (1989-90) (21 goals, 60 assists)
Most Points, Center Season	**148**	Pat LaFontaine (1992-93) (53 goals, 95 assists)
Most Points, Right Wing Season	**127**	Alexander Mogilny (1992-93) (76 goals, 51 assists)
Most Points, Left Wing Season	**95**	Richard Martin (1974-75) (52 goals, 43 assists)
Most Points, Rookie Season	**74**	Richard Martin (1971-72) (44 goals, 30 assists)
Most Shutouts, Season	**7**	Dominik Hasek (1993-94)
Most Goals, Game	**5**	Dave Andreychuk (Feb. 6/86)
Most Assists, Game	**5**	Gilbert Perreault (Feb. 1/76; Mar. 9/80; Jan. 4/84) Dale Hawerchuk (Jan. 15/92); Pat LaFontaine (Dec. 31/92; Feb. 10/93)
Most Points, Game	**7**	Gilbert Perreault (Feb. 1/76)

* NHL Record.

Coaching History

"Punch" Imlach, 1970-71; "Punch" Imlach, Floyd Smith and Joe Crozier, 1971-72; Joe Crozier, 1972-73 to 1973-74; Floyd Smith, 1974-75 to 1976-77; Marcel Pronovost, 1977-78; Marcel Pronovost and Billy Inglis, 1978-79; Scotty Bowman, 1979-80; Roger Neilson, 1980-81; Jim Roberts and Scotty Bowman, 1981-82; Scotty Bowman 1982-83 to 1984-85; Jim Schoenfeld and Scotty Bowman, 1985-86; Scotty Bowman, Craig Ramsay and Ted Sator, 1986-87; Ted Sator, 1987-88 to 1988-89; Rick Dudley, 1989-90 to 1990-91; Rick Dudley and John Muckler, 1991-92; John Muckler, 1992-93 to 1994-95; Ted Nolan, 1995-96.

Captains' History

Floyd Smith, 1970-71; Gerry Meehan, 1971-72 to 1973-74; Gerry Meehan and Jim Schoenfeld, 1974-75; Jim Schoenfeld, 1975-76 to 1976-77; Danny Gare, 1977-78 to 1980-81; Danny Gare and Gil Perreault, 1981-82; Gil Perreault, 1982-83 to 1985-86; Gil Perreault and Lindy Ruff, 1986-87; Lindy Ruff, 1987-88; Lindy Ruff and Mike Foligno, 1988-89; Mike Foligno, 1989-90. Mike Foligno and Mike Ramsey, 1990-91; Mike Ramsey, 1991-92; Mike Ramsey and Pat LaFontaine, 1992-93; Pat LaFontaine and Alexander Mogilny, 1993-94; Pat LaFontaine, 1994-95 to date.

General Managers' History

George "Punch" Imlach, 1970-71 to 1977-78; John Anderson (acting), 1978-79; Scotty Bowman, 1979-80 to 1985-86; Scotty Bowman and Gerry Meehan, 1986-87; Gerry Meehan, 1987-88 to 1992-93; John Muckler, 1993-94 to date.

Retired Numbers

11	Gilbert Perreault	1970-1987

All-time Record vs. Other Clubs

Regular Season

	At Home							On Road							Total						
	GP	W	L	T	GF	GA	PTS	GP	W	L	T	GF	GA	PTS	GP	W	L	T	GF	GA	PTS
Anaheim	1	1	0	0	4	2	2	1	1	0	0	3	0	2	2	2	0	0	7	2	4
Boston	84	41	29	14	316	263	96	83	24	48	11	253	341	59	167	65	77	25	569	604	155
Calgary	38	22	12	4	160	115	48	38	15	13	10	133	137	40	76	37	25	14	293	252	88
Chicago	45	28	11	6	174	116	62	43	15	22	6	120	138	36	88	43	33	12	294	254	98
Dallas	45	23	12	10	168	124	56	46	20	20	6	144	144	46	91	43	32	16	312	268	102
Detroit	45	31	7	7	209	124	69	47	18	24	5	145	176	41	92	49	31	12	354	300	110
Edmonton	23	9	9	5	95	90	23	22	4	16	2	59	97	10	45	13	25	7	154	187	33
Florida	4	3	1	0	14	4	6	3	2	1	0	10	5	4	7	5	2	0	24	9	10
Hartford	56	30	19	7	236	182	67	58	29	20	9	184	173	67	114	59	39	16	420	355	134
Los Angeles	45	22	15	8	183	141	52	46	21	17	8	162	158	50	91	43	32	16	345	299	102
Montreal	79	38	23	18	250	222	94	79	21	48	10	234	328	52	158	59	71	28	484	550	146
New Jersey	36	26	6	4	166	110	56	36	20	9	7	139	112	47	72	46	15	11	305	222	103
NY Islanders	43	24	13	6	156	125	54	43	18	18	7	125	125	43	86	42	31	13	281	250	97
NY Rangers	50	30	14	6	226	166	66	48	15	22	11	132	168	41	98	45	36	17	358	334	107
Ottawa	7	7	0	0	39	10	14	9	5	2	2	36	21	12	16	12	2	2	75	31	26
Philadelphia	45	22	17	6	159	138	50	49	11	30	8	131	182	30	94	33	47	14	290	320	80
Pittsburgh	51	25	12	14	222	146	64	50	15	22	13	174	194	43	101	40	34	27	396	340	107
Quebec	56	32	16	8	226	182	72	56	18	28	10	178	213	46	112	50	44	18	404	395	118
St. Louis	44	28	12	4	183	138	60	43	11	26	6	111	165	28	87	39	38	10	294	303	88
San Jose	4	4	0	0	21	16	8	3	1	1	1	16	12	3	7	5	1	1	37	28	11
Tampa Bay	5	2	2	1	13	17	5	5	4	1	0	14	8	8	10	6	3	1	27	25	13
Toronto	50	31	16	3	212	145	65	49	23	18	8	183	152	54	99	54	34	11	395	297	119
Vancouver	45	23	14	8	164	130	54	44	13	21	10	146	168	36	89	36	35	18	310	298	90
Washington	38	28	6	4	167	99	60	38	22	9	7	148	107	51	76	50	15	11	315	206	111
Winnipeg	22	19	1	2	104	53	40	22	11	9	2	82	71	24	44	30	10	4	186	124	64
Defunct Clubs	23	13	5	5	94	63	31	23	12	8	3	97	76	27	46	25	13	8	191	139	58
Totals	**984**	**562**	**272**	**150**	**3961**	**2921**	**1274**	**984**	**369**	**453**	**162**	**3159**	**3471**	**900**	**1968**	**931**	**725**	**312**	**7120**	**6392**	**2174**

Calgary totals include Atlanta, 1972-73 to 1979-80. Dallas totals include Minnesota, 1970-71 to 1992-93.
New Jersey totals include Kansas City, 1974-75 to 1975-76, and Colorado, 1976-77 to 1981-82.

Playoffs

	Series	W	L	GP	W	L	T	GF	GA	Last Mtg.	Round	Result
Boston	6	1	5	33	14	19	0	113	132	1993	DSF	W 4-0
Chicago	2	2	0	9	8	1	0	36	17	1980	QF	W 4-0
Dallas	2	1	1	7	3	4	0	28	26	1981	QF	L 1-4
Montreal	6	2	4	31	13	18	0	94	114	1993	DF	L 0-4
New Jersey	1	0	1	7	3	4	0	14	14	1994	CQF	L 3-4
NY Islanders	3	0	3	16	4	12	0	45	59	1980	SF	L 2-4
NY Rangers	1	1	0	3	2	1	0	11	6	1978	PR	W 2-1
Philadelphia	3	0	3	16	4	12	0	36	53	1995	CQF	L 1-4
Pittsburgh	1	0	1	3	1	2	0	9	9	1979	PR	L 1-2
Quebec	2	0	2	8	2	6	0	27	35	1985	DSF	L 2-3
St. Louis	1	1	0	3	2	1	0	7	8	1976	PR	W 2-1
Vancouver	2	2	0	7	6	1	0	28	14	1981	PR	W 3-0
Totals	**30**	**10**	**20**	**143**	**62**	**81**	**0**	**448**	**480**			

Playoff Results 1995-91

Year	Round	Opponent	Result	GF	GA
1995	CQF	Philadelphia	L 1-4	13	18
1994	CQF	New Jersey	L 3-4	14	14
1993	DF	Montreal	L 0-4	12	16
	DSF	Boston	W 4-0	19	12
1992	DSF	Boston	L 3-4	24	19
1991	DSF	Montreal	L 2-4	24	29

Abbreviations: Round: F – Final; **CF** – conference final; **CQF** – conference quarter-final; **CSF** – conference semi-final; **DF** – division final; **DSF** – division semi-final; **SF** – semi-final; **QF** – quarter-final; **PR** – preliminary round.

1994-95 Results

Jan.	20	at	NY Rangers	2-1		18	at	Ottawa	3-4
	22	at	Tampa Bay	5-2		19		Tampa Bay	1-6
	25		New Jersey	2-1		21		Pittsburgh	2-3
	27		Quebec	3-7		24		Florida	3-0
	28	at	Ottawa	2-2		26	at	Philadelphia	1-3
	31	at	New Jersey	1-2		28		Quebec	5-3
Feb.	2	at	Washington	1-0		30		Ottawa	7-0
	4	at	Philadelphia	2-4	**Apr.**	1	at	NY Islanders	5-1
	5		Tampa Bay	2-1		4		Hartford	6-3
	7		Washington	2-1		6	at	Boston	1-1
	11	at	NY Islanders	1-2		8	at	Hartford	2-4
	12		Boston	1-2		9		Boston	5-6
	15		NY Rangers	1-2		12	at	NY Rangers	1-3
	19	at	Pittsburgh	3-3		14	at	Quebec	2-5
	22		NY Islanders	3-3		16		Ottawa	2-1
	25	at	Hartford	3-1		18		Hartford	1-2
	26		NY Rangers	2-4		19	at	Boston	1-4
Mar.	2		Pittsburgh	6-3		23		Philadelphia	4-2
	4	at	Quebec	1-1		24	at	Tampa Bay	3-1
	5		Montreal	4-1		26		Florida	5-0
	8	at	Montreal	2-2		28	at	Washington	1-5
	11	at	Pittsburgh	2-6		29	at	Montreal	3-3
	14	at	Florida	2-1	**May**	1		Montreal	2-0
	16		NY Islanders	6-3		3		New Jersey	5-4

Entry Draft
Selections 1995-81

1995 Pick		1993 Pick		1991 Pick		1989 Pick		1987 Pick		1985 Pick		1983 Pick		1982 Pick	
14	Jay McKee	38	Denis Tsygurov	13	Philippe Boucher	14	Kevin Haller	1	Pierre Turgeon	14	Calle Johansson	5	Tom Barrasso	6	Phil Housley
16	Martin Biron	64	Ethan Philpott	35	Jason Dawe	56	John (Scott) Thomas	22	Brad Miller	35	Benoit Hogue	10	Normand Lacombe	9	Paul Cyr
42	Mark Dutiaume	116	Richard Safarik	57	Jason Young	77	Doug MacDonald	53	Andrew MacVicar	56	Keith Gretzky	11	Adam Creighton	16	Dave Andreychuk
68	Mathieu Sunderland	142	Kevin Pozzo	72	Peter Ambroziak	98	Ken Sutton	84	John Bradley	77	Dave Moylan	31	John Tucker	26	Mike Anderson
94	Matt Davidson	168	Sergei Petrenko	101	Steve Shields	107	Bill Pye	85	David Pergola	98	Ken Priestlay	34	Richard Hajdu	30	Jens Johansson
111	Marian Menhart	194	Mike Barrie	123	Sean O'Donnell	119	Mike Barkley	106	Chris Marshall	119	Joe Reekie	74	Daren Puppa	68	Timo Jutila
119	Kevin Popp	220	Barrie Moore	124	Brian Holzinger	161	Derek Plante	127	Paul Flanagan	140	Petri Matikainen	94	Jayson Meyer	79	Jeff Hamilton
123	Daniel Bienvenue	246	Chris Davis	145	Chris Snell	183	Donald Audette	148	Sean Dooley	161	Trent Kaese	114	Jim Hofford	100	Bob Logan
172	Brian Scott	272	Scott Nichol	162	Jiri Kuntos	194	Mark Astley	153	Tim Roberts	182	Jiri Sejba	134	Christian Ruuttu	111	Jeff Parker
198	Mike Zanutto			189	Tony Iob	203	John Nelson	169	Grant Tkachuk	203	Boyd Sutton	154	Don McSween	121	Jacob Gustavsson
224	Rob Skrlac	**1992** Pick		211	Spencer Meany	224	Todd Henderson	190	Ian Herbers	224	Guy Larose	174	Tim Hoover	142	Allen Bishop
		11	David Cooper	233	Mikhail Volkov	245	Michael Bavis	211	David Littman	245	Ken Baumgartner	194	Mark Ferner	163	Claude Verret
1994 Pick		35	Jozef Cierny	255	Michael Smith			232	Allan MacIsaac			214	Uwe Krupp	184	Rob Norman
17	Wayne Primeau	59	Ondrej Steiner			**1988** Pick				**1984** Pick		234	Marc Hamelin	205	Mike Craig
43	Curtis Brown	80	Dean Melanson	**1990** Pick		13	Joel Savage	**1986** Pick		18	Mikael Andersson	235	Kermit Salfi	226	Jim Plankers
69	Rumun Ndur	83	Matthew Barnaby	14	Brad May	55	Darcy Loewen	5	Shawn Anderson	39	Doug Trapp				
121	Sergei Klimentjev	107	Markus Ketterer	82	Brian McCarthy	76	Keith E. Carney	26	Greg Brown	60	Ray Sheppard			**1981** Pick	
147	Cal Benazic	108	Yuri Khmylev	97	Richard Smehlik	89	Alexander Mogilny	47	Bob Corkum	81	Bob Halkidis			17	Jiri Dudacek
168	Steve Plouffe	131	Paul Rushforth	100	Todd Bojcun	97	Robert Ray	56	Kevin Kerr	102	Joey Rampton			38	Hannu Virta
173	Shane Hnidy	179	Dean Tiltgen	103	Brad Pascall	106	David Di Vita	68	David Baseggio	123	James Gasseau			59	Jim Aldred
176	Steve Webb	203	Todd Simon	142	Viktor Gordiyuk	118	Mike McLaughlin	89	Larry Rooney	144	Darcy Wakaluk			60	Colin Chisholm
199	Bob Westerby	227	Rick Kowalsky	166	Milan Nedoma	139	Mike Griffith	110	Miguel Baldris	165	Orvar Stambert			80	Jeff Eatough
225	Craig Millar	251	Chris Clancy	187	Jason Winch	160	Daniel Ruoho	131	Mike Hartman	206	Brian McKinnon			83	Anders Wikberg
251	Mark Polak			208	Sylvain Naud	181	Wade Flaherty	152	Francois Guay	226	Grant Delcourt			101	Mauri Eivola
277	Shayne Wright			229	Kenneth Martin	223	Thomas Nieman	173	Shawn Whitham	247	Sean Baker			122	Ali Butorac
				250	Brad Rubachuk	244	Robert Wallwork	194	Kenton Rein					143	Heikki Leime
								215	Troy Arndt					164	Gates Orlando
														185	Venci Sebek
														206	Warren Harper

Club Directory

Memorial Auditorium
Buffalo, NY 14202
Phone **716/856-7300**
Outside Buffalo: **800/333-PUCK**
Ticket Office: 716/856-8100
FAX 716/856-2104
Capacity: 16,230

Board of Directors
Chairman of the Board . . . . Seymour H. Knox, III
Vice-Chairman of the Board and Counsel . . . . Robert O. Swados
Vice-Chairman of the Board . . . . Robert E. Rich, Jr.
Treasurer . . . . Joseph T.J. Stewart
Board of Directors . . . . Edwin C. Andrews, Peter C. Andrews,
Niagara Frontier Hockey, LP. George L. Collins, Jr. M.D., William C. Cox, III,
  (includes above listed officers) John B. Fisher, George T. Gregory,
  John E. Houghton, Seymour H. Knox, IV,
  John J. Rigas, Michael J. Rigas, Richard W. Rupp,
  Howard T. Saperston, Jr., Paul A. Schoellkopf,
  George Strawbridge, Jr., William H. Weeks

Administration
President/CEO . . . . Douglas G. Moss
Assistant to the President . . . . Seymour H. Knox, IV
Senior Vice-President/Administration . . . . George Bergantz
Senior Vice-President/Legal and Business Affairs . . . . Kevin Billet
Vice-President/Finance and
  Chief Financial Officer . . . . Dan DiPofi
Vice-President/Sales and Marketing . . . . Jeff Eisenberg
Consultant . . . . Northrup R. Knox
Administrative Assistants:
  President . . . . Elaine Burzynski
  General Manager . . . .
  Administration . . . . Verna B. Wojcik
Receptionists . . . . Olive Anticola, Evelyn Battleson

Hockey Department
General Manager . . . . John Muckler
Head Coach . . . . Ted Nolan
Director of Player Personnel . . . . Don Luce
Director of Player Evaluation . . . . Larry Carriere
Associate Coach . . . . Don Lever
Assistant Coach . . . . Terry Martin
Goaltender Consultant . . . . Mitch Korn
Director of Scouting . . . . Rudy Migay
Scouting Staff . . . . Don Barrie, Jim Benning, Jack Bowman,
  Ross Mahoney, Paul Merritt, Mike Racicot,
  Gleb Tchistyakov

Training/Medical
Head Athletic Trainer . . . . Jim Pizzutelli
Strength and Conditioning Coach . . . . Doug McKenney
Trainer . . . . Rip Simonick
Equipment Supervisor . . . . George Babcock
Club Doctor . . . . John L. Butsch, M.D.
Orthopedic Consultant . . . . John Marzo, M.D.
Club Dentist . . . . Daniel Yustin, D.D.S., M.S.
Team Psychologist . . . . Max Offenberger, Ph.D. & Dan Smith, Ph.D.

Public Relations
Director of Public Relations . . . . Jeff Holbrook
Director of Information . . . . Bruce Wawrzyniak
Media Relations Assistant . . . . Gil Chorbajian

Sales & Marketing
Director of Ticket Operations . . . . John Sinclair
Ticket Administrators . . . . Paul Barker, Jennifer Glowny, Christopher
  Makowski, Rose Thompson
Director of Sales and Marketing/Suite and
  Club Seating . . . . Karen Marsch
Administrative Assistant . . . . Melinda Lucier
Manager of Telemarketing Operations . . . . Chris Barlow
Manager of Account Services . . . . Marc Morgan
Account Services Representatives . . . . Sue Smith, Mike Tout
Area Sales Managers . . . . Jeffrey Krebs, Jim Meissner, Gary Rabinowitz
Special Projects . . . . Dave Forman, Jr.
Director of Community Relations . . . . Ken Martin, Jr.
Administrative Assistant . . . . Barb Blendowski
Director of Alumni Relations . . . . Larry Playfair
Director of Merchandising . . . . Julie Scully
Merchandise Manager . . . . Mike Kaminska
Distribution Manager . . . . Gerry Magill
Promotions Manager . . . . Matt Rabinowitz
Empire Sports Sales:
Vice President/Advertising . . . . Kerry Atkinson
Administrative Assistant . . . . Ann Miller
National Sales Manager . . . . Jim DiMino
Senior Account Manager . . . . Nick DiVico
Account Managers . . . . John Glynn, Nick Turano
Traffic Manager . . . . Cheryl Reukauf
Assistant Traffic Manager . . . . Terese Schmidle

Operations & Promotions
Director of Operations & Promotions . . . . Stan Makowski
Administrative Assistant . . . . Pat Chimera
Public Address Announcer . . . . Milt Ellis

Finance
Director of Finance . . . . John Cudmore
Assistant Finance Coordinator . . . . Elizabeth McPartland
Director of MIS . . . . Ken Bass
Controller . . . . TBA
Accounting Manager . . . . Chris Ivansitz
Finance Assistants . . . . Birgid Haensel, Mary Jones, Sally Lippert,
  Toni Jaruszewski

Sabreland
Manager . . . . Cliff Smith

Crossroads Arena Corporation
Executive Vice-President . . . . Larry Quinn
Project Director . . . . Carolyn Hoyt
Administrative Assistants . . . . Deidre Daniels, Debbie Driscoll
Project Accountant . . . . Scott Haima

Legal
Associate Counsel . . . . Helen Drew
Administrative Assistants . . . . Eleanore MacKenzie, Karen Young

TV & Radio
Director of Broadcast Services . . . . Jennifer Smith
Administrative Assistant . . . . Lisa Tzetzo
Television Producer – Live Telecasts . . . . Doug Walton
Television Director – Live Telecasts . . . . Phil Mollica
Television Producer – Marquee Programming . . . . . Tim Melligan
Production Manager . . . . Joe Guarnieri
Staff Cameraman . . . . Martin McCreary
TV Stations . . . . Empire Sports Network, WUTV Fox 29
TV Broadcast Team . . . . Rick Jeanneret (play-by-play),
  Jim Lorentz (color commentary),
  TBA (host)
Radio Flagship Stations . . . . WWKB AM-1520 & CJRN AM-710
Radio Broadcast Team . . . . TBA

General Information
Dimensions of Rink . . . . 193 feet by 84 feet
Location of Press Box . . . . Suspended from ceiling on west side
Club Colors . . . . Blue, Gold & White
Training Camp/Practice Site . . . . Sabreland/Wheatfield, NY
AHL Affiliate . . . . Rochester Americans

Calgary Flames

1994-95 Results: 24W-17L-7T 55PTS. First, Pacific Division

Schedule

Oct.	Sat.	7	at Tampa Bay		Sat.	6	Florida
	Sun.	8	at Florida		Wed.	10	Hartford
	Tues.	10	at Dallas		Fri.	12	Buffalo
	Sun.	15	at Chicago		Sun.	14	at Colorado
	Tues.	17	at Detroit		Tues.	16	at Los Angeles
	Thur.	19	at Ottawa		Wed.	17	at Anaheim
	Fri.	20	at Toronto		Wed.	24	NY Islanders
	Wed.	25	Colorado		Fri.	26	Dallas
	Fri.	27	Detroit		Tues.	30	Edmonton
	Sun.	29	at Anaheim	Feb.	Thur.	1	New Jersey
	Tues.	31	at Los Angeles		Sat.	3	Los Angeles
Nov.	Wed.	1	at Colorado		Tues.	6	Ottawa
	Sat.	4	Vancouver		Thur.	8	Washington
	Mon.	6	at NY Rangers		Sat.	10	Winnipeg
	Wed.	8	at New Jersey		Sun.	11	at Edmonton
	Thur.	9	at Philadelphia		Tues.	13	at Washington
	Sat.	11	Montreal		Thur.	15	at NY Islanders
	Tues.	14	Edmonton		Sat.	17	at Montreal
	Fri.	17	Colorado		Tues.	20	San Jose
	Sat.	18	at Colorado		Fri.	23	Anaheim
	Tues.	21	Anaheim		Sat.	24	Boston
	Fri.	24	Edmonton		Thur.	29	Pittsburgh
	Sun.	26	Chicago	Mar.	Sun.	3	at San Jose*
	Wed.	29	at San Jose		Thur.	7	at St. Louis
Dec.	Fri.	1	at Edmonton		Sat.	9	at Toronto
	Sun.	3	at Winnipeg		Tues.	12	St. Louis
	Tues.	5	St. Louis		Fri.	15	at Buffalo
	Sat.	9	Vancouver		Sun.	17	at Detroit*
	Mon.	11	Los Angeles		Wed.	20	at Chicago
	Wed.	13	at Dallas		Fri.	22	San Jose
	Thur.	14	at St. Louis		Sat.	23	at Vancouver
	Sat.	16	at Boston		Mon.	25	Toronto
	Tues.	19	at Pittsburgh		Wed.	27	Chicago
	Wed.	20	at Hartford		Fri.	29	Los Angeles
	Fri.	22	Detroit		Sun.	31	Winnipeg
	Tues.	26	at Vancouver	Apr.	Wed.	3	Vancouver
	Wed.	27	Toronto		Sat.	6	at Winnipeg
	Fri.	29	Philadelphia		Mon.	8	at Edmonton
	Sun.	31	NY Rangers		Tues.	9	at Dallas
Jan.	Tues.	2	Tampa Bay		Fri.	12	at San Jose
	Fri.	5	Anaheim		Sat.	13	at Vancouver

* Denotes afternoon game.

Home Starting Times:

Weeknights	. . . .	7:35 p.m.
Saturdays	. . . .	8:35 p.m.
Sundays	. . . .	6:05 p.m.
Except	Sat. Nov. 11	5:35 p.m.
	Sat. Jan. 6	6:05 p.m.
	Sat. Feb. 10	6:05 p.m.

Franchise date: June 24, 1980
Transferred from Atlanta to Calgary.

24th NHL Season

PACIFIC DIVISION

Calgary's Theoren Fleury finished seventh in goals in 1994-95, clicking for 29 goals in 47 games.

Year-by-Year Record

		Home			Road			Overall							
Season	GP	W	L	T	W	L	T	W	L	T	GF	GA	Pts.	Finished	Playoff Result
1994-95	48	15	7	2	9	10	5	24	17	7	163	135	55	1st, Pacific Div.	Lost Conf. Quarter-Final
1993-94	84	25	12	5	17	17	8	42	29	13	302	256	97	1st, Pacific Div.	Lost Conf. Quarter-Final
1992-93	84	23	14	5	20	16	6	43	30	11	322	282	97	2nd, Smythe Div.	Lost Div. Semi-Final
1991-92	80	19	14	7	12	23	5	31	37	12	296	305	74	5th, Smythe Div.	Out of Playoffs
1990-91	80	29	8	3	17	18	5	46	26	8	344	263	100	2nd, Smythe Div.	Lost Div. Semi-Final
1989-90	80	28	7	5	14	16	10	42	23	15	348	265	99	1st, Smythe Div.	Lost Div. Semi-Final
1988-89	**80**	**32**	**4**	**4**	**22**	**13**	**5**	**54**	**17**	**9**	**354**	**226**	**117**	**1st, Smythe Div.**	**Won Stanley Cup**
1987-88	80	26	11	3	22	12	6	48	23	9	397	305	105	1st, Smythe Div.	Lost Div. Final
1986-87	80	25	13	2	21	18	1	46	31	3	318	289	95	2nd, Smythe Div.	Lost Div. Semi-Final
1985-86	80	23	11	6	17	20	3	40	31	9	354	315	89	2nd, Smythe Div.	Lost Final
1984-85	80	23	11	6	18	16	6	41	27	12	363	302	94	3rd, Smythe Div.	Lost Div. Semi-Final
1983-84	80	22	11	7	12	21	7	34	32	14	311	314	82	2nd, Smythe Div.	Lost Div. Final
1982-83	80	21	12	7	11	22	7	32	34	14	321	317	78	2nd, Smythe Div.	Lost Div. Final
1981-82	80	20	11	9	9	23	8	29	34	17	334	345	75	3rd, Smythe Div.	Lost Div. Semi-Final
1980-81	80	25	5	10	14	22	4	39	27	14	329	298	92	3rd, Patrick Div.	Lost Semi-Final
1979-80*	80	18	15	7	17	17	6	35	32	13	282	269	83	4th, Patrick Div.	Lost Prelim. Round
1978-79*	80	25	11	4	16	20	4	41	31	8	327	280	90	4th, Patrick Div.	Lost Prelim. Round
1977-78*	80	20	13	7	14	14	12	34	27	19	274	252	87	3rd, Patrick Div.	Lost Prelim. Round
1976-77*	80	22	11	7	12	23	5	34	34	12	264	265	80	3rd, Patrick Div.	Lost Prelim. Round
1975-76*	80	19	14	7	16	19	5	35	33	12	262	237	82	3rd, Patrick Div.	Lost Prelim. Round
1974-75*	80	24	9	7	10	22	8	34	31	15	243	233	83	4th, Patrick Div.	Out of Playoffs
1973-74*	78	17	15	7	13	19	7	30	34	14	214	238	74	4th, West Div.	Lost Quarter-Final
1972-73*	78	16	16	7	9	22	8	25	38	15	191	239	65	7th, West Div.	Out of Playoffs

* Atlanta Flames

1995-96 Player Personnel

FORWARDS	HT	WT	S	Place of Birth	Date	1994-95 Club
DINGMAN, Chris	6-4	225	L	Edmonton, Alta.	7/6/76	Brandon
EISENHUT, Neil	6-1	190	L	Osoyoos, B.C.	2/9/67	Saint John-Calgary
FLEURY, Theoren	5-6	160	R	Oxbow, Sask.	6/29/68	Tappara-Calgary
HARPER, Kelly	6-2	180	R	Sudbury, Ont.	5/9/72	Huntington
HLUSHKO, Todd	5-11	185	L	Toronto, Ont.	2/7/70	Saint John-Calgary
KENNEDY, Sheldon	5-10	180	R	Elkhorn, Man.	6/15/69	Calgary
KOHN, Ladislav	5-10	175	L	Uherske Hradiste, Czech.	3/4/75	Swift Current-Saint John
KRUSE, Paul	6-0	202	L	Merritt, B.C.	3/15/70	Calgary
LABRAATEN, Jan	6-2	198	R	Karlstad, Sweden	2/17/77	Farjestad-Farjestad
MATTSSON, Jesper	6-0	185	R	Malmo, Sweden	5/13/75	Malmo
McCARTHY, Sandy	6-3	225	R	Toronto, Ont.	6/15/72	Calgary
MURRAY, Marty	5-9	170	L	Deloraine, Man.	2/16/75	Brandon
MURRAY, Michael	6-1	200	R	Cumberland, RI	4/18/71	Saint John
NIEUWENDYK, Joe	6-1	195	L	Oshawa, Ont.	9/10/66	Calgary
NYLANDER, Michael	5-11	190	L	Stockholm, Sweden	10/3/72	JyP HT-Calgary
PELUSO, Mike	6-0	200	R	Denver, CO	9/2/74	Minn.-Duluth
PEPLINSKI, Jim	6-3	210	R	Renfrew, Ont.	10/24/60	Calgary
PERRY, Jeff	6-0	195	L	Sarnia, Ont.	4/12/71	Saint John
ROBERTS, Gary	6-1	190	L	North York, Ont.	5/23/66	Calgary
STERN, Ron	6-0	195	R	Ste. Agathe, Que.	1/11/67	Calgary
STILLMAN, Cory	6-0	180	L	Peterborough, Ont.	12/20/73	Saint John-Calgary
STRUCH, David	5-10	180	L	Flin Flon, Man.	2/11/71	Saint John
SULLIVAN, Mike	6-2	190	L	Marshfield, MA	2/27/68	Calgary
SUNDBLAD, Niklas	6-1	200	R	Stockholm, Sweden	1/3/73	Saint John
TITOV, German	6-1	190	L	Moscow, USSR	10/16/65	TPS-Calgary
TORGAYEV, Pavel	6-1	190	L	Gorky, USSR	1/25/66	JyP HT
VIITAKOSKI, Vesa	6-3	215	L	Lappeenranta, Finland	2/13/71	Saint John-Calgary
WARD, Ed	6-3	205	R	Edmonton, Alta.	11/10/69	Cornwall-Calgary-Saint John
DEFENSEMEN						
ALLISON, Jamie	6-1	190	L	Lindsay, Ont.	5/13/75	Detroit (OHL)-Calgary
BOUCHARD, Joel	6-0	190	L	Montreal, Que.	1/23/74	Saint John-Calgary
CHIASSON, Steve	6-1	205	L	Barrie, Ont.	4/14/67	Calgary
DAHL, Kevin	5-11	190	R	Regina, Sask.	12/30/68	Calgary
HELENIUS, Sami	6-5	225	L	Helsinki, Finland	1/22/74	Saint John
HOUSLEY, Phil	5-10	185	L	St. Paul, MN	3/9/64	Grasshoppers-Calgary
MARSHALL, Bobby	6-1	190	L	North York, Ont.	4/11/72	Saint John
McCAMBRIDGE, Keith	6-2	205	L	Thompson, Man.	2/1/74	Swift Current-Kamloops
PATRICK, James	6-2	198	R	Winnipeg, Man.	6/14/63	Calgary
SIMPSON, Todd	6-3	215	L	Edmonton, Alta.	5/28/73	Saint John
YAWNEY, Trent	6-3	195	L	Hudson Bay, Sask.	9/29/65	Calgary
ZALAPSKI, Zarley	6-1	215	L	Edmonton, Alta.	4/22/68	Calgary

GOALTENDERS	HT	WT	C	Place of Birth	Date	1994-95 Club
KIDD, Trevor	6-2	190	L	Dugald, Man.	3/29/72	Calgary
MUZZATTI, Jason	6-1	190	L	Toronto, Ont.	2/3/70	Saint John-Calgary
ROLOSON, Dwayne	6-1	180	L	Simcoe, Ont.	10/12/69	Saint John
TABARACCI, Rick	6-1	180	L	Toronto, Ont.	1/2/69	Wsh-Chicago (IHL)-Cgy

General Manager

RISEBROUGH, DOUG
General Manager, Calgary Flames. Born in Guelph, Ont., January 29, 1954.

Doug Risebrough enters his fifth full NHL season as general manager of the Calgary Flames. After ending his 14-year NHL playing career with the Flames in 1987, Risebrough was named an assistant coach with Calgary and joined Terry Crisp behind the bench. Risebrough was appointed head coach of the Flames on May 18, 1990 and on May 16, 1991, he also assumed the role of general manager. Late in the 1991-92 campaign he directed his energies full-time to general manager, handing the coaching responsibilities over to Guy Charron for the balance of the season.

During his first season as an NHL head coach, Risebrough led the Flames to a fourth place overall finish in the NHL standings. Risebrough was Montreal's first selection, seventh overall, in the 1974 Amateur Draft. During his nine years with the Canadiens, he helped his club to four consecutive Stanley Cup championships between 1976 and 1979. He joined the Flames prior to the start of the club's 1982 training camp. During his NHL career, his clubs have won five Stanley Cup titles (1976-1979 and 1989 with Calgary) and two Presidents' Trophies (1987-88 and 1988-89).

NHL Coaching Record

		Regular Season					Playoffs			
Season	Team	Games	W	L	T	%	Games	W	L	%
1990-91	Calgary	80	46	26	8	.625	7	3	4	.429
1991-92	Calgary	64	25	30	9	.461	....	....	....	....
	NHL Totals	**144**	**71**	**56**	**17**	**.522**	**7**	**3**	**4**	**.429**

General Managers' History

Cliff Fletcher, 1972-73 to 1990-91; Doug Risebrough, 1991-92 to date.

1994-95 Scoring

* – rookie

Regular Season

Pos	#	Player	Team	GP	G	A	Pts	+/–	PIM	PP	SH	GW	GT	S	%
R	14	Theoren Fleury	CGY	47	29	29	58	6	112	9	2	5	0	173	16.8
C	25	Joe Nieuwendyk	CGY	46	21	29	50	11	33	3	0	4	0	122	17.2
D	6	Phil Housley	CGY	43	8	35	43	17	18	3	0	0	0	135	5.9
C	26	Robert Reichel	CGY	48	18	17	35	–2	28	5	0	2	0	160	11.3
D	33	Zarley Zalapski	CGY	48	4	24	28	9	46	1	0	1	0	76	5.3
D	21	Steve Chiasson	CGY	45	2	23	25	10	39	1	0	0	0	110	1.8
C	13	German Titov	CGY	40	12	12	24	6	16	3	2	3	0	88	13.6
C	29	Joel Otto	CGY	47	8	13	21	8	130	0	2	2	1	46	17.4
C	17	Wes Walz	CGY	39	6	12	18	7	11	4	0	1	0	73	8.2
L	12	Paul Kruse	CGY	45	11	5	16	13	141	0	0	2	0	52	21.2
R	23	Sheldon Kennedy	CGY	30	7	8	15	5	45	1	0	0	0	44	15.9
R	22	Ronnie Stern	CGY	39	9	4	13	4	163	1	0	0	0	69	13.0
D	4	Kevin Dahl	CGY	34	4	8	12	8	38	0	0	0	0	30	13.3
C	11	Kelly Kisio	CGY	12	7	4	11	2	6	5	1	0	0	26	26.9
C	32	Mike Sullivan	CGY	38	4	7	11	–2	14	0	0	2	0	31	12.9
R	16	Nikolai Borschevsky	TOR	19	0	5	5	3	0	0	0	0	0	28	0.0
			CGY	8	0	5	5	7	0	0	0	0	0	12	0.0
			TOTAL	27	0	10	10	10	0	0	0	0	0	40	0.0
D	5	James Patrick	CGY	43	0	10	10	–3	14	0	0	0	0	43	0.0
R	15	Sandy McCarthy	CGY	37	5	3	8	1	101	0	0	2	0	29	17.2
D	28	Leonard Esau	EDM	14	0	6	6	–8	15	0	0	0	0	17	0.0
			CGY	1	0	0	0	–2	0	0	0	0	0	4	0.0
			TOTAL	15	0	6	6	–10	15	0	0	0	0	21	0.0
D	39	Dan Keczmer	CGY	28	2	3	5	7	10	0	0	0	0	33	6.1
L	41	Alan May	DAL	27	1	1	2	1	106	0	0	0	0	23	4.3
			CGY	7	1	2	3	2	13	0	0	0	0	5	20.0
			TOTAL	34	2	3	5	3	119	0	0	0	0	28	7.1
D	3	Frank Musil	CGY	35	0	5	5	6	61	0	0	0	0	18	0.0
L	10	Gary Roberts	CGY	8	2	2	4	1	43	2	0	0	0	20	10.0
L	19	* Vesa Viitakoski	CGY	10	1	2	3	–1	6	1	0	0	0	6	16.7
R	42	* Ed Ward	CGY	2	1	1	2	–2	2	0	0	0	0	1	100.0
R	16	Mark Greig	CGY	8	1	1	2	1	2	0	0	0	0	5	20.0
C	20	* Cory Stillman	CGY	10	0	2	2	1	2	0	0	0	0	7	0.0
G	31	Rick Tabaracci	WSH	8	0	1	1	0	2	0	0	0	0	0	0.0
			CGY	5	0	1	1	0	0	0	0	0	0	0	0.0
			TOTAL	13	0	2	2	0	2	0	0	0	0	0	0.0
D	18	Trent Yawney	CGY	37	0	2	2	–4	108	0	0	0	0	20	0.0
C	38	* Todd Hlushko	CGY	2	0	1	1	1	2	0	0	0	0	3	0.0
L	24	Jim Peplinski	CGY	6	0	1	1	–2	11	0	0	0	0	5	0.0
C	92	Michael Nylander	CGY	6	0	1	1	1	2	0	0	0	0	2	0.0
G	37	Trevor Kidd	CGY	43	0	1	1	0	2	0	0	0	0	0	0.0
D	7	Steve Konroyd	CGY	1	0	0	0	0	0	0	0	0	0	0	0.0
G	36	* Jason Muzzatti	CGY	1	0	0	0	0	0	0	0	0	0	0	0.0
D	7	* Jamie Allison	CGY	1	0	0	0	0	0	0	0	0	0	0	0.0
D	34	* Joel Bouchard	CGY	2	0	0	0	0	0	0	0	0	0	0	0.0
C	35	Neil Eisenhut	CGY	3	0	0	0	0	0	0	0	0	0	2	0.0
L	28	Barry Nieckar	CGY	3	0	0	0	0	12	0	0	0	0	0	0.0
L	27	* Scott Morrow	CGY	4	0	0	0	0	0	0	0	0	0	1	0.0
G	1	* Andrei Trefilov	CGY	6	0	0	0	0	0	0	0	0	0	0	0.0

Goaltending

No.	Goaltender	GPI	Mins	Avg	W	L	T	EN	SO	GA	SA	S%
36	* Jason Muzzatti	1	10	.00	0	0	0	0	0	0	8	1.000
31	Rick Tabaracci	5	202	1.49	2	0	1	0	0	5	93	.946
37	Trevor Kidd	43	2463	2.61	22	14	6	4	3	107	1170	.909
1	* Andrei Trefilov	6	236	4.07	0	3	0	3	0	16	130	.877
	Totals	**48**	**2922**	**2.77**	**24**	**17**	**7**	**7**	**3**	**135**	**1408**	**.904**

Playoffs

Pos	#	Player	Team	GP	G	A	Pts	+/–	PIM	PP	SH	GW	OT	S	%
R	14	Theoren Fleury	CGY	7	7	7	14	8	2	2	1	0	0	40	17.5
D	6	Phil Housley	CGY	7	0	9	9	5	0	0	0	0	0	22	0.0
C	13	German Titov	CGY	7	5	3	8	1	10	0	1	0	0	14	35.7
C	32	Mike Sullivan	CGY	7	3	5	8	5	2	0	1	1	0	12	25.0
C	25	Joe Nieuwendyk	CGY	5	4	3	7	0	0	2	0	1	0	21	19.0
L	12	Paul Kruse	CGY	7	4	2	6	2	10	0	1	0	0	18	22.2
C	26	Robert Reichel	CGY	7	2	4	6	1	4	0	0	1	0	20	10.0
C	92	Michael Nylander	CGY	6	0	6	6	–3	2	0	0	0	0	13	0.0
C	11	Kelly Kisio	CGY	7	3	2	5	0	19	1	0	0	0	11	27.3
R	23	Sheldon Kennedy	CGY	7	3	1	4	3	16	0	1	0	0	19	15.8
R	22	Ronnie Stern	CGY	7	3	1	4	4	8	1	1	0	0	19	15.8
D	33	Zarley Zalapski	CGY	7	0	4	4	7	4	0	0	0	0	7	0.0
D	21	Steve Chiasson	CGY	7	1	2	3	9	9	1	0	0	0	16	6.3
C	29	Joel Otto	CGY	7	0	3	3	2	2	0	0	0	0	12	0.0
D	3	Frank Musil	CGY	5	0	1	1	0	0	0	0	0	0	3	0.0
D	5	James Patrick	CGY	5	0	1	1	–2	0	0	0	0	0	4	0.0
R	15	Sandy McCarthy	CGY	6	0	1	1	–2	17	0	0	0	0	0	0.0
D	39	Dan Keczmer	CGY	7	0	1	1	0	2	0	0	0	0	6	0.0
G	31	Rick Tabaracci	CGY	1	0	0	0	0	0	0	0	0	0	0	0.0
C	17	Wes Walz	CGY	1	0	0	0	0	0	0	0	0	0	1	0.0
C	38	* Todd Hlushko	CGY	1	0	0	0	0	2	0	0	0	0	0	0.0
D	18	Trent Yawney	CGY	2	0	0	0	–4	2	0	0	0	0	1	0.0
D	4	Kevin Dahl	CGY	3	0	0	0	–1	0	0	0	0	0	0	0.0
G	37	Trevor Kidd	CGY	7	0	0	0	0	0	0	0	0	0	0	0.0

Goaltending

No.	Goaltender	GPI	Mins	Avg	W	L	EN	SO	GA	SA	S%
31	Rick Tabaracci	1	19	0.00	0	0	0	0	0	9	1.000
37	Trevor Kidd	7	434	3.59	3	4	0	1	26	181	.856
	Totals	**7**	**454**	**3.44**	**3**	**4**	**0**	**1**	**26**	**190**	**.863**

Club Records

Team

(Figures in brackets for season records are games played; records for fewest points, wins, ties, losses, goals, goals against are for 70 or more games)

Most Points	117	1988-89 (80)
Most Wins	54	1988-89 (80)
Most Ties	19	1977-78 (80)
Most Losses	38	1972-73 (78)
Most Goals	397	1987-88 (80)
Most Goals Against	345	1981-82 (80)
Fewest Points	65	1972-73 (78)
Fewest Wins	25	1972-73 (78)
Fewest Ties	3	1986-87 (80)
Fewest Losses	17	1988-89 (80)
Fewest Goals	191	1972-73 (78)
Fewest Goals Against	226	1988-89 (80)

Longest Winning Streak

Overall .... 10 Oct. 14-Nov. 3/78

Home .... 9 Oct. 17-Nov. 15/78
Jan. 3-Feb. 5/89
Mar. 3-Apr. 1/90
Feb. 21-Mar. 14/91

Away .... 7 Nov. 10-Dec. 4/88

Longest Undefeated Streak

Over-all .... 13 Nov. 10-Dec. 8/88
(12 wins, 1 tie)

Home .... 18 Dec. 29/90-Mar. 14/91
(17 wins, 1 tie)

Away .... 9 Feb. 20-Mar. 21/88
(6 wins, 3 ties)
Nov. 11-Dec. 16/90
(6 wins, 3 ties)

Longest Losing Streak

Over-all .... 11 Dec. 14/85-Jan. 7/86

Home .... 4 Seven times
Away .... 9 Dec. 1/85-Jan. 12/86

Longest Winless Streak

Over-all .... 11 Dec. 14/85-Jan. 7/86
(11 losses)
Jan. 5-26/93
(9 losses, 2 ties)

Home .... 6 Nov. 25-Dec. 18/82
(5 losses, 1 tie)

Away .... 13 Feb. 3-Mar. 29/73
(10 losses, 3 ties)

Most Shutouts, Season	8	1974-75 (80)
Most PIM, Season	2,655	1991-92 (80)
Most Goals, Game	13	Feb. 10/93 (San Jose 1 at Calgary 13)

Individual

Most Seasons	13	Al MacInnis
Most Games	803	Al MacInnis
Most Goals, Career	314	Joe Nieuwendyk
Most Assists, Career	609	Al MacInnis
Most Points, Career	822	Al MacInnis (213 goals, 609 assists)
Most PIM, Career	2,405	Tim Hunter
Most Shutouts, Career	20	Dan Bouchard

Longest Consecutive
Games Streak .... 257 Brad Marsh
(Oct. 11/78-Nov. 10/81)

Most Goals, Season .... 66 Lanny McDonald (1982-83)

Most Assists, Season .... 82 Kent Nilsson (1980-81)

Most Points, Season .... 131 Kent Nilsson (1980-81)
(49 goals, 82 assists)

Most PIM, Season .... 375 Tim Hunter (1988-89)

Most Points, Defenseman
Season .... 103 Al MacInnis (1990-91)
(28 goals, 75 assists)

Most Points, Center

Season .... 131 Kent Nilsson (1980-81) (49 goals, 82 assists)

Most Points, Right Wing

Season .... 110 Joe Mullen (1988-89) (51 goals, 59 assists)

Most Points, Left Wing

Season .... 90 Gary Roberts (1991-92) (53 goals, 37 assists)

Most Points, Rookie

Season .... 92 Joe Nieuwendyk (1987-88) (51 goals, 41 assists)

Most Shutouts, Season	5	Dan Bouchard (1973-74) Phil Myre (1974-75)
Most Goals, Game	5	Joe Nieuwendyk (Jan. 11/89)
Most Assists, Game	6	Guy Chouinard (Feb. 25/81) Gary Suter (Apr. 4/86)
Most Points, Game	7	Sergei Makarov (Feb. 25/90)

Retired Numbers

9   Lanny McDonald   1981-1989

Coaching History

Bernie Geoffrion, 1972-73 to 1973-74; Bernie Geoffrion and Fred Creighton, 1974-75; Fred Creighton, 1975-76 to 1978-79; Al MacNeil, 1979-80 (Atlanta); 1980-81 to 1981-82 (Calgary); Bob Johnson, 1982-83 to 1986-87; Terry Crisp, 1987-88 to 1989-90; Doug Risebrough, 1990-91; Doug Risebrough and Guy Charron, 1991-92; Dave King, 1992-93 to 1994-95; Pierre Page, 1995-96.

All-time Record vs. Other Clubs

Regular Season

			At Home							On Road							Total				
	GP	W	L	T	GF	GA	PTS	GP	W	L	T	GF	GA	PTS	GP	W	L	T	GF	GA	PTS
Anaheim	5	3	2	0	15	14	6	6	3	2	1	17	13	7	11	6	4	1	32	27	13
Boston	38	15	20	3	144	140	33	39	10	24	5	107	138	25	77	25	44	8	251	278	58
Buffalo	38	13	15	10	137	133	36	38	12	22	4	115	160	28	76	25	37	14	252	293	64
Chicago	45	21	17	7	148	139	49	43	13	20	10	132	154	36	88	34	37	17	280	293	85
Dallas	44	27	6	11	177	116	65	44	17	21	6	147	162	40	88	44	27	17	324	278	105
Detroit	42	26	11	5	183	132	57	41	13	21	7	133	159	33	83	39	32	12	316	291	90
Edmonton	56	31	19	6	264	203	68	57	20	29	8	209	240	48	113	51	48	14	473	443	116
Florida	1	1	0	0	4	2	2	1	0	1	0	2	2	1	2	1	1	0	5	4	2
Hartford	22	17	4	1	118	75	35	22	12	7	3	90	75	27	44	29	11	4	208	150	62
Los Angeles	74	46	19	9	356	250	101	71	27	37	7	265	287	61	145	73	56	16	621	537	162
Montreal	37	11	21	5	120	135	27	38	11	21	6	94	135	28	75	22	42	11	214	270	55
New Jersey	36	27	4	5	172	93	59	37	23	11	3	144	109	49	73	50	15	8	316	202	108
NY Islanders	43	19	13	11	154	134	49	43	10	24	9	114	178	29	86	29	37	20	268	312	78
NY Rangers	43	24	10	9	196	134	57	44	20	19	5	160	156	45	87	44	29	14	356	290	102
Ottawa	2	2	0	0	18	4	4	2	1	0	1	7	3	3	4	3	0	1	25	6	7
Philadelphia	45	23	13	9	188	148	55	44	12	30	2	120	180	26	89	35	43	11	308	328	81
Pittsburgh	38	22	9	7	163	114	51	38	10	18	10	125	139	30	76	32	27	17	288	253	81
Quebec	23	13	4	6	103	72	32	22	9	7	6	90	93	24	45	22	11	12	193	165	56
St. Louis	44	23	18	3	161	132	49	45	18	20	7	141	161	43	89	41	38	10	302	293	92
San Jose	12	9	3	0	66	30	18	14	11	2	1	51	34	23	26	20	5	1	117	64	41
Tampa Bay	2	1	1	0	3	6	2	3	2	1	0	16	13	4	5	3	2	0	19	19	6
Toronto	44	27	12	5	195	143	59	44	17	18	7	163	162	41	88	44	30	12	358	305	100
Vancouver	74	51	13	10	330	207	112	74	31	27	16	253	267	78	148	82	40	26	583	474	190
Washington	32	22	6	4	140	77	48	33	13	15	5	121	127	31	65	35	21	9	261	204	79
Winnipeg	53	35	11	7	259	171	77	52	20	23	9	190	213	49	105	55	34	16	449	384	126
Defunct Clubs	13	8	4	1	51	34	17	13	7	3	3	43	33	17	26	15	7	4	94	67	34
Totals	906	517	255	134	3865	2838	1168	906	342	423	141	3048	3392	825	1812	859	678	275	6913	6230	1993

Calgary totals include Atlanta, 1972-73 to 1979-80. Dallas totals include Minnesota, 1972-73 to 1992-93.
New Jersey totals include Kansas City, 1974-75 to 1975-76, and Colorado, 1976-77 to 1981-82.

Captains' History

Keith McCreary, 1972-73 to 1974-75; Pat Quinn, 1975-76, 1976-77; Tom Lysiak, 1977-78, 1978-79; Jean Pronovost, 1979-80; Brad Marsh, 1980-81; Phil Russell, 1981-82, 1982-83; Lanny McDonald, Doug Risebrough (co-captains), 1983-84; Lanny McDonald, Doug Risebrough, Jim Peplinski (tri-captains), 1984-85 to 1986-87; Lanny McDonald, Jim Peplinski (co-captains), 1987-88; Lanny McDonald, Jim Peplinski, Tim Hunter (tri-captains), 1988-89; Brad McCrimmon, 1989-90; alternating captains, 1990-91; Joe Nieuwendyk, 1991-92 to date.

Playoffs

	Series	W	L	GP	W	L	T	GF	GA	Last Mtg.	Round	Result
Chicago	2	2	0	8	7	1	0	30	17	1989	CF	W 4-1
Dallas	1	0	1	6	2	4	0	18	25	1981	SF	L 2-4
Detroit	1	0	1	2	0	2	0	5	8	1978	PR	L 0-2
Edmonton	5	1	4	30	11	19	0	96	132	1991	DSF	L 2-4
Los Angeles	6	2	4	26	13	13	0	102	105	1993	DSF	L 2-4
Montreal	2	1	1	11	5	6	0	32	31	1989	F	W 4-2
NY Rangers	1	0	1	4	1	3	0	8	14	1980	PR	L 1-3
Philadelphia	2	1	1	11	4	7	0	28	43	1981	QF	W 4-3
St. Louis	2	1	0	7	4	3	0	28	22	1986	CF	W 4-3
San Jose	1	0	1	7	3	4	0	35	26	1995	CQF	L 3-4
Toronto	1	1	0	2	2	0	0	5	9	1979	PR	L 2-7
Vancouver	5	3	2	25	13	12	0	82	80	1994	CQF	L 3-4
Winnipeg	3	1	2	13	6	7	0	43	45	1987	DSF	L 2-4
Totals	31	12	19	152	69	83	0	522	557			

Playoff Results 1995-91

Year	Round	Opponent	Result	GF	GA
1995	CQF	San Jose	L 3-4	35	26
1994	CQF	Vancouver	L 3-4	20	23
1993	DSF	Los Angeles	L 2-4	28	33
1991	DSF	Edmonton	L 3-4	20	22

Abbreviations: Round: F – Final; CF – conference final; CQF – conference quarter-final; CSF – conference semi-final; DF – division final; DSF – division semi-final; SF – semi-final; QF – quarter-final; PR – preliminary round.

1994-95 Results

Jan.	20	at	Winnipeg	3-3	12	at	Dallas	4-4
	22	at	Detroit	4-1	15		Anaheim	0-5
	24	at	St. Louis	6-4	17		Winnipeg	8-4
	26	at	Detroit	1-5	19		San Jose	3-5
	28	at	Toronto	1-2	20	at	Edmonton	2-5
Feb.	1		Detroit	2-1	22		St. Louis	4-3
	3		Chicago	3-4	24		Detroit	3-2
	4		Toronto	4-1	26		Vancouver	3-3
	6		Winnipeg	4-5	28		Los Angeles	3-5
	9		Anaheim	5-1	31	at	Edmonton	6-2
	11	at	Dallas	6-0	Apr. 4		Chicago	3-2
	13	at	St. Louis	2-4	6		Los Angeles	7-4
	16	at	Chicago	2-2	8		Vancouver	2-4
	18		Dallas	3-2	10		San Jose	8-3
	20		Dallas	1-2	12	at	Los Angeles	4-1
	23	at	Los Angeles	3-3	13	at	Anaheim	2-2
	24	at	San Jose	3-0	15	at	Edmonton	4-2
	26	at	Anaheim	5-3	17		Los Angeles	5-2
	28		Edmonton	5-2	20	at	Vancouver	2-2
Mar.	2		Vancouver	2-2	24	at	Anaheim	1-2
	4	at	Toronto	2-3	25	at	San Jose	3-2
	5	at	Winnipeg	2-3	29		Toronto	2-2
	7	at	Chicago	6-3	30	at	Vancouver	4-6
	9	at	St. Louis	1-5	May 3		Edmonton	5-3

Entry Draft
Selections 1995-81

1995
Pick
20 Denis Gauthier Jr.
46 Pavel Smirnov
72 Rocky Thompson
98 Jan Labraaten
150 Clarke Wilm
176 Ryan Gillis
233 Steve Shirreffs

1994
Pick
19 Chris Dingman
45 Dmitri Ryabykin
77 Chris Clark
91 Ryan Duthie
97 Johan Finnstrom
107 Nils Ekman
123 Frank Appel
149 Patrick Haltia
175 Ladislav Kohn
201 Keith McCambridge
227 Jorgen Jonsson
253 Mike Peluso
279 Pavel Torgayev

1993
Pick
18 Jesper Mattsson
44 Jamie Allison
70 Dan Tompkins
95 Jason Smith
96 Marty Murray
121 Darryl Lafrance
122 John Emmons
148 Andreas Karlsson
200 Derek Sylvester
252 German Titov
278 Burke Murphy

1992
Pick
6 Cory Stillman
30 Chris O'Sullivan
54 Mathias Johansson
78 Robert Svehla
102 Sami Helenius
126 Ravil Yakubov
129 Joel Bouchard
150 Pavel Rajnoha
174 Ryan Mulhern
198 Brandon Carper
222 Jonas Hoglund
246 Andrei Potaichuk

1991
Pick
19 Niklas Sundblad
41 Francois Groleau
52 Sandy McCarthy
63 Brian Caruso
85 Steven Magnusson
107 Jerome Butler
129 Bobby Marshall
140 Matt Hoffman
151 Kelly Harper
173 David St. Pierre
195 David Struch
217 Sergei Zolotov
239 Marko Jantunen
261 Andrei Trefilov

1990
Pick
11 Trevor Kidd
26 Nicolas P. Perreault
32 Vesa Viitakoski
41 Etienne Belzile
62 Glen Mears
83 Paul Kruse
125 Chris Tschupp
146 Dmitri Frolov
167 Shawn Murray
188 Mike Murray
209 Rob Sumner
230 invalid claim
251 Leo Gudas

1989
Pick
24 Kent Manderville
42 Ted Drury
50 Veli-Pekka Kautonen
63 Corey Lyons
70 Robert Reichel
84 Ryan O'Leary
105 F. (Toby) Kearney
147 Alex Nikolic
168 Kevin Wortman
189 Sergei Gomolyako
210 Dan Sawyer
231 Alexander Yudin
252 Kenneth Kennholt

1988
Pick
21 Jason Muzzatti
42 Todd Harkins
84 Gary Socha
85 Thomas Forslund
90 Scott Matusovich
126 Jonas Bergqvist
147 Stefan Nilsson
168 Troy Kennedy
189 Brett Peterson
210 Guy Darveau
231 Dave Tretowicz
252 Sergei Priakhan

1987
Pick
19 Bryan Deasley
25 Stephane Matteau
40 Kevin Grant
61 Scott Mahoney
70 Tim Harris
103 Tim Corkery
124 Joe Aloi
145 Peter Ciavaglia
166 Theoren Fleury
187 Mark Osiecki
208 William Sedergren
229 Peter Hasselblad
250 Magnus Svensson

1986
Pick
16 George Pelawa
37 Brian Glynn
79 Tom Quinlan
100 Scott Bloom
121 John Parker
142 Rick Lessard
163 Mark Olsen
184 Warren Sharples
205 Doug Pickell
226 Anders Lindstrom
247 Antonin Stavjana

1985
Pick
17 Chris Biotti
27 Joe Nieuwendyk
38 Jeff Wenaas
59 Lane MacDonald
80 Roger Johansson
101 Esa Keskinen
122 Tim Sweeney
143 Stu Grimson
164 Nate Smith
185 Darryl Olsen
206 Peter Romberg
227 Alexander Kozhevnikov
248 Bill Gregoire

1984
Pick
12 Gary Roberts
33 Ken Sabourin
38 Paul Ranheim
75 Petr Rosol
96 Joel Paunio
117 Brett Hull
138 Kevan Melrose
159 Jiri Hrdina
180 Gary Suter
200 Petr Rucka
221 Stefan Jonsson
241 Rudolf Suchanek

1983
Pick
13 Dan Quinn
51 Brian Bradley
55 Perry Berezan
66 John Bekkers
71 Kevan Guy
77 Bill Claviter
91 Igor Liba
111 Grant Blair
131 Jeff Hogg
151 Chris MacDonald
171 Rob Kivell
191 Tom Pratt
211 Jaroslav Benak
231 Sergei Makarov

1982
Pick
29 Dave Reierson
37 Richard Kromm
51 Jim Laing
65 Dave Meszaros
72 Mark Lamb
93 Lou Kiriakou
114 Jeff Vaive
118 Mats Kihlstrom
135 Brad Ramsden
156 Roy Myllari
177 Ted Pearson
198 Jim Uens
219 Rick Erdall
240 Dale Thompson

1981
Pick
15 Allan MacInnis
56 Mike Vernon
78 Peter Madach
99 Mario Simioni
120 Todd Hooey
141 Rick Heppner
162 Dale Degray
183 George Boudreau
204 Bruce Eakin

Coach

PAGE, PIERRE
Coach, Calgary Flames.
Born in St. Hermas, Que., April 30, 1948.

Pierre Page was named the ninth head coach in Flames franchise history on July 17, 1995. For Page, his head coaching appointment returns him to the organization with whom he began his NHL coaching career.

Page joined the Calgary Flames in 1980-81 as an assistant coach to Al MacNeil. He served in that capacity through the 1981-82 season before accepting a position as head coach and general manager of the Flames top development club in Denver (two seasons), and later, Moncton (one season). In 1985-86, Page returned to Calgary as an assistant to head coach Bob Johnson and remained in that capacity through the 1987-88 season under Terry Crisp.

Page left the Flames following the 1987-88 season to become the head coach of the Minnesota North Stars. In his rookie season with Minnesota, the club posted a 27-37-16 record for 70-points, a 19-point improvement over the previous year and earned its first playoff berth since 1985-86. In 1989-90, the North Stars continued improving, finishing the season with 76 points (36-40-4).

After two seasons as head coach in Minnesota, Page was named general manager of the Quebec Nordiques on May 4, 1990. He added the Nordiques head coaching duties to his resume during 1991-92, replacing Dave Chambers 18 games into the season. Under Page's guidance, the Nordiques compiled their best record during the 1992-93 season, garnering a 56-point improvement and qualifying for the playoffs for the first time in six seasons. The 56-point improvement between the two seasons ranks as one of the largest improvements in NHL history. Page left the Nordiques following the 1993-94 season, serving as a pro scout with Toronto in 1994-95.

Before joining the Flames in 1980, Page was head coach of the Dalhousie University Tigers of the CIAU where in 1978-79, he guided his club to a second place finish in the national final. He also served as a guest coach with the 1980 Canadian Olympic Team and an assistant coach with Team Canada in the 1981 Canada Cup.

Club Directory

Canadian Airlines Saddledome
P.O. Box 1540 Station M
Calgary, Alberta T2P 3B9
Phone **403/777-2177**
FAX 403/777-2195
Capacity: 20,000

Owners Harley N. Hotchkiss, Byron J. Seaman, Daryl K. Seaman, Grant A. Bartlett, N. Murray Edwards, Ronald V. Joyce, Alvin G. Libin, Allan P. Markin, J.R. (Bud) McCaig

Management
NHL Chairman of the Board
  Cheif Executive Officer/Governor . . . . Harley Hotchkiss
Executive Vice-President/Alternate Governor . . . . . . Al Coates
Vice-President, General Manager . . . . Doug Risebrough
Vice-President, Business and Finance . . . . Clare Rhyasen
Vice-President, Marketing and Broadcasting. . . . . . . Lanny McDonald
Vice-President, General Manager Canadian
  Airlines Saddledome . . . . Jay Green

Hockey Club Personnel
Director of Hockey Operations . . . . Al MacNeil
Head Coach . . . . Pierre Page
Assistant Coaches. . . . . Don Hay, Guy Lapointe
Goaltending Consultant . . . . TBA
St. John Head Coach . . . . Paul Baxter
St. John Assistant Coach. TBA
St. John Trainer. . . . . Brian Patafie
Director of Amateur Scouting. . . . . Tom Thompson
Scouts. . . . . Ray Clearwater, Jiri Hrdina, Ian McKenzie
Pro Scout . . . . Nick Polano
Scouting Staff . . . . Glen Giovanucci, Larry Popein, Ernie Vargas, Paul McIntosh, Andres Steen
Secretary to CEO, Executive VP, and Finance . . . . . . Yvette Mutcheson
Secretary to General Manager and
  Hockey Operations . . . . Brenda Koyich

Administration
Controller. . . . . Michael Holditch
Assistant Controller . . . . Dorothy Stuart

Corporate Resources
Manager, Corporate Resources . . . . Brian Beavis

Marketing
Manager, Marketing and Special Events. . . . . Roger Lemire
Director, Executive Suites/Club Sales. . . . . Bob White
Director, Advertising and Publishing . . . . Pat Halls
Accounting Executive . . . . John Vidalin
Manager, Tickets . . . . Anne Marie Malarchuk

Public Relations
Director, Public Relations . . . . Rick Skaggs
Assistant Public Relations Director . . . . Mike Burke

Medical/Training Staff
Head Trainer. . . . . Jim (Bearcat) Murray
Equipment Manager. . . . . Bobby Stewart
Physiotherapist and Fitness Coordinator . . . . TBA
Dressing Room Attendants . . . . Ernie Minhinnett, Cliff Stewart, Craig Forester, Les Jarvis
Director of Medicine . . . . Dr. Terry Groves
Orthopedic Surgeon . . . . Dr. Lowell Van Zuiden
Team Dentist . . . . Dr. Bill Blair

Canadian Airlines Saddledome
Assistant Manager . . . . Libby Raines
Operations Manager. . . . . George Greenwood
Food Services Manager. . . . . Nancy Cleveland

Facility
Location of Press Boxes. . . . . Print – north side
                                    TV & Radio – south side
Dimensions of Rink . . . . 200 feet by 85 feet

Broadcast Stations
Radio . . . . 66 CFR Radio (660 AM)
Television . . . . Channels 2 & 7

Coaching Record

Season	Team	Regular Season					Playoffs			
		Games	W	L	T	%	Games	W	L	%
1978-79	Dalhousie (CIAU)	....	....	....	....	....	....	....	....	....
1982-83	Denver (CHL)	80	41	36	3	.531	6	2	4	.333
1983-84	Denver (CHL)	76	48	25	3	.651	6	2	4	.333
1984-85	Moncton (AHL)	80	32	40	8	.450	....	....	....	....
1988-89	Minnesota (NHL)	80	27	37	16	.438	5	1	4	.200
1989-90	Minnesota (NHL)	80	36	40	4	.475	7	3	4	.429
1991-92	Quebec (NHL)	62	17	34	11	.362	....	....	....	....
1992-93	Quebec (NHL)	84	47	27	10	.619	6	2	4	.333
1993-94	Quebec (NHL)	84	34	42	8	.452	....	....	....	....
	NHL Totals	390	161	180	49	.476	18	6	12	.333

Chicago Blackhawks

1994-95 Results: 24W-19L-5T 53PTS. Third, Central Division

Chicago's Bernie Nicholls returned to the top of the charts in 1994-95, leading the Hawks in goals (22) and points (51).

Schedule

Oct.	Sat.	7	at San Jose	Sat.	6	at Detroit
	Tues.	10	at Los Angeles	Sun.	7	Dallas
	Thur.	12	Pittsburgh	Tues.	9	at NY Islanders
	Sat.	14	at Hartford	Fri.	12	Anaheim
	Sun.	15	Calgary	Sun.	14	Los Angeles
	Tues.	17	at Florida	Wed.	17	Washington
	Thur.	19	Tampa Bay	Mon.	22	at Ottawa
	Sat.	21	at St. Louis	Wed.	24	at Toronto
	Sun.	22	Philadelphia	Thur.	25	San Jose
	Thur.	26	Toronto	Sat.	27	Detroit*
	Sat.	28	at Montreal	Wed.	31	at Edmonton
	Sun.	29	Buffalo	**Feb.** Sat.	3	at San Jose*
Nov.	Wed.	1	at Dallas	Sun.	4	at Anaheim
	Sun.	5	Colorado	Tues.	6	at Los Angeles
	Thur.	9	Vancouver	Thur.	8	at St. Louis
	Sat.	11	at Washington	Sat.	10	at Pittsburgh*
	Sun.	12	Edmonton	Thur.	15	Boston
	Tues.	14	at Winnipeg	Sun.	18	Edmonton*
	Thur.	16	NY Rangers	Thur.	22	St. Louis
	Sun.	19	San Jose	Fri.	23	at Winnipeg
	Wed.	22	at Colorado	Sun.	25	at Philadelphia
	Fri.	24	at Anaheim*	Thur.	29	Colorado
	Sun.	26	at Calgary	**Mar.** Fri.	1	at Colorado
	Tues.	28	at Edmonton	Sun.	3	Detroit
	Wed.	29	at Vancouver	Tues.	5	at Tampa Bay
Dec.	Sat.	2	at Winnipeg	Fri.	8	Los Angeles
	Wed.	6	at NY Rangers	Mon.	11	Florida
	Thur.	7	Ottawa	Thur.	14	Vancouver
	Sun.	10	Hartford	Sun.	17	NY Islanders*
	Wed.	13	at Detroit	Wed.	20	Calgary
	Fri.	15	Montreal	Fri.	22	at New Jersey
	Sun.	17	Winnipeg	Sun.	24	Anaheim*
	Wed.	20	at Toronto	Wed.	27	at Calgary
	Thur.	21	Toronto	Fri.	29	at Vancouver
	Sat.	23	at Dallas	Sun.	31	Dallas*
	Tues.	26	Dallas	**Apr.** Wed.	3	at Toronto
	Thur.	28	Winnipeg	Fri.	5	at Dallas
	Fri.	29	at Buffalo	Sun.	7	Detroit*
	Sun.	31	New Jersey	Thur.	11	Toronto
Jan.	Tues.	2	at Boston	Fri.	12	at Detroit
	Thur.	4	St. Louis	Sun.	14	St. Louis*

* Denotes afternoon game.

Home Starting Times:
Night games . . . . 7:30 p.m.
Matinees . . . . 2:00 p.m.
Except Thu. Oct. 12 . . . . 7:00 p.m.
Sun. Jan. 7 . . . . 7:00 p.m.
Sun. Mar. 3 . . . . 7:00 p.m.

Franchise date: September 25, 1926

CENTRAL DIVISION

70th NHL Season

Year-by-Year Record

		Home			Road			Overall							
Season	**GP**	**W**	**L**	**T**	**W**	**L**	**T**	**W**	**L**	**T**	**GF**	**GA**	**Pts.**	**Finished**	**Playoff Result**
1994-95	48	11	10	3	13	9	2	24	19	5	156	115	53	3rd, Central Div.	Lost Conf. Championship
1993-94	84	21	16	5	18	20	4	39	36	9	254	240	87	5th, Central Div.	Lost Conf. Quarter-Final
1992-93	84	25	11	6	22	14	6	47	25	12	279	230	106	1st, Norris Div.	Lost Div. Semi-Final
1991-92	80	23	9	8	13	20	7	36	29	15	257	236	87	2nd, Norris Div.	Lost Final
1990-91	80	28	8	4	21	15	4	49	23	8	284	211	106	1st, Norris Div.	Lost Div. Semi-Final
1989-90	80	25	13	2	16	20	4	41	33	6	316	294	88	1st, Norris Div.	Lost Conf. Championship
1988-89	80	16	14	10	11	27	2	27	41	12	297	335	66	4th, Norris Div.	Lost Conf. Championship
1987-88	80	21	17	2	9	24	7	30	41	9	284	328	69	3rd, Norris Div.	Lost Div. Semi-Final
1986-87	80	18	13	9	11	24	5	29	37	14	290	310	72	3rd, Norris Div.	Lost Div. Semi-Final
1985-86	80	23	12	5	16	21	3	39	33	8	351	349	86	1st, Norris Div.	Lost Div. Semi-Final
1984-85	80	22	16	2	16	19	5	38	35	7	309	299	83	2nd, Norris Div.	Lost Conf. Championship
1983-84	80	25	13	2	5	29	6	30	42	8	277	311	68	4th, Norris Div.	Lost Div. Semi-Final
1982-83	80	29	8	3	18	15	7	47	23	10	338	268	104	1st, Norris Div.	Lost Conf. Championship
1981-82	80	20	13	7	10	25	5	30	38	12	332	363	72	4th, Norris Div.	Lost Conf. Championship
1980-81	80	21	11	8	10	22	8	31	33	16	304	315	78	2nd, Smythe Div.	Lost Prelim. Round
1979-80	80	21	12	7	13	15	12	34	27	19	241	250	87	1st, Smythe Div.	Lost Quarter-Final
1978-79	80	18	12	10	11	24	5	29	36	15	244	277	73	1st, Smythe Div.	Lost Quarter-Final
1977-78	80	20	9	11	12	20	8	32	29	19	230	220	83	1st, Smythe Div.	Lost Quarter-Final
1976-77	80	19	16	5	7	27	6	26	43	11	240	298	63	3rd, Smythe Div.	Lost Prelim. Round
1975-76	80	17	15	8	15	15	10	32	30	18	254	261	82	1st, Smythe Div.	Lost Quarter-Final
1974-75	80	24	12	4	13	23	4	37	35	8	268	241	82	3rd, Smythe Div.	Lost Quarter-Final
1973-74	78	20	6	13	21	8	10	41	14	23	272	164	105	2nd, West Div.	Lost Semi-Final
1972-73	78	26	9	4	16	18	5	42	27	9	284	225	93	1st, West Div.	Lost Final
1971-72	78	28	3	8	18	14	7	46	17	15	256	166	107	1st, West Div.	Lost Semi-Final
1970-71	78	30	6	3	19	14	6	49	20	9	277	184	107	1st, West Div.	Lost Final
1969-70	76	26	7	5	19	15	4	45	22	9	250	170	99	1st, East Div.	Lost Semi-Final
1968-69	76	20	14	4	14	19	5	34	33	9	280	246	77	6th, East Div.	Out of Playoffs
1967-68	74	20	13	4	12	13	12	32	26	16	212	222	80	4th, East Div.	Lost Semi-Final
1966-67	70	24	5	6	17	12	6	41	17	12	264	170	94	1st,	Lost Semi-Final
1965-66	70	21	8	6	16	17	2	37	25	8	240	187	82	2nd,	Lost Semi-Final
1964-65	70	20	13	2	14	15	6	34	28	8	224	176	76	3rd,	Lost Final
1963-64	70	26	4	5	10	18	7	36	22	12	218	169	84	2nd,	Lost Semi-Final
1962-63	70	17	9	9	15	12	8	32	21	17	194	178	81	2nd,	Lost Semi-Final
1961-62	70	20	10	5	11	16	8	31	26	13	217	186	75	3rd,	Lost Final
1960-61	70	20	6	9	9	18	8	29	24	17	198	180	75	3rd,	**Won Stanley Cup**
1959-60	70	18	11	6	10	18	7	28	29	13	191	180	69	3rd,	Lost Semi-Final
1958-59	70	14	12	9	14	17	4	28	29	13	197	208	69	3rd,	Lost Semi-Final
1957-58	70	15	17	3	9	22	4	24	39	7	163	202	55	5th,	Out of Playoffs
1956-57	70	12	15	8	4	24	7	16	39	15	169	225	47	6th,	Out of Playoffs
1955-56	70	9	19	7	10	20	5	19	39	12	155	216	50	6th,	Out of Playoffs
1954-55	70	6	21	8	7	19	9	13	40	17	161	235	43	6th,	Out of Playoffs
1953-54	70	8	21	6	4	30	1	12	51	7	133	242	31	6th,	Out of Playoffs
1952-53	70	14	11	10	13	17	5	27	28	15	169	175	69	4th,	Lost Semi-Final
1951-52	70	9	19	7	8	25	2	17	44	9	158	241	43	6th,	Out of Playoffs
1950-51	70	8	22	5	5	25	5	13	47	10	171	280	36	6th,	Out of Playoffs
1949-50	70	13	18	4	9	20	6	22	38	10	203	244	54	6th,	Out of Playoffs
1948-49	60	13	12	5	8	19	3	21	31	8	173	211	50	5th,	Out of Playoffs
1947-48	60	10	17	3	10	17	3	20	34	6	195	225	46	6th,	Out of Playoffs
1946-47	60	10	17	3	9	20	1	19	37	4	193	274	42	6th,	Out of Playoffs
1945-46	50	15	5	5	8	15	2	23	20	7	200	178	53	3rd,	Lost Semi-Final
1944-45	50	9	14	2	4	16	5	13	30	7	141	194	33	5th,	Out of Playoffs
1943-44	50	15	6	4	7	17	1	22	23	5	178	187	49	4th,	Lost Final
1942-43	50*	14	3	8	3	15	7	17	18	15	179	180	49	5th,	Out of Playoffs
1941-42	48	15	8	1	7	15	2	22	23	3	145	155	47	4th,	Lost Quarter-Final
1940-41	48	11	10	3	5	13	6	16	25	7	112	139	39	5th,	Lost Semi-Final
1939-40	48	15	7	2	8	12	4	23	19	6	112	120	52	4th,	Lost Quarter-Final
1938-39	48	5	13	6	7	15	2	12	28	8	91	132	32	7th,	Out of Playoffs
1937-38	48	10	10	4	4	15	5	14	25	9	97	139	37	3rd, Amn. Div.	**Won Stanley Cup**
1936-37	48	8	13	3	6	14	4	14	27	7	99	131	35	4th, Amn. Div.	Out of Playoffs
1935-36	48	15	7	2	6	12	6	21	19	8	93	92	50	3rd, Amn. Div.	Lost Quarter-Final
1934-35	48	12	9	3	14	8	2	26	17	5	118	88	57	2nd, Amn. Div.	Lost Quarter-Final
1933-34	48	13	4	7	7	13	4	20	17	11	88	83	51	2nd, Amn. Div.	**Won Stanley Cup**
1932-33	48	12	7	5	4	13	7	16	20	12	88	101	44	4th, Amn. Div.	Out of Playoffs
1931-32	48	13	5	6	5	14	5	18	19	11	86	101	47	2nd, Amn. Div.	Lost Semi-Final
1930-31	44	13	8	1	11	9	2	24	17	3	108	78	51	2nd, Amn. Div.	Lost Final
1929-30	44	12	9	1	9	9	4	21	18	5	117	111	47	2nd, Amn. Div.	Lost Quarter-Final
1928-29	44	3	13	6	4	16	2	7	29	8	33	85	22	5th, Amn. Div.	Out of Playoffs
1927-28	44	2	18	2	5	16	1	7	34	3	68	134	17	5th, Amn. Div.	Out of Playoffs
1926-27	44	12	8	2	7	14	1	19	22	3	115	116	41	3rd, Amn. Div.	Lost Quarter-Final

1995-96 Player Personnel

FORWARDS	HT	WT	S	Place of Birth	Date	1994-95 Club
AMONTE, Tony	6-0	190	L	Hingham, MA	8/2/70	Fassa-Chicago
BLACK, James	5-11	185	L	Regina, Sask.	8/15/69	Las Vegas
CRAVEN, Murray	6-2	185	L	Medicine Hat, Alta.	7/20/64	Chicago
CUMMINS, Jim	6-2	203	R	Dearborn, MI	5/17/70	Tampa Bay-Chicago
DAZE, Eric	6-4	215	L	Montreal, Que.	7/2/75	Beauport-Chicago
DUBINSKY, Steve	6-0	190	L	Montreal, Que.	7/9/70	Indianapolis-Chicago
ENSON, Jim	6-3	191	L	Oshawa, Ont.	8/24/76	North Bay-Kitchener
GAUTHIER, Daniel	6-1	190	L	Charlemagne, Que.	5/17/70	Indianapolis-Chicago
GRIEVE, Brent	6-1	202	L	Oshawa, Ont.	5/9/69	Chicago
HUSKA, Ryan	6-2	194	L	Cranbrook, B.C.	7/2/75	Kamloops
HYMOVITZ, David	5-11	170	L	Boston, MA	5/30/74	Boston College
JOSEPHSON, Mike	5-11	195	L	Vancouver, B.C.	4/6/76	Kamloops-Lethbridge
KIMBLE, Darin	6-2	210	R	Lucky Lake, Sask.	11/22/68	Chicago
KIRTON, Scott	6-4	215	R	Penetanguishene, Ont.	10/4/71	North Dakota
KLIMOVICH, Sergei	6-3	189	R	Novosibirsk, USSR	3/8/74	Moscow D'amo-Indianapolis
KRIVOKRASOV, Sergei	5-10	195	L	Angarsk, USSR	4/15/74	Indianapolis-Chicago
LeCOMPTE, Eric	6-4	190	L	Montreal, Que.	4/4/75	Hull-St-Jean-Sher-Ind
LEROUX, Jean-Yves	6-2	193	L	Montreal, Que.	6/24/76	Beauport
MacINTYRE, Andy	6-1	190	L	Thunder Bay, Ont.	4/16/74	Columbus-Indianapolis
MANLOW, Eric	6-0	190	L	Belleville, Ont.	4/7/75	Kitchener-Detroit (OHL)
MARA, Rob	6-1	175	R	Boston, MA	9/25/75	Colgate
MILLER, Kip	5-10	190	L	Lansing, MI	6/11/69	Denver-NY Islanders
MOREAU, Ethan	6-2	205	L	Huntsville, Ont.	9/22/75	Niagara Falls-Sudbury
MURPHY, Joe	6-1	190	L	London, Ont.	10/16/67	Chicago
NABOKOV, Dmitri	6-2	209	R	Novosibirsk, USSR	1/4/77	Soviet Wings
NICHOLLS, Bernie	6-1	185	R	Haliburton, Ont.	6/24/61	Chicago
OATES, Matt	6-3	208	L	Evanston, IL	12/20/72	Columbus-Indianapolis
PETROV, Sergei	5-11	185	L	Leningrad, USSR	1/22/75	Minn.-Duluth
POMICHTER, Michael	6-1	222	L	New Haven, CT	9/10/73	Indianapolis
POULIN, Patrick	6-1	210	L	Vanier, Que.	4/23/73	Chicago
PROBERT, Bob	6-3	225	L	Windsor, Ont.	6/5/65	DID NOT PLAY
PROKOPEC, Mike	6-2	190	R	Toronto, Ont.	5/17/74	Indianapolis
PROSOFSKY, Tyler	5-11	175	L	Saskatoon, Sask.	2/19/76	Tacoma
PYSZ, Patrik	5-11	187	L	Nowy Targ, Poland	1/15/75	Augsburg
ROENICK, Jeremy	6-0	170	R	Boston, MA	1/17/70	Koln-Chicago
ROYER, Gaetan	6-3	193	R	Donnacona, Que.	3/13/76	Sherbrooke
SAVARD, Denis	5-10	175	R	Pointe Gatineau, Que.	2/4/61	Tampa Bay-Chicago
SHANTZ, Jeff	6-0	184	R	Duchess, Alta.	10/10/73	Indianapolis-Chicago
SUTTER, Brent	5-11	187	R	Viking, Alta.	6/10/62	Chicago
WHITE, Tom	6-1	185	L	Chicago, IL	8/25/75	Miami-Ohio

DEFENSEMEN	HT	WT	S	Place of Birth	Date	1994-95 Club
BUCHANAN, Jeff	5-10	165	R	Swift Current, Sask.	5/23/71	Atlanta-Indianapolis
CARNEY, Keith E.	6-2	205	L	Providence, RI	2/3/70	Chicago
CASSIDY, Bruce	5-11	176	L	Ottawa, Ont.	5/20/65	Indianapolis
CHELIOS, Chris	6-1	186	R	Chicago, IL	1/25/62	Biel-Chicago
DROPPA, Ivan	6-2	209	L	Liptovsky Mikulas, Czech.	2/1/72	Indianapolis
DUPUIS, Marc	5-11	176	L	Cornwall, Ont.	4/22/76	Belleville
KRIZ, Pavel	6-1	205	R	Nymburk, Czech.	1/2/77	Tri-City
LAFLAMME, Christian	6-1	195	R	St. Charles, Que.	11/24/76	Beauport
McKAY, Kevin	6-3	198	L	North Battleford, Sask.	1/4/77	Moose Jaw
MCLAREN, Steve	6-0	194	L	Owen Sound, Ont.	2/3/75	North Bay
RUSK, Mike	6-1	175	L	Milton, Ont.	4/26/75	Guelph
RUSSELL, Cam	6-4	195	L	Halifax, N.S.	1/12/69	Chicago
SEROWIK, Jeff	6-1	210	R	Manchester, NH	1/10/67	Providence (AHL)-Boston
SMITH, Steve	6-4	215	L	Glasgow, Scotland	4/30/63	Chicago
SUTER, Gary	6-0	200	L	Madison, WI	6/24/64	Chicago
THIESSEN, Travis	6-3	203	L	North Battleford, Sask.	7/11/72	Flint-Indianapolis-Saint John
VAN DYK, Chris	6-2	185	R	Welland, Ont.	2/18/77	Windsor
WEINRICH, Eric	6-1	210	L	Roanoke, VA	12/19/66	Chicago
WERENKA, Brad	6-2	210	L	Two Hills, Alta.	2/12/69	Milwaukee
WILFORD, Marty	6-0	216	L	Cobourg, Ont.	4/17/77	Oshawa

GOALTENDERS	HT	WT	C	Place of Birth	Date	1994-95 Club
BELFOUR, Ed	5-11	182	L	Carman, Man.	4/21/65	Chicago
HACKETT, Jeff	6-1	180	L	London, Ont.	6/1/68	Chicago
NOBLE, Tom	5-10	165	L	Quincy, MA	3/21/75	Boston U.
RACICOT, Andre	5-11	165	L	Rouyn-Noranda, Que.	6/9/69	Portland (AHL)-Phoenix
SOUCY, Christian	5-11	160	L	Gatineau, Que.	9/14/70	Indianapolis
WAITE, Jimmy	6-1	180	L	Sherbrooke, Que.	4/15/69	Chicago-Indianapolis
WEIBEL, Lars	6-0	178	L	Rapperswil, Switz.	5/20/74	Lugano

Coach

HARTSBURG, CRAIG
Coach, Chicago Blackhawks. Born in Stratford, Ont., June 29, 1959.

Craig Hartsburg was introduced as the 30th Head Coach in the history of the Chicago Blackhawks at a press conference on June 29, 1995. Hartsburg comes to the Blackhawks from the Guelph Storm (OHL), where he was named OHL Coach of the Year after leading the Storm to a 47-14-5 record.

Hartsburg received his first head coaching position at Guelph last season after spending four seasons as an assistant coach from 1990-94 with the Philadelphia Flyers and one season as an assistant coach with the Minnesota North Stars during the 1989-90 season.

Hartsburg played his entire 10-year NHL career with Minnesota. Known as an offensive-defenseman, Hartsburg was the North Stars' captain for six seasons, until injuries forced him to retire from active play on January 13, 1988.

Hartsburg lists winning the Canada Cup Championship in 1987 as his most memorable hockey moment. He participated in three NHL All-Star games (1980, 1982 and 1983) and also competed in three World Championship tournaments for Team Canada — and was chosen best defenseman of the 1987 World Championships. In February of 1992, Hartsburg was voted to the North Stars' 25th Anniversary Dream Team by Minnesota fans.

Hartsburg, who turned 36 on the day he was announced as head coach, and his wife Peggy have two children, Christopher and Katie.

1994-95 Scoring

* – rookie

Regular Season

Pos	#	Player	Team	GP	G	A	Pts	+/–	PIM	PP	SH	GW	GT	S	%
C	92	Bernie Nicholls	CHI	48	22	29	51	4	32	11	2	5	0	114	19.3
R	17	Joe Murphy	CHI	40	23	18	41	7	89	7	0	3	0	120	19.2
D	7	Chris Chelios	CHI	48	5	33	38	17	72	3	1	0	0	166	3.0
D	20	Gary Suter	CHI	48	10	27	37	14	42	5	0	0	0	144	6.9
R	10	Tony Amonte	CHI	48	15	20	35	7	41	6	1	3	1	105	14.3
C	27	Jeremy Roenick	CHI	33	10	24	34	5	14	5	0	1	0	93	10.8
L	44	Patrick Poulin	CHI	45	15	15	30	13	53	4	0	2	0	77	19.5
C	18	Denis Savard	T.B.	31	6	11	17	–6	10	1	0	1	0	56	10.7
			CHI	12	4	4	8	3	8	1	0	0	0	26	15.4
			TOTAL	43	10	15	25	–3	18	2	0	1	0	82	12.2
R	25 *	Sergei Krivokrasov	CHI	41	12	7	19	9	33	6	0	2	1	72	16.7
C	11	Jeff Shantz	CHI	45	6	12	18	11	33	0	2	0	0	58	10.3
C	12	Brent Sutter	CHI	47	7	8	15	6	51	1	0	1	0	65	10.8
R	33	Dirk Graham	CHI	40	4	9	13	2	42	1	1	0	0	68	5.9
D	2	Eric Weinrich	CHI	48	3	10	13	1	33	1	0	2	0	50	6.0
D	5	Steve Smith	CHI	48	1	12	13	6	128	0	0	0	0	43	2.3
L	32	Murray Craven	CHI	16	4	3	7	2	2	1	0	2	0	29	13.8
L	19	Brent Grieve	CHI	24	1	5	6	2	23	0	0	0	0	30	3.3
R	15	Jim Cummins	T.B.	10	1	0	1	–3	41	0	0	1	0	3	33.3
			CHI	27	3	1	4	–3	117	0	0	0	0	20	15.0
			TOTAL	37	4	1	5	–6	158	0	0	1	0	23	17.4
D	6	Gerald Diduck	VAN	22	1	3	4	–8	15	1	0	0	0	25	4.0
			CHI	13	1	0	1	3	48	0	0	0	0	17	5.9
			TOTAL	35	2	3	5	–5	63	1	0	0	0	42	4.8
D	8	Cam Russell	CHI	33	1	3	4	4	88	0	0	0	0	18	5.6
D	3	Greg Smyth	CHI	22	0	3	3	2	33	0	0	0	0	10	0.0
G	30	Ed Belfour	CHI	42	0	3	3	0	11	0	0	0	0	0	0.0
L	55 *	Eric Daze	CHI	4	1	1	2	2	2	0	0	0	0	1	100.0
D	26	Roger Johansson	CHI	11	1	0	1	1	6	0	0	0	0	10	10.0
D	4	Keith Carney	CHI	18	1	0	1	–1	11	0	0	1	0	14	7.1
L	34	Tony Horacek	CHI	19	0	1	1	–4	25	0	0	0	0	6	0.0
G	49	Jim Waite	S.J.	0	0	0	0	0	0	0	0	0	0	0	0.0
			CHI	2	0	0	0	0	0	0	0	0	0	0	0.0
			TOTAL	2	0	0	0	0	0	0	0	0	0	0	0.0
L	23 *	Daniel Gauthier	CHI	5	0	0	0	0	0	0	0	0	0	4	0.0
G	31	Jeff Hackett	CHI	7	0	0	0	0	0	0	0	0	0	0	0.0
R	29	Darin Kimble	CHI	14	0	0	0	–5	30	0	0	0	0	2	0.0
C	22	Steve Dubinsky	CHI	16	0	0	0	–5	8	0	0	0	0	16	0.0

Goaltending

No.	Goaltender	GPI	Mins	Avg	W	L	T	EN	SO	GA	SA	S%
30	Ed Belfour	42	2450	2.28	22	15	3	4	5	93	990	.906
31	Jeff Hackett	7	328	2.38	1	3	2	0	0	13	150	.913
49	Jim Waite	2	119	2.52	1	1	0	0	0	5	51	.902
	Totals	**48**	**2909**	**2.37**	**24**	**19**	**5**	**4**	**5**	**115**	**1195**	**.904**

Playoffs

Pos	#	Player	Team	GP	G	A	Pts	+/–	PIM	PP	SH	GW	OT	S	%
C	18	Denis Savard	CHI	16	7	11	18	12	10	3	0	0	0	39	17.9
R	17	Joe Murphy	CHI	16	9	3	12	–1	29	3	0	3	1	69	13.0
C	92	Bernie Nicholls	CHI	16	1	11	12	0	8	1	0	0	0	28	3.6
D	7	Chris Chelios	CHI	16	4	7	11	6	12	0	1	3	2	49	8.2
L	32	Murray Craven	CHI	16	5	5	10	2	4	0	0	1	0	28	17.9
D	20	Gary Suter	CHI	12	2	5	7	–1	10	1	0	0	0	43	4.7
R	10	Tony Amonte	CHI	16	3	3	6	3	10	0	0	0	0	32	9.4
D	2	Eric Weinrich	CHI	16	1	5	6	8	4	0	0	0	0	14	7.1
L	44	Patrick Poulin	CHI	16	4	1	5	1	8	1	0	0	0	30	13.3
R	33	Dirk Graham	CHI	16	2	3	5	6	8	0	0	1	0	21	9.5
C	11	Jeff Shantz	CHI	16	3	1	4	0	2	0	0	0	0	16	18.8
D	6	Gerald Diduck	CHI	16	1	3	4	–4	22	0	0	0	0	21	4.8
C	27	Jeremy Roenick	CHI	8	1	2	3	–2	16	0	0	0	0	13	7.7
C	12	Brent Sutter	CHI	16	1	2	3	1	4	0	0	0	0	23	4.3
D	8	Cam Russell	CHI	16	0	3	3	4	8	0	0	0	0	5	0.0
R	15	Jim Cummins	CHI	14	1	1	2	3	4	0	0	1	0	8	12.5
D	4	Keith Carney	CHI	4	0	1	1	0	0	0	0	0	0	1	0.0
D	5	Steve Smith	CHI	16	0	1	1	2	26	0	0	0	0	11	0.0
L	55 *	Eric Daze	CHI	16	0	1	1	–4	4	0	0	0	0	16	0.0
G	31	Jeff Hackett	CHI	2	0	0	0	0	0	0	0	0	0	0	0.0
R	25 *	Sergei Krivokrasov	CHI	10	0	0	0	0	8	0	0	0	0	4	0.0
G	30	Ed Belfour	CHI	16	0	0	0	0	6	0	0	0	0	0	0.0

Goaltending

No.	Goaltender	GPI	Mins	Avg	W	L	EN	SO	GA	SA	S%
30	Ed Belfour	16	1014	2.19	9	7	1	1	37	479	.923
31	Jeff Hackett	2	26	2.31	0	0	0	0	1	11	.909
	Totals	**16**	**1044**	**2.24**	**9**	**7**	**1**	**1**	**39**	**491**	**.921**

Coaching Record

		Regular Season					Playoffs			
Season	Team	Games	W	L	T	%	Games	W	L	%
1994-95	Guelph (OHL)	66	47	14	5	.750	14	10	4	.714

Club Records

Team

(Figures in brackets for season records are games played; records for fewest points, wins, ties, losses, goals, goals against are for 70 or more games)

Most Points	**107**	1970-71 (78) 1971-72 (78)
Most Wins	**49**	1970-71 (78) 1990-91 (80)
Most Ties	**23**	1973-74 (78)
Most Losses	**51**	1953-54 (70)
Most Goals	**351**	1985-86 (80)
Most Goals Against	**363**	1981-82 (80)
Fewest Points	**31**	1953-54 (70)
Fewest Wins	**12**	1953-54 (70)
Fewest Ties	**6**	1989-90 (80)
Fewest Losses	**14**	1973-74 (78)
Fewest Goals	***133**	1953-54 (70)
Fewest Goals Against	**164**	1973-74 (78)
Longest Winning Streak		
Over-all	**8**	Dec. 9-26/71; Jan. 4-21/81
Home	**13**	Nov. 11- Dec. 20/70
Away	**7**	Dec. 9-29/64
Longest Undefeated Streak		
Over-all	**15**	Jan. 14- Feb. 16/67 (12 wins, 3 ties)
Home	**18**	Oct. 11- Dec. 20/70 (16 wins, 2 ties)
Away	**12**	Oct. 29- Dec. 3/75 (6 wins, 9 ties)
Longest Losing Streak		
Over-all	**13**	Feb. 25- Oct. 11/51
Home	**11**	Feb. 8- Nov. 22/28
Away	**17**	Jan. 2- Oct. 7/54
Longest Winless Streak		
Over-all	**21**	Dec. 17/50- Jan. 28/51 (18 losses, 3 ties)
Home	***15**	Dec. 16/28- Feb. 28/29 (11 losses, 4 ties)
Away	**23**	Dec. 19/50- Oct. 11/51 (15 losses, 8 ties)
Most Shutouts, Season	**15**	1969-70 (76)
Most PIM, Season	**2,663**	1991-92 (80)
Most Goals, Game	**12**	Jan. 30/69 (Chi. 12 at Phil. 0)

Individual

Most Seasons	**22**	Stan Mikita
Most Games	**1,394**	Stan Mikita
Most Goals, Career	**604**	Bobby Hull
Most Assists, Career	**926**	Stan Mikita
Most Points, Career	**1,467**	Stan Mikita (541 goals, 926 assists)
Most PIM, Career	**1,442**	Keith Magnuson
Most Shutouts, Career	**74**	Tony Esposito
Longest Consecutive Games Streak	**884**	Steve Larmer (1982-83 to 1992-93)
Most Goals, Season	**58**	Bobby Hull (1968-69)
Most Assists, Season	**87**	Denis Savard (81-82, 87-88)
Most Points, Season	**131**	Denis Savard (1987-88) (44 goals, 87 assists)
Most PIM, Season	**408**	Mike Peluso (1991-92)
Most Points, Defenseman Season	**85**	Doug Wilson (1981-82) (39 goals, 46 assists)
Most Points, Center, Season	**131**	Denis Savard (1987-88) (44 goals, 87 assists)
Most Points, Right Wing, Season	**101**	Steve Larmer (1990-91) (44 goals, 57 assists)
Most Points, Left Wing, Season	**107**	Bobby Hull (1968-69) (58 goals, 49 assists)
Most Points, Rookie, Season	**90**	Steve Larmer (1982-83) (43 goals, 47 assists)
Most Shutouts, Season	**15**	Tony Esposito (1969-70)
Most Goals, Game	**5**	Grant Mulvey (Feb. 3/82)
Most Assists, Game	**6**	Pat Stapleton (Mar. 30/69)
Most Points, Game	**7**	Max Bentley (Jan. 28/43) Grant Mulvey (Feb. 3/82)

* NHL Record.

Coaching History

Pete Muldoon, 1926-27; Barney Stanley and Hugh Lehman, 1927-28; Herb Gardiner, 1928-29; Tom Shaughnessy and Bill Tobin, 1929-30; Dick Irvin, 1930-31; Dick Irvin and Bill Tobin, 1931-32; Emil Iverson, Godfrey Matheson and Tommy Gorman, 1932-33; Tommy Gorman, 1933-34; Clem Loughlin, 1934-35 to 1936-37; Bill Stewart, 1937-38; Bill Stewart and Paul Thompson, 1938-39; Paul Thompson, 1939-40 to 1943-44; Paul Thompson and Johnny Gottselig, 1944-45; Johnny Gottselig, 1945-46 to 1946-47; Johnny Gottselig and Charlie Conacher, 1947-48; Charlie Conacher, 1948-49, 1949-50; Ebbie Goodfellow, 1950-51 to 1951-52; Sid Abel, 1952-53 to 1953-54; Frank Eddolls, 1954-55; Dick Irvin, 1955-56; Tommy Ivan, 1956-57; Tommy Ivan and Rudy Pilous, 1957-58; Rudy Pilous, 1958-59 to 1962-63; Billy Reay, 1963-64 to 1975-76; Billy Reay and Bill White, 1976-77; Bob Pulford, 1977-78, 1978-79; Eddie Johnston, 1979-80; Keith Magnuson, 1980-81; Keith Magnuson and Bob Pulford, 1981-82; Orval Tessier, 1982-83 to 1983-84; Orval Tessier and Bob Pulford, 1984-85; Bob Pulford, 1985-86 to 1986-87; Bob Murdoch, 1987-88; Mike Keenan, 1988-89 to 1991-92; Darryl Sutter, 1992-93 to 1994-95; Craig Hartsburg, 1995-96.

Captains' History

Dick Irvin, 1926-27 to 1928-29; "Duke" Dutkowski, 1929-30; Ty Arbour, 1930-31; Cy Wentworth, 1931-32; Helge Bostrom, 1932-33; Chuck Gardiner, 1933-34; no captain, 1934-35; Johnny Gottselig, 1935-36 to 1939-40; Earl Seibert, 1940-41, 1941-42; Doug Bentley, 1942-43, 1943-44; Clint Smith 1944-45; John Mariucci, 1945-46; "Red" Hamill, 1946-47; John Mariucci, 1947-48; Gaye Stewart, 1948-49; Doug Bentley, 1949-50; Jack Stewart, 1950-51, 1951-52; Bill Gadsby, 1952-53, 1953-54; Gus Mortson, 1954-55 to 1956-57; no captain, 1957-58; Eddie Litzenberger, 1958-59 to 1960-61; Pierre Pilote, 1961-62 to 1967-68, no captain, 1968-69; Pat Stapleton, 1969-70; no captain, 1970-71 to 1974-75; Stan Mikita and "Pit" Martin, 1975-76; Stan Mikita, "Pit" Martin and Keith Magnuson, 1976-77; Keith Magnuson, 1977-78, 1978-79; Keith Magnuson, Terry Ruskowski, 1979-80; Terry Ruskowski, 1980-81, 1981-82; Darryl Sutter, 1982-83 to 1984-85; Darryl Sutter and Bob Murray, 1985-86; Darryl Sutter, 1986-87; no captain, 1987-88; Denis Savard and Dirk Graham, 1988-89; Dirk Graham, 1989-90 to 1994-95.

General Managers' History

Major Frederic McLaughlin, 1926-27 to 1941-42; Bill Tobin, 1942-43 to 1953-54; Tommy Ivan, 1954-55 to 1976-77; Bob Pulford, 1977-78 to 1989-90; Mike Keenan, 1990-91 to 1991-92; Mike Keenan and Bob Pulford, 1992-93; Bob Pulford, 1993-94 to date.

All-time Record vs. Other Clubs

Regular Season

	At Home							On Road							Total						
	GP	W	L	T	GF	GA	PTS	GP	W	L	T	GF	GA	PTS	GP	W	L	T	GF	GA	PTS
Anaheim	5	4	1	0	15	8	8	4	3	1	0	10	7	6	9	7	2	0	25	15	14
Boston	278	141	93	44	896	745	326	276	85	159	32	778	1003	202	554	226	252	76	1674	1748	528
Buffalo	43	22	15	6	138	120	50	45	11	28	6	116	174	28	88	33	43	12	254	294	78
Calgary	43	20	13	10	154	132	50	45	17	21	7	139	148	41	88	37	34	17	293	280	91
Dallas	89	58	21	10	368	231	126	91	39	40	12	296	309	90	180	97	61	22	664	540	216
Detroit	312	144	120	48	939	864	336	311	92	191	28	767	1066	212	623	236	311	76	1706	1930	548
Edmonton	26	14	9	3	110	103	31	27	12	14	1	105	114	25	53	26	23	4	215	217	56
Florida	1	0	0	1	4	4	1	1	1	0	0	3	2	2	2	1	0	1	7	6	3
Hartford	22	13	6	3	99	64	29	23	11	10	2	80	80	24	45	24	16	5	179	144	53
Los Angeles	57	29	20	8	222	173	66	56	26	24	6	197	192	58	113	55	44	14	419	365	124
Montreal	267	91	121	55	722	747	237	267	51	168	48	629	1037	150	534	142	289	103	1351	1784	387
New Jersey	39	22	9	8	163	112	52	38	14	15	9	115	114	37	77	36	24	17	278	226	89
NY Islanders	41	20	16	5	135	143	45	39	11	16	12	118	142	34	80	31	32	17	253	285	79
NY Rangers	278	124	112	42	848	777	290	279	109	116	54	790	827	272	557	233	228	96	1638	1604	562
Ottawa	2	1	0	1	7	5	3	2	2	0	0	5	2	4	4	3	0	1	12	7	7
Philadelphia	53	24	11	18	191	150	66	54	15	28	11	145	178	41	107	39	39	29	336	328	107
Pittsburgh	52	35	8	9	221	144	79	51	22	24	5	170	181	49	103	57	32	14	391	325	128
Quebec	23	14	7	2	94	74	30	22	9	9	4	89	94	22	45	23	16	6	183	168	52
St. Louis	93	55	26	12	373	285	122	90	29	44	17	278	309	75	183	84	70	29	651	594	197
San Jose	7	5	1	1	28	17	11	8	3	5	0	22	22	6	15	8	6	1	50	39	17
Tampa Bay	5	3	0	2	16	9	8	4	2	2	0	15	14	4	9	5	2	2	31	23	12
Toronto	302	153	109	40	935	786	346	301	89	160	52	773	1034	230	603	242	269	92	1708	1820	576
Vancouver	53	35	13	5	205	126	75	54	17	25	12	160	168	46	107	52	38	17	365	294	121
Washington	32	20	7	5	134	97	45	33	10	19	4	102	127	24	65	30	26	9	236	224	69
Winnipeg	29	21	5	3	142	84	45	30	11	16	3	105	118	25	59	32	21	6	247	202	70
Defunct Clubs	139	79	40	20	408	268	178	140	52	67	21	316	346	125	279	131	107	41	724	614	303
Totals	**2291**	**1147**	**783**	**361**	**7567**	**6268**	**2655**	**2291**	**743**	**1202**	**346**	**6323**	**7808**	**1832**	**4582**	**1890**	**1985**	**707**	**13890**	**14076**	**4487**

Calgary totals include Atlanta, 1972-73 to 1979-80. Dallas totals include Minnesota, 1967-68 to 1992-93.
New Jersey totals include Kansas City, 1974-75 to 1975-76, and Colorado, 1976-77 to 1981-82.

Playoffs

	Series	W	L	GP	W	L	T	GF	GA	Last Mtg.	Round	Result
Boston	6	1	5	22	5	16	1	63	97	1978	QF	L 0-4
Buffalo	2	0	2	9	1	8	0	17	36	1980	QF	L 0-4
Calgary	2	0	2	8	1	7	0	17	30	1989	CF	L 1-4
Dallas	6	4	2	33	19	14	0	119	119	1991	DSF	L 2-4
Detroit	14	8	6	69	38	31	0	210	190	1995	CF	L 1-4
Edmonton	4	1	3	20	8	12	0	77	102	1992	CF	W 4-0
Los Angeles	1	1	0	5	4	1	0	10	7	1974	QF	W 4-1
Montreal	17	5	12	81	29	50	2	185	261	1976	QF	L 0-4
NY Islanders	2	0	2	6	0	6	0	6	21	1979	QF	L 0-4
NY Rangers	5	4	1	24	14	10	0	66	54	1973	SF	W 4-1
Philadelphia	1	1	0	4	4	0	0	20	8	1971	QF	W 4-0
Pittsburgh	2	1	1	8	4	4	0	24	23	1992	F	L 0-4
St. Louis	9	7	2	45	27	18	0	166	129	1993	DSF	L 0-4
Toronto	9	3	6	38	15	22	1	89	111	1995	CQF	W 4-3
Vancouver	2	1	1	9	5	4	0	24	24	1995	CSF	W 4-0
Defunct Clubs	4	2	2	9	5	3	1	16	15			
Totals	**86**	**39**	**47**	**390**	**179**	**206**	**5**	**1109**	**1227**			

Playoff Results 1995-91

Year	Round	Opponent	Result	GF	GA
1995	CF	Detroit	L 1-4	12	13
	CSF	Vancouver	W 4-0	11	6
	CQF	Toronto	W 4-3	22	20
1994	CQF	Toronto	L 2-4	10	15
1993	DSF	St. Louis	L 0-4	6	13
1992	F	Pittsburgh	L 0-4	10	15
	CF	Edmonton	W 4-0	21	8
	DF	Detroit	W 4-0	11	6
	DSF	St. Louis	W 4-2	23	19
1991	DSF	Minnesota	L 2-4	16	23

Abbreviations: Round: F – Final;
CF – conference final; **CQF** – conference quarter-final;
CSF – conference semi-final; **DF** – division final;
DSF – division semi-final; **SF** – semi-final;
QF – quarter-final; **PR** – preliminary round.

1994-95 Results

Jan.	20	at	Detroit	1-4		13	at	Dallas	2-4
	23	at	Winnipeg	3-5		16		Vancouver	9-2
	25		Edmonton	5-1		19	at	Winnipeg	3-2
	27		Toronto	4-1		21	at	San Jose	7-3
	29	at	Los Angeles	6-3		23	at	Vancouver	3-1
	30	at	San Jose	1-2		26		Anaheim	5-2
Feb.	1	at	Edmonton	7-0		29		St. Louis	1-3
	3	at	Calgary	4-3		31		Toronto	3-3
	5	at	Vancouver	9-4	**Apr.**	2		Dallas	1-2
	7	at	Anaheim	3-0		4	at	Calgary	2-3
	9	at	St. Louis	5-0		5	at	Winnipeg	1-4
	13	at	Toronto	2-4		9		Detroit	1-4
	16		Calgary	2-2		12		San Jose	2-3
	19		Edmonton	4-1		14		Detroit	1-3
	20		San Jose	3-2		16	at	Dallas	0-2
	23		Detroit	2-4		17		Toronto	1-3
	26	at	Dallas	2-1		19		St. Louis	2-2
	28	at	Los Angeles	8-4		21		Winnipeg	1-2
Mar.	1	at	Anaheim	1-3		23	at	St. Louis	2-2
	3	at	Edmonton	5-2		25		Vancouver	4-3
	5		Anaheim	3-0		27		Dallas	5-1
	7		Calgary	3-6		30	at	Detroit	4-0
	9		Los Angeles	3-4	**May**	1		Winnipeg	3-2
	11	at	Toronto	2-2		3		Los Angeles	5-1

Entry Draft
Selections 1995-81

1995
Pick
19	Dimitri Nabokov
45	Christian Laflamme
71	Kevin McKay
82	Chris Van Dyk
97	Pavel Kriz
146	Marc Magliarditi
149	Marty Wilford
175	Steve Tardif
201	Casey Hankinson
227	Mike Pittman

1994
Pick
14	Ethan Moreau
40	Jean-Yves Leroux
85	Steve McLaren
118	Marc Dupuis
144	Jim Enson
170	Tyler Prosofsky
196	Mike Josephson
222	Lubomir Jandera
248	Lars Weibel
263	Rob Mara

1993
Pick
24	Eric Lecompte
50	Eric Manlow
54	Bogdan Savenko
76	Ryan Huska
90	Eric Daze
102	Patrik Pysz
128	Jonni Vauhkonen
180	Tom White
206	Sergei Petrov
232	Mike Rusk
258	Mike McGhan
284	Tom Noble

1992
Pick
12	Sergei Krivokrasov
36	Jeff Shantz
41	Sergei Klimovich
89	Andy MacIntyre
113	Tim Hogan
137	Gerry Skrypec
161	Mike Prokopec
185	Layne Roland
209	David Hymovitz
233	Richard Raymond

1991
Pick
22	Dean McAmmond
39	Michael Pomichter
44	Jamie Matthews
66	Bobby House
71	Igor Kravchuk
88	Zac Boyer
110	Maco Balkovec
112	Kevin St. Jacques
132	Jacques Auger
154	Scott Kirton
176	Roch Belley
198	Scott MacDonald
220	A. Andriyevsky
242	Mike Larkin
264	Scott Dean

1990
Pick
16	Karl Dykhuis
37	Ivan Droppa
79	Chris Tucker
121	Brett Stickney
124	Derek Edgerly
163	Hugo Belanger
184	Owen Lessard
205	Erik Peterson
226	Steve Dubinsky
247	Dino Grossi

1989
Pick
6	Adam Bennett
27	Michael Speer
48	Bob Kellogg
111	Tommi Pullola
132	Tracy Egeland
153	Milan Tichy
174	Jason Greyerbiehl
195	Matt Saunders
216	Mike Kozak
237	Michael Doneghey

1988
Pick
8	Jeremy Roenick
50	Trevor Dam
71	Stefan Elvenas
92	Joe Cleary
113	Justin Lafayette
134	Craig Woodcroft
155	Jon Pojar
176	Mathew Hentges
197	Daniel Maurice
218	Dirk Tenzer
239	Andreas Lupzig

1987
Pick
8	Jimmy Waite
29	Ryan McGill
50	Cam Russell
60	Mike Dagenais
92	Ulf Sandstrom
113	Mike McCormick
134	Stephen Tepper
155	John Reilly
176	Lance Werness
197	Dale Marquette
218	Bill Lacouture
239	Mike Lappin

1986
Pick
14	Everett Sanipass
35	Mark Kurzawski
77	Frantisek Kucera
98	Lonnie Loach
119	Mario Doyon
140	Mike Hudson
161	Marty Nanne
182	Geoff Benic
203	Glen Lowes
224	Chris Thayer
245	Sean Williams

1985
Pick
11	Dave Manson
53	Andy Helmuth
74	Dan Vincellette
87	Rick Herbert
95	Brad Belland
116	Jonas Heed
137	Victor Posa
158	John Reid
179	Richard LaPlante
200	Brad Hamilton
221	Ian Pound
242	Rick Braccia

1984
Pick
3	Ed Olczyk
45	Trent Yawney
66	Tommy Eriksson
90	Timo Lehkonen
101	Darin Sceviour
111	Chris Clifford
132	Mike Stapleton
153	Glen Greenough
174	Ralph DiFiorie
194	Joakim Persson
215	Bill Brown
224	David Mackey
235	Dan Williams

1983
Pick
18	Bruce Cassidy
39	Wayne Presley
59	Marc Bergevin
79	Tarek Howard
99	Kevin Robinson
115	Jari Torkki
119	Mark Lavarre
139	Scot Birnie
159	Kevin Paynter
179	Brian Noonan
199	Dominik Hasek
219	Steve Pepin

1982
Pick
7	Ken Yaremchuk
28	Rene Badeau
49	Tom McMurchy
70	Bill Watson
91	Brad Beck
112	Mark Hatcher
133	Jay Ness
154	Jeff Smith
175	Phil Patterson
196	Jim Camazzola
217	Mike James
238	Bob Andrea

1981
Pick
12	Tony Tanti
25	Kevin Griffin
54	Darrell Anholt
75	Perry Pelensky
96	Doug Chessell
117	Bill Schafhauser
138	Marc Centrone
159	Johan Mellstrom
180	John Benns
201	Sylvain Roy

General Manager

PULFORD, ROBERT JESSE (BOB)
Senior Vice President/General Manager, Chicago Blackhawks.
Born in Newton Robinson, Ont., March 31, 1936.

Bob Pulford has excelled at every aspect of the game of hockey: player, coach, general manager. In his playing career, which began in 1956, Pulford collected 643 points (281 goals, 362 assists) in 1,079 games. With the Toronto Maple Leafs in their glory-days of the Sixties, Pulford earned a Stanley Cup ring in the 1962, 1963, 1964 and 1967. Known as an outstanding penalty killer, he registered four 20-or-more goal seasons and played in the NHL All-Star Game six times. To this date, he ranks among the Maple Leafs' top ten in goals, assists, points, and games played.

Retiring from active play, Pulford accepted the position of head coach with the Los Angeles Kings in 1972. The team developed rapidly under his direction, and in the 1974-75 season, the Kings posted a 42-17-21 record for 105 points. For his efforts, Pulford was named NHL coach of the year.

Following five successful seasons in L.A., Pulford joined the Chicago Blackhawks on July 6, 1977, as head coach and general manager. He promptly led the Blackhawks to a first place finish in the Smythe Division and again earned the honor of being named coach of the year as voted by *The Hockey News*. The Chicago Blackhawks have won eight division titles with Pulford as general manager and coach, and the team has made the playoffs in each of his 17 seasons with the Hawks.

In June of 1990, William Wirtz, president of the Chicago Blackhawks, appointed Pulford the club's senior vice president.

In 1967, Pulford became first president of the NHL Players' Association. Today, he plays a key role acting as Alternate Governor for the team and sitting on the advisory committee to league ownership. On June 21, 1991, he was inducted into the Hockey Hall of Fame.

Pulford also served as head coach of Team USA during the 1976 Canada Cup. In the 1991 Canada Cup, he served as co-general manager for Team USA.

Club Directory

United Center
1901 W. Madison St.
Chicago, IL 60612
Phone **312/455-7000**
Capacity: 20,500

President	William W. Wirtz
Vice President & Assistant to the President	Thomas N. Ivan
Senior Vice President/General Manager	Robert J. Pulford
Vice President	Jack Davison
Assistant GM/Director of Player Personnel	Bob Murray
Head Coach	Craig Hartsburg
Assistant Coach	Lorne Henning
Assistant Coach	Dirk Graham
Goaltending Consultant	Vladislav Tretiak
Special Assignments	Darryl Sutter
Video Coach	Rob Pulford
Chief Amateur Scout	Michel Dumas
Amateur Scouting Staff	Kerry Davison, Bruce Franklin, Dave Lucas, Steve Lyons, Jim Walker
European Scouts	Jan Blomgren, Lars Norrman
Director of Team Services	Phil Thibodeau
Executive Assistant	Cindy Bodnarchuk
Receptionist/Secretary	Vicki Littleton

Medical Staff
Club Doctors	Louis Kolb, Howard Baim
Club Dentist	Robert Duresa
Head Trainer	Michael Gapski
Equipment Manager	Troy Parchman
Assistant Trainer	Lou Varga
Strength and Conditioning Coach	Mark Kling
Massage Therapist	Pawel Prylinski

Finance
Controller	Robert Rinkus
Assistant to the Controller	Penny Swenson
Staff Accountant	Dave Jorns
Accounting Secretary	Pat Dema

Public Relations/Marketing
Vice President of Marketing	Peter R. Wirtz
Director of Public Relations/Sales	Jim DeMaria
Director of Marketing/Merchandising	Jim Sofranko
Marketing Associate	Kelly Bodnarchuk
Director of Community Relations/PR Assistant	Barbara Davidson
Director of Publications/PR Assistant	Brad Freeman
Director of Game Night Operations/Special Events	Tom Finks

Ticketing
Ticket Manager	Jim Bare
Team Photographers	Ray Grabowski, Rob Grabowski
Organist	Frank Pellico
Location of Press Box	North Side of United Center
Dimensions of Rink	200 feet by 85 feet
Club Colors	Red,Black & White
Uniforms	Home – Base color white trimmed with black & red; Away – Base color red trimmed with black & white
Radio Station	WMVP (AM 1000)
Television Station	SportsChannel
Broadcasters	Pat Foley, Dale Tallon, Darren Pang, Brian Davis, Jim Blaney, Bill Gardner

Retired Numbers

1	Glenn Hall	1957-1967
9	Bobby Hull	1957-1972
21	Stan Mikita	1958-1980
35	Tony Esposito	1969-1984

NHL Coaching Record

Season	Team	Regular Season					Playoffs			
		Games	W	L	T	%	Games	W	L	%
1972-73	Los Angeles	78	31	36	11	.468	....	....	....	....
1973-74	Los Angeles	78	33	33	12	.500	5	1	4	.200
1974-75	Los Angeles	80	42	17	21	.656	3	1	2	.333
1975-76	Los Angeles	80	38	33	9	.531	9	5	4	.556
1976-77	Los Angeles	80	34	31	15	.519	9	4	5	.444
1977-78	Chicago	80	32	29	19	.519	4	0	4	.000
1978-79	Chicago	80	29	36	15	.456	4	0	4	.000
1981-82	Chicago	28	13	13	2	.500	15	8	7	.533
1984-85	Chicago	27	16	7	4	.667	15	9	6	.600
1985-86	Chicago	80	39	33	8	.538	3	0	3	.000
1986-87	Chicago	80	29	37	14	.450	4	0	4	.000
	NHL Totals	**771**	**336**	**305**	**130**	**.520**	**71**	**28**	**43**	**.394**

Colorado Avalanche

1994-95 Results: 30W-13L-5T 65PTS. First, Northeast Division

Schedule

Oct.	Fri.	6	Detroit		Mon.	8	at Boston
	Sat.	7	at Los Angeles		Wed.	10	Florida
	Mon.	9	Pittsburgh		Sun.	14	Calgary
	Wed.	11	Boston		Tues.	16	at Pittsburgh
	Fri.	13	at Washington		Wed.	17	at Detroit
	Sat.	14	at St. Louis		Mon.	22	NY Islanders
	Wed.	18	Washington		Thur.	25	Vancouver
	Mon.	23	Anaheim		Sat.	27	at San Jose*
	Wed.	25	at Calgary		Wed.	31	at Anaheim
	Fri.	27	Buffalo	Feb.	Thur.	1	Winnipeg
	Mon.	30	at Dallas		Sat.	3	NY Rangers*
Nov.	Wed.	1	Calgary		Mon.	5	Montreal
	Fri.	3	at Winnipeg		Wed.	7	Tampa Bay
	Sun.	5	at Chicago		Fri.	9	Hartford
	Thur.	9	Dallas		Sun.	11	at Philadelphia
	Sat.	11	at Vancouver		Thur.	15	at Tampa Bay
	Wed.	15	at Anaheim		Fri.	16	at Florida
	Fri.	17	at Calgary		Mon.	19	Edmonton
	Sat.	18	Calgary		Fri.	23	Los Angeles
	Mon.	20	at Edmonton		Sun.	25	Ottawa
	Wed.	22	Chicago		Mon.	26	Anaheim
	Sat.	25	at Montreal		Thur.	29	at Chicago
	Tues.	28	at NY Islanders	Mar.	Fri.	1	Chicago
	Wed.	29	at New Jersey		Sun.	3	Toronto
Dec.	Fri.	1	at NY Rangers		Tues.	5	San Jose
	Sun.	3	Dallas		Fri.	8	Detroit
	Tues.	5	San Jose		Sat.	9	at Vancouver
	Thur.	7	Edmonton		Wed.	13	at Anaheim
	Sat.	9	at Ottawa		Sun.	17	Edmonton
	Mon.	11	at Toronto		Tues.	19	at Vancouver
	Wed.	13	at Buffalo		Wed.	20	at Los Angeles
	Fri.	15	at Hartford		Fri.	22	at Detroit
	Mon.	18	Vancouver		Sun.	24	at Winnipeg*
	Wed.	20	at Edmonton		Wed.	27	Winnipeg
	Fri.	22	St. Louis		Thur.	28	at San Jose
	Sat.	23	at Los Angeles	Apr.	Wed.	3	St. Louis
	Tues.	26	at San Jose		Sat.	6	San Jose*
	Fri.	29	Toronto		Sun.	7	at Dallas*
Jan.	Wed.	3	New Jersey		Wed.	10	Anaheim
	Thur.	4	Philadelphia		Thur.	11	at St. Louis
	Sat.	6	at Toronto		Sun.	14	Los Angeles*

* Denotes afternoon game.

Home Starting Times:
Night games . . . . 7:00 p.m.
Matinees . . . . 1:00 p.m.
Except   Fri. Oct. 6 . . . . 6:00 p.m.
           Sat. Nov. 18 . . . . 8:30 p.m.

Franchise date: June 22, 1979
                 Transferred from Quebec to Denver,
                 June 21, 1995

PACIFIC DIVISION

17th NHL Season

Rookie sensation Peter Forsberg led all first-year NHL players in assists (35) and points (50) en route to winning the Calder Trophy.

Year-by-Year Record

		Home			Road			Overall							
Season	GP	W	L	T	W	L	T	W	L	T	GF	GA	Pts.	Finished	Playoff Result
1994-95*	48	19	1	4	11	12	1	30	13	5	185	134	65	1st, Northeast Div.	Lost Conf. Quarter-Final
1993-94*	84	19	17	6	15	25	2	34	42	8	277	292	76	5th, Northeast Div.	Out of Playoffs
1992-93*	84	23	17	2	24	10	8	47	27	10	351	300	104	2nd, Adams Div.	Lost Div. Semi-Final
1991-92*	80	18	19	3	2	29	9	20	48	12	255	318	52	5th, Adams Div.	Out of Playoffs
1990-91*	80	9	23	8	7	27	6	16	50	14	236	354	46	5th, Adams Div.	Out of Playoffs
1989-90*	80	8	26	6	4	35	1	12	61	7	240	407	31	5th, Adams Div.	Out of Playoffs
1988-89*	80	16	20	4	11	26	3	27	46	7	269	342	61	5th, Adams Div.	Out of Playoffs
1987-88*	80	15	23	2	17	20	3	32	43	5	271	306	69	5th, Adams Div.	Out of Playoffs
1986-87*	80	20	13	7	11	26	3	31	39	10	267	276	72	4th, Adams Div.	Lost Div. Final
1985-86*	80	23	13	4	20	18	2	43	31	6	330	289	92	1st, Adams Div.	Lost Div. Semi-Final
1984-85*	80	24	12	4	17	18	5	41	30	9	323	275	91	2nd, Adams Div.	Lost Conf. Championship
1983-84*	80	24	11	5	18	17	5	42	28	10	360	278	94	3th, Adams Div.	Lost Div. Final
1982-83*	80	23	10	7	11	24	5	34	34	12	343	336	80	4th, Adams Div.	Lost Div. Semi-Final
1981-82*	80	24	13	3	9	18	13	33	31	16	356	345	82	4th, Adams Div.	Lost Conf. Championship
1980-81*	80	18	11	11	12	21	7	30	32	18	314	318	78	4th, Adams Div.	Lost Prelim. Round
1979-80*	80	17	16	7	8	28	4	25	44	11	248	313	61	5th, Adams Div.	Out of Playoffs

* Quebec Nordiques

1995-96 Player Personnel

FORWARDS	HT	WT	S	Place of Birth	Date	1994-95 Club
BROUSSEAU, Paul	6-2	203	R	Pierrefonds, Que.	9/18/73	Cornwall
CLARK, Wendel	5-11	194	L	Kelvington, Sask.	10/25/66	Quebec
CORBET, Rene	6-0	187	L	Victoriaville, Que.	6/25/73	Cornwall-Quebec
DEADMARSH, Adam	6-0	195	R	Trail, B.C.	5/10/75	Portland (WHL)-Quebec
FORSBERG, Peter	6-0	190	L	Ornskoldsvik, Sweden	7/20/73	MoDo-Quebec
FRIEDMAN, Doug	6-1	189	L	Cape Elizabeth, ME	9/1/71	Cornwall
HUARD, Bill	6-1	215	L	Welland, Ont.	6/24/67	Ottawa-Quebec
KAMENSKY, Valeri	6-2	198	R	Voskresensk, USSR	4/18/66	Ambri-Quebec
KOVALENKO, Andrei	5-10	200	L	Balakovo, USSR	6/7/70	Togliatti-Quebec
LAPOINTE, Claude	5-9	181	L	Lachine, Que.	10/11/68	Quebec
MARHA, Josef	6-0	176	L	Havlickuv Brod, Czech.	6/2/76	Dukla Jihlava
MATTE, Christian	5-11	166	R	Hull, Que.	1/20/75	Granby-Cornwall
MURRAY, Troy	6-1	195	R	Calgary, Alta.	7/31/62	Ottawa-Pittsburgh
NOLAN, Owen	6-1	201	R	Belfast, Ireland	9/22/71	Quebec
RICCI, Mike	6-0	190	L	Scarborough, Ont.	10/27/71	Quebec
RUCINSKY, Martin	6-0	178	L	Most, Czech.	3/11/71	Litvinov-Quebec
SAKIC, Joe	5-11	185	L	Burnaby, B.C.	7/7/69	Quebec
SCHULTE, Paxton	6-2	217	L	Ionaway, Alta.	7/16/72	Cornwall
SIMON, Chris	6-3	219	L	Wawa, Ont.	1/30/72	Quebec
VEILLEUX, Eric	5-7	148	L	Quebec, Que.	2/20/72	Cornwall
WILSON, Landon	6-2	202	R	St. Louis, MO	3/13/75	North Dakota-Cornwall
YELLE, Stephane	6-1	162	L	Ottawa, Ont.	5/9/74	Cornwall
YOUNG, Scott	6-0	190	R	Clinton, MA	10/1/67	Landshut-Frankfurt-Quebec

DEFENSEMEN						
BELAK, Wade	6-4	213	R	Saskatoon, Sask.	7/3/76	Saskatoon-Cornwall
BREKKE, Brent	6-1	175	L	Minot, ND	8/16/71	Cornwall-Dayton
BRENNAN, Rich	6-2	200	R	Schenectady, NY	11/26/72	Boston U.
FINN, Steven	6-0	191	L	Laval, Que.	8/20/66	Quebec
FOOTE, Adam	6-1	202	R	Toronto, Ont.	7/10/71	Quebec
GUSAROV, Alexei	6-3	185	L	Leningrad, USSR	7/8/64	Quebec
KLEMM, Jon	6-3	200	R	Cranbrook, B.C.	1/8/70	Cornwall-Quebec
KRUPP, Uwe	6-6	235	R	Cologne, West Germany	6/24/65	Landshut-Quebec
LAUKKANEN, Janne	6-0	180	L	Lahti, Finland	3/19/70	Cornwall-Quebec
LEFEBVRE, Sylvain	6-2	205	L	Richmond, Que.	10/14/67	Quebec
LESCHYSHYN, Curtis	6-1	205	L	Thompson, Man.	9/21/69	Quebec
MILLER, Aaron	6-3	197	R	Buffalo, NY	8/11/71	Cornwall-Quebec
MYRVOLD, Anders	6-1	178	L	Lorenskog, Norway	8/12/75	Laval-Cornwall
PARROTT, Jeff	6-1	195	R	The Pas, Man.	4/6/71	Cornwall
SLANEY, John	6-0	185	L	St. John's, Nfld.	2/7/72	Washington-Portland (AHL)
WOLANIN, Craig	6-3	205	L	Grosse Pointe, MI	7/27/67	Quebec

GOALTENDERS	HT	WT	C	Place of Birth	Date	1994-95 Club
ELLIS, Aaron	6-1	170	L	Indianapolis, IN	5/13/74	Det (OHL)-Belv'le-Memphis
FISET, Stephane	6-1	195	L	Montreal, Que.	6/17/70	Quebec
SHULMISTRA, Richard	6-2	186	R	Sudbury, Ont.	4/1/71	Cornwall
THIBAULT, Jocelyn	5-11	170	L	Montreal, Que.	1/12/75	Sherbrooke-Quebec

General Manager

LACROIX, PIERRE
Executive Vice President of Hockey Operations and General Manager, Colorado Avalanche. Born in Montreal, Que., August 3, 1948.

Pierre Lacroix was appointed as the fourth General Manager in franchise history on May 24, 1994.

Following a 20-year career in world of hockey as a players' agent, he knows and understands the National Hockey League and he also knows the needs of today's players.

General Managers' History

Maurice Filion, 1979-80 to 1987-88; Martin Madden 1988-89; Martin Madden and Maurice Filion, 1989-90; Pierre Page, 1990-91 to 1993-94; Pierre Lacroix, 1994-95 to date.

Coaching History

Jacques Demers, 1979-80; Maurice Filion and Michel Bergeron, 1980-81; Michel Bergeron, 1981-82 to 1986-87; André Savard and Ron Lapointe, 1987-88; Ron Lapointe and Jean Perron, 1988-89; Michel Bergeron, 1989-90; Dave Chambers, 1990-91; Dave Chambers and Pierre Page, 1991-92; Pierre Page, 1992-93 to 1993-94; Marc Crawford, 1994-95 to date.

1994-95 Scoring
*– rookie

Regular Season

Pos	#	Player	Team	GP	G	A	Pts	+/-	PIM	PP	SH	GW	GT	S	%
C	19	Joe Sakic	QUE	47	19	43	62	7	30	3	2	5	0	157	12.1
C	21	* Peter Forsberg	QUE	47	15	35	50	17	16	3	0	3	0	86	17.4
R	11	Owen Nolan	QUE	46	30	19	49	21	46	13	2	8	0	137	21.9
R	48	Scott Young	QUE	48	18	21	39	9	14	3	3	0	0	167	10.8
C	9	Mike Ricci	QUE	48	15	21	36	5	40	9	0	1	1	73	20.5
L	17	Wendel Clark	QUE	37	12	18	30	−1	45	5	0	0	0	95	12.6
L	13	Valeri Kamensky	QUE	40	10	20	30	3	22	5	1	5	0	70	14.3
C	28	Bob Bassen	QUE	47	12	15	27	14	33	0	1	1	0	66	18.2
R	51	Andrei Kovalenko	QUE	45	14	10	24	−4	31	1	0	3	0	63	22.2
D	4	Uwe Krupp	QUE	44	6	17	23	14	20	3	0	1	1	102	5.9
R	18	* Adam Deadmarsh	QUE	48	9	8	17	16	56	0	0	1	0	48	18.8
D	7	Curtis Leschyshyn	QUE	44	2	13	15	29	20	0	0	0	0	43	4.7
D	2	Sylvain Lefebvre	QUE	48	2	11	13	13	17	0	0	0	0	81	2.5
C	47	Claude Lapointe	QUE	29	4	8	12	5	41	0	0	0	0	40	10.0
L	12	Chris Simon	QUE	29	3	9	12	14	106	0	0	0	0	33	9.4
L	25	Martin Rucinsky	QUE	20	3	6	9	5	14	0	0	0	0	32	9.4
D	6	Craig Wolanin	QUE	40	3	6	9	12	40	0	0	0	0	36	8.3
D	52	Adam Foote	QUE	35	0	7	7	17	52	0	0	0	0	24	0.0
L	15	Bill Huard	OTT	26	1	1	2	−2	64	0	0	0	0	15	6.7
			QUE	7	2	2	4	2	13	0	0	1	6	33.3
			TOTAL	33	3	3	6	0	77	0	0	1	21	14.3
R	23	Paul MacDermid	QUE	14	3	1	4	3	22	0	0	1	0	13	23.1
R	14	* Dwayne Norris	QUE	13	1	2	3	1	2	0	1	0	7	14.3
D	5	Alexei Gusarov	QUE	14	1	2	3	−1	6	0	0	1	0	7	14.3
L	20	* Rene Corbet	QUE	8	0	3	3	3	2	0	0	0	4	0.0
D	31	* Aaron Miller	QUE	9	0	3	3	2	6	0	0	0	12	0.0
D	22	* Janne Laukkanen	QUE	11	0	3	3	3	4	0	0	0	12	0.0
G	35	Stephane Fiset	QUE	32	0	3	3	0	2	0	0	0	0	0.0
D	29	Steven Finn	QUE	40	0	3	3	1	64	0	0	0	28	0.0
D	24	* Jon Klemm	QUE	4	1	0	1	3	4	0	0	0	5	20.0
G	1	* Garth Snow	QUE	2	0	0	0	0	0	0	0	0	0	0.0
G	41	Jocelyn Thibault	QUE	18	0	0	0	0	0	0	0	0	0	0.0

Goaltending

No.	Goaltender	GPI	Mins	Avg	W	L	T	EN	SO	GA	SA	S%
41	Jocelyn Thibault	18	898	2.34	12	2	2	0	1	35	423	.917
35	Stephane Fiset	32	1879	2.78	17	10	3	1	2	87	968	.910
1	* Garth Snow	2	119	5.55	1	1	0	0	0	11	63	.825
	Totals	**48**	**2908**	**2.76**	**30**	**13**	**5**	**1**	**3**	**134**	**1455**	**.908**

Playoffs

Pos	#	Player	Team	GP	G	A	Pts	+/-	PIM	PP	SH	GW	OT	S	%
R	48	Scott Young	QUE	6	3	3	6	3	2	0	1	0	0	12	25.0
C	28	Bob Bassen	QUE	5	2	4	6	2	0	0	0	0	0	10	20.0
C	21	* Peter Forsberg	QUE	6	2	4	6	2	4	1	0	0	0	13	15.4
C	19	Joe Sakic	QUE	6	4	1	5	−4	0	1	1	1	0	15	26.7
R	11	Owen Nolan	QUE	6	2	3	5	2	6	0	0	0	0	12	16.7
C	9	Mike Ricci	QUE	6	1	3	4	4	8	0	0	0	0	9	11.1
L	17	Wendel Clark	QUE	6	1	2	3	−6	6	0	0	0	0	18	5.6
D	6	Craig Wolanin	QUE	6	1	1	2	5	4	0	0	0	0	8	12.5
L	12	Chris Simon	QUE	6	1	1	2	−1	19	0	0	1	0	9	11.1
D	4	Uwe Krupp	QUE	6	0	2	2	−2	2	0	0	0	0	13	0.0
D	2	Sylvain Lefebvre	QUE	6	0	2	2	5	2	0	0	0	0	7	0.0
L	13	Valeri Kamensky	QUE	2	1	0	1	0	0	0	0	0	0	2	50.0
D	22	* Janne Laukkanen	QUE	6	1	0	1	−2	2	0	0	0	0	11	9.1
L	20	* Rene Corbet	QUE	2	0	1	1	1	0	0	0	0	0	0	0.0
D	7	Curtis Leschyshyn	QUE	3	0	1	1	−1	4	0	0	0	0	0	0.0
D	29	Steven Finn	QUE	4	0	1	1	−4	2	0	0	0	0	2	0.0
D	52	Adam Foote	QUE	6	0	1	1	−3	14	0	0	0	0	6	0.0
R	51	Andrei Kovalenko	QUE	6	0	1	1	−3	2	0	0	0	0	6	0.0
R	18	* Adam Deadmarsh	QUE	6	0	1	1	−3	0	0	0	0	0	6	0.0
L	15	Bill Huard	QUE	1	0	0	0	0	0	0	0	0	0	0	0.0
G	1	* Garth Snow	QUE	1	0	0	0	0	0	0	0	0	0	0	0.0
R	23	Paul MacDermid	QUE	3	0	0	0	0	0	0	0	0	0	1	0.0
G	41	Jocelyn Thibault	QUE	3	0	0	0	0	0	0	0	0	0	0	0.0
G	35	Stephane Fiset	QUE	4	0	0	0	0	0	0	0	0	0	0	0.0
C	47	Claude Lapointe	QUE	5	0	0	0	−1	4	0	0	0	0	0	0.0

Goaltending

No.	Goaltender	GPI	Mins	Avg	W	L	EN	SO	GA	SA	S%
41	Jocelyn Thibault	3	148	3.24	1	2	0	0	8	76	.895
35	Stephane Fiset	4	209	4.59	1	2	0	0	16	115	.861
1	* Garth Snow	1	9	6.67	0	0	0	0	1	3	.667
	Totals	**6**	**368**	**4.08**	**2**	**4**	**0**	**0**	**25**	**194**	**.871**

Captains' History

Marc Tardif, 1979-80, 1980-81; Robbie Ftorek and Andre Dupont, 1981-82; Mario Marois, 1982-83 to 1984-85; Mario Marois and Peter Stastny, 1985-86; Peter Stastny, 1986-87 to 1989-90; Joe Sakic and Steven Finn, 1990-91; Mike Hough, 1991-92; Joe Sakic, 1992-93 to date.

Retired Numbers

3	J.C. Tremblay	1972-1979
8	Marc Tardif	1979-1983
16	Michel Goulet	1979-1990

Club Records

Team

(Figures in brackets for season records are games played; records for fewest points, wins, ties, losses, goals, goals against are for 70 or more games)

Most Points	104	1992-93 (84)	
Most Wins	47	1992-93 (84)	
Most Ties	18	1980-81 (80)	
Most Losses	61	1989-90 (80)	
Most Goals	360	1983-84 (80)	
Most Goals Against	407	1989-90 (80)	
Fewest Points	31	1989-90 (80)	
Fewest Wins	12	1989-90 (80)	
Fewest Ties	5	1987-88 (80)	
Fewest Losses	27	1992-93 (84)	
Fewest Goals	236	1990-91 (80)	
Fewest Goals Against	275	1984-85 (80)	

Longest Winning Streak

Over-all	7	Four times
Home	10	Nov. 26/83-Jan. 10/84; Mar. 6-Apr. 16/95
Away	5	Feb. 28-Mar. 24, 1986

Longest Undefeated Streak

Over-all	11	Mar. 10-31/81 (7 wins, 4 ties)
Home	14	Nov. 19/83 Jan. 21/84 (11 wins, 3 ties)
Away	8	Feb. 17/81-Mar. 22/81 (6 wins, 2 ties)

Longest Losing Streak

Over-all	14	Oct. 21-Nov. 19/90
Home	8	Oct. 21-Nov. 24/90
Away	18	Jan. 18-Apr. 1/90

Longest Winless Streak

Over-all	17	Oct. 21-Nov. 25/90 (15 losses, 2 ties)
Home	11	Nov. 14-Dec. 26/89 (7 losses, 4 ties)
Away	33	Oct. 8/91-Feb. 27/92 (25 losses, 8 ties)

Most Shutouts, Season	6	1985-86 (80)
Most PIM, Season	2,104	1989-90 (80)
Most Goals, Game	12	Feb. 1/83 (Hfd. 3 at Que. 12) Oct. 20/84 (Que. 12 at Tor. 3)

Individual

Most Seasons	11	Michel Goulet
Most Games	813	Michel Goulet
Most Goals, Career	456	Michel Goulet
Most Assists, Career	668	Peter Stastny
Most Points, Career	1,048	Peter Stastny (380 goals, 668 assists)
Most PIM, Career	1,545	Dale Hunter
Most Shutouts, Career	6	Mario Gosselin
Longest Consecutive Games Streak	312	Dale Hunter (Oct. 9/80-Mar. 13/84)
Most Goals, Season	57	Michel Goulet (1982-83)
Most Assists, Season	93	Peter Stastny (1981-82)
Most Points, Season	139	Peter Stastny (1981-82) (46 goals, 93 assists)
Most PIM, Season	301	Gord Donnelly (1987-88)
Most Points, Defenseman, Season	82	Steve Duchesne (1992-93) (20 goals, 62 assists)
Most Points, Center, Season	139	Peter Stastny (1981-82) (46 goals, 93 assists)

Most Points, Right Wing, Season	103	Jacques Richard (1980-81) (52 goals, 51 assists)
Most Points, Left Wing, Season	121	Michel Goulet (1983-84) (56 goals, 65 assists)
Most Points, Rookie, Season	109	Peter Stastny (1980-81) (39 goals, 70 assists)
Most Shutouts, Season	4	Clint Malarchuk (1985-86)
Most Goals, Game	5	Mats Sundin (Mar. 5/92) Mike Ricci (Feb. 17/94)
Most Assists, Game	5	Anton Stastny (Feb. 22/81) Michel Goulet (Jan. 3/84) Owen Nolan (Mar. 5/92) Mike Ricci (Dec. 12/92)
Most Points, Game	8	Peter Stastny (Feb. 22/81) Anton Stastny (Feb. 22/81)

All-time Record vs. Other Clubs

Regular Season

			At Home						On Road						Total					
	GP	W	L	T	GF	GA	PTS	GP	W	L	T	GF	GA	PTS	GP	W	L	T	GF	GA	PTS
Anaheim	1	0	1	0	3	6	0	1	1	0	0	2	1	2	2	1	1	0	4	6	2
Boston	57	18	33	6	208	252	42	55	18	29	8	174	223	44	112	36	62	14	382	475	86
Buffalo	56	28	18	10	213	178	66	56	16	32	8	182	226	40	112	44	50	18	395	404	106
Calgary	22	7	9	6	93	90	20	23	4	13	6	72	103	14	45	11	22	12	165	193	34
Chicago	22	9	9	4	94	89	22	23	7	14	2	74	94	16	45	16	23	6	168	183	38
Dallas	23	16	5	2	107	62	34	22	7	13	2	72	88	16	45	23	18	4	179	150	50
Detroit	23	12	8	3	96	85	27	22	9	12	1	77	88	19	45	21	20	4	173	173	46
Edmonton	22	7	13	2	88	107	16	22	5	17	0	66	125	10	44	12	30	2	154	232	26
Florida	3	1	1	1	9	10	3	4	3	1	0	16	9	6	7	4	2	1	25	19	9
Hartford	57	34	16	7	246	173	75	55	21	23	11	193	189	53	112	55	39	18	439	362	128
Los Angeles	22	10	9	3	94	91	23	22	8	13	1	77	102	17	44	18	22	4	171	193	40
Montreal	57	27	26	4	191	207	58	56	12	36	8	176	242	32	113	39	62	12	367	449	90
New Jersey	26	14	9	3	106	83	31	28	12	14	2	102	118	26	54	26	23	5	208	201	57
NY Islanders	26	14	10	2	100	84	30	25	9	15	1	83	108	19	51	23	25	3	183	192	49
NY Rangers	27	14	10	3	114	107	31	25	6	16	3	71	107	15	52	20	26	6	185	214	46
Ottawa	8	8	0	0	47	21	16	10	5	3	2	49	33	12	18	13	3	2	96	54	28
Philadelphia	26	9	9	8	99	97	26	27	5	20	2	71	106	12	53	14	29	10	170	203	38
Pittsburgh	25	13	12	0	114	101	26	28	9	15	4	114	125	22	53	22	27	4	228	226	48
St. Louis	22	10	9	3	82	74	23	22	4	16	2	74	105	10	44	14	25	5	156	179	33
San Jose	3	3	0	0	17	9	6	4	2	2	0	21	20	4	7	5	2	0	38	29	10
Tampa Bay	5	4	1	0	25	12	8	5	1	4	0	14	19	2	10	5	5	0	39	31	10
Toronto	23	13	5	5	94	73	31	23	10	11	2	99	84	22	46	23	16	7	193	157	53
Vancouver	23	9	10	4	67	68	22	22	7	11	4	88	93	18	45	16	21	8	155	161	40
Washington	26	10	12	4	86	101	24	26	9	14	3	86	107	21	52	19	26	7	172	208	45
Winnipeg	23	10	10	3	93	95	23	22	7	10	5	87	94	19	45	17	20	8	180	189	42
Totals	**628**	**300**	**245**	**83**	**2486**	**2275**	**683**	**628**	**197**	**354**	**77**	**2139**	**2608**	**471**	**1256**	**497**	**599**	**160**	**4625**	**4883**	**1154**

Calgary totals include Atlanta, 1979-80. Dallas totals include Minnesota, 1979-80 to 1992-93.
New Jersey totals include Colorado, 1979-80 to 1981-82.

Playoffs

	Series	W	L	GP	W	L	T	GF	GA	Last Mtg.	Round	Result
Boston	2	1	1	11	5	6	0	36	37	1983	DSF	L 1-3
Buffalo	2	2	0	8	6	2	0	35	27	1985	DSF	W 3-2
Hartford	2	1	1	9	4	5	0	34	35	1987	DSF	W 4-2
Montreal	5	2	3	31	14	17	0	85	105	1993	DSF	L 2-4
NY Islanders	1	0	1	4	0	4	0	9	18	1982	CF	L 0-4
NY Rangers	1	0	1	6	2	4	0	19	25	1995	CQF	L 2-4
Philadelphia	2	0	2	11	4	7	0	29	39	1985	CF	L 2-4
Totals	**15**	**6**	**9**	**80**	**35**	**45**	**0**	**247**	**286**			

Playoff Results 1995-91

Year	Round	Opponent	Result	GF	GA
1995	CQF	NY Rangers	L 2-4	19	25
1993	DSF	Montreal	L 2-4	16	19

Abbreviations: Round: F – Final;
CF – conference final; **CQF** – conference quarter-final;
CSF – conference semi-final; **DF** – division final;
DSF – division semi-final; **SF** – semi-final;
QF – quarter-final; **PR** – preliminary round.

1994-95 Results

Jan.	21	at Philadelphia	3-1		11		NY Islanders	2-1
	24	Washington	5-1		16		Pittsburgh	3-2
	27	at Buffalo	7-3		18	at	Montreal	4-5
	28	NY Rangers	2-0		20		Florida	5-4
	31	Philadelphia	5-2		22		Boston	6-2
Feb.	2	at New Jersey	4-5		25		NY Rangers	2-1
	4	New Jersey	2-0		26	at	Montreal	11-4
	5	Hartford	3-1		28	at	Buffalo	3-5
	8	at Hartford	3-2		30	at	NY Rangers	5-4
	9	at Boston	4-3		31	at	Washington	4-6
	11	Ottawa	5-2	Apr.	2		Ottawa	7-5
	14	at NY Islanders	3-2		5	at	Montreal	5-6
	16	at Philadelphia	4-2		6		Montreal	3-2
	18	at Washington	2-4		8	at	Ottawa	2-2
	19	at Florida	4-5		12	at	Boston	4-0
	21	at Pittsburgh	4-5		14		Buffalo	5-2
	23	Philadelphia	6-6		16		Washington	4-2
	25	Boston	1-1		18	at	NY Islanders	2-5
	27	Pittsburgh	5-7		20	at	Tampa Bay	2-5
Mar.	1	Tampa Bay	3-2		22	at	Florida	2-4
	4	Buffalo	1-1		26		Montreal	1-1
	6	New Jersey	6-3		29		Tampa Bay	4-1
	7	at Pittsburgh	5-4		30	at	New Jersey	2-4
	9	at Hartford	1-2	May	3		Hartford	4-1

Entry Draft
Selections 1995-81

1995
Pick
25	Marc Denis
51	Nic Beaudoin
77	John Tripp
81	Tomi Kallio
159	Brent Johnson
155	John Cirjak
181	Dan Smith
207	Tomi Hirvonen
228	Chris George

1994
Pick
12	Wade Belak
22	Jeffrey Kealty
35	Josef Marha
61	Sebastien Bety
72	Chris Drury
87	Milan Hejduk
113	Tony Tuzzolino
139	Nicholas Windsor
165	Calvin Elfring
191	Jay Bertsch
217	Tim Thomas
243	Chris Pittman
285	Steven Low

1993
Pick
10	Jocelyn Thibault
14	Adam Deadmarsh
49	Ashley Buckberger
75	Bill Pierce
101	Ryan Tocher
127	Anders Myrvold
137	Nicholas Checco
153	Christian Matte
179	David Ling
205	Petr Franek
231	Vincent Auger
257	Mark Pivetz
283	John Hillman

1992
Pick
4	Todd Warriner
28	Paul Brousseau
29	Tuomas Gronman
52	Emmanuel Fernandez
76	Ian McIntyre
100	Charlie Wasley
124	Paxton Schulte
148	Martin LePage
172	Mike Jickling
196	Steve Passmore
220	Anson Carter
244	Aaron Ellis

1991
Pick
1	Eric Lindros
24	Rene Corbet
46	Richard Brennan
68	Dave Karpa
90	Patrick Labrecque
103	Bill Lindsay
134	Mikael Johansson
156	Janne Laukkanen
157	Aaron Asp
178	Adam Bartell
188	Brent Brekke
200	Paul Koch
222	Doug Friedman
244	Eric Meloche

1990
Pick
1	Owen Nolan
22	Ryan Hughes
43	Bradley Zavisha
106	Jeff Parrott
127	Dwayne Norris
148	Andrei Kovalenko
158	Alexander Karpovtsev
169	Pat Mazzoli
190	Scott Davis
211	Mika Stromberg
232	Wade Klippenstein

1989
Pick
1	Mats Sundin
22	Adam Foote
43	Stephane Morin
54	John Tanner
68	Niclas Andersson
76	Eric Dubois
85	Kevin Kaiser
106	Dan Lambert
127	Sergei Mylnikov
148	Paul Krake
169	Viacheslav Bykov
190	Andrei Khomutov
211	Byron Witkowski
232	Noel Rahn

1988
Pick
3	Curtis Leschyshyn
5	Daniel Dore
24	Stephane Fiset
45	Petri Aaltonen
66	Darin Kimble
87	Stephane Venne
108	Ed Ward
129	Valeri Kamensky
150	Sakari Lindfors
171	Dan Wiebe
213	Alexei Gusarov
234	Claude Lapointe

1987
Pick
9	Bryan Fogarty
15	Joe Sakic
51	Jim Sprott
72	Kip Miller
93	Rob Mendel
114	Garth Snow
135	Tim Hanus
156	Jake Enebak
177	Jaroslav Sevcik
183	Ladislav Tresl
198	Darren Nauss
219	Mike Williams

1986
Pick
18	Ken McRae
39	Jean-Marc Routhier
41	Stephane Guerard
81	Ron Tugnutt
102	Gerald Bzdel
117	Scott White
123	Morgan Samuelsson
134	Mark Vermette
144	Jean-Francois Nault
165	Keith Miller
186	Pierre Millier
207	Chris Lappin
228	Martin Latreille
249	Sean Boudreault

1985
Pick
15	David Latta
36	Jason Lafreniere
57	Max Middendorf
65	Peter Massey
78	David Espe
99	Bruce Major
120	Andy Akervik
141	Mike Oliverio
162	Mario Brunetta
183	Brit Peer
204	Tom Sasso
225	Gary Murphy
246	Jean Bois

1984
Pick
15	Trevor Stienburg
36	Jeff Brown
57	Steve Finn
78	Terry Perkins
120	Darren Cota
141	Henrik Cedergren
162	Jyrki Maki
183	Guy Ouellette
203	Ken Quinney
244	Peter Loob

1983
Pick
32	Yves Heroux
52	Bruce Bell
54	Iiro Jarvi
92	Luc Guenette
112	Brad Walcott
132	Craig Mack
152	Tommy Albelin
172	Wayne Groulx
192	Scott Shaunessy
232	Bo Berglund
239	Jindrich Kokrment

1982
Pick
13	David Shaw
34	Paul Gillis
55	Mario Gosselin
76	Jiri Lala
97	Phil Stanger
131	Daniel Poudrier
181	Mike Hough
202	Vincent Lukac
223	Andre Martin
244	Jozef Lukac
248	Jan Jasko

1981
Pick
11	Randy Moller
53	Jean-Marc Gaulin
74	Clint Malarchuk
95	Ed Lee
116	Mike Eagles
158	Andre Cote
179	Marc Brisebois
200	Kari Takko

Club Directory

McNichols Sports Arena
1635 Clay Street
Denver, Colorado 80204
Phone **303/893-6700**
FAX 303/893-0614
Capacity: 16,061

Owner	COMSAT Entertainment Group
President and Governor	Charlie Lyons
Alternate Governor	Pierre Lacroix

Hockey Operations
Executive Vice President of Hockey Operations and General Manager	Pierre Lacroix
Executive Assistant	Charlotte Grahame
Assistant General Manager	François Giguère
Administrative Assistant	Jill Darnell
Head Coach	Marc Crawford
Assistant Coach	Jacques Martin
Assistant Coach	Joel Quenneville
Goaltending Coach	Jacques Cloutier
Director of Media Relations and Team Services	Jean Martineau
Media Relations Assistant	Sally Christgau
Strength and Conditioning Coach	TBA
Director of Player Development	André Savard
Chief Scout	Dave Draper
Scouts	Yvon Gendron, Jan Janda, Bengt Lundholm, Brian MacDonald, Don McKenney, Orval Tessier
Pro Scout	TBA
Athletic Trainer	Pat Karns
Kinesiologist	Matthew Sokolowski
Equipment Manager	Rob McLean
Team Physician	Andrew Parker
Team Dentist	Steve Barker
Assistant Equipment Manager	Mike Kramer

Business Operations
Senior Executive Vice President/Business Operations	Gary Hunter
Executive Vice President	Shawn Hunter
Vice President/Chief Financial Officer	Mark Waggoner
Vice President/Broadcasting	Lou Personett

Finance
Controller	Jerry Girkin
Accountant	Loretta Harmon
Accountant	Karen Becker

Ticket Sales
Director of Ticket Operations	Kirk Dyer
Assistant Director of Ticket Operations	Ed Gow
Ticket Assistants	Flo Kunze, Lori Blanche

Sales/Game Operations
Director of Ticket Sales and Game Operations	Joe Levy
Sales Manager	Paul Andrews
Account Executives	Allison Levy, John Liotta, Amy Seltenreich, Nikki Lockton, Dan Sweeney, Jon Moore, Aimee Ahlers, Robert Kinnard
Sales Assistant	Sharon Chinn
Game Operations Coordinator	Tim McBride

Marketing/Corporate Partnership
Director of Marketing	Michael Blake
Director of Corporate Sales	Susan Cohig
Director of Corporate Services	Chris Whitney
Director of Special Events	Deb Dowling
Special Events Assistant	Becky Grupe
Senior Corporate Account Executives	Deanna Poyfair, Tracy Hartman
Corporate Account Executives	Todd Goldstein, Brian Jones, Mike Kurowski, Meredith Hall, Dave Smrek
Marketing Manager	Susan Buckley

Retail
Director of Retail Operations	Scott Franklin
Manager, Arena Retail	Alan Fey

Broadcasting
Broadcast Coordinator	Mark Hulsey
TV Play-by-play Announcer	TBA
TV Color Commentator	Peter McNab
Radio Play-by-play Announcer	Michael Haynes
Radio Color Commentator	Norm Jones

Creative Services
Creative Director	Daniel S. Price
Senior Art Director	Michael Beindorff
Art Director	Rich Fillmon

Community Relations
Director of Community Relations	Kathleen MacDonald
Community Funds Coordinator	Lou Carroll
Community Relations Program Coordinator	Carolyn Dugan
Community Relations Coordinator	Derek Williams
Community Relations Assistant	Meredith Kaplan

Administration
Director of Administration	Cheryl Miller
Director of Legal Services	Ron Sally
Receptionists	Heather Ellsworth, Valerie Millon-Whitlock

Coach

CRAWFORD, MARC
Coach, Colorado Avalanche. Born in Belleville, Ont., February 13, 1961.

On July 6th, 1994, Marc Crawford became the tenth head coach in franchise history. Last year, in his rookie season as an NHL head coach, Crawford led the Nordiques to a first place finish in the Eastern Conference and second place overall in the NHL. Crawford was named the 1995 coach of the year and awarded the Jack Adams Trophy.

After serving as the general manager and coach of the junior Cornwall Royals for two seasons, Crawford joined the Toronto Maple Leafs organization in 1991 as head coach of the St. John's Maple Leafs. In three seasons, he recorded 125 wins, 78 losses and 37 ties for a winning percentage of .598. In 1991-92, he led his team to the AHL finals. Crawford was named the AHL coach of the year in 1992. In 1992-93, his team won the Atlantic Division title with 41 wins and a total of 95 points.

Marc Crawford has been associated with professional hockey since the early 1980s. He played 176 games in the NHL, all with the Vancouver Canucks.

Coaching Record

Season	Team	Regular Season					Playoffs			
		Games	W	L	T	%	Games	W	L	%
1989-90	Cornwall (OHL)	66	24	38	4	.394	6	2	4	.333
1990-91	Cornwall (OHL)	66	23	42	1	.356	....	....	....	....
1991-92	St. John's (AHL)	80	39	29	12	.562	16	11	5	.688
1992-93	St. John's (AHL)	80	41	26	13	.594	9	4	5	.444
1993-94	St. John's (AHL)	80	45	23	12	.638	11	6	5	.545
1994-95	**Quebec (NHL)**	**48**	**30**	**13**	**5**	**.677**	**6**	**2**	**4**	**.333**
	NHL Totals	48	30	13	5	.677	6	2	4	.333

Dallas Stars

1994-95 Results: 17w-23L-8T 42PTS. Fifth, Central Division

Schedule

Oct.	Sat.	7	at Winnipeg	Sun.	14 at New Jersey
	Tues.	10	Calgary	Mon.	15 at Philadelphia
	Thur.	12	St. Louis	Wed.	17 Edmonton
	Sat.	14	Boston	Mon.	22 at Vancouver
	Tues.	17	Washington	Wed.	24 at Edmonton
	Thur.	19	at St. Louis	Fri.	26 at Calgary
	Sat.	21	Tampa Bay	Mon.	29 Winnipeg
	Tues.	24	Buffalo	Wed.	31 NY Rangers
	Thur.	26	Anaheim	**Feb.** Fri.	2 Vancouver
	Sat.	28	at San Jose*	Sun.	4 at NY Islanders
	Mon.	30	Colorado	Tues.	6 at St. Louis
Nov.	Wed.	1	Chicago	Wed.	7 Montreal
	Sat.	4	at Detroit*	Sat.	10 St. Louis*
	Wed.	8	Los Angeles	Sun.	11 Hartford*
	Thur.	9	at Colorado	Fri.	16 Edmonton
	Tues.	14	at Pittsburgh	Sun.	18 at Florida
	Wed.	15	at Buffalo	Mon.	19 at Tampa Bay
	Fri.	17	San Jose	Thur.	22 Ottawa
	Wed.	22	Vancouver	Sat.	24 at Toronto
	Sat.	25	New Jersey	Sun.	25 at Hartford
Dec.	Sat.	2	at Los Angeles	Wed.	28 Philadelphia
	Sun.	3	at Colorado	**Mar.** Thur.	2 Toronto
	Tues.	5	at Boston	Tues.	5 at Anaheim
	Thur.	7	at Detroit	Wed.	6 at San Jose
	Sat.	9	at Toronto	Mon.	11 at Montreal
	Mon.	11	at NY Rangers	Wed.	13 at Ottawa
	Wed.	13	Calgary	Fri.	15 at Toronto
	Fri.	15	Pittsburgh	Sun.	17 at Washington*
	Sun.	17	San Jose	Wed.	20 St. Louis
	Thur.	21	NY Islanders	Fri.	22 at Vancouver
	Sat.	23	Chicago	Sat.	23 at Los Angeles
	Tues.	26	at Chicago	Tues.	26 Winnipeg
	Thur.	28	at St. Louis	Thur.	28 Anaheim
	Fri.	29	Detroit	Sun.	31 at Chicago*
Jan.	Mon.	1	Toronto*	**Apr.** Wed.	3 at Winnipeg
	Wed.	3	at Detroit	Fri.	5 Chicago
	Fri.	5	Winnipeg	Sun.	7 Colorado*
	Sun.	7	at Chicago	Tues.	9 at Calgary
	Mon.	8	Los Angeles	Wed.	10 at Edmonton
	Wed.	10	Detroit	Fri.	12 at Anaheim
	Fri.	12	Florida	Sun.	14 Detroit*

* Denotes afternoon game.

Home Starting Times:
Weeknights . . . . 7:35 p.m.
Saturday and Sunday . . . . 7:05 p.m.
Matinees . . . . 1:05 p.m.

Franchise date: June 5, 1967
Transferred from Minnesota to Dallas
beginning with 1993-94 season.

**CENTRAL
DIVISION**

**29th
NHL
Season**

With his energetic forechecking and feistiness, rookie center Todd Harvey quickly became a fan favorite in Dallas.

Year-by-Year Record

Season	GP	Home W	L	T	Road W	L	T	Overall W	L	T	GF	GA	Pts.	Finished		Playoff Result
1994-95	48	9	10	5	8	13	3	17	23	8	136	135	42	5th,	Central Div.	Lost Conf. Quarter-Final
1993-94	84	23	12	7	19	17	6	42	29	13	286	265	97	3rd,	Central Div.	Lost Conf. Semi-Final
1992-93*	84	18	17	7	18	21	3	36	38	10	272	293	82	5th,	Norris Div.	Out of Playoffs
1991-92*	80	20	16	4	12	26	2	32	42	6	246	278	70	4th,	Norris Div.	Lost Div. Semi-Final
1990-91*	80	19	15	6	8	24	8	27	39	14	256	266	68	4th,	Norris Div.	Lost Final
1989-90*	80	26	12	2	10	28	2	36	40	4	284	291	76	4th,	Norris Div.	Lost Div. Semi-Final
1988-89*	80	17	15	8	10	22	8	27	37	16	258	278	70	3rd,	Norris Div.	Lost Div. Semi-Final
1987-88*	80	10	24	6	9	24	7	19	48	13	242	349	51	5th,	Norris Div.	Out of Playoffs
1986-87*	80	17	20	3	13	20	7	30	40	10	296	314	70	5th,	Norris Div.	Out of Playoffs
1985-86*	80	21	15	4	17	18	5	38	33	9	327	305	85	2nd,	Norris Div.	Lost Div. Semi-Final
1984-85*	80	14	19	7	11	24	5	25	43	12	268	321	62	4th,	Norris Div.	Lost Div. Final
1983-84*	80	22	14	4	17	17	6	39	31	10	345	344	88	1st,	Norris Div.	Lost Conf. Championship
1982-83*	80	23	6	11	17	18	5	40	24	16	321	290	96	2nd,	Norris Div.	Lost Div. Final
1981-82*	80	21	7	12	16	16	8	37	23	20	346	288	94	1st,	Norris Div.	Lost Div. Semi-Final
1980-81*	80	23	10	7	12	18	10	35	28	17	291	263	87	3rd,	Adams Div.	Lost Final
1979-80*	80	25	8	7	11	20	9	36	28	16	311	253	88	3rd,	Adams Div.	Lost Semi-Final
1978-79*	80	19	15	6	9	25	6	28	40	12	257	289	68	4th,	Adams Div.	Out Of Playoffs
1977-78*	80	12	24	4	6	29	5	18	53	9	218	325	45	5th,	Smythe Div.	Out of Playoffs
1976-77*	80	17	14	9	6	25	9	23	39	18	240	310	64	2nd,	Smythe Div.	Lost Prelim. Round
1975-76*	80	15	22	3	5	31	4	20	53	7	195	303	47	4th,	Smythe Div.	Out of Playoffs
1974-75*	80	17	20	3	6	30	4	23	50	7	221	341	53	4th,	Smythe Div.	Out of Playoffs
1973-74*	78	18	15	6	5	23	11	23	38	17	235	275	63	7th,	West Div.	Out of Playoffs
1972-73*	78	26	8	5	11	22	6	37	30	11	254	230	85	3rd,	West Div.	Lost Quarter-Final
1971-72*	78	22	11	6	15	18	6	37	29	12	212	191	86	2nd,	West Div.	Lost Quarter-Final
1970-71*	78	16	15	8	12	19	8	28	34	16	191	223	72	4th,	West Div.	Lost Quarter-Final
1969-70*	76	11	16	11	8	19	11	19	35	22	224	257	60	3rd,	West Div.	Lost Quarter-Final
1968-69*	76	11	21	6	7	22	9	18	43	15	189	270	51	6th,	West Div.	Out of Playoffs
1967-68*	74	17	12	8	10	20	7	27	32	15	191	226	69	4th,	West Div.	Lost Semi-Final

* Minnesota North Stars

1995-96 Player Personnel

FORWARDS	HT	WT	S	Place of Birth	Date	1994-95 Club
ADAMS, Greg	6-3	198	L	Nelson, B.C.	8/1/63	Vancouver-Dallas
BASSEN, Bob	5-10	180	L	Calgary, Alta.	5/6/65	Quebec
BOYER, Zac	6-1	199	R	Inuvik, N.W.T.	10/25/71	Kalamazoo-Dallas
BRADY, Neil	6-2	200	L	Montreal, Que.	4/12/68	Kalamazoo
BROTEN, Paul	5-11	188	R	Roseau, MN	10/27/65	Dallas
CHURLA, Shane	6-1	200	R	Fernie, B.C.	6/24/65	Dallas
DONNELLY, Mike	5-11	185	L	Detroit, MI	10/10/63	Los Angeles-Dallas
GAGNER, Dave	5-10	180	L	Chatham, Ont.	12/11/64	Courmaosta-Dallas
GILCHRIST, Brent	5-11	181	L	Moose Jaw, Sask.	4/3/67	Dallas
HARVEY, Todd	6-0	195	R	Hamilton, Ont.	2/17/75	Detroit (OHL)-Dallas
IGINLA, Jarome	6-1	193	R	Edmonton, Alta.	7/1/77	Kamloops
JINMAN, Lee	5-10	160	R	Toronto, Ont.	1/10/76	North Bay
KENNEDY, Mike	6-1	170	R	Vancouver, B.C.	4/13/72	Kalamazoo-Dallas
KESA, Dan	6-0	198	R	Vancouver, B.C.	11/23/71	Syracuse
KLATT, Trent	6-1	205	R	Robbinsdale, MN	1/30/71	Dallas
LANGENBRUNNER, Jamie	5-11	185	R	Duluth, MN	7/24/75	Peterborough-Dallas-Kalamazoo
LAWRENCE, Mark	6-4	215	R	Burlington, Ont.	1/27/72	Kalamazoo-Dallas
LEHTINEN, Jere	6-0	185	R	Espoo, Finland	6/24/73	TPS
LIND, Juha	5-11	160	L	Helsinki, Finland	1/2/74	Jokerit
MARSHALL, Grant	6-1	185	R	Mississauga, Ont.	6/9/73	Kalamazoo-Dallas
MILLEN, Corey	5-7	170	R	Cloquet, MN	3/30/64	New Jersey-Dallas
MITCHELL, Jeff	6-1	190	R	Wayne, MI	5/16/75	Detroit (OHL)
MODANO, Mike	6-3	190	L	Livonia, MI	6/7/70	Dallas
WRIGHT, Jamie	6-0	172	L	Kitchener, Ont.	5/13/76	Guelph

DEFENSEMEN						
BONNER, Craig	6-4	205	L	Edmonton, Alta.	5/20/72	Kalamazoo
CAVALLINI, Paul	6-1	202	L	Toronto, Ont.	10/13/65	Dallas
GUSEV, Sergei	6-1	195	L	Nizhny Tagil, USSR	7/31/75	CSK Samara
HATCHER, Derian	6-5	225	L	Sterling Heights, MI	6/4/72	Dallas
HATCHER, Kevin	6-4	225	R	Detroit, MI	9/9/66	Dallas
LALOR, Mike	6-0	200	L	Buffalo, NY	3/8/63	Dallas-Kalamazoo
LEDYARD, Grant	6-2	195	L	Winnipeg, Man.	11/19/61	Dallas
LUDWIG, Craig	6-3	217	L	Rhinelander, WI	3/15/61	Dallas
MATVICHUK, Richard	6-2	190	L	Edmonton, Alta.	2/5/73	Dallas-Kalamazoo
RICHARDS, Travis	6-1	185	L	Crystal, MN	3/22/70	Kalamazoo-Dallas
ZMOLEK, Doug	6-2	220	L	Rochester, MN	11/3/70	Dallas

GOALTENDERS	HT	WT	C	Place of Birth	Date	1994-95 Club
FERNANDEZ, Emmanuel	6-0	185	L	Etobicoke, Ont.	8/27/74	Kalamazoo
MOOG, Andy	5-8	170	L	Penticton, B.C.	2/18/60	Dallas
WAKALUK, Darcy	5-11	180	L	Pincher Creek, Alta.	3/14/66	Dallas
WILLIS, Jordan	5-9	155	L	Kincardine, Ont.	2/28/75	London

General Managers' History

Wren A. Blair, 1967-68 to 1973-74; Jack Gordon, 1974-75 to 1976-77; Lou Nanne, 1977-78 to 1987-88; Jack Ferreira, 1988-89 to 1989-90; Bob Clarke 1990-91 to 1991-92; Bob Gainey, 1992-93 to date.

Coaching History

Wren Blair, 1967-68; Wren Blair and John Muckler, 1968-69; Wren Blair and Charlie Burns, 1969-70; Jackie Gordon, 1970-71 to 1972-73; Jackie Gordon and Parker MacDonald, 1973-74; Jackie Gordon and Charlie Burns, 1974-75; Ted Harris, 1975-76, 1976-77; Ted Harris, André Beaulieu and Lou Nanne, 1977-78; Harry Howell and Glen Sonmor, 1978-79; Glen Sonmor, 1979-80 to 1981-82; Glen Sonmor and Murray Oliver, 1982-83; Bill Mahoney, 1983-84 to 1984-85; Lorne Henning, 1985-86; Lorne Henning and Glen Sonmor, 1986-87; Herb Brooks, 1987-88; Pierre Page, 1988-89 to 1989-90; Bob Gainey, 1990-91 to date.

Captains' History

Bob Woytowich, 1967-68; "Moose" Vasko, 1968-69; Claude Larose, 1969-70; Ted Harris, 1970-71 to 1973-74; Bill Goldsworthy, 1974-75, 1975-76; Bill Hogaboam, 1976-77; Nick Beverley, 1977-78; J.P. Parise, 1978-79; Paul Shmyr, 1979-80, 1980-81; Tim Young, 1981-82; Craig Hartsburg, 1982-83; Craig Hartsburg, Brian Bellows, 1983-84; Craig Hartsburg, 1984-85 to 1987-88; Curt Fraser, Bob Rouse and Curt Giles, 1988-89; Curt Giles, 1989-90 to 1990-91; Mark Tinordi, 1991-92 to 1993-94; Neal Broten and Derian Hatcher, 1994-95; Derian Hatcher, 1995-96.

Retired Numbers

8	Bill Goldsworthy	1967-1976
19	Bill Masterton	1967-1968

1994-95 Scoring

* – rookie

Regular Season

Pos	#	Player	Team	GP	G	A	Pts	+/-	PIM	PP	SH	GW	GT	S	%
C	15	Dave Gagner	DAL	48	14	28	42	2	42	7	0	2	1	138	10.1
C	9	Mike Modano	DAL	30	12	17	29	7	8	4	1	0	0	100	12.0
D	4	Kevin Hatcher	DAL	47	10	19	29	−4	66	3	0	2	1	138	7.2
L	11	Mike Donnelly	L.A.	9	1	1	2	−7	4	0	0	0	0	22	4.5
			DAL	35	11	14	25	3	29	3	0	3	0	94	11.7
			TOTAL	44	12	15	27	−4	33	3	0	3	0	116	10.3
C	6	Corey Millen	N.J.	17	2	3	5	2	8	0	0	0	0	30	6.7
			DAL	28	3	15	18	4	28	1	0	0	0	44	6.8
			TOTAL	45	5	18	23	6	36	1	0	0	0	74	6.8
R	22	Trent Klatt	DAL	47	12	10	22	−2	26	5	0	3	0	91	13.2
L	23	Greg Adams	VAN	31	5	10	15	1	12	2	2	0	0	56	8.9
			DAL	12	3	3	6	−4	4	1	0	0	0	16	18.8
			TOTAL	43	8	13	21	−3	16	3	2	0	0	72	11.1
C	10	* Todd Harvey	DAL	40	11	9	20	−3	67	2	0	1	0	64	17.2
L	39	* Mike Kennedy	DAL	44	6	12	18	4	33	2	0	0	0	76	7.9
D	12	Grant Ledyard	DAL	38	5	13	18	6	20	4	0	0	1	79	6.3
R	21	Paul Broten	DAL	47	7	9	16	−7	36	0	0	0	1	67	10.4
D	2	Derian Hatcher	DAL	47	5	11	16	3	105	0	2	0	0	74	6.8
C	16	Dean Evason	DAL	47	8	7	15	3	48	1	0	0	0	53	15.1
C	41	Brent Gilchrist	DAL	32	9	4	13	−3	16	1	3	1	0	70	12.9
D	14	Paul Cavallini	DAL	44	1	11	12	8	28	0	0	0	0	69	1.4
C	25	Peter Zezel	DAL	30	6	5	11	−6	19	0	0	1	0	47	12.8
D	3	Craig Ludwig	DAL	47	2	7	9	−6	61	0	0	0	0	55	3.6
D	5	Doug Zmolek	DAL	42	0	5	5	−6	67	0	0	0	0	28	0.0
R	27	Shane Churla	DAL	27	1	3	4	0	186	0	0	1	0	22	4.5
R	11	* Jarkko Varvio	DAL	5	1	1	2	1	0	1	0	0	0	9	11.1
D	24	Richard Matvichuk	DAL	14	0	2	2	−7	14	0	0	0	0	21	0.0
D	43	Gord Donnelly	DAL	16	1	0	1	1	52	0	0	0	0	9	11.1
R	29	* Grant Marshall	DAL	2	0	1	1	1	0	0	0	0	0	0	0.0
G	35	Andy Moog	DAL	31	0	1	1	0	14	0	0	0	0	0	0.0
R	37	Zac Boyer	DAL	1	0	0	0	0	0	0	0	0	0	1	0.0
G	30	* Emmanuel Fernandez	DAL	1	0	0	0	0	0	0	0	0	0	0	0.0
D	28	* Travis Richards	DAL	2	0	0	0	0	0	0	0	0	0	1	0.0
R	38	* Mark Lawrence	DAL	2	0	0	0	0	0	0	0	0	0	3	0.0
C	20	* Jamie Langenbrunner	DAL	2	0	0	0	2	0	0	0	0	0	1	0.0
G	1	* Mike Torchia	DAL	6	0	0	0	0	0	0	0	0	0	0	0.0
D	18	Mike Lalor	DAL	12	0	0	0	0	0	0	0	0	0	6	0.0
G	34	Darcy Wakaluk	DAL	15	0	0	0	0	4	0	0	0	0	0	0.0

Goaltending

No.	Goaltender	GPI	Mins	Avg	W	L	T	EN	SO	GA	SA	S%
35	Andy Moog	31	1770	2.44	10	12	7	1	2	72	846	.915
30	* Emmanuel Fernande	1	59	3.05	0	1	0	0	0	3	27	.889
34	Darcy Wakaluk	15	754	3.18	4	8	0	1	2	40	341	.883
1	* Mike Torchia	6	327	3.30	3	2	1	0	0	18	172	.895
	Totals	**48**	**2925**	**2.77**	**17**	**23**	**8**	**2**	**4**	**135**	**1388**	**.903**

Playoffs

Pos	#	Player	Team	GP	G	A	Pts	+/-	PIM	PP	SH	GW	OT	S	%
D	4	Kevin Hatcher	DAL	5	2	1	3	−4	2	1	0	1	0	18	11.1
R	21	Paul Broten	DAL	5	1	2	3	−2	2	0	0	0	0	6	16.7
C	16	Dean Evason	DAL	5	1	2	3	1	12	0	1	0	0	7	14.3
L	23	Greg Adams	DAL	5	2	0	2	1	0	0	0	0	0	14	14.3
C	15	Dave Gagner	DAL	5	1	1	2	0	4	1	0	0	0	10	10.0
D	14	Paul Cavallini	DAL	5	0	2	2	2	6	0	0	0	0	8	0.0
D	24	Richard Matvichuk	DAL	5	0	2	2	−3	4	0	0	0	0	6	0.0
C	25	Peter Zezel	DAL	3	1	0	1	0	0	0	0	0	0	3	33.3
C	6	Corey Millen	DAL	5	1	0	1	−1	2	0	0	0	0	2	50.0
R	22	Trent Klatt	DAL	5	1	0	1	0	0	1	0	0	0	4	25.0
D	3	Craig Ludwig	DAL	4	0	1	1	5	2	0	0	0	0	4	0.0
L	11	Mike Donnelly	DAL	5	0	1	1	0	6	0	0	0	0	6	0.0
C	41	Brent Gilchrist	DAL	5	0	1	1	−1	2	0	0	0	0	7	0.0
G	34	Darcy Wakaluk	DAL	1	0	0	0	0	0	0	0	0	0	0	0.0
R	37	Zac Boyer	DAL	2	0	0	0	0	0	0	0	0	0	1	0.0
D	18	Mike Lalor	DAL	3	0	0	0	2	2	0	0	0	0	1	0.0
D	12	Grant Ledyard	DAL	5	0	0	0	−2	2	0	0	0	0	4	0.0
R	27	Shane Churla	DAL	5	0	0	0	−1	20	0	0	0	0	2	0.0
G	35	Andy Moog	DAL	5	0	0	0	0	2	0	0	0	0	0	0.0
D	5	Doug Zmolek	DAL	5	0	0	0	−2	10	0	0	0	0	3	0.0
L	39	* Mike Kennedy	DAL	5	0	0	0	−1	9	0	0	0	0	3	0.0
C	10	* Todd Harvey	DAL	5	0	0	0	−1	9	0	0	0	0	7	0.0

Goaltending

No.	Goaltender	GPI	Mins	Avg	W	L	EN	SO	GA	SA	S%
34	Darcy Wakaluk	1	20	3.00	0	0	0	0	1	9	.889
35	Andy Moog	5	277	3.47	1	4	0	0	16	169	.905
	Totals	**5**	**300**	**3.40**	**1**	**4**	**0**	**0**	**17**	**178**	**.904**

Club Records

Team

(Figures in brackets for season records are games played; records for fewest points, wins, ties, losses, goals, goals against are for 70 or more games)

Most Points	97	1993-94 (84)
Most Wins	42	1993-94 (84)
Most Ties	22	1969-70 (76)
Most Losses	53	1975-76, 1977-78 (80)
Most Goals	346	1981-82 (80)
Most Goals Against	349	1987-88 (80)
Fewest Points	45	1977-78 (80)
Fewest Wins	18	1968-69 (76) 1977-78 (80)
Fewest Ties	4	1989-90 (80)
Fewest Losses	23	1981-82 (80)
Fewest Goals	189	1968-69 (76)
Fewest Goals Against	191	1971-72 (78)

Longest Winning Streak

Over-all	7	Mar. 16-28/80
Home	11	Nov. 4-Dec. 27/72
Away	7	Nov. 18-Dec. 5/92; Jan. 26-Feb. 21/94

Longest Undefeated Streak

Over-all	12	Feb. 18-Mar. 15/82 (9 wins, 3 ties)
Home	13	Oct. 28-Dec. 27/72 (12 wins, 1 tie) Nov. 21-Jan. 9/80 (10 wins, 3 ties) Jan. 17-Mar. 17/91 (11 wins, 2 ties)
Away	8	Jan. 26-Feb. 21/94 (7 wins, 1 tie)

Longest Losing Streak

Over-all	10	Feb. 1-20/76
Home	6	Jan. 17-Feb. 4/70
Away	8	Oct. 19-Nov. 13/75; Jan. 28-Mar. 3/88

Longest Winless Streak

Over-all	20	Jan. 15-Feb. 28/70 (15 losses, 5 ties)
Home	12	Jan. 17-Feb. 25/70 (8 losses, 4 ties)
Away	23	Oct. 25/74-Jan. 28/75 (19 losses, 4 ties)

Most Shutouts, Season	7	1972-73 (78)
Most PIM, Season	2,313	1987-88 (80)
Most Goals, Game	15	Nov. 11/81 (Wpg. 2 at Minn. 15)

Individual

Most Seasons	15	Neal Broten
Most Games	972	Neal Broten
Most Goals, Career	342	Brian Bellows
Most Assists, Career	586	Neal Broten
Most Points Career	852	Neal Broten (266 goals, 586 assists)
Most PIM, Career	1,715	Shane Churla
Most Shutouts, Career	26	Cesare Maniago
Longest Consecutive Games Streak	442	Danny Grant (Dec. 4/68-Apr. 7/74)
Most Goals, Season	55	Dino Ciccarelli (1981-82) Brian Bellows (1989-90)
Most Assists, Season	76	Neal Broten (1985-86)
Most Points, Season	114	Bobby Smith (1981-82) (43 goals, 71 assists)
Most PIM, Season	382	Basil McRae (1987-88)

Most Points, Defenseman

Season	77	Craig Hartsburg (1981-82) (17 goals, 60 assists)

Most Points, Center,

Season	114	Bobby Smith (1981-82) (43 goals, 71 assists)

Most Points, Right Wing,

Season	107	Dino Ciccarelli (1981-82) (55 goals, 52 assists)

Most Point, Left Wing,

Season	99	Brian Bellows (1989-90) (55 goals, 44 assists)

Most Points, Rookie,

Season	98	Neal Broten (1981-82) (38 goals, 60 assists)

Most Shutouts, Season	6	Cesare Maniago (1967-68)
Most Goals, Game	5	Tim Young (Jan. 15/79)
Most Assists, Game	5	Murray Oliver (Oct. 24/71) Larry Murphy (Oct. 17/89)
Most Points, Game	7	Bobby Smith (Nov. 11/81)

Records include Minnesota North Stars 1967-68 through 1992-93.

All-time Record vs. Other Clubs

Regular Season

			At Home							On Road							Total				
	GP	W	L	T	GF	GA	PTS	GP	W	L	T	GF	GA	PTS	GP	W	L	T	GF	GA	PTS
Anaheim	4	3	1	0	19	8	6	5	3	2	0	15	12	6	9	6	3	0	34	20	12
Boston	53	13	29	11	145	198	37	53	6	38	9	125	239	21	106	19	67	20	270	437	58
Buffalo	46	20	20	6	144	144	46	45	12	23	10	124	168	34	91	32	43	16	268	312	80
Calgary	44	21	17	6	162	147	48	44	6	27	11	116	177	23	88	27	44	17	278	324	71
Chicago	91	40	39	12	309	296	92	89	21	58	10	231	368	52	180	61	97	22	540	664	144
Detroit	86	45	27	14	323	261	104	85	30	43	12	290	346	72	171	75	70	26	613	607	176
Edmonton	27	9	12	6	97	96	24	26	4	16	6	85	127	14	53	13	28	12	182	223	38
Florida	1	0	0	1	4	4	1	1	1	0	0	5	4	2	2	1	0	1	9	8	3
Hartford	22	12	9	1	93	72	25	23	11	9	3	87	84	25	45	23	18	4	180	156	50
Los Angeles	61	36	16	9	252	173	81	60	18	27	15	180	216	51	121	54	43	24	432	389	132
Montreal	52	14	27	11	135	186	39	51	9	35	7	125	230	25	103	23	62	18	260	416	64
New Jersey	37	22	9	6	150	100	50	37	16	18	3	115	123	35	74	38	27	9	265	223	85
NY Islanders	39	14	19	6	114	148	34	39	9	22	8	111	154	26	78	23	41	14	225	302	60
NY Rangers	53	16	29	8	162	205	40	54	11	33	10	148	194	32	107	27	62	18	310	399	72
Ottawa	3	2	1	0	17	8	4	2	0	0	9	6	4	5	4	1	0	26	14	8	
Philadelphia	59	24	22	13	197	196	61	59	9	40	10	136	235	28	118	33	62	23	333	431	89
Pittsburgh	57	32	20	5	218	192	69	56	17	34	5	158	216	39	113	49	54	10	376	408	108
Quebec	22	13	7	2	88	72	28	23	5	16	2	62	107	12	45	18	23	4	150	179	40
St. Louis	95	43	34	18	329	282	104	97	26	53	18	276	359	70	192	69	87	36	605	641	174
San Jose	7	4	2	1	32	23	9	7	4	3	0	29	20	8	14	8	5	1	61	43	17
Tampa Bay	4	3	1	0	15	12	6	5	5	3	0	2	13	7	8	9	6	1	2	28	19	14
Toronto	86	43	32	11	334	286	97	89	29	45	15	284	325	73	175	72	77	26	618	611	170
Vancouver	53	30	13	10	212	153	70	53	19	24	10	166	204	48	106	49	37	20	378	357	118
Washington	32	14	10	8	122	94	36	33	13	13	7	105	106	33	65	27	23	15	227	200	69
Winnipeg	30	17	9	4	132	96	38	29	14	14	1	105	103	29	59	31	23	5	237	199	67
Defunct Clubs	33	19	8	6	123	86	44	32	10	16	6	84	105	26	65	29	24	12	207	191	70
Totals	**1097**	**509**	**413**	**175**	**3928**	**3538**	**1193**	**1097**	**308**	**609**	**180**	**3184**	**4235**	**796**	**2194**	**817**	**1022**	**355**	**7112**	**7773**	**1989**

Calgary totals include Atlanta, 1972-73 to 1979-80. Dallas totals include Minnesota, 1967-68 to 1992-93.
New Jersey totals include Kansas City, 1974-75 to 1975-76, and Colorado, 1976-77 to 1981-82.

Playoffs

	Series	W	L	GP	W	L	T	GF	GA	Last Mtg.	Round	Result
Boston	1	1	0	3	3	0	0	20	13	1981	PR	W 3-0
Buffalo	2	1	1	7	4	3	0	26	28	1981	QF	W 4-1
Calgary	1	1	0	6	4	2	0	25	18	1981	SF	W 4-2
Chicago	6	2	4	33	14	19	0	119	119	1991	DSF	W 4-2
Detroit	2	0	2	12	4	8	0	29	40	1995	CQF	L 1-4
Edmonton	2	1	1	9	4	5	0	30	36	1991	CF	W 4-1
Los Angeles	1	1	0	7	4	3	0	26	21	1968	QF	W 4-3
Montreal	2	1	1	13	6	7	0	37	48	1980	QF	W 4-3
NY Islanders	1	0	1	5	1	4	0	16	26	1981	F	L 1-4
Philadelphia	2	0	2	11	3	8	0	26	41	1980	SF	L 1-4
Pittsburgh	1	0	1	6	2	4	0	16	28	1991	F	L 2-4
St. Louis	10	5	5	56	30	26	0	174	162	1994	CQF	W 4-0
Toronto	2	2	0	7	6	1	0	35	26	1983	DSF	W 3-1
Vancouver	1	0	1	5	1	4	0	11	18	1994	CSF	L 1-4
Totals	**34**	**15**	**19**	**180**	**86**	**94**	**0**	**590**	**624**			

Playoff Results 1995-91

Year	Round	Opponent	Result	GF	GA
1995	CQF	Detroit	L 1-4	10	17
1994	CSF	Vancouver	L 1-4	11	18
	CQF	St. Louis	W 4-0	16	10
1992	DSF	Detroit	L 3-4	19	23
1991	F	Pittsburgh	L 2-4	16	28
	CF	Edmonton	W 4-1	20	14
	DF	St. Louis	W 4-2	22	17
	DSF	Chicago	W 4-2	23	16

Abbreviations: Round: F – Final;
CF – conference final; **CQF** – conference quarter-final;
CSF – conference semi-final; **DF** – division final;
DSF – division semi-final; **SF** – semi-final;
QF – quarter-final; **PR** – preliminary round.

1994-95 Results

Jan. 20	at	Vancouver	1-1	12		Calgary	4-4
24	at	Los Angeles	4-2	13		Chicago	4-2
25	at	Anaheim	4-1	16	at	Detroit	4-5
28	at	San Jose	2-3	22		Edmonton	4-4
30		Toronto	1-2	23		Edmonton	2-1
Feb. 1		Anaheim	9-2	27		St. Louis	2-3
2		San Jose	1-2	30	at	Detroit	2-3
4	at	St. Louis	4-7	Apr. 1		Detroit	2-3
8	at	Toronto	3-3	2	at	Chicago	2-1
11		Calgary	0-6	4	at	Vancouver	2-2
13		Winnipeg	4-7	6	at	Los Angeles	2-3
15		Los Angeles	1-3	7	at	Anaheim	2-0
18	at	Calgary	2-3	9	at	St. Louis	3-2
20	at	Calgary	2-1	11		Detroit	1-4
22	at	Edmonton	1-2	14	at	Toronto	1-2
24		Vancouver	3-3	16		Chicago	2-0
26		Chicago	1-2	17		Vancouver	2-2
28	at	Winnipeg	4-0	19		San Jose	5-5
Mar. 1	at	Edmonton	5-3	22		Toronto	6-4
3		Anaheim	4-0	23		Winnipeg	5-2
5		St. Louis	2-1	25		St. Louis	4-8
6		Los Angeles	8-2	27	at	Chicago	1-5
8	at	Toronto	2-3	29	at	Detroit	2-4
10	at	Winnipeg	3-4	May 1	at	San Jose	1-3

Entry Draft Selections 1995-81

1995
Pick
11 Jarome Iginla
37 Patrick Cote
63 Petr Buzek
69 Sergei Gusev
115 Wade Strand
141 Dominic Marleau
173 Jeff Dewar
193 Anatoli Kovesnikov
202 Sergei Luchinkin
219 Stephen Lowe

1994
Pick
20 Jason Botterill
46 Lee Jinman
98 Jamie Wright
124 Marty Turco
150 Yevgeny Petrochinin
228 Marty Flichel
254 Jimmy Roy
280 Chris Szysky

1993
Pick
9 Todd Harvey
35 Jamie Langenbrunner
87 Chad Lang
136 Rick Mrozik
139 Per Svartvadet
165 Jeremy Stasiuk
191 Rob Lurtsema
243 Jordan Willis
249 Bill Lang
269 Cory Peterson

1992
Pick
34 Jarkko Varvio
58 Jeff Bes
88 Jere Lehtinen
130 Michael Johnson
154 Kyle Peterson
178 Juha Lind
202 Lars Edstrom
226 Jeff Romfo
250 Jeffrey Moen

1991
Pick
8 Richard Matvichuk
74 Mike Torchia
97 Mike Kennedy
118 Mark Lawrence
137 Geoff Finch
174 MichaelBurkett
184 Derek Herlofsky
206 Tom Nemeth
228 Shayne Green
250 Jukka Suomalainen

1990
Pick
8 Derian Hatcher
50 Laurie Billeck
70 Cal McGowan
71 Frank Kovacs
92 Enrico Ciccone
113 Roman Turek
134 Jeff Levy
155 Doug Barrault
176 Joe Biondi
197 Troy Binnie
218 Ole-Eskild Dahlstrom
239 John McKersie

1989
Pick
7 Doug Zmolek
28 Mike Craig
60 Murray Garbutt
75 Jean-François Quintin
87 Pat MacLeod
91 Bryan Schoen
97 Rhys Hollyman
112 Scott Cashman
154 Jonathan Pratt
175 Kenneth Blum
196 Arturs Irbe
217 Tom Pederson
238 Helmut Balderis

1988
Pick
1 Mike Modano
40 Link Gaetz
43 Shaun Kane
64 Jeffrey Stop
148 Ken MacArthur
169 Travis Richards
190 Ari Matilainen
211 Grant Bischoff
232 Trent Andison

1987
Pick
6 David Archibald
35 Scott McCrady
48 Kevin Kaminski
73 John Weisbrod
88 Teppo Kivela
109 Darcy Norton
130 Timo Kulonen
151 Don Schmidt
172 Jarmo Myllys
193 Larry Olimb
214 Mark Felicio
235 Dave hields

1986
Pick
12 Warren Babe
30 Neil Wilkinson
33 Dean Kolstad
54 Eric Bennett
55 Rob Zettler
58 Brad Turner
75 Kirk Tomlinson
96 Jari Gronstrand
159 Scott Mathias
180 Lance Pitlick
201 Dan Keczmer
222 Garth Joy
243 Kurt Stahura

1985
Pick
51 Stephane Roy
69 Mike Berger
90 Dwight Mullins
111 MikeMullowney
132 Mike Kelfer
153 Ross Johnson
174 Tim Helmer
195 Gordon Ernst
216 Ladislav Lubina
237 Tommy Sjodin

1984
Pick
13 David Quinn
46 Ken Hodge
76 Miroslav Maly
89 Jiri Poner
97 Kari Takko
118 Gary McColgan
139 Vladimir Kyhos
160 Darin MacInnis
181 Duane Wahlin
201 Mike Orn
222 Tom Terwilliger
242 Mike Nightenale

1983
Pick
1 Brian Lawton
36 Malcolm Parks
38 Frantisek Musil
56 Mitch Messier
76 Brian Durand
96 Rich Geist
116 Tom McComb
136 Sean Toomey
156 Don Biggs
176 Paul Pulis
196 Milos Riha
212 Oldrich Valek
236 Paul Roff

1982
Pick
2 Brian Bellows
59 Wally Chapman
80 Rob Rouse
81 Dusan Pasek
101 Marty Wiitala
122 Todd Carlile
143 Victor Zhluktov
164 Paul Miller
185 Pat Micheletti
206 Arnold Kadlec
227 Scott Knutson

1981
Pick
13 Ron Meighan
27 Dave Donnelly
31 Mike Sands
33 Tom Hirsch
34 Dave Preuss
41 Jali Wahlsten
69 Terry Tait
76 Jim Malwitz
97 Kelly Hubbard
118 Paul Guay
139 Jim Archibald
160 Kari Kaervo
181 Scott Bjugstad
202 Steve Kudebeh

Coach and General Manager

GAINEY, BOB
Coach and General Manager, Dallas Stars.
Born in Peterborough, Ont., December 13, 1953.

Bob Gainey enters his sixth season behind the bench with both the longest consecutive tenure of any coach in Stars history as well as the current longest tenure with one team among his coaching peers in the NHL. After an inaugural year in Dallas in which Gainey led the Stars to a record-setting season with franchise marks in wins (42) and points (97), he rallied his team in the 1994-95 season to their second consecutive playoff berth and fourth in his five years coaching the Stars.

Gainey has been the general manager of the Stars since June, 1992 after being appointed head coach on June 19, 1990. The Stars improved their regular-season record in each of Gainey's first four seasons as coach, improving from 27 wins and 68 points his first year to the 42 wins and 97 points in 1993-94. In his first season, 1990-91, Gainey led the Stars through to the Stanley Cup Finals, surprising Chicago and St. Louis, the Stars eliminated defending champion Edmonton before bowing in six games to Pittsburgh.

Elected to the Hockey Hall of Fame in 1992, Gainey was Montreal's first choice (eighth overall) in the 1973 Amateur Draft. During his 16-year career with the Canadiens, Gainey was a member of five Stanley Cup-winning teams and was named the Conn Smythe Trophy winner in 1979. He was a four-time recipient of the Frank Selke Trophy (1978-81), awarded to the League's top defensive forward, and participated in four NHL All-Star Games (1977, 1978, 1980 and 1981). He served as team captain for eight seasons (1981-89). During his career, he played in 1,160 regular-season games, registering 239 goals and 262 assists for 501 points. In addition, he tallied 73 points (25-48-73) in 182 post-season games.

Coaching Record

		Regular Season					Playoffs			
Season	**Team**	**Games**	**W**	**L**	**T**	**%**	**Games**	**W**	**L**	**%**
1989-90	Epinal (France)	....	....	....	....	....	....	....	....	....
1990-91	**Minnesota (NHL)**	**80**	**27**	**39**	**14**	**.425**	**23**	**14**	**9**	**.643**
1991-92	**Minnesota (NHL)**	**80**	**32**	**42**	**6**	**.438**	**7**	**3**	**4**	**.429**
1992-93	**Minnesota (NHL)**	**84**	**36**	**38**	**10**	**.488**	....	....	....	....
1993-94	**Dallas (NHL)**	**84**	**42**	**29**	**13**	**.577**	**9**	**5**	**4**	**.556**
1994-95	**Dallas (NHL)**	**48**	**17**	**23**	**8**	**.438**	**5**	**1**	**4**	**.200**
	NHL Totals	**376**	**154**	**171**	**51**	**.477**	**44**	**23**	**21**	**.523**

Club Directory

Reunion Arena

Dallas Stars Hockey Club, Inc.
Dr Pepper StarCenter
211 Cowboys Parkway
Irving, TX 75063
Phone **214/868-2890**
FAX 214/868-2860
P.R. Office 214/868-2807 or 2818
Capacity: 16,924

Executive
Owner and Governor . . . . Norman N. Green
President and Alternate Governor. . . . . James R. Lites
Director, Board of Directors . . . . Denise Ilitch Lites
Vice President of Hockey Operations . . . . Bob Gainey
Vice President of Marketing and Broadcasting . . . . . William C. Strong
Vice President of Marketing and Promotion . . . . Jeff Cogen
Vice President and Chief Financial Officer. . . . . Rick McLaughlin
Vice President of Business Operations/
General Counsel . . . . Len Perna
Office Manager . . . . Rene Marshall
Assistant to the Chairman . . . . Lesa Moake
Assistant to the President . . . . Kim Smith

Hockey
General Manager/Head Coach . . . . Bob Gainey
Assistant General Manager. . . . . Les Jackson
Assistant Coaches. . . . . Doug Jarvis, Rick Wilson
Assistant to the General Manager . . . . Doug Armstrong
Director of Amateur Scouting. . . . . Craig Button
Chief Scout. . . . . Bob Gernander
Scout . . . . Tim Bernhardt
Pro Scout . . . . Doug Overton
Regional Scouts . . . . Brad Robson, Jeff Twohey, Ray Robson, David Volek, Kevin Pottle, Bob Richardson, Jim Pederson, David Korol, Hans Edlund, Evgeny Larionov
Director of Team Services . . . . Dan Stuchal
Head Athletic Trainer . . . . Dave Surprenant
Equipment Manager. . . . . Dave Smith
Equipment Manager. . . . . Lance Vogt
Strength Coach . . . . Norm Temnograd
Administrative Assistant . . . . Syndi Bennett

Public Relations
Director of Public Relations. . . . . Larry Kelly
Public Relations Manager . . . . Kurt Daniels
Graphics Manager . . . . Jaqueline Grisez

Ticket Sales
Director of Ticket Sales . . . . Brian Byrnes
Account Executives. . . . . Tom Fireoved, Devin Fogleman, Adam Green, Frank Hubach, Andrew Menter, Jamie Norman, Alison Smith, Todd Smith, Lacey Wadlington
Sales Coordinator . . . . Mary Shartouny
Sales/Marketing Assistant . . . . Melissa Hill

Advertising and Promotion
Director of Advertising and Promotion . . . . Christy Martinez
Manager of Events & Sponsor Services . . . . Lee Smith
Community Relations Assistant. . . . . Susan Turner

Merchandising
Director of Merchandising . . . . Steve Shilts
Retail Manager . . . . Tiffani McCallon
Merchandise Operations Manager . . . . Jeff Casanova
Warehouse Manager . . . . Oscar Garza
Mail Order Supervisor. . . . . Loren Krasner

Corporate Sales
Director of Corporate Sales. . . . . Dana Summers
Director of Advertising Sales. . . . . Jeff Buch

Broadcasting
Producer/Director . . . . Kevin Spivey
Announcers, TV/Radio . . . . Mike Fornes, Ralph Strangis
Annoucer, Arena . . . . Bill Oellerman
Manager, Broadcast and Sales Services . . . . Hilary Roberts

Finance
Director of Finance . . . . Therese Baird
Director of Box Office Operations. . . . . Augie Manfredo
Manager of Accounting . . . . Sharon Arellano
Senior Accountant . . . . Tim Montrose
Senior Accountant . . . . Debbie Lalone
Payroll Accountant . . . . Bonnie Winchester
Box Office Manager . . . . Jenny Cauhorn
Assistant Box Office Manager. . . . . Stacy Lesanto
Phone Room Supervisor . . . . Ben Marthaler
Accounting Assistant . . . . Cliff Johnson

StarCenter Division
Director of Business Operations . . . . Ed Reusch
Director of Building Operations . . . . Geoff Moore
Skating Programs Manager . . . . Peter Cain
Hockey Programs Manager. . . . . Jouni Lehtola
Director of Corporate Hospitality . . . . Jill Cogen
Corporate Hospitality Manager. . . . . Barbara Patten
Assistant Business Manager . . . . Lance Lankford
Assistant Marketing Manager. . . . . Rebecca Miller
Coordinator of Skating Programs . . . . Alex LaFave
Coordinator of Hockey Programs . . . . Louis Iglesias
Superintendent. . . . . Robert Santana

Operations
Receptionist . . . . Paula Monzo
Office Assistant. . . . . Wanda Kress
Practice Facility . . . . Dr Pepper StarCenter
Radio flagship station . . . . WBAP (820 AM)
TV Stations . . . . KDFW (Ch. 4), KDFI (Ch. 27), Prime Sports (Cable)
Colors. . . . . Black, Green, Gold and White

Detroit Red Wings

1994-95 Results: 33w-11l-4t 70pts. First, Central Division

Keith Primeau's combination of size, strength and skill has made him one of the NHL's dominant centers.

Schedule

Oct.	Fri.	6	at Colorado	Fri.	12	Los Angeles
	Sun.	8	at Edmonton	Sat.	13	at Washington
	Mon.	9	at Vancouver	Wed.	17	Colorado
	Fri.	13	Edmonton	Wed.	24	San Jose
	Sun.	15	at Winnipeg	Thur.	25	at Ottawa
	Tues.	17	Calgary	Sat.	27	at Chicago*
	Thur.	19	at New Jersey	Tues.	30	Toronto
	Sat.	21	Boston*	**Feb.** Sat.	3	Pittsburgh*
	Tues.	24	Ottawa	Tues.	6	Florida
	Fri.	27	at Calgary	Thur.	8	at Florida
	Mon.	30	at Winnipeg	Sat.	10	at Tampa Bay*
Nov.	Wed.	1	at Buffalo	Tues.	13	Los Angeles
	Thur.	2	at Boston	Thur.	15	Washington
	Sat.	4	Dallas*	Fri.	16	at St. Louis
	Tues.	7	Edmonton	Sun.	18	at Toronto*
	Sat.	11	at San Jose	Mon.	19	Vancouver
	Tues.	14	at Los Angeles	Thur.	22	Toronto
	Fri.	17	at Edmonton	Sat.	24	Tampa Bay
	Wed.	22	San Jose	Tues.	27	at NY Islanders
	Fri.	24	at Philadelphia*	Thur.	29	NY Islanders
	Sat.	25	NY Rangers	**Mar.** Sat.	2	Vancouver*
	Tues.	28	Montreal	Sun.	3	at Chicago
Dec.	Fri.	1	Anaheim	Wed.	6	at Hartford
	Sat.	2	at Montreal	Fri.	8	at Colorado
	Tues.	5	Philadelphia	Sun.	10	at Winnipeg
	Thur.	7	Dallas	Tues.	12	Winnipeg
	Fri.	8	at NY Rangers	Sun.	17	Calgary*
	Tues.	12	at St. Louis	Tues.	19	Toronto
	Wed.	13	Chicago	Wed.	20	at Toronto
	Fri.	15	New Jersey	Fri.	22	Colorado
	Wed.	20	at Anaheim	Sun.	24	at St. Louis
	Fri.	22	at Calgary	Mon.	25	Anaheim
	Sat.	23	at Vancouver	Wed.	27	Buffalo
	Tues.	26	St. Louis	Sun.	31	St. Louis*
	Fri.	29	at Dallas	**Apr.** Tues.	2	at San Jose
	Sun.	31	Hartford	Wed.	3	at Los Angeles
Jan.	Wed.	3	Dallas	Fri.	5	at Anaheim
	Fri.	5	at Pittsburgh	Sun.	7	at Chicago*
	Sat.	6	Chicago	Wed.	10	Winnipeg
	Mon.	8	Winnipeg	Fri.	12	Chicago
	Wed.	10	at Dallas	Sun.	14	at Dallas*

* Denotes afternoon game.

Home Starting Times:

Night games . . . . 7:35 p.m.
Saturday matinees . . . . 3:05 p.m.
Sundays. . . . . 3:05 p.m.
Except   Sun. Dec. 31 . . . . 7:35 p.m.

Franchise date: September 25, 1926

WESTERN CONFERENCE

CENTRAL DIVISION

70th NHL Season

Year-by-Year Record

		Home			Road			Overall							Playoff Result
Season	GP	W	L	T	W	L	T	W	L	T	GF	GA	Pts.	Finished	
1994-95	48	17	4	3	16	7	1	33	11	4	180	117	70	1st, Central Div.	Lost Final
1993-94	84	23	13	6	23	17	2	46	30	8	356	275	100	1st, Central Div.	Lost Conf. Quarter-Final
1992-93	84	25	14	3	22	14	6	47	28	9	369	280	103	2nd, Norris Div.	Lost Div. Semi-Final
1991-92	80	24	12	4	19	13	8	43	25	12	320	256	98	1st, Norris Div.	Lost Div. Final
1990-91	80	26	14	0	8	24	8	34	38	8	273	298	76	3rd, Norris Div.	Lost Div. Semi-Final
1989-90	80	20	14	6	8	24	8	28	38	14	288	323	70	5th, Norris Div.	Out of Playoffs
1988-89	80	20	14	6	14	20	6	34	34	12	313	316	80	1st, Norris Div.	Lost Div. Semi-Final
1987-88	80	24	10	6	17	18	5	41	28	11	322	269	93	1st, Norris Div.	Lost Conf. Championship
1986-87	80	20	14	6	14	22	4	34	36	10	260	274	78	2nd, Norris Div.	Lost Conf. Championship
1985-86	80	10	26	4	7	31	2	17	57	6	266	415	40	5th, Norris Div.	Out of Playoffs
1984-85	80	19	14	7	8	27	5	27	41	12	313	357	66	3rd, Norris Div.	Lost Div. Semi-Final
1983-84	80	18	20	2	13	22	5	31	42	7	298	323	69	3rd, Norris Div.	Lost Div. Semi-Final
1982-83	80	14	19	7	7	25	8	21	44	15	263	344	57	5th, Norris Div.	Out of Playoffs
1981-82	80	15	19	6	6	28	6	21	47	12	270	351	54	6th, Norris Div.	Out of Playoffs
1980-81	80	16	15	9	3	28	9	19	43	18	252	339	56	5th, Norris Div.	Out of Playoffs
1979-80	80	14	21	5	12	22	6	26	43	11	268	306	63	5th, Norris Div.	Out of Playoffs
1978-79	80	15	17	8	8	24	8	23	41	16	252	295	62	5th, Norris Div.	Out of Playoffs
1977-78	80	22	11	7	10	23	7	32	34	14	252	266	78	2nd, Norris Div.	Lost Quarter-Final
1976-77	80	12	22	6	4	33	3	16	55	9	183	309	41	5th, Norris Div.	Out of Playoffs
1975-76	80	17	15	8	9	29	2	26	44	10	226	300	62	4th, Norris Div.	Out of Playoffs
1974-75	80	17	17	6	6	28	6	23	45	12	259	335	58	4th, Norris Div.	Out of Playoffs
1973-74	78	21	12	6	8	27	4	29	39	10	255	319	68	6th, East Div.	Out of Playoffs
1972-73	78	22	12	5	15	17	7	37	29	12	265	243	86	5th, East Div.	Out of Playoffs
1971-72	78	25	11	3	8	24	7	33	35	10	261	262	76	5th, East Div.	Out of Playoffs
1970-71	78	17	15	7	5	30	4	22	45	11	209	308	55	7th, East Div.	Out of Playoffs
1969-70	76	20	11	7	20	10	8	40	21	15	246	199	95	3rd, East Div.	Lost Quarter-Final
1968-69	76	23	8	7	10	23	5	33	31	12	239	221	78	5th, East Div.	Out of Playoffs
1967-68	74	18	15	4	9	20	8	27	35	12	245	257	66	6th, East Div.	Out of Playoffs
1966-67	70	21	11	3	6	28	1	27	39	4	212	241	58	5th,	Out of Playoffs
1965-66	70	20	8	7	11	19	5	31	27	12	221	194	74	4th,	Lost Final
1964-65	70	25	7	3	15	16	4	40	23	7	224	175	87	1st,	Lost Semi-Final
1963-64	70	23	9	3	7	20	8	30	29	11	191	204	71	4th,	Lost Final
1962-63	70	19	10	6	13	15	7	32	25	13	200	194	77	4th,	Lost Final
1961-62	70	17	11	7	6	22	7	23	33	14	184	219	60	5th,	Out of Playoffs
1960-61	70	15	13	7	10	16	9	25	29	16	195	215	66	4th,	Lost Final
1959-60	70	18	14	3	8	15	12	26	29	15	186	197	67	4th,	Lost Semi-Final
1958-59	70	13	17	5	12	20	3	25	37	8	167	218	58	6th,	Out of Playoffs
1957-58	70	16	11	8	13	18	4	29	29	12	176	207	70	3rd,	Lost Semi-Final
1956-57	70	23	7	5	15	13	7	38	20	12	198	157	88	1st,	Lost Semi-Final
1955-56	70	21	6	8	9	18	8	30	24	16	183	148	76	2nd,	Lost Final
1954-55	**70**	**25**	**5**	**5**	**17**	**12**	**6**	**42**	**17**	**11**	**204**	**134**	**95**	**1st,**	**Won Stanley Cup**
1953-54	**70**	**24**	**4**	**7**	**13**	**15**	**7**	**37**	**19**	**14**	**191**	**132**	**88**	**1st,**	**Won Stanley Cup**
1952-53	70	20	5	10	16	11	8	36	16	18	222	133	90	1st,	Lost Semi-Final
1951-52	**70**	**24**	**7**	**4**	**20**	**7**	**8**	**44**	**14**	**12**	**215**	**133**	**100**	**1st,**	**Won Stanley Cup**
1950-51	70	25	3	7	19	10	6	44	13	13	236	139	101	1st,	Lost Semi-Final
1949-50	**70**	**19**	**9**	**7**	**18**	**10**	**7**	**37**	**19**	**14**	**229**	**164**	**88**	**1st,**	**Won Stanley Cup**
1948-49	60	21	6	3	13	13	4	34	19	7	195	145	75	1st,	Lost Final
1947-48	60	16	9	5	14	9	7	30	18	12	187	148	72	2nd,	Lost Final
1946-47	60	14	10	6	8	17	5	22	27	11	190	193	55	4th,	Lost Semi-Final
1945-46	50	16	5	4	4	15	6	20	20	10	146	159	50	4th,	Lost Semi-Final
1944-45	50	19	5	1	12	9	4	31	14	5	218	161	67	2nd,	Lost Final
1943-44	50	18	5	2	8	13	4	26	18	6	214	177	58	2nd,	Lost Semi-Final
1942-43	**50**	**16**	**4**	**5**	**9**	**10**	**6**	**25**	**14**	**11**	**169**	**124**	**61**	**1st,**	**Won Stanley Cup**
1941-42	48	14	7	3	5	18	1	19	25	4	140	147	42	5th,	Lost Final
1940-41	48	14	5	5	7	11	6	21	16	11	112	102	53	3rd,	Lost Final
1939-40	48	11	10	3	5	16	3	16	26	6	90	126	38	5th,	Lost Semi-Final
1938-39	48	14	8	2	4	16	4	18	24	6	107	128	42	5th,	Lost Semi-Final
1937-38	48	8	10	6	4	15	5	12	25	11	99	133	35	4th, Amn. Div.	Out of Playoffs
1936-37	**48**	**14**	**5**	**5**	**11**	**9**	**4**	**25**	**14**	**9**	**128**	**102**	**59**	**1st, Amn. Div.**	**Won Stanley Cup**
1935-36	**48**	**14**	**5**	**5**	**10**	**11**	**3**	**24**	**16**	**8**	**124**	**103**	**56**	**1st, Amn. Div.**	**Won Stanley Cup**
1934-35	48	11	8	5	8	14	2	19	22	7	127	114	45	4th, Amn. Div.	Out of Playoffs
1933-34	48	15	5	4	9	9	6	24	14	10	113	98	58	1st, Amn. Div.	Lost Final
1932-33*	48	17	3	4	8	12	4	25	15	8	111	93	58	2nd, Amn. Div.	Lost Semi-Final
1931-32	48	15	5	4	3	13	8	18	20	10	95	108	46	3rd, Amn. Div.	Lost Quarter-Final
1930-31**	44	10	7	5	6	14	2	16	21	7	102	105	39	4th, Amn. Div.	Out of Playoffs
1929-30	44	9	6	7	5	14	3	14	24	6	117	133	34	4th, Amn. Div.	Out of Playoffs
1928-29	44	11	6	5	8	10	4	19	16	9	72	63	47	3rd, Amn. Div.	Lost Quarter-Final
1927-28	44	13	8	1	6	11	5	19	19	6	88	79	44	4th, Amn. Div.	Out of Playoffs
1926-27***	44	6	15	1	6	13	3	12	28	4	76	105	28	5th, Amn. Div.	Out of Playoffs

* Team name changed to Red Wings. ** Team name changed to Falcons. *** Team named Cougars.

1995-96 Player Personnel

FORWARDS	HT	WT	S	Place of Birth	Date	1994-95 Club
BOWEN, Curtis	6-1	195	L	Kenora, Ont.	3/24/74	Adirondack
BROWN, Doug	5-10	185	R	Southborough, MA	6/12/64	Detroit
CASSELMAN, Mike	5-11	190	L	Morrisburg, Ont.	8/23/68	Adirondack
CICCARELLI, Dino	5-10	185	R	Sarnia, Ont.	2/8/60	Detroit
CLOUTIER, Sylvain	6-0	195	L	Mont-Laurier, Que.	2/13/74	Adirondack
DANDENAULT, Mathieu	6-0	174	R	Sherbrooke, Que.	2/3/76	Sherbrooke
DRAPER, Kris	5-11	185	L	Toronto, Ont.	5/24/71	Detroit
ERREY, Bob	5-10	185	L	Montreal, Que.	9/21/64	San Jose-Detroit
FEDOROV, Sergei	6-1	200	L	Pskov, USSR	12/13/69	Detroit
GRIMSON, Stu	6-5	227	L	Kamloops, B.C.	5/20/65	Anaheim-Detroit
HANKINSON, Ben	6-2	210	R	Edina, MN	5/1/69	New Jersey-Albany-Tampa Bay
JOHNSON, Greg	5-10	185	L	Thunder Bay, Ont.	3/16/71	Detroit
KNUBLE, Michael	6-3	208	R	Toronto, Ont.	7/4/72	U. of Michigan-Adirondack
KOZLOV, Vyacheslav	5-10	180	L	Voskresensk, USSR	5/3/72	CSKA-Detroit
LAPOINTE, Martin	5-11	200	R	Ville Ste. Pierre, Que.	9/12/73	Adirondack-Detroit
MacDONALD, Jason	6-0	195	R	Charlottetown, P.E.I.	4/1/74	Adirondack
MAJOR, Mark	6-3	223	L	Toronto, Ont.	3/20/70	Detroit (IHL)
McCARTY, Darren	6-1	210	R	Burnaby, B.C.	4/1/72	Detroit
MILLER, Kurtis	5-11	190	L	Bemidji, MN	6/1/70	Adirondack
PRIMEAU, Keith	6-4	210	L	Toronto, Ont.	11/24/71	Detroit
SHEPPARD, Ray	6-1	195	R	Pembroke, Ont.	5/27/66	Detroit
TAYLOR, Tim	6-1	185	L	Stratford, Ont.	2/6/69	Detroit
YZERMAN, Steve	5-11	185	R	Cranbrook, B.C.	5/9/65	Detroit
DEFENSEMEN						
BERGEVIN, Marc	6-1	197	L	Montreal, Que.	8/11/65	Tampa Bay
BLOEMBERG, Jeff	6-2	205	R	Listowel, Ont.	1/31/68	Adirondack
COFFEY, Paul	6-0	190	L	Weston, Ont.	6/1/61	Detroit
ERIKSSON, Anders	6-3	218	L	Bollnas, Sweden	1/9/75	MoDo
FETISOV, Viacheslav	6-1	220	L	Moscow, USSR	4/20/58	New Jersey-Spartak-Detroit
GOLUBOVSKY, Yan	6-3	183	R	Novosibirsk, USSR	3/9/76	Adirondack
KONSTANTINOV, Vladimir	5-11	190	R	Murmansk, USSR	3/19/67	Wedemark-Detroit
LIDSTROM, Nicklas	6-2	185	L	Vasteras, Sweden	4/28/70	Vasteras-Detroit
PUSHOR, Jamie	6-3	192	R	Lethbridge, Alta.	2/11/73	Adirondack
RAMSEY, Mike	6-3	195	L	Minneapolis, MN	12/3/60	Detroit
ROUSE, Bob	6-1	210	R	Surrey, B.C.	6/18/64	Detroit
WARD, Aaron	6-2	200	R	Windsor, Ont.	1/17/73	Adirondack-Detroit
GOALTENDERS	**HT**	**WT**	**C**	**Place of Birth**	**Date**	**1994-95 Club**
ARSENAULT, David	6-2	165	L	Frankfurt, Germany	3/21/77	St-Hyacinthe-Drummondville
ESSENSA, Bob	6-0	185	L	Toronto, Ont.	1/14/65	San Diego
HODSON, Kevin	6-0	182	L	Winnipeg, Man.	3/27/72	Adirondack
MARACLE, Norm	5-9	175	L	Belleville, Ont.	10/2/74	Adirondack
OSGOOD, Chris	5-10	160	L	Peace River, Alta.	11/26/72	Detroit-Adirondack

Director of Player Personnel/Coach

BOWMAN, WILLIAM SCOTT (SCOTTY)
Director of Player Personnel/Coach, Detroit Red Wings.
Born in Montreal, Que. September 18, 1933.

Scotty Bowman is in his third year behind the Red Wings' bench. 1995-96 will be his second season as Detroit's director of player personnel. This is the third time that Bowman has held a front-office position while working as an NHL head coach. Bowman holds the NHL regular-season record for coaching wins (913) and winning percentage (.656) and has also recorded more post-season victories than any other coach, compiling a 152-92 mark in playoff encounters.

He is the only coach to guide four different teams into the Stanley Cup Finals. Bowman's six Cup victories are second only to Montreal's Toe Blake. After guiding the St. Louis Blues into the championship round in three consecutive seasons from 1968-70, Bowman was appointed head coach of the Montreal Canadiens, who captured five Stanley Cup titles under Bowman's supervision.

Following an eight season term as the general manager of the Buffalo Sabres, and a brief stint as a commentator for CBC Television, Bowman joined the Pittsburgh Penguins as director of player development, but returned to coaching when head coach Bob Johnson became ill in September, 1991. Bowman was elected to the Hockey Hall of Fame as a builder in 1991.

NHL Coaching Record

		Regular Season					Playoffs			
Season	Team	Games	W	L	T	%	Games	W	L	%
1967-68	St. Louis	58	23	21	14	.517	18	8	10	.444
1968-69	St. Louis	76	37	25	14	.579	12	8	4	.667
1969-70	St. Louis	76	37	27	12	.566	16	8	8	.500
1970-71	St. Louis	28	13	10	5	.554	6	2	4	.333
1971-72	Montreal	78	46	16	16	.692	6	2	4	.333
1972-73	Montreal	78	52	10	16	.769	17	12	5	.706*
1973-74	Montreal	78	45	24	9	.635	6	2	4	.333
1974-75	Montreal	80	47	14	19	.706	11	6	5	.545
1975-76	Montreal	80	58	11	11	.794	13	12	1	.923*
1976-77	Montreal	80	60	8	12	.825	14	12	2	.857*
1977-78	Montreal	80	59	10	11	.806	15	12	3	.800*
1978-79	Montreal	80	52	17	11	.719	16	12	4	.750*
1979-80	Buffalo	80	47	17	16	.688	14	9	5	.643
1981-82	Buffalo	35	18	10	7	.614	4	1	3	.250
1982-83	Buffalo	80	38	29	13	.556	10	6	4	.600
1983-84	Buffalo	80	48	25	7	.644	3	0	3	.000
1984-85	Buffalo	80	38	28	14	.563	5	2	3	.400
1985-86	Buffalo	37	18	18	1	.500	....	....	....	....
1986-87	Buffalo	12	3	7	2	.333	....	....	....	....
1991-92	Pittsburgh	80	39	32	9	.544	21	16	5	.762*
1992-93	Pittsburgh	84	56	21	7	.708	12	7	5	.583
1993-94	Detroit	84	46	30	8	.595	7	3	4	.429
1994-95	Detroit	48	33	11	4	.729	18	12	6	.667
	NHL Totals	**1572**	**913**	**421**	**238**	**.656**	**244**	**152**	**92**	**.623**

* Stanley Cup win.

1994-95 Scoring

* – rookie

Regular Season

Pos	#	Player	Team	GP	G	A	Pts	+/–	PIM	PP	SH	GW	GT	S	%
D	77	Paul Coffey	DET	45	14	44	58	18	72	4	1	2	0	181	7.7
C	91	Sergei Fedorov	DET	42	20	30	50	6	24	7	3	5	0	147	13.6
R	22	Dino Ciccarelli	DET	42	16	27	43	12	39	6	0	3	0	106	15.1
L	55	Keith Primeau	DET	45	15	27	42	17	99	1	0	3	0	96	15.6
R	26	Ray Sheppard	DET	43	30	10	40	11	17	11	0	5	1	125	24.0
C	19	Steve Yzerman	DET	47	12	26	38	6	40	4	0	1	0	134	9.0
C	13	Vyacheslav Kozlov	DET	46	13	20	33	12	45	5	0	3	0	97	13.4
D	5	Nicklas Lidstrom	DET	43	10	16	26	15	6	7	0	0	0	90	11.1
R	17	Doug Brown	DET	45	9	12	21	14	16	1	1	2	0	69	13.0
L	21	Bob Errey	S.J.	13	2	2	4	4	27	0	0	0	0	19	10.5
			DET	30	6	11	17	9	31	0	0	1	0	53	11.3
			TOTAL	43	8	13	21	13	58	0	0	1	0	72	11.1
D	44	Viacheslav Fetisov	N.J.	4	0	1	1	–2	0	0	0	0	0	1	0.0
			DET	14	3	11	14	3	2	3	0	0	0	36	8.3
			TOTAL	18	3	12	15	1	2	3	0	0	0	37	8.1
L	11	Shawn Burr	DET	42	6	8	14	13	60	0	0	3	0	65	9.2
D	16	Vlad. Konstantinov	DET	47	3	11	14	10	101	0	0	0	0	57	5.3
R	25	Darren McCarty	DET	31	5	8	13	5	88	1	0	2	0	27	18.5
R	20	Martin Lapointe	DET	39	4	6	10	1	73	0	0	1	0	46	8.7
C	23	Greg Johnson	DET	22	3	5	8	1	14	2	0	0	0	32	9.4
C	33	Kris Draper	DET	36	2	6	8	1	22	0	0	0	0	44	4.5
D	3	Bob Rouse	DET	48	1	7	8	14	36	0	0	1	0	51	2.0
D	4	Mark Howe	DET	18	1	5	6	–3	10	0	0	1	0	14	7.1
C	18	Mike Krushelnyski	DET	20	2	3	5	3	6	0	0	0	0	20	10.0
C	37	* Tim Taylor	DET	22	0	4	4	3	16	0	0	0	0	21	0.0
D	2	Terry Carkner	DET	20	1	2	3	7	21	0	0	0	0	9	11.1
D	15	Mike Ramsey	DET	33	1	2	3	11	23	0	0	0	0	29	3.4
D	8	* Aaron Ward	DET	1	0	1	1	1	2	0	0	0	0	0	0.0
D	27	Mark Ferner	ANA	14	0	1	1	–4	6	0	0	0	0	15	0.0
			DET	3	0	0	0	0	0	0	0	0	0	1	0.0
			TOTAL	17	0	1	1	–4	6	0	0	0	0	16	0.0
L	32	Stu Grimson	ANA	31	0	1	1	–7	110	0	0	0	0	14	0.0
			DET	11	0	0	0	–4	37	0	0	0	0	4	0.0
			TOTAL	42	0	1	1	–11	147	0	0	0	0	18	0.0
C	14	Andrew McKim	DET	2	0	0	0	0	2	0	0	0	0	0	0.0
G	30	Chris Osgood	DET	19	0	0	0	0	2	0	0	0	0	0	0.0
G	29	Mike Vernon	DET	30	0	0	0	0	8	0	0	0	0	0	0.0

Goaltending

No.	Goaltender	GPI	Mins	Avg	W	L	T	EN	SO	GA	SA	S%
30	Chris Osgood	19	1087	2.26	14	5	0	0	1	41	496	.917
29	Mike Vernon	30	1807	2.52	19	6	4	0	1	76	710	.893
	Totals	**48**	**2900**	**2.42**	**33**	**11**	**4**	**0**	**2**	**117**	**1206**	**.903**

Playoffs

Pos	#	Player	Team	GP	G	A	Pts	+/–	PIM	PP	SH	GW	OT	S	%
C	91	Sergei Fedorov	DET	17	7	17	24	13	6	3	0	0	0	53	13.2
D	77	Paul Coffey	DET	18	6	12	18	4	10	2	1	0	0	74	8.1
C	13	Vyacheslav Kozlov	DET	18	9	7	16	12	10	1	0	4	1	45	20.0
D	5	Nicklas Lidstrom	DET	18	4	12	16	4	8	3	0	2	1	37	10.8
C	19	Steve Yzerman	DET	15	4	8	12	–2	0	2	0	1	0	37	10.8
R	17	Doug Brown	DET	18	4	8	12	14	2	0	1	1	0	27	14.8
R	22	Dino Ciccarelli	DET	16	9	2	11	–4	22	6	0	2	0	49	18.4
L	55	Keith Primeau	DET	17	4	5	9	–2	45	2	0	0	0	34	11.8
D	44	Viacheslav Fetisov	DET	18	0	8	8	1	14	0	0	0	0	31	0.0
R	26	Ray Sheppard	DET	17	4	3	7	–6	5	2	0	0	0	41	9.8
L	21	Bob Errey	DET	18	1	5	6	0	30	1	0	0	0	18	5.6
C	33	Kris Draper	DET	18	4	1	5	–2	12	0	1	1	0	22	18.2
R	25	Darren McCarty	DET	18	3	2	5	3	14	0	0	0	0	31	9.7
D	3	Bob Rouse	DET	18	0	3	3	2	8	0	0	0	0	16	0.0
D	16	Vlad. Konstantinov	DET	18	1	1	2	6	22	0	0	1	1	25	4.0
L	11	Shawn Burr	DET	16	0	2	2	–2	6	0	0	0	0	20	0.0
L	32	Stu Grimson	DET	11	1	0	1	0	26	0	0	0	0	3	33.3
R	20	Martin Lapointe	DET	2	0	1	1	1	8	0	0	0	0	0	0.0
C	37	* Tim Taylor	DET	6	0	1	1	–4	12	0	0	0	0	11	0.0
D	15	Mike Ramsey	DET	15	0	1	1	2	4	0	0	0	0	7	0.0
C	23	Greg Johnson	DET	1	0	0	0	1	0	0	0	0	0	0	0.0
G	30	Chris Osgood	DET	2	0	0	0	0	0	0	0	0	0	0	0.0
D	4	Mark Howe	DET	3	0	0	0	2	0	0	0	0	0	1	0.0
C	18	Mike Krushelnyski	DET	8	0	0	0	1	0	0	0	0	0	1	0.0
G	29	Mike Vernon	DET	18	0	0	0	0	0	0	0	0	0	0	0.0

Goaltending

No.	Goaltender	GPI	Mins	Avg	W	L	EN	SO	GA	SA	S%
30	Chris Osgood	2	68	1.76	0	0	0	0	2	25	.920
29	Mike Vernon	18	1063	2.31	12	6	1	1	41	370	.889
	Totals	**18**	**1133**	**2.33**	**12**	**6**	**1**	**1**	**44**	**396**	**.889**

Club Records

Team

(Figures in brackets for season records are games played; records for fewest points, wins, ties, losses, goals, goals against are for 70 or more games)

Most Points	103	1992-93 (84)
Most Wins	47	1992-93 (84)
Most Ties	18	1952-53 (70)
		1980-81 (80)
Most Losses	57	1985-86 (80)
Most Goals	369	1992-93 (84)
Most Goals Against	415	1985-86 (80)
Fewest Points	40	1985-86 (80)
Fewest Wins	16	1976-77 (80)
Fewest Ties	4	1966-67 (70)
Fewest Losses	13	1950-51 (70)
Fewest Goals	167	1958-59 (70)
Fewest Goals Against	132	1953-54 (70)

Longest Winning Streak
Over-all	9	Mar. 3-21/51; Feb. 27-Mar. 20/55
Home	14	Jan. 21-Mar. 25/65
Away	7	Mar. 25-Apr. 14/95

Longest Undefeated Streak
Over-all	15	Nov. 27-Dec. 28/52 (8 wins, 7 ties)
Home	18	Dec. 26/54-Mar. 20/55 (13 wins, 5 ties)
Away	15	Oct. 18-Dec. 20/51 (10 wins, 5 ties)

Longest Losing Streak
Over-all	14	Feb. 24-Mar. 25/82
Home	7	Feb. 20-Mar. 25/82
Away	14	Oct. 19-Dec. 21/66

Longest Winless Streak
Over-all	19	Feb. 26-Apr. 3/77 (18 losses, 1 tie)
Home	10	Dec. 11/85-Jan. 18/86 (9 losses, 1 tie)
Away	26	Dec. 15/76-Apr. 3/77 (23 losses, 3 ties)

Most Shutouts, Season	13	1953-54 (70)
Most. PIM, Season	2,393	1985-86 (80)
Most Goals, Game	15	Jan. 23/44 (NYR 0 at Det. 15)

Individual

Most Seasons	25	Gordie Howe
Most Games	1,687	Gordie Howe
Most Goals, Career	786	Gordie Howe
Most Assists, Career	1,023	Gordie Howe
Most Points, Career	1,809	Gordie Howe (786 goals, 1,023 assists)
Most PIM, Career	2,090	Bob Probert
Most Shutouts, Career	85	Terry Sawchuk
Longest Consecutive Games Streak	548	Alex Delvecchio (Dec. 13/56-Nov. 11/64)
Most Goals, Season	65	Steve Yzerman (1988-89)
Most Assists, Season	90	Steve Yzerman (1988-89)
Most Points, Season	155	Steve Yzerman (1988-89) (65 goals, 90 assists)
Most PIM, Season	398	Bob Probert (1987-88)
Most Points, Defenseman Season	77	Paul Coffey (1993-94) (14 goals, 63 assists)
Most Points, Center, Season	155	Steve Yzerman (1988-89) (65 goals, 90 assists)

Most Points, Right Wing, Season	103	Gordie Howe (1968-69) (44 goals, 59 assists)
Most Points, Left Wing, Season	105	John Ogrodnick (1984-85) (55 goals, 50 assists)
Most Points, Rookie, Season	87	Steve Yzerman (1983-84) (39 goals, 48 assists)
Most Shutouts, Season	12	Terry Sawchuk (1951-52; 1953-54; 1954-55) Glenn Hall (1955-56)
Most Goals, Game	6	Syd Howe (Feb. 3/44)
Most Assists, Game	*7	Billy Taylor (Mar. 16/47)
Most Points, Game	7	Carl Liscombe (Nov. 5/42) Don Grosso (Feb. 3/44) Billy Taylor (Mar. 16/47)

* NHL Record

Retired Numbers

1	Terry Sawchuk	1949-55, 57-64, 68-69
6	Larry Aurie	1927-1939
7	Ted Lindsay	1944-57, 64-65
9	Gordie Howe	1946-1971
10	Alex Delvecchio	1951-1973
12	Sid Abel	1938-43, 45-52

All-time Record vs. Other Clubs

Regular Season

		At Home						On Road						Total					
	GP	W	L	T	GF	GA	PTS	GP	W	L	T	GF	GA	PTS	GP	W	L	T	GF	GA	PTS
Anaheim	4	3	0	1	21	15	7	4	3	0	1	22	12	7	8	6	0	2	43	27	14
Boston	278	150	76	52	930	699	352	279	85	151	43	739	986	213	557	235	227	95	1669	1685	565
Buffalo	47	24	18	5	176	145	53	45	7	31	7	124	209	21	92	31	49	12	300	354	74
Calgary	41	21	13	7	159	133	49	42	11	26	5	132	183	27	83	32	39	12	291	316	76
Chicago	311	191	92	28	1066	767	410	312	120	144	48	864	939	288	623	311	236	76	1930	1706	698
Dallas	85	43	30	12	346	290	98	86	27	45	14	261	323	68	171	70	75	26	607	613	166
Edmonton	26	11	13	2	101	111	24	26	8	14	4	104	126	20	52	19	27	6	205	237	44
Florida	1	1	0	0	7	3	2	1	1	0	0	4	3	2	2	2	0	0	11	6	4
Hartford	23	10	7	6	88	68	26	22	7	14	1	60	85	15	45	17	21	7	148	153	41
Los Angeles	61	25	27	9	247	231	59	62	16	35	11	191	269	43	123	41	62	20	438	500	102
Montreal	274	125	96	53	782	703	303	274	62	169	43	608	978	167	548	187	265	96	1390	1681	470
New Jersey	32	18	12	2	138	114	38	33	10	15	8	95	118	28	65	28	27	10	233	232	66
NY Islanders	37	19	16	2	131	123	40	38	14	22	2	109	148	30	75	33	38	4	240	271	70
NY Rangers	278	158	75	45	978	689	361	276	87	131	58	710	852	232	554	245	206	103	1688	1541	593
Ottawa	2	2	0	0	13	5	4	2	1	1	0	7	7	2	4	3	1	0	20	12	6
Philadelphia	51	24	18	9	184	168	57	52	12	29	11	156	210	35	103	36	47	20	340	378	92
Pittsburgh	58	36	11	11	232	164	83	57	14	39	4	169	254	32	115	50	50	15	401	418	115
Quebec	22	12	9	1	88	77	25	23	8	12	3	85	96	19	45	20	21	4	173	173	44
St. Louis	85	35	37	13	309	280	83	86	25	48	13	241	317	63	171	60	85	26	550	597	146
San Jose	7	7	0	0	37	10	14	8	6	1	1	42	24	13	15	13	1	1	79	34	27
Tampa Bay	4	3	1	0	20	13	6	6	5	1	0	39	21	10	10	8	2	0	59	34	16
Toronto	304	158	101	45	905	741	361	303	98	161	44	804	1011	240	607	256	262	89	1709	1752	601
Vancouver	48	29	13	6	204	141	64	47	16	24	7	152	189	39	95	45	37	13	356	330	103
Washington	40	16	13	11	142	118	43	38	14	20	4	120	152	32	78	30	33	15	262	270	75
Winnipeg	31	17	10	4	135	110	38	31	8	12	8	86	95	24	59	25	22	12	221	205	62
Defunct Clubs	141	76	40	25	430	307	177	141	49	63	29	364	375	127	282	125	103	54	794	682	304
Totals	**2291**	**1214**	**728**	**349**	**7869**	**6225**	**2777**	**2291**	**714**	**1208**	**369**	**6288**	**7982**	**1797**	**4582**	**1928**	**1936**	**718**	**14157**	**14207**	**4574**

Calgary totals include Atlanta, 1972-73 to 1979-80. Dallas totals include Minnesota, 1967-68 to 1992-93.
New Jersey totals include Kansas City, 1974-75 to 1975-76, and Colorado, 1976-77 to 1981-82.

Playoffs

	Series	W	L	GP	W	L	T	GF	GA	Last Mtg.	Round	Result
Boston	7	3	4	33	14	19	0	98	96	1957	SF	L 1-4
Calgary	1	1	0	2	2	0	0	8	5	1978	PR	W 2-0
Chicago	14	6	8	69	31	38	0	190	210	1995	CF	W 4-1
Dallas	2	2	0	12	8	4	0	40	29	1995	CQF	W 4-1
Edmonton	2	0	2	10	2	8	0	26	39	1988	CF	L 1-4
Montreal	12	7	5	62	29	33	0	149	161	1978	QF	L 1-4
New Jersey	1	0	1	4	0	4	0	7	16	1995	F	L 0-4
NY Rangers	5	4	1	23	13	10	0	57	49	1950	F	W 4-3
St. Louis	3	1	2	16	8	8	0	53	51	1991	DF	L 3-4
San Jose	2	1	1	11	7	4	0	51	27	1995	CSF	W 4-0
Toronto	23	11	12	117	59	58	0	321	311	1993	DSF	L 3-4
Defunct Clubs	4	3	1	10	7	2	1	21	13			
Totals	**76**	**39**	**37**	**369**	**180**	**188**	**1**	**1021**	**1007**			

Playoff Results 1995-91

Year	Round	Opponent	Result	GF	GA
1995	F	New Jersey	L 0-4	7	16
	CF	Chicago	W 4-1	13	12
	CSF	San Jose	W 4-0	24	6
	CQF	Dallas	W 4-1	17	10
1994	CQF	San Jose	L 3-4	27	21
1993	DSF	Toronto	L 3-4	30	24
1992	DF	Chicago	L 0-4	6	11
	DSF	Minnesota	W 4-3	23	19
1991	DSF	St. Louis	L 3-4	20	24

Abbreviations: Round: F – Final;
CF – conference final; **CQF** – conference quarter-final;
CSF – conference semi-final; **DF** – division final;
DSF – division semi-final; **SF** – semi-final;
QF – quarter-final; **PR** – preliminary round.

1994-95 Results

Jan.	20		Chicago	4-1	16		Dallas	5-4
	22		Calgary	1-4	17		Vancouver	3-1
	24		Vancouver	6-3	22		Winnipeg	6-3
	26		Calgary	5-1	24	at	Calgary	2-3
	28		Edmonton	5-2	25	at	Vancouver	2-1
	30	at	Edmonton	4-2	28		Anaheim	6-4
Feb.	1	at	Calgary	1-2	30		Dallas	3-2
	3	at	Anaheim	5-2	**Apr.** 1	at	Dallas	3-2
	4	at	Los Angeles	3-4	2	at	St. Louis	3-3
	7		San Jose	6-0	5	at	San Jose	5-3
	10		Toronto	1-2	7	at	Toronto	4-2
	12		Los Angeles	4-4	9	at	Chicago	4-1
	15	at	Winnipeg	5-1	11	at	Dallas	4-1
	17		Edmonton	4-2	13		San Jose	3-0
	20	at	Toronto	4-2	14	at	Chicago	3-1
	22		Toronto	4-1	16	at	St. Louis	5-6
	23	at	Chicago	4-2	19		Winnipeg	5-5
	25		St. Louis	2-3	21		Anaheim	6-5
Mar.	2		Winnipeg	6-1	23	at	San Jose	5-1
	5	at	Edmonton	2-4	25	at	Los Angeles	1-5
	6	at	Vancouver	5-2	27	at	Winnipeg	3-2
	9	at	Anaheim	4-4	29		Dallas	4-2
	12	at	St. Louis	2-1	30		Chicago	0-4
	14		Los Angeles	5-2	**May** 3	at	St. Louis	3-2

Entry Draft
Selections 1995-81

1995 Pick		1991 Pick		1987 Pick		1984 Pick	
26	Maxim Kuznetsov	10	Martin Lapointe	11	Yves Racine	7	Shawn Burr
52	Philippe Audet	32	Jamie Pushor	32	Gordon Kruppke	28	Doug Houda
58	Darryl Laplante	54	Chris Osgood	41	Bob Wilkie	49	Milan Chalupa
104	Anatoly Ustugov	76	Michael Knuble	52	Dennis Holland	91	Mats Lundstrom
125	Chad Wilchynski	98	Dmitri Motkov	74	Mark Reimer	112	Randy Hansch
126	David Arsenault	142	Igor Malykhin	95	Radomir Brazda	133	Stefan Larsson
156	Tyler Perry	186	Jim Bermingham	116	Sean Clifford	152	Lars Karlsson
182	Per Eklund	208	Jason Firth	137	Mike Gober	154	Urban Nordin
208	Andrei Samokvalov	230	Bart Turner	158	Kevin Scott	175	Bill Shibicky
234	David Engblom	252	Andrew Miller	179	Mikko Haapakoski	195	Jay Rose
				200	Darin Bannister	216	Tim Kaiser
1994 Pick		**1990 Pick**		221	Craig Quinlan	236	Tom Nickolau
23	Yan Golubovsky	3	Keith Primeau	242	Tomas Jansson		
49	Mathieu Dandenault	45	Vyacheslav Kozlov			**1983 Pick**	
75	Sean Gillam	66	Stewart Malgunas	**1986 Pick**		4	Steve Yzerman
114	Frederic Deschenes	87	Tony Burns	1	Joe Murphy	25	Lane Lambert
127	Doug Battaglia	108	Claude Barthe	22	Adam Graves	46	Bob Probert
153	Pavel Agarkov	129	Jason York	43	Derek Mayer	68	David Korol
205	Jason Elliot	150	Wes McCauley	64	Tim Cheveldae	86	Petr Klima
231	Jeff Mikesch	171	Anthony Gruba	85	Johan Garpenlov	88	Joey Kocur
257	Tomas Holmstrom	192	Travis Tucker	106	Jay Stark	106	Chris Pusey
283	Toivo Suursoo	213	Brett Larson	127	Per Djoos	126	Bob Pierson
		234	John Hendry	148	Dean Morton	146	Craig Butz
1993 Pick				169	Marc Potvin	166	Dave Sikorski
22	Anders Eriksson	**1989 Pick**		190	Scott King	186	Stu Grimson
48	Jonathan Coleman	11	Mike Sillinger	211	Tom Bissett	206	Jeff Frank
74	Kevin Hilton	32	Bob Boughner	232	Peter Ekroth	226	Charles Chiatto
97	John Jakopin	53	Nicklas Lidstrom				
100	Benoit Larose	74	Sergei Fedorov	**1985 Pick**		**1982 Pick**	
126	Norm Maracle	95	Shawn McCosh	8	Brent Fedyk	17	Murray Craven
152	Tim Spitzig	116	Dallas Drake	29	Jeff Sharples	23	Yves Courteau
178	Yuri Yeresko	137	Scott Zygulski	50	Steve Chiasson	44	Carmine Vani
204	Vitezslav Skuta	158	Andy Suhy	71	Mark Gowans	66	Craig Coxe
230	Ryan Shanahan	179	Bob Jones	92	Chris Luongo	86	Brad Shaw
256	James Kosecki	200	Greg Bignell	113	Randy McKay	107	Claude Vilgrain
282	Gordon Hunt	204	Rick Judson	134	Thomas Bjur	128	Greg Hudas
		221	Vladimir Konstantinov	155	Mike Luckraft	149	Pat Lahey
1992 Pick		242	Joseph Frederick	176	Rob Schenna	170	Gary Cullen
22	Curtis Bowen	246	Jason Glickman	197	Erik Hamalainen	191	Brent Meckling
46	Darren McCarty			218	Bo Svanberg	212	Mike Stern
70	Sylvain Cloutier	**1988 Pick**		239	Mikael Lindman	233	Shaun Reagan
118	Mike Sullivan	17	Kory Kocur				
142	Jason MacDonald	38	Serge Anglehart			**1981 Pick**	
166	Greg Scott	47	Guy Dupuis			23	Claude Loiselle
183	Justin Krall	59	Petr Hrbek			44	Corrado Micalef
189	C.J. Denomme	80	Sheldon Kennedy			86	Larry Trader
214	Jeff Walker	143	Kelly Hurd			107	Gerard Gallant
238	Daniel McGillis	164	Brian McCormack			128	Greg Stefan
262	Ryan Bach	185	Jody Praznik			149	Rick Zombo
		206	Glen Goodall			170	Don Leblanc
		227	Darren Colbourne			191	Robert Nordmark
		248	Donald Stone				

Club Directory

Joe Louis Arena
600 Civic Center Drive
Detroit, Michigan 48226
Phone **(313) 396-7544**
FAX PR: (313) 567-0296
Capacity: 19,275

Owner/President	Mike Ilitch
Owner/Secretary-Treasurer	Marian Ilitch
Vice-Presidents	Atanas Ilitch, Christopher Ilitch
Senior Vice-President	Jim Devellano
Director of Player Personnel/Head Coach	Scotty Bowman
Assistant General Manager/Goaltending Consultant	Ken Holland
Assistant Coaches	Barry Smith, Dave Lewis
NHL Scout	Dan Belisle
Director of Player Development/AHL-IHL Scout	Jim Nill
Eastern Canada Scout	Joe McDonnell
Western Canada Scout	Wayne Meier
Eastern USA Scout	Mark Leach
Western USA Scout	Chris Coury
Director of European Scouting	Hakan Andersson
Czech Republic Scout	Vladimir HavLug
Controller	Paul MacDonald
General Sales Manager	Jack Johnson
Marketing Director	Ted Speers
Public Relations Director	Bill Jamieson
Broadcast Print/Sales Director	Amy Goan
Public Relations Assistants	Kathy Best, Karen Davis
Box Office Manager	Bob Kerlin
Season Ticket Sales Director	Brad Ebben
Executive Assistant	Nancy Beard
Accounting Assistant	Cathy Witzke
Athletic Trainer	John Wharton
Equipment Manager/Trainer	Paul Boyer
Assistant Equipment Manager	Tim Abbott
Team Physicians	Dr. John Finley, D.O., Dr. David Collon, M.D.
Team Dentist	Dr. C.J. Regula, D.M.D.
Team Ophthalmologist	Dr. Charles Slater, M.D.
Home Ice/Training Camp Site	Joe Louis Arena
Press Box & Radio-TV Booths	Jefferson Avenue side of arena, top of seats
Media Lounge	First-floor hallway near Red Wings' dressing room
Rink Dimensions	200 feet by 85 feet
Uniforms	Home: Base color white, trimmed in red
	Road: Base color red, trimmed in white
Radio flagship station	WJR-AM (760)
TV stations	WKBD (Channel 50); PASS Sports; Special Order Sports
Radio announcers	Ken Kal, Paul Woods
TV announcers	Dave Strader, Mickey Redmond

Senior Vice-President

DEVELLANO, JAMES (JIM)
Senior Vice-President, Detroit Red Wings.
Born in Toronto, Ont., January 18, 1943.

Jim Devellano is in his 14th season with the Red Wings and has played a major role in the team's success. He served eight years as general manager before being appointed senior vice-president.

Devellano, respected throughout the league as an astute judge of talent, scouts players on all levels and also helps the scouting staff to prepare for the Entry Draft. In addition, he is involved with administrative matters and serves as the team's alternate on the NHL's Board of Governors.

Devellano, who is in his 28th season in the NHL in various capacities, came to Detroit as general manager July 12, 1982, and built a team through the draft, trades and free agency that finished first in its division in five of the past eight seasons and won the Presidents' Trophy as the NHL's best club in 1994-95 regular-season play. He also developed a top farm club in Adirondack that under his direction, won the AHL's Calder Cup championship in 1986 and 1989.

Devellano, 52, didn't play professional hockey but worked in various levels of the game in his hometown of Toronto. He joined the St. Louis Blues as a scout in 1967 when the NHL expanded from six to 12 teams. The Blues reached the Stanley Cup Finals in each of their first three seasons.

When the New York Islanders were founded in 1972, Devellano came aboard and helped to build a club that won four consecutive Stanley Cup titles (1980-89). In 1979-80, he became g.m. of the Islanders' Indianapolis (CHL) farm club and was named minor league executive of the year by *The Hockey News* in his first year. He returned to Long Island in 1981 as the Islanders' asssistant g.m.

Mike Ilitch bought the Red Wings in June of 1982 and brought in Devellano the following month. Jim became a team vice-president December 30, 1985, and assumed his present position July 13, 1990.

"Jimmy D." is single and resides in Detroit.

General Managers' History

Art Duncan, 1926-27; Jack Adams, 1927-28 to 1961-62; Sid Abel, 1962-63 to 1969-70; Sid Abel and Ned Harkness, 1970-71; Ned Harkness, 1971-72 to 1973-74; Alex Delvecchio, 1974-75 to 1975-76; Alex Delvecchio and Ted Lindsay, 1976-77; Ted Lindsay, 1977-78 to 1979-80; Jimmy Skinner, 1980-81 to 1981-82; Jim Devellano, 1982-83 to 1989-90; Bryan Murray, 1990-91 to 1993-94; Jim Devellano (Senior Vice President), 1994-95 to date.

Coaching History

Art Duncan, 1926-27; Jack Adams, 1927-28 to 1946-47; Tommy Ivan, 1947-48 to 1953-54; Jimmy Skinner, 1954-55 to 1956-57; Jimmy Skinner and Sid Abel, 1957-58; Sid Abel, 1958-59 to 1967-68; Bill Gadsby, 1968-69; Bill Gadsby and Sid Abel, 1969-70; Ned Harkness and Doug Barkley, 1970-71; Doug Barkley and John Wilson, 1971-72; John Wilson, 1972-73; Ted Garvin and Alex Delvecchio, 1973-74; Alex Delvecchio, 1974-75; Doug Barkley and Alex Delvecchio, 1975-76; Alex Delvecchio and Larry Wilson, 1976-77; Bobby Kromm, 1977-78 to 1978-79; Bobby Kromm and Ted Lindsay, 1979-80; Ted Lindsay and Wayne Maxner, 1980-81; Wayne Maxner and Billy Dea, 1981-82; Nick Polano, 1982-83 to 1984-85; Harry Neale and Brad Park, 1985-86; Jacques Demers, 1986-87 to 1989-90; Bryan Murray, 1990-91 to 1992-93; Scotty Bowman, 1993-94 to date.

Captains' History

Art Duncan, 1926-27; Reg Noble, 1927-28 to 1929-30; George Hay, 1930-31; Carson Cooper, 1931-32; Larry Aurie, 1932-33; Herbie Lewis, 1933-34; Ebbie Goodfellow, 1934-35; Doug Young, 1935-36 to 1937-38; Ebbie Goodfellow, 1938-39 to 1940-41; Ebbie Goodfellow and Syd Howe, 1941-42; Sid Abel, 1942-43; "Mud" Bruneteau, Bill Hollett (co-captains), 1943-44; Bill Hollett, 1944-45; Bill Hollett and Sid Abel, 1945-46; Sid Abel, 1946-47 to 1951-52; Ted Lindsay, 1952-53 to 1955-56; Red Kelly, 1956-57, 1957-58; Gordie Howe, 1958-59 to 1961-62; Alex Delvecchio, 1962-63 to 1972-73; Alex Delvecchio, Nick Libett, Red Berenson, Gary Bergman, Ted Harris, Mickey Redmond, Larry Johnston, 1973-74; Marcel Dionne, 1974-75; Danny Grant, Terry Harper, 1975-76; Danny Grant, Dennis Polonich, 1976-77; Dan Maloney, Dennis Hextall, 1977-78; Dennis Hextall, Nick Libett, Paul Woods, 1978-79; Dale McCourt, 1979-80; Errol Thompson, Reed Larson, 1980-81; Reed Larson, 1981-82; Danny Gare, 1982-83 to 1985-86; Steve Yzerman, 1986-87 to date.

Edmonton Oilers

1994-95 Results: 17w-27l-4t 38pts. Fifth, Pacific Division

Year-by-Year Record

Season	GP	Home W	Home L	Home T	Road W	Road L	Road T	Overall W	Overall L	Overall T	GF	GA	Pts.	Finished	Playoff Result
1994-95	48	11	12	1	6	15	3	17	27	4	136	183	38	5th, Pacific Div.	Out of Playoffs
1993-94	84	17	22	3	8	23	11	25	45	14	261	305	64	6th, Pacific Div.	Out of Playoffs
1992-93	84	16	21	5	10	29	3	26	50	8	242	337	60	5th, Smythe Div.	Out of Playoffs
1991-92	80	22	13	5	14	21	5	36	34	10	295	297	82	3rd, Smythe Div.	Lost Conf. Championship
1990-91	80	22	15	3	15	22	3	37	37	6	272	272	80	3rd, Smythe Div.	Lost Conf. Championship
1989-90	**80**	**23**	**11**	**6**	**15**	**17**	**8**	**38**	**28**	**14**	**315**	**283**	**90**	**2nd, Smythe Div.**	**Won Stanley Cup**
1988-89	80	21	16	3	17	18	5	38	34	8	325	306	84	3rd, Smythe Div.	Lost Div. Semi-Final
1987-88	**80**	**28**	**8**	**4**	**16**	**17**	**7**	**44**	**25**	**11**	**363**	**288**	**99**	**2nd, Smythe Div.**	**Won Stanley Cup**
1986-87	**80**	**29**	**6**	**5**	**21**	**18**	**1**	**50**	**24**	**6**	**372**	**284**	**106**	**1st, Smythe Div.**	**Won Stanley Cup**
1985-86	80	32	6	2	24	11	5	56	17	7	426	310	119	1st, Smythe Div.	Lost Div. Final
1984-85	**80**	**26**	**7**	**7**	**23**	**13**	**4**	**49**	**20**	**11**	**401**	**298**	**109**	**1st, Smythe Div.**	**Won Stanley Cup**
1983-84	**80**	**31**	**5**	**4**	**26**	**13**	**1**	**57**	**18**	**5**	**446**	**314**	**119**	**1st, Smythe Div.**	**Won Stanley Cup**
1982-83	80	25	9	6	22	12	6	47	21	12	424	315	106	1st, Smythe Div.	Lost Final
1981-82	80	31	5	4	17	12	11	48	17	15	417	295	111	1st, Smythe Div.	Lost Div. Semi-Final
1980-81	80	17	13	10	12	22	6	29	35	16	328	327	74	4th, Smythe Div.	Lost Quarter-Final
1979-80	80	17	14	9	11	25	4	28	39	13	301	322	69	4th, Smythe Div.	Lost Prelim. Round

Schedule

Oct.	Sun.	8	Detroit
	Tues.	10	at St. Louis
	Fri.	13	at Detroit
	Sun.	15	at Philadelphia
	Tues.	17	at New Jersey
	Wed.	18	at Buffalo
	Sat.	21	Vancouver
	Sun.	22	San Jose
	Fri.	27	Winnipeg
	Tues.	31	New Jersey
Nov.	Wed.	1	at Vancouver
	Sat.	4	Toronto
	Tues.	7	at Detroit
	Thur.	9	at Florida
	Fri.	10	at Tampa Bay
	Sun.	12	at Chicago
	Tues.	14	at Calgary
	Wed.	15	Montreal
	Fri.	17	Detroit
	Mon.	20	Colorado
	Wed.	22	Anaheim
	Fri.	24	at Calgary
	Sun.	26	at Winnipeg
	Tues.	28	Chicago
Dec.	Fri.	1	Calgary
	Sat.	2	St. Louis
	Tues.	5	at Vancouver
	Thur.	7	at Colorado
	Sat.	9	at San Jose
	Sun.	10	at Anaheim
	Wed.	13	Vancouver
	Fri.	15	at Winnipeg
	Mon.	18	Ottawa
	Wed.	20	Colorado
	Fri.	22	at Washington
	Sat.	23	at Toronto
	Wed.	27	Philadelphia
	Fri.	29	Los Angeles
	Sat.	30	NY Rangers
Jan.	Wed.	3	Tampa Bay
	Fri.	5	Florida

	Sun.	7	Anaheim
	Tues.	9	Hartford
	Sat.	13	Buffalo
	Tues.	16	at St. Louis
	Wed.	17	at Dallas
	Wed.	24	Dallas
	Fri.	26	NY Islanders
	Tues.	30	at Calgary
	Wed.	31	Chicago
Feb.	Wed.	7	Washington
	Fri.	9	Vancouver
	Sun.	11	Calgary
	Wed.	14	Anaheim
	Fri.	16	at Dallas
	Sun.	18	at Chicago*
	Mon.	19	at Colorado
	Wed.	21	Los Angeles
	Fri.	23	Boston
	Sun.	25	at NY Islanders*
	Tues.	27	at Boston
	Wed.	28	at Hartford
Mar.	Fri.	1	Pittsburgh
	Sun.	3	St. Louis*
	Wed.	6	at Los Angeles
	Fri.	8	San Jose
	Wed.	13	at San Jose
	Sat.	16	at Los Angeles
	Sun.	17	at Colorado
	Tues.	19	at NY Rangers
	Thur.	21	at Pittsburgh
	Sat.	23	at Montreal
	Sun.	24	at Ottawa
	Wed.	27	Los Angeles
	Fri.	29	Winnipeg
	Sat.	30	Toronto
Apr.	Mon.	1	at Vancouver
	Wed.	3	at Anaheim
	Thur.	4	at San Jose
	Mon.	8	Calgary
	Wed.	10	Dallas
	Sat.	13	at Toronto

* Denotes afternoon game.

Home Starting Times:

Weeknights	7:30 p.m.
Saturdays	8:30 p.m.
Sundays	6:00 p.m.
Except	Sat. Nov. 4	5:30 p.m.
	Sat. Dec. 2	5:30 p.m.
	Sun. Mar. 3	2:00 p.m.

Franchise date: June 22, 1979

17th NHL Season

PACIFIC DIVISION

Despite his rookie status, Todd Marchant was used in a variety of roles in 1994-95, leading all Oiler rookies with two short-handed and two game-winning goals.

1995-96 Player Personnel

FORWARDS	HT	WT	S	Place of Birth	Date	1994-95 Club
ARNOTT, Jason	6-3	220	R	Collingwood, Ont.	10/11/74	Edmonton
BONSIGNORE, Jason	6-4	208	R	Rochester, NY	4/15/76	Niagara Falls-Sudbury-Edmonton
BREEN, George	6-2	200	R	Webster, MA	8/3/73	Providence
BUCHBERGER, Kelly	6-2	200	L	Langenburg, Sask.	12/2/66	Edmonton
CIERNY, Jozef	6-2	185	L	Zvolen, Czech.	5/13/74	Cape Breton
CIGER, Zdeno	6-1	190	L	Martin, Czech.	10/19/69	Dukla Trencin-Edmonton
COPELAND, Adam	6-1	185	R	St. Catharines, Ont.	6/5/76	Miami-Ohio
DeBRUSK, Louie	6-2	215	L	Cambridge, Ont.	3/19/71	Edmonton
GRIER, Michael	6-1	215	R	Detroit, MI	1/5/75	Boston U.
HAGGERTY, Ryan	6-1	185	L	Rye, NY	5/2/73	Boston College
INTRANUOVO, Ralph	5-8	185	L	East York, Ont.	12/11/73	Cape Breton-Edmonton
KELLY, Steve	6-1	190	L	Vancouver, B.C.	10/26/76	Prince Albert
LARAQUE, Georges	6-3	225	R	Montreal, Que.	12/7/76	St-Jean
LINDGREN, Mats	6-2	200	L	Skelleftea, Sweden	10/1/74	Farjestad
MARCHANT, Todd	6-0	180	L	Buffalo, NY	8/12/73	Cape Breton-Edmonton
McAMMOND, Dean	5-11	185	L	Grand Cache, Alta.	6/15/73	Edmonton
OLIVER, David	6-0	190	R	Sechelt, B.C.	4/17/71	Cape Breton-Edmonton
PADEN, Kevin	6-3	180	L	Woodhaven, MI	2/12/75	Windsor
SATAN, Miroslav	6-1	180	L	Topolcany, Czech.	10/22/74	C.B.-Det (IHL)-S.D.
SMYTH, Ryan	6-1	185	L	Banff, Alta.	2/21/76	Moose Jaw-Edmonton
THORNTON, Scott	6-3	210	L	London, Ont.	1/9/71	Edmonton
TUOMAINEN, Marko	6-3	203	R	Kuopio, Finland	4/25/72	Clarkson-Edmonton
VUJTEK, Vladimir	6-1	190	L	Ostrava, Czech.	2/17/72	Vitkovice-Cape Breton-Las Vegas
VYBORNY, David	5-10	174	L	Jihlava, Czech.	1/22/75	Cape Breton
WEIGHT, Doug	5-11	191	L	Warren, MI	1/21/71	Rosenheim-Edmonton
WHITE, Peter	5-11	200	L	Montreal, Que.	3/15/69	Cape Breton-Edmonton
WRIGHT, Tyler	5-11	185	R	Canora, Sask.	4/6/73	Cape Breton-Edmonton
DEFENSEMEN						
BENNETT, Adam	6-4	206	R	Georgetown, Ont.	3/30/71	Cape Breton
BONVIE, Dennis	5-11	210	R	Antigonish, N.S.	7/23/73	Cape Breton-Edmonton
DAMEWORTH, Chad	6-2	200	L	Marquette, MI	7/6/72	N. Michigan-Cape Breton
DeVRIES, Greg	6-3	218	L	Sundridge, Ont.	1/4/73	Cape Breton
FAFARD, Dominic	6-5	230	R	Longueuil, Que.	7/13/74	Whlng-C.B.-S.C.
KENNEDY, Dean	6-2	208	R	Redvers, Sask.	1/18/63	Edmonton
KRAVCHUK, Igor	6-1	200	L	Ufa, USSR	9/13/66	Edmonton
MARCHMENT, Bryan	6-1	205	L	Scarborough, Ont.	5/1/69	Edmonton
McGILL, Ryan	6-2	210	R	Prince Albert, Sask.	2/28/69	Philadelphia-Edmonton
MIRONOV, Boris	6-3	220	R	Moscow, USSR	3/21/72	Edmonton-Cape Breton
NEILSON, Corey	6-5	207	R	Oromocto, N.B.	8/22/76	North Bay
OLAUSSON, Fredrik	6-2	195	R	Dadesjo, Sweden	10/5/66	Edmonton-Ehrwald
POPE, Brent	6-3	214	R	Hamilton, Ont.	2/20/73	Cape Breton-Wheeling
RICHARDSON, Luke	6-4	210	L	Ottawa, Ont.	3/26/69	Edmonton
SLEGR, Jiri	6-1	205	L	Jihlava, Czech.	5/30/71	Litvinov-Vancouver-Edmonton
SNOPEK, Jan	6-3	212	R	Prague, Czech.	6/22/76	Oshawa
STAJDUHAR, Nick	6-2	195	L	Kitchener, Ont.	12/6/74	Cape Breton
SUTTON, Ken	6-0	200	L	Edmonton, Alta.	11/5/69	Buffalo-Edmonton
SYMES, Brad	6-2	210	L	Edmonton, Alta.	4/26/76	Portland (WHL)
ZHURIK, Alexander	6-3	195	L	Minsk, USSR	5/29/75	Kingston
ZIB, Lukas	6-1	198	R	Ceske Budejovice, Czech.	2/24/77	Budejovice

GOALTENDERS	HT	WT	C	Place of Birth	Date	1994-95 Club
BRATHWAITE, Fred	5-7	170	L	Ottawa, Ont.	11/24/72	Edmonton
GAGE, Joaquin	6-0	200	L	Vancouver, B.C.	10/19/73	Cape Breton-Edmonton
JOSEPH, Curtis	5-10	182	L	Keswick, Ont.	4/29/67	St. Louis
MINARD, Mike	6-3	205	L	Owen Sound, Ont.	11/1/76	Chilliwack
PASSMORE, Steve	5-9	165	L	Thunder Bay, Ont.	1/29/73	Cape Breton
RANFORD, Bill	5-11	185	L	Brandon, Man.	12/14/66	Edmonton
WICKENHEISER, Chris	6-1	185	L	Lethbridge, Alta.	1/20/76	Red Deer

General Managers' History

Larry Gordon, 1979-80; Glen Sather, 1980-81 to date.

Coaching History

Glen Sather, 1979-80; Bryan Watson and Glen Sather, 1980-81; Glen Sather, 1981-82 to 1988-89; John Muckler, 1989-90 to 1990-91; Ted Green, 1991-92 to 1992-93; Ted Green and Glen Sather, 1993-94; George Burnett and Ron Low, 1994-95; Ron Low, 1995-96.

Captains' History

Ron Chipperfield, 1979-80; Blair MacDonald and Lee Fogolin, 1980-81; Lee Fogolin, 1981-82 to 1982-83; Wayne Gretzky, 1983-84 to 1987-88; Mark Messier, 1988-89 to 1990-91; Kevin Lowe, 1991-92; Craig MacTavish, 1992-93 to 1993-94; Shayne Corson, 1994-95.

Retired Numbers

3	Al Hamilton	1972-1980

1994-95 Scoring

* – rookie

Regular Season

Pos	#	Player	Team	GP	G	A	Pts	+/–	PIM	PP	SH	GW	GT	S	%
C	39	Doug Weight	EDM	48	7	33	40	–17	69	1	0	1	0	104	6.7
C	7	Jason Arnott	EDM	42	15	22	37	–14	128	7	0	1	0	156	9.6
L	9	Shayne Corson	EDM	48	12	24	36	–17	86	2	0	1	0	131	9.2
R	20 *	David Oliver	EDM	44	16	14	30	–11	20	10	0	0	1	79	20.3
C	26 *	Todd Marchant	EDM	45	13	14	27	–3	32	3	2	2	0	95	13.7
L	16	Kelly Buchberger	EDM	48	7	17	24	0	82	2	1	5	0	73	9.6
C	17	Scott Thornton	EDM	47	10	12	22	–4	89	0	1	1	0	69	14.5
D	21	Igor Kravchuk	EDM	36	7	11	18	–15	29	3	1	0	0	93	7.5
C	25	Mike Stapleton	EDM	46	6	11	17	–12	21	3	0	2	0	59	10.2
D	22	Luke Richardson	EDM	46	3	10	13	–6	40	1	1	1	0	51	5.9
D	28	Jiri Slegr	VAN	19	1	5	6	0	32	0	0	1	0	42	2.4
			EDM	12	1	5	6	–5	14	1	0	0	0	27	3.7
			TOTAL	31	2	10	12	–5	46	1	0	1	0	69	2.9
R	18	Kirk Maltby	EDM	47	8	3	11	–11	49	0	2	1	1	73	11.0
D	32	Dean Kennedy	EDM	40	2	8	10	2	25	0	0	1	0	45	4.4
D	15	Fredrik Olausson	EDM	33	0	10	10	–4	20	0	0	0	0	52	0.0
D	2	Boris Mironov	EDM	29	1	7	8	–9	40	0	0	0	0	48	2.1
D	6	Ken Sutton	BUF	12	1	2	3	–2	30	0	0	1	0	12	8.3
			EDM	12	3	1	4	–1	12	0	0	0	0	28	10.7
			TOTAL	24	4	3	7	–3	42	0	0	1	0	40	10.0
C	27 *	Peter White	EDM	9	2	4	6	1	0	2	0	0	0	13	15.4
D	24	Bryan Marchment	EDM	40	1	5	6	–11	184	0	0	0	0	57	1.8
L	8	Zdeno Ciger	EDM	5	2	2	4	–1	0	1	0	1	0	10	20.0
C	38	Iain Fraser	DAL	4	0	0	0	–3	0	0	0	0	0	2	0.0
			EDM	9	3	0	3	3	0	0	0	0	0	5	60.0
			TOTAL	13	3	0	3	0	0	0	0	0	0	7	42.9
L	29	Louie Debrusk	EDM	34	2	0	2	–4	93	0	0	0	0	14	14.3
D	6	Gordon Mark	EDM	18	0	2	2	–9	35	0	0	0	0	21	0.0
G	30	Bill Ranford	EDM	40	0	2	2	0	2	0	0	0	0	0	0.0
C	23 *	Jason Bonsignore	EDM	1	1	0	1	–1	0	0	0	0	0	3	33.3
C	14	Kent Nilsson	EDM	6	1	0	1	–5	0	1	0	0	0	2	50.0
C	19	Tyler Wright	EDM	6	1	0	1	1	14	0	0	0	0	6	16.7
C	36 *	Ralph Intranuovo	EDM	1	0	1	1	1	0	0	0	0	0	1	0.0
G	1 *	Joaquin Gage	EDM	2	0	1	1	0	0	0	0	0	0	0	0.0
C	12	Micah Aivazoff	EDM	21	0	1	1	–2	2	0	0	0	0	6	0.0
D	43 *	Dennis Bonvie	EDM	2	0	0	0	0	0	0	0	0	0	0	0.0
L	10 *	Ryan Smyth	EDM	3	0	0	0	–1	0	0	0	0	0	2	0.0
R	33 *	Marko Tuomainen	EDM	4	0	0	0	0	0	0	0	0	0	5	0.0
L	37	Dean McAmmond	EDM	6	0	0	0	–1	0	0	0	0	0	3	0.0
G	31 *	Fred Brathwaite	EDM	14	0	0	0	0	0	0	0	0	0	0	0.0
D	34	Ryan McGill	PHI	12	0	0	0	0	13	0	0	0	0	2	0.0
			EDM	8	0	0	0	–4	8	0	0	0	0	6	0.0
			TOTAL	20	0	0	0	–4	21	0	0	0	0	8	0.0

Goaltending

No.	Goaltender	GPI	Mins	Avg	W	L	T	EN	SO	GA	SA	S%
30	Bill Ranford	40	2203	3.62	15	20	3	2	2	133	1134	.883
31	* Fred Brathwaite	14	601	3.99	2	5	1	1	0	40	292	.863
1	* Joaquin Gage	2	99	4.24	0	2	0	0	0	7	40	.825
	Totals	**48**	**2912**	**3.77**	**17**	**27**	**4**	**3**	**2**	**183**	**1469**	**.875**

Coach

LOW, RONALD ALBERT (RON)
Coach, Edmonton Oilers. Born in Birtle, Man., June 21, 1950.

After serving as an assistant coach with the Edmonton Oilers for six seasons, Ron Low became the team's fifth head coach when he was named to the position on April 6, 1995. Low relieved George Burnett after 35 games of the abbreviated 1994-95 season and guided the Oilers to a 5-7-1 (.423) record over the final 13 games of the campaign.

On August 3, 1989 Low was appointed to the Edmonton Oilers' coaching staff as an assistant coach. During his tenure in that role, he was a member of the 1990 Stanley Cup championship team.

Low first became involved with the Oilers as a player during the 1979-80 season when Edmonton obtained his rights from the Quebec Nordiques in exchange for Ron Chipperfield. Playing parts of four seasons with Edmonton from 1979-80 to 1982-83, Low compiled a record of 30-23-5 and a 4.03 goals-against average in 67 regular season games.

The Oilers were one of six teams the Birtle, Manitoba native played for in an 11-year NHL career that saw him tend goal for Toronto, Washington, Detroit, Quebec, Edmonton and New Jersey. From 1972-73 to 1984-85, he played 382 NHL games and registered a 4.28 goals-against average with four shutouts and a 102-203-37 record.

In 1985-86 he was named assistant playing coach of the Nova Scotia Oilers, Edmonton's American Hockey League affiliate. Following two years as an assistant coach he was named Nova Scotia's head coach in 1987-88 and kept that position when the team became the Cape Breton Oilers in 1988-89. Low compiled a 62-83-15 record as an AHL head coach before joining the NHL coaching ranks.

Ron and his wife, Linda, have one daughter, Alexandra Juliana, born in June of 1992, and are expecting their second child in September.

Coaching Record

		Regular Season					Playoffs			
Season	Team	Games	W	L	T	%	Games	W	L	%
1987-88	Nova Scotia (AHL)	80	35	36	9	.506	5	1	4	.200
1988-89	Cape Breton (AHL)	80	27	47	6	.375	....	....	....	....
1994-95	**Edmonton (NHL)**	**13**	**5**	**7**	**1**	**.423**	....	....	....	....
	NHL Totals	**13**	**5**	**7**	**1**	**.423**	....	....	....	....

Club Records

Team

(Figures in brackets for season records are games played; records for fewest points, wins, ties, losses, goals, goals against are for 70 or more games)

Most Points	119	1983-84 (80)
		1985-86 (80)
Most Wins	57	1983-84 (80)
Most Ties	16	1980-81 (80)
Most Losses	50	1992-93 (84)
Most Goals	*446	1983-84 (80)
Most Goals Against	327	1980-81 (80)
Fewest Points	60	1992-93 (84)
Fewest Wins	25	1993-94 (84)
Fewest Ties	5	1983-84 (80)
Fewest Losses	17	1981-82 (80)
		1985-86 (80)
Fewest Goals	242	1992-93 (84)
Fewest Goals Against	272	1990-91 (80)

Longest Winning Streak

Over-all	8	Five times
Home	8	Jan. 19/-
		Feb. 22/85;
		Feb. 24-
		Apr. 2/86
Away	8	Dec. 9/86-
		Jan. 17/87

Longest Undefeated Streak

Over-all	15	Oct. 11-
		Nov. 9/84
		(12 wins, 3 ties)
Home	14	Nov. 15/89-
		Jan. 6/90
		(11 wins, 3 ties)
Away	9	Jan. 17-
		Mar. 2/82
		(6 wins, 3 ties)
		Nov. 23/82-
		Jan. 18/83
		(7 wins, 2 ties)

Longest Losing Streak

Over-all	11	Oct. 16-
		Nov. 7/93
Home	9	Oct. 16-
		Nov. 24/93
Away	9	Nov. 25-
		Dec. 30/80

Longest Winless Streak

Over-all	14	Oct. 11-
		Nov. 7/93
		(13 losses, 1 tie)
Home	9	Oct. 16-
		Nov. 24/93
		(9 losses)
Away	9	Three times
Most Shutouts, Season	4	1987-88 (80)
Most PIM, Season	2,173	1987-88 (80)
Most Goals, Game	13	Nov. 19/83
		(NJ 4 at Edm. 13)
		Nov. 8/85
		(Van. 0 at Edm. 13)

Individual

Most Seasons	13	Kevin Lowe
Most Games	966	Kevin Lowe
Most Goals, Career	583	Wayne Gretzky
Most Assists, Career	1,086	Wayne Gretzky
Most Points, Career	1,669	Wayne Gretzky
		(583 goals, 1,086 assists)
Most PIM, Career	1,291	Kevin McClelland
Most Shutouts, Career	9	Grant Fuhr

Longest Consecutive

Games Streak	521	Craig MacTavish
		(Oct. 11/86-Jan. 2/93)
Most Goals, Season	*92	Wayne Gretzky
		(1981-82)
Most Assists, Season	*163	Wayne Gretzky
		(1985-86)
Most Points, Season	*215	Wayne Gretzky
		(1985-86)
		(52 goals, 163 assists)
Most PIM, Season	286	Steve Smith
		(1987-88)

Most Points, Defenseman,

Season	138	Paul Coffey
		(1985-86)
		(48 goals, 90 assists)

Most Points, Center,

Season	*215	Wayne Gretzky
		(1985-86)
		(52 goals, 163 assists)

Most Points, Right Wing,

Season	135	Jari Kurri
		(1984-85)
		(71 goals, 64 assists)

Most Points, Left Wing,

Season	106	Mark Messier
		(1982-83)
		(48 goals, 58 assists)

Most Points, Rookie,

Season	75	Jari Kurri
		(1980-81)
		(32 goals, 43 assists)
Most Shutouts, Season	4	Grant Fuhr
		(1987-88)
Most Goals, Game	5	Wayne Gretzky
		(Feb. 18/81, Dec. 30/81,
		Dec. 15/84, Dec. 6/87)
		Jari Kurri (Nov. 19/83)
		Pat Hughes (Feb. 3/84)
Most Assists, Game	*7	Wayne Gretzky
		(Feb. 15/80; Dec. 11/85;
		Feb. 14/86)
Most Points, Game	8	Wayne Gretzky
		(Nov. 19/83)
		Paul Coffey
		(Mar. 14/86)
		Wayne Gretzky
		(Jan. 4/84)

* NHL Record.

For the second consecutive season, Doug Weight led the Oilers in scoring, clicking for 40 points in 48 games.

All-time Record vs. Other Clubs

Regular Season

		At Home							On Road							Total					
	GP	W	L	T	GF	GA	PTS	GP	W	L	T	GF	GA	PTS	GP	W	L	T	GF	GA	PTS
Anaheim	5	2	3	0	10	14	4	5	1	4	0	14	19	2	10	3	7	0	24	33	6
Boston	22	8	11	3	76	76	19	23	4	17	2	63	107	10	45	12	28	5	139	183	29
Buffalo	22	16	4	2	97	59	34	23	9	9	5	90	95	23	45	25	13	7	187	154	57
Calgary	57	29	20	8	240	209	66	56	19	31	6	203	264	44	113	48	51	14	443	473	110
Chicago	27	14	12	1	114	105	29	26	9	14	3	103	110	21	53	23	26	4	217	215	50
Dallas	26	16	4	6	127	85	38	27	12	9	6	96	97	30	53	28	13	12	223	182	68
Detroit	26	14	8	4	126	104	32	26	13	11	2	111	101	28	52	27	19	6	237	205	60
Florida	1	0	1	0	3	5	0	1	0	1	0	4	4	1	2	0	1	1	7	9	1
Hartford	23	17	3	3	102	67	37	22	9	9	4	83	94	22	45	26	12	7	185	161	59
Los Angeles	57	29	15	13	287	224	71	57	23	22	12	251	247	58	114	52	37	25	538	471	129
Montreal	23	13	10	0	82	71	26	22	6	13	3	67	79	15	45	19	23	3	149	150	41
New Jersey	25	13	7	5	124	97	31	25	12	11	2	88	88	26	50	25	18	7	212	185	57
NY Islanders	23	14	5	4	93	70	32	23	5	10	8	92	99	18	46	19	15	12	185	169	50
NY Rangers	22	10	11	1	86	77	21	22	12	6	4	90	87	28	44	22	17	5	176	164	49
Ottawa	2	1	1	0	10	9	2	2	2	0	0	5	7	4	4	3	1	0	15	16	2
Philadelphia	22	13	5	4	83	63	30	23	6	16	1	67	102	13	45	19	21	5	150	165	43
Pittsburgh	23	18	4	1	125	80	37	23	12	10	1	110	90	25	46	30	14	2	235	170	62
Quebec	22	17	5	0	125	66	34	22	13	7	2	107	88	28	44	30	12	2	232	154	62
St. Louis	26	15	8	3	114	100	33	26	10	12	4	105	108	24	52	25	20	7	219	208	57
San Jose	13	10	1	2	59	31	22	12	3	8	1	29	48	7	25	13	9	3	88	79	29
Tampa Bay	3	3	0	0	9	6	6	3	2	1	0	6	13	1	6	3	2	1	15	19	7
Toronto	26	15	6	5	133	90	35	26	13	11	2	125	104	28	52	28	17	7	258	194	63
Vancouver	56	39	13	4	282	178	82	58	29	22	7	246	225	65	114	68	35	11	528	403	147
Washington	22	9	9	4	88	78	22	22	8	12	2	81	96	18	44	17	21	6	169	174	40
Winnipeg	54	33	17	4	246	182	70	53	29	20	4	247	218	62	107	62	37	8	493	400	132
Totals	**628**	**368**	**183**	**77**	**2841**	**2146**	**813**	**628**	**257**	**288**	**83**	**2483**	**2590**	**597**	**1256**	**625**	**471**	**160**	**5324**	**4736**	**1410**

Calgary totals include Atlanta, 1979-80. Dallas totals include Minnesota, 1979-80 to 1992-93.
New Jersey totals include Colorado, 1979-80 to 1981-82.

Playoffs

	Series	W	L	GP	W	L	T	GF	GA	Last Mtg.	Round	Result
Boston	2	2	0	9	8	1	0	41	20	1990	F	W 4-1
Calgary	5	4	1	30	19	11	0	132	96	1991	DSF	W 4-3
Chicago	4	3	1	20	12	8	0	102	77	1992	CF	L 0-4
Dallas	2	1	1	9	5	4	0	36	30	1991	CF	L 1-4
Detroit	2	2	0	10	8	2	0	39	26	1988	CF	W 4-1
Los Angeles	7	5	2	36	24	12	0	154	127	1992	DSF	W 4-2
Montreal	1	1	0	3	3	0	0	15	6	1981	PR	W 3-0
NY Islanders	3	1	2	15	6	9	0	47	58	1984	F	W 4-1
Philadelphia	3	2	1	15	8	7	0	49	44	1987	F	W 4-3
Vancouver	2	2	0	9	7	2	0	35	20	1992	DF	W 4-2
Winnipeg	6	6	0	26	22	4	0	120	75	1990	DSF	W 4-3
Totals	**37**	**29**	**8**	**180**	**120**	**60**	**0**	**770**	**579**			

Playoff Results 1995-91

Year	Round	Opponent	Result	GF	GA
1992	CF	Chicago	L 0-4	8	21
	DF	Vancouver	W 4-2	18	15
	DSF	Los Angeles	W 4-2	23	18
1991	CF	Minnesota	L 1-4	14	20
	DF	Los Angeles	W 4-2	21	20
	DSF	Calgary	W 4-3	22	20

Abbreviations: Round: F – Final;
CF – conference final; **CQF** – conference quarter-final;
CSF – conference semi-final; **DF** – division final;
DSF – division semi-final; **SF** – semi-final;
QF – quarter-final; **PR** – preliminary round.

1994-95 Results

Jan.	20		Anaheim	2-1	14		St. Louis	6-5
	22	at	Los Angeles	4-3	17		San Jose	5-3
	23	at	Anaheim	4-5	20		Calgary	5-2
	25	at	Chicago	1-5	22	at	Dallas	4-4
	28	at	Detroit	2-5	23	at	Dallas	1-2
	30		Detroit	2-4	26	at	St. Louis	1-5
Feb.	1		Chicago	0-7	27	at	Toronto	3-4
	3		Toronto	5-3	31		Calgary	2-6
	7	at	Vancouver	4-4	Apr. 1		Vancouver	1-5
	8		Winnipeg	3-3	3	at	Los Angeles	2-7
	10		San Jose	5-1	5	at	Anaheim	3-4
	12		Anaheim	2-0	7	at	San Jose	0-5
	15	at	Toronto	4-1	9		San Jose	2-5
	17	at	Detroit	2-4	13	at	Vancouver	6-4
	19	at	Chicago	1-4	15		Calgary	2-4
	20	at	St. Louis	0-4	17	at	Winnipeg	6-5
	22		Dallas	2-1	19		Los Angeles	2-0
	25		Los Angeles	3-4	21	at	Los Angeles	3-3
	28	at	Calgary	2-5	22	at	Vancouver	1-6
Mar.	1		Dallas	3-5	25	at	Winnipeg	5-3
	3		Chicago	2-4	27		St. Louis	2-3
	5		Detroit	4-2	29		Winnipeg	1-5
	8	at	San Jose	5-2	May 1		Toronto	5-6
	12		Vancouver	2-5	3	at	Calgary	3-5

Entry Draft
Selections 1995-81

1995
Pick
6	Steve Kelly
31	Georges Laraque
57	Lukas Zib
83	Mike Minard
109	Jan Snopek
161	Martin Cerven
187	Stephen Douglas
213	Jiri Antonin

1994
Pick
4	Jason Bonsignore
6	Ryan Smyth
32	Mike Watt
53	Corey Neilson
60	Brad Symes
79	Adam Copeland
95	Jussi Tarvainen
110	Jon Gaskins
136	Terry Marchant
160	Curtis Sheptak
162	Dmitri Shulga
179	Chris Wickenheiser
185	Rob Guinn
188	Jason Reid
214	Jeremy Jablonski
266	Ladislav Benysek

1993
Pick
7	Jason Arnott
16	Nick Stajduhar
33	David Vyborny
59	Kevin Paden
60	Alexander Kerch
111	Miroslav Satan
163	Alexander Zhurik
189	Martin Bakula
215	Brad Norton
241	Oleg Maltsev
267	Ilja Byakin

1992
Pick
13	Joe Hulbig
37	Martin Reichel
61	Simon Roy
65	Kirk Maltby
96	Ralph Intranuovo
109	Joaquin Gage
157	Steve Gibson
181	Kyuin Shim
190	Colin Schmidt
205	Marko Tuomainen
253	Bryan Rasmussen

1991
Pick
12	Tyler Wright
20	Martin Rucinsky
34	Andrew Verner
56	George Breen
78	Mario Nobili
93	Ryan Haggerty
144	David Oliver
166	Gary Kitching
210	Vegar Barlie
232	Evgeny Belosheikin
254	Juha Riihijarvi

1990
Pick
17	Scott Allison
38	Alexandre Legault
59	Joe Crowley
67	Joel Blain
101	Greg Louder
122	Keijo Sailynoja
143	Mike Power
164	Roman Mejzlik
185	Richard Zemlicka
206	Petr Korinek
227	invalid claim
248	Sami Nuutinen

1989
Pick
15	Jason Soules
36	Richard Borgo
78	Josef Beranek
92	Peter White
120	Anatoli Semenov
140	Davis Payne
141	Sergei Yashin
162	Darcy Martini
225	Roman Bozek

1988
Pick
19	Francois Leroux
39	Petro Koivunen
53	Trevor Sim
61	Collin Bauer
82	Cam Brauer
103	Don Martin
124	Len Barrie
145	Mike Glover
166	Shjon Podein
187	Tom Cole
208	Vladimir Zubkov
229	Darin MacDonald
250	Tim Tisdale

1987
Pick
21	Peter Soberlak
42	Brad Werenka
63	Geoff Smith
64	Peter Eriksson
105	Shaun Van Allen
126	Radek Toupal
147	Tomas Srsen
168	Age Ellingsen
189	Gavin Armstrong
210	Mike Tinkham
231	Jeff Pauletti
241	Jesper Duus
252	Igor Vyazmikin

1986
Pick
21	Kim Issel
42	Jamie Nichols
63	Ron Shudra
84	Dan Currie
105	David Haas
126	Jim Ennis
147	Ivan Matulik
168	Nicolas Beaulieu
189	Mike Greenlay
210	Matt Lanza
231	Mojmir Bozik
252	Tony Hand

1985
Pick
20	Scott Metcalfe
41	Todd Carnelley
62	Mike Ware
104	Tomas Kapusta
125	Brian Tessier
146	Shawn Tyers
167	Tony Fairfield
188	Kelly Buchberger
209	Mario Barbe
230	Peter Headon
251	John Haley

1984
Pick
21	Selmar Odelein
42	Daryl Reaugh
63	Todd Norman
84	Rich Novak
105	Richard Lambert
106	Emanuel Viveiros
126	Ivan Dornic
147	Heikki Riihijarvi
168	Todd Ewen
209	Joel Curtis
229	Simon Wheeldon
250	Darren Gani

1983
Pick
19	Jeff Beukeboom
40	Mike Golden
60	Mike Flanagan
80	Esa Tikkanen
120	Don Barber
140	Dale Derkatch
160	Ralph Vos
180	Dave Roach
200	Warren Yadlowski
220	John Miner
240	Steve Woodburn

1982
Pick
20	Jim Playfair
41	Steve Graves
62	Brent Loney
83	Jaroslav Pouzar
104	Dwayne Boettger
125	Raimo Summanen
146	Brian Small
167	Dean Clark
188	Ian Wood
209	Grant Dion
230	Chris Smith
251	Jeff Crawford

1981
Pick
8	Grant Fuhr
29	Todd Strueby
71	Paul Houck
92	Phil Drouillard
111	Steve Smith
113	Marc Habscheid
155	Mike Sturgeon
176	Miloslav Horava
197	Gord Sherven

General Manager

SATHER, GLEN CAMERON
President and General Manager, Edmonton Oilers.
Born in High River, Alta., Sept. 2, 1943.

The architect of the Edmonton Oilers' five Stanley Cup championships, Glen Sather is one of the most respected administrators in the NHL. The 1995-96 season is his 16th as general manager of the Oilers and his 20th with Edmonton since joining the organization in August of 1976.

Sather was the Oilers' coach and general manager for nine of the team's first ten seasons and returned to the coaching ranks in 1993-94, relieving Ted Green in late November. In 60 games, Sather guided the team to a 22-27-11 record. In 842 regular season games as coach, Sather has compiled a 464-268-110 record for a .616 winning percentage. He ranks seventh on the NHL's all-time coaching list while his .706 winning percentage in the playoffs is the best mark in NHL history.

Sather played for six different teams during his nine-year NHL career, registering 80 goals and 113 points in 660 games.

NHL Coaching Record

		Regular Season					Playoffs			
Season	Team	Games	W	L	T	%	Games	W	L	%
1979-80	Edmonton (NHL)	80	28	39	13	.431	3	0	3	.000
1980-81	Edmonton (NHL)	62	25	26	11	.492	9	5	4	.555
1981-82	Edmonton (NHL)	80	48	17	15	.694	5	2	3	.400
1982-83	Edmonton (NHL)	80	47	21	12	.663	16	11	5	.687
1983-84	Edmonton (NHL)	80	57	18	5	.744	19	15	4	.789*
1984-85	Edmonton (NHL)	80	49	20	11	.681	18	15	3	.833*
1985-86	Edmonton (NHL)	80	56	17	7	.744	10	6	4	.600
1986-87	Edmonton (NHL)	80	50	24	6	.663	21	16	5	.762*
1987-88	Edmonton (NHL)	80	44	25	11	.619	18	16	2	.889*
1988-89	Edmonton (NHL)	80	38	34	8	.538	7	3	4	.429
1993-94	Edmonton (NHL)	60	22	27	11	.458	....	....	....	....
	NHL Totals	842	464	268	110	.616	126	89	37	.706

* Stanley Cup win.

Club Directory

Edmonton Coliseum
7424 – 118 Avenue
Edmonton, Alberta T5B 4M9
Phone **403/474-8561**
Ticketing 403/471-2191
FAX 403/477-9625
Capacity: 17,111

Owner/Governor	Peter Pocklington
Alternate Governor	Glen Sather
General Counsel	Lorne Ruzicka
President/General Manager	Glen Sather
Exec. Vice-President/Assistant G.M.	Bruce MacGregor
Assistant to the President	Ted Green
Coach	Ron Low
Assistant Coaches	Kevin Primeau, Bob McCammon
Chief Scout	Barry Fraser
Director of Player Personnel/Hockey Operations	Kevin Prendergast
Director of Hockey Administration	Steve Pellegrini
Coordinator of Development	Curtis Brackenbury
Scouting Staff	Ed Chadwick, Lorne Davis, Bob Freeman, Harry Howell, Chris McCarthy, Curly Reeves, Brad Smith, Kent Nilsson, Brad MacGregor, Peter Mahovlich
Executive Secretary	Betsy Freedman
Receptionist/Secretary	Melahna Matan

Medical and Training Staff
Athletic Trainer/Therapist	Ken Lowe
Athletic Trainer	Barrie Stafford
Assistant Trainer	Lyle Kulchisky
Massage Therapist	Roland Kelly
Team Medical Chief of Staff/Director of Glen Sather Sports Medicine Clinic	Dr. David C. Reid
Team Physicians	Dr. Don Groot, Dr. Boris Boyko
Team Dentists	Dr. Tony Sneazwell, Dr. Brian Nord
Fitness Consultant	Dr. Art Quinney
Physical Therapy Consultant	Dr. Dave Magee
Team Acupuncturist	Dr. Steven Aung

Finance
Vice-President, Finance	Werner Baum
Accountants	Rhonda Holgersen, Terry Sperling
Executive Secretary	Lisa Colby

Public Relations
Director of Public Relations	Bill Tuele
Coordinator of Publications and Statistics	Steve Knowles
Director of Community Relations/Special Events	Trish Kerr
Public Relations Secretary	Fiona Liew

Marketing
Director of Marketing	Stew MacDonald
Manager of Properties Division	Darrell Holowaychuk
Marketing Secretary	Heather Allen
Assistant Properties Manager	Ray MacDonald
Administrative Assistant Properties	Julia Slade
Merchandising Clerk	Kerri Hill

Ticketing
Director of Ticketing Operations	Sheila MacDonald
Ticketing Operations	Sheila McCaskill, Marcella Kinsman
Group Ticket Sales Representative	Dave Semenko

Miscellaneous
Team Administration Offices	Edmonton Coliseum, Edmonton, Alta., Canada T5B 4M9
Location of Press Box	East Side at top (Radio/TV) West Side at top (Media)
Dimensions of Rink	200 feet by 85 feet
Club Colours	Blue, Orange, White
Team Uniforms	Home: Base colour white, trimmed with blue and orange Away: Base colour blue, trimmed with white and orange
Training Camp Site	Edmonton Coliseum, Edmonton, Alberta; Northlands Agricom, Edmonton, Alberta
Television Channel	CFRN (Channel 3, Cable 2) CBXT TV (Channel 5, Cable 4)
Radio Station	CFCW (790 AM)

Florida Panthers

1994-95 Results: 20W-22L-6T 46PTS. Fifth, Atlantic Division

Year-by-Year Record

Season	GP	Home W	Home L	Home T	Road W	Road L	Road T	Overall W	Overall L	Overall T	GF	GA	Pts.	Finished		Playoff Result
1994-95	48	9	12	3	11	10	3	20	22	6	115	127	46	5th,	Atlantic Div.	Out of Playoffs
1993-94	84	15	18	9	18	16	8	33	34	17	233	233	83	5th,	Atlantic Div.	Out of Playoffs

Schedule

Oct.	Sat.	7	at New Jersey*
	Sun.	8	Calgary
	Wed.	11	Montreal
	Fri.	13	Ottawa
	Sun.	15	NY Islanders
	Tues.	17	Chicago
	Sat.	21	Hartford
	Tues.	24	at Toronto
	Wed.	25	at Montreal
	Sat.	28	at Ottawa*
	Tues.	31	NY Islanders
Nov.	Thur.	2	at Philadelphia
	Fri.	3	at Washington
	Sun.	5	Tampa Bay
	Tues.	7	Philadelphia
	Thur.	9	Edmonton
	Sat.	11	Buffalo
	Tues.	14	Toronto
	Thur.	16	Vancouver
	Sat.	18	at Los Angeles
	Sun.	19	at Anaheim
	Tues.	21	New Jersey
	Sun.	26	Los Angeles
	Wed.	29	Philadelphia
Dec.	Fri.	1	at Pittsburgh
	Sat.	2	at Hartford
	Tues.	5	at Washington
	Thur.	7	Anaheim
	Sat.	9	Boston
	Mon.	11	at New Jersey
	Tues.	12	at NY Islanders
	Thur.	14	at Boston
	Sat.	16	at Tampa Bay
	Thur.	21	Winnipeg
	Sat.	23	New Jersey
	Thur.	28	Washington
	Sat.	30	at Pittsburgh
Jan.	Wed.	3	at Vancouver
	Fri.	5	at Edmonton
	Sat.	6	at Calgary
	Mon.	8	at San Jose

	Wed.	10	at Colorado
	Fri.	12	at Dallas
	Tues.	16	San Jose
	Mon.	22	at Philadelphia
	Tues.	23	at Washington
	Thur.	25	Montreal
	Sat.	27	Buffalo
	Mon.	29	Pittsburgh
	Wed.	31	at Buffalo
Feb.	Thur.	1	at Boston
	Sat.	3	at Tampa Bay*
	Tues.	6	at Detroit
	Thur.	8	Detroit
	Sun.	11	St. Louis
	Wed.	14	Philadelphia
	Fri.	16	Colorado
	Sun.	18	Dallas
	Wed.	21	at New Jersey
	Sat.	24	NY Rangers
	Sun.	25	at Buffalo
	Thur.	29	Washington
Mar.	Sat.	2	at Hartford
	Tues.	5	at St. Louis
	Thur.	7	at Winnipeg
	Sun.	10	Boston
	Mon.	11	at Chicago
	Wed.	13	at NY Rangers
	Sun.	17	New Jersey
	Tues.	19	Ottawa
	Thur.	21	NY Islanders*
	Sat.	23	at Tampa Bay
	Wed.	27	at NY Rangers
	Thur.	28	Pittsburgh
	Sat.	30	Tampa Bay
Apr.	Mon.	1	Hartford
	Wed.	3	at Ottawa
	Sat.	6	at Montreal
	Mon.	8	at NY Rangers
	Wed.	10	Tampa Bay
	Fri.	12	at NY Islanders
	Sun.	14	NY Rangers*

* Denotes afternoon game.

Home Starting Times:

Weeknights	7:35 p.m.
Sundays	6:05 p.m.
Except Sun. Oct. 8	7:35 p.m.
Sun. Mar. 10	7:35 p.m.
Sun. Apr. 14	3:00 p.m.

Franchise date: June 14, 1993

EASTERN
NHL
CONFERENCE

ATLANTIC
DIVISION

**3rd
NHL
Season**

The first player selected in the 1994 Entry Draft, 6'2" Ed Jovanovski earned his second consecutive OHL All-Star selection with the Windsor Spitfires in 1994-95. He is expected to join the the Panthers' defense corps in 1995-96.

1995-96 Player Personnel

FORWARDS	HT	WT	S	Place of Birth	Date	1994-95 Club
BARNES, Stu	5-11	174	R	Edmonton, Alta.	12/25/70	Florida
BELANGER, Jesse	6-0	186	R	St. Georges de Beauce, Que.	6/15/69	Florida
BUCKBERGER, Ashley	6-2	206	R	Esterhazy, Sask.	2/19/75	Swift Current-Kamloops
DVORAK, Radek	6-2	187	R	Tabor, Czech.	3/9/77	Budejovice
FITZGERALD, Tom	6-1	191	R	Melrose, MA	8/28/68	Florida
GARPENLOV, Johan	5-11	184	L	Stockholm, Sweden	3/21/68	San Jose-Florida
HARKINS, Brett	6-1	185	L	North Ridgeville, OH	7/2/70	Providence (AHL)-Boston
HOUGH, Mike	6-1	197	L	Montreal, Que.	2/6/63	Florida
HULL, Jody	6-2	195	R	Cambridge, Ont.	2/2/69	Florida
KONTOS, Chris	6-1	195	L	Toronto, Ont.	12/10/63	Cdn. National
KUDASHOV, Alexei	6-0	183	R	Elektrostal, USSR	7/21/71	St. John's
KUDELSKI, Bob	6-1	205	R	Springfield, MA	3/3/64	Florida
LINDEN, Jamie	6-3	185	R	Medicine Hat, Alta.	7/19/72	Cincinnati-Florida
LINDSAY, Bill	5-11	190	L	Big Fork, MT	5/17/71	Florida
LOWRY, Dave	6-1	200	L	Sudbury, Ont.	2/14/65	Florida
MELLANBY, Scott	6-1	199	R	Montreal, Que.	6/11/66	Florida
NEMIROVSKY, David	6-1	192	R	Toronto, Ont.	8/1/76	Ottawa (OHL)
NIEDERMAYER, Rob	6-2	201	L	Cassiar, B.C.	12/28/74	Medicine Hat-Florida
PODOLLAN, Jason	6-1	192	R	Vernon, B.C.	2/18/76	Spokane
SKRUDLAND, Brian	6-0	195	L	Peace River, Alta.	7/31/63	Florida
TOMLINSON, Dave	5-11	180	L	North Vancouver, B.C.	5/8/69	Cincinnati-Florida
TROMBLEY, Rhett	6-3	230	R	Regina, Sask.	8/9/74	Toledo-Las Vegas
WASHBURN, Steve	6-2	191	L	Ottawa, Ont.	4/10/75	Ottawa (OHL)-Cincinnati

DEFENSEMEN	HT	WT	S	Place of Birth	Date	1994-95 Club
ARMSTRONG, Chris	6-0	198	L	Regina, Sask.	6/26/75	Moose Jaw-Cincinnati
BOUGHNER, Bob	6-0	205	R	Windsor, Ont.	3/8/71	Cincinnati
BROWN, Keith	6-1	196	R	Corner Brook, Nfld.	5/6/60	Florida
CARKNER, Terry	6-3	210	L	Smiths Falls, Ont.	3/7/66	Detroit
DOYLE, Trevor	6-3	212	R	Ottawa, Ont.	1/1/74	Cincinnati
EAKINS, Dallas	6-2	195	L	Dade City, FL	2/27/67	Cincinnati-Florida
ESAU, Leonard	6-3	190	R	Meadow Lake, Sask.	6/3/68	Saint John-Edmonton-Calgary
GUSTAFSSON, Per	6-2	190	L	Osterham, Sweden	6/6/70	HV-71
JOHNSON, Mike	6-3	205	L	Halifax, N.S.	5/29/74	Cdn. National-Las Vegas
JOVANOVSKI, Ed	6-2	205	L	Windsor, Ont.	6/26/76	Windsor
LAUS, Paul	6-1	216	R	Beamsville, Ont.	9/26/70	Florida
MOLLER, Randy	6-2	210	R	Red Deer, Alta.	8/23/63	Florida
MURPHY, Gord	6-2	191	R	Willowdale, Ont.	3/23/67	Florida
SMITH, Geoff	6-3	194	L	Edmonton, Alta.	3/7/69	Florida
SVEHLA, Robert	6-1	190	R	Martin, Czech.	1/2/69	Malmo-Florida
SVENSSON, Magnus	5-11	180	L	Tranas, Sweden	3/1/63	Davos-Florida
WARRENER, Rhett	6-1	209	L	Shaunavon, Sask.	1/27/76	Saskatoon
WOOLLEY, Jason	6-0	188	L	Toronto, Ont.	7/27/69	Detroit (IHL)-Florida

GOALTENDERS	HT	WT	C	Place of Birth	Date	1994-95 Club
CHABOT, Frederic	5-11	175	L	Hebertville-Station, Que.	2/12/68	Cincinnati
FITZPATRICK, Mark	6-2	198	L	Toronto, Ont.	11/13/68	Florida
LORENZ, Danny	5-10	187	L	Murrayville, B.C.	12/12/69	Cincinnati
VANBIESBROUCK, John	5-8	176	L	Detroit, MI	9/4/63	Florida
WEEKES, Kevin	6-0	158	L	Toronto, Ont.	4/4/75	Ottawa (OHL)

1994-95 Scoring

*– rookie

Regular Season

Pos	#	Player	Team	GP	G	A	Pts	+/–	PIM	PP	SH	GW	GT	S	%
C	26	Jesse Belanger	FLA	47	15	14	29	-5	18	6	0	3	1	89	16.9
C	14	Stu Barnes	FLA	41	10	19	29	7	8	1	0	2	0	93	10.8
R	27	Scott Mellanby	FLA	48	13	12	25	-16	90	4	0	5	0	130	10.0
D	5	Gord Murphy	FLA	46	6	16	22	-14	24	5	0	0	0	94	6.4
L	10	Dave Lowry	FLA	45	10	10	20	-3	25	2	0	3	0	70	14.3
R	12	Jody Hull	FLA	46	11	8	19	-1	8	0	0	4	0	63	17.5
L	11	Bill Lindsay	FLA	48	10	9	19	1	46	0	1	0	0	63	15.9
R	21	Tom Fitzgerald	FLA	48	3	13	16	-3	31	0	0	0	0	78	3.8
C	20	Brian Skrudland	FLA	47	5	9	14	0	88	1	0	0	0	44	11.4
L	29	Johan Garpenlov	S.J.	13	1	2	3	-3	2	0	0	0	0	16	6.3
			FLA	27	3	9	12	4	0	0	0	0	0	28	10.7
			TOTAL	40	4	10	14	1	2	0	0	0	0	44	9.1
L	18	Mike Hough	FLA	48	6	7	13	1	38	0	0	2	0	58	10.3
D	6	Jason Woolley	FLA	34	4	9	13	-1	18	1	0	0	1	76	5.3
L	15	Gaetan Duchesne	S.J.	33	2	7	9	-6	16	0	0	0	0	48	4.2
			FLA	13	1	2	3	3	0	0	0	0	0	14	7.1
			TOTAL	46	3	9	12	-3	16	0	0	0	0	62	4.8
C	44	Rob Niedermayer	FLA	48	4	6	10	-13	36	1	0	0	0	58	6.9
R	22	Bob Kudelski	FLA	26	6	3	9	2	2	3	0	1	0	29	20.7
D	7	Brian Benning	FLA	24	1	7	8	-6	18	1	0	0	0	26	3.8
D	28	Magnus Svensson	FLA	19	2	5	7	5	10	1	0	0	0	41	4.9
L	19	Andrei Lomakin	FLA	31	1	6	7	-5	6	1	0	0	0	25	4.0
D	3	Paul Laus	FLA	37	0	7	7	12	138	0	0	0	0	18	0.0
D	25	Geoff Smith	FLA	47	2	4	6	-5	22	0	0	0	0	40	5.0
D	16	Randy Moller	FLA	17	0	3	3	-5	16	0	0	0	0	12	0.0
D	24 *	Robert Svehla	FLA	5	1	1	2	3	0	1	0	0	0	6	16.7
D	8	Dallas Eakins	FLA	17	0	1	1	2	35	0	0	0	0	3	0.0
D	2	Joe Cirella	FLA	20	0	1	1	-7	21	0	0	0	0	13	0.0
G	34	John Vanbiesbrouck	FLA	37	0	1	1	0	6	0	0	0	0	0	0.0
D	38	Stephane Richer	FLA	1	0	0	0	0	2	0	0	0	0	0	0.0
L	23	Jeff Daniels	FLA	3	0	0	0	0	0	0	0	0	0	0	0.0
R	42 *	Jamie Linden	FLA	4	0	0	0	-1	17	0	0	0	0	0	0.0
C	17	Dave Tomlinson	FLA	5	0	0	0	-2	0	0	0	0	0	4	0.0
D	4	Keith Brown	FLA	13	0	0	0	1	2	0	0	0	0	10	0.0
G	30	Mark Fitzpatrick	FLA	15	0	0	0	0	0	0	0	0	0	0	0.0

Goaltending

No.	Goaltender	GPI	Mins	Avg	W	L	T	EN	SO	GA	SA	S%
34	John Vanbiesbrouck	37	2087	2.47	14	15	4	4	4	86	1000	.914
30	Mark Fitzpatrick	15	819	2.64	6	7	2	1	2	36	361	.900
	Totals	48	2916	2.61	20	22	6	5	6	127	1366	.907

Mark Fitzpatrick combined with John Vanbiesbrouck to help the Panthers record a league-high six shutouts in 1994-95.

General Manager

MURRAY, BRYAN CLARENCE
General Manager, Florida Panthers.
Born in Shawville, Que., December 5, 1942.

Bryan Murray was named general manager of the Florida Panthers on August 1, 1994. He has five years experience as an NHL general manager. Prior to joining the Panthers, Bryan signed with the Detroit Red Wings on July 30, 1990 and held the dual role of general manager and head coach of the Red Wings his first three seasons in Detroit. During the 1993-94 season, as general manager, Murray helped guide the Red Wings to a 46-30-8 record (100 points) and a first place finish in the Central Division. In 328 games under Murray's control, the Wings won a total of 170 games while losing only 121 and tying 37, an average of 43 wins and 94 points a season. Prior to Murray's arrival, the Wings failed to make the playoffs in the previous four seasons. Murray, 51, left his mark in the NHL record book as a coach with a career record of 467-337-112 in 916 regular season games, placing him sixth on the all-time victory list. His .571 winning percentage has him tied for eighth with Billy Reay among those coaching 600 games or more.

Bryan has made his presence felt within the Panthers organization. He bolstered the Panthers defensive corps with the acquisition of defenseman Jason Woolley, from the Detroit Vipers (IHL), and European defensemen Magnus Svensson and Robert Svehla.

Murray broke into the NHL coaching ranks with the Washington Capitals on November 11, 1981. He spent the next 8 1/2 seasons with the Caps and was awarded the Jack Adams Award as NHL coach of the year in 1983-84 and captured the Patrick Division title in 1988-89 (the only first place finish in Capitals history). On January 15, 1990, he was replaced by his brother, Terry, who is currently the Flyers head coach.

NHL Coaching Record

		Regular Season					Playoffs			
Season	Team	Games	W	L	T	%	Games	W	L	%
1981-82	Washington	76	25	28	13	.477	....			....
1982-83	Washington	80	39	25	16	.588	4	1	3	.250
1983-84	Washington	80	48	27	5	.631	8	4	4	.500
1984-85	Washington	80	46	25	9	.631	5	2	3	.400
1985-86	Washington	80	50	23	7	.669	9	5	4	.556
1986-87	Washington	80	38	32	10	.538	7	3	4	.429
1987-88	Washington	80	38	33	9	.531	14	7	7	.500
1988-89	Washington	80	41	29	10	.575	6	2	4	.333
1989-90	Washington	46	18	24	4	.435	....			....
1990-91	Detroit	80	34	38	8	.475	7	3	4	.429
1991-92	Detroit	80	43	25	12	.613	11	4	7	.364
1992-93	Detroit	84	47	28	9	.613	7	3	4	.429
	NHL Totals	916	467	337	112	.571	78	34	44	.436

Club Records

Team

(Figures in brackets for season records are games played; records for fewest points, wins, ties, losses, goals, goals against are for 70 or more games)

Most Points	83	1993-94 (84)
Most Wins	33	1993-94 (84)
Most Ties	17	1993-94 (84)
Most Losses	34	1993-94 (84)
Most Goals	233	1993-94 (84)
Most Goals Against	233	1993-94 (84)
Fewest Points	83	1993-94 (84)
Fewest Wins	33	1993-94 (84)
Fewest Ties	17	1993-94 (84)
Fewest Losses	34	1993-94 (84)
Fewest Goals	233	1993-94 (84)
Fewest Goals Against	233	1993-94 (84)

Longest Winning Streak
Over-all 4   Jan. 16-Jan. 24/94
Home 2   Three times
Away 3   Nov. 7-Nov. 10/93 / Dec. 7-Dec. 10/93

Longest Undefeated Streak
Over-all 9   Jan. 8-Jan. 30/94
Home 5   Mar. 14-Mar. 21/94 (3 wins, 2 ties)
Away 7   Dec. 7-Dec. 29/93 (5 wins, 2 ties)

Longest Losing Streak
Over-all 5   Feb. 24-Mar. 4/94
Home 5   Feb. 20-Mar. 4/94
Away 3   Nov. 26-Dec. 5/93

Longest Winless Streak
Over-all 8   Mar. 28-Apr. 12/94 (4 losses, 4 ties)
Home 6   Mar. 21-Apr. 12/94 (3 losses, 3 ties)
Away 4   Jan. 3-Jan. 13/94 (2 losses, 2 ties)

Most Shutouts, Season 6   1994-95 (48)
Most PIM, Season 1,620   1993-94 (84)
Most Goals, Game 8   Jan. 24/94 (Mtl. 3 at Fla. 8)

Individual

Most Seasons 2   Several Players
Most Games 132   Bill Lindsay
Most Goals, Career 43   Scott Mellanby
Most Assists, Career 47   Jesse Belanger
Most Points, Career 85   Scott Mellanby (43 goals, 42 assists)
Most PIM, Career 247   Paul Laus
Most Shutouts, Career 5   John Vanbiesbrouck

Longest Consecutive Games Streak 132   Bill Lindsay
Most Goals, Season 30   Scott Mellanby (1993-94)
Most Assists, Season 33   Jesse Belanger (1993-94)
Most Points, Season 60   Scott Mellanby (1993-94) (30 goals, 30 assists)
Most PIM, Season 156   Brent Severyn (1993-94)
Most Shutouts, Season 4   John Vanbiesbrouck (1994-95)

Most Points, Defenseman
Season 43   Gord Murphy (1993-94) (14 goals, 29 assists)

Most Points, Center
Season 50   Jesse Belanger (1993-94) (17 goals, 33 assists)

Most Points, Right Wing
Season 60   Scott Mellanby (1993-94) (30 goals, 30 assists)

Most Points, Left Wing
Season 47   Andrei Lomakin (1993-94) (19 goals, 28 assists)

Most Points, Rookie
Season 50   Jesse Belanger (1993-94) (17 goals, 33 assists)

Most Goals, Game 2   Seventeen players
Most Assists, Game 3   Four players
Most Points, Game 4   Jesse Belanger (Jan. 19/94)

* NHL Record.

In addition to tying for the team lead in points, Stu Barnes led all Panther forwards with a plus/minus rating of +7.

All-time Record vs. Other Clubs

Regular Season

	At Home							On Road							Total						
	GP	W	L	T	GF	GA	PTS	GP	W	L	T	GF	GA	PTS	GP	W	L	T	GF	GA	PTS
Anaheim	1	1	0	0	4	2	2	1	1	0	0	3	2	2	2	2	0	0	7	4	4
Boston	3	1	2	0	8	7	2	4	2	1	1	8	6	5	7	3	3	1	16	13	7
Buffalo	3	1	2	0	5	10	2	4	1	3	0	4	14	2	7	2	5	0	9	24	4
Calgary	1	1	0	0	2	1	2	1	0	1	0	2	4	0	2	1	1	0	4	5	2
Chicago	1	0	1	0	2	3	0	1	0	0	1	4	4	1	2	0	1	1	6	7	1
Dallas	1	0	1	0	4	5	0	1	0	0	1	4	4	1	2	0	1	1	8	9	1
Detroit	1	0	1	0	3	4	0	1	0	1	0	3	7	0	2	0	2	0	6	11	0
Edmonton	1	0	0	1	4	4	1	1	1	0	0	5	3	2	2	1	0	1	9	7	3
Hartford	4	1	2	1	10	11	3	4	3	1	0	11	9	6	8	4	3	1	21	20	9
Los Angeles	1	0	0	1	2	2	1	1	1	0	0	6	5	2	2	1	0	1	8	7	3
Montreal	4	1	1	2	14	12	4	3	3	0	0	11	5	6	7	4	1	2	25	17	10
New Jersey	5	1	2	2	10	12	4	4	0	4	0	4	15	0	9	1	6	2	14	27	4
NY Islanders	4	2	2	0	11	11	4	5	3	1	1	12	9	7	9	5	3	1	23	20	11
NY Rangers	5	2	3	0	10	17	4	4	1	2	1	8	9	3	9	3	5	1	18	26	7
Ottawa	4	3	0	1	12	8	7	4	4	0	0	18	7	8	8	7	0	1	30	15	15
Philadelphia	4	1	3	0	12	14	2	5	1	2	2	14	13	4	9	2	5	2	26	27	6
Pittsburgh	4	1	3	0	11	12	2	4	1	2	1	10	14	3	8	2	5	1	21	26	5
Quebec	4	1	3	0	9	16	2	3	1	1	1	10	9	3	7	2	4	1	19	25	5
St. Louis	1	0	1	0	1	3	0	1	0	1	0	3	5	0	2	0	2	0	4	8	0
San Jose	1	0	0	1	3	3	1	1	0	1	0	2	2	0	2	0	1	1	5	5	1
Tampa Bay	4	3	0	1	13	7	7	5	3	1	1	12	6	7	9	6	1	2	25	13	14
Toronto	2	0	1	1	4	5	1	1	0	0	1	3	3	1	3	0	1	2	7	8	2
Vancouver	1	1	0	0	2	1	2	1	0	1	0	2	2	0	2	1	1	0	4	3	2
Washington	5	3	1	1	17	9	7	4	0	3	1	7	13	1	9	3	4	2	24	22	8
Winnipeg	1	0	1	0	2	5	0	1	0	0	1	2	2	1	2	0	1	1	4	7	1
Totals	66	24	30	12	175	184	60	66	29	26	11	173	176	69	132	53	56	23	348	360	129

1994-95 Results

Date		Opponent	Score		Date		Opponent	Score
Jan.	21	at NY Islanders	1-2			12	at Hartford	4-1
	23	Pittsburgh	5-6			14	Buffalo	1-2
	25	at Tampa Bay	2-3			16	Washington	5-1
	26	Tampa Bay	4-2			18	Philadelphia	3-4
	28	at Hartford	2-1			20	at Quebec	4-5
	30	at Boston	2-1			22	at Montreal	3-2
	31	NY Islanders	1-5			24	at Buffalo	0-3
Feb.	2	Montreal	1-1			26	Pittsburgh	2-0
	4	at Washington	2-3			29	Hartford	4-4
	7	at Pittsburgh	3-7		Apr.	2	at Tampa Bay	4-1
	9	at Philadelphia	3-0			5	NY Rangers	0-5
	11	Hartford	4-3			8	at NY Islanders	2-2
	12	New Jersey	2-4			12	at NY Islanders	1-3
	15	Ottawa	2-0			14	at Washington	0-3
	17	Boston	4-5			16	Tampa Bay	4-1
	19	Quebec	1-4			18	Philadelphia	1-3
	21	NY Rangers	3-5			20	New Jersey	1-0
	23	Montreal	2-5			22	Quebec	4-2
	25	at Ottawa	4-1			24	at Ottawa	5-1
	28	at NY Rangers	0-0			26	at Buffalo	0-5
Mar.	2	at Philadelphia	2-2			28	at New Jersey	1-3
	4	at New Jersey	1-6			30	Washington	2-2
	8	Ottawa	3-2		May	2	at NY Rangers	4-3
	11	at Boston	2-0			3	at Pittsburgh	4-3

Entry Draft
Selections 1995-93

1995 Pick		1994 Pick		1993 Pick	
10	Radek Dvorak	1	Ed Jovanovski	5	Rob Niedermayer
36	Aaron MacDonald	27	Rhett Warrener	41	Kevin Weekes
62	Mike O'Grady	31	Jason Podollan	57	Chris Armstrong
80	Dave Duerden	36	Ryan Johnson	67	Mikael Tjallden
88	Daniel Tjarnqvist	84	David Nemirovsky	78	Steve Washburn
114	Francois Cloutier	105	Dave Geris	83	Bill McCauley
166	Peter Worrell	157	Matt O'Dette	109	Todd MacDonald
192	Filip Kuba	183	Jasson Boudrias	135	Alain Nasreddine
218	David Lemanowicz	235	Tero Lehtera	161	Trevor Doyle
		261	Per Gustafsson	187	Briane Thompson
				213	Chad Cabana
				239	John Demarco
				265	Eric Montreuil

Coach

MacLEAN, DOUG
Coach, Florida Panthers. Born in Summerside, P.E.I., April 12, 1954.

MacLean, 41, brings nine years of National Hockey League experience to the Panthers bench. MacLean's NHL career began in 1986-87 when he was hired by St. Louis as an assistant to head coach Jacques Martin. MacLean spent two seasons in St. Louis, helping guide the Blues to first and second place finishes in the Norris Division, before becoming Bryan Murray's assistant coach in Washington at the start of the 1988-89 season.

MacLean spent two seasons in the Capitals' organization. He spent the entire 1988-89 season as Murray's assistant and began the '89-90 season in that capacity until he was named head coach of the Capitals' American Hockey League affiliate in Baltimore midway through the season. MacLean was Baltimore's head coach for the final 35 games of the '89-90 season and he compiled a record of 17-13-5, finishing third in the AHL's South Division with an overall record of 43-30-7.

The following season, 1990-91, MacLean left the Capitals' organization to become Murray's assistant coach in Detroit. MacLean spent two seasons behind the Red Wings bench, the second season as associate coach, and helped guide the Red Wings to third and first place finishes, respectively. In 1992-93, MacLean left the coaching ranks to concentrate on Detroit's player development. MacLean spent the 1992-93 and 1993-94 seasons as the Red Wings' assistant general manager, as well as general manager of the Adirondack Red Wings, Detroit's AHL affiliate. Through his eye for talent and his player evaluation expertise, the Red Wings finished second and first, respectively, in his two years developing talent, and this past season, with several of MacLean's acquisitions, Detroit advanced to the Stanley Cup Finals.

MacLean left the Detroit organization just prior to the start of the 1994-95 season and once again was reunited with Bryan Murray. MacLean became the Panthers director of player development and pro scout in October of 1994.

MacLean was born in Summerside, Prince Edward Island and played collegiate hockey at the University of P.E.I., where he graduated with a bachelors degree in education. Maclean also played for the Montreal Junior Canadiens, and in 1974 he was invited to attend the St. Louis Blues' training camp.

After his playing career, MacLean enrolled at the University of Western Ontario, where he received his masters degree in educational psychology. While attending Western Ontario, MacLean began his coaching career as an assistant with the London Knights of the Ontario Hockey League. Upon graduating from Western Ontario, MacLean returned home where he taught high school and became head coach of Summerside's junior A hockey team. In 1985-86, MacLean became head coach at the University of New Brunswick, and after only one season there, he was tabbed by Jacques Martin to join his coaching staff in St. Louis.

MacLean is married, and he and his wife, Jill, have two children, a son, Clark (7) and a daughter, MacKenzie (4).

Coaching Record

Season	Team	Games	Regular Season W	L	T	%	Playoffs Games	W	L	%
1985-86	U. of New Brunswick (CIAU)	22	8	14	0	.364	....	....	....	....
1989-90	Baltimore (AHL)	35	17	13	5	.557	12	6	6	.500

Club Directory

Chairman and CEO.	H. Wayne Huizenga
President & Governor	William A. Torrey
Vice President, Business/Mktg. & Alt. Governor	Dean J. Jordan
General Manager	Bryan Murray
Special Consultant	Richard C. Rochon
Executive Assistants to President.	Deanna Cocozzelli, Cathy Stevenson
Executive Assistant/Business & Marketing	Janine Shea
Executive Assistant to General Manager	Diana Marchand
Chief Financial Officer	Steve Dauria
Accounting Manager	Evelyn Lopez
Staff Accountants	Laura Barrera, Ana Carrasquilla
MIS Co-ordinator	Abe Betesh
Secretary, Chief Financial Officer	Jackie Ortega
Receptionist	Marilyn Klees

Hockey Operations

Director of Player Personnel	John Chapman
Assistant General Manager.	Chuck Fletcher
Head Coach	Doug MacLean
Assistant Coach	Lindy Ruff
Goaltending Coach.	Bill Smith
Eastern Scout	Ron Harris
European Scout	Matti Vaisanen
Amateur Scouts	Paul Henry, Tim Murray, Mike Abbamont
Athletic Trainer	David Smith
Equipment Manager	Mark Brennan
Associate Equipment Manager	Tim Leroy
Assistant to the Equipment Manager	Scott Tinkler
Training Facility Assistant	Andre Szucko
Team Services Assistant	Marni Share
Internist	Charles Posternack, M.D.
Orthopedic Surgeons	David E. Attarian, M.D., Stephen R. Southworth, M.D.
Plastic Surgeon	Harry K. Moon
Minor League Affiliates.	Carolina (AHL) and Cincinnati (IHL)

Communications Department

Director, Public/Media Relations	Greg Bouris
Public/Media Relations Associates	Kevin Dessart, Ron Colangelo
Manager of Archives.	Ed Krajewski
Secretary, Public/Media Relations & Community Services	Aza Krotz

Marketing Department

Director, Promotions & Special Projects	Declan J. Bolger
Director, Corporate Sales and Sponsorship	Kimberly Terranova
Director, Merchandise.	Ron Dennis
Coordinator, Corporate Sales and Sponsorship	Joe Valesco
Coordinator, Promotions & Youth Hockey	Elizabeth Ridley
Marketing Assistant	Brette Zalkin
Secretary, Corporate Sales and Sponsorship	Susan Gonzalez
Secretary, Promotions & Special Projects	Sandra Gale
Secretary, Merchandise.	Mary Lou Poag

Ticket Operations

Director, Ticket and Game Day Operations.	Steve Dangerfield
Manager, Ticket Operations	Scott Wampold
Sales Managers.	Greg Hanessian, Barry Cohen, Jeff Moss
Ticket Operations	Julian Smyle, Matt Coyne
Account Executives	Mike Nichols, Chris Trinceri

General Information

Arena Phone Number	(305) 530-4444
Location of Press Box	Mezzanine, Sec. 211
Dimensions of Rink	200 feet by 85 feet
Practice Arena	Gold Coast Ice Arena (305) 784-5500
Team Colors	Red, Navy Blue, Yellow-Gold
Television Station	Sunshine Network & UPN33
Television Announcers	Jeff Rimer, Denis Potvin, Paul Kennedy
Panthers Radio Network	WQAM, 560 AM
Radio Announcers	Chris Moore, Denis Potvin, Alain Chevrier
Panthers Spanish Radio.	WCMQ, 1210 AM
Spanish Announcer.	Arley Londono
Public Address Announcer	John DeMott

General Managers' History

Bob Clarke, 1993-94; Bryan Murray, 1994-95 to date.

Coaching History

Roger Neilson, 1993-94 to 1994-95; Doug MacLean, 1995-96.

Captains' History

Brian Skrudland, 1993-94 to date.

Hartford Whalers

1994-95 Results: 19w-24L-5T 43PTS. Fifth, Northeast Division

Year-by-Year Record

Season	GP	Home W	L	T	Road W	L	T	Overall W	L	T	GF	GA	Pts.	Finished		Playoff Result
1994-95	48	12	10	2	7	14	3	19	24	5	127	141	43	5th,	Northeast Div.	Out of Playoffs
1993-94	84	14	22	6	13	26	3	27	48	9	227	288	63	6th,	Northeast Div.	Out of Playoffs
1992-93	84	12	25	5	14	27	1	26	52	6	284	369	58	5th,	Adams Div.	Out of Playoffs
1991-92	80	13	17	10	13	24	3	26	41	13	247	283	65	4th,	Adams Div.	Lost Div. Semi-Final
1990-91	80	18	16	6	13	22	5	31	38	11	238	276	73	4th,	Adams Div.	Lost Div. Semi-Final
1989-90	80	17	18	5	21	15	4	38	33	9	275	268	85	4th,	Adams Div.	Lost Div. Semi-Final
1988-89	80	21	17	2	16	21	3	37	38	5	299	290	79	4th,	Adams Div.	Lost Div. Semi-Final
1987-88	80	21	14	5	14	24	2	35	38	7	249	267	77	4th,	Adams Div.	Lost Div. Semi-Final
1986-87	80	26	9	5	17	21	2	43	30	7	287	270	93	1st,	Adams Div.	Lost Div. Semi-Final
1985-86	80	21	17	2	19	19	2	40	36	4	332	302	84	4th,	Adams Div.	Lost Div. Final
1984-85	80	17	18	5	13	23	4	30	41	9	268	318	69	5th,	Adams Div.	Out of Playoffs
1983-84	80	19	16	5	9	26	5	28	42	10	288	320	66	5th,	Adams Div.	Out of Playoffs
1982-83	80	13	22	5	6	32	2	19	54	7	261	403	45	5th,	Adams Div.	Out of Playoffs
1981-82	80	13	17	10	8	24	8	21	41	18	264	351	60	5th,	Adams Div.	Out of Playoffs
1980-81	80	14	17	9	7	24	9	21	41	18	292	372	60	4th,	Norris Div.	Out of Playoffs
1979-80	80	22	12	6	5	22	13	27	34	19	303	312	73	4th,	Norris Div.	Lost Prelim. Round

Schedule

Oct.	Sat.	7	NY Rangers		Wed.	10	at Calgary
	Wed.	11	Anaheim		Fri.	12	at Winnipeg
	Sat.	14	Chicago		Tues.	16	Vancouver
	Mon.	16	at NY Rangers		Wed.	17	at NY Islanders
	Fri.	20	Pittsburgh		Wed.	24	at Buffalo
	Sat.	21	at Florida		Thur.	25	Los Angeles
	Wed.	25	St. Louis		Sat.	27	New Jersey
	Fri.	27	Montreal		Tues.	30	at San Jose
	Sat.	28	at Boston		Wed.	31	at Los Angeles
Nov.	Thur.	2	Ottawa	Feb.	Fri.	2	at Anaheim
	Sat.	4	at Ottawa		Wed.	7	at Vancouver
	Sun.	5	at Philadelphia		Fri.	9	at Colorado
	Tues.	7	San Jose		Sun.	11	at Dallas*
	Sat.	11	NY Rangers		Wed.	14	Boston
	Tues.	14	at New Jersey		Sat.	17	Buffalo
	Wed.	15	Ottawa		Wed.	21	Montreal
	Sat.	18	Philadelphia*		Fri.	23	at Pittsburgh
	Mon.	20	at Montreal		Sun.	25	Dallas
	Wed.	22	Montreal		Wed.	28	Edmonton
	Fri.	24	at Toronto	Mar.	Fri.	1	Winnipeg
	Sat.	25	Washington		Sat.	2	Florida
	Wed.	29	at Tampa Bay		Wed.	6	Detroit
Dec.	Fri.	1	at Buffalo		Fri.	8	Toronto
	Sat.	2	Florida		Sat.	9	at St. Louis
	Wed.	6	NY Islanders		Wed.	13	Pittsburgh
	Sat.	9	at Pittsburgh		Sat.	16	Buffalo
	Sun.	10	at Chicago		Mon.	18	Tampa Bay
	Wed.	13	Tampa Bay		Wed.	20	at Montreal
	Fri.	15	Colorado		Fri.	22	at Ottawa
	Sat.	16	at NY Islanders		Sat.	23	at Washington
	Mon.	18	at Montreal		Mon.	25	at Philadelphia
	Wed.	20	Calgary		Wed.	27	Boston
	Fri.	22	at NY Rangers		Sat.	30	NY Islanders*
	Sat.	23	Philadelphia	Apr.	Mon.	1	at Florida
	Thur.	28	at Pittsburgh		Wed.	3	at Tampa Bay
	Sat.	30	at Washington		Thur.	4	at New Jersey
	Sun.	31	at Detroit		Sat.	6	New Jersey*
Jan.	Wed.	3	Washington		Mon.	8	Pittsburgh
	Fri.	5	Ottawa		Thur.	11	at Boston
	Sat.	6	at Boston		Sat.	13	Boston*
	Tues.	9	at Edmonton		Sun.	14	at Buffalo

* Denotes afternoon game.

Home Starting Times:
Weeknights . . . . 7:00 p.m.
Saturdays . . . . 7:00 p.m.
Matinees . . . . 1:30 p.m.

Franchise date: June 22, 1979

EASTERN CONFERENCE NHL

NORTHEAST DIVISION

17th NHL Season

Despite playing only 46 games, defenseman Adam Burt enjoyed his finest offensive season in 1994-95, collecting seven goals and 11 assists.

1995-96 Player Personnel

FORWARDS	HT	WT	S	Place of Birth	Date	1994-95 Club
BALL, Matt	6-0	219	R	Toronto, Ont.	1/29/76	Detroit (OHL)
BES, Jeff	6-0	190	L	Tillsonburg, Ont.	7/31/73	Kalamazoo
BUCKLEY, Tom	6-1	204	L	Buffalo, NY	5/26/76	Detroit (OHL)
CARSON, Jimmy	6-1	200	R	Southfield, MI	7/20/68	Hartford
CASSELS, Andrew	6-0	192	L	Bramalea, Ont.	7/23/69	Hartford
DANIELS, Jeff	6-1	200	L	Oshawa, Ont.	6/24/68	Florida-Detroit (IHL)
DANIELS, Scott	6-3	200	L	Prince Albert, Sask.	9/19/69	Springfield-Hartford
DOMENICHELLI, Hnat	6-0	173	L	Edmonton, Alta.	2/17/76	Kamloops
DRURY, Ted	6-0	185	L	Boston, MA	9/13/71	Hartford-Springfield
HARDING, Mike	6-4	225	R	Edsow, Alta.	2/24/71	N. Michigan
JANSSENS, Mark	6-3	216	L	Surrey, B.C.	5/19/68	Hartford
JUNKIN, Dale	5-11	196	L	Oshawa, Ont.	5/23/73	Springfield
KAPANEN, Sami	5-10	169	L	Vantaa, Finland	6/14/73	HIFK
KRON, Robert	5-10	180	L	Brno, Czech.	2/27/67	Hartford
MacNEIL, Ian	6-2	171	L	Halifax, N.S.	4/27/77	Oshawa
MARTINS, Steve	5-9	175	L	Gatineau, Que.	4/13/72	Harvard
NIKOLISHIN, Andrei	5-11	180	L	Vorkuta, USSR	3/25/73	Moscow D'amo-Hartford
NIMIGON, Steve	6-1	185	R	Oshawa, Ont.	4/4/76	Niagara Falls
O'NEILL, Jeff	6-1	176	R	Richmond Hill, Ont.	2/23/76	Guelph
PETROVICKY, Robert	5-11	172	L	Kosice, Czech.	10/26/73	Springfield-Hartford
RANHEIM, Paul	6-0	195	R	St. Louis, MO	1/25/66	Hartford
RICE, Steven	6-0	215	R	Kitchener, Ont.	5/26/71	Hartford
SANDERSON, Geoff	6-0	185	L	Hay River, N.W.T.	2/1/72	HPK-Hartford
SECORD, Brian	5-11	179	L	Ridgetown, Ont.	6/19/75	Belleville
SHANAHAN, Brendan	6-3	215	R	Mimico, Ont.	1/23/69	Dusseldorf-St. Louis
SMYTH, Kevin	6-2	217	L	Banff, Alta.	11/22/73	Springfield-Hartford
STORM, Jim	6-2	200	L	Milford, MI	2/5/71	Hartford-Springfield
TURCOTTE, Darren	6-0	178	L	Boston, MA	3/2/68	Hartford
WREN, Bob	5-10	185	L	Preston, Ont.	9/16/74	Springfield-Richmond

DEFENSEMEN	HT	WT	S	Place of Birth	Date	1994-95 Club
BURT, Adam	6-0	190	L	Detroit, MI	1/15/69	Hartford
DIDUCK, Gerald	6-2	207	R	Edmonton, Alta.	4/6/65	Vancouver-Chicago
FEATHERSTONE, Glen	6-4	215	L	Toronto, Ont.	7/8/68	NY Rangers-Hartford
FEDOTOV, Sergei	6-1	185	L	Moscow, USSR	1/24/77	Moscow D'amo
GLYNN, Brian	6-4	224	L	Iserlohn, West Germany	11/23/67	Hartford
GODYNYUK, Alexander	6-0	207	L	Kiev, Ukraine	1/27/70	Hartford
HAMILTON, Hugh	6-1	175	L	Saskatoon, Sask.	2/11/77	Spokane
KUCERA, Frantisek	6-2	205	R	Prague, Czech.	2/3/68	Sparta Praha-Hartford
MALIK, Marek	6-5	190	L	Ostrava, Czech.	6/24/75	Springfield-Hartford
McBAIN, Jason	6-2	178	L	Ilion, NY	4/12/74	Springfield
McCRIMMON, Brad	5-11	197	L	Dodsland, Sask.	3/29/59	Hartford
MUELLER, Brian	5-11	225	L	Liverpool, NY	6/2/72	Clarkson
PRATT, Nolan	6-2	195	L	Fort McMurray, Alta.	8/14/75	Portland (WHL)
RISODORE, Ryan	6-4	192	L	Hamilton, Ont.	4/4/76	Guelph
STEVENS, John	6-1	195	L	Campbellton, N.B.	5/4/66	Springfield
STEWART, Michael	6-2	210	L	Calgary, Alta.	5/30/72	Binghamton-Springfield
WESLEY, Glen	6-1	195	L	Red Deer, Alta.	10/2/68	Hartford

GOALTENDERS	HT	WT	C	Place of Birth	Date	1994-95 Club
BURKE, Sean	6-4	210	L	Windsor, Ont.	1/29/67	Hartford
LEGACE, Manny	5-9	162	L	Toronto, Ont.	2/4/73	Springfield
REESE, Jeff	5-9	175	L	Brantford, Ont.	3/24/66	Hartford

Retired Numbers

2	Rick Ley	1972-1981
9	Gordie Howe	1977-1980
19	John McKenzie	1976-1979

1994-95 Scoring

* – rookie

Regular Season

Pos	#	Player	Team	GP	G	A	Pts	+/–	PIM	PP	SH	GW	GT	S	%
C	21	Andrew Cassels	HFD	46	7	30	37	–3	18	1	0	1	0	74	9.5
C	89	Darren Turcotte	HFD	47	17	18	35	1	22	3	1	3	0	121	14.0
C	8	Geoff Sanderson	HFD	46	18	14	32	–10	24	4	0	4	0	170	10.6
R	12	Steven Rice	HFD	40	11	10	21	2	61	4	0	1	1	57	19.3
L	28	Paul Ranheim	HFD	47	6	14	20	–3	10	0	0	1	0	73	8.2
D	4	Frantisek Kucera	HFD	48	3	17	20	3	30	0	0	1	0	73	4.1
C	33	Jimmy Carson	HFD	38	9	10	19	5	29	4	0	3	0	58	15.5
R	18	Robert Kron	HFD	37	10	8	18	–3	10	3	1	1	0	88	11.4
R	11 *	Andrei Nikolishin	HFD	39	8	10	18	7	10	1	1	0	0	57	14.0
D	6	Adam Burt	HFD	46	7	11	18	0	65	3	0	1	0	73	9.6
D	20	Glen Wesley	HFD	48	2	14	16	–6	50	1	0	1	0	125	1.6
D	44	Chris Pronger	HFD	43	5	9	14	–12	54	3	0	1	0	94	5.3
L	26	Jocelyn Lemieux	HFD	41	6	5	11	–7	32	0	0	1	0	78	7.7
C	13	Ted Drury	HFD	34	3	6	9	–3	21	0	0	0	0	31	9.7
C	22	Mark Janssens	HFD	46	2	5	7	–8	93	0	0	0	0	33	6.1
D	7	Brian Glynn	HFD	43	1	6	7	–2	32	0	0	0	0	35	2.9
L	14 *	Kevin Smyth	HFD	16	1	5	6	–3	13	0	0	0	0	20	5.0
C	32	Igor Chibirev	HFD	8	3	1	4	1	0	0	0	0	0	9	33.3
R	27	Kelly Chase	HFD	28	0	4	4	1	141	0	0	0	0	15	0.0
D	36	Glen Featherstone	NYR	6	1	0	1	0	18	0	0	0	0	6	16.7
			HFD	13	1	1	2	–7	32	0	0	0	0	16	6.3
			TOTAL	19	2	1	3	–7	50	0	0	0	0	22	9.1
L	24	Jim Storm	HFD	6	0	3	3	2	0	0	0	0	0	3	0.0
L	17 *	Scott Daniels	HFD	12	0	2	2	1	55	0	0	0	0	7	0.0
D	23 *	Marek Malik	HFD	1	0	1	1	0	0	0	0	0	0	0	0.0
D	10	Brad McCrimmon	HFD	33	0	1	1	7	42	0	0	0	0	13	0.0
G	1	Sean Burke	HFD	42	0	1	1	0	8	0	0	0	0	0	0.0
C	39	Robert Petrovicky	HFD	2	0	0	0	0	0	0	0	0	0	1	0.0
G	35	Jeff Reese	HFD	11	0	0	0	0	0	0	0	0	0	0	0.0
R	52	Jim Sandlak	HFD	13	0	0	0	–10	0	0	0	0	0	13	0.0
D	5	Alexander Godynyuk	HFD	14	0	0	0	1	8	0	0	0	0	16	0.0

Goaltending

No.	Goaltender	GPI	Mins	Avg	W	L	T	EN	SO	GA	SA	S%
1	Sean Burke	42	2418	2.68	17	19	4	6	0	108	1233	.912
35	Jeff Reese	11	477	3.27	2	5	1	1	0	26	234	.889
	Totals	**48**	**2914**	**2.90**	**19**	**24**	**5**	**7**	**0**	**141**	**1474**	**.904**

One of the NHL's top set-up artists, Andrew Cassels led the Whalers in assists (30) and points (37) during the 1994-95 campaign.

General Managers' History

Jack Kelly, 1979-80 to 1980-81; Larry Pleau, 1981-82 to 1982-83; Emile Francis, 1983-84 to 1988-89; Ed Johnston, 1989-90 to 1991-92; Brian Burke, 1992-93; Paul Holmgren, 1993-94; Jim Rutherford, 1994-95 to date.

Coaching History

Don Blackburn, 1979-80; Don Blackburn and Larry Pleau, 1980-81; Larry Pleau, 1981-82; Larry Kish, Larry Pleau and John Cuniff, 1982- 83; Jack "Tex" Evans, 1983-84 to 1986-87; Jack "Tex" Evans and Larry Pleau, 1987-88; Larry Pleau, 1988-89; Rick Ley, 1989-90 to 1990-91; Jim Roberts, 1991-92; Paul Holmgren, 1992-93; Paul Holmgren and Pierre Maguire, 1993-94; Paul Holmgren, 1994-95 to date.

Captains' History

Rick Ley, 1979-80; Rick Ley and Mike Rogers, 1980-81; Dave Keon, 1981-82; Russ Anderson, 1982-83; Mark Johnson, 1983-84; Mark Johnson and Ron Francis, 1984-85; Ron Francis, 1985-86 to 1990-91; Randy Ladouceur, 1991-92; Pat Verbeek, 1992-93 to 1994-95.

Club Records

Team

(Figures in brackets for season records are games played; records for fewest points, wins, ties, losses, goals, goals against are for 70 or more games)

Most Points	93	1986-87 (80)
Most Wins	43	1986-87 (80)
Most Ties	19	1979-80 (80)
Most Losses	54	1982-83 (80)
Most Goals	332	1985-86 (80)
Most Goals Against	403	1982-83 (80)
Fewest Points	45	1982-83 (80)
Fewest Wins	19	1982-83 (80)
Fewest Ties	4	1985-86 (80)
Fewest Losses	30	1986-87 (80)
Fewest Goals	227	1993-94 (84)
Fewest Goals Against	267	1987-88 (80)

Longest Winning Streak
Over-all .... 7 Mar. 16-29/85
Home .... 5 Mar. 17-29/85
Away .... 6 Nov. 10-
Dec. 7/90

Longest Undefeated Streak
Over-all .... 10 Jan. 20-
Feb. 10/82
(6 wins, 4 ties)
Home .... 7 Mar. 15-
Apr. 5/86
(5 wins, 2 ties)
Away .... 6 Jan. 23-Feb. 10/82
(3 wins, 3 ties);
Nov. 30-
Dec. 26/89
(5 wins, 1 tie);
Nov. 10-
Dec. 7/90
(6 wins)

Longest Losing Streak
Over-all .... 9 Feb. 19/83-
Mar. 8/83
Home .... 6 Feb. 19/83-
Mar. 12/83;
Feb. 10-
Mar. 3/85
Away .... 13 Dec. 18/82-
Feb. 5/83

Longest Winless Streak
Over-all .... 14 Jan. 4/92-
Feb. 9/92
(8 losses, 6 ties)
Home .... 13 Jan. 15-
Mar. 10/85
(11 losses, 2 ties)
Away .... 15 Nov. 11/79-
Jan. 9/80
(11 losses, 4 ties)
Most Shutouts, Season 5 1986-87 (80)
Most PIM, Season 2,354 1992-93 (84)
Most Goals, Game .... 11 Feb. 12/84
(Edm. 0 at Hfd. 11)
Oct. 19/85
(Mtl. 6 at Hfd. 11)
Jan. 17/86
(Que. 6 at Hfd. 11)
Mar. 15/86
(Chi. 4 at Hfd. 11)

Individual

Most Seasons .... 10 Ron Francis
Most Games .... 714 Ron Francis
Most Goals, Career ...... 264 Ron Francis
Most Assists, Career .... 557 Ron Francis
Most Points, Career ...... 821 Ron Francis
(264 goals, 557 assists)
Most PIM, Career .... 1,368 Torrie Robertson
Most Shutouts, Career .... 13 Mike Liut
Longest Consecutive
Games Streak .... 419 Dave Tippett
(Mar. 3/84-Oct. 7/89)
Most Goals, Season .... 56 Blaine Stoughton
(1979-80)
Most Assists, Season .... 69 Ron Francis
(1989-90)
Most Points, Season .... 105 Mike Rogers
(1979-80)
(44 goals, 61 assists)
(1980-81)
(40 goals, 65 assists)
Most PIM, Season .... 358 Torrie Robertson
(1985-86)
Most Points, Defenseman
Season .... 69 Dave Babych
(1985-86)
(14 goals, 55 assists)

Most Points, Center,
Season .... 105 Mike Rogers
(1979-80)
(44 goals, 61 assists)
Mike Rogers
(1980-81)
(40 goals, 65 assists)
Most Points, Right Wing,
Season .... 100 Blaine Stoughton
(1979-80)
(56 goals, 44 assists)
Most Points, Left Wing,
Season .... 89 Geoff Sanderson
(1992-93)
(46 goals, 43 assists)
Most Points, Rookie,
Season .... 72 Sylvain Turgeon
(1983-84)
(40 goals, 32 assists)
Most Shutouts, Season .... 4 Mike Liut
(1986-87)
Peter Sidorkiewicz
(1988-89)
Most Goals, Game .... 4 Jordy Douglas
(Feb. 3/80)
Ron Francis
(Feb. 12/84)
Most Assists, Game .... 6 Ron Francis
(Mar. 5/87)
Most Points, Game............ 6 Paul Lawless
(Jan. 4/87)
Ron Francis
(Mar. 5/87,
Oct. 8/89)

All-time Record vs. Other Clubs

Regular Season

		At Home							On Road							Total				
	GP	W	L	T	GF	GA	PTS	GP	W	L	T	GF	GA	PTS	GP	W	L	T	GF	GA	PTS
Anaheim	1	0	1	0	2	3	0	1	0	1	0	3	6	0	2	0	2	0	5	9	0
Boston	55	24	24	7	193	199	55	57	12	40	5	150	232	29	112	36	64	12	343	431	84
Buffalo	58	20	29	9	173	184	49	56	19	30	7	182	236	45	114	39	59	16	355	420	94
Calgary	22	7	12	3	75	90	17	22	4	17	1	75	118	9	44	11	29	4	150	208	26
Chicago	23	10	11	2	80	80	22	22	6	13	3	64	99	15	45	16	24	5	144	179	37
Dallas	23	9	11	3	84	87	21	22	9	12	1	72	93	19	45	18	23	4	156	180	40
Detroit	22	14	7	1	85	60	29	23	7	10	6	68	88	20	45	21	17	7	153	148	49
Edmonton	22	9	9	4	94	83	22	23	3	17	3	67	102	9	45	12	26	7	161	185	31
Florida	4	1	3	0	9	11	2	4	2	1	1	11	10	5	8	3	4	1	20	21	7
Los Angeles	23	12	8	3	90	94	27	22	6	13	3	87	100	15	45	18	21	6	177	194	42
Montreal	57	20	29	8	176	214	48	55	11	37	7	164	253	29	112	31	66	15	340	467	77
New Jersey	25	12	7	6	92	77	30	27	10	14	3	100	103	23	52	22	21	9	192	180	53
NY Islanders	27	12	11	4	101	102	28	25	7	15	3	64	96	17	52	19	26	7	165	198	45
NY Rangers	25	13	9	3	96	91	29	26	8	16	2	75	113	18	51	21	25	5	171	204	47
Ottawa	7	7	0	0	32	14	14	9	7	1	1	32	17	15	16	14	1	1	64	31	29
Philadelphia	26	10	12	4	105	110	24	25	7	17	1	73	104	15	51	17	29	5	178	214	39
Pittsburgh	27	14	12	1	119	107	29	26	10	13	3	110	122	23	53	24	25	4	229	229	52
Quebec	55	23	21	11	189	193	57	57	16	34	7	173	246	39	112	39	55	18	362	439	96
St. Louis	24	9	13	2	74	76	20	23	8	13	2	77	91	18	47	17	26	4	151	167	38
San Jose	4	2	2	0	13	10	4	3	1	2	0	14	19	2	7	3	4	0	27	29	6
Tampa Bay	5	4	1	0	16	11	8	5	1	4	0	10	17	2	10	5	5	0	26	28	10
Toronto	22	12	6	4	102	74	28	22	12	8	2	90	82	26	44	24	14	6	192	156	54
Vancouver	22	9	9	4	73	79	22	23	8	9	6	66	82	22	45	17	18	10	139	161	44
Washington	27	9	14	4	81	102	22	26	10	15	1	80	93	21	53	19	29	5	161	195	43
Winnipeg	22	11	6	5	92	71	27	24	11	12	1	88	86	23	46	22	18	6	180	157	50
Totals	**628**	**273**	**267**	**88**	**2246**	**2222**	**634**	**628**	**195**	**364**	**69**	**1995**	**2608**	**459**	**1256**	**468**	**631**	**157**	**4241**	**4830**	**1093**

Calgary totals include Atlanta, 1979-80. Dallas totals include Minnesota, 1979-80 to 1992-93.
New Jersey totals include Colorado, 1979-80 to 1981-82.

Playoffs

	Series	W	L	GP	W	L	T	GF	GA	Last Mtg.	Round	Result
Boston	2	0	2	13	5	8	0	38	47	1991	DSF	L 2-4
Montreal	5	0	5	27	8	19	0	70	96	1992	DSF	L 3-4
Quebec	2	1	1	9	5	4	0	35	34	1987	DSF	L 2-4
Totals	**9**	**1**	**8**	**49**	**18**	**31**	**0**	**143**	**177**			

Playoff Results 1995-91

Year	Round	Opponent	Result	GF	GA
1992	DSF	Montreal	L 3-4	18	21
1991	DSF	Boston	L 2-4	17	24

Abbreviations: Round: F – Final;
CF – conference final; **CQF** – conference quarter-final;
CSF – conference semi-final; **DF** – division final;
DSF – division semi-final; **SF** – semi-final;
QF – quarter-final; **PR** – preliminary round.

1994-95 Results

Jan.	21	Washington	1-1	12		Florida	1-4
	22	New Jersey	2-2	14		NY Islanders	6-4
	25	Ottawa	4-1	16	at	New Jersey	2-2
	26	at Philadelphia	2-3	20		Washington	0-5
	28	Florida	1-2	22		Philadelphia	4-3
Feb.	1	at Ottawa	2-1	25		NY Islanders	5-1
	4	at Boston	4-5	26	at	Washington	4-3
	5	at Quebec	1-3	29	at	Florida	4-4
	8	Quebec	2-3	31	at	Tampa Bay	0-2
	10	at Tampa Bay	3-4	**Apr.** 4	at	Buffalo	3-6
	11	at Florida	3-4	5	at	Pittsburgh	8-4
	13	at Montreal	2-2	8		Buffalo	4-2
	15	Montreal	4-1	9		Tampa Bay	0-3
	16	at Pittsburgh	2-5	12		Ottawa	4-2
	18	Pittsburgh	4-2	14		Montreal	4-3
	22	Boston	3-2	16	at	New Jersey	2-3
	24	at NY Rangers	2-1	18	at	Boston	2-1
	25	Buffalo	1-3	20	at	NY Rangers	3-6
	28	at Ottawa	6-3	21	at	Washington	3-6
Mar.	1	NY Rangers	2-5	23		Pittsburgh	2-4
	4	Tampa Bay	3-2	24	at	Montreal	4-3
	5	Boston	2-5	26	at	Boston	0-4
	7	at NY Islanders	1-3	28		Philadelphia	3-4
	9	Quebec	2-1	**May** 3	at	Quebec	1-4

Entry Draft
Selections 1995-81

1995
Pick
13	J-Sebastien Giguere
35	Sergei Fedotov
85	Ian MacNeil
87	Sami Kapanen
113	Hugh Hamilton
165	Byron Ritchie
191	Milan Kostolny
217	Mike Rucinski

1994
Pick
5	Jeff O'Neill
83	Hnat Domenichelli
109	Ryan Risidore
187	Tom Buckley
213	Ashlin Halfnight
230	Matt Ball
239	Brian Regan
265	Steve Nimigon

1993
Pick
2	Chris Pronger
72	Marek Malik
84	Trevor Roenick
115	Nolan Pratt
188	Emmanuel Legace
214	Dmitri Gorenko
240	Wes Swinson
266	Igor Chibirev

1992
Pick
9	Robert Petrovicky
47	Andrei Nikolishin
57	Jan Vopat
79	Kevin Smyth
81	Jason McBain
143	Jarret Reid
153	Ken Belanger
177	Konstantin Korotkov
201	Greg Zwakman
225	Steven Halko
249	Joacim Esbjors

1991
Pick
9	Patrick Poulin
31	Martin Hamrlik
53	Todd Hall
59	Mikael Nylander
75	Jim Storm
119	Mike Harding
141	Brian Mueller
163	Steve Yule
185	Chris Belanger
207	Jason Currie
229	Mike Santonelli
251	Rob Peters

1990
Pick
15	Mark Greig
36	Geoff Sanderson
57	Mike Lenarduzzi
78	Chris Bright
120	Cory Keenan
141	Jergus Baca
162	Martin D'Orsonnens
183	Corey Osmak
204	Espen Knutsen
225	Tommie Eriksen
246	Denis Chalifoux

1989
Pick
10	Robert Holik
52	Blair Atcheynum
73	Jim McKenzie
94	James Black
115	Jerome Bechard
136	Scott Daniels
157	Raymond Saumier
178	Michel Picard
199	Trevor Buchanan
220	John Battice
241	Peter Kasowski

1988
Pick
11	Chris Govedaris
32	Barry Richter
74	Dean Dyer
95	Scott Morrow
116	Corey Beaulieu
137	Kerry Russell
158	Jim Burke
179	Mark Hirth
200	Wayde Bucsis
221	Rob White
242	Dan Slatalla

1987
Pick
18	Jody Hull
39	Adam Burt
81	Terry Yake
102	Marc Rousseau
123	Jeff St. Cyr
144	Greg Wolf
165	John Moore
186	Joe Day
228	Kevin Sullivan
249	Steve Laurin

1986
Pick
11	Scott Young
32	Marc Laforge
74	Brian Chapman
95	Bill Horn
116	Joe Quinn
137	Steve Torrel
158	Ron Hoover
179	Robert Glasgow
200	Sean Evoy
221	Cal Brown
242	Brian Verbeek

1985
Pick
5	Dana Murzyn
26	Kay Whitmore
68	Gary Callaghan
110	Shane Churla
131	Chris Brant
152	Brian Puhalsky
173	Greg Dornbach
194	Paul Tory
215	Jerry Pawlowski
236	Bruce Hill

1984
Pick
11	Sylvain Cote
110	Mike Millar
131	Mike Vellucci
173	John Devereaux
193	Brent Regan
214	Jim Culhane
234	Pete Abric

1983
Pick
2	Sylvain Turgeon
20	David Jensen
23	Ville Siren
61	Leif Carlsson
64	Dave MacLean
72	Ron Chyzowski
104	Brian Johnson
124	Joe Reekie
143	Chris Duperron
144	James Falle
164	Bill Fordy
193	Reine Karlsson
204	Allan Acton
224	Darcy Kaminski

1982
Pick
14	Paul Lawless
35	Mark Paterson
56	Kevin Dineen
67	Ulf Samuelsson
88	Ray Ferraro
109	Randy Gilhen
130	Jim Johannson
151	Mickey Kramptoich
172	Kevin Skilliter
214	Martin Linse
235	Randy Cameron

1981
Pick
4	Ron Francis
61	Paul MacDermid
67	Michael Hoffman
93	Bill Maguire
103	Dan Bourbonnais
130	John Mokosak
151	Denis Dore
172	Jeff Poeschl
193	Larry Power

Club Directory

Hartford Whalers
242 Trumbull Street
Eighth Floor
Hartford, Connecticut 06103
Phone 860/728-3366
GM FAX 860/493-2423
FAX 860/522-7707
Capacity: 15,635

Ownership
Chief Executive Officer/Governor	Peter Karmanos Jr.
General Partner	Thomas Thewes
Chief Operating Officer/President/General Manager	Jim Rutherford

Hockey Operations
Vice President of Hockey Operations	Terry McDonnell
Head Coach	Paul Holmgren
Assistant Coach	Paul Maurice, Ted Sator
Strength and Conditioning Instructor	Jim McCrossin
Goaltending Consultant	Steve Weeks
Director of Pro Scouting	Kevin Maxwell
Director of Amateur Scouting	Sheldon Ferguson
Scouting Staff	Claude Larose, Willy Langer, Willy Lindstrom, Bruce Haralson, Ken Schinkel, Tony MacDonald, Larry Johnston, Yves Sansfacon, Bill Terry
Medical Trainer	Bud Gouveia
Equipment Managers	Skip Cunningham, Wally Tatimor
Assistant Equipment Managers	Bob Gorman, Rick Szuber
Executive Secretary, Hockey Operations	Cathy Merrick
Executive Secretary, Hockey Operations	Anne Sullivan

Administration
Senior Vice President of Marketing and Communications	Russ Gregory
Vice President of Finance and Administration	Mike Amendola
Vice President of Marketing and Sales	Rick Francis
Director of Advertising Sales	Kevin Bauer
Director of Sponsorship Sales	Bill McMinn
Director of Corporate Sales	Jim Jacen
Director of Communications/Team Services	John Forslund
Media Relations Manager	Chris Brown
Director of Community Relations	Mary Lynn Gorman
Director of Publications/Statistics	Frank Polnaszek
Consultant on Business Affairs	Lou Beer
Business Development Manager	Paula Fischer
Director of Amateur Hockey Development	Mike Veisor
Director of Ticket Operations	Jim Baldwin
Ticket Office Supervisors	Mike Barnes, Chris O'Connor
Ticket Sales Manager	Bryan Dooley
Senior Account Executive	David Keith

General Information
Radio Play-by-Play/Director of Broadcasting	Chuck Kaiton
Radio Color	Marty Howe
TV/Cable Play-by-Play	John Forslund
TV/Cable Commentator	Daryl Reaugh
Cable TV Outlet	SportsChannel - New England
Radio Network Flagship Station	WTIC-AM (1080)
Home Ice	Hartford Civic Center Veterans Memorial Coliseum
Dimensions of Rink	200 feet by 85 feet

General Manager

RUTHERFORD, JIM
General Manager, Hartford Whalers. Born in Beeton, Ont., February 17, 1949.

Years of work by Jim Rutherford and the KTR Limited Partnership were rewarded on June 28, 1994 when the Detroit, Michigan group was approved by the National Hockey League Board of Governors as the owners of the Hartford Whalers. KTR completed a $50 million deal with the Connecticut Development Authority to keep the only major professional sports team in the state.

Rutherford has extensive experience in youth hockey and junior programs, serving as director of hockey operations for Compuware Sports Corporation. As a former player, coach, and general manager, he earned much respect in the hockey world for his ability to develop players and produce winning programs.

As KTR Limited Partnership's point man, Rutherford led efforts to land an NHL expansion franchise. Based on Rutherford's experience in the sport and Compuware's success at the junior hockey level, the CDA and the State of Connecticut elected to sell the Whalers to KTR Limited Partnership.

Rutherford, 46, began his professional goaltending career in 1969, as a first-round selection of the Detroit Red Wings. He collected 14 career shutouts in his 13 seasons in the NHL for Pittsburgh, Toronto, Los Angeles and Detroit, serving as the Red Wings' player representative for five seasons. Rutherford also played for Team Canada in the World Championships in Vienna in 1977 and Moscow in 1979.

After his playing days with the Red Wings, Rutherford joined Compuware and guided Compuware Sports Corporation's purchase of the Windsor Spitfires of the Ontario Hockey League in April, 1984. Rutherford served as g.m. of the Spitfires from that season until 1987-88, and spent the 1986-87 season behind the bench as head coach. He was instrumental in guiding the Spitfires to the 1988 Memorial Cup finals.

On December 11, 1989, Rutherford brought the first American-based OHL franchise to Detroit, as the Ambassadors donned Compuware's orange and brown colors. Playing as the Jr. Red Wings until the spring of 1995, the OHL franchise is now known as the Detroit Jr. Whalers. In the Hartford area, Rutherford has created the CT Midget Whalers and also is involved with the Springfield Pics (now known as the Junior Whalers) of the Eastern Junior Hockey League.

With Detroit, Rutherford took over as coach for the 1991-92 OHL season, leading the Ambassadors to their first-ever playoff berth. As director of hockey operations, he then put together the 1993-94 Jr. Red Wings that won the Emms Division championship. Rutherford won the 1993 Executive of the Year Award in both the OHL and the Canadian Hockey League. He again won the OHL Executive of the Year Award in 1994.

Coach

HOLMGREN, PAUL
Coach, Hartford Whalers. Born in St. Paul, MN, December 2, 1955.

Paul Holmgren was reappointed coach of the Hartford Whalers, succeeding Pierre McGuire, on June 28, 1994. A sixth round draft selection of the Philadelphia Flyers in 1975, Holmgren spent nine years with the team before finishing his career with the Minnesota North Stars in 1985. The next season, he was named as assistant to Mike Keenan, spending three years in that role. In 1988, Holmgren became the first former-Flyer to be named head coach, serving in that capacity for four seasons. In Philadelphia, Holmgren compiled a 107-126-31 record before being replaced by Bill Dineen on December 4, 1991. He resigned as Whalers' coach on November 16, 1993 to concentrate on his duties as the club's general manager.

Coaching Record

Season	Team	Games	Regular Season W	L	T	%	Playoffs Games	W	L	%
1988-89	Philadelphia (NHL)	80	36	36	8	.500	19	10	9	.526
1989-90	Philadelphia (NHL)	80	30	39	11	.444	....	....	....	....
1990-91	Philadelphia (NHL)	80	33	37	10	.475	....	....	....	....
1991-92	Philadelphia (NHL)	24	8	14	2	.375	....	....	....	....
1992-93	Hartford (NHL)	84	26	52	6	.345	....	....	....	....
1993-94	Hartford (NHL)	17	4	11	2	.294	....	....	....	....
1994-95	Hartford (NHL)	48	19	24	5	.448	....	....	....	....
	NHL Totals	413	156	213	44	.431	19	10	9	.526

Los Angeles Kings

1994-95 Results: 16W-23L-9T 41PTS. Fourth, Pacific Division

Schedule

Oct.	Sat.	7	Colorado	Mon.	8	at Dallas
	Tues.	10	Chicago	Wed.	10	at Toronto
	Thur.	12	Vancouver	Fri.	12	at Detroit
	Sun.	15	at Vancouver	Sun.	14	at Chicago
	Wed.	18	Philadelphia	Tues.	16	Calgary
	Fri.	20	at Washington	Mon.	22	at NY Rangers
	Sat.	21	at Pittsburgh	Tues.	23	at New Jersey
	Mon.	23	at Montreal	Thur.	25	at Hartford
	Thur.	26	at Ottawa	Sat.	27	Anaheim*
	Sat.	28	at Toronto	Wed.	31	Hartford
	Tues.	31	Calgary	**Feb.** Thur.	1	at San Jose
Nov.	Thur.	2	NY Rangers	Sat.	3	at Calgary
	Sat.	4	New Jersey	Tues.	6	Chicago
	Tues.	7	at St. Louis	Thur.	8	Toronto
	Wed.	8	at Dallas	Sat.	10	San Jose*
	Sat.	11	Pittsburgh	Tues.	13	at Detroit
	Mon.	13	at Anaheim	Wed.	14	at Buffalo
	Tues.	14	Detroit	Sat.	17	Anaheim
	Thur.	16	NY Islanders	Mon.	19	Boston*
	Sat.	18	Florida	Wed.	21	at Edmonton
	Tues.	21	at Philadelphia	Fri.	23	at Colorado
	Wed.	22	at NY Islanders	Sat.	24	at St. Louis
	Fri.	24	at Boston*	Mon.	26	at Winnipeg
	Sun.	26	at Florida	Wed.	28	Tampa Bay
	Mon.	27	at Tampa Bay	**Mar.** Sat.	2	Montreal
	Thur.	30	Washington	Wed.	6	Edmonton
Dec.	Sat.	2	Dallas	Fri.	8	at Chicago
	Wed.	6	Winnipeg	Sun.	10	at Anaheim
	Sat.	9	St. Louis	Wed.	13	Buffalo
	Mon.	11	at Calgary	Sat.	16	Edmonton
	Wed.	13	Ottawa	Mon.	18	St. Louis
	Sat.	16	Toronto	Wed.	20	Colorado
	Wed.	20	Vancouver	Sat.	23	Dallas
	Fri.	22	at San Jose	Mon.	25	at Vancouver
	Sat.	23	Colorado	Wed.	27	at Edmonton
	Wed.	27	Anaheim	Fri.	29	at Calgary
	Fri.	29	at Edmonton	**Apr.** Mon.	3	Detroit
	Sun.	31	at Anaheim*	Sat.	6	Vancouver
Jan.	Wed.	3	Winnipeg	Wed.	10	San Jose
	Fri.	5	at San Jose	Fri.	12	at Winnipeg
	Sat.	6	San Jose	Sun.	14	at Colorado*

* Denotes afternoon game.

Home Starting Times:

Weeknights and Saturdays	7:30 p.m.
Matinees	1:00 p.m.
Except Sat. Jan. 27	12:00 p.m.
Sat. Feb. 10	12:00 p.m.

Franchise date: June 5, 1967

29th NHL Season

PACIFIC DIVISION

The play of Kelly Hrudey was a highlight of the Kings' 1994-95 season. The veteran netminder won 14 games and compiled a GAA of 3.14.

Year-by-Year Record

Season	GP	Home W	L	T	Road W	L	T	Overall W	L	T	GF	GA	Pts.	Finished		Playoff Result
1994-95	48	7	11	6	9	12	3	16	23	9	142	174	41	4th,	Pacific Div.	Out of Playoffs
1993-94	84	18	19	5	9	26	7	27	45	12	294	322	66	5th,	Pacific Div.	Out of Playoffs
1992-93	84	22	15	5	17	20	5	39	35	10	338	340	88	3rd,	Smythe Div.	Lost Final
1991-92	80	20	11	9	15	20	5	35	31	14	287	296	84	2nd,	Smythe Div.	Lost Div. Semi-Final
1990-91	80	26	9	5	20	15	5	46	24	10	340	254	102	1st,	Smythe Div.	Lost Div. Final
1989-90	80	21	16	3	13	23	4	34	39	7	338	337	75	4th,	Smythe Div.	Lost Div. Final
1988-89	80	25	12	3	17	19	4	42	31	7	376	335	91	2nd,	Smythe Div.	Lost Div. Final
1987-88	80	19	18	3	11	24	5	30	42	8	318	359	68	4th,	Smythe Div.	Lost Div. Semi-Final
1986-87	80	20	17	3	11	24	5	31	41	8	318	341	70	4th,	Smythe Div.	Lost Div. Semi-Final
1985-86	80	9	27	4	14	22	4	23	49	8	284	389	54	5th,	Smythe Div.	Out of Playoffs
1984-85	80	20	14	6	14	18	8	34	32	14	339	326	82	4th,	Smythe Div.	Lost Div. Semi-Final
1983-84	80	13	19	8	10	25	5	23	44	13	309	376	59	5th,	Smythe Div.	Out of Playoffs
1982-83	80	20	13	7	7	28	5	27	41	12	308	365	66	5th,	Smythe Div.	Out of Playoffs
1981-82	80	19	15	6	5	26	9	24	41	15	314	369	63	4th,	Smythe Div.	Lost Div. Final
1980-81	80	22	11	7	21	13	6	43	24	13	337	290	99	2nd,	Norris Div.	Lost Prelim. Round
1979-80	80	18	13	9	12	23	5	30	36	14	290	313	74	2nd,	Norris Div.	Lost Prelim. Round
1978-79	80	20	13	7	14	21	5	34	34	12	292	286	80	3rd,	Norris Div.	Lost Prelim. Round
1977-78	80	18	16	6	13	18	9	31	34	15	243	245	77	3rd,	Norris Div.	Lost Prelim. Round
1976-77	80	20	13	7	14	18	8	34	31	15	271	241	83	2nd,	Norris Div.	Lost Quarter-Final
1975-76	80	22	13	5	16	20	4	38	33	9	263	265	85	2nd,	Norris Div.	Lost Quarter-Final
1974-75	80	22	7	11	20	10	10	42	17	21	269	185	105	2nd,	Norris Div.	Lost Prelim. Round
1973-74	78	22	13	4	11	20	8	33	33	12	233	231	78	3rd,	West Div.	Lost Quarter-Final
1972-73	78	21	11	7	10	25	4	31	36	11	232	245	73	6th,	West Div.	Out of Playoffs
1971-72	78	14	23	2	6	26	7	20	49	9	206	305	49	7th,	West Div.	Out of Playoffs
1970-71	78	17	14	8	8	26	5	25	40	13	239	303	63	5th,	West Div.	Out of Playoffs
1969-70	76	12	22	4	2	30	6	14	52	10	168	290	38	6th,	West Div.	Out of Playoffs
1968-69	76	19	14	5	5	28	5	24	42	10	185	260	58	4th,	West Div.	Lost Semi-Final
1967-68	74	20	13	4	11	20	6	31	33	10	200	224	72	2nd,	West Div.	Lost Quarter-Final

1995-96 Player Personnel

FORWARDS	HT	WT	S	Place of Birth	Date	1994-95 Club
BOBACK, Michael	5-11	185	R	Mt. Clemens, MI	8/13/70	Portland (AHL)
BROWN, Kevin	6-1	212	R	Birmingham, England	5/11/74	Phoenix-Los Angeles
BYLSMA, Dan	6-2	215	L	Grand Rapids, MI	9/19/70	Phoenix
CONACHER, Pat	5-8	190	L	Edmonton, Alta.	5/1/59	Los Angeles
DRUCE, John	6-2	195	R	Peterborough, Ont.	2/23/66	Los Angeles
GRANATO, Tony	5-10	185	R	Downers Grove, IL	7/25/64	Los Angeles
GRETZKY, Wayne	6-0	180	L	Brantford, Ont.	1/26/61	Los Angeles
JOHNSON, Matt	6-5	230	L	Welland, Ont.	11/23/75	Peterborough-Los Angeles
KHRISTICH, Dimitri	6-2	195	R	Kiev, USSR	7/23/69	Washington
KURRI, Jari	6-1	195	R	Helsinki, Finland	5/18/60	Jokerit-Los Angeles
LACROIX, Eric	6-1	205	L	Montreal, Que.	7/15/71	St. John's-Phoenix-Los Angeles
LANG, Robert	6-2	189	R	Teplice, Czech.	12/19/70	Litvinov-Los Angeles
MacLEAN, Donald	6-2	174	L	Sydney, N.S.	1/14/77	Beauport
MORGAN, Jason	6-1	190	L	St. John's, Nfld.	10/9/76	Kitchener-Kingston
PERREAULT, Yanic	5-11	182	L	Sherbrooke, Que.	4/4/71	Phoenix-Los Angeles
POTOMSKI, Barry	6-2	215	L	Windsor, Ont.	11/24/72	Phoenix
REDMOND, Keith	6-3	208	L	Richmond Hill, Ont.	10/25/72	Phoenix
ROSA, Pavel	5-11	178	R	Most, Czech.	6/7/77	Litvinov
RYDMARK, Daniel	5-10	180	L	Vasteras, Sweden	2/23/70	Malmo
SHEVALIER, Jeff	5-11	185	L	Mississauga, Ont.	3/14/74	Phoenix-Los Angeles
SHUCHUK, Gary	5-11	190	R	Edmonton, Alta.	2/17/67	Los Angeles-Phoenix
SOULLIERE, Stephane	5-11	180	L	Greenfield Park, Que.	5/30/75	Oshawa-Sarnia-Guelph
TOCCHET, Rick	6-0	205	R	Scarborough, Ont.	4/9/64	Los Angeles
TODD, Kevin	5-10	180	L	Winnipeg, Man.	5/4/68	Los Angeles
TSYPLAKOV, Vladimir	6-2	194	L	Inta, USSR	4/18/69	Fort Wayne
VACHON, Nick	5-10	180	L	Montreal, Que.	7/20/72	Phoenix
YACHMENEV, Vitali	5-9	180	L	Chelyabinsk, USSR	1/8/75	North Bay-Phoenix

DEFENSEMEN						
BATYRSHIN, Ruslan	6-1	180	L	Moscow, USSR	2/19/75	Moscow D'amo
BERG, Aki-Petteri	6-3	200	L	Turku, Finland	7/28/77	TPS-Kiekko-67
BLAKE, Rob	6-3	215	R	Simcoe, Ont.	12/10/69	Los Angeles
BLOMSTEN, Arto	6-3	210	L	Vaasa, Finland	3/16/65	Springfield-Wpg-L.A.-Phoenix
BOUCHER, Philippe	6-2	189	R	St. Apollinaire, Que.	3/24/73	Rochester-Buffalo-Los Angeles
COWIE, Rob	6-0	195	L	Toronto, Ont.	11/3/67	Phoenix-Los Angeles
HOCKING, Justin	6-4	205	R	Stettler, Alta.	1/9/74	Syr-Port (AHL)-Knox-Phx
LAROSE, Benoit	6-0	200	L	Ottawa, Ont.	5/31/73	V'ville-Sher-Wichita-Tol
McSORLEY, Marty	6-1	225	R	Hamilton, Ont.	5/18/63	Los Angeles
O'DONNELL, Sean	6-2	224	L	Ottawa, Ont.	10/13/71	Phoenix-Los Angeles
PETIT, Michel	6-1	205	R	St. Malo, Que.	2/12/64	Los Angeles
SNELL, Chris	5-11	200	L	Regina, Sask.	5/12/71	Phoenix-Los Angeles
SYDOR, Darryl	6-0	205	L	Edmonton, Alta.	5/13/72	Los Angeles
TSYGUROV, Denis	6-3	198	L	Chelyabinsk, USSR	2/26/71	Togliatti-Buffalo-Los Angeles
VOPAT, Jan	6-0	198	L	Most, Czech.	3/22/73	Litvinov

GOALTENDERS	HT	WT	C	Place of Birth	Date	1994-95 Club
BEAUBIEN, Frederick	6-1	204	L	Lauzon, Que.	4/1/75	St-Hyacinthe
DAFOE, Byron	5-11	175	L	Sussex, England	2/25/71	Phoenix-Wsh-Portland (AHL)
HRUDEY, Kelly	5-10	189	L	Edmonton, Alta.	1/13/61	Los Angeles
STORR, Jamie	6-1	192	L	Brampton, Ont.	12/28/75	Owen Sound-L.A.-Windsor

Although he was plagued by injury through much of the 1994-95 season, Rob Blake still led all Kings defensemen with four powerplay goals.

1994-95 Scoring

* – rookie

Regular Season

Pos	#	Player	Team	GP	G	A	Pts	+/−	PIM	PP	SH	GW	GT	S	%
C	99	Wayne Gretzky	L.A.	48	11	37	48	−20	6	3	0	1	0	142	7.7
R	22	Rick Tocchet	L.A.	36	18	17	35	−8	70	7	1	3	0	95	18.9
C	7	Dan Quinn	L.A.	44	14	17	31	−3	32	2	0	4	3	78	17.9
L	17	Jari Kurri	L.A.	38	10	19	29	−17	24	2	0	1	0	84	11.9
L	21	Tony Granato	L.A.	33	13	11	24	9	68	2	0	3	0	106	12.3
D	25	Darryl Sydor	L.A.	48	4	19	23	−2	36	3	0	0	1	96	4.2
D	33	Marty McSorley	L.A.	41	3	18	21	−14	83	1	0	1	1	75	4.0
R	19	John Druce	L.A.	43	15	5	20	−3	20	3	0	1	0	75	20.0
L	44	Randy Burridge	WSH	2	0	0	0	0	2	0	0	0	0	2	0.0
			L.A.	38	4	15	19	−4	8	2	0	0	0	50	8.0
			TOTAL	40	4	15	19	−4	10	2	0	0	0	52	7.7
D	24	Michel Petit	L.A.	40	5	12	17	4	84	2	0	0	0	70	7.1
L	28	* Eric Lacroix	L.A.	45	9	7	16	2	54	2	1	1	0	64	14.1
L	15	Pat Conacher	L.A.	48	7	9	16	−9	12	0	1	0	0	64	10.9
C	13	Robert Lang	L.A.	36	4	8	12	−7	4	0	0	0	0	38	10.5
D	4	Rob Blake	L.A.	24	4	7	11	−16	38	4	0	1	0	76	5.3
C	12	Kevin Todd	L.A.	33	3	8	11	−5	12	0	0	1	0	34	8.8
L	14	Gary Shuchuk	L.A.	22	3	6	9	−2	6	0	0	0	0	16	18.8
D	29	* Chris Snell	L.A.	32	2	7	9	−7	22	0	2	0	0	45	4.4
D	77	Rob Cowie	L.A.	32	2	7	9	−6	20	0	0	0	0	39	5.1
C	39	* Yanic Perreault	L.A.	26	2	5	7	3	20	0	0	1	0	43	4.7
D	26	Philippe Boucher	BUF	9	1	4	5	6	0	0	0	0	0	15	6.7
			L.A.	6	1	0	1	−3	4	0	0	0	0	15	6.7
			TOTAL	15	2	4	6	3	4	0	0	0	0	30	6.7
R	8	* Kevin Brown	L.A.	23	2	3	5	−7	18	0	0	0	0	25	8.0
R	55	* Troy Crowder	L.A.	29	1	2	3	0	99	0	0	0	0	4	25.0
D	6	* Sean O'Donnell	L.A.	15	0	2	2	−2	49	0	0	0	0	12	0.0
L	10	* Jeff Shevalier	L.A.	1	1	0	1	1	0	0	0	0	0	1	100.0
L	34	* Matt Johnson	L.A.	14	1	0	1	0	102	0	0	0	0	4	25.0
D	35	Arto Blomsten	WPG	1	0	0	0	0	2	0	0	0	0	0	0.0
			L.A.	4	0	1	1	2	0	0	0	0	0	1	0.0
			TOTAL	5	0	1	1	2	2	0	0	0	0	1	0.0
L	27	Dave Thomlinson	L.A.	1	0	0	0	−1	0	0	0	0	0	0	0.0
D	5	Tim Watters	L.A.	1	0	0	0	−1	0	0	0	0	0	0	0.0
D	38	* Eric Lavigne	L.A.	1	0	0	0	−1	0	0	0	0	0	0	0.0
G	36	* Pauli Jaks	L.A.	1	0	0	0	0	0	0	0	0	0	0	0.0
R	9	Rob Brown	L.A.	2	0	0	0	−2	0	0	0	0	0	1	0.0
G	31	* Jamie Storr	L.A.	5	0	0	0	0	0	0	0	0	0	0	0.0
G	31	Grant Fuhr	BUF	3	0	0	0	0	2	0	0	0	0	0	0.0
			L.A.	14	0	0	0	0	2	0	0	0	0	0	0.0
			TOTAL	17	0	0	0	0	4	0	0	0	0	0	0.0
D	3	* Denis Tsygurov	BUF	4	0	0	0	−1	4	0	0	0	0	4	0.0
			L.A.	21	0	0	0	−2	11	0	0	0	0	16	0.0
			TOTAL	25	0	0	0	−3	15	0	0	0	0	20	0.0
G	32	Kelly Hrudey	L.A.	35	0	0	0	0	0	0	0	0	0	0	0.0

Goaltending

No.	Goaltender	GPI	Mins	Avg	W	L	T	EN	SO	GA	SA	S%
36	* Pauli Jaks	1	40	3.00	0	0	0	0	0	2	25	.920
32	Kelly Hrudey	35	1894	3.14	14	13	5	3	0	99	1099	.910
31	* Jamie Storr	5	263	3.88	1	3	1	1	0	17	152	.888
31	Grant Fuhr	14	698	4.04	1	7	3	3	0	47	379	.876
35	Robb Stauber	1	16	7.50	0	0	0	0	0	2	6	.667
	Totals	**48**	**2925**	**3.57**	**16**	**23**	**9**	**7**	**0**	**174**	**1668**	**.896**

General Managers' History

Larry Regan, 1967-68 to 1972-73; Larry Regan and Jake Milford, 1973-74; Jake Milford, 1974-75 to 1976-77; George Maguire, 1977-78 to 1982-83; George Maguire and Rogatien Vachon, 1983-84; Rogatien Vachon, 1984-85 to 1991-92; Nick Beverley, 1992-93 to 1993-94; Sam McMaster, 1994-95 to date.

Coaching History

"Red" Kelly, 1967-68 to 1968-69; Hal Laycoe and John Wilson, 1969-70; Larry Regan, 1970-71; Larry Regan and Fred Glover, 1971-72; Bob Pulford, 1972-73 to 1976-77; Ron Stewart, 1977-78; Bob Berry, 1978-79 to 1980-81; Parker MacDonald and Don Perry, 1981-82; Don Perry, 1982-83; Don Perry, Rogie Vachon and Roger Neilson, 1983-84; Pat Quinn, 1984-85 to 1985-86; Pat Quinn and Mike Murphy 1986-87; Mike Murphy, Rogie Vachon and Robbie Ftorek, 1987-88; Robbie Ftorek, 1988-89; Tom Webster, 1989-90 to 1991-92; Barry Melrose, 1992-93 to 1993-94; Barry Melrose and Rogie Vachon, 1994-95; Larry Robinson, 1995-96.

Captains' History

Bob Wall, 1967-68, 1968-69; Larry Cahan, 1969-70, 1970-71; Bob Pulford, 1971-72, 1972-73; Terry Harper, 1973-74, 1974-75; Mike Murphy, 1975-76 to 1980-81; Dave Lewis, 1981-82, 1982-83; Terry Ruskowski, 1983-84, 1984-85; Dave Taylor, 1985-86 to 1988-89; Wayne Gretzky, 1989-90 to 1991-92; Wayne Gretzky and Luc Robitaille, 1992-93; Wayne Gretzky, 1993-94 to date.

Retired Numbers

16	Marcel Dionne	1975-1987
18	Dave Taylor	1977-1994
30	Rogatien Vachon	1971-1978

Club Records

Team

(Figures in brackets for season records are games played; records for fewest points, wins, ties, losses, goals, goals against are for 70 or more games)

Most Points	**105**	1974-75 (80)
Most Wins	**46**	1990-91 (80)
Most Ties	**21**	1974-75 (80)
Most Losses	**52**	1969-70 (76)
Most Goals	**376**	1988-89 (80)
Most Goals Against	**389**	1985-86 (80)
Fewest Points	**38**	1969-70 (76)
Fewest Wins	**14**	1969-70 (76)
Fewest Ties	**7**	1988-89 (80) 1989-90 (80)
Fewest Losses	**17**	1974-75 (80)
Fewest Goals	**168**	1969-70 (76)
Fewest Goals Against	**185**	1974-75 (80)
Longest Winning Streak		
Over-all	**8**	Oct. 21-Nov. 7/72
Home	**12**	Oct. 10-Dec. 5/92
Away	**8**	Dec. 18/74-Jan. 16/75
Longest Undefeated Streak		
Over-all	**11**	Feb. 28-Mar. 24/74 (9 wins, 2 ties)
Home	**13**	Oct. 10-Dec. 8/92 (12 wins, 1 tie)
Away	**11**	Oct. 10-Dec. 11/74 (6 wins, 5 ties)
Longest Losing Streak		
Over-all	**10**	Feb. 22-Mar. 9/84
Home	**9**	Feb. 8-Mar. 12/86
Away	**12**	Jan. 11-Feb. 15/70
Longest Winless Streak		
Over-all	**17**	Jan. 29-Mar. 5/70 (13 losses, 4 ties)
Home	**9**	Jan. 29-Mar. 5/70 (8 losses, 1 tie) Feb. 8-Mar. 12/86 (9 losses)
Away	**21**	Jan. 11-Apr. 3/70 (17 losses, 4 ties)
Most Shutouts, Season	**9**	1974-75 (80)
Most PIM, Season	**2,228**	1990-91 (80)
Most Goals, Game	**12**	Nov. 28/84 (Van. 1 at L.A. 12)

Individual

Most Seasons	**17**	Dave Taylor
Most Games	**1,111**	Dave Taylor
Most Goals, Career	**550**	Marcel Dionne
Most Assists, Career	**757**	Marcel Dionne
Most Points Career	**1,307**	Marcel Dionne
Most PIM, Career	**1,698**	Marty McSorley
Most Shutouts, Career	**32**	Rogie Vachon
Longest Consecutive Games Streak	**324**	Marcel Dionne (Jan. 7/78-Jan. 9/82)
Most Goals, Season	**70**	Bernie Nicholls (1988-89)
Most Assists, Season	**122**	Wayne Gretzky (1990-91)
Most Points, Season	**168**	Wayne Gretzky (1988-89) (54 goals, 114 assists)
Most PIM, Season	**399**	Marty McSorley (1992-93)
Most Points, Defenseman Season	**76**	Larry Murphy (1980-81) (16 goals, 60 assists)
Most Points, Center, Season	**168**	Wayne Gretzky (1988-89) (54 goal, 114 assists)
Most Points, Right Wing, Season	**112**	Dave Taylor (1980-81) (47 goals, 65 assists)
Most Points, Left Wing, Season	***125**	Luc Robitaille (1992-93) (63 goals, 62 assists)
Most Points, Rookie, Season	**84**	Luc Robitaille (1986-87) (45 goals, 39 assists)
Most Shutouts, Season	**8**	Rogie Vachon (1976-77)
Most Goals, Game	**4**	Several players
Most Assists, Game	**6**	Bernie Nicholls (Dec. 1/88) Tomas Sandstrom (Oct. 9/93)
Most Points, Game	**8**	Bernie Nicholls (Dec. 1/88)

* NHL Record

All-time Record vs. Other Clubs

Regular Season

	At Home							On Road							Total						
	GP	W	L	T	GF	GA	PTS	GP	W	L	T	GF	GA	PTS	GP	W	L	T	GF	GA	PTS
Anaheim	6	3	2	1	16	14	7	5	2	2	1	14	18	5	11	5	4	2	30	32	12
Boston	53	18	30	5	185	203	41	54	10	41	3	149	261	23	107	28	71	8	334	464	64
Buffalo	46	17	21	8	158	162	42	45	15	22	8	141	183	38	91	32	43	16	299	345	80
Calgary	71	37	27	7	287	265	81	74	19	46	9	250	356	47	145	56	73	16	537	621	128
Chicago	56	24	26	6	192	197	54	57	20	29	8	173	222	48	113	44	55	14	365	419	102
Dallas	60	27	18	15	216	180	69	61	16	36	9	173	252	41	121	43	54	24	389	432	110
Detroit	62	35	16	11	269	191	81	61	27	25	9	231	247	63	123	62	41	20	500	438	144
Edmonton	57	22	23	12	247	251	56	57	15	29	13	224	287	43	114	37	52	25	471	538	99
Florida	1	0	1	0	5	6	0	1	0	0	1	2	2	1	2	0	1	1	7	8	1
Hartford	22	13	6	3	100	87	29	23	8	12	3	94	90	19	45	21	18	6	194	177	48
Montreal	58	15	34	9	178	234	39	57	7	39	11	147	265	25	115	22	73	20	325	499	64
New Jersey	35	26	3	6	189	107	58	35	15	15	5	130	121	35	70	41	18	11	319	228	93
NY Islanders	37	16	14	7	132	125	39	37	13	20	4	108	140	30	74	29	34	11	240	265	69
NY Rangers	52	20	23	9	174	187	49	51	15	31	5	150	207	35	103	35	54	14	324	394	84
Ottawa	2	2	0	0	15	6	4	2	1	1	0	5	7	2	4	3	1	0	20	13	6
Philadelphia	58	17	34	7	171	204	41	56	15	34	7	145	217	37	114	32	68	14	316	421	78
Pittsburgh	62	40	14	8	245	161	88	64	19	37	8	203	243	46	126	59	51	16	448	404	134
Quebec	22	13	8	1	102	77	27	22	9	10	3	91	94	21	44	22	18	4	193	171	48
St. Louis	60	32	19	9	225	172	73	60	14	39	7	159	233	35	120	46	58	16	384	405	108
San Jose	12	8	3	1	42	28	17	13	5	6	2	43	48	12	25	13	9	3	85	76	29
Tampa Bay	3	0	3	0	9	14	0	2	2	0	0	9	5	4	5	2	3	0	18	19	4
Toronto	58	31	19	8	209	169	70	57	17	30	10	193	234	44	115	48	49	18	402	403	114
Vancouver	79	41	28	10	327	264	92	77	25	40	12	258	311	62	156	66	68	22	585	575	154
Washington	39	23	12	4	159	123	50	38	15	17	6	140	166	36	77	38	29	10	299	289	86
Winnipeg	51	19	22	10	218	215	48	54	20	25	9	199	230	49	105	39	47	19	417	445	97
Defunct Clubs	35	27	6	2	141	76	56	34	11	14	9	91	109	31	69	38	20	11	232	185	87
Totals	**1097**	**526**	**412**	**159**	**4211**	**3718**	**1211**	**1097**	**335**	**600**	**162**	**3522**	**4548**	**832**	**2194**	**861**	**1012**	**321**	**7733**	**8266**	**2043**

Calgary totals include Atlanta, 1972-73 to 1979-80. Dallas totals include Minnesota, 1967-68 to 1992-93.
New Jersey totals include Kansas City, 1974-75 to 1975-76, and Colorado, 1976-77 to 1981-82.

Playoffs

	Series	W	L	GP	W	L	T	GF	GA	Last Mtg.	Round	Result
Boston	2	0	2	13	5	8	0	38	56	1977	QF	L 2-4
Calgary	6	4	2	26	13	13	0	105	112	1993	DSF	W 4-2
Chicago	1	0	1	5	1	4	0	7	10	1974	QF	L 1-4
Dallas	1	0	1	7	3	4	0	21	26	1968	QF	L 3-4
Edmonton	7	2	5	36	12	24	0	124	150	1992	DSF	L 2-4
Montreal	1	0	1	5	1	4	0	12	15	1993	F	L 1-4
NY Islanders	1	0	1	4	1	3	0	10	21	1980	PR	L 1-3
NY Rangers	2	0	2	6	1	5	0	14	32	1981	PR	L 1-3
St. Louis	1	0	1	4	0	4	0	5	16	1969	SF	L 0-4
Toronto	3	1	2	12	5	7	0	31	41	1993	CF	W 4-3
Vancouver	3	2	1	17	9	8	0	66	60	1993	DF	W 4-2
Defunct Clubs	1	1	0	7	4	3	0	23	25			
Totals	**29**	**10**	**19**	**142**	**55**	**87**	**0**	**459**	**568**			

Playoff Results 1995-91

Year	Round	Opponent	Result	GF	GA
1993	F	Montreal	L 1-4	12	15
	CF	Toronto	W 4-3	22	23
	DF	Vancouver	W 4-2	26	25
	DSF	Calgary	W 4-2	33	28
1992	DSF	Edmonton	L 2-4	18	23
1991	DF	Edmonton	L 2-4	20	21
	DSF	Vancouver	W 4-2	26	16

Abbreviations: Round: F – Final; **CF** – conference final; **CQF** – conference quarter-final; **CSF** – conference semi-final; **DF** – division final; **DSF** – division semi-final; **SF** – semi-final; **QF** – quarter-final; **PR** – preliminary round.

1994-95 Results

Jan.	20		Toronto	3-3		16		St. Louis	2-2
	22		Edmonton	3-4		18		Toronto	3-5
	24		Dallas	2-4		20		St. Louis	5-3
	26	at	St. Louis	1-3		21	at	Anaheim	3-3
	28		Winnipeg	4-2		25		San Jose	1-3
	29		Chicago	3-6		26	at	San Jose	7-3
Feb.	4		Detroit	4-3		28	at	Calgary	5-3
	5		Anaheim	2-3		29	at	Vancouver	2-5
	7	at	St. Louis	5-5	**Apr.**	1		Winnipeg	7-7
	11	at	Toronto	5-2		3		Edmonton	7-2
	12	at	Detroit	4-4		6		Dallas	3-2
	15	at	Dallas	3-1		7	at	Calgary	4-7
	17		San Jose	0-2		9	at	Anaheim	1-5
	18		Vancouver	2-6		12		Calgary	1-4
	20	at	Vancouver	2-8		16	at	San Jose	0-2
	23		Calgary	3-3		17	at	Calgary	2-5
	25	at	Edmonton	4-3		19	at	Edmonton	0-2
	28		Chicago	4-8		21		Edmonton	3-3
Mar.	4		Vancouver	4-5		23		Anaheim	2-2
	6	at	Dallas	2-8		25		Detroit	5-1
	9	at	Chicago	4-3		28	at	San Jose	0-4
	11	at	Winnipeg	4-2		30		Anaheim	2-1
	13	at	Toronto	4-1	**May**	2	at	Winnipeg	2-1
	14	at	Detroit	2-5		3	at	Chicago	1-5

Entry Draft
Selections 1995-81

1995 Pick	1991 Pick	1988 Pick	1984 Pick
3 Aki-Petteri Berg	42 Guy Leveque	7 Martin Gelinas	6 Craig Redmond
33 Donald MacLean	79 Keith Redmond	28 Paul Holden	24 Brian Wilks
50 Pavel Rosa	81 Alexei Zhitnik	49 John Van Kessel	48 John English
59 Vladimir Tsyplakov	108 Pauli Jaks	70 Rob Blake	69 Tom Glavine
118 Jason Morgan	130 Brett Seguin	91 Jeff Robison	87 Dave Grannis
137 Igor Melyakov	152 Kelly Fairchild	109 Micah Aivazoff	108 Greg Strome
157 Benoit Larose	196 Craig Brown	112 Robert Larsson	129 Tim Hanley
163 Juha Vuorivirta	218 Mattias Olsson	133 Jeff Kruesel	150 Shannon Deegan
215 Brian Stewart	240 Andre Bouliane	154 Timo Peltomaa	171 Luc Robitaille
	262 Michael Gaul	175 Jim Larkin	191 Jeff Crossman
1994 Pick		196 Brad Hyatt	212 Paul Kenny
7 Jamie Storr	**1990 Pick**	217 Doug Laprade	232 Brian Martin
33 Matt Johnson	7 Darryl Sydor	238 Joe Flanagan	
59 Vitali Yachmenev	28 Brandy Semchuk		**1983 Pick**
111 Chris Schmidt	49 Bob Berg	**1987 Pick**	47 Bruce Shoebottom
163 Luc Gagne	91 David Goverde	4 Wayne McBean	67 Guy Benoit
189 Andrew Dale	112 Erik Andersson	27 Mark Fitzpatrick	87 Bob LaForest
215 Jan Nemecek	133 Robert Lang	43 Ross Wilson	100 Garry Galley
241 Sergei Shalomai	154 Dean Hulett	90 Mike Vukonich	107 Dave Lundmark
	175 Denis LeBlanc	111 Greg Batters	108 Kevin Stevens
1993 Pick	196 Patrik Ross	174 Jeff Gawlicki	127 Tim Burgess
42 Shayne Toporowski	217 K.J. (Kevin) White	195 John Preston	147 Ken Hammond
68 Jeffrey Mitchell	238 Troy Mohns	216 Rostislav Vlach	167 Bruce Fishback
94 Bob Wren		237 Mikael Lindholm	187 Thomas Ahlen
105 Frederick Beaubien	**1989 Pick**		207 Miroslav Blaha
117 Jason Saal	39 Brent Thompson	**1986 Pick**	227 Chad Johnson
120 Tomas Vlasak	81 Jim Maher	2 Jimmy Carson	
146 Jere Karalahti	102 Eric Ricard	44 Denis Larocque	**1982 Pick**
172 Justin Martin	103 Thomas Newman	65 Sylvain Couturier	27 Mike Heidt
198 John-Tra Dillabough	123 Daniel Rydmark	86 Dave Guden	48 Steve Seguin
224 Martin Strbak	144 Ted Kramer	107 Robb Stauber	64 Dave Gans
250 Kimmo Timonen	165 Sean Whyte	128 Sean Krakiwsky	82 Dave Ross
276 Patrick Howald	182 Jim Giacin	149 Rene Chapdelaine	90 Darcy Roy
	186 Martin Maskarinec	170 Trevor Pochipinski	95 Ulf Isaksson
1992 Pick	207 Jim Hiller	191 Paul Kelly	132 Victor Nechaev
39 Justin Hocking	228 Steve Jaques	212 Russ Mann	153 Peter Helander
63 Sandy Allan	249 Kevin Sneddon	233 Brian Hayton	174 Dave Chartier
87 Kevin Brown			195 John Franzosa
111 Jeff Shevalier		**1985 Pick**	216 Ray Shero
135 Raymond Murray		9 Craig Duncanson	237 Mats Ulander
207 Magnus Wernblom		10 Dan Gratton	
231 Ryan Pisiak		30 Par Edlund	**1981 Pick**
255 Jukka Tiilikainen		72 Perry Florio	2 Doug Smith
		93 Petr Prajsler	39 Dean Kennedy
		135 Tim Flannigan	81 Marty Dallman
		156 John Hyduke	123 Brad Thompson
		177 Steve Horner	134 Craig Hurley
		219 Trent Ciprick	144 Peter Sawkins
		240 Marian Horwath	165 Dan Brennan
			186 Allan Tuer
			207 Jeff Baikie

Coach

ROBINSON, LARRY
Coach, Los Angeles Kings. Born in Winchester, Ont., June 2, 1951.

Larry Robinson became the 18th head coach of the Los Angeles Kings on July 26, 1995, replacing Barry Melrose (Rogie Vachon served as interim coach for the final seven games of 1994-95 season). He served as an assistant coach with the New Jersey Devils the previous two seasons, helping them win the Stanley Cup in 1995. One of the great defensemen in NHL history, Robinson enjoyed a stellar 20-year playing career with the Montreal Canadiens and the Kings (1972-73–1991-92). In his 17 seasons with Montreal, the Habs won five Stanley Cups, including four straight (1975-76–1978-79). Robinson played in 1,384 career games (9th all-time), scoring 208 goals, 750 assists (3rd all-time defenseman) and 958 points (4th all-time defenseman). In playoff action, he holds NHL records for most career games played (227) and most consecutive years in playoffs (20). Robinson's individual honors include two Norris Trophies as the NHL's top defenseman, a Conn Smythe Trophy as playoff MVP, three seasons each as a first team all-star and second team all-star, and 10 appearances in the NHL All-Star Game.

Club Directory

The Great Western Forum
3900 West Manchester Blvd.
Inglewood, California 90305
Phone **310/419-3160**
GM FAX 310/672-1490
PR FAX 310/673-8927
Capacity: 16,005

Executive
Chairman/Governor . . . . Joseph M. Cohen
President/Alternate Governor . . . . Rogatien Vachon
Executive Vice President . . . . Lester M. Wintz
Chief Financial Officer . . . . Michael Handelman
Executive Secretary to Chairman. . . . . Celeste Grant

Hockey Operations
General Manager/Alternate Governor . . . . Sam McMaster
Assistant General Manager/Director of
   Player Development . . . . Dave Taylor
Assistant to General Manager . . . . John Wolf
Executive Secretary to General Manager . . . . Marcia Galloway
Head Coach . . . . Larry Robinson
Assistant Coaches. . . . . John Perpich, Rick Green
Director of Amateur Scouting. . . . . Al Murray
Director of Pro Scouting . . . . Ace Bailey
Scouting Staff. . . . . Serge Aubry, Peter Brill, Gary Harker,
   Jan Lindegren, Vaclav Nedomansky, John
   Stanton
Video Coordinator . . . . Bill Gurney

Medical Staff
Trainer . . . . Pete Demers
Equipment Manager. . . . . Peter Millar
Assistant Equipment Manager . . . . Rick Garcia
Massage Therapist/Assistant Trainer . . . . Pete Radulovic
Team Physicians . . . . Kerlan/Jobe Orthopaedic Clinic directed by
   Dr. Ronald Kvitne
Internist . . . . Dr. Michael Mellman
Team Dentist . . . . Dr. Gordon Knuth

Communications/Public Relations
Director, Public Relations . . . . Rick Minch
Director, Communications . . . . Nick Salata
Manager, Communications . . . . Angela Ladd
Fundraising Coordinator . . . . Jim Fox
Public Relations Assistant . . . . Mike Altieri
Administrative Assistant, Communications/
   Public Relations . . . . Jill Berke
Receptionist . . . . Elizabeth Tutt

Personnel/Accounting
Director, Human Resources. . . . . Barbara Mendez
Controller . . . . Peter Mazur
Accounts Payable . . . . Emma Harris

Marketing/Advertising Sales
Executive Director, Sales . . . . Dennis Metz
Director, Marketing . . . . Sergio del Prado
Season Seat Account Executives . . . . Keith Jacobson, Andrew Silverman
Corporate Account Executive . . . . Bill Hirsch, Karen Marumoto
Manager, Marketing Services . . . . Susan Long
Marketing/Promotions Assistant . . . . Tami Cole
Assistant to Executive Vice President. . . . . Charlie Jacobs

Broadcasting
Play-by-Play Announcer, Television . . . . Bob Miller
Color Commentator, Television . . . . Jim Fox
Play-by-Play Announcer, Radio . . . . Nick Nickson
Color Commentator, Radio. . . . . TBA
Television Stations . . . . Prime Sports, Cable
   KTLA, Channel 5
Radio Station . . . . XTRA (690 AM)
Spanish Radio Station . . . . KWIZ (1480 AM)

Home Ice . . . . The Great Western Forum
Dimensions of Rink. . . . . 200 feet by 85 feet
Supervisor of Off-Ice Officials . . . . Bill Meuris
Public Address Announcer . . . . David Courtney
Organist . . . . Dan Stein
Videoboard Director . . . . Keith Harris
Colors . . . . Black, White and Silver
Training Camp . . . . Iceoplex, North Hills, CA
Location of Press Box . . . . West Colonnade, Sec. 28, Rows 1-12

General Manager

McMASTER, SAM
General Manager, Los Angeles Kings. Born in Vancouver, B.C., March 3, 1944.

Sam McMaster is entering his second season as general manager of the Los Angeles Kings in 1995-96. He was named the sixth general manager in Los Angeles franchise history on May 24, 1994. He spent the six years prior to his appointment as general manager and director of hockey operations for the Sudbury Wolves of the Ontario Hockey League, earning league executive of the year honors in 1991. Prior to his tenure at Sudbury, McMaster served as assistant director of player personnel for the Washington Capitals from 1985 to 1988. He was also general manager of the OHL's Sault Ste. Marie Greyhounds from 1980 to 1985. These Soo teams won over 70 percent of their games and captured three OHL titles.

Montreal Canadiens

1994-95 Results: 18W-23L-7T 43PTS. Sixth, Northeast Division

Right winger Mike Keane is the 21st player to wear the captain's "C" for the Montreal Canadiens

Schedule

Oct.	Sat.	7	Philadelphia	Wed.	10	Vancouver
	Wed.	11	at Florida	Fri.	12	at Pittsburgh
	Thur.	12	at Tampa Bay	Sat.	13	St. Louis
	Sat.	14	New Jersey	Wed.	17	at Ottawa
	Fri.	20	at NY Islanders	Mon.	22	Tampa Bay
	Sat.	21	Toronto	Thur.	25	at Florida
	Mon.	23	Los Angeles	Sat.	27	Winnipeg*
	Wed.	25	Florida	Sun.	28	Boston*
	Fri.	27	at Hartford	Wed.	31	Washington
	Sat.	28	Chicago	**Feb.** Thur.	1	at Philadelphia
	Tues.	31	at Boston	Sat.	3	at Toronto
Nov.	Wed.	1	at Washington	Mon.	5	at Colorado
	Sat.	4	Boston	Wed.	7	at Dallas
	Wed.	8	Anaheim	Sat.	10	Ottawa
	Sat.	11	at Calgary	Mon.	12	San Jose
	Sun.	12	at Vancouver	Thur.	15	at NY Rangers
	Wed.	15	at Edmonton	Sat.	17	Calgary
	Sat.	18	Ottawa	Wed.	21	at Hartford
	Mon.	20	Hartford	Fri.	23	at New Jersey
	Wed.	22	at Hartford	Sat.	24	Pittsburgh
	Sat.	25	Colorado	Mon.	26	at San Jose
	Tues.	28	at Detroit	Wed.	28	at Anaheim
	Wed.	29	at St. Louis	**Mar.** Sat.	2	at Los Angeles
Dec.	Sat.	2	Detroit	Sat.	9	Ottawa
	Wed.	6	New Jersey	Mon.	11	Dallas
	Thur.	7	at Pittsburgh	Wed.	13	at New Jersey
	Sat.	9	NY Rangers	Sat.	16	NY Rangers
	Tues.	12	at Winnipeg	Mon.	18	Buffalo
	Fri.	15	at Chicago	Wed.	20	Hartford
	Sat.	16	Philadelphia	Fri.	22	at Buffalo
	Mon.	18	Hartford	Sat.	23	Edmonton
	Wed.	20	at Buffalo	Mon.	25	NY Islanders
	Fri.	22	at Pittsburgh	Wed.	27	Washington
	Sat.	23	Pittsburgh	Thur.	28	at Boston
	Tues.	26	at Washington	Sat.	30	at Ottawa
	Thur.	28	at Tampa Bay	**Apr.** Mon.	1	Buffalo
	Sat.	30	at Ottawa	Wed.	3	Boston
Jan.	Wed.	3	at NY Rangers	Thur.	4	at Boston
	Thur.	4	at NY Islanders	Sat.	6	Florida
	Sat.	6	Buffalo	Thur.	11	at Philadelphia
	Mon.	8	Tampa Bay	Sat.	13	NY Islanders

* Denotes afternoon game.

Home Starting Times:
All games . . . . 7:35 p.m.
Except   Sat. Jan. 27 . . . . 1:30 p.m.
Sun. Jan. 28 . . . . 3:00 p.m.

Franchise date: November 22, 1917

79th NHL Season

NORTHEAST DIVISION

Year-by-Year Record

Season	GP	Home W	L	T	Road W	L	T	Overall W	L	T	GF	GA	Pts	Finished	Playoff Result
1994-95	48	15	5	4	3	18	3	18	23	7	125	148	43	6th, Northeast Div.	Out of Playoffs
1993-94	84	26	12	4	15	17	10	41	29	14	283	248	96	3rd, Northeast Div.	Lost Conf. Quarter-Final
1992-93	84	27	13	2	21	17	4	48	30	6	326	280	102	3rd, Adams Div.	Won Stanley Cup
1991-92	80	27	8	5	14	20	6	41	28	11	267	207	93	1st, Adams Div.	Lost Div. Final
1990-91	80	23	12	5	16	18	6	39	30	11	273	249	89	2nd, Adams Div.	Lost Div. Final
1989-90	80	26	8	6	15	20	5	41	28	11	288	234	93	3rd, Adams Div.	Lost Div. Final
1988-89	80	30	6	4	23	12	5	53	18	9	315	218	115	1st, Adams Div.	Lost Final
1987-88	80	26	8	6	19	14	7	45	22	13	298	238	103	1st, Adams Div.	Lost Div. Final
1986-87	80	27	9	4	14	20	6	41	29	10	277	241	92	1st, Adams Div.	Lost Conf. Championship
1985-86	80	25	11	4	15	22	3	40	33	7	330	280	87	2nd, Adams Div.	Won Stanley Cup
1984-85	80	24	10	6	17	17	6	41	27	12	309	262	94	1st, Adams Div.	Lost Div. Final
1983-84	80	19	19	2	16	21	3	35	40	5	286	295	75	4th, Adams Div.	Lost Conf. Championship
1982-83	80	25	6	9	17	18	5	42	24	14	350	286	98	2nd, Adams Div.	Lost Div. Semi-Final
1981-82	80	25	6	9	21	11	8	46	17	17	360	223	109	1st, Adams Div.	Lost Div. Semi-Final
1980-81	80	31	7	2	14	15	11	45	22	13	332	232	103	1st, Norris Div.	Lost Prelim. Round
1979-80	80	30	7	3	17	13	10	47	20	13	328	240	107	1st, Norris Div.	Lost Quarter-Final
1978-79	80	29	6	5	23	11	6	52	17	11	337	204	115	1st, Norris Div.	Won Stanley Cup
1977-78	80	32	4	4	27	6	7	59	10	11	359	183	129	1st, Norris Div.	Won Stanley Cup
1976-77	80	33	1	6	27	7	6	60	8	12	387	171	132	1st, Norris Div.	Won Stanley Cup
1975-76	80	32	3	5	26	8	6	58	11	11	337	174	127	1st, Norris Div.	Won Stanley Cup
1974-75	80	27	8	5	20	6	14	47	14	19	374	225	113	1st, Norris Div.	Lost Semi-Final
1973-74	78	24	12	3	21	12	6	45	24	9	293	240	99	2nd, East Div.	Lost Quarter-inal
1972-73	78	29	4	6	23	6	10	52	10	16	329	184	120	1st, East Div.	Won Stanley Cup
1971-72	78	29	3	7	17	13	9	46	16	16	307	205	108	3rd, East Div.	Lost Quarter-Final
1970-71	78	29	7	3	13	16	10	42	23	13	291	216	97	3rd, East Div.	Won Stanley Cup
1969-70	76	21	9	8	17	13	8	38	22	16	244	201	92	5th, East Div.	Out of Playoffs
1968-69	76	26	7	5	20	12	6	46	19	11	271	202	103	1st, East Div.	Won Stanley Cup
1967-68	74	26	5	6	16	17	4	42	22	10	236	167	94	1st, East Div.	Won Stanley Cup
1966-67	70	19	9	7	13	16	6	32	25	13	202	188	77	2nd,	Lost Final
1965-66	70	23	11	1	18	10	7	41	21	8	239	173	90	1st,	Won Stanley Cup
1964-65	70	20	8	7	16	15	4	36	23	11	211	185	83	2nd,	Won Stanley Cup
1963-64	70	22	7	6	14	14	7	36	21	13	209	167	85	1st,	Lost Semi-Final
1962-63	70	15	10	10	13	9	13	28	19	23	225	183	79	3rd,	Lost Semi-Final
1961-62	70	26	2	7	16	12	7	42	14	14	259	166	98	1st,	Lost Semi-Final
1960-61	70	24	6	5	17	13	5	41	19	10	254	188	92	1st,	Lost Semi-Final
1959-60	70	23	4	8	17	14	4	40	18	12	255	178	92	1st,	Won Stanley Cup
1958-59	70	21	8	6	18	10	7	39	18	13	258	158	91	1st,	Won Stanley Cup
1957-58	70	23	8	4	20	9	6	43	17	10	250	158	96	1st,	Won Stanley Cup
1956-57	70	23	6	6	12	17	6	35	23	12	210	155	82	2nd,	Won Stanley Cup
1955-56	70	29	5	1	16	10	9	45	15	10	222	131	100	1st,	Won Stanley Cup
1954-55	70	26	5	4	15	13	7	41	18	11	228	157	93	2nd,	Lost Final
1953-54	70	27	5	3	8	19	8	35	24	11	195	141	81	2nd,	Lost Final
1952-53	70	18	12	5	10	11	14	28	23	19	155	148	75	2nd,	Won Stanley Cup
1951-52	70	22	8	5	12	18	5	34	26	10	195	164	78	2nd,	Lost Final
1950-51	70	17	10	8	8	20	7	25	30	15	173	184	65	3rd,	Lost Final
1949-50	70	17	8	10	12	14	9	29	22	19	172	150	77	2nd,	Lost Semi-Final
1948-49	60	19	8	3	9	15	6	28	23	9	152	126	65	3rd,	Lost Semi-Final
1947-48	60	13	13	4	7	16	7	20	29	11	147	169	51	5th,	Out of Playoffs
1946-47	60	19	6	5	15	10	5	34	16	10	189	138	78	1st,	Lost Final
1945-46	50	16	6	3	12	11	2	28	17	5	172	134	61	1st,	Won Stanley Cup
1944-45	50	21	2	2	17	6	2	38	8	4	228	121	80	1st,	Lost Semi-Final
1943-44	50	22	0	3	16	5	4	38	5	7	234	109	83	1st,	Won Stanley Cup
1942-43	50	14	4	7	5	15	5	19	19	12	181	191	50	4th,	Lost Semi-Final
1941-42	48	12	10	2	6	17	1	18	27	3	134	173	39	6th,	Lost Quarter-Final
1940-41	48	11	9	4	5	17	2	16	26	6	121	147	38	6th,	Lost Quarter-Final
1939-40	48	5	14	5	5	19	0	10	33	5	90	167	25	7th,	Out of Playoffs
1938-39	48	8	11	5	7	13	4	15	24	9	115	146	39	6th,	Lost Quarter-Final
1937-38	48	13	4	7	5	13	6	18	17	13	123	128	49	3rd, Cdn. Div.	Lost Quarter-Final
1936-37	48	16	8	0	8	10	6	24	18	6	115	111	54	1st, Cdn. Div.	Lost Semi-Final
1935-36	48	5	11	8	6	15	3	11	26	11	82	123	33	4th, Cdn. Div.	Out of Playoffs
1934-35	48	11	11	2	8	12	4	19	23	6	110	145	44	3rd, Cdn. Div.	Lost Quarter-Final
1933-34	48	16	6	2	6	14	4	22	20	6	99	101	50	2nd, Cdn. Div.	Lost Quarter-Final
1932-33	48	15	5	4	3	20	1	18	25	5	92	115	41	3rd, Cdn. Div.	Lost Quarter-Final
1931-32	48	18	3	3	7	13	4	25	16	7	128	111	57	1st, Cdn. Div.	Lost Semi-Final
1930-31	44	15	3	4	11	7	4	26	10	8	129	89	60	1st, Cdn. Div.	Won Stanley Cup
1929-30	44	13	5	4	8	9	5	21	14	9	142	114	51	2nd, Cdn. Div.	Won Stanley Cup
1928-29	44	12	4	6	10	3	9	22	7	15	71	43	59	1st, Cdn. Div.	Lost Semi-Final
1927-28	44	12	7	3	14	4	4	26	11	7	116	48	59	1st, Cdn. Div.	Lost Semi-Final
1926-27	44	15	5	2	13	9	0	28	14	2	99	67	58	2nd, Cdn. Div.	Lost Semi-Final
1925-26	36	5	12	1	6	12	0	11	24	1	79	108	23	7th,	Out of Playoffs
1924-25	30	10	5	0	7	6	2	17	11	2	93	56	36	3rd,	Lost Final
1923-24	24	10	2	0	3	9	0	13	11	0	59	48	26	2nd,	Won Stanley Cup
1922-23	24	10	2	0	3	7	2	13	9	2	73	61	28	2nd,	Lost NHL Final
1921-22	24	8	3	1	4	8	0	12	11	1	88	94	25	3rd,	Out of Playoffs
1920-21	24	9	3	0	4	8	0	13	11	0	112	99	26	3rd and 2nd*	Out of Playoffs
1919-20	24	8	4	0	5	7	0	13	11	0	129	113	26	2nd and 3rd*	Out of Playoffs
1918-19	18	7	2	0	3	6	0	10	8	0	88	78	20	1st and 2nd*	Cup Final but no Decision
1917-18	22	8	3	0	5	6	0	13	9	0	115	84	26	1st and 3rd*	Lost NHL Final

* Season played in two halves with no combined standing at end.
From 1917-18 through 1925-26, NHL champions played against PCHA champions for Stanley Cup.

1995-96 Player Personnel

FORWARDS	HT	WT	S	Place of Birth	Date	1994-95 Club
BORDELEAU, Sebastien	5-10	180	R	Vancouver, B.C.	2/15/75	Hull
BRASHEAR, Donald	6-2	220	L	Bedford, IN	1/7/72	Fredericton-Montreal
BRUNET, Benoit	5-11	195	L	Pointe-Claire, Que.	8/24/68	Montreal
BURE, Valeri	5-10	168	R	Moscow, USSR	6/13/74	Fredericton-Montreal
BUREAU, Marc	6-1	198	R	Trois-Rivières, Que.	5/19/66	Tampa Bay
CAMPBELL, Jim	6-2	185	R	Worcester, MA	4/3/73	Fredericton
CONROY, Craig	6-2	198	R	Potsdam, NY	9/4/71	Fredericton-Montreal
CORPSE, Keli	5-11	175	L	London, Ont.	5/14/74	Cdn. National-Kingston
DAMPHOUSSE, Vincent	6-1	200	L	Montreal, Que.	12/17/67	Ratingen-Montreal
FERGUSON, Craig	5-11	190	L	Castro Valley, CA	4/8/70	Fredericton-Montreal
FLEMING, Gerry	6-5	253	L	Montreal, Que.	10/16/67	Fredericton-Montreal
FRASER, Scott	6-1	178	R	Moncton, N.B.	5/3/72	Fredericton-Wheeling
GRENIER, David	6-2	195	L	Montreal, Que.	2/5/75	Shawinigan
KEANE, Mike	5-10	185	R	Winnipeg, Man.	5/29/67	Montreal
KOIVU, Saku	5-9	165	L	Turku, Finland	11/23/74	TPS
KRAMER, Brady	6-2	180	L	Philadelphia, PA	6/13/73	Providence-Fredericton
LAMB, Mark	5-9	180	L	Ponteix, Sask.	8/3/64	Philadelphia-Montreal
MAJIC, Xavier	6-0	190	L	Fernie, B.C.	3/10/73	Wheeling-Fredericton
MURRAY, Chris	6-2	209	R	Port Hardy, B.C.	10/25/74	Fredericton-Montreal
PETROV, Oleg	5-8	175	L	Moscow, USSR	4/18/71	Montreal-Fredericton
RECCHI, Mark	5-10	185	L	Kamloops, B.C.	2/1/68	Philadelphia-Montreal
ROBERGE, Mario	5-11	193	L	Quebec City, Que.	1/25/64	Montreal-Fredericton
SARAULT, Yves	6-1	170	L	Valleyfield, Que.	12/23/72	Fredericton-Montreal
SAVAGE, Brian	6-1	195	L	Sudbury, Ont.	2/24/71	Montreal
SEVIGNY, Pierre	6-0	195	L	Trois-Rivières, Que.	9/8/71	Montreal
STEVENSON, Turner	6-3	220	R	Prince George, B.C.	5/18/72	Fredericton-Montreal
SYCHRA, Martin	6-1	180	L	Brno, Czech.	6/19/74	Fredericton
TUCKER, Darcy	5-10	170	L	Castor, Alta.	3/15/75	Kamloops
TURGEON, Pierre	6-1	195	L	Rouyn, Que.	8/29/69	NY Islanders-Montreal
DEFENSEMEN						
BERNARD, Louis	6-2	205	R	Victoriaville, Que.	7/10/74	Wheeling-Fredericton
BILODEAU, Brent	6-3	217	L	Dallas, TX	3/27/73	Fredericton
BRISEBOIS, Patrice	6-1	188	R	Montreal, Que.	1/27/71	Montreal
BROWN, Brad	6-3	218	R	Baie Verte, Nfld.	12/27/75	North Bay
DAIGNEAULT, Jean-Jacques	5-10	186	L	Montreal, Que.	10/12/65	Montreal
DARLING, Dion	6-3	205	L	Edmonton, Alta.	10/22/74	Fredericton-Wheeling
FITZPATRICK, Rory	6-1	195	R	Rochester, NY	1/11/75	Sudbury-Fredericton
GINGRAS, Gaston	6-1	200	L	Temiscamingue, Que.	2/13/59	Fredericton
KIPRUSOFF, Marko	6-0	195	L	Turku, Finland	6/6/72	TPS
LETANG, Alan	6-0	185	L	Renfrew, Ont.	9/4/75	Sarnia
MAGUIRE, Derek	5-10	210	R	Delbarton, NJ	12/9/71	Fredericton
MALAKHOV, Vladimir	6-3	220	L	Sverdlovsk, USSR	8/30/68	NY Islanders-Montreal
ODELEIN, Lyle	5-11	210	R	Quill Lake, Sask.	7/21/68	Montreal
POPOVIC, Peter	6-6	235	R	Koping, Sweden	2/10/68	Vasteras-Montreal
PROULX, Christian	6-0	185	L	Sherbrooke, Que.	12/10/73	Fredericton
QUINTAL, Stephane	6-3	215	R	Boucherville, Que.	10/22/68	Winnipeg
RACINE, Yves	6-0	205	L	Matane, Que.	2/7/69	Montreal
RIVET, Craig	6-1	190	R	North Bay, Ont.	9/13/74	Fredericton-Montreal
WIESEL, Adam	6-3	210	R	Holyoke, MA	1/25/75	Clarkson
WILKIE, David	6-2	210	R	Ellensburgh, WA	5/30/74	Fredericton-Montreal

GOALTENDERS	HT	WT	C	Place of Birth	Date	1994-95 Club
BROCHU, Martin	5-10	200	L	Anjou, Que.	3/10/73	Fredericton
LABRECQUE, Patrick	6-0	190	L	Laval, Que.	3/6/71	Fredericton-Wheeling
LAMOTHE, Marc	6-1	204	L	New Liskeard, Ont.	2/27/74	Fredericton-Wheeling
ROY, Patrick	6-0	192	L	Quebec City, Que.	10/5/65	Montreal

Coach

DEMERS, JACQUES
Coach, Montreal Canadiens. Born in Montreal, Que., August 25, 1944.

Named as the 21st head coach in the history of the Montreal Canadiens in July, 1992, Jacques Demers guided the Habs to their 24th Stanley Cup title in 1992-93, defeating the Los Angeles Kings in five games in the championship finals. Demers, who is the only man in NHL history to win coach of the year honors in back-to-back seasons when he was with Detroit, began his coaching career in Quebec's junior ranks before making his professional coaching debut with the WHA's Chicago Cougars in 1972-73. Eventually, Demers joined the Quebec Nordiques' organization and was that team's first coach when the club joined the NHL in 1979-80. In 1981, Demers was appointed as the head of the Nordiques' AHL farm affiliate in Fredericton, where he earned Executive of the Year honors in 1983. The following season, Demers returned to the NHL with the St. Louis Blues, where he spent three seasons as head coach.

Coaching Record

		Regular Season					Playoffs			
Season	Team	Games	W	L	T	%	Games	W	L	%
1975-76	Indianapolis (WHA)	80	35	39	6	.475	7	3	4	.429
1976-77	Indianapolis (WHA)	81	36	37	8	.494	9	5	4	.556
1977-78	Cincinnati (WHA)	80	35	42	3	.456	....	....	....	....
1978-79	Quebec (WHA)	80	41	34	5	.544	4	0	4	.000
1979-80	**Quebec (NHL)**	**80**	**25**	**44**	**11**	**.381**	....	....	....	....
1981-82	Fredericton (AHL)	80	20	55	5	.281	....	....	....	....
1982-83	Fredericton (AHL)	80	45	27	8	.544	12	6	6	.500
1983-84	**St. Louis (NHL)**	**80**	**32**	**41**	**7**	**.444**	**11**	**6**	**5**	**.545**
1984-85	**St. Louis (NHL)**	**80**	**37**	**31**	**12**	**.538**	**3**	**0**	**3**	**.000**
1985-86	**St. Louis (NHL)**	**80**	**37**	**34**	**9**	**.519**	**19**	**10**	**9**	**.526**
1986-87	**Detroit (NHL)**	**80**	**34**	**36**	**10**	**.488**	**16**	**9**	**7**	**.563**
1987-88	**Detroit (NHL)**	**80**	**41**	**28**	**11**	**.581**	**16**	**9**	**7**	**.563**
1988-89	**Detroit (NHL)**	**80**	**34**	**34**	**12**	**.500**	**6**	**2**	**4**	**.333**
1989-90	**Detroit (NHL)**	**80**	**28**	**38**	**14**	**.437**	....	....	....	....
1992-93	**Montreal (NHL)**	**84**	**48**	**30**	**6**	**.607**	**20**	**16**	**4**	**.800***
1993-94	**Montreal (NHL)**	**84**	**41**	**29**	**14**	**.571**	**7**	**3**	**4**	**.429**
1994-95	**Montreal (NHL)**	**48**	**18**	**23**	**7**	**.448**	....	....	....	....
	NHL Totals	**856**	**375**	**368**	**113**	**.504**	**98**	**55**	**43**	**.561**

* Stanley Cup win.

1994-95 Scoring

* – rookie

Regular Season

Pos	#	Player	Team	GP	G	A	Pts	+/–	PIM	PP	SH	GW	GT	S	%
R	8	Mark Recchi	PHI	10	2	3	5	–6	12	1	0	2	0	17	11.8
			MTL	39	14	29	43	–3	16	8	0	1	0	104	13.5
			TOTAL	49	16	32	48	–9	28	9	0	3	0	121	13.2
C	77	Pierre Turgeon	NYI	34	13	14	27	–12	10	3	2	2	0	93	14.0
			MTL	15	11	9	20	12	4	2	0	2	0	67	16.4
			TOTAL	49	24	23	47	0	14	5	2	4	0	160	15.0
L	25	Vincent Damphousse	MTL	48	10	30	40	15	42	4	0	4	0	123	8.1
L	22	Benoit Brunet	MTL	45	7	18	25	7	16	1	1	2	1	80	8.8
D	38	Vladimir Malakhov	NYI	26	3	13	16	–1	32	1	0	0	0	61	4.9
			MTL	14	1	4	5	–2	14	0	0	0	0	30	3.3
			TOTAL	40	4	17	21	–3	46	1	0	0	0	91	4.4
R	12	Mike Keane	MTL	48	10	10	20	5	15	1	0	0	0	75	13.3
C	49	* Brian Savage	MTL	37	12	7	19	5	27	0	0	0	0	64	18.8
L	23	Brian Bellows	MTL	41	8	8	16	–7	8	1	0	1	0	110	7.3
D	43	Patrice Brisebois	MTL	35	4	8	12	–2	26	0	0	2	0	67	6.0
D	29	Yves Racine	MTL	47	4	7	11	–1	42	2	0	1	0	63	6.3
D	24	Lyle Odelein	MTL	48	3	7	10	–13	152	0	0	0	0	74	4.1
D	48	J.J. Daigneault	MTL	45	3	5	8	2	40	0	0	0	0	36	8.3
R	30	* Turner Stevenson	MTL	41	6	1	7	0	86	0	0	1	0	35	17.1
D	44	Bryan Fogarty	MTL	21	5	2	7	–3	34	3	0	0	0	41	12.2
R	6	Oleg Petrov	MTL	12	2	3	5	–7	4	0	0	0	0	26	7.7
R	31	Ed Ronan	MTL	30	1	4	5	–7	12	0	0	0	0	14	7.1
D	34	Peter Popovic	MTL	33	0	5	5	–10	8	0	0	0	0	23	0.0
R	18	* Valeri Bure	MTL	24	3	1	4	–1	6	0	0	1	0	39	7.7
C	17	Mark Lamb	PHI	8	0	2	2	1	2	0	0	0	0	7	0.0
			MTL	39	1	0	1	–13	18	0	0	0	0	23	4.3
			TOTAL	47	1	2	3	–12	20	0	0	0	0	30	3.3
L	35	* Donald Brashear	MTL	20	1	1	2	–5	63	0	0	1	0	10	10.0
C	28	* Craig Conroy	MTL	6	1	0	1	–1	0	0	0	0	0	4	25.0
D	52	* Craig Rivet	MTL	5	0	1	1	2	5	0	0	0	0	2	0.0
L	26	* Yves Sarault	MTL	8	0	1	1	–1	0	0	0	0	0	9	0.0
G	33	Patrick Roy	MTL	43	0	1	1	0	20	0	0	0	0	0	0.0
C	46	* Craig Ferguson	MTL	1	0	0	0	0	0	0	0	0	0	3	0.0
D	56	* David Wilkie	MTL	1	0	0	0	0	0	0	0	0	0	0	0.0
R	57	Chris Murray	MTL	3	0	0	0	0	4	0	0	0	0	0	0.0
L	36	Gerry Fleming	MTL	6	0	0	0	–1	17	0	0	0	0	1	0.0
G	1	Ron Tugnutt	MTL	7	0	0	0	0	0	0	0	0	0	0	0.0
L	32	Mario Roberge	MTL	9	0	0	0	–2	34	0	0	0	0	0	0.0
L	20	Pierre Sevigny	MTL	19	0	0	0	–5	15	0	0	0	0	6	0.0

Goaltending

No.	Goaltender	GPI	Mins	Avg	W	L	T	EN	SO	GA	SA	S%
33	Patrick Roy	43	2566	2.97	17	20	6	3	1	127	1357	.906
1	Ron Tugnutt	7	346	3.12	1	3	1	0	0	18	172	.895
	Totals	**48**	**2921**	**3.04**	**18**	**23**	**7**	**3**	**1**	**148**	**1532**	**.903**

Although he played only 39 games with the Habs, Mark Recchi still led the club in goals (14) and points (43).

Captains' History

"Newsy" Lalonde, 1917-18 to 1920-21; Sprague Cleghorn, 1921-22 to 1924-25; Bill Couture, 1925-26; Sylvio Mantha, 1926-27 to 1931-32; George Hainsworth, 1932-33; Sylvio Mantha, 1933-34 to 1935-36; "Babe" Seibert, 1936-37 to 1938-39; Walter Buswell, 1939-40; "Toe" Blake, 1940-41 to 1946-47; "Toe" Blake and Bill Durnan, 1947-48; Emile Bouchard, 1948-49 to 1955-56; Maurice Richard, 1956-57 to 1959-60; Doug Harvey, 1960-61; Jean Beliveau, 1961-62 to 1970-71; Henri Richard, 1971-72 to 1974-75; Yvan Cournoyer, 1975-76 to 1978-79; Serge Savard, 1979-80, 1980-81; Bob Gainey, 1981-82 to 1988-89, Guy Carbonneau and Chris Chelios (co-captains), 1989-90; Guy Carbonneau, 1990-91 to 1993-94; Kirk Muller and Mike Keane, 1994-95; Mike Keane, 1995-96.

Club Records

Team

(Figures in brackets for season records are games played; records for fewest points, wins, ties, losses, goals, goals against are for 70 or more games)

Most Points	*132	1976-77 (80)
Most Wins	*60	1976-77 (80)
Most Ties	23	1962-63 (70)
Most Losses	40	1983-84 (80)
Most Goals	387	1976-77 (80)
Most Goals Against	295	1983-84 (80)
Fewest Points	65	1950-51 (70)
Fewest Wins	25	1950-51 (70)
Fewest Ties	5	1983-84 (80)
Fewest Losses	*8	1976-77 (80)
Fewest Goals	155	1952-53 (70)
Fewest Goals Against	*131	1955-56 (70)

Longest WinningStreak

Over-all	12	Jan. 6-Feb. 3/68
Home	13	Nov. 2/43-Jan. 8/44; Jan. 30-Mar. 26/77
Away	8	Dec. 18/77-Jan. 18/78; Jan. 21-Feb. 21/82

Longest Undefeated Streak

Over-all	28	Dec. 18/77-Feb. 23/78 (23 wins, 5 ties)
Home	*34	Nov. 1/76-Apr. 2/77 (28 wins, 6 ties)
Away	*23	Nov. 27/74-Mar. 12/75 (14 wins, 9 ties)

Longest Losing Streak

Over-all	12	Feb. 13/26-Mar. 13/26
Home	7	Dec. 16/39-Jan. 18/40
Away	10	Dec. 1/25-Feb. 2/26

Longest Winless Streak

Over-all	12	Feb. 13-Mar. 13/26 (12 losses); Nov. 28-Dec. 29/35 (8 losses, 4 ties)
Home	*15	Dec. 16/39-Mar. 7/40 (12 losses, 3 ties)
Away	12	Oct. 20-Dec. 13/51 (8 losses, 4 ties)

Most Shutouts, Season	*22	1928-29 (44)
Most PIM, Season	1,842	1987-88 (80)
Most Goals, Game	*16	Mar. 3/20 (Mt. 16 at Que. 3)

Individual

Most Seasons	20	Henri Richard, Jean Beliveau
Most Games	1,256	Henri Richard
Most Goals Career	544	Maurice Richard
Most Assists, Career	728	Guy Lafleur
Most Points Career	1,246	Guy Lafleur (518 goals, 728 assists)
Most PIM, Career	2,248	Chris Nilan
Most Shutouts, Career	75	George Hainsworth

Longest Consecutive Games Streak	560	Doug Jarvis (Oct. 8/75-Apr. 4/82)
Most Goals, Season	60	Steve Shutt (1976-77) Guy Lafleur (1977-78)
Most Assists, Season	82	Peter Mahovlich (1974-75)
Most Points, Season	136	Guy Lafleur (1976-77) (56 goals, 80 assists)
Most PIM, Season	358	Chris Nilan (1984-85)
Most Points, Defenseman Season	85	Larry Robinson (1976-77) (19 goals, 66 assists)

Most Points, Center, Season	117	Peter Mahovlich (1974-75) (35 goals, 82 assists)
Most Points, Right Wing, Season	136	Guy Lafleur (1976-77) (56 goals, 80 assists)
Most Points, Left Wing, Season	110	Mats Naslund (1985-86) (43 goals, 67 assists)
Most Points, Rookie, Season	71	Mats Naslund (1982-83) (26 goals, 45 assists) Kjell Dahlin (1985-86) (32 goals, 39 assists)
Most Shutouts, Season	*22	George Hainsworth (1928-29)
Most Goals, Game	6	Newsy Lalonde (Jan. 10/20)
Most Assists, Game	6	Elmer Lach (Feb. 6/43)
Most Points, Game	8	Maurice Richard 5G-3A (Dec. 28/44) Bert Olmstead 4G-4A (Jan. 9/54)

* NHL Record.

Retired Numbers

2	Doug Harvey	1947-1961
4	Aurèle Joliat	1922-1938
	Jean Béliveau	1950-1971
7	Howie Morenz	1923-1937
9	Maurice Richard	1942-1960
10	Guy Lafleur	1971-1984
16	Elmer Lach	1942-1954
	Henri Richard	1955-1975

All-time Record vs. Other Clubs

Regular Season

	At Home							On Road							Total						
	GP	W	L	T	GF	GA	PTS	GP	W	L	T	GF	GA	PTS	GP	W	L	T	GF	GA	PTS
Anaheim	1	1	0	0	4	1	2	1	0	0	5	2	2	2	2	0	0	9	3	4	
Boston	310	179	86	45	1056	720	403	311	114	144	53	840	924	281	621	293	230	98	1896	1644	684
Buffalo	79	48	21	10	328	234	106	79	23	38	18	222	250	64	158	71	59	28	550	484	170
Calgary	38	21	11	6	135	94	48	37	21	11	5	135	120	47	75	42	22	11	270	214	95
Chicago	267	168	51	48	1037	629	384	267	121	91	55	747	722	297	534	289	142	103	1784	1351	681
Dallas	51	35	9	7	230	125	77	52	27	14	11	186	135	65	103	62	23	18	416	260	142
Detroit	274	169	62	43	978	608	381	274	96	125	53	703	782	245	548	265	187	96	1681	1390	626
Edmonton	22	13	6	3	79	67	29	23	10	13	0	71	82	20	45	23	19	3	150	149	49
Florida	3	0	3	0	5	11	0	4	1	1	2	12	14	4	7	1	4	2	17	25	4
Hartford	55	37	11	7	253	164	81	57	29	20	8	214	176	66	112	66	31	15	467	340	147
Los Angeles	57	39	7	11	265	147	89	58	34	15	9	234	178	77	115	73	22	20	499	325	166
New Jersey	36	26	6	4	148	90	56	36	24	12	0	161	104	48	72	50	18	4	309	194	104
NY Islanders	42	24	11	7	162	130	55	42	19	19	4	128	141	42	84	43	30	11	290	271	97
NY Rangers	272	183	55	34	1074	626	400	272	109	110	53	793	789	271	544	292	165	87	1867	1415	671
Ottawa	9	7	2	0	32	24	14	7	6	1	0	29	20	12	16	13	3	0	61	44	26
Philadelphia	56	29	15	12	211	168	70	55	21	21	13	168	165	55	111	50	36	25	379	333	125
Pittsburgh	62	51	4	7	317	148	109	61	30	22	9	220	184	69	123	81	26	16	537	332	178
Quebec	56	36	12	8	242	176	80	57	26	27	4	207	191	56	113	62	39	12	449	367	136
St. Louis	52	38	8	6	235	134	82	51	27	10	14	183	129	68	103	65	18	20	418	263	150
San Jose	4	4	0	0	21	7	8	4	2	0	2	8	6	6	8	6	0	2	29	13	14
Tampa Bay	4	3	1	0	9	7	6	5	0	4	1	8	15	1	9	3	5	1	17	22	7
Toronto	314	191	83	40	1119	773	422	315	111	160	44	824	966	266	629	302	243	84	1943	1727	688
Vancouver	45	35	8	2	226	120	72	43	28	7	8	172	107	64	88	63	15	10	398	227	136
Washington	42	29	7	6	188	85	64	41	18	16	7	137	109	43	83	47	23	13	325	194	107
Winnipeg	22	20	2	0	119	51	40	22	9	8	5	84	71	23	44	29	10	5	203	122	63
Defunct Clubs	231	148	58	25	779	469	321	230	98	97	35	586	606	231	461	246	155	60	1365	1075	552
Totals	**2404**	**1534**	**539**	**331**	**9252**	**5808**	**3399**	**2404**	**1005**	**986**	**413**	**7077**	**6976**	**2423**	**4808**	**2539**	**1525**	**744**	**16329**	**12784**	**5822**

Calgary totals include Atlanta, 1972-73 to 1979-80. Dallas totals include Minnesota, 1967-68 to 1992-93.
New Jersey totals include Kansas City, 1974-75 to 1975-76, and Colorado, 1976-77 to 1981-82.

Playoffs

	Series	W	L	GP	W	L	T	GF	GA	Last Mtg.	Round	Result
Boston	28	21	7	139	87	52	0	430	339	1994	CQF	L 3-4
Buffalo	6	4	2	31	18	13	0	114	94	1993	DF	W 4-0
Calgary	2	1	1	11	6	5	0	31	32	1989	F	L 2-4
Chicago	17	12	5	81	50	29	2	261	185	1976	QF	W 4-0
Dallas	2	1	1	13	7	6	0	48	37	1980	QF	L 3-4
Detroit	12	5	7	62	33	29	0	161	149	1978	QF	W 4-1
Edmonton	1	0	1	3	0	3	0	6	15	1981	PR	L 0-3
Hartford	5	5	0	27	19	8	0	96	70	1992	DSF	W 4-3
Los Angeles	1	1	0	5	4	1	0	15	12	1993	F	W 4-1
NY Islanders	4	3	1	22	14	8	0	64	55	1993	CF	W 4-1
NY Rangers	13	7	6	55	32	21	2	171	139	1986	CF	W 4-1
Philadelphia	4	3	1	21	14	7	0	72	52	1989	CF	W 4-2
Quebec	5	2	3	31	17	14	0	105	85	1993	DSF	W 4-2
St. Louis	3	3	0	12	12	0	0	42	14	1977	QF	W 4-0
Toronto	15	8	7	71	42	29	0	215	160	1979	QF	W 4-0
Vancouver	1	1	0	5	4	1	0	20	9	1975	QF	W 4-1
Defunct Clubs	11*	6	4	28	15	9	4	70	71			
Totals	**130***	**84**	**45**	**617**	**374**	**235**	**8**	**1921**	**1518**			

* 1919 Final incomplete due to influenza epidemic.

Playoff Results 1995-91

Year	Round	Opponent	Result	GF	GA
1994	CQF	Boston	L 3-4	20	22
1993	**F**	**Los Angeles**	**W 4-1**	**15**	**12**
	CF	NY Islanders	W 4-1	16	11
	DF	Buffalo	W 4-0	16	12
	DSF	Quebec	W 4-2	19	16
1992	DF	Boston	L 0-4	8	14
	DSF	Hartford	W 4-3	21	18
1991	DF	Boston	L 3-4	18	18
	DSF	Buffalo	W 4-2	29	24

Abbreviations: Round: F – Final;
CF – conference final; **CQF** – conference quarter-final;
CSF – conference semi-final; **DF** – division final;
DSF – division semi-final; **SF** – semi-final;
QF – quarter-final; **PR** – preliminary round.

1994-95 Results

Jan.	21	at	NY Rangers	2-5	15		Pittsburgh	8-5
	25		Washington	2-0	16	at	Boston	0-6
	28		New Jersey	5-1	18		Quebec	5-4
	29		Philadelphia	2-2	20	at	Philadelphia	4-8
	31	at	Tampa Bay	1-4	22		Florida	2-3
Feb.	2	at	Florida	1-1	25		Ottawa	3-1
	4		NY Islanders	4-2	27	at	Tampa Bay	2-3
	7	at	Boston	4-7	**Apr.** 1	at	New Jersey	1-4
	8	at	Ottawa	4-2	3	at	Ottawa	5-4
	11	at	Pittsburgh	1-3	5		Quebec	6-5
	13		Hartford	2-2	6	at	Quebec	2-3
	15	at	Hartford	1-4	8		Pittsburgh	2-1
	16	at	NY Rangers	2-2	10		New Jersey	2-1
	18		NY Rangers	5-2	12	at	Philadelphia	2-3
	20		NY Islanders	3-2	14	at	Hartford	3-4
	23	at	Florida	5-2	15		Boston	2-3
	25		Philadelphia	0-7	17		Washington	5-2
	27	at	New Jersey	1-6	19		Ottawa	4-1
	28	at	NY Islanders	1-2	22		Tampa Bay	3-1
Mar.	4	at	Washington	1-5	24		Hartford	5-4
	5	at	Buffalo	1-4	26	at	Quebec	1-1
	8		Buffalo	2-2	29		Buffalo	3-3
	11		NY Rangers	3-1	**May** 1	at	Buffalo	0-2
	13	at	Pittsburgh	2-4	3		Boston	2-4

Entry Draft Selections 1995-81

1995

Pick	
8	Terry Ryan
60	Miroslav Guren
74	Martin Hohenberger
86	Jonathan Delisle
112	Niklas Anger
138	Boyd Olson
164	Stephane Robidas
190	Greg Hart
216	Eric Houde

1994

Pick	
18	Brad Brown
44	Jose Theodore
54	Chris Murray
70	Marko Kiprusoff
74	Martin Belanger
96	Arto Kuki
122	Jimmy Drolet
148	Joel Irving
174	Jessie Rezansoff
200	Peter Strom
226	Tomas Vokoun
252	Chris Aldous
278	Ross Parsons

1993

Pick	
21	Saku Koivu
47	Rory Fitzpatrick
73	Sebastien Bordeleau
85	Adam Wiesel
99	Jean-Francois Houle
113	Jeff Lank
125	Dion Darling
151	Darcy Tucker
177	David Ruhly
203	Alan Letang
229	Alexandre Duchesne
255	Brian Larochelle
281	Russell Guzior

1992

Pick	
20	David Wilkie
33	Valeri Bure
44	Keli Corpse
68	Craig Rivet
82	Louis Bernard
92	Marc Lamothe
116	Don Chase
140	Martin Sychra
164	Christian Proulx
188	Michael Burman
212	Earl Cronan
236	Trent Cavicchi
260	Hiroyuki Miura

1991

Pick	
17	Brent Bilodeau
28	Jim Campbll
43	Craig Darby
61	Yves Sarault
73	Vladimir Vujtek
83	Sylvain Lapointe
100	Brad Layzell
105	Tony Prpic
127	Oleg Petrov
149	Brady Kramer
171	Brian Savage
193	Scott Fraser
215	Greg MacEachern
237	Paul Lepler
259	Dale Hooper

1990

Pick	
12	Turner Stevenson
39	Ryan Kuwabara
58	Charles Poulin
60	Robert Guillet
81	Gilbert Dionne
102	Paul DiPietro
123	Craig Conroy
144	Stephen Rohr
165	Brent Fleetwood
186	Derek Maguire
207	Mark Kettelhut
228	John Uniac
249	Sergei Martynyuk

1989

Pick	
13	Lindsay Vallis
30	Patrice Brisebois
41	Steve Larouche
51	Pierre Sevigny
83	Andre Racicot
104	Marc Deschamps
146	Craig Ferguson
167	Patrick Lebeu
188	Roy Mitchell
209	Ed Henrich
230	Justin Duberman
251	Steve Cadieux

1988

Pick	
20	Eric Charron
34	Martin St. Amour
46	Neil Carnes
83	Patrik Kjellberg
93	Peter Popovic
104	Jean-Claude Bergeron
125	Patrik Carnback
146	Tim Chase
167	Sean Hill
188	Harijs Vitolinsh
209	Yuri Krivokhizha
230	Kevin Dahl
251	Dave Kunda

1987

Pick	
17	Andrew Cassels
33	John LeClair
38	Eric Desjardins
44	Mathieu Schneider
58	Francois Gravel
80	Kris Miller
101	Steve McCool
122	Les Kuntar
143	Rob Kelley
164	Will Geist
185	Eric Tremblay
206	Barry McKinlay
227	Ed Ronan
248	Bryan Herring

1986

Pick	
15	Mark Pederson
27	Benoit Brunet
57	Jyrki Lumme
78	Brent Bobyck
94	Eric Aubertin
99	Mario Milani
120	Steve Bisson
141	Lyle Odelein
162	Rick Hayward
183	Antonin Routa
204	Eric Bohemier
225	Charlie Moore
246	Karel Svoboda

1985

Pick	
12	Jose Charbonneau
16	Tom Chorske
33	Todd Richards
47	Rocky Dundas
75	Martin Desjardins
79	Brent Gilchrist
96	Tom Sagissor
117	Donald Dufresne
142	Ed Cristofoli
163	Mike Claringbull
184	Roger Beedon
198	Maurice Mansi
205	Chad Arthur
226	Mike Bishop
247	John Ferguson Jr.

1984

Pick	
5	Petr Svoboda
8	Shayne Corson
29	Stephane Richer
51	Patrick Roy
54	Graeme Bonar
65	Lee Brodeur
95	Gerald Johannson
116	Jim Nesich
137	Scott MacTavish
158	Brad McCughey
179	Eric Demers
199	Ron Annear
220	Dave Tanner
240	Troy Crosby

1983

Pick	
17	Alfie Turcotte
26	Claude Lemieux
27	Sergio Momesso
35	Todd Francis
45	Daniel Letendre
78	John Kordic
98	Dan Wurst
118	Arto Javanainen
138	Vladislav Tretiak
158	Rob Bryden
178	Grant MacKay
198	Thomas Rundqvist
218	Jeff Perpich
238	Jean-Guy Bergeron

1982

Pick	
19	Alain Heroux
31	Jocelyn Gauvreau
32	Kent Carlson
33	David Maley
40	Scott Sandelin
61	Scott Harlow
69	John Devoe
103	Kevin Houle
117	Ernie Vargas
124	Michael Dark
145	Hannu Jarvenpaa
150	Steve Smith
166	Tom Kolioupoulos
187	Brian Williams
208	Bob Emery
229	Darren Acheson
250	Bill Brauer

1981

Pick	
7	Mark Hunter
18	Gilbert Delorme
19	Jan Ingman
32	Lars Eriksson
40	Chris Chelios
46	Dieter Hegen
82	Kjell Dahlin
88	Steve Rooney
124	Tom Anastos
145	Tom Kurvers
166	Paul Gess
187	Scott Ferguson
208	Danny Burrows

General Manager

SAVARD, SERGE A.
Managing Director, Montreal Canadiens.
Born in Montreal, Que., January 22, 1946.

Serge Savard was elected to the Hockey Hall of Fame in 1986, following a brilliant 16 year career as a defenseman. He was appointed managing director of the Canadiens on April 28, 1983. Since then, the team has qualified for the playoffs in 11 of 12 seasons. Under the direction of Serge Savard, the Canadiens have won two Stanley Cups (1986, 1993), three Conference and four Division championships. As a player with Montreal, he was a member of eight Stanley Cup-winning teams. He won the Conn Smythe Trophy as MVP of the 1969 playoffs and the Bill Masterton Trophy in 1978-79. He was selected to the 1978-79 Second All-Star Team. He ended his playing career in Winnipeg in 1982-83. In 1994, Serge Savard was named an Officer of the Order of Canada.

General Managers' History

Joseph Cattarinich, 1909-1910; George Kennedy, 1910-11 to 1919-20; Leo Dandurand, 1920-21 to 1934-35; Ernest Savard, 1935-36; Cecil Hart, 1936-37 to 1938-39; Jules Dugal, 1939-40; Tom P. Gorman, 1940-41 to 1945-46; Frank J. Selke, 1946-47 to 1963-64; Sam Pollock, 1964-65 to 1977-78; Irving Grundman, 1978-79 to 1982-83; Serge Savard, 1983-84 to date.

Club Directory

Montreal Forum
2313 St. Catherine Street West
Montreal, Quebec H3H 1N2
Phone **514/932-2582**
FAX (Hockey) 514/932-8736
Team Services 514/989-2717
P.R. 514/932-9296
Media 514/932-8285
Capacity: 16,259 (standing 1,700)
Total: 17,959

Owner: The Molson Companies Limited

Chairman of the Board, President and Governor	Ronald Corey
Vice-President Hockey, Managing Director and Alternate Governor	Serge Savard
Vice-President, Forum Operations	Aldo Giampaolo
Vice-President, Finance and Administration	Fred Steer
Vice-President, Communications and Marketing Services	Bernard Brisset
Assistant Managing Director and Director of Scouting	André Boudrias
Administrative Assistant to the Managing Director	Phil Scheuer
Head Coach	Jacques Demers
Assistant Coaches	Jacques Laperrière, Charles Thiffault, Steve Shutt
Goaltending Instructor	François Allaire
Director of Team Services	Michele Lapointe
Pro Scout	Carol Vadnais
Director of Player Development and Scout	Claude Ruel
Chief Scout	Doug Robinson
Scouting Staff	Neil Armstrong, Scott Baker, Elmer Benning, Pierre Dorion, Pierre Mondou, Gerry O'Flaherty, Sakari Pietila, Richard Scammell, Antonin Routa
AHL Affiliation	Fredericton Canadiens
Governor	André Boudrias
Head Coach	Paulin Bordeleau
Assistant Coach	Luc Gauthier
Player/Assistant Coach	Mario Roberge
Director of Operations	Wayne Gamble
Medical and Training Staff	
Club Physician	Dr. D.G. Kinnear
Athletic Trainer	Gaétan Lefebvre
Assistant to the Athletic Trainer	John Shipman
Equipment Manager	Eddy Palchak
Assistants to the Equipment Manager	Pierre Gervais, Robert Boulanger, Pierre Ouellette
Marketing	
EFFIX Inc.	François-Xavier Seigneur
Communications	
Director of Communications	Donald Beauchamp
Assistant to the Director of Communications	Denis Dessureault
Executive Assistant	Normande Herget
Assistant — Communications	Frédérique Cardinal
Photo	Claude Rompré
Finance	
Director of Finance	François Trudel
Controller	Dennis McKinley
Administrative Supervisor	Dave Poulton
Manager of Financial Analysis and Control	Françoise Brault
Accountants	Gilles Viens, Paule Jolicoeur
Forum	
Building Manager	Alain Gauthier
Director of Security	TBA
Director of Events	Louise Laliberté
Director of Computer, Operations	Sylvain Roy
Director of Concessions	TBA
Director of Purchasing	Robert Loiseau
Director, Souvenir Boutiques	Yves Renaud
Ticketing	
Box Office Manager	Richard Primeau
Assistant to the Box Office Manager	Caterina D'Ascoli

Executive Assistants
President, Lise Beaudry; Managing Director, Donna Stuart; V.P. Forum Operations, Vicky Mercuri; V.P. Finance, Susan Cryans; Hockey, Claudine Crépin

Location of Press Box	Suspended above ice — West side
Location of Radio and TV booth	Suspended above ice — East side
Dimensions of rink	200 feet by 85 feet
Club colors	Red, White and Blue
Club trains at	Montreal Forum
Play-by-Play — Radio/TV	Dick Irvin, Jim Corsi (English) Claude Quenneville, René Pothier, André Côté, Pierre Houde (French)
TV Channels	CBFT (2), TQS (35) (French), CBMT (6) (English)
Cable TV	RDS (25)
Radio Stations	CBF (690) (French), CJAD (800) (English)

Coaching History

George Kennedy, 1917-18 to 1919-20; Léo Dandurand, 1920-21 to 1924-25; Cecil Hart, 1925-26 to 1931-32; "Newsy" Lalonde, 1932-33 to 1933-34; "Newsy" Lalonde and Léo Dandurand, 1934-35; Sylvio Mantha, 1935-36; Cecil Hart, 1936-37 to 1937-38; Cecil Hart and Jules Dugal, 1938-39; "Babe" Siebert, 1939*; "Pit" Lepine, 1939-40; Dick Irvin 1940-41 to 1954-55; "Toe" Blake, 1955-56 to 1967-68; Claude Ruel, 1968-69 to 1969-70; Claude Ruel and Al MacNeil, 1970-71; Scotty Bowman, 1971-72 to 1978-79; Bernie Geoffrion and Claude Ruel, 1979-80; Claude Ruel, 1980-81; Bob Berry, 1981-82 to 1982-83; Bob Berry and Jacques Lemaire, 1983-84; Jacques Lemaire, 1984-85; Jean Perron, 1985-86 to 1987-88; Pat Burns, 1988-89 to 1991-92; Jacques Demers, 1992-93 to date.

* Named coach in summer but died before 1939-40 season began.

New Jersey Devils

1994-95 Results: 22W-18L-8T 52PTS. Second, Atlantic Division

Schedule

Oct.	Sat.	7	Florida*		Thur.	11	San Jose
	Thur.	12	Winnipeg		Sat.	13	at Boston*
	Sat.	14	at Montreal		Sun.	14	Dallas
	Sun.	15	at Buffalo		Tue.	16	Boston
	Tues.	17	Edmonton		Tues.	23	Los Angeles
	Thur.	19	Detroit		Thur.	25	Washington
	Sat.	21	Ottawa		Sat.	27	at Hartford
	Wed.	25	Vancouver		Tues.	30	at Vancouver
	Sat.	28	Pittsburgh	Feb.	Thur.	1	at Calgary
	Tues.	31	at Edmonton		Sat.	3	at Ottawa
Nov.	Thur.	2	at San Jose		Wed.	7	Pittsburgh
	Sat.	4	at Los Angeles		Sat.	10	NY Rangers*
	Sun.	5	at Anaheim		Sun.	11	Anaheim
	Wed.	8	Calgary		Fri.	16	at Buffalo
	Sat.	11	Philadelphia*		Sun.	18	Washington*
	Sun.	12	at Philadelphia*		Mon.	19	at Philadelphia*
	Tues.	14	Hartford		Wed.	21	Florida
	Thur.	16	at Boston		Fri.	23	Montreal
	Sat.	18	Buffalo*		Sat.	24	at Washington
	Tues.	21	at Florida	Mar.	Fri.	1	NY Islanders
	Wed.	22	at Tampa Bay		Sat.	2	at Ottawa
	Sat.	25	at Dallas		Mon.	4	at NY Rangers
	Mon.	27	at NY Rangers		Wed.	6	at Toronto
	Wed.	29	Colorado		Sat.	9	at Pittsburgh*
Dec.	Fri.	1	Tampa Bay		Sun.	10	at Philadelphia
	Sat.	2	at NY Islanders		Wed.	13	Montreal
	Wed.	6	at Montreal		Fri.	15	Tampa Bay
	Thur.	7	Toronto		Sun.	17	at Florida
	Sat.	9	NY Islanders*		Wed.	20	Boston
	Mon.	11	Florida		Fri.	22	Chicago
	Fri.	15	at Detroit		Sat.	23	at NY Islanders
	Sat.	16	Buffalo		Tues.	26	at Tampa Bay
	Tues.	19	Philadelphia		Thur.	28	at St. Louis
	Thur.	21	at Tampa Bay		Sat.	30	at Pittsburgh*
	Sat.	23	at Florida	Apr.	Tues.	2	at NY Rangers
	Wed.	27	NY Islanders		Thur.	4	Hartford
	Fri.	29	at Winnipeg		Sat.	6	at Hartford*
	Sun.	31	at Chicago		Sun.	7	NY Rangers*
Jan.	Wed.	3	at Colorado		Wed.	10	Philadelphia
	Sat.	6	Washington		Thur.	11	at Washington
	Tues.	9	St. Louis		Sat.	13	Ottawa*

* Denotes afternoon game.

Home Starting Times:

Night games	7:35 p.m.
Matinees	1:05 p.m.
Except Sat. Feb. 10	3:05 p.m.
Sun. Apr. 7	3:05 p.m.

Franchise date: June 30, 1982
Transferred from Denver to New Jersey, previously transferred from Kansas City to Denver, Colorado.

ATLANTIC DIVISION

22nd NHL Season

Year-by-Year Record

		Home			Road			Overall							
Season	GP	W	L	T	W	L	T	W	L	T	GF	GA	Pts.	Finished	Playoff Result
1994-95	**48**	**14**	**4**	**6**	**8**	**14**	**2**	**22**	**18**	**8**	**136**	**121**	**52**	**2nd, Atlantic Div.**	**Won Stanley Cup**
1993-94	84	29	11	2	18	14	10	47	25	12	306	220	106	2nd, Atlantic Div.	Lost Conf. Championship
1992-93	84	24	14	4	16	23	3	40	37	7	308	299	87	4th, Patrick Div.	Lost Div. Semi-Final
1991-92	80	24	12	4	14	19	3	38	31	11	289	259	87	4th, Patrick Div.	Lost Div. Semi-Final
1990-91	80	23	10	7	9	23	8	32	33	15	272	264	79	4th, Patrick Div.	Lost Div. Semi-Final
1989-90	80	22	15	3	15	19	6	37	34	9	295	288	83	2nd, Patrick Div.	Lost Div. Semi-Final
1988-89	80	17	18	5	10	23	7	27	41	12	281	325	66	5th, Patrick Div.	Out of Playoffs
1987-88	80	23	16	1	15	20	5	38	36	6	295	296	82	4th, Patrick Div.	Lost Conf. Championship
1986-87	80	20	17	3	9	28	3	29	45	6	293	368	64	6th, Patrick Div.	Out of Playoffs
1985-86	80	17	21	2	11	28	1	28	49	3	300	374	59	6th, Patrick Div.	Out of Playoffs
1984-85	80	13	21	6	9	27	4	22	48	10	264	346	54	5th, Patrick Div.	Out of Playoffs
1983-84	80	10	28	2	7	28	5	17	56	7	231	350	41	5th, Patrick Div.	Out of Playoffs
1982-83	80	11	20	9	6	29	5	17	49	14	230	338	48	5th, Patrick Div.	Out of Playoffs
1981-82**	80	14	21	5	4	28	8	18	49	13	241	362	49	5th, Smythe Div.	Out of Playoffs
1980-81**	80	15	16	9	7	29	4	22	45	13	258	344	57	5th, Smythe Div.	Out of Playoffs
1979-80**	80	12	20	8	7	28	5	19	48	13	234	308	51	6th, Smythe Div.	Out of Playoffs
1978-79**	80	8	24	8	7	29	4	15	53	12	210	331	42	4th, Smythe Div.	Out of Playoffs
1977-78**	80	17	14	9	2	26	12	19	40	21	257	305	59	2nd, Smythe Div.	Lost Prelim. Round
1976-77**	80	12	20	8	8	26	6	20	46	14	226	307	54	5th, Smythe Div.	Out of Playoffs
1975-76*	80	8	24	8	4	32	4	12	56	12	190	351	36	5th, Smythe Div.	Out of Playoffs
1974-75*	80	12	20	8	3	34	5	15	54	11	184	328	41	5th, Smythe Div.	Out of Playoffs

** Kansas City Scouts. ** Colorado Rockies.*

One of only a handful of active players to have played at least ten years with one club, Ken Daneyko was a key contributor to the Devils' Stanley Cup title in 1995.

1995-96 Player Personnel

FORWARDS	HT	WT	S	Place of Birth	Date	1994-95 Club
ARMSTRONG, Bill H.	6-2	195	L	London, Ont.	6/25/66	Albany
BERTRAND, Eric	6-1	195	L	St. Ephrem, Que.	4/16/75	Granby
BROTEN, Neal	5-9	175	L	Roseau, MN	11/29/59	Dallas-New Jersey
BRULE, Steve	5-11	185	R	Montreal, Que.	1/15/75	St-Jean-Albany
BRYLIN, Sergei	5-9	175	L	Moscow, USSR	1/13/74	Albany-New Jersey
CARPENTER, Bob	6-0	200	L	Beverly, MA	7/13/63	New Jersey
CHORSKE, Tom	6-1	205	R	Minneapolis, MN	9/18/66	Milan Devils-New Jersey
CONN, Rob	6-2	200	R	Calgary, Alta.	9/3/68	Indianapolis-Albany
DOWD, Jim	6-1	190	R	Brick, NJ	12/25/68	New Jersey
ELIAS, Patrik	6-0	175	L	Trebic, Czech.	4/13/76	Kladno
GOSSELIN, David	6-0	175	R	Levis, Que.	6/22/77	Sherbrooke
GUERIN, Bill	6-2	200	R	Wilbraham, MA	11/9/70	New Jersey
HOLIK, Bobby	6-3	220	R	Jihlava, Czech.	1/1/71	New Jersey
HOUSE, Bobby	6-1	200	R	Whitehorse, Yukon	1/7/73	Columbus-Indianapolis-Albany
LEMIEUX, Claude	6-1	215	R	Buckingham, Que.	7/16/65	New Jersey
MacLEAN, John	6-0	200	R	Oshawa, Ont.	11/20/64	New Jersey
McCAULEY, Alyn	5-11	185	L	Brockville, Ont.	5/29/77	Ottawa (OHL)
McKAY, Randy	6-1	205	R	Montreal, Que.	1/25/67	New Jersey
OLIWA, Krzysztof	6-5	220	L	Tychy, Poland	4/12/73	Alb-Saint Jn-Ral-Det (IHL)
PEDERSON, Denis	6-2	190	R	Prince Albert, Sask.	9/10/75	Prince Albert-Albany
PELLERIN, Scott	5-11	180	L	Shediac, N.B.	1/9/70	Albany
PELUSO, Mike	6-4	220	L	Pengilly, MN	11/8/65	New Jersey
PERROTT, Nathan	6-0	215	R	Owen Sound, Ont.	12/8/76	Oshawa
REGNIER, Curt	6-2	220	L	Prince Albert, Sask.	1/24/72	Albany
RHEAUME, Pascal	6-1	185	L	Quebec, Que.	6/21/73	Albany
RICHER, Stephane J. J.	6-2	215	R	Ripon, Que.	6/7/66	New Jersey
ROCHEFORT, Richard	5-9	180	R	North Bay, Ont.	1/7/77	Sudbury
ROLSTON, Brian	6-2	185	L	Flint, MI	2/21/73	Albany-New Jersey
SHARIFIJANOV, Vadim	5-11	210	L	Ufa, USSR	12/23/75	CSKA-Albany
SIMPSON, Reid	6-1	211	L	Flin Flon, Man.	5/21/69	Albany-New Jersey
SULLIVAN, Steve	5-9	155	R	Timmons, Ont.	7/6/74	Albany
SYKORA, Petr	5-11	183	L	Plzen, Czech.	11/19/76	Detroit (IHL)
WILLIAMS, Jeff	6-0	175	L	Pointe-Claire, Que.	2/11/76	Guelph
YOUNG, Adam	6-4	222	L	Toronto, Ont.	1/15/75	Windsor
ZELEPUKIN, Valeri	5-11	190	L	Voskresensk, USSR	9/17/68	New Jersey
DEFENSEMEN						
ALBELIN, Tommy	6-1	190	L	Stockholm, Sweden	5/21/64	New Jersey
BOMBARDIR, Brad	6-2	190	L	Powell River, B.C.	5/5/72	Albany
CHAMBERS, Shawn	6-2	200	L	Royal Oaks, MI	10/11/66	Tampa Bay-New Jersey
DANEYKO, Ken	6-0	210	L	Windsor, Ont.	4/17/64	New Jersey
DEAN, Kevin	6-2	195	L	Madison, WI	4/1/69	Albany-New Jersey
GOSSELIN, Christian	6-4	205	L	St. Redempteur, Que.	8/21/76	St-Hyacinthe
HELMER, Bryan	6-1	190	R	Sault Ste. Marie, Ont.	7/15/72	Albany
HULSE, Cale	6-3	210	R	Edmonton, Alta.	11/10/73	Albany
KINNEAR, Geordie	6-1	200	L	Simcoe, Ont.	7/9/73	Albany
McALPINE, Chris	6-0	190	R	Roseville, MN	12/1/71	Albany-New Jersey
NIEDERMAYER, Scott	6-0	200	L	Edmonton, Alta.	8/31/73	New Jersey
PERSSON, Ricard	6-2	205	L	Ostersund, Sweden	8/24/69	Malmo-Albany
SMITH, Jason	6-3	195	R	Calgary, Alta.	11/2/73	New Jersey-Albany
SOURAY, Sheldon	6-2	210	L	Elk Point, Alta.	7/13/76	Tri-City-Victoria-Albany
STEVENS, Scott	6-2	210	L	Kitchener, Ont.	4/1/64	New Jersey

GOALTENDERS	HT	WT	C	Place of Birth	Date	1994-95 Club
BRODEUR, Martin	6-1	205	L	Montreal, Que.	5/6/72	New Jersey
DUNHAM, Michael	6-3	185	L	Johnson City, NY	6/1/72	Albany
HEINKE, Michael	5-11	165	L	Denville, NY	1/11/71	N. Hampshire
HENRY, Frederic	5-10	150	L	Cap-Rouge, Que.	8/9/77	Granby
MASON, Chris	5-11	180	L	Red Deer, Alta.	4/20/76	Prince George
SCHWAB, Corey	6-0	180	L	North Battleford, Sask.	11/4/70	Albany
SIDORKIEWICZ, Peter	5-9	180	L	Dabrowa Bialostocka, Pol.	6/29/63	Fort Wayne
TERRERI, Chris	5-8	160	L	Providence, RI	11/15/64	New Jersey

General Managers' History

(Kansas City) Sid Abel, 1974-75 to 1975-76; (Colorado) Ray Miron, 1976-77 to 1980-81; Billy MacMillan, 1981-82 to 1982-83; Billy MacMillan and Max McNab, 1983-84; Max McNab 1984-85 to 1986-87; Lou Lamoriello, 1987-88 to date.

The offensive sparkplug of the Devils' den, Stephane Richer led New Jersey in goals (23), points (39), shorthanded goals (2) and game-winning goals (5) in 1994-95.

1994-95 Scoring

* – rookie

Regular Season

Pos	#	Player	Team	GP	G	A	Pts	+/–	PIM	PP	SH	GW	GT	S	%
R	44	Stephane Richer	N.J.	45	23	16	39	8	10	1	2	5	1	133	17.3
C	9	Neal Broten	DAL	17	0	4	4	–8	4	0	0	0	0	29	0.0
			N.J.	30	8	20	28	9	20	2	0	3	0	43	18.6
			TOTAL	47	8	24	32	1	24	2	0	3	0	72	11.1
R	15	John MacLean	N.J.	46	17	12	29	13	32	2	1	0	0	139	12.2
R	12	Bill Guerin	N.J.	48	12	13	25	6	72	4	0	3	0	96	12.5
D	4	Scott Stevens	N.J.	48	2	20	22	4	56	1	0	1	0	111	1.8
D	29	Shawn Chambers	T.B.	24	2	12	14	0	6	1	0	0	0	44	4.5
			N.J.	21	2	5	7	2	6	1	0	0	0	23	8.7
			TOTAL	45	4	17	21	2	12	2	0	0	0	67	6.0
L	16	Bobby Holik	N.J.	48	10	10	20	9	18	0	0	2	0	84	11.9
R	22	Claude Lemieux	N.J.	45	6	13	19	2	86	1	0	1	0	117	5.1
D	27	Scott Niedermayer	N.J.	48	4	15	19	19	18	4	0	0	0	52	7.7
L	17	Tom Chorske	N.J.	42	10	8	18	–4	16	0	0	2	0	59	16.9
C	14 *	Brian Rolston	N.J.	40	7	11	18	5	17	2	0	3	0	92	7.6
L	19	Bob Carpenter	N.J.	41	5	11	16	–1	19	0	0	0	2	69	7.2
D	23	Bruce Driver	N.J.	41	4	12	16	–1	18	1	0	1	1	62	6.5
D	6	Tommy Albelin	N.J.	48	5	10	15	9	20	2	0	0	0	60	8.3
C	18 *	Sergei Brylin	N.J.	26	6	8	14	12	8	0	0	0	0	41	14.6
R	21	Randy McKay	N.J.	33	5	7	12	10	44	0	0	0	0	44	11.4
L	8	Mike Peluso	N.J.	46	2	9	11	5	167	0	0	1	0	27	7.4
R	20	Danton Cole	T.B.	26	3	3	6	–1	6	1	0	0	0	56	5.4
			N.J.	12	1	2	3	0	8	0	0	0	0	20	5.0
			TOTAL	38	4	5	9	–1	14	1	0	0	0	76	5.3
C	11	Jim Dowd	N.J.	10	1	4	5	–5	0	1	0	0	0	14	7.1
L	25	Valeri Zelepukin	N.J.	4	1	2	3	3	6	0	0	0	0	6	16.7
D	3	Ken Daneyko	N.J.	25	1	2	3	4	54	0	0	0	0	27	3.7
D	7 *	Chris McAlpine	N.J.	24	0	3	3	4	17	0	0	0	0	19	0.0
G	30	Martin Brodeur	N.J.	40	0	2	2	0	2	0	0	0	0	0	0.0
R	24 *	David Emma	N.J.	6	0	1	1	–2	0	0	0	0	0	4	0.0
D	28 *	Kevin Dean	N.J.	17	0	1	1	6	4	0	0	0	0	11	0.0
D	26	Jason Smith	N.J.	2	0	0	0	–3	0	0	0	0	0	5	0.0
L	33 *	Reid Simpson	N.J.	9	0	0	0	–1	27	0	0	0	0	5	0.0
D	5	Jaroslav Modry	N.J.	11	0	0	0	–1	0	0	0	0	0	10	0.0
G	31	Chris Terreri	N.J.	15	0	0	0	0	0	0	0	0	0	0	0.0

Goaltending

No.	Goaltender	GPI	Mins	Avg	W	L	T	EN	SO	GA	SA	S%
30	Martin Brodeur	40	2184	2.45	19	11	6	1	3	89	908	.902
31	Chris Terreri	15	734	2.53	3	7	2	0	0	31	309	.900
	Totals	**48**	**2926**	**2.48**	**22**	**18**	**8**	**1**	**3**	**121**	**1218**	**.901**

Playoffs

Pos	#	Player	Team	GP	G	A	Pts	+/–	PIM	PP	SH	GW	OT	S	%
R	44	Stephane Richer	N.J.	19	6	15	21	9	2	3	1	2	0	55	10.9
C	9	Neal Broten	N.J.	20	7	12	19	13	6	1	0	4	1	47	14.9
R	15	John MacLean	N.J.	20	5	13	18	8	14	2	0	0	0	57	8.8
R	22	Claude Lemieux	N.J.	20	13	3	16	12	20	0	0	3	0	65	20.0
R	21	Randy McKay	N.J.	19	8	4	12	5	11	2	0	2	1	30	26.7
D	27	Scott Niedermayer	N.J.	20	4	7	11	11	10	2	0	1	0	53	7.5
R	12	Bill Guerin	N.J.	20	3	8	11	6	30	1	0	0	0	28	10.7
D	29	Shawn Chambers	N.J.	20	4	5	9	2	2	2	0	0	0	36	11.1
L	16	Bobby Holik	N.J.	20	4	4	8	7	22	2	0	1	0	33	12.1
D	6	Tommy Albelin	N.J.	20	1	7	8	5	2	0	0	0	0	17	5.9
D	4	Scott Stevens	N.J.	20	1	7	8	10	24	0	0	1	0	54	1.9
D	23	Bruce Driver	N.J.	17	1	6	7	13	8	1	0	0	0	19	5.3
L	17	Tom Chorske	N.J.	17	1	5	6	–2	4	0	0	0	0	21	4.8
L	19	Bob Carpenter	N.J.	17	1	4	5	–1	6	1	0	0	0	21	4.8
C	14 *	Brian Rolston	N.J.	6	2	1	3	6	4	1	0	0	0	12	16.7
C	11	Jim Dowd	N.J.	11	2	1	3	3	8	0	0	1	0	12	16.7
C	18 *	Sergei Brylin	N.J.	12	1	2	3	1	4	0	0	0	0	11	9.1
L	25	Valeri Zelepukin	N.J.	18	1	2	3	1	12	0	0	1	0	12	8.3
L	8	Mike Peluso	N.J.	20	1	2	3	4	8	0	0	0	0	10	10.0
D	28 *	Kevin Dean	N.J.	3	0	2	2	0	0	0	0	0	0	4	0.0
D	3	Ken Daneyko	N.J.	20	1	0	1	9	22	0	0	0	0	11	9.1
G	30	Martin Brodeur	N.J.	20	0	1	1	0	6	0	0	0	0	0	0.0
R	20	Danton Cole	N.J.	1	0	0	0	–1	0	0	0	0	0	1	0.0
G	31	Chris Terreri	N.J.	1	0	0	0	0	0	0	0	0	0	0	0.0

Goaltending

No.	Goaltender	GPI	Mins	Avg	W	L	EN	SO	GA	SA	S%
31	Chris Terreri	1	8	0.00	0	0	0	0	0	2	1.000
30	Martin Brodeur	20	1222	1.67	16	4	0	3	34	463	.927
	Totals	**20**	**1232**	**1.66**	**16**	**4**	**0**	**3**	**34**	**465**	**.927**

Coaching History

(Kansas City) "Bep" Guidolin, 1974-75; "Bep" Guidolin, Sid Abel, and Eddie Bush, 1975-76; (Colorado) John Wilson, 1976-77; Pat Kelly, 1977-78; Pat Kelly and Aldo Guidolin, 1978-79; Don Cherry, 1979-80; Bill MacMillan, 1980-81; Bert Marshall and Marshall Johnston, 1981-82; (New Jersey) Bill MacMillan, 1982-83; Bill MacMillan and Tom McVie, 1983-84; Doug Carpenter, 1984-85 to 1986-87; Doug Carpenter and Jim Schoenfeld, 1987-88; Jim Schoenfeld, 1988-89; Jim Schoenfeld and John Cunniff, 1989-90; John Cunniff and Tom McVie, 1990-91; Tom McVie, 1991-92; Herb Brooks, 1992-93; Jacques Lemaire, 1993-94 to date.

Captains' History

Simon Nolet, 1974-75 to 1976-77; Wilf Paiement, 1977-78; Gary Croteau, 1978-79; Mike Christie, Rene Robert, Lanny McDonald, 1979-80; Lanny McDonald, 1980-81, Lanny McDonald, Rob Ramage, 1981-82; Don Lever, 1982-83; Don Lever and Mel Bridgman, 1983-84; Mel Bridgman, 1984-85 to 1986-87; Kirk Muller, 1987-88 to 1990-91; Bruce Driver, 1991-92; Scott Stevens, 1992-93 to date.

Club Records

Team

(Figures in brackets for season records are games played; records for fewest points, wins, ties, losses, goals, goals against are for 70 or more games)

Most Points	106	1993-94 (84)
Most Wins	47	1993-94 (84)
Most Ties	21	1977-78 (80)
Most Losses	56	1983-84 (80)
		1975-76 (80)
Most Goals	308	1992-93 (84)
Most Goals Against	374	1985-86 (80)
Fewest Points	*36	1975-76 (80)
	41	1983-84 (80)
Fewest Wins	*12	1975-76 (80)
	17	1982-83 (80)
		1983-84 (80)
Fewest Ties	3	1985-86 (80)
Fewest Losses	25	1993-94 (84)
Fewest Goals	*184	1974-75 (80)
	230	1982-83 (80)
Fewest Goals Against	220	1993-94 (84)

Longest Winning Streak

Over-all	7	Oct. 6- Oct. 23/93
Home	8	Oct. 9- Nov. 7/87
Away	4	Oct. 5-23/89 Dec. 31/91-Jan. 31/92 Nov. 5-Nov. 18/93

Longest Undefeated Streak

Over-all	9	Feb. 26- Mar. 13/94 (7 wins, 2 ties)
Home	10	Feb. 28- Mar. 29/94 (9 wins, 1 tie)
Away	8	Nov. 5- Dec. 2/93 (5 wins, 3 ties)

Longest Losing Streak

Over-all	*14	Dec. 30/75- Jan. 29/76
	10	Oct. 14- Nov. 4/83

Home	9	Dec. 22/85- Feb. 6/86
Away	12	Oct. 19/83- Dec. 1/83

Longest Winless Streak

Over-all	*27	Feb. 12- Apr. 4/76 (21 losses, 6 ties)
	18	Oct. 20- Nov. 26/82 (14 losses 4 ties)
Home	*14	Feb. 12- Mar. 30/76 (10 losses, 4 ties)
		Feb. 4- Mar. 31/79 (12 losses, 2 ties)
	9	Dec. 22/85- Feb. 6/86 (9 losses)
Away	*32	Nov. 12/77- Mar. 15/78 (22 losses, 10 ties)
	14	Dec. 26/82- Mar. 5/83 (13 losses, 1 tie)

Most Shutouts, Season	5	1993-94 (84)
Most PIM, Season	2,494	1988-89 (80)
Most Goals, Game	9	Seven times.

Individual

Most Seasons	12	Ken Daneyko, Bruce Driver
Most Games	752	John MacLean
Most Goals, Career	295	John MacLean
Most Assists, Career	335	Kirk Muller
Most Points, Career	588	John MacLean (295 goals, 293 assists)
Most PIM, Career	1,936	Ken Daneyko
Most Shutouts, Career	6	Chris Terreri, Martin Brodeur

Longest Consecutive

Games Streak	388	Ken Daneyko (Nov. 4/89-Mar. 29/94)
Most Goals, Season	46	Pat Verbeek (1987-88)

Most Assists, Season	60	Scott Stevens (1993-94)
Most Points, Season	94	Kirk Muller (1987-88; 37G, 57A)
Most PIM, Season	283	Ken Daneyko (1988-89)

Most Points, Defenseman

Season	78	Scott Stevens (1993-94; 18G, 60A)

Most Points, Center

Season	94	Kirk Muller (1987-88; 37G, 57A)

Most Points, Right Wing,

Season	*87	Wilf Paiement (1977-78; 31G, 56A)
	87	John MacLean (1988-89; 42G, 45A)

Most Points, Left Wing,

Season	86	Kirk Muller (1989-90; 30G, 56A)

Most Points, Rookie,

Season	63	Kevin Todd (1991-92; 21G, 42A)
Most Shutouts, Season	3	Sean Burke (1988-89) Martin Brodeur (1993-94, 1994-95)
Most Goals, Game	4	Bob MacMillan (Jan. 8/82) Pat Verbeek (Feb. 28/88)
Most Assists, Game	5	Kirk Muller (Mar. 25/87) Greg Adams (Oct. 10/86) Tom Kurvers (Feb. 13/89)
Most Points, Game	6	Kirk Muller (Nov. 29/86; 3G, 3A)

* Records include Kansas City Scouts and Colorado Rockies from 1974-75 through 1981-82

All-time Record vs. Other Clubs

Regular Season

		At Home						On Road						Total					
	GP	W	L	T	GF	GA	PTS	GP	W	L	T	GF	GA	PTS	GP	W	L	T	GF	GA	PTS
Anaheim	1	1	0	0	4	0	2	1	1	0	0	6	3	2	2	2	0	0	10	3	4
Boston	35	7	20	8	96	130	22	38	10	25	3	120	170	23	73	17	45	11	216	300	45
Buffalo	36	9	20	7	112	139	25	36	6	26	4	110	166	16	72	15	46	11	222	305	41
Calgary	37	11	23	3	109	144	25	36	4	27	5	93	172	13	73	15	50	8	202	316	38
Chicago	38	15	14	9	114	115	39	39	9	22	8	112	163	26	77	24	36	17	226	278	65
Dallas	37	18	16	3	123	115	39	37	9	22	6	100	150	24	74	27	38	9	223	265	63
Detroit	33	15	10	8	118	95	38	32	12	18	2	114	138	26	65	27	28	10	232	233	64
Edmonton	25	11	12	2	88	88	24	25	7	13	5	97	124	19	50	18	25	7	185	212	43
Florida	4	4	0	0	15	4	8	5	2	1	2	12	10	6	9	6	1	2	27	14	14
Hartford	27	14	10	3	103	100	31	25	7	12	6	77	92	20	52	21	22	9	180	192	51
Los Angeles	35	15	15	5	121	130	35	35	3	26	6	107	189	12	70	18	41	11	228	319	47
Montreal	36	12	24	0	104	161	24	36	6	26	4	90	148	16	72	18	50	4	194	309	40
NY Islanders	61	20	31	10	202	245	50	61	6	46	9	172	291	21	122	26	77	19	374	536	71
NY Rangers	62	27	31	4	212	234	58	61	16	37	8	194	271	40	123	43	68	12	406	505	98
Ottawa	5	5	0	0	24	11	10	6	4	1	1	22	11	9	11	9	1	1	46	22	19
Philadelphia	60	29	27	4	220	231	62	61	12	42	7	150	262	31	121	41	69	11	370	493	93
Pittsburgh	59	29	19	11	232	204	69	58	19	35	4	205	247	42	117	48	54	15	437	451	111
Quebec	28	14	12	2	118	102	30	26	9	14	3	83	106	21	54	23	26	5	201	208	51
St. Louis	39	17	15	7	128	114	41	38	8	25	5	118	172	21	77	25	40	12	246	286	62
San Jose	4	3	1	0	20	7	6	3	2	1	0	10	5	4	7	5	2	0	30	12	10
Tampa Bay	6	4	1	1	20	12	9	5	3	1	1	15	12	7	11	7	2	2	35	24	16
Toronto	32	13	10	9	120	103	35	33	6	24	3	107	151	15	65	19	34	12	227	254	50
Vancouver	41	18	17	6	130	137	42	41	6	24	11	118	160	23	82	24	41	17	248	297	65
Washington	58	24	27	7	187	187	55	59	16	40	3	177	255	35	117	40	67	10	364	442	90
Winnipeg	21	6	9	6	66	70	18	23	4	16	3	61	92	11	44	10	25	9	127	162	29
Defunct Clubs	8	4	2	2	25	19	10	3	3	3	0	19	27	7	16	6	5	5	44	46	17
Totals	**828**	**345**	**366**	**117**	**2811**	**2897**	**807**	**828**	**189**	**527**	**112**	**2489**	**3587**	**490**	**1656**	**534**	**893**	**229**	**5300**	**6484**	**1297**

Calgary totals include Atlanta, 1974-75 to 1979-80. Dallas totals include Minnesota, 1974-75 to 1992-93.
New Jersey totals include Kansas City, 1974-75 to 1975-76, and Colorado, 1976-77 to 1981-82.

Playoffs

	Series	W	L	GP	W	L	T	GF	GA	Last Mtg.	Round	Result
Boston	3	2	1	18	11	7	0	55	52	1995	CQF	W 4-1
Buffalo	1	1	0	7	4	3	0	14	14	1994	CQF	W 4-3
Detroit	1	1	0	4	4	0	0	16	7	1995	F	W 4-0
NY Islanders	1	1	0	6	4	2	0	23	18	1988	DSF	W 4-2
NY Rangers	2	0	2	14	6	8	0	41	46	1994	CF	L 3-4
Philadelphia	2	1	1	8	4	4	0	23	20	1995	CF	W 4-2
Pittsburgh	3	1	2	17	8	9	0	47	56	1995	CSF	W 4-1
Washington	2	1	1	13	6	7	0	43	44	1990	DSF	L 2-4
Totals	**15**	**8**	**7**	**87**	**47**	**40**	**0**	**262**	**257**			

Playoff Results 1995-91

Year	Round	Opponent	Result	GF	GA
1995	**F**	**Detroit**	**W 4-0**	**16**	**7**
	CF	Philadelphia	W 4-2	20	14
	CSF	Pittsburgh	W 4-1	17	8
	CQF	Boston	W 4-1	14	5
1994	CF	NY Rangers	L 3-4	16	18
	CSF	Boston	W 4-2	22	17
	CQF	Buffalo	W 4-3	14	14
1993	DSF	Pittsburgh	L 1-4	13	23
1992	DSF	NY Rangers	L 3-4	25	28
1991	DSF	Pittsburgh	L 3-4	17	25

Abbreviations: Round: F – Final;
CF – conference final; **CQF** – conference quarter-final;
CSF – conference semi-final; **DF** – division final;
DSF – division semi-final; **SF** – semi-final;
QF – quarter-final; **PR** – preliminary round.

1994-95 Results

Jan.	22	at	Hartford	2-2	14	Ottawa	4-2
	25	at	Buffalo	1-2	16	Hartford	2-2
	26	at	Boston	0-1	18	Tampa Bay	1-2
	28	at	Montreal	1-5	19	Boston	4-3
	31		Buffalo	2-1	22 at	NY Rangers	5-2
Feb.	2		Quebec	5-4	24 at	Pittsburgh	2-5
	4	at	Quebec	0-2	26 at	NY Islanders	5-5
	5		Pittsburgh	3-3	29 at	Ottawa	4-2
	9		NY Rangers	4-1	30 at	Philadelphia	4-3
	11		Philadelphia	1-3	**Apr.** 1	Montreal	4-1
	12	at	Florida	4-4	4	Tampa Bay	1-1
	15		Washington	4-2	5 at	Ottawa	2-0
	17		NY Islanders	2-2	9	NY Rangers	2-0
	18	at	NY Islanders	2-3	10 at	Montreal	1-2
	20	at	Washington	2-0	12 at	Washington	2-2
	23		Boston	2-3	14	NY Islanders	6-3
	25		Washington	3-3	16	Hartford	3-2
	27		Montreal	6-1	18 at	Tampa Bay	2-3
Mar.	2	at	Boston	2-7	20 at	Florida	0-1
	4		Florida	6-1	22	Philadelphia	3-4
	6	at	Quebec	3-6	26	Pittsburgh	3-3
	8	at	NY Rangers	4-6	28	Florida	3-1
	10	at	Tampa Bay	3-2	30	Quebec	4-2
	12	at	Philadelphia	3-4	**May** 3 at	Buffalo	4-5

Entry Draft
Selections 1995-81

1995
Pick
18	Petr Sykora
44	Nathan Perrott
70	Sergei Vyshedkevich
78	David Gosselin
79	Alyn McCauley
96	Henrik Rehnberg
122	Chris Mason
148	Adam Young
174	Richard Rochefort
200	Frederic Henry
226	Colin O'Hara

1994
Pick
25	Vadim Sharifijanov
51	Patrik Elias
71	Sheldon Souray
103	Zdenek Skorepa
129	Christian Gosselin
134	Ryan Smart
155	Luciano Caravaggio
181	Jeff Williams
207	Eric Bertrand
233	Steve Sullivan
259	Scott Swanjord
269	Mike Hanson

1993
Pick
13	Denis Pederson
32	Jay Pandolfo
39	Brendan Morrison
65	Krzysztof Oliwa
110	John Guirestante
143	Steve Brule
169	Nikolai Zavarukhin
195	Thomas Cullen
221	Judd Lambert
247	Jimmy Provencher
273	Michael Legg

1992
Pick
18	Jason Smith
42	Sergei Brylin
66	Cale Hulse
90	Vitali Tomilin
94	Scott McCabe
114	Ryan Black
138	Daniel Trebil
162	Geordie Kinnear
186	Stephane Yelle
210	Jeff Toms
234	Heath Weenk
258	Vladislav Yakovenko

1991
Pick
3	Scott Niedermayer
11	Brian Rolston
33	Donevan Hextall
55	Fredrik Lindqvist
77	Bradley Willner
121	Curt Regnier
143	David Craievich
165	Paul Wolanski
187	Daniel Reimann
231	Kevin Riehl
253	Jason Hehr

1990
Pick
20	Martin Brodeur
24	David Harlock
29	Chris Gotziaman
53	Michael Dunham
56	Brad Bombardir
64	Mike Bodnarchuk
95	Dean Malkoc
104	Petr Kuchyna
116	Lubomir Kolnik
137	Chris McAlpine
179	Jaroslav Modry
200	Corey Schwab
221	Valeri Zelepukin
242	Todd Reirden

1989
Pick
5	Bill Guerin
18	Jason Miller
26	Jarrod Skalde
47	Scott Pellerin
89	Mike Heinke
110	David Emma
152	Sergei Starikov
173	Andre Faust
215	Jason Simon
236	Peter Larsson

1988
Pick
12	Corey Foster
23	Jeff Christian
54	Zdeno Ciger
65	Matt Ruchty
75	Scott Luik
96	Chris Nelson
117	Chad Johnson
138	Chad Erickson
159	Bryan Lafort
180	Sergei Svetlov
201	Bob Woods
207	Alexander Semak
222	Charles Hughes
243	Michael Pohl

1987
Pick
2	Brendan Shanahan
23	Rickard Persson
65	Brian Sullivan
86	Kevin Dean
107	Ben Hankinson
128	Tom Neziol
149	Jim Dowd
170	John Blessman
191	Peter Fry
212	Alain Charland

1986
Pick
3	Neil Brady
24	Todd Copeland
45	Janne Ojanen
62	Marc Laniel
66	Anders Carlsson
108	Troy Crowder
129	Kevin Todd
150	Ryan Pardoski
171	Scott McCormack
192	Frederic Chabot
213	John Andersen
236	Doug Kirton

1985
Pick
3	Craig Wolanin
24	Sean Burke
32	Eric Weinrich
45	Myles O'Connor
66	Gregg Polak
108	Bill McMillan
129	Kevin Schrader
150	Ed Krayer
171	Jamie Huscroft
192	Terry Shold
213	Jamie McKinley
234	David Williams

1984
Pick
2	Kirk Muller
23	Craig Billington
44	Neil Davey
74	Paul Ysebaert
86	Jon Morris
107	Kirk McLean
128	Ian Ferguson
149	Vladimir Kames
170	Mike Roth
190	Mike Peluso
211	Jarkko Piiparinen
231	Chris Kiene

1983
Pick
6	John MacLean
24	Shawn Evans
85	Chris Terreri
105	Gordon Mark
125	Greg Evtushevski
145	Viacheslav Fetisov
165	Jay Octeau
185	Alexander Chernykh
205	Allan Stewart
225	Alexei Kasatonov

1982
Pick
8	Rocky Trottier
18	Ken Daneyko
43	Pat Verbeek
54	Dave Kasper
5	Scott Brydges
106	Mike Moher
127	Paul Fulcher
148	John Hutchings
169	Alan Hepple
190	Brent Shaw
207	Tony Gilliard
211	Scott Fusco
232	Dan Dorion

1981
Pick
5	Joe Cirella
26	Rich Chernomaz
48	Uli Hiemer
66	Gus Greco
87	Doug Speck
108	Bruce Driver
129	Jeff Larmer
150	Tony Arima
171	Tim Army
192	John Johannson

Coach

LEMAIRE, JACQUES GERARD
Coach, New Jersey Devils. Born in LaSalle, Quebec, September 7, 1945.

Jacques Lemaire is entering his third season as head coach of the New Jersey Devils. Last season Lemaire led the Devils to a record of 22-18-8 and their first Stanley Cup championship that included a four-game sweep in the finals. In 1993-94, his first season behind the Devils' bench, he led the team to a franchise record 106 points and guided the team to the Conference Finals for the first time since 1988. Lemaire was named the winner of the Jack Adams Award as the NHL's outstanding coach and was also honored by The Sporting News and The Hockey News. Lemaire, who served as the assistant to the managing director of the Montreal Canadiens for seven years, coached the Canadiens from February 24, 1984 to the end of the 1984-85 season. During his successful term as the Habs' coach, he led the team to the Conference Finals in 1984 and to a first place finish in the Adams Division in 1984-85.

A member of the Hockey Hall of Fame as a player, Lemaire coached Sierre of the Swiss League and Longueuil of the Quebec Major Junior Hockey League before joining the Canadiens' organization in 1983.

Coaching Record

		Regular Season					Playoffs		
Season	**Team**	**Games**	**W**	**L**	**T**	**%**	**Games**	**W**	**L**	**%**
1979-80	Sierre (Switzerland)				UNAVAILABLE				
1980-81	Sierre (Switzerland)				UNAVAILABLE				
1982-83	Longueuil (QMJHL)	70	37	29	4	.557	15	9	6	.600
1983-84	Montreal (NHL)	17	7	10	0	.412	15	9	6	.600
1984-85	Montreal (NHL)	80	41	27	12	.588	12	6	6	.500
1993-94	New Jersey (NHL)	84	47	25	12	.631	20	11	9	.550
1994-95	New Jersey (NHL)	48	22	18	8	.542	20	16	4	.800*
	NHL Totals	229	117	80	32	.581	67	42	25	.627

* Stanley Cup win.

Club Directory

Meadowlands Arena
P.O. Box 504
East Rutherford, NJ 07073
Phone **201/935-6050**
GM FAX 201/935-6898
FAX 201/935-2127
Capacity: 19,040

Chairman	John J. McMullen
President & General Manager	Louis A. Lamoriello
Senior Vice President, Finance	Chris Modrzynski
Vice President, General Counsel	Joseph C. Benedetti
Vice President, Ticket Operations	Terry Farmer
Vice President, Communications & Broadcasting	John Hewig
Vice President, Sales & Marketing	Michael G. McCall
Vice President, Operations & Human Resources	Peter McMullen
Executive Assistants to the President/GM	Marie Carnevale, Mary K. Morrison

Hockey Club Personnel
Head Coach	Jacques Lemaire
Assistant Coaches	Chris Nilan, Dennis Gendron
Goaltending Coach	Jacques Caron
Director of Scouting	David Conte
Scouting Staff	Claude Carrier, Glen Dirk, Milt Fisher, Ferny Flaman, Dan Labraaten, Chris Lamoriello, Yvon Lemaire, Joe Mahoney, Larry Perris, Marcel Pronovost, Lou Reycroft, Ed Thomlinson, Les Widdifield
Pro Scouting Staff	John Cunniff, Bob Hoffmeyer, Jan Ludvig
Scouting Staff Assistant	Callie A. Smith
Strength & Conditioning Coach	Michael Vasalani
Medical Trainer	Ted Schuch
Equipment Manager	Dave Nichols
Assistant Equipment Manager	Alex Abasto
Massage Therapist	Bob Huddleston
Team Cardiologist	Dr. Joseph Niznik
Team Dentist	Dr. H. Hugh Gardy
Team Orthopedists	Dr. Barry Fisher, Dr. Len Jaffe
Exercise Physiologist	Dr. Garret Caffrey
Physical Therapist	David Feniger
Video Consultant	Mitch Kaufman

Finance Department
Senior Director of Finance	Scott Struble
Staff Accountants	Gina Durante, Rob Geoffroy, Bill Rodriguez
Secretary	Eileen Musikant

Ticket Department
Director, Ticket Operations	Tom Bates
Director, Customer Service/Gold Circle	Gail DeRisi
Director, Group Sales	Neil Desormeaux

Marketing Department
Senior Director, Promotional Marketing	Ken Ferriter
Director, Ticket Sales	Kevin Morgan
Director, Promotions	Carol Kolbus
Coordinator, Game Entertainment	Joe Schilp
Account Managers	David Beck, Megan Gardner, Mike Kozak
Secretary	Karen Pietz

Communications Department
Senior Director, Media Relations	Mike Levine
Media Relations Assistants	Audra Ottimo, Gary Symmons
Merchandising Assistant	David Perricone
Community Relations	Seth Schachter
Receptionists	Jelsa Belotta, Pat Maione
Staff Assistant	Wayne Rose

Television/Radio
Television Outlet	SportsChannel
Broadcasters	Mike Emrick, Play-by-Play; Doug Sulliman, Color
Radio Outlet	WABC (770 AM)
Broadcasters	Mike Miller, Play-by-Play; TBA, Color
Dimensions of Rink	200 feet by 85 feet
Club Colors	Red, Black and White

General Manager

LAMORIELLO, LOU
President and General Manager, New Jersey Devils.
Born in Providence, Rhode Island, October 21, 1942.

Lou Lamoriello's life-long dedication to the game of hockey was rewarded in 1992 when he was named a recipient of the Lester Patrick Trophy for outstanding service to hockey in the United States. Lamoriello is entering his ninth season as president and general manager of the Devils following more than 20 years with Providence College as a player, coach and administrator. His trades, signings and draft choices helped lead the Devils to its first ever Stanley Cup championship in 1995. A member of the varsity hockey Friars during his undergraduate days, he became an assistant coach with the college club after graduating in 1963. Lamoriello was later named head coach and in the ensuing 15 years, led his teams to a 248-179-13 record, a .578 winning percentage and appearances in 10 post-season tournaments, including the 1983 NCAA Final Four. Lamoriello also served a five-year term as athletic director at Providence and was a co-founder of Hockey East, one of the strongest collegiate hockey conferences in the U.S. He remained as athletic director until he was hired as president of the Devils on April 30, 1987. He assumed the dual responsibility of general manager on September 10, 1987.

New York Islanders

1994-95 Results: 15W-28L-5T 35PTS. Seventh, Atlantic Division

Forced out of the lineup by injuries for all but 13 games in 1994-95, Darius Kasparaitis remains an important member of the Islanders' defense corps.

Schedule

Oct.	Sat.	7	at Boston		Mon.	15	Tampa Bay*
	Tues.	10	at Toronto		Wed.	17	Hartford
	Sat.	14	Philadelphia		Mon.	22	at Colorado
	Sun.	15	at Florida		Wed.	24	at Calgary
	Tues.	17	NY Rangers		Fri.	26	at Edmonton
	Fri.	20	Montreal		Sat.	27	at Vancouver
	Wed.	25	at Philadelphia		Tues.	30	Buffalo
	Thur.	26	Pittsburgh	**Feb.**	Sat.	3	at Washington
	Sat.	28	Philadelphia		Sun.	4	Dallas
	Tues.	31	at Florida		Tues.	6	NY Rangers
Nov.	Fri.	3	at Tampa Bay		Thur.	8	at NY Rangers
	Sat.	4	Washington		Sat.	10	Anaheim*
	Tues.	7	Vancouver		Mon.	12	Ottawa
	Fri.	10	at NY Rangers		Thur.	15	Calgary
	Sat.	11	St. Louis		Sat.	17	San Jose*
	Tues.	14	at San Jose		Thur.	22	at NY Rangers
	Thur.	16	at Los Angeles		Fri.	23	Tampa Bay
	Fri.	17	at Anaheim		Sun.	25	Edmonton*
	Wed.	22	Los Angeles		Tues.	27	Detroit
	Fri.	24	at Buffalo		Thur.	29	at Detroit
	Sat.	25	Tampa Bay	**Mar.**	Fri.	1	at New Jersey
	Tues.	28	Colorado		Sun.	3	Winnipeg*
	Thur.	30	at Ottawa		Tues.	5	Boston
Dec.	Sat.	2	New Jersey		Thur.	7	at Boston
	Tues.	5	Pittsburgh		Sat.	9	at Winnipeg*
	Wed.	6	at Hartford		Sat.	16	at Pittsburgh*
	Sat.	9	at New Jersey*		Sun.	17	at Chicago*
	Sun.	10	at Philadelphia		Tues.	19	at Philadelphia
	Tues.	12	Florida		Thur.	21	at Florida*
	Thur.	14	at Washington		Sat.	23	New Jersey
	Sat.	16	Hartford		Mon.	25	at Montreal
	Tues.	19	at St. Louis		Tues.	26	Washington
	Thur.	21	at Dallas		Sat.	30	at Hartford*
	Sat.	23	Washington		Sun.	31	NY Rangers*
	Tues.	26	Boston	**Apr.**	Tues.	2	Philadelphia
	Wed.	27	at New Jersey		Fri.	5	at Ottawa
	Sun.	31	at Buffalo		Sat.	6	Buffalo
Jan.	Thur.	4	Montreal		Mon.	8	at Tampa Bay
	Sat.	6	Ottawa		Wed.	10	at Pittsburgh
	Tues.	9	Chicago		Fri.	12	Florida
	Thur.	11	Toronto		Sat.	13	at Montreal

* Denotes afternoon game.

Home Starting Times:
Weeknights . . . . 7:30 p.m.
Saturdays and Sundays. . . . . 7:00 p.m.
Matinees . . . . 1:00 p.m.
Except Sun. Mar. 31 . . . . 3:00 p.m.

Franchise date: June 6, 1972

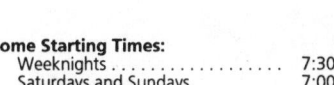

ATLANTIC DIVISION

24th NHL Season

Year-by-Year Record

		Home			Road			Overall						
Season	GP	W	L	T	W	L	T	W	L	T	GF	GA	Pts.	Finished	Playoff Result
1994-95	48	10	11	3	5	17	2	15	28	5	126	158	35	7th, Atlantic Div.	Out of Playoffs
1993-94	84	23	15	4	13	21	8	36	36	12	282	264	84	4th, Atlantic Div.	Lost Conf. Quarter-Final
1992-93	84	20	19	3	20	18	4	40	37	7	335	297	87	3rd, Patrick Div.	Lost Conf. Championship
1991-92	80	20	15	5	14	20	6	34	35	11	291	299	79	5th, Patrick Div.	Out of Playoffs
1990-91	80	15	19	6	10	26	4	25	45	10	223	290	60	6th, Patrick Div.	Out of Playoffs
1989-90	80	15	17	8	16	21	3	31	38	11	281	288	73	4th, Patrick Div.	Lost Div. Semi-Final
1988-89	80	19	18	3	9	29	2	28	47	5	265	325	61	6th, Patrick Div.	Out of Playoffs
1987-88	80	24	10	6	15	21	4	39	31	10	308	267	88	1st, Patrick Div.	Lost Div. Semi-Final
1986-87	80	20	15	5	15	18	7	35	33	12	279	281	82	3rd, Patrick Div.	Lost Div. Final
1985-86	80	22	11	7	17	18	5	39	29	12	327	284	90	3rd, Patrick Div.	Lost Div. Semi-Final
1984-85	80	26	11	3	14	23	3	40	34	6	345	312	86	3rd, Patrick Div.	Lost Div. Final
1983-84	80	28	11	1	22	15	3	50	26	4	357	269	104	1st, Patrick Div.	Lost Final
1982-83	**80**	**26**	**11**	**3**	**16**	**15**	**9**	**42**	**26**	**12**	**302**	**226**	**96**	**2nd, Patrick Div.**	**Won Stanley Cup**
1981-82	**80**	**33**	**3**	**4**	**21**	**13**	**6**	**54**	**16**	**10**	**385**	**250**	**118**	**1st, Patrick Div.**	**Won Stanley Cup**
1980-81	**80**	**23**	**6**	**11**	**25**	**12**	**3**	**48**	**18**	**14**	**355**	**260**	**110**	**1st, Patrick Div.**	**Won Stanley Cup**
1979-80	**80**	**26**	**9**	**5**	**13**	**19**	**8**	**39**	**28**	**13**	**281**	**247**	**91**	**2nd, Patrick Div.**	**Won Stanley Cup**
1978-79	80	31	3	6	20	12	8	51	15	14	358	214	116	1st, Patrick Div.	Lost Semi-Final
1977-78	80	29	3	8	19	14	7	48	17	15	334	210	111	1st, Patrick Div.	Lost Quarter-Final
1976-77	80	24	11	5	23	10	7	47	21	12	288	193	106	2nd, Patrick Div.	Lost Semi-Final
1975-76	80	24	8	8	18	13	9	42	21	17	297	190	101	2nd, Patrick Div.	Lost Semi-Final
1974-75	80	22	6	12	11	19	10	33	25	22	264	221	88	3rd, Patrick Div.	Lost Semi-Final
1973-74	78	13	17	9	6	24	9	19	41	18	182	247	56	8th, East Div.	Out of Playoffs
1972-73	78	10	25	4	2	35	2	12	60	6	170	347	30	8th, East Div.	Out of Playoffs

1995-96 Player Personnel

FORWARDS

Name	HT	WT	S	Place of Birth	Date	1994-95 Club
AIVAZOFF, Micah	6-0	195	L	Powell River, B.C.	5/4/69	Edmonton
ANDERSSON, Niclas	5-9	175	L	Kungalv, Sweden	5/20/71	Denver
ARMSTRONG, Derek	5-11	180	R	Ottawa, Ont.	4/23/73	Denver
BERTUZZI, Todd	6-3	227	L	Sudbury, Ont.	2/2/75	Guelph
DALGARNO, Brad	6-3	215	R	Vancouver, B.C.	8/11/67	NY Islanders
DARBY, Craig	6-3	180	R	Oneida, NY	9/26/72	Fredericton-Mtl-NYI
DEULING, Jarrett	5-11	194	L	Vernon, B.C.	3/4/74	Worcester
FLATLEY, Pat	6-2	197	R	Toronto, Ont.	10/3/63	NY Islanders
GREEN, Travis	6-2	200	R	Castlegar, B.C.	12/20/70	NY Islanders
HLAVAC, Jan	6-0	185	L	Prague, Czech.	9/20/76	HC Sparta
JOHANSSON, Andreas	5-10	198	L	Hofors, Sweden	5/19/73	Farjestad
KAMINSKY, Yan	6-1	176	L	Penza, USSR	7/28/71	Denver-NY Islanders
KING, Derek	6-1	203	L	Hamilton, Ont.	2/11/67	NY Islanders
LINDROS, Brett	6-4	215	R	London, Ont.	12/2/75	Kingston-NY Islanders
MacWILLIAM, Mike	6-4	230	L	Burnaby, B.C.		Denver
MARINUCCI, Chris	6-0	175	L	Grand Rapids, MN	12/29/71	Denver-NY Islanders
McINNIS, Marty	6-0	185	R	Hingham, MA.	6/2/70	NY Islanders
McKENZIE, Jim	6-3	205	L	Gull Lake, Sask.	11/3/69	Pittsburgh
MULLER, Kirk	6-0	205	L	Kingston, Ont.	2/8/66	Montreal-NY Islanders
NIECKAR, Barry	6-3	200	R	Rama, Sask.	12/16/67	Saint John-Calgary
ORSAGH, Vladimir	5-10	172	L	Banska Bystrica, Czech.	5/24/77	B. Bystrica
PALFFY, Zigmund	5-10	169	L	Skalica, Czech.	5/5/72	Denver-NY Islanders
PLANTE, Dan	5-11	198	R	St. Louis, MO	10/5/71	Denver
TAYLOR, Chris	6-0	185	L	Stratford, Ont.	3/6/72	Denver-NY Islanders
THOMAS, Steve	5-11	184	L	Stockport, England	7/15/63	NY Islanders
VASILIEV, Andrei	5-9	180	R	Voskresensk, USSR	3/30/72	Denver-NY Islanders
VUKOTA, Mick	6-2	195	R	Saskatoon, Sask.	9/14/66	NY Islanders

DEFENSEMEN

Name	HT	WT	S	Place of Birth	Date	1994-95 Club
BEERS, Bob	6-2	200	R	Pittsburgh, PA	5/20/67	NY Islanders
CHEBATURKIN, Vladimir	6-2	189	L	Tyumen, USSR	4/23/75	Elektrostal
CHYNOWETH, Dean	6-2	190	R	Calgary, Alta.	10/30/68	NY Islanders
DINEEN, Gord	6-0	195	R	Quebec City, Que.	9/21/62	Denver-NY Islanders
HERTER, Jason	6-1	190	R	Hafford, Sask.	10/2/70	Kalamazoo
HOLLAND, Jason	6-2	190	R	Morinville, Alta.	4/30/76	Kamloops
KASPARAITIS, Darius	5-11	195	L	Elektrenai, USSR	10/16/72	NY Islanders
LACHANCE, Scott	6-1	197	L	Charlottesville, VA	10/22/72	NY Islanders
LUKOWICH, Brad	6-1	170	L	Cranbrook, B.C.	8/12/76	Kamloops
LUONGO, Chris	6-0	199	R	Detroit, MI	3/17/67	Denver-NY Islanders
McCABE, Bryan	6-1	200	L	St. Catharines, Ont.	6/8/75	Spokane-Brandon
PILON, Richard	6-0	202	L	Saskatoon, Sask.	4/30/68	NY Islanders
REDDEN, Wade	6-2	193	L	Lloydminster, Sask.	6/12/77	Brandon
SCHNEIDER, Mathieu	5-11	189	L	New York, NY	6/12/69	Montreal-NY Islanders
SEVERYN, Brent	6-2	210	L	Vegreville, Alta.	2/22/66	Florida-NY Islanders
SMITH, Denis	6-1	210	L	Windsor, Ont.	5/13/77	Windsor
STRUDWICK, Jason	6-3	210	L	Edmonton, Alta.	7/17/75	Kamloops
TICHY, Milan	6-3	198	L	Plzen, Czech.	9/22/69	Denver-NY Islanders
VASKE, Dennis	6-2	210	L	Rockford, IL	10/11/67	NY Islanders
WIDMER, Jason	6-0	205	L	Calgary, Alta.	8/1/73	Worcester-Cdn. National-NYI

GOALTENDERS

Name	HT	WT	C	Place of Birth	Date	1994-95 Club
FICHAUD, Eric	5-11	165	L	Montreal, Que.	11/4/75	Chicoutimi
HNILICKA, Milan	6-0	180	L	Litomerice, Czech.	6/25/73	Denver
McARTHUR, Mark	5-11	189	L	Peterborough, Ont.	11/16/75	Guelph
McLENNAN, Jamie	6-0	190	L	Edmonton, Alta.	6/30/71	NY Islanders-Denver
PIETRANGELO, Frank	5-10	185	L	Niagara Falls, Ont.	12/17/64	Minnesota
SALO, Tommy	5-11	161	L	Surahammar, Sweden	2/1/71	Denver-NY Islanders
SODERSTROM, Tommy	5-9	165	L	Stockholm, Sweden	7/17/69	NY Islanders

1994-95 Scoring

* – rookie

Regular Season

Pos	#	Player	Team	GP	G	A	Pts	+/-	PIM	PP	SH	GW	GT	S	%
C	20	Ray Ferraro	NYI	47	22	21	43	1	30	2	0	1	2	94	23.4
D	72	Mathieu Schneider	MTL	30	5	15	20	−3	49	2	0	0	0	82	6.1
			NYI	13	3	6	9	−5	30	1	0	2	0	36	8.3
			TOTAL	43	8	21	29	−8	79	3	0	2	0	118	6.8
L	9	Kirk Muller	MTL	33	8	11	19	−21	33	3	0	1	1	81	9.9
			NYI	12	3	5	8	3	14	1	1	1	0	16	18.8
			TOTAL	45	11	16	27	−18	47	4	1	2	1	97	11.3
R	26	Patrick Flatley	NYI	45	7	20	27	9	12	1	0	1	0	81	8.6
L	32	Steve Thomas	NYI	47	11	15	26	−14	60	3	0	1	0	133	8.3
L	27	Derek King	NYI	43	10	16	26	−5	41	7	0	0	0	118	8.5
L	68	* Zigmund Palffy	NYI	33	10	7	17	3	6	1	0	1	0	75	13.3
C	18	Marty McInnis	NYI	41	9	7	16	−1	8	0	0	1	0	68	13.2
D	7	Scott Lachance	NYI	26	6	7	13	2	26	3	0	0	0	56	10.7
C	39	Travis Green	NYI	42	5	7	12	−10	25	0	0	0	0	59	8.5
D	37	Dennis Vaske	NYI	41	1	11	12	3	53	0	0	0	0	48	2.1
D	2	Bob Beers	NYI	22	2	7	9	−8	6	1	0	0	0	38	5.3
D	24	Brent Severyn	FLA	9	1	1	2	−3	37	1	0	0	0	10	10.0
			NYI	19	1	3	4	1	34	0	0	0	0	22	4.5
			TOTAL	28	2	4	6	−2	71	1	0	0	0	32	6.3
R	15	Brad Dalgarno	NYI	22	3	2	5	−8	14	1	1	0	1	18	16.7
C	17	* Chris Marinucci	NYI	12	1	4	5	−1	2	0	0	0	0	11	9.1
C	14	Ron Sutter	NYI	27	1	4	5	−8	21	0	0	1	0	29	3.4
R	75	* Brett Lindros	NYI	33	1	3	4	−8	100	0	0	1	0	35	2.9
D	6	Chris Luongo	NYI	47	1	3	4	−2	36	0	0	0	0	44	2.3
D	25	Paul Stanton	NYI	18	0	4	4	−6	9	0	0	0	0	28	0.0
C	28	Chris Taylor	NYI	10	0	3	3	1	2	0	0	0	0	13	0.0
L	34	* Yan Kaminsky	NYI	2	1	1	2	2	0	0	0	0	0	4	25.0
D	47	Richard Pilon	NYI	20	1	1	2	−3	40	0	0	0	0	11	9.1
C	10	* Craig Darby	MTL	10	0	2	2	−5	0	0	0	0	0	4	0.0
			NYI	3	0	0	0	−1	0	0	0	0	0	1	0.0
			TOTAL	13	0	2	2	−6	0	0	0	0	0	5	0.0
D	3	Dean Chynoweth	NYI	32	0	2	2	9	77	0	0	0	0	22	0.0
R	12	Mick Vukota	NYI	40	0	2	2	1	109	0	0	0	0	11	0.0
G	35	* Tommy Salo	NYI	6	0	1	1	0	0	0	0	0	0	0	0.0
C	10	Kip Miller	NYI	8	0	1	1	0	0	0	0	0	0	11	0.0
D	11	Darius Kasparaitis	NYI	13	0	1	1	−11	22	0	0	0	0	8	0.0
D	36	* Jason Widmer	NYI	1	0	0	0	−1	0	0	0	0	0	0	0.0
D	34	* Milan Tichy	NYI	2	0	0	0	−1	2	0	0	0	0	1	0.0
L	38	* Andrei Vasiliev	NYI	2	0	0	0	0	2	0	0	0	0	2	0.0
D	8	Gord Dineen	NYI	9	0	0	0	−5	2	0	0	0	0	4	0.0
L	9	Dave Chyzowski	NYI	13	0	0	0	−2	11	0	0	0	0	11	0.0
G	29	* Jamie McLennan	NYI	21	0	0	0	0	2	0	0	0	0	0	0.0
G	30	Tommy Soderstrom	NYI	26	0	0	0	0	0	0	0	0	0	0	0.0

Goaltending

No.	Goaltender	GPI	Mins	Avg	W	L	T	EN	SO	GA	SA	S%
35	* Tommy Salo	6	358	3.02	1	5	0	0	0	18	189	.905
30	Tommy Soderstrom	26	1350	3.11	8	12	3	2	1	70	717	.902
29	* Jamie McLennan	21	1185	3.39	6	11	2	1	0	67	539	.876
	Totals	48	2909	3.26	15	28	5	3	1	158	1448	.891

Coach

MILBURY, MIKE
Coach, New York Islanders. Born in Walpole, MA, June 17, 1952.

Milbury, 43, comes to the Islanders with 20 years of professional hockey experience with the Boston Bruins — as a player, assistant coach, assistant general manager, general manager and coach on both the NHL and AHL levels.

The Walpole, MA native joined the Boston organization after graduating from Colgate University with a degree in urban sociology and enjoyed a nine-year playing career with the team. He retired May 6, 1985 and took over as assistant coach. He returned to the ice late in the 1985-86 season when injuries decimated the Bruins' defense.

Milbury's playing career concluded on July 16, 1987 when he took over as coach of the Maine Mariners, Boston's top AHL affiliate. In his first year with the team he guided the Mariners to the AHL's Northern Division title and was named both AHL Coach of the Year and *The Hockey News* Minor League Coach of the Year.

He was named the assistant general manager and coach of the Boston Bruins May 16, 1989. In two years behind the bench Milbury was the NHL's most successful coach: He guided the Bruins to consecutive 100-point seasons and Adams Division titles, the 1990 Presidents' Trophy and Wales Conference championship, and an appearance in the Stanley Cup Finals in 1990. He earned coach of the year honors from both *The Hockey News* and *The Sporting News* for this effort.

Milbury and his wife, Debbie, have two sons, Owen and Luke, and two daughters, Alison and Caitlin.

Coaching Record

Season	Team	Regular Season					Playoffs			
		Games	W	L	T	%	Games	W	L	%
1987-88	Maine (AHL)	80	44	29	7	.594	10	5	5	.500
1988-89	Maine (AHL)	80	32	40	8	.450	....	....	....	....
1989-90	**Boston (NHL)**	80	46	25	9	.631	21	13	8	.619
1990-91	**Boston (NHL)**	80	44	24	12	.606	19	10	9	.526
	NHL Totals	160	90	49	21	.628	40	23	17	.575

Club Records

Team

(Figures in brackets for season records are games played; records for fewest points, wins, ties, losses, goals, goals against are for 70 or more games)

Most Points	118	1981-82 (80)	
Most Wins	54	1981-82 (80)	
Most Ties	22	1974-75 (80)	
Most Losses	60	1972-73 (78)	
Most Goals	385	1981-82 (80)	
Most Goals Against	347	1972-73 (78)	
Fewest Points	30	1972-73 (78)	
Fewest Wins	12	1972-73 (78)	
Fewest Ties	4	1983-84 (80)	
Fewest Losses	15	1978-79 (80)	
Fewest Goals	170	1972-73 (78)	
Fewest Goals Against	190	1975-76 (80)	

Longest Winning Streak

Over-all .... 15 Jan. 21/82-
Feb. 20/82

Home .... 14 Jan. 2/82-
Feb. 27/82

Away .... 8 Feb. 27/81-
Mar. 31/81

Longest Undefeated Streak

Over-all .... 15 Jan. 21-
Feb. 20/82
(15 wins)
Nov. 4-
Dec. 4/80
(13 wins, 2 ties)

Home .... 23 Oct. 17/78-
Jan. 27/79
(19 wins, 4 ties)
Jan. 2/82-
Apr. 3/82
(21 wins, 2 ties)

Away .... 8 Four times

Longest Losing Streak

Over-all .... 12 Dec. 27/72-
Jan. 18/73
Nov. 22-
Dec. 17/88

Home .... 5 Jan. 2-23/33
Feb. 28-
Mar. 19/74
Nov. 22-
Dec. 17/88

Away .... 15 Jan. 20-
Apr. 1/73

Longest Winless Streak

Over-all .... 15 Nov. 22-
Dec. 23/72
(12 losses, 3 ties)

Home .... 7 Oct. 14-
Nov. 21/72
(6 losses, 1 tie)
Nov. 28-
Dec. 23/72
(5 losses, 2 ties)
Feb. 13-
Mar. 13/90
(4 losses, 3 ties)

Away .... 20 Nov. 3/72-
Jan. 13/73
(19 losses, 1 tie)

Most Shutouts, Season 10 1975-76 (80)
Most PIM, Season 1,857 1986-87 (80)
Most Goals, Game .... 11 Dec. 20/83
(Pit. 3 at NYI 11)
Mar. 3/84
(NYI 11 at Tor. 6)

Individual

Most Seasons .... 17 Billy Smith
Most Games .... 1,123 Bryan Trottier
Most Goals, Career .... 573 Mike Bossy
Most Assists, Career .... 853 Bryan Trottier
Most Points, Career ...... 1,353 Bryan Trottier
(500 goals, 853 assists)
Most PIM, Career .... 1,466 Garry Howatt
Most Shutouts, Career .... 25 Glenn Resch
Longest Consecutive
Games Streak .... 576 Bill Harris
(Oct. 7/72-Nov. 30/79)
Most Goals, Season .... 69 Mike Bossy
(1978-79)
Most Assists, Season .... 87 Bryan Trottier
(1978-79)

Most Points, Season .... 147 Mike Bossy
(1981-82)
(64 goals, 83 assists)
Most PIM, Season .... 356 Brian Curran
(1986-87)
Most Points, Defenseman,
Season .... 101 Denis Potvin
(1978-79)
(31 goals, 70 assists)
Most Points, Center,
Season .... 134 Bryan Trottier
(1978-79)
(47 goals, 87 assists)
Most Points, Right Wing,
Season .... *147 Mike Bossy
(1981-82)
(64 goals, 83 assists)
Most Points, Left Wing,
Season .... 100 John Tonelli
(1984-85)
(42 goals, 58 assists)
Most Points, Rookie,
Season .... 95 Bryan Trottier
(1975-76)
(32 goals, 63 assists)
Most Shutouts, Season .... 7 Glenn Resch
(1975-76)
Most Goals, Game .... 5 Bryan Trottier
(Dec. 23/78;
Feb. 13/82)
John Tonelli
(Jan. 6/81)
Most Assists, Game .... 6 Mike Bossy
(Jan. 6/81)
Most Points, Game .... 8 Bryan Trottier
(Dec. 23/78)

* NHL Record.

Retired Numbers

5	Denis Potvin	1973-1988
22	Mike Bossy	1977-1987
23	Bob Nystrom	1972-1986
31	Billy Smith	1972-1989

All-time Record vs. Other Clubs

Regular Season

	At Home						On Road						Total					
	GP	W	L	T	GF	GA	PTS	GP	W	L	T	GF	GA	PTS	GP	W	L	T	GF	GA	PTS
Anaheim	1	0	1	0	0	3	0	1	1	0	0	4	3	2	2	1	1	0	4	6	2
Boston	43	16	23	4	136	148	36	41	9	23	9	115	161	27	84	25	46	13	251	309	63
Buffalo	43	18	18	7	125	125	43	43	13	24	6	125	156	32	86	31	42	13	250	281	75
Calgary	43	24	10	9	178	114	57	43	13	19	11	134	154	37	86	37	29	20	312	268	94
Chicago	39	16	11	12	142	118	44	41	16	20	5	143	135	37	80	32	31	17	285	253	81
Dallas	39	22	9	8	154	111	52	39	19	14	6	148	114	44	78	41	23	14	302	225	96
Detroit	38	22	14	2	148	109	46	37	16	19	2	123	131	34	75	38	33	4	271	240	80
Edmonton	23	10	5	8	99	92	28	23	5	14	4	70	93	14	46	15	19	12	169	185	42
Florida	5	1	3	1	9	12	3	4	2	2	0	11	11	4	9	3	5	1	20	23	7
Hartford	25	15	7	3	96	64	33	27	11	12	4	102	101	26	52	26	19	7	198	165	59
Los Angeles	37	20	13	4	140	108	44	37	14	16	7	125	132	35	74	34	29	11	265	240	79
Montreal	42	19	19	4	141	128	42	42	11	24	7	130	162	29	84	30	43	11	271	290	71
New Jersey	61	46	6	9	291	172	101	61	31	20	10	245	202	72	122	77	26	19	536	374	173
NY Rangers	73	49	18	6	314	223	104	72	21	43	8	219	286	50	145	70	61	14	533	509	154
Ottawa	6	2	2	2	26	19	6	5	2	2	1	22	13	5	11	4	4	3	48	32	11
Philadelphia	74	41	22	11	294	216	93	72	21	43	8	221	277	50	146	62	65	19	515	493	143
Pittsburgh	65	35	22	8	270	211	78	66	24	31	11	231	257	59	131	59	53	19	501	468	137
Quebec	25	15	9	1	108	83	31	26	10	14	2	84	100	22	51	25	23	3	192	183	53
St. Louis	41	23	8	10	161	98	56	40	17	16	7	134	146	41	81	40	24	17	295	244	97
San Jose	4	4	0	0	27	15	8	3	1	2	0	12	8	2	7	5	2	0	39	23	10
Tampa Bay	5	2	3	0	14	19	4	6	3	3	0	19	17	6	11	5	6	0	33	36	10
Toronto	38	22	13	3	166	117	47	40	20	17	3	149	135	43	78	42	30	6	315	252	90
Vancouver	39	22	9	8	150	102	52	41	20	18	3	138	135	43	80	42	27	11	288	237	95
Washington	61	37	23	1	252	193	75	61	27	25	9	206	195	63	122	64	48	10	458	388	138
Winnipeg	23	11	6	6	87	71	28	22	13	7	2	87	70	28	45	24	13	8	174	141	56
Defunct Clubs	13	11	0	2	75	33	24	13	4	4	5	35	41	12	26	15	5	6	110	74	36
Totals	906	503	274	129	3603	2704	1135	906	344	433	129	3032	3235	817	1812	847	707	258	6635	5939	1952

Calgary totals include Atlanta, 1972-73 to 1979-80. Dallas totals include Minnesota, 1972-73 to 1992-93.
New Jersey totals include Kansas City, 1974-75 to 1975-76, and Colorado, 1976-77 to 1981-82.

Playoffs

	Series	W	L	GP	W	L	T	GF	GA	Last Mtg.	Round	Result
Boston	2	2	0	11	8	3	0	49	35	1983	CF	W 4-2
Buffalo	3	3	0	16	12		0	59	45	1980	SF	W 4-2
Chicago	2	2	0	6	6	0	0	21	6	1979	QF	W 4-0
Dallas	1	1	0	5	4	1	0	26	16	1981	F	W 4-1
Edmonton	3	2	1	15	9	6	0	58	47	1984	F	L 1-4
Los Angeles	1	1	0	4	3	1	0	21	10	1980	PR	W 3-1
Montreal	4	1	3	22	8	14	0	55	64	1993	CF	L 1-4
New Jersey	1	0	1	6	2	4	0	18	23	1988	DSF	L 2-4
NY Rangers	8	5	3	39	20	19	0	129	132	1994	CQF	L 0-4
Philadelphia	4	1	3	25	11	14	0	69	83	1987	DF	L 3-4
Pittsburgh	3	3	0	19	11	8	0	67	58	1993	DF	W 4-3
Quebec	1	1	0	4	4	0	0	18	9	1982	CF	W 4-0
Toronto	2	1	1	10	6	4	0	33	20	1981	PR	W 3-0
Vancouver	2	2	0	6	6	0	0	26	14	1982	F	W 4-0
Washington	6	5	1	30	18	12	0	99	88	1993	DSF	W 4-2
Totals	43	30	13	218	128	90	0	748	650			

Playoff Results 1995-91

Year	Round	Opponent	Result	GF	GA
1994	CQF	NY Rangers	L 0-4	3	22
1993	CF	Montreal	L 1-4	11	16
	DF	Pittsburgh	W 4-3	24	27
	DSF	Washington	W 4-2	23	22

Abbreviations: Round: F – Final;
CF – conference final; **CQF** – conference quarter-final;
CSF – conference semi-final; **DF** – division final;
DSF – division semi-final; **SF** – semi-final;
QF – quarter-final; **PR** – preliminary round.

1994-95 Results

Jan.	21	Florida	2-1		14	at	Hartford	4-6
	22	Ottawa	3-3		16	at	Buffalo	3-6
	24	Philadelphia	4-3		18	at	Boston	3-4
	27 at	Washington	2-5		23		NY Rangers	1-0
	28	Tampa Bay	1-4		25	at	Hartford	1-5
	31 at	Florida	5-1		26		New Jersey	5-5
Feb.	2 at	Philadelphia	5-4		28	at	Pittsburgh	3-6
	4 at	Montreal	2-4		30		Boston	2-3
	7 at	Tampa Bay	2-5	Apr.	1		Buffalo	1-5
	9	Pittsburgh	2-5		4		Washington	4-5
	11	Buffalo	2-1		7	at	NY Rangers	4-3
	14	Quebec	2-3		8		Florida	2-2
	17 at	New Jersey	2-2		11	at	Tampa Bay	2-5
	18	New Jersey	3-2		12	at	Florida	3-1
	20 at	Montreal	2-3		14	at	New Jersey	3-6
	22 at	Buffalo	3-3		16		NY Rangers	2-3
	23	Tampa Bay	1-4		18		Quebec	5-2
	25	Pittsburgh	3-1		20	at	Philadelphia	1-2
	28	Montreal	2-1		22		Ottawa	2-3
Mar.	2	Washington	3-4		24	at	Boston	5-3
	5 at	Ottawa	1-3		26	at	Washington	5-6
	7	Hartford	3-1		28	at	NY Rangers	4-2
	9 at	Pittsburgh	2-4		29	at	Ottawa	3-4
	11 at	Quebec	1-2	May	2		Philadelphia	0-2

Entry Draft
Selections 1995-81

1995 Pick		1991 Pick		1987 Pick		1984 Pick	
2	Wade Redden	4	Scott Lachance	13	Dean Chynoweth	20	Duncan MacPherson
28	Jan Hlavac	26	Zigmund Palffy	34	Jeff Hackett	41	Bruce Melanson
41	Denis Smith	48	Jamie McLennan	55	Dean Ewen	62	Jeff Norton
106	Vladimir Orsagh	70	Milan Hnilicka	76	George Maneluk	70	Doug Wieck
158	Andrew Taylor	92	Steve Junker	97	Petr Vlk	83	Ari Haanpaa
210	David MacDonald	114	Robert Valicevic	118	Rob DiMaio	104	Mike Murray
211	Mike Broda	136	Andreas Johansson	139	Knut Walbye	125	Jim Wilharm
		158	Todd Sparks	160	Jeff Saterdalen	146	Kelly Murphy
1994 Pick		180	John Johnson	181	Shawn Howard	167	Franco Desantis
9	Brett Lindros	202	Robert Canavan	202	John Herlihy	187	Tom Warden
38	Jason Holland	224	Marcus Thuresson	223	Michael Erickson	208	David Volek
63	Jason Strudwick	246	Marty Schriner	244	Will Averill	228	Russ Becker
90	Brad Lukowich					249	Allister Brown
112	Mark McArthur	**1990 Pick**		**1986 Pick**			
116	Albert O'Connell	6	Scott Scissons	17	Tom Fitzgerald	**1983 Pick**	
142	Jason Stewart	27	Chris Taylor	38	Dennis Vaske	3	Pat LaFontaine
194	Mike Loach	48	Dan Plante	59	Bill Berg	16	Gerald Diduck
203	Peter Hogardh	90	Chris Marinucci	80	Shawn Byram	37	Garnet McKechney
220	Gord Walsh	111	Joni Lehto	101	Dean Sexsmith	57	Mike Neill
246	Kirk Dewaele	132	Michael Guilbert	104	Todd McLellan	65	Mikko Maklla
272	Dick Tarnstrom	153	Sylvain Fleury	122	Tony Schmalzbauer	84	Bob Caulfield
		174	John Joyce	138	Will Anderson	97	Ron Viglasi
1993 Pick		195	Richard Enga	143	Darin Illikainen	117	Darin Illikainen
23	Todd Bertuzzi	216	Martin Lacroix	164	Peter Harris	137	Jim Sprenger
40	Bryan McCabe	237	Andy Shirr	185	Jeff Jablonski	157	Dale Henry
66	Vladim Chebaturkin			206	Kerry Clark	177	Kevin Vescio
92	Warren Luhning	**1989 Pick**		227	Dan Beaudette	197	Dave Shellington
118	Tommy Salo	2	Dave Chyzowski	248	Paul Thompson	217	John Bjorkman
144	Peter Leboutillier	23	Travis Green			237	Peter McGeough
170	Darren Van Impe	44	Jason Zent	**1985 Pick**			
196	Rod Hinks	65	Brent Grieve	6	Brad Dalgarno	**1982 Pick**	
222	Daniel Johansson	86	Jace Reed	13	Derek King	21	Patrick Flatley
248	Stephane Larocque	90	Steve Young	34	Brad Lauer	42	Vern Smith
274	Carl Charland	99	Kevin O'Sullivan	55	Jeff Finley	63	Garry Lacey
		128	Jon Larson	76	Kevin Herom	84	Alan Kerr
1992 Pick		133	Brett Harkins	89	Tommy Hedlund	105	Rene Breton
5	Darius Kasparaitis	149	Phil Huber	97	Jeff Sveen	126	Roger Kortko
56	Jarrett Deuling	170	Matthew Robbins	118	Rod Dallman	147	John Tiano
104	Tomas Klimt	191	Vladimir Malakhov	139	Kurt Lackten	168	Todd Okerlund
105	Ryan Duthie	212	Kelly Ens	160	Hank Lammens	189	Gord Paddock
128	Derek Armstrong	233	Iain Fraser	181	Rich Wiest	210	Eric Faust
152	Vladimir Grachev			202	Real Arsenault	231	Pat Goff
159	Steve O'Rourke	**1988 Pick**		223	Mike Volpe	252	Jim Koudys
176	Jason Widmer	16	Kevin Cheveldayoff	244	Tony Grenier		
200	Daniel Paradis	29	Wayne Doucet			**1981 Pick**	
224	David Wainwright	37	Sean LeBrun			21	Paul Boutilier
248	Andrei Vasiljev	58	Danny Lorenz			42	Gord Dineen
		79	Andre Brassard			57	Ron Handy
		100	Paul Rutherford			63	Neal Coulter
		111	Pavel Gross			84	Todd Lumbard
		121	Jason Rathbone			94	Jacques Sylvestre
		142	Yves Gaucher			126	Chuck Brimmer
		163	Marty McInnis			147	Teppo Virta
		184	Jeff Blumer			168	Bill Dowd
		205	Jeff Kampersal			189	Scott MacLellan
		226	Phillip Neururer			210	Dave Randerson
		247	Joe Capprini				

Club Directory

Nassau Veterans'
Memorial Coliseum
Uniondale, NY 11553
Phone **516/794-4100**
GM FAX 516/542-9350
FAX 516/542-9348
Capacity: 16,297

Co-Chairmen	Robert Rosenthal, Stephen Walsh
Chief Operating Officer	Ralph Palleschi
Executive Vice-President	Paul Greenwood
Senior Vice-President & CFO	Arthur McCarthy
Consultant	John Krumpe
General Counsel	William Skehan

Hockey Staff

Vice-President/General Manager	Don Maloney
Vice-President of Hockey Operations	Al Arbour
Assistant General Manager/ Director of Player Personnel	Darcy Regier
Assistant to the General Manager	Gerry Ehman
Head Coach	Mike Milbury
Assistant Coach	Guy Charron
Goaltending Coach	Bob Froese
Director of Pro Scouting	Ken Morrow
Scouting Staff	Harry Boyd, Earl Ingarfield, Jim Madigan, Chris Pryor, Mario Saraceno
Administrative Assistants to the General Manager	Joanne Holewa, Pam Kamvakis
Video Coordinator	Bob Smith

Communications Staff

Vice-President/Communications	Patrick Calabria
Director of Amateur Hockey Development/ Alumni Relations	Bob Nystrom
Director of Community Relations	Maureen Brady
Director of Game Events	Tim Beach
Director of Media Relations	Ginger Killian Serby
Director of Publications	Chris Botta
Assistant Director of Media Relations	Eric Mirlis
Community Relations Assistant	Tom Bigliani

Sales and Administration

Vice-President/Media Sales	Arthur Adler
Controller	Ralph Sellitti
Assistant Controller	Ginna Cotton
Director of Administration	Joseph Dreyer
Director of Corporate Sales	Bill Kain
Director of Executive Suites	Tracy F. Matthews
Director of Marketing and Ticket Sales	Brian Edwards
Director of Merchandising	Mike Walsh
Director of Suite Operations	Sam Buonogura
Ticket Manager	Cathy Henning
Account Representatives	Tom Engel, Richard Gaudet, Scott Lindquist, Brian Rabinowitz, Eric Schiebe, Andy Smith, Bob Tobin
Accountants	Christine Bowler, Vincent Diorio, Sue Meares
Assistant Ticket Manager	Joy Rusciano
Administrative Assistant	Margie Barrett
Office Manager/Group Administrator	Kathleen Maloney
Executive Suite Coordinator	Rebecca Giardino
Receptionist	Colleen Touhey-Ramirez, Jennifer Guadagno

Medical and Training Staff

Athletic Trainer	Ed Tyburski
Equipment Manager	John Doolan
Assistant Trainer	Jerry Iannarelli
Assistant Equipment Manager	Joe McMahon
Team Orthopedists	Jeffrey Minkoff, M.D., Barry Simonson, M.D.
Team Internists	Gerald Cordani, M.D., Larry Smith, M.D.
Physical Therapist	Steve Wirth
Team Dentists	Bruce Michnik, D.D.S., Jan Sherman, D.D.S.

Team Information

Colors	Orange, blue, white, silver, Atlantic green
Television Coverage	SportsChannel
Announcers	Ed Westfall, Stan Fischler
Radio	WRCN – 94.3 & 103.9
Announcers	Barry Landers, Bob Nystrom

General Manager

MALONEY, DON
Vice-President/General Manager, New York Islanders.
Born in Lindsay, Ont., September 5, 1958.

Don Maloney became the second general manager in New York Islanders' history on August 17, 1992. After a 13-year playing career that included stays with the Rangers, Islanders and Whalers, Maloney joined the Islanders' organization in January, 1991 as a part-time assistant to coach Al Arbour and general manager Bill Torrey. The following season, he became assistant general manager, representing the team in contract discussions and organizing the Islanders' training camp itinerary. In his playing career, Maloney compiled 214 goals and 350 assists in 765 games.

General Managers' History

William A. Torrey, 1972-73 to 1991-92; Don Maloney, 1992-93 to date.

Coaching History

Phil Goyette and Earl Ingarfield, 1972-73; Al Arbour, 1973-74 to 1985-86; Terry Simpson, 1986-87 to 1987-88; Terry Simpson and Al Arbour, 1988-89; Al Arbour, 1989-90 to 1993-94; Lorne Henning, 1994-95; Mike Milbury, 1995-96.

Captains' History

Ed Westfall, 1972-73 to 1975-76; Ed Westfall, Clark Gillies, 1976-77; Clark Gillies, 1977-78, 1978-79; Denis Potvin, 1979-80 to 1986-87; Brent Sutter, 1987-88 to 1990-91; Brent Sutter and Patrick Flatley, 1991-92; Patrick Flatley, 1992-93 to date.

New York Rangers

1994-95 Results: 22W-23L-3T 47PTS. Fourth, Atlantic Division

For the third time in his four seasons in New York, Mark Messier led the Rangers in scoring, notching 53 points in 46 games.

Schedule

Oct.	Sat.	7	at Hartford
	Wed.	11	Winnipeg
	Sat.	14	at Toronto
	Mon.	16	Hartford
	Tues.	17	at NY Islanders
	Fri.	20	at Buffalo
	Sun.	22	Ottawa
	Tues.	24	Vancouver
	Thur.	26	at Tampa Bay
	Sun.	29	Toronto
	Tues.	31	at San Jose
Nov.	Thur.	2	at Los Angeles
	Fri.	3	at Anaheim
	Mon.	6	Calgary
	Wed.	8	Tampa Bay
	Fri.	10	NY Islanders
	Sat.	11	at Hartford
	Tues.	14	at St. Louis
	Thur.	16	at Chicago
	Fri.	17	at Winnipeg
	Tues.	21	Pittsburgh
	Wed.	22	at Pittsburgh
	Sat.	25	at Detroit
	Mon.	27	New Jersey
	Wed.	29	Buffalo
Dec.	Fri.	1	Colorado
	Sat.	2	at Ottawa
	Mon.	4	Anaheim
	Wed.	6	Chicago
	Fri.	8	Detroit
	Sat.	9	at Montreal
	Mon.	11	Dallas
	Wed.	13	Boston
	Fri.	15	at Buffalo
	Sat.	16	at Washington
	Mon.	18	Washington
	Thur.	21	at Philadelphia
	Fri.	22	Hartford
	Tues.	26	Ottawa
	Thur.	28	at Vancouver
	Sat.	30	at Edmonton

	Sun.	31	at Calgary
Jan.	Wed.	3	Montreal
	Fri.	5	at Washington
	Mon.	8	Washington
	Wed.	10	San Jose
	Sat.	13	at Philadelphia*
	Sun.	14	St. Louis
	Mon.	22	Los Angeles
	Wed.	24	Philadelphia
	Sat.	27	at Boston*
	Wed.	31	at Dallas
Feb.	Sat.	3	at Colorado*
	Tues.	6	at NY Islanders
	Thur.	8	NY Islanders
	Sat.	10	at New Jersey*
	Sun.	11	at Tampa Bay*
	Thur.	15	Montreal
	Sat.	17	at Ottawa
	Sun.	18	at Pittsburgh
	Thur.	22	NY Islanders
	Sat.	24	at Florida
	Wed.	28	Boston
Mar.	Fri.	1	Buffalo
	Mon.	4	New Jersey
	Thur.	7	at Tampa Bay
	Sat.	9	at Washington*
	Wed.	13	Florida
	Sat.	16	at Montreal
	Tues.	19	Edmonton
	Sat.	23	at Boston*
	Sun.	24	Pittsburgh
	Wed.	27	Florida
	Sun.	31	at NY Islanders*
Apr.	Tues.	2	New Jersey
	Thur.	4	at Philadelphia
	Fri.	5	Philadelphia
	Sun.	7	at New Jersey*
	Mon.	8	Florida
	Wed.	10	Washington
	Fri.	12	Tampa Bay
	Sun.	14	at Florida*

* Denotes afternoon game.

Home Starting Times:

All games	7:35 p.m.
Except Sun. Oct. 22	7:00 p.m.
Sun. Oct. 29	6:00 p.m.
Sun. Jan. 14	8:00 p.m.
Sun. Mar. 24	8:00 p.m.

Franchise date: May 15, 1926

EASTERN CONFERENCE

ATLANTIC DIVISION

70th NHL Season

Year-by-Year Record

Season	GP	Home W	L	T	Road W	L	T	Overall W	L	T	GF	GA	Pts.	Finished	Playoff Result
1994-95	48	11	10	3	11	13	0	22	23	3	139	134	47	4th, Atlantic Div.	Lost Conf. Semi-Final
1993-94	**84**	**28**	**8**	**6**	**24**	**16**	**2**	**52**	**24**	**8**	**299**	**231**	**112**	**1st, Atlantic Div.**	**Won Stanley Cup**
1992-93	84	20	17	5	14	22	6	34	39	11	304	308	79	6th, Patrick Div.	Out of Playoffs
1991-92	80	28	8	4	22	17	1	50	25	5	321	246	105	1st, Patrick Div.	Lost Div. Final
1990-91	80	22	11	7	14	20	6	36	31	13	297	265	85	2nd, Patrick Div.	Lost Div. Semi-Final
1989-90	80	20	11	9	16	20	4	36	31	13	279	267	85	1st, Patrick Div.	Lost Div. Final
1988-89	80	21	17	2	16	18	6	37	35	8	310	307	82	3rd, Patrick Div.	Lost Div. Semi-Final
1987-88	80	22	13	5	14	21	5	36	34	10	300	283	82	5th, Patrick Div.	Out of Playoffs
1986-87	80	18	18	4	16	20	4	34	38	8	307	323	76	4th, Patrick Div.	Lost Div. Semi-Final
1985-86	80	20	18	2	16	20	4	36	38	6	280	276	78	4th, Patick Div.	Lost Conf. Championship
1984-85	80	16	18	6	10	26	4	26	44	10	295	345	62	4th, Patrick Div.	Lost Div. Semi-Final
1983-84	80	27	12	1	15	17	8	42	29	9	314	304	93	4th, Patrick Div.	Lost Div. Semi-Final
1982-83	80	24	13	3	11	22	7	35	35	10	306	287	80	4th, Patrick Div.	Lost Div. Final
1981-82	80	19	15	6	20	12	8	39	27	14	316	306	92	2nd, Patrick Div.	Lost Div. Final
1980-81	80	17	13	10	13	23	4	30	36	14	312	317	74	4th, Patrick Div.	Lost Semi-Final
1979-80	80	22	10	8	16	22	2	38	32	10	308	284	86	3rd, Patrick Div.	Lost Quarter-Final
1978-79	80	19	13	8	21	16	3	40	29	11	316	292	91	3rd, Patrick Div.	Lost Final
1977-78	80	18	15	7	12	22	6	30	37	13	279	280	73	4th, Patrick Div.	Lost Prelim. Round
1976-77	80	17	18	5	12	19	9	29	37	14	272	310	72	4th, Patrick Div.	Out of Playoffs
1975-76	80	16	16	8	13	26	1	29	42	9	262	333	67	4th, Patrick Div.	Out of Playoffs
1974-75	80	21	11	8	16	18	6	37	29	14	319	276	88	2nd, Patrick Div.	Lost Prelim. Round
1973-74	78	26	7	6	14	17	8	40	24	14	300	251	94	3rd, East Div.	Lost Semi-Final
1972-73	78	26	8	5	21	15	3	47	23	8	297	208	102	3rd, East Div.	Lost Semi-Final
1971-72	78	26	6	7	22	11	6	48	17	13	317	192	109	2nd, East Div.	Lost Final
1970-71	78	30	2	7	19	16	4	49	18	11	259	177	109	2nd, East Div.	Lost Semi-Final
1969-70	76	22	8	8	16	14	8	38	22	16	246	189	92	4th, East Div.	Lost Quarter-Final
1968-69	76	27	7	4	14	19	5	41	26	9	231	196	91	3rd, East Div.	Lost Quarter-Final
1967-68	74	22	8	7	17	15	5	39	23	12	226	183	90	2nd, East Div.	Lost Quarter-Final
1966-67	70	18	12	5	12	16	7	30	28	12	188	189	72	4th,	Lost Semi-Final
1965-66	70	12	16	7	6	25	4	18	41	11	195	261	47	6th,	Out of Playoffs
1964-65	70	8	19	8	12	19	4	20	38	12	179	246	52	5th,	Out of Playoffs
1963-64	70	14	13	8	8	25	2	22	38	10	186	242	54	5th,	Out of Playoffs
1962-63	70	12	17	6	10	19	6	22	36	12	211	233	56	5th,	Out of Playoffs
1961-62	70	16	11	8	10	21	4	26	32	12	195	207	64	4th,	Lost Semi-Final
1960-61	70	15	15	5	7	23	5	22	38	10	204	248	54	5th,	Out of Playoffs
1959-60	70	10	15	10	7	23	5	17	38	15	187	247	49	6th,	Out of Playoffs
1958-59	70	14	16	5	12	16	7	26	32	12	201	217	64	5th,	Out of Playoffs
1957-58	70	14	15	6	18	10	7	32	25	13	195	188	77	2nd,	Lost Semi-Final
1956-57	70	15	12	8	11	18	6	26	30	14	184	227	66	4th,	Lost Semi-Final
1955-56	70	20	7	8	12	21	2	32	28	10	204	203	74	3rd,	Lost Semi-Final
1954-55	70	10	12	13	7	23	5	17	35	18	150	210	52	5th,	Out of Playoffs
1953-54	70	18	12	5	11	19	5	29	31	10	161	182	68	5th,	Out of Playoffs
1952-53	70	11	14	10	6	23	6	17	37	16	152	211	50	6th,	Out of Playoffs
1951-52	70	16	13	6	7	21	7	23	34	13	192	219	59	5th,	Out of Playoffs
1950-51	70	14	11	10	6	18	11	20	29	21	169	201	61	5th,	Out of Playoffs
1949-50	70	19	12	4	9	19	7	28	31	11	170	189	67	4th,	Lost Final
1948-49	60	13	12	5	5	19	6	18	31	11	133	172	47	6th,	Out of Playoffs
1947-48	60	11	12	7	10	14	6	21	26	13	176	201	55	4th,	Out of Playoffs
1946-47	60	11	14	5	11	18	1	22	32	6	167	186	50	5th,	Out of Playoffs
1945-46	50	8	12	5	5	16	4	13	28	9	144	191	35	6th,	Out of Playoffs
1944-45	50	7	11	7	4	18	3	11	29	10	154	247	32	6th,	Out of Playoffs
1943-44	50	4	17	4	2	22	1	6	39	5	162	310	17	6th,	Out of Playoffs
1942-43	50	7	13	5	4	18	3	11	31	8	161	253	30	6th,	Out of Playoffs
1941-42	48	15	8	1	14	9	1	29	17	2	177	143	60	1st,	Lost Semi-Final
1940-41	48	13	7	4	8	12	4	21	19	8	143	125	50	4th,	Lost Quarter-Final
1939-40	**48**	**17**	**4**	**3**	**10**	**7**	**7**	**27**	**11**	**10**	**136**	**77**	**64**	**2nd,**	**Won Stanley Cup**
1938-39	48	13	8	3	13	8	3	26	16	6	149	105	58	2nd,	Lost Semi-Final
1937-38	48	15	5	4	12	10	2	27	15	6	149	96	60	2nd, Amn. Div.	Lost Quarter-Final
1936-37	48	9	7	8	10	13	1	19	20	9	117	106	47	3rd, Amn. Div.	Lost Final
1935-36	48	11	6	7	8	11	5	19	17	12	91	96	50	4th, Amn. Div.	Out of Playoffs
1934-35	48	11	8	5	11	12	1	22	20	6	137	139	50	3rd, Amn. Div.	Lost Semi-Final
1933-34	48	11	7	6	10	12	2	21	19	8	120	113	50	3rd, Amn. Div.	Lost Quarter-Final
1932-33	**48**	**12**	**7**	**5**	**11**	**10**	**3**	**23**	**17**	**8**	**135**	**107**	**54**	**3rd, Amn. Div.**	**Won Stanley Cup**
1931-32	48	13	7	4	10	10	4	23	17	8	134	112	54	1st,	Lost Final
1930-31	44	10	9	3	9	7	6	19	16	9	106	87	47	3rd, Amn. Div.	Lost Semi-Final
1929-30	44	11	5	6	6	12	4	17	17	10	136	143	44	3rd, Amn. Div.	Lost Semi-Final
1928-29	44	12	6	4	9	7	6	21	13	10	72	65	52	2nd, Amn. Div.	Lost Final
1927-28	**44**	**10**	**8**	**4**	**9**	**8**	**5**	**19**	**16**	**9**	**94**	**79**	**47**	**2nd, Amn. Div.**	**Won Stanley Cup**
1926-27	44	13	5	4	12	8	5	25	13	6	95	72	56	1st, Amn. Div.	Lost Quarter-Final

1995-96 Player Personnel

FORWARDS	HT	WT	S	Place of Birth	Date	1994-95 Club
FERRARO, Chris	5-10	175	R	Port Jefferson, NY	1/24/73	Atlanta-Binghamton
FERRARO, Peter	5-10	175	R	Port Jefferson, NY	1/24/73	Atlanta-Binghamton
FERRARO, Ray	5-10	185	L	Trail, B.C.	8/23/64	NY Islanders
FLINTON, Eric	6-2	200	L	William Lake, B.C.	2/2/72	N. Hampshire
GERNANDER, Ken	5-10	180	L	Coleraine, MN	6/30/69	Binghamton
GRAVES, Adam	6-0	205	L	Toronto, Ont.	4/12/68	NY Rangers
JONES, Brad	6-0	195	L	Sterling Heights, MI	6/26/65	Springfield
KOVALEV, Alexei	6-0	205	L	Togliatti, USSR	2/24/73	Togliatti-NY Rangers
KUDINOV, Andrei	6-0	195	L	Chelyabinsk, USSR	6/28/70	Binghamton
KYPREOS, Nick	6-0	205	L	Toronto, Ont.	6/4/66	NY Rangers
LaFAYETTE, Nathan	6-1	194	R	New Westminster, B.C.	2/17/73	Syracuse-Vancouver-NY Rangers
LACROIX, Daniel	6-2	195	L	Montreal, Que.	3/11/69	Providence (AHL)-Bos-NYR
LANGDON, Darren	6-1	205	L	Deer Lake, Nfld.	1/8/71	Binghamton-NY Rangers
MATTEAU, Stephane	6-3	210	L	Rouyn-Noranda, Que.	9/2/69	NY Rangers
MESSIER, Mark	6-1	205	L	Edmonton, Alta.	1/18/61	NY Rangers
NEMCHINOV, Sergei	6-0	200	L	Moscow, USSR	1/14/64	NY Rangers
NIELSEN, Jeff	6-0	200	R	Grand Rapids, MN	9/20/71	Binghamton
PRESLEY, Wayne	5-11	180	R	Dearborn, MI	3/23/65	Buffalo
ROBITAILLE, Luc	6-1	195	L	Montreal, Que.	2/17/66	Pittsburgh
ROY, Jean-Yves	5-10	180	L	Rosemere, Que.	2/17/69	Binghamton-NY Rangers
STAROSTENKO, Dimitri	6-0	195	L	Minsk, USSR	3/18/73	Binghamton
SUNDSTROM, Niklas	6-0	185	L	Ornskoldsvik, Sweden	6/6/75	MoDo
VANDENBUSSCHE, Ryan	5-11	187	R	Simcoe, Ont.	2/28/73	St. John's
VERBEEK, Pat	5-9	190	R	Sarnia, Ont.	5/24/64	Hartford-NY Rangers

DEFENSEMEN						
BEUKEBOOM, Jeff	6-5	230	R	Ajax, Ont.	3/28/65	NY Rangers
BLOUIN, Sylvain	6-2	225	L	Montreal, Que.	5/21/74	Chicago-Charlotte-Binghamton
CAIRNS, Eric	6-5	225	L	Oakville, Ont.	6/27/74	Birmingham-Binghamton
DRIVER, Bruce	6-0	185	L	Toronto, Ont.	4/29/62	New Jersey
GALANOV, Maxim	6-1	175	L	Krasnoyarsk, USSR	3/13/74	Togliatti
KARPOVTSEV, Alexander	6-1	200	R	Moscow, USSR	4/7/70	Moscow D'amo-NY Rangers
KOMAROV, Pavel	6-1	180	L	Gorky, USSR	2/28/74	Torpedo Niz.-Binghamton
LEETCH, Brian	5-11	190	L	Corpus Christi, TX	3/3/68	NY Rangers
LIDSTER, Doug	6-0	190	R	Kamloops, B.C.	10/18/60	St. Louis
LOWE, Kevin	6-2	190	L	Lachute, Que.	4/15/59	NY Rangers
MALONE, Scott	6-0	195	L	Boston, MA	1/16/71	Birmingham-Binghamton
NORSTROM, Mattias	6-1	205	L	Mora, Sweden	1/2/72	Binghamton-NY Rangers
REID, Shawn	6-0	200	L	Toronto, Ont.	9/21/70	Fort Wayne-Binghamton
RICHTER, Barry	6-2	195	L	Madison, WI	9/11/70	Binghamton
SAMUELSSON, Ulf	6-1	195	L	Fagersta, Sweden	3/26/64	Leksand-Pittsburgh
SILVERMAN, Andrew	6-3	205	L	Beverly, MA	8/23/72	Binghamton-Charlotte
SOROCHAN, Lee	6-1	210	L	Edmonton, Alta.	9/9/75	Lethbridge-Saskatoon-Bing.
WERENKA, Darcy	6-1	205	R	Edmonton, Alta.	5/13/73	Binghamton

GOALTENDERS	HT	WT	C	Place of Birth	Date	1994-95 Club
HEALY, Glenn	5-10	185	L	Pickering, Ont.	8/23/62	NY Rangers
HILLEBRANDT, Jon	5-10	185	L	Cottage Grove, WI	12/18/71	Charlotte-San Diego-Binghamton
RAM, Jamie	5-11	175	L	Scarborough, Ont.	1/18/71	Binghamton
RICHTER, Mike	5-11	185	L	Abington, PA	9/22/66	NY Rangers
SHEPARD, Ken	5-10	192	L	Toronto, Ont.	1/20/74	Oshawa

General Manager

SMITH, NEIL

General Manager, New York Rangers. Born in Toronto, Ont., January 9, 1954.

Through his first six years at the helm of the Rangers, Neil Smith has enjoyed great success. The club has posted an overall record of 230-173-53, ranking sixth among NHL teams since 1989-90. New York has captured three divisional titles, two Presidents' Trophies and one Stanley Cup championship.

In 1993-94, the Rangers captured the fourth Stanley Cup in franchise history, defeating Vancouver four games to three. The championship was the culmination of a season in which New York set a club record with 52 wins and 112 points. The Rangers captured their second Presidents' Trophy in three years and became the first team since the Presidents' Trophy was established to win it, along with the Conference Championship and Stanley Cup in the same year. Following the season Neil was awarded with *The Hockey News* Executive of the Year Award.

In his first three seasons as general manager after joining the Rangers on July 17, 1989, New York enjoyed the best three consecutive finishes in club history.

On June 19, 1992, he was promoted to the position of president and general manager, becoming the ninth president in Rangers' history and the first president to also hold the title of general manager.

A native of Toronto, Ontario, Smith played junior hockey at Brockville, Ontario, before entering Western Michigan University where he became an All-American defenseman as a freshman and team captain in his second year.

After being selected by the New York Islanders in the NHL Amateur Draft and playing two seasons in the International Hockey League, Neil joined the Islanders scouting department during the '80-81 season. Following two seasons in that capacity, he joined the Detroit Red Wings in 1982 as director of professional scouting and soon after became director of their farm system.

Smith was then named director of scouting, and general manager/governor of the Adirondack Red Wings of the AHL, where he won two Calder Cup championships.

1994-95 Scoring

* – rookie

Regular Season

Pos	#	Player	Team	GP	G	A	Pts	+/–	PIM	PP	SH	GW	GT	S	%
C	11	Mark Messier	NYR	46	14	39	53	8	40	3	3	2	0	126	11.1
D	2	Brian Leetch	NYR	48	9	32	41	0	18	3	0	2	0	182	4.9
D	21	Sergei Zubov	NYR	38	10	26	36	–2	18	6	0	0	0	116	8.6
R	17	Pat Verbeek	HFD	29	7	11	18	0	53	3	0	0	1	75	9.3
			NYR	19	10	5	15	–2	18	4	0	2	0	56	17.9
			TOTAL	48	17	16	33	–2	71	7	0	2	1	131	13.0
C	9	Adam Graves	NYR	47	17	14	31	9	51	9	0	3	0	185	9.2
R	28	Steve Larmer	NYR	47	14	15	29	8	16	3	1	4	0	116	12.1
R	27	Alexei Kovalev	NYR	48	13	15	28	–6	30	1	1	1	0	103	12.6
R	16	Brian Noonan	NYR	45	14	13	27	–3	26	7	0	1	0	95	14.7
C	10	Petr Nedved	NYR	46	11	12	23	–1	26	1	0	3	0	123	8.9
C	13	Sergei Nemchinov	NYR	47	7	6	13	–6	16	0	0	3	0	67	10.4
D	25	A. Karpovtsev	NYR	47	4	8	12	–4	30	1	0	1	0	82	4.9
L	14	Troy Loney	NYI	26	5	4	9	0	23	2	0	1	0	45	11.1
			NYR	4	0	0	0	–2	0	0	0	0	0	2	0.0
			TOTAL	30	5	4	9	–2	23	2	0	1	0	47	10.6
D	24	Jay Wells	NYR	43	2	7	9	0	36	0	0	0	0	38	5.3
C	22	Nathan LaFayette	VAN	27	4	4	8	2	2	0	1	0	0	30	13.3
			NYR	12	0	0	0	1	0	0	0	0	0	5	0.0
			TOTAL	39	4	4	8	3	2	0	1	0	0	35	11.4
L	32	Stephane Matteau	NYR	41	3	5	8	–8	25	0	0	0	0	37	8.1
D	4	Kevin Lowe	NYR	44	1	7	8	–2	58	1	0	0	0	35	2.9
L	20	Mark Osborne	NYR	37	1	3	4	–2	19	0	0	0	0	32	3.1
L	19	Nick Kypreos	NYR	40	1	3	4	0	93	0	0	0	0	16	6.3
D	23	Jeff Beukeboom	NYR	44	1	3	4	3	70	0	0	0	0	29	3.4
R	26	Joey Kocur	NYR	48	1	2	3	–4	71	0	0	0	0	25	4.0
D	5	* Mattias Norstrom	NYR	9	0	3	3	2	2	0	0	0	0	4	0.0
L	15	* Darren Langdon	NYR	18	1	1	2	0	62	0	0	0	0	6	16.7
D	29	Joby Messier	NYR	10	0	2	2	2	18	0	0	0	0	4	0.0
G	30	Glenn Healy	NYR	17	0	2	2	0	2	0	0	0	0	0	0.0
R	8	* Jean-Yves Roy	NYR	3	1	0	1	–1	2	0	0	0	0	8	12.5
C	39	* Shawn McCosh	NYR	5	1	0	1	1	2	0	0	0	0	2	50.0
L	37	* Dan Lacroix	BOS	23	1	0	1	–2	38	0	0	0	0	14	7.1
			NYR	1	0	0	0	0	0	0	0	0	0	0	0.0
			TOTAL	24	1	0	1	–2	38	0	0	0	0	14	7.1
L	18	Mike Hartman	NYR	1	0	0	0	0	4	0	0	0	0	0	0.0
G	35	Mike Richter	NYR	35	0	0	0	0	2	0	0	0	0	0	0.0

Goaltending

No.	Goaltender	GPI	Mins	Avg	W	L	T	EN	SO	GA	SA	S%
30	Glenn Healy	17	888	2.36	8	6	1	0	1	35	377	.907
35	Mike Richter	35	1993	2.92	14	17	2	2	2	97	884	.890
	Totals	**48**	**2895**	**2.78**	**22**	**23**	**3**	**2**	**3**	**134**	**1263**	**.894**

Playoffs

Pos	#	Player	Team	GP	G	A	Pts	+/–	PIM	PP	SH	GW	OT	S	%
D	2	Brian Leetch	NYR	10	6	8	14	–1	8	3	0	1	0	46	13.0
C	11	Mark Messier	NYR	10	3	10	13	–11	8	2	0	1	0	26	11.5
R	27	Alexei Kovalev	NYR	10	4	7	11	2	10	0	0	0	0	23	17.4
D	21	Sergei Zubov	NYR	10	3	8	11	–9	2	1	0	0	0	34	8.8
R	17	Pat Verbeek	NYR	10	4	6	10	–8	20	3	0	0	0	29	13.8
C	13	Sergei Nemchinov	NYR	10	4	5	9	6	2	0	0	1	0	16	25.0
C	9	Adam Graves	NYR	10	4	4	8	–13	8	2	0	0	0	38	10.5
C	10	Petr Nedved	NYR	10	3	2	5	–4	6	2	0	0	0	28	10.7
R	28	Steve Larmer	NYR	10	2	2	4	–5	6	0	1	1	1	14	14.3
L	19	Nick Kypreos	NYR	10	0	2	2	3	6	0	0	0	0	9	0.0
L	20	Mark Osborne	NYR	7	1	0	1	1	2	0	0	0	0	2	50.0
D	25	A. Karpovtsev	NYR	8	1	0	1	–1	0	0	0	0	0	8	12.5
L	32	Stephane Matteau	NYR	9	0	1	1	–1	10	0	0	0	0	9	0.0
D	4	Kevin Lowe	NYR	10	0	1	1	–5	12	0	0	0	0	7	0.0
L	14	Troy Loney	NYR	1	0	0	0	0	0	0	0	0	0	0	0.0
D	5	* Mattias Norstrom	NYR	3	0	0	0	–1	0	0	0	0	0	1	0.0
G	30	Glenn Healy	NYR	5	0	0	0	0	0	0	0	0	0	0	0.0
R	16	Brian Noonan	NYR	5	0	0	0	0	8	0	0	0	0	5	0.0
G	35	Mike Richter	NYR	7	0	0	0	0	0	0	0	0	0	0	0.0
C	22	Nathan Lafayette	NYR	8	0	0	0	–1	2	0	0	0	0	1	0.0
D	23	Jeff Beukeboom	NYR	9	0	0	0	1	10	0	0	0	0	11	0.0
R	26	Joey Kocur	NYR	10	0	0	0	0	8	0	0	0	0	1	0.0
D	24	Jay Wells	NYR	10	0	0	0	–4	8	0	0	0	0	5	0.0

Goaltending

No.	Goaltender	GPI	Mins	Avg	W	L	EN	SO	GA	SA	S%
30	Glenn Healy	5	230	3.39	2	1	0	0	13	93	.860
35	Mike Richter	7	384	3.59	2	5	1	0	23	189	.878
	Totals	**10**	**616**	**3.60**	**4**	**6**	**1**	**0**	**37**	**283**	**.869**

General Managers' History

Lester Patrick, 1927-28 to 1945-46; Frank Boucher, 1946-47 to 1954-55; "Muzz" Patrick, 1955-56 to 1963-64; Emile Francis, 1964-65 to 1974-75; Emile Francis and John Ferguson, 1975-76; John Ferguson, 1976-77 to 1977-78; John Ferguson and Fred Shero, 1978-79; Fred Shero, 1979-80; Fred Shero and Craig Patrick, 1980-81; Craig Patrick, 1981-82 to 1985-86; Phil Esposito, 1986-87 to 1988-89; Neil Smith, 1989-90 to date.

Retired Numbers

1	Eddie Giacomin	1965-1976
7	Rod Gilbert	1960-1978

Club Records

Team

(Figures in brackets for season records are games played; records for fewest points, wins, ties, losses, goals, goals against are for 70 or more games)

Most Points **112** 1993-94 (84)
Most Wins **52** 1993-94 (84)
Most Ties **21** 1950-51 (70)
Most Losses **44** 1984-85 (80)
Most Goals **371** 1991-92 (80)
Most Goals Against **345** 1984-85 (80)
Fewest Points **47** 1965-66 (70)
Fewest Wins **17** 1952-53; 54-55; 59-60 (70)
Fewest Ties **5** 1991-92 (80)
Fewest Losses **17** 1971-72 (78)
Fewest Goals **150** 1954-55 (70)
Fewest Goals Against **177** 1970-71 (78)

Longest Winning Streak
Over-all .... **10** Dec. 19/39-Jan. 13/40; Jan. 19-Feb. 10/73
Home .... **14** Dec. 19/39-Feb. 25/40
Away .... **7** Jan. 12-Feb. 12/35; Oct. 28-Nov. 29/78

Longest Undefeated Streak
Over-all .... **19** Nov. 23/39-Jan. 13/40 (14 wins, 5 ties)
Home .... **26** Mar. 29/70-Feb. 2/71 (19 wins, 7 ties)
Away .... **11** Nov. 5/39-Jan. 13/40 (6 wins, 5 ties)

Longest Losing Streak
Over-all .... **11** Oct. 30-Nov. 27/43
Home .... **7** Oct. 20-Nov. 14/76; Mar. 24-Apr. 14/93
Away .... **10** Oct. 30-Dec. 23/43

Longest Winless Streak
Over-all .... **21** Jan. 23-Mar. 19/44 (17 losses, 4 ties)
Home .... **10** Jan. 30-Mar. 19/44 (7 losses, 3 ties)
Away .... **16** Oct. 9-Dec. 20/52 (12 losses, 4 ties)

Most Shutouts, Season **13** 1928-29 (44)
Most PIM, Season **2,018** 1989-90 (80)
Most Goals, Game .... **12** Nov. 21/71 (Cal. 1 at NYR 12)

Individual

Most Seasons .... **17** Harry Howell
Most Games .... **1,160** Harry Howell
Most Goals, Career .... **406** Rod Gilbert
Most Assists, Career .... **615** Rod Gilbert
Most Points, Career .... **1,021** Rod Gilbert (406 goals, 615 assists)
Most PIM, Career .... **1,226** Ron Greschner
Most Shutouts, Career .... **49** Ed Giacomin
Longest Consecutive Games Streak .... **560** Andy Hebenton (Oct. 7/55-Mar. 24/63)
Most Goals, Season .... **52** Adam Graves (1993-94)
Most Assists, Season .... **80** Brian Leetch (1991-92)
Most Points, Season .... **109** Jean Ratelle (1971-72) (46 goals, 63 assists)
Most PIM, Season .... **305** Troy Mallette (1989-90)
Most Points, Defenseman Season .... **102** Brian Leetch (1991-92) (22 goals, 80 assists)
Most Points, Center, Season .... **109** Jean Ratelle (1971-72) (46 goals, 63 assists)
Most Points, Right Wing, Season .... **97** Rod Gilbert (1971-72) (43 goals, 54 assists); Rod Gilbert (1974-75) (36 goals, 61 assists)
Most Points, Left Wing, Season .... **106** Vic Hadfield (1971-72) (50 goals, 56 assists)
Most Points, Rookie, Season .... **76** Mark Pavelich (1981-82) (33 goals, 43 assists)
Most Shutouts, Season .... **13** John Ross Roach (1928-29)
Most Goals, Game .... **5** Don Murdoch (Oct. 12/76); Mark Pavelich (Feb. 23/83)
Most Assists, Game .... **5** Walt Tkaczuk (Feb. 12/72); Rod Gilbert (Mar. 2/75; Mar. 30/75; Oct. 8/76); Don Maloney (Jan. 3/87)
Most Points, Game .... **7** Steve Vickers (Feb. 18/76)

Captains' History

Bill Cook, 1926-27 to 1936-37; Art Coulter, 1937-38 to 1941-42; Ott Heller, 1942-43 to 1944-45; Neil Colville 1945-46 to 1948-49; Buddy O'Connor, 1949-50; Frank Eddolls, 1950-51; Frank Eddolls and Allan Stanley, 1951-52; Allan Stanley, 1952-53; Allan Stanley and Don Raleigh, 1953-54; Don Raleigh, 1954-55; Harry Howell, 1955-56, 1956-57; George Sullivan, 1957-58 to 1960-61; Andy Bathgate, 1961-62, 1962-63; Andy Bathgate and Camille Henry, 1963-64; Camille Henry and Bob Nevin, 1964-65; Bob Nevin 1965-66 to 1970-71; Vic Hadfield, 1971-72 to 1973-74; Brad Park, 1974-75; Brad Park and Phil Esposito, 1975-76; Phil Esposito, 1976-77, 1977-78; Dave Maloney, 1978-79, 1979-80; Dave Maloney, Walt Tkaczuk and Barry Beck, 1980-81; Barry Beck, 1981-82 to 1985-86; Ron Greschner, 1986-87; Ron Greschner and Kelly Kisio, 1987-88; Kelly Kisio, 1988-89 to 1990-91; Mark Messier, 1991-92 to date.

All-time Record vs. Other Clubs

Regular Season

	At Home							On Road							Total						
	GP	W	L	T	GF	GA	PTS	GP	W	L	T	GF	GA	PTS	GP	W	L	T	GF	GA	PTS
Anaheim	1	0	1	0	2	4	0	1	0	1	0	2	3	0	2	0	2	0	4	7	0
Boston	284	123	107	54	863	797	300	280	89	151	40	781	1016	218	564	212	258	94	1644	1813	518
Buffalo	48	22	15	11	168	132	55	50	14	30	6	166	226	34	98	36	45	17	334	358	89
Calgary	44	19	20	5	156	160	43	43	10	24	9	134	196	29	87	29	44	14	290	356	72
Chicago	279	116	109	54	827	790	286	278	112	124	42	777	848	266	557	228	233	96	1604	1638	552
Dallas	54	33	11	10	194	148	76	53	29	16	8	205	162	66	107	62	27	18	399	310	142
Detroit	276	131	87	58	852	710	320	278	75	158	45	689	978	195	554	206	245	103	1541	1688	515
Edmonton	22	6	12	4	87	90	16	22	11	10	1	77	86	23	44	17	22	5	164	176	39
Florida	4	2	1	1	9	8	5	5	3	2	0	17	10	6	9	5	3	1	26	18	11
Hartford	26	16	8	2	113	75	34	25	9	13	3	91	96	21	51	25	21	5	204	171	55
Los Angeles	51	31	15	5	207	150	67	52	23	20	9	187	174	55	103	54	35	14	394	324	122
Montreal	272	110	109	53	789	793	273	272	55	183	34	626	1074	144	544	165	292	87	1415	1867	417
New Jersey	61	37	16	8	271	194	82	62	31	27	4	234	212	66	123	68	43	12	505	406	148
NY Islanders	72	43	21	8	286	219	94	73	18	49	6	223	314	42	145	61	70	14	509	533	136
Ottawa	5	5	0	0	25	10	10	5	5	0	0	21	11	10	10	10	0	0	46	21	20
Philadelphia	87	40	27	20	293	253	100	85	30	42	13	247	295	73	172	70	69	33	540	548	173
Pittsburgh	79	41	31	7	322	276	89	79	36	32	11	297	288	83	158	77	63	18	619	564	172
Quebec	25	16	6	3	107	71	35	27	10	14	3	107	114	23	52	26	20	6	214	185	58
St. Louis	53	42	6	5	228	120	89	55	26	21	8	183	163	60	108	68	27	13	411	283	149
San Jose	3	2	0	1	15	7	5	4	4	0	0	22	9	8	7	6	0	1	37	16	13
Tampa Bay	7	4	2	1	29	29	9	5	4	1	0	17	14	8	12	8	3	1	46	43	17
Toronto	268	111	101	56	821	785	278	267	78	151	38	692	920	194	535	189	252	94	1513	1705	472
Vancouver	47	35	7	5	215	117	75	45	31	11	3	187	144	65	92	66	18	8	402	261	140
Washington	62	32	24	6	256	225	70	63	24	31	8	213	245	56	125	56	55	14	469	470	126
Winnipeg	22	12	8	2	104	89	26	23	12	9	2	87	84	26	45	24	17	4	191	173	52
Defunct Clubs	139	87	30	22	460	290	196	139	82	34	23	441	291	187	278	169	64	45	901	581	383
Totals	**2291**	**1116**	**774**	**401**	**7699**	**6542**	**2633**	**2291**	**821**	**1154**	**316**	**6723**	**7973**	**1958**	**4582**	**1937**	**1928**	**717**	**14422**	**14515**	**4591**

Calgary totals include Atlanta, 1972-73 to 1979-80. Dallas totals include Minnesota, 1967-68 to 1992-93.
New Jersey totals include Kansas City, 1974-75 to 1975-76, and Colorado, 1976-77 to 1981-82.

Playoffs

	Series	W	L	GP	W	L	T	GF	GA	Last Mtg.	Round	Result
Boston	9	3	6	42	18	22	2	104	114	1973	QF	W 4-1
Buffalo	1	0	1	3	1	2	0	6	11	1978	PR	L 1-2
Calgary	1	1	0	4	3	1	0	14	8	1980	PR	W 3-1
Chicago	5	1	4	24	10	14	0	54	66	1973	SF	L 1-4
Detroit	5	1	4	23	10	13	0	49	57	1950	F	L 3-4
Los Angeles	2	2	0	6	5	1	0	32	14	1981	PR	W 3-1
Montreal	13	6	7	55	21	32	2	139	171	1986	CF	L 1-4
New Jersey	2	2	0	14	8	6	0	46	41	1994	CF	W 4-3
NY Islanders	8	3	5	39	19	20	0	132	129	1994	CQF	W 4-0
Philadelphia	9	4	5	42	19	23	0	140	137	1995	CSF	L 0-4
Pittsburgh	2	0	2	10	2	8	0	30	44	1992	DF	L 2-4
Quebec	1	1	0	6	4	2	0	25	19	1995	CQF	W 4-2
St. Louis	1	1	0	6	4	2	0	29	22	1981	QF	W 4-2
Toronto	8	5	3	35	19	16	0	86	86	1971	QF	W 4-2
Vancouver	1	1	0	7	4	3	0	21	19	1994	F	W 4-3
Washington	4	2	2	22	11	11	0	71	75	1994	CSF	W 4-1
Defunct	9	6	3	22	11	7	4	43	29			
Totals	**81**	**39**	**42**	**360**	**169**	**183**	**8**	**1021**	**1041**			

Playoff Results 1995-91

Year	Round	Opponent	Result	GF	GA
1995	CSF	Philadelphia	L 0-4	10	18
	CQF	Quebec	W 4-2	25	19
1994	F	Vancouver	W 4-3	21	19
	CF	New Jersey	W 4-3	18	16
	CSF	Washington	W 4-1	20	12
	CQF	NY Islanders	W 4-0	22	3
1992	DF	Pittsburgh	L 2-4	19	24
	DSF	New Jersey	W 4-3	28	25
1991	DSF	Washington	L 2-4	16	16

Abbreviations: Round: F – Final; **CF** – conference final; **CQF** – conference quarter-final; **CSF** – conference semi-final; **DF** – division final; **DSF** – division semi-final; **SF** – semi-final; **QF** – quarter-final; **PR** – preliminary round.

1994-95 Results

Jan.	20		Buffalo	1-2		8		New Jersey	6-4
	21		Montreal	5-2		11	at	Montreal	1-3
	23		Boston	1-2		15		Philadelphia	3-4
	25		Pittsburgh	2-3		18	at	Washington	1-4
	28	at	Quebec	0-2		22		New Jersey	2-5
	30		Ottawa	6-2		23	at	NY Islanders	0-1
Feb.	1	at	Pittsburgh	3-4		25	at	Quebec	1-2
	2		Tampa Bay	3-3		30		Quebec	4-5
	4	at	Ottawa	2-1	**Apr.**	1	at	Boston	3-2
	8		Washington	5-4		2	at	Philadelphia	2-4
	9	at	New Jersey	1-4		5	at	Florida	5-0
	11	at	Tampa Bay	3-2		7		NY Islanders	3-4
	15	at	Buffalo	2-1		9	at	New Jersey	0-2
	16		Montreal	2-2		12		Buffalo	3-1
	18	at	Montreal	2-5		14		Boston	5-3
	20	at	Tampa Bay	3-1		16	at	NY Islanders	3-2
	21	at	Florida	5-3		18	at	Pittsburgh	5-6
	24		Hartford	1-2		20		Hartford	3-2
	26	at	Buffalo	4-2		23	at	Boston	4-5
	28		Florida	0-0		24		Washington	5-4
Mar.	1	at	Hartford	5-2		26		Tampa Bay	6-4
	3		Philadelphia	5-3		28		NY Islanders	2-4
	5	at	Washington	2-4		30	at	Philadelphia	2-0
	6		Ottawa	4-3	**May**	2		Florida	3-4

Entry Draft
Selections 1995-81

1995
Pick
39 Christian Dube
65 Mike Martin
91 Marc Savard
110 Alexei Vasiliev
117 Dale Purinton
143 Peter Slamiar
169 Jeff Heil
195 Ilja Gorohov
221 Bob Maudie

1994
Pick
26 Dan Cloutier
52 Rudolf Vercik
78 Adam Smith
100 Alexander Korobolin
104 Sylvain Blouin
130 Martin Ethier
135 Yuri Litvinov
156 David Brosseau
182 Alexei Lazarenko
208 Craig Anderson
209 Vitali Yeremeyev
234 Eric Boulton
260 Radoslav Kropac
267 Jamie Butt
286 Kim Johnsson

1993
Pick
8 Niklas Sundstrom
34 Lee Sorochan
61 Maxim Galanov
86 Sergei Olimpiyev
112 Gary Roach
138 Dave Trofimenkoff
162 Sergei Kondrashkin
164 Todd Marchant
190 Eddy Campbell
216 Ken Shepard
242 Andrei Kudinov
261 Pavel Komarov
268 Maxim Smelnitsky

1992
Pick
24 Peter Ferraro
48 Mattias Norstrom
72 Eric Cairns
85 Chris Ferraro
120 Dmitri Starostenko
144 David Dal Grande
168 Matt Oates
192 Mickey Elick
216 Dan Brierley
240 Vladimir Vorobjev

1991
Pick
15 Alexei Kovalev
37 Darcy Werenka
96 Corey Machanic
125 Fredrik Jax
128 Barry Young
147 John Rushin
169 Corey Hirsch
191 Viacheslav Uvayev
213 Jamie Ram
235 Vitali Chinakhov
257 Brian Wiseman

1990
Pick
13 Michael Stewart
34 Doug Weight
55 John Vary
69 Jeff Nielsen
76 Rick Willis
85 Sergei Zubov
99 Lubos Rob
118 Jason Weinrich
139 Bryan Lonsinger
160 Todd Hedlund
181 Andrew Silverman
202 Jon Hillebrandt
223 Brett Lievers
244 Sergei Nemchinov

1989
Pick
20 Steven Rice
40 Jason Prosofsky
45 Rob Zamuner
49 Louie DeBrusk
67 Jim Cummins
88 Aaron Miller
118 Joby Messier
139 Greg Leahy
160 Greg Spenrath
181 Mark Bavis
202 Roman Oksyuta
223 Steve Locke
244 Ken MacDermid

1988
Pick
22 Troy Mallette
26 Murray Duval
68 Tony Amonte
99 Martin Bergeron
110 Dennis Vial
131 Mike Rosati
152 Eric Couvrette
173 Shorty Forrest
194 Paul Cain
202 Eric Fenton
215 Peter Fiorentino
236 Keith Slifstien

1987
Pick
10 Jayson More
31 Daniel Lacroix
46 Simon Gagne
69 Michael Sullivan
94 Eric O'Borsky
115 Ludek Cajka
136 Clint Thomas
157 Charles Wiegand
178 Eric Burrill
199 David Porter
205 Brett Barnett
220 Lance Marciano

1986
Pick
9 Brian Leetch
51 Bret Walter
53 Shawn Clouston
72 Mark Janssens
93 Jeff Bloemberg
114 Darren Turcotte
135 Robb Graham
156 Barry Chyzowski
177 Pat Scanlon
198 Joe Ranger
219 Russell Parent
240 Soren True

1985
Pick
7 Ulf Dahlen
28 Mike Richter
49 Sam Lindstahl
70 Pat Janostin
91 Brad Stephan
112 Brian McReynolds
133 Neil Pilon
154 Larry Bernard
175 Stephane Brochu
196 Steve Nemeth
217 Robert Burakowsky
238 Rudy Poeschek

1984
Pick
14 Terry Carkner
35 Raimo Helminen
77 Paul Broten
98 Clark Donatelli
119 Kjell Samuelsson
140 Thomas Hussey
161 Brian Nelson
182 Ville Kentala
188 Heinz Ehlers
202 Kevin Miller
223 Tom Lorentz
243 Scott Brower

1983
Pick
12 Dave Gagner
33 Randy Heath
49 Vesa Salo
53 Gordie Walker
73 Peter Andersson
93 Jim Andonoff
113 Bob Alexander
133 Steve Orth
153 Peter Marcov
173 Paul Jerrard
213 Bryan Walker
233 Ulf Nilsson

1982
Pick
15 Chris Kontos
36 Tomas Sandstrom
57 Corey Millen
78 Chris Jensen
120 Tony Granato
141 Sergei Kapustin
160 Brian Glynn
162 Jan Karlsson
183 Kelly Miller
193 Simo Saarinen
204 Bob Lowes
225 Andy Otto
246 Dwayne Robinson

1981
Pick
9 James Patrick
30 Jan Erixon
50 Peter Sundstrom
51 Mark Morrison
72 John Vanbiesbrouck
114 Eric Magnuson
135 Mike Guentzel
156 Ari Lahteenmaki
177 Paul Reifenberger
198 Mario Proulx

Club Directory

Madison Square Garden
14th Floor
2 Pennsylvania Plaza
New York, New York 10121
Phone **212/465-6000**
PR FAX 212/465-6494
Capacity: 18,200

Executive Management
President and General Manager . . . . Neil Smith
Executive Vice-President and General Counsel . . . . . Kenneth W. Munoz
Vice-President and Business Manager . . . . Francis P. Murphy
Governor . . . . Charles Dolan
Alternate Governors . . . . Neil Smith, David W. Checketts, Kenneth W. Munoz, Rand Araskog, James Dolan

Hockey Club Personnel
Assistant General Manager/Player Development . . . . Larry Pleau
Head Coach . . . . Colin Campbell
Assistant Coach . . . . Dick Todd
Assistant Coach . . . . Mike Murphy
Development Coach . . . . George Burnett
Assistant Development Coach . . . . Mike Busniak
Goaltending Analyst . . . . Sam St. Laurent
Scouting Staff . . . . Darwin Bennett, Tony Feltrin, Herb Hammond, Martin Madden, Kevin McDonald, Christer Rockstrom
Director of Business Administration . . . . John Gentile
Director of Team Operations . . . . Matthew Loughran
Scouting Manager . . . . Bill Short
Executive Administrative Assistant . . . . Barbara Cahill
Senior Secretary . . . . Nicole Wetzold

Medical/Training Staff
Team Physician and Orthopedic Surgeon . . . . Dr. Barton Nisonson
Assistant Team Physician . . . . Dr. Tony Maddalo
Medical Consultants . . . . Dr. Howard Chester, Dr. Frank Gardner, Dr. Ronald Weissman
Team Dentists . . . . Dr. Irwin Miller, Dr. Don Soloman
Sports Physiologist . . . . Howie Wenger
Medical Trainer . . . . Jim Ramsay
Equipment Manager . . . . Mike Folga
Massage Therapist . . . . Bruce Lifrieri
Lockerroom Assistant . . . . Benny Petrizzi
Video Assistant . . . . Gerry Dineen
Staff Assistant . . . . Brad Kolodny

Public Relations Department
Director of Public Relations . . . . Brooks Thomas
Assistant Director of Public Relations . . . . John Rosasco
Public Relations Assistant . . . . Rob Koch
Administrative Assistant . . . . Ann Marie Gilmartin

Marketing Department
Vice-President of Marketing . . . . Kevin Kennedy
Director of Community Relations . . . . Rod Gilbert
Promotions Manager . . . . Caroline Calabrese
Manager of Marketing Operations . . . . Jim Pfeifer
Manager of Event Presentation . . . . Jeanie Baumgartner

Home Ice . . . . Madison Square Garden
Press Facilities . . . . 33rd Street
Television Facilities . . . . 31st Street
Radio Facilities . . . . 33rd Street
Rink Dimensions . . . . 200 feet by 85 feet
Ends and Sides of Rink . . . . Plexiglass (8 feet)
Club Colors . . . . Blue, Red and White
Practice Facility . . . . Rye, New York
TV Announcers . . . . John Davidson, Sam Rosen, Al Trautwig
Radio Announcers . . . . Marv Albert, Sal Messina, Howie Rose
Television Outlets . . . . Madison Square Garden Cable Network
Radio Outlet . . . . MSG Radio – WFAN (66 AM), WEVD (1050 AM), WXPS (107.1 FM)

The New York Rangers Hockey Club is part of Madison Square Garden

Coach

CAMPBELL, COLIN
Coach, New York Rangers. Born in London, Ontario, January 28, 1953.

Colin Campbell begins his second season as head coach of the Rangers after being named to the post on August 9, 1994. He was promoted to the position after serving in various capacities over the previous five years, including assistant coach, associate coach and half of the 1992-93 season as head coach of the Rangers American Hockey League affiliate at Binghamton. Colin made his head coaching debut on January 20 vs. Buffalo and earned his first NHL victory on January 21 vs. Montreal.

Campbell, 42, began his coaching career in 1985-86 with Detroit, following his retirement as a player after the 1984-85 season. He worked a total of five seasons as a Red Wings assistant coach, one season under coach Harry Neale and four seasons under coach Jacques Demers.

The native of London, Ontario, joined the Rangers organization in August of 1990 as an assistant coach to Roger Neilson. He served in that role until January 4, 1993, when he became head coach of the Binghamton Rangers, New York's American Hockey League affiliate. He guided Binghamton to a record of 29-8-5, helping the club set AHL records for wins (57) and points (124) in a single season.

On June 21, 1993, Campbell was promoted to associate coach of New York, under head coach Mike Keenan, helping the Rangers capture the Presidents' Trophy, given to the team with the best regular-season record, and the Stanley Cup.

Before joining the coaching ranks, Campbell played 12 seasons of professional hockey as a defensive defenseman.

He played in a total of 636 NHL contests, collecting 25 goals and 103 assists for 128 points along with 1,292 penalty minutes.

Coaching Record

			Regular Season				Playoffs			
Season	Team	Games	W	L	T	%	Games	W	L	%
1992-93	Binghamton (AHL)	42	29	8	5	.750	14	7	7	.500
1994-95	**NY Rangers (NHL)**	**48**	**22**	**23**	**3**	**.490**	**10**	**4**	**6**	**.400**
	NHL Totals	48	22	23	3	.490	10	4	6	.400

Coaching History

Lester Patrick, 1926-27 to 1938-39; Frank Boucher, 1939-40 to 1947-48; Frank Boucher and Lynn Patrick, 1948-49; Lynn Patrick, 1949-50; Neil Colville, 1950-51; Neil Colville and Bill Cook, 1951-52; Bill Cook, 1952-53; Frank Boucher and "Muzz" Patrick, 1953-54; "Muzz" Patrick, 1954-55; Phil Watson, 1955-56 to 1958-59; Phil Watson and Alf Pike, 1959-60; Alf Pike, 1960-61; Doug Harvey, 1961-62; "Muzz" Patrick and George Sullivan, 1962-63; George Sullivan, 1963-64 to 1964-65; George Sullivan and Emile Francis, 1965-66; Emile Francis, 1966-67 to 1967-68; Bernie Geoffrion and Emile Francis, 1968-69; Emile Francis, 1969-70 to 1972-73; Larry Popein and Emile Francis, 1973-74; Emile Francis, 1974-75; Ron Stewart and John Ferguson, 1975-76; John Ferguson, 1976-77; Jean-Guy Talbot, 1977-78; Fred Shero, 1978-79 to 1979-80; Fred Shero and Craig Patrick, 1980-81; Herb Brooks, 1981-82 to 1983-84; Herb Brooks and Craig Patrick, 1984-85; Ted Sator, 1985-86; Ted Sator, Tom Webster and Phil Esposito 1986-87; Michel Bergeron, 1987-88; Michel Bergeron and Phil Esposito, 1988-89; Roger Neilson, 1989-90 to 1991-92; Roger Neilson and Ron Smith, 1992-93; Mike Keenan, 1993-94; Colin Campbell, 1994-95 to date.

Ottawa Senators

1994-95 Results: 9w-34l-5t 23pts. Seventh, Northeast Division

Year-by-Year Record

Season	GP	Home			Road			Overall							
		W	L	T	W	L	T	W	L	T	GF	GA	Pts.	Finished	Playoff Result
1994-95	48	5	16	3	4	18	2	9	34	5	117	174	23	7th, Northeast Div.	Out of Playoffs
1993-94	84	8	30	4	6	31	5	14	61	9	201	397	37	7th, Northeast Div.	Out of Playoffs
1992-93	84	9	29	4	1	41	0	10	70	4	202	395	24	6th, Adams Div.	Out of Playoffs

Schedule

Oct.	Sat.	7	Buffalo		Sat.	13	at Tampa Bay
	Fri.	13	at Florida		Wed.	17	Montreal
	Sun.	15	at Tampa Bay		Mon.	22	Chicago
	Thur.	19	Calgary		Wed.	24	Pittsburgh
	Sat.	21	at New Jersey		Thur.	25	Detroit
	Sun.	22	at NY Rangers		Sat.	27	Toronto
	Tues.	24	at Detroit		Mon.	29	St. Louis
	Thur.	26	Los Angeles		Wed.	31	Boston
	Sat.	28	Florida*	**Feb.**	Thur.	1	Washington
	Sun.	29	at Philadelphia		Sat.	3	New Jersey
Nov.	Thur.	2	at Hartford		Tues.	6	at Calgary
	Sat.	4	Hartford		Thur.	8	at Winnipeg
	Wed.	8	Pittsburgh		Sat.	10	at Montreal
	Thur.	9	at Boston		Mon.	12	at NY Islanders
	Sat.	11	Anaheim*		Thur.	15	San Jose
	Wed.	15	at Hartford		Sat.	17	NY Rangers
	Thur.	16	at Philadelphia		Tues.	20	at St. Louis
	Sat.	18	at Montreal		Thur.	22	at Dallas
	Sun.	19	at Buffalo		Sun.	25	at Colorado
	Wed.	22	Winnipeg		Wed.	28	Buffalo
	Sat.	25	Boston	**Mar.**	Fri.	1	Philadelphia
	Tues.	28	at Pittsburgh		Sat.	2	New Jersey
	Thur.	30	NY Islanders		Thur.	7	at Pittsburgh
Dec.	Sat.	2	NY Rangers		Sat.	9	at Montreal
	Tues.	5	at Toronto		Wed.	13	Dallas
	Thur.	7	at Chicago		Fri.	15	Vancouver
	Sat.	9	Colorado		Sun.	17	Tampa Bay*
	Tues.	12	at San Jose		Tues.	19	at Florida
	Wed.	13	at Los Angeles		Thur.	21	at Boston
	Fri.	15	at Anaheim		Fri.	22	Hartford
	Sun.	17	at Vancouver*		Sun.	24	Edmonton
	Mon.	18	at Edmonton		Wed.	27	Philadelphia
	Sat.	23	Buffalo		Fri.	29	at Washington
	Tues.	26	at NY Rangers		Sat.	30	Montreal
	Wed.	27	at Buffalo	**Apr.**	Mon.	1	Boston
	Sat.	30	Montreal		Wed.	3	Florida
	Sun.	31	Tampa Bay		Fri.	5	NY Islanders
Jan.	Wed.	3	at Pittsburgh		Sat.	6	Washington
	Fri.	5	at Hartford		Wed.	10	at Buffalo
	Sat.	6	at NY Islanders		Thur.	11	Pittsburgh
	Thur.	11	at Washington		Sat.	13	at New Jersey*

* Denotes afternoon game.

Home Starting Times:

Weeknights	7:30 p.m.
Saturdays	8:00 p.m.
Sundays	7:00 p.m.
Matinees	1:30 p.m.
Except Sat. Dec. 30	7:30 p.m.
Sat. Jan. 27	7:30 p.m.
Sat. Mar. 2	7:30 p.m.
Sat. Mar. 30	7:30 p.m.

Franchise date: December 16, 1991

NORTHEAST DIVISION

4th NHL Season

Fifteen-year veteran Don Beaupre provided the Ottawa Senators with high-quality netminding throughout the 1994-95 season.

1995-96 Player Personnel

FORWARDS	HT	WT	S	Place of Birth	Date	1994-95 Club
ALFREDSSON, Daniel	5-11	187	R	Grums, Sweden	12/11/72	V. Frolunda
ARCHIBALD, Dave	6-1	210	L	Chilliwack, B.C.	4/14/69	Ottawa
BONK, Radek	6-3	215	L	Krnov, Czech.	1/9/76	Las Vegas-Ottawa-P.E.I.
BOURQUE, Phil	6-1	196	L	Chelmsford, MA	6/8/62	Ottawa
CUNNEYWORTH, Randy	6-0	180	L	Etobicoke, Ont.	5/10/61	Ottawa
DAIGLE, Alexandre	6-0	185	L	Montreal, Que.	2/7/75	Victoriaville-Ottawa
DEMITRA, Pavol	6-0	189	L	Dubnica, Czech.	11/29/74	P.E.I.-Ottawa
ELYNUIK, Pat	6-0	185	R	Foam Lake, Sask.	10/30/67	Ottawa
GARDINER, Bruce	6-1	185	R	Barrie, Ont.	2/11/71	P.E.I.
GAUDREAU, Rob	5-11	185	R	Lincoln, RI	1/20/70	Ottawa
GUERARD, Daniel	6-4	185	R	LaSalle, Que.	4/9/74	P.E.I.-Ottawa
LAROUCHE, Steve	6-0	180	R	Rouyn, Que.	4/14/71	P.E.I.-Ottawa
LEVINS, Scott	6-4	210	R	Spokane, WA	1/30/70	Ottawa-P.E.I.
MALLETTE, Troy	6-2	210	L	Sudbury, Ont.	2/25/70	Ottawa-P.E.I.
MCCLEARY, Trent	6-0	180	L	Swift Current, Sask.	10/10/72	P.E.I.
McILWAIN, Dave	6-0	185	L	Seaforth, Ont.	1/9/67	Ottawa
PENNEY, Chad	6-0	195	L	Labrador City, Nfld.	9/18/73	P.E.I.
PICARD, Michel	5-11	190	L	Beauport, Que.	11/7/69	P.E.I.-Ottawa
QUINN, Dan	5-11	182	L	Ottawa, Ont.	6/1/65	Zug-Los Angeles
SAVOIE, Claude	5-11	200	R	Montreal, Que.	3/12/73	P.E.I.
STRAKA, Martin	5-10	178	L	Plzen, Czech.	9/3/72	Interconex Plzen-Pit-Ott
TORMANEN, Antti	6-1	198	L	Espoo, Finland	9/19/70	Jokerit
YASHIN, Alexei	6-3	215	R	Sverdlovsk, USSR	11/5/73	Las Vegas-Ottawa
ZENT, Jason	5-11	180	L	Buffalo, NY	4/15/71	P.E.I.

DEFENSEMEN						
BERARD, Bryan	6-1	190	L	Woonsocket, RI	3/5/77	Detroit (OHL)
BICANEK, Radim	6-1	195	L	Uherske Hradiste, Czech.	1/18/75	Belleville-Ottawa-P.E.I.
DAHLQUIST, Chris	6-1	195	L	Fridley, MN	12/14/62	Ottawa
DUCHESNE, Steve	5-11	195	L	Sept-Iles, Que.	6/30/65	St. Louis
HILL, Sean	6-0	195	R	Duluth, MN	2/14/70	Ottawa
HUFFMAN, Kerry	6-2	200	L	Peterborough, Ont.	1/3/68	Ottawa
LAPERRIERE, Daniel	6-1	195	L	Laval, Que.	3/28/69	Peoria-St. Louis-Ottawa
MODRY, Jaroslav	6-2	195	L	Ceske-Budejovice, Czech.	2/27/71	Budejovice-New Jersey-Albany
NECKAR, Stanislav	6-1	196	L	Ceske Budejovice, Czech.	12/22/75	Detroit (IHL)-Ottawa
PITLICK, Lance	6-0	180	R	Minneapolis, MN	11/5/67	P.E.I.-Ottawa
TRAVERSE, Patrick	6-3	200	L	Montreal, Que.	3/14/74	P.E.I.
VIAL, Dennis	6-2	218	L	Sault Ste. Marie, Ont.	4/10/69	Ottawa

GOALTENDERS	HT	WT	C	Place of Birth	Date	1994-95 Club
BALES, Michael	6-1	180	L	Prince Albert, Sask.	8/6/71	P.E.I.-Ottawa
BEAUPRE, Don	5-10	172	L	Waterloo, Ont.	9/19/61	Ottawa
CHARBONNEAU, Patrick	5-11	205	L	St-Jean sur Richelieu, Que.	7/22/75	Victoriaville-P.E.I.
LESLIE, Lance	5-10	160	L	Dawson Creek, B.C.	6/21/74	Thunder Bay-P.E.I.
MADELEY, Darrin	5-11	170	L	Holland Landing, Ont.	2/25/68	Ottawa-P.E.I.-Detroit (IHL)
CASSIVI, Frederic	6-3	193	L	Sorel, Que.	6/12/75	Halifax-St-Jean

1994-95 Scoring

*– rookie

Regular Season

Pos	#	Player	Team	GP	G	A	Pts	+/−	PIM	PP	SH	GW	GT	S	%
C	19	Alexei Yashin	OTT	47	21	23	44	−20	20	11	0	1	0	154	13.6
C	91	Alexandre Daigle	OTT	47	16	21	37	−22	14	4	1	2	0	105	15.2
L	61	Sylvain Turgeon	OTT	33	11	8	19	−1	29	2	0	1	0	83	13.3
R	82	Martin Straka	PIT	31	4	12	16	0	16	0	0	0	0	36	11.1
			OTT	6	1	1	2	−1	0	0	0	0	0	13	7.7
			TOTAL	37	5	13	18	−1	16	0	0	0	0	49	10.2
C	74	* Steve Larouche	OTT	18	8	7	15	−5	6	2	0	2	0	38	21.1
D	3	Sean Hill	OTT	45	1	14	15	−11	30	0	0	0	0	107	0.9
C	10	Rob Gaudreau	OTT	36	5	9	14	−16	8	0	0	0	0	65	7.7
L	49	Michel Picard	OTT	24	5	8	13	−1	14	1	0	0	0	33	15.2
R	26	Scott Levins	OTT	24	5	6	11	4	51	0	0	0	0	34	14.7
C	17	Dave McIlwain	OTT	43	5	6	11	−26	22	1	0	0	0	48	10.4
C	76	* Radek Bonk	OTT	42	3	8	11	−5	28	1	0	0	0	40	7.5
L	7	Randy Cunneyworth	OTT	48	5	5	10	−19	68	2	0	0	0	71	7.0
R	25	Pat Elynuik	OTT	41	3	7	10	−11	51	0	0	0	0	58	5.2
L	18	Troy Mallette	OTT	23	3	5	8	6	35	0	0	1	0	21	14.3
D	6	Chris Dahlquist	OTT	46	1	7	8	−30	36	1	0	0	0	45	2.2
L	78	* Pavol Demitra	OTT	16	4	3	7	−4	0	1	0	0	0	21	19.0
L	29	Phil Bourque	OTT	38	4	3	7	−17	20	0	0	0	0	34	11.8
D	5	Kerry Huffman	OTT	37	2	4	6	−17	46	2	0	0	0	68	2.9
C	15	David Archibald	OTT	14	2	2	4	−7	19	0	0	1	0	27	7.4
D	94	* Stanislav Neckar	OTT	48	1	3	4	−20	37	0	0	0	0	34	2.9
D	21	Dennis Vial	OTT	27	0	4	4	0	65	0	0	0	0	9	0.0
R	11	Evgeny Davydov	OTT	3	1	2	3	2	0	0	0	0	0	2	50.0
D	24	* Daniel Laperriere	STL	4	0	0	0	1	15	0	0	0	0	0	0.0
			OTT	13	1	1	2	−4	0	1	0	0	0	18	5.6
			TOTAL	17	1	1	2	−3	15	1	0	0	0	18	5.6
D	2	Jim Paek	OTT	29	0	2	2	−5	28	0	0	0	0	16	0.0
L	23	Claude Boivin	OTT	3	0	1	1	−1	6	0	0	0	0	0	0.0
D	56	Lance Pitlick	OTT	15	0	1	1	−5	6	0	0	0	0	11	0.0
G	35	* Mike Bales	OTT	1	0	0	0	0	0	0	0	0	0	0	0.0
D	4	Brad Shaw	OTT	2	0	0	0	3	0	0	0	0	0	3	0.0
R	46	* Daniel Guerard	OTT	2	0	0	0	0	0	0	0	0	0	0	0.0
G	30	Darrin Madeley	OTT	5	0	0	0	0	0	0	0	0	0	0	0.0
D	44	* Radim Bicanek	OTT	6	0	0	0	3	0	0	0	0	0	6	0.0
G	33	Don Beaupre	OTT	38	0	0	0	0	10	0	0	0	0	0	0.0

Goaltending

No.	Goaltender	GPI	Mins	Avg	W	L	T	EN	SO	GA	SA	S%
35	* Mike Bales	1	3	.00	0	0	0	0	0	0	1	1.000
33	Don Beaupre	38	2161	3.36	8	25	3	3	1	121	1167	.896
30	Darrin Madeley	5	255	3.53	1	3	0	1	0	15	147	.898
1	Craig Billington	9	472	4.07	0	6	2	2	0	32	240	.867
	Totals	48	2913	3.58	9	34	5	6	1	174	1561	.889

Alexei Yashin, left, and Sylvain Turgeon both reached double figures in goals during the 1994-95 season.

President and General Manager

SEXTON, RANDY JOHN
President and General Manager, Ottawa Senators.
Born in Brockville, Ont., July 24, 1959.

Randy Sexton was appointed general manager of the Ottawa Senators in April 1993, adding to his responsibilities of president and alternate governor.

As the club's general manager, Sexton signed more than 15 players from the 1992, 1993 and 1994 Entry Drafts, including young stars Alexandre Daigle, Stan Neckar, Radek Bonk and Radim Bicanek.

Prior to the 1994-95 season, he improved the club's goaltending by acquiring 14-year veteran Don Beaupre, who was eventually named the club's 1994-95 most valuable player. He also improved the club's offense with the acquisition of right winger Rob Gaudreau from the NHL Waiver Draft, as well as centre Martin Straka at the trading deadline. Sexton also bolstered the team's defence by trading for 23-year old Jaroslav Modry who was acquired from New Jersey on the day of the 1995 Entry Draft.

Sexton's post secondary education began at St. Lawrence University where he obtained a Bachelor of Science degree. He played for the St. Lawrence University varsity hockey team from 1978 to 1982, and served as team captain for his last two seasons. Sexton captured numerous awards including All-American honors, senior male athlete of the year, Brian "P" Doyle award, most valuable player and the coaches' award.

Sexton acted as assistant coach and recruiting co-ordinator with St. Lawrence from 1983 to 1985. He later received his Masters degree in Business Administration from Clarkson University, Potsdam, New York.

Club Records

Team

(Figures in brackets for season records are games played; records for fewest points, wins, ties, losses, goals, goals against are for 70 or more games)

Most Points	37	1993-94 (84)
Most Wins	14	1993-94 (84)
Most Ties	9	1993-94 (84)
Most Losses	70	1992-93 (84)
Most Goals	202	1992-93 (84)
Most Goals Against	397	1993-94 (84)
Fewest Points	24	1992-93 (84)
Fewest Wins	10	1992-93 (84)
Fewest Ties	4	1992-93 (84)
Fewest Losses	61	1993-94 (84)
Fewest Goals	201	1993-94 (84)
Fewest Goals Against	395	1992-93 (84)

Longest Winning Streak
Over-all .... 3 Oct. 30/93-
Nov. 5/93;
Apr. 26-29/95
Home .... 3 Mar. 23/94-
Apr. 6/94
Away .... 3 Oct. 30/93-
Nov. 5/93

Longest Undefeated Streak
Over-all .... 3 Four times
Home .... 4 Jan. 28/93-
Feb. 8/93 (3-0-1)
Away .... 3 Oct. 30-
Nov. 5/93

Longest Losing Streak
Over-all .... 14 Mar. 2/93-
Apr. 7/93
Home .... *11 Oct. 27-
Dec. 8/93
Away .... *38 Oct. 10/92-
Apr. 3/93**

Longest Winless Streak
Over-all .... 21 Oct. 10/92-
Nov. 23/92 (0-20-1)
Home .... 11 Oct. 27-
Dec. 8/93
Away .... *38 Oct. 10/92-
Apr. 3/93 (0-39-0)**

** NHL records do not include neutral site games

General Managers' History

Mel Bridgman, 1992-93; Randy Sexton, 1993-94 to date.

Coaching History

Rick Bowness, 1992-93 to date.

Captains' History

Laurie Boschman, 1992-93; Brad Shaw, Mark Lamb and Gord Dineen, 1993-94; Randy Cunneyworth, 1994-95.

Retired Numbers

8   Frank Finnigan   1924-1934

Most Shutouts, Season	1	1994-95 (48)
Most PIM, Season	1,716	1992-93 (84)
Most Goals, Game	7	Nov. 3/93 (Ott. 7 at Edm. 5)
		Nov. 5/93 (Ott. 7 at Wpg. 6)

Individual

Most Seasons	3	Five players
Most Games, Career	161	Norm Maciver
Most Goals, Career	51	Alexei Yashin
Most Assists, Career	73	Norm Maciver
Most Points, Career	123	Alexei Yashin (51 goals, 72 assists)
Most PIM, Career	318	Mike Peluso
Most Shutouts, Career	1	Don Beaupre
Longest Consecutive Games Streak	103	Brad Shaw (Oct. 31/92-Dec. 9/93)
Most Goals, Season	30	Alexei Yashin (1993-94)
Most Assists, Season	49	Alexei Yashin (1993-94)
Most Points, Season	79	Alexei Yashin (1993-94) (30 goals, 49 assists)
Most PIM, Season	318	Mike Peluso (1992-93)

Most Points, Defenseman Season	63	Norm Maciver (1992-93) (17 goals, 46 assists)
Most Points, Center Season	79	Alexei Yashin (1993-94) (30 goals, 49 assists)
Most Points, Right Wing Season	43	Dave McIlwain (1993-94) (17 goals, 26 assists)
Most Points, Left Wing Season	43	Sylvain Turgeon (1992-93) (25 goals, 18 assists)
Most Points, Rookie Season	79	Alexei Yashin (1993-94) (30 goals, 49 assists)
Most Shutouts, Season	1	Don Beaupre (1994-95)
Most Goals, Game	3	Eight times
Most Assists, Game	4	Alexei Yashin (Nov. 5/93)
Most Points, Game	5	Alexei Yashin (Nov. 3/93)

* NHL Record.

Alexander Daigle suited up with the Victoriaville Tigers, the Canadian National Junior Team and the Ottawa Senators during the 1994-95 campaign.

All-time Record vs. Other Clubs

Regular Season

	At Home							On Road							Total						
	GP	W	L	T	GF	GA	PTS	GP	W	L	T	GF	GA	PTS	GP	W	L	T	GF	GA	PTS
Anaheim	1	1	0	0	4	1	2	1	0	1	0	1	5	0	2	1	1	0	5	6	2
Boston	7	0	7	0	13	32	0	9	0	9	0	25	48	0	16	0	16	0	38	80	0
Buffalo	9	2	5	2	21	36	6	7	0	7	0	10	39	0	16	2	12	2	31	75	6
Calgary	2	0	1	1	2	7	1	2	0	2	0	4	18	0	4	0	3	1	6	25	1
Chicago	2	0	2	0	2	5	0	2	0	1	1	5	7	1	4	0	3	1	7	12	1
Dallas	2	0	2	0	6	9	0	3	1	2	0	8	17	2	5	1	4	0	14	26	2
Detroit	2	1	1	0	7	7	2	2	0	5	13	0		4	3	1	0	12	20	2
Edmonton	2	2	0	0	7	5	4	2	1	1	0	9	10	2	4	3	1	0	16	15	6
Florida	4	0	4	0	7	18	0	4	0	4	0	3	1	8	0	7	1	0	15	30	1
Hartford	9	1	7	1	17	32	3	7	0	7	0	14	32	0	16	1	14	1	31	64	3
Los Angeles	2	1	1	0	7	5	2	2	0	6	15	0		4	1	3	0	13	20	2
Montreal	7	1	6	0	20	29	2	9	2	7	0	24	32	4	16	3	13	0	44	61	6
New Jersey	6	1	4	1	11	22	3	5	0	5	0	11	24	0	11	1	9	1	22	46	3
NY Islanders	5	2	2	1	13	22	5	6	2	2	2	19	26	6	11	4	4	3	32	48	11
NY Rangers	5	0	5	0	11	21	0	5	0	5	0	10	25	0	10	0	10	0	21	46	0
Philadelphia	5	2	2	1	12	13	5	5	1	4	0	11	29	2	10	3	6	1	23	42	7
Pittsburgh	6	1	5	0	11	24	2	5	0	5	1	16	33	1	11	1	10	1	27	57	3
Quebec	10	3	5	2	33	49	8	8	0	8	0	21	47	0	18	3	13	2	54	96	8
St. Louis	2	0	2	0	2	15	0	2	0	6	12	0		4	0	0	8	27	0	
San Jose	2	2	0	0	9	6	4	2	1	1	0	4	4	2	4	3	1	0	13	10	6
Tampa Bay	5	1	4	0	12	16	2	5	2	3	0	10	13	4	10	3	7	0	22	29	6
Toronto	2	0	2	0	2	7	0	3	0	7	16	0		5	0	5	0	9	23	0
Vancouver	2	0	2	0	2	10	0	1	1	3	6	1		4	0	0	5	16	1	
Washington	5	1	3	1	20	26	3	6	0	5	1	13	33	1	11	1	8	2	33	59	4
Winnipeg	4	0	3	1	9	21	1	2	1	1	0	10	12	2	6	1	4	1	19	33	3
Totals	**108**	**22**	**75**	**11**	**260**	**438**	**55**	**108**	**11**	**90**	**7**	**260**	**528**	**29**	**216**	**33**	**165**	**18**	**520**	**966**	**84**

Dallas totals include Minnesota, 1992-93.

1994-95 Results

Jan.	22	at NY Islanders	3-3		18	Buffalo	4-3
	25	at Hartford	1-4		19	Pittsburgh	3-4
	27	at Pittsburgh	4-5		21	at Washington	0-1
	28	Buffalo	2-2		25	at Montreal	1-3
	30	at NY Rangers	2-6		26	Quebec	4-11
Feb.	1	Hartford	1-2		29	New Jersey	2-4
	2	at Boston	4-6		30	at Buffalo	0-7
	4	NY Rangers	1-2	**Apr.**	2	at Quebec	5-7
	6	Philadelphia	3-0		3	Montreal	2-2
	8	Montreal	2-4		5	New Jersey	0-2
	11	at Quebec	2-5		8	Quebec	2-2
	15	at Florida	0-2		10	Pittsburgh	3-4
	17	at Tampa Bay	2-1		12	at Hartford	2-5
	23	Washington	5-5		15	at Pittsburgh	2-5
	25	Florida	1-4		16	at Buffalo	1-2
	27	Boston	0-2		19	at Montreal	1-4
	28	Hartford	3-6		20	Boston	5-6
Mar.	2	Tampa Bay	2-3		22	at NY Islanders	3-2
	5	NY Islanders	3-1		24	Florida	1-5
	6	at NY Rangers	3-4		26	at Philadelphia	5-2
	8	at Florida	2-3		27	Tampa Bay	6-1
	10	at Washington	2-2		29	NY Islanders	2-2
	14	at New Jersey	2-4	**May**	1	at Boston	4-5
	16	Philadelphia	1-3		3	at Tampa Bay	4-3

Entry Draft
Selections 1995-92

1995 Pick		1994 Pick		1993 Pick		1992 Pick	
1	Bryan Berard	3	Radek Bonk	1	Alexandre Daigle	2	Alexei Yashin
27	Marc Moro	29	Stanislav Neckar	27	Radim Bicanek	25	Chad Penney
53	Brad Larsen	81	Bryan Masotta	53	Patrick Charbonneau	50	Patrick Traverse
89	Kevin Bolibruck	131	Mike Gaffney	91	Cosmo Dupaul	73	Radek Hamr
103	Kevin Boyd	133	Daniel Alfredsson	131	Rick Bodkin	98	Daniel Guerard
131	David Hruska	159	Doug Sproule	157	Sergei Poleschuk	121	Al Sinclair
183	Kaj Linna	210	Frederic Cassivi	183	Jason Disher	146	Jaroslav Miklenda
184	Ray Schultz	211	Danny Dupont	209	Toby Kvalevog	169	Jay Kenney
231	Erik Kaminski	237	Stephen MacKinnon	227	Pavol Demitra	194	Claude Savoie
		274	Antti Tormanen	235	Rick Schuwerk	217	Jake Grimes
						242	Tomas Jelinek
						264	Petter Ronnqvist

Twenty-year-old rookie rearguard Stanislav Neckar is a bright light on the Senators' horizon. He played two seasons with Ceske Budejovice in the Czech Republic before being drafted 29th overall by the Senators in 1994.

Coach

BOWNESS, RICK
Coach, Ottawa Senators. Born in Moncton, N.B., January 25, 1955.

Rick Bowness is entering his fourth season behind the Senators' bench. He is one of only two head coaches in NHL history to head an expansion team for its first three seasons. (Terry Crisp with Tampa Bay is the other.)

Rick was appointed the club's first head coach on June 15, 1992. He coached his 300th NHL game on March 19, 1995 vs. Pittsburgh. He has posted a 77-214-33 coaching record in 324 NHL games. His record with the Senators stands at 33-165-18 (216 games).

Prior to joining the Senators, Rick coached the Boston Bruins in 1991-92, guiding the team to a 39-32-12 record and a berth in the conference finals. The Moncton native began his coaching career with the AHL's Sherbrooke Jets as a player/coach in 1981, and returned to his hometown in 1987 as the coach and general manager of the Moncton Hawks, the Jets' AHL development team. In February 1989, Rick took over as interim coach of the Winnipeg Jets (28 games). Bowness then joined the Boston organization, coaching the AHL's Maine Mariners for two seasons before assuming head coaching duties for the Bruins for 1991-92.

Coaching Record

Season	Team	Regular Season					Playoffs			
		Games	W	L	T	%	Games	W	L	%
1987-88	Moncton (AHL)	80	27	45	8	.388	....	....	....	....
1988-89	Moncton (AHL)	53	28	20	5	.576	....	....	....	....
	Winnipeg (NHL)	**28**	**8**	**17**	**3**	**.340**	....	....	....	....
1989-90	Maine (AHL)	80	31	38	11	.457	....	....	....	....
1990-91	Maine (AHL)	80	34	34	12	.500	2	0	2	.000
1991-92	**Boston (NHL)**	**80**	**36**	**32**	**12**	**.525**	**15**	**8**	**7**	**.533**
1992-93	Ottawa (NHL)	84	10	70	4	.143	....	....	....	....
1993-94	Ottawa (NHL)	84	14	61	9	.220	....	....	....	....
1994-95	Ottawa (NHL)	48	9	34	5	.240	....	....	....	....
	NHL Totals	**324**	**77**	**214**	**33**	**.289**	**15**	**8**	**7**	**.533**

Club Directory

Palladium

Ottawa Senators
301 Moodie Drive
Suite 200
Nepean, Ontario
K2H 9C4
Phone **613/721-0115**
FAX 613/726-1419
Capacity: 10,575 Civic Centre
18,500 Palladium

Executive
Chairman, Governor and Chief Executive Officer . . . Rod Bryden
President, G.M. and Alternate Governor. . . . . Randy Sexton
Executive V-P, CFO and Alternate Governor . . . . . . Bernie Ashe
President, Palladium Corp. and Alternate Governor . Cyril Leeder

Assistants
Secretary to the Governor. . . . . Sharry Dozois
Secretary to the President. . . . . Allison Vaughan
Secretary to the Executive V-P . . . . Cheryl Blake
Secretary to the President, Palladuim Corporation . . Gail Martineau

Hockey Operations
Assistant General Manager. . . . . Ray Shero
Director of Player Personnel . . . . John Ferguson
Head Coach . . . . Rick Bowness
Assistant Coach . . . . Alain Vigneault
Assistant Coach . . . . Glenn "Chico" Resch
Director, Team and Business Development. . . . . . . Brad Marsh
Head Coach, Development Team . . . . Dave Allison
Assistant Coach, Development Team . . . . John Phelan
Head Equipment Trainer. Ed Georgica
Athletic Therapist . . . . Conrad Lackten
Assistant Trainer . . . . John Gervais
Director of Team Services . . . . Trevor Timmins
US Eastern Amateur Scout . . . . Paul Castron
Quebec Amateur Scout . . . . André Dupont
Ontario Amateur Scout. . . . . Tim Higgins
Professional Scout. . . . . Barry Long
Professional Scout. . . . . Pierre McGuire
Western Canada Scout. . . . . Bruce Southern
Team Doctor. . . . . Jamie Kissick M.D.
Strength and Conditioning Coach . . . . Mark Slater
Coordinator, Team and Business Development. . . . . Sherry Doiron

Team and Business Development
Coordinator, Team and Business Development. . . . . Sylvie Guénette-Craig
Community Relations Coordinator . . . . Marie Olney

Corporate Sales
Vice-President, Sales. . . . . Mark Bonneau
Corporate Sales Coordinator . . . . Christine Clancy
Manager of Sponsorship and Corporate Properties . Dan Quinn
Director, Outaouais Business Development. . . . . . . Enrico Valente
Senior Account Manager . . . . Brian Jokat
Senior Account Manager . . . . Darren McCartney
Corporate Account Manager . . . . Susan Ferguson
Corporate Account Manager . . . . Gina Gianetto
Corporate Account Manager . . . . Craig Purcell

Finance
Vice President, Finance . . . . Jim Ablett
Controller. . . . . Mark Goudie
Senior Accountant . . . . Lynda Rozon
Senior Accountant . . . . David Spooner
Payroll Supervisor . . . . Sandi Horner
Accounts Payable . . . . Anne Hersey
Accounts Payable . . . . Laurel Neill
Accounts Payable . . . . Lisa Saumure

Administration
Manager, Computer Services . . . . Sean Shrubsole
Office Coordinator . . . . Katrina Phelps
Receptionist . . . . Kelly MacCallum

Marketing
V-P, Corporate Marketing and Communications . . . John Owens
Vice-President, Marketing. . . . . Jim Steel
Merchandise Manager . . . . Bob Maxwell
Director of Publications . . . . Carl Lavigne
Art Director of Bodycheck Magazine . . . . Jean-Guy Brunet
Graphic Designer . . . . Kevin Caradonna
Marketing Coordinator. . . . . Krista Pogue

Media Relations
Director, Media Relations . . . . Laurent Benoit
Media Relations Assistant . . . . Dominick Saillant
Secretary, Media Relations . . . . Vivianne Slade
Club Historian. . . . . Jim McAuley

Ticketing and Event Services
Vice-President, Ticketing & Game-Day Operations . . Jeff Kyle
Secreaart, Ticketing & Game-Day Operations . . . . . Jody Thorson
Director of Operations & Guest Services . . . . Dave Dakers
Director of Promotions . . . . Patti Zebchuck
Ticket Sales Manager . . . . Pat Whalen
Season Ticket Service Manager . . . . Shawn Williams
Ticketing Coordinator. . . . . Tracey Drennan
Ticketing Sales Representative . . . . Jim Armstrong
Ticketing Sales Representative . . . . Gus Ayoub
Ticketing Sales Representative . . . . Ron Ayoub
Account Director . . . . Daniel Brazeau
Ticketing Sales Representative . . . . Robert Campagna
Ticketing Sales Representative . . . . Gianni Farinon
Guest Services Representative. . . . . Cindy Kruger
Secretary, Ticket Sales and Jr. Fan Club Coordinator Paulette Surette

Philadelphia Flyers

1994-95 Results: 28w-16L-4T 60PTS. First, Atlantic Division

Schedule

Oct.	Sat.	7	at Montreal
	Wed.	11	Washington
	Sat.	14	at NY Islanders
	Sun.	15	Edmonton
	Wed.	18	at Los Angeles
	Fri.	20	at Anaheim
	Sun.	22	at Chicago
	Wed.	25	NY Islanders
	Sat.	28	at NY Islanders
	Sun.	29	Ottawa
	Tues.	31	Tampa Bay
Nov.	Thur.	2	Florida
	Sat.	4	at Pittsburgh
	Sun.	5	Hartford
	Tues.	7	at Florida
	Thur.	9	Calgary
	Sat.	11	at New Jersey*
	Sun.	12	New Jersey*
	Tues.	14	at Washington
	Thur.	16	Ottawa
	Sat.	18	at Hartford*
	Sun.	19	Vancouver
	Tues.	21	Los Angeles
	Fri.	24	Detroit*
	Wed.	29	at Florida
	Thur.	30	Toronto
Dec.	Sun.	3	Boston
	Tues.	5	at Detroit
	Thur.	7	Buffalo
	Sun.	10	NY Islanders
	Thur.	14	Tampa Bay
	Sat.	16	at Montreal
	Sun.	17	Pittsburgh
	Tues.	19	at New Jersey
	Thur.	21	NY Rangers
	Sat.	23	at Hartford
	Wed.	27	at Edmonton
	Fri.	29	at Calgary
	Sun.	31	at Vancouver*
Jan.	Wed.	3	at San Jose
	Thur.	4	at Colorado

	Tues.	9	Anaheim
	Thur.	11	St. Louis
	Sat.	13	NY Rangers*
	Mon.	15	Dallas
	Mon.	22	Florida
	Wed.	24	at NY Rangers
	Sat.	27	at Pittsburgh*
	Sun.	28	at Washington*
Feb.	Thur.	1	Montreal
	Sat.	3	at St. Louis*
	Thur.	8	Buffalo
	Sat.	10	at Boston*
	Sun.	11	Colorado
	Wed.	14	at Florida
	Sat.	17	at Tampa Bay
	Mon.	19	New Jersey*
	Thur.	22	Washington
	Fri.	23	at Buffalo
	Sun.	25	Chicago
	Wed.	28	at Dallas
Mar.	Fri.	1	at Ottawa
	Sun.	3	at Washington*
	Sat.	9	at Boston*
	Sun.	10	New Jersey
	Wed.	13	Tampa Bay
	Sat.	16	Winnipeg
	Sun.	17	San Jose
	Tues.	19	NY Islanders
	Fri.	22	at Winnipeg
	Sat.	23	at Toronto
	Mon.	25	Hartford
	Wed.	27	at Ottawa
	Fri.	29	at Buffalo
	Sun.	31	Pittsburgh*
Apr.	Tues.	2	at NY Islanders
	Thur.	4	NY Rangers
	Fri.	5	at NY Rangers
	Sun.	7	Boston*
	Wed.	10	at New Jersey
	Thur.	11	Montreal
	Sun.	14	at Tampa Bay

* Denotes afternoon game.

Home Starting Times:

Weeknights	7:30 p.m.
Sundays	7:00 p.m.
Matinees	1:00 p.m.
Except Sun. Nov. 12	1:00 p.m.
Sun. Feb. 11	8:00 p.m.
Sun. Feb. 25	8:00 p.m.
Sun. Mar. 10	8:00 p.m.
Sun. Mar. 31	3:00 p.m.
Sun. Apr. 7	3:00 p.m.

Franchise date: June 5, 1967

ATLANTIC DIVISION

29th NHL Season

Traded to the Flyers on February 9, 1995, John LeClair established career-highs in goals (26), assists (28) and points (54) with his new club.

Year-by-Year Record

Season	GP	Home W	Home L	Home T	Road W	Road L	Road T	Overall W	Overall L	Overall T	GF	GA	Pts.	Finished		Playoff Result
1994-95	48	16	7	1	12	9	3	28	16	4	150	132	60	1st,	Atlantic Div.	Lost Conf. Championship
1993-94	84	19	20	3	16	19	7	35	39	10	294	314	80	6th,	Atlantic Div.	Out of Playoffs
1992-93	84	23	14	5	13	23	6	36	37	11	319	319	83	5th,	Patrick Div.	Out of Playoffs
1991-92	80	22	11	7	10	26	4	32	37	11	252	273	75	6th,	Patrick Div.	Out of Playoffs
1990-91	80	18	16	6	15	21	4	33	37	10	252	267	76	5th,	Patrick Div.	Out of Playoffs
1989-90	80	17	19	4	13	20	7	30	39	11	290	297	71	6th,	Patrick Div.	Out of Playoffs
1988-89	80	22	15	3	14	21	5	36	36	8	307	285	80	4th,	Patrick Div.	Lost Conf. Championship
1987-88	80	20	14	6	18	19	3	38	33	9	292	292	85	3rd,	Patrick Div.	Lost Div. Semi-Final
1986-87	80	29	9	2	17	17	6	46	26	8	310	245	100	1st,	Patrick Div.	Lost Final
1985-86	80	33	6	1	20	17	3	53	23	4	335	241	110	1st,	Patrick Div.	Lost Div. Semi-Final
1984-85	80	32	4	4	21	16	3	53	20	7	348	241	113	1st,	Patrick Div.	Lost Final
1983-84	80	25	10	5	19	16	5	44	26	10	350	290	98	3rd,	Patrick Div.	Lost Div. Semi-Final
1982-83	80	29	8	3	20	15	5	49	23	8	326	240	106	1st,	Patrick Div.	Lost Div. Semi-Final
1981-82	80	25	10	5	13	21	6	38	31	11	325	313	87	3rd,	Patrick Div.	Lost Div. Semi-Final
1980-81	80	23	9	8	18	15	7	41	24	15	313	249	97	2nd,	Patrick Div.	Lost Quarter-Final
1979-80	80	27	5	8	21	7	12	48	12	20	327	254	116	1st,	Patrick Div.	Lost Final
1978-79	80	26	10	4	14	15	11	40	25	15	281	248	95	2nd,	Patrick Div.	Lost Quarter-Final
1977-78	80	29	6	5	16	14	10	45	20	15	296	200	105	2nd,	Patrick Div.	Lost Semi-Final
1976-77	80	33	6	1	15	10	15	48	16	16	323	213	112	1st,	Patrick Div.	Lost Semi-Final
1975-76	80	36	2	2	15	11	14	51	13	16	348	209	118	1st,	Patrick Div.	Lost Final
1974-75	**80**	**32**	**6**	**2**	**19**	**12**	**9**	**51**	**18**	**11**	**293**	**181**	**113**	**1st,**	**Patrick Div.**	**Won Stanley Cup**
1973-74	**78**	**28**	**6**	**5**	**22**	**10**	**7**	**50**	**16**	**12**	**273**	**164**	**112**	**1st,**	**West Div.**	**Won Stanley Cup**
1972-73	78	27	8	4	10	22	7	37	30	11	296	256	85	2nd,	West Div.	Lost Semi-Final
1971-72	78	19	13	7	7	25	7	26	38	14	200	236	66	5th,	West Div.	Out of Playoffs
1970-71	78	20	10	9	8	23	8	28	33	17	207	225	73	3rd,	West Div.	Lost Quarter-Final
1969-70	76	11	14	13	6	21	11	17	35	24	197	225	58	5th,	West Div.	Out of Playoffs
1968-69	76	14	16	8	6	19	13	20	35	21	174	225	61	3rd,	West Div.	Lost Quarter-Final
1967-68	74	17	13	7	14	19	4	31	32	11	173	179	73	1st,	West Div.	Lost Quarter-Final

1995-96 Player Personnel

FORWARDS	HT	WT	S	Place of Birth	Date	1994-95 Club
ANTOSKI, Shawn	6-4	235	L	Brantford, Ont.	3/25/70	Vancouver-Philadelphia
BRIND'AMOUR, Rod	6-1	202	L	Ottawa, Ont.	8/9/70	Philadelphia
COLES, Bruce	5-9	183	L	Montreal, Que.	1/12/68	Johnstown-Hershey
CROWE, Philip	6-2	220	L	Nanton, Alta.	4/14/70	Hershey
DiMAIO, Rob	5-10	190	R	Calgary, Alta.	2/19/68	Philadelphia
DINEEN, Kevin	5-11	190	R	Quebec City, Que.	10/28/63	Houston-Philadelphia
DIONNE, Gilbert	6-0	194	L	Drummondville, Que.	9/19/70	Montreal-Philadelphia
DUPRE, Yanick	6-0	189	L	Montreal, Que.	11/20/72	Hershey-Philadelphia
FAUST, Andre	5-11	191	L	Joliette, Que.	10/7/69	Hershey
FEDYK, Brent	6-0	195	R	Yorkton, Sask.	3/8/67	Philadelphia
FORBES, Colin	6-3	190	L	New Westminster, B.C.	2/16/76	Portland (WHL)
HEALEY, Paul	6-2	185	R	Edmonton, Alta.	3/20/75	Prince Albert
HERPERGER, Chris	6-0	190	L	Esterhazy, Sask.	2/24/74	Seattle-Hershey
JUHLIN, Patrik	6-0	194	L	Huddinge, Sweden	4/24/70	Vasteras-Philadelphia
LeCLAIR, John	6-2	219	L	St. Albans, VT	7/5/69	Montreal-Philadelphia
LINDROS, Eric	6-4	229	R	London, Ont.	2/28/73	Philadelphia
MacTAVISH, Craig	6-1	195	L	London, Ont.	8/15/58	Philadelphia
MONTGOMERY, Jim	5-10	185	R	Montreal, Que.	6/30/69	Montreal-Philadelphia-Hershey
NORRIS, Clayton	6-2	205	R	Edmonton, Alta.	3/8/72	Hershey
OTTO, Joel	6-4	220	R	Elk River, MN	10/29/61	Calgary
PAQUIN, Patrice	6-2	192	L	St. Jerome, Que.	6/26/74	Beauport-St-Jean
PODEIN, Shjon	6-2	200	L	Rochester, MN	3/5/68	Philadelphia
PROSPAL, Vaclav	6-2	173	L	Ceske-Budejovice, Czech.	2/17/75	Hershey
RENBERG, Mikael	6-1	218	L	Pitea, Sweden	5/5/72	Lulea-Philadelphia
ROMANIUK, Russell	6-0	195	L	Winnipeg, Man.	6/9/70	Winnipeg-Springfield
SEMENOV, Anatoli	6-2	190	L	Moscow, USSR	3/5/62	Anaheim-Philadelphia
SITTLER, Ryan	6-2	195	L	London, Ont.	1/28/74	Hershey-Johnstown
ZAVISHA, Brad	6-2	205	L	Hines Creek, Alta.	1/4/72	Cape Breton-Hershey

DEFENSEMEN	HT	WT	S	Place of Birth	Date	1994-95 Club
BOULIN, Vladislav	6-4	196	L	Penza, USSR	5/18/72	Hershey
BOWEN, Jason	6-4	215	L	Port Alice, B.C.	11/9/73	Hershey-Philadelphia
BRIMANIS, Aris	6-3	210	R	Cleveland, OH	3/14/72	Hershey
DESJARDINS, Eric	6-1	200	R	Rouyn, Que.	6/14/69	Montreal-Philadelphia
DYKHUIS, Karl	6-3	195	L	Sept-Iles, Que.	7/8/72	Indianapolis-Hershey-Phi
HALLER, Kevin	6-2	183	L	Trochu, Alta.	12/5/70	Philadelphia
KORDIC, Dan	6-5	220	L	Edmonton, Alta.	4/18/71	Hershey
LANK, Jeff	6-3	185	L	Indian Head, Sask.	3/1/75	Prince Albert
SAMUELSSON, Kjell	6-6	235	R	Tyngsryd, Sweden	10/18/58	Pittsburgh
STAPLES, Jeff	6-2	207	L	Kitimat, B.C.	3/4/75	Brandon
SVOBODA, Petr	6-1	174	L	Most, Czech.	2/14/66	Litvinov-Buffalo-Philadelphia
THERIEN, Chris	6-3	230	L	Ottawa, Ont.	12/14/71	Hershey-Philadelphia

GOALTENDERS	HT	WT	C	Place of Birth	Date	1994-95 Club
HEXTALL, Ron	6-3	192	L	Brandon, Man.	5/3/64	Philadelphia
ISRAEL, Aaron	6-2	176	L	Boston, MA	6/4/73	Hershey-Johnstown
KUNTAR, Les	6-2	195	L	Elma, NY	7/28/69	Worcester-Hershey
LITTLE, Neil	6-1	175	L	Medicine Hat, Alta.	12/18/71	Hershey-Johnstown
ROUSSEL, Dominic	6-1	191	L	Hull, Que.	2/22/70	Philadelphia-Hershey
SNOW, Garth	6-3	200	L	Wrentham, MA	7/28/69	Cornwall-Quebec

General Managers' History

"Bud" Poile, 1967-68 to 1968-69; "Bud" Poile and Keith Allen, 1969-70; Keith Allen, 1970-71 to 1982-83; Bob McCammon, 1983-84; Bob Clarke, 1984-85 to 1989-90; Russ Farwell, 1990-91 to 1993-94; Bob Clarke, 1994-95 to date.

Coaching History

Keith Allen, 1967-68 to 1968-69; Vic Stasiuk, 1969-70 to 1970-71; Fred Shero, 1971-72 to 1977-78; Bob McCammon and Pat Quinn, 1978-79; Pat Quinn, 1979-80 to 1980-81; Pat Quinn and Bob McCammon, 1981-82; Bob McCammon, 1982-83 to 1983-84; Mike Keenan, 1984-85 to 1987-88; Paul Holmgren, 1988-89 to 1990-91; Paul Holmgren and Bill Dineen, 1991-92; Bill Dineen, 1992-93; Terry Simpson, 1993-94; Terry Murray, 1994-95 to date.

Captains' History

Lou Angotti, 1967-68; Ed Van Impe, 1968-69 to 1971-72; Ed Van Impe and Bobby Clarke, 1972-73; Bobby Clarke, 1973-74 to 1978-79; Mel Bridgman, 1979-80, 1980-81; Bill Barber, 1981-82; Bill Barber and Bobby Clarke, 1982-83; Bobby Clarke, 1983-84; Dave Poulin, 1984-85 to 1988-89; Dave Poulin and Ron Sutter, 1989-90; Ron Sutter, 1990-91; Rick Tocchet, 1991-92; no captain, 1992-93; Kevin Dineen, 1993-94; Eric Lindros, 1994-95 to date.

1994-95 Scoring

* – rookie

Regular Season

Pos	#	Player	Team	GP	G	A	Pts	+/–	PIM	PP	SH	GW	GT	S	%
C	88	Eric Lindros	PHI	46	29	41	70	27	60	7	0	4	1	144	20.1
L	19	Mikael Renberg	PHI	47	26	31	57	20	20	8	0	4	0	143	18.2
C	10	John Leclair	MTL	9	1	4	5	–1	10	1	0	0	0	18	5.6
			PHI	37	25	24	49	21	20	5	0	7	0	113	22.1
			TOTAL	46	26	28	54	20	30	6	0	7	0	131	19.8
C	17	Rod Brind'Amour	PHI	48	12	27	39	–4	33	4	1	2	0	86	14.0
D	37	Eric Desjardins	MTL	9	0	6	6	2	2	0	0	0	0	14	0.0
			PHI	34	5	18	23	10	12	1	0	1	0	79	6.3
			TOTAL	43	5	24	29	12	14	1	0	1	0	93	5.4
D	2	Dimitri Yushkevich	PHI	40	5	9	14	–4	47	3	1	1	0	80	6.3
R	11	Kevin Dineen	PHI	40	8	5	13	–1	39	4	0	2	0	55	14.5
D	6	* Chris Therien	PHI	48	3	10	13	8	38	1	0	0	0	53	5.7
R	18	Brent Fedyk	PHI	30	8	4	12	–2	14	3	0	2	0	41	19.5
C	14	Craig MacTavish	PHI	45	3	9	12	2	23	0	0	0	0	38	7.9
C	44	Anatoli Semenov	ANA	15	3	4	7	–10	4	2	0	0	0	33	9.1
			PHI	26	1	2	3	–2	6	0	0	0	0	36	2.8
			TOTAL	41	4	6	10	–12	10	2	0	0	0	69	5.8
C	25	Shjon Podein	PHI	44	3	7	10	–2	33	0	0	1	0	48	6.3
D	5	Kevin Haller	PHI	36	2	8	10	16	48	0	0	0	0	26	7.7
L	45	Gilbert Dionne	MTL	6	0	3	3	–3	2	0	0	0	0	4	0.0
			PHI	20	0	6	6	–1	2	0	0	0	0	29	0.0
			TOTAL	26	0	9	9	–4	4	0	0	0	0	33	0.0
D	24	Karl Dykhuis	PHI	33	2	6	8	7	37	1	0	1	0	46	4.3
D	23	Petr Svoboda	BUF	26	0	5	5	–5	60	0	0	0	0	22	0.0
			PHI	11	0	3	3	0	10	0	0	0	0	17	0.0
			TOTAL	37	0	8	8	–5	70	0	0	0	0	39	0.0
D	23	Petr Svoboda	PHI	37	0	8	8	–5	70	0	0	0	0	39	0.0
L	12	* Patrik Juhlin	PHI	42	4	3	7	–13	6	0	0	1	0	44	9.1
C	9	Rob Dimaio	PHI	36	3	1	4	8	53	0	0	0	1	34	8.8
R	21	Dave Brown	PHI	28	1	2	3	–1	53	0	0	0	0	8	12.5
C	22	Jim Montgomery	MTL	5	0	0	0	–2	2	0	0	0	0	3	0.0
			PHI	8	1	1	2	–2	6	0	0	0	0	10	10.0
			TOTAL	13	1	1	2	–4	8	0	0	0	0	13	7.7
D	20	Rob Zettler	PHI	32	0	1	1	–3	34	0	0	0	0	17	0.0
D	37	Shawn Anderson	PHI	1	0	0	0	0	0	0	0	0	0	0	0.0
D	23	Stewart Malgunas	PHI	4	0	0	0	–1	4	0	0	0	0	1	0.0
D	28	Jason Bowen	PHI	4	0	0	0	–2	0	0	0	0	0	2	0.0
G	33	Dominic Roussel	PHI	19	0	0	0	0	6	0	0	0	0	0	0.0
L	15	* Yanick Dupre	PHI	22	0	0	0	–7	8	0	0	0	0	21	0.0
G	27	Ron Hextall	PHI	31	0	0	0	0	13	0	0	0	0	0	0.0
L	8	Shawn Antoski	VAN	7	0	0	0	–4	46	0	0	0	0	4	0.0
			PHI	25	0	0	0	0	61	0	0	0	0	12	0.0
			TOTAL	32	0	0	0	–4	107	0	0	0	0	16	0.0

Goaltending

No.	Goaltender	GPI	Mins	Avg	W	L	T	EN	SO	GA	SA	S%
33	Dominic Roussel	19	1075	2.34	11	7	0	1	1	42	486	.914
27	Ron Hextall	31	1824	2.89	17	9	4	1	1	88	801	.890
	Totals	**48**	**2906**	**2.73**	**28**	**16**	**4**	**2**	**2**	**132**	**1289**	**.898**

Playoffs

Pos	#	Player	Team	GP	G	A	Pts	+/–	PIM	PP	SH	GW	OT	S	%
C	17	Rod Brind'Amour	PHI	15	6	9	15	5	8	2	1	1	0	28	21.4
C	88	Eric Lindros	PHI	12	4	11	15	7	18	0	0	1	1	28	14.3
L	19	Mikael Renberg	PHI	15	6	7	13	5	6	2	0	0	0	45	13.3
C	10	John Leclair	PHI	15	5	7	12	7	4	1	0	1	0	37	13.5
R	11	Kevin Dineen	PHI	15	6	4	10	2	18	1	0	1	0	24	25.0
D	37	Eric Desjardins	PHI	15	4	4	8	13	10	1	0	2	1	35	11.4
D	5	Kevin Haller	PHI	15	4	4	8	10	10	0	1	1	1	14	28.6
D	24	Karl Dykhuis	PHI	15	4	4	8	2	14	2	0	2	1	17	23.5
C	9	Rob Dimaio	PHI	15	2	4	6	3	4	0	1	1	0	8	25.0
C	44	Anatoli Semenov	PHI	15	2	4	6	3	0	0	0	0	0	13	15.4
D	2	Dimitri Yushkevich	PHI	15	1	5	6	–2	12	0	0	0	0	25	4.0
C	14	Craig MacTavish	PHI	15	1	4	5	–3	20	0	0	0	0	13	7.7
R	18	Brent Fedyk	PHI	9	2	2	4	2	8	0	0	0	0	9	22.2
C	25	Shjon Podein	PHI	15	1	3	4	2	10	0	0	0	0	10	10.0
D	23	Petr Svoboda	PHI	14	0	4	4	5	8	0	0	0	0	15	0.0
C	22	Jim Montgomery	PHI	7	1	0	1	2	2	0	0	0	0	3	33.3
L	12	* Patrik Juhlin	PHI	13	1	0	1	–1	2	0	0	0	0	14	7.1
L	8	Shawn Antoski	PHI	13	0	1	1	1	10	0	0	0	0	3	0.0
G	27	Ron Hextall	PHI	15	0	1	1	0	4	0	0	0	0	0	0.0
D	20	Rob Zettler	PHI	1	0	0	0	1	2	0	0	0	0	1	0.0
G	33	Dominic Roussel	PHI	1	0	0	0	0	0	0	0	0	0	0	0.0
R	21	Dave Brown	PHI	3	0	0	0	0	0	0	0	0	0	2	0.0
L	45	Gilbert Dionne	PHI	3	0	0	0	–1	4	0	0	0	0	2	0.0
D	6	* Chris Therien	PHI	15	0	0	0	–2	10	0	0	0	0	24	0.0

Goaltending

No.	Goaltender	GPI	Mins	Avg	W	L	EN	SO	GA	SA	S%
33	Dominic Roussel	1	23	0.00	0	0	0	0	0	8	1.000
27	Ron Hextall	15	897	2.81	10	5	1	0	42	437	.904
	Totals	**15**	**922**	**2.80**	**10**	**5**	**1**	**0**	**43**	**446**	**.904**

Retired Numbers

1	Bernie Parent	1967-1971 and 1973-1979
4	Barry Ashbee	1970-1974
7	Bill Barber	1972-1985
16	Bobby Clarke	1969-1984

Club Records

Team

(Figures in brackets for season records are games played; records for fewest points, wins, ties, losses, goals, goals against are for 70 or more games)

Most Points	118	1975-76 (80)
Most Wins	53	1984-85 (80)
		1985-86 (80)
Most Ties	*24	1969-70 (76)
Most Losses	39	1993-94 (84)
Most Goals	350	1983-84 (80)
Most Goals Against	319	1992-93 (84)
Fewest Points	58	1969-70 (76)
Fewest Wins	17	1969-70 (76)
Fewest Ties	4	1985-86 (80)
Fewest Losses	12	1979-80 (80)
Fewest Goals	173	1967-68 (74)
Fewest Goals Against	164	1973-74 (78)

Longest Winning Streak

Over-all	13	Oct. 19-Nov. 17/85
Home	*20	Jan. 4-Apr. 3/76
Away	8	Dec. 22/82-Jan. 16/83

Longest Undefeated Streak

Over-all	*35	Oct. 14/79-Jan. 6/80 (25 wins, 10 ties)
Home	26	Oct. 11/79-Feb. 3/80 (19 wins, 7 ties)
Away	16	Oct. 20/79-Jan. 6/80 (11 wins, 5 ties)

Longest Losing Streak

Over-all	6	Mar. 25-Apr. 4/70; Dec. 5-Dec. 17/92; Jan. 25-Feb. 5/94
Home	5	Jan. 30-Feb. 15/69
Away	8	Oct. 25-Nov. 26/72

Longest Winless Streak

Over-all	11	Nov. 21-Dec. 14/69 (9 losses, 2 ties) Dec. 10/70-Jan. 3/71 (9 losses, 2 ties)
Home	8	Dec. 19/68-Jan. 18/69 (4 losses, 4 ties)
Away	19	Oct. 23/71-Jan. 27/72 (15 losses, 4 ties)

Most Shutouts, Season	13	1974-75 (80)
Most PIM, Season	2,621	1980-81 (80)
Most Goals, Game	13	Mar. 22/84 (Pit. 4 at Phi. 13) Oct. 18/84 (Van. 2 at Phil. 13)

Individual

Most Seasons	15	Bobby Clarke
Most Games	1,144	Bobby Clarke
Most Goals, Career	420	Bill Barber
Most Assists, Career	852	Bobby Clarke
Most Points, Career	1,210	Bobby Clarke (358 goals, 852 assists)
Most PIM, Career	1,683	Rick Tocchet
Most Shutouts, Career	50	Bernie Parent

Longest Consecutive

Game Streak	287	Rick MacLeish (Oct. 6/72-Feb. 5/76)
Most Goals, Season	61	Reggie Leach (1975-76)
Most Assists, Season	89	Bobby Clarke (1974-75; 1975-76)
Most Points, Season	123	Mark Recchi (1992-93) (53 goals, 70 assists)
Most PIM, Season	*472	Dave Schultz (1974-75)

Most Points, Defenseman,

Season	82	Mark Howe (1985-86) (24 goals, 58 assists)

Most Points, Center,

Season	119	Bobby Clarke (1975-76) (30 goals, 89 assists)

Most Points, Right Wing,

Season	123	Mark Recchi (1992-93) (53 goals, 70 assists)

Most Points, Left Wing,

Season	112	Bill Barber (1975-76) (50 goals, 62 assists)

Most Points, Rookie,

Season	82	Mikael Renberg (1993-94) (38 goals, 44 assists)
Most Shutouts, Season	12	Bernie Parent (1973-74; 1974-75)
Most Goals, Game	4	Rick MacLeish (Feb. 13/73; Mar. 4/73) Tom Bladon (Dec. 11/77) Tim Kerr (Oct. 25/84, Jan. 17/85, Feb. 9/85, Nov. 20/86) Brian Propp (Dec. 2/86) Rick Tocchet (Feb. 27/88; Jan. 25/90) Kevin Dineen (Oct. 31/93)
Most Assists, Game	5	Bobby Clarke (Apr. 1/76) Eric Lindros (Mar. 10/94)
Most Points, Game	8	Tom Bladon (Dec. 11/77)

* NHL Record.

All-time Record vs. Other Clubs

Regular Season

	GP	W	L	T	GF	GA	PTS	GP	W	L	T	GF	GA	PTS	GP	W	L	T	GF	GA	PTS
			At Home							**On Road**							**Total**				
Anaheim	1	0	1		2	3	0	1	0	1	0	3	6	0	2	0	2	0	5	9	0
Boston	55	24	25	6	183	167	54	58	13	38	7	167	242	33	113	37	63	13	350	409	87
Buffalo	49	30	11	8	182	131	68	45	17	22	6	138	159	40	94	47	33	14	320	290	108
Calgary	44	30	12	2	180	120	62	45	13	23	9	148	188	35	89	43	35	11	328	308	97
Chicago	54	28	15	11	178	145	67	53	11	24	18	150	191	40	107	39	39	29	328	336	107
Dallas	59	40	9	10	235	136	90	59	22	24	13	196	197	57	118	62	33	23	431	333	147
Detroit	52	29	12	11	210	156	69	51	18	24	9	168	184	45	103	47	36	20	378	340	114
Edmonton	23	16	6	1	102	67	33	22	5	13	4	63	83	14	45	21	19	5	165	150	47
Florida	5	2	1	2	13	14	6	4	3	1	0	14	12	6	9	5	2	2	27	26	12
Hartford	25	17	7	1	104	73	35	26	12	10	4	110	105	28	51	29	17	5	214	178	63
Los Angeles	56	34	15	7	217	145	75	58	34	17	7	204	171	75	114	68	32	14	421	316	150
Montreal	55	21	21	13	165	168	55	56	15	29	12	168	211	42	111	36	50	25	333	379	97
New Jersey	61	42	12	7	262	150	91	60	27	29	4	231	220	58	121	69	41	11	493	370	149
NY Islanders	72	43	21	8	277	221	94	74	22	41	11	216	294	55	146	65	62	19	493	515	149
NY Rangers	85	42	30	13	295	247	97	87	27	40	20	253	293	74	172	69	70	33	548	540	171
Ottawa	5	4	1	0	29	11	8	5	2	2	1	13	12	5	10	6	3	1	42	23	13
Pittsburgh	85	63	15	7	370	219	133	84	31	36	17	270	289	79	169	94	51	24	640	508	212
Quebec	27	20	5	2	106	71	42	26	9	9	8	97	99	26	53	29	14	10	203	170	68
St. Louis	59	40	10	9	237	135	89	59	29	23	7	183	173	65	118	69	33	16	420	308	154
San Jose	3	2	1	0	12	7	4	4	4	3	1	0	14	5	7	2	0	26	16	10	
Tampa Bay	5	4	0	1	22	13	9	6	4	2	0	19	17	8	11	8	2	1	41	30	17
Toronto	52	33	11	8	211	123	74	52	20	19	13	177	180	53	104	53	30	21	388	303	127
Vancouver	45	30	14	1	202	135	61	45	24	10	11	174	131	59	90	54	24	12	376	266	120
Washington	63	37	22	4	242	182	78	60	27	22	11	215	211	65	123	64	44	15	457	393	143
Winnipeg	23	17	6	0	107	69	34	22	11	9	2	78	72	24	45	28	15	2	185	141	58
Defunct Clubs	34	24	4	6	137	67	54	35	13	14	8	102	89	34	69	37	18	14	239	156	88
Totals	1097	672	287	138	4280	2975	1482	1097	412		483	202	3571	3838	1026	2194	1084		770	340	7851	6813	2508

Calgary totals include Atlanta, 1972-73 to 1979-80. Dallas totals include Minnesota, 1967-68 to 1992-93.
New Jersey totals include Kansas City, 1974-75 to 1975-76, and Colorado, 1976-77 to 1981-82.

Playoffs

	Series	W	L	GP	W	L	T	GF	GA	Last Mtg.	Round	Result
Boston	4	2	2	20	9	11	0	57	60	1978	QF	L 1-4
Buffalo	3	3	0	16	12	4	0	53	36	1995	CQF	W 4-1
Calgary	2	1	1	11	7	4	0	43	28	1981	QF	L 3-4
Chicago	1	0	1	4	0	4	0	8	20	1971	QF	L 0-4
Dallas	2	2	0	11	8	3	0	41	26	1980	SF	W 4-1
Edmonton	3	1	2	15	7	8	0	44	49	1987	F	L 3-4
Montreal	4	1	3	21	6	15	0	52	72	1989	CF	L 2-4
New Jersey	2	1	1	8	4	4	0	20	23	1995	CF	L 2-4
NY Islanders	4	3	1	25	14	11	0	83	69	1987	DF	W 4-3
NY Rangers	9	5	4	42	23	19	0	137	140	1995	CSF	W 4-0
Pittsburgh	1	1	0	7	4	3	0	31	24	1989	CF	W 4-3
Quebec	2	2	0	11	7	4	0	39	29	1985	CF	W 4-2
St. Louis	2	0	2	11	3	8	0	20	34	1969	QF	L 0-4
Toronto	3	3	0	17	12	5	0	67	47	1977	QF	W 4-2
Vancouver	1	1	0	3	2	1	0	15	9	1979	PR	W 2-1
Washington	3	1	2	16	7	9	0	55	65	1989	DSF	W 4-2
Totals	46	27	19	238	126	112	0	765	731			

Playoff Results 1995-91

Year	Round	Opponent	Result	GF	GA
1995	CF	New Jersey	L 2-4	14	20
	CSF	NY Rangers	W 4-0	18	10
	CQF	Buffalo	W 4-1	18	13

Abbreviations: Round: F – Final; CF – conference final; CQF – conference quarter-final; CSF – conference semi-final; DF – division final; DSF – division semi-final; SF – semi-final; QF – quarter-final; PR – preliminary round.

Entry Draft
Selections 1995-81

1995
Pick
22 Brian Boucher
48 Shane Kenny
100 Radovan Somik
132 Dimitri Tertyshny
135 Jamie Sokolsky
152 Martin Spanhel
178 Martin Streit
204 Ruslan Shafikov
230 Jeff Lank

1994
Pick
62 Artem Anisimov
88 Adam Magarrell
101 Sebastien Vallee
140 Alexander Selivanov
166 Colin Forbes
192 Derek Diener
202 Raymond Giroux
218 Johan Hedberg
244 Andre Payette
270 Jan Lipiansky

1993
Pick
36 Janne Niinimaa
71 Vaclav Prospal
77 Milos Holan
114 Vladimir Krechin
140 Mike Crowley
166 Aaron Israel
192 Paul Healey
218 Tripp Tracy
226 E.J. Bradley
244 Jeffrey Staples
270 Kenneth Hemmenway

1992
Pick
7 Ryan Sittler
15 Jason Bowen
31 Denis Metlyuk
103 Vladislav Buljin
127 Roman Zolotov
151 Kirk Daubenspeck
175 Claude Jutras Jr.
199 Jonas Hakansson
223 Chris Herperger
247 Patrice Paquin

1991
Pick
6 Peter Forsberg
50 Yanick Dupre
86 Aris Brimanis
94 Yanick Degrace
116 Clayton Norris
122 Dmitri Yushkevich
138 Andrei Lomakin
182 James Bode
204 Josh Bartell
226 Neil Little
248 John Porco

1990
Pick
4 Mike Ricci
25 Chris Simon
40 Mikael Renberg
42 Terran Sandwith
44 Kimbi Daniels
46 Bill Armstrong
47 Chris Therien
52 Al Kinisky
88 Dan Kordic
109 Viacheslav Butsayev
151 Patrik Englund
172 Toni Porkka
193 Greg Hanson
214 Tommy Soderstrom
235 William Lund

1989
Pick
33 Greg Johnson
34 Patrik Juhlin
72 Reid Simpson
117 Niklas Eriksson
138 John Callahan Jr.
159 Sverre Sears
180 Glen Wisser
201 Al Kummu
222 Matt Brait
243 James Pollio

1988
Pick
14 Claude Boivin
35 Pat Murray
56 Craig Fisher
63 Dominic Roussel
77 Scott Lagrand
98 Edward O'Brien
119 Gordie Frantti
140 Jamie Cooke
161 Johan Salle
182 Brian Arthur
203 Jeff Dandreta
224 Scott Billey
245 Drahomir Kadlec

1987
Pick
20 Darren Rumble
30 Jeff Harding
62 Martin Hostak
83 Tomaz Eriksson
104 Bill Gall
125 Tony Link
146 Mark Strapon
167 Darryl Ingham
188 Bruce McDonald
209 Steve Morrow
230 Darius Rusnak
251 Dale Roehl

1986
Pick
20 Kerry Huffman
23 Jukka Seppo
28 Kent Hawley
83 Mark Bar
125 Steve Scheifele
146 Sami Wahlsten
167 Murray Baron
188 Blaine Rude
209 Shawn Sabol
230 Brett Lawrence
251 Daniel Stephano

1985
Pick
21 Glen Seabrooke
42 Bruce Rendall
48 Darryl Gilmour
63 Shane Whelan
84 Paul Marshall
105 Daril Holmes
126 Ken Alexander
147 Tony Horacek
168 Mike Cusack
189 Gordon Murphy
231 Rod Williams
252 Paul Maurice

1984
Pick
22 Greg Smyth
27 Scott Mellanby
37 Jeff Chychrun
43 Dave McLay
47 John Stevens
79 Dave Hanson
100 Brian Dobbin
121 John Dzikowski
142 Tom Allen
163 Luke Vitale
184 Bill Powers
204 Daryn Fersovitch
245 Juraj Bakos

1983
Pick
41 Peter Zezel
44 Derrick Smith
81 Alan Bourbeau
101 Jerome Carrier
121 Rick Tocchet
141 Bobby Mormina
161 Per-Erik Eklund
181 Rob Nichols
201 William McCormick
221 Brian Jopling
241 Harold Duvall

1982
Pick
4 Ron Sutter
46 Miroslav Dvorak
47 Bill Campbell
77 Mikael Hjalm
98 Todd Bergen
119 Ron Hextall
140 Dave Brown
161 Alain Lavigne
182 Magnus Roupe
203 Tom Allen
224 Rick Gal
245 Mark Vichorek

1981
Pick
16 Steve Smith
37 Rich Costello
47 Barry Tabobondung
58 Ken Strong
5 David Michayluk
79 Ken Latta
100 Justin Hanley
121 Andre Villeneuve
137 Vladimir Svitek
142 Gil Hudon
163 Steve Taylor
184 Len Hachborn
205 Steve Tsujiura

Coach

MURRAY, TERRY RODNEY
Coach, Philadelphia Flyers. Born in Shawville, Que., July 20, 1950.

Terry Murray was named as the tenth coach of the Philadelphia Flyers on June 23, 1994. He is the second former Flyer player to return to the team as head coach, joining Paul Holmgren, who coached the team from 1988-91. Prior to joining the Flyers, Murray served as the head coach of the Washington Capitals for five seasons from January 20, 1990 to January 27, 1994. As coach of the Capitals, Murray's team posted an overall record of 163-134-28 for a .545 winning percentage. After leaving the Capitals, Murray served as head coach of the Cincinnati Cyclones, the Florida Panthers' IHL affiliate, leading the team to a 17-7-4 record in 28 games. The Shawville, Quebec, native also spent six seasons as the head coach of the AHL's Baltimore Skipjacks.

Murray was selected 88th overall by California in the 1970 Amateur Draft. He enjoyed a successful playing career in both the NHL and American Hockey League. He led the Maine Mariners to two Calder Cup championships in 1977-78 and 1978-79, and was awarded the AHL's Eddie Shore Plaque as the league's outstanding defenseman in both seasons. He was an AHL First Team All-Star in three seasons, 1975-76, 1977-78 and 1978-79. Terry played in 302 NHL games over eight seasons, concluding his career with the Capitals in 1981-82. He was the first ex-Capital to coach the club.

Coaching Record

Season	Team	Games	Regular Season W	L	T	%	Playoffs Games	W	L	%
1988-89	Baltimore (AHL)	80	30	46	4	.400	....	....	....	....
1989-90	Baltimore (AHL)	44	26	17	1	.603	....	....	....	....
1989-90	**Washington (NHL)**	34	18	14	2	.559	15	8	7	.533
1990-91	**Washington (NHL)**	80	37	36	7	.506	11	5	6	.455
1991-92	**Washington (NHL)**	80	45	27	8	.613	7	3	4	.429
1992-93	**Washington (NHL)**	84	43	34	7	.554	6	2	4	.333
1993-94	**Washington (NHL)**	47	20	23	4	.468	....	....	....	....
	Cincinnati (IHL)	28	17	7	4	.679	11	6	5	.545
1994-95	**Philadelphia (NHL)**	48	28	16	4	.625	15	10	5	.667
	NHL Totals	373	191	150	32	.555	54	28	26	.519

Club Directory

CoreStates Spectrum
3601 South Broad St.
Philadelphia, PA 19148
Phone 215/465-4500
PR FAX 215/389-9403
Capacity: 17,380

Board of Directors
Ed Snider, Jay Snider, Joe Scott, Keith Allen, Fred Shabel, Sylvan Tobin, Bob Clarke, Sanford Lipstein, Ron Ryan

Majority Ownership	Ed Snider and family
Limited Partners	Sylvan and Fran Tobin
President and General Manager	Bob Clarke
Chairman of the Board, Emeritus	Joe Scott
Chief Operating Officer	Ron Ryan
Executive Vice-President	Keith Allen
Head Coach	Terry Murray
Assistant General Manager	John Blackwell
Assistant Coaches	Keith Acton, Tom Webster
Goaltending Coach	Rejean Lemelin
Director of Pro Scouting	Bill Barber
Chief Scout	Jerry Melnyk
Scouts	Bill Dineen, Inge Hammarstrom, Simon Nolet, Dennis Patterson, Vaclav Slansky, Evgeny Zimin
Head Trainer	Dave Settlemyre
Trainers	Jim Evers, Harry Bricker, Derek Settlemyre
Athletic Trainer	John Worley
Medical Staff	Arthur Bartolozzi, M.D., Gary Dorshimer, M.D., Jeff Hartzell, M.D., Guy Lanzi, D.D.S.
Director of Team Services	Joe Kadlec
Computer Analyst	David Gelberg
Vice-President, Finance	Dan Clemmens
Vice-President, Public Relations	Mark Piazza
Vice-President, Sales	Jack Betson
Director of Finance	Jeff Niessen
Controller	Michelle Hay
Payroll Accountant	Susann Schaffer
Director of Marketing	Eileen Smith
Manager, Season Ticket Sales	Steve Schiff
Manager, Media Relations	Zack Hill
Assistant Director of Public Relations	Joe Klugo
Public Relations Assistant	Linda Held
Director of Community Relations	Linda Panasci
Director of Youth Hockey	Greg Scott
Ticket Manager	Cecilia Baker
Sales/Marketing Assistant	Helen Hubbard
General Manager, Advertising/Sales	Dave Resnick
Sponsorship Manager	Carolyn Wollman
Flyers Sales Staff	Daniel Carchedi, Steve Coates, Jeff Kirk, Ivan Shlichtman, Joe Watson
Executive Assistants	Suzanne Carlin, Kim Clayton, Kathy Nasevich, Dianna Taylor
Receptionist	Aggie Preston
Television Announcers	Jim Jackson, Gary Dornhoefer
Radio Announcers	Steve Coates, TBA
Broadcast Consultant	Mike Finocchiaro
Broadcast Advisor	Gene Hart
Public Address Announcer	Lou Nolan
Television Outlets	WPHL-TV (Ch. 17), PRISM, SportsChannel Philadelphia
Radio Station (Flagship)	WIP-AM (610 AM)

General Manager

CLARKE, ROBERT EARLE (BOB)
General Manager, Philadelphia Flyers. Born in Flin Flon, Man., August 13, 1949.

Bob Clarke was named president and general manager of the Philadelphia Flyers on June 15, 1994. Prior to joining the Flyers' family, Clarke served as president and general manager of the Florida Panthers. In 1993-94, their first season in the NHL, the Panthers established NHL records for wins (33) and points (83) by an expansion franchise. Clarke also served as the vice president and general manager of the Minnesota North Stars from 1990-92, guiding the team to the Stanley Cup finals in 1990-91.

Clarke's appointment marks the second time he has served as the Flyers' general manager. The Flin Flon native was the Flyers' vice president and general manager from 1984-90, when the team posted a 256-177-47 record. During his six years as general manager, the Flyers won three divisional titles, two conference championships, reached the Stanley Cup semifinals three times and the Finals twice.

As a player, the former Philadelphia captain led his club to Stanley Cup championships in 1974 and 1975 and captured numerous individual awards, including the Hart Trophy as the League's most valuable player in 1973, 1975 and 1976. The four-time All-Star also received the Masterton Memorial Trophy (perseverance and dedication) in 1972 and the Frank J. Selke Trophy (top defensive forward) in 1983. He appeared in nine All-Star Games and was elected to the Hockey Hall of Fame in 1987. He was awarded the Lester Patrick Trophy in 1979-80 in recognition of his contribution to hockey in the United States. Clarke appeared in 1,144 regular-season games, recording 358 goals and 852 assists for 1,210 points. He also added 119 points in 136 playoff games.

Pittsburgh Penguins

1994-95 Results: 29w-16l-3t 61pts. Second, Northeast Division

Schedule

Oct.	Sat.	7	Toronto		Fri.	12	Montreal
	Mon.	9	at Colorado		Sat.	13	San Jose
	Thur.	12	at Chicago		Tues.	16	Colorado
	Sat.	14	Anaheim		Wed.	17	at Buffalo
	Fri.	20	at Hartford		Mon.	22	Boston
	Sat.	21	Los Angeles		Wed.	24	at Ottawa
	Thur.	26	at NY Islanders		Sat.	27	Philadelphia*
	Sat.	28	at New Jersey		Mon.	29	at Florida
Nov.	Wed.	1	Tampa Bay		Wed.	31	at Tampa Bay
	Fri.	3	at Buffalo	Feb.	Sat.	3	at Detroit*
	Sat.	4	Philadelphia		Tues.	6	Boston
	Wed.	8	at Ottawa		Wed.	7	at New Jersey
	Fri.	10	at San Jose		Sat.	10	Chicago*
	Sat.	11	at Los Angeles		Mon.	12	at Toronto
	Tues.	14	Dallas		Fri.	16	at Winnipeg
	Fri.	17	at Washington		Sun.	18	NY Rangers
	Sat.	18	Washington		Wed.	21	at Buffalo
	Tues.	21	at NY Rangers		Fri.	23	Hartford
	Wed.	22	NY Rangers		Sat.	24	at Montreal
	Sat.	25	Buffalo		Tues.	27	at Vancouver
	Tues.	28	Ottawa		Thur.	29	at Calgary
	Thur.	30	at Boston	Mar.	Fri.	1	at Edmonton
Dec.	Fri.	1	Florida		Tues.	5	Winnipeg
	Sun.	3	at Tampa Bay		Thur.	7	Ottawa
	Tues.	5	at NY Islanders		Sat.	9	New Jersey*
	Thur.	7	Montreal		Wed.	13	at Hartford
	Sat.	9	Hartford		Thur.	14	at Boston
	Wed.	13	at Anaheim		Sat.	16	NY Islanders*
	Fri.	15	at Dallas		Thur.	21	Edmonton
	Sun.	17	at Philadelphia		Sat.	23	Buffalo
	Tues.	19	Calgary		Sun.	24	at NY Rangers
	Fri.	22	Montreal		Tues.	26	St. Louis
	Sat.	23	at Montreal		Thur.	28	at Florida
	Tues.	26	Buffalo		Sat.	30	New Jersey*
	Thur.	28	Hartford		Sun.	31	at Philadelphia*
	Sat.	30	Florida	Apr.	Thur.	4	Washington
Jan.	Mon.	1	at Washington*		Sat.	6	Tampa Bay
	Wed.	3	Ottawa		Mon.	8	at Hartford
	Fri.	5	Detroit		Wed.	10	NY Islanders
	Sat.	6	at St. Louis		Thur.	11	at Ottawa
	Mon.	8	Vancouver		Sun.	14	at Boston*

* Denotes afternoon game.

Home Starting Times:

Weeknights	7:30 p.m.
Matinees	1:30 p.m.
Except Sat. Jan. 27	3:00 p.m.
Sat. Feb. 10	3:00 p.m.
Sun. Feb. 18	8:00 p.m.

Franchise date: June 5, 1967

NORTHEAST DIVISION

29th NHL Season

Year-by-Year Record

Season	GP	Home W	L	T	Road W	L	T	Overall W	L	T	GF	GA	Pts.	Finished		Playoff Result
1994-95	48	18	5	1	11	11	2	29	16	3	181	158	61	2nd,	Northeast Div.	Lost Conf. Semi-Final
1993-94	84	25	9	8	19	18	5	44	27	13	299	285	101	1st,	Northeast Div.	Lost Conf. Quarter-Final
1992-93	84	32	6	4	24	15	3	56	21	7	367	268	119	1st,	Patrick Div.	Lost Div. Final
1991-92	**80**	**21**	**13**	**6**	**18**	**19**	**3**	**39**	**32**	**9**	**343**	**308**	**87**	**3rd,**	**Patrick Div.**	**Won Stanley Cup**
1990-91	**80**	**25**	**12**	**3**	**16**	**21**	**3**	**41**	**33**	**6**	**342**	**305**	**88**	**1st,**	**Patrick Div.**	**Won Stanley Cup**
1989-90	80	22	15	3	10	25	5	32	40	8	318	359	72	5th,	Patrick Div.	Out of Playoffs
1988-89	80	24	13	3	16	20	4	40	33	7	347	349	87	2nd,	Patrick Div.	Lost Div. Final
1987-88	80	22	12	6	14	23	3	36	35	9	319	316	81	6th,	Patrick Div.	Out of Playoffs
1986-87	80	19	15	6	11	23	6	30	38	12	297	290	72	5th,	Patrick Div.	Out of Playoffs
1985-86	80	20	15	5	14	23	3	34	38	8	313	305	76	5th,	Patrick Div.	Out of Playoffs
1984-85	80	17	20	3	7	31	2	24	51	5	276	385	53	6th,	Patrick Div.	Out of Playoffs
1983-84	80	7	29	4	9	29	2	16	58	6	254	390	38	6th,	Patrick Div.	Out of Playoffs
1982-83	80	14	22	4	4	31	5	18	53	9	257	394	45	6th,	Patrick Div.	Out of Playoffs
1981-82	80	21	11	8	10	25	5	31	36	13	310	337	75	4th,	Patrick Div.	Lost Div. Semi-Final
1980-81	80	21	16	3	9	21	10	30	37	13	302	345	73	3rd,	Norris Div.	Lost Prelim. Round
1979-80	80	20	13	7	10	24	6	30	37	13	251	303	73	3rd,	Norris Div.	Lost Prelim. Round
1978-79	80	23	12	5	13	19	8	36	31	13	281	279	85	2nd,	Norris Div.	Lost Quarter-Final
1977-78	80	16	15	9	9	22	9	25	37	18	254	321	68	4th,	Norris Div.	Out of Playoffs
1976-77	80	22	12	6	12	21	7	34	33	13	240	252	81	3rd,	Norris Div.	Lost Prelim. Round
1975-76	80	23	11	6	12	22	6	35	33	12	339	303	82	3rd,	Norris Div.	Lost Prelim. Round
1974-75	80	25	5	10	12	23	5	37	28	15	326	289	89	3rd,	Norris Div.	Lost Quarter-Final
1973-74	78	15	18	6	13	23	3	28	41	9	242	273	65	5th,	West Div.	Out of Playoffs
1972-73	78	24	11	4	8	26	5	32	37	9	257	265	73	4th,	West Div.	Out of Playoffs
1971-72	78	18	15	6	8	23	8	26	38	14	220	258	66	4th,	West Div.	Lost Quarter-Final
1970-71	78	18	12	9	3	25	11	21	37	20	221	240	62	6th,	West Div.	Out of Playoffs
1969-70	76	17	13	8	9	25	4	26	38	12	182	238	64	2nd,	West Div.	Lost Semi-Final
1968-69	76	12	20	6	8	25	5	20	45	11	189	252	51	5th,	West Div.	Out of Playoffs
1967-68	74	15	12	10	12	22	3	27	34	13	195	216	67	5th,	West Div.	Out of Playoffs

In addition to reaching the 1,000-point mark during the 1994-95 season, Ron Francis won a trio of NHL honors: the Lady Byng Trophy, the Frank Selke Trophy and the Alka-Seltzer Plus Award.

1995-96 Player Personnel

FORWARDS	HT	WT	S	Place of Birth	Date	1994-95 Club
AUBIN, Serge	6-1	176	L	Val d'Or, Que.	2/15/75	Granby
BARRIE, Len	6-0	200	L	Kimberley, B.C.	6/4/69	Cleveland-Pittsburgh
BELOV, Oleg	6-0	185	L	Moscow, USSR	4/20/73	CSKA
CHRISTIAN, Jeff	6-1	195	L	Burlington, Ont.	7/30/70	Pittsburgh-Cleveland
CROWDER, Troy	6-4	220	R	Sudbury, Ont.	5/3/68	Los Angeles
DAVYDOV, Evgeny	6-0	200	R	Chelyabinsk, USSR	5/27/67	Ottawa-San Diego-Chicago
DZIEDZIC, Joe	6-3	200	L	Minneapolis, MN	12/18/71	Cleveland
FITZGERALD, Rusty	6-1	190	L	Minneapolis, MN	10/4/72	Minn.-Duluth-Cleveland-Pit
FRANCIS, Ron	6-2	200	L	Sault Ste. Marie, Ont.	3/1/63	Pittsburgh
HAWKINS, Todd	6-1	195	R	Kingston, Ont.	8/2/66	Cleveland-Minnesota
HRDINA, Jan	6-1	180	R	Hradec Kralove, Czech.	2/5/76	Seattle
JAGR, Jaromir	6-2	208	L	Kladno, Czech.	2/15/72	Kladno-Bolzano-Schalke-Pit
LAUER, Brad	6-0	195	L	Humboldt, Sask.	10/27/66	Cleveland
LEMIEUX, Mario	6-4	210	R	Montreal, Que.	10/5/65	DID NOT PLAY
MOROZOV, Alexei	6-1	178	L	Moscow, USSR	2/16/77	Soviet Wings
MURRAY, Glen	6-2	213	R	Halifax, N.S.	11/1/72	Boston
NASLUND, Markus	6-0	186	L	Ornskoldsvik, Sweden	7/30/73	Pittsburgh-Cleveland
NEDVED, Petr	6-3	195	L	Liberec, Czech.	12/9/71	NY Rangers
PARK, Richard	5-11	176	R	Seoul, S. Korea	5/27/76	Belleville-Pittsburgh
PATTERSON, Ed	6-2	213	R	Delta, B.C.	11/14/72	Cleveland
PITTIS, Domenic	5-11	180	L	Calgary, Alta.	10/1/74	Cleveland
ROCHE, Dave	6-4	224	L	Lindsay, Ont.	6/13/75	Windsor
SANDSTROM, Tomas	6-2	200	L	Jakobstad, Finland	9/4/64	Malmo-Pittsburgh
SAVOIA, Ryan	6-0	195	R	Thorold, Ont.	5/6/73	Brock U.-Cleveland
SMOLINSKI, Bryan	6-1	200	R	Toledo, OH	12/27/71	Boston
WELLS, Chris	6-6	215	L	Calgary, Alta.	11/12/75	Seattle-Cleveland
DEFENSEMEN						
ALLEN, Peter	6-2	185	R	Calgary, Alta.	3/6/70	Cdn. National
ANDRUSAK, Greg	6-1	190	R	Cranbrook, B.C.	11/14/69	Detroit (IHL)-Pit-Cleveland
BEREHOWSKY, Drake	6-1	211	R	Toronto, Ont.	1/3/72	Toronto-Pittsburgh
BERGQVIST, Stefan	6-3	216	L	Leksand, Sweden	3/10/75	London
BUTENSCHON, Sven	6-5	201	L	Itzehoe, West Germany	3/22/76	Brandon
FOSTER, Corey	6-3	204	L	Ottawa, Ont.	10/27/69	P.E.I.
JOSEPH, Chris	6-2	210	R	Burnaby, B.C.	9/10/69	Pittsburgh
KRIVCHENKOV, Alexei	6-0	185	L	Novosibirsk, USSR	6/11/74	CSKA
LEROUX, Francois	6-5	220	L	Ste.-Adele, Que.	4/18/70	P.E.I.-Pittsburgh
MACIVER, Norm	5-11	180	L	Thunder Bay, Ont.	9/8/64	Ottawa-Pittsburgh
McBEAN, Wayne	6-2	185	L	Calgary, Alta.	2/21/69	DID NOT PLAY
MIRONOV, Dmitri	6-2	214	R	Moscow, USSR	12/25/65	Toronto
MORAN, Ian	5-11	180	R	Cleveland, OH	8/24/72	Cleveland-Pittsburgh
PALMER, Drew	6-4	209	L	Wayzata, MN	1/10/76	Seattle
TAMER, Chris	6-2	185	L	Dearborn, MI	11/17/70	Cleveland-Pittsburgh
TOK, Chris	6-1	185	L	Grand Rapids, MN	3/19/73	U. Wisconsin
VORONOV, Sergei	6-2	200	L	Moscow, USSR	2/5/71	Moscow D'amo
ZUBOV, Sergei	6-1	200	R	Moscow, USSR	7/22/70	NY Rangers

GOALTENDERS	HT	WT	C	Place of Birth	Date	1994-95 Club
AUBIN, Jean-Sebastien	5-11	179	R	Montreal, Que.	7/19/77	Sherbrooke
BARRASSO, Tom	6-3	211	R	Boston, MA	3/31/65	Pittsburgh
DeROUVILLE, Philippe	6-1	185	L	Victoriaville, Que.	8/7/74	Cleveland-Pittsburgh
LALIME, Patrick	6-2	170	L	St. Bonaventure, Que.	7/7/74	Hampton Rds.-Cleveland
WREGGET, Ken	6-1	195	L	Brandon, Man.	3/25/64	Pittsburgh

Coach

JOHNSTON, ED
Coach, Pittsburgh Penguins. Born in Montreal, Que., November 24, 1935.

Ed Johnston has compiled the NHL's third best coaching record over the last two seasons, with a record of 73-43-16 in 132 games for a winning percentage of .614. He is the Penguins all-time leader among coaches in wins (152) and games (372). He began his second stint as coach of the Penguins in 1993-94 having previously coached the team, from 1980-81 to 1982-83, compiling a record of 79-126-35. He was named general manager of the club on May 27, 1983, a position he held for five seasons. During the 1988-89 season, his last with the Penguins, Johnston served as assistant general manager. In 1989, Johnston was named vice president and general manager of the Hartford Whalers, serving three seasons in Connecticut. During Johnston's first season in Hartford (1989-90), the Whalers recorded the second best record (38-33-9) in their NHL history.

Johnston played in the NHL for 16 seasons with Boston, Toronto, St. Louis and Chicago. He was a member of two Stanley Cup championship teams with the Boston Bruins, and was the last goaltender to play every minute of a season, when he played all 70 games in 1963-64 for the Bruins. Overall, Johnston played in 592 games, recording 236 wins, 32 shutouts and a 3.25 goals against average.

Coaching Record

		Regular Season					Playoffs			
Season	Team	Games	W	L	T	%	Games	W	L	%
1979-80	Chicago (NHL)	80	34	27	19	.544	7	3	4	.429
1980-81	Pittsburgh (NHL)	80	30	37	13	.456	5	2	3	.400
1981-82	Pittsburgh (NHL)	80	31	36	13	.469	5	2	3	.400
1982-83	Pittsburgh (NHL)	80	18	53	9	.281	....	....	....	....
1993-94	Pittsburgh (NHL)	84	44	27	13	.601	6	2	4	.333
1994-95	Pittsburgh (NHL)	48	29	16	3	.635	12	5	7	.417
	NHL Totals	452	186	196	70	.489	35	14	21	.400

Coaching History

George Sullivan, 1967-68 to 1968-69; Red Kelly, 1969-70 to 1971-72; Red Kelly and Ken Schinkel, 1972-73; Ken Schinkel and Marc Boileau, 1973-74; Marc Boileau, 1974-75; Marc Boileau and Ken Schinkel, 1975-76; Ken Schinkel, 1976-77; John Wilson, 1977-78 to 1979-80; Eddie Johnston, 1980-81 to 1982-83; Lou Angotti, 1983-84; Bob Berry, 1984-85 to 1986-87; Pierre Creamer, 1987-88; Gene Ubriaco, 1988-89; Gene Ubriaco and Craig Patrick, 1989-90; Bob Johnson, 1990-91 to 1991-92; Scotty Bowman, 1991-92 to 1992-93; Eddie Johnston, 1993-94 to date.

1994-95 Scoring

* – rookie

Regular Season

Pos	#	Player	Team	GP	G	A	Pts	+/–	PIM	PP	SH	GW	GT	S	%
R	68	Jaromir Jagr	PIT	48	32	38	70	23	37	8	3	7	0	192	16.7
C	10	Ron Francis	PIT	44	11	48	59	30	18	3	0	1	0	94	11.7
R	17	Tomas Sandstrom	PIT	47	21	23	44	1	42	4	1	3	1	116	18.1
L	20	Luc Robitaille	PIT	46	23	19	42	10	37	5	0	3	1	109	21.1
D	55	Larry Murphy	PIT	48	13	25	38	12	18	4	0	3	0	124	10.5
R	7	Joe Mullen	PIT	45	16	21	37	15	6	5	2	3	0	78	20.5
C	11	John Cullen	PIT	46	13	24	37	–4	66	2	0	1	0	88	14.8
L	25	Kevin Stevens	PIT	27	15	12	27	0	51	6	0	4	0	80	18.8
C	15	Shawn McEachern	PIT	44	13	13	26	4	22	1	2	1	0	97	13.4
D	22	Norm Maciver	OTT	28	4	7	11	–9	10	2	0	0	0	30	13.3
			PIT	13	0	9	9	7	6	0	0	0	0	20	0.0
			TOTAL	41	4	16	20	–2	16	2	0	0	0	50	8.0
C	12	Troy Murray	OTT	33	4	10	14	–1	16	0	0	1	0	38	10.5
			PIT	13	0	2	2	–1	23	0	0	0	0	7	0.0
			TOTAL	46	4	12	16	–2	39	0	0	1	0	45	8.9
D	5	Ulf Samuelsson	PIT	44	1	15	16	11	113	0	0	0	0	47	2.1
D	23	Chris Joseph	PIT	33	5	10	15	3	46	3	0	0	0	73	6.8
C	9	* Len Barrie	PIT	48	3	11	14	–4	66	0	0	1	0	37	8.1
C	16	Mike Hudson	PIT	40	2	9	11	–1	34	0	0	1	0	33	6.1
D	28	Kjell Samuelsson	PIT	41	1	6	7	8	54	0	0	0	0	37	2.7
D	4	Greg Hawgood	PIT	21	1	4	5	2	25	1	0	0	0	17	5.9
R	29	Markus Naslund	PIT	14	2	2	4	0	2	0	0	0	0	13	15.4
D	37	* Greg Andrusak	PIT	7	0	4	4	–1	6	0	0	0	0	7	0.0
L	33	Jim McKenzie	PIT	39	2	1	3	–7	63	0	0	1	0	16	12.5
D	2	* Chris Tamer	PIT	36	2	0	2	0	82	0	0	0	0	26	7.7
D	44	Drake Berehowsky	TOR	25	0	2	2	–10	15	0	0	0	0	12	0.0
			PIT	4	0	0	0	1	13	0	0	0	0	2	0.0
			TOTAL	29	0	2	2	–9	28	0	0	0	0	14	0.0
D	18	Francois Leroux	PIT	40	0	2	2	7	114	0	0	0	0	19	0.0
C	34	* Rusty Fitzgerald	PIT	4	1	0	1	2	0	0	0	0	0	5	20.0
C	26	* Richard Park	PIT	1	0	1	1	1	2	0	0	0	0	4	0.0
D	32	Peter Taglianetti	PIT	13	0	1	1	1	12	0	0	0	0	5	0.0
L	34	* Jeff Christian	PIT	1	0	0	0	0	0	0	0	0	0	2	0.0
G	30	* Philippe De Rouville	PIT	1	0	0	0	0	0	0	0	0	0	0	0.0
G	35	Tom Barrasso	PIT	2	0	0	0	0	0	0	0	0	0	0	0.0
G	1	Wendell Young	T.B.	0	0	0	0	0	0	0	0	0	0	0	0.0
			PIT	10	0	0	0	0	2	0	0	0	0	0	0.0
			TOTAL	10	0	0	0	0	2	0	0	0	0	0	0.0
G	31	Ken Wregget	PIT	38	0	0	0	0	14	0	0	0	0	0	0.0

Goaltending

No.	Goaltender	GPI	Mins	Avg	W	L	T	EN	SO	GA	SA	S%
30	* Philippe De Rouville	1	60	3.00	1	0	0	0	0	3	27	.889
31	Ken Wregget	38	2208	3.21	25	9	2	1	0	118	1219	.903
1	Wendell Young	10	497	3.26	3	6	0	1	0	27	255	.894
35	Tom Barrasso	2	125	3.84	0	1	1	0	0	8	75	.893
	Totals	**48**	**2901**	**3.27**	**29**	**16**	**3**	**2**	**0**	**158**	**1578**	**.900**

Playoffs

Pos	#	Player	Team	GP	G	A	Pts	+/–	PIM	PP	SH	GW	OT	S	%
C	10	Ron Francis	PIT	12	6	13	19	3	4	2	0	0	0	30	20.0
R	68	Jaromir Jagr	PIT	12	10	5	15	3	6	2	1	1	0	55	18.2
D	55	Larry Murphy	PIT	12	2	13	15	3	0	1	0	0	0	35	5.7
L	20	Luc Robitaille	PIT	12	7	4	11	5	26	0	0	2	1	33	21.2
L	25	Kevin Stevens	PIT	12	4	7	11	–5	21	3	0	1	0	32	12.5
R	17	Tomas Sandstrom	PIT	12	3	3	6	–5	16	2	0	0	0	22	13.6
D	22	Norm Maciver	PIT	12	1	4	5	–4	8	0	0	1	0	16	6.3
C	12	Troy Murray	PIT	12	2	1	3	–1	12	0	0	0	0	14	14.3
R	7	Joe Mullen	PIT	12	0	3	3	–5	4	0	0	0	0	12	0.0
D	23	Chris Joseph	PIT	10	1	1	2	–4	12	0	0	0	0	13	7.7
D	5	Ulf Samuelsson	PIT	7	0	2	2	2	8	0	0	0	0	5	0.0
C	11	John Cullen	PIT	9	0	2	2	–4	8	0	0	0	0	7	0.0
C	15	Shawn McEachern	PIT	11	0	2	2	–2	8	0	0	0	0	12	0.0
D	18	Francois Leroux	PIT	12	0	2	2	0	14	0	0	0	0	13	0.0
C	9	* Len Barrie	PIT	4	1	0	1	–6	8	1	0	0	0	2	50.0
D	28	Kjell Samuelsson	PIT	11	0	1	1	–4	32	0	0	0	0	5	0.0
D	44	Drake Berehowsky	PIT	1	0	0	0	–1	0	0	0	0	0	0	0.0
G	35	Tom Barrasso	PIT	2	0	0	0	0	2	0	0	0	0	0	0.0
C	26	* Richard Park	PIT	3	0	0	0	–1	2	0	0	0	0	5	0.0
D	32	Peter Taglianetti	PIT	4	0	0	0	–3	2	0	0	0	0	3	0.0
D	2	* Chris Tamer	PIT	4	0	0	0	–4	18	0	0	0	0	0	0.0
L	33	Jim McKenzie	PIT	5	0	0	0	0	4	0	0	0	0	0	0.0
C	34	* Rusty Fitzgerald	PIT	5	0	0	0	–1	4	0	0	0	0	0	0.0
D	37	* Ian Moran	PIT	8	0	0	0	0	0	0	0	0	0	1	0.0
C	16	Mike Hudson	PIT	11	0	0	0	–3	6	0	0	0	0	2	0.0
G	31	Ken Wregget	PIT	11	0	0	0	0	7	0	0	0	0	0	0.0

Goaltending

No.	Goaltender	GPI	Mins	Avg	W	L	EN	SO	GA	SA	S%
31	Ken Wregget	11	661	3.00	5	6	2	1	33	349	.905
35	Tom Barrasso	2	80	6.00	0	1	0	0	8	41	.805
	Totals	**12**	**743**	**3.47**	**5**	**7**	**2**	**1**	**43**	**392**	**.890**

Captains' History

Ab McDonald, 1967-68; no captain, 1968-69 to 1972-73; Ron Schock, 1973-74 to 1976-77; Jean Pronovost, 1977-78; Orest Kindrachuk, 1978-79 to 1980-81; Randy Carlyle, 1981-82 to 1983-84; Mike Bullard, 1984-85, 1985-86; Mike Bullard and Terry Ruskowski, 1986-87; Dan Frawley and Mario Lemieux, 1987-88; Mario Lemieux, 1988-89 to 1993-94; Ron Francis, 1994-95.

Club Records

Team

(Figures in brackets for season records are games played; records for fewest points, wins, ties, losses, goals, goals against are for 70 or more games)

Most Points	**119**	1992-93 (84)
Most Wins	**56**	1992-93 (84)
Most Ties	**20**	1970-71 (78)
Most Losses	**58**	1983-84 (80)
Most Goals	**367**	1992-93 (84)
Most Goals Against	**394**	1982-83 (80)
Fewest Points	**38**	1983-84 (80)
Fewest Wins	**16**	1983-84 (80)
Fewest Ties	**5**	1984-85 (80)
Fewest Losses	**21**	1992-93 (84)
Fewest Goals	**182**	1969-70 (76)
Fewest Goals Against	**216**	1967-68 (74)
Longest Winning Streak		
Over-all	***17**	Mar. 9-Apr. 10/93
Home	**11**	Jan. 5-Mar. 7/91
Away	**6**	Mar. 14-Apr. 9/93
Longest Undefeated Streak		
Over-all	**18**	Mar. 9-Apr. 14/93 (17 wins, 1 tie)
Home	**20**	Nov. 30/74-Feb. 22/75 (12 wins, 8 ties)
Away	**7**	Twice
Longest Losing Streak		
Over-all	**11**	Jan. 22/83-Feb. 10/83
Home	**7**	Oct. 8-29/83
Away	**18**	Dec. 23/82-Mar. 4/83
Longest Winless Streak		
Over-all	**18**	Jan. 2-Feb. 10/83 (17 losses, 1 tie)
Home	**11**	Oct. 8-Nov. 19/83 (9 losses, 2 ties)
Away	**18**	Oct. 25/70-Jan. 14/71 (11 losses, 7 ties) Dec. 23/82-Mar. 4/83 (18 losses)
Most Shutouts, Season	**6**	1967-68 (74) 1976-77 (80)
Most PIM, Season	***2,670**	1988-89 (80)
Most Goals, Game	**12**	Mar. 15/75 (Wash. 1 at Pit. 12) Dec. 26/91 (Tor. 1 at Pit. 12)

Individual

Most Seasons	**11**	Rick Kehoe
Most Games	**753**	Jean Pronovost
Most Goals, Career	**494**	Mario Lemieux
Most Assists, Career	**717**	Mario Lemieux
Most Points, Career	**1,211**	Mario Lemieux (494 goals, 717 assists)
Most PIM, Career	**980**	Troy Loney
Most Shutouts, Career	**11**	Les Binkley
Longest Consecutive Games Streak	**320**	Ron Schock (Oct. 24/73-Apr. 3/77)
Most Goals, Season	**85**	Mario Lemieux (1988-89)
Most Assists, Season	**114**	Mario Lemieux (1988-89)
Most Points, Season	**199**	Mario Lemieux (1988-89)
Most PIM, Season	**409**	Paul Baxter (1981-82)
Most Points, Defenseman, Season	**113**	Paul Coffey (1988-89) (30 goals, 83 assists)
Most Points, Center, Season	**199**	Mario Lemieux (1988-89) (85 goals, 114 assists)
Most Points, Right Wing, Season	**115**	Rob Brown (1988-89) (49 goals, 66 assists)
Most Points, Left Wing, Season	**123**	Kevin Stevens (1991-92) (54 goals, 69 assists)
Most Points, Rookie, Season	**100**	Mario Lemieux (1984-85) (43 goals, 57 assists)
Most Shutouts, Season	**6**	Les Binkley (1967-68)
Most Goals, Game	**5**	Mario Lemieux (Dec. 31/88)
Most Assists, Game	**6**	Ron Stackhouse (Mar. 8/75) Greg Malone (Nov. 28/79) Mario Lemieux (Oct. 15/88, Dec. 5/92)
Most Points, Game	**8**	Mario Lemieux (Oct. 15/88, Dec. 31/88)

* NHL Record.

Retired Numbers

21	Michel Brière	1969-1970

All-time Record vs. Other Clubs

Regular Season

	At Home							On Road							Total						
	GP	W	L	T	GF	GA	PTS	GP	W	L	T	GF	GA	PTS	GP	W	L	T	GF	GA	PTS
Anaheim	1	0	0	1	2	2	1	1	1	0	0	5	4	2	2	1	0	1	7	6	3
Boston	60	23	26	11	207	226	57	58	11	41	6	167	267	28	118	34	67	17	374	493	85
Buffalo	50	22	15	13	194	174	57	51	12	25	14	146	222	38	101	34	40	27	340	396	95
Calgary	38	18	10	10	139	125	46	38	9	22	7	114	163	25	76	27	32	17	253	288	71
Chicago	51	24	22	5	181	170	53	52	8	35	9	144	221	25	103	32	57	14	325	391	78
Dallas	56	34	17	5	216	158	73	57	20	32	5	192	218	45	113	54	49	10	408	376	118
Detroit	57	39	14	4	254	169	82	58	11	36	11	164	232	33	115	50	50	15	418	401	115
Edmonton	23	10	12	1	90	110	21	23	4	18	1	80	125	9	46	14	30	2	170	235	30
Florida	4	2	1	1	14	10	5	4	3	1	0	12	11	6	8	5	2	1	26	21	11
Hartford	26	13	10	3	122	110	29	27	12	14	1	107	119	25	53	25	24	4	229	229	54
Los Angeles	64	37	19	8	243	203	82	62	14	40	8	161	245	36	126	51	59	16	404	448	118
Montreal	61	22	30	9	184	220	53	62	4	51	7	148	317	15	123	26	81	16	332	537	68
New Jersey	58	35	19	4	247	205	74	59	19	29	11	204	232	49	117	54	48	15	451	437	123
NY Islanders	66	31	24	11	257	231	73	65	22	35	8	211	270	52	131	53	59	19	468	501	125
NY Rangers	79	32	36	11	288	297	75	79	31	41	7	276	322	69	158	63	77	18	564	619	144
Ottawa	7	6	0	1	33	16	13	6	5	1	0	24	11	10	13	11	1	1	57	27	23
Philadelphia	84	36	31	17	289	270	89	85	15	63	7	219	370	37	169	51	94	24	508	640	126
Quebec	28	15	9	4	125	114	34	25	12	13	0	101	114	24	53	27	22	4	226	228	58
St. Louis	56	25	19	12	209	172	62	57	13	38	6	154	228	32	113	38	57	18	363	400	94
San Jose	3	2	0	1	19	6	5	4	3	0	1	27	10	7	7	5	0	2	46	16	12
Tampa Bay	5	3	1	1	21	14	7	4	3	1	0	18	13	6	9	6	2	1	39	27	13
Toronto	54	28	20	6	223	176	62	53	17	25	11	178	220	45	107	45	45	17	401	396	107
Vancouver	43	28	8	7	194	144	63	43	20	20	3	165	159	43	86	48	28	10	359	303	106
Washington	65	33	26	6	261	223	72	68	27	35	6	258	299	60	133	60	61	12	519	522	132
Winnipeg	23	16	7	0	96	69	32	22	12	9	1	83	83	25	45	28	16	1	179	152	57
Defunct Clubs	35	22	6	7	148	93	51	34	13	10	11	108	101	37	69	35	16	18	256	194	88
Totals	**1097**	**556**	**382**	**159**	**4256**	**3707**	**1271**	**1097**	**321**	**635**	**141**	**3466**	**4576**	**783**	**2194**	**877**	**1017**	**300**	**7722**	**8283**	**2054**

Calgary totals include Atlanta, 1972-73 to 1979-80. Dallas totals include Minnesota, 1967-68 to 1992-93.
New Jersey totals include Kansas City, 1974-75 to 1975-76, and Colorado, 1976-77 to 1981-82.

Playoffs

	Series	W	L	GP	W	L	T	GF	GA	Last Mtg.	Round	Result
Boston	4	2	2	19	10	9	0	67	62	1992	CF	W 4-0
Buffalo	1	1	0	3	2	1	0	9	9	1979	PR	W 2-1
Chicago	2	1	1	8	4	4	0	23	24	1992	F	W 4-0
Dallas	1	1	0	6	4	2	0	28	16	1991	F	W 4-2
New Jersey	3	2	1	17	9	8	0	56	47	1995	CSF	L 1-4
NY Islanders	3	0	3	19	8	11	0	58	67	1993	DF	L 3-4
NY Rangers	2	2	0	10	8	2	0	43	30	1992	DF	W 4-2
Philadelphia	1	0	1	7	3	4	0	24	31	1989	DF	L 3-4
St. Louis	3	1	2	13	6	7	0	40	45	1981	PR	L 2-3
Toronto	2	0	2	6	2	4	0	13	21	1977	PR	L 1-2
Washington	4	3	1	25	14	11	0	85	86	1995	CQF	W 4-3
Defunct Clubs	1	1	0	4	4	0	0	13	6			
Totals	**27**	**14**	**13**	**137**	**74**	**63**	**0**	**459**	**444**			

Playoff Results 1995-91

Year	Round	Opponent	Result	GF	GA
1995	CSF	New Jersey	L 1-4	8	17
	CQF	Washington	W 4-3	29	26
1994	CQF	Washington	L 2-4	12	20
1993	DF	NY Islanders	L 3-4	27	24
	DSF	New Jersey	W 4-1	23	13
1992	**F**	**Chicago**	**W 4-0**	**15**	**10**
	CF	Boston	W 4-0	19	7
	DF	NY Rangers	W 4-2	24	19
	DSF	Washington	W 4-3	25	27
1991	**F**	**Minnesota**	**W 4-2**	**28**	**16**
	CF	Boston	W 4-2	27	18
	DF	Washington	W 4-1	19	13
	DSF	New Jersey	W 4-3	25	17

Abbreviations: Round: F – Final;
CF – conference final; **CQF** – conference quarter-final;
CSF – conference semi-final; **DF** – division final;
DSF – division semi-final; **SF** – semi-final;
QF – quarter-final; **PR** – preliminary round.

1994-95 Results

Jan.	20	at	Tampa Bay	5-3		11		Buffalo	6-2
	23	at	Florida	6-5		13		Montreal	4-2
	25	at	NY Rangers	3-2		15	at	Montreal	5-8
	27		Ottawa	5-4		16	at	Quebec	2-3
	29	at	Washington	4-1		19	at	Ottawa	4-3
Feb.	1		NY Rangers	4-3		21	at	Buffalo	3-2
	4		Tampa Bay	6-3		24		New Jersey	5-2
	5	at	New Jersey	3-3		26	at	Florida	0-2
	7		Florida	7-3		28		NY Islanders	6-3
	9	at	NY Islanders	5-2	**Apr.**	1		Philadelphia	3-2
	11		Montreal	3-1		5		Hartford	4-8
	14		Boston	5-3		8	at	Montreal	1-2
	16		Hartford	5-2		10	at	Ottawa	4-3
	18	at	Hartford	2-4		11		Washington	3-1
	19		Buffalo	3-3		15		Ottawa	5-2
	21		Quebec	5-4		16	at	Philadelphia	3-4
	24		Tampa Bay	2-4		18		NY Rangers	6-5
	25	at	NY Islanders	1-3		22		Washington	1-2
	27	at	Quebec	7-5		23	at	Hartford	4-2
Mar.	2	at	Buffalo	3-6		26	at	New Jersey	3-3
	4	at	Boston	4-3		28		Boston	4-1
	5	at	Philadelphia	2-6		30	at	Boston	2-5
	7		Quebec	4-5	**May**	2	at	Washington	2-7
	9		NY Islanders	4-2		3		Florida	3-4

Entry Draft
Selections 1995-81

1995
Pick
24 Alexei Morozov
76 J-Sebastien Aubin
102 Oleg Belov
128 Jan Hrdina
154 Alexei Kolkunov
180 Derrick Pyke
206 Sergei Voronov
232 Frank Ivankovic

1994
Pick
24 Chris Wells
50 Richard Park
57 Sven Butenschon
73 Greg Crozier
76 Alexei Krivchenkov
102 Thomas O'Connor
128 Clint Johnson
154 Valentin Morozov
161 Serge Aubin
180 Drew Palmer
206 Boris Zelenko
232 Jason Godbout
258 Mikhail Kazakevich
284 Brian Leitza

1993
Pick
26 Stefan Bergqvist
52 Domenic Pittis
62 Dave Roche
104 Jonas Andersson-Junkka
130 Chris Kelleher
156 Patrick Lalime
182 Sean Selmser
208 Larry McMorran
234 Timothy Harberts
260 Leonid Toropchenko
286 Hans Jonsson

1992
Pick
19 Martin Straka
43 Marc Hussey
67 Travis Thiessen
91 Todd Klassen
115 Philipp De Rouville
139 Artem Kopot
163 Jan Alinc
187 Fran Bussey
211 Brian Bonin
235 Brian Callahan

1991
Pick
16 Markus Naslund
38 Rusty Fitzgerald
60 Shane Peacock
82 Joe Tamminen
104 Robert Melanson
126 Brian Clifford
148 Ed Patterson
170 Peter McLaughlin
192 Jeff Lembke
214 Chris Tok
236 Paul Dyck
258 Pasi Huura

1990
Pick
5 Jaromir Jagr
61 Joe Dziedzic
68 Chris Tamer
89 Brian Farrell
107 Ian Moran
110 Denis Casey
130 Mika Valila
131 Ken Plaquin
145 Pat Neaton
152 Petteri Koskimaki
173 Ladislav Karabin
194 Timothy Fingerhut
215 Michael Thompson
236 Brian Bruininks

1989
Pick
16 Jamie Heward
37 Paul Laus
58 John Brill
79 Todd Nelson
100 Tom Nevers
121 Mike Markovich
126 Mike Needham
142 Patrick Schafhauser
163 Dave Shute
184 Andrew Wolf
205 Greg Hagen
226 Scott Farrell
247 Jason Smart

1988
Pick
4 Darrin Shannon
25 Mark Major
62 Daniel Gauthier
67 Mark Recchi
88 Greg Andrusak
130 Troy Mick
151 Jeff Blaeser
172 Rob Gaudreau
193 Donald Pancoe
214 Cory Laylin
235 Darren Stolk

1987
Pick
5 Chris Joseph
26 Richard Tabaracci
47 Jamie Leach
68 Risto Kurkinen
89 Jeff Waver
110 Shawn McEachern
131 Jim Bodden
152 Jiri Kucera
173 Jack MacDougall
194 Daryn McBride
215 Mark Carlson
236 Ake Lilljebjorn

1986
Pick
4 Zarley Zalapski
25 Dave Capuano
46 Brad Aitken
67 Rob Brown
88 Sandy Smith
109 Jeff Daniels
130 Doug Hobson
151 Steve Rohlik
172 Dave McLwain
193 Kelly Cain
214 Stan Drulia
235 Rob Wilson

1985
Pick
2 Craig Simpson
23 Lee Giffin
58 Bruce Racine
86 Steve Gotaas
107 Kevin Clemens
114 Stuart Marston
128 Steve Titus
149 Paul Stanton
170 Jim Paek
191 Steve Shaunessy
212 Doug Greschuk
233 Gregory Choules

1984
Pick
1 Mario Lemieux
9 Doug Bodger
16 Roger Belanger
64 Mark Teevens
85 Arto Javanainen
127 Tom Ryan
169 John Del Col
189 Steve Hurt
210 Jim Steen
230 Mark Ziliotto

1983
Pick
15 Bob Errey
22 Todd Charlesworth
58 Mike Rowe
63 Frank Pietrangelo
103 Patrick Emond
123 Paul Ames
163 Marty Ketola
183 Alec Haidy
203 Garth Hildebrand
223 Dave Goertz

1982
Pick
10 Rich Sutter
38 Tim Hrynewich
52 Troy Loney
94 Grant Sasser
136 Grant Couture
157 Peter Derksen
178 Greg Gravel
199 Stu Wenaas
220 Chris McCauley
241 Stan Bautch

1981
Pick
28 Steve Gatzos
49 Tom Thornbury
70 Norm Schmidt
109 Paul Edwards
112 Rod Buskas
133 Geoff Wilson
154 Mitch Lamoureux
175 Dean Defazio
196 David Hannan

General Manager

PATRICK, CRAIG
General Manager, Pittsburgh Penguins. Born in Detroit, MI, May 20, 1946.

Appointed general manager of the Penguins on December 5, 1989, Patrick's teams have since won two Stanley Cup titles (1991 and 1992), and the Presidents' Trophy (1993). Patrick has laid the groundwork for success through shrewd acquisitions and drafts; his trades for Ulf Samuelsson, Ron Francis, Rick Tocchet and Ken Wregget, and the drafting of Jaromir Jagr are all moves considered crucial to Pittsburgh's recent success.

A 1969 graduate of the University of Denver, Patrick was captain of the Pioneers' NCAA Championship hockey team that year. He returned to his alma mater in 1986 where he served as director of athletics and recreation for two years. Patrick served as administrative assistant to the president of the Amateur Hockey Association of the United States in 1980 and as an assistant coach/assistant general manager for the 1980 gold-medal winning U.S. Olympic hockey team. Before pursuing a coaching career, Patrick played professional hockey with Washington, Kansas City, St. Louis, Minnesota and California from 1971-79. In eight seasons, Patrick tallied 163 points (72-91-163) in 401 games.

NHL Coaching Record

| Season | Team | Regular Season | | | | | Playoffs | | | |
		Games	W	L	T	%	Games	W	L	%
1980-81	NY Rangers	59	26	23	10	.525	14	7	7	.500
1984-85	NY Rangers	35	11	22	2	.343	3	0	3	.000
1989-90	Pittsburgh	54	22	26	6	.463	....	....	....	....
	NHL Totals	**148**	**59**	**71**	**18**	**.459**	**17**	**7**	**10**	**.412**

General Managers' History

Jack Riley, 1967-68 to 1969-70; "Red" Kelly, 1970-71; "Red" Kelly and Jack Riley, 1971-72; Jack Riley, 1972-73; Jack Riley and Jack Button, 1973-74; Jack Button, 1974-75; Wren Blair, 1975-76; Wren A. Blair and Baz Bastien, 1976-77; Baz Bastien, 1977-78 to 1982-83; Ed Johnston, 1983-84 to 1987-88; Tony Esposito, 1988-89; Tony Esposito and Craig Patrick, 1989-90; Craig Patrick, 1990-91 to date.

Club Directory

Civic Arena
Pittsburgh, PA 15219
Phone **412/642-1300**
FAX 412/642-1859
Capacity: 17,181

Ownership	Howard L. Baldwin, Morris Belzberg, Thomas V. Ruta
Chairman of the Board & Governor	Howard L. Baldwin

Administration
President & Chief Operating Officer – PGH Sports Associates	Steve Ryan
President & Alternate Governor	Jack Kelley
Senior Executive Vice President	Bill Barnes
Executive Vice President & Chief Financial Officer	Donn Patton
Vice President and General Counsel	Greg Cribbs
Assistant to the President	Howard Baldwin, Jr.
Assistant Vice President of Operations	Nick Ruta
Executive Assistants	Elaine Heufelder, Paula Nichols
Administrative Assistant	Christine Black
Receptionist	Maryann Dayton

Hockey Operations
Executive Vice President & General Manager	Craig Patrick
Head Coach	Ed Johnston
Assistant Coaches	Rick Kehoe, Bryan Trottier
Goaltending Coach and Scout	Gilles Meloche
Head Scout	Greg Malone
Scouting Staff	Les Binkley, Charlie Hodge, Mark Kelley, Ralph Cox
Professional Scouts	Glenn Patrick, Phil Russell
Strength and Conditioning Coach	John Welday
Equipment Manager	Steve Latin
Trainer	Charles "Skip" Thayer
Team Physician	Dr. Charles Burke
Team Dentist	Dr. David Donatelli
Executive Assistant	Tracey Botsford
Assistant Equipment Manager	Paul Flati

Public and Community Relations
Vice President, Public & Community Relations	Phil Langan
Director of Public Relations	Cindy Himes
Director of Media Relations	Harry Sanders
Director of Amateur Hockey Development	George Kirk
Special Projects Coordinator	Jamie Belo
Assistant Media Relations Director	Steve Bovino
Public Relations Administrative Assistant	Renee Petrichevich

Finance
Controller	Kevin Hart
Assistant Controller	Bill Snyder
Accounting Staff	Eric Brandenburg, Barb Pilarski

Ticketing
Director of Ticket Sales	Jeff Mercer
Assistant Director of Ticket Sales	Stella Robertson
Box Office Manager	Carol Coulson
Assistant Box Office Manager	Debbie Campbell
Director of Suite Sales & Service	Chuck Saller
Marketing Representatives	Terri Dobos Young, Fred Traynor, Allison Quigley, Jon Jones

Sales and Communications
Director of Advertising Sales	Taylor Baldwin
Senior Account Representative	Richard Chmura
Director of Promotions & Advertising Sales Coordinator	Amy Novak
Advertising Sales Representatives	Bruce Weber, Steve Violetta
Director of Special Projects/Penvision	Bill Miller

Iceoplex at Southpointe
General Manager	Dave Hanson
Director of Ice Hockey	Alain Lemieux
Director of Skating	Suzanne Semanick
Director of Operations	Scott Baldwin
Assistant Director of Operations	Dan Kaschalk
Administrative Assistant	Nicole Kaschalk

General Information
Home Ice	Civic Arena
Dimensions of Rink	200 feet by 85 feet
Location of Press Box	West Side of Building
Team Colors	Black, Gold and White
Flagship Radio Station	WTAE (1250 AM)
TV Station	Prime Sports
Announcers	Mike Lange, Doug McLeod, Stan Savran, Paul Steigerwald
Practice Facility	Iceoplex at Southpointe
Minor League Affiliation	Cleveland Lumberjacks (IHL)

St. Louis Blues

1994-95 Results: 28W-15L-5T 61PTS. Second, Central Division

Schedule

Oct.	Sat.	7	at Washington		Thur.	11	at Philadelphia
	Tues.	10	Edmonton		Sat.	13	at Montreal
	Thur.	12	at Dallas		Sun.	14	at NY Rangers
	Sat.	14	Colorado		Tues.	16	Edmonton
	Tues.	17	Boston		Wed.	24	at Winnipeg
	Thur.	19	Dallas		Sat.	27	Tampa Bay*
	Sat.	21	Chicago		Mon.	29	at Ottawa
	Sun.	22	at Buffalo		Wed.	31	at Toronto
	Wed.	25	at Hartford	Feb.	Thur.	1	Vancouver
	Fri.	27	Anaheim		Sat.	3	Philadelphia*
	Sun.	29	Washington		Tues.	6	Dallas
Nov.	Wed.	1	at Anaheim		Thur.	8	Chicago
	Sat.	4	at San Jose		Sat.	10	at Dallas*
	Tues.	7	Los Angeles		Sun.	11	at Florida
	Fri.	10	Winnipeg		Tues.	13	at Tampa Bay
	Sat.	11	at NY Islanders		Fri.	16	Detroit
	Tues.	14	NY Rangers		Sun.	18	Winnipeg
	Thur.	16	San Jose		Tues.	20	Ottawa
	Sat.	18	at Boston		Thur.	22	at Chicago
	Tues.	21	at Toronto		Sat.	24	Los Angeles
	Thur.	23	Vancouver		Thur.	29	at Vancouver
	Sat.	25	Toronto	Mar.	Sun.	3	at Edmonton*
	Mon.	27	Buffalo		Tues.	5	Florida
	Wed.	29	Montreal		Thur.	7	Calgary
	Thur.	30	at Winnipeg		Sat.	9	Hartford
Dec.	Sat.	2	at Edmonton		Tues.	12	at Calgary
	Tues.	5	at Calgary		Fri.	15	at San Jose
	Fri.	8	at Vancouver		Sun.	17	at Anaheim
	Sat.	9	at Los Angeles		Mon.	18	at Los Angeles
	Tues.	12	Detroit		Wed.	20	at Dallas
	Thur.	14	Calgary		Fri.	22	Anaheim
	Sat.	16	San Jose		Sun.	24	Detroit
	Tues.	19	NY Islanders		Tues.	26	at Pittsburgh
	Fri.	22	at Colorado		Thur.	28	New Jersey
	Sat.	23	at Winnipeg		Sun.	31	at Detroit*
	Tues.	26	at Detroit	Apr.	Wed.	3	at Colorado
	Thur.	28	Dallas		Thur.	4	Toronto
	Sat.	30	Toronto		Sat.	6	at Toronto
Jan.	Thur.	4	at Chicago		Mon.	8	Winnipeg
	Sat.	6	Pittsburgh		Thur.	11	Colorado
	Tues.	9	at New Jersey		Sun.	14	at Chicago*

* Denotes afternoon game.

Home Starting Times:

Weeknights and Saturdays		7:35 p.m.
Sundays		6:05 p.m.
Matinees		2:05 p.m.
Except	Sat. Nov. 25	6:35 p.m.
	Tue. Dec. 12	8:05 p.m.
	Sat. Dec. 30	6:35 p.m.

Franchise date: June 5, 1967

CENTRAL DIVISION

29th NHL Season

Year-by-Year Record

Season	GP	Home W	L	T	Road W	L	T	Overall W	L	T	GF	GA	Pts.	Finished		Playoff Result
1994-95	48	16	6	2	12	9	3	28	15	5	178	135	61	2nd,	Central Div.	Lost Conf. Quarter-Final
1993-94	84	23	11	8	17	22	3	40	33	11	270	283	91	4th,	Central Div.	Lost Conf. Quarter-Final
1992-93	84	22	13	7	15	23	4	37	36	11	282	278	85	4th,	Norris Div.	Lost Div. Final
1991-92	80	25	12	3	11	21	8	36	33	11	279	266	83	3rd,	Norris Div.	Lost Div. Semi-Final
1990-91	80	24	9	7	23	13	4	47	22	11	310	250	105	2nd,	Norris Div.	Lost Div. Final
1989-90	80	20	15	5	17	19	4	37	34	9	295	279	83	2nd,	Norris Div.	Lost Div. Final
1988-89	80	22	11	7	11	24	5	33	35	12	275	285	78	2nd,	Norris Div.	Lost Div. Final
1987-88	80	18	17	5	16	21	3	34	38	8	278	294	76	2nd,	Norris Div.	Lost Div. Final
1986-87	80	21	12	7	11	21	8	32	33	15	281	293	79	1st,	Norris Div.	Lost Div. Semi-Final
1985-86	80	23	11	6	14	23	3	37	34	9	302	291	83	3rd,	Norris Div.	Lost Conf. Championship
1984-85	80	21	12	7	16	19	5	37	31	12	299	288	86	1st,	Norris Div.	Lost Div. Semi-Final
1983-84	80	23	14	3	9	27	4	32	41	7	293	316	71	2nd,	Norris Div.	Lost Div. Final
1982-83	80	16	16	8	9	24	7	25	40	15	285	316	65	4th,	Norris Div.	Lost Div. Semi-Final
1981-82	80	22	14	4	10	26	4	32	40	8	315	349	72	3rd,	Norris Div.	Lost Div. Final
1980-81	80	29	7	4	16	11	13	45	18	17	352	281	107	1st,	Smythe Div.	Lost Quarter-Final
1979-80	80	20	13	7	14	21	5	34	34	12	266	278	80	2nd,	Smythe Div.	Lost Prelim. Round
1978-79	80	14	20	6	4	30	6	18	50	12	249	348	48	3rd,	Smythe Div.	Out of Playoffs
1977-78	80	12	20	8	8	27	5	20	47	13	195	304	53	4th,	Smythe Div.	Out of Playoffs
1976-77	80	22	13	5	10	26	4	32	39	9	239	276	73	1st,	Smythe Div.	Lost Quarter-Final
1975-76	80	20	12	8	9	25	6	29	37	14	249	290	72	3rd,	Smythe Div.	Lost Prelim. Round
1974-75	80	23	13	4	12	18	10	35	31	14	269	267	84	2nd,	Smythe Div.	Lost Prelim. Round
1973-74	78	16	16	7	10	24	5	26	40	12	206	248	64	6th,	West Div.	Out of Playoffs
1972-73	78	21	11	7	11	23	5	32	34	12	233	251	76	4th,	West Div.	Lost Quarter-Final
1971-72	78	17	17	5	11	22	6	28	39	11	208	247	67	3rd,	West Div.	Lost Semi-Final
1970-71	78	23	7	9	11	18	10	34	25	19	223	208	87	2nd,	West Div.	Lost Quarter-Final
1969-70	76	24	9	5	13	18	7	37	27	12	224	179	86	1st,	West Div.	Lost Final
1968-69	76	21	8	9	16	17	5	37	25	14	204	157	88	1st,	West Div.	Lost Final
1967-68	74	18	12	7	9	19	9	27	31	16	177	191	70	3rd,	West Div.	Lost Final

Often assigned the task of checking and pestering his opponent's top offensive player, Esa Tikkanen has earned the nickname "the Grate One" due to his effectiveness at this often under-appreciated task. In 1994-95, he combined top-flight defensive play with scoring punch, finishing with 35 points for the Blues.

1995-96 Player Personnel

FORWARDS	HT	WT	S	Place of Birth	Date	1994-95 Club
AMBROSIO, Jeff	6-1	188	L	Toronto, Ont.	4/26/77	Belleville
CARBONNEAU, Guy	5-11	184	R	Sept-Iles, Que.	3/18/60	St. Louis
CHASSE, Denis	6-2	200	R	Montreal, Que.	2/7/70	St. Louis
CORSON, Shayne	6-1	200	L	Midland, Ont.	8/13/66	Edmonton
COURTNALL, Geoff	6-1	195	L	Duncan, B.C.	8/18/62	Vancouver
CREIGHTON, Adam	6-5	220	L	Burlington, Ont.	6/2/65	St. Louis
GILBERT, Greg	6-1	191	L	Mississauga, Ont.	1/22/62	St. Louis
HAMEL, Denis	6-2	188	L	Lachute, Que.	5/10/77	Chicoutimi
HANDZUS, Michal	6-3	191	L	Banska Bystrica, Czech.	3/11/77	B. Bystrica
HAWERCHUK, Dale	5-11	190	L	Toronto, Ont.	4/4/63	Buffalo
HECHT, Jochen	6-1	180	L	Mannheim, Germany	6/21/77	Mannheim
HULL, Brett	5-10	201	R	Belleville, Ont.	8/9/64	St. Louis
JOHNSON, Craig	6-2	197	L	St. Paul, MN	3/18/72	Peoria-St. Louis
KENADY, Chris	6-2	195	R	Mound, MN	4/10/73	U. of Denver
LACHANCE, Bob	5-11	180	R	Northampton, MA	2/1/74	Boston U.
LAPERRIERE, Ian	6-1	195	R	Montreal, Que.	1/19/74	Peoria-St. Louis
MAYERS, Jamal	6-0	190	R	Toronto, Ont.	10/24/74	W. Michigan
McRAE, Basil	6-2	210	L	Beaverton, Ont.	1/5/61	St. Louis-Peoria
NOONAN, Brian	6-1	200	R	Boston, MA	5/29/65	NY Rangers
ROBERTS, David	6-0	185	L	Alameda, CA	5/28/70	Peoria-St. Louis
ROY, Stephane	5-10	173•	L	Ste-Martine, Que.	1/26/76	Val d'Or
SAWYER, Kevin	6-2	205	L	Christina Lake, B.C.	2/21/74	Spokane
STASTNY, Peter	6-1	200	L	Bratislava, Czech.	9/18/56	St. Louis
STEPHAN, Marc	6-2	205	L	Burlington, Ont.	1/9/76	Tri-City
TARDIF, Patrice	6-2	202	L	Thetford Mines, Que.	10/30/70	Peoria-St. Louis
TIKKANEN, Esa	6-1	190	L	Helsinki, Finland	1/25/65	HIFK-St. Louis
TWIST, Tony	6-1	220	L	Sherwood Park, Alta.	5/9/68	St. Louis
VASILEVSKY, Alexander	5-11	190	L	Kiev, USSR	1/8/75	Victoria-Brandon
VOPAT, Roman	6-3	216	L	Litvinov, Czech.	4/21/76	Moose Jaw

DEFENSEMEN	HT	WT	S	Place of Birth	Date	1994-95 Club
BARON, Murray	6-3	215	L	Prince George, B.C.	6/1/67	St. Louis
DUFRESNE, Donald	6-1	206	R	Quebec City, Que.	4/10/67	St. Louis
FRYLEN, Edvin	6-0	211	L	Jarfalla, Sweden	12/23/75	Vasteras
GUNKO, Yuri	6-1	187	L	Kiev, USSR	2/28/72	Sokol Kiev
HAMRLIK, Martin	5-11	185	R	Gottwaldov, Czech.	5/6/73	Peoria
MacINNIS, Al	6-2	196	R	Inverness, N.S.	7/11/63	St. Louis
NORTON, Jeff	6-2	200	L	Acton, MA	11/25/65	San Jose-St. Louis
OLSSON, Christer	5-11	190	L	Arboga, Sweden	7/24/70	Brynas
PRONGER, Chris	6-5	220	L	Dryden, Ont.	10/10/74	Hartford
RIVERS, Jamie	6-0	190	L	Ottawa, Ont.	3/16/75	Sudbury
STAIOS, Steve	6-0	185	R	Hamilton, Ont.	7/28/73	Peoria
WELLS, Jay	6-1	210	L	Paris, Ont.	5/18/59	NY Rangers
ZOMBO, Rick	6-1	202	R	Des Plaines, IL	5/8/63	St. Louis

GOALTENDERS	HT	WT	C	Place of Birth	Date	1994-95 Club
BUZAK, Mike	6-3	183	L	Edson, Alta.	2/10/73	Michigan State
CASEY, Jon	5-10	155	L	Grand Rapids, MN	3/29/62	St. Louis
FUHR, Grant	5-9	190	R	Spruce Grove, Alta.	9/28/62	Buffalo-Los Angeles
RACINE, Bruce	6-0	170	L	Cornwall, Ont.	8/9/66	St. John's
ROCHE, Scott	6-4	220	L	Lindsay, Ont.	3/19/77	North Bay

General Managers' History

Lynn Patrick, 1967-68; Scotty Bowman, 1968-69 to 1970-71; Lynn Patrick, 1971-72; Sid Abel, 1972-73; Charles Catto, 1973-74; Gerry Ehman, 1974-75; Dennis Ball, 1975-76; Emile Francis, 1976-77 to 1982-83; Ron Caron, 1983-84 to 1993-94; Mike Keenan, 1994-95 to date.

Coaching History

Lynn Patrick and Scotty Bowman, 1967-68; Scotty Bowman, 1968-69 to 1969-70; Al Arbour and Scotty Bowman, 1970-71; Sid Abel, Bill McCreary and Al Arbour, 1971-72; Al Arbour and Jean-Guy Talbot, 1972-73; Jean-Guy Talbot and Lou Angotti, 1973-74; Lou Angotti, Lynn Patrck and Garry Young, 1974-75; Garry Young, Lynn Patrick and Leo Boivin, 1975-76; Emile Francis, 1976-77; Leo Boivin and Barclay Plager, 1977-78; Barclay Plager, 1978-79; Barclay Plager and Red Berenson, 1979-80; Red Berenson, 1980-81; Red Berenson and Emile Francis, 1981-82; Emile Francis and Barclay Plager, 1982-83; Jacques Demers, 1983-84 to 1985-86; Jacques Martin, 1986-87 to 1987-88. Brian Sutter, 1988-89 to 1991-92; Bob Plager and Bob Berry, 1992-93; Bob Berry, 1993-94; Mike Keenan, 1994-95 to date.

Captains' History

Al Arbour, 1967-68 to 1969-70; Red Berenson and Barclay Plager, 1970-71; Barclay Plager, 1971-72 to 1975-76; no captain, 1976-77; Red Berenson, 1977-78; Barry Gibbs, 1978-79; Brian Sutter, 1979-80 to 1987-88; Bernie Federko, 1988-89; Rick Meagher, 1989-90; Scott Stevens, 1990-91; Garth Butcher, 1991-92; Brett Hull, 1992-93 to date.

Retired Numbers

3	Bob Gassoff	1973-1977
8	Barclay Plager	1967-1977
11	Brian Sutter	1976-1988
24	Bernie Federko	1976-1989

1994-95 Scoring

Regular Season

*– rookie

Pos	#	Player	Team	GP	G	A	Pts	+/-	PIM	PP	SH	GW	GT	S	%
R	16	Brett Hull	STL	48	29	21	50	13	10	9	3	6	0	200	14.5
L	19	Brendan Shanahan	STL	45	20	21	41	7	136	6	2	6	0	153	13.1
D	28	Steve Duchesne	STL	47	12	26	38	29	36	1	0	1	0	116	10.3
L	10	Esa Tikkanen	STL	43	12	23	35	13	22	5	2	1	1	107	11.2
C	20	Adam Creighton	STL	48	14	20	34	17	74	3	0	1	0	81	17.3
D	5	Jeff Norton	S.J.	20	1	9	10	1	39	0	0	0	0	21	4.8
			STL	28	2	18	20	21	33	0	0	1	0	27	7.4
			TOTAL	48	3	27	30	22	72	0	0	1	0	48	6.3
D	2	Al MacInnis	STL	32	8	20	28	19	43	2	0	0	0	110	7.3
C	22	* Ian Laperriere	STL	37	13	14	27	12	85	1	0	1	0	53	24.5
R	9	Glenn Anderson	STL	36	12	14	26	9	37	0	0	3	0	54	22.2
L	7	Greg Gilbert	STL	46	11	14	25	22	11	0	0	3	0	57	19.3
C	14	Todd Elik	S.J.	22	7	10	17	3	18	4	0	1	0	50	14.0
			STL	13	2	4	6	5	4	0	0	1	2	26	7.7
			TOTAL	35	9	14	23	8	22	4	0	2	2	76	11.8
D	33	Bill Houlder	STL	41	5	13	18	16	20	1	0	0	0	59	8.5
R	27	* Denis Chasse	STL	47	7	9	16	12	133	1	0	0	0	48	14.6
C	21	Guy Carbonneau	STL	42	5	11	16	11	16	1	0	1	0	33	15.2
C	25	* Patrice Tardif	STL	27	3	10	13	4	29	1	0	0	0	46	6.5
L	15	* David Roberts	STL	19	6	5	11	2	10	3	0	2	1	41	14.6
L	12	Vitali Karamnov	STL	26	3	7	10	7	14	0	0	0	0	22	13.6
D	6	Doug Lidster	STL	37	2	7	9	9	12	1	0	0	0	37	5.4
L	23	* Craig Johnson	STL	15	3	3	6	4	6	0	0	0	0	19	15.8
D	4	Rick Zombo	STL	23	1	4	5	7	24	0	0	1	0	18	5.6
L	17	Basil McRae	STL	21	0	5	5	4	72	0	0	0	0	14	0.0
L	34	Murray Baron	STL	39	0	5	5	9	93	0	0	0	0	28	0.0
L	18	Tony Twist	STL	28	3	0	3	0	89	0	0	1	0	8	37.5
D	32	Donald Dufresne	STL	22	0	3	3	2	10	0	0	0	0	11	0.0
C	26	Peter Stastny	STL	6	1	1	2	1	0	0	0	0	0	9	11.1
G	29	* Geoff Sarjeant	STL	4	0	1	1	0	2	0	0	0	0	0	0.0
G	31	Curtis Joseph	STL	36	0	1	1	0	4	0	0	0	0	0	0.0
L	36	Philippe Bozon	STL	2	0	0	0	1	0	0	0	0	0	0	0.0
L	25	Vitali Prokhorov	STL	2	0	0	0	1	0	0	0	0	0	0	0.0
L	9	Denny Felsner	STL	3	0	0	0	-1	2	0	0	0	0	2	0.0
L	44	* Terry Hollinger	STL	5	0	0	0	-1	2	0	0	0	0	1	0.0
D	37	* Jeff Batters	STL	10	0	0	0	-5	21	0	0	0	0	3	0.0
G	30	Jon Casey	STL	19	0	0	0	0	0	0	0	0	0	0	0.0

Goaltending

No.	Goaltender	GPI	Mins	Avg	W	L	T	EN	SO	GA	SA	S%
30	Jon Casey	19	872	2.75	7	5	4	0	0	40	400	.900
31	Curtis Joseph	36	1914	2.79	20	10	1	0	1	89	904	.902
29	* Geoff Sarjeant	4	120	3.00	1	0	0	0	0	6	52	.885
	Totals	48	2912	2.78	28	15	5	0	1	135	1356	.900

Playoffs

Pos	#	Player	Team	GP	G	A	Pts	+/-	PIM	PP	SH	GW	OT	S	%
L	19	Brendan Shanahan	STL	5	4	5	9	2	14	1	0	1	0	23	17.4
R	16	Brett Hull	STL	7	6	2	8	0	0	2	0	0	0	34	17.6
R	27	* Denis Chasse	STL	7	1	7	8	7	23	0	0	0	0	10	10.0
C	14	Todd Elik	STL	7	4	3	7	1	2	1	1	0	0	20	20.0
D	2	Al MacInnis	STL	7	1	5	6	-3	10	0	0	0	0	22	4.5
L	10	Esa Tikkanen	STL	7	2	2	4	-1	20	1	0	0	0	19	10.5
D	28	Steve Duchesne	STL	7	0	4	4	0	0	0	0	0	0	22	0.0
C	22	* Ian Laperriere	STL	7	0	4	4	3	21	0	0	0	0	10	0.0
L	17	Basil McRae	STL	7	2	1	3	4	4	0	0	0	0	6	33.3
C	21	Guy Carbonneau	STL	7	1	2	3	3	6	0	0	0	0	6	16.7
L	7	Greg Gilbert	STL	7	0	3	3	6	0	0	0	0	0	9	0.0
C	20	Adam Creighton	STL	7	2	0	2	-1	16	1	0	1	0	17	11.8
D	33	Bill Houlder	STL	4	1	1	2	6	0	0	0	0	0	10	10.0
R	9	Glenn Anderson	STL	6	1	1	2	0	49	0	0	0	0	3	33.3
D	34	Murray Baron	STL	7	1	1	2	2	2	0	0	0	0	9	11.1
D	5	Jeff Norton	STL	7	1	1	2	1	11	0	0	0	0	13	7.7
G	31	Curtis Joseph	STL	7	0	1	1	0	0	0	0	0	0	0	0.0
L	18	Tony Twist	STL	1	0	0	0	0	6	0	0	0	0	1	0.0
L	23	* Craig Johnson	STL	1	0	0	0	0	2	0	0	0	0	1	0.0
G	30	Jon Casey	STL	2	0	0	0	0	0	0	0	0	0	0	0.0
L	12	Vitali Karamnov	STL	2	0	0	0	1	0	0	0	0	0	4	0.0
D	32	Donald Dufresne	STL	3	0	0	0	-1	4	0	0	0	0	2	0.0
D	4	Rick Zombo	STL	3	0	0	0	-1	2	0	0	0	0	2	0.0
D	6	Doug Lidster	STL	4	0	0	0	6	2	0	0	0	0	8	0.0
L	15	* David Roberts	STL	6	0	0	0	-5	4	0	0	0	0	11	0.0

Goaltending

No.	Goaltender	GPI	Mins	Avg	W	L	EN	SO	GA	SA	S%
31	Curtis Joseph	7	392	3.67	3	3	1	0	24	178	.865
30	Jon Casey	2	30	4.00	0	1	0	0	2	10	.800
	Totals	7	422	3.84	3	4	1	0	27	189	.857

Club Records

Team

(Figures in brackets for season records are games played; records for fewest points, wins, ties, losses, goals, goals against are for 70 or more games)

Most Points	107	1980-81 (80)
Most Wins	47	1990-91 (80)
Most Ties	19	1970-71 (78)
Most Losses	50	1978-79 (80)
Most Goals	352	1980-81 (80)
Most Goals Against	349	1981-82 (80)
Fewest Points	48	1978-79 (80)
Fewest Wins	18	1978-79 (80)
Fewest Ties	7	1983-84 (80)
Fewest Losses	18	1980-81 (80)
Fewest Goals	177	1967-68 (74)
Fewest Goals Against	157	1968-69 (76)

Longest Winning Streak

Over-all	7	Jan. 21- Feb. 3/88; Mar. 19-31/91
Home	9	Jan. 26- Feb. 26/91
Away	4	Four times

Longest Undefeated Streak

Over-all	12	Nov. 10- Dec. 8/68 (5 wins, 7 ties)
Home	11	Feb. 12- Mar. 19/69 (5 wins, 6 ties); Feb. 7- Mar. 29/75 (9 wins, 2 ties); Oct. 7- Nov. 26/93 (7 wins, 4 ties)
Away	7	Dec. 9-26/87 (4 wins, 3 ties)

Longest Losing Streak

Over-all	7	Nov. 12-26/67; Feb. 12-25/89
Home	5	Nov. 19- Dec. 6/77
Away	10	Jan. 20/82- Mar. 8/82

Longest Winless Streak

Over-all	12	Jan. 17- Feb. 15/78 (10 losses, 2 ties)
Home	7	Dec. 28/82- Jan. 25/83 (5 losses, 2 ties)
Away	17	Jan. 23- Apr. 7/74 (14 losses, 3 ties)

Most Shutouts, Season	13	1968-69 (76)
Most PIM, Season	2,041	1990-91 (80)
Most Goals, Game	11	Feb. 26/94 (St. L. 11 at Ott. 1)

Individual

Most Seasons	13	Bernie Federko
Most Games	927	Bernie Federko
Most Goals, Career	415	Brett Hull
Most Assists, Career	721	Bernie Federko
Most Points, Career	1,073	Bernie Federko
Most PIM, Career	1,786	Brian Sutter
Most Shutouts, Career	16	Glenn Hall
Longest Consecutive Games Streak	662	Garry Unger (Feb. 7/71-Apr. 8/79)
Most Goals, Season	86	Brett Hull (1990-91)
Most Assists, Season	90	Adam Oates (1990-91)
Most Points, Season	131	Brett Hull (1990-91) (86 goals, 45 assists)
Most PIM, Season	306	Bob Gassoff (1975-76)
Most Points, Defenseman Season	78	Jeff Brown (1992-93) (25 goals, 53 assists)
Most Points, Center, Season	115	Adam Oates (1990-91) (25 goals, 90 assists)
Most Points, Right Wing, Season	131	Brett Hull (1990-91) (86 goals, 45 assists)

Most Points, Left Wing, Season	102	Brendan Shanahan (1993-94) (52 goals, 50 assists)
Most Points, Rookie, Season	73	Jorgen Pettersson (1980-81) (37 goals, 36 assists)
Most Shutouts, Season	8	Glenn Hall (1968-69)
Most Goals, Game	6	Red Berenson (Nov. 7/68)
Most Assists, Game	5	Brian Sutter (Nov. 22/88) Bernie Federko (Feb. 27/88) Adam Oates (Jan. 26/91)
Most Points, Game	7	Red Berenson (Nov. 7/68) Garry Unger (Mar. 13/71)

All-time Record vs. Other Clubs
Regular Season

			At Home							On Road							Total				
	GP	W	L	T	GF	GA	PTS	GP	W	L	T	GF	GA	PTS	GP	W	L	T	GF	GA	PTS
Anaheim	4	3	1	0	20	11	6	4	3	1	0	13	9	6	8	6	2	0	33	20	12
Boston	52	21	22	9	163	181	51	51	11	33	7	138	225	29	103	32	55	16	301	406	80
Buffalo	43	26	11	6	165	111	58	44	12	28	4	138	183	28	87	38	39	10	303	294	86
Calgary	45	20	18	7	161	141	47	44	18	23	3	132	161	39	89	38	41	10	293	302	86
Chicago	90	44	29	17	309	278	105	93	26	55	12	285	373	64	183	70	84	29	594	651	169
Dallas	97	53	26	18	359	276	124	95	34	43	18	282	329	86	192	87	69	36	641	605	210
Detroit	86	48	25	13	317	241	109	85	37	35	13	280	309	87	171	85	60	26	597	550	196
Edmonton	26	12	10	4	108	105	28	26	8	15	3	100	114	19	52	20	25	7	208	219	47
Florida	1	1	0	0	5	3	2	1	1	0	0	3	1	2	2	2	0	0	8	4	4
Hartford	23	13	8	2	91	77	28	24	13	9	2	76	74	28	47	26	17	4	167	151	56
Los Angeles	60	39	14	7	233	159	85	60	19	32	9	172	225	47	120	58	46	16	405	384	132
Montreal	51	10	27	14	129	183	34	52	8	38	6	134	235	22	103	18	65	20	263	418	56
New Jersey	38	25	8	5	172	118	55	39	15	17	7	114	128	37	77	40	25	12	286	246	92
NY Islanders	40	16	17	7	146	134	39	41	8	23	10	98	161	26	81	24	40	17	244	295	65
NY Rangers	55	21	26	8	163	183	50	53	6	42	5	120	228	17	108	27	68	13	283	411	67
Ottawa	2	2	0	0	12	6	4	2	2	0	0	15	2	4	4	4	0	0	27	8	8
Philadelphia	59	23	29	7	173	183	53	59	10	40	9	135	237	29	118	33	69	16	308	420	82
Pittsburgh	57	38	13	6	228	154	82	56	19	25	12	172	209	50	113	57	38	18	400	363	132
Quebec	22	16	4	2	105	74	34	22	9	10	3	74	82	21	44	25	14	5	179	156	55
San Jose	9	8	1	0	39	19	16	6	6	0	0	23	11	12	15	14	1	0	62	30	28
Tampa Bay	4	3	1	0	18	13	6	5	2	2	1	18	17	5	9	5	3	1	36	30	11
Toronto	86	51	23	12	304	245	114	85	22	53	10	248	329	54	171	73	76	22	552	574	168
Vancouver	53	30	16	7	203	159	67	54	24	24	6	168	168	54	107	54	40	13	371	327	121
Washington	33	14	11	8	139	111	36	32	12	17	3	98	118	27	65	26	28	11	237	229	63
Winnipeg	29	14	7	8	118	91	36	31	9	16	6	94	109	24	60	23	23	14	212	200	60
Defunct Clubs	32	25	4	3	131	55	53	33	11	10	12	95	100	34	65	36	14	15	226	155	87
Totals	**1097**	**576**	**351**	**170**	**4011**	**3311**	**1322**	**1097**	**345**	**591**	**161**	**3225**	**4137**	**851**	**2194**	**921**	**942**	**331**	**7236**	**7448**	**2173**

Calgary totals include Atlanta, 1972-73 to 1979-80. Dallas totals include Minnesota, 1967-68 to 1992-93.
New Jersey totals include Kansas City, 1974-75 to 1975-76, and Colorado, 1976-77 to 1981-82.

Playoffs

	Series	W	L	GP	W	L	T	GF	GA	Last Mtg.	Round	Result
Boston	2	0	2	8	0	8	0	15	48	1972	SF	L 0-4
Buffalo	1	0	1	3	1	2	0	8	7	1976	PR	L 1-2
Calgary	1	0	1	7	3	4	0	22	28	1986	CF	L 3-4
Chicago	9	2	7	45	18	27	0	129	166	1993	DSF	W 4-0
Dallas	10	5	5	56	26	30	0	162	174	1994	CQF	L 0-4
Detroit	3	2	1	16	8	8	0	51	53	1991	DSF	W 4-3
Los Angeles	1	1	0	4	4	0	0	16	5	1969	SF	W 4-0
Montreal	3	0	3	12	0	12	0	14	42	1977	QF	L 0-4
NY Rangers	1	0	1	6	2	4	0	22	29	1981	QF	L 2-4
Philadelphia	2	2	0	11	8	3	0	34	20	1969	QF	W 4-0
Pittsburgh	3	2	1	13	7	6	0	45	40	1981	PR	W 3-2
Toronto	4	2	2	25	13	12	0	67	75	1993	DF	L 3-4
Vancouver	2	1	1	7	3	4	0	27	27	1995	CQF	L 3-4
Winnipeg	1	1	0	4	3	1	0	20	13	1982	DSF	W 3-1
Totals	**42**	**17**	**25**	**217**	**96**	**121**	**0**	**632**	**727**			

Playoff Results 1995-91

Year	Round	Opponent	Result	GF	GA
1995	CQF	Vancouver	L 3-4	27	27
1994	CQF	Dallas	L 0-4	10	16
1993	DF	Toronto	L 3-4	11	22
	DSF	Chicago	W 4-0	13	6
1992	DSF	Chicago	L 2-4	19	23
1991	DF	Minnesota	L 2-4	17	22
	DSF	Detroit	W 4-3	24	20

Abbreviations: Round: F – Final;
CF – conference final; **CQF** – conference quarter-final;
CSF – conference semi-final; **DF** – division final;
DSF – division semi-final; **SF** – semi-final;
QF – quarter-final; **PR** – preliminary round.

1994-95 Results

Jan.	20	at	San Jose	5-2	19	at	Anaheim	4-2
	21	at	Vancouver	7-1	20	at	Los Angeles	3-5
	24	at	Calgary	4-6	22	at	Calgary	3-4
	26		Los Angeles	3-1	26		Edmonton	5-1
	28		Vancouver	1-3	27	at	Dallas	3-2
	31		Anaheim	7-2	29	at	Chicago	3-1
Feb.	2	at	Winnipeg	4-1	31		San Jose	4-1
	4		Dallas	7-4	Apr. 2	at	Detroit	3-3
	7		Los Angeles	5-5	3		Toronto	5-2
	9		Chicago	0-5	5	at	Toronto	6-4
	11		Winnipeg	2-3	9		Dallas	2-3
	13		Calgary	4-2	11		Winnipeg	7-5
	17	at	Winnipeg	4-3	13	at	Winnipeg	2-5
	18	at	Toronto	1-3	16		Detroit	6-5
	20		Edmonton	4-0	18		Vancouver	4-1
	22		San Jose	4-3	19	at	Chicago	2-2
	25	at	Detroit	3-2	21		Toronto	3-1
	27		Toronto	3-2	23		Chicago	2-2
Mar.	5	at	Dallas	1-2	25	at	Dallas	8-4
	7		Anaheim	6-3	27	at	Edmonton	2-3
	9		Calgary	5-1	28	at	Vancouver	1-3
	12		Detroit	1-2	30	at	San Jose	4-3
	14	at	Edmonton	5-6	May 1	at	Anaheim	5-3
	16	at	Los Angeles	2-2	3		Detroit	2-3

Entry Draft
Selections 1995-81

1995
Pick
49	Jochen Hecht
75	Scott Roche
101	Michal Handzus
127	Jeff Ambrosio
153	Denis Hamel
179	J-Luc Grand-Pierre
205	Derek Bekar
209	Libor Zabransky

1994
Pick
68	Stephane Roy
94	Tyler Harlton
120	Edvin Frylen
172	Roman Vopat
198	Steve Noble
224	Marc Stephan
250	Kevin Harper
276	Scott Fankhouser

1993
Pick
37	Maxim Bets
63	Jamie Rivers
89	Jamal Mayers
141	Todd Kelman
167	Mike Buzak
193	Eric Boguniecki
219	Michael Grier
245	Libor Prochazka
271	Alexander Vasilevsky
275	Christer Olsson

1992
Pick
38	Igor Korolev
62	Vitali Karamnov
64	Vitali Prokhorov
86	Lee J. Leslie
134	Bob Lachance
158	Ian LaPerriere
160	Lance Burns
180	Igor Boldin
182	Nicholas Naumenko
206	Todd Harris
230	Yuri Gunko
259	Wade Salzman

1991
Pick
27	Steve Staios
64	Kyle Reeves
65	Nathan Lafayette
87	Grayden Reid
109	Jeff Callinan
131	Bruce Gardiner
153	Terry Hollinger
175	Christopher Kenady
197	Jed Fiebelkorn
219	Chris MacKenzie
241	Kevin Rappana
263	Mike Veisor

1990
Pick
33	Craig Johnson
54	Patrice Tardif
96	Jason Ruff
117	Kurtis Miller
138	Wayne Conlan
180	Parris Duffus
201	Steve Widmeyer
222	Joe Hawley
243	Joe Fleming

1989
Pick
9	Jason Marshall
31	Rick Corriveau
55	Denny Felsner
93	Daniel Laperriere
114	David Roberts
124	Derek Frenette
135	Jeff Batters
156	Kevin Plager
177	John Roderick
198	John Valo
219	Brian Lukowski

1988
Pick
9	Rod Brind' Amour
30	Adrien Plavsic
51	Rob Fournier
72	Jaan Luik
105	Dave Lacouture
114	Dan Fowler
135	Matt Hayes
156	John McCoy
177	Tony Twist
198	Bret Hedican
219	Heath DeBoer
240	Michael Francis

1987
Pick
12	Keith Osborne
54	Kevin Miehm
59	Robert Nordmark
75	Darin Smith
82	Andy Rymsha
117	Rob Robinson
138	Todd Crabtree
159	Guy Hebert
180	Robert Dumas
201	David Marvin
207	Andy Cesarski
222	Dan Rolfe
243	Ray Savard

1986
Pick
10	Jocelyn Lemieux
31	Mike Posma
52	Tony Hejna
73	Glen Featherstone
87	Michael Wolak
115	Mike O'Toole
136	Andy May
157	Randy Skarda
178	Martyn Ball
199	Rod Thacker
220	Terry MacLean
234	Bill Butler
241	David O'Brien

1985
Pick
37	Herb Raglan
44	Nelson Emerson
54	Ned Desmond
100	Dan Brooks
121	Rich Burchill
138	Pat Jablonski
159	Scott Brickey
180	Jeff Urban
201	Vince Guidotti
222	Ron Saatzer
243	Dave Jecha

1984
Pick
26	Brian Benning
32	Tony Hrkac
50	Toby Ducolon
53	Robert Dirk
56	Alan Perry
71	Graham Herring
92	Scott Paluch
113	Steve Tuttle
134	Cliff Ronning
148	Don Porter
155	Jim Vesey
176	Daniel Jomphe
196	Tom Tilley
217	Mark Cupolo
237	Mark Lanigan

1983
DID NOT DRAFT

1982
Pick
50	Mike Posavad
92	Scott Machej
113	Perry Ganchar
134	Doug Gilmour
155	Chris Delaney
176	Matt Christensen
197	John Shumski
218	Brian Ahern
239	Peter Smith

1981
Pick
20	Marty Ruff
36	Hakan Nordin
62	Gordon Donnelly
104	Mike Hickey
125	Peter Aslin
146	Erik Holmberg
167	Alain Vigneault
188	Dan Wood
209	Richard Zemlak

Club Directory

Kiel Center
1401 Clark Avenue
St. Louis, MO 63103-2709
Phone **314/622-2500**
FAX 314/622-2582
Capacity: 19,260

Board of Directors
Jerry Ritter, Robert M. Cox, Jr., H. Edwin Trusheim, Andrew E. Newman,
Horace Wilkins, Charles W. Mueller, Lee Liberman, John J. Quinn, Ted C. Wetterau

Executive
President and CEO	John J. Quinn
General Manager and Head Coach	Mike Keenan
Executive Vice-President	Ronald Caron
Vice-President, Sales	Bruce Affleck
Vice-President, Finance and Administration	Jerry Jasiek
Vice-President, Broadcast Sales	Matt Hyland
Executive Assistant to President	Lynn Diederichsen
Executive Assistant to General Manager	Janiece Chambers

Hockey Operations
Director of Amateur Player Personnel and Scouting	Ted Hampson
Assistant Director of Scouting	Jack Evans
Scouting Staff	Pat Ginnell, Matt Keator, Peter Stastny, Dick Cherry, Ken Williamson
Director of Professional Playing Personnel	Jim Pappin
Professional Scouts	Bob Plager, Rick Meagher
Associate Coaches	Bob Berry, Roger Nielson
Video Coordinator	Arne Pappin
Director of Team Services	Michael Caruso
General Manager/Head Coach, Worcester IceCats	Jim Roberts
Assistant Coach, Worcester IceCats	Paul Pickard

Medical Staff
Athletic Trainer	Ray Barile
Massage Therapist	Jeff Cope
Equipment Manager	Terry Roof
Assistant Equipment Manager	Mark Roof
Orthopedic Surgeon	Dr. Rick Lehman
Internist	Dr. Aaron Birenbaum
Dentist	Dr. Glenn Edwards
Optometrist	Dr. N. Rex Ghormley

Public Relations/Marketing
Director of Promotions/Community Relations	Stacy Solomon
Director of Public Relations	Adam Fell
Assistant Director of Public Relations	Michael Eiskant
Marketing/Public Relations Secretary	Donna Quirk
Receptionist	Pam Barrett

Finance/Sales
Director of Retail Operations	Andy Cotlar
Sales Representatives	Wes Edwards, John Casson, Tammy Iuli, Jill Mann, Paula Barnes
Accounting Staff	Craig Bryant, Marsha McBride, Jim Bergman

Miscellaneous
Television Stations	KPLR (Channel 11) and Prime Sports
Radio Station	KMOX (1120 AM)
Broadcasters	Ken Wilson, Joe Micheletti, Bruce Affleck, Ron Jacober
Team Colors	Blue, Gold & Red

General Manager and Coach

KEENAN, MICHAEL (MIKE)
General Manager and Coach, St. Louis Blues.
Born in Toronto, Ontario, October 21, 1949.

In his first season as general manager and head coach of the St. Louis Blues, Mike Keenan led the club to the third best record overall in the National Hockey League. The Blues regular season record of 28-15-5 (61 points) marked the third highest winning percentage (.635) in club history.

Keenan became the 18th head coach and ninth general manager in St. Louis Blues' history on July 18, 1994. In 772 career games, Keenan owns a 423-267-82 career coaching record. In 147 playoff games, Keenan sports a 84-63 mark, and has coached his team to the Stanley Cup Finals four times, leading the NY Rangers to their first Stanley Cup in 54 years in 1994. Keenan has guided his clubs to six division titles. He has finished with the best record in the National Hockey League three times with three different teams, averaging 44 wins and 96 points per season throughout his coaching career (minimum 80 game schedule).

He started in the NHL with Philadelphia in 1984-85, taking the Flyers from a third place finish the previous season to the best record in the NHL with 113 points. He coached the Flyers for three more seasons and posted a mark of 190-102-28 in 320 games. He then moved to Chicago in 1988-89 and coached the Blackhawks for four seasons and 320 games. He left in 1991-92 with a record of 153-126-41 having coached the Hawks to the NHL's best record in 1990-91 with 106 points and a Stanley Cup Final appearance in 1992. Keenan also served as the Blackhawks' general manager from 1989-90 to his departure in 1991-92.

Keenan joined the New York Rangers on April 17, 1993 and guided the club to its best record ever (52-24-8, 113PTS) and his first Stanley Cup championship.

Mike has one daughter, Gayla, and resides in St. Louis.

Coaching Record

			Regular Season				Playoffs			
Season	Team	Games	W	L	T	%	Games	W	L	%
1979-80	Peterborough (OHL)	68	47	20	1	.699	18	15	3	.833
1980-81	Rochester (AHL)	80	30	42	8	.425	....	....	....	....
1981-82	Rochester (AHL)	80	40	31	9	.556	9	4	5	.444
1982-83	Rochester (AHL)	80	46	25	9	.631	16	12	4	.750
1983-84	U. of Toronto (CIAU)	49	41	5	3	.867	....	....	....	....
1984-85	Philadelphia (NHL)	80	53	20	7	.706	19	12	7	.632
1985-86	Philadelphia (NHL)	80	53	23	4	.688	5	2	3	.400
1986-87	Philadelphia (NHL)	80	46	26	8	.625	26	15	11	.577
1987-88	Philadelphia (NHL)	80	38	33	9	.531	7	3	4	.429
1988-89	Chicago (NHL)	80	27	41	12	.413	16	9	7	.563
1989-90	Chicago (NHL)	80	41	33	6	.550	20	10	10	.500
1990-91	Chicago (NHL)	80	49	23	8	.663	6	2	4	.333
1991-92	Chicago (NHL)	80	36	29	15	.544	18	12	6	.667
1993-94	NY Rangers (NHL)	84	52	24	8	.667	23	16	7	.696*
1994-95	St. Louis (NHL)	48	28	15	5	.635	7	3	4	.429
	NHL Totals	772	423	267	82	.601	147	84	63	.571

* Stanley Cup win.

San Jose Sharks

1994-95 Results: 19W-25L-4T 42PTS. Third, Pacific Division

Year-by-Year Record

Season	GP	Home			Road			Overall						Finished		Playoff Result
		W	L	T	W	L	T	W	L	T	GF	GA	Pts.			
1994-95	48	10	13	1	9	12	3	19	25	4	129	161	42	3rd,	Pacific Div.	Lost Conf. Semi-Final
1993-94	84	19	13	10	14	22	6	33	35	16	252	265	82	3rd,	Pacific Div.	Lost Conf. Semi-Final
1992-93	84	8	33	1	3	38	1	11	71	2	218	414	24	6th,	Smythe Div.	Out of Playoffs
1991-92	80	14	23	3	3	35	2	17	58	5	219	359	39	6th,	Smythe Div.	Out of Playoffs

Schedule

Oct.	Sat.	7	Chicago		Wed.	10	at NY Rangers
	Thur.	12	Boston		Thur.	11	at New Jersey
	Sat.	14	Vancouver		Sat.	13	at Pittsburgh
	Tues.	17	at Toronto		Tues.	16	at Florida
	Thur.	19	at Winnipeg		Wed.	17	at Tampa Bay
	Sun.	22	at Edmonton		Wed.	24	at Detroit
	Wed.	25	Winnipeg		Thur.	25	at Chicago
	Sat.	28	Dallas*		Sat.	27	Colorado*
	Mon.	30	at Vancouver		Tues.	30	Hartford
	Tues.	31	NY Rangers	Feb.	Thur.	1	Los Angeles
Nov.	Thur.	2	New Jersey		Sat.	3	Chicago*
	Sat.	4	St. Louis		Mon.	5	Toronto
	Tues.	7	at Hartford		Sat.	10	at Los Angeles*
	Wed.	8	at Buffalo		Mon.	12	at Montreal
	Fri.	10	Pittsburgh		Wed.	14	at Toronto
	Sat.	11	Detroit		Thur.	15	at Ottawa
	Tues.	14	NY Islanders		Sat.	17	at NY Islanders*
	Thur.	16	at St. Louis		Tues.	20	at Calgary
	Fri.	17	at Dallas		Fri.	23	at Vancouver
	Sun.	19	at Chicago		Sun.	25	at Anaheim*
	Tues.	21	at Washington		Mon.	26	Montreal
	Wed.	22	at Detroit	Mar.	Fri.	1	Tampa Bay
	Sat.	25	Vancouver		Sun.	3	Calgary*
	Wed.	29	Calgary		Tues.	5	at Colorado
Dec.	Fri.	1	at Vancouver		Wed.	6	Dallas
	Sat.	2	Washington		Fri.	8	at Edmonton
	Tues.	5	at Colorado		Sun.	10	Buffalo*
	Thur.	7	Winnipeg		Wed.	13	Edmonton
	Sat.	9	Edmonton		Fri.	15	St. Louis
	Tues.	12	Ottawa		Sun.	17	at Philadelphia
	Thur.	14	Toronto		Mon.	18	at Boston
	Sat.	16	at St. Louis		Wed.	20	at Winnipeg
	Sun.	17	at Dallas		Fri.	22	at Calgary
	Tues.	19	at Anaheim		Thur.	28	Colorado
	Fri.	22	Los Angeles		Sun.	31	Anaheim*
	Tues.	26	Colorado	Apr.	Tues.	2	Detroit
	Fri.	29	at Anaheim		Thur.	4	at Edmonton
Jan.	Wed.	3	Philadelphia		Sat.	6	at Colorado*
	Fri.	5	Los Angeles		Sun.	7	Anaheim*
	Sat.	6	at Los Angeles		Wed.	10	at Los Angeles
	Mon.	8	Florida		Fri.	12	Calgary

* Denotes afternoon game.

Home Starting Times:

All games	. . . .	7:30 p.m.
Except	Sat. Oct. 28	12:00 p.m.
	Tue. Oct. 31	6:00 p.m.
	Sat. Jan. 27	12:00 p.m.
	Sat. Feb. 3	12:00 p.m.
	Sun. Mar. 3	2:00 p.m.
	Sun. Mar. 10	2:00 p.m.
	Sun. Mar. 31	12:00 p.m.
	Sun. Apr. 7	12:00 p.m.

Franchise date: May 9, 1990

WESTERN CONFERENCE

PACIFIC DIVISION

5th
NHL
Season

Craig Janney, obtained late in the 1994-95 season from St. Louis, provides the Sharks with depth and dependability at center.

1995-96 Player Personnel

FORWARDS	HT	WT	S	Place of Birth	Date	1994-95 Club
BAKER, Jamie	6-0	190	L	Ottawa, Ont.	8/31/66	San Jose
BROWN, David	6-5	222	R	Saskatoon, Sask.	10/12/62	Philadelphia
CALOUN, Jan	5-10	175	R	Usti-Nad-Labem, Czech.	12/20/72	Kansas City
CHERBAYEV, Alexander	6-1	190	L	Voskresensk, USSR	8/13/73	Kansas City
DAHLEN, Ulf	6-2	195	L	Ostersund, Sweden	1/12/67	San Jose
DONOVAN, Shean	6-2	190	R	Timmins, Ont.	1/22/75	Ottawa (OHL)-S.J.-Kansas City
FALLOON, Pat	5-11	190	R	Foxwarren, Man.	9/22/72	San Jose
FRIESEN, Jeff	6-0	185	L	Meadow Lake, Sask.	8/5/76	Regina-San Jose
GRILLO, Dean	6-2	210	R	Bemidji, MN	12/8/72	Kansas City
HAKANEN, Timo	6-2	190	L	Pori, Finland	3/26/77	Assat
JANNEY, Craig	6-1	190	L	Hartford, CT	9/26/67	St. Louis-San Jose
KOROLYUK, Alexander	5-9	170	L	Moscow, USSR	1/15/76	Soviet Wings
KOZLOV, Viktor	6-5	225	R	Togliatti, USSR	2/14/75	Moscow D'amo-S.J.-Kansas City
LARIONOV, Igor	5-9	170	L	Voskresensk, USSR	12/3/60	San Jose
MAKAROV, Sergei	5-11	185	L	Chelyabinsk, USSR	6/19/58	San Jose
MAKINEN, Marko	6-4	198	R	Turku, Finland	3/31/77	TPS-Kiekko-67
MILLER, Kevin	5-11	190	R	Lansing, MI	9/2/65	St. Louis-San Jose
NAZAROV, Andrei	6-5	230	R	Chelyabinsk, USSR	5/22/74	Kansas City-San Jose
NILSSON, Fredrik	6-1	200	L	Stockholm, Sweden	4/16/71	Kansas City
ODGERS, Jeff	6-0	195	R	Spy Hill, Sask.	5/31/69	San Jose
PELTONEN, Ville	5-11	172	L	Vantaa, Finland	5/24/73	HIFK
RIIHIJARVI, Teemu	6-6	202	L	Espoo, Finland	3/1/77	Espoo
ROED, Peter	5-10	210	L	St. Paul, MN	11/15/76	White Bear Lk.
TANCILL, Chris	5-10	185	L	Livonia, MI	2/7/68	Kansas City-San Jose
VARADA, Vaclav	6-0	198	L	Vsetin, Czech.	4/26/76	Tacoma
WHITNEY, Ray	5-9	160	R	Fort Saskatchewan, Alta.	5/8/72	San Jose
WOOD, Dody	5-11	181	L	Chetwynd, B.C.	3/10/72	Kansas City-San Jose
YEGOROV, Alexei	5-11	185	L	St. Petersburg, USSR	5/21/75	St. Peterburg-Fort Worth
DEFENSEMEN						
KROUPA, Vlastimil	6-3	210	L	Most, Czech.	4/27/75	Kansas City-San Jose
KYTE, Jim	6-5	210	L	Ottawa, Ont.	3/21/64	Las Vegas-San Jose
MORE, Jayson	6-1	200	R	Souris, Man.	1/12/69	San Jose
NIKOLOV, Angel	6-1	176	L	Most, Czech.	11/18/75	Litvinov
ODUYA, Fredrik	6-2	185	L	Stockholm, Sweden	5/31/75	Ottawa (OHL)
OSADCHY, Alexander	5-11	190	R	Kharkov, USSR	7/19/75	CSKA
OZOLINSH, Sandis	6-1	195	L	Riga, Latvia	8/3/72	San Jose
PEDERSON, Tom	5-9	175	R	Bloomington, MN	1/14/70	San Jose
RAGNARSSON, Marcus	6-1	200	L	Ostervala, Sweden	8/13/71	Djurgarden
RATHJE, Mike	6-6	220	L	Mannville, Alta.	5/11/74	San Jose-Kansas City
SYKORA, Michal	6-5	225	L	Pardubice, Czech.	7/5/73	Kansas City-San Jose

GOALTENDERS	HT	WT	C	Place of Birth	Date	1994-95 Club
FLAHERTY, Wade	6-0	170	L	Terrace, B.C.	1/11/68	San Jose
IRBE, Arturs	5-7	180	L	Riga, Latvia	2/2/67	San Jose
KIPRUSOFF, Miikka	6-0	176	L	Turku, Finland	10/26/76	TPS-TPS
NABOKOV, Yevgeni	6-0	180	L	Ust-Kamenogorsk, USSR	7/25/75	Moscow D'amo
TOSKALA, Vesa	5-9	172	L	Tampere, Finland	5/20/77	Ilves

Coach

CONSTANTINE, KEVIN
Head Coach, San Jose Sharks.
Born in International Falls, MN, December 27, 1958.

In 1994-95, head coach Kevin Constantine guided the San Jose Sharks to the NHL playoffs for the second consecutive season where he again engineered a first-round upset of a higher ranked post-season opponent. The team's series wins over Calgary last season and Detroit in 1993-94 rank as two of the biggest first-round upsets in NHL playoff history.

Having been successful at every level in his coaching career, it is no surprise that Constantine has quickly made his mark in the NHL. As a rookie head coach in 1993-94, he led the Sharks to a league-record 58-point improvement over the previous season and their first-ever playoff berth. He skilfully blended a diverse group of players hailing from across the hockey world.

Constantine was runner-up for the 1993-94 Jack Adams Award as NHL coach of the year, finishing behind New Jersey's Jacques Lemaire. He also received honorable mention as coach of the year in annual awards presented by *The Hockey News* in which he finished third in that voting behind Lemaire and Rangers coach Mike Keenan.

Constantine was named Sharks head coach on June 16, 1993 after two seasons as coach of the Kansas City Blades, San Jose's development affiliate and IHL champion in 1991-92.

He led Kansas City to a combined record of 102-48-14 (.659) from 1991 to 1993. His club recorded professional hockey's best mark of 56-22-4 in 1991-92, earning him IHL coach of the year honors.

Before being hired by the Sharks to coach at Kansas City, Constantine was an assistant coach with the IHL Kalamazoo Wings from 1988 to 1991. He also coached the U.S. National Junior Team to a fourth-place finish and a record of 4-2-1 at the 1991 IIHF World Junior Championships.

Coaching Record

		Regular Season					Playoffs			
Season	**Team**	**Games**	**W**	**L**	**T**	**%**	**Games**	**W**	**L**	**%**
1985-86	North Iowa (USHL)	48	17	31	0	.354	....	....	....	....
1987-88	Rochester (USHL)	48	39	7	2	.833	15	9	4 (2 ties)	.692
1991-92	Kansas City (IHL)	82	56	22	4	.707	15	12	3	.800
1992-93	Kansas City (IHL)	82	46	26	10	.622	12	6	6	.500
1993-94	**San Jose (NHL)**	**84**	**33**	**35**	**16**	**.488**	**14**	**7**	**7**	**.500**
1994-95	**San Jose (NHL)**	**48**	**19**	**25**	**4**	**.438**	**11**	**4**	**7**	**.364**
	NHL Totals	**132**	**52**	**60**	**20**	**.470**	**25**	**11**	**14**	**.440**

1994-95 Scoring

* – rookie

Regular Season

Pos	#	Player	Team	GP	G	A	Pts	+/–	PIM	PP	SH	GW	GT	S	%
R	22	Ulf Dahlen	S.J.	46	11	23	34	–2	11	4	1	4	0	85	12.9
C	15	Craig Janney	STL	8	2	5	7	3	0	1	0	0	0	9	22.2
			S.J.	27	5	15	20	–4	10	2	0	1	0	31	16.1
			TOTAL	35	7	20	27	–1	10	3	0	1	0	40	17.5
L	39	* Jeff Friesen	S.J.	48	15	10	25	–8	14	5	1	2	0	86	17.4
C	14	Ray Whitney	S.J.	39	13	12	25	–7	14	4	0	1	0	67	19.4
D	6	Sandis Ozolinsh	S.J.	48	9	16	25	–6	30	3	1	2	0	83	10.8
R	24	Sergei Makarov	S.J.	43	10	14	24	–4	40	1	0	1	1	56	17.9
C	7	Igor Larionov	S.J.	33	4	20	24	–3	14	0	0	1	0	69	5.8
R	8	Kevin Miller	STL	15	2	5	7	4	0	0	0	0	0	19	10.5
			S.J.	21	6	7	13	0	13	1	1	2	0	41	14.6
			TOTAL	36	8	12	20	4	13	1	1	2	0	60	13.3
R	17	Pat Falloon	S.J.	46	12	7	19	–4	25	0	0	3	0	91	13.2
D	41	Tom Pederson	S.J.	47	5	11	16	–14	31	0	0	0	2	59	8.5
C	18	Chris Tancill	S.J.	26	3	11	14	1	10	0	1	0	0	39	7.7
C	13	Jamie Baker	S.J.	43	7	4	11	–7	22	0	1	0	0	60	11.7
D	40	Mike Rathje	S.J.	42	2	7	9	–1	29	0	0	0	0	38	5.3
R	23	* Andrei Nazarov	S.J.	26	3	5	8	–1	94	0	0	0	0	19	15.8
R	36	Jeff Odgers	S.J.	48	4	3	7	–8	117	0	0	1	0	47	8.5
D	2	Jim Kyte	S.J.	18	2	5	7	–7	33	0	0	1	0	14	14.3
D	4	Jay More	S.J.	45	0	6	6	7	71	0	0	0	0	25	0.0
D	3	Ilya Byakin	S.J.	13	0	5	5	–9	14	0	0	0	0	19	0.0
D	38	* Michal Sykora	S.J.	16	0	4	4	6	10	0	0	0	0	6	0.0
C	09	V. Butsayev	S.J.	6	2	0	2	–2	0	0	0	0	0	6	33.3
R	47	* Viktor Kozlov	S.J.	16	2	0	2	–5	2	0	0	0	0	23	8.7
C	16	* Dody Wood	S.J.	9	1	1	2	0	29	0	0	0	0	5	20.0
D	26	Vlastimil Kroupa	S.J.	14	0	2	2	–7	16	0	0	0	0	4	0.0
D	44	Shawn Cronin	S.J.	29	0	2	2	0	61	0	0	0	0	12	0.0
G	31	Wade Flaherty	S.J.	18	0	1	1	0	0	0	0	0	0	0	0.0
R	42	* Shean Donovan	S.J.	14	0	0	0	–6	6	0	0	0	0	13	0.0
G	32	Arturs Irbe	S.J.	38	0	0	0	0	4	0	0	0	0	0	0.0

Goaltending

No.	Goaltender	GPI	Mins	Avg	W	L	T	EN	SO	GA	SA	S%
31	Wade Flaherty	18	852	3.10	5	6	1	2	1	44	455	.903
32	Arturs Irbe	38	2043	3.26	14	19	3	4	4	111	1056	.895
	Totals	**48**	**2904**	**3.33**	**19**	**25**	**4**	**6**	**5**	**161**	**1517**	**.894**

Playoffs

Pos	#	Player	Team	GP	G	A	Pts	+/–	PIM	PP	SH	GW	OT	S	%
R	22	Ulf Dahlen	S.J.	11	5	4	9	–13	0	3	0	1	1	19	26.3
C	7	Igor Larionov	S.J.	11	1	8	9	–4	2	0	0	0	0	19	5.3
C	14	Ray Whitney	S.J.	11	4	4	8	–3	2	0	0	1	1	15	26.7
D	40	Mike Rathje	S.J.	11	5	2	7	–15	4	5	0	0	0	18	27.8
C	15	Craig Janney	S.J.	11	3	4	7	–13	4	0	0	1	0	17	17.6
R	24	Sergei Makarov	S.J.	11	3	3	6	–3	4	0	0	0	0	8	37.5
L	39	* Jeff Friesen	S.J.	11	1	5	6	–9	4	0	0	0	0	21	4.8
D	6	Sandis Ozolinsh	S.J.	11	3	2	5	–13	6	1	0	0	0	15	20.0
D	41	Tom Pederson	S.J.	10	0	5	5	–14	8	0	0	0	0	14	0.0
R	17	Pat Falloon	S.J.	11	3	1	4	–6	0	0	0	0	0	24	12.5
C	13	Jamie Baker	S.J.	11	2	2	4	–7	12	0	0	1	0	20	10.0
D	4	Jay More	S.J.	11	0	4	4	0	6	0	0	0	0	11	0.0
C	18	Chris Tancill	S.J.	11	1	1	2	–7	8	0	0	0	0	16	6.3
R	36	Jeff Odgers	S.J.	11	1	1	2	0	23	0	0	0	0	5	20.0
D	2	Jim Kyte	S.J.	11	0	2	2	–1	14	0	0	0	0	8	0.0
R	42	* Shean Donovan	S.J.	7	0	1	1	–3	6	0	0	0	0	7	0.0
R	8	Kevin Miller	S.J.	6	0	0	0	–3	2	0	0	0	0	7	0.0
G	32	Arturs Irbe	S.J.	6	0	0	0	0	10	0	0	0	0	0	0.0
R	23	* Andrei Nazarov	S.J.	6	0	0	0	0	9	0	0	0	0	3	0.0
D	26	Vlastimil Kroupa	S.J.	6	0	0	0	–3	4	0	0	0	0	3	0.0
G	31	Wade Flaherty	S.J.	7	0	0	0	0	0	0	0	0	0	0	0.0
D	44	Shawn Cronin	S.J.	9	0	0	0	2	5	0	0	0	0	1	0.0

Goaltending

No.	Goaltender	GPI	Mins	Avg	W	L	EN	SO	GA	SA	S%
31	Wade Flaherty	7	377	4.93	2	3	0	0	31	221	.860
32	Arturs Irbe	6	316	5.13	2	4	1	0	27	184	.853
	Totals	**11**	**694**	**5.10**	**4**	**7**	**1**	**0**	**59**	**406**	**.855**

Coaching History

George Kingston, 1991-92 to 1992-93; Kevin Constantine, 1993-94 to date.

Club Records

Team

(Figures in brackets for season records are games played; records for fewest points, wins, ties, losses, goals, goals against are for 70 or more games)

Most Points	82	1993-94 (84)
Most Wins	33	1993-94 (84)
Most Ties	16	1993-94 (84)
Most Losses	*71	1992-93 (84)
Most Goals	252	1993-94 (84)
Most Goals Against	414	1992-93 (84)
Fewest Points	24	1992-93 (84)
Fewest Wins	11	1992-93 (84)
Fewest Ties	*2	1992-93 (84)
Fewest Losses	35	1993-94 (84)
Fewest Goals	218	1992-93 (84)
Fewest Goals Against	265	1993-94 (84)

Longest Winning Streak
Overall	7	Mar. 24-Apr. 5/94
Home	5	Jan. 21-Feb. 15/95
Away	4	Mar. 24-Apr. 5/94

Longest Undefeated Streak
Overall	9	Mar. 20-Apr. 5/94 (7 wins, 2 ties)
Home	6	Mar. 20-Apr. 13/94 (4 wins, 2 ties)
Away	5	Two times

Longest Losing Streak
Overall	*17	Jan. 4/93-Feb. 12/93
Home	9	Nov. 19/92-Dec. 19/92
Away	19	Nov. 27/92-Feb. 12/93

Longest Winless Streak
Overall	20	Dec. 29/92-Feb. 12/93 (0-19-1)
Home	9	Nov. 19/92-Dec. 18/92 (0-9-0)
Away	19	Nov. 27/92-Feb. 12/93 (0-19-0)

Most Shutouts, Season	5	1994-95 (48)
Most PIM, Season	2134	1992-93 (84)
Most Goals, Game	9	Mar. 29/94 (Wpg. 4 at S.J. 9)

Individual

Most Seasons	4	Pat Falloon, Jayson More, Jeff Odgers
Most Games, Career	256	Jeff Odgers
Most Goals, Career	73	Pat Falloon
Most Assists, Career	86	Johan Garpenlov, Pat Falloon
Most Points, Career	159	Pat Falloon (73 goals, 86 assists)
Most PIM, Career	809	Jeff Odgers
Most Shutouts, Career	8	Arturs Irbe

Longest Consecutive Games Streak	117	Doug Zmolek (Oct. 8/92-Dec. 15/93)
Most Goals, Season	30	Sergei Makarov (1993-94)
Most Assists, Season	52	Kelly Kisio (1992-93)
Most Points, Season	78	Kelly Kisio (1992-93) (26 goals, 52 assists)
Most PIM, Season	326	Link Gaetz (1991-92)
Most Shutouts, Season	4	Arturs Irbe (1994-95)
Most Points, Defenseman Season	64	Sandis Ozolnish (1993-94) (26 goals, 38 assists)
Most Points, Center, Season	78	Kelly Kisio (1992-93) (26 goals, 52 assists)
Most Points, Right Wing, Season	68	Sergei Makarov (1993-94) (30 goals, 38 assists)
Most Points, Left Wing, Season	66	Johan Garpenlov (1992-93) (22 goals, 44 assists)
Most Points, Rookie, Season	59	Pat Falloon (1991-92) (25 goals, 34 assists)
Most Goals, Game	3	Eight times
Most Assists, Game	4	Two times
Most Points, Game	4	Seventeen times

* NHL Record.

Entry Draft Selections 1995-91

1995
Pick
12	Teemu Riihijarvi
38	Peter Roed
64	Marko Makinen
90	Vesa Toskala
116	Miikka Kiprusoff
130	Michal Bros
140	Timo Hakanen
142	Jaroslav Kudrna
167	Brad Mehalko
168	Robert Jindrich
194	Ryan Kraft
220	Miiko Markkanen

1994
Pick
11	Jeff Friesen
37	Angel Nikolov
66	Alexei Yegorov
89	Vaclav Varada
115	Brian Swanson
141	Alexander Korolyuk
167	Sergei Gorbachev
193	Eric Landry
219	Yevgeny Nabokov
240	Tomas Pisa
245	Aniket Dhadphale
271	David Beauregard

1993
Pick
6	Viktor Kozlov
28	Shean Donovan
45	Vlastimil Kroupa
58	Ville Peltonen
80	Alexander Osadchy
106	Andrei Buschan
132	Petri Varis
154	Fredrik Oduya
158	Anatoli Filatov
184	Todd Holt
210	Jonas Forsberg
236	Jeff Salajko
262	Jamie Matthews

1992
Pick
3	Mike Rathje
10	Andrei Nazarov
51	Alexander Cherbajev
75	Jan Caloun
99	Marcus Ragnarsson
123	Michal Sykora
147	Eric Bellerose
171	Ryan Smith
195	Chris Burns
219	A. Kholomeyev
243	Victor Ignatjev

1991
Pick
2	Pat Falloon
23	Ray Whitney
30	Sandis Ozolinsh
45	Dody Wood
67	Kerry Toporowski
89	Dan Ryder
111	Fredrik Nilsson
133	Jaroslav Otevrel
155	Dean Grillo
177	Corwin Saurdiff
199	Dale Craigwell
221	Aaron Kriss
243	Mikhail Kravets

General Managers' History

Jack Ferreira, 1991-92; Office of the General Manager: Chuck Grillo (V.P. Director of Player Personnel) and Dean Lombardi (V.P. Director of Hockey Operations), 1992-93 to date.

Captains' History

Doug Wilson, 1991-92 to 1992-93; Bob Errey, 1993-94; Bob Errey and Jeff Odgers, 1994-95; Jeff Odgers, 1995-96.

All-time Record vs. Other Clubs

Regular Season

		At Home						On Road						Total				
	GP	W	L	T	GF	GA	PTS	GP	W	L	T	GF	GA	PTS	GP	W	L	T	GF	GA	PTS
Anaheim	5	3	2	0	17	15	6	6	4	2	0	20	16	8	11	7	4	0	37	31	14
Boston	3	0	2	1	4	13	1	3	0	3	0	10	14	0	6	0	5	1	14	27	1
Buffalo	3	1	1	1	12	16	3	4	0	4	0	16	21	0	7	1	5	1	28	37	3
Calgary	14	2	11	1	34	51	5	12	3	9	0	30	66	6	26	5	20	1	64	117	11
Chicago	8	5	3	0	22	22	10	7	1	5	1	17	28	3	15	6	8	1	39	50	13
Dallas	7	3	4	0	20	29	6	7	2	4	1	23	32	5	14	5	8	1	43	61	11
Detroit	8	1	6	1	24	42	3	7	0	7	0	10	37	0	15	1	13	1	34	79	3
Edmonton	12	8	3	1	48	29	17	13	1	10	2	31	59	4	25	9	13	3	79	88	21
Florida	1	1	0	0	2	1	2	1	0	0	1	3	3	1	2	1	0	1	5	4	3
Hartford	3	2	1	0	19	14	4	4	2	2	0	10	13	4	7	4	3	0	29	27	8
Los Angeles	13	6	5	2	48	43	14	12	3	8	1	28	42	7	25	9	13	3	76	85	21
Montreal	4	0	2	2	6	8	2	4	0	4	0	7	21	0	8	0	6	2	13	29	2
New Jersey	3	1	2	0	5	10	2	4	0	4	1	7	20	2	7	2	5	1	12	30	4
NY Islanders	3	2	1	0	8	12	4	4	0	4	0	15	27	0	7	2	5	0	23	39	4
NY Rangers	4	0	4	0	9	22	0	3	0	2	1	7	15	1	7	0	6	1	16	37	1
Ottawa	2	1	1	0	4	4	2	2	0	2	0	6	9	0	4	1	3	0	10	13	2
Philadelphia	4	1	3	0	9	14	2	3	0	2	1	7	12	2	7	1	5	1	16	26	4
Pittsburgh	4	0	3	1	10	27	1	3	0	3	0	6	19	1	7	0	6	1	16	46	2
Quebec	4	2	2	0	20	21	4	3	0	3	0	9	17	0	7	2	5	0	29	38	4
St. Louis	6	0	6	0	11	23	0	9	1	8	0	19	39	2	15	1	14	0	30	62	2
Tampa Bay	3	0	3	0	9	13	0	3	2	1	0	5	7	4	6	2	4	0	14	20	4
Toronto	8	3	4	1	16	20	7	7	2	4	1	14	27	5	15	5	8	2	30	47	12
Vancouver	13	4	7	2	39	47	10	12	2	9	1	27	50	5	25	6	16	3	66	97	15
Washington	3	0	3	0	7	12	0	3	1	2	0	7	12	2	6	1	5	0	14	24	2
Winnipeg	10	5	3	2	46	40	12	12	3	7	2	35	45	8	22	8	10	4	81	85	20
Totals	**148**	**51**	**82**	**15**	**449**	**548**	**117**	**148**	**29**	**107**	**12**	**369**	**651**	**70**	**296**	**80**	**189**	**27**	**818**	**1199**	**187**

Dallas totals include Minnesota, 1991-92 to 1992-93.

Playoffs

	Series	W	L	GP	W	L	T	GF	GA	Last Mtg.	Round	Result
Calgary	1	1	0	7	4	3	0	26	35	1995	CQF	W 4-3
Detroit	2	1	1	11	4	7	0	27	51	1995	CSF	L 0-4
Toronto	1	0	1	7	3	4	0	21	26	1994	CSF	L 3-4
Totals	**4**	**2**	**2**	**25**	**11**	**14**	**0**	**74**	**112**			

Playoff Results 1995-91

Year	Round	Opponent	Result	GF	GA
1995	CSF	Detroit	L 0-4	6	24
	CQF	Calgary	W 4-3	26	35
1994	CSF	Toronto	L 3-4	21	26
	CQF	Detroit	W 4-3	21	27

Abbreviations: Round: F – Final;
CF – conference final; **CQF** – conference quarter-final;
CSF – conference semi-final; **DF** – division final;
DSF – division semi-final; **SF** – semi-final;
QF – quarter-final; **PR** – preliminary round.

1994-95 Results

Jan. 20		St. Louis	2-5	19	at	Calgary	5-3
21		Toronto	3-2	21		Chicago	3-7
25		Winnipeg	4-0	23	at	Anaheim	3-6
28		Dallas	3-2	25	at	Los Angeles	3-1
30		Chicago	2-1	26		Los Angeles	3-7
Feb. 2	at	Dallas	2-1	28		Winnipeg	6-5
4	at	Winnipeg	3-3	31	at	St. Louis	1-4
6	at	Toronto	3-7	Apr. 2	at	Anaheim	4-5
7	at	Detroit	0-6	5		Detroit	3-5
10	at	Edmonton	1-5	7		Edmonton	5-0
11	at	Vancouver	1-1	9	at	Edmonton	5-2
15		Vancouver	3-1	10	at	Calgary	3-8
17	at	Los Angeles	2-0	12	at	Chicago	3-2
18		Anaheim	3-6	13	at	Detroit	0-3
20	at	Chicago	2-3	16		Los Angeles	2-0
22	at	St. Louis	3-4	17	at	Anaheim	5-5
24		Calgary	0-3	19	at	Dallas	5-5
26		Vancouver	1-5	23		Detroit	1-5
28	at	Vancouver	4-3	25		Calgary	2-3
Mar. 2	at	Toronto	4-3	26	at	Anaheim	5-2
4	at	Winnipeg	2-4	28		Los Angeles	4-0
8		Edmonton	2-5	30		St. Louis	3-4
15		Toronto	1-2	May 1		Dallas	3-1
17	at	Edmonton	3-5	3		Vancouver	3-3

Office of the General Manager

LOMBARDI, DEAN
Executive Vice President and Director of Hockey Operations, San Jose Sharks.
Born in Holyoke, Massachusetts, March 5, 1958.

Dean Lombardi enters his eighth year in the National Hockey League and his sixth with the Sharks. Before joining the Sharks, he spent two seasons as assistant general manager with the Minnesota North Stars.

Lombardi, 37, oversees and is well versed in contract negotiations and knowledge of the NHL's business and legal workings. In 1994-95, he worked with NHL owners and agents to bring about a settlement in the league's labor stoppage, re-signed veteran players and brought talented newcomers into the Sharks fold.

His constant search for Stanley Cup success led to some difficult personnel decisions in 1994-95, but also to another visit to the second round of the playoffs (one of only four teams to do so over the past two seasons).

He was, and continues to be, instrumental in constructing key trades, including the March 1995 acquisitions of Craig Janney and Kevin Miller.

Lombardi was one of the NHL's groundbreakers in negotiating the release of players under contract to European clubs. His research has assisted relations between the NHL and the Russian Ice Hockey Federation.

On the ice, Lombardi was captain during his final two seasons at the University of New Haven where he earned the school's student/athlete of the year award. He also was named to the Junior All-America team in 1978 while playing for the Springfield (MA) Olympics.

GRILLO, CHUCK
Executive Vice President and Director of Player Personnel, San Jose Sharks.
Born in Hibbing, Minnesota, July 24, 1939.

Moving into his 16th NHL season and sixth with the Sharks is Chuck Grillo who supervises the club's scouting department and player development program.

Grillo was promoted to executive vice president on March 23, 1995. He had been a vice president since June 26, 1992. He served as director of pro scouting from 1988-90 with the Minnesota North Stars, preceded by eight years as a scout for the New York Rangers.

One of only two U.S.-born player personnel directors in the NHL, Grillo is noted for his ability to recognize talent and implement innovative ideas for player development. He has participated in the NHL draft process since 1981. His contributions have led to the selection of 39 players who are established NHL performers, and nearly 30 others who either have NHL experience or are on the verge of breaking into the league. Out of 14 first-round selections for whom he has been responsible, all 14 have become NHL regulars.

Grillo, 56, also is owner and operator of a successful hockey camp in Nisswa, MN. Many athletes at the camp have gone on to become players, coaches and trainers in the NHL.

Grillo spent 16 years as a high school hockey and baseball coach, taking teams to the Minnesota state tournament on 11 occasions.

He is working toward a doctorate in educational administration from Bemidji State University.

Club Directory

San Jose Arena
525 West Santa Clara Street
P.O. Box 1240
San Jose, California 95113
Phone **408/287-7070**
FAX 408/999-5797
Capacity: 17,190

Executive Staff
Majority Owner & Chairman	George Gund III
Co-Owner	Gordon Gund
President & Chief Executive Officer	Arthur L. Savage
Exec. Vice President, Director of Player Personnel	Chuck Grillo
Exec. Vice President, Chief Operating Officer	Greg Jamison
Exec. Vice President, Building Operations	Frank Jirik
Exec. Vice President, Development	Matt Levine
Exec. Vice President, Director of Hockey Operations	Dean Lombardi
Vice Chairman	Tom McEnery
Vice President, Chief Financial Officer	Gregg Olson
Chief of Staff to President & CEO	Karen C. Shiraki
Executive Assistant to President & CEO	Dawn Beres

Hockey
Head Coach	Kevin Constantine
Assistant Coach & Ass't to the Dir. of Hockey Oper.	Wayne Thomas
Assistant Coach	Drew Remenda
Assistant Coach	Vasily Tikhonov
Strength & Conditioning Coach	Steve Millard
Coaching Staff Assistant	Derek Eisler
Head Coach, Kansas City Blades	Jim Wiley
Assistant Coach, Kansas City Blades	Mark Kaufman
Assistant to the Director of Player Personnel	Joe Will
Director of Hockey Administration	Brenda Will
Professional/Amateur Scout	Tim Burke
Scout and Player Development	Pat Funk
Scout and Player Development	Rob Grillo
Area Scouts	Tim Gorski (Alaska), George Gund III (International), Steve Harrison (Minor pro), Konstantin Krylov (Russia), Erkki Liesmaki (Finland), Dimitri Lopuchin (Fitness consultant), Karel Masopust (Czech. Republic), Jack Morganstern (New England), Dan Summers (Manitoba)
Video Scouting Coordinator	Bob Friedlander
Head Trainer	Tom Woodcock
Equipment Manager	Bob Crocker, Jr.
Assistant Equipment Manager	Sergei Tchekmarev
Travel Coordinator	Steve Perry
Equipment Assistant	Jason Rude
Head Trainer, Kansas City Blades	Les Lundberg
Team Physician	Arthur J. Ting, M.D.
Team Dentist	Robert Bonahoom, D.D.S.
Team Vision Specialist	Vincent S. Zuccaro, O.D., F.A.A.O.
Medical Staff	Warren King, M.D., James Klint, M.D., Will Straw, M.D.

Business Operations
Vice President, Broadcast & Media Marketing	Malcolm Bordelon
Director of Media Relations	Ken Arnold
Director of Ticket Sales	Rich Muschell
Director of Community Development	Lori Smith
Director of Broadcasting	Mark Stulberger

Director of Marketing	Elaine Sullivan-Digre
Director of Event Services	Diane Bloom
Executive Assistant	Michelle Simmons
Account Service Managers	Annie Chan-Zien, Elizabeth Smith, Paul Solby, Gene Wiggins
Assistant Director of Media Relations	Paul Turner
Ticket Manager	Mary Enriquez
Media Marketing Managers	Jim Josel, Don Olvarado, Ted Atlee
Manager, Educational Marketing	J.D. Kershaw
Media Relations Assistant	Roger Ross
Suite Hospitality Managers	Pat Swan, Coleen Duncan
Sponsorship Services Coordinator	Valerie Bigelow
Promotions and Broadcast Coordinator	Patti Sircus
Tour Administrator	Dianna Carthew
Assistant Ticket Manager	John Castro
Assistant, Community Development	Lou Siville
S.J. Arena Administrative Marketing Assistant	Beth Brigino
Assistant, Executive Suite Services	Steward Diner
Ticket Sales Assistant	Kris Lyon
Assistant, Event Services	Anna Saalfield
Mascot Coordinator	Jason Minsky
Mascot	S.J. Sharkie

Development
Executive Assistant	Joyce Coppola

Finance
Manager, Accounting	Colleen Baker
Manager, Budget & Analysis	Steve Calamia
Manager, Information Systems	Alex Ignacio
Manager, Taxation & GGIII Accounting	Ken Caveney
Staff Accountant, Arena	Sarah McEnery
Staff Accountant, Sharks	Elaine Rappaport
Accounting Associate, Payroll	Sue Feachen
Accounting Associate, GGIII Accounting	Diane Rubino
Sytems Support Analyst	Wee Yap
Exec. Assistant/Human Resources Coordinator	Carol Ross

Building Operations
Vice President	Jim Goddard
Director of Guest Services	Colleen Reilly
Director of Ticket Operations	Daniel DeBoer
Executive Assistant	Chris Palmer
Ticket Office Manager	Judy Jones
Facilities Technical Director	Bob McCrobie
Building Services Managers	Bruce Tharaldson
Building Services Managers	John Jordan
Building Services Managers	Blair Engelbrekt
Building Services Coordinator	George Gund IV
Building Services Coordinator	Greg Gund
Mailroom Coordinator	Helen Howen
Administrative Assistants	Beth Ganeff, Cathy Hancock

Aramark
General Manager	Dale Haynes
Concessions Manager	Julie Whoriskey
Financial Controller	Larry Tokarski
Restaurant Manager/Executive Chef	Jurgen Pauer
Merchandise Manager	Dawn Haney
Suites/Catering Manager	Judy Moline

Miscellaneous
Team Colors	Pacific Teal, Gray, Black, White
Dimensions of Rink	200 feet by 85 feet
Television Stations	KICU-TV 36, SportsChannel
Radio Network Flagship	KFRC (610-AM) or (99.7-FM)
Spanish Language Radio Netewerk Flagship	KLOK (1170-AM)
Play-By-Play (Radio)	Dan Rusanowsky
Play-By-Play (Television)	Randy Hahn
Play-By-Play (Spanish Radio)	Erwin Higueros
Color Commentator (Television)	Pete Stemkowski
Color Commentator (Radio)	Chris Collins
P.A. Announcer	TBA
Organist	Dieter Ruehle

Tampa Bay Lightning

1994-95 Results: 17w-28L-3T 37PTS. Sixth, Atlantic Division

Year-by-Year Record

Season	GP	Home			Road			Overall					Pts.	Finished		Playoff Result
		W	L	T	W	L	T	W	L	T	GF	GA				
1994-95	48	10	14	0	7	14	3	17	28	3	120	144	37	6th,	Atlantic Div.	Out of Playoffs
1993-94	84	14	22	6	16	21	5	30	43	11	224	251	71	7th,	Atlantic Div.	Out of Playoffs
1992-93	84	12	27	7	11	27	4	23	54	7	245	332	53	6th,	Norris Div.	Out of Playoffs

Schedule

Oct.	Sat.	7	Calgary
	Thur.	12	Montreal
	Sat.	14	at Washington
	Sun.	15	Ottawa
	Tues.	17	at Winnipeg
	Thur.	19	at Chicago
	Sat.	21	at Dallas
	Thur.	26	NY Rangers
	Sat.	28	Washington
	Tues.	31	at Philadelphia
Nov.	Wed.	1	at Pittsburgh
	Fri.	3	NY Islanders
	Sun.	5	at Florida
	Wed.	8	at NY Rangers
	Fri.	10	Edmonton
	Sun.	12	Buffalo
	Tues.	14	Boston
	Thur.	16	Toronto
	Sat.	18	Vancouver
	Wed.	22	New Jersey
	Fri.	24	at Washington
	Sat.	25	at NY Islanders
	Mon.	27	Los Angeles
	Wed.	29	Hartford
Dec.	Fri.	1	at New Jersey
	Sun.	3	Pittsburgh
	Wed.	6	Anaheim
	Fri.	8	Boston
	Sun.	10	at Buffalo
	Wed.	13	at Hartford
	Thur.	14	at Philadelphia
	Sat.	16	Florida
	Tues.	19	Winnipeg
	Thur.	21	New Jersey
	Sat.	23	at Boston
	Thur.	28	Montreal
	Sun.	31	at Ottawa
Jan.	Tues.	2	at Calgary
	Wed.	3	at Edmonton
	Sat.	6	at Vancouver
	Mon.	8	at Montreal

	Sat.	13	Ottawa
	Mon.	15	at NY Islanders*
	Wed.	17	San Jose
	Mon.	22	at Montreal
	Thur.	25	at Boston
	Sat.	27	at St. Louis*
	Wed.	31	Pittsburgh
Feb.	Sat.	3	Florida*
	Sun.	4	at Buffalo*
	Wed.	7	at Colorado
	Sat.	10	Detroit*
	Sun.	11	NY Rangers*
	Tues.	13	St. Louis
	Thur.	15	Colorado
	Sat.	17	Philadelphia
	Mon.	19	Dallas
	Wed.	21	at Toronto
	Fri.	23	at NY Islanders
	Sat.	24	at Detroit
	Wed.	28	at Los Angeles
Mar.	Fri.	1	at San Jose
	Sun.	3	at Anaheim
	Tues.	5	Chicago
	Thur.	7	NY Rangers
	Sun.	10	Washington*
	Wed.	13	at Philadelphia
	Fri.	15	at New Jersey
	Sun.	17	at Ottawa*
	Mon.	18	at Hartford
	Thur.	21	Washington
	Sat.	23	Florida
	Tues.	26	New Jersey
	Sat.	30	at Florida
	Sun.	31	at Washington
Apr.	Wed.	3	Hartford
	Fri.	5	Buffalo
	Sat.	6	at Pittsburgh
	Mon.	8	NY Islanders
	Wed.	10	at Florida
	Fri.	12	at NY Rangers
	Sun.	14	Philadelphia*

* Denotes afternoon game.

Home Starting Times:

Weeknights	7:35 p.m.
Matinees	3:05 p.m.
Except Mon. Feb. 19	5:05 p.m.
Sun. Mar. 10	1:35 p.m.

Franchise date: December 16, 1991

4th NHL Season

ATLANTIC DIVISION

The first player selected in the 1993 Entry Draft, Roman Hamrlik led the Lightning with seven powerplay goals in 1994-95.

1995-96 Player Personnel

FORWARDS	HT	WT	S	Place of Birth	Date	1994-95 Club
ANDERSSON, Mikael	5-11	185	L	Malmo, Sweden	5/10/66	V. Frolunda-Tampa Bay
BELLOWS, Brian	5-11	210	R	St. Catharines, Ont.	9/1/64	Montreal
BRADLEY, Brian	5-10	177	R	Kitchener, Ont.	1/21/65	Tampa Bay
BURR, Shawn	6-1	195	L	Sarnia, Ont.	7/1/66	Detroit
CAMPEAU, Christian	5-10	180	R	Verdun, Que.	6/2/71	Atlanta
CLOUTIER, Colin	6-3	224	L	Winnipeg, Man.	1/27/76	Brandon
EGELAND, Allan	6-0	184	L	Lethbridge, Alta.	1/31/73	Atlanta
GAVEY, Aaron	6-1	175	L	Sudbury, Ont.	2/22/74	Atlanta
GERVAIS, Shawn	6-0	190	L	Falher, Alta.	7/12/76	Seattle
GOLOKHVASTOV, Konstantin	6-1	185	R	Dneprodzerzinsk, USSR	2/6/77	Moscow D'amo
GRATTON, Chris	6-3	212	L	Brantford, Ont.	7/5/75	Tampa Bay
KACIR, Marian	6-1	183	L	Hodonin, Czech.	9/29/74	Charlotte-Nashville-Chicago (IHL)
KLIMA, Petr	6-0	190	R	Chomutov, Czech.	12/23/64	Wolfsburg-ZPS Zlin-Tampa Bay
LANGKOW, Daymond	5-10	170	L	Edmonton, Alta	9/27/76	Tri-City
MACDONALD, Tom	5-11	190	L	Toronto, Ont.	4/14/74	Nashville
MYHRES, Brantt	6-3	220	R	Edmonton, Alta.	3/18/74	Atlanta-Tampa Bay
PERSHIN, Eduard	6-0	191	L	Nizhnekamsk, USSR	9/1/77	Moscow D'amo
PETERSON, Brent	6-3	200	L	Calgary, Alta.	7/20/72	Michigan Tech
POESCHEK, Rudy	6-2	210	R	Kamloops, B.C.	9/29/66	Tampa Bay
RUFF, Jason	6-2	192	L	Kelowna, B.C.	1/27/70	Atlanta
SELIVANOV, Alexander	6-1	187	L	Moscow, USSR	3/23/71	Atlanta-Chicago (IHL)-Tampa Bay
SEMAK, Alexander	5-10	180	R	Ufa, USSR	2/11/66	Ufa Salavat-N.J.-T.B.
SMIRNOV, Yuri	5-11	172	L	Moscow, USSR	1/10/76	Spartak
TOMS, Jeff	6-3	180	L	Swift Current, Sask.	6/4/74	Atlanta
TUCKER, John	6-0	200	R	Windsor, Ont.	9/29/64	Tampa Bay
WIEMER, Jason	6-1	215	L	Kimberley, B.C.	4/14/76	Portland (WHL)-Tampa Bay
WILLIS, Shane	6-0	170	R	Edmonton, Alta.	6/13/77	Prince Albert
YSEBAERT, Paul	6-1	190	L	Sarnia, Ont.	5/15/66	Chicago-Tampa Bay
ZAMUNER, Rob	6-2	202	L	Oakville, Ont.	9/17/69	Tampa Bay
DEFENSEMEN						
BANNISTER, Drew	6-1	193	R	Belleville, Ont.	9/4/74	Atlanta
BARANOV, Alexei	6-1	174	R	Lipetsk, USSR	6/3/76	Moscow D'amo
CHARRON, Eric	6-3	192	L	Verdun, Que.	1/14/70	Tampa Bay
CICCONE, Enrico	6-4	210	L	Montreal, Que.	4/10/70	Tampa Bay
CROSS, Cory	6-5	212	L	Lloydminster, Alta.	1/3/71	Atlanta-Tampa Bay
DUBOIS, Eric	6-0	195	R	Montreal, Que.	5/9/70	Atlanta
HALKIDIS, Bob	5-11	205	L	Toronto, Ont.	3/5/66	Detroit-Tampa Bay
HAMRLIK, Roman	6-2	202	L	Gottwaldov, Czech.	4/12/74	ZPS Zlin-Tampa Bay
HOULDER, Bill	6-3	218	L	Thunder Bay, Ont.	3/11/67	St. Louis
LAPORTE, Alexandre	6-3	210	R	Cowansville, Que.	5/1/75	St-Hyacinthe-Drummondville
LIPUMA, Chris	6-0	183	L	Bridgeview, IL	3/23/71	Atlanta-Tampa Bay-Nashville
MAILLET, Chris	6-5	188	L	Moncton, NB	1/28/76	Red Deer
McBAIN, Mike	6-1	191	L	Kimberley, B.C.	1/12/77	Red Deer
PLAVSIC, Adrien	6-1	200	L	Montreal, Que.	1/13/70	Vancouver-Tampa Bay
RABY, Mathieu	6-2	204	R	Hull, Que.	1/19/75	Victoriaville-Sherbrooke
SHAW, David	6-2	205	R	St. Thomas, Ont.	5/25/64	Boston

GOALTENDERS	HT	WT	C	Place of Birth	Date	1994-95 Club
BERGERON, Jean-Claude	6-2	192	L	Hauterive, Que.	10/14/68	Atlanta-Tampa Bay
MOSS, Tyler	6-0	168	R	Ottawa, Ont.	6/29/75	Kingston
PUPPA, Daren	6-3	205	R	Kirkland Lake, Ont.	3/23/65	Tampa Bay
WILKINSON, Derek	6-0	160	L	Lasalle, Que.	7/29/74	Atlanta

1994-95 Scoring

* – rookie

Regular Season

Pos	#	Player	Team	GP	G	A	Pts	+/-	PIM	PP	SH	GW	GT	S	%
C	19	Brian Bradley	T.B.	46	13	27	40	–6	42	3	0	2	0	111	11.7
L	15	Paul Ysebaert	CHI	15	4	5	9	4	6	0	0	1	0	23	17.4
			T.B.	29	8	11	19	–1	12	0	0	0	0	70	11.4
			TOTAL	44	12	16	28	3	18	0	0	1	0	93	12.9
C	77	Chris Gratton	T.B.	46	7	20	27	–2	89	2	0	0	0	91	7.7
R	85	Petr Klima	T.B.	47	13	13	26	–13	26	4	0	3	0	75	17.3
R	14	John Tucker	T.B.	46	12	13	25	–10	14	2	0	1	0	81	14.8
D	44	Roman Hamrlik	T.B.	48	12	11	23	–18	86	7	1	2	0	134	9.0
C	27	Alexander Semak	N.J.	19	2	6	8	–4	13	0	0	0	0	32	6.3
			T.B.	22	5	5	10	–3	12	0	0	1	0	39	12.8
			TOTAL	41	7	11	18	–7	25	0	0	1	0	71	9.9
R	29	* Alexander Selivanov	T.B.	43	10	6	16	–2	14	4	0	3	0	94	10.6
L	7	Rob Zamuner	T.B.	43	9	6	15	–3	24	0	3	1	0	74	12.2
C	28	Marc Bureau	T.B.	48	2	12	14	–8	30	0	1	0	1	72	2.8
L	34	Mikael Andersson	T.B.	36	4	7	11	–3	4	0	0	0	0	36	11.1
D	39	Enrico Ciccone	T.B.	41	2	4	6	3	225	0	0	0	0	43	4.7
D	25	Marc Bergevin	T.B.	44	2	4	6	–6	51	0	1	0	0	32	6.3
D	4	* Cory Cross	T.B.	43	1	5	6	–6	41	0	0	1	0	35	2.9
D	21	Bob Halkidis	DET	4	0	1	1	2	6	0	0	0	0	0	0.0
			T.B.	27	1	3	4	–12	40	0	0	0	0	25	4.0
			TOTAL	31	1	4	5	–10	46	0	0	0	0	25	4.0
L	9	* Jason Wiemer	T.B.	36	1	4	5	–2	44	0	0	0	0	10	10.0
D	3	* Eric Charron	T.B.	45	1	4	5	1	26	0	0	0	0	33	3.0
D	6	Adrien Plavsic	VAN	3	0	1	1	3	4	0	0	0	0	11	0.0
			T.B.	15	2	1	3	5	4	0	0	0	0	24	8.3
			TOTAL	18	2	2	4	8	8	0	0	0	0	35	5.7
R	33	* Brantt Myhres	T.B.	15	2	0	2	–2	81	0	0	1	0	4	50.0
D	20	Rudy Poeschek	T.B.	25	1	1	2	0	92	0	0	0	0	14	7.1
R	16	* Ben Hankinson	N.J.	8	0	0	0	–6	7	0	0	0	0	8	0.0
			T.B.	18	0	2	2	1	6	0	0	0	0	18	0.0
			TOTAL	26	0	2	2	–5	13	0	0	0	0	26	0.0
C	49	* Brent Gretzky	T.B.	3	0	1	1	–2	0	0	0	0	0	1	0.0
G	93	Daren Puppa	T.B.	36	0	1	1	0	2	0	0	0	0	0	0.0
L	17	Gerard Gallant	T.B.	1	0	0	0	0	0	0	0	0	0	1	0.0
D	26	Chris Lipuma	T.B.	1	0	0	0	2	0	0	0	0	0	1	0.0
G	30	J.C. Bergeron	T.B.	17	0	0	0	0	2	0	0	0	0	0	0.0

Goaltending

No.	Goaltender	GPI	Mins	Avg	W	L	T	EN	SO	GA	SA	S%
93	Daren Puppa	36	2013	2.68	14	19	2	4	1	90	946	.905
30	J.C. Bergeron	17	883	3.33	3	9	1	1	1	49	374	.869
	Totals	**48**	**2906**	**2.97**	**17**	**28**	**3**	**5**	**2**	**144**	**1325**	**.891**

General Manager

ESPOSITO, PHIL
General Manager, Tampa Bay Lightning.
Born in Sault Ste. Marie, Ont., February 20, 1942.

Phil Esposito, who headed up Tampa Bay's successful campaign to obtain an NHL franchise, was rewarded for his hard work when the Lightning were granted a berth in the NHL, beginning with the 1992-93 season. After an 18-year Hall-of-Fame career that included eight All-Star selections as well as winning the Hart Trophy twice and the Art Ross Trophy five times, Esposito was named vice president and general manager of the NY Rangers in 1986, remaining in that role until the start of the 1989-90 season. He also doubled as coach during the 1986-87 campaign and took over the bench duties again at the conclusion of 1988-89. Esposito, who began his career with Chicago and finished his playing days with the NY Rangers, had his most productive days with the Boston Bruins, winning a pair of Stanley Cup titles while establishing numerous team records, including most goals (76) and points (152) in a single season. In 1968-69, he became the first NHL player to record 100 points in a season.

NHL Coaching Record

		Regular Season					Playoffs			
Season	Team	Games	W	L	T	%	Games	W	L	%
1986-87	NY Rangers (NHL)	43	24	19	0	.558	6	2	4	.333
1988-89	NY Rangers (NHL)	2	0	2	0	.000	4	0	4	.000
	NHL Totals	**45**	**24**	**21**	**0**	**.533**	**10**	**2**	**8**	**.200**

General Managers' History

Phil Esposito, 1992-93 to date.

Coaching History

Terry Crisp, 1992-93 to date.

Captains' History

No captain, 1992-93 to date.

Coach

CRISP, TERRY
Coach, Tampa Bay Lightning. Born in Parry Sound, Ont., May 28, 1943.

After a two-year absence, Terry Crisp returned to the NHL's coaching ranks to become the first coach of the Tampa Bay Lightning. Crisp, who won two Stanley Cups as a member of the Philadelphia Flyers, played 11 years in the NHL for the Bruins, Blues, Islanders and Flyers. After retiring in 1976, he joined the Flyers' organization as an assistant coach, serving two terms before leaving to coach the OHL's Sault Ste. Marie Greyhounds. With the Greyhounds, Crisp won three regular-season crowns and twice earned the nod as the league's coach of the year. In 1985, Crisp accepted a coaching position with the Calgary Flames' top AHL farm affiliate in Moncton and spent two seasons with the Golden Flames before being elevated to the head coaching position with their parent club. Crisp led Calgary to its best finish in 1988-89, winning 54 games and capturing the franchise's first Stanley Cup championship after a six-game final series win over the Montreal Canadiens. After being released by the Flames, Crisp joined the Canadian National Team program as an assistant coach and was with the club when Team Canada won a silver medal at the 1992 Olympics.

Coaching Record

		Regular Season					Playoffs				
Season	Team	Games	W	L	T	%	Games	W	L	T	%
1979-80	S.S. Marie (OHL)	68	22	45	1	.331	....	....	....	....	....
1980-81	S.S. Marie (OHL)	68	47	19	2	.706	19	8	7	4	.526
1981-82	S.S. Marie (OHL)	68	40	25	3	.610	13	4	6	3	.423
1982-83	S.S. Marie (OHL)	70	48	21	1	.693	16	7	6	3	.531
1983-84	S.S. Marie (OHL)	70	38	28	4	.571	16	8	4	4	.625
1984-85	S.S. Marie (OHL)	66	54	11	1	.826	16	12	2	2	.813
1985-86	Moncton (AHL)	80	34	34	12	.500	10	5	5	0	.500
1986-87	Moncton (AHL)	80	43	31	6	.575	6	2	4	0	.333
1987-88	**Calgary (NHL)**	**80**	**48**	**23**	**9**	**.656**	**9**	**4**	**5**	**0**	**.444**
1988-89	**Calgary (NHL)**	**80**	**54**	**17**	**9**	**.731**	**22**	**16**	**6**	**0**	**.727***
1989-90	**Calgary (NHL)**	**80**	**42**	**23**	**15**	**.619**	**6**	**2**	**4**	**0**	**.333**
1992-93	**Tampa Bay (NHL)**	**84**	**23**	**54**	**7**	**.315**	....	....	....	....	....
1993-94	**Tampa Bay (NHL)**	**84**	**30**	**43**	**11**	**.423**	....	....	....	....	....
1994-95	**Tampa Bay (NHL)**	**48**	**17**	**28**	**3**	**.385**	....	....	....	....	....
	NHL Totals	**456**	**214**	**188**	**54**	**.529**	**37**	**22**	**15**	**0**	**.595**

* Stanley Cup win.

Club Records

Team

(Figures in brackets for season records are games played; records for fewest points, wins, ties, losses, goals, goals against are for 70 or more games)

Most Points	71	1993-94 (84)
Most Wins	30	1993-94 (84)
Most Ties	11	1993-94 (84)
Most Losses	54	1992-93 (84)
Most Goals	245	1992-93 (84)
Most Goals Against	332	1992-93 (84)
Fewest Points	53	1992-93 (84)
Fewest Wins	23	1992-93 (84)
Fewest Ties	7	1992-93 (84)
Fewest Losses	43	1993-94 (84)
Fewest Goals	224	1993-94 (84)
Fewest Goals Against	251	1993-94 (84)

Longest Winning Streak
- Overall ... 4 ... Nov. 7-13/92
- Home ... 4 ... Jan. 25-Feb. 4/95
- Away ... 3 ... Dec. 3-7/93

Longest Undefeated Streak
- Overall ... 6 ... Nov. 3-13/92 (5 wins, 1 tie)
- Home ... 3 ... Nov. 3-13/92 (3 wins)
- Away ... 6 ... Dec. 28/93-Jan. 12/94 (5 wins, 1 tie)

Longest Losing Streak
- Overall ... 8 ... Mar. 9-28/93
- Home ... 6 ... Mar. 9-Apr. 11/93
- Away ... 6 ... Apr. 14-29/95

Longest Winless Streak
- Overall ... 8 ... Mar. 9-28/93 (8 losses)
- Home ... 9 ... Mar. 9-Apr. 10/93 (8 losses, 1 tie)
- Away ... 8 ... Feb. 3-Mar. 23/93

Most Shutouts, Season	5	1993-94 (84)
Most PIM, Season	1,625	1992-93 (84)
Most Goals, Game	7	Three times

Individual

Most Seasons	3	Several players
Most Games, Career	205	Marc Bergevin
Most Goals, Career	79	Brian Bradley
Most Assists, Career	111	Brian Bradley
Most Points, Career	190	Brian Bradley (79 goals, 111 assists)
Most PIM, Career	292	Roman Hamrlik
Most Shutouts, Career	5	Daren Puppa
Longest Consecutive Games Streak	106	Chris Gratton
Most Goals, Season	42	Brian Bradley (1992-93)
Most Assists, Season	44	Brian Bradley (1992-93)
Most Points, Season	86	Brian Bradley (1992-93)
Most PIM, Season	225	Enrico Ciccone (1994-95)
Most Shutouts, Season	4	Daren Puppa (1993-94)
Most Points, Defenseman Season	39	Shawn Chambers (1992-93)
Most Points, Center, Season	86	Brian Bradley (1992-93)
Most Points, Right Wing, Season	56	John Tucker (1992-93)
Most Points, Left Wing, Season	51	Chris Kontos (1992-93)
Most Points, Rookie, Season	43	Rob Zamuner (1992-93) Chris Gratton (1993-94)
Most Goals, Game	4	Chris Kontos (Oct. 7/92)
Most Assists, Game	4	Joe Reekie (Oct. 7/92) Marc Bureau (Dec. 16/92)
Most Points, Game	6	Doug Crossman (Nov. 11/92)

For the third consecutive season, Brian Bradley led the Lightning in scoring, notching 40 points in 46 games.

One of the Lightning's top special team players, Rob Zamuner led the club with three shorthanded goals in 1994-95.

All-time Record vs. Other Clubs

Regular Season

	At Home							On Road							Total						
	GP	W	L	T	GF	GA	PTS	GP	W	L	T	GF	GA	PTS	GP	W	L	T	GF	GA	PTS
Anaheim	1	0	1	0	1	4	0	1	1	0	0	4	2	2	2	1	1	0	5	6	2
Boston	5	1	2	2	14	15	4	4	1	2	1	8	11	3	9	2	4	3	22	26	7
Buffalo	5	1	4	0	8	14	2	5	2	2	1	17	13	5	10	3	6	1	25	27	7
Calgary	3	1	2	0	13	16	2	2	1	1	0	6	3	2	5	2	3	0	19	19	4
Chicago	5	2	3	0	14	15	4	5	0	3	2	9	16	2	10	2	6	2	23	31	6
Dallas	5	0	3	2	7	13	2	4	1	3	0	12	15	2	9	1	6	2	19	28	4
Detroit	6	1	5	0	21	39	2	4	1	3	0	13	20	2	10	2	8	0	34	59	4
Edmonton	3	2	0	1	13	6	5	3	0	3	0	6	9	0	6	2	3	1	19	15	5
Florida	5	1	3	1	6	12	3	4	3	0	1	7	13	7	9	4	3	2	13	25	10
Hartford	5	4	1	0	17	10	8	5	1	4	0	11	16	2	10	5	5	0	28	26	10
Los Angeles	2	0	2	0	5	9	0	3	3	0	0	14	9	6	5	3	2	0	19	18	6
Montreal	5	4	0	1	15	8	9	4	0	2	2	7	9	2	9	4	2	3	22	17	11
New Jersey	5	1	3	1	12	15	3	6	1	4	1	12	20	3	11	2	7	2	24	35	6
NY Islanders	6	3	3	0	17	19	6	5	3	2	0	19	14	6	11	6	5	0	36	33	12
NY Rangers	5	1	4	0	14	17	2	7	2	4	1	29	29	5	12	3	8	1	43	46	7
Ottawa	5	3	2	0	13	10	6	5	4	1	0	16	12	8	10	7	3	0	29	22	14
Philadelphia	6	2	4	0	17	19	4	5	4	0	1	13	22	9	11	6	4	1	30	41	13
Pittsburgh	4	1	3	0	13	18	2	5	2	5	0	14	21	4	9	3	6	0	27	39	6
Quebec	5	4	1	0	19	14	8	5	0	3	2	12	25	2	10	4	4	2	31	39	10
St. Louis	5	2	2	1	17	18	5	4	1	3	0	13	18	2	9	3	5	1	30	36	7
San Jose	3	1	2	0	7	5	2	2	3	0	0	13	9	6	5	4	2	0	20	14	8
Toronto	5	1	4	0	8	18	2	3	3	0	0	14	24	6	8	4	4	0	22	42	8
Vancouver	2	0	2	0	5	8	0	3	3	0	0	17	14	6	5	3	2	0	22	22	6
Washington	5	0	5	0	6	19	0	6	2	3	1	16	20	5	11	2	8	1	22	39	5
Winnipeg	3	0	3	0	10	14	0	3	2	1	0	9	8	4	6	2	4	0	19	22	4
Totals	**108**	**36**	**63**	**9**	**292**	**355**	**81**	**108**	**34**	**62**	**12**	**297**	**372**	**80**	**216**	**70**	**125**	**21**	**589**	**727**	**161**

Dallas totals include Minnesota, 1992-93.

1994-95 Results

Jan.	20	Pittsburgh	3-5		12	at Washington	1-3
	22	Buffalo	2-5		13	Washington	0-3
	25	Florida	3-2		18	at New Jersey	2-1
	26	at Florida	2-4		19	at Buffalo	6-1
	28	at NY Islanders	4-1		24	Boston	3-4
	31	Montreal	4-1		27	Montreal	3-2
Feb.	2	at NY Rangers	3-3		29	Washington	2-4
	4	at Pittsburgh	3-6		31	Hartford	2-0
	5	at Buffalo	1-2	Apr.	2	Florida	1-4
	7	NY Islanders	5-2		4	at New Jersey	1-1
	10	Hartford	4-3		6	at Philadelphia	4-5
	11	NY Rangers	2-3		8	at Boston	1-5
	14	Philadelphia	2-5		9	at Hartford	3-0
	17	Ottawa	1-2		11	NY Islanders	5-2
	18	Boston	3-1		14	at Philadelphia	2-3
	20	NY Rangers	1-3		16	at Florida	1-4
	23	at NY Islanders	4-1		18	New Jersey	3-2
	24	at Pittsburgh	4-2		20	Quebec	5-2
	26	at Washington	1-1		22	at Montreal	1-3
Mar.	1	at Quebec	2-8		24	Buffalo	1-3
	2	at Ottawa	3-2		26	at NY Rangers	4-6
	4	at Hartford	2-3		27	at Ottawa	1-6
	7	Philadelphia	3-4		29	at Quebec	1-4
	10	New Jersey	2-3	May	3	Ottawa	3-4

Entry Draft
Selections 1995-92

1995 Pick		1994 Pick		1993 Pick		1992 Pick	
5	Daymond Langkow	8	Jason Wiemer	3	Chris Gratton	1	Roman Hamrlik
30	Mike McBain	34	Colin Cloutier	29	Tyler Moss	26	Drew Bannister
56	Shane Willis	55	Vadim Epanchintsev	55	Allan Egeland	49	Brent Gretzky
108	Konsta Golokhvastov	86	Dmitri Klevakin	81	Marian Kacir	74	Aaron Gavey
134	Eduard Pershin	137	Daniel Juden	107	Ryan Brown	97	Brantt Myhres
160	Cory Murphy	138	Bryce Salvador	133	Kiley Hill	122	Martin Tanguay
186	Joe Cardarelli	164	Chris Maillet	159	Mathieu Raby	145	Derek Wilkinson
212	Zac Bierk	190	Alexei Baranov	185	Ryan Nauss	170	Dennis Maxwell
		216	Yuri Smirnov	211	Alexandre Laporte	193	Andrew Kemper
		242	Shawn Gervais	237	Brett Duncan	218	Marc Tardif
		268	Brian White	263	Mark Szoke	241	Tom MacDonald

Chris Gratton enjoyed a productive season in 1994-95, collecting 27 points with a +/– rating of -2, the best mark among Tampa Bay centermen.

Club Directory

ThunderDome

501 East Kennedy Boulevard
Suite 175
Tampa, FL 33602
Phone **813/229-2658**
FAX 813/229-3350

Capacity: 26,000

Lightning Partners, Ltd
General Partner . . . . Lightning Partners, Inc.
Limited Partners . . . . Lightning International, Inc.
Tokyo Tower Development Co., Ltd
Nippon Meat Packers, Inc.
Estate of John Chase
Equity Resources Group of
Indian River County, Inc.
James Murphy
Tampa Bay Hockey Group Partners, Ltd.
Board of Directors . . . . Takashi Okubo, Majority Owner and Chairman,
Phil Esposito, Yasukiyo Hiyashiyama, David
LeFevre, Fukusaboro Maeda, Tadashide Oku,
Saburo (Steve) Oto, Chris Phillips, Reece Smith,
Jr., Yoshiuki Sugioka

Executive Staff
Majority Owner and President . . . . Takashi Okubo
President, CEO and Alternate Governor . . . . Saburo (Steve) Oto
Governor . . . . David LeFevre
General Manager and Alternate Governor . . . . Phil Esposito
Executive Vice President and Alternate Governor . . Chris Phillips
Executive Vice President and Alternate Governor . . Mel Lowell

Hockey Operations
President of Hockey Operations Group . . . . Phil Esposito
Director of Hockey Operations . . . . Tony Esposito
Counsel . . . . Henry Lee Paul – Lazzara & Paul, P.A.
Head Coach . . . . Terry Crisp
Associate Coach . . . . Wayne Cashman
Strength and Conditioning Coach . . . . Chris Reichart
Head Scout . . . . Don Murdoch
Scouting Staff . . . . Angelo Bumbacco, Jacques Campeau,
Jake Goertzen, Doug Macauley, Richard
Rose, Luke Williams
Head Trainer . . . . Larry Ness
Equipment Manager . . . . Jocko Cayer
Assistant Trainer . . . . Bill Cronin
Director of Team Services . . . . Carrie Esposito
Administrative Assistant . . . . Teresa P. Huffman
Administrative Assistant . . . . Kathy Skelton

Ice System Supervisor . . . . Tim Friedenberger
Operations Manager . . . . Michael Wall
Video Coordinator . . . . Duncan McMillian

Finance
Chief Financial Officer . . . . Frank Sato
Accounting Manager . . . . Vincent Ascanio
Executive Administrative Assistant . . . . Evelyn Hicks
Accounting Assistant . . . . Kevin Annison
Accounting Assistant . . . . Kris Swofford

Marketing and Sales
Director of Sales . . . . Paul D'Aiuto
Promotions Manager . . . . Nichole Reckner
Sales Representative . . . . Karl Nickel
Marketing Assistant . . . . Kimberly Hargreaves
Director of Fan Services . . . . Steve Woznick
Director of Merchandising . . . . Kevin L. Murphy

Ticket Operations
Vice President/Ticket Operations . . . . Jeff Morander
Ticket Office Manager . . . . Kevin Brooks
Assistant Ticket Office Manager . . . . Keven Smith
Ticket Office Representatives . . . . April Blackmon, Dan Pekarek
Season Ticket Service Manager . . . . Dan Froehlich
Ticket Sales Manager . . . . Bill Makris
Group Sales Manager . . . . Ray Mihara
Senior Sales Representatives . . . . Keith Brennan, Brendan Cunningham
Regional Sales Representative . . . . Jon Roman
Sales Representative . . . . Jason Baumgarten

Communications
Vice President/Communications . . . . Gerry Helper
Media Relations Manager . . . . Barry Hanrahan
Publications Manager . . . . Becky D'Aiuto
Communications Assistant . . . . Carrie Schuldt
Director of Amateur Hockey . . . . Nigel Kirwan
Receptionist . . . . Kim Pryor

Medical Staff
Team Physician . . . . Dr. David Leffers
Team Dentist . . . . Dr. Joseph Spoto

Game Night Staff
Team Photographer . . . . Jonathan Hayt
Off-ice Officials . . . . Jim Galluzzi, Ron Brace, Gerry Dollmont,
Ralph Emery, Chuck Fontana, Rich Galipault,
Mark Losier, Tony Mancuso, Jeff Maust, Mike
Rees, Gary Reilly, Bill Shapiro, John Supak, Rich
Wasilewski
Game Summary . . . . Rick Pratt
NHL Commercial Coordinator . . . . David Rice
P.A. Announcer . . . . Paul Porter
Game Night Music . . . . Mike Oliviero
Scoreboard Operation . . . . Todd Schirmer, Bill Heald

Television and Radio
Television Stations . . . . Sunshine Network, WTOG-TV 44 &
Lightning Television Network
Broadcasters . . . . John Kelly and Bobby Taylor
Radio Station . . . . WFNS 910 AM and WSUN 620 AM
Broadcasters . . . . Larry Hirsch and Bobby Taylor

Team Information
Home Arena . . . . ThunderDome
Seating Capacity 26,000
Rink Dimensions . . . . 200 feet by 85 feet
Team Colors . . . . Black, Blue, Silver and White
Training Camp Site . . . . The Lakeland Center, Lakeland, Florida

Toronto Maple Leafs

1994-95 Results: 21w-19L-8T 50PTS. Fourth, Central Division

Schedule

Oct. Sat.	7	at Pittsburgh	
Tues.	10	NY Islanders	
Sat.	14	NY Rangers	
Tues.	17	San Jose	
Fri.	20	Calgary	
Sat.	21	at Montreal	
Tues.	24	Florida	
Thur.	26	at Chicago	
Sat.	28	Los Angeles	
Sun.	29	at NY Rangers	
Nov. Wed.	1	at Winnipeg	
Fri.	3	at Vancouver	
Sat.	4	at Edmonton	
Tues.	7	Anaheim	
Fri.	10	Washington	
Sat.	11	at Boston	
Tues.	14	at Florida	
Thur.	16	at Tampa Bay	
Sat.	18	Winnipeg	
Tues.	21	St. Louis	
Fri.	24	Hartford	
Sat.	25	at St. Louis	
Tues.	28	at Winnipeg	
Thur.	30	at Philadelphia	
Dec. Sat.	2	Anaheim	
Tues.	5	Ottawa	
Thur.	7	at New Jersey	
Sat.	9	Dallas	
Mon.	11	Colorado	
Thur.	14	at San Jose	
Sat.	16	at Los Angeles	
Sun.	17	at Anaheim	
Wed.	20	Chicago	
Thur.	21	at Chicago	
Sat.	23	Edmonton	
Wed.	27	at Calgary	
Fri.	29	at Colorado	
Sat.	30	at St. Louis	
Jan. Mon.	1	at Dallas*	
Wed.	3	Boston	
Fri.	5	at Buffalo	

Sat.	6	Colorado	
Wed.	10	Los Angeles	
Thur.	11	at NY Islanders	
Sat.	13	Vancouver	
Wed.	17	Winnipeg	
Wed.	24	Chicago	
Sat.	27	at Ottawa	
Tues.	30	at Detroit	
Wed.	31	St. Louis	
Feb. Sat.	3	Montreal	
Mon.	5	at San Jose	
Wed.	7	at Anaheim	
Thur.	8	at Los Angeles	
Sat.	10	Buffalo	
Mon.	12	Pittsburgh	
Wed.	14	San Jose	
Fri.	16	at Washington	
Sun.	18	Detroit*	
Wed.	21	Tampa Bay	
Thur.	22	at Detroit	
Sat.	24	Dallas	
Wed.	28	at Winnipeg	
Mar. Sat.	2	at Dallas	
Sun.	3	at Colorado	
Wed.	6	New Jersey	
Fri.	8	at Hartford	
Sat.	9	Calgary	
Wed.	13	Winnipeg	
Fri.	15	Dallas	
Sun.	17	Vancouver*	
Tues.	19	at Detroit	
Wed.	20	Detroit	
Sat.	23	Philadelphia	
Mon.	25	at Calgary	
Wed.	27	at Vancouver	
Sat.	30	at Edmonton	
Apr. Wed.	3	Chicago	
Thur.	4	at St. Louis	
Sat.	6	at St. Louis	
Thur.	11	at Chicago	
Sat.	13	Edmonton	

Denotes afternoon game.

Home Starting Times:
Weeknights . . . . 7:35 p.m.
Saturdays . . . . 7:35 p.m.
Sundays . . . . 1:35 p.m.

Franchise date: November 22, 1917

WESTERN NHL CONFERENCE

CENTRAL DIVISION

79th NHL Season

Obtained from Quebec in June, 1994, Mats Sundin led the Leafs in goals (23), points (47), powerplay goals (9), shots (173) and game-winning goals (4) in 1994-95.

Year-by-Year Record

Season	GP	Home W	L	T	Road W	L	T	Overall W	L	T	GF	GA	Pts	Finished		Playoff Result
1994-95	48	15	7	2	6	12	6	21	19	8	135	146	50	4th,	Central Div.	Lost Conf. Quarter-Final
1993-94	84	23	15	4	20	14	8	43	29	12	280	243	98	2nd,	Central Div.	Lost Conf. Championship
1992-93	84	25	11	6	19	18	5	44	29	11	288	241	99	3rd,	Norris Div.	Lost Conf. Championship
1991-92	80	21	16	3	9	27	4	30	43	7	234	294	67	5th,	Norris Div.	Out of Playoffs
1990-91	80	15	21	4	8	25	7	23	46	11	241	318	57	5th,	Norris Div.	Out of Playoffs
1989-90	80	24	14	2	14	24	2	38	38	4	337	358	80	3rd,	Norris Div.	Lost Div. Semi-Final
1988-89	80	15	20	5	13	26	1	28	46	6	259	342	62	5th,	Norris Div.	Out of Playoffs
1987-88	80	14	20	6	7	29	4	21	49	10	273	345	52	4th,	Norris Div.	Lost Div. Semi-Final
1986-87	80	22	14	4	10	28	2	32	42	6	286	319	70	4th,	Norris Div.	Lost Div. Final
1985-86	80	16	21	3	9	27	4	25	48	7	311	386	57	4th,	Norris Div.	Lost Div. Final
1984-85	80	10	28	2	10	24	6	20	52	8	253	358	48	5th,	Norris Div.	Out of Playoffs
1983-84	80	17	16	7	9	29	2	26	45	9	303	387	61	5th,	Norris Div.	Out of Playoffs
1982-83	80	20	15	5	8	24	8	28	40	12	293	330	68	3rd,	Norris Div.	Lost Div. Semi-Final
1981-82	80	12	20	8	8	24	8	20	44	16	298	380	56	5th,	Norris Div.	Out of Playoffs
1980-81	80	14	21	5	14	16	10	28	37	15	322	367	71	5th,	Adams Div.	Lost Prelim. Round
1979-80	80	17	19	4	18	21	1	35	40	5	304	327	75	4th,	Adams Div.	Lost Prelim. Round
1978-79	80	20	12	8	14	21	5	34	33	13	267	252	81	3rd,	Adams Div.	Lost Quarter-Final
1977-78	80	21	13	6	20	16	4	41	29	10	271	237	92	3rd,	Adams Div.	Lost Semi-Final
1976-77	80	18	13	9	15	19	6	33	32	15	301	285	81	3rd,	Adams Div.	Lost Quarter-Final
1975-76	80	23	12	5	11	19	10	34	31	15	294	276	83	3rd,	Adams Div.	Lost Quarter-Final
1974-75	80	19	12	9	12	21	7	31	33	16	280	309	78	3rd,	Adams Div.	Lost Quarter-Final
1973-74	78	21	11	7	14	16	9	35	27	16	274	230	86	4th,	East Div.	Lost Quarter-Final
1972-73	78	20	12	7	7	29	3	27	41	10	247	279	64	6th,	East Div.	Out of Playoffs
1971-72	78	21	11	7	12	20	7	33	31	14	209	208	80	4th,	East Div.	Lost Quarter-Final
1970-71	78	24	9	6	13	24	2	37	33	8	248	211	82	4th,	East Div.	Lost Quarter-Final
1969-70	76	18	13	7	11	21	6	29	34	13	222	242	71	6th,	East Div.	Out of Playoffs
1968-69	76	20	8	10	15	18	5	35	26	15	234	217	85	4th,	East Div.	Lost Quarter-Final
1967-68	74	24	9	4	9	22	6	33	31	10	209	176	75	5th,	East Div.	Out of Playoffs
1966-67	70	21	8	6	11	19	5	32	27	11	204	211	75	3rd,		**Won Stanley Cup**
1965-66	70	22	9	4	12	16	7	34	25	11	208	187	79	3rd,		Lost Semi-Final
1964-65	70	17	15	3	13	11	11	30	26	14	204	173	74	4th,		Lost Semi-Final
1963-64	70	22	7	6	11	18	6	33	25	12	192	172	78	3rd,		**Won Stanley Cup**
1962-63	70	21	8	6	14	15	6	35	23	12	221	180	82	1st,		**Won Stanley Cup**
1961-62	70	25	5	5	12	17	6	37	22	11	232	180	85	2nd,		**Won Stanley Cup**
1960-61	70	21	6	8	18	13	4	39	19	12	234	176	90	2nd,		Lost Semi-Final
1959-60	70	20	9	6	15	17	3	35	26	9	199	195	79	2nd,		Lost Final
1958-59	70	17	13	5	10	19	6	27	32	11	189	201	65	4th,		Lost Final
1957-58	70	12	16	7	9	22	4	21	38	11	192	226	53	6th,		Out of Playoffs
1956-57	70	12	16	7	9	18	8	21	34	15	174	192	57	5th,		Out of Playoffs
1955-56	70	19	10	6	5	23	7	24	33	13	153	181	61	4th,		Lost Semi-Final
1954-55	70	14	10	11	10	14	11	24	24	22	147	135	70	3rd,		Lost Semi-Final
1953-54	70	22	6	7	10	18	7	32	24	14	152	131	78	3rd,		Lost Semi-Final
1952-53	70	17	12	6	10	18	7	27	30	13	156	167	67	5th,		Out of Playoffs
1951-52	70	17	10	8	12	15	8	29	25	16	168	157	74	3rd,		Lost Semi-Final
1950-51	70	22	8	5	19	8	8	41	16	13	212	138	95	2nd,		**Won Stanley Cup**
1949-50	70	18	9	8	13	18	4	31	27	12	176	173	74	3rd,		Lost Semi-Final
1948-49	60	12	8	10	10	17	3	22	25	13	147	161	57	4th,		**Won Stanley Cup**
1947-48	60	22	3	5	10	12	8	32	15	13	182	143	77	1st,		**Won Stanley Cup**
1946-47	60	20	8	2	11	11	8	31	19	10	209	172	72	2nd,		**Won Stanley Cup**
1945-46	50	10	13	2	9	11	5	19	24	7	174	185	45	5th,		Out of Playoffs
1944-45	50	13	9	3	11	13	1	24	22	4	183	161	52	3rd,		**Won Stanley Cup**
1943-44	50	13	11	1	10	12	3	23	23	4	214	174	50	3rd,		Lost Semi-Final
1942-43	50	17	6	2	5	13	7	22	19	9	198	159	53	3rd,		Lost Semi-Final
1941-42	48	18	6	0	9	12	3	27	18	3	158	136	57	2nd,		**Won Stanley Cup**
1940-41	48	16	5	3	12	11	1	28	14	6	145	99	62	2nd,		Lost Semi-Final
1939-40	48	15	8	1	10	14	0	25	17	6	134	110	56	3rd,		Lost Final
1938-39	48	13	8	3	6	12	6	19	20	9	114	107	47	3rd,		Lost Final
1937-38	48	13	6	5	11	9	4	24	15	9	151	127	57	1st,	Cdn. Div.	Lost Quarter-Final
1936-37	48	14	9	1	8	12	4	22	21	5	119	115	49	3rd,	Cdn. Div.	Lost Quarter-Final
1935-36	48	15	4	5	8	15	1	23	19	6	126	106	52	2nd,	Cdn. Div.	Lost Final
1934-35	48	16	6	2	14	8	2	30	14	4	157	111	64	1st,	Cdn. Div.	Lost Final
1933-34	48	19	2	3	7	11	6	26	13	9	174	119	61	1st,	Cdn. Div.	Lost Semi-Final
1932-33	48	16	4	4	8	14	2	24	18	6	119	111	54	1st,	Cdn. Div.	Lost Final
1931-32	48	17	4	3	6	14	4	23	18	7	155	127	53	2nd,	Cdn. Div.	**Won Stanley Cup**
1930-31	44	15	4	3	7	9	6	22	13	9	118	99	53	2nd,	Cdn. Div.	Lost Quarter-Final
1929-30	44	10	8	4	7	13	2	17	21	6	116	124	40	4th,	Cdn. Div.	Out of Playoffs
1928-29	44	15	5	2	6	13	3	21	18	5	85	69	47	3rd,	Cdn. Div.	Lost Semi-Final
1927-28	44	9	8	5	9	10	3	18	18	8	89	88	44	4th,	Cdn. Div.	Out of Playoffs
1926-27*	44	10	10	2	5	14	3	15	24	5	79	94	35	5th,	Cdn. Div.	Out of Playoffs
1925-26	36	11	5	2	1	16	1	12	21	3	92	114	27	6th,		Out of Playoffs
1924-25	30	10	5	0	9	6	0	19	11	0	90	84	38	2nd,		Lost NHL S-Final
1923-24	24	7	5	0	3	9	0	10	14	0	59	85	20	3rd,		Out of Playoffs
1922-23	24	10	1	1	3	9	0	13	10	1	82	88	27	3rd,		Out of Playoffs
1921-22	24	8	4	0	5	6	1	13	10	1	98	97	27	2nd,		**Won Stanley Cup**
1920-21	24	9	3	0	6	6	0	15	9	0	105	100	30	2nd and 1st***		Lost NHL Final
1919-20**	24	8	4	0	4	9	0	12	12	0	119	106	24	3rd and 2nd***		Out of Playoffs
1918-19	24	5	4	0	0	9	0	5	13	0	64	92	10	3rd and 3rd***		Out of Playoffs
1917-18	22	10	1	0	3	8	0	13	9	0	108	109	26	2nd and 1st***		**Won Stanley Cup**

* Name changed from St. Patricks to Maple Leafs.   ** Name changed from Arenas to St. Patricks.
*** Season played in two halves with no combined standing at end.

1995-96 Player Personnel

FORWARDS	HT	WT	S	Place of Birth	Date	1994-95 Club
ANDREYCHUK, Dave	6-3	220	R	Hamilton, Ont.	9/29/63	Toronto
BAUMGARTNER, Ken	6-1	205	L	Flin Flon, Man.	3/11/66	Toronto
BELANGER, Ken	6-4	225	L	Sault Ste. Marie, Ont.	5/14/74	St. John's-Toronto
BEREZIN, Sergei	5-10	172	R	Voskresensk, USSR	11/5/71	Koln
BERG, Bill	6-1	205	L	St. Catharines, Ont.	10/21/67	Toronto
BUTLER, Rob	6-2	180	L	Winnipeg, Manitoba	3/31/76	Green Bay-Sioux City
BUTZ, Rob	6-3	191	L	Dewberry, Alta.	2/24/75	Prince George-Tri-City
CLARKE, Wayne	6-2	188	R	Sterling, Ont.	8/30/72	RPI
CONVERY, Brandon	6-1	182	R	Kingston, Ont.	2/4/74	St. John's
CRAIG, Mike	6-1	180	R	St. Mary's, Ont.	6/6/71	Toronto
DE RUITER, Chris	6-2	190	R	Kingston, Ont.	2/27/74	Clarkson
DEYELL, Mark	5-11	170	R	Regina, Sask.	3/26/76	Saskatoon
DI PIETRO, Paul	5-8	179	R	Sault Ste. Marie, Ont.	9/8/70	Montreal-Toronto
DOMI, Tie	5-10	200	R	Windsor, Ont.	11/1/69	Winnipeg-Toronto
FAIRCHILD, Kelly	5-11	180	L	Hibbing, MN	4/9/73	St. John's
FERGUSON, Kyle	6-3	215	R	Toronto, Ont.	8/12/73	Michigan Tech
GARTNER, Mike	6-0	187	R	Ottawa, Ont.	10/29/59	Toronto
GILMOUR, Doug	5-11	172	L	Kingston, Ont.	6/25/63	Rapperswil-Toronto
HAGGERTY, Sean	6-1	186	L	Rye, NY	2/11/76	Detroit (OHL)
HAKANSSON, Mikael	6-1	196	L	Stockholm, Sweden	5/31/74	MoDo
HENDRICKSON, Darby	6-0	185	L	Richfield, MN	8/28/72	St. John's-Toronto
HOGUE, Benoit	5-10	194	L	Repentigny, Que.	10/28/66	NY Islanders-Toronto
HUDSON, Mike	6-1	205	L	Guelph, Ont.	2/6/67	Pittsburgh
KELLEY, Jonathan	6-0	180	R	Brighton, MA	6/25/73	Princeton
KOLESAR, Mark	6-1	188	R	Brampton, Ont.	1/23/73	St. John's
KUCHARCIK, Tomas	6-2	200	L	Vlasim, Czech.	5/10/70	Plzen
MANDERVILLE, Kent	6-3	207	L	Edmonton, Alta.	4/12/71	Toronto
MODIN, Fredrik	6-3	202	L	Sundsvall, Sweden	10/8/74	Brynas
MOMESSO, Sergio	6-3	215	L	Montreal, Que.	9/4/65	Milan Devils-Vancouver
NEDVED, Zdenek	6-0	180	L	Lany, Czech.	3/3/75	Sudbury-Toronto
NOLAN, Doug	6-1	185	L	Quincy, MA	1/5/76	Catholic Mem.
PEPPERALL, Ryan	6-1	178	R	Niagara Falls, Ont.	1/26/77	Kitchener
PROCHAZKA, Martin	5-11	180	R	Slany, Czech.	3/3/72	Kladno
RYCHEL, Warren	6-0	202	L	Tecumseh, Ont.	5/12/67	Los Angeles-Toronto
SUNDIN, Mats	6-4	215	R	Bromma, Sweden	2/13/71	Djurgarden-Toronto
TOPOROWSKI, Shayne	6-2	216	R	Paddockwood, Sask.	8/6/75	Prince Albert
VINCENT, Paul	6-4	200	L	Utica, NY	1/4/75	Sea-Swft-St.J's
WALBY, Steffon	6-1	198	R	Madison, WI	11/22/72	St. John's
WARE, Mike	6-2	193	L	Toronto, Ont.	2/27/74	Kingston-St. John's
WARRINER, Todd	6-1	188	L	Blenheim, Ont.	1/3/74	St. John's-Toronto
WOOD, Randy	6-0	195	L	Princeton, NJ	10/12/63	Toronto
DEFENSEMEN						
BUTCHER, Garth	6-0	204	R	Regina, Sask.	1/8/63	Toronto
CULL, Trent	6-3	210	L	Brampton, Ont.	9/27/73	St. John's
DEMPSEY, Nathan	6-0	170	L	Spruce Grove, Alta.	7/14/74	St. John's
ELLETT, Dave	6-2	205	L	Cleveland, OH	3/30/64	Toronto
GILL, Todd	6-0	180	L	Cardinal, Ont.	11/9/65	Toronto
GODBOUT, Daniel	6-2	195	L	Grand Falls, N.B.	3/20/75	Kitchener
GRONVALL, Janne	6-3	195	L	Rauma, Finland	7/17/73	St. John's
HARLOCK, David	6-2	205	L	Toronto, Ont.	3/16/71	St. John's-Toronto
HEWARD, Jamie	6-2	207	R	Regina, Sask.	3/30/71	Cdn. National
JONSSON, Kenny	6-3	195	L	Angelholm, Sweden	10/6/74	Rogle-St. John's-Toronto
LAPIN, Mikhail	6-2	190	L	Moscow, USSR	5/12/75	W. Michigan
LEHOUX, Guy	5-11	210	L	Disraeli, Que.	10/19/71	St. John's
MACOUN, Jamie	6-2	200	L	Newmarket, Ont.	8/17/61	Toronto
MARTIN, Matt	6-3	205	L	Hamden, CT	4/30/71	St. John's-Toronto
MULLIN, Kory	6-2	185	L	Lethbridge, Alta.	5/24/75	Lethbridge
MURPHY, Larry	6-2	210	R	Scarborough, Ont.	3/8/61	Pittsburgh
RAJAMAKI, Tommi	6-2	180	L	Pori, Finland	2/29/76	Assat Jr.-Assat
SIMONOV, Sergei	6-3	194	L	Saratov, USSR	5/20/74	Magnitogorsk
TREMBLAY, Yanick	6-2	178	R	Pointe-aux-Trembles, Que.	11/15/75	Beauport
WARE, Jeff	6-4	220	L	Toronto, Ont.	5/19/77	Oshawa
WHITE, Kam	6-3	211	L	Chicago, IL	2/13/76	Sarnia-North Bay
YUSHKEVICH, Dimitri	5-11	208	R	Yaroslavl, USSR	11/19/71	Torpedo Yaro.-Philadelphia
ZETTLER, Rob	6-3	200	L	Sept Iles, Que.	3/8/68	Philadelphia
GOALTENDERS	**HT**	**WT**	**C**	**Place of Birth**	**Date**	**1994-95 Club**
BONNER, Doug	5-10	175	L	Tacoma, WA	10/15/76	Seattle
COUSINEAU, Marcel	5-9	180	L	Delson, Que.	4/30/73	St. John's
JABLONSKI, Pat	6-0	180	R	Toledo, OH	6/20/67	Chicago (IHL)-Houston
POTVIN, Felix	6-0	190	L	Anjou, Que.	6/23/71	Toronto
RHODES, Damian	6-0	190	L	St. Paul, MN	5/28/69	Toronto
SAAL, Jason	5-11	175	L	Sterling Heights, MI	2/1/75	Detroit (OHL)

General Managers' History

Conn Smythe, 1927-28 to 1956-57; "Hap" Day, 1957-58; "Punch" Imlach, 1958-59 to 1968-69; Jim Gregory, 1969-70 to 1978-79; "Punch" Imlach, 1979-80 to 1980-81; "Punch" Imlach and Gerry McNamara, 1981-82; Gerry McNamara, 1982-83 to 1987-88; Gord Stellick, 1988-89; Floyd Smith, 1989-90 to 1990-91; Cliff Fletcher, 1991-92 to date.

Coaching History

Conn Smythe, 1927-28 to 1929-30; Conn Smythe and Art Duncan, 1930-31; Art Duncan and Dick Irvin, 1931-32; Dick Irvin, 1932-33 to 1939-40; "Hap" Day, 1940-41 to 1949-50; Joe Primeau, 1950-51 to 1952-53; "King" Clancy, 1953-54 to 1955-56; Howie Meeker, 1956-57; Billy Reay, 1957-58; Billy Reay and "Punch" Imlach, 1958-59; "Punch" Imlach, 1959-60 to 1968-69; John McLellan, 1969-70 to 1970-71; John McLellan and "King" Clancy, 1971-72; John McLellan, 1972-73; "Red" Kelly, 1973-74 to 1976-77; Roger Neilson, 1977-78 to 1978-79; Floyd Smith, Dick Duff and "Punch" Imlach, 1979-80; "Punch" Imlach, Joe Crozier and Mike Nykoluk, 1980-81; Mike Nykoluk, 1981-82 to 1983-84; Dan Maloney, 1984-85 to 1985-86; John Brophy, 1986-87 to 1987-88; John Brophy and George Armstrong, 1988-89; Doug Carpenter, 1989-90; Doug Carpenter and Tom Watt, 1990-91; Tom Watt, 1991-92; Pat Burns, 1992-93 to date.

1994-95 Scoring

* – rookie

Regular Season

Pos	#	Player	Team	GP	G	A	Pts	+/–	PIM	PP	SH	GW	GT	S	%
C	13	Mats Sundin	TOR	47	23	24	47	–5	14	9	0	4	1	173	13.3
L	14	Dave Andreychuk	TOR	48	22	16	38	–7	34	8	0	2	2	168	13.1
C	7	Mike Ridley	TOR	48	10	27	37	1	14	2	2	1	1	88	11.4
C	93	Doug Gilmour	TOR	44	10	23	33	–5	26	3	0	1	1	73	13.7
D	23	Todd Gill	TOR	47	7	25	32	–8	64	3	1	2	0	82	8.5
L	24	Randy Wood	TOR	48	13	11	24	7	34	1	1	2	0	125	10.4
R	11	Mike Gartner	TOR	38	12	8	20	0	6	2	1	1	1	91	13.2
D	15	Dmitri Mironov	TOR	33	5	12	17	6	28	2	0	0	0	68	7.4
C	32	Benoit Hogue	NYI	33	6	4	10	0	34	1	0	1	1	50	12.0
			TOR	12	3	3	6	0	0	1	0	1	0	16	18.8
			TOTAL	45	9	7	16	0	34	2	0	2	1	66	13.6
D	4	Dave Ellett	TOR	33	5	10	15	–6	26	3	0	1	0	84	6.0
C	25	Paul Dipietro	MTL	22	4	5	9	–3	4	0	0	1	1	41	9.8
			TOR	12	1	1	2	–6	6	0	0	0	0	19	5.3
			TOTAL	34	5	6	11	–9	10	0	0	1	1	60	8.3
R	9	Mike Craig	TOR	37	5	5	10	–21	12	1	0	1	0	61	8.2
D	34	Jamie Macoun	TOR	46	2	8	10	–6	75	1	0	0	0	84	2.4
R	28	Tie Domi	WPG	31	4	4	8	–6	128	0	0	0	0	34	11.8
			TOR	9	0	1	1	1	31	0	0	0	0	12	0.0
			TOTAL	40	4	5	9	–5	159	0	0	0	0	46	8.7
D	19	* Kenny Jonsson	TOR	39	2	7	9	–8	16	0	0	1	0	50	4.0
D	2	Garth Butcher	TOR	45	1	7	8	–5	59	0	0	0	0	24	4.2
L	21	Warren Rychel	L.A.	7	0	0	0	–5	19	0	0	0	0	7	0.0
			TOR	26	1	6	7	1	101	0	0	0	0	34	2.9
			TOTAL	33	1	6	7	–4	120	0	0	0	0	41	2.4
L	10	Bill Berg	TOR	32	5	1	6	–11	26	0	0	2	0	57	8.8
D	3	Grant Jennings	PIT	25	0	4	4	2	36	0	0	0	0	16	0.0
			TOR	10	0	2	2	–6	7	0	0	0	0	9	0.0
			TOTAL	35	0	6	6	–4	43	0	0	0	0	25	0.0
R	25	Terry Yake	TOR	19	3	2	5	1	2	1	0	2	0	26	11.5
R	12	Dixon Ward	TOR	22	0	3	3	–4	31	0	0	0	0	15	0.0
R	20	Rich Sutter	CHI	15	0	0	0	1	28	0	0	0	0	17	0.0
			T.B.	4	0	0	0	0	0	0	0	0	0	3	0.0
			TOR	18	0	3	3	–7	10	0	0	0	0	19	0.0
			TOTAL	37	0	3	3	–6	38	0	0	0	0	39	0.0
C	16	* Darby Hendrickson	TOR	8	0	1	1	0	4	0	0	0	0	4	0.0
L	18	Kent Manderville	TOR	36	0	1	1	–2	22	0	0	0	0	43	0.0
D	28	* David Harlock	TOR	1	0	0	0	–1	0	0	0	0	0	0	0.0
R	45	* Zdenek Nedved	TOR	1	0	0	0	0	2	0	0	0	0	0	0.0
L	22	Ken Baumgartner	TOR	2	0	0	0	0	5	0	0	0	0	1	0.0
L	43	* Ken Belanger	TOR	3	0	0	0	0	9	0	0	0	0	1	0.0
L	8	* Todd Warriner	TOR	5	0	0	0	–3	0	0	0	0	0	1	0.0
G	1	* Damian Rhodes	TOR	13	0	0	0	0	4	0	0	0	0	0	0.0
D	33	* Matt Martin	TOR	15	0	0	0	2	13	0	0	0	0	14	0.0
G	29	Felix Potvin	TOR	36	0	0	0	0	4	0	0	0	0	0	0.0

Goaltending

No.	Goaltender	GPI	Mins	Avg	W	L	T	EN	SO	GA	SA	S%
1	* Damian Rhodes	13	760	2.68	6	6	1	2	0	34	404	.916
29	Felix Potvin	36	2144	2.91	15	13	7	6	0	104	1120	.907
	Totals	**48**	**2920**	**3.00**	**21**	**19**	**8**	**8**	**0**	**146**	**1532**	**.905**

Playoffs

Pos	#	Player	Team	GP	G	A	Pts	+/–	PIM	PP	SH	GW	OT	S	%
C	13	Mats Sundin	TOR	7	5	4	9	–2	4	2	0	1	0	27	18.5
C	93	Doug Gilmour	TOR	7	0	6	6	2	6	0	0	0	0	8	0.0
L	14	Dave Andreychuk	TOR	7	3	2	5	3	25	2	0	0	0	19	15.8
C	7	Mike Ridley	TOR	7	3	1	4	–3	2	1	0	1	0	11	27.3
R	11	Mike Gartner	TOR	5	2	2	4	4	2	0	0	0	0	10	20.0
D	15	Dmitri Mironov	TOR	6	2	1	3	–1	2	1	0	0	0	11	18.2
D	34	Jamie Macoun	TOR	7	1	2	3	0	8	0	0	0	0	15	6.7
D	23	Todd Gill	TOR	7	0	3	3	–4	6	0	0	0	0	16	0.0
L	24	Randy Wood	TOR	7	2	0	2	–2	6	1	0	1	1	14	14.3
C	25	Paul Dipietro	TOR	7	1	1	2	–3	0	0	0	0	0	9	11.1
D	4	Dave Ellett	TOR	7	0	2	2	–5	0	0	0	0	0	18	0.0
R	28	Tie Domi	TOR	7	1	0	1	–2	0	0	0	0	0	7	14.3
R	9	Mike Craig	TOR	2	0	1	1	0	2	0	0	0	0	7	0.0
L	10	Bill Berg	TOR	7	0	1	1	–3	4	0	0	0	0	6	0.0
L	21	Warren Rychel	TOR	3	0	0	0	–2	0	0	0	0	0	2	0.0
D	3	Grant Jennings	TOR	4	0	0	0	–3	0	0	0	0	0	4	0.0
R	20	Rich Sutter	TOR	4	0	0	0	–3	2	0	0	0	0	0	0.0
D	19	* Kenny Jonsson	TOR	4	0	0	0	–2	0	0	0	0	0	3	0.0
C	32	Benoit Hogue	TOR	7	0	0	0	–4	6	0	0	0	0	6	0.0
D	2	Garth Butcher	TOR	7	0	0	0	0	8	0	0	0	0	6	0.0
L	18	Kent Manderville	TOR	7	0	0	0	–3	6	0	0	0	0	6	0.0
G	29	Felix Potvin	TOR	7	0	0	0	0	0	0	0	0	0	0	0.0

Goaltending

No.	Goaltender	GPI	Mins	Avg	W	L	EN	SO	GA	SA	S%
29	Felix Potvin	7	424	2.83	3	4	2	1	20	253	.921
	Totals	**7**	**430**	**3.07**	**3**	**4**	**2**	**1**	**22**	**255**	**.914**

Captains' History

"Hap" Day, 1927-28 to 1936-37; Charlie Conacher, 1937-38; Red Horner, 1938-39, 1939-40; Syl Apps, 1940-41 to 1942-43; Bob Davidson, 1943-44, 1944-45; Syl Apps, 1945-46 to 1947-48; Ted Kennedy, 1948-49 to 1954-55; Sid Smith, 1955-56; Jim Thomson, Ted Kennedy, 1956-57; George Armstrong, 1957-58 to 1968-69; Dave Keon, 1969-70 to 1974-75; Darryl Sittler, 1975-76 to 1980-81; Rick Vaive, 1981-82 to 1985-86; no captain, 1986-87 to 1988-89; Rob Ramage, 1989-90 to 1990-91; Wendel Clark, 1991-92 to 1993-94; Doug Gilmour, 1994-95 to date.

Club Records

Team

(Figures in brackets for season records are games played; records for fewest points, wins, ties, losses, goals, goals against are for 70 or more games)

Most Points	99	1992-93 (84)
Most Wins	44	1992-93 (84)
Most Ties	22	1954-55 (70)
Most Losses	52	1984-85 (80)
Most Goals	337	1989-90 (80)
Most Goals Against	387	1983-84 (80)
Fewest Points	48	1984-85 (80)
Fewest Wins	20	1981-82, 1984-85 (80)
Fewest Ties	4	1989-90 (80)
Fewest Losses	16	1950-51 (70)
Fewest Goals	147	1954-55 (70)
Fewest Goals Against	*131	1953-54 (70)

Longest Winning Streak

Over-all	10	Oct. 7-28/93
Home	9	Nov. 11-Dec. 26/53
Away	7	Nov. 14-Dec. 15/40 Dec. 4/60-Jan. 5/61

Longest Undefeated Streak

Over-all	11	Oct. 15-Nov. 8/50 (8 wins, 3 ties) Jan. 6-Feb. 1/94 (7 wins, 4 ties)
Home	18	Nov. 28/33-Mar. 10/34 (15 wins, 3 ties) Oct. 31/53-Jan. 23/54 (16 wins, 2 ties)
Away	9	Nov. 30/47-Jan. 11/48 (4 wins, 5 ties)

Longest Losing Streak

Over-all	10	Jan. 15-Feb. 8/67
Home	7	Nov. 10-Dec. 5/84 Jan. 26-Feb. 25/85
Away	11	Feb. 20/-Apr. 1/88

Longest Winless Streak

Over-all	15	Dec. 26/87-Jan. 25/88 (11 losses, 4 ties)
Home	11	Dec. 19/87-Jan. 25/88 (7 losses, 4 ties)
Away	18	Oct. 6/82-Jan. 5/83 (13 losses, 5 ties)

Most Shutouts, Season	13	1953-54 (70)
Most PIM, Season	2,419	1989-90 (80)
Most Goals, Game	14	Mar. 16/57 (NYR 1 at Tor. 14)

Individual

Most Seasons	21	George Armstrong
Most Games	1,187	George Armstrong
Most Goals, Career	389	Darryl Sittler
Most Assists, Career	620	Borje Salming
Most Points, Career	916	Darryl Sittler (389 goals, 527 assists)
Most PIM, Career	1,670	Dave Williams
Most Shutouts, Career	62	Turk Broda
Longest Consecutive Games Streak	486	Tim Horton (Feb. 11/61-Feb. 4/68)
Most Goals, Season	54	Rick Vaive (1981-82)
Most Assists, Season	95	Doug Gilmour (1992-93)
Most Points, Season	127	Doug Gilmour (1992-93) (32 goals, 95 assists)
Most PIM, Season	351	Dave Williams (1977-78)

Most Points, Defenseman Season	79	Ian Turnbull (1976-77) (22 goals, 57 assists)
Most Points, Center Season	127	Doug Gilmour (1992-93) (32 goals, 95 assists)
Most Points, Right Wing, Season	97	Wilf Paiement (1980-81) (40 goals, 57 assists)
Most Points, Left Wing, Season	99	Dave Andreychuk (1993-94) (53 goals, 46 assists)
Most Points, Rookie, Season	66	Peter Ihnacak (1982-83) (28 goals, 38 assists)
Most Shutouts, Season	13	Harry Lumley (1953-54)
Most Goals, Game	6	Corb Denneny (Jan. 26/21) Darryl Sittler (Feb. 7/76)
Most Assists, Game	6	Babe Pratt (Jan. 8/44) Doug Gilmour (Feb. 13/93)
Most Points, Game	*10	Darryl Sittler (Feb. 7/76)

* NHL Record.

Retired Numbers

5	Bill Barilko	1946-1951
6	Irvine "Ace" Bailey	1927-1934

Honored Numbers

1	"Turk" Broda	1936-43, 45-52
	Johnny Bower	1958-70
9	Ted Kennedy	1942-1955, 56-57
10	Syl Apps	1936-1948

All-time Record vs. Other Clubs

Regular Season

			At Home						On Road						Total				
	GP	W	L	T	GF	GA	PTS	GP	W	L	T	GF	GA	PTS	GP	W	L	T	GF	GA	PTS
Anaheim	4	2	1		9	7	5	4	1	2	1	9	15	3	8	3	3	2	18	22	8
Boston	280	147	86	47	953	728	341	280	82	151	47	749	924	211	560	229	237	94	1702	1652	552
Buffalo	49	18	23	8	152	183	44	50	16	31	3	145	212	35	99	34	54	11	297	395	79
Calgary	42	18	17	7	162	163	43	44	12	27	5	143	195	29	86	30	44	12	305	358	72
Chicago	301	160	89	52	1034	773	372	302	109	153	40	786	935	258	603	269	242	92	1820	1708	630
Dallas	89	45	29	15	325	284	105	86	32	43	11	286	334	75	175	77	72	26	611	618	180
Detroit	303	161	98	44	1011	804	366	304	101	158	45	741	905	247	607	262	256	89	1752	1709	613
Edmonton	26	11	13	2	104	125	24	26	6	15	5	90	133	17	52	17	28	7	194	258	41
Florida	1	1	0	0	6	3	2	1	0	1	0	5	4	3	2	1	1	0	11	7	5
Hartford	22	8	12	2	82	90	18	22	6	12	4	74	102	16	44	14	24	6	156	192	34
Los Angeles	57	30	17	10	234	193	70	58	19	31	8	169	209	46	115	49	48	18	403	402	116
Montreal	315	160	111	44	954	824	364	314	83	191	40	773	1119	206	629	243	302	84	1727	1943	570
New Jersey	33	24	6	3	151	107	51	32	10	13	9	103	120	29	65	34	19	12	254	227	80
NY Islanders	40	17	20	3	135	149	37	38	13	22	3	117	166	29	78	30	42	6	252	315	66
NY Rangers	267	151	78	38	920	692	340	268	101	111	56	785	821	258	535	252	189	94	1705	1513	598
Ottawa	3	3	0	0	16	7	6	2	2	0	0	7	2	4	5	5	0	0	23	9	10
Philadelphia	52	19	20	13	180	177	51	52	11	33	8	123	211	30	104	30	53	21	303	388	81
Pittsburgh	53	25	17	11	220	178	61	54	20	28	6	176	223	46	107	45	45	17	396	401	107
Quebec	23	11	10	2	84	99	24	23	5	13	5	73	94	15	46	16	23	7	157	193	39
St. Louis	85	53	22	10	329	248	116	86	23	51	12	245	304	58	171	76	73	22	574	552	174
San Jose	7	4	2	1	27	14	9	8	4	3	1	20	16	9	15	8	5	2	47	30	18
Tampa Bay	7	4	3	0	24	14	8	5	4	1	0	18	8	8	12	8	4	0	42	22	16
Vancouver	49	22	18	9	188	169	53	47	14	25	8	152	161	36	96	36	43	17	340	330	89
Washington	34	19	11	4	164	122	42	35	12	21	2	96	132	26	69	31	32	6	260	254	68
Winnipeg	30	13	16	1	116	122	27	29	10	14	5	117	130	25	59	23	30	6	233	252	52
Defunct Clubs	232	158	53	21	860	515	337	233	84	120	29	607	745	197	465	242	173	50	1467	1260	534
Totals	**2404**	**1284**	**772**	**348**	**8440**	**6790**	**2916**	**2404**	**781**	**1269**	**354**	**6609**	**8220**	**1916**	**4808**	**2065**	**2041**	**702**	**15049**	**15010**	**4832**

Calgary totals include Atlanta, 1972-73 to 1979-80. Dallas totals include Minnesota, 1967-68 to 1992-93.
New Jersey totals include Kansas City, 1974-75 to 1975-76, and Colorado, 1976-77 to 1981-82.

Playoffs

	Series	W	L	GP	W	L	T	GF	GA	Last Mtg.	Round	Result
Boston	13	8	5	62	31	30	1	150	153	1974	QF	L 0-4
Calgary	1	1	0	2	2	0	0	9	5	1979	PR	W 2-0
Chicago	9	6	3	38	22	15	1	111	89	1995	CQF	L 3-4
Dallas	2	0	2	7	1	6	0	26	35	1983	DSF	L 1-3
Detroit	23	12	11	117	58	59	0	311	321	1993	DSF	W 4-3
Los Angeles	3	2	1	12	7	5	0	41	31	1993	CF	L 3-4
Montreal	15	7	8	71	29	42	0	160	215	1979	QF	L 0-4
NY Islanders	2	1	1	10	4	6	0	20	33	1981	PR	L 0-3
NY Rangers	8	3	5	35	16	19	0	86	86	1971	QF	L 2-4
Philadelphia	3	0	3	17	5	12	0	47	67	1977	QF	L 2-4
Pittsburgh	2	2	0	6	4	2	0	21	13	1977	PR	W 2-1
St. Louis	4	2	2	25	12	13	0	75	67	1993	DF	W 4-3
San Jose	1	1	0	7	4	3	0	26	21	1994	CSF	W 4-3
Vancouver	1	0	1	5	1	4	0	9	16	1994	CF	L 1-4
Defunct	8	6	2	24	12	10	2	59	57			
Totals	**95**	**51**	**44**	**438**	**208**	**226**	**4**	**1151**	**1209**			

Playoff Results 1995-91

Year	Round	Opponent	Result	GF	GA
1995	CQF	Chicago	L 3-4	20	22
1994	CF	Vancouver	L 1-4	9	16
	CSF	San Jose	W 4-3	26	21
	CQF	Chicago	W 4-2	15	10
1993	CF	Los Angeles	L 3-4	23	22
	DF	St. Louis	W 4-3	22	11
	DSF	Detroit	W 4-3	24	30

Abbreviations: Round: F – Final;
CF – conference final; **CQF** – conference quarter-final;
CSF – conference semi-final; **DF** – division final;
DSF – division semi-final; **SF** – semi-final;
QF – quarter-final; **PR** – preliminary round.

Entry Draft Selections 1995-81

1995 Pick		1991 Pick		1988 Pick		1984 Pick	
15	Jeff Ware	47	Yanic Perreault	6	Scott Pearson	4	Al Iafrate
54	Ryan Pepperall	69	Terry Chitaroni	27	Tie Domi	25	Todd Gill
139	Doug Bonner	102	Alexei Kudashov	48	Peter Ing	67	Jeff Reese
145	Yannick Tremblay	113	Jeff Perry	69	Ted Crowley	88	Jack Capuano
171	Marek Melenovsky	120	Alexander Kuzminsky	88	Leonard Esau	109	Joseph Fabian
197	Mark Murphy	135	Martin Prochazka	132	Matt Mallgrave	130	Joe McInnis
223	Danlil Markov	160	Dmitri Mironov	153	Roger Elvenas	151	Derek Laxdal
		164	Robb McIntyre	174	Mike Delay	172	Dan Turner
1994 Pick		167	Tomas Kucharcik	195	David Sacco	192	David Buckley
16	Eric Fichaud	179	Guy Lehoux	216	Mike Gregorio	213	Mikael Wurst
48	Sean Haggerty	201	Gary Miller	237	Peter DeBoer	233	Peter Slanina
64	Fredrik Modin	223	Jonathan Kelley				
126	Mark Deyell	245	Chris O'Rourke	**1987** Pick		**1983** Pick	
152	Kam White			7	Luke Richardson	7	Russ Courtnall
178	Tommi Rajamaki	**1990** Pick		28	Daniel Marois	28	Jeff Jackson
204	Rob Butler	10	Drake Berehowsky	49	John McIntyre	48	Allan Bester
256	Sergei Berezin	31	Felix Potvin	71	Joe Sacco	83	Dan Hodgson
282	Doug Nolan	73	Darby Hendrickson	91	Mike Eastwood	128	Cam Plante
		80	Greg Walters	112	Damian Rhodes	148	Paul Bifano
1993 Pick		115	Alexander Godynyuk	133	Trevor Jobe	168	Cliff Albrecht
12	Kenny Jonsson	136	Eric Lacroix	154	Chris Jensen	184	Greg Rolston
19	Landon Wilson	157	Dan Stiver	175	Brian Blad	188	Brian Ross
123	Zdenek Nedved	178	Robert Horyna	196	Ron Bernacci	208	Mike Tomlak
149	Paul Vincent	199	Rob Chebator	217	Ken Alexander	228	Ron Choules
175	Jeff Andrews	220	Scott Malone	238	Alex Weinrich		
201	David Brumby	241	Nick Vachon			**1982** Pick	
253	Kyle Ferguson			**1986** Pick		3	Gary Nylund
279	Mikhail Lapin	**1989** Pick		6	Vincent Damphousse	24	Gary Leeman
		3	Scott Thornton	36	Darryl Shannon	25	Peter Ihnacak
1992 Pick		12	Rob Pearson	48	Sean Boland	45	Ken Wregget
8	Brandon Convery	21	Steve Bancroft	69	Kent Hulst	73	Vladimir Ruzicka
23	Grant Marshall	66	Matt Martin	90	Scott Taylor	87	Eduard Uvira
77	Nikolai Borschevsky	96	Keith Carney	111	Stephane Giguere	99	Sylvain Charland
95	Mark Raiter	108	David Burke	132	Danny Hie	108	Ron Dreger
101	Janne Gronvall	125	Michael Doers	153	Stephen Brennan	115	Craig Kales
106	Chris Deruiter	129	Keith Merkler	174	Brian Bellefeuille	129	Dom Campedelli
125	Mikael Hakansson	150	Derek Langille	195	Sean Davidson	139	Jeff Triano
149	Patrik Augusta	171	Jeffrey St. Laurent	216	Mark Holick	171	Miroslav Ihnacak
173	Ryan Vandenbussche	192	Justin Tomberlin	237	Brian Hoard	192	Leigh Verstraete
197	Wayne Clarke	213	Mike Jackson			213	Tim Loven
221	Sergei Simonov	234	Steve Chartrand	**1985** Pick		234	Jim Appleby
245	Nathan Dempsey			1	Wendel Clark		
				22	Ken Spangler	**1981** Pick	
				43	Dave Thomlinson	6	Jim Benning
				64	Greg Vey	24	Gary Yaremchuk
				85	Jeff Serowik	55	Ernie Godden
				106	Jiri Latal	90	Normand LeFrancois
				127	Tim Bean	102	Barry Brigley
				148	Andy Donahue	132	Andrew Wright
				169	Todd Whittemore	153	Richard Turmel
				190	Bob Reynolds	174	Greg Barber
				211	Tim Armstrong	195	Marc Magnan
				232	Mitch Murphy		

Club Directory

Maple Leaf Gardens
60 Carlton Street
Toronto, Ontario M5B 1L1
Phone **416/977-1641**
FAX 416/977-5364
Capacity: 15,746 (standing 100)

Board of Directors
Brian P. Bellmore, Robert G. Bertram, William T. Brock, J. Donald Crump, George J. Engman, Terence V. Kelly, Q.C., Ted Nikolaou, W. Ron Pringle, Steve A. Stavro, George E. Whyte, Q.C.

Chairman of the Board and CEO	Steve A. Stavro
President, Chief Operating Officer and General Manager	Cliff Fletcher
Secretary-Treasurer	J. Donald Crump
Alternate Governors	Cliff Fletcher, Brian P. Bellmore
Assistant General Manager	Bill Watters
Special Consultant to the President	Darryl Sittler
Director of Scouting and Player Personnel	Nick Beverley
Director of Business Operations and Communications	Bob Stellick
Head Coach	Pat Burns
Assistant Coach	Mike Kitchen
Assistant Coach	Rick Wamsley
Director of Professional Development	Floyd Smith
Scouts	George Armstrong, John Choyce, Anders Hedberg, Peter Johnson, Garth Malarchuk, Dan Marr, Mark Hillier, Dick Bouchard, Jack Gardiner, Bob Johnson, Ernie Gare, Doug Woods
Media Relations Coordinator	Pat Park
Administrative Assistants	Mary Speck, Brenda Powers
Communications Coordinator	Casey Vanden Heuvel
Community Relations Coordinators	Kristy Fletcher, Angela McManus
Executive Assistant to the President and G.M.	Shelley Bernardo
Head Athletic Therapist	Chris Broadhurst
Athletic Therapist	Brent Smith
Trainers	Brian Papineau, Dave Aleo
Vice President of Building Operations	Brian Conacher
Director of Marketing	Bill Cluff
Controller	Ian Clarke
Assistant Controller	Paul Franck
Marketing and Promotions Manager	Denis Cordick
Marketing Representative	Chris Reed
Luxury Suites Coordinator	Nancy Read
Retail Operations Manager	Jeff Newman
Box Office Manager	Donna Henderson
Building Manager	Wayne Gillespie
Team Doctors	Dr. Michael Clarfield, Dr. Darrell Ogilvie-Harris, Dr. Leith Douglas, Dr. Michael Easterbrook, Dr. Simon McGrail
Team Dentist	Dr. Ernie Lewis
Team Psychologist	Robert Offenberger, Ph.D.
Head Off Ice Official	Joe Lamantia
AHL Affiliate	St. John's Maple Leafs
Head Coach – St. John's	Tom Watt

Coach

BURNS, PAT
Coach, Toronto Maple Leafs. Born in St-Henri, Que., April 4, 1952.

Since the 1993 post-season, the Maple Leafs' total of 46 playoff games ranks second only to the Vancouver Canucks. It's no coincidence that Pat Burns has been at the helm of the Maple Leafs since that time.

Under Burns' guidance in his first campaign, Toronto set single-season club records in 1992-93 for most wins (44), points (99), home ice wins (25), playoff victories (11), and playoff games (21). The Maple Leafs improved 32 points from the previous season. For his efforts, Burns won the 1992-93 Jack Adams Award as NHL coach of the year.

In 1993-94, the Maple Leafs surpassed 40 wins in consecutive seasons for the first time, as the club was the only NHL team to reach the Conference Championships in both 1993 and 1994. A league-record 10-game winning streak to start 1993-94 vaulted the team to the top of the NHL's overall standings for much of the first half of that season.

He is just the third multiple Jack Adams winner, joining Pat Quinn of the Canucks and Jacques Demers of the Canadiens. Burns also joins Quinn as the only coaches to win the award with two different teams.

Burns, 43, coached the Hull Olympiques for four seasons beginning in 1983-84. He joined the Sherbrooke Canadiens for the 1987-88 season. After one season, Burns was elevated to the head coaching job with Montreal. He led the Canadiens to a berth in the Stanley Cup Finals in his rookie season, earning his first Jack Adams Award. He coached in Montreal for four seasons prior to joining the Leafs.

Coaching Record

Season	Team	Games	Regular Season W	L	T	%	Games	Playoffs W	L	%
1983-84	Hull (QMJHL)	70	25	45	0	.357	....	....	....	....
1984-85	Hull (QMJHL)	68	33	34	1	.493	5	1	4	.200
1985-86	Hull (QMJHL)	72	54	18	0	.750	15	15	0	1.000
1986-87	Hull (QMJHL)	70	26	39	5	.407	8	4	4	.500
1987-88	Sherbrooke (AHL)	80	42	34	4	.550	6	2	4	.333
1988-89	**Montreal (NHL)**	80	53	18	9	.719	21	14	7	.667
1989-90	**Montreal (NHL)**	80	41	28	11	.581	11	5	6	.455
1990-91	**Montreal (NHL)**	80	39	30	11	.556	13	7	6	.538
1991-92	**Montreal (NHL)**	80	41	28	11	.581	11	4	7	.364
1992-93	**Toronto (NHL)**	84	44	29	11	.589	21	11	10	.524
1993-94	**Toronto (NHL)**	84	43	29	12	.583	18	9	9	.500
1994-95	**Toronto (NHL)**	48	21	19	8	.521	7	3	4	.429
	NHL Totals	536	282	181	73	.594	102	53	49	.520

General Manager

FLETCHER, CLIFF
President, General Manager and Chief Operating Officer, Toronto Maple Leafs. Born in Montreal, Que., August 16, 1935.

Cliff Fletcher's progressive approach has brought Maple Leaf fans three consecutive seasons of better than .500% hockey for the first time since 1976-79. His commitment to bring championship hockey back to Toronto is evidenced by his six trades consumated at the past two Entry Drafts. The past three post-seasons have produced 23 playoff games at Maple Leaf Gardens. By combining the tasks of chief operating officer, president and general manager since July 1, 1991, Cliff has restored the winning tradition on the ice. Off the ice, his vision includes fostering a solid relationship with the community and the club's alumni.

In 1992-93, the Maple Leafs set club regular-season standards with 44 wins and 99 points en route to gaining the Norris Division playoff championship in some of the most memorable hockey played at Maple Leaf Gardens in years. Appearances in the NHL Conference Championships in 1993 and 1994 were the team's first since 1978, and the Leafs fell just one goal shy of reaching the Stanley Cup Finals in 1993. The organization's success in 1992-93 earned Fletcher *The Hockey News'* Man of the Year and Executive of the Year awards.

A native of Montreal, Fletcher was the general manager of the Atlanta/Calgary Flames in their first 19 years in the NHL. He orchestrated the start-up of the Atlanta franchise in February 1972, and in the off-season of 1980, organized its transfer to Calgary. In the Flames' 11 seasons in Calgary with Fletcher at the helm, the club captured the Stanley Cup in 1989 and won the Presidents' Trophy and the Campbell Conference titles twice.

Fletcher's hockey career began with the Montreal Junior Canadiens as he scouted for 10 years in Sam Pollock's system. From there he became St. Louis' Eastern Canada scout in 1967 which proceded his appointment to the assistant general manager's post with the Blues. Cliff Fletcher's hockey clubs have missed the playoffs only three times in the past 26 seasons and he has been involved in five Stanley Cup Finals (two with Calgary in 1986 and 1989 and three with St. Louis in 1968, 1969 and 1970).

Cliff and his wife Boots make their home in Rosedale, Ontario. The couple have a son, Chuck, and a daughter, Kristy.

Vancouver Canucks

1994-95 Results: 18W-18L-12T 48PTS. Second, Pacific Division

Year-by-Year Record

		Home			Road			Overall						
Season	GP	W	L	T	W	L	T	W	L	T	GF	GA	Pts.	Finished	Playoff Result
1994-95	48	10	8	6	8	10	6	18	18	12	153	148	48	2nd, Pacific Div.	Lost Conf. Semi-Final
1993-94	84	20	19	3	21	21	0	41	40	3	279	276	85	2nd, Pacific Div.	Lost Final
1992-93	84	27	11	4	19	18	5	46	29	9	346	278	101	1st, Smythe Div.	Lost Div. Final
1991-92	80	23	10	7	19	16	5	42	26	12	285	250	96	1st, Smythe Div.	Lost Div. Final
1990-91	80	18	17	5	10	26	4	28	43	9	243	315	65	4th, Smythe Div.	Lost Div. Semi-Final
1989-90	80	13	16	11	12	25	3	25	41	14	245	306	64	5th, Smythe Div.	Out of Playoffs
1988-89	80	19	15	6	14	24	2	33	39	8	251	253	74	4th, Smythe Div.	Lost Div. Semi-Final
1987-88	80	15	20	5	10	26	4	25	46	9	272	320	59	5th, Smythe Div.	Out of Playoffs
1986-87	80	17	19	4	12	24	4	29	43	8	282	314	66	5th, Smythe Div.	Out of Playoffs
1985-86	80	17	18	5	6	26	8	23	44	13	282	333	59	4th, Smythe Div.	Lost Div. Semi-Final
1984-85	80	15	21	4	10	25	5	25	46	9	284	401	59	5th, Smythe Div.	Out of Playoffs
1983-84	80	20	16	4	12	23	5	32	39	9	306	328	73	3rd, Smythe Div.	Lost Div. Semi-Final
1982-83	80	20	12	8	10	23	7	30	35	15	303	309	75	3rd, Smythe Div.	Lost Div. Semi-Final
1981-82	80	20	8	12	10	25	5	30	33	17	290	286	77	2nd, Smythe Div.	Lost Final
1980-81	80	17	12	11	11	20	9	28	32	20	289	301	76	3rd, Smythe Div.	Lost Prelim. Round
1979-80	80	14	17	9	13	20	7	27	37	16	256	281	70	3rd, Smythe Div.	Lost Prelim. Round
1978-79	80	15	18	7	10	24	6	25	42	13	217	291	63	2nd, Smythe Div.	Lost Prelim. Round
1977-78	80	13	15	12	7	28	5	20	43	17	239	320	57	3rd, Smythe Div.	Out of Playoffs
1976-77	80	13	21	6	12	21	7	25	42	13	235	294	63	4th, Smythe Div.	Out of Playoffs
1975-76	80	22	11	7	11	21	8	33	32	15	271	272	81	2nd, Smythe Div.	Lost Prelim. Round
1974-75	80	23	12	5	15	20	5	38	32	10	271	254	86	1st, Smythe Div.	Lost Quarter-Final
1973-74	78	14	18	7	10	25	4	24	43	11	224	296	59	7th, East Div.	Out of Playoffs
1972-73	78	17	18	4	5	29	5	22	47	9	233	339	53	7th, East Div.	Out of Playoffs
1971-72	78	14	20	5	6	30	3	20	50	8	203	297	48	7th, East Div.	Out of Playoffs
1970-71	78	17	18	4	7	28	4	24	46	8	229	296	56	6th, East Div.	Out of Playoffs

Schedule

Oct.	Mon.	9	Detroit		Sat.	13	at Toronto
	Thur.	12	at Los Angeles		Mon.	15	at Boston*
	Sat.	14	at San Jose		Tues.	16	at Hartford
	Sun.	15	Los Angeles		Mon.	22	Dallas
	Wed.	18	at Anaheim		Wed.	24	Anaheim
	Sat.	21	at Edmonton		Thur.	25	at Colorado
	Tues.	24	at NY Rangers		Sat.	27	NY Islanders
	Wed.	25	at New Jersey		Tues.	30	New Jersey
	Sat.	28	Winnipeg	Feb.	Thur.	1	at St. Louis
	Mon.	30	San Jose		Fri.	2	at Dallas
Nov.	Wed.	1	Edmonton		Sun.	4	at Winnipeg*
	Fri.	3	Toronto		Wed.	7	Hartford
	Sat.	4	at Calgary		Fri.	9	at Edmonton
	Tues.	7	at NY Islanders		Sat.	10	Washington
	Thur.	9	at Chicago		Tues.	13	Winnipeg
	Sat.	11	Colorado		Thur.	15	Anaheim
	Sun.	12	Montreal		Sat.	17	Boston
	Thur.	16	at Florida		Mon.	19	at Detroit
	Sat.	18	at Tampa Bay		Wed.	21	at Winnipeg
	Sun.	19	at Philadelphia		Fri.	23	San Jose
	Wed.	22	at Dallas		Tues.	27	Pittsburgh
	Thur.	23	at St. Louis		Thur.	29	St. Louis
	Sat.	25	at San Jose	Mar.	Sat.	2	at Detroit*
	Wed.	29	Chicago		Sun.	3	at Buffalo*
Dec.	Fri.	1	San Jose		Wed.	6	Buffalo
	Tues.	5	Edmonton		Sat.	9	Colorado
	Fri.	8	St. Louis		Tues.	12	at Washington
	Sat.	9	at Calgary		Thur.	14	at Chicago
	Wed.	13	at Edmonton		Fri.	15	at Ottawa
	Sun.	17	Ottawa*		Sun.	17	at Toronto*
	Mon.	18	at Colorado		Tues.	19	Colorado
	Wed.	20	at Los Angeles		Fri.	22	Dallas
	Fri.	22	at Anaheim		Sat.	23	Calgary
	Sat.	23	Detroit		Mon.	25	Los Angeles
	Tues.	26	Calgary		Wed.	27	Toronto
	Thur.	28	NY Rangers		Fri.	29	Chicago
	Sun.	31	Philadelphia*	Apr.	Mon.	1	Edmonton
Jan.	Wed.	3	Florida		Wed.	3	at Calgary
	Sat.	6	Tampa Bay		Sat.	6	at Los Angeles
	Mon.	8	at Pittsburgh		Mon.	8	at Anaheim
	Wed.	10	at Montreal		Sat.	13	Calgary

* Denotes afternoon game.

Home Starting Times:

All games				7:30 p.m.
Except	Sun. Nov. 12			5:00 p.m.
	Sun. Dec. 17			2:00 p.m.
	Sun. Dec. 31			2:00 p.m.

Franchise date: May 22, 1970

WESTERN
NHL CONFERENCE

**26th
NHL
Season**

**PACIFIC
DIVISION**

The Vancouver Canucks have reunited former junior linemates Pavel Bure, left, and Alexander Mogilny for 1995-96. Mogilny was obtained from Buffalo in a trade that was announced from the floor of the 1995 Entry Draft on July 8, 1995.

1995-96 Player Personnel

FORWARDS	HT	WT	S	Place of Birth	Date	1994-95 Club
BADDUKE, John	6-2	195	R	Watson, Sask.	6/21/72	Syracuse
BERANEK, Josef	6-2	185	L	Litvinov, Czechoslovakia	10/25/69	Vsetin-Philadelphia-Vancouver
BOHONOS, Lonny	5-11	190	R	Winnipeg, Man.	5/20/73	Syracuse
BURE, Pavel	5-10	189	L	Moscow, USSR	3/31/71	Landshut-Spartak-Vancouver
COURVILLE, Larry	6-1	180	L	Timmins, Ont.	4/2/75	Sarnia-Oshawa
FELSNER, Denny	6-0	195	L	Warren, MI	4/29/70	Peoria-St. Louis
GELINAS, Martin	5-11	195	L	Shawinigan, Que.	6/5/70	Vancouver
GIRARD, Rick	5-11	175	L	Edmonton, Alta.	5/1/74	Syracuse
HUNTER, Tim	6-2	202	R	Calgary, Alta.	9/10/60	Vancouver
KUZNETSOV, Yuri	5-11	176	L	Omak, USSR	8/10/71	Syracuse
LONEY, Brian	6-2	200	R	Winnipeg, Man.	8/9/72	Syracuse
McINTYRE, John	6-1	190	L	Ravenswood, Ont.	4/29/69	Vancouver
MOGILNY, Alexander	5-11	187	L	Khabarovsk, USSR	2/18/69	Spartak-Buffalo
NASH, Tyson	6-0	180	L	Edmonton, Alta.	3/11/75	Kamloops
ODJICK, Gino	6-3	210	L	Maniwaki, Que.	9/7/70	Vancouver
OKSIUTA, Roman	6-3	229	L	Murmansk, USSR	8/21/70	Cape Breton-Edmonton-Van
POLASEK, Libor	6-3	220	R	Vitkovice, Czech.	4/22/74	Syracuse-South Carolina
RIDLEY, Mike	6-0	195	L	Winnipeg, Man.	7/8/63	Toronto
RONNING, Cliff	5-8	170	L	Burnaby, B.C.	10/1/65	Vancouver
RUCHTY, Matthew	6-1	225	L	Kitchener, Ont.	11/27/69	Albany
SAVENKO, Bogdan	6-1	192	R	Kiev, USSR	11/20/74	Indianapolis
STEVENS, Rod	5-10	175	L	Fort St. John, B.C.	4/5/74	Syracuse
STOJANOV, Alek	6-4	220	L	Windsor, Ont.	4/25/73	Syracuse-Vancouver
TRUMBLEY, Rob	5-10	174	R	Regina, Sask.	8/9/74	Moose Jaw
DEFENSEMEN						
AUCOIN, Adrian	6-1	194	R	Ottawa, Ont.	7/3/73	Syracuse-Vancouver
BABYCH, Dave	6-2	215	L	Edmonton, Alta.	5/23/61	Vancouver
BROWN, Jeff	6-1	204	R	Ottawa, Ont.	4/30/66	Vancouver
CULLIMORE, Jassen	6-5	225	L	Simcoe, Ont.	12/4/72	Syracuse-Vancouver
HEDICAN, Bret	6-2	195	L	St. Paul, MN	8/10/70	Vancouver
LUMME, Jyrki	6-1	205	L	Tampere, Finland	7/16/66	Ilves-Vancouver
MALKOC, Dean	6-3	200	L	Vancouver, B.C.	1/26/70	Albany-Indianapolis
McALLISTER, Chris	6-7	238	L	Saskatoon, Sask.	6/16/75	Saskatoon
MURZYN, Dana	6-2	200	L	Calgary, Alta.	12/9/66	Vancouver
NAMESTNIKOV, Yevgeny	5-11	190	R	Arzamis-Ig, USSR	10/9/71	Syracuse-Vancouver
OKTYABREV, Artur	5-11	183	L	Irkutsk, USSR	11/26/73	CSKA-Syracuse
ROBERTSSON, Bert	6-2	198	L	Sodertalje, Sweden	6/30/74	Sodertalje
ROHLIN, Leif	6-1	198	L	Vasteras, Sweden	2/26/68	Vasteras
TULLY, Brent	6-3	195	R	Peterborough, Ont.	3/26/74	Syracuse
WALKER, Scott	5-9	180	R	Montreal, Que.	7/19/73	Syracuse-Vancouver
WOTTON, Mark	5-11	187	L	Foxwarren, Man.	11/16/73	Syracuse-Vancouver

GOALTENDERS	HT	WT	C	Place of Birth	Date	1994-95 Club
FOUNTAIN, Mike	6-1	176	L	North York, Ont.	1/26/72	Syracuse
HIRSCH, Corey	5-10	160	L	Medicine Hat, Alta.	7/1/72	Binghamton
McLEAN, Kirk	6-0	195	L	Willowdale, Ont.	6/26/66	Vancouver
MIGNACCA, Sonny	5-8	178	L	Winnipeg, Man.	1/4/74	Syracuse

General Manager

QUINN, PAT
President and General Manager, Vancouver Canucks.
Born in Hamilton, Ont., January 29, 1943.

After guiding the Vancouver Canucks to their third straight season with 40+ wins and a berth in the Stanley Cup Finals in 1994, Pat Quinn stepped down as the most successful coach in club history. In 1994-95, he completed his eighth season with the organization, concentrating on his duties as president, general manager and alternate governor.

When Quinn joined the Canucks in 1987, he inherited a team that had endured 11 consecutive losing seasons. In just five years, he turned the club around, posting the franchise's first 40-win campaign in 1991-92. He has also earned a reputation as an outstanding judge of talent and a shrewd negotiator, acquiring numerous players that have helped the club through deals at the NHL's annual trading deadline. He was named *The Hockey News* Executive of the Year in 1992 and was runner-up for the award in 1994. Last season, he received the Jake Milford Award recognizing his contributions to hockey in British Columbia.

In three-and-a-half seasons as head coach, Quinn posted a .554 winning percentage and a record of 132-108-28, four victories shy of the club's coaching record. Under Quinn, the Canucks set single-season records for wins (48) and points (101) in 1992-93.

Quinn accepted the position of Vancouver's president and g.m. on January 9, 1987 and officially became the club's seventh g.m. on May 1, 1987. He added the coaching portfolio on January 31, 1991. In 1992, he won the Jack Adams Award as the NHL's coach of the year for the second time in his career and is one of only two coaches to win the award with two different teams.

He previously coached in Los Angeles from 1984 to 1987 and in Philadelphia from 1978 to 1982. In 1979-80, his Flyers were the NHL's top team (48-12-20) and posted a 35-game undefeated streak, earning Quinn his first NHL coach of the year honors. After leaving the Flyers, Quinn earned his law degree from Delaware Law School. As a player, he was an NHL defenseman who played 606 games over nine years with Vancouver, Toronto and Atlanta. An original member of the 1970-71 Canucks, he finished his NHL career with 18 goals, 113 assists and 950 penalty minutes.

NHL Coaching Record

		Regular Season					Playoffs			
Season	Team	Games	W	L	T	%	Games	W	L	%
1978-79	Philadelphia	30	18	8	4	.667	8	3	5	.375
1979-80	Philadelphia	80	48	12	20	.725	19	13	6	.684
1980-81	Philadelphia	80	41	24	15	.606	12	6	6	.500
1981-82	Philadelphia	72	34	29	9	.535	....	....	....	....
1984-85	Los Angeles	80	34	32	14	.513	3	0	3	.000
1985-86	Los Angeles	80	23	49	8	.338	....	....	....	....
1986-87	Los Angeles	42	18	20	4	.476	....	....	....	....
1990-91	Vancouver	26	9	13	4	.423	6	2	4	.333
1991-92	Vancouver	80	42	26	12	.600	13	6	7	.462
1992-93	Vancouver	84	46	29	9	.601	12	6	6	.500
1993-94	Vancouver	84	41	40	3	.506	24	15	9	.625
	NHL Totals	**738**	**354**	**282**	**102**	**.549**	**97**	**51**	**46**	**.526**

1994-95 Scoring

* – rookie

Regular Season

Pos	#	Player	Team	GP	G	A	Pts	+/–	PIM	PP	SH	GW	GT	S	%
L	10	Pavel Bure	VAN	44	20	23	43	–8	47	6	2	2	0	198	10.1
C	16	Trevor Linden	VAN	48	18	22	40	–5	40	9	0	1	3	129	14.0
R	9	Russ Courtnall	DAL	32	7	10	17	–8	13	2	0	1	0	90	7.8
			VAN	13	4	14	18	10	4	0	2	1	0	42	9.5
			TOTAL	45	11	24	35	2	17	2	2	2	0	132	8.3
L	14	Geoff Courtnall	VAN	45	16	18	34	2	81	7	0	1	0	144	11.1
C	42	Josef Beranek	PHI	14	5	5	10	3	2	1	0	0	0	39	12.8
			VAN	37	8	13	21	–10	28	2	0	0	1	95	8.4
			TOTAL	51	13	18	31	–7	30	3	0	0	1	134	9.7
D	22	Jeff Brown	VAN	33	8	23	31	–2	16	3	0	0	0	111	7.2
L	27	Sergio Momesso	VAN	48	10	15	25	–2	65	6	0	1	0	82	12.2
C	7	Cliff Ronning	VAN	41	6	19	25	–4	27	3	0	2	0	93	6.5
L	23	Martin Gelinas	VAN	46	13	10	23	8	36	1	0	4	0	75	17.3
R	28 *	Roman Oksiuta	EDM	26	11	2	13	–14	8	5	0	0	0	52	21.2
			VAN	12	5	2	7	2	2	1	0	1	0	15	33.3
			TOTAL	38	16	4	20	–12	10	6	0	1	0	67	23.9
C	20	Christian Ruuttu	CHI	20	2	5	7	3	6	0	0	1	0	25	8.0
			VAN	25	5	6	11	11	23	0	0	1	0	19	26.3
			TOTAL	45	7	11	18	14	29	0	0	2	0	44	15.9
D	21	Jyrki Lumme	VAN	36	5	12	17	4	26	3	0	1	0	78	6.4
D	44	Dave Babych	VAN	40	3	11	14	–13	18	1	0	0	0	58	5.2
D	3	Bret Hedican	VAN	45	2	11	13	–3	34	0	0	0	0	56	3.6
C	33 *	Mike Peca	VAN	33	6	6	12	–6	30	2	0	1	1	46	13.0
L	29	Gino Odjick	VAN	23	4	5	9	–3	109	0	0	0	0	35	11.4
D	5	Dana Murzyn	VAN	40	0	8	8	14	129	0	0	0	0	29	0.0
R	19	Tim Hunter	VAN	34	3	2	5	1	120	0	0	0	0	17	17.6
C	15	John McIntyre	VAN	28	0	4	4	–3	37	0	0	0	0	6	0.0
D	34 *	Jassen Cullimore	VAN	34	1	2	3	–2	39	0	0	0	0	30	3.3
D	2 *	Yevgeny Namestnikov	VAN	16	0	3	3	2	4	0	0	0	0	18	0.0
R	9	Gary Leeman	VAN	10	2	0	2	–3	0	0	0	1	0	14	14.3
D	6 *	Adrian Aucoin	VAN	1	1	0	1	1	0	0	0	0	0	2	50.0
R	20	Jose Charbonneau	VAN	3	1	0	1	0	0	0	0	0	0	2	50.0
R	36 *	Dane Jackson	VAN	3	1	0	1	0	4	0	0	0	0	6	16.7
G	35	Kay Whitmore	VAN	11	0	1	1	0	7	0	0	0	0	0	0.0
D	24 *	Scott Walker	VAN	11	0	1	1	0	33	0	0	0	0	8	0.0
G	1	Kirk McLean	VAN	40	0	1	1	0	4	0	0	0	0	0	0.0
D	4 *	Mark Wotton	VAN	1	0	0	0	1	0	0	0	0	0	2	0.0
R	25 *	Alek Stojanov	VAN	4	0	0	0	–2	13	0	0	0	0	1	0.0

Goaltending

No.	Goaltender	GPI	Mins	Avg	W	L	T	EN	SO	GA	SA	S%
1	Kirk McLean	40	2374	2.75	18	12	10	1	1	109	1140	.904
35	Kay Whitmore	11	558	3.98	0	6	2	1	0	37	279	.867
	Totals	**48**	**2942**	**3.02**	**18**	**18**	**12**	**2**	**1**	**148**	**1421**	**.896**

Playoffs

Pos	#	Player	Team	GP	G	A	Pts	+/–	PIM	PP	SH	GW	OT	S	%
L	10	Pavel Bure	VAN	11	7	6	13	–1	10	2	2	0	0	39	17.9
R	9	Russ Courtnall	VAN	11	4	8	12	1	21	0	2	1	0	27	14.8
C	7	Cliff Ronning	VAN	11	3	5	8	–5	2	1	0	2	1	20	15.0
D	21	Jyrki Lumme	VAN	11	2	6	8	0	8	1	0	0	0	23	8.7
C	16	Trevor Linden	VAN	11	2	6	8	–1	12	1	0	0	0	19	10.5
L	14	Geoff Courtnall	VAN	11	4	2	6	–8	34	3	1	1	0	31	12.9
R	28 *	Roman Oksiuta	VAN	10	2	3	5	0	0	1	0	0	0	9	22.2
L	27	Sergio Momesso	VAN	11	3	1	4	–5	16	1	0	0	0	11	27.3
D	44	Dave Babych	VAN	11	2	2	4	–8	14	1	1	0	0	16	12.5
D	22	Jeff Brown	VAN	5	1	3	4	2	2	0	0	0	0	11	9.1
C	20	Christian Ruuttu	VAN	9	1	1	2	–3	0	0	1	0	0	12	8.3
C	42	Josef Beranek	VAN	11	1	1	2	–7	12	0	0	0	0	21	4.8
D	3	Bret Hedican	VAN	11	0	2	2	–5	6	0	0	0	0	6	0.0
D	6 *	Adrian Aucoin	VAN	4	1	0	1	–1	0	1	0	0	0	2	50.0
L	23	Martin Gelinas	VAN	3	0	1	1	1	0	0	0	0	0	5	0.0
C	33 *	Mike Peca	VAN	5	0	1	1	0	8	0	0	0	0	7	0.0
D	5	Dana Murzyn	VAN	8	0	1	1	–1	22	0	0	0	0	9	0.0
G	1	Kirk McLean	VAN	11	0	1	1	0	0	0	0	0	0	0	0.0
G	35	Kay Whitmore	VAN	1	0	0	0	0	0	0	0	0	0	0	0.0
D	2 *	Yevgeny Namestnikov	VAN	1	0	0	0	0	2	0	0	0	0	0	0.0
L	29	Gino Odjick	VAN	5	0	0	0	–2	47	0	0	0	0	7	0.0
R	25 *	Alek Stojanov	VAN	5	0	0	0	0	2	0	0	0	0	1	0.0
D	4 *	Mark Wotton	VAN	5	0	0	0	0	4	0	0	0	0	2	0.0
R	36 *	Dane Jackson	VAN	6	0	0	0	–2	10	0	0	0	0	2	0.0
R	19	Tim Hunter	VAN	11	0	0	0	–3	22	0	0	0	0	3	0.0
D	34 *	Jassen Cullimore	VAN	11	0	0	0	–4	12	0	0	0	0	9	0.0

Goaltending

No.	Goaltender	GPI	Mins	Avg	W	L	EN	SO	GA	SA	S%
1	Kirk McLean	11	660	3.27	4	7	0	0	36	336	.893
35	Kay Whitmore	1	20	6.00	0	0	0	0	2	18	.889
	Totals	**11**	**683**	**3.34**	**4**	**7**	**0**	**0**	**38**	**354**	**.893**

General Managers' History

Normand Robert Poile, 1970-71 to 1972-73; Hal Laycoe, 1973-74; Phil Maloney, 1974-75 to 1976-77; Jake Milford, 1977-78 to 1981-82; Harry Neale, 1982-83 to 1984-85; Jack Gordon, 1985-86 to 1986-87; Pat Quinn, 1987-88 to date.

Club Records

Team

(Figures in brackets for season records are games played; records for fewest points, wins, ties, losses, goals, goals against are for 70 or more games)

Most Points	101	1992-93 (84)
Most Wins	46	1992-93 (84)
Most Ties	20	1980-81 (80)
Most Losses	50	1971-72 (78)
Most Goals	346	1992-93 (84)
Most Goals Against	401	1984-85 (80)
Fewest Points	48	1971-72 (78)
Fewest Wins	20	1971-72 (78)
		1977-78 (80)
Fewest Ties	3	1993-94 (84)
Fewest Losses	26	1991-92 (80)
Fewest Goals	203	1971-72 (78)
Fewest Goals Against	250	1991-92 (80)

Longest Winning Streak

Over-all	7	Feb. 10-23/89
Home	9	Nov. 6- Dec. 9/92
Away	5	Jan. 14-25/92

Longest Undefeated Streak

Over-all	10	Mar. 5-25/77 (5 wins, 5 ties)
Home	18	Oct. 30/92 Jan. 18/93 (16 wins, 2 ties)
Away	5	Four times

Longest Losing Streak

Over-all	9	Four times
Home	6	Dec. 18/70- Jan. 20/71 Nov. 3-18/78
Away	12	Nov. 28/81- Feb. 6/82

Longest Winless Streak

Over-all	13	Nov. 9- Dec. 7/73 (10 losses, 3 ties)
Home	11	Dec. 18/70- Feb. 6/71 (10 losses, 1 tie)
Away	20	Jan. 2/86- Apr. 2/86 (14 losses, 6 ties)

Most Shutouts, Season	8	1974-75 (80)
Most PIM, Season	2,326	1992-93 (84)
Most Goals, Game	11	Mar. 28/71 (Cal. 5 at Van. 11) Nov. 25/86 (L.A. 5 at Van. 11) Mar. 1/92 (Cgy. 0 at Van. 11)

Individual

Most Seasons	13	Stan Smyl
Most Games	896	Stan Smyl
Most Goals, Career	262	Stan Smyl
Most Assists, Career	411	Stan Smyl
Most Points, Career	673	Stan Smyl (262 goals, 411 assists)
Most PIM, Career	1,668	Garth Butcher
Most Shutouts, Career	17	Kirk McLean

Longest Consecutive

Games Streak	437	Don Lever (Oct. 7/72-Jan. 14/78)
Most Goals, Season	60	Pavel Bure (1992-93, 1993-94)
Most Assists, Season	62	André Boudrias (1974-75)
Most Points, Season	110	Pavel Bure (1992-93) (60 goals, 50 assists)
Most PIM, Season	370	Gino Odjick (1992-93)

Most Points, Defenseman,

Season	63	Doug Lidster (1986-87) (12 goals, 51 assists)

Most Points, Center,

Season	91	Patrik Sundstrom (1983-84) (38 goals, 53 assists)

Most Points, Right Wing,

Season	110	Pavel Bure (1992-93) (60 goals, 50 assists)

Most Points, Left Wing,

Season	81	Darcy Rota (1982-83) (42 goals, 39 assists)

Most Points, Rookie,

Season	60	Ivan Hlinka (1981-82) (23 goals, 37 assists) Pavel Bure (1991-92) (34 goals, 26 assists)

Most Shutouts, Season	6	Gary Smith (1974-75)
Most Goals, Game	4	Several players
Most Assists, Game	6	Patrik Sundstrom (Feb. 29/84)
Most Points, Game	7	Patrik Sundstrom (Feb. 29/84)

All-time Record vs. Other Clubs

Regular Season

	At Home							On Road							Total						
	GP	W	L	T	GF	GA	PTS	GP	W	L	T	GF	GA	PTS	GP	W	L	T	GF	GA	PTS
Anaheim	6	4	2	0	23	15	8	5	3	1	1	11	10	7	11	7	3	1	34	25	15
Boston	44	14	22	8	149	187	36	43	4	35	4	96	194	12	87	18	57	12	245	381	48
Buffalo	44	21	13	10	168	146	52	45	14	23	8	130	164	36	89	35	36	18	298	310	88
Calgary	74	27	31	16	267	253	70	74	13	51	10	207	330	36	148	40	82	26	474	583	106
Chicago	54	25	17	12	168	160	62	53	13	35	5	126	205	31	107	38	52	17	294	365	93
Dallas	53	24	19	10	204	166	58	53	13	30	10	153	212	36	106	37	49	20	357	378	94
Detroit	47	24	16	7	189	152	55	48	13	29	6	141	204	32	95	37	45	13	330	356	87
Edmonton	58	22	29	7	225	246	51	56	13	39	4	178	282	30	114	35	68	11	403	528	81
Florida	1	0	1	0	1	2	0	1	0	1	0	1	2	0	2	0	2	0	2	4	0
Hartford	23	9	8	6	82	66	24	22	9	9	4	79	73	22	45	18	17	10	161	139	46
Los Angeles	77	40	25	12	311	258	92	79	28	41	10	264	327	66	156	68	66	22	575	585	158
Montreal	43	7	28	8	107	172	22	45	8	35	2	120	226	18	88	15	63	10	227	398	40
New Jersey	41	24	6	11	160	118	59	41	17	18	6	137	130	40	82	41	24	17	297	248	99
NY Islanders	41	18	20	3	135	138	39	39	9	22	8	102	150	26	80	27	42	11	237	288	65
NY Rangers	45	11	31	3	144	187	25	47	7	35	5	117	215	19	92	18	66	8	261	402	44
Ottawa	2	1	0	1	6	3	3	2	2	0	0	10	2	4	4	3	0	1	16	5	7
Philadelphia	45	10	24	11	131	174	31	45	1	35	9	135	202	29	90	24	54	12	266	376	60
Pittsburgh	43	20	20	3	159	165	43	43	8	28	7	144	194	23	86	28	48	10	303	359	66
Quebec	22	11	7	4	93	88	26	23	10	9	4	68	67	24	45	21	16	8	161	155	50
St. Louis	54	24	24	6	168	168	54	53	16	30	7	159	203	39	107	40	54	13	327	371	93
San Jose	12	9	2	1	50	27	19	13	7	4	2	47	39	16	25	16	6	3	97	66	35
Tampa Bay	3	3	0	0	14	3	6	2	0	2	0	8	5	4	5	5	0	0	22	8	10
Toronto	47	25	14	8	161	152	58	49	18	22	9	169	188	45	96	43	36	17	330	340	103
Washington	32	15	13	4	109	103	34	33	11	18	4	103	111	26	65	26	31	8	212	214	60
Winnipeg	54	31	15	8	211	156	70	51	18	25	8	195	202	44	105	49	40	16	406	358	114
Defunct Clubs	19	14	3	2	82	48	30	19	10	8	1	71	68	21	38	24	11	3	153	116	51
Totals	**984**	**433**	**390**	**161**	**3517**	**3353**	**1027**	**984**	**280**	**578**	**126**	**2971**	**4005**	**686**	**1968**	**713**	**968**	**287**	**6488**	**7358**	**1713**

Calgary totals include Atlanta, 1972-73 to 1979-80. Dallas totals include Minnesota, 1970-71 to 1992-93.
New Jersey totals include Kansas City, 1974-75 to 1975-76, and Colorado, 1976-77 to 1981-82.

Playoffs

	Series	W	L	GP	W	L	T	GF	GA	Last Mtg.	Round	Result
Buffalo	2	0	2	7	1	6	0	14	28	1981	PR	L 0-3
Calgary	5	2	3	25	12	13	0	80	82	1994	CQF	W 4-3
Chicago	2	1	1	9	4	5	0	24	24	1995	CSF	L 0-4
Dallas	1	1	0	5	4	1	0	18	11	1994	CSF	W 4-1
Edmonton	2	0	2	9	2	7	0	20	35	1992	DF	L 2-4
Los Angeles	3	1	2	17	10	7	0	60	66	1993	DF	L 2-4
Montreal	1	0	1	5	1	4	0	9	20	1975	QF	L 1-4
NY Islanders	2	0	2	6	0	6	0	14	26	1982	F	L 0-4
NY Rangers	1	0	1	7	3	4	0	19	21	1994	F	L 3-4
Philadelphia	1	0	1	3	1	2	0	9	15	1979	PR	L 1-2
St. Louis	1	1	0	7	4	3	0	27	27	1995	CQF	W 4-3
Toronto	1	1	0	5	4	1	0	16	9	1994	CF	W 4-1
Winnipeg	2	2	0	13	8	5	0	34	33	1993	DSF	W 4-2
Totals	**24**	**9**	**15**	**118**	**52**	**66**	**0**	**360**	**398**			

Playoff Results 1995-91

Year	Round	Opponent	Result	GF	GA
1995	CSF	Chicago	L 0-4	6	11
	CQF	St. Louis	W 4-3	27	27
1994	F	NY Rangers	L 3-4	19	21
	CF	Toronto	W 4-1	16	9
	CSF	Dallas	W 4-1	18	11
	CQF	Calgary	W 4-3	23	20
1993	DF	Los Angeles	L 2-4	25	26
	DSF	Winnipeg	W 4-2	21	17
1992	DF	Edmonton	L 2-4	15	18
	DSF	Winnipeg	W 4-3	29	17
1991	DSF	Los Angeles	L 2-4	16	26

Abbreviations: Round: F – Final;
CF – conference final; **CQF** – conference quarter-final;
CSF – conference semi-final; **DF** – division final;
DSF – division semi-final; **SF** – semi-final;
QF – quarter-final; **PR** – preliminary round.

1994-95 Results

Jan. 20		Dallas	1-1	16	at	Chicago	2-9
21		St. Louis	1-7	17	at	Detroit	1-3
24	at	Detroit	3-6	21		Toronto	3-1
25	at	Toronto	2-6	23		Chicago	1-3
28	at	St. Louis	1-4	25		Detroit	1-2
Feb. 1		Toronto	4-4	26	at	Calgary	0-2
5		Chicago	4-9	29		Los Angeles	5-2
7		Edmonton	4-4	31		Anaheim	6-1
9		Winnipeg	5-1	**Apr.** 1	at	Edmonton	5-1
11		San Jose	1-1	4		Dallas	2-2
15	at	San Jose	1-3	7	at	Winnipeg	4-7
17	at	Anaheim	2-2	8	at	Calgary	4-2
18	at	Los Angeles	6-2	11		Anaheim	5-0
20		Los Angeles	8-2	13		Edmonton	4-6
22		Winnipeg	1-4	15	at	Anaheim	3-1
24	at	Dallas	3-3	17	at	Dallas	2-2
26	at	San Jose	5-1	18	at	St. Louis	1-4
28		San Jose	3-4	20		Calgary	2-2
Mar. 2	at	Calgary	2-2	22		Edmonton	6-1
4	at	Los Angeles	5-4	25	at	Chicago	3-4
6		Detroit	2-5	28	at	Toronto	2-5
11		Anaheim	5-3	28		St. Louis	3-1
12	at	Edmonton	5-2	30		Calgary	6-4
14	at	Winnipeg	3-3	**May** 3	at	San Jose	3-3

Entry Draft
Selections 1995-81

1995
Pick
40 Chris McAllister
61 Larry Courville
66 Peter Schaefer
92 Lloyd Shaw
120 Todd Norman
144 Brent Sopel
170 Stewart Bodtker
196 Tyler Willis
222 Jason Cugnet

1994
Pick
13 Mattias Ohlund
39 Robb Gordon
42 Dave Scatchard
65 Chad Allan
92 Mike Dubinsky
117 Yanick Dube
169 Yuri Kuznetsov
195 Rob Trumbley
221 Bill Muckalt
247 Tyson Nash
273 Robert Longpre

1993
Pick
20 Mike Wilson
46 Rick Girard
98 Dieter Kochan
124 Scott Walker
150 Troy Creurer
176 Yevgeny Babariko
202 Sean Tallaire
254 Bert Robertsson
280 Sergei Tkachenko

1992
Pick
21 Libor Polasek
40 Mike Peca
45 Michael Fountain
69 Jeff Connolly
93 Brent Tully
110 Brian Loney
117 Adrian Aucoin
141 Jason Clark
165 Scott Hollis
213 Sonny Mignacca
237 Mark Wotton
261 Aaron Boh

1991
Pick
7 Alex Stojanov
29 Jassen Cullimore
51 Sean Pronger
95 Danny Kesa
117 Evgeny Namestnikov
139 Brent Thurston
161 Eric Johnson
183 David Neilson
205 Brad Barton
227 Jason Fitzsimmons
249 Xavier Majic

1990
Pick
2 Petr Nedved
18 Shawn Antoski
23 Jiri Slegr
65 Darin Bader
86 Gino Odjick
128 Daryl Filipek
149 Paul O'Hagan
170 Mark Cipriano
191 Troy Neumier
212 Tyler Ertel
233 Karri Kivi

1989
Pick
8 Jason Herter
29 Robert Woodward
71 Brett Hauer
113 Pavel Bure
134 James Revenberg
155 Rob Sangster
176 Sandy Moger
197 Gus Morschauser
218 Hayden O'Rear
239 Darcy Cahill
248 Jan Bergman

1988
Pick
2 Trevor Linden
33 Leif Rohlin
44 Dane Jackson
107 Corrie D'Alessio
122 Phil Von Stefenelli
128 Dixon Ward
149 Greg Geldart
170 Roger Akerstrom
191 Paul Constantin
212 Chris Wolanin
233 Stefan Nilsson

1987
Pick
24 Rob Murphy
45 Steve Veilleux
66 Doug Torrel
87 Sean Fabian
108 Garry Valk
129 Todd Fanning
150 Viktor Tumenev
171 Craig Daly
192 John Fletcher
213 Roger Hansson
233 Neil Eisenhut
234 Matt Evo

1986
Pick
7 Dan Woodley
49 Don Gibson
70 Ronnie Stern
91 Eric Murano
112 Steve Herniman
133 Jon Helgeson
154 Jeff Noble
175 Matt Merton
196 Marc Lyons
217 Todd Hawkins
238 Vladimir Krutov

1985
Pick
4 Jim Sandlak
25 Troy Gamble
46 Shane Doyle
67 Randy Siska
88 Robert Kron
109 Martin Hrstka
130 Brian McFarlane
151 Hakan Ahlund
172 Curtis Hunt
193 Carl Valimont
214 Igor Larionov
235 Darren Taylor

1984
Pick
10 J.J. Daigneault
31 Jeff Rohlicek
52 Dave Saunders
55 Landis Chaulk
58 Mike Stevens
73 Brian Bertuzzi
94 Brett MacDonald
115 Jeff Korchinski
136 Blaine Chrest
157 Jim Agnew
178 Rex Grant
198 Ed Lowney
219 Doug Clarke
239 Ed Kister

1983
Pick
9 Cam Neely
30 Dave Bruce
50 Scott Tottle
70 Tim Lorentz
90 Doug Quinn
110 Dave Lowry
130 Terry Maki
150 John Labatt
170 Allan Measures
190 Roger Grillo
210 Steve Kayser
230 Jay Mazur

1982
Pick
11 Michel Petit
53 Yves Lapointe
71 Shawn Kilroy
116 Taylor Hall
137 Parie Proft
158 Newell Brown
179 Don McLaren
200 Al Raymond
221 Steve Driscoll
242 Shawn Green

1981
Pick
10 Garth Butcher
52 Jean-Marc Lanthier
73 Wendell Young
105 Moe Lemay
115 Stu Kulak
136 Bruce Holloway
157 Petri Skriko
178 Frank Caprice
199 Rejean Vignola

Coaching History

Hal Laycoe, 1970-71 to 1971-72; Vic Stasiuk, 1972-73; Bill McCreary and Phil Maloney, 1973-74; Phil Maloney, 1974-75 to 1975-76; Phil Maloney and Orland Kurtenbach, 1976-77; Orland Kurtenbach, 1977-78; Harry Neale, 1978-79 to 1980-81; Harry Neale and Roger Neilson, 1981-82; Roger Neilson 1982-83; Roger Neilson and Harry Neale, 1983-84; Harry Neale and Bill Laforge, 1984-85; Tom Watt, 1985-86, 1986-87; Bob McCammon, 1987-88 to 1989-90. Bob McCammon and Pat Quinn, 1990-91; Pat Quinn, 1991-92 to 1993-94; Rick Ley, 1994-95 to date.

Captains' History

Orland Kurtenbach, 1970-71 to 1973-74; no captain, 1974-75; Andre Boudrias, 1975-76; Chris Oddleifson, 1976-77; Don Lever, 1977-78; Don Lever and Kevin McCarthy, 1978-79; Kevin McCarthy, 1979-80 to 1981-82; Stan Smyl, 1982-83 to 1989-90; Dan Quinn, Doug Lidster and Trevor Linden, 1990-91; Trevor Linden, 1991-92 to date.

Retired Numbers

12 Stan Smyl 1978-1991

Club Directory

General Motors Place
800 Griffiths Way
Vancouver, B.C.
Phone **604/899-4600**
FAX 604/899-4640
Capacity: 19,056

Orca Bay Sports & Entertainment
Chairman, Chief Executive Officer . . . . Arthur Griffiths
Vice Chairman . . . . John E. McCaw, Jr.
President, Chief Operating Officer . . . . John Chapple
Deputy Chairman and General Counsel . . . . Michael Korenberg
Executive Vice President . . . . Stanley McCammon
Executive Vice President, Business . . . . Tod Leiweke
Vice President, Consumer Sales . . . . John Rizzardini

Hockey Operations
President, General Manager, Alternate Governor . . . Pat Quinn
Vice President, Hockey Operations . . . . George McPhee
Vice President, Finance and Administration . . . . Carlos Mascarenhas
Vice President, Communications,
  Assistant to President. . . . . Steve Tambellini
Director of Corporate Sales and Promotions. . . . . . . Ric Thomsen
Director, Customer Sales and Service . . . . John Rocha
Director, Player Development/Scouting. . . . . Mike Penny
Manager, Hockey Information . . . . Devin Smith
Public and Community Relations Manager . . . . Veronica Varhaug
Game Presentation . . . . Jane Bremner
Head Coach . . . . Rick Ley
Assistant Coaches . . . . Glen Hanlon, Stan Smyl
Strength and Conditioning Coach . . . . Peter Twist
Head Coach, Syracuse Crunch . . . . Jack McIlhargey
Assistant Coach, Syracuse Crunch . . . . Curt Fraser
Director of Pro Scouting . . . . Murray Oliver
Scouting Information Coordinator . . . . Frank Provenzano
Scouts. . . . . Ron Delorme, Jack McCartan, Noel Price,
  Ken Slater, Jack Birch, Ross Mahoney, Mike
  Backman, Sergei Chibisov, Jim Eagle, Thomas
  Gradin, Ed McColgan, Ray Miron, Al McDonald
Medical Trainer. . . . . Larry Ashley
Massage Therapist . . . . Dave Schima
Equipment Trainers. . . . . Pat O'Neill, Darren Granger
Team Doctors . . . . Dr. Ross Davidson, Dr. Doug Clement
Team Dentist . . . . Dr. David Lawson

Miscellaneous Information
Rink Dimensions . . . . 200 feet by 85 feet
Club Colors. . . . . White, Black, Red and Gold
Radio Affiliation . . . . CKNW Radio (980 AM)
T.V. Affiliation . . . . BCTV (Channel 8)

Coach

LEY, RICK
Coach, Vancouver Canucks. Born in Orillia, Ont., November 2, 1948.

After serving three years as an assistant coach with Pat Quinn, Rick Ley was promoted to head coach of the Vancouver Canucks on August 10, 1994. He is the 12th head coach in franchise history. He inherited a team that won 40+ games each of the past three seasons and, in 1994, advanced to the Stanley Cup Finals for the first time in 12 years.

Ley was previously head coach of the Hartford Whalers for two seasons, where he posted records of 31-38-11 in 1991 and 38-33-9 in 1990, the best winning percentage in Whaler history. In nine seasons as a head coach in professional hockey, Ley has posted a lifetime record of 378-255-55 for a .589 winning percentage. Four times under his direction, teams have posted 50-or-more wins in a single season.

Prior to coaching Hartford, Ley was with the Canuck organization as head coach of the team's IHL affiliate, the Milwaukee Admirals, guiding them to a 54-23-5 record in 1988-89. Ley also coached the IHL's Muskegon Lumberjacks to four first place finishes from 1984 to 1988. In 1984-85, after guiding the Lumberjacks to the Turner Cup championship, Ley shared IHL coach of the year honors.

A former defenseman, Ley retired in 1981 after 13 seasons in the NHL and WHA with Toronto and New England/Hartford, including six as Whalers captain. Often described as the "heart and soul" of the Whalers, Ley was named the WHA's top defenseman in 1978-79 with New England and was a key member of Team Canada '74, comprised of WHA stars who played against the Soviet Union. He remains one of only three players in Whalers franchise history to have his jersey retired (#2), joining Gordie Howe and John McKenzie. Drafted by the Toronto Maple Leafs as an underage junior in 1968 (16th overall), Ley captained the Niagara Falls Flyers to a Memorial Cup championship in his final junior season.

Coaching Record

| Season | Team | Regular Season | | | | | Playoffs | | | |
		Games	W	L	T	%	Games	W	L	%
1982-83	Binghamton (AHL)	44	22	17	5	.534	5	1	4	.200
1983-84	Mohawk Valley (ACHL)	75	29	39	7	.433	5	1	4	.200
1984-85	Muskegon (IHL)	82	50	29	3	.628	17	11	6	.647
1985-86	Muskegon (IHL)	82	50	32	0	.610	14	12	2	.857
1986-87	Muskegon (IHL)	82	47	30	5	.604	15	10	5	.667
1987-88	Muskegon (IHL)	82	58	14	10	.768	6	2	4	.333
1988-89	Milwaukee (IHL)	82	54	23	5	.689	11	5	6	.455
1989-90	**Hartford (NHL)**	80	38	33	9	.531	7	3	4	.429
1990-91	**Hartford (NHL)**	80	31	38	11	.456	6	2	4	.333
1994-95	**Vancouver (NHL)**	48	18	18	12	.500	11	4	7	.364
	NHL Totals	208	87	89	32	.495	24	9	15	.375

Washington Capitals

1994-95 Results: 22W-18L-8T 52PTS. Third, Atlantic Division

Schedule

Oct.	Sat.	7	St. Louis		Thur.	11	Ottawa
	Wed.	11	at Philadelphia		Sat.	13	Detroit
	Fri.	13	Colorado		Tues.	16	Winnipeg
	Sat.	14	Tampa Bay		Wed.	17	at Chicago
	Tues.	17	at Dallas		Tues.	23	Florida
	Wed.	18	at Colorado		Thur.	25	at New Jersey
	Fri.	20	Los Angeles		Fri.	26	Buffalo
	Thur.	26	at Boston		Sun.	28	Philadelphia*
	Sat.	28	at Tampa Bay		Wed.	31	at Montreal
	Sun.	29	at St. Louis	Feb.	Thur.	1	at Ottawa
Nov.	Wed.	1	Montreal		Sat.	3	NY Islanders
	Fri.	3	Florida		Wed.	7	at Edmonton
	Sat.	4	at NY Islanders		Thur.	8	at Calgary
	Tues.	7	Boston		Sat.	10	at Vancouver
	Fri.	10	at Toronto		Tues.	13	Calgary
	Sat.	11	Chicago		Thur.	15	at Detroit
	Tues.	14	Philadelphia		Fri.	16	Toronto
	Fri.	17	Pittsburgh		Sun.	18	at New Jersey*
	Sat.	18	at Pittsburgh		Thur.	22	at Philadelphia
	Tues.	21	San Jose		Sat.	24	New Jersey
	Fri.	24	Tampa Bay		Thur.	29	at Florida
	Sat.	25	at Hartford	Mar.	Sat.	2	at Boston*
	Wed.	29	at Anaheim		Sun.	3	Philadelphia*
	Thur.	30	at Los Angeles		Sat.	9	NY Rangers*
Dec.	Sat.	2	at San Jose		Sun.	10	at Tampa Bay*
	Tues.	5	Florida		Tues.	12	Vancouver
	Fri.	8	at Buffalo		Fri.	15	Boston
	Sun.	10	at Winnipeg		Sun.	17	Dallas*
	Thur.	14	NY Islanders		Tues.	19	Anaheim
	Sat.	16	NY Rangers		Thur.	21	at Tampa Bay
	Mon.	18	at NY Islanders		Sat.	23	Hartford
	Fri.	22	Edmonton		Tues.	26	at NY Islanders
	Sat.	23	at NY Islanders		Wed.	27	at Montreal
	Tues.	26	Montreal		Fri.	29	Ottawa
	Thur.	28	at Florida		Sun.	31	Tampa Bay
	Sat.	30	Hartford	Apr.	Wed.	3	at Buffalo
Jan.	Mon.	1	Pittsburgh*		Thur.	4	at Pittsburgh
	Wed.	3	at Hartford		Sat.	6	at Ottawa
	Fri.	5	NY Rangers		Wed.	10	at NY Rangers
	Sat.	6	at New Jersey		Thur.	11	New Jersey
	Mon.	8	at NY Rangers		Sat.	13	Buffalo

* Denotes afternoon game.

Rookie goaltending sensation Jim Carey is the first player nominated for rookie-of-the-year honors in two different leagues in the same season. He won the Dudley "Red" Garrett Memorial Trophy as the AHL's top first-year player and was a finalist for the NHL's Calder Trophy in 1994-95.

Home Starting Times:

Weeknights and Saturdays	7:30 p.m.
Fridays	8:00 p.m.
Matinees	1:30 p.m.
Except Fri. Nov. 24.	7:30 p.m.
Sun. Jan. 28	12:00 p.m.
Sun. Mar. 31	6:00 p.m.

Franchise date: June 11, 1974

ATLANTIC DIVISION

22nd NHL Season

Year-by-Year Record

Season	GP	Home W	L	T	Road W	L	T	Overall W	L	T	GF	GA	Pts.	Finished		Playoff Result
1994-95	48	15	6	3	7	12	5	22	18	8	136	120	52	3rd,	Atlantic Div.	Lost Conf. Quarter-Final
1993-94	84	17	16	9	22	19	1	39	35	10	277	263	88	3rd,	Atlantic Div.	Lost Conf. Semi-Final
1992-93	84	21	15	6	22	19	1	43	34	7	325	286	93	2nd,	Patrick Div.	Lost Div. Semi-Final
1991-92	80	25	12	3	20	15	5	45	27	8	330	275	98	2nd,	Patrick Div.	Lost Div. Semi-Final
1990-91	80	21	14	5	16	22	2	37	36	7	258	258	81	3rd,	Patrick Div.	Lost Div. Final
1989-90	80	19	18	3	17	20	3	36	38	6	284	275	78	3rd,	Patrick Div.	Lost Conf. Championship
1988-89	80	25	12	3	16	17	7	41	29	10	305	259	92	1st,	Patrick Div.	Lost Div. Semi-Final
1987-88	80	22	14	4	16	19	5	38	33	9	281	249	85	2nd,	Patrick Div.	Lost Div. Final
1986-87	80	22	15	3	16	17	7	38	32	10	285	278	86	2nd,	Patrick Div.	Lost Div. Semi-Final
1985-86	80	30	8	2	20	15	5	50	23	7	315	272	107	2nd,	Patrick Div.	Lost Div. Final
1984-85	80	27	11	2	19	14	7	46	25	9	322	240	101	2nd,	Patrick Div.	Lost Div. Semi-Final
1983-84	80	26	11	3	22	16	2	48	27	5	308	226	101	2nd,	Patrick Div.	Lost Div. Final
1982-83	80	22	12	6	17	13	10	39	25	16	306	283	94	3rd,	Patrick Div.	Lost Div. Semi-Final
1981-82	80	16	16	8	10	25	5	26	41	13	319	338	65	5th,	Patrick Div.	Out of Playoffs
1980-81	80	16	17	7	10	19	11	26	36	18	286	317	70	5th,	Patrick Div.	Out of Playoffs
1979-80	80	20	14	6	7	26	7	27	40	13	261	293	67	5th,	Patrick Div.	Out of Playoffs
1978-79	80	15	19	6	9	22	9	24	41	15	273	338	63	4th,	Norris Div.	Out of Playoffs
1977-78	80	10	23	7	7	26	7	17	49	14	195	321	48	5th,	Norris Div.	Out of Playoffs
1976-77	80	17	15	8	7	27	6	24	42	14	221	307	62	4th,	Norris Div.	Out of Playoffs
1975-76	80	6	26	8	5	33	2	11	59	10	224	394	32	5th,	Norris Div.	Out of Playoffs
1974-75	80	7	28	5	1	39	0	8	67	5	181	446	21	5th,	Norris Div.	Out of Playoffs

1995-96 Player Personnel

FORWARDS	HT	WT	S	Place of Birth	Date	1994-95 Club
ALLISON, Jason	6-3	205	R	North York, Ont.	5/29/75	London-Wsh-Portland (AHL)
BERUBE, Craig	6-1	205	L	Calahoo, Alta.	12/17/65	Washington
BONDRA, Peter	6-1	200	L	Luck, USSR	2/7/68	Kosice-Washington
CHERREY, Scott	6-2	205	L	Drayton, Ont.	5/27/76	North Bay
CHURCH, Brad	6-1	210	L	Dauphin, Man.	11/14/76	Prince Albert
EAGLES, Mike	5-10	190	L	Sussex, N.B.	3/7/63	Winnipeg-Washington
ELOMO, Miikka	6-0	180	L	Turku, Finland	4/21/77	Kiekko-67-TPS
GENDRON, Martin	5-9	190	R	Valleyfield, Que.	2/15/74	Portland (AHL)-Washington
GRATTON, Benoit	5-10	163	L	Montreal, Que.	12/28/76	Laval
HAY, Dwayne	6-1	183	L	London, Ont.	2/11/77	Guelph
HUNTER, Dale	5-10	198	L	Petrolia, Ont.	7/31/60	Washington
JONES, Keith	6-0	200	L	Brantford, Ont.	11/8/68	Washington
JUNEAU, Joe	6-0	195	R	Pont-Rouge, Que.	1/5/68	Washington
KAMINSKI, Kevin	5-10	190	L	Churchbridge, Sask.	3/13/69	Portland (AHL)-Washington
KHARLAMOV, Alexander	5-10	180	L	Moscow, USSR	9/23/75	CSKA
KONOWALCHUK, Steve	6-1	195	L	Salt Lake City, UT	11/11/72	Washington
MILLER, Kelly	5-11	197	L	Lansing, MI	3/3/63	Washington
NELSON, Jeff	6-0	190	L	Prince Albert, Sask.	12/18/72	Portland (AHL)-Washington
PANKEWICZ, Greg	6-0	185	R	Drayton Valley, Alta.	10/6/70	P.E.I.
PEAKE, Pat	6-1	195	R	Rochester, MI	5/28/73	Washington-Portland (AHL)
PEARSON, Rob	6-3	198	R	Oshawa, Ont.	3/8/71	Washington
PIVONKA, Michal	6-2	195	L	Kladno, Czech.	1/28/66	Klagenfurt-Washington
POIRIER, Joel	6-1	190	L	Richmond Hill, Ont.	1/15/75	Windsor
REJA, Daniel	6-2	180	L	Toronto, Ont.	5/16/76	London-Belleville
USTORF, Stefan	6-0	185	L	Kaufbeuren, Germany	1/3/74	Portland (AHL)
ZEDNIK, Richard	5-11	172	L	Bystrica, Czech.	1/6/76	Portland (WHL)
DEFENSEMEN						
ALEXEEV, Alexander	6-0	216	L	Kiev, USSR	3/21/74	Tacoma
BAUMGARTNER, Nolan	6-1	200	R	Calgary, Alta.	3/23/76	Kamloops
BIALOWAS, Frank	5-11	220	L	Winnipeg, Man.	9/25/70	St. John's
BOILEAU, Patrick	6-0	190	R	Montreal, Que.	2/22/75	Laval
CORT, Joel	6-3	227	L	Hamilton, Ont.	4/30/77	Guelph
COTE, Sylvain	6-0	190	R	Quebec City, Que.	1/19/66	Washington
GONCHAR, Sergei	6-2	212	L	Chelyabinsk, USSR	4/13/74	Portland (AHL)-Washington
JEAN, Yanick	6-1	198	L	Alma, Que.	11/26/75	Chicoutimi
JOBIN, Frederic	6-0	210	L	Montreal, Que.	1/28/77	Laval
JOHANSSON, Calle	5-11	200	L	Goteborg, Sweden	2/14/67	Kloten-Washington
JOHNSON, Jim	6-1	190	L	New Hope, MN	8/9/62	Washington
KLEE, Ken	6-1	205	R	Indianapolis, IN	4/24/71	Portland (AHL)-Washington
MEKESHKIN, Dimitri	6-2	186	L	Izhevsk, USSR	1/29/76	Omsk
POAPST, Steve	6-0	200	L	Cornwall, Ont.	1/3/69	Portland (AHL)
REEKIE, Joe	6-3	220	L	Victoria, B.C.	2/22/65	Washington
STACEY, Brian	6-2	190	L	East York, Ont.	6/28/75	London-Sudbury
TERTYSHNY, Sergei	6-0	187	L	Chelyabinsk, USSR	6/3/70	Portland (AHL)
THERIAULT, Joel	6-3	201	R	Montreal, Que.	10/30/76	St-Jean-Beauport
TINORDI, Mark	6-4	213	L	Red Deer, Alta.	5/9/66	Washington
ULANOV, Igor	6-1	205	L	Krasnokamsk, USSR	10/1/69	Winnipeg-Washington
WITT, Brendan	6-1	205	L	Humbolt, Sask.	2/20/75	

GOALTENDERS	HT	WT	C	Place of Birth	Date	1994-95 Club
CAREY, Jim	6-2	205	L	Dorchester, MA	5/31/74	Portland (AHL)-Washington
CHARPENTIER, Sebastien	5-9	161	L	Drummondville, Que.	4/18/77	Laval
KOLZIG, Olaf	6-3	225	L	Johannesburg, South Africa	4/9/70	Washington-Portland (AHL)
TORCHIA, Mike	5-11	215	L	Toronto, Ont.	2/23/72	Kalamazoo-Dallas

General Manager

POILE, DAVID
Vice-President, General Manager and Alternate Governor, Washington Capitals. Born in Toronto, Ont., February 14, 1949.

Fourteen years and 522 wins ago, the Washington Capitals were a struggling franchise that had never made the playoffs. Today, the franchise can look back on 13 consecutive playoff appearances as one of the NHL's most successful clubs.

On August 30, 1982, David Poile was named general manager of the Capitals. His reconstruction of the franchise began just 11 days later, when he acquired Rod Langway from the Montreal Canadiens. Over the next 13 seasons, the Capitals never finished lower than third place in their division, while making the playoffs each year.

Washington has recorded a 522-385-112 mark in the Poile era, fifth among all NHL teams in that span. The Capitals won their first Patrick Division crown in 1989, and advanced to the Wales Conference finals in 1990.

Poile is now the third longest serving general manager with one team, trailing only Boston's Harry Sinden and Edmonton's Glen Sather. In the last eight seasons, other deals have brought players including Mark Tinordi, Sylvain Cote, Joe Juneau, Kelly Miller, and Dale Hunter to Washington. The draft has put Jim Carey, Michal Pivonka, Peter Bondra, Dimitri Khristich, Steve Konowalchuk, Keith Jones and Sergei Gonchar into the team's lineup.

David was honored as *The Sporting News* NHL Executive of the Year his first two seasons with the Capitals. David began his hockey management career with the Atlanta Flames. He served as assistant general manager to the Flames, a position he held for six seasons prior to joining the Capitals.

His responsibilities do not end in Washington, as he is a member of the NHL's general managers committee. He was a driving force behind the NHL's adoption of an instant replay rule for the 1991-92 season. His leadership on this issue, combined with his growing influence in the NHL, led to his being named the *Inside Hockey* Man of the Year for 1992.

David's father, Norman "Bud" Poile, played seven seasons in the NHL and was general manager of the Philadelphia Flyers and Vancouver Canucks. Bud was a co-winner of the 1989 Lester Patrick Award, and was inducted into the Hockey Hall of Fame in 1990.

David, 46, and his wife Elizabeth make their year-round home in Maryland with their children, Brian and Lauren.

1994-95 Scoring

* – rookie

Regular Season

Pos	#	Player	Team	GP	G	A	Pts	+/–	PIM	PP	SH	GW	GT	S	%
R	12	Peter Bondra	WSH	47	34	9	43	9	24	12	6	3	1	177	19.2
C	90	Joe Juneau	WSH	44	5	38	43	–1	8	3	0	0	1	70	7.1
C	20	Michal Pivonka	WSH	46	10	23	33	3	50	4	2	2	0	80	12.5
D	6	Calle Johansson	WSH	46	5	26	31	–6	35	4	0	2	0	112	4.5
L	8	Dimitri Khristich	WSH	48	12	14	26	0	41	8	0	2	2	92	13.0
C	22	Steve Konowalchuk	WSH	46	11	14	25	7	44	3	3	3	0	88	12.5
L	10	Kelly Miller	WSH	48	10	13	23	5	6	2	0	1	0	70	14.3
C	32	Dale Hunter	WSH	45	8	15	23	–4	101	3	0	1	0	73	11.0
R	26	Keith Jones	WSH	40	14	6	20	–2	65	1	0	4	0	85	16.5
D	3	Sylvain Cote	WSH	47	5	14	19	2	53	1	0	2	0	124	4.0
D	4	Jim Johnson	WSH	47	0	13	13	6	43	0	0	0	0	46	0.0
D	24	Mark Tinordi	WSH	42	3	9	12	–5	71	2	0	1	0	71	4.2
C	9	Dave Poulin	WSH	29	4	5	9	2	10	0	2	0	1	30	13.3
C	36	Mike Eagles	WPG	27	2	1	3	–13	40	0	0	0	0	13	15.4
			WSH	13	1	3	4	2	8	0	0	0	0	15	6.7
			TOTAL	40	3	4	7	–11	48	0	0	0	0	28	10.7
D	17	* Sergei Gonchar	WSH	31	2	5	7	4	22	0	0	0	0	38	5.3
D	29	Joe Reekie	WSH	48	1	6	7	10	97	0	0	0	0	52	1.9
L	27	Craig Berube	WSH	43	2	4	6	–5	173	0	0	0	0	22	9.1
R	25	Rob Pearson	WSH	32	0	6	6	–6	96	0	0	0	0	34	0.0
D	44	Igor Ulanov	WPG	19	1	3	4	–2	27	0	0	0	0	13	7.7
			WSH	3	0	1	1	3	2	0	0	0	0	0	0.0
			TOTAL	22	1	4	5	1	29	0	0	0	0	13	7.7
D	2	* Ken Klee	WSH	23	3	1	4	2	41	0	0	0	0	18	16.7
C	14	Pat Peake	WSH	18	0	4	4	–6	12	0	0	0	0	30	0.0
R	34	* Martin Gendron	WSH	8	2	1	3	3	2	0	0	0	0	11	18.2
C	41	* Jason Allison	WSH	12	2	1	3	–3	6	2	0	0	0	9	22.2
D	28	John Slaney	WSH	16	0	3	3	–3	6	0	0	0	0	21	0.0
C	23	* Kevin Kaminski	WSH	27	1	1	2	–6	102	0	0	1	0	12	8.3
C	15	* Jeff Nelson	WSH	10	1	0	1	–2	2	0	0	0	0	4	25.0
G	35	* Byron Dafoe	WSH	4	0	0	0	0	0	0	0	0	0	0	0.0
G	37	* Olaf Kolzig	WSH	14	0	0	0	0	4	0	0	0	0	0	0.0
G	30	* Jim Carey	WSH	28	0	0	0	0	0	0	0	0	0	0	0.0

Goaltending

No.	Goaltender	GPI	Mins	Avg	W	L	T	EN	SO	GA	SA	S%
30	* Jim Carey	28	1604	2.13	18	6	3	2	4	57	654	.913
31	Rick Tabaracci	8	394	2.44	1	3	2	0	0	16	147	.891
37	* Olaf Kolzig	14	724	2.49	2	8	2	4	0	30	305	.902
35	* Byron Dafoe	4	187	3.53	1	1	1	0	0	11	80	.863
	Totals	**48**	**2922**	**2.46**	**22**	**18**	**8**	**6**	**4**	**120**	**1192**	**.899**

Playoffs

Pos	#	Player	Team	GP	G	A	Pts	+/–	PIM	PP	SH	GW	OT	S	%
R	12	Peter Bondra	WSH	7	5	3	8	0	10	2	0	1	0	23	21.7
C	32	Dale Hunter	WSH	7	4	4	8	0	24	2	0	0	0	13	30.8
R	26	Keith Jones	WSH	7	4	4	8	–1	22	1	0	0	0	14	28.6
C	90	Joe Juneau	WSH	7	2	6	8	–2	2	0	0	0	0	16	12.5
C	22	Steve Konowalchuk	WSH	7	2	5	7	2	12	0	1	0	0	18	11.1
L	8	Dimitri Khristich	WSH	7	1	4	5	4	0	0	0	0	0	13	7.7
C	20	Michal Pivonka	WSH	7	1	4	5	2	21	0	0	0	0	9	11.1
D	6	Calle Johansson	WSH	7	3	1	4	6	0	1	0	0	0	21	14.3
D	17	* Sergei Gonchar	WSH	7	2	2	4	8	2	0	0	1	0	15	13.3
D	3	Sylvain Cote	WSH	7	1	3	4	–9	2	0	0	0	0	16	6.3
L	10	Kelly Miller	WSH	7	0	3	3	–2	4	0	0	0	0	5	0.0
C	36	Mike Eagles	WSH	7	0	2	2	1	4	0	0	0	0	6	0.0
D	4	Jim Johnson	WSH	7	0	2	2	3	8	0	0	0	0	9	0.0
R	25	Rob Pearson	WSH	3	1	0	1	0	17	0	0	1	0	5	20.0
D	24	Mark Tinordi	WSH	1	0	0	0	–2	2	0	0	0	0	2	0.0
G	35	* Byron Dafoe	WSH	1	0	0	0	0	0	0	0	0	0	0	0.0
G	37	* Olaf Kolzig	WSH	2	0	0	0	0	0	0	0	0	0	0	0.0
C	9	Dave Poulin	WSH	2	0	0	0	–1	0	0	0	0	0	3	0.0
D	44	Igor Ulanov	WSH	2	0	0	0	0	4	0	0	0	0	1	0.0
C	23	* Kevin Kaminski	WSH	5	0	0	0	–1	36	0	0	0	0	1	0.0
L	27	Craig Berube	WSH	7	0	0	0	–3	29	0	0	0	0	4	0.0
D	29	Joe Reekie	WSH	7	0	0	0	–4	2	0	0	0	0	3	0.0
D	2	* Ken Klee	WSH	7	0	0	0	1	4	0	0	0	0	10	0.0
G	30	* Jim Carey	WSH	7	0	0	0	0	4	0	0	0	0	0	0.0

Goaltending

No.	Goaltender	GPI	Mins	Avg	W	L	EN	SO	GA	SA	S%
37	* Olaf Kolzig	2	44	1.36	1	0	0	0	1	21	.952
35	* Byron Dafoe	1	20	3.00	0	0	0	0	1	3	.667
30	* Jim Carey	7	358	4.19	2	4	2	0	25	151	.834
	Totals	**7**	**425**	**4.09**	**3**	**4**	**2**	**0**	**29**	**177**	**.836**

Captains' History

Doug Mohns, 1974-75; Bill Clement and Yvon Labre, 1975-76; Yvon Labre, 1976-77, 1977-78; Guy Charron, 1978-79; Ryan Walter, 1979-80 to 1981-82; Rod Langway, 1982-83 to 1991-92; Rod Langway and Kevin Hatcher, 1992-93; Kevin Hatcher, 1993-94; Dale Hunter, 1994-95 to date.

General Managers' History

Milt Schmidt, 1974-75; Milt Schmidt and Max McNab, 1975-76; Max McNab, 1976-77 to 1980-81; Max McNab and Roger Crozier, 1981-82; David Poile, 1982-83 to date.

Retired Numbers

7	Yvon Labre	1973-1981

Club Records

Team

(Figures in brackets for season records are games played; records for fewest points, wins, ties, losses, goals, goals against are for 70 or more games)

Most Points	107	1985-86 (80)
Most Wins	50	1985-86 (80)
Most Ties	18	1980-81 (80)
Most Losses	67	1974-75 (80)
Most Goals	330	1991-92 (80)
Most Goals Against	*446	1974-75 (80)
Fewest Points	*21	1974-75 (80)
Fewest Wins	*8	1974-75 (80)
Fewest Ties	5	1974-75 (80)
		1983-84 (80)
Fewest Losses	23	1985-86 (80)
Fewest Goals	181	1974-75 (80)
Fewest Goals Against	226	1983-84 (80)

Longest Winning Streak

Over-all	10	Jan. 27-
		Feb. 18/84
Home	8	Feb. 1-
		Mar. 11/86
		Mar. 3-
		April 1/89
Away	6	Feb. 26-
		Apr. 1/84

Longest Undefeated Streak

Over-all	14	Nov. 24-
		Dec. 23/82
		(9 wins, 5 ties)
Home	13	Nov. 25/92-
		Feb. 2/93
		(9 wins, 4 ties)
Away	10	Nov. 24/82-
		Jan. 8/83
		(6 wins, 4 ties)

Longest Losing Streak

Over-all	*17	Feb. 18-
		Mar. 26/75
Home	*11	Feb. 18-
		Mar. 30/75
Away	37	Oct. 9/74-
		Mar. 26/75

Longest Winless Streak

Over-all	25	Nov. 29/75-
		Jan. 21/76
		(22 losses, 3 ties)
Home	14	Dec. 3/75-
		Jan. 21/76
		(11 losses, 3 ties)
Away	37	Oct. 9/74-
		Mar. 26/75
		(37 losses)
Most Shutouts, Season	8	1983-84 (80)
Most PIM, Season	2,204	1989-90 (80)
Most Goals, Game	12	Feb. 6/90
		(Que. 2 at Wash. 12)

Individual

Most Seasons	11	Rod Langway
Most Games	758	Mike Gartner
Most Goals, Career	397	Mike Gartner
Most Assists, Career	392	Mike Gartner
Most Points, Career	789	Mike Gartner
		(397 goals, 392 assists)
Most PIM, Career	1,630	Scott Stevens
Most Shutouts, Career	12	Don Beaupre

Longest Consecutive
Games Streak 422   Bob Carpenter

Most Goals, Season	60	Dennis Maruk
		(1981-82)
Most Assists, Season	76	Dennis Maruk
		(1981-82)
Most Points, Season	136	Dennis Maruk
		(1981-82)
		(60 goals, 76 assists)
Most PIM, Season	339	Alan May
		(1989-90)

Most Points, Defenseman,
Season 81   Larry Murphy
(1986-87)
(23 goals, 58 assists)

Most Points, Center,
Season 136   Dennis Maruk
(1981-82)
(60 goals, 76 assists)

Most Points, Right Wing,
Season 102   Mike Gartner
(1984-85)
(50 goals, 52 assists)

Most Points, Left Wing,
Season 87   Ryan Walter
(1981-82)
(38 goals, 49 assists)

Most Points, Rookie,
Season 67   Bobby Carpenter
(1981-82)
(32 goals, 35 assists)
Chris Valentine
(1981-82)
(30 goals, 37 assists)

Most Shutouts, Season	5	Don Beaupre
		(1990-91)
Most Goals, Game	5	Bengt Gustafsson
		(Jan. 8/84)
		Peter Bondra
		(Feb. 5/94)
Most Assists, Game	6	Mike Ridley
		(Jan. 7/89)
Most Points, Game	7	Dino Ciccarelli
		(Mar. 18/89)

* NHL Record.

All-time Record vs. Other Clubs
Regular Season

		At Home							On Road							Total				
	GP	W	L	T	GF	GA	PTS	GP	W	L	T	GF	GA	PTS	GP	W	L	T	GF	GA	PTS
Anaheim	1	1	0	0	3	0	2	1	1	0	0	5	2	2	2	2	0	0	8	2	4
Boston	37	10	19	8	112	141	28	38	10	23	5	107	158	25	75	20	42	13	219	299	53
Buffalo	38	9	22	7	107	148	25	38	6	28	4	99	167	16	76	15	50	11	206	315	41
Calgary	33	15	13	5	127	121	35	32	6	22	4	77	140	16	65	21	35	9	204	261	51
Chicago	33	19	10	4	127	102	42	32	7	20	5	97	134	19	65	26	30	9	224	236	61
Dallas	33	13	13	7	106	105	33	32	10	14	8	94	122	28	65	23	27	15	200	227	61
Detroit	38	20	14	4	152	120	44	40	13	16	11	118	142	37	78	33	30	15	270	262	81
Edmonton	22	12	8	2	96	81	26	22	9	9	4	78	88	22	44	21	17	6	174	169	48
Florida	4	3	0	1	13	7	7	5	1	3	1	9	17	3	9	4	3	2	22	24	10
Hartford	26	15	10	1	93	80	31	27	14	9	4	102	81	32	53	29	19	5	195	161	63
Los Angeles	38	17	15	6	166	140	40	39	12	23	4	123	159	28	77	29	38	10	289	299	68
Montreal	41	16	18	7	109	137	39	42	7	29	6	85	188	20	83	23	47	13	194	325	59
New Jersey	59	40	16	3	255	177	83	58	27	24	7	187	187	61	117	67	40	10	442	364	144
NY Islanders	61	25	27	9	195	206	59	61	23	37	1	193	252	47	122	48	64	10	388	458	106
NY Rangers	63	31	24	8	245	213	70	62	24	32	6	225	256	54	125	55	56	14	470	469	124
Ottawa	6	5	0	1	33	13	11	5	3	1	1	26	20	7	11	8	1	2	59	33	18
Philadelphia	60	22	27	11	211	215	55	63	22	37	4	182	242	48	123	44	64	15	393	457	103
Pittsburgh	68	35	27	6	299	258	76	65	26	33	6	223	261	58	133	61	60	12	522	519	134
Quebec	26	14	9	3	107	86	31	26	12	10	4	101	86	28	52	26	19	7	208	172	59
St. Louis	32	17	12	3	118	98	37	33	11	14	8	111	139	30	65	28	26	11	229	237	67
San Jose	3	2	1	0	12	7	4	3	0	0	2	7	6	5	6	1	0	3	24	14	10
Tampa Bay	6	2	1	3	20	16	7	5	5	0	0	19	6	10	11	7	1	3	39	22	17
Toronto	35	21	12	2	132	96	44	34	11	19	4	122	164	26	69	32	31	6	254	260	70
Vancouver	33	18	11	4	111	103	40	32	13	15	4	103	109	30	65	31	26	8	214	212	70
Winnipeg	22	15	5	2	104	70	32	23	6	12	5	83	90	17	45	21	17	7	187	160	49
Defunct Clubs	10	2	8	0	28	42	4	10	4	5	1	30	39	9	20	6	13	1	58	81	13
Totals	**828**	**399**	**322**	**107**	**3081**	**2782**	**905**	**828**	**286**	**435**	**107**	**2611**	**3256**	**679**	**1656**	**685**	**757**	**214**	**5692**	**6038**	**1584**

Calgary totals include Atlanta, 1974-75 to 1979-80. Dallas totals include Minnesota, 1974-75 to 1992-93.
New Jersey totals include Kansas City, 1974-75 to 1975-76, and Colorado, 1976-77 to 1981-82.

Playoffs

	Series	W	L	GP	W	L	T	GF	GA	Last Mtg.	Round	Result
Boston	1	0	1	4	0	4	0	6	15	1990	CF	L 0-4
New Jersey	2	1	1	13	7	6	0	44	43	1990	DSF	W 4-2
NY Islanders	6	1	5	30	12	18	0	88	89	1993	DSF	L 2-4
NY Rangers	4	2	2	22	11	11	0	75	71	1994	CSF	L 1-4
Philadelphia	3	2	1	16	9	7	0	65	55	1989	DSF	L 2-4
Pittsburgh	4	1	3	25	11	14	0	86	85	1995	CQF	L 3-4
Totals	**20**	**7**	**13**	**110**	**50**	**60**	**0**	**364**	**368**			

Playoff Results 1995-91

Year	Round	Opponent	Result	GF	GA
1995	CSF	Pittsburgh	L 3-4	26	29
1994	CSF	NY Rangers	L 1-4	12	20
	CQF	Pittsburgh	W 4-2	20	12
1993	DSF	NY Islanders	L 2-4	22	23
1992	DSF	Pittsburgh	L 3-4	27	25
1991	DF	Pittsburgh	L 1-4	13	19
	DSF	NY Rangers	W 4-2	16	16

Abbreviations: Round: F – Final;
CF – conference final; **CQF** – conference quarter-final;
CSF – conference semi-final; **DF** – division final;
DSF – division semi-final; **SF** – semi-final;
QF – quarter-final; **PR** – preliminary round.

1994-95 Results

Jan.	21	at	Hartford	1-1	13	at Tampa Bay	3-0
	24	at	Quebec	1-5	16	at Florida	1-5
	25	at	Montreal	0-2	18	NY Rangers	4-1
	27		NY Islanders	5-2	20	at Hartford	5-0
	29		Pittsburgh	1-4	21	Ottawa	1-0
Feb.	2		Buffalo	0-1	25	Philadelphia	2-2
	4		Florida	3-2	26	Hartford	3-4
	7	at	Buffalo	1-2	29	at Tampa Bay	4-2
	8	at	NY Rangers	4-5	31	Quebec	6-4
	11	at	Boston	1-1	**Apr.** 2	Boston	2-1
	13	at	Philadelphia	3-5	4	at NY Islanders	5-4
	15	at	New Jersey	2-4	8	Philadelphia	1-3
	18		Quebec	4-2	11	at Pittsburgh	1-3
	20		New Jersey	0-2	12	New Jersey	1-2
	23	at	Ottawa	5-5	14	Florida	3-0
	25	at	New Jersey	3-3	16	at Quebec	2-4
	26		Tampa Bay	1-1	17	at Montreal	2-5
	28	at	Philadelphia	2-4	21	Hartford	6-3
Mar.	2	at	NY Islanders	4-3	22	at Pittsburgh	2-1
	4		Montreal	5-1	24	at NY Rangers	4-5
	5		NY Rangers	4-2	26	NY Islanders	6-5
	7	at	Boston	3-1	28	Buffalo	5-1
	10		Ottawa	2-2	30	at Florida	2-2
	12		Tampa Bay	3-1	**May** 2	Pittsburgh	7-2

Entry Draft
Selections 1995-81

1995
Pick
17 Brad Church
23 Miikka Elomo
43 Dwayne Hay
93 Sebasti Charpentier
95 Joel Theriault
105 Benoit Gratton
124 Joel Cort
147 Frederick Jobin
199 Vasili Turkovsky
225 Scott Swanson

1994
Pick
10 Nolan Baumgartner
15 Alexander Kharlamov
41 Scott Cherrey
93 Matthew Herr
119 Yanick Jean
145 Dmitri Mekeshkin
171 Daniel Reja
197 Chris Patrick
223 John Tuohy
249 Richard Zednik
275 Sergei Tertyshny

1993
Pick
11 Brendan Witt
17 Jason Allison
69 Patrick Boileau
147 Frank Banham
173 Daniel Hendrickson
174 Andrew Brunette
199 Joel Poirier
225 Jason Gladney
251 Mark Seliger
277 Dany Bousquet

1992
Pick
14 Sergei Gonchar
32 Jim Carey
53 Stefan Ustorf
71 Martin Gendron
119 John Varga
167 Mark Matier
191 Mike Mathers
215 Brian Stagg
239 Gregory Callahan
263 Billy Jo MacPherson

1991
Pick
14 Pat Peake
21 Trevor Halverson
25 Eric Lavigne
36 Jeff Nelson
58 Steve Konowalchuk
80 Justin Morrison
146 Dave Morissette
168 Rick Corriveau
190 Trevor Duhaime
209 Rob Leask
212 Carl LeBlanc
234 Rob Puchniak
256 Bill Kovacs

1990
Pick
9 John Slaney
30 Rod Pasma
51 Chris Longo
72 Randy Pearce
93 Brian Sakic
94 Mark Ouimet
114 Andrei Kovalev
135 Roman Kontsek
156 Peter Bondra
159 Steve Martell
177 Ken Klee
198 Michael Boback
219 Alan Brown
240 Todd Hlushko

1989
Pick
19 Olaf Kolzig
35 Byron Dafoe
59 Jim Mathieson
61 Jason Woolley
82 Trent Klatt
145 Dave Lorentz
166 Dean Holoien
187 Victor Gervais
208 Jiri Vykoukal
229 Andrei Sidorov
250 Ken House

1988
Pick
15 Reginald Savage
36 Tim Taylor
41 Wade Bartley
57 Duane Derksen
78 Rob Krauss
120 Dmitri Khristich
141 Keith Jones
144 Brad Schlegel
162 Todd Hilditch
183 Petr Pavlas
192 Mark Sorensen
204 Claudio Scremin
225 Chris Venkus
246 Ron Pascucci

1987
Pick
36 Jeff Ballantyne
57 Steve Maltais
78 Tyler Larter
99 Pat Beauchesne
120 Rich Defreitas
141 Devon Oleniuk
162 Thomas Sjogren
204 Chris Clarke
225 Milos Vanik
240 Dan Brettschneider
246 Ryan Kummu

1986
Pick
19 Jeff Greenlaw
40 Steve Seftel
60 Shawn Simpson
61 Jimmy Hrivnak
82 Erin Ginnell
103 John Purves
124 Stefan Nilsson
145 Peter Choma
166 Lee Davidson
187 Tero Toivola
208 Bobby Bobcock
229 John Schratz
250 Scott McCrory

1985
Pick
19 Yvon Corriveau
40 John Druce
61 Rob Murray
82 Bill Houlder
83 Larry Shaw
103 Claude Dumas
124 Doug Stromback
145 Jamie Nadjiwan
166 Mark Haarmann
187 Steve Hollett
208 Dallas Eakins
229 Steve Hrynewich
250 Frank DiMuzio

1984
Pick
17 Kevin Hatcher
34 Steve Leach
59 Michal Pivonka
80 Kris King
122 Vito Cramarossa
143 Timo Iljina
164 Frank Joo
185 Jim Thomson
205 Paul Cavallini
225 Mikhail Tatarinov
246 Per Schedrin

1983
Pick
75 Tim Bergland
95 Martin Bouliane
135 Dwaine Hutton
155 Marty Abrams
175 David Cowan
195 Yves Beaudoin
215 Alain Raymond
216 Anders Huss

1982
Pick
5 Scott Stevens
58 Milan Novy
89 Dean Evason
110 Ed Kastelic
152 Wally Schreiber
173 Jamie Reeve
194 Juha Nurmi
215 Wayne Prestage
236 Jon Holden
247 Marco Kallas

1981
Pick
3 Bob Carpenter
45 Eric Calder
68 Tony Kellin
89 Mike Siltala
91 Peter Sidorkiewicz
110 Jim McGeough
131 Risto Jalo
152 Gaetan Duchesne
173 George White
194 Chris Valentine

Coach

SCHOENFELD, JAMES GRANT (JIM)
Coach, Washington Capitals. Born in Galt, Ont., September 4, 1952.

Jim enters his second full season as Capitals' head coach. In 1994-95, the Capitals rebounded from a slow start to record the second-best record in the Eastern Conference over the season's final six weeks before falling to Pittsburgh in the playoffs.

Jim was named the Capitals' tenth head coach on January 27, 1994 and made his coaching debut that night in Buffalo. Under his inspirational leadership, the Capitals recorded a 19-12-6 record, finishing seventh in the Conference.

He served as head coach of the New Jersey Devils from January 26, 1988 to November 6, 1990. Schoenfeld led the Devils to their first playoff appearance in 1988, and took the club to within one game of the Stanley Cup Finals. He also was head coach for the Buffalo Sabres from June 11, 1985 to January 15, 1986, when general manager Scotty Bowman elected to resume his coaching career.

Schoenfeld played 13 years in the National Hockey League with Buffalo, Detroit and Boston. In 719 games, he tallied 51 goals, 204 assists and 1,132 penalty minutes. He was named to the NHL's Second All-Star Team in 1979-80 and finished third in Norris Trophy voting that season. Schoenfeld also appeared in the 1977 and 1980 NHL All-Star games, and was selected to play in the 1979 Challenge Cup.

Schoenfeld and wife Theresa live in Maryland and have four children, Justin, Katie, Adam and Nathan.

Coaching Record

Season	Team	Regular Season					Playoffs			
		Games	W	L	T	%	Games	W	L	%
1984-85	Rochester (AHL)	25	17	6	2	.720	....	....	....	....
1985-86	Buffalo (NHL)	43	19	19	5	.500	....	....	....	....
1987-88	New Jersey (NHL)	30	17	12	1	.583	20	11	9	.550
1988-89	New Jersey (NHL)	80	27	41	12	.413	....	....	....	....
1989-90	New Jersey (NHL)	14	6	6	2	.500	....	....	....	....
1993-94	Washington (NHL)	37	19	12	6	.595	11	5	6	.455
1994-95	Washington (NHL)	48	22	18	8	.542	7	3	4	.429
	NHL Totals	**252**	**110**	**108**	**34**	**.504**	**38**	**19**	**19**	**.500**

Club Directory

USAir Arena
1 Harry S Truman Drive
Landover, Maryland 20785
Phone **301/386-7000**
PR FAX 301/386-7012
Capacity: 18,130

Board of Directors
David P. Bindeman, Stuart L. Bindeman, James A. Cafritz, A. James Clark, Albert Cohen, J. Martin Irving, R. Robert Linowes, Arthur K. Mason, Dr. Jack Meshel, David M. Osnos, Richard M. Patrick

Management
Chairman . . . . Abe Pollin
President and Governor . . . . Richard M. Patrick
Legal Counsel and Alternate Governors . . . . David M. Osnos, Peter O'Malley
Vice-President of Finance . . . . Edmund Stelzer

Hockey Department
Vice-President, G.M. and Alternate Governor . . . . . David Poile
Director of Player Personnel . . . . Jack Button
Head Coach . . . . Jim Schoenfeld
Assistant Coaches . . . . Keith Allain, Tod Button
Head Coach, Portland Pirates . . . . Barry Trotz
Assistant Coach, Portland Pirates . . . . Paul Gardner
Admin. Assistant to the V.P. and G.M. . . . . Pat Young
Team Services . . . . Todd Warren
Assistant to the Hockey Department . . . . Larissa Cason
Piney Orchard Staff . . . . Alex Walker
Scouts . . . . Robert Atrill, Craig Channell, Gilles Cote, Archie Henderson, Hugh Rogers, Bob Schmidt, Shawn Simpson

Medical and Training Staff
Head Trainer . . . . Stan Wong
Assistant Trainer/Head Equipment Manager . . . . . . Doug Shearer
Assistant Equipment Manager . . . . Craig Leydig
Assistant to the Equipment Manager . . . . Rick Harper
Strength and Conditioning Coach . . . . Frank Costello
Massage Therapist . . . . Curt Millar
Team Nutritionist . . . . Dr. Pat Mann
Team Physicians . . . . Dr. Richard Grossman, Dr. Stephen Haas, Dr. Carl MacCartee, Dr. Frank Melograna
Team Ophthamologist . . . . Dr. Michael Herr
Team Optometrists . . . . Dr. Ron Berger, Dr. Harry Wachs
Team Dentist . . . . Dr. Howard Salob

Accounting Department
Controller . . . . Aggie Ballard
Accounting Assistants . . . . Kathleen Brady, Crystal Coffren, Deborah Kostakos, Melanie Loveless

WASHINGTON SPORTS
President . . . . Susan O'Malley
Ex. Vice President . . . . Wes Unseld

Communications Department
Vice President of Communications . . . . Matt Williams
Public Relations Director . . . . Nancy Yasharoff
Public Relations Manager . . . . Dan Kaufman
Creative Services Editor . . . . Jim Delaney
Creative Services Assistant . . . . Rick Braunstein
Communications Coordinator . . . . Julie Hensley

Community Relations Department
Vice President of Community Relations . . . . Judy Holland
Director of Special Programs . . . . Yvon Labre
Assistant Director of Community Relations . . . . . . Tara Greco
Community Relations Manager . . . . Nicol Addison
Administrative Assistant . . . . Kathy Moriarty

Assistant Director of Game Operations . . . . Chris Mulcahy
Game Operations Assistant . . . . Rory Ingram
Game Day Coordinator . . . . TBA

Sales
Vice President of Sales . . . . Rick Moreland
Director of Sales . . . . Jerry Murphy
Regional Sales Managers . . . . Bryan Maust, John Oakes, Ron Potter
Account Executives . . . . Scott Bershadsky, Tim Bronaugh, Darren Bruening, Todd Freundlich, Don Gore, Sean Martin, Tim Munchmeyer, Melissa Tindall, Scott Tippins, Brian Walsh

Customer Service/Promotions
Ex. Dir. of Customer Service/Advertising/
  Marketing/Promotions . . . . Rhonda Ballute
Director of Customer Service . . . . Joanne Kowalski
Asst. Director of Advertising/Promotions . . . . Terri Maruca
Asst. Director of Customer Service . . . . Kerry Gregg
Special Events Coordinator . . . . Cathy Tessier
Sales Coordinator . . . . Gina Spear
Customer Service, Box Office . . . . Jason Sheer
Receptionist . . . . Nancy Woodall
Assistant to the Vice President, Washington Sports . Aidan Duffy
Sales Secretary . . . . Tonya Turner
Administrative Assistant . . . . Janice Toepper

Coaching History

Jim Anderson, ''Red'' Sullivan and Milt Schmidt, 1974-75; Milt Schmidt and Tom McVie, 1975-76; Tom McVie, 1976-77 to 1977-78; Danny Belisle, 1978-79; Danny Belisle and Gary Green, 1979-80; Gary Green, 1980-81; Gary Green, Roger Crozier and Bryan Murray, 1981-82; Bryan Murray, 1982-83 to 1988-89; Bryan Murray and Terry Murray, 1989-90; Terry Murray, 1990-91 to 1992-93; Terry Murray and Jim Schoenfeld, 1993-94; Jim Schoenfeld, 1994-95 to date.

Winnipeg Jets

1994-95 Results: 16W-25L-7T 39PTS. Sixth, Central Division

The only player to register a five-goal game in 1994-95, Alexei Zhamnov also was selected to the NHL's Second All-Star Team.

Schedule

Oct.	Sat.	7	Dallas	Wed.	10	Buffalo	
	Mon.	9	Anaheim	Fri.	12	Hartford	
	Wed.	11	at NY Rangers	Sun.	14	Anaheim	
	Thur.	12	at New Jersey	Tues.	16	at Washington	
	Sun.	15	Detroit	Wed.	17	at Toronto	
	Tues.	17	Tampa Bay	Wed.	24	St. Louis	
	Thur.	19	San Jose	Sat.	27	at Montreal*	
	Sun.	22	at Anaheim	Mon.	29	at Dallas	
	Wed.	25	at San Jose	**Feb.**	Thur.	1	at Colorado
	Fri.	27	at Edmonton	Sun.	4	Vancouver*	
	Sat.	28	at Vancouver	Thur.	8	Ottawa	
	Mon.	30	Detroit	Sat.	10	at Calgary	
Nov.	Wed.	1	Toronto	Tues.	13	at Vancouver	
	Fri.	3	Colorado	Fri.	16	Pittsburgh	
	Sun.	5	at Buffalo	Sun.	18	at St. Louis	
	Fri.	10	at St. Louis	Wed.	21	Vancouver	
	Tues.	14	Chicago	Fri.	23	Chicago	
	Fri.	17	NY Rangers	Mon.	26	Los Angeles	
	Sat.	18	at Toronto	Wed.	28	Toronto	
	Tues.	21	at Boston	**Mar.**	Fri.	1	at Hartford
	Wed.	22	at Ottawa	Sun.	3	at NY Islanders*	
	Sun.	26	Edmonton	Tues.	5	at Pittsburgh	
	Tues.	28	Toronto	Thur.	7	Florida	
	Thur.	30	St. Louis	Sat.	9	NY Islanders*	
Dec.	Sat.	2	Chicago	Sun.	10	Detroit	
	Sun.	3	Calgary	Tues.	12	at Detroit	
	Wed.	6	at Los Angeles	Wed.	13	at Toronto	
	Thur.	7	at San Jose	Sat.	16	at Philadelphia	
	Sun.	10	Washington	Wed.	20	San Jose	
	Tues.	12	Montreal	Fri.	22	Philadelphia	
	Fri.	15	Edmonton	Sun.	24	Colorado*	
	Sun.	17	at Chicago	Tues.	26	at Dallas	
	Tues.	19	at Tampa Bay	Wed.	27	at Colorado	
	Thur.	21	at Florida	Fri.	29	at Edmonton	
	Sat.	23	St. Louis	Sun.	31	at Calgary	
	Thur.	28	at Chicago	**Apr.**	Wed.	3	Dallas
	Fri.	29	New Jersey	Sat.	6	Calgary	
	Sun.	31	Boston*	Mon.	8	at St. Louis	
Jan.	Wed.	3	at Los Angeles	Wed.	10	at Detroit	
	Fri.	5	at Dallas	Fri.	12	Los Angeles	
	Mon.	8	at Detroit	Sun.	14	at Anaheim	

* Denotes afternoon game.

Home Starting Times:

Weeknights	7:35 p.m.
Saturdays and Sundays	6:35 p.m.
Matinees	2:05 p.m.
Except Mon. Oct. 9	7:05 p.m.
Sun. Dec. 31	4:30 p.m.

Franchise date: June 22, 1979

CENTRAL DIVISION

17th NHL Season

Year-by-Year Record

		Home			Road			Overall							
Season	GP	W	L	T	W	L	T	W	L	T	GF	GA	Pts.	Finished	Playoff Result
1994-95	48	10	10	4	6	15	3	16	25	7	157	177	39	6th, Central Div.	Out of Playoffs
1993-94	84	15	23	4	9	28	5	24	51	9	245	344	57	6th, Central Div.	Out of Playoffs
1992-93	84	23	16	3	17	21	4	40	37	7	322	320	87	4th, Smythe Div.	Lost Div. Semi-Final
1991-92	80	20	14	6	13	18	9	33	32	15	251	244	81	4th, Smythe Div.	Lost Div. Semi-Final
1990-91	80	17	18	5	9	25	6	26	43	11	260	288	63	5th, Smythe Div.	Out of Playoffs
1989-90	80	22	13	5	15	19	6	37	32	11	298	290	85	3rd, Smythe Div.	Lost Div. Semi-Final
1988-89	80	17	18	5	9	24	7	26	42	11	300	355	64	5th, Smythe Div.	Out of Playoffs
1987-88	80	20	14	6	13	22	5	33	36	11	292	310	77	3rd, Smythe Div.	Lost Div. Semi-Final
1986-87	80	25	12	3	15	20	5	40	32	8	279	271	88	3rd, Smythe Div.	Lost Div. Final
1985-86	80	18	19	3	8	28	4	26	47	7	295	372	59	3rd, Smythe Div.	Lost Div. Semi-Final
1984-85	80	21	13	6	22	14	4	43	27	10	358	332	96	2nd, Smythe Div.	Lost Div. Final
1983-84	80	17	15	8	14	23	3	31	38	11	340	374	73	4th, Smythe Div.	Lost Div. Semi-Final
1982-83	80	22	16	2	11	23	6	33	39	8	311	333	74	4th, Smythe Div.	Lost Div. Semi-Final
1981-82	80	18	13	9	15	20	5	33	33	14	319	332	80	2nd, Norris Div.	Lost Div. Semi-Final
1980-81	80	7	25	8	2	32	6	9	57	14	246	400	32	6th, Smythe Div.	Out of Playoffs
1979-80	80	13	19	8	7	30	3	20	49	11	214	314	51	5th, Smythe Div.	Out of Playoffs

1995-96 Player Personnel

FORWARDS	HT	WT	S	Place of Birth	Date	1994-95 Club
BUDAYEV, Alexei	6-2	183	R	Pavlov Posad, USSR	4/24/75	Elektrostal-Red Deer
DEAZELEY, Mark	6-4	240	L	North York, Ont.	4/8/72	Springfield-Toledo
DOAN, Shane	6-1	215	R	Halkirk, Alta.	10/10/76	Kamloops
DRAKE, Dallas	6-0	180	L	Trail, B.C.	2/4/69	Winnipeg
EASTWOOD, Mike	6-3	205	R	Ottawa, Ont.	7/1/67	Toronto-Winnipeg
EMERSON, Nelson	5-11	175	R	Hamilton, Ont.	8/17/67	Winnipeg
GILHEN, Randy	6-0	190	L	Zweibrucken, W. Germany	6/13/63	Winnipeg
GOVEDARIS, Chris	6-0	200	L	Toronto, Ont.	2/2/70	Milwaukee-Adirondack
GROSEK, Michal	6-2	180	R	Vyskov, Czech.	6/1/75	Springfield-Winnipeg
GUSMANOV, Ravil	6-3	185	L	Naberezhnye Chelny, USSR	7/25/72	Springfield
HANSEN, Tavis	6-1	180	R	Prince Albert, Sask.	6/17/75	Tacoma-Winnipeg
KING, Kris	5-11	208	L	Bracebridge, Ont.	2/18/66	Winnipeg
KOROLEV, Igor	6-1	187	L	Moscow, USSR	9/6/70	Moscow D'amo-Winnipeg
MARTIN, Craig	6-2	215	R	Amherst, N.S.	1/21/71	Winnipeg-Springfield
MURRAY, Rob	6-1	180	R	Toronto, Ont.	4/4/67	Springfield-Winnipeg
OLCZYK, Ed	6-1	205	L	Chicago, IL	8/16/66	NY Rangers-Winnipeg
SELANNE, Teemu	6-0	200	R	Helsinki, Finland	7/3/70	Jokerit-Winnipeg
SHANNON, Darrin	6-2	210	L	Barrie, Ont.	12/8/69	Winnipeg
SIMON, Jason	6-1	190	L	Sarnia, Ont.	3/21/69	Denver
STAPLETON, Mike	5-10	183	R	Sarnia, Ont.	5/5/66	Edmonton
TKACHUK, Keith	6-2	210	L	Melrose, MA	3/28/72	Winnipeg
ZHAMNOV, Alexei	6-1	195	L	Moscow, USSR	10/1/70	Winnipeg

DEFENSEMEN						
CHEREDARYK, Steve	6-2	197	L	Calgary, Alta.	11/20/75	Medicine Hat-Springfield
FINLEY, Jeff	6-2	204	L	Edmonton, Alta.	4/14/67	Hershey
MALGUNAS, Stewart	6-0	200	L	Prince George, B.C.	4/21/70	Philadelphia-Hershey
MANSON, Dave	6-2	202	L	Prince Albert, Sask.	1/27/67	Winnipeg
MULLER, Mike	6-2	205	L	Fairview, MN	9/18/71	Springfield
NUMMINEN, Teppo	6-1	190	R	Tampere, Finland	7/3/68	TuTo-Winnipeg
QUINT, Deron	6-1	182	L	Durham, NH	3/12/76	Seattle
SHANNON, Darryl	6-2	200	L	Barrie, Ont.	6/21/68	Winnipeg
THOMPSON, Brent	6-2	200	L	Calgary, Alta.	1/9/71	Winnipeg
VISHEAU, Mark	6-4	200	R	Burlington, Ont.	6/27/73	Springfield
WILKINSON, Neil	6-3	190	R	Selkirk, Man.	8/15/67	Winnipeg

GOALTENDERS	HT	WT	C	Place of Birth	Date	1994-95 Club
CHEVELDAE, Tim	5-10	195	L	Melville, Sask.	2/15/68	Winnipeg
DUFFUS, Parris	6-1	192	L	Denver, CO	1/27/70	Peoria
KHABIBULIN, Nikolai	6-1	176	L	Sverdlovsk, USSR	1/13/73	Springfield-Winnipeg
LANGKOW, Scott	5-11	190	L	Sherwood Park, Alta.	4/21/75	Portland (WHL)

1994-95 Scoring

*– rookie

Regular Season

Pos	#	Player	Team	GP	G	A	Pts	+/–	PIM	PP	SH	GW	GT	S	%
C	10	Alexei Zhamnov	WPG	48	30	35	65	5	20	9	0	4	0	155	19.4
L	7	Keith Tkachuk	WPG	48	22	29	51	–4	152	7	2	2	1	129	17.1
R	8	Teemu Selanne	WPG	45	22	26	48	1	2	8	2	1	1	167	13.2
R	19	Nelson Emerson	WPG	48	14	23	37	–12	26	4	1	1	0	122	11.5
R	23	Igor Korolev	WPG	45	8	22	30	1	10	1	0	1	0	85	9.4
C	18	Dallas Drake	WPG	43	8	18	26	–6	30	0	0	1	0	66	12.1
D	4	Stephane Quintal	WPG	43	6	17	23	0	78	3	0	2	0	107	5.6
D	27	Teppo Numminen	WPG	42	5	16	21	12	16	2	0	0	0	86	5.8
C	32	Mike Eastwood	TOR	36	5	5	10	–12	32	0	0	0	0	38	13.2
			WPG	13	3	6	9	3	4	0	0	0	0	17	17.6
			TOTAL	49	8	11	19	–9	36	0	0	0	0	55	14.5
D	3	Dave Manson	WPG	44	3	15	18	–20	139	2	0	1	0	104	2.9
C	25	Thomas Steen	WPG	31	5	10	15	–13	14	2	0	0	0	32	15.6
D	24	Darryl Shannon	WPG	40	5	9	14	1	48	0	1	0	0	42	11.9
C	16	Ed Olczyk	NYR	20	2	1	3	–2	4	1	0	0	0	29	6.9
			WPG	13	2	8	10	1	8	1	0	0	0	27	7.4
			TOTAL	33	4	9	13	–1	12	2	0	0	0	56	7.1
C	15	Randy Gilhen	WPG	44	5	6	11	–17	52	0	1	1	0	47	10.6
L	34	Darrin Shannon	WPG	19	5	3	8	–6	14	3	0	1	0	26	19.2
L	17	Kris King	WPG	48	4	2	6	0	85	0	0	0	0	58	6.9
D	2	Neil Wilkinson	WPG	40	1	4	5	–26	75	0	0	0	0	25	4.0
L	75	*Michal Grosek	WPG	24	2	2	4	–3	21	0	0	1	0	27	7.4
R	36	Greg Brown	WPG	9	0	3	3	1	17	0	0	0	0	12	0.0
C	12	Rob Murray	WPG	10	0	2	2	1	2	0	0	0	0	5	0.0
D	42	Oleg Mikulchik	WPG	25	0	2	2	10	12	0	0	0	0	5	0.0
R	28	*Craig Martin	WPG	20	0	1	1	–4	19	0	0	0	0	3	0.0
G	35	*N. Khabibulin	WPG	26	0	1	1	0	4	0	0	0	0	0	0.0
G	29	Tim Cheveldae	WPG	30	0	1	1	0	2	0	0	0	0	0	0.0
C	47	*Tavis Hansen	WPG	1	0	0	0	0	0	0	0	0	0	0	0.0
R	37	John Leblanc	WPG	2	0	0	0	0	0	0	0	0	0	2	0.0
C	38	Luciano Borsato	WPG	4	0	0	0	–1	0	0	0	0	0	3	0.0
L	21	Russ Romaniuk	WPG	6	0	0	0	–3	0	0	0	0	0	3	0.0
D	22	Brent Thompson	WPG	29	0	0	0	–17	78	0	0	0	0	16	0.0

Goaltending

No.	Goaltender	GPI	Mins	Avg	W	L	T	EN	SO	GA	SA	S%
35	*N. Khabibulin	26	1339	3.41	8	9	4	1	0	76	723	.895
29	Tim Cheveldae	30	1571	3.70	8	16	3	3	0	97	818	.881
	Totals	**48**	**2923**	**3.63**	**16**	**25**	**7**	**4**	**0**	**177**	**1545**	**.885**

Coach

SIMPSON, TERRY
Coach, Winnipeg Jets. Born in Brantford, Ont., August 30, 1943.

Simpson enters his first full season as the Jets' head coach, after serving as an assistant coach for the club for one season. Following his appointment late last season, the Jets posted a 7-7-1 record.

Simpson returned to the Jets' coaching staff last year after one season as the Philadelphia Flyers' head coach. Under Simpson's direction, the Flyers posted a 35-39-10 record. Prior to being named head coach of the Flyers in May of 1993, he spent three seasons as an assistant coach with the Jets. During the 1991-92 season, Terry, a defensive specialist, was instrumental in helping the Jets achieve the NHL's third best over-all team defense and penalty killing ratings. Before joining the Jets, the Brantford, Ontario native served as the head coach of the New York Islanders in 1986-87 and 1987-88 and part of the 1988-89 season. In two-plus seasons behind the Islanders' bench, he compiled a 81-82-24 record including a Patrick Division championship in 1987-88.

Prior to coaching the Islanders, Simpson coached the Prince Albert Raiders of the Saskatchewan Junior League for ten years before the team moved up to the Western Hockey League. In four years of competition in the WHL, his teams compiled a record of 167-112-9. He provided the Raiders with tremendous leadership and guided the 1984-85 team to a Memorial Cup, symbolic of junior hockey supremacy in Canada. Terry was also a member of the Canadian National Junior Team coaching staff for three years (1984-86), the last two as head coach. The Canadians won a gold medal in 1985 and a silver medal in 1986.

Simpson also is the majority owner of the Red Deer Rebels of the WHL.

Terry and his wife, Eunice "Red" reside in Charleswood, Manitoba. They have two daughters, Tracie and Kelly.

Coaching Record

Season	Team	Regular Season Games	W	L	T	%	Playoffs Games	W	L	%
1982-83	Prince Albert (WHL)	72	16	55	1	.229	....	....	....	....
1983-84	Prince Albert (WHL)	72	41	29	2	.583	5	1	4	.200
1984-85	Prince Albert (WHL)	72	58	11	3	.826	13	12	1	.923
1985-86	Prince Albert (WHL)	72	52	17	3	.743	20	15	5	.750
1986-87	NY Islanders (NHL)	80	35	33	12	.513	14	7	7	.500
1987-88	NY Islanders (NHL)	80	39	31	10	.550	6	2	4	.333
1988-89	NY Islanders (NHL)	27	7	18	2	.296	....	....	....	....
1993-94	Philadelphia (NHL)	84	35	39	10	.476	....	....	....	....
1994-95	Winnipeg (NHL)	15	7	7	1	.500	....	....	....	....
	NHL Totals	**286**	**123**	**128**	**35**	**.491**	**20**	**9**	**11**	**.450**

General Managers' History

John Ferguson, 1979-80 to 1987-88; John Ferguson and Mike Smith, 1988-89; Mike Smith, 1989-90 to 1992-93; Mike Smith and John Paddock, 1993-94; John Paddock, 1994-95 to date.

Coaching History

Tom McVie and Bill Sutherland, 1979-80; Tom McVie, Bill Sutherland and Mike Smith, 1980-81; Tom Watt, 1981-82 to 1982-83; Tom Watt and Barry Long, 1983-84; Barry Long, 1984-85; Barry Long and John Ferguson, 1985-86; Dan Maloney, 1986-87 to 1987-88, Dan Maloney and Rick Bowness 1988-89; Bob Murdoch, 1989-90, 1990-91; John Paddock, 1991-92 to 1993-94; John Paddock and Terry Simpson, 1994-95; Terry Simpson, 1995-96.

Captains' History

Lars-Erik Sjoberg, 1979-80; Morris Lukowich, 1980-81; Dave Christian, 1981-82; Dave Christian and Lucien DeBlois, 1982-83; Lucien DeBlois, 1983-84; Dale Hawerchuk, 1984-85 to 1988-89; Randy Carlyle, Dale Hawerchuk and Thomas Steen (tri-captains), 1989-90; Randy Carlyle and Thomas Steen (co-captains), 1990-91; Troy Murray, 1991-92; Troy Murray and Dean Kennedy, 1992-93; Dean Kennedy and Keith Tkachuk, 1993-94; Keith Tkachuk, 1994-95 to date.

Retired Numbers

9	Bobby Hull	1972-1980
25	Thomas Steen	1981-1995

Club Records

Team

(Figures in brackets for season records are games played; records for fewest points, wins, ties, losses, goals, goals against are for 70 or more games)

Most Points	96	1984-85 (80)
Most Wins	43	1984-85 (80)
Most Ties	15	1991-92 (80)
Most Losses	57	1980-81 (80)
Most Goals	358	1984-85 (80)
Most Goals Against	400	1980-81 (80)
Fewest Points	32	1980-81 (80)
Fewest Wins	9	1980-81 (80)
Fewest Ties	7	1985-86 (80)
		1992-93 (84)
Fewest Losses	27	1984-85 (80)
Fewest Goals	214	1979-80 (80)
Fewest Goals Against	244	1991-92 (80)

Longest Winning Streak

Over-all	9	Mar. 8-27/85
Home	9	Dec. 27/92-Jan. 23/93
Away	8	Feb. 25-Apr. 6/85

Longest Undefeated Streak

Over-all	13	Mar. 8-Apr. 7/85 (10 wins, 3 ties)
Home	11	Dec. 23/83 Feb. 5/84 (6 wins, 5 ties)
Away	9	Feb. 25-Apr. 7/85 (8 wins, 1 tie)

Longest Losing Streak

Over-all	10	Nov. 30-Dec. 20/80 Feb. 6-25/94
Home	5	Oct. 29-Nov. 13/93
Away	13	Jan. 26-Apr. 14/94

Longest Winless Streak

Over-all	*30	Oct. 19-Dec. 20/80 (23 losses, 7 ties)
Home	14	Oct. 19-Dec. 14/80 (9 losses, 5 ties)

Away	18	Oct. 10-Dec. 20/80 (16 losses, 2 ties)
Most Shutouts, Season	7	1991-92 (80)
Most PIM, Season	2,278	1987-88 (80)
Most Goals, Game	12	Feb. 25/85 (Wpg. 12 at NYR. 5)

Individual

Most Seasons	14	Thomas Steen
Most Games	950	Thomas Steen
Most Goals, Career	379	Dale Hawerchuk
Most Assists, Career	553	Thomas Steen
Most Points, Career	929	Dale Hawerchuk (379 goals, 550 assists)
Most PIM, Career	1,338	Laurie Boschman
Most Shutouts, Career	14	Bob Essensa
Longest Consecutive Games Streak	475	Dale Hawerchuk (Dec. 19/82-Dec. 10/88)
Most Goals, Season	76	Teemu Selanne (1992-93)
Most Assists, Season	79	Phil Housley (1992-93)
Most Points, Season	132	Teemu Selanne (1992-93) (76 goals, 56 assists)
Most PIM, Season	347	Tie Domi (1993-94)
Most Points, Defenseman Season	97	Phil Housley (1992-93) (18 goals, 79 assists)
Most Points, Center, Season	130	Dale Hawerchuk (1984-85) (53 goals, 77 assists)
Most Points, Right Wing, Season	132	Teemu Selanne (1992-93) (76 goals, 56 assists)
Most Points, Left Wing, Season	92	Morris Lukowich (1981-82) (43 goals, 49 assists)

Most Points, Rookie, Season	*132	Teemu Selanne (1992-93) (76 goals, 56 assists)
Most Shutouts, Season	5	Bob Essensa (1991-92)
Most Goals, Game	5	Willy Lindstrom (Mar. 2/82) Alexei Zhamnov (Apr. 1/95)
Most Assists, Game	5	Dale Hawerchuk (Mar. 6/84, Mar. 18/89, Mar. 4/90) Phil Housley (Jan. 18/93)
Most Points, Game	6	Willy Lindstrom (Mar. 2/82) Dale Hawerchuk (Dec. 14/83, Mar. 5/88, Mar. 18/89) Thomas Steen (Oct. 24/84) Eddie Olczyk (Dec. 21/91)

* NHL Record.

All-time Record vs. Other Clubs

Regular Season

			At Home						On Road						Total				
	GP	W	L	T	GF	GA	PTS	GP	W	L	T	GF	GA	PTS	GP	W	L	T	GF	GA	PTS
Anaheim	4	1	3	0	13	15	2	4	0	4	0	6	14	0	8	1	7	0	19	29	2
Boston	23	9	12	2	83	86	20	22	3	16	3	70	105	9	45	12	28	5	153	191	29
Buffalo	22	9	11	2	71	82	20	22	1	19	2	53	104	4	44	10	30	4	124	186	24
Calgary	52	23	20	9	213	190	55	53	11	35	7	171	259	29	105	34	55	16	384	449	84
Chicago	30	16	11	3	118	105	35	29	5	21	3	84	142	13	59	21	32	6	202	247	48
Dallas	29	14	14	1	103	105	29	30	9	17	4	96	132	22	59	23	31	5	199	237	51
Detroit	28	12	8	8	95	86	32	31	10	17	4	110	135	24	59	22	25	12	205	221	56
Edmonton	53	20	29	4	218	247	44	54	17	33	4	182	246	38	107	37	62	8	400	493	82
Florida	2	0	2	0	4	8	0	1	1	0	0	5	2	2	3	1	2	0	9	10	2
Hartford	24	12	11	1	86	88	25	22	6	11	5	71	92	17	46	18	22	6	157	180	42
Los Angeles	54	25	20	9	230	199	59	51	22	19	10	215	218	54	105	47	39	19	445	417	113
Montreal	22	8	9	5	71	84	21	22	2	20	0	51	119	4	44	10	29	5	122	203	25
New Jersey	23	16	4	3	92	61	35	21	9	6	6	70	66	24	44	25	10	9	162	127	59
NY Islanders	22	7	13	2	70	87	16	23	6	11	6	71	87	18	45	13	24	8	141	174	34
NY Rangers	23	9	12	2	84	87	20	22	8	12	2	89	104	18	45	17	24	4	173	191	38
Ottawa	2	1	1	0	12	10	2	4	3	0	1	21	9	7	6	4	1	1	33	19	9
Philadelphia	22	9	11	2	72	78	20	23	6	17	0	69	107	12	45	15	28	2	141	185	32
Pittsburgh	22	9	12	1	83	83	19	23	7	16	0	69	96	14	45	16	28	1	152	179	33
Quebec	22	10	7	5	94	87	25	23	10	10	3	95	93	23	45	20	17	8	189	180	48
St. Louis	31	16	9	6	109	94	38	29	7	14	8	91	118	22	60	23	23	14	200	212	60
San Jose	12	7	3	2	45	35	16	10	3	5	2	40	46	8	22	10	8	4	85	81	24
Tampa Bay	3	1	2	0	8	9	2	3	3	0	0	14	10	6	6	4	2	0	22	19	8
Toronto	29	14	10	5	130	117	33	30	6	13	1	122	116	13	59	20	23	6	252	233	66
Vancouver	51	25	18	8	202	195	58	54	15	31	8	156	211	38	105	40	49	16	358	406	96
Washington	23	12	6	5	90	83	29	22	5	15	2	70	104	12	45	17	21	7	160	187	41
Totals	**628**	**285**	**258**	**85**	**2396**	**2321**	**655**	**628**	**185**	**362**	**81**	**2091**	**2735**	**451**	**1256**	**470**	**620**	**166**	**4487**	**5056**	**1106**

Calgary totals include Atlanta, 1979-80. Dallas totals include Minnesota, 1979-80 to 1992-93.
New Jersey totals include Colorado, 1979-80 to 1981-82.

Playoffs

	Series	W	L	GP	W	L	T	GF	GA	Last Mtg.	Round	Result
Calgary	3	2	1	13	7	6	0	45	43	1987	DSF	W 4-2
Edmonton	6	0	6	26	4	22	0	75	120	1990	DSF	L 3-4
St. Louis	1	0	1	4	1	3	0	13	20	1982	DSF	L 1-3
Vancouver	2	0	2	13	5	8	0	34	50	1993	DSF	L 2-4
Totals	**12**	**2**	**10**	**56**	**17**	**39**	**0**	**167**	**233**			

Playoff Results 1995-91

Year	Round	Opponent	Result	GF	GA
1993	DSF	Vancouver	L 2-4	17	21
1992	DSF	Vancouver	L 3-4	17	29

Abbreviations: Round: F – Final;
CF – conference final; **CQF** – conference quarter-final;
CSF – conference semi-final; **DF** – division final;
DSF – division semi-final; **SF** – semi-final;
QF – quarter-final; **PR** – preliminary round.

1994-95 Results

Jan.	20		Calgary	3-3	14		Vancouver	3-3
	21		Anaheim	3-4	17	at	Calgary	4-8
	23		Chicago	5-3	19		Chicago	2-3
	25	at	San Jose	0-4	22	at	Detroit	3-6
	27	at	Anaheim	2-3	24	at	Toronto	2-3
	28	at	Los Angeles	2-4	25		Toronto	3-3
Feb.	2		St. Louis	4-5	28	at	San Jose	5-6
	4		San Jose	3-3	30	at	Los Angeles	7-7
	6	at	Calgary	5-4	Apr.	1	at	Los Angeles	7-7
	8	at	Edmonton	3-3	5		Chicago	4-1
	9	at	Vancouver	1-5	7		Vancouver	7-4
	11	at	St. Louis	3-2	8	at	Toronto	3-4
	13	at	Dallas	7-4	11	at	St. Louis	5-7
	15		Detroit	1-5	13		St. Louis	5-2
	17		St. Louis	3-4	15		Toronto	5-1
	22	at	Vancouver	4-1	17		Edmonton	5-6
	24		Anaheim	4-2	19	at	Detroit	5-5
	25	at	Toronto	2-5	21	at	Chicago	2-1
	28		Dallas	0-4	23	at	Dallas	2-5
Mar.	2	at	Detroit	1-6	25		Edmonton	3-5
	4		San Jose	4-2	27		Detroit	4-3
	5		Calgary	3-2	29	at	Edmonton	5-1
	10		Dallas	4-3	May	1	at	Chicago	2-3
	11		Los Angeles	2-4	2		Los Angeles	1-2

Entry Draft Selections 1995-81

1995
Pick
7 Shane Doan
32 Marc Chouinard
34 Jason Doig
67 Brad Isbister
84 Jason Kurtz
121 Brian Elder
136 Sylvain Daigle
162 Paul Traynor
188 Jaroslav Obsut
189 Frederik Loven
214 Rob Deciantis

1994
Pick
30 Deron Quint
56 Dorian Anneck
58 Tavis Hansen
82 Steve Cheredaryk
108 Craig Mills
143 Steve Vezina
146 Chris Kibermanis
186 Ramil Saifullin
212 Henrik Smangs
238 Mike Mader
264 Jason Issel

1993
Pick
15 Mats Lindgren
31 Scott Langkow
43 Alexei Budayev
79 Ruslan Batyrshin
93 Ravil Gusmanov
119 Larry Courville
145 Michal Grosek
171 Martin Woods
197 Adrian Murray
217 Vladimir Potapov
223 Ilja Stashenkov
228 Harijs Vitolinsh
285 Russell Hewson

1992
Pick
17 Sergei Bautin
27 Boris Mironov
60 Jeremy Stevenson
84 Mark Visheau
132 Alexander Alexeyev
155 Artur Oktyabrev
156 Andrei Raisky
204 Nikolai Khaibulin
228 Yevgeny Garanin
229 Teemu Numminen
252 Andrei Karpovtsev
254 Ivan Vologzhaninov

1991
Pick
5 Aaron Ward
49 Dmitri Filimonov
91 Juha Ylonen
99 Yan Kaminsky
115 Jeff Sebastian
159 Jeff Ricciardi
181 Sean Gauthier
203 Igor Ulanov
225 Jason Jennings
247 Sergei Sorokin

1990
Pick
19 Keith Tkachuk
35 Mike Muller
74 Roman Meluzin
75 Scott Levins
77 Alexei Zhamnov
98 Craig Martin
119 Daniel Jardemyr
140 John Lilley
161 Henrik Andersson
182 Rauli Raitanen
203 Mika Alatalo
224 Sergei Selyanin
245 Keith Morris

1989
Pick
4 Stu Barnes
25 Dan Ratushny
46 Jason Cirone
62 Kris Draper
64 Mark Brownschidle
69 Alain Roy
109 Dan Bylsma
130 Pekka Peltola
131 Doug Evans
151 Jim Solly
172 Stephane Gauvin
193 Joe Larson
214 Bradley Podiak
235 Evgeny Davydov
240 Sergei Kharin

1988
Pick
10 Teemu Selanne
31 Russell Romaniuk
52 Stephane Beauregard
73 Brian Hunt
94 Anthony Joseph
101 Benoit Lebeau
115 Ronald Jones
127 Markus Akerblom
136 Jukka Marttila
157 Mark Smith
178 Mike Helber
199 Pavel Kostichkin
220 Kevin Heise
241 Kyle Galloway

1987
Pick
16 Bryan Marchment
37 Patrik Erickson
79 Don McLennan
96 Ken Gernander
100 Darrin Amundson
121 Joe Harwell
142 Tod Hartje
163 Markku Kyllonen
184 Jim Fernholz
226 Roger Rougelot
247 Hans Goran Elo

1986
Pick
8 Pat Elynuik
29 Teppo Numminen
50 Esa Palosaari
71 Hannu Jarvenpaa
92 Craig Endean
113 Robertson Bateman
155 Frank Furlan
176 Mark Green
197 John Blue
218 Matt Cote
239 Arto Blomsten

1985
Pick
18 Ryan Stewart
39 Roger Ohman
60 Daniel Berthiaume
81 Fredrik Olausson
102 John Borrell
123 Danton Cole
144 Brent Mowery
165 Tom Draper
186 Nevin Kardum
207 Dave Quigley
228 Chris Norton
249 Anssi Melametsa

1984
Pick
30 Peter Douris
68 Chris Mills
72 Sean Clement
93 Scott Schneider
99 Brent Severyn
114 Gary Lorden
135 Luciano Borsato
156 Brad Jones
177 Gord Whitaker
197 Rick Forst
218 Mike Warus
238 Jim Edmonds

1983
Pick
8 Andrew McBain
14 Bobby Dollas
29 Brad Berry
43 Peter Taglianetti
69 Bob Essensa
89 Harry Armstrong
109 Joel Baillargeon
129 Iain Duncan
149 Ron Pessetti
169 Todd Flichel
189 Cory Wright
209 Eric Cormier
229 Jamie Husgen

1982
Pick
12 Jim Kyte
74 Tom Martin
75 Dave Ellett
96 Tim Mishler
138 Derek Ray
159 Guy Gosselin
180 Tom Ward
201 Mike Savage
222 Bob Shaw
243 Jan Urban Ericson

1981
Pick
1 Dale Hawerchuk
22 Scott Arniel
43 Jyrki Seppa
64 Kirk McCaskill
85 Marc Behrend
106 Bob O'Connor
127 Peter Nilsson
148 Dan McFaul
169 Greg Dick
190 Vladimir Kadlec
211 Dave Kirwin

General Manager

PADDOCK, JOHN
General Manager, Winnipeg Jets.
Born in Brandon, Man., June 9, 1954.

John Paddock was named the interim general manager of the Winnipeg Jets on January 19, 1994, replacing Mike Smith who was the g.m. from 1988-93. On June 3, 1994, Paddock was officially named the Jets' g.m. and head coach. He is the Jets' third general manager since joining the NHL in 1979 and the fifth g.m. in the club's history.

Paddock has excelled at every level of hockey. As a player and a coach, he has been a winner. In his professional career (1975-1983), Paddock played 87 games in the NHL with Washington, Philadelphia and Quebec. In the American Hockey League, he played 445 games, recording 132 goals and 141 assists for 273 points and 1291 penalty minutes. He was a fierce competitor who helped Maine win an American Hockey League championship in 1978-79 with his hard-nosed, physical style of play.

Paddock, a 41-year-old native of Oak River, Manitoba, was named head coach of the Jets on June 17, 1991 after coaching one season at Binghamton, NY, the New York Rangers' AHL affiliate. On April 5, 1995, Paddock handed the head coach's portfolio to veteran coach Terry Simpson, enabling him to devote full attention to his general manager's duties. In four seasons with the Jets, Paddock posted a coaching record of 106-138-37. He was the first Jets coach to lead the team to two consecutive winning seasons ('91-92 and '92-93). His coaching career began with Maine of the AHL in 1983 and continued with a move to Hershey to work for the Philadelphia Flyers organization between 1985 and 1989. Paddock won Calder Cups in both Maine and Hershey and was a two-time recipient of the Louis A.R. Pieri Memorial Award as coach of the year in the AHL. In 1989-90, Paddock moved to Philadelphia to become the Flyers' assistant general manager under Bobby Clarke.

This season, Paddock will continue his efforts to assemble a winning team comprised of players who exemplify his own characteristics: hard work, dedication, pride and commitment to excellence.

John and his wife, Jill reside in Charleswood, Manitoba, with their four daughters, Jenny, Sally, Anna and Alyssa.

Club Directory

Offices:
Winnipeg Jets
10th Floor, 1661 Portage Ave.
Winnipeg, Manitoba R3J 3T7
Phone **204/982-5387**
FAX 204/788-4668
Winnipeg Arena
15-1430 Maroons Road
Winnipeg, Manitoba R3G 0L5
Capacity: 15,393

Board of Directors
Barry L. Shenkarow, Bill Davis, Marvin Shenkarow, Harvey Secter, Barry McQueen, Steve Bannatyne, Dick Archer
President & Governor .... Barry L. Shenkarow
Alternate Governor .... Bill Davis

Hockey Operations
General Manager .... John Paddock
Assistant General Manager/VP Of Hockey Operations .... Mike O'Hearn
Head Coach .... Terry Simpson
Assistant Coach .... Perry Pearn
Assistant Coach .... Randy Carlyle
Goaltending Coach .... Pete Peeters
Director of Hockey Information .... Igor Kuperman
Director of Scouting .... Bill Lesuk
Assistant Director of Scouting .... Joe Yannetti
Scouts .... Connie Broden, Sean Coady, Timo Sutinen, Boris Yemeljanov, Larry Hornung, Evzen Slansky, Vaughn Karpan
Executive Assistant to General Manager .... Brenda Thompson
Administrative Assistant, Hockey Operations .... Sacha Palmer

Communications
Public Relations/Director of Corporate & Public Relations/Executive Director of Winnipeg Jets Goals for Kids Foundation .... Lori Summers
Director of Media & Player Relations .... Richard Nairn
Statistician & Publications Co-ordinator .... Jeffrey Hecht
Administrative Assistant – President & Winnipeg Jets Goals For Kids Foundation .... Maryann Mazepa
Special Events Co-ordinator .... Teresa Bastian

Finance & Administration
Vice President of Finance & Administration .... Don Binda
Director of Ticket Operations .... Dianne Gabbs
Ticket Operations Assistant .... Georgie Jorowski
Information Systems Consultant .... Doug Bergman
Director of Team Services .... Murray Harding
Controller .... Joe Leibfried
Assistant Accountants .... Bryan Braun, Robert Thorsten,
Accounting Assistant .... Lynda Sweetland
Jets' All Sports Store Managers .... Jennifer Zalnasky, Mike Delorme
Pro Shop Manager .... Dave Blackmore
Administrative Consultant .... Laurence Gilman
Receptionist .... Devon Wingate

Marketing
Director of Corporate Sales .... Gord Dmytriw
Director of Ticket Sales .... Hartley Miller
Graphic Design/DeskTop Publishing .... Roberta Rackal
Group Promotions Coordinator .... Patti Martens
Account Executive .... Laurie Kepron
Account Executive .... Dave MacLean

Dressing Room
Athletic Trainers .... Phil Walker, Gord Hart
Equipment Managers .... Craig Heisinger, Stan Wilson
Team Physician .... Dr. Brian Lukie
Team Dentist .... Dr. Gene Solmundson

Team Information
Team Colours .... Blue, Red & White
Dimensions of Rink .... 200 feet by 85 feet
Seating Capacity 15,393
Training Camp .... Winnipeg
Press Box Location .... East Side
TV Channel .... CKND TV
Radio Station .... CJOB AM 680
Play-by-Play (Radio) .... Kelly Moore

NHL Coaching Record

		Regular Season					Playoffs			
Season	Team	Games	W	L	T	%	Games	W	L	%
1991-92	Winnipeg	80	33	32	15	.506	7	3	4	.429
1992-93	Winnipeg	84	40	37	7	.518	6	2	4	.333
1993-94	Winnipeg	84	24	51	9	.339	....	....	....	....
1994-95	Winnipeg	33	9	18	6	.364	....	....	....	....
	NHL Totals	**281**	**106**	**138**	**37**	**.443**	**13**	**5**	**8**	**.385**

1994-95 Final Statistics

Standings

Abbreviations: GA – goals against; **GF** – goals for; **GP** – games played; **L** – losses;
PTS – points; **T** – ties; **W** – wins; **%** – percentage of games won.

EASTERN CONFERENCE
Northeast Division

	GP	W	L	T	GF	GA	PTS	%
Quebec	48	30	13	5	185	134	65	.677
Pittsburgh	48	29	16	3	181	158	61	.635
Boston	48	27	18	3	150	127	57	.594
Buffalo	48	22	19	7	130	119	51	.531
Hartford	48	19	24	5	127	141	43	.448
Montreal	48	18	23	7	125	148	43	.448
Ottawa	48	9	34	5	117	174	23	.240

Atlantic Division

	GP	W	L	T	GF	GA	PTS	%
Philadelphia	48	28	16	4	150	132	60	.625
New Jersey	48	22	18	8	136	121	52	.542
Washington	48	22	18	8	136	120	52	.542
NY Rangers	48	22	23	3	139	134	47	.490
Florida	48	20	22	6	115	127	46	.479
Tampa Bay	48	17	28	3	120	144	37	.385
NY Islanders	48	15	28	5	126	158	35	.365

WESTERN CONFERENCE
Central Division

	GP	W	L	T	GF	GA	PTS	%
Detroit	48	33	11	4	180	117	70	.729
St. Louis	48	28	15	5	178	135	61	.635
Chicago	48	24	19	5	156	115	53	.552
Toronto	48	21	19	8	135	146	50	.521
Dallas	48	17	23	8	136	135	42	.438
Winnipeg	48	16	25	7	157	177	39	.406

Pacific Division

	GP	W	L	T	GF	GA	PTS	%
Calgary	48	24	17	7	163	135	55	.573
Vancouver	48	18	18	12	153	148	48	.500
San Jose	48	19	25	4	129	161	42	.438
Los Angeles	48	16	23	9	142	174	41	.427
Edmonton	48	17	27	4	136	183	38	.396
Anaheim	48	16	27	5	125	164	37	.385

Philadelphia's Mikael Renberg finished among the NHL's leaders in goals, assists, points and powerplay goals.

INDIVIDUAL LEADERS

Goal Scoring

Player	Team	GP	G
Peter Bondra	Wsh.	47	34
Jaromir Jagr	Pit.	48	32
Ray Sheppard	Det.	43	30
Owen Nolan	Que.	46	30
Alexei Zhamnov	Wpg.	48	30
Eric Lindros	Phi.	46	29
Theoren Fleury	Cgy.	47	29
Brett Hull	St. L.	48	29
Cam Neely	Bos.	42	27
John LeClair	Mtl.-Phi.	46	26
Mikael Renberg	Phi.	47	26

Assists

Player	Team	GP	A
Ron Francis	Pit.	44	48
Paul Coffey	Det.	45	44
Joe Sakic	Que.	47	43
Eric Lindros	Phi.	46	41
Adam Oates	Bos.	48	41
Mark Messier	NYR	46	39
Joe Juneau	Wsh.	44	38
Jaromir Jagr	Pit.	48	38

Power-play Goals

Player	Team	GP	PP
Cam Neely	Bos.	42	16
Donald Audette	Buf.	46	13
Owen Nolan	Que.	46	13
Alexander Mogilny	Buf.	44	12
Peter Bondra	Wsh.	47	12
Ray Sheppard	Det.	43	11
Alexei Yashin	Ott.	47	11
Bernie Nicholls	Chi.	48	11

Short-handed Goals

Player	Team	GP	SH
Peter Bondra	Wsh.	47	6
Wayne Presley	Buf.	46	5
Brent Gilchrist	Dal.	32	3
Sergei Fedorov	Det.	42	3
Rob Zamuner	T.B.	43	3
Mark Messier	NYR	46	3
Steve Konowalchuk	Wsh.	46	3
Brett Hull	St. L.	48	3
Jaromir Jagr	Pit.	48	3
Scott Young	Que.	48	3

Game-winning Goals

Player	Team	GP	GW
Owen Nolan	Que.	46	8
Donald Audette	Buf.	46	7
John LeClair	Mtl.-Phi.	46	7
Jaromir Jagr	Pit.	48	7

Game-tying Goals

Player	Team	GP	GT
Dan Quinn	L.A.	44	3
Trevor Linden	Van.	48	3
Todd Elik	S.J.-St. L.	35	2
Bob Carpenter	N.J.	41	2
Ray Ferraro	NYI	47	2
Tom Pederson	S.J.	47	2
Dave Andreychuk	Tor.	48	2
Dimitri Khristich	Wsh.	48	2

Shots

Player	Team	GP	S
Ray Bourque	Bos.	46	210
Brett Hull	St. L.	48	200
Pavel Bure	Van.	44	198
Jaromir Jagr	Pit.	48	192
Adam Graves	NYR	47	185

Shooting Percentage
(minimum 48 shots)

Player	Team	GP	G	S	%
Ian Laperriere	St. L.	37	13	53	24.5
Ray Sheppard	Det.	43	30	125	24.0
Roman Oksiuta	Edm.-Van.	38	16	67	23.9
Ray Ferraro	NYI	47	22	94	23.4

Penalty Minutes

Player	Team	GP	PIM
Enrico Ciccone	T.B.	41	225
Shane Churla	Dal.	27	186
Bryan Marchment	Edm.	40	184
Craig Berube	Wsh.	43	173
Rob Ray	Buf.	47	173

Plus/Minus

Player	Team	GP	+/-
Ron Francis	Pit.	44	30
Curtis Leschyshyn	Que.	44	29
Steve Duchesne	St. L.	47	29
Eric Lindros	Phi.	46	27
Jaromir Jagr	Pit.	48	23

Individual Leaders

Abbreviations: * ** – rookie eligible for Calder Trophy; **A – assists; **G** – goals; **GP** – games played; **GT** – game-tying goals;
GW – game-winning goals; **PIM** – penalties in minutes; **PP** – power play goals; **Pts** – points; **S** – shots on goal; **SH** – short-handed goals;
% – percentage of shots on goal resulting in goals; **+/–** – difference between Goals For (**GF**) scored when a player is on the ice with his
team at even strength or short-handed and Goals Against (**GA**) scored when the same player is on the ice with his team at even strength
or on a power play.

Individual Scoring Leaders for Art Ross Trophy

Player	Team	GP	G	A	Pts	+/–	PIM	PP	SH	GW	GT	S	%
Jaromir Jagr	Pittsburgh	48	32	38	70	23	37	8	3	7	0	192	16.7
Eric Lindros	Philadelphia	46	29	41	70	27	60	7	0	4	1	144	20.1
Alexei Zhamnov	Winnipeg	48	30	35	65	5	20	9	0	4	0	155	19.4
Joe Sakic	Quebec	47	19	43	62	7	30	3	2	5	0	157	12.1
Ron Francis	Pittsburgh	44	11	48	59	30	18	3	0	1	0	94	11.7
Theoren Fleury	Calgary	47	29	29	58	6	112	9	2	5	0	173	16.8
Paul Coffey	Detroit	45	14	44	58	18	72	4	1	2	0	181	7.7
Mikael Renberg	Philadelphia	47	26	31	57	20	20	8	0	4	0	143	18.2
John LeClair	Mtl.-Phi.	46	26	28	54	20	30	6	0	7	0	131	19.8
Mark Messier	NY Rangers	46	14	39	53	8	40	3	3	2	0	126	11.1
Adam Oates	Boston	48	12	41	53	–11	8	4	1	2	0	109	11.0
Bernie Nicholls	Chicago	48	22	29	51	4	32	11	2	5	0	114	19.3
Keith Tkachuk	Winnipeg	48	22	29	51	–4	152	7	2	2	1	129	17.1
Brett Hull	St. Louis	48	29	21	50	13	10	9	3	6	0	200	14.5
Joe Nieuwendyk	Calgary	46	21	29	50	11	33	3	0	4	0	122	17.2
Sergei Fedorov	Detroit	42	20	30	50	6	24	7	3	5	0	147	13.6
*Peter Forsberg	Quebec	47	15	35	50	17	16	3	0	3	0	86	17.4
Owen Nolan	Quebec	46	30	19	49	21	46	13	2	8	0	137	21.9
Teemu Selanne	Winnipeg	45	22	26	48	1	2	8	2	1	0	167	13.2
Mark Recchi	Phi.-Mtl.	49	16	32	48	–9	28	9	0	3	0	121	13.2
Wayne Gretzky	Los Angeles	48	11	37	48	–20	6	3	0	1	0	142	7.7
Pierre Turgeon	NYI.-Mtl.	49	24	23	47	0	14	5	2	4	0	160	15.0
Mats Sundin	Toronto	47	23	24	47	–5	14	9	0	4	1	173	13.3
Alexander Mogilny	Buffalo	44	19	28	47	0	36	12	0	2	1	148	12.8
Tomas Sandstrom	Pittsburgh	47	21	23	44	1	42	4	1	3	1	116	18.1
Alexei Yashin	Ottawa	47	21	23	44	–20	20	11	0	1	0	154	13.6

Defensemen Scoring Leaders

Player	Team	GP	G	A	Pts	+/–	PIM	PP	SH	GW	GT	S	%
Paul Coffey	Detroit	45	14	44	58	18	72	4	1	2	0	181	7.7
Ray Bourque	Boston	46	12	31	43	3	20	9	0	2	0	210	5.7
Phil Housley	Calgary	43	8	35	43	17	18	3	0	0	0	135	5.9
Brian Leetch	NY Rangers	48	9	32	41	0	18	3	0	2	0	182	4.9
Larry Murphy	Pittsburgh	48	13	25	38	12	18	4	0	3	0	124	10.5
Steve Duchesne	St. Louis	47	12	26	38	29	36	1	0	1	0	116	10.3
Chris Chelios	Chicago	48	5	33	38	17	72	3	1	0	0	166	3.0
Gary Suter	Chicago	48	10	27	37	14	42	5	0	0	0	144	6.9
Sergei Zubov	NY Rangers	38	10	26	36	–2	18	6	0	0	0	116	8.6
Todd Gill	Toronto	47	7	25	32	–8	64	3	1	2	0	82	8.5
Garry Galley	Phi.-Buf.	47	3	29	32	4	30	2	0	0	0	97	3.1
Jeff Brown	Vancouver	33	8	23	31	–2	16	3	0	0	0	111	7.2
Calle Johansson	Washington	46	5	26	31	–6	35	4	0	2	0	112	4.5

CONSECUTIVE SCORING STREAKS

Goals

Games	Player	Team	G
7	Peter Bondra	Washington	10
7	Ray Sheppard	Detroit	10
6	Joe Murphy	Chicago	8
6	Kelly Kisio	Calgary	7
6	Eric Lindros	Philadelphia	6
5	Owen Nolan	Quebec	7
5	Sylvain Turgeon	Ottawa	7
5	Dino Ciccarelli	Detroit	6
5	Keith Jones	Washington	6
5	*Jeff Friesen	San Jose	6
5	John Cullen	Pittsburgh	5
5	Jaromir Jagr	Pittsburgh	5
5	Alexander Mogilny	Buffalo	5
5	Mikael Renberg	Philadelphia	5
5	Sergei Zubov	NY Rangers	5

Assists

Games	Player	Team	A
8	Mark Messier	NY Rangers	19
8	Phil Housley	Calgary	11
8	Eric Lindros	Philadelphia	11
7	Joe Juneau	Washington	14
7	Mikael Renberg	Philadelphia	12
7	Russ Courtnall	Dal.-Van.	9
7	Dino Ciccarelli	Detroit	8
7	Garry Galley	Phi.-Buf.	8
7	Pat Lafontaine	Buffalo	8
6	Neal Broten	Dal.-N.J.	7
6	Stephane Richer	New Jersey	7
6	Denis Savard	Tampa Bay	7
6	Ulf Dahlen	San Jose	6
6	Wayne Gretzky	Los Angeles	6

Points

Games	Player	Team	G	A	PTS
14	Pierre Turgeon	NYI-Mtl.	11	10	21
14	Eric Lindros	Philadelphia	10	11	21
13	Ron Francis	Pittsburgh	5	18	23
13	Paul Coffey	Detroit	6	15	21
13	Mikael Renberg	Philadelphia	9	9	18
12	John LeClair	Mtl.-Phi.	9	9	18
11	Dino Ciccarelli	Detroit	7	10	17
10	Eric Lindros	Philadelphia	9	13	22
10	Wendel Clark	Quebec	8	6	14
10	Brett Hull	St. Louis	6	7	13

Peter Bondra, below, followed in the footsteps of
fellow European sharpshooters Alexander Mogilny
and Pavel Bure to lead the NHL with 34 goals in
1994-95. Buffalo sniper Donald Audette, right,
ranked second among NHL powerplay specialists
by scoring 13 goals when the Sabres
enjoyed the man advantage.

Boston's Mariusz Czerkawski finished third among NHL freshmen in powerplay assists, fifth in powerplay points and second in shots.

Individual Rookie Scoring Leaders

Rookie	Team	GP	G	A	Pts	+/-	PIM	PP	SH	GW	GT	S	%
Peter Forsberg	Quebec	47	15	35	50	17	16	3	0	3	0	86	17.4
Paul Kariya	Anaheim	47	18	21	39	-17	4	7	1	3	1	134	13.4
David Oliver	Edmonton	44	16	14	30	-11	20	10	0	0	1	79	20.3
Ian Laperriere	St. Louis	37	13	14	27	12	85	1	0	1	0	53	24.5
Todd Marchant	Edmonton	45	13	14	27	-3	32	3	2	2	0	95	13.7
Mariusz Czerkawski	Boston	47	12	14	26	4	31	1	0	2	0	126	9.5
Jeff Friesen	San Jose	48	15	10	25	-8	14	5	1	2	0	86	17.4
Roman Oksiuta	Edm.-Van.	38	16	4	20	-12	10	6	0	1	0	67	23.9
Todd Harvey	Dallas	40	11	9	20	-3	67	2	0	1	0	64	17.2
Brian Savage	Montreal	37	12	7	19	5	27	0	0	0	0	64	18.8
Sergei Krivokrasov	Chicago	41	12	7	19	9	33	6	0	2	1	72	16.7

Goal Scoring

Name	Team	GP	G
Paul Kariya	Anaheim	47	18
Roman Oksiuta	Edm.-Van.	38	16
David Oliver	Edmonton	44	16
Peter Forsberg	Quebec	47	15
Jeff Friesen	San Jose	48	15
Ian Laperriere	St. Louis	37	13
Todd Marchant	Edmonton	45	13
Brian Savage	Montreal	37	12
Sergei Krivokrasov	Chicago	41	12
Mariusz Czerkawski	Boston	47	12

Assists

Name	Team	GP	A
Peter Forsberg	Quebec	47	35
Paul Kariya	Anaheim	47	21
Ian Laperriere	St. Louis	37	14
David Oliver	Edmonton	44	14
Todd Marchant	Edmonton	45	14
Mariusz Czerkawski	Boston	47	14
Mike Kennedy	Dallas	44	12
Brian Rolston	New Jersey	40	11
Steve Rucchin	Anaheim	43	11
Len Barrie	Pittsburgh	48	11

Power Play Goals

Name	Team	GP	PP
David Oliver	Edmonton	44	10
Paul Kariya	Anaheim	47	7
Roman Oksiuta	Edm.-Van.	38	6
Sergei Krivokrasov	Chicago	41	6
Jeff Friesen	San Jose	48	5
Alexander Selivano	Tampa Bay	43	4
David Roberts	St. Louis	19	3
Todd Marchant	Edmonton	45	3
Peter Forsberg	Quebec	47	3

Short Hand Goals

Name	Team	GP	SH
Chris Snell	Los Angeles	32	2
Todd Marchant	Edmonton	45	2
Oleg Tverdovsky	Anaheim	36	1
Andrei Nikolishin	Hartford	39	1
Eric Lacroix	Los Angeles	45	1
Paul Kariya	Anaheim	47	1
Jeff Friesen	San Jose	48	1

Game Winning Goals

Name	Team	GP	GW
Brian Rolston	New Jersey	40	3
Alexander Selivano	Tampa Bay	43	3
Peter Forsberg	Quebec	47	3
Paul Kariya	Anaheim	47	3
Steve Larouche	Ottawa	18	2
David Roberts	St. Louis	19	2
Sergei Krivokrasov	Chicago	41	2
Todd Marchant	Edmonton	45	2
Mariusz Czerkawski	Boston	47	2
Jeff Friesen	San Jose	48	2

Game Tying Goals

Name	Team	GP	GT
David Roberts	St. Louis	19	1
Mike Peca	Vancouver	33	1
Jon Rohloff	Boston	34	1
Sergei Krivokrasov	Chicago	41	1
David Oliver	Edmonton	44	1
Paul Kariya	Anaheim	47	1
Adam Deadmarsh	Quebec	48	1

Shots

Name	Team	GP	S
Paul Kariya	Anaheim	47	134
Mariusz Czerkawski	Boston	47	126
Todd Marchant	Edmonton	45	95
Alexander Selivano	Tampa Bay	43	94
Milos Holan	Anaheim	25	93
Brian Rolston	New Jersey	40	92
Peter Forsberg	Quebec	47	86
Jeff Friesen	San Jose	48	86

Shooting Percentage

(minimum 48 shots)

Name	Team	GP	G	S	%
Ian Laperriere	St. Louis	37	13	53	24.5
Roman Oksiuta	Edm.-Van.	38	16	67	23.9
David Oliver	Edmonton	44	16	79	20.3
Brian Savage	Montreal	37	12	64	18.8
Adam Deadmarsh	Quebec	48	9	48	18.8
Peter Forsberg	Quebec	47	15	86	17.4
Jeff Friesen	San Jose	48	15	86	17.4
Todd Harvey	Dallas	40	11	64	17.2

Plus/Minus

Name	Team	GP	+/-
Peter Forsberg	Quebec	47	17
Adam Deadmarsh	Quebec	48	16
Sergei Brylin	New Jersey	26	12
Ian Laperriere	St. Louis	37	12
Denis Chasse	St. Louis	47	12
Sergei Krivokrasov	Chicago	41	9
Chris Therien	Philadelphia	48	8
Andrei Nikolishin	Hartford	39	7
Steve Rucchin	Anaheim	43	7

Three-or-More-Goal Games

Player	Team	Date	Final Score	G
Jason Arnott	Edmonton	Mar. 20	Cgy. 2 Edm.5	3
Donald Audette	Buffalo	Mar. 30	Ott. 0 Buf. 7	3
Josef Beranek	Philadelphia	Feb. 02	NYI 5 Phi. 4	3
Peter Bondra	Washington	Apr. 21	Hfd. 3 Wsh.6	3
Pavel Bure	Vancouver	Apr. 11	Ana. 0 Van. 5	3
Igor Chibirev	Hartford	Apr. 05	Hfd. 8 Pit. 4	3
Wendel Clark	Quebec	Feb. 09	Que. 4 Bos. 3	3
Russ Courtnall	Vancouver	Apr. 22	Edm. 1 Van. 6	3
Alexandre Daigle	Ottawa	Mar. 26	Que.11 Ott. 4	3
Nelson Emerson	Winnipeg	Mar. 28	Wpg.5 S.J. 6	3
Sergei Fedorov	Detroit	Feb. 12	L.A. 4 Det. 4	4
Tony Granato	Los Angeles	Apr. 03	Edm.2 L.A. 7	3
Adam Graves	NY Rangers	Jan. 30	Ott. 2 NYR 6	3
*Todd Harvey	Dallas	Apr. 22	Tor. 4 Dal. 6	3
Brett Hull	St. Louis	Feb. 04	Dal. 4 St.L. 7	3
Brett Hull	St. Louis	Apr. 16	Det. 5 St.L. 6	4
Jaromir Jagr	Pittsburgh	Feb. 14	Bos. 3 Pit. 5	3
Uwe Krupp	Quebec	Mar. 01	T.B. 2 Que.8	3
*Steve Larouche	Ottawa	Apr. 03	Mtl. 5 Ott. 4	3
John LeClair	Philadelphia	Feb. 14	Phi. 5 T.B. 2	3
John LeClair	Philadelphia	Feb. 25	Phi. 7 Mtl. 0	3
Eric Lindros	Philadelphia	Feb. 23	Phi. 6 Que.6	3
Eric Lindros	Philadelphia	Mar. 18	Phi. 4 Fla. 3	3
Eric Lindros	Philadelphia	Mar. 20	Mtl. 4 Phi. 8	3
Cam Neely	Boston	Jan. 22	Phi. 1 Bos. 4	3
Cam Neely	Boston	Apr. 23	NYR 4 Bos. 5	3
Bernie Nicholls	Chicago	Feb. 05	Chi. 9 Van. 4	4
Bernie Nicholls	Chicago	Feb. 28	Chi. 8 L.A. 4	4
Bernie Nicholls	Chicago	Mar. 21	Chi. 7 S.J. 3	3
Joe Nieuwendyk	Calgary	Apr. 10	S.J. 3 Cgy. 8	3
Owen Nolan	Quebec	Mar. 06	N.J. 3 Que.6	3
Owen Nolan	Quebec	Mar. 30	Que. 5 NYR 4	3

Player	Team	Date	Final Score	G
Owen Nolan	Quebec	Apr. 02	Ott. 5 Que. 7	3
Brian Noonan	NY Rangers	Mar. 01	NYR 5 Hfd. 2	3
*David Oliver	Edmonton	Mar. 22	Edm. 4 Dal. 4	3
Steven Rice	Hartford	Mar. 29	Hfd. 4 Fla. 4	3
Luc Robitaille	Pittsburgh	Feb. 16	Hfd. 2 Pit. 5	4
Geoff Sanderson	Hartford	Feb. 15	Mtl. 1 Hfd. 4	3
Ray Sheppard	Detroit	Jan. 24	Van. 3 Det. 6	3
Bryan Smolinski	Boston	Mar. 02	N.J. 2 Bos. 7	3
Ronnie Stern	Calgary	Mar. 12	Cgy. 4 Dal. 4	3
German Titov	Calgary	Feb. 04	Tor. 1 Cgy. 4	3
Rick Tocchet	Los Angeles	Feb. 04	Det. 3 L.A. 4	3
Pierre Turgeon	Montreal	Apr. 17	Wsh.2 Mtl. 5	3
Alexei Yashin	Ottawa	Feb. 23	Wsh.5 Ott. 5	3
Scott Young	Quebec	Mar. 26	Que.11 Ott. 4	3
Alexei Zhamnov	Winnipeg	Feb. 11	Wpg.3 St.L. 2	3
Alexei Zhamnov	Winnipeg	Apr. 01	Wpg.7 L.A. 7	5

NOTE: *48 Three-or-more-goal games recorded in 1994-95.*

Pierre Turgeon, below, was the only member of the Montreal Canadiens to register a hat-trick in 1994-95, notching three goals against Washington on April 17, 1995. Ken Wregget, left, took over the starting goaltender's job in Pittsburgh when Tom Barrasso was injured early in the season. He led the NHL with 25 victories in 1994-95.

Goaltending Leaders

Minimum 13 games

Goals Against Average

Goaltender	Team	GPI	Mins	GA	Avg
Dominik Hasek	Buffalo	41	2416	85	2.11
Rick Tabaracci	Wsh.-Cgy.	13	596	21	2.11
*Jim Carey	Washington	28	1604	57	2.13
Chris Osgood	Detroit	19	1087	41	2.26
Ed Belfour	Chicago	42	2450	93	2.28

Save Percentage

Goaltender	Team	GPI	MINS	GA	SA	S%	W	L	T
Dominik Hasek	Buffalo	41	2416	85	1221	.930	19	14	7
Chris Osgood	Detroit	19	1087	41	496	.917	14	5	0
Jocelyn Thibault	Quebec	18	898	35	423	.917	12	2	2
Andy Moog	Dallas	31	1770	72	846	.915	10	12	7
*Damian Rhodes	Toronto	13	760	34	404	.915	6	6	1

Wins

Goaltender	Team	GPI	MINS	W	L	T
Ken Wregget	Pittsburgh	38	2208	25	9	2
Ed Belfour	Chicago	42	2450	22	15	3
Trevor Kidd	Calgary	43	2463	22	14	6
Curtis Joseph	St. Louis	36	1914	20	10	1
Mike Vernon	Detroit	30	1807	19	6	4
*Blaine Lacher	Boston	35	1965	19	11	2
Martin Brodeur	New Jersey	40	2184	19	11	6
Dominik Hasek	Buffalo	41	2416	19	14	7

Shutouts

Goaltender	Team	GPI	MINS	SO	W	L	T
Dominik Hasek	Buffalo	41	2416	5	19	14	7
Ed Belfour	Chicago	42	2450	5	22	15	3
*Jim Carey	Washington	28	1604	4	18	6	3
*Blaine Lacher	Boston	35	1965	4	19	11	2
Arturs Irbe	San Jose	38	2043	4	14	19	3
J. Vanbiesbrouck	Florida	37	2087	4	14	15	4

Team-by-Team Point Totals

1990-91 to 1994-95

(Ranked by five-year winning %)

	94-95	93-94	92-93	91-92	90-91	W%
Pittsburgh	61	101	119	87	88	.606
Detroit	70	100	103	98	76	.594
Boston	57	97	109	84	100	.594
Chicago	53	87	106	87	106	.584
NY Rangers	47	112	79	105	85	.569
St. Louis	61	91	85	83	105	.565
Calgary	55	97	97	74	100	.563
Montreal	43	96	102	93	89	.563
Washington	52	88	93	98	81	.548
New Jersey	52	106	87	87	79	.547
Vancouver	48	85	101	96	65	.525
Buffalo	51	95	86	74	81	.515
Los Angeles	41	66	88	84	102	.507
Philadelphia	60	80	83	75	76	.497
Toronto	50	98	99	67	57	.493
Florida	46	83	–	–	–	.489
Dallas	42	97	82	70	68	.477
NY Islanders	35	84	87	79	60	.459
Quebec	65	76	104	52	46	.456
Winnipeg	39	57	87	81	63	.435
Edmonton	38	64	60	82	80	.431
Anaheim	37	71	–	–	–	.409
Hartford	43	63	58	65	73	.402
Tampa Bay	37	71	53	–	–	.373
San Jose	42	82	24	39	–	.316
Ottawa	23	37	24	–	–	.194

Team Record When Scoring First Goal of a Game

Team	GP	FG	W	L	T
Detroit	48	27	22	3	2
Quebec	48	27	20	6	1
Philadelphia	48	25	18	4	3
Calgary	48	24	17	2	5
Toronto	48	30	16	8	6
Buffalo	48	27	15	5	7
Florida	48	26	16	6	4
Vancouver	48	27	15	6	6
New Jersey	48	25	15	5	5
Washington	48	23	15	5	3
Chicago	48	24	15	6	3
Boston	48	25	16	9	0
St. Louis	48	21	15	4	2
San Jose	48	23	14	8	1
NY Rangers	48	24	14	9	1
Dallas	48	29	12	12	5
Anaheim	48	20	13	5	2
Tampa Bay	48	28	13	13	2
Los Angeles	48	23	12	7	4
Hartford	48	23	11	7	5
Pittsburgh	48	20	13	7	0
Montreal	48	22	12	8	2
Winnipeg	48	22	10	10	2
Edmonton	48	18	10	7	1
NY Islanders	48	19	7	12	0
Ottawa	48	21	6	13	2

Team Plus/Minus Differential

Team	GF	PPGF	Net GF	GA	PPGA	Net GA	Goal Differential
St. Louis	178	36	142	135	46	89	+ 53
Quebec	185	45	140	134	38	96	+ 44
Detroit	180	52	128	117	28	89	+ 39
Pittsburgh	181	42	139	158	46	112	+ 27
Calgary	163	39	124	135	37	98	+ 26
Chicago	156	52	104	115	36	79	+ 25
New Jersey	136	22	114	121	28	93	+ 21
Philadelphia	150	40	110	132	37	95	+ 15
Washington	136	45	91	120	34	86	+ 5
Boston	150	46	104	127	24	103	+ 1
NY Rangers	139	40	99	134	34	100	– 1
Buffalo	130	45	85	119	32	87	– 2
Vancouver	153	47	106	148	39	109	– 3
Dallas	136	39	97	135	34	101	– 4
Hartford	127	30	97	141	37	104	– 7
Florida	115	29	86	127	32	95	– 9
NY Islanders	126	28	98	158	46	112	– 14
Montreal	125	28	97	148	37	111	– 14
Anaheim	125	23	102	164	47	117	– 15
San Jose	129	24	105	161	39	122	– 17
Tampa Bay	120	25	95	144	32	112	– 17
Toronto	135	37	98	146	28	118	– 20
Winnipeg	157	42	115	177	40	137	– 22
Los Angeles	142	35	107	174	42	132	– 25
Edmonton	136	42	94	183	52	131	– 37
Ottawa	117	31	86	174	39	135	– 49

Team Record when Leading, Trailing, Tied

Team	Leading after 1 period W	L	T	Leading after 2 periods W	L	T	Trailing after 1 period W	L	T	Trailing after 2 periods W	L	T	Tied after 1 period W	L	T	Tied after 2 periods W	L	T
Anaheim	9	1	1	14	2	1	2	19	2	0	24	2	5	7	2	2	1	2
Boston	14	2	0	16	1	0	6	5	1	3	12	0	7	11	2	8	5	3
Buffalo	15	4	5	14	1	1	3	8	0	0	13	2	4	7	2	8	5	4
Calgary	13	2	2	21	2	4	3	10	1	2	12	1	8	5	4	1	3	2
Chicago	16	5	2	19	0	0	1	10	1	1	13	1	7	4	2	6	4	4
Dallas	7	4	2	13	2	2	3	8	3	0	14	3	7	11	3	4	7	3
Detroit	20	1	2	26	0	2	3	6	2	2	10	1	10	4	0	5	1	1
Edmonton	10	3	0	10	2	0	2	19	1	1	22	4	5	5	3	6	3	0
Florida	9	5	3	11	2	1	1	13	1	1	16	0	10	4	2	8	4	5
Hartford	11	3	2	11	1	1	4	11	0	1	17	1	4	10	3	7	6	3
Los Angeles	13	1	3	14	0	3	0	18	1	1	21	5	3	4	5	1	2	1
Montreal	12	3	0	12	1	3	3	12	3	2	18	2	3	8	4	4	4	2
New Jersey	12	4	2	10	0	4	2	6	2	2	8	2	8	8	4	10	10	2
NY Islanders	5	4	1	12	3	0	4	16	3	1	21	1	6	8	1	2	4	4
NY Rangers	9	4	1	15	0	1	5	10	0	3	11	0	8	9	2	4	12	2
Ottawa	5	4	0	6	2	1	1	22	3	0	19	1	3	8	2	3	13	3
Philadelphia	17	2	1	15	0	2	8	10	1	0	12	2	3	4	2	13	4	0
Pittsburgh	9	3	0	21	1	1	7	8	1	2	12	2	13	5	2	6	3	0
Quebec	15	2	1	24	2	0	3	8	1	0	8	2	12	3	4	6	3	3
St. Louis	15	0	0	19	0	1	9	8	2	2	10	1	4	7	3	7	5	3
San Jose	12	3	1	15	1	1	4	15	2	1	20	0	3	7	1	3	4	3
Tampa Bay	9	6	1	15	2	2	2	13	1	1	19	0	6	9	1	1	7	1
Toronto	11	4	2	17	1	1	1	9	1	1	15	1	9	6	5	3	6	6
Vancouver	15	2	4	15	1	4	0	13	3	1	16	2	3	3	5	2	1	6
Washington	10	3	1	17	0	1	0	10	0	0	13	3	12	5	7	5	5	4
Winnipeg	6	5	2	13	1	3	3	12	2	0	19	1	7	8	3	3	5	3

Team Statistics

TEAMS' HOME-AND-ROAD RECORD

Northeast Division

			Home									Road				
	GP	W	L	T	GF	GA	PTS	%	GP	W	L	T	GF	GA	PTS	%
QUE	24	19	1	4	95	50	42	.875	24	11	12	1	90	84	23	.479
PIT	24	18	5	1	103	71	37	.771	24	11	11	2	78	87	24	.500
BOS	24	15	7	2	82	55	32	.667	24	12	11	1	68	72	25	.521
BUF	24	15	8	1	80	58	31	.646	24	7	11	6	50	61	20	.417
HFD	24	12	10	2	64	65	26	.542	24	7	14	3	63	76	17	.354
MTL	24	15	5	4	78	59	34	.708	24	3	18	3	47	89	9	.188
OTT	24	5	16	3	62	84	13	.271	24	4	18	2	55	90	10	.208
Total	168	99	52	17	564	442	215	.640	168	55	95	18	451	559	128	.381

Atlantic Division

	GP	W	L	T	GF	GA	PTS	%	GP	W	L	T	GF	GA	PTS	%
PHI	24	16	7	1	77	64	33	.688	24	12	9	3	73	68	27	.563
N.J.	24	14	4	6	78	50	34	.708	24	8	14	2	58	71	18	.375
WSH	24	15	6	3	75	48	33	.688	24	7	12	5	61	72	19	.396
NYR	24	11	10	3	80	72	25	.521	24	11	13	0	59	62	22	.458
FLA	24	9	12	3	60	69	21	.438	24	11	10	3	55	58	25	.521
T.B.	24	10	14	0	63	69	20	.417	24	7	14	3	57	75	17	.354
NYI	24	10	11	3	60	66	23	.479	24	5	17	2	66	92	12	.250
Total	168	85	64	19	493	438	189	.563	168	61	89	18	429	498	140	.417

Central Division

	GP	W	L	T	GF	GA	PTS	%	GP	W	L	T	GF	GA	PTS	%
DET	24	17	4	3	97	59	37	.771	24	16	7	1	83	58	33	.688
ST.L.	24	16	6	2	92	60	34	.708	24	12	9	3	86	75	27	.563
CHI	24	11	10	3	73	57	25	.521	24	13	9	2	83	58	28	.583
TOR	24	15	7	2	77	65	32	.667	24	6	12	6	58	81	18	.375
DAL	24	9	10	5	77	72	23	.479	24	8	13	3	59	63	19	.396
WPG	24	10	10	4	81	77	24	.500	24	6	15	3	76	100	15	.313
Total	144	78	47	19	497	390	175	.608	144	61	65	18	445	435	140	.486

Pacific Division

	GP	W	L	T	GF	GA	PTS	%	GP	W	L	T	GF	GA	PTS	%
CGY	24	15	7	2	90	68	32	.667	24	9	10	5	73	67	23	.479
VAN	24	10	8	6	83	70	26	.542	24	8	10	6	70	78	22	.458
S.J.	24	10	13	1	65	78	21	.438	24	9	12	3	64	83	21	.438
L.A.	24	7	11	6	75	84	20	.417	24	9	12	3	67	90	21	.438
EDM	24	11	12	1	69	84	23	.479	24	6	15	3	67	99	15	.313
ANA	24	11	9	4	69	68	26	.542	24	5	18	1	56	96	11	.229
Total	144	64	60	20	451	452	148	.514	144	46	77	21	397	513	113	.392
Total	624	326	223	75	2005	1722	727	.583	624	223	326	75	1722	2005	521	.417

TEAMS' DIVISIONAL RECORD

Northeast Division

		Against Own Division									Against Other Divisions						
	GP	W	L	T	GF	GA	PTS	%	GP	W	L	T	GF	GA	PTS	%
QUE	24	14	6	4	97	68	32	.667	24	16	7	1	88	66	33	.688
PIT	24	15	8	1	94	83	31	.646	24	14	8	2	87	75	30	.625
BOS	24	15	7	2	83	68	32	.667	24	12	11	1	67	59	25	.521
BUF	24	8	10	6	69	67	22	.458	24	14	9	1	61	52	29	.604
HFD	24	13	10	1	71	67	27	.563	24	6	14	4	56	74	16	.333
MTL	24	8	12	4	66	79	20	.417	24	10	11	3	59	69	23	.479
OTT	24	1	21	2	60	108	4	.083	24	8	13	3	57	66	19	.396
Total	168	74	74	20	540	540	168	.500	168	80	73	15	475	461	175	.521

Atlantic Division

	GP	W	L	T	GF	GA	PTS	%	GP	W	L	T	GF	GA	PTS	%
PHI	24	16	6	2	76	61	34	.708	24	12	10	2	74	71	26	.542
N.J.	24	12	8	4	72	55	28	.583	24	10	10	4	64	66	24	.500
WSH	24	11	9	4	70	65	26	.542	24	11	9	4	66	55	26	.542
NYR	24	11	11	2	70	70	24	.500	24	11	12	1	69	64	23	.479
FLA	24	7	13	4	49	63	18	.375	24	13	9	2	66	64	28	.583
T.B.	24	7	14	3	58	70	17	.354	24	10	14	0	62	74	20	.417
NYI	24	9	12	3	66	77	21	.438	24	6	16	2	60	81	14	.292
Total	168	73	73	22	461	461	168	.500	168	73	80	15	461	475	161	.479

Central Division

	GP	W	L	T	GF	GA	PTS	%	GP	W	L	T	GF	GA	PTS	%
DET	24	17	5	2	87	56	36	.750	24	16	6	2	93	61	34	.708
ST.L.	24	13	8	3	81	72	29	.604	24	15	7	2	97	63	32	.667
CHI	24	7	13	4	52	60	18	.375	24	17	6	1	104	55	35	.729
TOR	24	10	10	4	62	71	24	.500	24	11	9	4	73	75	26	.542
DAL	24	8	15	1	65	77	17	.354	24	9	8	7	71	58	25	.521
WPG	24	9	13	2	77	88	20	.417	24	7	12	5	80	89	19	.396
Total	144	64	64	16	424	424	144	.500	144	75	48	21	518	401	171	.594

Pacific Division

	GP	W	L	T	GF	GA	PTS	%	GP	W	L	T	GF	GA	PTS	%
CGY	24	13	8	3	86	68	29	.604	24	11	9	4	77	67	26	.542
VAN	24	14	4	6	96	55	34	.708	24	4	14	6	57	93	14	.292
S.J.	24	10	12	2	67	77	22	.458	24	9	13	2	62	84	20	.417
L.A.	24	5	15	4	60	88	14	.292	24	11	8	5	82	86	27	.563
EDM	24	9	13	2	70	89	20	.417	24	8	14	2	66	94	18	.375
ANA	24	11	10	3	68	70	25	.521	24	5	17	2	57	94	12	.250
Total	144	62	62	20	447	447	144	.500	144	48	75	21	401	518	117	.406

TEAM STREAKS

Consecutive Wins

Games	Team	From	To
9	Philadelphia	Apr. 2	Apr. 22
8	Philadelphia	Mar. 5	Mar. 20
7	Pittsburgh	Jan. 20	Feb. 4
7	Quebec	Feb. 4	Feb. 16
6	Detroit	Apr. 5	Apr. 14
5	Quebec	Jan. 21	Jan. 31
5	San Jose	Jan. 21	Feb. 2
5	Chicago	Feb. 1	Feb. 9
5	Pittsburgh	Feb. 7	Feb. 16
5	Detroit	Feb. 15	Feb. 23
5	Dallas	Feb. 28	Mar. 6
5	Detroit	Mar. 12	Mar. 22
5	Chicago	Mar. 16	Mar. 26
5	Chicago	Apr. 25	May 3

Consecutive Home Wins

Games	Team	From	To
10	Quebec	Mar. 6	Apr. 16
7	Pittsburgh	Jan. 27	Feb. 16
7	Detroit	Mar. 2	Mar. 30
6	Quebec	Jan. 24	Feb. 11
6	St. Louis	Feb. 13	Mar. 9
6	Pittsburgh	Mar. 9	Apr. 1
6	Philadelphia	Apr. 2	Apr. 20
6	San Jose	Jan. 21	Feb. 15
5	Philadelphia	Mar. 5	Mar. 26
5	NY Rangers	Apr. 12	Apr. 26
5	Washington	Apr. 14	May 2
5	Boston	Apr. 19	May 1

Consecutive Road Wins

Games	Team	From	To
7	Detroit	Mar. 25	Apr. 14
5	Chicago	Feb. 1	Feb. 9
4	Pittsburgh	Jan. 20	Jan. 29
4	Quebec	Feb. 8	Feb. 16
4	NY Rangers	Feb. 20	Mar. 1
4	Philadelphia	Mar. 7	Mar. 18
3	Winnipeg	Feb. 11	Feb. 22
3	Detroit	Feb. 15	Feb. 23
3	Washington	Mar. 2	Mar. 13
3	Los Angeles	Mar. 9	Mar. 13
3	Chicago	Mar. 19	Mar. 23
3	Washington	Mar. 20	Apr. 4
3	New Jersey	Mar. 29	Apr. 5
3	Philadelphia	Apr. 8	Apr. 22

Consecutive Undefeated

Games	Team	W	T	From	To
13	Pittsburgh	12	1	Jan. 20	Feb. 16
11	Detroit	10	1	Mar. 25	Apr. 14
9	Philadelphia	9	0	Apr. 2	Apr. 22
8	Philadelphia	8	0	Mar. 5	Mar. 20
7	Quebec	7	0	Feb. 4	Feb. 16
7	Washington	6	1	Mar. 2	Mar. 13
7	Detroit	6	1	Mar. 6	Mar. 22
7	New Jersey	5	2	Mar. 26	Apr. 9
7	St. Louis	6	1	Mar. 26	Apr. 5
6	San Jose	5	1	Jan. 21	Feb. 4
6	Edmonton	4	2	Feb. 3	Feb. 15
6	Detroit	5	1	Feb. 12	Feb. 23
6	St. Louis	4	2	Apr. 16	Apr. 25
6	Chicago	5	1	Apr. 23	May 3

Consecutive Home Undefeated

Games	Team	W	T	From	To
15	Quebec	13	2	Mar. 1	May 3
12	Detroit	10	2	Mar. 2	Apr. 29
9	Pittsburgh	8	1	Jan. 27	Feb. 21
8	Quebec	6	2	Jan. 24	Feb. 25
8	Washington	5	3	Feb. 26	Mar. 25
7	Montreal	5	2	Jan. 25	Feb. 20
7	Philadelphia	6	1	Feb. 28	Mar. 26
7	Dallas	5	2	Mar. 3	Mar. 23
6	St. Louis	6	0	Feb. 13	Mar. 9
6	Pittsburgh	6	0	Mar. 9	Apr. 1
6	New Jersey	5	1	Mar. 19	Apr. 16
6	Philadelphia	6	0	Apr. 2	Apr. 20

Consecutive Road Undefeated

Games	Team	W	T	From	To
8	Vancouver	4	4	Feb. 17	Mar. 14
7	Detroit	7	0	Mar. 25	Apr. 14
6	Pittsburgh	5	1	Jan. 20	Feb. 9
5	Chicago	5	0	Feb. 1	Feb. 9

TEAM PENALTIES

Abbreviations: GP – games played; **PEN** – total penalty minutes including bench minutes; **BMI** – total bench minor minutes; **AVG** – average penalty minutes/game calculated by dividing total penalty minutes by games played

Team	GP	PEN	BMI	AVG
ANA	48	731	16	15.2
PHI	48	741	6	15.4
TOR	48	744	12	15.5
OTT	48	749	8	15.6
FLA	48	770	8	16.0
QUE	48	770	4	16.0
NYR	48	781	4	16.3
N.J.	48	787	14	16.4
BOS	48	793	6	16.5
MTL	48	840	10	17.5
S.J.	48	840	18	17.5
NYI	48	901	4	18.8
HFD	48	915	2	19.1
DET	48	932	10	19.4
L.A.	48	978	18	20.4
BUF	48	1022	4	21.3
PIT	48	1036	10	21.6
T.B.	48	1040	10	21.7
ST.L.	48	1077	16	22.4
VAN	48	1093	6	22.8
DAL	48	1117	10	23.3
CHI	48	1123	8	23.4
WSH	48	1144	16	23.8
WPG	48	1141	16	23.8
EDM	48	1183	12	24.6
CGY	48	1249	18	26.0
TOTAL	**624**	**24497**	**266**	**39.3**

The NHL's most productive offensive defenseman, Paul Coffey led the NHL in powerplay assists (27) and powerplay points (31) during the 1994-95 season.

TEAMS' POWER PLAY RECORD

Abbreviations: ADV – total advantages; **PPGF** – power-play goals for; **%** – calculated by dividing number of power-play goals by total advantages.

Home

	Team	GP	ADV	PPGF	%
1	DET	24	119	32	26.9
2	NYR	24	111	28	25.2
3	PHI	24	100	24	24.0
4	CHI	24	97	22	22.7
5	PIT	24	110	25	22.7
6	HFD	24	89	20	22.5
7	QUE	24	104	23	22.1
8	BUF	24	118	26	22.0
9	BOS	24	120	25	20.8
10	VAN	24	121	25	20.7
11	WSH	24	117	23	19.7
12	TOR	24	104	20	19.2
13	L.A.	24	112	21	18.8
14	N.J.	24	84	15	17.9
15	DAL	24	136	24	17.6
16	CGY	24	106	18	17.0
17	ST.L.	24	121	20	16.5
18	OTT	24	118	19	16.1
19	EDM	24	138	22	15.9
20	WPG	24	102	16	15.7
21	MTL	24	89	14	15.7
22	FLA	24	126	17	13.5
23	ANA	24	98	13	13.3
24	S.J.	24	114	14	12.3
25	NYI	24	83	10	12.0
26	T.B.	24	94	11	11.7
	TOTAL	**624**	**2831**	**527**	**18.6**

Road

Team	GP	ADV	PPGF	%
QUE	24	82	22	26.8
CHI	24	115	30	26.1
BOS	24	91	21	23.1
WPG	24	117	26	22.2
DET	24	96	20	20.8
WSH	24	109	22	20.2
CGY	24	105	21	20.0
NYI	24	95	18	18.9
VAN	24	117	22	18.8
MTL	24	83	14	16.9
T.B.	24	83	14	16.9
EDM	24	121	20	16.5
ST.L.	24	99	16	16.2
L.A.	24	88	14	15.9
PHI	24	104	16	15.4
BUF	24	124	19	15.3
PIT	24	111	17	15.3
TOR	24	114	17	14.9
NYR	24	89	12	13.5
DAL	24	112	15	13.4
FLA	24	96	12	12.5
OTT	24	97	12	12.4
HFD	24	85	10	11.8
S.J.	24	89	10	11.2
ANA	24	104	10	9.6
N.J.	24	80	7	8.8
TOTAL	**624**	**2606**	**437**	**16.8**

Overall

Team	GP	ADV	PPGF	%
CHI	48	212	52	24.5
DET	48	215	52	24.2
QUE	48	186	45	24.2
BOS	48	211	46	21.8
NYR	48	200	40	20.0
WSH	48	226	45	19.9
VAN	48	238	47	19.7
PHI	48	204	40	19.6
WPG	48	219	42	19.2
PIT	48	221	42	19.0
BUF	48	242	45	18.6
CGY	48	211	39	18.5
L.A.	48	200	35	17.5
HFD	48	174	30	17.2
TOR	48	218	37	17.0
ST.L.	48	220	36	16.4
MTL	48	172	28	16.3
EDM	48	259	42	16.2
DAL	48	248	39	15.7
NYI	48	178	28	15.7
OTT	48	215	31	14.4
T.B.	48	177	25	14.1
N.J.	48	164	22	13.4
FLA	48	222	29	13.1
S.J.	48	203	24	11.8
ANA	48	202	23	11.4
TOTAL	**624**	**5437**	**964**	**17.7**

SHORT HAND GOALS FOR

Home

	Team	GP	SHGF
1	BUF	24	10
2	WPG	24	7
3	WSH	24	7
4	EDM	24	5
5	QUE	24	5
6	CGY	24	5
7	CHI	24	5
8	ST.L.	24	5
9	NYR	24	4
10	T.B.	24	4
11	VAN	24	4
12	TOR	24	4
13	PIT	24	4
14	DET	24	3
15	HFD	24	2
16	PHI	24	2
17	BOS	24	2
18	N.J.	24	2
19	S.J.	24	1
20	OTT	24	1
21	L.A.	24	1
22	NYI	24	0
23	FLA	24	0
24	ANA	24	0
25	MTL	24	0
	TOTAL	**624**	**85**

Road

Team	GP	SHGF
WSH	24	6
L.A.	24	5
S.J.	24	5
PIT	24	4
ANA	24	4
QUE	24	4
NYI	24	4
BUF	24	3
EDM	24	3
VAN	24	3
CHI	24	2
CGY	24	2
ST.L.	24	2
T.B.	24	2
DET	24	2
DAL	24	1
TOR	24	1
FLA	24	1
MTL	24	1
N.J.	24	1
BOS	24	1
HFD	24	1
NYR	24	0
PHI	24	0
OTT	24	0
WPG	24	0
TOTAL	**624**	**59**

Overall

Team	GP	SHGF
BUF	48	13
WSH	48	13
QUE	48	9
PIT	48	8
EDM	48	8
CHI	48	7
WPG	48	7
CGY	48	7
VAN	48	7
ST.L.	48	7
T.B.	48	6
S.J.	48	6
NYR	48	5
DET	48	5
L.A.	48	5
TOR	48	5
ANA	48	4
DAL	48	4
NYI	48	4
HFD	48	3
BOS	48	3
N.J.	48	3
PHI	48	2
FLA	48	1
MTL	48	1
OTT	48	1
TOTAL	**624**	**144**

TEAMS' PENALTY KILLING RECORD

Abbreviations: TSH – total times short-handed; **PPGA** – power-play goals against; **%** – calculated by dividing times short minus power-play goals against by times short.

Home

	TEAM	GP	TSH	PPGA	%
1	WSH	24	98	12	87.8
2	BOS	24	96	12	87.5
3	T.B.	24	109	14	87.2
4	BUF	24	105	14	86.7
5	DAL	24	113	16	85.8
6	TOR	24	80	12	85.0
7	PIT	24	98	15	84.7
8	DET	24	104	16	84.6
9	PHI	24	84	13	84.5
10	QUE	24	97	15	84.5
11	CHI	24	106	17	84.0
12	VAN	24	103	17	83.5
13	WPG	24	114	19	83.3
14	N.J.	24	77	13	83.1
15	CGY	24	122	21	82.8
16	L.A.	24	109	19	82.6
17	MTL	24	92	16	82.6
18	S.J.	24	96	17	82.3
19	NYR	24	101	18	82.2
20	ANA	24	92	17	81.5
21	NYI	24	98	19	80.6
22	FLA	24	93	18	80.6
23	OTT	24	94	19	79.8
24	HFD	24	87	18	79.3
25	ST.L.	24	120	25	79.2
26	EDM	24	118	25	78.8
	TOTAL	**624**	**2606**	**437**	**83.2**

Road

TEAM	GP	TSH	PPGA	%
DET	24	102	12	88.2
CGY	24	127	16	87.4
BOS	24	87	12	86.2
FLA	24	98	14	85.7
NYR	24	110	16	85.5
TOR	24	105	16	84.8
CHI	24	122	19	84.4
BUF	24	115	18	84.3
VAN	24	133	22	83.5
DAL	24	105	18	82.9
WPG	24	121	21	82.6
WSH	24	122	22	82.0
ST.L.	24	113	21	81.4
T.B.	24	96	18	81.3
OTT	24	105	20	81.0
HFD	24	98	19	80.6
S.J.	24	112	22	80.4
L.A.	24	112	23	79.5
N.J.	24	72	15	79.2
MTL	24	99	21	78.8
QUE	24	106	23	78.3
PHI	24	109	24	78.0
EDM	24	115	27	76.5
NYI	24	115	27	76.5
PIT	24	131	31	76.3
ANA	24	101	30	70.3
TOTAL	**624**	**2831**	**527**	**81.4**

Overall

TEAM	GP	TSH	PPGA	%
BOS	48	183	24	86.9
DET	48	206	28	86.4
BUF	48	220	32	85.5
CGY	48	249	37	85.1
TOR	48	185	28	84.9
WSH	48	220	34	84.5
T.B.	48	205	32	84.4
DAL	48	218	34	84.4
CHI	48	228	36	84.2
NYR	48	211	34	83.9
VAN	48	236	39	83.5
FLA	48	191	32	83.2
WPG	48	235	40	83.0
S.J.	48	208	39	81.3
QUE	48	203	38	81.3
N.J.	48	149	28	81.2
L.A.	48	221	42	81.0
PHI	48	193	37	80.8
MTL	48	191	37	80.6
OTT	48	199	40	80.4
ST.L.	48	233	46	80.3
HFD	48	185	37	80.0
PIT	48	229	46	79.9
NYI	48	213	46	78.4
EDM	48	233	52	77.7
ANA	48	193	47	75.6
TOTAL	**624**	**5437**	**964**	**82.3**

SHORT HAND GOALS AGAINST

Home

	Team	GP	SHGA
1	QUE	24	0
2	ST.L.	24	0
3	NYR	24	1
4	HFD	24	1
5	BOS	24	1
6	FLA	24	1
7	MTL	24	1
8	CHI	24	1
9	PIT	24	1
10	WSH	24	1
11	T.B.	24	2
12	DET	24	2
13	VAN	24	2
14	CGY	24	2
15	TOR	24	2
16	N.J.	24	2
17	WPG	24	2
18	EDM	24	3
19	S.J.	24	3
20	ANA	24	3
21	BUF	24	3
22	DAL	24	3
23	OTT	24	4
24	PHI	24	5
25	L.A.	24	6
26	NYI	24	6
	TOTAL	**624**	**59**

Road

Team	GP	SHGA
CGY	24	1
WSH	24	1
N.J.	24	1
CHI	24	1
ST.L.	24	2
MTL	24	2
OTT	24	2
L.A.	24	2
NYR	24	2
S.J.	24	3
PIT	24	3
TOR	24	3
QUE	24	3
BOS	24	3
WPG	24	3
T.B.	24	3
BUF	24	4
DAL	24	4
PHI	24	4
ANA	24	5
FLA	24	5
EDM	24	5
HFD	24	5
NYI	24	5
DET	24	5
VAN	24	6
TOTAL	**624**	**85**

Overall

Team	GP	SHGA
ST.L.	48	2
WSH	48	2
NYR	48	3
CHI	48	3
CGY	48	3
MTL	48	3
QUE	48	3
N.J.	48	3
PIT	48	4
BOS	48	5
T.B.	48	5
S.J.	48	5
TOR	48	5
WPG	48	6
HFD	48	6
FLA	48	6
OTT	48	7
BUF	48	7
DET	48	7
DAL	48	7
EDM	48	8
ANA	48	8
L.A.	48	8
PHI	48	8
VAN	48	10
NYI	48	11
TOTAL	**624**	**144**

Overtime Results

1985-86 to 1994-95

Team	94-95 GP	W	L	T	93-94 GP	W	L	T	92-93 GP	W	L	T	91-92 GP	W	L	T	90-91 GP	W	L	T	89-90 GP	W	L	T	88-89 GP	W	L	T	87-88 GP	W	L	T	86-87 GP	W	L	T	85-86 GP	W	L	T
ANA	7	2	0	5																																				
BOS	8	2	3	3	17	2	2	13	15	5	3	7	20	6	2	12	17	5	0	12	14	3	2	9	19	3	2	14	14	4	4	6	12	2	3	7	17	2	3	12
BUF	9	1	1	7	13	0	4	9	18	4	4	10	16	2	2	12	24	3	2	19	15	4	3	8	13	2	4	7	12	0	1	11	13	1	4	8	9	1	2	6
CGY	9	1	1	7	18	3	2	13	19	4	4	11	19	2	5	12	15	3	4	8	21	3	3	15	17	5	3	9	15	2	4	9	4	1	0	3	12	1	2	9
CHI	7	2	0	5	16	2	5	9	16	1	3	12	19	2	2	15	12	3	1	8	10	2	2	6	17	2	3	12	15	4	2	9	15	1	0	14	12	3	1	8
DAL	9	0	1	8	22	6	3	13	10	0	0	10	8	0	2	6	17	0	3	14	11	3	4	4	17	0	1	16	16	1	2	13	14	2	2	10	15	4	2	9
DET	4	0	0	4	15	5	2	8	11	2	0	9	16	3	1	12	14	2	4	8	17	2	1	14	16	3	1	12	15	4	3	8	17	2	5	10	13	2	5	6
EDM	7	1	2	4	21	1	6	14	17	5	4	8	12	0	2	10	15	4	5	6	20	5	1	14	15	4	3	8	16	3	2	11	14	5	3	6	14	5	2	7
FLA	9	0	3	6	24	2	5	17																																
HFD	9	4	0	5	14	4	1	9	18	3	9	6	18	2	3	13	18	2	5	11	9	0	0	9	10	1	4	5	12	3	2	7	9	2	0	7	7	1	2	4
L.A.	9	0	0	9	18	3	3	12	13	2	1	10	16	1	1	14	16	4	2	10	12	3	2	7	14	6	1	7	12	1	3	8	12	2	2	8	14	3	3	8
MTL	10	1	2	7	19	3	2	14	14	5	3	6	20	6	3	11	17	3	3	11	17	4	2	11	11	2	0	9	16	1	2	13	16	2	4	10	14	1	6	7
N.J.	11	1	2	8	14	1	1	12	11	4	0	7	17	2	4	11	17	1	1	15	16	3	4	9	17	1	4	12	12	4	2	6	13	3	4	6	10	4	3	3
NYI	7	1	1	5	19	5	2	12	13	3	3	7	16	3	2	11	15	2	3	10	16	3	2	11	11	3	3	5	13	3	0	10	20	5	3	12	17	4	1	12
NYR	3	0	0	3	12	3	1	8	17	2	4	11	11	5	1	5	16	1	2	13	17	2	2	13	10	1	1	8	11	0	1	10	19	5	6	8	13	0	7	6
OTT	7	1	1	5	17	4	4	9	10	0	6	4																												
PHI	8	3	1	4	18	3	5	10	17	4	2	11	17	2	4	11	11	1	0	10	18	2	5	11	14	1	5	8	13	1	3	9	10	1	1	8	9	4	1	4
PIT	5	1	1	3	19	4	2	13	10	3	0	7	12	2	1	9	14	3	3	8	10	2	1	7	16	5	2	9	21	5	4	12	14	3	3	8				
QUE	6	1	0	5	8	0	0	8	15	4	1	10	17	0	5	12	18	1	3	14	8	0	1	7	10	2	1	7	9	2	2	5	14	0	4	10				
ST.L.	7	1	1	5	17	4	2	11	17	2	4	11	15	2	2	11	18	3	4	11	15	2	4	9	16	3	1	12	14	2	4	8	21	4	2	15	17	5	3	9
S.J.	5	1	0	4	19	2	1	16	10	3	5	2	9	1	3	5																								
T.B.	7	2	2	3	18	3	4	11	14	3	4	7																												
TOR	8	0	0	8	17	4	1	12	13	1	1	11	11	4	0	7	17	4	2	11	11	3	4	4	11	1	4	6	13	1	2	10	13	3	4	6	17	4	6	7
VAN	13	0	1	12	12	5	4	3	10	1	0	9	17	4	1	12	15	3	3	9	21	2	5	14	14	2	4	8	11	0	2	9	10	2	0	8	16	1	2	13
WSH	9	0	1	8	14	2	2	10	11	2	2	7	12	2	2	8	14	4	3	7	9	2	1	6	16	2	4	10	15	2	4	9	17	5	2	10	11	4	0	7
WPG	9	0	2	7	15	1	5	9	11	2	2	7	20	1	4	15	14	1	2	11	19	4	4	11	20	6	2	12	21	8	2	11	11	2	1	8	8	0	1	7
Totals	**101**	**26**		**75**	**214**	**74**		**140**	**165**	**65**		**100**	**169**	**52**		**117**	**166**	**54**		**112**	**155**	**55**		**100**	**149**	**52**		**97**	**146**	**49**		**97**	**148**	**55**		**93**	**135**	**56**		**79**

1994-95
Home Team Wins: 16
Visiting Team Wins: 10

1994-95 Penalty Shots

Scored

Benoit Hogue (NY Islanders) scored against Ron Hextall (Philadelphia), January 24. Final score: Philadelphia 3 at NY Islanders 4.

Mats Sundin (Toronto) scored against Arturs Irbe (San Jose), March 15. Final score: Toronto 2 at San Jose 1.

Dan Quinn (Los Angeles) scored against Mikhail Shtalenkov (Anaheim), March 21. Final score: Los Angeles 3 at Anaheim 3.

Although Winnipeg's rookie netminder Nikolai Khabibulin turned aside Bob Errey's penalty shot on March 22, 1995, the Red Wings downed the Jets 6-3.

Stopped

Sean Burke (Hartford) stopped Michal Pivonka (Washington), January 21. Final score: Washington 1 at Hartford 1.

Don Beaupre (Ottawa) stopped Mark Recchi (Philadelphia), February 6. Final score: Philadelphia 0 at Ottawa 3.

Trevor Kidd (Calgary) stopped Teemu Selanne (Winnipeg), February 6. Final score: Winnipeg 5 at Calgary 4.

Kelly Hrudey (Los Angeles) stopped Sergei Fedorov (Detroit), February 12. Final score: Los Angeles 4 at Detroit 4.

Mike Richter (NY Rangers) stopped Steve Konowalchuk (Washington), March 5. Final score: NY Rangers 2 at Washington 4.

Andrei Trefilov (Calgary) stopped Jeremy Roenick (Chicago), March 7. Final score: Calgary 6 at Chicago 3.

Dominik Hasek (Buffalo) stopped Mark Recchi (Montreal), March 8. Final score: Buffalo 2 at Montreal 2.

Kelly Hrudey (Los Angeles) stopped Dirk Graham (Chicago), March 9. Final score: Los Angeles 4 at Chicago 3.

Jocelyn Thibault (Quebec) stopped Martin Straka (Pittsburgh), March 16. Final score: Pittsburgh 2 at Quebec 3.

Damian Rhodes (Toronto) stopped Geoff Courtnall (Vancouver), March 21. Final score: Toronto 1 at Vancouver 3.

Nikolai Khabibulin (Winnipeg) stopped Bob Errey (Detroit), March 22. Final score: Winnipeg 3 at Detroit 6.

Bill Ranford (Edmonton) stopped Brett Hull (St. Louis), March 26. Final score: Edmonton 1 at St. Louis 5.

Chris Osgoode (Detroit) stopped Dave Gagner (Dallas), April 1. Final score: Detroit 3 at Dallas 2.

Tim Cheveldae (Winnipeg) stopped Dave Andreychuk (Toronto), April 8. Final score: Winnipeg 3 at Toronto 4.

Summary
17 penalty shots resulted in 3 goals.

NHL Record Book

Year-By-Year Final Standings & Leading Scorers

*Stanley Cup winner

1917-18

Team	GP	W	L	T	GF	GA	PTS
Montreal	22	13	9	0	115	84	26
*Toronto	22	13	9	0	108	109	26
Ottawa	22	9	13	0	102	114	18
**Mtl. Wanderers	6	1	5	0	17	35	2

**Montreal Arena burned down and Wanderers forced to withdraw from League. Canadiens and Toronto each counted a win for defaulted games with Wanderers.

Leading Scorers

Player	Club	GP	G	A	PTS
Malone, Joe	Montreal	20	44	—	44
Denneny, Cy	Ottawa	22	36	—	36
Noble, Reg	Toronto	20	28	—	28
Lalonde, Newsy	Montreal	14	23	—	23
Denneny, Corbett	Toronto	21	20	—	20
Pitre, Didier	Montreal	19	17	—	17
Cameron, Harry	Toronto	20	17	—	17
Darragh, Jack	Ottawa	18	14	—	14
Hyland, Harry	Mtl.W., Ott.	16	14	—	14
Skinner, Alf	Toronto	19	13	—	13
Gerard, Eddie	Ottawa	21	13	—	13

1918-19

Team	GP	W	L	T	GF	GA	PTS
Ottawa	18	12	6	0	71	53	24
Montreal	18	10	8	0	88	78	20
Toronto	18	5	13	0	64	92	10

Leading Scorers

Player	Club	GP	G	A	PTS	PIM
Lalonde, Newsy	Montreal	17	21	9	30	40
Cleghorn, Odie	Montreal	17	23	6	29	33
Denneny, Cy	Ottawa	18	18	4	22	43
Nighbor, Frank	Ottawa	18	18	4	22	27
Pitre, Didier	Montreal	17	14	4	18	9
Skinner, Alf	Toronto	17	12	3	15	26
Cameron, Harry	Tor., Ott.	14	11	3	14	35
Noble, Reg	Toronto	17	11	3	14	35
Darragh, Jack	Ottawa	14	12	1	13	27
Randall, Ken	Toronto	14	7	6	13	27

1919-20

Team	GP	W	L	T	GF	GA	PTS
*Ottawa	24	19	5	0	121	64	38
Montreal	24	13	11	0	129	113	26
Toronto	24	12	12	0	119	106	24
Quebec	24	4	20	0	91	177	8

Leading Scorers

Player	Club	GP	G	A	PTS	PIM
Malone, Joe	Quebec	24	39	9	48	12
Lalonde, Newsy	Montreal	23	36	6	42	33
Denneny, Corbett	Toronto	23	23	12	35	18
Nighbor, Frank	Ottawa	23	26	7	33	18
Noble, Reg	Toronto	24	24	7	31	51
Darragh, Jack	Ottawa	22	22	5	27	22
Arbour, Amos	Montreal	20	22	4	26	10
Wilson, Cully	Toronto	23	21	5	26	79
Broadbent, Punch	Ottawa	20	19	4	23	39
Cleghorn, Odie	Montreal	21	19	3	22	30
Pitre, Didier	Montreal	22	15	7	22	6

All-Time Standings of NHL Teams

(ranked by percentage)

Active Clubs

Team	Games	Wins	Losses	Ties	Goals For	Goals Against	Points	%	First Season
Montreal	4808	2539	1525	744	16329	12784	5822	.605	1917-18
Philadelphia	2194	1084	770	340	7851	6813	2508	.572	1967-68
Edmonton	1256	625	471	160	5324	4736	1410	.561	1979-80
Boston	4648	2240	1722	686	15375	13822	5166	.556	1924-25
Buffalo	1968	931	725	312	7120	6392	2174	.552	1970-71
Calgary	1812	859	678	275	6913	6230	1993	.550	1972-73
NY Islanders	1812	847	707	258	6635	5939	1952	.539	1972-73
Toronto	4808	2065	2041	702	15049	15010	4832	.502	1917-18
NY Rangers	4582	1937	1928	717	14422	14515	4591	.501	1926-27
Detroit	4582	1928	1936	718	14157	14207	4574	.499	1926-27
St. Louis	2194	921	942	331	7236	7448	2173	.495	1967-68
Chicago	4582	1890	1985	707	13890	14076	4487	.490	1926-27
Florida	132	53	56	23	348	360	129	.489	1993-94
Washington	1656	685	757	214	5692	6038	1584	.478	1974-75
Pittsburgh	2194	877	1017	300	7722	8283	2054	.468	1967-68
Los Angeles	2194	861	1012	321	7733	8266	2043	.466	1967-68
Colorado	1256	497	599	160	4625	4883	1154	.459	1979-80
Dallas	2194	817	1022	355	7112	7773	1989	.453	1967-68
Winnipeg	1256	470	620	166	4487	5056	1106	.440	1979-80
Hartford	1256	468	631	157	4241	4830	1093	.435	1979-80
Vancouver	1968	713	968	287	6488	7358	1713	.435	1970-71
Anaheim	132	49	73	10	354	415	108	.409	1993-94
New Jersey	1656	534	893	229	5300	6484	1297	.392	1974-75
Tampa Bay	216	70	125	21	589	727	161	.373	1992-93
San Jose	296	80	189	27	818	1199	187	.316	1991-92
Ottawa	216	33	165	18	520	966	84	.194	1992-93

Defunct Clubs

Team	Games	Wins	Losses	Ties	Goals For	Goals Against	Points	%	First Season	Last Season
Ottawa Senators	542	258	221	63	1458	1333	579	.534	1917-18	1933-34
Montreal Maroons	622	271	260	91	1474	1405	633	.509	1924-25	1937-38
NY/Brooklyn Americans	784	255	402	127	1643	2182	637	.406	1925-26	1941-42
Hamilton Tigers	126	47	78	1	414	475	95	.377	1920-21	1924-25
Cleveland Barons	160	47	87	26	470	617	120	.375	1976-77	1977-78
Pittsburgh Pirates	212	67	122	23	376	519	157	.370	1925-26	1929-30
Calif./Oakland Seals	698	182	401	115	1826	2580	479	.343	1967-68	1975-76
St. Louis Eagles	48	11	31	6	86	144	28	.292	1934-35	1934-35
Quebec Bulldogs	24	4	20	0	91	177	8	.167	1919-20	1919-20
Montreal Wanderers	6	1	5	0	17	35	2	.167	1917-18	1917-18
Philadelphia Quakers	44	4	36	4	76	184	12	.136	1930-31	1930-31

Calgary totals include Atlanta, 1972-73 to 1979-80.
Dallas totals include Minnesota, 1967-68 to 1992-93.
Detroit totals include Cougars, 1926-27 to 1928-29, and Falcons, 1929-30 to 1931-32.
New Jersey totals include Kansas City, 1974-75 to 1975-76, and Colorado, 1976-77 to 1981-82.
Toronto totals include Arenas, 1917-18 to 1918-19, and St. Patricks, 1919-20 to 1925-56.
Colorado totals include Quebec, 1979-80 to 1994-95.

1920-21

Team	GP	W	L	T	GF	GA	PTS
Toronto	24	15	9	0	105	100	30
*Ottawa	24	14	10	0	97	75	28
Montreal	24	13	11	0	112	99	26
Hamilton	24	6	18	0	92	132	12

Leading Scorers

Player	Club	GP	G	A	PTS	PIM
Lalonde, Newsy	Montreal	24	33	8	41	36
Denneny, Cy	Ottawa	24	34	5	39	0
Dye, Babe	Ham., Tor.	24	35	2	37	32
Malone, Joe	Hamilton	20	30	4	34	2
Cameron, Harry	Toronto	24	18	9	27	35
Noble, Reg	Toronto	24	20	6	26	54
Prodgers, Goldie	Hamilton	23	18	8	26	8
Denneny, Corbett	Toronto	20	17	6	23	27
Nighbor, Frank	Ottawa	24	18	3	21	10
Berlinquette, Louis	Montreal	24	12	9	21	24

1921-22

Team	GP	W	L	T	GF	GA	PTS
Ottawa	24	14	8	2	106	84	30
*Toronto	24	13	10	1	98	97	27
Montreal	24	12	11	1	88	94	25
Hamilton	24	7	17	0	88	105	14

Leading Scorers

Player	Club	GP	G	A	PTS	PIM
Broadbent, Punch	Ottawa	24	32	14	46	24
Denneny, Cy	Ottawa	22	27	12	39	18
Dye, Babe	Toronto	24	30	7	37	18
Malone, Joe	Hamilton	24	25	7	32	4
Cameron, Harry	Toronto	24	19	8	27	18
Denneny, Corbett	Toronto	24	19	7	26	28
Noble, Reg	Toronto	24	17	8	25	10
Cleghorn, Odie	Montreal	23	21	3	24	26
Cleghorn, Sprague	Montreal	24	17	7	24	63
Reise, Leo	Hamilton	24	9	14	23	8

1922-23

Team	GP	W	L	T	GF	GA	PTS
*Ottawa	24	14	9	1	77	54	29
Montreal	24	13	9	2	73	61	28
Toronto	24	13	10	1	82	88	27
Hamilton	24	6	18	0	81	110	12

Leading Scorers

Player	Club	GP	G	A	PTS	PIM
Dye, Babe	Toronto	22	26	11	37	19
Denneny, Cy	Ottawa	24	21	10	31	20
Adams, Jack	Toronto	23	19	9	28	42
Boucher, Billy	Montreal	24	23	4	27	52
Cleghorn, Odie	Montreal	24	19	7	26	14
Roach, Mickey	Hamilton	23	17	8	25	8
Boucher, George	Ottawa	23	15	9	24	44
Joliat, Aurel	Montreal	24	13	9	22	31
Noble, Reg	Toronto	24	12	10	22	41
Wilson, Cully	Hamilton	23	16	3	19	46

1923-24

Team	GP	W	L	T	GF	GA	PTS
Ottawa	24	16	8	0	74	54	32
*Montreal	24	13	11	0	59	48	26
Toronto	24	10	14	0	59	85	20
Hamilton	24	9	15	0	63	68	18

Leading Scorers

Player	Club	GP	G	A	PTS	PIM
Denneny, Cy	Ottawa	21	22	1	23	10
Boucher, Billy	Montreal	23	16	6	22	33
Joliat, Aurel	Montreal	24	15	5	20	19
Dye, Babe	Toronto	19	17	2	19	23
Boucher, George	Ottawa	21	14	5	19	28
Burch, Billy	Hamilton	24	16	2	18	4
Clancy, King	Ottawa	24	9	8	17	18
Adams, Jack	Toronto	22	13	3	16	49
Morenz, Howie	Montreal	24	13	3	16	20
Noble, Reg	Toronto	23	12	3	15	23

1924-25

Team	GP	W	L	T	GF	GA	PTS
Hamilton	30	19	10	1	90	60	39
Toronto	30	19	11	0	90	84	38
Montreal	30	17	11	2	93	56	36
Ottawa	30	17	12	1	83	66	35
Mtl. Maroons	30	9	19	2	45	65	20
Boston	30	6	24	0	49	119	12

Leading Scorers

Player	Club	GP	G	A	PTS	PIM
Dye, Babe	Toronto	29	38	6	44	41
Denneny, Cy	Ottawa	28	27	15	42	16
Joliat, Aurel	Montreal	24	29	11	40	85
Morenz, Howie	Montreal	30	27	7	34	31
Boucher, Billy	Montreal	30	18	13	31	92
Adams, Jack	Toronto	27	21	8	29	66
Burch, Billy	Hamilton	27	20	4	24	10
Green, Red	Hamilton	30	19	4	23	63
Herberts, Jimmy	Boston	30	17	5	22	50
Day, Hap	Toronto	26	10	12	22	27

1925-26

Team	GP	W	L	T	GF	GA	PTS
Ottawa	36	24	8	4	77	42	52
*Mtl. Maroons	36	20	11	5	91	73	45
Pittsburgh	36	19	16	1	82	70	39
Boston	36	17	15	4	92	85	38
NY Americans	36	12	20	4	68	89	28
Toronto	36	12	21	3	92	114	27
Montreal	36	11	24	1	79	108	23

Leading Scorers

Player	Club	GP	G	A	PTS	PIM
Stewart, Nels	Mtl. Maroons	36	34	8	42	119
Denneny, Cy	Ottawa	36	24	12	36	18
Cooper, Carson	Boston	36	28	3	31	10
Herberts, Jimmy	Boston	36	26	5	31	47
Morenz, Howie	Montreal	31	23	3	26	39
Adams, Jack	Toronto	36	21	5	26	52
Joliat, Aurel	Montreal	35	17	9	26	52
Burch, Billy	NY Americans	36	22	3	25	33
Smith, Hooley	Ottawa	28	16	9	25	53
Nighbor, Frank	Ottawa	35	12	13	25	40

1926-27

Canadian Division

Team	GP	W	L	T	GF	GA	PTS
*Ottawa	44	30	10	4	86	69	64
Montreal	44	28	14	2	99	67	58
Mtl. Maroons	44	20	20	4	71	68	44
NY Americans	44	17	25	2	82	91	36
Toronto	44	15	24	5	79	94	35

American Division

Team	GP	W	L	T	GF	GA	PTS
New York	44	25	13	6	95	72	56
Boston	44	21	20	3	97	89	45
Chicago	44	19	22	3	115	116	41
Pittsburgh	44	15	26	3	79	108	33
Detroit	44	12	28	4	76	105	28

Leading Scorers

Player	Club	GP	G	A	PTS	PIM
Cook, Bill	New York	44	33	4	37	58
Irvin, Dick	Chicago	43	18	18	36	34
Morenz, Howie	Montreal	44	25	7	32	49
Fredrickson, Frank	Det., Bos.	41	18	13	31	46
Dye, Babe	Chicago	41	25	5	30	14
Bailey, Ace	Toronto	42	15	13	28	82
Boucher, Frank	New York	44	13	15	28	17
Burch, Billy	NY Americans	43	19	8	27	40
Oliver, Harry	Boston	42	18	6	24	17
Keats, Gordon	Bos., Det.	42	16	8	24	52

1927-28

Canadian Division

Team	GP	W	L	T	GF	GA	PTS
Montreal	44	26	11	7	116	48	59
Mtl. Maroons	44	24	14	6	96	77	54
Ottawa	44	20	14	10	78	57	50
Toronto	44	18	18	8	89	88	44
NY Americans	44	11	27	6	63	128	28

American Division

Team	GP	W	L	T	GF	GA	PTS
Boston	44	20	13	11	77	70	51
*New York	44	19	16	9	94	79	47
Pittsburgh	44	19	17	8	67	76	46
Detroit	44	19	19	6	88	79	44
Chicago	44	7	34	3	68	134	17

Leading Scorers

Player	Club	GP	G	A	PTS	PIM
Morenz, Howie	Montreal	43	33	18	51	66
Joliat, Aurel	Montreal	44	28	11	39	105
Boucher, Frank	New York	44	23	12	35	15
Hay, George	Detroit	42	22	13	35	20
Stewart, Nels	Mtl. Maroons	41	27	7	34	104
Gagne, Art	Montreal	44	20	10	30	75
Cook, Fred	New York	44	14	14	28	45
Carson, Bill	Toronto	32	20	6	26	36
Finnigan, Frank	Ottawa	38	20	5	25	34
Cook, Bill	New York	43	18	6	24	42
Keats, Gordon	Det., Chi..	38	14	10	24	60

1928-29

Canadian Division

Team	GP	W	L	T	GF	GA	PTS
Montreal	44	22	7	15	71	43	59
NY Americans	44	19	13	12	53	53	50
Toronto	44	21	18	5	85	69	47
Ottawa	44	14	17	13	54	67	41
Mtl. Maroons	44	15	20	9	67	65	39

American Division

Team	GP	W	L	T	GF	GA	PTS
*Boston	44	26	13	5	89	52	57
New York	44	21	13	10	72	65	52
Detroit	44	19	16	9	72	63	47
Pittsburgh	44	9	27	8	46	80	26
Chicago	44	7	29	8	33	85	22

Leading Scorers

Player	Club	GP	G	A	PTS	PIM
Bailey, Ace	Toronto	44	22	10	32	78
Stewart, Nels	Mtl. Maroons	44	21	8	29	74
Cooper, Carson	Detroit	43	18	9	27	14
Morenz, Howie	Montreal	42	17	10	27	47
Blair, Andy	Toronto	44	12	15	27	41
Boucher, Frank	New York	44	10	16	26	8
Oliver, Harry	Boston	43	17	6	23	24
Cook, Bill	New York	43	15	8	23	41
Ward, Jimmy	Mtl. Maroons	43	14	8	22	46
Seven players tied with 19 points						

1929-30

Canadian Division

Team	GP	W	L	T	GF	GA	PTS
Mtl. Maroons	44	23	16	5	141	114	51
*Montreal	44	21	14	9	142	114	51
Ottawa	44	21	15	8	138	118	50
Toronto	44	17	21	6	116	124	40
NY Americans	44	14	25	5	113	161	33

American Division

Team	GP	W	L	T	GF	GA	PTS
Boston	44	38	5	1	179	98	77
Chicago	44	21	18	5	117	111	47
New York	44	17	17	10	136	143	44
Detroit	44	14	24	6	117	133	34
Pittsburgh	44	5	36	3	102	185	13

Leading Scorers

Player	Club	GP	G	A	PTS	PIM
Weiland, Cooney	Boston	44	43	30	73	27
Boucher, Frank	New York	42	26	36	62	16
Clapper, Dit	Boston	44	41	20	61	48
Cook, Bill	New York	44	29	30	59	56
Kilrea, Hec	Ottawa	44	36	22	58	72
Stewart, Nels	Mtl. Maroons	44	39	16	55	81
Morenz, Howie	Montreal	44	40	10	50	72
Himes, Norm	NY Americans	44	28	22	50	15
Lamb, Joe	Ottawa	44	29	20	49	119
Gainor, Norm	Boston	42	18	31	49	39

1930-31

Canadian Division

Team	GP	W	L	T	GF	GA	PTS
*Montreal	44	26	10	8	129	89	60
Toronto	44	22	13	9	118	99	53
Mtl. Maroons	44	20	18	6	105	106	46
NY Americans	44	18	16	10	76	74	46
Ottawa	44	10	30	4	91	142	24

American Division

Team	GP	W	L	T	GF	GA	PTS
Boston	44	28	10	6	143	90	62
Chicago	44	24	17	3	108	78	51
New York	44	19	16	9	106	87	47
Detroit	44	16	21	7	102	105	39
Philadelphia	44	4	36	4	76	184	12

Leading Scorers

Player	Club	GP	G	A	PTS	PIM
Morenz, Howie	Montreal	39	28	23	51	49
Goodfellow, Ebbie	Detroit	44	25	23	48	32
Conacher, Charlie	Toronto	37	31	12	43	78
Cook, Bill	New York	43	30	12	42	39
Bailey, Ace	Toronto	40	23	19	42	46
Primeau, Joe	Toronto	38	9	32	41	18
Stewart, Nels	Mtl. Maroons	42	25	14	39	75
Boucher, Frank	New York	44	12	27	39	20
Weiland, Cooney	Boston	44	25	13	38	14
Cook, Fred	New York	44	18	17	35	72
Joliat, Aurel	Montreal	43	13	22	35	73

1931-32

Canadian Division

Team	GP	W	L	T	GF	GA	PTS
Montreal	48	25	16	7	128	111	57
*Toronto	48	23	18	7	155	127	53
Mtl. Maroons	48	19	22	7	142	139	45
NY Americans	48	16	24	8	95	142	40

American Division

Team	GP	W	L	T	GF	GA	PTS
New York	48	23	17	8	134	112	54
Chicago	48	18	19	11	86	101	47
Detroit	48	18	20	10	95	108	46
Boston	48	15	21	12	122	117	42

Leading Scorers

Player	Club	GP	G	A	PTS	PIM
Jackson, Harvey	Toronto	48	28	25	53	63
Primeau, Joe	Toronto	46	13	37	50	25
Morenz, Howie	Montreal	48	24	25	49	46
Conacher, Charlie	Toronto	44	34	14	48	66
Cook, Bill	New York	48	34	14	48	33
Trottier, Dave	Mtl. Maroons	48	26	18	44	94
Smith, Reg	Mtl. Maroons	43	11	33	44	49
Siebert, Albert	Mtl. Maroons	48	21	18	39	64
Clapper, Dit	Boston	48	17	22	39	21
Joliat, Aurel	Montreal	48	15	24	39	46

Bill Cook gave the New York Rangers instant credibility by winning the NHL scoring title in 1926-27, the Broadway Blueshirts' first season in the NHL.

1932-33

Canadian Division

Team	GP	W	L	T	GF	GA	PTS
Toronto	48	24	18	6	119	111	54
Mtl. Maroons	48	22	20	6	135	119	50
Montreal	48	18	25	5	92	115	41
NY Americans	48	15	22	11	91	118	41
Ottawa	48	11	27	10	88	131	32

American Division

Team	GP	W	L	T	GF	GA	PTS
Boston	48	25	15	8	124	88	58
Detroit	48	25	15	8	111	93	58
*New York	48	23	17	8	135	107	54
Chicago	48	16	20	12	88	101	44

Leading Scorers

Player	Club	GP	G	A	PTS	PIM
Cook, Bill	New York	48	28	22	50	51
Jackson, Harvey	Toronto	48	27	17	44	43
Northcott, Lawrence	Mtl. Maroons	48	22	21	43	30
Smith, Reg	Mtl. Maroons	48	20	21	41	66
Haynes, Paul	Mtl. Maroons	48	16	25	41	18
Joliat, Aurel	Montreal	48	18	21	39	53
Barry, Marty	Boston	48	24	13	37	40
Cook, Fred	New York	48	22	15	37	35
Stewart, Nels	Boston	47	18	18	36	62
Morenz, Howie	Montreal	46	14	21	35	32
Gagnon, Johnny	Montreal	48	12	23	35	64
Shore, Eddie	Boston	48	8	27	35	102
Boucher, Frank	New York	47	7	28	35	4

1933-34

Canadian Division

Team	GP	W	L	T	GF	GA	PTS
Toronto	48	26	13	9	174	119	61
Montreal	48	22	20	6	99	101	50
Mtl. Maroons	48	19	18	11	117	122	49
NY Americans	48	15	23	10	104	132	40
Ottawa	48	13	29	6	115	143	32

American Division

Team	GP	W	L	T	GF	GA	PTS
Detroit	48	24	14	10	113	98	58
*Chicago	48	20	17	11	88	83	51
New York	48	21	19	8	120	113	50
Boston	48	18	25	5	111	130	41

Leading Scorers

Player	Club	GP	G	A	PTS	PIM
Conacher, Charlie	Toronto	42	32	20	52	38
Primeau, Joe	Toronto	45	14	32	46	8
Boucher, Frank	New York	48	14	30	44	4
Barry, Marty	Boston	48	27	12	39	12
Dillon, Cecil	New York	48	13	26	39	10
Stewart, Nels	Boston	48	21	17	38	68
Jackson, Harvey	Toronto	38	20	18	38	38
Joliat, Aurel	Montreal	48	22	15	37	27
Smith, Reg	Mtl. Maroons	47	18	19	37	58
Thompson, Paul	Chicago	48	20	16	36	17

1934-35

Canadian Division

Team	GP	W	L	T	GF	GA	PTS
Toronto	48	30	14	4	157	111	64
*Mtl. Maroons	48	24	19	5	123	92	53
Montreal	48	19	23	6	110	145	44
NY Americans	48	12	27	9	100	142	33
St. Louis	48	11	31	6	86	144	28

American Division

Team	GP	W	L	T	GF	GA	PTS
Boston	48	26	16	6	129	112	58
Chicago	48	26	17	5	118	88	57
New York	48	22	20	6	137	139	50
Detroit	48	19	22	7	127	114	45

Leading Scorers

Player	Club	GP	G	A	PTS	PIM
Conacher, Charlie	Toronto	47	36	21	57	24
Howe, Syd	St.L., Det.	50	22	25	47	34
Aurie, Larry	Detroit	48	17	29	46	24
Boucher, Frank	New York	48	13	32	45	2
Jackson, Harvey	Toronto	42	22	22	44	27
Lewis, Herb	Detroit	47	16	27	43	26
Chapman, Art	NY Americans	47	9	34	43	4
Barry, Marty	Boston	48	20	20	40	33
Schriner, Sweeney	NY Americans	48	18	22	40	6
Stewart, Nels	Boston	47	21	18	39	45
Thompson, Paul	Chicago	48	16	23	39	20

1935-36

Canadian Division

Team	GP	W	L	T	GF	GA	PTS
Mtl. Maroons	48	22	16	10	114	106	54
Toronto	48	23	19	6	126	106	52
NY Americans	48	16	25	7	109	122	39
Montreal	48	11	26	11	82	123	33

American Division

Team	GP	W	L	T	GF	GA	PTS
*Detroit	48	24	16	8	124	103	56
Boston	48	22	20	6	92	83	50
Chicago	48	21	19	8	93	92	50
New York	48	19	17	12	91	96	50

Leading Scorers

Player	Club	GP	G	A	PTS	PIM
Schriner, Sweeney	NY Americans	48	19	26	45	8
Barry, Marty	Detroit	48	21	19	40	16
Thompson, Paul	Chicago	45	17	23	40	19
Thoms, Bill	Toronto	48	23	15	38	29
Conacher, Charlie	Toronto	44	23	15	38	74
Smith, Reg	Mtl. Maroons	47	19	19	38	75
Romnes, Doc	Chicago	48	13	25	38	6
Chapman, Art	NY Americans	47	10	28	38	14
Lewis, Herb	Detroit	45	14	23	37	25
Northcott, Lawrence	Mtl. Maroons	48	15	21	36	41

1936-37

Canadian Division

Team	GP	W	L	T	GF	GA	PTS
Montreal	48	24	18	6	115	111	54
Mtl. Maroons	48	22	17	9	126	110	53
Toronto	48	22	21	5	119	115	49
NY Americans	48	15	29	4	122	161	34

American Division

Team	GP	W	L	T	GF	GA	PTS
*Detroit	48	25	14	9	128	102	59
Boston	48	23	18	7	120	110	53
New York	48	19	20	9	117	106	47
Chicago	48	14	27	7	99	131	35

Leading Scorers

Player	Club	GP	G	A	PTS	PIM
Schriner, Sweeney	NY Americans	48	21	25	46	17
Apps, Syl	Toronto	48	16	29	45	10
Barry, Marty	Detroit	48	17	27	44	6
Aurie, Larry	Detroit	45	23	20	43	20
Jackson, Harvey	Toronto	46	21	19	40	12
Gagnon, Johnny	Montreal	48	20	16	36	38
Gracie, Bob	Mtl. Maroons	47	11	25	36	18
Stewart, Nels	Bos., NYA	43	23	12	35	37
Thompson, Paul	Chicago	47	17	18	35	28
Cowley, Bill	Boston	46	13	22	35	4

1937-38

Canadian Division

Team	GP	W	L	T	GF	GA	PTS
Toronto	48	24	15	9	151	127	57
NY Americans	48	19	18	11	110	111	49
Montreal	48	18	17	13	123	128	49
Mtl. Maroons	48	12	30	6	101	149	30

American Division

Team	GP	W	L	T	GF	GA	PTS
Boston	48	30	11	7	142	89	67
New York	48	27	15	6	149	96	60
*Chicago	48	14	25	9	97	139	37
Detroit	48	12	25	11	99	133	35

Leading Scorers

Player	Club	GP	G	A	PTS	PIM
Drillon, Gord	Toronto	48	26	26	52	4
Apps, Syl	Toronto	47	21	29	50	9
Thompson, Paul	Chicago	48	22	22	44	14
Mantha, Georges	Montreal	47	23	19	42	12
Dillon, Cecil	New York	48	21	18	39	6
Cowley, Bill	Boston	48	17	22	39	8
Schriner, Sweeney	NY Americans	49	21	17	38	22
Thoms, Bill	Toronto	48	14	24	38	14
Smith, Clint	New York	48	14	23	37	0
Stewart, Nels	NY Americans	48	19	17	36	29
Colville, Neil	New York	45	17	19	36	11

1938-39

Team	GP	W	L	T	GF	GA	PTS
*Boston	48	36	10	2	156	76	74
New York	48	26	16	6	149	105	58
Toronto	48	19	20	9	114	107	47
NY Americans	48	17	21	10	119	157	44
Detroit	48	18	24	6	107	128	42
Montreal	48	15	24	9	115	146	39
Chicago	48	12	28	8	91	132	32

Leading Scorers

Player	Club	GP	G	A	PTS	PIM
Blake, Hector	Montreal	48	24	23	47	10
Schriner, Sweeney	NY Americans	48	13	31	44	20
Cowley, Bill	Boston	34	8	34	42	2
Smith, Clint	New York	48	21	20	41	2
Barry, Marty	Detroit	48	13	28	41	4
Apps, Syl	Toronto	44	15	25	40	4
Anderson, Tom	NY Americans	48	13	27	40	14
Gottselig, Johnny	Chicago	48	16	23	39	15
Haynes, Paul	Montreal	47	5	33	38	27
Conacher, Roy	Boston	47	26	11	37	12
Carr, Lorne	NY Americans	46	19	18	37	16
Colville, Neil	New York	48	18	19	37	12
Watson, Phil	New York	48	15	22	37	42

1939-40

Team	GP	W	L	T	GF	GA	PTS
Boston	48	31	12	5	170	98	67
*New York	48	27	11	10	136	77	64
Toronto	48	25	17	6	134	110	56
Chicago	48	23	19	6	112	120	52
Detroit	48	16	26	6	90	126	38
NY Americans	48	15	29	4	106	140	34
Montreal	48	10	33	5	90	167	25

Leading Scorers

Player	Club	GP	G	A	PTS	PIM
Schmidt, Milt	Boston	48	22	30	52	37
Dumart, Woody	Boston	48	22	21	43	16
Bauer, Bob	Boston	48	17	26	43	2
Drillon, Gord	Toronto	43	21	19	40	13
Cowley, Bill	Boston	48	13	27	40	24
Hextall, Bryan	New York	48	24	15	39	52
Colville, Neil	New York	48	19	19	38	22
Howe, Syd	Detroit	46	14	23	37	17
Blake, Hector	Montreal	48	17	19	36	48
Armstrong, Murray	NY Americans	48	16	20	36	12

1940-41

Team	GP	W	L	T	GF	GA	PTS
*Boston	48	27	8	13	168	102	67
Toronto	48	28	14	6	145	99	62
Detroit	48	21	16	11	112	102	53
New York	48	21	19	8	143	125	50
Chicago	48	16	25	7	112	139	39
Montreal	48	16	26	6	121	147	38
NY Americans	48	8	29	11	99	186	27

Leading Scorers

Player	Club	GP	G	A	PTS	PIM
Cowley, Bill	Boston	46	17	45	62	16
Hextall, Bryan	New York	48	26	18	44	16
Drillon, Gord	Toronto	42	23	21	44	2
Apps, Syl	Toronto	41	20	24	44	6
Patrick, Lynn	New York	48	20	24	44	12
Howe, Syd	Detroit	48	20	24	44	8
Colville, Neil	New York	48	14	28	42	28
Wiseman, Eddie	Boston	48	16	24	40	10
Bauer, Bobby	Boston	48	17	22	39	2
Schriner, Sweeney	Toronto	48	24	14	38	6
Conacher, Roy	Boston	40	24	14	38	7
Schmidt, Milt	Boston	44	13	25	38	23

1941-42

Team	GP	W	L	T	GF	GA	PTS
New York	48	29	17	2	177	143	60
*Toronto	48	27	18	3	158	136	57
Boston	48	25	17	6	160	118	56
Chicago	48	22	23	3	145	155	47
Detroit	48	19	25	4	140	147	42
Montreal	48	18	27	3	134	173	39
Brooklyn	48	16	29	3	133	175	35

Leading Scorers

Player	Club	GP	G	A	PTS	PIM
Hextall, Bryan	New York	48	24	32	56	30
Patrick, Lynn	New York	47	32	22	54	18
Grosso, Don	Detroit	48	23	30	53	13
Watson, Phil	New York	48	15	37	52	48
Abel, Sid	Detroit	48	18	31	49	45
Blake, Hector	Montreal	47	17	28	45	19
Thoms, Bill	Chicago	47	15	30	45	8
Drillon, Gord	Toronto	48	23	18	41	6
Apps, Syl	Toronto	38	18	23	41	0
Anderson, Tom	Brooklyn	48	12	29	41	54

1942-43

Team	GP	W	L	T	GF	GA	PTS
*Detroit	50	25	14	11	169	124	61
Boston	50	24	17	9	195	176	57
Toronto	50	22	19	9	198	159	53
Montreal	50	19	19	12	181	191	50
Chicago	50	17	18	15	179	180	49
New York	50	11	31	8	161	253	30

Leading Scorers

Player	Club	GP	G	A	PTS	PIM
Bentley, Doug	Chicago	50	33	40	73	18
Cowley, Bill	Boston	48	27	45	72	10
Bentley, Max	Chicago	47	26	44	70	2
Patrick, Lynn	New York	50	22	39	61	28
Carr, Lorne	Toronto	50	27	33	60	15
Taylor, Billy	Toronto	50	18	42	60	2
Hextall, Bryan	New York	50	27	32	59	28
Blake, Hector	Montreal	48	23	36	59	28
Lach, Elmer	Montreal	45	18	40	58	14
O'Connor, Herb	Montreal	50	15	43	58	2

1943-44

Team	GP	W	L	T	GF	GA	PTS
*Montreal	50	38	5	7	234	109	83
Detroit	50	26	18	6	214	177	58
Toronto	50	23	23	4	214	174	50
Chicago	50	22	23	5	178	187	49
Boston	50	19	26	5	223	268	43
New York	50	6	39	5	162	310	17

Leading Scorers

Player	Club	GP	G	A	PTS	PIM
Cain, Herb	Boston	48	36	46	82	4
Bentley, Doug	Chicago	50	38	39	77	22
Carr, Lorne	Toronto	50	36	38	74	9
Liscombe, Carl	Detroit	50	36	37	73	17
Lach, Elmer	Montreal	48	24	48	72	23
Smith, Clint	Chicago	50	23	49	72	4
Cowley, Bill	Boston	36	30	41	71	12
Mosienko, Bill	Chicago	50	32	38	70	10
Jackson, Art	Boston	49	28	41	69	8
Bodnar, Gus	Toronto	50	22	40	62	18

1944-45

Team	GP	W	L	T	GF	GA	PTS
Montreal	50	38	8	4	228	121	80
Detroit	50	31	14	5	218	161	67
*Toronto	50	24	22	4	183	161	52
Boston	50	16	30	4	179	219	36
Chicago	50	13	30	7	141	194	33
New York	50	11	29	10	154	247	32

Leading Scorers

Player	Club	GP	G	A	PTS	PIM
Lach, Elmer	Montreal	50	26	54	80	37
Richard, Maurice	Montreal	50	50	23	73	36
Blake, Hector	Montreal	49	29	38	67	15
Cowley, Bill	Boston	49	25	40	65	12
Kennedy, Ted	Toronto	49	29	25	54	14
Mosienko, Bill	Chicago	50	28	26	54	0
Carveth, Joe	Detroit	50	26	28	54	6
DeMarco, Albert	New York	50	24	30	54	10
Smith, Clint	Chicago	50	23	31	54	0
Howe, Syd	Detroit	46	17	36	53	6

1945-46

Team	GP	W	L	T	GF	GA	PTS
*Montreal	50	28	17	5	172	134	61
Boston	50	24	18	8	167	156	56
Chicago	50	23	20	7	200	178	53
Detroit	50	20	20	10	146	159	50
Toronto	50	19	24	7	174	185	45
New York	50	13	28	9	144	191	35

Leading Scorers

Player	Club	GP	G	A	PTS	PIM
Bentley, Max	Chicago	47	31	30	61	6
Stewart, Gaye	Toronto	50	37	15	52	8
Blake, Hector	Montreal	50	29	21	50	2
Smith, Clint	Chicago	50	26	24	50	2
Richard, Maurice	Montreal	50	27	21	48	50
Mosienko, Bill	Chicago	40	18	30	48	12
DeMarco, Albert	New York	50	20	27	47	20
Lach, Elmer	Montreal	50	13	34	47	34
Kaleta, Alex	Chicago	49	19	27	46	17
Taylor, Billy	Toronto	48	23	18	41	14
Horeck, Pete	Chicago	50	20	21	41	34

1946-47

Team	GP	W	L	T	GF	GA	PTS
Montreal	60	34	16	10	189	138	78
*Toronto	60	31	19	10	209	172	72
Boston	60	26	23	11	190	175	63
Detroit	60	22	27	11	190	193	55
New York	60	22	32	6	167	186	50
Chicago	60	19	37	4	193	274	42

Leading Scorers

Player	Club	GP	G	A	PTS	PIM
Bentley, Max	Chicago	60	29	43	72	12
Richard, Maurice	Montreal	60	45	26	71	69
Taylor, Billy	Detroit	60	17	46	63	35
Schmidt, Milt	Boston	59	27	35	62	40
Kennedy, Ted	Toronto	60	28	32	60	27
Bentley, Doug	Chicago	52	21	34	55	18
Bauer, Bob	Boston	58	30	24	54	4
Conacher, Roy	Detroit	60	30	24	54	6
Mosienko, Bill	Chicago	59	25	27	52	2
Dumart, Woody	Boston	60	24	28	52	12

1947-48

Team	GP	W	L	T	GF	GA	PTS
*Toronto	60	32	15	13	182	143	77
Detroit	60	30	18	12	187	148	72
Boston	60	23	24	13	167	168	59
New York	60	21	26	13	176	201	55
Montreal	60	20	29	11	147	169	51
Chicago	60	20	34	6	195	225	46

Leading Scorers

Player	Club	GP	G	A	PTS	PIM
Lach, Elmer	Montreal	60	30	31	61	72
O'Connor, Buddy	New York	60	24	36	60	8
Bentley, Doug	Chicago	60	20	37	57	16
Stewart, Gaye	Tor., Chi.	61	27	29	56	83
Bentley, Max	Chi., Tor.	59	26	28	54	14
Poile, Bud	Tor., Chi.	58	25	29	54	17
Richard, Maurice	Montreal	53	28	25	53	89
Apps, Syl	Toronto	55	26	27	53	12
Lindsay, Ted	Detroit	60	33	19	52	95
Conacher, Roy	Chicago	52	22	27	49	4

1948-49

Team	GP	W	L	T	GF	GA	PTS
Detroit	60	34	19	7	195	145	75
Boston	60	29	23	8	178	163	66
Montreal	60	28	23	9	152	126	65
*Toronto	60	22	25	13	147	161	57
Chicago	60	21	31	8	173	211	50
New York	60	18	31	11	133	172	47

Leading Scorers

Player	Club	GP	G	A	PTS	PIM
Conacher, Roy	Chicago	60	26	42	68	8
Bentley, Doug	Chicago	58	23	43	66	38
Abel, Sid	Detroit	60	28	26	54	49
Lindsay, Ted	Detroit	50	26	28	54	97
Conacher, Jim	Det., Chi.	59	26	23	49	43
Ronty, Paul	Boston	60	20	29	49	11
Watson, Harry	Toronto	60	26	19	45	0
Reay, Billy	Montreal	60	22	23	45	33
Bodnar, Gus	Chicago	59	19	26	45	14
Peirson, John	Boston	59	22	21	43	45

1949-50

Team	GP	W	L	T	GF	GA	PTS
*Detroit	70	37	19	14	229	164	88
Montreal	70	29	22	19	172	150	77
Toronto	70	31	27	12	176	173	74
New York	70	28	31	11	170	189	67
Boston	70	22	32	16	198	228	60
Chicago	70	22	38	10	203	244	54

Leading Scorers

Player	Club	GP	G	A	PTS	PIM
Lindsay, Ted	Detroit	69	23	55	78	141
Abel, Sid	Detroit	69	34	35	69	46
Howe, Gordie	Detroit	70	35	33	68	69
Richard, Maurice	Montreal	70	43	22	65	114
Ronty, Paul	Boston	70	23	36	59	8
Conacher, Roy	Chicago	70	25	31	56	16
Bentley, Doug	Chicago	64	20	33	53	28
Peirson, John	Boston	57	27	25	52	49
Prystai, Metro	Chicago	65	29	22	51	31
Guidolin, Bep	Chicago	70	17	34	51	42

The dynamic trio of Ted Lindsay, right, Sid Abel, center, and Gordie Howe finished 1-2-3 respectively in the scoring race during the 1949-50 season.

Toronto's Ted Kennedy, seen here blasting the puck past Detroit's Terry Sawchuk, captured the Hart Trophy as the NHL's most valuable player in 1954-55.

1950-51

Team	GP	W	L	T	GF	GA	PTS
Detroit	70	44	13	13	236	139	101
*Toronto	70	41	16	13	212	138	95
Montreal	70	25	30	15	173	184	65
Boston	70	22	30	18	178	197	62
New York	70	20	29	21	169	201	61
Chicago	70	13	47	10	171	280	36

Leading Scorers

Player	Club	GP	G	A	PTS	PIM
Howe, Gordie	Detroit	70	43	43	86	74
Richard, Maurice	Montreal	65	42	24	66	97
Bentley, Max	Toronto	67	21	41	62	34
Abel, Sid	Detroit	69	23	38	61	30
Schmidt, Milt	Boston	62	22	39	61	33
Kennedy, Ted	Toronto	63	18	43	61	32
Lindsay, Ted	Detroit	67	24	35	59	110
Sloan, Tod	Toronto	70	31	25	56	105
Kelly, Red	Detroit	70	17	37	54	24
Smith, Sid	Toronto	70	30	21	51	10
Gardner, Cal	Toronto	66	23	28	51	42

1951-52

Team	GP	W	L	T	GF	GA	PTS
*Detroit	70	44	14	12	215	133	100
Montreal	70	34	26	10	195	164	78
Toronto	70	29	25	16	168	157	74
Boston	70	25	29	16	162	176	66
New York	70	23	34	13	192	219	59
Chicago	70	17	44	9	158	241	43

Leading Scorers

Player	Club	GP	G	A	PTS	PIM
Howe, Gordie	Detroit	70	47	39	86	78
Lindsay, Ted	Detroit	70	30	39	69	123
Lach, Elmer	Montreal	70	15	50	65	36
Raleigh, Don	New York	70	19	42	61	14
Smith, Sid	Toronto	70	27	30	57	6
Geoffrion, Bernie	Montreal	67	30	24	54	66
Mosienko, Bill	Chicago	70	31	22	53	10
Abel, Sid	Detroit	62	17	36	53	32
Kennedy, Ted	Toronto	70	19	33	52	33
Schmidt, Milt	Boston	69	21	29	50	57
Peirson, John	Boston	68	20	30	50	30

1952-53

Team	GP	W	L	T	GF	GA	PTS
Detroit	70	36	16	18	222	133	90
*Montreal	70	28	23	19	155	148	75
Boston	70	28	29	13	152	172	69
Chicago	70	27	28	15	169	175	69
Toronto	70	27	30	13	156	167	67
New York	70	17	37	16	152	211	50

Leading Scorers

Player	Club	GP	G	A	PTS	PIM
Howe, Gordie	Detroit	70	49	46	95	57
Lindsay, Ted	Detroit	70	32	39	71	111
Richard, Maurice	Montreal	70	28	33	61	112
Hergesheimer, Wally	New York	70	30	29	59	10
Delvecchio, Alex	Detroit	70	16	43	59	28
Ronty, Paul	New York	70	16	38	54	20
Prystai, Metro	Detroit	70	16	34	50	12
Kelly, Red	Detroit	70	19	27	46	8
Olmstead, Bert	Montreal	69	17	28	45	83
Mackell, Fleming	Boston	65	27	17	44	63
McFadden, Jim	Chicago	70	23	21	44	29

1953-54

Team	GP	W	L	T	GF	GA	PTS
*Detroit	70	37	19	14	191	132	88
Montreal	70	35	24	11	195	141	81
Toronto	70	32	24	14	152	131	78
Boston	70	32	28	10	177	181	74
New York	70	29	31	10	161	182	68
Chicago	70	12	51	7	133	242	31

Leading Scorers

Player	Club	GP	G	A	PTS	PIM
Howe, Gordie	Detroit	70	33	48	81	109
Richard, Maurice	Montreal	70	37	30	67	112
Lindsay, Ted	Detroit	70	26	36	62	110
Geoffrion, Bernie	Montreal	54	29	25	54	87
Olmstead, Bert	Montreal	70	15	37	52	85
Kelly, Red	Detroit	62	16	33	49	18
Reibel, Earl	Detroit	69	15	33	48	18
Sandford, Ed	Boston	70	16	31	47	42
Mackell, Fleming	Boston	67	15	32	47	60
Mosdell, Ken	Montreal	67	22	24	46	64
Ronty, Paul	New York	70	13	33	46	18

1954-55

Team	GP	W	L	T	GF	GA	PTS
*Detroit	70	42	17	11	204	134	95
Montreal	70	41	18	11	228	157	93
Toronto	70	24	24	22	147	135	70
Boston	70	23	26	21	169	188	67
New York	70	17	35	18	150	210	52
Chicago	70	13	40	17	161	235	43

Leading Scorers

Player	Club	GP	G	A	PTS	PIM
Geoffrion, Bernie	Montreal	70	38	37	75	57
Richard, Maurice	Montreal	67	38	36	74	125
Beliveau, Jean	Montreal	70	37	36	73	58
Reibel, Earl	Detroit	70	25	41	66	15
Howe, Gordie	Detroit	64	29	33	62	68
Sullivan, George	Chicago	69	19	42	61	51
Olmstead, Bert	Montreal	70	10	48	58	103
Smith, Sid	Toronto	70	33	21	54	14
Mosdell, Ken	Montreal	70	22	32	54	82
Lewicki, Danny	New York	70	29	24	53	8

1955-56

Team	GP	W	L	T	GF	GA	PTS
*Montreal	70	45	15	10	222	131	100
Detroit	70	30	24	16	183	148	76
New York	70	32	28	10	204	203	74
Toronto	70	24	33	13	153	181	61
Boston	70	23	34	13	147	185	59
Chicago	70	19	39	12	155	216	50

Leading Scorers

Player	Club	GP	G	A	PTS	PIM
Beliveau, Jean	Montreal	70	47	41	88	143
Howe, Gordie	Detroit	70	38	41	79	100
Richard, Maurice	Montreal	70	38	33	71	89
Olmstead, Bert	Montreal	70	14	56	70	94
Sloan, Tod	Toronto	70	37	29	66	100
Bathgate, Andy	New York	70	19	47	66	59
Geoffrion, Bernie	Montreal	59	29	33	62	66
Reibel, Earl	Detroit	68	17	39	56	10
Delvecchio, Alex	Detroit	70	25	26	51	24
Creighton, Dave	New York	70	20	31	51	43
Gadsby, Bill	New York	70	9	42	51	84

1956-57

Team	GP	W	L	T	GF	GA	PTS
Detroit	70	38	20	12	198	157	88
*Montreal	70	35	23	12	210	155	82
Boston	70	34	24	12	195	174	80
New York	70	26	30	14	184	227	66
Toronto	70	21	34	15	174	192	57
Chicago	70	16	39	15	169	225	47

Leading Scorers

Player	Club	GP	G	A	PTS	PIM
Howe, Gordie	Detroit	70	44	45	89	72
Lindsay, Ted	Detroit	70	30	55	85	103
Beliveau, Jean	Montreal	69	33	51	84	105
Bathgate, Andy	New York	70	27	50	77	60
Litzenberger, Ed	Chicago	70	32	32	64	48
Richard, Maurice	Montreal	63	33	29	62	74
McKenney, Don	Boston	69	21	39	60	31
Moore, Dickie	Montreal	70	29	29	58	56
Richard, Henri	Montreal	63	18	36	54	71
Ullman, Norm	Detroit	64	16	36	52	47

1957-58

Team	GP	W	L	T	GF	GA	PTS
*Montreal	70	43	17	10	250	158	96
New York	70	32	25	13	195	188	77
Detroit	70	29	29	12	176	207	70
Boston	70	27	28	15	199	194	69
Chicago	70	24	39	7	163	202	55
Toronto	70	21	38	11	192	226	53

Leading Scorers

Player	Club	GP	G	A	PTS	PIM
Moore, Dickie	Montreal	70	36	48	84	65
Richard, Henri	Montreal	67	28	52	80	56
Bathgate, Andy	New York	65	30	48	78	42
Howe, Gordie	Detroit	64	33	44	77	40
Horvath, Bronco	Boston	67	30	36	66	71
Litzenberger, Ed	Chicago	70	32	30	62	63
Mackell, Fleming	Boston	70	20	40	60	72
Beliveau, Jean	Montreal	55	27	32	59	93
Delvecchio, Alex	Detroit	70	21	38	59	22
McKenney, Don	Boston	70	28	30	58	22

1958-59

Team	GP	W	L	T	GF	GA	PTS
*Montreal	70	39	18	13	258	158	91
Boston	70	32	29	9	205	215	73
Chicago	70	28	29	13	197	208	69
Toronto	70	27	32	11	189	201	65
New York	70	26	32	12	201	217	64
Detroit	70	25	37	8	167	218	58

Leading Scorers

Player	Club	GP	G	A	PTS	PIM
Moore, Dickie	Montreal	70	41	55	96	61
Beliveau, Jean	Montreal	64	45	46	91	67
Bathgate, Andy	New York	70	40	48	88	48
Howe, Gordie	Detroit	70	32	46	78	57
Litzenberger, Ed	Chicago	70	33	44	77	37
Geoffrion, Bernie	Montreal	59	22	44	66	30
Sullivan, George	New York	70	21	42	63	56
Hebenton, Andy	New York	70	33	29	62	8
McKenney, Don	Boston	70	32	30	62	20
Sloan, Tod	Chicago	59	27	35	62	79

1959-60

Team	GP	W	L	T	GF	GA	PTS
*Montreal	70	40	18	12	255	178	92
Toronto	70	35	26	9	199	195	79
Chicago	70	28	29	13	191	180	69
Detroit	70	26	29	15	186	197	67
Boston	70	28	34	8	220	241	64
New York	70	17	38	15	187	247	49

Leading Scorers

Player	Club	GP	G	A	PTS	PIM
Hull, Bobby	Chicago	70	39	42	81	68
Horvath, Bronco	Boston	68	39	41	80	60
Beliveau, Jean	Montreal	60	34	40	74	57
Bathgate, Andy	New York	70	26	48	74	28
Richard, Henri	Montreal	70	30	43	73	66
Howe, Gordie	Detroit	70	28	45	73	46
Geoffrion, Bernie	Montreal	59	30	41	71	36
McKenney, Don	Boston	70	20	49	69	28
Stasiuk, Vic	Boston	69	29	39	68	121
Prentice, Dean	New York	70	32	34	66	43

1960-61

Team	GP	W	L	T	GF	GA	PTS
Montreal	70	41	19	10	254	188	92
Toronto	70	39	19	12	234	176	90
*Chicago	70	29	24	17	198	180	75
Detroit	70	25	29	16	195	215	66
New York	70	22	38	10	204	248	54
Boston	70	15	42	13	176	254	43

Leading Scorers

Player	Club	GP	G	A	PTS	PIM
Geoffrion, Bernie	Montreal	64	50	45	95	29
Béliveau, Jean	Montreal	69	32	58	90	57
Mahovlich, Frank	Toronto	70	48	36	84	131
Bathgate, Andy	New York	70	29	48	77	22
Howe, Gordie	Detroit	64	23	49	72	30
Ullman, Norm	Detroit	70	28	42	70	34
Kelly, Red	Toronto	64	20	50	70	12
Moore, Dickie	Montreal	57	35	34	69	62
Richard, Henri	Montreal	70	24	44	68	91
Delvecchio, Alex	Detroit	70	27	35	62	26

1961-62

Team	GP	W	L	T	GF	GA	PTS
Montreal	70	42	14	14	259	166	98
*Toronto	70	37	22	11	232	180	85
Chicago	70	31	26	13	217	186	75
New York	70	26	32	12	195	207	64
Detroit	70	23	33	14	184	219	60
Boston	70	15	47	8	177	306	38

Leading Scorers

Player	Club	GP	G	A	PTS	PIM
Hull, Bobby	Chicago	70	50	34	84	35
Bathgate, Andy	New York	70	28	56	84	44
Howe, Gordie	Detroit	70	33	44	77	54
Mikita, Stan	Chicago	70	25	52	77	97
Mahovlich, Frank	Toronto	70	33	38	71	87
Delvecchio, Alex	Detroit	70	26	43	69	18
Backstrom, Ralph	Montreal	66	27	38	65	29
Ullman, Norm	Detroit	70	26	38	64	54
Hay, Bill	Chicago	60	11	52	63	34
Provost, Claude	Montreal	70	33	29	62	22

"Eddie the Entertainer" sneaks behind the Leaf defense for a scoring opportunity but Johnny Bower stacks the pads and slams the door on the Rangers' Shack.

1962-63

Team	GP	W	L	T	GF	GA	PTS
*Toronto	70	35	23	12	221	180	82
Chicago	70	32	21	17	194	178	81
Montreal	70	28	19	23	225	183	79
Detroit	70	32	25	13	200	194	77
New York	70	22	36	12	211	233	56
Boston	70	14	39	17	198	281	45

Leading Scorers

Player	Club	GP	G	A	PTS	PIM
Howe, Gordie	Detroit	70	38	48	86	100
Bathgate, Andy	New York	70	35	46	81	54
Mikita, Stan	Chicago	65	31	45	76	69
Mahovlich, Frank	Toronto	67	36	37	73	56
Richard, Henri	Montreal	67	23	50	73	57
Beliveau, Jean	Montreal	69	18	49	67	68
Bucyk, John	Boston	69	27	39	66	36
Delvecchio, Alex	Detroit	70	20	44	64	8
Hull, Bobby	Chicago	65	31	31	62	27
Oliver, Murray	Boston	65	22	40	62	38

1963-64

Team	GP	W	L	T	GF	GA	PTS
Montreal	70	36	21	13	209	167	85
Chicago	70	36	22	12	218	169	84
*Toronto	70	33	25	12	192	172	78
Detroit	70	30	29	11	191	204	71
New York	70	22	38	10	186	242	54
Boston	70	18	40	12	170	212	48

Leading Scorers

Player	Club	GP	G	A	PTS	PIM
Mikita, Stan	Chicago	70	39	50	89	146
Hull, Bobby	Chicago	70	43	44	87	50
Beliveau, Jean	Montreal	68	28	50	78	42
Bathgate, Andy	NYR, Tor.	71	19	58	77	34
Howe, Gordie	Detroit	69	26	47	73	70
Wharram, Ken	Chicago	70	39	32	71	18
Oliver, Murray	Boston	70	24	44	68	41
Goyette, Phil	New York	67	24	41	65	15
Gilbert, Rod	New York	70	24	40	64	62
Keon, Dave	Toronto	70	23	37	60	6

1964-65

Team	GP	W	L	T	GF	GA	PTS
Detroit	70	40	23	7	224	175	87
*Montreal	70	36	23	11	211	185	83
Chicago	70	34	28	8	224	176	76
Toronto	70	30	26	14	204	173	74
New York	70	20	38	12	179	246	52
Boston	70	21	43	6	166	253	48

Leading Scorers

Player	Club	GP	G	A	PTS	PIM
Mikita, Stan	Chicago	70	28	59	87	154
Ullman, Norm	Detroit	70	42	41	83	70
Howe, Gordie	Detrot	70	29	47	76	104
Hull, Bobby	Chicago	61	39	32	71	32
Delvecchio, Alex	Detroit	68	25	42	67	16
Provost, Claude	Montreal	70	27	37	64	28
Gilbert, Rod	New York	70	25	36	61	52
Pilote, Pierre	Chicago	68	14	45	59	162
Bucyk, John	Boston	68	26	29	55	24
Backstrom, Ralph	Montreal	70	25	30	55	41
Esposito, Phil	Chicago	70	23	32	55	44

1965-66

Team	GP	W	L	T	GF	GA	PTS
*Montreal	70	41	21	8	239	173	90
Chicago	70	37	25	8	240	187	82
Toronto	70	34	25	11	208	187	79
Detroit	70	31	27	12	221	194	74
Boston	70	21	43	6	174	275	48
New York	70	18	41	11	195	261	47

Leading Scorers

Player	Club	GP	G	A	PTS	PIM
Hull, Bobby	Chicago	65	54	43	97	70
Mikita, Stan	Chicago	68	30	48	78	58
Rousseau, Bobby	Montreal	70	30	48	78	20
Beliveau, Jean	Montreal	67	29	48	77	50
Howe, Gordie	Detroit	70	29	46	75	83
Ullman, Norm	Detroit	70	31	41	72	35
Delvecchio, Alex	Detroit	70	31	38	69	16
Nevin, Bob	New York	69	29	33	62	10
Richard, Henri	Montreal	62	22	39	61	47
Oliver, Murray	Boston	70	18	42	60	30

1966-67

Team	GP	W	L	T	GF	GA	PTS
Chicago	70	41	17	12	264	170	94
Montreal	70	32	25	13	202	188	77
*Toronto	70	32	27	11	204	211	75
New York	70	30	28	12	188	189	72
Detroit	70	27	39	4	212	241	58
Boston	70	17	43	10	182	253	44

Leading Scorers

Player	Club	GP	G	A	PTS	PIM
Mikita, Stan	Chicago	70	35	62	97	12
Hull, Bobby	Chicago	66	52	28	80	52
Ullman, Norm	Detroit	68	26	44	70	26
Wharram, Ken	Chicago	70	31	34	65	21
Howe, Gordie	Detroit	69	25	40	65	53
Rousseau, Bobby	Montreal	68	19	44	63	58
Esposito, Phil	Chicago	69	21	40	61	40
Goyette, Phil	New York	70	12	49	61	6
Mohns, Doug	Chicago	61	25	35	60	58
Richard, Henri	Montreal	65	21	34	55	28
Delvecchio, Alex	Detroit	70	17	38	55	10

In this photo from the 1967-68 season, Bruins' goaltender Gerry Cheevers sneaks a backward glance at a young Bobby Orr as the rookie defenseman gathers momentum before launching one of his patented end-to-end rushes.

1967-68

East Division

Team	GP	W	L	T	GF	GA	PTS
*Montreal	74	42	22	10	236	167	94
New York	74	39	23	12	226	183	90
Boston	74	37	27	10	259	216	84
Chicago	74	32	26	16	212	222	80
Toronto	74	33	31	10	209	176	76
Detroit	74	27	35	12	245	257	66

West Division

Team	GP	W	L	T	GF	GA	PTS
Philadelphia	74	31	32	11	173	179	73
Los Angeles	74	31	33	10	200	224	72
St. Louis	74	27	31	16	177	191	70
Minnesota	74	27	32	15	191	226	69
Pittsburgh	74	27	34	13	195	216	67
Oakland	74	15	42	17	153	219	47

Leading Scorers

Player	Club	GP	G	A	PTS	PIM
Mikita, Stan	Chicago	72	40	47	87	14
Esposito, Phil	Boston	74	35	49	84	21
Howe, Gordie	Detroit	74	39	43	82	53
Ratelle, Jean	New York	74	32	46	78	18
Gilbert, Rod	New York	73	29	48	77	12
Hull, Bobby	Chicago	71	44	31	75	39
Ullman, Norm	Det., Tor.	71	35	37	72	28
Delvecchio, Alex	Detroit	74	22	48	70	14
Bucyk, John	Boston	72	30	39	69	8
Wharram, Ken	Chicago	74	27	42	69	18

1968-69

East Division

Team	GP	W	L	T	GF	GA	PTS
*Montreal	76	46	19	11	271	202	103
Boston	76	42	18	16	303	221	100
New York	76	41	26	9	231	196	91
Toronto	76	35	26	15	234	217	85
Detroit	76	33	31	12	239	221	78
Chicago	76	34	33	9	280	246	77

West Division

Team	GP	W	L	T	GF	GA	PTS
St. Louis	76	37	25	14	204	157	88
Oakland	76	29	36	11	219	251	69
Philadelphia	76	20	35	21	174	225	61
Los Angeles	76	24	42	10	185	260	58
Pittsburgh	76	20	45	11	189	252	51
Minnesota	76	18	43	5	189	270	51

Leading Scorers

Player	Club	GP	G	A	PTS	PIM
Esposito, Phil	Boston	74	49	77	126	79
Hull, Bobby	Chicago	74	58	49	107	48
Howe, Gordie	Detroit	76	44	59	103	58
Mikita, Stan	Chicago	74	30	67	97	52
Hodge, Ken	Boston	75	45	45	90	75
Cournoyer, Yvan	Montreal	76	43	44	87	31
Delvecchio, Alex	Detroit	72	25	58	83	8
Berenson, Red	St. Louis	76	35	47	82	43
Beliveau, Jean	Montreal	69	33	49	82	55
Mahovlich, Frank	Detroit	76	49	29	78	38
Ratelle, Jean	New York	75	32	46	78	26

1969-70

East Division

Team	GP	W	L	T	GF	GA	PTS
Chicago	76	45	22	9	250	170	99
*Boston	76	40	17	19	277	216	99
Detroit	76	40	21	15	246	199	95
New York	76	38	22	16	246	189	92
Montreal	76	38	22	16	244	201	92
Toronto	76	29	34	13	222	242	71

West Division

Team	GP	W	L	T	GF	GA	PTS
St. Louis	76	37	27	12	224	179	86
Pittsburgh	76	26	38	12	182	238	64
Minnesota	76	19	35	22	224	257	60
Oakland	76	22	40	14	169	243	58
Philadelphia	76	17	35	24	197	225	58
Los Angeles	76	14	52	10	168	290	38

Leading Scorers

Player	Club	GP	G	A	PTS	PIM
Orr, Bobby	Boston	76	33	87	120	125
Esposito, Phil	Boston	76	43	56	99	50
Mikita, Stan	Chicago	76	39	47	86	50
Goyette, Phil	St. Louis	72	29	49	78	16
Tkaczuk, Walt	New York	76	27	50	77	38
Ratelle, Jean	New York	75	32	42	74	28
Berenson, Red	St. Louis	67	33	39	72	38
Parise, Jean-Paul	Minnesota	74	24	48	72	72
Howe, Gordie	Detroit	76	31	40	71	58
Mahovlich, Frank	Detroit	74	38	32	70	59
Balon, Dave	New York	76	33	37	70	100
McKenzie, John	Boston	72	29	41	70	114

1970-71

East Division

Team	GP	W	L	T	GF	GA	PTS
Boston	78	57	14	7	399	207	121
New York	78	49	18	11	259	177	109
*Montreal	78	42	23	13	291	216	97
Toronto	78	37	33	8	248	211	82
Buffalo	78	24	39	15	217	291	63
Vancouver	78	24	46	8	229	296	56
Detroit	78	22	45	11	209	308	55

West Division

Team	GP	W	L	T	GF	GA	PTS
Chicago	78	49	20	9	277	184	107
St. Louis	78	34	25	19	223	208	87
Philadelphia	78	28	33	17	207	225	73
Minnesota	78	28	34	16	191	223	72
Los Angeles	78	25	40	13	239	303	63
Pittsburgh	78	21	37	20	221	240	62
California	78	20	53	5	199	320	45

Leading Scorers

Player	Club	GP	G	A	PTS	PIM
Esposito, Phil	Boston	78	76	76	152	71
Orr, Bobby	Boston	78	37	102	139	91
Bucyk, John	Boston	78	51	65	116	8
Hodge, Ken	Boston	78	43	62	105	113
Hull, Bobby	Chicago	78	44	52	96	32
Ullman, Norm	Toronto	73	34	51	85	24
Cashman, Wayne	Boston	77	21	58	79	100
McKenzie, John	Boston	65	31	46	77	120
Keon, Dave	Toronto	76	38	38	76	4
Beliveau, Jean	Montreal	70	25	51	76	40
Stanfield, Fred	Boston	75	24	52	76	12

1971-72

East Division

Team	GP	W	L	T	GF	GA	PTS
*Boston	78	54	13	11	330	204	119
New York	78	48	17	13	317	192	109
Montreal	78	46	16	16	307	205	108
Toronto	78	33	31	14	209	208	80
Detroit	78	33	35	10	261	262	76
Buffalo	78	16	43	19	203	289	51
Vancouver	78	20	50	8	203	297	48

West Division

Team	GP	W	L	T	GF	GA	PTS
Chicago	78	46	17	15	256	166	107
Minnesota	78	37	29	12	212	191	86
St. Louis	78	28	39	11	208	247	67
Pittsburgh	78	26	38	14	220	258	66
Philadelphia	78	26	38	14	200	236	66
California	78	21	39	18	216	288	60
Los Angeles	78	20	49	9	206	305	49

Leading Scorers

Player	Club	GP	G	A	PTS	PIM
Esposito, Phil	Boston	76	66	67	133	76
Orr, Bobby	Boston	76	37	80	117	106
Ratelle, Jean	New York	63	46	63	109	4
Hadfield, Vic	New York	78	50	56	106	142
Gilbert, Rod	New York	73	43	54	97	64
Mahovlich, Frank	Montreal	76	43	53	96	36
Hull, Bobby	Chicago	78	50	43	93	24
Cournoyer, Yvan	Montreal	73	47	36	83	15
Bucyk, John	Boston	78	32	51	83	4
Clarke, Bobby	Philadelphia	78	35	46	81	87
Lemaire, Jacques	Montreal	77	32	49	81	26

1972-73

East Division

Team	GP	W	L	T	GF	GA	PTS
*Montreal	78	52	10	16	329	184	120
Boston	78	51	22	5	330	235	107
NY Rangers	78	47	23	8	297	208	102
Buffalo	78	37	27	14	257	219	88
Detroit	78	37	29	12	265	243	86
Toronto	78	27	41	10	247	279	64
Vancouver	78	22	47	9	233	339	53
NY Islanders	78	12	60	6	170	347	30

West Division

Team	GP	W	L	T	GF	GA	PTS
Chicago	78	42	27	9	284	225	93
Philadelphia	78	37	30	11	296	256	85
Minnesota	78	37	30	11	254	230	85
St. Louis	78	32	34	12	233	251	76
Pittsburgh	78	32	37	9	257	265	73
Los Angeles	78	31	36	11	232	245	73
Atlanta	78	25	38	15	191	239	65
California	78	16	46	16	213	323	48

Leading Scorers

Player	Club	GP	G	A	PTS	PIM
Esposito, Phil	Boston	78	55	75	130	87
Clarke, Bobby	Philadelphia	78	37	67	104	80
Orr, Bobby	Boston	63	29	72	101	99
MacLeish, Rick	Philadelphia	78	50	50	100	69
Lemaire, Jacques	Montreal	77	44	51	95	16
Ratelle, Jean	NY Rangers	78	41	53	94	12
Redmond, Mickey	Detroit	76	52	41	93	24
Bucyk, John	Boston	78	40	53	93	12
Mahovlich, Frank	Montreal	78	38	55	93	51
Pappin, Jim	Chicago	76	41	51	92	82

1973-74

East Division

Team	GP	W	L	T	GF	GA	PTS
Boston	78	52	17	9	349	221	113
Montreal	78	45	24	9	293	240	99
NY Rangers	78	40	24	14	300	251	94
Toronto	78	35	27	16	274	230	86
Buffalo	78	32	34	12	242	250	76
Detroit	78	29	39	10	255	319	68
Vancouver	78	24	43	11	224	296	59
NY Islanders	78	19	41	18	182	247	56

West Division

Team	GP	W	L	T	GF	GA	PTS
*Philadelphia	78	50	16	12	273	164	112
Chicago	78	41	14	23	272	164	105
Los Angeles	78	33	33	12	233	231	78
Atlanta	78	30	34	14	214	238	74
Pittsburgh	78	28	41	9	242	273	65
St. Louis	78	26	40	12	206	248	64
Minnesota	78	23	38	17	235	275	63
California	78	13	55	10	195	342	36

Leading Scorers

Player	Club	GP	G	A	PTS	PIM
Esposito, Phil	Boston	78	68	77	145	58
Orr, Bobby	Boston	74	32	90	122	82
Hodge, Ken	Boston	76	50	55	105	43
Cashman, Wayne	Boston	78	30	59	89	111
Clarke, Bobby	Philadelphia	77	35	52	87	113
Martin, Rick	Buffalo	78	52	34	86	38
Apps, Syl	Pittsburgh	75	24	61	85	37
Sittler, Darryl	Toronto	78	38	46	84	55
MacDonald, Lowell	Pittsburgh	78	43	39	82	14
Park, Brad	NY Rangers	78	25	57	82	148
Hextall, Dennis	Minnesota	78	20	62	82	138

1974-75
PRINCE OF WALES CONFERENCE
Norris Division

Team	GP	W	L	T	GF	GA	PTS
Montreal	80	47	14	19	374	225	113
Los Angeles	80	42	17	21	269	185	105
Pittsburgh	80	37	28	15	326	289	89
Detroit	80	23	45	12	259	335	58
Washington	80	8	67	5	181	446	21

Adams Division

Team	GP	W	L	T	GF	GA	PTS
Buffalo	80	49	16	15	354	240	113
Boston	80	40	26	14	345	245	94
Toronto	80	31	33	16	280	309	78
California	80	19	48	13	212	316	51

CLARENCE CAMPBELL CONFERENCE
Patrick Division

Team	GP	W	L	T	GF	GA	PTS
*Philadelphia	80	51	18	11	293	181	113
NY Rangers	80	37	29	14	319	276	88
NY Islanders	80	33	25	22	264	221	88
Atlanta	80	34	31	15	243	233	83

Smythe Division

Team	GP	W	L	T	GF	GA	PTS
Vancouver	80	38	32	10	271	254	86
St. Louis	80	35	31	14	269	267	84
Chicago	80	37	35	8	268	241	82
Minnesota	80	23	50	7	221	341	53
Kansas City	80	15	54	11	184	328	41

Leading Scorers

Player	Club	GP	G	A	PTS	PIM
Orr, Bobby	Boston	80	46	89	135	101
Esposito, Phil	Boston	79	61	66	127	62
Dionne, Marcel	Detroit	80	47	74	121	14
Lafleur, Guy	Montreal	70	53	66	119	37
Mahovlich, Pete	Montreal	80	35	82	117	64
Clarke, Bobby	Philadelphia	80	27	89	116	125
Robert, Rene	Buffalo	74	40	60	100	75
Gilbert, Rod	NY Rangers	76	36	61	97	22
Perreault, Gilbert	Buffalo	68	39	57	96	36
Martin, Rick	Buffalo	68	52	43	95	72

1975-76
PRINCE OF WALES CONFERENCE
Norris Division

Team	GP	W	L	T	GF	GA	PTS
*Montreal	80	58	11	11	337	174	127
Los Angeles	80	38	33	9	263	265	85
Pittsburgh	80	35	33	12	339	303	82
Detroit	80	26	44	10	226	300	62
Washington	80	11	59	10	224	394	32

Adams Division

Team	GP	W	L	T	GF	GA	PTS
Boston	80	48	15	17	313	237	113
Buffalo	80	46	21	13	339	240	105
Toronto	80	34	31	15	294	276	83
California	80	27	42	11	250	278	65

CLARENCE CAMPBELL CONFERENCE
Patrick Division

Team	GP	W	L	T	GF	GA	PTS
Philadelphia	80	51	13	16	348	209	118
NY Islanders	80	42	21	17	297	190	101
Atlanta	80	35	33	12	262	237	82
NY Rangers	80	29	42	9	262	333	67

Smythe Division

Team	GP	W	L	T	GF	GA	PTS
Chicago	80	32	30	18	254	261	82
Vancouver	80	33	32	15	271	272	81
St. Louis	80	29	37	14	249	290	72
Minnesota	80	20	53	7	195	303	47
Kansas City	80	12	56	12	190	351	36

Leading Scorers

Player	Club	GP	G	A	PTS	PIM
Lafleur, Guy	Montreal	80	56	69	125	36
Clarke, Bobby	Philadelphia	76	30	89	119	13
Perreault, Gilbert	Buffalo	80	44	69	113	36
Barber, Bill	Philadelphia	80	50	62	112	104
Larouche, Pierre	Pittsburgh	76	53	58	111	33
Ratelle, Jean	Bos., NYR	80	36	69	105	18
Mahovlich, Pete	Montreal	80	34	71	105	76
Pronovost, Jean	Pittsburgh	80	52	52	104	24
Sittler, Darryl	Toronto	79	41	59	100	90
Apps, Syl	Pittsburgh	80	32	67	99	24

1976-77
PRINCE OF WALES CONFERENCE
Norris Division

Team	GP	W	L	T	GF	GA	PTS
*Montreal	80	60	8	12	387	171	132
Los Angeles	80	34	31	15	271	241	83
Pittsburgh	80	34	33	13	240	252	81
Washington	80	24	42	14	221	307	62
Detroit	80	16	55	9	183	309	41

Adams Division

Team	GP	W	L	T	GF	GA	PTS
Boston	80	49	23	8	312	240	106
Buffalo	80	48	24	8	301	220	104
Toronto	80	33	32	15	301	285	81
Cleveland	80	25	42	13	240	292	63

CLARENCE CAMPBELL CONFERENCE
Patrick Division

Team	GP	W	L	T	GF	GA	PTS
Philadelphia	80	48	16	16	323	213	112
NY Islanders	80	47	21	12	288	193	106
Atlanta	80	34	34	12	264	265	80
NY Rangers	88	29	37	14	272	310	72

Smythe Division

Team	GP	W	L	T	GF	GA	PTS
St. Louis	80	32	39	9	239	276	73
Minnesota	80	23	39	18	240	310	64
Chicago	80	26	43	11	240	298	63
Vancouver	80	25	42	13	235	294	63
Colorado	80	20	46	14	226	307	54

Leading Scorers

Player	Club	GP	G	A	PTS	PIM
Lafleur, Guy	Montreal	80	56	80	136	20
Dionne, Marcel	Los Angeles	80	53	69	122	12
Shutt, Steve	Montreal	80	60	45	105	28
MacLeish, Rick	Philadelphia	79	49	48	97	42
Perreault, Gilbert	Buffalo	80	39	56	95	30
Young, Tim	Minnesota	80	29	66	95	58
Ratelle, Jean	Boston	78	33	61	94	2
McDonald, Lanny	Toronto	80	46	44	90	77
Sittler, Darryl	Toronto	73	38	52	90	89
Clarke, Bobby	Philadelphia	80	27	63	90	71

1977-78
PRINCE OF WALES CONFERENCE
Norris Division

Team	GP	W	L	T	GF	GA	PTS
*Montreal	80	59	10	11	359	183	129
Detroit	80	32	34	14	252	266	78
Los Angeles	80	31	34	15	243	245	77
Pittsburgh	80	25	37	18	254	321	68
Washington	80	17	49	14	195	321	48

Adams Division

Team	GP	W	L	T	GF	GA	PTS
Boston	80	51	18	11	333	218	113
Buffalo	80	44	19	17	288	215	105
Toronto	80	41	29	10	271	237	92
Cleveland	80	22	45	13	230	325	57

CLARENCE CAMPBELL CONFERENCE
Patrick Division

Team	GP	W	L	T	GF	GA	PTS
NY Islanders	80	48	17	15	334	210	111
Philadelphia	80	45	20	15	296	200	105
Atlanta	80	34	27	19	274	252	87
NY Rangers	80	30	37	13	279	280	73

Smythe Division

Team	GP	W	L	T	GF	GA	PTS
Chicago	80	32	29	19	230	220	83
Colorado	80	19	40	21	257	305	59
Vancouver	80	20	43	17	239	320	57
St. Louis	80	20	47	13	195	304	53
Minnesota	80	18	53	9	218	325	45

Leading Scorers

Player	Club	GP	G	A	PTS	PIM
Lafleur, Guy	Montreal	79	60	72	132	26
Trottier, Bryan	NY Islanders	77	46	77	123	46
Sittler, Darryl	Toronto	80	45	72	117	100
Lemaire, Jacques	Montreal	76	36	61	97	14
Potvin, Denis	NY Islanders	80	30	64	94	81
Bossy, Mike	NY Islanders	73	53	38	91	6
O'Reilly, Terry	Boston	77	29	61	90	211
Perreault, Gilbert	Buffalo	79	41	48	89	20
Clarke, Bobby	Philadelphia	71	21	68	89	83
McDonald, Lanny	Toronto	74	47	40	87	54
Paiement, Wilf	Colorado	80	31	56	87	114

1978-79
PRINCE OF WALES CONFERENCE
Norris Division

Team	GP	W	L	T	GF	GA	PTS
*Montreal	80	52	17	11	337	204	115
Pittsburgh	80	36	31	13	281	279	85
Los Angeles	80	34	34	12	292	286	80
Washington	80	24	41	15	273	338	63
Detroit	80	23	41	16	252	295	62

Adams Division

Team	GP	W	L	T	GF	GA	PTS
Boston	80	43	23	14	316	270	100
Buffalo	80	36	28	16	280	263	88
Toronto	80	34	33	13	267	252	81
Minnesota	80	28	40	12	257	289	68

CLARENCE CAMPBELL CONFERENCE
Patrick Division

Team	GP	W	L	T	GF	GA	PTS
NY Islanders	80	51	15	14	358	214	116
Philadelphia	80	40	25	15	281	248	95
NY Rangers	80	40	29	11	316	292	91
Atlanta	80	41	31	8	327	280	90

Smythe Division

Team	GP	W	L	T	GF	GA	PTS
Chicago	80	29	36	15	244	277	73
Vancouver	80	25	42	13	217	291	63
St. Louis	80	18	50	12	249	348	48
Colorado	80	15	53	12	210	331	42

Leading Scorers

Player	Club	GP	G	A	PTS	PIM
Trottier, Bryan	NY Islanders	76	47	87	134	50
Dionne, Marcel	Los Angeles	80	59	71	130	30
Lafleur, Guy	Montreal	80	52	77	129	28
Bossy, Mike	NY Islanders	80	69	57	126	25
MacMillan, Bob	Atlanta	79	37	71	108	14
Chouinard, Guy	Atlanta	80	50	57	107	14
Potvin, Denis	NY Islanders	73	31	70	101	58
Federko, Bernie	St. Louis	74	31	64	95	14
Taylor, Dave	Los Angeles	78	43	48	91	124
Gillies, Clark	NY Islanders	75	35	56	91	68

Michel "Bunny" Larocque was the NHL's finest backup goaltender during the 1970s. In 1975-76, he compiled a superb 16-1-3 won-lost-tied record for the powerhouse Montreal Canadiens.

1979-80

PRINCE OF WALES CONFERENCE
Norris Division

Team	GP	W	L	T	GF	GA	PTS
Montreal	80	47	20	13	328	240	107
Los Angeles	80	30	36	14	290	313	74
Pittsburgh	80	30	37	13	251	303	73
Hartford	80	27	34	19	303	312	73
Detroit	80	26	43	11	268	306	63

Adams Division

Team	GP	W	L	T	GF	GA	PTS
Buffalo	80	47	17	16	318	201	110
Boston	80	46	21	13	310	234	105
Minnesota	80	36	28	16	311	253	88
Toronto	80	35	40	5	304	327	75
Quebec	80	25	44	11	248	313	61

CLARENCE CAMPBELL CONFERENCE
Patrick Division

Team	GP	W	L	T	GF	GA	PTS
Philadelphia	80	48	12	20	327	254	116
*NY Islanders	80	39	28	13	281	247	91
NY Rangers	80	38	32	10	308	284	86
Atlanta	80	35	32	13	282	269	83
Washington	80	27	40	13	261	293	67

Smythe Division

Team	GP	W	L	T	GF	GA	PTS
Chicago	80	34	27	19	241	250	87
St. Louis	80	34	34	12	266	278	80
Vancouver	80	27	37	16	256	281	70
Edmonton	80	28	39	13	301	322	69
Winnipeg	80	20	49	11	214	314	51
Colorado	80	19	48	13	234	308	51

Leading Scorers

Player	Club	GP	G	A	PTS	PIM
Dionne, Marcel	Los Angeles	80	53	84	137	32
Gretzky, Wayne	Edmonton	79	51	86	137	21
Lafleur, Guy	Montreal	74	50	75	125	12
Perreault, Gilbert	Buffalo	80	40	66	106	57
Rogers, Mike	Hartford	80	44	61	105	10
Trottier, Bryan	NY Islanders	78	42	62	104	68
Simmer, Charlie	Los Angeles	64	56	45	101	65
Stoughton, Blaine	Hartford	80	56	44	100	16
Sittler, Darryl	Toronto	73	40	57	97	62
MacDonald, Blair	Edmonton	80	46	48	94	6
Federko, Bernie	St. Louis	79	38	56	94	24

Dave Taylor, who was selected 210th overall in the 1975 Amateur Draft, compiled back-to-back 100-point seasons in 1980-81 and 1981-82.

1980-81

PRINCE OF WALES CONFERENCE
Norris Division

Team	GP	W	L	T	GF	GA	PTS
Montreal	80	45	22	13	332	232	103
Los Angeles	80	43	24	13	337	290	99
Pittsburgh	80	30	37	13	302	345	73
Hartford	80	21	41	18	292	372	60
Detroit	80	19	43	18	252	339	56

Adams Division

Team	GP	W	L	T	GF	GA	PTS
Buffalo	80	39	20	21	327	250	99
Boston	80	37	30	13	316	272	87
Minnesota	80	35	28	17	291	263	87
Quebec	80	30	32	18	314	318	78
Toronto	80	28	37	15	322	367	71

CLARENCE CAMPBELL CONFERENCE
Patrick Division

Team	GP	W	L	T	GF	GA	PTS
*NY Islanders	80	48	18	14	355	260	110
Philadelphia	80	41	24	15	313	249	97
Calgary	80	39	27	14	329	298	92
NY Rangers	80	30	36	14	312	317	74
Washington	80	26	36	18	286	317	70

Smythe Division

Team	GP	W	L	T	GF	GA	PTS
St. Louis	80	45	18	17	352	281	107
Chicago	80	31	33	16	304	315	78
Vancouver	80	28	32	20	289	301	76
Edmonton	80	29	35	16	328	327	74
Colorado	80	22	45	13	258	344	57
Winnipeg	80	9	57	14	246	400	32

Leading Scorers

Player	Club	GP	G	A	PTS	PIM
Gretzky, Wayne	Edmonton	80	55	109	164	28
Dionne, Marcel	Los Angeles	80	58	77	135	70
Nilsson, Kent	Calgary	80	49	82	131	26
Bossy, Mike	NY Islanders	79	68	51	119	32
Taylor, Dave	Los Angeles	72	47	65	112	130
Stastny, Peter	Quebec	77	39	70	109	37
Simmer, Charlie	Los Angeles	65	56	49	105	62
Rogers, Mike	Hartford	80	40	65	105	32
Federko, Bernie	St. Louis	78	31	73	104	47
Richard, Jacques	Quebec	78	52	51	103	39
Middleton, Rick	Boston	80	44	59	103	16
Trottier, Bryan	NY Islanders	73	31	72	103	74

1981-82

CLARENCE CAMPBELL CONFERENCE
Norris Division

Team	GP	W	L	T	GF	GA	PTS
Minnesota	80	37	23	20	346	288	94
Winnipeg	80	33	33	14	319	332	80
St. Louis	80	32	40	8	315	349	72
Chicago	80	30	38	12	332	363	72
Toronto	80	20	44	16	298	380	56
Detroit	80	21	47	12	270	351	54

Smythe Division

Team	GP	W	L	T	GF	GA	PTS
Edmonton	80	48	17	15	417	295	111
Vancouver	80	30	33	17	290	286	77
Calgary	80	29	34	17	334	345	75
Los Angeles	80	24	41	15	314	369	63
Colorado	80	18	49	13	241	362	49

PRINCE OF WALES CONFERENCE
Adams Division

Team	GP	W	L	T	GF	GA	PTS
Montreal	80	46	17	17	360	223	109
Boston	80	43	27	10	323	285	96
Buffalo	80	39	26	15	307	273	93
Quebec	80	33	31	16	356	345	82
Hartford	80	21	41	18	264	351	60

Patrick Division

Team	GP	W	L	T	GF	GA	PTS
*NY Islanders	80	54	16	10	385	250	118
NY Rangers	80	39	27	14	316	306	92
Philadelphia	80	38	31	11	325	313	87
Pittsburgh	80	31	36	13	310	337	75
Washington	80	26	41	13	319	338	65

Leading Scorers

Player	Club	GP	G	A	PTS	PIM
Gretzky, Wayne	Edmonton	80	92	120	212	26
Bossy, Mike	NY Islanders	80	64	83	147	22
Stastny, Peter	Quebec	80	46	93	139	91
Maruk, Dennis	Washington	80	60	76	136	128
Trottier, Bryan	NY Islanders	80	50	79	129	88
Savard, Denis	Chicago	80	32	87	119	82
Dionne, Marcel	Los Angeles	78	50	67	117	50
Smith, Bobby	Minnesota	80	43	71	114	82
Ciccarelli, Dino	Minnesota	76	55	51	106	138
Taylor, Dave	Los Angeles	78	39	67	106	130

1982-83

CLARENCE CAMPBELL CONFERENCE
Norris Division

Team	GP	W	L	T	GF	GA	PTS
Chicago	80	47	23	10	338	268	104
Minnesota	80	40	24	16	321	290	96
Toronto	80	28	40	12	293	330	68
St. Louis	80	25	40	15	285	316	65
Detroit	80	21	44	15	263	344	57

Smythe Division

Team	GP	W	L	T	GF	GA	PTS
Edmonton	80	47	21	12	424	315	106
Calgary	80	32	34	14	321	317	78
Vancouver	80	30	35	15	303	309	75
Winnipeg	80	33	39	8	311	333	74
Los Angeles	80	27	41	12	308	365	66

PRINCE OF WALES CONFERENCE
Adams Division

Team	GP	W	L	T	GF	GA	PTS
Boston	80	50	20	10	327	228	110
Montreal	80	42	24	14	350	286	98
Buffalo	80	38	29	13	318	285	89
Quebec	80	34	34	12	343	336	80
Hartford	80	19	54	7	261	403	45

Patrick Division

Team	GP	W	L	T	GF	GA	PTS
Philadelphia	80	49	23	8	326	240	106
*NY Islanders	80	42	26	12	302	226	96
Washington	80	39	25	16	306	283	94
NY Rangers	80	35	35	10	306	287	80
New Jersey	80	17	49	14	230	338	48
Pittsburgh	80	18	53	9	257	394	45

Leading Scorers

Player	Club	GP	G	A	PTS	PIM
Gretzky, Wayne	Edmonton	80	71	125	196	59
Stastny, Peter	Quebec	75	47	77	124	78
Savard, Denis	Chicago	78	35	86	121	99
Bossy, Mike	NY Islanders	79	60	58	118	20
Dionne, Marcel	Los Angeles	80	56	51	107	22
Pederson, Barry	Boston	77	46	61	107	47
Messier, Mark	Edmonton	77	48	58	106	72
Goulet, Michel	Quebec	80	57	48	105	51
Anderson, Glenn	Edmonton	72	48	56	104	70
Nilsson, Kent	Calgary	80	46	58	104	10
Kurri, Jari	Edmonton	80	45	59	104	22

A three-time All-Star during the 1980s, Mark Howe collected a career-high 24 goals and 82 points in the 1985-86 season.

1983-84

CLARENCE CAMPBELL CONFERENCE
Norris Division

Team	GP	W	L	T	GF	GA	PTS
Minnesota	80	39	31	10	345	344	88
St. Louis	80	32	41	7	293	316	71
Detroit	80	31	42	7	298	323	69
Chicago	80	30	42	8	277	311	68
Toronto	80	26	45	9	303	387	61

Smythe Division

Team	GP	W	L	T	GF	GA	PTS
*Edmonton	80	57	18	5	446	314	119
Calgary	80	34	32	14	311	314	82
Vancouver	80	32	39	9	306	328	73
Winnipeg	80	31	38	11	340	374	73
Los Angeles	80	23	44	13	309	376	59

PRINCE OF WALES CONFERENCE
Adams Division

Team	GP	W	L	T	GF	GA	PTS
Boston	80	49	25	6	336	261	104
Buffalo	80	48	25	7	315	257	103
Quebec	80	42	28	10	360	278	94
Montreal	80	35	40	5	286	295	75
Hartford	80	28	42	10	288	320	66

Patrick Division

Team	GP	W	L	T	GF	GA	PTS
NY Islanders	80	50	26	4	357	269	104
Washington	80	48	27	5	308	226	101
Philadelphia	80	44	26	10	350	290	98
NY Rangers	80	42	29	9	314	304	93
New Jersey	80	17	56	7	231	350	41
Pittsburgh	80	16	58	6	254	390	38

Leading Scorers

Player	Club	GP	G	A	PTS	PIM
Gretzky, Wayne	Edmonton	74	87	118	205	39
Coffey, Paul	Edmonton	80	40	86	126	104
Goulet, Michel	Quebec	75	56	65	121	76
Stastny, Peter	Quebec	80	46	73	119	73
Bossy, Mike	NY Islanders	67	51	67	118	8
Pederson, Barry	Boston	80	39	77	116	64
Kurri, Jari	Edmonton	64	52	61	113	14
Trottier, Bryan	NY Islanders	68	40	71	111	59
Federko, Bernie	St. Louis	79	41	66	107	43
Middleton, Rick	Boston	80	47	58	105	14

1984-85

CLARENCE CAMPBELL CONFERENCE
Norris Division

Team	GP	W	L	T	GF	GA	PTS
St. Louis	80	37	31	12	299	288	86
Chicago	80	38	35	7	309	299	83
Detroit	80	27	41	12	313	357	66
Minnesota	80	25	43	12	268	321	62
Toronto	80	20	52	8	253	358	48

Smythe Division

Team	GP	W	L	T	GF	GA	PTS
*Edmonton	80	49	20	11	401	298	109
Winnipeg	80	43	27	10	358	332	96
Calgary	80	41	27	12	363	302	94
Los Angeles	80	34	32	14	339	326	82
Vancouver	80	25	46	9	284	401	59

PRINCE OF WALES CONFERENCE
Adams Division

Team	GP	W	L	T	GF	GA	PTS
Montreal	80	41	27	12	309	262	94
Quebec	80	41	30	9	323	275	91
Buffalo	80	38	28	14	290	237	90
Boston	80	36	34	10	303	287	82
Hartford	80	30	41	9	268	318	69

Patrick Division

Team	GP	W	L	T	GF	GA	PTS
Philadelphia	80	53	20	7	348	241	113
Washington	80	46	25	9	322	240	101
NY Islanders	80	40	34	6	345	312	86
NY Rangers	80	26	44	10	295	345	62
New Jersey	80	22	48	10	264	346	54
Pittsburgh	80	24	51	5	276	385	53

Leading Scorers

Player	Club	GP	G	A	PTS	PIM
Gretzky, Wayne	Edmonton	80	73	135	208	52
Kurri, Jari	Edmonton	73	71	64	135	30
Hawerchuk, Dale	Winnipeg	80	53	77	130	74
Dionne, Marcel	Los Angeles	80	46	80	126	46
Coffey, Paul	Edmonton	80	37	84	121	97
Bossy, Mike	NY Islanders	76	58	59	117	38
Ogrodnick, John	Detroit	79	55	50	105	30
Savard, Denis	Chicago	79	38	67	105	56
Federko, Bernie	St. Louis	76	30	73	103	27
Gartner, Mike	Washington	80	50	52	102	7

1985-86

CLARENCE CAMPBELL CONFERENCE
Norris Division

Team	GP	W	L	T	GF	GA	PTS
Chicago	80	39	33	8	351	349	86
Minnesota	80	38	33	9	327	305	85
St. Louis	80	37	34	9	302	291	83
Toronto	80	25	48	7	311	386	57
Detroit	80	17	57	6	266	415	40

Smythe Division

Team	GP	W	L	T	GF	GA	PTS
Edmonton	80	56	17	7	426	310	119
Calgary	80	40	31	9	354	315	89
Winnipeg	80	26	47	7	295	372	59
Vancouver	80	23	44	13	282	333	59
Los Angeles	80	23	49	8	284	389	54

PRINCE OF WALES CONFERENCE
Adams Division

Team	GP	W	L	T	GF	GA	PTS
Quebec	80	43	31	6	330	289	92
*Montreal	80	40	33	7	330	280	87
Boston	80	37	31	12	311	288	86
Hartford	80	40	36	4	332	302	84
Buffalo	80	37	37	6	296	291	80

Patrick Division

Team	GP	W	L	T	GF	GA	PTS
Philadelphia	80	53	23	4	335	241	110
Washington	80	50	23	7	315	272	107
NY Islanders	80	39	29	12	327	284	90
NY Rangers	80	36	38	6	280	276	78
Pittsburgh	80	34	38	8	313	305	76
New Jersey	80	28	49	3	300	374	59

Leading Scorers

Player	Club	GP	G	A	PTS	PIM
Gretzky, Wayne	Edmonton	80	52	163	215	52
Lemieux, Mario	Pittsburgh	79	48	93	141	43
Coffey, Paul	Edmonton	79	48	90	138	120
Kurri, Jari	Edmonton	78	68	63	131	22
Bossy, Mike	NY Islanders	80	61	62	123	14
Stastny, Peter	Quebec	76	41	81	122	60
Savard, Denis	Chicago	80	47	69	116	111
Naslund, Mats	Montreal	80	43	67	110	16
Hawerchuk, Dale	Winnipeg	80	46	59	105	44
Broten, Neal	Minnesota	80	29	76	105	47

1986-87

CLARENCE CAMPBELL CONFERENCE
Norris Division

Team	GP	W	L	T	GF	GA	PTS
St. Louis	80	32	33	15	281	293	79
Detroit	80	34	36	10	260	274	78
Chicago	80	29	37	14	290	310	72
Toronto	80	32	42	6	286	319	70
Minnesota	80	30	40	10	296	314	70

Smythe Division

Team	GP	W	L	T	GF	GA	PTS
*Edmonton	80	50	24	6	372	284	106
Calgary	80	46	31	3	318	289	95
Winnipeg	80	40	32	8	279	271	88
Los Angeles	80	31	41	8	318	341	70
Vancouver	80	29	43	8	282	314	66

PRINCE OF WALES CONFERENCE
Adams Division

Team	GP	W	L	T	GF	GA	PTS
Hartford	80	43	30	7	287	270	93
Montreal	80	41	29	10	277	241	92
Boston	80	39	34	7	301	276	85
Quebec	80	31	39	10	267	276	72
Buffalo	80	28	44	8	280	308	64

Patrick Division

Team	GP	W	L	T	GF	GA	PTS
Philadelphia	80	46	26	8	310	245	100
Washington	80	38	32	10	285	278	86
NY Islanders	80	35	33	12	279	281	82
NY Rangers	80	34	38	8	307	323	76
Pittsburgh	80	30	38	12	297	290	72
New Jersey	80	29	45	6	293	368	64

Leading Scorers

Player	Club	GP	G	A	PTS	PIM
Gretzky, Wayne	Edmonton	79	62	121	183	28
Kurri, Jari	Edmonton	79	54	54	108	41
Lemieux, Mario	Pittsburgh	63	54	53	107	57
Messier, Mark	Edmonton	77	37	70	107	73
Gilmour, Doug	St. Louis	80	42	63	105	58
Ciccarelli, Dino	Minnesota	80	52	51	103	92
Hawerchuk, Dale	Winnipeg	80	47	53	100	54
Goulet, Michel	Quebec	75	49	47	96	61
Kerr, Tim	Philadelphia	75	58	37	95	57
Bourque, Ray	Boston	78	23	72	95	36

1987-88

CLARENCE CAMPBELL CONFERENCE
Norris Division

Team	GP	W	L	T	GF	GA	PTS
Detroit	80	41	28	11	322	269	93
St. Louis	80	34	38	8	278	294	76
Chicago	80	30	41	9	284	328	69
Toronto	80	21	49	10	273	345	52
Minnesota	80	19	48	13	242	349	51

Smythe Division

Team	GP	W	L	T	GF	GA	PTS
Calgary	80	48	23	9	397	305	105
*Edmonton	80	44	25	11	363	288	99
Winnipeg	80	33	36	11	292	310	77
Los Angeles	80	30	42	8	318	359	68
Vancouver	80	25	46	9	272	320	59

PRINCE OF WALES CONFERENCE
Adams Division

Team	GP	W	L	T	GF	GA	PTS
Montreal	80	45	22	13	298	238	103
Boston	80	44	30	6	300	251	94
Buffalo	80	37	32	11	283	305	85
Hartford	80	35	38	7	249	267	77
Quebec	80	32	43	5	271	306	69

Patrick Division

Team	GP	W	L	T	GF	GA	PTS
NY Islanders	80	39	31	10	308	267	88
Washington	80	38	33	9	281	249	85
Philadelphia	80	38	33	9	292	292	85
New Jersey	80	38	36	6	295	296	82
NY Rangers	80	36	34	10	300	283	82
Pittsburgh	80	36	35	9	319	316	81

Leading Scorers

Player	Club	GP	G	A	PTS	PIM
Lemieux, Mario	Pittsburgh	76	70	98	168	92
Gretzky, Wayne	Edmonton	64	40	109	149	24
Savard, Denis	Chicago	80	44	87	131	95
Hawerchuk, Dale	Winnipeg	80	44	77	121	59
Robitaille, Luc	Los Angeles	80	53	58	111	82
Stastny, Peter	Quebec	76	46	65	111	69
Messier, Mark	Edmonton	77	37	74	111	103
Carson, Jimmy	Los Angeles	80	55	52	107	45
Loob, Hakan	Calgary	80	50	56	106	47
Goulet, Michel	Quebec	80	48	58	106	56

1988-89

CLARENCE CAMPBELL CONFERENCE
Norris Division

Team	GP	W	L	T	GF	GA	PTS
Detroit	80	34	34	12	313	316	80
St. Louis	80	33	35	12	275	285	78
Minnesota	80	27	37	16	258	278	70
Chicago	80	27	41	12	297	335	66
Toronto	80	28	46	6	259	342	62

Smythe Division

Team	GP	W	L	T	GF	GA	PTS
*Calgary	80	54	17	9	354	226	117
Los Angeles	80	42	31	7	376	335	91
Edmonton	80	38	34	8	325	306	84
Vancouver	80	33	39	8	251	253	74
Winnipeg	80	26	42	12	300	355	64

PRINCE OF WALES CONFERENCE
Adams Division

Team	GP	W	L	T	GF	GA	PTS
Montreal	80	53	18	9	315	218	115
Boston	80	37	29	14	289	256	88
Buffalo	80	38	35	7	291	299	83
Hartford	80	37	38	5	299	290	79
Quebec	80	27	46	7	269	342	61

Patrick Division

Team	GP	W	L	T	GF	GA	PTS
Washington	80	41	29	10	305	259	92
Pittsburgh	80	40	33	7	347	349	87
NY Rangers	80	37	35	8	310	307	82
Philadelphia	80	36	36	8	307	285	80
New Jersey	80	27	41	12	281	325	66
NY Islanders	80	28	47	5	265	325	61

Leading Scorers

Player	Club	GP	G	A	PTS	PIM
Lemieux, Mario	Pittsburgh	76	85	114	199	100
Gretzky, Wayne	Los Angeles	78	54	114	168	26
Yzerman, Steve	Detroit	80	65	90	155	61
Nicholls, Bernie	Los Angeles	79	70	80	150	96
Brown, Rob	Pittsburgh	68	49	66	115	118
Coffey, Paul	Pittsburgh	75	30	83	113	193
Mullen, Joe	Calgary	79	51	59	110	16
Kurri, Jari	Edmonton	76	44	58	102	69
Carson, Jimmy	Edmonton	80	49	51	100	36
Robitaille, Luc	Los Angeles	78	46	52	98	65

1989-90

CLARENCE CAMPBELL CONFERENCE
Norris Division

Team	GP	W	L	T	GF	GA	PTS
Chicago	80	41	33	6	316	294	88
St. Louis	80	37	34	9	295	279	83
Toronto	80	38	38	4	337	358	80
Minnesota	80	36	40	4	284	291	76
Detroit	80	28	38	14	288	323	70

Smythe Division

Team	GP	W	L	T	GF	GA	PTS
Calgary	80	42	23	15	348	265	99
*Edmonton	80	38	28	14	315	283	90
Winnipeg	80	37	32	11	298	290	85
Los Angeles	80	34	39	7	338	337	75
Vancouver	80	25	41	14	245	306	64

PRINCE OF WALES CONFERENCE
Adams Division

Team	GP	W	L	T	GF	GA	PTS
Boston	80	46	25	9	289	232	101
Buffalo	80	45	27	8	286	248	98
Montreal	80	41	28	11	288	234	93
Hartford	80	38	33	9	275	268	85
Quebec	80	12	61	7	240	407	31

Patrick Division

Team	GP	W	L	T	GF	GA	PTS
NY Rangers	80	36	31	13	279	267	85
New Jersey	80	37	34	9	295	288	83
Washington	80	36	38	6	284	275	78
NY Islanders	80	31	38	11	281	288	73
Pittsburgh	80	32	40	8	318	359	72
Philadelphia	80	30	39	11	290	297	71

Leading Scorers

Player	Club	GP	G	A	PTS	PIM
Gretzky, Wayne	Los Angeles	73	40	102	142	42
Messier, Mark	Edmonton	79	45	84	129	79
Yzerman, Steve	Detroit	79	62	65	127	79
Lemieux, Mario	Pittsburgh	59	45	78	123	78
Hull, Brett	St. Louis	80	72	41	113	24
Nicholls, Bernie	L.A., NYR	79	39	73	112	86
Turgeon, Pierre	Buffalo	80	40	66	106	29
LaFontaine, Pat	NY Islanders	74	54	51	105	38
Coffey, Paul	Pittsburgh	80	29	74	103	95
Sakic, Joe	Quebec	80	39	63	102	27
Oates, Adam	St. Louis	80	23	79	102	30

1990-91

CLARENCE CAMPBELL CONFERENCE
Norris Division

Team	GP	W	L	T	GF	GA	PTS
Chicago	80	49	23	8	284	211	106
St. Louis	80	47	22	11	310	250	105
Detroit	80	34	38	8	273	298	76
Minnesota	80	27	39	14	256	266	68
Toronto	80	23	46	11	241	318	57

Smythe Division

Team	GP	W	L	T	GF	GA	PTS
Los Angeles	80	46	24	10	340	254	102
Calgary	80	46	26	8	344	263	100
Edmonton	80	37	37	6	272	272	80
Vancouver	80	28	43	9	243	315	65
Winnipeg	80	26	43	11	260	288	63

PRINCE OF WALES CONFERENCE
Adams Division

Team	GP	W	L	T	GF	GA	PTS
Boston	80	44	24	12	299	264	100
Montreal	80	39	30	11	273	249	89
Buffalo	80	31	30	19	292	278	81
Hartford	80	31	38	11	238	276	73
Quebec	80	16	50	14	236	354	46

Patrick Division

Team	GP	W	L	T	GF	GA	PTS
*Pittsburgh	80	41	33	6	342	305	88
NY Rangers	80	36	31	13	297	265	85
Washington	80	37	36	7	258	258	81
New Jersey	80	32	33	15	272	264	79
Philadelphia	80	33	37	10	252	267	76
NY Islanders	80	25	45	10	223	290	60

Leading Scorers

Player	Club	GP	G	A	PTS	PIM
Gretzky, Wayne	Los Angeles	78	41	122	163	16
Hull, Brett	St. Louis	78	86	45	131	22
Oates, Adam	St. Louis	61	25	90	115	29
Recchi, Mark	Pittsburgh	78	40	73	113	48
Cullen, John	Pit., Hfd.	78	39	71	110	101
Sakic, Joe	Quebec	80	48	61	109	24
Yzerman, Steve	Detroit	80	51	57	108	34
Fleury, Theo	Calgary	79	51	53	104	136
MacInnis, Al	Calgary	78	28	75	103	90
Larmer, Steve	Chicago	80	44	57	101	79

1991-92

CLARENCE CAMPBELL CONFERENCE
Norris Division

Team	GP	W	L	T	GF	GA	PTS
Detroit	80	43	25	12	320	256	98
Chicago	80	36	29	15	257	236	87
St. Louis	80	36	33	11	279	266	83
Minnesota	80	32	42	6	246	278	70
Toronto	80	30	43	7	234	294	67

Smythe Division

Team	GP	W	L	T	GF	GA	PTS
Vancouver	80	42	26	12	285	250	96
Los Angeles	80	35	31	14	287	296	84
Edmonton	80	36	34	10	295	297	82
Winnipeg	80	33	32	15	251	244	81
Calgary	80	31	37	12	296	305	74
San Jose	80	17	58	5	219	359	39

PRINCE OF WALES CONFERENCE
Adams Division

Team	GP	W	L	T	GF	GA	PTS
Montreal	80	41	28	11	267	207	93
Boston	80	36	32	12	270	275	84
Buffalo	80	31	37	12	289	299	74
Hartford	80	26	41	13	247	283	65
Quebec	80	20	48	12	255	318	52

Patrick Division

Team	GP	W	L	T	GF	GA	PTS
NY Rangers	80	50	25	5	321	246	105
Washington	80	45	27	8	330	275	98
*Pittsburgh	80	39	32	9	343	308	87
New Jersey	80	38	31	11	289	259	87
NY Islanders	80	34	35	11	291	299	79
Philadelphia	80	32	37	11	252	273	75

Leading Scorers

Player	Club	GP	G	A	PTS	PIM
Lemieux, Mario	Pittsburgh	64	44	87	131	94
Stevens, Kevin	Pittsburgh	80	54	69	123	254
Gretzky, Wayne	Los Angeles	74	31	90	121	34
Hull, Brett	St. Louis	73	70	39	109	48
Robitaille, Luc	Los Angeles	80	44	63	107	95
Messier, Mark	NY Rangers	79	35	72	107	76
Roenick, Jeremy	Chicago	80	53	50	103	23
Yzerman, Steve	Detroit	79	45	58	103	64
Leetch, Brian	NY Rangers	80	22	80	102	26
Oates, Adam	St. L., Bos.	80	20	79	99	22

1992-93
CLARENCE CAMPBELL CONFERENCE
Norris Division

Team	GP	W	L	T	GF	GA	PTS
Chicago	84	47	25	12	279	230	106
Detroit	84	47	28	9	369	280	103
Toronto	84	44	29	11	288	241	99
St. Louis	84	37	36	11	282	278	85
Minnesota	84	36	38	10	272	293	82
Tampa Bay	84	23	54	7	245	332	53

Smythe Division

Team	GP	W	L	T	GF	GA	PTS
Vancouver	84	46	29	9	346	278	101
Calgary	84	43	30	11	322	282	97
Los Angeles	84	39	35	10	338	340	88
Winnipeg	84	40	37	7	322	320	87
Edmonton	84	26	50	8	242	337	60
San Jose	84	11	71	2	218	414	24

PRINCE OF WALES CONFERENCE
Adams Division

Team	GP	W	L	T	GF	GA	PTS
Boston	84	51	26	7	332	268	109
Quebec	84	47	27	10	351	300	104
*Montreal	84	48	30	6	326	280	102
Buffalo	84	38	36	10	335	297	86
Hartford	84	26	52	6	284	369	58
Ottawa	84	10	70	4	202	395	24

Patrick Division

Team	GP	W	L	T	GF	GA	PTS
Pittsburgh	84	56	21	7	367	268	119
Washington	84	43	34	7	325	286	93
NY Islanders	84	40	37	7	335	297	87
New Jersey	84	40	37	7	308	299	87
Philadelphia	84	36	37	11	319	319	83
NY Rangers	84	34	39	11	304	308	79

Leading Scorers

Player	Club	GP	G	A	PTS	PIM
Lemieux, Mario	Pittsburgh	60	69	91	160	38
LaFontaine, Pat	Buffalo	84	53	95	148	63
Oates, Adam	Boston	84	45	97	142	32
Yzerman, Steve	Detroit	84	58	79	137	44
Selanne, Teemu	Winnipeg	84	76	56	132	45
Turgeon, Pierre	NY Islanders	83	58	74	132	26
Mogilny, Alexander	Buffalo	77	76	51	127	40
Gilmour, Doug	Toronto	83	32	95	127	100
Robitaille, Luc	Los Angeles	84	63	62	125	100
Recchi, Mark	Philadelphia	84	53	70	123	95

1993-94
EASTERN CONFERENCE
Northeast Division

Team	GP	W	L	T	GF	GA	PTS
Pittsburgh	84	44	27	13	299	285	101
Boston	84	42	29	13	289	252	97
Montreal	84	41	29	14	283	248	96
Buffalo	84	43	32	9	282	218	95
Quebec	84	34	42	8	277	292	76
Hartford	84	27	48	9	227	288	63
Ottawa	84	14	61	9	201	397	37

Atlantic Division

Team	GP	W	L	T	GF	GA	PTS
*NY Rangers	84	52	24	8	299	231	112
New Jersey	84	47	25	12	306	220	106
Washington	84	39	35	10	277	263	88
NY Islanders	84	36	36	12	282	264	84
Florida	84	33	34	17	233	233	83
Philadelphia	84	35	39	10	294	314	80
Tampa Bay	84	30	43	11	224	251	71

WESTERN CONFERENCE
Central Division

Team	GP	W	L	T	GF	GA	PTS
Detroit	84	46	30	8	356	275	100
Toronto	84	43	29	12	280	243	98
Dallas	84	42	29	13	286	265	97
St. Louis	84	40	33	11	270	283	91
Chicago	84	39	36	9	254	240	87
Winnipeg	84	24	51	9	245	344	57

Pacific Division

Team	GP	W	L	T	GF	GA	PTS
Calgary	84	42	29	13	302	256	97
Vancouver	84	41	40	3	279	276	85
San Jose	84	33	35	16	252	265	82
Anaheim	84	33	46	5	229	251	71
Los Angeles	84	27	45	12	294	322	66
Edmonton	84	25	45	14	261	305	64

Leading Scorers

Player	Club	GP	G	A	PTS	PIM
Gretzky, Wayne	Los Angeles	81	38	92	130	20
Fedorov, Sergei	Detroit	82	56	64	120	34
Oates, Adam	Boston	77	32	80	112	45
Gilmour, Doug	Toronto	83	27	84	111	105
Bure, Pavel	Vancouver	76	60	47	107	86
Roenick, Jeremy	Chicago	84	46	61	107	125
Recchi, Mark	Philadelphia	84	40	67	107	46
Shanahan, Brendan	St. Louis	81	52	50	102	211
Andreychuk, Dave	Toronto	83	53	46	99	98
Jagr, Jaromir	Pittsburgh	80	32	67	99	61

1994-95
EASTERN CONFERENCE
Northeast Division

Team	GP	W	L	T	GF	GA	PTS
Quebec	48	30	13	5	185	134	65
Pittsburgh	48	29	16	3	181	158	61
Boston	48	27	18	3	150	127	57
Buffalo	48	22	19	7	130	119	51
Hartford	48	19	24	5	127	141	43
Montreal	48	18	23	7	125	148	43
Ottawa	48	9	34	5	117	174	23

Atlantic Division

Team	GP	W	L	T	GF	GA	PTS
Philadelphia	48	28	16	4	150	132	60
*New Jersey	48	22	18	8	136	121	52
Washington	48	22	18	8	136	120	52
NY Rangers	48	22	23	3	139	134	47
Florida	48	20	22	6	115	127	46
Tampa Bay	48	17	28	3	120	144	37
NY Islanders	48	15	28	5	126	158	35

WESTERN CONFERENCE
Central Division

Team	GP	W	L	T	GF	GA	PTS
Detroit	48	33	11	4	180	117	70
St. Louis	48	28	15	5	178	135	61
Chicago	48	24	19	5	156	115	53
Toronto	48	21	19	8	135	146	50
Dallas	48	17	23	8	136	135	42
Winnipeg	48	16	25	7	157	177	39

Pacific Division

Team	GP	W	L	T	GF	GA	PTS
Calgary	48	24	17	7	163	135	55
Vancouver	48	18	18	12	153	148	48
San Jose	48	19	25	4	129	161	42
Los Angeles	48	16	23	9	142	174	41
Edmonton	48	17	27	4	136	183	38
Anaheim	48	16	27	5	125	164	37

Leading Scorers

Player	Club	GP	G	A	PTS	PIM
Jagr, Jaromir	Pittsburgh	48	32	38	70	37
Lindros, Eric	Philadelphia	46	29	41	70	60
Zhamnov, Alexei	Winnipeg	48	30	35	65	20
Sakic, Joe	Quebec	47	19	43	62	30
Francis, Ron	Pittsburgh	44	11	48	59	18
Fleury, Theoren	Calgary	47	29	29	58	112
Coffey, Paul	Detroit	45	14	44	58	72
Renberg, Mikael	Philadelphia	47	26	31	57	20
LeClair, John	Mtl., Phi.	46	26	28	54	30
Messier, Mark	NY Rangers	46	14	39	53	40
Oates, Adam	Boston	48	12	41	53	8

Note: Detailed statistics for 1994-95 are listed in the Final Statistics, 1994-95 section of the **NHL Guide & Record Book. See page 117.**

Buffalo Sabres' captain Pat LaFontaine finished as the NHL's second-leading scorer in 1992-93, notching career-highs in goals (53), assists (95) and points (148).

Team Records

BEST WINNING PERCENTAGE, ONE SEASON:
  .875 —Boston Bruins, 1929-30. 38w-5L-1T. 77PTS in 44GP
  .830 —Montreal Canadiens, 1943-44. 38w-5L-7T. 83PTS in 50GP
  .825 —Montreal Canadiens, 1976-77. 60w-8L-12T. 132PTS in 80GP
  .806 —Montreal Canadiens, 1977-78. 59w-10L-11T. 129PTS in 80GP
  .800 —Montreal Canadiens, 1944-45. 38w-8L-4T. 80PTS in 50GP

MOST POINTS, ONE SEASON:
  132 —Montreal Canadiens, 1976-77. 60w-8L-12T. 80GP
  129 —Montreal Canadiens, 1977-78. 59w-10L-11T. 80GP
  127 —Montreal Canadiens, 1975-76. 58w-11L-11T. 80GP

FEWEST POINTS, ONE SEASON:
  8 —Quebec Bulldogs, 1919-20. 4w-20L-0T. 24GP
  10 —Toronto Arenas, 1918-19. 5w-13L-0T. 18GP
  12 —Hamilton Tigers, 1920-21. 6w-18L-0T. 24GP
    —Hamilton Tigers, 1922-23. 6w-18L-0T. 24GP
    —Boston Bruins, 1924-25. 6w-24L-0T. 30GP
    —Philadelphia Quakers, 1930-31. 4w-36L-4T. 44GP

FEWEST POINTS, ONE SEASON (MINIMUM 70-GAME SCHEDULE):
  21 —Washington Capitals, 1974-75. 8w-67L-5T. 80GP
  24 —Ottawa Senators, 1992-93. 10w-70L-4T. 84GP
    —San Jose Sharks, 1992-93. 11w-71L-2T. 84GP
  30 —NY Islanders, 1972-73. 12w-60L-6T. 78GP

WORST WINNING PERCENTAGE, ONE SEASON:
  .131 —Washington Capitals, 1974-75. 8w-67L-5T. 21PTS in 80GP
  .136 —Philadelphia Quakers, 1930-31. 4w-36L-4T. 12PTS in 44GP
  .143 —Ottawa Senators, 1992-93. 10w-70L-4T. 24PTS in 84GP
  .143 —San Jose Sharks, 1992-93. 11w-71L-2T. 24PTS in 84GP
  .148 —Pittsburgh Pirates, 1929-30. 5w-36L-3T. 13PTS in 44GP

MOST WINS, ONE SEASON:
  60 —Montreal Canadiens, 1976-77. 80GP
  59 —Montreal Canadiens, 1977-78. 80GP
  58 —Montreal Canadiens, 1975-76. 80GP

FEWEST WINS, ONE SEASON:
  4 —Quebec Bulldogs, 1919-20. 24GP
    —Philadelphia Quakers, 1930-31. 44GP
  5 —Toronto Arenas, 1918-19. 18GP
    —Pittsburgh Pirates, 1929-30. 44GP

FEWEST WINS, ONE SEASON (MINIMUM 70-GAME SCHEDULE):
  8 —Washington Capitals, 1974-75. 80GP
  9 —Winnipeg Jets, 1980-81. 80GP
  10 —Ottawa Senators, 1992-93. 84GP

MOST LOSSES, ONE SEASON:
  71 —San Jose Sharks, 1992-93. 84GP
  70 —Ottawa Senators, 1992-93. 84GP
  67 —Washington Capitals, 1974-75. 80GP
  61 —Quebec Nordiques, 1989-90. 80GP
    —Ottawa Senators, 1993-94. 84GP

FEWEST LOSSES, ONE SEASON:
  5 —Ottawa Senators, 1919-20. 24GP
    —Boston Bruins, 1929-30. 44GP
    —Montreal Canadiens, 1943-44. 50GP

FEWEST LOSSES, ONE SEASON (MINIMUM 70-GAME SCHEDULE):
  8 —Montreal Canadiens, 1976-77. 80GP
  10 —Montreal Canadiens, 1972-73. 78GP
    —Montreal Canadiens, 1977-78. 80GP
  11 —Montreal Canadiens, 1975-76. 80GP

MOST TIES, ONE SEASON:
  24 —Philadelphia Flyers, 1969-70. 76GP
  23 —Montreal Canadiens, 1962-63. 70GP
    —Chicago Blackhawks, 1973-74. 78GP

FEWEST TIES, ONE SEASON (Since 1926-27):
  1 —Boston Bruins, 1929-30. 44GP
  2 —NY Americans, 1926-27. 44GP
    —Montreal Canadiens, 1926-27. 44GP
    —Boston Bruins, 1938-39. 48GP
    —NY Rangers, 1941-42. 48GP
    —San Jose Sharks, 1992-93. 84GP

FEWEST TIES, ONE SEASON (MINIMUM 70-GAME SCHEDULE):
  2 —San Jose Sharks, 1992-93. 84GP
  3 —New Jersey Devils, 1985-86. 80GP
    —Calgary Flames, 1986-87. 80GP
    —Vancouver Canucks, 1993-94. 84GP

MOST HOME WINS, ONE SEASON:
  36 —Philadelphia Flyers, 1975-76. 40GP
  33 —Boston Bruins, 1970-71. 39GP
    —Boston Bruins, 1973-74. 39GP
    —Montreal Canadiens, 1976-77. 40GP
    —Philadelphia Flyers, 1976-77. 40GP
    —NY Islanders, 1981-82. 40GP
    —Philadelphia Flyers, 1985-86. 40GP

MOST ROAD WINS, ONE SEASON:
  27 —Montreal Canadiens, 1976-77. 40GP
    —Montreal Canadiens, 1977-78. 40GP
  26 —Boston Bruins, 1971-72. 39GP
    —Montreal Canadiens, 1975-76. 40GP
    —Edmonton Oilers, 1983-84. 40GP

MOST HOME LOSSES, ONE SEASON:
  *32 —San Jose Sharks, 1992-93. 41GP
  29 —Pittsburgh Penguins, 1983-84. 40GP
  * —Ottawa Senators, 1993-94. 41GP

MOST ROAD LOSSES, ONE SEASON:
  *40 —Ottawa Senators, 1992-93. 41GP
  39 —Washington Capitals, 1974-75. 40GP
  37 —California Seals, 1973-74. 39GP
  * —San Jose Sharks, 1992-93. 41GP

MOST HOME TIES, ONE SEASON:
  13 —NY Rangers, 1954-55. 35GP
    —Philadelphia Flyers, 1969-70. 38GP
    —California Seals, 1971-72. 39GP
    —California Seals, 1972-73. 39GP
    —Chicago Blackhawks, 1973-74. 39GP

MOST ROAD TIES, ONE SEASON:
  15 —Philadelphia Flyers, 1976-77. 40GP
  14 —Montreal Canadiens, 1952-53. 35GP
    —Montreal Canadiens, 1974-75. 40GP
    —Philadelphia Flyers, 1975-76. 40GP

FEWEST HOME WINS, ONE SEASON:
  2 —Chicago Blackhawks, 1927-28. 22GP
  3 —Boston Bruins, 1924-25. 15GP
    —Chicago Blackhawks, 1928-29. 22GP
    —Philadelphia Quakers, 1930-31. 22GP

FEWEST HOME WINS, ONE SEASON (MINIMUM 70-GAME SCHEDULE):
  6 —Chicago Blackhawks, 1954-55. 35GP
    —Washington Capitals, 1975-76. 40GP
  7 —Boston Bruins, 1962-63. 35GP
    —Washington Capitals, 1974-75. 40GP
    —Winnipeg Jets, 1980-81. 40GP
    —Pittsburgh Penguins, 1983-84. 40GP

FEWEST ROAD WINS, ONE SEASON:
  0 —Toronto Arenas, 1918-19. 9GP
    —Quebec Bulldogs, 1919-20. 12GP
    —Pittsburgh Pirates, 1929-30. 22GP
  1 —Hamilton Tigers, 1921-22. 12GP
    —Toronto St. Patricks, 1925-26. 18GP
    —Philadelphia Quakers, 1930-31. 22GP
    —NY Americans, 1940-41. 24GP
    —Washington Capitals, 1974-75. 40GP
  * —Ottawa Senators, 1992-93. 41GP

FEWEST ROAD WINS, ONE SEASON (MINIMUM 70-GAME SCHEDULE):
  1 —Washington Capitals, 1974-75. 40GP
  * **—Ottawa Senators,** 1992-93. 41GP
  2 —Boston Bruins, 1960-61. 35GP
    —Los Angeles Kings, 1969-70. 38GP
    —NY Islanders, 1972-73. 39GP
    —California Seals, 1973-74. 39GP
    —Colorado Rockies, 1977-78. 40GP
    —Winnipeg Jets, 1980-81. 40GP
    —Quebec Nordiques, 1991-92. 40GP

FEWEST HOME LOSSES, ONE SEASON:
  0 —Ottawa Senators, 1922-23. 12GP
    —Montreal Canadiens, 1943-44. 25GP
  1 —Toronto Arenas, 1917-18. 11GP
    —Ottawa Senators, 1918-19. 9GP
    —Ottawa Senators, 1919-20. 12GP
    —Toronto St. Patricks, 1922-23. 12GP
    —Boston Bruins, 1929-30 and 1930-31. 22GP
    —Montreal Canadiens, 1976-77. 40GP
    —Quebec Nordiques, 1994-95. 24GP

FEWEST HOME LOSSES, ONE SEASON (MINIMUM 70-GAME SCHEDULE):
  1 —Montreal Canadiens, 1976-77. 40GP
  2 —Montreal Canadiens, 1961-62. 35GP
    —NY Rangers, 1970-71. 39GP
    —Philadelphia Flyers, 1975-76. 40GP

---

* Does not include neutral site games

FEWEST ROAD LOSSES, ONE SEASON:
 3 —Montreal Canadiens, 1928-29. 22GP
 4 —Ottawa Senators, 1919-20. 12GP
  —Montreal Canadiens, 1927-28. 22GP
  —Boston Bruins, 1929-30. 20GP
  —Boston Bruins, 1940-41. 24GP

FEWEST ROAD LOSSES, ONE SEASON (MINIMUM 70-GAME SCHEDULE):
 6 —Montreal Canadiens, 1972-73. 39GP
  —Montreal Canadiens, 1974-75. 40GP
  —Montreal Canadiens, 1977-78. 40GP
 7 —Detroit Red Wings, 1951-52. 35GP
  —Montreal Canadiens, 1976-77. 40GP
  —Philadelphia Flyers, 1979-80. 40GP

LONGEST WINNING STREAK:
 17 Games —Pittsburgh Penguins, Mar. 9, 1993 - Apr. 10, 1993.
 15 Games —NY Islanders, Jan. 21, 1982 - Feb. 20, 1982.
 14 Games —Boston Bruins, Dec. 3, 1929 - Jan. 9, 1930.
 13 Games —Boston Bruins, Feb. 23, 1971 - Mar. 20, 1971.
  —Philadelphia Flyers, Oct. 19, 1985 - Nov. 17, 1985.

LONGEST WINNING STREAK FROM START OF SEASON:
 10 Games —Toronto Maple Leafs, 1993-94.
 8 Games —Toronto Maple Leafs, 1934-35.
  —Buffalo Sabres, 1975-76.
 7 Games —Edmonton Oilers, 1983-84.
  —Quebec Nordiques, 1985-86.
  —Pittsburgh Penguins, 1986-87.
  —Pittsburgh Penguins, 1994-95.

LONGEST WINNING STREAK, INCLUDING PLAYOFFS:
 15 Games —Detroit Red Wings, Feb. 27, 1955 - Apr. 5, 1955. Nine
  regular-season games, six playoff games.

LONGEST HOME WINNING STREAK FROM START OF SEASON:
 11 Games —Chicago Blackhawks, 1963-64
 10 Games —Ottawa Senators, 1925-26
 9 Games —Montreal Canadiens, 1953-54
  —Chicago Blackhawks, 1971-72
 8 Games —Boston Bruins, 1983-84
  —Philadelphia Flyers, 1986-87
  —New Jersey Devils, 1987-88

LONGEST HOME WINNING STREAK (ONE SEASON):
 20 Games —Boston Bruins, Dec. 3, 1929 - Mar. 18, 1930.
  —Philadelphia Flyers, Jan. 4, 1976 - Apr. 3, 1976.

LONGEST HOME WINNING STREAK, INCLUDING PLAYOFFS:
 24 Games —Philadelphia Flyers, Jan. 4, 1976 - Apr. 25, 1976. 20 regular-season
  games, 4 playoff games.

LONGEST ROAD WINNING STREAK (ONE SEASON):
 10 Games —Buffalo Sabres, Dec. 10, 1983 - Jan. 23, 1984.
 8 Games —Boston Bruins, Feb. 17, 1972 - Mar. 8, 1972.
  —Los Angeles Kings, Dec. 18, 1974 - Jan. 16, 1975.
  —Montreal Canadiens, Dec. 18, 1977 - Jan. 18. 1978.
  —NY Islanders, Feb. 27, 1981 - Mar. 29, 1981.
  —Montreal Canadiens, Jan. 21, 1982 - Feb. 21, 1982.
  —Philadelphia Flyers, Dec. 22, 1982 - Jan. 16, 1983.
  —Winnipeg Jets, Feb. 25, 1985 - Apr. 6, 1985.
  —Edmonton Oilers, Dec. 9, 1986 - Jan. 17, 1987.
  —Boston Bruins, Mar. 15, 1993 - Apr. 14, 1993.

LONGEST UNDEFEATED STREAK (ONE SEASON):
 35 Games —Philadelphia Flyers, Oct. 14, 1979 - Jan. 6, 1980. 25W-10T.
 28 Games —Montreal Canadiens, Dec. 18, 1977 - Feb. 23, 1978. 23W-5T.
 23 Games —Boston Bruins, Dec. 22, 1940 - Feb. 23, 1941. 15W-8T.
  —Philadelphia Flyers, Jan. 29, 1976 - Mar. 18, 1976. 17W-6T.

LONGEST UNDEFEATED STREAK FROM START OF SEASON:
 15 Games —Edmonton Oilers, 1984-85. 12W-3T.
 14 Games —Montreal Canadiens, 1943-44. 11W-3T.
 13 Games —Montreal Canadiens, 1972-73. 9W-4T.
  —Pittsburgh Penguins, 1994-95. 12W-1T.

LONGEST HOME UNDEFEATED STREAK (ONE SEASON):
 34 Games —Montreal Canadiens, Nov. 1, 1976 - Apr. 2, 1977. 28W-6T.
 27 Games —Boston Bruins, Nov. 22, 1970 - Mar. 20, 1971. 26W-1T.

LONGEST HOME UNDEFEATED STREAK, INCLUDING PLAYOFFS:
 38 Games —Montreal Canadiens, Nov. 1, 1976 - Apr. 26, 1977. 28W-6T in
  regular season and 4W in playoffs).

LONGEST ROAD UNDEFEATED STREAK (ONE SEASON):
 23 Games —Montreal Canadiens, Nov. 27, 1974 - Mar. 12, 1975. 14W-9T.
 17 Games —Montreal Canadiens, Dec. 18, 1977 - Mar. 1, 1978. 14W-3T.
 16 Games —Philadelphia Flyers, Oct. 20, 1979 - Jan. 6, 1980. 11W-5T.

LONGEST LOSING STREAK (ONE SEASON):
 17 Games —Washington Capitals, Feb. 18, 1975 - Mar. 26, 1975.
  —San Jose Sharks, Jan. 4, 1993 - Feb. 12, 1993.
 15 Games —Philadelphia Quakers, Nov. 29, 1930 - Jan. 8, 1931.

LONGEST LOSING STREAK FROM START OF SEASON:
 11 Games —NY Rangers, 1943-44.
 7 Games —Montreal Canadiens, 1938-39.
  —Chicago Blackhawks, 1947-48.
  —Washington Capitals, 1983-84.

LONGEST HOME LOSING STREAK (ONE SEASON):
 11 Games —Boston Bruins, Dec. 8, 1924 - Feb. 17, 1925.
  —Washington Capitals, Feb. 18, 1975 - Mar. 30, 1975.
  —Ottawa Senators, Oct. 27, 1993 - Dec. 8, 1993.

LONGEST ROAD LOSING STREAK (ONE SEASON):
 *38 Games —Ottawa Senators, Oct. 10, 1992 - Apr. 3, 1993.
 37 Games —Washington Capitals, Oct. 9, 1974 - Mar. 26, 1975.
 * – Does not include neutral site games.

LONGEST WINLESS STREAK (ONE SEASON):
 30 Games —Winnipeg Jets, Oct. 19, 1980 - Dec. 20, 1980. 23L-7T.
 27 Games —Kansas City Scouts, Feb. 12, 1976 - Apr. 4, 1976. 21L-6T.
 25 Games —Washington Capitals, Nov. 29, 1975 - Jan. 21, 1976. 22L-3T.

LONGEST WINLESS STREAK FROM START OF SEASON:
 15 Games —NY Rangers, 1943-44. 14L-1T
 12 Games —Pittsburgh Pirates, 1927-28. 9L-3T
 11 Games —Minnesota North Stars, 1973-74. 5L-6T

LONGEST HOME WINLESS STREAK (ONE SEASON):
 15 Games —Chicago Blackhawks, Dec. 16, 1928 - Feb. 28, 1929. 11L-4T.
  —Montreal Canadiens, Dec. 16, 1939 - Mar. 7, 1940. 12L-3T.

LONGEST ROAD WINLESS STREAK (ONE SEASON):
 *38 Games —Ottawa Senators, Oct. 10, 1992 - Apr. 3, 1993. 38L-0T.
 37 Games —Washington Capitals, Oct. 9, 1974 - Mar. 26, 1975. 37L-0T.
 * – Does not include neutral site games.

LONGEST NON-SHUTOUT STREAK:
 264 Games —Calgary Flames, Nov. 12, 1981 - Jan. 9, 1985.
 262 Games —Los Angeles Kings, Mar. 15, 1986 - Oct. 25, 1989.
 244 Games —Washington Capitals, Oct. 31, 1989 - Nov. 11, 1993.
 230 Games —Quebec Nordiques, Feb. 10, 1980 - Jan. 13, 1983.
 229 Games —Edmonton Oilers, Mar. 15, 1981 - Feb. 11, 1984.

LONGEST NON-SHUTOUT STREAK INCLUDING PLAYOFFS:
 264 Games —Los Angeles Kings, Mar. 15 1986 - Apr. 6, 1989.
   (5 playoff games in 1987; 5 in 1988; 2 in 1989)
 262 Games —Chicago Blackhawks, Mar. 14, 1970 - Feb. 21, 1973. (8 playoff
   games in 1970; 18 in 1971; 8 in 1972.)
 251 Games —Quebec Nordiques, Feb. 10, 1980 - Jan. 13, 1983. (5 playoff games
   in 1981; 16 in 1982).
 245 Games —Pittsburgh Penguins, Jan. 7, 1989 - Oct. 26, 1991. (11 playoff games
   in 1989; 23 in 1991).

MOST CONSECUTIVE GAMES SHUT OUT:
 8 —Chicago Blackhawks, 1928-29.

MOST SHUTOUTS, ONE SEASON:
 22 —Montreal Canadiens, 1928-29. All by George Hainsworth. 44GP
 16 —NY Americans, 1928-29. Roy Worters had 13; Flat Walsh 3. 44GP
 15 —Ottawa Senators, 1925-26. All by Alex Connell. 36GP
  —Ottawa Senators, 1927-28. All by Alex Connell. 44GP
  —Boston Bruins, 1927-28. All by Hal Winkler. 44GP
  —Chicago Blackhawks, 1969-70. All by Tony Esposito. 76GP

MOST GOALS, ONE SEASON:
 446 —Edmonton Oilers, 1983-84. 80GP
 426 —Edmonton Oilers, 1985-86. 80GP
 424 —Edmonton Oilers, 1982-83. 80GP
 417 —Edmonton Oilers, 1981-82. 80GP
 401 —Edmonton Oilers, 1984-85. 80GP

HIGHEST GOALS-PER-GAME AVERAGE, ONE SEASON:
 5.58 —Edmonton Oilers, 1983-84. 446G in 80GP.
 5.38 —Montreal Canadiens, 1919-20. 129G in 24GP.
 5.33 —Edmonton Oilers, 1985-86. 426G in 80GP.
 5.30 —Edmonton Oilers, 1982-83. 424G in 80GP.
 5.23 —Montreal Canadiens, 1917-18. 115G in 22GP.

FEWEST GOALS, ONE SEASON:
 33 —Chicago Blackhawks, 1928-29. 44GP
 45 —Montreal Maroons, 1924-25. 30GP
 46 —Pittsburgh Pirates, 1928-29. 44GP

FEWEST GOALS, ONE SEASON (MINIMUM 70-GAME SCHEDULE):
 133 —Chicago Blackhawks, 1953-54. 70GP
 147 —Toronto Maple Leafs, 1954-55. 70GP
  —Boston Bruins, 1955-56. 70GP
 150 —NY Rangers, 1954-55. 70GP

LOWEST GOALS-PER-GAME AVERAGE, ONE SEASON:
 .75 —Chicago Blackhawks, 1928-29. 33G in 44GP.
 1.05 —Pittsburgh Pirates, 1928-29. 46G in 44GP.
 1.20 —NY Americans, 1928-29. 53G in 44GP.

MOST GOALS AGAINST, ONE SEASON:
 446 —Washington Capitals, 1974-75. 80GP
 415 —Detroit Red Wings, 1985-86. 80GP
 414 —San Jose Sharks, 1992-93. 84GP
 407 —Quebec Nordiques, 1989-90. 80GP
 403 —Hartford Whalers, 1982-83. 80GP

HIGHEST GOALS-AGAINST-PER-GAME AVERAGE, ONE SEASON:
 7.38 —Quebec Bulldogs, 1919-20, 177GA vs. in 24GP.
 6.20 —NY Rangers, 1943-44, 310GA vs. in 50GP.
 5.58 —Washington Capitals, 1974-75, 446GA vs. in 80GP.

FEWEST GOALS AGAINST, ONE SEASON:
42 —Ottawa Senators, 1925-26. 36GP
43 —Montreal Canadiens, 1928-29. 44GP
48 —Montreal Canadiens, 1923-24. 24GP
—Montreal Canadiens, 1927-28. 44GP

FEWEST GOALS AGAINST, ONE SEASON (MINIMUM 70-GAME SCHEDULE):
131 —Toronto Maple Leafs, 1953-54. 70GP
—Montreal Canadiens, 1955-56. 70GP
132 —Detroit Red Wings, 1953-54. 70GP
133 —Detroit Red Wings, 1951-52. 70GP
—Detroit Red Wings, 1952-53. 70GP

LOWEST GOALS-AGAINST-PER-GAME AVERAGE, ONE SEASON:
.98 —Montreal Canadiens, 1928-29. 43GA vs. in 44GP.
1.09 —Montreal Canadiens, 1927-28. 48GA vs. in 44GP.
1.17 —Ottawa Senators, 1925-26. 42GA vs. in 36GP.

MOST POWER-PLAY GOALS, ONE SEASON:
119 —Pittsburgh Penguins, 1988-89. 80GP
113 —Detroit Red Wings, 1992-93. 84GP
111 —NY Rangers, 1987-88. 80GP
110 —Pittsburgh Penguins, 1987-88. 80GP
—Winnipeg Jets, 1987-88, 80GP

MOST POWER-PLAY GOALS AGAINST, ONE SEASON:
122 —Chicago Blackhawks, 1988-89. 80GP
120 —Pittsburgh Penguins, 1987-88. 80GP
115 —New Jersey Devils, 1988-89. 80GP
—Ottawa Senators, 1992-93. 84GP
114 —Los Angeles Kings, 1992-93. 84GP
113 —San Jose Sharks, 1992-93. 84GP

MOST SHORTHAND GOALS, ONE SEASON:
36 —Edmonton Oilers, 1983-84. 80GP
28 —Edmonton Oilers, 1986-87. 80GP
27 —Edmonton Oilers, 1985-86. 80GP
—Edmonton Oilers, 1988-89. 80GP

MOST SHORTHAND GOALS AGAINST, ONE SEASON:
22 —Pittsburgh Penguins, 1984-85. 80GP
—Minnesota North Stars, 1991-92. 80GP
21 —Calgary Flames, 1984-85. 80GP
—Pittsburgh Penguins, 1989-90. 80GP
20 —Minnesota North Stars, 1982-83. 80GP
—Quebec Nordiques, 1985-86. 80GP
—Tampa Bay Lightning, 1993-94. 84GP

MOST ASSISTS, ONE SEASON:
737 —Edmonton Oilers, 1985-86. 80GP
736 —Edmonton Oilers, 1983-84. 80GP
706 —Edmonton Oilers, 1981-82. 80GP

FEWEST ASSISTS, ONE SEASON:
45 —NY Rangers, 1926-27. 44GP

FEWEST ASSISTS, ONE SEASON (MINIMUM 70-GAME SCHEDULE):
206 —Chicago Blackhawks, 1953-54. 70GP

MOST SCORING POINTS, ONE SEASON:
1,182 —Edmonton Oilers, 1983-84. 80GP
1,163 —Edmonton Oilers, 1985-86. 80GP
1,123 —Edmonton Oilers, 1981-82. 80GP

MOST 50-OR-MORE-GOAL SCORERS, ONE SEASON:
3 —Edmonton Oilers, 1983-84. Wayne Gretzky, 87; Glenn Anderson, 54; Jari Kurri, 52 80GP.
—Edmonton Oilers, 1985-86. Jari Kurri, 68; Glenn Anderson, 54; Wayne Gretzky, 52. 80GP.
2 —Boston Bruins, 1970-71. Phil Esposito, 76; John Bucyk, 51. 78GP
—Boston Bruins, 1973-74. Phil Esposito, 68; Ken Hodge, 50. 78GP
—Philadelphia Flyers, 1975-76. Reggie Leach, 61; Bill Barber, 50. 80GP
—Pittsburgh Penguins, 1975-76. Pierre Larouche, 53; Jean Pronovost, 52. 80GP
—Montreal Canadiens, 1976-77. Steve Shutt, 60; Guy Lafleur, 56. 80GP
—Los Angeles Kings, 1979-80. Charlie Simmer, 56; Marcel Dionne, 53. 80GP
—Montreal Canadiens, 1979-80. Pierre Larouche, 50; Guy Lafleur, 50. 80GP
—Los Angeles Kings, 1980-81. Marcel Dionne, 58; Charlie Simmer, 56. 80GP
—Edmonton Oilers, 1981-82. Wayne Gretzky, 92; Mark Messier, 50. 80GP
—NY Islanders, 1981-82. Mike Bossy, 64; Bryan Trottier, 50. 80GP
—Edmonton Oilers, 1984-85. Wayne Gretzky, 73; Jari Kurri, 71. 80GP
—Washington Capitals, 1984-85. Bob Carpenter, 53; Mike Gartner, 50. 80GP
—Edmonton Oilers, 1986-87. Wayne Gretzky, 62; Jari Kurri, 54. 80GP
—Calgary Flames, 1987-88. Joe Nieuwendyk, 51; Hakan Loob, 50. 80GP
—Los Angeles Kings, 1987-88. Jimmy Carson, 55; Luc Robitaille, 53. 80GP
—Los Angeles Kings, 1988-89. Bernie Nicholls, 70; Wayne Gretzky, 54. 80GP
—Calgary Flames, 1988-89. Joe Nieuwendyk, 51; Joe Mullen, 51. 80GP
—Buffalo Sabres, 1992-93. Alexander Mogilny, 76; Pat Lafontaine, 53. 84GP
—Pittsburgh Penguins, 1992-93. Mario Lemieux, 69; Kevin Stevens, 55. 84GP
—St. Louis Blues, 1992-93. Brett Hull, 54; Brendan Shanahan, 51. 84GP
—St. Louis Blues, 1993-94. Brett Hull, 57; Brendan Shanahan, 52. 84GP
—Detroit Red Wings, 1993-94. Sergei Fedorov, 56; Ray Sheppard, 52. 84GP

MOST 40-OR-MORE-GOAL SCORERS, ONE SEASON:
4 —Edmonton Oilers, 1982-83. Wayne Gretzky, 71; Glenn Anderson, 48; Mark Messier, 48; Jari Kurri, 45. 80GP
—Edmonton Oilers, 1983-84. Wayne Gretzky, 87; Glenn Anderson, 54; Jari Kurri, 52; Paul Coffey, 40. 80GP
—Edmonton Oilers, 1984-85. Wayne Gretzky, 73; Jari Kurri, 71; Mike Krushelnyski, 43; Glenn Anderson, 42. 80GP
—Edmonton Oilers, 1985-86. Jari Kurri, 68; Glenn Anderson, 54; Wayne Gretzky, 52; Paul Coffey, 48. 80GP
—Calgary Flames, 1987-88. Joe Nieuwendyk, 51; Hakan Loob, 50; Mike Bullard, 48; Joe Mullen, 40. 80GP
3 —Boston Bruins, 1970-71. Phil Esposito, 76; John Bucyk, 51; Ken Hodge, 43. 78GP
—NY Rangers, 1971-72. Vic Hadfield, 50; Jean Ratelle, 46; Rod Gilbert, 43. 78GP
—Buffalo Sabres, 1975-76. Danny Gare, 50; Rick Martin, 49; Gilbert Perreault, 44. 80GP
—Montreal Canadiens, 1979-80. Guy Lafleur, 50; Pierre Larouche, 50; Steve Shutt, 47. 80GP
—Buffalo Sabres, 1979-80. Danny Gare, 56; Rick Martin, 45; Gilbert Perreault, 40. 80GP
—Los Angeles Kings, 1980-81. Marcel Dionne, 58; Charlie Simmer, 56; Dave Taylor, 47. 80GP
—Los Angeles Kings, 1984-85. Marcel Dionne, 46; Bernie Nicholls, 46; Dave Taylor, 41. 80GP
—NY Islanders, 1984-85. Mike Bossy, 58; Brent Sutter, 42; John Tonelli; 42. 80GP
—Chicago Blackhawks, 1985-86. Denis Savard, 47; Troy Murray, 45; Al Secord, 40. 80GP
—Chicago Blackhawks, 1987-88. Denis Savard, 44; Rick Vaive, 43; Steve Larmer, 41. 80GP
—Edmonton Oilers, 1987-88. Craig Simpson, 43; Jari Kurri, 43; Wayne Gretzky, 40. 80GP
—Los Angeles Kings, 1988-89. Bernie Nicholls, 70; Wayne Gretzky 54; Luc Robitaille, 46. 80GP
—Los Angeles Kings, 1990-91. Luc Robitaille, 45; Tomas Sandstrom, 45; Wayne Gretzky 41. 80GP
—Pittsburgh Penguins, 1991-92. Kevin Stevens, 54; Mario Lemieux, 44; Joe Mullen, 42. 80GP
—Pittsburgh Penguins, 1992-93. Mario Lemieux, 69; Kevin Stevens, 55; Rick Tocchet, 48. 84GP
—Calgary Flames, 1993-94. Gary Roberts, 41; Robert Reichel, 40; Theoren Fleury, 40. 84GP

Bob Pulford (20) and Jim Neilson (15) battle for possession of a rebound in the Rangers' crease as Ed Giacomin attempts to poke the puck away from the onrushing Leaf forwards.

MOST 30-OR-MORE GOAL SCORERS, ONE SEASON:
6 —**Buffalo Sabres,** 1974-75. Rick Martin, 52; Rene Robert, 40; Gilbert
    Perreault, 39; Don Luce, 33; Rick Dudley, Danny Gare, 31 each. 80GP.
  —**NY Islanders,** 1977-78, Mike Bossy, 53; Bryan Trottier, 46; Clark Gillies, 35;
    Denis Potvin, Bob Nystrom, Bob Bourne, 30 each. 80GP.
  —**Winnipeg Jets,** 1984-85. Dale Hawerchuk, 53; Paul MacLean, 41; Laurie
    Boschman, 32; Brian Mullen, 32; Doug Smail, 31; Thomas Steen, 30. 80GP.
5 —Chicago Blackhawks, 1968-69. 76GP.
  —Boston Bruins, 1970-71. 78GP.
  —Montreal Canadiens, 1971-72. 78GP.
  —Philadelphia Flyers, 1972-73. 78GP.
  —Boston Bruins, 1973-74. 78GP.
  —Montreal Canadiens, 1974-75. 80GP.
  —Montreal Canadiens, 1975-76. 80GP.
  —Pittsburgh Penguins, 1975-76. 80GP.
  —NY Islanders, 1978-79. 80GP.
  —Detroit Red Wings, 1979-80. 80GP.
  —Philadelphia Flyers, 1979-80. 80GP.
  —NY Islanders, 1980-81. 80GP.
  —St. Louis Blues, 1980-81. 80GP.
  —Chicago Blackhawks, 1981-82. 80GP.
  —Edmonton Oilers, 1981-82. 80GP.
  —Montreal Canadiens, 1981-82. 80GP.
  —Quebec Nordiques, 1981-82. 80GP.
  —Washington Capitals, 1981-82. 80GP.
  —Edmonton Oilers, 1982-83. 80GP.
  —Edmonton Oilers, 1983-84. 80GP.
  —Edmonton Oilers, 1984-85. 80GP.
  —Los Angeles Kings, 1984-85. 80GP.
  —Edmonton Oilers, 1985-86. 80GP.
  —Edmonton Oilers, 1986-87. 80GP.
  —Edmonton Oilers, 1987-88. 80GP.
  —Edmonton Oilers, 1988-89. 80GP.
  —Detroit Red Wings, 1991-92. 80GP.
  —NY Rangers, 1991-92. 80GP.
  —Pittsburgh Penguins, 1991-92. 80GP.
  —Detroit Red Wings, 1992-93. 84GP.
  —Pittsburgh Penguins, 1992-93. 84GP.

MOST 20-OR-MORE GOAL SCORERS, ONE SEASON:
11 —**Boston Bruins,** 1977-78; Peter McNab, 41; Terry O'Reilly, 29; Bobby
    Schmautz, Stan Jonathan, 27 each; Jean Ratelle, Rick Middleton, 25 each;
    Wayne Cashman, 24; Gregg Sheppard, 23; Brad Park, 22; Don Marcotte,
    Bob Miller, 20 each. 80GP.
10 —Boston Bruins, 1970-71. 78GP.
  —Montreal Canadiens, 1974-75. 80GP.
  —St. Louis Blues, 1980-81. 80GP.

MOST 100 OR-MORE-POINT SCORERS, ONE SEASON:
4 —**Boston Bruins,** 1970-71, Phil Esposito, 76G-76A-152PTS; Bobby Orr,
    37G-102A-139PTS; John Bucyk, 51G-65A-116PTS; Ken Hodge,
    43G-62A-105PTS. 78GP.
  —**Edmonton Oilers,** 1982-83, Wayne Gretzky, 71G-125A-196PTS; Mark
    Messier, 48G-58A-106PTS; Glenn Anderson, 48G-56A-104PTS; Jari Kurri,
    45G-59A-104PTS. 80GP.
  —**Edmonton Oilers,** 1983-84, Wayne Gretzky, 87G-118A-205PTS; Paul Coffey,
    40G-86A-126PTS; Jari Kurri, 52G-61A-113PTS; Mark Messier, 37G-64A-101PTS.
    80GP.
  —**Edmonton Oilers,** 1985-86, Wayne Gretzky, 52G-163A-215PTS; Paul Coffey,
    48G-90A-138PTS; Jari Kurri, 68G-63A-131PTS; Glenn Anderson, 54G-48A-102PTS.
    80GP.
  —**Pittsburgh Penguins,** 1992-93, Mario Lemieux, 69G-91A-160PTS; Kevin
    Stevens, 55G-56A-111PTS; Rick Tocchet, 48G-61A-109PTS; Ron Francis,
    24G-76A-100PTS. 84GP.
3 —Boston Bruins, 1973-74, Phil Esposito, 68G-77A-145PTS; Bobby Orr,
    32G-90A-122PTS; Ken Hodge, 50G-55A-105PTS. 78GP.
  —NY Islanders, 1978-79, Bryan Trottier, 47G-87A-134PTS; Mike Bossy,
    69G-57A-126PTS; Denis Potvin, 31G-70A-101PTS. 80GP.
  —Los Angeles Kings, 1980-81, Marcel Dionne, 58G-77A-135PTS; Dave Taylor, 47
    G-65A-112PTS; Charlie Simmer, 56G-49A-105PTS. 80GP.
  —Edmonton Oilers, 1984-85, Wayne Gretzky, 73G-135A-208PTS; Jari Kurri,
    71G-64A-135PTS; Paul Coffey, 37G-84A-121PTS. 80GP.
  —NY Islanders, 1984-85. Mike Bossy, 58G-59A-117PTS; Brent Sutter,
    42G-60A-102PTS; John Tonelli, 42G-58A-100PTS. 80GP.
  —Edmonton Oilers, 1986-87, Wayne Gretzky, 62G-121A-183PTS; Jari Kurri,
    54G-54A-108PTS; Mark Messier, 37G-70A-107PTS. 80GP.
  —Pittsburgh Penguins, 1988-89, Mario Lemieux, 85G-114A-199PTS; Rob Brown,
    49G-66A-115PTS; Paul Coffey, 30G-83A-113PTS. 80GP.

MOST PENALTY MINUTES, ONE SEASON:
2,713 —**Buffalo Sabres,** 1991-92. 80GP.
2,670 —Pittsburgh Penguins, 1988-89. 80GP.
2,663 —Chicago Blackhawks, 1991-92. 80GP.
2,643 —Calgary Flames, 1991-92. 80GP.
2,621 —Philadelphia Flyers, 1980-81. 80GP.

MOST GOALS, BOTH TEAMS, ONE GAME:
21 —**Montreal Canadiens, Toronto St. Patricks,** at Montreal, Jan. 10, 1920.
    Montreal won 14-7.
  —**Edmonton Oilers, Chicago Blackhawks,** at Chicago, Dec. 11, 1985.
    Edmonton won 12-9.
20 —Edmonton Oilers, Minnesota North Stars, at Edmonton, Jan. 4, 1984.
    Edmonton won 12-8.
  —Toronto Maple Leafs, Edmonton Oilers, at Toronto, Jan. 8, 1986. Toronto
    won 11-9.
19 —Montreal Wanderers, Toronto Arenas, at Montreal, Dec. 19, 1917. Montreal
    won 10-9.
  —Montreal Canadiens, Quebec Bulldogs, at Quebec, Mar. 3, 1920, Montreal
    won 16-3.
  —Montreal Canadiens, Hamilton Tigers, at Montreal, Feb. 26, 1921. Montreal
    won 13-6.
  —Boston Bruins, NY Rangers, at Boston, Mar. 4, 1944, Boston won 10-9.
  —Boston Bruins, Detroit Red Wings, at Detroit, Mar. 16, 1944. Detroit won
    10-9.
  —Vancouver Canucks, Minnesota North Stars, at Vancouver, Oct. 7, 1983.
    Vancouver won 10-9.

MOST GOALS, ONE TEAM, ONE GAME:
16 —**Montreal Canadiens,** Mar. 3, 1920, at Quebec. Defeated Quebec Bulldogs
    16-3.

MOST CONSECUTIVE GOALS, ONE TEAM, ONE GAME:
15 —**Detroit Red Wings,** Jan. 23, 1944, at Detroit. Defeated NY Rangers 15-0.

MOST POINTS, BOTH TEAMS, ONE GAME:
62 —**Edmonton Oilers, Chicago Blackhawks,** at Chicago, Dec. 11, 1985.
    Edmonton won 12-9. Edmonton had 24A, Chicago, 17.
53 —Quebec Nordiques, Washington Capitals, at Washington, Feb. 22, 1981.
    Quebec won 11-7. Quebec had 22A, Washington, 13.
  —Edmonton Oilers, Minnesota North Stars, at Edmonton, Jan. 4, 1984.
    Edmonton won 12-8. Edmonton had 20A, Minnesota 13.
  —Minnesota North Stars, St. Louis Blues, at St. Louis, Jan. 27, 1984. Minnesota
    won 10-8. Minnesota had 19A, St. Louis 16.
  —Toronto Maple Leafs, Edmonton Oilers, at Toronto, Jan. 8, 1986. Toronto
    won 11-9. Toronto had 17A, Edmonton 16.
52 —Mtl. Maroons, NY Americans, at New York, Feb. 18, 1936. 8-8 tie. New York
    had 20A, Montreal 16. (3A allowed for each goal.)
  —Vancouver Canucks, Minnesota North Stars, at Vancouver, Oct. 7, 1983.
    Vancouver won 10-9. Vancouver had 16A, Minnesota 17.

On February 16, 1952, Montreal's
Elmer Lach recorded career point
#549 to pass Bill Cowley and become
the NHL's all-time leading scorer.

MOST POINTS, ONE TEAM, ONE GAME:

40 — Buffalo Sabres, Dec. 21, 1975, at Buffalo. Buffalo defeated Washington 14-2, receiving 26A.

39 — Minnesota North Stars, Nov. 11, 1981, at Minnesota. Minnesota defeated Winnipeg 15-2, receiving 24A.

37 — Detroit Red Wings, Jan. 23, 1944, at Detroit. Detroit defeated NY Rangers 15-0, receiving 22A.
— Toronto Maple Leafs, Mar. 16, 1957, at Toronto. Toronto defeated NY Rangers 14-1, receiving 23A.
— Buffalo Sabres, Feb. 25, 1978, at Cleveland. Buffalo defeated Cleveland 13-3, receiving 24A.
— Calgary Flames, Feb. 10, 1993, at Calgary. Calgary defeated San Jose 13-1, receiving 24A.

MOST SHOTS, BOTH TEAMS, ONE GAME:

141 — **NY Americans, Pittsburgh Pirates,** Dec. 26, 1925, at New York. NY Americans, who won game 3-1, had 73 shots; Pit. Pirates, 68 shots.

MOST SHOTS, ONE TEAM, ONE GAME:

83 — **Boston Bruins,** March 4, 1941, at Boston. Boston defeated Chicago 3-2.

73 — NY Americans, Dec. 26, 1925, at New York. NY Americans defeated Pit. Pirates 3-1.
— Boston Bruins, March 21, 1991, at Boston. Boston tied Quebec 3-3.

72 — Boston Bruins, Dec. 10, 1970, at Boston. Boston defeated Buffalo 8-2.

MOST PENALTIES, BOTH TEAMS, ONE GAME:

85 Penalties — **Edmonton Oilers (44), Los Angeles Kings (41)** at Los Angeles, Feb. 28, 1990. Edmonton received 26 minors, 7 majors, 6 10-minute misconducts, 4 game misconducts and 1 match penalty; Los Angeles received 26 minors, 9 majors, 3 10-minute misconducts and 3 game misconducts.

MOST PENALTY MINUTES, BOTH TEAMS, ONE GAME:

406 Minutes — **Minnesota North Stars, Boston Bruins** at Boston, Feb. 26, 1981. Minnesota received 18 minors, 13 majors, 4 10-minute misconducts and 7 game misconducts; a total of 211PIM. Boston received 20 minors, 13 majors, 3 10-minute misconducts and six game misconducts; a total of 195PIM.

MOST PENALTIES, ONE TEAM, ONE GAME:

44 — **Edmonton Oilers**, Feb. 28, 1990, at Los Angeles. Edmonton received 26 minors, 7 majors, 6 10-minute misconducts, 4 game misconducts and 1 match penalty.

42 — Minnesota North Stars, Feb. 26, 1981, at Boston. Minnesota received 18 minors, 13 majors, 4 10-minute misconducts and 7 game misconducts.
— Boston Bruins, Feb. 26, 1981, at Boston vs. Minnesota. Boston received 20 minors, 13 majors, 3 10-minute misconducts and 7 game misconducts.

MOST PENALTY MINUTES, ONE TEAM, ONE GAME:

211 — **Minnesota North Stars**, Feb. 26, 1981, at Boston. Minnesota received 18 minors, 13 majors, 4 10-minute misconducts and 7 game misconducts.

MOST GOALS, BOTH TEAMS, ONE PERIOD:

12 — **Buffalo Sabres, Toronto Maple Leafs,** at Buffalo, March 19, 1981, second period. Buffalo scored 9 goals, Toronto 3. Buffalo won 14-4.
— **Edmonton Oilers, Chicago Blackhawks,** at Chicago, Dec. 11, 1985, second period. Edmonton scored 6 goals, Chicago 6. Edmonton won 12-9.

10 — NY Rangers, NY Americans, at NY Americans, March 16, 1939, third period. NY Rangers scored 7 goals, NY Americans 3. NY Rangers won 11-5.
— Toronto Maple Leafs, Detroit Red Wings, at Detroit, March 17, 1946, third period. Toronto scored 6 goals, Detroit 4. Toronto won 11-7.
— Vancouver Canucks, Buffalo Sabres, at Buffalo, Jan. 8, 1976, third period. Buffalo scored 6 goals, Vancouver 4. Buffalo won 8-5.
— Buffalo Sabres, Montreal Canadiens, at Montreal, Oct. 26, 1982, first period. Montreal scored 5 goals, Buffalo 5. 7-7 tie.
— Boston Bruins, Quebec Nordiques, at Quebec, Dec. 7, 1982, second period. Quebec scored 6 goals, Boston 4. Quebec won 10-5.
— Calgary Flames, Vancouver Canucks, at Vancouver, Jan. 16, 1987, first period. Vancouver scored 6 goals, Calgary 4. Vancouver won 9-5.
— Winnipeg Jets, Detroit Red Wings, at Detroit, Nov. 25, 1987, third period. Detroit scored 7 goals, Winnipeg 3. Detroit won 10-8.
— Chicago Blackhawks, St. Louis Blues, at St. Louis, March 15, 1988, third period. Chicago scored 5 goals, St. Louis 5. 7-7 tie.

MOST GOALS, ONE TEAM, ONE PERIOD:

9 — **Buffalo Sabres,** March 19, 1981, at Buffalo, second period during 14-4 win over Toronto.

8 — Detroit Red Wings, Jan. 23, 1944, at Detroit, third period during 15-0 win over NY Rangers.
— Boston Bruins, March 16, 1969, at Boston, second period during 11-3 win over Toronto.
— NY Rangers, Nov. 21, 1971, at New York, third period during 12-1 win over California.
— Philadelphia Flyers, March 31, 1973, at Philadelphia, second period during 10-2 win over NY Islanders.
— Buffalo Sabres, Dec. 21, 1975, at Buffalo, third period during 14-2 win over Washington.
— Minnesota North Stars, Nov. 11, 1981, at Minnesota, second period during 15-2 win over Winnipeg.
— Pittsburgh Penguins, Dec. 17, 1991, at Pittsburgh, second period during 10-2 win over San Jose.

MOST POINTS, BOTH TEAMS, ONE PERIOD:

35 — **Edmonton, Oilers, Chicago Blackhawks,** at Chicago, Dec. 11, 1985, second period. Edmonton had 6G, 12A; Chicago, 6G, 11A. Edmonton won 12-9.

31 — Buffalo Sabres, Toronto Maple Leafs, at Buffalo, March 19, 1981, second period. Buffalo had 9G, 14A; Toronto, 3G, 5A. Buffalo won 14-4.

29 — Winnipeg Jets, Detroit Red Wings, at Detroit, Nov. 25, 1987, third period. Detroit had 7G, 13A; Winnipeg had 3G, 6A. Detroit won 10-8.
— Chicago Blackhawks, St. Louis Blues, at St. Louis, March 15, 1988, third period. St. Louis had 5G, 10A; Chicago had 5G, 9A. 7-7 tie.

Andrew McBain was one of three Winnipeg Jets to score at least 20 powerplay goals during the 1987-88 season. McBain and Dale Hawerchuk notched 20 powerplay markers each, while Paul MacLean connected 22 times with the man advantage.

Lee Fogolin recorded a goal and an assist in Edmonton's 12-9 victory over Chicago on December 11, 1985, a wild shootout that saw the two teams combine for an NHL record 62 scoring points.

MOST POINTS, ONE TEAM, ONE PERIOD:

23 —NY Rangers, Nov. 21, 1971, at New York, third period during 12-1 win over California. NY Rangers scored 8g and 15a.

—Buffalo Sabres, Dec. 21, 1975, at Buffalo, third period during 14-2 win over Washington. Buffalo scored 8g and 15a.

—Buffalo Sabres, March 19, 1981, at Buffalo, second period, during 14-4 win over Toronto. Buffalo scored 9g and 14a.

22 —Detroit Red Wings, Jan. 23, 1944, at Detroit, third period during 15-0 win over NY Rangers. Detroit scored 8g and 14a.

—Boston Bruins, March 16, 1969, at Boston, second period during 11-3 win over Toronto Maple Leafs. Boston scored 8g and 14a.

—Minnesota North Stars, Nov. 11, 1981, at Minnesota, second period during 15-2 win over Winnipeg. Minnesota scored 8g and 14a.

—Pittsburgh Penguins, Dec. 17, 1991, at Pittsburgh, second period during 10-2 win over San Jose. Pittsburgh scored 8g and 14a.

MOST SHOTS, ONE TEAM, ONE PERIOD:

33 —Boston Bruins, March 4, 1941, at Boston, second period. Boston defeated Chicago 3-2.

MOST PENALTIES, BOTH TEAMS, ONE PERIOD:

67 —Minnesota North Stars, Boston Bruins, at Boston, Feb. 26, 1981, first period. Minnesota received 15 minors, 8 majors, 4 10-minute misconducts and 7 game misconducts, a total of 34 penalties. Boston had 16 minors, 8 majors, 3 10-minute misconducts and 6 game misconducts, a total of 33 penalties.

MOST PENALTY MINUTES, BOTH TEAMS, ONE PERIOD:

372 —Los Angeles Kings, Philadelphia Flyers at Philadelphia, March 11, 1979, first period. Philadelphia received 4 minors, 8 majors, 6 10-minute misconducts and 8 game misconducts for 188 minutes. Los Angeles received 2 minors, 8 majors, 6 10-minute misconducts and 8 game misconducts for 184 minutes.

MOST PENALTIES, ONE TEAM, ONE PERIOD:

34 —Minnesota North Stars, Feb. 26, 1981, at Boston, first period. 15 minors, 8 majors, 4 10-minute misconducts, 7 game misconducts.

MOST PENALTY MINUTES, ONE TEAM, ONE PERIOD:

188 —Philadelphia Flyers, March 11, 1979, at Philadelphia vs. Los Angeles, first period. Flyers received 4 minors, 8 majors, 6 10-minute misconducts and 8 game misconducts.

FASTEST SIX GOALS, BOTH TEAMS

3 Minutes, 15 Seconds — Montreal Canadiens, Toronto Maple Leafs, at Montreal, Jan. 4, 1944, first period. Montreal scored 4G, Toronto 2. Montreal won 6-3.

FASTEST FIVE GOALS, BOTH TEAMS:

1 Minute, 24 Seconds — Chicago Blackhawks, Toronto Maple Leafs, at Toronto, Oct. 15, 1983, second period. Scorers were: Gaston Gingras, Toronto, 16:49; Denis Savard, Chicago, 17:12; Steve Larmer, Chicago, 17:27; Savard, 17:42; and John Anderson, Toronto, 18:13. Toronto won 10-8.

1 Minute, 39 Seconds — Detroit Red Wings, Toronto Maple Leafs, at Toronto, Nov. 15, 1944, third period. Scorers were: Ted Kennedy, Toronto, 10:36 and 10:55; Hal Jackson, Detroit, 11:48; Steve Wochy, Detroit, 12:02; Don Grosso, Detroit, 12:15. Detroit won 8-4.

FASTEST FIVE GOALS, ONE TEAM:

2 Minutes, 7 Seconds — Pittsburgh Penguins, at Pittsburgh, Nov. 22, 1972, third period. Scorers: Bryan Hextall, 12:00; Jean Pronovost, 12:18; Al McDonough, 13:40; Ken Schinkel, 13:49; Ron Schock, 14:07. Pittsburgh defeated St. Louis 10-4.

2 Minutes, 37 seconds — NY Islanders, at New York, Jan. 26, 1982, first period. Scorers: Duane Sutter, 1:31; John Tonelli, 2:30; Bryan Trottier, 2:46; Bryan Trottier, 3:31; Duane Sutter, 4:08. NY Islanders defeated Pittsburgh 9-2.

2 Minutes, 55 seconds — Boston Bruins, at Boston, Dec. 19, 1974. Scorers: Bobby Schmautz, 19:13 (first period); Ken Hodge, 0:18; Phil Esposito, 0:43; Don Marcotte, 0:58; John Bucyk, 2:08 (second period). Boston defeated NY Rangers 11-3.

FASTEST FOUR GOALS, BOTH TEAMS:

53 Seconds — Chicago Blackhawks, Toronto Maple Leafs, at Toronto, Oct. 15, 1983, second period. Scorers were: Gaston Gingras, Toronto, 16:49; Denis Savard, Chicago, 17:12; Steve Larmer, Chicago, 17:27; and Savard at 17:42. Toronto won 10-8.

57 Seconds — Quebec Nordiques, Detroit Red Wings, at Quebec, Jan. 27, 1990, first period. Scorers were: Paul Gillis, Quebec, 18:01; Claude Loiselle, Quebec, 18:12; Joe Sakic, Quebec, 18:27; and Jimmy Carson, Detroit, 18:58. Detroit won 8-6.

1 Minute, 1 Second — Colorado Rockies, NY Rangers, at New York, Jan. 15, 1980, first period. Scorers were: Doug Sulliman, NY Rangers, 7:52; Ed Johnstone, NY Rangers, 7:57; Warren Miller, NY Rangers, 8:20; Rob Ramage, Colorado, 8:53. 6-6 tie.

— Chicago Blackhawks, Toronto Maple Leafs, at Toronto, Oct. 15, 1983, second period. Scorers were: Denis Savard, Chicago, 17:12; Steve Larmer, Chicago, 17:27; Savard, 17:42; John Anderson, Toronto, 18:13. Toronto won 10-8.

FASTEST FOUR GOALS, ONE TEAM:

1 Minute, 20 Seconds — Boston Bruins, at Boston, Jan. 21, 1945, second period. Scorers were: Bill Thoms at 6:34; Frank Mario at 7:08 and 7:27; and Ken Smith at 7:54. Boston defeated NY Rangers 14-3.

FASTEST THREE GOALS, BOTH TEAMS:

15 Seconds — Minnesota North Stars, NY Rangers, at Minnesota, Feb. 10, 1983, second period. Scorers were: Mark Pavelich, NY Rangers, 19:18; Ron Greschner, NY Rangers, 19:27; Willi Plett, Minnesota, 19:33. Minnesota won 7-5.

18 Seconds — Montreal Canadiens, NY Rangers, at Montreal, Dec. 12, 1963, first period. Scorers were: Dave Balon, Montreal, 0:58; Gilles Tremblay, Montreal, 1:04; Camille Henry, NY Rangers, 1:16. Montreal won 6-4.

18 Seconds — California Golden Seals, Buffalo Sabres, at California, Feb. 1, 1976, third period. Scorers were: Jim Moxey, California, 19:38; Wayne Merrick, California, 19:45; Danny Gare, Buffalo, 19:56. Buffalo won 9-5.

FASTEST THREE GOALS, ONE TEAM:

20 Seconds — Boston Bruins, at Boston, Feb. 25, 1971, third period. John Bucyk scored at 4:50, Ed Westfall at 5:02 and Ted Green at 5:10. Boston defeated Vancouver 8-3.

21 Seconds — Chicago Blackhawks, at New York, March 23, 1952, third period. Bill Mosienko scored all three goals, at 6:09, 6:20 and 6:30. Chicago defeated NY Rangers 7-6.

21 Seconds — Washington Capitals, at Washington, Nov. 23, 1990, first period. Michal Pivonka scored at 16:18 and Stephen Leach scored at 16:29 and 16:39. Washington defeated Pittsburgh 7-3.

FASTEST THREE GOALS FROM START OF PERIOD, BOTH TEAMS:

1 Minute, 5 seconds — Hartford Whalers, Montreal Canadiens, at Montreal, March 11, 1989, second period. Scorers were: Kevin Dineen, Hartford, 0:11; Guy Carbonneau, Montreal, 0:36; Petr Svoboda, Montreal, 1:05. Montreal won 5-3.

FASTEST THREE GOALS FROM START OF PERIOD, ONE TEAM:

53 Seconds — Calgary Flames, at Calgary, Feb. 10, 1993, third period. Scorers were: Gary Suter at 0:17, Chris Lindbergh at 0:40, Ron Stern at 0:53. Calgary defeated San Jose 13-1.

FASTEST TWO GOALS, BOTH TEAMS:

2 Seconds — St. Louis Blues, Boston Bruins, at Boston, Dec. 19, 1987, third period. Scorers were: Ken Linseman, Boston, at 19:50; Doug Gilmour, St. Louis, at 19:52. St. Louis won 7-5.

3 Seconds — Chicago Blackhawks, Minnesota North Stars, at Minnesota, November 5, 1988, third period. Scorers were: Steve Thomas, Chicago, at 6:03; Dave Gagner, Minnesota, at 6:06. 5-5 tie.

FASTEST TWO GOALS, ONE TEAM:

4 Seconds — Montreal Maroons, at Montreal, Jan. 3, 1931, third period. Nels Stewart scored both goals, at 8:24 and 8:28. Mtl. Maroons defeated Boston 5-3.

— Buffalo Sabres, at Buffalo, Oct. 17, 1974, third period. Scorers were: Lee Fogolin at 14:55 and Don Luce at 14:59. Buffalo defeated California 6-1.

— Toronto Maple Leafs, at Quebec, December 29, 1988, third period. Scorers were: Ed Olczyk at 5:24 and Gary Leeman at 5:28. Toronto defeated Quebec 6-5.

— Calgary Flames, at Quebec, October 17, 1989, third period. Scorers were: Doug Gilmour at 19:45 and Paul Ranheim at 19:49. Calgary and Quebec tied 8-8.

FASTEST TWO GOALS FROM START OF PERIOD, BOTH TEAMS:

14 Seconds — NY Rangers, Quebec Nordiques, at Quebec, Nov. 5, 1983, third period. Scorers were: Andre Savard, Quebec, 0:08; Pierre Larouche, NY Rangers, 0:14. 4-4 tie.

26 Seconds — Buffalo Sabres, St. Louis Blues, at Buffalo, Jan. 3, 1993, third period. Scorers: Alexander Mogilny, Buffalo, 0:08; Philippe Bozon, St. Louis, 0:26. Buffalo won 6-5.

28 Seconds — Boston Bruins, Montreal Canadiens, at Montreal, Oct. 11, 1989, third period. Scorers: Jim Wiemer, Boston 0:10; Tom Chorske, Montreal 0:28. Montreal won 4-2.

FASTEST TWO GOALS FROM START OF GAME, ONE TEAM:

24 Seconds — Edmonton Oilers, March 28, 1982, at Los Angeles. Mark Messier, at 0:14 and Dave Lumley, at 0:24, scored in first period. Edmonton defeated Los Angeles 6-2.

29 Seconds — Pittsburgh Penguins, Dec. 6, 1981, at Pittsburgh. George Ferguson, at 0:17 and Greg Malone, at 0:29, scored in first period. Pittsburgh defeated Chicago 6-4.

32 Seconds — Calgary Flames, March 11, 1987, at Hartford. Doug Risebrough at 0:09, and Colin Patterson, at 0:32, in first period. Calgary defeated Hartford 6-1.

FASTEST TWO GOALS FROM START OF PERIOD, ONE TEAM:

21 Seconds — Chicago Blackhawks, Nov. 5, 1983, at Minnesota, second period. Ken Yaremchuk scored at 0:12 and Darryl Sutter at 0:21. Minnesota defeated Chicago 10-5.

30 Seconds — Washington Capitals, Jan. 27, 1980, at Washington, second period. Mike Gartner at 0:08 and Bengt Gustafsson at 0:30. Washington defeated NY Islanders 7-1.

31 Seconds — Buffalo Sabres, Jan. 10, 1974, at Buffalo, third period. Rene Robert scored at 0:21 and Rick Martin at 0:30. Buffalo defeated NY Rangers 7-2.

— NY Islanders, Feb. 22, 1986, at New York, third period. Roger Kortko scored at 0:10 and Bob Bourne at 0:31. NY Islanders defeated Detroit 5-2.

NHL Individual Scoring Records – History

Six individual scoring records stand as benchmarks in the history of the game: most goals, single-season and career; most assists, single-season and career; and most points, single-season and career. The evoultion of these six records is traced here, beginning with 1917-18, the NHL's first season.

MOST GOALS, ONE SEASON

44 – Joe Malone, Montreal, 1917-18.
Scored goal #44 against Toronto's Harry Holmes on March 2, 1918 and finished season with 44 goals.

50 – Maurice Richard, Montreal, 1944-45.
Scored goal #45 against Toronto's Frank McCool on February 25, 1945 and finished the season with 50 goals.

50 – Bernie Geoffrion, Montreal, 1960-61.
Scored goal #50 against Toronto's Cesare Maniago on March 16, 1961 and finished the season with 50 goals.

50 – Bobby Hull, Chicago, 1961-62.
Scored goal #50 against NY Rangers' Gump Worsley on March 25, 1962 and finished the season with 50 goals.

54 – Bobby Hull, Chicago, 1965-66.
Scored goal #51 against NY Rangers' Cesare Maniago on March 12, 1966 and finished the season with 54 goals.

58 – Bobby Hull, Chicago, 1968-69.
Scored goal #55 against Boston's Gerry Cheevers on March 20, 1969 and finished the season with 58 goals.

76 – Phil Esposito, Boston, 1970-71.
Scored goal #59 against Los Angeles' Denis DeJordy on March 11, 1971 and finished the season with 76 goals.

92 – Wayne Gretzky, Edmonton, 1981-82.
Scored goal #77 against Buffalo's Don Edwards on February 24, 1982 and finished the season with 92 goals.

Using a combination of size, strength and a rapier-like release, Phil Esposito led the NHL's goal-scoring parade for six consecutive seasons.

MOST ASSISTS, ONE SEASON

9 – Newsy Lalonde, Montreal, 1918-19.
14 – Leo Reise Sr., Hamilton, 1921-22.
14 – Punch Broadbent, Ottawa, 1921-22.
15 – Cy Denneny, Ottawa, 1924-25.
18 – Dick Irvin, Chicago, 1926-27.
18 – Howie Morenz, Montreal, 1927-28.
36 – Frank Boucher, NY Rangers, 1929-30.
37 – Joe Primeau, Toronto, 1931-32.
45 – Bill Cowley, Boston, 1940-41.
45 – Bill Cowley, Boston, 1942-43.
49 – Clint Smith, Chicago, 1943-44.
54 – Elmer Lach, Montreal, 1944-45.
55 – Ted Lindsay, Detroit, 1949-50.
56 – Bert Olmstead, Montreal, 1955-56.
58 – Jean Beliveau, Montreal, 1960-61.
58 – Andy Bathgate, NY Rangers/Toronto, 1963-64.
59 – Stan Mikita, Chicago, 1964-65.
62 – Stan Mikita, Chicago, 1966-67.
77 – Phil Esposito, Boston, 1968-69.
87 – Bobby Orr, Boston, 1969-70.
102 – Bobby Orr, Boston, 1970-71.
109 – Wayne Gretzky, Edmonton, 1980-81.
120 – Wayne Gretzky, Edmonton, 1981-82.
125 – Wayne Gretzky, Edmonton, 1982-83.
135 – Wayne Gretzky, Edmonton, 1984-85.
163 – Wayne Gretzky, Edmonton, 1985-86.

Cy Denneny was the first NHL player to reach the 100-goal and 300-point milestones, on-ice achievements that remained in the NHL record book until the 1930s.

Dickie Moore established an NHL single-season scoring record when he notched 96 points for the Montreal Canadiens during the 1958-59 season.

MOST POINTS, ONE SEASON

44 – Joe Malone, Montreal, 1917-18.
48 – Joe Malone, Montreal, 1919-20.
51 – Howie Morenz, Montreal, 1927-28.
73 – Cooney Weiland, Boston, 1929-30.
73 – Doug Bentley, Chicago, 1942-43.
82 – Herb Cain, Boston, 1943-44.
86 – Gordie Howe, Detroit, 1950-51.
95 – Gordie Howe, Detroit, 1952-53.
96 – Dickie Moore, Montreal, 1958-59.
97 – Bobby Hull, Chicago, 1965-66.
97 – Stan Mikita, Chicago, 1966-67.
126 – Phil Esposito, Boston, 1968-69.
152 – Phil Esposito, Boston, 1970-71.
212 – Wayne Gretzky, Edmonton, 1981-82.
215 – Wayne Gretzky, Edmonton, 1985-86.

MOST GOALS, CAREER

44 – Joe Malone, 1917-18, Montreal.
   Malone led the NHL in goals in the league's first season and
   finished with 44 goals in 22 games in 1917-18.

54 – Cy Denneny, 1918-19, Ottawa.
   Denneny passed Malone during the 1918-19 season, finishing the
   year with a two-year total of 54 goals. He held the career goal-
   scoring mark until 1919-20.

146 – Joe Malone, Montreal, Quebec Bulldogs, Hamilton.
   Malone passed Denneny in 1919-20 and remained the NHL's career
   goal-scoring leader until his retirement. He finished with a career
   total of 146 goals.

246 – Cy Denneny, Ottawa, Boston.
   Denneny passed Malone with goal #147 in 1922-23 and remained
   the NHL's career goal-scoring leader until his retirement. He
   finished with a career total of 246 goals.

270 – Howie Morenz, Montreal, NY Rangers, Chicago.
   Morenz passed Denneny with goal #247 in 1933-34 and finished
   his career with 270 goals.

324 – Nels Stewart, Montreal Maroons, Boston, NY Americans.
   Stewart passed Morenz with goal #271 in 1936-37 and remained
   the NHL's career goal-scoring leader until his retirement. He
   finished his career with 324 goals.

544 – Maurice Richard, Montreal.
   Richard passed Nels Stewart with goal #325 on Nov. 8, 1952 and
   remained the NHL's career goal-scoring leader until his retirement.
   He finished his career with 544 goals.

801 – Gordie Howe, Detroit, Hartford.
   Howe passed Richard with goal #545 on Nov. 10, 1963 and
   remained the NHL's career goal-scoring leader until his retirement.
   He finished his career with 801 goals.

814 – Wayne Gretzky, Edmonton, Los Angeles.
   Gretzky passed Gordie Howe with goal #802 on March 23, 1994.
   He is the current career goal-scoring leader with 814.

*The holder of 17 different single-season records,
Wayne Gretzky led the league in goals, assists and
points in six of his first eight years in the league.*

MOST ASSISTS, CAREER (minimum 100 assists)

Note: Assists were not tabulated in 1917-18, the NHL's first season. Newsy
Lalonde of the Canadiens was the NHL's first career (and single-season) assist
leader, recording nine in 1918-19

100 – Frank Boucher, Ottawa, NY Rangers.
   In 1930-31, Boucher became the first NHL player to reach the
   100-assist milestone.

262 – Frank Boucher, Ottawa, NY Rangers.
   Boucher retired as the NHL's career assist leader in 1938 with
   252. He returned to the NHL in 1943-44 and remained the NHL's
   career assist leader until he was overtaken by Bill Cowley in
   1943-44. He finished his career with 262 assists.

353 – Bill Cowley, St. Louis Eagles, Boston.
   Cowley passed Boucher with assist #263 in 1943-44. He retired
   as the NHL's career assist leader in 1947 with 353.

408 – Elmer Lach, Montreal.
   Lach passed Cowley with assist #354 in 1951-52. He retired as
   the NHL's career assist leader in 1953 with 408.

1,049 – Gordie Howe, Detroit, Hartford.
   Howe passed Lach with assist #409 in 1957-58. He retired as the
   NHL's career assist leader in 1980 with 1,049.

1,692 – Wayne Gretzky, Edmonton, Los Angeles.
   Gretzky passed Howe with assist #1,050 in 1988-89. He is the
   current career assist leader with 1,692.

*A two-time winner of the Hart Trophy as the NHL's most
valuable player, Bill Cowley was the third player in
League history to record 500 career points.*

MOST POINTS, CAREER (minimum 100 points)

100 – Joe Malone, Montreal, Quebec Bulldogs, Hamilton.
In 1920-21, Malone became the first player in NHL history to record 100 points.

200 – Cy Denneny, Ottawa.
In 1923-24, Denneny became the first player in NHL history to record 200 points.

300 – Cy Denneny, Ottawa.
In 1926-27, Denneny became the first player in NHL history to record 300 points.

315 – Cy Denneny, Ottawa, Boston.
Denneny retired as the NHL's career point-scoring leader in 1929 with 315 points.

467 – Howie Morenz, Montreal, Chicago, NY Rangers.
Morenz passed Cy Denneny with point #316 in 1931-32. At the time his career ended in 1937, he was the NHL's career point-scoring leader with 467 points.

515 – Nels Stewart, Montreal Maroons, Boston, NY Americans.
Stewart passed Morenz with point #468 in 1938-39. He retired as the NHL's career point-scoring leader in 1940 with 515 points.

528 – Syd Howe, Ottawa, Philadelphia Quakers, Toronto, St. Louis Eagles, Detroit.
Howe passed Nels Stewart with point #516 on March 8, 1945. He retired as the NHL's career point-scoring leader in 1946 with 528 points.

548 – Bill Cowley, St. Louis Eagles, Boston.
Cowley passed Syd Howe with point #529 on Feb. 12, 1947. He retired as the NHL's career point-scoring leader in 1947 with 548 points.

610 – Elmer Lach, Montreal.
Lach passed Bill Cowley with point #549 on Feb. 23, 1952. He remained the NHL's career point-scoring leader until he was overtaken by Maurice Richard in 1953-54. He finished his career with 623 points.

946 – Maurice Richard, Montreal.
Richard passed teammate Elmer Lach with point #611 on Dec. 12, 1953. He remained the NHL's career point-scoring leader until he was overtaken by Gordie Howe in 1959-60. He finished his career with 965 points.

1,850 – Gordie Howe, Detroit, Hartford.
Howe passed Richard with point #947 on Jan. 16, 1960. He retired as the NHL's career point-scoring leader in 1980 with 1,850 points.

2,506 – Wayne Gretzky, Edmonton, Los Angeles.
Gretzky passed Howe with point #1,851 on Oct. 15, 1989. He is the current career point-scoring leader with 2,506.

Gordie Howe, seen here after eclipsing Maurice Richard's career goal-scoring mark on November 10, 1963, still holds or shares seven regular-season and playoff career records.

Individual Records

Career

MOST SEASONS:
26 —Gordie Howe, Detroit, 1946-47 – 1970-71; Hartford, 1979-80.
24 —Alex Delvecchio, Detroit, 1950-51 – 1973-74.
—Tim Horton, Toronto, NY Rangers, Pittsburgh, Buffalo, 1949-50, 1951-52 – 1973-74.
23 —John Bucyk, Detroit, Boston, 1955-56 – 1977-78.
22 —Dean Prentice, NY Rangers, Boston, Detroit, Pittsburgh, Minnesota, 1952-53 – 1973-74.
—Doug Mohns, Boston, Chicago, Minnesota, Atlanta, Washington, 1953-54 – 1974-75.
—Stan Mikita, Chicago, 1958-59 – 1979-80.

MOST GAMES:
1,767 —Gordie Howe, Detroit, 1946-47 – 1970-71; Hartford, 1979-80.
1,549 —Alex Delvecchio, Detroit, 1950-51 – 1973-74.
1,540 —John Bucyk, Detroit, Boston, 1955-56 – 1977-78.

MOST GOALS:
814 —Wayne Gretzky, Edmonton, Los Angeles, in 16 seasons, 1,173GP.
801 —Gordie Howe, Detroit, Hartford, in 26 seasons, 1,767GP.
731 —Marcel Dionne, Detroit, Los Angeles, NY Rangers, in 18 seasons, 1,348GP.
717 —Phil Esposito, Chicago, Boston, NY Rangers, in 18 seasons, 1,282GP.
629 —Mike Gartner, Washington, Minnesota, NY Rangers, Toronto, in 16 seasons, 1,208GP.

HIGHEST GOALS-PER-GAME AVERAGE, CAREER
(AMONG PLAYERS WITH 200 OR MORE GOALS):
.825 —Mario Lemieux, Pittsburgh, 494G, 599GP, from 1984-85 – 1993-94.
.767 —Cy Denneny, Ottawa, Boston, 250G, 326GP, from 1917-18 – 1928-29.
.762 —Mike Bossy, NY Islanders, 573G, 752GP, from 1977-78 – 1986-87.
.752 —Brett Hull, Calgary, St. Louis, 442G, 588GP, from 1986-87 – 1994-95.
.694 —Wayne Gretzky, Edmonton, Los Angeles, 814G, 1,173GP, from 1979-80 – 1994-95.

MOST ASSISTS:
1,692 —Wayne Gretzky, Edmonton, Los Angeles, in 16 seasons, 1,173GP.
1,049 —Gordie Howe, Detroit, Hartford in 26 seasons, 1,767GP.
1,040 —Marcel Dionne, Detroit, Los Angeles, NY Rangers, in 18 seasons, 1,348GP.
978 —Paul Coffey, Edmonton, Pittsburgh, Los Angeles, Detroit, in 15 seasons, 1,078GP.
926 —Stan Mikita, Chicago, in 22 seasons, 1,394GP.

HIGHEST ASSIST-PER-GAME AVERAGE, CAREER
(AMONG PLAYERS WITH 300 OR MORE ASSISTS):
1.442 —Wayne Gretzky, Edmonton, Los Angeles, 1,692A, 1,173GP from 1979-80 – 1994-95.
1.197 —Mario Lemieux, Pittsburgh, 717A, 599GP from 1984-85 – 1993-94.
.982 —Bobby Orr, Boston, Chicago, 645A, 657GP from 1966-67 – 1978-79.
.907 —Paul Coffey, Edmonton, Pittsburgh, Los Angeles, Detroit, 978A, 1,078GP from 1980-81 – 1994-95.
.904 —Adam Oates, Detroit, St. Louis, Boston, 611A, 676GP from 1984-85 – 1994-95.

MOST POINTS:
2,506 —Wayne Gretzky, Edmonton, Los Angeles, in 16 seasons, 1,173GP (814G-1,692A).
1,850 —Gordie Howe, Detroit, Hartford, in 26 seasons, 1,767GP (801G-1049A).
1,771 —Marcel Dionne, Detroit, Los Angeles, NY Rangers, in 18 seasons, 1,348GP (731G-1,040A).
1,590 —Phil Esposito, Chicago, Boston, NY Rangers in 18 seasons, 1,282GP (717G-873A).
1,467 —Stan Mikita, Chicago in 22 seasons, 1,394GP (541G-926A).

HIGHEST POINTS-PER-GAME AVERAGE, CAREER:
(AMONG PLAYERS WITH 500 OR MORE POINTS):
2.136 —Wayne Gretzky, Edmonton, Los Angeles, 2,506PTS (814G-1,692A), 1,173GP from 1979-80 – 1994-95.
2.022 —Mario Lemieux, Pittsburgh, 1,211PTS (494G-717A), 599GP from 1984-85 – 1993-94.
1.497 —Mike Bossy, NY Islanders, 1,126PTS (573G-553A), 752GP from 1978-79 – 1986-87.
1.393 —Bobby Orr, Boston, Chicago, 915PTS (270G-645A), 657GP from 1966-67 – 1978-79.
1.346 —Steve Yzerman, Detroit, 1,160PTS (481G-679A), 862GP from 1983-84 – 1994-95.

MOST GOALS BY A CENTER, CAREER
814 —Wayne Gretzky, Edmonton, Los Angeles, in 16 seasons.
731 —Marcel Dionne, Detroit, Los Angeles, NY Rangers, in 18 seasons
717 —Phil Esposito, Chicago, Boston, NY Rangers, in 18 seasons.
541 —Stan Mikita, Chicago, in 22 seasons.
524 —Bryan Trottier, NY Islanders, Pittsburgh, in 18 seasons.

MOST ASSISTS BY A CENTER, CAREER;
1,692 —Wayne Gretzky, Edmonton, Los Angeles, in 16 seasons.
1,040 —Marcel Dionne, Detroit, Los Angeles, NY Rangers, in 18 seasons.
926 —Stan Mikita, Chicago, in 22 seasons.
901 —Bryan Trottier, NY Islanders, Pittsburgh, in 18 seasons.
877 —Mark Messier, Edmonton, NY Rangers, in 16 seasons.

Stan Mikita, seen here receiving a gift from a representative of the Czechoslovakian National Team on January 4, 1963, ranks fourth on the NHL's all-time scoring register with 1,467 career points.

MOST POINTS BY A CENTER, CAREER:
2,506 —Wayne Gretzky, Edmonton, Los Angeles, in 16 seasons.
1,771 —Marcel Dionne, Detroit, Los Angeles, NY Rangers, in 18 seasons.
1,590 —Phil Esposito, Chicago, Boston, NY Rangers, in 18 seasons.
1,467 —Stan Mikita, Chicago, in 22 seasons
1,425 —Bryan Trottier, NY Islanders, Pittsburgh, in 18 seasons.

MOST GOALS BY A LEFT WING, CAREER:
610 —Bobby Hull, Chicago, Winnipeg, Hartford, in 16 seasons.
556 —John Bucyk, Detroit, Boston, in 23 seasons.
548 —Michel Goulet, Quebec, Chicago, in 15 seasons.
533 —Frank Mahovlich, Toronto, Detroit, Montreal, in 18 seasons.
448 —Dave Andreychuk, Buffalo, Toronto, in 13 seasons.

MOST ASSISTS BY A LEFT WING, CAREER:
813 —John Bucyk, Detroit, Boston, in 23 seasons.
604 —Michel Goulet, Quebec, Chicago, in 15 seasons.
579 —Brian Propp, Philadelphia, Boston, Minnesota, Hartford, in 15 seasons.
570 —Frank Mahovlich, Toronto, Detroit, Montreal, in 18 seasons.
560 —Bobby Hull, Chicago, Winnipeg, Hartford, in 16 seasons.

MOST POINTS BY A LEFT WING, CAREER:
1,369 —John Bucyk, Detroit, Boston, in 23 seasons.
1,170 —Bobby Hull, Chicago, Winnipeg, Hartford, in 16 seasons.
1,152 —Michel Goulet, Quebec, Chicago, in 15 seasons.
1,103 —Frank Mahovlich, Toronto, Detroit, Montreal, in 18 seasons.
1,004 —Brian Propp, Philadelphia, Boston, Minnesota, Hartford, in 15 seasons.

MOST GOALS BY A RIGHT WING, CAREER:
801 —Gordie Howe, Detroit, Hartford, in 26 seasons.
629 —Mike Gartner, Washington, Minnesota, NY Rangers, Toronto, in 16 seasons.
573 —Mike Bossy, NY Islanders, in 10 seasons.
565 —Jari Kurri, Edmonton, Los Angeles, in 14 seasons.
560 —Guy Lafleur, Montreal, NY Rangers, Quebec, in 17 seasons.

MOST ASSISTS BY A RIGHT WING, CAREER:
1,049 —Gordie Howe, Detroit, Hartford, in 26 seasons.
793 —Guy Lafleur, Montreal, NY Rangers, Quebec, in 17 seasons.
731 —Jari Kurri, Edmonton, Los Angeles, in 14 seasons.
638 —Dave Taylor, Los Angeles, in 17 seasons.
624 —Andy Bathgate, NY Rangers, Toronto, Detroit, Pittsburgh in 17 seasons.

MOST POINTS BY A RIGHT WING, CAREER:
1,850 —Gordie Howe, Detroit, Hartford, in 26 seasons.
1,353 —Guy Lafleur, Montreal, NY Rangers, Quebec, in 17 seasons.
1,296 —Jari Kurri, Edmonton, Los Angeles, in 14 seasons.
1,191 —Mike Gartner, Washington, Minnesota, NY Rangers, Toronto, in 16 seasons.

Bob Sweeney (42) is known for saving his best for when it counts the most. Of the 22 game-winning goals he has collected in his nine-year career, a record-tying seven of them have come in overtime.

MOST GOALS BY A DEFENSEMAN, CAREER:
358 — Paul Coffey, Edmonton, Pittsburgh, Los Angeles, Detroit, in 15 seasons.
323 — Ray Bourque, Boston, in 16 seasons.
310 — Denis Potvin, NY Islanders, in 15 seasons.
270 — Bobby Orr, Boston, Chicago, in 12 seasons.
257 — Phil Housley, Buffalo, Winnipeg, St. Louis, Calgary, in 13 seasons.

MOST ASSISTS BY A DEFENSEMAN, CAREER:
978 — Paul Coffey, Edmonton, Pittsburgh, Los Angeles, Detroit, in 15 seasons.
908 — Ray Bourque, Boston, in 16 seasons.
750 — Larry Robinson, Montreal, Los Angeles, in 20 seasons.
742 — Denis Potvin, NY Islanders, in 15 seasons.
712 — Larry Murphy, Los Angeles, Washington, Minnesota, Pittsburgh, in 15 seasons.

MOST POINTS BY A DEFENSEMAN, CAREER:
1,336 — Paul Coffey, Edmonton, Pittsburgh, Los Angeles, Detroit, in 15 seasons.
1,231 — Ray Bourque, Boston, in 16 seasons.
1,052 — Denis Potvin, NY Islanders, in 15 seasons.
958 — Larry Robinson, Montreal, Los Angeles, in 20 seasons.
945 — Larry Murphy, Los Angeles, Washington, Minnesota, Pittsburgh, in 15 seasons.

MOST OVERTIME GOALS, CAREER:
7 — Mario Lemieux, Pittsburgh.
— **Jari Kurri,** Edmonton.
— **Tomas Sandstrom,** NY Rangers, Los Angeles.
— **Bob Sweeney,** Boston, Buffalo.
— **Murray Craven,** Philadelphia, Hartford, Vancouver, Chicago.

MOST OVERTIME ASSISTS, CAREER:
12 — Wayne Gretzky, Edmonton, Los Angeles.
10 — Mario Lemieux, Pittsburgh.
— Mark Messier, Edmonton, NY Rangers.
— Adam Oates, Detroit, St. Louis, Boston.
9 — Bernie Federko, St. Louis.
— Dale Hawerchuk, Winnipeg, Buffalo.
— Doug Gilmour, St. Louis, Calgary, Toronto.

MOST OVERTIME POINTS, CAREER:
17 — Mario Lemieux, Pittsburgh, 7G-10A
15 — Mark Messier, Edmonton, NY Rangers. 5G-10A
14 — Wayne Gretzky, Edmonton, Los Angeles. 2G-12A
13 — Jari Kurri, Edmonton, Los Angeles. 7G-6A
— Paul MacLean, Winnipeg, Detroit, St. Louis. 6G-7A
— Dale Hawerchuk, Winnipeg, Buffalo. 4G-9A

MOST PENALTY MINUTES:
3,966 — Dave Williams, Toronto, Vancouver, Detroit, Los Angeles, Hartford, in 14 seasons, 962GP.
3,106 — Dale Hunter, Quebec, Washington, in 15 seasons, 1,099GP.
3,043 — Chris Nilan, Monteal, NY Rangers, Boston, in 13 seasons, 688GP.
2,889 — Tim Hunter, Calgary, Quebec, Vancouver, in 14 seasons, 709GP.
2,723 — Marty McSorley, Pittsburgh, Edmonton, Los Angeles, in 12 seasons, 707GP.

MOST GAMES, INCLUDING PLAYOFFS:
1,924 — Gordie Howe, Detroit, Hartford, 1,767 regular-season and 157 playoff games.
1,670 — Alex Delvecchio, Detroit, 1,549 regular-season and 121 playoff games.
1,664 — John Bucyk, Detroit, Boston, 1,540 regular-season and 124 playoff games.

MOST GOALS, INCLUDING PLAYOFFS:
924 — Wayne Gretzky, Edmonton, Los Angeles, 814 regular-season and 110 playoff goals.
869 — Gordie Howe, Detroit, Hartford, 801 regular-season goals and 68 playoff goals.
778 — Phil Esposito, Chicago, Boston, NY Rangers, 717 regular-season and 61 playoff goals.
752 — Marcel Dionne, Detroit, Los Angeles, NY Rangers, 731 regular-season and 21 playoff goals.

MOST ASSISTS, INCLUDING PLAYOFFS:
1,928 — Wayne Gretzky, Edmonton, Los Angeles, 1,692 regular-season and 236 playoff assists.
1,141 — Gordie Howe, Detroit, Hartford, 1,049 regular-season and 92 playoff assists.
1,097 — Paul Coffey, Edmonton, Pittsburgh, Los Angeles, Detroit, 978 regular-season and 119 playoff assists.
1,064 — Marcel Dionne, Detroit, Los Angeles, NY Rangers, 1,040 regular-season and 24 playoff assists.
1,047 — Mark Messier, Edmonton, NY Rangers, 877 regular-season and 170 playoff assists.

MOST POINTS, INCLUDING PLAYOFFS:
2,852 — Wayne Gretzky, Edmonton, Los Angeles, 2,506 regular-season and 346 playoff points.
2,010 — Gordie Howe, Detroit, Hartford, 1,850 regular-season and 160 playoff assists.
1,816 — Marcel Dionne, Detroit, Los Angeles, NY Rangers, 1,771 regular-season and 45 playoff points.
1,727 — Phil Esposito, Chicago, Boston, NY Rangers, 1,590 regular-season and 137 playoff points.
1,641 — Mark Messier, Edmonton, NY Rangers, 1,369 regular-season and 272 playoff points.

MOST PENALTY MINUTES, INCLUDING PLAYOFFS:
4,421 — Dave Williams, Toronto, Vancouver, Detroit, Los Angeles, Hartford, 3,966 in regular season; 455 in playoffs.
3,743 — Dale Hunter, Quebec, Washington, 3,106 in regular-season; 637 in playoffs.
3,584 — Chris Nilan, Montreal, NY Rangers, Boston, 3,043 in regular-season; 541 in playoffs.
3,315 — Tim Hunter, Calgary, Quebec, Vancouver, 2,889 regular-season; 426 in playoffs.
3,095 — Marty McSorley, Pittsburgh, Edmonton, Los Angeles, 2,723 in regular-season; 372 in playoffs.

MOST CONSECUTIVE GAMES:
964 — Doug Jarvis, Montreal, Washington, Hartford, from Oct. 8, 1975 – Oct. 10, 1987.
914 — Garry Unger, Toronto, Detroit, St. Louis, Atlanta from Feb. 24, 1968, – Dec. 21, 1979.
884 — Steve Larmer, Chicago, from Oct. 6, 1982 to April 16, 1993.
776 — Craig Ramsay, Buffalo, from March 27, 1973, – Feb. 10, 1983.
630 — Andy Hebenton, NY Rangers, Boston, nine complete 70-game seasons from 1955-56 – 1963-64.

MOST GAMES APPEARED IN BY A GOALTENDER, CAREER:
971 — Terry Sawchuk, Detroit, Boston, Toronto, Los Angeles, NY Rangers from 1949-50 – 1969-70.
906 — Glenn Hall, Detroit, Chicago, St. Louis from 1952-53 – 1970-71.
886 — Tony Esposito, Montreal, Chicago from 1968-69 – 1983-84.
860 — Lorne "Gump" Worsley, NY Rangers, Montreal, Minnesota from 1952-53 – 1973-74.

MOST CONSECUTIVE COMPLETE GAMES BY A GOALTENDER:
502 — Glenn Hall, Detroit, Chicago. Played 502 games from beginning of 1955-56 season - first 12 games of 1962-63. In his 503rd straight game, Nov. 7, 1962, at Chicago, Hall was removed from the game against Boston with a back injury in the first period.

MOST SHUTOUTS BY A GOALTENDER, CAREER:
103 — Terry Sawchuk, Detroit, Boston, Toronto, Los Angeles, NY Rangers in 21 seasons.
94 — George Hainsworth, Montreal Canadiens, Toronto in 10 seasons.
84 — Glenn Hall, Detroit, Chicago, St. Louis in 16 seasons.

MOST THREE-OR-MORE GOAL GAMES, CAREER:
49 — Wayne Gretzky, Edmonton, Los Angeles, in 15 seasons, 36 three-goal games, 9 four-goal games, 4 five-goal games.
39 — Mike Bossy, NY Islanders, in 10 seasons, 30 three-goal games, 9 four-goal games.
32 — Phil Esposito, Chicago, Boston, NY Rangers, in 18 seasons, 27 three-goal games, 5 four-goal games.
31 — Mario Lemieux, Pittsburgh, in 10 seasons, 21 three-goal games, 8 four-goal games and 2 five-goal games.
28 — Bobby Hull, Chicago, Winnipeg, Hartford, in 16 seasons, 24 three-goal games, 4 four-goal games.
— Marcel Dionne, Detroit, Los Angeles, NY Rangers, in 18 seasons, 25 three-goal games, 3 four-goal games.
26 — Cy Denneny, Ottawa in 12 seasons. 20 three-goal games, 5 four-goal games, 1 six-goal game.
— Maurice Richard, Montreal, in 18 seasons, 23 three-goal games, 2 four-goal games, 1 five-goal game.

MOST 20-OR-MORE GOAL SEASONS:
22 — Gordie Howe, Detroit, Hartford in 26 seasons.
17 — Marcel Dionne, Detroit, Los Angeles, NY Rangers, in 18 seasons.
16 — Phil Esposito, Chicago, Boston, NY Rangers, in 18 seasons.
— Norm Ullman, Detroit, Toronto, in 19 seasons.
— John Bucyk, Detroit, Boston, in 22 seasons.
15 — Frank Mahovlich, Toronto, Detroit, Montreal in 17 seasons.
— Gilbert Perreault, Buffalo, in 17 seasons.
— Mike Gartner, Washington, Minnesota, NY Rangers, Toronto, in 16 seasons.

MOST CONSECUTIVE 20-OR-MORE GOAL SEASONS:
22 — Gordie Howe, Detroit, 1949-50 – 1970-71.
17 — Marcel Dionne, Detroit, Los Angeles, NY Rangers, 1971-72 – 1987-88.
16 — Phil Esposito, Chicago, Boston, NY Rangers, 1964-65 – 1979-80.
15 — Mike Gartner, Washington, Minnesota, NY Rangers, Toronto, 1979-80 – 1993-94.
14 — Maurice Richard, Montreal, 1943-44 – 1956-57.
— Stan Mikita, Chicago, 1961-62 – 1974-75.
— Michel Goulet, Quebec, Chicago, 1979-80 – 1992-93.
13 — Bobby Hull, Chicago, 1959-60 – 1971-72.
— Guy Lafleur, Montreal, 1971-72 – 1983-84.
— Bryan Trottier, NY Islanders, 1975-76 – 1987-88.
— Wayne Gretzky, Edmonton, Los Angeles, 1979-80 – 1991-92.
— Ron Francis, Hartford, Pittsburgh, 1981-82 – 1993-94.

MOST 30-OR-MORE GOAL SEASONS:
15 — Mike Gartner, Washington, Minnesota, NY Rangers, Toronto in 16 seasons.
14 — Gordie Howe, Detroit, Hartford in 26 seasons.
— Marcel Dionne, Detroit, Los Angeles, NY Rangers in 18 seasons.
— Wayne Gretzky, Edmonton, Los Angeles in 16 seasons.
13 — Bobby Hull, Chicago, Winnipeg, Hartford in 16 seasons.
— Phil Esposito, Chicago, Boston, NY Rangers in 18 seasons.

Leaf coach Punch Imlach shows star forward Frank Mahovlich a "hat trick" during one of Mahovlich's fifteen 20-goal seasons.

MOST CONSECUTIVE 30-OR-MORE GOAL SEASONS:
15 — Mike Gartner, Washington, Minnesota, NY Rangers, Toronto, 1979-80 – 1993-94.
13 — Bobby Hull, Chicago, 1959-60 – 1971-72.
— Phil Esposito, Boston, NY Rangers, 1967-68 – 1979-80.
— Wayne Gretzky, Edmonton, Los Angeles, 1979-80 – 1991-92.
12 — Marcel Dionne, Detroit, Los Angeles, 1974-75 – 1985-86.
10 — Darryl Sittler, Toronto, Philadelphia, 1973-74 – 1982-83.
— Mike Bossy, NY Islanders, 1977-78 – 1986-87.
— Jari Kurri, Edmonton, 1980-81 – 1989-90.

MOST 40-OR-MORE GOAL SEASONS:
12 — Wayne Gretzky, Edmonton, Los Angeles, in 16 seasons.
10 — Marcel Dionne, Detroit, Los Angeles, NY Rangers, in 18 seasons.
9 — Mike Bossy, NY Islanders, in 10 seasons.
— Mike Gartner, Washington, Minnesota, NY Rangers, Toronto, in 16 seasons.
8 — Bobby Hull, Chicago, Winnipeg, Hartford, in 16 seasons.
— Phil Esposito, Chicago, Boston, NY Rangers, in 18 seasons.
— Jari Kurri, Edmonton, Los Angeles, in 14 seasons.
— Luc Robitaille, Los Angeles, Pittsburgh, in 9 seasons.

MOST CONSECUTIVE 40-OR-MORE GOAL SEASONS:
12 — Wayne Gretzky, Edmonton, Los Angeles, 1979-80 – 1990-91.
9 — Mike Bossy, NY Islanders, 1977-78 – 1985-86.
8 — Luc Robitaille, Los Angeles, 1986-87 – 1993-94.
7 — Phil Esposito, Boston, 1968-69 – 1974-75.
— Michel Goulet, Quebec, 1981-82 – 1987-88.
— Jari Kurri, Edmonton, 1982-83 – 1988-89.
6 — Guy Lafleur, Montreal, 1974-75 – 1979-80.
— Joe Mullen, St. Louis, Calgary, 1983-84 – 1988-89.
— Mario Lemieux, Pittsburgh, 1984-85 – 1989-90.
— Steve Yzerman, Detroit, 1987-88 – 1992-93.
— Brett Hull, St. Louis, 1988-89 – 1993-94.

MOST 50-OR-MORE GOAL SEASONS:
9 — Mike Bossy, NY Islanders, in 10 seasons.
— Wayne Gretzky, Edmonton, Los Angeles, in 16 seasons.
6 — Guy Lafleur, Montreal, NY Rangers, Quebec, in 17 seasons.
— Marcel Dionne, Detroit, Los Angeles, NY Rangers, in 18 seasons.
5 — Bobby Hull, Chicago, Winnipeg, Hartford, in 16 seasons.
— Phil Esposito, Chicago, Boston, NY Rangers, in 18 seasons.
— Brett Hull, Calgary, St. Louis, in 9 seasons.

MOST CONSECUTIVE 50-OR-MORE GOAL SEASONS:
9 — Mike Bossy, NY Islanders, 1977-78 – 1985-86.
8 — Wayne Gretzky, Edmonton, 1979-80 – 1986-87.
6 — Guy Lafleur, Montreal, 1974-75 – 1979-80.
5 — Phil Esposito, Boston, 1970-71 – 1974-75.
— Marcel Dionne, Los Angeles, 1978-79 – 1982-83.
— Brett Hull, St. Louis, 1989-90 – 1993-94.

MOST 60-OR-MORE GOAL SEASONS:
5 — Mike Bossy, NY Islanders, in 10 seasons.
— Wayne Gretzky, Edmonton, Los Angeles, in 16 seasons.
4 — Phil Esposito, Chicago, Boston, NY Rangers, in 18 seasons.

MOST CONSECUTIVE 60-OR-MORE GOAL SEASONS:
4 — Wayne Gretzky, Edmonton, 1981-82 – 1984-85.
3 — Mike Bossy, NY Islanders, 1980-81 – 1982-83.
— Brett Hull, St. Louis, 1989-90 – 1991-92.
2 — Phil Esposito, Boston, 1970-71 – 1971-72, 1973-74 – 1974-75.
— Jari Kurri, Edmonton, 1984-85 – 1985-86.
— Mario Lemieux, Pittsburgh, 1987-88 – 1988-89.
— Steve Yzerman, Detroit, 1988-89 – 1989-90.
— Pavel Bure, Vancouver, 1992-93 – 1993-94.

MOST 100-OR-MORE POINT SEASONS:
14 — Wayne Gretzky, Edmonton, Los Angeles, 1979-80 – 1991-92; 1993-94.
 8 — Marcel Dionne, Detroit, 1974-75; Los Angeles, 1976-77; 1978-79 – 1982-83; 1984-85.
  — Mario Lemieux, Pittsburgh, 1984-85 – 1989-90; 1991-92; 1992-93.
 7 — Mike Bossy, NY Islanders, 1978-79; 1980-81 – 1985-86.
  — Peter Stastny, Quebec, 1980-81 – 1985-86; 1987-88.
 6 — Phil Esposito, Boston, 1968-69; 1970-71 – 1974-75.
  — Bobby Orr, Boston, 1969-70 – 1974-75.
  — Guy Lafleur, Montreal, 1974-75 – 1979-80.
  — Bryan Trottier, NY Islanders, 1977-78 – 1981-82; 1983-84.
  — Dale Hawerchuk, Winnipeg, 1981-82; 1983-84 – 1987-88.
  — Jari Kurri, Edmonton, 1982-83 – 1986-87; 1988-89.
  — Mark Messier, Edmonton, 1982-83 – 1983-84; 1986-87 – 1987-88; 1989-90; NY Rangers, 1991-92.
  — Steve Yzerman, Detroit, 1987-88 – 1992-93.

MOST CONSECUTIVE 100-OR-MORE POINT SEASONS:
13 — Wayne Gretzky, Edmonton, Los Angeles, 1979-80 – 1991-92.
 6 — Bobby Orr, Boston, 1969-70 – 1974-75.
  — Guy Lafleur, Montreal, 1974-75 – 1979-80.
  — Mike Bossy, NY Islanders, 1980-81 – 1985-86.
  — Peter Stastny, Quebec, 1980-81 – 1985-86.
  — Mario Lemieux, Pittsburgh, 1984-85 – 1989-90.
  — Steve Yzerman, Detroit, 1987-88 – 1992-93.

MOST 40-OR-MORE WIN SEASONS BY A GOALTENDER:
3 — Jacques Plante, Montreal, NY Rangers, St. Louis, Toronto, Boston in 18 seasons.
 2 — Terry Sawchuck, Detroit, Boston, Toronto, Los Angeles, NY Rangers in 21 seasons.
  — Bernie Parent, Boston, Philadelphia, Toronto in 13 seasons.
  — Ken Dryden, Montreal, in 8 seasons.
  — Ed Belfour, Chicago, in 6 seasons.

MOST CONSECUTIVE 40-OR-MORE WIN SEASONS BY A GOALTENDER:
2 — Terry Sawchuk, Detroit, 1950-51 – 1951-52.
  — Bernie Parent, Philadelphia, 1973-74 – 1974-75.
  — Ken Dryden, Montreal, 1975-76 – 1976-77.

MOST 30-OR-MORE WIN SEASONS BY A GOALTENDER:
8 — Tony Esposito, Montreal, Chicago in 16 seasons.
 7 — Jacques Plante, Montreal, NY Rangers, St. Louis, Toronto, Boston in 18 seasons.
  — Ken Dryden, Montreal, in 8 seasons.
 6 — Glenn Hall, Detroit, Chicago, St. Louis in 18 seasons.

MOST CONSECUTIVE 30-OR-MORE WIN SEASONS BY A GOALTENDER:
7 — Tony Esposito, Chicago, 1969-70 – 1975-76.
 6 — Jacques Plante, Montreal, 1954-55 – 1959-60.
 5 — Ken Dryden, Montreal, 1974-75 – 1978-79.
 4 — Terry Sawchuk, Detroit, 1950-51 – 1953-54.
  — Ed Giacomin, NY Rangers, 1966-67 – 1969-70.

Single Season

MOST GOALS, ONE SEASON:
92 — Wayne Gretzky, Edmonton, 1981-82. 80 game schedule.
 87 — Wayne Gretzky, Edmonton, 1983-84. 80 game schedule.
 86 — Brett Hull, St. Louis, 1990-91. 80 game schedule.
 85 — Mario Lemieux, Pittsburgh, 1988-89. 80 game schedule.
 76 — Phil Esposito, Boston, 1970-71. 78 game schedule.
  — Alexander Mogilny, Buffalo, 1992-93. 84 game schedule.
  — Teemu Selanne, Winnipeg, 1992-93. 84 game schedule.
 73 — Wayne Gretzky, Edmonton, 1984-85. 80 game schedule.
 72 — Brett Hull, St. Louis, 1989-90. 80 game schedule.
 71 — Jari Kurri, Edmonton, 1984-85 80 game schedule.
  — Wayne Gretzky, Edmonton, 1982-83. 80 game schedule.
 70 — Mario Lemieux, Pittsburgh, 1987-1988. 80 game schedule.
  — Bernie Nicholls, Los Angeles, 1988-89. 80 game schedule.
  — Brett Hull, St. Louis, 1991-92. 80 game schedule.

MOST ASSISTS, ONE SEASON:
163 — Wayne Gretzky, Edmonton , 1985-86. 80 game schedule.
 135 — Wayne Gretzky, Edmonton, 1984-85. 80 game schedule.
 125 — Wayne Gretzky, Edmonton, 1982-83. 80 game schedule.
 122 — Wayne Gretzky, Los Angeles, 1990-91. 80 game schedule.
 121 — Wayne Gretzky, Edmonton, 1986-87. 80 game schedule.
 120 — Wayne Gretzky, Edmonton, 1981-82. 80 game schedule.
 118 — Wayne Gretzky, Edmonton, 1983-84. 80 game schedule.
 114 — Wayne Gretzky, Los Angeles, 1988-89. 80 game schedule.
  — Mario Lemieux, Pittsburgh, 1988-89. 80 game schedule.
 109 — Wayne Gretzky, Edmonton, 1980-81. 80 game schedule.
  — Wayne Gretzky, Edmonton, 1987-88. 80 game schedule.
 102 — Bobby Orr, Boston, 1970-71. 78 game schedule.
  — Wayne Gretzky, Los Angeles, 1989-90. 80 game schedule.

MOST POINTS, ONE SEASON:
215 — Wayne Gretzky, Edmonton, 1985-86. 80 game schedule.
 212 — Wayne Gretzky, Edmonton, 1981-82. 80 game schedule.
 208 — Wayne Gretzky, Edmonton, 1984-85. 80 game schedule.
 205 — Wayne Gretzky, Edmonton, 1983-84. 80 game schedule.
 199 — Mario Lemieux, Pittsburgh, 1988-89. 80 game schedule.
 196 — Wayne Gretzky, Edmonton, 1982-83. 80 game schedule.
 183 — Wayne Gretzky, Edmonton, 1986-87. 80 game schedule.
 168 — Mario Lemieux, Pittsburgh, 1987-88. 80 game schedule.
  — Wayne Gretzky, Los Angeles, 1988-89. 80 game schedule.
 164 — Wayne Gretzky, Edmonton, 1980-81. 80 game schedule.
 163 — Wayne Gretzky, Los Angeles, 1990-91. 80 game schedule.
 160 — Mario Lemieux, Pittsburgh, 1992-93. 84 game schedule.
 155 — Steve Yzerman, Detroit, 1988-89. 80 game schedule.

MOST THREE-OR-MORE GOAL GAMES, ONE SEASON:
10 — Wayne Gretzky, Edmonton, 1981-82. 6 three-goal games, 3 four-goal games, 1 five-goal game.
  — Wayne Gretzky, Edmonton, 1983-84. 6 three-goal games, 4 four-goal games.
 9 — Mike Bossy, NY Islanders, 1980-81. 6 three-goal games, 3 four-goal games.
  — Mario Lemieux, Pittsburgh, 1988-89. 7 three-goal games, 1 four-goal game, 1 five-goal game.
 8 — Brett Hull, St. Louis, 1991-92. 8 three-goal games.
 7 — Joe Malone, Montreal, 1917-18. 2 three-goal games, 2 four-goal games, 3 five-goal games.
  — Phil Esposito, Boston, 1970-71. 7 three-goal games.
  — Rick Martin, Buffalo, 1975-76. 6 three-goal games, 1 four-goal game.
  — Alexander Mogilny, Buffalo, 1992-93. 5 three-goal games, 2 four-goal games.

HIGHEST GOALS-PER-GAME AVERAGE, ONE SEASON (AMONG PLAYERS WITH 20-OR-MORE GOALS):
2.20 — Joe Malone, Montreal, 1917-18, with 44G in 20GP.
 1.64 — Cy Denneny, Ottawa, 1917-18, with 36G in 22GP.
  — Newsy Lalonde, Montreal, 1917-18, with 23G in 14GP.
 1.63 — Joe Malone, Qebec, 1919-20, with 39G in 24GP.
 1.57 — Newsy Lalonde, Montreal, 1919-20, with 36G in 23GP.
 1.50 — Joe Malone, Hamilton, 1920-21, with 30G in 20GP.

HIGHEST GOALS-PER-GAME AVERAGE, ONE SEASON (AMONG PLAYERS WITH 50-OR-MORE GOALS):
1.18 — Wayne Gretzky, Edmonton, 1983-84, with 87G in 74GP.
 1.15 — Wayne Gretzky, Edmonton, 1981-82, with 92G in 80GP.
  — Mario Lemieux, Pittsburgh, 1992-93, with 69G in 60GP.
 1.12 — Mario Lemieux, Pittsburgh, 1988-89, with 85G in 76GP.
 1.10 — Brett Hull, St. Louis, 1990-91, with 86G in 78GP.
 1.02 — Cam Neely, Boston, 1993-94, with 50G in 49GP.
 1.00 — Maurice Richard, Montreal, 1944-45, with 50G in 50GP.
  .99 — Alexander Mogilny, Buffalo, 1992-93, with 76G in 77GP.
  .97 — Phil Esposito, Boston, 1970-71, with 76G in 78GP.
  — Jari Kurri, Edmonton, 1984-85, with 71G in 73GP.

Jacques Plante, who donned the pads for five different NHL teams in his 21-year career, is the only goaltender to record three 40-win seasons.

HIGHEST ASSISTS-PER-GAME AVERAGE, ONE SEASON
(AMONG PLAYERS WITH 35-OR-MORE ASSISTS):
2.04 — Wayne Gretzky, Edmonton, 1985-86, with 163A in 80GP.
1.70 — Wayne Grezky, Edmonton, 1987-88, with 109A in 64GP.
1.69 — Wayne Gretzky, Edmonton, 1984-85, with 135A in 80GP.
1.59 — Wayne Gretzky, Edmonton, 1983-84, with 118A in 74GP.
1.56 — Wayne Gretzky, Edmonton, 1982-83, with 125A in 80GP.
1.56 — Wayne Gretzky, Los Angeles, 1990-91, with 122A in 78GP.
1.53 — Wayne Gretzky, Edmonton, 1986-87, with 121A in 79GP.
1.52 — Mario Lemieux, Pittsburgh, 1992-93, with 91A in 60GP.
1.50 — Wayne Gretzky, Edmonton, 1981-82, with 120A in 80GP.
1.50 — Mario Lemieux, Pittsburgh, 1988-89, with 114A in 76GP.

HIGHEST POINTS-PER-GAME AVERAGE, ONE SEASON
(AMONG PLAYERS WITH 50-OR-MORE POINTS):
2.77 — Wayne Gretzky, Edmonton, 1983-84, with 205PTS in 74GP.
2.69 — Wayne Gretzky, Edmonton, 1985-86, with 215PTS in 80GP.
2.67 — Mario Lemieux, Pittsburgh, 1992-93, with 160PTS in 60GP.
2.65 — Wayne Gretzky, Edmonton, 1981-82, with 212PTS in 80GP.
2.62 — Mario Lemieux, Pittsburgh, 1988-89, with 199PTS in 78GP.
2.60 — Wayne Gretzky, Edmonton, 1984-85, with 208PTS in 80GP.
2.45 — Wayne Gretzky, Edmonton, 1982-83, with 196PTS in 80GP.
2.33 — Wayne Gretzky, Edmonton, 1987-88, with 149PTS in 64GP.
2.32 — Wayne Gretzky, Edmonton, 1986-87, with 183PTS in 79GP.
2.18 — Mario Lemieux, Pittsburgh, 1987-88 with 168PTS in 77GP.
2.15 — Wayne Gretzky, Los Angeles, 1988-89, with 168PTS in 78GP.
2.09 — Wayne Gretzky, Los Angeles, 1990-91, with 163 PTS in 78GP.
2.08 — Mario Lemieux, Pittsburgh, 1989-90, with 123 PTS in 59GP.
2.05 — Wayne Gretzky, Edmonton, 1980-81, with 164PTS in 80GP.

MOST GOALS, ONE SEASON, INCLUDING PLAYOFFS:
100 — Wayne Gretzky, Edmonton, 1983-84, 87G in 74 regular-season games and 13G in 19 playoff games.
97 — Wayne Gretzky, Edmonton, 1981-82, 92G in 80 regular-season games and 5G in 5 playoff games.
— Mario Lemieux, Pittsburgh, 1988-89, 85G in 76 regular-season games and 12G in 11 playoff games.
— Brett Hull, St. Louis, 1990-91, 86G in 78 regular-season games and 11G in 13 playoff games.
90 — Wayne Gretzky, Edmonton, 1984-85, 73G in 80 regular season games and 17G in 18 playoff games.
— Jari Kurri, Edmonton, 1984-85, 71G in 80 regular season games and 19G in 18 playoff games.
85 — Mike Bossy, NY Islanders, 1980-81, 68G in 79 regular-season games and 17G in 18 playoff games.
— Brett Hull, St. Louis, 1989-90, 72G in 80 regular season games and 13G in 12 playoff games.
83 — Wayne Gretzky, Edmonton, 1982-83, 71G in 73 regular-season games and 12G in 16 playoff games.
— Alexander Mogilny, Buffalo, 1992-93, 76G in 77 regular-season games and 7G in 7 playoff games.
81 — Mike Bossy, NY Islanders, 1981-82, 64G in 80 regular-season games and 17G in 19 playoff games.

MOST ASSISTS, ONE SEASON, INCLUDING PLAYOFFS:
174 — Wayne Gretzky, Edmonton, 1985-86, 163A in 80 regular-season games and 11A in 10 playoff games.
165 — Wayne Gretzky, Edmonton, 1984-85, 135A in 80 regular-season games and 30A in 18 playoff games.
151 — Wayne Gretzky, Edmonton, 1982-83, 125A in 80 regular-season games and 26A in 16 playoff games.
150 — Wayne Gretzky, Edmonton, 1986-87, 121A in 79 regular-season games and 29A in 21 playoff games.
140 — Wayne Gretzky, Edmonton, 1983-84, 118A in 74 regular-season games and 22A in 19 playoff games.
— Wayne Gretzky, Edmonton, 1987-88, 109A in 64 regular-season games and 31A in 19 playoff games.
133 — Wayne Gretzky, Los Angeles, 1990-91, 122A in 78 regular-season games and 11A in 12 playoff games.
131 — Wayne Gretzky, Los Angeles, 1988-89, 114A in 78 regular-season games and 17A in 11 playoff games.
127 — Wayne Gretzky, Edmonton, 1981-82, 120A in 80 regular-season games and 7A in 5 playoff games.
123 — Wayne Gretzky, Edmonton, 1980-81, 109A in 80 regular-season games and 14A in 9 playoff games.
121 — Mario Lemieux, Pittsburgh, 1988-89, 114A in 76 regular-season games and 7A in 11 playoff games.

MOST POINTS, ONE SEASON, INCLUDING PLAYOFFS:
255 — Wayne Gretzky, Edmonton, 1984-85, 208PTS in 80 regular-season games and 47PTS in 18 playoff games.
240 — Wayne Gretzky, Edmonton, 1983-84, 205PTS in 74 regular-season games and 35PTS in 19 playoff games.
234 — Wayne Gretzky, Edmonton, 1982-83, 196PTS in 80 regular-season games and 38PTS in 16 playoff games.
— Wayne Gretzky, Edmonton, 1985-86, 215PTS in 80 regular-season games and 19PTS in 10 playoff games.
224 — Wayne Gretzky, Edmonton, 1981-82, 212PTS in 80 regular-season games and 12PTS in 5 playoff games.
218 — Mario Lemieux, Pittsburgh, 1988-89, 199PTS in 76 regular-season games and 19PTS in 11 playoff games.
217 — Wayne Gretzky, Edmonton, 1986-87, 183PTS in 79 regular-season games and 34PTS in 21 playoff games.
192 — Wayne Gretzky, Edmonton, 1987-88, 149PTS in 64 regular-season games and 43PTS in 19 playoff games.
190 — Wayne Gretzky, Los Angeles, 1988-89, 168PTS in 78 regular-season games and 22PTS in 11 playoff games.
185 — Wayne Gretzky, Edmonton, 1980-81, 164PTS in 80 regular-season games and 21PTS in 9 playoff games.

MOST GOALS, ONE SEASON, BY A DEFENSEMAN:
48 — Paul Coffey, Edmonton, 1985-86. 80 game schedule.
46 — Bobby Orr, Boston, 1974-75. 80 game schedule.
40 — Paul Coffey, Edmonton, 1983-84. 80 game schedule.
39 — Doug Wilson, Chicago, 1981-82. 80 game schedule.
37 — Bobby Orr, Boston, 1970-71. 78 game schedule.
— Bobby Orr, Boston, 1971-72. 78 game schedule.
— Paul Coffey, Edmonton, 1984-85 80 game schedule..
34 — Kevin Hatcher, Washington, 1992-93. 84 game schedule.
33 — Bobby Orr, Boston, 1969-70. 76 game schedule.
32 — Bobby Orr, Boston, 1973-74. 78 game schedule.

MOST GOALS, ONE SEASON, BY A CENTER:
92 — Wayne Gretzky, Edmonton, 1981-82. 80 game schedule.
87 — Wayne Gretzky, Edmonton, 1983-84. 80 game schedule.
85 — Mario Lemieux, Pittsburgh, 1988-89. 80 game schedule.
76 — Phil Esposito, Boston, 1970-71. 78 game schedule.
73 — Wayne Gretzky, Edmonton, 1984-85. 80 game schedule.
71 — Wayne Gretzky, Edmonton, 1982-83. 80 game schedule.
70 — Mario Lemieux, Pittsburgh, 1987-88. 80 game schedule.
— Bernie Nicholls, Los Angeles, 1988-89. 80 game schedule.

Kevin Hatcher, who joined the Dallas Stars in 1994-95 after ten years with the Washington Capitals, is one of only six NHL defensemen to have scored 30 goals in a single season.

MOST GOALS, ONE SEASON, BY A RIGHT WINGER:
- 86 — **Brett Hull**, St. Louis, 1990-91. 80 game schedule.
- 76 — Alexander Mogilny, Buffalo, 1992-93. 84 game schedule.
  — Teemu Selanne, Winnipeg, 1992-93. 84 game schedule.
- 72 — Brett Hull, St. Louis, 1989-90. 80 game schedule.
- 71 — Jari Kurri, Edmonton, 1984-85. 80 game schedule.
- 70 — Brett Hull, St. Louis, 1991-92. 80 game schedule.
- 69 — Mike Bossy, NY Islanders, 1978-79. 80 game schedule.
- 68 — Jari Kurri, Edmonton, 1985-86. 80 game schedule..
  — Mike Bossy, NY Islanders, 1980-81. 80 game schedule.
- 66 — Lanny McDonald, Calgary, 1982-83. 80 game schedule.
- 64 — Mike Bossy, NY Islanders, 1981-82. 80 game schedule.
- 61 — Reggie Leach, Philadelphia, 1975-76. 80 game schedule.
  — Mike Bossy, NY Islanders, 1985-86. 80 game schedule.

MOST GOALS, ONE SEASON, BY A LEFT WINGER:
- 63 — **Luc Robitaille**, Los Angeles, 1992-93. 84 game schedule.
- 60 — Steve Shutt, Montreal, 1976-77. 80 game schedule.
- 58 — Bobby Hull, Chicago, 1968-69. 76 game schedule.
- 57 — Michel Goulet, Quebec, 1982-83. 80 game schedule.
- 56 — Charlie Simmer, Los Angeles, 1979-80. 80 game schedule.
  — Charlie Simmer, Los Angeles, 1980-81. 80 game schedule.
  — Michel Goulet, Quebec, 1983-84. 80 game schedule.
- 55 — Michel Goulet, Quebec, 1984-85. 80 game schedule.
  — John Ogrodnick, Detroit, 1984-85. 80 game schedule.
  — Kevin Stevens, Pittsburgh, 1992-93. 84 game schedule.

MOST GOALS, ONE SEASON, BY A ROOKIE:
- 76 — **Teemu Selanne**, Winnipeg, 1992-93. 84 game schedule.
- 53 — Mike Bossy, NY Islanders, 1977-78. 80 game schedule.
- 51 — Joe Nieuwendyk, Calgary, 1987-88. 80 game schedule.
- 45 — Dale Hawerchuk, Winnipeg, 1981-82. 80 game schedule.
  — Luc Robitaille, Los Angeles, 1986-87. 80 game schedule.
- 44 — Richard Martin, Buffalo, 1971-72. 78 game schedule.
  — Barry Pederson, Boston, 1981-82. 80 game schedule.
- 43 — Steve Larmer, Chicago, 1982-83. 80 game schedule.
  — Mario Lemieux, Pittsburgh, 1984-85. 80 game schedule.

MOST GOALS, ONE SEASON, BY A ROOKIE DEFENSEMAN:
- 23 — **Brian Leetch**, NY Rangers, 1988-89. 80 game schedule.
- 22 — Barry Beck, Colorado, 1977-78. 80 game schedule.
- 19 — Reed Larson, Detroit, 1977-78. 80 game schedule.
  — Phil Housley, Buffalo, 1982-83. 80 game schedule.

MOST ASSISTS, ONE SEASON, BY A DEFENSEMAN:
- 102 — **Bobby Orr**, Boston, 1970-71. 78 game schedule.
- 90 — Paul Coffey, Edmonton, 1985-86. 80 game schedule.
- 90 — Bobby Orr, Boston, 1973-74. 78 game schedule.
- 89 — Bobby Orr, Boston, 1974-75. 80 game schedule.

MOST ASSISTS, ONE SEASON, BY A CENTER:
- 163 — **Wayne Gretzky,** Edmonton, 1985-86. 80 game schedule.
- 135 — Wayne Gretzky, Edmonton, 1984-85. 80 game schedule.
- 125 — Wayne Gretzky, Edmonton, 1982-83. 80 game schedule.
- 122 — Wayne Gretzky, Los Angeles, 1990-91. 80 game schedule.
- 121 — Wayne Gretzky, Edmonton, 1986-87. 80 game schedule.
- 120 — Wayne Gretzky, Edmonton, 1981-82. 80 game schedule.
- 118 — Wayne Gretzky, Edmonton, 1983-84. 80 game schedule.
- 114 — Wayne Gretzky, Edmonton, 1988-89. 80 game schedule.
  — Mario Lemieux, Pittsburgh, 1988-89. 80 game schedule.
- 109 — Wayne Gretzky, Edmonton, 1980-81. 80 game schedule.
  — Wayne Gretzky, Edmonton, 1987-88. 80 game schedule.

MOST ASSISTS, ONE SEASON, BY A RIGHT WINGER:
- 83 — **Mike Bossy,** NY Islanders, 1981-82. 80 game schedule.
- 80 — Guy Lafleur, Montreal, 1976-77. 80 game schedule.
- 77 — Guy Lafleur, Montreal, 1978-79. 80 game schedule.

MOST ASSISTS, ONE SEASON, BY A LEFT WINGER:
- 70 — **Joe Juneau,** Boston, 1992-93. 84 game schedule.
- 69 — Kevin Stevens, Pittsburgh, 1991-92. 80 game schedule.
- 67 — Mats Naslund, Montreal, 1985-86. 80 game schedule.
- 65 — John Bucyk, Boston, 1970-71. 78 game schedule.
  — Michel Goulet, Quebec, 1983-84. 80 game schedule.
- 64 — Mark Messier, Edmonton, 1983-84. 80 game schedule.
- 63 — Luc Robitaille, Los Angeles, 1991-92. 80 game schedule.

*Phil Housley, right, is the only defenseman to jump directly
from high school to the NHL. He scored 19 goals as a rookie
in 1982-83. Bobby Orr, below, seen here in his last season as
a junior with the Oshawa Generals, still holds the mark for
most assists by a defenseman in a single season.*

MOST ASSISTS, ONE SEASON, BY A ROOKIE:
70 — Peter Stastny, Quebec, 1980-81. 80 game schedule.
— Joe Juneau, Boston, 1992-93. 84 game schedule.
63 — Bryan Trottier, NY Islanders, 1975-76. 80 game schedule.
62 — Sergei Makarov, Calgary, 1989-90. 80 game schedule.
60 — Larry Murphy, Los Angeles, 1980-81. 80 game schedule.

MOST ASSISTS, ONE SEASON, BY A ROOKIE DEFENSEMAN:
60 — Larry Murphy, Los Angeles, 1980-81. 80 game schedule.
55 — Chris Chelios, Montreal, 1984-85. 80 game schedule.
50 — Stefan Persson, NY Islanders, 1977-78. 80 game schedule.
— Gary Suter, Calgary, 1985-86, 80 game schedule..
49 — Nicklas Lidstrom, Detroit, 1991-92. 80 game schedule.
48 — Raymond Bourque, Boston, 1979-80. 80 game schedule.
— Brian Leetch, NY Rangers, 1988-89. 80 game schedule.

MOST POINTS, ONE SEASON, BY A DEFENSEMAN:
139 — Bobby Orr, Boston, 1970-71. 78 game schedule.
138 — Paul Coffey, Edmonton,1985-86. 80 game schedule.
135 — Bobby Orr, Boston, 1974-75. 80 game schedule.
126 — Paul Coffey, Edmonton, 1983-84. 80 game schedule.
122 — Bobby Orr, Boston, 1973-74. 78 game schedule.

MOST POINTS, ONE SEASON, BY A CENTER:
215 — Wayne Gretzky, Edmonton, 1985-86. 80 game schedule.
212 — Wayne Gretzky, Edmonton, 1981-82. 80 game schedule.
208 — Wayne Gretzky, Edmonton, 1984-85. 80 game schedule.
205 — Wayne Gretzky, Edmonton, 1983-84. 80 game schedule.
199 — Mario Lemieux, Pittsburgh, 1988-89. 80 game schedule.
196 — Wayne Gretzky, Edmonton, 1982-83. 80 game schedule.
183 — Wayne Gretzky, Edmonton, 1986-87. 80 game schedule.
168 — Mario Lemieux, Pittsburgh, 1987-88. 80 game schedule.
— Wayne Gretzky, Los Angeles, 1988-89. 80 game schedule.
164 — Wayne Gretzky, Edmonton, 1980-81. 80 game schedule.
163 — Wayne Gretzky, Los Angeles, 1990-91. 80 game schedule.

MOST POINTS, ONE SEASON, BY A RIGHT WINGER:
147 — Mike Bossy, NY Islanders, 1981-82. 80 game schedule.
136 — Guy Lafleur, Montreal, 1976-77. 80 game schedule.
135 — Jari Kurri, Edmonton, 1984-85. 80 game schedule.
132 — Guy Lafleur, Montreal, 1977-78. 80 game schedule.
— Teemu Selanne, Winnipeg, 1992-93. 84 game schedule.

MOST POINTS, ONE SEASON, BY A LEFT WINGER:
125 — Luc Robitaille, Los Angeles, 1992-93. 84 game schedule.
123 — Kevin Stevens, Pittsburgh, 1991-92. 80 game schedule.
121 — Michel Goulet, Quebec, 1983-84. 80 game schedule.
116 — John Bucyk, Boston, 1970-71. 78 game schedule.
112 — Bill Barber, Philadelphia, 1975-76. 80 game schedule.

MOST POINTS, ONE SEASON, BY A ROOKIE:
132 — Teemu Selanne, Winnipeg, 1992-93, 84 game schedule.
109 — Peter Stastny, Quebec, 1980-81. 80 game schedule.
103 — Dale Hawerchuk, Winnipeg, 1981-82. 80 game schedule.
102 — Joe Juneau, Boston, 1992-93. 84 game schedule.
100 — Mario Lemieux, Pittsburgh, 1984-85. 80 game schedule.

MOST POINTS, ONE SEASON, BY A ROOKIE DEFENSEMAN:
76 — Larry Murphy, Los Angeles, 1980-81. 80 game schedule.
71 — Brian Leetch, NY Rangers, 1988-89. 80 game schedule.
68 — Gary Suter, Calgary, 1985-86. 80 game schedule.
66 — Phil Housley, Buffalo, 1982-83. 80 game schedule.
65 — Raymond Bourque, Boston, 1979-80. 80 game schedule.
64 — Chris Chelios, Montreal, 1984-85. 80 game schedule.

MOST POINTS, ONE SEASON, BY A GOALTENDER:
14 — Grant Fuhr, Edmonton, 1983-84. (14A)
9 — Curtis Joseph, St. Louis, 1991-92. (9A)
8 — Mike Palmateer, Washington, 1980-81. (8A)
— Grant Fuhr, Edmonton, 1987-88. (8A)
— Ron Hextall, Philadelphia, 1988-89. (8A)
— Tom Barrasso, Pittsburgh, 1992-93. (8A)
7 — Ron Hextall, Philadelphia, 1987-88. (1G-6A)
— Mike Vernon, Calgary, 1987-88. (7A)

MOST POWER-PLAY GOALS, ONE SEASON:
34 — Tim Kerr, Philadelphia, 1985-86. 80 game schedule.
32 — Dave Andreychuk, Buffalo, Toronto, 1992-93. 84 game schedule.
31 — Joe Nieuwendyk, Calgary, 1987-88. 80 game schedule.
— Mario Lemieux, Pittsburgh, 1988-89. 80 game schedule.
29 — Michel Goulet, Quebec, 1987-88. 80 game schedule.
— Brett Hull, St. Louis, 1990-91. 80 game schedule.
— Brett Hull, St. Louis, 1992-93. 84 game schedule.

MOST SHORTHAND GOALS, ONE SEASON:
13 — Mario Lemieux, Pittsburgh, 1988-89. 80 game schedule.
12 — Wayne Gretzky, Edmonton, 1983-84. 80 game schedule.
11 — Wayne Gretzky, Edmonton, 1984-85. 80 game schedule.
10 — Marcel Dionne, Detroit, 1974-75. 80 game schedule.
— Mario Lemieux, Pittsburgh, 1987-88. 80 game schedule.
— Dirk Graham, Chicago, 1988-89. 80 game schedule.

*Dirk Graham, the Selke Trophy winner in 1990-91,
led the NHL with 10 shorthanded goals in 1988-89.
The NHL's single-season record—13 by Mario Lemieux—
was set that same season.*

MOST SHOTS ON GOAL, ONE SEASON:
  550 — Phil Esposito, Boston, 1970-71. 78 game schedule.
  426 — Phil Esposito, Boston, 1971-72. 78 game schedule.
  414 — Bobby Hull, Chicago, 1968-69. 76 game schedule.

MOST PENALTY MINUTES, ONE SEASON:
  472 — Dave Schultz, Philadelphia, 1974-75.
  409 — Paul Baxter, Pittsburgh, 1981-82.
  408 — Mike Peluso, Chicago, 1991-92.
  405 — Dave Schultz, Los Angeles, Pittsburgh, 1977-78.

MOST SHUTOUTS, ONE SEASON:
  22 — George Hainsworth, Montreal, 1928-29. 44GP
  15 — Alex Connell, Ottawa, 1925-26. 36GP
    — Alex Connell, Ottawa, 1927-28. 44GP
    — Hal Winkler, Boston, 1927-28. 44GP
    — Tony Esposito, Chicago, 1969-70. 63GP
  14 — George Hainsworth, Montreal, 1926-27. 44GP

LONGEST WINNING STREAK, ONE SEASON, BY A GOALTENDER:
  17 — Gilles Gilbert, Boston, 1975-76.
  14 — Don Beaupre, Minnesota, 1985-86.
    — Ross Brooks, Boston, 1973-74.
    — Tiny Thompson, Boston, 1929-30.
    — Tom Barrasso, Pittsburgh, 1992-93.

LONGEST UNDEFEATED STREAK BY A GOALTENDER:
  32 Games — Gerry Cheevers, Boston, 1971-72. 24w-8T.
  31 Games — Pete Peeters, Boston, 1982-83. 26w-5T.
  27 Games — Pete Peeters, Philadelphia, 1979-80. 22w-5T.
  23 Games — Frank Brimsek, Boston, 1940-41. 15w-8T.
    — Glenn Resch, NY Islanders, 1978-79. 15w-8T.
    — Grant Fuhr, Edmonton, 1981-82. 15w-8T.

MOST GAMES, ONE SEASON, BY A GOALTENDER:
  75 — Grant Fuhr, Edmonton, 1987-88.
  74 — Ed Belfour, Chicago, 1990-91.
    — Arturs Irbe, San Jose, 1993-94.
  73 — Bernie Parent, Philadelphia, 1973-74.
  72 — Gary Smith, Vancouver, 1974-75.
    — Don Edwards, Buffalo, 1977-78.
    — Tim Cheveldae, Detroit, 1991-92.

During the 1991-92 season, New York Ranger rearguard Brian Leetch recorded assists in 15 consecutive games, establishing the fourth longest streak in NHL history.

MOST WINS, ONE SEASON, BY A GOALTENDER:
  47 — Bernie Parent, Philadelphia, 1973-74.
  44 — Bernie Parent, Philadelphia, 1974-75.
    — Terry Sawchuk, Detroit, 1950-51.
    — Terry Sawchuk, Detroit, 1951-52.

LONGEST SHUTOUT SEQUENCE BY A GOALTENDER:
  461 Minutes, 29 Seconds — Alex Connell, Ottawa, 1927-28, six consecutive
    shutouts. (Forward passing not permitted in attacking zones in 1927-1928.)
  343 Minutes, 5 Seconds — George Hainsworth, Montreal, 1928-29, four consecutive
    shutouts.
  324 Minutes, 40 Seconds — Roy Worters, NY Americans, 1930-31, four consecutive
    shutouts.
  309 Minutes, 21 Seconds — Bill Durnan, Montreal, 1948-49, four consecutive shutouts.

MOST GOALS, 50 GAMES FROM START OF SEASON:
  61 — Wayne Gretzky, Edmonton, 1981-82. Oct. 7, 1981 - Jan. 22, 1982.
    (80-game schedule)
    — Wayne Gretzky, Edmonton, 1983-84. Oct. 5, 1983 - Jan. 25, 1984.
    (80-game schedule)
  54 — Mario Lemieux, Pittsburgh, 1988-89. Oct. 7, 1988 - Jan. 31, 1989. (80-game
    schedule)
  53 — Wayne Gretzky, Edmonton, 1984-85. Oct. 11, 1984 - Jan. 28, 1985.
    (80-game schedule).
  52 — Brett Hull, St. Louis, 1990-91. Oct. 4, 1990 - Jan. 26, 1991. (80-game
    schedule).
  50 — Maurice Richard, Montreal, 1944-45. Oct. 28, 1944 - March 18, 1945.
    (50-game schedule)
    — Mike Bossy, NY Islanders, 1980-81. Oct. 11, 1980 - Jan. 24, 1981. (80-game
    schedule)
    — Brett Hull, St. Louis, 1991-92. Oct. 5, 1991 – Jan 28, 1992. (80 game
    schedule)

LONGEST CONSECUTIVE POINT-SCORING STREAK
FROM START OF SEASON:
  51 Games — Wayne Gretzky, Edmonton, 1983-84. 61G-92A-153PTS during
    streak which was stopped by goaltender Markus Mattsson and
    Los Angeles on Jan. 28, 1984.

LONGEST CONSECUTIVE POINT SCORING STREAK:
  51 Games — Wayne Gretzky, Edmonton, 1983-84. 61G-92A-153PTS during streak.
  46 Games — Mario Lemieux, Pittsburgh, 1989-90. 39G-64A-103PTS during streak.
  39 Games — Wayne Gretzky, Edmonton, 1985-86. 33G-75A-108PTS during streak.
  30 Games — Wayne Gretzky, Edmonton, 1982-83. 24G52A76PTS during streak.
    — Mats Sundin, Quebec, 1992-93. 21G-25A-46PTS during streak.
  28 Games — Guy Lafleur, Montreal, 1976-77. 19G-42A-61PTS during streak.
    — Wayne Gretzky, Edmonton, 1984-85. 20G-43A-63PTS during streak.
    — Mario Lemieux, Pittsburgh, 1985-86. 21G-38A-59PTS during streak.
    — Paul Coffey, Edmonton, 1985-86. 16G-39A-55PTS during streak.
    — Steve Yzerman, Detroit, 1988-89. 29G-36A-65PTS during streak.

LONGEST CONSECUTIVE POINT-SCORING STREAK BY A DEFENSEMAN:
  28 Games — Paul Coffey, Edmonton, 1985-86. 16G-39A-55PTS during streak.
  19 Games — Ray Bourque, Boston, 1987-88. 6G-21A-27PTS during streak.
  17 Games — Ray Bourque, Boston, 1984-85. 4G-24A-28PTS during streak.
    — Brian Leetch, NY Rangers, 1991-92. 5G-24A-29PTS during streak.
  16 Games — Gary Suter, Calgary, 1987-88. 8G-17A-25PTS during streak.
  15 Games — Bobby Orr, Boston, 1970-71. 10G-23A-33PTS during streak.
    — Bobby Orr, Boston, 1973-74. 8G-15A-23PTS during streak.
    — Steve Duchesne, Quebec, 1992-93. 4G-17A-21PTS during streak.

LONGEST CONSECUTIVE GOAL-SCORING STREAK:
  16 Games — Harry (Punch) Broadbent, Ottawa, 1921-22.
    25 goals during streak.
  14 Games — Joe Malone, Montreal, 1917-18. 35 goals during streak.
  13 Games — Newsy Lalonde, Montreal, 1920-21. 24 goals during streak.
    — Charlie Simmer, Los Angeles, 1979-80. 17 goals during streak.
  12 Games — Cy Denneny, Ottawa, 1917-18. 23 goals during streak.
    — Dave Lumley, Edmonton, 1981-82. 15 goals during streak.
    — Mario Lemieux, Pittsburgh, 1992-93. 18 goals during streak.

LONGEST CONSECUTIVE ASSIST-SCORING STREAK:
  23 Games — Wayne Gretzky, Los Angeles, 1990-91. 48A during streak.
  18 Games — Adam Oates, Boston, 1992-93. 28A during streak.
  17 Games — Wayne Gretzky, Edmonton, 1983-84. 38A during streak.
    — Paul Coffey, Edmonton, 1985-86. 27A during streak.
    — Wayne Gretzky, Los Angeles, 1989-90. 35A during streak.
  15 Games — Jari Kurri, Edmonton, 1983-84. 21A during streak.
    — Brian Leetch, NY Rangers, 1991-92. 23A during streak.

Single Game

MOST GOALS, ONE GAME:
  7 — Joe Malone, Quebec Bulldogs, Jan. 31, 1920, at Quebec. Quebec 10,
    Toronto 6.
  6 — Newsy Lalonde, Montreal, Jan. 10, 1920, at Montreal. Montreal 14,
    Toronto 7.
    — Joe Malone, Quebec Bulldogs, March 10, 1920, at Quebec. Quebec 10,
    Ottawa 4.
    — Corb Denneny, Toronto, Jan. 26, 1921, at Toronto. Toronto 10, Hamilton 3.
    — Cy Denneny, Ottawa, March 7, 1921, at Ottawa. Ottawa 12, Hamilton 5.
    — Syd Howe, Detroit, Feb. 3, 1944, at Detroit. Detroit 12, NY Rangers 2.
    — Red Berenson, St. Louis, Nov. 7, 1968, at Philadelphia. St. Louis 8,
    Philadelphia 0
    — Darryl Sittler, Toronto, Feb. 7, 1976, at Toronto. Toronto 11, Boston 4.

MOST GOALS, ONE ROAD GAME:

6 —Red Berenson, St. Louis, Nov. 7, 1968, at Philadelphia. St. Louis 8, Philadelphia 0.

5 —Joe Malone, Montreal, Dec. 19, 1917, at Ottawa. Montreal 9, Ottawa 4.
—Redvers Green, Hamilton, Dec. 5, 1924, at Toronto. Hamilton 10, Toronto 3.
—Babe Dye, Toronto, Dec. 22, 1924, at Boston. Toronto 10, Boston 2.
—Harry Broadbent, Mtl. Maroons, Jan. 7, 1925, at Hamilton. Mtl. Maroons 6, Hamilton 2.
—Don Murdoch, NY Rangers, Oct. 12, 1976, at Minnesota. NY Rangers 10, Minnesota 4.
—Tim Young, Minnesota, Jan. 15, 1979, at NY Rangers. Minnesota 8, NY Rangers 4.
—Willy Lindstrom, Winnipeg, March 2, 1982, at Philadelphia. Winnipeg 7, Philadelphia 6.
—Bengt Gustafsson, Washington, Jan. 8, 1984, at Philadelphia. Washington 7, Philadelphia 1.
—Wayne Gretzky, Edmonton, Dec. 15, 1984, at St. Louis. Edmonton 8, St. Louis 2.
—Dave Andreychuk, Buffalo, Feb. 6, 1986, at Boston. Buffalo 8, Boston 6.
—Mats Sundin, Quebec, Mar. 5, 1992, at Hartford. Quebec 10, Hartford 4.
—Mario Lemieux, Pittsburgh, Apr. 9, 1993, at New York. Pittsburgh 10, NY Rangers 4.
—Mike Ricci, Quebec, Feb. 17, 1994, at San Jose. Quebec 8, San Jose 2.
—Alexei Zhamnov, Winnipeg, Apr. 1, 1995, at Los Angeles. Winnipeg 7, Los Angeles 7.

MOST ASSISTS, ONE GAME:

7 —Billy Taylor, Detroit, March 16, 1947, at Chicago. Detroit 10, Chicago 6.
—Wayne Gretzky, Edmonton, Feb. 15, 1980, at Edmonton. Edmonton 8, Washington 2.
—Wayne Gretzky, Edmonton, Dec. 11, 1985, at Chicago. Edmonton 12, Chicago 9.
—Wayne Gretzky, Edmonton, Feb. 14, 1986, at Edmonton. Edmonton 8, Quebec 2.

6 —Elmer Lach, Montreal, Feb. 6, 1943.
—Walter (Babe) Pratt, Toronto, Jan. 8, 1944.
—Don Grosso, Detroit, Feb. 3, 1944.
—Pat Stapleton, Chicago, March 30, 1969.
—Ken Hodge, Boston, Feb. 9, 1971.
—Bobby Orr, Boston, Jan. 1, 1973.
—Ron Stackhouse, Pittsburgh, March 8, 1975.
—Greg Malone, Pittsburgh, Nov. 28, 1979.
—Mike Bossy, NY Islanders, Jan. 6, 1981.
—Guy Chouinard, Calgary, Feb. 25, 1981.
—Mark Messier, Edmonton, Jan. 4, 1984.
—Patrik Sundstrom, Vancouver, Feb 29, 1984.
—Wayne Gretzky, Edmonton, Dec. 20, 1985.
—Paul Coffey, Edmonton, March 14, 1986.
—Gary Suter, Calgary, Apr. 4, 1986.
—Ron Francis, Hartford, March 5, 1987.
—Mario Lemieux, Pittsburgh, Oct. 15, 1988.
—Bernie Nicholls, Los Angeles, Dec. 1, 1988.
—Mario Lemieux, Pittsburgh, Dec. 31, 1988.
—Mario Lemieux, Pittsburgh, Dec. 5, 1992.
—Doug Gilmour, Toronto, Feb. 13, 1993.
—Tomas Sandstrom, Los Angeles, Oct. 9, 1993.

MOST ASSISTS, ONE ROAD GAME:

7 —Billy Taylor, Detroit, March 16, 1947, at Chicago. Detroit 10, Chicago 6.
—Wayne Gretzky, Edmonton, Dec. 11, 1985, at Chicago. Edmonton 12, Chicago 9.

6 —Bobby Orr, Boston, Jan. 1, 1973, at Vancouver. Boston 8, Vancouver 2.
—Patrik Sundstrom, Vancouver, Feb. 29, 1984, at Pittsburgh. Vancouver 9, Pittsburgh 5.
—Mario Lemieux, Pittsburgh, Dec. 5, 1992, at San Jose. Pittsburgh 9, San Jose 4.

MOST POINTS, ONE GAME:

10 —Darryl Sittler, Toronto, Feb. 7, 1976, at Toronto, 6G-4A. Toronto 11, Boston 4.
8 —Maurice Richard, Montreal, Dec. 28, 1944, at Montreal, 5G-3A. Montreal 9, Detroit 1.
—Bert Olmstead, Montreal, Jan. 9, 1954, at Montreal, 4G-4A. Montreal 12, Chicago 1.
—Tom Bladon, Philadelphia, Dec. 11, 1977, at Philadelphia, 4G-4A. Philadelphia 11, Cleveland 1.
—Bryan Trottier, NY Islanders, Dec. 23, 1978, at New York, 5G-3A. NY Islanders 9, NY Rangers 4.
—Peter Stastny, Quebec, Feb. 22, 1981, at Washington, 4G-4A. Quebec 11, Washington 7.
—Anton Stastny, Quebec, Feb. 22, 1981, at Washington, 3G-5A. Quebec 11, Washington 7.
—Wayne Gretzky, Edmonton, Nov. 19, 1983, at Edmonton, 3G-5A. Edmonton 13, New Jersey 4.
—Wayne Gretzky, Edmonton, Jan. 4, 1984, at Edmonton, 4G-4A. Edmonton 12 Minnesota 8.
—Paul Coffey, Edmonton, March 14, 1986, at Edmonton, 2G-6A. Edmonton 12, Detroit 3.
—Mario Lemieux, Pittsburgh, Oct. 15, 1988, at Pittsburgh, 2G-6A. Pittsburgh 9, St. Louis 2.
—Mario Lemieux, Pittsburgh, Dec. 31, 1988, at Pittsburgh, 5G-3A. Pittsburgh 8, New Jersey 6.
—Bernie Nicholls, Los Angeles, Dec. 1, 1988, at Los Angeles, 2G-6A. Los Angeles 9, Toronto 3.

Bert Olmstead, right, is seen here teaching the troops in the Maple Leaf dressing room. On January 9, 1954, Olmstead became the second player in NHL history to collect eight points in a single game.

Goaltender Jeff Reese, who started his career with Toronto before moving on to Calgary and Hartford, established an NHL record by assisting on three goals in Calgary's 13-1 win over San Jose on February 10, 1993.

MOST POINTS, ONE ROAD GAME:

8 — Peter Stastny, Quebec, Feb. 22, 1981, at Washington, 4G-4A. Quebec 11, Washington 7.
— **Anton Stastny,** Quebec, Feb. 22, 1981, at Washington, 3G-5A. Quebec 11, Washington 7.
7 — Billy Taylor, Detroit, March 16, 1947, at Chicago, 7A. Detroit 10, Chicago 6.
— Red Berenson, St. Louis, Nov. 7, 1968, at Philadelphia, 6G-1A. St. Louis 8, Philadelphia 0.
— Gilbert Perreault, Buffalo, Feb. 1, 1976, at California, 2G-5A. Buffalo 9, California 5.
— Peter Stastny, Quebec, April 1, 1982, at Boston, 3G-4A. Quebec 8, Boston 5.
— Wayne Gretzky, Edmonton, Nov. 6, 1983, at Winnipeg, 4G-3A. Edmonton 8, Winnipeg 5.
— Patrik Sundstrom, Vancouver, Feb. 29, 1984, at Pittsburgh, 1G-6A. Vancouver 9, Pittsburgh 5.
— Wayne Gretzky, Edmonton, Dec. 11, 1985, at Chicago. 7A, Edmonton 12, Chicago 9.
— Mario Lemieux, Pittsburgh, Jan. 21, 1989, at Edmonton, 2G, 5A. Pittsburgh 7, Edmonton 4.
— Cam Neely, Boston, Oct. 16, 1988, at Chicago, 3G, 4A. Boston 10, Chicago 3.
— Dino Ciccarelli, Washington, March 18, 1989, at Hartford, 4G, 3A. Washington 8, Hartford 2.
— Mats Sundin, Quebec, Mar. 5, 1992, at Hartford, 5G, 2A. Quebec 10, Hartford 4.
— Mario Lemieux, Pittsburgh, Dec. 5, 1992, at San Jose, 1G, 6A. Pittsburgh 9, San Jose 4.

MOST GOALS, ONE GAME, BY A DEFENSEMAN:

5 — Ian Turnbull, Toronto, Feb. 2, 1977, at Toronto. Toronto 9, Detroit 1.
4 — Harry Cameron, Toronto, Dec. 26, 1917, at Toronto. Toronto 7, Montreal 5.
— Harry Cameron, Montreal, March 3, 1920, at Quebec City. Montreal 16, Que. Bulldogs 3.
— Sprague Cleghorn, Montreal, Jan. 14, 1922, at Montreal. Montreal 10, Hamilton 6.
— Johnny McKinnon, Pit. Pirates, Nov. 19, 1929, at Pittsburgh. Pit. Pirates 10, Toronto 5.
— Hap Day, Toronto, Nov. 19, 1929, at Pittsburgh. Pit. Pirates 10, Toronto 5.
— Tom Bladon, Philadelphia, Dec. 11, 1977, at Philadelphia. Philadelphia 11, Cleveland 1.
— Ian Turnbull, Los Angeles, Dec. 12, 1981, at Los Angeles. Los Angeles 7, Vancouver 5.
— Paul Coffey, Edmonton, Oct. 26, 1984, at Calgary. Edmonton 6, Calgary 5.

MOST GOALS BY ONE PLAYER IN HIS FIRST NHL GAME:

3 — Alex Smart, Montreal, Jan. 14, 1943, at Montreal. Montreal 5, Chicago 1.
— **Real Cloutier,** Quebec, Oct. 10, 1979, at Quebec. Atlanta 5, Quebec 3.

MOST GOALS, ONE GAME, BY A PLAYER IN HIS FIRST NHL SEASON:

5 — Howie Meeker, Toronto, Jan. 8, 1947, at Toronto. Toronto 10, Chicago 4.
— **Don Murdoch,** NY Rangers, Oct. 12, 1976, at Minnesota. NY Rangers 10, Minnesota 4.

MOST ASSISTS, ONE GAME, BY A DEFENSEMAN:

6 — Babe Pratt, Toronto, Jan. 8, 1944, at Toronto. Toronto 12, Boston 3.
— **Pat Stapleton,** Chicago, March 30, 1969, at Chicago. Chicago 9, Detroit 5.
— **Bobby Orr,** Boston, Jan. 1, 1973, at Vancouver, Boston 8, Vancouver 2.
— **Ron Stackhouse,** Pittsburgh, March 8, 1975, at Pittsburgh. Pittsburgh 8, Philadelphia 2.
— **Paul Coffey,** Edmonton, Mar. 14, 1986, at Edmonton. Edmonton 12, Detroit 3.
— **Gary Suter,** Calgary, Apr. 4, 1986, at Calgary. Calgary 9, Edmonton 3.

MOST ASSISTS BY ONE PLAYER IN HIS FIRST NHL GAME:

4 — Earl (Dutch) Reibel, Detroit, Oct. 8, 1953, at Detroit. Detroit 4, NY Rangers 1.
— **Roland Eriksson,** Minnesota, Oct. 6, 1976, at New York. NY Rangers 6, Minnesota 5.
3 — Al Hill, Philadelphia, Feb. 14, 1977, at Philadelphia. Philadelphia 6, St. Louis 4.

MOST ASSISTS, ONE GAME, BY A PLAYER IN HIS FIRST NHL SEASON:

7 — Wayne Gretzky, Edmonton, Feb. 15, 1980, at Edmonton. Edmonton 8, Washington 2.
6 — Gary Suter, Calgary, Apr. 4, 1986, at Calgary. Calgary 9, Edmonton 3.

MOST ASSISTS, ONE GAME, BY A GOALTENDER:

3 — Jeff Reese, Calgary, Feb. 10, 1993, at Calgary. Calgary 13, San Jose 1.

MOST POINTS, ONE GAME, BY A DEFENSEMAN:

8 — Tom Bladon, Philadelphia, Dec. 11, 1977, at Philadelphia. 4G-4A. Philadelphia 11, Cleveland 1.
— **Paul Coffey,** Edmonton, Mar. 14, 1986, at Edmonton. 2G-6A. Edmonton 12, Detroit 3.
7 — Bobby Orr, Boston, Nov. 15, 1973, at Boston, 3G-4A. Boston 10, NY Rangers 2.

MOST POINTS BY ONE PLAYER IN HIS FIRST NHL GAME:

5 — Al Hill, Philadelphia, Feb. 14, 1977, at Philadelphia. 2G-3A. Philadelphia 6, St. Louis 4.
4 — Alex Smart, Montreal, Jan. 14, 1943, at Montreal, 3G-1A. Montreal 5, Chicago 1.
— Earl (Dutch) Reibel, Detroit, Oct. 8, 1953, at Detroit. 4A. Detroit 4, NY Rangers 1.
— Roland Eriksson, Minnesota, Oct. 6, 1976 at New York. 4A. NY Rangers 6, Minnesota 5.

MOST POINTS, ONE GAME, BY A PLAYER IN HIS FIRST NHL SEASON:
8 — Peter Stastny, Quebec, Feb. 22, 1981, at Washington. 4G-4A. Quebec 11, Washington 7.
— Anton Stastny, Quebec, Feb. 22, 1981, at Washington. 3G-5A. Quebec 11, Washington 7.
7 — Wayne Gretzky, Edmonton, Feb. 15, 1980, at Edmonton. 7A. Edmonton 8, Washington 2.
— Sergei Makarov, Calgary, Feb. 25, 1990, at Calgary, 2G-5A. Calgary 10, Edmonton 4.
6 — Wayne Gretzky, Edmonton, March 29, 1980, at Toronto. 2G-4A. Edmonton 8, Toronto 5.
— Gary Suter, Calgary, Apr. 4, 1986, at Calgary. 6A. Calgary 9, Edmonton 3.

MOST PENALTIES, ONE GAME:
10 — Chris Nilan, Boston, March 31, 1991, at Boston against Hartford. 6 minors, 2 majors, 1 10-minute misconduct, 1 game misconduct.
9 — Jim Dorey, Toronto, Oct. 16, 1968, at Toronto against Pittsburgh. 4 minors, 2 majors, 2 10-minute misconducts, 1 game misconduct.
— Dave Schultz, Pittsburgh, Apr. 6, 1978, at Detroit. 5 minors, 2 majors, 2 10-minute misconducts.
— Randy Holt, Los Angeles, Mar. 11, 1979, at Philadelphia. 1 minor, 3 majors, 2 10-minute misconducts, 3 game misconducts.
— Russ Anderson, Pittsburgh, Jan. 19, 1980, at Pittsburgh. 3 minors, 3 majors, 3 game misconducts.
— Kim Clackson, Quebec, March 8, 1981, at Quebec. 4 minors, 3 majors, 2 game misconducts.
— Terry O'Reilly, Boston, Dec. 19, 1984 at Hartford. 5 minors, 3 majors, 1 game misconduct.
— Larry Playfair, Los Angeles, Dec. 9, 1986, at NY Islanders. 6 minors, 2 majors, 1 10-minute misconduct.
— Marty McSorley, Los Angeles, Apr. 14, 1992, at Vancouver. 5 minors, 2 majors, 1 10-minute misconduct, 1 game misconduct.

MOST PENALTY MINUTES, ONE GAME:
67 — Randy Holt, Los Angeles, Mar. 11, 1979, at Philadelphia. 1 minor, 3 majors, 2 10-minute misconducts, 3 game misconducts.
55 — Frank Bathe, Philadelphia, Mar. 11, 1979, at Philadelphia. 3 majors, 2 10-minute misconducts, 2 game misconducts.
51 — Russ Anderson, Pittsburgh, Jan. 19, 1980, at Pittsburgh. 3 minors, 3 majors, 3 game misconducts.

MOST GOALS, ONE PERIOD:
4 — Harvey (Busher) Jackson, Toronto, Nov. 20, 1934, at St. Louis, third period. Toronto 5, St. Louis Eagles 2.
— Max Bentley, Chicago, Jan. 28, 1943, at Chicago, third period. Chicago 10, NY Rangers 1.
— Clint Smith, Chicago, March 4, 1945, at Chicago, third period. Chicago 6, Montreal 4.
— Red Berenson, St. Louis, Nov. 7, 1968, at Philadelphia, second period. St. Louis 8, Philadelphia 0.
— Wayne Gretzky, Edmonton, Feb. 18, 1981, at Edmonton, third period. Edmonton 9, St. Louis 2.
— Grant Mulvey, Chicago, Feb. 3, 1982, at Chicago, first period. Chicago 9, St. Louis 5.
— Bryan Trottier, NY Islanders, Feb. 13, 1982, at New York, second period. NY Islanders 8, Philadelphia 2.
— Al Secord, Chicago, Jan. 7, 1987 at Chicago, second period. Chicago 6, Toronto 4.
— Joe Nieuwendyk, Calgary, Jan. 11, 1989, at Calgary, second period. Calgary 8, Winnipeg 3.
— Peter Bondra, Washington, Feb. 5, 1994, at Washington, first period. Washington 6, Tampa Bay 3.

MOST ASSISTS, ONE PERIOD:
5 — Dale Hawerchuk, Winnipeg, Mar. 6, 1984, at Los Angeles, second period. Winnipeg 7, Los Angeles 3.
4 — Four assists have been recorded in one period on 44 occasions since Buddy O'Connor of Montreal first accomplished the feat vs. NY Rangers on Nov. 8, 1942. Most recent player, Adam Oates of Boston (Mar. 24, 1994 vs Anaheim).

MOST POINTS, ONE PERIOD:
6 — Bryan Trottier, NY Islanders, Dec. 23, 1978, at NY Islanders, second period. 3G, 3A. NY Islanders 9, NY Rangers 4.
5 — Les Cunningham, Chicago, Jan. 28, 1940, at Chicago, third period. 2G, 3A. Chicago 8, Montreal 1.
— Max Bentley, Chicago, Jan. 28, 1943, at Chicago, third period. 4G, 1A, Chicago 10, NY Rangers 1.
— Leo Labine, Boston, Nov. 28, 1954, at Boston, second period. 3G, 2A. Boston 6, Detroit 2.
— Darryl Sittler, Toronto, Feb. 7, 1976, at Toronto, second period. 3G, 2A. Toronto 11, Boston 4.
— Dale Hawerchuk, Winnipeg, Mar. 6, 1984, at Los Angeles, second period. 5A. Winnipeg 7, Los Angeles 3.
— Jari Kurri, Edmonton, October 26, 1984 at Edmonton, second period. Edmonton 8, Los Angeles 2.
— Pat Elynuik, Winnipeg, Jan. 20, 1989, at Winnipeg, second period. 2G, 3A. Winnipeg 7, Pittsburgh 3.
— Ray Ferraro, Hartford, Dec. 9, 1989, at Hartford, first period. 3G, 2A. Hartford 7, New Jersey 3.
— Stephane Richer, Montreal, Feb. 14, 1990, at Montreal, first period. 2G, 3A. Montreal 10, Vancouver 1.
— Cliff Ronning, Vancouver, Apr. 15, 1993, at Los Angeles, third period. 3G, 2A. Vancouver 8, Los Angeles 6.

MOST PENALTIES, ONE PERIOD:
9 — Randy Holt, Los Angeles, Mar. 11, 1979, at Philadelphia, first period. 1 minor, 3 majors, 2 10-minute misconducts, 3 game misconducts.

MOST PENALTY MINUTES, ONE PERIOD:
67 — Randy Holt, Los Angeles, Mar. 11, 1979, at Philadelphia, first period. 1 minor, 3 majors, 2 10-minute misconducts, 3 game misconducts.

FASTEST GOAL BY A ROOKIE IN HIS FIRST NHL GAME:
15 Seconds — Gus Bodnar, Toronto, Oct. 30, 1943. Toronto 5, NY Rangers 2.
18 Seconds — Danny Gare, Buffalo, Oct. 10, 1974. Buffalo 9, Boston 5.
20 Seconds — Alexander Mogilny, Buffalo, Oct. 5, 1989. Buffalo 4, Quebec 3.

FASTEST GOAL FROM START OF A GAME:
5 Seconds — Doug Smail, Winnipeg, Dec. 20, 1981, at Winnipeg. Winnipeg 5, St. Louis 4.
— Bryan Trottier, NY Islanders, Mar. 22, 1984, at Boston. NY Islanders 3, Boston 3
— Alexander Mogilny, Buffalo, Dec. 21, 1991, at Toronto. Buffalo 4, Toronto 1.
6 Seconds — Henry Boucha, Detroit, Jan. 28, 1973, at Montreal. Detroit 4, Montreal 2.
— Jean Pronovost, Pittsburgh, March 25, 1976, at St. Louis. St. Louis 5, Pittsburgh 2.
7 Seconds — Charlie Conacher, Toronto, Feb. 6, 1932, at Toronto. Toronto 6, Boston 0.
— Danny Gare, Buffalo, Dec. 17, 1978, at Buffalo. Buffalo 6, Vancouver 3.
— Dave Williams, Los Angeles, Feb. 14, 1987 at Los Angeles. Los Angeles 5, Harford 2.
8 Seconds — Ron Martin, NY Americans, Dec. 4, 1932, at New York. NY Americans 4, Montreal 2.
— Chuck Arnason, Colorado, Jan. 28, 1977, at Atlanta. Colorado 3, Atlanta 3.
— Wayne Gretzky, Edmonton, Dec. 14, 1983, at New York. Edmonton 9, NY Rangers 4
— Gaetan Duchesne, Washington, Mar. 14, 1987, at St. Louis. Washington 3, St. Louis 3.
— Tim Kerr, Philadelphia, March 7, 1989, at Philadelphia. Philadelphia 4, Edmonton 4.
— Grant Ledyard, Buffalo, Dec. 4, 1991, at Winnipeg. Buffalo 4, Winnipeg 4.
— Brent Sutter, Chicago, Feb. 5, 1995, at Vancouver. Chicago 9, Vancouver 4.

FASTEST GOAL FROM START OF A PERIOD:
4 Seconds — Claude Provost, Montreal, Nov. 9, 1957, at Montreal, second period. Montreal 4, Boston 2.
— Denis Savard, Chicago, Jan. 12, 1986, at Chicago, third period. Chicago 4, Hartford 2.

FASTEST TWO GOALS:
4 Seconds — Nels Stewart, Mtl. Maroons, Jan. 3, 1931, at Montreal at 8:24 and 8:28, third period. Mtl. Maroons 5, Boston 3.
5 Seconds — Pete Mahovlich, Montreal, Feb. 20, 1971, at Montreal at 12:16 and 12:21, third period. Montreal 7, Chicago 1.
6 Seconds — Jim Pappin, Chicago, Feb. 16, 1972, at Chicago at 2:57 and 3:03, third period. Chicago 3, Philadelphia 3.
— Ralph Backstrom, Los Angeles, Nov. 2, 1972, at Los Angeles at 8:30 and 8:36, third period. Los Angeles 5, Boston 2.
— Lanny McDonald, Calgary, Mar. 22, 1984, at Calgary at 16:23 and 16:29, first period. Detroit 6, Calgary 4.
— Sylvain Turgeon, Hartford, Mar. 28, 1987, at Hartford at 13:59 and 14:05, second period. Hartford 5, Pittsburgh 4.

FASTEST THREE GOALS:
21 Seconds — Bill Mosienko, Chicago, March 23, 1952, at New York, against goaltender Lorne Anderson. Mosienko scored at 6:09, 6:20 and 6:30 of third period, all with both teams at full strength. Chicago 7, NY Rangers 6.
44 Seconds — Jean Béliveau, Montreal, Nov. 5, 1955, at Montreal, against goaltender Terry Sawchuk. Béliveau scored at :42, 1:08 and 1:26 of second period, all with Montreal holding a 6-4 man advantage. Montreal 4, Boston 2.

FASTEST THREE ASSISTS:
21 Seconds — Gus Bodnar, Chicago, March 23, 1952, at New York, Bodnar assisted on Bill Mosienko's three goals at 6:09, 6:20, 6:30 of third period. Chicago 7, NY Rangers 6.
44 Seconds — Bert Olmstead, Montreal, Nov. 5, 1955, at Montreal against Boston. Olmstead assisted on Jean Béliveau's three goals at :42, 1:08 and 1:26 of second period. Montreal 4, Boston 2.

Active NHL Players' Three-or-More-Goal Games

Regular Season

Teams named are the ones the players were with at the time of their multiple-scoring games. Players listed alphabetically.

Bryan Smolinski connected for his first NHL hat-trick on March 2, 1995 in the Bruins' 7-2 victory over the New Jersey Devils.

Player	Team	3-Goals	4-Goals	5-Goals
Adams, Greg	Vancouver	1	1	—
Amonte, Tony	NY Rangers	1	—	—
Anderson, Glenn	Edm., Tor.	18	3	—
Andersson, Mikael	Tampa Bay	1	—	—
Andreychuk, Dave	Buf., Tor.	7	2	1
Arnott, Jason	Edmonton	1	—	—
Audette, Donald	Buffalo	1	—	—
Babych, Dave	Vancouver	1	—	—
Barnes, Stu	Winnipeg	1	—	—
Barr, Dave	St. L., Det.	2	—	—
Bellows, Brian	Min., Mtl.	5	3	—
Beranek, Josef	Philadelphia	1	—	—
Bondra, Peter	Washington	2	—	1
Bourque, Phil	Pittsburgh	1	—	—
Bourque, Ray	Boston	1	—	—
Bradley, Brian	Tampa Bay	1	—	—
Brickley, Andy	Pit., Bos.	2	—	—
Brind'Amour, Rod	Philadelphia	1	—	—
Broten, Neal	Minnesota	6	—	—
Broten, Paul	NY Rangers	1	—	—
Brown, Rob	Pittsburgh	7	—	—
Buchberger, Kelly	Edmonton	1	—	—
Bure, Pavel	Vancouver	5	1	—
Burr, Shawn	Detroit	3	—	—
Burridge, Randy	Bos., Wsh.	4	—	—
Butsayev, Viacheslav	Philadelphia	1	—	—
Carbonneau, Guy	Montreal	1	1	—
Carpenter, Bob	Wsh., Bos.	2	1	—
Carson, Jimmy	L.A., Edm., Det.	9	1	—
Cavallini, Gino	St. Louis	1	—	—
Chibirev, Igor	Hartford	1	—	—
Christian, Dave	Wpg., Wsh.	2	—	—
Ciccarelli, Dino	Min., Wsh.	14	4	1
Clark, Wendel	Tor., Que.	7	1	—
Coffey, Paul	Edmonton	4	1	—
Corson, Shayne	Mtl., Edm.	3	—	—
Courtnall, Geoff	Bos., Wsh.	2	—	—
Courtnall, Russ	Tor., Mtl., Min., Van.	4	—	—
Craven, Murray	Philadelphia	3	—	—
Creighton, Adam	Buf., Chi.	2	—	—
Crossman, Doug	Tampa Bay	1	—	—
Cullen, John	Pit., Hfd.	3	—	—
Cunneyworth, R.	Pittsburgh	1	1	—
Dahlen, Ulf	NYR, Min., S.J.	4	—	—
Daigle, Alexandre	Ottawa	1	—	—
Damphousse, V.	Tor., Edm., Mtl.	7	1	—
Davydov, Evgeny	Winnipeg	1	—	—
Dineen, Kevin	Hfd., Phi.	9	1	—
Dionne, Gilbert	Montreal	1	—	—
Donnelly, Mike	Los Angeles	2	—	—
Druce, John	Wsh., L.A.	2	—	—
Duchesne, Steve	L.A., Phi., St.L.	3	—	—
Emerson, Nelson	Winnipeg	1	—	—
Errey, Bob	Pittsburgh	1	—	—
Evason, Dean	Hartford	1	—	—
Fedorov, Sergei	Detroit	1	1	—
Ferraro, Ray	Hfd., NYI	6	1	—
Flatley, Patrick	NY Islanders	2	1	—
Fleury, Theo	Calgary	7	—	—
Fogarty, Bryan	Quebec	1	—	—
Francis, Ron	Hartford	8	1	—
Gagner, Dave	Min., Dal.	3	1	—
Gallant, Gerard	Detroit	4	—	—
Garpenlov, Johan	Det., S.J.	1	1	—
Gartner, Mike	Wsh., Min., NYR	14	2	—
Gaudreau, Rob	San Jose	3	—	—
Gelinas, Martin	Edmonton	1	—	—
Gilbert, Greg	NY Islanders	2	—	—
Gilchrist, Brent	Montreal	1	—	—
Gilmour, Doug	St.L., Tor.	3	—	—
Graham, Dirk	Minnesota	1	—	—
Granato, Tony	NYR, L.A.	4	1	—
Graves, Adam	Edm., NYR	5	—	—
Green, Travis	NY Islanders	1	—	—
Gretzky, Wayne	Edm., L.A.	36	9	4
Grieve, Brent	Edmonton	1	—	—
Hannan, Dave	Edmonton	1	—	—
Harvey, Todd	Dallas	1	—	—
Hatcher, Kevin	Washington	1	—	—
Hawerchuk, Dale	Wpg., Buf.	13	—	—
Heinze, Stephen	Boston	1	—	—
Hogue, Benoit	NY Islanders	1	—	—
Holik, Bobby	New Jersey	2	—	—
Horacek, Tony	Philadelphia	1	—	—
Housley, Phil	Buffalo	2	—	—
Howe, Mark	Hartford	1	—	—
Hull, Brett	Cgy., St. L.	22	1	—

Player	Team	3-Goal	4-Goal	5-Goal
Hull, Jody	Hartford	1	—	—
Hunter, Dale	Que., Wsh.	4	—	—
Jagr, Jaromir	Pittsburgh	2	—	—
Janney, Craig	Bos., St. L.	3	—	—
Juneau, Joe	Boston	1	—	—
Khmylev, Yuri	Buffalo	1	—	—
Khristich, Dimitri	Washington	2	—	—
King, Derek	NY Islanders	4	1	—
Klima, Petr	Det., Edm.	6	—	—
Kontos, Chris	Tampa Bay	—	1	—
Kovalenko, Andrei	Quebec	1	—	—
Kovalev, Alexei	NY Rangers	1	—	—
Kozlov, Vyacheslav	Detroit	1	—	—
Krupp, Uwe	Quebec	1	—	—
Krushelnyski, Mike	Edmonton	1	—	—
Krygier, Todd	Washington	1	—	—
Kudelski, Robert	L.A., Ott.	4	—	—
Kurri, Jari	Edm., L.A.	20	1	1
LaFontaine, Pat	NYI, Buf.	12	—	—
Larionov, Igor	Van., S.J.	4	—	—
Larmer, Steve	Chicago	9	—	—
Larouche, Steve	Ottawa	1	—	—
Lavoie, Dominic	Los Angeles	1	—	—
Lebeau, Stephan	Montreal	1	—	—
LeClair, John	Philadelphia	2	—	—
Leeman, Gary	Tor., Cgy.	5	—	—
Lemieux, Claude	Mtl., N.J.	4	—	—
Lemieux, Jocelyn	Chicago	2	—	—
Lemieux, Mario	Pittsburgh	21	8	2
Linden, Trevor	Vancouver	3	—	—
Lindros, Eric	Philadelphia	7	—	—
MacInnis, Al	Calgary	1	—	—
MacLean, John	New Jersey	6	—	—
MacTavish, Craig	Edmonton	2	—	—
Makarov, Sergei	Cgy., S.J.	4	—	—
Makela, Mikko	NY Islanders	1	—	—
Marois, Daniel	Toronto	3	—	—
McPhee, Mike	Montreal	3	—	—
Messier, Mark	Edm., NYR	12	4	—
Miller, Kevin	Det., St.L.	3	—	—
Modano, Mike	Min., Dal.	2	—	—
Mogilny, Alexander	Buffalo	8	2	—
Momesso, Sergio	Montreal	1	—	—
Mullen, Joe	St. L., Cgy., Pit.	7	4	—
Muller, Kirk	N.J., Mtl.	6	—	—
Murray, Troy	Chicago	4	—	—
Murzyn, Dana	Calgary	1	—	—
Neely, Cam	Boston	13	—	—
Nemchinov, Sergei	NY Rangers	1	—	—
Nicholls, Bernie	L.A., N.J., Chi.	14	4	—
Nieuwendyk, Joe	Calgary	7	2	1
Nolan, Owen	Quebec	7	—	—
Noonan, Brian	Chi., NYR	3	1	—
Nylander, Michael	Hartford	1	—	—
Oates, Adam	Boston	5	—	—
Odelein, Lyle	Montreal	1	—	—
Olczyk, Ed	Tor., NYR	3	—	—
Oliver, David	Edmonton	1	—	—
Osborne, Mark	Detroit	1	—	—
Otto, Joel	Calgary	2	—	—
Petrov, Oleg	Montreal	1	—	—
Pivonka, Michal	Washington	1	—	—
Plante, Derek	Buffalo	1	—	—
Poulin, Dave	Philadelphia	5	—	—
Presley, Wayne	Chicago	1	—	—
Probert, Bob	Detroit	1	—	—
Prokhorov, Vitali	St. Louis	1	—	—
Quinn, Dan	Pit., Van.	4	—	—

Player	Team	3-Goal	4-Goal	5-Goal
Ranheim, Paul	Calgary	1	—	—
Recchi, Mark	Pittsburgh	1	—	—
Reichel, Robert	Calgary	3	—	—
Renberg, Mikael	Philadelphia	1	—	—
Ricci, Mike	Quebec	—	—	1
Rice, Steven	Hartford	1	—	—
Richer, Stephane	Mtl., N.J.	7	1	—
Ridley, Mike	NYR, Wsh.	3	1	—
Roberts, Gary	Calgary	6	1	—
Robitaille, Luc	L.A., Pit.	9	3	—
Roenick, Jeremy	Chicago	4	3	—
Ronning, Cliff	St.L., Van.	2	—	—
Sakic, Joe	Quebec	4	1	—
Sanderson, Geoff	Hartford	3	—	—
Sandlak, Jim	Vancouver	1	—	—
Sandstrom, Tomas	NYR, L.A.	7	1	—
Savard, Denis	Chi., Mtl.	12	—	—
Selanne, Teemu	Winnipeg	6	1	—
Semak, Alexander	New Jersey	1	—	—
Shanahan, Brendan	N.J., St.L.	6	—	—
Sheppard, Ray	Buf., Det.	6	—	—
Simpson, Craig	Pit., Edm.	3	—	—
Smith, Derrick	Philadelphia	1	—	—
Smolinski, Bryan	Boston	1	—	—
Stastny, Peter	Que., N.J.	15	2	—
Steen, Thomas	Winnipeg	4	—	—
Stern, Ronnie	Calgary	3	—	—
Stevens, Kevin	Pittsburgh	8	2	—
Straka, Martin	Pittsburgh	1	—	—
Sundin, Mats	Quebec	3	—	1
Sutter, Brent	NY Islanders	6	—	—
Sutter, Rich	Vancouver	1	—	—
Sweeney, Bob	Boston	1	—	—
Thomas, Steve	Chi., NYI	4	2	—
Tikkanen, Esa	Edmonton	3	—	—
Titov, German	Calgary	1	—	—
Tkachuk, Keith	Winnipeg	1	—	—
Tocchet, Rick	Phi., Pit., L.A.	10	2	—
Tucker, John	Buffalo	1	—	—
Turcotte, Darren	NY Rangers	4	—	—
Turgeon, Pierre	Buf., NYI, Mtl.	11	—	—
Turgeon, Sylvain	Hfd., N.J., Ott.	5	—	—
Verbeek, Pat	N.J., Hfd.	8	1	—
Vukota, Mick	NY Islanders	1	—	—
Wesley, Glen	Boston	1	—	—
Wood, Randy	NY Islanders	1	—	—
Yake, Terry	Anaheim	1	—	—
Yashin, Alexei	Ottawa	2	—	—
Young, Scott	Quebec	1	—	—
Yzerman, Steve	Detroit	17	1	—
Ysebaert, Paul	Detroit	1	—	—
Zezel, Peter	Philadelphia	1	—	—
Zhamnov, Alexei	Winnipeg	3	—	1

Top 100 All-Time Goal-Scoring Leaders

* active player

(figures in parentheses indicate ranking of top 10 by goals per game)

Player	Seasons	Games	Goals	Goals per game	
* 1. Wayne Gretzky, Edm., L.A.	16	1173	814	.694	(4)
2. Gordie Howe, Det., Hfd.	26	1767	801	.453	
3. Marcel Dionne, Det., L.A., NYR	18	1348	731	.542	
4. Phil Esposito, Chi., Bos., NYR.	18	1282	717	.559	(10)
* 5. Mike Gartner, Wsh., Min., NYR, Tor.	16	1208	629	.521	
6. Bobby Hull, Chi., Wpg., Hfd.	16	1063	610	.574	(6)
7. Mike Bossy, NYI.	10	752	573	.762	(2)
* 8. Jari Kurri, Edm., L.A.	14	1028	565	.550	
9. Guy Lafleur, Mtl., NYR, Que.	17	1126	560	.497	
10. John Bucyk, Det., Bos.,	23	1540	556	.361	
11. Michel Goulet, Que., Chi.	15	1089	548	.503	
12. Maurice Richard, Mtl.	18	978	544	.556	
13. Stan Mikita, Chi.	22	1394	541	.388	
14. Frank Mahovlich, Tor., Det., Mtl.	18	1181	533	.451	
* 15. Dino Ciccarelli, Min., Wsh., Det.	15	1015	529	.521	
16. Bryan Trottier, NYI, Pit.	18	1279	524	.410	
17. Gilbert Perreault, Buf.	17	1191	512	.430	
18. Jean Beliveau, Mtl.	20	1125	507	.451	
19. Lanny McDonald, Tor., Col., Cgy.	16	1111	500	.450	
* 20. Mario Lemieux, Pit.	10	599	494	.825	(1)
* 21. Glenn Anderson, Edm., Tor., NYR, St.L.	15	1097	492	.448	
* 22. Mark Messier, Edm., NYR	16	1127	492	.437	
23. Jean Ratelle, NYR, Bos.	21	1281	491	.383	
24. Norm Ullman, Det., Tor.	20	1410	490	.348	
* 25. Dale Hawerchuk, Wpg., Buf.	14	1055	489	.464	
* 26. Joe Mullen, St.L., Cgy., Pit.	14	971	487	.502	
27. Darryl Sittler, Tor., Phi., Det.	15	1096	484	.442	
* 28. Steve Yzerman, Det.	12	862	481	.558	
29. Alex Delvecchio, Det.	24	1549	456	.294	
* 30. Denis Savard, Chi., Mtl., T.B.	15	1063	451	.424	
* 31. Peter Stastny, Que., N.J., St.L.	15	977	450	.461	
* 32. Dave Andreychuk, Buf., Tor.	13	925	448	.484	
33. Rick Middleton, NYR, Bos.	14	1005	448	.446	
* 34. Brett Hull, Cgy., St.L.	9	588	442	.752	(3)
35. Rick Vaive, Van., Tor., Chi., Buf.	13	876	441	.503	
36. Steve Larmer, Chi., NYR.	15	1006	441	.438	
* 37. Bernie Nicholls, L.A., NYR, Edm., N.J., Chi.	14	933	438	.469	
38. Dave Taylor, L.A.	17	1111	431	.388	
39. Yvan Cournoyer, Mtl.	16	968	428	.442	
40. Brian Propp, Phi., Bos., Min., Hfd.	15	1016	425	.418	
41. Steve Shutt, Mtl., L.A.	13	930	424	.456	
* 42. Brian Bellows, Min., Mtl.	13	953	423	.444	
43. Bill Barber, Phi.	12	903	420	.465	
* 44. Luc Robitaille, L.A., Pit.	9	686	415	.605	(5)
45. Garry Unger, Tor., Det., St.L., Atl., L.A., Edm.	16	1105	413	.374	
46. Rod Gilbert, NYR	18	1065	406	.381	
* 47. Pat LaFontaine, NYI, Buf.	12	709	403	.568	(7)
48. John Ogrodnick, Det., Que., NYR	14	928	402	.433	
49. Dave Keon, Tor., Hfd.	18	1296	396	.306	
50. Pierre Larouche, Pit., Mtl., Hfd., NYR	14	812	395	.486	
51. Bernie Geoffrion, Mtl., NYR	16	883	393	.445	
52. Jean Pronovost, Wsh., Pit., Atl.	14	998	391	.392	
53. Dean Prentice, Pit., Min., Det., NYR, Bos.	22	1378	391	.284	
54. Rick Martin, Buf., L.A.	11	685	384	.561	(9)
55. Reggie Leach, Bos., Cal., Phi., Det.	13	934	381	.408	
56. Ted Lindsay, Det., Chi.	17	1068	379	.355	
57. Butch Goring, L.A., NYI, Bos.	16	1107	375	.339	
* 58. Pat Verbeek, N.J., Hfd., NYR	13	915	372	.407	
59. Rick Kehoe, Tor., Pit.	14	906	371	.409	
60. Tim Kerr, Phi., NYR, Hfd.	13	655	370	.565	(8)
* 61. Cam Neely, Van., Bos.	12	677	369	.545	
62. Bernie Federko, St.L., Det.	14	1000	369	.369	
63. Jacques Lemaire, Mtl.	12	853	366	.429	
64. Peter McNab, Buf., Bos., Van., N.J.	14	954	363	.381	
65. Ivan Boldirev, Bos., Cal., Chi., Atl., Van., Det.	15	1052	361	.343	
* 66. Paul Coffey, Edm., Pit., L.A., Det.	15	1078	358	.332	
67. Bobby Clarke, Phi.	15	1144	358	.313	
68. Henri Richard, Mtl.	20	1256	358	.285	
69. Bobby Smith, Min., Mtl.	15	1077	357	.331	
70. Dennis Maruk, Cal., Clev., Min., Wsh.	14	888	356	.401	
71. Wilf Paiement, K.C. Col., Tor., Que., NYR, Buf., Pit.	14	946	356	.376	
72. Mike Foligno, Det., Buf., Tor., Fla.	15	1018	355	.349	
73. Danny Gare, Buf., Det., Edm.	13	827	354	.428	
74. Rick MacLeish, Phi., Hfd., Pit., Det.	14	846	349	.413	
* 75. Ron Francis, Hfd., Pit.	14	1008	349	.346	
76. Andy Bathgate, NYR, Tor., Det., Pit.	17	1069	349	.326	
77. Charlie Simmer, Cal., Cle., L.A., Bos., Pit.	14	712	342	.480	

Bob Nevin (11) buries one of his 307 career goals behind Detroit's Terry Sawchuk during the 1962-63 season.

Player	Seasons	Games	Goals	Goals per game
* 78. Brent Sutter, NYI, Chi.	15	940	341	.363
* 79. Dave Christian, Wpg., Wsh., Bos., St.L., Chi.	15	1009	340	.337
80. Ron Ellis, Tor.	16	1034	332	.321
81. Mike Bullard, Pit., Cgy., St.L., Phi., Tor.	11	727	329	.453
82. Ken Hodge, Chi., Bos., NYR	13	881	328	.372
83. John Tonelli, NYI, Cgy., L.A., Chi., Que.	14	1028	325	.316
84. Nels Stewart, Mtl.M., Bos., NYA.	15	650	324	.498
* 85. Stephane J. J. Richer, Mtl., N.J.	11	690	324	.470
86. Paul MacLean, St.L., Wpg., Det.	11	719	324	.451
87. Pit Martin, Det., Bos., Chi., Van.	17	1101	324	.294
88. Vic Hadfield, NYR, Pit.	16	1002	323	.322
* 89. Ray Bourque, Bos.	16	1146	323	.282
90. Tony McKegney, Buf., Que., Min., NYR, St. L., Det., Chi.	13	912	320	.351
91. Clark Gillies, NYI, Buf.	14	958	319	.333
* 92. Tomas Sandstrom, NYR, L.A., Pit.	11	716	317	.443
* 93. Joe Nieuwendyk, Cgy.	9	577	314	.544
* 94. Doug Gilmour, St.L., Cgy., Tor.	12	900	314	.349
95. Don Lever, Van., Atl., Cgy., Col., N.J., Buf.	15	1020	313	.307
96. Denis Potvin, NYI	15	1060	310	.292
* 97. Rick Tocchet, Phi., Pit., L.A.	11	717	309	.431
98. Bob Nevin, Tor., NYR, Min., L.A.	18	1128	307	.272
99. Brian Sutter, St.L.	12	779	303	.389
100. Dennis Hull, Chi., Det.	14	959	303	.316

Top 100 Active Goal-Scoring Leaders

Player	Games	Goals	Goals per game
1. **Wayne Gretzky**, Edm., L.A.	1173	**814**	.694
2. **Mike Gartner**, Wsh., Min., NYR, Tor.	1208	**629**	.521
3. **Jari Kurri**, Edm., L.A.	1028	**565**	.550
4. **Dino Ciccarelli**, Min., Wsh., Det.	1015	**529**	.521
5. **Mario Lemieux**, Pit.	599	**494**	.825
6. **Glenn Anderson**, Edm., Tor., NYR, St.L.	1097	**492**	.448
7. **Mark Messier**, Edm., NYR	1127	**492**	.437
8. **Dale Hawerchuk**, Wpg., Buf.	1055	**489**	.464
9. **Joe Mullen**, St.L., Cgy., Pit.	971	**487**	.502
10. **Steve Yzerman**, Det.	862	**481**	.558
11. **Denis Savard**, Chi., Mtl., T.B.	1063	**451**	.424
12. **Peter Stastny**, Que., N.J., St.L.	977	**450**	.461
13. **Dave Andreychuk**, Buf., Tor.	925	**448**	.484
14. **Brett Hull**, Cgy., St.L.	588	**442**	.752
15. **Steve Larmer**, Chi., NYR	1006	**441**	.438
16. **Bernie Nicholls**, L.A., NYR, Edm., N.J., Chi.	933	**438**	.469
17. **Brian Bellows**, Min., Mtl.	953	**423**	.444
18. **Luc Robitaille**, L.A., Pit.	686	**415**	.605
19. **Pat LaFontaine**, NYI, Buf.	709	**403**	.568
20. **Pat Verbeek**, N.J., Hfd., NYR	915	**372**	.407
21. **Cam Neely**, Van., Bos.	677	**369**	.545
22. **Paul Coffey**, Edm., Pit., L.A., Det.	1078	**358**	.332
23. **Ron Francis**, Hfd., Pit.	1008	**349**	.346
24. **Brent Sutter**, NYI, Chi.	940	**341**	.363
25. **Dave Christian**, Wpg., Wsh., Bos., St.L., Chi.	1009	**340**	.337
26. **Stephane J. J. Richer**, Mtl., N.J.	690	**324**	.470
27. **Ray Bourque**, Bos.	1146	**323**	.282
28. **Tomas Sandstrom**, NYR, L.A., Pit.	716	**317**	.443
29. **Joe Nieuwendyk**, Cgy.	577	**314**	.544
30. **Doug Gilmour**, St.L., Cgy., Tor.	900	**314**	.349
31. **Rick Tocchet**, Phi., Pit., L.A.	717	**309**	.431
32. **Kevin Dineen**, Hfd., Phi.	747	**302**	.404
33. **Bob Carpenter**, Wsh., NYR, L.A., Bos., N.J.	942	**300**	.318
34. **John MacLean**, N.J.	752	**295**	.392
35. **Kirk Muller**, N.J., Mtl., NYI	835	**292**	.350
36. **Petr Klima**, Det., Edm., T.B.	673	**288**	.428
37. **Geoff Courtnall**, Bos., Edm., Wsh., St.L., Van.	788	**288**	.365
38. **Dale Hunter**, Que., Wsh.	1099	**286**	.260
39. **Pierre Turgeon**, Buf., NYI, Mtl.	592	**280**	.473
40. **Jimmy Carson**, L.A., Edm., Det., Van., Hfd.	615	**274**	.446
41. **Neal Broten**, Min., Dal., N.J.	1002	**274**	.273
42. **Ray Ferraro**, Hfd., NYI	758	**273**	.360
43. **Steve Thomas**, Tor., Chi., NYI	667	**269**	.403
44. **Sylvain Turgeon**, Hfd., N.J., Mtl., Ott.	669	**269**	.402
45. **Ed Olczyk**, Chi., Tor., Wpg., NYR	751	**267**	.356
46. **Mike Ridley**, NYR, Wsh., Tor.	754	**266**	.353
47. **Kent Nilsson**, Atlanta, Cgy., Min., Edm.	553	**264**	.477
48. **Thomas Steen**, Wpg.	950	**264**	.278
49. **Phil Housley**, Buf., Wpg., St.L., Cgy.	909	**257**	.283
50. **Dan Quinn**, Cgy., Pit., Van., St.L., Phi., Min., Ott., L.A.	726	**253**	.348
51. **Kevin Stevens**, Pit.	458	**251**	.548
52. **Mats Naslund**, Mtl., Bos.	651	**251**	.386
53. **Greg Adams**, N.J., Van., Dal.	687	**249**	.362
54. **Craig Simpson**, Pit., Edm., Buf.	634	**247**	.390
55. **Vincent Damphousse**, Tor., Edm., Mtl.	690	**245**	.355
56. **Brendan Shanahan**, N.J., St.L.	558	**244**	.437
57. **Dave Gagner**, NYR, Min., Dal.	644	**244**	.379
58. **Russ Courtnall**, Tor., Mtl., Min., Dal., Van.	772	**242**	.313
59. **Mike Krushelnyski**, Bos., Edm., L.A., Tor., Det.	897	**241**	.269
60. **Ray Sheppard**, Buf., NYR, Det.	487	**238**	.489
61. **Jeremy Roenick**, Chi.	458	**235**	.513
62. **Gary Roberts**, Cgy.	550	**235**	.427
63. **Joe Sakic**, Que.	508	**234**	.461
64. **Larry Murphy**, L.A., Wsh., Min., Pit.	1152	**233**	.202
65. **Theoren Fleury**, Cgy.	488	**232**	.475
66. **Kelly Kisio**, Det., NYR, S.J., Cgy.	761	**229**	.301
67. **Guy Carbonneau**, Mtl., St.L.	954	**226**	.237
68. **Murray Craven**, Det., Phi., Hfd., Van., Chi.	801	**224**	.280
69. **Mark Recchi**, Pit., Phi., Mtl.	464	**223**	.481
70. **Troy Murray**, Chi., Wpg., Ott., Pit.	852	**223**	.262
71. **Claude Lemieux**, Mtl., N.J.	634	**222**	.350
72. **Al MacInnis**, Cgy., St.L.	835	**221**	.265
73. **Wendel Clark**, Tor., Que.	500	**220**	.440
74. **Dirk Graham**, Min., Chi.	772	**219**	.284
75. **Esa Tikkanen**, Edm., NYR, St.L.	663	**214**	.323
76. **Mark Osborne**, Det., NYR, Tor., Wpg.	919	**212**	.231
77. **Alexander Mogilny**, Buf.	381	**211**	.554
78. **Gerard Gallant**, Det., T.B.	615	**211**	.343
79. **Adam Oates**, Det., St.L., Bos.	676	**211**	.312
80. **Craig MacTavish**, Bos., Edm., NYR, Phi.	975	**206**	.211
81. **Dave Poulin**, Phi., Bos., Wsh.	724	**205**	.283
82. **Ulf Dahlen**, NYR, Min., Dal., S.J.	554	**201**	.363
83. **Mike McPhee**, Mtl., Min., Dal.	744	**200**	.269

Neal Broten, who scored eight goals for the New Jersey Devils in the 1994-95 season, currently stands 41st among active goal scorers in the NHL.

Player	Games	Goals	Goals per game
84. **Gary Leeman**, Tor., Cgy., Mtl., Van.	665	**199**	.299
85. **Trevor Linden**, Van.	529	**198**	.374
86. **Mark Howe**, Hfd., Phi., Det.	929	**197**	.212
87. **Peter Zezel**, Phi., St.L., Wsh., Tor., Dal.	692	**196**	.283
88. **Mike Modano**, Min., Dal.	423	**185**	.437
89. **Ron Sutter**, Phi., St.L., Que., NYI	782	**184**	.235
90. **Gaetan Duchesne**, Wsh., Que., Min., S.J., Fla.	1028	**179**	.174
91. **Derek King**, NYI	507	**176**	.347
92. **Adam Creighton**, Buf., Chi., NYI, T.B., St.L.	628	**175**	.279
93. **Pavel Bure**, Van.	268	**174**	.649
94. **Tony Granato**, NYR, L.A.	446	**174**	.390
95. **John Tucker**, Buf., Wsh., NYI, T.B.	593	**174**	.293
96. **Shayne Corson**, Mtl., Edm.	612	**174**	.284
97. **Sergei Fedorov**, Det.	354	**173**	.489
98. **Joel Otto**, Cgy.	730	**167**	.229
99. **Scott Mellanby**, Phi., Edm., Fla.	632	**164**	.259
100. **Randy Wood**, NYI, Buf., Tor.	600	**161**	.268

Top 100 All-Time Assist Leaders

* active player

(figures in parentheses indicate ranking of top 10 in order of assists per game)

	Player	Seasons	Games	Assists	Assist per game	
* 1.	Wayne Gretzky, Edm., L.A.	16	1173	**1692**	1.442	(1)
2.	Gordie Howe, Det., Hfd.	26	1767	**1049**	.594	
3.	Marcel Dionne, Det., L.A., NYR	18	1348	**1040**	.772	
* 4.	Paul Coffey, Edm., Pit., L.A., Det.	15	1078	**978**	.907	(4)
5.	Stan Mikita, Chi.	22	1394	**926**	.664	
* 6.	Ray Bourque, Bos.	16	1146	**908**	.792	(7)
7.	Bryan Trottier, NYI, Pit.	18	1279	**901**	.704	
* 8.	Mark Messier, Edm., NYR	16	1127	**877**	.778	
9.	Phil Esposito, Chi., Bos., NYR	18	1282	**873**	.681	
10.	Bobby Clarke, Phi.	15	1144	**852**	.745	
* 11.	Dale Hawerchuk, Wpg., Buf.	14	1055	**825**	.782	(10)
12.	Alex Delvecchio, Det.	24	1549	**825**	.533	
13.	Gilbert Perreault, Buf.	17	1191	**814**	.683	
14.	John Bucyk, Det., Bos.,	23	1540	**813**	.528	
* 15.	Denis Savard, Chi., Mtl., T.B.	15	1063	**812**	.764	
16.	Guy Lafleur, Mtl., NYR, Que.	17	1126	**793**	.704	
* 17.	Peter Stastny, Que., N.J., St.L.	15	977	**789**	.808	(6)
* 18.	Ron Francis, Hfd., Pit.	14	1008	**789**	.783	(9)
19.	Jean Ratelle, NYR, Bos.	21	1281	**776**	.606	
20.	Bernie Federko, St.L., Det.	14	1000	**761**	.761	
21.	Larry Robinson, Mtl., L.A.	20	1384	**750**	.542	
22.	Denis Potvin, NYI.	15	1060	**742**	.700	
23.	Norm Ullman, Det., Tor.	20	1410	**739**	.524	
* 24.	Jari Kurri, Edm., L.A.	14	1028	**731**	.711	
* 25.	Mario Lemieux, Pit.	10	599	**717**	1.197	(2)
26.	Jean Beliveau, Mtl.	20	1125	**712**	.633	
* 27.	Larry Murphy, L.A., Wsh., Min., Pit.	15	1152	**712**	.618	
28.	Henri Richard, Mtl.	20	1256	**688**	.548	
29.	Brad Park, NYR, Bos., Det.	17	1113	**683**	.614	
* 30.	Steve Yzerman, Det.	12	862	**679**	.788	(8)
31.	Bobby Smith, Min., Mtl.	15	1077	**679**	.630	
* 32.	Doug Gilmour, St.L., Cgy., Tor.	12	900	**655**	.728	
33.	Bobby Orr, Bos., Chi.	12	657	**645**	.982	(3)
34.	Dave Taylor, L.A.	17	1111 •	**638**	.574	
35.	Darryl Sittler, Tor., Phi., Det.	15	1096	**637**	.581	
36.	Borje Salming, Tor., Det.	17	1148	**637**	.555	
* 37.	Bernie Nicholls, L.A., NYR, Edm., N.J., Chi.	14	933	**636**	.682	
* 38.	Al MacInnis, Cgy., St.L.	14	835	**629**	.753	
* 39.	Phil Housley, Buf., Wpg., St.L., Cgy.	13	909	**625**	.688	
40.	Andy Bathgate, NYR, Tor., Det., Pit.	17	1069	**624**	.584	
41.	Rod Gilbert, NYR	18	1065	**615**	.577	
* 42.	Dale Hunter, Que., Wsh.	15	1099	**614**	.559	
* 43.	Adam Oates, Det., St.L., Bos.	10	676	**611**	.904	(5)
* 44.	Neal Broten, Min., Dal., N.J.	15	1002	**606**	.605	
45.	Michel Goulet, Que., Chi.	15	1089	**604**	.555	
* 46.	Glenn Anderson, Edm., Tor., NYR, St.L.	15	1097	**593**	.541	
47.	Doug Wilson, Chi., S.J.	16	1024	**590**	.576	
48.	Dave Keon, Tor., Hfd.	18	1296	**590**	.455	
49.	Brian Propp, Phi., Bos., Min., Hfd.	15	1016	**579**	.570	
50.	Steve Larmer, Chi., NYR.	15	1006	**571**	.568	
51.	Frank Mahovlich, Tor., Det., Mtl.	18	1181	**570**	.483	
* 52.	Mike Gartner, Wsh., Min., NYR, Tor.	16	1208	**562**	.465	
53.	Bobby Hull, Chi., Wpg., Hfd.	16	1063	**560**	.527	
54.	Mike Bossy, NYI.	10	752	**553**	.735	
55.	Thomas Steen, Wpg.	14	950	**553**	.582	
56.	Ken Linseman, Phi., Edm., Bos., Tor.	14	860	**551**	.641	
57.	Tom Lysiak, Atl., Chi.	13	919	**551**	.600	
* 58.	Mark Howe, Hfd., Phi., Det.	16	929	**545**	.587	
* 59.	Scott Stevens, Wsh., St.L., N.J.	13	959	**542**	.565	
60.	Red Kelly, Det., Tor.	20	1316	**542**	.412	
61.	Rick Middleton, NYR, Bos.	14	1005	**540**	.537	
* 62.	Joe Mullen, St.L., Cgy., Pit.	14	971	**539**	.555	
* 63.	Dino Ciccarelli, Min., Wsh., Det.	15	1015	**528**	.520	
* 64.	Dave Babych, Wpg., Hfd., Van.	15	970	**523**	.539	
65.	Dennis Maruk, Cal., Clev., Min., Wsh.	14	888	**522**	.588	
66.	Wayne Cashman, Bos.	17	1027	**516**	.502	
67.	Butch Goring, L.A., NYI, Bos.	16	1107	**513**	.463	
68.	John Tonelli, NYI, Cgy., L.A., Chi., Que.	14	1028	**511**	.497	
69.	Lanny McDonald, Tor., Col., Cgy.	16	1111	**506**	.455	
70.	Ivan Boldirev, Bos., Cal., Chi., Atl., Van., Det.	15	1052	**505**	.480	
71.	Randy Carlyle, Tor., Pit., Wpg.	17	1055	**499**	.473	
* 72.	Dave Andreychuk, Buf., Tor.	13	925	**498**	.538	
73.	Pete Mahovlich, Det., Mtl., Pit.	16	884	**485**	.549	
74.	Pit Martin, Det., Bos., Chi., Van.	17	1101	**485**	.441	
* 75.	Kirk Muller, N.J., Mtl., NYI	11	835	**483**	.578	
* 76.	Brian Bellows, Min., Mtl.	13	953	**474**	.497	
77.	Ken Hodge, Chi., Bos., NYR	13	881	**472**	.536	
78.	Ted Lindsay, Det., Chi.	17	1068	**472**	.442	
* 79.	Chris Chelios, Mtl., Chi.	12	767	**471**	.614	
80.	Jacques Lemaire, Mtl.	12	853	**469**	.550	

Though Bobby Hull was best known for his goal-scoring abilities, he was also a nifty passer, registering 560 assists during his 16-year NHL career.

	Player	Seasons	Games	Assists	Assists per game
81.	Dean Prentice, Pit., Min., Det., NYR, Bos.	22	1378	**469**	.340
* 82.	Gary Suter, Cgy., Chi.	10	681	**467**	.686
83.	Phil Goyette, Mtl., NYR, St.L., Buf.	16	941	**467**	.496
84.	Bill Barber, Phi.	12	903	**463**	.513
85.	Reed Larson, Det., Bos., Edm., NYI, Min., Buf.	14	904	**463**	.512
86.	Doug Mohns, Bos., Chi., Min., Atl., Wsh.	22	1390	**462**	.332
87.	Bobby Rousseau, Mtl., Min., NYR.	15	942	**458**	.486
88.	Wilf Paiement, K.C. Col., Tor., Que., NYR, Buf., Pit.	14	946	**458**	.484
89.	Murray Oliver, Det., Bos., Tor., Min.	17	1127	**454**	.403
90.	Doug Harvey, Mtl., NYR, Det., St.L.	20	1113	**452**	.406
91.	Guy Lapointe, Mtl., St.L., Bos.	16	884	**451**	.510
92.	Walt Tkaczuk, NYR.	14	945	**451**	.477
93.	Peter McNab, Buf., Bos., Van., N.J.	14	954	**450**	.472
* 94.	Pat LaFontaine, NYI, Buf.	12	709	**449**	.633
95.	Mel Bridgman, Phi., Cgy., N.J., Det., Van.	14	977	**449**	.460
96.	Bill Gadsby, Chi., NYR, Det.	20	1248	**437**	.350
97.	Yvan Cournoyer, Mtl.	16	968	**435**	.449
* 98.	Dave Christian, Wpg., Wsh., Bos., St.L., Chi.	15	1009	**433**	.429
99.	Ron Greschner, NYR.	16	982	**431**	.439
* 100.	Luc Robitaille, L.A., Pit.	9	686	**430**	.627

Top 100 Active Assist Leaders

Player	Games	Assists	Assists per game
1. **Wayne Gretzky**, Edm., L.A.	1173	**1692**	1.442
2. **Paul Coffey**, Edm., Pit., L.A., Det.	1078	**978**	.907
3. **Ray Bourque**, Bos.	1146	**908**	.792
4. **Mark Messier**, Edm., NYR	1127	**877**	.778
5. **Dale Hawerchuk**, Wpg., Buf.	1055	**825**	.782
6. **Denis Savard**, Chi., Mtl., T.B.	1063	**812**	.764
7. **Peter Stastny**, Que., N.J., St.L.	977	**789**	.808
8. **Ron Francis**, Hfd., Pit.	1008	**789**	.783
9. **Jari Kurri**, Edm., L.A.	1028	**731**	.711
10. **Mario Lemieux**, Pit.	599	**717**	1.197
11. **Larry Murphy**, L.A., Wsh., Min., Pit.	1152	**712**	.618
12. **Steve Yzerman**, Det.	862	**679**	.788
13. **Doug Gilmour**, St.L., Cgy., Tor.	900	**655**	.728
14. **Bernie Nicholls**, L.A., NYR, Edm., N.J., Chi.	933	**636**	.682
15. **Al MacInnis**, Cgy., St.L.	835	**629**	.753
16. **Phil Housley**, Buf., Wpg., St.L., Cgy.	909	**625**	.688
17. **Dale Hunter**, Que., Wsh.	1099	**614**	.559
18. **Adam Oates**, Det., St.L., Bos.	676	**611**	.904
19. **Neal Broten**, Min., Dal., N.J.	1002	**606**	.605
20. **Glenn Anderson**, Edm., Tor., NYR, St.L.	1097	**593**	.541
21. **Steve Larmer**, Chi., NYR	1006	**571**	.568
22. **Mike Gartner**, Wsh., Min., NYR, Tor.	1208	**562**	.465
23. **Thomas Steen**, Wpg.	950	**553**	.582
24. **Mark Howe**, Hfd., Phi., Det.	929	**545**	.587
25. **Scott Stevens**, Wsh., St.L., N.J.	959	**542**	.565
26. **Joe Mullen**, St.L., Cgy., Pit.	971	**539**	.555
27. **Dino Ciccarelli**, Min., Wsh., Det.	1015	**528**	.520
28. **Dave Babych**, Wpg., Hfd., Van.	970	**523**	.539
29. **Dave Andreychuk**, Buf., Tor.	925	**498**	.538
30. **Kirk Muller**, N.J., Mtl., NYI	835	**483**	.578
31. **Brian Bellows**, Min., Mtl.	953	**474**	.497
32. **Chris Chelios**, Mtl., Chi.	767	**471**	.614
33. **Gary Suter**, Cgy., Chi.	681	**467**	.686
34. **Pat LaFontaine**, NYI, Buf.	709	**449**	.633
35. **Dave Christian**, Wpg., Wsh., Bos., St.L., Chi.	1009	**433**	.429
36. **Luc Robitaille**, L.A., Pit.	686	**430**	.627
37. **Kelly Kisio**, Det., NYR, S.J., Cgy.	761	**429**	.564
38. **Brent Sutter**, NYI, Chi.	940	**426**	.453
39. **Kent Nilsson**, Atlanta, Cgy., Min., Edm.	553	**422**	.763
40. **Mike Ridley**, NYR, Wsh., Tor.	754	**419**	.556
41. **Murray Craven**, Det., Phi., Hfd., Van., Chi.	801	**408**	.509
42. **Pierre Turgeon**, Buf., NYI, Mtl.	592	**403**	.681
43. **Vincent Damphousse**, Tor., Edm., Mtl.	690	**401**	.581
44. **Craig Janney**, Bos., St.L., S.J.	475	**398**	.838
45. **James Patrick**, NYR, Hfd., Cgy.	776	**395**	.509
46. **Joe Sakic**, Que.	508	**392**	.772
47. **Dan Quinn**, Cgy., Pit., Van., St.L., Phi., Min., Ott., L.A.	726	**384**	.529
48. **Mats Naslund**, Mtl., Bos.	651	**383**	.588
49. **Tomas Sandstrom**, NYR, L.A., Pit.	716	**378**	.528
50. **Brian Leetch**, NYR	485	**375**	.773
51. **Ed Olczyk**, Chi., Tor., Wpg., NYR	751	**372**	.495
52. **Bob Carpenter**, Wsh., NYR, L.A., Bos., N.J.	942	**371**	.394
53. **Rick Tocchet**, Phi., Pit., L.A.	717	**367**	.512
54. **Pat Verbeek**, N.J., Hfd., NYR	915	**367**	.401
55. **Russ Courtnall**, Tor., Mtl., Min., Dal., Van.	772	**365**	.473
56. **Doug Bodger**, Pit., Buf.	762	**360**	.472
57. **Jeff Brown**, Que., St.L., Van.	610	**359**	.589
58. **Doug Crossman**, Chi., Phi., L.A., NYI, Hfd., Det., T.B., St.L.	914	**359**	.393
59. **Gordie Roberts**, Hfd., Min., Phi., St.L., Pit., Bos.	1097	**359**	.327
60. **Charlie Huddy**, Edm., L.A., Buf.	952	**349**	.367
61. **Dave Ellett**, Wpg., Tor.	785	**347**	.442
62. **Steve Duchesne**, L.A., Phi., Que., St.L.	625	**342**	.547
63. **Peter Zezel**, Phi., St.L., Wsh., Tor., Dal.	692	**341**	.493
64. **Troy Murray**, Chi., Wpg., Ott., Pit.	852	**340**	.399
65. **Guy Carbonneau**, Mtl., St.L.	954	**337**	.353
66. **Geoff Courtnall**, Bos., Edm., Wsh., St.L., Van.	788	**336**	.426
67. **Mark Recchi**, Pit., Phi., Mtl.	464	**334**	.720
68. **Kevin Lowe**, Edm., NYR	1130	**329**	.291
69. **Tom Kurvers**, Mtl., Buf., N.J., Tor., Van., NYI, Ana.	659	**328**	.498
70. **Mike Krushelnyski**, Bos., Edm., L.A., Tor., Det.	897	**328**	.366
71. **Michal Pivonka**, Wsh.	629	**325**	.517
72. **Dave Poulin**, Phi., Bos., Wsh.	724	**325**	.449
73. **Garry Galley**, L.A., Wsh., Bos., Phi., Buf.	740	**321**	.434
74. **Pat Flatley**, NYI	656	**319**	.486
75. **Mark Osborne**, Det., NYR, Tor., Wpg.	919	**319**	.347
76. **Esa Tikkanen**, Edm., NYR, St.L.	663	**318**	.480
77. **Kevin Dineen**, Hfd., Phi.	747	**318**	.426
78. **Bruce Driver**, N.J.	702	**316**	.450
79. **Ray Ferraro**, Hfd., NYI	758	**316**	.417
80. **Brad McCrimmon**, Bos., Phi., Cgy., Det., Hfd.	1127	**311**	.276
81. **Brett Hull**, Cgy., St.L.	588	**308**	.524

John MacLean, the New Jersey Devils' career-leader in games played, goals and points, also ranks among the top-100 active players in assists.

Player	Games	Assists	Assists per game
82. **Steve Thomas**, Tor., Chi., NYI	667	**308**	.462
83. **Joe Nieuwendyk**, Cgy.	577	**302**	.523
84. **Christian Ruuttu**, Buf., Chi., Van.	621	**298**	.480
85. **Kevin Hatcher**, Wsh., Dal.	732	**296**	.404
86. **Al Iafrate**, Tor., Wsh., Bos.	740	**295**	.399
87. **Jeremy Roenick**, Chi.	458	**294**	.642
88. **John MacLean**, N.J.	752	**293**	.390
89. **Ron Sutter**, Phi., St.L., Que., NYI	782	**293**	.375
90. **John Cullen**, Pit., Hfd., Tor.	471	**292**	.620
91. **Dave Gagner**, NYR, Min., Dal.	644	**290**	.450
92. **Stephane J. J. Richer**, Mtl., N.J.	690	**290**	.420
93. **Theoren Fleury**, Cgy.	488	**288**	.590
94. **Jimmy Carson**, L.A., Edm., Det., Van., Hfd.	615	**286**	.465
95. **Cam Neely**, Van., Bos.	677	**279**	.412
96. **Fredrik Olausson**, Wpg., Edm.	584	**278**	.476
97. **Kevin Stevens**, Pit.	458	**276**	.603
98. **Brendan Shanahan**, N.J., St.L.	558	**276**	.495
99. **Steve Smith**, Edm., Chi.	644	**274**	.425
100. **Keith Brown**, Chi., Fla.	876	**274**	.313

Top 100 All-Time Point Leaders

* active player

(figures in parentheses indicate ranking of top 10 in order of points per game)

Joe Mullen reached two historical milestones during the 1994-95 season. In addition to playing in his 1,000th game, he became the first U.S.-born player in NHL history to reach the 1,000-point plateau.

	Player	Seasons	Games	Goals	Assists	Points	Goals per game
* 1.	Wayne Gretzky, Edm., L.A. .	16	1173	814	1692	**2506**	2.136 (1)
2.	Gordie Howe, Det., Hfd. . . .	26	1767	801	1049	**1850**	1.046
3.	Marcel Dionne, Det., L.A., NYR	18	1348	731	1040	**1771**	1.313 (6)
4.	Phil Esposito, Chi., Bos., NYR	18	1282	717	873	**1590**	1.240
5.	Stan Mikita, Chi.	22	1394	541	926	**1467**	1.052
6.	Bryan Trottier, NYI, Pit. . .	18	1279	524	901	**1425**	1.114
* 7.	Mark Messier, Edm., NYR . .	16	1127	492	877	**1369**	1.214
8.	John Bucyk, Det., Bos., ...	23	1540	556	813	**1369**	.889
9.	Guy Lafleur, Mtl., NYR, Que.	17	1126	560	793	**1353**	1.201
* 10.	Paul Coffey, Edm., Pit., L.A., Det.	15	1078	358	978	**1336**	1.239
11.	Gilbert Perreault, Buf.	17	1191	512	814	**1326**	1.113
* 12.	Dale Hawerchuk, Wpg., Buf.	14	1055	489	825	**1314**	1.245(10)
* 13.	Jari Kurri, Edm., L.A.	14	1028	565	731	**1296**	1.260 (9)
14.	Alex Delvecchio, Det.	24	1549	456	825	**1281**	.827
15.	Jean Ratelle, NYR, Bos.	21	1281	491	776	**1267**	.989
* 16.	Denis Savard, Chi., Mtl., T.B.	15	1063	451	812	**1263**	1.188
* 17.	Peter Stastny, Que., N.J., St.L.	15	977	450	789	**1239**	1.268 (8)
* 18.	Ray Bourque, Bos.	16	1146	323	908	**1231**	1.074
19.	Norm Ullman, Det., Tor. . . .	20	1410	490	739	**1229**	.872
20.	Jean Beliveau, Mtl.	20	1125	507	712	**1219**	1.083
* 21.	Mario Lemieux, Pit.	10	599	494	717	**1211**	2.021 (2)
22.	Bobby Clarke, Phi.	15	1144	358	852	**1210**	1.057
* 23.	Mike Gartner, Wsh., Min., NYR, Tor.	16	1208	629	562	**1191**	.986
24.	Bobby Hull, Chi., Wpg., Hfd.	16	1063	610	560	**1170**	1.100
* 25.	Steve Yzerman, Det.	12	862	481	679	**1160**	1.345 (5)
26.	Michel Goulet, Que., Chi. . .	15	1089	548	604	**1152**	1.057
* 27.	Ron Francis, Hfd., Pit.	14	1008	349	789	**1138**	1.128
28.	Bernie Federko, St.L., Det. . .	14	1000	369	761	**1130**	1.130
29.	Mike Bossy, NYI	10	752	573	553	**1126**	1.497 (3)
30.	Darryl Sittler, Tor., Phi., Det.	15	1096	484	637	**1121**	1.022
31.	Frank Mahovlich, Tor., Det., Mtl.	18	1181	533	570	**1103**	.934
* 32.	Glenn Anderson, Edm., Tor., NYR, St.L.	15	1097	492	593	**1085**	.989
* 33.	Bernie Nicholls, L.A., NYR, Edm., N.J., Chi.	14	933	438	636	**1074**	1.151
34.	Dave Taylor, L.A.	17	1111	431	638	**1069**	.962
* 35.	Dino Ciccarelli, Min., Wsh., Det.	15	1015	529	528	**1057**	1.041
36.	Denis Potvin, NYI	15	1060	310	742	**1052**	.992
37.	Henri Richard, Mtl.	20	1256	358	688	**1046**	.833
38.	Bobby Smith, Min., Mtl. . . .	15	1077	357	679	**1036**	.962
* 39.	Joe Mullen, St.L., Cgy., Pit. . .	14	971	487	539	**1026**	1.056
40.	Rod Gilbert, NYR	18	1065	406	615	**1021**	.959
41.	Steve Larmer, Chi., NYR. . . .	15	1006	441	571	**1012**	1.005
42.	Lanny McDonald, Tor., Col., Cgy.	16	1111	500	506	**1006**	.905
43.	Brian Propp, Phi., Bos., Min., Hfd.	15	1016	425	579	**1004**	.988
44.	Rick Middleton, NYR, Bos. . .	14	1005	448	540	**988**	.983
45.	Dave Keon, Tor., Hfd. . . .	18	1296	396	590	**986**	.761
46.	Andy Bathgate, NYR, Tor., Det., Pit.	17	1069	349	624	**973**	.910
* 47.	Doug Gilmour, St.L., Cgy., Tor.	12	900	314	655	**969**	1.076
48.	Maurice Richard, Mtl.	18	978	544	421	**965**	.987
49.	Larry Robinson, Mtl., L.A. . .	20	1384	208	750	**958**	.692
* 50.	Dave Andreychuk, Buf., Tor.	13	925	448	498	**946**	1.022
* 51.	Larry Murphy, L.A., Wsh., Min., Pit.	15	1152	233	712	**945**	.820
52.	Bobby Orr, Bos., Chi.	12	657	270	645	**915**	1.392 (4)
* 53.	Dale Hunter, Que., Wsh. . . .	15	1099	286	614	**900**	.819
* 54.	Brian Bellows, Min., Mtl. . . .	13	953	423	474	**897**	.941
55.	Brad Park, NYR, Bos., Det. . .	17	1113	213	683	**896**	.805
56.	Butch Goring, L.A., NYI, Bos.	16	1107	375	513	**888**	.802
57.	Bill Barber, Phi.	12	903	420	463	**883**	.978
* 58.	Phil Housley, Buf., Wpg., St.L., Cgy.	13	909	257	625	**882**	.970
* 59.	Neal Broten, Min., Dal., N.J. .	15	1002	274	606	**880**	.878
60.	Dennis Maruk, Cal., Clev., Min., Wsh.	14	888	356	522	**878**	.989
61.	Ivan Boldirev, Bos., Cal., Chi., Atl., Van., Det.	15	1052	361	505	**866**	.823
62.	Yvan Cournoyer, Mtl.	16	968	428	435	**863**	.892
63.	Dean Prentice, Pit., Min., Det., NYR, Bos.	22	1378	391	469	**860**	.624
* 64.	Pat LaFontaine, NYI, Buf. . . .	12	709	403	449	**852**	1.201
65.	Ted Lindsay, Det., Chi.	17	1068	379	472	**851**	.797
* 66.	Al MacInnis, Cgy., St.L. . . .	14	835	221	629	**850**	1.017
* 67.	Luc Robitaille, L.A., Pit. . . .	9	686	415	430	**845**	1.231

	Player	Seasons	Games	Goals	Assists	Points	Points per game
68.	Tom Lysiak, Atl., Chi.	13	919	292	551	**843**	.917
69.	John Tonelli, NYI, Cgy., L.A., Chi., Que.	14	1028	325	511	**836**	.813
70.	Jacques Lemaire, Mtl.	12	853	366	469	**835**	.979
71.	John Ogrodnick, Det., Que., NYR.	14	928	402	425	**827**	.891
72.	Doug Wilson, Chi., S.J. . . .	16	1024	237	590	**827**	.808
73.	Red Kelly, Det., Tor.	20	1316	281	542	**823**	.625
* 74.	Adam Oates, Det., St.L., Bos. .	10	676	211	611	**822**	1.215
75.	Pierre Larouche, Pit., Mtl., Hfd., NYR.	14	812	395	427	**822**	1.012
76.	Bernie Geoffrion, Mtl., NYR .	16	883	393	429	**822**	.931
77.	Steve Shutt, Mtl., L.A. . . .	13	930	424	393	**817**	.878
78.	Thomas Steen, Wpg.	14	950	264	553	**817**	.860
79.	Wilf Paiement, K.C. Col., Tor., Que., NYR, Buf., Pit. . . .	14	946	356	458	**814**	.860
80.	Peter McNab, Buf., Bos., Van., N.J. . . .	14	954	363	450	**813**	.852
81.	Pit Martin, Det., Bos., Chi., Van. . . .	17	1101	324	485	**809**	.735
82.	Ken Linseman, Phi., Edm., Bos., Tor. . . .	14	860	256	551	**807**	.938
83.	Garry Unger, Tor., Det., St.L., Atl., L.A., Edm. . . .	16	1105	413	391	**804**	.728
84.	Ken Hodge, Chi., Bos., NYR .	13	881	328	472	**800**	.908
85.	Wayne Cashman, Bos.	17	1027	277	516	**793**	.772
86.	Rick Vaive, Van., Tor., Chi., Buf. . . .	13	876	441	347	**788**	.900
87.	Borje Salming, Tor., Det. . . .	17	1148	150	637	**787**	.686
* 88.	Kirk Muller, N.J., Mtl., NYI . .	11	835	292	483	**775**	.928
89.	Jean Pronovost, Wsh., Pit., Atl. . . .	14	998	391	383	**774**	.776
90.	Pete Mahovlich, Det., Mtl., Pit. . . .	16	884	288	485	**773**	.874
* 91.	Dave Christian, Wpg., Wsh., Bos., St.L., Chi.	15	1009	340	433	**773**	.766
92.	Rick Kehoe, Tor., Pit.	14	906	371	396	**767**	.847
* 93.	Brent Sutter, NYI, Chi. . . .	15	940	341	426	**767**	.816
94.	Rick MacLeish, Phi., Hfd., Pit., Det. . . .	14	846	349	410	**759**	.897
* 95.	Brett Hull, Cgy., St.L. . . .	9	588	442	308	**750**	1.275 (7)
* 96.	Mark Howe, Hfd., Phi., Det. .	16	929	197	545	**742**	.799
* 97.	Pat Verbeek, N.J., Hfd., NYR.	13	915	372	367	**739**	.808
98.	Murray Oliver, Det., Bos., Tor., Min.	17	1127	274	454	**728**	.646
99.	Mike Foligno, Det., Buf., Tor., Fla.	15	1018	355	372	**727**	.714
100.	Bob Nevin, Tor., NYR, Min., L.A.	18	1128	307	419	**726**	.644

Top 100 Active Points Leaders

	Player	Games	Goals	Assists	Points	Points per game
1.	**Wayne Gretzky**, Edm., L.A.	1173	814	1692	**2506**	2.136
2.	**Mark Messier**, Edm., NYR	1127	492	877	**1369**	1.215
3.	**Paul Coffey**, Edm., Pit., L.A., Det.	1078	358	978	**1336**	1.239
4.	**Dale Hawerchuk**, Wpg., Buf.	1055	489	825	**1314**	1.245
5.	**Jari Kurri**, Edm., L.A.	1028	565	731	**1296**	1.261
6.	**Denis Savard**, Chi., Mtl., T.B.	1063	451	812	**1263**	1.188
7.	**Peter Stastny**, Que., N.J., St.L.	977	450	789	**1239**	1.268
8.	**Ray Bourque**, Bos.	1146	323	908	**1231**	1.074
9.	**Mario Lemieux**, Pit.	599	494	717	**1211**	2.022
10.	**Mike Gartner**, Wsh., Min., NYR, Tor.	1208	629	562	**1191**	.986
11.	**Steve Yzerman**, Det.	862	481	679	**1160**	1.346
12.	**Ron Francis**, Hfd., Pit.	1008	349	789	**1138**	1.129
13.	**Glenn Anderson**, Edm., Tor., NYR, St.L.	1097	492	593	**1085**	.989
14.	**Bernie Nicholls**, L.A., NYR, Edm., N.J., Chi.	933	438	636	**1074**	1.151
15.	**Dino Ciccarelli**, Min., Wsh., Det.	1015	529	528	**1057**	1.041
16.	**Joe Mullen**, St.L., Cgy., Pit.	971	487	539	**1026**	1.057
17.	**Steve Larmer**, Chi., NYR	1006	441	571	**1012**	1.006
18.	**Doug Gilmour**, St.L., Cgy., Tor.	900	314	655	**969**	1.077
19.	**Dave Andreychuk**, Buf., Tor.	925	448	498	**946**	1.023
20.	**Larry Murphy**, L.A., Wsh., Min., Pit.	1152	233	712	**945**	.820
21.	**Dale Hunter**, Que., Wsh.	1099	286	614	**900**	.819
22.	**Brian Bellows**, Min., Mtl.	953	423	474	**897**	.941
23.	**Phil Housley**, Buf., Wpg., St.L., Cgy.	909	257	625	**882**	.970
24.	**Neal Broten**, Min., Dal., N.J.	1002	274	606	**880**	.878
25.	**Pat LaFontaine**, NYI, Buf.	709	403	449	**852**	1.202
26.	**Al MacInnis**, Cgy., St.L.	835	221	629	**850**	1.018
27.	**Luc Robitaille**, L.A., Pit.	686	415	430	**845**	1.232
28.	**Adam Oates**, Det., St.L., Bos.	676	211	611	**822**	1.216
29.	**Thomas Steen**, Wpg.	950	264	553	**817**	.860
30.	**Kirk Muller**, N.J., Mtl., NYI	835	292	483	**775**	.928
31.	**Dave Christian**, Wpg., Wsh., Bos., St.L., Chi.	1009	340	433	**773**	.766
32.	**Brent Sutter**, NYI, Chi.	940	341	426	**767**	.816
33.	**Brett Hull**, Cgy., St.L.	588	442	308	**750**	1.276
34.	**Mark Howe**, Hfd., Phi., Det.	929	197	545	**742**	.799
35.	**Pat Verbeek**, N.J., Hfd., NYR	915	372	367	**739**	.808
36.	**Tomas Sandstrom**, NYR, L.A., Pit.	716	317	378	**695**	.971
37.	**Scott Stevens**, Wsh., St.L., N.J.	959	152	542	**694**	.724
38.	**Kent Nilsson**, Atlanta, Cgy., Min., Edm.	553	264	422	**686**	1.241
39.	**Mike Ridley**, NYR, Wsh., Tor.	754	266	419	**685**	.908
40.	**Pierre Turgeon**, Buf., NYI, Mtl.	592	280	403	**683**	1.154
41.	**Rick Tocchet**, Phi., Pit., L.A.	717	309	367	**676**	.943
42.	**Bob Carpenter**, Wsh., NYR, L.A., Bos., N.J.	942	300	371	**671**	.712
43.	**Kelly Kisio**, Det., NYR, S.J., Cgy.	761	229	429	**658**	.865
44.	**Dave Babych**, Wpg., Hfd., Van.	970	132	523	**655**	.675
45.	**Cam Neely**, Van., Bos.	677	369	279	**648**	.957
46.	**Vincent Damphousse**, Tor., Edm., Mtl.	690	245	401	**646**	.936
47.	**Ed Olczyk**, Chi., Tor., Wpg., NYR	751	267	372	**639**	.851
48.	**Dan Quinn**, Cgy., Pit., Van., St.L., Phi., Min., Ott., L.A.	726	253	384	**637**	.877
49.	**Mats Naslund**, Mtl., Bos.	651	251	383	**634**	.974
50.	**Murray Craven**, Det., Phi., Hfd., Van., Chi.	801	224	408	**632**	.789
51.	**Joe Sakic**, Que.	508	234	392	**626**	1.232
52.	**Geoff Courtnall**, Bos., Edm., Wsh., St.L., Van.	788	288	336	**624**	.792
53.	**Kevin Dineen**, Hfd., Phi.	747	302	318	**620**	.830
54.	**Joe Nieuwendyk**, Cgy.	577	314	302	**616**	1.068
55.	**Stephane J. J. Richer**, Mtl., N.J.	690	324	290	**614**	.890
56.	**Gary Suter**, Cgy., Chi.	681	140	467	**607**	.891
57.	**Russ Courtnall**, Tor., Mtl., Min., Dal., Van.	772	242	365	**607**	.786
58.	**Chris Chelios**, Mtl., Chi.	767	129	471	**600**	.782
59.	**Ray Ferraro**, Hfd., NYI	758	273	316	**589**	.777
60.	**John MacLean**, N.J.	752	295	293	**588**	.782
61.	**Steve Thomas**, Tor., Chi., NYI	667	269	308	**577**	.865
62.	**Mike Krushelnyski**, Bos., Edm., L.A., Tor., Det.	897	241	328	**569**	.634
63.	**Troy Murray**, Chi., Wpg., Ott., Pit.	852	223	340	**563**	.661
64.	**Guy Carbonneau**, Mtl., St.L.	954	226	337	**563**	.590
65.	**Jimmy Carson**, L.A., Edm., Det., Van., Hfd.	615	274	286	**560**	.911
66.	**Mark Recchi**, Pit., Phi., Mtl.	464	223	334	**557**	1.200
67.	**Peter Zezel**, Phi., St.L., Wsh., Tor., Dal.	692	196	341	**537**	.776
68.	**Craig Janney**, Bos., St.L., S.J.	475	138	398	**536**	1.128
69.	**Dave Gagner**, NYR, Min., Dal.	644	244	290	**534**	.829
70.	**Esa Tikkanen**, Edm., NYR, St.L.	663	214	318	**532**	.802
71.	**Mark Osborne**, Det., NYR, Tor., Wpg.	919	212	319	**531**	.578
72.	**Dave Poulin**, Phi., Bos., Wsh.	724	205	325	**530**	.732
73.	**Jeremy Roenick**, Chi.	458	235	294	**529**	1.155
74.	**Kevin Stevens**, Pit.	458	251	276	**527**	1.151
75.	**Theoren Fleury**, Cgy.	488	232	288	**520**	1.066
76.	**Brendan Shanahan**, N.J., St.L.	558	244	276	**520**	.932
77.	**Greg Adams**, N.J., Van., Dal.	687	249	271	**520**	.757
78.	**James Patrick**, NYR, Hfd., Cgy.	776	114	395	**509**	.656
79.	**Petr Klima**, Det., Edm., T.B.	673	288	218	**506**	.752
80.	**Jeff Brown**, Que., Van., St.L.	610	142	359	**501**	.821
81.	**Steve Duchesne**, L.A., Phi., Que., St.L.	625	157	342	**499**	.798
82.	**Craig Simpson**, Pit., Edm., Buf.	634	247	250	**497**	.784

Kevin Stevens, who was traded to the Boston Bruins on August 2, 1995, has averaged 1.51 points-per-game in eight NHL seasons.

	Player	Games	Goals	Assists	Points	Points per game
83.	**Sylvain Turgeon**, Hfd., N.J., Mtl., Ott.	669	269	226	**495**	.740
84.	**Dirk Graham**, Min., Chi.	772	219	270	**489**	.633
85.	**Brian Leetch**, NYR	485	112	375	**487**	1.004
86.	**Dave Ellett**, Wpg., Tor.	785	139	347	**486**	.619
87.	**Gerard Gallant**, Det., T.B.	615	211	269	**480**	.780
88.	**Ron Sutter**, Phi., St.L., Que., NYI	782	184	293	**477**	.610
89.	**Michal Pivonka**, Wsh.	629	150	325	**475**	.755
90.	**Pat Flatley**, NYI	656	152	319	**471**	.718
91.	**Gary Leeman**, Tor., Cgy., Mtl., Van.	665	199	266	**465**	.699
92.	**Doug Crossman**, Chi., Phi., L.A., NYI, Hfd., Det., T.B., St.L.	914	105	359	**464**	.508
93.	**Gary Roberts**, Cgy.	550	235	228	**463**	.842
94.	**Craig MacTavish**, Bos., Edm., NYR, Phi.	975	206	253	**459**	.471
95.	**Kevin Hatcher**, Wsh., Dal.	732	159	296	**455**	.622
96.	**Doug Bodger**, Pit., Buf.	762	89	360	**449**	.589
97.	**Claude Lemieux**, Mtl., N.J.	634	222	226	**448**	.707
98.	**John Cullen**, Pit., Hfd., Tor.	471	153	292	**445**	.945
99.	**Alexander Mogilny**, Buf.	381	211	233	**444**	1.165
100.	**Charlie Huddy**, Edm., L.A., Buf.	952	94	349	**443**	.465

All-Time Games Played Leaders

Regular Season

* active player

Player	Team	Seasons	GP
1. Gordie Howe	Detroit	25	1,687
	Hartford	1	80
	Total	**26**	**1,767**
2. Alex Delvecchio	**Detroit**	**24**	**1,549**
3. John Bucyk	Detroit	2	104
	Boston	21	1,436
	Total	**23**	**1,540**
4. Tim Horton	Toronto	19¾	1,185
	NY Rangers	1¼	93
	Pittsburgh	1	44
	Buffalo	2	124
	Total	**24**	**1,446**
5. Harry Howell	NY Rangers	17	1,160
	California	1½	83
	Los Angeles	2½	168
	Total	**21**	**1,411**
6. Norm Ullman	Detroit	12½	875
	Toronto	7½	535
	Total	**20**	**1,410**
7. Stan Mikita	**Chicago**	**22**	**1,394**
8. Doug Mohns	Boston	11	710
	Chicago	6½	415
	Minnesota	2½	162
	Atlanta	1	28
	Washington	1	75
	Total	**22**	**1,390**
9. Larry Robinson	Montreal	17	1,202
	Los Angeles	3	182
	Total	**20**	**1,384**
10. Dean Prentice	NY Rangers	10½	666
	Boston	3	170
	Detroit	3½	230
	Pittsburgh	2	144
	Minnesota	3	168
	Total	**22**	**1,378**
11. Ron Stewart	Toronto	13	838
	Boston	2	126
	St. Louis	½	19
	NY Rangers	4	306
	Vancouver	1	42
	NY Islanders	½	22
	Total	**21**	**1,353**
12. Marcel Dionne	Detroit	4	309
	Los Angeles	11¾	921
	NY Rangers	2¼	118
	Total	**18**	**1,348**
13. Red Kelly	Detroit	12½	846
	Toronto	7½	470
	Total	**20**	**1,316**
14. Dave Keon	Toronto	15	1,062
	Hartford	3	234
	Total	**18**	**1,296**
15. Phil Esposito	Chicago	4	235
	Boston	8¼	625
	NY Rangers	5¾	422
	Total	**18**	**1,282**
16. Jean Ratelle	NY Rangers	15¼	862
	Boston	5¾	419
	Total	**21**	**1,281**
17. Bryan Trottier	NY Islanders	15	1,123
	Pittsburgh	3	156
	Total	**18**	**1,279**
18. Henri Richard	**Montreal**	**20**	**1,256**
19. Bill Gadsby	Chicago	8½	468
	NY Rangers	6½	457
	Detroit	5	323
	Total	**20**	**1,248**
20. Allan Stanley	NY Rangers	6¼	307
	Chicago	1¾	111
	Boston	2	129
	Toronto	9	633
	Philadelphia	1	64
	Total	**21**	**1,244**
21. Eddie Westfall	Boston	11	734
	NY Islanders	7	493
	Total	**18**	**1,227**
22. Eric Nesterenko	Toronto	5	206
	Chicago	16	1,013
	Total	**21**	**1,219**
* 23. Mike Gartner	Washington	9¾	758
	Minnesota	1	80
	NY Rangers	4	322
	Toronto	1¼	48
	Total	**16**	**1,208**
24. Marcel Pronovost	Detroit	16	983
	Toronto	5	223
	Total	**21**	**1,206**
25. Gilbert Perreault	**Buffalo**	**17**	**1,191**
26. George Armstrong	**Toronto**	**21**	**1,187**

Player	Team	Seasons	GP
27. Frank Mahovlich	Toronto	11¾	720
	Detroit	2¾	198
	Montreal	3½	263
	Total	**18**	**1,181**
28. Don Marshall	Montreal	10	585
	NY Rangers	7	479
	Buffalo	1	62
	Toronto	1	50
	Total	**19**	**1,176**
* 29. Wayne Gretzky	Edmonton	9	696
	Los Angeles	7	477
	Total	**16**	**1,173**
30. Bob Gainey	**Montreal**	**16**	**1,160**
* 31. Larry Murphy	Los Angeles	3¼	242
	Washington	5½	453
	Minnesota	1¾	121
	Pittsburgh	4½	336
	Total	**15**	**1,152**
32. Leo Boivin	Toronto	3¼	137
	Boston	11½	717
	Detroit	1¼	85
	Pittsburgh	1½	114
	Minnesota	1½	97
	Total	**19**	**1,150**
33. Borje Salming	Toronto	16	1,099
	Detroit	1	49
	Total	**17**	**1,148**
* 34. Ray Bourque	**Boston**	**16**	**1,146**
35. Bobby Clarke	**Philadelphia**	**15**	**1,144**
* 36. Kevin Lowe	Edmonton	13	966
	NY Rangers	3	164
	Total	**16**	**1,130**
37. Bob Nevin	Toronto	5¾	250
	NY Rangers	7¼	505
	Minnesota	2	138
	Los Angeles	3	235
	Total	**18**	**1,128**
38. Murray Oliver	Detroit	2½	101
	Boston	6½	429
	Toronto	3	226
	Minnesota	5	371
	Total	**17**	**1,127**

Player	Team	Seasons	GP
* 39. Brad McCrimmon	Boston	3	228
	Philadelphia	5	367
	Calgary	3	231
	Detroit	3	203
	Hartford	2	98
	Total	**16**	**1,127**
* 40. Mark Messier	Edmonton	12	851
	NY Rangers	4	276
	Total	**16**	**1,127**
41. Guy Lafleur	Montreal	14	961
	NY Rangers	1	67
	Quebec	2	98
	Total	**17**	**1,126**
42. Jean Beliveau	**Montreal**	**20**	**1,125**
43. Doug Harvey	Montreal	14	890
	NY Rangers	3	151
	Detroit	1	2
	St. Louis	1	70
	Total	**19**	**1,113**
44. Brad Park	NY Rangers	7½	465
	Boston	7½	501
	Detroit	2	147
	Total	**17**	**1,113**
45. Lanny McDonald	Toronto	6½	477
	Colorado	1¾	142
	Calgary	7¾	441
	Total	**16**	**1,111**
46. Dave Taylor	**Los Angeles**	**17**	**1,111**
47. Butch Goring	Los Angeles	10¾	736
	NY Islanders	4¾	332
	Boston	½	39
	Total	**16**	**1,107**
48. Garry Unger	Toronto	½	15
	Detroit	3	216
	St. Louis	8½	662
	Atlanta	1	79
	Los Angeles	¾	58
	Edmonton	2¼	75
	Total	**16**	**1,105**
49. Pit Martin	Detroit	3¼	119
	Boston	1¾	111
	Chicago	10¼	740
	Vancouver	1¾	131
	Total	**17**	**1,101**

Red Kelly, seen here celebrating the Toronto Maple Leafs' Stanley Cup victory over the Detroit Red Wings on April 16, 1963, played 1,316 games in his 20-year career.

Player	Team	Seasons	GP
* 50. Dale Hunter	Quebec	7	523
	Washington	8	576
	Total	**15**	**1,099**
* 51. Gordie Roberts	Hartford	1½	107
	Minnesota	7	555
	Philadelphia	¼	11
	St. Louis	2½	166
	Pittsburgh	1¾	134
	Boston	2	124
	Total	**15**	**1,097**
* 52. Glenn Anderson	Edmonton	11	828
	Toronto	2¾	221
	NY Rangers	¼	12
	St. Louis	1	36
	Total	**15**	**1,097**
53. Darryl Sittler	Toronto	11½	844
	Philadelphia	2½	191
	Detroit	1	61
	Total	**15**	**1,096**
54. Michel Goulet	Quebec	10¾	813
	Chicago	4¼	276
	Total	**15**	**1,089**
55. Carol Vadnais	Montreal	2	42
	Oakland	2	152
	California	1¾	94
	Boston	3½	263
	NY Rangers	6¾	485
	New Jersey	1	51
	Total	**17**	**1,087**
56. Brad Marsh	Atlanta	2	160
	Calgary	1¼	97
	Philadelphia	6¾	514
	Toronto	2¾	181
	Detroit	1¼	75
	Ottawa	1	59
	Total	**15**	**1,086**
57. Bob Pulford	Toronto	14	947
	Los Angeles	2	132
	Total	**16**	**1,079**
* 58. Paul Coffey	Edmonton	7	532
	Pittsburgh	4¾	331
	Los Angeles	¾	60
	Detroit	2½	155
	Total	**15**	**1,078**
59. Bobby Smith	Minnesota	8¼	572
	Montreal	6¾	505
	Total	**15**	**1,077**
60. Craig Ramsay	Buffalo	14	1,070
61. Andy Bathgate	NY Rangers	11¾	719
	Toronto	1¼	70
	Detroit	2	130
	Pittsburgh	2	150
	Total	**17**	**1,069**
62. Ted Lindsay	Detroit	14	862
	Chicago	3	206
	Total	**17**	**1,068**
63. Terry Harper	Montreal	10	554
	Los Angeles	3	234
	Detroit	4	252
	St. Louis	1	11
	Colorado	1	15
	Total	**19**	**1,066**
64. Rod Gilbert	NY Rangers	18	1,065
65. Bobby Hull	Chicago	15	1,036
	Winnipeg	⅔	18
	Hartford	⅓	9
	Total	**16**	**1,063**
* 66. Denis Savard	Chicago	10¼	748
	Montreal	3	210
	Tampa Bay	1¾	105
	Total	**15**	**1,063**
67. Denis Potvin	NY Islanders	15	1,060
68. Jean Guy Talbot	Montreal	13	791
	Minnesota	¼	4
	Detroit	½	32
	St. Louis	2½	172
	Buffalo	¾	57
	Total	**17**	**1,056**
69. Randy Carlyle	Toronto	2	94
	Pittsburgh	5¾	397
	Winnipeg	9¼	564
	Total	**17**	**1,055**
* 70. Dale Hawerchuk	Winnipeg	9	713
	Buffalo	5	342
	Total	**14**	**1,055**

Player	Team	Seasons	GP
71. Ivan Boldirev	Boston	1¼	13
	California	2¾	191
	Chicago	4¾	384
	Atlanta	1	65
	Vancouver	2¾	216
	Detroit	2½	183
	Total	**15**	**1,052**
72. Eddie Shack	NY Rangers	2¼	141
	Toronto	8¾	504
	Boston	2	120
	Los Angeles	1¼	84
	Buffalo	1½	111
	Pittsburgh	1¼	87
	Total	**17**	**1,047**
73. Rob Ramage	Colorado	3	234
	St. Louis	5¾	441
	Calgary	1¼	80
	Toronto	2	160
	Minnesota	1	34
	Tampa Bay	¾	66
	Montreal	½	14
	Philadelphia	¾	15
	Total	**15**	**1,044**
74. Serge Savard	Montreal	15	917
	Winnipeg	2	123
	Total	**17**	**1,040**
75. Ron Ellis	Toronto	16	1,034
76. Harold Snepsts	Vancouver	11¾	781
	Minnesota	1	71
	Detroit	3	120
	St. Louis	1¼	61
	Total	**17**	**1,033**
77. Ralph Backstrom	Montreal	14½	844
	Los Angeles	2¼	172
	Chicago	¼	16
	Total	**17**	**1,032**
78. Dick Duff	Toronto	9¾	582
	NY Rangers	¾	43
	Montreal	5	305
	Los Angeles	¾	39
	Buffalo	1¾	61
	Total	**18**	**1,030**
79. John Tonelli	NY Islanders	7¾	584
	Calgary	2¼	161
	Los Angeles	3	231
	Chicago	¾	33
	Quebec	¼	19
	Total	**14**	**1,028**
* 80. Jari Kurri	Edmonton	10	754
	Los Angeles	4	274
	Total	**14**	**1,028**
* 81. Gaetan Duchesne	Washington	6	451
	Quebec	2	150
	Minnesota	4	297
	San Jose	1¾	117
	Florida	¼	13
	Total	**14**	**1,028**
82. Wayne Cashman	Boston	17	1,027
83. Doug Wilson	Chicago	14	938
	San Jose	2	86
	Total	**16**	**1,024**
84. Jim Neilson	NY Rangers	12	810
	California	2	98
	Cleveland	2	115
	Total	**16**	**1,023**
85. Keith Acton	Montreal	4¼	228
	Minnesota	4¼	343
	Edmonton	1	72
	Philadelphia	4½	303
	Washington	¼	6
	NY Islanders	¾	71
	Total	**15**	**1,023**
* 86. Mike Ramsey	Buffalo	13¾	911
	Pittsburgh	1¼	77
	Detroit	1	33
	Total	**16**	**1,021**
87. Don Lever	Vancouver	7⅔	593
	Atlanta	⅓	28
	Calgary	1¼	85
	Colorado	¾	59
	New Jersey	3	216
	Buffalo	2	39
	Total	**15**	**1,020**
88. Mike Foligno	Detroit	2½	186
	Buffalo	9	664
	Toronto	2¾	129
	Florida	¾	39
	Total	**15**	**1,018**

Player	Team	Seasons	GP
89. Phil Russell	Chicago	6¾	504
	Atlanta	1¼	93
	Calgary	3	229
	New Jersey	2¾	172
	Buffalo	1¼	18
	Total	**15**	**1,016**
90. Brian Propp	Philadelphia	10¾	790
	Boston	¼	14
	Minnesota	3	147
	Hartford	1	65
	Total	**15**	**1,016**
91. Laurie Boschman	Toronto	2¾	187
	Edmonton	1	73
	Winnipeg	7¼	526
	New Jersey	2	153
	Ottawa	1	70
	Total	**14**	**1,009**
92. Dave Christian	Winnipeg	4	230
	Washington	6½	504
	Boston	1½	128
	St. Louis	1	78
	Chicago	2	69
	Total	**15**	**1,009**
93. Dave Lewis	NY Islanders	6¾	514
	Los Angeles	3¼	221
	New Jersey	3	209
	Detroit	2	64
	Total	**15**	**1,008**
94. Bob Murray	Chicago	15	1,008
* 95. Ron Francis	Hartford	9¾	714
	Pittsburgh	4¼	294
	Total	**14**	**1,008**
96. Jim Roberts	Montreal	9⅔	611
	St. Louis	5⅓	395
	Total	**15**	**1,006**
97. Steve Larmer	Chicago	13	891
	NY Rangers	2	115
	Total	**15**	**1,006**
98. Claude Provost	Montreal	15	1,005
99. Rick Middleton	NY Rangers	2	124
	Boston	12	881
	Total	**14**	**1,005**
100. Ryan Walter	Washington	4	307
	Montreal	9	604
	Vancouver	2	92
	Total	**15**	**1,003**
101. Vic Hadfield	NY Rangers	13	839
	Pittsburgh	3	163
	Total	**16**	**1,002**
*102. Neal Broten	Minnesota	13	876
	Dallas	1½	96
	New Jersey	½	30
	Total	**15**	**1,002**
*103. Jay Wells	Los Angeles	9	604
	Philadelphia	1¾	126
	Buffalo	2	85
	NY Rangers	3¼	186
	Total	**16**	**1,001**
104. Bernie Federko	St. Louis	14	927
	Detroit	1	73
	Total	**15**	**1,000**

Steve Larmer joined Neal Broten, Gaetan Duchesne, Jay Wells, Jari Kurri, Mike Ramsey, Joe Mullen, Dino Ciccarelli and Ron Francis as elite members of the 1,000 games-played club in 1994-95.

Goaltending Records

All-Time Shutout Leaders

Goaltender	Team	Seasons	Games	Shutouts
Terry Sawchuk	Detroit	14	734	85
(1949-1970)	Boston	2	102	11
	Toronto	3	91	4
	Los Angeles	1	36	2
	NY Rangers	1	8	1
	Total	21	971	**103**
George Hainsworth	Montreal	7½	318	75
(1926-1937)	Toronto	3½	146	19
	Total	11	464	**94**
Glenn Hall	Detroit	4	148	17
(1952-1971)	Chicago	10	618	51
	St. Louis	4	140	16
	Total	18	906	**84**
Jacques Plante	Montreal	11	556	58
(1952-1973)	NY Rangers	2	98	5
	St. Louis	2	69	10
	Toronto	2¾	106	7
	Boston	¼	8	2
	Total	18	837	**82**
Tiny Thompson	Boston	10¼	468	74
(1928-1940)	Detroit	1¾	85	7
	Total	12	553	**81**
Alex Connell	Ottawa	8	293	64
(1924-1937)	Detroit	1	48	6
	NY Americans	1	1	0
	Mtl. Maroons	2	75	11
	Total	12	417	**81**
Tony Esposito	Montreal	1	13	2
(1968-1984)	Chicago	15	873	74
	Total	16	886	**76**
Lorne Chabot	NY Rangers	2	80	21
(1926-1937)	Toronto	5	214	33
	Montreal	1	47	8
	Chicago	1	48	8
	Mtl. Maroons	1	16	2
	NY Americans	1	6	1
	Total	11	411	**73**
Harry Lumley	Detroit	6½	324	26
(1943-1960)	NY Rangers	½	1	0
	Chicago	2	134	5
	Toronto	4	267	34
	Boston	3	78	6
	Total	16	804	**71**
Roy Worters	Pittsburgh Pirates	3	123	22
(1925-1937)	NY Americans	9	360	44
	* Montreal		1	0
	Total	12	484	**66**
Turk Broda	Toronto	14	629	62
(1936-1952)				
John Roach	Toronto	7	223	13
(1921-1935)	NY Rangers	4	89	30
	Detroit	3	180	15
	Total	14	492	**58**

Goaltender	Team	Seasons	Games	Shutouts
Clint Benedict	Ottawa	7	158	19
(1917-1930)	Mtl. Maroons	6	204	38
	Total	13	362	**57**
Bernie Parent	Boston	2	57	1
(1965-1979)	Philadelphia	9½	486	50
	Toronto	1½	65	4
	Total	13	608	**55**
Ed Giacomin	NY Rangers	10¼	539	49
(1965-1978)	Detroit	2¾	71	5
	Total	13	610	**54**
David Kerr	Mtl. Maroons	3	101	11
(1930-1941)	NY Americans	1	1	0
	NY Rangers	7	324	40
	Total	11	426	**51**
Rogie Vachon	Montreal	5¼	206	13
(1966-1982)	Los Angeles	6¾	389	32
	Detroit	2	109	4
	Boston	2	91	2
	Total	16	795	**51**
Ken Dryden	Montreal	8	397	**46**
(1970-1979)				
Gump Worsley	NY Rangers	10	583	24
(1952-1974)	Montreal	6½	172	16
	Minnesota	4½	107	3
	Total	21	862	**43**
Charlie Gardiner	Chicago	7	316	**42**
(1927-1934)				
Frank Brimsek	Boston	9	444	35
(1938-1950)	Chicago	1	70	5
	Total	10	514	**40**
Johnny Bower	NY Rangers	3	77	5
(1953-1970)	Toronto	12	475	32
	Total	15	552	**37**
Bill Durnan	Montreal	7	383	**34**
(1943-1950)				
Eddie Johnston	Boston	11	444	27
(1962-1978)	Toronto	1	26	1
	St. Louis	3⅔	118	4
	Chicago	⅓	4	0
	Total	16	592	**32**
Roger Crozier	Detroit	7	313	20
(1963-1977)	Buffalo	6	202	10
	Washington	1	3	0
	Total	14	518	**30**
Cesare Maniago	Toronto	1	7	0
(1960-1978)	Montreal	1	14	0
	NY Rangers	2	34	2
	Minnesota	9	420	26
	Vancouver	2	93	2
	Total	15	568	**30**

*Played 1 game for Canadiens in 1929-30.

Ten or More Shutouts, One Season

Number of Shutouts	Goaltender	Team	Season	Length of Schedule
22	George Hainsworth	Montreal	1928-29	44
15	Alex Connell	Ottawa	1925-26	36
	Alex Connell	Ottawa	1927-28	44
	Hal Winkler	Boston	1927-28	44
	Tony Esposito	Chicago	1969-70	76
14	George Hainsworth	Montreal	1926-27	44
13	Clint Benedict	Mtl. Maroons	1926-27	44
	Alex Connell	Ottawa	1926-27	44
	George Hainsworth	Montreal	1927-28	44
	John Roach	NY Rangers	1928-29	44
	Roy Worters	NY Americans	1928-29	44
	Harry Lumley	Toronto	1953-54	70
12	Tiny Thompson	Boston	1928-29	44
	Lorne Chabot	Toronto	1928-29	44
	Chuck Gardiner	Chicago	1930-31	44
	Terry Sawchuk	Detroit	1951-52	70
	Terry Sawchuk	Detroit	1953-54	70
	Terry Sawchuk	Detroit	1954-55	70
	Glenn Hall	Detroit	1955-56	70
	Bernie Parent	Philadelphia	1973-74	78
	Bernie Parent	Philadelphia	1974-75	80
11	Lorne Chabot	NY Rangers	1927-28	44
	Harry Holmes	Detroit	1927-28	44
	Clint Benedict	Mtl. Maroons	1928-29	44
	Joe Miller	Pittsburgh Pirates	1928-29	44
	Tiny Thompson	Boston	1932-33	48
	Terry Sawchuk	Detroit	1950-51	70
10	Lorne Chabot	NY Rangers	1926-27	44
	Roy Worters	Pittsburgh Pirates	1927-28	44
	Clarence Dolson	Detroit	1928-29	44
	John Roach	Detroit	1932-33	48
	Chuck Gardiner	Chicago	1933-34	48
	Tiny Thompson	Boston	1935-36	48
	Frank Brimsek	Boston	1938-39	48
	Bill Durnan	Montreal	1948-49	60
	Gerry McNeil	Montreal	1952-53	70
	Harry Lumley	Toronto	1952-53	70
	Tony Esposito	Chicago	1973-74	78
	Ken Dryden	Montreal	1976-77	80

All-Time Win Leaders

(Minimum 200 Wins)

Wins	Goaltender	GP	Decisions	Mins.	Losses	Ties	%
447	Terry Sawchuk	971	950	57,205	330	173	.562
434	Jacques Plante	837	827	49,553	246	147	.614
423	Tony Esposito	886	881	52,585	306	152	.566
407	Glenn Hall	906	897	53,484	327	163	.545
355	Rogie Vachon	795	773	46,298	291	127	.541
335	Gump Worsley	862	839	50,232	353	151	.489
333	Harry Lumley	804	802	48,107	326	143	.504
313 *	Andy Moog	582	544	32,848	160	71	.641
305	Billy Smith	680	643	38,431	233	105	.556
302	Turk Broda	629	627	38,173	224	101	.562
294	Mike Liut	663	639	38,155	271	74	.518
290 *	Grant Fuhr	596	556	33,647	195	71	.585
289	Ed Giacomin	610	592	35,693	206	97	.570
286	Dan Bouchard	655	631	37,919	232	113	.543
284	Tiny Thompson	553	553	34,174	194	75	.581
277 *	Patrick Roy	529	508	30,658	166	65	.609
270	Bernie Parent	608	588	35,136	197	121	.562
270	Gilles Meloche	788	752	45,401	351	131	.446
267 *	Mike Vernon	497	406	28,385	161	55	.725
266 *	Tom Barrasso	548	524	31,555	197	61	.566
261 *	Don Beaupre	622	582	35,120	246	75	.513
258	Ken Dryden	397	389	23,352	57	74	.758
252	Frank Brimsek	514	514	31,210	182	80	.568
251	Johnny Bower	552	535	32,077	194	90	.553
246	George Hainsworth	465	465	29,415	145	74	.609
246	Pete Peeters	489	452	27,699	155	51	.601
244 *	Kelly Hrudey	565	525	32,016	210	71	.532
236	Reggie Lemelin	507	461	28,006	162	63	.580
236	Eddie Johnston	592	573	34,209	256	81	.483
235 *	John Vanbiesbrouck	543	514	30,907	217	62	.518
231	Glenn Resch	571	537	32,279	224	82	.507
230	Gerry Cheevers	418	407	24,394	103	74	.656
218	John Roach	491	491	30,423	204	69	.514
215	Greg Millen	604	588	35,377	284	89	.441
208	Bill Durnan	383	382	22,945	112	62	.626
208	Don Edwards	459	437	26,181	155	74	.561
206	Lorne Chabot	411	411	25,309	140	65	.580
206	Roger Crozier	518	472	28,567	196	70	.511
204	Rick Wamsley	407	381	23,123	131	46	.596
203	David Kerr	426	426	26,519	148	75	.565
203 *	Ron Hextall	431	410	24,631	161	46	.551

* active player

Active Shutout Leaders

(Minimum 12 Shutouts)

Goaltender	Teams	Seasons	Games	Shutouts
Patrick Roy	Montreal	11	529	**28**
Ed Belfour	Chicago	7	332	**28**
Tom Barrasso	Buffalo, Pittsburgh	12	548	**21**
John Vanbiesbrouck	NY Rangers, Florida	13	543	**21**
Andy Moog	Edm., Bos., Dal.	15	582	**21**
Kirk McLean	New Jersey, Vancouver	10	404	**17**
Jon Casey	Min., Bos., St.L.	10	401	**16**
Kelly Hrudey	NY Islanders, Los Angeles	12	565	**16**
Don Beaupre	Min., Wsh., Ott.	15	622	**16**
Bob Essensa	Winnipeg, Detroit	6	294	**15**
Grant Fuhr	Edm., Tor., Buf., L.A.	14	596	**14**
Dominik Hasek	Chicago, Buffalo	5	152	**13**
Daren Puppa	Buf., Tor., T.B.	10	322	**12**
Clint Malarchuk	Que., Wsh., Buf.	10	338	**12**

Active Goaltending Leaders

(Ranked by winning percentage; minimum 250 games played)

Goaltender	Teams	Seasons	GP	Decisions	W	L	T	Winning %
Andy Moog	Edm., Bos., Dal.	15	582	544	313	160	71	.641
Mike Vernon	Calgary, Detroit	12	497	483	267	161	55	.610
Patrick Roy	Montreal	11	529	508	277	166	65	.609
Mike Richter	NY Rangers	6	250	228	125	78	25	.603
Ed Belfour	Chicago	7	332	314	168	106	40	.599
Grant Fuhr	Edm., Tor., Buf., L.A.	14	596	556	290	195	71	.585
Curtis Joseph	St. Louis	6	280	267	137	96	34	.577
Tom Barrasso	Buffalo, Pittsburgh	12	548	524	266	197	61	.566
Ron Hextall	Phi., Que., NYI	9	431	410	203	161	46	.551
Tim Cheveldae	Detroit, Winnipeg	7	308	292	141	117	34	.541
Kelly Hrudey	NY Islanders, Los Angeles	12	565	525	244	210	71	.532
Daren Puppa	Buf., Tor., T.B.	10	322	296	138	122	36	.527
Jon Casey	Min., Bos., St.L.	10	401	366	165	146	55	.526
John Vanbiesbrouck	NY Rangers, Florida	13	543	514	235	217	62	.518
Clint Malarchuk	Que., Wsh., Buf.	10	338	316	141	130	45	.517
Don Beaupre	Min., Wsh., Ott.	15	622	582	261	246	75	.513
Chris Terreri	New Jersey	8	264	236	103	101	32	.504
Bob Essensa	Winnipeg, Detroit	6	294	275	120	121	34	.498
Kirk McLean	New Jersey, Vancouver	10	404	391	171	174	46	.496
Glenn Healy	L.A., NYI, NYR	9	305	282	121	134	27	.477
Bill Ranford	Boston, Edmonton	10	441	407	169	190	48	.474
Ken Wregget	Tor., Phi., Pit.	12	421	388	161	190	37	.463
Sean Burke	New Jersey, Hartford	7	301	283	112	136	35	.458

Goals Against Average Leaders

(minimum 13 games played, 1994-95; minimum 27 games played, 1992-93 to 1993-94; 25 games played, 1926-27 to 1991-92; 15 games played, 1917-18 to 1925-26.)

Season	Goaltender and Club	GP	Mins.	GA	SO	AVG.
1994-95	Dominik Hasek, Buffalo	41	2,416	85	5	2.11
1993-94	Dominik Hasek, Buffalo	58	3,358	109	7	1.95
1992-93	Felix Potvin, Toronto	48	2,781	116	2	2.50
1991-92	Patrick Roy, Montreal	67	3,935	155	5	2.36
1990-91	Ed Belfour, Chicago	74	4,127	170	4	2.47
1989-90	Mike Liut, Hartford, Washington	37	2,161	91	4	2.53
1988-89	Patrick Roy, Montreal	48	2,744	113	4	2.47
1987-88	Pete Peeters, Washington	35	1,896	88	2	2.78
1986-87	Brian Hayward, Montreal	37	2,178	102	1	2.81
1985-86	Bob Froese, Philadelphia	51	2,728	116	5	2.55
1984-85	Tom Barrasso, Buffalo	54	3,248	144	5	2.66
1983-84	Pat Riggin, Washington	41	2,299	102	4	2.66
1982-83	Pete Peeters, Boston	62	3,611	142	8	2.36
1981-82	Denis Herron, Montreal	27	1,547	68	3	2.64
1980-81	Richard Sevigny, Montreal	33	1,777	71	2	2.40
1979-80	Bob Sauve, Buffalo	32	1,880	74	4	2.36
1978-79	Ken Dryden, Montreal	47	2,814	108	5	2.30
1977-78	Ken Dryden, Montreal	52	3,071	105	5	2.05
1976-77	Michel Larocque, Montreal	26	1,525	53	4	2.09
1975-76	Ken Dryden, Montreal	62	3,580	121	8	2.03
1974-75	Bernie Parent, Philadelphia	68	4,041	137	12	2.03
1973-74	Bernie Parent, Philadelphia	73	4,314	136	12	1.89
1972-73	Ken Dryden, Montreal	54	3,165	119	6	2.26
1971-72	Tony Esposito, Chicago	48	2,780	82	9	1.77
1970-71	Jacques Plante, Toronto	40	2,329	73	4	1.88
1969-70	Ernie Wakely, St. Louis	30	1,651	58	4	2.11
1968-69	Jacques Plante, St. Louis	37	2,139	70	5	1.96
1967-68	Gump Worsley, Montreal	40	2,213	73	6	1.98
1966-67	Glenn Hall, Chicago	32	1,664	66	2	2.38
1965-66	Johnny Bower, Toronto	35	1,998	75	3	2.25
1964-65	Johnny Bower, Toronto	34	2,040	81	3	2.38
1963-64	Johnny Bower, Toronto	51	3,009	106	5	2.11
1962-63	Jacques Plante, Montreal	56	3,320	138	5	2.49
1961-62	Jacques Plante, Montreal	70	4,200	166	4	2.37
1960-61	Johnny Bower, Toronto	58	3,480	145	2	2.50
1959-60	Jacques Plante, Montreal	69	4,140	175	3	2.54
1958-59	Jacques Plante, Montreal	67	4,000	144	9	2.16
1957-58	Jacques Plante, Montreal	57	3,386	119	9	2.11
1956-57	Jacques Plante, Montreal	61	3,660	123	9	2.02

Season	Goaltender and Club	GP	Mins.	GA	SO	AVG.
1955-56	Jacques Plante, Montreal	64	3,840	119	7	1.86
1954-55	Terry Sawchuk, Detroit	68	4,080	132	12	1.94
1953-54	Harry Lumley, Toronto	69	4,140	128	13	1.86
1952-53	Terry Sawchuk, Detroit	63	3,780	120	9	1.90
1951-52	Terry Sawchuk, Detroit	70	4,200	133	12	1.90
1950-51	Al Rollins, Toronto	40	2,367	70	5	1.77
1949-50	Bill Durnan, Montreal	64	3,840	141	8	2.20
1948-49	Bill Durnan, Montreal	60	3,600	126	10	2.10
1947-48	Turk Broda, Toronto	60	3,600	143	5	2.38
1946-47	Bill Durnan, Montreal	60	3,600	138	4	2.30
1945-46	Bill Durnan, Montreal	40	2,400	104	4	2.60
1944-45	Bill Durnan, Montreal	50	3,000	121	1	2.42
1943-44	Bill Durnan, Montreal	50	3,000	109	2	2.18
1942-43	Johnny Mowers, Detroit	50	3,010	124	6	2.47
1941-42	Frank Brimsek, Boston	47	2,930	115	3	2.35
1940-41	Turk Broda, Toronto	48	2,970	99	5	2.00
1939-40	Dave Kerr, NY Rangers	48	3,000	77	8	1.54
1938-39	Frank Brimsek, Boston	43	2,610	68	10	1.56
1937-38	Tiny Thompson, Boston	48	2,970	89	7	1.80
1936-37	Normie Smith, Detroit	48	2,980	102	6	2.05
1935-36	Tiny Thompson, Boston	48	2,930	82	10	1.68
1934-35	Lorne Chabot, Chicago	48	2,940	88	8	1.80
1933-34	Wilf Cude, Detroit, Montreal	30	1,920	47	5	1.47
1932-33	Tiny Thompson, Boston	48	3,000	88	11	1.76
1931-32	Chuck Gardiner, Chicago	48	2,989	92	4	1.85
1930-31	Roy Worters, NY Americans	44	2,760	74	8	1.61
1929-30	Tiny Thompson, Boston	44	2,680	98	3	2.19
1928-29	George Hainsworth, Montreal	44	2,800	43	22	0.92
1927-28	George Hainsworth, Montreal	44	2,730	48	13	1.05
1926-27	Clint Benedict, Mtl. Maroons	43	2,748	65	13	1.42
1925-26	Alex Connell, Ottawa	36	2,251	42	15	1.12
1924-25	Georges Vezina, Montreal	30	1,860	56	5	1.81
1923-24	Georges Vezina, Montreal	24	1,459	48	3	1.97
1922-23	Clint Benedict, Ottawa	24	1,478	54	4	2.19
1921-22	Clint Benedict, Ottawa	24	1,508	84	2	3.34
1920-21	Clint Benedict, Ottawa	24	1,457	75	2	3.09
1919-20	Clint Benedict, Ottawa	24	1,444	64	5	2.66
1918-19	Clint Benedict, Ottawa	18	1,113	53	2	2.86
1917-18	Georges Vezina, Montreal	21	1,282	84	1	3.93

All-Time NHL Coaching Register

Regular Season, 1917-95

(figures in parentheses indicate ranking of top 25 in order of games coached)

Coach	Team	Games	Wins	Losses	Ties	%	Cup Wins	Seasons
Abel, Sid (6)	Chicago	140	39	79	22	.357	0	1952-54
	Detroit	811	340	339	132	.501	0	1957-68, 1969-70
	St. Louis	10	3	6	1	.350	0	1971-72
	Kansas City	3	0	3	0	.000	0	1975-76
	Total	**963**	**382**	**426**	**155**	**.477**	**0**	**1952-76**
Adams, Jack (5)	Toronto St. Pats	18	10	7	1	.583	0	1922-23
	Detroit	964	413	390	161	.512	3	1927-44
	Total	**982**	**423**	**397**	**162**	**.513**	**3**	**1922-44**
Allen, Keith	Philadelphia	150	51	67	32	.447	0	1967-69
Anderson, Jim	Washington	54	4	45	5	.120	0	1974-75
Angotti, Lou	St. Louis	32	6	20	6	.281	0	1973-75
	Pittsburgh	80	16	58	6	.238	0	1983-84
	Total	**112**	**22**	**78**	**12**	**.250**	**0**	**1973-84**
Arbour, Al (1)	St. Louis	107	42	40	25	.509	0	1970-71, 1971-73
	NY Islanders	1499	739	537	223	.567	4	1973-86, 1988-94
	Total	**1606**	**781**	**577**	**248**	**.564**	**4**	**1970-94**
Armstrong, George	Toronto	47	17	26	4	.404	0	1988-89
Barkley, Doug	Detroit	77	20	46	11	.331	0	1970-72, 1975-76
Beaulieu, Andre	Minnesota	31	6	22	3	.242	0	1977-78
Belisle, Danny	Washington	96	28	51	17	.380	0	1978-80
Berenson, Red	St. Louis	204	100	72	32	.569	0	1979-82
Bergeron, Michel (14)	Quebec	634	265	283	86	.486	0	1980-87, 1989-90
	NY Rangers	158	73	67	18	.519	0	1987-89
	Total	**792**	**338**	**350**	**104**	**.492**	**0**	**1980-89**
Berry, Bob (10)	Los Angeles	240	107	94	39	.527	0	1978-81
	Montreal	223	116	71	36	.601	0	1981-84
	Pittsburgh	240	88	127	25	.419	0	1984-87
	St. Louis	157	73	63	21	.532	0	1992-94
	Total	**860**	**384**	**355**	**121**	**.517**	**0**	**1978-94**
Blackburn, Don	Hartford	140	42	63	35	.425	0	1979-81
Blair, Wren	Minnesota	147	48	65	34	.442	0	1967-70
Blake, Toe (9)	Montreal	914	500	255	159	.634	8	1955-68
Bolieau, Marc	Pittsburgh	151	66	61	24	.517	0	1973-76
Boivin, Leo	St. Louis	97	28	53	16	.371	0	1975-76, 1977-78
Boucher, Frank	NY Rangers	525	179	263	83	.420	1	1939-49, 1953-54
Boucher, George	Mtl. Maroons	12	6	5	1	.542	0	1930-31
	Ottawa	48	13	29	6	.333	0	1933-34
	St.L. Eagles	35	9	20	6	.343	0	1934-35
	Boston	70	22	32	16	.429	0	1949-50
	Total	**165**	**50**	**86**	**29**	**.391**	**0**	**1930-50**
Bowman, Scott (2)	St. Louis	238	110	83	45	.557	0	1967-70, 1970-71
	Montreal	634	419	110	105	.744	5	1971-79
	Buffalo	404	210	134	60	.594	0	1979-80, 1981-85, 1985-87
	Pittsburgh	164	95	53	16	.628	1	1991-93
	Detroit	132	79	41	12	.644	0	1993-95
	Total	**1572**	**913**	**421**	**238**	**.656**	**6**	**1967-94**
Bowness, Rick	Winnipeg	28	8	17	3	.339	0	1988-89
	Boston	80	36	32	12	.525	0	1991-92
	Ottawa	216	33	165	18	.194	0	1992-95
	Total	**324**	**77**	**214**	**33**	**.289**	**0**	**1991-95**
Brooks, Herb	NY Rangers	285	131	113	41	.532	0	1981-85
	Minnesota	80	19	48	13	.319	0	1987-88
	New Jersey	84	40	37	7	.518	0	1992-93
	Total	**449**	**190**	**198**	**61**	**.491**	**0**	**1981-93**
Brophy, John	Toronto	160	53	91	16	.381	0	1986-88
Burnett, George	Edmonton	35	12	20	3	.386	0	1994-95
Burns, Charlie	Minnesota	86	22	50	14	.337	0	1969-70, 1974-75
Burns, Pat	Montreal	320	174	104	42	.609	0	1988-92
	Toronto	216	108	77	31	.572	0	1992-95
	Total	**536**	**282**	**181**	**73**	**.594**	**0**	**1988-95**
Bush, Eddie	Kansas City	32	1	23	8	.156	0	1975-76
Colin Campbell	NY Rangers	48	22	23	3	.490	0	1994-95
Doug Carpenter	New Jersey	290	100	166	24	.386	0	1984-88
	Toronto	91	39	47	5	.456	0	1989-91
	Total	**381**	**139**	**213**	**29**	**.403**	**0**	**1984-91**
Carroll, Dick	Toronto Arenas	40	18	22	0	.450	1	1917-19
	Toronto St. Pats	24	15	9	0	.625	0	1920-21
	Total	**64**	**33**	**31**	**0**	**.516**	**1**	**1917-21**
Cashman, Wayne	NY Rangers	2	0	2	0	.000	0	1986-87
Chambers, Dave	Quebec	98	19	64	15	.270	0	1990-92
Charron, Guy	Calgary	16	6	7	3	.469	0	1991-92
Cheevers, Gerry	Boston	376	204	126	46	.604	0	1980-85
Cherry, Don	Boston	400	231	105	64	.658	0	1974-79
	Colorado	80	19	48	13	.319	0	1979-80
	Total	**480**	**250**	**153**	**77**	**.601**	**0**	**1974-80**
Clancy, King	Mtl. Maroons	18	6	11	1	.361	0	1937-38
	Toronto	235	96	94	45	.504	0	1953-56, 1966-67, 1971-72
	Total	**253**	**102**	**105**	**46**	**.494**	**0**	**1937-72**
Clapper, Dit	Boston	230	102	88	40	.530	0	1945-49
Cleghorn, Odie	Pit. Pirates	168	62	86	20	.429	0	1925-29
Colville, Neil	NY Rangers	93	26	41	26	.419	0	1950-52
Conacher, Charlie	Chicago	162	56	84	22	.414	0	1947-50
Conacher, Lionel	NY Americans	44	14	25	5	.375	0	1929-30
Constantine, Kevin	San Jose	132	52	60	20	.470	0	1993-95
Cook, Bill	NY Rangers	117	34	59	24	.393	0	1951-53
Crawford, Marc	Quebec	48	30	13	5	.677	0	1994-95
Creamer, Pierre	Pittsburgh	80	36	35	9	.506	0	1987-88
Creighton, Fred	Atlanta	348	156	136	56	.529	0	1974-79
	Boston	73	40	20	13	.637	0	1979-80
	Total	**421**	**196**	**156**	**69**	**.548**	**0**	**1974-80**
Crisp, Terry	Calgary	240	144	63	33	.669	1	1987-90
	Tampa Bay	216	70	125	21	.373	0	1992-95
	Total	**456**	**214**	**188**	**54**	**.529**	**1**	**1987-95**
Crozier, Joe	Buffalo	192	77	80	35	.492	0	1971-74
	Toronto	40	13	22	5	.388	0	1980-81
	Total	**232**	**90**	**102**	**40**	**.474**	**0**	**1971-81**
Crozier, Roger	Washington	1	0	1	0	.000	0	1981-82
Cunniff, John	Hartford	13	3	9	1	.269	0	1982-83
	New Jersey	133	59	56	18	.511	0	1989-91
	Total	**146**	**62**	**65**	**19**	**.490**	**0**	**1983-91**
Dandurand, Leo	Montreal	158	82	68	8	.544	1	1920-25, 1934-35
Day, Hap	Toronto	546	259	206	81	.549	5	1940-50
Dea, Bill	Detroit	100	32	57	11	.375	0	1975-77, 1981-82
Delvecchio, Alex	Detroit	156	53	82	21	.407	0	1973-77
Demers, Jacques (11)	Quebec	80	25	44	11	.381	0	1979-80
	St. Louis	240	106	106	28	.500	0	1983-86
	Detroit	320	137	136	47	.502	0	1986-90
	Montreal	216	107	82	27	.558	1	1992-95
	Total	**856**	**375**	**368**	**113**	**.504**	**1**	**1979-95**
Denneny, Cy	Boston	44	26	13	5	.648	1	1928-29
	Ottawa	48	11	27	10	.333	0	1932-33
	Total	**92**	**37**	**40**	**15**	**.484**	**1**	**1928-33**
Dineen, Bill	Philadelphia	140	60	60	20	.500	0	1991-93

Dick Irvin, who guided the Chicago Black Hawks, Toronto Maple Leafs and the Montreal Canadiens into the Stanley Cup Finals, stood behind the bench in 1,437 regular-season games.

Coach	Team	Games	Wins	Losses	Ties	%	Cup Wins	Seasons
Dudley, Rick	Buffalo	188	85	72	31	.535	0	1989-92
Duff, Dick	Toronto	2	0	2	0	.000	0	1979-80
Dugal, Jules	Montreal	18	9	6	3	.583	0	1938-39
Duncan, Art	Detroit	33	10	21	2	.333	0	1926-27
	Toronto	47	21	16	10	.553	0	1930-32
	Total	**80**	**31**	**37**	**12**	**.463**	**0**	**1926-32**
Dutton, Red	NY Americans	336	106	180	50	.390	0	1935-42
Eddolls, Frank	Chicago	70	13	40	17	.307	0	1954-55
Esposito, Phil	NY Rangers	45	24	21	0	.533	0	1986-87, 1988-89
Evans, Jack (23)	California	80	27	42	11	.406	0	1975-76
	Cleveland	160	47	87	26	.375	0	1976-78
	Hartford	374	163	174	37	.485	0	1983-88
	Total	**614**	**237**	**303**	**74**	**.446**	**0**	**1975-88**
Fashoway, Gordie	Oakland	10	4	5	1	.450	0	1967-68
Ferguson, John	NY Rangers	121	43	59	19	.434	0	1975-77
	Winnipeg	14	7	6	1	.536	0	1985-86
	Total	**135**	**50**	**65**	**20**	**.444**	**0**	**1975-86**
Filion, Maurice	Quebec	6	1	3	2	.333	0	1980-81
Francis, Emile (15)	NY Rangers	654	347	209	98	.606	0	1965-68, 1968-73, 1973-75
	St. Louis	124	46	64	14	.427	0	1976-77, 1981-83
	Total	**778**	**393**	**273**	**112**	**.577**	**0**	**1965-83**
Frederickson, Frank	Pit. Pirates	44	5	36	3	.148	0	1929-30
Ftorek, Robbie	Los Angeles	132	65	56	11	.534	0	1987-89
Gadsby, Bill	Detroit	78	35	31	12	.526	0	1968-69
Gainey, Bob	Minnesota	244	95	119	30	.451	0	1990-93
	Dallas	132	59	52	21	.527	0	1993-95
	Total	**376**	**154**	**171**	**51**	**.477**	**0**	**1990-95**
Gardiner, Herb	Chicago	44	7	29	8	.250	0	1928-29
Gardner, Jimmy	Hamilton	30	19	10	1	.650	0	1924-25
Garvin, Ted	Detroit	11	2	8	1	.227	0	1973-74
Geoffrion, Bernie	NY Rangers	43	22	18	3	.547	0	1968-69
	Atlanta	208	77	92	39	.464	0	1972-75
	Montreal	30	15	9	6	.600	0	1979-80
	Total	**281**	**114**	**119**	**48**	**.491**	**0**	**1968-80**
Gerard, Eddie	Ottawa	22	9	13	0	.409	0	1917-18
	Mtl. Maroons	284	129	112	43	.530	1	1924-29, 1932-34
	NY Americans	102	34	50	18	.422	0	1930-32
	St.L. Eagles	13	2	11	0	.154	0	1934-35
	Total	**421**	**174**	**186**	**61**	**.486**	**1**	**1917-35**
Gill, David	Ottawa	132	64	41	27	.587	1	1926-29
Glover, Fred	California	356	96	207	53	.344	0	1968-72, 1972-74
	Los Angeles	68	18	42	8	.324	0	1971-72
	Total	**424**	**114**	**249**	**61**	**.341**	**0**	**1968-74**
Goodfellow, Ebbie	Chicago	140	30	91	19	.282	0	1950-52
Gordon, Jackie	Minnesota	289	116	123	50	.488	0	1970-74, 1974-75
Goring, Butch	Boston	93	42	38	13	.522	0	1985-87
Gorman, Tommy	NY Americans	80	31	33	16	.488	0	1925-26, 1928-29
	Chicago	73	28	28	17	.500	1	1932-34
	Mtl. Maroons	174	74	71	29	.509	1	1934-38
	Total	**327**	**133**	**132**	**62**	**.502**	**2**	**1925-38**
Gottselig, Johnny	Chicago	187	62	104	21	.388	0	1944-48
Goyette, Phil	NY Islanders	48	6	38	4	.167	0	1972-73
Green, Gary	Washington	157	50	78	29	.411	0	1979-82
Green, Pete	Ottawa	186	117	61	8	.651	3	1919-26
Green, Wilf	NY Americans	44	11	27	6	.318	0	1927-28
Green, Ted	Edmonton	188	65	102	21	.402	0	1991-94
Guidolin, Aldo	Colorado	59	12	39	8	.271	0	1978-79
Guidolin, Bep	Boston	104	72	23	9	.736	0	1972-74
	Kansas City	125	26	84	15	.268	0	1974-76
	Total	**229**	**98**	**107**	**24**	**.480**	**0**	**1972-76**
Harkness, Ned	Detroit	38	12	22	4	.368	0	1970-71
Harris, Ted	Minnesota	179	48	104	27	.344	0	1975-78
Hart, Cecil	Montreal	430	207	149	74	.567	2	1925-32, 1936-39
Harvey, Doug	NY Rangers	70	26	32	12	.457	0	1961-62
Heffernan, Frank	Toronto St. Pats	12	5	7	0	.417	0	1919-20
Henning, Lorne	Minnesota	158	68	72	18	.487	0	1985-87
	NY Islanders	48	15	28	5	.365	0	1994-95
	Total	**206**	**83**	**100**	**23**	**.459**	**0**	**1985-95**
Holmgren, Paul	Philadelphia	264	107	126	31	.464	0	1988-92
	Hartford	149	49	87	13	.372	0	1992-95
	Total	**413**	**156**	**213**	**44**	**.431**	**0**	**1988-95**
Howell, Harry	Minnesota	11	3	6	2	.364	0	1978-79
Imlach, Punch (7)	Toronto	760	363	274	123	.559	4	1958-69, 1979-80
	Buffalo	119	32	62	25	.374	0	1970-72
	Total	**879**	**395**	**336**	**148**	**.534**	**4**	**1958-80**
Ingarfield, Earl	NY Islanders	30	6	22	2	.233	0	1972-73
Inglis, Bill	Buffalo	56	28	18	10	.589	0	1978-79
Irvin, Dick (3)	Chicago	114	43	56	15	.443	0	1930-31, 1955-56
	Toronto	427	216	152	59	.575	1	1931-40
	Montreal	896	431	313	152	.566	3	1940-55
	Total	**1437**	**690**	**521**	**226**	**.559**	**4**	**1930-55**
Ivan, Tommy (25)	Detroit	470	262	118	90	.653	3	1947-54
	Chicago	103	26	56	21	.354	0	1956-58
	Total	**573**	**288**	**174**	**111**	**.599**	**3**	**1947-58**
Iverson, Emil	Chicago	71	26	28	17	.486	0	1931-33
Johnson, Bob	Calgary	400	193	155	52	.548	0	1982-87
	Pittsburgh	80	41	33	6	.550	1	1990-91
	Total	**480**	**234**	**188**	**58**	**.548**	**1**	**1982-91**
Johnson, Tom	Boston	208	142	43	23	.738	1	1970-73
Johnston, Eddie	Chicago	80	34	27	19	.544	0	1979-80
	Pittsburgh	372	152	169	51	.477	0	1980-83, 1993-95
	Total	**452**	**186**	**196**	**70**	**.489**	**0**	**1979-95**
Johnston, Marshall	California	69	13	45	11	.268	0	1973-75
	Colorado	56	15	32	9	.348	0	1981-82
	Total	**125**	**28**	**77**	**20**	**.304**	**0**	**1973-82**
Keats, Duke	Detroit	11	2	7	2	.273	0	1926-27
Keenan, Mike (16)	Philadelphia	320	190	102	28	.638	0	1984-88
	Chicago	320	153	126	41	.542	0	1988-92
	NY Rangers	84	52	24	8	.667	0	1993-94
	St. Louis	48	28	15	5	.635	0	1994-95
	Total	**772**	**423**	**267**	**82**	**.601**	**0**	**1984-95**
Kelly, Pat	Colorado	101	22	54	25	.342	0	1977-79
Kelly, Red (19)	Los Angeles	150	55	75	20	.433	0	1967-69
	Pittsburgh	274	90	132	52	.423	0	1969-73
	Toronto	318	133	123	62	.516	0	1973-77
	Totals	**742**	**278**	**330**	**134**	**.465**	**0**	**1967-77**
Kennedy, George	Montreal	64	36	28	0	.563	0	1917-20
King, Dave	Calgary	216	109	76	31	.576	0	1992-95
Kingston, George	San Jose	164	28	129	7	.192	0	1991-93
Kish, Larry	Hartford	49	12	32	5	.296	0	1982-83
Kromm, Bobby	Detroit	231	79	111	41	.431	0	1977-80
Kurtenbach, Orland	Vancouver	125	36	62	27	.396	0	1976-78
LaForge, Bill	Vancouver	20	4	14	2	.250	0	1984-85
Lalonde, Newsy	NY Americans	44	17	25	2	.409	0	1926-27
	Ottawa	88	31	45	12	.420	0	1929-31
	Montreal	112	45	53	14	.464	0	1932-35
	Totals	**244**	**93**	**123**	**28**	**.439**	**0**	**1926-35**
Lapointe, Ron	Quebec	89	33	50	6	.404	0	1987-89
Laycoe, Hal	Los Angeles	24	5	18	1	.229	0	1969-70
	Vancouver	156	44	96	16	.333	0	1970-72
	Totals	**180**	**49**	**114**	**17**	**.319**	**0**	**1969-72**
Lehman, Hugh	Chicago	21	3	17	1	.167	0	1927-28
Lemaire, Jacques	Montreal	97	48	37	12	.557	0	1983-85
	New Jersey	132	69	43	20	.598	1	1993-95
	Total	**229**	**117**	**80**	**32**	**.581**	**1**	**1983-95**
Lepine, Pit	Montreal	48	10	33	5	.260	0	1939-40
Lesueur, Percy	Hamilton	24	9	15	0	.375	0	1923-24
Ley, Rick	Hartford	160	69	71	20	.494	0	1989-91
	Vancouver	48	18	18	12	.500	0	1994-95
	Total	**208**	**87**	**89**	**32**	**.495**	**0**	**1989-95**
Lindsay, Ted	Detroit	20	3	14	3	.225	0	1980-81
Long, Barry	Winnipeg	205	87	93	25	.485	0	1983-86
Loughlin, Clem	Chicago	144	61	63	20	.493	0	1934-37
Low, Ron	Edmonton	13	5	7	1	.423	0	1994-95
MacDonald, Parker	Minnesota	61	20	30	11	.418	0	1973-74
	Los Angeles	42	13	24	5	.369	0	1981-82
	Total	**103**	**33**	**54**	**16**	**.398**	**0**	**1973-82**
MacMillan, Billy	Colorado	80	22	45	13	.356	0	1980-81
	New Jersey	100	19	67	14	.260	0	1982-84
	Total	**180**	**41**	**112**	**27**	**.303**	**0**	**1980-83**
MacNeil, Al	Montreal	55	31	15	9	.645	1	1970-71
	Atlanta	80	35	32	13	.519	0	1979-80
	Calgary	160	68	61	31	.522	0	1980-82
	Total	**295**	**134**	**108**	**53**	**.544**	**1**	**1970-82**
Mahoney, Bill	Minnesota	93	42	39	12	.516	0	1983-85
Magnuson, Keith	Chicago	132	49	57	26	.470	0	1980-82
Maguire, Pierre	Hartford	67	23	37	7	.396	0	1993-94
Maloney, Dan	Toronto	160	45	100	15	.328	0	1984-86
	Winnipeg	212	91	93	28	.495	0	1986-89
	Total	**372**	**136**	**193**	**43**	**.423**	**0**	**1984-89**
Maloney, Phil	Vancouver	232	95	105	32	.478	0	1973-77
Mantha, Sylvio	Montreal	48	11	26	11	.344	0	1935-36
Marshall, Bert	Colorado	24	3	17	4	.208	0	1981-82
Martin, Jacques	St. Louis	160	66	71	23	.484	0	1986-88
Maxner, Wayne	Detroit	129	34	68	27	.368	0	1980-82
McCammon, Bob	Philadelphia	218	119	68	31	.617	0	1978-79, 1981-84
	Vancouver	294	102	156	36	.408	0	1987-91
	Total	**511**	**221**	**223**	**67**	**.498**	**0**	**1978-91**
McCreary, Bill	St. Louis	24	6	14	4	.333	0	1971-72
	Vancouver	41	9	25	7	.305	0	1973-74
	California	32	8	20	4	.313	0	1974-75
	Total	**97**	**23**	**59**	**15**	**.314**	**0**	**1971-75**
McLellan, John	Toronto	295	117	136	42	.468	0	1969-73
McVie, Tom	Washington	204	49	122	33	.321	0	1975-78
	Winnipeg	105	20	67	18	.276	0	1979-80, 1980-81
	New Jersey	153	57	74	22	.444	0	1983-84, 1990-92
	Total	**462**	**126**	**263**	**73**	**.352**	**0**	**1975-92**
Meeker, Howie	Toronto	70	21	34	15	.407	0	1956-57
Melrose, Barry	Los Angeles	209	79	101	29	.447	0	1992-95
Milbury, Mike	Boston	160	90	49	21	.628	0	1989-91
Muckler, John	Minnesota	35	6	23	6	.257	0	1968-69
	Edmonton	160	75	65	20	.531	1	1989-91
	Buffalo	268	125	109	34	.530	0	1991-95
	Total	**463**	**206**	**197**	**60**	**.510**	**1**	**1968-95**
Muldoon, Pete	Chicago	44	19	22	3	.466	0	1926-27
Munro, Dunc	Mtl. Maroons	76	37	29	10	.553	0	1929-31
Murdoch, Bob	Chicago	80	30	41	9	.431	0	1987-88
	Winnipeg	160	63	75	22	.463	0	1989-91
	Total	**240**	**93**	**116**	**31**	**.452**	**0**	**1987-91**

Coach	Team	Games	Wins	Losses	Ties	%	Cup Wins	Seasons
Murphy, Mike	Los Angeles	65	20	37	8	.369	0	1986-88
Murray, Bryan (8)	Washington	672	343	246	83	.572	0	1981-90
	Detroit	244	124	91	29	.568	0	1990-93
	Total	**916**	**467**	**337**	**112**	**.571**	**0**	**1981-93**
Murray, Terry	Washington	325	163	134	28	.545	0	1989-94
	Philadelphia	48	28	16	4	.625	0	1994-95
	Total	**373**	**191**	**150**	**32**	**.555**	**0**	**1989-95**
Nanne, Lou	Minnesota	29	7	18	4	.310	0	1977-78
Neale, Harry	Vancouver	407	142	189	76	.442	0	1978-82
	Detroit	35	8	23	4	.286	0	1985-86
	Total	**442**	**150**	**212**	**80**	**.430**	**0**	**1978-82, 1983-84, 1984-85**
Neilson, Roger (13)	Toronto	160	75	62	23	.541	0	1977-79
	Buffalo	80	39	20	21	.619	0	1980-81
	Vancouver	133	51	61	21	.462	0	1982-84
	Los Angeles	28	8	17	3	.339	0	1983-84
	NY Rangers	280	141	104	35	.566	0	1989-93
	Florida	132	53	56	23	.489	0	1993-95
	Total	**813**	**367**	**320**	**126**	**.529**	**0**	**1977-95**
Nykoluk, Mike	Toronto	280	89	144	47	.402	0	1980-84
Oliver, Murray	Minnesota	40	21	11	8	.625	0	1981-83
Olmstead, Bert	Oakland	64	11	37	16	.297	0	1967-68
O'Reilly, Terry	Boston	227	115	86	26	.564	0	1986-89
Paddock, John	Winnipeg	281	106	138	37	.443	0	1991-95
Page, Pierre	Minnesota	160	63	77	20	.456	0	1988-90
	Quebec	230	98	103	29	.489	0	1991-94
	Total	**390**	**161**	**180**	**49**	**.476**	**0**	**1988-94**
Park, Brad	Detroit	45	9	34	2	.222	0	1985-86
Patrick, Craig	NY Rangers	94	37	45	12	.457	0	1980-81, 1984-85
	Pittsburgh	54	22	26	6	.463	0	1989-90
	Total	**148**	**59**	**71**	**18**	**.459**	**0**	**1980-89**
Patrick, Frank	Boston	96	48	36	12	.563	0	1934-36
Patrick, Lester (24)	NY Rangers	604	281	216	107	.554	2	1926-39
Patrick, Lynn	NY Rangers	107	40	51	16	.449	0	1948-50
	Boston	310	117	130	63	.479	0	1950-55
	St. Louis	26	8	15	3	.365	0	1967-68, 1974-75, 1975-76
	Total	**443**	**165**	**186**	**82**	**.465**	**0**	**1948-76**
Patrick, Muzz	NY Rangers	135	44	65	26	.422	0	1953-55, 1962-63
Perron, Jean	Montreal	240	126	84	30	.588	1	1985-88
	Quebec	47	16	26	5	.394	0	1988-89
	Total	**287**	**142**	**110**	**35**	**.556**	**1**	**1985-89**
Perry, Don	Los Angeles	168	52	85	31	.402	0	1981-84
Pike, Alf	NY Rangers	125	36	67	22	.376	0	1959-61
Pilous, Rudy	Chicago	387	162	151	74	.514	1	1958-63
Plager, Barclay	St. Louis	178	49	96	33	.368	0	1977-80, 1982-83
Plager, Bob	St. Louis	11	4	6	1	.409	0	1992-93
Pleau, Larry	Hartford	224	81	117	26	.420	0	1980-83, 1987-89
Polano, Nick	Detroit	240	79	127	34	.400	0	1982-85
Popein, Larry	NY Rangers	41	18	14	9	.549	0	1973-74
Powers, Eddie	Toronto St. Pats	114	54	56	4	.491	1	1921-22, 1923-26
Primeau, Joe	Toronto	210	97	71	42	.562	1	1950-53
Pronovost, Marcel	Buffalo	104	52	29	23	.611	0	1977-79
	Detroit	9	2	7	0	.222	0	1979-80
	Total	**113**	**54**	**36**	**23**	**.580**	**0**	**1977-80**
Pulford, Bob (17)	Los Angeles	396	178	150	68	.535	0	1972-77
	Chicago	375	158	155	62	.504	0	1977-79, 1981-82, 1984-87
	Total	**771**	**336**	**305**	**130**	**.520**	**0**	**1972-87**
Querrie, Charlie	Toronto St. Pats	6	3	3	0	.500	0	1922-23
Quinn, Mike	Quebec Bulldogs	24	4	20	0	.167	0	1919-20
Quinn, Pat (20)	Philadelphia	262	141	73	48	.630	0	1978-82
	Los Angeles	202	75	101	26	.436	0	1984-87
	Vancouver	274	138	108	28	.555	0	1990-94
	Total	**738**	**354**	**282**	**102**	**.549**	**0**	**1978-94**
Ramsay, Craig	Buffalo	21	4	15	2	.238	0	1986-87
Reay, Billy (4)	Toronto	90	26	50	14	.367	0	1957-59
	Chicago	1012	516	335	161	.589	0	1963-77
	Total	**1102**	**542**	**385**	**175**	**.571**	**0**	**1957-77**
Regan, Larry	Los Angeles	88	27	47	14	.386	0	1970-72
Risebrough, Doug	Calgary	144	71	56	17	.552	0	1990-92
Roberts, Jim	Buffalo	45	21	16	8	.556	0	1981-82
	Hartford	80	26	41	13	.406	0	1991-92
	Total	**125**	**47**	**56**	**22**	**.464**	**0**	**1981-92**
Ross, Art (22)	Mtl. Wanderers	6	1	5	0	.167	0	1917-18
	Hamilton	24	6	18	0	.250	0	1922-23
	Boston	698	354	254	90	.572	1	1924-28, 1929-34, 1936-39, 1941-45
	Total	**728**	**361**	**277**	**90**	**.558**	**1**	**1917-45**
Ruel, Claude	Montreal	305	172	82	51	.648	1	1968-71, 1979-81
Sather, Glen (12)	Edmonton	842	464	268	110	.616	4	1979-80, 1980-89, 1993-94
Sator, Ted	NY Rangers	99	41	48	10	.465	0	1985-87
	Buffalo	207	96	89	22	.517	0	1986-89
	Total	**306**	**137**	**137**	**32**	**.500**	**0**	**1985-88**
Savard, Andre	Quebec	24	10	13	1	.438	0	1987-88
Schinkel, Ken	Pittsburgh	203	83	92	28	.478	0	1972-74, 1975-77
Schmidt, Milt (18)	Boston	726	245	360	121	.421	0	1954-61, 1962-66
	Washington	43	5	33	5	.174	0	1974-76
	Total	**769**	**250**	**393**	**126**	**.407**	**0**	**1954-66**
Schonfeld, Jim	Buffalo	43	19	19	5	.500	0	1985-86
	New Jersey	124	50	59	15	.464	0	1987-90
	Washington	85	41	30	14	.565	0	1993-95
	Total	**209**	**91**	**89**	**29**	**.505**	**0**	**1985-95**
Shaughnessy, Tom	Chicago	21	10	8	3	.548	0	1929-30
Shero, Fred (21)	Philadelphia	554	308	151	95	.642	2	1971-78
	NY Rangers	180	82	74	24	.522	0	1978-81
	Total	**734**	**390**	**225**	**119**	**.612**	**2**	**1971-81**
Simpson, Joe	NY Americans	144	42	72	30	.396	0	1932-35
Simpson, Terry	NY Islanders	187	81	82	24	.497	0	1986-89
	Winnipeg	1	0	1	0	.000	0	1992-93
	Philadelphia	84	35	39	10	.476	0	1993-94
	Winnipeg	15	7	7	1	.500	0	1994-95
	Total	**271**	**116**	**121**	**34**	**.491**	**0**	**1986-95**
Sinden, Harry	Boston	330	151	121	58	.545	1	1966-70, 1979-80, 1984-85
Skinner, Jimmy	Detroit	247	123	78	46	.591	1	1954-58
Smeaton, Cooper	Phi. Quakers	44	4	36	4	.136	0	1930-31
Smith, Alf	Ottawa	18	12	6	0	.667	1	1918-19
Smith, Floyd	Buffalo	241	143	62	36	.668	0	1974-77
	Toronto	68	30	33	5	.478	0	1979-80
	Total	**309**	**173**	**95**	**41**	**.626**	**0**	**1971-80**
Smith, Mike	Winnipeg	23	2	17	4	.174	0	1980-81
Smith, Ron	NY Rangers	44	15	22	7	.420	0	1992-93
Smythe, Conn	Toronto	178	72	81	25	.475	0	1926-30
Sonmor, Glen	Minnesota	416	174	161	81	.516	0	1978-83, 1984-85, 1986-87
Sproule, Harry	Toronto St. Pats	12	7	5	0	.583	0	1919-20
Stanley, Barney	Chicago	23	4	17	2	.217	0	1927-28
Stasiuk, Vic	Philadelphia	154	45	68	41	.425	0	1969-71
	California	75	21	38	16	.387	0	1971-72
	Vancouver	78	22	47	9	.340	0	1972-73
	Total	**307**	**88**	**153**	**66**	**.394**	**0**	**1969-73**
Stewart, Bill	Chicago	69	22	35	12	.406	1	1937-39
Stewart, Ron	NY Rangers	39	15	20	4	.436	0	1975-76
	Los Angeles	80	31	34	15	.481	0	1977-78
	Total	**119**	**46**	**54**	**19**	**.466**	**0**	**1975-78**
Sullivan, Red	NY Rangers	196	58	103	35	.385	0	1962-66
	Pittsburgh	150	47	79	24	.393	0	1967-69
	Washington	19	2	17	0	.105	0	1974-75
	Total	**365**	**107**	**199**	**59**	**.374**	**0**	**1962-75**
Sutherland, Bill	Winnipeg	32	7	22	3	.266	0	1979-80, 1980-81
Sutter, Brian	St. Louis	320	153	124	43	.545	0	1988-92
	Boston	216	120	73	23	.609	0	1992-95
	Total	**488**	**246**	**179**	**63**	**.569**	**0**	**1988-95**
Sutter, Darryl	Chicago	216	110	80	26	.569	0	1992-95
Talbot, Jean-Guy	St. Louis	120	52	53	15	.496	0	1972-74
	NY Rangers	80	30	37	13	.456	0	1977-78
	Total	**200**	**82**	**90**	**28**	**.480**	**0**	**1972-78**
Tessier, Orval	Chicago	213	99	93	21	.514	0	1982-85
Thompson, Paul	Chicago	272	104	127	41	.458	0	1938-45
Thompson, Percy	Hamilton	48	14	34	0	.292	0	1920-22
Tobin, Bill	Chicago	23	11	10	2	.522	0	1929-30
Ubriaco, Gene	Pittsburgh	106	50	47	9	.514	0	1988-90
Vachon, Rogie	Los Angeles	8	4	2	2	.625	0	1983-84, 1987-88, 1994-95
Watson, Bryan	Edmonton	18	4	9	5	.361	0	1980-81
Watson, Phil	NY Rangers	294	118	124	52	.490	0	1955-60
	Boston	84	16	55	13	.268	0	1961-63
	Total	**378**	**134**	**179**	**65**	**.440**	**0**	**1955-64**
Watt, Tom	Winnipeg	181	72	85	24	.464	0	1981-84
	Vancouver	160	52	87	21	.391	0	1985-87
	Toronto	149	52	80	17	.406	0	1990-92
	Total	**490**	**176**	**252**	**62**	**.422**	**0**	**1981-92**
Webster, Tom	NY Rangers	16	5	7	4	.438	0	1986-87
	Los Angeles	240	115	94	31	.544	0	1989-92
	Total	**256**	**120**	**101**	**35**	**.537**	**0**	**1986-92**
Weiland, Cooney	Boston	96	58	20	18	.698	1	1939-41
White, Bill	Chicago	46	16	24	6	.413	0	1976-77
Wilson, Johnny	Los Angeles	52	9	34	9	.260	0	1969-70
	Detroit	145	67	56	22	.538	0	1971-73
	Colorado	80	20	46	14	.338	0	1976-77
	Pittsburgh	240	91	105	44	.471	0	1977-80
	Total	**517**	**187**	**241**	**89**	**.448**	**0**	**1969-80**
Wilson, Larry	Detroit	36	3	29	4	.139	0	1976-77
Wilson, Ron	Anaheim	132	49	73	10	.409	0	1993-95
Young, Garry	California	12	2	7	3	.292	0	1972-73
	St. Louis	98	41	41	16	.500	0	1974-76
	Total	**110**	**43**	**48**	**19**	**.477**	**0**	**1972-76**

Coaching greats: Scott Bowman, top has directed four different teams into the Stanley Cup Finals during 19 years behind the bench. Don Cherry, center, led the Boston Bruins into the finals in 1977 and 1978. Mervyn "Red" Dutton coached the New York Americans for eight seasons before succeeding Frank Calder as NHL president in 1943.

All-Time Penalty-Minute Leaders

* active player

(Regular season. Minimum 1,500 minutes)

Player	Teams	Seasons	Games	Penalty Minutes	Mins. per game
Dave Williams,	Tor., Van., Det., L.A., Hfd.	14	962	3966	4.12
*Dale Hunter,	Que., Wsh.	15	1099	3106	2.83
Chris Nilan,	Mtl., NYR, Bos.	13	688	3043	4.42
*Tim Hunter,	Cgy., Que., Van.	14	709	2889	4.07
*Marty McSorley,	Pit., Edm., L.A.	12	707	2723	3.85
Willi Plett,	Atl., Cgy., Min., Bos.	13	834	2572	3.08
*Basil McRae,	Que., Tor., Det., Min., St.L.	14	550	2405	4.37
*Garth Butcher,	Van., St.L., Que., Tor.	14	897	2302	2.57
Dave Schultz,	Phi., L.A., Pit., Buf.	9	535	2294	4.29
*Jay Wells,	L.A., Phi., Buf., NYR	16	1001	2279	2.28
Laurie Boschman,	Tor., Edm., Wpg., N.J., Ott.	14	1009	2265	2.24
Rob Ramage,	Col., St.L., Cgy., Tor., Min., T.B., Mtl., Phi.	15	1044	2226	2.13
Bryan Watson,	Mtl., Det., Cal., Pit., St.L., Wsh.	16	878	2212	2.52
*Joey Kocur,	Det., NYR.	11	639	2202	3.45
*Rick Tocchet,	Phi., Pit., L.A.	11	717	2190	3.05
*Scott Stevens,	Wsh., St.L., N.J.	13	959	2190	2.28
*Pat Verbeek,	N.J., Hfd., NYR	13	915	2105	2.30
Terry O'Reilly,	Boston.	14	891	2095	2.35
Al Secord,	Chi., Tor., Phi.	12	766	2093	2.73
*Bob Probert,	Detroit.	9	474	2090	4.41
*Gord Donnelly,	Que., Wpg., Buf., Dal.	12	554	2069	3.73
Mike Foligno,	Det., Buf., Tor., Fla.	15	1018	2049	2.01
Phil Russell,	Chi., Atl., Cgy., N.J., Buf.	15	1016	2038	2.01
Harold Snepsts,	Van., Min., Det., St.L.	17	1033	2009	1.94
Andre Dupont,	NYR, St.L., Phi., Que.	13	810	1986	2.45
*Shane Churla,	Hfd., Cgy., Min., Dal.	9	388	1964	5.06
*Dave Manson,	Chi., Edm., Wpg.	9	606	1935	3.19
*Ken Daneyko,	N.J.	12	716	1933	2.70
*Ulf Samuelsson,	Hfd., Pit.	11	740	1914	2.59
*Steve Smith,	Edm., Chi.	11	644	1900	2.95
*Craig Berube,	Phi., Tor., Cgy., Wsh.	9	515	1899	3.69
Garry Howatt,	NYI, Hfd., N.J.	12	720	1836	2.55
Carol Vadnais,	Mtl., Oak., Cal., Bos., NYR, N.J.	17	1087	1813	1.67
Larry Playfair,	Buf., L.A.	11	688	1812	2.63
Ted Lindsay,	Det., Chi.	17	1068	1808	1.69
Jim Korn,	Det., Tor., Buf., N.J., Cgy.	10	597	1801	3.02
*Chris Chelios,	Mtl., Chi.	12	767	1786	2.33
Brian Sutter,	St. Louis.	12	779	1786	2.29
Bob McGill,	Tor., Chi., S.J., Det., NYI, Hfd.	13	705	1766	2.50
Wilf Paiement,	K.C., Col., Tor., Que., NYR, Buf., Pit.	14	946	1757	1.86
Torrie Robertson,	Wsh., Hfd., Det.	10	442	1751	3.96
Mario Marois,	NYR, Van., Que., Win., St.L.	15	955	1746	1.83
*Dave Brown,	Phi., Edm.	13	692	1743	2.52
Ken Linseman,	Phi., Edm., Bos., Tor.	14	860	1727	2.01
Jay Miller,	Bos., L.A.	7	446	1723	3.86
*Mick Vukota,	NY Islanders	8	461	1702	3.69
*Randy Moller,	Que., NYR, Buf., Fla.	14	815	1692	2.08
Gordie Howe,	Det., Hfd.	26	1767	1685	0.95
Paul Holmgren,	Phi., Min.	10	527	1684	3.20
*Gerard Gallant,	Det., T.B.	11	615	1674	2.72
Kevin McClelland,	Pit., Edm., Det., Tor., Wpg.	12	588	1672	2.84
*Gary Roberts,	Calgary	9	550	1658	3.01
*Joel Otto,	Calgary.	11	730	1642	2.25
Jerry Korab,	Chi., Van., Buf., L.A.	15	975	1629	1.67
Mel Bridgman,	Phi., Cgy., N.J., Det., Van.	14	977	1625	1.66
Tim Horton,	Tor., NYR, Pit., Buf.	24	1446	1611	1.11
Dave Taylor,	Los Angeles	17	1111	1589	1.43
*Gordie Roberts,	Hfd., Min., Phi., St.L., Pit., Bos.	15	1097	1582	1.44
Paul Baxter,	Que., Pit., Cgy.	8	472	1564	3.31
Glen Cochrane,	Phi., Van., Chi., Edm.	9	411	1556	3.79
*Michel Petit,	Van., NYR, Que., Tor., Cgy., L.A.	13	703	1556	2.21
Stan Smyl,	Vancouver.	13	896	1556	1.74
Mike Milbury,	Boston.	12	754	1552	2.06
*Ken Baumgartner,	L.A., NYI, Tor.	8	406	1551	3.82
Dave Hutchison,	L.A., Tor., Chi., N.J.	10	534	1550	2.65
*Paul Coffey,	Edm., Pit., L.A., Det.	15	1078	1546	1.43
Doug Risebrough,	Mtl., Cgy.	14	740	1542	2.03
Bill Gadsby,	Chi., NYR, Det.	20	1249	1539	1.23
*Steven Finn,	Quebec	10	605	1514	2.50
*Kevin Dineen,	Hfd., Phi.	11	747	1512	2.02
*Ron Stern,	Van., Cgy.	8	362	1500	4.14

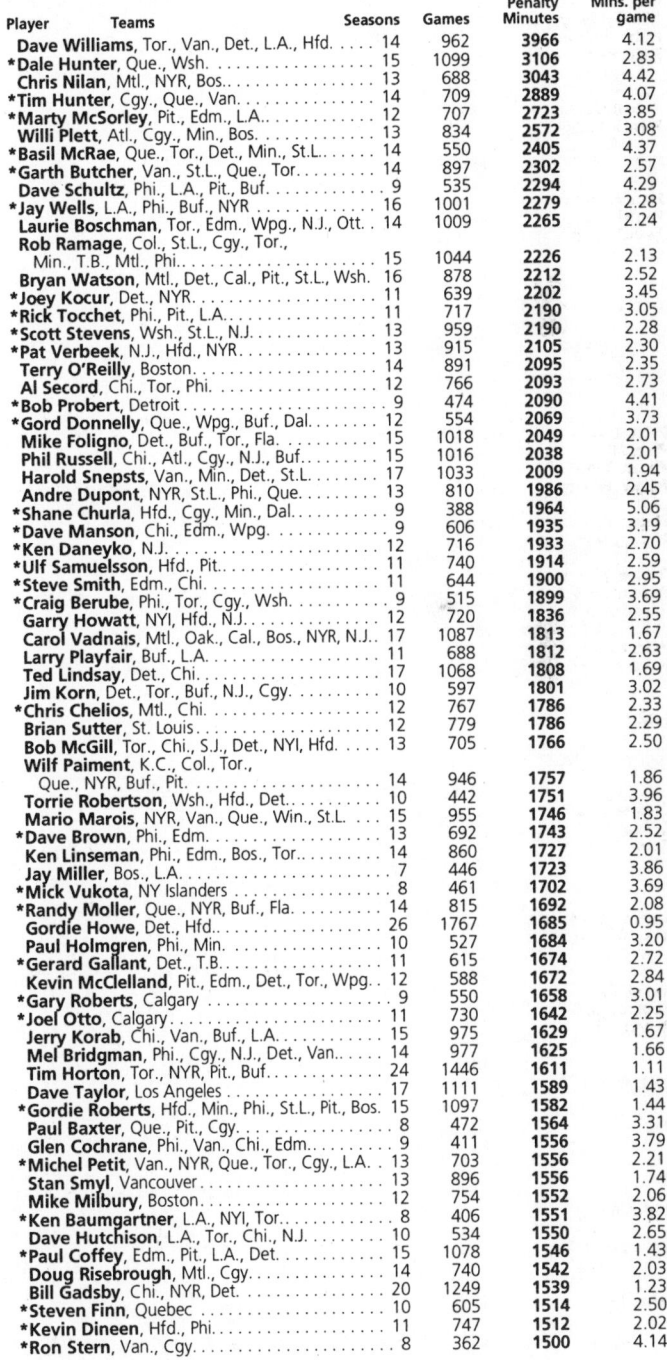

One Season Scoring Records

Goals-Per-Game Leaders, One Season

(Among players with 20 goals or more in one season)

Player	Team	Season	Games	Goals	Average
Joe Malone	Montreal	1917-18	20	44	2.20
Cy Denneny	Ottawa	1917-18	22	36	1.64
Newsy Lalonde	Montreal	1917-18	14	23	1.64
Joe Malone	Quebec	1919-20	24	39	1.63
Newsy Lalonde	Montreal	1919-20	23	36	1.57
Joe Malone	Hamilton	1920-21	20	30	1.50
Babe Dye	Ham., Tor.	1920-21	24	35	1.46
Cy Denneny	Ottawa	1920-21	24	34	1.42
Reg Noble	Toronto	1917-18	20	28	1.40
Newsy Lalonde	Montreal	1920-21	24	33	1.38
Odie Cleghorn	Montreal	1918-19	17	23	1.35
Harry Broadbent	Ottawa	1921-22	24	32	1.33
Babe Dye	Toronto	1924-25	29	38	1.31
Babe Dye	Toronto	1921-22	24	30	1.25
Newsy Lalonde	Montreal	1918-19	17	21	1.24
Cy Denneny	Ottawa	1921-22	22	27	1.23
Aurel Joliat	Montreal	1924-25	24	29	1.21
Wayne Gretzky	Edmonton	1983-84	74	87	1.18
Babe Dye	Toronto	1922-23	22	26	1.18
Wayne Gretzky	Edmonton	1981-82	80	92	1.15
Mario Lemieux	Pittsburgh	1992-93	60	69	1.15
Frank Nighbor	Ottawa	1919-20	23	26	1.13
Mario Lemieux	Pittsburgh	1988-89	76	85	1.12
Brett Hull	St. Louis	1990-91	78	86	1.10
Amos Arbour	Montreal	1919-20	20	22	1.10
Cy Denneny	Ottawa	1923-24	21	22	1.05
Joe Malone	Hamilton	1921-22	24	25	1.04
Billy Boucher	Montreal	1922-23	24	25	1.04
Cam Neely	Boston	1993-94	49	50	1.02
Maurice Richard	Montreal	1944-45	50	50	1.00
Howie Morenz	Montreal	1924-25	30	30	1.00
Reg Noble	Toronto	1919-20	24	24	1.00
Corbett Denneny	Toronto	1919-20	23	23	1.00
Jack Darragh	Ottawa	1919-20	22	22	1.00
Alexander Mogilny	Buffalo	1992-93	77	76	.99
Cooney Weiland	Boston	1929-30	44	43	.98
Phil Esposito	Boston	1970-71	78	76	.97
Jari Kurri	Edmonton	1984-85	73	71	.97

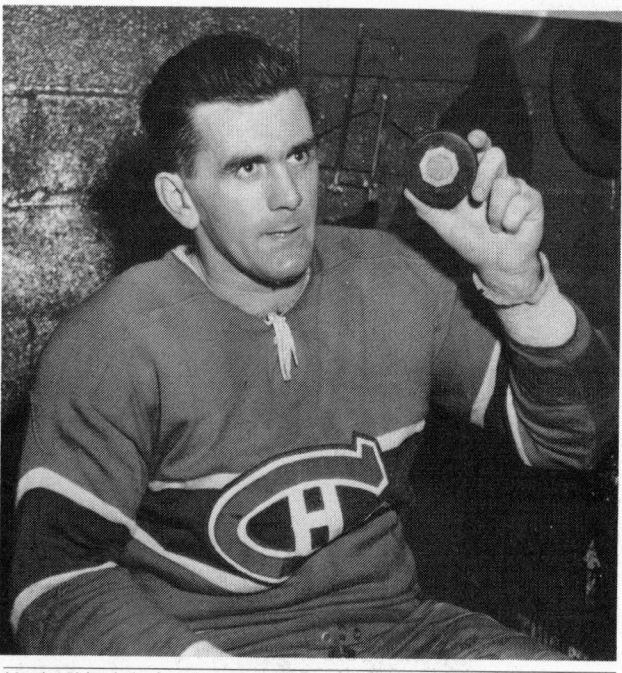

Maurice Richard, the first player to score 50 goals in 50 games, displays the puck he fired past Toronto goaltender Harry Lumley to tie Nels Stewart on the NHL's all-time goal scoring ladder on October 29, 1952.

Penalty Leaders

* Match Misconduct penalty not included in total penalty minutes.
** Three Match Misconduct penalties not included in total penalty minutes.
1946-47 was the first season that a Match penalty was automaticaly written into the player's total penalty minutes as 20 minutes. Now all penalties, Match, Game Misconduct, and Misconduct, are written as 10 minutes. Penalty minutes not calculated in 1917-18.

Season	Player and Club	GP	PIM	Season	Player and Club	GP	PIM	Season	Player and Club	GP	PIM
1994-95	Enrico Ciccone, Tampa Bay	41	225	1968-69	Forbes Kennedy, Phi., Tor.	77	219	1942-43	Jimmy Orlando, Detroit	40	89*
1993-94	Tie Domi, Winnipeg	81	347	1967-68	Barclay Plager, St. Louis	49	153	1941-42	Jimmy Orlando, Detroit	48	81**
1992-93	Marty McSorley, Los Angeles	81	399	1966-67	John Ferguson, Montreal	67	177	1940-41	Jimmy Orlando, Detroit	48	99
1991-92	Mike Peluso, Chicago	63	408	1965-66	Reg Fleming, Bos., NYR	69	166	1939-40	Red Horner, Toronto	30	87
1990-91	Rob Ray, Buffalo	66	350	1964-65	Carl Brewer, Toronto	70	177	1938-39	Red Horner, Toronto	48	85
1989-90	Basil McRae, Minnesota	66	351	1963-64	Vic Hadfield, NY Rangers	69	151	1937-38	Red Horner, Toronto	47	82*
1988-89	Tim Hunter, Calgary	75	375	1962-63	Howie Young, Detroit	64	273	1936-37	Red Horner, Toronto	48	124
1987-88	Bob Probert, Detroit	74	398	1961-62	Lou Fontinato, Montreal	54	167	1935-36	Red Horner, Toronto	43	167
1986-87	Tim Hunter, Calgary	73	361	1960-61	Pierre Pilote, Chicago	70	165	1934-35	Red Horner, Toronto	46	125
1985-86	Joey Kocur, Detroit	59	377	1959-60	Carl Brewer, Toronto	67	150	1933-34	Red Horner, Toronto	42	126*
1984-85	Chris Nilan, Montreal	77	358	1958-59	Ted Lindsay, Chicago	70	184	1932-33	Red Horner, Toronto	48	144
1983-84	Chris Nilan, Montreal	76	338	1957-58	Lou Fontinato, NY Rangers	70	152	1931-32	Red Dutton, NY Americans	47	107
1982-83	Randy Holt, Washington	70	275	1956-57	Gus Mortson, Chicago	70	147	1930-31	Harvey Rockburn, Detroit	42	118
1981-82	Paul Baxter, Pittsburgh	76	409	1955-56	Lou Fontinato, NY Rangers	70	202	1929-30	Joe Lamb, Ottawa	44	119
1980-81	Dave Williams, Vancouver	77	343	1954-55	Fern Flaman, Boston	70	150	1928-29	Red Dutton, Mtl. Maroons	44	139
1979-80	Jimmy Mann, Winnipeg	72	287	1953-54	Gus Mortson, Chicago	68	132	1927-28	Eddie Shore, Boston	44	165
1978-79	Dave Williams, Toronto	77	298	1952-53	Maurice Richard, Montreal	70	112	1926-27	Nels Stewart, Mtl. Maroons	44	133
1977-78	Dave Schultz, L.A., Pit.	74	405	1951-52	Gus Kyle, Boston	69	127	1925-26	Bert Corbeau, Toronto	36	121
1976-77	Dave Williams, Toronto	77	338	1950-51	Gus Mortson, Toronto	60	142	1924-25	Billy Boucher, Montreal	30	92
1975-76	Steve Durbano, Pit., K.C.	69	370	1949-50	Bill Ezinicki, Toronto	67	144	1923-24	Bert Corbeau, Toronto	24	55
1974-75	Dave Schultz, Philadelphia	76	472	1948-49	Bill Ezinicki, Toronto	52	145	1922-23	Billy Boucher, Montreal	24	52
1973-74	Dave Schultz, Philadelphia	73	348	1947-48	Bill Barilko, Toronto	57	147	1921-22	Sprague Cleghorn, Montreal	24	63
1972-73	Dave Schultz, Philadelphia	76	259	1946-47	Gus Mortson, Toronto	60	133	1920-21	Bert Corbeau, Montreal	24	86
1971-72	Bryan Watson, Pittsburgh	75	212	1945-46	Jack Stewart, Detroit	47	73	1919-20	Cully Wilson, Toronto	23	79
1970-71	Keith Magnuson, Chicago	76	291	1944-45	Pat Egan, Boston	48	86	1918-19	Joe Hall, Montreal	17	85
1969-70	Keith Magnuson, Chicago	76	213	1943-44	Mike McMahon, Montreal	42	98				

Assists-Per-Game Leaders, One Season

(Among players with 35 assists or more in one season)

Player	Team	Season	Games	Assists	Average
Wayne Gretzky	Edmonton	1985-86	80	163	2.04
Wayne Gretzky	Edmonton	1987-88	64	109	1.70
Wayne Gretzky	Edmonton	1984-85	80	135	1.69
Wayne Gretzky	Edmonton	1983-84	74	118	1.59
Wayne Gretzky	Edmonton	1982-83	80	125	1.56
Wayne Gretzky	Los Angeles	1990-91	78	122	1.56
Wayne Gretzky	Edmonton	1986-87	79	121	1.53
Mario Lemieux	Pittsburgh	1992-93	60	91	1.52
Wayne Gretzky	Edmonton	1981-82	80	120	1.50
Mario Lemieux	Pittsburgh	1988-89	76	114	1.50
Adam Oates	St. Louis	1990-91	61	90	1.48
Wayne Gretzky	Los Angeles	1988-89	78	114	1.46
Wayne Gretzky	Los Angeles	1989-90	73	102	1.40
Wayne Gretzky	Edmonton	1980-81	80	109	1.36
Mario Lemieux	Pittsburgh	1991-92	64	87	1.36
Mario Lemieux	Pittsburgh	1989-90	59	78	1.32
Bobby Orr	Boston	1970-71	78	102	1.31
Mario Lemieux	Pittsburgh	1987-88	77	98	1.27
Bobby Orr	Boston	1973-74	74	90	1.22
Wayne Gretzky	Los Angeles	1991-92	74	90	1.22
Mario Lemieux	Pittsburgh	1985-86	79	93	1.18
Bobby Clarke	Philadelphia	1975-76	76	89	1.17
Peter Stastny	Quebec	1981-82	80	93	1.16
Adam Oates	Boston	1992-93	84	97	1.15
Doug Gilmour	Toronto	1992-93	83	95	1.14
Wayne Gretzky	Los Angeles	1993-94	81	92	1.14
Paul Coffey	Edmonton	1985-86	79	90	1.14
Bobby Orr	Boston	1969-70	76	87	1.14
Bryan Trottier	NY Islanders	1978-79	76	87	1.14
Bobby Orr	Boston	1972-73	63	72	1.14
Bill Cowley	Boston	1943-44	36	41	1.14
Pat LaFontaine	Buffalo	1992-93	84	95	1.13
Steve Yzerman	Detroit	1988-89	80	90	1.13
Paul Coffey	Pittsburgh	1987-88	46	52	1.13
Bobby Orr	Boston	1974-75	80	89	1.11
Bobby Clarke	Philadelphia	1974-75	80	89	1.11
Paul Coffey	Pittsburgh	1988-89	75	83	1.11
Wayne Gretzky	Los Angeles	1992-93	45	49	1.11
Denis Savard	Chicago	1982-83	78	86	1.10
Ron Francis	Pittsburgh	**1994-95**	44	48	1.09
Denis Savard	Chicago	1981-82	80	87	1.09
Denis Savard	Chicago	1987-88	80	87	1.09
Wayne Gretzky	Edmonton	1979-80	79	86	1.09
Paul Coffey	Edmonton	1983-84	80	86	1.08
Elmer Lach	Montreal	1944-45	50	54	1.08
Peter Stastny	Quebec	1985-86	76	81	1.07
Mark Messier	Edmonton	1989-90	79	84	1.06
Paul Coffey	Edmonton	1984-85	80	84	1.05
Marcel Dionne	Los Angeles	1979-80	80	84	1.05
Bobby Orr	Boston	1971-72	76	80	1.05
Mike Bossy	NY Islanders	1981-82	80	83	1.04
Adam Oates	Boston	1993-94	77	80	1.04
Phil Esposito	Boston	1968-69	74	77	1.04
Bryan Trottier	NY Islanders	1983-84	68	71	1.04
Pete Mahovlich	Montreal	1974-75	80	82	1.03
Kent Nilsson	Calgary	1980-81	80	82	1.03
Peter Stastny	Quebec	1982-83	75	77	1.03
Doug Gilmour	Toronto	1993-94	83	84	1.01
Bernie Nicholls	Los Angeles	1988-89	79	80	1.01
Guy Lafleur	Montreal	1979-80	74	75	1.01
Guy Lafleur	Montreal	1976-77	80	80	1.00
Marcel Dionne	Los Angeles	1984-85	80	80	1.00
Brian Leetch	NY Rangers	1991-92	80	80	1.00
Bryan Trottier	NY Islanders	1977-78	77	77	1.00
Mike Bossy	NY Islanders	1983-84	67	67	1.00
Jean Ratelle	NY Rangers	1971-72	63	63	1.00
Steve Yzerman	Detroit	1993-94	58	58	1.00
Ron Francis	Hartford	1985-86	53	53	1.00
Guy Chouinard	Calgary	1980-81	52	52	1.00
Elmer Lach	Montreal	1943-44	48	48	1.00

Mario Lemieux, who is scheduled to return to active duty during the 1995-96 campaign, has averaged more than one assist per game in six of his ten NHL seasons.

Points-Per-Game Leaders, One Season

(Among players with 50 points or more in one season)

Player	Team	Season	Games	Points	Average	Player	Team	Season	Games	Points	Average
Wayne Gretzky	Edmonton	1983-84	74	205	2.77	Cooney Weiland	Boston	1929-30	44	73	1.66
Wayne Gretzky	Edmonton	1985-86	80	215	2.69	Alexander Mogilny	Buffalo	1992-93	77	127	1.65
Mario Lemieux	Pittsburgh	1992-93	60	160	2.67	Peter Stastny	Quebec	1982-83	75	124	1.65
Wayne Gretzky	Edmonton	1981-82	80	212	2.65	Bobby Orr	Boston	1973-74	74	122	1.65
Mario Lemieux	Pittsburgh	1988-89	76	199	2.62	Kent Nilsson	Calgary	1980-81	80	131	1.64
Wayne Gretzky	Edmonton	1984-85	80	208	2.60	Wayne Gretzky	Los Angeles	1991-92	74	121	1.64
Wayne Gretzky	Edmonton	1982-83	80	196	2.45	Denis Savard	Chicago	1987-88	80	131	1.64
Wayne Gretzky	Edmonton	1987-88	64	149	2.33	Steve Yzerman	Detroit	1992-93	84	137	1.63
Wayne Gretzky	Edmonton	1986-87	79	183	2.32	Marcel Dionne	Los Angeles	1978-79	80	130	1.63
Mario Lemieux	Pittsburgh	1987-88	77	168	2.18	Dale Hawerchuk	Winnipeg	1984-85	80	130	1.63
Wayne Gretzky	Los Angeles	1988-89	78	168	2.15	Mark Messier	Edmonton	1989-90	79	129	1.63
Wayne Gretzky	Los Angeles	1990-91	78	163	2.09	Bryan Trottier	NY Islanders	1983-84	68	111	1.63
Mario Lemieux	Pittsburgh	1989-90	59	123	2.08	Pat LaFontaine	Buffalo	1991-92	57	93	1.63
Wayne Gretzky	Edmonton	1980-81	80	164	2.05	Charlie Simmer	Los Angeles	1980-81	65	105	1.62
Mario Lemieux	Pittsburgh	1991-92	64	131	2.05	Guy Lafleur	Montreal	1978-79	80	129	1.61
Bill Cowley	Boston	1943-44	36	71	1.97	Bryan Trottier	NY Islanders	1981-82	80	129	1.61
Phil Esposito	Boston	1970-71	78	152	1.95	Phil Esposito	Boston	1974-75	79	127	1.61
Wayne Gretzky	Los Angeles	1989-90	73	142	1.95	Steve Yzerman	Detroit	1989-90	79	127	1.61
Steve Yzerman	Detroit	1988-89	80	155	1.94	Peter Stastny	Quebec	1985-86	76	122	1.61
Bernie Nicholls	Los Angeles	1988-89	79	150	1.90	Michel Goulet	Quebec	1983-84	75	121	1.61
Adam Oates	St. Louis	1990-91	61	115	1.89	Wayne Gretzky	Los Angeles	1993-94	81	130	1.60
Phil Esposito	Boston	1973-74	78	145	1.86	Bryan Trottier	NY Islanders	1977-78	77	123	1.60
Jari Kurri	Edmonton	1984-85	73	135	1.85	Bobby Orr	Boston	1972-73	63	101	1.60
Mike Bossy	NY Islanders	1981-82	80	147	1.84	Guy Chouinard	Calgary	1980-81	52	83	1.60
Mario Lemieux	Pittsburgh	1985-86	79	141	1.78	Elmer Lach	Montreal	1944-45	50	80	1.60
Bobby Orr	Boston	1970-71	78	139	1.78	Pierre Turgeon	NY Islanders	1992-93	83	132	1.59
Jari Kurri	Edmonton	1983-84	64	113	1.77	Steve Yzerman	Detroit	1987-88	64	102	1.59
Pat LaFontaine	Buffalo	1992-93	84	148	1.76	Mike Bossy	NY Islanders	1978-79	80	126	1.58
Bryan Trottier	NY Islanders	1978-79	76	134	1.76	Paul Coffey	Edmonton	1983-84	80	126	1.58
Mike Bossy	NY Islanders	1983-84	67	118	1.76	Marcel Dionne	Los Angeles	1984-85	80	126	1.58
Paul Coffey	Edmonton	1985-86	79	138	1.75	Bobby Orr	Boston	1969-70	76	120	1.58
Phil Esposito	Boston	1971-72	76	133	1.75	Charlie Simmer	Los Angeles	1979-80	64	101	1.58
Peter Stastny	Quebec	1981-82	80	139	1.74	Teemu Selanne	Winnipeg	1992-93	84	132	1.57
Wayne Gretzky	Edmonton	1979-80	79	137	1.73	Bobby Clarke	Philadelphia	1975-76	76	119	1.57
Jean Ratelle	NY Rangers	1971-72	63	109	1.73	Guy Lafleur	Montreal	1975-76	80	125	1.56
Marcel Dionne	Los Angeles	1979-80	80	137	1.71	Dave Taylor	Los Angeles	1980-81	72	112	1.56
Herb Cain	Boston	1943-44	48	82	1.71	Denis Savard	Chicago	1982-83	78	121	1.55
Guy Lafleur	Montreal	1976-77	80	136	1.70	Mike Bossy	NY Islanders	1985-86	80	123	1.54
Dennis Maruk	Washington	1981-82	80	136	1.70	Bobby Orr	Boston	1971-72	76	117	1.54
Phil Esposito	Boston	1968-69	74	126	1.70	Kevin Stevens	Pittsburgh	1991-92	80	123	1.54
Guy Lafleur	Montreal	1974-75	70	119	1.70	Mike Bossy	NY Islanders	1984-85	76	117	1.54
Mario Lemieux	Pittsburgh	1986-87	63	107	1.70	Kevin Stevens	Pittsburgh	1992-93	72	111	1.54
Adam Oates	Boston	1992-93	84	142	1.69	Doug Bentley	Chicago	1943-44	50	77	1.54
Bobby Orr	Boston	1974-75	80	135	1.69	Doug Gilmour	Toronto	1992-93	83	127	1.53
Marcel Dionne	Los Angeles	1980-81	80	135	1.69	Marcel Dionne	Los Angeles	1976-77	80	122	1.53
Guy Lafleur	Montreal	1977-78	78	132	1.69	Eric Lindros	Philadelphia	**1994-95**	46	70	1.52
Guy Lafleur	Montreal	1979-80	74	125	1.69	Marcel Dionne	Detroit	1974-75	80	121	1.51
Rob Brown	Pittsburgh	1988-89	68	115	1.69	Dale Hawerchuk	Winnipeg	1987-88	80	121	1.51
Jari Kurri	Edmonton	1985-86	78	131	1.68	Paul Coffey	Pittsburgh	1988-89	75	113	1.51
Brett Hull	St. Louis	1990-91	78	131	1.68	Cam Neely	Boston	1993-94	49	74	1.51
Phil Esposito	Boston	1972-73	78	130	1.67						

Herb Cain (#4, shown here with Boston manager Art Ross and teammate Bobby Bauer) entered the record book during the 1943-44 season when he averaged 1.71 points per game. Cain's 82 points established a new NHL record, bettering Doug Bentley's mark of 73 points recorded in 1942-43.

Minnesota left wing Danny Grant scored 34 goals for the North Stars in 1968-69 and won the Calder Trophy as the league's top rookie. Though he was still considered a rookie in 1968-69, Grant had also played 22 games for the Stanley-Cup winning Montreal Canadiens in 1967-68.

Rookie Scoring Records

All-Time Top 50 Goal-Scoring Rookies

	Rookie	Team	Position	Season	GP	G	A	PTS
1.	* Teemu Selanne	Winnipeg	Right wing	1992-93	84	76	56	132
2.	* Mike Bossy	NY Islanders	Right wing	1977-78	73	53	38	91
3.	* Joe Nieuwendyk	Calgary	Center	1987-88	75	51	41	92
4.	* Dale Hawerchuk	Winnipeg	Center	1981-82	80	45	58	103
	* Luc Robitaille	Los Angeles	Left wing	1986-87	79	45	39	84
6.	Rick Martin	Buffalo	Left wing	1971-72	73	44	30	74
	Barry Pederson	Boston	Center	1981-82	80	44	48	92
8.	* Steve Larmer	Chicago	Right wing	1982-83	80	43	47	90
	* Mario Lemieux	Pittsburgh	Center	1984-85	73	43	57	100
10.	Eric Lindros	Philadelphia	Center	1992-93	61	41	34	75
11.	Darryl Sutter	Chicago	Left wing	1980-81	76	40	22	62
	Sylvain Turgeon	Hartford	Left wing	1983-84	76	40	32	72
	Warren Young	Pittsburgh	Left wing	1984-85	80	40	32	72
14.	Eric Vail	Atlanta	Left wing	1974-75	72	39	21	60
	Anton Stastny	Quebec	Left wing	1980-81	80	39	46	85
	* Peter Stastny	Quebec	Center	1980-81	77	39	70	109
	Steve Yzerman	Detroit	Center	1983-84	80	39	48	87
18.	* Gilbert Perreault	Buffalo	Center	1970-71	78	38	34	72
	Neal Broten	Minnesota	Center	1981-82	73	38	60	98
	Ray Sheppard	Buffalo	Right wing	1987-88	74	38	27	65
	Mikael Renberg	Philadelphia	Left wing	1993-94	83	38	44	82
22.	Jorgen Pettersson	St. Louis	Left wing	1980-81	62	37	36	73
	Jimmy Carson	Los Angeles	Centre	1986-87	80	37	42	79
24.	Mike Foligno	Detroit	Right wing	1979-80	80	36	35	71
	Mike Bullard	Pittsburgh	Center	1981-82	75	36	27	63
	Paul MacLean	Winnipeg	Right wing	1981-82	74	36	25	61
	Tony Granato	NY Rangers	Right wing	1988-89	78	36	27	63
28.	Marian Stastny	Quebec	Right wing	1981-82	74	35	54	89
	Brian Bellows	Minnesota	Right wing	1982-83	78	35	30	65
	Tony Amonte	NY Rangers	Right wing	1991-92	79	35	34	69
31.	Nels Stewart	Mtl. Maroons	Center	1925-26	36	34	8	42
	* Danny Grant	Minnesota	Left wing	1968-69	75	34	31	65
	Norm Ferguson	Oakland	Right wing	1968-69	76	34	20	54
	Brian Propp	Philadelphia	Left wing	1979-80	80	34	41	75
	Wendel Clark	Toronto	Left wing	1985-86	66	34	11	45
	* Pavel Bure	Vancouver	Right wing	1991-92	65	34	26	60
37.	* Willi Plett	Atlanta	Right wing	1976-77	64	33	23	56
	Dale McCourt	Detroit	Center	1977-78	76	33	39	72
	Mark Pavelich	NY Rangers	Center	1981-82	79	33	43	76
	Ron Flockhart	Philadelphia	Center	1981-82	72	33	39	72
	Steve Bozek	Los Angeles	Center	1981-82	71	33	23	56
	Jason Arnott	Edmonton	Center	1993-94	78	33	35	68
43.	Bill Mosienko	Chicago	Right wing	1943-44	50	32	38	70
	Michel Bergeron	Detroit	Right wing	1975-76	72	32	27	59
	* Bryan Trottier	NY Islanders	Center	1975-76	80	32	63	95
	Don Murdoch	NY Rangers	Right wing	1976-77	59	32	24	56
	Jari Kurri	Edmonton	Left wing	1980-81	75	32	43	75
	Bobby Carpenter	Washington	Center	1981-82	80	32	35	67
	Kjell Dahlin	Montreal	Right wing	1985-86	77	32	39	71
	Petr Klima	Detroit	Left wing	1985-86	74	32	24	56
	Darren Turcotte	NY Rangers	Right wing	1989-90	76	32	34	66
	Joe Juneau	Boston	Center	1992-93	84	32	70	102

All-Time Top 50 Point-Scoring Rookies

	Rookie	Team	Position	Season	GP	G	A	PTS
1.	* Teemu Selanne	Winnipeg	Right wing	1992-93	84	76	56	132
2.	* Peter Stastny	Quebec	Center	1980-81	77	39	70	109
3.	* Dale Hawerchuk	Winnipeg	Center	1981-82	80	45	58	103
4.	Joe Juneau	Boston	Center	1992-93	84	32	70	102
5.	* Mario Lemieux	Pittsburgh	Center	1984-85	73	43	57	100
6.	Neal Broten	Minnesota	Center	1981-82	73	38	60	98
7.	* Bryan Trottier	NY Islanders	Center	1975-76	80	32	63	95
8.	Barry Pederson	Boston	Center	1981-82	80	44	48	92
	* Joe Nieuwendyk	Calgary	Center	1987-88	75	51	41	92
10.	* Mike Bossy	NY Islanders	Right wing	1977-78	73	53	38	91
11.	* Steve Larmer	Chicago	Right wing	1982-83	80	43	47	90
12.	Marian Stastny	Quebec	Right wing	1981-82	74	35	54	89
13.	Steve Yzerman	Detroit	Center	1983-84	80	39	48	87
14.	* Sergei Makarov	Calgary	Right wing	1989-90	80	24	62	86
15.	Anton Stastny	Quebec	Left wing	1980-81	80	39	46	85
16.	* Luc Robitaille	Los Angeles	Left wing	1986-87	79	45	39	84
17.	Mikael Renberg	Philadelphia	Left wing	1993-94	83	38	44	82
18.	Jimmy Carson	Los Angeles	Center	1986-87	80	37	42	79
	Sergei Fedorov	Detroit	Center	1990-91	77	31	48	79
	Alexei Yashin	Ottawa	Center	1993-94	83	30	49	79
21.	Marcel Dionne	Detroit	Center	1971-72	78	28	49	77
22.	Larry Murphy	Los Angeles	Defense	1980-81	80	16	60	76
	Mark Pavelich	NY Rangers	Center	1981-82	79	33	43	76
	Dave Poulin	Philadelphia	Center	1983-84	73	31	45	76
25.	Brian Propp	Philadelphia	Left wing	1979-80	80	34	41	75
	Jari Kurri	Edmonton	Left wing	1980-81	75	32	43	75
	Denis Savard	Chicago	Center	1980-81	76	28	47	75
	Mike Modano	Minnesota	Center	1989-90	80	29	46	75
	Eric Lindros	Philadelphia	Center	1992-93	61	41	34	75
30.	Rick Martin	Buffalo	Left wing	1971-72	73	44	30	74
	* Bobby Smith	Minnesota	Center	1978-79	80	30	44	74
32.	Jorgen Pettersson	St. Louis	Left wing	1980-81	62	37	36	73
33.	* Gilbert Perreault	Buffalo	Center	1970-71	78	38	34	72
	Dale McCourt	Detroit	Center	1977-78	76	33	39	72
	Ron Flockhart	Philadelphia	Center	1981-82	72	33	39	72
	Sylvain Turgeon	Hartford	Left wing	1983-84	76	40	32	72
	Warren Young	Pittsburgh	Left wing	1984-85	80	40	32	72
	Carey Wilson	Calgary	Center	1984-85	74	24	48	72
	Alexei Zhamnov	Winnipeg	Center	1992-93	68	25	47	72
40.	Mike Foligno	Detroit	Right wing	1979-80	80	36	35	71
	Dave Christian	Winnipeg	Center	1980-81	80	28	43	71
	Mats Naslund	Montreal	Left wing	1982-83	74	26	45	71
	Kjell Dahlin	Montreal	Right wing	1985-86	77	32	39	71
	* Brian Leetch	NY Rangers	Defense	1988-89	68	23	48	71
45.	Bill Mosienko	Chicago	Right wing	1943-44	50	32	38	70
46.	Roland Eriksson	Minnesota	Center	1976-77	80	25	44	69
	Tony Amonte	NY Rangers	Right wing	1991-92	79	35	34	69
48.	Jude Drouin	Minnesota	Center	1970-71	75	16	52	68
	Pierre Larouche	Pittsburgh	Center	1974-75	79	31	37	68
	Ron Francis	Hartford	Center	1981-82	59	25	43	68
	* Gary Suter	Calgary	Defense	1985-86	80	18	50	68
	Jason Arnott	Edmonton	Center	1993-94	84	33	35	68

* Calder Trophy Winner

The first member of the Pittsburgh Penguins to score 50 goals in a season, Jean Pronovost, left, was also the fourth-oldest player to reach the coveted milestone when he scored his 50th on Boston goaltender Gilles Gilbert on March 24, 1976. Below, left: Bobby Hull, seen here wearing #7 during the 1961-62 season, used his devastating combination of speed and strength, to reach the 50-goal plateau five times in his 16-year NHL career. Below: The "Golden Brett", who has registered five 50-goal seasons, has been the NHL's top sharpshooter in the 1990s, slipping 296 shots past opposition netminders since the start of the 1990-91 season.

50-Goal Seasons

Player	Team	Date of 50th Goal	Score			Goaltender	Player's Game No.	Team Game No.	Total Goals	Total Games	Age When First 50th Scored (Yrs. & Mos.)
Maurice Richard	Mtl.	18-3-45	Mtl. 4	at	Bos. 2	Harvey Bennett	50	50	50	50	23.7
Bernie Geoffrion	Mtl.	16-3-61	Tor. 2	at	Mtl. 5	Cesare Maniago	62	68	50	64	30.1
Bobby Hull	Chi.	25-3-62	Chi. 1	at	NYR 4	Gump Worsley	70	70	50	70	23.2
Bobby Hull	Chi.	2-3-66	Det. 4	at	Chi. 5	Hank Bassen	52	57	54	65	
Bobby Hull	Chi.	18-3-67	Chi. 5	at	Tor. 9	Bruce Gamble	63	66	52	66	
Bobby Hull	Chi.	5-3-69	NYR 4	at	Chi. 4	Ed Giacomin	64	66	58	74	
Phil Esposito	Bos.	20-2-71	Bos. 4	at	L.A. 5	Denis DeJordy	58	58	76	78	29.0
John Bucyk	Bos.	16-3-71	Bos. 11	at	Det. 4	Roy Edwards	69	69	51	78	35.1
Phil Esposito	Bos.	20-2-72	Bos. 3	at	Chi. 1	Tony Esposito	60	60	66	76	
Bobby Hull	Chi.	2-4-72	Det. 1	at	Chi. 6	Andy Brown	78	78	50	78	
Vic Hadfield	NYR	2-4-72	Mtl. 6	at	NYR 5	Denis DeJordy	78	78	50	78	31.6
Phil Esposito	Bos.	25-3-73	Buf. 1	at	Bos. 6	Roger Crozier	75	75	55	78	
Mickey Redmond	Det.	27-3-73	Det. 8	at	Tor. 1	Ron Low	73	75	52	76	25.3
Rick MacLeish	Phi.	1-4-73	Phi. 4	at	Pit. 5	Cam Newton	78	78	50	78	23.2
Phil Esposito	Bos.	20-2-74	Bos. 5	at	Min. 5	Cesare Maniago	56	56	68	78	
Mickey Redmond	Det.	23-3-74	NYR 3	at	Det 5	Ed Giacomin	69	71	51	76	
Ken Hodge	Bos.	6-4-74	Bos. 2	at	Mtl. 6	Michel Larocque	75	77	50	78	29.10
Rick Martin	Buf.	7-4-74	St. L. 2	at	Buf. 5	Wayne Stephenson	78	78	52	78	22.9
Phil Esposito	Bos.	8-2-75	Bos. 8	at	Det. 5	Jim Rutherford	54	54	61	79	
Guy Lafleur	Mtl.	29-3-75	K.C. 1	at	Mtl. 4	Denis Herron	66	76	53	70	23.6
Danny Grant	Det.	2-4-75	Wsh. 3	at	Det. 8	John Adams	78	78	50	80	29.2
Rick Martin	Buf.	3-4-75	Bos. 2	at	Buf. 4	Ken Broderick	67	79	52	68	
Reggie Leach	Phi.	14-3-76	Atl. 1	at	Phi. 6	Daniel Bouchard	69	69	61	80	25.11
Jean Pronovost	Pit.	24-3-76	Bos. 5	at	Pit. 5	Gilles Gilbert	74	74	52	80	31.3
Guy Lafleur	Mtl.	27-3-76	K.C. 2	at	Mtl. 8	Denis Herron	76	76	56	80	
Bill Barber	Phi.	3-4-76	Buf. 2	at	Phi. 5	Al Smith	79	79	50	80	23.9
Pierre Larouche	Pit.	3-4-76	Wsh. 5	at	Pit. 4	Ron Low	75	79	53	76	20.5
Danny Gare	Buf.	4-4-76	Tor. 2	at	Buf. 5	Gord McRae	79	80	50	79	21.11
Steve Shutt	Mtl.	1-3-77	Mtl. 5	at	NYI 4	Glenn Resch	65	65	60	80	24.8
Guy Lafleur	Mtl.	6-3-77	Mtl. 1	at	Buf. 4	Don Edwards	68	68	56	80	
Marcel Dionne	L.A.	2-4-77	Min. 2	at	L.A. 7	Pete LoPresti	79	79	53	80	25.8
Guy Lafleur	Mtl.	8-3-78	Wsh. 3	at	Mtl. 4	Jim Bedard	63	65	60	78	
Mike Bossy	NYI	1-4-78	Wsh. 2	at	NYI 3	Bernie Wolfe	69	76	53	73	21.2
Mike Bossy	NYI	24-2-79	Det. 1	at	NYI 3	Rogie Vachon	58	58	69	80	
Marcel Dionne	L.A.	11-3-79	L.A. 3	at	Phi. 6	Wayne Stephenson	68	68	59	80	
Guy Lafleur	Mtl.	31-3-79	Pit. 3	at	Mtl. 5	Denis Herron	76	76	52	80	
Guy Chouinard	Atl.	6-4-79	NYR 2	at	Atl. 9	John Davidson	79	79	50	80	22.5
Marcel Dionne	L.A.	12-3-80	L.A. 2	at	Pit. 4	Nick Ricci	70	70	53	80	
Mike Bossy	NYI	16-3-80	NYI 6	at	Chi. 1	Tony Esposito	68	71	51	75	
Charlie Simmer	L.A.	19-3-80	Det. 3	at	L.A. 4	Jim Rutherford	57	73	56	64	26.0
Pierre Larouche	Mtl.	25-3-80	Chi. 4	at	Mtl. 8	Tony Esposito	72	75	50	73	
Danny Gare	Buf.	27-3-80	Det. 1	at	Buf. 10	Jim Rutherford	71	75	56	76	
Blaine Stoughton	Hfd.	28-3-80	Hfd. 4	at	Van. 4	Glen Hanlon	75	75	56	80	27.0
Guy Lafleur	Mtl.	2-4-80	Mtl. 7	at	Det. 2	Rogie Vachon	72	78	50	74	
Wayne Gretzky	Edm.	2-4-80	Min. 1	at	Edm. 1	Gary Edwards	78	79	51	79	19.2
Reggie Leach	Phi.	3-4-80	Wsh. 2	at	Phi. 4	(empty net)	75	79	50	76	
Mike Bossy	NYI	24-1-81	Que. 3	at	NYI 7	Ron Grahame	50	50	68	79	
Charlie Simmer	L.A.	26-1-81	L.A. 7	at	Que. 5	Michel Dion	51	51	56	65	
Marcel Dionne	L.A.	8-3-81	L.A. 4	at	Wpg. 3	Markus Mattsson	68	68	58	80	
Wayne Babych	St. L.	12-3-81	St. L. 3	at	Mtl. 4	Richard Sevigny	70	68	54	78	22.9
Wayne Gretzky	Edm.	15-3-81	Edm. 3	at	Cgy. 3	Pat Riggin	69	69	55	80	
Rick Kehoe	Pit.	16-3-81	Pit. 7	at	Edm. 6	Eddie Mio	70	70	55	80	29.7
Jacques Richard	Que.	29-3-81	Mtl. 0	at	Que. 4	Richard Sevigny	76	75	52	78	28.6
Dennis Maruk	Wsh.	5-4-81	Det. 2	at	Wsh. 7	Larry Lozinski	80	80	50	80	25.3
Wayne Gretzky	Edm.	30-12-81	Phi. 5	at	Edm. 7	(empty net)	39	39	92	80	
Dennis Maruk	Wsh.	21-2-82	Wpg. 3	at	Wsh. 6	Doug Soetaert	61	61	60	80	
Mike Bossy	NYI	4-3-82	Tor. 1	at	NYI 10	Michel Larocque	66	66	64	80	
Dino Ciccarelli	Min.	8-3-82	St. L. 1	at	Min. 8	Mike Liut	67	68	55	76	21.7
Rick Vaive	Tor.	24-3-82	St. L. 3	at	Tor. 4	Mike Liut	72	75	54	77	22.10
Rick Middleton	Bos.	28-3-82	Bos. 5	at	Buf. 9	Paul Harrison	72	77	51	75	28.11
Blaine Stoughton	Hfd.	28-3-82	Min. 5	at	Hfd. 2	Gilles Meloche	76	76	52	80	28.3
Marcel Dionne	L.A.	30-3-82	Cgy. 7	at	L.A. 5	Pat Riggin	75	77	50	78	
Mark Messier	Edm.	31-3-82	L.A. 3	at	Edm. 7	Mario Lessard	78	79	50	78	21.3
Bryan Trottier	NYI	3-4-82	Phi. 3	at	NYI 6	Pete Peeters	79	79	50	80	25.9
Lanny McDonald	Cgy.	18-2-83	Cgy. 1	at	Buf. 5	Bob Sauve	60	60	66	80	30.0
Wayne Gretzky	Edm.	19-2-83	Edm. 10	at	Pit. 7	Nick Ricci	60	60	71	80	
Michel Goulet	Que.	5-3-83	Hfd. 3	at	Que. 10	Mike Veisor	67	67	57	80	22.11
Mike Bossy	NYI	12-3-83	Wsh. 2	at	NYI 6	Al Jensen	70	71	60	79	
Marcel Dionne	L.A.	17-3-83	Que. 3	at	L.A. 4	Daniel Bouchard	71	71	56	80	
Al Secord	Chi.	20-3-83	Tor. 3	at	Chi. 7	Mike Palmateer	73	73	54	80	25.0
Rick Vaive	Tor.	30-3-83	Tor. 4	at	Det. 2	Gilles Gilbert	76	78	51	78	
Wayne Gretzky	Edm.	7-1-84	Hfd. 3	at	Edm. 5	Greg Millen	42	42	87	74	
Michel Goulet	Que.	8-3-84	Que. 8	at	Pit. 6	Denis Herron	63	69	56	75	
Rick Vaive	Tor.	14-3-84	Min. 3	at	Tor. 3	Gilles Meloche	69	72	52	76	
Mike Bullard	Pit.	14-3-84	Pit. 6	at	L.A. 7	Markus Mattsson	71	72	51	76	23.0

Rick Martin

Rick Middleton

Rick Vaive

Gary Leeman

Pavel Bure

Mike Modano

Player	Team	Date of 50th Goal	Score		Goaltender	Player's Game No.	Team Game No.	Total Goals	Total Games	Age When First 50th Scored (Yrs. & Mos.)
Jari Kurri	Edm.	15-3-84	Edm. 2	at Mtl. 3	Rick Wamsley	57	73	52	64	23.10
Glenn Anderson	Edm.	21-3-84	Hfd. 3	at Edm. 5	Greg Millen	76	76	54	80	23.6
Tim Kerr	Phi.	22-3-84	Pit. 4	at Phi. 13	Denis Herron	74	75	54	79	24.3
Mike Bossy	NYI	31-3-84	NYI 3	at Wsh. 1	Pat Riggin	67	79	51	67	
Wayne Gretzky	Edm.	26-1-85	Pit. 3	at Edm. 6	Denis Herron	49	49	73	80	
Jari Kurri	Edm.	3-2-85	Hfd. 3	at Edm. 6	Greg Millen	50	53	71	73	
Mike Bossy	NYI	5-3-85	Phi. 5	at NYI 4	Bob Froese	61	65	58	76	
Tim Kerr	Phi.	7-3-85	Wsh. 6	at Phi. 9	Pat Riggin	63	65	54	74	
John Ogrodnick	Det.	13-3-85	Det. 6	at Edm. 7	Grant Fuhr	69	69	55	79	25.9
Bob Carpenter	Wsh.	21-3-85	Wsh. 2	at Mtl. 3	Steve Penney	72	72	53	80	21.9
Michel Goulet	Que.	6-3-85	Buf. 3	at Que. 4	Tom Barrasso	62	73	55	69	
Dale Hawerchuk	Wpg.	29-3-85	Chi. 5	at Wpg. 5	W. Skorodenski	77	77	53	80	21.1
Mike Gartner	Wsh.	7-4-85	Pit. 3	at Wsh. 7	Brian Ford	80	80	50	80	25.5
Jari Kurri	Edm.	4-3-86	Edm. 6	at Van. 2	Richard Brodeur	63	65	68	78	
Mike Bossy	NYI	11-3-86	Cgy. 4	at NYI 8	Rejean Lemelin	67	67	61	80	
Glenn Anderson	Edm.	14-3-86	Det. 3	at Edm. 12	Greg Stefan	63	71	54	72	
Michel Goulet	Que.	17-3-86	Que. 8	at Mtl. 6	Patrick Roy	67	72	53	75	
Wayne Gretzky	Edm.	18-3-86	Wpg. 2	at Edm. 6	Brian Hayward	72	72	52	80	
Tim Kerr	Phi.	20-3-86	Pit. 1	at Phi. 5	Roberto Romano	68	72	58	76	
Wayne Gretzky	Edm.	4-2-87	Edm. 6	at Min. 5	Don Beaupre	55	55	62	79	
Tim Kerr	Phi.	17-3-87	NYR 1	at Phi. 4	J. Vanbiesbrouck	67	71	58	75	
Jari Kurri	Edm.	17-3-87	N.J. 4	at Edm. 7	Craig Billington	69	70	54	79	
Mario Lemieux	Pit.	12-3-87	Que. 3	at Pit. 6	Mario Gosselin	53	70	54	63	21.5
Dino Ciccarelli	Min.	7-3-87	Pit. 7	at Min. 3	Gilles Meloche	66	66	52	80	
Mario Lemieux	Pit.	2-2-88	Wsh. 2	at Pit. 3	Pete Peeters	51	54	70	77	
Steve Yzerman	Det.	1-3-88	Buf. 0	at Det. 4	Tom Barrasso	64	64	50	64	22.10
Joe Nieuwendyk	Cgy.	12-3-88	Buf. 4	at Cgy. 10	Tom Barrasso	66	70	51	75	21.5
Craig Simpson	Edm.	15-3-88	Buf. 4	at Edm. 6	Jacques Cloutier	71	71	56	80	21.1
Jimmy Carson	L.A.	26-3-88	Chi. 5	at L.A. 9	Darren Pang	77	77	55	88	19.7
Luc Robitaille	L.A.	1-4-88	L.A. 6	at Cgy. 3	Mike Vernon	79	79	53	80	21.10
Hakan Loob	Cgy.	3-4-88	Min. 1	at Cgy. 4	Don Beaupre	80	80	50	80	27.9
Stephane Richer	Mtl.	3-4-88	Mtl. 4	at Buf. 4	Tom Barrasso	72	80	50	72	21.10
Mario Lemieux	Pit.	20-1-89	Pit. 3	at Wpg. 7	Eldon Reddick	44	46	85	76	
Bernie Nicholls	L.A.	28-1-89	Edm. 7	at L.A. 6	Grant Fuhr	51	51	70	79	27.7
Steve Yzerman	Det.	5-2-89	Det. 6	at Wpg. 2	Eldon Reddick	55	55	65	80	
Wayne Gretzky	L.A.	4-3-89	Phi. 2	at L.A. 6	Ron Hextall	66	67	54	78	
Joe Nieuwendyk	Cgy.	21-3-89	NYI 1	at Cgy. 4	Mark Fitzpatrick	72	74	51	77	
Joe Mullen	Cgy.	31-3-89	Wpg. 1	at Cgy. 4	Bob Essensa	78	79	51	79	32.1
Brett Hull	St. L.	6-2-90	Tor. 4	at St. L. 6	Jeff Reese	54	54	72	80	25.6
Steve Yzerman	Det.	24-2-90	Det. 3	at NYI 3	Glenn Healy	63	63	62	79	
Cam Neely	Bos.	10-3-90	Bos. 3	at NYI 3	Mark Fitzpatrick	69	71	55	76	24.9
Brian Bellows	Min.	22-3-90	Min. 5	at Det. 1	Tim Cheveldae	75	75	55	80	25.
Pat LaFontaine	NYI	24-3-90	NYI 5	at Edm. 5	Bill Ranford	71	77	54	74	25.1
Luc Robitaille	L.A.	21-3-90	L.A. 3	at Van. 6	Kirk McLean	79	79	52	80	
Stephane Richer	Mtl.	24-3-90	Mtl. 4	at Hfd. 7	Peter Sidorkiewicz	75	77	51	75	
Gary Leeman	Tor.	28-3-90	NYI 6	at Tor. 3	Mark Fitzpatrick	78	78	51	80	26.1
Brett Hull	St. L.	25-1-91	St. L. 9	at Det. 4	Dave Gagnon	49	49	86	78	
Cam Neely	Bos.	26-3-91	Bos. 7	at Que. 4	empty net	67	78	51	69	
Theoren Fleury	Cgy.	26-3-91	Van. 2	at Cgy. 7	Bob Mason	77	77	51	79	22.9
Steve Yzerman	Det.	30-3-91	NYR 5	at Det. 6	Mike Richter	79	79	51	80	
Brett Hull	St. L.	28-1-92	St. L. 3	at L.A. 3	Kelly Hrudey	50	50	70	73	
Kevin Stevens	Pit.	24-3-92	Pit. 3	at Det. 4	Tim Cheveldae	74	74	54	80	26.11
Gary Roberts	Cgy.	31-3-92	Edm. 2	at Cgy. 5	Bill Ranford	73	77	53	76	25.10
Jeremy Roenick	Chi.	7-3-92	Chi. 2	at Bos. 1	Daniel Berthiaume	67	67	53	80	22.2
Alexander Mogilny	Buf.	3-2-93	Hfd. 2	at Buf. 3	Sean Burke	46	53	76	77	23.11
Teemu Selanne	Wpg.	28-2-93	Min. 6	at Wpg. 7	Darcy Wakaluk	63	63	76	84	22.6
Pavel Bure	Van.	1-3-93	Van. 5	at Buf. 2*	Grant Fuhr	63	63	60	83	21.11
Steve Yzerman	Det.	10-3-93	Det. 6	at Edm. 3	Bill Ranford	70	70	58	84	
Luc Robitaille	L.A.	15-3-93	L.A. 4	at Buf. 2	Grant Fuhr	69	69	63	84	
Brett Hull	St. L.	20-3-93	St. L. 2	at L.A. 3	Robb Stauber	73	73	54	80	
Mario Lemieux	Pit.	21-3-93	Pit. 6	at Edm. 4**	Ron Tugnutt	48	72	69	60	
Kevin Stevens	Pit.	21-3-93	Pit. 6	at Edm. 4**	Ron Tugnutt	62	72	55	72	
Dave Andreychuk	Tor.	23-3-93	Tor. 5	at Wpg. 4	Bob Essensa	72	73	54	83	29.6
Pat LaFontaine	Buf.	28-3-93	Ott. 1	at Buf. 3	Peter Sidorkiewicz	75	75	53	84	
Pierre Turgeon	NYI	2-4-93	NYI 3	at NYR 2	Mike Richter	75	76	58	83	23.8
Mark Recchi	Phi.	3-4-93	T.B. 2	at Phi. 6	J-C Bergeron	77	77	53	84	25.2
Jeremy Roenick	Chi.	15-4-93	Tor. 2	at Chi. 3	Felix Potvin	84	84	50	84	
Brendan Shanahan	St. L.	15-4-93	T.B. 5	at St. L. 6	Pat Jablonski	71	84	51	71	24.3
Cam Neely	Bos.	7-3-94	Wsh. 3	at Bos. 6	Don Beaupre	44	66	50	49	
Sergei Fedorov	Det.	15-3-94	Van. 2	at Det. 5	Kirk McLean	67	69	56	82	24.3
Pavel Bure	Van.	23-3-94	Van. 4	at L.A. 3	empty net	65	73	60	76	
Adam Graves	NYR	23-3-94	NYR 5	at Edm. 3	Bill Ranford	74	74	51	84	25.11
Dave Andreychuk	Tor	24-3-94	S.J. 2	at Tor. 1	Arturs Irbe	73	74	53	83	
Brett Hull	St.L.	25-3-94	Dal. 3	at St.L. 5	Andy Moog	71	74	52	81	
Ray Sheppard	Det.	29-3-94	Hfd. 2	at Det. 6	Sean Burke	74	76	52	82	27.10
Brendan Shanahan	St. L.	12-4-94	St.L. 5	at Dal. 9	Andy Moog	80	83	52	81	
Mike Modano	Dal.	12-4-94	St.L. 5	at Dal. 9	Curtis Joseph	75	83	50	76	23.11

* neutral site game played at Hamilton; ** neutral site game played at Cleveland

100-Point Seasons

Player	Team	Date of 100th Point	G or A	Score		Player's Game No.	Team Game No.	Points G - A PTS	Total Games	Age when first 100th point scored (Yrs. & Mos.)
Phil Esposito	Bos.	2-3-69	(G)	Pit. 0	at Bos. 4	60	62	49-77 — 126	74	27.1
Bobby Hull	Chi.	20-3-69	(G)	Chi. 5	at Bos. 5	71	71	58-49 — 107	76	30.2
Gordie Howe	Det.	30-3-69	(G)	Det. 5	at Chi. 9	76	76	44-59 — 103	76	41.0
Bobby Orr	Bos.	15-3-70	(G)	Det. 5	at Bos. 5	67	67	33-87 — 120	76	22.11
Phil Esposito	Bos.	6-2-71	(A)	Buf. 3	at Bos. 4	51	51	76-76 — 152	78	
Bobby Orr	Bos.	22-2-71	(A)	Bos. 4	at L.A. 5	58	58	37-102 — 139	78	
John Bucyk	Bos.	13-3-71	(A)	Bos. 6	at Van. 3	68	68	51-65 — 116	78	35.10
Ken Hodge	Bos.	21-3-71	(A)	Buf. 7	at Bos. 5	72	72	43-62 — 105	78	26.9
Jean Ratelle	NYR	18-2-72	(A)	NYR 2	at Cal. 2	58	58	46-63 — 109	63	31.4
Phil Esposito	Bos.	19-2-72	(A)	Bos. 6	at Min. 4	59	59	66-67 — 133	76	
Bobby Orr	Bos.	2-3-72	(A)	Van. 3	at Bos. 7	64	64	37-80 — 117	76	
Vic Hadfield	NYR	25-3-72	(A)	NYR 3	at Mtl. 3	74	74	50-56 — 106	78	31.5
Phil Esposito	Bos.	3-3-73	(A)	Bos. 1	at Mtl. 5	64	64	55-75 — 130	78	
Bobby Clarke	Phi.	29-3-73	(G)	Atl. 2	at Phi. 4	76	76	37-67 — 104	78	23.7
Bobby Orr	Bos.	31-3-73	(G)	Bos. 3	at Tor. 7	62	77	29-72 — 101	63	
Rick MacLeish	Phi.	1-4-73	(G)	Phi. 4	at Pit. 5	78	78	50-50 — 100	78	23.3
Phil Esposito	Bos.	13-2-74	(A)	Bos. 9	at Cal. 6	53	53	68-77 — 145	78	
Bobby Orr	Bos.	12-3-74	(A)	Buf. 0	at Bos. 4	62	66	32-90 — 122	74	
Ken Hodge	Bos.	24-3-74	(A)	Mtl. 3	at Bos. 6	72	72	50-55 — 105	76	
Phil Esposito	Bos.	8-2-75	(A)	Bos. 8	at Det. 5	54	54	61-66 — 127	79	
Bobby Orr	Bos.	13-2-75	(A)	Bos. 1	at Buf. 3	57	57	46-89 — 135	80	
Guy Lafleur	Mtl.	7-3-75	(G)	Wsh. 4	at Mtl. 8	56	66	53-66 — 119	70	24.6
Pete Mahovlich	Mtl.	9-3-75	(A)	Mtl. 5	at NYR 3	67	67	35-82 — 117	80	29.5
Marcel Dionne	Det.	9-3-75	(A)	Det. 5	at Phi. 8	67	67	47-74 — 121	80	23.7
Bobby Clarke	Phi.	22-3-75	(A)	Min. 0	at Phi. 4	72	72	27-89 — 116	80	
Rene Robert	Buf.	5-4-75	(A)	Buf. 4	at Tor. 2	74	80	40-60 — 100	74	26.4
Guy Lafleur	Mtl.	10-3-76	(G)	Mtl. 5	at Chi. 1	69	69	56-69 — 125	80	
Bobby Clarke	Phi.	11-3-76	(A)	Buf. 1	at Phi. 6	64	68	30-89 — 119	76	
Bill Barber	Phi.	18-3-76	(A)	Van. 2	at Phi. 3	71	71	50-62 — 112	80	23.8
Gilbert Perreault	Buf.	21-3-76	(A)	K.C. 1	at Buf. 3	73	73	44-69 — 113	80	25.4
Pierre Larouche	Pit.	24-3-76	(A)	Bos. 5	at Pit. 5	70	74	53-58 — 111	76	20.4
Pete Mahovlich	Mtl.	28-3-76	(A)	Mtl. 2	at Bos. 2	77	77	34-71 — 105	80	
Jean Ratelle	Bos.	30-3-76	(G)	Buf. 4	at Bos. 4	77	77	36-69 — 105	80	
Jean Pronovost	Pit.	3-4-76	(A)	Wsh. 5	at Pit. 4	79	79	52-52 — 104	80	30.4
Darryl Sittler	Tor.	3-4-76	(A)	Bos. 4	at Tor. 2	78	79	41-59 — 100	79	26.7
Guy Lafleur	Mtl.	26-2-77	(A)	Clev. 3	at Mtl. 5	63	63	56-80 — 136	80	
Marcel Dionne	L.A.	5-3-77	(G)	Pit. 3	at L.A. 4	67	67	53-69 — 122	80	
Steve Shutt	Mtl.	27-3-77	(A)	Mtl. 6	at Det. 0	77	77	60-45 — 105	80	24.9
Bryan Trottier	NYI	25-2-78	(A)	Chi. 1	at NYI 7	59	60	46-77 — 123	77	21.7
Guy Lafleur	Mtl.	28-2-78	(G)	Det. 3	at Mtl. 9	69	61	60-72 — 132	78	
Darryl Sittler	Tor.	12-3-78	(A)	Tor. 7	at Pit. 1	67	67	45-72 — 117	80	
Guy Lafleur	Mtl.	27-2-79	(A)	Mtl. 3	at NYI 7	61	61	52-77 — 129	80	
Bryan Trottier	NYI	6-3-79	(A)	Buf. 3	at NYI 2	59	63	47-87 — 134	76	
Marcel Dionne	L.A.	8-3-79	(G)	L.A. 4	at Buf. 6	66	66	59-71 — 130	80	
Mike Bossy	NYI	11-3-79	(G)	NYI 4	at Bos. 4	66	66	69-57 — 126	80	22.2
Bob MacMillan	Atl.	15-3-79	(A)	Atl. 4	at Phi. 5	68	69	37-71 — 108	79	26.6
Guy Chouinard	Atl.	30-3-79	(A)	L.A. 3	at Atl. 5	75	75	50-57 — 107	80	22.5
Denis Potvin	NYI	8-4-79	(A)	NYI 5	at NYR 2	73	80	31-70 — 101	73	25.5
Marcel Dionne	L.A.	6-2-80	(A)	L.A. 3	at Hfd. 7	53	53	53-84 — 137	80	
Guy Lafleur	Mtl.	10-2-80	(A)	Mtl. 3	at Bos. 2	55	55	50-75 — 125	74	
Wayne Gretzky	Edm.	24-2-80	(A)	Bos. 4	at Edm. 2	61	62	51-86 — 137	79	19.2
Bryan Trottier	NYI	30-3-80	(A)	NYI 9	at Que. 6	75	77	42-62 — 104	78	
Gilbert Perreault	Buf.	1-4-80	(A)	Buf. 5	at Atl. 2	77	77	40-66 — 106	80	
Mike Rogers	Hfd.	4-4-80	(A)	Que. 2	at Hfd. 9	79	79	44-61 — 105	80	25.5
Charlie Simmer	L.A.	5-4-80	(A)	Van. 5	at L.A. 3	64	80	56-45 — 101	64	26.0
Blaine Stoughton	Hfd.	6-4-80	(A)	Det. 3	at Hfd. 5	80	80	56-44 — 100	80	27.0
Wayne Gretzky	Edm.	6-2-81	(G)	Wpg. 4	at Edm. 10	53	53	55-109 — 164	80	
Marcel Dionne	L.A.	12-2-81	(A)	L.A. 5	at Chi. 5	58	58	58-77 — 135	80	
Charlie Simmer	L.A.	14-2-81	(A)	Bos. 5	at L.A. 4	59	59	56-49 — 105	65	
Kent Nilsson	Cgy.	27-2-81	(G)	Hfd. 1	at Cgy. 5	64	64	49-82 — 131	80	24.6
Mike Bossy	NYI	3-3-81	(G)	Edm. 8	at NYI 8	65	66	68-51 — 119	79	
Dave Taylor	L.A.	14-3-81	(G)	Min. 4	at L.A. 10	63	70	47-65 — 112	72	25.3
Mike Rogers	Hfd.	22-3-81	(G)	Tor. 3	at Hfd. 3	74	74	40-65 — 105	80	
Bernie Federko	St. L.	28-3-81	(A)	Buf. 4	at St. L. 7	74	76	31-73 — 104	78	24.10
Rick Middleton	Bos.	28-3-81	(A)	Chi. 2	at Bos. 5	76	76	44-59 — 103	80	27.4
Jacques Richard	Que.	29-3-81	(G)	Mtl. 0	at Que. 4	75	76	52-51 — 103	78	28.6
Bryan Trottier	NYI	29-3-81	(G)	NYI 1	at Wsh. 4	69	76	31-72 — 103	73	
Peter Stastny	Que.	29-3-81	(G)	Mtl. 0	at Que. 4	73	76	39-70 — 109	77	24.6
Wayne Gretzky	Edm.	27-12-81	(G)	L.A. 3	at Edm. 10	38	38	92-120 — 212	80	
Mike Bossy	NYI	13-2-82	(A)	Phi. 2	at NYI 8	55	55	64-83 — 147	80	
Peter Stastny	Que.	16-2-82	(A)	Wpg. 3	at Que. 7	60	60	46-93 — 139	80	
Dennis Maruk	Wsh.	20-2-82	(G)	Wsh. 3	at Min. 7	60	60	60-76 — 136	80	26.3
Bryan Trottier	NYI	23-2-82	(A)	Chi. 1	at NYI 5	61	61	50-79 — 129	80	
Denis Savard	Chi.	27-2-82	(A)	Chi. 5	at L.A. 3	64	64	32-87 — 119	80	21.1
Bobby Smith	Min.	3-3-82	(A)	Det. 4	at Min. 6	66	66	43-71 — 114	80	24.1
Marcel Dionne	L.A.	6-3-82	(G)	L.A. 6	at Hfd. 7	64	66	50-67 — 117	78	
Dave Taylor	L.A.	20-3-82	(A)	Pit. 5	at L.A. 7	71	72	39-67 — 106	78	
Dale Hawerchuk	Wpg.	24-3-82	(G)	L.A. 3	at Wpg.	74	74	45-58 — 103	80	18.11
Dino Ciccarelli	Min.	27-3-82	(G)	Min. 6	at Bos. 5	72	76	55-52 — 107	76	21.8
Glenn Anderson	Edm.	28-3-82	(G)	Edm. 6	at L.A. 2	78	78	38-67 — 105	80	21.7
Mike Rogers	NYR	2-4-82	(G)	Pit. 7	at NYR 5	79	79	38-65 — 103	80	

Ken Hodge

Paul MacLean

Barry Pederson

A slick skater and a precise passer, Bernie Federko, right, was the first player in NHL history to record 50-or-more assists in 10 consecutive seasons. Doug Gilmour, below, was dismissed by many scouts as being too small to play in the NHL. He proved the skeptics wrong by reaching the 100-point mark three times, including a 105-point effort with the St. Louis Blues in 1986-87. Below, right: Dale Hawerchuk, who reached the 100-point plateau in six of his first seven seasons in the NHL, is one of the hockey's most resilient performers. Until groin and leg injuries forced him to miss 25 games in 1994-95, he had never missed more than five games in any one of his 14 NHL seasons.

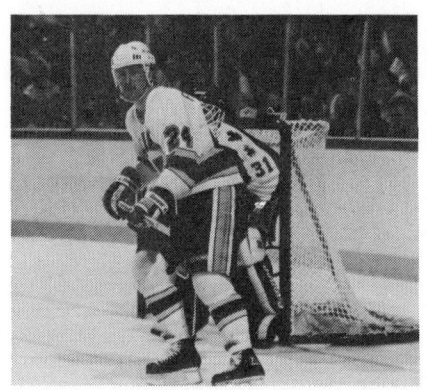

100-Point Seasons — *continued*

Player	Team	Date of 100th Point	G or A	Score		Player's Game No.	Team Game No.	Points G - A — PTS	Total Games	Age when first 100th point scored (Yrs. & Mos.)
Wayne Gretzky	Edm.	5-1-83	(A)	Edm. 8	at Wpg. 3	42	42	71-125 — 196	80	
Mike Bossy	NYI	3-3-83	(A)	Tor. 1	at NYI. 5	66	67	60-58 — 118	79	
Peter Stastny	Que.	5-3-83	(A)	Hfd. 3	at Que. 10	62	67	47-77 — 124	75	
Denis Savard	Chi.	6-3-83	(G)	Mtl. 4	at Chi. 5	65	67	35-86 — 121	78	
Mark Messier	Edm.	23-3-83	(G)	Edm. 4	at Wpg. 7	73	76	48-58 — 106	77	22.2
Barry Pederson	Bos.	26-3-83	(A)	Hfd. 4	at Bos. 7	73	76	46-61 — 107	77	22.0
Marcel Dionne	L.A.	26-3-83	(A)	Edm. 9	at L.A. 3	75	75	56-51 — 107	80	
Michel Goulet	Que.	27-3-83	(A)	Que. 6	at Buf. 6	77	77	57-48 — 105	80	22.11
Glenn Anderson	Edm.	29-3-83	(A)	Edm. 7	at Van. 4	70	78	48-56 — 104	72	
Jari Kurri	Edm.	29-3-83	(A)	Edm. 7	at Van. 4	78	78	45-59 — 104	80	22.10
Kent Nilsson	Cgy.	29-3-83	(G)	L.A. 3	at Cgy. 5	78	78	46-58 — 104	80	
Wayne Gretzky	Edm.	18-12-83	(G)	Edm. 7	at Wpg. 5	34	34	87-118 — 205	74	
Paul Coffey	Edm.	4-3-84	(A)	Mtl. 1	at Edm. 6	68	68	40-86 — 126	80	22.9
Michel Goulet	Que.	4-3-84	(A)	Que. 1	at Buf. 1	62	67	56-65 — 121	75	
Jari Kurri	Edm.	7-3-84	(G)	Chi. 4	at Edm. 7	53	69	52-61 — 113	64	
Peter Stastny	Que.	8-3-84	(A)	Que. 8	at Pit. 6	69	69	46-73 — 119	80	
Mike Bossy	NYI	8-3-84	(G)	Tor. 5	at NYI 9	56	68	51-67 — 118	67	
Barry Pederson	Bos.	14-3-84	(A)	Bos. 4	at Det. 2	71	71	39-77 — 116	80	
Bryan Trottier	NYI	18-3-84	(G)	Que. 1	at Hfd. 5	62	73	40-71 — 111	68	
Bernie Federko	St. L.	20-3-84	(A)	Wpg. 3	at St. L. 9	75	76	41-66 — 107	79	
Rick Middleton	Bos.	27-3-84	(G)	Bos. 6	at Que. 4	77	77	47-58 — 105	80	
Dale Hawerchuk	Wpg.	27-3-84	(G)	Wpg. 3	at L.A. 3	77	77	37-65 — 102	80	
Mark Messier	Edm.	27-3-84	(G)	Edm. 9	at Cgy. 2	72	79	37-64 — 101	73	
Wayne Gretzky	Edm.	29-12-84	(A)	Det. 3	at Edm. 6	35	35	73-135 — 208	80	
Jari Kurri	Edm.	29-1-85	(G)	Edm. 4	at Cgy. 2	48	51	71-64 — 135	73	
Mike Bossy	NYI	23-2-85	(G)	Bos. 1	at NYI 7	56	60	58-59 — 117	76	
Dale Hawerchuk	Wpg.	25-2-85	(A)	Wpg. 12	at NYR 5	64	64	53-77 — 130	80	
Marcel Dionne	L.A.	5-3-85	(A)	Pit. 0	at L.A. 6	66	66	46-80 — 126	80	22.10
Brent Sutter	NYI	12-3-85	(A)	NYI 6	at St. L. 5	68	68	42-60 — 102	72	
John Ogrodnick	Det.	22-3-85	(A)	NYR 3	at Det. 5	73	73	55-50 — 105	79	25.9
Paul Coffey	Edm.	26-3-85	(G)	Edm. 7	at NYI 5	74	74	37-84 — 121	80	
Denis Savard	Chi.	29-3-85	(A)	Chi. 5	at Wpg. 5	75	76	38-67 — 105	79	
Peter Stastny	Que.	2-4-85	(A)	Bos. 4	at Que. 6	74	77	32-68 — 100	75	
Bernie Federko	St. L.	4-4-85	(A)	NYR 5	at St. L. 4	74	78	30-73 — 103	76	
John Tonelli	NYI	6-4-85	(G)	NJ 5	at NYI 5	80	80	42-58 — 100	80	28.1
Paul MacLean	Wpg.	6-4-85	(A)	Wpg. 6	at Edm. 5	78	79	41-60 — 101	79	27.1
Mike Gartner	Wsh.	7-4-85	(A)	Pit. 3	at Wsh. 7	80	80	50-52 — 102	80	25.6
Bernie Nicholls	L.A.	6-4-85	(A)	Van. 4	at L.A. 4	80	80	46-54 — 100	80	22.9
Mario Lemieux	Pit.	7-4-85	(G)	Pit. 3	at Wsh. 7	73	80	43-57 — 100	73	19.6
Wayne Gretzky	Edm.	4-1-86	(A)	Hfd. 3	at Edm. 4	39	39	52-163 — 215	80	
Mario Lemieux	Pit.	15-2-86	(G)	Van. 4	at Pit. 9	55	56	48-93 — 141	79	
Paul Coffey	Edm.	19-2-86	(A)	Tor. 5	at Edm. 9	59	60	48-90 — 138	79	
Jari Kurri	Edm.	2-3-86	(G)	Phi. 1	at Edm. 2	62	64	68-63 — 131	78	
Peter Stastny	Que.	1-3-86	(A)	Buf. 8	at Que. 4	66	68	41-81 — 122	76	
Mike Bossy	NYI	8-3-86	(G)	Wsh. 6	at NYI 2	65	65	61-62 — 123	80	
Denis Savard	Chi.	12-3-86	(A)	Buf. 7	at Chi. 6	69	69	47-69 — 116	80	
Mats Naslund	Mtl.	13-3-86	(A)	Mtl. 2	at Bos. 3	70	70	43-67 — 110	80	26.4
Michel Goulet	Que.	24-3-86	(A)	Que. 1	at Min. 0	70	75	53-50 — 103	75	
Glenn Anderson	Edm.	25-3-86	(G)	Edm. 7	at Det. 2	66	74	54-48 — 102	72	
Neal Broten	Min.	26-3-86	(A)	Min. 6	at Tor. 1	76	76	29-76 — 105	80	26.4
Dale Hawerchuk	Wpg.	31-3-86	(A)	Wpg. 5	at L.A. 2	78	78	46-59 — 105	80	
Bernie Federko	St. L.	5-4-86	(G)	Chi. 5	at St. L. 7	79	79	34-68 — 102	80	
Wayne Gretzky	Edm.	11-1-87	(A)	Cgy. 3	at Edm. 5	42	42	62-121 — 183	79	
Jari Kurri	Edm.	14-3-87	(A)	Buf. 3	at Edm. 5	67	68	54-54 — 108	79	
Mario Lemieux	Pit.	18-3-87	(A)	St. L. 4	at Pit. 5	55	72	54-53 — 107	63	
Mark Messier	Edm.	19-3-87	(A)	Edm. 4	at Cgy. 5	71	71	37-70 — 107	77	
Doug Gilmour	St. L.	2-4-87	(A)	Buf. 3	at St. L. 5	78	78	42-63 — 105	80	23.10
Dino Ciccarelli	Min.	30-3-87	(A)	NYR 6	at Min. 5	78	78	52-51 — 103	80	
Dale Hawerchuk	Wpg.	5-4-87	(A)	Wpg. 3	at Cgy. 1	80	80	47-53 — 100	80	
Mario Lemieux	Pit.	20-1-88	(G)	Pit. 8	at Chi. 3	45	48	70-98 — 168	77	
Wayne Gretzky	Edm.	11-2-88	(A)	Edm. 7	at Van. 2	43	56	40-109 — 149	64	
Denis Savard	Chi.	12-2-88	(A)	St. L. 3	at Chi. 4	57	57	44-87 — 131	80	
Dale Hawerchuk	Wpg.	23-2-88	(G)	Wpg. 4	at Pit. 3	61	61	44-77 — 121	80	
Steve Yzerman	Det.	27-2-88	(A)	Det. 4	at Que. 5	63	63	50-52 — 102	64	22.10
Peter Stastny	Que.	8-3-88	(A)	Hfd. 4	at Que. 6	63	67	46-65 — 111	76	
Mark Messier	Edm.	15-3-88	(A)	Buf. 4	at Edm. 6	68	71	37-74 — 111	77	
Jimmy Carson	L.A.	26-3-88	(A)	Chi. 5	at L.A. 9	77	77	55-52 — 107	80	19.8
Hakan Loob	Cgy.	26-3-88	(A)	Van. 1	at Cgy. 6	76	76	50-56 — 106	80	27.9
Mike Bullard	Cgy.	26-3-88	(A)	Van. 1	at Cgy. 6	76	76	48-55 — 103	79	27.1
Michel Goulet	Que.	27-3-88	(A)	Pit. 6	at Que. 3	76	76	48-58 — 106	80	
Luc Robitaille	L.A.	30-3-88	(G)	Cgy. 7	at L.A. 9	78	78	53-58 — 111	80	22.1
Mario Lemieux	Pit.	31-12-88	(A)	N.J. 6	at Pit. 8	36	38	85-114 — 199	76	
Wayne Gretzky	L.A.	21-1-89	(A)	L.A. 4	at Hfd. 5	47	48	54-114 — 168	78	
Steve Yzerman	Det.	27-1-89	(G)	Tor. 1	at Det. 8	50	50	65-90 — 155	80	
Bernie Nicholls	L.A.	21-1-89	(A)	L.A. 4	at Hfd. 5	48	48	70-80 — 150	79	
Rob Brown	Pit.	16-3-89	(A)	Pit. 2	at N.J. 1	60	72	49-66 — 115	68	20.11
Paul Coffey	Pit.	20-3-89	(A)	Pit. 2	at Min. 7	69	74	30-83 — 113	75	
Joe Mullen	Cgy.	23-3-89	(A)	L.A. 2	at Cgy. 4	74	75	51-59 — 110	79	32.1
Jari Kurri	Edm.	29-3-89	(A)	Edm. 5	at Van. 4	75	79	44-58 — 102	76	
Jimmy Carson	Edm.	2-4-89	(A)	Edm. 2	at Cgy. 4	80	80	49-51 — 100	80	
Mario Lemieux	Pit.	28-1-90	(G)	Pit. 2	at Buf. 7	50	50	45-78 — 123	59	
Wayne Gretzky	L.A.	30-1-90	(A)	N.J. 2	at L.A. 5	51	51	40-102 — 142	73	
Steve Yzerman	Det.	19-2-90	(A)	Mtl. 2	at Det. 5	61	61	62-65 — 127	79	
Mark Messier	Edm.	20-2-90	(A)	Edm. 4	at Van. 2	62	62	45-84 — 129	79	
Brett Hull	St. L.	3-3-90	(A)	NYI 4	at St. L. 5	67	67	72-41 — 113	80	25.7
Bernie Nicholls	NYR	12-3-90	(A)	L.A. 6	at NYR 2	70	71	39-73 — 112	79	
Pierre Turgeon	Buf.	25-3-90	(G)	N.J. 4	at Buf. 3	76	76	40-66 — 106	80	20.7

Mats Naslund

Jimmy Carson

Craig Janney

Steve Yzerman

Sergei Fedorov

100-Point Seasons — *continued*

Player	Team	Date of 100th Point	G or A	Score		Player's Game No.	Team Game No.	Points G - A PTS	Total Games	Age when first 100th point scored (Yrs. & Mos.)
Paul Coffey	Pit.	25-3-90	(A)	Pit. 2	at Hfd. 4	77	77	29-74 — 103	80	
Pat LaFontaine	NYI	27-3-90	(G)	Cgy. 4	at NYI 2	72	78	54-51 — 105	74	25.1
Adam Oates	St. L.	29-3-90	(G)	Pit 4	at St. L. 5	79	79	23-79 — 102	80	27.7
Joe Sakic	Que.	31-3-90	(G)	Hfd. 3	at Que. 2	79	79	39-63 — 102	80	20.8
Ron Francis	Hfd.	31-3-90	(G)	Hfd. 3	at Que. 2	79	79	32-69 — 101	80	27.0
Luc Robitaille	L.A.	1-4-91	(A)	L.A. 4	at Cgy. 8	80	80	52-49 — 101	80	
Wayne Gretzky	L.A.	30-1-91	(A)	N.J. 4	at L.A. 2	50	51	41-122 — 163	78	
Brett Hull	St. L.	23-2-91	(G)	Bos. 2	at St. L. 9	60	62	86-45 — 131	78	
Mark Recchi	Pit.	5-3-91	(G)	Van. 1	at Pit. 4	66	67	40-73 — 113	78	23.1
Steve Yzerman	Det.	10-3-91	(G)	Det. 4	at St. L. 1	72	72	51-57 — 108	80	
John Cullen	Hfd.	16-3-91	(G)	N.J. 2	at Hfd. 6	71	71	39-71 — 110	78	26.7
Adam Oates	St. L.	17-3-91	(A)	St. L. 4	at Chi. 6	54	73	25-90 — 115	61	
Joe Sakic	Que.	19-3-91	(G)	Edm. 7	at Que. 6	74	74	48-61 — 109	80	
Steve Larmer	Chi.	24-3-91	(A)	Min. 4	at Chi. 5	76	76	44-57 — 101	80	29.9
Theoren Fleury	Cgy.	26-3-91	(A)	Van. 2	at Cgy. 7	77	77	51-53 — 104	79	22.9
Al MacInnis	Cgy.	28-3-91	(A)	Edm. 4	at Cgy. 7	78	78	28-75 — 103	78	27.8
Brett Hull	St. L.	2-3-92	(G)	St. L. 5	at Van. 3	66	66	70-39 — 109	73	
Wayne Gretzky	L.A.	3-3-92	(A)	Phi. 1	at L.A. 4	60	66	31-90 — 121	74	
Kevin Stevens	Pit.	7-3-92	(A)	Pit. 3	at L.A. 5	66	66	54-69 — 123	80	26.11
Mario Lemieux	Pit.	10-03-92	(G)	Cgy. 2	at Pit. 5	53	67	44-87 — 131	64	
Luc Robitaille	L.A.	17-3-92	(G)	Wpg. 4	at L.A. 5	73	73	44-63 — 107	80	
Mark Messier	NYR	22-3-92	(G)	N.J. 3	at NYR 6	74	75	35-72 — 107	79	
Jeremy Roenick	Chi.	29-3-92	(A)	Tor. 1	at Chi. 5	77	77	53-50 — 103	80	22.2
Steve Yzerman	Det.	14-4-92	(G)	Det. 7	at Min. 4	79	80	45-58 — 103	79	
Brian Leetch	NYR	16-4-92	(G)	Pit. 1	at NYR 7	80	80	22-80 — 102	80	24.1
Mario Lemieux	Pit.	31-12-92	(G)	Tor. 3	at Pit. 3	38	39	69-91 — 160	60	
Pat LaFontaine	Buf.	10-2-93	(A)	Buf. 6	at Wpg. 2	55	55	53-95 — 148	84	
Adam Oates	Bos.	14-2-93	(A)	Bos. 3	at T.B. 3	58	58	45-97 — 142	84	
Steve Yzerman	Det.	24-2-93	(A)	Det. 7	at Buf. 10	64	64	58-79 — 137	84	
Pierre Turgeon	NYI	28-2-93	(G)	NYI 7	at Hfd. 6	62	63	58-74 — 132	83	
Doug Gilmour	Tor.	3-3-93	(A)	Min. 1	at Tor. 3	64	64	32-95 — 127	83	
Alexander Mogilny	Buf.	5-3-93	(A)	Hfd. 4	at Buf. 2	58	65	76-51 — 127	77	24.1
Mark Recchi	Phi.	7-3-93	(G)	Phi. 3	at N.J. 7	66	66	53-70 — 123	84	
Teemu Selanne	Wpg.	9-3-93	(G)	Wpg. 4	at T.B. 2	68	68	76-56 — 132	84	22.7
Luc Robitaille	L.A.	15-3-93	(A)	L.A. 4	at Buf. 2	69	69	63-62 — 125	84	
Kevin Stevens	Pit.	23-3-93	(A)	S.J. 2	at Pit. 7	63	73	55-56 — 111	72	
Mats Sundin	Que.	27-3-93	(A)	Phi. 3	at Que. 8	71	75	47-67 — 114	80	22.1
Pavel Bure	Van.	1-4-93	(G)	Van. 5	at T.B. 3	77	77	60-50 — 110	83	22.0
Jeremy Roenick	Chi.	4-4-93	(G)	St. L. 4	at Chi. 5	79	79	50-57 — 107	84	
Craig Janney	St. L.	4-4-93	(A)	St. L. 4	at Chi. 5	79	79	24-82 — 106	84	25.7
Rick Tocchet	Pit.	7-4-93	(G)	Mtl. 3	at Pit. 4	77	81	48-61 — 109	80	28.11
Joe Sakic	Que.	8-4-93	(A)	Que. 2	at Bos. 6	75	81	48-57 — 105	78	
Ron Francis	Pit.	9-4-93	(A)	Pit. 10	at NYR 4	82	82	24-76 — 100	84	
Brett Hull	St. L.	11-4-93	(G)	Min. 1	at St. L. 5	78	82	54-47 — 101	80	
Theoren Fleury	Cgy.	11-4-93	(A)	Cgy. 3	at Van. 6	82	82	34-66 — 100	83	
Joe Juneau	Bos.	14-4-93	(A)	Bos. 4	at Ott. 2	84	84	32-70 — 102	84	25.3
Wayne Gretzky	L.A.	14-2-94	(A)	Bos. 3	at L.A. 2	56	56	38-92 — 130	81	
Sergei Fedorov	Det.	1-3-94	(A)	Cgy. 2	at Det. 5	63	63	56-64 — 120	82	24.2
Doug Gilmour	Tor.	23-3-94	(A)	Tor. 1	at Fla. 1	74	74	27-84 — 111	83	
Adma Oates	Bos.	26-3-94	(A)	Mtl. 3	at Bos. 6	68	75	32-80 — 112	77	
Mark Recchi	Phi.	27-3-94	(A)	Ana. 3	at Phi. 2	76	76	40-67 — 107	84	
Pavel Bure	Van.	28-3-94	(A)	Tor. 2	at Van. 3	68	76	60-47 — 107	76	
Brendan Shanahan	St.L.	12-4-94	(G)	St.L. 5	at Dal. 9	80	83	52-50 — 102	81	25.2

Five-or-more-Goal Games

Player	Team	Date	Score		Opposing Goaltender
SEVEN GOALS					
Joe Malone	Quebec Bulldogs	Jan. 31/20	Tor. 6	at Que. 10	Ivan Mitchell
SIX GOALS					
Newsy Lalonde	Montreal	Jan. 10/20	Tor. 7	at Mtl. 14	Ivan Mitchell
Joe Malone	Quebec Bulldogs	Mar. 10/20	Ott. 4	at Que. 10	Clint Benedict
Corb Denneny	Toronto St. Pats	Jan. 26/21	Ham. 3	at Tor. 10	Howard Lockhart
Cy Denneny	Ottawa Senators	Mar. 7/21	Ham. 5	at Ott. 12	Howard Lockhart
Syd Howe	Detroit	Feb. 3/44	NYR 2	at Det. 12	Ken McAuley
Red Berenson	St. Louis	Nov. 7/68	St. L. 8	at Phil 0	Doug Favell
Darryl Sittler	Toronto	Feb. 7/76	Bos. 4	at Tor. 11	Dave Reece
FIVE GOALS					
Joe Malone	Montreal	Dec. 19/17	Mtl. 7	at Ott. 4	Clint Benedict
Harry Hyland	Mtl. Wanderers	Dec. 19/17	Tor. 9	at Mtl. W. 10	Arthur Brooks
Joe Malone	Montreal	Jan. 12/18	Ott. 4	at Mtl. 9	Clint Benedict
Joe Malone	Montreal	Feb. 2/18	Tor. 2	at Mtl. 11	Harry Holmes
Mickey Roach	Toronto St. Pats	Mar. 6/20	Que. 2	at Tor. 11	Frank Brophy
Newsy Lalonde	Montreal	Feb. 16/21	Ham. 5	at Mtl. 10	Howard Lockhart
Babe Dye	Toronto St. Pats	Dec. 16/22	Mtl. 2	at Tor. 7	Georges Vezina
Redvers Green	Hamilton Tigers	Dec. 5/24	Ham. 10	at Tor. 3	John Roach
Babe Dye	Toronto St. Pats	Dec. 22/24	Tor. 10	at Bos. 1	Charlie Stewart
Harry Broadbent	Mtl. Maroons	Jan. 7/25	Ham. 2	at Ham. 2	Vernon Forbes
Pit Lepine	Montreal	Dec. 14/29	Ott. 4	at Mtl. 6	Alex Connell
Howie Morenz	Montreal	Mar. 18/30	NYA 3	at Mtl. 8	Roy Worters
Charlie Conacher	Toronto	Jan. 19/32	NYA 3	at Tor. 11	Roy Worters
Ray Getliffe	Montreal	Feb. 6/43	Bos. 3	at Mtl. 8	Frank Brimsek
Maurice Richard	Montreal	Dec. 28/44	Det. 1	at Mtl. 9	Harry Lumley
Howie Meeker	Toronto	Jan. 8/47	Chi. 4	at Tor. 10	Paul Bibeault
Bernie Geoffrion	Montreal	Feb. 19/55	NYR 2	at Mtl. 10	Gump Worsley
Bobby Rousseau	Montreal	Feb. 1/64	Det. 3	at Mtl. 9	Roger Crozier
Yvan Cournoyer	Montreal	Feb. 15/75	Chi. 3	at Mtl. 12	Mike Veisor
Don Murdoch	NY Rangers	Oct. 12/76	NYR 10	at Min. 4	Gary Smith
Ian Turnbull	Toronto	Feb. 2/77	Det. 1	at Tor. 9	Ed Giacomin (2) Jim Rutherford (3)
Bryan Trottier	NY Islanders	Dec. 23/78	NYR 4	at NYI 9	Wayne Thomas (4) John Davidson (1)

Player	Team	Date	Score		Opposing Goaltender
Tim Young	Minnesota	Jan. 15/79	Min. 8	at NYR 1	Doug Soetaert (3) Wayne Thomas (2)
John Tonelli	NY Islanders	Jan. 6/81	Tor. 3	at NYI 6	Jiri Crha (4) empty net (1)
Wayne Gretzky	Edmonton	Feb. 18/81	St. L. 2	at Edm. 9	Mike Liut (3) Ed Staniowski (2)
Wayne Gretzky	Edmonton	Dec. 30/81	Phi. 5	at Edm. 7	Pete Peeters (4) empty net (1)
Grant Mulvey	Chicago	Feb. 3/82	St. L. 5	at Chi. 9	Mike Liut (4) Gary Edwards (1)
Bryan Trottier	NY Islanders	Feb. 13/82	Phi. 2	at NYI 8	Pete Peeters
Willy Lindstrom	Winnipeg	Mar. 2/82	Wpg. 7	at Phi. 6	Pete Peeters
Mark Pavelich	NY Rangers	Feb. 23/82	Hfd. 3	at NYR 11	Greg Millen
Jari Kurri	Edmonton	Nov. 19/83	N.J. 4	at Edm. 13	Glenn Resch (3) Ron Low (2)
Bengt Gustafsson	Washington	Jan. 8/84	Wsh. 7	at Phi. 1	Pelle Lindbergh
Pat Hughes	Edmonton	Feb. 3/84	Cgy. 5	at Edm. 10	Don Edwards (3) Rejean Lemelin (2)
Wayne Gretzky	Edmonton	Dec. 15/84	Edm. 8	at St. L. 2	Rick Wamsley (4) Mike Liut(1)
Dave Andreychuk	Buffalo	Feb. 6/86	Buf. 8	at Bos. 6	Pat Riggin (1) Doug Keans (4)
Wayne Gretzky	Edmonton	Dec. 6/87	Min. 4	at Edm. 10	Don Beaupre (4) Kari Takko (1)
Mario Lemieux	Pittsburgh	Dec. 31/88	N.J. 6	at Pit. 8	Bob Sauve (3) Chris Terreri (2)
Joe Nieuwendyk	Calgary	Jan. 11/89	Wpg. 3	at Cgy. 8	Daniel Berthiaume
Mats Sundin	Quebec	Mar. 5/92	Que. 10	at Hfd. 4	Peter Sidorkiewicz (3) Kay Whitmore (2)
Mario Lemieux	Pittsburgh	Apr. 9/93	Pit. 10	at NYR 4	Corey Hirsch (3) Mike Richter (2)
Peter Bondra	Washington	Feb. 5/94	T.B. 3	at Wsh. 6	Darren Puppa (4) Pat Jablonski (1)
Mike Ricci	Quebec	Feb. 17/94	S.J. 2	at Que. 8	Arturs Irbe (3) Jimmy Waite (2)
Alexei Zhamnov	Winnipeg	Apr. 1/95	Wpg. 7	at L.A. 7	Kelly Hrudey (3) Grant Fuhr (2)

Left: Frank Mahovlich, The "Big M", was the first player to collect his 500th goal and his 1,000th point in the same NHL season, reaching both milestones in 1972-73. Washington forward Bengt Gustafsson, below left, had the night of his hockey life on January 8, 1984 when he blasted five shots past Philadelphia's Pelle Lindbergh to became the first Capital to register a five-goal game. Below: The "Roadrunner", Yvan Cournoyer, became the first NHL player since former teammate Bobby Rousseau to notch five goals in a single game when he slipped five pucks past Chicago's Mike Veisor on February 15, 1974.

Players' 500th Goals

Player	Team	Date	Game No.		Score	Opposing Goaltender	Total Goals	Total Games
Maurice Richard	Montreal	Oct. 19/57	863	Chi. 1	at Mtl. 3	Glenn Hall	544	978
Gordie Howe	Detroit	Mar. 14/62	1,045	Det. 2	at NYR 3	Gump Worsley	801	1,767
Bobby Hull	Chicago	Feb. 21/70	861	NYR. 2	at Chi. 4	Ed Giacomin	610	1,063
Jean Béliveau	Montreal	Feb. 11/71	1,101	Min. 2	at Mtl. 6	Gilles Gilbert	507	1,125
Frank Mahovlich	Montreal	Mar. 21/73	1,105	Van. 2	at Mtl. 3	Dunc Wilson	533	1,181
Phil Esposito	Boston	Dec. 22/74	803	Det. 4	at Bos. 5	Jim Rutherford	717	1,282
John Bucyk	Boston	Oct. 30/75	1,370	St. L. 2	at Bos. 3	Yves Bélanger	556	1,540
Stan Mikita	Chicago	Feb. 27/77	1,221	Van. 4	at Chi. 3	Cesare Maniago	541	1,394
Marcel Dionne	Los Angeles	Dec. 14/82	887	L.A. 2	at Wsh. 7	Al Jensen	731	1,348
Guy Lafleur	Montreal	Dec. 20/83	918	Mtl. 6	at N.J. 0	Glenn Resch	560	1,126
Mike Bossy	NY Islanders	Jan. 2/86	647	Bos. 5	at NYI 7	empty net	573	752
Gilbert Perreault	Buffalo	Mar. 9/86	1,159	NJ 3	at Buf. 4	Alain Chevrier	512	1,191
*Wayne Gretzky	Edmonton	Nov. 22/86	575	Van. 2	at Edm. 5	empty net	814	1,173
Lanny McDonald	Calgary	Mar. 21/89	1,107	NYI 1	at Cgy. 4	Mark Fitzpatrick	500	1,111
Bryan Trottier	NY Islanders	Feb. 13/90	1,104	Cgy. 4	at NYI 2	Rick Wamsley	524	1,279
*Mike Gartner	NY Rangers	Oct. 14/91	936	Wsh. 5	at NYR 3	Mike Liut	629	1,208
Michel Goulet	Chicago	Feb. 16/92	951	Cgy. 5	at Chi. 5	Jeff Reese	548	1,089
*Jari Kurri	Los Angeles	Oct. 17/92	833	Bos. 6	at L.A. 8	empty net	565	1,028
*Dino Ciccarelli	Detroit	Jan. 8/94	946	Det. 6	at L.A. 3	Kelly Hrudey	529	1,015

* Active

Dino Ciccarelli, who set a rookie record for post-season points during the 1981 playoffs, scored his 500th goal and recorded his 1,000th career point during the 1993-94 season.

Players' 1,000th Points

Player	Team	Date	Game No.	G or A		Score	Total Points G A PTS	Total Games
Gordie Howe	Detroit	Nov. 27/60	938	(A)	Tor. 0	at Det. 2	801-1,049–1,850	1,767
Jean Béliveau	Montreal	Mar. 3/68	911	(G)	Mtl. 2	at Det. 5	507-712–1,219	1,125
Alex Delvecchio	Detroit	Feb. 16/69	1,143	(A)	LA 3	at Det. 6	456-825–1,281	1,549
Bobby Hull	Chicago	Dec. 12/70	909	(A)	Minn. 3	at Chi. 5	610-560–1,170	1,063
Norm Ullman	Toronto	Oct. 16/71	1,113	(A)	NYR 5	at Tor. 3	490-739–1,229	1,410
Stan Mikita	Chicago	Oct. 15/72	924	(A)	St.L. 3	at Chi. 1	541-926–1,467	1,394
John Bucyk	Boston	Nov. 9/72	1,144	(G)	Det. 3	at Bos. 8	556-813–1,369	1,540
Frank Mahovlich	Montreal	Feb. 17/73	1,090	(A)	Phi. 1	at Mtl. 6	533-570–1,103	1,181
Henri Richard	Montreal	Dec. 20/73	1,194	(A)	Mtl. 2	at Buf. 2	358-688–1,046	1,256
Phil Esposito	Boston	Feb. 15/74	745	(A)	Bos. 4	at Van. 2	717-873–1,590	1,282
Rod Gilbert	NY Rangers	Feb. 19/77	1,027	(A)	NYR 2	at NYI 5	406-615–1,021	1,065
Jean Ratelle	Boston	Apr. 3/77	1,007	(A)	Tor. 4	at Bos. 7	491-776–1,267	1,281
Marcel Dionne	Los Angeles	Jan. 7/81	740	(G)	L.A. 5	at Hfd. 3	731-1,040–1,771	1,348
Guy Lafleur	Montreal	Mar. 4/81	720	(A)	Mtl. 9	at Wpg. 3	560-793–1,353	1,126
Bobby Clarke	Philadelphia	Mar. 19/81	922	(G)	Bos. 3	at Phi. 5	358-852–1,210	1,144
Gilbert Perreault	Buffalo	Apr. 3/82	871	(A)	Buf. 5	at Mtl.4	512-814–1,326	1,191
Darryl Sittler	Philadelphia	Jan. 20/83	927	(A)	Cgy 2	at Phi. 5	484-637–1,121	1,096
*Wayne Gretzky	Edmonton	Dec. 19/84	424	(A)	L.A. 3	at Edm. 7	814-1,692–2,506	1,173
Bryan Trottier	NY Islanders	Jan. 29/85	726	(G)	Min. 4	at NYI 4	524-901–1,425	1,279
Mike Bossy	NY Islanders	Jan. 24/86	656	(A)	NYI 7	at Wsh. 5	573-553–1,126	752
Denis Potvin	NY Islanders	Apr. 4/87	987	(G)	Buf. 6	at NYI 6	310-742–1,052	1,060
Bernie Federko	St. Louis	Mar 19/88	855	(A)	Hfd. 5	at St.L. 3	369-761–1,130	1,000
Lanny McDonald	Calgary	Mar. 7/89	1,101	(G)	Wpg. 5	at Cgy. 9	500-506–1,006	1,111
*Peter Stastny	Quebec	Oct. 19/89	682	(G)	Que. 5	at Chi. 3	450-789–1,239	977
*Jari Kurri	Edmonton	Jan. 2/90	716	(A)	Edm. 6	at St.L. 4	565-731–1,296	1,028
*Denis Savard	Chicago	Mar. 11/90	727	(A)	St.L. 6	at Chi. 4	451-812–1,263	1,063
*Paul Coffey	Pittsburgh	Dec. 22/90	770	(A)	Pit. 4	at NYI 3	358-978–1,336	1,078
*Mark Messier	Edmonton	Jan. 13/91	822	(A)	Edm. 5	at Phi. 3	492-877–1,369	1,127
Dave Taylor	Los Angeles	Feb. 5/91	930	(A)	L.A. 3	at Phi. 2	431-638–1,069	1,111
Michel Goulet	Chicago	Feb. 23/91	878	(G)	Chi. 3	at Min. 3	548-604–1,152	1,089
*Dale Hawerchuk	Buffalo	Mar. 8/91	781	(G)	Chi. 5	at Buf. 3	489-825–1,314	1,055
Bobby Smith	Minnesota	Nov. 30/91	986	(A)	Min. 4	at Tor. 3	357-679–1,036	1,077
*Mike Gartner	NY Rangers	Jan. 4/92	971	(G)	NYR 4	at N.J. 6	629-562–1,191	1,208
*Ray Bourque	Boston	Feb. 29/92	933	(A)	Wsh. 5	at Bos. 5	323-908–1,231	1,146
*Mario Lemieux	Pittsburgh	Mar. 24/92	513	(A)	Pit. 3	at Det. 4	494-717–1,211	599
*Glenn Anderson	Toronto	Feb. 22/93	954	(G)	Tor. 8	at Van. 1	492-593–1,085	1,097
*Steve Yzerman	Detroit	Feb. 24/93	737	(A)	Det. 7	at Buf. 10	481-679–1,160	862
*Ron Francis	Pittsburgh	Oct. 28/93	893	(G)	Que. 7	at Pit. 3	349-789–1,138	1,008
*Bernie Nicholls	New Jersey	Feb. 13/94	858	(G)	N.J. 3	at T.B. 3	438-636–1,074	933
*Dino Ciccarelli	Detroit	Mar. 9/94	957	(G)	Det. 5	at Cgy. 1	529-528–1,057	1,015
Brian Propp	Hartford	Mar. 19/94	1,008	(G)	Hfd. 5	at Phi. 3	425-578–1,003	1,016
*Joe Mullen	Pittsburgh	Feb. 7/95	935	(A)	Fla. 3	at Pit. 7	487-539–1,026	971
Steve Larmer	NY Rangers	Mar. 8/95	983	(A)	N.J. 4	at NYR 6	441-571–1,012	1,006

* Active

Brian Propp, who began his career with the Philadelphia Flyers in 1979-80, reached the 1,000-point mark in Hartford's 5-3 win over his former teammates on March 19, 1994.

Individual Awards

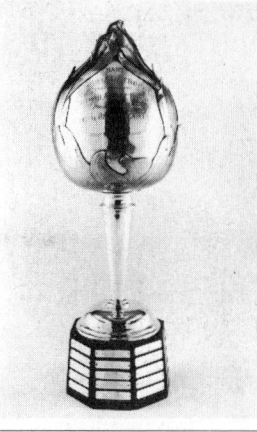

Hart Memorial Trophy

Art Ross Trophy

Calder Memorial Trophy

James Norris Memorial Trophy

HART MEMORIAL TROPHY

An annual award "to the player adjudged to be the most valuable to his team". Winner selected in poll by Professional Hockey Writers' Association in the 26 NHL cities at the end of the regular schedule. The winner receives $10,000 and the runners-up $6,000 and $4,000.

History: The Hart Memorial Trophy was presented by the National Hockey League in 1960 after the original Hart Trophy was retired to the Hockey Hall of Fame. The original Hart Trophy was donated to the NHL in 1923 by Dr. David A. Hart, father of Cecil Hart, former manager-coach of the Montreal Canadiens.

1994-95 Winner: Eric Lindros, Philadelphia Flyers.
Runners-up: Jaromir Jagr, Pittsburgh Penguins
Dominik Hasek, Buffalo Sabres

Lindros was a top-three selection on all 15 ballots, attracting 10 first-place votes and four second place tallies for 63 points, ahead of Pittsburgh right wing Jaromir Jagr (27 points) and Buffalo goaltender Dominik Hasek (23).

In his third NHL season, Lindros finished second in League scoring in 1994-95 with 70 points (28-41-70) behind Jaromir Jagr, who also tallied 70 points but scored more goals. Lindros led his team in points, goals, assists, plus-minus, shots and shooting percentage to help the Flyers reach the Stanley Cup playoffs for the first time since 1989. Lindros became the youngest winner of the Hart Trophy (22 years, four months) since Wayne Gretzky, who captured the first of his nine Hart Trophies at 19 years, five months in 1980.

CALDER MEMORIAL TROPHY

An annual award "to the player selected as the most proficient in his first year of competition in the National Hockey League." Winner selected in poll by Professional Hockey Writers' Association at the end of the regular schedule. The winner receives $10,000 and the runners-up $6,000 and $4,000.

History: From 1936-37 until his death in 1943, Frank Calder, NHL President, bought a trophy each year to be given permanently to the outstanding rookie. After Calder's death, the NHL presented the Calder Memorial Trophy in his memory and the trophy is to be kept in perpetuity. To be eligible for the award, a player cannot have played more than 25 games in any single preceding season nor in six or more games in each of any two preceding seasons in any major professional league. Beginning in 1990-91, to be eligible for this award a player must not have attained his twenty-sixth birthday by September 15th of the season in which he is eligible.

1994-95 Winner: Peter Forsberg, Quebec Nordiques
Runners-up: Jim Carey, Washington Capitals
Paul Kariya, Mighty Ducks of Anaheim

Center Peter Forsberg of the Quebec Nordiques was selected as the winner of the Calder Memorial Trophy in 1994-95. Forsberg was named on all 15 ballots, receiving 13 first-place votes and two second-place tallies, for a total of 71 points. Washington's Jim Carey also polled top-three votes on all 15 ballots, finishing with 41 points to take second place in the voting.

Forsberg made his NHL debut after spending four years with MoDo in the Swedish League and was obtained by the Nordiques in a trade with Philadelphia, who had selected him sixth overall in the 1991 Entry Draft. Forsberg led all rookie scorers in 1994-95 with 50 points (15-35-50) in 47 games, and was first among rookies in plus-minus (+17).

He is the first Swedish player to be named a Calder winner, surpassing the top-three finishes of countrymen Mikael Renberg (3rd, 1994), Nicklas Lidstrom (2nd, 1992) and Kjell Dahlin (3rd, 1986).

ART ROSS TROPHY

An annual award "to the player who leads the league in scoring points at the end of the regular season." The winner receives $10,000 and the runners-up $6,000 and $4,000.

History: Arthur Howie Ross, former manager-coach of Boston Bruins, presented the trophy to the National Hockey League in 1947. If two players finish the schedule with the same number of points, the trophy is awarded in the following manner: 1. Player with most goals. 2. Player with fewer games played. 3. Player scoring first goal of the season.

1994-95 Winner: Jaromir Jagr, Pittsburgh Penguins
Runners-up: Eric Lindros, Philadelphia Flyers
Alexei Zhamnov, Winnipeg Jets

Jaromir Jagr of the Pittsburgh Penguins won the first Art Ross Trophy of his career in 1994-95, recording totals of 32 goals and 38 assists for 70 points. Eric Lindros of the Philadelphia Flyers finished second to Jagr with 29 goals and 41 assists for 70 points. Jagr won the Art Ross Trophy by virtue of having scored more goals than Lindros. Alexei Zhamnov of the Winnipeg Jets finished third in scoring with 30 goals and 35 assists for 65 points.

JAMES NORRIS MEMORIAL TROPHY

An annual award "to the defense player who demonstrates throughout the season the greatest all-round ability in the position." Winner selected in poll by Professional Hockey Writers' Association at the end of the regular schedule. The winner receives $10,000 and the runners-up $6,000 and $4,000.

History: The James Norris Memorial Trophy was presented in 1953 by the four children of the late James Norris in memory of the former owner-president of the Detroit Red Wings.

1994-95 Winner: Paul Coffey, Detroit Red Wings
Runners-up: Chris Chelios, Chicago Blackhawks
Ray Bourque, Boston Bruins

Paul Coffey of the Detroit Red Wings won his third career Norris Trophy in 1994-95. Coffey was a top-three selection on all 15 ballots, receiving 12 first-place votes, to outdistance second-place Chris Chelios of the Chicago Blackhawks. Chelios earned 39 points, garnering two first-place votes, and was mentioned on 13 of 15 ballots.

In his second full season with the Red Wings, Coffey led all defensemen in scoring in 1994-95, recording 58 points (14-44-58) in 45 games. He was the League's only defenseman to lead his team in scoring and he also led the Red Wings in plus-minus with a plus-18 rating.

Coffey became the sixth defenseman in NHL history to be a three-time winner of the Norris Trophy, joining Bobby Orr (eight times), Doug Harvey (seven), Ray Bourque (five), Pierre Pilote (three) and Denis Potvin (three). Coffey previously won consecutive Norris Trophies in 1985 and 1986 as a member of the Edmonton Oilers.

Vezina Trophy

Lady Byng Memorial Trophy

Frank J. Selke Trophy

Conn Smythe Trophy

VEZINA TROPHY

An annual award "to the goalkeeper adjudged to be the best at his position" **as voted by the general managers of each of the 26 clubs.** Over-all winner receives $10,000, runners-up $6,000 and $4,000.

History: Leo Dandurand, Louis Letourneau and Joe Cattarinich, former owners of the Montreal Canadiens, presented the trophy to the National Hockey League in 1926-27 in memory of Georges Vezina, outstanding goalkeeper of the Canadiens who collapsed during an NHL game November 28, 1925, and died of tuberculosis a few months later. Until the 1981-82 season, the goalkeeper(s) of the team allowing the fewest number of goals during the regular-season were awarded the Vezina Trophy.

1994-95 Winner: **Dominik Hasek, Buffalo Sabres**
      Runners-up: **Ed Belfour, Chicago Blackhawks**
                  Jim Carey, Washington Capitals

Hasek was a clear choice in the voting, capturing 17 of a possible 26 first-place votes and receiving votes on 24 of 26 ballots. Ed Belfour of the Chicago Blackhawks and Washington's Jim Carey staged a close race for second place, each finishing with 25 points with Belfour placing second based on a higher number of first-place votes.

Hasek enjoyed another outstanding campaign in 1994-95, posting a 19-14-7 record and tying for the League lead in goals-against average (2.11) and shutouts (five). He led all goaltenders in save percentage (.930) for the second consecutive season.

Hasek becomes the second goaltender since 1981-82 to win the Vezina Trophy in consecutive years, joining Montreal's Patrick Roy, who accomplished the feat in 1989 and 1990.

LADY BYNG MEMORIAL TROPHY

An annual award "to the player adjudged to have exhibited the best type of **sportsmanship and gentlemanly conduct combined with a high standard of** **playing ability."** Winner selected in poll by Professional Hockey Writers' Association at the end of the regular schedule. The winner receives $10,000 and the runners-up $6,000 and $4,000.

History: Lady Byng, wife of Canada's Governor-General at the time, presented the Lady Byng Trophy in 1925. After Frank Boucher of New York Rangers won the award seven times in eight seasons, he was given the trophy to keep and Lady Byng donated another trophy in 1936. After Lady Byng's death in 1949, the National Hockey League presented a new trophy, changing the name to Lady Byng Memorial Trophy.

1994-95 Winner: **Ron Francis, Pittsburgh Penguins**
      Runners-up: **Adam Oates, Boston Bruins**
                  Alexei Zhamnov, Winnipeg Jets

Francis was named on 14 of the 15 ballots, receiving 50 points to edge second-place finisher Adam Oates of the Boston Bruins, who tallied 40 points. 1994-95 was the third consecutive year Oates has finished as runner-up for the Lady Byng Trophy.

Francis appeared in 44 games for the Penguins, finishing fifth in the League in scoring with 59 points (11-48-59). He captured the NHL Alka-Seltzer Plus Award with the NHL's best plus-minus rating of +30. Francis was assessed only 18 minutes in penalties during the regular season. Francis becomes the second Penguins player to have won the Lady Byng Trophy, joining Rick Kehoe who won in 1981.

FRANK J. SELKE TROPHY

An annual award "to the forward who best excels in the defensive aspects of **the game."** Winner selected in poll by Professional Hockey Writers' Association at the end of the regular schedule. The winner receives $10,000 and the runners-up $6,000 and $4,000.

History: Presented to the National Hockey League in 1977 by the Board of Governors of the NHL in honour of Frank J. Selke, one of the great architects of NHL championship teams.

1994-95 Winner: **Ron Francis, Pittsburgh Penguins**
      Runners-up: **Esa Tikkanen, St. Louis Blues**
                  Joel Otto, Calgary Flames

In the closest race among all trophies this season, Francis received 50 points and was named on 14 of 15 ballots to edge Esa Tikkanen of the St. Louis Blues (48 points, named on 14 of 15 ballots).

Francis appeared in 44 games for the Penguins, capturing the Alka-Seltzer Plus Award with the NHL's best plus-minus rating of +30 and remaining one of the League's most effective face-off men. In addition to his defensive play he was also an offensive threat, finishing fifth in the League in scoring with 59 points (11-48-59).

CONN SMYTHE TROPHY

An annual award "to the most valuable player for his team in the playoffs." Winner selected by the Professional Hockey Writers' Association at the conclusion of the final game in the Stanley Cup Finals. The winner receives $10,000.

History: Presented by Maple Leaf Gardens Limited in 1964 to honor Conn Smythe, the former coach, manager, president and owner-governor of the Toronto Maple Leafs.

1994-95 Winner: **Claude Lemieux, New Jersey Devils**

New Jersey right winger Claude Lemieux topped all playoff scorers with 13 goals in 20 playoff games. He was a spark plug for the Devils in each playoff round en route to the Stanley Cup. He scored three power-play goals and finished the 1995 playoffs with a plus/minus rating of +12.

WILLIAM M. JENNINGS TROPHY

An annual award "to the goalkeeper(s) having played a minimum of 25 games **for the team with the fewest goals scored against it."** Winners selected on regular-season play. Overall winner receives $10,000, runners-up $6,000 and $4,000.

History: The Jennings Trophy was presented in 1981-82 by the National Hockey League's Board of Governors to honor the late William M. Jennings, longtime governor and president of the New York Rangers and one of the great builders of hockey in the United States.

1994-95 Winner: **Ed Belfour, Chicago Blackhawks**
      Runners-up: **Mike Vernon, Chris Osgood, Detroit Red Wings**
                  Dominik Hasek, Buffalo Sabres

Belfour collected the Jennings Trophy for the third time in his career, having also captured the award in 1991 and 1993. Belfour is the sole recipient by virtue of having played in 42 of the Chicago Blackhawks' 48 games. The Hawks allowed only 115 goals-against this season, two fewer than second-place Detroit with 117. Belfour posted a 22-15-3 record, 2.28 goals against average and tied for the League lead with five shutouts.

William M. Jennings Trophy

Jack Adams Award

Bill Masterton Trophy

Lester Patrick Trophy

Lester B. Pearson Award

JACK ADAMS AWARD

An annual award presented by the National Hockey League Broadcasters' Association to "the NHL coach adjudged to have contributed the most to his team's success." Winner selected by poll among members of the NHL Broadcasters' Association at the end of the regular season. The winner receives $1,000 from the NHLBA.

History: The award was presented by the NHL Broadcasters' Association in 1974 to commemorate the late Jack Adams, coach and general manager of the Detroit Red Wings, whose lifetime dedication to hockey serves as an inspiration to all who aspire to further the game.

1994-95 Winner: **Marc Crawford, Quebec Nordiques**
      Runners-up: **Scotty Bowman, Detroit Red Wings**
                  Terry Murray, Philadelphia Flyers

Crawford polled 34 of a possible 70 first-place votes in posting a total of 239 points to finish ahead of second-place Scott Bowman of the Detroit Red Wings, who finished with 160 points. Bowman was named on 50 of 70 ballots, including 17 first-place votes, for 160 points.

Crawford led the Quebec Nordiques to the best record in the Eastern Conference with a 30-13-5 record in 48 games. The club's winning percentage climbed from .452 in 1993-94 to .677 in 1994-95. Quebec also cut its goals-against average from 3.46 to 2.76 in the process.

Crawford is the first rookie coach to win the Jack Adams Award since Montreal's Pat Burns in 1989 and is the sixth rookie coach overall to have captured the award since it was inaugurated in 1974. Other first-year NHL coaches to have won the award include Bobby Kromm (Detroit, 1978), Tom Watt (Winnipeg, 1982), Orval Tessier (Chicago, 1983) and Mike Keenan (Philadelphia, 1985).

BILL MASTERTON MEMORIAL TROPHY

An annual award under the trusteeship of the Professional Hockey Writers' Association to "the National Hockey League player who best exemplifies the qualities of perseverance, sportsmanship and dedication to hockey." Winner selected by poll among the 26 chapters of the PHWA at the end of the regular season. A $2,500 grant from the PHWA is awarded annually to the Bill Masterton Scholarship Fund, based in Bloomington, MN, in the name of the Masterton Trophy winner.

History: The trophy was presented by the NHL Writers' Association in 1968 to commemorate the late William Masterton, a player of the Minnesota North Stars, who exhibited to a high degree the qualities of perseverance, sportsmanship and dedication to hockey, and who died January 15, 1968.

1994-95 Winner: **Pat LaFontaine, Buffalo Sabres**
      Runners-up: **Kevin Dineen, Philadelphia Flyers**
                  Steve Smith, Chicago Blackhawks

Pat LaFontaine returned to NHL play on March 16, 1995, following 16 months of rehabilitation from a torn anterior cruciate ligament in his right knee suffered in November, 1993. Following knee surgery in December, 1993, LaFontaine embarked on a rigorous exercise and therapy program to get back in the Sabres lineup. His hard work paid off in 1994-95 when he made a successful return, finishing the season with 27 points (12-15-27) in 22 games and reached an NHL Milestone by scoring his 400th career regular-season goal on April 14 versus Quebec.

LESTER PATRICK TROPHY

An annual award "for outstanding service to hockey in the United States." Eligible recipients are players, officials, coaches, executives and referees. Winner selected by an award committee consisting of the President of the NHL, an NHL Governor, a representative of the New York Rangers, a member of the Hockey Hall of Fame Builder's section, a member of the Hockey Hall of Fame Player's section, a member of the U.S. Hockey Hall of Fame, a member of the NHL Broadcasters' Association and a member of the Professional Hockey Writers' Association. Each except the League President is rotated annually. The winner receives a miniature of the trophy.

History: Presented by the New York Rangers in 1966 to honor the late Lester Patrick, longtime general manager and coach of the New York Rangers, whose teams finished out of the playoffs only once in his first 16 years with the club.

1994-95 Winners: **Joe Mullen**
                        Brian Mullen
                        Bob Fleming

New York City natives Joe and Brian Mullen, brothers who have had lengthy and successful National Hockey League careers, along with long-time amateur hockey executive Bob Fleming, were named the 1995 recipients of the Lester Patrick Award for outstanding service to hockey in the United States.

Following an all-star career at Boston College, Joe Mullen signed with the St. Louis Blues as a free agent in August, 1979 and by 1981-82 was an integral part of the Blues' attack. His lengthy list of accomplishments over his 14-season NHL career with St. Louis, Calgary and Pittsburgh includes three Stanley Cup championships, two with Pittsburgh and one with Calgary; six consecutive 40-goal seasons; two Lady Byng Trophies and three All-Star Game appearances. During this past season, Mullen became the first U.S.-born player in NHL history to reach the milestone of 1,000 career points.

Brian Mullen, five years Joe's junior, attended the University of Wisconsin playing for coach Bob Johnson, and helped his club win the NCAA Championship in 1981 and reach the Final in 1982. He was selected by the Winnipeg Jets in the 1980 NHL draft and joined the club in 1982-83. In 11 NHL seasons with Winnipeg, NY Rangers, San Jose and NY Islanders, Mullen played in 832 games, scoring 260 goals and 362 assists for 622 points. In August, 1993, his NHL career was interrupted after suffering a stroke and he underwent surgery the following month to repair a small hole in his heart. He announced his retirement from active play during the 1994-95 season and currently works in the NY Islanders' front office.

Bob Fleming, a native of Rochester, Minnesota, has contributed at every level of amateur hockey in the United States during his long and distinguished career. A director of USA Hockey since 1963, he served as vice president from 1971 to 1981. Fleming has been a member of the Team USA Hockey Management Committee since 1969, acting as Chairman since 1990, served as Director at the United States Hockey Hall of Fame in Eveleth, Minnesota from 1970 to 1979 and was President of the Minnesota Amateur Hockey Association from 1958 to 1970.

LESTER B. PEARSON AWARD

An annual award presented to the NHL's outstanding player as selected by the members of the National Hockey League Players' Association. The winner receives $10,000.

History: The award was presented in 1970-71 by the NHLPA in honor of the late Lester B. Pearson, former Prime Minister of Canada.

1994-95 Winner: **Eric Lindros, Philadelphia Flyers**

Eric Lindros led the Flyers as its top scorer and team captain in 1994-95. Lindros tied for the League lead in points (70) and finished with a plus/minus rating of +27.

King Clancy Memorial Trophy

Alka-Seltzer Plus Award

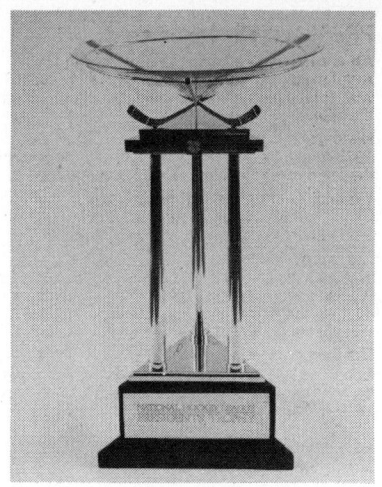

Presidents' Trophy

KING CLANCY MEMORIAL TROPHY

An annual award "to the player who best exemplifies leadership qualities on and off the ice and has made a noteworthy humanitarian contribution in his community." The winner receives $3,000 and the runner-up $1,000.

History: The King Clancy Memorial Trophy was presented to the National Hockey League by the Board of Governors in 1988 to honor the late Frank "King" Clancy.

1994-95 Winner: **Joe Nieuwendyk, Calgary Flames**
Runner-up: **Doug Gilmour, Toronto Maple Leafs**

Nieuwendyk enjoyed another productive season in 1994-95, his ninth in a Calgary uniform, finishing second on the team in scoring. He is now the Flames' all-time leading career goal scorer (314). As team captain over the last four seasons, Nieuwendyk has played a central role in team promotions and encourages the support of his teammates. Nieuwendyk's work in his community includes involvement with the Calgary unit of the Society for the Prevention of Cruelty to Animals (SPCA). He has acted as a spokesperson and participated in annual awareness programs and promotional campaigns. He has also been the honorary chairman of the Foothills Hospital Foundation since 1991, assisting with projects such as the hospital's NeoNatal Unit and the Burn Unit.

ALKA-SELTZER PLUS AWARD

An annual award "to the player, having played a minimum of 60 games (34 games in 1994-95), who leads the League in plus/minus statistics" at the end of the regular season. Miles, Inc. will contribute $5,000 on behalf of the winner to the charity of his choice and $1000 on behalf of each individual team winner.

History: The award was presented to the NHL in 1989-90 by Miles, Inc., to recognize the League leader in plus-minus statistics. Plus-minus statistics are calculated by giving a player a "plus" when on-ice for an even-strength or shorthand goal scored by his team. He receives a "minus" when on-ice for an even-strength or shorthand goal scored by the opposing team. A plus-minus award has been presented since the 1982-83 season.

1994-95 Winner: Ron Francis, Pittsburgh Penguins

Pittsburgh forward Ron Francis was the NHL's leader in +/– rankings in 1994-95 with a total of +30 in 44 games played. The second highest +/– figure belonged to Quebec's Curtis Leschyshyn and St. Louis' Steve Duchesne who each finished with a rating of +29. Team +/– leaders for 1994-95 were: Anaheim, Steve Rucchin; Boston, Dave Reid; Buffalo, Yuri Khmylev; Calgary, Phil Housley; Chicago, Chris Chelios; Dallas, Paul Cavallini; Detroit, Paul Coffey; Edmonton, Dean Kennedy; Florida, Paul Laus; Hartford, Andrei Nikolishin; Los Angeles, Michel Petit; Montreal, Vincent Damphousse; New Jersey, Scott Niedermayer, NY Islanders, Pat Flatley; NY Rangers, Adam Graves; Ottawa, Radek Bonk; Philadelphia, Eric Lindros; Pittsburgh, Ron Francis; Quebec, Curtis Leschyshyn; San Jose, Jay More; St. Louis, Steve Duchesne; Tampa Bay, Enrico Ciccone; Toronto, Randy Wood; Vancouver, Dana Murzyn; Washington, Joe Reekie; Winnipeg, Teppo Numminen.

NHL AWARD MONEY BREAKDOWN

(Players on each club determine how team award money is divided.)

TEAM AWARDS

Stanley Cup Playoffs	Number of Clubs	Share Per Club	Total
Conference Quarter-Final Losers	8	$ 175,000	$1,400,000
Conference Semi-Final Losers	4	350,000	1,400,000
Conference Championship Losers	2	550,000	1,100,000
Stanley Cup Loser	1	825,000	825,000
Stanley Cup Winners	1	1,250,000	1,250,000
TOTAL PLAYOFF AWARD MONEY			$5,975,000

Final Standings, Regular Season	Number of Clubs	Share Per Club	Total
Presidents' Trophy			
Club's Share	1	$ 100,000	$ 100,000
Players' Share	1	250,000	250,000
Division Winners	4	425,000	1,700,000
Division Second Place	4	200,000	800,000
TOTAL REGULAR SEASON AWARD MONEY			$2,850,000

INDIVIDUAL AWARDS	Winner	First Runner-up	Second Runner-up
Hart, Calder, Norris, Ross, Vezina, Byng, Selke, Jennings, Masterton Trophies	$10,000	$6,000	$4,000
Conn Smythe Trophy	$10,000		
King Clancy Memorial Award	$ 3,000	$1,000	
TOTAL INDIVIDUAL AWARD MONEY			$194,000

ALL-STARS	Number of winners	Per Player	Total
First Team All-Stars	6	$10,000	$ 60,000
Second Team All-Stars	6	5,000	$ 30,000
TOTAL ALL-STAR AWARD MONEY			$ 90,000
TOTAL ALL AWARDS			**$9,109,000**

PRESIDENTS' TROPHY

An annual award to the club finishing the regular-season with the best overall record. The winner receives $200,000, to be split evenly between the team and its players.

History: Presented to the National Hockey League in 1985-86 by the NHL Board of Governors to recognize the team compiling the top regular-season record.

1994-95 Winner: Detroit Red Wings
Runners-up: Quebec Nordiques
Pittsburgh Penguins

The Detroit Red Wings won their first Presidents' Trophy in team history in 1994-95, compiling the NHL's best regular-season record of 33-11-4 for 70 points. It marks the first time since the 1964-65 season that the Red Wings finished with the best record in the NHL.

The Quebec Nordiques finished second with a 30-13-5 record for 65 points while the Pittsburgh Penguins had the third-best regular season mark with a record of 29-16-3 for 61 points.

PRESIDENTS' TROPHY

	Winner	Runner-up
1995	Detroit Red Wings	Quebec Nordiques
1994	New York Rangers	New Jersey Devils
1993	Pittsburgh Penguins	Boston Bruins
1992	New York Rangers	Washington Capitals
1991	Chicago Blackhawks	St. Louis Blues
1990	Boston Bruins	Calgary Flames
1989	Calgary Flames	Montreal Canadiens
1988	Calgary Flames	Montreal Canadiens
1987	Edmonton Oilers	Philadelphia Flyers
1986	Edmonton Oilers	Philadelphia Flyers

1994-95 NHL Player of the Week Award Winners

Player of the Week

Week Ending	Player	Team
Jan. 30	**Stephane Fiset**	Quebec
Feb. 6	**Chris Chelios**	Chicago
Feb. 13	**Jaromir Jagr**	Pittsburgh
Feb. 20	**Sean Burke**	Hartford
Feb. 27	**John LeClair**	Philadelphia
Mar. 6	**Andy Moog**	St. Louis
	Darcy Wakaluk	Dallas
March 13	**Jim Carey**	Washington
March 20	**Eric Lindros**	Philadelphia
March 27	**Trevor Kidd**	Calgary
Apr. 3	**Owen Nolan**	Quebec
Apr. 10	**Martin Brodeur**	New Jersey
Apr. 17	**Paul Coffey**	Detroit
Apr. 24	**Cam Neely**	Boston
May 1	**Ed Belfour**	Chicago

Player of the Month

Month	Player	Team
Feb.	**Jaromir Jagr**	Pittsburgh
Mar.	**Jim Carey**	Washington
Apr.	**Paul Coffey**	Detroit

1994-95 Upper Deck/NHL Rookie of the Month Award

Month	Player	Team
Feb.	**Blaine Lacher**	Boston
Mar.	**Jim Carey**	Washington
Apr.	**Peter Forsberg**	Quebec

NATIONAL HOCKEY LEAGUE INDIVIDUAL AWARD WINNERS

ART ROSS TROPHY

	Winner	Runner-up
1995	Jaromir Jagr, Pit.	Eric Lindros, Phi.
1994	Wayne Gretzky, L.A.	Sergei Fedorov, Det.
1993	Mario Lemieux, Pit.	Pat LaFontaine, Buf.
1992	Mario Lemieux, Pit.	Kevin Stevens, Pit.
1991	Wayne Gretzky, L.A.	Brett Hull, St.L.
1990	Wayne Gretzky, L.A.	Mark Messier, Edm.
1989	Mario Lemieux, Pit.	Wayne Gretzky, L.A.
1988	Mario Lemieux, Pit.	Wayne Gretzky, Edm.
1987	Wayne Gretzky, Edm.	Jari Kurri, Edm.
1986	Wayne Gretzky, Edm.	Mario Lemieux, Pit.
1985	Wayne Gretzky, Edm.	Jari Kurri, Edm.
1984	Wayne Gretzky, Edm.	Paul Coffey, Edm.
1983	Wayne Gretzky, Edm.	Peter Stastny, Que.
1982	Wayne Gretzky, Edm.	Mike Bossy, NYI
1981	Wayne Gretzky, Edm.	Marcel Dionne, L.A.
1980	Marcel Dionne, L.A.	Wayne Gretzky, Edm.
1979	Bryan Trottier, NYI	Marcel Dionne, L.A.
1978	Guy Lafleur, Mtl.	Bryan Trottier, NYI
1977	Guy Lafleur, Mtl.	Marcel Dionne, L.A.
1976	Guy Lafleur, Mtl.	Bobby Clarke, Phi.
1975	Bobby Orr, Bos.	Phil Esposito, Bos.
1974	Phil Esposito, Bos.	Bobby Orr, Bos.
1973	Phil Esposito, Bos.	Bobby Clarke, Phi.
1972	Phil Esposito, Bos.	Bobby Orr, Bos.
1971	Phil Esposito, Bos.	Bobby Orr, Bos.
1970	Bobby Orr, Bos.	Phil Esposito, Bos.
1969	Phil Esposito, Bos.	Bobby Hull, Chi.
1968	Stan Mikita, Chi.	Phil Esposito, Bos.
1967	Stan Mikita, Chi.	Bobby Hull, Chi.
1966	Bobby Hull, Chi.	Stan Mikita, Chi.
1965	Stan Mikita, Chi.	Norm Ullman, Det.
1964	Stan Mikita, Chi.	Bobby Hull, Chi.
1963	Gordie Howe, Det.	Andy Bathgate, NYR
1962	Bobby Hull, Chi.	Andy Bathgate, NYR
1961	Bernie Geoffrion, Mtl.	Jean Beliveau, Mtl.
1960	Bobby Hull, Chi.	Bronco Horvath, Bos.
1959	Dickie Moore, Mtl.	Jean Beliveau, Mtl.
1958	Dickie Moore, Mtl.	Henri Richard, Mtl.
1957	Gordie Howe, Det.	Ted Lindsay, Det.
1956	Jean Beliveau, Mtl.	Gordie Howe, Det.
1955	Bernie Geoffrion, Mtl.	Maurice Richard, Mtl.
1954	Gordie Howe, Det.	Maurice Richard, Mtl.
1953	Gordie Howe, Det.	Ted Lindsay, Det.
1952	Gordie Howe, Det.	Ted Lindsay, Det.
1951	Gordie Howe, Det.	Maurice Richard, Mtl.
1950	Ted Lindsay, Det.	Sid Abel, Det.
1949	Roy Conacher, Chi.	Doug Bentley, Chi.
1948	Elmer Lach, Mtl.	Buddy O'Connor, NYR
1947*	Max Bentley, Chi.	Maurice Richard, Mtl.
1946	Max Bentley, Chi.	Gaye Stewart, Tor.
1945	Elmer Lach, Mtl.	Maurice Richard, Mtl.
1944	Herbie Cain, Bos.	Doug Bentley, Chi.
1943	Doug Bentley, Chi.	Bill Cowley, Bos.
1942	Bryan Hextall, NYR	Lynn Patrick, NYR
1941	Bill Cowley, Bos.	Bryan Hextall, NYR
1940	Milt Schmidt, Bos.	Woody Dumart, Bos.
1939	Toe Blake, Mtl.	Dave Schriner, NYA
1938	Gordie Drillon, Tor.	Syl Apps, Tor.
1937	Dave Schriner, NYA	Syl Apps, Tor.
1936	Dave Schriner, NYA	Marty Barry, Det.
1935	Charlie Conacher, Tor.	Syd Howe, St.L-Det.
1934	Charlie Conacher, Tor.	Joe Primeau, Tor.
1933	Bill Cook, NYR	Harvey Jackson, Tor.
1932	Harvey Jackson, Tor.	Joe Primeau, Tor.
1931	Howie Morenz, Mtl.	Ebbie Goodfellow, Det.
1930	Cooney Weiland, Bos.	Frank Boucher, NYR
1929	Ace Bailey, Tor.	Nels Stewart, Mtl.M
1928	Howie Morenz, Mtl.	Aurel Joliat, Mtl.
1927	Bill Cook, NYR	Dick Irvin, Chi.
1926	Nels Stewart, Mtl.M.	Cy Denneny, Ott.
1925	Babe Dye, Tor.	Cy Denneny, Ott.
1924	Cy Denneny, Ott.	Billy Boucher, Mtl.
1923	Babe Dye, Tor.	Cy Denneny, Ott.
1922	Punch Broadbent, Ott.	Cy Denneny, Ott.
1921	Newsy Lalonde, Mtl.	Cy Denneny, Ott.
1920	Joe Malone, Que.	Newsy Lalonde, Mtl.
1919	Newsy Lalonde, Mtl.	Odie Cleghorn, Mtl.
1918	Joe Malone, Mtl.	Cy Denneny, Ott.

* Trophy first awarded in 1948.
Scoring leaders listed from 1918 to 1947.

KING CLANCY MEMORIAL TROPHY WINNERS

1995	Joe Nieuwendyk	Calgary
1994	Adam Graves	NY Rangers
1993	Dave Poulin	Boston
1992	Ray Bourque	Boston
1991	Dave Taylor	Los Angeles
1990	Kevin Lowe	Edmonton
1989	Bryan Trottier	NY Islanders
1988	Lanny McDonald	Calgary

HART TROPHY

	Winner	Runner-up
1995	Eric Lindros, Phi.	Jaromir Jagr, Pit.
1994	Sergei Fedorov, Det.	Dominik Hasek, Buf.
1993	Mario Lemieux, Pit.	Doug Gilmour, Tor.
1992	Mark Messier, NYR	Patrick Roy, Mtl.
1991	Brett Hull, St.L.	Wayne Gretzky, L.A.
1990	Mark Messier, Edm.	Ray Bourque, Bos.
1989	Wayne Gretzky, L.A.	Mario Lemieux, Pit.
1988	Mario Lemieux, Pit.	Grant Fuhr, Edm.
1987	Wayne Gretzky, Edm.	Ray Bourque, Bos.
1986	Wayne Gretzky, Edm.	Mario Lemieux, Pit.
1985	Wayne Gretzky, Edm.	Dale Hawerchuk, Wpg.
1984	Wayne Gretzky, Edm.	Rod Langway, Wsh.
1983	Wayne Gretzky, Edm.	Pete Peeters, Bos.
1982	Wayne Gretzky, Edm.	Bryan Trottier, NYI
1981	Wayne Gretzky, Edm.	Mike Liut, St.L.
1980	Wayne Gretzky, Edm.	Marcel Dionne, L.A.
1979	Bryan Trottier, NYI	Guy Lafleur, Mtl
1978	Guy Lafleur, Mtl.	Bryan Trottier, NYI
1977	Guy Lafleur, Mtl.	Bobby Clarke, Phi.
1976	Bobby Clarke, Phi.	Denis Potvin, NYI
1975	Bobby Clarke, Phi.	Rogatien Vachon, L.A.
1974	Phil Esposito, Bos.	Bernie Parent, Phi.
1973	Bobby Clarke, Phi.	Phil Esposito, Bos.
1972	Bobby Orr, Bos.	Ken Dryden, Mtl.
1971	Bobby Orr, Bos.	Phil Esposito, Bos.
1970	Bobby Orr, Bos.	Tony Esposito, Chi.
1969	Phil Esposito, Bos.	Jean Beliveau, Mtl.
1968	Stan Mikita, Chi.	Jean Beliveau, Mtl.
1967	Stan Mikita, Chi.	Ed Giacomin, NYR
1966	Bobby Hull, Chi.	Jean Beliveau, Mtl.
1965	Bobby Hull, Chi.	Norm Ullman, Det.
1964	Jean Beliveau, Mtl.	Bobby Hull, Chi.
1963	Gordie Howe, Det.	Stan Mikita, Chi.
1962	Jacques Plante, Mtl.	Doug Harvey, NYR
1961	Bernie Geoffrion, Mtl.	Johnny Bower, Tor.
1960	Gordie Howe, Det.	Bobby Hull, Chi.
1959	Andy Bathgate, NYR	Gordie Howe, Det.
1958	Gordie Howe, Det.	Andy Bathgate, NYR
1957	Gordie Howe, Det.	Jean Beliveau, Mtl.
1956	Jean Beliveau, Mtl.	Tod Sloan, Tor.
1955	Ted Kennedy, Tor.	Harry Lumley, Tor.
1954	Al Rollins, Chi.	Red Kelly, Det.
1953	Gordie Howe, Det.	Al Rollins, Chi.
1952	Gordie Howe, Det.	Elmer Lach, Mtl.
1951	Milt Schmidt, Bos.	Maurice Richard, Mtl.
1950	Charlie Rayner, NYR	Ted Kennedy, Tor.
1949	Sid Abel, Det.	Bill Durnan, Mtl.
1948	Buddy O'Connor, NYR	Frank Brimsek, Bos.
1947	Maurice Richard, Mtl.	Milt Schmidt, Bos.
1946	Max Bentley, Chi.	Gaye Stewart, Tor.
1945	Elmer Lach, Mtl.	Maurice Richard, Mtl.
1944	Babe Pratt, Tor.	Bill Cowley, Bos.
1943	Bill Cowley, Bos.	Doug Bentley, Chi.
1942	Tom Anderson, Bro.	Syl Apps, Tor.
1941	Bill Cowley, Bos.	Dit Clapper, Bos.
1940	Ebbie Goodfellow, Det.	Syl Apps, Tor.
1939	Toe Blake, Mtl.	Syl Apps, Tor.
1938	Eddie Shore, Bos.	Paul Thompson, Chi.
1937	Babe Siebert, Mtl.	Lionel Conacher, Mtl.M
1936	Eddie Shore, Bos.	Hooley Smith, Mtl.M
1935	Eddie Shore, Bos.	Charlie Conacher, Tor.
1934	Aurel Joliat, Mtl.	Lionel Conacher, Chi.
1933	Eddie Shore, Bos.	Bill Cook, NYR
1932	Howie Morenz, Mtl.	Ching Johnson, NYR
1931	Howie Morenz, Mtl.	Eddie Shore, Bos.
1930	Nels Stewart, Mtl.M.	Lionel Hitchman, Bos.
1929	Roy Worters, NYA	Ace Bailey, Tor.
1928	Howie Morenz, Mtl.	Roy Worters, Pit.
1927	Herb Gardiner, Mtl.	Bill Cook, NYR
1926	Nels Stewart, Mtl.M.	Sprague Cleghorn, Bos.
1925	Billy Burch, Ham.	Howie Morenz, Mtl.
1924	Frank Nighbor, Ott.	Sprague Cleghorn, Mtl.

FRANK J. SELKE TROPHY WINNERS

	Winner	Runner-up
1995	Ron Francis, Pit.	Esa Tikkanen, St.L.
1994	Sergei Fedorov, Det.	Doug Gilmour, Tor.
1993	Doug Gilmour, Tor.	Dave Poulin, Bos.
1992	Guy Carbonneau, Mtl.	Sergei Fedorov, Det.
1991	Dirk Graham, Chi.	Esa Tikkanen, Edm.
1990	Rick Meagher, St.L.	Guy Carbonneau, Mtl.
1989	Guy Carbonneau, Mtl.	Esa Tikkanen, Edm.
1988	Guy Carbonneau, Mtl.	Steve Kasper, Bos.
1987	Dave Poulin, Phi.	Guy Carbonneau, Mtl.
1986	Troy Murray, Chi.	Ron Sutter, Phi.
1985	Craig Ramsay, Buf.	Doug Jarvis, Wsh.
1984	Doug Jarvis, Wsh.	Bryan Trottier, NYI
1983	Bobby Clarke, Phi.	Jari Kurri, Edm.
1982	Steve Kasper, Bos.	Bob Gainey, Mtl.
1981	Bob Gainey, Mtl.	Craig Ramsay, Buf.
1980	Bob Gainey, Mtl.	Craig Ramsay, Buf.
1979	Bob Gainey, Mtl.	Don Marcotte, Bos.
1978	Bob Gainey, Mtl.	Craig Ramsay, Buf.

LADY BYNG TROPHY

Winner	Runner-up
1995 Ron Francis, Pit.	Adam Oates, Bos.
1994 Wayne Gretzky, L.A.	Adam Oates, Bos.
1993 Pierre Turgeon, NYI	Adam Oates, Bos.
1992 Wayne Gretzky, L.A.	Joe Sakic, Que.
1991 Wayne Gretzky, L.A.	Brett Hull, St.L.
1990 Brett Hull, St.L.	Wayne Gretzky, L.A.
1989 Joe Mullen, Cgy.	Wayne Gretzky, L.A.
1988 Mats Naslund, Mtl.	Wayne Gretzky, Edm.
1987 Joe Mullen, Cgy.	Wayne Gretzky, Edm.
1986 Mike Bossy, NYI	Jari Kurri, Edm.
1985 Jari Kurri, Edm.	Joe Mullen, St.L.
1984 Mike Bossy, NYI	Rick Middleton, Bos.
1983 Mike Bossy, NYI	Rick Middleton, Bos.
1982 Rick Middleton, Bos.	Mike Bossy, NYI
1981 Rick Kehoe, Pit.	Wayne Gretzky, Edm.
1980 Wayne Gretzky, Edm.	Marcel Dionne, L.A.
1979 Bob MacMillan, Atl.	Marcel Dionne, L.A.
1978 Butch Goring, L.A.	Peter McNab, Bos.
1977 Marcel Dionne, L.A.	Jean Ratelle, Bos.
1976 Jean Ratelle, NYR-Bos.	Jean Pronovost, Pit.
1975 Marcel Dionne, Det.	John Bucyk, Bos.
1974 John Bucyk, Bos.	Lowell MacDonald, Pit.
1973 Gilbert Perreault, Buf.	Jean Ratelle, NYR
1972 Jean Ratelle, NYR	John Bucyk, Bos.
1971 John Bucyk, Bos.	Dave Keon, Tor.
1970 Phil Goyette, St.L.	John Bucyk, Bos.
1969 Alex Delvecchio, Det.	Ted Hampson, Oak.
1968 Stan Mikita, Chi.	John Bucyk, Bos.
1967 Stan Mikita, Chi.	Dave Keon, Tor.
1966 Alex Delvecchio, Det.	Bobby Rousseau, Mtl.
1965 Bobby Hull, Chi.	Alex Delvecchio, Det.
1964 Ken Wharram, Chi.	Dave Keon, Tor.
1963 Dave Keon, Tor.	Camille Henry, NYR
1962 Dave Keon, Tor.	Claude Provost, Mtl.
1961 Red Kelly, Tor.	Norm Ullman, Det.
1960 Don McKenney, Bos.	Andy Hebenton, NYR
1959 Alex Delvecchio, Det.	Andy Hebenton, NYR
1958 Camille Henry, NYR	Don Marshall, Mtl.
1957 Andy Hebenton, NYR	Earl Reibel, Det.
1956 Earl Reibel, Det.	Floyd Curry, Mtl.
1955 Sid Smith, Tor.	Danny Lewicki, NYR
1954 Red Kelly, Det.	Don Raleigh, NYR
1953 Red Kelly, Det.	Wally Hergesheimer, NYR
1952 Sid Smith, Tor.	Red Kelly, Det.
1951 Red Kelly, Det.	Woody Dumart, Bos.
1950 Edgar Laprade, NYR	Red Kelly, Det.
1949 Bill Quackenbush, Det.	Harry Watson, Tor.
1948 Buddy O'Connor, NYR	Syl Apps, Tor.
1947 Bobby Bauer, Bos.	Syl Apps, Tor.
1946 Toe Blake, Mtl.	Clint Smith, Chi.
1945 Bill Mosienko, Chi.	Syd Howe, Det.
1944 Clint Smith, Chi.	Herb Cain, Bos.
1943 Max Bentley, Chi.	Buddy O'Connor, Mtl.
1942 Syl Apps, Tor.	Gordie Drillon, Tor.
1941 Bobby Bauer, Bos.	Gordie Drillon, Tor.
1940 Bobby Bauer, Bos.	Clint Smith, NYR
1939 Clint Smith, NYR	Marty Barry, Det.
1938 Gordie Drillon, Tor.	Clint Smith, NYR
1937 Marty Barry, Det.	Gordie Drillon, Tor.
1936 Doc Romnes, Chi.	Dave Schriner, NYA
1935 Frank Boucher, NYR	Russ Blinco, Mtl.M
1934 Frank Boucher, NYR	Joe Primeau, Tor.
1933 Frank Boucher, NYR	Joe Primeau, Tor.
1932 Joe Primeau, Tor.	Frank Boucher, NYR
1931 Frank Boucher, NYR	Normie Himes, NYA
1930 Frank Boucher, NYR	Normie Himes, NYA
1929 Frank Boucher, NYR	Harry Darragh, Pit.
1928 Frank Boucher, NYR	George Hay, Det.
1927 Billy Burch, NYA	Dick Irvin, Chi.
1926 Frank Nighbor, Ott.	Billy Burch, NYA
1925 Frank Nighbor, Ott.	none

VEZINA TROPHY

Winner	Runner-up
1995 Dominik Hasek, Buf.	Ed Belfour, Chi.
1994 Dominik Hasek, Buf.	John Vanbiesbrouck, Fla.
1993 Ed Belfour, Chi.	Tom Barrasso, Pit.
1992 Patrick Roy, Mtl.	Kirk McLean, Van.
1991 Ed Belfour, Chi.	Patrick Roy, Mtl.
1990 Patrick Roy, Mtl.	Daren Puppa, Buf.
1989 Patrick Roy, Mtl.	Mike Vernon, Cgy.
1988 Grant Fuhr, Edm.	Tom Barrasso, Buf.
1987 Ron Hextall, Phi.	Mike Liut, Hfd.
1986 John Vanbiesbrouck, NYR	Bob Froese, Phi.
1985 Pelle Lindbergh, Phi.	Tom Barrasso, Buf.
1984 Tom Barrasso, Buf.	Rejean Lemelin, Cgy.
1983 Pete Peeters, Bos.	Roland Melanson, NYI
1982 Bill Smith, NYI	Grant Fuhr, Edm.
1981 Richard Sevigny, Mtl.	Pete Peeters, Phi.
Denis Herron, Mtl.	Rick St. Croix, Phi.
Michel Larocque, Mtl.	
1980 Bob Sauve, Buf.	Gerry Cheevers, Bos.
Don Edwards, Buf.	Gilles Gilbert, Bos.
1979 Ken Dryden, Mtl.	Glenn Resch, NYI
Michel Larocque, Mtl.	Bill Smith, NYI
1978 Ken Dryden, Mtl.	Bernie Parent, Phi.
Michel Larocque	Wayne Stephenson, Phi.
1977 Ken Dryden, Mtl.	Glenn Resch, NYI
Michel Larocque, Mtl.	Bill Smith, NYI
1976 Ken Dryden, Mtl.	Glenn Resch, NYI
	Bill Smith, NYI
1975 Bernie Parent, Phi.	Rogie Vachon, L.A.
	Gary Edwards, L.A.
1974 Bernie Parent, Phi. (tie)	Gilles Gilbert, Bos.
Tony Esposito, Chi. (tie)	
1973 Ken Dryden, Mtl.	Ed Giacomin, NYR
	Gilles Villemure, NYR
1972 Tony Esposito, Chi.	Cesare Maniago, Min.
Gary Smith, Chi.	Lorne Worsley, Min.
1971 Ed Giacomin, NYR	Tony Esposito, Chi.
Gilles Villemure, NYR	
1970 Tony Esposito, Chi.	Jacques Plante, St.L.
	Ernie Wakely, St.L.
1969 Jacques Plante, St.L.	Ed Giacomin, NYR
Glenn Hall, St.L.	
1968 Lorne Worsley, Mtl.	Johnny Bower, Tor.
Rogatien Vachon, Mtl.	Bruce Gamble, Tor.
1967 Glenn Hall, Chi.	Charlie Hodge, Mtl.
Denis Dejordy, Chi.	
1966 Lorne Worsley, Mtl.	Glenn Hall, Chi.
Charlie Hodge, Mtl.	
1965 Terry Sawchuk, Tor.	Roger Crozier, Det.
Johnny Bower, Tor.	
1964 Charlie Hodge, Mtl.	Glenn Hall, Chi.
1963 Glenn Hall, Chi.	Johnny Bower, Tor.
	Don Simmons, Tor.
1962 Jacques Plante, Mtl.	Johnny Bower, Tor.
1961 Johnny Bower, Tor.	Glenn Hall, Chi.
1960 Jacques Plante, Mtl.	Glenn Hall, Chi.
1959 Jacques Plante, Mtl.	Johnny Bower, Tor.
	Ed Chadwick, Tor.
1958 Jacques Plante, Mtl.	Lorne Worsley, NYR
	Marcel Paille, NYR
1957 Jacques Plante, Mtl.	Glenn Hall, Det.
1956 Jacques Plante, Mtl.	Glenn Hall, Det.
1955 Terry Sawchuk, Det.	Harry Lumley, Tor.
1954 Harry Lumley, Tor.	Terry Sawchuk, Det.
1953 Terry Sawchuk, Det.	Gerry McNeil, Mtl.
1952 Terry Sawchuk, Det.	Al Rollins, Tor.
1951 Al Rollins, Tor.	Terry Sawchuk, Det.
1950 Bill Durnan, Mtl.	Harry Lumley, Det.
1949 Bill Durnan, Mtl.	Harry Lumley, Det.
1948 Turk Broda, Tor.	Harry Lumley, Det.
1947 Bill Durnan, Mtl.	Turk Broda, Tor.
1946 Bill Durnan, Mtl.	Frank Brimsek, Bos.
1945 Bill Durnan, Mtl.	Frank McCool, Tor. (tie)
	Harry Lumley, Det. (tie)
1944 Bill Durnan, Mtl.	Paul Bibeault, Tor.
1943 Johnny Mowers, Det.	Turk Broda, Tor.
1942 Frank Brimsek, Bos.	Turk Broda, Tor.
1941 Turk Broda, Tor.	Frank Brimsek, Bos. (tie)
	Johnny Mowers, Det. (tie)
1940 Dave Kerr, NYR	Frank Brimsek, Bos.
1939 Frank Brimsek, Bos.	Dave Kerr, NYR
1938 Tiny Thompson, Bos.	Dave Kerr, NYR
1937 Normie Smith, Det.	Dave Kerr, NYR
1936 Tiny Thompson, Bos.	Mike Karakas, Chi.
1935 Lorne Chabot, Chi.	Alex Connell, Mtl.M
1934 Charlie Gardiner, Chi.	Wilf Cude, Det.
1933 Tiny Thompson, Bos.	John Roach, Det.
1932 Charlie Gardiner, Chi.	Alex Connell, Det.
1931 Roy Worters, NYA	Charlie Gardiner, Chi.
1930 Tiny Thompson, Bos.	Charlie Gardiner, Chi.
1929 George Hainsworth, Mtl.	Tiny Thompson, Bos.
1928 George Hainsworth, Mtl.	Alex Connell, Ott.
1927 George Hainsworth, Mtl.	Clint Benedict, Mtl.M

BILL MASTERTON TROPHY WINNERS

1995 Pat LaFontaine	Buffalo
1994 Cam Neely	Boston
1993 Mario Lemieux	Pittsburgh
1992 Mark Fitzpatrick	NY Islanders
1991 Dave Taylor	Los Angeles
1990 Gord Kluzak	Boston
1989 Tim Kerr	Philadelphia
1988 Bob Bourne	Los Angeles
1987 Doug Jarvis	Hartford
1986 Charlie Simmer	Boston
1985 Anders Hedberg	NY Rangers
1984 Brad Park	Detroit
1983 Lanny McDonald	Calgary
1982 Glenn Resch	Colorado
1981 Blake Dunlop	St. Louis
1980 Al MacAdam	Minnesota
1979 Serge Savard	Montreal
1978 Butch Goring	Los Angeles
1977 Ed Westfall	NY Islanders
1976 Rod Gilbert	NY Rangers
1975 Don Luce	Buffalo
1974 Henri Richard	Montreal
1973 Lowell MacDonald	Pittsburgh
1972 Bobby Clarke	Philadelphia
1971 Jean Ratelle	NY Rangers
1970 Pit Martin	Chicago
1969 Ted Hampson	Oakland
1968 Claude Provost	Montreal

CALDER MEMORIAL TROPHY WINNERS

Winner	Runner-up
1995 Peter Forsberg, Que.	Jim Carey, Wsh.
1994 Martin Brodeur, N.J.	Jason Arnott, Edm.
1993 Teemu Selanne, Wpg.	Joe Juneau, Bos.
1992 Pavel Bure, Van.	Nicklas Lidstrom, Det
1991 Ed Belfour, Chi.	Sergei Fedorov, Det.
1990 Sergei Makarov, Cgy.	Mike Modano, Min.
1989 Brian Leetch, NYR	Trevor Linden, Van.
1988 Joe Nieuwendyk, Cgy.	Ray Sheppard, Buf.
1987 Luc Robitaille, L.A.	Ron Hextall, Phi.
1986 Gary Suter, Cgy.	Wendel Clark, Tor.
1985 Mario Lemieux, Pit.	Chris Chelios, Mtl.
1984 Tom Barrasso, Buf.	Steve Yzerman, Det.
1983 Steve Larmer, Chi.	Phil Housley, Buf.
1982 Dale Hawerchuk, Wpg.	Barry Pederson, Bos.
1981 Peter Stastny, Que.	Larry Murphy, L.A.
1980 Ray Bourque, Bos.	Mike Foligno, Det.
1979 Bobby Smith, Min	Ryan Walter, Wsh.
1978 Mike Bossy, NYI	Barry Beck, Col.
1977 Willi Plett, Atl.	Don Murdoch, NYR
1976 Bryan Trottier, NYI	Glenn Resch, NYI
1975 Eric Vail, Atl.	Pierre Larouche, Pit.
1974 Denis Potvin, NYI	Tom Lysiak, Atl.
1973 Steve Vickers, NYR	Bill Barber, Phi.
1972 Ken Dryden, Mtl.	Rick Martin, Buf.
1971 Gilbert Perreault, Buf.	Jude Drouin, Min.
1970 Tony Esposito, Chi.	Bill Fairbairn, NYR
1969 Danny Grant, Min.	Norm Ferguson, Oak.
1968 Derek Sanderson, Bos.	Jacques Lemaire, Mtl.
1967 Bobby Orr, Bos.	Ed Van Impe, Chi.
1966 Brit Selby, Tor.	Bert Marshall, Tor.
1965 Roger Crozier, Det.	Ron Ellis, Tor.
1964 Jacques Laperriere, Mtl.	John Ferguson, Mtl.
1963 Kent Douglas, Tor.	Doug Barkley, Det.
1962 Bobby Rousseau, Mtl.	Cliff Pennington, Bos.
1961 Dave Keon, Tor.	Bob Nevin, Tor.
1960 Bill Hay, Chi.	Murray Oliver, Det.
1959 Ralph Backstrom, Mtl.	Carl Brewer, Tor.
1958 Frank Mahovlich, Tor.	Bobby Hull, Chi.
1957 Larry Regan, Bos.	Ed Chadwick, Tor.
1956 Glenn Hall, Det.	Andy Hebenton, NYR
1955 Ed Litzenberger, Chi.	Don McKenney, Bos.
1954 Camille Henry, NYR	Earl Reibel, Det.
1953 Lorne Worsley, NYR	Gordie Hannigan, Tor.
1952 Bernie Geoffrion, Mtl.	Hy Buller, NYR
1951 Terry Sawchuk, Det.	Al Rollins, Tor.
1950 Jack Gelineau, Bos.	Phil Maloney, Bos.
1949 Pentti Lund, NYR	Allan Stanley, NYR
1948 Jim McFadden, Det.	Pete Babando, Bos.
1947 Howie Meeker, Tor.	Jimmy Conacher, Det.
1946 Edgar Laprade, NYR	George Gee, Chi.
1945 Frank McCool, Tor.	Ken Smith, Bos.
1944 Gus Bodnar, Tor.	Bill Durnan, Mtl.
1943 Gaye Stewart, Tor.	Glen Harmon, Mtl.
1942 Grant Warwick, NYR	Buddy O'Connor, Mtl.
1941 Johnny Quilty, Mtl.	Johnny Mowers, Det.
1940 Kilby MacDonald, NYR	Wally Stanowski, Det.
1939 Frank Brimsek, Bos.	Roy Conacher, Bos.
1938 Cully Dahlstrom, Chi.	Murph Chamberlain, Tor.
1937 Syl Apps, Tor.	Gordie Drillon, Tor.
1936 Mike Karakas, Chi.	Bucko McDonald, Det.
1935 Dave Schriner, NYA	Bert Connolly, NYR
1934 Russ Blinko, Mtl.M	
1933 Carl Voss, Det.	

CONN SMYTHE TROPHY WINNERS

Year	Winner	Team
1995	Claude Lemieux	New Jersey
1994	Brian Leetch	NY Rangers
1993	Patrick Roy	Montreal
1992	Mario Lemieux	Pittsburgh
1991	Mario Lemieux	Pittsburgh
1990	Bill Ranford	Edmonton
1989	Al MacInnis	Calgary
1988	Wayne Gretzky	Edmonton
1987	Ron Hextall	Philadelphia
1986	Patrick Roy	Montreal
1985	Wayne Gretzky	Edmonton
1984	Mark Messier	Edmonton
1983	Bill Smith	NY Islanders
1982	Mike Bossy	NY Islanders
1981	Butch Goring	NY Islanders
1980	Bryan Trottier	NY Islanders
1979	Bob Gainey	Montreal
1978	Larry Robinson	Montreal
1977	Guy Lafleur	Montreal
1976	Reggie Leach	Philadelphia
1975	Bernie Parent	Philadelphia
1974	Bernie Parent	Philadelphia
1973	Yvan Cournoyer	Montreal
1972	Bobby Orr	Boston
1971	Ken Dryden	Montreal
1970	Bobby Orr	Boston
1969	Serge Savard	Montreal
1968	Glenn Hall	St. Louis
1967	Dave Keon	Toronto
1966	Roger Crozier	Detroit

JAMES NORRIS TROPHY WINNERS

Year	Winner	Runner-up
1995	Paul Coffey, Det.	Chris Chelios, Chi.
1994	Ray Bourque, Bos.	Scott Stevens, N.J.
1993	Chris Chelios, Chi.	Ray Bourque, Bos.
1992	Brian Leetch, NYR	Ray Bourque, Bos.
1991	Ray Bourque, Bos.	Al MacInnis, Cgy.
1990	Ray Bourque, Bos.	Al MacInnis, Cgy.
1989	Chris Chelios, Mtl	Paul Coffey, Pit.
1988	Ray Bourque, Bos.	Scott Stevens, Wsh.
1987	Ray Bourque, Bos.	Mark Howe, Phi.
1986	Paul Coffey, Edm.	Mark Howe, Phi.
1985	Paul Coffey, Edm.	Ray Bourque, Bos.
1984	Rod Langway, Wsh.	Paul Coffey, Edm.
1983	Rod Langway, Wsh.	Mark Howe, Phi.
1982	Doug Wilson, Chi.	Ray Bourque, Bos.
1981	Randy Carlyle, Pit.	Denis Potvin, NYI
1980	Larry Robinson, Mtl.	Borje Salming, Tor.
1979	Denis Potvin, NYI	Larry Robinson, Mtl.
1978	Denis Potvin, NYI	Brad Park, Bos.
1977	Larry Robinson, Mtl.	Borje Salming, Tor.
1976	Denis Potvin, NYI	Brad Park, NYR-Bos.
1975	Bobby Orr, Bos.	Denis Potvin, NYI
1974	Bobby Orr, Bos.	Brad Park, NYR
1973	Bobby Orr, Bos.	Guy Lapointe, Mtl.
1972	Bobby Orr, Bos.	Brad Park, NYR
1971	Bobby Orr, Bos.	Brad Park, NYR
1970	Bobby Orr, Bos.	Brad Park, NYR
1969	Bobby Orr, Bos.	Tim Horton, Tor.
1968	Bobby Orr, Bos.	J.C. Tremblay, Mtl
1967	Harry Howell, NYR	Pierre Pilote, Chi.
1966	Jacques Laperriere, Mtl.	Pierre Pilote, Chi.
1965	Pierre Pilote, Chi.	Jacques Laperriere, Mtl.
1964	Pierre Pilote, Chi.	Tim Horton, Tor.
1963	Pierre Pilote, Chi.	Carl Brewer, Tor.
1962	Doug Harvey, NYR	Pierre Pilote, Chi.
1961	Doug Harvey, Mtl.	Marcel Pronovost, Det.
1960	Doug Harvey, Mtl.	Allan Stanley, Tor.
1959	Tom Johnson, Mtl.	Bill Gadsby, NYR
1958	Doug Harvey, Mtl.	Bill Gadsby, NYR
1957	Doug Harvey, Mtl.	Red Kelly, Det.
1956	Doug Harvey, Mtl.	Bill Gadsby, NYR
1955	Doug Harvey, Mtl.	Red Kelly, Det.
1954	Red Kelly, Det.	Doug Harvey, Mtl.

LESTER PATRICK TROPHY WINNERS

1995	Joe Mullen
	Brian Mullen
	Bob Fleming
1994	Wayne Gretzky
	Robert Ridder
1993	*Frank Boucher
	*Mervyn (Red) Dutton
	Bruce McNall
	Gil Stein
1992	Al Arbour
	Art Berglund
	Lou Lamoriello
1991	Rod Gilbert
	Mike Ilitch
1990	Len Ceglarski
1989	Dan Kelly
	Lou Nanne
	*Lynn Patrick
	Bud Poile
1988	Keith Allen
	Fred Cusick
	Bob Johnson
1987	*Hobey Baker
	Frank Mathers
1986	John MacInnes
	Jack Riley
1985	Jack Butterfield
	Arthur M. Wirtz
1984	John A. Ziegler Jr.
	*Arthur Howie Ross
1983	Bill Torrey
1982	Emile P. Francis
1981	Charles M. Schulz
1980	Bobby Clarke
	Edward M. Snider
	Frederick A. Shero
	1980 U.S. Olympic Hockey Team
1979	Bobby Orr
1978	Phil Esposito
	Tom Fitzgerald
	William T. Tutt
	William W. Wirtz
1977	John P. Bucyk
	Murray A. Armstrong
	John Mariucci
1976	Stanley Mikita
	George A. Leader
	Bruce A. Norris
1975	Donald M. Clark
	William L. Chadwick
	Thomas N. Ivan
1974	Alex Delvecchio
	Murray Murdoch
	*Weston W. Adams, Sr.
	*Charles L. Crovat
1973	Walter L. Bush, Jr.
1972	Clarence S. Campbell
	John A. "Snooks" Kelly
	Ralph "Cooney" Weiland
	*James D. Norris
1971	William M. Jennings
	*John B. Sollenberger
	*Terrance G. Sawchuk
1970	Edward W. Shore
	*James C. V. Hendy
1969	Robert M. Hull
	*Edward J. Jeremiah
1968	Thomas F. Lockhart
	*Walter A. Brown
	*Gen. John R. Kilpatrick
1967	Gordon Howe
	*Charles F. Adams
	*James Norris, Sr.
1966	J.J. "Jack" Adams
	* awarded posthumously

WILLIAM M. JENNINGS TROPHY WINNERS

Year	Winner	Runner-up
1995	Ed Belfour, Chi.	Mike Vernon, Det.
		Chris Osgood
1994	Dominik Hasek, Buf.	Martin Brodeur, N.J.
	Grant Fuhr	Chris Terreri
1993	Ed Belfour, Chi.	Felix Potvin, Tor.
		Grant Fuhr
1992	Patrick Roy, Mtl.	Ed Belfour, Chi.
1991	Ed Belfour, Chi.	Patrick Roy, Mtl.
1990	Andy Moog, Bos.	Patrick Roy, Mtl.
	Rejean Lemelin	Brian Hayward
1989	Patrick Roy, Mtl.	Mike Vernon, Cgy.
	Brian Hayward	Rick Wamsley
1988	Patrick Roy, Mtl.	Clint Malarchuk, Wsh.
	Brian Hayward	Pete Peeters
1987	Patrick Roy, Mtl.	Ron Hextall, Phi.
	Brian Hayward	
1986	Bob Froese, Phi.	Al Jensen, Wsh.
	Darren Jensen	Pete Peeters
1985	Tom Barrasso, Buf.	Pat Riggin, Wsh.
	Bob Sauve	
1984	Al Jensen, Wsh.	Tom Barrasso, Buf.
	Pat Riggin	Bob Sauve
1983	Roland Melanson, NYI	Pete Peeters, Bos.
	Bill Smith	
1982	Rick Wamsley, Mtl.	Billy Smith, NYI
	Denis Herron	Roland Melanson

LESTER B. PEARSON AWARD WINNERS

Year	Winner	Team
1995	Eric Lindros	Philadelphia
1994	Sergei Fedorov	Detroit
1993	Mario Lemieux	Pittsburgh
1992	Mark Messier	NY Rangers
1991	Brett Hull	St. Louis
1990	Mark Messier	Edmonton
1989	Steve Yzerman	Detroit
1988	Mario Lemieux	Pittsburgh
1987	Wayne Gretzky	Edmonton
1986	Mario Lemieux	Pittsburgh
1985	Wayne Gretzky	Edmonton
1984	Wayne Gretzky	Edmonton
1983	Wayne Gretzky	Edmonton
1982	Wayne Gretzky	Edmonton
1981	Mike Liut	St. Louis
1980	Marcel Dionne	Los Angeles
1979	Marcel Dionne	Los Angeles
1978	Guy Lafleur	Montreal
1977	Guy Lafleur	Montreal
1976	Guy Lafleur	Montreal
1975	Bobby Orr	Boston
1974	Phil Esposito	Boston
1973	Bobby Clarke	Philadelphia
1972	Jean Ratelle	NY Rangers
1971	Phil Esposito	Boston

JACK ADAMS AWARD WINNERS

Year	Winner	Runner-up
1995	Marc Crawford, Que.	Scotty Bowman, Det.
1994	Jacques Lemaire, N.J.	Kevin Constantine, S.J.
1993	Pat Burns, Tor.	Brian Sutter, Bos.
1992	Pat Quinn, Van.	Roger Neilson, NYR
1991	Brian Sutter, St.L.	Tom Webster, L.A.
1990	Bob Murdoch, Wpg.	Mike Milbury, Bos.
1989	Pat Burns, Mtl.	Bob McCammon, Van.
1988	Jacques Demers, Det.	Terry Crisp, Cgy.
1987	Jacques Demers, Det.	Jack Evans, Hfd.
1986	Glen Sather, Edm.	Jacques Demers, St.L.
1985	Mike Keenan, Phi.	Barry Long, Wpg.
1984	Bryan Murray, Wsh.	Scotty Bowman, Buf.
1983	Orval Tessier, Chi.	
1982	Tom Watt, Wpg.	
1981	Red Berenson, St.L.	Bob Berry, L.A.
1980	Pat Quinn, Phi.	
1979	Al Arbour, NYI	Fred Shero, NYR
1978	Bobby Kromm, Det.	Don Cherry, Bos.
1977	Scotty Bowman, Mtl.	Tom McVie, Wsh.
1976	Don Cherry, Bos.	
1975	Bob Pulford, L.A.	
1974	Fred Shero, Phi.	

ALKA-SELTZER PLUS AWARD WINNERS

1995	Ron Francis	Pittsburgh
1994	Scott Stevens	New Jersey
1993	Mario Lemieux	Pittsburgh
1992	Paul Ysebaert	Detroit
1991	Marty McSorley	Los Angeles
	Theoren Fleury	Calgary
1990	Paul Cavallini	St. Louis

NHL Amateur and Entry Draft

History

Year	Site	Date	Total Players Drafted
1963	Queen Elizabeth Hotel	June 5	21
1964	Queen Elizabeth Hotel	June 11	24
1965	Queen Elizabeth Hotel	April 27	11
1966	Mount Royal Hotel	April 25	24
1967	Queen Elizabeth Hotel	June 7	18
1968	Queen Elizabeth Hotel	June 13	24
1969	Queen Elizabeth Hotel	June 12	84
1970	Queen Elizabeth Hotel	June 11	115
1971	Queen Elizabeth Hotel	June 10	117
1972	Queen Elizabeth Hotel	June 8	152
1973	Mount Royal Hotel	May 15	168
1974	NHL Montreal Office	May 28	247
1975	NHL Montreal Office	June 3	217
1976	NHL Montreal Office	June 1	135
1977	NHL Montreal Office	June 14	185
1978	Queen Elizabeth Hotel	June 15	234
1979	Queen Elizabeth Hotel	August 9	126
1980	Montreal Forum	June 11	210
1981	Montreal Forum	June 10	211
1982	Montreal Forum	June 9	252
1983	Montreal Forum	June 8	242
1984	Montreal Forum	June 9	250
1985	Toronto Convention Centre	June 15	252
1986	Montreal Forum	June 21	252
1987	Joe Louis Sports Arena	June 13	252
1988	Montreal Forum	June 11	252
1989	Metropolitan Sports Center	June 17	252
1990	B. C. Place	June 16	250
1991	Memorial Auditorium	June 9	264
1992	Montreal Forum	June 20	264
1993	Colisée de Québec	June 26	286
1994	Hartford Civic Center	June 28-29	286
1995	Edmonton Coliseum	July 8	234

* The NHL Amateur Draft became the NHL Entry Draft in 1979

Defenseman Bryan Berard was chosen first overall in the 1995 Entry Draft by the Ottawa Senators. A talented, smooth-skating rearguard, Berard helped lead the Detroit Jr. Red Wings to the OHA title in 1994-95 by collecting 75 points in 58 games.

First Selections

Year	Player	Pos	Drafted By	Drafted From	Age
1969	Rejean Houle	LW	Montreal	Jr. Canadiens	19.8
1970	Gilbert Perreault	C	Buffalo	Jr. Canadiens	19.7
1971	Guy Lafleur	RW	Montreal	Quebec Remparts	19.9
1972	Billy Harris	RW	NY Islanders	Toronto Marlboros	20.4
1973	Denis Potvin	D	NY Islanders	Ottawa 67's	19.7
1974	Greg Joly	D	Washington	Regina Pats	20.0
1975	Mel Bridgman	C	Philadelphia	Victoria Cougars	20.1
1976	Rick Green	D	Washington	London Knights	20.3
1977	Dale McCourt	C	Detroit	St. Catharines Fincups	20.4
1978	Bobby Smith	C	Minnesota	Ottawa 67's	20.4
1979	Bob Ramage	D	Colorado	London Knights	20.5
1980	Doug Wickenheiser	C	Montreal	Regina Pats	19.2
1981	Dale Hawerchuk	C	Winnipeg	Cornwall Royals	18.2
1982	Gord Kluzak	D	Boston	Nanaimo Islanders	18.3
1983	Brian Lawton	C	Minnesota	Mount St. Charles HS	18.11
1984	Mario Lemieux	C	Pittsburgh	Laval Voisins	18.8
1985	Wendel Clark	LW/D	Toronto	Saskatoon Blades	18.7
1986	Joe Murphy	C	Detroit	Michigan State	18.8
1987	Pierre Turgeon	C	Buffalo	Granby Bisons	17.10
1988	Mike Modano	C	Minnesota	Prince Albert Raiders	18.0
1989	Mats Sundin	RW	Quebec	Nacka (Sweden)	18.4
1990	Owen Nolan	RW	Quebec	Cornwall Royals	18.4
1991	Eric Lindros	C	Quebec	Oshawa Generals	18.3
1992	Roman Hamrlik	D	Tampa Bay	ZPS Zlin (Czech.)	18.2
1993	Alexandre Daigle	C	Ottawa	Victoriaville Tigres	18.5
1994	Ed Jovanovski	D	Florida	Windsor Spitfires	18.0
1995	Bryan Berard	D	Ottawa	Detroit Jr. Red Wings	18.4

Draft Summary

Following is a summary of the number of players drafted from the Ontario Hockey League (OHL), Western Hockey League (WHL), Quebec Major Junior Hockey League (QMJHL), United States Colleges, United States High Schools, European Leagues and other Leagues throughout North America since 1969:

	OHL	WHL	QMJHL	US Coll.	US HS	International	Other
1969	36	20	11	7	0	1	9
1970	51	22	13	16	0	0	13
1971	41	28	13	22	0	0	13
1972	46	44	30	21	0	0	11
1973	56	49	24	25	0	0	14
1974	69	66	40	41	0	6	25
1975	55	57	28	59	0	6	12
1976	47	33	18	26	0	8	3
1977	42	44	40	49	0	5	5
1978	59	48	22	73	0	16	16
1979	48	37	19	15	0	6	1
1980	73	41	24	42	7	13	10
1981	59	37	28	21	17	32	17
1982	60	55	17	20	47	35	18
1983	57	41	24	14	35	34	37
1984	55	38	16	22	44	40	36
1985	59	47	15	20	48	31	31
1986	66	32	22	22	40	28	42
1987	32	36	17	40	69	38	20
1988	32	30	22	48	56	39	25
1989	39	44	16	48	47	38	20
1990	39	33	14	38	57	53	16
1991	43	40	25	43	37	55	21
1992	57	45	22	9	25	84	22
1993	60	44	23	17	33	78	31
1994	45	66	28	6	28	80	33
1995	54	55	35	5	2	69	14
Total	1380	1132	606	769	592	795	515

Total Drafted, 1969-1995: 5,789

Ontario Hockey League

Club	'69	'70	'71	'72	'73	'74	'75	'76	'77	'78	'79	'80	'81	'82	'83	'84	'85	'86	'87	'88	'89	'90	'91	'92	'93	'94	'95	Total
Peterborough	5	5	4	5	9	4	8	1	4	6	9	10	3	5	7	3	9	2	5	2	2	4	3	4	4	2	5	130
Oshawa	5	4	3	5	5	7	6	6	1	3	3	2	9	5	5	6	6	6	3	2	4	2	4	4	4	1	10	121
Kitchener	1	6	2	8	4	13	3	1	3	4	4	4	5	5	8	4	6	3	2	1	7	5	3	1	4	2	4	113
Ottawa	2	4	3	4	6	5	6	5	5	5	3	8	4	9	2	2	3	3	2	1	–	5	5	6	4	1	1	104
London	4	9	1	5	6	6	3	5	4	3	6	2	5	5	3	7	1	3	2	6	3	3	1	3	4	1	1	102
S.S. Marie	–	–	–	–	4	5	2	5	1	5	3	3	8	1	6	4	5	7	1	2	3	1	2	7	3	4	3	85
Sudbury	–	–	–	–	6	6	4	5	4	4	3	7	2	4	–	2	5	3	1	–	1	2	8	2	10	2	2	83
Kingston	–	–	–	–	–	4	4	6	4	9	2	8	5	2	1	3	3	4	1	1	–	2	2	3	5	2	3	74
Niagara Falls	4	2	1	4	–	–	–	–	2	3	5	8	6	6	–	–	–	–	–	–	4	4	4	4	4	3	2	66
Windsor	–	–	–	–	–	–	–	2	1	4	2	3	5	3	2	2	3	7	–	5	2	1	–	3	–	3	4	52
North Bay	–	–	–	–	–	–	–	–	–	–	–	–	–	–	4	4	3	3	3	3	1	4	2	5	2	7	2	43
Guelph	–	–	–	–	–	–	–	–	–	–	–	–	–	–	1	5	3	8	2	–	4	–	–	2	2	7	5	39
Belleville	–	–	–	–	–	–	–	–	–	–	–	–	–	–	3	4	4	5	2	–	4	2	1	4	–	3	3	35
Detroit	–	–	–	–	–	–	–	–	–	–	–	–	–	–	–	–	–	–	–	–	–	–	2	2	7	2	6	19
Owen Sound	–	–	–	–	–	–	–	–	–	–	–	–	–	–	–	–	–	–	–	–	–	1	1	2	4	3	2	13
Sarnia	–	–	–	–	–	–	–	–	–	–	–	–	–	–	–	–	–	–	–	–	–	–	–	–	–	–	1	1
Teams no longer operating																												
Toronto	3	7	6	5	6	8	4	4	7	5	4	10	2	6	4	4	3	4	1	2	2	–	–	–	–	–	–	97
Hamilton	2	3	5	4	6	4	7	3	–	8	1	–	–	–	–	–	3	6	4	4	–	–	2	–	–	–	–	62
St. Catharines	5	5	8	5	4	7	8	4	6	–	–	–	–	–	–	–	–	–	–	–	–	–	–	–	–	–	–	52
Cornwall	–	–	–	–	–	–	–	–	–	–	–	–	–	7	4	3	2	2	3	3	2	3	3	5	–	–	–	37
Brantford	–	–	–	–	–	–	–	–	–	–	3	8	5	2	7	2	–	–	–	–	–	–	–	–	–	–	–	27
Montreal	5	6	8	1	–	–	–	–	–	–	–	–	–	–	–	–	–	–	–	–	–	–	–	–	–	–	–	20
Newmarket	–	–	–	–	–	–	–	–	–	–	–	–	–	–	–	–	–	–	–	–	–	–	–	–	3	2	–	5

Year	Total Ontario Drafted	Total Players Drafted	Ontario %
1969	36	84	42.9
1970	51	115	44.3
1971	41	117	35.0
1972	46	152	30.3
1973	56	168	33.3
1974	69	247	27.9
1975	55	217	25.3
1976	47	135	34.8
1977	42	185	22.7
1978	59	234	25.2
1979	48	126	38.1
1980	73	210	34.8
1981	59	211	28.0
1982	60	252	23.8
1983	57	242	23.6
1984	55	250	22.0
1985	59	252	23.4
1986	66	252	26.2
1987	32	252	12.7
1988	32	252	12.7
1989	39	252	15.5
1990	39	250	15.6
1991	43	264	16.3
1992	57	264	21.6
1993	60	286	21.0
1994	45	286	15.7
1995	54	234	23.1
Total	**1380**	**5789**	**23.8**

Western Hockey League

Club	'69	'70	'71	'72	'73	'74	'75	'76	'77	'78	'79	'80	'81	'82	'83	'84	'85	'86	'87	'88	'89	'90	'91	'92	'93	'94	'95	Total
Regina	–	–	5	5	1	8	5	3	1	4	1	3	5	6	8	4	4	3	2	–	5	1	–	4	–	3	2	83
Saskatoon	1	–	1	3	8	4	5	3	4	1	2	2	3	5	5	3	1	5	4	4	3	2	2	3	2	4	2	82
Portland	–	–	–	–	–	–	–	–	4	8	7	8	6	7	7	5	2	4	3	1	4	1	1	4	4	3	2	81
Medicine Hat	–	–	–	4	6	4	5	3	5	4	–	4	2	1	2	1	6	2	5	1	4	1	3	3	1	6	2	75
Brandon	–	3	1	5	2	7	4	–	3	1	10	5	2	2	1	3	2	1	3	3	–	1	1	1	2	5	6	74
Kamloops	–	–	–	–	–	4	4	4	4	–	–	–	–	2	4	4	4	4	3	1	5	4	6	3	2	9	5	72
Lethbridge	–	–	–	–	–	–	3	2	3	5	4	1	4	7	2	1	5	1	–	3	3	4	7	3	4	3	3	68
Seattle	–	–	–	–	–	–	–	–	–	4	2	3	–	6	–	1	3	1	2	4	2	6	3	2	4	5	5	53
Prince Albert	–	–	–	–	–	–	–	–	–	–	–	–	–	4	2	2	6	6	1	3	3	4	6	2	5	3	4	51
Swift Current	1	–	1	–	3	6	–	–	–	–	–	–	–	–	–	–	–	–	5	2	2	2	1	1	5	4	4	37
Spokane	–	–	–	–	–	–	–	–	–	–	–	–	1	–	–	–	–	–	1	3	2	1	5	7	4	4	4	32
Moose Jaw	–	–	–	–	–	–	–	–	–	–	–	–	–	–	–	–	4	1	3	–	3	1	2	3	2	3	4	26
Tri-Cities	–	–	–	–	–	–	–	–	–	–	–	–	–	–	–	–	–	–	–	–	4	3	3	5	2	2	6	25
Tacoma	–	–	–	–	–	–	–	–	–	–	–	–	–	–	–	–	–	–	–	–	–	–	–	3	2	5	2	12
Red Deer	–	–	–	–	–	–	–	–	–	–	–	–	–	–	–	–	–	–	–	–	–	–	–	–	3	5	2	10
Prince George	–	–	–	–	–	–	–	–	–	–	–	–	–	–	–	–	–	–	–	–	–	–	–	–	–	–	2	2
Teams no longer operating																												
Victoria	–	–	–	2	2	5	7	4	3	3	1	8	6	2	3	4	2	1	2	4	4	2	–	1	2	2	–	70
Calgary	3	5	2	7	4	8	4	4	4	3	–	2	5	4	3	3	3	2	–	–	–	–	–	–	–	–	–	66
New Westm'r	–	–	–	6	8	7	9	5	8	6	5	1	–	–	–	2	1	1	2	1	–	–	–	–	–	–	–	62
Flin Flon	4	4	5	2	4	7	4	3	1	5	–	–	–	–	–	–	–	–	–	–	–	–	–	–	–	–	–	39
Winnipeg	3	2	4	2	5	4	4	–	4	–	–	–	1	4	1	–	–	–	–	–	–	–	–	–	–	–	–	34
Edmonton	4	4	5	6	6	2	3	2	–	–	2	–	–	–	–	–	–	–	–	–	–	–	–	–	–	–	–	34
Billings	–	–	–	–	–	–	–	–	–	4	3	4	2	–	–	–	–	–	–	–	–	–	–	–	–	–	–	13
Estevan	4	4	4	–	–	–	–	–	–	–	–	–	–	–	–	–	–	–	–	–	–	–	–	–	–	–	–	12
Kelowna	–	–	–	–	–	–	–	–	–	–	–	–	–	–	2	4	5	–	–	–	–	–	–	–	–	–	–	11
Nanaimo	–	–	–	–	–	–	–	–	–	–	–	–	–	5	1	–	–	–	–	–	–	–	–	–	–	–	–	6
Vancouver	–	–	–	2	–	–	–	–	–	–	–	–	–	–	–	–	–	–	–	–	–	–	–	–	–	–	–	2

Year	Total Western Drafted	Total Players Drafted	Western %
1969	20	84	23.8
1970	22	115	19.1
1971	28	117	23.9
1972	44	152	28.9
1973	49	168	29.2
1974	66	247	26.7
1975	57	217	26.3
1976	33	135	24.4
1977	44	185	23.8
1978	48	234	20.5
1979	37	126	29.4
1980	41	210	19.5
1981	37	211	17.5
1982	55	252	21.8
1983	41	242	16.9
1984	37	250	14.8
1985	48	252	19.0
1986	32	252	12.7
1987	36	252	14.3
1988	30	252	11.9
1989	44	252	17.5
1990	33	250	13.2
1991	40	264	15.2
1992	45	264	17.0
1993	44	286	15.4
1994	66	286	23.0
1995	55	234	23.5
Total	**1132**	**5789**	**19.5**

Quebec Major Junior Hockey League

Club	'69	'70	'71	'72	'73	'74	'75	'76	'77	'78	'79	'80	'81	'82	'83	'84	'85	'86	'87	'88	'89	'90	'91	'92	'93	'94	'95	Total
Shawinigan	3	2	1	6	1	5	3	–	3	–	–	2	2	5	5	2	–	2	1	–	2	–	2	3	1	1	2	54
Sherbrooke	–	–	2	2	4	3	7	5	6	3	4	1	5	2	–	–	–	–	–	–	–	–	–	–	3	2	4	53
Laval	–	–	–	1	–	2	1	1	4	2	1	–	–	2	1	2	–	5	3	1	3	3	4	1	2	5	4	48
Hull	–	–	–	–	–	–	3	2	2	3	–	3	1	–	3	1	–	4	3	2	2	3	3	3	3	1	3	45
Drummondville	2	4	1	4	2	1	–	–	–	–	–	–	–	–	–	1	2	2	2	4	1	–	4	2	2	1	4	39
Chicoutimi	–	–	–	–	–	1	–	–	5	1	1	3	6	1	3	–	3	1	2	2	1	1	–	1	1	3	2	38
Verdun	–	1	1	2	–	–	–	–	–	1	3	3	–	–	3	3	–	3	0	3	1	–	–	3	–	–	–	27
Granby	–	–	–	–	–	–	–	–	–	–	–	–	–	2	1	3	2	2	4	–	2	–	2	–	1	5	2	26
St. Jean	–	–	–	–	–	–	–	–	–	–	–	–	–	–	2	–	1	1	0	3	1	–	3	1	2	1	1	16
Victoriaville	–	–	–	–	–	–	–	–	–	–	–	–	–	–	–	–	–	–	–	4	–	1	–	2	6	1	1	15
Beauport	–	–	–	–	–	–	–	–	–	–	–	–	–	–	–	–	–	–	–	–	–	–	1	3	1	3	7	15
St. Hyacinthe	–	–	–	–	–	–	–	–	–	–	–	–	–	–	–	–	–	–	–	–	–	3	1	2	1	4	–	11
Val D'Or	–	–	–	–	–	–	–	–	–	–	–	–	–	–	–	–	–	–	–	–	–	–	–	–	–	1	2	3
Halifax	–	–	–	–	–	–	–	–	–	–	–	–	–	–	–	–	–	–	–	–	–	–	–	–	–	–	3	3
Teams no longer operating																												
Quebec	1	1	2	4	6	6	1	3	7	1	3	2	2	1	2	2	3	–	–	–	–	–	–	–	–	–	–	47
Trois Rivieres	–	1	2	2	2	2	3	2	6	3	2	2	2	1	3	–	3	–	1	3	3	1	2	1	–	–	–	47
Cornwall	2	1	2	6	4	8	1	3	1	6	1	5	5	–	–	–	–	–	–	–	–	–	–	–	–	–	–	45
Montreal	–	–	–	–	4	4	8	1	3	2	4	3	–	3	–	–	–	–	–	–	–	–	–	–	–	–	–	32
Sorel	2	3	1	3	1	8	1	1	3	–	–	–	5	–	–	–	–	–	–	–	–	–	–	–	–	–	–	28
Longueuil	–	–	–	–	–	–	–	–	–	–	–	–	–	–	1	2	1	2	1	–	–	2	3	–	–	–	–	12
St. Jerome	1	–	1	–	–	–	–	–	–	–	–	–	–	–	–	–	–	–	–	–	–	–	–	–	–	–	–	2

Year	Total Quebec Drafted	Total Players Drafted	Quebec %
1969	11	84	13.1
1970	13	115	11.3
1971	13	117	11.1
1972	30	152	19.7
1973	24	168	14.3
1974	40	247	16.2
1975	28	217	12.9
1976	18	135	13.3
1977	40	185	21.6
1978	22	234	9.4
1979	19	126	15.1
1980	24	210	11.4
1981	28	211	13.3
1982	17	252	6.7
1983	24	242	9.9
1984	16	250	6.4
1985	15	252	5.9
1986	22	252	8.7
1987	17	252	6.7
1988	22	252	8.7
1989	16	252	6.3
1990	14	250	5.6
1991	25	264	9.5
1992	22	264	8.3
1993	23	286	8.0
1994	28	286	9.7
1995	35	234	14.9
Total	**606**	**5789**	**10.4**

United States Colleges

Club	'69	'70	'71	'72	'73	'74	'75	'76	'77	'78	'79	'80	'81	'82	'83	'84	'85	'86	'87	'88	'89	'90	'91	'92	'93	'94	'95	Total
Minnesota	1	3	2	–	–	9	4	4	5	5	2	3	1	1	1	–	–	2	1	1	1	–	–	–	–	–	2	48
Michigan Tech	–	–	3	1	2	5	4	4	1	2	1	4	–	1	–	2	2	2	1	1	2	1	2	–	1	2	–	44
Michigan	1	–	–	–	2	2	3	3	1	6	–	4	–	–	–	1	1	–	1	2	3	5	4	2	1	1	–	43
Wisconsin	–	1	2	4	5	4	4	2	3	–	1	–	3	2	–	1	1	–	1	–	1	–	1	–	–	–	–	36
Boston U.	–	4	–	–	1	1	1	1	4	5	1	–	1	–	–	1	1	2	2	3	1	2	2	1	1	–	1	36
Denver	1	3	2	4	2	3	1	2	2	2	2	1	–	1	–	–	1	2	4	1	1	–	–	–	–	–	–	35
Michigan State	–	–	1	–	1	1	1	1	–	–	–	2	–	2	–	2	–	1	1	4	4	5	4	1	1	1	–	33
North Dakota	2	3	3	1	4	2	1	–	1	2	3	3	1	–	1	–	–	–	–	2	1	1	–	–	–	–	–	31
Providence	–	–	–	–	–	3	2	3	4	–	5	4	1	2	–	1	1	–	–	–	1	–	–	–	–	–	–	27
Clarkson	–	–	2	2	1	–	2	–	2	–	2	1	1	1	–	–	1	1	1	3	2	1	1	–	–	–	–	27
New Hampshire	–	–	–	1	1	3	6	–	4	1	1	2	1	1	1	2	–	–	1	–	–	–	–	–	–	–	–	25
Cornell	–	–	–	2	1	1	–	1	1	1	–	1	1	1	–	1	2	–	1	2	5	2	–	–	–	–	–	23
Bowling Green	–	–	–	–	–	1	3	2	1	1	1	1	–	–	1	–	–	–	3	2	1	3	1	–	–	–	–	21
Colorado	2	1	–	–	–	1	3	1	2	2	–	1	–	–	3	–	1	–	1	–	2	–	–	–	–	–	1	21
W. Michigan	–	–	–	–	–	–	–	2	–	–	2	–	–	2	2	–	2	1	1	1	1	4	–	2	–	–		20
Lake Superior	–	–	–	1	1	1	–	–	3	–	–	–	–	–	1	–	3	–	3	2	3	1	–	1	–	–		20
Notre Dame	–	–	2	3	–	7	2	–	3	1	1	–	–	–	–	–	–	–	–	–	–	–	–	–	–	–		19
RPI	–	–	–	–	1	–	–	1	3	–	1	2	1	1	–	1	–	2	2	–	–	3	1	–	–	–		19
St. Lawrence	–	–	–	–	–	1	–	1	4	–	–	–	3	–	1	1	1	1	1	1	2	–	1	–	–	–		19
Harvard	–	–	2	–	–	–	2	–	2	2	2	–	–	–	1	1	–	2	–	1	1	2	–	–	2	1	–	19
Boston College	–	1	–	–	–	–	1	1	–	5	–	2	1	1	–	–	–	1	2	–	2	–	–	–	–	–	–	17
Northern Mich.	–	–	–	–	–	–	–	–	–	4	–	1	2	1	–	–	–	4	1	2	–	1	–	–	–	–		16
Vermont	–	–	–	–	1	–	4	–	1	1	–	1	1	–	1	1	2	–	–	1	–	–	1	–	–	1	–	16
Miami of Ohio	–	–	–	–	–	–	–	–	–	–	–	–	–	–	–	1	–	2	4	2	–	2	1	1	–	–		13
Minn.-Duluth	–	–	2	1	–	–	–	–	1	1	–	–	1	–	–	–	–	–	–	2	1	2	1	–	–	–		12
Ohio State	–	–	–	–	–	–	–	–	2	1	–	–	–	–	–	1	–	2	2	–	1	1	1	1	–	–		12
Brown	–	–	–	1	2	1	–	3	2	–	1	–	–	–	1	–	–	–	–	–	–	–	1	–	–	–		11
Colgate	–	–	–	–	–	1	–	–	2	1	–	–	–	–	–	–	–	1	1	2	2	–	–	–	1	–		10
Yale	–	–	1	–	1	–	–	2	–	1	–	–	–	–	1	2	–	1	–	–	–	1	–	–				10
Maine	–	–	–	–	–	–	–	–	–	–	1	1	–	1	1	–	3	2	1	–	1	–	–	1	–	–		10
Northeastern	–	–	–	–	1	–	–	1	–	1	–	1	–	1	1	–	–	1	1	–	–	–	–	–				8
Princeton	–	–	–	–	–	1	–	1	–	1	1	1	–	1	–	–	–	1	–	1	–	–	–	1	–	–		8
Ferris State	–	–	–	–	–	–	–	–	–	–	–	–	–	–	–	–	2	1	1	1	2	–	–	–	–	–		7
St. Louis	–	–	–	–	1	2	–	1	2	–	–	–	–	–	–	–	–	–	–	–	–	–	–	–	–	–		6
U. of Ill.-Chi.	–	–	–	–	–	–	–	–	–	–	–	–	1	–	2	1	2	–	–	–	–	–	–	–	–			6
Pennsylvania	–	–	–	1	2	1	–	–	–	1	–	–	–	–	–	–	–	–	–	–	–	–	–	–	–			5
Dartmouth	–	–	–	1	–	–	–	–	1	–	1	–	–	–	–	1	–	–	–	1	–	–	–	–	–			5
Union College	–	–	–	–	–	–	–	–	4	–	–	–	–	–	–	–	–	–	–	–	–	–	–	–	–			4
Lowell	–	–	–	–	–	–	1	1	–	1	–	–	1	–	–	–	–	–	–	–	–	–	–	–	–			4
Merrimack	–	–	–	–	–	–	–	1	–	–	–	–	–	1	–	1	–	–	1	–	–	–	–	–				4
Alaska-Anchorage	–	–	–	–	–	–	–	–	–	–	–	–	–	–	–	–	–	2	1	–	1	–	–	–				4
Babson College	–	–	–	–	–	–	–	–	–	–	–	–	–	1	–	1	1	–	–	–	–	–	–	–				3
Alaska-Fairbanks	–	–	–	–	–	–	–	–	–	–	–	–	–	–	–	–	–	1	1	–	–	–	–	–				2
Salem State	–	–	–	–	–	1	–	–	–	–	–	–	–	–	–	–	–	–	–	–	–	–	–	–				1
Bemidji State	–	1	–	–	–	–	–	–	–	–	–	–	–	–	–	–	–	–	–	–	–	–	–	–				1
San Diego U.	–	–	–	–	–	–	–	–	–	–	–	–	–	1	–	–	–	–	–	–	–	–	–	–				1
Greenway	–	–	–	–	–	–	–	–	–	–	–	–	–	–	–	–	1	–	–	–	–	–	–	–				1
St. Anselen College	–	–	–	–	–	–	–	–	–	–	–	–	–	–	–	–	1	–	–	–	–	–	–	–				1
Hamilton College	–	–	–	–	–	–	–	–	–	–	–	–	–	–	–	–	1	–	–	–	–	–	–	–				1
St. Thomas	–	–	–	–	–	–	–	–	–	–	–	–	–	–	–	–	–	1	–	–	–	–	–	–				1
St. Cloud State	–	–	–	–	–	–	–	–	–	–	–	–	–	–	–	–	–	1	–	–	–	–	–	–				1
Amer. Int'l College	–	–	–	–	–	–	–	–	–	–	–	–	–	–	–	–	–	–	1	–	–	–	–	–				1
Wisc.-River Falls	–	–	–	–	–	–	–	–	–	–	–	–	–	–	–	–	–	–	–	–	–	–	–	–	–	1		1

Year	Total College Drafted	Total Players Drafted	College %
1969	7	84	8.3
1970	16	115	13.9
1971	22	117	18.8
1972	21	152	13.8
1973	25	168	14.9
1974	41	247	16.6
1975	59	217	26.7
1976	26	135	19.3
1977	49	185	26.5
1978	73	234	31.2
1979	15	126	11.9
1980	42	210	20.0
1981	21	211	10.0
1982	20	252	7.9
1983	14	242	5.8
1984	22	250	8.8
1985	20	252	7.9
1986	22	252	8.7
1987	40	252	15.9
1988	48	252	19.0
1989	48	252	19.0
1990	38	250	15.2
1991	43	264	16.3
1992	9	264	3.4
1993	17	286	5.9
1994	6	286	2.1
1995	5	234	2.1
Total	**769**	**5789**	**13.3**

United States High Schools (selected)

Club	'80	'81	'82	'83	'84	'85	'86	'87	'88	'89	'90	'91	'92	'93	'94	'95	Total
Northwood Prep (NY)	–	–	2	1	–	2	2	4	1	1	3	1	–	1	1	–	19
Belmont Hill (MA)	–	–	–	1	–	2	1	3	2	1	2	–	1	–	–	–	16
Edina (MN)	–	1	4	2	2	–	–	1	2	2	1	–	1	–	–	–	16
Hill-Murray (MN)	–	–	–	–	3	–	3	3	–	2	3	–	–	–	1	–	15
Cushing Acad. (MA)	–	–	–	–	1	–	–	3	2	3	1	–	2	2	–		14
Mount St. Charles (RI)	–	1	–	3	1	–	2	1	2	1	1	–	–	–	–	–	12
Cilver Mil. Acad. (IN)	–	–	–	–	–	–	2	1	2	2	1	2	2	–			12
Catholic Memorial (MA)	–	–	–	–	–	2	–	1	1	2	–	–	2	1	2	–	11
Canterbury (CT)	–	–	–	–	–	–	2	–	3	–	2	–	2	1	–	–	10
Matignon (MA)	1	1	1	–	3	–	–	3	–	–	–	1	–	–	–	–	10
Roseau (MN)	1	–	1	1	1	–	1	–	–	–	1	3	1	–	–	–	10

Year	Total USHS Drafted	Total Players Drafted	USHS %
1980	7	210	3.3
1981	17	211	8.1
1982	47	252	18.6
1983	35	242	14.5
1984	44	250	17.6
1985	48	252	19.1
1986	40	252	15.9
1987	69	252	27.4
1988	56	252	22.2
1989	47	252	18.7
1990	57	250	22.8
1991	37	264	14.0
1992	25	264	9.5
1993	33	286	11.5
1994	28	286	9.7
1995	2	234	0.9
Total	**592**	**5789**	**10.2**

International

Country	'69	'70	'71	'72	'73	'74	'75	'76	'77	'78	'79	'80	'81	'82	'83	'84	'85	'86	'87	'88	'89	'90	'91	'92	'93	'94	'95	Total
Sweden	–	–	–	–	–	5	2	5	2	8	5	9	14	14	10	14	16	9	15	14	9	7	11	11	18	17	8	223
USSR/CIS	–	–	–	–	–	–	1	–	2	–	–	3	5	1	2	1	2	11	18	14	25	45	31	35	27			223
Czech Republic and Slovakia	–	–	–	–	–	–	–	2	1	–	4	139	8	6	11	5	8	21	9	17	15	18	21					181
Finland	1	–	–	1	3	2	3	2	–	4	12	5	9	10	4	10	6	7	3	9	6	8	9	8	12			134
Germany	–	–	–	–	–	–	–	2	–	–	2	1	2	1	–	1	2	–	1	–	1	1	3	1	1			19
Norway	–	–	–	–	–	–	–	–	–	–	–	–	–	–	–	–	–	2	–	2	1	–	–					5
Switzerland	–	–	–	–	–	1	–	–	–	–	–	–	–	–	–	–	–	–	–	–	1	–	2	1	–			5
Denmark	–	–	–	–	–	–	–	–	–	–	–	–	–	–	1	1	–	–	–	–	–	–	–					2
Scotland	–	–	–	–	–	–	–	–	–	–	–	–	–	–	–	1	–	–	–	–	–	–	–					1
Poland	–	–	–	–	–	–	–	–	–	–	–	–	–	–	–	–	–	–	–	–	–	–	1	–	–			1
Japan	–	–	–	–	–	–	–	–	–	–	–	–	–	–	–	–	–	–	–	–	–	1	–	–	–			1

Sweden

Club	'74	'75	'76	'77	'78	'79	'80	'81	'82	'83	'84	'85	'86	'87	'88	'89	'90	'91	'92	'93	'94	'95	Total
Djurgarden Stockholm	1	1	1	–	–	1	2	–	1	2	1	–	1	2	–	1	1	2	1	1	–	3	22
Leksand	1	–	1	–	1	–	2	2	1	1	2	1	2	1	–	2	–	2	–	2	2	–	18
Farjestad Karlstad	–	–	2	2	–	1	2	1	1	2	–	–	1	–	1	2	1	–	2	19
AIK Solna	–	–	1	–	1	1	–	2	3	1	–	4	–	–	–	1	1	1	–	1	–	17
MoDo Hockey Ornskoldsvik	–	–	1	–	1	–	1	–	2	–	1	–	–	2	2	5	–	–	15
Brynas Gavle	1	–	–	1	1	1	1	–	1	2	–	4	–	–	–	–	–	1	–	13
Sodertalje	–	–	1	–	1	1	1	2	2	2	–	2	–	–	1	–	13
Vastra Frolunda Goteborg	–	–	–	–	–	–	2	1	–	1	1	–	1	–	1	3	1	11
Skelleftea	–	1	1	–	–	1	1	2	1	–	–	–	–	–	9
Vasteras	–	–	–	–	–	–	–	–	–	–	2	2	1	1	–	1	1	–	8
Rogle Angelholm	–	–	–	–	–	–	–	–	1	2	–	–	2	2	1	8
Lulea	–	–	–	1	1	–	1	1	1	–	1	–	–	6
Sundsvall Timra[1]	–	–	1	2	–	1	1	–	–	–	1	–	6
HV 71 Jonkoping	–	–	–	1	–	–	–	1	1	–	1	2	–	5
Bjorkloven Umea	–	2	1	–	1	–	1	–	–	–	–	5
Orebro	–	1	1	–	1	–	–	1	–	–	4
Nacka	–	–	1	1	–	–	1	–	1	–	4
Hammarby Stockholm	–	–	–	–	–	–	1	–	1	1	1	4
Malmo	–	–	–	1	–	–	1	1	–	3
Falun	–	–	1	–	1	–	–	1	–	3
Team Kiruna	–	–	–	–	1	–	–	1	1	3
Boden	1	–	–	–	1	–	1	–	3
Pitea	–	–	1	–	1	–	1	–	3
Mora	–	–	–	1	–	–	1	2
Troja	–	–	1	–	1	–	2
Ostersund	–	–	–	1	–	1
Almtuna	–	–	–	–	1	1
Danderyd Hockey	–	–	1	–	1
Fagersta	–	1	–	1
Huddinge	–	–	1	1
Karskoga	–	1	–	1
Stocksund	–	–	1	1
S/G Hockey 83 Gavle	–	1	–	1
Talje	–	1	1
Tunabro	1	–	1
Uppsala	–	1	1
Grums	–	1	–	1
Vallentuna	–	1	1

Former club names: [1]–Timra

Russia/C.I.S.

Club	'74	'75	'76	'77	'78	'79	'80	'81	'82	'83	'84	'85	'86	'87	'88	'89	'90	'91	'92	'93	'94	'95	Total
CSKA Moscow	–	–	–	–	1	–	–	1	4	–	1	1	5	8	3	4	7	3	5	2	46
Dynamo Moscow	–	–	–	–	–	–	–	–	2	3	4	7	10	2	1	7	36
Krylja Sovetov Moscow	–	–	–	–	–	–	–	1	1	2	4	3	1	5	3	20
Spartak Moscow	–	–	–	–	1	–	1	–	1	–	–	1	4	–	6	1	15
Traktor Chelyabinsk	–	–	–	–	–	–	–	2	–	–	2	7	1	1	13
Sokol Kiev	–	–	–	–	–	1	–	1	–	1	2	3	–	1	–	2	11
Pardaugava Riga[1]	–	1	–	–	–	–	–	1	2	–	1	4	1	–	10
Khimik Voskresensk	–	–	–	–	–	–	–	1	3	1	2	–	1	–	9
Torpedo Yaroslavl	–	–	–	–	–	–	–	1	2	–	–	1	5	9
SKA St. Peterburg[2]	–	–	–	1	–	–	–	2	1	–	1	–	6
Dynamo-2 Moscow	–	–	–	–	–	–	2	1	2	–	5
Salavat Yulayev Ufa	–	–	–	–	–	–	2	2	1	5
Torpedo Ust Kamenogorsk	–	–	–	–	–	1	1	2	1	5
Tivali Minsk[3]	–	–	–	–	1	–	2	1	–	4
Kristall Elektrostal	–	–	–	–	–	3	–	3
Lada Togliatti	–	–	–	1	2	–	3
Torpedo Nizhny Novgorod[4]	–	–	–	1	–	2	–	3
Avangard Omsk	–	–	–	–	3	–	3
Verstal Cherepovets[5]	–	–	–	1	1	–	1	3
Molot Perm	–	–	–	1	1	2
Argus Moscow	–	–	1	–	1
Dizelist Penza	–	–	1	–	1
Dynamo Kharkov	–	1	–	–	1
Izhorets St. Peterburg	–	–	1	–	1
Khimik Novopolotsk	–	–	1	–	1
Kristall Saratov	–	–	1	–	1
Krylja Sovetov-2 Moscow	–	–	1	–	1
Itil Kazan	–	–	1	–	1
Mechel Chelyabinsk	–	–	1	–	1
CSKA-2 Moscow	–	–	–	1	1
Torpedo-2 Yaroslavl	–	–	–	1	1
CSK VVS Samara	–	–	–	1	1

Former club names: [1]–Dynamo Riga, HC Riga, [2]–SKA Leningrad, [3]–Dynamo Minsk, [4]–Torpedo Gorky, [5]–Metallurg Cherepovets

Year	Total International Drafted	Total Players Drafted	International %
1969	1	84	1.2
1970	0	115	0
1971	0	117	0
1972	0	152	0
1973	0	168	0
1974	6	247	2.4
1975	6	217	2.8
1976	8	135	5.9
1977	5	185	2.7
1978	16	234	6.8
1979	6	126	4.8
1980	13	210	6.2
1981	32	211	15.2
1982	35	252	13.9
1983	34	242	14.0
1984	40	250	17.6
1985	31	252	12.3
1986	28	252	11.1
1987	38	252	15.1
1988	39	252	15.5
1989	38	252	15.1
1990	53	250	21.2
1991	55	264	20.8
1992	84	264	31.4
1993	78	286	27.3
1994	80	286	27.9
1995	69	234	29.5
Total	**795**	**5789**	**13.7**

Note: Players drafted in the International category played outside North America in their draft year. European-born players drafted from the OHL, QMJHL, WHL or U.S. Colleges are not counted as International players. See Country of Origin, below.

1995 Entry Draft Analysis

Country of Origin

Country	Players Drafted
Canada	138
Russia	24
Czech Republic	21
USA	16
Finland	13
Sweden	8
Slovakia	7
Ukraine	3
Germany	2
Kazahkstan	1
Austria	1

Position

Position	Players Drafted
Defense	80
Center	47
Left Wing	42
Right Wing	38
Goaltender	27

Birth Year

Year	Players Drafted
1977	131
1976	71
1975	22
1974	1
1973	4
1972	1
1971	2
1970	1
1969	1

Czech Republic and Slovakia

Club	'69	'70	'71	'72	'73	'74	'75	'76	'77	'78	'79	'80	'81	'82	'83	'84	'85	'86	'87	'88	'89	'90	'91	'92	'93	'94	'95	Total
Dukla Jihlava	-	-	-	-	-	-	-	-	-	-	-	-	-	2	4	3	1	-	3	1	1	3	2	1	1	1	2	25
Chemopetrol Litvinov[1]	-	-	-	-	-	-	-	-	-	-	-	-	3	1	2	-	-	-	2	2	1	3	2	4	2	-	-	22
Sparta Praha	-	-	-	-	-	-	-	-	-	-	-	-	-	1	-	2	1	1	1	2	1	2	-	1	1	-	1	14
HC Ceske Budejovice[6]	-	-	-	-	-	-	-	-	-	-	-	-	-	2	1	1	-	1	-	-	1	2	-	-	1	2	3	14
HC Kladno[7]	-	-	-	-	-	-	-	-	-	-	-	-	-	2	1	-	1	-	1	-	-	1	2	-	1	1	1	11
Slovan Bratislava	-	-	-	-	-	-	-	1	1	-	-	-	2	-	-	-	1	1	1	-	-	1	-	-	3	-	-	11
ZPS Zlin[2]	-	-	-	-	-	-	-	-	-	-	-	-	-	-	-	-	1	-	1	1	1	-	2	2	1	-	2	11
Dukla Trencin	-	-	-	-	-	-	-	-	-	-	-	-	-	-	-	1	-	-	-	1	1	2	-	2	2	-	1	10
HC Vitkovice[8]	-	-	-	-	-	-	1	-	-	-	1	-	-	-	-	-	-	-	-	-	-	1	-	1	3	1	1	9
HC Kosice[3]	-	-	-	-	-	-	-	-	-	-	-	-	1	2	-	2	1	-	-	2	-	-	-	-	-	-	-	8
Interconex Plzen[9]	-	-	-	-	-	-	-	-	-	-	-	-	-	-	-	-	-	1	-	-	1	1	3	-	-	1	1	8
HC Pardubice[4]	-	-	-	-	-	-	-	-	-	-	-	-	-	-	2	-	2	-	1	-	-	-	-	-	-	2	1	8
Zetor Brno	-	-	-	-	-	-	-	-	-	-	-	-	-	-	-	-	1	3	-	2	1	-	-	-	-	-	-	7
HC Olomouc[5]	-	-	-	-	-	-	-	-	-	-	-	-	-	-	-	-	-	-	-	-	-	2	-	1	-	1	2	6
AC Nitra	-	-	-	-	-	-	-	-	-	-	-	-	-	-	-	-	-	-	-	2	-	1	-	-	-	-	-	3
ZTS Martin	-	-	-	-	-	-	-	-	-	-	-	-	-	-	-	1	-	-	-	-	-	-	-	-	-	-	2	3
Slavia Praha	-	-	-	-	-	-	-	-	-	-	-	-	-	-	-	-	1	-	-	-	-	-	-	1	-	-	-	2
ZTK Zvolen	-	-	-	-	-	-	-	-	-	-	-	-	-	-	-	-	-	-	-	-	-	-	1	-	-	1	-	2
IS Banska Bystrica	-	-	-	-	-	-	-	-	-	-	-	-	-	-	-	-	-	-	-	-	-	-	-	-	-	1	1	2
Ingstav Brno	-	-	-	-	-	-	-	-	-	-	-	-	-	-	-	1	-	-	-	-	-	-	-	-	-	-	-	1
Partizan Liptovsky Mikulas	-	-	-	-	-	-	-	-	-	-	-	-	-	-	-	-	-	-	-	-	1	-	-	-	-	-	-	1
VTJ Pisek	-	-	-	-	-	-	-	-	-	-	-	-	-	-	-	-	-	-	-	-	1	-	-	-	-	-	-	1
ZPA Presov	-	-	-	-	-	-	-	-	-	-	-	-	-	-	-	-	-	-	-	-	-	-	-	-	1	-	-	1
Banik Sokolov	-	-	-	-	-	-	-	-	-	-	-	-	-	-	-	-	-	-	-	-	-	-	-	-	-	-	1	1

Former club names: [1]–CHZ Litvinov, [2]–TJ Gottwaldov, TJ Zlin, [3]–VSZ Kosice, [4]–Tesla Pardubice, [5]–DS Olomouc, [6]–Motor Ceske Budejovice, [7]–Poldi Kladno, [8]–TJ Vitkovice, [9]–Skoda Plzen

Finland

Club	'69	'70	'71	'72	'73	'74	'75	'76	'77	'78	'79	'80	'81	'82	'83	'84	'85	'86	'87	'88	'89	'90	'91	'92	'93	'94	'95	Total
TPS Turku	-	-	-	-	-	-	-	-	-	-	-	1	6	-	-	1	1	-	-	-	-	-	-	-	3	2	3	17
HIFK Helsinki	1	-	-	-	-	-	1	-	1	-	-	1	1	2	2	1	-	-	2	1	-	-	-	-	2	-	1	16
Ilves Tampere	-	-	-	-	-	-	-	1	2	-	-	2	-	2	2	-	1	-	1	-	1	1	-	-	-	-	2	15
Jokerit Helsinki	-	-	-	-	-	-	-	-	-	-	2	1	-	1	-	1	1	2	-	3	-	1	-	-	-	-	-	12
Assat Pori	-	-	-	-	2	-	-	-	-	-	-	1	-	2	2	-	-	-	1	-	1	-	-	-	1	1	1	12
Tappara Tampere	-	-	-	-	-	-	-	1	-	-	-	2	-	-	-	4	1	-	1	-	-	-	-	-	-	-	1	10
Karpat Oulu	-	-	-	-	-	-	-	-	1	-	1	-	1	-	2	2	-	-	-	1	-	1	-	-	-	-	-	9
Lukko Rauma	-	-	-	-	-	-	2	1	-	-	-	-	2	1	-	-	1	-	-	1	-	1	-	-	-	-	-	9
Kiekko-Espoo	-	-	-	-	-	-	-	-	-	-	-	-	-	-	-	-	-	-	-	1	1	2	-	2	-	1	1	8
Reipas Lahti	-	-	-	-	-	-	-	-	-	-	-	1	1	1	-	-	-	-	-	-	2	-	1	-	-	-	-	6
KalPa Kuopio	-	-	-	-	-	-	-	-	-	-	-	-	-	-	-	-	-	-	-	-	-	-	1	2	-	1	-	4
HPK Hameenlinna	-	-	-	-	-	-	-	-	-	-	-	-	-	-	-	-	-	-	1	-	-	2	-	-	-	-	-	3
Kiekoo-67 Turku	-	-	-	-	-	-	-	-	-	-	-	-	-	-	-	-	-	-	-	-	-	-	-	-	-	-	3	3
SaiPa Lappeenranta	-	-	-	-	-	-	-	-	-	-	-	-	1	-	-	-	-	-	-	-	1	-	-	-	-	-	-	2
Sapko Savonlinna	-	-	-	-	-	-	-	-	-	-	-	-	-	-	-	-	-	1	1	-	-	-	-	-	-	-	-	2
Sport Vaasa	-	-	-	-	-	-	-	-	-	-	-	-	-	-	-	-	-	-	1	1	-	-	-	-	-	-	-	2
GrIFK Kauniainen	-	-	-	-	-	-	-	-	-	-	-	-	-	-	-	-	-	-	-	1	-	-	-	-	-	-	-	1
JyP HT Jyvaskyla	-	-	-	-	-	-	-	-	-	-	-	-	-	-	-	-	-	-	-	-	1	-	-	-	-	-	-	1
Koo Koo Kouvola	-	-	-	-	-	-	-	-	-	-	-	-	-	-	-	-	-	-	-	-	-	-	1	-	-	-	-	1
S-Kiekko Seinajoki	-	-	-	-	-	-	-	-	-	-	-	-	-	-	-	1	-	-	-	-	-	-	-	-	-	-	-	1

Dave Babych, right, seen here celebrating a goal during his five-season stint with the Hartford Whalers, was drafted second overall in the 1980 Entry Draft by the Winnipeg Jets. Yuri Khmylev, below, who split the 1994-95 season between the Soviet Wings and the Buffalo Sabres, was the 108th player selected in the 1992 Entry Draft.

First Round Draft Selections, 1995

1. OTTAWA • **BRYAN BERARD** • D
The fourth U.S.-born player to be selected first overall in the NHL Entry Draft, Bryan Berard had an outstanding season in 1994-95. The 6'1" rearguard was named the OHL's rookie of the year and the league's best defenseman after collecting 20 goals and 74 points for the Detroit Jr. Red Wings. Berard also represented the United States at the 1995 World Junior Championships, notching one assist in seven games.

2. NY ISLANDERS • **WADE REDDEN** • D
A strong skating defenseman with deceptive speed and a hard, accurate shot, Wade Redden was a WHL East Second Team All-Star in 1994-95. Redden, who compiled a plus/minus rating of +49 during the 1994-95 campaign, finished seventh in scoring among WHL defensemen with 14 goals and 46 assists for the Brandon Wheat Kings. The WHL's rookie of the year in 1993-94, Redden also played for Team Canada at the 1995 World Junior Hockey Championships.

3. LOS ANGELES • **AKI-PETTERI BERG** • D
The first Finnish-born player to be selected among the top five at the NHL Entry Draft, Aki-Petteri Berg has the speed, size and skill to be a dominant blueliner in the NHL. Blessed with soft hands and excellent vision, the 6'3" Berg played the majority of the 1994-95 season with Kiekko '67, but did see limited action with TPS of the Finnish elite league.

4. ANAHEIM • **CHAD KILGER** • C
A strong, power forward blessed with both size and skill, Chad Kilger had an outstanding season with the OHL's Kingston Frontenacs, collecting 42 goals and 53 assists. The Midget player of the year in 1992-93 when he notched 66 points for Cornwall, Kilger has become known as one the best skaters in the OHL as well as being named one of the league's elite prospects. He played in the CHL All-Star Game in 1994-95 and was Kingston's nominee for Scholastic Player of the Year.

5. TAMPA BAY • **DAYMOND LANGKOW** • C
Daymond Langkow had a superb season for the Tri-City Americans in 1994-95, leading the WHL in goals (67) and points (140). In his three years with Tri-City, Langkow improved his goal, assist and point totals in each season. In addition to being a talented scorer, Langkow is also known for his defensive skills, using his strong work ethic and tenacious forechecking ability to become a team leader.

6. EDMONTON • **STEVE KELLY** • C
A creative two-way forward, Steve Kelly has the ability to control the boards at one end of the rink and lead a scoring charge at the other. In his three seasons with the Prince Albert Raiders, Kelly has shown steady improvement in all areas of his play. In 1994-95, Kelly scored 31 goals, including six game-winning markers, and added 41 assists. He was also named Prince Albert's Scholastic Player of the Year.

7. WINNIPEG • **SHANE DOAN** • RW
Highly regarded prospect Shane Doan had another fine season with the Kamloops Blazers in 1994-95, finishing third in team scoring with 37 goals and 94 points. Winner of the WHL's "Diamond in the Rough" award in 1992-93, Doan has progressed steadily in his junior career, improving from a 19-point season in 1993 to the 94-point campaign in 1995. A strong skater and dedicated team leader, Doan won the Stafford Smythe Memorial Trophy as the MVP of the 1995 Memorial Cup.

8. MONTREAL • **TERRY RYAN** • LW
Years of patience and hard work finally paid off for Newfoundland native Terry Ryan when he was selected by Montreal in the 1995 Entry Draft. Ryan, who left home at age 15 and moved from Canada's Atlantic Coast to the USA's Pacific Northwest to pursue his career, was drafted by Tri-City of the WHL in 1993. He finished third in team scoring in 1994-95 with 50 goals and 60 assists. He collected 11 game-winning goals in 1994-95 and finished third in playoff scoring with 12 goals and 27 points.

9. BOSTON • **KYLE McLAREN** • D
With his lanky 6'4" frame and long, smooth strides, Kyle McLaren is a prototype NHL defenseman. A member of the Tacoma Rockets for the past two seasons, McLaren compiled 13 goals and 19 assists in 47 games in 1994-95 and added two points in four playoff games. A top-scoring bantam rearguard with Lethbridge, McLaren plays the game with a combination of controlled aggression and finesse.

10. FLORIDA • **RADEK DVORAK** • LW
Although he was sidelined for most of the 1994-95 schedule with a broken hand, Radek Dvorak still had a fine season with Ceske Budejovice of the Czech Extraleague, collecting eight points in 10 games. A speedy right winger with terrific stickhandling and skating ability, Dvorak played for the Czech Junior team at the 1995 World Junior Championships and the Four Nations tournament.

11. DALLAS • **JAROME IGINLA** • C
A multi-talented athlete who was also an all-star catcher with the Canadian National Junior baseball team, Jarome Iginla is also a highly-prized right winger with the Kamloops Blazers. After scoring only eight goals in his rookie junior season, Iginla had a tremendous sophomore campaign, collecting 33 goals and 71 points. Iginla, who won the George Parsons Trophy for sportsmanship, had a plus/minus rating of +25 in 1994-95.

12. SAN JOSE • **TEEMU RIIHIJARVI** • RW
At 6'6", Finnish native Teemu Riihijarvi was the tallest player selected in the first round of the 1995 Entry Draft. For the past two seasons, Riihijarvi has played for Kiekko-Espoo's junior and senior clubs, receiving the bulk of his playing time with the junior squad. In 1994-95, he notched 10 goals and four assists in 30 games of junior competition and added one goal in 13 games with the senior team.

13. HARTFORD • **JEAN-SEBASTIEN GIGUERE** • G
One of the top young goaltenders in Quebec, Jean-Sebastien Giguere was a midget all-star and winner of the Ken Dryden Award as his league's top goaltender in 1992-93 when he backstopped his team to the Quebec AAA championship. In his first season of major junior play, Giguere was a QMJHL First Team All-Star with a goals-against average of 3.21 in 25 games. In 1994-95, he helped lead the expansion Halifax Mooseheads into the playoffs with 14 wins and a 3.94 GAA in 47 games.

14. BUFFALO • **JAY McKEE** • D
A hard-hitting rearguard who stresses the defensive aspect of his position, Jay McKee was named the Niagara Falls Thunder's best defenseman and the OHL's Central Division's best bodychecker in 1994-95. McKee will need to put more muscle on his slender 6'2½" frame, but he already has great acceleration and a competitive mean streak that adds to his tenacious nature. In 1994-95, this Kingston native collected nine goals and 19 assists in 65 games with the Thunder.

15. TORONTO • **JEFF WARE** • D
The second member of the Ware family to join the Toronto organization, Jeff Ware was named to the Ontario Under-17 All-Star Team in 1993-94 when he patrolled the blueline for the Jr. A Wexford Raiders. He enjoyed an impressive rookie season in the OHL in 1994-95, earning a berth on the OHL's All-Rookie Team as a member of the Oshawa Generals. He collected 13 points in 55 games and played for the OHL in the CHL All-Star Challenge.

16. BUFFALO • **MARTIN BIRON** • G
Martin Biron had a tremendous rookie season with Beauport of the Quebec Major Junior League in 1994-95, winning a trio of prestigious awards. Biron was named the top goaltender for 1994-95 in both the Canadian Hockey League and the QMJHL and also earned a berth on the QMJHL's All-Rookie Team. During the 1994-95 campaign, Biron led all Quebec junior goaltenders with a 2.48 goals-against average, 29 victories and three shutouts.

17. WASHINGTON • **BRAD CHURCH** • LW
Mixing physical intimidation with aggressive defensive play has made Brad Church one of the WHL's top prospects. In his first junior season, Church was named the Prince Albert Raiders' top rookie after compiling 33 goals and 53 points in 61 games. A strong skater who uses his size and strength to knock opponents off their game and off the puck, Church's totals slipped slightly in 1994-95, but he finished the season by collecting 15 points in 15 post-season games.

18. NEW JERSEY • **PETR SYKORA** • C
A member of the Czech National Junior Team in 1994 and 1995, Petr Sykora sustained a serious shoulder injury only 29 games into the 1994-95 season. At 17 years and 71 days of age, he became the youngest player to ever skate in the IHL when he moved to North America late in the 1993-94 season and appeared in 13 games for Cleveland. He later signed with the Detroit Vipers, notching 29 points in 1994-95 before suffering his season-ending injury.

19. CHICAGO • **DMITRI NABOKOV** • C/LW
Despite being only 18 years old, Dmitri Nabokov has already played two years with the Soviet Wings in the Russian National League. Although he needs to improve his skating skills, Nabokov is a natural scorer who can carry the puck through traffic. In 1994-95, he scored 15 goals and added 12 assists in 49 games for the fourth-highest total on the team. The 6'2", 209 pound forward was rated as one of the best prospects in Russia.

20. CALGARY • **DENIS GAUTHIER** • D
In his three seasons with the Drummondville Voltigeurs, Denis Gauthier has matured into one of the most complete rearguards in the QMJHL. A hard-hitting physical blueliner who plays a "stay-at-home" style, Gauthier had his finest offensive season in 1994-95, scoring seven goals and earning 31 assists in 64 games. The QMJHL's Player of the Month for December, 1994, Gauthier was named Drummondville's Defensive Player of the Year for 1994-95.

21. BOSTON • **SEAN BROWN** • D
Named one of the top defensive defensemen in the Ontario Hockey League in a coaches' poll, Sean Brown had a productive sophomore season with the Belleville Bulls. A hard-working, "clean-up-your-own-zone-first" blueliner, Brown's mobility and strength allows him to neutralize opponents with crushing bodychecks. In 1994-95, Brown collected 18 points and 200 penalty minutes in 58 games with the Bulls.

22. PHILADELPHIA • **BRIAN BOUCHER** • G
An outstanding goaltender with Mount St. Charles high school where he compiled a goals-against average of less than 1.00 in both 1992-93 and 1993-94, Brian Boucher continued his fine play in goal with the Tri-City Americans in 1994-95. His 3.29 GAA was the sixth lowest in the WHL while his save percentage of .907 was the second-best in the league. Named the CHL's Rookie of the Month in December, 1994, Boucher also earned the nod as Tri-City's Scholastic Player of the Year.

23. WASHINGTON • **MIIKA ELOMO** • C
One of Finland's finest young prospects and a natural goal scorer, Miika Elomo was the third Finn selected in the first round of the 1995 Entry Draft. Elomo, who was the youngest member of the Finnish Team at the 1995 World Junior Championships, spent the 1994-95 season with Kiekko-67, where he notched nine goals in only 14 games. An excellent skater with tremendous straightaway speed, Elomo played for the TPS junior team in 1993-94, scoring seven goals.

24. PITTSBURGH • **ALEXEI MOROZOV** • RW
Another outstanding forward from Moscow's Soviet Wings, Alexei Morozov had a fine season in 1994-95, collecting 27 points in 48 games. Morozov made his first-division debut as a 16-year old in 1993-94, and although he failed to register a point in seven games, his skills and enthusiasm earned a full-time spot on the team in 1994-95. He was a linemate of Dmitri Nabokov, who was drafted 19th.

25. COLORADO • **MARC DENIS** • G
Marc Denis was the third goaltender from the Quebec Major Junior Hockey League to be selected in the first round of the 1995 Entry Draft. After rapidly rising through Quebec's AAA bantam and midget programs, Denis joined the Chicoutimi Sagueneens and won 17 games with a goals-against average of 3.48. His save percentage of .893 was the fifth-best mark in the QMJHL in 1994-95.

26. DETROIT • **MAXIM KUZNETSOV** • D
A strapping 6'5" rearguard who enjoys the physical side of the game, Maxim Kuznetsov is a stay-at-home defenseman who was the last player cut from the Russian National Under-18 Team in 1995. In 1994-95, he spent the majority of the season with the Moscow Dynamo's junior club, but was called up to the senior squad for 11 games. Kuznetsov was bothered by small injuries in 1994-95.

Players selected second through tenth in the 1995 NHL Entry Draft:
Top row, left to right: 2. Wade Redden, D, NY Islanders; 3. Aki-Petteri Berg, D, L.A. Kings
Second row: 4. Chad Kilger, C, Anaheim, 5. Daymond Langkow, C, Tampa Bay.
Third row: 6. Steve Kelly, C, Edmonton; 7. Shane Doan, RW, Winnipeg.
Fourth row: 8. Terry Ryan, LW, Montreal; 9. Kyle McLaren, D, Boston.
Bottom row: 10. Radek Dvorak, LW, Florida.

1995 Entry Draft

Transferred draft choice notation:

Example: Col.-Ana. represents a draft choice transferred **from** Colorado **to** Anaheim.

Pick	Player	Claimed By	Amateur Club	Position
ROUND # 1				
1	BERARD, Bryan	Ott.	Detroit	D
2	REDDEN, Wade	NYI	Brandon	D
3	BERG, Aki-Petteri	L.A.	Kiekko-67 Turku	D
4	KILGER, Chad	Ana.	Kingston	C
5	LANGKOW, Daymond	T.B.	Tri-City	C
6	KELLY, Steve	Edm.	Prince Albert	C
7	DOAN, Shane	Wpg.	Kamloops	RW
8	RYAN, Terry	Mtl.	Tri-City	LW
9	McLAREN, Kyle	Hfd.-Bos.	Tacoma	D
10	DVORAK, Radek	Fla.	HC Ceske Budejovice	W
11	IGINLA, Jarome	Dal.	Kamloops	C
12	RIIHIJARVI, Teemu	S.J.	Kiekko-Espoo Jr.	LW
13	GIGUERE, J-Sebastien	NYR-Hfd.	Halifax	G
14	McKEE, Jay	Van.-Buf.	Niagara Falls	D
15	WARE, Jeff	Tor.	Oshawa	D
16	BIRON, Martin	Buf.	Beauport	G
17	CHURCH, Brad	Wsh.	Prince Albert	LW
18	SYKORA, Petr	N.J.	Detroit	C
19	NABOKOV, Dmitri	Chi.	Krylja Sovetov	C
20	GAUTHIER, Denis Jr.	Cgy.	Drummondville	D
21	BROWN, Sean	Bos.	Belleville	D
22	BOUCHER, Brian	Phi.	Tri-City	G
23	ELOMO, Miika	St.L.-Wsh.	Kiekko-67 Turku	LW
24	MOROZOV, Alexei	Pit.	Krylja Sovetov	RW
25	DENIS, Marc	Col.	Chicoutimi	G
26	KUZNETSOV, Maxim	Det.	Dynamo Moscow	D
ROUND # 2				
27	MORO, Marc	Ott.	Kingston	D
28	HLAVAC, Jan	NYI	Sparta Praha	LW
29	WESENBERG, Brian	Ana.	Guelph	RW
30	McBAIN, Mike	T.B.	Red Deer	D
31	LARAQUE, Georges	Edm.	St-Jean	RW
32	CHOUINARD, Marc	Wpg.	Beauport	C
33	MacLEAN, Donald	L.A.	Beauport	C
34	DOIG, Jason	Mtl.-Wpg.	Laval	D
35	FEDOTOV, Sergei	Hfd.	Dynamo Moscow	D
36	MacDONALD, Aaron	Fla.	Swift Current	G
37	COTE, Patrick	Dal.	Beauport	LW
38	ROED, Peter	S.J.	White Bear Lake	C
39	DUBE, Christian	NYR	Sherbrooke	C
40	McALLISTER, Chris	Van.	Saskatoon	D
41	SMITH, Denis (D.J.)	Tor.-NYI	Windsor	D
42	DUTIAUME, Mark	Buf.	Brandon	LW
43	HAY, Dwayne	Wsh.	Guelph	LW
44	PERROTT, Nathan	N.J.	Oshawa	RW
45	LAFLAMME, Christian	Chi.	Beauport	D
46	SMIRNOV, Pavel	Cgy.	Molot Perm	RW/C
47	SCHAFER, Paxton	Bos.	Medicine Hat	G
48	KENNY, Shane	Phi.	Owen Sound	D
49	HECHT, Jochen	St.L.	Mannheim	C
50	ROSA, Pavel	Pit.-L.A.	Chemopetrol Litvinov Jr.	RW
51	BEAUDOIN, Nic	Col.	Detroit	LW
52	AUDET, Philippe	Det.	Granby	LW
ROUND # 3				
53	LARSEN, Brad	Ott.	Swift Current	LW
54	PEPPERALL, Ryan	NYI-Tor.	Kitchener	RW
55	LECLERC, Mike	Ana.	Brandon	LW
56	WILLIS, Shane	T.B.	Prince Albert	RW
57	ZIB, Lukas	Edm.	HC Ceske Budejovice	D
58	LAPLANTE, Darryl	Wpg.-Det.	Moose Jaw	C
59	TSYPLAKOV, Vladimir	L.A.	Fort Wayne	LW
60	GUREN, Miloslav	Mtl.	ZPS Zlin	D
61	COURVILLE, Larry	Hfd.-Chi.-Van.	Oshawa	LW
62	O'GRADY, Mike	Fla.	Lethbridge	D
63	BUZEK, Petr	Dal.	Dukla Jihlava	D
64	MAKINEN, Marko	S.J.	TPS Jr. Turku	RW
65	MARTIN, Mike	NYR	Windsor	D
66	SCHAEFER, Peter	Van.	Brandon	LW
67	ISBISTER, Brad	Tor.-Wpg.	Portland	RW
68	SUNDERLAND, Mathieu	Buf.	Drummondville	RW
69	GUSEV, Sergei	Wsh.-Wpg.-Dal.	CSK VVS Samara	D
70	VYSHEDKEVICH, Sergei	N.J.	Dynamo Moscow	D
71	McKAY, Kevin	Chi.	Moose Jaw	D
72	THOMPSON, Rocky	Cgy.	Medicine Hat	D
73	McCAULEY, Bill	Bos.	Detroit	C
74	HOHENBERGER, Martin	Phi.-Mtl.	Prince George	LW
75	ROCHE, Scott	St.L.	North Bay	G
76	AUBIN, J-Sebastien	Pit.	Sherbrooke	G
77	TRIPP, John	Col.	Oshawa	RW
78	GOSSELIN, David	Det.-N.J.	Sherbrooke	RW

ROUND # 4

No.	Name	Team	Club	Pos
79	McCAULEY, Alyn	Ott.-N.J.	Ottawa	C
80	DUERDEN, Dave	NYI-Fla.	Peterborough	LW
81	KALLIO, Tomi	Ana.-Col.	Kiekko-67 Turku	LW
82	VAN DYK, Chris	T.B.-Ana.-Chi.	Windsor	D
83	MINARD, Mike	Edm.	Chilliwack T-II Jr. A	G
84	KURTZ, Justin	Wpg.	Brandon	D
85	MacNEIL, Ian	L.A.-Hfd.	Oshawa	C
86	DELISLE, Jonathan	Mtl.	Hull	RW
87	KAPANEN, Sami	Hfd.	HIFK Helsinki	LW
88	TJARNQVIST, Daniel	Fla.	Rogle Angelholm	D
89	BOLIBRUCK, Kevin	Dal.-Fla.-Ott.	Peterborough	D
90	TOSKALA, Vesa	S.J.	Ilves Jr. Tampere	G
91	SAVARD, Marc	NYR	Oshawa	C
92	SHAW, Lloyd	Van.	Seattle	D
93	CHARPENTIER, Sebasti	Tor.-Wsh.	Laval	G
94	DAVIDSON, Matt	Buf.	Portland	RW
95	THERIAULT, Joel	Wsh.	Beauport	D
96	REHNBERG, Henrik	N.J.	Farjestad Jr. Karlstad	D
97	KRIZ, Pavel	Chi.	Tri-City	D
98	LABRAATEN, Jan	Cgy.	Farjestad Jr. Karlstad	LW
99	MANN, Cameron	Bos.	Peterborough	RW
100	SOMIK, Radovan	Phi.	ZTS Martin	LW
101	HANDZUS, Michal	St.L.	IS Banska Bystrica	C
102	BELOV, Oleg	Pit.	CSKA Moscow	C
103	BOYD, Kevin	Col.-Ott.	London	LW
104	USTYUGOV, Anatoli	Det.	Torpedo Yaroslavl	LW

ROUND # 5

No.	Name	Team	Club	Pos
105	GRATTON, Benoit	Ott.-Wsh.	Laval	C
106	ORSAGH, Vladimir	NYI	IS Banska Bystrica	RW
107	NIKULIN, Igor	Ana.	Severstal Cherepovets	RW
108	GOLOKHVASTOV, Konstantin	T.B.	Dynamo Moscow	RW
109	SNOPEK, Jan	Edm.	Oshawa	D
110	VASILJEV, Alexei	Wpg.-NYR	Torpedo-2 Yaroslavl	D
111	MENHART, Marian	L.A.-Buf.	Chemopetrol Litvinov Jr.	D
112	ANGER, Niklas	Mtl.	Djurgarden Jr. Stockholm	RW
113	HAMILTON, Hugh	Hfd.	Spokane	D
114	CLOUTIER, Francois	Fla.	Hull	LW
115	STRAND, Wade	Dal.	Regina	D
116	KIPRUSOFF, Miikka	S.J.	TPS Jr. Turku	G
117	PURINTON, Dale	NYR	Tacoma	D
118	MORGAN, Jason	Van.-Dal.-L.A.	Kingston	C
119	POPP, Kevin	Tor.-Buf.	Seattle	D
120	NORMAN, Todd	Buf.-Van.	Guelph	LW
121	ELDER, Brian	Wsh.-Wpg.	Brandon	G
122	MASON, Chris	N.J.	Prince George	G
123	BIENVENUE, Daniel	Chi.-Buf.	Val d'Or	LW
124	CORT, Joel	Cgy.-Wsh.	Guelph	D
125	WILCHYNSKI, Chad	Bos.-Det.	Regina	D
126	ARSENAULT, David	Phi.-Det.	Drummondville	G
127	AMBROSIO, Jeff	St.L.	Belleville	LW
128	HRDINA, Jan	Pit.	Seattle	C
129	JOHNSON, Brent	Col.	Owen Sound	G
130	BROS, Michal	Det.-S.J.	HC Olomouc Jr.	C

ROUND # 6

No.	Name	Team	Club	Pos
131	HRUSKA, David	Ott.	Banik Sokolov	RW
132	TERTYSHNY, Dmitri	NYI-Phi.	Traktor Chelyabinsk	D
133	LEBOUTILLIER, Peter	Ana.	Red Deer	RW
134	PERSHIN, Eduard	T.B.	Dynamo Moscow	RW
135	SOKOLSKY, Jamie	Edm.-Phi.	Belleville	D
136	DAIGLE, Sylvain	Wpg.	Shawinigan	G
137	MELYAKOV, Igor	L.A.	Torpedon Yaroslavl	RW
138	OLSON, Boyd	Mtl.	Tri-City	C
139	BONNER, Doug	Hfd.-Tor.	Seattle	G
140	HAKANEN, Timo	Fla.-S.J.	Assat Jr. Porri	C
141	MARLEAU, Dominic	Dal.	Victoriaville	D
142	KUDRNA, Jaroslav	S.J.	Penticton T-II Jr. A	LW
143	SLAMIAR, Peter	NYR	ZTK Zvolen Jr.	LW
144	SOPEL, Brent	Van.	Swift Current	D
145	TREMBLAY, Yannick	Tor.	Beauport	D
146	MAGLIARDITI, Marc	Buf.-Chi.	Des Moines Jr. A	G
147	JOBIN, Frederick	Wsh.	Laval	D
148	YOUNG, Adam	N.J.	Windsor	D
149	WILFORD, Marty	Chi.	Oshawa	D
150	WILM, Clarke	Cgy.	Saskatoon	C
151	SHALDYBIN, Yevgeny	Bos.	Torpedo Yaroslavl	D
152	SPANHEL, Martin	Phi.	ZPS Zlin Jr.	LW
153	HAMEL, Denis	St.L.-Ana.-St.L.	Chicoutimi	LW
154	KOLKUNOV, Alexei	Pit.	Krylja Sovetov	C
155	CIRJAK, John	Col.	Spokane	RW
156	PERRY, Tyler	Det.	Seattle	C

ROUND # 7

No.	Name	Team	Club	Pos
157	LAROSE, Benoit	Ott.-L.A.	Sherbrooke	D
158	TAYLOR, Andrew	NYI	Detroit	LW
159	LAPLANTE, Mike	Ana.	Calgary Royals	D
160	MURPHY, Cory	T.B.	Sault Ste. Marie	D
161	CERVEN, Martin	Edm.	Dukla Trencin Jr.	C
162	TRAYNOR, Paul	Wpg.	Kitchener	D
163	VUORIVIRTA, Juha	L.A.	Tappara Tampere	C
164	ROBIDAS, Stephane	Mtl.	Shawinigan	D
165	RITCHIE, Byron	Hfd.	Lethbridge	C
166	WORRELL, Peter	Fla.	Hull	LW
167	MEHALKO, Brad	Dal.-S.J.	Lethbridge	RW
168	JINDRICH, Robert	S.J.	Plzen	D
169	HEIL, Jeff	NYR	Wisconsin/River Fall	G
170	BODTKER, Stewart	Van.	Colorado College	C
171	MELENOVSKY, Marek	Tor.	Dukla Jr. Jihlava	C
172	SCOTT, Brian	Buf.	Kitchener	LW
173	DEWAR, Jeff	Wsh.-Dal.	Moose Jaw	RW
174	ROCHEFORT, Richard	N.J.	Sudbury	C
175	GILLIS, Steve	Chi.	Drummondville	C
176	GILLIS, Ryan	Cgy.	North Bay	D
177	AXELSSON, Per Johan	Bos.	V. Frolunda Jr. Goteborg	LW
178	STREIT, Martin	Phi.	HC Olomouc Jr.	LW
179	GRAND-PIERRE, J-Luc	St.L.	Val d'Or	D
180	PYKE, Derrick	Pit.	Halifax	RW
181	SMITH, Dan	Col.	University of B.C.	D
182	EKLUND, Per	Det.	Djurgarden Stockholm	LW

ROUND # 8

No.	Name	Team	Club	Pos
183	LINNA, Kaj	Ott.	Boston University	D
184	SCHULTZ, Ray	NYI-Bos.-Ott.	Tri-City	D
185	KARPENKO, Igor	Ana.	Sokol Kiev	G
186	CARDARELLI, Joe	T.B.	Spokane	LW
187	DOUGLAS, Stephen	Edm.	Niagara Falls	D
188	OBSUT, Jaroslav	Wpg.	North Battleford	D
189	LOVEN, Frederik	L.A.-Wpg.	Djurgarden Jr. Stockholm	C
190	HART, Greg	Mtl.	Kamloops	RW
191	KOSTOLNY, Milan	Hfd.	Detroit	RW
192	KUBA, Filip	Fla.	HC Vitkovice Jr.	D
193	KOVESHNIKOV, Anatoli	Dal.	Sokol Kiev	RW
194	KRAFT, Ryan	S.J.	U. of Minnesota	C
195	GOROKHOV, Ilja	NYR	Torpedo Jaroslavl	D
196	WILLIS, Tyler	Van.	Swift Current	RW
197	MURPHY, Mark	Tor.	Stratford Jr. B	LW
198	ZANUTTO, Mike	Buf.	Oshawa	C
199	TURKOVSKY, Vasili	Wsh.	CSKA Moscow	G
200	HENRY, Frederic	N.J.	Granby	G
201	HANKINSON, Casey	Chi.	U. of Minnesota	LW
202	LUCHINKIN, Sergei	Cgy.-Dal.	Dynamo Moscow	RW
203	ZHUKOV, Sergei	Bos.	Torpedo Yaroslavl	D
204	SHAFIKOV, Ruslan	Phi.	Salavat Yulayev ufa	C
205	BEKAR, Derek	St.L.	Powell River T-II Jr. A	C
206	VORONOV, Sergei	Pit.	Dynamo Moscow	C
207	HIRVONEN, Tomi	Col.	Ilves Jr. Tampere	C
208	SAMOKHALOV, Andrei	Det.	Torp. Ust-Kamenogorsk	RW

ROUND # 9

No.	Name	Team	Club	Pos
209	ZABRANSKY, Libor	Ott.-St.L.	HC Ceske Budejovice	D
210	MacDONALD, David	NYI	Sudbury	G
211	BRODA, Mike	Ana.-NYI	Moose Jaw	LW
212	BIERK, Zac	T.B.	Peterborough	G
213	ANTONIN, Jiri	Edm.	HC Pardubice	D
214	DECIANTIS, Rob	Wpg.	Kitchener	C
215	STEWART, Brian	L.A.	Sault Ste. Marie	C
216	HOUDE, Eric	Mtl.	Halifax	C
217	RUCINSKI, Mike	Hfd.	Detroit	D
218	LEMANOWICZ, David	Fla.	Spokane	G
219	LOWE, Stephen	Dal.	Sault Ste. Marie	C
220	MARKKANEN, Mikko	S.J.	TPS Jr. Turku	RW
221	MAUDIE, Bob	NYR	Kamloops	C
222	CUGNET, Jason	Van.	Kelowna T-II Jr. A	G
223	MARKOV, Daniil	Tor.	Spartak Moscow	D
224	SKRLAC, Rob	Buf.	Kamloops	LW
225	SWANSON, Scott	Wsh.	Omaha Jr. A	D
226	O'HARA, Colin	N.J.	Winnipeg T-II Jr. A	D
227	PITTMAN, Mike	Chi.	Guelph	C
228	GEORGE, Chris	Cgy.-Col.	Sarnia	RW
229	MURPHY, Jonathan	Bos.	Peterborough	G
230	LANK, Jeff	Phi.	Prince Albert	D
231	KASMINSKI, Erik	St.L.-Ott.	Cleveland	RW
232	IVANKOVIC, Frank	Pit.	Oshawa	G
233	SHIRREFFS, Steve	Col.-Cgy.	Hotchkiss	D
234	ENGBLOM, David	Det.	Vallentuna	C

Draft Choices, 1994-69

1994

FIRST ROUND

Selection	Claimed By	Amateur Club	
1. JOVANOVSKI, Ed	Fla.	Windsor	D
2. TVERDOVSKY, Oleg	Ana.	Soviet Wings	D
3. BONK, Radek	Ott.	Las Vegas	C
4. BONSIGNORE, Jason	Wpg.-Edm.	Niagara Falls	C
5. O'NEILL, Jeff	Hfd.	Guelph	C
6. SMYTH, Ryan	Edm.	Moose Jaw	LW
7. STORR, Jamie	L.A.	Owen Sound	G
8. WIEMER, Jason	T.B.	Portland	LW
9. LINDROS, Brett	Que.-NYI	Kingston	RW
10. BAUMGARTNER, Nolan	Phi.-Que.-Tor.-Wsh.	Kamloops	D
11. FRIESEN, Jeff	S.J.	Regina	LW
12. BELAK, Wade	NYI-Que.	Saskatoon	D
13. OHLUND, Mattias	Van.	Pitea	D
14. MOREAU, Ethan	Chi.	Niagara Falls	LW
15. KHARLAMOV, Alexander	Wsh.	CSKA Moscow	C
16. FICHAUD, Eric	St.L.-Wsh.-Tor.	Chicoutimi	G
17. PRIMEAU, Wayne	Buf.	Owen Sound	C
18. BROWN, Brad	Mtl.	North Bay	C
19. DINGMAN, Chris	Cgy.	Brandon	LW
20. BOTTERILL, Jason	Dal.	U. of Michigan	LW
21. RYABCHIKOV, Evgeni	Bos.	Molot Perm	G
22. KEALTY, Jeffrey	Tor.-Que.	Catholic Memorial	D
23. GOLUBOVSKY, Yan	Det.	CSKA Jr. Moscow	D
24. WELLS, Chris	Pit.	Seattle	G
25. SHARIFIJANOV, Vadim	N.J.	Salavat Yulayev ufa	RW
26. CLOUTIER, Dan	NYR	Sault Ste. Marie	G

SECOND ROUND

Selection	Claimed By	Amateur Club	
27. WARRENER, Rhett	Fla.	Saskatoon	D
28. DAVIDSSON, Johan	Ana.	HV 71	C
29. NECKAR, Stanislav	Ott.	Ceske Budejovice	D
30. QUINT, Deron	Wpg.	Seattle	D
31. PODOLLAN, Jason	Hfd.-Fla.	Spokane	C
32. WATT, Mike	Edm.	Stratford Jr. B	LW
33. JOHNSON, Matt	L.A.	Peterborough	LW
34. CLOUTIER, Colin	T.B.	Brandon	C
35. MARHA, Josef	Que.	Dukla Jihlava	C
36. JOHNSON, Ryan	Phi.-Fla.	Thunder Bay Jr. A	C
37. NIKOLOV, Angel	S.J.	Litvinov	D
38. HOLLAND, Jason	NYI	Kamloops	D
39. GORDON, Robb	Van.	Powell River Jr. A	C
40. LEROUX, Jean-Yves	Chi.	Beauport	LW
41. CHERREY, Scott	Wsh.	North Bay	LW
42. SCATCHARD, Dave	St.L.-Van.	Portland	C
43. BROWN, Curtis	Buf.	Moose Jaw	C
44. THEODORE, Jose	Mtl.	St-Jean	G
45. RYABYKIN, Dmitri	Cgy.	Dynamo-2	D
46. JINMAN, Lee	Dal.	North Bay	C
47. GONEAU, Daniel	Bos.	Laval	LW
48. HAGGERTY, Sean	Tor.	Detroit	LW
49. DANDENAULT, Mathieu	Det.	Sherbrooke	RW
50. PARK, Richard	Pit.	Belleville	C
51. ELIAS, Patrik	N.J.	Kladno	LW
52. VERCIK, Rudolf	NYR	Slovan Bratislava	LW

1993

FIRST ROUND

Selection	Claimed By	Amateur Club	
1. DAIGLE, Alexandre	Ott.	Victoriaville	C
2. PRONGER, Chris	S.J.-Hfd.	Peterborough	D
3. GRATTON, Chris	T.B.	Kingston	C
4. KARIYA, Paul	Ana.	University of Maine	LW
5. NIEDERMAYER, Rob	Fla.	Medicine Hat	C
6. KOZLOV, Viktor	Hfd.-S.J.	Dynamo Moscow	LW
7. ARNOTT, Jason	Edm.	Oshawa	C
8. SUNDSTROM, Niklas	NYR	MoDo	LW
9. HARVEY, Todd	Dal.	Detroit	C
10. THIBAULT, Jocelyn	Phi.-Que.	Sherbrooke	G
11. WITT, Brendan	St. L.-Wsh.	Seattle	D
12. JONSSON, Kenny	Buf.-Tor.	Rogle Angelholm	D
13. PEDERSON, Denis	N.J.	Prince Albert	C
14. DEADMARSH, Adam	NYI-Que.	Portland	C
15. LINDGREN, Mats	Wpg.	Skelleftea	C
16. STAJDUHAR, Nick	L.A.-Edm.	London	D
17. ALLISON, Jason	Wsh.	London	C
18. MATTSSON, Jesper	Cgy.	Malmo	C
19. WILSON, Landon	Tor.	Dubuque Jr. A	RW
20. WILSON, Mike	Van.	Sudbury	D
21. KOIVU, Saku	Mtl.	TPS Turku	C
22. ERIKSSON, Anders	Det.	MoDo	D
23. BERTUZZI, Todd	Que.-NYI	Guelph	C
24. LECOMPTE, Eric	Chi.	Hull	LW
25. ADAMS, Kevyn	Bos.	Miami-Ohio	C
26. BERGQVIST, Stefan	Pit.	Leksand	D

SECOND ROUND

Selection	Claimed By	Amateur Club	
27. BICANEK, Radim	Ott.	Dukla Jihlava	D
28. DONOVAN, Shean	S.J.	Ottawa	RW
29. MOSS, Tyler	T.B.	Kingston	G
30. TSULYGIN, Nikolai	Ana.	Salavat Yulalev Ufa	D
31. LANGKOW, Scott	Fla.-Wpg.	Portland	G
32. PANDOLFO, Jay	Hfd.-N.J.	Boston University	LW
33. VYBORNY, David	Edm.	Sparta Praha	C
34. SOROCHAN, Lee	NYR	Lethbridge	D
35. LANGENBRUNNER, Jamie	Dal.	Cloquet	C
36. NIINIMAA, Janne	Phi.	Karpat Oulu	D
37. BETS, Maxim	St. L.	Spokane	LW
38. TSYGUROV, Denis	Buf.	Lada Togliatti	D
39. MORRISON, Brendan	N.J.	Penticton T-II Jr. A	C
40. McCABE, Bryan	NYI	Spokane	D
41. WEEKES, Kevin	Wpg.-Fla.	Owen Sound	G
42. TOPOROWSKI, Shayne	L.A.	Prince Albert	RW
43. BUDAYEV, Alexei	Wsh.-Wpg.	Kristall Elektrostal	C
44. ALLISON, Jamie	Cgy.	Detroit	D
45. KROUPA, Vlastimil	Tor.-Hfd.-S.J.	Chemopetrol Litvinov	D
46. GIRARD, Rick	Van.	Swift Current	C
47. FITZPATRICK, Rory	Mtl.	Sudbury	D
48. COLEMAN, Jonathan	Det.	Andover Academy	D
49. BUCKBERGER, Ashley	Que.	Swift Current	RW
50. MANLOW, Eric	Chi.	Kitchener	C
51. ALVEY, Matt	Bos.	Springfield Jr. B	RW
52. PITTIS, Domenic	Pit.	Lethbridge	C

1992

FIRST ROUND

Selection	Claimed By	Amateur Club	
1. HAMRLIK, Roman	T.B.	ZPS Zlin (Czech.)	D
2. YASHIN, Alexei	Ott.	Dynamo Moscow (CIS)	C
3. RATHJE, Mike	S.J.	Medicine Hat	D
4. WARRINER, Todd	Que.	Windsor	LW
5. KASPARAITIS, Darius	Tor.-NYI	Dynamo Moscow (CIS)	D
6. STILLMAN, Cory	Cgy.	Windsor	C
7. SITTLER, Ryan	Phi.	Nichols	LW
8. CONVERY, Brandon	NYI-Tor.	Sudbury	C
9. PETROVICKY, Robert	Hfd.	Dukla Trencin (Czech.)	C
10. NAZAROV, Andrei	Min.-S.J.	Dynamo Moscow	LW
11. COOPER, David	Buf.	Medicine Hat	D
12. KRIVOKRASOV, Sergei	Wpg.-Chi.	CSKA Moscow (CIS)	RW
13. HULBIG, Joe	Edm.	St. Sebastian's	LW
14. GONCHAR, Sergei	St.L.-Wsh.	Chelybinsk (CIS)	D
15. BOWEN, Jason	L.A.-Pit.-Phi.	Tri-City	LW
16. KVARTALNOV, Dmitri	Bos.	San Diego	LW
17. BAUTIN, Sergei	Chi.-Wpg.	Dynamo Moscow (CIS)	D
18. SMITH, Jason	N.J.	Regina	D
19. STRAKA, Martin	Pit.	Skoda Plzen (Czech.)	C
20. WILKIE, David	Mtl.	Kamloops	D
21. POLASEK, Libor	Van.	TJ Vitkovice (Czech.)	C
22. BOWEN, Curtis	Det.	Ottawa	LW
23. MARSHALL, Grant	Wsh.-Tor.	Ottawa	RW
24. FERRARO, Peter	NYR	Waterloo Jr. A	C

SECOND ROUND

Selection	Claimed By	Amateur Club	
25. PENNEY, Chad	Ott.	North Bay	LW
26. BANNISTER, Drew	T.B.	Sault-Ste-Marie	D
27. MIRANOV, Boris	S.J.-Chi.-Wpg.	CSKA Moscow (CIS)	D
28. BROUSSEAU, Paul	Que.	Hull	RW
29. GRONMAN, Toumas	Tor.-Que.	Tacoma	D
30. O'SULLIVAN, Chris	Cgy.	Catholic Memorial	D
31. METLYUK, Denis	Phi.	Lada Togliatti (CIS)	C
32. CAREY, Jim	NYI-Tor.-Wsh.	Catholic Memorial	G
33. BURE, Valeri	Hfd.-Mtl.	Spokane	LW
34. VARVIO, Jarkko	Min.	HPK (Finland)	RW
35. CIERNY, Jozef	Buf.	ZTK Zvolen (Czech.)	LW
36. SHANTZ, Jeff	Wpg.-Chi.	Regina	C
37. REICHEL, Martin	Edm.	Freiburg (Germany)	RW
38. KOROLEV, Igor	St.L.	Dynamo Moscow	RW
39. HOCKING, Justin	L.A.	Spokane	D
40. PECA, Mike	Bos.-Van.	Ottawa	C
41. KLIMOVICH, Sergei	Chi.	Dynamo Moscow	C
42. BRYLIN, Sergei	N.J.	CSKA Moscow (CIS)	C
43. HUSSEY, Marc	Pit.	Moose Jaw	D
44. CORPSE, Keli	Mtl.	Kingston	C
45. FOUNTAIN, Michael	Van.	Oshawa	G
46. McCARTY, Darren	Det.	Belleville	RW
47. NIKOLISHIN, Andrei	Wsh.-Hfd.	Dynamo Moscow	LW
48. NORSTROM, Mattias	NYR	AIK (Sweden)	D

1991

FIRST ROUND

Selection	Claimed By	Amateur Club	
1. LINDROS, Eric	Que.	Oshawa	C
2. FALLOON, Pat	S.J.	Spokane	RW
3. NIEDERMAYER, Scott	Tor.-N.J.	Kamloops	D
4. LACHANCE, Scott	NYI	Boston University	D
5. WARD, Aaron	Wpg.	U. of Michigan	D
6. FORSBERG, Peter	Phi.	MoDo (Sweden)	C
7. STOJANOV, Alex	Van.	Hamilton	RW
8. MATVICHUK, Richard	Min.	Saskatoon	D
9. POULIN, Patrick	Hfd.	St.-Hyacinthe	LW
10. LAPOINTE, Martin	Det.	Laval	RW
11. ROLSTON, Brian	N.J.	Detroit Comp. Jr. A	C
12. WRIGHT, Tyler	Edm.	Swift Current	C
13. BOUCHER, Phillipe	Buf.	Granby	D
14. PEAKE, Pat	Wsh.	Detroit	C
15. KOVALEV, Alexei	NYR	D'amo Moscow	RW
16. NASLUND, Markus	Pit.	MoDo	RW
17. BILODEAU, Brent	Mtl.	Seattle	D
18. MURRAY, Glen	Bos.	Sudbury	RW
19. SUNDBLAD, Niklas	Cgy.	AIK (Sweden)	RW
20. RUCINSKY, Martin	L.A.-Edm.	CHZ Litvinov (Czech.)	LW
21. HALVERSON, Trevor	St.L.-Wsh.	North Bay	LW
22. McAMMOND, Dean	Chi.	Prince Albert	C

SECOND ROUND

Selection	Claimed By	Amateur Club	
23. WHITNEY, Ray	S.J.	Spokane	C
24. CORBET, Rene	Que.	Drummondville	LW
25. LAVIGNE, Eric	Tor.-Que.-Wsh.	Hull	D
26. PALFFY, Zigmund	NYI	AC Nitra (Czech.)	LW
27. STAIOS, Steve	Wpg.-St.L.	Niagara Falls	D
28. CAMPBELL, Jim	Phi.-Mtl.	Northwood Prep	C
29. CULLIMORE, Jassen	Van.	Peterborough	D
30. OZOLINSH, Sandis	Min.-S.J.	Dynamo Riga (USSR)	D
31. HAMRLIK, Martin	Hfd.	TJ Zin (Czech.)	D
32. PUSHOR, Jamie	Det.	Lethbridge	D
33. HEXTALL, Donevan	N.J.	Prince Albert	LW
34. VERNER, Andrew	Edm.	Peterborough	G
35. DAWE, Jason	Buf.	Peterborough	LW
36. NELSON, Jeff	Wsh.	Prince Albert	C
37. WERENKA, Darcy	NYR	Lethbridge	D
38. FITZGERALD, Rusty	Pit.	Duluth East HS	C
39. POMICHTER, Michael	Mtl.-Chi.	Springfield Jr. B	C
40. STUMPEL, Jozef	Bos.	AC Nitra (Czech.)	RW
41. GROLEAU, Francois	Cgy.	Shawinigan	D
42. LEVEQUE, Guy	L.A.	Cornwall	C
43. DARBY, Craig	St.L.-Mtl.	Albany Academy	C
44. MATTHEWS, Jamie	Chi.	Sudbury	C

1990

FIRST ROUND

Selection	Claimed By	Amateur Club	
1. NOLAN, Owen	Que.	Cornwall	RW
2. NEDVED, Petr	Van.	Seattle	C
3. PRIMEAU, Keith	Det.	Niagara Falls	C
4. RICCI, Mike	Phi.	Peterborough	C
5. JAGR, Jaromir	Pit.	Poldi Kladno (Czech.)	LW
6. SCISSONS, Scott	NYI	Saskatoon	C
7. SYDOR, Darryl	L.A.	Kamloops	D
8. HATCHER, Derian	Min.	North Bay	D
9. SLANEY, John	Wsh.	Cornwall	D
10. BEREHOWSKY, Drake	Tor.	Kingston	D
11. KIDD, Trevor	N.J.-Cgy.	Brandon	G
12. STEVENSON, Turner	St.L.-Mtl.	Seattle	RW
13. STEWART, Michael	NYR	Michigan State	D
14. MAY, Brad	Wpg.-Buf.	Niagara Falls	LW
15. GREIG, Mark	Hfd.	Lethbridge	RW
16. DYKHUIS, Karl	Chi.	Hull	D
17. ALLISON, Scott	Edm.	Prince Albert	C
18. ANTOSKI, Shawn	Mtl.-St.L.-Van.	North Bay	LW
19. TKACHUK, Keith	Buf.-Wpg.	Malden Catholic	LW
20. BRODEUR, Martin	Cgy.-N.J.	St. Hyacinthe	G
21. SMOLINSKI, Bryan	Bos.	Michigan State	C

SECOND ROUND

Selection	Claimed By	Amateur Club	
22. HUGHES, Ryan	Que.	Cornell	C
23. SLEGR, Jiri	Van.	CHZ Litvinov (Czech.)	D
24. HARLOCK, David	Det.-Cgy.-N.J.	U. of Michigan	D
25. SIMON, Chris	Phi.	Ottawa	LW
26. PERREAULT, Nicolas P.	Pit.-Cgy.	Hawkesbury Jr. A	D
27. TAYLOR, Chris	NYI	London	C
28. SEMCHUK, Brandy	L.A.	Canadian National	RW
29. GOTZIAMAN, Chris	Min.-Cgy.-N.J.	Roseau	RW
30. PASMA, Rod	Wsh.	Cornwall	D
31. POTVIN, Felix	Tor.	Chicoutimi	G
32. VIITAKOSKI, Vesa	N.J.-Cgy.	SaiPa (Finland)	LW
33. JOHNSON, Craig	St.L.	Hill-Murray HS	C
34. WEIGHT, Doug	NYR	Lake Superior	C
35. MULLER, Mike	Wpg.	Wayzata	D
36. SANDERSON, Geoff	Hfd.	Swift Current	C
37. DROPPA, Ivan	Chi.	Partizan (Czech.)	D
38. LEGAULT, Alexandre	Edm.	Boston University	RW
39. KUWABARA, Ryan	Mtl.	Ottawa	RW
40. RENBERG, Mikael	Buf.-Phi.	Pitea (Sweden)	LW
41. BELZILE, Etienne	Cgy.	Cornell	D
42. SANDWITH, Terran	Bos.-Phi.	Tri-Cities	D

1989

FIRST ROUND

Selection	Claimed By	Amateur Club	
1. SUNDIN, Mats	Que.	Nacka (Sweden)	RW
2. CHYZOWSKI, Dave	NYI	Kamloops	LW
3. THORNTON, Scott	Tor.	Belleville	C
4. BARNES, Stu	Wpg.	Tri-Cities	C
5. GUERIN, Bill	N.J.	Springfield Jr. B	RW
6. BENNETT, Adam	Chi.	Sudbury	D
7. ZMOLEK, Doug	Min.	John Marshall	D
8. HERTER, Jason	Van.	U. of North Dakota	D
9. MARSHALL, Jason	St.L.	Vernon Jr. A	D
10. HOLIK, Robert	Hfd.	Dukla Jihlava (Czech.)	C
11. SILLINGER, Mike	Det.	Regina	C
12. PEARSON, Rob	Phi.-Tor.	Belleville	RW
13. VALLIS, Lindsay	NYR-Mtl.	Seattle	RW
14. HALLER, Kevin	Buf.	Regina	D
15. SOULES, Jason	Edm.	Niagara Falls	D
16. HEWARD, Jamie	Pit.	Regina	RW
17. STEVENSON, Shayne	Bos.	Kitchener	RW
18. MILLER, Jason	L.A.-Edm.-N.J.	Medicine Hat	C
19. KOLZIG, Olaf	Wsh.	Tri-Cities	G
20. RICE, Steven	Mtl.-NYR	Kitchener	RW
21. BANCROFT, Steve	Cgy.-Tor.	Belleville	D

SECOND ROUND

Selection	Claimed By	Amateur Club	
22. FOOTE, Adam	Que.	Sault Ste. Marie	D
23. GREEN, Travis	NYI	Spokane	C
24. MANDERVILLE, Kent	Tor.-Cgy.	Notre Dame Jr. A	LW
25. RATUSHNY, Dan	Wpg.	Cornell	D
26. SKALDE, Jarrod	N.J.	Oshawa	C
27. SPEER, Michael	Chi.	Guelph	D
28. CRAIG, Mike	Min.	Oshawa	RW
29. WOODWARD, Robert	Van.	Deerfield	LW
30. BRISEBOIS, Patrice	St.L.-Mtl.	Laval	D
31. CORRIVEAU, Rick	Hfd.-St.L.	London	D
32. BOUGHNER, Bob	Det.	Sault-Ste. Marie	D
33. JOHNSON, Greg	Phi.	Thunder Bay Jr. A	C
34. JUHLIN, Patrik	NYR-Phi.	Vasteras (Sweden)	LW
35. DAFOE, Byron	Buf.-Wsh.	Portland	G
36. BORGO, Richard	Edm.	Kitchener	G
37. LAUS, Paul	Pit.	Niagara Falls	D
38. PARSON, Mike	Bos.	Guelph	G
39. THOMPSON, Brent	L.A.	Medicine Hat	D
40. PROSOFSKY, Jason	Wsh.-NYR	Medicine Hat	RW
41. LAROUCHE, Steve	Mtl.	Trois-Rivieres	C
42. DRURY, Ted	Cgy.	Fairfield Prep	C

1988

FIRST ROUND

Selection	Claimed By	Amateur Club	
1. MODANO, Mike	Min.	Prince Albert	C
2. LINDEN, Trevor	Van.	Medicine Hat	RW
3. LESCHYSHYN, Curtis	Que.	Saskatoon	D
4. SHANNON, Darrin	Pit.	Windsor	LW
5. DORE, Daniel	NYR-Que.	Drummondville	RW
6. PEARSON, Scott	Tor.	Kingston	LW
7. GELINAS, Martin	L.A.	Hull	LW
8. ROENICK, Jeremy	Chi.	Thayer Academy	C
9. BRIND'AMOUR, Rod	St.L.	Notre Dame Jr. A	C
10. SELANNE, Teemu	Wpg.	Jokerit (Finland)	RW
11. GOVEDARIS, Chris	Hfd.	Toronto	LW
12. FOSTER, Corey	N.J.	Peterborough	D
13. SAVAGE, Joel	Buf.	Victoria	RW
14. BOIVIN, Claude	Phi.	Drummondville	LW
15. SAVAGE, Reginald	Wsh.	Victoriaville	C
16. CHEVELDAYOFF, Kevin	NYI	Brandon	D
17. KOCUR, Kory	Det.	Saskatoon	RW
18. CIMETTA, Robert	Bos.	Toronto	LW
19. LEROUX, Francois	Edm.	St. Jean	D
20. CHARRON, Eric	Mtl.	Trois-Rivieres	D
21. MUZZATTI, Jason	Cgy.	Michigan State	G

SECOND ROUND

Selection	Claimed By	Amateur Club	
22. MALLETTE, Troy	Min.-NYR	Sault Ste. Marie	C
23. CHRISTIAN, Jeff	Van.-N.J.	London	LW
24. FISET, Stephane	Que.	Victoriaville	G
25. MAJOR, Mark	Pit.	North Bay	D
26. DUVAL, Murray	NYR	Spokane	RW
27. DOMI, Tie	Tor.	Peterborough	RW
28. HOLDEN, Paul	L.A.	London	D
29. DOUCET, Wayne	Chi.-NYI	Hamilton	LW
30. PLAVSIC, Adrien	St.L.	U. of New Hampshire	D
31. ROMANIUK, Russell	Wpg.	St. Boniface Jr. A	LW
32. RICHTER, Barry	Hfd.	Culver Academy	D
33. ROHLIN, Leif	N.J.-Van.	Vasteras (Sweden)	D
34. ST. AMOUR, Martin	Buf.-Mtl.	Verdun	LW
35. MURRAY, Pat	Phi.	Michigan State	LW
36. TAYLOR, Tim	Wsh.	London	C
37. LEBRUN, Sean	NYI	New Westminster	LW
38. ANGLEHART, Serge	Det.	Drummondville	D
39. KOIVUNEN, Petro	Bos.-Edm.	Espoo (Finland)	C
40. GAETZ, Link	Edm.-Min.	Spokane	D
41. BARTLEY, Wade	Mtl.-St.L.-Wsh.	Dauphin Jr. A	D
42. HARKINS, Todd	Cgy.	Miami-Ohio	RW

1987

FIRST ROUND

Selection	Claimed By	Amateur Club	
1. TURGEON, Pierre	Buf.	Granby	C
2. SHANAHAN, Brendan	N.J.	London	C
3. WESLEY, Glen	Van.-Bos.	Portland	D
4. McBEAN, Wayne	Min.-L.A.	Medicine Hat	D
5. JOSEPH, Chris	Pit.	Seattle	D
6. ARCHIBALD, David	L.A.-Min.	Portland	C/LW
7. RICHARDSON, Luke	Tor.	Peterborough	D
8. WAITE, Jimmy	Chi.	Chicoutimi	G
9. FOGARTY, Bryan	Que.	Kingston	D
10. MORE, Jayson	NYR	New Westminster	D
11. RACINE, Yves	Det.	Longueuil	D
12. OSBORNE, Keith	St.L.	North Bay	RW
13. CHYNOWETH, Dean	NYI	Medicine Hat	D
14. QUINTAL, Stephane	Bos.	Granby	D
15. SAKIC, Joe	Wsh.-Que.	Swift Current	C
16. MARCHMENT, Bryan	Wpg.	Belleville	D
17. CASSELS, Andrew	Mtl.	Ottawa	C
18. HULL, Jody	Hfd.	Peterborough	RW
19. DEASLEY, Bryan	Cgy.	U. of Michigan	LW
20. RUMBLE, Darren	Phi.	Kitchener	D
21. SOBERLAK, Peter	Edm.	Swift Current	LW

SECOND ROUND

Selection	Claimed By	Amateur Club	
22. MILLER, Brad	Buf.	Regina	D
23. PERSSON, Rickard	N.J.	Ostersund (Sweden)	D
24. MURPHY, Rob	Van.	Laval	C
25. MATTEAU, Stephane	Min.-Cgy.	Hull	LW
26. TABARACCI, Richard	Pit.	Cornwall	G
27. FITZPATRICK, Mark	L.A.	Medicine Hat	G
28. MAROIS, Daniel	Tor.	Chicoutimi	RW
29. McGILL, Ryan	Chi.	Swift Current	D
30. HARDING, Jeff	Que.-Phi.	St. Michael's Jr. B	LW
31. LACROIX, Daniel	NYR	Granby	LW
32. KRUPPKE, Gordon	Det.	Prince Albert	D
33. LECLAIR, John	St.L.-Mtl.	Bellows Academy	D
34. HACKETT, Jeff	NYI	Oshawa	G
35. McCRADY, Scott	Bos.-Min.	Medicine Hat	D
36. BALLANTYNE, Jeff	Wsh.	Ottawa	D
37. ERICKSSON, Patrik	Wpg.	Brynas (Sweden)	C
38. DESJARDINS, Eric	Mtl.	Granby	D
39. BURT, Adam	Hfd.	North Bay	D
40. GRANT, Kevin	Cgy.	Kitchener	D
41. WILKIE, Bob	Phi.-Det.	Swift Current	D
42. WERENKA, Brad	Edm.	N. Michigan	D

1986

FIRST ROUND

Selection	Claimed By	Amateur Club	
1. MURPHY, Joe	Det.	Michigan State	C
2. CARSON, Jimmy	L.A.	Verdun	C
3. BRADY, Neil	N.J.	Medicine Hat	C
4. ZALAPSKI, Zarley	Pit.	Canadian National	D
5. ANDERSON, Shawn	Buf.	Canadian National	D
6. DAMPHOUSSE, Vincent	Tor.	Laval	LW
7. WOODLEY, Dan	Van.	Portland	C
8. ELYNUIK, Pat	Wpg.	Prince Albert	RW
9. LEETCH, Brian	NYR	Avon Old Farms HS	D
10. LEMIEUX, Jocelyn	St.L.	Laval	RW
11. YOUNG, Scott	Hfd.	Boston University	RW
12. BABE, Warren	Min.	Lethbridge	LW
13. JANNEY, Craig	Bos.	Boston College	C
14. SANIPASS, Everett	Chi.	Verdun	LW
15. PEDERSON, Mark	Mtl.	Medicine Hat	LW
16. PELAWA, George	Cgy.	Bemidji HS	RW
17. FITZGERALD, Tom	NYI	Austin Prep	C
18. McRAE, Ken	Que.	Sudbury	C
19. GREENLAW, Jeff	Wsh.	Canadian National	LW
20. HUFFMAN, Kerry	Phi.	Guelph	D
21. ISSEL, Kim	Edm.	Prince Albert	RW

SECOND ROUND

Selection	Claimed By	Amateur Club	
22. GRAVES, Adam	Det.	Windsor	C
23. SEPPO, Jukka	L.A.-Phi.	Sport (Finland)	LW
24. COPELAND, Todd	N.J.	Belmont Hill HS	D
25. CAPUANO, Dave	Pit.	Mt. St. Charles HS	C
26. BROWN, Greg	Buf.	St. Mark's	D
27. BRUNET, Benoit	Tor.-Mtl.	Hull	LW
28. HAWLEY, Kent	Van.-Phi.	Ottawa	C
29. NUMMINEN, Teppo	Wpg.	Tappara (Finland)	D
30. WILKINSON, Neil	NYR-Min.	Selkirk	D
31. POSMA, Mike	St.L.	Buffalo Jr. A	D
32. LaFORGE, Marc	Hfd.	Kingston	D
33. KOLSTAD, Dean	Min.	Prince Albert	D
34. TIRKKONEN, Pekka	Bos.	SaPKo (Finland)	C
35. KURZAWSKI, Mark	Chi.	Windsor	D
36. SHANNON, Darryl	Mtl.-Tor.	Windsor	D
37. GLYNN, Brian	Cgy.	Saskatoon	D
38. VASKE, Dennis	NYI	Armstrong HS	D
39. ROUTHIER, Jean-Marc	Que.	Hull	RW
40. SEFTEL, Steve	Wsh.	Kingston	LW
41. GUERARD, Stephane	Phi.-Que.	Shawinigan	D
42. NICHOLS, Jamie	Edm.	Portland	LW

1985

FIRST ROUND

Selection	Claimed By	Amateur Club	
1. CLARK, Wendel	Tor.	Saskatoon	D
2. SIMPSON, Craig	Pit.	Michigan State	C
3. WOLANIN, Craig	N.J.	Kitchener	D
4. SANDLAK, Jim	Van.	London	RW
5. MURZYN, Dana	Hfd.	Calgary	D
6. DALGARNO, Brad	Min.-NYI	Hamilton	RW
7. DAHLEN, Ulf	NYR	Ostersund (Sweden)	C
8. FEDYK, Brent	Det.	Regina	RW
9. DUNCANSON, Craig	L.A.	Sudbury	LW
10. GRATTON, Dan	Bos.-L.A.	Oshawa	C
11. MANSON, David	Chi.	Prince Albert	D
12. CHARBONNEAU, Jose	St.L.-Mtl.	Drummondville	RW
13. KING, Derek	NYI	Sault Ste. Marie	LW
14. JOHANSSON, Calle	Buf.	V. Frolunda (Sweden)	D
15. LATTA, Dave	Que.	Kitchener	LW
16. CHORSKE, Tom	Mtl.	Minneapolis SW HS	LW
17. BIOTTI, Chris	Cgy.	Belmont Hill HS	D
18. STEWART, Ryan	Wpg.	Kamloops	C
19. CORRIVEAU, Yvon	Wsh.	Toronto	LW
20. METCALFE, Scott	Edm.	Kingston	LW
21. SEABROOKE, Glen	Phi.	Peterborough	C

SECOND ROUND

Selection	Claimed By	Amateur Club	
22. SPANGLER, Ken	Tor.	Calgary	D
23. GIFFIN, Lee	Pit.	Oshawa	RW
24. BURKE, Sean	N.J.	Toronto	G
25. GAMBLE, Troy	Van.	Medicine Hat	G
26. WHITMORE, Kay	Hfd.	Peterborough	G
27. NIEUWENDYK, Joe	Min.-Cgy.	Cornell	C
28. RICHTER, Mike	NYR	Northwood Prep.	G
29. SHARPLES, Jeff	Det.	Kelowna	D
30. EDLUND, Par	L.A.	Bjorkloven (Sweden)	RW
31. COTE, Alain	Bos.	Quebec	D
32. WEINRICH, Eric	Chi.-N.J.	North Yarmouth	D
33. RICHARD, Todd	Mtl.	Armstrong HS	D
34. LAUER, Brad	NYI	Regina	RW
35. HOGUE, Benoit	Buf.	St-Jean	C
36. LAFRENIERE, Jason	Que.	Hamilton	C
37. RAGLAN, Herb	Mtl.-St.L.	Kingston	RW
38. WENAAS, Jeff	Cgy.	Medicine Hat	C
39. OHMAN, Roger	Wpg.	Leksand (Sweden)	D
40. DRUCE, John	Wsh.	Peterborough	RW
41. CARNELLEY, Todd	Edm.	Kamloops	D
42. RENDALL, Bruce	Phi.	Chatham	LW

1984

FIRST ROUND

Selection	Claimed By	Amateur Club	
1. LEMIEUX, Mario	Pit.	Laval	C
2. MULLER, Kirk	N.J.	Cdn-Nat.-Guelph	C
3. OLCZYK, Ed	L.A.-Chi.	U.S. National	RW
4. IAFRATE, Al	Tor.	U.S. National-Belleville	D
5. SVOBODA, Petr	Hfd.-Mtl.	CHZ (Czech.)	D
6. REDMOND, Craig	Chi.-L.A.	Canadian National	D
7. BURR, Shawn	Det.	Kitchener	C
8. CORSON, Shayne	St.L.-Mtl.	Brantford	C
9. BODGER, Doug	Wpg.-Pit.	Kamloops Jr. A	D
10. DAIGNEAULT, J.J.	Van.	Cdn. Nat.-Longueuil	D
11. COTE, Sylvain	Mtl.-Hfd.	Quebec	D
12. ROBERTS, Gary	Cgy.	Ottawa	LW
13. QUINN, David	Min.	Kent HS	D
14. CARKNER, Terry	NYR	Peterborough	D
15. STIENBURG, Trevor	Que.	Guelph	C
16. BELANGER, Roger	Phi.-Pit.	Kingston	C
17. HATCHER, Kevin	Wsh.	North Bay	D
18. ANDERSSON, Mikael	Buf.	V. Frolunda (Sweden)	C
19. PASIN, Dave	Bos.	Prince Albert	RW
20. MacPHERSON, Duncan	NYI	Saskatoon	D
21. ODELEIN, Selmar	Edm.	Regina	D

SECOND ROUND

Selection	Claimed By	Amateur Club	
22. SMYTH, Greg	Phi.	London	D
23. BILLINGTON, Craig	N.J.	Belleville	G
24. WILKS, Brian	L.A.	Kitchener	C
25. GILL, Todd	Tor.	Windsor	D
26. BENNING, Brian	Hfd.-St.L.	Portland	D
27. MELLANBY, Scott	Chi.-Phi.	Henry Carr Jr. B	RW
28. HOUDA, Doug	Det.	Calgary	D
29. RICHER, Stephane	St.L.-Mtl.	Granby	C
30. DOURIS, Peter	Wpg.	U. of New Hampshire	C
31. ROHLICEK, Jeff	Van.	Portland	LW
32. HRKAC, Anthony	Mtl.-St.L.	Orillia Jr. A	C
33. SABOURIN, Ken	Cgy.	Sault Ste. Marie	D
34. LEACH, Stephen	Min.-Wsh.	Matignon HS	RW
35. HELMINEN, Raimo	NYR	Ilves (Finland)	C
36. BROWN, Jeff	Que.	Sudbury	D
37. CHYCHRUN, Jeff	Phi.	Kingston	D
38. RANHEIM, Paul	Wsh.-Cgy.	Edina Hornets HS	C
39. TRAPP, Doug	Buf.	Regina	LW
40. PODLOSKI, Ray	Bos.	Portland	C
41. MELANSON, Bruce	NYI	Oshawa	RW
42. REAUGH, Daryl	Edm.	Kamloops Jr. A	G

1983

FIRST ROUND

Selection	Claimed By	Amateur Club	
1. LAWTON, Brian	Pit.-Min.	Mount St. Charles HS	C
2. TURGEON, Sylvain	Hfd.	Hull	C
3. LaFONTAINE, Pat	N.J.-NYI	Verdun	C
4. YZERMAN, Steve	Det.	Peterborough	C
5. BARRASSO, Tom	St.L.-Buf.	Acton-Boxboro HS	G
6. MacLEAN, John	L.A.-N.J.	Oshawa	RW
7. COURTNALL, Russ	Tor.	Victoria	C
8. McBAIN, Andrew	Wpg.	North Bay	RW
9. NEELY, Cam	Van.	Portland	RW
10. LACOMBE, Normand	Cgy.-Buf.	U. of New Hampshire	RW
11. CREIGHTON, Adam	Que.-Buf.	Ottawa	C
12. GAGNER, Dave	NYR	Brantford	C
13. QUINN, Dan	Buf.-Cgy.	Belleville	C
14. DOLLAS, Bobby	Wsh.-Wpg.	Laval	D
15. ERREY, Bob	Min.-Pit.	Peterborough	LW
16. DIDUCK, Gerald	NYI	Lethbridge	D
17. TURCOTTE, Alfie	Mtl.	Portland	C
18. CASSIDY, Bruce	Chi.	Ottawa	D
19. BEUKEBOOM, Jeff	Edm.	Sault Ste. Marie	D
20. JENSEN, David	Phi.-Hfd.	Lawrence	C
21. MARKWART, Nevin	Bos.	Regina	LW

SECOND ROUND

Selection	Claimed By	Amateur Club	
22. CHARLESWORTH, Todd	Pit.	Oshawa	D
23. SIREN, Ville	Hfd.	Ilves (Finland)	D
24. EVANS, Shawn	N.J.	Peterborough	D
25. LAMBERT, Lane	Det.	Saskatoon	RW
26. LEMIEUX, Claude	St.L.-Mtl.	Trois-Rivières	RW
27. MOMESSO, Sergio	L.A.-Mtl.	Shawinigan	C
28. JACKSON, Jeff	Tor.	Brantford	LW
29. BERRY, Brad	Wpg.	St. Albert	D
30. BRUCE, Dave	Van.	Kitchener	RW
31. TUCKER, John	Cgy.-Buf.	Kitchener	C
32. HEROUX, Yves	Que.	Chicoutimi	RW
33. HEATH, Randy	NYR	Portland	LW
34. HAJDU, Richard	Wsh.-Buf.	Kamloops Jr. A	LW
35. FRANCIS, Todd	Mtl.	Brantford	RW
36. PARKS, Malcolm	Min.	St. Albert	C
37. McKECHNEY, Garnet	NYI	Kitchener	RW
38. MUSIL, Frantisek	Mtl.-Min.	Tesla (Czech.)	D
39. PRESLEY, Wayne	Chi.	Kitchener	RW
40. GOLDEN, Mike	Edm.	Reading HS	C
41. ZEZEL, Peter	Phi.	Toronto	C
42. JOHNSTON, Greg	Bos.	Toronto	RW

1982

FIRST ROUND

Selection	Claimed By	Amateur Club	
1. KLUZAK, Gord	Col.-Bos.	Nanaimo	D
2. BELLOWS, Brian	Det.-Min.	Kitchener	RW
3. NYLUND, Gary	Tor.	Portland	D
4. SUTTER, Ron	Hfd.-Phi.	Lethbridge	C
5. STEVENS, Scott	L.A.-Wsh.	Kitchener	D
6. HOUSLEY, Phil	Wsh.-Buf.	S. St. Paul HS	D
7. YAREMCHUK, Ken	Chi.	Portland	C
8. TROTTIER, Rocky	St.L.-N.J.	Nanaimo	RW
9. CYR, Paul	Cgy.-Buf.	Victoria	LW
10. SUTTER, Rich	Pit.	Lethbridge	RW
11. PETIT, Michel	Van.	Sherbrooke	D
12. KYTE, Jim	Wpg.	Cornwall	D
13. SHAW, David	Que.	Kitchener	D
14. LAWLESS, Paul	Phi.-Hfd.	Windsor	LW
15. KONTOS, Chris	NYR	Toronto	C
16. ANDREYCHUK, Dave	Buf.	Oshawa	LW
17. CRAVEN, Murray	Min.-Det.	Medicine Hat	C
18. DANEYKO, Ken	Bos.-N.J.	Seattle	D
19. HEROUX, Alain	Mtl.	Chicoutimi	LW
20. PLAYFAIR, Jim	Edm.	Portland	D
21. FLATLEY, Pat	NYI	U. of Wisconsin	RW

SECOND ROUND

Selection	Claimed By	Amateur Club	
22. CURRAN, Brian	Col.-Bos.	Portland	D
23. COURTEAU, Yves	Det.	Laval	RW
24. LEEMAN, Gary	Tor.	Regina	D
25. IHNACAK, Peter	Hfd.-Tor.	Sparta (Czech.)	C
26. ANDERSON, Mike	L.A.-Buf.	N. St. Paul HS	C
27. HEIDT, Mike	Wsh.-L.A.	Calgary	D
28. BADEAU, Rene	St.L.-Chi.	Quebec	D
29. REIERSON, Dave	Cgy.	Prince Albert	D
30. JOHANSSON, Jens	Buf.	Pitea (Sweden)	D
31. GAUVREAU, Jocelyn	Pit.-Mtl.	Granby	D
32. CARLSON, Kent	Van.-Mtl.	St. Lawrence University	D
33. MALEY, David	Wpg.-Mtl.	Edina HS	C
34. GILLIS, Paul	Que.	Niagara Falls	C
35. PATERSON, Mark	Phi.-Hfd.	Ottawa	D
36. SANDSTROM, Tomas	NYR	Farjestads (Sweden)	RW
37. KROMM, Richard	Buf.-Cgy.	Portland	LW
38. HRYNEWICH, Tim	Min.-Pit.	Sudbury	LW
39. BYERS, Lyndon	Bos.	Regina	RW
40. SANDELIN, Scott	Mtl.	Hibbing HS	D
41. GRAVES, Steve	Edm.	Sault Ste. Marie	C
42. SMITH, Vern	NYI	Lethbridge	D

1981

FIRST ROUND

Selection	Claimed By	Amateur Club	
1. HAWERCHUK, Dale	Wpg.	Cornwall	C
2. SMITH, Doug	Det.-L.A.	Ottawa	C
3. CARPENTER, Bobby	Col.-Wsh.	St. John's HS	C
4. FRANCIS, Ron	Hfd.	Sault Ste. Marie	C
5. CIRELLA, Joe	Wsh.-Col.	Oshawa	D
6. BENNING, Jim	Tor.	Portland	D
7. HUNTER, Mark	Pit.-Mtl.	Brantford	RW
8. FUHR, Grant	Edm.	Victoria	G
9. PATRICK, James	NYR	Prince Albert	D
10. BUTCHER, Garth	Van.	Regina	D
11. MOLLER, Randy	Que.	Lethbridge	D
12. TANTI, Tony	Chi.	Oshawa	RW
13. MEIGHAN, Ron	Min.	Niagara Falls	D
14. LEVEILLE, Normand	Bos.	Chicoutimi	LW
15. MacINNIS, Allan	Cgy.	Kitchener	D
16. SMITH, Steve	Phi.	Sault Ste. Marie	D
17. DUDACEK, Jiri	Buf.	Poldi Kladno (Czech.)	RW
18. DELORME, Gilbert	L.A.-Mtl.	Chicoutimi	D
19. INGMAN, Jan	Mtl.	Farjestad (Sweden)	LW
20. RUFF, Marty	St.L.	Lethbridge	D
21. BOUTILIER, Paul	NYI	Sherbrooke	D

SECOND ROUND

Selection	Claimed By	Amateur Club	
22. ARNIEL, Scott	Wpg.	Cornwall	LW
23. LOISELLE, Claude	Det.	Windsor	C
24. YAREMCHUK, Gary	Col.-Tor.	Portland	C
25. GRIFFIN, Kevin	Hfd.-Chi.	Portland	LW
26. CHERNOMAZ, Rich	Wsh.-Col.	Victoria	C
27. DONNELLY, Dave	Tor.-Min.	St. Albert	C
28. GATZOS, Steve	Pit.	Sault Ste. Marie	RW
29. STRUEBY, Todd	Edm.	Regina	LW
30. ERIXON, Jan	NYR	Skelleftea (Sweden)	RW
31. SANDS, Mike	Van.-Min.	Sudbury	G
32. ERIKSSON, Lars	Que.-Mtl.	Brynas (Sweden)	G
33. HIRSCH, Tom	Chi.-Min.	Patrick Henry HS	D
34. PREUSS, Dave	Min.	St. Thomas Academy	RW
35. DUFOUR, Luc	Bos.	Chicoutimi	RW
36. NORDIN, Hakan	Cgy.-St.L.	Farjestad (Sweden)	D
37. COSTELLO, Rich	Phi.	Natick HS	C
38. VIRTA, Hannu	Buf.	TPS (Finland)	D
39. KENNEDY, Dean	L.A.	Brandon	D
40. CHELIOS, Chris	Mtl.	Moose Jaw	D
41. WAHLSTEN, Jali	St.L.-Min.	TPS (Finland)	C
42. DINEEN, Gord	NYI	Sault Ste. Marie	D

1980

FIRST ROUND

Selection	Claimed By	Amateur Club	
1. WICKENHEISER, Doug	Col.-Mtl.	Regina	C
2. BABYCH, Dave	Wpg.	Portland	D
3. SAVARD, Denis	Que.-Chi.	Montreal	C
4. MURPHY, Larry	Det.-L.A.	Peterborough	D
5. VEITCH, Darren	Wsh.	Regina	D
6. COFFEY, Paul	Edm.	Kitchener	D
7. LANZ, Rick	Van.	Oshawa	D
8. ARTHUR, Fred	Hfd.	Cornwall	D
9. BULLARD, Mike	Pit.	Brantford	C
10. FOX, Jimmy	L.A.	Ottawa	RW
11. BLAISDELL, Mike	Tor.-Det.	Regina	RW
12. WILSON, Rik	St.L.	Kingston	D
13. CYR, Denis	Cgy.	Montreal	RW
14. MALONE, Jim	NYR	Toronto	C
15. DUPONT, Jerome	Chi.	Toronto	D
16. PALMER, Brad	Min.	Victoria	LW
17. SUTTER, Brent	NYI	Red Deer	C
18. PEDERSON, Barry	Bos.	Victoria	C
19. GAGNE, Paul	Mtl.-Col.	Windsor	LW
20. PATRICK, Steve	Buf.	Brandon	RW
21. STOTHERS, Mike	Phi.	Kingston	D

SECOND ROUND

Selection	Claimed By	Amateur Club	
22. WARD, Joe	Col.	Seattle	C
23. MANTHA, Moe	Wpg.	Toronto	D
24. ROCHEFORT, Normand	Que.	Quebec	D
25. MUNI, Craig	Det.-Tor.	Kingston	D
26. McGILL, Bob	Wsh.-Tor.	Victoria	D
27. NATTRESS, Ric	Edm.-Mtl.	Brantford	D
28. LUDZIK, Steve	Van.-Chi.	Niagara Falls	C
29. GALARNEAU, Michel	Hfd.	Hull	C
30. SOLHEIM, Ken	Pit.-Chi.	Medicine Hat	LW
31. CURTALE, Tony	L.A.-Cgy.	Brantford	D
32. LaVALLEE, Kevin	Tor.-Cgy.	Brantford	LW
33. TERRION, Greg	St.L.-L.A.	Brantford	LW
34. MORRISON, Dave	Cgy.-L.A.	Peterborough	RW
35. ALLISON, Mike	NYR	Sudbury	LW
36. DAWES, Len	Chi.	Victoria	D
37. BEAUPRE, Don	Min.	Sudbury	G
38. HRUDEY, Kelly	NYI	Medicine Hat	G
39. KONROYD, Steve	Cgy.	Oshawa	D
40. CHABOT, John	Mtl.	Hull	C
41. MOLLER, Mike	Buf.	Lethbridge	RW
42. FRASER, Jay	Phi.	Ottawa	LW

1979

FIRST ROUND

Selection	Claimed By	Amateur Club	
1. RAMAGE, Rob	Col.	London	D
2. TURNBULL, Perry	St.L.	Portland	C
3. FOLIGNO, Mike	Det.	Sudbury	RW
4. GARTNER, Mike	Wsh.	Niagara Falls	RW
5. VAIVE, Rick	Van.	Sherbrooke	RW
6. HARTSBURG, Craig	Min.	Sault St. Marie	D
7. BROWN, Keith	Chi.	Portland	D
8. BOURQUE, Raymond	L.A.-Bos.	Verdun	D
9. BOSCHMAN, Laurie	Tor.	Brandon	C
10. McCARTHY, Tom	Wsh.-Min.	Oshawa	LW
11. RAMSEY, Mike	Buf.	U. of Minnesota	D
12. REINHART, Paul	Atl.	Kitchener	D
13. SULLIMAN, Doug	NYR	Kitchener	RW
14. PROPP, Brian	Phi.	Brandon	LW
15. McCRIMMON, Brad	Bos.	Brandon	D
16. WELLS, Jay	Mtl.-L.A.	Kingston	D
17. SUTTER, Duane	NYI	Lethbridge	RW
18. ALLISON, Ray	Hfd.	Brandon	RW
19. MANN, Jimmy	Wpg.	Sherbrooke	RW
20. GOULET, Michel	Que.	Quebec	LW
21. LOWE, Kevin	Edm.	Quebec	D

SECOND ROUND

Selection	Claimed By	Amateur Club	
22. WESLEY, Blake	Col.-Phi.	Portland	D
23. PEROVICH, Mike	St.L.-Atl.	Brandon	D
24. RAUSSE, Errol	Det.-Wsh.	Seattle	LW
25. JONSSON, Tomas	Wsh.-NYI	MoDo AIK (Sweden)	D
26. ASHTON, Brent	Van.	Saskatoon	LW
27. GINGRAS, Gaston	Min.-Mtl.	Hamilton	D
28. TRIMPER, Tim	Chi.	Peterborough	LW
29. HOPKINS, Dean	L.A.	London	RW
30. HARDY, Mark	Tor.-L.A.	Montreal	D
31. MARSHALL, Paul	Wsh.-Pit.	Brantford	LW
32. RUFF, Lindy	Buf.	Lethbridge	D
33. RIGGIN, Pat	Atl.	London	G
34. HOSPODAR, Ed	NYR	Ottawa	D
35. LINDBERGH, Pelle	Phi.	AIK Solna (Sweden)	G
36. MORRISON, Doug	Bos.	Lethbridge	RW
37. NASLUND, Mats	Mtl.	Brynas IFK (Sweden)	LW
38. CARROLL, Billy	NYI	London	C
39. SMITH, Stuart	Hfd.	Peterborough	D
40. CHRISTIAN, Dave	Wpg.	U. of North Dakota	C
41. HUNTER, Dale	Que.	Sudbury	C
42. BROTEN, Neal	Min.	U. of Minnesota	C

1978

FIRST ROUND

Selection	Claimed By	Amateur Club	
1. SMITH, Bobby	Min.	Ottawa	C
2. WALTER, Ryan	Wsh.	Seattle	LW
3. BABYCH, Wayne	St.L.	Portland	RW
4. DERLAGO, Bill	Van.	Brandon	C
5. GILLIS, Mike	Col.	Kingston	LW
6. WILSON, Behn	Pit.-Phi.	Kingston	D
7. LINSEMAN, Ken	NYR-Phi.	Kingston	C
8. GEOFFRION, Danny	L.A.-Mtl.	Cornwall	RW
9. HUBER, Willie	Det.	Hamilton	D
10. HIGGINS, Tim	Chi.	Ottawa	RW
11. MARSH, Brad	Atl.	London	D
12. PETERSON, Brent	Tor.-Det.	Portland	C
13. PLAYFAIR, Larry	Buf.	Portland	D
14. LUCAS, Danny	Phi.	Sault Ste. Marie	RW
15. TAMBELLINI, Steve	NYI	Lethbridge	C
16. SECORD, Al	Bos.	Hamilton	LW
17. HUNTER, Dave	Mtl.	Sudbury	LW
18. COULIS, Tim	Wsh.	Hamilton	LW

SECOND ROUND

Selection	Claimed By	Amateur Club	
19. PAYNE, Steve	Min.	Ottawa	LW
20. MULVEY, Paul	Wsh.	Portland	RW
21. QUENNEVILLE, Joel	Tor.	Windsor	D
22. FRASER, Curt	Van.	Victoria	LW
23. MacKINNON, Paul	Wsh.	Peterborough	D
24. CHRISTOFF, Steve	Min.	U. of Minnesota	C
25. MEEKER, Mike	Pit.	Peterborough	RW
26. MALONEY, Don	NYR	Kitchener	LW
27. MALINOWSKI, Merlin	Col.	Medicine Hat	C
28. HICKS, Glenn	Det.	Flin Flon	LW
29. LECUYER, Doug	Chi.	Portland	LW
30. YAKIWCHUK, Dale	Mtl.	Portland	C
31. JENSEN, Al	Det.	Hamilton	G
32. McKEGNEY, Tony	Buf.	Kingston	LW
33. SIMURDA, Mike	Phi.	Kingston	RW
34. JOHNSTON, Randy	NYI	Peterborough	D
35. NICOLSON, Graeme	Bos.	Cornwall	D
36. CARTER, Ron	Mtl.	Sherbrooke	RW

1977

FIRST ROUND

Selection	Claimed By	Amateur Club	
1. McCOURT, Dale	Det.	St. Catharines	C
2. BECK, Barry	Col.	New Westminster	D
3. PICARD, Robert	Wsh.	Montreal	D
4. GILLIS, Jere	Van.	Sherbrooke	LW
5. CROMBEEN, Mike	Cle.	Kingston	RW
6. WILSON, Doug	Chi.	Ottawa	D
7. MAXWELL, Brad	Min.	New Westminster	D
8. DEBLOIS, Lucien	NYR	Sorel	C
9. CAMPBELL, Scott	St.L.	London	D
10. NAPIER, Mark	Atl.-Mtl.	Toronto	RW
11. ANDERSON, John	Tor.	Toronto	RW
12. JOHANSEN, Trevor	Pit.-Tor.	Toronto	D
13. DUGUAY, Ron	L.A.-NYR	Sudbury	C
14. SEILING, Ric	Buf.	St. Catharines	RW
15. BOSSY, Mike	NYI	Laval	RW
16. FOSTER, Dwight	Bos.	Kitchener	C/RW
17. McCARTHY, Kevin	Phi.	Winnipeg	D
18. DUPONT, Norm	Mtl.	Montreal	C

SECOND ROUND

Selection	Claimed By	Amateur Club	
19. SAVARD, Jean	Det.-Chi.	Quebec	C
20. ZAHARKO, Miles	Col.-Atl.	New Westminister	D
21. LOFTHOUSE, Mark	Wsh.	New Westminster	RW
22. BANDURA, Jeff	Van.	Portland	D
23. CHICOINE, Daniel	Cle.	Sherbrooke	RW
24. GLADNEY, Bob	Chi.-Tor.	Oshawa	D
25. SEMENKO, Dave	Min.	Brandon	LW
26. KEATING, Mike	NYR	St. Catherines	LW
27. LABATTE, Neil	St.L.	Toronto	D
28. LAURENCE, Don	Atl.	Kitchener	C
29. SAGANIUK, Rocky	Tor.	Lethbridge	RW
30. HAMILTON, Jim	Pit.	London	RW
31. HILL, Brian	L.A.-Atl.	Medicine Hat	RW
32. ARESHENKOFF, Ron	Buf.	Medicine Hat	C
33. TONELLI, John	NYI	Toronto	LW
34. PARRO, Dave	Bos.	Saskatoon	G
35. GORENCE, Tom	Phi.	U. of Minnesota	RW
36. LANGWAY, Rod	Mtl.	U. of New Hampshire	D

1976

FIRST ROUND

Selection	Claimed By	Amateur Club	
1. GREEN, Rick	K.C.-Wsh.	London	D
2. CHAPMAN, Blair	Pit.	Saskatoon	RW
3. SHARPLEY, Glen	Min.	Hull	C
4. WILLIAMS, Fred	Det.	Saskatoon	C
5. JOHANSSON, Bjorn	Cal.	Sweden	D
6. MURDOCH, Don	NYR	Medicine Hat	RW
7. FEDERKO, Bernie	St.L.	Saskatoon	C
8. SHAND, Dave	Van.-Atl.	Peterborough	D
9. CLOUTIER, Real	Chi.	Quebec	RW
10. PHILLIPOFF, Harold	Atl.	New Westminster	LW
11. GARDNER, Paul	Pit.-K.C.	Oshawa	C
12. LEE, Peter	Tor.-Mtl.	Ottawa	RW
13. SCHUTT, Rod	L.A.-Mtl.	Sudbury	LW
14. McKENDRY, Alex	NYI	Sudbury	LW
15. CARROLL, Greg	Buf.-Wsh.	Medicine Hat	C
16. PACHAL, Clayton	Bos.	New Westminster	C
17. SUZOR, Mark	Phi.	Kingston	D
18. BAKER, Bruce	Mtl.	Ottawa	RW

SECOND ROUND

Selection	Claimed By	Amateur Club	
19. MALONE, Greg	Wsh.-Pit.	Oshawa	C
20. SUTTER, Brian	K.C.-St.L.	Lethbridge	LW
21. CLIPPINGDALE, Steve	Min.-L.A.	New Westminster	LW
22. LARSON, Reed	Det.	U. of Minnesota	D
23. STENLUND, Vern	Cal.	London	C
24. FARRISH, Dave	NYR	Sudbury	D
25. SMRKE, John	St.L.	Toronto	LW
26. MANNO, Bob	Van.	St. Catharines	D
27. McDILL, Jeff	Chi.	Victoria	RW
28. SIMPSON, Bobby	Atl.	Sherbrooke	LW
29. MARSH, Peter	Pit.	Sherbrooke	RW
30. CARLYLE, Randy	Tor.	Sudbury	D
31. ROBERTS, Jim	L.A.-Min.	Ottawa	LW
32. KASZYCKI, Mike	NYI	Sault Ste. Marie	C
33. KOWAL, Joe	Buf.	Hamilton	LW
34. GLOECKNER, Larry	Bos.	Victoria	D
35. CALLANDER, Drew	Phi.	Regina	C
36. MELROSE, Barry	Mtl.	Kamloops	D

1975

FIRST ROUND

Selection	Claimed By	Amateur Club	
1. BRIDGMAN, Mel	Wsh.-Phi.	Victoria	C
2. DEAN, Barry	K.C.	Medicine Hat	LW
3. KLASSEN, Ralph	Cal.	Saskatoon	C
4. MAXWELL, Brian	Min.	Medicine Hat	D
5. LAPOINTE, Rick	Det.	Victoria	D
6. ASHBY, Don	Tor.	Calgary	C
7. VAYDIK, Greg	Chi.	Medicine Hat	C
8. MULHERN, Richard	Atl.	Sherbrooke	D
9. SADLER, Robin	St.L.-Mtl.	Edmonton	D
10. BLIGHT, Rick	Van.	Brandon	RW
11. PRICE, Pat	NYI	Saskatoon	D
12. DILLON, Wayne	NYR	Toronto	C
13. LAXTON, Gord	Pit.	New Westminster	G
14. HALWARD, Doug	Bos.	Peterborough	D
15. MONDOU, Pierre	L.A.-Mtl.	Montreal	C
16. YOUNG, Tim	Mtl.-L.A.	Ottawa	C
17. SAUVE, Bob	Buf.	Laval	G
18. FORSYTH, Alex	Phi.-Wsh.	Kingston	C

SECOND ROUND

Selection	Claimed By	Amateur Club	
19. SCAMURRA, Peter	Wsh.	Peterborough	D
20. CAIRNS, Don	K.C.	Victoria	LW
21. MARUK, Dennis	Cal.	London	C
22. ENGBLOM, Brian	Min.-Mtl.	U. of Wisconsin	D
23. ROLLINS, Jerry	Det.	Winnipeg	D
24. JARVIS, Doug	Tor.	Peterborough	C
25. ARNDT, Daniel	Chi.	Saskatoon	LW
26. BOWNESS, Rick	Atl.	Montreal	RW
27. STANIOWSKI, Ed	St.L.	Regina	G
28. GASSOFF, Brad	Van.	Kamloops	D
29. SALVIAN, David	NYI	St. Catharines	RW
30. SOETAERT, Doug	NYR	Edmonton	G
31. ANDERSON, Russ	Pit.	U. of Minnesota	D
32. SMITH, Barry	Bos.	New Westminster	C
33. BUCYK, Terry	L.A.	Lethbridge	RW
34. GREENBANK, Kelvin	Mtl.	Winnipeg	RW
35. BREITENBACH, Ken	Buf.	St. Catharines	D
36. MASTERS, Jamie	Phi.-St.L.	Ottawa	D

1974

FIRST ROUND

Selection	Claimed By	Amateur Club	
1. JOLY, Greg	Wsh.	Regina	D
2. PAIEMENT, Wilfred	K.C.	St. Catharines	RW
3. HAMPTON, Rick	Cal.	St. Catharines	D
4. GILLIES, Clark	NYI	Regina	LW
5. CONNOR, Cam	Van.-Mtl.	Flin Flon	RW
6. HICKS, Doug	Min.	Flin Flon	D
7. RISEBROUGH, Doug	St.L.-Mtl.	Kitchener	C
8. LAROUCHE, Pierre	Pit.	Sorel	C
9. LOCHEAD, Bill	Det.	Oshawa	LW
10. CHARTRAW, Rick	Atl.-Mtl.	Kitchener	D
11. FOGOLIN, Lee	Buf.	Oshawa	D
12. TREMBLAY, Mario	L.A.-Mtl.	Montreal	RW
13. VALIQUETTE, Jack	Tor.	Sault Ste. Marie	C
14. MALONEY, Dave	NYR	Kitchener	D
15. McTAVISH, Gord	Mtl.	Sudbury	C
16. MULVEY, Grant	Chi.	Calgary	RW
17. CHIPPERFIELD, Ron	Phi.-Cal.	Brandon	C
18. LARWAY, Don	Bos.	Swift Current	RW

SECOND ROUND

Selection	Claimed By	Amateur Club	
19. MARSON, Mike	Wsh.	Sudbury	LW
20. BURDON, Glen	K.C.	Regina	C
21. AFFLECK, Bruce	Cal.	U. of Denver	D
22. TROTTIER, Bryan	NYI	Swift Current	C
23. SEDLBAUER, Ron	Van.	Kitchener	LW
24. NANTAIS, Rick	Min.	Quebec	LW
25. HOWE, Mark	St.L.-Bos.	Toronto	D
26. HESS, Bob	Pit.-St.L.	New Westminster	D
27. COSSETTE, Jacques	Det.-Pit.	Sorel	RW
28. CHOUINARD, Guy	Atl.	Quebec	C
29. GARE, Danny	Buf.	Calgary	RW
30. MacGREGOR, Gary	L.A.-Mtl.	Cornwall	C
31. WILLIAMS, Dave	Tor.	Swift Current	LW
32. GRESCHNER, Ron	NYR	New Westminster	D
33. LUPIEN, Gilles	Mtl.	Montreal	D
34. DAIGLE, Alain	Chi.	Trois-Rivières	RW
35. McLEAN, Don	Phi.	Sudbury	D
36. STURGEON, Peter	Bos.	Kitchener	LW

1973

FIRST ROUND

Selection	Claimed By	Amateur Club	
1. POTVIN, Denis	NYI	Ottawa	D
2. LYSIAK, Tom	Cal.-Mtl.-Atl.	Medicine Hat	C
3. VERVERGAERT, Dennis	Van.	London	RW
4. McDONALD, Lanny	Tor.	Medicine Hat	RW
5. DAVIDSON, John	Atl.-Mtl.-St.L.	Calgary	G
6. SAVARD, Andre	L.A.-Bos.	Quebec	C
7. STOUGHTON, Blaine	Pit.	Flin Flon	RW
8. GAINEY, Bob	St.L.-Mtl.	Peterborough	LW
9. DAILEY, Bob	Min.-Mtl.-Van.	Toronto	D
10. NEELY, Bob	Phi.-Tor.	Peterborough	LW
11. RICHARDSON, Terry	Det.	New Westminster	G
12. TITANIC, Morris	Buf.	Sudbury	LW
13. ROTA, Darcy	Chi.	Edmonton	LW
14. MIDDLETON, Rick	NYR	Oshawa	RW
15. TURNBULL, Ian	Bos.-Tor.	Ottawa	D
16. MERCREDI, Vic	Mtl.-Atl.	New Westminster	C

SECOND ROUND

Selection	Claimed By	Amateur Club	
17. GOLDUP, Glen	NYI-Mtl.	Toronto	RW
18. DUNLOP, Blake	Cal.-Min.	Ottawa	C
19. BORDELEAU, Paulin	Van.	Toronto	RW
20. GOODENOUGH, Larry	Tor.-Phi.	London	D
21. VAIL, Eric	Atl.	Sudbury	LW
22. MARRIN, Peter	L.A.-Mtl.	Toronto	C
23. BIANCHIN, Wayne	Pit.	Flin Flon	LW
24. PESUT, George	St.L.	Saskatoon	D
25. ROGERS, John	Min.	Edmonton	RW
26. LEVINS, Brent	Phi.	Swift Current	
27. CAMPBELL, Colin	Det.-Pit.	Peterborough	D
28. LANDRY, Jean	Buf.	Quebec	D
29. THOMAS, Reg	Chi.	London	LW
30. HICKEY, Pat	NYR	Hamilton	LW
31. JONES, Jim	Bos.	Peterborough	RW
32. ANDRUFF, Ron	Mtl.	Flin Flon	C

1972

FIRST ROUND

Selection	Claimed By	Amateur Club	
1. HARRIS, Billy	NYI	Toronto	RW
2. RICHARD, Jacques	Atl.	Quebec	LW
3. LEVER, Don	Van.	Niagara Falls	C
4. SHUTT, Steve	L.A.-Mtl.	Toronto	LW
5. SCHOENFELD, Jim	Buf.	Niagara Falls	D
6. LAROCQUE, Michel	Cal.-Mtl.	Ottawa	G
7. BARBER, Bill	Phi.	Kitchener	LW
8. GARDNER, Dave	Pit.-Min.-Mtl.	Toronto	C
9. MERRICK, Wayne	St.L.	Ottawa	C
10. BLANCHARD, Albert	Det.-NYR	Kitchener	LW
11. FERGUSON, George	Tor.	Toronto	C
12. BYERS, Jerry	Min.	Kitchener	LW
13. RUSSELL, Phil	Chi.	Edmonton	D
14. VAN BOXMEER, John	Mtl.	Guelph	D
15. MacMILLAN, Bobby	NYR	St. Catharines	RW
16. BLOOM, Mike	Bos.	St. Catharines	LW

SECOND ROUND

Selection	Claimed By	Amateur Club	
17. HENNING Lorne	NYI	New Westminster	C
18. BIALOWAS, Dwight	Atl.	Regina	D
19. McSHEFFREY, Brian	Van.	Ottawa	RW
20. KOZAK, Don	L.A.	Edmonton	RW
21. SACHARUK, Larry	Buf.-NYR	Saskatoon	D
22. CASSIDY, Tom	Cal.	Kitchener	C
23. BLADON, Tom	Phi.	Edmonton	D
24. LYNCH, Jack	Pit.	Oshawa	D
25. CARRIERE, Larry	St.L.-Buf.	Loyola College	D
26. GUITE, Pierre	Det.	St. Catharines	LW
27. OSBURN, Randy	Tor.	London	LW
28. WEIR, Stan	Min.-Cal.	Medicine Hat	C
29. OGILVIE, Brian	Chi.	Edmonton	C
30. LUKOWICH, Bernie	Mtl.-Pit.	New Westminster	RW
31. VILLEMURE, Rene	NYR	Shawinigan	LW
32. ELDER, Wayne	Bos.	London	D

1971

FIRST ROUND

Selection	Claimed By	Amateur Club	
1. LAFLEUR, Guy	Cal.-Mtl.	Quebec	RW
2. DIONNE, Marcel	Det.	St. Catharines	C
3. GUEVREMONT, Jocelyn	Van.	Montreal	D
4. CARR, Gene	Pit.-St.L.	Flin Flon	C
5. MARTIN, Rick	Buf.	Montreal	LW
6. JONES, Ron	L.A.-Bos.	Edmonton	D
7. ARNASON, Chuck	Min.-Mtl.	Flin Flon	RW
8. WRIGHT, Larry	Phi.	Regina	C
9. PLANTE, Pierre	Tor.-Phi.	Drummondville	RW
10. VICKERS, Steve	St.L.-NYR	Toronto	LW
11. WILSON, Murray	Mtl.	Ottawa	LW
12. SPRING, Dan	Chi.	Edmonton	C
13. DURBANO, Steve	NYR	Toronto	D
14. O'REILLY, Terry	Bos.	Oshawa	RW

SECOND ROUND

Selection	Claimed By	Amateur Club	
15. BAIRD, Ken	Cal.	Flin Flon	D
16. BOUCHA, Henry	Det.	U.S. Nationals	C
17. LALONDE, Bobby	Van.	Montreal	C
18. McKENZIE, Brian	Pit.	St. Catharines	LW
19. RAMSAY, Craig	Buf.	Peterborough	LW
20. ROBINSON, Larry	L.A.-Mtl.	Kitchener	D
21. NORRISH, Rod	Min.	Regina	LW
22. KEHOE, Rick	Phi.-Tor.	Hamilton	RW
23. FORTIER, Dave	Tor.	St. Catharines	D
24. DEGUISE, Michel	St.L.-Mtl.	Sorel	G
25. FRENCH, Terry	Mtl.	Ottawa	C
26. KRYSKOW, Dave	Chi.	Edmonton	LW
27. WILLIAMS, Tom	NYR	Hamilton	LW
28. RIDLEY, Curt	Bos.	Portage	G

1970

FIRST ROUND

Selection	Claimed By	Amateur Club	
1. PERREAULT, Gilbert	Buf.	Montreal	C
2. TALLON, Dale	Van.	Toronto	D
3. LEACH, Reg	L.A.-Bos.	Flin Flon	LW
4. MacLEISH, Rick	Phi.-Bos.	Peterborough	C
5. MARTINIUK, Ray	Oak.-Mtl.	Flin Flon	G
6. LEFLEY, Chuck	Min.-Mtl.	Canadian Nationals	C
7. POLIS, Greg	Pit.	Estevan	LW
8. SITTLER, Darryl	Tor.	London	C
9. PLUMB, Ron	Bos.	Peterborough	D
10. ODDLEIFSON, Chris	St.L.-Oak.	Winnipeg	C
11. GRATTON, Norm	Mtl.-NYR	Montreal	LW
12. LAJEUNESSE, Serge	Det.	Montreal	RW
13. STEWART, Bob	Bos.	Oshawa	D
14. MALONEY, Dan	Chi.	London	LW

SECOND ROUND

Selection	Claimed By	Amateur Club	
15. DEADMARSH, Butch	Buf.	Brandon	LW
16. HARGREAVES, Jim	Van.	Winnipeg	D
17. HARVEY, Fred	L.A.-Min.	Hamilton	RW
18. CLEMENT, Bill	Phi.	Ottawa	C
19. LAFRAMBOISE, Pete	Oak.	Ottawa	C
20. BARRETT, Fred	Min.	Toronto	D
21. STEWART, John	Pit.	Flin Flon	LW
22. THOMPSON, Errol	Tor.	Charlottetown	LW
23. KEOGAN, Murray	St.L.	U. of Minnesota	C
24. McDONOUGH, Al	Mtl.-L.A.	St. Catharines	RW
25. MURPHY, Mike	NYR	Toronto	RW
26. GUINDON, Bobby	Det.	Montreal	LW
27. BOUCHARD, Dan	Bos.	London	G
28. ARCHAMBAULT, Mike	Chi.	Drummondville	LW

1969

FIRST ROUND

Selection	Claimed By	Amateur Club	
1. HOULE, Rejean	Mtl.	Montreal	LW
2. TARDIF, Marc	Mtl.	Montreal	LW
3. TANNAHILL, Don	Min.-Bos.	Niagara Falls	LW
4. SPRING, Frank	Pit.-Bos.	Edmonton	RW
5. REDMOND, Dick	L.A.-Mtl.-Min.	St. Catharines	D
6. CURRIER, Bob	Phi.	Cornwall	C
7. FEATHERSTONE, Tony	Oak.	Peterborough	RW
8. DUPONT, André	St.L.-NYR	Montreal	D
9. MOSER, Ernie	Det.-Tor.	Estevan	RW
10. RUTHERFORD, Jim	Det.	Hamilton	G
11. BOLDIREV, Ivan	Bos.	Oshawa	C
12. JARRY, Pierre	NYR	Ottawa	LW
13. BORDELEAU, J.-P.	Chi.	Montreal	RW
14. O'BRIEN, Dennis	Min.	St. Catharines	D

SECOND ROUND

Selection	Claimed By	Amateur Club	
15. KESSELL, Rick	Pit.	Oshawa	C
16. HOGANSON, Dale	L.A.	Estevan	D
17. CLARKE, Bobby	Phi.	Flin Flon	C
18. STACKHOUSE, Ron	Oak.	Peterborough	D
19. LOWE, Mike	St.L.	Loyola College	
20. BRINDLEY, Doug	Tor.	Niagara Falls	C
21. GARWASIUK, Ron	Det.	Regina	LW
22. QUOQUOCHI, Art	Bos.	Montreal	
23. WILSON, Bert	NYR	London	LW
24. ROMANCHYCH, Larry	Chi.	Flin Flon	RW
25. GILBERT, Gilles	Min.	London	G
26. BRIERE, Michel	Pit.	Shawinigan Falls	C
27. BODDY, Greg	L.A.	Edmonton	D
28. BROSSART, Bill	Phi.	Estevan	D

NHL All-Stars

Active Players' All-Star Selection Records

GOALTENDERS

Player	First Team Selections	Second Team Selections	Total
Patrick Roy	(3) 1988-89; 1989-90; 1991-92.	(2) 1987-88; 1990-91.	5
Ed Belfour	(2) 1990-91; 1992-93.	(1) 1994-95	3
Tom Barrasso	(1) 1983-84.	(2) 1984-85; 1992-93.	3
Dominik Hasek	(2) 1993-94; 1994-95.	(0)	2
Grant Fuhr	(1) 1987-88.	(1) 1981-82.	2
J.Vanbiesbrouck	(1) 1985-86.	(1) 1993-94.	2
Ron Hextall	(1) 1986-87.	(0)	1
Mike Vernon	(0)	(1) 1988-89	1
Daren Puppa	(0)	(1) 1989-90.	1
Kirk McLean	(0)	(1) 1991-92.	1

DEFENSEMEN

Player	First Team Selections	Second Team Selections	Total
Ray Bourque	(11) 1979-80; 1981-82; 1983-84; 1984-85; 1986-87; 1987-88; 1989-90; 1990-91; 1991-92; 1992-93; 1993-94.	(5) 1980-81; 1982-83; 1985-86; 1988-89; 1994-95.	16
Paul Coffey	(4) 1984-85; 1985-86; 1988-89; 1994-95.	(4) 1981-82; 1982-83; 1983-84; 1989-90.	8
Al MacInnis	(2) 1989-90; 1990-91.	(3) 1986-87; 1988-89; 1993-94.	5
Chris Chelios	(3) 1988-89; 1992-93; 1994-95.	(1) 1990-91.	4
Mark Howe	(3) 1982-83; 1985-86; 1986-87.	(0)	3
Scott Stevens	(2) 1987-88; 1993-94.	(2) 1991-92	3
Brian Leetch	(1) 1991-92.	(2) 1990-91; 1993-94.	3
Larry Murphy	(0)	(3) 1986-87; 1992-93; 1994-95.	3
Gary Suter	(0)	(1) 1987-88.	1
Brad McCrimmon	(0)	(1) 1987-88.	1
Phil Housley	(0)	(1) 1991-92	1
Al Iafrate	(0)	(1) 1992-93	1

CENTERS

Player	First Team Selections	Second Team Selections	Total
Wayne Gretzky	(8) 1980-81; 1981-82; 1982-83; 1983-84; 1984-85; 1985-86; 1986-87; 1990-91.	(5) 1979-80; 1987-88; 1988-89; 1989-90; 1993-94.	13
Mario Lemieux	(3) 1987-88; 1988-89; 1992-93.	(3) 1985-86; 1986-87; 1991-92.	6
Bryan Trottier	(2) 1977-78; 1978-79.	(2) 1981-82; 1983-84.	4
Mark Messier	(2) 1989-90; 1991-92.	(0)	2
Sergei Fedorov	(1) 1993-94.	(0)	1
Eric Lindros	(1) 1994-95.	(0)	1
Denis Savard	(0)	(1) 1982-83.	1
Dale Hawerchuk	(0)	(1) 1984-85.	1
Adam Oates	(0)	(1) 1990-91.	1
Pat LaFontaine	(0)	(1) 1992-93	1
Alexei Zhamnov	(0)	(1) 1994-95.	1

RIGHT WINGERS

Player	First Team Selections	Second Team Selections	Total
Jari Kurri	(2) 1984-85; 1986-87.	(3) 1983-84; 1985-86; 1988-89.	5
Cam Neely	(0)	(4) 1987-88; 1989-90; 1990-91; 1993-94.	4
Brett Hull	(3) 1989-90; 1990-91; 1991-92.	(0)	3
Joe Mullen	(1) 1988-89.	(0)	1
Teemu Selanne	(1) 1992-93.	(0)	1
Pavel Bure	(1) 1993-94.	(0)	1
Jaromir Jagr	(1) 1994-95.	(0)	1
Mark Recchi	(0)	(1) 1991-92.	1
Alexander Mogilny	(0)	(1) 1992-93.	1
Theoren Fleury	(0)	(1) 1994-95.	1

LEFT WINGERS

Player	First Team Selections	Second Team Selections	Total
Luc Robitaille	(5) 1987-88; 1988-89; 1989-90; 1990-91; 1992-93.	(2) 1986-87; 1991-92.	7
Michel Goulet	(3) 1983-84; 1985-86; 1986-87.	(2) 1982-83; 1987-88.	5
Mark Messier	(2) 1981-82; 1982-83.	(1) 1983-84.	3
Kevin Stevens	(1) 1991-92.	(2) 1990-91; 1992-93.	3
Brendan Shanahan	(1) 1993-94.	(0)	1
John LeClair	(1) 1994-95.	(0)	1
Gerard Gallant	(0)	(1) 1988-89.	1
Brian Bellows	(0)	(1) 1989-90.	1
Adam Graves	(0)	(1) 1993-94.	1
Keith Tkachuk	(0)	(1) 1994-95.	1

Leading NHL All-Stars   1930-95

Player	Pos	Team	NHL Seasons	First Team Selections	Second Team Selections	Total Selections
Howe, Gordie	RW	Detroit	26	12	9	21
* Bourque, Ray	D	Boston	16	11	5	16
Richard, Maurice	RW	Montreal	18	8	6	14
* Gretzky, Wayne	C	Edm., L.A.	16	8	5	13
Hull, Bobby	LW	Chicago	16	10	2	12
Harvey, Doug	D	Mtl., NYR	19	10	1	11
Hall, Glenn	G	Chi., St.L.	18	7	4	11
Beliveau, Jean	C	Montreal	20	6	4	10
Seibert, Earl	D	NYR, Chi	15	4	6	10
Orr, Bobby	D	Boston	12	8	1	9
Lindsay, Ted	LW	Detroit	17	8	1	9
Mahovlich, Frank	LW	Tor., Det., Mtl.	18	3	6	9
Shore, Eddie	D	Boston	14	7	1	8
Mikita, Stan	C	Chicago	22	6	2	8
Kelly, Red	D	Detroit	20	6	2	8
Esposito, Phil	C	Boston	18	6	2	8
Pilote, Pierre	D	Chicago	14	5	3	8
* Coffey, Paul	D	Edm., Pit., Det.	15	4	4	8
Brimsek, Frank	G	Boston	10	2	6	8
Bossy, Mike	RW	NY Islanders	10	5	3	8
* Robitaille, Luc	LW	Los Angeles	9	5	2	7
Potvin, Denis	D	NY Islanders	15	5	2	7
Park, Brad	D	NYR, Bos.	17	5	2	7
Plante, Jacques	G	Mtl-Tor	18	3	4	7
Gadsby, Bill	D	Chi., NYR, Det.	20	3	4	7
Sawchuk, Terry	G	Detroit	21	3	4	7
Durnan, Bill	G	Montreal	7	6	0	6
Lafleur, Guy	RW	Montreal	16	6	0	6
Dryden, Ken	G	Montreal	8	5	1	6
* Lemieux, Mario	C	Pittsburgh	10	3	3	6
Robinson, Larry	D	Montreal	20	3	3	6
Horton, Tim	D	Toronto	24	3	3	6
Salming, Borje	D	Toronto	17	1	5	6
Cowley, Bill	C	Boston	13	4	1	5
* Messier, Mark	LW/C	Edm., NYR	16	4	1	5
Jackson, Harvey	LW	Toronto	15	4	1	5
Goulet, Michel	LW	Quebec	15	3	2	5
Conacher, Charlie	RW	Toronto	12	3	2	5
Stewart, Jack	D	Detroit	12	3	2	5
Lach, Elmer	C	Montreal	14	3	2	5
Quackenbush, Bill	D	Det., Bos.	14	3	2	5
Blake, Toe	LW	Montreal	15	3	2	5
Esposito, Tony	G	Chicago	16	3	2	5
* Roy, Patrick	G	Montreal	11	2	3	5
Reardon, Ken	D	Montreal	7	2	3	5
* Kurri, Jari	RW	Edmonton	14	2	3	5
Apps, Syl	C	Toronto	10	2	3	5
Giacomin, Ed	G	NY Rangers	13	2	3	5

*   Active

Position Leaders in All-Star Selections

Position	Player	First Team	Second Team	Total
GOAL	Glenn Hall	7	4	11
	Frank Brimsek	2	6	8
	Jacques Plante	3	4	7
	Terry Sawchuk	3	4	7
	Bill Durnan	6	0	6
	Ken Dryden	5	1	6
DEFENSE	* Ray Bourque	11	4	15
	Doug Harvey	10	1	11
	Earl Seibert	4	6	10
	Bobby Orr	8	1	9
	Eddie Shore	7	1	8
	Red Kelly	6	2	8
	Pierre Pilote	5	3	8
	* Paul Coffey	4	4	8

Position	Player	First Team	Second Team	Total
LEFT WING	Bobby Hull	10	2	12
	Ted Lindsay	8	1	9
	Frank Mahovlich	3	6	9
	* Luc Robitaille	5	2	7
	Harvey Jackson	4	1	5
	Michel Goulet	3	2	5
	Toe Blake	3	2	5
RIGHT WING	Gordie Howe	12	9	21
	Maurice Richard	8	6	14
	Mike Bossy	5	3	8
	Guy Lafleur	6	0	6
	Charlie Conacher	3	2	5
CENTER	* Wayne Gretzky	8	5	13
	Jean Beliveau	6	4	10
	Stan Mikita	6	2	8
	Phil Esposito	6	2	8
	* Mario Lemieux	3	3	6
	Bill Cowley	4	1	5
	Elmer Lach	3	2	5
	Syl Apps	2	3	5

* active player

All-Star Teams

1930-95

Voting for the NHL All-Star Team is conducted among the representatives of the Professional Hockey Writers' Association at the end of the season.

Following is a list of the First and Second All-Star Teams since their inception in 1930-31.

First Team		Second Team
1994-95		
Hasek, Dominik, Buf.	G	Belfour, Ed, Chi.
Coffey, Paul, Det.	D	Bourque, Ray, Bos.
Chelios, Chris, Chi.	D	Murphy, Larry, Pit.
Lindros, Eric, Phi.	C	Zhamnov, Alexei, Wpg.
Jagr, Jaromir, Pit.	RW	Fleury, Theoren, Cgy.
LeClair, John, Mtl., Phi.	LW	Tkachuk, Keith, Wpg.
1993-94		
Hasek, Dominik, Buf.	G	Vanbiesbrouck, John, Fla.
Bourque, Ray, Bos.	D	MacInnis, Al, Cgy.
Stevens, Scott, N.J.	D	Leetch, Brian, NYR
Fedorov, Sergei, Det.	C	Gretzky, Wayne, L.A.
Bure, Pavel, Van.	RW	Neely, Cam, Bos.
Shanahan, Brendan, St. L.	LW	Graves, Adam, NYR
1992-93		
Belfour, Ed, Chi.	G	Barrasso, Tom, Pit.
Chelios, Chris, Chi.	D	Murphy, Larry, Pit.
Bourque, Ray, Bos.	D	Iafrate, Al, Wsh.
Lemieux, Mario, Pit.	C	LaFontaine, Pat, NYI
Selanne, Teemu, Wpg.	RW	Mogilny, Alexander, Buf.
Robitaille, Luc, L.A.	LW	Stevens, Kevin, Pit.
1991-92		
Roy, Patrick, Mtl.	G	McLean, Kirk, Van.
Leetch, Brian, NYR	D	Housley, Phil, Wpg.
Bourque, Ray, Bos.	D	Stevens, Scott, N.J.
Messier, Mark, NYR	C	Lemieux, Mario, Pit.
Hull, Brett, St. L.	RW	Recchi, Mark, Pit., Phi.
Stevens, Kevin, Pit.	LW	Robitaille, Luc, L.A.
1990-91		
Belfour, Ed, Chi.	G	Roy, Patrick, Mtl.
Bourque, Ray, Bos.	D	Chelios, Chris, Chi.
MacInnis, Al, Cgy.	D	Leetch, Brian, NYR
Gretzky, Wayne, L.A.	C	Oates, Adam, St. L.
Hull, Brett, St. L.	RW	Neely, Cam, Bos.
Robitaille, Luc, L.A.	LW	Stevens, Kevin, Pit.
1989-90		
Roy, Patrick, Mtl.	G	Puppa, Daren, Buf.
Bourque, Ray, Bos.	D	Coffey, Paul, Pit.
MacInnis, Al, Cgy.	D	Wilson, Doug, Chi.
Messier, Mark, Edm.	C	Gretzky, Wayne, L.A.
Hull, Brett, St. L.	RW	Neely, Cam, Bos.
Robitaille, Luc, L.A.	LW	Bellows, Brian, Min.
1988-89		
Roy, Patrick, Mtl.	G	Vernon, Mike, Cgy.
Chelios, Chris, Mtl.	D	MacInnis, Al, Cgy.
Coffey, Paul, Pit.	D	Bourque, Ray, Bos.
Lemieux, Mario, Pit.	C	Gretzky, Wayne, L.A.
Mullen, Joe, Cgy.	RW	Kurri, Jari, Edm.
Robitaille, Luc, L.A.	LW	Gallant, Gerard, Det.
1987-88		
Fuhr, Grant, Edm.	G	Roy, Patrick, Mtl.
Bourque, Ray, Bos.	D	Suter, Gary, Cgy.
Stevens, Scott, Wsh.	D	McCrimmon, Brad, Cgy.
Lemieux, Mario, Pit.	C	Gretzky, Wayne, Edm.
Loob, Hakan, Cgy.	RW	Neely, Cam, Bos.
Robitaille, Luc, L.A.	LW	Goulet, Michel, Que.

First Team		Second Team
1986-87		
Hextall, Ron, Phi.	G	Liut, Mike, Hfd.
Bourque, Ray, Bos.	D	Murphy, Larry, Wsh.
Howe, Mark, Phi.	D	MacInnis, Al, Cgy.
Gretzky, Wayne, Edm.	C	Lemieux, Mario, Pit.
Kurri, Jari, Edm.	RW	Kerr, Tim, Phi.
Goulet, Michel, Que.	LW	Robitaille, Luc, L.A.
1985-86		
Vanbiesbrouck, J., NYR	G	Froese, Bob, Phi.
Coffey, Paul, Edm.	D	Robinson, Larry, Mtl.
Howe, Mark, Phi.	D	Bourque, Ray, Bos.
Gretzky, Wayne, Edm.	C	Lemieux, Mario, Pit.
Bossy, Mike, NYI	RW	Kurri, Jari, Edm.
Goulet, Michel, Que.	LW	Naslund, Mats, Mtl.

First Team		Second Team
1984-85		
Lindbergh, Pelle, Phi.	G	Barrasso, Tom, Buf.
Coffey, Paul, Edm.	D	Langway, Rod, Wsh.
Bourque, Ray, Bos.	D	Wilson, Doug, Chi.
Gretzky, Wayne, Edm.	C	Hawerchuk, Dale, Wpg.
Kurri, Jari, Edm.	RW	Bossy, Mike, NYI
Ogrodnick, John, Det.	LW	Tonelli, John, NYI
1983-84		
Barrasso, Tom, Buf.	G	Riggin, Pat, Wsh.
Langway, Rod, Wsh.	D	Coffey, Paul, Edm.
Bourque, Ray, Bos.	D	Potvin, Denis, NYI
Gretzky, Wayne, Edm.	C	Trottier, Bryan, NYI
Bossy, Mike, NYI	RW	Kurri, Jari, Edm.
Goulet, Michel, Que.	LW	Messier, Mark, Edm.

Ed Belfour, who won his third Jennings Trophy award in 1994-95, also earned his third post-season All-Star berth when he was selected to the NHL's Second All-Star Team.

First Team		Second Team

1982-83
	Pos	
Peeters, Pete, Bos.	G	Melanson, Roland, NYI
Howe, Mark, Phi.	D	Bourque, Ray, Bos.
Langway, Rod, Wsh.	D	Coffey, Paul, Edm.
Gretzky, Wayne, Edm.	C	Savard, Denis, Chi.
Bossy, Mike, NYI	RW	McDonald, Lanny, Cgy.
Messier, Mark, Edm.	LW	Goulet, Michel, Que.

1981-82
Smith, Bill, NYI	G	Fuhr, Grant, Edm.
Wilson, Doug, Chi.	D	Coffey, Paul, Edm.
Bourque, Ray, Bos.	D	Engblom, Brian, Mtl.
Gretzky, Wayne, Edm.	C	Trottier, Bryan, NYI
Bossy, Mike, NYI	RW	Middleton, Rick, Bos.
Messier, Mark, Edm.	LW	Tonelli, John, NYI

1980-81
Liut, Mike, St.L.	G	Lessard, Mario, L.A.
Potvin, Denis, NYI	D	Robinson, Larry, Mtl.
Carlyle, Randy, Pit.	D	Bourque, Ray, Bos.
Gretzky, Wayne, Edm.	C	Dionne, Marcel, L.A.
Bossy, Mike, NYI	RW	Taylor, Dave, L.A.
Simmer, Charlie, L.A.	LW	Barber, Bill, Phi.

1979-80
Esposito, Tony, Chi.	G	Edwards, Don, Buf.
Robinson, Larry, Mtl.	D	Salming, Borje, Tor.
Bourque, Ray, Bos.	D	Schoenfeld, Jim, Buf.
Dionne, Marcel, L.A.	C	Gretzky, Wayne, Edm.
Lafleur, Guy, Mtl.	RW	Gare, Danny, Buf.
Simmer, Charlie, L.A.	LW	Shutt, Steve, Mtl.

1978-79
Dryden, Ken, Mtl.	G	Resch, Glenn, NYI
Potvin, Denis, NYI	D	Salming, Borje, Tor.
Robinson, Larry, Mtl.	D	Savard, Serge, Mtl.
Trottier, Bryan, NYI	C	Dionne, Marcel, L.A.
Lafleur, Guy, Mtl.	RW	Bossy, Mike, NYI
Gillies, Clark, NYI	LW	Barber, Bill, Phi.

1977-78
Dryden, Ken, Mtl.	G	Edwards, Don, Buf.
Potvin, Denis, NYI	D	Robinson, Larry, Mtl.
Park, Brad, Bos.	D	Salming, Borje, Tor.
Trottier, Bryan, NYI	C	Sittler, Darryl, Tor.
Lafleur, Guy, Mtl.	RW	Bossy, Mike, NYI
Gillies, Clark, NYI	LW	Shutt, Steve, Mtl.

1976-77
Dryden, Ken, Mtl.	G	Vachon, Rogatien, L.A.
Robinson, Larry, Mtl.	D	Potvin, Denis, NYI
Salming, Borje, Tor.	D	Lapointe, Guy, Mtl.
Dionne, Marcel, L.A.	C	Perreault, Gilbert, Buf.
Lafleur, Guy, Mtl.	RW	McDonald, Lanny, Tor.
Shutt, Steve, Mtl.	LW	Martin, Richard, Buf.

1975-76
Dryden, Ken, Mtl.	G	Resch, Glenn, NYI
Potvin, Denis, NYI	D	Salming, Borje, Tor.
Park, Brad, Bos.	D	Lapointe, Guy, Mtl.
Clarke, Bobby, Phi.	C	Perreault, Gilbert, Buf.
Lafleur, Guy, Mtl.	RW	Leach, Reggie, Phi.
Barber, Bill, Phi.	LW	Martin, Richard, Buf.

1974-75
Parent, Bernie, Phi.	G	Vachon, Rogie, L.A.
Orr, Bobby, Bos.	D	Lapointe, Guy, Mtl.
Potvin, Denis, NYI	D	Salming, Borje, Tor.
Clarke, Bobby, Phi.	C	Esposito, Phil, Bos.
Lafleur, Guy, Mtl.	RW	Robert, René, Buf.
Martin, Richard, Buf.	LW	Vickers, Steve, NYR

1973-74
Parent, Bernie, Phi.	G	Esposito, Tony, Chi.
Orr, Bobby, Bos.	D	White, Bill, Chi.
Park, Brad, NYR	D	Ashbee, Barry, Phi.
Esposito, Phil, Bos.	C	Clarke, Bobby, Phi.
Hodge, Ken, Bos.	RW	Redmond, Mickey, Det.
Martin, Richard, Buf.	LW	Cashman, Wayne, Bos.

1972-73
Dryden, Ken, Mtl.	G	Esposito, Tony, Chi.
Orr, Bobby, Bos.	D	Park, Brad, NYR
Lapointe, Guy, Mtl.	D	White, Bill, Chi.
Esposito, Phil, Bos.	C	Clarke, Bobby, Phi.
Redmond, Mickey, Det.	RW	Cournoyer, Yvan, Mtl.
Mahovlich, Frank, Mtl.	LW	Hull, Dennis, Chi.

1971-72
Esposito, Tony, Chi.	G	Dryden, Ken, Mtl.
Orr, Bobby, Bos.	D	White, Bill, Chi.
Park, Brad, NYR	D	Stapleton, Pat, Chi.
Esposito, Phil, Bos.	C	Ratelle, Jean, NYR
Gilbert, Rod, NYR	RW	Cournoyer, Yvan, Mtl.
Hull, Bobby, Chi.	LW	Hadfield, Vic, NYR

1970-71
Giacomin, Ed, NYR	G	Plante, Jacques, Tor.
Orr, Bobby, Bos.	D	Park, Brad, NYR
Tremblay, J.C., Mtl.	D	Stapleton, Pat, Chi.
Esposito, Phil, Bos.	C	Keon, Dave, Tor.
Hodge, Ken, Bos.	RW	Cournoyer, Yvan, Mtl.
Bucyk, John, Bos.	LW	Hull, Bobby, Chi.

1969-70
Esposito, Tony, Chi.	G	Giacomin, Ed, NYR
Orr, Bobby, Bos.	D	Brewer, Carl, Det.
Park, Brad, NYR	D	Laperriere, Jacques, Mtl.
Esposito, Phil, Bos.	C	Mikita, Stan, Chi.
Howe, Gordie, Det.	RW	McKenzie, John, Bos.
Hull, Bobby, Chi.	LW	Mahovlich, Frank, Det.

1968-69
Hall, Glenn, St.L.	G	Giacomin, Ed, NYR
Orr, Bobby, Bos.	D	Green, Ted, Bos.
Horton, Tim, Tor.	D	Harris, Ted, Mtl.
Esposito, Phil, Bos.	C	Béliveau, Jean, Mtl.
Howe, Gordie, Det.	RW	Cournoyer, Yvan, Mtl.
Hull, Bobby, Chi.	LW	Mahovlich, Frank, Det.

1967-68
Worsley, Lorne, Mtl.	G	Giacomin, Ed, NYR
Orr, Bobby, Bos.	D	Tremblay, J.C., Mtl.
Horton, Tim, Tor.	D	Neilson, Jim, NYR
Mikita, Stan, Chi.	C	Esposito, Phil, Bos.
Howe, Gordie, Det.	RW	Gilbert, Rod, NYR
Hull, Bobby, Chi.	LW	Bucyk, John, Bos.

1966-67
Giacomin, Ed, NYR	G	Hall, Glenn, Chi.
Pilote, Pierre, Chi.	D	Horton, Tim, Tor.
Howell, Harry, NYR	D	Orr, Bobby, Bos.
Mikita, Stan, Chi.	C	Ullman, Norm, Det.
Wharram, Ken, Chi.	RW	Howe, Gordie, Det.
Hull, Bobby, Chi.	LW	Marshall, Don, NYR

1965-66
Hall, Glenn, Chi.	G	Worsley, Lorne, Mtl.
Laperriere, Jacques, Mtl.	D	Stanley, Allan, Tor.
Pilote, Pierre, Chi.	D	Stapleton, Pat, Chi.
Mikita, Stan, Chi.	C	Béliveau, Jean, Mtl.
Howe, Gordie, Det.	RW	Rousseau, Bobby, Mtl.
Hull, Bobby, Chi.	LW	Mahovlich, Frank, Tor.

1964-65
Crozier, Roger, Det.	G	Hodge, Charlie, Mtl.
Pilote, Pierre, Chi.	D	Gadsby, Bill, Det.
Laperriere, Jacques, Mtl.	D	Brewer, Carl, Tor.
Ullman, Norm, Det.	C	Mikita, Stan, Chi.
Provost, Claude, Mtl.	RW	Howe, Gordie, Det.
Hull, Bobby, Chi.	LW	Mahovlich, Frank, Tor.

1963-64
Hall, Glenn, Chi.	G	Hodge, Charlie, Mtl.
Pilote, Pierre, Chi.	D	Vasko, Elmer, Chi.
Horton, Tim, Tor.	D	Laperriere, Jacques, Mtl.
Mikita, Stan, Chi.	C	Béliveau, Jean, Mtl.
Wharram, Ken, Chi.	RW	Howe, Gordie, Det.
Hull, Bobby, Chi.	LW	Mahovlich, Frank, Tor.

1962-63
Hall, Glenn, Chi.	G	Sawchuk, Terry, Det.
Pilote, Pierre, Chi.	D	Horton, Tim, Tor.
Brewer, Carl, Tor.	D	Vasko, Elmer, Chi.
Mikita, Stan, Chi.	C	Richard, Henri, Mtl.
Howe, Gordie, Det.	RW	Bathgate, Andy, NYR
Mahovlich, Frank, Tor.	LW	Hull, Bobby, Chi.

1961-62
Plante, Jacques, Mtl.	G	Hall, Glenn, Chi.
Harvey, Doug, NYR	D	Brewer, Carl, Tor.
Talbot, Jean-Guy, Mtl.	D	Pilote, Pierre, Chi.
Mikita, Stan, Chi.	C	Keon, Dave, Tor.
Bathgate, Andy, NYR	RW	Howe, Gordie, Det.
Hull, Bobby, Chi.	LW	Mahovlich, Frank, Tor.

1960-61
Bower, Johnny, Tor.	G	Hall, Glenn, Chi.
Harvey, Doug, Mtl.	D	Stanley, Allan, Tor.
Pronovost, Marcel, Det.	D	Pilote, Pierre, Chi.
Béliveau, Jean, Mtl.	C	Richard, Henri, Mtl.
Geoffrion, Bernie, Mtl.	RW	Howe, Gordie, Det.
Mahovlich, Frank, Tor.	LW	Moore, Dickie, Mtl.

1959-60
Hall, Glenn, Chi.	G	Plante, Jacques, Mtl.
Harvey, Doug, Mtl.	D	Stanley, Allan, Tor.
Pronovost, Marcel, Det.	D	Pilote, Pierre, Chi.
Béliveau, Jean, Mtl.	C	Horvath, Bronco, Bos.
Howe, Gordie, Det.	RW	Geoffrion, Bernie, Mtl.
Hull, Bobby, Chi.	LW	Prentice, Dean, NYR

1958-59
Plante, Jacques, Mtl.	G	Sawchuk, Terry, Det.
Johnson, Tom, Mtl.	D	Pronovost, Marcel, Det.
Gadsby, Bill, NYR	D	Harvey, Doug, Mtl.
Béliveau, Jean, Mtl.	C	Richard, Henri, Mtl.
Bathgate, Andy, NYR	RW	Howe, Gordie, Det.
Moore, Dickie, Mtl.	LW	Delvecchio, Alex, Det.

1957-58
Hall, Glenn, Chi.	G	Plante, Jacques, Mtl.
Harvey, Doug, Mtl.	D	Flaman, Fern, Bos.
Gadsby, Bill, NYR	D	Pronovost, Marcel, Det.
Richard, Henri, Mtl.	C	Béliveau, Jean, Mtl.
Howe, Gordie, Det.	RW	Bathgate, Andy, NYR
Moore, Dickie, Mtl.	LW	Henry, Camille, NYR

1956-57
Hall, Glenn, Det.	G	Plante, Jacques, Mtl.
Harvey, Doug, Mtl.	D	Flaman, Fern, Bos.
Kelly, Red, Det.	D	Gadsby, Bill, NYR
Béliveau, Jean, Mtl.	C	Litzenberger, Eddie, Chi.
Howe, Gordie, Det.	RW	Richard, Maurice, Mtl.
Lindsay, Ted, Det.	LW	Chevrefils, Real, Bos.

First Team		Second Team

1955-56

First Team	Pos	Second Team
Plante, Jacques, Mtl.	G	Hall, Glenn, Det.
Harvey, Doug, Mtl.	D	Kelly, Red, Det.
Gadsby, Bill, NYR	D	Johnson, Tom, Mtl.
Béliveau, Jean, Mtl.	C	Sloan, Tod, Tor.
Richard, Maurice, Mtl.	RW	Howe, Gordie, Det.
Lindsay, Ted, Det.	LW	Olmstead, Bert, Mtl.

1954-55

First Team	Pos	Second Team
Lumley, Harry, Tor.	G	Sawchuk, Terry, Det.
Harvey, Doug, Mtl.	D	Goldham, Bob, Det.
Kelly, Red, Det.	D	Flaman, Fern, Bos.
Béliveau, Jean, Mtl.	C	Mosdell, Ken, Mtl.
Richard, Maurice, Mtl.	RW	Geoffrion, Bernie, Mtl.
Smith, Sid, Tor.	LW	Lewicki, Danny, NYR

1953-54

First Team	Pos	Second Team
Lumley, Harry, Tor.	G	Sawchuk, Terry, Det.
Kelly, Red, Det.	D	Gadsby, Bill, Chi.
Harvey, Doug, Mtl.	D	Horton, Tim, Tor.
Mosdell, Ken, Mtl.	C	Kennedy, Ted, Tor.
Howe, Gordie, Det.	RW	Richard, Maurice, Mtl.
Lindsay, Ted, Det.	LW	Sandford, Ed, Bos.

1952-53

First Team	Pos	Second Team
Sawchuk, Terry, Det.	G	McNeil, Gerry, Mtl.
Kelly, Red, Det.	D	Quackenbush, Bill, Bos.
Harvey, Doug, Mtl.	D	Gadsby, Bill, Chi.
Mackell, Fleming, Bos.	C	Delvecchio, Alex, Det.
Howe, Gordie, Det.	RW	Richard, Maurice, Mtl.
Lindsay, Ted, Det.	LW	Olmstead, Bert, Mtl.

1951-52

First Team	Pos	Second Team
Sawchuk, Terry, Det.	G	Henry, Jim, Bos.
Kelly, Red, Det.	D	Buller, Hy, NYR
Harvey, Doug, Mtl.	D	Thomson, Jim, Tor.
Lach, Elmer, Mtl.	C	Schmidt, Milt, Bos.
Howe, Gordie, Det.	RW	Richard, Maurice, Mtl.
Lindsay, Ted, Det.	LW	Smith, Sid, Tor.

1950-51

First Team	Pos	Second Team
Sawchuk, Terry, Det.	G	Rayner, Chuck, NYR
Kelly, Red, Det.	D	Thomson, Jim, Tor.
Quackenbush, Bill, Bos.	D	Reise, Leo, Det.
Schmidt, Milt, Bos.	C	Abel, Sid, Det.
	(tied)	Kennedy, Ted, Tor.
Howe, Gordie, Det.	RW	Richard, Maurice, Mtl.
Lindsay, Ted, Det.	LW	Smith, Sid, Tor.

1949-50

First Team	Pos	Second Team
Durnan, Bill, Mtl.	G	Rayner, Chuck, NYR
Mortson, Gus, Tor.	D	Reise, Leo, Det.
Reardon, Kenny, Mtl.	D	Kelly, Red, Det.
Abel, Sid, Det.	C	Kennedy, Ted, Tor.
Richard, Maurice, Mtl.	RW	Howe, Gordie, Det.
Lindsay, Ted, Det.	LW	Leswick, Tony, NYR

1948-49

First Team	Pos	Second Team
Durnan, Bill, Mtl.	G	Rayner, Chuck, NYR
Quackenbush, Bill, Det.	D	Harmon, Glen, Mtl.
Stewart, Jack, Det.	D	Reardon, Kenny, Mtl.
Abel, Sid, Det.	C	Bentley, Doug, Chi.
Richard, Maurice, Mtl.	RW	Howe, Gordie, Det.
Conacher, Roy, Chi.	LW	Lindsay, Ted, Det.

1947-48

First Team	Pos	Second Team
Broda, W. "Turk", Tor.	G	Brimsek, Frank, Bos.
Quackenbush, Bill, Det.	D	Reardon, Kenny, Mtl.
Stewart, Jack, Det.	D	Colville, Neil, NYR
Lach, Elmer, Mtl.	C	O'Connor, "Buddy", NYR
Richard, Maurice, Mtl.	RW	Poile, "Bud", Chi.
Lindsay, Ted, Det.	LW	Stewart, Gaye, Chi.

1946-47

First Team	Pos	Second Team
Durnan, Bill, Mtl.	G	Brimsek, Frank, Bos.
Reardon, Kenny, Mtl.	D	Stewart, Jack, Det.
Bouchard, Emile, Mtl.	D	Quackenbush, Bill, Det.
Schmidt, Milt, Bos.	C	Bentley, Max, Chi.
Richard, Maurice, Mtl.	RW	Bauer, Bobby, Bos.
Bentley, Doug, Chi.	LW	Dumart, Woody, Bos.

1945-46

First Team	Pos	Second Team
Durnan, Bill, Mtl.	G	Brimsek, Frank, Bos.
Crawford, Jack, Bos.	D	Reardon, Kenny, Mtl.
Bouchard, Emile, Mtl.	D	Stewart, Jack, Det.
Bentley, Max, Chi.	C	Lach, Elmer, Mtl.
Richard, Maurice, Mtl.	RW	Mosienko, Bill, Chi.
Stewart, Gaye, Tor.	LW	Blake, "Toe", Mtl.
Irvin, Dick, Mtl.	Coach	Gottselig, John, Chi.

1944-45

First Team	Pos	Second Team
Durnan, Bill, Mtl.	G	Karakas, Mike, Chi.
Bouchard, Emile, Mtl.	D	Harmon, Glen, Mtl.
Hollett, Bill, Det.	D	Pratt, "Babe", Bos.
Lach, Elmer, Mtl.	C	Cowley, Bill, Bos.
Richard, Maurice, Mtl.	RW	Mosienko, Bill, Chi.
Blake, "Toe", Mtl.	LW	Howe, Syd, Det.
Irvin, Dick, Mtl.	Coach	Adams, Jack, Det.

1943-44

First Team	Pos	Second Team
Durnan, Bill, Mtl.	G	Bibeault, Paul, Tor.
Seibert, Earl, Chi.	D	Bouchard, Emile, Mtl.
Pratt, "Babe", Tor.	D	Clapper, "Dit", Bos.
Cowley, Bill, Bos.	C	Lach, Elmer, Mtl.
Carr, Lorne, Tor.	RW	Richard, Maurice, Mtl.
Bentley, Doug, Chi.	LW	Cain, Herb, Bos.
Irvin, Dick, Mtl.	Coach	Day, "Hap", Tor.

1942-43

First Team	Pos	Second Team
Mowers, Johnny, Det.	G	Brimsek, Frank, Bos.
Seibert, Earl, Chi.	D	Crawford, Jack, Bos.
Stewart, Jack, Det.	D	Hollett, Bill, Bos.
Cowley, Bill, Bos.	C	Apps, Syl, Tor.
Carr, Lorne, Tor.	RW	Hextall, Bryan, NYR
Bentley, Doug, Chi.	LW	Patrick, Lynn, NYR
Adams, Jack, Det.	Coach	Ross, Art, Bos.

1941-42

First Team	Pos	Second Team
Brimsek, Frank, Bos.	G	Broda, W. "Turk", Tor.
Seibert, Earl, Chi.	D	Egan, Pat, Bro.
Anderson, Tommy, Bro.	D	McDonald, Bucko, Tor.
Apps, Syl, Tor.	C	Watson, Phil, NYR
Hextall, Bryan, NYR	RW	Drillon, Gord, Tor.
Patrick, Lynn, NYR	LW	Abel, Sid, Det.
Boucher, Frank, NYR	Coach	Thompson, Paul, Chi.

1940-41

First Team	Pos	Second Team
Broda, W. "Turk", Tor.	G	Brimsek, Frank, Bos.
Clapper, "Dit", Bos.	D	Seibert, Earl, Chi.
Stanowski, Wally, Tor.	D	Heller, Ott, NYR
Cowley, Bill, Bos.	C	Apps, Syl, Tor.
Hextall, Bryan, NYR	RW	Bauer, Bobby, Bos.
Schriner, Dave, Tor.	LW	Dumart, Woody, Bos.
Weiland, "Cooney", Bos.	Coach	Irvin, Dick, Mtl.

1939-40

First Team	Pos	Second Team
Kerr, Dave, NYR	G	Brimsek, Frank, Bos.
Clapper, "Dit", Bos.	D	Coulter, Art, NYR
Goodfellow, Ebbie, Det.	D	Seibert, Earl, Chi.
Schmidt, Milt, Bos.	C	Colville, Neil, NYR
Hextall, Bryan, NYR	RW	Bauer, Bobby, Bos.
Blake, "Toe", Mtl.	LW	Dumart, Woody, Bos.
Thompson, Paul, Chi.	Coach	Boucher, Frank, NYR

1938-39

First Team	Pos	Second Team
Brimsek, Frank, Bos.	G	Robertson, Earl, NYA
Shore, Eddie, Bos.	D	Seibert, Earl, Chi.
Clapper, "Dit", Bos.	D	Coulter, Art, NYR
Apps, Syl, Tor.	C	Colville, Neil, NYR
Drillon, Gord, Tor.	RW	Bauer, Bobby, Bos.
Blake, "Toe", Mtl.	LW	Gottselig, Johnny, Chi.
Ross, Art, Bos.	Coach	Dutton, "Red", NYA

1937-38

First Team	Pos	Second Team
Thompson, "Tiny", Bos.	G	Kerr, Dave, NYR
Shore, Eddie, Bos.	D	Coulter, Art, NYR
Siebert, "Babe", Mtl.	D	Seibert, Eart, Chi.
Cowley, Bill, Bos.	C	Apps, Syl, Tor.
Dillon, Cecil, NYR	RW	Dillon, Cecil, NYR
Drillon, Gord, Tor.	(tied)	Drillon, Gord, Tor.
Thompson, Paul, Chi.	LW	Blake, Toe, Mtl.
Patrick, Lester, NYR	Coach	Ross, Art, Bos.

1936-37

First Team	Pos	Second Team
Smith, Norm, Det.	G	Cude, Wilf, Mtl.
Siebert, "Babe", Mtl.	D	Seibert, Earl, Chi.
Goodfellow, Ebbie, Det.	D	Conacher, Lionel, Mtl. M.
Barry, Marty, Det.	C	Chapman, Art, NYA
Aurie, Larry, Det.	RW	Dillon, Cecil, NYR
Jackson, Harvey, Tor.	LW	Schriner, Dave, NYA
Adams, Jack, Det.	Coach	Hart, Cecil, Mtl.

1935-36

First Team	Pos	Second Team
Thompson, "Tiny", Bos.	G	Cude, Wilf, Mtl.
Shore, Eddie, Bos.	D	Seibert, Earl, Chi.
Siebert, "Babe", Bos.	D	Goodfellow, Ebbie, Det.
Smith, "Hooley", Mtl. M.	C	Thoms, Bill, Tor.
Conacher, Charlie, Tor.	RW	Dillon, Cecil, NYR
Schriner, Dave, NYA	LW	Thompson, Paul, Chi.
Patrick, Lester, NYR	Coach	Gorman, T.P., Mtl. M.

1934-35

First Team	Pos	Second Team
Chabot, Lorne, Chi.	G	Thompson, "Tiny", Bos.
Shore, Eddie, Bos.	D	Wentworth, Cy, Mtl. M.
Seibert, Earl, NYR	D	Coulter, Art, Chi.
Boucher, Frank, NYR	C	Weiland, "Cooney", Det.
Conacher, Charlie, Tor.	RW	Clapper, "Dit", Bos.
Jackson, Harvey, Tor.	LW	Joliat, Aurel, Mtl.
Patrick, Lester, NYR	Coach	Irvin, Dick, Tor.

1933-34

First Team	Pos	Second Team
Gardiner, Charlie, Chi.	G	Worters, Roy, NYA
Clancy, "King", Tor.	D	Shore, Eddie, Bos.
Conacher, Lionel, Chi.	D	Johnson, "Ching", NYR
Boucher, Frank, NYR	C	Primeau, Joe, Tor.
Conacher, Charlie, Tor.	RW	Cook, Bill, NYR
Jackson, Harvey, Tor.	LW	Joliat, Aurel, Mtl.
Patrick, Lester, NYR	Coach	Irvin, Dick, Tor.

1932-33

First Team	Pos	Second Team
Roach, John Ross, Det.	G	Gardiner, Charlie, Chi.
Shore, Eddie, Bos.	D	Clancy, "King", Tor.
Johnson, "Ching", NYR	D	Conacher, Lionel, Mtl. M.
Boucher, Frank, NYR	C	Morenz, Howie, Mtl.
Cook, Bill, NYR	RW	Conacher, Charlie, Tor.
Northcott, "Baldy", Mtl M.	LW	Jackson, Harvey, Tor.
Patrick, Lester, NYR	Coach	Irvin, Dick, Tor.

1931-32

First Team	Pos	Second Team
Gardiner, Charlie, Chi.	G	Worters, Roy, NYA
Shore, Eddie, Bos.	D	Mantha, Sylvio, Mtl.
Johnson, "Ching", NYR	D	Clancy, "King", Tor.
Morenz, Howie, Mtl.	C	Smith, "Hooley", Mtl. M.
Cook, Bill, NYR	RW	Conacher, Charlie, Tor.
Jackson, Harvey, Tor.	LW	Joliat, Aurel, Mtl.
Patrick, Lester, NYR	Coach	Irvin, Dick, Mtl.

1930-31

First Team	Pos	Second Team
Gardiner, Charlie, Chi.	G	Thompson, "Tiny", Bos.
Shore, Eddie, Bos.	D	Mantha, Sylvio, Mtl.
Clancy, "King", Tor.	D	Johnson, "Ching", NYR
Morenz, Howie, Mtl.	C	Boucher, Frank, NYR
Cook, Bill, NYR	RW	Clapper, "Dit", Bos.
Joliet, Aurel, Mtl.	LW	Cook, "Bun", NYR
Patrick, Lester, NYR	Coach	Irvin, Dick, Chi.

All-Star Game Results

Year	Venue	Score	Coaches	Attendance
1994	NY Rangers	Eastern 9, Western 8	Jacques Demers, Barry Melrose	18,200
1993	Montreal	Wales 16, Campbell 6	Scotty Bowman, Mike Keenan	17,137
1992	Philadelphia	Campbell 10, Wales 6	Bob Gainey, Scotty Bowman	17,380
1991	Chicago	Campbell 11, Wales 5	John Muckler, Mike Milbury	18,472
1990	Pittsburgh	Wales 12, Campbell 7	Pat Burns, Terry Crisp	16,236
1989	Edmonton	Campbell 9, Wales 5	Glen Sather, Terry O'Reilly	17,503
1988	St. Louis	Wales 6, Campbell 5 OT	Mike Keenan, Glen Sather	17,878
1986	Hartford	Wales 4, Campbell 3 OT	Mike Keenan, Glen Sather	15,100
1985	Calgary	Wales 6, Campbell 4	Al Arbour, Glen Sather	16,825
1984	New Jersey	Wales 7, Campbell 6	Al Arbour, Glen Sather	18,939
1983	NY Islanders	Campbell 9, Wales 3	Roger Neilson, Al Arbour	15,230
1982	Washington	Wales 4, Campbell 2	Al Arbour, Glen Sonmor	18,130
1981	Los Angeles	Campbell 4, Wales 1	Pat Quinn, Scotty Bowman	15,761
1980	Detroit	Wales 6, Campbell 3	Scotty Bowman, Al Arbour	21,002
1978	Buffalo	Wales 3, Campbell 2 OT	Scotty Bowman, Fred Shero	16,433
1977	Vancouver	Wales 4, Campbell 3	Scotty Bowman, Fred Shero	15,607
1976	Philadelphia	Wales 7, Campbell 5	Floyd Smith, Fred Shero	16,436
1975	Montreal	Wales 7, Campbell 1	Bep Guidolin, Fred Shero	16,080
1974	Chicago	West 6, East 4	Billy Reay, Scotty Bowman	16,426
1973	New York	East 5, West 4	Tom Johnson, Billy Reay	16,986
1972	Minnesota	East 3, West 2	Al MacNeil, Billy Reay	15,423
1971	Boston	West 2, East 1	Scotty Bowman, Harry Sinden	14,790
1970	St. Louis	East 4, West 1	Claude Ruel, Scotty Bowman	16,587
1969	Montreal	East 3, West 3	Toe Blake, Scotty Bowman	16,260
1968	Toronto	Toronto 4, All-Stars 3	Punch Imlach, Toe Blake	15,753
1967	Montreal	Montreal 3, All-Stars 0	Toe Blake, Sid Abel	14,284
1965	Montreal	All-Stars 5, Montreal 2	Billy Reay, Toe Blake	13,529
1964	Toronto	All-Stars 3, Toronto 3	Sid Abel, Punch Imlach	14,232
1963	Toronto	All-Stars 3, Toronto 3	Sid Abel, Punch Imlach	14,034
1962	Toronto	Toronto 4, All-Stars 1	Punch Imlach, Rudy Pilous	14,236
1961	Chicago	All-Stars 3, Chicago 1	Sid Abel, Rudy Pilous	14,534
1960	Montreal	All-Stars 2, Montreal 1	Punch Imlach, Toe Blake	13,949
1959	Montreal	Montreal 6, All-Stars 1	Toe Blake, Punch Imlach	13,818
1958	Montreal	Montreal 6, All-Stars 3	Toe Blake, Milt Schmidt	13,989
1957	Montreal	All-Stars 5, Montreal 3	Milt Schmidt, Toe Blake	13,003
1956	Montreal	All-Stars 1, Montreal 1	Jim Skinner, Toe Blake	13,095
1955	Detroit	Detroit 3, All-Stars 1	Jim Skinner, Dick Irvin	10,111
1954	Detroit	All-Stars 2, Detroit 2	King Clancy, Jim Skinner	10,689
1953	Montreal	All-Stars 3, Montreal 1	Lynn Patrick, Dick Irvin	14,153
1952	Detroit	1st team 1, 2nd team 1	Tommy Ivan, Dick Irvin	10,680
1951	Toronto	1st team 2, 2nd team 2	Joe Primeau, Hap Day	11,469
1950	Detroit	Detroit 7, All-Stars 1	Tommy Ivan, Lynn Patrick	9,166
1949	Toronto	All-Stars 3, Toronto 1	Tommy Ivan, Hap Day	13,541
1948	Chicago	All-Stars 3, Toronto 1	Tommy Ivan, Hap Day	12,794
1947	Toronto	All-Stars 4, Toronto 3	Dick Irvin, Hap Day	14,169

There was no All-Star contest during the calendar year of 1966 because the game was moved from the start of season to mid-season. In 1979, the Challenge Cup series between the Soviet Union and Team NHL replaced the All-Star Game. In 1987, Rendez-Vous '87, two games between the Soviet Union and Team NHL replaced the All-Star Game. Rendez-Vous '87 scores: game one, NHL All-Stars 4, Soviet Union 3; game two, Soviet Union 5, NHL All-Stars 3. There was no All-Star Game in 1995 due to a labor disruption.

The 1996 All-Star Game will be played in Boston's new FleetCenter on Saturday, January 20, 1996 at 8:00 p.m.

NHL/UPPER DECK ALL-ROOKIE TEAM

Voting for the NHL/Upper Deck All-Rookie Team is conducted among the representatives of the Professional Hockey Writers' Association at the end of the season. The rookie all-star team was first selected for the 1982-83 season.

1994-95

Jim Carey, Washington	Goal
Chris Therien, Philadelphia	Defense
Kenny Jonsson, Toronto	Defense
Peter Forsberg, Quebec	Forward
Jeff Friesen, San Jose	Forward
Paul Kariya, Anaheim	Forward

1993-94

Martin Brodeur, New Jersey	Goal
Chris Pronger, Hartford	Defense
Boris Mironov, Wpg., Edm.	Defense
Jason Arnott, Edmonton	Center
Mikael Renberg, Philadelphia	Wing
Oleg Petrov, Montreal	Wing

1991-92

Dominik Hasek, Chicago	Goal
Nicklas Lidstrom, Detroit	Defense
Vladimir Konstantinov, Detroit	Defense
Kevin Todd, New Jersey	Center
Tony Amonte, NY Rangers	Right Wing
Gilbert Dionne, Montreal	Left Wing

1989-90

Bob Essensa, Winnipeg	Goal
Brad Shaw, Hartford	Defense
Geoff Smith, Edmonton	Defense
Mike Modano, Minnesota	Center
Sergei Makarov, Calgary	Right Wing
Rod Brind'Amour, St. Louis	Left Wing

1992-93

Felix Potvin, Toronto	Goal
Vladimir Malakhov, NY Islanders	Defense
Scott Niedermayer, New Jersey	Defense
Eric Lindros, Philadelphia	Center
Teemu Selanne, Winnipeg	Wing
Joe Juneau, Boston	Wing

1990-91

Ed Belfour, Chicago	Goal
Eric Weinrich, New Jersey	Defense
Rob Blake, Los Angeles	Defense
Sergei Fedorov, Detroit	Center
Ken Hodge, Boston	Right Wing
Jaromir Jagr, Pittsburgh	Left Wing

1988-89

Peter Sidorkiewicz, Hartford	Goal
Brian Leetch, NY Rangers	Defense
Zarley Zalapski, Pittsburgh	Defense
Trevor Linden, Vancouver	Center
Tony Granato, NY Rangers	Right Wing
David Volek, NY Islanders	Left Wing

1987-88

Darren Pang, Chicago	Goal
Glen Wesley, Boston	Defense
Calle Johansson, Buffalo	Defense
Joe Nieuwendyk, Calgary	Center
Ray Sheppard, Buffalo	Right Wing
Iain Duncan, Winnipeg	Left Wing

1985-86

Patrick Roy, Montreal	Goal
Gary Suter, Calgary	Defense
Dana Murzyn, Hartford	Defense
Mike Ridley, NY Rangers	Center
Kjell Dahlin, Montreal	Right Wing
Wendel Clark, Toronto	Left Wing

1983-84

Tom Barrasso, Buffalo	Goal
Thomas Eriksson, Philadelphia	Defense
Jamie Macoun, Calgary	Defense
Steve Yzerman, Detroit	Center
Hakan Loob, Calgary	Right Wing
Sylvain Turgeon, Hartford	Left Wing

1986-87

Ron Hextall, Philadelphia	Goal
Steve Duchesne, Los Angeles	Defense
Brian Benning, St. Louis	Defense
Jimmy Carson, Los Angeles	Center
Jim Sandlak, Vancouver	Right Wing
Luc Robitaille, Los Angeles	Left Wing

1984-85

Steve Penney, Montreal	Goal
Chris Chelios, Montreal	Defense
Bruce Bell, Quebec	Defense
Mario Lemieux, Pittsburgh	Center
Tomas Sandstrom, NY Rangers	Right Wing
Warren Young, Pittsburgh	Left Wing

1982-83

Pelle Lindbergh, Philadelphia	Goal
Scott Stevens, Washington	Defense
Phil Housley, Buffalo	Defense
Dan Daoust, Montreal/Toronto	Center
Steve Larmer, Chicago	Right Wing
Mats Naslund, Montreal	Left Wing

All-Star Game Records 1947 through 1994

TEAM RECORDS

MOST GOALS, BOTH TEAMS, ONE GAME:
22 — Wales 16, Campbell 6, 1993 at Montreal
19 — Wales 12, Campbell 7, 1990 at Pittsburgh
17 — East 9, West 8, 1994 at NY Rangers
16 — Campbell 11, Wales 5, 1991 at Chicago
— Campbell 10, Wales 6, 1992 at Philadelphia
14 — Campbell 9, Wales 5, 1989 at Edmonton
13 — Wales 7, Campbell 6, 1984 at New Jersey
12 — Campbell 9, Wales 3, 1983 at NY Islanders
— Wales 7, Campbell 5, 1976 at Philadelphia

FEWEST GOALS, BOTH TEAMS, ONE GAME:
2 — NHL All-Stars 1, Montreal Canadiens 1, 1956 at Montreal
— First Team All-Stars 1, Second Team All-Stars 1, 1952 at Detroit
3 — West 2, East 1, 1971 at Boston
— Montreal Canadiens 3, NHL All-Stars 0, 1967 at Montreal
— NHL All-Stars 2, Montreal Canadiens 1, 1960 at Montreal

MOST GOALS, ONE TEAM, ONE GAME:
16 — Wales 16, Campbell 6, 1993 at Montreal
12 — Wales 12, Campbell 7, 1990 at Pittsburgh
11 — Campbell 11, Wales 5, 1991 at Chicago
10 — Campbell 10, Wales 6, 1992 at Philadelphia
9 — Campbell 9, Wales 3, 1983 at NY Islanders
— Campbell 9, Wales 5, 1989 at Edmonton
— East 9, West 8, 1994 at NY Rangers

FEWEST GOALS, ONE TEAM, ONE GAME:
0 — NHL All-Stars 0, Montreal Canadiens 3, 1967 at Montreal
1 — 17 times (1981, 1975, 1971, 1970, 1962, 1961, 1960, 1959, both teams 1956, 1955, 1953, both teams 1952, 1950, 1949, 1948)

MOST SHOTS, BOTH TEAMS, ONE GAME (SINCE 1955):
102 — 1994 at NY Rangers — East 9 (56 shots)
West 8 (46 shots)
90 — 1993 at Montreal — Wales 16 (49 shots),
Campbell 6 (41 shots)
87 — 1990 at Pittsburgh — Wales 12 (45 shots),
Campbell 7 (42 shots)
83 — 1992 at Philadelphia — Campbell 10 (42 shots),
Wales 6 (41 shots)
82 — 1991 at Chicago — Campbell 11 (41 shots),
Wales 5 (41 shots)

FEWEST SHOTS, BOTH TEAMS, ONE GAME (SINCE 1955):
52 — 1978 at Buffalo — Campbell 2 (12 shots)
Wales 3 (40 shots)
53 — 1960 at Montreal — NHL All-Stars 2 (27 shots)
Montreal Canadiens 1 (26 shots)
55 — 1956 at Montreal — NHL All-Stars 1 (28 shots)
Montreal Canadiens 1 (27 shots)
— 1971 at Boston — West 2 (28 shots)
East 1 (27 shots)

MOST SHOTS, ONE TEAM, ONE GAME (SINCE 1955):
56 — 1994 at NY Rangers — East (9-8 vs. West)
49 — 1993 at Montreal — Wales (16-6 vs. Campbell)
46 — 1994 at NY Rangers — West (8-9 vs. East)
45 — 1990 at Pittsburgh — Wales (12-7 vs. Campbell)
44 — 1955 at Detroit — Detroit Red Wings (3-1 vs. NHL All-Stars)
— 1970 at St. Louis — East (4-1 vs. West)
43 — 1981 at Los Angeles — Campbell (4-1 vs. Wales)

FEWEST SHOTS, ONE TEAM, ONE GAME (SINCE 1955):
12 — 1978 at Buffalo — Campbell (2-3 vs. Wales)
17 — 1970 at St. Louis — West (1-4 vs. East)
23 — 1961 at Chicago — Chicago Black Hawks (1-3 vs. NHL All-Stars)
24 — 1976 at Philadelphia — Campbell (5-7 vs. Wales)

MOST POWER-PLAY GOALS, BOTH TEAMS, ONE GAME (SINCE 1950):
3 — 1953 at Montreal — NHL All-Stars 3 (2 power-play goals),
Montreal Canadiens 1 (1 power-play goal)
— 1954 at Detroit — NHL All-Stars 2 (1 power-play goal)
Detroit Red Wings 2 (2 power-play goals)
— 1958 at Montreal — NHL All-Stars 3 (1 power-play goal)
Montreal Canadiens 6 (2 power-play goals)

FEWEST POWER-PLAY GOALS, BOTH TEAMS, ONE GAME (SINCE 1950):
0 — 14 times (1952, 1959, 1960, 1967, 1968, 1969, 1972, 1973, 1976, 1980, 1981, 1984, 1985, 1992, 1994)

FASTEST TWO GOALS, BOTH TEAMS, FROM START OF GAME:
37 seconds — 1970 at St. Louis — Jacques Laperriere of East scored at 20 seconds and Dean Prentice of West scored at 37 seconds. Final score: East 4, West 1.
3:37 — 1993 at Montreal — Mike Gartner scored at 3:15 and at 3:37 for Wales. Final score: Wales 16, Campbell 6.
4:08 — 1963 at Toronto — Frank Mahovlich scored for Toronto Maple Leafs at 2:22 of first period and Henri Richard scored at 4:08 for NHL All-Stars. Final score: NHL All-Stars 3, Toronto Maple Leafs 3.

FASTEST TWO GOALS, BOTH TEAMS:
10 seconds — 1976 at Philadelphia — Dennis Ververgaert scored at 4:33 and at 4:43 of third period for Campbell. Final score: Wales 7, Campbell 5.
14 seconds — 1989 at Edmonton. Steve Yzerman and Gary Leeman scored at 17:21 and 17:35 of second period for Campbell. Final score: Campbell 9, Wales 5.
16 seconds — 1990 at Pittsburgh. Kirk Muller of Wales scored at 8:47 of second period and Al MacInnis of Campbell scored at 9:03. Final score: Wales 12, Campbell 7.

FASTEST THREE GOALS, BOTH TEAMS:
1:08 — 1993 at Montreal — all by Wales — Mike Gartner scored at 3:15 and at 3:37 of first period; Peter Bondra scored at 4:23. Final score: Wales 16, Campbell 6.
1:14 — 1994 at NY Rangers — Bob Kudelski scored at 9:46 of first period for East; Sergei Fedorov scored at 10:20 for West; Eric Lindros scored at 11:00 for East. Final score: East 9, West 8.
1:25 — 1992 at Philadelphia — Bryan Trottier scored at 4:03 of third period for Wales; Brian Bellows scored at 4:50 for Campbell; Alexander Mogilny scored at 5:28 for Wales. Final score: Campbell 10, Wales 6.

FASTEST FOUR GOALS, BOTH TEAMS:
3:29 — 1994 at NY Rangers — Jeremy Roenick scored at 7:31 of first period for West; Bob Kudelski scored at 9:46 of first period for East; Sergei Fedorov scored at 10:20 for West; Eric Lindros scored at 11:00 for East. Final score: East 9, West 8.
3:35 — 1994 at NY Rangers — Bob Kudelski scored at 9:46 of first period for East; Sergei Fedorov scored at 10:20 for West; Eric Lindros scored at 11:00 for East; Brendan Shanahan scored at 13:21 for West. Final score: East 9, West 8.
3:40 — 1993 at Montreal — Pierre Turgeon scored at 15:51 of third period for Wales; Teemu Selanne scored at 17:03 for Campbell; Pavel Bure at 18:44 and 19:31 for Campbell. Final score: Wales 16, Campbell 6.

FASTEST TWO GOALS, ONE TEAM, FROM START OF GAME:
3:37 — 1993 at Montreal — Wales — Mike Gartner scored at 3:15 and at 3:37. Final socre: Wales 16, Campbell 6.
4:19 — 1980 at Detroit — Wales — Larry Robinson scored at 3:58 and Steve Payne scored at 4:19. Final score: Wales 6, Campbell 3.
4:38 — 1971 at Boston — West — Chico Maki scored at 36 seconds and Bobby Hull scored at 4:38. Final score: West 2, East 1.

FASTEST TWO GOALS, ONE TEAM:
10 seconds — 1976 at Philadelphia — Campbell — Dennis Ververgaert scored at 4:33 and at 4:43 of third period. Final score: Wales 7, Campbell 5.
14 seconds — 1989 at Edmonton — Campbell — Steve Yzerman and Gary Leeman scored at 17:21 and 17:35 of second period. Final score: Campbell 9, Wales 5.
17 seconds — 1993 at Montreal — Wales — Pierre Turgeon scored at 13:05 of first period and Mike Gartner scored at 13:22. Final score: Wales 16, Campbell 6.

FASTEST THREE GOALS, ONE TEAM:
1:08 — 1993 at Montreal — Wales — Mike Gartner scored at 3:15 and 3:37 of first period; Peter Bondra scored at 4:23. Final socre: Wales 16, Campbell 6.
1:32 — 1980 at Detroit — Wales — Ron Stackhouse scored at 11:40 of third period; Craig Hartsburg scored at 12:40; Reed Larson scored at 13:12. Final score: Wales 6, Campbell 3.
1:42 — 1993 at Montreal — Wales — Alexander Mogilny scored at 11:40 of first period; Pierre Turgeon scored at 13:05; Mike Gartner scored at 13:22. Final score: Wales 16, Campbell 6.

FASTEST FOUR GOALS, ONE TEAM:
4:19 — 1992 at Philadelphia — Campbell — Brian Bellows scored at 7:40 of second period, Jeremy Roenick scored at 8:13, Theoren Fleury scored at 11:06, Brett Hull scored at 11:59. Final score: Campbell 10, Wales 6.
4:26 — 1980 at Detroit — Wales — Ron Stackhouse scored at 11:40 of third period; Craig Hartsburg scored at 12:40; Reed Larson scored at 13:12; Real Cloutier scored at 16:06. Final score: Wales 6, Campbell 3.
5:34 — 1993 at Montreal — Campbell — Doug Gilmour scored at 13:57 of third period; Teemu Selanne scored at 17:03; Pavel Bure at 18:44 and 19:31. Final score: Wales 16, Campbell 6.

MOST GOALS, BOTH TEAMS, ONE PERIOD:
9 — 1990 at Pittsburgh — First Period — Wales (7), Campbell (2). Final score: Wales 12, Campbell 7.
8 — 1992 at Philadelphia — Second period — Campbell (6), Wales (2). Final Score: Campbell 10, Wales 6.
— 1993 at Montreal — Second period — Wales (6), Campbell (2).
Final score: Wales 16, Campbell 6.
— 1993 at Montreal — Third period — Wales (4), Campbell (4).
Final score: Wales 16, Campbell 6.

MOST GOALS, ONE TEAM, ONE PERIOD:
7 — 1990 at Pittsburgh — First period — Wales. Final score: Wales 12, Campbell 7.
6 — 1983 at NY Islanders — Third period — Campbell.
Final score: Campbell 9, Wales 3.
— 1992 at Philadelphia — Second Period — Campbell.
Final score: Campbell 10, Wales 6.
— 1993 at Montreal — First period — Wales.
Final score: Wales 16, Campbell 6.
— 1993 at Montreal — Second period — Wales.
Final score: Wales 16, Campbell 6.

MOST SHOTS, BOTH TEAMS, ONE PERIOD:
39 — 1994 at NY Rangers — Second period — West (21) East (18).
Final score: East 9, West 8.
36 — 1990 at Pittsburgh — Third period — Campbell (22), Wales (14).
Final score: Wales 12, Campbell 7.
— 1994 at NY Rangers — First period — East (19), West (17).
Final score: East 9, West 8.

MOST SHOTS, ONE TEAM, ONE PERIOD:
22 — 1990 at Pittsburgh — Third period — Campbell.
Final score: Wales 12, Campbell 7.
— 1991 at Chicago — Third Period — Wales.
Final score: Campbell 11, Wales 5.
— 1993 at Montreal — First period — Wales.
Final score: Wales 16, Campbell 6.
20 — 1970 at St. Louis — Third period — East. Final score: East 4, West 1.

FEWEST SHOTS, BOTH TEAMS, ONE PERIOD:
9 — 1971 at Boston — Third period — East (2), West (7).
Final score: West 2, East 1.
— 1980 at Detroit — Second period — Campbell (4), Wales (5).
Final score: Wales 6, Campbell 3.
13 — 1982 at Washington — Third period — Campbell (6), Wales (7).
Final score: Wales 4, Campbell 2.
14 — 1978 at Buffalo — First period — Campbell (7), Wales (7).
Final score: Wales 3, Campbell 2.
— 1986 at Hartford — First period — Campbell (6), Wales (8).
Final score: Wales 4, Campbell 3.

FEWEST SHOTS, ONE TEAM, ONE PERIOD:
2 — 1971 at Boston   Third period   East
Final score: West 2, East 1
— 1978 at Buffalo   Second period   Campbell
Final score: Wales 3, Campbell 2
3 — 1978 at Buffalo   Third period   Campbell
Final score: Wales 3, Campbell 2
4 — 1955 at Detroit   First period   NHL All-Stars
Final score: Detroit Red Wings 3, NHL All-Stars 1
4 — 1980 at Detroit   Second period   Campbell
Final score: Wales 6, Campbell 3

A group of the NHL's finest talent including (l-r) Tommy Ivan, "Black" Jack Stewart, Elmer Lach, Bill Quackenbush, Walter "Turk" Broda, Maurice "Rocket" Richard and "Terrible" Ted Lindsay receive accolades from NHL president Clarence Campbell prior to the NHL's second annual All-Star Game on November 3, 1948.

INDIVIDUAL RECORDS

Career

MOST GAMES PLAYED:
23 — **Gordie Howe** from 1948 through 1980
15 — Frank Mahovlich from 1959 through 1974
13 — Jean Beliveau from 1953 through 1969
— Alex Delvecchio from 1953 through 1967
— Doug Harvey from 1951 through 1969
— Maurice Richard from 1947 through 1959
— Wayne Gretzky from 1980 through 1993
— Ray Bourque from 1981 through 1994

MOST GOALS:
12 — **Wayne Gretzky** in 14GP
10 — Gordie Howe in 23GP
9 — Mario Lemieux in 6GP
8 — Frank Mahovlich in 15GP
7 — Maurice Richard in 13GP
6 — Mike Gartner in 6GP

MOST ASSISTS:
11 — **Ray Bourque** in 13GP
10 — Adam Oates in 4GP
— Joe Sakic in 5GP
9 — Gordie Howe in 23GP
— Larry Robinson in 10GP
7 — Doug Harvey in 13GP
— Guy Lafleur in 5GP
— Paul Coffey in 12GP
— Wayne Gretzky in 14GP

MOST POINTS:
19 — Gordie Howe (10G-9A in 23GP)
— Wayne Gretzky (12G-7A in 14GP)
15 — Mario Lemieux (9G-6A in 6GP)
13 — Frank Mahovlich (8G-5A in 15GP)
— Ray Bourque (2G-11A in 13GP)
11 — Adam Oates (1G-10A in 4GP)
— Joe Sakic (1G-10A in 5GP)
10 — Bobby Hull (5G-5A in 12GP)
— Ted Lindsay (5G-5A in 11GP)
— Luc Robitaille (5G-5A in 6GP)
— Larry Robinson (1G-9A in 10GP)

MOST PENALTY MINUTES:
27 — Gordie Howe in 23GP
21 — Gus Mortson in 9GP
16 — Harry Howell in 7GP

MOST POWER-PLAY GOALS:
6 — **Gordie Howe** in 23GP
3 — Bobby Hull in 12GP
2 — Maurice Richard in 13GP

Game

MOST GOALS, ONE GAME:
4 — **Wayne Gretzky**, Campbell, 1983
— **Mario Lemieux**, Wales, 1990
— **Vince Damphousse**, Campbell, 1991
— **Mike Gartner**, Wales, 1993
3 — Ted Lindsay, Detroit Red Wings, 1950
— Mario Lemieux, Wales, 1988
— Pierre Turgeon, Wales, 1993
2 — Wally Hergesheimer, NHL All-Stars, 1953
— Earl Reibel, Detroit Red Wings, 1955
— Andy Bathgate, NHL All-Stars, 1958
— Maurice Richard, Montreal Canadiens, 1958
— Frank Mahovlich, Toronto Maple Leafs, 1963
— Gordie Howe, NHL All-Stars, 1965
— John Ferguson, Montreal Canadiens, 1967
— Frank Mahovlich, East All-Stars, 1969
— Greg Polis, West All-Stars, 1973
— Syl Apps, Wales, 1975
— Dennis Ververgaert, Campbell, 1976
— Richard Martin, Wales, 1977
— Lanny McDonald, Wales, 1977
— Mike Bossy, Wales, 1982
— Pierre Larouche, Wales, 1984
— Mario Lemieux, Wales 1985
— Brian Propp, Wales, 1986
— Luc Robitaille, Campbell, 1988
— Joe Mullen, Campbell, 1989
— Pierre Turgeon, Wales, 1990
— Kirk Muller, Wales, 1990
— Luc Robitaille, Campbell, 1990
— Pat LaFontaine, Wales, 1991
— Brett Hull, Campbell, 1992
— Theoren Fleury, Campbell, 1992
— Rick Tocchet, Wales, 1993
— Pavel Bure, Campbell, 1993
— Sandis Ozolinsh, West All-Stars, 1994
— Brendan Shanahan, West All-Stars, 1994
— Bob Kudelski, East All-Stars, 1994
— Alexei Yashin, East All-Stars, 1994

MOST ASSISTS, ONE GAME:
5 — Mats Naslund, Wales, 1988
4 — Ray Bourque, Wales, 1985
— Adam Oates, Campbell, 1991
— Adam Oates, Wales, 1993
— Mark Recchi, Wales, 1993
— Pierre Turgeon, East All-Stars, 1994
3 — Dickie Moore, Montreal Canadiens, 1958
— Doug Harvey, Montreal Canadiens, 1959
— Guy Lafleur, Wales, 1975
— Pete Mahovlich, Wales, 1976
— Mark Messier, Campbell, 1983
— Rick Vaive, Campbell, 1984
— Mark Johnson, Wales, 1984
— Don Maloney, Wales, 1984
— Mike Krushelnyski, Campbell, 1985
— Mario Lemieux, Wales, 1988
— Brett Hull, Campbell, 1990
— Luc Robitaille, Campbell, 1992
— Joe Sakic, Wales, 1993

MOST POINTS, ONE GAME:
6 — Mario Lemieux, Wales, 1988 (3G-3A)
5 — Mats Naslund, Wales, 1988 (5A)
— Adam Oates, Campbell, 1991 (1G-4A)
— Mike Gartner, Wales, 1993 (4G-1A)
— Mark Recchi, Wales, 1993 (1G-4A)
— Pierre Turgeon, Wales, 1993 (3G-2A)

MOST GOALS, ONE PERIOD:
4 — Wayne Gretzky, Campbell, Third period, 1983
3 — Mario Lemieux, Wales, First period, 1990
— Vince Damphousse, Campbell, Third period, 1991
— Mike Gartner, Wales, First period, 1993
2 — Ted Lindsay, Detroit Red Wings, First period, 1950
— Wally Hergesheimer, NHL All-Stars, First period, 1953
— Andy Bathgate, NHL All-Stars, Third period, 1958
— Frank Mahovlich, Toronto Maple Leafs, First period, 1963
— Dennis Ververgaert, Campbell, Third period, 1976
— Richard Martin, Wales, Third period, 1977
— Pierre Turgeon, Wales, First period, 1990
— Luc Robitaille, Campbell, Third period, 1990
— Theoren Fleury, Campbell, Second period, 1992
— Brett Hull, Campbell, Second period, 1992
— Rick Tocchet, Wales, Second period, 1993
— Pavel Bure, Campbell, Third period, 1993

MOST ASSISTS, ONE PERIOD:
4 — Adam Oates, Wales, First period, 1993
3 — Mark Messier, Campbell, Third period, 1983

MOST POINTS, ONE PERIOD:
4 — Wayne Gretzky, Campbell, Third period, 1983 (4G)
— Mike Gartner, Wales, First period, 1993 (3G-1A)
— Adam Oates, Wales, First period, 1993 (4A)
3 — Gordie Howe, NHL All-Stars, Second period, 1965 (1G-2A)
— Pete Mahovlich, Wales, First period, 1976 (1G-2A)
— Mark Messier, Campbell, Third period, 1983 (3A)
— Mario Lemieux, Wales, Second period, 1988 (1G-2A)
— Mario Lemieux, Wales, First period, 1990 (3G)
— Vince Damphousse, Campbell, Third period, 1991 (3G)
— Mark Recchi, Wales, Second period, 1993 (1G-2A)

FASTEST GOAL FROM START OF GAME:
19 seconds — Ted Lindsay, Detroit Red Wings, 1950
20 seconds — Jacques Laperriere, East All-Stars, 1970
21 seconds — Mario Lemieux, Wales, 1990
36 seconds — Chico Maki, West All-Stars, 1971
37 seconds — Dean Prentice, West All-Star, 1970

FASTEST GOAL FROM START OF A PERIOD:
19 seconds — Ted Lindsay, Detroit Red Wings, 1950 (first period)
       — **Rick Tocchet**, Wales, 1993 (second period)
20 seconds — Jacques Laperriere, East, 1970 (first period)
21 seconds — Mario Lemieux, Wales, 1990 (first period)
26 seconds — Wayne Gretzky, Campbell, 1982 (second period)
28 seconds — Maurice Richard, NHL All-Stars, 1947 (third period)

FASTEST TWO GOALS (ONE PLAYER) FROM START OF GAME:
3:37 — Mike Gartner, Wales, 1993, at 3:15 and 3:37.
5:25 — Wally Hergesheimer, NHL All-Stars, 1953, at 4:06 and 5:25.
12:11 — Frank Mahovlich, Toronto, 1963, at 2:22 and 12:11.

FASTEST TWO GOALS (ONE PLAYER) FROM START OF A PERIOD:
3:37 — Mike Gartner, Wales, 1993, at 3:15 and 3:37 of first period.
4:43 — Dennis Ververgaert, Campbell, 1976, at 4:33 and 4:43 of third period.
4:57 — Rick Tocchet, Wales, 1993, at :19 and 4:57 of second period.

FASTEST TWO GOALS (ONE PLAYER):
10 seconds — Dennis Ververgaert, Campbell, 1976. Scored at 4:33 and 4:43 of third period.
22 seconds — Mike Gartner, Wales, 1993. Scored at 3:15 and 3:37 of first period.
47 seconds — Pavel Bure, Campbell, 1993. Scored at 18:44 and 19:31 of third period.

Goaltenders

MOST GAMES PLAYED:
13 — Glenn Hall from 1955-1969
11 — Terry Sawchuk from 1950-1968
8 — Jacques Plante from 1956-1970
6 — Tony Esposito from 1970-1980
— Ed Giacomin from 1967-1973
— Grant Fuhr from 1982-1989

MOST GOALS AGAINST:
22 — Glenn Hall in 13GP
21 — Mike Vernon in 5GP
19 — Terry Sawchuk in 11GP
18 — Jacques Plante in 8GP

BEST GOALS-AGAINST-AVERAGE AMONG THOSE WITH AT LEAST TWO GAMES PLAYED:
0.68 — Gilles Villemure in 3GP
1.02 — Frank Brimsek in 2GP
1.59 — Johnny Bower in 4GP
1.64 — Lorne "Gump" Worsley in 4GP
1.98 — Gerry McNeil in 3GP
2.03 — Don Edwards in 2GP
2.44 — Terry Sawchuk in 11GP

MOST MINUTES PLAYED:
467 — Terry Sawchuk in 11GP
421 — Glenn Hall in 13GP
370 — Jacques Plante in 8GP
209 — Turk Broda in 4GP
182 — Ed Giacomin in 6GP
177 — Grant Fuhr in 6GP
165 — Tony Esposito in 6GP

Eddie Shore greets Ace Bailey prior to the start of the NHL's first All-Star Game. Shore's hit on Bailey during a Leaf-Bruin tilt on December 12, 1933 ended the future Hall-of-Famers career, prompting the league to hold a game in his benefit on February 14, 1934.

Hockey Hall of Fame

Location: BCE Place, at the corner of Front and Yonge Streets in the heart of downtown Toronto. Easy access from all major highways running into Toronto. Close to TTC and Union Station.

Telephone: administration (416) 360-7735; information (416) 360-7765.

Summer and Christmas/March break hours: Monday to Saturday 9:30 a.m. to 6 p.m.; Sunday 10:00 a.m. to 6 p.m.

Fall/Winter/Spring hours (except Christmas/March break): Monday to Friday 10 a.m. to 5 p.m.; Saturday 9:30 a.m. to 6 p.m.; Sunday 10:30 a.m. to 5 p.m. The Hockey Hall of Fame can be booked for private functions after hours.

History: The Hockey Hall of Fame was established in 1943. Members were first honored in 1945. On August 26, 1961, the Hockey Hall of Fame opened its doors to the public in a building located on the grounds of the Canadian National Exhibition in Toronto. The Hockey Hall of Fame relovated to its new site at BCE Place and welcomed the hockey world on June 18, 1993.

Honor Roll: There are 300 Honored Members in the Hockey Hall of Fame. 205 have been inducted as players, 82 as builders and 13 as Referees/Linesmen. In addition, there are 53 media honorees. Additional Honored Members will be inducted November 20, 1995.

(Year of induction to the Hockey Hall of Fame is indicated in brackets after each Member's names).

Founding Sponsors: Special thanks to Blockbuster Video, Bell Canada, Coca-Cola Canada, Household Finance, Ford of Canada, Imperial Oil, Molson Breweries, London Life, TSN/RDS and The Toronto Sun.

PLAYERS

Abel, Sidney Gerald 1969
* Adams, John James "Jack" 1959
  Apps, Charles Joseph Sylvanus "Syl" 1961
  Armstrong, George Edward 1975
* Bailey, Irvine Wallace "Ace" 1975
* Bain, Donald H. "Dan" 1945
* Baker, Hobart "Hobey" 1945
  Barber, William Charles "Bill" 1990
* Barry, Martin J. "Marty" 1965
  Bathgate, Andrew James "Andy" 1978
  Béliveau, Jean Arthur 1972
* Benedict, Clinton S. 1965
* Bentley, Douglas Wagner 1964
* Bentley, Maxwell H. L. 1966
* Blake, Hector "Toe" 1966
  Boivin, Leo Joseph 1986
* Boon, Richard R. "Dickie" 1952
  Bossy, Michael 1991
  Bouchard, Emile Joseph "Butch" 1966
* Boucher, Frank 1958
* Boucher, George "Buck" 1960
  Bower, John William 1976
* Bowie, Russell 1945
  Brimsek, Francis Charles 1966
* Broadbent, Harry L. "Punch" 1962
* Broda, Walter Edward "Turk" 1967
  Bucyk, John Paul 1981
* Burch, Billy 1974
* Cameron, Harold Hugh "Harry" 1962
  Cheevers, Gerald Michael "Gerry" 1985
* Clancy, Francis Michael "King" 1958
* Clapper, Aubrey "Dit" 1947
  Clarke, Robert "Bobby" 1987
* Cleghorn, Sprague 1958
* Colville, Neil MacNeil 1967
* Conacher, Charles W. 1961
* Conacher, Lionel Pretoria 1994
* Connell, Alex 1958
* Cook, William Osser 1952
  Coulter, Arthur Edmund 1974
  Cournoyer, Yvan Serge 1982
* Cowley, William Mailes 1968
* Crawford, Samuel Russell "Rusty" 1962
* Darragh, John Proctor "Jack" 1962
* Davidson, Allan M. "Scotty" 1950
* Day, Clarence Henry "Hap" 1961
  Delvecchio, Alex 1977
* Denneny, Cyril "Cy" 1959
  Dionne, Marcel 1992
* Drillon, Gordon Arthur 1975
* Drinkwater, Charles Graham 1950
  Dryden, Kenneth Wayne 1983

Dumart, Woodrow "Woody" 1992
* Dunderdale, Thomas 1974
* Durnan, William Ronald 1964
* Dutton, Mervyn A. "Red" 1958
* Dye, Cecil Henry "Babe" 1970
  Esposito, Anthony James "Tony" 1988
  Esposito, Philip Anthony 1984
* Farrell, Arthur F. 1965
  Flaman, Ferdinand Charles "Fern" 1990
* Foyston, Frank 1958
* Frederickson, Frank 1958
  Gadsby, William Alexander 1970
  Gainey, Bob 1992
* Gardiner, Charles Robert "Chuck" 1945
* Gardiner, Herbert Martin "Herb" 1958
* Gardner, James Henry "Jimmy" 1962
  Geoffrion, Jos. A. Bernard "Boom Boom" 1972
* Gerard, Eddie 1945
  Giacomin, Edward "Eddie" 1987
  Gilbert, Rodrigue Gabriel "Rod" 1982
* Gilmour, Hamilton Livingstone "Billy" 1962
* Goheen, Frank Xavier "Moose" 1952
* Goodfellow, Ebenezer R. "Ebbie" 1963
* Grant, Michael "Mike" 1950
* Green, Wilfred "Shorty" 1962
* Griffis, Silas Seth "Si" 1950
* Hainsworth, George 1961
  Hall, Glenn Henry 1975
* Hall, Joseph Henry 1961
* Harvey, Douglas Norman 1973
* Hay, George 1958
* Hern, William Milton "Riley" 1962
* Hextall, Bryan Aldwyn 1969
* Holmes, Harry "Hap" 1972
* Hooper, Charles Thomas "Tom" 1962
  Horner, George Reginald "Red" 1965
* Horton, Miles Gilbert "Tim" 1977
  Howe, Gordon 1972
* Howe, Sydney Harris 1965
  Howell, Henry Vernon "Harry" 1979
  Hull, Robert Marvin 1983
* Hutton, John Bower "Bouse" 1962
* Hyland, Harry M. 1962
* Irvin, James Dickenson "Dick" 1958
* Jackson, Harvey "Busher" 1971
* Johnson, Ernest "Moose" 1952
* Johnson, Ivan "Ching" 1958
  Johnson, Thomas Christian 1970
* Joliat, Aurel 1947
* Keats, Gordon "Duke" 1958
  Kelly, Leonard Patrick "Red" 1969
  Kennedy, Theodore Samuel "Teeder" 1966

Keon, David Michael 1986
  Lach, Elmer James 1966
  Lafleur, Guy Damien 1988
* Lalonde, Edouard Charles "Newsy" 1950
  Laperriere, Jacques 1987
  Lapointe, Guy 1993
  Laprade, Edgar 1993
* Laviolette, Jean Baptiste "Jack" 1962
* Lehman, Hugh 1958
  Lemaire, Jacques Gerard 1984
* LeSueur, Percy 1961
* Lewis, Herbert A. 1989
  Lindsay, Robert Blake Theodore "Ted" 1966
  Lumley, Harry 1980
* MacKay, Duncan "Mickey" 1952
  Mahovlich, Frank William 1981
* Malone, Joseph "Joe" 1950
* Mantha, Sylvio 1960
* Marshall, John "Jack" 1965
* Maxwell, Fred G. "Steamer" 1962
  McDonald, Lanny 1992
* McGee, Frank 1945
* McGimsie, William George "Billy" 1962
* McNamara, George 1958
  Mikita, Stanley 1983
  Moore, Richard Winston 1974
* Moran, Patrick Joseph "Paddy" 1958
* Morenz, Howie 1945
* Mosienko, William "Billy" 1965
* Nighbor, Frank 1947
* Noble, Edward Reginald "Reg" 1962
* O'Connor, Herbert William "Buddy" 1988
* Oliver, Harry 1967
  Olmstead, Murray Bert "Bert" 1985
  Orr, Robert Gordon 1979
  Parent, Bernard Marcel 1984
  Park, Douglas Bradford "Brad" 1988
* Patrick, Joseph Lynn 1980
* Patrick, Lester 1947
  Perreault, Gilbert 1990
* Phillips, Tommy 1945
  Pilote, Joseph Albert Pierre Paul 1975
* Pitre, Didier "Pit" 1962
* Plante, Joseph Jacques Omer 1978
  Potvin, Denis 1991
* Pratt, Walter "Babe" 1966
* Primeau, A. Joseph 1963
  Pronovost, Joseph René Marcel 1978
  Pulford, Bob 1991
* Pulford, Harvey 1945
  Quackenbush, Hubert George "Bill" 1976
* Rankin, Frank 1961

BUILDERS

* Adams, Weston W. 1972
* Aheam, Thomas Franklin "Frank" 1962
* Ahearne, John Francis "Bunny" 1977
* Allan, Sir Montagu (C.V.O.) 1945
  Allen, Keith 1992
* Ballard, Harold Edwin 1977
* Bauer, Father David 1989
* Bickell, John Paris 1978
  Bowman, Scott 1991
* Brown, George V. 1961
* Brown, Walter A. 1962
* Buckland, Frank 1975
  Bush, Walter 1994
  Butterfield, Jack Arlington 1980
* Calder, Frank 1947
* Campbell, Angus D. 1964
* Campbell, Clarence Sutherland 1966
* Cattarinich, Joseph 1977
* Dandurand, Joseph Viateur "Leo" 1963
  Dilio, Francis Paul 1964
* Dudley, George S. 1958
* Dunn, James A. 1968
  Eagleson, Robert Alan 1989
  Francis, Emile 1982
* Gibson, Dr. John L. "Jack" 1976
* Gorman, Thomas Patrick "Tommy" 1963
* Griffiths, Frank A. 1993
* Hanley, William 1986
* Hay, Charles 1974
* Hendy, James C. 1968
* Hewitt, Foster 1965
* Hewitt, William Abraham 1947
* Hume, Fred J. 1962
* Imlach, George "Punch" 1984
  Ivan, Thomas N. 1974
* Jennings, William M. 1975
* Johnson, Bob 1992
* Juckes, Gordon W. 1979
* Kilpatrick, Gen. John Reed 1960
  Knox, Seymour H. III 1993
* Leader, George Alfred 1969
  LeBel, Robert 1970
* Lockhart, Thomas F. 1965
* Loicq, Paul 1961
* Mariucci, John 1985
  Mathers, Frank 1992
* McLaughlin, Major Frederic 1963
* Milford, John "Jake" 1984
  Molson, Hon. Hartland de Montarville 1973
* Nelson, Francis 1947
* Norris, Bruce A. 1969
* Norris, Sr., James 1958
* Norris, James Dougan 1962
* Northey, William M. 1947
* O'Brien, John Ambrose 1962
  O'Neill, Brian 1994
  Page, Fred 1993
* Patrick, Frank 1958
* Pickard, Allan W. 1958
* Pilous, Rudy 1985
  Poile, Norman "Bud" 1990
  Pollock, Samuel Patterson Smyth 1978
* Raymond, Sen. Donat 1958
* Robertson, John Ross 1947
* Robinson, Claude C. 1947
* Ross, Philip D. 1976
* Selke, Frank J. 1960
  Sinden, Harry James 1983
* Smith, Frank D. 1962
* Smythe, Conn 1958
  Snider, Edward M. 1988
* Stanley of Preston, Lord (G.C.B.) 1945
* Sutherland, Cap. James T. 1947
* Tarasov, Anatoli V. 1974
* Turner, Lloyd 1958
* Tutt, William Thayer 1978
* Voss, Carl Potter 1974
* Waghorn, Fred C. 1961
* Wirtz, Arthur Michael 1971
  Wirtz, William W. "Bill" 1976
  Ziegler, John A. Jr. 1987

REFEREES/LINESMEN

  Armstrong, Neil 1991
  Ashley, John George 1981
  Chadwick, William L. 1964
  D'Amico, John 1993
* Elliott, Chaucer 1961
* Hayes, George William 1988
* Hewitson, Robert W. 1963
* Ion, Fred J. "Mickey" 1961
  Pavelich, Matt 1987
* Rodden, Michael J. "Mike" 1962
* Smeaton, J. Cooper 1961
  Storey, Roy Alvin "Red" 1967
  Udvari, Frank Joseph 1973

*Deceased

Ratelle, Joseph Gilbert Yvan Jean "Jean" 1985
Rayner, Claude Earl "Chuck" 1973
Reardon, Kenneth Joseph 1966
Richard, Joseph Henri 1979
Richard, Joseph Henri Maurice "Rocket" 1961
* Richardson, George Taylor 1950
* Roberts, Gordon 1971
* Ross, Arthur Howie 1945
* Russel, Blair 1965
* Russell, Ernest 1965
* Ruttan, J.D. "Jack" 1962
  Savard, Serge A. 1986
* Sawchuk, Terrance Gordon "Terry" 1971
* Scanlan, Fred 1965
  Schmidt, Milton Conrad "Milt" 1961
* Schriner, David "Sweeney" 1962
* Seibert, Earl Walter 1963
* Seibert, Oliver Levi 1961
* Shore, Edward W. "Eddie" 1947
  Shutt, Stephen 1993
* Siebert, Albert C. "Babe" 1964
* Simpson, Harold Edward "Bullet Joe" 1962
  Sittler, Darryl Glen 1989
* Smith, Alfred E. 1962
  Smith, Clint 1991
* Smith, Reginald "Hooley" 1972
* Smith, Thomas James 1973
  Smith, William John "Billy" 1993
  Stanley, Allan Herbert 1981
* Stanley, Russell "Barney" 1962
* Stewart, John Sherratt "Black Jack" 1964
* Stewart, Nelson "Nels" 1962
* Stuart, Bruce 1961
* Stuart, Hod 1945
* Taylor, Frederic "Cyclone" (O.B.E.) 1947
* Thompson, Cecil R. "Tiny" 1959
  Tretiak, Vladislav 1989
* Trihey, Col. Harry J. 1950
  Ullman, Norman V. Alexander "Norm" 1982
* Vezina, Georges 1945
* Walker, John Phillip "Jack" 1960
* Walsh, Martin "Marty" 1962
* Watson, Harry E. 1962
  Watson, Harry 1994
* Weiland, Ralph "Cooney" 1971
* Westwick, Harry 1962
* Whitcroft, Fred 1962
* Wilson, Gordon Allan "Phat" 1962
  Worsley, Lorne John "Gump" 1980
* Worters, Roy 1969

United States Hockey Hall of Fame

The United States Hockey Hall of Fame is located in Eveleth, Minnesota, 60 miles north of Duluth, on Highway 53. The facility is open Monday to Saturday 9 a.m. to 5 p.m. and Sundays 11 a.m to 5 p.m.; Adult $3.00; Seniors $2.00; Juniors 13-17 $1.50; and Children 6-12 $1.25; Children under 6 free. Group rates available.

The Hall was dedicated and opened on June 21, 1973, largely as the result of the work of D. Kelly Campbell, Chairman of the Eveleth Civic Association's Project H Committee. There are now 89 enshrinees consisting of 54 players, 19 coaches, 16 administrators, and one referee. New members are inducted annually in October and must have made a significant contribution toward hockey in the United States through the vehicle of their careers. Support for the Hall comes from sponsorship and membership programs, grants from the hockey community, and government agencies.

PLAYERS

* Abel, Clarence "Taffy"
* Baker, Hobart "Hobey"
Bartholome, Earl
Bessone, Peter
Blake, Robert
Boucha, Henry
Brimsek, Frank
Cavanough, Joe
* Chaisson, Ray
Chase, John P.
Christian, Roger
Christian, William "Bill"
Cleary, Robert
Cleary, William
* Conroy, Anthony
Dahlstrom, Carl "Cully"
DesJardins, Victor
Desmond, Richard
* Dill, Robert
Everett, Doug
Ftorek, Robbie
* Garrison, John B.
Garrity, Jack
* Goheen, Frank "Moose"
Grant, Wally
Harding, Austin "Austie"
Iglehart, Stewart
Johnson, Virgil
Karakas, Mike
Kirrane, Jack
* Lane, Myles J.
Langevin, David R.
* Linder, Joseph
* LoPresti, Sam L.
* Mariucci, John
Matchefts, John
Mayasich, John
McCartan, Jack
Moe, William
Morrow, Ken
* Moseley, Fred
* Murray, Hugh "Muzz" Sr.
* Nelson, Hubert "Hub"
Olson , Eddie
* Owen, Jr., George
* Palmer, Winthrop
Paradise, Robert
Purpur, Clifford "Fido"
Riley, William
* Romnes, Elwin "Doc"
Rondeau, Richard
* Williams, Thomas
* Winters, Frank "Coddy"
* Yackel, Ken

COACHES

* Almquist, Oscar
Bessone, Amo
Brooks, Herbert
Ceglarski, Len
* Fullerton, James
* Gordon, Malcolm K.
Harkness, Nevin D. "Ned"
Heyliger, Victor
Ikola, Willard
* Jeremiah, Edward J.
* Johnson, Bob
* Kelley, John "Snooks"
Kelley, John H. "Jack"
Pleban, John "Connie"
Riley, Jack
* Ross, Larry
* Thompson, Clifford, R.
* Stewart, William
* Winsor, Alfred "Ralph"

ADMINISTRATORS

* Brown, George V.
* Brown, Walter A.
Bush, Walter
Clark, Donald
Claypool, James
* Gibson, J.C. "Doc"
* Jennings, William M.
* Kahler, Nick
* Lockhart, Thomas F.
Marvin, Cal
Ridder, Robert
Schulz, Charles M.
Trumble, Harold
* Tutt, William Thayer
Wirtz, William W. "Bill"
* Wright, Lyle Z.

REFEREE

Chadwick, William

*Deceased

Robbie Ftorek, who compiled four 100-point seasons in the WHA in addition to suiting up for the Detroit Red Wings, Quebec Nordiques and New York Rangers in the NHL, is an honored member of the United States Hockey Hall of Fame.

Results

CONFERENCE QUARTER-FINALS
(Best-of-seven series)

Eastern Conference

Series 'A'
Sat. May 6	NY Rangers 4	at	Quebec 5
Mon. May 8	NY Rangers 8	at	Quebec 3
Wed. May 10	Quebec 3	at	NY Rangers 4
Fri. May 12	Quebec 2	at	NY Rangers 3 OT
Sun. May 14	NY Rangers 2	at	Quebec 4
Tue. May 16	Quebec 2	at	NY Rangers 4

NY Rangers won series 4-2

Series 'B'
Sun. May 7	Buffalo 3	at	Philadelphia 4 OT
Mon. May 8	Buffalo 1	at	Philadelphia 3
Wed. May 10	Philadelphia 1	at	Buffalo 3
Fri. May 12	Philadelphia 4	at	Buffalo 2
Sun. May 14	Buffalo 4	at	Philadelphia 6

Philadelphia won series 4-1

Series 'C'
Sat. May 6	Washington 5	at	Pittsburgh 4
Mon. May 8	Washington 3	at	Pittsburgh 5
Wed. May 10	Pittsburgh 2	at	Washington 6
Fri. May 12	Pittsburgh 2	at	Washington 6
Sun. May 14	Washington 5	at	Pittsburgh 6 OT
Tue. May 16	Pittsburgh 7	at	Washington 1
Thu. May 18	Washington 0	at	Pittsburgh 3

Pittsburgh won series 4-3

Series 'D'
Sun. May 7	New Jersey 5	at	Boston 0
Mon. May 8	New Jersey 3	at	Boston 0
Wed. May 10	Boston 3	at	New Jersey 2
Fri. May 12	Boston 0	at	New Jersey 1 OT
Sun. May 14	New Jersey 3	at	Boston 2

New Jersey won series 4-1

Western Conference

Series 'E'
Sun. May 7	Dallas 3	at	Detroit 4
Tue. May 9	Dallas 1	at	Detroit 4
Thu. May 11	Detroit 5	at	Dallas 1
Sun. May 14	Detroit 1	at	Dallas 4
Mon. May 15	Dallas 1	at	Detroit 3

Detroit won series 4-1

Series 'F'
Sun. May 7	San Jose 5	at	Calgary 4
Tue. May 9	San Jose 5	at	Calgary 4 OT
Thu. May 11	Calgary 9	at	San Jose 2
Sat. May 13	Calgary 6	at	San Jose 4
Mon. May 15	San Jose 0	at	Calgary 5
Wed. May 17	Calgary 3	at	San Jose 5
Fri. May 19	San Jose 5	at	Calgary 4 OT

San Jose won series 4-3

Series 'G'
Sun. May 7	Vancouver 1	at	St. Louis 2
Tue. May 9	Vancouver 5	at	St. Louis 3
Thu. May 11	St. Louis 1	at	Vancouver 6
Sat. May 13	St. Louis 5	at	Vancouver 2
Mon. May 15	Vancouver 6	at	St. Louis 5 OT
Wed. May 17	St. Louis 8	at	Vancouver 2
Fri. May 19	Vancouver 5	at	St. Louis 3

Vancouver won series 4-3

Series 'H'
Sun. May 7	Toronto 5	at	Chicago 3
Tue. May 9	Toronto 3	at	Chicago 0
Thu. May 11	Chicago 3	at	Toronto 2
Sat. May 13	Chicago 3	at	Toronto 1
Mon. May 15	Toronto 2	at	Chicago 4
Wed. May 17	Chicago 4	at	Toronto 5 OT
Fri. May 19	Toronto 2	at	Chicago 5

Chicago won series 4-3

CONFERENCE SEMI-FINALS
(Best-of-seven series)

Eastern Conference

Series 'I'
Sun. May 21	NY Rangers 4	at	Philadelphia 5 OT
Mon. May 22	NY Rangers 3	at	Philadelphia 4 OT
Wed. May 24	Philadelphia 5	at	NY Rangers 2
Fri. May 26	Philadelphia 4	at	NY Rangers 1

Philadelphia won series 4-0

Series 'J'
Sat. May 20	New Jersey 2	at	Pittsburgh 3
Mon. May 22	New Jersey 4	at	Pittsburgh 2
Wed. May 24	Pittsburgh 1	at	New Jersey 5
Fri. May 26	Pittsburgh 1	at	New Jersey 2 OT
Sun. May 28	New Jersey 4	at	Pittsburgh 1

New Jersey won series 4-1

Western Conference

Series 'K'
Sun. May 21	San Jose 0	at	Detroit 6
Tue. May 23	San Jose 2	at	Detroit 6
Thu. May 25	Detroit 6	at	San Jose 2
Sat. May 27	Detroit 6	at	San Jose 2

Detroit won series 4-0

Series 'L'
Sun. May 21	Vancouver 1	at	Chicago 2 OT
Tue. May 23	Vancouver 0	at	Chicago 2
Thu. May 25	Chicago 3	at	Vancouver 2 OT
Sat. May 27	Chicago 4	at	Vancouver 3 OT

Chicago won series 4-0

CONFERENCE FINALS
(Best-of-seven series)

Eastern Conference

Series 'M'
Sat. Jun. 3	New Jersey 4	at	Philadelphia 1
Mon. Jun. 5	New Jersey 5	at	Philadelphia 2
Wed. Jun. 7	Philadelphia 3	at	New Jersey 2 OT
Sat. Jun. 10	Philadelphia 4	at	New Jersey 2
Sun. Jun. 11	New Jersey 3	at	Philadelphia 2
Tue. Jun. 13	Philadelphia 2	at	New Jersey 4

New Jersey won series 4-2

Western Conference

Series 'N'
Thu. Jun. 1	Chicago 1	at	Detroit 2 OT
Sun. Jun. 4	Chicago 2	at	Detroit 3
Tue. Jun. 6	Detroit 4	at	Chicago 3 OT
Thu. Jun. 8	Detroit 2	at	Chicago 5
Sun. Jun. 11	Chicago 1	at	Detroit 2 OT

Detroit won series 4-1

STANLEY CUP CHAMPIONSHIP
(Best-of-seven series)

Series 'O'
Sat. Jun. 17	New Jersey 2	at	Detroit 1
Tue. Jun. 20	New Jersey 4	at	Detroit 2
Thu. Jun. 22	Detroit 2	at	New Jersey 5
Sat. Jun. 24	Detroit 2	at	New Jersey 5

New Jersey won series 4-0

1995 Stanley Cup Playoffs

Team Playoff Records

	GP	W	L	GF	GA	%
New Jersey	20	16	4	67	34	.800
Detroit	18	12	6	61	44	.667
Philadelphia	15	10	5	50	43	.667
Chicago	16	9	7	45	39	.563
Pittsburgh	12	5	7	37	43	.417
NY Rangers	10	4	6	35	37	.400
Vancouver	11	4	7	33	38	.364
San Jose	11	4	7	32	59	.364
Calgary	7	3	4	35	26	.429
St. Louis	7	3	4	27	27	.429
Toronto	7	3	4	20	22	.429
Washington	7	3	4	26	29	.429
Quebec	6	2	4	19	25	.333
Buffalo	5	1	4	13	18	.200
Dallas	5	1	4	10	17	.200
Boston	5	1	4	5	14	.200

Individual Leaders

Abbreviations: * – rookie eligible for Calder Trophy; **A** – assists; **G** – goals; **GP** – Games Played; **OT** – overtime goals; **GW** – game-winning goals; **PIM** – penalties in minutes; **PP** – power play goals; **Pts** – points; **S** – shots on goal; **SH** – short-handed goals; **%** – percentage shots resulting in goals; **+/–** – difference between Goals For (**GF**) scored when a player is on the ice with his team at even strength or short-handed and Goals Against (**GA**) scored when the same player is on the ice with his team at even strength or on a power play.

Playoff Scoring Leaders

Player	Team	GP	G	A	Pts	+/–	PIM	PP	SH	GW	OT	S	%
Sergei Fedorov	Detroit	17	7	17	24	13	6	3	0	0	0	53	13.2
Stephane Richer	New Jersey	19	6	15	21	9	2	3	1	2	0	55	10.9
Neal Broten	New Jersey	20	7	12	19	13	6	1	0	4	1	47	14.9
Ron Francis	Pittsburgh	12	6	13	19	3	4	2	0	0	0	30	20.0
Denis Savard	Chicago	16	7	11	18	12	10	3	0	0	0	39	17.9
Paul Coffey	Detroit	18	6	12	18	4	10	2	1	0	0	74	8.1
John MacLean	New Jersey	20	5	13	18	8	14	2	0	0	0	57	8.8
Claude Lemieux	New Jersey	20	13	3	16	12	20	0	0	3	0	65	20.0
Vyacheslav Kozlov	Detroit	18	9	7	16	12	10	1	0	4	1	45	20.0
Nicklas Lidstrom	Detroit	18	4	12	16	4	8	3	0	2	1	37	10.8
Jaromir Jagr	Pittsburgh	12	10	5	15	3	6	2	1	1	0	55	18.2
Rod Brind'Amour	Philadelphia	15	6	9	15	5	8	2	1	1	0	28	21.4
Eric Lindros	Philadelphia	12	4	11	15	7	18	0	0	1	1	28	14.3
Larry Murphy	Pittsburgh	12	2	13	15	3	0	1	0	0	0	35	5.7
Theoren Fleury	Calgary	7	7	7	14	8	2	2	1	0	0	40	17.5
Brian Leetch	NY Rangers	10	6	8	14	–1	8	3	0	1	0	46	13.0
Pavel Bure	Vancouver	11	7	6	13	–1	10	2	2	0	0	39	17.9
Mikael Renberg	Philadelphia	15	6	7	13	5	6	2	0	0	0	45	13.3
Mark Messier	NY Rangers	10	3	10	13	–11	8	2	0	1	0	26	11.5
Joe Murphy	Chicago	16	9	3	12	–1	29	3	0	3	1	69	13.0
Randy McKay	New Jersey	19	8	4	12	5	11	2	0	2	1	30	26.7
John LeClair	Philadelphia	15	5	7	12	7	4	1	0	1	0	37	13.5
Russ Courtnall	Vancouver	11	4	8	12	1	21	0	2	1	0	27	14.8
Steve Yzerman	Detroit	15	4	8	12	–2	0	2	0	1	0	37	10.8
Doug Brown	Detroit	18	4	8	12	14	2	0	1	1	0	27	14.8
Bernie Nicholls	Chicago	16	1	11	12	0	8	1	0	0	0	28	3.6

Playoff Defensemen Scoring Leaders

Player	Team	GP	G	A	Pts	+/–	PIM	PP	SH	GW	OT	S	%
Paul Coffey	Detroit	18	6	12	18	4	10	2	1	0	0	74	8.1
Nicklas Lidstrom	Detroit	18	4	12	16	4	8	3	0	2	1	37	10.8
Larry Murphy	Pittsburgh	12	2	13	15	3	0	1	0	0	0	35	5.7
Brian Leetch	NY Rangers	10	6	8	14	–1	8	3	0	1	0	46	13.0
Chris Chelios	Chicago	16	4	7	11	6	12	0	1	3	2	49	8.2
Scott Niedermayer	New Jersey	20	4	7	11	11	10	2	0	1	0	53	7.5
Sergei Zubov	NY Rangers	10	3	8	11	–9	2	1	0	0	0	34	8.8
Shawn Chambers	New Jersey	20	4	5	9	2	2	2	0	0	0	36	11.1
Phil Housley	Calgary	7	0	9	9	5	0	0	0	0	0	22	.0

GOALTENDING LEADERS

Goals Against Average

Goaltender	Team	GPI	Mins.	GA	Avg.
*Olaf Kolzig	Washington	2	44	1	1.36
Martin Brodeur	New Jersey	20	1222	34	1.67
Chris Osgood	Detroit	2	68	2	1.76
Ed Belfour	Chicago	16	1014	37	2.19
Mike Vernon	Detroit	18	1063	41	2.31
Jeff Hackett	Chicago	2	26	1	2.31

Wins

Goaltender	Team	GPI	Mins.	W	L
Martin Brodeur	New Jersey	20	1222	16	4
Mike Vernon	Detroit	18	1063	12	6
Ron Hextall	Philadelphia	15	897	10	5
Ed Belfour	Chicago	16	1014	9	7
Ken Wregget	Pittsburgh	11	661	5	6

Save Percentage

Goaltender	Team	GPI	Mins.	GA	SA	S%	W	L
Dominic Roussel	Philadelphia	1	23	0	8	1.000	0	0
Rick Tabaracci	Calgary	1	19	0	9	1.000	0	0
Chris Terreri	New Jersey	1	8	0	2	1.000	0	0
*Olaf Kolzig	Washington	2	44	1	21	.952	1	0
Martin Brodeur	New Jersey	20	1222	34	463	.927	16	4
Ed Belfour	Chicago	16	1014	37	479	.923	9	7
Felix Potvin	Toronto	7	424	20	253	.920	3	4
Chris Osgood	Detroit	2	68	2	25	.920	0	0

Shutouts

Goaltender	Team	GPI	Mins.	SO
Martin Brodeur	New Jersey	20	1222	3
Felix Potvin	Toronto	7	424	1
Trevor Kidd	Calgary	7	434	1
Ken Wregget	Pittsburgh	11	661	1
Ed Belfour	Chicago	16	1014	1
Mike Vernon	Detroit	18	1063	1

Goal Scoring

Name	Team	GP	G
Claude Lemieux	New Jersey	20	13
Jaromir Jagr	Pittsburgh	12	10
Dino Ciccarelli	Detroit	16	9
Joe Murphy	Chicago	16	9
Vyacheslav Kozlov	Detroit	18	9
Randy McKay	New Jersey	19	8
Theoren Fleury	Calgary	7	7
Pavel Bure	Vancouver	11	7
Luc Robitaille	Pittsburgh	12	7
Denis Savard	Chicago	16	7
Sergei Fedorov	Detroit	17	7
Neal Broten	New Jersey	20	7
Brett Hull	St. Louis	7	6

Assists

Name	Team	GP	A
Sergei Fedorov	Detroit	17	17
Stephane Richer	New Jersey	19	15
Ron Francis	Pittsburgh	12	13
Larry Murphy	Pittsburgh	12	13
John MacLean	New Jersey	20	13
Paul Coffey	Detroit	18	12
Nicklas Lidstrom	Detroit	18	12
Neal Broten	New Jersey	20	12
Eric Lindros	Philadelphia	12	11
Bernie Nicholls	Chicago	16	11
Denis Savard	Chicago	16	11

Power-play Goals

Name	Team	GP	PP
Dino Ciccarelli	Detroit	16	6
Mike Rathje	San Jose	11	5
Brian Leetch	NY Rangers	10	3

Game-winning Goals

Name	Team	GP	GW
Vyacheslav Kozlov	Detroit	18	4
Neal Broten	New Jersey	20	4
Chris Chelios	Chicago	16	3
Joe Murphy	Chicago	16	3
Claude Lemieux	New Jersey	20	3
Cliff Ronning	Vancouver	11	2

Short-handed Goals

Name	Team	GP	SH
Russ Courtnall	Vancouver	11	2
Pavel Bure	Vancouver	11	2
Dean Evason	Dallas	5	1
Wayne Presley	Buffalo	5	1

Overtime Goals

Name	Team	GP	OT
Chris Chelios	Chicago	16	2
Randy Wood	Toronto	7	1
Steve Larmer	NY Rangers	10	1
Ulf Dahlen	San Jose	11	1
Cliff Ronning	Vancouver	11	1

Shots

Name	Team	GP	S
Paul Coffey	Detroit	18	74
Joe Murphy	Chicago	16	69
Claude Lemieux	New Jersey	20	65
John MacLean	New Jersey	20	57
Jaromir Jagr	Pittsburgh	12	55

Plus/Minus

Name	Team	GP	+/–
Doug Brown	Detroit	18	14
Eric Desjardins	Philadelphia	15	13
Bruce Driver	New Jersey	17	13
Sergei Fedorov	Detroit	17	13
Neal Broten	New Jersey	20	13

Team Statistics

TEAMS' HOME-AND-ROAD RECORD

	Home						Road					
	GP	W	L	GF	GA	%	GP	W	L	GF	GA	%
N.J.	9	6	3	28	18	.667	11	10	1	39	16	.909
DET	10	8	2	33	17	.800	8	4	4	28	27	.500
PHI	8	5	3	27	27	.625	7	5	2	23	16	.714
CHI	8	5	3	24	19	.625	8	4	4	21	20	.500
PIT	7	4	3	24	23	.571	5	1	4	13	20	.200
NYR	5	3	2	14	16	.600	5	1	4	21	21	.200
VAN	5	1	4	15	21	.200	6	3	3	18	17	.500
S.J.	5	1	4	15	30	.200	6	3	3	17	29	.500
CGY	4	1	3	17	15	.250	3	2	1	18	11	.667
ST.L.	4	1	3	13	17	.250	3	2	1	14	10	.667
TOR	3	1	2	8	10	.333	4	2	2	12	12	.500
WSH	3	2	1	13	11	.667	4	1	3	13	18	.250
QUE	3	2	1	12	14	.667	3	0	3	7	11	.000
BUF	2	1	1	5	5	.500	3	0	3	8	13	.000
DAL	2	1	1	5	6	.500	3	0	3	5	11	.000
BOS	3	0	3	2	11	.000	2	1	1	3	3	.500
TOTAL	**81**	**42**	**39**	**255**	**260**	**.519**	**81**	**39**	**42**	**260**	**255**	**.481**

TEAMS' POWER-PLAY RECORD

Abbreviations: **Adv**-total advantages; **PPGF**-power play goals for; **%** arrived by dividing number of power-play goals by total advantages.

	Home					Road					Overall			
	Team	GP	ADV	PPGF	%	Team	GP	ADV	PPGF	%	Team	GP	ADV	PPGF	%
1	DET	10	43	13	30.2	NYR	5	23	11	47.8	NYR	10	46	13	28.3
2	CGY	4	18	5	27.8	N.J.	11	39	12	30.8	N.J.	20	72	18	25.0
3	PIT	7	31	8	25.8	TOR	4	15	4	26.7	DET	18	89	22	24.7
4	VAN	5	32	8	25.0	S.J.	6	24	5	20.8	CGY	7	31	7	22.6
5	DAL	2	11	2	18.2	BOS	2	5	1	20.0	VAN	11	57	12	21.1
6	N.J.	9	33	6	18.2	DET	8	46	9	19.6	TOR	7	36	7	19.4
7	S.J.	5	24	4	16.7	PHI	7	31	5	16.1	PIT	12	58	11	19.0
8	ST.L.	4	26	4	15.4	VAN	6	25	4	16.0	S.J.	11	48	9	18.8
9	TOR	3	21	3	14.3	CGY	3	13	2	15.4	WSH	7	44	6	13.6
10	WSH	3	24	3	12.5	CHI	8	33	5	15.2	ST.L.	7	45	6	13.3
11	CHI	8	35	4	11.4	WSH	4	20	3	15.0	CHI	16	68	9	13.2
12	PHI	8	39	4	10.3	BUF	3	15	2	13.3	PHI	15	70	9	12.9
13	BUF	2	11	1	9.1	PIT	5	27	3	11.1	BUF	5	26	3	11.5
14	NYR	5	23	2	8.7	ST.L.	3	19	2	10.5	DAL	5	26	3	11.5
15	QUE	3	13	1	7.7	QUE	3	12	1	8.3	BOS	5	20	2	10.0
16	BOS	3	15	1	6.7	DAL	3	15	1	6.7	QUE	6	25	2	8.0
	TOTAL	**81**	**399**	**69**	**17.3**		**81**	**362**	**70**	**19.3**		**81**	**761**	**139**	**18.3**

TEAMS' PENALTY KILLING RECORD

Abbreviations: **TSH** – Total times short-handed; **PPGA** – power-play goals against; **%** arrived by dividing times short minus power-play goals against by times short.

	Home					Road					Overall			
	Team	GP	TSH	PPGA	%	Team	GP	TSH	PPGA	%	Team	GP	TSH	PPGA	%
1	VAN	5	35	3	91.4	TOR	4	16	0	100.0	TOR	7	27	2	92.6
2	N.J.	9	33	4	87.9	BUF	3	17	1	94.1	NYR	10	50	5	90.0
3	NYR	5	24	3	87.5	QUE	3	16	1	93.8	BUF	5	26	3	88.5
4	S.J.	5	21	3	85.7	NYR	5	26	2	92.3	VAN	11	66	8	87.9
5	WSH	3	20	3	85.0	PIT	5	32	4	87.5	N.J.	20	74	10	86.5
6	CHI	8	35	6	82.9	CHI	8	40	5	87.5	CHI	16	75	11	85.3
7	DET	10	35	6	82.9	PHI	7	28	4	85.7	PIT	12	61	10	83.6
8	TOR	3	11	2	81.8	N.J.	11	41	6	85.4	DET	18	78	14	82.1
9	CGY	4	16	3	81.3	VAN	6	31	5	83.9	CGY	7	31	6	80.6
10	PIT	7	29	6	79.3	BOS	2	6	1	83.3	PHI	15	66	15	77.3
11	ST.L.	4	19	4	78.9	DET	8	43	8	81.4	WSH	7	42	10	76.2
12	BUF	2	9	2	77.8	CGY	3	15	3	80.0	QUE	6	29	7	75.9
13	PHI	8	38	11	71.1	ST.L.	3	24	7	70.8	ST.L.	7	43	11	74.4
14	DAL	2	13	4	69.2	DAL	3	17	5	70.6	S.J.	11	46	13	71.7
15	BOS	3	11	4	63.6	WSH	4	22	7	68.2	BOS	5	17	5	70.6
16	QUE	3	13	6	53.8	S.J.	6	25	10	60.0	DAL	5	30	9	70.0
	TOTAL	**81**	**362**	**70**	**80.7**		**81**	**399**	**69**	**82.7**		**81**	**761**	**139**	**81.7**

SHORT-HANDED GOALS

	For			Against		
Team	Games	Goals	Team	Games	Goals	
VAN	11	7	CGY	7	0	
CGY	7	6	DAL	5	0	
PHI	15	3	DET	18	1	
DET	18	3	CHI	16	1	
QUE	6	2	PHI	15	1	
BUF	5	1	PIT	12	1	
DAL	5	1	VAN	11	1	
WSH	7	1	WSH	7	1	
ST.L.	7	1	TOR	7	1	
NYR	10	1	QUE	6	1	
PIT	12	1	BUF	5	1	
CHI	16	1	BOS	5	1	
N.J.	20	1	N.J.	20	2	
BOS	5	0	NYR	10	3	
TOR	7	0	ST.L.	7	6	
S.J.	11	0	S.J.	11	8	
TOTAL	**81**	**29**	**TOTAL**	**81**	**29**	

TEAM PENALTIES

Abbreviations: **GP** – games played; **PEN** – total penalty minutes, including bench penalties; **BMI** – total bench penalty minutes; **AVG** – average penalty minutes per game.

Team	GP	PEN	BMI	AVG
BOS	5	47	2	9.4
N.J.	20	227	2	11.4
S.J.	11	135	2	12.3
PHI	15	186	2	12.4
CHI	16	203	0	12.7
TOR	7	89	0	12.7
NYR	10	138	2	13.8
DET	18	264	0	14.7
QUE	6	89	2	14.8
CGY	7	111	0	15.9
BUF	5	80	0	16.0
DAL	5	95	0	19.0
PIT	12	236	4	19.7
VAN	11	272	6	24.7
ST.L.	7	210	2	30.0
WSH	7	213	4	30.4
TOTAL	**81**	**2595**	**28**	**32.0**

Sergei Fedorov led all playoff performers in assists (17) and points (24) as the Detroit Red Wings reached the Stanley Cup Finals for the first time since 1966.

The New Jersey Devils swept past the Detroit Red Wings in four straight games to win the first Stanley Cup championship in the franchise's history.

Stanley Cup Record Book

History: The Stanley Cup, the oldest trophy competed for by professional athletes in North America, was donated by Frederick Arthur, Lord Stanley of Preston and son of the Earl of Derby, in 1893. Lord Stanley purchased the trophy for 10 guineas ($50 at that time) for presentation to the amateur hockey champions of Canada. Since 1910, when the National Hockey Association took possession of the Stanley Cup, the trophy has been the symbol of professional hockey supremacy. It has been competed for only by NHL teams since 1926 and has been under the exclusive control of the NHL since 1946.

Stanley Cup Standings

1918-95
(ranked by Cup wins)

Teams	Cup Wins	Yrs.	Series	Wins	Losses	Games	Wins	Losses	Ties	Goals For	Goals Against	Winning %
Montreal	23*	69	130**	84	45	617	374	235	8	1921	1518	.613
Toronto	13	57	95	51	44	438	208	226	4	1151	1209	.479
Detroit	7	44	76	39	37	369	180	188	1	1021	1007	.489
Boston	5	56	97	46	51	471	227	238	6	1389	1400	.488
Edmonton	5	13	37	29	8	180	120	60	0	770	579	.667
NY Rangers	4	46	81	39	42	360	169	183	8	1021	1041	.481
NY Islanders	4	17	43	30	13	218	128	90	0	748	650	.587
Chicago	3	50	86	39	47	390	179	206	5	1127	1242	.465
Philadelphia	2	21	46	27	19	238	126	112	0	765	731	.529
Pittsburgh	2	15	27	14	13	137	74	63	0	455	448	.540
Calgary*	1	20	31	12	19	152	69	83	0	522	557	.454
New Jersey**	1	8	15	8	7	87	47	40	0	266	253	.540
St. Louis	0	25	42	17	25	217	96	121	0	632	727	.442
Los Angeles	0	19	29	10	19	142	55	87	0	459	568	.387
Buffalo	0	20	30	10	20	143	62	81	0	448	480	.434
Dallas***	0	19	34	15	19	180	86	94	0	591	624	.478
Vancouver	0	15	24	9	15	118	52	66	0	360	398	.441
Washington	0	13	20	7	13	110	50	60	0	364	368	.455
Winnipeg	0	10	12	2	10	56	17	39	0	167	233	.304
Colorado****	0	9	15	6	9	80	35	45	0	247	286	.438
Hartford	0	8	9	1	8	49	18	31	0	143	177	.367
San Jose	0	2	4	2	2	25	11	14	0	74	112	.440

*Montreal also won the Stanley Cup in 1916.
**1919 final incomplete due to influenza epidemic.
***Includes totals of Atlanta 1972-80.
****Includes totals of Colorado 1976-82.
*****Includes totals of Minnesota 1967-93.
******Includes totals of Quebec 1979-95.

Stanley Cup Winners Prior to Formation of NHL in 1917

Season	Champions	Manager	Coach
1916-17	Seattle Metropolitans	Pete Muldoon	Pete Muldoon
1915-16	Montreal Canadiens	George Kennedy	George Kennedy
1914-15	Vancouver Millionaires	Frank Patrick	Frank Patrick
1913-14	Toronto Blueshirts	Jack Marshall	Scotty Davidson*
1912-13**	Quebec Bulldogs	M.J. Quinn	Joe Malone*
1911-12	Quebec Bulldogs	M.J. Quinn	C. Nolan
1910-11	Ottawa Senators		Bruce Stuart*
1909-10	Montreal Wanderers	R. R. Boon	Pud Glass*
1908-09	Ottawa Senators		Bruce Stuart*
1907-08	Montreal Wanderers	R. R. Boon	Cecil Blachford
1906-07	Montreal Wanderers (March)	R. R. Boon	Cecil Blachford
1906-07	Kenora Thistles (January)	F.A. Hudson	Tommy Phillips*
1905-06	Montreal Wanderers		Cecil Blachford*
1904-05	Ottawa Silver Seven		A. T. Smith
1903-04	Ottawa Silver Seven		A. T. Smith
1902-03	Ottawa Silver Seven		A. T. Smith
1901-02	Montreal A.A.A.		C. McKerrow
1900-01	Winnipeg Victorias		D. H. Bain
1899-1900	Montreal Shamrocks		H.J. Trihey*
1898-99	Montreal Shamrocks		H.J. Trihey*
1897-98	Montreal Victorias		F. Richardson
1896-97	Montreal Victorias		Mike Grant*
1895-96	Montreal Victorias (December, 1896)		Mike Grant*
1895-96	Winnipeg Victorias (February)		J.C. G. Armytage
1894-95	Montreal Victorias		Mike Grant*
1893-94	Montreal A.A.A.		
1892-93	Montreal A.A.A.		

** Victoria defeated Quebec in challenge series. No official recognition.
* In the early years the teams were frequently run by the Captain. *Indicates Captain

Stanley Cup Winners

Year	W&L in Finals	Winner	Coach	Finalist	Coach
1995	4-0	New Jersey	Jacques Lemaire	Detroit	Scotty Bowman
1994	4-3	NY Rangers	Mike Keenan	Vancouver	Pat Quinn
1993	4-1	Montreal	Jacques Demers	Los Angeles	Barry Melrose
1992	4-0	Pittsburgh	Scotty Bowman	Chicago	Mike Keenan
1991	4-2	Pittsburgh	Bob Johnson	Minnesota	Bob Gainey
1990	4-1	Edmonton	John Muckler	Boston	Mike Milbury
1989	4-2	Calgary	Terry Crisp	Montreal	Pat Burns
1988	4-0	Edmonton	Glen Sather	Boston	Terry O'Reilly
1987	4-3	Edmonton	Glen Sather	Philadelphia	Mike Keenan
1986	4-1	Montreal	Jean Perron	Calgary Flames	Bob Johnson
1985	4-1	Edmonton	Glen Sather	Philadelphia	Mike Keenan
1984	4-1	Edmonton	Glen Sather	NY Islanders	Al Arbour
1983	4-0	NY Islanders	Al Arbour	Edmonton	Glen Sather
1982	4-0	NY Islanders	Al Arbour	Vancouver	Roger Neilson
1981	4-1	NY Islanders	Al Arbour	Minnesota	Glen Sonmor
1980	4-2	NY Islanders	Al Arbour	Philadelphia	Pat Quinn
1979	4-1	Montreal	Scotty Bowman	NY Rangers	Fred Shero
1978	4-2	Montreal	Scotty Bowman	Boston	Don Cherry
1977	4-0	Montreal	Scotty Bowman	Boston	Don Cherry
1976	4-0	Montreal	Scotty Bowman	Philadelphia	Fred Shero
1975	4-2	Philadelphia	Fred Shero	Buffalo Sabres	Floyd Smith
1974	4-2	Philadelphia	Fred Shero	Boston	Bep Guidolin
1973	4-2	Montreal	Scotty Bowman	Chicago	Billy Reay
1972	4-2	Boston	Tom Johnson	NY Rangers	Emile Francis
1971	4-3	Montreal	Al MacNeil	Chicago	Billy Reay
1970	4-0	Boston	Harry Sinden	St. Louis	Scotty Bowman
1969	4-0	Montreal	Claude Ruel	St. Louis	Scotty Bowman
1968	4-0	Montreal	Toe Blake	St. Louis	Scotty Bowman
1967	4-2	Toronto	Punch Imlach	Montreal	Toe Blake
1966	4-2	Montreal	Toe Blake	Detroit	Sid Abel
1965	4-3	Montreal	Toe Blake	Chicago	Billy Reay
1964	4-3	Toronto	Punch Imlach	Detroit	Sid Abel
1963	4-1	Toronto	Punch Imlach	Detroit	Sid Abel
1962	4-2	Toronto	Punch Imlach	Chicago	Rudy Pilous
1961	4-2	Chicago	Rudy Pilous	Detroit	Sid Abel
1960	4-3	Montreal	Toe Blake	Toronto	Punch Imlach
1959	4-1	Montreal	Toe Blake	Toronto	Punch Imlach
1958	4-2	Montreal	Toe Blake	Boston	Milt Schmidt
1957	4-1	Montreal	Toe Blake	Boston	Milt Schmidt
1956	4-1	Montreal	Toe Blake	Detroit	Jimmy Skinner
1955	4-3	Detroit	Jimmy Skinner	Montreal	Dick Irvin
1954	4-3	Detroit	Tommy Ivan	Montreal	Dick Irvin
1953	4-1	Montreal	Dick Irvin	Boston	Lynn Patrick
1952	4-0	Detroit	Tommy Ivan	Montreal	Dick Irvin
1951	4-1	Toronto	Joe Primeau	Montreal	Dick Irvin
1950	4-3	Detroit	Tommy Ivan	NY Rangers	Lynn Patrick
1949	4-0	Toronto	Hap Day	Detroit	Tommy Ivan
1948	4-0	Toronto	Hap Day	Detroit	Tommy Ivan
1947	4-2	Toronto	Hap Day	Montreal	Dick Irvin
1946	4-1	Montreal	Dick Irvin	Boston	Dit Clapper
1945	4-3	Toronto	Hap Day	Detroit	Jack Adams
1944	4-0	Montreal	Dick Irvin	Chicago	Paul Thompson
1943	4-0	Detroit	Jack Adams	Boston	Art Ross
1942	4-3	Toronto	Hap Day	Detroit	Jack Adams
1941	4-0	Boston	Cooney Weiland	Detroit	Ebbie Goodfellow
1940	4-2	NY Rangers	Frank Boucher	Toronto	Dick Irvin
1939	4-1	Boston	Art Ross	Toronto	Dick Irvin
1938	3-1	Chicago	Bill Stewart	Toronto	Dick Irvin
1937	3-2	Detroit	Jack Adams	NY Rangers	Lester Patrick
1936	3-1	Detroit	Jack Adams	Toronto	Dick Irvin
1935	3-0	Mtl. Maroons	Tommy Gorman	Toronto	Dick Irvin
1934	3-1	Chicago	Tommy Gorman	Detroit	Herbie Lewis
1933	3-1	NY Rangers	Lester Patrick	Toronto	Dick Irvin
1932	3-0	Toronto	Dick Irvin	NY Rangers	Lester Patrick
1931	3-2	Montreal	Cecil Hart	Chicago	Dick Irvin
1930	2-0	Montreal	Cecil Hart	Boston	Art Ross
1929	2-0	Boston	Cy Denneny	NY Rangers	Lester Patrick
1928	3-2	NY Rangers	Lester Patrick	Mtl. Maroons	Eddie Gerard
1927	2-0-2	Ottawa	Dave Gill	Boston	Art Ross

The National Hockey League assumed control of Stanley Cup competition after 1926

Year	W&L in Finals	Winner	Coach	Finalist	Coach
1926	3-1	Mtl. Maroons	Eddie Gerard	Victoria	Lester Patrick
1925	3-1	Victoria	Lester Patrick	Montreal	Leo Dandurand
1924	2-0 / 2-0	Montreal	Leo Dandurand	Cgy. Tigers / Van. Maroons	— / —
1923	2-0 / 3-1	Ottawa	Pete Green	Edm. Eskimos / Van. Maroons	— / —
1922	3-2	Tor. St. Pats	Eddie Powers	Van. Millionaires	Frank Patrick
1921	3-2	Ottawa	Pete Green	Van. Millionaires	Frank Patrick
1920	3-2	Ottawa	Pete Green	Seattle	
1919	2-2-1	No decision - series between Montreal and Seattle cancelled due to influenza epidemic			
1918	3-2	Tor. Arenas	Dick Carroll	Van. Millionaires	Frank Patrick

Championship Trophies

PRINCE OF WALES TROPHY

Beginning with the 1993-94 season, the club which advances to the Stanley Cup Finals as the winner of the Eastern Conference Championship is presented with the Prince of Wales Trophy.

History: His Royal Highness, the Prince of Wales, donated the trophy to the National Hockey League in 1924. From 1927-28 through 1937-38, the award was presented to the team finishing first in the American Division of the NHL. From 1938-39, when the NHL reverted to one section, to 1966-67, it was presented to the team winning the NHL regular season championship. With expansion in 1967-68, it again became a divisional trophy, awarded to the regular season champions of the East Division through to the end of the 1973-74 season. Beginning in 1974-75, it was awarded to the regular-season winner of the conference bearing the name of the trophy. From 1981-82 to 1992-93 the trophy was presented to the playoff champion in the Wales Conference. Since 1993-94, the trophy has been presented to the playoff champion in the Eastern Conference.

1994-95 Winner: New Jersey Devils

The New Jersey Devils won their first Prince of Wales Trophy on June 13, 1995 after defeating the Philadelphia Flyers 4-2 in game six of the Eastern Conference Championship series. Before defeating the Flyers, the Devils had series wins over the Boston Bruins and the Pittsburgh Penguins.

PRINCE OF WALES TROPHY WINNERS

1994-95	**New Jersey Devils**	1958-59	Montreal Canadiens
1993-94	New York Rangers	1957-58	Montreal Canadiens
1992-93	Montreal Canadiens	1956-57	Detroit Red Wings
1991-92	Pittsburgh Penguins	1955-56	Montreal Canadiens
1990-91	Pittsburgh Penguins	1954-55	Detroit Red Wings
1989-90	Boston Bruins	1953-54	Detroit Red Wings
1988-89	Montreal Canadiens	1952-53	Detroit Red Wings
1987-88	Boston Bruins	1951-52	Detroit Red Wings
1986-87	Philadelphia Flyers	1950-51	Detroit Red Wings
1985-86	Montreal Canadiens	1949-50	Detroit Red Wings
1984-85	Philadelphia Flyers	1948-49	Detroit Red Wings
1983-84	New York Islanders	1947-48	Toronto Maple Leafs
1982-83	New York Islanders	1946-47	Montreal Canadiens
1981-82	New York Islanders	1945-46	Montreal Canadiens
1980-81	Montreal Canadiens	1944-45	Montreal Canadiens
1979-80	Buffalo Sabres	1943-44	Montreal Canadiens
1978-79	Montreal Canadiens	1942-43	Detroit Red Wings
1977-78	Montreal Canadiens	1941-42	New York Rangers
1976-77	Montreal Canadiens	1940-41	Boston Bruins
1975-76	Montreal Canadiens	1939-40	Boston Bruins
1974-75	Buffalo Sabres	1938-39	Boston Bruins
1973-74	Boston Bruins	1937-38	Boston Bruins
1972-73	Montreal Canadiens	1936-37	Detroit Red Wings
1971-72	Boston Bruins	1935-36	Detroit Red Wings
1970-71	Boston Bruins	1934-35	Boston Bruins
1969-70	Chicago Blackhawks	1933-34	Detroit Red Wings
1968-69	Montreal Canadiens	1932-33	Boston Bruins
1967-68	Montreal Canadiens	1931-32	New York Rangers
1966-67	Chicago Blackhawks	1930-31	Boston Bruins
1965-66	Montreal Canadiens	1929-30	Boston Bruins
1964-65	Detroit Red Wings	1928-29	Boston Bruins
1963-64	Montreal Canadiens	1927-28	Boston Bruins
1962-63	Toronto Maple Leafs	1926-27	Ottawa Senators
1961-62	Montreal Canadiens	1925-26	Montreal Maroons
1960-61	Montreal Canadiens	1924-25	Montreal Canadiens
1959-60	Montreal Canadiens	1923-24	Montreal Canadiens

Prince of Wales Trophy

Clarence S. Campbell Bowl

Stanley Cup

CLARENCE S. CAMPBELL BOWL

Beginning with the 1993-94 season, the club which advances to the Stanley Cup Finals as the winner of the Western Conference Championship is presented with the Clarence S. Campbell Bowl.

History: Presented by the member clubs in 1968 for perpetual competition by the National Hockey League in recognition of the services of Clarence S. Campbell, President of the NHL from 1946 to 1977. From 1967-68 through 1973-74, the trophy was awarded to the regular season champions of the West Division. Beginning in 1974-75, it was awarded to the regular-season winner of the conference bearing the name of the trophy. From 1981-82 to 1992-93 the trophy was presented to the playoff champion in the Campbell Conference. Since 1993-94, the trophy has been presented to the playoff champion in the Western Conference. The trophy itself is a hallmark piece made of sterling silver and was crafted by a British silversmith in 1878.

1994-95 Winner: Detroit Red Wings

The Detroit Red Wings won their first Clarence S. Campbell Bowl on June 11, 1995 after defeating the Chicago Blackhawks 2-1 in game five of the Western Conference Championship series. Before defeating the Blackhawks, the Red Wings had series wins over the Dallas Stars and the San Jose Sharks.

CLARENCE S. CAMPBELL BOWL WINNERS

1994-95	**Detroit Red Wings**	1980-81	New York Islanders
1993-94	Vancouver Canucks	1979-80	Philadelphia Flyers
1992-93	Los Angeles Kings	1978-79	New York Islanders
1991-92	Chicago Blackhawks	1977-78	New York Islanders
1990-91	Minnesota North Stars	1976-77	Philadelphia Flyers
1989-90	Edmonton Oilers	1975-76	Philadelphia Flyers
1988-89	Calgary Flames	1974-75	Philadelphia Flyers
1987-88	Edmonton Oilers	1973-74	Philadelphia Flyers
1986-87	Edmonton Oilers	1972-73	Chicago Blackhawks
1985-86	Calgary Flames	1971-72	Chicago Blackhawks
1984-85	Edmonton Oilers	1970-71	Chicago Blackhawks
1983-84	Edmonton Oilers	1969-70	St. Louis Blues
1982-83	Edmonton Oilers	1968-69	St. Louis Blues
1981-82	Vancouver Canucks	1967-68	Philadelphia Flyers

Stanley Cup Winners:

Rosters and Final Series Scores

1994-95 — New Jersey Devils — R. Scott Stevens (Captain), Tommy Albelin, Martin Brodeur, Neil Broten, Sergei Brylin, Robert E. Carpenter, Jr., Shawn Chambers, Tom Chorske, Danton Cole, Ken Daneyko, Kevin Dean, Jim Dowd, Bruce Driver (Alternate Captain), Bill Guerin, Bobby Holik, Claude Lemieux, John MacLean (Alternate Captain), Chris McAlpine, Randy McKay, Scott Niedermayer, Mike Peluso, Stephane J.J. Richer, Brian Rolston, Chris Terreri, Valeri Zelepukin, Dr. John J. McMullen (Owner/Chairman), Peter S. McMullen (Owner), Lou Lamoriello (President/General Manager), Jacques Lemaire (Head Coach), Jacques Caron (Goaltender Coach), Dennis Gendron (Assistant Coach), Larry Robinson (Assistant Coach), Robbie Ftorek (AHL Coach), Alex Abasto (Assistant Equipment Manager), Bob Huddleston (Massage Therapist), David Nichols (Equipment Manager), Ted Schuch (Medical Trainer), Mike Vasalani (Strength Coach), David Conte (Director of Scouting) Claude Carrier (Scout), Milt Fisher (Scout), Dan Labraaten (Scout), Marcel Pronovost (Scout).
Scores: June 17 at Detroit — New Jersey 2, Detroit 1; June 20 at Detroit — New Jersey 4, Detroit 2; June 22 at New Jersey — New Jersey 5, Detroit 2; June 24 at New Jersey — New Jersey 5, Detroit 2.

1993-94 — New York Rangers — Mark Messier (Captain), Brian Leetch, Kevin Lowe, Adam Graves, Steve Larmer, Glenn Anderson, Jeff Beukeboom, Greg Gilbert, Mike Hartman, Glenn Healy, Mike Hudson, Alexander Karpovtsev, Joe Kocur, Alexei Kovalev, Nick Kypreos, Doug Lidster, Stephane Matteau, Craig MacTavish, Sergei Nemchinov, Brian Noonan, Ed Olczyk, Mike Richter, Esa Tikkanen, Jay Wells, Sergei Zubov, Neil Smith (President, General Manager and Governor), Robert Gutkowski, Stanley Jaffe, Kenneth Munoz (Governors), Larry Pleau (Assistant General Manager), Mike Keenan (Head Coach), Colin Campbell (Associate Coach), Dick Todd (Assistant Coach), Matthew Loughren (Manager, Team Operations), Barry Watkins (Director, Communications), Christer Rockstrom, Tony Feltrin, Martin Madden, Herb Hammond, Darwin Bennett (Scouts), Dave Smith, Joe Murphy, Mike Folga, Bruce Lifrieri (Trainers).
Scores: May 31 at New York — Vancouver 3, NY Rangers 2; June 2 at New York — NY Rangers 3, Vancouver 1; June 4 at Vancouver — NY Rangers 5, Vancouver 1; June 7 at Vancouver — NY Rangers 4, Vancouver 2; June 9 at New York — Vancouver 6 at NY Rangers 3; June 11 at Vancouver — Vancouver 4, NY Rangers 1; June 14 at New York — NY Rangers 3, Vancouver 2.

1992-93 — Montreal Canadiens — Guy Carbonneau (Captain), Patrick Roy, Mike Keane, Eric Desjardins, Stephan Lebeau, Mathieu Schneider, Jean-Jacques Daigneault, Denis Savard, Lyle Odelein, Todd Ewen, Kirk Muller, John LeClair, Gilbert Dionne, Benoit Brunet, Patrice Brisebois, Paul Di Pietro, Andre Racicot, Donald Dufresne, Mario Roberge, Sean Hill, Ed Ronan, Kevin Haller, Vincent Damphousse, Brian Bellows, Gary Leeman, Rob Ramage, Ronald Corey (President), Serge Savard (Managing Director & Vice-President Hockey), Jacques Demers (Head Coach), Jacques Laperriere (Assistant Coach), Charles Thiffault (Assistant Coach), Francois Allaire (Goaltending Instructor), Jean Béliveau (Senior Vice-President, Corporate Affairs), Fred Steer (Vice-President, Finance & Adminstration), Aldo Giampaolo (Vice-President, Operations), Bernard Brisset (Vice-President, Marketing & Communications), André Boudrias (Assistant to the Managing Director & Director of Scouting), Jacques Lemaire (Assistant to the Managing Director), Gaeten Lefebvre (Athletic Trainer), John Shipman (Assistant to the Athletic Trainer), Eddy Palchak (Equipment Manager), Pierre Gervais (Assistant to the Equipment Manager), Robert Boulanger (Assistant to the Equipment Manager), Pierre Ouellete (Assistant to the Equipment Manager).
Scores: June 1 at Montreal — Los Angeles 4, Montreal 1; June 2 at Montreal — Montreal 3, Los Angeles 2; June 5 at Los Angeles — Montreal 4, Los Angeles 3; June 7 at Los Angeles — Montreal 3, Los Angeles 2; June 9 at Montreal — Montreal 4, Los Angeles 1.

1991-92 — Pittsburgh Penguins — Mario Lemieux (Captain), Ron Francis, Bryan Trottier, Kevin Stevens, Bob Errey, Phil Bourque, Troy Loney, Rick Tocchet, Joe Mullen, Jaromir Jagr, Jiri Hrdina, Shawn McEachern, Ulf Samuelsson, Kjell Samuelsson, Larry Murphy, Gord Roberts, Jim Paek, Paul Stanton, Tom Barrasso, Ken Wregget, Jay Caufield, Jamie Leach, Wendell Young, Grant Jennings, Peter Taglianetti, Jock Callander, Dave Michayluk, Mike Needham, Jeff Chychrun, Ken Priestlay, Jeff Daniels, Howard Baldwin (Owner and President), Morris Belzberg (Owner), Thomas Ruta (Owner), Donn Patton (Executive Vice President and Chief Financial Officer), Paul Martha (Executive Vice President and General Counsel), Craig Patrick (Executive Vice President and General Manager), Bob Johnson (Coach), Scotty Bowman (Director of Player Development and Coach), Barry Smith, Rick Kehoe, Pierre McGuire, Gilles Meloche, Rick Paterson (Assistant Coaches), Steve Latin (Equipment Manager), Skip Thayer (Trainer), John Welday (Strength and Conditioning Coach), Greg Malone, Les Binkley, Charlie Hodge, John Gill, Ralph Cox (Scouts).
Scores: May 26 at Pittsburgh — Pittsburgh 5, Chicago 4; May 28 at Pittsburgh — Pittsburgh 3, Chicago 1; May 30 at Chicago — Pittsburgh 1, Chicago 0; June 1 at Chicago — Pittsburgh 6, Chicago 5.

1990-91 — Pittsburgh Penguins — Mario Lemieux (Captain), Paul Coffey, Randy Hillier, Bob Errey, Tom Barrasso, Phil Bourque, Jay Caufield, Ron Francis, Randy Gilhen, Jiri Hrdina, Jaromir Jagr, Grant Jennings, Troy Loney, Joe Mullen, Larry Murphy, Jim Paek, Frank Pietrangelo, Barry Pederson, Mark Recchi, Gordie Roberts, Ulf Samuelsson, Paul Stanton, Kevin Stevens, Peter Taglianetti, Bryan Trottier, Scott Young, Wendell Young, Edward J. DeBartolo, Sr. (Owner), Marie D. DeBartolo York (President), Paul Martha (Vice-President & General Counsel), Craig Patrick (General Manager), Scotty Bowman (Director of Player Development & Recruitment), Bob Johnson (Coach), Rick Kehoe (Assistant Coach), Gilles Meloche (Goaltending Coach & Scout), Rick Paterson (Assistant Coach), Barry Smith (Assistant Coach), Steve Latin (Equipment Manager), Skip Thayer (Trainer), John Welday (Strength & Conditioning Coach), Greg Malone (Scout).
Scores: May 15 at Pittsburgh — Minnesota 5, Pittsburgh 4; May 17 at Pittsburgh — Pittsburgh 4, Minnesota 1; May 19 at Minnesota — Minnesota 3, Pittsburgh 1; May 21 at Minnesota — Pittsburgh 5, Minnesota 3; May 23 at Pittsburgh — Pittsburgh 6, Minnesota 4; May 25 at Minnesota — Pittsburgh 8, Minnesota 0.

1989-90 — Edmonton Oilers — Kevin Lowe, Steve Smith, Jeff Beukeboom, Mark Lamb, Joe Murphy, Glenn Anderson, Mark Messier, Adam Graves, Craig MacTavish, Kelly Buchberger, Jari Kurri, Craig Simpson, Martin Gelinas, Randy Gregg, Charlie Huddy, Geoff Smith, Reijo Ruotsalainen, Craig Muni, Bill Ranford, Dave Brown, Eldon Reddick, Petr Klima, Esa Tikkanen, Grant Fuhr, Peter Pocklington (Owner), Glen Sather (President/General Manager), John Muckler (Coach), Ted Green (Co-Coach), Ron Low (Ass't Coach), Bruce MacGregor (Ass't General Manager), Barry Fraser (Director of Player Personnel), John Blackwell (Director of Operations, AHL), Ace Bailey, Ed Chadwick, Lorne Davis, Harry Howell, Matti Vaisanen and Albert Reeves (Scouts), Bill Tuele (Director of Public Relations), Dr. Gordon Cameron (Medical Chief of Staff), Dr. David Reid (Team Physician), Barrie Stafford (Athletic Trainer), Ken Lowe (Athletic Therapist), Stuart Poirier (Massage Therapist), Lyle Kulchisky (Ass't Trainer).
Scores: May 15 at Boston — Edmonton 3, Boston 2; May 18 at Boston — Edmonton 7, Boston 2; May 20 at Edmonton — Boston 2, Edmonton 1; May 22 at Edmonton — Edmonton 5, Boston 1; May 24 at Boston — Edmonton 4, Boston 1.

1988-89 — Calgary Flames — Mike Vernon, Rick Wamsley, Al MacInnis, Brad McCrimmon, Dana Murzyn, Ric Nattress, Joe Mullen, Lanny McDonald (Co-captain), Gary Roberts, Colin Patterson, Hakan Loob, Theoren Fleury, Jiri Hrdina, Tim Hunter (Ass't captain), Gary Suter, Mark Hunter, Jim Peplinski (Co-captain), Joe Nieuwendyk, Brian MacLellan, Joel Otto, Jamie Macoun, Doug Gilmour, Rob Ramage. Norman Green, Harley Hotchkiss, Norman Kwong, Sonia Scurfield, B.J. Seaman, D.K. Seaman (Owners), Cliff Fletcher (President and General Manager), Al MacNeil (Ass't General Manager), Al Coates (Ass't to the President), Terry Crisp (Head Coach), Doug Risebrough, Tom Watt (Ass't Coaches), Glenn Hall (Goaltending Consultant), Jim Murray (Trainer), Bob Stewart (Equipment Manager), Al Murray (Ass't Trainer).
Scores: May 14 at Calgary — Calgary 3, Montreal 2; May 17 at Calgary— Montreal 4, Calgary 2; May 19 at Montreal — Montreal 4, Calgary 3; May 21 at Montreal — Calgary 4, Montreal 2; May 23 at Calgary — Calgary 3, Montreal 2; May 25 at Montreal — Calgary 4, Montreal 2.

1987-88 — Edmonton Oilers — Keith Acton, Glenn Anderson, Jeff Beukeboom, Geoff Courtnall, Grant Fuhr, Randy Gregg, Wayne Gretzky, Dave Hannan, Charlie Huddy, Mike Krushelnyski, Jari Kurri, Normand Lacombe, Kevin Lowe, Craig MacTavish, Kevin McClelland, Marty McSorley, Mark Messier, Craig Muni, Bill Ranford, Craig Simpson, Steve Smith, Esa Tikkanen, Peter Pocklington (Owner), Glen Sather (General Manager/Coach), John Muckler (Co-Coach), Ted Green (Ass't Coach), Bruce MacGregor (Ass't Director of Player Personnel), Bill Tuele (Director of Public Relations), Dr. Gordon Cameron (Team Physician), Peter Millar (Athletic Therapist), Barrie Stafford (Trainer), Juergen Mers (Massage Therapist), Lyle Kulchisky (Ass't Trainer).
Scores: May 18 at Edmonton — Edmonton 2, Boston 1; May 20 at Edmonton — Edmonton 4, Boston 2; May 22 at Boston — Edmonton 6, Boston 3; May 24 at Boston — Boston 3, Edmonton 3 (suspended due to power failure); May 26 at Edmonton — Edmonton 6, Boston 3.

Tom Barrasso appeared in every game for the Pittsburgh Penguins during the 1991 playoffs, including the clubs record-setting 14-game winning streak.

1986-87 — Edmonton Oilers — Glenn Anderson, Jeff Beukeboom, Kelly Buchberger, Paul Coffey, Grant Fuhr, Randy Gregg, Wayne Gretzky, Charlie Huddy, Dave Hunter, Mike Krushelnyski, Jari Kurri, Moe Lemay, Kevin Lowe, Craig MacTavish, Kevin McClelland, Marty McSorley, Mark Messier, Andy Moog, Craig Muni, Kent Nilsson, Jaroslav Pouzar, Reijo Ruotsalainen, Steve Smith, Esa Tikkanen, Peter Pocklington (Owner), Glen Sather (General Manager/Coach), John Muckler (Co-Coach), Ted Green (Ass't. Coach), Ron Low (Ass't. Coach), Bruce MacGregor (Ass't. General Manager), Barry Fraser (Director of Player Personnel), Peter Millar (Athletic Therapist), Barrie Stafford (Trainer), Lyle Kulchisky (Ass't Trainer).
Scores: May 17 at Edmonton — Edmonton 4, Philadelphia 3; May 20 at Edmonton — Edmonton 3, Philadelphia 2; May 22 at Philadelphia — Philadelphia 5, Edmonton 3; May 24 at Philadelphia — Edmonton 4, Philadelphia 1; May 26 at Edmonton — Philadelphia 4, Edmonton 3; May 28 at Philadelphia — Philadelphia 3, Edmonton 2; May 31 at Edmonton — Edmonton 3, Philadelphia 1.

1985-86 — Montreal Canadiens — Bob Gainey, Doug Soetaert, Patrick Roy, Rick Green, David Maley, Ryan Walter, Serge Boisvert, Mario Tremblay, Bobby Smith, Craig Ludwig, Tom Kurvers, Kjell Dahlin, Larry Robinson, Guy Carbonneau, Chris Chelios, Petr Svoboda, Mats Naslund, Lucien DeBlois, Steve Rooney, Gaston Gingras, Mike Lalor, Chris Nilan, John Kordic, Claude Lemieux, Mike McPhee, Brian Skrudland, Stephane Richer, Ronald Corey (President), Serge Savard (General Manager), Jean Perron (Coach), Jacques Laperrière (Ass't. Coach), Jean Béliveau (Vice President), Francois-Xavier Seigneur (Vice President), Fred Steer (Vice President), Jacques Lemaire (Ass't. General Manager), André Boudrias (Ass't. General Manager), Claude Ruel, Yves Belanger (Athletic Therapist), Gaetan Lefebvre (Ass't. Athletic Therapist), Eddy Palchek (Trainer), Sylvain Toupin (Ass't. Trainer).
Scores: May 16 at Calgary — Calgary 5, Montreal 3; May 18 at Calgary — Montreal 3, Calgary 2; May 20 at Montreal — Montreal 5, Calgary 3; May 22 at Montreal — Montreal 1, Calgary 0; May 24 at Calgary — Montreal 4, Calgary 3.

1984-85 — Edmonton Oilers — Glenn Anderson, Bill Carroll, Paul Coffey, Lee Fogolin, Grant Fuhr, Randy Gregg, Wayne Gretzky, Charlie Huddy, Pat Hughes, Dave Hunter, Don Jackson, Mike Krushelnyski, Jari Kurri, Willy Lindstrom, Kevin Lowe, Dave Lumley, Kevin McClelland, Larry Melnyk, Mark Messier, Andy Moog, Mark Napier, Jaroslav Pouzar, Dave Semenko, Esa Tikkanen, Peter Pocklington (Owner), Glen Sather (General Manager/Coach), John Muckler (Ass't. Coach), Ted Green (Ass't. Coach), Bruce MacGregor (Ass't. General Manager), Barry Fraser (Director of Player Personnel/Chief Scout), Peter Millar (Athletic Therapist), Barrie Stafford, Lyle Kulchisky (Trainers).
Scores: May 21 at Philadelphia — Philadelphia 4, Edmonton 1; May 23 at Philadelphia — Edmonton 3, Philadelphia 1; May 25 at Edmonton — Edmonton 4, Philadelphia 3; May 28 at Edmonton — Edmonton 5, Philadelphia 3; May 30 at Edmonton — Edmonton 8, Philadelphia 3.

1983-84 — Edmonton Oilers — Glenn Anderson, Paul Coffey, Pat Conacher, Lee Fogolin, Grant Fuhr, Randy Gregg, Wayne Gretzky, Charlie Huddy, Pat Hughes, Dave Hunter, Don Jackson, Jari Kurri, Willy Lindstrom, Ken Linseman, Kevin Lowe, Dave Lumley, Kevin McClelland, Mark Messier, Andy Moog, Jaroslav Pouzar, Dave Semenko, Peter Pocklington (Owner), Glen Sather (General Manager/Coach), John Muckler (Ass't. Coach), Ted Green (Ass't. Coach), Bruce MacGregor (Ass't. General Manager), Barry Fraser (Director of Player Personnel/Chief Scout), Peter Millar (Athletic Therapist), Barrie Stafford (Trainer)
Scores: May 10 at New York — Edmonton 1, NY Islanders 0; May 12 at New York — NY Islanders 6, Edmonton 1; May 15 at Edmonton — Edmonton 7, NY Islanders 2; May 17 at Edmonton — Edmonton 7, NY Islanders 2; May 19 at Edmonton — Edmonton 5, NY Islanders 2.

1982-83 — New York Islanders — Mike Bossy, Bob Bourne, Paul Boutilier, Bill Carroll, Greg Gilbert, Clark Gillies, Butch Goring, Mats Hallin, Tomas Jonsson, Anders Kallur, Gord Lane, Dave Langevin, Mike McEwen, Roland Melanson, Wayne Merrick, Ken Morrow, Bob Nystrom, Stefan Persson, Denis Potvin, Bill Smith, Brent Sutter, Duane Sutter, John Tonelli, Bryan Trottier, Al Arbour (coach), Lorne Henning (ass't coach), Bill Torrey (general manager), Ron Waske, Jim Pickard (trainers)
Scores: May 10 at Edmonton — NY Islanders 2, Edmonton 0; May 12 at Edmonton — NY Islanders 6, Edmonton 3; May 14 at New York — NY Islanders 5, Edmonton 1; May 17 at New York — NY Islanders 4, Edmonton 2

1981-82 — New York Islanders — Mike Bossy, Bob Bourne, Bill Carroll, Butch Goring, Greg Gilbert, Clark Gillies, Tomas Jonsson, Anders Kallur, Gord Lane, Dave Langevin, Hector Marini, Mike McEwen, Roland Melanson, Wayne Merrick, Ken Morrow, Bob Nystrom, Stefan Persson, Denis Potvin, Bill Smith, Brent Sutter, Duane Sutter, John Tonelli, Bryan Trottier, Al Arbour (coach), Lorne Henning (ass't coach), Bill Torrey (general manager), Ron Waske, Jim Pickard (trainers)
Scores: May 8 at New York — NY Islanders 6, Vancouver 5; May 11 at New York — NY Islanders 6, Vancouver 4; May 13 at Vancouver — NY Islanders 3, Vancouver 0; May 16 at Vancouver — NY Islanders 3, Vancouver 1

1980-81 — New York Islanders — Denis Potvin, Mike McEwen, Ken Morrow, Gord Lane, Bob Lorimer, Stefan Persson, Dave Langevin, Mike Bossy, Bryan Trottier, Butch Goring, Wayne Merrick, Clark Gillies, John Tonelli, Bob Nystrom, Bill Carroll, Bob Bourne, Hector Marini, Anders Kallur, Duane Sutter, Garry Howatt, Lorne Henning, Bill Smith, Roland Melanson, Al Arbour (coach), Bill Torrey (general manager), Ron Waske, Jim Pickard (trainers).
Scores: May 12 at New York — NY Islanders 6, Minnesota 3; May 14 at New York — NY Islanders 6, Minnesota 3; May 17 at Minnesota — NY Islanders 7, Minnesota 5; May 19 at Minnesota— Minnesota 4, NY Islanders 2; May 21 at New York — NY Islanders 5, Minnesota 1.

1979-80 — New York Islanders — Gord Lane, Jean Potvin, Bob Lorimer, Denis Potvin, Stefan Persson, Ken Morrow, Dave Langevin, Duane Sutter, Garry Howatt, Clark Gillies, Lorne Henning, Wayne Merrick, Bob Bourne, Steve Tambellini, Bryan Trottier, Mike Bossy, Bob Nystrom, John Tonelli, Anders Kallur, Butch Goring, Alex McKendry, Glenn Resch, Billy Smith, Al Arbour (coach), Bill Torrey (general manager), Ron Waske, Jim Pickard (trainers).
Scores: May 13 at Philadelphia — NY Islanders 4, Philadelphia 3; May 15 at Philadelphia — Philadelphia 8, NY Islanders 3; May 17 at New York — NY Islanders 6, Philadelphia 2; May 19 at New York — NY Islanders 5, Philadelphia 2; May 22 at Philadelphia — Philadelphia 6, NY Islanders 3; May 24 at New York — NY Islanders 5, Philadelphia 4.

1978-79 — Montreal Canadiens — Ken Dryden, Larry Robinson, Serge Savard, Guy Lapointe, Brian Engblom, Gilles Lupien, Rick Chartraw, Guy Lafleur, Steve Shutt, Jacques Lemaire, Yvan Cournoyer, Réjean Houle, Pierre Mondou, Bob Gainey, Doug Jarvis, Yvon Lambert, Doug Risebrough, Pierre Larouche, Mario Tremblay, Cam Connor, Pat Hughes, Rod Langway, Mark Napier, Michel Larocque, Richard Sévigny, Scotty Bowman (coach), Irving Grundman (managing director), Eddy Palchak, Pierre Meilleur (trainers).
Scores: May 13 at Montreal — NY Rangers 4, Montreal 1; May 15 at Montreal — Montreal 6, NY Rangers 2; May 17 at New York — Montreal 4, NY Rangers 1; May 19 at New York — Montreal 4, NY Rangers 3; May 21 at Montreal — Montreal 4, NY Rangers 1.

1977-78 — Montreal Canadiens — Ken Dryden, Larry Robinson, Serge Savard, Guy Lapointe, Bill Nyrop, Pierre Bouchard, Brian Engblom, Gilles Lupien, Rick Chartraw, Guy Lafleur, Steve Shutt, Jacques Lemaire, Yvan Cournoyer, Réjean Houle, Pierre Mondou, Bob Gainey, Doug Jarvis, Yvon Lambert, Doug Risebrough, Pierre Larouche, Mario Tremblay, Michel Larocque, Murray Wilson, Scotty Bowman (coach), Sam Pollock (general manager), Eddy Palchak, Pierre Meilleur (trainers).
Scores: May 13 at Montreal — Montreal 4, Boston 1; May 16 at Montreal — Montreal 3, Boston 2; May 18 at Boston — Boston 4, Montreal 0; May 21 at Boston — Boston 4, Montreal 3; May 23 at Montreal — Montreal 4, Boston 1; May 25 at Boston — Montreal 4, Boston 1.

1976-77 — Montreal Canadiens — Ken Dryden, Guy Lapointe, Larry Robinson, Serge Savard, Jimmy Roberts, Rick Chartraw, Bill Nyrop, Pierre Bouchard, Brian Engblom, Yvan Cournoyer, Guy Lafleur, Jacques Lemaire, Steve Shutt, Pete Mahovlich, Murray Wilson, Doug Jarvis, Yvon Lambert, Bob Gainey, Doug Risebrough, Mario Tremblay, Rejean Houle, Pierre Mondou, Mike Polich, Michel Larocque, Scotty Bowman (coach), Sam Pollock (general manager), Eddy Palchak, Pierre Meilleur (trainers).
Scores: May 7 at Montreal — Montreal 7, Boston 3; May 10 at Montreal — Montreal 3, Boston 0; May 12 at Boston — Montreal 4, Boston 2; May 14 at Boston — Montreal 2, Boston 1.

1975-76 — Montreal Canadiens — Ken Dryden, Serge Savard, Guy Lapointe, Larry Robinson, Bill Nyrop, Pierre Bouchard, Jim Roberts, Guy Lafleur, Steve Shutt, Pete Mahovlich, Yvan Cournoyer, Jacques Lemaire, Yvon Lambert, Bob Gainey, Doug Jarvis, Doug Risebrough, Murray Wilson, Mario Tremblay, Rick Chartraw, Michel Larocque, Scotty Bowman (coach), Sam Pollock (general manager), Eddy Palchak, Pierre Meilleur (trainers).
Scores: May 9 at Montreal — Montreal 4, Philadelphia 3; May 11 at Montreal — Montreal 2, Philadelphia 1; May 13 at Philadelphia — Montreal 3, Philadelphia 2; May 16 at Philadelphia — Montreal 5, Philadelphia 3.

1974-75 — Philadelphia Flyers — Bernie Parent, Wayne Stephenson, Ed Van Impe, Tom Bladon, André Dupont, Joe Watson, Jim Watson, Ted Harris, Larry Goodenough, Rick MacLeish, Bobby Clarke, Bill Barber, Reggie Leach, Gary Dornhoefer, Ross Lonsberry, Bob Kelly, Terry Crisp, Don Saleski, Dave Schultz, Orest Kindrachuk, Bill Clement, Fred Shero (coach), Keith Allen (general manager), Frank Lewis, Jim McKenzie (trainers).
Scores: May 15 at Philadelphia — Philadelphia 4, Buffalo 1; May 18 at Philadelphia — Philadelphia 2, Buffalo 1; May 20 at Buffalo — Buffalo 5, Philadelphia 4; May 22 at Buffalo — Buffalo 4, Philadelphia 2; May 25 at Philadelphia — Philadelphia 5, Buffalo 1; May 27 at Buffalo — Philadelphia 2, Buffalo 0.

1973-74 — Philadelphia Flyers — Bernie Parent, Ed Van Impe, Tom Bladon, André Dupont, Joe Watson, Jim Watson, Barry Ashbee, Bill Barber, Dave Schultz, Don Saleski, Gary Dornhoefer, Terry Crisp, Bobby Clarke, Simon Nolet, Ross Lonsberry, Rick MacLeish, Bill Flett, Orest Kindrachuk, Bill Clement, Bob Kelly, Bruce Cowick, Al MacAdam, Bobby Taylor, Fred Shero (coach), Keith Allen (general manager), Frank Lewis, Jim McKenzie (trainers).
Scores: May 7 at Boston — Boston 3, Philadelphia 2; May 9 at Boston — Philadelphia 3, Boston 2; May 12 at Philadelphia — Philadelphia 4, Boston 1; May 14 at Philadelphia — Philadelphia 4, Boston 2; May 16 at Boston — Boston 5, Philadelphia 1; May 19 at Philadelphia — Philadelphia 1, Boston 0.

1972-73 — Montreal Canadiens — Ken Dryden, Guy Lapointe, Serge Savard, Larry Robinson, Jacques Laperrière, Bob Murdoch, Pierre Bouchard, Jim Roberts, Yvan Cournoyer, Frank Mahovlich, Jacques Lemaire, Pete Mahovlich, Marc Tardif, Henri Richard, Réjean Houle, Guy Lafleur, Chuck Lefley, Claude Larose, Murray Wilson, Steve Shutt, Michel Plasse, Scotty Bowman (coach), Sam Pollock (general manager), Ed Palchak, Bob Williams (trainers).
Scores: April 29 at Montreal — Montreal 8, Chicago 3; May 1 at Montreal — Montreal 4, Chicago 1; May 3 at Chicago — Chicago 7, Montreal 4; May 6 at Chicago — Montreal 4, Chicago 0; May 8 at Montreal — Chicago 8, Montreal 7; May 10 at Chicago — Montreal 6, Chicago 4.

1971-72 — Boston Bruins — Gerry Cheevers, Ed Johnston, Bobby Orr, Ted Green, Carol Vadnais, Dallas Smith, Don Awrey, Phil Esposito, Ken Hodge, John Bucyk, Mike Walton, Wayne Cashman, Garnet Bailey, Derek Sanderson, Fred Stanfield, Ed Westfall, John McKenzie, Don Marcotte, Garry Peters, Chris Hayes, Tom Johnson (coach), Milt Schmidt (general manager), Dan Canney, John Forristall (trainers).
Scores: April 30 at Boston — Boston 6, NY Rangers 5; May 2 at Boston — Boston 2, NY Rangers 1; May 4 at New York — NY Rangers 5, Boston 2; May 7 at New York — Boston 3, NY Rangers 2; May 9 at Boston — NY Rangers 3, Boston 2; May 11 at New York — Boston 3, NY Rangers 0.

1970-71 — Montreal Canadiens — Ken Dryden, Rogatien Vachon, Jacques Laperrière, Jean-Claude Tremblay, Guy Lapointe, Terry Harper, Pierre Bouchard, Jean Béliveau, Marc Tardif, Yvan Cournoyer, Réjean Houle, Claude Larose, Henri Richard, Phil Roberto, Pete Mahovlich, Leon Rochefort, John Ferguson, Bobby Sheehan, Jacques Lemaire, Frank Mahovlich, Bob Murdoch, Chuck Lefley, Al MacNeil (coach), Sam Pollock (general manager), Yvon Belanger, Ed Palchak (trainers).
Scores: May 4 at Chicago — Chicago 2, Montreal 1; May 6 at Chicago — Chicago 5, Montreal 3; May 9 at Montreal — Montreal 4, Chicago 2; May 11 at Montreal — Montreal 5, Chicago 2; May 13 at Chicago — Chicago 2, Montreal 0; May 16 at Montreal — Montreal 4, Chicago 3; May 18 at Chicago — Montreal 3, Chicago 2.

1969-70 — Boston Bruins — Gerry Cheevers, Ed Johnston, Bobby Orr, Rick Smith, Dallas Smith, Bill Speer, Gary Doak, Don Awrey, Phil Esposito, Ken Hodge, John Bucyk, Wayne Carleton, Wayne Cashman, Derek Sanderson, Fred Stanfield, Ed Westfall, John McKenzie, Jim Lorentz, Don Marcotte, Bill Lesuk, Dan Schock, Harry Sinden (coach), Milt Schmidt (general manager), Dan Canney, John Forristall (trainers).
Scores: May 3 at St. Louis — Boston 6, St. Louis 1; May 5 at St. Louis — Boston 6, St. Louis 2; May 7 at Boston — Boston 4, St. Louis 1; May 10 at Boston — Boston 4, St. Louis 3.

1968-69 — Montreal Canadiens — Lorne Worsley, Rogatien Vachon, Jacques Laperrière, Jean-Claude Tremblay, Ted Harris, Serge Savard, Terry Harper, Larry Hillman, Jean Béliveau, Ralph Backstrom, Dick Duff, Yvan Cournoyer, Claude Provost, Bobby Rousseau, Henri Richard, John Ferguson, Christian Bordeleau, Mickey Redmond, Jacques Lemaire, Lucien Grenier, Tony Esposito, Claude Ruel (coach), Sam Pollock (general manager), Larry Aubut, Eddy Palchak (trainers).
Scores: April 27 at Montreal — Montreal 3, St. Louis 1; April 29 at Montreal — Montreal 3, St. Louis 1; May 1 at St. Louis — Montreal 4, St. Louis 0; May 4 at St. Louis — Montreal 2, St. Louis 1.

1967-68 — Montreal Canadiens — Lorne Worsley, Rogatien Vachon, Jacques Laperrière, Jean-Claude Tremblay, Ted Harris, Serge Savard, Terry Harper, Carol Vadnais, Jean Béliveau, Gilles Tremblay, Ralph Backstrom, Dick Duff, Claude Larose, Yvan Cournoyer, Claude Provost, Bobby Rousseau, Henri Richard, John Ferguson, Danny Grant, Jacques Lemaire, Mickey Redmond, Toe Blake (coach), Sam Pollock (general manager), Larry Aubut, Eddy Palchak (trainers).
Scores: May 5 at St. Louis — Montreal 3, St. Louis 2; May 7 at St. Louis — Montreal 1, St. Louis 0; May 9 at Montreal — Montreal 4, St. Louis 3; May 11 at Montreal — Montreal 3, St. Louis 2.

1966-67 — Toronto Maple Leafs — Johnny Bower, Terry Sawchuk, Larry Hillman, Marcel Pronovost, Tim Horton, Bob Baun, Aut Erickson, Allan Stanley, Red Kelly, Ron Ellis, George Armstrong, Pete Stemkowski, Dave Keon, Mike Walton, Jim Pappin, Bob Pulford, Brian Conacher, Eddie Shack, Frank Mahovlich, Milan Marcetta, Larry Jeffrey, Bruce Gamble, Punch Imlach (manager-coach), Bob Haggart (trainer).
Scores: April 20 at Montreal — Toronto 2, Montreal 6; April 22 at Montreal — Toronto 3, Montreal 0; April 25 at Toronto — Toronto 3, Montreal 2; April 27 at Toronto — Toronto 2, Montreal 6; April 29 at Montreal — Toronto 4, Montreal 1; May 2 at Toronto — Toronto 3, Montreal 1.

1965-66 — Montreal Canadiens — Lorne Worsley, Charlie Hodge, Jean-Claude Tremblay, Ted Harris, Jean-Guy Talbot, Terry Harper, Jacques Laperrière, Noel Price, Jean Béliveau, Ralph Backstrom, Dick Duff, Gilles Tremblay, Claude Larose, Yvan Cournoyer, Claude Provost, Bobby Rousseau, Henri Richard, Dave Balon, John Ferguson, Leon Rochefort, Jim Roberts, Toe Blake (coch), Sam Pollock (general manager), Larry Aubut, Andy Galley (trainers).
Scores: April 24 at Montreal — Detroit 3, Montreal 2; April 26 at Montreal — Detroit 5, Montreal 2; April 28 at Detroit — Montreal 4, Detroit 2; May 1 at Detroit — Montreal 2, Detroit 1; May 3 at Montreal — Montreal 5, Detroit 1; May 5 at Detroit — Montreal 3, Detroit 2.

1964-65 — Montreal Canadiens — Lorne Worsley, Charlie Hodge, Jean-Claude Tremblay, Ted Harris, Jean-Guy Talbot, Terry Harper, Jacques Laperrière, Jean Gauthier, Noel Picard, Jean Béliveau, Ralph Backstrom, Dick Duff, Claude Larose, Yvan Cournoyer, Claude Provost, Bobby Rousseau, Henri Richard, Dave Balon, John Ferguson, Red Berenson, Jim Roberts, Toe Blake (coach), Sam Pollock (general manager), Larry Aubut, Andy Galley (trainers).
Scores: April 17 at Montreal — Montreal 3, Chicago 2; April 20 at Montreal — Montreal 2, Chicago 0; April 22 at Chicago — Montreal 1, Chicago 3; April 25 at Chicago — Montreal 1, Chicago 5; April 7 at Montreal — Montreal 6, Chicago 0; April 29 at Chicago — Montreal 1, Chicago 2; May 1 at Montreal — Montreal 4, Chicago 0.

1963-64 — Toronto Maple Leafs — Johnny Bower, Carl Brewer, Tim Horton, Bob Baun, Allan Stanley, Larry Hillman, Al Arbour, Red Kelly, Gerry Ehman, Andy Bathgate, George Armstrong, Ron Stewart, Dave Keon, Billy Harris, Don McKenney, Jim Pappin, Bob Pulford, Eddie Shack, Frank Mahovlich, Eddie Litzenberger, Punch Imlach (manager-coach), Bob Haggert (trainer).
Scores April 11 at Toronto — Toronto 3, Detroit 2; April 14 at Toronto — Toronto 3, Detroit 4; April 16 at Detroit — Detroit 4, Toronto 4; April 18 at Detroit — Toronto 4, Detroit 2; April 21 at Toronto — Toronto 1, Detroit 2; April 23 at Detroit — Toronto 4, Detroit 3; April 25 at Toronto — Toronto 4, Detroit 0.

1962-63 — Toronto Maple Leafs — Johnny Bower, Don Simmons, Carl Brewer, Tim Horton, Kent Douglas, Allan Stanley, Bob Baun, Larry Hillman, Red Kelly, Dick Duff, George Armstrong, Bob Nevin, Ron Stewart, Dave Keon, Billy Harris, Bob Pulford, Eddie Shack, Ed Litzenberger, Frank Mahovlich, John MacMillan, Punch Imlach (manager-coach), Bob Haggert (trainer).
Scores: April 9 at Toronto — Toronto 4, Detroit 2; April 11 at Toronto — Toronto 4, Detroit 2; April 14 at Detroit — Toronto 3, Detroit 4; April 16 at Detroit — Toronto 4, Detroit 2; April 18 at Toronto — Toronto 3, Detroit 1.

1961-62 — Toronto Maple Leafs — Johnny Bower, Don Simmons, Carl Brewer, Tim Horton, Bob Baun, Allan Stanley, Al Arbour, Larry Hillman, Red Kelly, Dick Duff, George Armstrong, Frank Mahovlich, Bob Nevin, Ron Stewart, Bill Harris, Bert Olmstead, Bob Pulford, Eddie Shack, Dave Keon, Ed Litzenberger, John MacMillan, Punch Imlach (manager-coach), Bob Haggert (trainer).
Scores: April 10 at Toronto — Toronto 4, Chicago 1; April 12 at Toronto — Toronto 3, Chicago 2; April 15 at Chicago — Toronto 0, Chicago 3; April 17 at Chicago — Toronto 1, Chicago 4; April 19 at Toronto —Toronto 8, Chicago 4; April 22 at Chicago — Toronto 2, Chicago 1.

1960-61 — Chicago Black Hawks — Glenn Hall, Al Arbour, Pierre Pilote, Elmer Vasko, Jack Evans, Dollard St. Laurent, Reg Fleming, Tod Sloan, Ron Murphy, Eddie Litzenberger, Bill Hay, Bobby Hull, Ab McDonald, Eric Nesterenko, Ken Wharram, Earl Balfour, Stan Mikita, Murray Balfour, Chico Maki, Wayne Hicks, Tommy Ivan (manager), Rudy Pilous (coach), Nick Garen (trainer).
Scores: April 6 at Chicago — Chicago 3, Detroit 2; April 8 at Detroit — Detroit 3, Chicago 2; April 10 at Chicago — Chicago 3, Detroit 1; April 12 at Detroit — Detroit 2, Chicago 1; April 14 at Chicago — Chicago 6, Detroit 3; April 16 at Detroit — Chicago 5, Detroit 1.

1959-60 — Montreal Canadiens — Jacques Plante, Charlie Hodge, Doug Harvey, Tom Johnson, Bob Turner, Jean-Guy Talbot, Albert Langlois, Ralph Backstrom, Jean Béliveau, Marcel Bonin, Bernie Geoffrion, Phil Goyette, Bill Hicke, Don Marshall, Ab McDonald, Dickie Moore, André Pronovost, Claude Provost, Henri Richard, Maurice Richard, Frank Selke (manager), Toe Blake (coach), Hector Dubois, Larry Aubut (trainers).
Scores: April 7 at Montreal — Montreal 4, Toronto 2; April 9 at Montreal — Montreal 2, Toronto 1; April 12 at Toronto — Montreal 5, Toronto 2; April 14 at Toronto — Montreal 4, Toronto 0.

1958-59 — Montreal Canadiens — Jacques Plante, Charlie Hodge, Doug Harvey, Tom Johnson, Bob Turner, Jean-Guy Talbot, Albert Langlois, Bernie Geoffrion, Ralph Backstrom, Bill Hicke, Maurice Richard, Dickie Moore, Claude Provost, Henri Richard, Marcel Bonin, Phil Goyette, Don Marshall, André Pronovost, Jean Béliveau, Frank Selke (manager), Toe Blake (coach), Hector Dubois, Larry Aubut (trainers).
Scores: April 9 at Montreal — Montreal 5, Toronto 3; April 11 at Montreal — Montreal 3, Toronto 1; April 14 at Toronto — Toronto 3, Montreal 2; April 16 at Toronto — Montreal 3, Toronto 2; April 18 at Montreal — Montreal 5, Toronto 3.

1957-58 — Montreal Canadiens — Jacques Plante, Gerry McNeil, Doug Harvey, Tom Johnson, Bob Turner, Dollard St-Laurent, Jean-Guy Talbot, Albert Langlois, Jean Béliveau, Bernie Geoffrion, Maurice Richard, Dickie Moore, Claude Provost, Floyd Curry, Bert Olmstead, Henri Richard, Marcel Bonin, Phil Goyette, Don Marshall, André Pronovost, Connie Broden, Frank Selke (manager), Toe Blake (coach), Hector Dubois, Larry Aubut (trainers).
Scores: April 8 at Montreal —Montreal 2, Boston 1; April 10 at Montreal — Boston 5, Montreal 2; April 13 at Boston — Montreal 3, Boston 0; April 15 at Boston — Boston 3, Montreal 1; April 17 at Montreal — Montreal 3, Boston 2; April 20 at Boston — Montreal 5, Boston 3.

Johnny Bower gets a blocker on this drive off the stick of Detroit's Norm Ullman during game two of the 1964 Stanley Cup Finals.

1956-57 — Montreal Canadiens — Jacques Plante, Gerry McNeil, Doug Harvey, Tom Johnson, Bob Turner, Dollard St. Laurent, Jean-Guy Talbot, Jean Béliveau, Bernie Geoffrion, Floyd Curry, Dickie Moore, Maurice Richard, Claude Provost, Bert Olmstead, Henri Richard, Phil Goyette, Don Marshall, André Pronovost, Connie Broden, Frank Selke (manager), Toe Blake (coach), Hector Dubois, Larry Aubut (trainers).
Scores: April 6, at Montreal — Montreal 5, Boston 1; April 9, at Montreal — Montreal 1, Boston 0; April 11, at Boston — Montreal 4, Boston 2; April 14, at Boston — Boston 2, Montreal 0; April 16, at Montreal — Montreal 5, Boston 1.

1955-56 — Montreal Canadiens — Jacques Plante, Doug Harvey, Emile Bouchard, Bob Turner, Tom Johnson, Jean-Guy Talbot, Dollard St. Laurent, Jean Béliveau, Bernie Geoffrion, Bert Olmstead, Floyd Curry, Jackie Leclair, Maurice Richard, Dickie Moore, Henri Richard, Ken Mosdell, Don Marshall, Claude Provost, Frank Selke (manager), Toe Blake (coach), Hector Dubois (trainer).
Scores: March 31, at Montreal — Montreal 6, Detroit 4; April 3, at Montreal — Montreal 5, Detroit 1; April 5, at Detroit — Detroit 3, Montreal 1; April 8, at Detroit — Montreal 3, Detroit 0; April 10, at Montreal — Montreal 3, Detroit 1.

1954-55 — Detroit Red Wings — Terry Sawchuk, Red Kelly, Bob Goldham, Marcel Pronovost, Ben Woit, Jim Hay, Larry Hillman, Ted Lindsay, Tony Leswick, Gordie Howe, Alex Delvecchio, Marty Pavelich, Glen Skov, Earl Reibel, John Wilson, Bill Dineen, Vic Stasiuk, Marcel Bonin, Jack Adams (manager), Jimmy Skinner (coach), Carl Mattson (trainer).
Scores: April 3, at Detroit — Detroit 4, Montreal 2; April 5, at Detroit — Detroit 7, Montreal 1; April 7 at Montreal — Montreal 4, Detroit 2; April 9, at Montreal — Montreal 5, Detroit 3; April 10, at Detroit — Detroit 5, Montreal 1; April 12, at Montreal — Montreal 6, Detroit 3; April 14, at Detroit — Detroit 3, Montreal 1.

1953-54 — Detroit Red Wings — Terry Sawchuk, Red Kelly, Bob Goldham, Ben Woit, Marcel Pronovost, Al Arbour, Keith Allen, Ted Lindsay, Tony Leswick, Gordie Howe, Marty Pavelich, Alex Delvecchio, Metro Prystai, Glen Skov, John Wilson, Bill Dineen, Jim Peters, Earl Reibel, Vic Stasiuk, Jack Adams (manager), Tommy Ivan (coach), Carl Mattson (trainer).
Scores: April 4, at Detroit — Detroit 3, Montreal 1; April 6, at Detroit — Montreal 3, Detroit 1; April 8, at Montreal — Detroit 5, Montreal 2; April 10, at Montreal — Detroit 2, Montreal 0; April 11, at Detroit — Montreal 1, Detroit 0; April 13, at Montreal — Montreal 4, Detroit 1; April 16, at Detroit — Detroit 2, Montreal 1.

1952-53 — Montreal Canadiens — Gerry McNeil, Jacques Plante, Doug Harvey, Emile Bouchard, Tom Johnson, Dollard St. Laurent, Bud MacPherson, Maurice Richard, Elmer Lach, Bert Olmstead, Bernie Geoffrion, Floyd Curry, Paul Masnick, Billy Reay, Dickie Moore, Ken Mosdell, Dick Gamble, Johnny McCormack, Lorne Davis, Calum McKay, Eddie Mazur, Frank Selke (manager), Dick Irvin (coach), Hector Dubois (trainer).
Scores: April 9, at Montreal — Montreal 4, Boston 2; April 11, at Montreal — Boston 4, Montreal 1; April 12, at Boston — Montreal 3, Boston 0; April 14, at Boston — Montreal 7, Boston 3; April 16, at Montreal — Montreal 1, Boston 0.

1951-52 — Detroit Red Wings — Terry Sawchuk, Bob Goldham, Ben Woit, Red Kelly, Leo Reise, Marcel Pronovost, Ted Lindsay, Tony Leswick, Gordie Howe, Marty Pavelich, Sid Abel, Glen Skov, Alex Delvecchio, John Wilson, Vic Stasiuk, Larry Zeidel, Jack Adams (manager) Tommy Ivan (coach), Carl Mattson (trainer).
Scores: April 10, at Montreal — Detroit 3, Montreal 1; April 12 at Montreal — Detroit 2, Montreal 1; April 13, at Detroit — Detroit 3, Montreal 0; April 15, at Detroit — Detroit 3, Montreal 0.

1950-51 — Toronto Maple Leafs — Turk Broda, Al Rollins, Jim Thomson, Gus Mortson, Bill Barilko, Bill Juzda, Fern Flaman, Hugh Bolton, Ted Kennedy, Sid Smith, Tod Sloan, Cal Gardner, Howie Meeker, Harry Watson, Max Bentley, Joe Klukay, Danny Lewicki, Ray Timgren, Fleming Mackell, Johnny McCormack, Bob Hassard, Conn Smythe (manager), Joe Primeau (coach), Tim Daly (trainer).
Scores: April 11, at Toronto — Toronto 3, Montreal 2; April 14, at Toronto — Montreal 3, Toronto 2; April 17, at Montreal — Toronto 2, Montreal 1; April 19, at Montreal — Toronto 3, Montreal 2; April 21, at Toronto — Toronto 3, Montreal 2.

1949-50 — Detroit Red Wings — Harry Lumley, Jack Stewart, Leo Reise, Clare Martin, Al Dewsbury, Lee Fogolin, Marcel Pronovost, Red Kelly, Ted Lindsay, Sid Abel, Gordie Howe, George Gee, Jimmy Peters, Marty Pavelich, Jim McFadden, Pete Babando, Max McNab, Gerry Couture, Joe Carveth, John Wilson, Larry Wilson, Jack Adams (manager), Tommy Ivan (coach), Carl Mattson (trainer).
Scores: April 11, at Detroit — Detroit 4, NY Rangers 1; April 13, at Toronto* — NY Rangers 3, Detroit 1; April 15, at Toronto — Detroit 4, NY Rangers 0; April 18, at Detroit — NY Rangers 4, Detroit 3; April 20, at Detroit — NY Rangers 2, Detroit 1; April 22, at Detroit — Detroit 5, NY Rangers 4; April 23, at Detroit — Detroit 4, NY Rangers 3.
* Ice was unavailable in Madison Square Garden and Rangers elected to play second and third games on Toronto ice.

1948-49 — Toronto Maple Leafs — Turk Broda, Jim Thomson, Gus Mortson, Bill Barilko, Garth Boesch, Bill Juzda, Ted Kennedy, Howie Meeker, Vic Lynn, Harry Watson, Bill Ezinicki, Cal Gardner, Max Bentley, Joe Klukay, Sid Smith, Don Metz, Ray Timgren, Fleming Mackell, Harry Taylor, Bob Dawes, Tod Sloan, Conn Smythe (manager), Hap Day (coach), Tim Daly (trainer).
Scores: April 8, at Detroit — Toronto 3, Detroit 2; April 10, at Detroit — Toronto 3, Detroit 1; April 13, at Toronto — Toronto 3, Detroit 1; April 16, at Toronto — Toronto 3, Detroit 1.

1947-48 — Toronto Maple Leafs — Turk Broda, Jim Thomson, Wally Stanowski, Garth Boesch, Bill Barilko, Gus Mortson, Phil Samis, Syl Apps, Bill Ezinicki, Harry Watson, Ted Kennedy, Howie Meeker, Vic Lynn, Nick Metz, Max Bentley, Joe Klukay, Les Costello, Don Metz, Sid Smith, Conn Smythe (manager), Hap Day (coach), Tim Daly (trainer).
Scores: April 7, at Toronto — Toronto 5, Detroit 3; April 10, at Toronto — Toronto 4, Detroit 2; April 11, at Detroit — Toronto 2, Detroit 0; April 14, at Detroit — Toronto 7, Detroit 2.

Ralph Backstrom, left, and Dick Duff celebrate the Montreal Canadiens' 4-0 victory over the Chicago Black Hawks in game seven of the 1965 Stanley Cup Finals.

1946-47 — Toronto Maple Leafs — Turk Broda, Garth Boesch, Gus Mortson, Jim Thomson, Wally Stanowski, Bill Barilko, Harry Watson, Bud Poile, Ted Kennedy, Syl Apps, Don Metz, Nick Metz, Bill Ezinicki, Vic Lynn, Howie Meeker, Gaye Stewart, Joe Klukay, Gus Bodnar, Bob Goldham, Conn Smythe (manager), Hap Day (coach), Tim Daly (trainer).
Scores: April 8, at Montreal — Montreal 6, Toronto 0; April 10, at Montreal — Toronto 4, Montreal 0; April 12, at Toronto — Toronto 4, Montreal 2; April 15, at Toronto — Toronto 2, Montreal 1; April 17, at Montreal — Montreal 3, Toronto 1; April 19, at Toronto — Toronto 2, Montreal 1.

1945-46 — Montreal Canadiens — Elmer Lach, Toe Blake, Maurice Richard, Bob Fillion, Dutch Hiller, Murph Chamberlain, Ken Mosdell, Buddy O'Connor, Glen Harmon, Jim Peters, Emile Bouchard, Bill Reay, Ken Reardon, Leo Lamoureux, Frank Eddolls, Gerry Plamondon, Bill Durnan, Tommy Gorman (manager), Dick Irvin (coach), Ernie Cook (trainer).
Scores: March 30, at Montreal — Montreal 4, Boston 3; April 2, at Montreal — Montreal 3, Boston 2; April 4, at Boston — Montreal 4, Boston 2; April 7, at Boston — Boston 3, Montreal 2; April 9, at Montreal — Montreal 6, Boston 3.

1944-45 — Toronto Maple Leafs — Don Metz, Frank McCool, Wally Stanowski, Reg Hamilton, Elwyn Morris, Johnny McCreedy, Tommy O'Neill, Ted Kennedy, Babe Pratt, Gus Bodnar, Art Jackson, Jack McLean, Mel Hill, Nick Metz, Bob Davidson, Dave Schriner, Lorne Carr, Conn Smythe (manager), Frank Selke (business manager), Hap Day (coach), Tim Daly (trainer).
Scores: April 6, at Detroit — Toronto 1, Detroit 0; April 8, at Detroit — Toronto 2, Detroit 0; April 12, at Toronto — Toronto 1, Detroit 0; April 14, at Toronto — Detroit 5, Toronto 3; April 19, at Detroit — Detroit 2, Toronto 0; April 21, at Toronto — Detroit 1, Toronto 0; April 22, at Detroit — Toronto 2, Detroit 1.

1943-44 — Montreal Canadiens — Toe Blake, Maurice Richard, Elmer Lach, Ray Getliffe, Murph Chamberlain, Phil Watson, Emile Bouchard, Glen Harmon, Buddy O'Connor, Jerry Heffernan, Mike McMahon, Leo Lamoureux, Fernand Majeau, Bob Fillion, Bill Durnan, Tommy Gorman (manager), Dick Irvin (coach), Ernie Cook (trainer).
Scores: April 4, at Montreal — Montreal 5, Chicago 1; April 6, at Chicago — Montreal 3, Chicago 1; April 9, at Chicago — Montreal 3, Chicago 2; April 13, at Montreal — Montreal 5, Chicago 4.

1942-43 — Detroit Red Wings — Jack Stewart, Jimmy Orlando, Sid Abel, Alex Motter, Harry Watson, Joe Carveth, Mud Bruneteau, Eddie Wares, Johnny Mowers, Cully Simon, Don Grosso, Carl Liscombe, Connie Brown, Syd Howe, Les Douglas, Hal Jackson, Joe Fisher, Jack Adams (manager), Ebbie Goodfellow (playing-coach), Honey Walker (trainer).
Scores: April 1, at Detroit — Detroit 6, Boston 2; April 4, at Detroit — Detroit 4, Boston 3; April 7, at Boston — Detroit 4, Boston 0; April 8, at Boston — Detroit 2, Boston 0.

1941-42 — Toronto Maple Leafs — Wally Stanowski, Syl Apps, Bob Goldham, Gord Drillon, Hank Goldup, Ernie Dickens, Dave Schriner, Bucko McDonald, Bob Davidson, Nick Metz, Bingo Kampman, Don Metz, Gaye Stewart, Turk Broda, Johnny McCreedy, Lorne Carr, Pete Langelle, Billy Taylor, Conn Smythe (manager), Hap Day (coach), Frank Selke (business manager), Tim Daly (trainer).
Scores: April 4, at Toronto — Detroit 3, Toronto 2; April 7, at Toronto — Detroit 4, Toronto 2; April 9, at Detroit — Detroit 5, Toronto 2; April 12, at Detroit — Toronto 4, Detroit 3; April 14, at Toronto — Toronto 9, Detroit 3; April 16, at Detroit — Toronto 3, Detroit 0; April 18, at Toronto — Toronto 3, Detroit 1.

1940-41 — Boston Bruins — Bill Cowley, Des Smith, Dit Clapper, Frank Brimsek, Flash Hollett, John Crawford, Bobby Bauer, Pat McReavy, Herb Cain, Mel Hill, Milt Schmidt, Woody Dumart, Roy Conacher, Terry Reardon, Art Jackson, Eddie Wiseman, Art Ross (manager), Cooney Weiland (coach), Win Green (trainer).
Scores: April 6, at Boston — Detroit 2, Boston 3; April 8, at Boston — Detroit 1, Boston 2; April 10, at Detroit — Boston 4, Detroit 2; April 12, at Detroit — Boston 3, Detroit 1.

1939-40 — New York Rangers — Dave Kerr, Art Coulter, Ott Heller, Alex Shibicky, Mac Colville, Neil Colville, Phil Watson, Lynn Patrick, Clint Smith, Muzz Patrick, Babe Pratt, Bryan Hextall, Kilby Macdonald, Dutch Hiller, Alf Pike, Sanford Smith, Lester Patrick (manager), Frank Boucher (coach), Harry Westerby (trainer).
Scores: April 2, at New York — NY Rangers 2, Toronto 1; April 3, at New York — NY Rangers 6, Toronto 2; April 6, at Toronto — NY Rangers 1, Toronto 2; April 9, at Toronto — NY Rangers 0, Toronto 3; April 11, at Toronto — NY Rangers 2, Toronto 1; April 13, at Toronto — NY Rangers 3, Toronto 2.

1938-39 — Boston Bruins — Bobby Bauer, Mel Hill, Flash Hollett, Roy Conacher, Gord Pettinger, Milt Schmidt, Woody Dumart, Jack Crawford, Ray Getliffe, Frank Brimsek, Eddie Shore, Dit Clapper, Bill Cowley, Jack Portland, Red Hamill, Cooney Weiland, Art Ross (manager-coach), Win Green (trainer).
Scores: April 6, at Boston — Toronto 1, Boston 2; April 9, at Boston — Toronto 3, Boston 2; April 11, at Toronto — Toronto 1, Boston 3; April 13 at Toronto — Toronto 0, Boston 2; April 16, at Boston — Toronto 1, Boston 3.

1937-38 — Chicago Black Hawks — Art Wiebe, Carl Voss, Hal Jackson, Mike Karakas, Mush March, Jack Shill, Earl Seibert, Cully Dahlstrom, Alex Levinsky, Johnny Gottselig, Lou Trudel, Pete Palangio, Bill MacKenzie, Doc Romnes, Paul Thompson, Roger Jenkins, Alf Moore, Bert Connolly, Virgil Johnson, Paul Goodman, Bill Stewart (manager-coach), Eddie Froelich (trainer).
Scores: April 5, at Toronto — Chicago 3, Toronto 1; April 7, at Toronto — Chicago 1, Toronto 5; April 10 at Chicago — Chicago 2, Toronto 1; April 12, at Chicago — Chicago 4, Toronto 1.

1936-37 — Detroit Red Wings — Normie Smith, Pete Kelly, Larry Aurie, Herbie Lewis, Hec Kilrea, Mud Bruneteau, Syd Howe, Wally Kilrea, Jimmy Franks, Bucko McDonald, Gordon Pettinger, Ebbie Goodfellow, Johnny Gallagher, Scotty Bowman, Johnny Sorrell, Marty Barry, Earl Robertson, Johnny Sherf, Howard Mackie, Jack Adams (manager-coach), Honey Walker (trainer).
Scores: April 6, at New York — Detroit 1, NY Rangers 5; April 8, at Detroit — Detroit 4, NY Rangers 2; April 11, at Detroit — Detroit 0, NY Rangers 1; April 13, at Detroit — Detroit 1, NY Rangers 0; April 15, at Detroit — Detroit 3, NY Rangers 0.

1935-36 — Detroit Red Wings — Johnny Sorrell, Syd Howe, Marty Barry, Herbie Lewis, Mud Bruneteau, Wally Kilrea, Hec Kilrea, Gordon Pettinger, Bucko McDonald, Scotty Bowman, Pete Kelly, Doug Young, Ebbie Goodfellow, Normie Smith, Jack Adams (manager-coach), Honey Walker (trainer).
Scores: April 5, at Detroit — Detroit 3, Toronto 1; April 7, at Detroit — Detroit 9, Toronto 4; April 9, at Toronto — Detroit 3, Toronto 4; April 11, at Toronto — Detroit 3, Toronto 2.

1934-35 — Montreal Maroons — Marvin (Cy) Wentworth, Alex Connell, Toe Blake, Stew Evans, Earl Robinson, Bill Miller, Dave Trottier, Jimmy Ward, Larry Northcott, Hooley Smith, Russ Blinco, Allan Shields, Sammy McManus, Gus Marker, Bob Gracie, Herb Cain, Tommy Gorman (manager), Lionel Conacher (coach), Bill O'Brien (trainer).
Scores: April 4, at Toronto — Mtl. Maroons 3, Toronto 2; April 6, at Toronto — Mtl. Maroons 3, Toronto 1; April 9, at Montreal — Mtl. Maroons 4, Toronto 1.

1933-34 — Chicago Black Hawks — Taffy Abel, Lolo Couture, Lou Trudel, Lionel Conacher, Paul Thompson, Leroy Goldsworthy, Art Coulter, Roger Jenkins, Don McFayden, Tommy Cook, Doc Romnes, Johnny Gottselig, Mush March, Johnny Sheppard, Chuck Gardiner (captain), Bill Kendall, Tommy Gorman (manager-coach), Eddie Froelich (trainer).
Scores: April 3, at Detroit — Chicago 2, Detroit 1; April 5, at Detroit — Chicago 4, Detroit 1; April 8, at Chicago — Detroit 5, Chicago 2; April 10, at Chicago — Chicago 1, Detroit 0.

1932-33 — New York Rangers — Ching Johnson, Butch Keeling, Frank Boucher, Art Somers, Babe Siebert, Bun Cook, Andy Aitkenhead, Ott Heller, Ozzie Asmundson, Gord Pettinger, Doug Brennan, Cecil Dillon, Bill Cook (captain), Murray Murdoch, Earl Seibert, Lester Patrick (manager-coach), Harry Westerby (trainer).
Scores: April 4, at New York — NY Rangers 5, Toronto 1; April 8, at Toronto — NY Rangers 3, Toronto 1; April 11, at Toronto — Toronto 3, NY Rangers 2; April 13, at Toronto — NY Rangers 1, Toronto 0.

1931-32 — Toronto Maple Leafs — Charlie Conacher, Harvey Jackson, King Clancy, Andy Blair, Red Horner, Lorne Chabot, Alex Levinsky, Joe Primeau, Hal Darragh, Hal Cotton, Frank Finnigan, Hap Day, Ace Bailey, Bob Gracie, Fred Robertson, Earl Miller, Conn Smythe (manager), Dick Irvin (coach), Tim Daly (trainer).
Scores: April 5 at New York — Toronto 6, NY Rangers 4; April 7, at Boston* — Toronto 6, NY Rangers 2; April 9, at Toronto — Toronto 6, NY Rangers 4.
* Ice was unavailable in Madison Square Garden and Rangers elected to play the second game on neutral ice.

1930-31 — Montreal Canadiens — George Hainsworth, Wildor Larochelle, Marty Burke, Sylvio Mantha, Howie Morenz, Johnny Gagnon, Aurel Joliat, Armand Mondou, Pit Lepine, Albert Leduc, Georges Mantha, Art Lesieur, Nick Wasnie, Bert McCaffrey, Gus Rivers, Jean Pusie, Léo Dandurand (manager), Cecil Hart (coach), Ed Dufour (trainer).
Scores: April 3, at Chicago — Montreal 2, Chicago 1; April 5, at Chicago — Chicago 2, Montreal 1; April 9, at Montreal — Chicago 3, Montreal 2; April 11, at Montreal — Montreal 4, Chicago 2; April 14, at Montreal — Montreal 2, Chicago 0.

1929-30 — Montreal Canadiens — George Hainsworth, Marty Burke, Sylvio Mantha, Howie Morenz, Bert McCaffrey, Aurel Joliat, Albert Leduc, Pit Lepine, Wildor Larochelle, Nick Wasnie, Gerald Carson, Armand Mondou, Georges Mantha, Gus Rivers, Léo Dandurand (manager), Cecil Hart (coach), Ed Dufour (trainer).
Scores: April 1 at Boston — Montreal 3, Boston 0; April 3 at Montreal — Montreal 4, Boston 3.

1928-29 — Boston Bruins — Cecil (Tiny) Thompson, Eddie Shore, Lionel Hitchman, Perk Galbraith, Eric Pettinger, Frank Fredrickson, Mickey Mackay, Red Green, Dutch Gainor, Harry Oliver, Eddie Rodden, Dit Clapper, Cooney Weiland, Lloyd Klein, Cy Denneny, Bill Carson, George Owen, Myles Lane, Art Ross (manager-coach), Win Green (trainer).
Scores: March 28 at Boston — Boston 2, NY Rangers 0; March 29 at New York — Boston 2, NY Rangers 1.

1927-28 — New York Rangers — Lorne Chabot, Taffy Abel, Leon Bourgault, Ching Johnson, Bill Cook, Bun Cook, Frank Boucher, Billy Boyd, Murray Murdoch, Paul Thompson, Alex Gray, Joe Miller, Patsy Callighen, Lester Patrick (manager-coach), Harry Westerby (trainer).
Scores: April 5 at Montreal — Mtl. Maroons 2, NY Rangers 0; April 7 at Montreal — NY Rangers 2, Mtl. Maroons 1; April 10 at Montreal — Mtl. Maroons 2, NY Rangers 1; April 12 at Montreal — NY Rangers 1, Mtl. Maroons 0; April 14 at Montreal — NY Rangers 2, Mtl. Maroons 1.

1926-27 — Ottawa Senators — Alex Connell, King Clancy, George (Buck) Boucher, Ed Gorman, Frank Finnigan, Alex Smith, Hec Kilrea, Hooley Smith, Cy Denneny, Frank Nighbor, Jack Adams, Milt Halliday, Dave Gill (manager-coach).
Scores: April 7 at Boston — Ottawa 0, Boston 0; April 9 at Boston — Ottawa 3, Boston 1; April 11 at Ottawa — Boston 1, Ottawa 1; April 13 at Ottawa — Ottawa 3, Boston 1.

1925-26 — Montreal Maroons — Clint Benedict, Reg Noble, Frank Carson, Dunc Munro, Nels Stewart, Harry Broadbent, Babe Siebert, Dinny Dinsmore, Bill Phillips, Hobart (Hobie) Kitchen, Sammy Rothschield, Albert (Toots) Holway, Shorty Horne, Bern Brophy, Eddie Gerard (manager-coach), Bill O'Brien (trainer).
Scores: March 30 at Montreal — Mtl. Maroons 3, Victoria 0; April 1 at Montreal — Mtl. Maroons 3, Victoria 0; April 3 at Montreal — Victoria 3, Mtl. Maroons 2; April 6 at Montreal — Mtl. Maroons 2, Victoria 0.

The series in the spring of 1926 ended the annual playoffs between the champions of the East and the champions of the West. Since 1926-27 the annual playoffs in the National Hockey League have decided the Stanley Cup champions.

1924-25 — Victoria Cougars — Harry (Happy) Holmes, Clem Loughlin, Gordie Fraser, Frank Fredrickson, Jack Walker, Harold (Gizzy) Hart, Harold (Slim) Halderson, Frank Foyston, Wally Elmer, Harry Meeking, Jocko Anderson, Lester Patrick (manager-coach).
Scores: March 21 at Victoria — Victoria 5, Montreal 2; March 23 at Vancouver — Victoria 3, Montreal 1; March 27 at Victoria — Montreal 4, Victoria 2; March 30 at Victoria — Victoria 6, Montreal 1.

1923-24 — Montreal Canadiens — Georges Vezina, Sprague Cleghorn, Billy Couture, Howie Morenz, Aurel Joliat, Billy Boucher, Odie Cleghorn, Sylvio Mantha, Bobby Boucher, Billy Bell, Billy Cameron, Joe Malone, Charles Fortier, Leo Dandurand (manager-coach).
Scores: March 18 at Montreal — Montreal 3, Van. Maroons 2; March 20 at Montreal — Montreal 2, Van. Maroons 1. March 22 at Montreal — Montreal 6, Cgy. Tigers 1; March 25 at Ottawa* — Montreal 3, Cgy. Tigers 0.

* Game transferred to Ottawa to benefit from artificial ice surface.

1922-23 — Ottawa Senators — George (Buck) Boucher, Lionel Hitchman, Frank Nighbor, King Clancy, Harry Helman, Clint Benedict, Jack Darragh, Eddie Gerard, Cy Denneny, Harry Broadbent, Tommy Gorman (manager), Pete Green (coach), F. Dolan (trainer).
Scores: March 16 at Vancouver — Ottawa 1, Van. Maroons 0; March 19 at Vancouver — Van. Maroons 4, Ottawa 1; March 23 at Vancouver — Ottawa 3, Van. Maroons 2; March 26 at Vancouver — Ottawa 5, Van. Maroons 1; March 29 at Vancouver — Ottawa 2, Edm. Eskimos 1; March 31 at Vancouver — Ottawa 1, Edm. Eskimos 0.

Toronto St. Pats' sharpshooter Cecil "Babe" Dye still holds the NHL record for most goals in a Stanley Cup final series. In the 1922 championship series against Vancouver, the colorful Dye left his mark in the NHL record book with a nine-goal performance.

1921-22 — Toronto St. Pats — Ted Stackhouse, Corb Denneny, Rod Smylie, Lloyd Andrews, John Ross Roach, Harry Cameron, Bill (Red) Stuart, Cecil (Babe) Dye, Ken Randall, Reg Noble, Eddie Gerard (borrowed for one game from Ottawa), Stan Jackson, Nolan Mitchell, Charlie Querrie (manager), Eddie Powers (coach).
Scores: March 17 at Toronto — Van. Millionaires 4, Toronto 3; March 20 at Toronto — Toronto 2, Van. Millionaires 1; March 23 at Toronto — Van. Millionaires 3, Toronto 0; March 25 at Toronto — Toronto 6, Van. Millionaires 0; March 28 at Toronto — Toronto 5, Van. Millionaires 1.

1920-21 — Ottawa Senators — Jack McKell, Jack Darragh, Morley Bruce, George (Buck) Boucher, Eddie Gerard, Clint Benedict, Sprague Cleghorn, Frank Nighbor, Harry Broadbent, Cy Denneny, Leth Graham, Tommy Gorman (manager), Pete Green (coach), F. Dolan (trainer).
Scores: March 21 at Vancouver — Van. Millionaires 2, Ottawa 1; March 24 at Vancouver — Ottawa 4, Van. Millionaires 3; March 28 at Vancouver — Ottawa 3, Van. Millionaires 2; March 31 at Vancouver — Van. Millionaires 3, Ottawa 2; April 4 at Vancouver — Ottawa 2, Van. Millionaires 1.

1919-20 — Ottawa Senators — Jack McKell, Jack Darragh, Morley Bruce, Horrace Merrill, George (Buck) Boucher, Eddie Gerard, Clint Benedict, Sprague Cleghorn, Frank Nighbor, Harry Broadbent, Cy Denneny, Price, Tommy Gorman (manager), Pete Green (coach).
Scores: March 22 at Ottawa — Ottawa 3, Seattle 2; March 24 at Ottawa — Ottawa 3, Seattle 0; March 27 at Ottawa — Seattle 3, Ottawa 1; March 30 at Toronto* — Seattle 5, Ottawa 2; April 1 at Toronto* — Ottawa 6, Seattle 1.
* Games transferred to Toronto to benefit from artificial ice surface.

1918-19 — No decision, Series halted by Spanish influenza epidemic, illness of several players and death of Joe Hall of Montreal Canadiens from flu. Five games had been played when the series was halted, each team having won two and tied one. The results are shown:
Scores: March 19 at Seattle — Seattle 7, Montreal 0; March 22 at Seattle — Montreal 4, Seattle 2; March 24 at Seattle — Seattle 7, Montreal 2; March 26 at Seattle — Montreal 0, Seattle 0; March 30 at Seattle — Montreal 4, Seattle 3.

1917-18 — Toronto Arenas — Rusty Crawford, Harry Meeking, Ken Randall, Corb Denneny, Harry Cameron, Jack Adams, Alf Skinner, Harry Mummery, Harry (Happy) Holmes, Reg Noble, Sammy Hebert, Jack Marks, Jack Coughlin, Neville, Charlie Querrie (manager), Dick Carroll (coach), Frank Carroll (trainer).
Scores: March 20 at Toronto — Toronto 5, Van. Millionaires 3; March 23 at Toronto — Van. Millionaires 6, Toronto 4; March 26 at Toronto — Toronto 6, Van. Millionaires 3; March 28 at Toronto — Van. Millionaires 8, Toronto 1; March 30 at Toronto — Toronto 2, Van. Millionaires 1.

1916-17 — Seattle Metropolitans — Harry (Happy) Holmes, Ed Carpenter, Cully Wilson, Jack Walker, Bernie Morris, Frank Foyston, Roy Rickey, Jim Riley, Bobby Rowe (captain), Peter Muldoon (manager).
Scores: March 17 at Seattle — Montreal 8, Seattle 4; March 20 at Seattle — Seattle 6, Montreal 1; March 23 at Seattle — Seattle 4, Montreal 1; March 25 at Seattle — Seattle 9, Montreal 1.

1915-16 — Montreal Canadiens — Georges Vezina, Bert Corbeau, Jack Laviolette, Newsy Lalonde, Louis Berlinguette, Goldie Prodgers, Howard McNamara, Didier Pitre, Skene Ronan, Amos Arbour, Georges Poulin, Jacques Fournier, George Kennedy (manager).
Scores: March 20 at Montreal — Portland 2, Montreal 0; March 22 at Montreal — Montreal 2, Portland 1; March 25 at Montreal — Montreal 6, Portland 3; March 28 at Montreal — Portland 6, Montreal 5; March 30 at Montreal — Montreal 2, Portland 1.

1914-15 — Vancouver Millionaires — Kenny Mallen, Frank Nighbor, Fred (Cyclone) Taylor, Hughie Lehman, Lloyd Cook, Mickey MacKay, Barney Stanley, Jim Seaborn, Si Griffis (captain), Jean Matz, Frank Patrick (playing manager).
Scores: March 22 at Vancouver — Van. Millionaires 6, Ottawa 2; March 24 at Vancouver — Van. Millionaires 8, Ottawa 3; March 26 at Vancouver — Van. Millionaires 12, Ottawa 3.

1913-14 — Toronto Blueshirts — Con Corbeau, F. Roy McGiffen, Jack Walker, George McNamara, Cully Wilson, Frank Foyston, Harry Cameron, Harry (Happy) Holmes, Alan M. Davidson (captain), Harriston, Jack Marshall (playing-manager), Frank and Dick Carroll (trainers).
Scores: March 14 at Toronto — Toronto 5, Victoria 2; March 17 at Toronto — Toronto 6, Victoria 5; March 19 at Toronto — Toronto 2, Victoria 1.

1912-13 — Quebec Bulldogs — Joe Malone, Joe Hall, Paddy Moran, Harry Mummery, Tommy Smith, Jack Marks, Russell Crawford, Billy Creighton, Jeff Malone, Rocket Power, M.J. Quinn (manager), D. Beland (trainer).
Scores: March 8 at Quebec — Que. Bulldogs 14, Sydney 3; March 10 at Quebec — Que. Bulldogs 6, Sydney 2.

Victoria challenged Quebec but the Bulldogs refused to put the Stanley Cup in competition so the two teams played an exhibition series with Victoria winning two games to one by scores of 7-5, 3-6, 6-1. It was the first meeting between the Eastern champions and the Western champions. The following year, and until the Western Hockey League disbanded after the 1926 playoffs, the Cup went to the winner of the series between East and West.

1911-12 — Quebec Bulldogs — Goldie Prodgers, Joe Hall, Walter Rooney, Paddy Moran, Jack Marks, Jack McDonald, Eddie Oatman, George Leonard, Joe Malone (captain), C. Nolan (coach), M.J. Quinn (manager), D. Beland (trainer).
Scores: March 11 at Quebec — Que. Bulldogs 9, Moncton 3; March 13 at Quebec — Que. Bulldogs 8, Moncton 0.

Prior to 1912, teams could challenge the Stanley Cup champions for the title, thus there was more than one Championship Series played in most of the seasons between 1894 and 1911.

1910-11 — Ottawa Senators — Hamby Shore, Percy LeSueur, Jack Darragh, Bruce Stuart, Marty Walsh, Bruce Ridpath, Fred Lake, Albert (Dubby) Kerr, Alex Currie, Horace Gaul.
Scores: March 13 at Ottawa — Ottawa 7, Galt 4; March 16 at Ottawa — Ottawa 13, Port Arthur 4.

1909-10 — Montreal Wanderers — Cecil W. Blachford, Ernie (Moose) Johnson, Ernie Russell, Riley Hern, Harry Hyland, Jack Marshall, Frank (Pud) Glass (captain), Jimmy Gardner, R. R. Boon (manager).
Scores: March 12 at Montreal — Mtl. Wanderers 7, Berlin (Kitchener) 3.

1908-09 — Ottawa Senators — Fred Lake, Percy LeSueur, Fred (Cyclone) Taylor, H.L. (Billy) Gilmour, Albert Kerr, Edgar Dey, Marty Walsh, Bruce Stuart (captain).
Scores: Ottawa, as champions of the Eastern Canada Hockey Association took over the Stanley Cup in 1909 and, although a challenge was accepted by the Cup trustees from Winnipeg Shamrocks, games could not be arranged because of the lateness of the season. No other challenges were made in 1909. The following season — 1909-10 — however, the Senators accepted two challenges as defending Cup Champions. The first was against Galt in a two-game, total-goals series, and the second against Edmonton, also a two-game, total-goals series. Results: January 5 at Ottawa —Ottawa 12, Galt 3; January 7 at Ottawa — Ottawa 3, Galt 1. January 18 at Ottawa — Ottawa 8, Edm. Eskimos 4; January 20 at Ottawa — Ottawa 13, Edm. Eskimos 7.

1907-08 — Montreal Wanderers — Riley Hern, Art Ross, Walter Smaill, Frank (Pud) Glass, Bruce Stuart, Ernie Russell, Ernie (Moose) Johnson, Cecil Blachford (captain), Tom Hooper, Larry Gilmour, Ernie Liffiton, R.R. Boon (manager).
Scores: Wanderers accepted four challenges for the Cup: January 9 at Montreal — Mtl. Wanderers 9, Ott. Victorias 3; January 13 at Montreal — Mtl. Wanderers 13, Ott. Victorias 1; March 10 at Montreal — Mtl. Wanderers 11, Wpg. Maple Leafs 5; March 12 at Montreal — Mtl. Wanderers 9, Wpg. Maple Leafs 3; March 14 at Montreal — Mtl. Wanderers 6, Toronto (OPHL) 4. At start of following season, 1908-09, Wanderers were challenged by Edmonton. Results: December 28 at Montreal — Mtl. Wanderers 7, Edm. Eskimos 3; December 30 at Montreal — Edm. Eskimos 7, Mtl. Wanderers 6. Total goals: Mtl. Wanderers 13, Edm. Eskimos 10.

1906-07 — (March) **— Montreal Wanderers —** W. S. (Billy) Strachan, Riley Hern, Lester Patrick, Hod Stuart, Frank (Pud) Glass, Ernie Russell, Cecil Blachford (captain), Ernie (Moose) Johnson, Rod Kennedy, Jack Marshall, R.R. Boon (manager).
Scores: March 23 at Winnipeg — Mtl. Wanderers 7, Kenora 2; March 25 at Winnipeg — Kenora 6, Mtl. Wanderers 5. Total goals: Mtl. Wanderers 12, Kenora 8.

1906-07 — (January) **— Kenora Thistles —** Eddie Geroux, Art Ross, Si Griffis, Tom Hooper, Billy McGimsie, Roxy Beaudro, Tom Phillips.
Scores: January 17 at Montreal — Kenora 4, Mtl. Wanderers 2; Jan. 21 at Montreal — Kenora 8, Mtl. Wanderers 6.

1905-06 — (March) **— Montreal Wanderers —** Henri Menard, Billy Strachan, Rod Kennedy, Lester Patrick, Frank (Pud) Glass, Ernie Russell, Ernie (Moose) Johnson, Cecil Blachford (captain), Josh Arnold, R.R. Boon (manager).
Scores: March 14 at Montreal — Mtl. Wanderers 9, Ottawa 1; March 17 at Ottawa — Ottawa 9, Mtl. Wanderers 3. Total goals: Mtl. Wanderers 12, Ottawa 10. Wanderers accepted a challenge from New Glasgow, N.S., prior to the start of the 1906-07 season. Results: December 27 at Montreal — Mtl. Wanderers 10, New Glasgow 3; December 29 at Montreal — Mtl. Wanderers 7, New Glasgow 2.

1905-06 — (February) **— Ottawa Silver Seven —** Harvey Pulford (captain), Arthur Moore, Harry Westwick, Frank McGee, Alf Smith (playing coach), Billy Gilmour, Billy Hague, Percy LeSueur, Harry Smith, Tommy Smith, Dion, Ebbs.
Scores: February 27 at Ottawa — Ottawa 16, Queen's University 7; February 28 at Ottawa — Ottawa 12, Queen's University 7; March 6 at Ottawa — Ottawa 6, Smiths Falls 5; March 8 at Ottawa — Ottawa 8, Smiths Falls 2.

1904-05 — Ottawa Silver Seven — Dave Finnie, Harvey Pulford (captain), Arthur Moore, Harry Westwick, Frank McGee, Alf Smith (playing coach), Billy Gilmour, Frank White, Horace Gaul, Hamby Shore, Bones Allen.
Scores: January 13 at Ottawa — Ottawa 9, Dawson City 2; January 16 at Ottawa — Ottawa 23, Dawson City 2; March 7 at Ottawa — Rat Portage 9, Ottawa 3; March 9 at Ottawa — Ottawa 4, Rat Portage 2; March 11 at Ottawa — Ottawa 5, Rat Portage 4.

1903-04 — Ottawa Silver Seven — S.C. (Suddy) Gilmour, Arthur Moore, Frank McGee, J.B. (Bouse) Hutton, H.L. (Billy) Gilmour, Jim McGee, Harry Westwick, E. H. (Harvey) Pulford (captain), Scott, Alf Smith (playing coach).
Scores: December 30 at Ottawa — Ottawa 9, Wpg. Rowing Club 1; January 1 at Ottawa — Wpg. Rowing Club 6, Ottawa 2; January 4 at Ottawa — Ottawa 2, Wpg. Rowing Club 0. February 23 at Ottawa — Ottawa 6, Tor. Marlboros 3; February 25 at Ottawa — Ottawa 11, Tor. Marlboros 2; March 2 at Montreal — Ottawa 5, Mtl. Wanderers 5. Following the tie game, a new two-game series was ordered to be played in Ottawa but the Wanderers refused unless the tie game was replayed in Montreal. When no settlement could be reached, the series was abandoned and Ottawa retained the Cup and accepted a two-game challenge from Brandon. Results: (both games at Ottawa), March 9, Ottawa 6, Brandon 3; March 11, Ottawa 9, Brandon 3.

1902-03 — (March) **— Ottawa Silver Seven —** S.C. (Suddy) Gilmour, P.T. (Percy) Sims, J.B. (Bouse) Hutton, D.J. (Dave) Gilmour, H.L. (Billy) Gilmour, Harry Westwick, Frank McGee, F.H. Wood, A.A. Fraser, Charles D. Spittal, E.H. (Harvey) Pulford (captain), Arthur Moore, Alf Smith (coach.)
Scores: March 7 at Montreal — Ottawa 1, Mtl. Victorias 1; March 10 at Ottawa — Ottawa 8, Mtl. Victorias 0. Total goals: Ottawa 9, Mtl. Victorias 1; March 12 at Ottawa — Ottawa 6, Rat Portage 2; March 14 at Ottawa — Ottawa 4, Rat Portage 2.

1902-03 — (February) **— Montreal AAA —** Tom Hodge, R.R. (Dickie) Boon, W.C. (Billy) Nicholson, Tom Phillips, Art Hooper, W.J. (Billy) Bellingham, Charles A. Liffiton, Jack Marshall, Jim Gardner, Cecil Blachford, George Smith.
Scores: January 29 at Montreal — Mtl. AAA 8, Wpg. Victorias 1; January 31 at Montreal — Wpg. Victorias 2, Mtl. AAA 2; February 2 at Montreal — Wpg. Victorias 4, Mtl. AAA 2; February 4 at Montreal — Mtl. AAA 5, Wpg. Victorias 1.

1901-02 — (March) **— Montreal AAA —** Tom Hodge, R.R. (Dickie) Boon, William C. (Billy) Nicholson, Archie Hooper, W.J. (Billy) Bellingham, Charles A. Liffiton, Jack Marshall, Roland Elliott, Jim Gardner.
Scores: March 13 at Winnipeg — Wpg. Victorias 1, Mtl. AAA 0; March 15 at Winnipeg — Mtl. AAA 5, Wpg. Victorias 0; March 17 at Winnipeg — Mtl. AAA 2, Wpg. Victorias 1.

1901-02 — (January) **— Winnipeg Victorias —** Burke Wood, A.B. (Tony) Gingras, Charles W. Johnstone, R.M. (Rod) Flett, Magnus L. Flett, Dan Bain (captain), Fred Scanlon, F. Cadham, G. Brown.
Scores: January 21 at Winnipeg — Wpg. Victorias 5, Tor Wellingtons 3; January 23 at Winnipeg — Wpg. Victorias 5, Tor. Wellingtons 3.

1900-01 — Winnipeg Victorias — Burke Wood, Jack Marshall, A.B. (Tony) Gingras, Charles W. Johnstone, R.M. (Rod) Flett, Magnus L. Flett, Dan Bain (captain), G. Brown.
Scores: January 29 at Montreal — Wpg. Victorias 4, Mtl. Shamrocks 3; January 31 at Montreal — Wpg. Victorias 2, Mtl. Shamrocks 1.

1899-1900 — Montreal Shamrocks — Joe McKenna, Frank Tansey, Frank Wall, Art Farrell, Fred Scanlon, Harry Trihey (captain), Jack Brannen.
Scores: February 12 at Montreal — Mtl. Shamrocks 4, Wpg. Victorias 3; February 14 at Montreal — Wpg. Victorias 3, Mtl. Shamrocks 2; February 16 at Montreal — Mtl. Shamrocks 5, Wpg. Victorias 4; March 5 at Montreal — Mtl. Shamrocks 10, Halifax 2; March 7 at Montreal — Mtl. Shamrocks 11, Halifax 0.

1898-99 — (March) **— Montreal Shamrocks —** Jim McKenna, Frank Tansey, Frank Wall, Harry Trihey (captain), Art Farrell, Fred Scanlon, Jack Brannen, John Dobby, Charles Hoerner.
Scores: March 14 at Montreal — Mtl. Shamrocks 6, Queen's University 2.

1898-99 — (February) **— Montreal Victorias —** Gordon Lewis, Mike Grant, Graham Drinkwater, Cam Davidson, Bob McDougall, Ernie McLea, Frank Richardson, Jack Ewing, Russell Bowie, Douglas Acer, Fred McRobie.
Scores: February 15 at Montreal — Mtl. Victorias 2, Wpg. Victorias 1; February 18 at Montreal — Mtl. Victorias 3, Wpg. Victorias 2.

1897-98 — Montreal Victorias — Gordon Lewis, Hartland McDougall, Mike Grant, Graham Drinkwater, Cam Davidson, Bob McDougall, Ernie McLea, Frank Richardson (captain), Jack Ewing. The Victorias as champions of the Amateur Hockey Association, retained the Cup and were not called upon to defend it.

1896-97 — Montreal Victorias — Gordon Lewis, Harold Henderson, Mike Grant (captain), Cam Davidson, Graham Drinkwater, Robert McDougall, Ernie McLea, Shirley Davidson, Hartland McDougall, Jack Ewing, Percy Molson, David Gillilan, McLellan.
Scores: December 27 at Montreal — Mtl. Victorias 15, Ott. Capitals 2.

1895-96 — (December) **— Montreal Victorias —** Harold Henderson, Mike Grant (captain), Robert McDougall, Graham Drinkwater, Shirley Davidson, Ernie McLea, Robert Jones, Cam Davidson, David Gillilan, Stanley Willett.
Scores: December 30 at Winnipeg — Mtl. Victorias 6, Wpg. Victorias 5.

1895-96 — (February) **— Winnipeg Victorias —** G.H. Merritt, Rod Flett, Fred Higginbotham, Jack Armitage (captain), C.J. (Tote) Campbell, Dan Bain, Charles Johnstone, H. Howard.
Scores: February 14 at Montreal — Wpg. Victorias 2, Mtl. Victorias 0.

1894-95 — Montreal Victorias — Robert Jones, Harold Henderson, Mike Grant (captain), Shirley Davidson, Bob McDougall, Norman Rankin, Graham Drinkwater, Roland Elliot, William Pullan, Hartland McDougall, Jim Fenwick, A. McDougall. Montreal Victorias, as champions of the Amateur Hockey Association, were prepared to defend the Stanley Cup. However, the Stanley Cup trustees had already accepted a challenge match between the 1894 champion Montreal AAA and Queen's University. It was declared that if Montreal AAA defeated Queen's University, Montreal Victorias would be declared Stanley Cup champions. If Queen's University won, the Cup would go to the university club. In a game played March 9, 1895, Montreal AAA defeated Queen's University 5-1. As a result, Montreal Victorias were awarded the Stanley Cup.

1893-94 — Montreal AAA — Herbert Collins, Allan Cameron, George James, Billy Barlow, Clare Mussen, Archie Hodgson, Haviland Routh, Alex Irving, James Stewart, A.C. (Toad) Wand, A. Kingan.
Scores: March 17 at Mtl. Victorias — Mtl. AAA 3, Mtl. Victorias 2; March 22 at Montreal — Mtl. AAA 3, Ott. Capitals 1.

1892-93 — Montreal AAA — Tom Paton, James Stewart, Allan Cameron, Haviland Routh, Archie Hodgson, Billy Barlow, A.B. Kingan, G.S. Lowe.
In accordance with the terms governing the presentation of the Stanley Cup, it was awarded for the first time to the Montreal AAA as champions of the Amateur Hockey Association in 1893. Once Montreal AAA had been declared holders of the Stanley Cup, any Canadian hockey team could challenge for the trophy.

All-Time NHL Playoff Formats

1917-18 — The regular-season was split into two halves. The winners of both halves faced each other in a two-game, total-goals series for the NHL championship and the right to meet the PCHA champion in the best-of-five Stanley Cup Finals.

1918-19 — Same as 1917-18, except that the Stanley Cup Finals was extended to a best-of-seven series.

1919-20 — Same as 1917-1918, except that Ottawa won both halves of the split regular-season schedule to earn an automatic berth into the best-of-five Stanley Cup Finals against the PCHA champions.

1921-22 — The top two teams at the conclusion of the regular-season faced each other in a two-game, total-goals series for the NHL championship. The NHL champion then moved on to play the winner of the PCHA-WCHL playoff series in the best-of-five Stanley Cup Finals.

1922-23 — The top two teams at the conclusion of the regular-season faced each other in a two-game, total-goals series for the NHL championship. The NHL champion then moved on to play the PCHA champion in the best-of-three Stanley Cup Semi-Finals, and the winner of the Semi-Finals played the WCHL champion, which had been given a bye, in the best-of-three Stanley Cup Finals.

1923-24 — The top two teams at the conclusion of the regular-season faced each other in a two-game, total-goals series for the NHL championship. The NHL champion then moved to play the loser of the PCHA-WCHL playoff (the winner of the PCHA-WCHL playoff earned a bye into the Stanley Cup Finals) in the best-of-three Stanley Cup Semi-Finals. The winner of this series met the PCHA-WCHL playoff winner in the best-of-three Stanley Cup Finals.

1924-25 — The first place team (Hamilton) at the conclusion of the regular-season was supposed to play the winner of a two-game, total goals series between the second (Toronto) and third (Montreal) place clubs. However, Hamilton refused to abide by this new format, demanding greater compensation than offered by the League. Thus, Toronto and Montreal played their two-game, total-goals series, and the winner (Montreal) earned the NHL title and then played the WCHL champion (Victoria) in the best-of-five Stanley Cup Finals.

1925-26 — The format which was intended for 1924-25 went into effect. The winner of the two-game, total-goals series between the second and third place teams squared off against the first place team in the two-game, total-goals NHL championship series. The NHL champion then moved on to play the WHL champion in the best-of-five Stanley Cup Finals.

After the 1925-26 season, the NHL was the only major professional hockey league still in existence and consequently took over sole control of the Stanley Cup competition.

1926-27 — The 10-team league was divided into two divisions — Canadian and American — of five teams apiece. In each division, the winner of the two-game, total-goals series between the second and third place teams faced the first place team in a two-game, total-goals series for the division title. The two division title winners then met in the best-of-five Stanley Cup Finals.

1928-29 — Both first place teams in the two divisions played each other in a best-of-five series. Both second place teams in the two divisions played each other in a two-game, total-goals series as did the two third place teams. The winners of these latter two series then played each other in a best-of-three series for the right to meet the winner of the series between the two first place clubs. This Stanley Cup Final was a best-of-three.

Series A: First in Canadian Division versus first in American (best-of-five)
Series B: Second in Canadian Division versus second in American (two-game, total-goals)
Series C: Third in Canadian Division versus third in American (two-game, total-goals)
Series D: Winner of Series B versus winner of Series C (best-of-three)
Series E: Winner of Series A versus winner of Series D (best of three) for Stanley Cup

1931-32 — Same as 1928-29, except that Series D was changed to a two-game, total-goals format and Series E was changed to best of five.

1936-37 — Same as 1931-32, except that Series B, C, and D were each best-of-three.

1938-39 — With the NHL reduced to seven teams, the two-division system was replaced by one seven-team league. Based on final regular-season standings, the following playoff format was adopted:

Series A: First versus Second (best-of-seven)
Series B: Third versus Fourth (best-of-three)
Series C: Fifth versus Sixth (best-of-three)
Series D: Winner of Series B versus winner of Series C (best-of-three)
Series E: Winner of Series A versus winner of Series D (best-of-seven)

1942-43 — With the NHL reduced to six teams (the "original six"), only the top four finishers qualified for playoff action. The best-of-seven Semi-Finals pitted Team #1 vs Team #3 and Team #2 vs Team #4. The winners of each Semi-Final series met in the best-of-seven Stanley Cup Finals.

1967-68 — When it doubled in size from 6 to 12 teams, the NHL once again was divided into two divisions — East and West — of six teams apiece. The top four clubs in each division qualified for the playoffs (all series were best-of-seven):

Series A: Team #1 (East) vs Team #3 (East)
Series B: Team #2 (East) vs Team #4 (East)
Series C: Team #1 (West) vs Team #3 (West)
Series D: Team #2 (West) vs Team #4 (West)
Series E: Winner of Series A vs winner of Series B
Series F: Winner of Series C vs winner of Series D
Series G: Winner of Series E vs Winner of Series F

1970-71 — Same as 1967-68 except that Series E matched the winners of Series A and D, and Series F matched the winners of Series B and C.

1971-72 — Same as 1970-71, except that Series A and C matched Team #1 vs #4, and Series B and D matched Team #2 vs Team #3.

1974-75 — With the League now expanded to 18 teams in four divisions, a completely new playoff format was introduced. First, the #2 and #3 teams in each of the four divisions were pooled together in the Preliminary round. These eight (#2 and #3) clubs were ranked #1 to #8 based on regular-season record:

Series A: Team #1 vs Team #8 (best-of-three)
Series B: Team #2 vs Team #7 (best-of-three)
Series C: Team #3 vs Team #6 (best-of-three)
Series D: Team #4 vs Team #5 (best-of-three)
The winners of this Preliminary round then pooled together with the four division winners, which had received byes into this Quarter-Final round. These eight teams were again ranked #1 to #8 based on regular-season record:
Series E: Team #1 vs Team #8 (best-of-seven)
Series F: Team #2 vs Team #7 (best-of-seven)
Series G: Team #3 vs Team #6 (best-of-seven)
Series H: Team #4 vs Team #5 (best-of-seven)
The four Quarter-Finals winners, which moved on to the Semi-Finals, were then ranked #1 to #4 based on regular season record:
Series I: Team #1 vs Team #4 (best-of-seven)
Series J: Team #2 vs Team #3 (best-of-seven)
Series K: Winner of Series I vs winner of Series J (best-of-seven)

1977-78 — Same as 1974-75, except that the Preliminary round consisted of the #2 teams in the four divisions and the next four teams based on regular-season record (not their standings within their divisions).

1979-80 — With the addition of four WHA franchises, the League expanded its playoff structure to include 16 of its 21 teams. The four first place teams in the four divisions automatically earned playoff berths. Among the 17 other clubs, the top 12, according to regular-season record, also earned berths. All 16 teams were then pooled together and ranked #1 to #16 based on regular-season record:

Series A: Team #1 vs Team #16 (best-of-five)
Series B: Team #2 vs Team #15 (best-of-five)
Series C: Team #3 vs Team #14 (best-of-five)
Series D: Team #4 vs Team #13 (best-of-five)
Series E: Team #5 vs Team #12 (best-of-five)
Series F: Team #6 vs Team #11 (best-of-five)
Series G: Team #7 vs Team #10 (best-of-five)
Series H: Team #8 vs Team # 9 (best-of-five)
The eight Preliminary round winners, ranked #1 to #8 based on regular-season record, moved on to the Quarter-Finals:
Series I: Team #1 vs Team #8 (best-of-seven)
Series J: Team #2 vs Team #7 (best-of-seven)
Series K: Team #3 vs Team #6 (best-of-seven)
Series L: Team #4 vs Team #5 (best-of-seven)
The eight Quarter-Finals winners, ranked #1 to #4 based on regular-season record, moved on to the semi-finals:
Series M: Team #1 vs Team #4 (best-of-seven)
Series N: Team #2 vs Team #3 (best-of-seven)
Series O: Winner of Series M vs winner of Series N (best-of-seven)

1981-82 — The first four teams in each division earned playoff berths. In each division, the first-place team opposed the fourth-place team and the second-place team opposed the third-place team in a best-of-five Division Semi-Final series (DSF). In each division, the two winners of the DSF met in a best-of-seven Division Final series (DF). The two winners in each conference met in a best-of-seven Conference Final series (CF). In the Prince of Wales Conference, the Adams Division winner opposed the Patrick Division winner; in the Clarence Campbell Conference, the Smythe Division winner opposed the Norris Division winner. The two CF winners met in a best-of-seven Stanley Cup Final (F) series.

1986-87 — Division Semi-Final series changed from best-of-five to best-of-seven.

1993-94 — The NHL's playoff draw conference-based rather than division-based. At the conclusion of the regular season, the top eight teams in each of the Eastern and Western Conferences qualify for the playoffs. The teams that finish in first place in each of the League's divisions are seeded first and second in each conference's playoff draw and are assured of home ice advantage in the first two playoff rounds. The remaining teams are seeded based on their regular-season point totals. In each conference, the team seeded #1 plays #8; #2 vs. #7; #3 vs. #6; and #4 vs. #5. All series are best-of-seven with home ice rotating on a 2-2-1-1-1 basis, with the exception of matchups between Central and Pacific Division teams. These matchups will be played on a 2-3-2 basis to reduce travel. In a 2-3-2 series, the team with the most points will have its choice to start the series at home or on the road. The Eastern Conference champion will face the Western Conference champion in the Stanley Cup Final.

1994-95 — Same as 1993-94, except that in first, second or third-round playoff series involving Central and Pacific Division teams, the team with the better record has the choice of using either a 2-3-2 or a 2-2-1-1-1 format. When a 2-3-2 format is selected, the higher-ranked team also has the choice of playing games 1, 2, 6 and 7 at home or playing games 3, 4 and 5 at home. The format for the Stanley Cup Final remains 2-2-1-1-1.

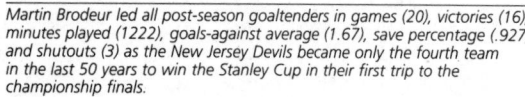

Martin Brodeur led all post-season goaltenders in games (20), victories (16), minutes played (1222), goals-against average (1.67), save percentage (.927) and shutouts (3) as the New Jersey Devils became only the fourth team in the last 50 years to win the Stanley Cup in their first trip to the championship finals.

Team Records

1918-1995

MOST STANLEY CUP CHAMPIONSHIPS:
23 — Montreal Canadiens 1924-30-31-44-46-53-56-57-58-59-60-65-66-68-69-71-73-76-77-78-79-86-93
13 — Toronto Maple Leafs 1918-22-32-42-45-47-48-49-51-62-63-64-67
7 — Detroit Red Wings 1936-37-43-50-52-54-55

MOST FINAL SERIES APPEARANCES:
32 — Montreal Canadiens in 78-year history.
21 — Toronto Maple Leafs in 78-year history.
19 — Detroit Red Wings in 69-year history.

MOST YEARS IN PLAYOFFS:
69 — Montreal Canadiens in 78-year history.
57 — Toronto Maple Leafs in 78-year history.
56 — Boston Bruins in 71-year history.

MOST CONSECUTIVE STANLEY CUP CHAMPIONSHIPS:
5 — Montreal Canadiens (1956-57-58-59-60)
4 — Montreal Canadiens (1976-77-78-79)
 — NY Islanders (1980-81-82-83)

MOST CONSECUTIVE FINAL SERIES APPEARANCES:
10 — Montreal Canadiens (1951-60, inclusive)
5 — Montreal Canadiens (1965-69, inclusive)
 — NY Islanders, (1980-84, inclusive)

MOST CONSECUTIVE PLAYOFF APPEARANCES:
28 — Boston Bruins (1968-95, inclusive)
26 — Chicago Blackhawks (1970-95, inclusive)
24 — Montreal Canadiens (1971-94, inclusive)
21 — Montreal Canadiens (1949-69, inclusive)
20 — Detroit Red Wings (1939-58, inclusive)

MOST GOALS BOTH TEAMS, ONE PLAYOFF SERIES:
69 — Edmonton Oilers, Chicago Blackhawks in 1985 CF. Edmonton won best-of-seven series 4-2, outscoring Chicago 44-25.
62 — Chicago Blackhawks, Minnesota North Stars in 1985 DF. Chicago won best-of-seven series 4-2, outscoring Minnesota 33-29.
61 — Los Angeles Kings, Calgary Flames in 1993 DSF. Los Angeles won best-of-seven series 4-2, outscoring Calgary 33-28.
 — San Jose Sharks, Calgary Flames in 1995 CQF. San Jose won best-of-seven series 4-3, while being outscored 35-26.

MOST GOALS ONE TEAM, ONE PLAYOFF SERIES:
44 — Edmonton Oilers in 1985 CF. Edmonton won best-of-seven series 4-2, outscoring Chicago 44-25.
35 — Edmonton Oilers in 1983 DF. Edmonton won best-of-seven series 4-1, outscoring Calgary 35-13.
 — Calgary Flames in 1995 CQF. Calgary lost best-of-seven series 3-4, outscoring San Jose 35-26.

MOST GOALS, BOTH TEAMS, TWO-GAME SERIES:
17 — Toronto St. Patricks, Montreal Canadiens in 1918 NHL F. Toronto won two-game total goal series 10-7.
15 — Boston Bruins, Chicago Blackhawks in 1927 QF. Boston won two-game total goal series 10-5.
 — Pittsburgh Penguins, St. Louis Blues in 1975 PR. Pittsburgh won best-of-three series 2-0, outscoring St. Louis 9-6.

MOST GOALS, ONE TEAM, TWO-GAME SERIES:
11 — Buffalo Sabres in 1977 PR. Buffalo won best-of-three series 2-0, outscoring Minnesota 11-3.
 — Toronto Maple Leafs in 1978 PR. Toronto won best-of-three series 2-0, outscoring Los Angeles 11-3.
10 — Boston Bruins in 1927 QF. Boston won two-game total goal series 10-5.

MOST GOALS, BOTH TEAMS, THREE-GAME SERIES:
33 — Minnesota North Stars, Boston Bruins in 1981 PR. Minnesota won best-of-five series 3-0, outscoring Boston 20-13.
31 — Chicago Blackhawks, Detroit Red Wings in 1985 DSF. Chicago won best-of-five series 3-0, outscoring Detroit 23-8.
28 — Toronto Maple Leafs, NY Rangers in 1932 F. Toronto won best-of-five series 3-0, outscoring New York 18-10.

MOST GOALS, ONE TEAM, THREE-GAME SERIES:
23 — Chicago Blackhawks in 1985 DSF. Chicago won best-of-five series 3-0, outscoring Detroit 23-8.
20 — Minnesota North Stars in 1981 PR. Minnesota won best-of-five series 3-0, outscoring Boston 20-13.
 — NY Islanders in 1981 PR. New York won best-of-five series 3-0, outscoring Toronto 20-4.

MOST GOALS, BOTH TEAMS, FOUR-GAME SERIES:
36 — Boston Bruins, St. Louis Blues in 1972 SF. Boston won best-of-seven series 4-0, outscoring St. Louis 28-8.
 — **Edmonton Oilers, Chicago Blackhawks** in 1983 CF. Edmonton won best-of-seven series 4-0, outscoring Chicago 25-11.
 — **Minnesota North Stars, Toronto Maple Leafs** in 1983 DSF. Minnesota won best-of-five series 3-1; teams tied in scoring 18-18.
35 — NY Rangers, Los Angeles Kings in 1981 PR. NY Rangers won best-of-five series 3-1, outscoring Los Angeles 23-12.

MOST GOALS, ONE TEAM, FOUR-GAME SERIES:
  28 — Boston Bruins in 1972 SF. Boston won best-of-seven series 4-0, outscoring
    St. Louis 28-8.

MOST GOALS, BOTH TEAMS, FIVE-GAME SERIES:
  52 — Edmonton Oilers, Los Angeles Kings in 1987 DSF. Edmonton won
    best-of-seven series 4-1, outscoring Los Angeles 32-20.
  50 — Los Angeles Kings, Edmonton Oilers in 1982 DSF. Los Angeles won best-of-five
    series 3-2, outscoring Edmonton 27-23.
  48 — Edmonton Oilers, Calgary Flames in 1983 DF. Edmonton won best-of-seven
    series 4-1, outscoring Calgary 35-13.
    — Calgary Flames, Los Angeles Kings in 1988 DSF. Calgary won best-of-seven
    series 4-1, outscoring Los Angeles 30-18.

MOST GOALS, ONE TEAM, FIVE-GAME SERIES:
  35 — Edmonton Oilers in 1983 DF. Edmonton won best-of-seven series 4-1,
    outscoring Calgary 35-13.
  32 — Edmonton Oilers in 1987 DSF. Edmonton won best-of-seven series 4-1,
    outscoring Los Angeles 32-20.
  28 — NY Rangers in 1979 QF. NY Rangers won best-of-seven series 4-1, outscoring
    Philadelphia 28-8.
  27 — Philadelphia Flyers in 1980 SF. Philadelphia won best-of-seven series 4-1,
    outscoring Minnesota 27-14.
    — Los Angeles Kings, in 1982 DSF. Los Angeles won best-of-five series 3-2,
    outscoring Edmonton 27-23.

MOST GOALS, BOTH TEAMS, SIX-GAME SERIES:
  69 — Edmonton Oilers, Chicago Blackhawks in 1985 CF. Edmonton won
    best-of-seven series 4-2, outscoring Chicago 44-25.
  62 — Chicago Blackhawks, Minnesota North Stars in 1985 DF. Chicago won
    best-of-seven series 4-2, outscoring Minnesota 33-29.
  61 — Los Angeles Kings, Calgary Flames in 1993 DSF. Los Angeles won best-of-seven
    series 4-2, outscoring Calgary 33-28.

MOST GOALS, ONE TEAM, SIX-GAME SERIES:
  44 — Edmonton Oilers in 1985 CF. Edmonton won best-of-seven series 4-2,
    outscoring Chicago 44-25.
  33 — Chicago Blackhawks in 1985 DF. Chicago won best-of-seven series 4-2,
    outscoring Minnesota 33-29.
    — Montreal Canadiens in 1973 F. Montreal won best-of-seven series 4-2,
    outscoring Chicago 33-23.
    — Los Angeles Kings in 1993 DSF. Los Angeles won best-of-seven series 4-2,
    outscoring Calgary 33-28.

MOST GOALS, BOTH TEAMS, SEVEN-GAME SERIES:
  61 — San Jose Sharks, Calgary Flames in 1995 CQF. San Jose won best-of-seven
    series 4-3, while being outscored 35-26.
  60 — Edmonton Oilers, Calgary Flames in 1984 DF. Edmonton won best-of-seven
    series 4-3, outscoring Calgary 33-27.

MOST GOALS, ONE TEAM, SEVEN-GAME SERIES:
  35 — Calgary Flames in 1995 CQF. Calgary lost best-of-seven series 3-4, outscoring
    San Jose 35-26.
  33 — Philadelphia Flyers in 1976 QF. Philadelphia won best-of-seven series 4-3,
    outscoring Toronto 33-23.
    — Boston Bruins in 1983 DF. Boston won best-of-seven series 4-3, outscoring
    Buffalo 33-23.
    — Edmonton Oilers in 1984 DF. Edmonton won best-of-seven series 4-3,
    outscoring Calgary 33-27.

FEWEST GOALS, BOTH TEAMS, TWO-GAME SERIES:
  1 — NY Rangers, NY Americans, in 1929 SF. NY Rangers defeated NY Americans
    1-0 in two-game, total-goal series.
    — **Mtl. Maroons, Chicago Blackhawks** in 1935 SF. Mtl. Maroons defeated
    Chicago 1-0 in two-game, total-goal series.

FEWEST GOALS, ONE TEAM, TWO-GAME SERIES:
  0 — NY Americans in 1929 SF. Lost two-game total-goal series 1-0 against NY
    Rangers.
    — **Chicago Blackhawks** in 1935 SF. Lost two-game total-goal series 1-0 against
    Mtl. Maroons.
    — **Mtl. Maroons** in 1937 SF. Lost best-of-three series 2-0 to NY Rangers while
    being outscored 5-0.
    — **NY Americans** in 1939 QF. Lost best-of-three series 2-0 to Toronto while
    being outscored 6-0.

FEWEST GOALS, BOTH TEAMS, THREE-GAME SERIES:
  7 — Boston Bruins, Montreal Canadiens in 1929 SF. Boston won best-of-five
    series 3-0, outscoring Montreal 5-2.
    — **Detroit Red Wings, Mtl. Maroons** in 1936 SF. Detroit won best-of-five series
    3-0, outscoring Mtl. Maroons 6-1.

FEWEST GOALS, ONE TEAM, THREE-GAME SERIES:
  1 — Mtl. Maroons in 1936 SF. Lost best-of-five series 3-0 to Detroit and were
    outscored 6-1.

FEWEST GOALS, BOTH TEAMS, FOUR-GAME SERIES:
  9 — Toronto Maple Leafs, Boston Bruins in 1935 SF. Toronto won best-of-five
    series 3-1, outscoring Boston 7-2.

FEWEST GOALS, ONE TEAM, FOUR-GAME SERIES:
  2 — Boston Bruins in 1935 SF. Toronto won best-of-five series 3-1, outscoring
    Boston 7-2.
    — **Montreal Canadiens** in 1952 F. Detroit won best-of-seven series 4-0,
    outscoring Montreal 11-2.

FEWEST GOALS, BOTH TEAMS, FIVE-GAME SERIES:
  11 — NY Rangers, Mtl. Maroons in 1928 F. NY Rangers won best-of-five series
    3-2, while outscored by Mtl. Maroons 6-5.

FEWEST GOALS, ONE TEAM, FIVE-GAME SERIES:
  5 — NY Rangers in 1928 F. NY Rangers won best-of-five series 3-2, while
    outscored by Mtl. Maroons 6-5.

FEWEST GOALS, BOTH TEAMS, SIX-GAME SERIES:
  22 — Toronto Maple Leafs, Boston Bruins in 1951 SF. Toronto won best-of-seven
    series 4-1 with 1 tie, outscoring Boston 17-5.

FEWEST GOALS, ONE TEAM, SIX-GAME SERIES:
  5 — Boston Bruins in 1951 SF. Toronto won best-of-seven series 4-1 with 1 tie,
    outscoring Boston 17-5.

FEWEST GOALS, BOTH TEAMS, SEVEN-GAME SERIES:
  18 — Toronto Maple Leafs, Detroit Red Wings in 1945 F. Toronto won
    best-of-seven series 4-3; teams tied in scoring 9-9.

FEWEST GOALS, ONE TEAM, SEVEN-GAME SERIES:
  9 — Toronto Maple Leafs, in 1945 F. Toronto won best-of- seven series 4-3;
    teams tied in scoring 9-9.
    — **Detroit Red Wings,** in 1945 F. Toronto won best-of-seven series 4-3; teams
    tied in scoring 9-9.

MOST GOALS, BOTH TEAMS, ONE GAME:
  18 — Los Angeles Kings, Edmonton Oilers at Edmonton, April 7, 1982.
    Los Angeles 10, Edmonton 8. Los Angeles won best-of-five DSF 3-2.
  17 — Pittsburgh Penguins, Philadelphia Flyers at Pittsburgh, April 25, 1989.
    Pittsburgh 10, Philadelphia 7. Philadelphia won best-of-seven DF 4-3.
  16 — Edmonton Oilers, Los Angeles Kings at Edmonton, April 9, 1987. Edmonton
    13, Los Angeles 3. Edmonton won best-of-seven DSF 4-1.
    — Los Angeles Kings, Calgary Flames at Los Angeles, April 10, 1990.
    Los Angeles 12, Calgary 4. Los Angeles won best-of-seven DF 4-2.

MOST GOALS, ONE TEAM, ONE GAME:
  13 — Edmonton Oilers at Edmonton, April 9, 1987. Edmonton 13, Los Angeles 3.
    Edmonton won best-of-seven DSF 4-1.
  12 — Los Angeles Kings at Los Angeles, April 10, 1990. Los Angeles 12, Calgary 4.
    Los Angeles won best-of-seven DSF 4-2.
  11 — Montreal Canadiens at Montreal, March 30, 1944. Montreal 11, Toronto 0.
    Canadiens won best-of-seven SF 4-1.
    — Edmonton Oilers at Edmonton May 4, 1985. Edmonton 11, Chicago 2.
    Edmonton won best-of-seven CF 4-2.

MOST GOALS, BOTH TEAMS, ONE PERIOD:
  9 — NY Rangers, Philadelphia Flyers, April 24, 1979, at Philadelphia, third
    period. NY Rangers won 8-3 scoring six of nine third-period goals.
    — **Los Angeles Kings, Calgary Flames** at Los Angeles, April 10, 1990, second
    period. Los Angeles won game 12-4, scoring five of nine second-period goals.
  8 — Chicago Blackhawks, Montreal Canadiens at Montreal, May 8, 1973, in the
    second period. Chicago won 8-7 scoring five of eight second-period goals.
    — Chicago Blackhawks, Edmonton Oilers at Chicago, May 12, 1985 in the first
    period. Chicago won 8-6, scoring five of eight first-period goals.
    — Edmonton Oilers, Winnipeg Jets at Edmonton, April 6, 1988 in the third period.
    Edmonton won 7-4, scoring six of eight third period goals.
    — Hartford Whalers, Montreal Canadiens at Hartford, April 10, 1988 in the third
    period. Hartford won 7-5, scoring five of eight third period goals.

MOST GOALS, ONE TEAM, ONE PERIOD:
  7 — Montreal Canadiens, March 30, 1944, at Montreal in third period, during
    11-0 win against Toronto.

LONGEST OVERTIME:
116 Minutes, 30 Seconds — Detroit Red Wings, Mtl. Maroons at Montreal,
  March 24, 25, 1936. Detroit 1, Mtl. Maroons 0. Mud Bruneteau scored,
  assisted by Hec Kilrea, at 16:30 of sixth overtime period, or after 176 minutes,
  30 seconds from start of game, which ended at 2:25 a.m. Detroit won
  best-of-five SF 3-0.

SHORTEST OVERTIME:
  9 Seconds — Montreal Canadiens, Calgary Flames, at Calgary, May 18,
    1986. Montreal won 3-2 on Brian Skrudland's goal and captured the
    best-of-seven F 4-1.
  11 Seconds — NY Islanders, NY Rangers, at NY Rangers, April 11, 1975. NY
    Islanders won 4-3 on Jean-Paul Parise's goal and captured the best-of-three PR
    2-1.

MOST OVERTIME GAMES, ONE PLAYOFF YEAR:
  28 — 1993. Of 85 games played, 28 went into overtime.
  18 — 1994. Of 90 games played, 18 went into overtime.
    — 1995. Of 81 games played, 18 went into overtime.

FEWEST OVERTIME GAMES, ONE PLAYOFF YEAR:
  0 — 1963. None of the 16 games went into overtime, the only year since 1926 that
    no overtime was required in any playoff series.

MOST OVERTIME-GAME VICTORIES, ONE TEAM, ONE PLAYOFF YEAR:
  10 — Montreal Canadiens, 1993. Two against Quebec in the DSF; three against
    Buffalo in the DF; two against NY Islanders in the CF; and three against
    Los Angeles in the F. Montreal played 20 games.
  6 — NY Islanders, 1980. One against Los Angeles in the PR; two against Boston in
    the QF; one against Buffalo in the SF; and two against Philadelphia in the F.
    Islanders played 21 games.
    — Vancouver Canucks, 1994. Three against Calgary in the CQF; one against
    Dallas in the CSF; one against Toronto in the CF; and one against NY Rangers
    in the F. Vancouver played 24 games.

MOST OVERTIME GAMES, FINAL SERIES:
  5 — Toronto Maple Leafs,, Montreal Canadiens in 1951. Toronto defeated
    Montreal 4-1 in best-of-seven series.

MOST OVERTIME GAMES, SEMI-FINAL SERIES:

4 — Toronto Maple Leafs, Boston Bruins in 1933. Toronto won best-of-five series 3-2.
— **Boston Bruins, NY Rangers** in 1939. Boston won best-of-seven series 4-3.
— **St. Louis Blues, Minnesota North Stars** in 1968. St. Louis won best-of-seven series 4-3.

MOST GAMES PLAYED BY ALL TEAMS, ONE PLAYOFF YEAR:

92 — 1991. There were 51 DSF, 24 DF, 11 CF and 6 F games.
90 — 1994. There were 48 CQF, 23 CSF, 12 CF and 7 F games.
87 — 1987. There were 44 DSF, 25 DF, 11 CF and 7 F games.
86 — 1992. There were 54 DSF, 20 DF, 8 CF and 4 F games.

MOST GAMES PLAYED, ONE TEAM, ONE PLAYOFF YEAR:

26 — Philadelphia Flyers, 1987. Won DSF 4-2 against NY Rangers, DF 4-3 against NY Islanders, CF 4-2 against Montreal, and lost F 4-3 against Edmonton.
24 — Pittsburgh Penguins, 1991. Won DSF 4-3 against New Jersey, DF 4-1 against Washington, CF 4-2 against Boston, and F 4-2 against Minnesota.
— Los Angeles Kings, 1993. Won DSF 4-2 against Calgary, DF 4-2 against Vancouver, CF 4-3 against Toronto, and lost F 4-1 against Montreal.
— Vancouver Canucks, 1994. Won CQF 4-3 against Calgary, CSF 4-1 against Dallas, CF 4-1 against Toronto, and lost F 4-3 against NY Rangers.

MOST ROAD VICTORIES, ONE TEAM, ONE PLAYOFF YEAR:

10 — New Jersey Devils, 1995. Won three at Boston in CQF; two at Pittsburgh in CSF; three at Philadelphia in CF; and two at Detroit in F series.
8 — NY Islanders, 1980. Won two at Los Angeles in PR; three at Boston in QF; two at Buffalo in SF; and one at Philadelphia in F series.
— Philadelphia Flyers, 1987. Won two at NY Rangers in DSF; two at NY Islanders in DF; three at Montreal in CF; and one at Edmonton in F series.
— Edmonton Oilers, 1990. Won one at Winnipeg in DSF; two at Los Angeles in DF; two at Chicago in CF and three at Boston in F series.
— Pittsburgh Penguins, 1992. Won two at Washington in DSF; two at NY Rangers in DF; two at Boston in CF; and two at Chicago in F series.
— Vancouver Canucks, 1994. Won three at Calgary in CQF; two at Dallas in CSF; one at Toronto in CF; and two at NY Rangers in F series.

MOST HOME VICTORIES, ONE TEAM, ONE PLAYOFF YEAR:

11 — Edmonton Oilers, 1988
10 — Edmonton Oilers, 1985 in 10 home-ice games.
— Montreal Canadiens, 1986.
— Montreal Canadiens, 1993.
9 — Philadelphia Flyers, 1974.
— Philadelphia Flyers, 1980.
— NY Islanders, 1981.
— NY Islanders, 1983.
— Edmonton Oilers, 1984.
— Edmonton Oilers, 1987.
— Calgary Flames, 1989.
— Pittsburgh Penguins, 1991.
— NY Rangers, 1994.

MOST ROAD VICTORIES, ALL TEAMS, ONE PLAYOFF YEAR:

46 — 1987. Of 87 games played, road teams won 46 (22 DSF, 14 DF, 8 CF and 2 Stanley Cup final).

MOST CONSECUTIVE PLAYOFF GAME VICTORIES:

14 — Pittsburgh Penguins. Streak started May 9, 1992, at Pittsburgh with a 5-4 in fourth game of a DF series against NY Rangers, won by Pittsburgh 4-2. Continued with a four-game sweep over Boston in the 1992 CF and a four-game win over Chicago in the 1992 F. Pittsburgh then won the first three games of the 1993 DSF versus New Jersey. New Jersey ended the streak April 25, 1993, at New Jersey with a 4-1 win.
12 — Edmonton Oilers. Streak began May 15, 1984 at Edmonton with a 7-2 win over NY Islanders in third game of F series, and ended May 9, 1985 when Chicago defeated Edmonton 5-2 at Chicago. Included in the streak were three wins over the NY Islanders, in 1984, three over Los Angeles, four over Winnipeg and two over Chicago, all in 1985.
11 — Montreal Canadiens. Streak began April 16, 1959, at Toronto with 3-2 win in fourth game of F series, won by Montreal 4-1, and ended March 23, 1961, when Chicago defeated Montreal 4-3 in second game of SF series. Included in streak were eight straight victories in 1960.
— Montreal Canadiens. Streak began April 28, 1968, at Montreal with 4-3 win in fifth game of SF series, won by Montreal 4-1, and ended April 17, 1969, at Boston when Boston defeated them 5-0 in third game of SF series. Included in the streak were four straight wins over St. Louis in the 1968 F and four straight wins over NY Rangers in a 1969 QF series.
— Boston Bruins. Streak began April 14, 1970, at Boston with 3-2 victory over NY Rangers in fifth game of a QF series, won by Boston 4-2. It continued with a four-game victory over Chicago in the 1970 SF and a four-game win over St. Louis in the 1970 F. Boston then won the first game of a 1971 QF series against Montreal. Montreal ended the streak April 8, 1971, at Boston with a 7-5 victory.
— Montreal Canadiens. Streak started May 6, 1976, at Montreal with 5-2 win in fifth game of a SF series against NY Islanders, won by Montreal 4-1. Continued with a four-game sweep over Philadelphia in the 1976 F and a four-game win against St. Louis in the 1977 QF. Montreal won the first two games of a 1977 SF series against the NY Islanders before NY Islanders ended the streak, April 2, 1977 at New York with a 5-3 victory.
— Chicago Blackhawks. Streak started April 24, 1992, at St. Louis with a 5-3 win in fourth game of a DSF series against St. Louis, won by Chicago 4-2. Continued with a four-game sweep over Detroit in the 1992 DF and a four-game win over Edmonton in the 1992 CF. Pittsburgh ended the streak May 26, 1992, at Pittsburgh with a 5-4 victory.

Doug Mohns (#2) and Bill Gadsby watch as Stan Mikita finds himself all alone in front of Detroit netminder Roger Crozier during game seven of the 1965 Stanley Cup semi-finals. A split-second later, Mikita deposited Mohns' pass behind Crozier to give the Black Hawks a 4-2 win and a berth in the 1965 finals.

MOST CONSECUTIVE VICTORIES, ONE PLAYOFF YEAR:

11 — Chicago Blackhawks in 1992. Chicago won last three games of best-of-seven DSF against St. Louis to win series 4-2 and then defeated Detroit 4-0 in best-of-seven DF and Edmonton 4-0 in best-of-seven CF.
— **Pittsburgh Penguins** in 1992. Pittsburgh won last three games of best-of-seven DF against NY Rangers to win series 4-2 and then defeated Boston 4-0 in best-of-seven CF and Chicago 4-0 in best-of-seven F.
— **Montreal Canadiens** in 1993. Montreal won last four games of best-of-seven DSF against Quebec to win series 4-2, defeated Buffalo 4-0 in best-of-seven DF and won first three games of CF against NY Islanders.

LONGEST PLAYOFF LOSING STREAK:

16 Games — Chicago Blackhawks. Streak started in 1975 QF against Buffalo when Chicago lost last two games. Then Chicago lost four games to Montreal in 1976 QF; two games to NY Islanders in 1977 PR; four games to Boston in 1978 QF and four games to NY Islanders in 1979 QF. Streak ended on April 8, 1980 when Chicago defeated St. Louis 3-2 in the opening game of their 1980 PR series.
12 Games — Toronto Maple Leafs. Streak started on April 16, 1979 as Toronto lost four straight games in a QF series against Montreal. Continued with three-game PR defeats versus Philadelphia and NY Islanders in 1980 and 1981 respectively. Toronto failed to qualify for the 1982 playoffs and lost the first two games of a 1983 DSF against Minnesota. Toronto ended the streak with a 6-3 win against the North Stars on April 9, 1983.
10 Games — NY Rangers. Streak started in 1968 QF against Chicago when NY Rangers lost last four games and continued through 1969 (four straight losses to Montreal in QF) and 1970 (two straight losses to Boston in QF) before ending with a 4-3 win against Boston, at New York, April 11, 1970.
— Philadelphia Flyers. Streak started on April 18, 1968, the last game in the 1968 QF series against St. Louis, and continued through 1969 (four straight losses to St. Louis in QF), 1971 (four straight losses to Chicago in QF) and 1973 (opening game loss to Minnesota in QF) before ending with a 4-1 win against Minnesota, at Philadelphia, April 5, 1973.
— Chicago Blackhawks. Streak started on May 26, 1992 as Chicago lost four straight games in the F to Pittsburgh. Continued with four straight losses to St. Louis in 1993 DSF. Chicago lost the first two games of 1994 CQF to Toronto before ending the streak with a 5-4 win against Toronto on April 23, 1994.

MOST SHUTOUTS, ONE PLAYOFF YEAR, ALL TEAMS:
 16 — 1994. Of 90 games played, NY Rangers and Vancouver had 4 each, Toronto had 3, Buffalo had 2, while Washington, Detroit and New Jersey had 1 each.
 12 — **1992.** Of 86 games played, Detroit, Edmonton and Vancouver had 2 each, while Boston, Buffalo, Chicago, Montreal, NY Rangers and Pittsburgh had 1 each.

FEWEST SHUTOUTS, ONE PLAYOFF YEAR, ALL TEAMS:
 0 — 1959. 18 games played.

MOST SHUTOUTS, BOTH TEAMS, ONE SERIES:
 5 — 1945 F, Toronto Maple Leafs, Detroit Red Wings. Toronto had 3 shutouts, Detroit 2. Toronto won best-of-seven series 4-3.
 — **1950 SF, Toronto Maple Leafs, Detroit Red Wings.** Toronto had 3 shutouts, Detroit 2. Detroit won best-of-seven series 4-3.

MOST PENALTIES, BOTH TEAMS, ONE SERIES:
 219 — New Jersey Devils, Washington Capitals in 1988 DF won by New Jersey 4-3. New Jersey received 98 minors, 11 majors, 9 misconducts and 1 match penalty. Washington received 80 minors, 11 majors, 8 misconducts and 1 match penalty.

MOST PENALTY MINUTES, BOTH TEAMS, ONE SERIES:
 656 — New Jersey Devils, Washington Capitals in 1988 DF won by New Jersey 4-3. New Jersey had 351 minutes; Washington 305.

MOST PENALTIES, ONE TEAM, ONE SERIES:
 119 — New Jersey Devils in 1988 DF versus Washington. New Jersey received 98 minors, 11 majors, 9 misconducts and 1 match penalty.

MOST PENALTY MINUTES, ONE TEAM, ONE SERIES:
 351 — New Jersey Devils in 1988 DF versus Washington. Series won by New Jersey 4-3.

MOST PENALTY MINUTES, BOTH TEAMS, ONE GAME:
 298 Minutes — Detroit Red Wings, St. Louis Blues, at St. Louis, April 12, 1991. Detroit received 33 penalties for 152 minutes; St. Louis 33 penalties for 146 minutes. St. Louis won 6-1.
 267 Minutes — NY Rangers, Los Angeles Kings, at Los Angeles, April 9, 1981. NY Rangers received 31 penalties for 142 minutes; Los Angeles 28 penalties for 125 minutes. Los Angeles won 5-4.

MOST PENALTIES, BOTH TEAMS, ONE GAME:
 66 — Detroit Red Wings, St. Louis Blues, at St. Louis, April 12, 1991. Detroit received 33 penalties; St. Louis 33. St. Louis won 6-1.
 62 — New Jersey Devils, Washington Capitals, at New Jersey, April 22, 1988. New Jersey received 32 penalties; Washington 30. New Jersey won 10-4.

MOST PENALTIES, ONE TEAM, ONE GAME:
 33 — Detroit Red Wings, at St. Louis, April 12,1991. St. Louis won 6-1.
 — **St. Louis Blues,** at St. Louis, April 12, 1991. St. Louis won 6-1.
 32 — New Jersey Devils, at Washington, April 22,1988. New Jersey won 10-4.
 31 — NY Rangers, at Los Angeles, April 9, 1981. Los Angeles won 5-4.
 30 — Philadelphia Flyers, at Toronto, April 15, 1976. Toronto won 5-4.

MOST PENALTY MINUTES, ONE TEAM, ONE GAME:
 152 — Detroit Red Wings, at St. Louis, April 12, 1991. St. Louis won 6-1.
 146 — St. Louis Blues, at St. Louis, April 12, 1991. St. Louis won 6-1.
 142 — NY Rangers, at Los Angeles, April 9, 1981. Los Angeles won 5-4.

MOST PENALTIES, BOTH TEAMS, ONE PERIOD:
 43 — NY Rangers, Los Angeles Kings, April 9, 1981, at Los Angeles, first period. NY Rangers had 24 penalties; Los Angeles 19. Los Angeles won 5-4.

MOST PENALTY MINUTES, BOTH TEAMS, ONE PERIOD:
 248 — NY Islanders, Boston Bruins, April 17, 1980, first period, at Boston. Each team received 124 minutes. Islanders won 5-4.

MOST PENALTIES, ONE TEAM, ONE PERIOD: (AND) MOST PENALTY MINUTES, ONE TEAM, ONE PERIOD:
 24 Penalties; 125 Minutes — NY Rangers, April 9, 1981, at Los Angeles, first period. Los Angeles won 5-4.

FEWEST PENALTIES, BOTH TEAMS, BEST-OF-SEVEN SERIES:
 19 — Detroit Red Wings, Toronto Maple Leafs in 1945 F, won by Toronto 4-3. Detroit received 10 minors. Toronto 9 minors.

FEWEST PENALTIES, ONE TEAM, BEST-OF-SEVEN SERIES:
 9 — Toronto Maple Leafs in 1945 F, won by Toronto 4-3 against Detroit.

MOST POWER-PLAY GOALS BY ALL TEAMS, ONE PLAYOFF YEAR:
 199 — 1988 in 83 games.

MOST POWER-PLAY GOALS, ONE TEAM, ONE PLAYOFF YEAR:
 35 — Minnesota North Stars, 1991 in 23 games.
 32 — Edmonton Oilers, 1988 in 18 games.
 31 — NY Islanders, 1981, in 18 games.

MOST POWER-PLAY GOALS, BOTH TEAMS, ONE SERIES:
 21 — NY Islanders, Philadelphia Flyers in 1980 F, won by NY Islanders 4-2. NY Islanders had 15 and Flyers 6.
 — **NY Islanders, Edmonton Oilers** in 1981 QF, won by NY Islanders 4-2. NY Islanders had 13 and Edmonton 8.
 — **Philadelphia Flyers, Pittsburgh Penguins** in 1989 DF, won by Philadelphia 4-3. Philadelphia had 11 and Pittsburgh 10.
 — **Minnesota North Stars, Chicago Blackhawks** in 1991 DSF, won by Minnesota 4-2. Minnesota had 15 and Chicago 6.
 20 — Toronto Maple Leafs, Philadelphia Flyers in 1976 QF series won by Philadelphia 4-3. Toronto had 12 power-pay goals; Philadelphia 8.

MOST POWER-PLAY GOALS, ONE TEAM, ONE SERIES:
 15 — NY Islanders in 1980 F against Philadelphia. NY Islanders won series 4-2.
 — **Minnesota North Stars** in 1991 DSF against Chicago. Minnesota won series 4-2.
 13 — NY Islanders in 1981 QF against Edmonton. NY Islanders won series 4-2.
 — Calgary Flames in 1986 CF against St. Louis. Calgary won series 4-3.
 12 — Toronto Maple Leafs in 1976 QF series won by Philadelphia 4-3.

MOST POWER-PLAY GOALS, BOTH TEAMS, ONE GAME:
 8 — Minnesota North Stars, St. Louis Blues, April 24, 1991 at Minnesota. Minnesota had 4, St. Louis 4. Minnesota won 8-4.
 7 — Minnesota North Stars, Edmonton Oilers, April 28, 1984 at Minnesota. Minnesota had 4, Edmonton 3. Edmonton won 8-5.
 — Philadelphia Flyers, NY Rangers, April 13, 1985 at New York. Philadelphia had 4, NY Rangers 3. Philadelphia won 6-5.
 — Edmonton Oilers, Chicago Blackhawks, May 14, 1985 at Edmonton. Chicago had 5, Edmonton 2. Edmonton won 10-5.
 — Edmonton Oilers, Los Angeles Kings, April 9, 1987 at Edmonton. Edmonton had 5, Los Angeles 2. Edmonton won 13-3.
 — Vancouver Canucks, Calgary Flames, April 9, 1989 at Vancouver. Vancouver had 4, Calgary 3. Vancouver won 5-3.

MOST POWER-PLAY GOALS, ONE TEAM, ONE GAME:
 6 — Boston Bruins, April 2, 1969, at Boston against Toronto. Boston won 10-0.

MOST POWER-PLAY GOALS, BOTH TEAMS, ONE PERIOD:
 5 — Minnesota North Stars, Edmonton Oilers, April 28, 1984, second period, at Minnesota. Minnesota had 4 and Edmonton 1. Edmonton won 8-5.
 — **Vancouver Canucks, Calgary Flames,** April 9, 1989, third period at Vancouver. Vancouver had 3 and Calgary 2. Vancouver won 5-3.
 — **Minnesota North Stars, St. Louis Blues,** April 24, 1991, second period, at Minnesota. Minnesota had 4 and St. Louis 1. Minnesota won 8-4.

MOST POWER-PLAY GOALS, ONE TEAM, ONE PERIOD:
 4 — Toronto Maple Leafs, March 26, 1936, second period against Boston at Toronto. Toronto won 8-3.
 — **Minnesota North Stars,** April 28, 1984, second period against Edmonton at Minnesota. Edmonton won 8-5.
 — **Boston Bruins,** April 11, 1991, third period against Hartford at Boston. Boston won 6-1.
 — **Minnesota North Stars,** April 24, 1991, second period against St. Louis at Minnesota. Minnesota won 8-4.

MOST SHORTHAND GOALS BY ALL TEAMS, ONE PLAYOFF YEAR:
 33 — 1988, in 83 games.

MOST SHORTHAND GOALS, ONE TEAM, ONE PLAYOFF YEAR:
 10 — Edmonton Oilers 1983, in 16 games.
 9 — NY Islanders, 1981, in 19 games.
 8 — Philadelphia Flyers, 1989, in 19 games.
 7 — NY Islanders, 1980, in 21 games.
 — Chicago Blackhawks, 1989, in 16 games.
 — Vancouver Canucks, 1995, in 11 games.

Stefan Persson scored three of the New York Islanders' record-setting 15 powerplay goals during the 1980 Stanley Cup Finals against the Philadelphia Flyers.

MOST SHORTHAND GOALS, BOTH TEAMS, ONE SERIES:

7 — **Boston Bruins (4), NY Rangers (3),** in 1958 SF, won by Boston 4-2.
— **Edmonton Oilers (5), Calgary Flames (2),** in 1983 DF won by Edmonton 4-1.
— **Vancouver Canucks (6), St. Louis Blues (1),** in 1995 CQF won by Vancouver 4-3.

MOST SHORTHAND GOALS, ONE TEAM, ONE SERIES:

6 — **Calgary Flames** in 1995 against San Jose in best-of-seven CQF won by San Jose 4-3.
— **Vancouver Canucks** in 1995 against St. Louis in best-of-seven CQF won by Vancouver 4-3.
5 — **Edmonton Oilers** in 1983 against Calgary in best-of-seven DF won by Edmonton 4-1.
— **NY Rangers** in 1979 against Philadelphia in best-of-seven QF, won by NY Rangers 4-1.

MOST SHORTHAND GOALS, BOTH TEAMS, ONE GAME:

4 — **NY Islanders, NY Rangers,** April 17, 1983 at NY Rangers. NY Islanders had 3 shorthand goals, NY Rangers 1. NY Rangers won 7-6.
— **Boston Bruins, Minnesota North Stars,** April 11, 1981, at Minnesota. Boston had 3 shorthand goals, Minnesota 1. Minnesota won 6-3.
— **San Jose Sharks, Toronto Maple Leafs,** May 8, 1994 at San Jose. Toronto had 3 shorthanded goals, San Jose 1. Toronto won 8-3.
3 — **Toronto Maple Leafs, Detroit Red Wings,** April 5, 1947, at Toronto. Toronto had 2 shorthand goals, Detroit 1. Toronto won 6-1.
— **NY Rangers, Boston Bruins,** April 1, 1958, at Boston. NY Rangers had 2 shorthand goals, Boston 1. NY Rangers won 5-2.
— **Minnesota North Stars, Philadelphia Flyers,** May 4, 1980, at Minnesota. Minnesota had 2 shorthand goals, Philadelphia 1. Philadelphia won 5-3.
— **Edmonton Oilers, Winnipeg Jets,** April 9, 1988 at Winnipeg. Winnipeg had 2 shorthand goals, Edmonton 1. Winnipeg won 6-4.
— **New Jersey Devils, NY Islanders,** April 14, 1988 at New Jersey. NY Islanders had 2 shorthand goals, New Jersey 1. New Jersey won 6-5.

MOST SHORTHAND GOALS, ONE TEAM, ONE GAME:

3 — **Boston Bruins,** April 11, 1981, at Minnesota. Minnesota won 6-3.
— **NY Islanders,** April 17, 1983, at NY Rangers. NY Rangers won 7-6.
— **Toronto Maple Leafs,** May 8, 1994, at San Jose. Toronto won 8-3.

MOST SHORTHAND GOALS, BOTH TEAMS, ONE PERIOD:

3 — **Toronto Maple Leafs, Detroit Red Wings,** April 5, 1947, at Toronto, first period. Toronto had 2 shorthand goals, Detroit 1. Toronto won 6-1.
— **Toronto Maple Leafs, San Jose Sharks,** May 8, 1994, at San Jose, third period. Toronto had 2 shorthanded goals, San Jose 1. Toronto won 8-3.

MOST SHORTHAND GOALS ONE TEAM, ONE PERIOD:

2 — **Toronto Maple Leafs,** April 5, 1947, at Toronto against Detroit, first period. Toronto won 6-1.
— **Toronto Maple Leafs,** April 13, 1965, at Toronto against Montreal, first period. Montreal won 4-3.
— **Boston Bruins,** April 20, 1969, at Boston against Montreal, first period. Boston won 3-2.
— **Boston Bruins,** April 8, 1970, at Boston against NY Rangers, second period. Boston won 8-2.
— **Boston Bruins,** April 30, 1972, at Boston against NY Rangers, first period. Boston won 6-5.
— **Chicago Blackhawks,** May 3, 1973, at Chicago against Montreal, first period. Chicago won 7-4.
— **Montreal Canadiens,** April 23, 1978, at Detroit, first period. Montreal won 8-0.
— **NY Islanders,** April 8, 1980, at New York against Los Angeles, second period. NY Islanders won 8-1.
— **Los Angeles Kings,** April 9, 1980, at NY Islanders, first period. Los Angeles won 6-3.
— **Boston Bruins,** April 13, 1980, at Pittsburgh, second period. Boston won 8-3.
— **Minnesota North Stars,** May 4, 1980, at Minnesota against Philadelphia, second period. Philadelphia won 5-3.
— **Boston Bruins,** April 11, 1981, at Minnesota, third period. Minnesota won 6-3.
— **NY Islanders,** May 12, 1981, at New York against Minnesota, first period. NY Islanders won 6-3.
— **Montreal Canadiens,** April 7, 1982, at Montreal against Quebec, third period. Montreal won 5-1.
— **Edmonton Oilers,** April 24, 1983, at Edmonton against Chicago, third period. Edmonton won 8-4.
— **Winnipeg Jets,** April 14, 1985, at Calgary, second period. Winnipeg won 5-3.
— **Boston Bruins,** April 6, 1988 at Boston against Buffalo, first period. Boston won 7-3.
— **NY Islanders,** April 14, 1988 at New Jersey, third period. New Jersey won 6-5.
— **Detroit Red Wings,** April 29, 1993 at Toronto, second period. Detroit won 7-3.
— **Toronto Maple Leafs,** May 8, 1994 at San Jose, third period. Toronto won 8-3.
— **Calgary Flames,** May 11, 1995 at San Jose, first period. Calgary won 9-2.
— **Vancouver Canucks,** May 15, 1995 at St. Louis, second period. Vancouver won 6-5.

Chicago penalty-killing specialist Wayne Presley scored three short-handed goals during the 1989 playoffs.

A group of victorious Toronto Maple Leafs, from left to right: Bob Pulford, Brian Conacher, Pete Stemkowski, Larry Hillman, Milan Marcetta, Larry Jeffrey (with crutches), Marcel Pronovost and Mike Walton surround captain George Armstrong after the Leafs clinched the Stanley Cup on May 2, 1967.

FASTEST TWO GOALS, BOTH TEAMS:
5 Seconds — Pittsburgh Penguins, Buffalo Sabres at Buffalo, April 14, 1979. Gilbert Perreault scored for Buffalo at 12:59 and Jim Hamilton for Pittsburgh at 13:04 of first period. Pittsburgh won 4-3 and best-of-three PR 2-1.
8 Seconds — Minnesota North Stars, St. Louis Blues at Minnesota, April 9, 1989. Bernie Federko scored for St. Louis at 2:28 of third period and Perry Berezan at 2:36 for Minnesota. Minnesota won 5-4. St. Louis won best-of-seven DSF 4-1.
9 Seconds — NY Islanders, Washington Capitals at Washington, April 10, 1986. Bryan Trottier scored for New York at 18:26 of second period and Scott Stevens at 18:35 for Washington. Washington won 5-2, and won best-of-five DSF 3-0.
10 Seconds — Washington Capitals, New Jersey Devils at New Jersey, April 5, 1990. Pat Conacher scored for New Jersey at 8:02 of second period and Dale Hunter at 8:12 for Washington. Washington won 5-4, and won best-of-seven DSF 4-2.
— Calgary Flames, Edmonton Oilers at Edmonton, April 8, 1991. Joe Nieuwendyk scored for Calgary at 2:03 of first period and Esa Tikkanen at 2:13 for Edmonton. Edmonton won 4-3, and won best-of-seven DSF 4-3.

FASTEST TWO GOALS, ONE TEAM:
5 Seconds — Detroit Red Wings at Detroit, April 11, 1965, against Chicago. Norm Ullman scored at 17:35 and 17:40, second period. Detroit won 4-2. Chicago won best-of-seven SF 4-3.

FASTEST THREE GOALS, BOTH TEAMS:
21 Seconds — Edmonton Oilers, Chicago Blackhawks at Edmonton, May 7, 1985. Behn Wilson scored for Chicago at 19:22 of third period, Jari Kurri at 19:36 and Glenn Anderson at 19:43 for Edmonton. Edmonton won 7-3 and best-of-seven CF 4-2.
30 Seconds — Chicago Blackhawks, Pittsburgh Penguins at Chicago, June 1, 1992. Dirk Graham scored for Chicago at 6:21 of first period, Kevin Stevens for Pittsburgh at 6:33 and Graham for Chicago at 6:51. Pittsburgh won 6-5 and best-of-seven F 4-0.
31 Seconds — Edmonton Oilers, Philadelphia Flyers at Edmonton, May 25, 1985. Wayne Gretzky scored for Edmonton at 1:10 and 1:25 of first period, Derrick Smith scored for Philadelphia at 1:41. Edmonton won 4-3 and best-of-seven F 4-1.

FASTEST THREE GOALS, ONE TEAM:
23 Seconds — Toronto Maple Leafs at Toronto, April 12, 1979, against Atlanta Flames. Darryl Sittler scored at 4:04 of first period and again at 4:16 and Ron Ellis at 4:27. Leafs won 7-4 and best-of-three PR 2-0.
38 Seconds — NY Rangers at New York, April 12, 1986. Jim Wiemer scored at 12:29 of third period, Bob Brooke at 12:43 and Ron Grescher at 13:07. NY Rangers won 5-2 and best-of-five DSF 3-2.
56 Seconds — Montreal Canadiens at Detroit, April 6, 1954. Dickie Moore scored at 15:03 of first period, Maurice Richard at 15:28 and again at 15:59. Montreal won 3-1. Detroit won best-of-seven F 4-3.

FASTEST FOUR GOALS, BOTH TEAMS:
1 Minute, 33 Seconds — Philadelphia Flyers, Toronto Maple Leafs at Philadelphia, April 20, 1976. Don Saleski of Philadelphia scored at 10:04 of second period; Bob Neely, Toronto, 10:42; Gary Dornhoefer, Philadelphia, 11:24; and Don Saleski, 11:37. Philadelphia won 7-1 and best-of-seven QF series 4-3.
1 minute, 34 seconds — Montreal Canadiens, Calgary Flames at Montreal, May 20, 1986. Joel Otto of Calgary scored at 17:59 of first period; Bobby Smith, Montreal, 18:25; Mats Naslund, Montreal, 19:17; and Bob Gainey, Montreal, 19:33. Montreal won 5-3 and best-of-seven F series 4-1.
1 Minute, 38 Seconds — Boston Bruins, Philadelphia Flyers at Philadelphia, April 26, 1977. Gregg Sheppard of Boston scored at 14:01 of second period; Mike Milbury, Boston, 15:01; Gary Dornhoefer, Philadelphia, 15:16; and Jean Ratelle, Boston, 15:39. Boston won 5-4 and best-of-seven SF series 4-0.

FASTEST FOUR GOALS, ONE TEAM:
2 Minutes, 35 Seconds — Montreal Canadiens at Montreal, March 30, 1944, against Toronto. Toe Blake scored at 7:58 of third period and again at 8:37; Maurice Richard, 9:17; Ray Getliffe, 10:33. Montreal won 11-0 and best-of-seven SF 4-1.

FASTEST FIVE GOALS, BOTH TEAMS:
3 Minutes, 6 Seconds — Chicago Blackhawks, Minnesota North Stars, at Chicago April 21, 1985. Keith Brown scored for Chicago at 1:12, second period; Ken Yaremchuk, Chicago, 1:27; Dino Ciccarelli, Minnesota, 2:48; Tony McKegney, Minnesota, 4:07; and Curt Fraser, Chicago, 4:18. Chicago won 6-2 and best-of-seven DF 4-2.
3 Minutes, 20 Seconds — Minnesota North Stars, Philadelphia Flyers, at Philadelphia, April 29, 1980. Paul Shmyr scored for Minnesota at 13:20, first period; Steve Christoff, Minnesota, 13:59; Ken Linseman, Philadelphia, 14:54; Tom Gorence, Philadelphia, 15:36; and Linseman, 16:40. Minnesota won 6-5. Philadelphia won best-of-seven SF 4-1.
4 Minutes, 19 Seconds — Toronto Maple Leafs, NY Rangers at Toronto, April 9, 1932. Ace Bailey scored for Toronto at 15:07, third period; Fred Cook, NY Rangers, 16:32; Bob Gracie, Toronto, 17:36; Frank Boucher, NY Rangers, 18:26 and again at 19:26. Toronto won 6-4 and best-of-five F 3-0.

FASTEST FIVE GOALS, ONE TEAM:
3 Minutes, 36 Seconds — Montreal Canadiens at Montreal, March 30, 1944, against Toronto. Toe Blake scored at 7:58 of third period and again at 8:37; Maurice Richard, 9:17; Ray Getliffe, 10:33; and Buddy O'Connor, 11:34. Canadiens won 11-0 and best-of-seven SF 4-1.

MOST THREE-OR-MORE GOAL GAMES BY ALL TEAMS, ONE PLAYOFF YEAR:
12 — **1983** in 66 games.
— **1988** in 83 games.
11 — 1985 in 70 games.
— 1992 in 86 games.

MOST THREE-OR-MORE GOAL GAMES, ONE TEAM, ONE PLAYOFF YEAR:
6 — **Edmonton Oilers in 16 games, 1983.**
— **Edmonton Oilers in 18 games, 1985.**

Individual Records

Career

MOST YEARS IN PLAYOFFS:
20 — Gordie Howe, Detroit, Hartford (1947-58 incl.; 60-61; 63-66 incl.; 70 & 80)
— Larry Robinson, Montreal, Los Angeles (1973-92 incl.)
19 — Red Kelly, Detroit, Toronto
18 — Stan Mikita, Chicago
— Henri Richard, Montreal

MOST CONSECUTIVE YEARS IN PLAYOFFS:
20 — Larry Robinson, Montreal, Los Angeles (1973-1992, inclusive).
17 — Brad Park, NY Rangers, Boston, Detroit (1969-1985, inclusive).
16 — Jean Beliveau, Montreal (1954-69, inclusive).
— Ray Bourque, Boston (1980-95, inclusive).

MOST PLAYOFF GAMES:
227 — Larry Robinson, Montreal, Los Angeles
221 — Bryan Trottier, NY Islanders, Pittsburgh
214 — Glenn Anderson, Edmonton, Toronto, NY Rangers, St. Louis
210 — Mark Messier, Edmonton, NY Rangers
202 — Kevin Lowe, Edmonton, NY Rangers

MOST POINTS IN PLAYOFFS (CAREER):
346 — Wayne Gretzky, Edmonton, Los Angeles, 110G, 236A
272 — Mark Messier, Edmonton, NY Rangers, 102G, 170A
222 — Jari Kurri, Edmonton, Los Angeles, 102G, 120A
209 — Glenn Anderson, Edmonton, Toronto, NY Rangers, St. Louis, 92G, 117A
184 — Bryan Trottier, NY Islanders, Pittsburgh 71G, 113A

MOST GOALS IN PLAYOFFS (CAREER):
110 — Wayne Gretzky, Edmonton, Los Angeles
102 — Jari Kurri, Edmonton, Los Angeles
102 — Mark Messier, Edmonton, NY Rangers
92 — Glenn Anderson, Edmonton, Toronto, NY Rangers, St. Louis
85 — Mike Bossy, NY Islanders

MOST ASSISTS IN PLAYOFFS (CAREER):
236 — Wayne Gretzky, Edmonton, Los Angeles
170 — Mark Messier, Edmonton, NY Rangers
120 — Jari Kurri, Edmonton, Los Angeles
119 — Paul Coffey, Edmonton, Pittsburgh, Los Angeles, Detroit
117 — Glenn Anderson, Edmonton, Toronto, NY Rangers, St. Louis

MOST OVERTIME GOALS IN PLAYOFFS (CAREER):
6 — Maurice Richard, Montreal (1 in 1946; 3 in 1951; 1 in 1957; 1 in 1958.)
4 — Bob Nystrom, NY Islanders
— Dale Hunter, Quebec, Washington
— Glenn Anderson, Edmonton, Toronto
— Wayne Gretzky, Edmonton, Los Angeles
— Stephane Richer, Montreal, New Jersey
3 — Mel Hill, Boston
— Rene Robert, Buffalo
— Danny Gare, Buffalo
— Jacques Lemaire, Montreal
— Bobby Clarke, Philadelphia
— Terry O'Reilly, Boston
— Mike Bossy, NY Islanders
— Steve Payne, Minnesota
— Ken Morrow, NY Islanders
— Lanny McDonald, Toronto, Calgary
— Peter Stastny, Quebec
— Dino Ciccarelli, Minnesota, Washington
— Russ Courtnall, Montreal
— Kirk Muller, Montreal
— Greg Adams, Vancouver
— Joe Murphy, Edmonton, Chicago

MOST POWER-PLAY GOALS IN PLAYOFFS (CAREER):
35 — Mike Bossy, NY Islanders
30 — Wayne Gretzky, Edmonton, Los Angeles
28 — Dino Ciccarelli, Minnesota, Washington, Detroit
27 — Denis Potvin, NY Islanders
26 — Jean Beliveau, Montreal
25 — Jari Kurri, Edmonton, Los Angeles
— Mario Lemieux, Pittsburgh
24 — Bobby Smith, Minnesota, Montreal
— Cam Neely, Vancouver, Boston
23 — Glenn Anderson, Edmonton, Toronto, NY Rangers
— Brian Propp, Philadelphia, Boston, Minnesota

MOST SHORTHAND GOALS IN PLAYOFFS (CAREER):
14 — Mark Messier, Edmonton, NY Rangers
11 — Wayne Gretzky, Edmonton, Los Angeles
9 — Jari Kurri, Edmonton, Los Angeles
8 — Ed Westfall, Boston, NY Islanders
— Hakan Loob, Calgary

MOST GAME-WINNING GOALS IN PLAYOFFS (CAREER):
21 — Wayne Gretzky, Edmonton, Los Angeles
18 — Maurice Richard, Montreal
17 — Mike Bossy, NY Islanders
16 — Glenn Anderson, Edmonton, Toronto, NY Rangers
15 — Jean Beliveau, Montreal
— Yvan Cournoyer, Montreal

MOST THREE-OR-MORE-GOAL GAMES IN PLAYOFFS (CAREER):
8 — Wayne Gretzky, Edmonton. Six three-goal games; two four-goal games.
7 — Maurice Richard, Montreal. Four three-goal games; two four-goal games; one five-goal game.
— Jari Kurri, Edmonton. Six three-goal games; one four-goal game.
6 — Dino Ciccarelli, Minnesota, Washington, Detroit. Five three-goal games; one four-goal game.
5 — Mike Bossy, NY Islanders. Four three-goal games; one four-goal game.

MOST PENALTY MINUTES IN PLAYOFFS (CAREER):
637 — Dale Hunter, Quebec, Washington
541 — Chris Nilan, Montreal, NY Rangers, Boston
466 — Willi Plett, Atlanta, Calgary, Minnesota, Boston
455 — Dave Williams, Toronto, Vancouver, Los Angeles
436 — Glenn Anderson, Edmonton, Toronto, NY Rangers, St. Louis

MOST SHUTOUTS IN PLAYOFFS (CAREER):
15 — Clint Benedict, Ottawa, Mtl. Maroons
14 — Jacques Plante, Montreal, St. Louis
13 — Turk Broda, Toronto
12 — Terry Sawchuk, Detroit, Toronto, Los Angeles

MOST PLAYOFF GAMES APPEARED IN BY A GOALTENDER (CAREER):
132 — Bill Smith, NY Islanders
119 — Grant Fuhr, Edmonton, Buffalo
116 — Andy Moog, Edmonton, Boston, Dallas
115 — Glenn Hall, Detroit, Chicago, St. Louis
114 — Patrick Roy, Montreal
112 — Jacques Plante, Montreal, St. Louis, Toronto, Boston
— Ken Dryden, Montreal

MOST MINUTES PLAYED BY A GOALTENDER (CAREER):
7,645 — Bill Smith, NY Islanders
7,002 — Grant Fuhr, Edmonton, Buffalo
6,964 — Patrick Roy, Montreal
6,899 — Glenn Hall, Detroit, Chicago, St. Louis
6,846 — Ken Dryden, Montreal

Single Playoff Year

MOST POINTS, ONE PLAYOFF YEAR:
47 — Wayne Gretzky, Edmonton, in 1985. 17 goals, 30 assists in 18 games.
44 — Mario Lemieux, Pittsburgh, in 1991. 16 goals, 28 assists in 23 games.
43 — Wayne Gretzky, Edmonton, in 1988. 12 goals, 31 assists in 19 games.
40 — Wayne Gretzky, Los Angeles, in 1993. 15 goals, 25 assists in 24 games.
38 — Wayne Gretzky, Edmonton, in 1983. 12 goals, 26 assists in 16 games.
37 — Paul Coffey, Edmonton, in 1985. 12 goals, 25 assists in 24 games.
35 — Mike Bossy, NY Islanders, in 1981. 17 goals, 18 assists in 18 games.
— Wayne Gretzky, Edmonton, in 1984. 13 goals, 22 assists in 19 games.
— Mark Messier, Edmonton, in 1988. 11 goals, 23 assists in 19 games.
— Doug Gilmour, Toronto, in 1993. 10 goals, 25 assists in 21 games.
34 — Wayne Gretzky, Edmonton, in 1987. 5 goals, 29 assists in 21 games.
— Mark Recchi, Pittsburgh, in 1991. 10 goals, 24 assists in 24 games.
— Mario Lemieux, Pittsburgh, in 1992. 16 goals, 18 assists in 15 games.
— Brian Leetch, NY Rangers, in 1994. 11 goals, 23 assists in 23 games.

MOST POINTS BY A DEFENSEMAN, ONE PLAYOFF YEAR:
37 — Paul Coffey, Edmonton, in 1985. 12 goals, 25 assists in 18 games.
34 — Brian Leetch, NY Rangers, in 1994. 11 goals, 23 assists in 23 games.
31 — Al MacInnis, Calgary, in 1989. 7 goals, 24 assists in 18 games.
25 — Denis Potvin, NY Islanders, in 1981. 8 goals, 17 assists in 18 games.
— Ray Bourque, Boston, in 1991. 7 goals, 18 assists in 19 games.

MOST POINTS BY A ROOKIE, ONE PLAYOFF YEAR:
21 — Dino Ciccarelli, Minnesota, in 1981. 14 goals, 7 assists in 19 games.
20 — Don Maloney, NY Rangers, in 1979. 7 goals, 13 assists in 18 games.

LONGEST CONSECUTIVE POINT-SCORING STREAK, ONE PLAYOFF YEAR:
18 games — Bryan Trottier, NY Islanders, 1981. 11 goals, 18 assists, 29 points.
17 games — Wayne Gretzky, Edmonton, 1988. 12 goals, 29 assists, 41 points.
— Al MacInnis, Calgary, 1989. 7 goals, 17 assists, 24 points.

**LONGEST CONSECUTIVE POINT-SCORING STREAK,
MORE THAN ONE PLAYOFF YEAR:**
27 games — Bryan Trottier, NY Islanders, 1980, 1981 and 1982. 7 games in 1980 (3 G, 5 A, 8 PTS), 18 games in 1981 (11 G, 18 A, 29 PTS), and two games in 1982 (2 G, 3 A, 5 PTS). Total points, 42.
19 games — Wayne Gretzky, Edmonton, Los Angeles 1988 and 1989. 17 games in 1988 (12 G, 29 A, 41 PTS with Edmonton), 2 games in 1989 (1 G, 2 A, 3 PTS with Los Angeles). Total points, 44.
18 games — Phil Esposito, Boston, 1970 and 1971. 13 G, 20 A, 33 PTS.

MOST GOALS, ONE PLAYOFF YEAR:
19 — Reggie Leach, Philadelphia, 1976. 16 games.
 — Jari Kurri, Edmonton, 1985. 18 games.
17 — Newsy Lalonde, Montreal, 1919. 10 games.
 — Mike Bossy, NY Islanders, 1981. 18 games.
 — Steve Payne, Minnesota, 1981. 19 games.
 — Mike Bossy, NY Islanders, 1982. 19 games.
 — Mike Bossy, NY Islanders, 1983. 19 games.
 — Wayne Gretzky, Edmonton, 1985. 18 games.
 — Kevin Stevens, Pittsburgh, 1991. 24 games.

MOST GOALS BY A DEFENSEMAN, ONE PLAYOFF YEAR:
12 — Paul Coffey, Edmonton, 1985. 18 games.
11 — Brian Leetch, NY Rangers, 1994. 23 games.
 9 — Bobby Orr, Boston, 1970. 14 games.
 — Brad Park, Boston, 1978. 15 games.
 8 — Denis Potvin, NY Islanders, 1981. 18 games.
 — Raymond Bourque, Boston, 1983. 17 games.
 — Denis Potvin, NY Islanders, 1983. 20 games.
 — Paul Coffey, Edmonton, 1984. 19 games

MOST GOALS BY A ROOKIE, ONE PLAYOFF YEAR:
14 — Dino Ciccarelli, Minnesota, 1981. 19 games.
11 — Jeremy Roenick, Chicago, 1990. 20 games.
10 — Claude Lemieux, Montreal, 1986. 20 games.
 9 — Pat Flatley, NY Islanders, 1984. 21 games
 8 — Steve Christoff, Minnesota, 1980. 14 games.
 — Brad Palmer, Minnesota, 1981. 19 games.
 — Mike Krushelnyski, Boston, 1983. 17 games.
 — Bob Joyce, Boston, 1988. 23 games.

MOST GAME-WINNING GOALS, ONE PLAYOFF YEAR:
5 — Mike Bossy, NY Islanders, 1983. 19 games.
 — Jari Kurri, Edmonton, 1987. 21 games.
 — Bobby Smith, Minnesota, 1991. 23 games.
 — Mario Lemieux, Pittsburgh, 1992. 15 games.

MOST OVERTIME GOALS, ONE PLAYOFF YEAR:
3 — Mel Hill, Boston, 1939. All against NY Rangers in best-of-seven SF, won by Boston 4-3.
 — Maurice Richard, Montreal, 1951. 2 against Detroit in best-of-seven SF, won by Montreal 4-2; 1 against Toronto best-of-seven F, won by Toronto 4-1.

MOST POWER-PLAY GOALS, ONE PLAYOFF YEAR:
9 — Mike Bossy, NY Islanders, 1981. 18 games against Toronto, Edmonton, NY Rangers and Minnesota.
 — Cam Neely, Boston, 1991. 19 games against Hartford, Montreal, Pittsburgh.
 8 — Tim Kerr, Philadelphia, 1989. 19 games.
 — John Druce, Washington, 1990. 15 games.
 — Brian Propp, Minnesota, 1991. 23 games.
 — Mario Lemieux, Pittsburgh, 1992. 15 games.
 7 — Michel Goulet, Quebec, 1985. 17 games.
 — Mark Messier, Edmonton, 1988. 19 games.
 — Mario Lemieux, Pittsburgh, 1989. 11 games.
 — Brett Hull, St. Louis, 1990. 12 games.
 — Kevin Stevens, Pittsburgh, 1991. 24 games.

MOST SHORTHAND GOALS, ONE PLAYOFF YEAR:
3 — Derek Sanderson, Boston, 1969. 1 against Toronto in QF, won by Boston 4-0; 2 against Montreal in SF, won by Montreal, 4-2.
 — Bill Barber, Philadelphia, 1980. All against Minnesota in SF, won by Philadelphia 4-1.
 — Lorne Henning, NY Islanders, 1980. 1 against Boston in QF won by NY Islanders 4-1; 1 against Buffalo in SF, won by NY Islanders 4-2, 1 against Philadelphia in F, won by NY Islanders 4-2.
 — Wayne Gretzky, Edmonton, 1983. 2 against Winnipeg in DSF won by Edmonton 3-0; 1 against Calgary in DF, won by Edmonton 4-1.
 — Wayne Presley, Chicago, 1989. All against Detroit in DSF won by Chicago 4-2.

MOST THREE-OR-MORE GOAL GAMES, ONE PLAYOFF YEAR:
4 — Jari Kurri, Edmonton, 1985. 1 four-goal game, 3 three-goal games.
 3 — Mark Messier, Edmonton, 1983. 3 three-goal games.
 — Mike Bossy, NY Islanders, 1983. 1 four-goal game, 2 three-goal games
 2 — Newsy Lalonde, Montreal, 1919. 1 five-goal game, 1 four-goal game.
 — Maurice Richard, Montreal, 1944. 1 five-goal game; 1 three-goal game.
 — Doug Bentley, Chicago, 1944. 2 three-goal games.
 — Norm Ullman, Detroit, 1964. 2 three-goal games.
 — Phil Esposito, Boston, 1970. 2 three-goal games.
 — Pit Martin, Chicago, 1973. 2 three-goal games.
 — Rick MacLeish, Philadelphia, 1975. 2 three-goal games.
 — Lanny McDonald, Toronto, 1977. 1 three-goal game; 1 four-goal game.
 — Wayne Gretzky, Edmonton, 1981. 2 three-goal games.
 — Wayne Gretzky, Edmonton, 1983. 2 four-goal games.
 — Wayne Gretzky, Edmonton, 1985. 2 three-goal games.
 — Petr Klima, Detroit, 1988. 2 three-goal games.
 — Cam Neely, Boston, 1991. 2 three-goal games.

LONGEST CONSECUTIVE GOAL-SCORING STREAK, ONE PLAYOFF YEAR:
9 Games — Reggie Leach, Philadelphia, 1976. Streak started April 17 at Toronto and ended May 9 at Montreal. He scored one goal in each of seven games; two in one game; and five in another; a total of 14 goals.

MOST ASSISTS, ONE PLAYOFF YEAR:
31 — Wayne Gretzky, Edmonton, 1988. 19 games.
30 — Wayne Gretzky, Edmonton, 1985. 18 games.
29 — Wayne Gretzky, Edmonton, 1987. 21 games.
28 — Mario Lemieux, Pittsburgh, 1991. 23 games.
26 — Wayne Gretzky, Edmonton, 1983. 16 games.
25 — Paul Coffey, Edmonton, 1985. 18 games.
 — Wayne Gretzky, Los Angeles, 1993. 24 games.
 — Doug Gilmour, Toronto, 1993. 21 games.

MOST ASSISTS BY A DEFENSEMAN, ONE PLAYOFF YEAR:
25 — Paul Coffey, Edmonton, 1985. 18 games.
24 — Al MacInnis, Calgary, 1989. 22 games.
23 — Brian Leetch, NY Rangers, 1994. 23 games.
19 — Bobby Orr, Boston, 1972. 15 games.
18 — Ray Bourque, Boston, 1988. 23 games.
 — Ray Bourque, Boston, 1991. 19 games.
 — Larry Murphy, Pittsburgh, 1991. 23 games.

MOST MINUTES PLAYED BY A GOALTENDER, ONE PLAYOFF YEAR:
1,544 — Kirk McLean, Vancouver, 1994. 24 games.
1,540 — Ron Hextall, Philadelphia, 1987. 26 games.
1,477 — Mike Richter, NY Rangers, 1994. 23 games.
1,401 — Bill Ranford, Edmonton, 1990. 22 games.
1,381 — Mike Vernon, Calgary, 1989. 22 games.

MOST WINS BY A GOALTENDER, ONE PLAYOFF YEAR:
16 — Grant Fuhr, Edmonton, 1988. 19 games.
 — Mike Vernon, Calgary, 1989. 22 games.
 — Bill Ranford, Edmonton, 1990. 22 games.
 — Tom Barrasso, Pittsburgh, 1992. 21 games.
 — Patrick Roy, Montreal, 1993. 20 games.
 — Mike Richter, NY Rangers, 1994. 23 games.
 — Martin Brodeur, New Jersey, 1995. 20 games.
15 — Bill Smith, NY Islanders, 1980. 20 games.
 — Bill Smith, NY Islanders, 1982. 18 games.
 — Grant Fuhr, Edmonton, 1985. 18 games.
 — Patrick Roy, Montreal, 1986. 20 games.
 — Ron Hextall, Philadelphia, 1987. 26 games.
 — Kirk McLean, Vancouver, 1994. 24 games.

MOST CONSECUTIVE WINS BY A GOALTENDER, ONE PLAYOFF YEAR:
11 — Ed Belfour, Chicago, 1992. 3 wins against St. Louis in DSF, won by Chicago 4-2; 4 wins against Detroit in DF, won by Chicago 4-0; and 4 wins against Edmonton in CF, won by Chicago 4-0.
 — Tom Barrasso, Pittsburgh, 1992. 3 wins against NY Rangers in DF, won by Pittsburgh 4-2; 4 wins against Boston in CF, won by Pittsburgh 4-0; and 4 wins against Chicago in F, won by Pittsburgh 4-0.
 — Patrick Roy, Montreal, 1993. 4 wins against Quebec in DSF, won by Montreal 4-2; 4 wins against Buffalo in DF, won by Montreal 4-0; and 3 wins against NY Islanders in CF, won by Montreal 4-1.

MOST SHUTOUTS, ONE PLAYOFF YEAR:
4 — Clint Benedict, Mtl. Maroons, 1926. 8 games.
 — Clint Benedict, Mtl. Maroons, 1928. 9 games.
 — Dave Kerr, NY Rangers, 1937. 9 games.
 — Frank McCool, Toronto, 1945. 13 games.
 — Terry Sawchuk, Detroit, 1952. 8 games.
 — Bernie Parent, Philadelphia, 1975. 17 games.
 — Ken Dryden, Montreal, 1977. 14 games.
 — Mike Richter, NY Rangers, 1994. 23 games.
 — Kirk McLean, Vancouver, 1994. 24 games.

MOST CONSECUTIVE SHUTOUTS:
3 — Clint Benedict, Mtl. Maroons, 1926. Benedict shut out Ottawa 1-0, Mar. 27; he then shut out Victoria twice, 3-0, Mar. 30; 3-0, Apr. 1. Mtl. Maroons won NHL F vs. Ottawa 2 goals to 1 and won the best-of-five F vs. Victoria 3-1.
 — John Roach, NY Rangers, 1929. Roach shutout NY Americans twice, 0-0, Mar. 19; 1-0, Mar. 21; he then shutout Toronto 1-0, Mar. 24. NY Rangers won QF vs. NY Americans 1 goal to 0 and won the best-of-three SF vs. Toronto 2-0.
 — Frank McCool, Toronto, 1945. McCool shut out Detroit 1-0, April 6; 2-0, April 8; 1-0, April 12. Toronto won the best-of-seven F 4-3.

LONGEST SHUTOUT SEQUENCE:
248 Minutes, 32 Seconds — Norm Smith, Detroit, 1936. In best-of-five SF, Smith shut out Mtl. Maroons 1-0, March 24, in 116:30 overtime; shut out Maroons 3-0 in second game, March 26; and was scored against at 12:02 of first period, March 29, by Gus Marker. Detroit won SF 3-0.

Left: The Philadelphia Flyers mob goaltender Bernie Parent after blanking the Boston Bruins 1-0 to win the 1974 Stanley Cup Finals. The Flyers were the first Cup winner from the "Second Six" teams that joined the NHL in 1967. Below: George Armstrong sealed the fate of the Detroit Red Wings when he slipped this shot past Terry Sawchuk at the 15:26 mark of the third period to give the Leafs a commanding 4-0 lead in the seventh and deciding game of the 1964 Stanley Cup Finals.

One-Series Records

MOST POINTS IN FINAL SERIES:
- **13 — Wayne Gretzky, Edmonton,** in 1988, 4 games plus suspended game vs. Boston. 3 goals, 10 assists.
- 12 — Gordie Howe, Detroit, in 1955, 7 games vs. Montreal. 5 goals, 7 assists.
  - — Yvan Cournoyer, Montreal, in 1973, 6 games vs. Chicago. 6 goals, 6 assists.
  - — Jacques Lemaire, Montreal, in 1973, 6 games vs. Chicago. 3 goals, 9 assists.
  - — Mario Lemieux, Pittsburgh, in 1991, 5 games vs. Minnesota. 5 goals, 7 assists.

MOST GOALS IN FINAL SERIES:
- **9 — Babe Dye, Toronto,** in 1922, 5 games vs. Van. Millionaires.
- 8 — Alf Skinner, Toronto, in 1918, 5 games vs. Van. Millionaires.
- 7 — Jean Beliveau, Montreal, in 1956, during 5 games vs. Detroit.
  - — Mike Bossy, NY Islanders, in 1982, during 4 games vs. Vancouver.
  - — Wayne Gretzky, Edmonton, in 1985, during 5 games vs. Philadelphia.

MOST ASSISTS IN FINAL SERIES:
- **10 — Wayne Gretzky, Edmonton,** in 1988, 4 games plus suspended game vs. Boston.
- 9 — Jacques Lemaire, Montreal, in 1973, 6 games vs. Chicago.
  - — Wayne Gretzky, Edmonton, in 1987, 7 games vs. Philadelphia.
  - — Larry Murphy, Pittsburgh, in 1991, 6 games vs. Minnesota.

MOST POINTS IN ONE SERIES (OTHER THAN FINAL):
- **19 — Rick Middleton, Boston,** in 1983 DF, 7 games vs. Buffalo. 5 goals, 14 assists.
- 18 — Wayne Gretzky, Edmonton, in 1985 CF, 6 games vs. Chicago. 4 goals, 14 assists.
- 17 — Mario Lemieux, Pittsburgh, in 1992 DSF, 6 games vs. Washington. 7 goals, 10 assists.
- 16 — Barry Pederson, Boston, in 1983 DF, 7 games vs. Buffalo. 7 goals, 9 assists.
  - — Doug Gilmour, Toronto, in 1994 CSF, 7 games vs. San Jose. 3 goals, 13 assists.
- 15 — Jari Kurri, Edmonton, in 1985 CF, 6 games vs. Chicago. 12 goals, 3 assists.
  - — Wayne Gretzky, Edmonton, in 1987 DSF, 5 games vs. Los Angeles. 2 goals, 13 assists.
  - — Tim Kerr, Philadelphia, in 1989 DF, 7 games vs. Pittsburgh. 10 goals, 5 assists.
  - — Mario Lemieux, Pittsburgh, in 1991 CF, 6 games vs. Boston. 6 goals, 9 assists.

MOST GOALS IN ONE SERIES (OTHER THAN FINAL):
- **12 — Jari Kurri, Edmonton,** in 1985 CF, 6 games vs. Chicago.
- 11 — Newsy Lalonde, Montreal, in 1919 NHL F, 5 games vs. Ottawa.
- 10 — Tim Kerr, Philadelphia, in 1989 DF, 7 games vs. Pittsburgh.
- 9 — Reggie Leach, Philadelphia, in 1976 SF, 5 games vs. Boston.
  - — Bill Barber, Philadelphia, in 1980 SF, 5 games vs. Minnesota.
  - — Mike Bossy, NY Islanders, in 1983 CF, 6 games vs. Boston.
  - — Mario Lemieux, Pittsburgh, in 1989 DF, 7 games vs. Philadelphia.

MOST ASSISTS IN ONE SERIES (OTHER THAN FINAL):
- **14 — Rick Middleton, Boston,** in 1983 DF, 7 games vs. Buffalo.
  - **— Wayne Gretzky, Edmonton,** in 1985 CF, 6 games vs. Chicago.
- 13 — Wayne Gretzky, Edmonton, in 1987 DSF, 5 games vs. Los Angeles.
  - — Doug Gilmour, Toronto, in 1994 CSF, 7 games vs. San Jose.
- 11 — Mark Messier, Edmonton, in 1989 DSF, 7 games vs. Los Angeles.
  - — Al MacInnis, Calgary, in 1984 DF, 7 games vs. Edmonton.
  - — Mike Ridley, Washington, in 1992 DSF, 7 games vs. Pittsburgh.
  - — Ron Francis, Pittsburgh, in 1995 CQF, 7 games vs. Washington.
- 10 — Fleming Mackell, Boston, in 1958 SF, 6 games vs. NY Rangers.
  - — Stan Mikita, Chicago, in 1962 SF, 6 games vs. Montreal.
  - — Bob Bourne, NY Islanders, in 1983 DF, 6 games vs. NY Rangers.
  - — Wayne Gretzky, Edmonton, in 1988 DSF, 5 games vs. Winnipeg.
  - — Mario Lemieux, Pittsburgh, in 1992 DSF, 6 games vs. Washington.

MOST GAME-WINNING GOALS, ONE PLAYOFF SERIES:
- **4 — Mike Bossy, NY Islanders,** 1983, CF vs. Boston, won by NY Islanders 4-2.

MOST OVERTIME GOALS, ONE PLAYOFF SERIES:
- **3 — Mel Hill, Boston,** 1939, SF vs. NY Rangers, won by Boston 4-3. Hill scored at 59:25 overtime March 21 for a 2-1 win; at 8:24, March 23 for a 3-2 win; and at 48:00, April 2 for a 2-1 win.

MOST POWER-PLAY GOALS, ONE PLAYOFF SERIES:
- **6 — Chris Kontos, Los Angeles,** 1989, DSF vs. Edmonton, won by Los Angeles 4-3.
- 5 — Andy Bathgate, Detroit, 1966, SF vs. Chicago, won by Detroit 4-2.
  - — Denis Potvin, NY Islanders, 1981, QF vs. Edmonton, won by NY Islanders 4-2.
  - — Ken Houston, Calgary, 1981, QF vs. Philadelphia, won by Calgary 4-3.
  - — Rick Vaive, Chicago, 1988, DSF vs. St. Louis, won by St. Louis 4-1.
  - — Tim Kerr, Philadelphia, 1989, DF vs. Pittsburgh, won by Philadelphia 4-3.
  - — Mario Lemieux, Pittsburgh, 1989, DF vs. Philadelphia, won by Philadelphia 4-3.
  - — John Druce, Washington, 1990, DF vs. NY Rangers won by Washington 4-1.
  - — Pat LaFontaine, Buffalo, 1992, DSF vs. Boston won by Boston 4-3.

MOST SHORTHAND GOALS, ONE PLAYOFF SERIES:
- **3 — Bill Barber, Philadelphia,** 1980, SF vs. Minnesota, won by Philadelphia 4-1.
  - **— Wayne Presley, Chicago,** 1989, DSF vs. Detroit, won by Chicago 4-2.
- 2 — Mac Colville, NY Rangers, 1940, SF vs. Boston, won by NY Rangers 4-2.
  - — Jerry Toppazzini, Boston, 1958, SF vs. NY Rangers, won by Boston 4-2.
  - — Dave Keon, Toronto, 1963, F vs. Detroit, won by Toronto 4-1.
  - — Bob Pulford, Toronto, 1964, F vs. Detroit, won by Toronto 4-3.
  - — Serge Savard, Montreal, 1968, F vs. St. Louis, won by Montreal 4-0.
  - — Derek Sanderson, Boston, 1969, SF vs. Montreal, won by Montreal 4-2.
  - — Bryan Trottier, NY Islanders, 1980, PR vs. Los Angeles, won by NY Islanders 3-1.
  - — Bobby Lalonde, Boston, 1981, PR vs. Minnesota, won by Minnesota 3-0.
  - — Butch Goring, NY Islanders, 1981, SF vs. NY Rangers, won by NY Islanders 4-0.
  - — Wayne Gretzky, Edmonton, 1983, DSF vs. Winnipeg, won by Edmonton 3-0.
  - — Mark Messier, Edmonton, 1983, DF vs. Calgary, won by Edmonton 4-1.
  - — Jari Kurri, Edmonton, 1983, CF vs. Chicago, won by Edmonton 4-0.
  - — Wayne Gretzky, Edmonton, 1985, DF vs. Winnipeg, won by Edmonton 4-0.
  - — Kevin Lowe, Edmonton, 1987, F vs. Philadelphia, won by Edmonton 4-3.
  - — Bob Gould, Washington, 1988, DSF vs. Philadelphia, won by Washington 4-3.
  - — Dave Poulin, Philadelphia, 1989, DF vs. Pittsburgh, won by Philadelphia 4-3.
  - — Russ Courtnall, Montreal, 1991, DF vs. Boston, won by Boston 4-3.
  - — Sergei Fedorov, Detroit, 1992 DSF vs. Minnesota, won by Detroit 4-3.
  - — Mark Messier, NY Rangers, 1992, DSF vs. New Jersey, won by NY Rangers 4-3.
  - — Tom Fitzgerald, NY Islanders, 1993, DF vs. Pittsburgh, won by NY Islanders 4-3.
  - — Mark Osborne, Toronto, 1994, CSF vs. San Jose, won by Toronto 4-3.

MOST THREE-OR-MORE-GOAL GAMES, ONE PLAYOFF SERIES:
3 — **Jari Kurri, Edmonton** 1985, CF vs. Chicago won by Edmonton 4-2. Kurri scored 3 G May 7 at Edmonton in 7-3 win, 3 G May 14 in 10-5 win and 4 G May 16 at Chicago in 8-2 win.
2 — Doug Bentley, Chicago, 1944, SF vs. Detroit, won by Chicago 4-1. Bentley scored 3 G Mar. 28 at Chicago in 7-1 win and 3 G Mar. 30 at Detroit in 5-2 win.
 — Norm Ullman, Detroit, 1964, SF vs. Chicago, won by Detroit 4-3. Ullman scored 3 G Mar. 29 at Chicago in 7-1 win and 3 G April 7 at Detroit in 7-2 win.
 — Mark Messier, Edmonton, 1983, DF vs. Calgary won by Edmonton 4-1. Messier scored 4 G April 14 at Edmonton in 6-3 win and 3 G April 17 at Calgary in 10-2 win.
 — Mike Bossy, NY Islanders, 1983, CF vs. Boston won by NY Islanders 4-2. Bossy scored 3 G May 3 at New York in 8-3 win and 4 G on May 7 at New York in 8-4 win.

Single Playoff Game Records

MOST POINTS, ONE GAME:
8 — **Patrik Sundstrom, New Jersey,** April 22, 1988 at New Jersey during 10-4 win over Washington. Sundstrom had 3 goals, 5 assists.
 — **Mario Lemieux, Pittsburgh,** April 25, 1989 at Pittsburgh during 10-7 win over Philadelphia. Lemieux had 5 goals, 3 assists.
7 — Wayne Gretzky, Edmonton, April 17, 1983 at Calgary during 10-2 win. Gretzky had 4 goals, 3 assists.
 — Wayne Gretzky, Edmonton, April 25,1985 at Winnipeg during 8-3 win. Gretzky had 3 goals, 4 assists.
 — Wayne Gretzky, Edmonton, April 9, 1987, at Edmonton during 13-3 win over Los Angeles. Gretzky had 1 goal, 6 assists.
6 — Dickie Moore, Montreal, March 25, 1954, at Montreal during 8-1 win over Boston. Moore had 2 goals, 4 assists.
 — Phil Esposito, Boston, April 2, 1969, at Boston during 10-0 win over Toronto. Esposito had 4 goals, 2 assists.
 — Darryl Sittler, Toronto, April 22, 1976, at Toronto during 8-5 win over Philadelphia. Sittler had 5 goals, 1 assist.
 — Guy Lafleur, Montreal, April 11, 1977, at Montreal during 7-2 victory vs. St. Louis. Lafleur had 3 goals, 3 assists.
 — Mikko Leinonen, NY Rangers, April 8, 1982, at New York during 7-3 win over Philadelphia. Leinonen had 6 assists.
 — Paul Coffey, Edmonton, May 14, 1985 at Edmonton during 10-5 win over Chicago. Coffey had 1 goal, 5 assists.
 — John Anderson, Hartford, April 12, 1986 at Hartford during 9-4 win over Quebec. Anderson had 2 goals, 4 assists.
 — Mario Lemieux, Pittsburgh, April 23, 1992 at Pittsburgh during 6-4 win over Washington. Lemieux had 3 goals, 3 assists.

MOST POINTS BY A DEFENSEMAN, ONE GAME:
6 — **Paul Coffey, Edmonton,** May 14, 1985 at Edmonton vs. Chicago. 1 goal, 5 assists. Edmonton won 10-5.
5 — Eddie Bush, Detroit, April 9, 1942, at Detroit vs. Toronto. 1 goal, 4 assists. Detroit won 5-2.
 — Bob Dailey, Philadelphia, May 1, 1980, at Philadelphia vs. Minnesota. 1 goal, 4 assists. Philadelphia won 7-0.
 — Denis Potvin, NY Islanders, April 17, 1981, at New York vs. Edmonton. 3 goals, 2 assists. NY Islanders won 6-3.
 — Risto Siltanen, Quebec, April 14, 1987 at Hartford. 5 assists. Quebec won 7-5.

MOST GOALS, ONE GAME:
5 — **Newsy Lalonde, Montreal,** March 1, 1919, at Montreal. Final score: Montreal 6, Ottawa 3.
 — **Maurice Richard, Montreal,** March 23, 1944, at Montreal. Final score: Montreal 5, Toronto 1.
 — **Darryl Sittler, Toronto,** April 22, 1976, at Toronto. Final score: Toronto 8, Philadelphia 5.
 — **Reggie Leach, Philadelphia,** May 6, 1976, at Philadelphia. Final score: Philadelphia 6, Boston 3.
 — **Mario Lemieux, Pittsburgh,** April 25, 1989 at Pittsburgh. Final score: Pittsburgh 10, Philadelphia 7.

MOST GOALS BY A DEFENSEMAN, ONE GAME:
3 — **Bobby Orr, Boston,** April 11, 1971 at Montreal. Final score: Boston 5, Montreal 2.
 — **Dick Redmond, Chicago,** April 4, 1973 at Chicago. Final score: Chicago 7, St. Louis 1.
 — **Denis Potvin, NY Islanders,** April 17, 1981 at New York. Final score: NY Islanders 6, Edmonton 3.
 — **Paul Reinhart, Calgary,** April 14, 1983 at Edmonton. Final score: Edmonton 6, Calgary 3.
 — **Paul Reinhart, Calgary,** April 8, 1984 at Vancouver. Final score: Calgary 5, Vancouver 1.
 — **Doug Halward, Vancouver,** April 7, 1984 at Vancouver. Final score: Vancouver 7, Calgary 0.
 — **Al Iafrate, Washington,** April 26, 1993 at Washington. Final score: Washington 6, NY Islanders 4.
 — **Eric Desjardins, Montreal,** June 3, 1993 at Montreal. Final score: Montreal 3, Los Angeles 2.
 — **Gary Suter, Chicago,** April 24, 1994, at Chicago. Final score: Chicago 4, Toronto 3.
 — **Brian Leetch, NY Rangers,** May 22, 1995 at Philadelphia. Final score: Philadelphia 4, NY Rangers 3.

MOST POWER-PLAY GOALS, ONE GAME:
3 — **Syd Howe, Detroit,** March 23, 1939, at Detroit vs. Montreal, Detroit won 7-3.
 — **Sid Smith, Toronto,** April 10, 1949, at Detroit. Toronto won 3-1.
 — **Phil Esposito, Boston,** April 2, 1969, at Boston vs. Toronto. Boston won 10-0.
 — **John Bucyk, Boston,** April 21, 1974, at Boston vs. Chicago. Boston won 8-6.
 — **Denis Potvin, NY Islanders,** April 17, 1981, at New York vs. Edmonton. NY Islanders won 6-3.
 — **Tim Kerr, Philadelphia,** April 13, 1985, at NY Rangers. Philadelphia won 6-5.
 — **Jari Kurri, Edmonton,** April 9, 1987, at Edmonton vs. Los Angeles. Edmonton won 13-3.
 — **Mark Johnson, New Jersey,** April 22, 1988, at New Jersey vs. Washington. New Jersey won 10-4.
 — **Dino Ciccarelli, Detroit,** April 29, 1993, at Toronto, in 7-3 win by Detroit.
 — **Dino Ciccarelli, Detroit,** May 11, 1995, at Dallas, in 5-1 win by Detroit.

MOST SHORTHAND GOALS, ONE GAME:
2 — **Dave Keon, Toronto,** April 18, 1963, at Toronto, in 3-1 win vs. Detroit.
 — **Bryan Trottier, NY Islanders,** April 8, 1980 at New York, in 8-1 win vs. Los Angeles.
 — **Bobby Lalonde, Boston,** April 11, 1981 at Minnesota, in 6-3 win by Minnesota.
 — **Wayne Gretzky, Edmonton,** April 6, 1983 at Edmonton, in 6-3 win vs. Winnipeg.
 — **Jari Kurri, Edmonton,** April 24, 1983, at Edmonton, in 8-3 win vs. Chicago.
 — **Mark Messier, NY Rangers,** April 21, 1992, at New York, in 7-3 loss vs. New Jersey.
 — **Tom Fitzgerald, NY Islanders,** May 8, 1993, at Long Island, in 6-5 win vs. Pittsburgh.

MOST ASSISTS, ONE GAME:
6 — **Mikko Leinonen, NY Rangers,** April 8, 1982, at New York. Final score: NY Rangers 7, Philadelphia 3.
 — **Wayne Gretzky, Edmonton,** April 9, 1987, at Edmonton. Final score: Edmonton 13, Los Angeles 3.
5 — Toe Blake, Montreal, March 23, 1944, at Montreal. Final score: Montreal 5, Toronto 1.
 — Maurice Richard, Montreal, March 27, 1956, at Montreal. Final score: Montreal 7, NY Rangers 0.
 — Bert Olmstead, Montreal, March 30, 1957, at Montreal. Final score: Montreal 8, NY Rangers 3.
 — Don McKenney, Boston, April 5, 1958, at Boston. Final score: Boston 8, NY Rangers 2.
 — Stan Mikita, Chicago, April 4, 1973, at Chicago. Final score: Chicago 7, St. Louis 1.
 — Wayne Gretzky, Edmonton, April 8, 1981, at Montreal. Final score: Edmonton 6, Montreal 3.
 — Paul Coffey, Edmonton, May 14, 1985, at Edmonton. Final score: Edmonton 10, Chicago 5.
 — Doug Gilmour, St. Louis, April 15, 1986, at Minnesota. Final score: St. Louis 6, Minnesota 3.
 — Risto Siltanen, Quebec, April 14, 1987 at Hartford. Final score: Quebec 7, Hartford 5.
 — Patrik Sundstrom, New Jersey, April 22, 1988, at New Jersey. Final score: New Jersey 10, Washington 4.

MOST PENALTY MINUTES, ONE GAME:
42 — **Dave Schultz, Philadelphia,** April 22, 1976, at Toronto. One minor, 2 majors, 1 10-minute misconduct and 2 game-misconducts. Final score: Toronto 8, Philadelphia 5.

MOST PENALTIES, ONE GAME:
8 — **Forbes Kennedy, Toronto,** April 2, 1969, at Boston. Four minors, 2 majors, 1 10-minute misconduct, 1 game misconduct. Final score: Boston 10, Toronto 0.
 — **Kim Clackson, Pittsburgh,** April 14, 1980, at Boston. Five minors, 2 majors, 1 10-minute misconduct. Final score: Boston 6, Pittsburgh 2

MOST POINTS, ONE PERIOD:
4 — **Maurice Richard, Montreal,** March 29, 1945, at Montreal vs. Toronto. Third period, 3 goals, 1 assist. Final score: Montreal 10, Toronto 3.
 — **Dickie Moore, Montreal,** March 25, 1954, at Montreal vs. Boston. First period, 2 goals, 2 assists. Final score: Montreal 8, Boston 1.
 — **Barry Pederson, Boston,** April 8, 1982, at Boston vs. Buffalo. Second period, 3 goals, 1 assist. Final score: Boston 7, Buffalo 3.
 — **Peter McNab, Boston,** April 11, 1982, at Buffalo. Second period, 1 goal, 3 assists. Final score: Boston 5, Buffalo 2.
 — **Tim Kerr, Philadelphia,** April 13, 1985 at New York. Second period, 4 goals. Final score: Philadelphia 6, Rangers 5.
 — **Ken Linseman, Boston,** April 14, 1985 at Boston vs. Montreal. Second period, 2 goals, 2 assists. Final score: Boston 7, Montreal 6.
 — **Wayne Gretzky, Edmonton,** April 12, 1987, at Los Angeles. Third period, 1 goal, 3 assists. Final score: Edmonton 6, Los Angeles 3.
 — **Glenn Anderson, Edmonton,** April 6, 1988, at Edmonton vs. Winnipeg. Third period, 3 goals, 1 assist. Final score: Edmonton 7, Winnipeg 4.
 — **Mario Lemieux, Pittsburgh,** April 25, 1989, at Pittsburgh vs. Philadelphia. First period, 4 goals. Final score: Pittsburgh 10, Philadelphia 7.
 — **Dave Gagner, Minnesota,** April 8, 1991, at Minnesota vs. Chicago. First period, 2 goals, 2 assists. Final score: Chicago 6, Minnesota 5.
 — **Mario Lemieux, Pittsburgh,** April 23, 1992, at Pittsburgh vs. Washington. Second period, 2 goals, 2 assists. Final score: Pittsburgh 6, Washington 4.

MOST GOALS, ONE PERIOD:
4 — Tim Kerr, Philadelphia, April 13, 1985, at New York vs. NY Rangers, second period. Final score: Philadelphia 6, NY Rangers 5.
— **Mario Lemieux, Pittsburgh,** April 25, 1989, at Pittsburgh vs. Philadelphia, first period. Final score: Pittsburgh 10, Philadelphia 7.
3 — Harvey (Busher) Jackson, Toronto, April 5, 1932, at New York vs. NY Rangers, second period. Final score: Toronto 6, NY Rangers 4.
— Maurice Richard, Montreal, March 23, 1944, at Montreal vs. Toronto, second period. Final score: Montreal 5, Toronto 1.
— Maurice Richard, Montreal, March 29, 1945, at Montreal vs. Toronto, third period. Final score: Montreal 10, Toronto 3.
— Maurice Richard, Montreal, April 6, 1957 at Montreal vs. Boston, second period. Final score: Montreal 5, Boston 1.
— Ted Lindsay, Detroit, April 5, 1955, at Detroit vs. Montreal, second period. Final score: Detroit 7, Montreal 1.
— Red Berenson, St. Louis, April 15, 1969, at St. Louis vs. Los Angeles, second period. Final score: St. Louis 4, Los Angeles 0.
— Jacques Lemaire, Montreal, April 20, 1971, at Montreal vs. Minnesota, second period. Final score: Montreal 7, Minnesota 2.
— Rick MacLeish, Philadelphia, April 11, 1974, at Philadelphia vs. Atlanta, second period. Final score: Philadelphia 5, Atlanta 1.
— Tom Williams, Los Angeles, April 14, 1974, at Los Angeles vs. Chicago, third period. Final score: Los Angeles 5, Chicago 1.
— Darryl Sittler, Toronto, April 22, 1976, at Toronto vs. Philadelphia, second period. Final score: Toronto 8, Philadelphia 5.
— Reggie Leach, Philadelphia, May 6, 1976, at Philadelphia vs. Boston, second period. Final score: Philadelphia 6, Boston 3.
— Bobby Schmautz, Boston, April 11, 1977, at Boston vs. Los Angeles, first period. Final score: Boston 8, Los Angeles 3.
— George Ferguson, Toronto, April 11, 1978, at Toronto vs. Los Angeles, third period. Final score: Toronto 7, Los Angeles 3.
— Barry Pederson, Boston, April 8, 1982, at Boston vs. Buffalo, second period. Final score: Boston 7, Buffalo 3.
— Peter Stastny, Quebec, April 5, 1983, at Boston, first period. Final score: Boston 4, Quebec 3.
— Wayne Gretzky, Edmonton, April 6, 1983 at Edmonton, second period. Final score: Edmonton 6, Winnipeg 3.
— Mike Bossy, NY Islanders, May 7, 1983 at New York, second period. Final score: NY Islanders 8, Boston 4.
— Dave Andreychuk, Buffalo, April 14, 1985, at Buffalo vs. Quebec, third period. Final score: Buffalo 7, Quebec 4.
— Wayne Gretzky, Edmonton, May 25, 1985, at Edmonton vs. Philadelphia, first period. Final score: Edmonton 4, Philadelphia 3.
— Glenn Anderson, Edmonton, April 6, 1988, at Edmonton vs. Winnipeg, third period. Final score: Edmonton 7, Winnipeg 4.
— Tim Kerr, Philadelphia, April 19, 1989, at Pittsburgh vs. Penguins, first period. Final score: Philadelphia 4, Pittsburgh 2.
— Petr Klima, Edmonton, May 4, 1991, at Edmonton vs. Minnesota, first period. Final score: Edmonton 7, Minnesota 2.
— Dino Ciccarelli, Washington, April 25, 1992, at Pittsburgh, third period. Final score: Washington 7, Pittsburgh 2.
— Kevin Stevens, Pittsburgh, May 17, 1992, at Boston, first period. Final score: Pittsburgh 5, Boston 1.
— Dirk Graham, Chicago, June 1, 1992, at Chicago vs. Pittsburgh, first period. Final score: Pittsburgh 6, Chicago 5.
— Ray Ferraro, NY Islanders, April 26, 1993, at Washington, third period. Final score: Washington 6, NY Islanders 4.
— Mark Messier, NY Rangers, May 25, 1994, at New Jersey, third period. Final score: NY Rangers 4, New Jersey 2.
— Brendan Shanahan, St. Louis, May 13, 1995, at Vancouver, second period. Final score: St. Louis 5, Vancouver 2.

MOST POWER-PLAY GOALS, ONE PERIOD:
3 — Tim Kerr, Philadelphia, April 13, 1985 at New York, second period in 6-5 win vs. NY Rangers.
2 — Two power-play goals have been scored by one player in one period on 43 occasions. Charlie Conacher of Toronto was the first to score two power-play goals in one period, setting the mark on Mar. 26, 1936. Dmitri Mironov of Toronto is the most recent to equal this mark with two power-play goals in the second period at Toronto, May 18, 1994. Final score: Vancouver 4, Toronto 3.

MOST SHORTHAND GOALS, ONE PERIOD:
2 — Bryan Trottier, NY Islanders, April 8, 1980, second period at New York in 8-1 win vs. Los Angeles.
— **Bobby Lalonde, Boston,** April 11, 1981, third period at Minnesota in 6-3 win by Minnesota.
— **Jari Kurri, Edmonton,** April 24, 1983, third period at Edmonton in 8-4 win vs. Chicago.

MOST ASSISTS, ONE PERIOD:
3 — Three assists by one player in one period of a playoff game has been recorded on 62 occasions. Vyacheslav Kozlov of the Detroit Red Wings is the most recent to equal this mark with 3 assists in the third period at Detroit, May 21, 1995. Final score: Detroit 6, San Jose 0.
Wayne Gretzky has had 3 assists in one period 5 times; Ray Bourque, 3 times; Toe Blake, Jean Beliveau, Doug Harvey and Bobby Orr, twice. Nick Metz of Toronto was the first player to be credited with 3 assists in one period of a playoff game Mar. 21, 1941 at Toronto vs. Boston.

MOST PENALTIES, ONE PERIOD AND MOST PENALTY MINUTES, ONE PERIOD:
6 Penalties; 39 Minutes — Ed Hospodar, NY Rangers, April 9, 1981, at Los Angeles, first period. Two minors, 1 major, 1 10-minute misconduct, 2 game misconducts. Final score: Los Angeles 5, NY Rangers 4.

FASTEST TWO GOALS:
5 Seconds — Norm Ullman, Detroit, at Detroit, April 11, 1965, vs. Chicago and goaltender Glenn Hall. Ullman scored at 17:35 and 17:40 of second period. Detroit won 4-2.

FASTEST GOAL FROM START OF GAME:
6 Seconds — Don Kozak, Los Angeles, April 17, 1977, at Los Angeles vs. Boston and goaltender Gerry Cheevers. Los Angeles won 7-4.
7 Seconds — Bob Gainey, Montreal, May 5, 1977, at New York vs. NY Islanders and goaltender Glenn Resch. Montreal won 2-1.
— Terry Murray, Philadelphia, April 12, 1981, at Quebec vs. goaltender Dan Bouchard. Quebec won 4-3 in overtime.
8 Seconds — Stan Smyl, Vancouver, April 7, 1982, at Vancouver vs. Calgary and goaltender Pat Riggin. Vancouver won 5-3.

FASTEST GOAL FROM START OF PERIOD (OTHER THAN FIRST):
6 Seconds — Pelle Eklund, Phiadelphia, April 25, 1989, at Pittsburgh vs. goaltender Tom Barrasso, second period. Pittsburgh won 10-7.
9 Seconds — Bill Collins, Minnesota, April 9, 1968, at Minnesota vs. Los Angeles and goaltender Wayne Rutledge, third period. Minnesota won 7-5.
— Dave Balon, Minnesota, April 25, 1968, at St. Louis vs. goaltender Glenn Hall, third period. Minnesota won 5-1.
— Murray Oliver, Minnesota, April 8, 1971, at St. Louis vs. goaltender Ernie Wakely, third period. St. Louis won 4-2.
— Clark Gillies, NY Islanders, April 15, 1977, at Buffalo vs. goaltender Don Edwards, third period. NY Islanders won 4-3.
— Eric Vail, Atlanta, April 11, 1978, at Atlanta vs. Detroit and goaltender Ron Low, third period. Detroit won 5-3.
— Stan Smyl, Vancouver, April 10, 1979, at Philadelphia vs. goaltender Wayne Stephenson, third period. Vancouver won 3-2.
— Wayne Gretzky, Edmonton, April 6, 1983, at Edmonton vs. Winnipeg and goaltender Brian Hayward, second period. Edmonton won 6-3.
— Mark Messier, Edmonton, April 16, 1984, at Calgary vs. goaltender Don Edwards, third period. Edmonton won 5-3.
— Brian Skrudland, Montreal, May 18, 1986 at Calgary vs. goaltender Mike Vernon, overtime. Montreal won 3-2.

FASTEST TWO GOALS FROM START OF GAME:
1 Minute, 8 Seconds — Dick Duff, Toronto, April 9, 1963 at Toronto vs. Detroit and goaltender Terry Sawchuk. Duff scored at 49 seconds and 1:08. Final score: Toronto 4, Detroit 2.

FASTEST TWO GOALS FROM START OF PERIOD:
35 Seconds — Pat LaFontaine, NY Islanders, May 19, 1984 at Edmonton vs. goaltender Andy Moog. LaFontaine scored at 13 and 35 seconds of third period. Final score: Edmonton 5, NY Islanders 2.

Early Playoff Records

1893-1918
Team Records

MOST GOALS, BOTH TEAMS, ONE GAME:
25 — Ottawa Silver Seven, Dawson City at Ottawa, Jan. 16, 1905. Ottawa 23, Dawson City 2. Ottawa won best-of-three series 2-0.

MOST GOALS, ONE TEAM, ONE GAME:
23 — Ottawa Silver Seven at Ottawa, Jan. 16, 1905. Ottawa defeated Dawson City 23-2.

MOST GOALS, BOTH TEAMS, BEST-OF-THREE SERIES:
42 — Ottawa Silver Seven, Queen's University at Ottawa, 1906. Ottawa defeated Queen's 16-7, Feb. 27, and 12-7, Feb. 28.

MOST GOALS, ONE TEAM, BEST-OF-THREE SERIES:
32 — Ottawa Silver Seven in 1905 at Ottawa. Defeated Dawson City 9-2, Jan. 13, and 23-2, Jan. 16.

MOST GOALS, BOTH TEAMS, BEST-OF-FIVE SERIES:
39 — Toronto Arenas, Vancouver Millionaires at Toronto, 1918. Toronto won 5-3, Mar. 20; 6-3, Mar. 26; 2-1, Mar. 30. Vancouver won 6-4, Mar. 23, and 8-1, Mar. 28. Toronto scored 18 goals; Vancouver 21.

MOST GOALS, ONE TEAM, BEST-OF-FIVE SERIES:
26 — Vancouver Millionaires in 1915 at Vancouver. Defeated Ottawa Senators 6-2, Mar. 22; 8-3, Mar. 24; and 12-3 Mar. 26.

Individual Records

MOST GOALS IN PLAYOFFS:
63 — Frank McGee, Ottawa Silver Seven, in 22 playoff games. Seven goals in four games, 1903; 21 goals in eight games, 1904; 18 goals in four games, 1905; 17 goals in six games, 1906.

MOST GOALS, ONE PLAYOFF SERIES:
15 — Frank McGee, Ottawa Silver Seven, in two games in 1905 at Ottawa. Scored one goal, Jan. 13, in 9-2 victory over Dawson City and 14 goals, Jan. 16, in 23-2 victory.

MOST GOALS, ONE PLAYOFF GAME:
14 — Frank McGee, Ottawa Silver Seven, Jan. 16, 1905 at Ottawa in 23-2 victory over Dawson City.

FASTEST THREE GOALS:
40 Seconds — Marty Walsh, Ottawa Senators, at Ottawa, March 16, 1911, at 3:00, 3:10, and 3:40 of third period. Ottawa defeated Port Arthur 13-4.

Denis Savard returned to the Chicago Blackhawks in April, 1995 and became the 10th player in NHL history to collect 100 post-season assists.

All-Time Playoff Goal Leaders since 1918

(40 or more goals)

Player	Teams	Yrs.	GP	G
* Wayne Gretzky	Edm., L.A.	14	180	110
* Jari Kurri	Edm., L.A.	12	174	102
* Mark Messier	Edm., NYR	15	210	102
* Glenn Anderson	Edm., Tor., NYR, St.L.	14	214	92
Mike Bossy	NY Islanders	10	129	85
Maurice Richard	Montreal	15	133	82
Jean Beliveau	Montreal	17	162	79
Bryan Trottier	NYI, Pit.	17	221	71
Gordie Howe	Det., Hfd.	20	157	68
* Dino Ciccarelli	Min., Wsh., Det.	13	124	67
* Denis Savard	Chi., Mtl.	14	153	65
Yvan Cournoyer	Montreal	12	147	64
Brian Propp	Phi., Bos., Min.	13	160	64
Bobby Smith	Min., Mtl.	13	184	64
Bobby Hull	Chi., Hfd.	14	119	62
Phil Esposito	Chi., Bos., NYR	15	130	61
Jacques Lemaire	Montreal	11	145	61
* Joe Mullen	St.L., Cgy., Pit.	14	142	60
Stan Mikita	Chicago	18	155	59
* Brett Hull	Cgy., St.L.	10	79	58
Guy Lafleur	Mtl., NYR	14	128	58
Bernie Geoffrion	Mtl., NYR	16	132	58
* Cam Neely	Van., Bos.	9	93	57
* Esa Tikkanen	Edm., NYR, St.L.	10	144	57
* Mario Lemieux	Pittsburgh	5	66	56
Steve Larmer	Chi., NYR	13	140	56
Denis Potvin	NY Islanders	14	185	56
Rick MacLeish	Phi., Pit., Det.	11	114	54
Bill Barber	Philadelphia	11	129	53
* Paul Coffey	Edm., Pit., L.A., Det.	13	155	53
* Stephane Richer	Mtl., N.J.	10	123	52
* Claude Lemieux	Mtl., N.J.	10	136	52
Frank Mahovlich	Tor., Det., Mtl.	14	137	51
Steve Shutt	Mtl., L.A.	12	99	50
Henri Richard	Montreal	18	180	49
* Doug Gilmour	St.L., Cgy., Tor.	11	130	48
Reggie Leach	Bos., Phi.	8	94	47
Ted Lindsay	Det., Chi.	16	133	47
Clark Gillies	NYI, Buf.	13	164	47
Dickie Moore	Mtl., Tor. St.L.	14	135	46
Rick Middleton	NYR, Bos.	12	114	45
Lanny McDonald	Tor., Cgy.	13	117	44
* Kevin Stevens	Pit.	6	86	43
Ken Linseman	Phi., Edm., Bos.	11	113	43
Bobby Clarke	Philadelphia	13	136	42
* Luc Robitaille	L.A., Pit.	8	85	41
* Brian Bellows	Min., Mtl.	10	105	41
John Bucyk	Det., Bos.	14	124	41
Tim Kerr	Phi., NYR	10	81	40
* Bernie Nicholls	L.A., NYR, Edm., N.J., Chi.	11	102	40
Peter McNab	Bos., Van.	10	107	40
Bob Bourne	NYI, L.A.	13	139	40
* Dale Hunter	Que., Wsh.	15	140	40
John Tonelli	NYI, Cgy., L.A.	13	172	40

* — Active player.

All-Time Playoff Assist Leaders since 1918

(60 or more assists)

Player	Teams	Yrs.	GP	A
* Wayne Gretzky	Edm., L.A.	14	180	236
* Mark Messier	Edm., NYR	15	210	170
* Jari Kurri	Edm., L.A.	12	174	120
* Paul Coffey	Edm., Pit., L.A., Det.	13	155	119
* Glenn Anderson	Edm., Tor., NYR, St.L.	14	214	117
Larry Robinson	Mtl., L.A.	20	227	116
Bryan Trottier	NYI, Pit.	17	221	113
Denis Potvin	NY Islanders	14	185	108
* Ray Bourque	Boston	16	157	106
* Denis Savard	Chi., Mtl.	14	153	105
* Doug Gilmour	St.L., Cgy., Tor.	11	130	104
Jean Beliveau	Montreal	17	162	97
Bobby Smith	Min., Mtl.	13	184	96
Gordie Howe	Det., Hfd.	20	157	92
Stan Mikita	Chicago	18	155	91
Brad Park	NYR, Bos., Det.	17	161	90
* Larry Murphy	L.A., Wsh., Min., Pit.	14	142	86
Chris Chelios	Mtl., Chi.	12	148	84
Brian Propp	Phi., Bos., Min.	13	160	84
* Adam Oates	Det., St.L., Bos.	9	200	84
* Al MacInnis	Cgy., St.L.	11	102	82
Henri Richard	Montreal	18	180	80
Jacques Lemaire	Montreal	11	145	78
* Craig Janney	Bos., St.L., S.J.	8	101	78
Ken Linseman	Phi., Edm., Bos.	11	113	77
Bobby Clarke	Philadelphia	13	136	77
Guy Lafleur	Mtl., NYR	14	128	76
Phil Esposito	Chi., Bos., NYR	15	130	76
Mike Bossy	NY Islanders	10	129	75
Steve Larmer	Chi., NYR	13	140	75
John Tonelli	NYI, Cgy., L.A.	13	172	75
* Peter Stastny	Que., N.J., St.L.	12	93	72
Gilbert Perreault	Buffalo	11	90	70
* Ron Francis	Hfd., Pit.	10	108	69
Alex Delvecchio	Detroit	14	121	69
Bobby Hull	Chi., Hfd.	14	119	67
Frank Mahovlich	Tor., Det., Mtl.	14	137	67
* Mario Lemieux	Pittsburgh	5	66	66
Bobby Orr	Boston	8	74	66
Bernie Federko	St. Louis	11	91	66
Jean Ratelle	NYR, Bos.	15	123	66
* Scott Stevens	Wsh., St. L., N.J.	13	132	66
* Charlie Huddy	Edm., L.A., Buf.	13	170	66
Dickie Moore	Mtl., Tor., St.L.	14	135	64
Doug Harvey	Mtl., NYR, St.L.	15	137	64
* Dale Hunter	Que., Wsh.	15	140	64
Yvan Cournoyer	Montreal	12	147	63
John Bucyk	Det., Bos.	14	124	62
* Neal Broten	Min., Dal., N.J.	12	133	62
Doug Wilson	Chicago	12	95	61
* Bernie Nicholls	L.A., NYR, Edm., N.J., Chi.	11	102	60
* Brian Bellows	Min., Mtl.	10	105	60

All-Time Playoff Point Leaders since 1918

(100 or more points)

Player	Teams	Yrs.	GP	G	A	Pts.
* Wayne Gretzky	Edm., L.A.	14	180	110	236	346
* Mark Messier	Edm., NYR	15	210	102	170	272
* Jari Kurri	Edm., L.A.	12	174	102	120	222
* Glenn Anderson	Edm., Tor., NYR., St.L.	14	214	92	117	209
Bryan Trottier	NYI, Pit.	17	221	71	113	184
Jean Beliveau	Montreal	17	162	79	97	176
* Paul Coffey	Edm., Pit., L.A., Det.	13	155	53	119	172
* Denis Savard	Chi., Mtl.	14	153	65	105	170
Denis Potvin	NY Islanders	14	185	56	108	164
Mike Bossy	NY Islanders	10	129	85	75	160
Gordie Howe	Det., Hfd.	20	157	68	92	160
Bobby Smith	Min., Mtl.	13	184	64	96	160
* Doug Gilmour	St.L., Cgy., Tor.	11	130	48	104	152
Stan Mikita	Chicago	18	155	59	91	150
Brian Propp	Phi., Bos., Min.	13	160	64	84	148
Larry Robinson	Mtl., L.A.	20	227	28	116	144
Jacques Lemaire	Montreal	11	145	61	78	139
* Ray Bourque	Boston	16	157	33	106	139
Phil Esposito	Chi., Bos., NYR	15	130	61	76	137
Guy Lafleur	Mtl., NYR	14	128	58	76	134
Steve Larmer	Chi., NYR	13	140	56	75	131
Bobby Hull	Chi., Hfd.	14	119	62	67	129
Henri Richard	Montreal	18	180	49	80	129
Yvan Cournoyer	Montreal	12	147	64	63	127
Maurice Richard	Montreal	15	133	82	44	126
Brad Park	NYR, Bos., Det.	17	161	35	90	125
* Mario Lemieux	Pittsburgh	5	66	56	66	122
Ken Linseman	Phi., Edm., Bos.	11	113	43	77	120
Bobby Clarke	Philadelphia	13	136	42	77	119
Bernie Geoffrion	Mtl., NYR	16	132	58	60	118
Frank Mahovlich	Tor., Det., Mtl.	14	137	51	67	118
* Larry Murphy	L.A., Wsh., Min., Pit.	14	142	30	86	116
John Tonelli	NYI, Cgy., L.A.	13	172	40	75	115
* Adam Oates	Det., St.L., Bos.	9	↑00	30	84	114
* Chris Chelios	Mtl., Chi.	12	148	28	84	112
* Dino Ciccarelli	Min., Wsh., Det.	13	124	67	43	110
Dickie Moore	Mtl., Tor., St.L.	14	135	46	64	110
* Esa Tikkanen	Edm., NYR, St.L.	10	144	57	52	109
* Al MacInnis	Cgy., St.L.	11	102	26	82	108
Bill Barber	Philadelphia	11	129	53	55	108
Rick MacLeish	Phi., Pit., Det.	11	114	54	53	107
* Joe Mullen	St.L., Cgy., Pit.	14	142	60	46	106
* Peter Stastny	Que., N.J., St.L.	12	93	33	72	105
* Ron Francis	Hfd., Pit.	10	108	35	69	104
Alex Delvecchio	Detroit	14	121	35	69	104
* Dale Hunter	Que., Wsh.	15	140	40	64	104
Gilbert Perreault	Buffalo	11	90	33	70	103
John Bucyk	Det., Bos.	14	124	41	62	103
Bernie Federko	St. Louis	11	91	35	66	101
* Craig Janney	Bos., St. L., S.J.	8	101	23	78	101
* Brian Bellows	Min., Mtl.	10	105	41	60	101
* Kevin Stevens	Pit.	6	36	43	57	100
* Bernie Nicholls	L.A., NYR, Edm., N.J., Chi.	11	102	40	60	100
Rick Middleton	NYR, Bos.	12	114	45	55	100

Three-or-more-Goal Games, Playoffs 1918–1995

Player	Team	Date	City	Total Goals	Opposing Goaltender	Score	
Wayne Gretzky (8)	Edm.	Apr. 11/81	Edm.	3	Richard Sevigny	Edm. 6	Mtl. 2
		Apr. 19/81	Edm.	3	Billy Smith	Edm. 5	NYI 2
		Apr. 6/83	Edm.	4	Brian Hayward	Edm. 6	Wpg. 3
		Apr. 17/83	Cgy.	4	Rejean Lemelin	Edm. 10	Cgy. 2
		Apr. 25/85	Wpg.	3	Bryan Hayward (2) Marc Behrend (1)	Edm. 8	Wpg. 3
		May 25/85	Edm.	3	Pelle Lindbergh	Edm. 4	Phi. 3
		Apr. 24/86	Cgy.	3	Mike Vernon	Edm. 7	Cgy. 4
	L.A.	May 29/93	Tor.	3	Felix Potvin	L.A. 5	Tor. 4
Maurice Richard (7)	Mtl.	Mar. 23/44	Mtl.	5	Paul Bibeault	Mtl. 5	Tor. 1
		Apr. 7/44	Chi.	3	Mike Karakas	Mtl. 3	Chi. 1
		Mar. 29/45	Mtl.	4	Frank McCool	Mtl. 10	Tor. 3
		Apr. 14/53	Bos.	3	Gord Henry	Mtl. 7	Bos. 3
		Mar. 20/56	Mtl.	3	Lorne Worsley	Mtl. 7	NYR 1
		Apr. 6/57	Mtl.	4	Don Simmons	Mtl. 5	Bos. 1
		Apr. 1/58	Det.	3	Terry Sawchuk	Mtl. 4	Det. 3
Jari Kurri (7)	Edm.	Apr. 4/84	Edm.	3	Doug Soetaert (1) Mike Veisor (2)	Edm. 9	Wpg. 2
		Apr. 25/85	Wpg.	3	Bryan Hayward (2) Marc Behrend (1)	Edm. 8	Wpg. 3
		May 7/85	Edm.	3	Murray Bannerman	Edm. 7	Chi. 3
		May 14/85	Edm.	3	Murray Bannerman	Edm. 10	Chi. 5
		May 16/85	Chi.	4	Murray Bannerman	Edm. 8	Chi. 2
		Apr. 9/87	Edm.	4	Roland Melanson (2) Daren Eliot (2)	Edm. 13	L.A. 3
		May 18/90	Bos.	3	Andy Moog (2) Rejean Lemelin (1)	Edm. 7	Bos. 2
Dino Ciccarelli (6)	Min.	May 5/81	Min.	3	Pat Riggin	Min. 7	Cgy. 4
		Apr. 10/82	Min.	3	Murray Bannerman	Min. 7	Chi. 1
	Wsh.	Apr. 5/90	N.J.	3	Sean Burke	Wsh. 5	N.J. 4
		Apr. 25/92	Pit.	4	Tom Barrasso (1) Ken Wregget (3)	Wsh. 7	Pit. 2
	Det.	Apr. 29/93	Tor.	3	Felix Potvin (2) Daren Puppa (1)	Det. 7	Tor. 3
		May 11/95	Dal.	3	Andy Moog (2) Darcy Wakaluk (1)	Det. 5	Dal. 1
Mike Bossy (5)	NYI	Apr. 16/79	NYI	3	Tony Esposito	NYI 6	Chi. 2
		May 8/82	NYI	3	Richard Brodeur	NYI 6	Van. 5
		Apr. 10/83	Wsh.	3	Al Jensen	NYI 6	Wsh. 3
		May 3/83	NYI	3	Pete Peeters	NYI 8	Bos. 3
		May 7/83	NYI	4	Pete Peeters	NYI 8	Bos. 4
Phil Esposito (4)	Bos.	Apr. 2/69	Bos.	4	Bruce Gamble	Bos. 10	Tor. 0
		Apr. 8/70	Bos.	3	Ed Giacomin	Bos. 8	NYR 2
		Apr. 19/70	Chi.	3	Tony Esposito	Bos. 6	Chi. 3
		Apr. 8/75	Bos.	3	Tony Esposito (2) Michel Dumas (1)	Bos. 8	Chi. 2
Mark Messier (4)	Edm.	Apr. 14/83	Edm.	4	Rejean Lemelin	Edm. 6	Cgy. 3
		Apr. 17/83	Cgy.	3	Rejean Lemelin (1) Don Edwards (2)	Edm. 10	Cgy. 2
		Apr. 26/83	Edm.	3	Murray Bannerman	Edm. 8	Chi. 2
	NYR	May 25/94	N.J.	3	Martin Brodeur (2) ENG (1)	NYR 4	N.J. 2
Bernie Geoffrion (3)	Mtl.	Mar. 27/52	Mtl.	3	Jim Henry	Mtl. 4	Bos. 0
		Apr. 7/55	Mtl.	3	Terry Sawchuk	Mtl. 4	Det. 2
		Mar. 30/57	Mtl.	3	Lorne Worsley	Mtl. 8	NYR 3
Norm Ullman (3)	Det.	Mar. 29/64	Chi.	3	Glenn Hall	Det. 5	Chi. 4
		Apr. 7/64	Det.	3	Glenn Hall (2) Denis DeJordy (1)	Det. 7	Chi. 2
		Apr. 11/65	Det.	3	Glenn Hall	Det. 4	Chi. 2
John Bucyk (3)	Bos.	May 3/70	St. L.	3	Jacques Plante (1) Ernie Wakely (2)	Bos. 6	St. L. 1
		Apr. 20/72	Bos.	3	Jacques Caron (1) Ernie Wakely (2)	Bos. 10	St. L. 2
		Apr. 21/74	Bos.	3	Tony Esposito	Bos. 8	Chi. 6
Rick MacLeish (3)	Phil	Apr. 11/74	Phil	3	Phil Myre	Phi. 5	Atl. 1
		Apr. 13/75	Phil	3	Gord McRae	Phi. 6	Tor. 3
		May 13/75	Phil	3	Glenn Resch	Phi. 4	NYI 1
Denis Savard (3)	Chi.	Apr. 19/82	Chi.	3	Mike Liut	Chi. 7	StL. 4
		Apr. 10/86	Chi.	4	Ken Wregget	Tor. 6	Chi. 4
		Apr. 9/88	St. L.	3	Greg Millen	Chi. 6	St. L. 3
Tim Kerr (3)	Phi.	Apr. 13/85	NYR	4	Glen Hanlon	Phi. 6	NYR 5
		Apr. 20/87	Phi.	3	Kelly Hrudey	Phi. 4	NYI 2
		Apr. 19/89	Pit.	3	Tom Barrasso	Phi. 4	Pit. 2
Cam Neely (3)	Bos.	Apr. 9/87	Mtl.	3	Patrick Roy	Mtl. 4	Bos. 3
		Apr. 5/91	Bos.	3	Peter Sidorkiewicz	Bos. 4	Hfd. 3
		Apr. 25/91	Bos.	3	Patrick Roy	Bos. 4	Mtl. 1
Petr Klima (3)	Det.	Apr. 7/88	Tor.	3	Alan Bester (2) Ken Wregett (1)	Det. 6	Tor. 2
		Apr. 21/88	St. L.	3	Greg Millen	Det. 6	St. L. 0
	Edm.	May 4/91	Edm.	3	Jon Casey	Edm. 7	Min. 2
Esa Tikkanen (3)	Edm.	May 22/88	Edm.	3	Rejean Lemelin	Edm. 6	Bos. 3
		Apr. 16/91	Cgy.	3	Mike Vernon	Edm. 5	Cgy. 4
		Apr. 26/92	L.A.	3	Kelly Hrudey	Edm. 5	L.A. 2
Newsy Lalonde (2)	Mtl.	Mar. 1/19	Mtl.	5	Clint Benedict	Mtl. 6	Ott. 3
		Mar. 22/19	Sea.	4	Harry Holmes	Mtl. 4	Sea. 2
Howie Morenz (2)	Mtl.	Mar. 22/24	Mtl.	3	Charles Reid	Mtl. 6	Cgy.T. 1
		Mar. 27/25	Mtl.	3	Harry Holmes	Mtl. 4	Vic. 2
Toe Blake (2)	Mtl.	Mar. 22/38	Mtl.	3	Mike Karakas	Mtl. 6	Chi. 4
		Mar. 26/46	Chi.	3	Mike Karakas	Mtl. 7	Chi. 2
Doug Bentley (2)	Chi.	Mar. 28/44	Chi.	3	Connie Dion	Chi. 7	Det. 1
		Mar. 30/44	Det.	3	Connie Dion	Chi. 5	Det. 2

Player	Team	Date	City	Total Goals	Opposing Goaltender	Score	
Ted Kennedy (2)	Tor.	Apr. 14/45	Tor.	3	Harry Lumley	Det. 5	Tor. 3
		Mar. 27/48	Tor.	4	Frank Brimsek	Tor. 5	Bos. 3
Bobby Hull (2)	Chi.	Apr. 7/63	Det.	3	Terry Sawchuk	Det. 7	Chi. 4
		Apr. 9/72	Pitt	3	Jim Rutherford	Chi. 6	Pit. 5
F. St. Marseille (2)	St. L.	Apr. 28/70	St. L.	3	Al Smith	St. L. 5	Pit. 0
		Apr. 6/72	Min.	3	Cesare Maniago	Min. 6	St. L. 5
Pit Martin (2)	Chi.	Apr. 4/73	Chi.	3	W. Stephenson	Chi. 7	St. L. 1
		May 10/73	Chi.	3	Ken Dryden	Mtl. 6	Chi. 4
Yvan Cournoyer (2)	Mtl.	Apr. 5/73	Mtl.	3	Dave Dryden	Mtl. 7	Buf. 3
		Apr. 11/74	Mtl.	3	Ed Giacomin	Mtl. 4	NYR 1
Guy Lafleur (2)	Mtl.	May 1/75	Mtl.	3	Roger Crozier (1) Gerry Desjardins (2)	Mtl. 7	Buf. 0
		Apr. 11/77	Mtl.	3	Ed Staniowski	Mtl. 7	St. L. 2
Lanny McDonald (2)	Tor.	Apr. 9/77	Pitt	3	Denis Herron	Tor. 5	Pit. 2
		Apr. 17/77	Tor.	4	W. Stephenson	Phi. 6	Tor. 5
Butch Goring (2)	L.A.	Apr. 9/77	L.A.	3	Phil Myre	L.A. 4	Atl. 2
	NYI	May 17/81	Min.	3	Gilles Meloche	NYI 7	Min. 5
Bryan Trottier (2)	NYI	Apr. 8/80	NYI	3	Doug Keans	NYI 8	L.A. 1
		Apr. 9/81	NYI	3	Michel Larocque	NYI 5	Tor. 1
Bill Barber (2)	Phil	May 4/80	Min.	4	Gilles Meloche	Phi. 5	Min. 3
		Apr. 9/81	Phil	3	Dan Bouchard	Phi. 8	Que. 5
Brian Propp (2)	Phi.	Apr. 22/81	Phi.	3	Pat Riggin	Phi. 9	Cgy. 4
		Apr. 21/85	Phi.	3	Billy Smith	Phi. 5	NYI 2
Paul Reinhart (2)	Cgy	Apr. 14/83	Edm.	3	Andy Moog	Edm. 6	Cgy. 3
		Apr. 8/84	Van	3	Richard Brodeur	Cgy. 5	Van. 1
Peter Stastny (2)	Que.	Apr. 5/83	Bos.	3	Pete Peeters	Bos. 4	Que. 3
		Apr. 11/87	Que.	3	Mike Liut (2) Steve Weeks (1)	Que. 5	Hfd. 1
Glenn Anderson (2)	Edm.	Apr. 26/83	Edm.	4	Murray Bannerman	Edm. 8	Chi. 2
		Apr. 6/88	Wpg.	3	Daniel Berthiaume	Edm. 7	Wpg. 4
Michel Goulet (2)	Que.	Apr. 23/85	Que.	3	Steve Penney	Que. 7	Mtl. 6
		Apr. 12/87	Que.	3	Mike Liut	Que. 4	Hfd. 1
Peter Zezel (2)	Phi.	Apr. 13/86	NYR	3	J. Vanbiesbrouck	Phi. 7	NYR 1
	St. L.	Apr. 11/89	St. L.	3	Jon Casey (2) Kari Takko (1)	St. L. 6	Min. 1
Steve Yzerman (2)	Det.	Apr. 6/89	Det.	3	Alain Chevrier	Chi. 5	Det. 4
		Apr. 4/91	St. L.	3	Vincent Riendeau (2) Pat Jablonski (1)	Det. 6	St. L. 3
Mario Lemieux (2)	Pit.	Apr. 25/89	Pit.	5	Ron Hextall	Pit. 10	Phi. 7
		Apr. 23/92	Pit.	3	Don Beaupre	Pit. 6	Wsh. 4
Mike Gartner (2)	NYR	Apr. 13/90	NYR	3	Mark Fitzpatrick (2) Glenn Healy (1)	NYR 6	NYI 5
		Apr. 27/92	NYR	3	Chris Terreri	NYR 8	N.J. 5
Geoff Courtnall (2)	Van.	Apr. 4/91	L.A.	3	Kelly Hrudey	Van. 6	L.A. 5
		Apr. 30/92	Van.	3	Rick Tabaracci	Van. 5	Win. 5
Harry Meeking	Tor.	Mar. 11/18	Tor.	3	Georges Vezina	Tor. 7	Mtl. 3
Alf Skinner	Tor.	Mar. 23/18	Tor.	3	Hugh Lehman	Van.M. 6	Tor. 4
Joe Malone	Mtl.	Feb. 23/19	Mtl.	3	Clint Benedict	Mtl. 8	Ott. 4
Odie Cleghorn	Mtl.	Feb. 27/19	Ott.	3	Clint Benedict	Mtl. 5	Ott. 3
Jack Darragh	Ott.	Apr. 1/20	Tor.	3	Harry Holmes	Ott. 6	Sea. 1
George Boucher	Ott.	Mar. 10/21	Ott.	3	Jake Forbes	Ott. 5	Tor. 0
Babe Dye	Tor.	Mar. 28/22	Tor.	4	Hugh Lehman	Tor. 5	Van.M. 1
Perk Galbraith	Bos.	Mar. 31/27	Bos.	3	Hugh Lehman	Bos. 4	Chi. 4
Busher Jackson	Tor.	Apr. 5/32	NYR	3	John Ross Roach	Tor. 6	NYR 4
Frank Boucher	NYR	Apr. 9/32	Tor.	3	Lorne Chabot	Tor. 6	NYR 4
Charlie Conacher	Tor.	Mar. 26/36	Tor.	3	Tiny Thompson	Tor. 8	Bos. 3
Syd Howe	Det.	Mar. 23/39	Det.	3	Claude Bourque	Det. 7	Mtl. 3
Bryan Hextall	NYR	Apr. 3/40	NYR	3	Turk Broda	NYR 6	Tor. 2
Joe Benoit	Mtl.	Mar. 22/41	Mtl.	3	Sam LoPresti	Mtl. 4	Chi. 3
Syl Apps	Tor.	Mar. 25/41	Tor.	3	Frank Brimsek	Tor. 7	Bos. 2
Jack McGill	Bos.	Mar. 29/42	Bos.	3	Johnny Mowers	Det. 6	Bos. 4
Don Metz	Tor.	Apr. 14/42	Tor.	3	Johnny Mowers	Tor. 9	Det. 3
Mud Bruneteau	Det.	Apr. 1/43	Det.	3	Frank Brimsek	Det. 6	Bos. 2
Don Grosso	Det.	Apr. 7/43	Bos.	3	Frank Brimsek	Det. 4	Bos. 0
Carl Liscombe	Det.	Apr. 3/45	Bos.	4	Paul Bibeault	Det. 5	Bos. 3
Billy Reay	Mtl.	Apr. 1/47	Bos.	4	Frank Brimsek	Mtl. 5	Bos. 1
Gerry Plamondon	Mtl.	Mar. 24/49	Det.	3	Harry Lumley	Mtl. 4	Det. 3
Sid Smith	Tor.	Apr. 10/49	Det.	3	Harry Lumley	Tor. 3	Det. 1
Pentti Lund	NYR	Apr. 2/50	NYR	3	Bill Durnan	NYR 4	Mtl. 1
Ted Lindsay	Det.	Apr. 5/55	Det.	4	Charlie Hodge (1) Jacques Plante (3)	Det. 7	Mtl. 1
Gordie Howe	Det.	Apr. 10/55	Det.	3	Jacques Plante	Det. 5	Mtl. 1
Phil Goyette	Mtl.	Mar. 25/58	Mtl.	3	Terry Sawchuk	Mtl. 8	Det. 1
Jerry Toppazzini	Bos.	Apr. 5/58	Bos.	3	Lorne Worsley	Bos. 8	NYR 2
Bob Pulford	Tor.	Apr. 19/62	Tor.	3	Glenn Hall	Tor. 8	Chi. 4
Dave Keon	Tor.	Apr. 9/64	Mtl.	3	Charlie Hodge	Tor. 3	Mtl. 1
Henri Richard	Mtl.	Apr. 20/67	Mtl.	3	Terry Sawchuk (2) Johnny Bower (1)	Mtl. 6	Tor. 2
Rosaire Paiement	Phi.	Apr. 13/68	Phi.	3	Glenn Hall (1) Seth Martin (2)	Phi. 6	St. L. 1
Jean Beliveau	Mtl.	Apr. 20/68	Mtl.	3	Denis DeJordy	Mtl. 4	Chi. 1
Red Berenson	St. L.	Apr. 15/69	St. L.	3	Gerry Desjardins	St. L. 4	L.A. 0
Ken Schinkel	Pit.	Apr. 11/70	Oak.	3	Gary Smith	Pit. 5	Oak. 2
Jim Pappin	Chi.	Apr. 11/71	Phi.	3	Bruce Gamble	Chi. 6	Phi. 2
Bobby Orr	Bos.	Apr. 11/71	Mtl.	3	Ken Dryden	Bos. 5	Mtl. 2
Jacques Lemaire	Mtl.	Apr. 20/71	Mtl.	3	Lorne Worsley	Mtl. 7	Min. 2
Vic Hadfield	NYR	Apr. 22/71	NYR	3	Tony Esposito	NYR 4	Chi. 1
Fred Stanfield	Bos.	Apr. 18/72	Bos.	3	Jacques Caron	Bos. 6	St. L. 1
Ken Hodge	Bos.	Apr. 30/72	Bos.	3	Ed Giacomin	Bos. 6	NYR 5
Steve Vickers	NYR	Apr. 10/73	Bos.	3	Ross Brooks (2) Ed Johnston (1)	NYR 6	Bos. 3
Dick Redmond	Chi.	Apr. 4/73	Chi.	3	Wayne Stephenson	Chi. 7	St. L. 1
Tom Williams	L.A.	Apr. 14/74	L.A.	3	Mike Veisor	L.A. 5	Chi. 1

Player	Team	Date	City	Total Goals	Opposing Goaltender	Score	
Marcel Dionne	L.A.	Apr. 15/76	L.A.	3	Gilles Gilbert	L.A. 6	Bos. 4
Don Saleski	Phi.	Apr. 20/76	Phi.	3	Wayne Thomas	Phi. 7	Tor. 1
Darryl Sittler	Tor.	Apr. 22/76	Tor.	5	Bernie Parent	Tor. 8	Phi. 5
Reggie Leach	Phi.	May 6/76	Phi.	3	Gilles Gilbert	Phi. 6	Bos. 3
Jim Lorentz	Buf.	Apr. 7/77	Min.	3	Pete LoPresti (2) Gary Smith (1)	Buf. 7	Min. 1
Bobby Schmautz	Bos.	Apr. 11/77	Bos.	3	Rogatien Vachon	Bos. 8	L.A. 3
Billy Harris	NYI	Apr. 23/77	Mtl.	3	Ken Dryden	Mtl. 4	NYI 3
George Ferguson	Tor.	Apr. 11/78	Tor.	3	Rogatien Vachon	Tor. 7	L.A. 3
Jean Ratelle	Bos.	May 3/79	Bos.	3	Ken Dryden	Bos. 4	Mtl. 3
Stan Jonathan	Bos.	May 8/79	Bos.	3	Ken Dryden	Bos. 5	Mtl. 2
Ron Duguay	NYR	Apr. 20/80	NYR	3	Pete Peeters	NYR 4	Phi. 2
Steve Shutt	Mtl.	Apr. 22/80	Mtl.	3	Gilles Meloche	Mtl. 6	Min. 2
Gilbert Perreault	Buf.	May 6/80	NYI	3	Billy Smith (2) ENG (1)	Buf. 7	NYI 4
Paul Holmgren	Phi.	May 15/80	Phil	3	Billy Smith	Phi. 8	NYI 3
Steve Payne	Min.	Apr. 8/81	Min.	3	Rogatien Vachon	Min. 5	Bos. 4
Denis Potvin	NYI	Apr. 17/81	NYI	3	Andy Moog	NYI 6	Edm. 3
Barry Pederson	Bos.	Apr. 8/82	Bos.	3	Don Edwards	Bos. 7	Buf. 3
Duane Sutter	NYI	Apr. 15/83	NYI	3	Glen Hanlon	NYI 5	NYR 0
Doug Halward	Van.	Apr. 7/84	Van.	3	Rejean Lemelin (2) Don Edwards (1)	Van. 7	Cgy. 0
Jorgen Pettersson	St. L.	Apr. 8/84	Det.	3	Ed Mio	St. L. 3	Det. 2
Clark Gillies	NYI	May 12/84	NYI	3	Grant Fuhr	NYI 6	Edm. 1
Ken Linseman	Bos.	Apr. 14/85	Bos.	3	Steve Penney	Bos. 7	Mtl. 6
Dave Andreychuk	Buf.	Apr. 14/85	Buf.	3	Dan Bouchard	Que. 4	Buf. 7
Greg Paslawski	StL.	Apr. 15/86	Min.	3	Don Beaupre	St. L. 6	Min. 3
Doug Risebrough	Cgy.	May 4/86	Cgy.	3	Rick Wamsley	Cgy. 8	St. L. 2
Mike McPhee	Mtl.	Apr. 11/87	Bos.	3	Doug Keans	Mtl. 5	Bos. 4
John Ogrodnick	Que.	Apr. 14/87	Hfd.	3	Mike Liut	Que. 7	Hfd. 5
Pelle Eklund	Phi.	May 10/87	Mtl.	3	Patrick Roy (1) Bryan Hayward (2)	Phi. 6	Mtl. 3
John Tucker	Buf.	Apr. 9/88	Bos.	4	Andy Moog	Buf. 6	Bos. 2
Tony Hrkac	St. L.	Apr. 10/88	St. L.	4	Darren Pang	St. L. 6	Chi. 5
Hakan Loob	Cgy.	Apr. 10/88	Cgy.	3	Glenn Healy	Cgy. 7	L.A. 3
Ed Olczyk	Tor.	Apr. 12/88	Tor.	3	Greg Stefan (2) Glen Hanlon (1)	Tor. 6	Det. 5
Aaron Broten	N.J.	Apr. 20/88	N.J.	3	Pete Peeters	N.J. 5	Wsh. 2
Mark Johnson	N.J.	Apr. 22/88	Wsh.	4	Pete Peeters	N.J. 10	Wsh. 4
Patrik Sundstrom	N.J.	Apr. 22/88	Wsh.	3	Pete Peeters (2) Clint Malarchuk (1)	N.J. 10	Wsh. 4
Bob Brooke	Min.	Apr. 5/89	St. L.	3	Greg Millen	St. L. 4	Min. 3
Chris Kontos	L.A.	Apr. 6/89	L.A.	3	Grant Fuhr	L.A. 5	Edm. 2
Wayne Presley	Chi.	Apr. 13/89	Chi.	3	Greg Stefan (1) Glen Hanlon (2)	Chi. 7	Det. 1
Tony Granato	L.A.	Apr. 10/90	L.A.	3	Mike Vernon (1) Rick Wamsley (2)	L.A. 12	Cgy. 4
Tomas Sandstrom	L.A.	Apr. 10/90	L.A.	3	Mike Vernon (1) Rick Wamsley (2)	L.A. 12	Cgy. 4
Dave Taylor	L.A.	Apr. 10/90	L.A.	3	Mike Vernon (1) Rick Wamsley (2)	L.A. 12	Cgy. 4
Bernie Nicholls	NYR	Apr. 19/90	NYR	3	Mike Liut	NYR 7	Wsh. 3
John Druce	Wsh.	Apr. 21/90	NYR	3	John Vanbiesbrouck	Wsh. 6	NYR 3
Adam Oates	St. L.	Apr. 12/91	St. L.	3	Tim Chevaldae	St. L. 6	Det. 1
Luc Robitaille	L.A.	Apr. 26/91	L.A.	3	Grant Fuhr	L.A. 5	Edm. 2
Ron Francis	Pit.	May 9/92	Pit.	3	Mike Liut (2) John V'brouck (1)	Pit. 5	NYR. 4
Dirk Graham	Chi.	June 1/92	Chi.	3	Tom Barrasso	Pit. 5	Chi. 2
Joe Murphy	Edm.	May 6/92	Edm.	3	Kirk McLean	Edm. 5	Van. 2
Ray Sheppard	Det.	Apr. 24/92	Min.	3	Jon Casey	Min. 5	Det. 2
Kevin Stevens	Pit.	May 21/92	Bos.	4	Andy Moog	Pit. 5	Bos. 2
Pavel Bure	Van.	Apr. 18/93	Wpg.	3	Rick Tabaracci	Van. 8	Wpg. 3
Brian Noonan	Chi.	Apr. 18/93	Chi.	3	Curtis Joseph	St. L. 4	Chi. 3
Dale Hunter	Wsh.	Apr. 20/93	Wsh.	3	Glenn Healy	NYI 5	Wsh. 4
Teemu Selanne	Wpg.	Apr. 23/93	Wpg.	3	Kirk McLean	Wpg. 5	Van. 4
Ray Ferraro	NYI	Apr. 26/93	Wsh.	3	Don Beaupre	Wsh. 6	NYI 4
Al Iafrate	Wsh.	Apr. 26/93	Wsh.	3	Glenn Healy (2) Mark Fitzpatrick (1)	Wsh. 6	NYI 4
Paul Di Pietro	Mtl.	Apr. 28/93	Mtl.	3	Ron Hextall	Mtl. 6	Que. 2
Wendel Clark	Tor.	May 27/93	L.A.	3	Kelly Hrudey	L.A. 5	Tor. 4
Eric Desjardins	Mtl.	Jun. 3/93	Mtl.	3	Kelly Hrudey	Mtl. 3	L.A. 2
Tony Amonte	Chi.	Apr. 23/94	Chi.	4	Felix Potvin	Chi. 5	Tor. 4
Gary Suter	Chi.	Apr. 24/94	Chi.	3	Felix Potvin	Chi. 4	Tor. 3
Ulf Dahlen	S.J.	May 6/94	S.J.	3	Felix Potvin	S.J. 5	Tor. 2
Joe Sakic	Que.	May 6/95	Que.	3	Mike Richter	Que. 5	NYR 4
Mike Sullivan	Cgy.	May 11/95	S.J.	3	Arturs Irbe (2) Wade Flaherty (1)	Cgy. 9	S.J. 2
Theoren Fleury	Cgy.	May 13/95	S.J.	3	Arturs Irbe (3) ENG (1)	Cgy. 6	S.J. 4
Brendan Shanahan	St. L.	May 13/95	Van.	3	Kirk McLean	St. L. 5	Van. 2
John LeClair	Phi.	May 21/95	Phi.	3	Mike Richter	Phi. 5	NYR 4
Brian Leetch	NYR	May 22/95	Phi.	3	Ron Hextall	Phi. 4	NYR 3

Leading Playoff Scorers, 1918–1995

Season	Player and Club	Games Played	Goals	Assists	Points
1994-95	Sergei Fedorov, Detroit	17	7	17	24
1993-94	Brian Leetch, NY Rangers	23	11	23	34
1992-93	Wayne Gretzky, Los Angeles	24	15	25	40
1991-92	Mario Lemieux, Pittsburgh	15	16	18	34
1990-91	Mario Lemieux, Pittsburgh	23	16	28	44
1989-90	Craig Simpson, Edmonton	22	16	15	31
	Mark Messier, Edmonton	22	9	22	31
1988-89	Al MacInnis, Calgary	22	7	24	31
1987-88	Wayne Gretzky, Edmonton	19	12	31	43
1986-87	Wayne Gretzky, Edmonton	21	5	29	34
1985-86	Doug Gilmour, St. Louis	19	9	12	21
	Bernie Federko, St. Louis	19	7	14	21
1984-85	Wayne Gretzky, Edmonton	18	17	30	47
1983-84	Wayne Gretzky, Edmonton	19	13	22	35
1982-83	Wayne Gretzky, Edmonton	16	12	26	38
1981-82	Bryan Trottier, NY Islanders	19	6	23	29
1980-81	Mike Bossy, NY Islanders	18	17	18	35
1979-80	Bryan Trottier, NY Islanders	21	12	17	29
1978-79	Jacques Lemaire, Montreal	16	11	12	23
	Guy Lafleur, Montreal	16	10	13	23
1977-78	Guy Lafleur, Montreal	15	10	11	21
	Larry Robinson, Montreal	15	4	17	21
1976-77	Guy Lafleur, Montreal	14	9	17	26
1975-76	Reggie Leach, Philadelphia	16	19	5	24
1974-75	Rick MacLeish, Philadelphia	17	11	9	20
1973-74	Rick MacLeish, Philadelphia	17	13	9	22
1972-73	Yvan Cournoyer, Montreal	17	15	10	25
1971-72	Phil Esposito, Boston	15	9	15	24
	Bobby Orr, Boston	15	5	19	24
1970-71	Frank Mahovlich, Montreal	20	14	13	27
1969-70	Phil Esposito, Boston	14	13	14	27
1968-69	Phil Esposito, Boston	10	8	10	18
1967-68	Bill Goldsworthy, Minnesota	14	8	7	15
1966-67	Jim Pappin, Toronto	12	7	8	15
1965-66	Norm Ullman, Detroit	12	6	9	15
1964-65	Bobby Hull, Chicago	14	10	7	17
1963-64	Gordie Howe, Detroit	14	9	10	19
1962-63	Gordie Howe, Detroit	11	7	9	16
	Norm Ullman, Detroit	11	4	12	16
1961-62	Stan Mikita, Chicago	12	6	15	21
1960-61	Gordie Howe, Detroit	11	4	11	15
	Pierre Pilote, Chicago	12	3	12	15
1959-60	Henri Richard, Montreal	8	3	9	12
	Bernie Geoffrion, Montreal	8	2	10	12
1958-59	Dickie Moore, Montreal	11	5	12	17
1957-58	Fleming Mackell, Boston	12	5	14	19
1956-57	Bernie Geoffrion, Montreal	11	11	7	18
1955-56	Jean Béliveau, Montreal	10	12	7	19
1954-55	Gordie Howe, Detroit	11	9	11	20
1953-54	Dickie Moore, Montreal	11	5	8	13
1952-53	Ed Sanford, Boston	11	8	3	11
1951-52	Ted Lindsay, Detroit	8	5	2	7
	Floyd Curry, Detroit	11	4	3	7
	Metro Prystai, Detroit	8	2	5	7
	Gordie Howe, Detroit	8	2	5	7
1950-51	Maurice Richard, Montreal	11	9	4	13
	Max Bentley, Toronto	11	2	11	13
1949-50	Pentti Lund, NY Rangers	12	6	5	11
1948-49	Gordie Howe, Detroit	11	8	3	11
1947-48	Ted Kennedy, Toronto	9	8	6	14
1946-47	Maurice Richard, Montreal	10	6	5	11
1945-46	Elmer Lach, Montreal	9	5	12	17
1944-45	Joe Carveth, Detroit	14	5	6	11
1943-44	Toe Blake, Montreal	9	7	11	18
1942-43	Carl Liscombe, Detroit	10	6	8	14
1941-42	Don Grosso, Detroit	12	8	6	14
1940-41	Milt Schmidt, Boston	11	5	6	11
1939-40	Phil Watson, NY Rangers	12	3	6	9
	Neil Colville, NY Rangers	12	2	7	9
1938-39	Bill Cowley, Boston	12	3	11	14
1937-38	Johnny Gottselig, Chicago	10	5	3	8
1936-37	Marty Barry, Detroit	10	4	7	11
1935-36	Buzz Boll, Toronto	9	7	3	10
1934-35	Baldy Northcott, Mtl. Maroons	7	4	1	5
	Harvey Jackson, Toronto	7	3	2	5
	Marvin Wentworth, Mtl. Maroons	7	3	2	5
1933-34	Larry Aurie, Detroit	9	3	7	10
1932-33	Cecil Dillon, NY Rangers	8	8	2	10
1931-32	Frank Boucher, NY Rangers	7	3	6	9
1930-31	Cooney Weiland, Boston	5	6	3	9
1929-30	Marty Barry, Boston	6	3	3	6
	Cooney Weiland, Boston	6	1	5	6
1928-29	Andy Blair, Toronto	4	3	0	3
	Butch Keeling, NY Rangers	6	3	0	3
	Ace Bailey, Toronto	4	1	2	3
1927-28	Frank Boucher, NY Rangers	9	7	3	10
1926-27	Harry Oliver, Boston	8	4	2	6
	Perk Galbraith, Boston	8	3	3	6
	Frank Fredrickson, Boston	8	2	4	6
1925-26	Nels Stewart, Mtl. Maroons	8	6	3	9
1924-25	Howie Morenz, Montreal	6	7	1	8
1923-24	Howie Morenz, Montreal	6	7	2	9
1922-23	Punch Broadbent, Ottawa	8	6	1	7
1921-22	Babe Dye, Toronto	7	11	2	13
1920-21	Cy Denneny, Ottawa	7	4	2	6
1919-20	Frank Nighbor, Ottawa	5	6	1	7
	Jack Darragh, Ottawa	5	5	2	7
1918-19	Newsy Lalonde, Montreal	10	17	1	18
1917-18	Alf Skinner, Toronto	7	8	1	9

Overtime Games since 1918

Abbreviations: Teams/Cities: — **Atl.** - Atlanta; **Bos.** - Boston; **Buf.** - Buffalo; **Cgy.** - Calgary; **Cgy. T.** - Calgary Tigers (Western Canada Hockey League); **Chi.** - Chicago; **Col.** - Colorado; **Dal.** - Dallas; **Det.** - Detroit; **Edm.** - Edmonton; **Edm. E.** - Edmonton Eskimos (WCHL); **Hfd.** - Hartford; **K.C.** - Kansas City; **L.A.** - Los Angeles; **Min.** - Minnesota; **Mtl.** - Montreal; **Mtl.M.** - Montreal Maroons; **N.J.** - New Jersey; **NYA** - NY Americans; **NYI** - New York Islanders; **NYR** - New York Rangers; **Oak.** - Oakland; **Ott.** - Ottawa; **Phi.** - Philadelphia; **Pit.** - Pittsburgh; **Que.** - Quebec; **St. L.** - St. Louis; **Sea.** - Seattle Metropolitans (Pacific Coast Hockey Association); **S.J.** - San Jose; **Tor.** - Toronto; **Van.** - Vancouver; **Van. M** - Vancouver Millionaires (PCHA); **Vic.** - Victoria Cougars (WCHL); **Wpg.** - Winnipeg; **Wsh.** - Washington.

SERIES — **CF** - conference final; **CSF** - conference semi-final; **CQF** - conference quarter-final; **DF** - division final; **DSF** - division semi-final; **F** - final; **PR** - preliminary round; **QF** - quarter final; **SF** - semi-final.

Date	City	Series	Score		Scorer	Overtime	Series Winner
Mar. 26/19	Sea.	F	Mtl. 0	Sea. 0	no scorer	20:00	
Mar. 29/19	Sea.	F	Mtl. 4	Sea. 3	Odie Cleghorn	15:57	
Mar. 21/22	Tor.	F	Tor 2	Van.M. 1	Babe Dye	4:50	Tor.
Mar. 29/23	Van.	F	Ott. 2	Edm.E. 1	Cy Denneny	2:08	Ott.
Mar. 31/27	Mtl.	QF	Mtl. 1	Mtl. M. 0	Howie Morenz	12:05	Mtl.
Apr. 7/27	Bos.	F	Ott. 0	Bos. 0	no scorer	20:00	Ott.
Apr. 11/27	Ott.	F	Bos. 1	Ott. 1	no scorer	20:00	Ott.
Apr. 3/28	Mtl.	QF	Mtl. M. 1	Mtl. 0	Russ Oatman	8:20	Mtl. M.
Apr. 7/28	Mtl.	F	NYR 2	Mtl. M. 1	Frank Boucher	7:05	NYR
Mar. 21/29	NY	QF	NYR 1	NYA 0	Butch Keeling	29:50	NYR
Mar. 26/29	Tor.	SF	NYR 2	Tor. 1	Frank Boucher	2:03	NYR
Mar. 20/30	Mtl.	SF	Bos. 2	Mtl. M. 1	Harry Oliver	45:35	Bos.
Mar. 25/30	Bos.	SF	Mtl. M. 1	Bos. 0	Archie Wilcox	26:27	Bos.
Mar. 26/30	Mtl.	QF	Chi. 2	Mtl. 2	Howie Morenz (Mtl.)	51:43	Mtl.
Mar. 28/30	Mtl.	SF	Mtl. 2	NYR 1	Gus Rivers	68:52	Mtl.
Mar. 24/31	Bos.	SF	Bos. 5	Mtl. 4	Cooney Weiland	18:56	Mtl.
Mar. 26/31	Chi.	QF	Chi. 2	Tor. 1	Steward Adams	19:20	Chi.
Mar. 28/31	Mtl.	SF	Mtl. 4	Bos. 3	Georges Mantha	5:10	Mtl.
Apr. 1/31	Mtl.	SF	Mtl. 3	Bos. 2	Wildor Larochelle	19:00	Mtl.
Apr. 5/31	Chi.	F	Chi. 2	Mtl. 1	Johnny Gottselig	24:50	Mtl.
Apr. 9/31	Mtl.	F	Chi. 3	Mtl. 2	Cy Wentworth	53:50	Mtl.
Mar. 26/32	Mtl.	SF	NYR 4	Mtl. 3	Fred Cook	59:32	NYR
Apr. 2/32	Tor.	SF	Tor. 3	Mtl. M. 2	Bob Gracie	17:59	Tor.
Mar. 25/33	Bos.	SF	Bos. 2	Tor. 1	Marty Barry	14:14	Tor.
Mar. 28/33	Bos.	SF	Tor. 1	Bos. 0	Busher Jackson	15:03	Tor.
Mar. 30/33	Tor.	SF	Bos. 2	Tor. 1	Eddie Shore	4:23	Tor.
Apr. 3/33	Tor.	SF	Tor. 1	Bos. 0	Ken Doraty	104:46	Tor.
Apr. 13/33	Tor.	F	NYR 1	Tor. 0	Bill Cook	7:33	NYR
Mar. 22/34	Tor.	SF	Det. 2	Tor. 1	Herbie Lewis	1:33	Det.
Mar. 25/34	Chi.	QF	Chi. 1	Mtl. 1	Mush March (Chi)	11:05	Chi.
Apr. 3/34	Det.	F	Chi. 2	Det. 1	Paul Thompson	21:10	Chi.
Apr. 10/34	Chi.	F	Chi. 1	Det. 0	Mush March	30:05	Chi.
Mar. 23/35	Bos.	SF	Bos. 1	Tor. 0	Dit Clapper	33:26	Tor.
Mar. 26/35	Chi.	QF	Mtl. M. 1	Chi. 0	Baldy Northcott	4:02	Mtl. M.
Mar. 30/35	Tor.	SF	Tor. 2	Bos. 1	Pep Kelly	1:36	Tor.
Apr. 4/35	Tor.	F	Mtl. M. 3	Tor. 2	Dave Trottier	5:28	Mtl. M.
Mar. 24/36	Mtl.	SF	Det. 1	Mtl. M. 0	Mud Bruneteau	116:30	Det.
Apr. 9/36	Tor.	F	Tor. 4	Det. 3	Buzz Boll	0:31	Det.
Mar. 25/37	NY	QF	NYR 2	Tor. 1	Babe Pratt	13:05	NYR
Apr. 1/37	Mtl.	SF	Det. 2	Mtl. 1	Hec Kilrea	51:49	Det.
Mar. 22/38	NY	QF	NYA 2	NYR 1	Johnny Sorrell	21:25	NYA
Mar. 24/38	Tor.	SF	Tor. 1	Bos. 0	George Parsons	21:31	Tor.
Mar. 26/38	Mtl.	QF	Chi. 3	Mtl. 2	Paul Thompson	11:49	Chi.
Mar. 27/38	NY	QF	NYA 3	NYR 2	Lorne Carr	60:40	NYA
Mar. 29/38	Bos.	SF	Tor. 3	Bos. 2	Gord Drillon	10:04	Tor.
Mar. 31/38	Chi.	SF	Chi. 1	NYA 0	Cully Dahlstrom	33:01	Chi.
Mar. 21/39	NY	SF	Bos. 2	NYR 1	Mel Hill	59:25	Bos.
Mar. 23/39	Bos.	SF	Bos. 3	NYR 2	Mel Hill	8:24	Bos.
Mar. 26/39	Det.	QF	Det. 1	Mtl. 0	Marty Barry	7:47	Det.
Mar. 30/39	Bos.	SF	NYR 2	Bos. 1	Clint Smith	17:19	Bos.
Apr. 1/39	Tor.	SF	Tor. 5	Det. 4	Gord Drillon	5:42	Tor.
Apr. 2/39	Bos.	SF	Bos. 2	NYR 1	Mel Hill	48:00	Bos.
Apr. 9/39	Bos.	F	Tor. 3	Bos. 2	Doc Romnes	10:38	Bos.
Mar. 19/40	Det.	QF	Det. 2	NYA 1	Syd Howe	0:25	Det.
Mar. 19/40	Tor.	QF	Tor. 3	Chi. 2	Syl Apps	6:35	Tor.
Apr. 2/40	NY	F	NYR 2	Tor. 1	Alf Pike	15:30	NYR
Apr. 11/40	Tor.	F	NYR 2	Tor. 1	Muzz Patrick	31:43	NYR
Apr. 13/40	Tor.	F	NYR 3	Tor. 2	Bryan Hextall	2:07	NYR
Mar. 20/41	Det.	QF	Det. 2	NYR 1	Gus Giesebrecht	12:01	Det.
Mar. 22/41	Mtl.	QF	Mtl. 4	Chi. 3	Charlie Sands	34:04	Chi.
Mar. 29/41	Bos.	SF	Tor. 2	Bos. 1	Pete Langelle	17:31	Bos.
Mar. 30/41	Chi.	SF	Det. 2	Chi. 1	Gus Giesebrecht	9:15	Det.
Mar. 22/42	Chi.	QF	Bos. 2	Chi. 1	Des Smith	6:51	Bos.
Mar. 21/43	Bos.	SF	Bos. 5	Mtl. 4	Don Gallinger	12:30	Bos.
Mar. 23/43	Det.	SF	Tor. 3	Det. 2	Jack McLean	70:18	Det.
Mar. 25/43	Mtl.	SF	Bos. 3	Mtl. 2	Harvey Jackson	3:20	Bos.
Mar. 30/43	Tor.	SF	Det. 3	Tor. 2	Adam Brown	9:21	Det.
Mar. 30/43	Bos.	SF	Bos. 5	Mtl. 4	Ab DeMarco	3:41	Bos.
Apr. 13/44	Mtl.	F	Mtl. 5	Chi. 4	Toe Blake	9:12	Mtl.
Mar. 27/45	Tor.	SF	Tor. 4	Mtl. 3	Gus Bodnar	12:36	Tor.
Mar. 29/45	Det.	SF	Det. 3	Bos. 2	Mud Bruneteau	17:12	Det.
Apr. 21/45	Tor.	F	Det. 1	Tor. 0	Ed Bruneteau	14:16	Tor.
Mar. 28/46	Bos.	SF	Bos. 4	Det. 3	Don Gallinger	9:51	Bos.
Mar. 30/46	Mtl.	F	Mtl. 4	Bos. 3	Maurice Richard	9:08	Mtl.
Apr. 2/46	Mtl.	F	Mtl. 3	Bos. 2	Jim Peters	16:55	Mtl.
Apr. 7/46	Bos.	F	Bos. 3	Mtl. 2	Terry Reardon	15:13	Mtl.
Mar. 26/47	Tor.	SF	Tor. 3	Det. 2	Howie Meeker	3:05	Tor.
Mar. 27/47	Mtl.	SF	Mtl. 2	Bos. 1	Ken Mosdell	5:38	Mtl.
Apr. 3/47	Mtl.	SF	Mtl. 4	Bos. 3	John Quilty	36:40	Mtl.
Apr. 15/47	Tor.	F	Tor. 2	Mtl. 1	Syl Apps	16:36	Tor.
Mar. 24/48	Tor.	SF	Tor. 5	Bos. 4	Nick Metz	17:03	Tor.
Mar. 22/49	Det.	SF	Det. 2	Mtl. 1	Max McNab	44:52	Det.
Mar. 24/49	Det.	SF	Mtl. 4	Det. 3	Gerry Plamondon	2:59	Det.
Mar. 26/49	Tor.	SF	Bos. 5	Tor. 4	Woody Dumart	16:14	Tor.
Apr. 8/49	Det.	F	Tor. 3	Det. 2	Joe Klukay	17:31	Tor.
Apr. 4/50	Tor.	SF	Det. 2	Tor. 1	Leo Reise	20:38	Det.
Apr. 4/50	Mtl.	SF	Mtl. 3	NYR 2	Elmer Lach	15:19	Mtl.
Apr. 9/50	Det.	SF	Det. 1	Tor. 0	Leo Reise	8:39	Det.
Apr. 18/50	Det.	F	NYR 4	Det. 3	Don Raleigh	8:34	Det.
Apr. 20/50	Det.	F	NYR 2	Det. 1	Don Raleigh	1:38	Det.
Apr. 23/50	Det.	F	Det. 4	NYR 3	Pete Babando	28:31	Det.
Mar. 27/51	Det.	SF	Mtl. 3	Det. 2	Maurice Richard	61:09	Mtl.
Mar. 29/51	Det.	SF	Mtl. 1	Det. 0	Maurice Richard	42:20	Mtl.
Mar. 31/51	Tor.	SF	Bos. 1	Tor. 1	no scorer	20:00	Tor.
Apr. 11/51	Tor.	F	Tor. 3	Mtl. 2	Sid Smith	5:51	Tor.
Apr. 14/51	Tor.	F	Mtl. 3	Tor. 2	Maurice Richard	2:55	Tor.
Apr. 17/51	Mtl.	F	Tor. 2	Mtl. 1	Ted Kennedy	4:47	Tor.
Apr. 19/51	Mtl.	F	Tor. 3	Mtl. 2	Harry Watson	5:15	Tor.
Apr. 21/51	Tor.	F	Tor. 3	Mtl. 2	Bill Barilko	2:53	Tor.
Apr. 6/52	Bos.	SF	Mtl. 3	Bos. 2	Paul Masnick	27:49	Mtl.
Mar. 29/53	Bos.	SF	Bos. 2	Det. 1	Jack McIntyre	12:29	Bos.
Mar. 29/53	Chi.	SF	Chi. 2	Mtl. 1	Al Dewsbury	5:18	Mtl.
Apr. 16/53	Mtl.	F	Mtl. 1	Bos. 0	Elmer Lach	1:22	Mtl.
Apr. 1/54	Det.	SF	Det. 4	Tor. 3	Ted Lindsay	21:01	Det.
Apr. 11/54	Det.	F	Mtl. 1	Det. 0	Ken Mosdell	5:45	Det.
Apr. 16/54	Det.	F	Det. 2	Mtl. 1	Tony Leswick	4:29	Det.
Mar. 29/55	Bos.	SF	Mtl. 4	Bos. 3	Don Marshall	3:05	Mtl.
Mar. 24/56	Tor.	SF	Det. 5	Tor. 4	Ted Lindsay	4:22	Det.
Mar. 28/57	NY	SF	NYR 4	Mtl. 3	Andy Hebenton	13:38	Mtl.
Apr. 4/57	Mtl.	SF	Mtl. 4	NYR 3	Maurice Richard	1:11	Mtl.
Mar. 27/58	NY	SF	Bos. 4	NYR 3	Jerry Toppazzini	4:46	Bos.
Mar. 30/58	Det.	SF	Mtl. 2	Det. 1	André Pronovost	11:52	Mtl.
Apr. 17/58	Mtl.	F	Mtl. 3	Bos. 2	Maurice Richard	5:45	Mtl.
Mar. 28/59	Tor.	SF	Tor. 3	Bos. 2	Gerry Ehman	5:02	Tor.
Mar. 31/59	Tor.	SF	Tor. 3	Bos. 2	Frank Mahovlich	11:21	Tor.
Apr. 14/59	Tor.	F	Tor. 3	Mtl. 2	Dick Duff	10:06	Mtl.
Mar. 26/60	Mtl.	SF	Mtl. 4	Chi. 3	Doug Harvey	8:38	Mtl.
Mar. 27/60	Det.	SF	Tor. 5	Det. 4	Frank Mahovlich	43:00	Tor.
Mar. 29/60	Det.	SF	Det. 2	Tor. 1	Gerry Melnyk	1:54	Tor.
Mar. 22/61	Tor.	SF	Tor. 3	Det. 2	George Armstrong	24:51	Det.
Mar. 26/61	Chi.	SF	Chi. 2	Mtl. 1	Murray Balfour	52:12	Chi.
Apr. 5/62	Tor.	SF	Tor. 3	NYR 2	Red Kelly	24:23	Tor.
Apr. 2/64	Det.	SF	Chi. 3	Det. 2	Murray Balfour	8:21	Det.
Apr. 14/64	Tor.	F	Det. 4	Tor. 3	Larry Jeffrey	7:52	Tor.
Apr. 23/64	Det.	F	Tor. 4	Det. 3	Bobby Baun	1:43	Tor.
Apr. 6/65	Tor.	SF	Tor. 3	Mtl. 2	Dave Keon	4:17	Mtl.
Apr. 13/65	Tor.	SF	Mtl. 4	Tor. 3	Claude Provost	16:33	Mtl.
May 5/66	Det.	F	Mtl. 3	Det. 2	Henri Richard	2:20	Mtl.
Apr. 13/67	NY	SF	Mtl. 2	NYR 1	John Ferguson	6:28	Mtl.
Apr. 25/67	Tor.	F	Tor. 3	Mtl. 2	Bob Pulford	28:26	Tor.
Apr. 10/68	St. L.	QF	St. L. 3	Phi. 2	Larry Keenan	24:10	St. L.
Apr. 16/68	St. L.	QF	Phi. 2	St. L. 1	Don Blackburn	31:18	St. L.
Apr. 16/68	Min.	QF	Min. 4	L.A. 3	Milan Marcetta	9:11	Min.
Apr. 22/68	Min.	SF	Min. 3	St. L. 2	Parker MacDonald	3:41	St. L.
Apr. 27/68	St. L.	SF	St. L. 4	Min. 3	Gary Sabourin	1:32	St. L.
Apr. 28/68	Mtl.	SF	Mtl. 4	Chi. 3	Jacques Lemaire	2:14	Mtl.
Apr. 29/68	St. L.	SF	St. L. 3	Min. 2	Bill McCreary	17:27	St. L.
May 3/68	St. L.	SF	St. L. 2	Min. 1	Ron Schock	22:50	St. L.
May 5/68	St. L.	F	Mtl. 3	St. L. 2	Jacques Lemaire	1:41	Mtl.
May 9/68	Mtl.	F	Mtl. 4	St. L. 3	Bobby Rousseau	1:13	Mtl.
Apr. 2/69	Oak.	QF	L.A. 5	Oak. 4	Ted Irvine	0:19	L.A.
Apr. 10/69	Mtl.	SF	Mtl. 3	Bos. 2	Ralph Backstrom	0:42	Mtl.
Apr. 13/69	Mtl.	SF	Mtl. 4	Bos. 3	Mickey Redmond	4:55	Mtl.
Apr. 24/69	Bos.	SF	Mtl. 2	Bos. 1	Jean Béliveau	31:28	Mtl.
Apr. 12/70	Oak.	QF	Pit. 3	Oak. 2	Michel Briere	8:28	Pit.
May 10/70	Bos.	F	Bos. 4	St. L. 3	Bobby Orr	0:40	Bos.
Apr. 15/71	Tor.	QF	NYR 2	Tor. 1	Bob Nevin	9:07	NYR
Apr. 18/71	Chi.	SF	NYR 2	Chi. 1	Pete Stemkowski	1:37	Chi.
Apr. 27/71	Chi.	SF	Chi. 3	NYR 2	Bobby Hull	6:35	Chi.
Apr. 29/71	NY	SF	NYR 3	Chi. 2	Pete Stemkowski	41:29	Chi.
May 4/71	Chi.	F	Chi. 2	Mtl. 1	Jim Pappin	21:11	Mtl.
Apr. 6/72	Bos.	QF	Tor. 4	Bos. 3	Jim Harrison	2:58	Bos.
Apr. 6/72	Min.	QF	Min. 6	St. L. 5	Bill Goldsworthy	1:36	St. L.
Apr. 9/72	Pit.	QF	Chi. 6	Pit. 5	Pit Martin	0:12	Chi.
Apr. 16/72	Min.	QF	St. L. 2	Min. 1	Kevin O'Shea	10:07	St. L.
Apr. 1/73	Mtl.	QF	Buf. 3	Mtl. 2	René Robert	9:18	Mtl.
Apr. 10/73	Phi.	QF	Phi. 3	Min. 2	Gary Dornhoefer	8:35	Phi.
Apr. 14/73	Mtl.	SF	Phi. 5	Mtl. 4	Rick MacLeish	2:56	Mtl.
Apr. 17/73	Mtl.	SF	Mtl. 4	Phi. 3	Larry Robinson	6:45	Mtl.
Apr. 14/74	Tor.	QF	Bos. 4	Tor. 3	Ken Hodge	1:27	Bos.
Apr. 14/74	Atl.	QF	Phi. 4	Atl. 3	Dave Schultz	5:40	Phi.
Apr. 16/74	Mtl.	QF	NYR 3	Mtl. 2	Ron Harris	4:07	NYR
Apr. 23/74	Chi.	SF	Chi. 4	Bos. 3	Jim Pappin	3:48	Bos.
Apr. 28/74	NY	SF	NYR 2	Phi. 1	Rod Gilbert	4:20	Phi.
May 9/74	Bos.	F	Phi. 3	Bos. 2	Bobby Clarke	12:01	Phi.
Apr. 8/75	L.A.	PR	L.A. 3	Tor. 2	Mike Murphy	8:53	Tor.
Apr. 10/75	Tor.	PR	Tor. 3	L.A. 2	Blaine Stoughton	10:19	Tor.
Apr. 10/75	Chi.	PR	Chi. 4	Bos. 3	Ivan Boldirev	7:33	Chi.
Apr. 11/75	NY	PR	NYI 4	NYR 3	Jean-Paul Parise	0:11	NYI
Apr. 19/75	Tor.	QF	Phi. 4	Tor. 3	André Dupont	1:45	Phi.
Apr. 17/75	Chi.	QF	Chi. 5	Buf. 4	Stan Mikita	2:31	Buf.
Apr. 22/75	Mtl.	QF	Mtl. 5	Van. 4	Guy Lafleur	17:06	Mtl.
May 1/75	Phi.	SF	Phi. 5	NYI 4	Bobby Clarke	2:56	Phi.
May 7/75	NYI	SF	NYI 4	Phi. 3	Jude Drouin	1:53	Phi.
Apr. 27/75	Buf.	SF	Buf. 6	Mtl. 5	Danny Gare	4:42	Buf.
May 6/75	Buf.	SF	Buf. 5	Mtl. 4	René Robert	5:56	Buf.
May 20/75	Buf.	F	Buf. 5	Phi. 4	René Robert	18:29	Phi.
Apr. 8/76	Buf.	PR	Buf. 3	St. L. 2	Danny Gare	11:43	Buf.
Apr. 9/76	Buf.	PR	Buf. 2	St. L. 1	Don Luce	14:27	Buf.
Apr. 13/76	Bos.	QF	L.A. 3	Bos. 2	Butch Goring	0:27	Bos.
Apr. 13/76	Buf.	QF	Buf. 3	NYI 2	Danny Gare	14:04	NYI
Apr. 22/76	L.A.	QF	L.A. 4	Bos. 3	Butch Goring	18:28	Bos.
Apr. 29/76	Phi.	SF	Phi. 2	Bos. 1	Reggie Leach	13:38	Phi.
Apr. 15/77	Tor.	QF	Phi. 4	Tor. 3	Rick MacLeish	2:55	Phi.
Apr. 17/77	Tor.	QF	Phi. 6	Tor. 5	Reggie Leach	19:10	Phi.
Apr. 24/77	Phi.	SF	Bos. 4	Phi. 3	Rick Middleton	2:57	Bos.
Apr. 26/77	Phi.	SF	Bos. 5	Phi. 4	Terry O'Reilly	30:07	Bos.
May 3/77	Mtl.	SF	NYI 4	Mtl. 3	Billy Harris	3:58	Mtl.
May 14/77	Bos.	F	Mtl. 2	Bos. 1	Jacques Lemaire	4:32	Mtl.

Date	City	Series	Score		Scorer	Overtime	Series Winner
Apr. 11/78	Phi.	PR	Phi. 3	Col. 2	Mel Bridgman	0:23	Phi.
Apr. 13/78	NY	PR	NYR 4	Buf. 3	Don Murdoch	1:37	Buf.
Apr. 19/78	Bos.	QF	Bos. 4	Chi. 3	Terry O'Reilly	1:50	Bos.
Apr. 19/78	NYI	QF	NYI 3	Tor. 2	Mike Bossy	2:50	Tor.
Apr. 21/78	Chi.	QF	Bos. 4	Chi. 3	Peter McNab	10:17	Bos.
Apr. 25/78	NYI	QF	NYI 2	Tor. 1	Bob Nystrom	8:02	Tor.
Apr. 29/78	NYI	QF	Tor. 2	NYI 1	Lanny McDonald	4:13	Tor.
May 2/78	Bos.	SF	Bos. 3	Phi. 2	Rick Middleton	1:43	Bos.
May 16/78	Mtl.	F	Mtl. 3	Bos. 2	Guy Lafleur	13:09	Mtl.
May 21/78	Bos.	F	Bos. 4	Mtl. 3	Bobby Schmautz	6:22	Mtl.
Apr. 12/79	L.A.	PR	NYR 2	L.A. 1	Phil Esposito	6:11	NYR
Apr. 14/79	Buf.	PR	Pit. 4	Buf. 3	George Ferguson	0:47	Pit.
Apr. 16/79	Phi.	QF	Phi. 3	NYR 2	Ken Linseman	0:44	NYR
Apr. 18/79	NYI	QF	NYI 1	Chi. 0	Mike Bossy	2:31	NYI
Apr. 21/79	Tor.	QF	Mtl. 4	Tor. 3	Cam Connor	25:25	Mtl.
Apr. 22/79	Tor.	QF	Mtl. 5	Tor. 4	Larry Robinson	4:14	Mtl.
Apr. 28/79	NYI	SF	NYI 4	NYR 3	Denis Potvin	8:02	NYR
May 3/79	NY	SF	NYI 3	NYR 2	Bob Nystrom	3:40	NYR
May 3/79	Bos.	SF	Bos. 4	Mtl. 3	Jean Ratelle	3:46	Mtl.
May 10/79	Mtl.	SF	Mtl. 5	Bos. 4	Yvon Lambert	9:33	Mtl.
May 19/79	NY	F	Mtl. 4	NYR 3	Serge Savard	7:25	Mtl.
Apr. 8/80	NY	PR	NYR 2	Atl. 1	Steve Vickers	0:33	NYR
Apr. 8/80	Phi.	PR	Phi. 4	Edm. 3	Bobby Clarke	8:06	Phi.
Apr. 8/80	Chi.	PR	Chi. 3	St. L. 2	Doug Lecuyer	12:34	Chi.
Apr. 11/80	Hfd.	PR	Mtl. 4	Hfd. 3	Yvon Lambert	0:29	Mtl.
Apr. 11/80	Tor.	PR	Min. 4	Tor. 3	Al MacAdam	0:32	Min.
Apr. 11/80	L.A.	PR	NYI 4	L.A. 3	Ken Morrow	6:55	NYI
Apr. 11/80	Edm.	PR	Phi. 3	Edm. 2	Ken Linseman	23:56	Phi.
Apr. 16/80	Bos.	QF	NYI 2	Bos. 1	Clark Gillies	1:02	NYI
Apr. 17/80	Bos.	QF	NYI 5	Bos. 4	Bob Bourne	1:24	NYI
Apr. 21/80	NYI	QF	Bos. 4	NYI 3	Terry O'Reilly	17:13	NYI
May 1/80	Buf.	SF	NYI 2	Buf. 1	Bob Nystrom	21:20	NYI
May 13/80	Phi.	F	NYI 4	Phi. 3	Denis Potvin	4:07	NYI
May 24/80	NYI	F	NYI 5	Phi. 4	Bob Nystrom	7:11	NYI
Apr. 8/81	Buf.	PR	Buf. 3	Van. 2	Alan Haworth	5:00	Buf.
Apr. 8/81	Bos.	PR	Min. 5	Bos. 4	Steve Payne	3:34	Min.
Apr. 11/81	Chi.	PR	Cgy. 5	Chi. 4	Willi Plett	35:17	Cgy.
Apr. 12/81	Que.	PR	Que. 4	Phi. 3	Dale Hunter	0:37	Phi.
Apr. 14/81	St. L.	PR	St. L. 4	Pit. 3	Mike Crombeen	25:16	St. L.
Apr. 16/81	Buf.	QF	Min. 4	Buf. 3	Steve Payne	0:22	Min.
Apr. 20/81	Min.	QF	Buf. 5	Min. 4	Craig Ramsay	16:32	Min.
Apr. 20/81	Edm.	QF	NYI 5	Edm. 4	Ken Morrow	5:41	NYI
Apr. 7/82	Min.	DSF	Chi. 3	Min. 2	Greg Fox	3:34	Chi.
Apr. 8/82	Edm.	DSF	Edm. 3	L.A. 2	Wayne Gretzky	6:20	L.A.
Apr. 8/82	Van.	DSF	Van. 2	Cgy. 1	Dave Williams	14:20	Van.
Apr. 10/82	Pit.	DSF	Pit. 2	NYI 1	Rick Kehoe	4:14	NYI
Apr. 10/82	L.A.	DSF	L.A. 6	Edm. 5	Daryl Evans	2:35	L.A.
Apr. 13/82	Mtl.	DSF	Que. 3	Mtl. 2	Dale Hunter	0:22	Que.
Apr. 13/82	NY	DSF	NYI 4	Pit. 3	John Tonelli	6:19	NYI
Apr. 16/82	Van.	DF	L.A. 3	Van. 2	Steve Bozek	4:33	Van.
Apr. 18/82	Que.	DF	Que. 3	Bos. 2	Wilf Paiement	11:44	Que.
Apr. 18/82	NY	DF	NYI 4	NYR 3	Bryan Trottier	3:00	NYI
Apr. 18/82	L.A.	DF	Van. 4	L.A. 3	Colin Campbell	1:23	Van.
Apr. 21/82	St. L.	DF	St. L. 3	Chi. 2	Bernie Federko	3:28	Chi.
Apr. 23/82	Que.	DF	Bos. 6	Que. 5	Peter McNab	10:54	Que.
Apr. 27/82	Chi.	CF	Van. 2	Chi. 1	Jim Nill	28:58	Van.
May 1/82	Que.	CF	NYI 5	Que. 4	Wayne Merrick	16:52	NYI
May 8/82	NYI	F	NYI 6	Van. 5	Mike Bossy	19:58	NYI
Apr. 5/83	Bos.	DSF	Bos. 4	Que. 3	Barry Pederson	1:46	Bos.
Apr. 6/83	Cgy.	DSF	Cgy. 4	Van. 3	Eddy Beers	12:27	Cgy.
Apr. 7/83	Min.	DSF	Min. 5	Tor. 4	Bobby Smith	5:03	Min.
Apr. 10/83	Tor.	DSF	Min. 5	Tor. 4	Dino Ciccarelli	8:05	Min.
Apr. 10/83	Van.	DSF	Cgy. 4	Van. 3	Greg Meredith	1:06	Cgy.
Apr. 18/83	Min.	DF	Chi. 4	Min. 3	Rich Preston	10:34	Chi.
Apr. 24/83	Bos.	DF	Bos. 3	Buf. 2	Brad Park	1:52	Bos.
Apr. 5/84	Edm.	DSF	Edm. 5	Wpg. 4	Randy Gregg	0:21	Edm.
Apr. 7/84	Det.	DSF	St. L. 4	Det. 3	Mark Reeds	37:07	St. L.
Apr. 8/84	Det.	DSF	St. L. 3	Det. 2	Jorgen Pettersson	2:42	St. L.
Apr. 10/84	NYI	DSF	NYI 3	NYR 2	Ken Morrow	8:56	NYI
Apr. 13/84	Min.	DF	St. L. 4	Min. 3	Doug Gilmour	16:16	Min.
Apr. 13/84	Edm.	DF	Cgy. 6	Edm. 5	Carey Wilson	3:42	Edm.
Apr. 13/84	NYI	DF	NYI 5	Wsh. 4	Anders Kallur	7:35	NYI
Apr. 16/84	Mtl.	DF	Que. 4	Mtl. 3	Bo Berglund	3:00	Mtl.
Apr. 20/84	Cgy.	DF	Cgy. 5	Edm. 4	Lanny McDonald	1:04	Edm.
Apr. 22/84	Min.	DF	Min. 4	St. L. 3	Steve Payne	6:00	Min.
Apr. 10/85	Phi.	DSF	Phi. 5	NYR 4	Mark Howe	8:01	Phi.

Maurice Richard, seen here scoring his 542nd career goal, scored the last overtime goal of his career on April 17, 1958 giving the Montreal Canadiens a 3-2 final series win over the Boston Bruins.

Date	City	Series	Score		Scorer	Overtime	Series Winner
Apr. 10/85	Wsh.	DSF	Wsh. 4	NYI 3	Alan Haworth	2:28	NYI
Apr. 10/85	Edm.	DSF	Edm. 3	L.A. 2	Lee Fogolin	3:01	Edm.
Apr. 10/85	Wpg.	DSF	Wpg. 5	Cgy. 4	Brian Mullen	7:56	Wpg.
Apr. 11/85	Wsh.	DSF	Wsh. 2	NYI 1	Mike Gartner	21:23	NYI
Apr. 13/85	L.A.	DSF	Edm. 4	L.A. 3	Glenn Anderson	0:46	Edm.
Apr. 18/85	Mtl.	DF	Que. 2	Mtl. 1	Mark Kumpel	12:23	Que.
Apr. 23/85	Que.	DF	Que. 7	Mtl. 6	Dale Hunter	18:36	Que.
May 2/85	Mtl.	DF	Que. 3	Mtl. 2	Peter Stastny	2:22	Que.
Apr. 25/85	Min.	DF	Chi. 7	Min. 6	Darryl Sutter	21:57	Chi.
Apr. 28/85	Chi.	DF	Min. 5	Chi. 4	Dennis Maruk	1:14	Chi.
Apr. 30/85	Min.	DF	Chi. 6	Min. 5	Darryl Sutter	15:41	Chi.
May 5/85	Que.	CF	Que. 2	Phi. 1	Peter Stastny	6:20	Phi.
Apr. 9/86	Que.	DSF	Hfd. 3	Que. 2	Sylvain Turgeon	2:36	Hfd.
Apr. 12/86	Wpg.	DSF	Cgy. 4	Wpg. 3	Lanny McDonald	8:25	Cgy.
Apr. 17/86	Wsh.	DF	NYR 4	Wsh. 3	Brian MacLellan	1:16	NYR
Apr. 20/86	Edm.	DF	Edm. 6	Cgy. 5	Glenn Anderson	1:04	Cgy.
Apr. 23/86	Hfd.	DF	Hfd. 2	Mtl. 1	Kevin Dineen	1:07	Mtl.
Apr. 23/86	NYR	DF	NYR 6	Wsh. 5	Bob Brooke	2:40	NYR
Apr. 26/86	St L.	DF	St L. 4	Tor. 3	Mark Reeds	7:11	St L.
Apr. 29/86	Mtl.	DF	Mtl. 2	Hfd. 1	Claude Lemieux	5:55	Mtl.
May 5/86	NYR	CF	Mtl. 4	NYR 3	Claude Lemieux	9:41	Mtl.
May 12/86	St L.	CF	St L. 6	Cgy. 5	Doug Wickenheiser	7:30	Cgy.
May 18/86	Cgy.	F	Mtl. 3	Cgy. 2	Brian Skrudland	0:09	Mtl.
Apr. 8/87	Hfd.	DSF	Hfd. 3	Que. 2	Paul MacDermid	2:20	Que.
Apr. 9/87	Mtl.	DSF	Mtl. 4	Bos. 3	Mats Naslund	2:38	Mtl.
Apr. 9/87	St. L.	DSF	Tor. 3	St. L. 2	Rick Lanz	10:17	Tor.
Apr. 11/87	Wpg.	DSF	Cgy. 3	Wpg. 2	Mike Bullard	3:53	Wpg.
Apr. 11/87	Chi.	DSF	Det. 4	Chi. 3	Shawn Burr	4:51	Det.
Apr. 16/87	Que.	DSF	Que. 5	Hfd. 4	Peter Stastny	6:05	Que.
Apr. 18/87	Wsh.	DSF	NYI 3	Wsh. 2	Pat LaFontaine	68:47	NYI
Apr. 21/87	Edm.	DF	Edm. 3	Wpg. 2	Glenn Anderson	0:36	Edm.
Apr. 26/87	Que.	DF	Mtl. 3	Que. 2	Mats Naslund	5:30	Mtl.
Apr. 27/87	Tor.	DF	Tor. 3	Det. 2	Mike Allison	9:31	Det.
May 4/87	Phi.	CF	Phi. 4	Mtl. 3	Ilkka Sinislao	9:11	Phi.
May 20/87	Edm.	F	Edm. 3	Phi. 2	Jari Kurri	6:50	Edm.
Apr. 6/88	NYI	DSF	NYI 4	N.J. 3	Pat LaFontaine	6:11	N.J.
Apr. 10/88	Phi.	DSF	Phi. 5	Wsh. 4	Murray Craven	1:18	Wsh.
Apr. 10/88	N.J.	DSF	NYI 5	N.J. 4	Brent Sutter	15:07	N.J.
Apr. 10/88	Buf.	DSF	Buf. 6	Bos. 5	John Tucker	5:32	Bos.
Apr. 12/88	Det.	DSF	Tor. 6	Det. 5	Ed Olczyk	0:34	Det.
Apr. 16/88	Wsh.	DSF	Wsh. 5	Phi. 4	Dale Hunter	5:57	Wsh.
Apr. 21/88	Cgy.	DF	Edm. 5	Cgy. 4	Wayne Gretzky	7:54	Edm.
May 4/88	Bos.	CF	N.J. 3	Bos. 2	Doug Brown	17:46	Bos.
May 9/88	Det.	CF	Edm. 4	Det. 3	Jari Kurri	11:02	Edm.
Apr. 5/89	St. L.	DSF	St. L. 4	Min. 3	Brett Hull	11:55	St. L.
Apr. 5/89	Cgy.	DSF	Van. 4	Cgy. 3	Paul Reinhart	2:47	Cgy.
Apr. 6/89	St. L.	DSF	St. L. 4	Min. 3	Rick Meagher	5:30	St. L.
Apr. 6/89	Det.	DSF	Chi. 5	Det. 4	Duane Sutter	14:36	Chi.
Apr. 8/89	Hfd.	DSF	Mtl. 5	Hfd. 4	Stephane Richer	5:01	Mtl.
Apr. 8/89	Phi.	DSF	Wsh. 4	Phi. 3	Kelly Miller	0:51	Phi.
Apr. 9/89	Hfd.	DSF	Mtl. 4	Hfd. 3	Russ Courtnall	15:12	Mtl.
Apr. 15/89	Cgy.	DSF	Cgy. 4	Van. 3	Joel Otto	19:21	Cgy.
Apr. 18/89	Cgy.	DF	Cgy. 4	L.A. 3	Doug Gilmour	7:47	Cgy.
Apr. 19/89	Mtl.	DF	Mtl. 3	Bos. 2	Bobby Smith	12:24	Mtl.
Apr. 20/89	St. L.	DF	St. L. 5	Chi. 4	Tony Hrkac	33:49	Chi.
Apr. 21/89	Phi.	DF	Pit. 4	Phi. 3	Phil Bourque	12:08	Phi.
May 8/89	Chi.	CF	Cgy. 2	Chi. 1	Al MacInnis	15:05	Cgy.
May 9/89	Mtl.	CF	Phi. 2	Mtl. 1	Dave Poulin	5:02	Mtl.
May 19/89	Mtl.	F	Mtl. 4	Cgy. 3	Ryan Walter	38:08	Cgy.
Apr. 5/90	N.J.	DSF	Wsh. 5	N.J. 4	Dino Ciccarelli	5:34	Wsh.
Apr. 6/90	Edm.	DSF	Edm. 3	Wpg. 2	Mark Lamb	4:21	Edm.
Apr. 8/90	Tor.	DSF	St. L. 6	Tor. 5	Sergio Momesso	6:04	St. L.
Apr. 8/90	L.A.	DSF	L.A. 2	Cgy. 1	Tony Granato	8:37	L.A.
Apr. 9/90	Mtl.	DSF	Mtl. 2	Buf. 1	Brian Skrudland	12:35	Mtl.
Apr. 9/90	NYI	DSF	NYI 4	NYR 3	Brent Sutter	20:59	NYR
Apr. 10/90	Wpg.	DSF	Wpg. 4	Edm. 3	Dave Ellett	21:08	Edm.
Apr. 14/90	L.A.	DSF	L.A. 4	Cgy. 3	Mike Krushelnyski	23:14	L.A.
Apr. 15/90	Hfd.	DSF	Hfd. 3	Bos. 2	Kevin Dineen	12:30	Bos.
Apr. 21/90	Bos.	DF	Bos. 5	Mtl. 4	Garry Galley	3:42	Bos.
Apr. 24/90	L.A.	DF	Edm. 6	L.A. 5	Joe Murphy	4:42	Edm.
Apr. 25/90	Wsh.	DF	Wsh. 4	NYR 3	Rod Langway	0:34	Wsh.
Apr. 27/90	NYR	DF	Wsh. 2	NYR 1	John Druce	6:48	Wsh.
May 15/90	Bos.	F	Edm. 3	Bos. 2	Petr Klima	55:13	Edm.
Apr. 4/91	Chi.	DSF	Min. 4	Chi. 3	Brian Propp	4:14	Min.
Apr. 5/91	Pit.	DSF	Pit. 5	N.J. 4	Jaromir Jagr	8:52	Pit.
Apr. 6/91	L.A.	DSF	L.A. 3	Van. 2	Wayne Gretzky	11:08	L.A.
Apr. 8/91	Van.	DSF	Van. 2	L.A. 1	Cliff Ronning	3:12	L.A.
Apr. 11/91	NYR	DSF	Wsh. 5	NYR 4	Dino Ciccarelli	6:44	Wsh.
Apr. 11/91	Mtl.	DSF	Mtl. 4	Buf. 3	Russ Courtnall	5:56	Mtl.
Apr. 14/91	Edm.	DSF	Cgy. 2	Edm. 1	Theo Fleury	4:40	Edm.
Apr. 16/91	Cgy.	DSF	Edm. 5	Cgy. 4	Esa Tikkanen	6:58	Edm.
Apr. 18/91	L.A.	DF	L.A. 4	Edm. 3	Luc Robitaille	2:13	Edm.
Apr. 19/91	Bos.	DF	Mtl. 4	Bos. 3	Stephane Richer	0:27	Bos.
Apr. 19/91	Pit.	DF	Pit. 7	Wsh. 6	Kevin Stevens	8:10	Pit.
Apr. 20/91	L.A.	DF	Edm. 4	L.A. 3	Petr Klima	24:48	Edm.
Apr. 22/91	Edm.	DF	Edm. 4	L.A. 3	Esa Tikkanen	20:48	Edm.
Apr. 27/91	Mtl.	DF	Mtl. 3	Bos. 2	Shayne Corson	17:47	Bos.
Apr. 28/91	Edm.	DF	Edm. 4	L.A. 3	Craig MacTavish	16:57	Edm.
May 3/91	Bos.	CF	Bos. 5	Pit. 4	Vladimir Ruzicka	8:14	Pit.
Apr. 21/92	Bos.	DSF	Bos. 3	Buf. 2	Adam Oates	11:14	Bos.
Apr. 22/92	Min.	DSF	Det. 5	Min. 4	Yves Racine	1:15	Det.
Apr. 22/92	St. L.	DSF	St. L. 5	Chi. 4	Brett Hull	23:33	Chi.
Apr. 25/92	Buf.	DSF	Bos. 5	Buf. 4	Ted Donato	2:08	Bos.
Apr. 28/92	Min.	DSF	Det. 1	Min. 0	Sergei Fedorov	16:13	Det.
Apr. 29/92	Hfd.	DSF	Hfd. 2	Mon. 1	Yvon Corriveau	0:24	Mtl.
May 1/92	Mtl.	DSF	Mtl. 3	Hfd. 2	Russ Courtnall	25:26	Mtl.
May 3/92	Van.	DF	Edm. 4	Van. 3	Joe Murphy	8:36	Edm.
May 5/92	Mtl.	DF	Bos. 3	Mtl. 2	Peter Douris	3:12	Bos.
May 7/92	Pit.	DF	NYR 6	Pit. 5	Kris King	1:29	Pit.
May 9/92	Pit.	DF	Pit. 5	NYR 4	Ron Francis	2:47	Pit.
May 17/92	Pit.	CF	Pit. 4	Bos. 3	Jaromir Jagr	9:44	Pit.
May 20/92	Edm.	CF	Chi. 4	Edm. 3	Jeremy Roenick	2:45	Chi.
Apr. 18/93	Bos.	DSF	Buf. 5	Bos. 4	Bob Sweeney	11:03	Buf.

Date	City	Series	Score		Scorer	Overtime	Series Winner
Apr. 18/93	Que.	DSF	Que. 3	Mtl. 2	Scott Young	16:49	Mtl.
Apr. 20/93	Wsh.	DSF	NYI 5	Wsh. 4	Brian Mullen	34:50	NYI
Apr. 22/93	Mtl.	DSF	Mtl. 2	Que. 1	Vincent Damphousse	10:30	Mtl.
Apr. 22/93	Buf.	DSF	Buf. 4	Bos. 3	Yuri Khmylev	1:05	Buf.
Apr. 22/93	NYI	DSF	NYI 4	Wsh. 3	Ray Ferraro	4:46	NYI
Apr. 24/93	Buf.	DSF	Buf. 6	Bos. 5	Brad May	4:48	Buf.
Apr. 24/93	NYI	DSF	NYI 4	Wsh. 3	Ray Ferraro	25:40	NYI
Apr. 25/93	St. L.	DSF	St. L. 4	Chi. 3	Craig Janney	10:43	St. L.
Apr. 26/93	Que.	DSF	Mtl. 5	Que. 4	Kirk Muller	8:17	Mtl.
Apr. 27/93	Det.	DSF	Tor. 5	Det. 4	Mike Foligno	2:05	Tor.
Apr. 27/93	Van.	DSF	Wpg. 4	Van. 3	Teemu Selanne	6:18	Van.
Apr. 29/93	Wpg.	DSF	Van. 4	Wpg. 3	Greg Adams	4:30	Van.
May 1/93	Det.	DSF	Tor. 4	Det. 3	Nikolai Borschevsky	2:35	Tor.
May 3/93	Tor.	DF	Tor. 2	St. L. 1	Doug Gilmour	23:16	Tor.
May 4/93	Mtl.	DF	Mtl. 4	Buf. 3	Guy Carbonneau	2:50	Mtl.
May 5/93	Tor.	DF	St. L. 2	Tor. 1	Jeff Brown	23:03	Tor.
May 6/93	Buf.	DF	Mtl. 4	Buf. 3	Gilbert Dionne	8:28	Mtl.
May 8/93	Buf.	DF	Mtl. 4	Buf. 3	Kirk Muller	11:37	Mtl.
May 11/93	Van.	DF	L.A. 4	Van. 3	Gary Shuchuk	26:31	L.A.
May 14/93	Pit.	DF	NYI 4	Pit. 3	Dave Volek	5:16	NYI
May 18/93	Mtl.	CF	Mtl. 4	NYI 3	Stephan Lebeau	26:21	Mtl.
May 20/93	NYI	CF	Mtl. 2	NYI 1	Guy Carbonneau	12:34	Mtl.
May 25/93	Tor.	CF	Tor. 3	L.A. 2	Glenn Anderson	19:20	L.A.
May 27/93	L.A.	CF	L.A. 5	Tor. 4	Wayne Gretzky	1:41	L.A.
Jun. 3/93	Mtl.	F	Mtl. 3	L.A. 2	Eric Desjardins	0:51	Mtl.
Jun. 5/93	L.A.	F	Mtl. 4	L.A. 3	John LeClair	0:34	Mtl.
Jun. 7/93	L.A.	F	Mtl. 3	L.A. 2	John LeClair	14:37	Mtl.
Apr. 20/94	Tor.	CQF	Tor. 1	Chi. 0	Todd Gill	2:15	Tor.
Apr. 22/94	St. L.	CQF	Dal. 5	St. L. 4	Paul Cavallini	8:34	Dal.
Apr. 24/94	Chi.	CQF	Chi. 4	Tor. 3	Jeremy Roenick	1:23	Tor.
Apr. 25/94	Bos.	CQF	Mtl. 2	Bos. 1	Kirk Muller	17:18	Bos.
Apr. 26/94	Cgy.	CQF	Van. 2	Cgy. 1	Geoff Courtnall	7:15	Van.
Apr. 27/94	Buf.	CQF	Buf. 1	N.J. 0	Dave Hannan	65:43	N.J.
Apr. 28/94	Van.	CQF	Van. 3	Cgy. 2	Trevor Linden	16:43	Van.
Apr. 30/94	Cgy.	CQF	Van. 4	Cgy. 3	Pavel Bure	22:20	Van.
May 3/94	N.J.	CSF	Bos. 6	N.J. 5	Don Sweeney	9:08	N.J.
May 7/94	Bos.	CSF	N.J. 5	Bos. 4	Stephane Richer	14:19	N.J.
May 8/94	Van.	CSF	Van. 2	Dal. 1	Sergio Momesso	11:01	Van.
May 12/94	Tor.	CSF	Tor. 3	S.J. 2	Mike Gartner	8:53	Tor.
May 15/94	NYR	CF	N.J. 4	NYR 3	Stephane Richer	35:23	NYR
May 16/94	Tor.	CF	Tor. 3	Van. 2	Peter Zezel	16:55	Van.
May 19/94	N.J.	CF	NYR 3	N.J. 2	Stephane Matteau	26:13	NYR
May 24/94	Van.	CF	Van. 4	Tor. 3	Greg Adams	20:14	Van.
May 27/94	NYR	CF	NYR 2	N.J. 1	Stephane Matteau	24:24	NYR
May 31/94	NYR	F	Van. 3	NYR 2	Greg Adams	19:26	NYR
May 7/95	Phi.	CQF	Phi. 4	Buf. 3	Karl Dykhuis	10:06	Phi.
May 9/95	Cgy.	CQF	S.J. 5	Cgy. 4	Ulf Dahlen	12:21	S.J.
May 12/95	NYR	CQF	NYR 3	Que. 2	Steve Larmer	8:09	NYR
May 12/95	N.J.	CQF	N.J. 1	Bos. 0	Randy McKay	8:51	N.J.
May 14/95	Pit.	CQF	Pit. 6	Wsh. 5	Luc Robitaille	4:30	Pit.
May 15/95	St. L.	CQF	Van. 6	St. L. 5	Cliff Ronning	1:48	Van.
May 17/95	Tor.	CQF	Tor. 5	Chi. 4	Randy Wood	10:00	Chi.
May 19/95	Cgy.	CQF	S.J. 5	Cgy. 4	Ray Whitney	21:54	S.J.
May 21/95	Phi.	CSF	Phi. 5	NYR 4	Eric Desjardins	7:03	Phi.
May 21/95	Chi.	CSF	Chi. 2	Van. 1	Joe Murphy	9:04	Chi.
May 22/95	Phi.	CSF	Phi. 4	NYR 3	Kevin Haller	0:25	Phi.
May 25/95	Van.	CSF	Chi. 3	Van. 2	Chris Chelios	6:22	Chi.
May 26/95	N.J.	CSF	N.J. 2	Pit. 1	Neal Broten	18:36	N.J.
May 27/95	Van.	CSF	Chi. 4	Van. 3	Chris Chelios	5:35	Chi.
Jun. 1/95	Det.	CF	Det. 2	Chi. 1	Nicklas Lidstrom	1:01	Det.
Jun. 6/95	Chi.	CF	Det. 4	Chi. 3	Vladimir Konstantinov	29:25	Det.
Jun. 7/95	N.J.	CF	Phi. 3	N.J. 2	Eric Lindros	4:19	N.J.
Jun. 11/95	Det.	CF	Det. 2	Chi. 1	Vyacheslav Kozlov	22:25	Det.

Left: Ray Whitney scored at 1:54 of the second overtime period in game seven of the Western Conference Quarter-Finals to give the San Jose Sharks a 5-4 victory over the Calgary Flames. Right: Karl Dykhuis scored the first overtime goal of the 1994-95 playoffs, sneaking a shot past Buffalo's Dominik Hasek to give the Philadelphia Flyers a 4-3 win over the Sabres in game one of the Eastern Conference Quarter-Finals.

Jacques Lemaire, left, Frank Boucher, center, and Toe Blake have scored a
Stanley Cup-winning goal and coached a Stanley Cup-winning team.

Stanley Cup
Coaching Records

Coaches listed in order of total games coached in playoffs. Minimum: 65 games.

Coach	Team	Years	Series	W	L	G	W	L	T	Cups	%
Bowman, Scott	St. Louis	4	10	6	4	52	26	26	0	0	.500
	Montreal	8	19	16	3	98	70	28	0	5	.714
	Buffalo	5	8	3	5	36	18	18	0	0	.500
	Pittsburgh	2	6	5	1	33	23	10	0	1	.696
	Detroit	2	5	3	2	25	15	10	0	0	.600
	Total	**21**	**48**	**33**	**15**	**244**	**152**	**92**	**0**	**6**	**.623**
Arbour, Al	St. Louis	1	2	1	1	11	4	7	0	0	.364
	NY Islanders	15	40	29	11	198	119	79	0	4	.601
	Total	**16**	**42**	**30**	**12**	**209**	**123**	**86**	**0**	**4**	**.589**
Irvin, Dick	Chicago	1	3	2	1	9	5	3	1	0	.611
	Toronto	9	20	12	8	66	33	32	1	1	.508
	Montreal	14	22	11	11	115	62	53	0	3	.539
	Total	**24**	**45**	**25**	**20**	**190**	**100**	**88**	**2**	**4**	**.532**
Keenan, Mike	Philadelphia	4	10	6	4	57	32	25	0	0	.561
	Chicago	4	11	7	4	60	33	27	0	0	.550
	NY Rangers	1	4	4	0	23	16	7	0	1	.695
	St. Louis	1	1	0	1	7	3	4	0	0	.428
	Total	**10**	**26**	**17**	**9**	**147**	**84**	**63**	**0**	**1**	**.571**
Sather, Glen	Edmonton	10	27	21	6	*126	89	37	0	4	.706
Blake, Toe	Montreal	13	23	18	5	119	82	37	0	8	.689
Reay, Billy	Chicago	12	22	10	12	117	57	60	0	0	.487
Shero, Fred	Philadelphia	6	16	12	4	83	48	35	0	2	.578
	NY Rangers	2	5	3	2	25	13	12	0	0	.520
	Total	**8**	**21**	**15**	**6**	**108**	**61**	**47**	**0**	**2**	**.565**
Adams, Jack	Detroit	15	27	15	12	105	52	52	1	3	.500
Demers, Jacques	St. Louis	3	6	3	3	33	16	17	0	0	.485
	Detroit	3	7	4	3	38	20	18	0	0	.526
	Montreal	2	5	4	1	27	19	8	0	1	.704
	Total	**8**	**18**	**11**	**7**	**98**	**55**	**43**	**0**	**1**	**.561**
Quinn, Pat	Philadelphia	3	8	5	3	39	22	17	0	0	.564
	Los Angeles	1	1	0	1	3	0	3	0	0	.000
	Vancouver	4	9	5	4	55	29	26	0	0	.527
	Total	**8**	**18**	**10**	**8**	**97**	**51**	**46**	**0**	**0**	**.525**
Burns, Pat	Montreal	4	10	6	4	56	30	26	0	0	.535
	Toronto	3	7	4	3	46	23	23	0	0	.500
	Total	**7**	**17**	**10**	**7**	**102**	**53**	**49**	**0**	**0**	**.519**
Francis, Emile	NY Rangers	9	14	5	9	75	34	41	0	0	.453
	St. Louis	3	4	1	3	18	6	12	0	0	.333
	Total	**12**	**18**	**6**	**12**	**93**	**40**	**53**	**0**	**0**	**.430**

Coach	Team	Years	Series	W	L	G	W	L	T	Cups	%
Imlach, Punch	Toronto	11	17	10	7	92	44	48	0	4	.478
Day, Hap	Toronto	9	14	10	4	80	49	31	0	5	.613
Murray, Bryan	Washington	7	10	3	7	53	24	29	0	0	.452
	Detroit	3	4	1	3	25	10	15	0	0	.400
	Total	**10**	**14**	**4**	**10**	**78**	**34**	**44**	**0**	**0**	**.435**
Johnson, Bob	Calgary	5	10	5	5	52	25	27	0	0	.481
	Pittsburgh	1	4	4	0	24	16	8	0	1	.666
	Total	**6**	**14**	**9**	**5**	**76**	**41**	**35**	**0**	**1**	**.539**
Abel, Sid	Chicago	1	1	0	1	7	3	4	0	0	.429
	Detroit	8	12	4	8	69	29	40	0	0	.420
	Total	**9**	**13**	**4**	**9**	**76**	**32**	**44**	**0**	**0**	**.421**
Ross, Art	Boston	12	19	9	10	70	32	33	5	1	.493
Bergeron, Michel	Quebec	7	13	6	7	68	31	37	0	0	.456
Lemaire, Jacques	Montreal	2	5	3	2	27	15	12	0	0	.555
	New Jersey	2	7	6	1	40	27	13	0	1	.675
	Total	**4**	**12**	**9**	**3**	**67**	**42**	**25**	**0**	**1**	**.626**
Muckler, John	Edmonton	2	7	6	1	40	25	15	0	1	.625
	Buffalo	4	5	1	4	27	11	16	0	0	.407
	Total	**6**	**12**	**7**	**5**	**67**	**36**	**31**	**0**	**1**	**.537**
Ivan, Tommy	Detroit	7	12	8	4	67	36	31	0	3	.537
Neilson, Roger	Toronto	2	5	3	2	19	8	11	0	0	.421
	Buffalo	1	2	1	1	8	4	4	0	0	.500
	Vancouver	2	5	3	2	21	12	9	0	0	.571
	NY Rangers	2	3	1	2	19	8	11	0	0	.421
	Total	**7**	**15**	**8**	**7**	**67**	**32**	**35**	**0**	**0**	**.473**
Pulford, Bob	Los Angeles	4	6	2	4	26	11	15	0	0	.423
	Chicago	5	9	4	5	41	17	24	0	0	.415
	Total	**9**	**15**	**6**	**9**	**67**	**28**	**39**	**0**	**0**	**.418**
Patrick, Lester	NY Rangers	12	24	14	10	65	31	26	8	2	.538

* Does not include suspended game, May 24, 1988.

Penalty Shots in Stanley Cup Playoff Games

Date	Player	Goaltender	Scored	Final Score				Series
Mar. 25/37	Lionel Conacher, Mtl. Maroons	Tiny Thompson, Boston	No	Mtl. M. 0	at	Bos.	4	QF
Apr. 15/37	Alex Shibicky, NY Rangers	Earl Robertson, Detroit	No	NYR 0	at	Det.	3	F
Apr. 13/44	Virgil Johnson, Chicago	Bill Durnan, Montreal	No	Chi. 4	at	Mtl.	5*	F
Apr. 9/68	Wayne Connelly, Minnesota	Terry Sawchuk, Los Angeles	Yes	L.A. 5	at	Min.	7	QF
Apr. 27/68	Jim Roberts, St. Louis	Cesare Maniago, Minnesota	No	St. L. 4	at	Min.	3	SF
May 16/71	Frank Mahovlich, Montreal	Tony Esposito, Chicago	No	Chi. 3	at	Mtl.	4	F
May 7/75	Bill Barber, Philadelphia	Glenn Resch, NY Islanders	No	Phi. 3	at	NYI	4*	SF
Apr. 20/79	Mike Walton, Chicago	Glenn Resch, NY Islanders	No	NYI 4	at	Chi.	0	QF
Apr. 9/81	Peter McNab, Boston	Don Beaupre, Minnesota	No	Min. 5	at	Bos.	4*	PR
Apr. 17/81	Anders Hedberg, NY Rangers	Mike Liut, St. Louis	Yes	NYR 6	at	St. L.	4	QF
Apr. 9/83	Denis Potvin, NY Islanders	Pat Riggin, Washington	No	NYI 6	at	Wsh.	2	DSF
Apr. 28/84	Wayne Gretzky, Edmonton	Don Beaupre, Minnesota	Yes	Edm. 8	at	Min.	5	CF
May 1/84	Mats Naslund, Montreal	Bill Smith, NY Islanders	No	Mtl. 1	at	NYI	3	CF
Apr. 14/85	Bob Carpenter, Washington	Bill Smith, NY Islanders	No	Wsh. 4	at	NYI.	6	DF
May 28/85	Ron Sutter, Philadelphia	Grant Fuhr, Edmonton	No	Phi. 3	at	Edm.	5	F
May 30/85	Dave Poulin, Philadelphia	Grant Fuhr, Edmonton	No	Phi. 3	at	Edm.	8	F
Apr. 9/88	John Tucker, Buffalo	Andy Moog, Boston	Yes	Bos. 2	at	Buf.	6	DSF
Apr. 9/88	Petr Klima, Detroit	Allan Bester, Toronto	Yes	Det. 6	at	Tor.	3	DSF
Apr. 8/89	Neal Broten, Minnesota	Greg Millen, St. Louis	Yes	St. L. 5	at	Min.	3	DSF
Apr. 4/90	Al MacInnis, Calgary	Kelly Hrudey, Los Angeles	Yes	L.A. 5	at	Cgy.	3	DSF
Apr. 5/90	Randy Wood, NY Islanders	Mike Richter, NY Rangers	No	NYI 1	at	NYR	2	DSF
May 3/90	Kelly Miller, Washington	Andy Moog, Boston	No	Wsh. 3	at	Bos.	5	CF
May 18/90	Petr Klima, Edmonton	Rejean Lemelin, Boston	No	Edm. 7	at	Bos.	2	F
Apr. 6/91	Basil McRae, Minnesota	Ed Belfour, Chicago	Yes	Min. 2	at	Chi.	5	DSF
Apr. 10/91	Steve Duchesne, Los Angeles	Kirk McLean, Vancouver	Yes	L.A. 6	at	Van.	1	DSF
May 11/92	Jaromir Jagr, Pittsburgh	John Vanbiesbrouck, NYR	Yes	Pit. 3	at	NYR	2	DF
May 13/92	Shawn McEachern, Pittsburgh	John Vanbiesbrouck, NYR	No	NYR 1	at	Pit.	5	DF
June 7/94	Pavel Bure, Vancouver	Mike Richter, NYR	No	NYR 4	at	Van.	2	F
May 9/95	Patrick Poulin, Chicago	Felix Potvin, Toronto	No	Tor. 3	at	Chi.	0	CQF
May 10/95	Michal Pivonka, Washington	Tom Barrasso, Pittsburgh	No	Pit. 2	at	Wsh.	6	CQF

* Game was decided in overtime, but shot taken during regulation time.

Ten Longest Overtime Games

Date	City	Series	Score				Scorer	Overtime	Series Winner
Mar. 24/36	Mtl.	SF	Det. 1		Mtl. M.	0	Mud Bruneteau	116:30	Det.
Apr. 3/33	Tor.	SF	Tor. 1		Bos.	0	Ken Doraty	104:46	Tor.
Mar. 23/43	Det.	SF	Tor. 3		Det.	2	Jack McLean	70:18	Det.
Mar. 28/30	Mtl.	SF	Mtl. 2		NYR	1	Gus Rivers	68:52	Mtl.
Apr. 18/87	Wsh.	DSF	NYI 3		Wsh.	2	Pat LaFontaine	68:47	NYI
Apr. 27/94	Buf.	CQF	Buf. 1		N.J.	0	Dave Hannan	65:43	N.J.
Mar. 27/51	Det.	SF	Mtl. 3		Det.	2	Maurice Richard	61:09	Mtl.
Mar. 27/38	NY	QF	NYA 3		NYR	2	Lorne Carr	60:40	NYA
Mar. 26/32	Mtl.	SF	NYR 4		Mtl.	3	Fred Cook	59:32	NYR
Mar. 21/39	NY	SF	Bos. 2		NYR	1	Mel Hill	59:25	Bos.

Two penalty shots were taken in the 1995 playoffs. Although Michal Pivonka, above, was stopped by Pittsburgh's Tom Barrasso, the Capitals held on for a 6–2 victory in game three of the Penguins-Capitals Eastern Conference Quarter-Final series. Felix Potvin, below, stopped Chicago's Patrick Poulin on a penalty shot in game two of the Western Quarter-Finals, preserving his shutout in a 3–0 victory for the Leafs.

Overtime Record of Current Teams

(Listed by number of OT games played)

	Overall				Home					Road				
Team	GP	W	L	T	GP	W	L	T	Last OT Game	GP	W	L	T	Last OT Game
Montreal	115	66	47	2	53	35	17	1	Jun. 3/93	62	31	30	1	Apr. 25/94
Boston	93	36	54	3	43	20	22	1	May 9/94	50	16	32	2	May 12/94
Toronto	87	44	42	1	55	28	26	1	May 17/95	32	16	16	0	May 24/94
NY Rangers	59	27	32	0	25	11	14	0	May 12/95	34	16	18	0	May 22/95
Chicago	56	26	28	2	26	14	11	1	Jun. 6/95	30	12	17	1	Jun. 11/95
Detroit	54	25	29	0	33	12	21	0	Jun. 1/95	21	13	8	0	Jun. 6/95
NY Islanders	38	29	9	0	17	14	3	0	May 20/93	21	15	6	0	May 18/93
Philadelphia	38	22	16	0	16	11	5	0	May 22/95	22	11	11	0	Jun. 7/95
St. Louis	33	19	14	0	17	13	4	0	May 15/95	16	6	10	0	May 5/93
Los Angeles	30	12	18	0	16	8	8	0	Jun. 7/93	14	4	10	0	Jun. 3/93
* Calgary	29	11	18	0	13	4	9	0	May 19/95	16	7	9	0	Apr. 28/94
Buffalo	28	14	14	0	17	11	6	0	Apr. 27/94	11	3	8	0	May 7/95
Vancouver	28	13	15	0	12	5	7	0	May 27/95	16	8	8	0	May 21/95
** Dallas	28	12	16	0	14	5	9	0	Apr. 28/92	14	7	7	0	May 8/94
Edmonton	27	17	10	0	14	9	5	0	May 20/92	13	8	5	0	May 3/92
*** Colorado	19	10	9	0	11	6	5	0	Apr. 26/93	8	4	4	0	May 12/95
Washington	18	8	10	0	7	4	3	0	Apr. 20/93	11	4	7	0	May 14/95
Pittsburgh	16	9	7	0	9	6	3	0	May 14/95	7	3	4	0	May 26/95
**** New Jersey	15	5	10	0	7	2	5	0	Jun. 7/95	8	3	5	0	May 27/94
Hartford	11	5	6	0	7	4	3	0	Apr. 29/92	4	1	3	0	May 1/92
Winnipeg	9	4	5	0	5	2	3	0	Apr. 29/93	4	2	2	0	Apr. 27/93
San Jose	3	2	1	0	0	0	0	0		3	2	1	0	May 19/95

*Totals include those of Atlanta 1972-80.
**Totals include those of Minnesota 1967-93.
***Totals include those of Quebec 1979-95.
****Totals include those of Kansas City and Colorado 1974-82.

Key to Player and Goaltender Registers

Demographics: Position, shooting side (catching hand for goaltenders), height, weight, place and date of birth are found on first line. Draft information, if any, is located on second line.

Major Junior, NCAA, minor pro, senior European and NHL clubs form a permanent part of each player's data panel. If a player sees action with more than one club in any of the above categories, a separate line is included for each one.

High school, prep school, Tier II junior, European junior and U.S. junior listings are deleted if a player accumulates two or more years of Major Junior, NCAA or senior European experience.

Canadian and U.S. National and Olympic Team statistics are also listed. For Europeans, Olympic Team participation is included as a separate line if a player joins an NHL club at the conclusion of the Games.

Some data is unavailable at press time. Readers are encouraged to contribute.
See page 5 for contact names and addresses.

Player's NHL organization as of August 17, 1995. This includes players under contract, unsigned draft choices and other players on reserve lists. Free agents as of August 17, 1995 show a blank here.

The complete career data panels of players with NHL experience who announced their retirement before the start of the 1995-96 season are included in the 1995-96 Player Register. These newly-retired players also show a blank here.

Each NHL club's minor-pro affiliates are listed at the bottom of this page.

Footnotes are listed below player's year-by-year data and indicate league awards and all-star selections. Letter corresponding to footnote is placed beside the season in which awards or all-star selections were received.

PLAYER, JOHN SAMPLE (PLAY-uhr) **S.J.**

Center. Shoots left, 6'1", 200 lbs.   Born, Neepawa, Man., April 14, 1974.
(Pittsburgh's 3rd choice, 62nd overall in the 1992 Entry Draft).

				Regular Season					Playoffs			
Season	Club	League	GP	G	A	TP	PIM	GP	G	A	TP	PIM
1990-91	Brandon	WHL	66	15	13	28	17	4	3	1	4	6
1991-92	Brandon	WHL	72	36	30	66	72	12	4	5	9	12
1992-93ab	Brandon	WHL	70	47	59	106	83	16	*16	8	*24	14
1993-94	**Pittsburgh**	**NHL**	**10**	**1**	**2**	**3**	**6**	....	....	....	....	....
	Cleveland	IHL	64	31	22	53	71	5	3	2	5	8
1994-95	**Montreal**	**NHL**	**24**	**7**	**6**	**13**	**42**	**1**	**0**	**0**	**0**	**0**
	Fredericton	AHL	47	41	31	72	106	....	....	....	....	....
	NHL Totals		**34**	**8**	**8**	**16**	**48**	**1**	**0**	**0**	**0**	**0**

a WHL East Second All-Star Team (1993)
b Won Stafford Smythe Memorial Trophy (Memorial Cup MVP) (1993)

Traded to **Montreal** by **Pittsburgh** for Montreal's third round choice in 1996 Entry Draft, June 14, 1994. Signed as a free agent by **San Jose**, August 3, 1995.

All trades, free agent signings and other transactions involving NHL clubs are listed in chronological order. Players selected by NHL clubs after re-entering the NHL Entry Draft are noted here. NHL All-Star Game appearances are listed above trade notes.

Asterisk (*) indicates league leader in this statistical category.

NHL Clubs and Minor League Affiliates 1995-96

NHL CLUB	MINOR LEAGUE AFFILIATE
Anaheim	Baltimore Bandits (IHL)
	Raleigh IceCaps (ECHL)
Boston	Providence Bruins (AHL)
	Charlotte Checkers (ECHL)
Buffalo	Rochester Americans (AHL)
	South Carolina Stingrays (ECHL)
Calgary	Saint John Flames (AHL)
Chicago	Indianapolis Ice (IHL)
	Columbus Chill (ECHL)
Colorado	Cornwall Aces (AHL)
Dallas	Michigan K-Wings (IHL)
	Dayton Bombers (ECHL)
Detroit	Adirondack Red Wings (AHL)
	Toledo Storm (ECHL)
Edmonton	Cape Breton Oilers (AHL)
	Wheeling Thunderbirds (ECHL)
Florida	Carolina Monarchs (AHL)
	Cincinnati Cyclones (IHL)
	Birmingham Bulls (ECHL)
Hartford	Springfield Falcons (AHL)
	Richmond Renegades (ECHL)
Los Angeles	Phoenix Roadrunners (IHL)
	Richmond Renegades (ECHL)
	Knoxville Cherokees (ECHL)

NHL CLUB	MINOR LEAGUE AFFILIATE
Montreal	Fredericton Canadiens (AHL)
	Wheeling Thunderbirds (ECHL)
New Jersey	Albany River Rats (AHL)
	Raleigh IceCaps (ECHL)
NY Islanders	Worcester Icecats (AHL)
	Utah Grizzlies (IHL)
	Tallahassee Tiger Sharks (ECHL)
NY Rangers	Binghamton Rangers (AHL)
Ottawa	P.E.I. Senators (AHL)
	Thunder Bay Senators (ColHL)
Philadelphia	Hershey Bears (AHL)
Pittsburgh	Cleveland Lumberjacks (IHL)
	Hampton Roads Admirals (ECHL)
St. Louis	Worcester Icecats (AHL)
San Jose	Kansas City Blades (IHL)
	Mobile Mysticks (ECHL)
Tampa Bay	Atlanta Knights (IHL)
	Nashville Knights (ECHL)
Toronto	St. John's Maple Leafs (AHL)
Vancouver	Syracuse Crunch (AHL)
Washington	Portland Pirates (AHL)
	Hampton Roads Admirals (ECHL)
Winnipeg	Springfield Falcons (AHL)
	Minnesota Moose (IHL)

Pronunciation of Player's Name

United Press International phonetic style.

AY	long A as in mate
A	short A as in cat
AI	nasal A as on air
AH	short A as in father
AW	broad A as in talk
EE	long E as in meat
EH	short E as in get
UH	hollow E as in "the"
AY	French long E with acute accent as in Pathe
IH	middle E as in pretty
EW	EW dipthong as in few
IGH	long I as in time
EE	French long I as in machine
IH	short I as in pity
OH	long O as in note
AH	short O as in hot
AW	broad O as in fought
OO	long double OO as in fool
UH	short double O as in ouch
OW	OW dipthong as in how
EW	long U as in mule
OO	long U as in rule
U	middle U as in put
UH	short U as in shut or hurt
K	hard C as in cat
S	soft C as in cease
SH	soft CH as in machine
CH	hard CH or TCH as in catch
Z	hard S as in decrease
S	soft S as in sun
G	hard G as in gang
J	soft G as in general
ZH	soft J as in French version of Joliet

Late Additions to Player Register

CASSIDY, BRUCE   CHI.

Defense. Shoots left. 5'11", 176 lbs.   Born, Ottawa, Ont., May 20, 1965.
(Chicago's 1st choice, 18th overall, in 1983 Entry Draft).

			Regular Season					Playoffs				
Season	Club	Lea	GP	G	A	TP	PIM	GP	G	A	TP	PIM
1982-83	Ottawa	OHL	70	25	86	111	33	9	3	9	12	10
1983-84	**Chicago**	**NHL**	**1**	**0**	**0**	**0**	**0**	....	....	....	....	....
a	Ottawa	OHL	67	27	68	95	58	13	6	16	22	6
1984-85	Ottawa	OHL	28	13	27	40	15	....	....	....	....	....
1985-86	**Chicago**	**NHL**	**1**	**0**	**0**	**0**	**0**	....	....	....	....	....
	Nova Scotia	AHL	4	0	0	0	0	....	....	....	....	....
1986-87	**Chicago**	**NHL**	**2**	**0**	**0**	**0**	**0**	....	....	....	....	....
	Nova Scotia	AHL	19	2	8	10	4	....	....	....	....	....
	Cdn. Olympic	....	12	3	6	9	4	....	....	....	....	....
	Saginaw	IHL	10	2	13	15	6	2	1	1	2	0
1987-88	**Chicago**	**NHL**	**21**	**3**	**10**	**13**	**6**	....	....	....	....	....
	Saginaw	IHL	60	9	37	46	59	10	2	3	5	19
1988-89	**Chicago**	**NHL**	**9**	**0**	**2**	**2**	**4**	**1**	**0**	**0**	**0**	**0**
b	Saginaw	IHL	72	16	64	80	80	6	0	2	2	6
1989-90	**Chicago**	**NHL**	**2**	**1**	**1**	**2**	**0**	....	....	....	....	....
b	Indianapolis	IHL	75	11	46	57	56	14	1	10	11	20
1990-91	Alleghe	Italy	36	23	52	75	20	10	7	8	15	2
1992-93	Alleghe	Italy	36	24	47	71	....	8	5	9	14	
1992-93	Alleghe	Italy	36	23	51	74	....	8	4	10	14	
1993-94	Kaufbeuren	Ger.	33	9	12	21	....	4	1	2	3	....
1994-95	Indianapolis	IHL	29	2	13	15	16	....	....	....	....	....
	NHL Totals		**36**	**4**	**13**	**17**	**10**	**1**	**0**	**0**	**0**	**0**

a OHL Second All-Star Team (1984)
b IHL First All-Star Team (1989, 1990)
Signed as a free agent by **Chicago**, July 28, 1994.

HICKS, ALEX   ANA.

Defense. Shoots left. 6'1", 195 lbs.   Born, Calgary, Alta., September 4, 1969.

			Regular Season					Playoffs				
Season	Club	Lea	GP	G	A	TP	PIM	GP	G	A	TP	PIM
1992-93	Toledo	ECHL	50	26	34	60	100	16	5	10	15	79
1993-94	Toledo	ECHL	60	31	49	80	240	14	10	10	20	56
1994-95	Las Vegas	IHL	79	24	42	66	212	9	2	4	6	47

Signed as a free agent by **Anaheim**, August 23, 1995.

WEBB, STEVE   BUF.

Right wing. Shoots right. 5'11", 205 lbs.   Born, Peterborough, Ont., April 30, 1975.
(Buffalo's 8th choice, 176th overall, in 1994 Entry Draft).

			Regular Season					Playoffs				
Season	Club	Lea	GP	G	A	TP	PIM	GP	G	A	TP	PIM
1992-93	Windsor	OHL	63	14	25	39	181	....	....	....	....	....
1993-94	Windsor	OHL	33	6	15	21	117	....	....	....	....	....
	Peterborough	OHL	2	0	1	1	9	6	1	1	2	10
1994-95	Peterborough	OHL	42	8	16	24	109	11	3	3	6	22

WHITE, BRIAN   T.B.

Defense. Shoots right. 6'1", 180 lbs.   Born, Winchester, MA, February 7, 1976.
(Tampa Bay's 11th choice, 268th overall, in 1994 Entry Draft).

			Regular Season					Playoffs				
Season	Club	Lea	GP	G	A	TP	PIM	GP	G	A	TP	PIM
1993-94	Arlington	HS	26	7	28	35	24	....	....	....	....	....
1994-95	U. of Maine	H.E.	28	1	1	2	16	....	....	....	....	....

Trade Notes and Free Agent Signings

DRIVER, BRUCE Signed as a free agent by NY Rangers, August 24, 1995.

FELSNER, DENNY Signed as a free agent by Vancouver, August 30, 1995.

FLINTON, ERIC Signed as a free agent by NY Rangers, August 22, 1995.

HUDSON, MIKE Signed as a free agent by Toronto, August 28, 1995.

JENNINGS, GRANT Signed as a free agent by Buffalo, August 29, 1995.

MAJOR, MARK Signed as a free agent by Detroit, August, 1995.

NEDVED, PETR Traded to Pittsburgh by NY Rangers with Sergei Zubov for Luc Robitaille and Ulf Samuelsson, August 31, 1995.

RACICOT, ANDRE Signed as a free agent by Chicago, August 29, 1995.

ROBITAILLE, LUC Traded to NY Rangers by Pittsburgh with Ulf Samuelsson for Petr Nedved and Sergei Zubov, August 31, 1995.

SAMUELSSON, ULF Traded to NY Rangers by Pittsburgh with Luc Robitaille for Petr Nedved and Sergei Zubov, August 31, 1995.

WARD, DIXON Signed as a free agent by Buffalo, August 24, 1995.

YUSHKEVICH, DIMITRI Traded to Toronto by Philadelphia with Philadelphia's second round choice in 1996 Entry Draft for Toronto's first round choice in 1996 Entry Draft, Los Angeles' fourth round choice (previously acquired by Toronto) in 1996 Entry Draft and Toronto's second round choice in 1997 Entry Draft, August 30, 1995.

ZUBOV, SERGEI Traded to Pittsburgh by NY Rangers with Petr Nedved for Luc Robitaille and Ulf Samuelsson, August 31, 1995.

1995-96 Player Register

Note: The 1995-96 Player Register lists forwards and defensemen only. Goaltenders are listed separately. The Player Register lists every skater who appeared in an NHL game in the 1994-95 season, every skater drafted in the first six rounds of the 1994 and 1995 Entry Drafts, players on NHL Reserve Lists and other players. Trades and roster changes are current as of August 17, 1995.

Abbreviations: A – assists; **G** – goals; **GP** – games played; **Lea** – league; **PIM** – penalties in minutes; **TP** – total points; * – league-leading total.

Pronunciations courtesy of the NHL Broadcasters' Association and Igor Kuperman, Winnipeg Jets

Goaltender Register begins on page 423.

LEAGUES:

ACHL	Atlantic Coast Hockey League
AHL	American Hockey League
AJHL	Alberta Junior Hockey League
Alp.	Alpenliga
AUAA	Atlantic Universities Athletic Association
BCJHL	British Columbia Junior Hockey League
CCHA	Central Collegiate Hockey Association
CHL	Central Hockey League
CIAU	Canadian Interuniversity Athletic Union
COJHL	Central Ontario Junior Hockey League
ColHL	Colonial Hockey League
CWUAA	Canada West Universities Athletic Association
ECAC	Eastern Collegiate Athletic Association
ECHL	East Coast Hockey League
EJHL	Eastern Junior Hockey League
G.N.	Great Northern
GPAC	Great Plains Athletic Conference
H.E.	Hockey East
HS	High School
IHL	International Hockey League
Jr.	Junior
MJHA	(New York) Metropolitan Junior Hockey Association
MJHL	Manitoba Junior Hockey League
NAJHL	North American Junior Hockey League
NCAA	National Collegiate Athletic Association
NHL	**National Hockey League**
OHA	Ontario Hockey Association
OHL	Ontario Hockey League
OMJHL	Ontario Major Junior Hockey League
OPJHL	Ontario Provincial Junior Hockey League
OUAA	Ontario Universities Athletic Association
QJHL	Quebec Junior Hockey League
QMJHL	Quebec Major Junior Hockey League
SJHL	Saskatchewan Junior Hockey League
SOHL	Southern Ontario Hockey League
USHL	United States Hockey League (Junior)
WCHA	Western Collegiate Hockey Association
WHA	World Hockey Association
WHL	Western Hockey League

AALTO, ANTTI (AL-toh, AN-tee) ANA.

Center. Shoots left. 6'2", 185 lbs. Born, Lappeenranta, Finland, March 4, 1975.
(Anaheim's 6th choice, 134th overall, in 1993 Entry Draft).

			Regular Season					Playoffs				
Season	**Club**	**Lea**	**GP**	**G**	**A**	**TP**	**PIM**	**GP**	**G**	**A**	**TP**	**PIM**
1991-92	SaiPa	Fin. 2	20	6	6	12	20	....	....	....	....	....
1992-93	SaiPa	Fin. 2	23	6	8	14	14	....	....	....	....	....
	TPS	Fin.	1	0	0	0	0	....	....	....	....	....
1993-94	TPS	Fin.	33	5	9	14	16	10	1	1	2	4
1994-95	TPS	Fin.	44	11	7	18	18	5	0	1	1	2

AALTONEN, PETRI (AL-tuh-nehn) COL.

Center. Shoots left. 5'10", 185 lbs. Born, Tampere, Finland, May 31, 1970.
(Quebec's 4th choice, 45th overall, in 1988 Entry Draft).

			Regular Season					Playoffs				
Season	**Club**	**Lea**	**GP**	**G**	**A**	**TP**	**PIM**	**GP**	**G**	**A**	**TP**	**PIM**
1988-89	HIFK	Fin.	2	0	0	0	0	....	....	....	....	....
1989-90	HIFK	Fin.	3	0	0	0	0	....	....	....	....	....
1990-91	HIFK	Fin.	43	6	9	15	12	3	1	1	2	0
1991-92	Tappara	Fin.	36	3	4	7	18	....	....	....	....	....
1992-93	Vantaa	Fin. 2	33	15	11	26	50	....	....	....	....	....
1993-94	Tappara	Fin.	25	2	4	6	12	....	....	....	....	....
	Karhu-Kissat	Fin. 2	9	3	7	10	50	....	....	....	....	....
1994-95	Haukat	Fin. 2	39	19	24	43	115	3	0	1	1	4

ADAMS, GREG DAL.

Left wing. Shoots left. 6'3", 198 lbs. Born, Nelson, B.C., August 1, 1963.

			Regular Season					Playoffs				
Season	**Club**	**Lea**	**GP**	**G**	**A**	**TP**	**PIM**	**GP**	**G**	**A**	**TP**	**PIM**
1982-83	N. Arizona	NCAA	29	14	21	35	19	....	....	....	....	....
1983-84	N. Arizona	NCAA	26	44	29	73	24	....	....	....	....	....
1984-85	**New Jersey**	**NHL**	**36**	**12**	**9**	**21**	**14**	....	....	....	....	....
	Maine	AHL	41	15	20	35	12	11	3	4	7	0
1985-86	**New Jersey**	**NHL**	**78**	**35**	**42**	**77**	**30**	....	....	....	....	....
1986-87	**New Jersey**	**NHL**	**72**	**20**	**27**	**47**	**19**	....	....	....	....	....
1987-88	**Vancouver**	**NHL**	**80**	**36**	**40**	**76**	**30**	....	....	....	....	....
1988-89	**Vancouver**	**NHL**	**61**	**19**	**14**	**33**	**24**	**7**	**2**	**3**	**5**	**2**
1989-90	**Vancouver**	**NHL**	**65**	**30**	**20**	**50**	**18**	....	....	....	....	....
1990-91	**Vancouver**	**NHL**	**55**	**21**	**24**	**45**	**10**	**5**	**0**	**0**	**0**	**2**
1991-92	**Vancouver**	**NHL**	**76**	**30**	**27**	**57**	**26**	**6**	**0**	**2**	**2**	**4**
1992-93	**Vancouver**	**NHL**	**53**	**25**	**31**	**56**	**14**	**12**	**7**	**6**	**13**	**6**
1993-94	**Vancouver**	**NHL**	**68**	**13**	**24**	**37**	**20**	**23**	**6**	**8**	**14**	**2**
1994-95	**Vancouver**	**NHL**	**31**	**5**	**10**	**15**	**12**	....	....	....	....	....
	Dallas	**NHL**	**12**	**3**	**3**	**6**	**4**	**5**	**2**	**0**	**2**	**0**
	NHL Totals		**687**	**249**	**271**	**520**	**221**	**58**	**17**	**19**	**36**	**16**

Played in NHL All-Star Game (1988)

Signed as a free agent by **New Jersey**, June 25, 1984. Traded to **Vancouver** by **New Jersey** with Kirk McLean for Patrik Sundstrom and Vancouver's fourth round choice (Matt Ruchty) in 1988 Entry Draft, September 10, 1987. Traded to **Dallas** by **Vancouver** with Dan Kesa and Vancouver's fifth round choice (later traded to Los Angeles — Los Angeles selected Jason Morgan) in 1995 Entry Draft for Russ Courtnall, April 7, 1995.

ADAMS, KEVYN BOS.

Center. Shoots right. 6'1", 182 lbs. Born, Washington, D.C., October 8, 1974.
(Boston's 1st choice, 25th overall, in 1993 Entry Draft).

			Regular Season					Playoffs				
Season	**Club**	**Lea**	**GP**	**G**	**A**	**TP**	**PIM**	**GP**	**G**	**A**	**TP**	**PIM**
1992-93	Miami-Ohio	CCHA	40	17	15	32	18	....	....	....	....	....
1993-94	Miami-Ohio	CCHA	36	15	28	43	24	....	....	....	....	....
1994-95a	Miami-Ohio	CCHA	38	20	29	49	30	....	....	....	....	....

a CCHA Second All-Star Team (1995)

AGARKOV, PAVEL (ah-GAHR-kohv) DET.

Right wing. Shoots left. 5'11", 167 lbs. Born, Moscow, USSR, April 23, 1975.
(Detroit's 6th choice, 153rd overall, in 1994 Entry Draft).

			Regular Season					Playoffs				
Season	**Club**	**Lea**	**GP**	**G**	**A**	**TP**	**PIM**	**GP**	**G**	**A**	**TP**	**PIM**
1993-94	Soviet Wings	CIS	27	2	0	2	12	....	....	....	....	....
1994-95	Shawinigan	QMJHL	55	19	26	45	34	14	7	5	12	10

AHLUND, HAKAN VAN.

Right wing. Shoots left. 6', 194 lbs. Born, Orebro, Sweden, August 16, 1967.
(Vancouver's 8th choice, 151st overall, in 1985 Entry Draft).

			Regular Season					Playoffs				
Season	**Club**	**Lea**	**GP**	**G**	**A**	**TP**	**PIM**	**GP**	**G**	**A**	**TP**	**PIM**
1983-84	Orebro	Swe. 2	1	0	1	1	0	....	....	....	....	....
1984-85	Orebro	Swe. 2	25	2	6	8	10	....	....	....	....	....
1985-86	Orebro	Swe. 2	20	5	4	9	10	2	0	0	0	0
1986-87	Orebro	Swe. 2	27	16	9	25	6	6	0	3	3	6
1987-88	Orebro	Swe. 2	36	24	23	47	29	6	3	4	7	7
1988-89	Malmo	Swe. 2	35	20	27	47	44	....	....	....	....	....
1989-90	Malmo	Swe. 2	35	12	38	50	30	....	....	....	....	....
1990-91	Malmo	Swe.	39	9	18	27	46	2	0	0	0	0
1991-92	Malmo	Swe.	38	5	12	17	48	10	2	2	4	8
1992-93	Malmo	Swe.	33	5	10	15	30	6	2	1	3	6
1993-94	Malmo	Swe.	37	7	7	14	26	10	4	3	7	13
1994-95	Malmo	Swe.	37	4	10	14	26	9	4	5	9	10

AIVAZOFF, MICAH (A-vuh-zahf, MIGH-kuh) NYI

Center. Shoots left. 6', 195 lbs. Born, Powell River, B.C., May 4, 1969.
(Los Angeles' 6th choice, 109th overall, in 1988 Entry Draft).

			Regular Season					Playoffs				
Season	**Club**	**Lea**	**GP**	**G**	**A**	**TP**	**PIM**	**GP**	**G**	**A**	**TP**	**PIM**
1986-87	Victoria	WHL	72	18	39	57	112	5	1	0	1	2
1987-88	Victoria	WHL	69	26	57	83	79	8	3	4	7	14
1988-89	Victoria	WHL	70	35	65	100	136	8	5	7	12	2
1989-90	New Haven	AHL	77	20	39	59	71	....	....	....	....	....
1990-91	New Haven	AHL	79	11	29	40	84	....	....	....	....	....
1991-92	Adirondack	AHL	61	9	20	29	50	19	2	8	10	25
1992-93	Adirondack	AHL	79	32	53	85	100	11	8	6	14	10
1993-94	**Detroit**	**NHL**	**59**	**4**	**4**	**8**	**38**	....	....	....	....	....
1994-95	**Edmonton**	**NHL**	**21**	**0**	**1**	**1**	**2**	....	....	....	....	....
	NHL Totals		**80**	**4**	**5**	**9**	**40**	....	....	....	....	....

Signed as a free agent by **Detroit**, March 18, 1993. Claimed by **Pittsburgh** from **Detroit** in NHL Waiver Draft, January 18, 1995. Claimed by **Edmonton** from **Pittsburgh** in NHL Waiver Draft, January 18, 1995. Signed as a free agent by **NY Islanders**, August 10, 1995.

AKERSTROM, ROGER (OHK-uhr-struhm) VAN.

Defense. Shoots left. 5'11", 189 lbs. Born, Lulea, Sweden, April 5, 1967.
(Vancouver's 8th choice, 170th overall, in 1988 Entry Draft).

			Regular Season					Playoffs				
Season	**Club**	**Lea**	**GP**	**G**	**A**	**TP**	**PIM**	**GP**	**G**	**A**	**TP**	**PIM**
1987-88	Lulea	Swe.	34	4	3	7	28	....	....	....	....	....
1988-89	Lulea	Swe.	38	6	12	18	32	....	....	....	....	....
1989-90	Lulea	Swe.	36	5	10	15	44	5	3	2	5	2
1990-91	Lulea	Swe.	37	2	10	12	38	5	0	1	1	6
1991-92	Vasteras	Swe.	39	3	9	12	20	....	....	....	....	....
1992-93	Vasteras	Swe.	37	13	13	26	36	3	0	0	0	6
1993-94	Vasteras	Swe.	36	5	4	9	37	4	2	1	3	4
1994-95	Lulea	Swe.	39	5	16	21	38	8	1	1	2	12

ALATALO, MIKA WPG.

Left wing. Shoots left. 5'11", 185 lbs. Born, Oulu, Finland, June 11, 1971.
(Winnipeg's 11th choice, 203rd overall, in 1990 Entry Draft).

			Regular Season					Playoffs				
Season	**Club**	**Lea**	**GP**	**G**	**A**	**TP**	**PIM**	**GP**	**G**	**A**	**TP**	**PIM**
1988-89	KooKoo	Fin.	34	8	6	14	10	....	....	....	....	....
1989-90	KooKoo	Fin.	41	3	5	8	22	....	....	....	....	....
1990-91	Lukko	Fin.	39	10	1	11	10	....	....	....	....	....
1991-92	Lukko	Fin.	43	20	17	37	32	2	0	0	0	0
1992-93	Lukko	Fin.	48	16	19	35	38	3	0	0	0	0
1993-94	Lukko	Fin.	45	19	15	34	77	9	2	2	4	4
1994-95	TPS	Fin.	44	23	13	36	79	13	2	5	7	8

ALBELIN, TOMMY (AL-buh-LEEN) N.J.

Defense. Shoots left. 6'1", 190 lbs. Born, Stockholm, Sweden, May 21, 1964.
(Quebec's 7th choice, 152nd overall, in 1983 Entry Draft).

			Regular Season					Playoffs				
Season	Club	Lea	GP	G	A	TP	PIM	GP	G	A	TP	PIM
1982-83	Djurgarden	Swe.	19	2	5	7	4	6	1	0	1	2
1983-84	Djurgarden	Swe.	30	9	5	14	26	4	0	1	1	2
1984-85	Djurgarden	Swe.	32	9	8	17	22	8	2	1	3	4
1985-86	Djurgarden	Swe.	35	4	8	12	26	....	....	....	....	....
1986-87	Djurgarden	Swe.	33	7	5	12	49	2	0	0	0	0
1987-88	**Quebec**	**NHL**	**60**	**3**	**23**	**26**	**47**	....	....	....	....	....
1988-89	**Quebec**	**NHL**	**14**	**2**	**4**	**6**	**27**	....	....	....	....	....
	Halifax	AHL	8	2	5	7	4	....	....	....	....	....
	New Jersey	**NHL**	**46**	**7**	**24**	**31**	**40**	....	....	....	....	....
1989-90	**New Jersey**	**NHL**	**68**	**6**	**23**	**29**	**63**	....	....	....	....	....
1990-91	**New Jersey**	**NHL**	**47**	**2**	**12**	**14**	**44**	**3**	**0**	**1**	**1**	**2**
	Utica	AHL	14	4	2	6	10	....	....	....	....	....
1991-92	**New Jersey**	**NHL**	**19**	**0**	**4**	**4**	**4**	**1**	**1**	**1**	**2**	**0**
	Utica	AHL	11	4	6	10	4	....	....	....	....	....
1992-93	**New Jersey**	**NHL**	**36**	**1**	**5**	**6**	**14**	**5**	**2**	**0**	**2**	**0**
1993-94	**New Jersey**	**NHL**	**62**	**2**	**17**	**19**	**36**	**20**	**2**	**5**	**7**	**14**
	Albany	AHL	4	0	2	2	17	....	....	....	....	....
1994-95	**New Jersey**	**NHL**	**48**	**5**	**10**	**15**	**20**	**20**	**1**	**7**	**8**	**2**
	NHL Totals		**400**	**28**	**122**	**150**	**295**	**49**	**6**	**14**	**20**	**18**

Traded to **New Jersey** by **Quebec** for New Jersey's fourth round choice (Niclas Andersson) in 1989 Entry Draft, December 12, 1988.

ALDOUS, CHRIS MTL.

Defense. Shoots left. 6'3", 181 lbs. Born, Massena, NY, November 19, 1975.
(Montreal's 12th choice, 252nd overall, in 1994 Entry Draft).

			Regular Season					Playoffs				
Season	Club	Lea	GP	G	A	TP	PIM	GP	G	A	TP	PIM
1993-94	Northwood	HS	41	9	42	51	18	....	....	....	....	....
1994-95	RPI	ECAC	31	0	1	1	4	....	....	....	....	....

ALEXEEV, ALEXANDER WSH.

Defense. Shoots left. 6', 216 lbs. Born, Kiev, USSR, March 21, 1974.
(Winnipeg's 5th choice, 132nd overall, in 1992 Entry Draft).

			Regular Season					Playoffs				
Season	Club	Lea	GP	G	A	TP	PIM	GP	G	A	TP	PIM
1990-91	Sokol Kiev	USSR	5	0	0	0	2	....	....	....	....	....
1991-92	Sokol Kiev	CIS	25	1	5	6	22	....	....	....	....	....
1992-93	Tacoma	WHL	44	3	33	36	67	7	2	7	9	4
1993-94a	Tacoma	WHL	64	12	48	60	106	8	0	5	5	9
1994-95a	Tacoma	WHL	54	14	32	46	55	4	0	3	3	4

a WHL West Second All-Star Team (1994, 1995)

Signed as a free agent by **Washington**, April 8, 1995.

ALFREDSSON, DANIEL (AHL-frehd-suhn) OTT.

Right wing. Shoots right. 5'11", 187 lbs. Born, Grums, Sweden, December 11, 1972.
(Ottawa's 5th choice, 133rd overall, in 1994 Entry Draft).

			Regular Season					Playoffs				
Season	Club	Lea	GP	G	A	TP	PIM	GP	G	A	TP	PIM
1991-92	Molndal	Swe. 2	32	12	8	20	43	....	....	....	....	....
1992-93	V. Frolunda	Swe.	20	1	5	6	8	....	....	....	....	....
1993-94	V. Frolunda	Swe.	39	20	10	30	18	4	1	1	2	....
1994-95	V. Frolunda	Swe.	22	7	11	18	22	....	....	....	....	....

ALINC, JAN (AH-lihnch, YAHN) PIT.

Center. Shoots left. 6'2", 190 lbs. Born, Most, Czech., May 27, 1972.
(Pittsburgh's 7th choice, 163rd overall, in 1992 Entry Draft).

			Regular Season					Playoffs				
Season	Club	Lea	GP	G	A	TP	PIM	GP	G	A	TP	PIM
1990-91	Litvinov	Czech.	7	1	1	2	....	....	....	....	....	....
1991-92	Litvinov	Czech.	45	21	16	37	24	....	....	....	....	....
1992-93	Litvinov	Czech.	36	16	13	29	....	....	....	....	....	....
1993-94	Litvinov	Czech.	36	16	25	41	....	4	1	4	5	....
1994-95	Litvinov	Czech.	42	16	32	48	50	4	3	2	5	2

ALLAN, CHAD VAN.

Defense. Shoots left. 6'1", 192 lbs. Born, Saskatoon, Sask., July 12, 1976.
(Vancouver's 4th choice, 65th overall, in 1994 Entry Draft).

			Regular Season					Playoffs				
Season	Club	Lea	GP	G	A	TP	PIM	GP	G	A	TP	PIM
1991-92	Saskatoon	WHL	1	0	0	0	2	....	....	....	....	....
1992-93	Saskatoon	WHL	69	2	10	12	67	9	0	0	0	25
1993-94	Saskatoon	WHL	70	6	16	22	123	16	1	1	2	21
1994-95a	Saskatoon	WHL	63	14	29	43	95	9	0	3	3	2

a WHL East First All-Star Team (1995)

ALLEN, PETER PIT.

Defense. Shoots right. 6'2", 185 lbs. Born, Calgary, Alta., March 6, 1970.
(Boston's 1st choice, 24th overall, in 1991 Supplemental Draft).

			Regular Season					Playoffs				
Season	Club	Lea	GP	G	A	TP	PIM	GP	G	A	TP	PIM
1989-90	Yale	ECAC	26	2	4	6	16	....	....	....	....	....
1990-91	Yale	ECAC	17	0	6	6	14	....	....	....	....	....
1991-92	Yale	ECAC	26	5	13	18	26	....	....	....	....	....
1992-93	Yale	ECAC	30	3	15	18	32	....	....	....	....	....
1993-94	Richmond	ECHL	52	2	16	18	62	....	....	....	....	....
	P.E.I.	AHL	6	0	1	1	6	....	....	....	....	....
1994-95	Cdn. National	....	52	5	15	20	36	....	....	....	....	....

Signed as a free agent by **Pittsburgh**, August 10, 1995.

ALLISON, JAMIE CGY.

Defense. Shoots left. 6'1", 190 lbs. Born, Lindsay, Ont., May 13, 1975.
(Calgary's 2nd choice, 44th overall, in 1993 Entry Draft).

			Regular Season					Playoffs				
Season	Club	Lea	GP	G	A	TP	PIM	GP	G	A	TP	PIM
1991-92	Windsor	OHL	59	4	8	12	70	4	1	1	2	2
1992-93	Detroit	OHL	61	0	13	13	64	15	2	5	7	23
1993-94	Detroit	OHL	40	2	22	24	69	17	2	9	11	35
1994-95	Detroit	OHL	50	1	14	15	119	18	2	7	9	35
	Calgary	**NHL**	**1**	**0**	**0**	**0**	**0**	....	....	....	....	....
	NHL Totals		**1**	**0**	**0**	**0**	**0**	....	....	....	....	....

ALLISON, JASON WSH.

Center. Shoots right. 6'3", 205 lbs. Born, North York, Ont., May 29, 1975.
(Washington's 2nd choice, 17th overall, in 1993 Entry Draft).

			Regular Season					Playoffs				
Season	Club	Lea	GP	G	A	TP	PIM	GP	G	A	TP	PIM
1991-92	London	OHL	65	11	19	30	15	7	0	0	0	0
1992-93	London	OHL	66	42	76	118	50	12	7	13	20	8
1993-94	**Washington**	**NHL**	**2**	**0**	**1**	**1**	**0**	....	....	....	....	....
abc	London	OHL	56	55	87	*142	68	5	2	13	15	13
	Portland	AHL	....	....	....	....	....	6	2	1	3	0
1994-95	London	OHL	15	15	21	36	43	....	....	....	....	....
	Washington	**NHL**	**12**	**2**	**1**	**3**	**6**	....	....	....	....	....
	Portland	AHL	8	5	4	9	2	7	3	8	11	2
	NHL Totals		**14**	**2**	**2**	**4**	**6**	....	....	....	....	....

a OHL First All-Star Team (1994)
b Canadian Major Junior First All-Star Team (1994)
c Canadian Major Junior Player of the Year (1994)

ALLISON, SCOTT

Center. Shoots left. 6'4", 194 lbs. Born, St. Boniface, Man., April 22, 1972.
(Edmonton's 1st choice, 17th overall, in 1990 Entry Draft).

			Regular Season					Playoffs				
Season	Club	Lea	GP	G	A	TP	PIM	GP	G	A	TP	PIM
1988-89	Prince Albert	WHL	51	6	9	15	37	3	0	0	0	0
1989-90	Prince Albert	WHL	66	22	16	38	73	11	1	4	5	8
1990-91	Prince Albert	WHL	30	5	5	10	57	....	....	....	....	....
	Portland	WHL	44	5	17	22	105	....	....	....	....	....
1991-92	Moose Jaw	WHL	72	37	45	82	238	3	1	1	2	25
1992-93	Cape Breton	AHL	49	3	5	8	34	....	....	....	....	....
	Wheeling	ECHL	6	3	3	6	8	....	....	....	....	....
1993-94	Cape Breton	AHL	75	19	14	33	202	3	0	1	1	2
1994-95	Cape Breton	AHL	58	6	14	20	104	....	....	....	....	....

ALVEY, MATT BOS.

Right wing. Shoots right. 6'5", 195 lbs. Born, Troy, NY, May 15, 1975.
(Boston's 2nd choice, 51st overall, in 1993 Entry Draft).

			Regular Season					Playoffs				
Season	Club	Lea	GP	G	A	TP	PIM	GP	G	A	TP	PIM
1993-94	Lake Superior	CCHA	41	6	8	14	16	....	....	....	....	....
1994-95	Lake Superior	CCHA	25	4	7	11	32	....	....	....	....	....

AMBROSIO, JEFF ST.L.

Left wing. Shoots left. 6'1", 188 lbs. Born, Toronto, Ont., April 26, 1977.
(St. Louis' 4th choice, 127th overall, in 1995 Entry Draft).

			Regular Season					Playoffs				
Season	Club	Lea	GP	G	A	TP	PIM	GP	G	A	TP	PIM
1993-94	Belleville	OHL	59	13	17	30	18	11	1	0	1	6
1994-95	Belleville	OHL	47	10	10	20	10	16	1	7	8	8

AMBROZIAK, PETER BUF.

Left wing. Shoots left. 6', 206 lbs. Born, Toronto, Ont., September 15, 1971.
(Buffalo's 4th choice, 72nd overall, in 1991 Entry Draft).

			Regular Season					Playoffs				
Season	Club	Lea	GP	G	A	TP	PIM	GP	G	A	TP	PIM
1990-91	Ottawa	OHL	62	30	32	62	56	17	15	9	24	24
1991-92	Ottawa	OHL	49	32	49	81	50	11	3	7	10	33
	Rochester	AHL	2	0	1	1	0	....	....	....	....	....
1992-93	Rochester	AHL	50	8	10	18	37	12	4	3	7	16
1993-94	Rochester	AHL	22	3	4	7	53	....	....	....	....	....
1994-95	Rochester	AHL	46	14	11	25	35	4	0	0	0	6
	Buffalo	**NHL**	**12**	**0**	**1**	**1**	**0**	....	....	....	....	....
	NHL Totals		**12**	**0**	**1**	**1**	**0**	....	....	....	....	....

AMONTE, TONY (eh-MAHN-tee) CHI.

Right wing. Shoots left. 6', 190 lbs. Born, Hingham, MA, August 2, 1970.
(NY Rangers' 3rd choice, 68th overall, in 1988 Entry Draft).

			Regular Season					Playoffs				
Season	Club	Lea	GP	G	A	TP	PIM	GP	G	A	TP	PIM
1989-90	Boston U.	H.E.	41	25	33	58	52	....	....	....	....	....
1990-91ab	Boston U.	H.E.	38	31	37	68	82	....	....	....	....	....
	NY Rangers	**NHL**	....	....	....	....	....	**2**	**0**	**2**	**2**	**2**
1991-92c	**NY Rangers**	**NHL**	**79**	**35**	**34**	**69**	**55**	**13**	**3**	**6**	**9**	**2**
1992-93	**NY Rangers**	**NHL**	**83**	**33**	**43**	**76**	**49**	....	....	....	....	....
1993-94	**NY Rangers**	**NHL**	**72**	**16**	**22**	**38**	**31**	....	....	....	....	....
	Chicago	**NHL**	**7**	**1**	**3**	**4**	**6**	**6**	**4**	**2**	**6**	**4**
1994-95	Fassa	Italy	14	22	16	38	10	....	....	....	....	....
	Chicago	**NHL**	**48**	**15**	**20**	**35**	**41**	**16**	**3**	**3**	**6**	**10**
	NHL Totals		**289**	**100**	**122**	**222**	**182**	**37**	**10**	**13**	**23**	**18**

a Hockey East Second All-Star Team (1991)
b NCAA Final Four All-Tournament Team (1991)
c NHL/Upper Deck All-Rookie Team (1992)

Traded to **Chicago** by **NY Rangers** with the rights to Matt Oates for Stephane Matteau and Brian Noonan, March 21, 1994.

ANDERSON, CRAIG NYR

Defense. Shoots left. 6'1", 171 lbs. Born, Minneapolis, MN, January 6, 1976.
(NY Rangers' 10th choice, 208th overall, in 1994 Entry Draft).

			Regular Season					Playoffs				
Season	Club	Lea	GP	G	A	TP	PIM	GP	G	A	TP	PIM
1993-94	Park Center	HS	24	24	18	42	....	....	....	....	....	....
1994-95	U. Wisconsin	WCHA				DID NOT PLAY						

ANDERSON, GLENN

Right wing. Shoots left. 6'1", 190 lbs. Born, Vancouver, B.C., October 2, 1960.
(Edmonton's 3rd choice, 69th overall, in 1979 Entry Draft).

			Regular Season					Playoffs				
Season	Club	Lea	GP	G	A	TP	PIM	GP	G	A	TP	PIM
1978-79	U. of Denver	WCHA	40	26	29	55	58	....	....	....	....	....
1979-80	Seattle	WHL	7	5	5	10	4	....	....	....	....	....
	Cdn. Olympic	....	49	21	21	42	46	....	....	....	....	....
1980-81	**Edmonton**	**NHL**	**58**	**30**	**23**	**53**	**24**	**9**	**5**	**7**	**12**	**12**
1981-82	**Edmonton**	**NHL**	**80**	**38**	**67**	**105**	**71**	**5**	**2**	**5**	**7**	**8**
1982-83	**Edmonton**	**NHL**	**72**	**48**	**56**	**104**	**70**	**16**	**10**	**10**	**20**	**32**
1983-84	**Edmonton**	**NHL**	**80**	**54**	**45**	**99**	**65**	**19**	**6**	**11**	**17**	**33**
1984-85	**Edmonton**	**NHL**	**80**	**42**	**39**	**81**	**69**	**18**	**10**	**16**	**26**	**38**
1985-86	**Edmonton**	**NHL**	**72**	**54**	**48**	**102**	**90**	**10**	**8**	**3**	**11**	**14**
1986-87	**Edmonton**	**NHL**	**80**	**35**	**38**	**73**	**65**	**21**	**14**	**13**	**27**	**59**
1987-88	**Edmonton**	**NHL**	**80**	**38**	**50**	**88**	**58**	**19**	**9**	**16**	**25**	**49**
1988-89	**Edmonton**	**NHL**	**79**	**16**	**48**	**64**	**93**	**7**	**1**	**2**	**3**	**8**
1989-90	**Edmonton**	**NHL**	**73**	**34**	**38**	**72**	**107**	**22**	**10**	**12**	**22**	**20**
1990-91	**Edmonton**	**NHL**	**74**	**24**	**31**	**55**	**59**	**18**	**6**	**7**	**13**	**41**
1991-92	**Toronto**	**NHL**	**72**	**24**	**33**	**57**	**100**	....	....	....	....	....
1992-93	**Toronto**	**NHL**	**76**	**22**	**43**	**65**	**117**	**21**	**7**	**11**	**18**	**31**
1993-94	**Toronto**	**NHL**	**73**	**17**	**18**	**35**	**50**	....	....	....	....	....
	NY Rangers	**NHL**	**12**	**4**	**2**	**6**	**12**	**23**	**3**	**3**	**6**	**42**
1994-95	Augsburg	Ger.	5	6	2	8	10	....	....	....	....	....
	Lukko	Fin.	4	1	1	2	0	....	....	....	....	....
	Cdn. National	....	26	11	8	19	40	....	....	....	....	....
	St. Louis	**NHL**	**36**	**12**	**14**	**26**	**37**	**6**	**1**	**1**	**2**	***49**
	NHL Totals		**1097**	**492**	**593**	**1085**	**1087**	**214**	**92**	**117**	**209**	**436**

Played in NHL All-Star Game (1984-86, 1988)

Traded to **Toronto** by **Edmonton** with Grant Fuhr and Craig Berube for Vincent Damphousse, Peter Ing, Scott Thornton, Luke Richardson, future considerations and cash, September 19, 1991. Traded to **NY Rangers** by **Toronto** with the rights to Scott Malone and Toronto's fourth round choice (Alexander Korobolin) in 1994 Entry Draft for Mike Gartner, March 21, 1994. Signed as a free agent by **St. Louis**, February 13, 1995

ANDERSON, SHAWN

Defense. Shoots left. 6'1", 200 lbs. Born, Montreal, Que., February 7, 1968.
(Buffalo's 1st choice, 5th overall, in 1986 Entry Draft).

			Regular Season					Playoffs				
Season	Club	Lea	GP	G	A	TP	PIM	GP	G	A	TP	PIM
1985-86	Maine	H.E.	16	5	8	13	22	....	....	....	....	....
	Cdn. National	....	33	2	6	8	16	....	....	....	....	....
1986-87	**Buffalo**	**NHL**	**41**	**2**	**11**	**13**	**23**	....	....	....	....	....
	Rochester	AHL	15	2	5	7	11	....	....	....	....	....
1987-88	**Buffalo**	**NHL**	**23**	**1**	**2**	**3**	**17**	....	....	....	....	....
	Rochester	AHL	22	5	16	21	19	6	0	0	0	0
1988-89	**Buffalo**	**NHL**	**33**	**2**	**10**	**12**	**18**	**5**	**0**	**1**	**1**	**4**
	Rochester	AHL	31	5	14	19	24	....	....	....	....	....
1989-90	**Buffalo**	**NHL**	**16**	**1**	**3**	**4**	**8**	....	....	....	....	....
	Rochester	AHL	39	2	16	18	41	9	1	0	1	4
1990-91	**Quebec**	**NHL**	**31**	**3**	**10**	**13**	**21**	....	....	....	....	....
	Halifax	AHL	4	0	1	1	2	....	....	....	....	....
1991-92	Weiswasser	Ger.	38	7	15	22	83	....	....	....	....	....
1992-93	**Washington**	**NHL**	**60**	**2**	**6**	**8**	**18**	**6**	**0**	**0**	**0**	**0**
	Baltimore	AHL	10	1	5	6	8	....	....	....	....	....
1993-94	**Washington**	**NHL**	**50**	**0**	**9**	**9**	**12**	**8**	**1**	**0**	**1**	**12**
1994-95	**Philadelphia**	**NHL**	**1**	**0**	**0**	**0**	**0**	....	....	....	....	....
	Hershey	AHL	31	9	21	30	18	6	2	3	5	19
	NHL Totals		**255**	**11**	**51**	**62**	**117**	**19**	**1**	**1**	**2**	**16**

Traded to **Washington** by **Buffalo** for Bill Houlder, September 30, 1990. Claimed by **Quebec** from **Washington** in NHL Waiver Draft, October 1, 1990. Traded to **Winnipeg** by **Quebec** for Sergei Kharin, October 22, 1991. Traded to **Washington** by **Winnipeg** for future considerations, October 23, 1991. Signed as a free agent by **Philadelphia**, August 16, 1994.

ANDERSSON, ERIK — L.A.

Right wing. Shoots left. 6'2", 187 lbs. Born, Stockholm, Sweden, August 19, 1971.
(Los Angeles' 5th choice, 112th overall, in 1990 Entry Draft).

			Regular Season					Playoffs				
Season	Club	Lea	GP	G	A	TP	PIM	GP	G	A	TP	PIM
1989-90	Danderyd	Swe. 2	30	14	5	19	16	....	....	....	....	....
1990-91	AIK	Swe.	32	1	1	2	10	....	....	....	....	....
1991-92	AIK	Swe.	3	0	0	0	0	....	....	....	....	....
1992-93						DID NOT PLAY						
1993-94	U. of Denver	WCHA	38	10	20	30	26	....	....	....	....	....
1994-95	U. of Denver	WCHA	42	12	19	31	42	....	....	....	....	....

ANDERSSON, MIKAEL (AN-duhr-suhn) — T.B.

Left wing. Shoots left. 5'11", 185 lbs. Born, Malmo, Sweden, May 10, 1966.
(Buffalo's 1st choice, 18th overall, in 1984 Entry Draft).

			Regular Season					Playoffs				
Season	Club	Lea	GP	G	A	TP	PIM	GP	G	A	TP	PIM
1982-83	V. Frolunda	Swe.	1	1	0	1	0	....	....	....	....	....
1983-84	V. Frolunda	Swe.	18	0	3	3	6	....	....	....	....	....
1984-85	V. Frolunda	Swe. 2	30	16	11	27	18	6	3	2	5	2
1985-86	**Buffalo**	**NHL**	**32**	**1**	**9**	**10**	**4**	....	....	....	....	....
	Rochester	AHL	20	10	4	14	6	....	....	....	....	....
1986-87	**Buffalo**	**NHL**	**16**	**0**	**3**	**3**	**0**	....	....	....	....	....
	Rochester	AHL	42	6	20	26	14	9	1	2	3	2
1987-88	**Buffalo**	**NHL**	**37**	**3**	**20**	**23**	**10**	**1**	**1**	**0**	**1**	**0**
	Rochester	AHL	35	12	24	36	16	....	....	....	....	....
1988-89	**Buffalo**	**NHL**	**14**	**0**	**1**	**1**	**4**	....	....	....	....	....
	Rochester	AHL	56	18	33	51	12	....	....	....	....	....
1989-90	**Hartford**	**NHL**	**50**	**13**	**24**	**37**	**6**	**5**	**0**	**3**	**3**	**2**
1990-91	**Hartford**	**NHL**	**41**	**4**	**7**	**11**	**8**	....	....	....	....	....
	Springfield	AHL	26	7	22	29	10	18	*10	8	18	12
1991-92	**Hartford**	**NHL**	**74**	**18**	**29**	**47**	**14**	**7**	**0**	**2**	**2**	**6**
1992-93	**Tampa Bay**	**NHL**	**77**	**16**	**11**	**27**	**14**	....	....	....	....	....
1993-94	**Tampa Bay**	**NHL**	**76**	**13**	**12**	**25**	**23**	....	....	....	....	....
1994-95	V. Frolunda	Swe.	7	1	0	1	31	....	....	....	....	....
	Tampa Bay	**NHL**	**36**	**4**	**7**	**11**	**4**	....	....	....	....	....
	NHL Totals		**453**	**72**	**123**	**195**	**87**	**13**	**1**	**5**	**6**	**8**

Claimed by **Hartford** from **Buffalo** in NHL Waiver Draft, October 2, 1989. Signed as a free agent by **Tampa Bay**, June 29, 1992.

ANDERSSON, NICLAS (AN-duhr-suhn) — NYI

Left wing. Shoots left. 5'9", 175 lbs. Born, Kungalv, Sweden, May 20, 1971.
(Quebec's 5th choice, 68th overall, in 1989 Entry Draft).

			Regular Season					Playoffs				
Season	Club	Lea	GP	G	A	TP	PIM	GP	G	A	TP	PIM
1987-88	V. Frolunda	Swe. 2	15	5	5	10	6	8	6	4	10	4
1988-89	V. Frolunda	Swe. 2	30	13	24	37	24	....	....	....	....	....
1989-90	V. Frolunda	Swe.	38	10	21	31	14	....	....	....	....	....
1990-91	V. Frolunda	Swe.	22	6	10	16	16	....	....	....	....	....
1991-92	Halifax	AHL	57	8	26	34	41	....	....	....	....	....
1992-93	**Quebec**	**NHL**	**3**	**0**	**1**	**1**	**2**	....	....	....	....	....
	Halifax	AHL	76	32	50	82	42	....	....	....	....	....
1993-94	Cornwall	AHL	42	18	34	52	8	....	....	....	....	....
1994-95	Denver	IHL	66	22	39	61	28	15	8	13	21	10
	NHL Totals		**3**	**0**	**1**	**1**	**2**	....	....	....	....	....

Signed as a free agent by **NY Islanders**, July 15, 1994.

ANDERSSON, PETER

Defense. Shoots left. 6', 196 lbs. Born, Orebro, Sweden, August 29, 1965.
(NY Rangers' 5th choice, 73rd overall, in 1983 Entry Draft).

			Regular Season					Playoffs				
Season	Club	Lea	GP	G	A	TP	PIM	GP	G	A	TP	PIM
1983-84	Farjestad	Swe.	36	4	7	11	22	....	....	....	....	....
1984-85	Farjestad	Swe.	35	5	12	17	24	....	....	....	....	....
1985-86	Farjestad	Swe.	34	6	10	16	18	....	....	....	....	....
1986-87	Farjestad	Swe.	32	9	8	17	32	....	....	....	....	....
1987-88	Farjestad	Swe.	38	14	20	34	44	....	....	....	....	....
1988-89	Farjestad	Swe.	33	6	17	23	44	....	....	....	....	....
1989-90	Malmo	Swe.	33	15	25	40	32	....	....	....	....	....
1990-91	Malmo	Swe.	34	9	17	26	26	....	....	....	....	....
1991-92	Malmo	Swe.	40	12	20	32	80	....	....	....	....	....
1992-93	**NY Rangers**	**NHL**	**31**	**4**	**11**	**15**	**18**	....	....	....	....	....
	Binghamton	AHL	27	11	22	33	16	....	....	....	....	....
1993-94	**NY Rangers**	**NHL**	**8**	**1**	**1**	**2**	**2**	....	....	....	....	....
	Florida	**NHL**	**8**	**1**	**1**	**2**	**0**	....	....	....	....	....
1994-95	Malmo	Swe.	27	1	9	10	18	9	5	0	5	16
	NHL Totals		**47**	**6**	**13**	**19**	**20**	....	....	....	....	....

Traded to **Florida** by **NY Rangers** for Florida's ninth round choice (Vitali Yeremeyev) in 1994 Entry Draft, March 21, 1994.

ANDERSSON-JUNKKA, JONAS — PIT.

Defense. Shoots right. 6'2", 170 lbs. Born, Kiruna, Sweden, May 4, 1975.
(Pittsburgh's 4th choice, 104th overall, in 1993 Entry Draft).

			Regular Season					Playoffs				
Season	Club	Lea	GP	G	A	TP	PIM	GP	G	A	TP	PIM
1991-92	Kiruna	Swe. 2	1	0	0	0	0	....	....	....	....	....
1992-93	Kiruna	Swe. 2	30	3	7	10	32	....	....	....	....	....
1993-94	Kiruna	Swe. 2	32	6	10	16	84	....	....	....	....	....
1994-95	V. Frolunda	Swe.	19	0	2	2	2	....	....	....	....	....

ANDREYCHUK, DAVE (AN-druh-chuhk) — TOR.

Left wing. Shoots right. 6'3", 220 lbs. Born, Hamilton, Ont., September 29, 1963.
(Buffalo's 3rd choice, 16th overall, in 1982 Entry Draft).

			Regular Season					Playoffs				
Season	Club	Lea	GP	G	A	TP	PIM	GP	G	A	TP	PIM
1980-81	Oshawa	OHA	67	22	22	44	80	10	3	2	5	20
1981-82	Oshawa	OHL	67	57	43	100	71	3	1	4	5	16
1982-83	**Buffalo**	**NHL**	**43**	**14**	**23**	**37**	**16**	**4**	**1**	**0**	**1**	**4**
	Oshawa	OHL	14	8	24	32	6	....	....	....	....	....
1983-84	**Buffalo**	**NHL**	**78**	**38**	**42**	**80**	**42**	**2**	**0**	**1**	**1**	**2**
1984-85	**Buffalo**	**NHL**	**64**	**31**	**30**	**61**	**54**	**5**	**4**	**2**	**6**	**4**
1985-86	**Buffalo**	**NHL**	**80**	**36**	**51**	**87**	**61**	....	....	....	....	....
1986-87	**Buffalo**	**NHL**	**77**	**25**	**48**	**73**	**46**	....	....	....	....	....
1987-88	**Buffalo**	**NHL**	**80**	**30**	**48**	**78**	**112**	**6**	**2**	**4**	**6**	**0**
1988-89	**Buffalo**	**NHL**	**56**	**28**	**24**	**52**	**40**	**5**	**0**	**3**	**3**	**0**
1989-90	**Buffalo**	**NHL**	**73**	**40**	**42**	**82**	**42**	**6**	**2**	**5**	**7**	**2**
1990-91	**Buffalo**	**NHL**	**80**	**36**	**33**	**69**	**32**	**6**	**2**	**2**	**4**	**8**
1991-92	**Buffalo**	**NHL**	**80**	**41**	**50**	**91**	**71**	**7**	**1**	**3**	**4**	**12**
1992-93	**Buffalo**	**NHL**	**52**	**29**	**32**	**61**	**48**	....	....	....	....	....
	Toronto	**NHL**	**31**	**25**	**13**	**38**	**8**	**21**	**12**	**7**	**19**	**35**
1993-94	**Toronto**	**NHL**	**83**	**53**	**46**	**99**	**98**	**18**	**5**	**5**	**10**	**16**
1994-95	**Toronto**	**NHL**	**48**	**22**	**16**	**38**	**34**	**7**	**3**	**2**	**5**	**25**
	NHL Totals		**925**	**448**	**498**	**946**	**704**	**87**	**32**	**34**	**66**	**108**

Played in NHL All-Star Game (1990, 1994)

Traded to **Toronto** by **Buffalo** with Daren Puppa and Buffalo's first round choice (Kenny Jonsson) in 1993 Entry Draft for Grant Fuhr and Toronto's fifth round choice (Kevin Popp) in 1995 Entry Draft, February 2, 1993.

ANDRUSAK, GREG (AN-druh-sak) — PIT.

Defense. Shoots right. 6'1", 190 lbs. Born, Cranbrook, B.C., November 14, 1969.
(Pittsburgh's 5th choice, 88th overall, in 1988 Entry Draft).

			Regular Season					Playoffs				
Season	Club	Lea	GP	G	A	TP	PIM	GP	G	A	TP	PIM
1987-88	Minn.-Duluth	WCHA	37	4	5	9	42	....	....	....	....	....
1988-89	Minn.-Duluth	WCHA	35	4	8	12	74	....	....	....	....	....
	Cdn. National	....	2	0	0	0	0	....	....	....	....	....
1989-90	Minn.-Duluth	WCHA	35	5	29	34	74	....	....	....	....	....
1990-91	Cdn. National	....	53	4	11	15	34	....	....	....	....	....
1991-92a	Minn.-Duluth	WCHA	36	7	27	34	125	....	....	....	....	....
1992-93	Cleveland	IHL	55	3	22	25	78	2	0	0	0	2
	Muskegon	ColHL	2	0	3	3	7	....	....	....	....	....
1993-94	**Pittsburgh**	**NHL**	**3**	**0**	**0**	**0**	**2**	....	....	....	....	....
	Cleveland	IHL	69	13	26	39	109	....	....	....	....	....
1994-95	Detroit	IHL	37	5	26	31	50	....	....	....	....	....
	Pittsburgh	**NHL**	**7**	**0**	**4**	**4**	**6**	....	....	....	....	....
	Cleveland	IHL	8	0	8	8	14	....	....	....	....	....
	NHL Totals		**10**	**0**	**4**	**4**	**8**	....	....	....	....	....

a WCHA First All-Star Team (1992)

ANGER, NIKLAS — MTL.

Right wing. Shoots left. 6'1", 185 lbs. Born, Gavle, Sweden, July 31, 1977.
(Montreal's 5th choice, 112th overall, in 1995 Entry Draft).

			Regular Season					Playoffs				
Season	Club	Lea	GP	G	A	TP	PIM	GP	G	A	TP	PIM
1994-95	Djurgarden	Swe. Jr.	30	14	12	26	26	....	....	....	....	....
	Djurgarden	Swe.	1	0	0	0	0	....	....	....	....	....

ANISIMOV, ARTEM (ah-NIH-sih-mohv) PHI.

Defense. Shoots left. 6'1", 187 lbs. Born, Kazan, USSR, July 27, 1976.
(Philadelphia's 1st choice, 62nd overall, in 1994 Entry Draft).

			Regular Season					Playoffs				
Season	Club	Lea	GP	G	A	TP	PIM	GP	G	A	TP	PIM
1993-94	Itil Kazan	CIS	38	0	1	1	12	5	0	0	0	0
1994-95	Kazan	CIS	46	3	2	5	55	1	0	0	0	0

ANNECK, DORIAN WPG.

Center. Shoots left. 6'1", 183 lbs. Born, Winnipeg, Man., April 24, 1976.
(Winnipeg's 2nd choice, 56th overall, in 1994 Entry Draft).

			Regular Season					Playoffs				
Season	Club	Lea	GP	G	A	TP	PIM	GP	G	A	TP	PIM
1992-93	Victoria	WHL	63	5	6	11	19	....	....	....	....	....
1993-94	Victoria	WHL	71	26	53	79	30	....	....	....	....	....
1994-95	Prince George	WHL	47	18	38	56	12	....	....	....	....	....
	Tri-City	WHL	3	0	0	0	0	....	....	....	....	....

ANTOSKI, SHAWN (an-TAW-skee) PHI.

Left wing. Shoots left. 6'4", 235 lbs. Born, Brantford, Ont., March 25, 1970.
(Vancouver's 2nd choice, 18th overall, in 1990 Entry Draft).

			Regular Season					Playoffs				
Season	Club	Lea	GP	G	A	TP	PIM	GP	G	A	TP	PIM
1987-88	North Bay	OHL	52	3	4	7	163	....	....	....	....	....
1988-89	North Bay	OHL	57	6	21	27	201	9	5	3	8	24
1989-90	North Bay	OHL	59	25	31	56	201	5	1	2	3	17
1990-91	**Vancouver**	**NHL**	**2**	**0**	**0**	**0**	**0**	....	....	....	....	....
	Milwaukee	IHL	62	17	7	24	330	5	1	2	3	10
1991-92	**Vancouver**	**NHL**	**4**	**0**	**0**	**0**	**29**	....	....	....	....	....
	Milwaukee	IHL	52	17	16	33	346	5	2	0	2	20
1992-93	**Vancouver**	**NHL**	**2**	**0**	**0**	**0**	**0**	....	....	....	....	....
	Hamilton	AHL	41	3	4	7	172	....	....	....	....	....
1993-94	**Vancouver**	**NHL**	**55**	**1**	**2**	**3**	**190**	**16**	**0**	**1**	**1**	**36**
1994-95	**Vancouver**	**NHL**	**7**	**0**	**0**	**0**	**46**	....	....	....	....	....
	Philadelphia	**NHL**	**25**	**0**	**0**	**0**	**61**	**13**	**0**	**1**	**1**	**10**
	NHL Totals		**95**	**1**	**2**	**3**	**326**	**29**	**0**	**2**	**2**	**46**

Traded to **Philadelphia** by **Vancouver** for Josef Beranek, February 15, 1995.

APPEL, FRANK (AHP-pehl) CGY.

Defense. Shoots left. 6'4", 210 lbs. Born, Dusseldorf, West Germany, May 12, 1976.
(Calgary's 7th choice, 123rd overall, in 1994 Entry Draft).

			Regular Season					Playoffs				
Season	Club	Lea	GP	G	A	TP	PIM	GP	G	A	TP	PIM
1993-94	Dusseldorf	Ger.	4	0	0	0	4	....	....	....	....	....
1994-95	Eisbaren Berlin	Ger.	12	0	0	0	4	....	....	....	....	....

ARCHIBALD, DAVE OTT.

Center/Left wing. Shoots left. 6'1", 210 lbs. Born, Chilliwack, B.C., April 14, 1969.
(Minnesota's 1st choice, 6th overall, in 1987 Entry Draft).

			Regular Season					Playoffs				
Season	Club	Lea	GP	G	A	TP	PIM	GP	G	A	TP	PIM
1984-85	Portland	WHL	47	7	11	18	10	3	0	2	2	0
1985-86	Portland	WHL	70	29	35	64	56	15	6	7	13	11
1986-87	Portland	WHL	65	50	57	107	40	20	10	18	28	11
1987-88	**Minnesota**	**NHL**	**78**	**13**	**20**	**33**	**26**	....	....	....	....	....
1988-89	**Minnesota**	**NHL**	**72**	**14**	**19**	**33**	**14**	**5**	**0**	**1**	**1**	**0**
1989-90	**Minnesota**	**NHL**	**12**	**1**	**5**	**6**	**6**	....	....	....	....	....
	NY Rangers	**NHL**	**19**	**2**	**3**	**5**	**6**	....	....	....	....	....
	Flint	IHL	41	14	38	52	16	4	3	2	5	0
1990-91	Cdn. National	....	29	19	12	31	20	....	....	....	....	....
1991-92	Cdn. National	....	58	20	43	63	64	....	....	....	....	....
	Cdn. Olympic	....	8	7	1	8	18	....	....	....	....	....
	Bolzano	....	5	4	3	7	16	7	8	5	13	7
1992-93	Binghamton	AHL	8	6	3	9	10	....	....	....	....	....
	Ottawa	**NHL**	**44**	**9**	**6**	**15**	**32**	....	....	....	....	....
1993-94	**Ottawa**	**NHL**	**33**	**10**	**8**	**18**	**14**	....	....	....	....	....
1994-95	**Ottawa**	**NHL**	**14**	**2**	**2**	**4**	**19**	....	....	....	....	....
	NHL Totals		**272**	**51**	**63**	**114**	**117**	**5**	**0**	**1**	**1**	**0**

Traded to **NY Rangers** by **Minnesota** for Jayson More, November 1, 1989. Traded to **Ottawa** by **NY Rangers** for Ottawa's fifth round choice (later traded to Los Angeles — Los Angeles selected Frederick Beaubien) in 1993 Entry Draft, November 5, 1992.

ARMSTRONG, BILL

Defense. Shoots left. 6'5", 220 lbs. Born, Richmond Hill, Ont., May 18, 1970.
(Philadelphia's 6th choice, 46th overall, in 1990 Entry Draft).

			Regular Season					Playoffs				
Season	Club	Lea	GP	G	A	TP	PIM	GP	G	A	TP	PIM
1987-88	Toronto	OHL	64	1	10	11	99	....	....	....	....	....
1988-89	Toronto	OHL	64	1	16	17	82	....	....	....	....	....
1989-90	Hamilton	OHL	18	0	2	2	38	....	....	....	....	....
	Niagara Falls	OHL	4	0	1	1	13	....	....	....	....	....
	Oshawa	OHL	41	2	8	10	115	17	0	7	7	39
1990-91	Hershey	AHL	56	1	9	10	117	....	....	....	....	....
1991-92	Hershey	AHL	80	2	14	16	159	3	0	0	0	2
1992-93	Hershey	AHL	80	2	10	12	205	....	....	....	....	....
1993-94	Providence	AHL	66	0	7	7	200	....	....	....	....	....
1994-95	Providence	AHL	75	3	10	13	244	13	0	2	2	8

Signed as a free agent by **Boston**, July 22, 1993.

ARMSTRONG, BILL H. N.J.

Center. Shoots left. 6'2", 195 lbs. Born, London, Ont., June 25, 1966.

			Regular Season					Playoffs				
Season	Club	Lea	GP	G	A	TP	PIM	GP	G	A	TP	PIM
1986-87	W. Michigan	CCHA	43	13	20	33	86	....	....	....	....	....
1987-88	W. Michigan	CCHA	41	22	17	39	88	....	....	....	....	....
1988-89	W. Michigan	CCHA	40	23	19	42	97	....	....	....	....	....
1989-90	Hershey	AHL	58	10	6	16	99	....	....	....	....	....
1990-91	**Philadelphia**	**NHL**	**1**	**0**	**1**	**1**	**0**	....	....	....	....	....
	Hershey	AHL	70	36	27	63	150	6	2	8	10	19
1991-92	Hershey	AHL	64	26	22	48	186	6	2	2	4	6
1992-93	Cincinnati	IHL	42	14	11	25	99	....	....	....	....	....
	Utica	AHL	32	18	21	39	60	....	....	....	....	....
1993-94	Albany	AHL	74	32	50	82	188	....	....	....	....	....
1994-95	Albany	AHL	76	32	47	79	115	13	6	5	11	20
	NHL Totals		**1**	**0**	**1**	**1**	**0**	....	....	....	....	....

Signed as a free agent by **Philadelphia**, May 16, 1989. Signed as a free agent by **New Jersey**, March 21, 1993.

ARMSTRONG, CHRIS FLA.

Defense. Shoots left. 6', 198 lbs. Born, Regina, Sask., June 26, 1975.
(Florida's 3rd choice, 57th overall, in 1993 Entry Draft).

			Regular Season					Playoffs				
Season	Club	Lea	GP	G	A	TP	PIM	GP	G	A	TP	PIM
1991-92	Moose Jaw	WHL	43	2	7	9	19	4	0	0	0	0
1992-93	Moose Jaw	WHL	67	9	35	44	104	....	....	....	....	....
1993-94ab	Moose Jaw	WHL	64	13	55	68	54	....	....	....	....	....
	Cincinnati	IHL	1	0	0	0	0	10	1	3	4	2
1994-95c	Moose Jaw	WHL	66	17	54	71	61	10	2	12	14	22
	Cincinnati	IHL	....	....	....	....	....	9	1	3	4	10

a WHL East First All-Star Team (1994)
b Canadian Major Junior Second All-Star Team (1994)
c WHL East Second All-Star Team (1995)

ARMSTRONG, DEREK NYI

Center. Shoots right. 5'11", 180 lbs. Born, Ottawa, Ont., April 23, 1973.
(NY Islanders' 5th choice, 128th overall, in 1992 Entry Draft).

			Regular Season					Playoffs				
Season	Club	Lea	GP	G	A	TP	PIM	GP	G	A	TP	PIM
1991-92	Sudbury	OHL	66	31	54	85	22	9	2	2	4	2
1992-93	Sudbury	OHL	66	44	62	106	56	14	9	10	19	26
1993-94	**NY Islanders**	**NHL**	**1**	**0**	**0**	**0**	**0**	....	....	....	....	....
	Salt Lake	IHL	76	23	35	58	61	....	....	....	....	....
1994-95	Denver	IHL	59	13	18	31	65	6	0	2	2	0
	NHL Totals		**1**	**0**	**0**	**0**	**0**	....	....	....	....	....

ARNOTT, JASON (AHR-nawt) EDM.

Center. Shoots right. 6'3", 220 lbs. Born, Collingwood, Ont., October 11, 1974.
(Edmonton's 1st choice, 7th overall, in 1993 Entry Draft).

			Regular Season					Playoffs				
Season	Club	Lea	GP	G	A	TP	PIM	GP	G	A	TP	PIM
1991-92	Oshawa	OHL	57	9	15	24	12	....	....	....	....	....
1992-93	Oshawa	OHL	56	41	57	98	74	13	9	9	18	20
1993-94a	**Edmonton**	**NHL**	**78**	**33**	**35**	**68**	**104**	....	....	....	....	....
1994-95	**Edmonton**	**NHL**	**42**	**15**	**22**	**37**	**128**	....	....	....	....	....
	NHL Totals		**120**	**48**	**57**	**105**	**232**	....	....	....	....	....

a NHL/Upper Deck All-Rookie Team (1994)

ASTLEY, MARK BUF.

Defense. Shoots left. 5'11", 185 lbs. Born, Calgary, Alta., March 30, 1969.
(Buffalo's 9th choice, 194th overall, in 1989 Entry Draft).

			Regular Season					Playoffs				
Season	Club	Lea	GP	G	A	TP	PIM	GP	G	A	TP	PIM
1988-89	Lake Superior	CCHA	42	3	12	15	26	....	....	....	....	....
1989-90	Lake Superior	CCHA	43	7	25	32	29	....	....	....	....	....
1990-91a	Lake Superior	CCHA	45	19	27	46	50	....	....	....	....	....
1991-92bcd	Lake Superior	CCHA	39	11	36	47	65	....	....	....	....	....
	Cdn. National	....	11	2	2	4	6	....	....	....	....	....
1992-93	Lugano	Switz.	30	10	12	22	57	....	....	....	....	....
	Cdn. National	....	22	4	14	18	14	....	....	....	....	....
1993-94	Ambri	Switz.	23	5	9	14	17	....	....	....	....	....
	Cdn. National	....	13	4	8	12	6	....	....	....	....	....
	Cdn. Olympic	....	8	0	1	1	4	....	....	....	....	....
	Buffalo	**NHL**	**1**	**0**	**0**	**0**	**0**	....	....	....	....	....
1994-95	Rochester	AHL	46	5	24	29	49	3	0	2	2	2
	Buffalo	**NHL**	**14**	**2**	**1**	**3**	**12**	**2**	**0**	**0**	**0**	**0**
	NHL Totals		**15**	**2**	**1**	**3**	**12**	**2**	**0**	**0**	**0**	**0**

a CCHA Second All-Star Team (1991)
b CCHA First All-Star Team (1992)
c NCAA West First All-American Team (1992)
d NCAA All-Tournament Team (1992)

AUBIN, SERGE PIT.

Center. Shoots left. 6'1", 176 lbs. Born, Val d'Or, Que., February 15, 1975.
(Pittsburgh's 9th choice, 161st overall, in 1994 Entry Draft).

			Regular Season					Playoffs				
Season	Club	Lea	GP	G	A	TP	PIM	GP	G	A	TP	PIM
1992-93	Drummondville	QMJHL	65	16	34	50	30	8	0	1	1	16
1993-94	Granby	QMJHL	63	42	32	74	80	7	2	3	5	8
1994-95	Granby	QMJHL	60	37	73	110	55	11	8	15	23	4

AUCOIN, ADRIAN (oh-KWEHN) VAN.

Defense. Shoots right. 6'1", 194 lbs. Born, Ottawa, Ont., July 3, 1973.
(Vancouver's 7th choice, 117th overall, in 1992 Entry Draft).

			Regular Season					Playoffs				
Season	Club	Lea	GP	G	A	TP	PIM	GP	G	A	TP	PIM
1991-92	Boston U.	H.E.	32	2	10	12	60	....	....	....	....	....
1992-93	Cdn. National	....	42	8	10	18	71	....	....	....	....	....
1993-94	Cdn. National	....	59	5	12	17	80	....	....	....	....	....
	Cdn. Olympic	....	4	0	0	0	2	....	....	....	....	....
	Hamilton	AHL	13	1	2	3	19	4	0	2	2	6
1994-95	Syracuse	AHL	71	13	18	31	52	....	....	....	....	....
	Vancouver	**NHL**	**1**	**1**	**0**	**1**	**0**	**4**	**1**	**0**	**1**	**0**
	NHL Totals		**1**	**1**	**0**	**1**	**0**	**4**	**1**	**0**	**1**	**0**

AUDET, PHILIPPE DET.

Left wing. Shoots left. 6'2", 175 lbs. Born, Ottawa, Ont., June 4, 1977.
(Detroit's 2nd choice, 52nd overall, in 1995 Entry Draft).

			Regular Season					Playoffs				
Season	Club	Lea	GP	G	A	TP	PIM	GP	G	A	TP	PIM
1993-94	Trois-Rivières	Midget	34	22	21	43	90	....	....	....	....	....
1994-95	Granby	QMJHL	62	19	17	36	93	13	2	5	7	10

AUDETTE, DONALD   (aw-DEHT)   **BUF.**

Right wing. Shoots right. 5'8", 175 lbs.   Born, Laval, Que., September 23, 1969.
(Buffalo's 8th choice, 183rd overall, in 1989 Entry Draft).

			Regular Season					Playoffs				
Season	Club	Lea	GP	G	A	TP	PIM	GP	G	A	TP	PIM
1986-87	Laval	QMJHL	66	17	22	39	36	14	2	6	8	10
1987-88	Laval	QMJHL	63	48	61	109	56	14	7	12	19	20
1988-89a	Laval	QMJHL	70	76	85	161	123	17	17	12	29	43
1989-90bc	Rochester	AHL	70	42	46	88	78	15	9	8	17	29
	Buffalo	**NHL**	....	....	....	....	....	2	0	0	0	0
1990-91	**Buffalo**	**NHL**	8	4	3	7	4	....	....	....	....	....
	Rochester	AHL	5	4	0	4	2	....	....	....	....	....
1991-92	**Buffalo**	**NHL**	63	31	17	48	75	....	....	....	....	....
1992-93	**Buffalo**	**NHL**	44	12	7	19	51	8	2	2	4	6
	Rochester	AHL	6	8	4	12	10	....	....	....	....	....
1993-94	**Buffalo**	**NHL**	77	29	30	59	41	7	0	1	1	6
1994-95	**Buffalo**	**NHL**	46	24	13	37	27	5	1	1	2	4
	NHL Totals		**238**	**100**	**70**	**170**	**198**	**22**	**3**	**4**	**7**	**16**

a QMJHL First All-Star Team (1989)
b AHL First All-Star Team (1990)
c Won Dudley "Red" Garret Memorial Trophy (Top Rookie - AHL) (1990)

AUGER, VINCENT   (OH-zhay, VIHN-cehnt)   **COL.**

Center. Shoots left. 5'10", 175 lbs.   Born, Quebec, Que., March 7, 1975.
(Quebec's 11th choice, 231st overall, in 1993 Entry Draft).

			Regular Season					Playoffs				
Season	Club	Lea	GP	G	A	TP	PIM	GP	G	A	TP	PIM
1993-94	Cornell	ECAC	29	11	13	24	33	....	....	....	....	....
1994-95			DID NOT PLAY									

AUGUSTA, PATRIK   (ah-GOOS-tuh, pa-TREEK)

Right wing. Shoots left. 5'10", 170 lbs.   Born, Jihlava, Czech., November 13, 1969.
(Toronto's 8th choice, 149th overall, in 1992 Entry Draft).

			Regular Season					Playoffs				
Season	Club	Lea	GP	G	A	TP	PIM	GP	G	A	TP	PIM
1988-89	Dukla Jihlava	Czech.	15	3	1	4	4	....	....	....	....	....
1989-90	Dukla Jihlava	Czech.	46	12	12	24	....	....	....	....	....	....
1990-91	Dukla Jihlava	Czech.	51	20	23	43	....	....	....	....	....	....
1991-92	Dukla Jihlava	Czech.	42	16	16	32	26	....	....	....	....	....
1992-93	St. John's	AHL	75	32	45	77	74	8	3	3	6	23
1993-94	**Toronto**	**NHL**	2	0	0	0	0	....	....	....	....	....
a	St. John's	AHL	77	*53	43	96	105	11	4	8	12	4
1994-95	St. John's	AHL	71	37	32	69	98	4	2	0	2	7
	NHL Totals		**2**	**0**	**0**	**0**	**0**					

a AHL Second All-Star Team (1994)

BABARIKO, JEVGENI   (boh-bah-RIH-koh)   **VAN.**

Center. Shoots left. 6'1", 183 lbs.   Born, Gorky, USSR, March 3, 1974.
(Vancouver's 6th choice, 176th overall, in 1993 Entry Draft).

			Regular Season					Playoffs				
Season	Club	Lea	GP	G	A	TP	PIM	GP	G	A	TP	PIM
1991-92	Torpedo Niz.	CIS	17	5	0	5	4	....	....	....	....	....
1992-93	Torpedo Niz.	CIS	13	1	0	1	4	....	....	....	....	....
1993-94	Torpedo Niz.	CIS	44	3	5	8	12	....	....	....	....	....
1994-95	Torpedo Niz.	CIS	41	10	4	14	12	5	0	2	2	0

BABYCH, DAVE   (BAB-itch)   **VAN.**

Defense. Shoots left. 6'2", 215 lbs.   Born, Edmonton, Alta., May 23, 1961.
(Winnipeg's 1st choice, 2nd overall, in 1980 Entry Draft).

			Regular Season					Playoffs				
Season	Club	Lea	GP	G	A	TP	PIM	GP	G	A	TP	PIM
1978-79	Portland	WHL	67	20	59	79	63	25	7	22	29	22
1979-80a	Portland	WHL	50	22	60	82	71	8	1	10	11	2
1980-81	**Winnipeg**	**NHL**	69	6	38	44	90	....	....	....	....	....
1981-82	**Winnipeg**	**NHL**	79	19	49	68	92	4	1	2	3	29
1982-83	**Winnipeg**	**NHL**	79	13	61	74	56	3	0	0	0	0
1983-84	**Winnipeg**	**NHL**	66	18	39	57	62	3	1	1	2	0
1984-85	**Winnipeg**	**NHL**	78	13	49	62	78	8	2	7	9	6
1985-86	**Winnipeg**	**NHL**	19	4	12	16	14	....	....	....	....	....
	Hartford	**NHL**	62	10	43	53	36	8	1	3	4	14
1986-87	**Hartford**	**NHL**	66	8	33	41	44	6	1	1	2	14
1987-88	**Hartford**	**NHL**	71	14	36	50	54	6	3	2	5	2
1988-89	**Hartford**	**NHL**	70	6	41	47	54	4	1	5	6	2
1989-90	**Hartford**	**NHL**	72	6	37	43	62	7	1	2	3	0
1990-91	**Hartford**	**NHL**	8	0	6	6	4	....	....	....	....	....
1991-92	**Vancouver**	**NHL**	75	5	24	29	63	13	2	6	8	10
1992-93	**Vancouver**	**NHL**	43	3	16	19	44	12	2	5	7	6
1993-94	**Vancouver**	**NHL**	73	4	28	32	52	24	3	5	8	12
1994-95	**Vancouver**	**NHL**	40	3	11	14	18	11	2	2	4	14
	NHL Totals		**970**	**132**	**523**	**655**	**823**	**109**	**20**	**41**	**61**	**109**

a WHL First All-Star Team (1980)
Played in NHL All-Star Game (1983, 1984)

Traded to **Hartford** by **Winnipeg** for Ray Neufeld, November 21, 1985. Claimed by **Minnesota** from **Hartford** in Expansion Draft, May 30, 1991. Traded to **Vancouver** by **Minnesota** for Tom Kurvers, June 22, 1991.

BADDUKE, JOHN   **VAN.**

Right wing. Shoots right. 6'2", 195 lbs.   Born, Watson, Sask., June 21, 1972.

			Regular Season					Playoffs				
Season	Club	Lea	GP	G	A	TP	PIM	GP	G	A	TP	PIM
1988-89	Regina	WHL	8	0	0	0	4	....	....	....	....	....
1989-90	Victoria	WHL	49	1	2	3	138	....	....	....	....	....
1990-91	Victoria	WHL	66	8	9	17	305	....	....	....	....	....
1991-92	Portland	WHL	67	6	13	19	*335	6	1	1	2	42
1992-93	Portland	WHL	71	12	14	26	*367	16	3	4	7	57
1993-94	Hamilton	AHL	55	6	8	14	*356	4	0	1	1	18
	Columbus	ECHL	7	0	3	3	60	....	....	....	....	....
	Brantford	ColHL	1	1	0	1	2	....	....	....	....	....
1994-95	Syracuse	AHL	44	6	0	6	334	....	....	....	....	....

Signed as a free agent by **Vancouver**, February 2, 1994.

BAKER, JAMIE   **S.J.**

Center. Shoots left. 6', 190 lbs.   Born, Ottawa, Ont., August 31, 1966.
(Quebec's 2nd choice, 8th overall, in 1988 Supplemental Draft).

			Regular Season					Playoffs				
Season	Club	Lea	GP	G	A	TP	PIM	GP	G	A	TP	PIM
1985-86	St. Lawrence	ECAC	31	9	16	25	52	....	....	....	....	....
1986-87	St. Lawrence	ECAC	32	8	24	32	59	....	....	....	....	....
1987-88	St. Lawrence	ECAC	34	26	24	50	38	....	....	....	....	....
1988-89	St. Lawrence	ECAC	13	11	16	27	16	....	....	....	....	....
1989-90	**Quebec**	**NHL**	1	0	0	0	0	....	....	....	....	....
	Halifax	AHL	74	17	43	60	47	6	0	0	0	7
1990-91	**Quebec**	**NHL**	18	2	0	2	8	....	....	....	....	....
	Halifax	AHL	50	14	22	36	85	....	....	....	....	....
1991-92	**Quebec**	**NHL**	52	7	10	17	32	....	....	....	....	....
	Halifax	AHL	9	5	0	5	12	....	....	....	....	....
1992-93	**Ottawa**	**NHL**	76	19	29	48	54	....	....	....	....	....
1993-94	**San Jose**	**NHL**	65	12	5	17	38	14	3	2	5	30
1994-95	**San Jose**	**NHL**	43	7	4	11	22	11	2	2	4	12
	NHL Totals		**255**	**47**	**48**	**95**	**154**	**25**	**5**	**4**	**9**	**42**

Signed as a free agent by **Ottawa**, September 2, 1992. Signed as a free agent by **San Jose**, September 11, 1993.

BALL, MATT   **HFD.**

Right wing. Shoots right. 6', 219 lbs.   Born, Toronto, Ont., January 29, 1976.
(Hartford's 6th choice, 230th overall, in 1994 Entry Draft).

			Regular Season					Playoffs				
Season	Club	Lea	GP	G	A	TP	PIM	GP	G	A	TP	PIM
1993-94	Detroit	OHL	43	3	7	10	11	17	2	0	2	0
1994-95	Detroit	OHL	64	35	44	79	84	21	9	19	28	22

BANCROFT, STEVE

Defense. Shoots left. 6'1", 214 lbs.   Born, Toronto, Ont., October 6, 1970.
(Toronto's 3rd choice, 21st overall, in 1989 Entry Draft).

			Regular Season					Playoffs				
Season	Club	Lea	GP	G	A	TP	PIM	GP	G	A	TP	PIM
1987-88	Belleville	OHL	56	1	8	9	42	....	....	....	....	....
1988-89	Belleville	OHL	66	7	30	37	99	5	0	2	2	10
1989-90	Belleville	OHL	53	10	33	43	135	11	3	9	12	38
1990-91	Newmarket	AHL	9	0	3	3	22	....	....	....	....	....
	Maine	AHL	53	2	12	14	46	2	0	0	0	2
1991-92	Maine	AHL	26	1	3	4	45	....	....	....	....	....
	Indianapolis	IHL	36	8	23	31	49	....	....	....	....	....
1992-93	**Chicago**	**NHL**	1	0	0	0	0	....	....	....	....	....
	Indianapolis	IHL	53	10	35	45	138	....	....	....	....	....
	Moncton	AHL	21	3	13	16	16	5	0	0	0	16
1993-94	Cleveland	IHL	33	2	12	14	58	....	....	....	....	....
1994-95	Detroit	IHL	6	1	3	4	0	....	....	....	....	....
	Fort Wayne	IHL	50	7	17	24	100	....	....	....	....	....
	St. John's	AHL	4	2	0	2	2	5	0	3	3	8
	NHL Totals		**1**	**0**	**0**	**0**	**0**					

Traded to **Boston** by **Toronto** for Rob Cimetta, November 9, 1990. Traded to **Chicago** by **Boston** with Boston's eleventh round choice (later traded to Winnipeg — Winnipeg selected Russel Hewson) in 1993 Entry Draft for Chicago's eleventh round choice (Eugene Pavlov) in 1992 Entry Draft, January 9, 1992. Traded to **Winnipeg** by **Chicago** with future considerations for Troy Murray, February 21, 1993. Claimed by **Florida** from **Winnipeg** in Expansion Draft, June 24, 1993. Signed as a free agent by **Pittsburgh**, August 2, 1993.

BANNISTER, DREW   **T.B.**

Defense. Shoots right. 6'1", 193 lbs.   Born, Belleville, Ont., September 4, 1974.
(Tampa Bay's 2nd choice, 26th overall, in 1992 Entry Draft).

			Regular Season					Playoffs				
Season	Club	Lea	GP	G	A	TP	PIM	GP	G	A	TP	PIM
1990-91	S.S. Marie	OHL	41	2	8	10	51	4	0	0	0	0
1991-92	S.S. Marie	OHL	64	4	21	25	122	16	3	10	13	36
1992-93a	S.S. Marie	OHL	59	5	28	33	114	18	2	7	9	12
1993-94b	S.S. Marie	OHL	58	7	43	50	108	14	6	9	15	20
1994-95	Atlanta	IHL	72	5	7	12	74	5	0	2	2	22

a Memorial Cup All-Star Team (1993)
b OHL Second All-Star Team (1994)

BARANOV, ALEXEI   **T.B.**

Defense. Shoots right. 6'1", 174 lbs.   Born, Lipetsk, USSR, June 3, 1976.
(Tampa Bay's 8th choice, 190th overall, in 1994 Entry Draft).

			Regular Season					Playoffs				
Season	Club	Lea	GP	G	A	TP	PIM	GP	G	A	TP	PIM
1993-94	Mosc. D'amo 2	CIS 3			UNAVAILABLE							
1994-95	Moscow D'amo	CIS	1	0	0	0	0	....	....	....	....	....

BARNABY, MATTHEW   **BUF.**

Left wing. Shoots left. 6', 170 lbs.   Born, Ottawa, Ont., May 4, 1973.
(Buffalo's 5th choice, 83rd overall, in 1992 Entry Draft).

			Regular Season					Playoffs				
Season	Club	Lea	GP	G	A	TP	PIM	GP	G	A	TP	PIM
1990-91	Beauport	QMJHL	52	9	5	14	262	....	....	....	....	....
1991-92	Beauport	QMJHL	63	29	37	66	*476	....	....	....	....	....
1992-93	**Buffalo**	**NHL**	2	1	0	1	10	1	0	1	1	4
	Victoriaville	QMJHL	65	44	67	111	*448	6	2	4	6	44
1993-94	**Buffalo**	**NHL**	35	2	4	6	106	3	0	0	0	17
	Rochester	AHL	42	10	32	42	153	....	....	....	....	....
1994-95	Rochester	AHL	56	21	29	50	274	....	....	....	....	....
	Buffalo	**NHL**	23	1	1	2	116	....	....	....	....	....
	NHL Totals		**60**	**4**	**5**	**9**	**232**	**4**	**0**	**1**	**1**	**21**

BARNES, STU — FLA.

Center. Shoots right. 5'11", 174 lbs. Born, Edmonton, Alta., December 25, 1970.
(Winnipeg's 1st choice, 4th overall, in 1989 Entry Draft).

			Regular Season					Playoffs				
Season	Club	Lea	GP	G	A	TP	PIM	GP	G	A	TP	PIM
1987-88	N. Westminster	WHL	71	37	64	101	88	5	2	3	5	6
1988-89a	Tri-City	WHL	70	59	82	141	117	7	6	5	11	10
1989-90	Tri-City	WHL	63	52	92	144	165	7	1	5	6	26
1990-91	Cdn. National	....	53	22	27	49	68	....	....	....	....	....
1991-92	**Winnipeg**	**NHL**	**46**	**8**	**9**	**17**	**26**	....	....	....	....	....
	Moncton	AHL	30	13	19	32	10	11	3	9	12	6
1992-93	**Winnipeg**	**NHL**	**38**	**12**	**10**	**22**	**10**	**6**	**1**	**3**	**4**	**2**
	Moncton	AHL	42	23	31	54	58	....	....	....	....	....
1993-94	**Winnipeg**	**NHL**	**18**	**5**	**4**	**9**	**8**	....	....	....	....	....
	Florida	**NHL**	**59**	**18**	**20**	**38**	**30**	....	....	....	....	....
1994-95	**Florida**	**NHL**	**41**	**10**	**19**	**29**	**8**	....	....	....	....	....
	NHL Totals		**202**	**53**	**62**	**115**	**82**	**6**	**1**	**3**	**4**	**2**

a WHL West Second All-Star Team (1989)

Traded to **Florida** by **Winnipeg** with St. Louis' sixth round choice (previously acquired by Winnipeg — later traded to Edmonton — later traded to Winnipeg — Winnipeg selected Chris Kibermanis) for Randy Gilhen, November 25, 1993.

BARON, MURRAY — ST.L.

Defense. Shoots left. 6'3", 215 lbs. Born, Prince George, B.C., June 1, 1967.
(Philadelphia's 7th choice, 167th overall, in 1986 Entry Draft).

			Regular Season					Playoffs				
Season	Club	Lea	GP	G	A	TP	PIM	GP	G	A	TP	PIM
1986-87	North Dakota	WCHA	41	4	10	14	62	....	....	....	....	....
1987-88	North Dakota	WCHA	41	1	10	11	95	....	....	....	....	....
1988-89	North Dakota	WCHA	40	2	6	8	92	....	....	....	....	....
	Hershey	AHL	9	0	3	3	8	....	....	....	....	....
1989-90	**Philadelphia**	**NHL**	**16**	**2**	**2**	**4**	**12**	....	....	....	....	....
	Hershey	AHL	50	0	10	10	101	....	....	....	....	....
1990-91	**Philadelphia**	**NHL**	**67**	**8**	**8**	**16**	**74**	....	....	....	....	....
	Hershey	AHL	6	2	3	5	0	....	....	....	....	....
1991-92	**St. Louis**	**NHL**	**67**	**3**	**8**	**11**	**94**	**2**	**0**	**0**	**0**	**2**
1992-93	**St. Louis**	**NHL**	**53**	**2**	**2**	**4**	**59**	**11**	**0**	**0**	**0**	**12**
1993-94	**St. Louis**	**NHL**	**77**	**5**	**9**	**14**	**123**	**4**	**0**	**0**	**0**	**10**
1994-95	**St. Louis**	**NHL**	**39**	**0**	**5**	**5**	**93**	**7**	**1**	**1**	**2**	**2**
	NHL Totals		**319**	**20**	**34**	**54**	**455**	**24**	**1**	**1**	**2**	**26**

Traded to **St. Louis** by **Philadelphia** with Ron Sutter for Dan Quinn and Rod Brind'Amour, September 22, 1991.

BARR, DAVE

Right wing. Shoots right. 6'1", 195 lbs. Born, Toronto, Ont., November 30, 1960.

			Regular Season					Playoffs				
Season	Club	Lea	GP	G	A	TP	PIM	GP	G	A	TP	PIM
1979-80	Lethbridge	WHL	60	16	38	54	47	....	....	....	....	....
1980-81	Lethbridge	WHL	72	26	62	88	106	10	4	10	14	4
1981-82	**Boston**	**NHL**	**2**	**0**	**0**	**0**	**0**	**5**	**1**	**0**	**1**	**0**
	Erie	AHL	76	18	48	66	29	....	....	....	....	....
1982-83	**Boston**	**NHL**	**10**	**1**	**1**	**2**	**7**	**10**	**0**	**0**	**0**	**2**
	Baltimore	AHL	72	27	51	78	67	....	....	....	....	....
1983-84	**NY Rangers**	**NHL**	**6**	**0**	**0**	**0**	**2**	....	....	....	....	....
	Tulsa	CHL	50	28	37	65	24	....	....	....	....	....
	St. Louis	**NHL**	**1**	**0**	**0**	**0**	**0**	....	....	....	....	....
1984-85	**St. Louis**	**NHL**	**75**	**16**	**18**	**34**	**32**	**2**	**0**	**0**	**0**	**2**
1985-86	**St. Louis**	**NHL**	**72**	**13**	**38**	**51**	**70**	**11**	**1**	**1**	**2**	**14**
1986-87	**St. Louis**	**NHL**	**2**	**0**	**0**	**0**	**0**	....	....	....	....	....
	Hartford	**NHL**	**30**	**2**	**4**	**6**	**19**	....	....	....	....	....
	Detroit	**NHL**	**37**	**13**	**13**	**26**	**49**	**13**	**1**	**0**	**1**	**14**
1987-88	**Detroit**	**NHL**	**51**	**14**	**26**	**40**	**58**	**16**	**5**	**7**	**12**	**22**
1988-89	**Detroit**	**NHL**	**73**	**27**	**32**	**59**	**69**	**6**	**3**	**1**	**4**	**6**
1989-90	**Detroit**	**NHL**	**62**	**10**	**25**	**35**	**45**	....	....	....	....	....
	Adirondack	AHL	9	1	14	15	17	....	....	....	....	....
1990-91	**Detroit**	**NHL**	**70**	**18**	**22**	**40**	**55**	....	....	....	....	....
1991-92	**New Jersey**	**NHL**	**41**	**6**	**12**	**18**	**32**	....	....	....	....	....
	Utica	AHL	1	0	0	0	7	....	....	....	....	....
1992-93	**New Jersey**	**NHL**	**62**	**6**	**8**	**14**	**61**	**5**	**1**	**0**	**1**	**6**
1993-94	**Dallas**	**NHL**	**20**	**2**	**5**	**7**	**21**	**3**	**0**	**1**	**1**	**4**
	Kalamazoo	IHL	4	3	2	5	5	....	....	....	....	....
1994-95	Kalamazoo	IHL	66	18	41	59	77	16	1	4	5	8
	NHL Totals		**614**	**128**	**204**	**332**	**520**	**71**	**12**	**10**	**22**	**70**

Signed as a free agent by **Boston**, September 28, 1981. Traded to **NY Rangers** by **Boston** for Dave Silk, October 5, 1983. Traded to **St. Louis** by **NY Rangers** with NY Rangers' third round choice (Alan Perry) in the 1984 Entry Draft for Larry Patey and Bob Brooke, March 5, 1984. Traded to **Hartford** by **St. Louis** for Tim Bothwell, October 21, 1986. Traded to **Detroit** by **Hartford** for Randy Ladouceur, January 12, 1987. Acquired by **New Jersey** from **Detroit** with Randy McKay as compensation for Detroit's signing of free agent Troy Crowder, September 9, 1991. Signed as a free agent by **Dallas**, August 28, 1993.

BARRAULT, DOUG (buh-ROH)

Right wing. Shoots right. 6'2", 205 lbs. Born, Golden, B.C., April 21, 1970.
(Minnesota's 8th choice, 155th overall, in 1990 Entry Draft).

			Regular Season					Playoffs				
Season	Club	Lea	GP	G	A	TP	PIM	GP	G	A	TP	PIM
1988-89	Lethbridge	WHL	57	14	13	27	34	....	....	....	....	....
1989-90	Lethbridge	WHL	54	14	16	30	36	19	7	3	10	0
1990-91a	Lethbridge	WHL	4	2	2	4	16	....	....	....	....	....
	Seattle	WHL	61	42	42	84	69	6	5	3	8	4
1991-92	Kalamazoo	IHL	60	5	14	19	26	....	....	....	....	....
1992-93	**Minnesota**	**NHL**	**2**	**0**	**0**	**0**	**2**	....	....	....	....	....
	Kalamazoo	IHL	78	32	34	66	74	....	....	....	....	....
1993-94	**Florida**	**NHL**	**2**	**0**	**0**	**0**	**0**	....	....	....	....	....
	Cincinnati	IHL	75	36	28	64	59	9	8	2	10	0
1994-95	Cincinnati	IHL	74	20	40	60	57	10	2	6	8	20
	NHL Totals		**4**	**0**	**0**	**0**	**2**	....	....	....	....	....

a WHL West Second All-Star Team (1991)

Claimed by **Florida** from **Dallas** in Expansion Draft, June 24, 1993.

BARRIE, LEN — PIT.

Center. Shoots left. 6', 200 lbs. Born, Kimberley, B.C., June 4, 1969.
(Edmonton's 7th choice, 124th overall, in 1988 Entry Draft).

			Regular Season					Playoffs				
Season	Club	Lea	GP	G	A	TP	PIM	GP	G	A	TP	PIM
1985-86	Calgary	WHL	32	3	0	3	18	....	....	....	....	....
1986-87	Calgary	WHL	34	13	13	26	81	....	....	....	....	....
	Victoria	WHL	34	7	6	13	92	5	0	1	1	15
1987-88	Victoria	WHL	70	37	49	86	192	8	2	0	2	29
1988-89	Victoria	WHL	67	39	48	87	157	7	5	2	7	23
1989-90	**Philadelphia**	**NHL**	**1**	**0**	**0**	**0**	**0**	....	....	....	....	....
a	Kamloops	WHL	70	*85	*100	*185	108	17	*14	23	*37	24
1990-91	Hershey	AHL	63	26	32	58	60	7	4	0	4	12
1991-92	Hershey	AHL	75	42	43	85	78	3	0	2	2	32
1992-93	**Philadelphia**	**NHL**	**8**	**2**	**2**	**4**	**9**	....	....	....	....	....
	Hershey	AHL	61	31	45	76	162	....	....	....	....	....
1993-94	**Florida**	**NHL**	**2**	**0**	**0**	**0**	**0**	....	....	....	....	....
b	Cincinnati	IHL	77	45	71	116	246	11	8	13	21	60
1994-95	Cleveland	IHL	28	13	30	43	137	....	....	....	....	....
	Pittsburgh	**NHL**	**48**	**3**	**11**	**14**	**66**	**4**	**1**	**0**	**1**	**8**
	NHL Totals		**59**	**5**	**13**	**18**	**75**	**4**	**1**	**0**	**1**	**8**

a WHL West First All-Star Team (1990)
b IHL Second All-Star Team (1994)

Signed as a free agent by **Philadelphia**, February 28, 1990. Signed as a free agent by **Florida**, July 20, 1993. Signed as a free agent by **Pittsburgh**, August 15, 1994.

BARRIE, MIKE — BUF.

Center. Shoots right. 6'1", 170 lbs. Born, Kelowna, B.C., March 16, 1974.
(Buffalo's 6th choice, 194th overall, in 1993 Entry Draft).

			Regular Season					Playoffs				
Season	Club	Lea	GP	G	A	TP	PIM	GP	G	A	TP	PIM
1991-92	Victoria	WHL	54	15	15	30	165	....	....	....	....	....
1992-93	Victoria	WHL	70	31	39	70	244	....	....	....	....	....
1993-94	Red Deer	WHL	19	11	14	25	53	....	....	....	....	....
	Seattle	WHL	48	24	28	52	119	9	5	3	8	14
	Rochester	AHL	....	....	....	....	....	3	0	1	1	0
1994-95	Rochester	AHL	16	1	3	4	40	....	....	....	....	....
	S. Carolina	ECHL	39	8	14	22	122	....	....	....	....	....

BARTELL, JOSH — PHI.

Defense. Shoots left. 6'3", 205 lbs. Born, Syracuse, NY, April 14, 1973.
(Philadelphia's 9th choice, 204th overall, in 1991 Entry Draft).

			Regular Season					Playoffs				
Season	Club	Lea	GP	G	A	TP	PIM	GP	G	A	TP	PIM
1992-93	Clarkson	ECAC	22	1	0	1	24	....	....	....	....	....
1993-94	Clarkson	ECAC	29	1	2	3	42	....	....	....	....	....
1994-95	Clarkson	ECAC	29	0	3	3	77	....	....	....	....	....

BASSEN, BOB — DAL.

Center. Shoots left. 5'10", 180 lbs. Born, Calgary, Alta., May 6, 1965.

			Regular Season					Playoffs				
Season	Club	Lea	GP	G	A	TP	PIM	GP	G	A	TP	PIM
1982-83	Medicine Hat	WHL	4	3	2	5	0	3	0	0	0	4
1983-84	Medicine Hat	WHL	72	29	29	58	93	14	5	11	16	12
1984-85a	Medicine Hat	WHL	65	32	50	82	143	10	2	8	10	39
1985-86	**NY Islanders**	**NHL**	**11**	**2**	**1**	**3**	**6**	**3**	**0**	**1**	**1**	**0**
	Springfield	AHL	54	13	21	34	111	....	....	....	....	....
1986-87	**NY Islanders**	**NHL**	**77**	**7**	**10**	**17**	**89**	**14**	**1**	**2**	**3**	**21**
1987-88	**NY Islanders**	**NHL**	**77**	**6**	**16**	**22**	**99**	**6**	**0**	**1**	**1**	**23**
1988-89	**NY Islanders**	**NHL**	**19**	**1**	**4**	**5**	**21**	....	....	....	....	....
	Chicago	**NHL**	**49**	**4**	**12**	**16**	**62**	**10**	**1**	**1**	**2**	**34**
1989-90	**Chicago**	**NHL**	**6**	**1**	**1**	**2**	**8**	**1**	**0**	**0**	**0**	**2**
b	Indianapolis	IHL	73	22	32	54	179	12	3	8	11	33
1990-91	**St. Louis**	**NHL**	**79**	**16**	**18**	**34**	**183**	**13**	**1**	**3**	**4**	**24**
1991-92	**St. Louis**	**NHL**	**79**	**7**	**25**	**32**	**167**	**6**	**0**	**2**	**2**	**4**
1992-93	**St. Louis**	**NHL**	**53**	**9**	**10**	**19**	**63**	**11**	**0**	**0**	**0**	**10**
1993-94	**St. Louis**	**NHL**	**46**	**2**	**7**	**9**	**44**	....	....	....	....	....
	Quebec	**NHL**	**37**	**11**	**8**	**19**	**55**	....	....	....	....	....
1994-95	**Quebec**	**NHL**	**47**	**12**	**15**	**27**	**33**	**5**	**2**	**4**	**6**	**0**
	NHL Totals		**580**	**78**	**127**	**205**	**830**	**69**	**5**	**14**	**19**	**118**

a WHL First All-Star Team (1985)
b IHL First All-Star Team (1990)

Signed as a free agent by **NY Islanders**, October 19, 1984. Traded to **Chicago** by **NY Islanders** with Steve Konroyd for Marc Bergevin and Gary Nylund, November 25, 1988. Claimed by **St. Louis** from **Chicago** in NHL Waiver Draft, October 1, 1990. Traded to **Quebec** by **St. Louis** with Garth Butcher and Ron Sutter for Steve Duchesne and Denis Chasse, January 23, 1994. Signed as a free agent by **Dallas**, August 10, 1995.

BATES, SHAWN — BOS.

Center. Shoots right. 5'11", 160 lbs. Born, Melrose, MA, April 3, 1975.
(Boston's 4th choice, 103rd overall, in 1993 Entry Draft).

			Regular Season					Playoffs				
Season	Club	Lea	GP	G	A	TP	PIM	GP	G	A	TP	PIM
1993-94	Boston U.	H.E.	41	10	19	29	24	....	....	....	....	....
1994-95a	Boston U.	H.E.	38	18	12	30	48	....	....	....	....	....

a NCAA Final Four All-Tournament Team (1995)

BATTAGLIA, DOUG — DET.

Left wing. Shoots left. 6'1", 185 lbs. Born, Newmarket, Ont., October 26, 1975.
(Detroit's 5th choice, 127th overall, in 1994 Entry Draft).

			Regular Season					Playoffs				
Season	Club	Lea	GP	G	A	TP	PIM	GP	G	A	TP	PIM
1993-94	Brockville	Jr. A	47	35	39	74	212	....	....	....	....	....
1994-95	RPI	ECAC	34	1	4	5	57	....	....	....	....	....

BATTAGLIA, JON — ANA.

Left wing. Shoots left. 6'2", 185 lbs. Born, Chicago, IL, December 13, 1975.
(Anaheim's 6th choice, 132nd overall, in 1994 Entry Draft).

			Regular Season					Playoffs				
Season	Club	Lea	GP	G	A	TP	PIM	GP	G	A	TP	PIM
1993-94	Caledon	Jr. A	44	15	33	48	104	....	....	....	....	....
1994-95	Lake Superior	CCHA	38	6	14	20	34	....	....	....	....	....

BATTERS, JEFF

Defense. Shoots right. 6'2", 215 lbs. Born, Victoria, B.C., October 23, 1970.
(St. Louis' 7th choice, 135th overall, in 1989 Entry Draft).

			Regular Season					Playoffs				
Season	Club	Lea	GP	G	A	TP	PIM	GP	G	A	TP	PIM
1988-89	Alaska-Anch.	G.N.	33	8	14	22	123	....	....	....	....	....
1989-90	Alaska-Anch.	G.N.	34	6	9	15	102	....	....	....	....	....
1990-91	Alaska-Anch.	G.N.	39	16	14	30	90	....	....	....	....	....
1991-92	Alaska-Anch.	G.N.	33	6	16	22	84	....	....	....	....	....
1992-93	Peoria	IHL	74	5	18	23	113	4	0	0	0	10
1993-94	**St. Louis**	**NHL**	**6**	**0**	**0**	**0**	**7**	....	....	....	....	....
	Peoria	IHL	59	3	9	12	175	6	0	0	0	18
1994-95	Peoria	IHL	42	0	11	11	128	5	0	1	1	18
	St. Louis	**NHL**	**10**	**0**	**0**	**0**	**21**	....	....	....	....	....
	NHL Totals		**16**	**0**	**0**	**0**	**28**	....	....	....	....	....

BATYRSHIN, RUSLAN (ba-TEER-shihn) L.A.

Defense. Shoots left. 6'1", 180 lbs. Born, Moscow, USSR, February 19, 1975.
(Winnipeg's 4th choice, 79th overall, in 1993 Entry Draft).

			Regular Season					Playoffs				
Season	Club	Lea	GP	G	A	TP	PIM	GP	G	A	TP	PIM
1991-92	Mosc.D'amo-2	CIS 3	40	0	2	2	52	....	....	....	....	....
1992-93	Mosc.D'amo-2	CIS 2			UNAVAILABLE							
1993-94	Moscow D'amo	CIS	10	0	0	0	10	3	0	0	0	22
1994-95	Moscow D'amo	CIS	36	2	2	4	65	12	1	1	2	6

Rights traded to **Los Angeles** by **Winnipeg** with Winnipeg's second round choice in 1996 Entry Draft for Brent Thompson and future considerations, August 8, 1994.

BAUMGARTNER, KEN TOR.

Left wing. Shoots left. 6'1", 205 lbs. Born, Flin Flon, Man., March 11, 1966.
(Buffalo's 12th choice, 245th overall, in 1985 Entry Draft).

			Regular Season					Playoffs				
Season	Club	Lea	GP	G	A	TP	PIM	GP	G	A	TP	PIM
1984-85	Prince Albert	WHL	60	3	9	12	252	13	1	3	4	89
1985-86	Prince Albert	WHL	70	4	23	27	277	20	3	9	12	112
1986-87	New Haven	AHL	13	0	3	3	99	6	0	0	0	60
1987-88	**Los Angeles**	**NHL**	**30**	**2**	**3**	**5**	**189**	**5**	**0**	**1**	**1**	**28**
	New Haven	AHL	48	1	5	6	181	....	....	....	....	....
1988-89	**Los Angeles**	**NHL**	**49**	**1**	**3**	**4**	**288**	**5**	**0**	**0**	**0**	**8**
	New Haven	AHL	10	1	3	4	26	....	....	....	....	....
1989-90	**Los Angeles**	**NHL**	**12**	**1**	**0**	**1**	**28**	....	....	....	....	....
	NY Islanders	**NHL**	**53**	**0**	**5**	**5**	**194**	**4**	**0**	**0**	**0**	**27**
1990-91	**NY Islanders**	**NHL**	**78**	**1**	**6**	**7**	**282**	....	....	....	....	....
1991-92	**NY Islanders**	**NHL**	**44**	**0**	**1**	**1**	**202**	....	....	....	....	....
	Toronto	**NHL**	**11**	**0**	**0**	**0**	**23**	....	....	....	....	....
1992-93	**Toronto**	**NHL**	**63**	**1**	**0**	**1**	**155**	**7**	**1**	**0**	**1**	**0**
1993-94	**Toronto**	**NHL**	**64**	**4**	**4**	**8**	**185**	**10**	**0**	**0**	**0**	**18**
1994-95	**Toronto**	**NHL**	**2**	**0**	**0**	**0**	**5**	....	....	....	....	....
	NHL Totals		**406**	**10**	**22**	**32**	**1551**	**31**	**1**	**1**	**2**	**81**

Traded to **Los Angeles** by **Buffalo** with Sean McKenna and Larry Playfair for Brian Engblom and Doug Smith, January 29, 1986. Traded to **NY Islanders** by **Los Angeles** with Hubie McDonough for Mikko Makela, November 29, 1989. Traded to **Toronto** by **NY Islanders** with Dave McLlwain for Daniel Marois and Claude Loiselle, March 10, 1992.

BAUMGARTNER, NOLAN WSH.

Defense. Shoots right. 6'1", 200 lbs. Born, Calgary, Alta., March 23, 1976.
(Washington's 1st choice, 10th overall, in 1994 Entry Draft).

			Regular Season					Playoffs				
Season	Club	Lea	GP	G	A	TP	PIM	GP	G	A	TP	PIM
1992-93	Kamloops	WHL	43	0	5	5	30	11	1	1	2	0
1993-94a	Kamloops	WHL	69	13	42	55	109	19	3	14	17	33
1994-95abcd	Kamloops	WHL	62	8	36	44	71	21	4	13	17	16

a Memorial Cup All-Star Team (1994, 1995)
b WHL West First All-Star Team (1995)
c Canadian Major Junior First All-Star Team (1995)
d Canadian Major Junior Defenseman of the Year (1995)

BAUTIN, SERGEI (BOW-tin)

Defense. Shoots left. 6'3", 200 lbs. Born, Rogachev, USSR, March 11, 1967.
(Winnipeg's 1st choice, 17th overall, in 1992 Entry Draft).

			Regular Season					Playoffs				
Season	Club	Lea	GP	G	A	TP	PIM	GP	G	A	TP	PIM
1990-91	Moscow D'amo	USSR	33	2	0	2	28	....	....	....	....	....
1991-92	Moscow D'amo	CIS	37	1	3	4	88	....	....	....	....	....
1992-93	**Winnipeg**	**NHL**	**71**	**5**	**18**	**23**	**96**	**6**	**0**	**0**	**0**	**2**
1993-94	**Winnipeg**	**NHL**	**59**	**0**	**7**	**7**	**78**	....	....	....	....	....
	Detroit	**NHL**	**1**	**0**	**0**	**0**	**0**	....	....	....	....	....
	Adirondack	AHL	9	1	5	6	6	....	....	....	....	....
1994-95	Adirondack	AHL	32	0	10	10	57	1	0	0	0	4
	NHL Totals		**131**	**5**	**25**	**30**	**174**	**6**	**0**	**0**	**0**	**2**

Traded to **Detroit** by **Winnipeg** with Bob Essensa for Tim Cheveldae and Dallas Drake, March 8, 1994.

BAWA, ROBIN (BAH-wah)

Right wing. Shoots right. 6'2", 214 lbs. Born, Chemainus, B.C., March 26, 1966.

			Regular Season					Playoffs				
Season	Club	Lea	GP	G	A	TP	PIM	GP	G	A	TP	PIM
1982-83	Kamloops	WHL	66	10	24	34	17	7	1	2	3	0
1983-84	Kamloops	WHL	64	16	28	44	40	13	4	2	6	4
1984-85	Kamloops	WHL	52	6	19	25	45	15	4	9	13	14
1985-86	Kamloops	WHL	63	29	43	72	78	16	5	13	18	4
1986-87a	Kamloops	WHL	62	57	56	113	91	13	6	7	13	22
1987-88	Fort Wayne	IHL	55	12	27	39	239	6	1	3	4	24
1988-89	Baltimore	AHL	75	23	24	47	205	....	....	....	....	....
1989-90	**Washington**	**NHL**	**5**	**1**	**0**	**1**	**6**	....	....	....	....	....
	Baltimore	AHL	61	7	18	25	189	11	1	2	3	49
1990-91	Fort Wayne	IHL	72	21	26	47	381	18	4	4	8	87
1991-92	**Vancouver**	**NHL**	**2**	**0**	**0**	**0**	**0**	**1**	**0**	**0**	**0**	**0**
	Milwaukee	IHL	70	27	14	41	238	5	2	2	4	8
1992-93	Hamilton	AHL	23	3	4	7	58	....	....	....	....	....
	San Jose	**NHL**	**42**	**5**	**0**	**5**	**47**	....	....	....	....	....
	Kansas City	IHL	5	2	0	2	20	....	....	....	....	....
1993-94	**Anaheim**	**NHL**	**12**	**0**	**1**	**1**	**7**	....	....	....	....	....
	San Diego	IHL	25	6	15	21	54	6	0	0	0	52
1994-95	Kalamazoo	IHL	71	22	12	34	184	....	....	....	....	....
	Milwaukee	IHL	4	1	1	2	19	15	1	5	6	48
	NHL Totals		**61**	**6**	**1**	**7**	**60**	**1**	**0**	**0**	**0**	**0**

a WHL West All-Star Team (1987)

Signed as a free agent by **Washington**, May 22, 1987. Traded to **Vancouver** by **Washington** for cash, July 31, 1991. Traded to **San Jose** by **Vancouver** for Rick Lessard, December 15, 1992. Claimed by **Anaheim** from **San Jose** in Expansion Draft, June 24, 1993. Signed as a free agent by **Dallas**, July 22, 1994.

BEAUDOIN, NIC (BOH-dwehn) COL.

Left wing. Shoots left. 6'3", 205 lbs. Born, Ottawa, Ont., December 25, 1976.
(Colorado's 2nd choice, 51st overall, in 1995 Entry Draft).

			Regular Season					Playoffs				
Season	Club	Lea	GP	G	A	TP	PIM	GP	G	A	TP	PIM
1993-94	Detroit	OHL	63	9	18	27	32	17	1	2	3	13
1994-95	Detroit	OHL	11	1	3	4	16	21	5	7	12	16

BEAUFAIT, MARK

Center. Shoots right. 5'9", 170 lbs. Born, Livonia, MI, May 13, 1970.
(San Jose's 2nd choice, 7th overall, in 1991 Supplemental Draft).

			Regular Season					Playoffs				
Season	Club	Lea	GP	G	A	TP	PIM	GP	G	A	TP	PIM
1988-89	N. Michigan	WCHA	11	2	1	3	2	....	....	....	....	....
1989-90	N. Michigan	WCHA	34	10	14	24	12	....	....	....	....	....
1990-91	N. Michigan	WCHA	47	19	30	49	18	....	....	....	....	....
1991-92	N. Michigan	WCHA	39	31	44	75	43	....	....	....	....	....
1992-93	**San Jose**	**NHL**	**5**	**1**	**0**	**1**	**0**	....	....	....	....	....
	Kansas City	IHL	66	19	40	59	22	9	1	1	2	8
1993-94	U.S. National	....	51	22	29	51	36	....	....	....	....	....
	U.S. Olympic	....	8	1	4	5	2	....	....	....	....	....
	Kansas City	IHL	21	12	9	21	18	....	....	....	....	....
1994-95	San Diego	IHL	68	24	39	63	22	5	2	2	4	2
	NHL Totals		**5**	**1**	**0**	**1**	**0**	....	....	....	....	....

BEDDOES, CLAYTON BOS.

Center. Shoots left. 5'11", 190 lbs. Born, Bentley, Alta., November 10, 1970.

			Regular Season					Playoffs				
Season	Club	Lea	GP	G	A	TP	PIM	GP	G	A	TP	PIM
1990-91	Lake Superior	CCHA	45	14	28	42	26	....	....	....	....	....
1991-92	Lake Superior	CCHA	38	14	26	40	24	....	....	....	....	....
1992-93	Lake Superior	CCHA	43	18	40	58	30	....	....	....	....	....
1993-94ab	Lake Superior	CCHA	44	23	31	54	56	....	....	....	....	....
1994-95	Providence	AHL	65	16	20	36	39	13	3	1	4	18

a CCHA Second All-Star Team (1994)
b NCAA West Second All-American Team (1994)

Signed as a free agent by **Boston**, June 2, 1994.

BEERS, BOB NYI

Defense. Shoots right. 6'2", 200 lbs. Born, Pittsburgh, PA, May 20, 1967.
(Boston's 10th choice, 210th overall, in 1985 Entry Draft).

			Regular Season					Playoffs				
Season	Club	Lea	GP	G	A	TP	PIM	GP	G	A	TP	PIM
1985-86	N. Arizona	NCAA	28	11	39	50	96	....	....	....	....	....
1986-87	U. of Maine	H.E.	38	0	13	13	45	....	....	....	....	....
1987-88	U. of Maine	H.E.	41	3	11	14	72	....	....	....	....	....
1988-89ab	U. of Maine	H.E.	44	10	27	37	53	....	....	....	....	....
1989-90	**Boston**	**NHL**	**3**	**0**	**1**	**1**	**6**	**14**	**1**	**1**	**2**	**18**
	Maine	AHL	74	7	36	43	63	....	....	....	....	....
1990-91	**Boston**	**NHL**	**16**	**0**	**1**	**1**	**10**	**6**	**0**	**0**	**0**	**4**
	Maine	AHL	36	2	16	18	21	....	....	....	....	....
1991-92	**Boston**	**NHL**	**31**	**0**	**5**	**5**	**29**	**1**	**0**	**0**	**0**	**0**
	Maine	AHL	33	6	23	29	24	....	....	....	....	....
1992-93	Providence	AHL	6	1	2	3	10	....	....	....	....	....
	Tampa Bay	**NHL**	**64**	**12**	**24**	**36**	**70**	....	....	....	....	....
	Atlanta	IHL	1	0	0	0	0	....	....	....	....	....
1993-94	**Tampa Bay**	**NHL**	**16**	**1**	**5**	**6**	**12**	....	....	....	....	....
	Edmonton	**NHL**	**66**	**10**	**27**	**37**	**74**	....	....	....	....	....
1994-95	**NY Islanders**	**NHL**	**22**	**2**	**7**	**9**	**6**	....	....	....	....	....
	NHL Totals		**218**	**25**	**70**	**95**	**207**	**21**	**1**	**1**	**2**	**22**

a Hockey East Second All-Star Team (1989)
b NCAA East Second All-American Team (1989)

Traded to **Tampa Bay** by **Boston** for Stephane Richer, October 28, 1992. Traded to **Edmonton** by **Tampa Bay** for Chris Joseph, November 11, 1993. Signed as a free agent by **NY Islanders**, August 29, 1994.

BELAK, WADE COL.

Defense. Shoots right. 6'4", 213 lbs. Born, Saskatoon, Sask., July 3, 1976.
(Quebec's 1st choice, 12th overall, in 1994 Entry Draft).

			Regular Season					Playoffs				
Season	Club	Lea	GP	G	A	TP	PIM	GP	G	A	TP	PIM
1992-93	N. Battleford	Midget	50	5	15	20	146	....	....	....	....	....
	Saskatoon	WHL	7	0	0	0	23	7	0	0	0	0
1993-94	Saskatoon	WHL	69	4	13	17	226	16	2	2	4	43
1994-95	Saskatoon	WHL	72	4	14	18	290	9	0	0	0	36
	Cornwall	AHL	....	....	....	....	....	11	1	2	3	40

BELANGER, JESSE (buh-LAWN-zhay) FLA.

Center. Shoots right. 6', 186 lbs. Born, St. Georges de Beauce, Que., June 15, 1969.

			Regular Season					Playoffs				
Season	Club	Lea	GP	G	A	TP	PIM	GP	G	A	TP	PIM
1987-88	Granby	QMJHL	69	33	43	76	10	5	3	3	6	0
1988-89	Granby	QMJHL	67	40	63	103	26	4	0	5	5	0
1989-90	Granby	QMJHL	67	53	54	107	53	....	....	....	....	....
1990-91	Fredericton	AHL	75	40	58	98	30	6	2	4	6	0
1991-92	**Montreal**	**NHL**	**4**	**0**	**0**	**0**	**0**	....	....	....	....	....
	Fredericton	AHL	65	30	41	71	26	7	3	3	6	2
1992-93	**Montreal**	**NHL**	**19**	**4**	**2**	**6**	**4**	**9**	**0**	**1**	**1**	**0**
	Fredericton	AHL	39	19	32	51	24	....	....	....	....	....
1993-94	**Florida**	**NHL**	**70**	**17**	**33**	**50**	**16**	....	....	....	....	....
1994-95	**Florida**	**NHL**	**47**	**15**	**14**	**29**	**18**	....	....	....	....	....
	NHL Totals		**140**	**36**	**49**	**85**	**38**	**9**	**0**	**1**	**1**	**0**

Signed as a free agent by **Montreal**, October 3, 1990. Claimed by **Florida** from **Montreal** in Expansion Draft, June 24, 1993.

BELANGER, KEN (buh-LAWN-zhay) TOR.

Left wing. Shoots left. 6'4", 225 lbs. Born, Sault Ste. Marie, Ont., May 14, 1974.
(Hartford's 7th choice, 153rd overall, in 1992 Entry Draft).

			Regular Season					Playoffs				
Season	Club	Lea	GP	G	A	TP	PIM	GP	G	A	TP	PIM
1991-92	Ottawa	OHL	51	4	4	8	174	11	0	0	0	24
1992-93	Ottawa	OHL	34	6	12	18	139	....	....	....	....	....
	Guelph	OHL	29	10	14	24	86	5	2	1	3	14
1993-94	Guelph	OHL	55	11	22	33	185	9	2	3	5	30
1994-95	St. John's	AHL	47	5	5	10	246	4	0	0	0	30
	Toronto	**NHL**	**3**	**0**	**0**	**0**	**9**	....	....	....	....	....
	NHL Totals		**3**	**0**	**0**	**0**	**9**	....	....	....	....	....

Traded to **Toronto** by **Hartford** for Toronto's ninth round choice (Matt Ball) in 1994 Entry Draft, March 18, 1994.

BELANGER, MARTIN (buh-LAWN-zhay) MTL.

Defense. Shoots right. 6', 205 lbs. Born, Lasalle, Que., February 3, 1976.
(Montreal's 5th choice, 74th overall, in 1994 Entry Draft).

			Regular Season					Playoffs				
Season	Club	Lea	GP	G	A	TP	PIM	GP	G	A	TP	PIM
1992-93	Granby	QMJHL	49	2	19	21	24	....	....	....	....	....
1993-94	Granby	QMJHL	63	8	32	40	49	7	0	1	1	28
1994-95	Granby	QMJHL	43	0	11	11	32	12	0	1	1	6

BELLOWS, BRIAN T.B.

Left wing. Shoots right. 5'11", 210 lbs. Born, St. Catharines, Ont., September 1, 1964.
(Minnesota's 1st choice, 2nd overall, in 1982 Entry Draft).

			Regular Season					Playoffs				
Season	Club	Lea	GP	G	A	TP	PIM	GP	G	A	TP	PIM
1980-81	Kitchener	OHA	66	49	67	116	23	16	14	13	27	13
1981-82ab	Kitchener	OHL	47	45	52	97	23	15	16	13	29	11
1982-83	**Minnesota**	**NHL**	**78**	**35**	**30**	**65**	**27**	**9**	**5**	**4**	**9**	**18**
1983-84	**Minnesota**	**NHL**	**78**	**41**	**42**	**83**	**66**	**16**	**2**	**12**	**14**	**6**
1984-85	**Minnesota**	**NHL**	**78**	**26**	**36**	**62**	**72**	**9**	**2**	**4**	**6**	**9**
1985-86	**Minnesota**	**NHL**	**77**	**31**	**48**	**79**	**46**	**5**	**5**	**0**	**5**	**16**
1986-87	**Minnesota**	**NHL**	**65**	**26**	**27**	**53**	**34**	....	....	....	....	....
1987-88	**Minnesota**	**NHL**	**77**	**40**	**41**	**81**	**81**	....	....	....	....	....
1988-89	**Minnesota**	**NHL**	**60**	**23**	**27**	**50**	**55**	**5**	**2**	**3**	**5**	**8**
1989-90c	**Minnesota**	**NHL**	**80**	**55**	**44**	**99**	**72**	**7**	**4**	**3**	**7**	**10**
1990-91	**Minnesota**	**NHL**	**80**	**35**	**40**	**75**	**43**	**23**	**10**	**19**	**29**	**30**
1991-92	**Minnesota**	**NHL**	**80**	**30**	**45**	**75**	**41**	**7**	**4**	**4**	**8**	**14**
1992-93	**Montreal**	**NHL**	**82**	**40**	**48**	**88**	**44**	**18**	**6**	**9**	**15**	**18**
1993-94	**Montreal**	**NHL**	**77**	**33**	**38**	**71**	**36**	**6**	**1**	**2**	**3**	**2**
1994-95	**Montreal**	**NHL**	**41**	**8**	**8**	**16**	**8**	....	....	....	....	....
	NHL Totals		**953**	**423**	**474**	**897**	**625**	**105**	**41**	**60**	**101**	**131**

a OHL First All-Star Team (1982)
b Won George Parsons Trophy (Memorial Cup Tournament Most Sportsmanlike Player) (1982)
c NHL Second All-Star Team (1990)

Played in NHL All-Star Game (1984, 1988, 1992)

Traded to **Montreal** by **Minnesota** for Russ Courtnall, August 31, 1992. Traded to **Tampa Bay** by **Montreal** for Marc Bureau, June 30, 1995.

BELOV, OLEG PIT.

Center. Shoots left. 6', 185 lbs. Born, Moscow, USSR, April 20, 1973.
(Pittsburgh's 3rd choice, 102nd overall, in 1995 Entry Draft).

			Regular Season					Playoffs				
Season	Club	Lea	GP	G	A	TP	PIM	GP	G	A	TP	PIM
1991-92	CSKA	CIS	1	0	0	0	2	....	....	....	....	....
1992-93	CSKA	CIS	42	7	4	11	18	....	....	....	....	....
1993-94	CSKA	CIS	46	14	8	22	18	3	1	0	1	2
1994-95	CSKA	CIS	46	21	18	39	51	....	....	....	....	....

BENAZIC, CAL BUF.

Defense. Shoots left. 6'3", 187 lbs. Born, Mackenzie, B.C., September 29, 1975.
(Buffalo's 5th choice, 147th overall, in 1994 Entry Draft).

			Regular Season					Playoffs				
Season	Club	Lea	GP	G	A	TP	PIM	GP	G	A	TP	PIM
1993-94	Medicine Hat	WHL	64	2	15	17	157	3	0	0	0	15
1994-95	Medicine Hat	WHL	71	9	23	32	166	5	0	1	1	19
	Rochester	AHL	2	0	0	0	0	....	....	....	....	....

BENNETT, ADAM EDM.

Defense. Shoots right. 6'4", 206 lbs. Born, Georgetown, Ont., March 30, 1971.
(Chicago's 1st choice, 6th overall, in 1989 Entry Draft).

			Regular Season					Playoffs				
Season	Club	Lea	GP	G	A	TP	PIM	GP	G	A	TP	PIM
1988-89	Sudbury	OHL	66	7	22	29	133	....	....	....	....	....
1989-90	Sudbury	OHL	65	18	43	61	116	7	1	2	3	23
1990-91a	Sudbury	OHL	54	21	29	50	123	5	1	2	3	11
	Indianapolis	IHL	3	0	1	1	12	2	0	0	0	0
1991-92	**Chicago**	**NHL**	**5**	**0**	**0**	**0**	**12**	....	....	....	....	....
	Indianapolis	IHL	59	4	10	14	89	....	....	....	....	....
1992-93	**Chicago**	**NHL**	**16**	**0**	**2**	**2**	**8**	....	....	....	....	....
	Indianapolis	IHL	39	8	16	24	69	2	0	0	0	2
1993-94	**Edmonton**	**NHL**	**48**	**3**	**6**	**9**	**49**	....	....	....	....	....
	Cape Breton	AHL	7	2	5	7	7	....	....	....	....	....
1994-95	Cape Breton	AHL	10	0	3	3	6	....	....	....	....	....
	NHL Totals		**69**	**3**	**8**	**11**	**69**	....	....	....	....	....

a OHL Second All-Star Team (1991)

Traded to **Edmonton** by **Chicago** for Kevin Todd, October 7, 1993.

BENNING, BRIAN

Defense. Shoots left. 6', 195 lbs. Born, Edmonton, Alta., June 10, 1966.
(St. Louis' 1st choice, 26th overall, in 1984 Entry Draft).

			Regular Season					Playoffs				
Season	Club	Lea	GP	G	A	TP	PIM	GP	G	A	TP	PIM
1983-84	Portland	WHL	38	6	41	47	108	....	....	....	....	....
1984-85	**St. Louis**	**NHL**	**4**	**0**	**2**	**2**	**0**	....	....	....	....	....
	Kamloops	WHL	17	3	18	21	26	....	....	....	....	....
1985-86	Cdn. National	....	60	6	13	19	43	....	....	....	....	....
	St. Louis	**NHL**	....	....	....	....	....	**6**	**1**	**2**	**3**	**13**
1986-87a	**St. Louis**	**NHL**	**78**	**13**	**36**	**49**	**110**	**6**	**0**	**4**	**4**	**9**
1987-88	**St. Louis**	**NHL**	**77**	**8**	**29**	**37**	**107**	**10**	**1**	**6**	**7**	**25**
1988-89	**St. Louis**	**NHL**	**66**	**8**	**26**	**34**	**102**	**7**	**1**	**1**	**2**	**11**
1989-90	**St. Louis**	**NHL**	**7**	**1**	**1**	**2**	**2**	....	....	....	....	....
	Los Angeles	**NHL**	**48**	**5**	**18**	**23**	**104**	**7**	**0**	**2**	**2**	**10**
1990-91	**Los Angeles**	**NHL**	**61**	**7**	**24**	**31**	**127**	**12**	**0**	**5**	**5**	**6**
1991-92	**Los Angeles**	**NHL**	**53**	**2**	**30**	**32**	**99**	....	....	....	....	....
	Philadelphia	**NHL**	**22**	**2**	**12**	**14**	**35**	....	....	....	....	....
1992-93	**Philadelphia**	**NHL**	**37**	**9**	**17**	**26**	**93**	....	....	....	....	....
	Edmonton	**NHL**	**18**	**1**	**7**	**8**	**59**	....	....	....	....	....
1993-94	**Florida**	**NHL**	**73**	**6**	**24**	**30**	**107**	....	....	....	....	....
1994-95	**Florida**	**NHL**	**24**	**1**	**7**	**8**	**18**	....	....	....	....	....
	NHL Totals		**568**	**63**	**233**	**296**	**963**	**48**	**3**	**20**	**23**	**74**

a NHL All-Rookie Team (1987)

Traded to **Los Angeles** by **St Louis** for Los Angeles' third round choice (Kyle Reeves) in 1991 Entry Draft, November 10, 1989. Traded to **Pittsburgh** by **Los Angeles** with Jeff Chychrun and Los Angeles' first round choice (later traded to Philadelphia — Philadelphia selected Jason Bowen) in 1992 Entry Draft for Paul Coffey, February 19, 1992. Traded to **Philadelphia** by **Pittsburgh** with Mark Recchi and Los Angeles' first round choice (previously acquired by Pittsburgh — Philadelphia selected Jason Bowen) in 1992 Entry Draft for Rick Tocchet, Kjell Samuelsson, Ken Wregget and Philadelphia's third round choice (Dave Roche) in 1993 Entry Draft, February 19, 1992. Traded to **Edmonton** by **Philadelphia** for Greg Hawgood and Josef Beranek, January 16, 1993. Signed as a free agent by **Florida**, July 13, 1993.

BERANEK, JOSEF (buh-RAH-nehk, JOH-sehf) VAN.

Left wing. Shoots left. 6'2", 185 lbs. Born, Litvinov, Czechoslovakia, October 25, 1969.
(Edmonton's 3rd choice, 78th overall, in 1989 Entry Draft).

			Regular Season					Playoffs				
Season	Club	Lea	GP	G	A	TP	PIM	GP	G	A	TP	PIM
1987-88	Litvinov	Czech.	14	7	4	11	12	....	....	....	....	....
1988-89	Litvinov	Czech.	32	18	10	28	47	....	....	....	....	....
1989-90	Dukla Trencin	Czech.	49	19	23	42	....	....	....	....	....	....
1990-91	Litvinov	Czech.	58	29	31	60	98	....	....	....	....	....
1991-92	**Edmonton**	**NHL**	**58**	**12**	**16**	**28**	**18**	**12**	**2**	**1**	**3**	**0**
1992-93	**Edmonton**	**NHL**	**26**	**2**	**6**	**8**	**28**	....	....	....	....	....
	Cape Breton	AHL	6	1	2	3	8	....	....	....	....	....
	Philadelphia	**NHL**	**40**	**13**	**12**	**25**	**50**	....	....	....	....	....
1993-94	**Philadelphia**	**NHL**	**80**	**28**	**21**	**49**	**85**	....	....	....	....	....
1994-95	Vsetin	Czech.	16	7	7	14	26	....	....	....	....	....
	Philadelphia	**NHL**	**14**	**5**	**5**	**10**	**2**	....	....	....	....	....
	Vancouver	**NHL**	**37**	**8**	**13**	**21**	**28**	**11**	**1**	**1**	**2**	**12**
	NHL Totals		**255**	**68**	**73**	**141**	**211**	**23**	**3**	**2**	**5**	**12**

Traded to **Philadelphia** by **Edmonton** with Greg Hawgood for Brian Benning, January 16, 1993. Traded to **Vancouver** by **Philadelphia** for Shawn Antoski, February 15, 1995.

BERARD, BRYAN OTT.

Defense. Shoots left. 6'1", 190 lbs. Born, Woonsocket, RI, March 5, 1977.
(Ottawa's 1st choice, 1st overall, in 1995 Entry Draft).

			Regular Season					Playoffs				
Season	Club	Lea	GP	G	A	TP	PIM	GP	G	A	TP	PIM
1993-94	Mt. St. Charles	HS	32	11	36	47	5	....	....	....	....	....
1994-95abc	Detroit	OHL	58	20	55	75	97	21	4	20	24	38

a OHL First All-Star Team (1995)
b Canadian Major Junior First All-Star Team (1995)
c Canadian Major Junior Rookie of the Year (1995)

BEREHOWSKY, DRAKE (beh-reh-HOW-skee) PIT.

Defense. Shoots right. 6'1", 211 lbs. Born, Toronto, Ont., January 3, 1972.
(Toronto's 1st choice, 10th overall, in 1990 Entry Draft).

			Regular Season					Playoffs				
Season	Club	Lea	GP	G	A	TP	PIM	GP	G	A	TP	PIM
1988-89	Kingston	OHL	63	7	39	46	85	....	....	....	....	....
	Cdn. National	....	1	0	0	0	0	....	....	....	....	....
1989-90	Kingston	OHL	9	3	11	14	28	....	....	....	....	....
1990-91	**Toronto**	**NHL**	**8**	**0**	**1**	**1**	**25**	....	....	....	....	....
	Kingston	OHL	13	5	13	18	38	....	....	....	....	....
	North Bay	OHL	26	7	23	30	51	10	2	7	9	21
1991-92	**Toronto**	**NHL**	**1**	**0**	**0**	**0**	**0**	....	....	....	....	....
ab	North Bay	OHL	62	19	63	82	147	21	7	24	31	22
	St. John's	AHL	....	....	....	....	....	6	0	5	5	21
1992-93	**Toronto**	**NHL**	**41**	**4**	**15**	**19**	**61**	....	....	....	....	....
	St. John's	AHL	28	10	17	27	38	....	....	....	....	....
1993-94	**Toronto**	**NHL**	**49**	**2**	**8**	**10**	**63**	....	....	....	....	....
	St. John's	AHL	18	3	12	15	40	....	....	....	....	....
1994-95	**Toronto**	**NHL**	**25**	**0**	**2**	**2**	**15**	....	....	....	....	....
	Pittsburgh	**NHL**	**4**	**0**	**0**	**0**	**13**	**1**	**0**	**0**	**0**	**0**
	NHL Totals		**128**	**6**	**26**	**32**	**177**	**1**	**0**	**0**	**0**	**0**

a Canadian Major Junior Defenseman of the Year (1992)
b OHL First All-Star Team (1992)

Traded to **Pittsburgh** by **Toronto** for Grant Jennings, April 7, 1995.

BEREZIN, SERGEI TOR.

Right wing. Shoots right. 5'10", 172 lbs. Born, Voskresensk, USSR, November 5, 1971.
(Toronto's 8th choice, 256th overall, in 1994 Entry Draft).

			Regular Season					Playoffs				
Season	Club	Lea	GP	G	A	TP	PIM	GP	G	A	TP	PIM
1990-91	Khimik	USSR	30	6	2	8	4	....	....	....	....	....
1991-92	Khimik	CIS	36	7	5	12	10	....	....	....	....	....
1992-93	Khimik	CIS	38	9	3	12	12	2	1	0	1	0
1993-94	Khimik	CIS	40	31	10	41	16	3	2	0	2	2
1994-95	Koln	Ger.	43	38	19	57	8	18	17	8	25	14

BERG, AKI-PETTERI L.A.

Defense. Shoots left. 6'3", 200 lbs. Born, Turku, Finland, July 28, 1977.
(Los Angeles' 1st choice, 3rd overall, in 1995 Entry Draft).

			Regular Season					Playoffs				
Season	Club	Lea	GP	G	A	TP	PIM	GP	G	A	TP	PIM
1993-94	TPS	Fin.	6	0	6	6	4	....	....	....	....	....
1994-95	TPS	Fin.	5	0	0	0	4	....	....	....	....	....
	Kiekko-67	Fin. 2	28	3	9	12	34	....	....	....	....	....

BERG, BILL — TOR.

Left wing. Shoots left. 6'1", 205 lbs. Born, St. Catharines, Ont., October 21, 1967.
(NY Islanders' 3rd choice, 59th overall, in 1986 Entry Draft).

			Regular Season					Playoffs				
Season	Club	Lea	GP	G	A	TP	PIM	GP	G	A	TP	PIM
1985-86	Toronto	OHL	64	3	35	38	143	4	0	0	0	19
	Springfield	AHL	4	1	1	2	4	....	....	....	....	....
1986-87	Toronto	OHL	57	3	15	18	138	....	....	....	....	....
1987-88	Springfield	AHL	76	6	26	32	148	....	....	....	....	....
	Peoria	IHL	5	0	1	1	8	7	0	3	3	31
1988-89	**NY Islanders**	**NHL**	**7**	**1**	**2**	**3**	**10**	....	....	....	....	....
	Springfield	AHL	69	17	32	49	122	....	....	....	....	....
1989-90	Springfield	AHL	74	12	42	54	74	15	5	12	17	35
1990-91	**NY Islanders**	**NHL**	**78**	**9**	**14**	**23**	**67**	....	....	....	....	....
1991-92	**NY Islanders**	**NHL**	**47**	**5**	**9**	**14**	**28**	....	....	....	....	....
	Capital Dist.	AHL	3	0	2	2	16	....	....	....	....	....
1992-93	**NY Islanders**	**NHL**	**22**	**6**	**3**	**9**	**49**	....	....	....	....	....
	Toronto	**NHL**	**58**	**7**	**8**	**15**	**54**	**21**	**1**	**1**	**2**	**18**
1993-94	**Toronto**	**NHL**	**83**	**8**	**11**	**19**	**93**	**18**	**1**	**2**	**3**	**10**
1994-95	**Toronto**	**NHL**	**32**	**5**	**1**	**6**	**26**	**7**	**0**	**1**	**1**	**4**
	NHL Totals		**327**	**41**	**48**	**89**	**327**	**46**	**2**	**4**	**6**	**32**

Claimed on waivers by **Toronto** from **NY Islanders**, December 3, 1992.

BERGEVIN, MARC — DET.

Defense. Shoots left. 6'1", 197 lbs. Born, Montreal, Que., August 11, 1965.
(Chicago's 3rd choice, 59th overall, in 1983 Entry Draft).

			Regular Season					Playoffs				
Season	Club	Lea	GP	G	A	TP	PIM	GP	G	A	TP	PIM
1982-83	Chicoutimi	QMJHL	64	3	27	30	113	....	....	....	....	....
1983-84	Chicoutimi	QMJHL	70	10	35	45	125	....	....	....	....	....
	Springfield	AHL	7	0	1	1	2	....	....	....	....	....
1984-85	**Chicago**	**NHL**	**60**	**0**	**6**	**6**	**54**	**6**	**0**	**3**	**3**	**2**
	Springfield	AHL	....	....	....	....	....	4	0	0	0	0
1985-86	**Chicago**	**NHL**	**71**	**7**	**7**	**14**	**60**	**3**	**0**	**0**	**0**	**0**
1986-87	**Chicago**	**NHL**	**66**	**4**	**10**	**14**	**66**	**3**	**1**	**0**	**1**	**2**
1987-88	**Chicago**	**NHL**	**58**	**1**	**6**	**7**	**85**	....	....	....	....	....
	Saginaw	IHL	10	2	7	9	20	....	....	....	....	....
1988-89	**Chicago**	**NHL**	**11**	**0**	**0**	**0**	**18**	....	....	....	....	....
	NY Islanders	**NHL**	**58**	**2**	**13**	**15**	**62**	....	....	....	....	....
1989-90	**NY Islanders**	**NHL**	**18**	**0**	**4**	**4**	**30**	....	....	....	....	....
	Springfield	AHL	47	7	16	23	66	17	2	11	13	16
1990-91	Capital Dist.	AHL	7	0	5	5	6	....	....	....	....	....
	Hartford	**NHL**	**4**	**0**	**0**	**0**	**4**	....	....	....	....	....
	Springfield	AHL	58	4	23	27	85	18	0	7	7	26
1991-92	**Hartford**	**NHL**	**75**	**7**	**17**	**24**	**64**	**5**	**0**	**0**	**0**	**2**
1992-93	**Tampa Bay**	**NHL**	**78**	**2**	**12**	**14**	**66**	....	....	....	....	....
1993-94	**Tampa Bay**	**NHL**	**83**	**1**	**15**	**16**	**87**	....	....	....	....	....
1994-95	**Tampa Bay**	**NHL**	**44**	**2**	**4**	**6**	**51**	....	....	....	....	....
	NHL Totals		**626**	**26**	**94**	**120**	**647**	**17**	**1**	**3**	**4**	**6**

Traded to **NY Islanders** by **Chicago** with Gary Nylund for Steve Konroyd and Bob Bassen, November 25, 1988. Traded to **Hartford** by **NY Islanders** for Hartford's fifth round choice (Ryan Duthie) in 1992 Entry Draft, October 30, 1990. Signed as a free agent by **Tampa Bay**, July 9, 1992. Traded to **Detroit** by **Tampa Bay** with Ben Hankinson for Shawn Burr and Detroit's third round choice (later traded to Boston) in 1996 Entry Draft, August 17, 1995.

BERGLAND, TIM

Right wing. Shoots right. 6'3", 194 lbs. Born, Crookston, MN, January 11, 1965.
(Washington's 1st choice, 75th overall, in 1983 Entry Draft).

			Regular Season					Playoffs				
Season	Club	Lea	GP	G	A	TP	PIM	GP	G	A	TP	PIM
1983-84	U. Minnesota	WCHA	24	4	11	15	4	....	....	....	....	....
1984-85	U. Minnesota	WCHA	34	5	9	14	8	....	....	....	....	....
1985-86	U. Minnesota	WCHA	48	11	16	27	26	....	....	....	....	....
1986-87	U. Minnesota	WCHA	49	18	17	35	48	....	....	....	....	....
1987-88	Fort Wayne	IHL	13	2	1	3	9	....	....	....	....	....
	Binghamton	AHL	63	21	26	47	31	4	0	0	0	0
1988-89	Baltimore	AHL	78	24	29	53	39	....	....	....	....	....
1989-90	**Washington**	**NHL**	**32**	**2**	**5**	**7**	**31**	**15**	**1**	**1**	**2**	**10**
	Baltimore	AHL	47	12	19	31	55	....	....	....	....	....
1990-91	**Washington**	**NHL**	**47**	**5**	**9**	**14**	**21**	**11**	**1**	**1**	**2**	**12**
	Baltmore	AHL	15	8	9	17	16	....	....	....	....	....
1991-92	**Washington**	**NHL**	**22**	**1**	**4**	**5**	**2**	....	....	....	....	....
	Baltimore	AHL	11	6	10	16	5	....	....	....	....	....
1992-93	**Tampa Bay**	**NHL**	**27**	**3**	**3**	**6**	**11**	....	....	....	....	....
	Atlanta	IHL	49	18	21	39	26	9	3	3	6	10
1993-94	**Tampa Bay**	**NHL**	**51**	**6**	**5**	**11**	**6**	....	....	....	....	....
	Atlanta	IHL	19	6	7	13	6	....	....	....	....	....
	Washington	**NHL**	**3**	**0**	**0**	**0**	**4**	....	....	....	....	....
1994-95	Chicago	IHL	81	12	21	33	70	3	1	2	3	4
	NHL Totals		**182**	**17**	**26**	**43**	**75**	**26**	**2**	**2**	**4**	**22**

Claimed by **Tampa Bay** from **Washington** in Expansion Draft, June 18, 1992. Claimed on waivers by **Washington** from **Tampa Bay**, March 19, 1994.

BERGQVIST, STEFAN — PIT.

Defense. Shoots left. 6'3", 216 lbs. Born, Leksand, Sweden, March 10, 1975.
(Pittsburgh's 1st choice, 26th overall, in 1993 Entry Draft).

			Regular Season					Playoffs				
Season	Club	Lea	GP	G	A	TP	PIM	GP	G	A	TP	PIM
1992-93	Leksand	Swe.	15	0	0	0	6	....	....	....	....	....
1993-94	Leksand	Swe.	6	0	0	0	0	....	....	....	....	....
1994-95	London	OHL	64	3	17	20	93	4	0	0	0	5

BERNARD, LOUIS — MTL.

Defense. Shoots right. 6'2", 205 lbs. Born, Victoriaville, Que., July 10, 1974.
(Montreal's 5th choice, 82nd overall, in 1992 Entry Draft).

			Regular Season					Playoffs				
Season	Club	Lea	GP	G	A	TP	PIM	GP	G	A	TP	PIM
1991-92	Drummondville	QMJHL	70	8	24	32	59	4	0	1	1	4
1992-93	Drummondville	QMJHL	68	8	38	46	78	10	0	4	4	14
1993-94	Sherbrooke	QMJHL	65	10	31	41	107	12	1	2	3	10
1994-95	Wheeling	ECHL	20	1	5	6	26	....	....	....	....	....
	Fredericton	AHL	31	2	1	3	34	1	0	0	0	0

BERRY, BRAD

Defense. Shoots left. 6'2", 190 lbs. Born, Bashaw, Alta., April 1, 1965.
(Winnipeg's 3rd choice, 29th overall, in 1983 Entry Draft).

			Regular Season					Playoffs				
Season	Club	Lea	GP	G	A	TP	PIM	GP	G	A	TP	PIM
1983-84	North Dakota	WCHA	32	2	7	9	8	....	....	....	....	....
1984-85	North Dakota	WCHA	40	4	26	30	26	....	....	....	....	....
1985-86	North Dakota	WCHA	40	6	29	35	26	....	....	....	....	....
	Winnipeg	**NHL**	**13**	**1**	**0**	**1**	**10**	**3**	**0**	**0**	**0**	**0**
1986-87	**Winnipeg**	**NHL**	**52**	**2**	**8**	**10**	**60**	**7**	**0**	**1**	**1**	**14**
1987-88	**Winnipeg**	**NHL**	**48**	**0**	**6**	**6**	**75**	....	....	....	....	....
	Moncton	AHL	10	1	3	4	14	....	....	....	....	....
1988-89	**Winnipeg**	**NHL**	**38**	**0**	**9**	**9**	**45**	....	....	....	....	....
	Moncton	AHL	38	3	16	19	39	....	....	....	....	....
1989-90	**Winnipeg**	**NHL**	**12**	**1**	**2**	**3**	**6**	**1**	**0**	**0**	**0**	**0**
	Moncton	AHL	38	1	9	10	58	....	....	....	....	....
1990-91	Brynas	Swe.	38	3	1	4	38	....	....	....	....	....
	Cdn. National	....	4	0	1	1	0	....	....	....	....	....
1991-92	**Minnesota**	**NHL**	**7**	**0**	**0**	**0**	**6**	**2**	**0**	**0**	**0**	**2**
	Kalamazoo	IHL	65	5	18	23	90	5	2	0	2	6
1992-93	**Minnesota**	**NHL**	**63**	**0**	**3**	**3**	**109**	....	....	....	....	....
1993-94	**Dallas**	**NHL**	**8**	**0**	**0**	**0**	**12**	....	....	....	....	....
	Kalamazoo	IHL	45	3	19	22	91	1	0	0	0	0
1994-95	Kalamazoo	IHL	65	4	11	15	146	1	0	0	0	0
	NHL Totals		**241**	**4**	**28**	**32**	**323**	**13**	**0**	**1**	**1**	**16**

Signed as a free agent by **Minnesota**, October 4, 1991.

BERTRAND, ERIC — N.J.

Left wing. Shoots left. 6'1", 195 lbs. Born, St. Ephrem, Que., April 16, 1975.
(New Jersey's 9th choice, 207th overall, in 1994 Entry Draft).

			Regular Season					Playoffs				
Season	Club	Lea	GP	G	A	TP	PIM	GP	G	A	TP	PIM
1992-93	Granby	QMJHL	64	10	15	25	82	....	....	....	....	....
1993-94	Granby	QMJHL	60	11	15	26	151	6	1	0	1	18
1994-95	Granby	QMJHL	56	14	26	40	268	13	3	8	11	50

BERTSCH, JAY — COL.

Right wing. Shoots right. 6'2", 208 lbs. Born, Lethbridge, Alta., July 14, 1976.
(Quebec's 10th choice, 191st overall, in 1994 Entry Draft).

			Regular Season					Playoffs				
Season	Club	Lea	GP	G	A	TP	PIM	GP	G	A	TP	PIM
1992-93	Lethbridge	WHL	49	3	2	5	80	1	0	0	0	0
1993-94	Lethbridge	WHL	36	1	6	7	61	....	....	....	....	....
	Spokane	WHL	29	5	4	9	87	3	0	0	0	16
1994-95	Spokane	WHL	47	5	7	12	147	9	3	0	3	34

BERTUZZI, TODD (buhr-TOO-zee) — NYI

Center. Shoots left. 6'3", 227 lbs. Born, Sudbury, Ont., February 2, 1975.
(NY Islanders' 1st choice, 23rd overall, in 1993 Entry Draft).

			Regular Season					Playoffs				
Season	Club	Lea	GP	G	A	TP	PIM	GP	G	A	TP	PIM
1991-92	Guelph	OHL	47	7	14	21	145	....	....	....	....	....
1992-93	Guelph	OHL	59	27	32	59	164	5	2	2	4	6
1993-94	Guelph	OHL	61	28	54	82	165	9	2	6	8	30
1994-95a	Guelph	OHL	62	54	65	119	58	14	*15	18	33	41

a OHL Second All-Star team (1995)

BERUBE, CRAIG (buh-ROO-bee) — WSH.

Left wing. Shoots left. 6'1", 205 lbs. Born, Calahoo, Alta., December 17, 1965.

			Regular Season					Playoffs				
Season	Club	Lea	GP	G	A	TP	PIM	GP	G	A	TP	PIM
1982-83	Kamloops	WHL	4	0	0	0	0	....	....	....	....	....
1983-84	N. Westminster	WHL	70	11	20	31	104	8	1	2	3	5
1984-85	N. Westminster	WHL	70	25	44	69	191	10	3	2	5	4
1985-86	Kamloops	WHL	32	17	14	31	119	....	....	....	....	....
	Medicine Hat	WHL	34	14	16	30	95	25	7	8	15	102
1986-87	**Philadelphia**	**NHL**	**7**	**0**	**0**	**0**	**57**	**5**	**0**	**0**	**0**	**17**
	Hershey	AHL	63	7	17	24	325	....	....	....	....	....
1987-88	**Philadelphia**	**NHL**	**27**	**3**	**2**	**5**	**108**	....	....	....	....	....
	Hershey	AHL	31	5	9	14	119	....	....	....	....	....
1988-89	**Philadelphia**	**NHL**	**53**	**1**	**1**	**2**	**199**	**16**	**0**	**0**	**0**	**56**
	Hershey	AHL	7	0	2	2	19	....	....	....	....	....
1989-90	**Philadelphia**	**NHL**	**74**	**4**	**14**	**18**	**291**	....	....	....	....	....
1990-91	**Philadelphia**	**NHL**	**74**	**8**	**9**	**17**	**293**	....	....	....	....	....
1991-92	**Toronto**	**NHL**	**40**	**5**	**7**	**12**	**109**	....	....	....	....	....
	Calgary	**NHL**	**36**	**1**	**4**	**5**	**155**	....	....	....	....	....
1992-93	**Calgary**	**NHL**	**77**	**4**	**8**	**12**	**209**	**6**	**0**	**1**	**1**	**21**
1993-94	**Washington**	**NHL**	**84**	**7**	**7**	**14**	**305**	**8**	**0**	**0**	**0**	**21**
1994-95	**Washington**	**NHL**	**43**	**2**	**4**	**6**	**173**	**7**	**0**	**0**	**0**	**29**
	NHL Totals		**515**	**35**	**56**	**91**	**1899**	**42**	**0**	**1**	**1**	**144**

Signed as a free agent by **Philadelphia**, March 19, 1986. Traded to **Edmonton** by **Philadelphia** with Craig Fisher and Scott Mellanby for Dave Brown, Corey Foster and Jari Kurri, May 30, 1991. Traded to **Toronto** by **Edmonton** with Grant Fuhr and Glenn Anderson for Vincent Damphousse, Peter Ing, Scott Thornton, Luke Richardson, future considerations and cash, September 19, 1991. Traded to **Calgary** by **Toronto** with Alexander Godynyuk, Gary Leeman, Michel Petit and Jeff Reese for Doug Gilmour, Jamie Macoun, Ric Nattress, Rick Wamsley and Kent Manderville, January 2, 1992. Traded to **Washington** by **Calgary** for Washington's fifth round choice (Darryl Lafrance) in 1993 Entry Draft, June 26, 1993.

BES, JEFF — HFD.

Center. Shoots left. 6', 190 lbs. Born, Tillsonburg, Ont., July 31, 1973.
(Minnesota's 2nd choice, 58th overall, in 1992 Entry Draft).

			Regular Season					Playoffs				
Season	Club	Lea	GP	G	A	TP	PIM	GP	G	A	TP	PIM
1990-91	Hamilton	OHL	66	23	47	70	53	4	1	4	5	4
1991-92	Guelph	OHL	62	40	62	102	123	....	....	....	....	....
1992-93	Guelph	OHL	59	48	67	115	128	5	3	5	8	4
	Kalamazoo	IHL	3	1	3	4	6	....	....	....	....	....
1993-94	Dayton	ECHL	2	2	0	2	12	....	....	....	....	....
	Kalamazoo	IHL	30	2	12	14	30	....	....	....	....	....
1994-95	Kalamazoo	IHL	52	8	17	25	47	....	....	....	....	....

Claimed on waivers by **Hartford** from **Dallas**, July 29, 1995.

BETS, MAXIM (BEHTS, MAKS-eem) ANA.

Left wing. Shoots left. 6'1", 185 lbs. Born, Chelyabinsk, USSR, January 31, 1974.
(St. Louis' 1st choice, 37th overall, in 1993 Entry Draft).

			Regular Season					Playoffs				
Season	Club	Lea	GP	G	A	TP	PIM	GP	G	A	TP	PIM
1991-92	Chelyabinsk	CIS	25	1	1	2	8	....	....	....	....	....
1992-93	Spokane	WHL	54	49	57	106	130	9	5	6	11	20
1993-94	Spokane	WHL	63	46	70	116	111	3	1	1	2	12
	Anaheim	**NHL**	**3**	**0**	**0**	**0**	**0**	....	....	....	....	....
	San Diego	IHL	....	....	....	....	....	9	0	2	2	0
1994-95	San Diego	IHL	36	2	6	8	31	....	....	....	....	....
	Worcester	AHL	9	1	1	2	6	....	....	....	....	....
	NHL Totals		**3**	**0**	**0**	**0**	**0**	....	....	....	....	....

Traded to **Anaheim** by **St. Louis** with St. Louis' sixth round choice (later traded back to St. Louis — St. Louis selected Denis Hamel) in 1995 Entry Draft for Alexei Kasatonov, March 21, 1994.

BETY, SEBASTIEN (BEE-tee) COL.

Defense. Shoots left. 6'2", 201 lbs. Born, St-Bernard Beauce, Que., May 6, 1976.
(Quebec's 4th choice, 61st overall, in 1994 Entry Draft).

			Regular Season					Playoffs				
Season	Club	Lea	GP	G	A	TP	PIM	GP	G	A	TP	PIM
1992-93	Drummondville	QMJHL	70	1	21	22	126	10	1	2	3	24
1993-94	Drummondville	QMJHL	67	3	8	11	164	10	0	0	0	17
1994-95	Drummondville	QMJHL	22	1	7	8	77	....	....	....	....	....
	Chicoutimi	QMJHL	24	4	9	13	109	13	1	5	6	46

BEUKEBOOM, JEFF (BOO-kuh-BOOM) NYR

Defense. Shoots right. 6'5", 230 lbs. Born, Ajax, Ont., March 28, 1965.
(Edmonton's 1st choice, 19th overall, in 1983 Entry Draft).

			Regular Season					Playoffs				
Season	Club	Lea	GP	G	A	TP	PIM	GP	G	A	TP	PIM
1982-83	S.S. Marie	OHL	70	0	25	25	143	16	1	4	5	46
1983-84	S.S. Marie	OHL	61	6	30	36	178	16	1	7	8	43
1984-85a	S.S. Marie	OHL	37	4	20	24	85	16	4	6	10	47
1985-86	Nova Scotia	AHL	77	9	20	29	175	....	....	....	....	....
	Edmonton	**NHL**	....	....	....	....	....	**1**	**0**	**0**	**0**	**4**
1986-87	**Edmonton**	**NHL**	**44**	**3**	**8**	**11**	**124**	....	....	....	....	....
	Nova Scotia	AHL	14	1	7	8	35	....	....	....	....	....
1987-88	**Edmonton**	**NHL**	**73**	**5**	**20**	**25**	**201**	**7**	**0**	**0**	**0**	**16**
1988-89	**Edmonton**	**NHL**	**36**	**0**	**5**	**5**	**94**	**1**	**0**	**0**	**0**	**2**
	Cape Breton	AHL	8	0	4	4	36	....	....	....	....	....
1989-90	**Edmonton**	**NHL**	**46**	**1**	**12**	**13**	**86**	**2**	**0**	**0**	**0**	**0**
1990-91	**Edmonton**	**NHL**	**67**	**3**	**7**	**10**	**150**	**18**	**1**	**3**	**4**	**28**
1991-92	**Edmonton**	**NHL**	**18**	**0**	**5**	**5**	**78**	....	....	....	....	....
	NY Rangers	**NHL**	**56**	**1**	**10**	**11**	**122**	**13**	**2**	**3**	**5**	**47**
1992-93	**NY Rangers**	**NHL**	**82**	**2**	**17**	**19**	**153**	....	....	....	....	....
1993-94	**NY Rangers**	**NHL**	**68**	**8**	**8**	**16**	**170**	**22**	**0**	**6**	**6**	**50**
1994-95	**NY Rangers**	**NHL**	**44**	**1**	**3**	**4**	**70**	**9**	**0**	**0**	**0**	**10**
	NHL Totals		**534**	**24**	**95**	**119**	**1248**	**73**	**3**	**12**	**15**	**157**

a OHL First All-Star Team (1985)

Traded to **NY Rangers** by **Edmonton** for David Shaw, November 12, 1991.

BIALOWAS, FRANK (bigh-uh-LOH-uhs) WSH.

Defense. Shoots left. 5'11", 220 lbs. Born, Winnipeg, Man., September 25, 1970.

			Regular Season					Playoffs				
Season	Club	Lea	GP	G	A	TP	PIM	GP	G	A	TP	PIM
1991-92	Roanoke	ECHL	23	4	2	6	150	3	0	0	0	4
1992-93	Richmond	ECHL	60	3	18	21	261	1	0	0	0	2
	St. John's	AHL	7	1	0	1	28	1	0	0	0	0
1993-94	St. John's	AHL	69	2	8	10	352	7	0	3	3	25
	Toronto	**NHL**	**3**	**0**	**0**	**0**	**12**	....	....	....	....	....
1994-95	St. John's	AHL	51	2	3	5	277	4	0	0	0	12
	NHL Totals		**3**	**0**	**0**	**0**	**12**	....	....	....	....	....

Signed as a free agent by **Toronto**, March 20, 1994. Signed as a free agent by **Washington**, August 10, 1995.

BICANEK, RADIM (BEE-chah-nehk) OTT.

Defense. Shoots left. 6'1", 195 lbs. Born, Uherske Hradiste, Czech., January 18, 1975.
(Ottawa's 2nd choice, 27th overall, in 1993 Entry Draft).

			Regular Season					Playoffs				
Season	Club	Lea	GP	G	A	TP	PIM	GP	G	A	TP	PIM
1992-93	Dukla Jihlava	Czech.	43	2	3	5	....	....	....	....	....	....
1993-94	Belleville	OHL	63	16	27	43	49	12	2	8	10	21
1994-95	Belleville	OHL	49	13	26	39	61	16	6	5	11	30
	Ottawa	**NHL**	**6**	**0**	**0**	**0**	**0**	....	....	....	....	....
	P.E.I.	AHL	....	....	....	....	....	3	0	1	1	0
	NHL Totals		**6**	**0**	**0**	**0**	**0**	....	....	....	....	....

BIENVENUE, DANIEL BUF.

Left wing. Shoots left. 6', 195 lbs. Born, Val d'Or, Que., June 10, 1977.
(Buffalo's 8th choice, 123rd overall, in 1995 Entry Draft).

			Regular Season					Playoffs				
Season	Club	Lea	GP	G	A	TP	PIM	GP	G	A	TP	PIM
1993-94	Chicoutimi	QMJHL	42	2	7	9	4	....	....	....	....	....
1994-95	Val d'Or	QMJHL	67	27	14	41	40	....	....	....	....	....

BIGGS, DON

Center. Shoots right. 5'8", 185 lbs. Born, Mississauga, Ont., April 7, 1965.
(Minnesota's 9th choice, 156th overall, in 1983 Entry Draft).

			Regular Season					Playoffs				
Season	Club	Lea	GP	G	A	TP	PIM	GP	G	A	TP	PIM
1982-83	Oshawa	OHL	70	22	53	75	145	16	3	6	9	17
1983-84	Oshawa	OHL	58	31	60	91	149	7	4	4	8	18
1984-85	**Minnesota**	**NHL**	**1**	**0**	**0**	**0**	**0**	....	....	....	....	....
	Springfield	AHL	6	0	3	3	0	2	1	0	1	0
	Oshawa	OHL	60	48	69	117	105	5	3	4	7	6
1985-86	Springfield	AHL	28	15	16	31	46	....	....	....	....	....
	Nova Scotia	AHL	47	6	23	29	36	....	....	....	....	....
1986-87	Nova Scotia	AHL	80	22	25	47	165	5	1	2	3	4
1987-88	Hershey	AHL	77	38	41	79	151	12	5	*11	*16	22
1988-89	Hershey	AHL	76	36	67	103	158	11	5	9	14	30
1989-90	**Philadelphia**	**NHL**	**11**	**2**	**0**	**2**	**8**	....	....	....	....	....
	Hershey	AHL	66	39	53	92	125	....	....	....	....	....
1990-91	Rochester	AHL	65	31	57	88	115	15	9	*14	*23	14
1991-92	Binghamton	AHL	74	32	50	82	122	11	3	7	10	8
1992-93abc	Binghamton	AHL	78	54	*84	*138	112	14	3	9	12	32
1993-94	Cincinnati	IHL	80	30	59	89	128	11	8	9	17	29
1994-95	Cincinnati	IHL	77	27	49	76	152	10	1	9	10	29
	NHL Totals		**12**	**2**	**0**	**2**	**8**	....	....	....	....	....

a Won Les Cunningham Plaque (MVP - AHL) (1993)
b Won John B. Sollenberger Trophy (Top Scorer - AHL) (1993)
c AHL First All-Star Team (1993)

Traded to **Edmonton** by **Minnesota** with Gord Sherven for Marc Habscheid, Don Barber and Emanuel Viveiros, December 20, 1985. Signed as a free agent by **Philadelphia**, July 17, 1987. Traded to **NY Rangers** by **Philadelphia** for future considerations, August 8, 1991.

BILODEAU, BRENT (BIHL-uh-DOH) MTL.

Defense. Shoots left. 6'3", 217 lbs. Born, Dallas, TX, March 27, 1973.
(Montreal's 1st choice, 17th overall, in 1991 Entry Draft).

			Regular Season					Playoffs				
Season	Club	Lea	GP	G	A	TP	PIM	GP	G	A	TP	PIM
1989-90	Seattle	WHL	68	14	29	43	170	13	3	5	8	31
1990-91	Seattle	WHL	55	7	18	25	145	6	1	0	1	12
1991-92a	Seattle	WHL	7	1	2	3	43	....	....	....	....	....
	Swift Current	WHL	56	10	47	57	118	8	2	3	5	11
1992-93a	Swift Current	WHL	59	11	57	68	77	17	5	14	19	18
1993-94	Fredericton	AHL	72	2	5	7	89	....	....	....	....	....
1994-95	Fredericton	AHL	50	4	8	12	146	12	3	3	6	28

a WHL East Second All-Star Team (1992, 1993)

BLACK, JAMES CHI.

Center. Shoots left. 5'11", 185 lbs. Born, Regina, Sask., August 15, 1969.
(Hartford's 4th choice, 94th overall, in 1989 Entry Draft).

			Regular Season					Playoffs				
Season	Club	Lea	GP	G	A	TP	PIM	GP	G	A	TP	PIM
1987-88	Portland	WHL	72	30	50	80	50	....	....	....	....	....
1988-89	Portland	WHL	71	45	51	96	57	19	13	6	19	28
1989-90	**Hartford**	**NHL**	**1**	**0**	**0**	**0**	**0**	....	....	....	....	....
	Binghamton	AHL	80	37	35	72	34	....	....	....	....	....
1990-91	**Hartford**	**NHL**	**1**	**0**	**0**	**0**	**0**	....	....	....	....	....
	Springfield	AHL	79	35	61	96	34	18	9	9	18	6
1991-92	**Hartford**	**NHL**	**30**	**4**	**6**	**10**	**10**	....	....	....	....	....
	Springfield	AHL	47	15	25	40	33	10	3	2	5	18
1992-93	**Minnesota**	**NHL**	**10**	**2**	**1**	**3**	**4**	....	....	....	....	....
	Kalamazoo	IHL	63	25	45	70	40	....	....	....	....	....
1993-94	**Dallas**	**NHL**	**13**	**2**	**3**	**5**	**2**	....	....	....	....	....
	Buffalo	**NHL**	**2**	**0**	**0**	**0**	**0**	....	....	....	....	....
	Rochester	AHL	45	19	32	51	28	4	2	3	5	0
1994-95	Las Vegas	IHL	78	29	44	73	54	10	1	6	7	4
	NHL Totals		**57**	**8**	**10**	**18**	**16**	....	....	....	....	....

Traded to **Minnesota** by **Hartford** for Mark Janssens, September 3, 1992. Traded to **Buffalo** by **Dallas** with Dallas' seventh round choice (Steve Webb) in 1994 Entry Draft for Gord Donnelly, December 15, 1993. Signed as a free agent by **Chicago**, August 10, 1995.

BLAKE, ROB L.A.

Defense. Shoots right. 6'3", 215 lbs. Born, Simcoe, Ont., December 10, 1969.
(Los Angeles' 4th choice, 70th overall, in 1988 Entry Draft).

			Regular Season					Playoffs				
Season	Club	Lea	GP	G	A	TP	PIM	GP	G	A	TP	PIM
1987-88	Bowling Green	CCHA	43	5	8	13	88	....	....	....	....	....
1988-89a	Bowling Green	CCHA	46	11	21	32	140	....	....	....	....	....
1989-90bc	Bowling Green	CCHA	42	23	36	59	140	....	....	....	....	....
	Los Angeles	**NHL**	**4**	**0**	**0**	**0**	**4**	**8**	**1**	**3**	**4**	**4**
1990-91d	**Los Angeles**	**NHL**	**75**	**12**	**34**	**46**	**125**	**12**	**1**	**4**	**5**	**26**
1991-92	**Los Angeles**	**NHL**	**57**	**7**	**13**	**20**	**102**	**6**	**2**	**1**	**3**	**12**
1992-93	**Los Angeles**	**NHL**	**76**	**16**	**43**	**59**	**152**	**23**	**4**	**6**	**10**	**46**
1993-94	**Los Angeles**	**NHL**	**84**	**20**	**48**	**68**	**137**	....	....	....	....	....
1994-95	**Los Angeles**	**NHL**	**24**	**4**	**7**	**11**	**38**	....	....	....	....	....
	NHL Totals		**320**	**59**	**145**	**204**	**558**	**49**	**8**	**14**	**22**	**88**

a CCHA Second All-Star Team (1989)
b CCHA First All-Star Team (1990)
c NCAA West First All-American Team (1990)
d NHL/Upper Deck All-Rookie Team (1991)

Played in NHL All-Star Game (1994)

BLOEMBERG, JEFF (BLOOM-buhrg) DET.

Defense. Shoots right. 6'2", 205 lbs. Born, Listowel, Ont., January 31, 1968.
(NY Rangers' 5th choice, 93rd overall, in 1986 Entry Draft).

			Regular Season					Playoffs				
Season	Club	Lea	GP	G	A	TP	PIM	GP	G	A	TP	PIM
1985-86	North Bay	OHL	60	2	11	13	76	8	1	2	3	9
1986-87	North Bay	OHL	60	5	13	18	91	21	1	6	7	13
1987-88	Colorado	IHL	5	0	0	0	0	11	1	0	1	8
	North Bay	OHL	46	9	26	35	60	4	1	4	5	2
1988-89	**NY Rangers**	**NHL**	**9**	**0**	**0**	**0**	**0**	....	....	....	....	....
	Denver	IHL	64	7	22	29	55	1	0	0	0	0
1989-90	**NY Rangers**	**NHL**	**28**	**3**	**3**	**6**	**25**	**7**	**0**	**3**	**3**	**5**
	Flint	IHL	41	7	14	21	24	....	....	....	....	....
1990-91	**NY Rangers**	**NHL**	**3**	**0**	**2**	**2**	**0**	....	....	....	....	....
a	Binghamton	AHL	77	16	46	62	28	10	0	6	6	10
1991-92	**NY Rangers**	**NHL**	**3**	**0**	**1**	**1**	**0**	....	....	....	....	....
	Binghamton	AHL	66	6	41	47	22	11	1	10	11	10
1992-93	Cape Breton	AHL	76	6	45	51	34	16	5	10	15	10
1993-94	Springfield	AHL	78	8	28	36	36	6	0	3	3	8
1994-95	Adirondack	AHL	44	5	19	24	10	4	0	0	0	0
	NHL Totals		**43**	**3**	**6**	**9**	**25**	**7**	**0**	**3**	**3**	**5**

a AHL Second All-Star Team (1991)

Claimed by **Tampa Bay** from **NY Rangers** in Expansion Draft, June 18, 1992. Traded to **Edmonton** by **Tampa Bay** for future considerations, September 25, 1992. Signed as a free agent by **Hartford**, August 9, 1993. Signed as a free agent by **Detroit**, May 9, 1995.

BLOMSTEN, ARTO (BLOOM-stehn) L.A.

Defense. Shoots left. 6'3", 210 lbs. Born, Vaasa, Finland, March 16, 1965.
(Winnipeg's 11th choice, 239th overall, in 1986 Entry Draft).

			Regular Season					Playoffs				
Season	Club	Lea	GP	G	A	TP	PIM	GP	G	A	TP	PIM
1983-84	Djurgarden	Swe.	3	0	0	0	4	....	....	....	....	....
1984-85	Djurgarden	Swe.	19	3	1	4	22	8	0	0	0	8
1985-86	Djurgarden	Swe.	8	0	3	3	6	....	....	....	....	....
1986-87	Djurgarden	Swe.	29	2	4	6	28	....	....	....	....	....
1987-88	Djurgarden	Swe.	39	12	6	18	36	2	1	0	1	0
1988-89	Djurgarden	Swe.	40	10	9	19	38	....	....	....	....	....
1989-90	Djurgarden	Swe.	36	5	21	26	28	8	0	1	1	6
1990-91	Djurgarden	Swe.	38	2	9	11	38	7	2	1	3	12
1991-92	Djurgarden	Swe.	39	6	8	14	34	10	2	0	2	8
1992-93	Djurgarden	Swe.	40	4	16	20	52	....	....	....	....	....
1993-94	**Winnipeg**	**NHL**	**18**	**0**	**2**	**2**	**6**	....	....	....	....	....
	Moncton	AHL	44	6	27	33	25	20	4	10	14	8
1994-95	Springfield	AHL	27	3	16	19	20	....	....	....	....	....
	Winnipeg	**NHL**	**1**	**0**	**0**	**0**	**2**	....	....	....	....	....
	Los Angeles	**NHL**	**4**	**0**	**1**	**1**	**0**	....	....	....	....	....
	Phoenix	IHL	2	1	2	3	0	8	3	6	9	6
	NHL Totals		**23**	**0**	**3**	**3**	**8**	....	....	....	....	....

Traded to **Los Angeles** by **Winnipeg** for Los Angeles' eighth round choice (Frederik Loven) in 1995 Entry Draft and a conditional draft choice in 1995 Entry Draft, March 27, 1995.

BLOUIN, SYLVAIN (bluh-WEHN) NYR

Defense. Shoots left. 6'2", 225 lbs. Born, Montreal, Que., May 21, 1974.
(NY Rangers' 5th choice, 104th overall, in 1994 Entry Draft).

			Regular Season					Playoffs				
Season	Club	Lea	GP	G	A	TP	PIM	GP	G	A	TP	PIM
1991-92	Laval	QMJHL	28	0	0	0	23	9	0	0	0	35
1992-93	Laval	QMJHL	68	0	10	10	373	13	1	0	1	*66
1993-94	Laval	QMJHL	62	18	22	40	*492	21	4	13	17	*177
1994-95	Chicago	IHL	1	0	0	0	2	....	....	....	....	....
	Charlotte	ECHL	50	5	7	12	280	3	0	0	0	6
	Binghamton	AHL	10	1	0	1	46	2	0	0	0	24

BOBACK, MICHAEL L.A.

Center. Shoots right. 5'11", 185 lbs. Born, Mt. Clemens, MI, August 13, 1970.
(Washington's 12th choice, 198th overall, in 1990 Entry Draft).

			Regular Season					Playoffs				
Season	Club	Lea	GP	G	A	TP	PIM	GP	G	A	TP	PIM
1988-89	Providence	H.E.	38	21	27	48	26	....	....	....	....	....
1989-90a	Providence	H.E.	31	13	29	42	28	....	....	....	....	....
1990-91	Providence	H.E.	26	15	24	39	6	....	....	....	....	....
1991-92b	Providence	H.E.	36	24	*48	*72	34	....	....	....	....	....
1992-93	Baltimore	AHL	69	11	68	79	14	5	3	3	6	6
1993-94	Portland	AHL	68	16	43	59	50	17	10	17	*27	4
1994-95	Portland	AHL	32	14	36	50	20	5	1	4	5	2

a Hockey East Second All-Star Team (1990)
b Hockey East First All-Star Team (1992)

Signed as a free agent by **Los Angeles**, July 10, 1995.

BODGER, DOUG BUF.

Defense. Shoots left. 6'2", 213 lbs. Born, Chemainus, B.C., June 18, 1966.
(Pittsburgh's 2nd choice, 9th overall, in 1984 Entry Draft).

			Regular Season					Playoffs				
Season	Club	Lea	GP	G	A	TP	PIM	GP	G	A	TP	PIM
1982-83a	Kamloops	WHL	72	26	66	92	98	7	0	5	5	2
1983-84	Kamloops	WHL	70	21	77	98	90	17	2	15	17	12
1984-85	**Pittsburgh**	**NHL**	**65**	**5**	**26**	**31**	**67**	....	....	....	....	....
1985-86	**Pittsburgh**	**NHL**	**79**	**4**	**33**	**37**	**63**	....	....	....	....	....
1986-87	**Pittsburgh**	**NHL**	**76**	**11**	**38**	**49**	**52**	....	....	....	....	....
1987-88	**Pittsburgh**	**NHL**	**69**	**14**	**31**	**45**	**103**	....	....	....	....	....
1988-89	**Pittsburgh**	**NHL**	**10**	**1**	**4**	**5**	**7**	....	....	....	....	....
	Buffalo	**NHL**	**61**	**7**	**40**	**47**	**52**	**5**	**1**	**1**	**2**	**11**
1989-90	**Buffalo**	**NHL**	**71**	**12**	**36**	**48**	**64**	**6**	**1**	**5**	**6**	**6**
1990-91	**Buffalo**	**NHL**	**58**	**5**	**23**	**28**	**54**	**4**	**0**	**1**	**1**	**0**
1991-92	**Buffalo**	**NHL**	**73**	**11**	**35**	**46**	**108**	**7**	**2**	**1**	**3**	**2**
1992-93	**Buffalo**	**NHL**	**81**	**9**	**45**	**54**	**87**	**8**	**2**	**3**	**5**	**0**
1993-94	**Buffalo**	**NHL**	**75**	**7**	**32**	**39**	**76**	**7**	**0**	**3**	**3**	**6**
1994-95	**Buffalo**	**NHL**	**44**	**3**	**17**	**20**	**47**	**5**	**0**	**4**	**4**	**0**
	NHL Totals		**762**	**89**	**360**	**449**	**780**	**42**	**6**	**18**	**24**	**25**

a WHL Second All-Star Team (1983)

Traded to **Buffalo** by **Pittsburgh** wih Darrin Shannon for Tom Barrasso and Buffalo's third round choice (Joe Dziedzic) in 1990 Entry Draft, November 12, 1988.

BOGUNIECKI, ERIC ST.L.

Center. Shoots right. 5'8", 192 lbs. Born, New Haven, CT, May 6, 1975.
(St. Louis' 6th choice, 193rd overall, in 1993 Entry Draft).

			Regular Season					Playoffs				
Season	Club	Lea	GP	G	A	TP	PIM	GP	G	A	TP	PIM
1993-94	N. Hampshire	H.E.	40	17	16	33	66	....	....	....	....	....
1994-95	N. Hampshire	H.E.	34	12	16	28	62	....	....	....	....	....

BOHONOS, LONNY (boh-HOH-nohz) VAN.

Right wing. Shoots right. 5'11", 190 lbs. Born, Winnipeg, Man., May 20, 1973.

			Regular Season					Playoffs				
Season	Club	Lea	GP	G	A	TP	PIM	GP	G	A	TP	PIM
1991-92	Moose Jaw	WHL	8	1	1	2	0	....	....	....	....	....
1992-93	Seattle	WHL	46	13	13	26	27	....	....	....	....	....
	Portland	WHL	27	20	17	37	16	15	8	13	21	19
1993-94ab	Portland	WHL	70	*62	*90	*152	80	10	8	11	19	13
1994-95	Syracuse	AHL	67	30	45	75	71	....	....	....	....	....

a WHL West First All-Star Team (1994)
b Canadian Major Junior First All-Star Team (1994)

Signed as a free agent by **Vancouver**, May 31, 1994.

BOILEAU, PATRICK WSH.

Defense. Shoots right. 6', 190 lbs. Born, Montreal, Que., February 22, 1975.
(Washington's 3rd choice, 69th overall, in 1993 Entry Draft).

			Regular Season					Playoffs				
Season	Club	Lea	GP	G	A	TP	PIM	GP	G	A	TP	PIM
1992-93	Laval	QMJHL	69	4	19	23	73	13	1	2	3	10
1993-94	Laval	QMJHL	64	13	57	70	56	21	1	7	8	24
1994-95	Laval	QMJHL	38	8	25	33	46	20	4	16	20	24

BOIVIN, CLAUDE (BOY-vihn)

Left wing. Shoots left. 6'2", 200 lbs. Born, Ste. Foy, Que., March 1, 1970.
(Philadelphia's 1st choice, 14th overall, in 1988 Entry Draft).

			Regular Season					Playoffs				
Season	Club	Lea	GP	G	A	TP	PIM	GP	G	A	TP	PIM
1987-88	Drummondville	QMJHL	63	23	26	49	233	17	5	3	8	74
1988-89	Drummondville	QMJHL	63	20	36	56	218	4	0	2	2	27
1989-90	Laval	QMJHL	59	24	51	75	309	13	7	13	20	59
1990-91	Hershey	AHL	65	13	32	45	159	7	1	5	6	28
1991-92	**Philadelphia**	**NHL**	**58**	**5**	**13**	**18**	**187**	....	....	....	....	....
	Hershey	AHL	20	4	5	9	96	....	....	....	....	....
1992-93	**Philadelphia**	**NHL**	**30**	**5**	**4**	**9**	**76**	....	....	....	....	....
1993-94	**Philadelphia**	**NHL**	**26**	**1**	**1**	**2**	**57**	....	....	....	....	....
	Hershey	AHL	4	1	6	7	6	....	....	....	....	....
	Ottawa	**NHL**	**15**	**1**	**0**	**1**	**38**	....	....	....	....	....
1994-95	**Ottawa**	**NHL**	**3**	**0**	**1**	**1**	**6**	....	....	....	....	....
	P.E.I.	AHL	22	10	9	19	89	9	1	2	3	32
	NHL Totals		**132**	**12**	**19**	**31**	**364**	....	....	....	....	....

Traded to **Ottawa** by **Philadelphia** with Kirk Daubenspeck for Mark Lamb, March 5, 1994.

BOLIBRUCK, KEVIN OTT.

Defense. Shoots left. 6'1", 197 lbs. Born, Peterborough, Ont., February 8, 1977.
(Ottawa's 4th choice, 89th overall, in 1995 Entry Draft).

			Regular Season					Playoffs				
Season	Club	Lea	GP	G	A	TP	PIM	GP	G	A	TP	PIM
1993-94	Thorold	Jr. B	38	6	18	24	78	....	....	....	....	....
1994-95	Peterborough	OHL	66	2	16	18	88	11	1	1	2	14

BOMBARDIR, BRAD N.J.

Defense. Shoots left. 6'2", 190 lbs. Born, Powell River, B.C., May 5, 1972.
(New Jersey's 5th choice, 56th overall, in 1990 Entry Draft).

			Regular Season					Playoffs				
Season	Club	Lea	GP	G	A	TP	PIM	GP	G	A	TP	PIM
1990-91	North Dakota	WCHA	33	3	6	9	18	....	....	....	....	....
1991-92	North Dakota	WCHA	35	3	14	17	54	....	....	....	....	....
1992-93	North Dakota	WCHA	38	8	15	23	34	....	....	....	....	....
1993-94	North Dakota	WCHA	38	5	17	22	38	....	....	....	....	....
1994-95	Albany	AHL	77	5	22	27	22	14	0	3	3	6

BONDRA, PETER WSH.

Right wing. Shoots left. 6'1", 200 lbs. Born, Luck, USSR, February 7, 1968.
(Washington's 9th choice, 156th overall, in 1990 Entry Draft).

			Regular Season					Playoffs				
Season	Club	Lea	GP	G	A	TP	PIM	GP	G	A	TP	PIM
1986-87	VSZ Kosice	Czech.	32	4	5	9	24	....	....	....	....	....
1987-88	VSZ Kosice	Czech.	45	27	11	38	20	....	....	....	....	....
1988-89	VSZ Kosice	Czech.	40	30	10	40	20	....	....	....	....	....
1989-90	VSZ Kosice	Czech.	49	36	19	55	....	....	....	....	....	....
1990-91	**Washington**	**NHL**	**54**	**12**	**16**	**28**	**47**	**4**	**0**	**1**	**1**	**2**
1991-92	**Washington**	**NHL**	**71**	**28**	**28**	**56**	**42**	**7**	**6**	**2**	**8**	**4**
1992-93	**Washington**	**NHL**	**83**	**37**	**48**	**85**	**70**	**6**	**0**	**6**	**6**	**0**
1993-94	**Washington**	**NHL**	**69**	**24**	**19**	**43**	**40**	**9**	**2**	**4**	**6**	**4**
1994-95	Kosice	Slov.	2	1	0	1	0	....	....	....	....	....
	Washington	**NHL**	**47**	***34**	**9**	**43**	**24**	**7**	**5**	**3**	**8**	**10**
	NHL Totals		**324**	**135**	**120**	**255**	**223**	**33**	**13**	**16**	**29**	**20**

Played in NHL All-Star Game (1993)

BONIN, BRIAN PIT.

Center. Shoots left. 5'10", 175 lbs. Born, White Bear Lake, MN, November 28, 1973.
(Pittsburgh's 9th choice, 211th overall, in 1992 Entry Draft).

			Regular Season					Playoffs				
Season	Club	Lea	GP	G	A	TP	PIM	GP	G	A	TP	PIM
1992-93	U. Minnesota	WCHA	38	10	18	28	10	....	....	....	....	....
1993-94	U. Minnesota	WCHA	42	24	20	44	14	....	....	....	....	....
1994-95ab	U. Minnesota	WCHA	44	32	31	*63	28	....	....	....	....	....

a WCHA First All-Star Team (1995)
b NCAA West First All-American Team (1995)

BONK, RADEK (BOHNK) OTT.

Center. Shoots left. 6'3", 215 lbs. Born, Krnov, Czech., January 9, 1976.
(Ottawa's 1st choice, 3rd overall, in 1994 Entry Draft).

			Regular Season					Playoffs				
Season	Club	Lea	GP	G	A	TP	PIM	GP	G	A	TP	PIM
1992-93	ZPS Zlin	Czech.	30	5	5	10	10	....	....	....	....	....
1993-94a	Las Vegas	IHL	76	42	45	87	208	5	1	2	3	10
1994-95	Las Vegas	IHL	33	7	13	20	62	....	....	....	....	....
	Ottawa	**NHL**	**42**	**3**	**8**	**11**	**28**	....	....	....	....	....
	P.E.I.	AHL	....	....	....	....	....	1	0	0	0	0
	NHL Totals		**42**	**3**	**8**	**11**	**28**	....	....	....	....	....

a Won Garry F. Longman Memorial Trophy (Top Rookie - IHL) (1994)

BONNER, CRAIG — DAL.

Defense. Shoots left. 6'4", 205 lbs. Born, Edmonton, Alta., May 20, 1972.

			Regular Season					Playoffs				
Season	Club	Lea	GP	G	A	TP	PIM	GP	G	A	TP	PIM
1989-90	Kamloops	WHL	64	1	17	18	77	17	1	2	3	0
1990-91	Kamloops	WHL	45	5	13	18	59	1	0	0	0	0
1991-92	Kamloops	WHL	67	15	28	43	122	3	0	0	0	8
1992-93	Kamloops	WHL	72	8	43	51	143	13	2	5	7	14
1993-94	Kalamazoo	IHL	20	0	2	2	49	1	0	0	0	0
1994-95	Kalamazoo	IHL	23	0	3	3	42	....	....	....	....	....

Signed as a free agent by **Dallas**, July 19, 1994.

BONSIGNORE, JASON (bohn-SEE-nohr) — EDM.

Center. Shoots right. 6'4", 208 lbs. Born, Rochester, NY, April 15, 1976.
(Edmonton's 1st choice, 4th overall, in 1994 Entry Draft).

			Regular Season					Playoffs				
Season	Club	Lea	GP	G	A	TP	PIM	GP	G	A	TP	PIM
1992-93	Newmarket	OHL	66	22	20	42	6	7	0	3	3	0
1993-94	Newmarket	OHL	17	7	17	24	22	....	....	....	....	....
	U.S. National	....	5	0	2	2	0	....	....	....	....	....
	Niagara Falls	OHL	41	15	47	62	41	....	....	....	....	....
1994-95	Niagara Falls	OHL	26	12	21	33	51	....	....	....	....	....
	Sudbury	OHL	23	15	14	29	45	17	13	10	23	12
	Edmonton	**NHL**	**1**	**1**	**0**	**1**	**0**	....	....	....	....	....
	NHL Totals		**1**	**1**	**0**	**1**	**0**	....	....	....	....	....

BONVIE, DENNIS — EDM.

Defense. Shoots right. 5'11", 210 lbs. Born, Antigonish, N.S., July 23, 1973.

			Regular Season					Playoffs				
Season	Club	Lea	GP	G	A	TP	PIM	GP	G	A	TP	PIM
1991-92	Kitchener	OHL	7	1	1	2	23	....	....	....	....	....
	North Bay	OHL	49	0	12	12	261	21	0	1	1	91
1992-93	North Bay	OHL	64	3	21	24	*316	5	0	0	0	34
1993-94	Cape Breton	AHL	63	1	10	11	278	4	0	0	0	11
1994-95	Cape Breton	AHL	74	5	15	20	422	....	....	....	....	....
	Edmonton	**NHL**	**2**	**0**	**0**	**0**	**0**	....	....	....	....	....
	NHL Totals		**2**	**0**	**0**	**0**	**0**	....	....	....	....	....

Signed as a free agent by **Edmonton**, August 25, 1994.

BORDELEAU, SEBASTIEN (BOHR-duh-loh) — MTL.

Center. Shoots right. 5'10", 180 lbs. Born, Vancouver, B.C., February 15, 1975.
(Montreal's 3rd choice, 73rd overall, in 1993 Entry Draft).

			Regular Season					Playoffs				
Season	Club	Lea	GP	G	A	TP	PIM	GP	G	A	TP	PIM
1991-92	Hull	QMJHL	62	26	32	58	91	5	0	3	3	23
1992-93	Hull	QMJHL	60	18	39	57	95	10	3	8	11	20
1993-94	Hull	QMJHL	60	26	57	83	147	17	6	14	20	26
1994-95a	Hull	QMJHL	68	52	76	128	142	18	*13	19	*32	25

a QMJHL First All-Star Team (1995)

BORSATO, LUCIANO (bohr-SAH-toh, LOO-chee-AH-noh)

Center. Shoots right. 5'11", 190 lbs. Born, Richmond Hill, Ont., January 7, 1966.
(Winnipeg's 7th choice, 135th overall, in 1984 Entry Draft).

			Regular Season					Playoffs				
Season	Club	Lea	GP	G	A	TP	PIM	GP	G	A	TP	PIM
1984-85	Clarkson	ECAC	33	15	17	32	37	....	....	....	....	....
1985-86	Clarkson	ECAC	28	14	17	31	44	....	....	....	....	....
1986-87	Clarkson	ECAC	31	16	41	57	55	....	....	....	....	....
1987-88ab	Clarkson	ECAC	33	15	29	44	38	....	....	....	....	....
	Moncton	AHL	3	1	1	2	0	....	....	....	....	....
1988-89	Moncton	AHL	6	2	5	7	4	....	....	....	....	....
	Tappara	Fin.	44	31	36	67	69	7	0	3	3	4
1989-90	Moncton	AHL	1	1	0	1	0	....	....	....	....	....
1990-91	**Winnipeg**	**NHL**	**1**	**0**	**1**	**1**	**2**	....	....	....	....	....
	Moncton	AHL	41	14	24	38	40	9	3	7	10	22
1991-92	**Winnipeg**	**NHL**	**56**	**15**	**21**	**36**	**45**	**1**	**0**	**0**	**0**	**0**
	Moncton	AHL	14	2	7	9	39	....	....	....	....	....
1992-93	**Winnipeg**	**NHL**	**67**	**15**	**20**	**35**	**38**	**6**	**1**	**0**	**1**	**4**
1993-94	**Winnipeg**	**NHL**	**75**	**5**	**13**	**18**	**28**	....	....	....	....	....
1994-95	**Winnipeg**	**NHL**	**4**	**0**	**0**	**0**	**0**	....	....	....	....	....
	Springfield	AHL	22	9	11	20	14	....	....	....	....	....
	NHL Totals		**203**	**35**	**55**	**90**	**113**	**7**	**1**	**0**	**1**	**4**

a ECAC Second All-Star Team (1988)
b NCAA East Second All-American Team (1988)

BORSCHEVSKY, NIKOLAI (bohr-SHEHV-skee)

Right wing. Shoots left. 5'9", 180 lbs. Born, Tomsk, USSR, January 12, 1965.
(Toronto's 3rd choice, 77th overall, in 1992 Entry Draft).

			Regular Season					Playoffs				
Season	Club	Lea	GP	G	A	TP	PIM	GP	G	A	TP	PIM
1983-84	Moscow D'amo	USSR	34	4	5	9	4	....	....	....	....	....
1984-85	Moscow D'amo	USSR	34	5	9	14	6	....	....	....	....	....
1985-86	Moscow D'amo	USSR	31	6	4	10	4	....	....	....	....	....
1986-87	Moscow D'amo	USSR	28	1	4	5	8	....	....	....	....	....
1987-88	Moscow D'amo	USSR	37	11	7	18	6	....	....	....	....	....
1988-89	Moscow D'amo	USSR	43	7	8	15	18	....	....	....	....	....
1989-90	Spartak	USSR	48	17	25	42	8	....	....	....	....	....
1990-91	Spartak	USSR	45	19	16	35	16	....	....	....	....	....
1991-92	Spartak	CIS	40	25	14	39	16	....	....	....	....	....
1992-93	**Toronto**	**NHL**	**78**	**34**	**40**	**74**	**28**	**16**	**2**	**7**	**9**	**0**
1993-94	**Toronto**	**NHL**	**45**	**14**	**20**	**34**	**10**	**15**	**2**	**2**	**4**	**4**
1994-95	Spartak	CIS	9	5	1	6	14	....	....	....	....	....
	Toronto	**NHL**	**19**	**0**	**5**	**5**	**0**	....	....	....	....	....
	Calgary	**NHL**	**8**	**0**	**5**	**5**	**0**	....	....	....	....	....
	NHL Totals		**150**	**48**	**70**	**118**	**38**	**31**	**4**	**9**	**13**	**4**

Traded to **Calgary** by **Toronto** for Calgary's sixth round choice in 1996 Entry Draft, April 6, 1995.

BOTTERILL, JASON (BOH-tuhr-ihl) — DAL.

Left wing. Shoots left. 6'3", 205 lbs. Born, Edmonton, Alta., May 19, 1976.
(Dallas' 1st choice, 20th overall, in 1994 Entry Draft).

			Regular Season					Playoffs				
Season	Club	Lea	GP	G	A	TP	PIM	GP	G	A	TP	PIM
1993-94	U. of Michigan	CCHA	36	20	19	39	94	....	....	....	....	....
1994-95	U. of Michigan	CCHA	34	14	14	28	117	....	....	....	....	....

BOUCHARD, JOEL — CGY.

Defense. Shoots left. 6', 190 lbs. Born, Montreal, Que., January 23, 1974.
(Calgary's 7th choice, 129th overall, in 1992 Entry Draft).

			Regular Season					Playoffs				
Season	Club	Lea	GP	G	A	TP	PIM	GP	G	A	TP	PIM
1990-91	Longueuil	QMJHL	53	3	19	22	34	8	1	0	1	11
1991-92	Verdun	QMJHL	70	9	20	29	55	19	1	7	8	20
1992-93	Verdun	QMJHL	60	10	49	59	126	4	0	2	2	4
1993-94a	Verdun	QMJHL	60	15	55	70	62	4	1	0	1	6
	Saint John	AHL	1	0	0	0	0	2	0	0	0	0
1994-95	Saint John	AHL	77	6	25	31	63	5	1	0	1	4
	Calgary	**NHL**	**2**	**0**	**0**	**0**	**0**	....	....	....	....	....
	NHL Totals		**2**	**0**	**0**	**0**	**0**	....	....	....	....	....

a QMJHL First All-Star Team (1994)

BOUCHER, PHILIPPE — L.A.

Defense. Shoots right. 6'2", 189 lbs. Born, St. Apollinaire, Que., March 24, 1973.
(Buffalo's 1st choice, 13th overall, in 1991 Entry Draft).

			Regular Season					Playoffs				
Season	Club	Lea	GP	G	A	TP	PIM	GP	G	A	TP	PIM
1990-91ab	Granby	QMJHL	69	21	46	67	92	....	....	....	....	....
1991-92	Granby	QMJHL	49	22	37	59	47	....	....	....	....	....
b	Laval	QMJHL	16	7	11	18	36	10	5	6	11	8
1992-93	**Buffalo**	**NHL**	**18**	**0**	**4**	**4**	**14**	....	....	....	....	....
	Laval	QMJHL	16	12	15	27	37	13	6	15	21	12
	Rochester	AHL	5	4	3	7	8	3	0	1	1	2
1993-94	**Buffalo**	**NHL**	**38**	**6**	**8**	**14**	**29**	**7**	**1**	**1**	**2**	**2**
	Rochester	AHL	31	10	22	32	51	....	....	....	....	....
1994-95	Rochester	AHL	43	14	27	41	26	....	....	....	....	....
	Buffalo	**NHL**	**9**	**1**	**4**	**5**	**0**	....	....	....	....	....
	Los Angeles	**NHL**	**6**	**1**	**0**	**1**	**4**	....	....	....	....	....
	NHL Totals		**71**	**8**	**16**	**24**	**47**	**7**	**1**	**1**	**2**	**2**

a Canadian Major Junior Rookie of the Year (1991)
b QMJHL Second All-Star Team (1991, 1992)

Traded to **Los Angeles** by **Buffalo** with Denis Tsygurov and Grant Fuhr for Alexei Zhitnik, Robb Stauber, Charlie Huddy and Los Angeles' fifth round choice (Marian Menhart) in 1995 Entry Draft, February 14, 1995.

BOUDRIAS, JASON — FLA.

Center. Shoots right. 6', 195 lbs. Born, Val D'or, Que., February 16, 1976.
(Florida's 8th choice, 183rd overall, in 1994 Entry Draft).

			Regular Season					Playoffs				
Season	Club	Lea	GP	G	A	TP	PIM	GP	G	A	TP	PIM
1993-94	Laval	QMJHL	61	17	25	42	62	21	5	9	14	10
1994-95	Laval	QMJHL	52	24	37	61	43	20	10	17	27	2

BOUGHNER, BOB (BOOG-nuhr) — FLA.

Defense. Shoots right. 6', 205 lbs. Born, Windsor, Ont., March 8, 1971.
(Detroit's 2nd choice, 32nd overall, in 1989 Entry Draft).

			Regular Season					Playoffs				
Season	Club	Lea	GP	G	A	TP	PIM	GP	G	A	TP	PIM
1988-89	S.S. Marie	OHL	64	6	15	21	182	....	....	....	....	....
1989-90	S.S. Marie	OHL	49	7	23	30	122	....	....	....	....	....
1990-91	S.S. Marie	OHL	64	13	33	46	156	14	2	9	11	35
1991-92	Toledo	ECHL	28	3	10	13	79	5	2	0	2	15
	Adirondack	AHL	1	0	0	0	7	....	....	....	....	....
1992-93	Adirondack	AHL	69	1	16	17	190	....	....	....	....	....
1993-94	Adirondack	AHL	72	8	14	22	292	10	1	1	2	18
1994-95	Cincinnati	IHL	81	2	14	16	192	10	0	0	0	18

Signed as a free agent by **Florida**, July 25, 1994.

BOULIN, VLADISLAV — PHI.

Defense. Shoots left. 6'4", 196 lbs. Born, Penza, USSR, May 18, 1972.
(Philadelphia's 5th choice, 103rd overall, in 1992 Entry Draft).

			Regular Season					Playoffs				
Season	Club	Lea	GP	G	A	TP	PIM	GP	G	A	TP	PIM
1992-93	Moscow D'amo	CIS	32	2	1	3	55	4	0	0	0	2
1993-94	Moscow D'amo	CIS	43	4	2	6	36	7	0	1	1	16
1994-95	Hershey	AHL	52	1	7	8	30	....	....	....	....	....

BOULTON, ERIC — NYR

Left wing. Shoots left. 6', 201 lbs. Born, Halifax, N.S., August 17, 1976.
(NY Rangers' 12th choice, 234th overall, in 1994 Entry Draft).

			Regular Season					Playoffs				
Season	Club	Lea	GP	G	A	TP	PIM	GP	G	A	TP	PIM
1993-94	Oshawa	OHL	45	4	3	7	149	5	0	0	0	16
1994-95	Oshawa	OHL	27	7	5	12	125	....	....	....	....	....
	Sarnia	OHL	24	3	7	10	134	4	0	1	1	10

BOURQUE, PHIL (BOHRK) — OTT.

Left wing. Shoots left. 6'1", 196 lbs. Born, Chelmsford, MA, June 8, 1962.

			Regular Season					Playoffs				
Season	Club	Lea	GP	G	A	TP	PIM	GP	G	A	TP	PIM
1980-81	Kingston	OHL	47	4	4	8	46	6	0	0	0	10
1981-82	Kingston	OHL	67	11	40	51	111	4	0	0	0	0
1982-83	Baltimore	AHL	65	1	15	16	93	....	....	....	....	....
1983-84	**Pittsburgh**	**NHL**	**5**	**0**	**1**	**1**	**12**	....	....	....	....	....
	Baltimore	AHL	58	5	17	22	96	....	....	....	....	....
1984-85	Baltimore	AHL	79	6	15	21	164	13	2	5	7	23
1985-86	**Pittsburgh**	**NHL**	**4**	**0**	**0**	**0**	**2**	....	....	....	....	....
	Baltimore	AHL	74	8	18	26	226	....	....	....	....	....
1986-87	**Pittsburgh**	**NHL**	**22**	**2**	**3**	**5**	**32**	....	....	....	....	....
	Baltimore	AHL	49	15	16	31	183	....	....	....	....	....
1987-88	**Pittsburgh**	**NHL**	**21**	**4**	**12**	**16**	**20**	....	....	....	....	....
ab	Muskegon	IHL	52	16	36	52	66	6	1	2	3	16
1988-89	**Pittsburgh**	**NHL**	**80**	**17**	**26**	**43**	**97**	**11**	**4**	**1**	**5**	**66**
1989-90	**Pittsburgh**	**NHL**	**76**	**22**	**17**	**39**	**108**	....	....	....	....	....
1990-91	**Pittsburgh**	**NHL**	**78**	**20**	**14**	**34**	**106**	**24**	**6**	**7**	**13**	**16**
1991-92	**Pittsburgh**	**NHL**	**58**	**10**	**16**	**26**	**58**	**21**	**3**	**4**	**7**	**25**
1992-93	**NY Rangers**	**NHL**	**55**	**6**	**14**	**20**	**39**	....	....	....	....	....
1993-94	**NY Rangers**	**NHL**	**16**	**0**	**1**	**1**	**8**	....	....	....	....	....
	Ottawa	**NHL**	**11**	**2**	**3**	**5**	**0**	....	....	....	....	....
1994-95	**Ottawa**	**NHL**	**38**	**4**	**3**	**7**	**20**	....	....	....	....	....
	NHL Totals		**464**	**87**	**110**	**197**	**502**	**56**	**13**	**12**	**25**	**107**

a IHL First All-Star Team (1988)
b Won Governor's Trophy (Outstanding Defenseman - IHL) (1988)

Signed as a free agent by **Pittsburgh**, October 4, 1982. Signed as a free agent by **NY Rangers**, August 31, 1992. Traded to **Ottawa** by **NY Rangers** for future considerations, March 21, 1994.

BOURQUE, RAY (BOHRK) BOS.

Defense. Shoots left. 5'11", 215 lbs. Born, Montreal, Que., December 28, 1960.
(Boston's 1st choice, 8th overall, in 1979 Entry Draft).

			Regular Season					Playoffs				
Season	Club	Lea	GP	G	A	TP	PIM	GP	G	A	TP	PIM
1976-77	Sorel	QJHL	69	12	36	48	61	....	....	....	....	....
1977-78	Verdun	QJHL	72	22	57	79	90	4	2	1	3	0
1978-79	Verdun	QJHL	63	22	71	93	44	11	3	16	19	18
1979-80ab	**Boston**	**NHL**	**80**	**17**	**48**	**65**	**73**	**10**	**2**	**9**	**11**	**27**
1980-81c	**Boston**	**NHL**	**67**	**27**	**29**	**56**	**96**	**3**	**0**	**1**	**1**	**2**
1981-82b	**Boston**	**NHL**	**65**	**17**	**49**	**66**	**51**	**9**	**1**	**5**	**6**	**16**
1982-83c	**Boston**	**NHL**	**65**	**22**	**51**	**73**	**20**	**17**	**8**	**15**	**23**	**10**
1983-84b	**Boston**	**NHL**	**78**	**31**	**65**	**96**	**57**	**3**	**0**	**2**	**2**	**0**
1984-85b	**Boston**	**NHL**	**73**	**20**	**66**	**86**	**53**	**5**	**0**	**3**	**3**	**4**
1985-86c	**Boston**	**NHL**	**74**	**19**	**58**	**77**	**68**	**3**	**0**	**0**	**0**	**0**
1986-87bd	**Boston**	**NHL**	**78**	**23**	**72**	**95**	**36**	**4**	**1**	**2**	**3**	**0**
1987-88bd	**Boston**	**NHL**	**78**	**17**	**64**	**81**	**72**	**23**	**3**	**18**	**21**	**26**
1988-89c	**Boston**	**NHL**	**60**	**18**	**43**	**61**	**52**	**10**	**0**	**4**	**4**	**6**
1989-90bd	**Boston**	**NHL**	**76**	**19**	**65**	**84**	**50**	**17**	**5**	**12**	**17**	**16**
1990-91bd	**Boston**	**NHL**	**76**	**21**	**73**	**94**	**75**	**19**	**7**	**18**	**25**	**12**
1991-92be	**Boston**	**NHL**	**80**	**21**	**60**	**81**	**56**	**12**	**3**	**6**	**9**	**12**
1992-93b	**Boston**	**NHL**	**78**	**19**	**63**	**82**	**40**	**4**	**1**	**0**	**1**	**2**
1993-94bd	**Boston**	**NHL**	**72**	**20**	**71**	**91**	**58**	**13**	**2**	**8**	**10**	**0**
1994-95c	**Boston**	**NHL**	**46**	**12**	**31**	**43**	**20**	**5**	**0**	**3**	**3**	**0**
	NHL Totals		**1146**	**323**	**908**	**1231**	**877**	**157**	**33**	**106**	**139**	**133**

a Won Calder Memorial Trophy (1980)
b NHL First All-Star Team (1980, 1982, 1984, 1985, 1987, 1988, 1990, 1991, 1992, 1993, 1994)
c NHL Second All-Star Team (1981, 1983, 1986, 1989, 1995)
d Won James Norris Memorial Trophy (1987, 1988, 1990, 1991, 1994)
e Won King Clancy Memorial Trophy (1992)

Played in NHL All-Star Game (1981-86, 1988-94)

BOUSQUET, DANY (boos-KEHT) WSH.

Center. Shoots left. 5'11", 155 lbs. Born, Montreal, Que., April 3, 1973.
(Washington's 10th choice, 277th overall, in 1993 Entry Draft).

			Regular Season					Playoffs				
Season	Club	Lea	GP	G	A	TP	PIM	GP	G	A	TP	PIM
1993-94	Penticton	BCJHL	58	76	76	152	78	....	....	....	....	....
1994-95	Dalhousie	AUAA	26	16	27	43	54	5	9	4	13	8

BOWEN, CURTIS (BOW-ehn) DET.

Left wing. Shoots left. 6'1", 195 lbs. Born, Kenora, Ont., March 24, 1974.
(Detroit's 1st choice, 22nd overall, in 1992 Entry Draft).

			Regular Season					Playoffs				
Season	Club	Lea	GP	G	A	TP	PIM	GP	G	A	TP	PIM
1990-91	Ottawa	OHL	42	12	14	26	31	....	....	....	....	....
1991-92	Ottawa	OHL	65	31	45	76	94	11	3	7	10	11
1992-93	Ottawa	OHL	21	9	19	28	51	....	....	....	....	....
1993-94	Ottawa	OHL	52	25	37	62	98	17	8	13	21	14
1994-95	Adirondack	AHL	64	6	11	17	71	4	0	2	2	4

BOWEN, JASON (BOW-ehn) PHI.

Defense. Shoots left. 6'4", 215 lbs. Born, Port Alice, B.C., November 9, 1973.
(Philadelphia's 2nd choice, 15th overall, in 1992 Entry Draft).

			Regular Season					Playoffs				
Season	Club	Lea	GP	G	A	TP	PIM	GP	G	A	TP	PIM
1989-90	Tri-City	WHL	61	8	5	13	129	7	0	3	3	4
1990-91	Tri-City	WHL	60	7	13	20	252	6	2	2	4	18
1991-92	Tri-City	WHL	19	5	3	8	135	5	0	1	1	42
1992-93	**Philadelphia**	**NHL**	**7**	**1**	**0**	**1**	**2**	....	....	....	....	....
	Tri-City	WHL	62	10	12	22	219	3	1	1	2	18
1993-94	**Philadelphia**	**NHL**	**56**	**1**	**5**	**6**	**87**	....	....	....	....	....
1994-95	Hershey	AHL	55	5	5	10	116	6	0	0	0	46
	Philadelphia	**NHL**	**4**	**0**	**0**	**0**	**0**	....	....	....	....	....
	NHL Totals		**67**	**2**	**5**	**7**	**89**	....	....	....	....	....

BOYD, KEVIN OTT.

Left wing. Shoots left. 6'3", 195 lbs. Born, Newmarket, Ont., May 19, 1977.
(Ottawa's 5th choice, 103rd overall, in 1995 Entry Draft).

			Regular Season					Playoffs				
Season	Club	Lea	GP	G	A	TP	PIM	GP	G	A	TP	PIM
1993-94	Newmarket	Jr. A	30	2	7	9	51	....	....	....	....	....
1994-95	London	OHL	65	5	5	10	125	4	0	0	0	0

BOYER, ZAC DAL.

Right wing. Shoots right. 6'1", 199 lbs. Born, Inuvik, N.W.T., October 25, 1971.
(Chicago's 4th choice, 88th overall, in 1991 Entry Draft).

			Regular Season					Playoffs				
Season	Club	Lea	GP	G	A	TP	PIM	GP	G	A	TP	PIM
1988-89	Kamloops	WHL	42	10	17	27	22	16	9	8	17	10
1989-90	Kamloops	WHL	71	24	47	71	163	17	4	4	8	8
1990-91	Kamloops	WHL	64	45	60	105	58	12	6	10	16	8
1991-92	Kamloops	WHL	70	40	69	109	90	17	9	*20	*29	16
1992-93	Indianapolis	IHL	59	7	14	21	26	....	....	....	....	....
1993-94	Indianapolis	IHL	54	13	12	25	67	....	....	....	....	....
1994-95	Kalamazoo	IHL	22	9	7	16	22	15	3	9	12	8
	Dallas	**NHL**	**1**	**0**	**0**	**0**	**0**	**2**	**0**	**0**	**0**	**0**
	NHL Totals		**1**	**0**	**0**	**0**	**0**	**2**	**0**	**0**	**0**	**0**

Signed as a free agent by **Dallas**, July 25, 1994.

BOZON, PHILIPPE (boh-ZOHN)

Left wing. Shoots left. 5'10", 185 lbs. Born, Chamonix, France, November 30, 1966.

			Regular Season					Playoffs				
Season	Club	Lea	GP	G	A	TP	PIM	GP	G	A	TP	PIM
1984-85	St-Jean	QMJHL	67	32	50	82	82	5	0	5	5	4
1985-86a	St-Jean	QMJHL	65	59	52	111	72	10	10	6	16	16
	Peoria	IHL	....	....	....	....	....	5	1	0	1	0
1986-87	Peoria	IHL	28	4	11	15	17	....	....	....	....	....
	St-Jean	QMJHL	25	20	21	41	75	8	5	5	10	30
1987-88	Mont-Blanc	France	18	11	15	26	34	10	15	6	21	6
1988-89	Mont Blanc	France	18	11	18	29	18	11	11	17	28	38
1989-90	Grenoble	France	36	45	38	83	34	6	4	3	7	2
1990-91	Grenoble	France	26	22	16	38	16	10	7	8	15	8
1991-92	Chamonix	France	10	12	8	20	20	....	....	....	....	....
	St. Louis	**NHL**	**9**	**1**	**3**	**4**	**4**	**6**	**1**	**0**	**1**	**27**
1992-93	**St. Louis**	**NHL**	**54**	**6**	**6**	**12**	**55**	**9**	**1**	**0**	**1**	**0**
	Peoria	IHL	4	3	2	5	2	....	....	....	....	....
1993-94	**St. Louis**	**NHL**	**80**	**9**	**16**	**25**	**42**	**4**	**0**	**0**	**0**	**4**
1994-95	**St. Louis**	**NHL**	**1**	**0**	**0**	**0**	**0**	....	....	....	....	....
	Grenoble	France	UNAVAILABLE									
	NHL Totals		**144**	**16**	**25**	**41**	**101**	**19**	**2**	**0**	**2**	**31**

a QMJHL Second All-Star Team (1986)

Signed as a free agent by **St. Louis**, September 29, 1985.

BRADLEY, BRIAN T.B.

Center. Shoots right. 5'10", 177 lbs. Born, Kitchener, Ont., January 21, 1965.
(Calgary's 2nd choice, 51st overall, in 1983 Entry Draft).

			Regular Season					Playoffs				
Season	Club	Lea	GP	G	A	TP	PIM	GP	G	A	TP	PIM
1982-83	London	OHL	67	37	82	119	37	3	1	0	1	0
1983-84	London	OHL	49	40	60	100	24	4	2	4	6	0
1984-85	London	OHL	32	27	49	76	22	8	5	10	15	4
1985-86	**Calgary**	**NHL**	**5**	**0**	**1**	**1**	**0**	**1**	**0**	**0**	**0**	**0**
	Moncton	AHL	59	23	42	65	40	10	6	9	15	4
1986-87	**Calgary**	**NHL**	**40**	**10**	**18**	**28**	**16**	....	....	....	....	....
	Moncton	AHL	20	12	16	28	8	....	....	....	....	....
1987-88	Cdn. National	....	47	18	19	37	42	....	....	....	....	....
	Cdn. Olympic	....	7	0	4	4	0	....	....	....	....	....
	Vancouver	**NHL**	**11**	**3**	**5**	**8**	**6**	....	....	....	....	....
1988-89	**Vancouver**	**NHL**	**71**	**18**	**27**	**45**	**42**	**7**	**3**	**4**	**7**	**10**
1989-90	**Vancouver**	**NHL**	**67**	**19**	**29**	**48**	**65**	....	....	....	....	....
1990-91	**Vancouver**	**NHL**	**44**	**11**	**20**	**31**	**42**	....	....	....	....	....
	Toronto	**NHL**	**26**	**0**	**11**	**11**	**20**	....	....	....	....	....
1991-92	**Toronto**	**NHL**	**59**	**10**	**21**	**31**	**48**	....	....	....	....	....
1992-93	**Tampa Bay**	**NHL**	**80**	**42**	**44**	**86**	**92**	....	....	....	....	....
1993-94	**Tampa Bay**	**NHL**	**78**	**24**	**40**	**64**	**56**	....	....	....	....	....
1994-95	**Tampa Bay**	**NHL**	**46**	**13**	**27**	**40**	**42**	....	....	....	....	....
	NHL Totals		**527**	**150**	**243**	**393**	**429**	**8**	**3**	**4**	**7**	**10**

Played in NHL All-Star Game (1993, 1994)

Traded to **Vancouver** by **Calgary** with Peter Bakovic and Kevin Guy for Craig Coxe, March 6, 1988. Traded to **Toronto** by **Vancouver** for Tom Kurvers, January 12, 1991. Claimed by **Tampa Bay** from **Toronto** in Expansion Draft, June 18, 1992.

BRADLEY, E.J. PHI.

Center. Shoots left. 5'10", 182 lbs. Born, New Hyde Park, NY, January 2, 1975.
(Philadelphia's 9th choice, 226th overall, in 1993 Entry Draft).

			Regular Season					Playoffs				
Season	Club	Lea	GP	G	A	TP	PIM	GP	G	A	TP	PIM
1993-94	Tabor Aca.	HS	48	33	37	70	....	....	....	....	....	....
1994-95	U. Wisconsin	WCHA	40	3	4	7	22	....	....	....	....	....

BRADY, NEIL DAL.

Center. Shoots left. 6'2", 200 lbs. Born, Montreal, Que., April 12, 1968.
(New Jersey's 1st choice, 3rd overall, in 1986 Entry Draft).

			Regular Season					Playoffs				
Season	Club	Lea	GP	G	A	TP	PIM	GP	G	A	TP	PIM
1984-85	Calgary	Midget	37	25	50	75	75	....	....	....	....	....
	Medicine Hat	WHL	....	....	....	....	....	3	0	0	0	2
1985-86	Medicine Hat	WHL	72	21	60	81	104	21	9	11	20	23
1986-87	Medicine Hat	WHL	57	19	64	83	126	18	1	4	5	25
1987-88	Medicine Hat	WHL	61	16	35	51	110	15	0	3	3	19
1988-89	Utica	AHL	75	16	21	37	56	4	0	3	3	0
1989-90	**New Jersey**	**NHL**	**19**	**1**	**4**	**5**	**13**	....	....	....	....	....
	Utica	AHL	38	10	13	23	21	5	0	1	1	10
1990-91	**New Jersey**	**NHL**	**3**	**0**	**0**	**0**	**0**	....	....	....	....	....
	Utica	AHL	77	33	63	96	91	....	....	....	....	....
1991-92	**New Jersey**	**NHL**	**7**	**1**	**0**	**1**	**4**	....	....	....	....	....
	Utica	AHL	33	12	30	42	28	....	....	....	....	....
1992-93	**Ottawa**	**NHL**	**55**	**7**	**17**	**24**	**57**	....	....	....	....	....
	New Haven	AHL	8	6	3	9	2	....	....	....	....	....
1993-94	Kalamazoo	IHL	43	10	16	26	188	5	1	1	2	10
	Dallas	**NHL**	**5**	**0**	**1**	**1**	**21**	....	....	....	....	....
1994-95	Kalamazoo	IHL	70	13	45	58	140	15	5	14	19	22
	NHL Totals		**89**	**9**	**22**	**31**	**95**	....	....	....	....	....

Traded to **Ottawa** by **New Jersey** for future considerations, September 3, 1992. Signed as a free agent by **Dallas**, December 3, 1993.

BRASHEAR, DONALD (bra-SHEER) MTL.

Left wing. Shoots left. 6'2", 220 lbs. Born, Bedford, IN, January 7, 1972.

			Regular Season					Playoffs				
Season	Club	Lea	GP	G	A	TP	PIM	GP	G	A	TP	PIM
1989-90	Longueuil	QMJHL	64	12	14	26	169	7	0	0	0	11
1990-91	Longueuil	QMJHL	68	12	26	38	195	8	0	3	3	33
1991-92	Verdun	QMJHL	65	18	24	42	283	18	4	2	6	98
1992-93	Fredericton	AHL	76	11	3	14	261	5	0	0	0	8
1993-94	**Montreal**	**NHL**	**14**	**2**	**2**	**4**	**34**	**2**	**0**	**0**	**0**	**0**
	Fredericton	AHL	62	38	28	66	250	....	....	....	....	....
1994-95	Fredericton	AHL	29	10	9	19	182	17	7	5	12	77
	Montreal	**NHL**	**20**	**1**	**1**	**2**	**63**	....	....	....	....	....
	NHL Totals		**34**	**3**	**3**	**6**	**97**	**2**	**0**	**0**	**0**	**0**

Signed as a free agent by **Montreal**, July 28, 1992.

BREEN, GEORGE EDM.

Right wing. Shoots right. 6'2", 200 lbs. Born, Webster, MA, August 3, 1973.
(Edmonton's 4th choice, 56th overall, in 1991 Entry Draft).

			Regular Season					Playoffs				
Season	Club	Lea	GP	G	A	TP	PIM	GP	G	A	TP	PIM
1991-92	Providence	H.E.	36	8	4	12	24	....	....	....	....	....
1992-93	Providence	H.E.	31	11	7	18	45	....	....	....	....	....
1993-94	Providence	H.E.	32	8	14	22	22	....	....	....	....	....
1994-95	Providence	H.E.	36	17	18	35	51	....	....	....	....	....

BREKKE, BRENT — COL.

Defense. Shoots left. 6'1", 175 lbs. Born, Minot, ND, August 16, 1971.
(Quebec's 9th choice, 188th overall, in 1991 Entry Draft).

			Regular Season					Playoffs				
Season	Club	Lea	GP	G	A	TP	PIM	GP	G	A	TP	PIM
1990-91	W. Michigan	CCHA	38	1	8	9	57	....	....	....	....	....
1991-92	W. Michigan	CCHA	36	1	10	11	68	....	....	....	....	....
1992-93	W. Michigan	CCHA	38	3	2	5	42	....	....	....	....	....
1993-94	W. Michigan	CCHA	39	4	25	29	76	....	....	....	....	....
1994-95	Cornwall	AHL	29	1	0	1	24	1	0	0	0	4
	Dayton	ECHL	24	1	7	8	31	....	....	....	....	....

BRENNAN, RICH — COL.

Defense. Shoots right. 6'2", 200 lbs. Born, Schenectady, NY, November 26, 1972.
(Quebec's 3rd choice, 46th overall, in 1991 Entry Draft).

			Regular Season					Playoffs				
Season	Club	Lea	GP	G	A	TP	PIM	GP	G	A	TP	PIM
1991-92	Boston U.	H.E.	30	4	13	17	50	....	....	....	....	....
1992-93	Boston U.	H.E.	40	9	11	20	68	....	....	....	....	....
1993-94ab	Boston U.	H.E.	41	8	27	35	82	....	....	....	....	....
1994-95	Boston U.	H.E.	31	5	22	27	56	....	....	....	....	....

a Hockey East First All-Star Team (1994)
b NCAA East Second All-American Team (1994)

BRICKLEY, ANDY

Left wing/Center. Shoots left. 5'11", 200 lbs. Born, Melrose, MA, August 9, 1961.
(Philadelphia's 10th choice, 210th overall, in 1980 Entry Draft).

			Regular Season					Playoffs				
Season	Club	Lea	GP	G	A	TP	PIM	GP	G	A	TP	PIM
1979-80	N. Hampshire	ECAC	27	15	17	32	8	....	....	....	....	....
1980-81	N. Hampshire	ECAC	31	27	25	52	16	....	....	....	....	....
1981-82ab	N. Hampshire	ECAC	35	26	27	53	6	....	....	....	....	....
1982-83	**Philadelphia**	**NHL**	**3**	**1**	**1**	**2**	**0**	....	....	....	....	....
c	Maine	AHL	76	29	54	83	10	17	9	5	14	0
1983-84	Springfield	AHL	7	1	5	6	2	....	....	....	....	....
	Pittsburgh	**NHL**	**50**	**18**	**20**	**38**	**9**	....	....	....	....	....
	Baltimore	AHL	4	0	5	5	2	....	....	....	....	....
1984-85	**Pittsburgh**	**NHL**	**45**	**7**	**15**	**22**	**10**	....	....	....	....	....
	Baltimore	AHL	31	13	14	27	8	15	*10	8	18	0
1985-86	Maine	AHL	60	26	34	60	20	5	0	4	4	0
1986-87	**New Jersey**	**NHL**	**51**	**11**	**12**	**23**	**8**	....	....	....	....	....
1987-88	**New Jersey**	**NHL**	**45**	**8**	**14**	**22**	**14**	**4**	**0**	**1**	**1**	**4**
	Utica	AHL	9	5	8	13	4	....	....	....	....	....
1988-89	**Boston**	**NHL**	**71**	**13**	**22**	**35**	**20**	**10**	**0**	**2**	**2**	**0**
1989-90	**Boston**	**NHL**	**43**	**12**	**28**	**40**	**8**	**2**	**0**	**0**	**0**	**0**
1990-91	**Boston**	**NHL**	**40**	**2**	**9**	**11**	**8**	....	....	....	....	....
	Maine	AHL	17	8	17	25	2	1	0	0	0	0
1991-92	**Boston**	**NHL**	**23**	**10**	**17**	**27**	**2**	....	....	....	....	....
	Maine	AHL	14	5	15	20	2	....	....	....	....	....
1992-93	**Winnipeg**	**NHL**	**12**	**0**	**2**	**2**	**2**	**1**	**1**	**1**	**2**	**0**
	Moncton	AHL	38	15	36	51	10	5	4	2	6	0
1993-94	**Winnipeg**	**NHL**	**2**	**0**	**0**	**0**	**0**	....	....	....	....	....
	Moncton	AHL	53	20	39	59	20	19	8	*19	*27	4
1994-95	Denver	IHL	58	15	35	50	16	16	5	*25	*30	2
	NHL Totals		**385**	**82**	**140**	**222**	**81**	**17**	**1**	**4**	**5**	**4**

a ECAC First All-Star Team (1982)
b NCAA All-American Team (1982)
c AHL Second All-Star Team (1983)

Traded to **Pittsburgh** by **Philadelphia** with Mark Taylor, Ron Flockhart, Philadelphia's first round (Roger Belanger) and third round (later traded to Vancouver — Vancouver selected Mike Stevens) choices in 1984 Entry Draft for Rich Sutter and Pittsburgh's second round (Greg Smyth) and third round (David McLay) choices in 1984 Entry Draft, October 23, 1983. Signed as a free agent by **New Jersey**, July 8, 1986. Claimed by **Boston** from **New Jersey** in NHL Waiver Draft, October 3, 1988. Signed as a free agent by **Winnipeg**, November 11, 1992. Signed as a free agent by **NY Islanders**, July 27, 1994.

BRIERLEY, DAN — NYR

Defense. Shoots left. 6'2", 185 lbs. Born, Nashua, NH, January 23, 1974.
(NY Rangers' 9th choice, 216th overall, in 1992 Entry Draft).

			Regular Season					Playoffs				
Season	Club	Lea	GP	G	A	TP	PIM	GP	G	A	TP	PIM
1992-93	Yale	ECAC	29	0	7	7	32	....	....	....	....	....
1993-94	Yale	ECAC	27	3	7	10	60	....	....	....	....	....
1994-95	Yale	ECAC	26	5	8	13	44	....	....	....	....	....

BRIMANIS, ARIS — PHI.

Defense. Shoots right. 6'3", 210 lbs. Born, Cleveland, OH, March 14, 1972.
(Philadelphia's 4th choice, 86th overall, in 1991 Entry Draft).

			Regular Season					Playoffs				
Season	Club	Lea	GP	G	A	TP	PIM	GP	G	A	TP	PIM
1990-91	Bowling Green	CCHA	38	3	6	9	42	....	....	....	....	....
1991-92	Bowling Green	CCHA	32	2	9	11	38	....	....	....	....	....
1992-93	Brandon	WHL	71	8	50	58	110	4	2	1	3	7
1993-94	**Philadelphia**	**NHL**	**1**	**0**	**0**	**0**	**0**	....	....	....	....	....
	Hershey	AHL	75	8	15	23	65	11	2	3	5	12
1994-95	Hershey	AHL	76	8	17	25	68	6	1	1	2	14
	NHL Totals		**1**	**0**	**0**	**0**	**0**	....	....	....	....	....

BRIND'AMOUR, ROD — (BRIHND-uh-MOHR) PHI.

Center. Shoots left. 6'1", 202 lbs. Born, Ottawa, Ont., August 9, 1970.
(St. Louis' 1st choice, 9th overall, in 1988 Entry Draft).

			Regular Season					Playoffs				
Season	Club	Lea	GP	G	A	TP	PIM	GP	G	A	TP	PIM
1988-89	Michigan State	CCHA	42	27	32	59	63	....	....	....	....	....
	St. Louis	**NHL**	....	....	....	....	....	**5**	**2**	**0**	**2**	**4**
1989-90a	**St. Louis**	**NHL**	**79**	**26**	**35**	**61**	**46**	**12**	**5**	**8**	**13**	**6**
1990-91	**St. Louis**	**NHL**	**78**	**17**	**32**	**49**	**93**	**13**	**2**	**5**	**7**	**10**
1991-92	**Philadelphia**	**NHL**	**80**	**33**	**44**	**77**	**100**	....	....	....	....	....
1992-93	**Philadelphia**	**NHL**	**81**	**37**	**49**	**86**	**89**	....	....	....	....	....
1993-94	**Philadelphia**	**NHL**	**84**	**35**	**62**	**97**	**85**	....	....	....	....	....
1994-95	**Philadelphia**	**NHL**	**48**	**12**	**27**	**39**	**33**	**15**	**6**	**9**	**15**	**8**
	NHL Totals		**450**	**160**	**249**	**409**	**446**	**45**	**15**	**22**	**37**	**28**

a NHL All-Rookie Team (1990)

Played in NHL All-Star Game (1992)

Traded to **Philadelphia** by **St. Louis** with Dan Quinn for Ron Sutter and Murray Baron, September 22, 1991.

BRISEBOIS, PATRICE — (BREES-bwah, pa-TREEZ) MTL.

Defense. Shoots right. 6'1", 188 lbs. Born, Montreal, Que., January 27, 1971.
(Montreal's 2nd choice, 30th overall, in 1989 Entry Draft).

			Regular Season					Playoffs				
Season	Club	Lea	GP	G	A	TP	PIM	GP	G	A	TP	PIM
1987-88	Laval	QMJHL	48	10	34	44	95	6	0	2	2	2
1988-89	Laval	QMJHL	50	20	45	65	95	17	8	14	22	45
1989-90a	Laval	QMJHL	56	18	70	88	108	13	7	9	16	26
1990-91	**Montreal**	**NHL**	**10**	**0**	**2**	**2**	**4**	....	....	....	....	....
bcd	Drummondville	QMJHL	54	17	44	61	72	14	6	18	24	49
1991-92	**Montreal**	**NHL**	**26**	**2**	**8**	**10**	**20**	**11**	**2**	**4**	**6**	**6**
	Fredericton	AHL	53	12	27	39	51	....	....	....	....	....
1992-93	**Montreal**	**NHL**	**70**	**10**	**21**	**31**	**79**	**20**	**0**	**4**	**4**	**18**
1993-94	**Montreal**	**NHL**	**53**	**2**	**21**	**23**	**63**	**7**	**0**	**4**	**4**	**6**
1994-95	**Montreal**	**NHL**	**35**	**4**	**8**	**12**	**26**	....	....	....	....	....
	NHL Totals		**194**	**18**	**60**	**78**	**192**	**38**	**2**	**12**	**14**	**30**

a QMJHL Second All-Star Team (1990)
b Canadian Major Junior Defenseman of the Year (1991)
c QMJHL First All-Star Team (1991)
d Memorial Cup All-Star Team (1991)

BRISKE, BYRON — ANA.

Defense. Shoots right. 6'2", 194 lbs. Born, Humboldt, Sask., January 23, 1976.
(Anaheim's 4th choice, 80th overall, in 1994 Entry Draft).

			Regular Season					Playoffs				
Season	Club	Lea	GP	G	A	TP	PIM	GP	G	A	TP	PIM
1992-93	Victoria	WHL	66	1	10	11	110	....	....	....	....	....
1993-94	Red Deer	WHL	61	6	21	27	174	....	....	....	....	....
1994-95	Red Deer	WHL	48	4	17	21	116	....	....	....	....	....
	Tri-City	WHL	15	0	1	1	22	13	0	0	0	18

BROS, MICHAL — S.J.

Center. Shoots right. 6'1", 195 lbs. Born, Olomouc, Czech., January 25, 1976.
(San Jose's 6th choice, 130th overall, in 1995 Entry Draft).

			Regular Season					Playoffs				
Season	Club	Lea	GP	G	A	TP	PIM	GP	G	A	TP	PIM
1994-95	Olomouc	Czech. Jr.	34	29	32	61	....	....	....	....	....	....

BROSSEAU, DAVID — NYR

Center. Shoots right. 6'2", 189 lbs. Born, Montreal, Que., January 16, 1976.
(NY Rangers' 8th choice, 156th overall, in 1994 Entry Draft).

			Regular Season					Playoffs				
Season	Club	Lea	GP	G	A	TP	PIM	GP	G	A	TP	PIM
1992-93	Shawinigan	QMJHL	56	5	4	9	28	....	....	....	....	....
1993-94	Shawinigan	QMJHL	65	27	26	53	62	5	3	0	3	2
1994-95	Shawinigan	QMJHL	39	28	20	48	65	....	....	....	....	....
	Granby	QMJHL	26	9	6	15	37	13	2	2	4	4

BROTEN, NEAL — (BRAH-tuhn) N.J.

Center. Shoots left. 5'9", 175 lbs. Born, Roseau, MN, November 29, 1959.
(Minnesota's 3rd choice, 42nd overall, in 1979 Entry Draft).

			Regular Season					Playoffs				
Season	Club	Lea	GP	G	A	TP	PIM	GP	G	A	TP	PIM
1978-79	U. Minnesota	WCHA	40	21	50	71	18	....	....	....	....	....
1979-80	U.S. National	....	55	25	30	55	20	....	....	....	....	....
	U.S. Olympic	....	7	2	1	3	2	....	....	....	....	....
1980-81ab	U. Minnesota	WCHA	36	17	54	71	56	....	....	....	....	....
	Minnesota	**NHL**	**3**	**2**	**0**	**2**	**12**	**19**	**1**	**7**	**8**	**9**
1981-82	**Minnesota**	**NHL**	**73**	**38**	**60**	**98**	**42**	**4**	**0**	**2**	**2**	**0**
1982-83	**Minnesota**	**NHL**	**79**	**32**	**45**	**77**	**43**	**9**	**1**	**6**	**7**	**10**
1983-84	**Minnesota**	**NHL**	**76**	**28**	**61**	**89**	**43**	**16**	**5**	**5**	**10**	**4**
1984-85	**Minnesota**	**NHL**	**80**	**19**	**37**	**56**	**39**	**9**	**2**	**5**	**7**	**10**
1985-86	**Minnesota**	**NHL**	**80**	**29**	**76**	**105**	**47**	**5**	**3**	**2**	**5**	**2**
1986-87	**Minnesota**	**NHL**	**46**	**18**	**35**	**53**	**33**	....	....	....	....	....
1987-88	**Minnesota**	**NHL**	**54**	**9**	**30**	**39**	**32**	....	....	....	....	....
1988-89	**Minnesota**	**NHL**	**68**	**18**	**38**	**56**	**57**	**5**	**2**	**2**	**4**	**4**
1989-90	**Minnesota**	**NHL**	**80**	**23**	**62**	**85**	**45**	**7**	**2**	**2**	**4**	**18**
1990-91	**Minnesota**	**NHL**	**79**	**13**	**56**	**69**	**26**	**23**	**9**	**13**	**22**	**6**
1991-92	Preussen	Ger.	8	3	5	8	2	....	....	....	....	....
	Minnesota	**NHL**	**76**	**8**	**26**	**34**	**16**	**7**	**1**	**5**	**6**	**2**
1992-93	**Minnesota**	**NHL**	**82**	**12**	**21**	**33**	**22**	....	....	....	....	....
1993-94	**Dallas**	**NHL**	**79**	**17**	**35**	**52**	**62**	**9**	**2**	**1**	**3**	**6**
1994-95	**Dallas**	**NHL**	**17**	**0**	**4**	**4**	**4**	....	....	....	....	....
	New Jersey	**NHL**	**30**	**8**	**20**	**28**	**20**	**20**	**7**	**12**	**19**	**6**
	NHL Totals		**1002**	**274**	**606**	**880**	**543**	**133**	**35**	**62**	**97**	**77**

a WCHA First All-Star Team (1981)
b Won Hobey Baker Memorial Award (Top U.S. Collegiate Player) (1981)

Played in NHL All-Star Game (1983-86)

Traded to **New Jersey** by **Dallas** for Corey Millen, February 27, 1995.

BROTEN, PAUL — (BRAH-tuhn) DAL.

Right wing. Shoots right. 5'11", 188 lbs. Born, Roseau, MN, October 27, 1965.
(NY Rangers' 3rd choice, 77th overall, in 1984 Entry Draft).

			Regular Season					Playoffs				
Season	Club	Lea	GP	G	A	TP	PIM	GP	G	A	TP	PIM
1984-85	U. Minnesota	WCHA	44	8	8	16	26	....	....	....	....	....
1985-86	U. Minnesota	WCHA	38	6	16	22	24	....	....	....	....	....
1986-87	U. Minnesota	WCHA	48	17	22	39	52	....	....	....	....	....
1987-88	U. Minnesota	WCHA	38	18	21	39	42	....	....	....	....	....
1988-89	Denver	IHL	77	28	31	59	133	4	0	2	2	6
1989-90	**NY Rangers**	**NHL**	**32**	**5**	**3**	**8**	**26**	**6**	**1**	**1**	**2**	**2**
	Flint	IHL	28	17	9	26	55	....	....	....	....	....
1990-91	**NY Rangers**	**NHL**	**28**	**4**	**6**	**10**	**18**	**5**	**0**	**0**	**0**	**2**
	Binghamton	AHL	8	2	2	4	4	....	....	....	....	....
1991-92	**NY Rangers**	**NHL**	**74**	**13**	**15**	**28**	**102**	**13**	**1**	**2**	**3**	**10**
1992-93	**NY Rangers**	**NHL**	**60**	**5**	**9**	**14**	**48**	....	....	....	....	....
1993-94	**Dallas**	**NHL**	**64**	**12**	**12**	**24**	**30**	**9**	**1**	**1**	**2**	**2**
1994-95	**Dallas**	**NHL**	**47**	**7**	**9**	**16**	**36**	**5**	**1**	**2**	**3**	**2**
	NHL Totals		**305**	**46**	**54**	**100**	**260**	**38**	**4**	**6**	**10**	**18**

Claimed by **Dallas** from **NY Rangers** in NHL Waiver Draft, October 3, 1993.

BROUSSEAU, PAUL — COL.

Right wing. Shoots right. 6'2", 203 lbs. Born, Pierrefonds, Que., September 18, 1973.
(Quebec's 2nd choice, 28th overall, in 1992 Entry Draft).

			Regular Season					Playoffs				
Season	Club	Lea	GP	G	A	TP	PIM	GP	G	A	TP	PIM
1989-90	Chicoutimi	QMJHL	57	17	24	41	32	7	0	3	3	0
1990-91	Trois-Rivières	QMJHL	67	30	66	96	48	6	3	2	5	2
1991-92	Hull	QMJHL	57	35	61	96	54	6	3	5	8	10
1992-93	Hull	QMJHL	59	27	48	75	49	10	7	8	15	6
1993-94	Cornwall	AHL	69	18	26	44	35	1	0	0	0	0
1994-95	Cornwall	AHL	57	19	17	36	29	7	2	1	3	10

BROWN, BRAD — MTL.

Defense. Shoots right. 6'3", 218 lbs. Born, Baie Verte, Nfld., December 27, 1975.
(Montreal's 1st choice, 18th overall, in 1994 Entry Draft).

			Regular Season					Playoffs				
Season	Club	Lea	GP	G	A	TP	PIM	GP	G	A	TP	PIM
1991-92	North Bay	OHL	49	2	9	11	170	18	0	6	6	43
1992-93	North Bay	OHL	61	4	9	13	228	2	0	2	2	13
1993-94	North Bay	OHL	66	8	24	32	196	18	3	12	15	33
1994-95	North Bay	OHL	64	8	38	46	172	6	1	4	5	8

BROWN, CURTIS — BUF.

Center. Shoots left. 6', 182 lbs. Born, Unity, Sask., February 12, 1976.
(Buffalo's 2nd choice, 43rd overall, in 1994 Entry Draft).

			Regular Season					Playoffs				
Season	Club	Lea	GP	G	A	TP	PIM	GP	G	A	TP	PIM
1992-93	Moose Jaw	WHL	71	13	16	29	30	....	....	....	....	....
1993-94	Moose Jaw	WHL	72	27	38	65	82	....	....	....	....	....
1994-95a	Moose Jaw	WHL	70	51	53	104	63	10	8	7	15	20
	Buffalo	**NHL**	**1**	**1**	**1**	**2**	**2**	....	....	....	....	....
	NHL Totals		**1**	**1**	**1**	**2**	**2**	....	....	....	....	....

a WHL East First All-Star Team (1995)

BROWN, DAVID — S.J.

Right wing. Shoots right. 6'5", 222 lbs. Born, Saskatoon, Sask., October 12, 1962.
(Philadelphia's 7th choice, 140th overall, in 1982 Entry Draft).

			Regular Season					Playoffs				
Season	Club	Lea	GP	G	A	TP	PIM	GP	G	A	TP	PIM
1980-81	Spokane	WHL	9	2	2	4	21	....	....	....	....	....
1981-82	Saskatoon	WHL	62	11	33	44	344	5	1	0	1	4
1982-83	**Philadelphia**	**NHL**	**2**	**0**	**0**	**0**	**5**	....	....	....	....	....
	Maine	AHL	71	8	6	14	*418	16	0	0	0	*107
1983-84	**Philadelphia**	**NHL**	**19**	**1**	**5**	**6**	**98**	**2**	**0**	**0**	**0**	**12**
	Springfield	AHL	59	17	14	31	150	....	....	....	....	....
1984-85	**Philadelphia**	**NHL**	**57**	**3**	**6**	**9**	**165**	**11**	**0**	**0**	**0**	**59**
1985-86	**Philadelphia**	**NHL**	**76**	**10**	**7**	**17**	**277**	**5**	**0**	**0**	**0**	**16**
1986-87	**Philadelphia**	**NHL**	**62**	**7**	**3**	**10**	**274**	**26**	**1**	**2**	**3**	**59**
1987-88	**Philadelphia**	**NHL**	**47**	**12**	**5**	**17**	**114**	**7**	**1**	**0**	**1**	**27**
1988-89	**Philadelphia**	**NHL**	**50**	**0**	**3**	**3**	**100**	....	....	....	....	....
	Edmonton	**NHL**	**22**	**0**	**2**	**2**	**56**	**7**	**0**	**0**	**0**	**6**
1989-90	**Edmonton**	**NHL**	**60**	**0**	**6**	**6**	**145**	**3**	**0**	**0**	**0**	**0**
1990-91	**Edmonton**	**NHL**	**58**	**3**	**4**	**7**	**160**	**16**	**0**	**1**	**1**	**30**
1991-92	**Philadelphia**	**NHL**	**70**	**4**	**2**	**6**	**81**	....	....	....	....	....
1992-93	**Philadelphia**	**NHL**	**70**	**0**	**2**	**2**	**78**	....	....	....	....	....
1993-94	**Philadelphia**	**NHL**	**71**	**1**	**4**	**5**	**137**	....	....	....	....	....
1994-95	**Philadelphia**	**NHL**	**28**	**1**	**2**	**3**	**53**	**3**	**0**	**0**	**0**	**0**
	NHL Totals		**692**	**42**	**51**	**93**	**1743**	**80**	**2**	**3**	**5**	**209**

Traded to **Edmonton** by **Philadelphia** for Keith Acton and Edmonton's fifth round choice (Dimitri Yushkevich) in 1991 Entry Draft, February 7, 1989. Traded to **Philadelphia** by **Edmonton** with Corey Foster and Jari Kurri for Craig Fisher, Scott Mellanby and Craig Berube, May 30, 1991. Signed as a free agent by **San Jose**, August 10, 1995.

BROWN, DOUG — DET.

Right wing. Shoots right. 5'10", 185 lbs. Born, Southborough, MA, June 12, 1964.

			Regular Season					Playoffs				
Season	Club	Lea	GP	G	A	TP	PIM	GP	G	A	TP	PIM
1982-83	Boston College	ECAC	22	9	8	17	0	....	....	....	....	....
1983-84	Boston College	ECAC	38	11	10	21	6	....	....	....	....	....
1984-85a	Boston College	H.E.	45	37	31	68	10	....	....	....	....	....
1985-86a	Boston College	H.E.	38	16	40	56	16	....	....	....	....	....
1986-87	**New Jersey**	**NHL**	**4**	**0**	**1**	**1**	**0**	....	....	....	....	....
	Maine	AHL	73	24	34	58	15	....	....	....	....	....
1987-88	**New Jersey**	**NHL**	**70**	**14**	**11**	**25**	**20**	**19**	**5**	**1**	**6**	**6**
	Utica	AHL	2	0	2	2	2	....	....	....	....	....
1988-89	**New Jersey**	**NHL**	**63**	**15**	**10**	**25**	**15**	....	....	....	....	....
	Utica	AHL	4	1	4	5	0	....	....	....	....	....
1989-90	**New Jersey**	**NHL**	**69**	**14**	**20**	**34**	**16**	**6**	**0**	**1**	**1**	**2**
1990-91	**New Jersey**	**NHL**	**58**	**14**	**16**	**30**	**4**	**7**	**2**	**2**	**4**	**2**
1991-92	**New Jersey**	**NHL**	**71**	**11**	**17**	**28**	**27**	....	....	....	....	....
1992-93	**New Jersey**	**NHL**	**15**	**0**	**5**	**5**	**2**	....	....	....	....	....
	Utica	AHL	25	11	17	28	8	....	....	....	....	....
1993-94	**Pittsburgh**	**NHL**	**77**	**18**	**37**	**55**	**18**	**6**	**0**	**0**	**0**	**2**
1994-95	**Detroit**	**NHL**	**45**	**9**	**12**	**21**	**16**	**18**	**4**	**8**	**12**	**2**
	NHL Totals		**472**	**95**	**129**	**224**	**118**	**56**	**11**	**12**	**23**	**14**

a Hockey East First All-Star Team (1985, 1986)

Signed as a free agent by **New Jersey**, August 6, 1986. Signed as a free agent by **Pittsburgh**, September 28, 1993. Claimed by **Detroit** from **Pittsburgh** in NHL Waiver Draft, January 18, 1995.

BROWN, GREG

Defense. Shoots right. 6', 185 lbs. Born, Hartford, CT, March 7, 1968.
(Buffalo's 2nd choice, 26th overall, in 1986 Entry Draft).

			Regular Season					Playoffs				
Season	Club	Lea	GP	G	A	TP	PIM	GP	G	A	TP	PIM
1986-87	Boston College	H.E.	37	10	27	37	22	....	....	....	....	....
1987-88	U.S. National	....	55	6	29	35	22	....	....	....	....	....
	U.S. Olympic	....	6	0	4	4	2	....	....	....	....	....
1988-89abc	Boston College	H.E.	40	9	34	43	24	....	....	....	....	....
1989-90abc	Boston College	H.E.	42	5	35	40	42	....	....	....	....	....
1990-91	**Buffalo**	**NHL**	**39**	**1**	**2**	**3**	**35**	....	....	....	....	....
	Rochester	AHL	31	6	17	23	16	14	1	4	5	8
1991-92	Rochester	AHL	56	8	30	38	25	16	1	5	6	4
	U.S. National	....	8	0	0	0	5	....	....	....	....	....
	U.S. Olympic	....	7	0	0	0	2	....	....	....	....	....
1992-93	**Buffalo**	**NHL**	**10**	**0**	**1**	**1**	**6**	....	....	....	....	....
	Rochester	AHL	61	11	38	49	46	16	3	8	11	14
1993-94	**Pittsburgh**	**NHL**	**36**	**3**	**8**	**11**	**28**	**6**	**0**	**1**	**1**	**4**
	San Diego	IHL	42	8	25	33	26	....	....	....	....	....
1994-95	Cleveland	IHL	28	5	14	19	22	....	....	....	....	....
	Winnipeg	**NHL**	**9**	**0**	**3**	**3**	**17**	....	....	....	....	....
	NHL Totals		**94**	**4**	**14**	**18**	**86**	**6**	**0**	**1**	**1**	**4**

a Hockey East First All-Star Team (1989, 1990)
b Hockey East Player of the Year (1989, 1990)
c NCAA East First All-American Team (1989, 1990)

Signed as a free agent by **Pittsburgh**, September 29, 1993. Traded to **Winnipeg** by **Pittsburgh** for a conditional eighth round choice in 1996 Entry Draft, April 7, 1995.

BROWN, JEFF — VAN.

Defense. Shoots right. 6'1", 204 lbs. Born, Ottawa, Ont., April 30, 1966.
(Quebec's 2nd choice, 36th overall, in 1984 Entry Draft).

			Regular Season					Playoffs				
Season	Club	Lea	GP	G	A	TP	PIM	GP	G	A	TP	PIM
1982-83	Sudbury	OHL	65	9	37	46	39	....	....	....	....	....
1983-84	Sudbury	OHL	68	17	60	77	39	....	....	....	....	....
1984-85	Sudbury	OHL	56	16	48	64	26	....	....	....	....	....
1985-86	**Quebec**	**NHL**	**8**	**3**	**2**	**5**	**6**	**1**	**0**	**0**	**0**	**0**
a	Sudbury	OHL	45	22	28	50	24	4	0	2	2	11
	Fredericton	AHL	....	....	....	....	....	1	0	1	1	0
1986-87	**Quebec**	**NHL**	**44**	**7**	**22**	**29**	**16**	**13**	**3**	**3**	**6**	**2**
	Fredericton	AHL	26	2	14	16	16	....	....	....	....	....
1987-88	**Quebec**	**NHL**	**78**	**16**	**36**	**52**	**64**	....	....	....	....	....
1988-89	**Quebec**	**NHL**	**78**	**21**	**47**	**68**	**62**	....	....	....	....	....
1989-90	**Quebec**	**NHL**	**29**	**6**	**10**	**16**	**18**	....	....	....	....	....
	St. Louis	**NHL**	**48**	**10**	**28**	**38**	**37**	**12**	**2**	**10**	**12**	**4**
1990-91	**St. Louis**	**NHL**	**67**	**12**	**47**	**59**	**39**	**13**	**3**	**9**	**12**	**6**
1991-92	**St. Louis**	**NHL**	**80**	**20**	**39**	**59**	**38**	**6**	**2**	**1**	**3**	**2**
1992-93	**St. Louis**	**NHL**	**71**	**25**	**53**	**78**	**58**	**11**	**3**	**8**	**11**	**6**
1993-94	**St. Louis**	**NHL**	**63**	**13**	**47**	**60**	**46**	....	....	....	....	....
	Vancouver	**NHL**	**11**	**1**	**5**	**6**	**10**	**24**	**6**	**9**	**15**	**37**
1994-95	**Vancouver**	**NHL**	**33**	**8**	**23**	**31**	**16**	**5**	**1**	**3**	**4**	**2**
	NHL Totals		**610**	**142**	**359**	**501**	**410**	**85**	**20**	**43**	**63**	**59**

a OHL First All-Star Team (1986)

Traded to **St Louis** by **Quebec** for Tony Hrkac and Greg Millen, December 13, 1989. Traded to **Vancouver** by **St. Louis** with Bret Hedican and Nathan Lafayette for Craign Janney, March 21, 1994.

BROWN, KEITH — FLA.

Defense. Shoots right. 6'1", 196 lbs. Born, Corner Brook, Nfld., May 6, 1960.
(Chicago's 1st choice, 7th overall, in 1979 Entry Draft).

			Regular Season					Playoffs				
Season	Club	Lea	GP	G	A	TP	PIM	GP	G	A	TP	PIM
1977-78	Portland	WHL	72	11	53	64	51	8	0	3	3	2
1978-79a	Portland	WHL	70	11	85	96	75	25	3	*30	33	21
1979-80	**Chicago**	**NHL**	**76**	**2**	**18**	**20**	**27**	**6**	**0**	**0**	**0**	**4**
1980-81	**Chicago**	**NHL**	**80**	**9**	**34**	**43**	**80**	**3**	**0**	**2**	**2**	**2**
1981-82	**Chicago**	**NHL**	**33**	**4**	**20**	**24**	**26**	**4**	**0**	**2**	**2**	**5**
1982-83	**Chicago**	**NHL**	**50**	**4**	**27**	**31**	**20**	**7**	**0**	**0**	**0**	**11**
1983-84	**Chicago**	**NHL**	**74**	**10**	**25**	**35**	**94**	**5**	**0**	**1**	**1**	**10**
1984-85	**Chicago**	**NHL**	**56**	**1**	**22**	**23**	**55**	**11**	**2**	**7**	**9**	**31**
1985-86	**Chicago**	**NHL**	**70**	**11**	**29**	**40**	**87**	**3**	**0**	**1**	**1**	**9**
1986-87	**Chicago**	**NHL**	**73**	**4**	**23**	**27**	**86**	**4**	**0**	**1**	**1**	**6**
1987-88	**Chicago**	**NHL**	**24**	**3**	**6**	**9**	**45**	**5**	**0**	**2**	**2**	**10**
1988-89	**Chicago**	**NHL**	**74**	**2**	**16**	**18**	**84**	**13**	**1**	**3**	**4**	**25**
1989-90	**Chicago**	**NHL**	**67**	**5**	**20**	**25**	**87**	**18**	**0**	**4**	**4**	**43**
1990-91	**Chicago**	**NHL**	**45**	**1**	**10**	**11**	**55**	**6**	**1**	**0**	**1**	**8**
1991-92	**Chicago**	**NHL**	**57**	**6**	**10**	**16**	**69**	**14**	**0**	**8**	**8**	**18**
1992-93	**Chicago**	**NHL**	**33**	**2**	**6**	**8**	**39**	**4**	**0**	**1**	**1**	**2**
1993-94	**Florida**	**NHL**	**51**	**4**	**8**	**12**	**60**	....	....	....	....	....
1994-95	**Florida**	**NHL**	**13**	**0**	**0**	**0**	**2**	....	....	....	....	....
	NHL Totals		**876**	**68**	**274**	**342**	**916**	**103**	**4**	**32**	**36**	**184**

a WHL First All-Star Team (1979)

Traded to **Florida** by **Chicago** for Darin Kimble, September 30, 1993.

BROWN, KEVIN — L.A.

Right wing. Shoots right. 6'1", 212 lbs. Born, Birmingham, England, May 11, 1974.
(Los Angeles' 3rd choice, 87th overall, in 1992 Entry Draft).

			Regular Season					Playoffs				
Season	Club	Lea	GP	G	A	TP	PIM	GP	G	A	TP	PIM
1991-92	Belleville	OHL	66	24	24	48	52	5	1	4	5	8
1992-93a	Belleville	OHL	6	2	5	7	4	....	....	....	....	....
	Detroit	OHL	56	48	86	134	76	15	10	18	28	18
1993-94bc	Detroit	OHL	57	54	81	135	85	17	14	*26	*40	28
1994-95	Phoenix	IHL	48	19	31	50	64	....	....	....	....	....
	Los Angeles	**NHL**	**23**	**2**	**3**	**5**	**18**	....	....	....	....	....
	NHL Totals		**23**	**2**	**3**	**5**	**18**	....	....	....	....	....

a OHL Second All-Star Team (1993)
b OHL First All-Star Team (1994)
c Canadian Major Junior Second All-Star Team (1994)

BROWN, ROB

Right wing. Shoots left. 5'11", 185 lbs.   Born, Kingston, Ont., April 10, 1968.
(Pittsburgh's 4th choice, 67th overall, in 1986 Entry Draft).

			Regular Season					Playoffs				
Season	Club	Lea	GP	G	A	TP	PIM	GP	G	A	TP	PIM
1984-85	Kamloops	WHL	60	29	50	79	95	15	8	8	26	28
1985-86a	Kamloops	WHL	69	58	*115	*173	171	16	*18	*28	*46	14
1986-87ab	Kamloops	WHL	63	*76	*136	*212	101	5	6	5	11	6
1987-88	Pittsburgh	NHL	51	24	20	44	56	....	....	....	....	....
1988-89	Pittsburgh	NHL	68	49	66	115	118	11	5	3	8	22
1989-90	Pittsburgh	NHL	80	33	47	80	102	....	....	....	....	....
1990-91	Pittsburgh	NHL	25	6	10	16	31	....	....	....	....	....
	Hartford	NHL	44	18	24	42	101	5	1	0	1	7
1991-92	Hartford	NHL	42	16	15	31	39	....	....	....	....	....
	Chicago	NHL	25	5	11	16	34	8	2	4	6	4
1992-93	Chicago	NHL	15	1	6	7	33	....	....	....	....	....
	Indianapolis	IHL	19	14	19	33	32	2	0	1	1	2
1993-94	Dallas	NHL	1	0	0	0	0	....	....	....	....	....
cde	Kalamazoo	IHL	79	42	*113	*155	188	5	1	3	4	6
1994-95f	Phoenix	IHL	69	34	73	107	135	9	4	12	16	0
	Los Angeles	NHL	2	0	0	0	0	....	....	....	....	....
	NHL Totals		353	152	199	351	514	24	8	7	15	33

a WHL First All-Star Team (1986, 1987)
b Canadian Major Junior Player of the Year (1987)
c IHL First All-Star Team (1994)
d Won Leo P. Lamoureux Memorial Trophy (Top Scorer - IHL) (1994)
e Won James Gatschene Memorial Trophy (MVP - IHL) (1994)
f IHL Second All-Star Team (1995)

Played in NHL All-Star Game (1989)

Traded to **Hartford** by Pittsburgh for Scott Young, December 21, 1990. Traded to **Chicago** by **Hartford** for Steve Konroyd, January 24, 1992. Signed as a free agent by **Dallas**, August 12, 1993. Signed as a free agent by **Los Angeles**, June 14, 1994.

BROWN, SEAN   BOS.

Defense. Shoots left. 6'3", 196 lbs.   Born, Oshawa, Ont., November 5, 1976.
(Boston's 2nd choice, 21st overall, in 1995 Entry Draft).

			Regular Season					Playoffs				
Season	Club	Lea	GP	G	A	TP	PIM	GP	G	A	TP	PIM
1993-94	Belleville	OHL	28	1	2	3	53	8	0	0	0	17
1994-95	Belleville	OHL	58	2	16	18	200	16	4	2	6	*67

BRUCE, DAVID

Left wing. Shoots right. 5'11", 190 lbs.   Born, Thunder Bay, Ont., October 7, 1964.
(Vancouver's 2nd choice, 30th overall, in 1983 Entry Draft).

			Regular Season					Playoffs				
Season	Club	Lea	GP	G	A	TP	PIM	GP	G	A	TP	PIM
1982-83	Kitchener	OHL	67	36	35	71	199	12	7	9	16	27
1983-84	Kitchener	OHL	62	52	40	92	203	10	5	8	13	20
1984-85	Fredericton	AHL	56	14	11	25	104	5	0	0	0	37
1985-86	Vancouver	NHL	12	0	1	1	14	1	0	0	0	0
	Fredericton	AHL	66	25	16	41	151	2	0	1	1	12
1986-87	Vancouver	NHL	50	9	7	16	109	....	....	....	....	....
	Fredericton	AHL	17	7	6	13	73	....	....	....	....	....
1987-88	Vancouver	NHL	28	7	3	10	57	....	....	....	....	....
	Fredericton	AHL	30	27	18	45	115	....	....	....	....	....
1988-89	Vancouver	NHL	53	7	7	14	65	....	....	....	....	....
1989-90a	Milwaukee	IHL	68	40	35	75	148	6	5	3	8	0
1990-91	St. Louis	NHL	12	1	2	3	14	2	0	0	0	2
ab	Peoria	IHL	60	*64	52	116	78	18	*18	11	*29	40
1991-92	San Jose	NHL	60	22	16	38	46	....	....	....	....	....
	Kansas City	IHL	7	5	5	10	6	....	....	....	....	....
1992-93	San Jose	NHL	17	2	3	5	33	....	....	....	....	....
1993-94	San Jose	NHL	2	0	0	0	0	....	....	....	....	....
	Kansas City	IHL	72	40	24	64	115	....	....	....	....	....
1994-95	Kansas City	IHL	63	33	25	58	80	....	....	....	....	....
	NHL Totals		234	48	39	87	338	3	0	0	0	2

a IHL First All-Star Team (1990, 1991)
b Won James Gatschene Memorial Trophy (MVP - IHL) (1991)

Signed as a free agent by **St. Louis**, July 6, 1990. Claimed by **San Jose** from **St. Louis** in Expansion Draft, May 30, 1991.

BRULE, STEVE   (broo-LAY)   N.J.

Center. Shoots right. 5'11", 185 lbs.   Born, Montreal, Que., January 15, 1975.
(New Jersey's 6th choice, 143rd overall, in 1993 Entry Draft).

			Regular Season					Playoffs				
Season	Club	Lea	GP	G	A	TP	PIM	GP	G	A	TP	PIM
1992-93	St-Jean	QMJHL	70	33	47	80	46	4	0	0	0	9
1993-94	St-Jean	QMJHL	66	41	64	105	46	5	2	1	3	0
1994-95a	St-Jean	QMJHL	69	44	64	108	42	7	3	4	7	8
	Albany	AHL	3	1	4	5	0	14	9	5	14	4

a QMJHL Second All-Star Team (1995)

BRUNET, BENOIT   (broo-NAY, BEHN-wah)   MTL.

Left wing. Shoots left. 5'11", 195 lbs.   Born, Pointe-Claire, Que., August 24, 1968.
(Montreal's 2nd choice, 27th overall, in 1986 Entry Draft).

			Regular Season					Playoffs				
Season	Club	Lea	GP	G	A	TP	PIM	GP	G	A	TP	PIM
1985-86	Hull	QMJHL	71	33	37	70	81	....	....	....	....	....
1986-87a	Hull	QMJHL	60	43	67	110	105	6	7	5	12	8
1987-88	Hull	QMJHL	62	54	89	143	131	10	3	10	13	11
1988-89	Montreal	NHL	2	0	1	1	0	....	....	....	....	....
b	Sherbrooke	AHL	73	41	76	117	95	6	2	0	2	4
1989-90	Sherbrooke	AHL	72	32	35	67	82	12	8	7	15	20
1990-91	Montreal	NHL	17	1	3	4	0	....	....	....	....	....
	Fredericton	AHL	24	13	18	31	16	6	5	6	11	2
1991-92	Montreal	NHL	18	4	6	10	14	....	....	....	....	....
	Fredericton	AHL	6	7	9	16	27	....	....	....	....	....
1992-93	Montreal	NHL	47	10	15	25	19	20	2	8	10	8
1993-94	Montreal	NHL	71	10	20	30	20	7	1	4	5	16
1994-95	Montreal	NHL	45	7	18	25	16	....	....	....	....	....
	NHL Totals		200	32	63	95	69	27	3	12	15	24

a QMJHL Second All-Star Team (1987)
b AHL First All-Star Team (1989)

BRUNETTE, ANDREW

Left wing. Shoots left. 6', 212 lbs.   Born, Sudbury, Ont., August 24, 1973.
(Washington's 6th choice, 174th overall, in 1993 Entry Draft).

			Regular Season					Playoffs				
Season	Club	Lea	GP	G	A	TP	PIM	GP	G	A	TP	PIM
1990-91	Owen Sound	OHL	63	15	20	35	15	....	....	....	....	....
1991-92	Owen Sound	OHL	66	51	47	98	42	5	5	0	5	8
1992-93ab	Owen Sound	OHL	66	*62	*100	*162	91	8	8	6	14	16
1993-94	Portland	AHL	23	9	11	20	10	2	0	1	1	0
	Hampton	ECHL	20	12	18	30	32	7	7	6	13	18
1994-95c	Portland	AHL	79	30	50	80	53	7	3	3	6	10

a OHL First All-Star Team (1993)
b Canadian Major Junior Second All-Star Team (1993)
c AHL Second All-Star Team (1995)

BRYLIN, SERGEI   (BRIH-lin)   N.J.

Center. Shoots left. 5'9", 175 lbs.   Born, Moscow, USSR, January 13, 1974.
(New Jersey's 2nd choice, 42nd overall, in 1992 Entry Draft).

			Regular Season					Playoffs				
Season	Club	Lea	GP	G	A	TP	PIM	GP	G	A	TP	PIM
1991-92	CSKA	CIS	44	1	6	7	4	....	....	....	....	....
1992-93	CSKA	CIS	42	5	4	9	36	....	....	....	....	....
1993-94	CSKA	CIS	39	4	6	10	36	3	1	0	1	2
	Russian Pen's	IHL	13	4	5	9	18	....	....	....	....	....
1994-95	Albany	AHL	63	19	35	54	78	....	....	....	....	....
	New Jersey	NHL	26	6	8	14	8	12	1	2	3	4
	NHL Totals		26	6	8	14	8	12	1	2	3	4

BUCHANAN, JEFF   CHI.

Defense. Shoots right. 5'10", 165 lbs.   Born, Swift Current, Sask., May 23, 1971.

			Regular Season					Playoffs				
Season	Club	Lea	GP	G	A	TP	PIM	GP	G	A	TP	PIM
1989-90	Saskatoon	WHL	66	7	12	19	96	9	0	2	2	2
1990-91	Saskatoon	WHL	69	10	26	36	123	....	....	....	....	....
1991-92	Saskatoon	WHL	72	17	37	54	145	22	10	14	24	39
1992-93	Atlanta	IHL	68	4	18	22	282	9	0	0	0	26
1993-94	Atlanta	IHL	76	5	24	29	253	14	0	1	1	20
1994-95	Atlanta	IHL	4	0	1	1	9	....	....	....	....	....
	Indianapolis	IHL	25	3	9	12	63	....	....	....	....	....

Signed as a free agent by **Tampa Bay**, July 13, 1992. Traded to **Chicago** by **Tampa Bay** with Jim Cummins and Tom Tilley for Paul Ysebaert and Rich Sutter, February 22, 1995.

BUCHBERGER, KELLY   (BUK-buhr-guhr)   EDM.

Left wing. Shoots left. 6'2", 200 lbs.   Born, Langenburg, Sask., December 2, 1966.
(Edmonton's 8th choice, 188th overall, in 1985 Entry Draft).

			Regular Season					Playoffs				
Season	Club	Lea	GP	G	A	TP	PIM	GP	G	A	TP	PIM
1984-85	Moose Jaw	WHL	51	12	17	29	114	....	....	....	....	....
1985-86	Moose Jaw	WHL	72	14	22	36	206	13	11	4	15	37
1986-87	Nova Scotia	AHL	70	12	20	32	257	5	0	1	1	23
	Edmonton	NHL	....	....	....	....	....	3	0	1	1	5
1987-88	Edmonton	NHL	19	1	0	1	81	....	....	....	....	....
	Nova Scotia	AHL	49	21	23	44	206	2	0	0	0	11
1988-89	Edmonton	NHL	66	5	9	14	234	....	....	....	....	....
1989-90	Edmonton	NHL	55	2	6	8	168	19	0	5	5	13
1990-91	Edmonton	NHL	64	3	1	4	160	12	2	1	3	25
1991-92	Edmonton	NHL	79	20	24	44	157	16	1	4	5	32
1992-93	Edmonton	NHL	83	12	18	30	133	....	....	....	....	....
1993-94	Edmonton	NHL	84	3	18	21	199	....	....	....	....	....
1994-95	Edmonton	NHL	48	7	17	24	82	....	....	....	....	....
	NHL Totals		498	53	93	146	1214	50	3	11	14	75

BUCKBERGER, ASHLEY   FLA.

Right wing. Shoots right. 6'2", 206 lbs.   Born, Esterhazy, Sask., February 19, 1975.
(Quebec's 3rd choice, 49th overall, in 1993 Entry Draft).

			Regular Season					Playoffs				
Season	Club	Lea	GP	G	A	TP	PIM	GP	G	A	TP	PIM
1991-92	Swift Current	WHL	67	23	22	45	38	8	2	1	3	2
1992-93	Swift Current	WHL	72	23	44	67	41	17	6	7	13	6
1993-94	Swift Current	WHL	67	42	45	87	42	7	0	1	1	6
1994-95	Swift Current	WHL	53	23	37	60	51	....	....	....	....	....
	Kamloops	WHL	21	9	13	22	13	19	7	11	18	22

Signed as a free agent by **Florida**, August 3, 1995.

BUCKLEY, TOM   HFD.

Center. Shoots left. 6'1", 204 lbs.   Born, Buffalo, NY, May 26, 1976.
(Hartford's 4th choice, 187th overall, in 1994 Entry Draft).

			Regular Season					Playoffs				
Season	Club	Lea	GP	G	A	TP	PIM	GP	G	A	TP	PIM
1993-94	St. Joseph	HS	17	17	18	35	40	....	....	....	....	....
1994-95	Detroit	OHL	64	30	36	66	49	21	10	9	19	8

BUDAYEV, ALEXEI   WPG.

Center. Shoots right. 6'2", 183 lbs.   Born, Pavlov Posad, USSR, April 24, 1975.
(Winnipeg's 3rd choice, 43rd overall, in 1993 Entry Draft).

			Regular Season					Playoffs				
Season	Club	Lea	GP	G	A	TP	PIM	GP	G	A	TP	PIM
1993-94	Elektrostal	CIS 2	46	6	5	11	26	....	....	....	....	....
1994-95	Elektrostal	CIS	25	2	1	3	12	....	....	....	....	....
	Red Deer	WHL	30	15	12	27	6	....	....	....	....	....

BURE, PAVEL (boo-RAY) VAN.

Right wing. Shoots left. 5'10", 189 lbs. Born, Moscow, USSR, March 31, 1971.
(Vancouver's 4th choice, 113th overall, in 1989 Entry Draft).

			Regular Season					Playoffs				
Season	Club	Lea	GP	G	A	TP	PIM	GP	G	A	TP	PIM
1987-88	CSKA	USSR	5	1	1	2	0	....	....	....	....	....
1988-89a	CSKA	USSR	32	17	9	26	8	....	....	....	....	....
1989-90	CSKA	USSR	46	14	10	24	20	....	....	....	....	....
1990-91	CSKA	USSR	44	35	11	46	24	....	....	....	....	....
1991-92b	Vancouver	NHL	65	34	26	60	30	13	6	4	10	14
1992-93	Vancouver	NHL	83	60	50	110	69	12	5	7	12	8
1993-94c	Vancouver	NHL	76	*60	47	107	86	24	*16	15	31	40
1994-95	Landshut	Ger.	1	3	0	3	2	....	....	....	....	....
	Spartak	CIS	1	2	0	2	2	....	....	....	....	....
	Vancouver	NHL	44	20	23	43	47	11	7	6	13	10
	NHL Totals		268	174	146	320	232	60	34	32	66	72

a Named Soviet National League Rookie-of-the-Year (1989)
b Won Calder Memorial Trophy (1992)
c NHL First All-Star Team (1994)

Played in NHL All-Star Game (1993, 1994)

BURE, VALERI (boo-RAY) MTL.

Right wing. Shoots right. 5'10", 168 lbs. Born, Moscow, USSR, June 13, 1974.
(Montreal's 2nd choice, 33rd overall, in 1992 Entry Draft).

			Regular Season					Playoffs				
Season	Club	Lea	GP	G	A	TP	PIM	GP	G	A	TP	PIM
1990-91	CSKA	USSR	3	0	0	0	0	....	....	....	....	....
1991-92	Spokane	WHL	53	27	22	49	78	10	11	6	17	10
1992-93a	Spokane	WHL	66	68	79	147	49	9	6	11	17	14
1993-94b	Spokane	WHL	59	40	62	102	48	3	5	3	8	2
1994-95	Fredericton	AHL	45	23	25	48	32	....	....	....	....	....
	Montreal	NHL	24	3	1	4	6	....	....	....	....	....
	NHL Totals		24	3	1	4	6	....	....	....	....	....

a WHL West First All-Star Team (1993)
b WHL West Second All-Star Team (1994)

BUREAU, MARC (BEWR-oh) MTL.

Center. Shoots right. 6'1", 198 lbs. Born, Trois-Rivières, Que., May 19, 1966.

			Regular Season					Playoffs				
Season	Club	Lea	GP	G	A	TP	PIM	GP	G	A	TP	PIM
1983-84	Chicoutimi	QMJHL	56	6	16	22	14	....	....	....	....	....
1984-85	Chicoutimi	QMJHL	41	30	25	55	15	....	....	....	....	....
	Granby	QMJHL	27	20	45	65	14	....	....	....	....	....
1985-86	Granby	QMJHL	19	6	17	23	36	....	....	....	....	....
	Chicoutimi	QMJHL	44	30	45	75	33	9	3	7	10	10
1986-87	Longueuil	QMJHL	66	54	58	112	68	20	17	20	37	12
1987-88	Salt Lake	IHL	69	7	20	27	86	7	0	3	3	8
1988-89	Salt Lake	IHL	76	28	36	64	119	14	7	5	12	31
1989-90	Calgary	NHL	5	0	0	0	4	....	....	....	....	....
a	Salt Lake	IHL	67	43	48	91	173	11	4	8	12	0
1990-91	Calgary	NHL	5	0	0	0	2	....	....	....	....	....
a	Salt Lake	IHL	54	40	48	88	101	....	....	....	....	....
	Minnesota	NHL	9	0	6	6	4	23	3	2	5	20
1991-92	Minnesota	NHL	46	6	4	10	50	5	0	0	0	14
	Kalamazoo	IHL	7	2	8	10	2	....	....	....	....	....
1992-93	Tampa Bay	NHL	63	10	21	31	111	....	....	....	....	....
1993-94	Tampa Bay	NHL	75	8	7	15	30	....	....	....	....	....
1994-95	Tampa Bay	NHL	48	2	12	14	30	....	....	....	....	....
	NHL Totals		251	26	50	76	231	28	3	2	5	34

a IHL Second All-Star Team (1990, 1991)

Signed as a free agent by **Calgary**, May 19, 1987. Traded to **Minnesota** by **Calgary** for Minnesota's third round choice (Sandy McCarthy) in 1991 Entry Draft, March 5, 1991. Claimed on waivers by **Tampa Bay** from **Minnesota**, October 16, 1992. Traded to **Montreal** by **Tampa Bay** for Brian Bellows, June 30, 1995.

BURR, SHAWN T.B.

Left wing/Center. Shoots left. 6'1", 195 lbs. Born, Sarnia, Ont., July 1, 1966.
(Detroit's 1st choice, 7th overall, in 1984 Entry Draft).

			Regular Season					Playoffs				
Season	Club	Lea	GP	G	A	TP	PIM	GP	G	A	TP	PIM
1983-84	Kitchener	OHL	68	41	44	85	50	16	5	12	17	22
1984-85	Detroit	NHL	9	0	0	0	2	....	....	....	....	....
	Adirondack	AHL	4	0	0	0	2	....	....	....	....	....
	Kitchener	OHL	48	24	42	66	50	4	3	3	6	2
1985-86	Detroit	NHL	5	1	0	1	4	....	....	....	....	....
	Adirondack	AHL	3	2	2	4	2	17	5	7	12	32
a	Kitchener	OHL	59	60	67	127	104	5	2	3	5	8
1986-87	Detroit	NHL	80	22	25	47	107	16	7	2	9	20
1987-88	Detroit	NHL	78	17	23	40	97	9	3	1	4	14
1988-89	Detroit	NHL	79	19	27	46	78	6	1	2	3	6
1989-90	Detroit	NHL	76	24	32	56	82	....	....	....	....	....
	Adirondack	AHL	3	4	2	6	2	....	....	....	....	....
1990-91	Detroit	NHL	80	20	30	50	112	7	0	4	4	15
1991-92	Detroit	NHL	79	19	32	51	118	11	1	5	6	10
1992-93	Detroit	NHL	80	10	25	35	74	7	2	1	3	2
1993-94	Detroit	NHL	51	10	12	22	31	7	2	0	2	6
1994-95	Detroit	NHL	42	6	8	14	60	16	0	2	2	6
	NHL Totals		659	148	214	362	765	79	16	17	33	79

a OHL Second All-Star Team (1986)

Traded to **Tampa Bay** by **Detroit** with Detroit's third round choice (later traded to Boston) in 1996 Entry Draft for Marc Bergevin for Shawn Burr, August 17, 1995.

BURRIDGE, RANDY

Left wing. Shoots left. 5'9", 185 lbs. Born, Fort Erie, Ont., January 7, 1966.
(Boston's 7th choice, 157th overall, in 1985 Entry Draft).

			Regular Season					Playoffs				
Season	Club	Lea	GP	G	A	TP	PIM	GP	G	A	TP	PIM
1983-84	Peterborough	OHL	55	6	7	13	44	8	3	2	5	7
1984-85	Peterborough	OHL	66	49	57	106	88	17	9	16	25	18
1985-86	Boston	NHL	52	17	25	42	28	3	0	4	4	12
	Peterborough	OHL	17	15	11	26	23	3	1	3	4	2
	Moncton	AHL	....	....	....	....	....	3	0	2	2	2
1986-87	Boston	NHL	23	1	4	5	16	2	1	0	1	2
	Moncton	AHL	47	26	41	67	139	3	1	2	3	30
1987-88	Boston	NHL	79	27	28	55	105	23	2	10	12	16
1988-89	Boston	NHL	80	31	30	61	39	10	5	2	7	6
1989-90	Boston	NHL	63	17	15	32	47	21	4	11	15	14
1990-91	Boston	NHL	62	15	13	28	40	19	0	3	3	39
1991-92	Washington	NHL	66	23	44	67	50	2	0	1	1	0
1992-93	Washington	NHL	4	0	0	0	0	4	1	0	1	0
	Baltimore	AHL	2	0	1	1	2	....	....	....	....	....
1993-94	Washington	NHL	78	25	17	42	73	11	0	2	2	12
1994-95	Washington	NHL	2	0	0	0	2	....	....	....	....	....
	Los Angeles	NHL	38	4	15	19	8	....	....	....	....	....
	NHL Totals		547	160	191	351	408	95	13	33	46	101

Played in NHL All-Star Game (1992)

Traded to **Washington** by **Boston** for Stephen Leach, June 21, 1991. Traded to **Los Angeles** by **Washington** for Warren Rychel, February 10, 1995.

BURT, ADAM HFD.

Defense. Shoots left. 6', 190 lbs. Born, Detroit, MI, January 15, 1969.
(Hartford's 2nd choice, 39th overall, in 1987 Entry Draft).

			Regular Season					Playoffs				
Season	Club	Lea	GP	G	A	TP	PIM	GP	G	A	TP	PIM
1985-86	North Bay	OHL	49	0	11	11	81	10	0	0	0	24
1986-87	North Bay	OHL	57	4	27	31	138	24	1	6	7	68
1987-88	Binghamton	AHL	....	....	....	....	....	2	1	1	2	0
a	North Bay	OHL	66	17	53	70	176	2	0	3	3	6
1988-89	Hartford	NHL	5	0	0	0	6	....	....	....	....	....
	Binghamton	AHL	5	0	2	2	13	....	....	....	....	....
	North Bay	OHL	23	4	11	15	45	12	2	12	14	12
1989-90	Hartford	NHL	63	4	8	12	105	2	0	0	0	0
1990-91	Hartford	NHL	42	2	7	9	63	....	....	....	....	....
	Springfield	AHL	9	1	3	4	22	....	....	....	....	....
1991-92	Hartford	NHL	66	9	15	24	93	2	0	0	0	0
1992-93	Hartford	NHL	65	6	14	20	116	....	....	....	....	....
1993-94	Hartford	NHL	63	1	17	18	75	....	....	....	....	....
1994-95	Hartford	NHL	46	7	11	18	65	....	....	....	....	....
	NHL Totals		350	29	72	101	523	4	0	0	0	0

a OHL Second All-Star Team (1988)

BUSSEY, FRAN PIT.

Center. Shoots left. 6'3", 190 lbs. Born, Duluth, MN, July 9, 1974.
(Pittsburgh's 8th choice, 187th overall, in 1992 Entry Draft).

			Regular Season					Playoffs				
Season	Club	Lea	GP	G	A	TP	PIM	GP	G	A	TP	PIM
1993-94	U. of Wisconsin	WCHA	DID NOT PLAY									
1994-95	U. of Wisconsin	WCHA	DID NOT PLAY									

BUTCHER, GARTH TOR.

Defense. Shoots right. 6', 204 lbs. Born, Regina, Sask., January 8, 1963.
(Vancouver's 1st choice, 10th overall, in 1981 Entry Draft).

			Regular Season					Playoffs				
Season	Club	Lea	GP	G	A	TP	PIM	GP	G	A	TP	PIM
1979-80	Regina	WHL	13	0	4	4	20	....	....	....	....	....
1980-81a	Regina	WHL	69	9	77	86	230	11	5	17	22	60
1981-82	Vancouver	NHL	5	0	0	0	9	1	0	0	0	0
a	Regina	WHL	65	24	68	92	318	19	3	17	20	95
1982-83	Vancouver	NHL	55	1	13	14	104	3	1	0	1	2
1983-84	Vancouver	NHL	28	2	0	2	34	....	....	....	....	....
	Fredericton	AHL	25	4	13	17	43	6	0	2	2	19
1984-85	Vancouver	NHL	75	3	9	12	152	....	....	....	....	....
	Fredericton	AHL	3	1	0	1	11	....	....	....	....	....
1985-86	Vancouver	NHL	70	4	7	11	188	3	0	0	0	0
1986-87	Vancouver	NHL	70	5	15	20	207	....	....	....	....	....
1987-88	Vancouver	NHL	80	6	17	23	285	....	....	....	....	....
1988-89	Vancouver	NHL	78	0	20	20	227	7	1	1	2	22
1989-90	Vancouver	NHL	80	6	14	20	205	....	....	....	....	....
1990-91	Vancouver	NHL	69	6	12	18	257	....	....	....	....	....
	St. Louis	NHL	13	0	4	4	32	13	2	1	3	54
1991-92	St. Louis	NHL	68	5	15	20	189	5	1	2	3	16
1992-93	St. Louis	NHL	84	5	10	15	211	11	1	1	2	20
1993-94	St. Louis	NHL	43	1	6	7	76	....	....	....	....	....
	Quebec	NHL	34	3	9	12	67	....	....	....	....	....
1994-95	Toronto	NHL	45	1	7	8	59	7	0	0	0	8
	NHL Totals		897	48	158	206	2302	50	6	5	11	122

a WHL First All-Star Team (1981, 1982)

Played in NHL All-Star Game (1993)

Traded to **St. Louis** by **Vancouver** with Dan Quinn for Geoff Courtnall, Robert Dirk, Sergio Momesso, Cliff Ronning and St Louis' fifth round choice (Brian Loney) in 1992 Entry Draft, March 5, 1991. Traded to **Quebec** by **St. Louis** with Ron Sutter and Bob Bassen for Steve Duchesne and Denis Chasse, January 23, 1994. Traded to **Toronto** by **Quebec** with Mats Sundin, Todd Warriner and Philadelphia's first round choice (previously acquired by Quebec — later traded to Washington — Washington selected Nolan Baumgartner) in 1994 Entry Draft for Wendel Clark, Sylvain Lefebvre, Landon Wilson and Toronto's first round choice (Jeffrey Kealty) in 1994 Entry Draft, June 28, 1994.

BUTENSCHON, SVEN (BUH-tehn-shohn) PIT.

Defense. Shoots left. 6'5", 201 lbs. Born, Itzehoe, West Germany, March 22, 1976.
(Pittsburgh's 3rd choice, 57th overall, in 1994 Entry Draft).

			Regular Season					Playoffs				
Season	Club	Lea	GP	G	A	TP	PIM	GP	G	A	TP	PIM
1993-94	Brandon	WHL	70	3	19	22	51	4	0	0	0	6
1994-95	Brandon	WHL	21	1	5	6	44	18	1	2	3	11

BUTLER, ROB TOR.

Left wing. Shoots left. 6'2", 180 lbs. Born, Winnipeg, Manitoba, March 31, 1976.
(Toronto's 7th choice, 204th overall, in 1994 Entry Draft).

			Regular Season					Playoffs				
Season	Club	Lea	GP	G	A	TP	PIM	GP	G	A	TP	PIM
1994-95	Green Bay	USHL	14	4	4	8	60	....	....	....	....	....
	Sioux City	USHL	29	12	12	24	220	....	....	....	....	....

BUTSAYEV, VIACHESLAV (boot-SIGH-yehf)

Center. Shoots left. 6'2", 200 lbs. Born, Togliatti, USSR, June 13, 1970.
(Philadelphia's 10th choice, 109th overall, in 1990 Entry Draft).

			Regular Season					Playoffs				
Season	Club	Lea	GP	G	A	TP	PIM	GP	G	A	TP	PIM
1989-90	CSKA	USSR	48	14	4	18	30	....	....	....	....	....
1990-91	CSKA	USSR	46	14	9	23	32	....	....	....	....	....
1991-92	CSKA	CIS	36	12	13	25	26	....	....	....	....	....
1992-93	CSKA	CIS	5	3	4	7	6	....	....	....	....	....
	Philadelphia	**NHL**	**52**	**2**	**14**	**16**	**61**	....	....	....	....	....
	Hershey	AHL	24	8	10	18	51	....	....	....	....	....
1993-94	**Philadelphia**	**NHL**	**47**	**12**	**9**	**21**	**58**	....	....	....	....	....
	San Jose	**NHL**	**12**	**0**	**2**	**2**	**10**	....	....	....	....	....
1994-95	Togliatti	CIS	9	2	6	8	6	....	....	....	....	....
	San Jose	**NHL**	**6**	**2**	**0**	**2**	**0**	....	....	....	....	....
	Kansas City	IHL	13	3	4	7	12	3	0	0	0	2
	NHL Totals		**117**	**16**	**25**	**41**	**129**	....	....	....	....	....

Traded to **San Jose** by **Philadelphia** for Rob Zettler, February 1, 1994.

BUTT, JAMIE — NYR

Left wing. Shoots left. 5'11", 180 lbs. Born, Richmond, B.C., April 4, 1976.
(NY Rangers' 14th choice, 267th overall, in 1994 Entry Draft).

			Regular Season					Playoffs				
Season	Club	Lea	GP	G	A	TP	PIM	GP	G	A	TP	PIM
1992-93	Tacoma	WHL	21	1	2	3	46	5	1	0	1	13
1993-94	Tacoma	WHL	64	8	13	21	214	8	1	3	4	18
1994-95	Tacoma	WHL	44	1	4	5	140	4	0	0	0	5

BUTZ, ROB — TOR.

Left wing. Shoots left. 6'3", 191 lbs. Born, Dewberry, Alta., February 24, 1975.

			Regular Season					Playoffs				
Season	Club	Lea	GP	G	A	TP	PIM	GP	G	A	TP	PIM
1992-93	Victoria	WHL	67	7	11	18	64	....	....	....	....	....
1993-94	Victoria	WHL	72	24	24	48	161	....	....	....	....	....
	St. John's	AHL	5	0	0	0	26	....	....	....	....	....
1994-95	Prince George	WHL	32	12	18	30	83	....	....	....	....	....
	Tri-City	WHL	17	4	8	12	38	17	4	5	9	22

Signed as a free agent by **Toronto**, April 1, 1993.

BUZEK, PETR — DAL.

Defense. Shoots left. 6', 183 lbs. Born, Jihlava, Czech., April 26, 1977.
(Dallas' 3rd choice, 63rd overall, in 1995 Entry Draft).

			Regular Season					Playoffs				
Season	Club	Lea	GP	G	A	TP	PIM	GP	G	A	TP	PIM
1993-94	Dukla Jihlava	Czech.	3	0	0	0	....	....	....	....	....	....
1994-95	Dukla Jihlava	Czech.	43	2	5	7	47	2	0	0	0	2

BYAKIN, ILYA

Defense. Shoots left. 5'9", 185 lbs. Born, Sverdlovsk, USSR, February 2, 1963.
(Edmonton's 11th choice, 267th overall, in 1993 Entry Draft).

			Regular Season					Playoffs				
Season	Club	Lea	GP	G	A	TP	PIM	GP	G	A	TP	PIM
1983-84	Spartak	USSR	44	9	12	21	26	....	....	....	....	....
1984-85	Spartak	USSR	46	7	11	18	56	....	....	....	....	....
1985-86	Spartak	USSR	34	8	7	15	41	....	....	....	....	....
1986-87					DID NOT PLAY							
1987-88	Sverdlovsk	USSR	30	10	10	20	37	....	....	....	....	....
1988-89	Sverdlovsk	USSR	40	11	9	20	53	....	....	....	....	....
1989-90	Sverdlovsk	USSR	27	14	7	21	20	....	....	....	....	....
1990-91	CSKA	USSR	29	4	7	11	20	....	....	....	....	....
1991-92	Rapperswil	Switz.2	36	27	40	67	36	....	....	....	....	....
1992-93	Landshut	Ger.	44	12	19	31	43	6	5	6	11	6
1993-94	**Edmonton**	**NHL**	**44**	**8**	**20**	**28**	**30**	....	....	....	....	....
	Cape Breton	AHL	12	2	9	11	8	....	....	....	....	....
1994-95	Yekaterinburg	CIS	4	3	2	5	14	....	....	....	....	....
	San Jose	**NHL**	**13**	**0**	**5**	**5**	**14**	....	....	....	....	....
	Kansas City	IHL	1	0	2	2	0	16	4	10	14	43
	NHL Totals		**57**	**8**	**25**	**33**	**44**	....	....	....	....	....

Signed as a free agent by **San Jose**, September 18, 1994.

BYKOV, VIACHESLAV (BIH-kahf) — COL.

Center. Shoots left. 5'8", 175 lbs. Born, Chelyabinsk, USSR, July 24, 1960.
(Quebec's 11th choice, 169th overall, in 1989 Entry Draft).

			Regular Season					Playoffs				
Season	Club	Lea	GP	G	A	TP	PIM	GP	G	A	TP	PIM
1979-80	Chelyabinsk	USSR	3	2	0	2	0	....	....	....	....	....
1980-81	Chelyabinsk	USSR	48	26	16	42	4	....	....	....	....	....
1981-82	Chelyabinsk	USSR	44	20	16	36	14	....	....	....	....	....
1982-83	CSKA	USSR	44	22	22	44	10	....	....	....	....	....
1983-84	CSKA	USSR	44	22	11	33	12	....	....	....	....	....
1984-85	CSKA	USSR	36	21	14	35	4	....	....	....	....	....
1985-86	CSKA	USSR	36	10	10	20	6	....	....	....	....	....
1986-87	CSKA	USSR	40	18	15	33	10	....	....	....	....	....
1987-88	CSKA	USSR	47	17	30	47	26	....	....	....	....	....
1988-89	CSKA	USSR	40	16	20	36	10	....	....	....	....	....
1989-90	CSKA	USSR	48	21	16	37	12	....	....	....	....	....
1990-91	Fribourg	Switz.	36	35	49	84	....	8	8	14	22	....
1991-92	Fribourg	Switz.	34	38	47	85	24	14	4	14	18	10
1992-93	Fribourg	Switz.	35	25	50	75	14	....	....	....	....	....
1993-94	Fribourg	Switz.	36	30	44	74	6	11	11	20	31	2
1994-95	Fribourg	Switz.	30	24	51	75	35	8	6	4	10	4

BYLSMA, DAN — L.A.

Left wing. Shoots left. 6'2", 215 lbs. Born, Grand Rapids, MI, September 19, 1970.
(Winnipeg's 7th choice, 109th overall, in 1989 Entry Draft).

			Regular Season					Playoffs				
Season	Club	Lea	GP	G	A	TP	PIM	GP	G	A	TP	PIM
1988-89	Bowling Green	CCHA	32	3	7	10	10	....	....	....	....	....
1989-90	Bowling Green	CCHA	44	13	17	30	30	....	....	....	....	....
1990-91	Bowling Green	CCHA	40	9	12	21	48	....	....	....	....	....
1991-92	Bowling Green	CCHA	34	11	14	25	24	....	....	....	....	....
1992-93	Greensboro	ECHL	60	25	35	60	66	1	0	1	1	10
	Rochester	AHL	2	0	1	1	0	....	....	....	....	....
1993-94	Greensboro	ECHL	25	14	16	30	52	....	....	....	....	....
	Albany	AHL	3	0	1	1	2	....	....	....	....	....
	Moncton	AHL	50	12	16	28	25	21	3	4	7	31
1994-95	Phoenix	IHL	81	19	23	42	41	9	4	4	8	4

Signed as a free agent by **Los Angeles**, July 7, 1994.

CABANA, CHAD — FLA.

Left wing. Shoots left. 6'1", 200 lbs. Born, Bonnyville, Alta., October 1, 1974.
(Florida's 11th choice, 213th overall, in 1993 Entry Draft).

			Regular Season					Playoffs				
Season	Club	Lea	GP	G	A	TP	PIM	GP	G	A	TP	PIM
1991-92	Tri-City	WHL	57	5	8	13	145	4	0	1	1	21
1992-93	Tri-City	WHL	68	19	23	42	104	4	1	0	1	10
1993-94	Tri-City	WHL	67	27	33	60	201	4	2	0	2	24
1994-95	Tri-City	WHL	68	25	34	59	252	17	10	11	21	47

CAIRNS, ERIC — NYR

Defense. Shoots left. 6'5", 225 lbs. Born, Oakville, Ont., June 27, 1974.
(NY Rangers' 3rd choice, 72nd overall, in 1992 Entry Draft).

			Regular Season					Playoffs				
Season	Club	Lea	GP	G	A	TP	PIM	GP	G	A	TP	PIM
1991-92	Detroit	OHL	64	1	11	12	232	7	0	0	0	31
1992-93	Detroit	OHL	64	3	13	16	194	15	0	3	3	24
1993-94	Detroit	OHL	59	7	35	42	204	17	0	4	4	46
1994-95	Birmingham	ECHL	11	1	3	4	49	....	....	....	....	....
	Binghamton	AHL	27	0	3	3	134	9	1	1	2	28

CALLAHAN, BRIAN — PIT.

Center. Shoots left. 6'1", 190 lbs. Born, Melrose, MA, July 13, 1974.
(Pittsburgh's 10th choice, 235th overall, in 1992 Entry Draft).

			Regular Season					Playoffs				
Season	Club	Lea	GP	G	A	TP	PIM	GP	G	A	TP	PIM
1993-94	Boston College	H.E.	36	11	11	22	58	....	....	....	....	....
1994-95	Boston College	H.E.	34	10	1	11	58	....	....	....	....	....

CALLAHAN, GREG — WSH.

Defense. Shoots left. 6'3", 200 lbs. Born, Chestnut Hill, MA, April 25, 1973.
(Washington's 9th choice, 239th overall, in 1992 Entry Draft).

			Regular Season					Playoffs				
Season	Club	Lea	GP	G	A	TP	PIM	GP	G	A	TP	PIM
1992-93	Boston College	H.E.	38	1	4	5	49	....	....	....	....	....
1993-94	Boston College	H.E.	24	3	2	5	65	....	....	....	....	....
1994-95	Boston College	H.E.	33	1	6	7	89	....	....	....	....	....

CALOUN, JAN (CHAH-loon) — S.J.

Right wing. Shoots right. 5'10", 175 lbs. Born, Usti-Nad-Labem, Czech., December 20, 1972.
(San Jose's 4th choice, 75th overall, in 1992 Entry Draft).

			Regular Season					Playoffs				
Season	Club	Lea	GP	G	A	TP	PIM	GP	G	A	TP	PIM
1990-91	Litvinov	Czech.	50	28	19	47	12	....	....	....	....	....
1991-92	Litvinov	Czech.	46	39	13	52	24	....	....	....	....	....
1992-93	Litvinov	Czech.	47	45	22	67	....	....	....	....	....	....
1993-94	Litvinov	Czech.	38	25	17	42	....	4	2	2	4	....
1994-95	Kansas City	IHL	76	34	39	73	50	21	13	10	23	18

CAMPBELL, ED — NYR

Defense. Shoots left. 6'2", 212 lbs. Born, Worcester, MA, November 26, 1974.
(NY Rangers' 9th choice, 190th overall, in 1993 Entry Draft).

			Regular Season					Playoffs				
Season	Club	Lea	GP	G	A	TP	PIM	GP	G	A	TP	PIM
1993-94	Lowell	H.E.	40	8	16	24	114	....	....	....	....	....
1994-95	Lowell	H.E.	34	6	24	30	105	....	....	....	....	....

CAMPBELL, JIM — MTL.

Center. Shoots right. 6'2", 185 lbs. Born, Worcester, MA, April 3, 1973.
(Montreal's 2nd choice, 28th overall, in 1991 Entry Draft).

			Regular Season					Playoffs				
Season	Club	Lea	GP	G	A	TP	PIM	GP	G	A	TP	PIM
1991-92	Hull	QMJHL	64	41	44	85	51	6	7	3	10	8
1992-93	Hull	QMJHL	50	42	29	71	66	8	11	4	15	43
1993-94	U.S. National	....	56	24	33	57	59	....	....	....	....	....
	U.S. Olympic	....	8	0	0	0	6	....	....	....	....	....
	Fredericton	AHL	19	6	17	23	6	....	....	....	....	....
1994-95	Fredericton	AHL	77	27	24	51	103	12	0	7	7	8

CAMPEAU, CHRISTIAN — T.B.

Right wing. Shoots right. 5'10", 180 lbs. Born, Verdun, Que., June 2, 1971.

			Regular Season					Playoffs				
Season	Club	Lea	GP	G	A	TP	PIM	GP	G	A	TP	PIM
1990-91	Granby	QMJHL	69	16	27	43	128	....	....	....	....	....
1991-92	Rouen	France	16	3	5	8	12	....	....	....	....	....
1992-93	Atlanta	IHL	66	3	5	8	40	3	0	0	0	2
1993-94	Atlanta	IHL	65	8	9	17	74	14	1	0	1	2
1994-95	Atlanta	IHL	76	10	13	23	96	5	1	0	1	11

Signed as a free agent by **Tampa Bay**, July 10, 1992.

CAPUANO, DEAN (ca-PEW-a-noh) — BOS.

Defense. Shoots right. 6'1", 175 lbs. Born, Providence, RI, November 3, 1971.
(Boston's 10th choice, 210th overall, in 1990 Entry Draft).

			Regular Season					Playoffs				
Season	Club	Lea	GP	G	A	TP	PIM	GP	G	A	TP	PIM
1990-91	Providence	H.E.	19	3	5	8	6	....	....	....	....	....
1991-92	Providence	H.E.	3	0	0	0	0	....	....	....	....	....
1992-93	Merrimack	H.E.				DID NOT PLAY						
1993-94	Merrimack	H.E.	19	0	6	6	20	....	....	....	....	....
1994-95						DID NOT PLAY						

CARBONNEAU, GUY (KAR-buhn-oh, GEE) ST.L.

Center. Shoots right. 5'11", 184 lbs. Born, Sept-Iles, Que., March 18, 1960.
(Montreal's 4th choice, 44th overall, in 1979 Entry Draft).

			Regular Season					Playoffs				
Season	Club	Lea	GP	G	A	TP	PIM	GP	G	A	TP	PIM
1976-77	Chicoutimi	QJHL	59	9	20	29	8	4	1	0	1	0
1977-78	Chicoutimi	QJHL	70	28	55	83	60	....	....	....	....	....
1978-79	Chicoutimi	QJHL	72	62	79	141	47	4	2	1	3	4
1979-80	Chicoutimi	QJHL	72	72	110	182	66	12	9	15	24	28
	Nova Scotia	AHL	....	....	....	....	....	2	1	1	2	2
1980-81	**Montreal**	**NHL**	**2**	**0**	**1**	**1**	**0**	....	....	....	....	....
	Nova Scotia	AHL	78	35	53	88	87	6	1	3	4	9
1981-82	Nova Scotia	AHL	77	27	67	94	124	9	2	7	9	8
1982-83	**Montreal**	**NHL**	**77**	**18**	**29**	**47**	**68**	**3**	**0**	**0**	**0**	**2**
1983-84	**Montreal**	**NHL**	**78**	**24**	**30**	**54**	**75**	**15**	**4**	**3**	**7**	**12**
1984-85	**Montreal**	**NHL**	**79**	**23**	**34**	**57**	**43**	**12**	**4**	**3**	**7**	**8**
1985-86	**Montreal**	**NHL**	**80**	**20**	**36**	**56**	**57**	**20**	**7**	**5**	**12**	**35**
1986-87	**Montreal**	**NHL**	**79**	**18**	**27**	**45**	**68**	**17**	**3**	**8**	**11**	**20**
1987-88a	**Montreal**	**NHL**	**80**	**17**	**21**	**38**	**61**	**11**	**0**	**4**	**4**	**2**
1988-89a	**Montreal**	**NHL**	**79**	**26**	**30**	**56**	**44**	**21**	**4**	**5**	**9**	**10**
1989-90	**Montreal**	**NHL**	**68**	**19**	**36**	**55**	**37**	**11**	**2**	**3**	**5**	**6**
1990-91	**Montreal**	**NHL**	**78**	**20**	**24**	**44**	**63**	**13**	**1**	**5**	**6**	**10**
1991-92a	**Montreal**	**NHL**	**72**	**18**	**21**	**39**	**39**	**11**	**1**	**1**	**2**	**6**
1992-93	**Montreal**	**NHL**	**61**	**4**	**13**	**17**	**20**	**20**	**3**	**3**	**6**	**10**
1993-94	**Montreal**	**NHL**	**79**	**14**	**24**	**38**	**48**	**7**	**1**	**3**	**4**	**4**
1994-95	**St. Louis**	**NHL**	**42**	**5**	**11**	**16**	**16**	**7**	**1**	**2**	**3**	**6**
	NHL Totals		**954**	**226**	**337**	**563**	**639**	**168**	**31**	**45**	**76**	**131**

a Won Frank J. Selke Trophy (1988, 1989, 1992)

Traded to **St. Louis** by **Montreal** for Jim Montgomery, August 19, 1994.

CARKNER, TERRY FLA.

Defense. Shoots left. 6'3", 210 lbs. Born, Smiths Falls, Ont., March 7, 1966.
(NY Rangers' 1st choice, 14th overall, in 1984 Entry Draft).

			Regular Season					Playoffs				
Season	Club	Lea	GP	G	A	TP	PIM	GP	G	A	TP	PIM
1983-84	Peterborough	OHL	58	4	19	23	77	8	0	6	6	13
1984-85a	Peterborough	OHL	64	14	47	61	125	17	2	10	12	11
1985-86b	Peterborough	OHL	54	12	32	44	106	16	1	7	8	17
1986-87	**NY Rangers**	**NHL**	**52**	**2**	**13**	**15**	**118**	**1**	**0**	**0**	**0**	**0**
	New Haven	AHL	12	2	6	8	56	3	1	0	1	0
1987-88	**Quebec**	**NHL**	**63**	**3**	**24**	**27**	**159**	....	....	....	....	....
1988-89	**Philadelphia**	**NHL**	**78**	**11**	**32**	**43**	**149**	**19**	**1**	**5**	**6**	**28**
1989-90	**Philadelphia**	**NHL**	**63**	**4**	**18**	**22**	**169**	....	....	....	....	....
1990-91	**Philadelphia**	**NHL**	**79**	**7**	**25**	**32**	**204**	....	....	....	....	....
1991-92	**Philadelphia**	**NHL**	**73**	**4**	**12**	**16**	**195**	....	....	....	....	....
1992-93	**Philadelphia**	**NHL**	**83**	**3**	**16**	**19**	**150**	....	....	....	....	....
1993-94	**Detroit**	**NHL**	**68**	**1**	**6**	**7**	**130**	**7**	**0**	**0**	**0**	**4**
1994-95	**Detroit**	**NHL**	**20**	**1**	**2**	**3**	**21**	....	....	....	....	....
	NHL Totals		**579**	**36**	**148**	**184**	**1295**	**27**	**1**	**5**	**6**	**32**

a OHL Second All-Star Team (1985)
b OHL First All-Star Team (1986)

Traded to **Quebec** by **NY Rangers** with Jeff Jackson for John Ogrodnick and David Shaw, September 30, 1987. Traded to **Philadelphia** by **Quebec** for Greg Smyth and Philadelphia's third round choice (John Tanner) in the 1989 Entry Draft, July 25, 1988. Traded to **Detroit** by **Philadelphia** for Yves Racine and Detroit's fourth round choice (Sebastien Vallee) in 1994 Entry Draft, October 5, 1993. Signed as a free agent by **Florida**, August 17, 1995.

CARNBACK, PATRIK (KAHRN-buhk) ANA.

Center. Shoots left. 6', 187 lbs. Born, Goteborg, Sweden, February 1, 1968.
(Montreal's 7th choice, 125th overall, in 1988 Entry Draft).

			Regular Season					Playoffs				
Season	Club	Lea	GP	G	A	TP	PIM	GP	G	A	TP	PIM
1986-87	V. Frolunda	Swe. 2	28	3	1	4	4	....	....	....	....	....
1987-88	V. Frolunda	Swe. 2	33	16	19	35	24	11	4	5	9	8
1988-89	V. Frolunda	Swe. 2	53	39	36	75	52	....	....	....	....	....
1989-90	V. Frolunda	Swe.	40	26	27	53	34	....	....	....	....	....
1990-91	V. Frolunda	Swe.	22	10	9	19	46	28	15	24	39	24
1991-92	V. Frolunda	Swe.	33	17	22	39	32	3	1	5	6	20
1992-93	**Montreal**	**NHL**	**6**	**0**	**0**	**0**	**2**	....	....	....	....	....
	Fredericton	AHL	45	20	37	57	45	5	0	3	3	14
1993-94	**Anaheim**	**NHL**	**73**	**12**	**11**	**23**	**54**	....	....	....	....	....
1994-95	V. Frolunda	Swe.	14	2	6	8	20	....	....	....	....	....
	Anaheim	**NHL**	**41**	**6**	**15**	**21**	**32**	....	....	....	....	....
	NHL Totals		**120**	**18**	**26**	**44**	**88**	....	....	....	....	....

Traded to **Anaheim** by **Montreal** with Todd Ewen for Anaheim's third round choice (Chris Murray) in 1994 Entry Draft, August 10, 1993.

CARNEY, KEITH E. CHI.

Defense. Shoots left. 6'2", 205 lbs. Born, Providence, RI, February 3, 1970.
(Buffalo's 3rd choice, 76th overall, in 1988 Entry Draft).

			Regular Season					Playoffs				
Season	Club	Lea	GP	G	A	TP	PIM	GP	G	A	TP	PIM
1988-89	U. of Maine	H.E.	40	4	22	26	24	....	....	....	....	....
1989-90ab	U. of Maine	H.E.	41	3	41	44	43	....	....	....	....	....
1990-91cd	U. of Maine	H.E.	40	7	49	56	38	....	....	....	....	....
1991-92	U.S. National	....	49	2	17	19	16	....	....	....	....	....
	Buffalo	**NHL**	**14**	**1**	**2**	**3**	**18**	**7**	**0**	**3**	**3**	**0**
	Rochester	AHL	24	1	10	11	2	2	0	2	2	0
1992-93	**Buffalo**	**NHL**	**30**	**2**	**4**	**6**	**55**	**8**	**0**	**3**	**3**	**6**
	Rochester	AHL	41	5	21	26	32	....	....	....	....	....
1993-94	**Buffalo**	**NHL**	**7**	**1**	**3**	**4**	**4**	....	....	....	....	....
	Chicago	**NHL**	**30**	**3**	**5**	**8**	**35**	**6**	**0**	**1**	**1**	**4**
	Indianapolis	IHL	28	0	14	14	20	....	....	....	....	....
1994-95	**Chicago**	**NHL**	**18**	**1**	**0**	**1**	**11**	**4**	**0**	**1**	**1**	**0**
	NHL Totals		**99**	**8**	**14**	**22**	**123**	**25**	**0**	**8**	**8**	**10**

a Hockey East Second All-Star Team (1990)
b NCAA East Second All-American Team (1990)
c Hockey East First All-Star Team (1991)
d NCAA East First All-American Team (1991)

Traded to **Chicago** by **Buffalo** with Buffalo's sixth round choice (Marc Magliarditi) in 1995 Entry Draft for Craig Muni and Chicago's fifth round choice (Daniel Bienvenue) in 1995 Entry Draft, October 27, 1993.

CARPENTER, BOB N.J.

Center. Shoots left. 6', 200 lbs. Born, Beverly, MA, July 13, 1963.
(Washington's 1st choice, 3rd overall, in 1981 Entry Draft).

			Regular Season					Playoffs				
Season	Club	Lea	GP	G	A	TP	PIM	GP	G	A	TP	PIM
1980-81	St. John's	HS	18	14	24	38	....	....	....	....	....	....
1981-82	**Washington**	**NHL**	**80**	**32**	**35**	**67**	**69**	....	....	....	....	....
1982-83	**Washington**	**NHL**	**80**	**32**	**37**	**69**	**64**	**4**	**1**	**0**	**1**	**2**
1983-84	**Washington**	**NHL**	**80**	**28**	**40**	**68**	**51**	**8**	**2**	**1**	**3**	**25**
1984-85	**Washington**	**NHL**	**80**	**53**	**42**	**95**	**87**	**5**	**1**	**4**	**5**	**8**
1985-86	**Washington**	**NHL**	**80**	**27**	**29**	**56**	**105**	**9**	**5**	**4**	**9**	**12**
1986-87	**Washington**	**NHL**	**22**	**5**	**7**	**12**	**21**	....	....	....	....	....
	NY Rangers	**NHL**	**28**	**2**	**8**	**10**	**20**	....	....	....	....	....
	Los Angeles	**NHL**	**10**	**2**	**3**	**5**	**6**	**5**	**1**	**2**	**3**	**2**
1987-88	**Los Angeles**	**NHL**	**71**	**19**	**33**	**52**	**84**	**5**	**1**	**1**	**2**	**0**
1988-89	**Los Angeles**	**NHL**	**39**	**11**	**15**	**26**	**16**	....	....	....	....	....
	Boston	**NHL**	**18**	**5**	**9**	**14**	**10**	**8**	**1**	**1**	**2**	**4**
1989-90	**Boston**	**NHL**	**80**	**25**	**31**	**56**	**97**	**21**	**4**	**6**	**10**	**39**
1990-91	**Boston**	**NHL**	**29**	**8**	**8**	**16**	**22**	**1**	**0**	**1**	**1**	**2**
1991-92	**Boston**	**NHL**	**60**	**25**	**23**	**48**	**46**	**8**	**0**	**1**	**1**	**6**
1992-93	**Washington**	**NHL**	**68**	**11**	**17**	**28**	**65**	**6**	**1**	**4**	**5**	**6**
1993-94	**New Jersey**	**NHL**	**76**	**10**	**23**	**33**	**51**	**20**	**1**	**7**	**8**	**20**
1994-95	**New Jersey**	**NHL**	**41**	**5**	**11**	**16**	**19**	**17**	**1**	**4**	**5**	**6**
	NHL Totals		**942**	**300**	**371**	**671**	**833**	**117**	**19**	**36**	**55**	**132**

Played in NHL All-Star Game (1985)

Traded to **NY Rangers** by **Washington** with Washington's second round choice (Jason Prosofsky) in 1989 Entry Draft for Bob Crawford, Kelly Miller and Mike Ridley, January 1, 1987. Traded to **Los Angeles** by **NY Rangers** with Tom Laidlaw for Jeff Crossman, Marcel Dionne and Los Angeles' third round choice (later traded to Minnesota — Minnesota selected Murray Garbutt) in 1989 Entry Draft. Traded to **Boston** by **Los Angeles** for Steve Kasper, January 23, 1989. Signed as a free agent by **Washington**, June 30, 1992. Signed as a free agent by **New Jersey**, September 30, 1993.

CARPER, BRANDON CGY.

Defense. Shoots left. 6'2", 200 lbs. Born, Highland Park, IL, April 2, 1972.
(Calgary's 9th choice, 198th overall, in 1992 Entry Draft).

			Regular Season					Playoffs				
Season	Club	Lea	GP	G	A	TP	PIM	GP	G	A	TP	PIM
1991-92	Bowling Green	CCHA	34	2	16	18	44	....	....	....	....	....
1992-93	Bowling Green	CCHA	41	7	20	27	72	....	....	....	....	....
1993-94	Bowling Green	CCHA	36	3	9	12	62	....	....	....	....	....
1994-95	Bowling Green	CCHA	23	2	11	13	60	....	....	....	....	....

CARSON, JIMMY HFD.

Center. Shoots right. 6'1", 200 lbs. Born, Southfield, MI, July 20, 1968.
(Los Angeles' 1st choice, 2nd overall, in 1986 Entry Draft).

			Regular Season					Playoffs				
Season	Club	Lea	GP	G	A	TP	PIM	GP	G	A	TP	PIM
1984-85	Verdun	QMJHL	68	44	72	116	12	14	9	17	26	12
1985-86a	Verdun	QMJHL	69	70	83	153	46	5	2	6	8	0
1986-87b	**Los Angeles**	**NHL**	**80**	**37**	**42**	**79**	**22**	**5**	**1**	**2**	**3**	**6**
1987-88	**Los Angeles**	**NHL**	**80**	**55**	**52**	**107**	**45**	**5**	**5**	**3**	**8**	**4**
1988-89	**Edmonton**	**NHL**	**80**	**49**	**51**	**100**	**36**	**7**	**2**	**1**	**3**	**6**
1989-90	**Edmonton**	**NHL**	**4**	**1**	**2**	**3**	**0**	....	....	....	....	....
	Detroit	**NHL**	**44**	**20**	**16**	**36**	**8**	....	....	....	....	....
1990-91	**Detroit**	**NHL**	**64**	**21**	**25**	**46**	**28**	**7**	**2**	**1**	**3**	**4**
1991-92	**Detroit**	**NHL**	**80**	**34**	**35**	**69**	**30**	**11**	**2**	**3**	**5**	**0**
1992-93	**Detroit**	**NHL**	**52**	**25**	**26**	**51**	**18**	....	....	....	....	....
	Los Angeles	**NHL**	**34**	**12**	**10**	**22**	**14**	**18**	**5**	**4**	**9**	**2**
1993-94	**Los Angeles**	**NHL**	**25**	**4**	**7**	**11**	**2**	....	....	....	....	....
	Vancouver	**NHL**	**34**	**7**	**10**	**17**	**22**	**2**	**0**	**1**	**1**	**0**
1994-95	**Hartford**	**NHL**	**38**	**9**	**10**	**19**	**29**	....	....	....	....	....
	NHL Totals		**615**	**274**	**286**	**560**	**254**	**55**	**17**	**15**	**32**	**22**

a QMJHL Second All-Star Team (1986)
b Named to NHL All-Rookie Team (1987)

Played in NHL All-Star Game (1989)

Traded to **Edmonton** by **Los Angeles** with Martin Gelinas, Los Angeles' first round choices in 1989 (later traded to New Jersey — New Jersey selected Jason Miller), 1991 (Martin Rucinsky) and 1993 (Nick Stajduhar) Entry Drafts and cash for Wayne Gretzky, Mike Krushelnyski and Marty McSorley, August 9, 1988. Traded to **Detroit** by **Edmonton** with Kevin McClelland and Edmonton's fifth round choice (later traded to Montreal — Montreal selected Brad Layzell) in 1991 Entry Draft for Petr Klima, Joe Murphy, Adam Graves and Jeff Sharples, November 2, 1989. Traded to **Los Angeles** by **Detroit** with Marc Potvin and Gary Shuchuk for Paul Coffey, Sylvain Couturier and Jim Hiller, January 29, 1993. Traded to **Vancouver** by **Los Angeles** for Dixon Ward and a conditional draft choice in 1995 Entry Draft, January 8, 1994. Signed as a free agent by **Hartford**, July 15, 1994.

CARTER, ANSON COL.

Center. Shoots right. 6'1", 175 lbs. Born, Toronto, Ont., June 6, 1974.
(Quebec's 10th choice, 220th overall, in 1992 Entry Draft).

			Regular Season					Playoffs				
Season	Club	Lea	GP	G	A	TP	PIM	GP	G	A	TP	PIM
1992-93	Michigan State	CCHA	34	15	7	22	20	....	....	....	....	....
1993-94a	Michigan State	CCHA	39	30	24	54	36	....	....	....	....	....
1994-95ab	Michigan State	CCHA	39	34	17	51	40	....	....	....	....	....

a CCHA First All-Star Team (1994, 1995)
b NCAA West Second All-American Team (1995)

CARTER, JOHN

Left wing. Shoots left. 5'10", 181 lbs. Born, Winchester, MA, May 3, 1963.

			Regular Season					Playoffs				
Season	Club	Lea	GP	G	A	TP	PIM	GP	G	A	TP	PIM
1982-83	RPI	ECAC	29	16	22	38	33	....	....	....	....	....
1983-84	RPI	ECAC	38	35	39	74	52	....	....	....	....	....
1984-85	RPI	ECAC	37	43	29	72	52	....	....	....	....	....
1985-86	RPI	ECAC	27	23	18	41	68	....	....	....	....	....
	Boston	**NHL**	**3**	**0**	**0**	**0**	**0**	....	....	....	....	....
1986-87	**Boston**	**NHL**	**8**	**0**	**1**	**1**	**0**	....	....	....	....	....
	Moncton	AHL	58	25	30	55	60	6	2	3	5	5
1987-88	**Boston**	**NHL**	**4**	**0**	**1**	**1**	**2**	....	....	....	....	....
	Maine	AHL	76	38	38	76	145	10	4	4	8	44
1988-89	**Boston**	**NHL**	**44**	**12**	**10**	**22**	**24**	**10**	**1**	**2**	**3**	**6**
	Maine	AHL	24	13	6	19	12	....	....	....	....	....
1989-90	**Boston**	**NHL**	**76**	**17**	**22**	**39**	**26**	**21**	**6**	**3**	**9**	**45**
	Maine	AHL	2	2	2	4	2	....	....	....	....	....
1990-91	**Boston**	**NHL**	**50**	**4**	**7**	**11**	**68**	....	....	....	....	....
	Maine	AHL	16	5	9	14	16	1	0	0	0	10
1991-92	**San Jose**	**NHL**	**4**	**0**	**0**	**0**	**0**	....	....	....	....	....
	Kansas City	IHL	42	11	15	26	116	15	6	9	15	18
1992-93	**San Jose**	**NHL**	**55**	**7**	**9**	**16**	**81**	....	....	....	....	....
	Kansas City	IHL	9	4	2	6	14	....	....	....	....	....
1993-94	Providence	AHL	47	11	5	16	82	....	....	....	....	....
1994-95	Worcester	AHL	64	18	9	27	96	....	....	....	....	....
	NHL Totals		**244**	**40**	**50**	**90**	**201**	**31**	**7**	**5**	**12**	**51**

Signed as a free agent by **Boston**, March 27, 1986. Signed as a free agent by **San Jose**, August 22, 1991.

CASSELMAN, MIKE — DET.

Center. Shoots left. 5'11", 190 lbs. Born, Morrisburg, Ont., August 23, 1968.
(Detroit's 1st choice, 3rd overall, in 1990 Supplemental Draft).

			Regular Season					Playoffs				
Season	Club	Lea	GP	G	A	TP	PIM	GP	G	A	TP	PIM
1987-88	Clarkson	ECAC	24	4	1	5	....	....	....	....	....	....
1988-89	Clarkson	ECAC	31	3	14	17	....	....	....	....	....	....
1989-90	Clarkson	ECAC	34	22	21	43	69	....	....	....	....	....
1990-91	Clarkson	ECAC	40	19	35	54	44	....	....	....	....	....
1991-92a	Toledo	ECHL	61	39	60	99	83	5	0	1	1	6
	Adirondack	AHL	1	0	0	0	0	....	....	....	....	....
1992-93	Adirondack	AHL	60	12	19	31	27	8	3	3	6	0
	Toledo	ECHL	3	0	1	1	2	....	....	....	....	....
1993-94	Adirondack	AHL	77	17	38	55	34	12	2	4	6	10
1994-95	Adirondack	AHL	60	17	43	60	42	4	0	0	0	2

a ECHL Second All-Star Team (1992)

CASSELS, ANDREW (KAS-uhls) — HFD.

Center. Shoots left. 6', 192 lbs. Born, Bramalea, Ont., July 23, 1969.
(Montreal's 1st choice, 17th overall, in 1987 Entry Draft).

			Regular Season					Playoffs				
Season	Club	Lea	GP	G	A	TP	PIM	GP	G	A	TP	PIM
1986-87	Ottawa	OHL	66	26	66	92	28	11	5	9	14	7
1987-88a	Ottawa	OHL	61	48	*103	*151	39	16	8	*24	*32	13
1988-89a	Ottawa	OHL	56	37	97	134	66	12	5	10	15	10
1989-90	**Montreal**	**NHL**	**6**	**2**	**0**	**2**	**2**	....	....	....	....	....
	Sherbrooke	AHL	55	22	45	67	25	12	2	11	13	6
1990-91	**Montreal**	**NHL**	**54**	**6**	**19**	**25**	**20**	**8**	**0**	**2**	**2**	**2**
1991-92	**Hartford**	**NHL**	**67**	**11**	**30**	**41**	**18**	**7**	**2**	**4**	**6**	**6**
1992-93	**Hartford**	**NHL**	**84**	**21**	**64**	**85**	**62**	....	....	....	....	....
1993-94	**Hartford**	**NHL**	**79**	**16**	**42**	**58**	**37**	....	....	....	....	....
1994-95	**Hartford**	**NHL**	**46**	**7**	**30**	**37**	**18**	....	....	....	....	....
	NHL Totals		**336**	**63**	**185**	**248**	**157**	**15**	**2**	**6**	**8**	**8**

a OHL First All-Star Team (1988,1989)

Traded to **Hartford** by **Montreal** for Hartford's second round choice (Valeri Bure) in 1992 Entry Draft, September 17, 1991.

CAVALLINI, GINO

Left wing. Shoots left. 6'1", 215 lbs. Born, Toronto, Ont., November 24, 1962.

			Regular Season					Playoffs				
Season	Club	Lea	GP	G	A	TP	PIM	GP	G	A	TP	PIM
1982-83	Bowling Green	CCHA	40	8	16	24	52	....	....	....	....	....
1983-84	Bowling Green	CCHA	43	25	23	48	16	....	....	....	....	....
1984-85	**Calgary**	**NHL**	**27**	**6**	**10**	**16**	**14**	**3**	**0**	**0**	**0**	**4**
	Moncton	AHL	51	29	19	48	28	....	....	....	....	....
1985-86	**Calgary**	**NHL**	**27**	**7**	**7**	**14**	**26**	....	....	....	....	....
	Moncton	AHL	4	3	2	5	7	....	....	....	....	....
	St. Louis	**NHL**	**30**	**6**	**5**	**11**	**36**	**17**	**4**	**5**	**9**	**10**
1986-87	**St. Louis**	**NHL**	**80**	**18**	**26**	**44**	**54**	**6**	**3**	**1**	**4**	**2**
1987-88	**St. Louis**	**NHL**	**64**	**15**	**17**	**32**	**62**	**10**	**5**	**5**	**10**	**19**
1988-89	**St. Louis**	**NHL**	**74**	**20**	**23**	**43**	**79**	**9**	**0**	**2**	**2**	**17**
1989-90	**St. Louis**	**NHL**	**80**	**15**	**15**	**30**	**77**	**12**	**1**	**3**	**4**	**12**
1990-91	**St. Louis**	**NHL**	**78**	**8**	**27**	**35**	**81**	**13**	**1**	**3**	**4**	**2**
1991-92	**St. Louis**	**NHL**	**48**	**9**	**7**	**16**	**40**	....	....	....	....	....
	Quebec	**NHL**	**18**	**1**	**7**	**8**	**4**	....	....	....	....	....
1992-93	**Quebec**	**NHL**	**67**	**9**	**15**	**24**	**34**	**4**	**0**	**0**	**0**	**0**
1993-94	Milwaukee	IHL	78	43	35	78	64	4	3	4	7	6
1994-95a	Milwaukee	IHL	80	53	35	88	54	15	7	2	9	10
	NHL Totals		**593**	**114**	**159**	**273**	**507**	**74**	**14**	**19**	**33**	**66**

a IHL Second All-Star Team (1995)

Signed as a free agent by **Calgary**, May 16, 1984. Traded to **St. Louis** by **Calgary** with Eddy Beers and Charles Bourgeois for Joe Mullen, Terry Johnson and Rik Wilson, February 1, 1986. Claimed on waivers by **Quebec** from **St. Louis**, February 27, 1992.

CAVALLINI, PAUL — DAL.

Defense. Shoots left. 6'1", 202 lbs. Born, Toronto, Ont., October 13, 1965.
(Washington's 9th choice, 205th overall, in 1984 Entry Draft).

			Regular Season					Playoffs				
Season	Club	Lea	GP	G	A	TP	PIM	GP	G	A	TP	PIM
1984-85	Providence	H.E.	37	4	10	14	52	....	....	....	....	....
1985-86	Cdn. National	....	52	1	11	12	95	....	....	....	....	....
	Binghamton	AHL	15	3	4	7	20	6	0	2	2	56
1986-87	**Washington**	**NHL**	**6**	**0**	**2**	**2**	**8**	....	....	....	....	....
	Binghamton	AHL	66	12	24	36	188	13	2	7	9	35
1987-88	**Washington**	**NHL**	**24**	**2**	**3**	**5**	**66**	....	....	....	....	....
	St. Louis	**NHL**	**48**	**4**	**7**	**11**	**86**	**10**	**1**	**6**	**7**	**26**
1988-89	**St. Louis**	**NHL**	**65**	**4**	**20**	**24**	**128**	**10**	**2**	**2**	**4**	**14**
1989-90a	**St. Louis**	**NHL**	**80**	**8**	**39**	**47**	**106**	**12**	**2**	**3**	**5**	**20**
1990-91	**St. Louis**	**NHL**	**67**	**10**	**25**	**35**	**89**	**13**	**2**	**3**	**5**	**20**
1991-92	**St. Louis**	**NHL**	**66**	**10**	**25**	**35**	**95**	**4**	**0**	**1**	**1**	**6**
1992-93	**St. Louis**	**NHL**	**11**	**1**	**4**	**5**	**10**	....	....	....	....	....
	Washington	**NHL**	**71**	**5**	**8**	**13**	**46**	**6**	**0**	**2**	**2**	**18**
1993-94	**Dallas**	**NHL**	**74**	**11**	**33**	**44**	**82**	**9**	**1**	**8**	**9**	**4**
1994-95	**Dallas**	**NHL**	**44**	**1**	**11**	**12**	**28**	**5**	**0**	**2**	**2**	**6**
	NHL Totals		**556**	**56**	**177**	**233**	**744**	**69**	**8**	**27**	**35**	**114**

a Won Alka-Seltzer Plus Award (1990)

Played in NHL All-Star Game (1990)

Traded to **St. Louis** by **Washington** for Montreal's second round choice (previously acquired by St. Louis — Washington selected Wade Bartley) in 1988 Entry Draft, December 11, 1987. Traded to **Washington** by **St. Louis** for Kevin Miller, November 2, 1992. Traded to **Dallas** by **Washington** for future considerations (Enrico Ciccone, June 25, 1993), June 20, 1993.

CHALIFOUX, DENIS (SHAL-ih-foo)

Center. Shoots right. 5'8", 165 lbs. Born, Laval, Que., February 28, 1971.
(Hartford's 11th choice, 246th overall, in 1990 Entry Draft).

			Regular Season					Playoffs				
Season	Club	Lea	GP	G	A	TP	PIM	GP	G	A	TP	PIM
1989-90	Laval	QMJHL	70	41	68	109	32	14	*14	14	*28	14
1990-91a	Laval	QMJHL	67	38	79	117	77	4	1	1	2	4
1991-92	Springfield	AHL	66	17	20	37	26	4	1	0	1	4
1992-93	Springfield	AHL	64	17	27	44	22	15	5	8	13	14
1993-94	Springfield	AHL	44	14	38	52	24	....	....	....	....	....
1994-95	Worcester	AHL	65	21	32	53	32	....	....	....	....	....

a QMJHL Second All-Star Team (1991)

CHAMBERS, SHAWN — N.J.

Defense. Shoots left. 6'2", 200 lbs. Born, Royal Oaks, MI, October 11, 1966.
(Minnesota's 1st choice, 4th overall, in 1987 Supplemental Draft).

			Regular Season					Playoffs				
Season	Club	Lea	GP	G	A	TP	PIM	GP	G	A	TP	PIM
1985-86	Alaska-Fair.	G.N.	25	15	21	36	34	....	....	....	....	....
1986-87	Alaska-Fair.	G.N.	28	8	29	37	84	....	....	....	....	....
	Seattle	WHL	28	8	25	33	58	....	....	....	....	....
	Fort Wayne	IHL	12	2	6	8	0	10	1	4	5	5
1987-88	**Minnesota**	**NHL**	**19**	**1**	**7**	**8**	**21**	....	....	....	....	....
	Kalamazoo	IHL	19	1	6	7	22	....	....	....	....	....
1988-89	**Minnesota**	**NHL**	**72**	**5**	**19**	**24**	**80**	**3**	**0**	**2**	**2**	**0**
1989-90	**Minnesota**	**NHL**	**78**	**8**	**18**	**26**	**81**	**7**	**2**	**1**	**3**	**10**
1990-91	**Minnesota**	**NHL**	**29**	**1**	**3**	**4**	**24**	**23**	**0**	**7**	**7**	**16**
	Kalamazoo	IHL	3	1	1	2	0	....	....	....	....	....
1991-92	**Washington**	**NHL**	**2**	**0**	**0**	**0**	**2**	....	....	....	....	....
	Baltimore	AHL	5	2	3	5	9	....	....	....	....	....
1992-93	**Tampa Bay**	**NHL**	**55**	**10**	**29**	**39**	**36**	....	....	....	....	....
	Atlanta	IHL	6	0	2	2	18	....	....	....	....	....
1993-94	**Tampa Bay**	**NHL**	**66**	**11**	**23**	**34**	**23**	....	....	....	....	....
1994-95	**Tampa Bay**	**NHL**	**24**	**2**	**12**	**14**	**6**	....	....	....	....	....
	New Jersey	**NHL**	**21**	**2**	**5**	**7**	**6**	**20**	**4**	**5**	**9**	**2**
	NHL Totals		**366**	**40**	**116**	**156**	**279**	**53**	**6**	**15**	**21**	**28**

Traded to **Washington** by **Minnesota** for Steve Maltais and Trent Klatt, June 21, 1991. Claimed by **Tampa Bay** from **Washington** in Expansion Draft, June 18, 1992. Traded to **New Jersey** by **Tampa Bay** with Danton Cole for Alexander Semak and Ben Hankinson, March 14, 1995.

CHARBONNEAU, JOSE (SHAHR-buh-noh, JOH-see)

Right wing. Shoots right. 6', 195 lbs. Born, Ferme-Neuve, Que., November 21, 1966.
(Montreal's 1st choice, 12th overall, in 1985 Entry Draft).

			Regular Season					Playoffs				
Season	Club	Lea	GP	G	A	TP	PIM	GP	G	A	TP	PIM
1983-84	Drummondville	QMJHL	65	31	59	90	110	....	....	....	....	....
1984-85	Drummondville	QMJHL	46	34	40	74	91	12	5	10	15	20
1985-86	Drummondville	QMJHL	57	44	45	89	158	23	16	20	36	40
1986-87	Sherbrooke	AHL	72	14	27	41	94	16	5	12	17	17
1987-88	**Montreal**	**NHL**	**16**	**0**	**2**	**2**	**6**	**8**	**0**	**0**	**0**	**4**
	Sherbrooke	AHL	55	30	35	65	108	....	....	....	....	....
1988-89	**Montreal**	**NHL**	**9**	**1**	**3**	**4**	**6**	....	....	....	....	....
	Sherbrooke	AHL	33	13	15	28	95	....	....	....	....	....
	Vancouver	**NHL**	**13**	**0**	**1**	**1**	**6**	....	....	....	....	....
	Milwaukee	IHL	13	8	5	13	46	10	3	2	5	23
1989-90	Milwaukee	IHL	65	23	38	61	137	5	0	1	1	8
1990-91	Cdn. National	....	56	22	29	51	54	....	....	....	....	....
1991-92					DID NOT PLAY							
1992-93	Cdn. National	....	1	0	0	0	0	....	....	....	....	....
1993-94	**Vancouver**	**NHL**	**30**	**7**	**7**	**14**	**49**	**3**	**1**	**0**	**1**	**4**
	Hamilton	AHL	7	3	2	5	8	....	....	....	....	....
1994-95	**Vancouver**	**NHL**	**3**	**1**	**0**	**1**	**0**	....	....	....	....	....
	Las Vegas	IHL	27	8	12	20	102	9	1	1	2	71
	NHL Totals		**71**	**9**	**13**	**22**	**67**	**11**	**1**	**0**	**1**	**8**

Traded to **Vancouver** by **Montreal** for Dan Woodley, January 25, 1989. Signed as a free agent by **Vancouver**, October 3, 1993.

CHARRON, ERIC — T.B.

Defense. Shoots left. 6'3", 192 lbs. Born, Verdun, Que., January 14, 1970.
(Montreal's 1st choice, 20th overall, in 1988 Entry Draft).

			Regular Season					Playoffs				
Season	Club	Lea	GP	G	A	TP	PIM	GP	G	A	TP	PIM
1987-88	Trois-Rivières	QMJHL	67	3	13	16	135	....	....	....	....	....
1988-89	Trois-Rivières	QMJHL	38	2	16	18	111	....	....	....	....	....
	Verdun	QMJHL	28	2	15	17	66	....	....	....	....	....
	Sherbrooke	AHL	1	0	0	0	0	....	....	....	....	....
1989-90	St-Hyacinthe	QMJHL	68	13	38	51	152	11	3	4	7	67
	Sherbrooke	AHL	....	....	....	....	....	2	0	0	0	0
1990-91	Fredericton	AHL	71	1	11	12	108	2	1	0	1	29
1991-92	Fredericton	AHL	59	2	11	13	98	6	1	0	1	4
1992-93	**Montreal**	**NHL**	**3**	**0**	**0**	**0**	**2**	....	....	....	....	....
	Fredericton	AHL	54	3	13	16	93	....	....	....	....	....
	Atlanta	IHL	11	0	2	2	12	3	0	1	1	6
1993-94	**Tampa Bay**	**NHL**	**4**	**0**	**0**	**0**	**2**	....	....	....	....	....
	Atlanta	IHL	66	5	18	23	144	14	1	4	5	28
1994-95	**Tampa Bay**	**NHL**	**45**	**1**	**4**	**5**	**26**	....	....	....	....	....
	NHL Totals		**52**	**1**	**4**	**5**	**30**					

Traded to **Tampa Bay** by **Montreal** with Alain Cote and future considerations (Donald Dufresne, June 18, 1993) for Rob Ramage, March 20, 1993.

CHARTIER, SCOTT — (SHAR-tee-yayr) ANA.

Defense. Shoots right. 6'1", 200 lbs. Born, St. Lazare, Man., January 19, 1972.

			Regular Season					Playoffs				
Season	Club	Lea	GP	G	A	TP	PIM	GP	G	A	TP	PIM
1992-93	W. Michigan	CCHA	38	6	23	29	84	....	....	....	....	....
1993-94	San Diego	IHL	49	2	6	8	84	4	0	0	0	6
1994-95	Greensboro	ECHL	30	6	14	20	82	18	2	3	5	41
	San Diego	IHL	8	0	0	0	0	....	....	....	....	....

Signed as a free agent by **Anaheim**, July 30, 1993.

CHASE, DON — MTL.

Center. Shoots right. 5'11", 190 lbs. Born, Springfield, MA, March 17, 1974.
(Montreal's 7th choice, 116th overall, in 1992 Entry Draft).

			Regular Season					Playoffs				
Season	Club	Lea	GP	G	A	TP	PIM	GP	G	A	TP	PIM
1992-93	Boston College	H.E.	38	7	5	12	48	....	....	....	....	....
1993-94	Boston College	H.E.	35	14	13	27	58	....	....	....	....	....
1994-95	Boston College	H.E.	35	19	12	31	74	....	....	....	....	....

CHASE, KELLY

Right wing. Shoots right. 5'11", 195 lbs. Born, Porcupine Plain, Sask., October 25, 1967.

			Regular Season					Playoffs				
Season	Club	Lea	GP	G	A	TP	PIM	GP	G	A	TP	PIM
1985-86	Saskatoon	WHL	57	7	18	25	172	10	3	4	7	37
1986-87	Saskatoon	WHL	68	17	29	46	285	11	2	8	10	37
1987-88	Saskatoon	WHL	70	21	34	55	*343	9	3	5	8	32
1988-89	Peoria	IHL	38	14	7	21	278	....	....	....	....	....
1989-90	**St. Louis**	**NHL**	**43**	**1**	**3**	**4**	**244**	9	1	0	1	46
	Peoria	IHL	10	1	2	3	76	....	....	....	....	....
1990-91	**St. Louis**	**NHL**	**2**	**1**	**0**	**1**	**15**	6	0	0	0	18
	Peoria	IHL	61	20	34	54	406	10	4	3	7	61
1991-92	**St. Louis**	**NHL**	**46**	**1**	**2**	**3**	**264**	1	0	0	0	7
1992-93	**St. Louis**	**NHL**	**49**	**2**	**5**	**7**	**204**	....	....	....	....	....
1993-94	**St. Louis**	**NHL**	**68**	**2**	**5**	**7**	**278**	4	0	1	1	6
1994-95	**Hartford**	**NHL**	**28**	**0**	**4**	**4**	**141**	....	....	....	....	....
	NHL Totals		**236**	**7**	**19**	**26**	**1146**	**20**	**1**	**1**	**2**	**77**

Signed as a free agent by **St. Louis**, February 23, 1988. Claimed by **Hartford** from **St. Louis** in NHL Waiver Draft, January 18, 1995.

CHASSE, DENIS — (shah-SAY) ST.L.

Right wing. Shoots right. 6'2", 200 lbs. Born, Montreal, Que., February 7, 1970.

			Regular Season					Playoffs				
Season	Club	Lea	GP	G	A	TP	PIM	GP	G	A	TP	PIM
1987-88	St-Jean	QMJHL	13	0	1	1	2	1	0	0	0	0
1988-89	Verdun	QMJHL	38	12	12	24	61	....	....	....	....	....
	Drummondville	QMJHL	30	15	16	31	77	3	0	2	2	28
1989-90	Drummondville	QMJHL	34	14	29	43	85	....	....	....	....	....
	Chicoutimi	QMJHL	33	19	27	46	105	7	7	4	11	50
1990-91	Drummondville	QMJHL	62	47	54	101	246	13	9	11	20	56
1991-92	Halifax	AHL	73	26	35	61	254	....	....	....	....	....
1992-93	Halifax	AHL	75	35	41	76	242	....	....	....	....	....
1993-94	Cornwall	AHL	48	27	39	66	194	....	....	....	....	....
	St. Louis	**NHL**	**3**	**0**	**1**	**1**	**15**	....	....	....	....	....
1994-95	**St. Louis**	**NHL**	**47**	**7**	**9**	**16**	**133**	7	1	7	8	23
	NHL Totals		**50**	**7**	**10**	**17**	**148**	**7**	**1**	**7**	**8**	**23**

Signed as a free agent by **Quebec**, May 14, 1991. Traded to **St. Louis** by **Quebec** with Steve Duchesne for Garth Butcher, Ron Sutter and Bob Bassen, January 23, 1994.

CHECCO, NICHOLAS — (CHEH-koh) COL.

Center. Shoots left. 5'11", 185 lbs. Born, Minneapolis, MN, November 18, 1974.
(Quebec's 7th choice, 137th overall, in 1993 Entry Draft).

			Regular Season					Playoffs				
Season	Club	Lea	GP	G	A	TP	PIM	GP	G	A	TP	PIM
1993-94	U. Minnesota	WCHA	41	7	5	12	28	....	....	....	....	....
1994-95	U. Minnesota	WCHA	43	14	11	25	46	....	....	....	....	....

CHELIOS, CHRIS — (CHELL-EE-ohs) CHI.

Defense. Shoots right. 6'1", 186 lbs. Born, Chicago, IL, January 25, 1962.
(Montreal's 5th choice, 40th overall, in 1981 Entry Draft).

			Regular Season					Playoffs				
Season	Club	Lea	GP	G	A	TP	PIM	GP	G	A	TP	PIM
1981-82	U. Wisconsin	WCHA	43	6	43	49	50	....	....	....	....	....
1982-83ab	U. Wisconsin	WCHA	26	9	17	26	50	....	....	....	....	....
1983-84	U.S. National	....	60	14	35	49	58	....	....	....	....	....
	U.S. Olympic	....	6	0	4	4	8	....	....	....	....	....
	Montreal	**NHL**	**12**	**0**	**2**	**2**	**12**	15	1	9	10	17
1984-85c	**Montreal**	**NHL**	**74**	**9**	**55**	**64**	**87**	9	2	8	10	17
1985-86	**Montreal**	**NHL**	**41**	**8**	**26**	**34**	**67**	20	2	9	11	49
1986-87	**Montreal**	**NHL**	**71**	**11**	**33**	**44**	**124**	17	4	9	13	38
1987-88	**Montreal**	**NHL**	**71**	**20**	**41**	**61**	**172**	11	3	1	4	29
1988-89de	**Montreal**	**NHL**	**80**	**15**	**58**	**73**	**185**	21	4	15	19	28
1989-90	**Montreal**	**NHL**	**53**	**9**	**22**	**31**	**136**	5	0	1	1	8
1990-91f	**Chicago**	**NHL**	**77**	**12**	**52**	**64**	**192**	6	1	7	8	46
1991-92	**Chicago**	**NHL**	**80**	**9**	**47**	**56**	**245**	18	6	15	21	37
1992-93de	**Chicago**	**NHL**	**84**	**15**	**58**	**73**	**282**	4	0	2	2	14
1993-94	**Chicago**	**NHL**	**76**	**16**	**44**	**60**	**212**	6	1	1	2	8
1994-95	Biel	Switz.	3	0	3	3	4	....	....	....	....	....
d	**Chicago**	**NHL**	**48**	**5**	**33**	**38**	**72**	16	4	7	11	12
	NHL Totals		**767**	**129**	**471**	**600**	**1786**	**148**	**28**	**84**	**112**	**303**

a WCHA Second All-Star Team (1983)
b NCAA All-Tournament Team (1983)
c NHL All-Rookie Team (1985)
d NHL First All-Star Team (1989, 1993, 1995)
e Won Norris Trophy (1989, 1993)
f NHL Second All-Star Team (1991)

Played in NHL All-Star Game (1985, 1990-94)

Traded to **Chicago** by **Montreal** with Montreal's second round choice (Michael Pomichter) in 1991 Entry Draft for Denis Savard, June 29, 1990.

CHERBATURKIN, VLADIMIR — NYI

Defense. Shoots left. 6'2", 189 lbs. Born, Tyumen, USSR, April 23, 1975.
(NY Islanders' 3rd choice, 66th overall, in 1993 Entry Draft).

			Regular Season					Playoffs				
Season	Club	Lea	GP	G	A	TP	PIM	GP	G	A	TP	PIM
1993-94	Elektrostal	CIS 2	42	4	4	8	38	....	....	....	....	....
1994-95	Elektrostal	CIS	52	2	6	8	90	....	....	....	....	....

CHERBAYEV, ALEXANDER — (chuhr-BIGH-ehv) S.J.

Left wing. Shoots left. 6'1", 190 lbs. Born, Voskresensk, USSR, August 13, 1973.
(San Jose's 3rd choice, 51st overall, in 1992 Entry Draft).

			Regular Season					Playoffs				
Season	Club	Lea	GP	G	A	TP	PIM	GP	G	A	TP	PIM
1990-91	Khimik	USSR	16	2	2	4	0	....	....	....	....	....
1991-92	Khimik	CIS	38	3	3	6	14	....	....	....	....	....
1992-93	Khimik	CIS	33	18	9	27	74	2	1	0	1	0
1993-94	Kansas City	IHL	43	17	15	32	100	....	....	....	....	....
1994-95	Kansas City	IHL	62	17	28	45	56	11	0	2	2	10

CHEREDARYK, STEVE — WPG.

Defense. Shoots left. 6'2", 197 lbs. Born, Calgary, Alta., November 20, 1975.
(Winnipeg's 4th choice, 82nd overall, in 1994 Entry Draft).

			Regular Season					Playoffs				
Season	Club	Lea	GP	G	A	TP	PIM	GP	G	A	TP	PIM
1992-93	Medicine Hat	WHL	67	1	9	10	88	10	0	1	1	16
1993-94	Medicine Hat	WHL	72	3	35	38	151	3	0	1	1	9
1994-95	Medicine Hat	WHL	70	3	26	29	193	5	0	1	1	13
	Springfield	AHL	3	0	1	1	0	....	....	....	....	....

CHERNOMAZ, RICH — (CHUHR-noh-mas)

Right wing. Shoots right. 5'8", 185 lbs. Born, Selkirk, Man., September 1, 1963.
(Colorado's 2nd choice, 26th overall, in 1981 Entry Draft).

			Regular Season					Playoffs				
Season	Club	Lea	GP	G	A	TP	PIM	GP	G	A	TP	PIM
1980-81	Victoria	WHL	72	49	64	113	92	15	11	15	26	38
1981-82	**Colorado**	**NHL**	**2**	**0**	**0**	**0**	**0**	....	....	....	....	....
	Victoria	WHL	49	36	62	98	69	4	1	2	3	13
1982-83a	Victoria	WHL	64	71	53	124	113	12	10	5	15	18
1983-84	**New Jersey**	**NHL**	**7**	**2**	**1**	**3**	**2**	....	....	....	....	....
	Maine	AHL	69	17	29	46	39	2	0	1	1	0
1984-85	**New Jersey**	**NHL**	**3**	**0**	**2**	**2**	**2**	....	....	....	....	....
	Maine	AHL	64	17	34	51	64	10	2	2	4	4
1985-86	Maine	AHL	78	21	28	49	82	5	0	0	0	2
1986-87	**New Jersey**	**NHL**	**25**	**6**	**4**	**10**	**8**	....	....	....	....	....
	Maine	AHL	58	35	27	62	65	....	....	....	....	....
1987-88	**Calgary**	**NHL**	**2**	**1**	**0**	**1**	**0**	....	....	....	....	....
b	Salt Lake	IHL	73	48	47	95	122	18	4	14	18	30
1988-89	**Calgary**	**NHL**	**1**	**0**	**0**	**0**	**0**	....	....	....	....	....
	Salt Lake	IHL	81	33	68	101	122	14	7	5	12	47
1989-90	Salt Lake	IHL	65	39	35	74	170	11	6	6	12	32
1990-91b	Salt Lake	IHL	81	39	58	97	213	4	3	1	4	8
1991-92	**Calgary**	**NHL**	**11**	**0**	**0**	**0**	**6**	....	....	....	....	....
	Salt Lake	IHL	66	20	40	60	201	5	1	2	3	10
1992-93	Salt Lake	IHL	76	26	48	74	172	....	....	....	....	....
1993-94cd	St. John's	AHL	78	45	65	110	199	11	5	11	16	18
1994-95	St. John's	AHL	77	24	45	69	235	5	1	1	2	8
	NHL Totals		**51**	**9**	**7**	**16**	**18**					

a WHL First All-Star Team (1983)
b IHL Second All-Star Team (1988, 1991)
c AHL First All-Star Team (1994)
d Won Les Cunningham Plaque (MVP - AHL) (1994)

Signed as a free agent by **Calgary**, August 4, 1987. Signed as a free agent by **Toronto**, August 3, 1993.

CHERREY, SCOTT — WSH.

Left wing. Shoots left. 6'2", 205 lbs. Born, Drayton, Ont., May 27, 1976.
(Washington's 3rd choice, 41st overall, in 1994 Entry Draft).

			Regular Season					Playoffs				
Season	Club	Lea	GP	G	A	TP	PIM	GP	G	A	TP	PIM
1993-94	North Bay	OHL	63	15	26	41	45	18	5	3	8	10
1994-95	North Bay	OHL	62	16	32	48	78	6	1	3	4	4

CHERVYAKOV, DENIS (CHAIR-vuh-kahf)

Defense. Shoots left. 6', 185 lbs. Born, Leningrad, USSR, April 20, 1970.
(Boston's 9th choice, 256th overall, in 1992 Entry Draft).

			Regular Season					Playoffs				
Season	Club	Lea	GP	G	A	TP	PIM	GP	G	A	TP	PIM
1990-91	Leningrad	USSR	28	2	1	3	40	....	....	....	....	....
1991-92	Riga	CIS	14	0	1	1	12	....	....	....	....	....
1992-93	**Boston**	**NHL**	**2**	**0**	**0**	**0**	**2**	....	....	....	....	....
	Providence	AHL	48	4	12	16	99	....	....	....	....	....
	Atlanta	IHL	1	0	0	0	0	....	....	....	....	....
1993-94	Providence	AHL	58	2	16	18	128	....	....	....	....	....
1994-95	Providence	AHL	65	1	18	19	130	10	0	2	2	14
	NHL Totals		**2**	**0**	**0**	**0**	**2**	....	....	....	....	....

CHIASSON, STEVE (CHAY-sahn) CGY.

Defense. Shoots left. 6'1", 205 lbs. Born, Barrie, Ont., April 14, 1967.
(Detroit's 3rd choice, 50th overall, in 1985 Entry Draft).

			Regular Season					Playoffs				
Season	Club	Lea	GP	G	A	TP	PIM	GP	G	A	TP	PIM
1984-85	Guelph	OHL	61	8	22	30	139	....	....	....	....	....
1985-86a	Guelph	OHL	54	12	30	42	126	18	10	10	20	37
1986-87	**Detroit**	**NHL**	**45**	**1**	**4**	**5**	**73**	**2**	**0**	**0**	**0**	**19**
1987-88	**Detroit**	**NHL**	**29**	**2**	**9**	**11**	**57**	**9**	**2**	**2**	**4**	**31**
	Adirondack	AHL	23	6	11	17	58	....	....	....	....	....
1988-89	**Detroit**	**NHL**	**65**	**12**	**35**	**47**	**149**	**5**	**2**	**1**	**3**	**6**
1989-90	**Detroit**	**NHL**	**67**	**14**	**28**	**42**	**114**	....	....	....	....	....
1990-91	**Detroit**	**NHL**	**42**	**3**	**17**	**20**	**80**	**5**	**3**	**1**	**4**	**19**
1991-92	**Detroit**	**NHL**	**62**	**10**	**24**	**34**	**136**	**11**	**1**	**5**	**6**	**12**
1992-93	**Detroit**	**NHL**	**79**	**12**	**50**	**62**	**155**	**7**	**2**	**2**	**4**	**19**
1993-94	**Detroit**	**NHL**	**82**	**13**	**33**	**46**	**122**	**7**	**2**	**3**	**5**	**2**
1994-95	**Calgary**	**NHL**	**45**	**2**	**23**	**25**	**39**	**7**	**1**	**2**	**3**	**9**
	NHL Totals		**516**	**69**	**223**	**292**	**925**	**53**	**13**	**16**	**29**	**117**

a Won Stafford Smythe Memorial Trophy (Memorial Cup Tournament MVP) (1986)

Played in NHL All-Star Game (1993)

Traded to **Calgary** by **Detroit** for Mike Vernon, June 29, 1994.

CHIBIREV, IGOR (CHEE-bihr-ehv)

Center. Shoots left. 6', 180 lbs. Born, Kiev, USSR, April 19, 1968.
(Hartford's 8th choice, 266th overall, in 1993 Entry Draft).

			Regular Season					Playoffs				
Season	Club	Lea	GP	G	A	TP	PIM	GP	G	A	TP	PIM
1987-88	CSKA	USSR	29	5	1	6	8	....	....	....	....	....
1988-89	CSKA	USSR	34	7	9	16	16	....	....	....	....	....
1989-90	CSKA	USSR	46	8	2	10	12	....	....	....	....	....
1990-91	CSKA	USSR	40	10	9	19	4	....	....	....	....	....
1991-92	CSKA	CIS	38	21	17	38	46	....	....	....	....	....
1992-93	Fort Wayne	IHL	60	33	36	69	2	12	*7	13	20	2
1993-94	**Hartford**	**NHL**	**37**	**4**	**11**	**15**	**2**	....	....	....	....	....
	Springfield	AHL	36	28	23	51	4	....	....	....	....	....
1994-95	Fort Wayne	IHL	56	34	28	62	10	....	....	....	....	....
	Hartford	**NHL**	**8**	**3**	**1**	**4**	**0**	....	....	....	....	....
	NHL Totals		**45**	**7**	**12**	**19**	**2**	....	....	....	....	....

CHORSKE, TOM (CHOHR-skee) N.J.

Right wing. Shoots right. 6'1", 205 lbs. Born, Minneapolis, MN, September 18, 1966.
(Montreal's 2nd choice, 16th overall, in 1985 Entry Draft).

			Regular Season					Playoffs				
Season	Club	Lea	GP	G	A	TP	PIM	GP	G	A	TP	PIM
1985-86	U. Minnesota	WCHA	39	6	4	10	16	....	....	....	....	....
1986-87	U. Minnesota	WCHA	47	20	22	42	20	....	....	....	....	....
1987-88	U.S. National	....	36	9	16	25	24	....	....	....	....	....
1988-89a	U. Minnesota	WCHA	37	25	24	49	28	....	....	....	....	....
1989-90	**Montreal**	**NHL**	**14**	**3**	**1**	**4**	**2**	....	....	....	....	....
	Sherbrooke	AHL	59	22	24	46	54	12	4	4	8	8
1990-91	**Montreal**	**NHL**	**57**	**9**	**11**	**20**	**32**	....	....	....	....	....
1991-92	**New Jersey**	**NHL**	**76**	**19**	**17**	**36**	**32**	**7**	**0**	**3**	**3**	**4**
1992-93	**New Jersey**	**NHL**	**50**	**7**	**12**	**19**	**25**	**1**	**0**	**0**	**0**	**0**
	Utica	AHL	6	1	4	5	2	....	....	....	....	....
1993-94	**New Jersey**	**NHL**	**76**	**21**	**20**	**41**	**32**	**20**	**4**	**3**	**7**	**0**
1994-95	Milan Devils	Italy	7	11	5	16	6	....	....	....	....	....
	New Jersey	**NHL**	**42**	**10**	**8**	**18**	**16**	**17**	**1**	**5**	**6**	**4**
	NHL Totals		**315**	**69**	**69**	**138**	**139**	**45**	**5**	**11**	**16**	**8**

a WCHA First All-Star Team (1989)

Traded to **New Jersey** by **Montreal** with Stephane Richer for Kirk Muller and Roland Melanson, September 20, 1991.

CHOUINARD, MARC WPG.

Center. Shoots right. 6'5", 187 lbs. Born, Charlesbourg, Ont., May 5, 1977.
(Winnipeg's 2nd choice, 32nd overall, in 1995 Entry Draft).

			Regular Season					Playoffs				
Season	Club	Lea	GP	G	A	TP	PIM	GP	G	A	TP	PIM
1993-94	Beauport	QMJHL	62	11	19	30	23	13	2	5	7	2
1994-95	Beauport	QMJHL	68	24	40	64	32	18	1	6	7	4

CHRISTIAN, DAVE

Right wing. Shoots right. 5'11", 175 lbs. Born, Warroad, MN, May 12, 1959.
(Winnipeg's 2nd choice, 40th overall, in 1979 Entry Draft).

			Regular Season					Playoffs				
Season	Club	Lea	GP	G	A	TP	PIM	GP	G	A	TP	PIM
1977-78	North Dakota	WCHA	38	8	16	24	14	....	....	....	....	....
1978-79	North Dakota	WCHA	40	22	24	46	22	....	....	....	....	....
1979-80	U.S. National	....	59	10	20	30	26	....	....	....	....	....
	U.S. Olympic	....	7	0	8	8	6	....	....	....	....	....
	Winnipeg	**NHL**	**15**	**8**	**10**	**18**	**2**	....	....	....	....	....
1980-81	**Winnipeg**	**NHL**	**80**	**28**	**43**	**71**	**22**	....	....	....	....	....
1981-82	**Winnipeg**	**NHL**	**80**	**25**	**51**	**76**	**28**	**4**	**0**	**1**	**1**	**2**
1982-83	**Winnipeg**	**NHL**	**55**	**18**	**26**	**44**	**23**	**3**	**0**	**0**	**0**	**0**
1983-84	**Washington**	**NHL**	**80**	**29**	**52**	**81**	**28**	**8**	**5**	**4**	**9**	**5**
1984-85	**Washington**	**NHL**	**80**	**26**	**43**	**69**	**14**	**5**	**1**	**1**	**2**	**0**
1985-86	**Washington**	**NHL**	**80**	**41**	**42**	**83**	**15**	**9**	**4**	**4**	**8**	**0**
1986-87	**Washington**	**NHL**	**76**	**23**	**27**	**50**	**8**	**7**	**1**	**3**	**4**	**6**
1987-88	**Washington**	**NHL**	**80**	**37**	**21**	**58**	**26**	**14**	**5**	**6**	**11**	**6**
1988-89	**Washington**	**NHL**	**80**	**34**	**31**	**65**	**12**	**6**	**1**	**1**	**2**	**0**
1989-90	**Washington**	**NHL**	**28**	**3**	**8**	**11**	**4**	....	....	....	....	....
	Boston	**NHL**	**50**	**12**	**17**	**29**	**8**	**21**	**4**	**1**	**5**	**4**
1990-91	**Boston**	**NHL**	**78**	**32**	**21**	**53**	**41**	**19**	**8**	**4**	**12**	**4**
1991-92	**St. Louis**	**NHL**	**78**	**20**	**24**	**44**	**41**	**4**	**3**	**0**	**3**	**0**
1992-93	**Chicago**	**NHL**	**60**	**4**	**14**	**18**	**12**	**1**	**0**	**0**	**0**	**0**
1993-94	**Chicago**	**NHL**	**9**	**0**	**3**	**3**	**0**	**1**	**0**	**0**	**0**	**0**
	Indianapolis	IHL	40	8	18	26	6	....	....	....	....	....
1994-95	Minnesota	IHL	81	38	42	80	16	3	0	1	1	0
	NHL Totals		**1009**	**340**	**433**	**773**	**284**	**102**	**32**	**25**	**57**	**27**

Played in NHL All-Star Game (1991)

Traded to **Washington** by **Winnipeg** for Washington's first round choice (Bob Dollas) in the 1983 Entry Draft, June 8, 1983. Traded to **Boston** by **Washington** for Bob Joyce, December 13, 1989. Acquired by **St. Louis** from **Boston** with Boston's third round choice (Vitali Prokhorov) in 1992 Entry Draft and Boston's seventh round choice (Lance Burns) in 1992 Entry Draft as compensation for Boston's free agent signings of Glen Featherstone and Dave Thomlinson, July 30, 1991. Claimed by **Chicago** from **St. Louis** in NHL Waiver Draft, October 4, 1992.

CHRISTIAN, JEFF PIT.

Left wing. Shoots left. 6'1", 195 lbs. Born, Burlington, Ont., July 30, 1970.
(New Jersey's 2nd choice, 23rd overall, in 1988 Entry Draft).

			Regular Season					Playoffs				
Season	Club	Lea	GP	G	A	TP	PIM	GP	G	A	TP	PIM
1987-88	London	OHL	64	15	29	44	154	9	1	5	6	27
1988-89	London	OHL	60	27	30	57	221	20	3	4	7	56
1989-90	London	OHL	18	14	7	21	64	....	....	....	....	....
	Owen Sound	OHL	37	19	26	45	145	10	6	7	13	43
1990-91	Utica	AHL	80	24	42	66	165	....	....	....	....	....
1991-92	**New Jersey**	**NHL**	**2**	**0**	**0**	**0**	**2**	....	....	....	....	....
	Utica	AHL	76	27	24	51	198	4	0	0	0	16
1992-93	Utica	AHL	22	4	6	10	39	....	....	....	....	....
	Hamilton	AHL	11	2	5	7	35	....	....	....	....	....
	Cincinnati	IHL	36	5	12	17	113	....	....	....	....	....
1993-94	Albany	AHL	76	34	43	77	227	5	1	2	3	19
1994-95	**Pittsburgh**	**NHL**	**1**	**0**	**0**	**0**	**0**	....	....	....	....	....
	Cleveland	IHL	56	13	24	37	126	2	0	1	1	8
	NHL Totals		**3**	**0**	**0**	**0**	**2**	....	....	....	....	....

Signed as a free agent by **Pittsburgh**, August 2, 1994.

CHURCH, BRAD WSH.

Left wing. Shoots left. 6'1", 210 lbs. Born, Dauphin, Man., November 14, 1976.
(Washington's 1st choice, 17th overall, in 1995 Entry Draft).

			Regular Season					Playoffs				
Season	Club	Lea	GP	G	A	TP	PIM	GP	G	A	TP	PIM
1993-94	Prince Albert	WHL	61	33	20	53	197	....	....	....	....	....
1994-95	Prince Albert	WHL	62	26	24	50	184	15	6	9	15	32

CHURLA, SHANE DAL.

Right wing. Shoots right. 6'1", 200 lbs. Born, Fernie, B.C., June 24, 1965.
(Hartford's 4th choice, 110th overall, in 1985 Entry Draft).

			Regular Season					Playoffs				
Season	Club	Lea	GP	G	A	TP	PIM	GP	G	A	TP	PIM
1983-84	Medicine Hat	WHL	48	3	7	10	115	14	1	5	6	41
1984-85	Medicine Hat	WHL	70	14	20	34	370	9	1	0	1	55
1985-86	Binghamton	AHL	52	4	10	14	306	3	0	0	0	22
1986-87	**Hartford**	**NHL**	**20**	**0**	**1**	**1**	**78**	**2**	**0**	**0**	**0**	**42**
	Binghamton	AHL	24	1	5	6	249	....	....	....	....	....
1987-88	**Hartford**	**NHL**	**2**	**0**	**0**	**0**	**14**	....	....	....	....	....
	Binghamton	AHL	25	5	8	13	168	....	....	....	....	....
	Calgary	**NHL**	**29**	**1**	**5**	**6**	**132**	**7**	**0**	**1**	**1**	**17**
1988-89	**Calgary**	**NHL**	**5**	**0**	**0**	**0**	**25**	....	....	....	....	....
	Salt Lake	IHL	32	3	13	16	278	....	....	....	....	....
	Minnesota	**NHL**	**13**	**1**	**0**	**1**	**54**	....	....	....	....	....
1989-90	**Minnesota**	**NHL**	**53**	**2**	**3**	**5**	**292**	**7**	**0**	**0**	**0**	**44**
1990-91	**Minnesota**	**NHL**	**40**	**2**	**2**	**4**	**286**	**22**	**2**	**1**	**3**	**90**
1991-92	**Minnesota**	**NHL**	**57**	**4**	**1**	**5**	**278**	....	....	....	....	....
1992-93	**Minnesota**	**NHL**	**73**	**5**	**16**	**21**	**286**	....	....	....	....	....
1993-94	**Dallas**	**NHL**	**69**	**6**	**7**	**13**	**333**	**9**	**1**	**3**	**4**	**35**
1994-95	**Dallas**	**NHL**	**27**	**1**	**3**	**4**	**186**	**5**	**0**	**0**	**0**	**20**
	NHL Totals		**388**	**22**	**38**	**60**	**1964**	**52**	**3**	**5**	**8**	**248**

Traded to **Calgary** by **Hartford** with Dana Murzyn for Neil Sheehy, Carey Wilson, and the rights to Lane MacDonald, January 3, 1988. Traded to **Minnesota** by **Calgary** with Perry Berezan for Brian MacLellan and Minnesota's fourth round choice (Robert Reichel) in 1989 Entry Draft, March 4, 1989. Claimed by **San Jose** from **Minnesota** in Dispersal Draft, May 30, 1991. Traded to **Minnesota** by **San Jose** for Kelly Kisio, June 3, 1991.

CHYNOWETH, DEAN (shih-NOWTH) NYI

Defense. Shoots right. 6'2", 190 lbs.   Born, Calgary, Alta., October 30, 1968.
(NY Islanders' 1st choice, 13th overall, in 1987 Entry Draft).

			Regular Season					Playoffs				
Season	Club	Lea	GP	G	A	TP	PIM	GP	G	A	TP	PIM
1985-86	Medicine Hat	WHL	69	3	12	15	208	17	3	2	5	52
1986-87	Medicine Hat	WHL	67	3	18	21	285	13	4	2	6	28
1987-88	Medicine Hat	WHL	64	1	21	22	274	16	0	6	6	*87
1988-89	**NY Islanders**	**NHL**	**6**	**0**	**0**	**0**	**48**	....	....	....	....	....
1989-90	**NY Islanders**	**NHL**	**20**	**0**	**2**	**2**	**39**	....	....	....	....	....
	Springfield	AHL	40	0	7	7	98	17	0	4	4	36
1990-91	**NY Islanders**	**NHL**	**25**	**1**	**1**	**2**	**59**	....	....	....	....	....
	Capital Dist.	AHL	44	1	5	6	176	....	....	....	....	....
1991-92	**NY Islanders**	**NHL**	**11**	**1**	**0**	**1**	**23**	....	....	....	....	....
	Capital Dist.	AHL	43	4	6	10	164	6	1	1	2	39
1992-93	Capital Dist.	AHL	52	3	10	13	197	4	0	1	1	9
1993-94	**NY Islanders**	**NHL**	**39**	**0**	**4**	**4**	**122**	**2**	**0**	**0**	**0**	**2**
	Salt Lake	IHL	5	0	1	1	33	....	....	....	....	....
1994-95	**NY Islanders**	**NHL**	**32**	**0**	**2**	**2**	**77**	....	....	....	....	....
	NHL Totals		**133**	**2**	**9**	**11**	**368**	**2**	**0**	**0**	**0**	**2**

CHYZOWSKI, DAVID (chih-ZOW-skee)

Left wing. Shoots left. 6'1", 190 lbs.   Born, Edmonton, Alta., July 11, 1971.
(NY Islanders' 1st choice, 2nd overall, in 1989 Entry Draft).

			Regular Season					Playoffs				
Season	Club	Lea	GP	G	A	TP	PIM	GP	G	A	TP	PIM
1987-88	Kamloops	WHL	66	16	17	33	117	18	2	4	6	26
1988-89a	Kamloops	WHL	68	56	48	104	139	16	15	13	28	32
1989-90	**NY Islanders**	**NHL**	**34**	**8**	**6**	**14**	**45**	....	....	....	....	....
	Springfield	AHL	4	0	0	0	7	....	....	....	....	....
	Kamloops	WHL	4	5	2	7	17	17	11	6	17	46
1990-91	**NY Islanders**	**NHL**	**56**	**5**	**9**	**14**	**61**	....	....	....	....	....
	Capital Dist.	AHL	7	3	6	9	22	....	....	....	....	....
1991-92	**NY Islanders**	**NHL**	**12**	**1**	**1**	**2**	**17**	....	....	....	....	....
	Capital Dist.	AHL	55	15	18	33	121	6	1	1	2	23
1992-93	Capital Dist.	AHL	66	15	21	36	177	3	2	0	2	0
1993-94	**NY Islanders**	**NHL**	**3**	**1**	**0**	**1**	**4**	**2**	**0**	**0**	**0**	**0**
	Salt Lake	IHL	66	27	13	40	151	....	....	....	....	....
1994-95	**NY Islanders**	**NHL**	**13**	**0**	**0**	**0**	**11**	....	....	....	....	....
	Kalamazoo	IHL	4	0	4	4	8	16	9	5	14	27
	NHL Totals		**118**	**15**	**16**	**31**	**138**	**2**	**0**	**0**	**0**	**0**

a   WHL West All-Star Team (1989)

CIAVAGLIA, PETER (see-a-VIHG-lee-a)

Center. Shoots left. 5'10", 173 lbs.   Born, Albany, NY, July 15, 1969.
(Calgary's 8th choice, 145th overall, in 1987 Entry Draft).

			Regular Season					Playoffs				
Season	Club	Lea	GP	G	A	TP	PIM	GP	G	A	TP	PIM
1987-88	Harvard	ECAC	30	10	23	33	16	....	....	....	....	....
1988-89a	Harvard	ECAC	34	15	48	63	36	....	....	....	....	....
1989-90	Harvard	ECAC	28	17	18	35	22	....	....	....	....	....
1990-91ab	Harvard	ECAC	27	24	*38	*62	2	....	....	....	....	....
1991-92	**Buffalo**	**NHL**	**2**	**0**	**0**	**0**	**0**	....	....	....	....	....
	Rochester	AHL	77	37	61	98	16	6	2	5	7	6
1992-93	**Buffalo**	**NHL**	**3**	**0**	**0**	**0**	**0**	....	....	....	....	....
	Rochester	AHL	64	35	67	102	32	17	9	16	25	12
1993-94	Leksand	Swe.	39	14	18	32	34	4	1	2	3	0
	U.S. National	....	18	2	9	11	6	....	....	....	....	....
	U.S. Olympic	....	8	2	4	6	0	....	....	....	....	....
1994-95	Detroit	IHL	73	22	59	81	83	5	1	1	2	6
	NHL Totals		**5**	**0**	**0**	**0**	**0**	....	....	....	....	....

a   ECAC Second All-Star Team (1989, 1991)
b   NCAA East Second All-American Team (1991)
Signed as a free agent by **Buffalo**, August 30, 1991.

CICCARELLI, DINO (sih-sih-REHL-ee) DET.

Right wing. Shoots right. 5'10", 185 lbs.   Born, Sarnia, Ont., February 8, 1960.

			Regular Season					Playoffs				
Season	Club	Lea	GP	G	A	TP	PIM	GP	G	A	TP	PIM
1977-78a	London	OHA	68	72	70	142	49	9	6	10	16	6
1978-79	London	OHA	30	8	11	19	35	7	3	5	8	0
1979-80	London	OHA	62	50	53	103	72	5	2	6	8	15
1980-81	**Minnesota**	**NHL**	**32**	**18**	**12**	**30**	**29**	**19**	**14**	**7**	**21**	**25**
	Oklahoma City	CHL	48	32	25	57	45	....	....	....	....	....
1981-82	**Minnesota**	**NHL**	**76**	**55**	**51**	**106**	**138**	**4**	**3**	**1**	**4**	**2**
1982-83	**Minnesota**	**NHL**	**77**	**37**	**38**	**75**	**94**	**9**	**4**	**6**	**10**	**11**
1983-84	**Minnesota**	**NHL**	**79**	**38**	**33**	**71**	**58**	**16**	**4**	**5**	**9**	**27**
1984-85	**Minnesota**	**NHL**	**51**	**15**	**17**	**32**	**41**	**9**	**3**	**3**	**6**	**8**
1985-86	**Minnesota**	**NHL**	**75**	**44**	**45**	**89**	**51**	**5**	**0**	**1**	**1**	**6**
1986-87	**Minnesota**	**NHL**	**80**	**52**	**51**	**103**	**88**	....	....	....	....	....
1987-88	**Minnesota**	**NHL**	**67**	**41**	**45**	**86**	**79**	....	....	....	....	....
1988-89	**Minnesota**	**NHL**	**65**	**32**	**27**	**59**	**64**	....	....	....	....	....
	Washington	**NHL**	**11**	**12**	**3**	**15**	**12**	**6**	**3**	**3**	**6**	**12**
1989-90	**Washington**	**NHL**	**80**	**41**	**38**	**79**	**122**	**8**	**8**	**3**	**11**	**6**
1990-91	**Washington**	**NHL**	**54**	**21**	**18**	**39**	**66**	**11**	**5**	**4**	**9**	**22**
1991-92	**Washington**	**NHL**	**78**	**38**	**38**	**76**	**78**	**7**	**5**	**4**	**9**	**14**
1992-93	**Detroit**	**NHL**	**82**	**41**	**56**	**97**	**81**	**7**	**4**	**2**	**6**	**16**
1993-94	**Detroit**	**NHL**	**66**	**28**	**29**	**57**	**73**	**7**	**5**	**2**	**7**	**14**
1994-95	**Detroit**	**NHL**	**42**	**16**	**27**	**43**	**39**	**16**	**9**	**2**	**11**	**22**
	NHL Totals		**1015**	**529**	**528**	**1057**	**1113**	**124**	**67**	**43**	**110**	**185**

a   OHA Second All-Star Team (1978)
Played in NHL All-Star Game (1982, 1983, 1989)
Signed as a free agent by **Minnesota**, September 28, 1979. Traded to **Washington** by **Minnesota** with Bob Rouse for Mike Gartner and Larry Murphy, March 7, 1989. Traded to **Detroit** by **Washington** for Kevin Miller, June 20, 1992.

CICCONE, ENRICO (CHIH-koh-nee) T.B.

Defense. Shoots left. 6'4", 210 lbs.   Born, Montreal, Que., April 10, 1970.
(Minnesota's 5th choice, 92nd overall, in 1990 Entry Draft).

			Regular Season					Playoffs				
Season	Club	Lea	GP	G	A	TP	PIM	GP	G	A	TP	PIM
1987-88	Shawinigan	QMJHL	61	2	12	14	324	....	....	....	....	....
1988-89	Shawinigan	QMJHL	34	7	11	18	132	....	....	....	....	....
	Trois-Rivières	QMJHL	24	0	7	7	153	....	....	....	....	....
1989-90	Trois-Rivières	QMJHL	40	4	24	28	227	3	0	0	0	15
1990-91	Kalamazoo	IHL	57	4	9	13	384	4	0	1	1	32
1991-92	**Minnesota**	**NHL**	**11**	**0**	**0**	**0**	**48**	....	....	....	....	....
	Kalamazoo	IHL	53	4	16	20	406	10	0	1	1	58
1992-93	**Minnesota**	**NHL**	**31**	**0**	**1**	**1**	**115**	....	....	....	....	....
	Kalamazoo	IHL	13	1	3	4	50	....	....	....	....	....
	Hamilton	AHL	6	1	3	4	44	....	....	....	....	....
1993-94	**Washington**	**NHL**	**46**	**1**	**1**	**2**	**174**	....	....	....	....	....
	Portland	AHL	6	0	0	0	27	....	....	....	....	....
	Tampa Bay	**NHL**	**11**	**0**	**1**	**1**	**52**	....	....	....	....	....
1994-95	**Tampa Bay**	**NHL**	**41**	**2**	**4**	**6**	***225**	....	....	....	....	....
	NHL Totals		**140**	**3**	**7**	**10**	**614**	....	....	....	....	....

Traded to **Washington** by **Dallas** to complete June 20, 1993 trade which sent Paul Cavallini to Dallas for future considerations, June 25, 1993. Traded to **Tampa Bay** by **Washington** with Washington's third round choice (later traded to Anaheim — Anaheim selected Craig Reichert) in 1994 Entry Draft and the return of future draft choices transferred in the Pat Elynuik trade for Joe Reekie, March 21, 1994.

CICHOCKI, CHRIS (chih-HAH-kee)

Right wing. Shoots right. 5'11", 185 lbs.   Born, Detroit, MI, September 17, 1963.

			Regular Season					Playoffs				
Season	Club	Lea	GP	G	A	TP	PIM	GP	G	A	TP	PIM
1982-83	Michigan Tech	CCHA	36	12	10	22	10	....	....	....	....	....
1983-84	Michigan Tech	CCHA	40	25	20	45	36	....	....	....	....	....
1984-85	Michigan Tech	CCHA	40	30	24	54	14	....	....	....	....	....
1985-86	**Detroit**	**NHL**	**59**	**10**	**11**	**21**	**21**	....	....	....	....	....
	Adirondack	AHL	9	4	4	8	6	....	....	....	....	....
1986-87	**Detroit**	**NHL**	**2**	**0**	**0**	**0**	**2**	....	....	....	....	....
	Adirondack	AHL	55	31	34	65	27	....	....	....	....	....
	Maine	AHL	7	2	2	4	0	....	....	....	....	....
1987-88	**New Jersey**	**NHL**	**5**	**1**	**0**	**1**	**2**	....	....	....	....	....
	Utica	AHL	69	36	30	66	66	....	....	....	....	....
1988-89	**New Jersey**	**NHL**	**2**	**0**	**1**	**1**	**2**	....	....	....	....	....
	Utica	AHL	59	32	31	63	50	5	0	1	1	2
1989-90	Utica	AHL	11	3	1	4	10	....	....	....	....	....
	Binghamton	AHL	60	21	26	47	22	....	....	....	....	....
1990-91	Binghamton	AHL	80	35	30	65	70	9	0	4	4	2
1991-92	Binghamton	AHL	75	28	29	57	132	6	5	4	9	4
1992-93	Binghamton	AHL	65	23	29	52	78	9	3	2	5	25
1993-94	Cincinnati	IHL	69	22	20	42	101	11	2	2	4	12
1994-95	Cincinnati	IHL	75	22	30	52	50	8	0	3	3	6
	NHL Totals		**68**	**11**	**12**	**23**	**27**	....	....	....	....	....

Signed as a free agent by **Detroit**, June 28, 1985. Traded to **New Jersey** by **Detroit** with Detroit's third round choice (later traded to Buffalo – Buffalo selected Andrew MacVicar) in 1987 Entry Draft for Mel Bridgman, March 9, 1987. Traded to **Hartford** by **New Jersey** for Jim Thomson, October 31, 1989. Signed as a free agent by **NY Rangers**, September 6, 1990.

CIERNY, JOZEF (chee-ER-nee) EDM.

Left wing. Shoots left. 6'2", 185 lbs.   Born, Zvolen, Czech., May 13, 1974.
(Buffalo's 2nd choice, 35th overall, in 1992 Entry Draft).

			Regular Season					Playoffs				
Season	Club	Lea	GP	G	A	TP	PIM	GP	G	A	TP	PIM
1991-92	ZTK Zvolen	Czech.2	26	10	3	13	8	....	....	....	....	....
1992-93	Rochester	AHL	54	27	27	54	36	....	....	....	....	....
1993-94	**Edmonton**	**NHL**	**1**	**0**	**0**	**0**	**0**	....	....	....	....	....
	Cape Breton	AHL	73	30	27	57	88	4	1	1	2	4
1994-95	Cape Breton	AHL	73	28	24	52	58	....	....	....	....	....
	NHL Totals		**1**	**0**	**0**	**0**	**0**	....	....	....	....	....

Traded to **Edmonton** by **Buffalo** with Buffalo's fourth round choice (Jussi Tarvainen) in 1994 Entry Draft for Craig Simpson, September 1, 1993.

CIGER, ZDENO (SEE-gur) EDM.

Left wing. Shoots left. 6'1", 190 lbs.   Born, Martin, Czech., October 19, 1969.
(New Jersey's 3rd choice, 54th overall, in 1988 Entry Draft).

			Regular Season					Playoffs				
Season	Club	Lea	GP	G	A	TP	PIM	GP	G	A	TP	PIM
1987-88	Dukla Trencin	Czech.	8	3	4	7	2	....	....	....	....	....
1988-89	Dukla Trencin	Czech.	43	18	13	31	18	....	....	....	....	....
1989-90	Dukla Trencin	Czech.	53	18	28	46	....	....	....	....	....	....
1990-91	**New Jersey**	**NHL**	**45**	**8**	**17**	**25**	**8**	**6**	**0**	**2**	**2**	**4**
	Utica	AHL	8	5	4	9	2	....	....	....	....	....
1991-92	**New Jersey**	**NHL**	**20**	**6**	**5**	**11**	**10**	**7**	**2**	**4**	**6**	**0**
1992-93	**New Jersey**	**NHL**	**27**	**4**	**8**	**12**	**2**	....	....	....	....	....
	Edmonton	**NHL**	**37**	**9**	**15**	**24**	**6**	....	....	....	....	....
1993-94	**Edmonton**	**NHL**	**84**	**22**	**35**	**57**	**8**	....	....	....	....	....
1994-95	Dukla Trencin	Slov.	34	23	25	48	8	9	2	9	11	2
	Edmonton	**NHL**	**5**	**2**	**2**	**4**	**0**	....	....	....	....	....
	NHL Totals		**218**	**51**	**82**	**133**	**34**	**13**	**2**	**6**	**8**	**4**

Traded to **Edmonton** by **New Jersey** with Kevin Todd for Bernie Nicholls, January 13, 1993.

CIRELLA, JOE (suh-REHL-uh)

Defense. Shoots right. 6'3", 210 lbs. Born, Hamilton, Ont., May 9, 1963.
(Colorado's 1st choice, 5th overall, in 1981 Entry Draft).

			Regular Season					Playoffs				
Season	Club	Lea	GP	G	A	TP	PIM	GP	G	A	TP	PIM
1980-81	Oshawa	OHA	56	5	31	36	220	11	0	2	2	41
1981-82	**Colorado**	**NHL**	**65**	**7**	**12**	**19**	**52**	....	....	....	....	....
	Oshawa	OHL	3	0	1	1	0	11	7	10	17	32
1982-83	**New Jersey**	**NHL**	**2**	**0**	**1**	**1**	**4**	....	....	....	....	....
a	Oshawa	OHL	56	13	55	68	110	17	4	16	20	37
1983-84	**New Jersey**	**NHL**	**79**	**11**	**33**	**44**	**137**	....	....	....	....	....
1984-85	**New Jersey**	**NHL**	**66**	**6**	**18**	**24**	**141**	....	....	....	....	....
1985-86	**New Jersey**	**NHL**	**66**	**6**	**23**	**29**	**147**	....	....	....	....	....
1986-87	**New Jersey**	**NHL**	**65**	**9**	**22**	**31**	**111**	....	....	....	....	....
1987-88	**New Jersey**	**NHL**	**80**	**8**	**31**	**39**	**191**	**19**	**0**	**7**	**7**	**49**
1988-89	**New Jersey**	**NHL**	**80**	**3**	**19**	**22**	**155**	....	....	....	....	....
1989-90	**Quebec**	**NHL**	**56**	**4**	**14**	**18**	**67**	....	....	....	....	....
1990-91	**Quebec**	**NHL**	**39**	**2**	**10**	**12**	**59**	....	....	....	....	....
	NY Rangers	**NHL**	**19**	**1**	**0**	**1**	**52**	**6**	**0**	**2**	**2**	**26**
1991-92	**NY Rangers**	**NHL**	**67**	**3**	**12**	**15**	**121**	**13**	**0**	**4**	**4**	**23**
1992-93	**NY Rangers**	**NHL**	**55**	**3**	**6**	**9**	**85**	....	....	....	....	....
1993-94	**Florida**	**NHL**	**63**	**1**	**9**	**10**	**99**	....	....	....	....	....
1994-95	**Florida**	**NHL**	**20**	**0**	**1**	**1**	**21**	....	....	....	....	....
	NHL Totals		**822**	**64**	**211**	**275**	**1442**	**38**	**0**	**13**	**13**	**98**

a OHL First All-Star Team (1983)

Played in NHL All-Star Game (1984)

Traded to **Quebec** by **New Jersey** with Claude Loiselle and New Jersey's eighth round choice (Alexander Karpovtsev) in 1990 Entry Draft for Walt Poddubny and Quebec's fourth round choice (Mike Bodnarchuk) in 1990 Entry Draft, June 17, 1989. Traded to **NY Rangers** by **Quebec** for Aaron Miller and NY Rangers' fifth round choice (Bill Lindsay) in 1991 Entry Draft, January 17, 1991. Claimed by **Florida** from **NY Rangers** in Expansion Draft, June 24, 1993.

CIRJAK, JOHN — COL.

Center. Shoots right. 6'2", 180 lbs. Born, Vancouver, B.C., February 10, 1977.
(Colorado's 6th choice, 155th overall, in 1995 Entry Draft).

			Regular Season					Playoffs				
Season	Club	Lea	GP	G	A	TP	PIM	GP	G	A	TP	PIM
1993-94	Spokane	WHL	44	2	5	7	22	3	0	0	0	0
1994-95	Spokane	WHL	69	21	37	58	58	11	4	11	15	11

CIRONE, JASON (suh-ROHN)

Center. Shoots left. 5'9", 185 lbs. Born, Toronto, Ont., February 21, 1971.
(Winnipeg's 3rd choice, 46th overall, in 1989 Entry Draft).

			Regular Season					Playoffs				
Season	Club	Lea	GP	G	A	TP	PIM	GP	G	A	TP	PIM
1987-88	Cornwall	OHL	53	12	11	23	41	11	1	2	3	4
1988-89	Cornwall	OHL	64	39	44	83	67	17	19	8	27	14
1989-90	Cornwall	OHL	32	22	41	63	56	6	4	2	6	14
1990-91	Cornwall	OHL	40	31	29	60	66	....	....	....	....	....
	Windsor	OHL	23	27	23	50	31	11	9	8	17	14
1991-92	**Winnipeg**	**NHL**	**3**	**0**	**0**	**0**	**2**	....	....	....	....	....
	Moncton	AHL	64	32	27	59	124	10	1	1	2	8
1992-93	Asiago	Alp.	25	24	14	38	36	....	....	....	....	....
	Asiago	Italy	16	6	5	11	18	2	1	5	6	18
1993-94	Cincinnati	IHL	26	4	2	6	61	....	....	....	....	....
	Birmingham	ECHL	11	3	3	6	45	10	8	8	16	*67
1994-95	Cincinnati	IHL	74	22	15	37	170	9	1	1	2	14
	NHL Totals		**3**	**0**	**0**	**0**	**2**	....	....	....	....	....

Traded to **Florida** by **Winnipeg** for Dave Tomlinson, August 3, 1993.

CLARK, CHRIS — CGY.

Right wing. Shoots right. 6', 190 lbs. Born, Manchester, CT, March 8, 1976.
(Calgary's 3rd choice, 77th overall, in 1994 Entry Draft).

			Regular Season					Playoffs				
Season	Club	Lea	GP	G	A	TP	PIM	GP	G	A	TP	PIM
1993-94	Springfield	Jr. B	35	31	26	57	185	....	....	....	....	....
1994-95	Clarkson	ECAC	32	12	11	23	92	....	....	....	....	....

CLARK, JASON — VAN.

Center. Shoots left. 6'1", 185 lbs. Born, Belmont, Ont., May 6, 1972.
(Vancouver's 8th choice, 141st overall, in 1992 Entry Draft).

			Regular Season					Playoffs				
Season	Club	Lea	GP	G	A	TP	PIM	GP	G	A	TP	PIM
1992-93	Bowling Green	CCHA	40	10	17	27	42	....	....	....	....	....
1993-94	Bowling Green	CCHA	37	10	18	28	39	....	....	....	....	....
1994-95	Bowling Green	CCHA	37	17	22	39	50	....	....	....	....	....

CLARK, KERRY

Right wing. Shoots right. 6'1", 190 lbs. Born, Kelvington, Sask., August 21, 1968.
(NY Islanders' 12th choice, 206th overall, in 1986 Entry Draft).

			Regular Season					Playoffs				
Season	Club	Lea	GP	G	A	TP	PIM	GP	G	A	TP	PIM
1985-86	Regina	WHL	23	4	4	8	58	....	....	....	....	....
	Saskatoon	WHL	39	5	8	13	104	13	2	2	4	33
1986-87	Saskatoon	WHL	54	12	10	22	229	8	0	1	1	23
1987-88	Saskatoon	WHL	67	15	11	26	241	10	2	2	4	16
1988-89	Springfield	AHL	63	7	7	14	264	....	....	....	....	....
	Indianapolis	IHL	3	0	1	1	12	....	....	....	....	....
1989-90	Springfield	AHL	21	0	1	1	73	....	....	....	....	....
	Phoenix	IHL	38	4	8	12	262	....	....	....	....	....
1990-91	Salt Lake	IHL	62	14	14	28	372	4	1	1	2	12
1991-92	Salt Lake	IHL	74	12	14	26	266	5	1	0	1	34
1992-93	Salt Lake	IHL	64	14	15	29	255	....	....	....	....	....
1993-94	Portland	AHL	55	9	5	14	309	5	0	0	0	26
1994-95	Portland	AHL	57	9	12	21	282	1	0	0	0	0

Signed as a free agent by **Calgary**, July 23, 1990. Signed as a free agent by **Washington**, September 23, 1994.

CLARK, WENDEL — COL.

Left wing. Shoots left. 5'11", 194 lbs. Born, Kelvington, Sask., October 25, 1966.
(Toronto's 1st choice, 1st overall, in 1985 Entry Draft).

			Regular Season					Playoffs				
Season	Club	Lea	GP	G	A	TP	PIM	GP	G	A	TP	PIM
1983-84	Saskatoon	WHL	72	23	45	68	225	....	....	....	....	....
1984-85a	Saskatoon	WHL	64	32	55	87	253	3	3	3	6	7
1985-86b	**Toronto**	**NHL**	**66**	**34**	**11**	**45**	**227**	**10**	**5**	**1**	**6**	**47**
1986-87	**Toronto**	**NHL**	**80**	**37**	**23**	**60**	**271**	**13**	**6**	**5**	**11**	**38**
1987-88	**Toronto**	**NHL**	**28**	**12**	**11**	**23**	**80**	....	....	....	....	....
1988-89	**Toronto**	**NHL**	**15**	**7**	**4**	**11**	**66**	....	....	....	....	....
1989-90	**Toronto**	**NHL**	**38**	**18**	**8**	**26**	**116**	**5**	**1**	**1**	**2**	**19**
1990-91	**Toronto**	**NHL**	**63**	**18**	**16**	**34**	**152**	....	....	....	....	....
1991-92	**Toronto**	**NHL**	**43**	**19**	**21**	**40**	**123**	....	....	....	....	....
1992-93	**Toronto**	**NHL**	**66**	**17**	**22**	**39**	**193**	**21**	**10**	**10**	**20**	**51**
1993-94	**Toronto**	**NHL**	**64**	**46**	**30**	**76**	**115**	**18**	**9**	**7**	**16**	**24**
1994-95	**Quebec**	**NHL**	**37**	**12**	**18**	**30**	**45**	**6**	**1**	**2**	**3**	**6**
	NHL Totals		**500**	**220**	**164**	**384**	**1388**	**73**	**32**	**26**	**58**	**185**

a WHL East First All-Star Team (1985)
b NHL All-Rookie Team (1986)

Played in NHL All-Star Game (1986)

Traded to **Quebec** by **Toronto** with Sylvain Lefebvre, Landon Wilson and Toronto's first round choice (Jeffrey Kealty) in 1994 Entry Draft for Mats Sundin, Garth Butcher, Todd Warriner and Philadelphia's first round choice (previously acquired by Quebec — later traded to Washington — Washington selected Nolan Baumgartner) in 1994 Entry Draft, June 28, 1994.

CLARKE, WAYNE — TOR.

Right wing. Shoots right. 6'2", 188 lbs. Born, Sterling, Ont., August 30, 1972.
(Toronto's 9th choice, 197th overall, in 1992 Entry Draft).

			Regular Season					Playoffs				
Season	Club	Lea	GP	G	A	TP	PIM	GP	G	A	TP	PIM
1991-92	RPI	ECAC	33	12	17	29	28	....	....	....	....	....
1992-93	RPI	ECAC	32	13	16	29	23	....	....	....	....	....
1993-94	RPI	ECAC	36	22	17	39	24	....	....	....	....	....
1994-95	RPI	ECAC	32	15	14	29	28	....	....	....	....	....

CLIFFORD, BRIAN — PIT.

Center. Shoots right. 6', 185 lbs. Born, Buffalo, NY, June 18, 1973.
(Pittsburgh's 6th choice, 126th overall, in 1991 Entry Draft).

			Regular Season					Playoffs				
Season	Club	Lea	GP	G	A	TP	PIM	GP	G	A	TP	PIM
1992-93	Michigan State	CCHA	34	15	7	22	20	....	....	....	....	....
1993-94	Michigan State	CCHA	35	6	4	10	22	....	....	....	....	....
1994-95	Michigan State	CCHA	17	2	5	7	8	....	....	....	....	....

CLOUTIER, COLIN (clootz-YAY) — T.B.

Center. Shoots left. 6'3", 224 lbs. Born, Winnipeg, Man., January 27, 1976.
(Tampa Bay's 2nd choice, 34th overall, in 1994 Entry Draft).

			Regular Season					Playoffs				
Season	Club	Lea	GP	G	A	TP	PIM	GP	G	A	TP	PIM
1992-93	Brandon	WHL	60	11	15	26	138	4	0	0	0	18
1993-94	Brandon	WHL	30	10	13	23	102	11	2	5	7	23
1994-95	Brandon	WHL	47	16	27	43	170	16	5	6	11	47

CLOUTIER, FRANCOIS (clootz-YAY) — FLA.

Left wing. Shoots left. 6'2", 206 lbs. Born, Sherbrooke, Que., April 28, 1977.
(Florida's 6th choice, 114th overall, in 1995 Entry Draft).

			Regular Season					Playoffs				
Season	Club	Lea	GP	G	A	TP	PIM	GP	G	A	TP	PIM
1993-94	Hull	QMJHL	7	0	0	0	2	....	....	....	....	....
1994-95	Hull	QMJHL	58	15	5	20	70	17	2	4	6	36

CLOUTIER, SYLVAIN (clootz-YAY) — DET.

Center. Shoots left. 6', 195 lbs. Born, Mont-Laurier, Que., February 13, 1974.
(Detroit's 3rd choice, 70th overall, in 1992 Entry Draft).

			Regular Season					Playoffs				
Season	Club	Lea	GP	G	A	TP	PIM	GP	G	A	TP	PIM
1991-92	Guelph	OHL	62	35	31	66	74	....	....	....	....	....
1992-93	Guelph	OHL	44	26	29	55	78	5	0	5	5	14
1993-94	Guelph	OHL	66	45	71	116	127	9	7	9	16	32
	Adirondack	AHL	2	0	2	2	2	....	....	....	....	....
1994-95	Adirondack	AHL	71	7	26	33	144	....	....	....	....	....

COFFEY, PAUL — DET.

Defense. Shoots left. 6', 190 lbs. Born, Weston, Ont., June 1, 1961.
(Edmonton's 1st choice, 6th overall, in the 1980 Draft).

			Regular Season					Playoffs				
Season	Club	Lea	GP	G	A	TP	PIM	GP	G	A	TP	PIM
1978-79	S.S. Marie	OHA	68	17	72	89	103	....	....	....	....	....
1979-80a	S.S. Marie	OHA	23	10	21	31	63	....	....	....	....	....
	Kitchener	OHA	52	19	52	71	130	....	....	....	....	....
1980-81	**Edmonton**	**NHL**	**74**	**9**	**23**	**32**	**130**	**9**	**4**	**3**	**7**	**22**
1981-82b	**Edmonton**	**NHL**	**80**	**29**	**60**	**89**	**106**	**5**	**1**	**1**	**2**	**6**
1982-83b	**Edmonton**	**NHL**	**80**	**29**	**67**	**96**	**87**	**16**	**7**	**7**	**14**	**14**
1983-84b	**Edmonton**	**NHL**	**80**	**40**	**86**	**126**	**104**	**19**	**8**	**14**	**22**	**21**
1984-85cd	**Edmonton**	**NHL**	**80**	**37**	**84**	**121**	**97**	**18**	**12**	**25**	**37**	**44**
1985-86cd	**Edmonton**	**NHL**	**79**	**48**	**90**	**138**	**120**	**10**	**1**	**9**	**10**	**30**
1986-87	**Edmonton**	**NHL**	**59**	**17**	**50**	**67**	**49**	**17**	**3**	**8**	**11**	**30**
1987-88	**Pittsburgh**	**NHL**	**46**	**15**	**52**	**67**	**93**	....	....	....	....	....
1988-89d	**Pittsburgh**	**NHL**	**75**	**30**	**83**	**113**	**195**	**11**	**2**	**13**	**15**	**31**
1989-90b	**Pittsburgh**	**NHL**	**80**	**29**	**74**	**103**	**95**	....	....	....	....	....
1990-91	**Pittsburgh**	**NHL**	**76**	**24**	**69**	**93**	**128**	**12**	**2**	**9**	**11**	**6**
1991-92	**Pittsburgh**	**NHL**	**54**	**10**	**54**	**64**	**62**	....	....	....	....	....
	Los Angeles	**NHL**	**10**	**1**	**4**	**5**	**25**	**6**	**4**	**3**	**7**	**2**
1992-93	**Los Angeles**	**NHL**	**50**	**8**	**49**	**57**	**50**	....	....	....	....	....
	Detroit	**NHL**	**30**	**4**	**26**	**30**	**27**	**7**	**2**	**9**	**11**	**2**
1993-94	**Detroit**	**NHL**	**80**	**14**	**63**	**77**	**106**	**7**	**1**	**6**	**7**	**8**
1994-95cd	**Detroit**	**NHL**	**45**	**14**	**44**	**58**	**72**	**18**	**6**	**12**	**18**	**10**
	NHL Totals		**1078**	**358**	**978**	**1336**	**1546**	**155**	**53**	**119**	**172**	**226**

a OHA Second All-Star Team (1980)
b NHL Second All-Star Team (1982, 1983, 1984, 1990)
c Won James Norris Memorial Trophy (1985, 1986, 1995)
d NHL First All-Star Team (1985, 1986, 1989, 1995)

Played in NHL All-Star Game (1982-86, 1988-94)

Traded to **Pittsburgh** by **Edmonton** with Dave Hunter and Wayne Van Dorp for Craig Simpson, Dave Hannan, Moe Mantha and Chris Joseph, November 24, 1987. Traded to **Los Angeles** by **Pittsburgh** for Brian Benning, Jeff Chychrun and Los Angeles' first round choice (later traded to Philadelphia — Philadelphia selected Jason Bowen) in 1992 Entry Draft, February 19, 1992. Traded to **Detroit** by **Los Angeles** with Sylvain Couturier and Jim Hiller for Jimmy Carson, Marc Potvin and Gary Shuchuk, January 29, 1993.

COLE, DANTON

Center/Right wing. Shoots right. 5'11", 185 lbs. Born, Pontiac, MI, January 10, 1967.
(Winnipeg's 6th choice, 123rd overall, in 1985 Entry Draft).

			Regular Season					Playoffs				
Season	Club	Lea	GP	G	A	TP	PIM	GP	G	A	TP	PIM
1985-86	Michigan State	CCHA	43	11	10	21	22	....	....	....	....	....
1986-87	Michigan State	CCHA	44	9	15	24	16	....	....	....	....	....
1987-88	Michigan State	CCHA	46	20	36	56	38	....	....	....	....	....
1988-89	Michigan State	CCHA	47	29	33	62	46	....	....	....	....	....
1989-90	**Winnipeg**	**NHL**	**2**	**1**	**1**	**2**	**0**	....	....	....	....	....
	Moncton	AHL	80	31	42	73	18	....	....	....	....	....
1990-91	**Winnipeg**	**NHL**	**66**	**13**	**11**	**24**	**24**	....	....	....	....	....
	Moncton	AHL	3	1	1	2	0	....	....	....	....	....
1991-92	**Winnipeg**	**NHL**	**52**	**7**	**5**	**12**	**32**	....	....	....	....	....
1992-93	**Tampa Bay**	**NHL**	**67**	**12**	**15**	**27**	**23**	....	....	....	....	....
	Atlanta	IHL	1	1	0	1	2	....	....	....	....	....
1993-94	**Tampa Bay**	**NHL**	**81**	**20**	**23**	**43**	**32**	....	....	....	....	....
1994-95	**Tampa Bay**	**NHL**	**26**	**3**	**3**	**6**	**6**	....	....	....	....	....
	New Jersey	**NHL**	**12**	**1**	**2**	**3**	**8**	**1**	**0**	**0**	**0**	**0**
	NHL Totals		**306**	**57**	**60**	**117**	**125**	**1**	**0**	**0**	**0**	**0**

Traded to **Tampa Bay** by **Winnipeg** for future considerations, June 19, 1992. Traded to **New Jersey** by **Tampa Bay** with Shawn Chambers for Alexander Semak and Ben Hankinson, March 14, 1995.

COLEMAN, JON — DET.

Defense. Shoots right. 6'1", 190 lbs. Born, Boston, MA, March 9, 1975.
(Detroit's 2nd choice, 48th overall, in 1993 Entry Draft).

			Regular Season					Playoffs				
Season	Club	Lea	GP	G	A	TP	PIM	GP	G	A	TP	PIM
1993-94	Boston U.	H.E.	29	1	14	15	26	....	....	....	....	....
1994-95	Boston U.	H.E.	40	5	23	28	42	....	....	....	....	....

COLES, BRUCE — PHI.

Left wing. Shoots left. 5'9", 183 lbs. Born, Montreal, Que., January 12, 1968.
(Montreal's 1st choice, 23rd overall, in 1990 Supplemental Draft).

			Regular Season					Playoffs				
Season	Club	Lea	GP	G	A	TP	PIM	GP	G	A	TP	PIM
1987-89	RPI	ECAC	32	16	23	39	48	....	....	....	....	....
1988-89	RPI	ECAC	27	8	14	22	66	....	....	....	....	....
1989-90	RPI	ECAC.	34	*28	24	52	142	....	....	....	....	....
1990-91	RPI	ECAC	31	23	29	52	145	....	....	....	....	....
1991-92	Winston-Salem	ECHL	16	2	6	8	37	....	....	....	....	....
	Johnstown	ECHL	43	32	45	77	113	6	3	1	4	12
1992-93	Johnstown	ECHL	28	28	26	54	61	5	1	3	4	29
	Cdn. National	....	27	9	22	31	20	....	....	....	....	....
1993-94	Johnstown	ECHL	24	23	20	43	56	3	0	1	1	10
1994-95	Johnstown	ECHL	29	20	25	45	56	....	....	....	....	....
	Hershey	AHL	51	16	25	41	73	6	1	5	6	14

Signed as a free agent by **Philadelphia**, May 31, 1995

CONACHER, PAT — (KAH-nuh-kuhr) — L.A.

Left wing. Shoots left. 5'8", 190 lbs. Born, Edmonton, Alta., May 1, 1959.
(NY Rangers' 3rd choice, 76th overall, in 1979 Entry Draft).

			Regular Season					Playoffs				
Season	Club	Lea	GP	G	A	TP	PIM	GP	G	A	TP	PIM
1977-78	Billings	WHL	72	31	44	75	105	20	15	14	29	22
1978-79	Billings	WHL	39	25	37	62	50	....	....	....	....	....
	Saskatoon	WHL	33	15	32	47	37	....	....	....	....	....
1979-80	**NY Rangers**	**NHL**	**17**	**0**	**5**	**5**	**4**	**3**	**0**	**1**	**1**	**2**
	New Haven	AHL	53	11	14	25	43	7	1	1	2	4
1980-81						DID NOT PLAY						
1981-82	Springfield	AHL	77	23	22	45	38	....	....	....	....	....
1982-83	**NY Rangers**	**NHL**	**5**	**0**	**1**	**1**	**4**	....	....	....	....	....
	Tulsa	CHL	63	29	28	57	44	....	....	....	....	....
1983-84	**Edmonton**	**NHL**	**45**	**2**	**8**	**10**	**31**	**3**	**1**	**0**	**1**	**2**
	Moncton	AHL	28	7	16	23	30	....	....	....	....	....
1984-85	Nova Scotia	AHL	68	20	45	65	44	6	3	2	5	0
1985-86	**New Jersey**	**NHL**	**2**	**0**	**2**	**2**	**2**	....	....	....	....	....
	Maine	AHL	69	15	30	45	83	5	1	1	2	11
1986-87	Maine	AHL	56	12	14	26	47	....	....	....	....	....
1987-88	**New Jersey**	**NHL**	**24**	**2**	**5**	**7**	**12**	**17**	**2**	**2**	**4**	**14**
	Utica	AHL	47	14	33	47	32	....	....	....	....	....
1988-89	**New Jersey**	**NHL**	**55**	**7**	**5**	**12**	**14**	....	....	....	....	....
1989-90	**New Jersey**	**NHL**	**19**	**3**	**3**	**6**	**4**	**5**	**1**	**0**	**1**	**10**
	Utica	AHL	57	13	36	49	53	....	....	....	....	....
1990-91	**New Jersey**	**NHL**	**49**	**5**	**11**	**16**	**27**	**7**	**0**	**2**	**2**	**2**
	Utica	AHL	4	0	1	1	6	....	....	....	....	....
1991-92	**New Jersey**	**NHL**	**44**	**7**	**3**	**10**	**16**	**7**	**1**	**1**	**2**	**4**
1992-93	**Los Angeles**	**NHL**	**81**	**9**	**8**	**17**	**20**	**24**	**6**	**4**	**10**	**6**
1993-94	**Los Angeles**	**NHL**	**77**	**15**	**13**	**28**	**71**	....	....	....	....	....
1994-95	**Los Angeles**	**NHL**	**48**	**7**	**9**	**16**	**12**	....	....	....	....	....
	NHL Totals		**466**	**57**	**73**	**130**	**217**	**66**	**11**	**10**	**21**	**40**

Signed as a free agent by **Edmonton**, October 4, 1983. Signed as a free agent by **New Jersey,** August 14, 1985. Traded to **Los Angeles** by **New Jersey** for future considerations, September 3, 1992.

CONLAN, WAYNE — ST.L.

Center. Shoots right. 5'10", 180 lbs. Born, New Haven, CT, January 9, 1972.
(St. Louis' 5th choice, 138th overall, in 1990 Entry Draft).

			Regular Season					Playoffs				
Season	Club	Lea	GP	G	A	TP	PIM	GP	G	A	TP	PIM
1991-92	U. of Maine	H.E.	22	8	1	9	10	....	....	....	....	....
1992-93	U. of Maine	H.E.	3	0	3	3	0	....	....	....	....	....
1993-94	U. of Maine	H.E.	29	7	9	16	28	....	....	....	....	....
1994-95	U. of Maine	H.E.	26	3	8	11	4	....	....	....	....	....

CONN, ROB — N.J.

Left/Right wing. Shoots right. 6'2", 200 lbs. Born, Calgary, Alta., September 3, 1968.

			Regular Season					Playoffs				
Season	Club	Lea	GP	G	A	TP	PIM	GP	G	A	TP	PIM
1988-89	Alaska-Anch.	G.N.	33	21	17	38	46	....	....	....	....	....
1989-90	Alaska-Anch.	G.N.	34	27	21	48	46	....	....	....	....	....
1990-91	Alaska-Anch.	G.N.	43	28	32	60	53	....	....	....	....	....
1991-92	**Chicago**	**NHL**	**2**	**0**	**0**	**0**	**2**	....	....	....	....	....
	Indianapolis	IHL	72	19	16	35	100	....	....	....	....	....
1992-93	Indianapolis	IHL	75	13	14	27	81	5	0	1	1	6
1993-94	Indianapolis	IHL	51	16	11	27	46	....	....	....	....	....
1994-95	Indianapolis	IHL	10	4	4	8	11	....	....	....	....	....
	Albany	AHL	68	35	32	67	76	14	4	6	10	16
	NHL Totals		**2**	**0**	**0**	**0**	**2**	....	....	....	....	....

Signed as a free agent by **Chicago**, July 31, 1991. Traded to **New Jersey** by **Chicago** for Dean Malkoc, January 30, 1995.

CONROY, AL

Center. Shoots right. 5'8", 170 lbs. Born, Calgary, Alta., January 17, 1966.

			Regular Season					Playoffs				
Season	Club	Lea	GP	G	A	TP	PIM	GP	G	A	TP	PIM
1986-87	Rapperswill	Switz.	36	30	32	62	0	....	....	....	....	....
	Rochester	AHL	13	4	4	8	40	13	1	3	4	50
1987-88	Varese	Italy	36	25	39	64	....	....	....	....	....	....
	Adirondack	AHL	13	5	8	13	20	11	1	3	4	41
1988-89	Dortmund	W. Ger.	46	53	78	131	....	....	....	....	....	....
1989-90	Adirondack	AHL	77	23	33	56	147	5	0	0	0	20
1990-91	Adirondack	AHL	80	26	39	65	172	2	1	1	2	0
1991-92	**Philadelphia**	**NHL**	**31**	**2**	**9**	**11**	**74**	....	....	....	....	....
	Hershey	AHL	47	17	28	45	90	6	4	2	6	12
1992-93	**Philadelphia**	**NHL**	**21**	**3**	**2**	**5**	**17**	....	....	....	....	....
	Hershey	AHL	60	28	32	60	130	....	....	....	....	....
1993-94	**Philadelphia**	**NHL**	**62**	**4**	**3**	**7**	**65**	....	....	....	....	....
1994-95	Detroit	IHL	71	18	40	58	151	....	....	....	....	....
	Houston	IHL	9	3	4	7	17	4	1	2	3	8
	NHL Totals		**114**	**9**	**14**	**23**	**156**	....	....	....	....	....

Signed as a free agent by **Detroit**, August 16, 1989. Signed as a free agent by **Philadelphia**, August 21, 1991.

CONROY, CRAIG — MTL.

Center. Shoots right. 6'2", 198 lbs. Born, Potsdam, NY, September 4, 1971.
(Montreal's 7th choice, 123rd overall, in 1990 Entry Draft).

			Regular Season					Playoffs				
Season	Club	Lea	GP	G	A	TP	PIM	GP	G	A	TP	PIM
1990-91	Clarkson	ECAC	40	8	21	29	24	....	....	....	....	....
1991-92	Clarkson	ECAC	31	19	17	36	36	....	....	....	....	....
1992-93	Clarkson	ECAC	35	10	23	33	26	....	....	....	....	....
1993-94abc	Clarkson	ECAC	34	26	*40	*66	46	....	....	....	....	....
1994-95	Fredericton	AHL	55	26	18	44	29	11	7	3	10	6
	Montreal	**NHL**	**6**	**1**	**0**	**1**	**0**	....	....	....	....	....
	NHL Totals		**6**	**1**	**0**	**1**	**0**	....	....	....	....	....

a ECAC First All-Star Team (1994)
b NCAA East First All-American Team (1994)
c NCAA Final Four All-Tournament Team (1994)

CONVERY, BRANDON — TOR.

Center. Shoots right. 6'1", 182 lbs. Born, Kingston, Ont., February 4, 1974.
(Toronto's 1st choice, 8th overall, in 1992 Entry Draft).

			Regular Season					Playoffs				
Season	Club	Lea	GP	G	A	TP	PIM	GP	G	A	TP	PIM
1990-91	Sudbury	OHL	56	26	22	48	18	5	1	1	2	2
1991-92	Sudbury	OHL	44	40	26	66	44	5	3	2	5	4
1992-93	Sudbury	OHL	7	7	9	16	6	....	....	....	....	....
	Niagara Falls	OHL	51	38	39	77	24	4	1	3	4	4
	St. John's	AHL	3	0	0	0	0	5	0	1	1	0
1993-94	Niagara Falls	OHL	29	24	29	53	30	....	....	....	....	....
	Belleville	OHL	23	16	19	35	22	12	4	10	14	13
	St. John's	AHL	....	....	....	....	....	1	0	0	0	0
1994-95	St. John's	AHL	76	34	37	71	43	5	2	2	4	4

COOPER, DAVID — BUF.

Defense. Shoots left. 6'2", 204 lbs. Born, Ottawa, Ont., November 2, 1973.
(Buffalo's 1st choice, 11th overall, in 1992 Entry Draft).

			Regular Season					Playoffs				
Season	Club	Lea	GP	G	A	TP	PIM	GP	G	A	TP	PIM
1989-90	Medicine Hat	WHL	61	4	11	15	65	3	0	2	2	2
1990-91	Medicine Hat	WHL	64	12	31	43	66	11	1	3	4	23
1991-92a	Medicine Hat	WHL	72	17	47	64	176	4	1	4	5	8
1992-93	Medicine Hat	WHL	63	15	50	65	88	10	2	2	4	32
	Rochester	AHL	....	....	....	....	....	2	0	0	0	2
1993-94	Rochester	AHL	68	10	25	35	82	4	1	1	2	2
1994-95	Rochester	AHL	21	2	4	6	48	....	....	....	....	....
	S. Carolina	ECHL	39	9	19	28	90	9	3	8	11	24

a WHL East First All-Star Team (1992)

COPELAND, ADAM — EDM.

Right wing. Shoots right. 6'1", 185 lbs. Born, St. Catharines, Ont., June 5, 1976.
(Edmonton's 6th choice, 79th overall, in 1994 Entry Draft).

			Regular Season					Playoffs				
Season	Club	Lea	GP	G	A	TP	PIM	GP	G	A	TP	PIM
1993-94	Burlington	Jr. A	39	28	44	72	55	....	....	....	....	....
1994-95	Miami-Ohio	CCHA	39	6	4	10	28	....	....	....	....	....

COPELAND, TODD

Defense. Shoots left. 6'2", 210 lbs. Born, Ridgewood, NJ, May 18, 1967.
(New Jersey's 2nd choice, 24th overall, in 1986 Entry Draft).

			Regular Season					Playoffs				
Season	Club	Lea	GP	G	A	TP	PIM	GP	G	A	TP	PIM
1986-87	U. of Michigan	CCHA	34	2	11	13	59	....	....	....	....	....
1987-88	U. of Michigan	CCHA	41	3	10	13	58	....	....	....	....	....
1988-89	U. of Michigan	CCHA	39	5	14	19	102	....	....	....	....	....
1989-90	U. of Michigan	CCHA	34	6	16	22	62	....	....	....	....	....
1990-91	Utica	AHL	79	6	24	30	53	....	....	....	....	....
1991-92	Utica	AHL	80	4	23	27	98	4	2	2	4	2
1992-93	Utica	AHL	16	3	2	5	10	....	....	....	....	....
	Moncton	AHL	16	1	4	5	16	5	1	3	4	2
1993-94	Moncton	AHL	80	4	17	21	158	19	0	1	1	54
1994-95	Rochester	AHL	77	4	12	16	152	5	1	0	1	14

Signed as a free agent by **Winnipeg**, September 17, 1993. Signed as a free agent by **Buffalo**, July 7, 1994.

CORBET, RENE — (cohr-BAY, ruh-NAY) — COL.

Left wing. Shoots left. 6', 187 lbs. Born, Victoriaville, Que., June 25, 1973.
(Quebec's 2nd choice, 24th overall, in 1991 Entry Draft).

			Regular Season					Playoffs				
Season	Club	Lea	GP	G	A	TP	PIM	GP	G	A	TP	PIM
1990-91	Drummondville	QMJHL	45	25	40	65	34	14	11	6	17	15
1991-92	Drummondville	QMJHL	56	46	50	96	90	4	1	2	3	17
1992-93ab	Drummondville	QMJHL	63	*79	69	*148	143	10	7	13	20	16
1993-94	**Quebec**	**NHL**	**9**	**1**	**1**	**2**	**0**	....	....	....	....	....
c	Cornwall	AHL	68	37	40	77	56	13	7	2	9	18
1994-95	Cornwall	AHL	65	33	24	57	79	12	2	8	10	27
	Quebec	**NHL**	**8**	**0**	**3**	**3**	**2**	**2**	**0**	**1**	**1**	**0**
	NHL Totals		**17**	**1**	**4**	**5**	**2**	**2**	**0**	**1**	**1**	**0**

a QMJHL First All-Star Team (1993)
b Canadian Major Junior First All-Star Team (1993)
c Won Dudley "Red" Garrett Memorial Trophy (Top Rookie - AHL) (1994)

CORCORAN, BRIAN — ANA.

Defense. Shoots left. 6'2", 247 lbs. Born, Baldwinsville, NY, April 23, 1972.

			Regular Season					Playoffs				
Season	Club	Lea	GP	G	A	TP	PIM	GP	G	A	TP	PIM
1993-94	U. Mass.	NCAA	15	1	7	8	24					
1994-95	U. Mass.	H.E.	20	3	3	6	40					

Signed as a free agent by **Anaheim**, March 29, 1995.

CORKUM, BOB — ANA.

Center. Shoots right. 6'2", 185 lbs. Born, Salisbury, MA, December 18, 1967.
(Buffalo's 3rd choice, 47th overall, in 1986 Entry Draft).

			Regular Season					Playoffs				
Season	Club	Lea	GP	G	A	TP	PIM	GP	G	A	TP	PIM
1985-86	U. of Maine	H.E.	39	7	26	33	53					
1986-87	U. of Maine	H.E.	35	18	11	29	24					
1987-88	U. of Maine	H.E.	40	14	18	32	64					
1988-89	U. of Maine	H.E.	45	17	31	48	64					
1989-90	**Buffalo**	**NHL**	**8**	**2**	**0**	**2**	**4**	**5**	**1**	**0**	**1**	**4**
	Rochester	AHL	43	8	11	19	45	12	2	5	7	16
1990-91	Rochester	AHL	69	13	21	34	77	15	4	4	8	4
1991-92	**Buffalo**	**NHL**	**20**	**2**	**4**	**6**	**21**	**4**	**1**	**0**	**1**	**0**
	Rochester	AHL	52	16	12	28	47	8	0	6	6	8
1992-93	**Buffalo**	**NHL**	**68**	**6**	**4**	**10**	**38**	**5**	**0**	**0**	**0**	**2**
1993-94	**Anaheim**	**NHL**	**76**	**23**	**28**	**51**	**18**					
1994-95	**Anaheim**	**NHL**	**44**	**10**	**9**	**19**	**25**					
	NHL Totals		**216**	**43**	**45**	**88**	**106**	**14**	**2**	**0**	**2**	**6**

Claimed by **Anaheim** from **Buffalo** in Expansion Draft, June 24, 1993.

CORPSE, KELI — (KOHRPS, KAL-ee) MTL.

Center. Shoots left. 5'11", 175 lbs. Born, London, Ont., May 14, 1974.
(Montreal's 3rd choice, 44th overall, in 1992 Entry Draft).

			Regular Season					Playoffs				
Season	Club	Lea	GP	G	A	TP	PIM	GP	G	A	TP	PIM
1990-91	Kingston	OHL	58	18	33	51	34					
1991-92	Kingston	OHL	65	31	52	83	20					
1992-93	Kingston	OHL	54	32	75	107	45	16	9	*20	29	10
	Cdn. National	....	1	0	0	0	2					
1993-94a	Kingston	OHL	63	42	84	126	55	6	1	7	8	2
1994-95	Cdn. National	....	32	10	7	17	16					
	Kingston	OHL	25	12	41	53	6	6	4	9	13	10

a OHL Second All-Star Team (1994)

CORRIVEAU, YVON — (KOHR-ih-voh, IGH-vihn)

Left wing. Shoots left. 6'1", 195 lbs. Born, Welland, Ont., February 8, 1967.
(Washington's 1st choice, 19th overall, in 1985 Entry Draft).

			Regular Season					Playoffs				
Season	Club	Lea	GP	G	A	TP	PIM	GP	G	A	TP	PIM
1984-85	Toronto	OHL	59	23	28	51	65	3	0	0	0	5
1985-86	**Washington**	**NHL**	**2**	**0**	**0**	**0**	**0**	**4**	**0**	**3**	**3**	**2**
	Toronto	OHL	59	54	36	90	75	4	1	1	2	0
1986-87	**Washington**	**NHL**	**17**	**1**	**1**	**2**	**24**					
	Toronto	OHL	23	14	19	33	23					
	Binghamton	AHL	7	0	0	0	2	8	0	1	1	0
1987-88	**Washington**	**NHL**	**44**	**10**	**9**	**19**	**84**	**13**	**1**	**2**	**3**	**30**
	Binghamton	AHL	35	15	14	29	64					
1988-89	**Washington**	**NHL**	**33**	**3**	**2**	**5**	**62**	**1**	**0**	**0**	**0**	**0**
	Baltimore	AHL	33	16	23	39	65					
1989-90	**Washington**	**NHL**	**50**	**9**	**6**	**15**	**50**					
	Hartford	**NHL**	**13**	**4**	**1**	**5**	**22**	**4**	**1**	**0**	**1**	**0**
1990-91	**Hartford**	**NHL**	**23**	**1**	**1**	**2**	**18**					
	Springfield	AHL	44	17	25	42	10	18	*10	6	16	31
1991-92	**Hartford**	**NHL**	**38**	**12**	**8**	**20**	**36**	**7**	**3**	**2**	**5**	**18**
	Springfield	AHL	39	26	15	41	40					
1992-93	**San Jose**	**NHL**	**20**	**3**	**7**	**10**	**0**					
	Hartford	**NHL**	**37**	**5**	**5**	**10**	**14**					
1993-94	**Hartford**	**NHL**	**3**	**0**	**0**	**0**	**0**					
	Springfield	AHL	71	42	39	81	53	6	7	3	10	20
1994-95	Minnesota	IHL	62	18	24	42	26	3	1	1	2	0
	NHL Totals		**280**	**48**	**40**	**88**	**310**	**29**	**5**	**7**	**12**	**50**

Traded to **Hartford** by **Washington** for Mike Liut, March 6, 1990. Traded to **Washington** by **Hartford** to complete June 15, 1992 deal in which Mark Hunter and future considerations were traded to Washington for Nick Kypreos, August 20, 1992. Claimed by **San Jose** from **Washington** in NHL Waiver Draft, October 4, 1992. Traded to **Hartford** by **San Jose** to complete October 9, 1992 trade in which Michel Picard was traded to San Jose for future considerations, January 21, 1993.

CORSON, SHAYNE — ST.L.

Left wing. Shoots left. 6'1", 200 lbs. Born, Midland, Ont., August 13, 1966.
(Montreal's 2nd choice, 8th overall, in 1984 Entry Draft).

			Regular Season					Playoffs				
Season	Club	Lea	GP	G	A	TP	PIM	GP	G	A	TP	PIM
1983-84	Brantford	OHL	66	25	46	71	165	6	4	1	5	26
1984-85	Hamilton	OHL	54	27	63	90	154	11	3	7	10	19
1985-86	**Montreal**	**NHL**	**3**	**0**	**0**	**0**	**2**					
	Hamilton	OHL	47	41	57	98	153					
1986-87	**Montreal**	**NHL**	**55**	**12**	**11**	**23**	**144**	**17**	**6**	**5**	**11**	**30**
1987-88	**Montreal**	**NHL**	**71**	**12**	**27**	**39**	**152**	**3**	**1**	**0**	**1**	**12**
1988-89	**Montreal**	**NHL**	**80**	**26**	**24**	**50**	**193**	**21**	**4**	**5**	**9**	**65**
1989-90	**Montreal**	**NHL**	**76**	**31**	**44**	**75**	**144**	**11**	**2**	**8**	**10**	**20**
1990-91	**Montreal**	**NHL**	**71**	**23**	**24**	**47**	**138**	**13**	**9**	**6**	**15**	**36**
1991-92	**Montreal**	**NHL**	**64**	**17**	**36**	**53**	**118**	**10**	**2**	**5**	**7**	**15**
1992-93	**Edmonton**	**NHL**	**80**	**16**	**31**	**47**	**209**					
1993-94	**Edmonton**	**NHL**	**64**	**25**	**29**	**54**	**118**					
1994-95	**Edmonton**	**NHL**	**48**	**12**	**24**	**36**	**86**					
	NHL Totals		**612**	**174**	**250**	**424**	**1304**	**75**	**24**	**29**	**53**	**178**

Played in NHL All-Star Game (1990, 1994)

Traded to **Edmonton** by **Montreal** with Brent Gilchrist and Vladimir Vujtek for Vincent Damphousse and Edmonton's fourth round choice (Adam Wiesel) in 1993 Entry Draft, August 27, 1992. Signed as a free agent by **St. Louis**, July 28, 1995.

CORT, JOEL — WSH.

Defense. Shoots left. 6'3", 227 lbs. Born, Hamilton, Ont., April 30, 1977.
(Washington's 7th choice, 124th overall, in 1995 Entry Draft).

			Regular Season					Playoffs				
Season	Club	Lea	GP	G	A	TP	PIM	GP	G	A	TP	PIM
1993-94	Hamilton	Midget	45	3	14	17	115					
1994-95	Guelph	OHL	29	1	3	4	20					

COTE, PATRICK — DAL.

Left wing. Shoots left. 6'3", 199 lbs. Born, Lasalle, Que., January 24, 1975.
(Dallas' 2nd choice, 37th overall, in 1995 Entry Draft).

			Regular Season					Playoffs				
Season	Club	Lea	GP	G	A	TP	PIM	GP	G	A	TP	PIM
1993-94	Beauport	QMJHL	48	2	4	6	230	12	1	0	1	61
1994-95	Beauport	QMJHL	56	20	20	40	314	17	8	8	16	115

COTE, SYLVAIN — (KOH-tay) WSH.

Defense. Shoots right. 6', 190 lbs. Born, Quebec City, Que., January 19, 1966.
(Hartford's 1st choice, 11th overall, in 1984 Entry Draft).

			Regular Season					Playoffs				
Season	Club	Lea	GP	G	A	TP	PIM	GP	G	A	TP	PIM
1982-83	Quebec	QMJHL	66	10	24	34	50					
1983-84	Quebec	QMJHL	66	15	50	65	89	5	1	1	2	0
1984-85	**Hartford**	**NHL**	**67**	**3**	**9**	**12**	**17**					
1985-86	**Hartford**	**NHL**	**2**	**0**	**0**	**0**	**0**					
a	Hull	QMJHL	26	10	33	43	14	13	6	*28	34	22
	Binghamton	AHL	12	2	4	6	0					
1986-87	**Hartford**	**NHL**	**67**	**2**	**8**	**10**	**20**	**2**	**0**	**2**	**2**	**2**
1987-88	**Hartford**	**NHL**	**67**	**7**	**21**	**28**	**30**	**6**	**1**	**1**	**2**	**4**
1988-89	**Hartford**	**NHL**	**78**	**8**	**9**	**17**	**49**	**3**	**0**	**1**	**1**	**4**
1989-90	**Hartford**	**NHL**	**28**	**4**	**2**	**6**	**14**	**5**	**0**	**0**	**0**	**2**
1990-91	**Hartford**	**NHL**	**73**	**7**	**12**	**19**	**17**	**6**	**0**	**2**	**2**	**2**
1991-92	**Washington**	**NHL**	**78**	**11**	**29**	**40**	**31**	**7**	**1**	**2**	**3**	**4**
1992-93	**Washington**	**NHL**	**77**	**21**	**29**	**50**	**34**	**6**	**1**	**1**	**2**	**4**
1993-94	**Washington**	**NHL**	**84**	**16**	**35**	**51**	**66**	**9**	**1**	**8**	**9**	**6**
1994-95	**Washington**	**NHL**	**47**	**5**	**14**	**19**	**53**	**7**	**1**	**3**	**4**	**2**
	NHL Totals		**668**	**84**	**168**	**252**	**331**	**51**	**5**	**20**	**25**	**30**

a QMJHL First All-Star Team (1986).

Traded to **Washington** by **Hartford** for Washington's second round choice (Andrei Nikolishin) in 1992 Entry Draft, September 8, 1991.

COURTNALL, GEOFF — ST.L.

Left wing. Shoots left. 6'1", 195 lbs. Born, Duncan, B.C., August 18, 1962.

			Regular Season					Playoffs				
Season	Club	Lea	GP	G	A	TP	PIM	GP	G	A	TP	PIM
1980-81	Victoria	WHL	11	3	4	7	6	15	2	1	3	7
1981-82	Victoria	WHL	72	35	57	90	100	4	1	0	1	2
1982-83	Victoria	WHL	71	41	73	114	186	12	6	7	13	42
1983-84	**Boston**	**NHL**	**4**	**0**	**0**	**0**	**0**					
	Hershey	AHL	74	14	12	26	51					
1984-85	**Boston**	**NHL**	**64**	**12**	**16**	**28**	**82**	**5**	**0**	**2**	**2**	**7**
	Hershey	AHL	9	8	4	12	4					
1985-86	**Boston**	**NHL**	**64**	**21**	**16**	**37**	**61**	**3**	**0**	**0**	**0**	**2**
	Moncton	AHL	12	8	8	16	6					
1986-87	**Boston**	**NHL**	**65**	**13**	**23**	**36**	**117**	**1**	**0**	**0**	**0**	**0**
1987-88	**Boston**	**NHL**	**62**	**32**	**26**	**58**	**108**					
	Edmonton	**NHL**	**12**	**4**	**4**	**8**	**15**	**19**	**0**	**3**	**3**	**23**
1988-89	**Washington**	**NHL**	**79**	**42**	**38**	**80**	**112**	**6**	**2**	**5**	**7**	**12**
1989-90	**Washington**	**NHL**	**80**	**35**	**39**	**74**	**104**	**15**	**4**	**9**	**13**	**32**
1990-91	**St. Louis**	**NHL**	**66**	**27**	**30**	**57**	**56**					
	Vancouver	**NHL**	**11**	**6**	**2**	**8**	**8**	**6**	**3**	**5**	**8**	**4**
1991-92	**Vancouver**	**NHL**	**70**	**23**	**34**	**57**	**116**	**12**	**6**	**8**	**14**	**20**
1992-93	**Vancouver**	**NHL**	**84**	**31**	**46**	**77**	**167**	**12**	**4**	**10**	**14**	**12**
1993-94	**Vancouver**	**NHL**	**82**	**26**	**44**	**70**	**123**	**24**	**9**	**10**	**19**	**51**
1994-95	**Vancouver**	**NHL**	**45**	**16**	**18**	**34**	**81**	**11**	**4**	**2**	**6**	**34**
	NHL Totals		**788**	**288**	**336**	**624**	**1150**	**114**	**32**	**54**	**86**	**197**

Signed as a free agent by **Boston**, July 6, 1983. Traded to **Edmonton** by **Boston** with Bill Ranford and future considerations for Andy Moog, March 8, 1988. Rights traded to **Washington** by **Edmonton** for Greg C. Adams, July 22, 1988. Traded to **St. Louis** by **Washington** for Peter Zezel and Mike Lalor, July 13, 1990. Traded to **Vancouver** by **St. Louis** with Robert Dirk, Sergio Momesso, Cliff Ronning and St. Louis' fifth round choice (Brian Loney) in 1992 Entry Draft for Dan Quinn and Garth Butcher, March 5, 1991. Signed as a free agent by **St. Louis**, July 14, 1995.

COURTNALL, RUSS

Right wing. Shoots right. 5'11", 185 lbs. Born, Duncan, B.C., June 2, 1965.
(Toronto's 1st choice, 7th overall, in 1983 Entry Draft).

			Regular Season					Playoffs				
Season	Club	Lea	GP	G	A	TP	PIM	GP	G	A	TP	PIM
1982-83	Victoria	WHL	60	36	61	97	33	12	11	7	18	6
1983-84	Victoria	WHL	32	29	37	66	63					
	Cdn. National	....	16	4	7	11	10					
	Cdn. Olympic	....	7	1	3	4	2					
	Toronto	**NHL**	**14**	**3**	**9**	**12**	**6**					
1984-85	**Toronto**	**NHL**	**69**	**12**	**10**	**22**	**44**					
1985-86	**Toronto**	**NHL**	**73**	**22**	**38**	**60**	**52**	**10**	**3**	**6**	**9**	**8**
1986-87	**Toronto**	**NHL**	**79**	**29**	**44**	**73**	**90**	**13**	**3**	**4**	**7**	**11**
1987-88	**Toronto**	**NHL**	**65**	**23**	**26**	**49**	**47**	**6**	**2**	**1**	**3**	**0**
1988-89	**Toronto**	**NHL**	**9**	**1**	**1**	**2**	**4**					
	Montreal	**NHL**	**64**	**22**	**17**	**39**	**15**	**21**	**8**	**5**	**13**	**18**
1989-90	**Montreal**	**NHL**	**80**	**27**	**32**	**59**	**27**	**11**	**5**	**1**	**6**	**10**
1990-91	**Montreal**	**NHL**	**79**	**26**	**50**	**76**	**29**	**13**	**8**	**3**	**11**	**7**
1991-92	**Montreal**	**NHL**	**27**	**7**	**14**	**21**	**6**	**10**	**1**	**1**	**2**	**4**
1992-93	**Minnesota**	**NHL**	**84**	**36**	**43**	**79**	**49**					
1993-94	**Dallas**	**NHL**	**84**	**23**	**57**	**80**	**59**	**9**	**1**	**8**	**9**	**0**
1994-95	**Dallas**	**NHL**	**32**	**7**	**10**	**17**	**13**					
	Vancouver	**NHL**	**13**	**4**	**14**	**18**	**4**	**11**	**4**	**8**	**12**	**21**
	NHL Totals		**772**	**242**	**365**	**607**	**445**	**104**	**35**	**37**	**72**	**79**

Played in NHL All-Star Game (1994)

Traded to **Montreal** by **Toronto** for John Kordic and Montreal's sixth round choice (Michael Doers) in 1989 Entry Draft, November 7, 1988. Traded to **Minnesota** by **Montreal** for Brian Bellows, August 31, 1992. Traded to **Vancouver** by **Dallas** for Greg Adams, Dan Kesa and Vancouver's fifth round choice (later traded to Los Angeles — Los Angeles selected Jason Morgan) in 1995 Entry Draft, April 7, 1995.

COURVILLE, LARRY — VAN.

Left wing. Shoots left. 6'1", 180 lbs. Born, Timmins, Ont., April 2, 1975.
(Winnipeg's 6th choice, 119th overall, in 1993 Entry Draft).

			Regular Season					Playoffs				
Season	Club	Lea	GP	G	A	TP	PIM	GP	G	A	TP	PIM
1991-92	Cornwall	OHL	60	8	12	20	80	6	0	0	0	8
1992-93	Newmarket	OHL	64	21	18	39	181	7	0	6	6	14
1993-94	Newmarket	OHL	39	20	19	39	134					
	Moncton	AHL	8	2	0	2	37	10	2	2	4	27
1994-95a	Sarnia	OHL	16	9	9	18	58					
	Oshawa	OHL	28	25	30	55	72	7	4	10	14	10

a OHL Second All-Star Team (1995)

Re-entered NHL Entry Draft, **Vancouver's** 2nd choice, 61st overall in 1995 Entry Draft.

COUTURIER, SYLVAIN (koo-TOOR-ee-yah, SIHL-vay)

Center. Shoots left. 6'2", 205 lbs. Born, Greenfield Park, Que., April 23, 1968.
(Los Angeles' 3rd choice, 65th overall, in 1986 Entry Draft).

			Regular Season					Playoffs				
Season	Club	Lea	GP	G	A	TP	PIM	GP	G	A	TP	PIM
1985-86	Laval	QMJHL	68	21	37	58	64	14	1	7	8	28
1986-87	Laval	QMJHL	67	39	51	90	77	13	12	14	26	19
1987-88	Laval	QMJHL	67	70	67	137	115	....	....	....	....	....
1988-89	Los Angeles	NHL	16	1	3	4	2	....	....	....	....	....
	New Haven	AHL	44	18	20	38	33	10	2	2	4	11
1989-90	New Haven	AHL	50	9	8	17	47	....	....	....	....	....
1990-91	Los Angeles	NHL	3	0	1	1	0	....	....	....	....	....
	Phoenix	IHL	66	50	37	87	49	10	8	2	10	10
1991-92	Los Angeles	NHL	14	3	1	4	2	....	....	....	....	....
	Phoenix	IHL	39	19	20	39	68	....	....	....	....	....
1992-93	Phoenix	IHL	38	23	16	39	63	....	....	....	....	....
	Adirondack	AHL	29	17	17	34	12	11	3	5	8	10
	Fort Wayne	IHL	....	....	....	....	....	4	2	3	5	2
1993-94	Milwaukee	IHL	80	41	51	92	123	4	1	2	3	2
1994-95	Milwaukee	IHL	77	31	41	72	77	15	1	4	5	10
	NHL Totals		33	4	5	9	4	....	....	....	....	....

Traded to **Detroit** by **Los Angeles** with Paul Coffey and Jim Hiller for Jimmy Carson, Marc Potvin and Gary Shuchuk, January 29, 1993.

COWIE, ROB L.A.

Defense. Shoots left. 6', 195 lbs. Born, Toronto, Ont., November 3, 1967.

			Regular Season					Playoffs				
Season	Club	Lea	GP	G	A	TP	PIM	GP	G	A	TP	PIM
1987-88	Northeastern	H.E.	36	7	8	15	38	....	....	....	....	....
1988-89a	Northeastern	H.E.	36	7	34	41	60	....	....	....	....	....
1989-90bc	Northeastern	H.E.	34	14	31	45	54	....	....	....	....	....
1990-91a	Northeastern	H.E.	33	18	23	41	56	....	....	....	....	....
1991-92	Moncton	AHL	64	11	30	41	89	5	1	1	2	0
1992-93	Moncton	AHL	67	12	20	32	91	5	3	5	8	2
1993-94d	Springfield	AHL	78	17	57	74	124	6	3	6	9	4
1994-95	Phoenix	IHL	51	14	33	47	71	....	....	....	....	....
	Los Angeles	NHL	32	2	7	9	20	....	....	....	....	....
	NHL Totals		32	2	7	9	20	....	....	....	....	....

a Hockey East Second All-Star Team (1989,1991)
b Hockey East First All-Star Team (1990)
c NCAA East First All-American Team (1990)
d AHL Second All-Star Team (1994)

Signed as a free agent by **Winnipeg**, July 4, 1991. Signed as a free agent by **Hartford**, August 9, 1993. Signed as a free agent by **Los Angeles**, July 8,1994.

CRAIG, MIKE TOR.

Right wing. Shoots right. 6'1", 180 lbs. Born, St. Mary's, Ont., June 6, 1971.
(Minnesota's 2nd choice, 28th overall, in 1989 Entry Draft).

			Regular Season					Playoffs				
Season	Club	Lea	GP	G	A	TP	PIM	GP	G	A	TP	PIM
1987-88	Oshawa	OHL	61	6	10	16	39	7	7	0	1	11
1988-89	Oshawa	OHL	63	36	36	72	34	6	3	1	4	6
1989-90	Oshawa	OHL	43	36	40	76	85	17	10	16	26	46
1990-91	Minnesota	NHL	39	8	4	12	32	10	1	1	2	20
1991-92	Minnesota	NHL	67	15	16	31	155	4	1	0	1	7
1992-93	Minnesota	NHL	70	15	23	38	106	....	....	....	....	....
1993-94	Dallas	NHL	72	13	24	37	139	4	0	0	0	2
1994-95	Toronto	NHL	37	5	5	10	12	2	0	1	1	2
	NHL Totals		285	56	72	128	444	20	2	2	4	31

Signed as a free agent by **Toronto**, July 29, 1994.

CRAIGWELL, DALE

Center. Shoots left. 5'11", 180 lbs. Born, Toronto, Ont., April 24, 1971.
(San Jose's 11th choice, 199th overall, in 1991 Entry Draft).

			Regular Season					Playoffs				
Season	Club	Lea	GP	G	A	TP	PIM	GP	G	A	TP	PIM
1988-89	Oshawa	OHL	55	9	14	23	15	....	....	....	....	....
1989-90	Oshawa	OHL	64	22	41	63	39	17	7	7	14	11
1990-91	Oshawa	OHL	56	27	68	95	34	16	7	16	23	9
1991-92	San Jose	NHL	32	5	11	16	8	....	....	....	....	....
	Kansas City	IHL	48	6	19	25	29	12	4	7	11	4
1992-93	San Jose	NHL	8	3	1	4	4	....	....	....	....	....
	Kansas City	IHL	60	15	38	53	24	12	*7	5	12	2
1993-94	San Jose	NHL	58	3	6	9	16	....	....	....	....	....
	Kansas City	IHL	5	3	1	4	0	....	....	....	....	....
1994-95			DID NOT PLAY – INJURED									
	NHL Totals		98	11	18	29	28	....	....	....	....	....

CRAVEN, MURRAY CHI.

Left wing. Shoots left. 6'2", 185 lbs. Born, Medicine Hat, Alta., July 20, 1964.
(Detroit's 1st choice, 17th overall, in 1982 Entry Draft).

			Regular Season					Playoffs				
Season	Club	Lea	GP	G	A	TP	PIM	GP	G	A	TP	PIM
1980-81	Medicine Hat	WHL	69	5	10	15	18	5	0	0	0	2
1981-82	Medicine Hat	WHL	72	35	46	81	49	....	....	....	....	....
1982-83	Detroit	NHL	31	4	7	11	6	....	....	....	....	....
	Medicine Hat	WHL	28	17	29	46	35	....	....	....	....	....
1983-84	Detroit	NHL	15	0	4	4	6	....	....	....	....	....
	Medicine Hat	WHL	48	38	56	94	53	4	5	3	8	4
1984-85	Philadelphia	NHL	80	26	35	61	30	19	4	6	10	11
1985-86	Philadelphia	NHL	78	21	33	54	34	5	0	3	3	4
1986-87	Philadelphia	NHL	77	19	30	49	38	12	3	1	4	9
1987-88	Philadelphia	NHL	72	30	46	76	58	7	2	5	7	4
1988-89	Philadelphia	NHL	51	9	28	37	52	1	0	0	0	0
1989-90	Philadelphia	NHL	76	25	50	75	42	....	....	....	....	....
1990-91	Philadelphia	NHL	77	19	47	66	53	....	....	....	....	....
1991-92	Philadelphia	NHL	12	3	3	6	8	....	....	....	....	....
	Hartford	NHL	61	24	30	54	38	7	3	3	6	6
1992-93	Hartford	NHL	67	25	42	67	20	....	....	....	....	....
	Vancouver	NHL	10	0	10	10	12	12	4	6	10	4
1993-94	Vancouver	NHL	78	15	40	55	30	22	4	9	13	18
1994-95	Chicago	NHL	16	4	3	7	2	16	5	5	10	4
	NHL Totals		801	224	408	632	429	101	25	38	63	60

Traded to **Philadelphia** by **Detroit** with Joe Paterson for Darryl Sittler, October 10, 1984. Traded to **Hartford** by **Philadelphia** with Philadelphia's fourth round choice (Kevin Smyth) in 1992 Entry Draft for Kevin Dineen, November 13, 1991. Traded to **Vancouver** by **Hartford** with Vancouver's fifth round choice (previously acquired by Hartford — Vancouver selected Scott Walker) in 1993 Entry Draft for Robert Kron, Vancouver's third round choice (Marek Malik) in 1993 Entry Draft and future considerations (Jim Sandlak, May 17, 1993), March 22, 1993. Traded to **Chicago** by **Vancouver** for Christian Ruutu, March 10, 1995.

CREIGHTON, ADAM (KRAY-ton) ST.L.

Center. Shoots left. 6'5", 220 lbs. Born, Burlington, Ont., June 2, 1965.
(Buffalo's 3rd choice, 11th overall, in 1983 Entry Draft).

			Regular Season					Playoffs				
Season	Club	Lea	GP	G	A	TP	PIM	GP	G	A	TP	PIM
1981-82	Ottawa	OHL	60	15	27	42	73	17	7	1	8	40
1982-83	Ottawa	OHL	68	44	46	90	88	9	0	2	2	12
1983-84	Buffalo	NHL	7	2	2	4	4	....	....	....	....	....
a	Ottawa	OHL	56	42	49	91	79	13	16	11	27	28
1984-85	Buffalo	NHL	30	2	8	10	33	....	....	....	....	....
	Rochester	AHL	6	5	3	8	2	5	2	1	3	20
	Ottawa	OHL	10	4	14	18	23	5	6	2	8	11
1985-86	Buffalo	NHL	19	1	1	2	2	....	....	....	....	....
	Rochester	AHL	32	17	21	38	27	....	....	....	....	....
1986-87	Buffalo	NHL	56	18	22	40	26	....	....	....	....	....
1987-88	Buffalo	NHL	36	10	17	27	87	....	....	....	....	....
1988-89	Buffalo	NHL	24	7	10	17	44	....	....	....	....	....
	Chicago	NHL	43	15	14	29	92	15	5	6	11	44
1989-90	Chicago	NHL	80	34	36	70	224	20	3	6	9	59
1990-91	Chicago	NHL	72	22	29	51	135	6	0	1	1	10
1991-92	Chicago	NHL	11	6	6	12	16	....	....	....	....	....
	NY Islanders	NHL	66	15	9	24	102	....	....	....	....	....
1992-93	Tampa Bay	NHL	83	19	20	39	110	....	....	....	....	....
1993-94	Tampa Bay	NHL	53	10	10	20	37	....	....	....	....	....
1994-95	St. Louis	NHL	48	14	20	34	74	7	2	0	2	16
	NHL Totals		628	175	204	379	986	48	10	13	23	129

a Won Stafford Smythe Memorial Trophy (Memorial Cup Tournament MVP) (1984)

Traded to **Chicago** by **Buffalo** for Rick Vaive, December 26, 1988. Traded to **NY Islanders** by **Chicago** with Steve Thomas for Brent Sutter and Brad Lauer, October 25, 1991. Claimed by **Tampa Bay** from **NY Islanders** in NHL Waiver Draft, October 4, 1992. Traded to **St. Louis** by **Tampa Bay** for Tom Tilley, October 6, 1994.

CREURER, TROY (KRUH-yuhr) VAN.

Defense. Shoots left. 6'1", 185 lbs. Born, Weyburn, Sask., May 2, 1975.
(Vancouver's 5th choice, 158th overall, in 1993 Entry Draft).

			Regular Season					Playoffs				
Season	Club	Lea	GP	G	A	TP	PIM	GP	G	A	TP	PIM
1993-94	St. Lawrence	ECAC	31	5	10	15	22	....	....	....	....	....
1994-95	St. Lawrence	ECAC	33	1	11	12	30	....	....	....	....	....

CRONAN, EARL MTL.

Left wing. Shoots left. 6'1", 195 lbs. Born, Warwick, RI, January 2, 1973.
(Montreal's 11th choice, 212th overall, in 1992 Entry Draft).

			Regular Season					Playoffs				
Season	Club	Lea	GP	G	A	TP	PIM	GP	G	A	TP	PIM
1992-93	Colgate	ECAC	33	8	9	17	40	....	....	....	....	....
1993-94	Colgate	ECAC	32	14	17	31	80	....	....	....	....	....
1994-95	Colgate	ECAC	37	21	20	41	81	....	....	....	....	....

CRONIN, SHAWN

Defense. Shoots left. 6'2", 225 lbs. Born, Joliet, IL, August 20, 1963.

			Regular Season					Playoffs				
Season	Club	Lea	GP	G	A	TP	PIM	GP	G	A	TP	PIM
1982-83	Ill.-Chicago	CCHA	36	1	5	6	52	....	....	....	....	....
1983-84	Ill.-Chicago	CCHA	32	0	4	4	41	....	....	....	....	....
1984-85	Ill.-Chicago	CCHA	31	2	6	8	52	....	....	....	....	....
1985-86	Ill.-Chicago	CCHA	35	3	8	11	70	....	....	....	....	....
1986-87	Salt Lake	IHL	53	8	16	24	118	....	....	....	....	....
	Binghamton	AHL	12	0	1	1	60	10	0	0	0	41
1987-88	Binghamton	AHL	65	3	8	11	212	4	0	0	0	15
1988-89	Washington	NHL	1	0	0	0	0	....	....	....	....	....
	Baltimore	AHL	75	3	9	12	267	....	....	....	....	....
1989-90	Winnipeg	NHL	61	0	4	4	243	5	0	0	0	7
1990-91	Winnipeg	NHL	67	1	5	6	189	....	....	....	....	....
1991-92	Winnipeg	NHL	65	0	4	4	271	4	0	0	0	6
1992-93	Philadelphia	NHL	35	2	1	3	37	....	....	....	....	....
	Hershey	AHL	7	0	1	1	12	....	....	....	....	....
1993-94	San Jose	NHL	34	0	2	2	76	14	1	0	1	20
1994-95	San Jose	NHL	29	0	2	2	61	9	0	0	0	5
	NHL Totals		292	3	18	21	877	32	1	0	1	38

Signed as a free agent by **Hartford**, March, 1986. Signed as a free agent by **Washington**, June 6, 1988. Signed as a free agent by **Philadelphia**, June 12, 1989. Traded to **Winnipeg** by **Philadelphia** for future considerations (Keith Acton and Pete Peeters were traded to Philadelphia for Toronto's fifth round choice (previously acquired by Philadelphia — Winnipeg selected Juha Ylonen), October 3, 1989), July 21, 1989. Traded to **Quebec** by **Winnipeg** for Dan Lambert, August 25, 1992. Claimed by **Philadelphia** from **Quebec** in NHL Waiver Draft, October 4, 1992. Traded to **San Jose** by **Philadelphia** for cash, August 5, 1993.

CROSS, CORY T.B.

Defense. Shoots left. 6'5", 212 lbs. Born, Lloydminster, Alta., January 3, 1971.
(Tampa Bay's 1st choice, 1st overall, in 1992 Supplemental Draft).

			Regular Season					Playoffs				
Season	Club	Lea	GP	G	A	TP	PIM	GP	G	A	TP	PIM
1989-90	U. of Alberta	CWUAA	UNAVAILABLE									
1990-91	U. of Alberta	CWUAA	20	2	5	7	16	....	....	....	....	....
1991-92	U. of Alberta	CWUAA	41	4	11	15	82	....	....	....	....	....
1992-93	U. of Alberta	CWUAA	43	11	28	39	105	....	....	....	....	....
	Atlanta	IHL	7	0	1	1	2	4	0	0	0	6
1993-94	Tampa Bay	NHL	5	0	0	0	6	....	....	....	....	....
	Atlanta	IHL	70	4	14	18	72	9	1	2	3	14
1994-95	Atlanta	IHL	41	5	10	15	67	....	....	....	....	....
	Tampa Bay	NHL	43	1	5	6	41	....	....	....	....	....
	NHL Totals		48	1	5	6	47	....	....	....	....	....

CROSSMAN, DOUG

Defense. Shoots left. 6'2", 190 lbs. Born, Peterborough, Ont., June 30, 1960.
(Chicago's 6th choice, 112th overall, in 1979 Entry Draft).

			Regular Season					Playoffs				
Season	Club	Lea	GP	G	A	TP	PIM	GP	G	A	TP	PIM
1977-78	Ottawa	OHA	65	4	17	21	17	....	....	....	....	....
1978-79	Ottawa	OHA	67	12	51	63	65	4	1	3	4	0
1979-80	Ottawa	OHA	66	20	96	116	48	11	7	6	13	19
1980-81	Chicago	NHL	9	0	2	2	2	....	....	....	....	....
	New Brunswick	AHL	70	13	43	56	90	13	5	6	11	36
1981-82	Chicago	NHL	70	12	28	40	24	11	0	3	3	4
1982-83	Chicago	NHL	80	13	40	53	46	13	3	7	10	6
1983-84	Philadelphia	NHL	78	7	28	35	63	3	0	0	0	0
1984-85	Philadelphia	NHL	80	4	33	37	65	19	4	6	10	38
1985-86	Philadelphia	NHL	80	6	37	43	55	5	0	1	1	4
1986-87	Philadelphia	NHL	78	9	31	40	29	26	4	14	18	31
1987-88	Philadelphia	NHL	76	9	29	38	43	7	1	1	2	8
1988-89	Los Angeles	NHL	74	10	15	25	53	2	0	1	1	2
	New Haven	AHL	3	0	0	0	0	....	....	....	....	....
1989-90	NY Islanders	NHL	80	15	44	59	54	5	0	1	1	6
1990-91	NY Islanders	NHL	16	1	6	7	12	....	....	....	....	....
	Hartford	NHL	41	4	19	23	19	....	....	....	....	....
	Detroit	NHL	17	3	4	7	17	6	0	5	5	6
1991-92	Detroit	NHL	26	0	8	8	14	....	....	....	....	....
1992-93	Tampa Bay	NHL	40	8	21	29	18	....	....	....	....	....
	St. Louis	NHL	19	2	7	9	10	....	....	....	....	....
1993-94	St. Louis	NHL	50	2	7	9	10	....	....	....	....	....
	Peoria	IHL	8	3	5	8	0	....	....	....	....	....
1994-95	Denver	IHL	77	6	43	49	31	17	3	6	9	7
	NHL Totals		914	105	359	464	534	97	12	39	51	105

Traded to **Philadelphia** by **Chicago** with Chicago's second round choice (Scott Mellanby) in 1984 Entry Draft for Behn Wilson, June 8, 1983. Traded to **Los Angeles** by **Philadelphia** for Jay Wells, September 29, 1988. Traded to **NY Islanders** by **Los Angeles** to complete February 22, 1989, transaction in which Mark Fitzpatrick, Wayne McBean and future considerations were traded to **NY Islanders** by **Los Angeles** for Kelly Hrudey, May 23, 1989. Traded to **Hartford** by **NY Islanders** for Ray Ferraro, November 13, 1990. Traded to **Detroit** by **Hartford** for Doug Houda, February 20, 1991. Traded to **Quebec** by **Detroit** with Dennis Vial for cash, June 15, 1992. Claimed by **Tampa Bay** from **Quebec** in Expansion Draft, June 18, 1992. Traded to **St. Louis** by **Tampa Bay** with Basil McRae and Tampa Bay's fourth round choice in 1996 Entry Draft for Jason Ruff and future considerations, January 28, 1993.

CROWDER, TROY — PIT.

Right wing. Shoots right. 6'4", 220 lbs. Born, Sudbury, Ont., May 3, 1968.
(New Jersey's 6th choice, 108th overall, in 1986 Entry Draft).

			Regular Season					Playoffs				
Season	Club	Lea	GP	G	A	TP	PIM	GP	G	A	TP	PIM
1985-86	Hamilton	OHL	56	4	4	8	178	....	....	....	....	....
1986-87	Belleville	OHL	21	5	5	10	52	....	....	....	....	....
	North Bay	OHL	35	6	11	17	90	23	3	9	12	99
1987-88	North Bay	OHL	9	1	2	3	44	....	....	....	....	....
	Belleville	OHL	46	12	27	39	103	6	2	3	5	24
	Utica	AHL	3	0	0	0	36	....	....	....	....	....
	New Jersey	NHL	....	....	....	....	....	1	0	0	0	12
1988-89	Utica	AHL	62	6	4	10	152	2	0	0	0	25
1989-90	New Jersey	NHL	10	0	0	0	23	2	0	0	0	10
	Nashville	ECHL	3	0	0	0	15	....	....	....	....	....
1990-91	New Jersey	NHL	59	6	3	9	182	....	....	....	....	....
1991-92	Detroit	NHL	7	0	0	0	35	1	0	0	0	0
1992-93			DID NOT PLAY – INJURED									
1993-94			DID NOT PLAY									
1994-95	Los Angeles	NHL	29	1	2	3	99	....	....	....	....	....
	NHL Totals		105	7	5	12	339	4	0	0	0	22

Signed as a free agent by **Detroit**, August 27, 1991. Signed as a free agent by **Los Angeles**, August 31, 1994. Signed as a free agent by **Pittsburgh**, August 10, 1995.

CROWE, PHILIP — PHI.

Left wing. Shoots left. 6'2", 220 lbs. Born, Nanton, Alta., April 14, 1970.

			Regular Season					Playoffs				
Season	Club	Lea	GP	G	A	TP	PIM	GP	G	A	TP	PIM
1991-92	Adirondack	AHL	6	1	0	1	29	....	....	....	....	....
	Columbus	ECHL	32	4	7	11	145	....	....	....	....	....
	Toledo	ECHL	2	0	0	0	0	5	0	0	0	58
1992-93	Phoenix	IHL	53	3	3	6	190	....	....	....	....	....
1993-94	Fort Wayne	IHL	5	0	1	1	26	....	....	....	....	....
	Phoenix	IHL	2	0	0	0	0	....	....	....	....	....
	Los Angeles	NHL	31	0	2	2	77	....	....	....	....	....
1994-95	Hershey	AHL	46	11	6	17	132	6	0	1	1	19
	NHL Totals		31	0	2	2	77	....	....	....	....	....

Signed as a free agent by **Los Angeles**, November 8, 1993. Signed as a free agent by **Philadelphia**, July 19, 1994.

CROWLEY, MIKE — PHI.

Defense. Shoots left. 5'11", 175 lbs. Born, Bloomington, MN, July 4, 1975.
(Philadelphia's 5th choice, 140th overall, in 1993 Entry Draft).

			Regular Season					Playoffs				
Season	Club	Lea	GP	G	A	TP	PIM	GP	G	A	TP	PIM
1993-94	Bloom.-Jeff.	HS	28	23	54	77	26	....	....	....	....	....
1994-95	U. Minnesota	WCHA	41	11	27	38	60	....	....	....	....	....

CROWLEY, TED — BOS.

Defense. Shoots right. 6'2", 188 lbs. Born, Concord, MA, May 3, 1970.
(Toronto's 4th choice, 69th overall, in 1988 Entry Draft).

			Regular Season					Playoffs				
Season	Club	Lea	GP	G	A	TP	PIM	GP	G	A	TP	PIM
1989-90	Boston College	H.E.	39	7	24	31	34	....	....	....	....	....
1990-91ab	Boston College	H.E.	39	12	24	36	61	....	....	....	....	....
1991-92	U.S. National	....	42	6	7	13	65	....	....	....	....	....
	St. John's	AHL	29	5	4	9	33	10	3	1	4	11
1992-93	St. John's	AHL	79	19	38	57	41	9	2	2	4	4
1993-94	U.S. National	....	48	9	13	22	80	....	....	....	....	....
	U.S. Olympic	....	8	0	2	2	8	....	....	....	....	....
	Hartford	NHL	21	1	2	3	10	....	....	....	....	....
1994-95	Chicago	IHL	53	8	23	31	68	....	....	....	....	....
	Houston	IHL	23	4	9	13	35	3	0	1	1	0
	NHL Totals		21	1	2	3	10	....	....	....	....	....

a Hockey East First All-Star Team (1991)
b NCAA East Second All-American Team (1991)

Traded to **Hartford** by **Toronto** for Mark Greig and Hartford's sixth round choice (later traded to NY Rangers — NY Rangers selected Yuri Litvinov) in 1994 Entry Draft, January 25, 1994. Signed as a free agent by **Boston**, August 9, 1995.

CROZIER, GREG — PIT.

Left wing. Shoots left. 6'4", 200 lbs. Born, Calgary, Alta., July 6, 1976.
(Pittsburgh's 4th choice, 73rd overall, in 1994 Entry Draft).

			Regular Season					Playoffs				
Season	Club	Lea	GP	G	A	TP	PIM	GP	G	A	TP	PIM
1993-94	Lawrence	HS	18	22	26	48	12	....	....	....	....	....
1994-95	Lawrence	HS	31	45	32	77	22	....	....	....	....	....

CULL, TRENT — TOR.

Defense. Shoots left. 6'3", 210 lbs. Born, Brampton, Ont., September 27, 1973.

			Regular Season					Playoffs				
Season	Club	Lea	GP	G	A	TP	PIM	GP	G	A	TP	PIM
1989-90	Owen Sound	OHL	57	0	5	5	53	12	0	2	2	11
1990-91	Owen Sound	OHL	24	1	2	3	19	....	....	....	....	....
	Windsor	OHL	33	1	6	7	34	11	0	0	0	8
1991-92	Windsor	OHL	32	0	6	6	66	....	....	....	....	....
	Kingston	OHL	18	0	0	0	31	....	....	....	....	....
1992-93	Kingston	OHL	60	11	28	39	144	16	2	8	10	37
1993-94	Kingston	OHL	50	2	30	32	147	6	0	1	1	6
1994-95	St. John's	AHL	43	0	1	1	53	....	....	....	....	....

Signed as a free agent by **Toronto**, June 4, 1994.

CULLEN, JOHN

Center. Shoots right. 5'10", 180 lbs. Born, Puslinch, Ont., August 2, 1964.
(Buffalo's 2nd choice, 10th overall, in 1986 Supplemental Draft).

			Regular Season					Playoffs				
Season	Club	Lea	GP	G	A	TP	PIM	GP	G	A	TP	PIM
1983-84	Boston U.	ECAC	40	23	33	56	28	....	....	....	....	....
1984-85a	Boston U.	H.E.	41	27	32	59	46	....	....	....	....	....
1985-86ab	Boston U.	H.E.	43	25	49	74	54	....	....	....	....	....
1986-87c	Boston U.	H.E.	36	23	29	52	35	....	....	....	....	....
1987-88defg	Flint	IHL	81	48	*109	*157	113	16	11	*15	26	16
1988-89	Pittsburgh	NHL	79	12	37	49	112	11	3	6	9	28
1989-90	Pittsburgh	NHL	72	32	60	92	138	....	....	....	....	....
1990-91	Pittsburgh	NHL	65	31	63	94	83	....	....	....	....	....
	Hartford	NHL	13	8	8	16	18	6	2	7	9	10
1991-92	Hartford	NHL	77	26	51	77	141	7	2	1	3	12
1992-93	Hartford	NHL	19	5	4	9	58	....	....	....	....	....
	Toronto	NHL	47	13	28	41	53	12	2	3	5	0
1993-94	Toronto	NHL	53	13	17	30	67	3	0	0	0	0
1994-95	Pittsburgh	NHL	46	13	24	37	66	9	0	2	2	8
	NHL Totals		471	153	292	445	736	48	9	19	28	58

a Hockey East First All-Star Team (1985, 1986)
b NCAA East Second All-American Team (1986)
c Hockey East Second All-Star Team (1987)
d IHL First All-Star Team (1988)
e Won James Gatschene Memorial Trophy (MVP - IHL) (1988)
f Shared Garry F. Longman Memorial Trophy (Top Rookie - IHL) with Ed Belfour (1988)
g Won Leo P. Lamoureux Memorial Trophy (Top Scorer - IHL) (1988)

Played in NHL All-Star Game (1991, 1992)

Signed as a free agent by **Pittsburgh**, June 21, 1988. Traded to **Hartford** by **Pittsburgh** with Jeff Parker and Zarley Zalapski for Ron Francis, Grant Jennings and Ulf Samuelsson, March 4, 1991. Traded to **Toronto** by **Hartford** for future considerations, November 24, 1992. Signed as a free agent by **Pittsburgh**, August 3, 1994.

CULLEN, THOMAS — N.J.

Defense. Shoots left. 6'1", 205 lbs. Born, Mississauga, Ont., July 14, 1975.
(New Jersey's 8th choice, 195th overall, in 1993 Entry Draft).

			Regular Season					Playoffs				
Season	Club	Lea	GP	G	A	TP	PIM	GP	G	A	TP	PIM
1993-94	St. Lawrence	ECAC	23	1	3	4	32	....	....	....	....	....
1994-95	St. Lawrence	ECAC	32	9	19	28	67	....	....	....	....	....

CULLIMORE, JASSEN — VAN.

Defense. Shoots left. 6'5", 225 lbs. Born, Simcoe, Ont., December 4, 1972.
(Vancouver's 2nd choice, 29th overall, in 1991 Entry Draft).

			Regular Season					Playoffs				
Season	Club	Lea	GP	G	A	TP	PIM	GP	G	A	TP	PIM
1989-90	Peterborough	OHL	59	2	6	8	61	11	0	2	2	8
1990-91	Peterborough	OHL	62	8	16	24	74	4	1	0	1	7
1991-92a	Peterborough	OHL	54	9	37	46	65	10	3	6	9	8
1992-93	Hamilton	AHL	56	5	7	12	60	....	....	....	....	....
1993-94	Hamilton	AHL	71	8	20	28	86	3	0	1	1	2
1994-95	Syracuse	AHL	33	2	7	9	66	....	....	....	....	....
	Vancouver	NHL	34	1	2	3	39	11	0	0	0	12
	NHL Totals		34	1	2	3	39	11	0	0	0	12

a OHL Second All-Star Team (1992)

CUMMINS, JIM — CHI.

Right wing. Shoots right. 6'2", 203 lbs. Born, Dearborn, MI, May 17, 1970.
(NY Rangers' 5th choice, 67th overall, in 1989 Entry Draft).

			Regular Season					Playoffs				
Season	Club	Lea	GP	G	A	TP	PIM	GP	G	A	TP	PIM
1988-89	Michigan State	CCHA	30	3	8	11	98	....	....	....	....	....
1989-90	Michigan State	CCHA	41	8	7	15	94	....	....	....	....	....
1990-91	Michigan State	CCHA	34	9	6	15	110	....	....	....	....	....
1991-92	Detroit	NHL	1	0	0	0	7	....	....	....	....	....
	Adirondack	AHL	65	7	13	20	338	5	0	0	0	19
1992-93	Detroit	NHL	7	1	1	2	58	....	....	....	....	....
	Adirondack	AHL	43	16	4	20	179	9	3	1	4	4
1993-94	Philadelphia	NHL	22	1	2	3	71	....	....	....	....	....
	Hershey	AHL	17	6	6	12	70	....	....	....	....	....
	Tampa Bay	NHL	4	0	0	0	13	....	....	....	....	....
	Atlanta	IHL	7	4	5	9	14	13	1	2	3	90
1994-95	Tampa Bay	NHL	10	1	0	1	41	....	....	....	....	....
	Chicago	NHL	27	3	1	4	117	14	1	1	2	4
	NHL Totals		71	6	4	10	307	14	1	1	2	4

Traded to **Detroit** by **NY Rangers** with Kevin Miller and Dennis Vial for Joey Kocur and Per Djoos, March 5, 1991. Traded to **Philadelphia** by **Detroit** with Philadelphia's fourth round choice (previously acquired by Detroit — later traded to Boston — Boston selected Charles Paquette) in 1993 Entry Draft for Greg Johnson and Philadelphia's fifth round choice (Frederic Deschenes) in 1994 Entry Draft, June 20, 1993. Traded to **Tampa Bay** by **Philadelphia** with Philadelphia's fourth round choice in 1995 Entry Draft for Rob DiMaio, March 18, 1994. Traded to **Chicago** by **Tampa Bay** with Tom Tilley and Jeff Buchanan for Paul Ysebaert and Rich Sutter, February 22, 1995.

CUNNEYWORTH, RANDY — OTT.

Left wing. Shoots left. 6', 180 lbs. Born, Etobicoke, Ont., May 10, 1961.
(Buffalo's 9th choice, 167th overall, in 1980 Entry Draft).

			Regular Season					Playoffs				
Season	Club	Lea	GP	G	A	TP	PIM	GP	G	A	TP	PIM
1979-80	Ottawa	OHA	63	16	25	41	145	11	0	1	1	13
1980-81	Buffalo	NHL	1	0	0	0	2	....	....	....	....	....
	Rochester	AHL	1	0	1	1	2	....	....	....	....	....
	Ottawa	OHA	67	54	74	128	240	15	5	8	13	35
1981-82	Buffalo	NHL	20	2	4	6	47	....	....	....	....	....
	Rochester	AHL	57	12	15	27	86	9	4	0	4	30
1982-83	Rochester	AHL	78	23	33	56	111	16	4	4	8	35
1983-84	Rochester	AHL	54	18	17	35	85	17	5	5	10	55
1984-85	Rochester	AHL	72	30	38	68	148	5	2	1	3	16
1985-86	Pittsburgh	NHL	75	15	30	45	74	....	....	....	....	....
1986-87	Pittsburgh	NHL	79	26	27	53	142	....	....	....	....	....
1987-88	Pittsburgh	NHL	71	35	39	74	141	....	....	....	....	....
1988-89	Pittsburgh	NHL	70	25	19	44	156	11	3	5	8	26
1989-90	Winnipeg	NHL	28	5	6	11	34	....	....	....	....	....
	Hartford	NHL	43	9	9	18	41	4	0	0	0	2
1990-91	Hartford	NHL	32	9	5	14	49	1	0	0	0	0
	Springfield	AHL	2	0	0	0	5	....	....	....	....	....
1991-92	Hartford	NHL	39	7	10	17	71	7	3	0	3	9
1992-93	Hartford	NHL	39	5	4	9	63	....	....	....	....	....
1993-94	Hartford	NHL	63	9	8	17	87	....	....	....	....	....
	Chicago	NHL	16	4	3	7	13	6	0	0	0	8
1994-95	Ottawa	NHL	48	5	5	10	68	....	....	....	....	....
	NHL Totals		624	156	169	325	988	29	6	5	11	45

Traded to **Pittsburgh** by **Buffalo** with Mike Moller for Pat Hughes, October 4, 1985. Traded to **Winnipeg** by **Pittsburgh** with Rick Tabaracci and Dave McLlwain for Jim Kyte, Andrew McBain and Randy Gilhen, June 17, 1989. Traded to **Hartford** by **Winnipeg** for Paul MacDermid, December 13, 1989. Traded to **Chicago** by **Hartford** with Gary Suter and Hartford's third round choice (later traded to Vancouver — Vancouver selected Larry Courville) in 1995 Entry Draft for Frantisek Kucera and Jocelyn Lemieux, March 11, 1994. Signed as a free agent by **Ottawa**, July 15, 1994.

CURRAN, BRIAN

Defense. Shoots left. 6'5", 220 lbs. Born, Toronto, Ont., November 5, 1963.
(Boston's 2nd choice, 22nd overall, in 1982 Entry Draft).

			Regular Season					Playoffs				
Season	Club	Lea	GP	G	A	TP	PIM	GP	G	A	TP	PIM
1980-81	Portland	WHL	59	2	28	30	275	7	0	1	1	13
1981-82	Portland	WHL	51	2	16	18	132	14	1	7	8	63
1982-83	Portland	WHL	56	1	30	31	187	14	1	3	4	57
1983-84	Boston	NHL	16	1	1	2	57	3	0	0	0	7
	Hershey	AHL	23	0	2	2	94	....	....	....	....	....
1984-85	Boston	NHL	56	0	1	1	158	....	....	....	....	....
	Hershey	AHL	4	0	0	0	19	....	....	....	....	....
1985-86	Boston	NHL	43	2	5	7	192	2	0	0	0	4
1986-87	NY Islanders	NHL	68	0	10	10	356	8	0	0	0	51
1987-88	NY Islanders	NHL	22	0	1	1	68	....	....	....	....	....
	Springfield	AHL	8	1	0	1	43	....	....	....	....	....
	Toronto	NHL	7	0	1	1	19	6	0	0	0	41
1988-89	Toronto	NHL	47	1	4	5	185	....	....	....	....	....
1989-90	Toronto	NHL	72	2	9	11	301	5	0	1	1	19
1990-91	Toronto	NHL	4	0	0	0	7	....	....	....	....	....
	Newmarket	AHL	6	0	1	1	32	....	....	....	....	....
	Buffalo	NHL	17	0	1	1	43	....	....	....	....	....
	Rochester	AHL	10	0	0	0	36	....	....	....	....	....
1991-92	Buffalo	NHL	3	0	0	0	14	....	....	....	....	....
	Rochester	AHL	36	0	3	3	122	....	....	....	....	....
1992-93	Cape Breton	AHL	61	2	24	26	223	12	0	3	3	12
1993-94	Washington	NHL	26	1	0	1	61	....	....	....	....	....
	Portland	AHL	46	1	6	7	247	15	0	1	1	59
1994-95	Portland	AHL	59	2	10	12	328	7	0	0	0	24
	NHL Totals		381	7	33	40	1461	24	0	1	1	122

Signed as a free agent by **NY Islanders**, August 29, 1987. Traded to **Toronto** by **NY Islanders** for Toronto's sixth round choice (Pavel Gross) in 1988 Entry Draft, March 8, 1988. Traded to **Buffalo** by **Toronto** with Lou Franceschetti for Mike Foligno and Buffalo's eighth round choice (Thomas Kucharcik) in 1991 Entry Draft, December 17, 1990. Signed as a free agent by **Edmonton**, October 27, 1992. Signed as a free agent by **Washington**, October 21, 1993.

CURRIE, DAN

Left wing. Shoots left. 6'2", 195 lbs. Born, Burlington, Ont., March 15, 1968.
(Edmonton's 4th choice, 84th overall, in 1986 Entry Draft).

			Regular Season					Playoffs				
Season	Club	Lea	GP	G	A	TP	PIM	GP	G	A	TP	PIM
1985-86	S.S. Marie	OHL	66	21	24	45	37	....	....	....	....	....
1986-87	S.S. Marie	OHL	66	31	52	83	53	4	2	1	3	2
1987-88	Nova Scotia	AHL	3	4	2	6	0	5	4	3	7	0
	S.S. Marie	OHL	57	50	59	109	53	6	3	9	12	4
1988-89	Cape Breton	AHL	77	29	36	65	29	....	....	....	....	....
1989-90	Cape Breton	AHL	77	36	40	76	28	6	4	4	8	0
1990-91	Edmonton	NHL	5	0	0	0	0	....	....	....	....	....
	Cape Breton	AHL	71	47	45	92	51	4	3	1	4	8
1991-92	Edmonton	NHL	7	1	0	1	0	....	....	....	....	....
a	Cape Breton	AHL	66	*50	42	92	39	5	4	5	9	4
1992-93	Edmonton	NHL	5	0	0	0	4	....	....	....	....	....
b	Cape Breton	AHL	75	57	41	98	73	16	7	4	11	29
1993-94	Los Angeles	NHL	5	1	1	2	0	....	....	....	....	....
	Phoenix	IHL	74	37	49	86	96	....	....	....	....	....
1994-95	Phoenix	IHL	16	2	6	8	8	....	....	....	....	....
	Minnesota	IHL	54	18	35	53	34	3	0	0	0	2
	NHL Totals		22	2	1	3	4	....	....	....	....	....

a AHL Second All-Star Team (1992)
b AHL First All-Star Team (1993)

Signed as a free agent by **Los Angeles**, July 16, 1993.

CZERKAWSKI, MARIUSZ — (chehr-KAWV-skee) BOS.

Right wing. Shoots right. 6', 195 lbs. Born, Radomsko, Poland, April 13, 1972.
(Boston's 5th choice, 106th overall, in 1991 Entry Draft).

			Regular Season					Playoffs				
Season	Club	Lea	GP	G	A	TP	PIM	GP	G	A	TP	PIM
1990-91	GKS Tychy	Poland	24	25	15	40	....	....	....	....	....	....
1991-92	Djurgarden	Swe.	39	8	5	13	4	3	0	0	0	2
1992-93	Hammarby	Swe. 2	32	39	30	69	74	....	....	....	....	....
1993-94	Djurgarden	Swe.	39	13	21	34	20	6	3	1	4	2
	Boston	NHL	4	2	1	3	0	13	3	3	6	4
1994-95	Kiekko-Espoo	Fin.	7	9	3	12	10	....	....	....	....	....
	Boston	NHL	47	12	14	26	31	5	1	0	1	0
	NHL Totals		51	14	15	29	31	18	4	3	7	4

DAGENAIS, MIKE — (DA-shuh-NAY)

Defense. Shoots left. 6'3", 200 lbs. Born, Gloucester, Ont., July 22, 1969.
(Chicago's 4th choice, 60th overall, in 1987 Entry Draft).

			Regular Season					Playoffs				
Season	Club	Lea	GP	G	A	TP	PIM	GP	G	A	TP	PIM
1985-86	Peterborough	OHL	45	1	3	4	40	....	....	....	....	....
1986-87	Peterborough	OHL	56	1	17	18	66	12	4	1	5	20
1987-88	Peterborough	OHL	66	11	23	34	125	12	1	1	2	31
1988-89	Peterborough	OHL	62	14	23	37	122	13	3	3	6	12
1989-90	Peterborough	OHL	44	14	26	40	74	12	4	1	5	18
1990-91	Indianapolis	IHL	76	13	14	27	115	4	0	0	0	4
1991-92	Halifax	AHL	69	11	21	32	143	....	....	....	....	....
1992-93	Cincinnati	IHL	69	14	22	36	128	....	....	....	....	....
1993-94	Cleveland	IHL	65	8	18	26	120	....	....	....	....	....
1994-95	Cleveland	IHL	38	3	5	8	84	....	....	....	....	....
	Peoria	IHL	2	0	0	0	2	7	0	2	2	20

Signed as a free agent by **Pittsburgh**, August 26, 1993.

DAHL, KEVIN — (DAHL) CGY.

Defense. Shoots right. 5'11", 190 lbs. Born, Regina, Sask., December 30, 1968.
(Montreal's 12th choice, 230th overall, in 1988 Entry Draft).

			Regular Season					Playoffs				
Season	Club	Lea	GP	G	A	TP	PIM	GP	G	A	TP	PIM
1986-87	Bowling Green	CCHA	32	2	6	8	54	....	....	....	....	....
1987-88	Bowling Green	CCHA	44	2	23	25	78	....	....	....	....	....
1988-89	Bowling Green	CCHA	46	9	26	35	51	....	....	....	....	....
1989-90	Bowling Green	CCHA	43	8	22	30	74	....	....	....	....	....
1990-91	Fredericton	AHL	32	1	15	16	45	9	0	1	1	11
	Winston-Salem	ECHL	36	7	17	24	58	....	....	....	....	....
1991-92	Cdn. National	....	45	2	15	17	44	....	....	....	....	....
	Cdn. Olympic	....	8	2	0	2	6	....	....	....	....	....
	Salt Lake	IHL	13	0	2	2	12	5	0	0	0	13
1992-93	Calgary	NHL	61	2	9	11	56	6	0	2	2	8
1993-94	Calgary	NHL	33	0	3	3	23	6	0	0	0	4
	Saint John	AHL	2	0	0	0	0	....	....	....	....	....
1994-95	Calgary	NHL	34	4	8	12	38	3	0	0	0	0
	NHL Totals		128	6	20	26	117	15	0	2	2	12

Signed as a free agent by **Calgary**, July 27, 1991.

DAHLEN, ULF — (DAH-lehn) S.J.

Right wing. Shoots left. 6'2", 195 lbs. Born, Ostersund, Sweden, January 12, 1967.
(NY Rangers' 1st choice, 7th overall, in 1985 Entry Draft).

			Regular Season					Playoffs				
Season	Club	Lea	GP	G	A	TP	PIM	GP	G	A	TP	PIM
1983-84	Ostersund	Swe. 2	36	15	11	26	10	....	....	....	....	....
1984-85	Ostersund	Swe. 2	36	33	26	59	20	....	....	....	....	....
1985-86	Bjorkloven	Swe.	22	4	3	7	8	....	....	....	....	....
1986-87	Bjorkloven	Swe.	31	9	12	21	20	6	6	2	8	4
1987-88	NY Rangers	NHL	70	29	23	52	26	....	....	....	....	....
	Colorado	IHL	2	2	2	4	0	....	....	....	....	....
1988-89	NY Rangers	NHL	56	24	19	43	50	4	0	0	0	0
1989-90	NY Rangers	NHL	63	18	18	36	30	....	....	....	....	....
	Minnesota	NHL	13	2	4	6	0	7	1	4	5	2
1990-91	Minnesota	NHL	66	21	18	39	6	15	2	6	8	4
1991-92	Minnesota	NHL	79	36	30	66	10	7	0	3	3	2
1992-93	Minnesota	NHL	83	35	39	74	6	....	....	....	....	....
1993-94	Dallas	NHL	65	19	38	57	10	....	....	....	....	....
	San Jose	NHL	13	6	6	12	0	14	6	2	8	0
1994-95	San Jose	NHL	46	11	23	34	11	11	5	4	9	0
	NHL Totals		554	201	218	419	149	58	14	19	33	8

Traded to **Minnesota** by **NY Rangers** with Los Angeles' fourth round choice (previously acquired by NY Rangers — Minnesota selected Cal McGowan) in 1990 Entry Draft and future considerations for Mike Gartner, March 6, 1990. Traded to **San Jose** by **Dallas** with Dallas' seventh round choice (Brad Mehalko) in 1995 Entry Draft for Doug Zmolek, Mike Lalor and cash, March 19, 1994.

DAHLQUIST, CHRIS — (DAHL-kwist) OTT.

Defense. Shoots left. 6'1", 195 lbs. Born, Fridley, MN, December 14, 1962.

			Regular Season					Playoffs				
Season	Club	Lea	GP	G	A	TP	PIM	GP	G	A	TP	PIM
1981-82	Lake Superior	CCHA	39	4	10	14	62	....	....	....	....	....
1982-83	Lake Superior	CCHA	35	0	12	12	63	....	....	....	....	....
1983-84	Lake Superior	CCHA	40	4	19	23	76	....	....	....	....	....
1984-85	Lake Superior	CCHA	32	4	10	14	18	....	....	....	....	....
1985-86	Pittsburgh	NHL	5	1	2	3	2	....	....	....	....	....
	Baltimore	AHL	65	4	21	25	64	....	....	....	....	....
1986-87	Pittsburgh	NHL	19	0	1	1	20	....	....	....	....	....
	Baltimore	AHL	51	1	16	17	50	....	....	....	....	....
1987-88	Pittsburgh	NHL	44	3	6	9	69	....	....	....	....	....
1988-89	Pittsburgh	NHL	43	1	5	6	42	2	0	0	0	0
	Muskegon	IHL	10	3	6	9	14	....	....	....	....	....
1989-90	Pittsburgh	NHL	62	4	10	14	56	....	....	....	....	....
	Muskegon	IHL	6	1	1	2	8	....	....	....	....	....
1990-91	Pittsburgh	NHL	22	1	2	3	30	....	....	....	....	....
	Minnesota	NHL	42	2	6	8	33	23	1	6	7	20
1991-92	Minnesota	NHL	74	1	13	14	68	7	0	0	0	6
1992-93	Calgary	NHL	74	3	7	10	66	6	3	1	4	4
1993-94	Calgary	NHL	77	1	11	12	52	1	0	0	0	0
1994-95	Ottawa	NHL	46	1	7	8	36	....	....	....	....	....
	NHL Totals		508	18	70	88	474	39	4	7	11	30

Signed as a free agent by **Pittsburgh**, May 7, 1985. Traded to **Minnesota** by **Pittsburgh** with Jim Johnson for Larry Murphy and Peter Taglianetti, December 11, 1990. Claimed by **Calgary** from **Minnesota** in NHL Waiver Draft, October 4, 1992. Signed as a free agent by **Ottawa**, July 4, 1994.

DAIGLE, ALEXANDRE — (DAYG) OTT.

Center. Shoots left. 6', 185 lbs. Born, Montreal, Que., February 7, 1975.
(Ottawa's 1st choice, 1st overall, in 1993 Entry Draft).

			Regular Season					Playoffs				
Season	Club	Lea	GP	G	A	TP	PIM	GP	G	A	TP	PIM
1991-92ab	Victoriaville	QMJHL	66	35	75	110	63	....	....	....	....	....
1992-93c	Victoriaville	QMJHL	53	45	92	137	85	6	5	6	11	4
1993-94	Ottawa	NHL	84	20	31	51	40	....	....	....	....	....
1994-95	Victoriaville	QMJHL	18	14	20	34	16	....	....	....	....	....
	Ottawa	NHL	47	16	21	37	14	....	....	....	....	....
	NHL Totals		131	36	52	88	54	....	....	....	....	....

a QMJHL Second All-Star Team (1992)
b Canadian Major Junior Rookie of the Year (1992)
c QMJHL First All-Star Team (1993)

DAIGNEAULT, JEAN-JACQUES (J.J.) (DAYN-yoh) MTL.

Defense. Shoots left. 5'10", 186 lbs. Born, Montreal, Que., October 12, 1965.
(Vancouver's 1st choice, 10th overall, in 1984 Entry Draft).

			Regular Season					Playoffs				
Season	Club	Lea	GP	G	A	TP	PIM	GP	G	A	TP	PIM
1981-82	Laval	QMJHL	64	4	25	29	41	18	1	3	4	2
1982-83a	Longueuil	QMJHL	70	26	58	84	58	15	4	11	15	35
1983-84	Cdn. National	....	55	5	14	19	40	....	....	....	....	....
	Cdn. Olympic	....	7	1	1	2	0	....	....	....	....	....
	Longueuil	QMJHL	10	2	11	13	6	14	3	13	16	30
1984-85	**Vancouver**	**NHL**	**67**	**4**	**23**	**27**	**69**	....	....	....	....	....
1985-86	**Vancouver**	**NHL**	**64**	**5**	**23**	**28**	**45**	**3**	**0**	**2**	**2**	**0**
1986-87	**Philadelphia**	**NHL**	**77**	**6**	**16**	**22**	**56**	**9**	**1**	**0**	**1**	**0**
1987-88	**Philadelphia**	**NHL**	**28**	**2**	**2**	**4**	**12**	....	....	....	....	....
	Hershey	AHL	10	1	5	6	8	....	....	....	....	....
1988-89	Hershey	AHL	12	0	10	10	13	....	....	....	....	....
	Sherbrooke	AHL	63	10	33	43	48	6	1	3	4	2
1989-90	**Montreal**	**NHL**	**36**	**2**	**10**	**12**	**14**	**9**	**0**	**0**	**0**	**2**
	Sherbrooke	AHL	28	8	19	27	18	....	....	....	....	....
1990-91	**Montreal**	**NHL**	**51**	**3**	**16**	**19**	**31**	**5**	**0**	**1**	**1**	**0**
1991-92	**Montreal**	**NHL**	**79**	**4**	**14**	**18**	**36**	**11**	**0**	**3**	**3**	**4**
1992-93	**Montreal**	**NHL**	**66**	**8**	**10**	**18**	**57**	**20**	**1**	**3**	**4**	**22**
1993-94	**Montreal**	**NHL**	**68**	**2**	**12**	**14**	**73**	**7**	**0**	**1**	**1**	**12**
1994-95	**Montreal**	**NHL**	**45**	**3**	**5**	**8**	**40**	....	....	....	....	....
	NHL Totals		**581**	**39**	**131**	**170**	**433**	**64**	**2**	**10**	**12**	**40**

a QMJHL First All-Star Team (1983)

Traded to **Philadelphia** by **Vancouver** with Vancouver's second round choice (Kent Hawley) in 1986 Entry Draft for Dave Richter, Rich Sutter and Vancouver's third round choice (previously acquired by Philadelphia — Vancouver selected Don Gibson) in 1986 Entry Draft, June 6, 1986. Traded to **Montreal** by **Philadelphia** for Scott Sandelin, November 7, 1988.

DALE, ANDREW L.A.

Center. Shoots left. 6'1", 196 lbs. Born, Sudbury, Ont., February 16, 1976.
(Los Angeles' 6th choice, 189th overall, in 1994 Entry Draft).

			Regular Season					Playoffs				
Season	Club	Lea	GP	G	A	TP	PIM	GP	G	A	TP	PIM
1993-94	Sudbury	OHL	53	8	13	21	21	9	0	3	3	4
1994-95	Sudbury	OHL	65	21	30	51	99	18	2	9	11	37

DALGARNO, BRAD NYI

Right wing. Shoots right. 6'3", 215 lbs. Born, Vancouver, B.C., August 11, 1967.
(NY Islanders' 1st choice, 6th overall, in 1985 Entry Draft).

			Regular Season					Playoffs				
Season	Club	Lea	GP	G	A	TP	PIM	GP	G	A	TP	PIM
1984-85	Hamilton	OHA	66	23	30	53	86	....	....	....	....	....
1985-86	**NY Islanders**	**NHL**	**2**	**1**	**0**	**1**	**0**	....	....	....	....	....
	Hamilton	OHL	54	22	43	65	79	....	....	....	....	....
1986-87	Hamilton	OHL	60	27	32	59	100	....	....	....	....	....
	NY Islanders	**NHL**	....	....	....	....	....	**1**	**0**	**1**	**1**	**0**
1987-88	**NY Islanders**	**NHL**	**38**	**2**	**8**	**10**	**58**	**4**	**0**	**0**	**0**	**19**
	Springfield	AHL	39	13	11	24	76	....	....	....	....	....
1988-89	**NY Islanders**	**NHL**	**55**	**11**	**10**	**21**	**86**	....	....	....	....	....
1989-90						DID NOT PLAY						
1990-91	**NY Islanders**	**NHL**	**41**	**3**	**12**	**15**	**24**	....	....	....	....	....
	Capital Dist.	AHL	27	6	14	20	26	....	....	....	....	....
1991-92	**NY Islanders**	**NHL**	**15**	**2**	**1**	**3**	**12**	....	....	....	....	....
	Capital Dist.	AHL	14	7	8	15	34	....	....	....	....	....
1992-93	**NY Islanders**	**NHL**	**57**	**15**	**17**	**32**	**62**	**18**	**2**	**2**	**4**	**14**
	Capital Dist.	AHL	19	10	4	14	16	....	....	....	....	....
1993-94	**NY Islanders**	**NHL**	**73**	**11**	**19**	**30**	**62**	**4**	**0**	**1**	**1**	**4**
1994-95	**NY Islanders**	**NHL**	**22**	**3**	**2**	**5**	**14**	....	....	....	....	....
	NHL Totals		**303**	**48**	**69**	**117**	**318**	**27**	**2**	**4**	**6**	**37**

DAL GRANDE, DAVID NYR

Defense. Shoots left. 6'5", 195 lbs. Born, Ottawa, Ont., July 8, 1974.
(NY Rangers' 6th choice, 144th overall, in 1992 Entry Draft).

			Regular Season					Playoffs				
Season	Club	Lea	GP	G	A	TP	PIM	GP	G	A	TP	PIM
1992-93	Notre Dame	CCHA	22	1	1	2	10	....	....	....	....	....
1993-94	Notre Dame	CCHA	32	2	4	6	20	....	....	....	....	....
1994-95	Notre Dame	CCHA	36	4	12	16	46	....	....	....	....	....

DAMEWORTH, CHAD EDM.

Defense. Shoots left. 6'2", 200 lbs. Born, Marquette, MI, July 6, 1972.
(Edmonton's 1st choice, 6th overall, in 1994 Supplemental Draft).

			Regular Season					Playoffs				
Season	Club	Lea	GP	G	A	TP	PIM	GP	G	A	TP	PIM
1991-92	N. Michigan	WCHA	13	0	2	2	8	....	....	....	....	....
1992-93	N. Michigan	WCHA	29	0	2	2	22	....	....	....	....	....
1993-94	N. Michigan	WCHA	36	0	4	4	26	....	....	....	....	....
1994-95	N. Michigan	WCHA	39	0	4	4	46	....	....	....	....	....
	Cape Breton	AHL	1	0	0	0	0	....	....	....	....	....

DAMPHOUSSE, VINCENT (DAHM-fooz) MTL.

Left wing. Shoots left. 6'1", 200 lbs. Born, Montreal, Que., December 17, 1967.
(Toronto's 1st choice, 6th overall, in 1986 Entry Draft).

			Regular Season					Playoffs				
Season	Club	Lea	GP	G	A	TP	PIM	GP	G	A	TP	PIM
1983-84	Laval	QMJHL	66	29	36	65	25	....	....	....	....	....
1984-85	Laval	QMJHL	68	35	68	103	62	....	....	....	....	....
1985-86a	Laval	QMJHL	69	45	110	155	70	14	9	27	36	12
1986-87	**Toronto**	**NHL**	**80**	**21**	**25**	**46**	**26**	**12**	**1**	**5**	**6**	**8**
1987-88	**Toronto**	**NHL**	**75**	**12**	**36**	**48**	**40**	**6**	**0**	**1**	**1**	**10**
1988-89	**Toronto**	**NHL**	**80**	**26**	**42**	**68**	**75**	....	....	....	....	....
1989-90	**Toronto**	**NHL**	**80**	**33**	**61**	**94**	**56**	**5**	**0**	**2**	**2**	**2**
1990-91	**Toronto**	**NHL**	**79**	**26**	**47**	**73**	**65**	....	....	....	....	....
1991-92	**Edmonton**	**NHL**	**80**	**38**	**51**	**89**	**53**	**16**	**6**	**8**	**14**	**8**
1992-93	**Montreal**	**NHL**	**84**	**39**	**58**	**97**	**98**	**20**	**11**	**12**	**23**	**16**
1993-94	**Montreal**	**NHL**	**84**	**40**	**51**	**91**	**75**	**7**	**1**	**2**	**3**	**8**
1994-95	Ratingen	Ger.	11	5	7	12	24	....	....	....	....	....
	Montreal	**NHL**	**48**	**10**	**30**	**40**	**42**	....	....	....	....	....
	NHL Totals		**690**	**245**	**401**	**646**	**530**	**66**	**19**	**30**	**49**	**52**

a QMJHL Second All-Star Team (1986)

Played in NHL All-Star Game (1991, 1992)

Traded to **Edmonton** by **Toronto** with Peter Ing, Scott Thornton, Luke Richardson, future considerations and cash for Grant Fuhr, Glenn Anderson and Craig Berube, September 19, 1991. Traded to **Montreal** by **Edmonton** with Edmonton's fourth round choice (Adam Wiesel) in 1993 Entry Draft for Shayne Corson, Brent Gilchrist and Vladimir Vujtek, August 27, 1992.

DANDENAULT, MATHIEU (DAHN-deh-noh) DET.

Right wing. Shoots right. 6', 174 lbs. Born, Sherbrooke, Que., February 3, 1976.
(Detroit's 2nd choice, 49th overall, in 1994 Entry Draft).

			Regular Season					Playoffs				
Season	Club	Lea	GP	G	A	TP	PIM	GP	G	A	TP	PIM
1993-94	Sherbrooke	QMJHL	67	17	36	53	67	12	4	10	14	12
1994-95	Sherbrooke	QMJHL	67	37	70	107	76	7	1	7	8	10

DANEYKO, KEN (DAN-ee-KOH) N.J.

Defense. Shoots left. 6', 210 lbs. Born, Windsor, Ont., April 17, 1964.
(New Jersey's 2nd choice, 18th overall, in 1982 Entry Draft).

			Regular Season					Playoffs				
Season	Club	Lea	GP	G	A	TP	PIM	GP	G	A	TP	PIM
1980-81	Spokane	WHL	62	6	13	19	40	4	0	0	0	6
1981-82	Spokane	WHL	26	1	11	12	147	....	....	....	....	....
	Seattle	WHL	38	1	22	23	151	14	1	9	10	49
1982-83	Seattle	WHL	69	17	43	60	150	4	1	3	4	14
1983-84	**New Jersey**	**NHL**	**11**	**1**	**4**	**5**	**17**	....	....	....	....	....
	Kamloops	WH	19	6	28	34	52	17	4	9	13	28
1984-85	**New Jersey**	**NHL**	**1**	**0**	**0**	**0**	**10**	....	....	....	....	....
	Maine	AHL	80	4	9	13	206	11	1	3	4	36
1985-86	**New Jersey**	**NHL**	**44**	**0**	**10**	**10**	**100**	....	....	....	....	....
	Maine	AHL	21	3	2	5	75	....	....	....	....	....
1986-87	**New Jersey**	**NHL**	**79**	**2**	**12**	**14**	**183**	....	....	....	....	....
1987-88	**New Jersey**	**NHL**	**80**	**5**	**7**	**12**	**239**	**20**	**1**	**6**	**7**	**83**
1988-89	**New Jersey**	**NHL**	**80**	**5**	**5**	**10**	**283**	....	....	....	....	....
1989-90	**New Jersey**	**NHL**	**74**	**6**	**15**	**21**	**216**	**6**	**2**	**0**	**2**	**21**
1990-91	**New Jersey**	**NHL**	**80**	**4**	**16**	**20**	**249**	**7**	**0**	**1**	**1**	**10**
1991-92	**New Jersey**	**NHL**	**80**	**1**	**7**	**8**	**170**	**7**	**0**	**3**	**3**	**16**
1992-93	**New Jersey**	**NHL**	**84**	**2**	**11**	**13**	**236**	**5**	**0**	**0**	**0**	**8**
1993-94	**New Jersey**	**NHL**	**78**	**1**	**9**	**10**	**176**	**20**	**0**	**1**	**1**	**45**
1994-95	**New Jersey**	**NHL**	**25**	**1**	**2**	**3**	**54**	**20**	**1**	**0**	**1**	**22**
	NHL Totals		**716**	**28**	**98**	**126**	**1933**	**85**	**4**	**11**	**15**	**205**

DANIELS, JEFF HFD.

Left wing. Shoots left. 6'1", 200 lbs. Born, Oshawa, Ont., June 24, 1968.
(Pittsburgh's 6th choice, 109th overall, in 1986 Entry Draft).

			Regular Season					Playoffs				
Season	Club	Lea	GP	G	A	TP	PIM	GP	G	A	TP	PIM
1984-85	Oshawa	OHL	59	7	11	18	16	....	....	....	....	....
1985-86	Oshawa	OHL	62	13	19	32	23	6	0	1	1	0
1986-87	Oshawa	OHL	54	14	9	23	22	15	3	2	5	5
1987-88	Oshawa	OHL	64	29	39	68	59	4	2	3	5	0
1988-89	Muskegon	IHL	58	21	21	42	58	11	3	5	8	11
1989-90	Muskegon	IHL	80	30	47	77	39	6	1	1	2	7
1990-91	**Pittsburgh**	**NHL**	**11**	**0**	**2**	**2**	**2**	....	....	....	....	....
	Muskegon	IHL	62	23	29	52	18	5	1	3	4	2
1991-92	**Pittsburgh**	**NHL**	**2**	**0**	**0**	**0**	**0**	....	....	....	....	....
	Muskegon	IHL	44	19	16	35	38	10	5	4	9	9
1992-93	**Pittsburgh**	**NHL**	**58**	**5**	**4**	**9**	**14**	**12**	**3**	**2**	**5**	**0**
	Cleveland	IHL	3	2	1	3	0	....	....	....	....	....
1993-94	**Pittsburgh**	**NHL**	**63**	**3**	**5**	**8**	**20**	....	....	....	....	....
	Florida	**NHL**	**7**	**0**	**0**	**0**	**0**	....	....	....	....	....
1994-95	**Florida**	**NHL**	**3**	**0**	**0**	**0**	**0**	....	....	....	....	....
	Detroit	IHL	25	8	12	20	6	5	1	0	1	0
	NHL Totals		**144**	**8**	**11**	**19**	**36**	**12**	**3**	**2**	**5**	**0**

Traded to **Florida** by **Pittsburgh** for Greg Hawgood, March 19, 1994. Signed as a free agent by **Hartford**, July 18, 1995.

DANIELS, SCOTT HFD.

Left wing. Shoots left. 6'3", 200 lbs. Born, Prince Albert, Sask., September 19, 1969.
(Hartford's 6th choice, 136th overall, in 1989 Entry Draft).

			Regular Season					Playoffs				
Season	Club	Lea	GP	G	A	TP	PIM	GP	G	A	TP	PIM
1986-87	Kamloops	WHL	43	6	4	10	68	....	....	....	....	....
	N. Westminster	WHL	19	4	7	11	30	....	....	....	....	....
1987-88	N. Westminster	WHL	37	6	11	17	157	....	....	....	....	....
	Regina	WHL	19	2	3	5	83	....	....	....	....	....
1988-89	Regina	WHL	64	21	26	47	241	....	....	....	....	....
1989-90	Regina	WHL	52	28	31	59	171	....	....	....	....	....
1990-91	Springfield	AHL	40	2	6	8	121	....	....	....	....	....
	Louisville	ECHL	9	5	3	8	34	1	0	2	2	0
1991-92	Springfield	AHL	54	7	15	22	213	10	0	0	0	32
1992-93	**Hartford**	**NHL**	**1**	**0**	**0**	**0**	**19**	....	....	....	....	....
	Springfield	AHL	60	11	12	23	181	12	2	7	9	12
1993-94	Springfield	AHL	52	9	11	20	185	6	0	1	1	53
1994-95	Springfield	AHL	48	9	5	14	277	....	....	....	....	....
	Hartford	**NHL**	**12**	**0**	**2**	**2**	**55**	....	....	....	....	....
	NHL Totals		**13**	**0**	**2**	**2**	**74**	....	....	....	....	....

DANYLUK, CAM VAN.

Left wing. Shoots left. 6'4", 215 lbs. Born, Andrew, Alta., September 6, 1972.

			Regular Season					Playoffs				
Season	Club	Lea	GP	G	A	TP	PIM	GP	G	A	TP	PIM
1991-92	Spokana	WHL	6	0	4	4	37	....	....	....	....	....
	Brandon	WHL	5	3	0	3	16	....	....	....	....	....
	Medicine Hat	WHL	52	27	26	53	158	4	0	2	2	6
1992-93	Medicine Hat	WHL	57	29	19	48	214	10	9	5	14	29
1993-94	Hamilton	AHL	60	11	12	23	159	2	1	0	1	0
1994-95	Syracuse	AHL	12	1	3	4	19	....	....	....	....	....
	S. Carolina	ECHL	50	26	27	53	188	9	5	4	9	76

Signed as a free agent by **Vancouver**, April 21, 1993.

DARBY, CRAIG NYI

Center. Shoots right. 6'3", 180 lbs. Born, Oneida, NY, September 26, 1972.
(Montreal's 3rd choice, 43rd overall, in 1991 Entry Draft).

			Regular Season					Playoffs				
Season	Club	Lea	GP	G	A	TP	PIM	GP	G	A	TP	PIM
1991-92	Providence	H.E.	35	17	24	41	47	....	....	....	....	....
1992-93	Providence	H.E.	35	11	21	32	62	....	....	....	....	....
1993-94	Fredericton	AHL	66	23	33	56	51	....	....	....	....	....
1994-95	Fredericton	AHL	64	21	47	68	82	....	....	....	....	....
	Montreal	**NHL**	**10**	**0**	**2**	**2**	**0**	....	....	....	....	....
	NY Islanders	**NHL**	**3**	**0**	**0**	**0**	**0**	....	....	....	....	....
	NHL Totals		**13**	**0**	**2**	**2**	**0**	....	....	....	....	....

Traded to **NY Islanders** by **Montreal** with Kirk Muller and Mathieu Schneider for Pierre Turgeon and Vladimir Malakhov, April 5, 1995.

DARLING, DION — MTL.

Defense. Shoots left. 6'3", 205 lbs. Born, Edmonton, Alta., October 22, 1974.
(Montreal's 7th choice, 125th overall, in 1993 Entry Draft).

			Regular Season					Playoffs				
Season	Club	Lea	GP	G	A	TP	PIM	GP	G	A	TP	PIM
1991-92	St. Albert	AJHL	29	5	15	20	101	....	....	....	....	....
1992-93	Spokane	WHL	69	1	4	5	168	9	0	1	1	14
1993-94	Spokane	WHL	45	1	8	9	190	....	....	....	....	....
	Moose Jaw	WHL	23	4	6	10	96	....	....	....	....	....
	Wheeling	ECHL	3	0	1	1	7	9	0	1	1	14
1994-95	Fredericton	AHL	51	0	2	2	153	....	....	....	....	....
	Wheeling	ECHL	4	0	0	0	24	....	....	....	....	....

DAVIDSON, MATT — BUF.

Right wing. Shoots right. 6'2", 190 lbs. Born, Flin Flon, Man., August 9, 1977.
(Buffalo's 5th choice, 94th overall, in 1995 Entry Draft).

			Regular Season					Playoffs				
Season	Club	Lea	GP	G	A	TP	PIM	GP	G	A	TP	PIM
1993-94	Portland	WHL	59	4	12	16	18	10	0	0	0	4
1994-95	Portland	WHL	72	17	20	37	51	9	1	3	4	0

DAVIDSSON, JOHAN (DAH-vihd-suhn) — ANA.

Center. Shoots right. 5'11", 170 lbs. Born, Jonkoping, Sweden, January 6, 1976.
(Anaheim's 2nd choice, 28th overall, in 1994 Entry Draft).

			Regular Season					Playoffs				
Season	Club	Lea	GP	G	A	TP	PIM	GP	G	A	TP	PIM
1992-93	HV-71	Swe.	8	1	0	1	0	....	....	....	....	....
1993-94	HV-71	Swe.	38	2	5	7	4	....	....	....	....	....
1994-95	HV-71	Swe.	37	4	7	11	20	13	3	2	5	0

DAVYDOV, EVGENY (dah-VEE-dohv, yev-GEHN-ee) — PIT.

Left wing. Shoots right. 6', 200 lbs. Born, Chelyabinsk, USSR, May 27, 1967.
(Winnipeg's 14th choice, 235th overall, in 1989 Entry Draft).

			Regular Season					Playoffs				
Season	Club	Lea	GP	G	A	TP	PIM	GP	G	A	TP	PIM
1984-85	Chelyabinsk	USSR	5	1	0	1	2	....	....	....	....	....
1985-86	Chelyabinsk	USSR	39	11	5	16	22	....	....	....	....	....
1986-87	CSKA	USSR	32	11	2	13	8	....	....	....	....	....
1987-88	CSKA	USSR	44	16	7	23	18	....	....	....	....	....
1988-89	CSKA	USSR	35	9	7	16	4	....	....	....	....	....
1989-90	CSKA	USSR	44	17	6	23	16	....	....	....	....	....
1990-91	CSKA	USSR	44	10	10	20	26	....	....	....	....	....
1991-92	CSKA	CIS	27	13	12	25	14	....	....	....	....	....
	Winnipeg	**NHL**	**12**	**4**	**3**	**7**	**8**	**7**	**2**	**2**	**4**	**2**
1992-93	**Winnipeg**	**NHL**	**79**	**28**	**21**	**49**	**66**	**4**	**0**	**0**	**0**	**0**
1993-94	**Florida**	**NHL**	**21**	**2**	**6**	**8**	**8**	....	....	....	....	....
	Ottawa	**NHL**	**40**	**5**	**7**	**12**	**38**	....	....	....	....	....
1994-95	**Ottawa**	**NHL**	**3**	**1**	**2**	**3**	**0**	....	....	....	....	....
	San Diego	IHL	11	2	1	3	14	....	....	....	....	....
	Chicago	IHL	18	10	12	22	26	3	1	0	1	0
	NHL Totals		**155**	**40**	**39**	**79**	**120**	**11**	**2**	**2**	**4**	**2**

Traded to **Florida** by **Winnipeg** for Florida's fourth round choice (later traded to Edmonton — Edmonton selected Adam Copeland) in 1994 Entry Draft, September 30, 1993. Traded to **Ottawa** by **Florida** with Scott Levins, Florida's sixth round choice (Mike Gaffney) in 1994 Entry Draft and Dallas' fourth round choice (previously acquired by Florida — Ottawa selected Kevin Bolibruck) in 1995 Entry Draft for Bob Kudelski, January 6, 1994. Signed as a free agent by **Pittsburgh**, August 10, 1995.

DAWE, JASON (DAW) — BUF.

Left wing. Shoots left. 5'10", 195 lbs. Born, North York, Ont., May 29, 1973.
(Buffalo's 2nd choice, 35th overall, in 1991 Entry Draft).

			Regular Season					Playoffs				
Season	Club	Lea	GP	G	A	TP	PIM	GP	G	A	TP	PIM
1989-90	Peterborough	OHL	50	15	18	33	19	12	4	7	11	4
1990-91	Peterborough	OHL	66	43	27	70	43	4	3	1	4	0
1991-92	Peterborough	OHL	66	53	55	108	55	4	5	0	5	0
1992-93abc	Peterborough	OHL	59	58	68	126	80	21	18	33	51	18
	Rochester	AHL	....	....	....	....	....	3	1	0	1	0
1993-94	**Buffalo**	**NHL**	**32**	**6**	**7**	**13**	**12**	**6**	**0**	**1**	**1**	**6**
	Rochester	AHL	48	22	14	36	44	....	....	....	....	....
1994-95	Rochester	AHL	44	27	19	46	24	....	....	....	....	....
	Buffalo	**NHL**	**42**	**7**	**4**	**11**	**19**	**5**	**2**	**1**	**3**	**6**
	NHL Totals		**74**	**13**	**11**	**24**	**31**	**11**	**2**	**2**	**4**	**12**

a OHL First All-Star Team (1993)
b Canadian Major Junior Second All-Star Team (1993)
c Won George Parsons Trophy (Memorial Cup Tournament Most Sportsmanlike Player) (1993)

DAY, JOE

Left wing. Shoots left. 5'11", 180 lbs. Born, Chicago, IL, May 11, 1968.
(Hartford's 8th choice, 186th overall, in 1987 Entry Draft).

			Regular Season					Playoffs				
Season	Club	Lea	GP	G	A	TP	PIM	GP	G	A	TP	PIM
1986-87	St. Lawrence	ECAC	33	9	11	20	25	....	....	....	....	....
1987-88	St. Lawrence	ECAC	30	21	16	37	36	....	....	....	....	....
1988-89	St. Lawrence	ECAC	36	21	27	48	44	....	....	....	....	....
1989-90a	St. Lawrence	ECAC	32	19	26	45	30	....	....	....	....	....
1990-91	Springfield	AHL	75	24	29	53	82	18	5	5	10	27
1991-92	**Hartford**	**NHL**	**24**	**0**	**3**	**3**	**10**	....	....	....	....	....
	Springfield	AHL	50	33	25	58	92	....	....	....	....	....
1992-93	**Hartford**	**NHL**	**24**	**1**	**7**	**8**	**47**	....	....	....	....	....
	Springfield	AHL	33	15	20	35	118	15	0	8	8	40
1993-94	**NY Islanders**	**NHL**	**24**	**0**	**0**	**0**	**30**	....	....	....	....	....
	Salt Lake	IHL	33	16	10	26	153	....	....	....	....	....
1994-95	Detroit	IHL	32	16	10	26	126	5	0	2	2	21
	NHL Totals		**72**	**1**	**10**	**11**	**87**	....	....	....	....	....

a ECAC Second All-Star Team (1990)

Signed as a free agent by **NY Islanders**, August 24, 1993.

DAZE, ERIC (dah-ZAY) — CHI.

Left wing. Shoots left. 6'4", 215 lbs. Born, Montreal, Que., July 2, 1975.
(Chicago's 5th choice, 90th overall, in 1993 Entry Draft).

			Regular Season					Playoffs				
Season	Club	Lea	GP	G	A	TP	PIM	GP	G	A	TP	PIM
1992-93	Beauport	QMJHL	68	19	36	55	24	....	....	....	....	....
1993-94a	Beauport	QMJHL	66	59	48	107	31	15	16	8	24	2
1994-95ab	Beauport	QMJHL	57	54	45	99	20	16	9	12	21	23
	Chicago	**NHL**	**4**	**1**	**1**	**2**	**2**	**16**	**0**	**1**	**1**	**4**
	NHL Totals		**4**	**1**	**1**	**2**	**2**	**16**	**0**	**1**	**1**	**4**

a QMJHL First All-Star Team (1994, 1995)
b Canadian Major Junior Most Sportsmanlike Player of the Year (1995)

DEADMARSH, ADAM — COL.

Center. Shoots right. 6', 195 lbs. Born, Trail, B.C., May 10, 1975.
(Quebec's 2nd choice, 14th overall, in 1993 Entry Draft).

			Regular Season					Playoffs				
Season	Club	Lea	GP	G	A	TP	PIM	GP	G	A	TP	PIM
1991-92	Portland	WHL	68	30	30	60	81	6	3	3	6	13
1992-93	Portland	WHL	58	33	36	69	126	16	7	8	15	29
1993-94	Portland	WHL	65	43	56	99	212	10	9	8	17	33
1994-95	Portland	WHL	29	28	20	48	129	....	....	....	....	....
	Quebec	**NHL**	**48**	**9**	**8**	**17**	**56**	**6**	**0**	**1**	**1**	**0**
	NHL Totals		**48**	**9**	**8**	**17**	**56**	**6**	**0**	**1**	**1**	**0**

DEAN, KEVIN — N.J.

Defense. Shoots left. 6'2", 195 lbs. Born, Madison, WI, April 1, 1969.
(New Jersey's 4th choice, 86th overall, in 1987 Entry Draft).

			Regular Season					Playoffs				
Season	Club	Lea	GP	G	A	TP	PIM	GP	G	A	TP	PIM
1987-88	N. Hampshire	H.E.	27	1	6	7	34	....	....	....	....	....
1988-89	N. Hampshire	H.E.	34	1	12	13	28	....	....	....	....	....
1989-90	N. Hampshire	H.E.	39	2	6	8	42	....	....	....	....	....
1990-91	N. Hampshire	H.E.	31	10	12	22	22	....	....	....	....	....
	Utica	AHL	7	0	1	1	2	....	....	....	....	....
1991-92	Utica	AHL	23	0	3	3	6	....	....	....	....	....
	Cincinnati	ECHL	30	3	22	25	43	9	1	6	7	8
1992-93	Cincinnati	IHL	13	2	1	3	15	....	....	....	....	....
	Utica	AHL	57	2	16	18	76	5	1	0	1	8
1993-94	Albany	AHL	70	9	33	42	92	5	0	2	2	7
1994-95a	Albany	AHL	68	5	37	42	66	8	0	4	4	4
	New Jersey	**NHL**	**17**	**0**	**1**	**1**	**4**	**3**	**0**	**2**	**2**	**0**
	NHL Totals		**17**	**0**	**1**	**1**	**4**	**3**	**0**	**2**	**2**	**0**

a AHL First All-Star Team (1995)

DEAZELEY, MARK — WPG.

Left wing. Shoots left. 6'4", 240 lbs. Born, North York, Ont., April 8, 1972.

			Regular Season					Playoffs				
Season	Club	Lea	GP	G	A	TP	PIM	GP	G	A	TP	PIM
1989-90	Oshawa	OHL	27	3	1	4	56	....	....	....	....	....
1990-91	Oshawa	OHL	65	17	19	36	149	16	1	2	3	38
1991-92	Oshawa	OHL	66	19	21	40	215	7	0	0	0	16
1992-93	Toledo	ECHL	63	27	18	45	263	15	8	6	14	66
1993-94	Toledo	ECHL	57	41	36	77	231	14	*16	10	*26	37
	Fort Wayne	IHL	1	0	0	0	2	....	....	....	....	....
1994-95	Springfield	AHL	26	2	0	2	141	....	....	....	....	....
	Toledo	ECHL	14	5	1	6	136	....	....	....	....	....

Signed as a free agent by **Winnipeg**, June 17, 1994.

DEBRUSK, LOUIE (dah-BRUHSK) — EDM.

Left wing. Shoots left. 6'2", 215 lbs. Born, Cambridge, Ont., March 19, 1971.
(NY Rangers' 4th choice, 49th overall, in 1989 Entry Draft).

			Regular Season					Playoffs				
Season	Club	Lea	GP	G	A	TP	PIM	GP	G	A	TP	PIM
1988-89	London	OHL	59	11	11	22	149	19	1	1	2	43
1989-90	London	OHL	61	21	19	40	198	6	2	2	4	24
1990-91	London	OHL	61	31	33	64	*223	7	2	2	4	14
	Binghamton	AHL	2	0	0	0	7	2	0	0	0	9
1991-92	**Edmonton**	**NHL**	**25**	**2**	**1**	**3**	**124**	....	....	....	....	....
	Cape Breton	AHL	28	2	2	4	73	....	....	....	....	....
1992-93	**Edmonton**	**NHL**	**51**	**8**	**2**	**10**	**205**	....	....	....	....	....
1993-94	**Edmonton**	**NHL**	**48**	**4**	**6**	**10**	**185**	....	....	....	....	....
	Cape Breton	AHL	5	3	1	4	58	....	....	....	....	....
1994-95	**Edmonton**	**NHL**	**34**	**2**	**0**	**2**	**93**	....	....	....	....	....
	NHL Totals		**158**	**16**	**9**	**25**	**607**	....	....	....	....	....

Traded to **Edmonton** by **NY Rangers** with Bernie Nicholls and Steven Rice for Mark Messier and future considerations, October 4, 1991.

DEEKS, ALAIN — ANA.

Defense. Shoots right. 6'5", 230 lbs. Born, Hawkesbury, Ont., April 15, 1969.

			Regular Season					Playoffs				
Season	Club	Lea	GP	G	A	TP	PIM	GP	G	A	TP	PIM
1991-92	Columbus	ECHL	46	15	24	39	73	....	....	....	....	....
1992-93	Hamilton	AHL	18	0	6	6	6	....	....	....	....	....
	New Haven	AHL	1	0	0	0	0	....	....	....	....	....
	Columbus	ECHL	23	5	11	16	34	....	....	....	....	....
1993-94	P.E.I.	AHL	35	1	3	4	36	....	....	....	....	....
	Thunder Bay	ColHL	22	1	5	6	16	9	3	6	9	13
1994-95	Knoxville	ECHL	58	15	13	28	150	1	0	0	0	0
	Las Vegas	IHL	13	1	2	3	27	5	1	1	2	6

Signed as a free agent by **Ottawa**, July 2, 1993. Signed as a free agent by **Anaheim**, July 10, 1995.

DELISLE, JONATHAN — MTL.

Right wing. Shoots right. 5'10", 186 lbs. Born, Ste-Anne-des-Plaines, Que., June 30, 1977.
(Montreal's 4th choice, 86th overall, in 1995 Entry Draft).

			Regular Season					Playoffs				
Season	Club	Lea	GP	G	A	TP	PIM	GP	G	A	TP	PIM
1993-94	Verdun	QMJHL	61	16	17	33	130	4	0	1	1	14
1994-95	Hull	QMJHL	60	21	38	59	218	19	11	8	19	43

DEMITRA, PAVOL (deh-MIHT-rah) — OTT.

Left wing. Shoots left. 6', 189 lbs. Born, Dubnica, Czech., November 29, 1974.
(Ottawa's 9th choice, 227th overall, in 1993 Entry Draft).

			Regular Season					Playoffs				
Season	Club	Lea	GP	G	A	TP	PIM	GP	G	A	TP	PIM
1991-92	Spartak Dubnica	Czech. 2	28	13	10	23	12	....	....	....	....	....
1992-93	Dukla Trencin	Czech.	46	10	18	28		....	....	....	....	....
	CAPEH Dubnica	Czech. 2	4	3	0	3	....	....	....	....	....	....
1993-94	**Ottawa**	**NHL**	**12**	**1**	**1**	**2**	**4**	....	....	....	....	....
	P.E.I.	AHL	41	18	23	41	8	....	....	....	....	....
1994-95	P.E.I.	AHL	61	26	48	74	23	5	0	7	7	0
	Ottawa	**NHL**	**16**	**4**	**3**	**7**	**0**	....	....	....	....	....
	NHL Totals		**28**	**5**	**4**	**9**	**4**	....	....	....	....	....

DEMPSEY, NATHAN — TOR.

Defense. Shoots left. 6', 170 lbs. Born, Spruce Grove, Alta., July 14, 1974.
(Toronto's 11th choice, 148th overall, in 1992 Entry Draft).

			Regular Season					Playoffs				
Season	Club	Lea	GP	G	A	TP	PIM	GP	G	A	TP	PIM
1991-92	Regina	WHL	70	4	22	26	72	....	....	....	....	....
1992-93	Regina	WHL	72	12	29	41	95	13	3	8	11	14
	St. John's	AHL	....	....	....	....	....	2	0	0	0	0
1993-94a	Regina	WHL	56	14	36	50	100	4	0	0	0	4
1994-95	St. John's	AHL	74	7	30	37	91	5	1	0	1	11

a WHL East Second All-Star Team (1994)

DEPALMA, LARRY

Left wing. Shoots left. 6', 195 lbs. Born, Trenton, MI, October 27, 1965.

			Regular Season					Playoffs				
Season	Club	Lea	GP	G	A	TP	PIM	GP	G	A	TP	PIM
1984-85	N. Westminster	WHL	65	14	16	30	87	10	1	1	2	25
1985-86	Saskatoon	WHL	65	61	51	112	232	13	7	9	16	58
	Minnesota	**NHL**	**1**	**0**	**0**	**0**	**0**	....	....	....	....	....
1986-87	**Minnesota**	**NHL**	**56**	**9**	**6**	**15**	**219**	....	....	....	....	....
	Springfield	AHL	9	2	2	4	82	....	....	....	....	....
1987-88	**Minnesota**	**NHL**	**7**	**1**	**1**	**2**	**15**	....	....	....	....	....
	Baltimore	AHL	16	8	10	18	121	....	....	....	....	....
	Kalamazoo	IHL	22	6	11	17	215	....	....	....	....	....
1988-89	**Minnesota**	**NHL**	**43**	**5**	**7**	**12**	**102**	**2**	**0**	**0**	**0**	**6**
1989-90	Kalamazoo	IHL	36	7	14	21	218	4	1	1	2	32
1990-91	**Minnesota**	**NHL**	**14**	**3**	**0**	**3**	**26**	....	....	....	....	....
	Kalamazoo	IHL	55	27	32	59	160	11	5	4	9	25
1991-92	Kansas City	IHL	62	28	29	57	188	15	7	*13	20	34
1992-93	**San Jose**	**NHL**	**20**	**2**	**6**	**8**	**41**	....	....	....	....	....
	Kansas City	IHL	30	11	11	22	83	10	1	4	5	20
1993-94	Atlanta	IHL	21	10	10	20	109	....	....	....	....	....
	Salt Lake	IHL	34	4	12	16	125	....	....	....	....	....
	Las Vegas	IHL	1	0	0	0	17	....	....	....	....	....
	Pittsburgh	**NHL**	**7**	**1**	**0**	**1**	**5**	**1**	**0**	**0**	**0**	**0**
	Cleveland	IHL	9	4	1	5	49	....	....	....	....	....
1994-95	Cleveland	IHL	25	6	6	12	113	....	....	....	....	....
	San Diego	IHL	38	14	8	22	86	2	0	0	0	20
	NHL Totals		**148**	**21**	**20**	**41**	**408**	**3**	**0**	**0**	**0**	**6**

Signed as a free agent by **Minnesota**, May 12, 1986. Signed as a free agent by **San Jose**, August 30, 1991. Signed as a free agent by **NY Islanders**, November 29, 1993. Claimed on waivers by **Pittsburgh** from **NY Islanders**, March 9, 1994.

DE RUITER, CHRIS — TOR.

Right wing. Shoots right. 6'2", 190 lbs. Born, Kingston, Ont., February 27, 1974.
(Toronto's 6th choice, 106th overall, in 1992 Entry Draft).

			Regular Season					Playoffs				
Season	Club	Lea	GP	G	A	TP	PIM	GP	G	A	TP	PIM
1992-93	Clarkson	ECAC	32	2	5	7	40	....	....	....	....	....
1993-94	Clarkson	ECAC	33	4	10	14	42	....	....	....	....	....
1994-95	Clarkson	ECAC	34	10	14	24	78	....	....	....	....	....

DESANTIS, MARK — ANA.

Defense. Shoots right. 6', 205 lbs. Born, Brampton, Ont., January 12, 1972.

			Regular Season					Playoffs				
Season	Club	Lea	GP	G	A	TP	PIM	GP	G	A	TP	PIM
1989-90	Cornwall	OHL	59	3	17	20	79	6	0	2	2	13
1990-91	Cornwall	OHL	41	7	15	22	78	....	....	....	....	....
1991-92	Cornwall	OHL	66	10	45	55	105	6	1	2	3	7
1992-93a	Newmarket	OHL	66	19	70	89	131	7	3	11	14	14
1993-94	San Diego	IHL	54	5	10	15	95	....	....	....	....	....
1994-95	San Diego	IHL	8	0	0	0	23	....	....	....	....	....
	Greensboro	ECHL	57	10	34	44	196	15	0	4	4	71

a OHL First All-Star Team (1993)

Signed as a free agent by **Anaheim**, August 2, 1993.

DESJARDINS, ERIC (deh-ZHAHR-dai) — PHI.

Defense. Shoots right. 6'1", 200 lbs. Born, Rouyn, Que., June 14, 1969.
(Montreal's 3rd choice, 38th overall, in 1987 Entry Draft).

			Regular Season					Playoffs				
Season	Club	Lea	GP	G	A	TP	PIM	GP	G	A	TP	PIM
1986-87a	Granby	QMJHL	66	14	24	38	178	8	3	2	5	10
1987-88	Sherbrooke	AHL	3	0	0	0	6	4	0	2	2	2
b	Granby	QMJHL	62	18	49	67	138	5	0	3	3	10
1988-89	**Montreal**	**NHL**	**36**	**2**	**12**	**14**	**26**	**14**	**1**	**1**	**2**	**6**
1989-90	**Montreal**	**NHL**	**55**	**3**	**13**	**16**	**51**	**6**	**0**	**0**	**0**	**10**
1990-91	**Montreal**	**NHL**	**62**	**7**	**18**	**25**	**27**	**13**	**1**	**4**	**5**	**8**
1991-92	**Montreal**	**NHL**	**77**	**6**	**32**	**38**	**50**	**11**	**3**	**3**	**6**	**4**
1992-93	**Montreal**	**NHL**	**82**	**13**	**32**	**45**	**98**	**20**	**4**	**10**	**14**	**23**
1993-94	**Montreal**	**NHL**	**84**	**12**	**23**	**35**	**97**	**7**	**0**	**2**	**2**	**4**
1994-95	**Montreal**	**NHL**	**9**	**0**	**6**	**6**	**2**	....	....	....	....	....
	Philadelphia	**NHL**	**34**	**5**	**18**	**23**	**12**	**15**	**4**	**4**	**8**	**10**
	NHL Totals		**439**	**48**	**154**	**202**	**363**	**86**	**13**	**24**	**37**	**65**

a QMJHL Second All-Star Team (1987)
b QMJHL First All-Star Team (1988)

Played in NHL All-Star Game (1992)

Traded to **Philadelphia** by **Montreal** with Gilbert Dionne and John LeClair for Mark Recchi and Philadelphia's third round choice (Martin Hohenberger) in 1995 Entry Draft, February 9, 1995.

DEULING, JARRETT — NYI

Left wing. Shoots left. 5'11", 194 lbs. Born, Vernon, B.C., March 4, 1974.
(NY Islanders' 2nd choice, 56th overall, in 1992 Entry Draft).

			Regular Season					Playoffs				
Season	Club	Lea	GP	G	A	TP	PIM	GP	G	A	TP	PIM
1990-91	Kamloops	WHL	48	4	12	16	43	12	5	2	7	7
1991-92	Kamloops	WHL	68	28	26	54	79	17	10	6	16	18
1992-93	Kamloops	WHL	68	31	32	63	93	13	6	7	13	14
1993-94	Kamloops	WHL	70	44	59	103	171	18	*13	8	21	43
1994-95	Worcester	AHL	63	11	8	19	37	....	....	....	....	....

DE VRIES, GREG — EDM.

Defense. Shoots left. 6'3", 218 lbs. Born, Sundridge, Ont., January 4, 1973.

			Regular Season					Playoffs				
Season	Club	Lea	GP	G	A	TP	PIM	GP	G	A	TP	PIM
1991-92	Bowling Green	CCHA	24	0	3	3	20	....	....	....	....	....
1992-93	Niagara Falls	OHL	62	3	23	26	86	4	0	1	1	6
1993-94	Niagara Falls	OHL	64	5	40	45	135	....	....	....	....	....
	Cape Breton	AHL	9	0	0	0	11	1	0	0	0	0
1994-95	Cape Breton	AHL	77	5	19	24	68	....	....	....	....	....

Signed as a free agent by **Edmonton**, March 20, 1994.

DEWAELE, KIRK — NYI

Defense. Shoots left. 6', 187 lbs. Born, Calgary, Alta., March 24, 1976.
(NY Islanders' 11th choice, 246th overall, in 1994 Entry Draft).

			Regular Season					Playoffs				
Season	Club	Lea	GP	G	A	TP	PIM	GP	G	A	TP	PIM
1993-94	Lethbridge	WHL	53	0	7	7	35	9	0	0	0	5
1994-95	Lethbridge	WHL	71	3	18	21	123	....	....	....	....	....

DEYELL, MARK — TOR.

Center. Shoots right. 5'11", 170 lbs. Born, Regina, Sask., March 26, 1976.
(Toronto's 4th choice, 126th overall, in 1994 Entry Draft).

			Regular Season					Playoffs				
Season	Club	Lea	GP	G	A	TP	PIM	GP	G	A	TP	PIM
1993-94	Saskatoon	WHL	66	17	36	53	52	16	5	2	7	20
1994-95	Saskatoon	WHL	70	34	68	102	56	10	2	5	7	14

DHADPHALE, ANIKET (DAHD-phayl, AH-nee-keht) — S.J.

Center. Shoots left. 6'3", 185 lbs. Born, Ann Arbor, MI, April 26, 1976.
(San Jose's 11th choice, 245th overall, in 1994 Entry Draft).

			Regular Season					Playoffs				
Season	Club	Lea	GP	G	A	TP	PIM	GP	G	A	TP	PIM
1993-94	Marquette	Midget	50	58	36	94	95	....	....	....	....	....
1994-95	Stratford	Jr. B	46	31	33	64	74	....	....	....	....	....

DIDUCK, GERALD (DIH-duhk) — HFD.

Defense. Shoots right. 6'2", 207 lbs. Born, Edmonton, Alta., April 6, 1965.
(NY Islanders' 2nd choice, 16th overall, in 1983 Entry Draft).

			Regular Season					Playoffs				
Season	Club	Lea	GP	G	A	TP	PIM	GP	G	A	TP	PIM
1981-82	Lethbridge	WHL	71	1	15	16	81	12	0	3	3	27
1982-83	Lethbridge	WHL	67	8	16	24	151	20	3	12	15	49
1983-84	Lethbridge	WHL	65	10	24	34	133	5	1	4	5	27
	Indianapolis	IHL	....	....	....	....	....	10	1	6	7	19
1984-85	**NY Islanders**	**NHL**	**65**	**2**	**8**	**10**	**80**	....	....	....	....	....
1985-86	**NY Islanders**	**NHL**	**10**	**1**	**2**	**3**	**2**	....	....	....	....	....
	Springfield	AHL	61	6	14	20	173	....	....	....	....	....
1986-87	**NY Islanders**	**NHL**	**30**	**2**	**3**	**5**	**67**	**14**	**0**	**1**	**1**	**35**
	Springfield	AHL	45	6	8	14	120	....	....	....	....	....
1987-88	**NY Islanders**	**NHL**	**68**	**7**	**12**	**19**	**113**	**6**	**1**	**0**	**1**	**42**
1988-89	**NY Islanders**	**NHL**	**65**	**11**	**21**	**32**	**155**	....	....	....	....	....
1989-90	**NY Islanders**	**NHL**	**76**	**3**	**17**	**20**	**163**	**5**	**0**	**0**	**0**	**12**
1990-91	**Montreal**	**NHL**	**32**	**1**	**2**	**3**	**39**	....	....	....	....	....
	Vancouver	**NHL**	**31**	**3**	**7**	**10**	**66**	**6**	**1**	**0**	**1**	**11**
1991-92	**Vancouver**	**NHL**	**77**	**6**	**21**	**27**	**229**	**5**	**0**	**0**	**0**	**10**
1992-93	**Vancouver**	**NHL**	**80**	**6**	**14**	**20**	**171**	**12**	**4**	**2**	**6**	**12**
1993-94	**Vancouver**	**NHL**	**55**	**1**	**10**	**11**	**72**	**24**	**1**	**7**	**8**	**22**
1994-95	**Vancouver**	**NHL**	**22**	**1**	**3**	**4**	**15**	....	....	....	....	....
	Chicago	**NHL**	**13**	**1**	**0**	**1**	**48**	**16**	**1**	**3**	**4**	**22**
	NHL Totals		**624**	**45**	**120**	**165**	**1220**	**88**	**8**	**13**	**21**	**166**

Traded to **Montreal** by **NY Islanders** for Craig Ludwig, September 4, 1990. Traded to **Vancouver** by **Montreal** for Vancouver's fourth round choice (Vladimir Vujtek) in 1991 Entry Draft, January 12, 1991. Traded to **Chicago** by **Vancouver** for Bogdan Savenko and Hartford's third round choice (previously acquired by Chicago — Vancouver selected Larry Courville) in 1995 Entry Draft, April 7, 1995. Signed as a free agent by **Hartford**, August 1, 1995.

DIENER, DEREK — PHI.

Defense. Shoots left. 6'4", 185 lbs. Born, Saskatoon, Sask., July 13, 1976.
(Philadelphia's 6th choice, 192nd overall, in 1994 Entry Draft).

			Regular Season					Playoffs				
Season	Club	Lea	GP	G	A	TP	PIM	GP	G	A	TP	PIM
1992-93	Lethbridge	WHL	1	0	0	0	0	....	....	....	....	....
1993-94	Lethbridge	WHL	62	1	8	9	64	3	0	0	0	7
1994-95	Lethbridge	WHL	68	13	29	42	104	....	....	....	....	....

DILLABOUGH, TRAVIS — L.A.

Center. Shoots left. 6', 175 lbs. Born, Peterborough, Ont., June 20, 1975.
(Los Angeles' 9th choice, 198th overall, in 1993 Entry Draft).

			Regular Season					Playoffs				
Season	Club	Lea	GP	G	A	TP	PIM	GP	G	A	TP	PIM
1993-94	Providence	H.E.	33	4	8	12	42	....	....	....	....	....
1994-95	Providence	H.E.	37	3	11	14	48	....	....	....	....	....

DIMAIO, ROB (duh-MIGH-oh) — PHI.

Center. Shoots right. 5'10", 190 lbs. Born, Calgary, Alta., February 19, 1968.
(NY Islanders' 6th choice, 118th overall, in 1987 Entry Draft).

			Regular Season					Playoffs				
Season	Club	Lea	GP	G	A	TP	PIM	GP	G	A	TP	PIM
1986-87	Medicine Hat	WHL	70	27	43	70	130	20	7	11	18	46
1987-88a	Medicine Hat	WHL	54	47	43	90	120	14	12	19	*31	59
1988-89	**NY Islanders**	**NHL**	**16**	**1**	**0**	**1**	**30**	....	....	....	....	....
	Springfield	AHL	40	13	18	31	67	....	....	....	....	....
1989-90	**NY Islanders**	**NHL**	**7**	**0**	**0**	**0**	**2**	**1**	**1**	**0**	**1**	**4**
	Springfield	AHL	54	25	27	52	69	16	4	7	11	45
1990-91	**NY Islanders**	**NHL**	**1**	**0**	**0**	**0**	**0**	....	....	....	....	....
	Capital Dist.	AHL	12	3	4	7	22	....	....	....	....	....
1991-92	**NY Islanders**	**NHL**	**50**	**5**	**2**	**7**	**43**	....	....	....	....	....
1992-93	**Tampa Bay**	**NHL**	**54**	**9**	**15**	**24**	**62**	....	....	....	....	....
1993-94	**Tampa Bay**	**NHL**	**39**	**8**	**7**	**15**	**40**	....	....	....	....	....
	Philadelphia	**NHL**	**14**	**3**	**5**	**8**	**6**	....	....	....	....	....
1994-95	**Philadelphia**	**NHL**	**36**	**3**	**1**	**4**	**53**	**15**	**2**	**4**	**6**	**4**
	NHL Totals		**217**	**29**	**30**	**59**	**236**	**16**	**3**	**4**	**7**	**8**

a Won Stafford Smythe Memorial Trophy (Memorial Cup Tournament MVP) (1988)

Claimed by **Tampa Bay** from **NY Islanders** in Expansion Draft, June 18, 1992. Traded to **Philadelphia** by **Tampa Bay** for Jim Cummins and Philadelphia's fourth round choice in 1995 Entry Draft, March 18, 1994.

DINEEN, GORD — NYI

Defense. Shoots right. 6', 195 lbs. Born, Quebec City, Que., September 21, 1962.
(NY Islanders' 2nd choice, 42nd overall, in 1981 Entry Draft).

			Regular Season					Playoffs				
Season	Club	Lea	GP	G	A	TP	PIM	GP	G	A	TP	PIM
1980-81	S.S. Marie	OHA	68	4	26	30	158	19	1	7	8	58
1981-82	S.S. Marie	OHL	68	9	45	54	185	13	1	2	3	52
1982-83	**NY Islanders**	**NHL**	**2**	**0**	**0**	**0**	**4**	....	....	....	....	....
abc	Indianapolis	CHL	73	10	47	57	78	13	2	10	12	29
1983-84	**NY Islanders**	**NHL**	**43**	**1**	**11**	**12**	**32**	**9**	**1**	**1**	**2**	**28**
	Indianapolis	CHL	26	4	13	17	63	....	....	....	....	....
1984-85	**NY Islanders**	**NHL**	**48**	**1**	**12**	**13**	**89**	**10**	**0**	**0**	**0**	**26**
	Springfield	AHL	25	1	8	9	46	....	....	....	....	....
1985-86	**NY Islanders**	**NHL**	**57**	**1**	**8**	**9**	**81**	**3**	**0**	**0**	**0**	**2**
	Springfield	AHL	11	2	3	5	20	....	....	....	....	....
1986-87	**NY Islanders**	**NHL**	**71**	**4**	**10**	**14**	**110**	**7**	**0**	**4**	**4**	**4**
1987-88	**NY Islanders**	**NHL**	**57**	**4**	**12**	**16**	**62**	....	....	....	....	....
	Minnesota	**NHL**	**13**	**1**	**1**	**2**	**21**	....	....	....	....	....
1988-89	**Minnesota**	**NHL**	**2**	**0**	**1**	**1**	**2**	....	....	....	....	....
	Kalamazoo	IHL	25	2	6	8	49	....	....	....	....	....
	Pittsburgh	**NHL**	**38**	**1**	**2**	**3**	**42**	**11**	**0**	**2**	**2**	**8**
1989-90	**Pittsburgh**	**NHL**	**69**	**1**	**8**	**9**	**125**	....	....	....	....	....
1990-91	**Pittsburgh**	**NHL**	**9**	**0**	**0**	**0**	**4**	....	....	....	....	....
	Muskegon	IHL	40	1	14	15	57	5	0	2	2	0
1991-92	**Pittsburgh**	**NHL**	**1**	**0**	**0**	**0**	**0**	....	....	....	....	....
d	Muskegon	IHL	79	8	37	45	83	14	2	4	6	33
1992-93	**Ottawa**	**NHL**	**32**	**2**	**4**	**6**	**30**	....	....	....	....	....
	San Diego	IHL	41	6	23	29	36	....	....	....	....	....
1993-94	**Ottawa**	**NHL**	**77**	**0**	**21**	**21**	**89**	....	....	....	....	....
	San Diego	IHL	3	0	0	0	2	....	....	....	....	....
1994-95	Denver	IHL	68	5	27	32	75	17	1	6	7	8
	NY Islanders	**NHL**	**9**	**0**	**0**	**0**	**2**	....	....	....	....	....
	NHL Totals		**528**	**16**	**90**	**106**	**693**	**40**	**1**	**7**	**8**	**68**

a CHL First All-Star Team (1983)
b Won Bob Gassoff Trophy (CHL's Most Improved Defenseman) (1983)
c Won Bobby Orr Trophy (CHL's Top Defenseman) (1983)
d IHL First All-Star Team (1992)

Traded to **Minnesota** by **NY Islanders** for Chris Pryor and future considerations, March 8, 1988. Traded to **Pittsburgh** by **Minnesota** with Scott Bjugstad for Ville Siren and Steve Gotaas, December 17, 1988. Signed as a free agent by **Ottawa**, August 31, 1992. Signed as a free agent by **NY Islanders**, July 26, 1994.

DINEEN, KEVIN — PHI.

Right wing. Shoots right. 5'11", 190 lbs. Born, Quebec City, Que., October 28, 1963.
(Hartford's 3rd choice, 56th overall, in 1982 Entry Draft).

			Regular Season					Playoffs				
Season	Club	Lea	GP	G	A	TP	PIM	GP	G	A	TP	PIM
1981-82	U. of Denver	WCHA	26	10	10	20	70	....	....	....	....	....
1982-83	U. of Denver	WCHA	36	16	13	29	108	....	....	....	....	....
1983-84	Cdn. National	....	52	5	11	16	2	....	....	....	....	....
	Cdn Olympic	....	7	0	0	0	0	....	....	....	....	....
1984-85	**Hartford**	**NHL**	**57**	**25**	**16**	**41**	**120**	....	....	....	....	....
	Binghamton	AHL	25	15	8	23	41	....	....	....	....	....
1985-86	**Hartford**	**NHL**	**57**	**33**	**35**	**68**	**124**	**10**	**6**	**7**	**13**	**18**
1986-87	**Hartford**	**NHL**	**78**	**40**	**39**	**79**	**110**	**6**	**2**	**1**	**3**	**31**
1987-88	**Hartford**	**NHL**	**74**	**25**	**25**	**50**	**217**	**6**	**4**	**4**	**8**	**8**
1988-89	**Hartford**	**NHL**	**79**	**45**	**44**	**89**	**167**	**4**	**1**	**0**	**1**	**10**
1989-90	**Hartford**	**NHL**	**67**	**25**	**41**	**66**	**164**	**6**	**3**	**2**	**5**	**18**
1990-91a	**Hartford**	**NHL**	**61**	**17**	**30**	**47**	**104**	**6**	**1**	**0**	**1**	**16**
1991-92	**Hartford**	**NHL**	**16**	**4**	**2**	**6**	**23**	....	....	....	....	....
	Philadelphia	**NHL**	**64**	**26**	**30**	**56**	**130**	....	....	....	....	....
1992-93	**Philadelphia**	**NHL**	**83**	**35**	**28**	**63**	**201**	....	....	....	....	....
1993-94	**Philadelphia**	**NHL**	**71**	**19**	**23**	**42**	**113**	....	....	....	....	....
1994-95	Houston	IHL	17	6	4	10	42	....	....	....	....	....
	Philadelphia	**NHL**	**40**	**8**	**5**	**13**	**39**	**15**	**6**	**4**	**10**	**18**
	NHL Totals		**747**	**302**	**318**	**620**	**1512**	**53**	**23**	**18**	**41**	**119**

a Won Bud Light/NHL Man of the Year Award (1991)

Played in NHL All-Star Game (1988, 1989)

Traded to **Philadelphia** by **Hartford** for Murray Craven and Philadelphia's fourth round choice (Kevin Smyth) in 1992 Entry Draft, November 13, 1991.

DINGMAN, CHRIS — CGY.

Left wing. Shoots left. 6'4", 225 lbs. Born, Edmonton, Alta., July 6, 1976.
(Calgary's 1st choice, 19th overall, in 1994 Entry Draft).

			Regular Season					Playoffs				
Season	Club	Lea	GP	G	A	TP	PIM	GP	G	A	TP	PIM
1992-93	Brandon	WHL	50	10	17	27	64	4	0	0	0	0
1993-94	Brandon	WHL	45	21	20	41	77	13	1	7	8	39
1994-95	Brandon	WHL	66	40	43	83	201	3	1	0	1	9

DIONNE, GILBERT — (dee-AHN, ZHIHL-bair) — PHI.

Left wing. Shoots left. 6', 194 lbs. Born, Drummondville, Que., September 19, 1970.
(Montreal's 5th choice, 81st overall, in 1990 Entry Draft).

			Regular Season					Playoffs				
Season	Club	Lea	GP	G	A	TP	PIM	GP	G	A	TP	PIM
1988-89	Kitchener	OHL	66	11	33	44	13	5	1	1	2	4
1989-90	Kitchener	OHL	64	48	57	105	85	17	13	10	23	22
1990-91	**Montreal**	**NHL**	**2**	**0**	**0**	**0**	**0**	....	....	....	....	....
	Fredericton	AHL	77	40	47	87	62	9	6	5	11	8
1991-92a	**Montreal**	**NHL**	**39**	**21**	**13**	**34**	**10**	**11**	**3**	**4**	**7**	**10**
	Fredericton	AHL	29	19	27	46	20	....	....	....	....	....
1992-93	**Montreal**	**NHL**	**75**	**20**	**28**	**48**	**63**	**20**	**6**	**6**	**12**	**20**
	Fredericton	AHL	3	4	3	7	0	....	....	....	....	....
1993-94	**Montreal**	**NHL**	**74**	**19**	**26**	**45**	**31**	**5**	**1**	**2**	**3**	**0**
1994-95	**Montreal**	**NHL**	**6**	**0**	**3**	**3**	**2**	....	....	....	....	....
	Philadelphia	**NHL**	**20**	**0**	**6**	**6**	**2**	**3**	**0**	**0**	**0**	**4**
	NHL Totals		**216**	**60**	**76**	**136**	**108**	**39**	**10**	**12**	**22**	**34**

a NHL/Upper Deck All-Rookie Team (1992)

Traded to **Philadelphia** by **Montreal** with Eric Desjardins and John LeClair for Mark Recchi and Philadelphia's third round choice (Martin Hohenberger) in 1995 Entry draft, February 9, 1995.

DI PIETRO, PAUL — (dee-pee-AY-troh) — TOR.

Center. Shoots right. 5'8", 179 lbs. Born, Sault Ste. Marie, Ont., September 8, 1970.
(Montreal's 6th choice, 102nd overall, in 1990 Entry Draft).

			Regular Season					Playoffs				
Season	Club	Lea	GP	G	A	TP	PIM	GP	G	A	TP	PIM
1986-87	Sudbury	OHL	49	5	11	16	13	....	....	....	....	....
1987-88	Sudbury	OHL	63	25	42	67	27	....	....	....	....	....
1988-89	Sudbury	OHL	57	31	48	79	27	....	....	....	....	....
1989-90	Sudbury	OHL	66	56	63	119	57	7	3	6	9	7
1990-91	Fredericton	AHL	78	39	31	70	38	9	5	6	11	2
1991-92	**Montreal**	**NHL**	**33**	**4**	**6**	**10**	**25**	....	....	....	....	....
	Fredericton	AHL	43	26	31	57	52	7	3	4	7	8
1992-93	**Montreal**	**NHL**	**29**	**4**	**13**	**17**	**14**	**17**	**8**	**5**	**13**	**8**
	Fredericton	AHL	26	8	16	24	16	....	....	....	....	....
1993-94	**Montreal**	**NHL**	**70**	**13**	**20**	**33**	**37**	**7**	**2**	**4**	**6**	**2**
1994-95	**Montreal**	**NHL**	**22**	**4**	**5**	**9**	**4**	....	....	....	....	....
	Toronto	**NHL**	**12**	**1**	**1**	**2**	**6**	**7**	**1**	**1**	**2**	**0**
	NHL Totals		**166**	**26**	**45**	**71**	**86**	**31**	**11**	**10**	**21**	**10**

Traded to **Toronto** by **Montreal** for a conditional fourth round draft choice, April 6, 1995.

DIRK, ROBERT — ANA.

Defense. Shoots left. 6'4", 210 lbs. Born, Regina, Sask., August 20, 1966.
(St. Louis' 4th choice, 53rd overall, in 1984 Entry Draft).

			Regular Season					Playoffs				
Season	Club	Lea	GP	G	A	TP	PIM	GP	G	A	TP	PIM
1982-83	Regina	WHL	1	0	0	0	0	....	....	....	....	....
1983-84	Regina	WHL	62	2	10	12	64	23	1	12	13	24
1984-85	Regina	WHL	69	10	34	44	97	8	0	0	0	4
1985-86	Regina	WHL	72	19	60	79	140	10	3	5	8	8
1986-87	Peoria	IHL	76	5	17	22	155	....	....	....	....	....
1987-88	**St. Louis**	**NHL**	**7**	**0**	**1**	**1**	**16**	**6**	**0**	**1**	**1**	**2**
	Peoria	IHL	54	4	21	25	126	....	....	....	....	....
1988-89	**St. Louis**	**NHL**	**9**	**0**	**1**	**1**	**11**	....	....	....	....	....
	Peoria	IHL	22	0	2	2	54	....	....	....	....	....
1989-90	**St. Louis**	**NHL**	**37**	**1**	**1**	**2**	**128**	**3**	**0**	**0**	**0**	**0**
	Peoria	IHL	24	1	2	3	79	....	....	....	....	....
1990-91	**St. Louis**	**NHL**	**41**	**1**	**3**	**4**	**100**	....	....	....	....	....
	Peoria	IHL	3	0	0	0	2	....	....	....	....	....
	Vancouver	**NHL**	**11**	**1**	**0**	**1**	**20**	**6**	**0**	**0**	**0**	**13**
1991-92	**Vancouver**	**NHL**	**72**	**2**	**7**	**9**	**126**	**13**	**0**	**0**	**0**	**20**
1992-93	**Vancouver**	**NHL**	**69**	**4**	**8**	**12**	**150**	**9**	**0**	**0**	**0**	**6**
1993-94	**Vancouver**	**NHL**	**65**	**2**	**3**	**5**	**105**	....	....	....	....	....
	Chicago	**NHL**	**6**	**0**	**0**	**0**	**26**	**2**	**0**	**0**	**0**	**15**
1994-95	**Anaheim**	**NHL**	**38**	**1**	**3**	**4**	**56**	....	....	....	....	....
	NHL Totals		**355**	**12**	**27**	**39**	**738**	**39**	**0**	**1**	**1**	**56**

Traded to **Vancouver** by **St. Louis** with Geoff Courtnall, Sergio Momesso, Cliff Ronning and St. Louis' fifth round choice (Brian Loney) in 1992 Entry Draft for Dan Quinn and Garth Butcher, March 5, 1991. Traded to **Chicago** by **Vancouver** for Chicago's fourth round choice (Mike Dubinsky) in 1994 Entry Draft, March 21, 1994. Traded to **Anaheim** by **Chicago** for Tampa Bay's fourth round choice (previously acquired by Anaheim — Chicago selected Chris Van Dyk) in 1995 Entry Draft, July 12, 1994.

DISHER, JASON — OTT.

Defense. Shoots left. 6'2", 208 lbs. Born, Windsor, Ont., May 28, 1975.
(Ottawa's 7th choice, 183rd overall, in 1993 Entry Draft).

			Regular Season					Playoffs				
Season	Club	Lea	GP	G	A	TP	PIM	GP	G	A	TP	PIM
1992-93	Kingston	OHL	46	2	4	6	100	14	0	1	1	18
1993-94	Kingston	OHL	62	4	12	16	170	4	0	0	0	5
1994-95	Kingston	OHL	57	4	32	36	110	6	0	2	2	23

DOAN, SHANE — WPG.

Right wing. Shoots right. 6'1", 215 lbs. Born, Halkirk, Alta., October 10, 1976.
(Winnipeg's 1st choice, 7th overall, in 1995 Entry Draft).

			Regular Season					Playoffs				
Season	Club	Lea	GP	G	A	TP	PIM	GP	G	A	TP	PIM
1992-93	Kamloops	WHL	51	7	12	19	65	13	0	1	1	8
1993-94	Kamloops	WHL	52	24	24	48	88	....	....	....	....	....
1994-95ab	Kamloops	WHL	71	37	57	94	106	21	6	10	16	16

a Memorial Cup All-Star Team (1995)
b Won Stafford Smythe Memorial Trophy (Memorial Cup Tournament MVP) (1995)

DOIG, JASON — WPG.

Defense. Shoots right. 6'3", 216 lbs. Born, Montreal, Que., January 29, 1977.
(Winnipeg's 3rd choice, 34th overall, in 1995 Entry Draft).

			Regular Season					Playoffs				
Season	Club	Lea	GP	G	A	TP	PIM	GP	G	A	TP	PIM
1993-94	St-Jean	QMJHL	63	8	17	25	65	5	0	2	2	2
1994-95	Laval	QMJHL	55	13	42	55	259	20	4	13	17	39

DOLLAS, BOBBY — ANA.

Defense. Shoots left. 6'2", 212 lbs. Born, Montreal, Que., January 31, 1965.
(Winnipeg's 2nd choice, 14th overall, in 1983 Entry Draft).

			Regular Season					Playoffs				
Season	Club	Lea	GP	G	A	TP	PIM	GP	G	A	TP	PIM
1982-83a	Laval	QMJHL	63	16	45	61	144	11	5	5	10	23
1983-84	**Winnipeg**	**NHL**	**1**	**0**	**0**	**0**	**0**	....	....	....	....	....
	Laval	QMJHL	54	12	33	45	80	14	1	8	9	23
1984-85	**Winnipeg**	**NHL**	**9**	**0**	**0**	**0**	**0**	....	....	....	....	....
	Sherbrooke	AHL	8	1	3	4	4	17	3	6	9	17
1985-86	**Winnipeg**	**NHL**	**46**	**0**	**5**	**5**	**66**	**3**	**0**	**0**	**0**	**2**
	Sherbrooke	AHL	25	4	7	11	29	....	....	....	....	....
1986-87	Sherbrooke	AHL	75	6	18	24	87	16	2	4	6	13
1987-88	**Quebec**	**NHL**	**9**	**0**	**0**	**0**	**2**	....	....	....	....	....
	Moncton	AHL	26	4	10	14	20	....	....	....	....	....
	Fredericton	AHL	33	4	8	12	27	15	2	2	4	24
1988-89	**Quebec**	**NHL**	**16**	**0**	**3**	**3**	**16**	....	....	....	....	....
	Halifax	AHL	57	5	19	24	65	4	1	0	1	14
1989-90	Cdn. National	....	68	8	29	37	60	....	....	....	....	....
1990-91	**Detroit**	**NHL**	**56**	**3**	**5**	**8**	**20**	**7**	**1**	**0**	**1**	**13**
1991-92	**Detroit**	**NHL**	**27**	**3**	**1**	**4**	**20**	**2**	**0**	**1**	**1**	**0**
	Adirondack	AHL	19	1	6	7	33	18	7	4	11	22
1992-93	**Detroit**	**NHL**	**6**	**0**	**0**	**0**	**2**	....	....	....	....	....
c	Adirondack	AHL	64	7	36	43	54	11	3	8	11	8
1993-94	**Anaheim**	**NHL**	**77**	**9**	**11**	**20**	**55**	....	....	....	....	....
1994-95	**Anaheim**	**NHL**	**45**	**7**	**13**	**20**	**12**	....	....	....	....	....
	NHL Totals		**292**	**22**	**38**	**60**	**193**	**12**	**1**	**1**	**2**	**15**

a QMJHL Second All-Star Team (1983)
b Won Eddie Shore Plaque (AHL's Outstanding Defenseman) (1993)
c AHL First All-Star Team (1993)

Traded to **Quebec** by **Winnipeg** for Stu Kulak, December 17, 1987. Signed as a free agent by **Detroit**, October 18, 1990. Claimed by **Anaheim** from **Detroit** in Expansion Draft, June 24, 1993.

DOMENICHELLI, HNAT
HFD.

Center/Left wing. Shoots left. 6', 173 lbs.   Born, Edmonton, Alta., February 17, 1976.
(Hartford's 2nd choice, 83rd overall, in 1994 Entry Draft).

			Regular Season					Playoffs				
Season	Club	Lea	GP	G	A	TP	PIM	GP	G	A	TP	PIM
1992-93	Kamloops	WHL	45	12	8	20	15	11	1	1	2	2
1993-94	Kamloops	WHL	69	27	40	67	31	19	10	12	22	0
1994-95a	Kamloops	WHL	72	52	62	114	34	19	9	9	18	9

a WHL West Second All-Star Team (1995)

DOMI, TIE
(DOH-mee)   **TOR.**

Right wing. Shoots right. 5'10", 200 lbs.   Born, Windsor, Ont., November 1, 1969.
(Toronto's 2nd choice, 27th overall, in 1988 Entry Draft).

			Regular Season					Playoffs				
Season	Club	Lea	GP	G	A	TP	PIM	GP	G	A	TP	PIM
1986-87	Peterborough	OHL	18	1	1	2	79	....	....	....	....	....
1987-88	Peterborough	OHL	60	22	21	43	292	12	3	9	12	24
1988-89	Peterborough	OHL	43	14	16	30	175	17	10	9	19	70
1989-90	Toronto	NHL	2	0	0	0	42	....	....	....	....	....
	Newmarket	AHL	57	14	11	25	285	....	....	....	....	....
1990-91	NY Rangers	NHL	28	1	0	1	185	....	....	....	....	....
	Binghamton	AHL	25	11	6	17	219	7	3	2	5	16
1991-92	NY Rangers	NHL	42	2	4	6	246	6	1	1	2	32
1992-93	NY Rangers	NHL	12	2	0	2	95	....	....	....	....	....
	Winnipeg	NHL	49	3	10	13	249	6	1	0	1	23
1993-94	Winnipeg	NHL	81	8	11	19	*347	....	....	....	....	....
1994-95	Winnipeg	NHL	31	4	4	8	128	....	....	....	....	....
	Toronto	NHL	9	0	1	1	31	7	1	0	1	0
	NHL Totals		**254**	**20**	**30**	**50**	**1323**	**19**	**3**	**1**	**4**	**55**

Traded to **NY Rangers** by **Toronto** with Mark LaForest for Greg Johnston, June 28, 1990. Traded to **Winnipeg** by **NY Rangers** with Kris King for Ed Olczyk, December 28, 1992. Traded to **Toronto** by **Winnipeg** for Mike Eastwood and Toronto's third round choice (Brad Isbister) in 1995 Entry Draft, April 7, 1995.

DONATO, TED
(duh-NAH-toh)   **BOS.**

Left wing. Shoots left. 5'10", 181 lbs.   Born, Dedham, MA, April 28, 1969.
(Boston's 6th choice, 98th overall, in 1987 Entry Draft).

			Regular Season					Playoffs				
Season	Club	Lea	GP	G	A	TP	PIM	GP	G	A	TP	PIM
1987-88	Harvard	ECAC	28	12	14	26	24	....	....	....	....	....
1988-89	Harvard	ECAC	34	14	37	51	30	....	....	....	....	....
1989-90	Harvard	ECAC	16	5	6	11	34	....	....	....	....	....
1990-91a	Harvard	ECAC	27	19	*37	56	26	....	....	....	....	....
1991-92	U.S. National		52	11	22	33	24	....	....	....	....	....
	U.S. Olympic	....	8	4	3	7	8	....	....	....	....	....
	Boston	NHL	10	1	2	3	8	15	3	4	7	4
1992-93	Boston	NHL	82	15	20	35	61	4	0	1	1	....
1993-94	Boston	NHL	84	22	32	54	59	13	4	2	6	10
1994-95	TuTo	Fin.	14	5	5	10	47	....	....	....	....	....
	Boston	NHL	47	10	10	20	10	5	0	0	0	4
	NHL Totals		**223**	**48**	**64**	**112**	**138**	**37**	**7**	**7**	**14**	**18**

a ECAC First All-Star Team (1991)

DONNELLY, GORD

Defense. Shoots right. 6'1", 202 lbs.   Born, Montreal, Que., April 5, 1962.
(St. Louis' 3rd choice, 62nd overall, in 1981 Entry Draft).

			Regular Season					Playoffs				
Season	Club	Lea	GP	G	A	TP	PIM	GP	G	A	TP	PIM
1980-81	Sherbrooke	QMJHL	67	15	23	38	252	14	1	2	3	35
1981-82	Sherbrooke	QMJHL	60	8	41	49	250	22	2	7	9	106
1982-83	Salt Lake	CHL	67	3	12	15	222	6	1	1	2	8
1983-84	Quebec	NHL	38	0	5	5	60	....	....	....	....	....
	Fredericton	AHL	30	2	3	5	146	7	1	1	2	43
1984-85	Quebec	NHL	22	0	0	0	33	....	....	....	....	....
	Fredericton	AHL	42	1	5	6	134	6	0	1	1	25
1985-86	Quebec	NHL	36	2	2	4	85	1	0	0	0	0
	Fredericton	AHL	38	3	5	8	103	5	0	0	0	33
1986-87	Quebec	NHL	38	0	2	2	143	13	0	0	0	53
1987-88	Quebec	NHL	63	4	3	7	301	....	....	....	....	....
1988-89	Quebec	NHL	16	4	0	4	46	....	....	....	....	....
	Winnipeg	NHL	57	6	10	16	228	....	....	....	....	....
1989-90	Winnipeg	NHL	55	3	3	6	222	6	0	1	1	8
1990-91	Winnipeg	NHL	57	3	4	7	265	....	....	....	....	....
1991-92	Winnipeg	NHL	4	0	0	0	11	....	....	....	....	....
	Buffalo	NHL	67	2	3	5	305	6	0	1	1	0
1992-93	Buffalo	NHL	60	3	8	11	221	....	....	....	....	....
1993-94	Buffalo	NHL	7	0	0	0	31	....	....	....	....	....
	Dallas	NHL	18	0	1	1	66	....	....	....	....	....
1994-95	Kalamazoo	IHL	7	2	2	4	18	....	....	....	....	....
	Dallas	NHL	16	1	0	1	52	....	....	....	....	....
	NHL Totals		**554**	**28**	**41**	**69**	**2069**	**26**	**0**	**2**	**2**	**61**

Rights transferred to **Quebec** by **St. Louis** with rights to Claude Julien when St. Louis signed Jacques Demers as coach, August 19, 1983. Traded to **Winnipeg** by **Quebec** for Mario Marois, December 6, 1988. Traded to **Buffalo** by **Winnipeg** with Dave McLlwain, Winnipeg's fifth round choice (Yuri Khmylev) in 1992 Entry Draft and future considerations for Darrin Shannon, Mike Hartman and Dean Kennedy, October 11, 1991. Traded to **Dallas** by **Buffalo** for James Black and Dallas' seventh round choice (Steve Webb) in 1994 Entry Draft, December 15, 1993.

DONNELLY, MIKE
DAL.

Left wing. Shoots left. 5'11", 185 lbs.   Born, Detroit, MI, October 10, 1963.

			Regular Season					Playoffs				
Season	Club	Lea	GP	G	A	TP	PIM	GP	G	A	TP	PIM
1982-83	Michigan State	CCHA	24	7	13	20	8	....	....	....	....	....
1983-84	Michigan State	CCHA	44	18	14	32	40	....	....	....	....	....
1984-85	Michigan State	CCHA	44	26	21	47	48	....	....	....	....	....
1985-86ab	Michigan State	CCHA	44	*59	38	97	65	....	....	....	....	....
1986-87	NY Rangers	NHL	5	1	1	2	0	....	....	....	....	....
	New Haven	AHL	58	27	34	61	52	7	2	0	2	9
1987-88	NY Rangers	NHL	17	2	2	4	8	....	....	....	....	....
	Colorado	IHL	8	7	11	18	15	....	....	....	....	....
	Buffalo	NHL	40	6	8	14	44	....	....	....	....	....
1988-89	Buffalo	NHL	22	4	6	10	10	....	....	....	....	....
	Rochester	AHL	53	32	37	69	53	....	....	....	....	....
1989-90	Buffalo	NHL	12	1	2	3	8	....	....	....	....	....
	Rochester	AHL	68	43	55	98	71	16	*12	7	19	9
1990-91	Los Angeles	NHL	53	7	5	12	41	12	5	4	9	6
	New Haven	AHL	18	10	6	16	2	....	....	....	....	....
1991-92	Los Angeles	NHL	80	29	16	45	20	6	1	0	1	4
1992-93	Los Angeles	NHL	84	29	40	69	45	24	6	7	13	14
1993-94	Los Angeles	NHL	81	21	21	42	34	....	....	....	....	....
1994-95	Los Angeles	NHL	9	1	1	2	4	....	....	....	....	....
	Dallas	NHL	35	11	14	25	29	5	0	1	1	6
	NHL Totals		**438**	**112**	**116**	**228**	**243**	**47**	**12**	**12**	**24**	**30**

a CCHA First All-Star Team (1986)
b NCAA West First All-American Team (1986)

Signed as a free agent by **NY Rangers**, August 15, 1986. Traded to **Buffalo** by **NY Rangers** with Rangers' fifth round choice (Alexander Mogilny) in 1988 Entry Draft for Paul Cyr and Buffalo's tenth round choice (Eric Fenton) in 1988 Entry Draft, December 31, 1987. Traded to **Los Angeles** by **Buffalo** for Mikko Makela, September 30, 1990. Traded to **Dallas** by **Los Angeles** with Los Angeles' seventh round choice in 1996 Entry Draft for Dallas' fourth round choice (later traded to Washington) in 1996 Entry Draft, February 17, 1995.

DONOVAN, SHEAN
S.J.

Right wing. Shoots right. 6'2", 190 lbs.   Born, Timmins, Ont., January 22, 1975.
(San Jose's 2nd choice, 28th overall, in 1993 Entry Draft).

			Regular Season					Playoffs				
Season	Club	Lea	GP	G	A	TP	PIM	GP	G	A	TP	PIM
1991-92	Ottawa	OHL	58	11	8	19	14	11	1	0	1	5
1992-93	Ottawa	OHL	66	29	23	52	33	....	....	....	....	....
1993-94	Ottawa	OHL	62	35	49	84	63	17	10	11	21	14
1994-95	Ottawa	OHL	29	22	19	41	41	....	....	....	....	....
	San Jose	NHL	14	0	0	0	6	7	0	1	1	6
	Kansas City	IHL	5	0	2	2	7	14	5	3	8	23
	NHL Totals		**14**	**0**	**0**	**0**	**6**	**7**	**0**	**1**	**1**	**6**

DOPITA, JIRI
BOS.

Center. Shoots left. 6'3", 202 lbs.   Born, Sumperk, Czech., December 2, 1968.
(Boston's 4th choice, 133rd overall, in 1992 Entry Draft).

			Regular Season					Playoffs				
Season	Club	Lea	GP	G	A	TP	PIM	GP	G	A	TP	PIM
1989-90	Dukla Jihlava	Czech.	5	1	2	3	....	....	....	....	....	....
1990-91	Olomouc	Czech.	42	11	13	24	26	....	....	....	....	....
1991-92	Olomouc	Czech.	41	25	24	49	28	....	....	....	....	....
1992-93	Olomouc	Czech.	28	12	17	29	....	....	....	....	....	....
	Eisbaren Berlin	Ger.	11	7	8	15	49	....	....	....	....	....
1993-94	Eisbaren Berlin	Ger.	42	23	21	44	52	....	....	....	....	....
1994-95	Eisbaren Berlin	Ger.	42	28	40	68	55	....	....	....	....	....

DOURIS, PETER
(DOOR-ihs)   **ANA.**

Right wing. Shoots right. 6'1", 195 lbs.   Born, Toronto, Ont., February 19, 1966.
(Winnipeg's 1st choice, 30th overall, in 1984 Entry Draft).

			Regular Season					Playoffs				
Season	Club	Lea	GP	G	A	TP	PIM	GP	G	A	TP	PIM
1983-84	N. Hampshire	ECAC	37	19	15	34	14	....	....	....	....	....
1984-85	N. Hampshire	H.E.	42	27	24	51	34	....	....	....	....	....
1985-86	Winnipeg	NHL	11	0	0	0	0	....	....	....	....	....
	Cdn. Olympic		33	16	7	23	18	....	....	....	....	....
1986-87	Winnipeg	NHL	6	0	0	0	0	....	....	....	....	....
	Sherbrooke	AHL	62	14	28	42	24	17	7	*15	*22	16
1987-88	Winnipeg	NHL	4	0	2	2	0	1	0	0	0	0
	Moncton	AHL	73	42	37	79	53	....	....	....	....	....
1988-89	Peoria	IHL	81	28	41	69	32	4	1	2	3	0
1989-90	Boston	NHL	36	5	6	11	15	8	0	1	1	8
	Maine	AHL	38	17	20	37	14	....	....	....	....	....
1990-91	Boston	NHL	39	5	2	7	9	7	0	1	1	6
	Maine	AHL	35	16	15	31	9	2	3	0	3	2
1991-92	Boston	NHL	54	10	13	23	10	7	2	3	5	0
	Maine	AHL	12	4	3	7	2	....	....	....	....	....
1992-93	Boston	NHL	19	4	4	8	4	4	1	0	1	0
	Providence	AHL	50	29	26	55	12	....	....	....	....	....
1993-94	Anaheim	NHL	74	12	22	34	21	....	....	....	....	....
1994-95	Anaheim	NHL	46	10	11	21	12	....	....	....	....	....
	NHL Totals		**289**	**46**	**60**	**106**	**71**	**27**	**3**	**5**	**8**	**14**

Traded to **St. Louis** by **Winnipeg** for Kent Carlson and St. Louis' twelfth round choice (Sergei Kharin) in 1989 Entry Draft and St. Louis' fourth round choice (Scott Levins) in 1990 Entry Draft, September 29, 1988. Signed as a free agent by **Boston**, June 27, 1989. Signed as a free agent by **Anaheim**, July 22, 1993.

DOWD, JIM
N.J.

Center. Shoots right. 6'1", 190 lbs.   Born, Brick, NJ, December 25, 1968.
(New Jersey's 7th choice, 149th overall, in 1987 Entry Draft).

			Regular Season					Playoffs				
Season	Club	Lea	GP	G	A	TP	PIM	GP	G	A	TP	PIM
1987-88	Lake Superior	CCHA	45	18	27	45	16	....	....	....	....	....
1988-89	Lake Superior	CCHA	46	24	35	59	40	....	....	....	....	....
1989-90ab	Lake Superior	CCHA	46	25	*67	92	30	....	....	....	....	....
1990-91cd	Lake Superior	CCHA	44	24	*54	*78	53	....	....	....	....	....
1991-92	New Jersey	NHL	1	0	0	0	0	....	....	....	....	....
	Utica	AHL	78	17	42	59	47	4	2	2	4	4
1992-93	New Jersey	NHL	1	0	0	0	0	....	....	....	....	....
	Utica	AHL	78	27	45	72	62	5	1	7	8	10
1993-94	New Jersey	NHL	15	5	10	15	0	19	2	6	8	8
	Albany	AHL	58	26	37	63	76	....	....	....	....	....
1994-95	New Jersey	NHL	10	1	4	5	0	11	2	1	3	8
	NHL Totals		**27**	**6**	**14**	**20**	**0**	**30**	**4**	**7**	**11**	**16**

a CCHA Second All-Star Team (1990)
b NCAA West Second All-American Team (1990)
c CCHA First All-Star Team (1991)
d NCAA West First All-American Team (1991)

DOYLE, TREVOR — FLA.

Defense. Shoots right. 6'3", 212 lbs. Born, Ottawa, Ont., January 1, 1974.
(Florida's 9th choice, 161st overall, in 1993 Entry Draft).

			Regular Season					Playoffs				
Season	Club	Lea	GP	G	A	TP	PIM	GP	G	A	TP	PIM
1991-92	Kingston	OHL	26	0	1	1	19	....	....	....	....	....
1992-93	Kingston	OHL	62	1	8	9	148	16	2	3	5	25
1993-94	Kingston	OHL	53	2	12	14	246	3	0	0	0	4
1994-95	Cincinnati	IHL	52	0	3	3	139	6	0	0	0	13

DRAKE, DALLAS — WPG.

Center. Shoots left. 6', 180 lbs. Born, Trail, B.C., February 4, 1969.
(Detroit's 6th choice, 116th overall, in 1989 Entry Draft).

			Regular Season					Playoffs				
Season	Club	Lea	GP	G	A	TP	PIM	GP	G	A	TP	PIM
1988-89	N. Michigan	WCHA	38	17	22	39	22	....	....	....	....	....
1989-90	N. Michigan	WCHA	46	13	24	37	42	....	....	....	....	....
1990-91	N. Michigan	WCHA	44	22	36	58	89	....	....	....	....	....
1991-92ab	N. Michigan	WCHA	38	*39	41	*80	46	....	....	....	....	....
1992-93	**Detroit**	**NHL**	**72**	**18**	**26**	**44**	**93**	**7**	**3**	**3**	**6**	**6**
1993-94	**Detroit**	**NHL**	**47**	**10**	**22**	**32**	**37**	....	....	....	....	....
	Adirondack	AHL	1	2	0	2	0	....	....	....	....	....
	Winnipeg	**NHL**	**15**	**3**	**5**	**8**	**12**	....	....	....	....	....
1994-95	**Winnipeg**	**NHL**	**43**	**8**	**18**	**26**	**30**	....	....	....	....	....
	NHL Totals		**177**	**39**	**71**	**110**	**172**	**7**	**3**	**3**	**6**	**6**

a WCHA First All-Star Team (1992)
b NCAA West First All-American Team (1992)

Traded to **Winnipeg** by **Detroit** with Tim Cheveldae for Bob Essensa and Sergei Bautin, March 8, 1994.

DRAPER, KRIS — DET.

Center. Shoots left. 5'11", 185 lbs. Born, Toronto, Ont., May 24, 1971.
(Winnipeg's 4th choice, 62nd overall, in 1989 Entry Draft).

			Regular Season					Playoffs				
Season	Club	Lea	GP	G	A	TP	PIM	GP	G	A	TP	PIM
1988-89	Cdn. National	....	60	11	15	26	16	....	....	....	....	....
1989-90	Cdn. National	....	61	12	22	34	44	....	....	....	....	....
1990-91	**Winnipeg**	**NHL**	**3**	**1**	**0**	**1**	**5**	....	....	....	....	....
	Ottawa	OHL	39	19	42	61	35	17	8	11	19	20
	Moncton	AHL	7	2	1	3	2	....	....	....	....	....
1991-92	**Winnipeg**	**NHL**	**10**	**2**	**0**	**2**	**2**	**2**	**0**	**0**	**0**	**0**
	Moncton	AHL	61	11	18	29	113	4	0	1	1	6
1992-93	**Winnipeg**	**NHL**	**7**	**0**	**0**	**0**	**2**	....	....	....	....	....
	Moncton	AHL	67	12	23	35	40	5	2	2	4	18
1993-94	**Detroit**	**NHL**	**39**	**5**	**8**	**13**	**31**	**7**	**2**	**2**	**4**	**4**
	Adirondack	AHL	46	20	23	43	49	....	....	....	....	....
1994-95	**Detroit**	**NHL**	**36**	**2**	**6**	**8**	**22**	**18**	**4**	**1**	**5**	**12**
	NHL Totals		**95**	**10**	**14**	**24**	**62**	**27**	**6**	**3**	**9**	**16**

Traded to **Detroit** by **Winnipeg** for future considerations, June 30, 1993.

DRIVER, BRUCE — N.J.

Defense. Shoots left. 6', 185 lbs. Born, Toronto, Ont., April 29, 1962.
(Colorado's 6th choice, 108th overall, in 1981 Entry Draft).

			Regular Season					Playoffs				
Season	Club	Lea	GP	G	A	TP	PIM	GP	G	A	TP	PIM
1980-81	U. Wisconsin	WCHA	42	5	15	20	42	....	....	....	....	....
1981-82ab	U. Wisconsin	WCHA	46	7	37	44	84	....	....	....	....	....
1982-83c	U. Wisconsin	WCHA	49	19	42	61	100	....	....	....	....	....
1983-84	Cdn. National	....	61	11	17	28	44	....	....	....	....	....
	Cdn. Olympic	....	7	3	1	4	10	....	....	....	....	....
	New Jersey	**NHL**	**4**	**0**	**2**	**2**	**0**	....	....	....	....	....
	Maine	AHL	12	2	6	8	15	16	0	10	10	8
1984-85	**New Jersey**	**NHL**	**67**	**9**	**23**	**32**	**36**	....	....	....	....	....
1985-86	**New Jersey**	**NHL**	**40**	**3**	**15**	**18**	**32**	....	....	....	....	....
	Maine	AHL	15	4	7	11	16	....	....	....	....	....
1986-87	**New Jersey**	**NHL**	**74**	**6**	**28**	**34**	**36**	....	....	....	....	....
1987-88	**New Jersey**	**NHL**	**74**	**15**	**40**	**55**	**68**	**20**	**3**	**7**	**10**	**14**
1988-89	**New Jersey**	**NHL**	**27**	**1**	**15**	**16**	**24**	....	....	....	....	....
1989-90	**New Jersey**	**NHL**	**75**	**7**	**46**	**53**	**63**	**6**	**1**	**5**	**6**	**6**
1990-91	**New Jersey**	**NHL**	**73**	**9**	**36**	**45**	**62**	**7**	**1**	**2**	**3**	**12**
1991-92	**New Jersey**	**NHL**	**78**	**7**	**35**	**42**	**66**	**7**	**0**	**4**	**4**	**2**
1992-93	**New Jersey**	**NHL**	**83**	**14**	**40**	**54**	**66**	**5**	**1**	**3**	**4**	**4**
1993-94	**New Jersey**	**NHL**	**66**	**8**	**24**	**32**	**63**	**20**	**3**	**5**	**8**	**12**
1994-95	**New Jersey**	**NHL**	**41**	**4**	**12**	**16**	**18**	**17**	**1**	**6**	**7**	**8**
	NHL Totals		**702**	**83**	**316**	**399**	**534**	**82**	**10**	**32**	**42**	**58**

a WCHA First All-Star Team (1982)
b NCAA All-Tournament Team (1982)
c WCHA Second All-Star Team (1983)

DROLET, JIMMY — MTL.

Defense. Shoots left. 6', 168 lbs. Born, Vanier, Que., February 19, 1976.
(Montreal's 7th choice, 122nd overall, in 1994 Entry Draft).

			Regular Season					Playoffs				
Season	Club	Lea	GP	G	A	TP	PIM	GP	G	A	TP	PIM
1993-94	St-Hyacinthe	QMJHL	72	10	46	56	93	7	1	7	8	10
1994-95	St-Hyacinthe	QMJHL	68	9	27	36	126	5	0	2	2	12

DROPPA, IVAN — CHI.

Defense. Shoots left. 6'2", 209 lbs. Born, Liptovsky Mikulas, Czech., February 1, 1972.
(Chicago's 2nd choice, 37th overall, in 1990 Entry Draft).

			Regular Season					Playoffs				
Season	Club	Lea	GP	G	A	TP	PIM	GP	G	A	TP	PIM
1990-91	VSZ Kosice	Czech.	54	1	7	8	12	....	....	....	....	....
1991-92	VSZ Kosice	Czech.	43	4	9	13	24	....	....	....	....	....
1992-93	Indianapolis	IHL	77	14	29	43	92	5	0	1	1	2
1993-94	**Chicago**	**NHL**	**12**	**0**	**1**	**1**	**12**	....	....	....	....	....
	Indianapolis	IHL	55	9	10	19	71	....	....	....	....	....
1994-95	Indianapolis	IHL	67	5	28	33	91	....	....	....	....	....
	NHL Totals		**12**	**0**	**1**	**1**	**12**	....	....	....	....	....

DRUCE, JOHN — L.A.

Right wing. Shoots right. 6'2", 195 lbs. Born, Peterborough, Ont., February 23, 1966.
(Washington's 2nd choice, 40th overall, in 1985 Entry Draft).

			Regular Season					Playoffs				
Season	Club	Lea	GP	G	A	TP	PIM	GP	G	A	TP	PIM
1984-85	Peterborough	OHL	54	12	14	26	90	17	6	2	8	21
1985-86	Peterborough	OHL	49	22	24	46	84	16	0	5	5	34
1986-87	Binghamton	AHL	77	13	9	22	131	12	0	3	3	28
1987-88	Binghamton	AHL	68	32	29	61	82	1	0	0	0	0
1988-89	**Washington**	**NHL**	**48**	**8**	**7**	**15**	**62**	**1**	**0**	**0**	**0**	**0**
	Baltimore	AHL	16	2	11	13	10	....	....	....	....	....
1989-90	**Washington**	**NHL**	**45**	**8**	**3**	**11**	**52**	**15**	**14**	**3**	**17**	**23**
	Baltimore	AHL	26	15	16	31	38	....	....	....	....	....
1990-91	**Washington**	**NHL**	**80**	**22**	**36**	**58**	**46**	**11**	**1**	**1**	**2**	**7**
1991-92	**Washington**	**NHL**	**67**	**19**	**18**	**37**	**39**	**7**	**1**	**0**	**1**	**2**
1992-93	**Winnipeg**	**NHL**	**50**	**6**	**14**	**20**	**37**	**2**	**0**	**0**	**0**	**0**
1993-94	**Los Angeles**	**NHL**	**55**	**14**	**17**	**31**	**50**	....	....	....	....	....
	Phoenix	IHL	8	5	6	11	9	....	....	....	....	....
1994-95	**Los Angeles**	**NHL**	**43**	**15**	**5**	**20**	**20**	....	....	....	....	....
	NHL Totals		**388**	**92**	**100**	**192**	**306**	**36**	**16**	**4**	**20**	**32**

Traded to **Winnipeg** by **Washington** with Toronto's fourth round choice (previously acquired by Washington — later traded to Detroit — Detroit selected John Jakopin) in 1993 Entry Draft for Pat Elynuik, October 1, 1992. Signed as a free agent by Los Angeles, August 2, 1993.

DRURY, CHRIS — COL.

Center. Shoots right. 5'10", 180 lbs. Born, Trumbull, CT, August 20, 1976.
(Quebec's 5th choice, 72nd overall, in 1994 Entry Draft).

			Regular Season					Playoffs				
Season	Club	Lea	GP	G	A	TP	PIM	GP	G	A	TP	PIM
1993-94	Fairfield Prep.	HS	24	37	18	55	....	....	....	....	....	....
1994-95	Boston U.	H.E.	39	12	15	27	38	....	....	....	....	....

DRURY, TED (DROO-ree) — HFD.

Center. Shoots left. 6', 185 lbs. Born, Boston, MA, September 13, 1971.
(Calgary's 2nd choice, 42nd overall, in 1989 Entry Draft).

			Regular Season					Playoffs				
Season	Club	Lea	GP	G	A	TP	PIM	GP	G	A	TP	PIM
1989-90	Harvard	ECAC	17	9	13	22	10	....	....	....	....	....
1990-91	Harvard	ECAC	25	18	18	36	22	....	....	....	....	....
1991-92	U.S. National	....	53	11	23	34	30	....	....	....	....	....
	U.S. Olympic	....	7	1	1	2	0	....	....	....	....	....
1992-93ab	Harvard	ECAC	31	22	*41	*63	28	....	....	....	....	....
1993-94	**Calgary**	**NHL**	**34**	**5**	**7**	**12**	**26**	....	....	....	....	....
	U.S. National	....	11	1	4	5	11	....	....	....	....	....
	U.S. Olympic	....	7	1	2	3	2	....	....	....	....	....
	Hartford	**NHL**	**16**	**1**	**5**	**6**	**10**	....	....	....	....	....
1994-95	**Hartford**	**NHL**	**34**	**3**	**6**	**9**	**21**	....	....	....	....	....
	Springfield	AHL	2	0	1	1	0	....	....	....	....	....
	NHL Totals		**84**	**9**	**18**	**27**	**57**	....	....	....	....	....

a ECAC First All-Star Team (1993)
b NCAA East First All-America Team (1993)

Traded to **Hartford** by **Calgary** with Gary Suter and Paul Ranheim for James Patrick, Zarley Zalapski and Michael Nylander, March 10, 1994.

DUBE, CHRISTIAN (doo-BAY) — NYR

Center. Shoots right. 5'11", 170 lbs. Born, Sherbrooke, Que., April 25, 1977.
(NY Rangers' 1st choice, 39th overall, in 1995 Entry Draft).

			Regular Season					Playoffs				
Season	Club	Lea	GP	G	A	TP	PIM	GP	G	A	TP	PIM
1993-94	Sherbrooke	QMJHL	72	31	41	72	22	11	3	2	5	8
1994-95	Sherbrooke	QMJHL	71	36	65	101	43	7	1	7	8	8

DUBE, YANNICK (doo-BAY) — NYR

Center. Shoots right. 5'9", 170 lbs. Born, Gaspé, Que., June 14, 1974.
(Vancouver's 6th choice, 117th overall, in 1994 Entry Draft).

			Regular Season					Playoffs				
Season	Club	Lea	GP	G	A	TP	PIM	GP	G	A	TP	PIM
1991-92	Laval	QMJHL	65	14	19	33	8	10	0	2	2	2
1992-92	Laval	QMJHL	68	45	38	83	25	13	6	7	13	6
1993-94abcd	Laval	QMJHL	64	*66	75	*141	30	21	12	18	30	8
1994-95	Cdn. National	....	24	4	6	10	16	....	....	....	....	....
	Syracuse	AHL	39	10	11	21	8	....	....	....	....	....
	Laval	QMJHL	1	0	1	1	0	16	11	3	14	12

a QMJHL First All-Star Team (1994)
b Canadian Major Junior Second All-Star Team (1994)
c Canadian Major Junior Most Sportsmanlike Player of the Year (1994)
d Won George Parsons Trophy (Memorial Cup Tournament Most Sportsmanlike Player) (1994)

DUBINSKY, MIKE — VAN.

Right wing. Shoots right. 6'2", 185 lbs. Born, Sherwood Park, Alta., June 28, 1976.
(Vancouver's 5th choice, 92nd overall, in 1994 Entry Draft).

			Regular Season					Playoffs				
Season	Club	Lea	GP	G	A	TP	PIM	GP	G	A	TP	PIM
1992-93	Brandon	WHL	64	10	25	35	44	3	0	0	0	0
1993-94	Brandon	WHL	20	9	13	22	23	....	....	....	....	....
1994-95	Brandon	WHL	4	1	2	3	0	1	1	0	1	4

DUBINSKY, STEVE — CHI.

Center. Shoots left. 6', 190 lbs. Born, Montreal, Que., July 9, 1970.
(Chicago's 9th choice, 226th overall, in 1990 Entry Draft).

			Regular Season					Playoffs				
Season	Club	Lea	GP	G	A	TP	PIM	GP	G	A	TP	PIM
1989-90	Clarkson	ECAC	35	7	10	17	24	....	....	....	....	....
1990-91	Clarkson	ECAC	39	13	23	36	26	....	....	....	....	....
1991-92	Clarkson	ECAC	32	20	31	51	40	....	....	....	....	....
1992-93	Clarkson	ECAC	35	18	26	44	58	....	....	....	....	....
1993-94	**Chicago**	**NHL**	**27**	**2**	**6**	**8**	**16**	**6**	**0**	**0**	**0**	**10**
	Indianapolis	IHL	54	15	25	40	63	....	....	....	....	....
1994-95	Indianapolis	IHL	62	16	11	27	29	....	....	....	....	....
	Chicago	**NHL**	**16**	**0**	**0**	**0**	**8**	....	....	....	....	....
	NHL Totals		**43**	**2**	**6**	**8**	**24**	**6**	**0**	**0**	**0**	**10**

DUBOIS, ERIC — T.B.

Defense. Shoots right. 6', 195 lbs. Born, Montreal, Que., May 9, 1970.
(Quebec's 6th choice, 76th overall, in 1989 Entry Draft).

			Regular Season					Playoffs				
Season	Club	Lea	GP	G	A	TP	PIM	GP	G	A	TP	PIM
1986-87	Laval	QMJHL	61	1	17	18	29	....	....	....	....	....
1987-88	Laval	QMJHL	69	8	32	40	132	14	1	7	8	12
1988-89	Laval	QMJHL	68	15	44	59	126	17	1	11	12	55
1989-90	Laval	QMJHL	66	9	36	45	153	13	3	8	11	29
1990-91	Laval	QMJHL	57	15	45	60	122	13	3	5	8	29
1991-92	Halifax	AHL	14	0	0	0	8	....	....	....	....	....
	New Haven	AHL	1	0	0	0	2	....	....	....	....	....
	Greensboro	ECHL	36	7	17	24	62	11	4	4	8	40
1992-93	Oklahoma City	CHL	25	5	20	25	70	....	....	....	....	....
	Atlanta	IHL	43	3	9	12	44	9	0	0	0	10
1993-94	Atlanta	IHL	80	13	26	39	174	14	0	7	7	48
1994-95	Atlanta	IHL	56	3	25	28	56	5	0	3	3	24

Signed as a free agent by **Tampa Bay**, June 2, 1993.

DUCHESNE, GAETAN — (doo-SHAYN)

Left wing. Shoots left. 5'11", 200 lbs. Born, Les Saulles, Que., July 11, 1962.
(Washington's 8th choice, 152nd overall, in 1981 Entry Draft).

			Regular Season					Playoffs				
Season	Club	Lea	GP	G	A	TP	PIM	GP	G	A	TP	PIM
1979-80	Quebec	QJHL	46	9	28	37	22	5	0	2	2	9
1980-81	Quebec	QJHL	72	27	45	72	63	7	1	4	5	6
1981-82	**Washington**	**NHL**	**74**	**9**	**14**	**23**	**46**	....	....	....	....	....
1982-83	**Washington**	**NHL**	**77**	**18**	**19**	**37**	**52**	**4**	**1**	**1**	**2**	**4**
	Hershey	AHL	1	1	0	1	0	....	....	....	....	....
1983-84	**Washington**	**NHL**	**79**	**17**	**19**	**36**	**29**	**8**	**2**	**1**	**3**	**2**
1984-85	**Washington**	**NHL**	**67**	**15**	**23**	**38**	**32**	**5**	**0**	**1**	**1**	**7**
1985-86	**Washington**	**NHL**	**80**	**11**	**28**	**39**	**39**	**9**	**4**	**3**	**7**	**12**
1986-87	**Washington**	**NHL**	**74**	**17**	**35**	**52**	**53**	**7**	**3**	**0**	**3**	**14**
1987-88	**Quebec**	**NHL**	**80**	**24**	**23**	**47**	**83**	....	....	....	....	....
1988-89	**Quebec**	**NHL**	**70**	**8**	**21**	**29**	**56**	....	....	....	....	....
1989-90	**Minnesota**	**NHL**	**72**	**12**	**8**	**20**	**33**	**7**	**0**	**0**	**0**	**6**
1990-91	**Minnesota**	**NHL**	**68**	**9**	**9**	**18**	**18**	**23**	**2**	**3**	**5**	**34**
1991-92	**Minnesota**	**NHL**	**73**	**8**	**15**	**23**	**102**	**7**	**1**	**0**	**1**	**6**
1992-93	**Minnesota**	**NHL**	**84**	**16**	**13**	**29**	**30**	....	....	....	....	....
1993-94	**San Jose**	**NHL**	**84**	**12**	**18**	**30**	**28**	**14**	**1**	**4**	**5**	**12**
1994-95	**San Jose**	**NHL**	**33**	**2**	**7**	**9**	**16**	....	....	....	....	....
	Florida	**NHL**	**13**	**1**	**2**	**3**	**0**	....	....	....	....	....
	NHL Totals		**1028**	**179**	**254**	**433**	**617**	**84**	**14**	**13**	**27**	**97**

Traded to **Quebec** by **Washington** with Alan Haworth and Washington's first round choice (Joe Sakic) in 1987 Entry Draft for Clint Malarchuk and Dale Hunter, June 13, 1987. Traded to **Minnesota** by **Quebec** for Kevin Kaminski, June 19, 1989. Traded to **San Jose** by **Dallas** for San Jose's sixth round choice (later traded back to San Jose — San Jose selected Petri Varis) in 1993 Entry Draft, June 20, 1993. Traded to **Florida** by **San Jose** for Florida's sixth round choice (Timo Hakanen) in 1995 Entry Draft, April 7, 1995.

DUCHESNE, STEVE — (doo-SHAYN) OTT.

Defense. Shoots left. 5'11", 195 lbs. Born, Sept-Iles, Que., June 30, 1965.

			Regular Season					Playoffs				
Season	Club	Lea	GP	G	A	TP	PIM	GP	G	A	TP	PIM
1983-84	Drummondville	QMJHL	67	1	34	35	79	....	....	....	....	....
1984-85a	Drummondville	QMJHL	65	22	54	76	94	5	4	7	11	8
1985-86	New Haven	AHL	75	14	35	49	76	5	0	2	2	9
1986-87b	**Los Angeles**	**NHL**	**75**	**13**	**25**	**38**	**74**	**5**	**2**	**2**	**4**	**4**
1987-88	**Los Angeles**	**NHL**	**71**	**16**	**39**	**55**	**109**	**5**	**1**	**3**	**4**	**14**
1988-89	**Los Angeles**	**NHL**	**79**	**25**	**50**	**75**	**92**	**11**	**4**	**4**	**8**	**12**
1989-90	**Los Angeles**	**NHL**	**79**	**20**	**42**	**62**	**36**	**10**	**2**	**9**	**11**	**6**
1990-91	**Los Angeles**	**NHL**	**78**	**21**	**41**	**62**	**66**	**12**	**4**	**8**	**12**	**8**
1991-92	**Philadelphia**	**NHL**	**78**	**18**	**38**	**56**	**86**	....	....	....	....	....
1992-93	**Quebec**	**NHL**	**82**	**20**	**62**	**82**	**57**	**6**	**0**	**5**	**5**	**6**
1993-94	**St. Louis**	**NHL**	**36**	**12**	**19**	**31**	**14**	**4**	**0**	**2**	**2**	**2**
1994-95	**St. Louis**	**NHL**	**47**	**12**	**26**	**38**	**36**	**7**	**0**	**4**	**4**	**2**
	NHL Totals		**625**	**157**	**342**	**499**	**570**	**60**	**13**	**37**	**50**	**54**

a QMJHL First All-Star Team (1985)
b NHL All-Rookie Team (1987)

Played in NHL All-Star Game (1989, 1990, 1993)

Signed as a free agent by **Los Angeles,** October 1, 1984. Traded to **Philadelphia** by **Los Angeles** with Steve Kasper and Los Angeles' fourth round choice (Aris Brimanis) in 1991 Entry Draft for Jari Kurri and Jeff Chychrun, May 30, 1991. Traded to **Quebec** by **Philadelphia** with Peter Forsberg, Kerry Huffman, Mike Ricci, Ron Hextall, Chris Simon, Philadelphia's first choice in the 1993 (Jocelyn Thibault) and 1994 (later traded to Toronto — later traded to Washington — Washington selected Nolan Baumgartner) Entry Drafts and cash for Eric Lindros, June 30, 1992. Traded to **St. Louis** by **Quebec** with Denis Chasse for Garth Butcher, Ron Sutter and Bob Bassen, January 23, 1994. Traded to **Ottawa** by **St. Louis** for Ottawa's second round choice in 1996 Entry Draft, August 5, 1995.

DUERDEN, DAVE — FLA.

Left wing. Shoots left. 6'2", 201 lbs. Born, Oshawa, Ont., April 11, 1977.
(Florida's 4th choice, 80th overall, in 1995 Entry Draft).

			Regular Season					Playoffs				
Season	Club	Lea	GP	G	A	TP	PIM	GP	G	A	TP	PIM
1993-94	Wexford	Jr. A	46	17	27	44	26	....	....	....	....	....
1994-95	Peterborough	OHL	66	20	33	53	21	11	6	2	8	6

DUFRESNE, DONALD — (doo-FRAYN, DOH-nal) ST.L.

Defense. Shoots right. 6'1", 206 lbs. Born, Quebec City, Que., April 10, 1967.
(Montreal's 8th choice, 117th overall, in 1985 Entry Draft).

			Regular Season					Playoffs				
Season	Club	Lea	GP	G	A	TP	PIM	GP	G	A	TP	PIM
1983-84	Trois-Rivières	QMJHL	67	7	12	19	97	....	....	....	....	....
1984-85	Trois-Rivières	QMJHL	65	5	30	35	112	7	1	3	4	12
1985-86a	Trois-Rivières	QMJHL	63	8	32	40	160	1	0	0	0	0
1986-87a	Trois-Rivières	QMJHL	51	5	21	26	79	....	....	....	....	....
	Longueuil	QMJHL	16	0	8	8	18	20	1	8	9	38
1987-88	Sherbrooke	AHL	47	1	8	9	107	6	1	0	1	34
1988-89	**Montreal**	**NHL**	**13**	**0**	**1**	**1**	**43**	**6**	**1**	**1**	**2**	**4**
	Sherbrooke	AHL	47	0	12	12	170	....	....	....	....	....
1989-90	**Montreal**	**NHL**	**18**	**0**	**4**	**4**	**23**	**10**	**0**	**1**	**1**	**18**
	Sherbrooke	AHL	38	2	11	13	104	....	....	....	....	....
1990-91	**Montreal**	**NHL**	**53**	**2**	**13**	**15**	**55**	**10**	**0**	**1**	**1**	**21**
	Fredericton	AHL	10	1	4	5	35	1	0	0	0	0
1991-92	**Montreal**	**NHL**	**3**	**0**	**0**	**0**	**2**	....	....	....	....	....
	Fredericton	AHL	31	8	12	20	60	7	0	0	0	10
1992-93	**Montreal**	**NHL**	**32**	**1**	**2**	**3**	**32**	**2**	**0**	**0**	**0**	**0**
1993-94	**Tampa Bay**	**NHL**	**51**	**2**	**6**	**8**	**48**	....	....	....	....	....
	Los Angeles	**NHL**	**9**	**0**	**0**	**0**	**10**	....	....	....	....	....
1994-95	**St. Louis**	**NHL**	**22**	**0**	**3**	**3**	**10**	**3**	**0**	**0**	**0**	**4**
	NHL Totals		**201**	**5**	**29**	**34**	**223**	**31**	**1**	**3**	**4**	**47**

a QMJHL Second All-Star Team (1986, 1987)

Traded to **Tampa Bay** by **Montreal** to complete March 20, 1993 trade in which Rob Ramage was traded to Montreal for Eric Charron, Alain Cote and future considerations, June 20, 1993. Traded to **Los Angeles** by **Tampa Bay** for Los Angeles' sixth round choice (Daniel Juden) in 1994 Entry Draft, March 19, 1994. Claimed by **St. Louis** from **Los Angeles** in NHL Waiver Draft, January 18, 1995.

DUNCANSON, CRAIG

Left wing. Shoots left. 6', 190 lbs. Born, Sudbury, Ont., March 17, 1967.
(Los Angeles' 1st choice, 9th overall, in 1985 Entry Draft).

			Regular Season					Playoffs				
Season	Club	Lea	GP	G	A	TP	PIM	GP	G	A	TP	PIM
1983-84	Sudbury	OHL	62	38	38	76	176	....	....	....	....	....
1984-85	Sudbury	OHL	53	35	28	63	129	....	....	....	....	....
1985-86	**Los Angeles**	**NHL**	**2**	**0**	**1**	**1**	**0**	....	....	....	....	....
	Sudbury	OHL	21	12	17	29	55	....	....	....	....	....
	Cornwall	OHL	40	31	50	81	135	6	4	7	11	2
	New Haven	AHL	....	....	....	....	....	2	0	0	0	5
1986-87	**Los Angeles**	**NHL**	**2**	**0**	**0**	**0**	**24**	....	....	....	....	....
	Cornwall	OHL	52	22	45	67	88	5	4	3	7	20
1987-88	**Los Angeles**	**NHL**	**9**	**0**	**0**	**0**	**12**	....	....	....	....	....
	New Haven	AHL	57	15	25	40	170	....	....	....	....	....
1988-89	**Los Angeles**	**NHL**	**5**	**0**	**0**	**0**	**0**	....	....	....	....	....
	New Haven	AHL	69	25	39	64	200	17	4	8	12	60
1989-90	**Los Angeles**	**NHL**	**10**	**3**	**2**	**5**	**9**	....	....	....	....	....
	New Haven	AHL	51	17	30	47	152	....	....	....	....	....
1990-91	**Winnipeg**	**NHL**	**7**	**2**	**0**	**2**	**16**	....	....	....	....	....
	Moncton	AHL	58	16	34	50	107	9	3	11	14	31
1991-92	Baltimore	AHL	46	20	26	46	98	....	....	....	....	....
	Moncton	AHL	19	12	9	21	6	11	6	4	10	10
1992-93	**NY Rangers**	**NHL**	**3**	**0**	**1**	**1**	**0**	....	....	....	....	....
	Binghamton	AHL	69	35	59	94	126	14	7	5	12	9
1993-94	Binghamton	AHL	70	25	44	69	83	....	....	....	....	....
1994-95	Binghamton	AHL	62	21	43	64	105	11	4	4	8	16
	NHL Totals		**38**	**5**	**4**	**9**	**61**	....	....	....	....	....

Traded to **Minnesota** by **Los Angeles** for Daniel Berthiaume, September 6, 1990. Traded to **Winnipeg** by **Minnesota** for Brian Hunt, September 6, 1990. Traded to **Washington** by **Winnipeg** with Brent Hughes and Simon Wheeldon for Bob Joyce, Tyler Larter and Kent Paynter, May 21, 1991. Signed as a free agent by **NY Rangers**, September 4, 1992.

DUPAUL, COSMO — OTT.

Center. Shoots left. 6', 186 lbs. Born, Pointe-Claire, Que., April 11, 1975.
(Ottawa's 4th choice, 91st overall, in 1993 Entry Draft).

			Regular Season					Playoffs				
Season	Club	Lea	GP	G	A	TP	PIM	GP	G	A	TP	PIM
1992-93	Victoriaville	QMJHL	67	23	35	58	16	6	1	3	4	2
1993-94	Victoriaville	QMJHL	66	26	46	72	32	5	2	2	4	6
1994-95	Victoriaville	QMJHL	71	29	44	73	60	4	3	4	7	6
	P.E.I.	AHL	3	0	1	1	2	1	0	0	0	0

DUPONT, DANNY — OTT.

Defense. Shoots left. 6'4", 221 lbs. Born, Trois-Rivières, Que., July 19, 1975.
(Ottawa's 8th choice, 211th overall, in 1994 Entry Draft).

			Regular Season					Playoffs				
Season	Club	Lea	GP	G	A	TP	PIM	GP	G	A	TP	PIM
1993-94	Laval	QMJHL	48	1	2	3	219	8	0	0	0	9
1994-95	Halifax	QMJHL	27	1	5	6	*239	....	....	....	....	....
	Laval	QMJHL	7	0	1	1	*77	....	....	....	....	....
	Granby	QMJHL	16	2	2	4	*130	11	0	0	0	41

DUPRE, YANICK — (doo-PRAY, YAH-nihk) PHI.

Left wing. Shoots left. 6', 189 lbs. Born, Montreal, Que., November 20, 1972.
(Philadelphia's 2nd choice, 50th overall, in 1991 Entry Draft).

			Regular Season					Playoffs				
Season	Club	Lea	GP	G	A	TP	PIM	GP	G	A	TP	PIM
1989-90	Chicoutimi	QMJHL	24	5	9	14	27	....	....	....	....	....
	Drummondville	QMJHL	29	10	10	20	42	....	....	....	....	....
1990-91	Drummondville	QMJHL	58	29	38	67	87	11	8	5	13	33
1991-92	**Philadelphia**	**NHL**	**1**	**0**	**0**	**0**	**0**	....	....	....	....	....
	Drummondville	QMJHL	28	19	17	36	48	....	....	....	....	....
	Verdun	QMJHL	12	7	14	21	21	19	9	9	18	20
1992-93	Hershey	AHL	63	13	24	37	22	....	....	....	....	....
1993-94	Hershey	AHL	51	22	20	42	42	8	1	3	4	2
1994-95	Hershey	AHL	41	15	19	34	35	....	....	....	....	....
	Philadelphia	**NHL**	**22**	**0**	**0**	**0**	**8**	....	....	....	....	....
	NHL Totals		**23**	**0**	**0**	**0**	**8**	....	....	....	....	....

DUPUIS, MARC — CHI.

Defense. Shoots left. 5'11", 176 lbs. Born, Cornwall, Ont., April 22, 1976.
(Chicago's 4th choice, 118th overall, in 1994 Entry Draft).

			Regular Season					Playoffs				
Season	Club	Lea	GP	G	A	TP	PIM	GP	G	A	TP	PIM
1992-93	Belleville	OHL	64	2	10	12	34	7	0	5	5	10
1993-94	Belleville	OHL	66	7	25	32	37	12	2	3	5	6
1994-95	Belleville	OHL	66	5	40	45	24	16	1	7	8	4

DUTHIE, RYAN

Center. Shoots right. 5'10", 180 lbs. Born, Red Deer, Alta., September 2, 1974.
(NY Islanders' 4th choice, 105th overall, in 1992 Entry Draft).

			Regular Season					Playoffs				
Season	Club	Lea	GP	G	A	TP	PIM	GP	G	A	TP	PIM
1991-92	Spokane	WHL	67	23	37	60	119	10	5	10	15	18
1992-93	Spokane	WHL	60	26	58	84	122	9	7	2	9	8
1993-94a	Spokane	WHL	71	57	69	126	111	3	3	5	8	11
1994-95	Saint John	AHL	72	18	21	39	70	2	0	0	0	0

a WHL West First All-Star Team (1994)
Re-entered NHL Entry Draft. **Calgary's** 4th choice, 91st overall in 1994 Entry Draft.

DUTIAUME, MARK   BUF.

Left wing. Shoots left. 6', 200 lbs. Born, Winnipeg, Man., January 31, 1977.
(Buffalo's 3rd choice, 42nd overall, in 1995 Entry Draft).

			Regular Season					Playoffs				
Season	Club	Lea	GP	G	A	TP	PIM	GP	G	A	TP	PIM
1993-94	Tri-City	WHL	3	2	0	2	0	....	....	....	....	....
	Brandon	WHL	55	4	7	11	43	12	0	2	2	6
1994-95	Brandon	WHL	62	23	21	44	80	17	1	2	3	33

DVORAK, RADEK   (duh-VOHR-ak)   FLA.

Left wing. Shoots right. 6'2", 187 lbs. Born, Tabor, Czech., March 9, 1977.
(Florida's 1st choice, 10th overall, in 1995 Entry Draft).

			Regular Season					Playoffs				
Season	Club	Lea	GP	G	A	TP	PIM	GP	G	A	TP	PIM
1993-94	Budejovice	Czech.	8	0	0	0	0	....	....	....	....	....
1994-95	Budejovice	Czech.	10	3	5	8	2	9	5	1	6	....

DYKHUIS, KARL   (DIGH-kowz)   PHI.

Defense. Shoots left. 6'3", 195 lbs. Born, Sept-Iles, Que., July 8, 1972.
(Chicago's 1st choice, 16th overall, in 1990 Entry Draft).

			Regular Season					Playoffs				
Season	Club	Lea	GP	G	A	TP	PIM	GP	G	A	TP	PIM
1988-89	Hull	QMJHL	63	2	29	31	59	9	1	9	10	6
1989-90a	Hull	QMJHL	69	10	46	56	119	11	2	5	7	2
1990-91	Cdn. National	....	37	2	9	11	16	....	....	....	....	....
	Longueuil	QMJHL	3	1	4	4	6	8	2	5	7	6
1991-92	**Chicago**	NHL	6	1	3	4	4	....	....	....	....	....
	Cdn. National	....	19	1	2	3	16	....	....	....	....	....
	Verdun	QMJHL	29	5	19	24	55	17	0	12	12	14
1992-93	**Chicago**	NHL	12	0	5	5	0	....	....	....	....	....
	Indianapolis	IHL	59	5	18	23	76	5	1	1	2	8
1993-94	Indianapolis	IHL	73	7	25	32	132	....	....	....	....	....
1994-95	Indianapolis	IHL	52	2	21	23	63	....	....	....	....	....
	Hershey	AHL	1	0	0	0	0	....	....	....	....	....
	Philadelphia	NHL	33	2	6	8	37	15	4	4	8	14
	NHL Totals		51	3	14	17	41	15	4	4	8	14

a QMJHL First All-Star Team (1990)
Traded to **Philadelphia** by **Chicago** for Bob Wilkie and a possible conditional choice in 1997 Entry Draft, February 16, 1995.

DZIEDZIC, JOE   (zehd-ZIHK)   PIT.

Left wing. Shoots left. 6'3", 200 lbs. Born, Minneapolis, MN, December 18, 1971.
(Pittsburgh's 2nd choice, 61st overall, in 1990 Entry Draft).

			Regular Season					Playoffs				
Season	Club	Lea	GP	G	A	TP	PIM	GP	G	A	TP	PIM
1990-91	U. Minnesota	WCHA	20	6	4	10	26	....	....	....	....	....
1991-92	U. Minnesota	WCHA	34	8	9	17	68	....	....	....	....	....
1992-93	U. Minnesota	WCHA	41	11	14	25	62	....	....	....	....	....
1993-94	U. Minnesota	WCHA	18	7	10	17	48	....	....	....	....	....
1994-95	Cleveland	IHL	68	15	15	30	74	4	1	0	1	10

EAGLES, MIKE   WSH.

Center/Left wing. Shoots left. 5'10", 190 lbs. Born, Sussex, N.B., March 7, 1963.
(Quebec's 5th choice, 116th overall, in 1981 Entry Draft).

			Regular Season					Playoffs				
Season	Club	Lea	GP	G	A	TP	PIM	GP	G	A	TP	PIM
1980-81	Kitchener	OHA	56	11	27	38	64	18	4	2	6	36
1981-82	Kitchener	OHL	62	26	40	66	148	15	3	11	14	27
1982-83	**Quebec**	NHL	2	0	0	0	2	....	....	....	....	....
	Kitchener	OHL	58	26	36	62	133	12	5	7	12	27
1983-84	Fredericton	AHL	68	13	29	42	85	4	0	0	0	5
1984-85	Fredericton	AHL	36	4	20	24	80	3	0	0	0	2
1985-86	**Quebec**	NHL	73	11	12	23	49	3	0	0	0	2
1986-87	**Quebec**	NHL	73	13	19	32	55	4	1	0	1	10
1987-88	**Quebec**	NHL	76	10	10	20	74	....	....	....	....	....
1988-89	**Chicago**	NHL	47	5	11	16	44	....	....	....	....	....
1989-90	**Chicago**	NHL	23	1	2	3	34	....	....	....	....	....
	Indianapolis	IHL	24	11	13	24	47	13	*10	10	20	34
1990-91	**Winnipeg**	NHL	44	0	9	9	79	....	....	....	....	....
	Indianapolis	IHL	25	15	14	29	47	....	....	....	....	....
1991-92	**Winnipeg**	NHL	65	7	10	17	118	7	0	0	0	8
1992-93	**Winnipeg**	NHL	84	8	18	26	131	5	0	1	1	6
1993-94	**Winnipeg**	NHL	73	4	8	12	96	....	....	....	....	....
1994-95	**Winnipeg**	NHL	27	2	1	3	40	....	....	....	....	....
	Washington	NHL	13	1	3	4	8	7	0	2	2	4
	NHL Totals		600	62	103	165	730	26	1	3	4	30

Traded to **Chicago** by **Quebec** for Bob Mason, July 5, 1988. Traded to **Winnipeg** by **Chicago** for Winnipeg's fourth round choice (Igor Kravchuk) in 1991 Entry Draft, December 14, 1990. Traded to **Washington** by **Winnipeg** with Igor Ulanov for Washington's third (later traded to Dallas — Dallas selected Sergei Gusev) and fifth (Brian Elder) round choices in 1995 Entry Draft, April 7, 1995.

EAKINS, DALLAS   (EE-kins)   FLA.

Defense. Shoots left. 6'2", 195 lbs. Born, Dade City, FL, February 27, 1967.
(Washington's 11th choice, 208th overall, in 1985 Entry Draft).

			Regular Season					Playoffs				
Season	Club	Lea	GP	G	A	TP	PIM	GP	G	A	TP	PIM
1984-85	Peterborough	OHL	48	0	8	8	96	7	0	0	0	18
1985-86	Peterborough	OHL	60	6	16	22	134	16	0	1	1	30
1986-87	Peterborough	OHL	54	3	11	14	145	12	1	4	5	37
1987-88	Peterborough	OHL	64	11	27	38	129	12	3	12	15	16
1988-89	Baltimore	AHL	62	0	10	10	139	....	....	....	....	....
1989-90	Moncton	AHL	75	2	11	13	189	....	....	....	....	....
1990-91	Moncton	AHL	75	1	12	13	132	9	0	1	1	44
1991-92	Moncton	AHL	67	3	13	16	136	11	2	1	3	16
1992-93	**Winnipeg**	NHL	14	0	2	2	38	....	....	....	....	....
	Moncton	AHL	55	4	6	10	132	....	....	....	....	....
1993-94	**Florida**	NHL	1	0	0	0	0	....	....	....	....	....
	Cincinnati	IHL	80	1	18	19	143	8	0	1	1	41
1994-95	Cincinnati	IHL	59	6	12	18	69	....	....	....	....	....
	Florida	NHL	17	0	1	1	35	....	....	....	....	....
	NHL Totals		32	0	3	3	73	....	....	....	....	....

Signed as a free agent by **Winnipeg**, October 17, 1989. Signed as a free agent by **Florida**, July 8, 1993.

EASTWOOD, MIKE   WPG.

Center. Shoots right. 6'3", 205 lbs. Born, Ottawa, Ont., July 1, 1967.
(Toronto's 5th choice, 91st overall, in 1987 Entry Draft).

			Regular Season					Playoffs				
Season	Club	Lea	GP	G	A	TP	PIM	GP	G	A	TP	PIM
1987-88	W. Michigan	CCHA	42	5	8	13	14	....	....	....	....	....
1988-89	W. Michigan	CCHA	40	10	13	23	87	....	....	....	....	....
1989-90	W. Michigan	CCHA	40	25	27	52	36	....	....	....	....	....
1990-91a	W. Michigan	CCHA	42	29	32	61	84	....	....	....	....	....
1991-92	**Toronto**	NHL	9	0	2	2	4	....	....	....	....	....
	St. John's	AHL	61	18	25	43	28	16	9	10	19	16
1992-93	**Toronto**	NHL	12	1	6	7	21	10	1	2	3	8
	St. John's	AHL	60	24	35	59	32	....	....	....	....	....
1993-94	**Toronto**	NHL	54	8	10	18	28	18	3	2	5	12
1994-95	**Toronto**	NHL	36	5	5	10	32	....	....	....	....	....
	Winnipeg	NHL	13	3	6	9	4	....	....	....	....	....
	NHL Totals		124	17	29	46	89	28	4	4	8	20

a CCHA Second All-Star Team (1991)
Traded to **Winnipeg** by **Toronto** with Toronto's third round choice (Brad Isbister) in 1995 Entry Draft for Tie Domi, April 7, 1995.

EGELAND, ALLAN   T.B.

Center. Shoots left. 6', 184 lbs. Born, Lethbridge, Alta., January 31, 1973.
(Tampa Bay's 3rd choice, 55th overall, in 1993 Entry Draft).

			Regular Season					Playoffs				
Season	Club	Lea	GP	G	A	TP	PIM	GP	G	A	TP	PIM
1990-91	Lethbridge	WHL	67	2	16	18	57	9	0	0	0	0
1991-92	Tacoma	WHL	72	35	39	74	135	4	0	1	1	18
1992-93a	Tacoma	WHL	71	56	57	113	119	7	9	7	16	18
1993-94b	Tacoma	WHL	70	47	76	123	204	8	5	3	8	26
1994-95	Atlanta	IHL	60	8	16	24	112	5	0	1	1	16

a WHL West First All-Star Team (1993)
b WHL West Second All-Star Team (1994)

EISENHUT, NEIL   (IGHS-ihn-huht)   CGY.

Center. Shoots left. 6'1", 190 lbs. Born, Osoyoos, B.C., February 9, 1967.
(Vancouver's 11th choice, 238th overall, in 1987 Entry Draft).

			Regular Season					Playoffs				
Season	Club	Lea	GP	G	A	TP	PIM	GP	G	A	TP	PIM
1987-88	North Dakota	WCHA	42	12	20	32	14	....	....	....	....	....
1988-89	North Dakota	WCHA	41	22	16	38	20	....	....	....	....	....
1989-90	North Dakota	WCHA	45	22	32	54	46	....	....	....	....	....
1990-91	North Dakota	WCHA	20	9	15	24	10	....	....	....	....	....
1991-92	Milwaukee	IHL	76	13	23	36	26	2	1	2	3	0
1992-93	Hamilton	AHL	72	22	40	62	41	....	....	....	....	....
1993-94	**Vancouver**	NHL	13	1	3	4	21	....	....	....	....	....
	Hamilton	AHL	60	17	36	53	30	4	1	4	5	0
1994-95	Saint John	AHL	75	16	39	55	30	5	1	1	2	6
	Calgary	NHL	3	0	0	0	0	....	....	....	....	....
	NHL Totals		16	1	3	4	21	....	....	....	....	....

Signed as a free agent by **Calgary**, June 16, 1994.

EKMAN, NILS   (EHK-mahn)   CGY.

Left wing. Shoots left. 5'11", 167 lbs. Born, Stockholm, Sweden, March 11, 1976.
(Calgary's 6th choice, 107th overall, in 1994 Entry Draft).

			Regular Season					Playoffs				
Season	Club	Lea	GP	G	A	TP	PIM	GP	G	A	TP	PIM
1993-94	Hammarby	Swe. 2	18	7	2	9	4	....	....	....	....	....
1994-95	Hammarby	Swe. 2	29	10	7	17	18	....	....	....	....	....

ELFRING, CALVIN   COL.

Defense. Shoots left. 6', 170 lbs. Born, Lethbridge, Alta., April 23, 1976.
(Quebec's 9th choice, 165th overall, in 1994 Entry Draft).

			Regular Season					Playoffs				
Season	Club	Lea	GP	G	A	TP	PIM	GP	G	A	TP	PIM
1993-94	Powell River	BCJHL	58	21	45	66	80	....	....	....	....	....
1994-95	Colorado	WCHA	43	3	23	26	34	....	....	....	....	....

ELIAS, PATRIK   (EH-lih-ahsh)   N.J.

Left wing. Shoots left. 6', 175 lbs. Born, Trebic, Czech., April 13, 1976.
(New Jersey's 2nd choice, 51st overall, in 1994 Entry Draft).

			Regular Season					Playoffs				
Season	Club	Lea	GP	G	A	TP	PIM	GP	G	A	TP	PIM
1992-93	Kladno	Czech.	2	0	0	0	....	....	....	....	....	....
1993-94	Kladno	Czech.	15	1	2	3	....	11	2	2	4	....
1994-95	Kladno	Czech.	28	4	3	7	37	7	1	2	3	12

ELICK, MICKEY   NYR

Defense. Shoots left. 6'1", 180 lbs. Born, Calgary, Alta., March 17, 1974.
(NY Rangers' 8th choice, 192nd overall, in 1992 Entry Draft).

			Regular Season					Playoffs				
Season	Club	Lea	GP	G	A	TP	PIM	GP	G	A	TP	PIM
1992-93	U. Wisconsin	WCHA	33	1	6	7	24	....	....	....	....	....
1993-94	U. Wisconsin	WCHA	42	7	12	19	54	....	....	....	....	....
1994-95	U. Wisconsin	WCHA	43	5	24	29	52	....	....	....	....	....

ELIK, TODD (EHL-ihk) BOS.

Center. Shoots left. 6'2", 195 lbs. Born, Brampton, Ont., April 15, 1966.

			Regular Season					Playoffs				
Season	Club	Lea	GP	G	A	TP	PIM	GP	G	A	TP	PIM
1984-85	Kingston	OHL	34	14	11	25	6	....	....	....	....	....
	North Bay	OHL	23	4	6	10	2	4	2	0	2	0
1985-86	North Bay	OHL	40	12	34	46	20	10	7	6	13	0
1986-87	U. of Regina	CWUAA	27	26	34	60	137	....	....	....	....	....
	Cdn. National	....	1	0	0	0	0	....	....	....	....	....
1987-88	Colorado	IHL	81	44	56	100	83	12	8	12	20	9
1988-89	Denver	IHL	28	20	15	35	22	....	....	....	....	....
	New Haven	AHL	43	11	25	36	31	17	10	12	22	44
1989-90	**Los Angeles**	**NHL**	**48**	**10**	**23**	**33**	**41**	**10**	**3**	**9**	**12**	**10**
	New Haven	AHL	32	20	23	43	42	....	....	....	....	....
1990-91	**Los Angeles**	**NHL**	**74**	**21**	**37**	**58**	**58**	**12**	**2**	**7**	**9**	**6**
1991-92	**Minnesota**	**NHL**	**62**	**14**	**32**	**46**	**125**	**5**	**1**	**1**	**2**	**2**
1992-93	**Minnesota**	**NHL**	**46**	**13**	**18**	**31**	**48**	....	....	....	....	....
	Edmonton	**NHL**	**14**	**1**	**9**	**10**	**8**	....	....	....	....	....
1993-94	**Edmonton**	**NHL**	**4**	**0**	**0**	**0**	**6**	....	....	....	....	....
	San Jose	**NHL**	**75**	**25**	**41**	**66**	**89**	**14**	**5**	**5**	**10**	**12**
1994-95	**San Jose**	**NHL**	**22**	**7**	**10**	**17**	**18**	....	....	....	....	....
	St. Louis	**NHL**	**13**	**2**	**4**	**6**	**4**	**7**	**4**	**3**	**7**	**2**
	NHL Totals		**358**	**93**	**174**	**267**	**397**	**48**	**15**	**25**	**40**	**32**

Signed as a free agent by **NY Rangers**, February 26, 1988. Traded to **Los Angeles** by **NY Rangers** with Igor Liba, Michael Boyce and future considerations for Dean Kennedy and Denis Larocque, December 12, 1988. Traded to **Minnesota** by **Los Angeles** for Randy Gilhen, Charlie Huddy, Jim Thomson and NY Rangers' fourth round choice (previously acquired by Minnesota — Los Angeles selected Alexei Zhitnik) in 1991 Entry Draft, June 22, 1991. Traded to **Edmonton** by **Minnesota** for Brent Gilchrist, March 5, 1993. Claimed on waivers by **San Jose** from **Edmonton**, October 26, 1993. Traded to **St. Louis** by **San Jose** for Kevin Miller, March 23, 1995. Signed as a free agent by **Boston**, August 8, 1995.

ELLETT, DAVE TOR.

Defense. Shoots left. 6'2", 205 lbs. Born, Cleveland, OH, March 30, 1964.
(Winnipeg's 3rd choice, 75th overall, in 1982 Entry Draft).

			Regular Season					Playoffs				
Season	Club	Lea	GP	G	A	TP	PIM	GP	G	A	TP	PIM
1982-83	Bowling Green	CCHA	40	4	13	17	34	....	....	....	....	....
1983-84ab	Bowling Green	CCHA	43	15	39	54	96	....	....	....	....	....
1984-85	**Winnipeg**	**NHL**	**80**	**11**	**27**	**38**	**85**	**8**	**1**	**5**	**6**	**4**
1985-86	**Winnipeg**	**NHL**	**80**	**15**	**31**	**46**	**96**	**3**	**0**	**1**	**1**	**0**
1986-87	**Winnipeg**	**NHL**	**78**	**13**	**31**	**44**	**53**	**10**	**0**	**8**	**8**	**2**
1987-88	**Winnipeg**	**NHL**	**68**	**13**	**45**	**58**	**106**	**5**	**1**	**2**	**3**	**10**
1988-89	**Winnipeg**	**NHL**	**75**	**22**	**34**	**56**	**62**	....	....	....	....	....
1989-90	**Winnipeg**	**NHL**	**77**	**17**	**29**	**46**	**96**	**7**	**2**	**0**	**2**	**6**
1990-91	**Winnipeg**	**NHL**	**17**	**4**	**7**	**11**	**6**	....	....	....	....	....
	Toronto	**NHL**	**60**	**8**	**30**	**38**	**69**	....	....	....	....	....
1991-92	**Toronto**	**NHL**	**79**	**18**	**33**	**51**	**95**	....	....	....	....	....
1992-93	**Toronto**	**NHL**	**70**	**6**	**34**	**40**	**46**	**21**	**4**	**8**	**12**	**8**
1993-94	**Toronto**	**NHL**	**68**	**7**	**36**	**43**	**42**	**18**	**3**	**15**	**18**	**31**
1994-95	**Toronto**	**NHL**	**33**	**5**	**10**	**15**	**26**	**7**	**0**	**2**	**2**	**0**
	NHL Totals		**785**	**139**	**347**	**486**	**782**	**79**	**11**	**41**	**52**	**61**

a CCHA Second All-Star Team (1984)
b Named to NCAA All-Tournament Team (1984)

Played in NHL All-Star Game (1989, 1992)

Traded to **Toronto** by **Winnipeg** with Paul Fenton for Ed Olczyk and Mark Osborne, November 10, 1990.

ELOMO, MIIKKA (eh-LOH-moh, MEE-ka) WSH.

Left wing. Shoots left. 6', 180 lbs. Born, Turku, Finland, April 21, 1977.
(Washington's 2nd choice, 23rd overall, in 1995 Entry Draft).

			Regular Season					Playoffs				
Season	Club	Lea	GP	G	A	TP	PIM	GP	G	A	TP	PIM
1994-95	Kiekko-67	Fin. 2	14	9	2	11	39	....	....	....	....	....
	TPS	Fin. Jr.	14	3	8	11	24	....	....	....	....	....

ELYNUIK, PAT (EL-ih-NYUK) OTT.

Right wing. Shoots right. 6', 185 lbs. Born, Foam Lake, Sask., October 30, 1967.
(Winnipeg's 1st choice, 8th overall, in 1986 Entry Draft).

			Regular Season					Playoffs				
Season	Club	Lea	GP	G	A	TP	PIM	GP	G	A	TP	PIM
1984-85	Prince Albert	WHL	70	23	20	43	54	13	9	3	12	7
1985-86a	Prince Albert	WHL	68	53	53	106	62	20	7	9	16	17
1986-87a	Prince Albert	WHL	64	51	62	113	40	8	5	5	10	12
1987-88	**Winnipeg**	**NHL**	**13**	**1**	**3**	**4**	**12**	....	....	....	....	....
	Moncton	AHL	30	11	18	29	35	....	....	....	....	....
1988-89	**Winnipeg**	**NHL**	**56**	**26**	**25**	**51**	**29**	....	....	....	....	....
	Moncton	AHL	7	8	2	10	2	....	....	....	....	....
1989-90	**Winnipeg**	**NHL**	**80**	**32**	**42**	**74**	**83**	**7**	**2**	**4**	**6**	**2**
1990-91	**Winnipeg**	**NHL**	**80**	**31**	**34**	**65**	**73**	....	....	....	....	....
1991-92	**Winnipeg**	**NHL**	**60**	**25**	**25**	**50**	**65**	**7**	**2**	**2**	**4**	**4**
1992-93	**Washington**	**NHL**	**80**	**22**	**35**	**57**	**66**	**6**	**2**	**3**	**5**	**19**
1993-94	**Washington**	**NHL**	**4**	**1**	**1**	**2**	**0**	....	....	....	....	....
	Tampa Bay	**NHL**	**63**	**12**	**14**	**26**	**64**	....	....	....	....	....
1994-95	**Ottawa**	**NHL**	**41**	**3**	**7**	**10**	**51**	....	....	....	....	....
	NHL Totals		**477**	**153**	**186**	**339**	**443**	**20**	**6**	**9**	**15**	**25**

a WHL East All-Star Team (1986, 1987)

Traded to **Washington** by **Winnipeg** for John Druce and Toronto's fourth round choice (previously acquired by Washington — later traded to Detroit — Detroit selected John Jakopin) in 1993 Entry Draft, October 1, 1992. Traded to **Tampa Bay** by **Washington** for future draft choices, October 22, 1993. Signed as a free agent by **Ottawa**, June 21, 1994.

EMERSON, NELSON WPG.

Center. Shoots right. 5'11", 175 lbs. Born, Hamilton, Ont., August 17, 1967.
(St. Louis' 2nd choice, 44th overall, in 1985 Entry Draft).

			Regular Season					Playoffs				
Season	Club	Lea	GP	G	A	TP	PIM	GP	G	A	TP	PIM
1986-87	Bowling Green	CCHA	45	26	35	61	28	....	....	....	....	....
1987-88ab	Bowling Green	CCHA	45	34	49	83	54	....	....	....	....	....
1988-89c	Bowling Green	CCHA	44	22	46	68	46	....	....	....	....	....
1989-90bd	Bowling Green	CCHA	44	30	52	82	42	....	....	....	....	....
	Peoria	IHL	3	1	1	2	0	....	....	....	....	....
1990-91	**St. Louis**	**NHL**	**4**	**0**	**3**	**3**	**2**	....	....	....	....	....
ef	Peoria	IHL	73	36	79	115	91	17	9	12	21	16
1991-92	**St. Louis**	**NHL**	**79**	**23**	**36**	**59**	**66**	**6**	**3**	**3**	**6**	**21**
1992-93	**St. Louis**	**NHL**	**82**	**22**	**51**	**73**	**62**	**11**	**1**	**6**	**7**	**6**
1993-94	**Winnipeg**	**NHL**	**83**	**33**	**41**	**74**	**80**	....	....	....	....	....
1994-95	**Winnipeg**	**NHL**	**48**	**14**	**23**	**37**	**26**	....	....	....	....	....
	NHL Totals		**296**	**92**	**154**	**246**	**236**	**17**	**4**	**9**	**13**	**27**

a NCAA West Second All-American Team (1988)
b CCHA First All-Star Team (1988, 1990)
c CCHA Second All-Star Team (1989)
d NCAA West First All-American Team (1990)
e IHL First All-Star Team (1991)
f Won Garry F. Longman Memorial Trophy (Top Rookie - IHL) (1991)

Traded to **Winnipeg** by **St. Louis** with Stephane Quintal for Phil Housley, September 24, 1993.

EMMA, DAVID

Center. Shoots left. 5'11", 180 lbs. Born, Cranston, RI, January 14, 1969.
(New Jersey's 6th choice, 110th overall, in 1989 Entry Draft).

			Regular Season					Playoffs				
Season	Club	Lea	GP	G	A	TP	PIM	GP	G	A	TP	PIM
1987-88	Boston College	H.E.	30	19	16	35	30	....	....	....	....	....
1988-89	Boston College	H.E.	36	20	31	51	36	....	....	....	....	....
1989-90ab	Boston College	H.E.	42	38	34	*72	46	....	....	....	....	....
1990-91abcd	Boston College	H.E.	39	*35	46	*81	44	....	....	....	....	....
1991-92	U.S. National	....	55	15	16	31	32	....	....	....	....	....
	U.S. Olympic	....	6	0	1	1	6	....	....	....	....	....
	Utica	AHL	15	4	7	11	12	4	1	1	2	2
1992-93	**New Jersey**	**NHL**	**2**	**0**	**0**	**0**	**0**	....	....	....	....	....
	Utica	AHL	61	21	40	61	47	5	2	1	3	6
1993-94	**New Jersey**	**NHL**	**15**	**5**	**5**	**10**	**2**	....	....	....	....	....
	Albany	AHL	56	26	29	55	53	5	1	2	3	8
1994-95	**New Jersey**	**NHL**	**6**	**0**	**1**	**1**	**0**	....	....	....	....	....
	Albany	AHL	1	0	0	0	0	....	....	....	....	....
	NHL Totals		**23**	**5**	**6**	**11**	**2**	....	....	....	....	....

a Hockey East First All-Star Team (1990, 1991)
b NCAA East First All-American Team (1990, 1991)
c Hockey East Player of the Year (1991)
d Won Hobey Baker Memorial Award (Top U.S. Collegiate Player) (1991)

EMMONS, GARY

Center. Shoots right. 6', 185 lbs. Born, Winnipeg, Man., December 30, 1963.
(NY Rangers' 1st choice, 14th overall, in 1986 Supplemental Draft).

			Regular Season					Playoffs				
Season	Club	Lea	GP	G	A	TP	PIM	GP	G	A	TP	PIM
1983-84	N. Michigan	CCHA	40	28	21	49	42	....	....	....	....	....
1984-85	N. Michigan	CCHA	40	25	28	53	22	....	....	....	....	....
1985-86	N. Michigan	CCHA	36	45	30	75	34	....	....	....	....	....
1986-87	N. Michigan	CCHA	35	32	34	66	59	....	....	....	....	....
1987-88	Milwaukee	IHL	13	3	4	7	4	....	....	....	....	....
	Nova Scotia	AHL	59	18	27	45	22	....	....	....	....	....
1988-89	Cdn. National	....	49	16	26	42	42	....	....	....	....	....
1989-90	Kalamazoo	IHL	81	41	59	100	38	8	2	7	9	2
1990-91	Kalamazoo	IHL	62	25	33	58	26	11	5	8	13	6
1991-92	Kansas City	IHL	80	29	54	83	60	15	6	13	19	8
1992-93	Kansas City	IHL	80	37	44	81	80	12	*7	6	13	8
1993-94	**San Jose**	**NHL**	**3**	**1**	**0**	**1**	**0**	....	....	....	....	....
	Kansas City	IHL	63	20	49	69	28	....	....	....	....	....
1994-95	Kansas City	IHL	81	22	38	60	42	21	9	19	28	24
	NHL Totals		**3**	**1**	**0**	**1**	**0**					

Signed as a free agent by **Edmonton**, July 27, 1987. Signed as a free agent by **Minnesota**, July 11, 1989. Signed as a free agent by **San Jose**, October 19, 1993.

EMMONS, JOHN CGY.

Center. Shoots left. 6', 185 lbs. Born, San Jose, CA, August 17, 1974.
(Calgary's 7th choice, 122nd overall, in 1993 Entry Draft).

			Regular Season					Playoffs				
Season	Club	Lea	GP	G	A	TP	PIM	GP	G	A	TP	PIM
1992-93	Yale	ECAC	28	3	5	8	66	....	....	....	....	....
1993-94	Yale	ECAC	25	5	12	17	66	....	....	....	....	....
1994-95	Yale	ECAC	28	4	16	20	57	....	....	....	....	....

ENGLEHART, BRAD ANA.

Center. Shoots left. 5'11", 180 lbs. Born, Woodstock, N.B., September 16, 1975.
(Anaheim's 8th choice, 184th overall, in 1994 Entry Draft).

			Regular Season					Playoffs				
Season	Club	Lea	GP	G	A	TP	PIM	GP	G	A	TP	PIM
1993-94	Kimball Un.	HS	24	20	23	43	10	....	....	....	....	....
1994-95	U. Wisconsin	WCHA	29	6	6	12	42	....	....	....	....	....

ENGLUND, PATRIK PHI.

Left wing. Shoots left. 6', 185 lbs. Born, Stockholm, Sweden, June 3, 1970.
(Philadelphia's 11th choice, 151st overall, in 1990 Entry Draft).

			Regular Season					Playoffs				
Season	Club	Lea	GP	G	A	TP	PIM	GP	G	A	TP	PIM
1988-89	AIK	Swe.	19	2	3	5	6	....	....	....	....	....
1989-90	AIK	Swe.	31	11	7	18	2	3	0	0	0	12
1990-91	AIK	Swe.	40	9	6	15	6	....	....	....	....	....
1991-92	AIK	Swe.	39	8	5	13	8	3	0	0	0	0
1992-93	AIK	Swe.	22	3	1	4	8	....	....	....	....	....
1993-94	AIK	Swe.	35	14	25	39	18	....	....	....	....	....
1994-95	AIK	Swe.	39	11	12	23	18	....	....	....	....	....

ENSOM, JIM CHI.

Center. Shoots left. 6'3", 191 lbs. Born, Oshawa, Ont., August 24, 1976.
(Chicago's 5th choice, 144th overall, in 1994 Entry Draft).

			Regular Season					Playoffs				
Season	Club	Lea	GP	G	A	TP	PIM	GP	G	A	TP	PIM
1992-93	North Bay	OHL	65	7	17	24	70	5	1	0	1	7
1993-94	North Bay	OHL	44	16	20	36	67	16	4	5	9	6
1994-95	North Bay	OHL	44	13	30	43	49	....	....	....	....	....
	Kitchener	OHL	21	10	8	18	9	3	1	1	2	6

EPANCHINTSEV, VADIM (yeh-pahn-CHIHN-tsehv) **T.B.**

Center. Shoots left. 5'9", 165 lbs. Born, Orsk, USSR, March 16, 1976.
(Tampa Bay's 3rd choice, 55th overall, in 1994 Entry Draft).

			Regular Season					Playoffs				
Season	Club	Lea	GP	G	A	TP	PIM	GP	G	A	TP	PIM
1993-94	Spartak	CIS	46	6	5	11	16	3	0	1	1	0
1994-95	Spartak	CIS	43	4	8	12	24	....	....	....	....	....

ERIKSSON, ANDERS **DET.**

Defense. Shoots left. 6'3", 218 lbs. Born, Bollnas, Sweden, January 9, 1975.
(Detroit's 1st choice, 22nd overall, in 1993 Entry Draft).

			Regular Season					Playoffs				
Season	Club	Lea	GP	G	A	TP	PIM	GP	G	A	TP	PIM
1992-93	MoDo	Swe.	20	0	2	2	2	1	0	0	0	0
1993-94	MoDo	Swe.	38	2	8	10	42	11	0	0	0	8
1994-95	MoDo	Swe.	39	3	6	9	54	....	....	....	....	....

ERIKSSON, NIKLAS (AIR-ihk-suhn) **PHI.**

Center. Shoots left. 5'10", 183 lbs. Born, Vastervik, Sweden, February 17, 1969.
(Philadelphia's 4th choice, 117th overall, in 1989 Entry Draft).

			Regular Season					Playoffs				
Season	Club	Lea	GP	G	A	TP	PIM	GP	G	A	TP	PIM
1987-88	Leksand	Swe.	16	1	8	9	4	2	0	0	0	0
1988-89	Leksand	Swe.	33	18	12	30	22	....	....	....	....	....
1989-90	Leksand	Swe.	40	18	16	34	16	3	0	2	2	2
1990-91	Leksand	Swe.	8	2	2	4	2	....	....	....	....	....
1991-92	Leksand	Swe.	22	10	7	17	16	....	....	....	....	....
1992-93	Leksand	Swe.	37	6	19	25	28	2	0	1	1	2
1993-94	Leksand	Swe.	33	10	25	35	34	4	1	2	3	2
1994-95	Leksand	Swe.	39	17	26	43	32	4	1	2	3	4

ERREY, BOB (AIRY) **DET.**

Left wing. Shoots left. 5'10", 185 lbs. Born, Montreal, Que., September 21, 1964.
(Pittsburgh's 1st choice, 15th overall, in 1983 Entry Draft).

			Regular Season					Playoffs				
Season	Club	Lea	GP	G	A	TP	PIM	GP	G	A	TP	PIM
1981-82	Peterborough	OHL	68	29	31	60	39	9	3	1	4	9
1982-83a	Peterborough	OHL	67	53	47	100	74	4	1	3	4	7
1983-84	**Pittsburgh**	**NHL**	**65**	**9**	**13**	**22**	**29**	....	....	....	....	....
1984-85	**Pittsburgh**	**NHL**	**16**	**0**	**2**	**2**	**7**	....	....	....	....	....
	Baltimore	AHL	59	17	24	41	14	8	3	4	7	11
1985-86	**Pittsburgh**	**NHL**	**37**	**11**	**6**	**17**	**8**	....	....	....	....	....
	Baltimore	AHL	18	8	7	15	28	....	....	....	....	....
1986-87	**Pittsburgh**	**NHL**	**72**	**16**	**18**	**34**	**46**	....	....	....	....	....
1987-88	**Pittsburgh**	**NHL**	**17**	**3**	**6**	**9**	**18**	....	....	....	....	....
1988-89	**Pittsburgh**	**NHL**	**76**	**26**	**32**	**58**	**124**	**11**	**1**	**2**	**3**	**12**
1989-90	**Pittsburgh**	**NHL**	**78**	**20**	**19**	**39**	**109**	....	....	....	....	....
1990-91	**Pittsburgh**	**NHL**	**79**	**20**	**22**	**42**	**115**	**24**	**5**	**2**	**7**	**29**
1991-92	**Pittsburgh**	**NHL**	**78**	**19**	**16**	**35**	**119**	**14**	**3**	**0**	**3**	**10**
1992-93	**Pittsburgh**	**NHL**	**54**	**8**	**6**	**14**	**76**	....	....	....	....	....
	Buffalo	**NHL**	**8**	**1**	**3**	**4**	**4**	**4**	**0**	**1**	**1**	**10**
1993-94	**San Jose**	**NHL**	**64**	**12**	**18**	**30**	**126**	**14**	**3**	**2**	**5**	**10**
1994-95	**San Jose**	**NHL**	**13**	**2**	**2**	**4**	**27**	....	....	....	....	....
	Detroit	**NHL**	**30**	**6**	**11**	**17**	**31**	**18**	**1**	**5**	**6**	**30**
	NHL Totals		**687**	**153**	**174**	**327**	**839**	**85**	**13**	**12**	**25**	**101**

a OHL First All-Star Team (1983)

Traded to **Buffalo** by **Pittsburgh** for Mike Ramsey, March 22, 1993. Signed as a free agent by **San Jose**, August 17, 1993. Traded to **Detroit** by **San Jose** for Detroit's fifth round choice (Michal Bros) in 1995 Entry Draft, February 27, 1995.

ESAU, LEONARD (EE-saw) **FLA.**

Defense. Shoots right. 6'3", 190 lbs. Born, Meadow Lake, Sask., June 3, 1968.
(Toronto's 5th choice, 86th overall, in 1988 Entry Draft).

			Regular Season					Playoffs				
Season	Club	Lea	GP	G	A	TP	PIM	GP	G	A	TP	PIM
1988-89	St. Cloud	NCAA	35	12	27	39	69	....	....	....	....	....
1989-90	St. Cloud	NCAA	29	8	11	19	83	....	....	....	....	....
1990-91	Newmarket	AHL	76	4	14	18	28	....	....	....	....	....
1991-92	**Toronto**	**NHL**	**2**	**0**	**0**	**0**	**0**	....	....	....	....	....
	St. John's	AHL	78	9	29	38	68	13	0	2	2	14
1992-93	**Quebec**	**NHL**	**4**	**0**	**1**	**1**	**2**	....	....	....	....	....
	Halifax	AHL	75	11	31	42	79	....	....	....	....	....
1993-94	**Calgary**	**NHL**	**6**	**0**	**3**	**3**	**7**	....	....	....	....	....
	Saint John	AHL	75	12	36	48	129	7	2	2	4	6
1994-95	Saint John	AHL	54	13	27	40	73	5	0	2	2	0
	Edmonton	**NHL**	**14**	**0**	**6**	**6**	**15**	....	....	....	....	....
	Calgary	**NHL**	**1**	**0**	**0**	**0**	**0**	....	....	....	....	....
	NHL Totals		**27**	**0**	**10**	**10**	**24**	....	....	....	....	....

Traded to **Quebec** by **Toronto** for Ken McRae, July 21, 1992. Signed as a free agent by **Calgary**, September 6, 1993. Claimed by **Edmonton** from **Calgary** in NHL Waiver Draft, January 18, 1995. Claimed on waivers by **Calgary** from **Edmonton**, March 7, 1995. Signed as a free agent by **Florida**, July 27, 1995.

ESBJORS, JOACIM (ehs-BEE-yuhrs, yoh-AH-kihm) **HFD.**

Defense. Shoots left. 6'1", 194 lbs. Born, Goteborg, Sweden, July 4, 1970.
(Hartford's 11th choice, 249th overall, in 1992 Entry Draft).

			Regular Season					Playoffs				
Season	Club	Lea	GP	G	A	TP	PIM	GP	G	A	TP	PIM
1989-90	V. Frolunda	Swe.	24	0	4	4	23	....	....	....	....	....
1990-91	V. Frolunda	Swe.	22	1	5	6	16	....	....	....	....	....
1991-92	V. Frolunda	Swe.	40	9	9	18	22	3	1	0	1	2
1992-93	V. Frolunda	Swe.	20	1	6	7	26	....	....	....	....	....
1993-94	V. Frolunda	Swe.	38	4	7	11	44	4	0	0	0	2
1994-95	V. Frolunda	Swe.	22	1	4	5	22	....	....	....	....	....

ETHIER, MARTIN **NYR**

Defense. Shoots right. 6'1", 178 lbs. Born, Ste-Eustache, Que., September 3, 1976.
(NY Rangers' 6th choice, 130th overall, in 1994 Entry Draft).

			Regular Season					Playoffs				
Season	Club	Lea	GP	G	A	TP	PIM	GP	G	A	TP	PIM
1993-94	Beauport	QMJHL	61	4	19	23	53	15	0	3	3	32
1994-95	Beauport	QMJHL	68	4	26	30	125	18	0	5	5	53

EVASON, DEAN (EH-vih-suhn)

Center. Shoots right. 5'10", 180 lbs. Born, Flin Flon, Man., August 22, 1964.
(Washington's 3rd choice, 89th overall, in 1982 Entry Draft).

			Regular Season					Playoffs				
Season	Club	Lea	GP	G	A	TP	PIM	GP	G	A	TP	PIM
1980-81	Spokane	WHL	3	1	1	2	0	....	....	....	....	....
1981-82	Spokane	WHL	26	8	14	22	65	....	....	....	....	....
	Kamloops	WHL	44	21	55	76	47	4	2	1	3	0
1982-83	Kamloops	WHL	70	71	93	164	102	7	5	7	12	18
1983-84	**Washington**	**NHL**	**2**	**0**	**0**	**0**	**2**	....	....	....	....	....
a	Kamloops	WHL	57	49	88	137	89	17	*21	20	41	33
1984-85	**Washington**	**NHL**	**15**	**3**	**4**	**7**	**2**	....	....	....	....	....
	Hartford	**NHL**	**2**	**0**	**0**	**0**	**0**	....	....	....	....	....
	Binghamton	AHL	65	27	49	76	38	8	3	5	8	9
1985-86	**Hartford**	**NHL**	**55**	**20**	**28**	**48**	**65**	**10**	**1**	**4**	**5**	**10**
	Binghamton	AHL	26	9	17	26	29	....	....	....	....	....
1986-87	**Hartford**	**NHL**	**80**	**22**	**37**	**59**	**67**	**5**	**3**	**2**	**5**	**35**
1987-88	**Hartford**	**NHL**	**77**	**10**	**18**	**28**	**115**	**6**	**1**	**1**	**2**	**2**
1988-89	**Hartford**	**NHL**	**67**	**11**	**17**	**28**	**60**	**4**	**1**	**2**	**3**	**10**
1989-90	**Hartford**	**NHL**	**78**	**18**	**25**	**43**	**138**	**7**	**2**	**2**	**4**	**22**
1990-91	**Hartford**	**NHL**	**75**	**6**	**23**	**29**	**170**	**6**	**0**	**4**	**4**	**29**
1991-92	**San Jose**	**NHL**	**74**	**11**	**15**	**26**	**99**	....	....	....	....	....
1992-93	**San Jose**	**NHL**	**84**	**12**	**19**	**31**	**132**	....	....	....	....	....
1993-94	**Dallas**	**NHL**	**80**	**11**	**33**	**44**	**66**	**9**	**0**	**2**	**2**	**12**
1994-95	**Dallas**	**NHL**	**47**	**8**	**7**	**15**	**48**	**5**	**1**	**2**	**3**	**12**
	NHL Totals		**736**	**132**	**226**	**358**	**964**	**52**	**9**	**19**	**28**	**132**

a WHL First All-Star Team, West Division (1984)

Traded to **Hartford** by **Washington** with Peter Sidorkiewicz for David Jensen, March 12, 1985. Traded to **San Jose** by **Hartford** for Dan Keczmer, October 2, 1991. Traded to **Dallas** by **San Jose** for San Jose's sixth round choice (previously acquired by Dallas — San Jose selected Petri Varis) in 1993 Entry Draft, June 26, 1993.

EWEN, TODD (YOO-ihn) **ANA.**

Right wing. Shoots right. 6'2", 220 lbs. Born, Saskatoon, Sask., March 22, 1966.
(Edmonton's 9th choice, 168th overall, in 1984 Entry Draft).

			Regular Season					Playoffs				
Season	Club	Lea	GP	G	A	TP	PIM	GP	G	A	TP	PIM
1982-83	Kamloops	WHL	3	0	0	0	2	2	0	0	0	0
1983-84	N. Westminster	WHL	68	11	13	24	176	7	2	1	3	15
1984-85	N. Westminster	WHL	56	11	20	31	304	10	1	8	9	60
1985-86	N. Westminster	WHL	60	28	24	52	289	....	....	....	....	....
	Maine	AHL	....	....	....	....	....	3	0	0	0	7
1986-87	**St. Louis**	**NHL**	**23**	**2**	**0**	**2**	**84**	**4**	**0**	**0**	**0**	**23**
	Peoria	IHL	16	3	3	6	110	....	....	....	....	....
1987-88	**St. Louis**	**NHL**	**64**	**4**	**2**	**6**	**227**	**6**	**0**	**0**	**0**	**21**
1988-89	**St. Louis**	**NHL**	**34**	**4**	**5**	**9**	**171**	**2**	**0**	**0**	**0**	**21**
1989-90	**St. Louis**	**NHL**	**3**	**0**	**0**	**0**	**11**	....	....	....	....	....
	Peoria	IHL	2	0	0	0	12	....	....	....	....	....
	Montreal	**NHL**	**41**	**4**	**6**	**10**	**158**	**10**	**0**	**0**	**0**	**4**
1990-91	**Montreal**	**NHL**	**28**	**3**	**2**	**5**	**128**	....	....	....	....	....
1991-92	**Montreal**	**NHL**	**46**	**1**	**2**	**3**	**130**	**3**	**0**	**0**	**0**	**18**
1992-93	**Montreal**	**NHL**	**75**	**5**	**9**	**14**	**193**	**1**	**0**	**0**	**0**	**0**
1993-94	**Anaheim**	**NHL**	**76**	**9**	**9**	**18**	**272**	....	....	....	....	....
1994-95	**Anaheim**	**NHL**	**24**	**0**	**0**	**0**	**90**	....	....	....	....	....
	NHL Totals		**414**	**32**	**35**	**67**	**1464**	**26**	**0**	**0**	**0**	**87**

Traded to **St. Louis** by **Edmonton** for Shawn Evans, October 15, 1986. Traded to **Montreal** by **St. Louis** for future considerations, December 12, 1989. Traded to **Anaheim** by **Montreal** with Patrik Carnback for Anaheim's third round choice (Chris Murray) in 1994 Entry Draft, August 10, 1993.

FAFARD, DOMINIC **EDM.**

Defense. Shoots right. 6'5", 230 lbs. Born, Longueuil, Que., July 13, 1974.

			Regular Season					Playoffs				
Season	Club	Lea	GP	G	A	TP	PIM	GP	G	A	TP	PIM
1993-94	Victoriaville	QMJHL	72	6	32	38	70	5	0	1	1	6
1994-95	Wheeling	ECHL	39	2	8	10	44	....	....	....	....	....
	Cape Breton	AHL	1	0	0	0	0	....	....	....	....	....
	S. Carolina	ECHL	7	0	1	1	4	8	1	0	1	6

Signed as a free agent by **Edmonton**, September 30, 1994.

FAIR, QUINN **L.A.**

Defense. Shoots right. 6'1", 210 lbs. Born, Campbell River, B.C., May 23, 1973.
(Los Angeles' 1st choice, 7th overall, in 1994 Supplemental Draft).

			Regular Season					Playoffs				
Season	Club	Lea	GP	G	A	TP	PIM	GP	G	A	TP	PIM
1992-93	Kent State	CCHA	37	6	6	12	77	....	....	....	....	....
1993-94	Kent State	CCHA	39	11	13	24	92	....	....	....	....	....
1994-95	Bowling Green	CCHA	37	4	7	11	62	....	....	....	....	....

FAIRCHILD, KELLY **TOR.**

Center. Shoots left. 5'11", 180 lbs. Born, Hibbing, MN, April 9, 1973.
(Los Angeles' 7th choice, 152nd overall, in 1991 Entry Draft).

			Regular Season					Playoffs				
Season	Club	Lea	GP	G	A	TP	PIM	GP	G	A	TP	PIM
1991-92	U. Wisconsin	WCHA	37	11	10	21	45	....	....	....	....	....
1992-93	U. Wisconsin	WCHA	42	25	29	54	54	....	....	....	....	....
1993-94a	U. Wisconsin	WCHA	42	20	44	*64	81	....	....	....	....	....
1994-95	St. John's	AHL	53	27	23	50	51	4	0	2	2	4

a WCHA First All-Star Team (1994)

Traded to **Toronto** by **Los Angeles** with Dixon Ward, Guy Leveque and Shayne Toporowski for Eric Lacroix, Chris Snell and Toronto's fourth round choice in 1996 Entry Draft, October 3, 1994.

FALLOON, PAT (fah-LOON) **S.J.**

Right wing. Shoots right. 5'11", 190 lbs. Born, Foxwarren, Man., September 22, 1972.
(San Jose's 1st choice, 2nd overall, in 1991 Entry Draft).

			Regular Season					Playoffs				
Season	Club	Lea	GP	G	A	TP	PIM	GP	G	A	TP	PIM
1988-89	Spokane	WHL	72	22	56	78	41	....	....	....	....	....
1989-90	Spokane	WHL	71	60	64	124	48	6	5	8	13	4
1990-91abcd	Spokane	WHL	61	64	74	138	33	15	10	14	24	10
1991-92	**San Jose**	**NHL**	**79**	**25**	**34**	**59**	**16**	....	....	....	....	....
1992-93	**San Jose**	**NHL**	**41**	**14**	**14**	**28**	**12**	....	....	....	....	....
1993-94	**San Jose**	**NHL**	**83**	**22**	**31**	**53**	**18**	**14**	**1**	**2**	**3**	**6**
1994-95	**San Jose**	**NHL**	**46**	**12**	**7**	**19**	**25**	**11**	**3**	**1**	**4**	**0**
	NHL Totals		**249**	**73**	**86**	**159**	**71**	**25**	**4**	**3**	**7**	**6**

a WHL West First All-Star Team (1991)
b Canadian Major Junior Most Sportsmanlike Player of the Year (1991)
c Memorial Cup All-Star Team (1991)
d Won Stafford Smythe Memorial Trophy (Memorial Cup Tournament MVP) (1991)

FAUST, ANDRE — PHI.

Center. Shoots left. 5'11", 191 lbs. Born, Joliette, Que., October 7, 1969.
(New Jersey's 8th choice, 173rd overall, in 1989 Entry Draft).

			Regular Season					Playoffs				
Season	**Club**	**Lea**	**GP**	**G**	**A**	**TP**	**PIM**	**GP**	**G**	**A**	**TP**	**PIM**
1988-89	Princeton	ECAC	27	15	24	39	28	....	....	....	....	....
1989-90a	Princeton	ECAC	22	9	28	37	20	....	....	....	....	....
1990-91	Princeton	ECAC	26	15	22	37	51	....	....	....	....	....
1991-92a	Princeton	ECAC	27	14	21	35	38	....	....	....	....	....
1992-93	**Philadelphia**	**NHL**	**10**	**2**	**2**	**4**	**4**	....	....	....	....	....
	Hershey	AHL	62	26	25	51	71	....	....	....	....	....
1993-94	**Philadelphia**	**NHL**	**37**	**8**	**5**	**13**	**10**	....	....	....	....	....
	Hershey	AHL	13	6	7	13	10	10	4	3	7	26
1994-95	Hershey	AHL	55	12	28	40	72	6	1	5	6	12
	NHL Totals		**47**	**10**	**7**	**17**	**14**	....	....	....	....	....

a ECAC Second All-Star Team (1990, 1992)

Signed as a free agent by **Philadelphia**, October 5, 1992.

FEATHERSTONE, GLEN — HFD.

Defense. Shoots left. 6'4", 215 lbs. Born, Toronto, Ont., July 8, 1968.
(St. Louis' 4th choice, 73rd overall, in 1986 Entry Draft).

			Regular Season					Playoffs				
Season	**Club**	**Lea**	**GP**	**G**	**A**	**TP**	**PIM**	**GP**	**G**	**A**	**TP**	**PIM**
1985-86	Windsor	OHL	49	0	6	6	135	14	1	1	2	23
1986-87	Windsor	OHL	47	6	11	17	154	14	2	6	8	19
1987-88	Windsor	OHL	53	7	27	34	201	12	6	9	15	47
1988-89	**St. Louis**	**NHL**	**18**	**0**	**2**	**2**	**22**	**6**	**0**	**0**	**0**	**25**
	Peoria	IHL	37	5	19	24	97	....	....	....	....	....
1989-90	**St. Louis**	**NHL**	**58**	**0**	**12**	**12**	**145**	**12**	**0**	**2**	**2**	**47**
	Peoria	IHL	15	1	4	5	43	....	....	....	....	....
1990-91	**St. Louis**	**NHL**	**68**	**5**	**15**	**20**	**204**	**9**	**0**	**0**	**0**	**31**
1991-92	**Boston**	**NHL**	**7**	**1**	**0**	**1**	**20**	....	....	....	....	....
1992-93	**Boston**	**NHL**	**34**	**5**	**5**	**10**	**102**	....	....	....	....	....
	Providence	AHL	8	3	4	7	60	....	....	....	....	....
1993-94	**Boston**	**NHL**	**58**	**1**	**8**	**9**	**152**	**1**	**0**	**0**	**0**	**0**
1994-95	**NY Rangers**	**NHL**	**6**	**1**	**0**	**1**	**18**	....	....	....	....	....
	Hartford	**NHL**	**13**	**1**	**1**	**2**	**32**	....	....	....	....	....
	NHL Totals		**262**	**14**	**43**	**57**	**695**	**28**	**0**	**2**	**2**	**103**

Signed as a free agent by **Boston**, July 25, 1991. Traded to **NY Rangers** by **Boston** for Daniel Lacroix, August 19, 1994. Traded to **Hartford** by **NY Rangers** with Michael Stewart, NY Rangers' first round choice (Jean-Sebastien Giguere) in 1995 Entry Draft and fourth round choice in 1996 Entry Draft for Pat Verbeek, March 23, 1995.

FEDOROV, SERGEI — (FEH-duh-rahf) DET.

Center. Shoots left. 6'1", 200 lbs. Born, Pskov, USSR, December 13, 1969.
(Detroit's 4th choice, 74th overall, in 1989 Entry Draft).

			Regular Season					Playoffs				
Season	**Club**	**Lea**	**GP**	**G**	**A**	**TP**	**PIM**	**GP**	**G**	**A**	**TP**	**PIM**
1986-87	CSKA	USSR	29	6	6	12	12	....	....	....	....	....
1987-88	CSKA	USSR	48	7	9	16	20	....	....	....	....	....
1988-89	CSKA	USSR	44	9	8	17	35	....	....	....	....	....
1989-90	CSKA	USSR	48	19	10	29	22	....	....	....	....	....
1990-91a	**Detroit**	**NHL**	**77**	**31**	**48**	**79**	**66**	**7**	**1**	**5**	**6**	**4**
1991-92	**Detroit**	**NHL**	**80**	**32**	**54**	**86**	**72**	**11**	**5**	**5**	**10**	**8**
1992-93	**Detroit**	**NHL**	**73**	**34**	**53**	**87**	**72**	**7**	**3**	**6**	**9**	**23**
1993-94bcde	**Detroit**	**NHL**	**82**	**56**	**64**	**120**	**34**	**7**	**1**	**7**	**8**	**6**
1994-95	**Detroit**	**NHL**	**42**	**20**	**30**	**50**	**24**	**17**	**7**	***17**	***24**	**6**
	NHL Totals		**354**	**173**	**249**	**422**	**268**	**49**	**17**	**40**	**57**	**47**

a NHL/Upper Deck All-Rookie Team (1991)
b NHL First All-Star Team (1994)
c Won Frank J. Selke Trophy (1994)
d Won Lester B. Pearson Award (1994)
e Won Hart Trophy (1994)

Played in NHL All-Star Game (1992, 1994)

FEDOTOV, ANATOLI — (FEH-duh-tahf, AN-uh-TOH-lee)

Defense. Shoots left. 5'11", 178 lbs. Born, Saratov, USSR, May 11, 1966.
(Anaheim's 10th choice, 238th overall, in 1993 Entry Draft).

			Regular Season					Playoffs				
Season	**Club**	**Lea**	**GP**	**G**	**A**	**TP**	**PIM**	**GP**	**G**	**A**	**TP**	**PIM**
1985-86	Moscow D'amo	USSR	35	0	2	2	10	....	....	....	....	....
1986-87	Moscow D'amo	USSR	18	3	2	5	12	....	....	....	....	....
1987-88	Moscow D'amo	USSR	48	2	3	5	38	....	....	....	....	....
1988-89	Moscow D'amo	USSR	40	2	1	3	24	....	....	....	....	....
1989-90	Moscow D'amo	USSR	41	2	4	6	22	....	....	....	....	....
1990-91					DID NOT PLAY							
1991-92	Moscow D'amo	CIS	11	1	0	1	8	....	....	....	....	....
1992-93	**Winnipeg**	**NHL**	**1**	**0**	**2**	**2**	**0**	....	....	....	....	....
	Moncton	AHL	76	10	37	47	99	2	0	0	0	0
1993-94	**Anaheim**	**NHL**	**3**	**0**	**0**	**0**	**0**	....	....	....	....	....
	San Diego	IHL	66	14	12	26	42	8	0	1	1	6
1994-95	San Diego	IHL	53	5	12	17	16	....	....	....	....	....
	NHL Totals		**4**	**0**	**2**	**2**	**0**	....	....	....	....	....

FEDOTOV, SERGEI — HFD.

Defense. Shoots left. 6'1", 185 lbs. Born, Moscow, USSR, January 24, 1977.
(Hartford's 2nd choice, 35th overall, in 1995 Entry Draft).

			Regular Season					Playoffs				
Season	**Club**	**Lea**	**GP**	**G**	**A**	**TP**	**PIM**	**GP**	**G**	**A**	**TP**	**PIM**
1994-95	Moscow D'amo	CIS	8	0	0	0	2	....	....	....	....	....

FEDYK, BRENT — (FEH-dihk) PHI.

Left wing. Shoots right. 6', 195 lbs. Born, Yorkton, Sask., March 8, 1967.
(Detroit's 1st choice, 8th overall, in 1985 Entry Draft).

			Regular Season					Playoffs				
Season	**Club**	**Lea**	**GP**	**G**	**A**	**TP**	**PIM**	**GP**	**G**	**A**	**TP**	**PIM**
1983-84	Regina	WHL	63	15	28	43	30	23	8	7	15	6
1984-85	Regina	WHL	66	35	35	70	48	8	5	4	9	0
1985-86	Regina	WHL	50	43	34	77	47	5	0	1	1	0
1986-87	Regina	WHL	12	9	6	15	9	....	....	....	....	....
	Seattle	WHL	13	5	11	16	9	....	....	....	....	....
	Portland	WHL	11	5	4	9	6	14	5	6	11	0
1987-88	**Detroit**	**NHL**	**2**	**0**	**1**	**1**	**2**	....	....	....	....	....
	Adirondack	AHL	34	9	11	20	22	5	0	2	2	6
1988-89	**Detroit**	**NHL**	**5**	**2**	**0**	**2**	**0**	....	....	....	....	....
	Adirondack	AHL	66	40	28	68	33	15	7	8	15	23
1989-90	**Detroit**	**NHL**	**27**	**1**	**4**	**5**	**6**	....	....	....	....	....
	Adirondack	AHL	33	14	15	29	24	6	2	1	3	4
1990-91	**Detroit**	**NHL**	**67**	**16**	**19**	**35**	**38**	**6**	**1**	**0**	**1**	**2**
1991-92	**Detroit**	**NHL**	**61**	**5**	**8**	**13**	**42**	**1**	**0**	**0**	**0**	**2**
	Adirondack	AHL	1	0	2	2	0	....	....	....	....	....
1992-93	**Philadelphia**	**NHL**	**74**	**21**	**38**	**59**	**48**	....	....	....	....	....
1993-94	**Philadelphia**	**NHL**	**72**	**20**	**18**	**38**	**74**	....	....	....	....	....
1994-95	**Philadelphia**	**NHL**	**30**	**8**	**4**	**12**	**14**	**9**	**2**	**2**	**4**	**8**
	NHL Totals		**338**	**73**	**92**	**165**	**224**	**16**	**3**	**2**	**5**	**12**

Traded to **Philadelphia** by **Detroit** for Philadelphia's fourth round choice (later traded to Boston — Boston selected Charles Paquette) in 1993 Entry Draft, October 1, 1992.

FELSNER, DENNY

Left wing. Shoots left. 6', 195 lbs. Born, Warren, MI, April 29, 1970.
(St. Louis' 3rd choice, 55th overall, in 1989 Entry Draft).

			Regular Season					Playoffs				
Season	**Club**	**Lea**	**GP**	**G**	**A**	**TP**	**PIM**	**GP**	**G**	**A**	**TP**	**PIM**
1988-89	U. of Michigan	CCHA	39	30	19	49	22	....	....	....	....	....
1989-90	U. of Michigan	CCHA	33	27	16	43	24	....	....	....	....	....
1990-91ab	U. of Michigan	CCHA	46	*40	35	75	58	....	....	....	....	....
1991-92ac	U. of Michigan	CCHA	44	42	52	94	46	....	....	....	....	....
	St. Louis	**NHL**	**3**	**0**	**1**	**1**	**0**	**1**	**0**	**0**	**0**	**0**
1992-93	**St. Louis**	**NHL**	**6**	**0**	**3**	**3**	**2**	**9**	**2**	**3**	**5**	**2**
	Peoria	IHL	29	14	21	35	8	....	....	....	....	....
1993-94	**St. Louis**	**NHL**	**6**	**1**	**0**	**1**	**2**	....	....	....	....	....
	Peoria	IHL	6	8	3	11	14	....	....	....	....	....
1994-95	Peoria	IHL	25	10	12	22	14	8	2	3	5	0
	St. Louis	**NHL**	**3**	**0**	**0**	**0**	**2**	....	....	....	....	....
	NHL Totals		**18**	**1**	**4**	**5**	**6**	**10**	**2**	**3**	**5**	**2**

a CCHA First All-Star Team (1991, 1992)
b NCAA West Second All-American Team (1991)
c NCAA West First All-American Team (1992)

FERGUSON, CRAIG — MTL.

Right wing. Shoots left. 5'11", 190 lbs. Born, Castro Valley, CA, April 8, 1970.
(Montreal's 7th choice, 146th overall, in 1989 Entry Draft).

			Regular Season					Playoffs				
Season	**Club**	**Lea**	**GP**	**G**	**A**	**TP**	**PIM**	**GP**	**G**	**A**	**TP**	**PIM**
1988-89	Yale	ECAC	24	11	6	17	20	....	....	....	....	....
1989-90	Yale	ECAC	28	6	13	19	36	....	....	....	....	....
1990-91	Yale	ECAC	29	11	10	21	34	....	....	....	....	....
1991-92	Yale	ECAC	27	9	16	25	26	....	....	....	....	....
1992-93	Fredericton	AHL	55	15	13	28	20	5	0	1	1	2
	Wheeling	ECHL	9	6	5	11	24	....	....	....	....	....
1993-94	**Montreal**	**NHL**	**2**	**0**	**1**	**1**	**0**	....	....	....	....	....
	Fredericton	AHL	57	29	32	61	60	....	....	....	....	....
1994-95	Fredericton	AHL	80	27	35	62	62	17	6	2	8	6
	Montreal	**NHL**	**1**	**0**	**0**	**0**	**0**	....	....	....	....	....
	NHL Totals		**3**	**0**	**1**	**1**	**0**	....	....	....	....	....

FERGUSON, KYLE — TOR.

Right wing. Shoots right. 6'3", 215 lbs. Born, Toronto, Ont., August 12, 1973.
(Toronto's 7th choice, 253rd overall, in 1993 Entry Draft).

			Regular Season					Playoffs				
Season	**Club**	**Lea**	**GP**	**G**	**A**	**TP**	**PIM**	**GP**	**G**	**A**	**TP**	**PIM**
1992-93	Michigan Tech	WCHA	31	9	5	14	74	....	....	....	....	....
1993-94	Michigan Tech	WCHA	36	4	5	9	63	....	....	....	....	....
1994-95	Michigan Tech	WCHA	3	1	1	2	2	....	....	....	....	....

FERGUSON, SCOTT — EDM.

Defense. Shoots left. 6'1", 195 lbs. Born, Camrose, Alta., January 6, 1973.

			Regular Season					Playoffs				
Season	**Club**	**Lea**	**GP**	**G**	**A**	**TP**	**PIM**	**GP**	**G**	**A**	**TP**	**PIM**
1990-91	Kamloops	WHL	4	0	0	0	0	....	....	....	....	....
1991-92	Kamloops	WHL	62	4	10	14	138	12	0	2	2	21
1992-93	Kamloops	WHL	71	4	19	23	206	13	0	2	2	24
1993-94a	Kamloops	WHL	68	5	49	54	180	19	5	11	16	48
1994-95	Cape Breton	AHL	58	4	6	10	103	....	....	....	....	....
	Wheeling	ECHL	5	1	5	6	16	....	....	....	....	....

a WHL West Second All-Star Team (1994)

Signed as a free agent by **Edmonton**, June 2, 1994.

FERNER, MARK

Defense. Shoots left. 6', 193 lbs. Born, Regina, Sask., September 5, 1965.
(Buffalo's 12th choice, 194th overall, in 1983 Entry Draft).

			Regular Season					Playoffs				
Season	Club	Lea	GP	G	A	TP	PIM	GP	G	A	TP	PIM
1982-83	Kamloops	WHL	69	6	15	21	81	7	0	0	0	7
1983-84	Kamloops	WHL	72	9	30	39	169	14	1	8	9	20
1984-85a	Kamloops	WHL	69	15	39	54	91	15	4	9	13	21
1985-86	Rochester	AHL	63	3	14	17	87	....	....	....	....	....
1986-87	**Buffalo**	**NHL**	**13**	**0**	**3**	**3**	**9**	....	....	....	....	....
	Rochester	AHL	54	0	12	12	157	....	....	....	....	....
1987-88	Rochester	AHL	69	1	25	26	165	7	1	4	5	31
1988-89	**Buffalo**	**NHL**	**2**	**0**	**0**	**0**	**2**	....	....	....	....	....
	Rochester	AHL	55	0	18	18	97	....	....	....	....	....
1989-90	**Washington**	**NHL**	**2**	**0**	**0**	**0**	**0**	....	....	....	....	....
	Baltimore	AHL	74	7	28	35	76	11	1	2	3	21
1990-91	**Washington**	**NHL**	**7**	**0**	**1**	**1**	**4**	....	....	....	....	....
b	Baltimore	AHL	61	14	40	54	38	6	1	4	5	24
1991-92	Baltimore	AHL	57	7	38	45	67	....	....	....	....	....
	St. John's	AHL	15	1	8	9	6	14	2	14	16	38
1992-93	New Haven	AHL	34	5	7	12	69	....	....	....	....	....
	San Diego	IHL	26	0	15	15	34	11	1	2	3	8
1993-94	**Anaheim**	**NHL**	**50**	**3**	**5**	**8**	**30**	....	....	....	....	....
1994-95	San Diego	IHL	46	3	12	15	51	....	....	....	....	....
	Anaheim	**NHL**	**14**	**0**	**1**	**1**	**6**	....	....	....	....	....
	Detroit	**NHL**	**3**	**0**	**0**	**0**	**0**	....	....	....	....	....
	Adirondack	AHL	3	0	0	0	2	1	0	0	0	0
	NHL Totals		**91**	**3**	**10**	**13**	**51**	....	....	....	....	....

a WHL West First All-Star Team (1985)
b AHL Second All-Star Team (1991)

Traded to **Washington** by **Buffalo** for Scott McCrory, June 1, 1989. Traded to **Toronto** by **Washington** for future considerations, February 27, 1992. Signed as a free agent by **Ottawa**, August 6, 1992. Claimed by **Anaheim** from **Ottawa** in Expansion Draft, June 24, 1993. Traded to **Detroit** by **Anaheim** with Stu Grimson and Anaheim's sixth round choice in 1996 Entry Draft for Mike Sillinger and Jason York, April 4, 1995.

FERRARO, CHRIS — NYR

Right wing. Shoots right. 5'10", 175 lbs. Born, Port Jefferson, NY, January 24, 1973.
(NY Rangers' 4th choice, 85th overall, in 1992 Entry Draft).

			Regular Season					Playoffs				
Season	Club	Lea	GP	G	A	TP	PIM	GP	G	A	TP	PIM
1992-93	U. of Maine	H.E.	39	25	26	51	46	....	....	....	....	....
1993-94	U. of Maine	H.E.	4	0	1	1	8	....	....	....	....	....
	U.S. National	....	48	8	34	42	58	....	....	....	....	....
1994-95	Atlanta	IHL	54	13	14	27	72	....	....	....	....	....
	Binghamton	AHL	13	6	4	10	38	10	2	3	5	16

FERRARO, PETER — NYR

Center. Shoots right. 5'10", 175 lbs. Born, Port Jefferson, NY, January 24, 1973.
(NY Rangers' 1st choice, 24th overall, in 1992 Entry Draft).

			Regular Season					Playoffs				
Season	Club	Lea	GP	G	A	TP	PIM	GP	G	A	TP	PIM
1992-93	U. of Maine	H.E.	36	18	32	50	106	....	....	....	....	....
1993-94	U. of Maine	H.E.	4	3	6	9	16	....	....	....	....	....
	U.S. National	....	60	30	34	64	87	....	....	....	....	....
	U.S. Olympic	....	8	6	0	6	6	....	....	....	....	....
1994-95	Atlanta	IHL	61	15	24	39	118	....	....	....	....	....
	Binghamton	AHL	12	2	6	8	67	11	4	3	7	51

FERRARO, RAY — NYR

Center. Shoots left. 5'10", 185 lbs. Born, Trail, B.C., August 23, 1964.
(Hartford's 5th choice, 88th overall, in 1982 Entry Draft).

			Regular Season					Playoffs				
Season	Club	Lea	GP	G	A	TP	PIM	GP	G	A	TP	PIM
1982-83	Portland	WHL	50	41	49	90	39	14	14	10	24	13
1983-84a	Brandon	WHL	72	*108	84	*192	84	11	13	15	28	20
1984-85	**Hartford**	**NHL**	**44**	**11**	**17**	**28**	**40**	....	....	....	....	....
	Binghamton	AHL	37	20	13	33	29	....	....	....	....	....
1985-86	**Hartford**	**NHL**	**76**	**30**	**47**	**77**	**57**	**10**	**3**	**6**	**9**	**4**
1986-87	**Hartford**	**NHL**	**80**	**27**	**32**	**59**	**42**	**6**	**1**	**1**	**2**	**8**
1987-88	**Hartford**	**NHL**	**68**	**21**	**29**	**50**	**81**	**6**	**1**	**1**	**2**	**6**
1988-89	**Hartford**	**NHL**	**80**	**41**	**35**	**76**	**86**	**4**	**2**	**0**	**2**	**4**
1989-90	**Hartford**	**NHL**	**79**	**25**	**29**	**54**	**109**	**7**	**0**	**3**	**3**	**2**
1990-91	**Hartford**	**NHL**	**15**	**2**	**5**	**7**	**18**	....	....	....	....	....
	NY Islanders	**NHL**	**61**	**19**	**16**	**35**	**52**	....	....	....	....	....
1991-92	**NY Islanders**	**NHL**	**80**	**40**	**40**	**80**	**92**	....	....	....	....	....
1992-93	**NY Islanders**	**NHL**	**46**	**14**	**13**	**27**	**40**	**18**	**13**	**7**	**20**	**18**
	Capital Dist.	AHL	1	0	2	2	2	....	....	....	....	....
1993-94	**NY Islanders**	**NHL**	**82**	**21**	**32**	**53**	**83**	**4**	**1**	**0**	**1**	**6**
1994-95	**NY Islanders**	**NHL**	**47**	**22**	**21**	**43**	**30**	....	....	....	....	....
	NHL Totals		**758**	**273**	**316**	**589**	**730**	**55**	**21**	**18**	**39**	**48**

a WHL First All-Star Team (1984)

Played in NHL All-Star Game (1992)

Traded to **NY Islanders** by **Hartford** for Doug Crossman, November 13, 1990. Signed as a free agent by **NY Rangers**, August 9, 1995.

FETISOV, VIACHESLAV — (feh-TEE-sahf) DET.

Defense. Shoots left. 6'1", 220 lbs. Born, Moscow, USSR, April 20, 1958.
(New Jersey's 6th choice, 150th overall, in 1983 Entry Draft).

			Regular Season					Playoffs				
Season	Club	Lea	GP	G	A	TP	PIM	GP	G	A	TP	PIM
1974-75	CSKA	USSR	1	0	0	0	0	....	....	....	....	....
1976-77	CSKA	USSR	28	3	4	7	14	....	....	....	....	....
1977-78a	CSKA	USSR	35	9	18	27	46	....	....	....	....	....
1978-79	CSKA	USSR	29	10	19	29	40	....	....	....	....	....
1979-80	CSKA	USSR	37	10	14	24	46	....	....	....	....	....
1980-81	CSKA	USSR	48	13	16	29	44	....	....	....	....	....
1981-82ac	CSKA	USSR	46	15	26	41	20	....	....	....	....	....
1982-83a	CSKA	USSR	43	6	17	23	46	....	....	....	....	....
1983-84ab	CSKA	USSR	44	19	30	49	38	....	....	....	....	....
1984-85a	CSKA	USSR	20	13	12	25	6	....	....	....	....	....
1985-86abc	CSKA	USSR	40	15	19	34	12	....	....	....	....	....
1986-87ab	CSKA	USSR	39	13	20	33	18	....	....	....	....	....
1987-88ab	CSKA	USSR	46	18	17	35	26	....	....	....	....	....
1988-89	CSKA	USSR	23	9	8	17	18	....	....	....	....	....
1989-90	**New Jersey**	**NHL**	**72**	**8**	**34**	**42**	**52**	**6**	**0**	**2**	**2**	**10**
1990-91	**New Jersey**	**NHL**	**67**	**3**	**16**	**19**	**62**	**7**	**0**	**0**	**0**	**17**
	Utica	AHL	1	1	1	2	0	....	....	....	....	....
1991-92	**New Jersey**	**NHL**	**70**	**3**	**23**	**26**	**108**	**6**	**0**	**3**	**3**	**8**
1992-93	**New Jersey**	**NHL**	**76**	**4**	**23**	**27**	**158**	**5**	**0**	**2**	**2**	**4**
1993-94	**New Jersey**	**NHL**	**52**	**1**	**14**	**15**	**30**	**14**	**1**	**0**	**1**	**8**
1994-95	**New Jersey**	**NHL**	**4**	**0**	**1**	**1**	**0**	....	....	....	....	....
1994-95	Spartak	CIS	1	0	1	1	4	....	....	....	....	....
	Detroit	**NHL**	**14**	**3**	**11**	**14**	**2**	**18**	**0**	**8**	**8**	**14**
	NHL Totals		**355**	**22**	**122**	**144**	**412**	**56**	**1**	**15**	**16**	**61**

a Soviet National League All-Star Team (1979, 1980, 1982-88)
b Leningradskaya-Pravda Trophy (Top Scoring Defenseman) (1984, 1986-88)
c Soviet Player of the Year (1982, 1986, 1988)

Traded to **Detroit** by **New Jersey** for Detroit's third round choice (David Gosselin) in 1995 Entry Draft, April 3, 1995.

FIEBELKORN, JED — ST.L.

Right wing. Shoots right. 6'3", 220 lbs. Born, Minneapolis, MN, September 1, 1972.
(St. Louis' 9th choice, 197th overall, in 1991 Entry Draft).

			Regular Season					Playoffs				
Season	Club	Lea	GP	G	A	TP	PIM	GP	G	A	TP	PIM
1991-92	U. Minnesota	WCHA	7	0	0	0	10	....	....	....	....	....
1992-93	U. Minnesota	WCHA	34	8	5	13	42	....	....	....	....	....
1993-94	U. Minnesota	WCHA	39	5	6	11	65	....	....	....	....	....
1994-95	U. Minnesota	WCHA	40	4	9	13	119	....	....	....	....	....

FILATOV, ANATOLI — (fih-LAH-tohv) S.J.

Right wing. Shoots right. 5'10", 195 lbs. Born, Kamenogorsk, USSR, April 28, 1975.
(San Jose's 9th choice, 158th overall, in 1993 Entry Draft).

			Regular Season					Playoffs				
Season	Club	Lea	GP	G	A	TP	PIM	GP	G	A	TP	PIM
1992-93	Kamenogorsk	CIS	17	4	0	4	14	....	....	....	....	....
1993-94	Kamenogorsk	CIS	20	3	3	6	22	....	....	....	....	....
1994-95	Torpedo Ust	CIS	33	6	6	12	30	....	....	....	....	....
	Niagara Falls	OHL	12	2	3	5	6	....	....	....	....	....

FILIMONOV, DMITRI — (fih-lih-MAHN-ahf)

Defense. Shoots right. 6'4", 220 lbs. Born, Perm, USSR, October 14, 1971.
(Winnipeg's 2nd choice, 49th overall, in 1991 Entry Draft).

			Regular Season					Playoffs				
Season	Club	Lea	GP	G	A	TP	PIM	GP	G	A	TP	PIM
1990-91	Moscow D'amo	USSR	45	4	6	10	12	....	....	....	....	....
1991-92	Moscow D'amo	CIS	38	3	2	5	12	....	....	....	....	....
1992-93	Moscow D'amo	CIS	42	2	3	5	30	10	1	2	3	2
1993-94	**Ottawa**	**NHL**	**30**	**1**	**4**	**5**	**18**	....	....	....	....	....
	P.E.I.	AHL	48	10	16	26	14	....	....	....	....	....
1994-95	P.E.I.	AHL	32	6	19	25	14	9	0	1	1	2
	NHL Totals		**30**	**1**	**4**	**5**	**18**	....	....	....	....	....

Rights traded to **Ottawa** by **Winnipeg** for Ottawa's fourth round choice (Ruslam Batyrshin) in 1993 Entry Draft, March 14, 1993.

FINLEY, JEFF — WPG.

Defense. Shoots left. 6'2", 204 lbs. Born, Edmonton, Alta., April 14, 1967.
(NY Islanders' 4th choice, 55th overall, in 1985 Entry Draft).

			Regular Season					Playoffs				
Season	Club	Lea	GP	G	A	TP	PIM	GP	G	A	TP	PIM
1983-84	Portland	WHL	5	0	0	0	5	5	0	1	1	4
1984-85	Portland	WHL	69	6	44	50	57	6	1	2	3	2
1985-86	Portland	WHL	70	11	59	70	83	15	1	7	8	16
1986-87	Portland	WHL	72	13	53	66	113	20	1	*21	22	27
1987-88	**NY Islanders**	**NHL**	**10**	**0**	**5**	**5**	**15**	**1**	**0**	**0**	**0**	**2**
	Springfield	AHL	52	5	18	23	50	....	....	....	....	....
1988-89	**NY Islanders**	**NHL**	**4**	**0**	**0**	**0**	**6**	....	....	....	....	....
	Springfield	AHL	65	3	16	19	55	....	....	....	....	....
1989-90	**NY Islanders**	**NHL**	**11**	**0**	**1**	**1**	**0**	**5**	**0**	**2**	**2**	**2**
	Springfield	AHL	57	1	15	16	41	13	1	4	5	23
1990-91	**NY Islanders**	**NHL**	**11**	**0**	**0**	**0**	**4**	....	....	....	....	....
	Capital Dist.	AHL	67	10	34	44	34	....	....	....	....	....
1991-92	**NY Islanders**	**NHL**	**51**	**1**	**10**	**11**	**26**	....	....	....	....	....
	Capital Dist.	AHL	20	1	9	10	6	....	....	....	....	....
1992-93	Capital Dist.	AHL	61	6	29	35	34	4	0	1	1	0
1993-94	**Philadelphia**	**NHL**	**55**	**1**	**8**	**9**	**24**	....	....	....	....	....
1994-95	Hershey	AHL	36	2	9	11	33	6	0	1	1	8
	NHL Totals		**142**	**2**	**24**	**26**	**75**	**6**	**0**	**2**	**2**	**4**

Traded to **Ottawa** by **NY Islanders** for Chris Luongo, June 30, 1993. Signed as a free agent by **Philadelphia**, July 30, 1993. Traded to **Winnipeg** by **Philadelphia** for Russ Romaniuk, June 27, 1995.

FINN, SHANNON

Defense. Shoots left. 6'2", 190 lbs. Born, Brampton, Ont., January 25, 1972.
(Philadelphia's 1st choice, 10th overall, in 1993 Supplemental Draft).

			Regular Season					Playoffs				
Season	Club	Lea	GP	G	A	TP	PIM	GP	G	A	TP	PIM
1991-92	Ill.-Chicago	CCHA	36	6	14	20	80	....	....	....	....	....
1992-93	Ill.-Chicago	CCHA	36	6	13	19	48	....	....	....	....	....
1993-94	Ill.-Chicago	CCHA	39	5	22	27	42	....	....	....	....	....
1994-95	Ill.-Chicago	CCHA	37	9	24	33	40	....	....	....	....	....
	Cdn. National	....	9	0	2	2	2	....	....	....	....	....
	Minnesota	IHL	3	0	2	2	6	....	....	....	....	....

FINN, STEVEN — COL.

Defense. Shoots left. 6', 191 lbs. Born, Laval, Que., August 20, 1966.
(Quebec's 3rd choice, 57th overall, in 1984 Entry Draft).

			Regular Season					Playoffs				
Season	Club	Lea	GP	G	A	TP	PIM	GP	G	A	TP	PIM
1982-83	Laval	QMJHL	69	7	30	37	108	6	0	2	2	6
1983-84	Laval	QMJHL	68	7	39	46	159	14	1	6	7	27
1984-85a	Laval	QMJHL	61	20	33	53	169	....	....	....	....	....
	Fredericton	AHL	4	0	0	0	14	6	1	1	2	4
1985-86	**Quebec**	**NHL**	**17**	**0**	**1**	**1**	**28**	....	....	....	....	....
	Laval	QMJHL	29	4	15	19	111	14	6	16	22	57
1986-87	**Quebec**	**NHL**	**36**	**2**	**5**	**7**	**40**	**13**	**0**	**2**	**2**	**29**
	Fredericton	AHL	38	7	19	26	73	....	....	....	....	....
1987-88	**Quebec**	**NHL**	**75**	**3**	**7**	**10**	**198**	....	....	....	....	....
1988-89	**Quebec**	**NHL**	**77**	**2**	**6**	**8**	**235**	....	....	....	....	....
1989-90	**Quebec**	**NHL**	**64**	**3**	**9**	**12**	**208**	....	....	....	....	....
1990-91	**Quebec**	**NHL**	**71**	**6**	**13**	**19**	**228**	....	....	....	....	....
1991-92	**Quebec**	**NHL**	**65**	**4**	**7**	**11**	**194**	....	....	....	....	....
1992-93	**Quebec**	**NHL**	**80**	**5**	**9**	**14**	**160**	**6**	**0**	**1**	**1**	**8**
1993-94	**Quebec**	**NHL**	**80**	**4**	**13**	**17**	**159**	....	....	....	....	....
1994-95	**Quebec**	**NHL**	**40**	**0**	**3**	**3**	**64**	**4**	**0**	**1**	**1**	**2**
	NHL Totals		**605**	**29**	**73**	**102**	**1514**	**23**	**0**	**4**	**4**	**39**

a QMJHL Second All-Star Team (1985)

FINNSTROM, JOHAN (FIHN-struhm) — CGY.

Defense. Shoots left. 6'3", 205 lbs. Born, Broby, Sweden, March 27, 1976.
(Calgary's 5th choice, 97th overall, in 1994 Entry Draft).

			Regular Season					Playoffs				
Season	Club	Lea	GP	G	A	TP	PIM	GP	G	A	TP	PIM
1993-94	Rogle	Swe.	7	1	1	2	2	....	....	....	....	....
1994-95	Rogle	Swe.	19	0	0	0	10	....	....	....	....	....

FIORENTINO, PETER

Defense. Shoots right. 6'1", 205 lbs. Born, Niagara Falls, Ont., December 22, 1968.
(NY Rangers' 11th choice, 215th overall, in 1988 Entry Draft).

			Regular Season					Playoffs				
Season	Club	Lea	GP	G	A	TP	PIM	GP	G	A	TP	PIM
1985-86	S.S. Marie	OHL	58	1	6	7	87	....	....	....	....	....
1986-87	S.S. Marie	OHL	64	1	12	13	187	....	....	....	....	....
1987-88	S.S. Marie	OHL	65	5	27	32	252	6	2	2	4	21
1988-89	S.S. Marie	OHL	55	5	24	29	220	....	....	....	....	....
	Denver	IHL	10	0	0	0	39	4	0	0	0	24
1989-90	Flint	IHL	64	2	7	9	302	....	....	....	....	....
1990-91	Binghamton	AHL	55	2	11	13	361	1	0	0	0	0
1991-92	**NY Rangers**	**NHL**	**1**	**0**	**0**	**0**	**0**	....	....	....	....	....
	Binghamton	AHL	70	2	11	13	340	5	0	1	1	24
1992-93	Binghamton	AHL	64	9	5	14	286	13	0	3	3	22
1993-94	Binghamton	AHL	68	7	15	22	220	....	....	....	....	....
1994-95	Binghamton	AHL	66	9	16	25	183	2	0	1	1	11
	NHL Totals		**1**	**0**	**0**	**0**	**0**	....	....	....	....	....

FISHER, CRAIG

Center. Shoots left. 6'3", 180 lbs. Born, Oshawa, Ont., June 30, 1970.
(Philadelphia's 3rd choice, 56th overall, in 1988 Entry Draft).

			Regular Season					Playoffs				
Season	Club	Lea	GP	G	A	TP	PIM	GP	G	A	TP	PIM
1988-89	Miami-Ohio	CCHA	37	22	20	42	37	....	....	....	....	....
1989-90a	Miami-Ohio	CCHA	39	37	29	66	38	....	....	....	....	....
	Philadelphia	**NHL**	**2**	**0**	**0**	**0**	**0**	....	....	....	....	....
1990-91	**Philadelphia**	**NHL**	**2**	**0**	**0**	**0**	**0**	....	....	....	....	....
	Hershey	AHL	77	43	36	79	46	7	5	3	8	2
1991-92	Cape Breton	AHL	60	20	25	45	28	1	0	0	0	0
1992-93	Cape Breton	AHL	75	32	29	61	74	1	0	0	0	2
1993-94	Cape Breton	AHL	16	5	5	10	11	....	....	....	....	....
	Winnipeg	**NHL**	**4**	**0**	**0**	**0**	**2**	....	....	....	....	....
	Moncton	AHL	46	26	35	61	36	21	11	11	22	28
1994-95	Indianapolis	IHL	77	53	40	93	65	....	....	....	....	....
	NHL Totals		**8**	**0**	**0**	**0**	**2**	....	....	....	....	....

a CCHA First All-Star Team (1990)

Traded to **Edmonton** by **Philadelphia** with Scott Mellanby and Craig Berube for Dave Brown, Corey Foster and Jari Kurri, May 30, 1991. Traded to **Winnipeg** by **Edmonton** for cash, December 9, 1993. Signed as a free agent by **Chicago**, June 9, 1994.

FITZGERALD, RUSTY — PIT.

Center. Shoots left. 6'1", 190 lbs. Born, Minneapolis, MN, October 4, 1972.
(Pittsburgh's 2nd choice, 38th overall, in 1991 Entry Draft).

			Regular Season					Playoffs				
Season	Club	Lea	GP	G	A	TP	PIM	GP	G	A	TP	PIM
1991-92	Minn.-Duluth	WCHA	37	9	11	20	40	....	....	....	....	....
1992-93	Minn.-Duluth	WCHA	39	24	23	47	48	....	....	....	....	....
1993-94	Minn.-Duluth	WCHA	37	11	25	36	59	....	....	....	....	....
1994-95	Minn.-Duluth	WCHA	34	16	22	38	50	....	....	....	....	....
	Cleveland	IHL	2	0	1	1	0	3	3	0	3	6
	Pittsburgh	**NHL**	**4**	**1**	**0**	**1**	**0**	**5**	**0**	**0**	**0**	**4**
	NHL Totals		**4**	**1**	**0**	**1**	**0**	**5**	**0**	**0**	**0**	**4**

FITZGERALD, TOM — FLA.

Right wing/Center. Shoots right. 6'1", 191 lbs. Born, Melrose, MA, August 28, 1968.
(NY Islanders' 1st choice, 17th overall, in 1986 Entry Draft).

			Regular Season					Playoffs				
Season	Club	Lea	GP	G	A	TP	PIM	GP	G	A	TP	PIM
1986-87	Providence	H.E.	27	8	14	22	22	....	....	....	....	....
1987-88	Providence	H.E.	36	19	15	34	50	....	....	....	....	....
1988-89	**NY Islanders**	**NHL**	**23**	**3**	**5**	**8**	**10**	....	....	....	....	....
	Springfield	AHL	61	24	18	42	43	....	....	....	....	....
1989-90	**NY Islanders**	**NHL**	**19**	**2**	**5**	**7**	**4**	**4**	**1**	**0**	**1**	**4**
	Springfield	AHL	53	30	23	53	32	14	2	9	11	13
1990-91	**NY Islanders**	**NHL**	**41**	**5**	**5**	**10**	**24**	....	....	....	....	....
	Capital Dist.	AHL	27	7	7	14	50	....	....	....	....	....
1991-92	**NY Islanders**	**NHL**	**45**	**6**	**11**	**17**	**28**	....	....	....	....	....
	Capital Dist.	AHL	4	1	1	2	4	....	....	....	....	....
1992-93	**NY Islanders**	**NHL**	**77**	**9**	**18**	**27**	**34**	**18**	**2**	**5**	**7**	**18**
1993-94	**Florida**	**NHL**	**83**	**18**	**14**	**32**	**54**	....	....	....	....	....
1994-95	**Florida**	**NHL**	**48**	**3**	**13**	**16**	**31**	....	....	....	....	....
	NHL Totals		**336**	**46**	**71**	**117**	**185**	**22**	**3**	**5**	**8**	**22**

Claimed by **Florida** from **NY Islanders** in Expansion Draft, June 24, 1993.

FITZPATRICK, RORY — MTL.

Defense. Shoots right. 6'1", 195 lbs. Born, Rochester, NY, January 11, 1975.
(Montreal's 2nd choice, 47th overall, in 1993 Entry Draft).

			Regular Season					Playoffs				
Season	Club	Lea	GP	G	A	TP	PIM	GP	G	A	TP	PIM
1992-93	Sudbury	OHL	58	4	20	24	68	14	0	0	0	17
1993-94	Sudbury	OHL	65	12	34	46	112	10	2	5	7	10
1994-95	Sudbury	OHL	56	12	36	48	72	18	3	15	18	21
	Fredericton	AHL	....	....	....	....	....	10	1	2	3	5

FLATLEY, PAT (FLAT-lee) — NYI

Right wing. Shoots right. 6'2", 197 lbs. Born, Toronto, Ont., October 3, 1963.
(NY Islanders' 1st choice, 21st overall, in 1982 Entry Draft).

			Regular Season					Playoffs				
Season	Club	Lea	GP	G	A	TP	PIM	GP	G	A	TP	PIM
1981-82	U. Wisconsin	WCHA	17	10	9	19	40	....	....	....	....	....
1982-83ab	U. Wisconsin	WCHA	26	17	24	41	48	....	....	....	....	....
1983-84	Cdn. National	....	57	31	17	48	136	....	....	....	....	....
	Cdn. Olympic	....	7	3	3	6	70	....	....	....	....	....
	NY Islanders	**NHL**	**16**	**2**	**7**	**9**	**6**	**21**	**9**	**6**	**15**	**14**
1984-85	**NY Islanders**	**NHL**	**78**	**20**	**31**	**51**	**106**	**4**	**1**	**0**	**1**	**6**
1985-86	**NY Islanders**	**NHL**	**73**	**18**	**34**	**52**	**66**	**3**	**0**	**0**	**0**	**21**
1986-87	**NY Islanders**	**NHL**	**63**	**16**	**35**	**51**	**81**	**11**	**3**	**2**	**5**	**6**
1987-88	**NY Islanders**	**NHL**	**40**	**9**	**15**	**24**	**28**	....	....	....	....	....
1988-89	**NY Islanders**	**NHL**	**41**	**10**	**15**	**25**	**31**	....	....	....	....	....
	Springfield	AHL	2	1	1	2	2	....	....	....	....	....
1989-90	**NY Islanders**	**NHL**	**62**	**17**	**32**	**49**	**101**	**5**	**3**	**0**	**3**	**2**
1990-91	**NY Islanders**	**NHL**	**56**	**20**	**25**	**45**	**74**	....	....	....	....	....
1991-92	**NY Islanders**	**NHL**	**38**	**8**	**28**	**36**	**31**	....	....	....	....	....
1992-93	**NY Islanders**	**NHL**	**80**	**13**	**47**	**60**	**63**	**15**	**2**	**7**	**9**	**12**
1993-94	**NY Islanders**	**NHL**	**64**	**12**	**30**	**42**	**40**	....	....	....	....	....
1994-95	**NY Islanders**	**NHL**	**45**	**7**	**20**	**27**	**12**	....	....	....	....	....
	NHL Totals		**656**	**152**	**319**	**471**	**639**	**59**	**18**	**15**	**33**	**61**

a WCHA First All-Star Team (1983)
b Named to NCAA All-Tournament Team (1983)

FLEMING, GERRY — MTL.

Left wing. Shoots left. 6'5", 253 lbs. Born, Montreal, Que., October 16, 1967.

			Regular Season					Playoffs				
Season	Club	Lea	GP	G	A	TP	PIM	GP	G	A	TP	PIM
1990-91	U.P.E.I.	AUAA				UNAVAILABLE						
1991-92	Charlottetown	Sr.				UNAVAILABLE						
	Fredericton	AHL	37	4	6	10	133	1	0	0	0	7
1992-93	Fredericton	AHL	64	9	17	26	262	5	1	2	3	14
1993-94	**Montreal**	**NHL**	**5**	**0**	**0**	**0**	**25**	....	....	....	....	....
	Fredericton	AHL	46	6	16	22	188	....	....	....	....	....
1994-95	Fredericton	AHL	16	3	3	6	60	10	2	0	2	67
	Montreal	**NHL**	**6**	**0**	**0**	**0**	**17**	....	....	....	....	....
	NHL Totals		**11**	**0**	**0**	**0**	**42**	....	....	....	....	....

Signed as a free agent by **Montreal**, February 17, 1992.

FLEURY, THEOREN (FLUH-ree, THAIR-ihn) — CGY.

Right wing. Shoots right. 5'6", 160 lbs. Born, Oxbow, Sask., June 29, 1968.
(Calgary's 9th choice, 166th overall, in 1987 Entry Draft).

			Regular Season					Playoffs				
Season	Club	Lea	GP	G	A	TP	PIM	GP	G	A	TP	PIM
1984-85	Moose Jaw	WHL	71	29	46	75	82	....	....	....	....	....
1985-86	Moose Jaw	WHL	72	43	65	108	124	....	....	....	....	....
1986-87	Moose Jaw	WHL	66	61	68	129	110	9	7	9	16	34
1987-88	Moose Jaw	WHL	65	68	92	*160	235	....	....	....	....	....
	Salt Lake	IHL	2	3	4	7	7	8	11	5	16	16
1988-89	**Calgary**	**NHL**	**36**	**14**	**20**	**34**	**46**	**22**	**5**	**6**	**11**	**24**
	Salt Lake	IHL	40	37	37	74	81	....	....	....	....	....
1989-90	**Calgary**	**NHL**	**80**	**31**	**35**	**66**	**157**	**6**	**2**	**3**	**5**	**10**
1990-91a	**Calgary**	**NHL**	**79**	**51**	**53**	**104**	**136**	**7**	**2**	**5**	**7**	**14**
1991-92	**Calgary**	**NHL**	**80**	**33**	**40**	**73**	**133**	....	....	....	....	....
1992-93	**Calgary**	**NHL**	**83**	**34**	**66**	**100**	**88**	**6**	**5**	**7**	**12**	**27**
1993-94	**Calgary**	**NHL**	**83**	**40**	**45**	**85**	**186**	**7**	**6**	**4**	**10**	**5**
1994-95	Tappara	Fin.	10	8	9	17	22	....	....	....	....	....
b	**Calgary**	**NHL**	**47**	**29**	**29**	**58**	**112**	**7**	**7**	**7**	**14**	**2**
	NHL Totals		**488**	**232**	**288**	**520**	**858**	**55**	**27**	**32**	**59**	**82**

a Co-winner of Alka-Seltzer Plus Award with Marty McSorley (1991)
b NHL Second All-Star Team (1995)
Played in NHL All-Star Game (1991, 1992)

FLICHEL, MARTY (FLIGH-shuhl) — DAL.

Right wing. Shoots left. 5'11", 175 lbs. Born, Hodgeville, Sask., March 6, 1976.
(Dallas' 6th choice, 228th overall, in 1994 Entry Draft).

			Regular Season					Playoffs				
Season	Club	Lea	GP	G	A	TP	PIM	GP	G	A	TP	PIM
1992-93	Tacoma	WHL	61	21	20	41	19	7	0	0	0	8
1993-94	Tacoma	WHL	72	27	48	75	69	8	1	4	5	13
1994-95	Tacoma	WHL	67	25	53	78	81	4	2	3	5	8

FLINTON, ERIC — OTT.

Left wing. Shoots left. 6'2", 200 lbs. Born, William Lake, B.C., February 2, 1972.
(Ottawa's 1st choice, 1st overall, in 1993 Supplemental Draft).

			Regular Season					Playoffs				
Season	Club	Lea	GP	G	A	TP	PIM	GP	G	A	TP	PIM
1991-92	N. Hampshire	H.E.	36	6	4	10	10	....	....	....	....	....
1992-93	N. Hampshire	H.E.	37	18	18	36	14	....	....	....	....	....
1993-94	N. Hampshire	H.E.	40	16	25	41	36	....	....	....	....	....
1994-95a	N. Hampshire	H.E.	36	22	23	45	44	....	....	....	....	....

a Hockey East Second All-Star Team (1995)

FOGARTY, BRYAN

Defense. Shoots left. 6'2", 206 lbs. Born, Brantford, Ont., June 11, 1969.
(Quebec's 1st choice, 9th overall, in 1987 Entry Draft).

			Regular Season					Playoffs				
Season	Club	Lea	GP	G	A	TP	PIM	GP	G	A	TP	PIM
1985-86	Kingston	OHL	47	2	19	21	14	10	1	3	4	4
1986-87a	Kingston	OHL	56	20	50	70	46	12	2	3	5	5
1987-88	Kingston	OHL	48	11	36	47	50	....	....	....	....	....
1988-89abc	Niagara Falls	OHL	60	47	*108	*155	88	17	10	22	32	36
1989-90	**Quebec**	**NHL**	**45**	**4**	**10**	**14**	**31**	....	....	....	....	....
	Halifax	AHL	22	5	14	19	6	6	2	4	6	0
1990-91	**Quebec**	**NHL**	**45**	**9**	**22**	**31**	**24**	....	....	....	....	....
	Halifax	AHL	5	0	2	2	0	....	....	....	....	....
1991-92	**Quebec**	**NHL**	**20**	**3**	**12**	**15**	**16**	....	....	....	....	....
	Halifax	AHL	2	0	0	0	2	....	....	....	....	....
	New Haven	AHL	4	0	1	1	6	....	....	....	....	....
	Muskegon	IHL	8	2	4	6	30	....	....	....	....	....
1992-93	**Pittsburgh**	**NHL**	**12**	**0**	**4**	**4**	**4**	....	....	....	....	....
	Cleveland	IHL	15	2	5	7	8	3	0	1	1	17
1993-94	Atlanta	IHL	8	1	5	6	4	....	....	....	....	....
	Las Vegas	IHL	33	3	16	19	38	....	....	....	....	....
	Kansas City	IHL	3	2	1	3	2	....	....	....	....	....
	Montreal	**NHL**	**13**	**1**	**2**	**3**	**10**	....	....	....	....	....
1994-95	**Montreal**	**NHL**	**21**	**5**	**2**	**7**	**34**	....	....	....	....	....
	NHL Totals		**156**	**22**	**52**	**74**	**119**	....	....	....	....	....

a OHL First All-Star Team (1987, 1989)
b Canadian Major Junior Player of the Year (1989)
c Canadian Major Junior Defenseman of the Year (1989)

Traded to **Pittsburgh** by **Quebec** for Scott Young, March 10, 1992. Signed as a free agent by **Tampa Bay**, September 28, 1993. Signed as a free agent by **Montreal**, February 25, 1994.

FOOTE, ADAM — COL.

Defense. Shoots right. 6'1", 202 lbs. Born, Toronto, Ont., July 10, 1971.
(Quebec's 2nd choice, 22nd overall, in 1989 Entry Draft).

			Regular Season					Playoffs				
Season	Club	Lea	GP	G	A	TP	PIM	GP	G	A	TP	PIM
1988-89	S.S. Marie	OHL	66	7	32	39	120	....	....	....	....	....
1989-90	S.S. Marie	OHL	61	12	43	55	199	....	....	....	....	....
1990-91a	S.S. Marie	OHL	59	18	51	69	93	14	5	12	17	28
1991-92	**Quebec**	**NHL**	**46**	**2**	**5**	**7**	**44**	....	....	....	....	....
	Halifax	AHL	6	0	1	1	2	....	....	....	....	....
1992-93	**Quebec**	**NHL**	**81**	**4**	**12**	**16**	**168**	**6**	**0**	**1**	**1**	**2**
1993-94	**Quebec**	**NHL**	**45**	**2**	**6**	**8**	**67**	....	....	....	....	....
1994-95	**Quebec**	**NHL**	**35**	**0**	**7**	**7**	**52**	**6**	**0**	**1**	**1**	**14**
	NHL Totals		**207**	**8**	**30**	**38**	**331**	**12**	**0**	**2**	**2**	**16**

a OHL First All-Star Team (1991)

FORBES, COLIN — PHI.

Left wing. Shoots left. 6'3", 190 lbs. Born, New Westminster, B.C., February 16, 1976.
(Philadelphia's 5th choice, 166th overall, in 1994 Entry Draft).

			Regular Season					Playoffs				
Season	Club	Lea	GP	G	A	TP	PIM	GP	G	A	TP	PIM
1993-94	Sherwood Park	AJHL	47	18	22	40	76	....	....	....	....	....
1994-95	Portland	WHL	72	24	31	55	108	9	1	3	4	10

FORSBERG, PETER (FOHRS-buhrg) — COL.

Center. Shoots left. 6', 190 lbs. Born, Ornskoldsvik, Sweden, July 20, 1973.
(Philadelphia's 1st choice, 6th overall, in 1991 Entry Draft).

			Regular Season					Playoffs				
Season	Club	Lea	GP	G	A	TP	PIM	GP	G	A	TP	PIM
1990-91	MoDo	Swe.	23	7	10	17	22	....	....	....	....	....
1991-92	MoDo	Swe.	39	9	18	27	78	....	....	....	....	....
1992-93	MoDo	Swe.	39	23	24	47	92	3	4	1	5	0
1993-94	MoDo	Swe.	39	18	26	44	82	11	9	7	16	14
1994-95	MoDo	Swe.	11	5	9	14	20	....	....	....	....	....
ab	**Quebec**	**NHL**	**47**	**15**	**35**	**50**	**16**	**6**	**2**	**4**	**6**	**4**
	NHL Totals		**47**	**15**	**35**	**50**	**16**	**6**	**2**	**4**	**6**	**4**

a NHL/Upper Deck All-Rookie Team (1995)
b Won Calder Memorial Trophy (1995)

Traded to **Quebec** by **Philadelphia** with Steve Duchesne, Kerry Huffman, Mike Ricci, Ron Hextall, Chris Simon, Philadelphia's first choice in the 1993 (Jocelyn Thibault) and 1994 (later traded to Toronto — later traded to Washington — Washington selected Nolan Baumgartner) Entry Drafts and cash for Eric Lindros, June 30, 1992.

FOSTER, COREY — PIT.

Defense. Shoots left. 6'3", 204 lbs. Born, Ottawa, Ont., October 27, 1969.
(New Jersey's 1st choice, 12th overall, in 1988 Entry Draft).

			Regular Season					Playoffs				
Season	Club	Lea	GP	G	A	TP	PIM	GP	G	A	TP	PIM
1986-87	Peterborough	OHL	30	3	4	7	4	1	0	0	0	0
1987-88	Peterborough	OHL	66	13	31	44	58	11	5	9	14	13
1988-89	**New Jersey**	**NHL**	**2**	**0**	**0**	**0**	**0**	....	....	....	....	....
	Peterborough	OHL	55	14	42	56	42	17	1	17	18	12
1989-90	Cape Breton	AHL	54	7	17	24	32	1	0	0	0	0
1990-91	Cape Breton	AHL	67	14	11	25	51	4	2	4	6	4
1991-92	**Philadelphia**	**NHL**	**25**	**3**	**4**	**7**	**20**	....	....	....	....	....
	Hershey	AHL	19	5	9	14	26	6	1	1	2	5
1992-93	Hershey	AHL	80	9	25	34	102	....	....	....	....	....
1993-94	Hershey	AHL	66	21	37	58	96	9	2	5	7	10
1994-95	P.E.I.	AHL	78	13	34	47	61	11	2	5	7	12
	NHL Totals		**27**	**3**	**4**	**7**	**20**	....	....	....	....	....

Traded to **Edmonton** by **New Jersey** for Edmonton's first round choice (Jason Miller) in 1989 Entry Draft, June 17, 1989. Traded to **Philadelphia** by **Edmonton** with Dave Brown and Jari Kurri for Craig Fisher, Scott Mellanby and Craig Berube, May 30, 1991. Signed as a free agent by **Ottawa**, June 20, 1994. Signed as a free agent by **Pittsburgh**, August 7, 1995.

FRANCIS, RON — PIT.

Center. Shoots left. 6'2", 200 lbs. Born, Sault Ste. Marie, Ont., March 1, 1963.
(Hartford's 1st choice, 4th overall, in 1981 Entry Draft).

			Regular Season					Playoffs				
Season	Club	Lea	GP	G	A	TP	PIM	GP	G	A	TP	PIM
1980-81	S.S. Marie	OHA	64	26	43	69	33	19	7	8	15	34
1981-82	**Hartford**	**NHL**	**59**	**25**	**43**	**68**	**51**	....	....	....	....	....
	S.S. Marie	OHL	25	18	30	48	46	....	....	....	....	....
1982-83	**Hartford**	**NHL**	**79**	**31**	**59**	**90**	**60**	....	....	....	....	....
1983-84	**Hartford**	**NHL**	**72**	**23**	**60**	**83**	**45**	....	....	....	....	....
1984-85	**Hartford**	**NHL**	**80**	**24**	**57**	**81**	**66**	....	....	....	....	....
1985-86	**Hartford**	**NHL**	**53**	**24**	**53**	**77**	**24**	**10**	**1**	**2**	**3**	**4**
1986-87	**Hartford**	**NHL**	**75**	**30**	**63**	**93**	**45**	**6**	**2**	**2**	**4**	**6**
1987-88	**Hartford**	**NHL**	**80**	**25**	**50**	**75**	**87**	**6**	**2**	**5**	**7**	**2**
1988-89	**Hartford**	**NHL**	**69**	**29**	**48**	**77**	**36**	**4**	**0**	**2**	**2**	**0**
1989-90	**Hartford**	**NHL**	**80**	**32**	**69**	**101**	**73**	**7**	**3**	**3**	**6**	**8**
1990-91	**Hartford**	**NHL**	**67**	**21**	**55**	**76**	**51**	....	....	....	....	....
	Pittsburgh	**NHL**	**14**	**2**	**9**	**11**	**21**	**24**	**7**	**10**	**17**	**24**
1991-92	**Pittsburgh**	**NHL**	**70**	**21**	**33**	**54**	**30**	**21**	**8**	***19**	**27**	**6**
1992-93	**Pittsburgh**	**NHL**	**84**	**24**	**76**	**100**	**68**	**12**	**6**	**11**	**17**	**19**
1993-94	**Pittsburgh**	**NHL**	**82**	**27**	**66**	**93**	**62**	**6**	**0**	**2**	**2**	**6**
1994-95abc	**Pittsburgh**	**NHL**	**44**	**11**	***48**	**59**	**18**	**12**	**6**	**13**	**19**	**4**
	NHL Totals		**1008**	**349**	**789**	**1138**	**737**	**108**	**35**	**69**	**104**	**79**

a Won Alka-Seltzer Plus Award (1995)
b Won Frank J. Selke Trophy (1995)
c Won Lady Byng Trophy (1995)

Played in NHL All-Star Game (1983, 1985, 1990)

Traded to **Pittsburgh** by **Hartford** with Grant Jennings and Ulf Samuelsson for John Cullen, Jeff Parker and Zarley Zalapski, March 4, 1991.

FRASER, IAIN

Center. Shoots left. 5'10", 175 lbs. Born, Scarborough, Ont., August 10, 1969.
(NY Islanders' 12th choice, 233rd overall, in 1989 Entry Draft).

			Regular Season					Playoffs				
Season	Club	Lea	GP	G	A	TP	PIM	GP	G	A	TP	PIM
1986-87	Oshawa	OHL	5	1	2	3	0	....	....	....	....	....
1987-88	Oshawa	OHL	16	4	4	8	22	6	2	3	5	2
1988-89	Oshawa	OHL	62	33	57	90	87	6	2	8	10	12
1989-90ab	Oshawa	OHL	56	40	65	105	75	17	10	*22	32	8
1990-91	Capital Dist.	AHL	32	5	13	18	16	....	....	....	....	....
	Richmond	ECHL	3	1	1	2	0	....	....	....	....	....
1991-92	Capital Dist.	AHL	45	9	11	20	24	....	....	....	....	....
1992-93	**NY Islanders**	**NHL**	**7**	**2**	**2**	**4**	**2**	....	....	....	....	....
c	Capital Dist.	AHL	74	41	69	110	16	4	0	1	1	0
1993-94	**Quebec**	**NHL**	**60**	**17**	**20**	**37**	**23**	....	....	....	....	....
1994-95	**Dallas**	**NHL**	**4**	**0**	**0**	**0**	**0**	....	....	....	....	....
	Edmonton	**NHL**	**9**	**3**	**0**	**3**	**0**	....	....	....	....	....
	Denver	IHL	1	0	0	0	0	....	....	....	....	....
	NHL Totals		**80**	**22**	**22**	**44**	**25**	....	....	....	....	....

a Memorial Cup All-Star Team (1990)
b Won Stafford Smythe Memorial Trophy (Memorial Cup Tournament MVP) (1990)
c AHL Second All-Star Team (1993)

Signed as a free agent by **Quebec**, August 3, 1993. Traded to **Dallas** by **Quebec** for a conditional choice in 1996 Entry Draft, January 31, 1995. Claimed on waivers by **Edmonton** from **Dallas**, March 3, 1995.

FRASER, SCOTT — MTL.

Center. Shoots right. 6'1", 178 lbs. Born, Moncton, N.B., May 3, 1972.
(Montreal's 12th choice, 193rd overall, in 1991 Entry Draft).

			Regular Season					Playoffs				
Season	Club	Lea	GP	G	A	TP	PIM	GP	G	A	TP	PIM
1990-91	Dartmouth	ECAC	24	10	10	20	30	....	....	....	....	....
1991-92	Dartmouth	ECAC	24	11	7	18	60	....	....	....	....	....
1992-93	Cdn. National	....	5	1	0	1	0	....	....	....	....	....
a	Dartmouth	ECAC	26	21	23	44	13	....	....	....	....	....
1993-94	Dartmouth	ECAC	24	17	13	30	34	....	....	....	....	....
	Cdn. National	....	4	0	1	1	4	....	....	....	....	....
1994-95	Fredericton	AHL	65	23	25	48	36	16	3	5	8	14
	Wheeling	ECHL	8	4	2	6	8	....	....	....	....	....

a ECAC Second All-Star Team (1993)

FREDERICK, JOSEPH — DET.

Right wing. Shoots right. 6'1", 190 lbs. Born, St. Hubert, Que., August 6, 1969.
(Detroit's 13th choice, 242nd overall, in 1989 Entry Draft).

			Regular Season					Playoffs				
Season	Club	Lea	GP	G	A	TP	PIM	GP	G	A	TP	PIM
1990-91	N. Michigan	WCHA	40	9	11	20	77	....	....	....	....	....
1991-92	N. Michigan	WCHA	36	23	8	31	100	....	....	....	....	....
1992-93a	N. Michigan	WCHA	29	28	20	48	100	....	....	....	....	....
	Adirondack	AHL	5	0	1	1	2	8	0	0	0	6
1993-94	Adirondack	AHL	68	28	30	58	130	12	11	4	15	22
1994-95	Adirondack	AHL	71	27	28	55	124	4	0	0	0	10

a WCHA Second All-Star Team (1993)

FREER, MARK (FRIHR)

Center. Shoots left. 5'10", 180 lbs. Born, Peterborough, Ont., July 14, 1968.

			Regular Season					Playoffs				
Season	Club	Lea	GP	G	A	TP	PIM	GP	G	A	TP	PIM
1985-86	Peterborough	OHL	65	16	28	44	24	14	3	4	7	13
1986-87	**Philadelphia**	**NHL**	**1**	**0**	**1**	**1**	**0**	....	....	....	....	....
	Peterborough	OHL	65	39	43	82	44	12	2	6	8	5
1987-88	**Philadelphia**	**NHL**	**1**	**0**	**0**	**0**	**0**	....	....	....	....	....
	Peterborough	OHL	63	38	70	108	63	12	5	12	17	4
1988-89	**Philadelphia**	**NHL**	**5**	**0**	**1**	**1**	**0**	....	....	....	....	....
	Hershey	AHL	75	30	49	79	77	12	4	6	10	2
1989-90	**Philadelphia**	**NHL**	**2**	**0**	**0**	**0**	**0**	....	....	....	....	....
	Hershey	AHL	65	28	36	64	31	....	....	....	....	....
1990-91	Hershey	AHL	77	18	44	62	45	7	1	3	4	17
1991-92	**Philadelphia**	**NHL**	**50**	**6**	**7**	**13**	**18**	....	....	....	....	....
	Hershey	AHL	31	13	11	24	38	6	0	3	3	2
1992-93	**Ottawa**	**NHL**	**63**	**10**	**14**	**24**	**39**	....	....	....	....	....
1993-94	**Calgary**	**NHL**	**2**	**0**	**0**	**0**	**4**	....	....	....	....	....
	Saint John	AHL	77	33	53	86	45	7	2	4	6	16
1994-95	Houston	IHL	80	38	42	80	54	4	0	1	1	4
	NHL Totals		**124**	**16**	**23**	**39**	**61**	....	....	....	....	....

Signed as a free agent by **Philadelphia**, October 7, 1986. Claimed by **Ottawa** from **Philadelphia** in Expansion Draft, June 18, 1992. Signed as a free agent by **Calgary**, August 10, 1993.

FRIEDMAN, DOUG
COL.

Left wing. Shoots left. 6'1", 189 lbs.   Born, Cape Elizabeth, ME, September 1, 1971.
(Quebec's 11th choice, 222nd overall, in 1991 Entry Draft).

			Regular Season					Playoffs				
Season	Club	Lea	GP	G	A	TP	PIM	GP	G	A	TP	PIM
1990-91	Boston U.	H.E.	36	6	6	12	37	....	....	....	....	....
1991-92	Boston U.	H.E.	34	11	8	19	42	....	....	....	....	....
1992-93	Boston U.	H.E.	38	17	24	41	62	....	....	....	....	....
1993-94	Boston U.	H.E.	41	9	23	32	110	....	....	....	....	....
1994-95	Cornwall	AHL	55	6	9	15	56	3	0	0	0	0

FRIESEN, JEFF
(FREE-zuhn)   S.J.

Center. Shoots left. 6', 185 lbs.   Born, Meadow Lake, Sask., August 5, 1976.
(San Jose's 1st choice, 11th overall, in 1994 Entry Draft).

			Regular Season					Playoffs				
Season	Club	Lea	GP	G	A	TP	PIM	GP	G	A	TP	PIM
1991-92	Regina	WHL	4	3	1	4	2	....	....	....	....	....
1992-93	Regina	WHL	70	45	38	83	23	13	7	10	17	8
1993-94	Regina	WHL	66	51	67	118	48	4	3	2	5	2
1994-95	Regina	WHL	25	21	23	44	22	....	....	....	....	....
a	San Jose	NHL	48	15	10	25	14	11	1	5	6	4
	NHL Totals		48	15	10	25	14	11	1	5	6	4

a NHL/Upper Deck All-Rookie Team (1995)

FRYLEN, EDVIN
(FRYUH-lehn)   ST.L.

Defense. Shoots left. 6', 211 lbs.   Born, Jarfalla, Sweden, December 23, 1975.
(St. Louis' 3rd choice, 120th overall, in 1994 Entry Draft).

			Regular Season					Playoffs				
Season	Club	Lea	GP	G	A	TP	PIM	GP	G	A	TP	PIM
1991-92	Vasteras	Swe.	2	0	0	0	0	....	....	....	....	....
1992-93	Vasteras	Swe.	29	0	2	2	14	3	0	0	0	0
1993-94	Vasteras	Swe.	32	1	0	1	26	....	....	....	....	....
1994-95	Vasteras	Swe.	25	2	1	3	14	4	0	0	0	4

GAFFNEY, MIKE
OTT.

Defense. Shoots right. 6'1", 202 lbs.   Born, Worchester, MA, June 19, 1976.
(Ottawa's 4th choice, 131st overall, in 1994 Entry Draft).

			Regular Season					Playoffs				
Season	Club	Lea	GP	G	A	TP	PIM	GP	G	A	TP	PIM
1993-94	St. John's	HS	20	6	16	22	....	....	....	....	....	....
1994-95	Massachusetts	H.E.	33	1	4	5	38	....	....	....	....	....

GAGNE, LUC
(GAH-nyay)   L.A.

Right wing. Shoots right. 6'1", 190 lbs.   Born, Sturgeon Falls, Ont., May 4, 1976.
(Los Angeles' 5th choice, 163rd overall, in 1994 Entry Draft).

			Regular Season					Playoffs				
Season	Club	Lea	GP	G	A	TP	PIM	GP	G	A	TP	PIM
1993-94	Sudbury	OHL	11	3	1	4	2	....	....	....	....	....
	Newmarket	OHL	19	1	2	3	17	....	....	....	....	....
1994-95	Sudbury	OHL	66	19	25	44	29	16	5	4	9	11

GAGNER, DAVE
(GAH-nyay)   DAL.

Center. Shoots left. 5'10", 180 lbs.   Born, Chatham, Ont., December 11, 1964.
(NY Rangers' 1st choice, 12th overall, in 1983 Entry Draft).

			Regular Season					Playoffs				
Season	Club	Lea	GP	G	A	TP	PIM	GP	G	A	TP	PIM
1981-82	Brantford	OHL	68	30	46	76	31	11	3	6	9	6
1982-83a	Brantford	OHL	70	55	66	121	57	8	5	5	10	4
1983-84	Cdn. National	....	50	19	18	37	26	....	....	....	....	....
	Cdn. Olympic	....	7	5	2	7	6	....	....	....	....	....
	Brantford	OHL	12	7	13	20	4	6	0	4	4	6
1984-85	NY Rangers	NHL	38	6	6	12	16	....	....	....	....	....
	New Haven	AHL	38	13	20	33	23	....	....	....	....	....
1985-86	NY Rangers	NHL	32	4	6	10	19	....	....	....	....	....
	New Haven	AHL	16	10	11	21	11	4	1	2	3	2
1986-87	NY Rangers	NHL	10	1	4	5	12	....	....	....	....	....
	New Haven	AHL	56	22	41	63	50	7	1	5	6	18
1987-88	Minnesota	NHL	51	8	11	19	55	....	....	....	....	....
	Kalamazoo	IHL	14	16	10	26	26	....	....	....	....	....
1988-89	Minnesota	NHL	75	35	43	78	104	....	....	....	....	....
	Kalamazoo	IHL	1	0	1	1	4	....	....	....	....	....
1989-90	Minnesota	NHL	79	40	38	78	54	7	2	3	5	16
1990-91	Minnesota	NHL	73	40	42	82	114	23	12	15	27	28
1991-92	Minnesota	NHL	78	31	40	71	107	7	2	4	6	8
1992-93	Minnesota	NHL	84	33	43	76	143	....	....	....	....	....
1993-94	Dallas	NHL	76	32	29	61	83	9	5	1	6	2
1994-95	Courmaosta	Italy	3	0	0	0	0	....	....	....	....	....
	Courmaosta	Euro.	1	0	4	4	0	....	....	....	....	....
	Dallas	NHL	48	14	28	42	42	5	1	1	2	4
	NHL Totals		644	244	290	534	749	51	22	24	46	58

a OHL Second All-Star Team (1983)
Played in NHL All-Star Game (1991)

Traded to **Minnesota** by **NY Rangers** with Jay Caulfield for Jari Gronstrand and Paul Boutilier, October 8, 1987.

GALANOV, MAXIM
NYR

Defense. Shoots left. 6'1", 175 lbs.   Born, Krasnoyarsk, USSR, March 13, 1974.
(NY Rangers' 3rd choice, 61st overall, in 1993 Entry Draft).

			Regular Season					Playoffs				
Season	Club	Lea	GP	G	A	TP	PIM	GP	G	A	TP	PIM
1992-93	Togliatti	CIS	41	4	2	6	12	10	1	1	2	12
1993-94	Togliatti	CIS	7	1	0	1	4	12	1	0	1	8
1994-95	Togliatti	CIS	45	5	6	11	54	9	0	1	1	12

GALLANT, GERARD
(guh-LANT)

Left wing. Shoots left. 5'10", 190 lbs.   Born, Summerside, P.E.I., September 2, 1963.
(Detroit's 4th choice, 107th overall, in 1981 Entry Draft).

			Regular Season					Playoffs				
Season	Club	Lea	GP	G	A	TP	PIM	GP	G	A	TP	PIM
1980-81	Sherbrooke	QMJHL	68	41	59	100	265	14	6	13	19	46
1981-82	Sherbrooke	QMJHL	58	34	58	92	260	22	14	24	38	84
1982-83	St-Jean	QMJHL	33	28	25	53	139	....	....	....	....	....
	Verdun	QMJHL	29	26	49	75	105	15	14	19	33	84
1983-84	Adirondack	AHL	77	31	33	64	195	7	1	3	4	34
1984-85	Detroit	NHL	32	6	12	18	66	3	0	0	0	11
	Adirondack	AHL	46	18	29	47	131	....	....	....	....	....
1985-86	Detroit	NHL	52	20	19	39	106	....	....	....	....	....
1986-87	Detroit	NHL	80	38	34	72	216	16	8	6	14	43
1987-88	Detroit	NHL	73	34	39	73	242	16	6	9	15	55
1988-89a	Detroit	NHL	76	39	54	93	230	6	1	2	3	40
1989-90	Detroit	NHL	69	36	44	80	254	....	....	....	....	....
1990-91	Detroit	NHL	45	10	16	26	111	....	....	....	....	....
1991-92	Detroit	NHL	69	14	22	36	187	11	2	2	4	25
1992-93	Detroit	NHL	67	10	20	30	188	6	1	2	3	4
1993-94	Tampa Bay	NHL	51	4	9	13	74	....	....	....	....	....
1994-95	Tampa Bay	NHL	1	0	0	0	0	....	....	....	....	....
	Atlanta	IHL	16	3	3	6	31	....	....	....	....	....
	NHL Totals		615	211	269	480	1674	58	18	21	39	178

a NHL Second All-Star Team (1989).
Signed as a free agent by **Tampa Bay**, July 21, 1993.

GALLEY, GARRY
BUF.

Defense. Shoots left. 6', 204 lbs.   Born, Montreal, Que., April 16, 1963.
(Los Angeles' 4th choice, 100th overall, in 1983 Entry Draft).

			Regular Season					Playoffs				
Season	Club	Lea	GP	G	A	TP	PIM	GP	G	A	TP	PIM
1981-82	Bowling Green	CCHA	42	3	36	39	48	....	....	....	....	....
1982-83	Bowling Green	CCHA	40	17	29	46	40	....	....	....	....	....
1983-84ab	Bowling Green	CCHA	44	15	52	67	61	....	....	....	....	....
1984-85	Los Angeles	NHL	78	8	30	38	82	3	1	0	1	2
1985-86	Los Angeles	NHL	49	9	13	22	46	....	....	....	....	....
	New Haven	AHL	4	2	6	8	6	....	....	....	....	....
1986-87	Los Angeles	NHL	30	5	11	16	57	....	....	....	....	....
	Washington	NHL	18	1	10	11	10	2	0	0	0	0
1987-88	Washington	NHL	58	7	23	30	44	13	2	4	6	13
1988-89	Boston	NHL	78	8	21	29	80	9	0	1	1	33
1989-90	Boston	NHL	71	8	27	35	75	21	3	3	6	34
1990-91	Boston	NHL	70	6	21	27	84	16	1	5	6	17
1991-92	Boston	NHL	38	2	12	14	83	....	....	....	....	....
	Philadelphia	NHL	39	3	15	18	34	....	....	....	....	....
1992-93	Philadelphia	NHL	83	13	49	62	115	....	....	....	....	....
1993-94	Philadelphia	NHL	81	10	60	70	91	....	....	....	....	....
1994-95	Philadelphia	NHL	33	2	20	22	20	....	....	....	....	....
	Buffalo	NHL	14	1	9	10	10	5	0	3	3	4
	NHL Totals		740	83	321	404	831	69	7	16	23	103

a CCHA First All-Star Team (1984)
b NCAA All-American (1984)
Played in NHL All-Star Game (1991, 1994)

Traded to **Washington** by **Los Angeles** for Al Jensen, February 14, 1987. Signed as a free agent by **Boston**, July 8, 1988. Traded to **Philadelphia** by **Boston** with Wes Walz and Boston's third round choice (Milos Holan) in 1993 Entry Draft for Gord Murphy, Brian Dobbin, Philadelphia's third round choice (Sergei Zholtok) in 1992 Entry Draft and Philadelphia's fourth round choice (Charles Paquette) in 1993 Entry Draft, January 2, 1992. Traded to **Buffalo** by **Philadelphia** for Petr Svoboda, April 7, 1995.

GARANIN, YEVGENY
WPG.

Center. Shoots left. 6'4", 191 lbs.   Born, Voskresensk, USSR, August 3, 1973.
(Winnipeg's 9th choice, 228th overall, in 1992 Entry Draft).

			Regular Season					Playoffs				
Season	Club	Lea	GP	G	A	TP	PIM	GP	G	A	TP	PIM
1991-92	Khimik	CIS	1	1	0	1	0	....	....	....	....	....
1992-93	Khimik	CIS	34	5	4	9	10	1	0	0	0	2
1993-94	Khimik	CIS	46	6	4	10	12	3	0	0	0	0
1994-95	Khimik	CIS	50	19	8	27	6	2	0	0	0	0

GARDINER, BRUCE
OTT.

Center. Shoots right. 6'1", 185 lbs.   Born, Barrie, Ont., February 11, 1971.
(St. Louis' 6th choice, 131st overall, in 1991 Entry Draft).

			Regular Season					Playoffs				
Season	Club	Lea	GP	G	A	TP	PIM	GP	G	A	TP	PIM
1990-91	Colgate	ECAC	27	4	9	13	72	....	....	....	....	....
1991-92	Colgate	ECAC	23	7	8	15	77	....	....	....	....	....
1992-93	Colgate	ECAC	33	17	12	29	64	....	....	....	....	....
1993-94a	Colgate	ECAC	33	23	23	46	·68	....	....	....	....	....
	Peoria	IHL	3	0	0	0	0	....	....	....	....	....
1994-95	P.E.I.	AHL	72	17	20	37	132	7	4	1	5	4

a ECAC Second All-Star Team (1994)
Signed as a free agent by **Ottawa**, June 14, 1994.

GARPENLOV, JOHAN
(GAHR-pehn-LAHV, YOH-hahn)   FLA.

Left wing. Shoots left. 5'11", 184 lbs.   Born, Stockholm, Sweden, March 21, 1968.
(Detroit's 5th choice, 85th overall, in 1986 Entry Draft).

			Regular Season					Playoffs				
Season	Club	Lea	GP	G	A	TP	PIM	GP	G	A	TP	PIM
1986-87	Djurgarden	Swe.	29	5	8	13	22	2	0	0	0	0
1987-88	Djurgarden	Swe.	30	7	10	17	12	3	1	3	4	4
1988-89	Djurgarden	Swe.	36	12	19	31	20	8	3	4	7	10
1989-90	Djurgarden	Swe.	39	20	13	33	35	8	2	4	6	4
1990-91	Detroit	NHL	71	18	22	40	18	6	0	1	1	4
1991-92	Detroit	NHL	16	1	1	2	4	....	....	....	....	....
	Adirondack	AHL	9	3	3	6	6	....	....	....	....	....
	San Jose	NHL	12	5	6	11	4	....	....	....	....	....
1992-93	San Jose	NHL	79	22	44	66	56	....	....	....	....	....
1993-94	San Jose	NHL	80	18	35	53	28	14	4	6	10	6
1994-95	San Jose	NHL	13	1	1	2	2	....	....	....	....	....
	Florida	NHL	27	3	9	12	0	....	....	....	....	....
	NHL Totals		298	68	118	186	112	20	4	7	11	10

Traded to **San Jose** by **Detroit** for Bob McGill and Vancouver's eighth round choice (previously acquired by Detroit — San Jose selected C.J. Denomme) in 1992 Entry Draft, March 9, 1992. Traded to **Florida** by **San Jose** for a conditional choice in 1998 Entry Draft, March 3, 1995.

GARTNER, MIKE — TOR.

Right wing. Shoots right. 6', 187 lbs. Born, Ottawa, Ont., October 29, 1959.
(Washington's 1st choice, 4th overall, in 1979 Entry Draft).

			Regular Season					Playoffs				
Season	Club	Lea	GP	G	A	TP	PIM	GP	G	A	TP	PIM
1976-77	Niagara Falls	OHA	62	33	42	75	125	....	....	....	....	....
1977-78a	Niagara Falls	OHA	64	41	49	90	56	....	....	....	....	....
1978-79	Cincinnati	WHA	78	27	25	52	123	3	0	2	2	2
1979-80	**Washington**	**NHL**	**77**	**36**	**32**	**68**	**66**	....	....	....	....	....
1980-81	**Washington**	**NHL**	**80**	**48**	**46**	**94**	**100**	....	....	....	....	....
1981-82	**Washington**	**NHL**	**80**	**35**	**45**	**80**	**121**	....	....	....	....	....
1982-83	**Washington**	**NHL**	**73**	**38**	**38**	**76**	**54**	**4**	**0**	**0**	**0**	**4**
1983-84	**Washington**	**NHL**	**80**	**40**	**45**	**85**	**90**	**8**	**3**	**7**	**10**	**16**
1984-85	**Washington**	**NHL**	**80**	**50**	**52**	**102**	**71**	**5**	**4**	**3**	**7**	**9**
1985-86	**Washington**	**NHL**	**74**	**35**	**40**	**75**	**63**	**9**	**2**	**10**	**12**	**4**
1986-87	**Washington**	**NHL**	**78**	**41**	**32**	**73**	**61**	**7**	**4**	**3**	**7**	**14**
1987-88	**Washington**	**NHL**	**80**	**48**	**33**	**81**	**73**	**14**	**3**	**4**	**7**	**14**
1988-89	**Washington**	**NHL**	**56**	**26**	**29**	**55**	**71**	....	....	....	....	....
	Minnesota	**NHL**	**13**	**7**	**7**	**14**	**2**	**5**	**0**	**0**	**0**	**6**
1989-90	**Minnesota**	**NHL**	**67**	**34**	**36**	**70**	**32**	....	....	....	....	....
	NY Rangers	**NHL**	**12**	**11**	**5**	**16**	**6**	**10**	**5**	**3**	**8**	**12**
1990-91	**NY Rangers**	**NHL**	**79**	**49**	**20**	**69**	**53**	**6**	**1**	**1**	**2**	**0**
1991-92	**NY Rangers**	**NHL**	**76**	**40**	**41**	**81**	**55**	**13**	**8**	**8**	**16**	**4**
1992-93	**NY Rangers**	**NHL**	**84**	**45**	**23**	**68**	**59**	....	....	....	....	....
1993-94	**NY Rangers**	**NHL**	**71**	**28**	**24**	**52**	**58**	....	....	....	....	....
	Toronto	**NHL**	**10**	**6**	**6**	**12**	**4**	**18**	**5**	**6**	**11**	**14**
1994-95	**Toronto**	**NHL**	**38**	**12**	**8**	**20**	**6**	**5**	**2**	**2**	**4**	**2**
	NHL Totals		**1208**	**629**	**562**	**1191**	**1045**	**104**	**37**	**47**	**84**	**99**

a OHA First All-Star Team (1978)

Played in NHL All-Star Game (1980, 1985, 1986, 1988, 1990, 1993)

Traded to **Minnesota** by **Washington** with Larry Murphy for Dino Ciccarelli and Bob Rouse, March 7, 1989. Traded to **NY Rangers** by **Minnesota** for Ulf Dahlen, Los Angeles' fourth round choice (previously acquired by NY Rangers — Minnesota selected Cal McGowan) in 1990 Entry Draft and future considerations, March 6, 1990. Traded to **Toronto** by **NY Rangers** for Glenn Anderson, the rights to Scott Malone and Toronto's fourth round choice (Alexander Korobolin) in 1994 Entry Draft, March 21, 1994.

GASKINS, JON — EDM.

Defense. Shoots left. 6'3", 205 lbs. Born, Dallas, TX, January 11, 1976.
(Edmonton's 8th choice, 110th overall, in 1994 Entry Draft).

			Regular Season					Playoffs				
Season	Club	Lea	GP	G	A	TP	PIM	GP	G	A	TP	PIM
1993-94	Dubuque	USHL	30	6	13	19	52	....	....	....	....	....
1994-95	Michigan State	CCHA	28	1	5	6	18	....	....	....	....	....

GAUDREAU, ROB — (GUH-droh) OTT.

Right wing. Shoots right. 5'11", 185 lbs. Born, Lincoln, RI, January 20, 1970.
(Pittsburgh's 8th choice, 172nd overall, in 1988 Entry Draft).

			Regular Season					Playoffs				
Season	Club	Lea	GP	G	A	TP	PIM	GP	G	A	TP	PIM
1988-89	Providence	H.E.	42	28	29	57	32	....	....	....	....	....
1989-90	Providence	H.E.	32	20	18	38	12	....	....	....	....	....
1990-91a	Providence	H.E.	36	34	27	61	20	....	....	....	....	....
1991-92bc	Providence	H.E.	36	21	34	55	22	....	....	....	....	....
1992-93	**San Jose**	**NHL**	**59**	**23**	**20**	**43**	**18**	....	....	....	....	....
	Kansas City	IHL	19	8	6	14	6	....	....	....	....	....
1993-94	**San Jose**	**NHL**	**84**	**15**	**20**	**35**	**28**	**14**	**2**	**0**	**2**	**0**
1994-95	**Ottawa**	**NHL**	**36**	**5**	**9**	**14**	**8**	....	....	....	....	....
	NHL Totals		**179**	**43**	**49**	**92**	**54**	**14**	**2**	**0**	**2**	**0**

a Hockey East Second All-Star Team (1991)
b NCAA East Second All-American Team (1992)
c Hockey East First All-Star Team (1992)

Rights traded to **Minnesota** by **Pittsburgh** for Richard Zemlak, November 1, 1988. Claimed by **San Jose** from **Minnesota** in Dispersal Draft, May 30, 1991. Claimed by **Ottawa** from **San Jose** in NHL Waiver Draft, January 18, 1995.

GAUTHIER, DANIEL — (GOH-tyay) CHI.

Left wing. Shoots left. 6'1", 190 lbs. Born, Charlemagne, Que., May 17, 1970.
(Pittsburgh's 3rd choice, 62nd overall, in 1988 Entry Draft).

			Regular Season					Playoffs				
Season	Club	Lea	GP	G	A	TP	PIM	GP	G	A	TP	PIM
1986-87	Longueuil	QMJHL	64	23	22	45	23	18	4	5	9	15
1987-88	Victoriaville	QMJHL	66	43	47	90	53	5	2	1	3	0
1988-89	Victoriaville	QMJHL	64	41	75	116	84	16	12	17	29	30
1989-90	Victoriaville	QMJHL	62	45	69	114	32	16	8	*19	27	16
1990-91	Albany	IHL	1	1	0	1	0	....	....	....	....	....
ab	Knoxville	ECHL	61	41	*93	134	40	2	0	4	4	4
1991-92	Muskegon	IHL	68	19	18	37	28	9	3	6	9	8
1992-93	Cleveland	IHL	80	40	66	106	88	4	2	2	4	14
1993-94	Cincinnati	IHL	74	30	34	64	101	10	2	3	5	14
1994-95	Indianapolis	IHL	66	22	50	72	53	....	....	....	....	....
	Chicago	**NHL**	**5**	**0**	**0**	**0**	**0**	....	....	....	....	....
	NHL Totals		**5**	**0**	**0**	**0**	**0**	....	....	....	....	....

a ECHL First All-Star Team (1991)
b ECHL Rookie of the Year (1991)

Signed as a free agent by **Florida**, July 14, 1993. Signed as a free agent by **Chicago**, June 14, 1994.

GAUTHIER, DENIS — (GOH-tyay) CGY.

Defense. Shoots left. 6'2", 195 lbs. Born, Montreal, Que., October 1, 1976.
(Calgary's 1st choice, 20th overall, in 1995 Entry Draft).

			Regular Season					Playoffs				
Season	Club	Lea	GP	G	A	TP	PIM	GP	G	A	TP	PIM
1992-93	Drummondville	QMJHL	60	1	7	8	136	10	0	5	5	40
1993-94	Drummondville	QMJHL	60	0	7	7	176	9	2	0	2	41
1994-95	Drummondville	QMJHL	64	9	31	40	190	4	0	5	5	12

GAVEY, AARON — T.B.

Center. Shoots left. 6'1", 175 lbs. Born, Sudbury, Ont., February 22, 1974.
(Tampa Bay's 4th choice, 74th overall, in 1992 Entry Draft).

			Regular Season					Playoffs				
Season	Club	Lea	GP	G	A	TP	PIM	GP	G	A	TP	PIM
1991-92	S.S. Marie	OHL	48	7	11	18	27	19	5	1	6	10
1992-93	S.S. Marie	OHL	62	45	39	84	116	18	5	9	14	36
1993-94	S.S. Marie	OHL	60	42	60	102	116	14	11	10	21	22
1994-95	Atlanta	IHL	66	18	17	35	85	5	0	1	1	9

GEARY, DEREK — BOS.

Right wing. Shoots right. 6'3", 180 lbs. Born, Gloucester, MA, February 18, 1970.
(Boston's 5th choice, 123rd overall, in 1988 Entry Draft).

			Regular Season					Playoffs				
Season	Club	Lea	GP	G	A	TP	PIM	GP	G	A	TP	PIM
1991-92	Dartmouth	ECAC	26	7	6	13	30	....	....	....	....	....
1992-93	Dartmouth	ECAC	27	7	8	15	4	....	....	....	....	....
1993-94	Dartmouth	ECAC	26	3	6	9	16	....	....	....	....	....
1994-95			DID NOT PLAY									

GELINAS, MARTIN — (ZHEHL-in-nuh, MAHR-ta) VAN.

Left wing. Shoots left. 5'11", 195 lbs. Born, Shawinigan, Que., June 5, 1970.
(Los Angeles' 1st choice, 7th overall, in 1988 Entry Draft).

			Regular Season					Playoffs				
Season	Club	Lea	GP	G	A	TP	PIM	GP	G	A	TP	PIM
1987-88a	Hull	QMJHL	65	63	68	131	74	17	15	18	33	32
1988-89	**Edmonton**	**NHL**	**6**	**1**	**2**	**3**	**0**	....	....	....	....	....
	Hull	QMJHL	41	38	39	77	31	9	5	4	9	14
1989-90	**Edmonton**	**NHL**	**46**	**17**	**8**	**25**	**30**	**20**	**2**	**3**	**5**	**6**
1990-91	**Edmonton**	**NHL**	**73**	**20**	**20**	**40**	**34**	**18**	**3**	**6**	**9**	**25**
1991-92	**Edmonton**	**NHL**	**68**	**11**	**18**	**29**	**62**	**15**	**1**	**3**	**4**	**10**
1992-93	**Edmonton**	**NHL**	**65**	**11**	**12**	**23**	**30**	....	....	....	....	....
1993-94	**Quebec**	**NHL**	**31**	**6**	**6**	**12**	**8**	....	....	....	....	....
	Vancouver	**NHL**	**33**	**8**	**8**	**16**	**26**	**24**	**5**	**4**	**9**	**14**
1994-95	**Vancouver**	**NHL**	**46**	**13**	**10**	**23**	**36**	**3**	**0**	**1**	**1**	**0**
	NHL Totals		**368**	**87**	**84**	**171**	**226**	**80**	**11**	**17**	**28**	**55**

a Won George Parsons Trophy (Memorial Cup Tournament Most Sportsmanlike Player) (1988)

Traded to **Edmonton** by **Los Angeles** with Jimmy Carson and Los Angeles' first round choices in 1989, (acquired by New Jersey — New Jersey selected Jason Miller), 1991 (Martin Rucinsky) and 1993 (Nick Stajduhar) Entry Drafts and cash for Wayne Gretzky, Mike Krushelnyski and Marty McSorley, August 9, 1988. Traded to **Quebec** by **Edmonton** with Edmonton's sixth round choice (Nicholas Checco) in 1993 Entry Draft for Scott Pearson, June 20, 1993. Claimed on waivers by **Vancouver** from **Quebec**, January 15, 1994.

GENDRON, MARTIN — (ZHEHN-drawn) WSH.

Right wing. Shoots right. 5'9", 190 lbs. Born, Valleyfield, Que., February 15, 1974.
(Washington's 4th choice, 71st overall, in 1992 Entry Draft).

			Regular Season					Playoffs				
Season	Club	Lea	GP	G	A	TP	PIM	GP	G	A	TP	PIM
1990-91	St-Hyacinthe	QMJHL	55	34	23	57	33	4	1	2	3	0
1991-92a	St-Hyacinthe	QMJHL	69	*71	66	137	45	6	7	4	11	14
1992-93bc	St-Hyacinthe	QMJHL	63	73	61	134	44	....	....	....	....	....
	Baltimore	AHL	10	1	2	3	2	3	0	0	0	0
1993-94	Cdn. National	....	19	4	5	9	2	....	....	....	....	....
	Hull	QMJHL	37	39	36	75	18	20	*21	17	38	8
1994-95	Portland	AHL	72	36	32	68	54	4	5	1	6	2
	Washington	**NHL**	**8**	**2**	**1**	**3**	**2**	....	....	....	....	....
	NHL Totals		**8**	**2**	**1**	**3**	**2**	....	....	....	....	....

a QMJHL First All-Star Team (1992)
b QMJHL Second All-Star Team (1993)
c Canadian Major Junior First All-Star Team (1993)

GERIS, DAVE — FLA.

Defense. Shoots left. 6'5", 240 lbs. Born, North Bay, Ont., June 7, 1976.
(Florida's 6th choice, 105th overall, in 1994 Entry Draft).

			Regular Season					Playoffs				
Season	Club	Lea	GP	G	A	TP	PIM	GP	G	A	TP	PIM
1993-94	Windsor	OHL	63	0	6	6	121	3	0	0	0	6
1994-95	Windsor	OHL	65	5	11	16	135	10	1	6	7	21

GERNANDER, KEN — NYR

Center. Shoots left. 5'10", 180 lbs. Born, Coleraine, MN, June 30, 1969.
(Winnipeg's 4th choice, 96th overall, in 1987 Entry Draft).

			Regular Season					Playoffs				
Season	Club	Lea	GP	G	A	TP	PIM	GP	G	A	TP	PIM
1987-88	U. Minnesota	WCHA	44	14	14	28	14	....	....	....	....	....
1988-89	U. Minnesota	WCHA	44	9	11	20	2	....	....	....	....	....
1989-90	U. Minnesota	WCHA	44	32	17	49	24	....	....	....	....	....
1990-91	U. Minnesota	WCHA	44	23	20	43	24	....	....	....	....	....
1991-92	Fort Wayne	IHL	13	7	6	13	2	....	....	....	....	....
	Moncton	AHL	43	8	18	26	9	8	1	1	2	2
1992-93	Moncton	AHL	71	18	29	47	20	5	1	4	5	0
1993-94	Moncton	AHL	71	22	25	47	12	19	6	1	7	0
1994-95	Binghamton	AHL	80	28	25	53	24	11	2	2	4	6

Signed as a free agent by **NY Rangers**, July 4, 1994.

GERVAIS, SHAWN — T.B.

Center. Shoots left. 6', 190 lbs. Born, Falher, Alta., July 12, 1976.
(Tampa Bay's 10th choice, 242nd overall, in 1994 Entry Draft).

			Regular Season					Playoffs				
Season	Club	Lea	GP	G	A	TP	PIM	GP	G	A	TP	PIM
1993-94	Seattle	WHL	70	2	18	20	32	8	0	1	1	0
1994-95	Seattle	WHL	66	11	23	34	73	4	0	1	1	4

GILBERT, GREG — ST.L.

Left wing. Shoots left. 6'1", 191 lbs. Born, Mississauga, Ont., January 22, 1962.
(NY Islanders' 5th choice, 80th overall, in 1980 Entry Draft).

			Regular Season					Playoffs				
Season	Club	Lea	GP	G	A	TP	PIM	GP	G	A	TP	PIM
1979-80	Toronto	OHA	68	10	11	21	35	....	....	....	....	....
1980-81	Toronto	OHA	64	30	37	67	73	5	2	6	8	16
1981-82	**NY Islanders**	**NHL**	1	1	0	1	0	4	1	1	2	2
	Toronto	OHL	65	41	67	108	119	10	4	12	16	23
1982-83	**NY Islanders**	**NHL**	45	8	11	19	30	10	1	0	1	14
	Indianapolis	CHL	24	11	16	27	23	....	....	....	....	....
1983-84	**NY Islanders**	**NHL**	79	31	35	66	59	21	5	7	12	39
1984-85	**NY Islanders**	**NHL**	58	13	25	38	36	....	....	....	....	....
1985-86	**NY Islanders**	**NHL**	60	9	19	28	82	2	0	0	0	9
	Springfield	AHL	2	0	0	0	2	....	....	....	....	....
1986-87	**NY Islanders**	**NHL**	51	6	7	13	26	10	2	2	4	6
1987-88	**NY Islanders**	**NHL**	76	17	28	45	46	4	0	0	0	6
1988-89	**NY Islanders**	**NHL**	55	8	13	21	45	....	....	....	....	....
	Chicago	**NHL**	4	0	0	0	0	15	1	5	6	20
1989-90	**Chicago**	**NHL**	70	12	25	37	54	19	5	8	13	34
1990-91	**Chicago**	**NHL**	72	10	15	25	58	5	0	1	1	2
1991-92	**Chicago**	**NHL**	50	7	5	12	35	10	1	3	4	16
1992-93	**Chicago**	**NHL**	77	13	19	32	57	3	0	0	0	0
1993-94	**NY Rangers**	**NHL**	76	4	11	15	29	23	1	3	4	8
1994-95	**St. Louis**	**NHL**	46	11	14	25	11	7	0	3	3	6
	NHL Totals		820	150	227	377	568	133	17	33	50	162

Traded to **Chicago** by **NY Islanders** for Chicago's fifth round choice (Steve Young) in 1989 Entry Draft, March 7, 1989. Signed as a free agent by **NY Rangers**, July 29, 1993. Claimed by **St. Louis** from **NY Rangers** in NHL Waiver Draft, January 18, 1995.

GILCHRIST, BRENT — DAL.

Left wing. Shoots left. 5'11", 181 lbs. Born, Moose Jaw, Sask., April 3, 1967.
(Montreal's 6th choice, 79th overall, in 1985 Entry Draft).

			Regular Season					Playoffs				
Season	Club	Lea	GP	G	A	TP	PIM	GP	G	A	TP	PIM
1983-84	Kelowna	WHL	69	16	11	27	16	....	....	....	....	....
1984-85	Kelowna	WHL	51	35	38	73	58	6	5	2	7	8
1985-86	Spokane	WHL	52	45	45	90	57	9	6	7	13	19
1986-87	Spokane	WHL	46	45	55	100	71	5	2	7	9	6
	Sherbrooke	AHL	....	....	....	....	....	10	2	7	9	2
1987-88	Sherbrooke	AHL	77	26	48	74	83	6	1	3	4	6
1988-89	**Montreal**	**NHL**	49	8	16	24	16	9	1	1	2	10
	Sherbrooke	AHL	7	6	5	11	7	....	....	....	....	....
1989-90	**Montreal**	**NHL**	57	9	15	24	28	8	2	0	2	2
1990-91	**Montreal**	**NHL**	51	6	9	15	10	13	5	3	8	6
1991-92	**Montreal**	**NHL**	79	23	27	50	57	11	2	4	6	6
1992-93	**Edmonton**	**NHL**	60	10	10	20	47	....	....	....	....	....
	Minnesota	**NHL**	8	0	1	1	2	....	....	....	....	....
1993-94	**Dallas**	**NHL**	76	17	14	31	31	9	3	1	4	2
1994-95	**Dallas**	**NHL**	32	9	4	13	16	5	0	1	1	2
	NHL Totals		412	82	96	178	207	55	13	10	23	28

Traded to **Edmonton** by **Montreal** with Shayne Corson and Vladimir Vujtek for Vincent Damphousse and Edmonton's fourth round choice (Adam Wiesel) in 1993 Entry Draft, August 27, 1992. Traded to **Minnesota** by **Edmonton** for Todd Elik, March 5, 1993.

GILHEN, RANDY (GIHL-uhn) — WPG.

Center. Shoots left. 6', 190 lbs. Born, Zweibrucken, W. Germany, June 13, 1963.
(Hartford's 6th choice, 109th overall, in 1982 Entry Draft).

			Regular Season					Playoffs				
Season	Club	Lea	GP	G	A	TP	PIM	GP	G	A	TP	PIM
1980-81	Saskatoon	WHL	68	10	5	15	154	....	....	....	....	....
1981-82	Saskatoon	WHL	25	15	9	24	45	....	....	....	....	....
	Winnipeg	WHL	36	26	28	54	42	....	....	....	....	....
1982-83	**Hartford**	**NHL**	2	0	1	1	0	....	....	....	....	....
	Winnipeg	WHL	71	57	44	101	84	3	2	2	4	0
1983-84	Binghamton	AHL	73	8	12	20	72	....	....	....	....	....
1984-85	Salt Lake	IHL	57	20	20	40	28	....	....	....	....	....
	Binghamton	AHL	18	3	3	6	9	8	4	1	5	16
1985-86	Fort Wayne	IHL	82	44	40	84	48	15	10	8	18	6
1986-87	**Winnipeg**	**NHL**	2	0	0	0	0	....	....	....	....	....
	Sherbrooke	AHL	75	36	29	65	44	17	7	13	20	10
1987-88	**Winnipeg**	**NHL**	13	3	2	5	15	4	1	0	1	10
	Moncton	AHL	68	40	47	87	51	....	....	....	....	....
1988-89	**Winnipeg**	**NHL**	64	5	3	8	38	....	....	....	....	....
1989-90	**Pittsburgh**	**NHL**	61	5	11	16	54	....	....	....	....	....
1990-91	**Pittsburgh**	**NHL**	72	15	10	25	51	16	1	0	1	14
1991-92	**Los Angeles**	**NHL**	33	3	6	9	14	....	....	....	....	....
	NY Rangers	**NHL**	40	7	7	14	14	13	1	2	3	2
1992-93	**NY Rangers**	**NHL**	33	3	2	5	8	....	....	....	....	....
	Tampa Bay	**NHL**	11	0	2	2	6	....	....	....	....	....
1993-94	**Florida**	**NHL**	20	4	4	8	16	....	....	....	....	....
	Winnipeg	**NHL**	40	3	3	6	34	....	....	....	....	....
1994-95	**Winnipeg**	**NHL**	44	5	6	11	52	....	....	....	....	....
	NHL Totals		435	53	57	110	302	33	3	2	5	26

Signed as a free agent by **Winnipeg**, November 8, 1985. Traded to **Pittsburgh** by **Winnipeg** with Jim Kyte and Andrew McBain for Randy Cunneyworth, Rick Tabaracci and Dave McLlwain, June 17, 1989. Claimed by **Minnesota** from **Pittsburgh** in Expansion Draft, May 30, 1991. Traded to **Los Angeles** by **Minnesota** with Charlie Huddy, Jim Thomson and NY Rangers' fourth round choice (previously acquired by Minnesota — Los Angeles selected Alexei Zhitnik) in 1991 Entry Draft for Todd Elik, June 22, 1991. Traded to **NY Rangers** by **Los Angeles** for Corey Millen, December 23, 1991. Traded to **Tampa Bay** by **NY Rangers** for Mike Hartman, March 22, 1993. Claimed by **Florida** from **Tampa Bay** in Expansion Draft, June 24, 1993. Traded to **Winnipeg** by **Florida** for Stu Barnes and St. Louis' sixth round choice (previously acquired by Winnipeg — later traded to Edmonton — later traded to Winnipeg — Winnipeg selected Chris Kibermanis), November 25, 1993.

GILL, HAL — BOS.

Defense. Shoots left. 6'6", 200 lbs. Born, Concord, MA, April 6, 1975.
(Boston's 8th choice, 207th overall, in 1993 Entry Draft).

			Regular Season					Playoffs				
Season	Club	Lea	GP	G	A	TP	PIM	GP	G	A	TP	PIM
1993-94	Providence	H.E.	31	1	2	3	26	....	....	....	....	....
1994-95	Providence	H.E.	26	1	3	4	22	....	....	....	....	....

GILL, TODD (GIHL) — TOR.

Defense. Shoots left. 6', 180 lbs. Born, Cardinal, Ont., November 9, 1965.
(Toronto's 2nd choice, 25th overall, in 1984 Entry Draft).

			Regular Season					Playoffs				
Season	Club	Lea	GP	G	A	TP	PIM	GP	G	A	TP	PIM
1982-83	Windsor	OHL	70	12	24	36	108	3	0	0	0	11
1983-84	Windsor	OHL	68	9	48	57	184	3	1	1	2	10
1984-85	**Toronto**	**NHL**	10	1	0	1	13	....	....	....	....	....
	Windsor	OHL	53	17	40	57	148	4	0	1	1	14
1985-86	**Toronto**	**NHL**	15	1	2	3	28	1	0	0	0	0
	St. Catharines	AHL	58	8	25	33	90	10	1	6	7	17
1986-87	**Toronto**	**NHL**	61	4	27	31	92	13	2	2	4	42
	Newmarket	AHL	11	1	8	9	33	....	....	....	....	....
1987-88	**Toronto**	**NHL**	65	8	17	25	131	6	1	3	4	20
	Newmarket	AHL	2	0	1	1	2	....	....	....	....	....
1988-89	**Toronto**	**NHL**	59	11	14	25	72	....	....	....	....	....
1989-90	**Toronto**	**NHL**	48	1	14	15	92	5	0	3	3	16
1990-91	**Toronto**	**NHL**	72	2	22	24	113	....	....	....	....	....
1991-92	**Toronto**	**NHL**	74	2	15	17	91	....	....	....	....	....
1992-93	**Toronto**	**NHL**	69	11	32	43	66	21	1	10	11	26
1993-94	**Toronto**	**NHL**	45	4	24	28	44	18	1	5	6	37
1994-95	**Toronto**	**NHL**	47	7	25	32	64	7	0	3	3	6
	NHL Totals		565	52	192	244	806	71	5	26	31	147

GILLAM, SEAN — DET.

Defense. Shoots right. 6'2", 187 lbs. Born, Lethbridge, Alta., May 7, 1976.
(Detroit's 3rd choice, 75th overall, in 1994 Entry Draft).

			Regular Season					Playoffs				
Season	Club	Lea	GP	G	A	TP	PIM	GP	G	A	TP	PIM
1992-93	Spokane	WHL	70	6	27	33	121	10	0	2	2	10
1993-94	Spokane	WHL	70	7	17	24	106	3	0	0	0	6
1994-95a	Spokane	WHL	72	16	40	56	192	11	0	3	3	33

a WHL West Second All-Star Team (1995)

GILMOUR, DOUG — TOR.

Center. Shoots left. 5'11", 172 lbs. Born, Kingston, Ont., June 25, 1963.
(St. Louis' 4th choice, 134th overall, in 1982 Entry Draft).

			Regular Season					Playoffs				
Season	Club	Lea	GP	G	A	TP	PIM	GP	G	A	TP	PIM
1981-82	Cornwall	OHL	67	46	73	119	42	5	6	9	15	2
1982-83a	Cornwall	OHL	68	70	*107	*177	62	8	8	10	18	16
1983-84	**St. Louis**	**NHL**	80	25	28	53	57	11	2	9	11	10
1984-85	**St. Louis**	**NHL**	78	21	36	57	49	3	1	1	2	2
1985-86	**St. Louis**	**NHL**	74	25	28	53	41	19	9	12	*21	25
1986-87	**St. Louis**	**NHL**	80	42	63	105	58	6	2	2	4	16
1987-88	**St. Louis**	**NHL**	72	36	50	86	59	10	3	14	17	18
1988-89	**Calgary**	**NHL**	72	26	59	85	44	22	11	11	22	20
1989-90	**Calgary**	**NHL**	78	24	67	91	54	6	3	1	4	8
1990-91	**Calgary**	**NHL**	78	20	61	81	144	7	1	1	2	0
1991-92	**Calgary**	**NHL**	38	11	27	38	46	....	....	....	....	....
	Toronto	**NHL**	40	15	34	49	32	....	....	....	....	....
1992-93b	**Toronto**	**NHL**	83	32	95	127	100	21	10	*25	35	30
1993-94	**Toronto**	**NHL**	83	27	84	111	105	18	6	22	28	42
1994-95	Rapperswil	Switz.	9	2	13	15	16	....	....	....	....	....
	Toronto	**NHL**	44	10	23	33	26	7	0	6	6	6
	NHL Totals		900	314	655	969	815	130	48	104	152	177

a OHL First All-Star Team (1983)
b Won Frank J. Selke Trophy (1993)

Played in NHL All-Star Game (1993, 1994)

Traded to **Calgary** by **St. Louis** with Mark Hunter, Steve Bozek and Michael Dark for Mike Bullard, Craig Coxe and Tim Corkery, September 6, 1988. Traded to **Toronto** by **Calgary** with Jamie Macoun, Ric Nattress, Kent Manderville and Rick Wamsley for Gary Leeman, Alexander Godynyuk, Jeff Reese, Michel Petit and Craig Berube, January 2, 1992.

GINGRAS, GASTON — MTL.

Defense. Shoots left. 6'1", 200 lbs. Born, Temiscamingue, Que., February 13, 1959.

			Regular Season					Playoffs				
Season	Club	Lea	GP	G	A	TP	PIM	GP	G	A	TP	PIM
1976-77	Kitchener	OHA	59	13	62	75	134	3	0	1	1	6
1977-78	Kitchener	OHA	32	13	24	37	31	....	....	....	....	....
	Hamilton	OHA	29	11	19	30	37	15	3	11	14	13
1978-79	Birmingham	WHA	60	13	21	34	35	....	....	....	....	....
1979-80	Nova Scotia	AHL	30	11	27	38	17	....	....	....	....	....
	Montreal	**NHL**	34	3	7	10	18	10	1	6	7	8
1980-81	**Montreal**	**NHL**	55	5	16	21	22	1	1	0	1	0
	Montreal	**NHL**	34	6	18	24	28	5	0	1	1	0
1982-83	**Montreal**	**NHL**	22	1	8	9	8	....	....	....	....	....
	Toronto	**NHL**	45	10	18	28	10	3	1	2	3	2
1983-84	**Toronto**	**NHL**	59	7	20	27	16	....	....	....	....	....
1984-85	**Toronto**	**NHL**	5	0	2	2	0	....	....	....	....	....
	St. Catharines	AHL	36	7	12	19	13	....	....	....	....	....
	Sherbrooke	AHL	21	3	14	17	6	17	5	4	9	4
1985-86	**Montreal**	**NHL**	34	8	18	26	12	11	2	3	5	4
	Sherbrooke	AHL	42	11	20	31	14	....	....	....	....	....
1986-87	**Montreal**	**NHL**	66	11	34	45	21	5	0	2	2	0
1987-88	**Montreal**	**NHL**	2	0	1	1	2	....	....	....	....	....
	St. Louis	**NHL**	68	7	22	29	18	10	1	3	4	4
1988-89	**St. Louis**	**NHL**	52	3	10	13	6	7	0	1	1	2
1989-90	Biel	Switz.	36	17	20	37	....	6	3	3	6	....
1990-91	Biel	Switz.	13	1	7	8	....	....	....	....	....	....
1991-92	Lugano	Switz.	34	10	19	29	24	....	....	....	....	....
1992-93	Val Gardena	Italy	18	3	24	27	16	....	....	....	....	....
1993-94	Val Gardena	Italy	21	3	14	17	14	....	....	....	....	....
1994-95	Fredericton	AHL	19	3	6	9	4	17	2	12	14	8
	NHL Totals		476	61	174	235	161	52	6	18	24	20

Traded to **Toronto** by **Montreal** for Toronto's second round choice in either 1985 or 1986 Entry Draft, December 17, 1982. Traded to **Montreal** by **Toronto** for Larry Landon, February 14, 1985. Traded to **St. Louis** by **Montreal** for Larry Trader and future considerations, October 13, 1987. Signed as a free agent by **Montreal**, August 10, 1995.

GIRARD, RICK — VAN.

Center. Shoots left. 5'11", 175 lbs. Born, Edmonton, Alta., May 1, 1974.
(Vancouver's 2nd choice, 46th overall, in 1993 Entry Draft).

			Regular Season					Playoffs				
Season	Club	Lea	GP	G	A	TP	PIM	GP	G	A	TP	PIM
1991-92	Swift Current	WHL	45	14	17	31	6	8	2	0	2	2
1992-93ab	Swift Current	WHL	72	71	70	141	25	17	9	17	26	10
1993-94a	Swift Current	WHL	58	40	49	89	43	7	1	8	9	6
	Hamilton	AHL	1	1	1	2	0	....	....	....	....	....
1994-95	Syracuse	AHL	26	10	13	23	22	....	....	....	....	....

a WHL East First All-Star Team (1993, 1994)
b Canadian Major Junior Sportsmanlike Player of the Year (1993)

GIROUX, RAYMOND (jih-ROO) PHI.

Defense. Shoots left. 6', 165 lbs. Born, North Bay, Ont., July 20, 1976.
(Philadelphia's 7th choice, 202nd overall, in 1994 Entry Draft).

			Regular Season					Playoffs				
Season	Club	Lea	GP	G	A	TP	PIM	GP	G	A	TP	PIM
1993-94	Powasson	Jr. A	36	10	40	50	42	....	....	....	....	....
1994-95	Yale	ECAC	27	1	3	4	8	....	....	....	....	....

GLYNN, BRIAN (GLIHN) HFD.

Defense. Shoots left. 6'4", 224 lbs. Born, Iserlohn, West Germany, November 23, 1967.
(Calgary's 2nd choice, 37th overall, in 1986 Entry Draft).

			Regular Season					Playoffs				
Season	Club	Lea	GP	G	A	TP	PIM	GP	G	A	TP	PIM
1984-85	Saskatoon	WHL	12	1	0	1	2	3	0	0	0	0
1985-86	Saskatoon	WHL	66	7	25	32	131	13	0	3	3	30
1986-87	Saskatoon	WHL	44	2	26	28	163	11	1	3	4	19
1987-88	Calgary	NHL	67	5	14	19	87	1	0	0	0	0
1988-89	Calgary	NHL	9	0	1	1	19	....	....	....	....	....
	Salt Lake	IHL	31	3	10	13	105	14	3	7	10	31
1989-90	Calgary	NHL	1	0	0	0	0	....	....	....	....	....
ab	Salt Lake	IHL	80	17	44	61	164	....	....	....	....	....
1990-91	Salt Lake	IHL	8	1	3	4	18	....	....	....	....	....
	Minnesota	NHL	66	8	11	19	83	23	2	6	8	18
1991-92	Minnesota	NHL	37	2	12	14	24	....	....	....	....	....
	Edmonton	NHL	25	2	6	8	6	16	4	1	5	12
1992-93	Edmonton	NHL	64	4	12	16	60	....	....	....	....	....
1993-94	Ottawa	NHL	48	2	13	15	41	....	....	....	....	....
	Vancouver	NHL	16	0	0	0	12	17	0	3	3	10
1994-95	Hartford	NHL	43	1	6	7	32	....	....	....	....	....
	NHL Totals		376	24	75	99	364	57	6	10	16	40

a IHL First All-Star Team (1990)
b Won Governors' Trophy (Outstanding Defenseman - IHL) (1990)

Traded to **Minnesota** by **Calgary** for Frantisek Musil, October 26, 1990. Traded to **Edmonton** by **Minnesota** for David Shaw, January 21, 1992. Traded to **Ottawa** by **Edmonton** for Ottawa's eighth round choice (Rob Quinn) in 1994 Entry Draft, September 15, 1993. Claimed on waivers by **Vancouver** from **Ottawa**, February 5, 1994. Claimed by **Hartford** from **Vancouver** in NHL Waiver Draft, January 18, 1995.

GODBOUT, DANIEL TOR.

Defense. Shoots left. 6'2", 195 lbs. Born, Grand Falls, N.B., March 20, 1975.

			Regular Season					Playoffs				
Season	Club	Lea	GP	G	A	TP	PIM	GP	G	A	TP	PIM
1991-92	Belleville	OHL	60	1	8	9	44	5	0	1	1	5
1992-93	Belleville	OHL	65	2	17	19	66	7	0	1	1	4
1993-94	Belleville	OHL	66	0	15	15	45	12	0	1	1	10
1994-95	Kitchener	OHL	56	3	11	14	85	5	0	1	1	0

Signed as a free agent by **Toronto**, August 30, 1993.

GODBOUT, JASON PIT.

Defense. Shoots left. 5'11", 180 lbs. Born, , IN, August 5, 1976.
(Pittsburgh's 12th choice, 232nd overall, in 1994 Entry Draft).

			Regular Season					Playoffs				
Season	Club	Lea	GP	G	A	TP	PIM	GP	G	A	TP	PIM
1993-94	Hill-Murray	HS	25	18	26	44	....	....	....	....	....	....
1994-95	U. Minnesota	WCHA	32	1	4	5	28	....	....	....	....	....

GODYNYUK, ALEXANDER (goh-dih-NYOOK) HFD.

Defense. Shoots left. 6', 207 lbs. Born, Kiev, Ukraine, January 27, 1970.
(Toronto's 5th choice, 115th overall, in 1990 Entry Draft).

			Regular Season					Playoffs				
Season	Club	Lea	GP	G	A	TP	PIM	GP	G	A	TP	PIM
1986-87	Sokol Kiev	USSR	9	0	1	1	2	....	....	....	....	....
1987-88	Sokol Kiev	USSR	2	0	0	0	2	....	....	....	....	....
1988-89	Sokol Kiev	USSR	30	3	3	6	12	....	....	....	....	....
1989-90	Sokol Kiev	USSR	37	3	2	5	31	....	....	....	....	....
1990-91	Sokol Kiev	USSR	19	3	1	4	20	....	....	....	....	....
	Toronto	NHL	18	0	3	3	16	....	....	....	....	....
	Newmarket	AHL	11	0	1	1	29	....	....	....	....	....
1991-92	Toronto	NHL	31	3	6	9	59	....	....	....	....	....
	Calgary	NHL	6	0	1	1	4	....	....	....	....	....
	Salt Lake	IHL	17	2	1	3	24	....	....	....	....	....
1992-93	Calgary	NHL	27	3	4	7	19	....	....	....	....	....
1993-94	Florida	NHL	26	0	10	10	35	....	....	....	....	....
	Hartford	NHL	43	3	9	12	40	....	....	....	....	....
1994-95	Hartford	NHL	14	0	0	0	8	....	....	....	....	....
	NHL Totals		165	9	33	42	181	....	....	....	....	....

Traded to **Calgary** by **Toronto** with Craig Berube, Gary Leeman, Michel Petit and Jeff Reese for Doug Gilmour, Jamie Macoun, Ric Nattress, Rick Wamsley and Kent Manderville, January 2, 1992. Claimed by **Florida** from **Calgary** in Expansion Draft, June 24, 1993. Traded to **Hartford** by **Florida** for Jim McKenzie, December 16, 1993.

GOLDEN, RYAN BOS.

Center. Shoots left. 6'3", 197 lbs. Born, Boston, MA, October 15, 1974.
(Boston's 7th choice, 181st overall, in 1993 Entry Draft).

			Regular Season					Playoffs				
Season	Club	Lea	GP	G	A	TP	PIM	GP	G	A	TP	PIM
1993-94	Lowell	H.E.	14	0	3	3	12	....	....	....	....	....
1994-95	Lowell	H.E.	10	0	0	0	10	....	....	....	....	....

GOLOKHVASTOV, KONSTANTIN T.B.

Right wing. Shoots right. 6'1", 185 lbs. Born, Dneprodzerzinsk, USSR, February 6, 1977.
(Tampa Bay's 4th choice, 108th overall, in 1995 Entry Draft).

			Regular Season					Playoffs				
Season	Club	Lea	GP	G	A	TP	PIM	GP	G	A	TP	PIM
1994-95	Moscow D'amo	CIS	6	0	0	0	2	....	....	....	....	....

GOLUBOVSKY, YAN (goh-luh-BOHV-skee) DET.

Defense. Shoots right. 6'3", 183 lbs. Born, Novosibirsk, USSR, March 9, 1976.
(Detroit's 1st choice, 23rd overall, in 1994 Entry Draft).

			Regular Season					Playoffs				
Season	Club	Lea	GP	G	A	TP	PIM	GP	G	A	TP	PIM
1993-94	Mosc. D'amo 2	CIS 3				UNAVAILABLE						
	Russian Pen's	IHL	8	0	0	0	23	....	....	....	....	....
1994-95	Adirondack	AHL	57	4	2	6	39	....	....	....	....	....

GONCHAR, SERGEI (gohn-CHAR) WSH.

Defense. Shoots left. 6'2", 212 lbs. Born, Chelyabinsk, USSR, April 13, 1974.
(Washington's 1st choice, 14th overall, in 1992 Entry Draft).

			Regular Season					Playoffs				
Season	Club	Lea	GP	G	A	TP	PIM	GP	G	A	TP	PIM
1991-92	Chelyabinsk	CIS	31	1	0	1	6	....	....	....	....	....
1992-93	Moscow D'amo	CIS	31	1	3	4	70	10	0	0	0	12
1993-94	Moscow D'amo	CIS	44	4	5	9	36	10	0	3	3	14
	Portland	AHL	....	....	....	....	....	2	0	0	0	0
1994-95	Portland	AHL	61	10	32	42	67	....	....	....	....	....
	Washington	NHL	31	2	5	7	22	7	2	2	4	2
	NHL Totals		31	2	5	7	22	7	2	2	4	2

GONEAU, DANIEL BOS.

Left wing. Shoots left. 6'1", 196 lbs. Born, Montreal, Que., January 16, 1976.
(Boston's 2nd choice, 47th overall, in 1994 Entry Draft).

			Regular Season					Playoffs				
Season	Club	Lea	GP	G	A	TP	PIM	GP	G	A	TP	PIM
1992-93	Laval	QMJHL	62	16	25	41	44	13	0	4	4	4
1993-94	Laval	QMJHL	68	29	57	86	81	19	8	21	29	45
1994-95	Laval	QMJHL	56	16	31	47	78	20	5	10	15	33

GORBACHEV, SERGEI S.J.

Right wing. Shoots left. 6'1", 185 lbs. Born, Saratov, USSR, October 24, 1975.
(San Jose's 7th choice, 167th overall, in 1994 Entry Draft).

			Regular Season					Playoffs				
Season	Club	Lea	GP	G	A	TP	PIM	GP	G	A	TP	PIM
1993-94	Moscow D'amo	CIS 2	2	0	0	0	0	....	....	....	....	....
1994-95	Moscow D'amo	CIS	4	0	1	1	2	....	....	....	....	....

GORDIOUK, VIKTOR (gohr-dee-YOOK)

Left wing. Shoots right. 5'10", 176 lbs. Born, Odintsovo, USSR, April 11, 1970.
(Buffalo's 6th choice, 142nd overall, in 1990 Entry Draft).

			Regular Season					Playoffs				
Season	Club	Lea	GP	G	A	TP	PIM	GP	G	A	TP	PIM
1986-87	Soviet Wings	USSR	2	0	0	0	0	....	....	....	....	....
1987-88	Soviet Wings	USSR	26	2	2	4	6	....	....	....	....	....
1988-89	Soviet Wings	USSR	41	5	1	6	10	....	....	....	....	....
1989-90	Soviet Wings	USSR	48	11	4	15	24	....	....	....	....	....
1990-91	Soviet Wings	USSR	46	12	10	22	22	....	....	....	....	....
1991-92	Soviet Wings	CIS	42	16	7	23	24	....	....	....	....	....
1992-93	Buffalo	NHL	16	3	6	9	0	....	....	....	....	....
	Rochester	AHL	35	11	14	25	8	17	9	9	18	4
1993-94	Rochester	AHL	74	28	39	67	26	4	3	0	3	2
1994-95	Rochester	AHL	63	31	30	61	36	3	0	2	2	0
	Buffalo	NHL	10	0	2	2	0	....	....	....	....	....
	NHL Totals		26	3	8	11	0	....	....	....	....	....

GORDON, RHETT WPG.

Right wing. Shoots right. 5'11", 175 lbs. Born, Regina, Sask., August 26, 1976.

			Regular Season					Playoffs				
Season	Club	Lea	GP	G	A	TP	PIM	GP	G	A	TP	PIM
1992-93	Regina	WHL	2	1	0	1	2	4	0	0	0	0
1993-94	Regina	WHL	60	19	28	47	14	4	0	0	0	7
1994-95	Regina	WHL	71	36	43	79	64	4	2	2	4	0

Signed as a free agent by **Winnipeg**, September 29, 1994.

GORDON, ROBB VAN.

Center. Shoots right. 5'11", 170 lbs. Born, Murrayville, B.C., January 13, 1976.
(Vancouver's 2nd choice, 39th overall, in 1994 Entry Draft).

			Regular Season					Playoffs				
Season	Club	Lea	GP	G	A	TP	PIM	GP	G	A	TP	PIM
1993-94	Powell River	BCJHL	60	69	89	158	141	....	....	....	....	....
1994-95	U. of Michigan	CCHA	39	15	26	41	72	....	....	....	....	....

GORENKO, DMITRI (goh-REHN-koh) HFD.

Left wing. Shoots left. 6', 165 lbs. Born, Barnaul, USSR, February 13, 1975.
(Hartford's 6th choice, 214th overall, in 1993 Entry Draft).

			Regular Season					Playoffs				
Season	Club	Lea	GP	G	A	TP	PIM	GP	G	A	TP	PIM
1991-92	CSKA	CIS	14	0	1	1	6	....	....	....	....	....
1992-93	CSKA	CIS	42	3	0	3	20	....	....	....	....	....
1993-94	CSKA	CIS	40	5	1	6	28	3	1	0	1	2
1994-95	CSKA	CIS	33	5	2	7	35	....	....	....	....	....

GOSSELIN, CHRISTIAN N.J.

Defense. Shoots left. 6'4", 205 lbs. Born, St. Redempteur, Que., August 21, 1976.
(New Jersey's 5th choice, 129th overall, in 1994 Entry Draft).

			Regular Season					Playoffs				
Season	Club	Lea	GP	G	A	TP	PIM	GP	G	A	TP	PIM
1993-94	St-Hyacinthe	QMJHL	12	3	2	5	16	....	....	....	....	....
1994-95	St-Hyacinthe	QMJHL	60	5	10	15	202	5	0	0	0	11

GOSSELIN, DAVID N.J.

Right wing. Shoots right. 6', 175 lbs. Born, Levis, Que., June 22, 1977.
(New Jersey's 4th choice, 78th overall, in 1995 Entry Draft).

			Regular Season					Playoffs				
Season	Club	Lea	GP	G	A	TP	PIM	GP	G	A	TP	PIM
1993-94	St-Jean	Midget	44	26	19	45	62	4	2	1	3	0
1994-95	Sherbrooke	QMJHL	58	8	8	16	36	7	0	0	0	2

GOVEDARIS, CHRIS (goh-va-DAIR-us) WPG.

Left wing. Shoots left. 6', 200 lbs. Born, Toronto, Ont., February 2, 1970.
(Hartford's 1st choice, 11th overall, in 1988 Entry Draft).

			Regular Season					Playoffs				
Season	Club	Lea	GP	G	A	TP	PIM	GP	G	A	TP	PIM
1986-87	Toronto	OHL	64	36	28	64	148					
1987-88	Toronto	OHL	62	42	38	80	118	4	2	1	3	10
1988-89	Toronto	OHL	49	41	38	79	117	6	2	3	5	0
1989-90	**Hartford**	**NHL**	**12**	**0**	**1**	**1**	**6**	**2**	**0**	**0**	**0**	**2**
	Binghamton	AHL	14	3	3	6	4					
	Hamilton	OHL	23	11	21	32	53					
1990-91	**Hartford**	**NHL**	**14**	**1**	**3**	**4**	**4**					
	Springfield	AHL	56	26	36	62	133	9	2	5	7	36
1991-92	Springfield	AHL	43	14	25	39	55	11	3	2	5	25
1992-93	**Hartford**	**NHL**	**7**	**1**	**0**	**1**	**0**					
	Springfield	AHL	65	31	24	55	58	15	7	4	11	18
1993-94	**Toronto**	**NHL**	**12**	**2**	**2**	**4**	**14**	**2**	**0**	**0**	**0**	**0**
	St. John's	AHL	62	35	35	70	76	11	6	5	11	22
1994-95	Milwaukee	IHL	54	34	25	59	71					
	Adirondack	AHL	24	19	11	30	34	4	2	1	3	10
	NHL Totals		**45**	**4**	**6**	**10**	**24**	**4**	**0**	**0**	**0**	**2**

Signed as a free agent by **Toronto**, September 16, 1993. Signed as a free agent by **Winnipeg**, August 8, 1995.

GRACHEV, VLADIMIR NYI

Left wing. Shoots left. 6', 178 lbs. Born, Moscow, USSR, January 28, 1973.
(NY Islanders' 6th choice, 152nd overall, in 1992 Entry Draft).

			Regular Season					Playoffs				
Season	Club	Lea	GP	G	A	TP	PIM	GP	G	A	TP	PIM
1991-92	Mosc. D'amo 2	CIS 3	62	13	3	16	26					
1992-93	Moscow D'amo	CIS	33	2	1	3	26	7	0	0	0	2
1993-94	Moscow D'amo	CIS	36	4	3	7	10	6	0	0	0	4
1994-95	Moscow D'amo	CIS	48	13	8	21	20	14	7	2	9	10

GRAHAM, DIRK

Left/Right wing. Shoots right. 5'11", 198 lbs. Born, Regina, Sask., July 29, 1959.
(Vancouver's 5th choice, 89th overall, in 1979 Entry Draft).

			Regular Season					Playoffs				
Season	Club	Lea	GP	G	A	TP	PIM	GP	G	A	TP	PIM
1975-76	Regina	WCHL	2	0	0	0	0	6	1	1	2	5
1976-77	Regina	WCHL	65	37	28	65	66					
1977-78	Regina	WCHL	72	49	61	110	87	13	15	19	34	37
1978-79	Regina	WHL	71	48	60	108	252					
1979-80	Dallas	CHL	62	17	15	32	96					
1980-81	Fort Wayne	IHL	6	1	2	3	12					
a	Toledo	IHL	61	40	45	85	88					
1981-82	Toledo	IHL	72	49	56	105	68	13	10	11	*21	8
1982-83b	Toledo	IHL	78	70	55	125	88	11	13	7	*20	30
1983-84	**Minnesota**	**NHL**	**6**	**1**	**1**	**2**	**0**	**1**	**0**	**0**	**0**	**2**
c	Salt Lake	CHL	57	37	57	94	72	5	3	8	11	2
1984-85	**Minnesota**	**NHL**	**36**	**12**	**11**	**23**	**23**	**9**	**0**	**4**	**4**	**7**
	Springfield	AHL	37	20	28	48	41					
1985-86	**Minnesota**	**NHL**	**80**	**22**	**33**	**55**	**87**	**5**	**3**	**1**	**4**	**2**
1986-87	**Minnesota**	**NHL**	**76**	**25**	**29**	**54**	**142**					
1987-88	**Minnesota**	**NHL**	**28**	**7**	**5**	**12**	**39**					
	Chicago	**NHL**	**42**	**17**	**19**	**36**	**32**	**4**	**1**	**2**	**3**	**4**
1988-89	**Chicago**	**NHL**	**80**	**33**	**45**	**78**	**89**	**16**	**2**	**4**	**6**	**38**
1989-90	**Chicago**	**NHL**	**73**	**22**	**32**	**54**	**102**	**5**	**1**	**5**	**6**	**2**
1990-91d	**Chicago**	**NHL**	**80**	**24**	**21**	**45**	**88**	**6**	**1**	**2**	**3**	**17**
1991-92	**Chicago**	**NHL**	**80**	**17**	**30**	**47**	**89**	**18**	**7**	**5**	**12**	**8**
1992-93	**Chicago**	**NHL**	**84**	**20**	**17**	**37**	**139**	**4**	**0**	**0**	**0**	**0**
1993-94	**Chicago**	**NHL**	**67**	**15**	**18**	**33**	**45**	**6**	**0**	**1**	**1**	**4**
1994-95	**Chicago**	**NHL**	**40**	**4**	**9**	**13**	**42**	**16**	**2**	**3**	**5**	**8**
	NHL Totals		**772**	**219**	**270**	**489**	**917**	**90**	**17**	**27**	**44**	**92**

a IHL Second All-Star Team (1981)
b IHL First All-Star Team (1983)
c CHL First All-Star Team (1984)
d Won Frank J. Selke Trophy (1991)

Signed as a free agent by **Minnesota**, August 17, 1983. Traded to **Chicago** by **Minnesota** for Curt Fraser, January 4, 1988.

GRANATO, TONY L.A.

Left wing. Shoots right. 5'10", 185 lbs. Born, Downers Grove, IL, July 25, 1964.
(NY Rangers' 5th choice, 120th overall, in 1982 Entry Draft).

			Regular Season					Playoffs				
Season	Club	Lea	GP	G	A	TP	PIM	GP	G	A	TP	PIM
1983-84	U. Wisconsin	WCHA	35	14	17	31	48					
1984-85	U. Wisconsin	WCHA	42	33	34	67	94					
1985-86	U. Wisconsin	WCHA	33	25	24	49	36					
1986-87ab	U. Wisconsin	WCHA	42	28	45	73	64					
1987-88	U.S. National	....	49	40	31	71	55					
	U.S. Olympic	....	6	1	7	8	4					
	Colorado	IHL	22	13	14	27	36	8	9	4	13	16
1988-89c	**NY Rangers**	**NHL**	**78**	**36**	**27**	**63**	**140**	**4**	**1**	**1**	**2**	**21**
1989-90	**NY Rangers**	**NHL**	**37**	**7**	**18**	**25**	**77**					
	Los Angeles	**NHL**	**19**	**5**	**6**	**11**	**45**	**10**	**5**	**4**	**9**	**12**
1990-91	**Los Angeles**	**NHL**	**68**	**30**	**34**	**64**	**154**	**12**	**1**	**4**	**5**	**28**
1991-92	**Los Angeles**	**NHL**	**80**	**39**	**29**	**68**	**187**	**6**	**1**	**5**	**6**	**10**
1992-93	**Los Angeles**	**NHL**	**81**	**37**	**45**	**82**	**171**	**24**	**6**	**11**	**17**	**50**
1993-94	**Los Angeles**	**NHL**	**50**	**7**	**14**	**21**	**150**					
1994-95	**Los Angeles**	**NHL**	**33**	**13**	**11**	**24**	**68**					
	NHL Totals		**446**	**174**	**184**	**358**	**992**	**56**	**14**	**25**	**39**	**121**

a WCHA Second All-Star Team (1987)
b NCAA West Second All-American Team (1987)
c NHL All-Rookie Team (1989)

Traded to **Los Angeles** by **NY Rangers** with Tomas Sandstrom for Bernie Nicholls, January 20, 1990.

GRATTON, BENOIT WSH.

Left wing. Shoots left. 5'10", 163 lbs. Born, Montreal, Que., December 28, 1976.
(Washington's 6th choice, 105th overall, in 1995 Entry Draft).

			Regular Season					Playoffs				
Season	Club	Lea	GP	G	A	TP	PIM	GP	G	A	TP	PIM
1993-94	Laval	QMJHL	51	9	14	23	70	20	2	1	3	19
1994-95	Laval	QMJHL	71	30	58	88	199	20	8	*21	29	42

GRATTON, CHRIS T.B.

Center. Shoots left. 6'3", 212 lbs. Born, Brantford, Ont., July 5, 1975.
(Tampa Bay's 1st choice, 3rd overall, in 1993 Entry Draft).

			Regular Season					Playoffs				
Season	Club	Lea	GP	G	A	TP	PIM	GP	G	A	TP	PIM
1991-92	Kingston	OHL	62	27	29	66	37					
1992-93	Kingston	OHL	58	55	54	109	125	16	11	18	29	42
1993-94	**Tampa Bay**	**NHL**	**84**	**13**	**29**	**42**	**123**					
1994-95	**Tampa Bay**	**NHL**	**46**	**7**	**20**	**27**	**89**					
	NHL Totals		**130**	**20**	**49**	**69**	**212**					

GRAVES, ADAM NYR

Center. Shoots left. 6', 205 lbs. Born, Toronto, Ont., April 12, 1968.
(Detroit's 2nd choice, 22nd overall, in 1986 Entry Draft).

			Regular Season					Playoffs				
Season	Club	Lea	GP	G	A	TP	PIM	GP	G	A	TP	PIM
1985-86	Windsor	OHL	62	27	37	64	35	16	5	11	16	10
1986-87	Windsor	OHL	66	45	55	100	70	14	9	8	17	32
	Adirondack	AHL						5	0	1	1	0
1987-88	**Detroit**	**NHL**	**9**	**0**	**1**	**1**	**8**					
	Windsor	OHL	37	28	32	60	107	12	14	18	*32	16
1988-89	**Detroit**	**NHL**	**56**	**7**	**5**	**12**	**60**	**5**	**0**	**0**	**0**	**4**
	Adirondack	AHL	14	10	11	21	28	14	11	7	18	17
1989-90	**Detroit**	**NHL**	**13**	**0**	**1**	**1**	**13**					
	Edmonton	**NHL**	**63**	**9**	**12**	**21**	**123**	**22**	**5**	**6**	**11**	**17**
1990-91	**Edmonton**	**NHL**	**76**	**7**	**18**	**25**	**127**	**18**	**2**	**4**	**6**	**22**
1991-92	**NY Rangers**	**NHL**	**80**	**26**	**33**	**59**	**139**	**10**	**5**	**3**	**8**	**22**
1992-93	**NY Rangers**	**NHL**	**84**	**36**	**29**	**65**	**148**					
1993-94ab	**NY Rangers**	**NHL**	**84**	**52**	**27**	**79**	**127**	**23**	**10**	**7**	**17**	**24**
1994-95	**NY Rangers**	**NHL**	**47**	**17**	**14**	**31**	**51**	**10**	**4**	**4**	**8**	**8**
	NHL Totals		**512**	**154**	**140**	**294**	**796**	**88**	**26**	**24**	**50**	**97**

a NHL Second All-Star Team (1994)
b Won King Clancy Memorial Trophy (1994)

Played in NHL All-Star Game (1994)

Traded to **Edmonton** by **Detroit** with Petr Klima, Joe Murphy and Jeff Sharples for Jimmy Carson, Kevin McClelland and Edmonton's fifth round choice (later traded to Montreal — Montreal selected Brad Layzell) in 1991 Entry Draft, November 2, 1989. Signed as a free agent by **NY Rangers**, September 3, 1991.

GREEN, TRAVIS NYI

Center. Shoots right. 6'2", 200 lbs. Born, Castlegar, B.C., December 20, 1970.
(NY Islanders' 2nd choice, 23rd overall, in 1989 Entry Draft).

			Regular Season					Playoffs				
Season	Club	Lea	GP	G	A	TP	PIM	GP	G	A	TP	PIM
1986-87	Spokane	WHL	64	8	17	25	27	3	0	0	0	0
1987-88	Spokane	WHL	72	33	54	87	42	15	10	10	20	13
1988-89	Spokane	WHL	75	51	51	102	79					
1989-90	Spokane	WHL	50	45	44	89	80					
	Medicine Hat	WHL	25	15	24	39	19	3	0	0	0	2
1990-91	Capital Dist.	AHL	73	21	34	55	26					
1991-92	Capital Dist.	AHL	71	23	27	50	10	7	0	4	4	21
1992-93	**NY Islanders**	**NHL**	**61**	**7**	**18**	**25**	**43**	**12**	**3**	**1**	**4**	**6**
	Capital Dist.	AHL	20	12	11	23	39					
1993-94	**NY Islanders**	**NHL**	**83**	**18**	**22**	**40**	**44**	**4**	**0**	**0**	**0**	**2**
1994-95	**NY Islanders**	**NHL**	**42**	**5**	**7**	**12**	**25**					
	NHL Totals		**186**	**30**	**47**	**77**	**112**	**16**	**3**	**1**	**4**	**8**

GREENLAW, JEFF

Left wing. Shoots left. 6'1", 230 lbs. Born, Toronto, Ont., February 28, 1968.
(Washington's 1st choice, 19th overall, in 1986 Entry Draft).

			Regular Season					Playoffs				
Season	Club	Lea	GP	G	A	TP	PIM	GP	G	A	TP	PIM
1985-86	Cdn. Olympic	....	57	3	16	19	81					
1986-87	**Washington**	**NHL**	**22**	**0**	**3**	**3**	**44**					
	Binghamton	AHL	4	0	2	2	0					
1987-88	Binghamton	AHL	56	8	7	15	142	1	0	0	0	2
	Washington	**NHL**						**1**	**0**	**0**	**0**	**19**
1988-89	Baltimore	AHL	55	12	15	27	115					
1989-90	Baltimore	AHL	10	3	2	5	26	7	1	0	1	13
1990-91	**Washington**	**NHL**	**10**	**2**	**0**	**2**	**10**	**1**	**0**	**0**	**0**	**2**
	Baltimore	AHL	50	17	17	34	93	3	1	1	2	2
1991-92	**Washington**	**NHL**	**5**	**0**	**1**	**1**	**34**					
	Baltimore	AHL	37	6	8	14	57					
1992-93	**Washington**	**NHL**	**16**	**1**	**1**	**2**	**18**					
	Baltimore	AHL	49	12	14	26	66	7	3	1	4	0
1993-94	**Florida**	**NHL**	**4**	**0**	**1**	**1**	**2**					
	Cincinnati	IHL	55	14	15	29	85	11	2	2	4	28
1994-95	Cincinnati	IHL	67	10	21	31	117	10	2	0	2	22
	NHL Totals		**57**	**3**	**6**	**9**	**108**	**2**	**0**	**0**	**0**	**21**

Signed as a free agent by **Florida**, July 14, 1993.

GREIG, MARK (GREG)

Right wing. Shoots right. 5'11", 190 lbs. Born, High River, Alta., January 25, 1970.
(Hartford's 1st choice, 15th overall, in 1990 Entry Draft).

			Regular Season					Playoffs				
Season	Club	Lea	GP	G	A	TP	PIM	GP	G	A	TP	PIM
1987-88	Lethbridge	WHL	65	9	18	27	38					
1988-89	Lethbridge	WHL	71	36	72	108	113	8	5	5	10	16
1989-90a	Lethbridge	WHL	65	55	80	135	149	18	11	21	32	35
1990-91	**Hartford**	**NHL**	**4**	**0**	**0**	**0**	**0**					
	Springfield	AHL	73	32	55	87	73	17	2	6	8	22
1991-92	**Hartford**	**NHL**	**17**	**0**	**5**	**5**	**6**					
	Springfield	AHL	50	20	27	47	38	9	1	1	2	20
1992-93	**Hartford**	**NHL**	**22**	**1**	**7**	**8**	**27**					
	Springfield	AHL	55	20	38	58	86					
1993-94	**Hartford**	**NHL**	**31**	**4**	**5**	**9**	**31**					
	Springfield	AHL	4	0	4	4	21					
	Toronto	**NHL**	**13**	**2**	**2**	**4**	**10**					
	St. John's	AHL	9	4	6	10	0	11	4	2	6	26
1994-95	Saint John	AHL	67	31	50	81	82	2	0	1	1	0
	Calgary	**NHL**	**8**	**1**	**1**	**2**	**2**					
	NHL Totals		**95**	**8**	**20**	**28**	**76**					

a WHL East First All-Star Team (1990)

Traded to **Toronto** by **Hartford** with Hartford's sixth round choice (later traded to NY Rangers — NY Rangers selected Yuri Litvinov) in 1994 Entry Draft for Ted Crowley, January 25, 1994. Signed as a free agent by **Calgary**, August 9, 1994.

GRENIER, DAVID — MTL.

Left wing. Shoots left. 6'2", 195 lbs. Born, Montreal, Que., February 5, 1975.

			Regular Season					Playoffs				
Season	Club	Lea	GP	G	A	TP	PIM	GP	G	A	TP	PIM
1992-93	Shawinigan	QMJHL	63	1	4	5	120	....	....	....	....	....
1993-94	Shawinigan	QMJHL	67	13	37	40	115	5	1	1	2	8
1994-95	Shawinigan	QMJHL	67	16	24	40	190	15	1	2	3	40

Signed as a free agent by **Montreal**, September 14, 1993.

GRETZKY, BRENT — (GRETZ-kee)

Center. Shoots left. 5'10", 160 lbs. Born, Brantford, Ont., February 20, 1972.
(Tampa Bay's 3rd choice, 49th overall, in 1992 Entry Draft).

			Regular Season					Playoffs				
Season	Club	Lea	GP	G	A	TP	PIM	GP	G	A	TP	PIM
1989-90	Belleville	OHL	66	15	32	47	30	11	0	0	0	0
1990-91	Belleville	OHL	66	26	56	82	25	6	3	3	6	2
1991-92	Belleville	OHL	62	43	78	121	37	....	....	....	....	....
1992-93	Atlanta	IHL	77	20	34	54	84	9	3	2	5	8
1993-94	**Tampa Bay**	**NHL**	**10**	**1**	**2**	**3**	**2**	....	....	....	....	....
	Atlanta	IHL	54	17	23	40	30	14	1	1	2	2
1994-95	Atlanta	IHL	67	19	32	51	42	5	4	1	5	4
	Tampa Bay	**NHL**	**3**	**0**	**1**	**1**	**0**	....	....	....	....	....
	NHL Totals		**13**	**1**	**3**	**4**	**2**	....	....	....	....	....

GRETZKY, WAYNE — (GRETZ-kee) — L.A.

Center. Shoots left. 6', 180 lbs. Born, Brantford, Ont., January 26, 1961.

			Regular Season					Playoffs				
Season	Club	Lea	GP	G	A	TP	PIM	GP	G	A	TP	PIM
1976-77	Peterborough	OHA	3	0	3	3	0	....	....	....	....	....
1977-78a	S.S. Marie	OHA	64	70	112	182	14	13	6	20	26	0
1978-79	Indianapolis	WHA	8	3	3	6	0	....	....	....	....	....
bc	Edmonton	WHA	72	43	61	104	19	13	*10	10	*20	2
1979-80def	**Edmonton**	**NHL**	**79**	**51**	***86**	***137**	**21**	**3**	**2**	**1**	**3**	**0**
1980-81 dghij	**Edmonton**	**NHL**	**80**	**55**	***109**	***164**	**28**	**9**	**7**	**14**	**21**	**4**
1981-82 dghijklp	**Edmonton**	**NHL**	**80**	***92**	***120**	***212**	**26**	**5**	**5**	**7**	**12**	**8**
1982-83 dghilmn	**Edmonton**	**NHL**	**80**	***71**	***125**	***196**	**59**	**16**	**12**	***26**	***38**	**4**
1983-84 dghlp	**Edmonton**	**NHL**	**74**	***87**	***118**	***205**	**39**	**19**	**13**	***22**	***35**	**12**
1984-85 dghilmnopq	**Edmonton**	**NHL**	**80**	***73**	***135**	***208**	**52**	**18**	**17**	***30**	***47**	**4**
1985-86 dghijq	**Edmonton**	**NHL**	**80**	**52**	***163**	***215**	**46**	**10**	**8**	**11**	**19**	**2**
1986-87 dghlpq	**Edmonton**	**NHL**	**79**	***62**	***121**	***183**	**28**	**21**	**5**	***29**	***34**	**6**
1987-88fmo	**Edmonton**	**NHL**	**64**	**40**	***109**	**149**	**24**	**19**	**12**	***31**	***43**	**16**
1988-89dfr	**Los Angeles**	**NHL**	**78**	**54**	***114**	**168**	**26**	**11**	**5**	**17**	**22**	**0**
1989-90fh	**Los Angeles**	**NHL**	**73**	**40**	***102**	***142**	**42**	**7**	**3**	**7**	**10**	**0**
1990-91egh	**Los Angeles**	**NHL**	**78**	**41**	***122**	***163**	**16**	**12**	**4**	**11**	**15**	**2**
1991-92e	**Los Angeles**	**NHL**	**74**	**31**	***90**	**121**	**34**	**6**	**2**	**5**	**7**	**2**
1992-93	**Los Angeles**	**NHL**	**45**	**16**	**49**	**65**	**6**	**24**	***15**	***25**	***40**	**4**
1993-94efh	**Los Angeles**	**NHL**	**81**	**38**	***92**	***130**	**20**	....	....	....	....	....
1994-95	**Los Angeles**	**NHL**	**48**	**11**	**37**	**48**	**6**	....	....	....	....	....
	NHL Totals		**1173**	***814**	***1692**	***2506**	**473**	**180**	***110**	***236**	***346**	**64**

a OHA Second All-Star Team (1978)
b WHA Second All-Star Team (1979)
c Named WHA's Rookie of the Year (1979)
d Won Hart Trophy (1980, 1981, 1982, 1983, 1984, 1985, 1986, 1987, 1989)
e Won Lady Byng Trophy (1980, 1991, 1992, 1994)
f NHL Second All-Star Team (1980, 1988, 1989, 1990, 1994)
g NHL First All-Star Team (1981, 1982, 1983, 1984, 1985, 1986, 1987, 1991)
h Won Art Ross Trophy (1981, 1982, 1983, 1984, 1985, 1986, 1987, 1990, 1991, 1994)
i NHL record for assists in regular season (1981, 1982, 1983, 1985, 1986)
j NHL record for points in regular season (1981, 1982, 1986)
k NHL record for goals in regular season (1982)
l Won Lester B. Pearson Award (1982, 1983, 1984, 1985, 1987)
m NHL record for assists in one playoff year (1983, 1988)
n NHL record for points in one playoff year (1983, 1985)
o Won Conn Smythe Trophy (1985, 1988)
p NHL Plus/Minus Leader (1982, 1984, 1985, 1987)
q Selected Chrysler-Dodge/NHL Performer of the Year (1985, 1986, 1987)
r Won Dodge Performance of the Year Award (1989)

Played in NHL All-Star Game (1980-1986, 1988-94)

Reclaimed by **Edmonton** as an under-age junior prior to Expansion Draft, June 9, 1979. Claimed as priority selection by **Edmonton**, June 9, 1979. Traded to **Los Angeles** by **Edmonton** with Mike Krushelnyski and Marty McSorley for Jimmy Carson, Martin Gelinas, Los Angeles' first round choices in 1989 (acquired by New Jersey — New Jersey selected Jason Miller), 1991 (Martin Rucinsky) and 1993 (Nick Stajduhar) Entry Drafts and cash, August 9, 1988.

GRIER, MICHAEL — EDM.

Right wing. Shoots right. 6'1", 215 lbs. Born, Detroit, MI, January 5, 1975.
(St. Louis' 7th choice, 219th overall, in 1993 Entry Draft).

			Regular Season					Playoffs				
Season	Club	Lea	GP	G	A	TP	PIM	GP	G	A	TP	PIM
1993-94	Boston U.	H.E.	39	9	9	18	56	....	....	....	....	....
1994-95ab	Boston U.	H.E.	37	*29	26	55	85	....	....	....	....	....

a Hockey East First All-Star Team (1995)
b NCAA East First All-American Team (1995)

Rights traded to **Edmonton** by **St. Louis** with Curtis Joseph for St. Louis' first round choices (previously acquired by Edmonton) in 1996 and 1997 Entry Drafts, August 4, 1995.

GRIEVE, BRENT — CHI.

Left wing. Shoots left. 6'1", 202 lbs. Born, Oshawa, Ont., May 9, 1969.
(NY Islanders' 4th choice, 65th overall, in 1989 Entry Draft).

			Regular Season					Playoffs				
Season	Club	Lea	GP	G	A	TP	PIM	GP	G	A	TP	PIM
1986-87	Oshawa	OHL	60	9	19	28	102	24	3	8	11	22
1987-88	Oshawa	OHL	55	19	20	39	122	7	0	1	1	8
1988-89	Oshawa	OHL	49	34	33	67	105	6	4	3	7	4
1989-90	Oshawa	OHL	62	46	47	93	125	17	10	10	20	26
1990-91	Capital Dist.	AHL	61	14	13	27	80	....	....	....	....	....
	Kansas City	IHL	5	2	2	4	2	....	....	....	....	....
1991-92	Capital Dist.	AHL	74	34	32	66	84	7	3	1	4	16
1992-93	Capital Dist.	AHL	79	34	28	62	122	4	1	1	2	10
1993-94	**NY Islanders**	**NHL**	**3**	**0**	**0**	**0**	**7**	....	....	....	....	....
	Salt Lake	IHL	22	9	5	14	30	....	....	....	....	....
	Edmonton	**NHL**	**24**	**13**	**5**	**18**	**14**	....	....	....	....	....
	Cape Breton	AHL	20	10	11	21	14	4	2	4	6	16
1994-95	**Chicago**	**NHL**	**24**	**1**	**5**	**6**	**23**	....	....	....	....	....
	NHL Totals		**51**	**14**	**10**	**24**	**44**	....	....	....	....	....

Traded to **Edmonton**, by **NY Islanders** for Marc Laforge, December 15, 1993. Signed as a free agent by **Chicago**, July 7, 1994.

GRILLO, DEAN — S.J.

Right wing. Shoots right. 6'2", 210 lbs. Born, Bemidji, MN, December 8, 1972.
(San Jose's 9th choice, 155th overall, in 1991 Entry Draft).

			Regular Season					Playoffs				
Season	Club	Lea	GP	G	A	TP	PIM	GP	G	A	TP	PIM
1992-93	North Dakota	WCHA	29	7	4	11	14	....	....	....	....	....
1993-94	North Dakota	WCHA	38	11	14	25	14	....	....	....	....	....
1994-95	Kansas City	IHL	72	15	21	36	24	18	3	5	8	18

GRIMSON, STU — DET.

Left wing. Shoots left. 6'5", 227 lbs. Born, Kamloops, B.C., May 20, 1965.
(Detroit's 11th choice, 186th overall, in 1983 Entry Draft).

			Regular Season					Playoffs				
Season	Club	Lea	GP	G	A	TP	PIM	GP	G	A	TP	PIM
1982-83	Regina	WHL	48	0	1	1	105	5	0	0	0	14
1983-84	Regina	WHL	63	8	8	16	131	21	0	1	1	29
1984-85	Regina	WHL	71	24	32	56	248	8	1	2	3	14
1985-86	U. Manitoba	CWUAA	12	7	4	11	113	3	1	1	2	20
1986-87	U. Manitoba	CWUAA	29	8	8	16	67	14	4	2	6	28
1987-88	Salt Lake	IHL	38	9	5	14	268	....	....	....	....	....
1988-89	**Calgary**	**NHL**	**1**	**0**	**0**	**0**	**5**	....	....	....	....	....
	Salt Lake	IHL	72	9	18	27	397	14	2	3	5	86
1989-90	**Calgary**	**NHL**	**3**	**0**	**0**	**0**	**17**	....	....	....	....	....
	Salt Lake	IHL	62	8	8	16	319	4	0	0	0	8
1990-91	**Chicago**	**NHL**	**35**	**0**	**1**	**1**	**183**	**5**	**0**	**0**	**0**	**46**
1991-92	**Chicago**	**NHL**	**54**	**2**	**2**	**4**	**234**	**14**	**0**	**1**	**1**	**10**
	Indianapolis	IHL	5	1	1	2	17	....	....	....	....	....
1992-93	**Chicago**	**NHL**	**78**	**1**	**1**	**2**	**193**	**2**	**0**	**0**	**0**	**4**
1993-94	**Anaheim**	**NHL**	**77**	**1**	**5**	**6**	**199**	....	....	....	....	....
1994-95	**Anaheim**	**NHL**	**31**	**0**	**1**	**1**	**110**	....	....	....	....	....
	Detroit	**NHL**	**11**	**0**	**0**	**0**	**37**	**11**	**1**	**0**	**1**	**26**
	NHL Totals		**290**	**4**	**10**	**14**	**978**	**32**	**1**	**1**	**2**	**86**

Re-entered NHL Entry Draft. **Calgary's** 8th choice, 143rd overall, in 1985 Entry Draft.

Claimed on conditional waivers by **Chicago** from **Calgary**, October 1, 1990. Claimed by **Anaheim** from **Chicago** in Expansion Draft, June 24, 1993. Traded to **Detroit** by **Anaheim** with Mark Ferner and Anaheim's sixth round choice in 1996 Entry Draft for Mike Sillinger and Jason York, April 4, 1995.

GROLEAU, FRANCOIS

Defense. Shoots left. 6', 200 lbs. Born, Longueuil, Que., January 23, 1973.
(Calgary's 2nd choice, 41st overall, in 1991 Entry Draft).

			Regular Season					Playoffs				
Season	Club	Lea	GP	G	A	TP	PIM	GP	G	A	TP	PIM
1989-90a	Shawinigan	QMJHL	65	11	54	65	80	6	0	1	1	12
1990-91	Shawinigan	QMJHL	70	9	60	69	70	6	0	3	3	2
1991-92b	Shawinigan	QMJHL	65	8	70	78	74	10	5	15	20	8
1992-93	St-Jean	QMJHL	48	7	38	45	66	4	0	1	1	14
1993-94	Saint John	AHL	73	8	14	22	49	7	0	1	1	2
1994-95	Saint John	AHL	65	6	34	40	28	....	....	....	....	....
	Cornwall	AHL	8	1	2	3	7	14	2	7	9	16

a QMJHL Second All-Star Team (1990)
b QMJHL First All-Star Team (1992)

Traded to **Quebec** by **Calgary** for Ed Ward, March 23, 1995.

GRONMAN, TUOMAS — (GROHN-mahn) — COL.

Defense. Shoots right. 6'3", 198 lbs. Born, Viitasaari, Finland, March 22, 1974.
(Quebec's 3rd choice, 29th overall, in 1992 Entry Draft).

			Regular Season					Playoffs				
Season	Club	Lea	GP	G	A	TP	PIM	GP	G	A	TP	PIM
1991-92	Tacoma	WHL	61	5	18	23	102	4	0	1	1	2
1992-93	Lukko	Fin.	45	2	11	13	46	3	1	0	1	2
1993-94	Lukko	Fin.	44	4	12	16	60	9	0	1	1	14
1994-95	TPS	Fin.	47	4	20	24	66	13	2	2	4	43

GRONVALL, JANNE — (GROHN-vahl, YAH-neh) — TOR.

Defense. Shoots left. 6'3", 195 lbs. Born, Rauma, Finland, July 17, 1973.
(Toronto's 5th choice, 101st overall, in 1992 Entry Draft).

			Regular Season					Playoffs				
Season	Club	Lea	GP	G	A	TP	PIM	GP	G	A	TP	PIM
1989-90	Lukko	Fin.	5	0	0	0	0	....	....	....	....	....
1990-91	Lukko	Fin.	40	2	8	10	30	....	....	....	....	....
1991-92	Lukko	Fin.	42	2	6	8	40	2	0	0	0	2
1992-93	Tappara	Fin.	46	1	7	8	54	....	....	....	....	....
1993-94	Tappara	Fin.	47	2	9	11	54	10	0	4	4	31
	St. John's	AHL	....	....	....	....	....	9	0	0	0	2
1994-95	St. John's	AHL	76	8	29	37	75	5	0	0	0	0

GROSEK, MICHAL — WPG.

Left wing. Shoots right. 6'2", 180 lbs. Born, Vyskov, Czech., June 1, 1975.
(Winnipeg's 7th choice, 145th overall, in 1993 Entry Draft).

			Regular Season					Playoffs				
Season	Club	Lea	GP	G	A	TP	PIM	GP	G	A	TP	PIM
1992-93	ZPS Zlin	Czech.	17	1	3	4	....	....	....	....	....	....
1993-94	**Winnipeg**	**NHL**	**3**	**1**	**0**	**1**	**0**	....	....	....	....	....
	Tacoma	WHL	30	25	20	45	106	7	2	2	4	30
	Moncton	AHL	20	1	2	3	47	2	0	0	0	0
1994-95	Springfield	AHL	45	10	22	32	98	....	....	....	....	....
	Winnipeg	**NHL**	**24**	**2**	**2**	**4**	**21**	....	....	....	....	....
	NHL Totals		**27**	**3**	**2**	**5**	**21**	....	....	....	....	....

GROSS, PAVEL — (GROHSS) NYI

Right wing. Shoots right. 6'3", 195 lbs. Born, Ustin Ogroh, Czech., May 11, 1968.
(NY Islanders' 7th choice, 111th overall, in 1988 Entry Draft).

			Regular Season					Playoffs				
Season	Club	Lea	GP	G	A	TP	PIM	GP	G	A	TP	PIM
1987-88	Sparta Praha	Czech.	29	4	6	10	10	....	....	....	....	....
1988-89	Sparta Praha	Czech.	39	13	9	22	22	....	....	....	....	....
1989-90	Sparta Praha	Czech.	36	10	9	19	....	....	....	....	....	....
1990-91	Freiburg	Ger.	32	11	24	35	66	....	....	....	....	....
1991-92	Freiburg	Ger.	43	15	22	37	59	....	....	....	....	....
1992-93	Freiburg	Ger.	41	11	20	31	62	8	5	5	10	6
1993-94	Mannheim	Ger.	42	14	24	38	30	3	0	0	0	16
1994-95	Mannheim	Ger.	42	21	40	61	99	6	4	3	7	0

GRUDEN, JOHN — BOS.

Defense. Shoots left. 6', 189 lbs. Born, Hastings, MN, April 6, 1970.
(Boston's 7th choice, 168th overall, in 1990 Entry Draft).

			Regular Season					Playoffs				
Season	Club	Lea	GP	G	A	TP	PIM	GP	G	A	TP	PIM
1990-91	Ferris State	CCHA	37	4	11	15	27	....	....	....	....	....
1991-92	Ferris State	CCHA	37	9	14	23	24	....	....	....	....	....
1992-93	Ferris State	CCHA	41	16	14	30	58	....	....	....	....	....
1993-94ab	Ferris State	CCHA	38	11	25	36	52	....	....	....	....	....
	Boston	**NHL**	**7**	**0**	**1**	**1**	**2**	....	....	....	....	....
1994-95	**Boston**	**NHL**	**38**	**0**	**6**	**6**	**22**	....	....	....	....	....
	Providence	AHL	1	0	1	1	0	....	....	....	....	....
	NHL Totals		**45**	**0**	**7**	**7**	**24**	....	....	....	....	....

a CCHA First All-Star Team (1994)
b NCAA West First All-American Team (1994)

GUERARD, DANIEL — OTT.

Right wing. Shoots right. 6'4", 215 lbs. Born, LaSalle, Que., April 9, 1974.
(Ottawa's 5th choice, 98th overall, in 1992 Entry Draft).

			Regular Season					Playoffs				
Season	Club	Lea	GP	G	A	TP	PIM	GP	G	A	TP	PIM
1991-92	Victoriaville	QMJHL	31	5	16	21	66	....	....	....	....	....
1992-93	Verdun	QMJHL	58	31	26	57	131	4	1	1	2	17
	New Haven	AHL	2	2	1	3	0	....	....	....	....	....
1993-94	Verdun	QMJHL	53	31	34	65	169	4	3	1	4	4
	P.E.I.	AHL	3	0	0	0	17	....	....	....	....	....
1994-95	P.E.I.	AHL	68	20	22	42	95	6	0	1	1	16
	Ottawa	**NHL**	**2**	**0**	**0**	**0**	**0**	....	....	....	....	....
	NHL Totals		**2**	**0**	**0**	**0**	**0**	....	....	....	....	....

GUERIN, BILL — (GAIR-ihn) N.J.

Right wing. Shoots right. 6'2", 200 lbs. Born, Wilbraham, MA, November 9, 1970.
(New Jersey's 1st choice, 5th overall, in 1989 Entry Draft).

			Regular Season					Playoffs				
Season	Club	Lea	GP	G	A	TP	PIM	GP	G	A	TP	PIM
1989-90	Boston College	H.E.	39	14	11	25	54	....	....	....	....	....
1990-91	Boston College	H.E.	38	26	19	45	102	....	....	....	....	....
	U.S. National	....	46	12	15	27	67	....	....	....	....	....
1991-92	**New Jersey**	**NHL**	**5**	**0**	**1**	**1**	**9**	**6**	**3**	**0**	**3**	**4**
	Utica	AHL	22	13	10	23	6	4	1	3	4	14
1992-93	**New Jersey**	**NHL**	**65**	**14**	**20**	**34**	**63**	**5**	**1**	**1**	**2**	**4**
	Utica	AHL	18	10	7	17	47	....	....	....	....	....
1993-94	**New Jersey**	**NHL**	**81**	**25**	**19**	**44**	**101**	**17**	**2**	**1**	**3**	**35**
1994-95	**New Jersey**	**NHL**	**48**	**12**	**13**	**25**	**72**	**20**	**3**	**8**	**11**	**30**
	NHL Totals		**199**	**51**	**53**	**104**	**245**	**48**	**9**	**10**	**19**	**73**

GUNKO, YURI — ST.L.

Defense. Shoots left. 6'1", 187 lbs. Born, Kiev, USSR, February 28, 1972.
(St. Louis' 11th choice, 230th overall, in 1992 Entry Draft).

			Regular Season					Playoffs				
Season	Club	Lea	GP	G	A	TP	PIM	GP	G	A	TP	PIM
1990-91	Sokol Kiev	USSR	14	0	0	0	8	....	....	....	....	....
1991-92	Sokol Kiev	CIS	22	1	0	1	16	....	....	....	....	....
1992-93	Sokol Kiev	CIS	40	2	3	5	28	....	....	....	....	....
1993-94	Sokol Kiev	CIS	42	0	8	8	28	....	....	....	....	....
1994-95	Sokol Kiev	CIS	25	4	0	4	18	....	....	....	....	....

GUOLLA, STEPHEN — OTT.

Left wing. Shoots left. 6', 180 lbs. Born, Scarborough, Ont., March 15, 1973.
(Ottawa's 1st choice, 3rd overall, in 1994 Supplemental Draft).

			Regular Season					Playoffs				
Season	Club	Lea	GP	G	A	TP	PIM	GP	G	A	TP	PIM
1991-92	Michigan State	CCHA	33	4	9	13	8	....	....	....	....	....
1992-93	Michigan State	CCHA	39	19	35	54	6	....	....	....	....	....
1993-94ab	Michigan State	CCHA	41	23	46	69	16	....	....	....	....	....
1994-95	Michigan State	CCHA	40	16	35	51	16	....	....	....	....	....

a CCHA Second All-Star Team (1994)
b NCAA West Second All-American Team (1994)

GUREN, MILOSLAV — MTL.

Defense. Shoots left. 6'2", 202 lbs. Born, Uherske. Hradiste, Czech., September 24, 1976.
(Montreal's 2nd choice, 60th overall, in 1995 Entry Draft).

			Regular Season					Playoffs				
Season	Club	Lea	GP	G	A	TP	PIM	GP	G	A	TP	PIM
1993-94	ZPS Zlin	Czech.	22	1	5	6	....	3	0	0	0	....
1994-95	ZPS Zlin	Czech.	32	3	7	10	10	12	1	0	1	6

GUSAROV, ALEXEI — (goo-SAH-rahf) COL.

Defense. Shoots left. 6'3", 185 lbs. Born, Leningrad, USSR, July 8, 1964.
(Quebec's 11th choice, 213th overall, in 1988 Entry Draft).

			Regular Season					Playoffs				
Season	Club	Lea	GP	G	A	TP	PIM	GP	G	A	TP	PIM
1981-82	SKA Leningrad	USSR	20	1	2	3	16	....	....	....	....	....
1982-83	SKA Leningrad	USSR	42	2	1	3	32	....	....	....	....	....
1983-84	SKA Leningrad	USSR	43	2	3	5	32	....	....	....	....	....
1984-85	CSKA	USSR	36	3	2	5	26	....	....	....	....	....
1985-86	CSKA	USSR	40	3	5	8	30	....	....	....	....	....
1986-87	CSKA	USSR	38	4	7	11	24	....	....	....	....	....
1987-88	CSKA	USSR	39	3	2	5	28	....	....	....	....	....
1988-89	CSKA	USSR	42	5	4	9	37	....	....	....	....	....
1989-90	CSKA	USSR	42	4	7	11	42	....	....	....	....	....
1990-91	CSKA	USSR	15	0	0	0	12	....	....	....	....	....
	Quebec	**NHL**	**36**	**3**	**9**	**12**	**12**	....	....	....	....	....
	Halifax	AHL	2	0	3	3	2	....	....	....	....	....
1991-92	**Quebec**	**NHL**	**68**	**5**	**18**	**23**	**22**	....	....	....	....	....
	Halifax	AHL	3	0	0	0	0	....	....	....	....	....
1992-93	**Quebec**	**NHL**	**79**	**8**	**22**	**30**	**57**	**5**	**0**	**1**	**1**	**0**
1993-94	**Quebec**	**NHL**	**76**	**5**	**20**	**25**	**38**	....	....	....	....	....
1994-95	**Quebec**	**NHL**	**14**	**1**	**2**	**3**	**6**	....	....	....	....	....
	NHL Totals		**273**	**22**	**71**	**93**	**135**	**5**	**0**	**1**	**1**	**0**

GUSEV, SERGEI — DAL.

Defense. Shoots left. 6'1", 195 lbs. Born, Nizhny Tagil, USSR, July 31, 1975.
(Dallas' 4th choice, 69th overall, in 1995 Entry Draft).

			Regular Season					Playoffs				
Season	Club	Lea	GP	G	A	TP	PIM	GP	G	A	TP	PIM
1994-95	CSK Samara	CIS	50	3	5	8	58	....	....	....	....	....

GUSMANOV, RAVIL — WPG.

Left wing. Shoots left. 6'3", 185 lbs. Born, Naberezhnye Chelny, USSR, July 25, 1972.
(Winnipeg's 5th choice, 93rd overall, in 1993 Entry Draft).

			Regular Season					Playoffs				
Season	Club	Lea	GP	G	A	TP	PIM	GP	G	A	TP	PIM
1990-91	Chelyabinsk	USSR	15	0	0	0	10	....	....	....	....	....
1991-92	Chelyabinsk	CIS	38	4	4	8	20	....	....	....	....	....
1992-93	Chelyabinsk	CIS	39	15	8	23	30	8	4	0	4	2
1993-94	Chelyabinsk	CIS	43	18	9	27	51	6	4	3	7	10
1994-95	Springfield	AHL	72	18	15	33	14	....	....	....	....	....

GUSTAFSSON, PER — FLA.

Defense. Shoots left. 6'2", 190 lbs. Born, Osterham, Sweden, June 6, 1970.
(Florida's 10th choice, 261st overall, in 1994 Entry Draft).

			Regular Season					Playoffs				
Season	Club	Lea	GP	G	A	TP	PIM	GP	G	A	TP	PIM
1993-94	HV-71	Swe.	34	9	7	16	10	....	....	....	....	....
1994-95	HV-71	Swe.	38	10	6	16	14	13	7	5	12	8

GUZIOR, RUSSELL — MTL.

Center. Shoots right. 5'10", 165 lbs. Born, Chicago, IL, January 12, 1974.
(Montreal's 13th choice, 281st overall, in 1993 Entry Draft).

			Regular Season					Playoffs				
Season	Club	Lea	GP	G	A	TP	PIM	GP	G	A	TP	PIM
1993-94	Providence	H.E.	34	9	13	22	8	....	....	....	....	....
1994-95	Providence	H.E.	9	1	7	8	10	....	....	....	....	....

HAGGERTY, RYAN — EDM.

Center. Shoots left. 6'1", 185 lbs. Born, Rye, NY, May 2, 1973.
(Edmonton's 6th choice, 93rd overall, in 1991 Entry Draft).

			Regular Season					Playoffs				
Season	Club	Lea	GP	G	A	TP	PIM	GP	G	A	TP	PIM
1991-92	Boston College	H.E.	34	12	5	17	16	....	....	....	....	....
1992-93	Boston College	H.E.	32	6	5	11	12	....	....	....	....	....
1993-94	Boston College	H.E.	36	17	23	40	16	....	....	....	....	....
1994-95	Boston College	H.E.	35	23	22	45	20	....	....	....	....	....

HAGGERTY, SEAN — TOR.

Left wing. Shoots left. 6'1", 186 lbs. Born, Rye, NY, February 11, 1976.
(Toronto's 2nd choice, 48th overall, in 1994 Entry Draft).

			Regular Season					Playoffs				
Season	Club	Lea	GP	G	A	TP	PIM	GP	G	A	TP	PIM
1993-94	Detroit	OHL	60	31	32	63	21	17	9	10	19	11
1994-95a	Detroit	OHL	61	40	49	89	37	21	13	24	37	18

a Memorial Cup All-Star Team (1995)

HAKANEN, TIMO — S.J.

Center. Shoots left. 6'2", 190 lbs. Born, Pori, Finland, March 26, 1977.
(San Jose's 7th choice, 140th overall, in 1995 Entry Draft).

			Regular Season					Playoffs				
Season	Club	Lea	GP	G	A	TP	PIM	GP	G	A	TP	PIM
1994-95	Assat	Fin. Jr.	36	23	21	44	6	5	0	0	0	0

HAKANSSON, JONAS — PHI.

Left wing. Shoots right. 6'1", 202 lbs. Born, Malmo, Sweden, January 4, 1974.
(Philadelphia's 8th choice, 199th overall, in 1992 Entry Draft).

			Regular Season					Playoffs				
Season	Club	Lea	GP	G	A	TP	PIM	GP	G	A	TP	PIM
1990-91	Malmo	Swe.	8	0	0	0	0	1	0	0	0	0
1991-92	Malmo	Swe. Jr.			UNAVAILABLE							
1992-93	Malmo	Swe.	11	0	0	0	0	....	....	....	....	....
1993-94	Pantern	Swe. 2	26	9	5	14	20	....	....	....	....	....
1994-95	Pantern	Swe. 2	26	2	2	4	10	....	....	....	....	....

HAKANSSON, MIKAEL — TOR.

Center. Shoots left. 6'1", 196 lbs. Born, Stockholm, Sweden, May 31, 1974.
(Toronto's 7th choice, 125th overall, in 1992 Entry Draft).

			Regular Season					Playoffs				
Season	Club	Lea	GP	G	A	TP	PIM	GP	G	A	TP	PIM
1990-91	Nacka	Swe. 2	27	2	5	7	6	....	....	....	....	....
1991-92	Nacka	Swe. 2	29	3	15	18	24	....	....	....	....	....
1992-93	Djurgarden	Swe.	40	0	1	1	6	3	0	0	0	0
1993-94	Djurgarden	Swe.	37	3	3	6	12	4	0	0	0	0
1994-95	MoDo	Swe.	37	3	7	10	16	....	....	....	....	....

HALFNIGHT, ASHLIN — HFD.

Defense. Shoots left. 6', 180 lbs. Born, Toronto, Ont., March 14, 1975.
(Hartford's 5th choice, 213th overall, in 1994 Entry Draft).

			Regular Season					Playoffs				
Season	Club	Lea	GP	G	A	TP	PIM	GP	G	A	TP	PIM
1992-93	Cdn. National	....	3	1	0	1	2	....	....	....	....	....
1993-94	Harvard	ECAC	30	2	8	10	24	....	....	....	....	....
1994-95	Harvard	ECAC	24	5	15	20	42	....	....	....	....	....

HALKIDIS, BOB — (hal-KEE-dihs)

Defense. Shoots left. 5'11", 205 lbs. Born, Toronto, Ont., March 5, 1966.
(Buffalo's 4th choice, 81st overall, in 1984 Entry Draft).

			Regular Season					Playoffs				
Season	Club	Lea	GP	G	A	TP	PIM	GP	G	A	TP	PIM
1983-84	London	OHL	51	9	22	31	123	8	0	2	2	27
1984-85a	London	OHL	62	14	50	64	154	8	3	6	9	22
	Buffalo	**NHL**	....	....	....	....	....	**4**	**0**	**0**	**0**	**19**
1985-86	**Buffalo**	**NHL**	**37**	**1**	**9**	**10**	**115**	....	....	....	....	....
1986-87	**Buffalo**	**NHL**	**6**	**1**	**1**	**2**	**19**	....	....	....	....	....
	Rochester	AHL	59	1	8	9	144	8	0	0	0	43
1987-88	**Buffalo**	**NHL**	**30**	**0**	**3**	**3**	**115**	**4**	**0**	**0**	**0**	**22**
	Rochester	AHL	15	2	5	7	50	....	....	....	....	....
1988-89	**Buffalo**	**NHL**	**16**	**0**	**1**	**1**	**66**	....	....	....	....	....
	Rochester	AHL	16	0	6	6	64	....	....	....	....	....
1989-90	Rochester	AHL	18	1	13	14	70	....	....	....	....	....
	Los Angeles	**NHL**	**20**	**0**	**4**	**4**	**56**	**8**	**0**	**1**	**1**	**8**
	New Haven	AHL	30	3	17	20	67	....	....	....	....	....
1990-91	**Los Angeles**	**NHL**	**34**	**1**	**3**	**4**	**133**	**3**	**0**	**0**	**0**	**0**
	New Haven	AHL	7	1	3	4	10	....	....	....	....	....
	Phoenix	IHL	4	1	5	6	6	....	....	....	....	....
1991-92	**Toronto**	**NHL**	**46**	**3**	**3**	**6**	**145**	....	....	....	....	....
1992-93	St. John's	AHL	29	2	13	15	61	....	....	....	....	....
	Milwaukee	IHL	26	0	9	9	79	5	0	1	1	27
1993-94	**Detroit**	**NHL**	**28**	**1**	**4**	**5**	**93**	**1**	**0**	**0**	**0**	**2**
	Adirondack	AHL	15	0	6	6	46	....	....	....	....	....
1994-95	**Detroit**	**NHL**	**4**	**0**	**1**	**1**	**6**	....	....	....	....	....
	Tampa Bay	**NHL**	**27**	**1**	**3**	**4**	**40**	....	....	....	....	....
	NHL Totals		**248**	**8**	**32**	**40**	**788**	**20**	**0**	**1**	**1**	**51**

a OHL First All-Star Team (1985)

Traded to **Los Angeles** by **Buffalo** with future considerations for Dale DeGray and future considerations, November 24, 1989. Signed as a free agent by **Toronto**, July 24, 1991. Signed as a free agent by **Detroit**, September 2, 1993. Claimed on waivers by **Tampa Bay** from **Detroit**, February 10, 1995.

HALKO, STEVEN — HFD.

Defense. Shoots right. 6'1", 183 lbs. Born, Etobicoke, Ont., March 8, 1974.
(Hartford's 10th choice, 225th overall, in 1992 Entry Draft).

			Regular Season					Playoffs				
Season	Club	Lea	GP	G	A	TP	PIM	GP	G	A	TP	PIM
1992-93	U. of Michigan	CCHA	39	1	12	13	12	....	....	....	....	....
1993-94	U. of Michigan	CCHA	41	2	13	15	32	....	....	....	....	....
1994-95a	U. of Michigan	CCHA	39	2	14	16	20	....	....	....	....	....

a CCHA Second All-Star Team (1995)

HALL, TODD — HFD.

Defense. Shoots left. 6'1", 212 lbs. Born, Hamden, CT, January 22, 1973.
(Hartford's 3rd choice, 53rd overall, in 1991 Entry Draft).

			Regular Season					Playoffs				
Season	Club	Lea	GP	G	A	TP	PIM	GP	G	A	TP	PIM
1991-92	Boston College	H.E.	33	2	10	12	14	....	....	....	....	....
1992-93	Boston College	H.E.	34	2	10	12	22	....	....	....	....	....
1993-94	N. Hampshire	H.E.			DID NOT PLAY							
1994-95	N. Hampshire	H.E.	36	8	18	26	16	....	....	....	....	....

HALLER, KEVIN — (HAHL-ehr) PHI.

Defense. Shoots left. 6'2", 183 lbs. Born, Trochu, Alta., December 5, 1970.
(Buffalo's 1st choice, 14th overall, in 1989 Entry Draft).

			Regular Season					Playoffs				
Season	Club	Lea	GP	G	A	TP	PIM	GP	G	A	TP	PIM
1988-89	Regina	WHL	72	10	31	41	99	....	....	....	....	....
1989-90	**Buffalo**	**NHL**	**2**	**0**	**0**	**0**	**0**	....	....	....	....	....
a	Regina	WHL	58	16	37	53	93	11	2	9	11	16
1990-91	**Buffalo**	**NHL**	**21**	**1**	**8**	**9**	**20**	**6**	**1**	**4**	**5**	**10**
	Rochester	AHL	52	2	8	10	53	10	2	1	3	6
1991-92	**Buffalo**	**NHL**	**58**	**6**	**15**	**21**	**75**	....	....	....	....	....
	Rochester	AHL	4	0	0	0	18	....	....	....	....	....
	Montreal	**NHL**	**8**	**2**	**2**	**4**	**17**	**9**	**0**	**0**	**0**	**6**
1992-93	**Montreal**	**NHL**	**73**	**11**	**14**	**25**	**117**	**17**	**1**	**6**	**7**	**16**
1993-94	**Montreal**	**NHL**	**68**	**4**	**9**	**13**	**118**	**7**	**1**	**1**	**2**	**19**
1994-95	**Philadelphia**	**NHL**	**36**	**2**	**8**	**10**	**48**	**15**	**4**	**4**	**8**	**10**
	NHL Totals		**266**	**26**	**56**	**82**	**395**	**54**	**7**	**15**	**22**	**61**

a WHL East First All-Star Team (1990)

Traded to **Montreal** by **Buffalo** for Petr Svoboda, March 10, 1992. Traded to **Philadelphia** by **Montreal** for Yves Racine, June 29, 1994.

HALVERSON, TREVOR

Left wing. Shoots left. 6'1", 195 lbs. Born, White River, Ont., April 6, 1971.
(Washington's 2nd choice, 21st overall, in 1991 Entry Draft).

			Regular Season					Playoffs				
Season	Club	Lea	GP	G	A	TP	PIM	GP	G	A	TP	PIM
1989-90	North Bay	OHL	54	22	20	42	172	2	2	1	3	2
1990-91a	North Bay	OHL	64	59	36	95	128	10	3	6	9	4
1991-92	Baltimore	AHL	74	10	11	21	181	....	....	....	....	....
1992-93	Baltimore	AHL	67	19	21	40	170	2	1	0	1	0
	Hampton Rds.	ECHL	9	7	5	12	6	....	....	....	....	....
1993-94	San Diego	IHL	58	4	9	13	115	....	....	....	....	....
	Milwaukee	IHL	4	1	0	1	8	2	0	0	0	17
1994-95	Portland	AHL	5	0	1	1	9	....	....	....	....	....
	Hampton Rds.	ECHL	42	14	26	40	194	4	1	1	2	2

a OHL First All-Star Team (1991)

Claimed by **Anaheim** from **Washington** in Expansion Draft, June 24, 1993.

HAMEL, DENIS — ST.L.

Left wing. Shoots left. 6'2", 188 lbs. Born, Lachute, Que., May 10, 1977.
(St. Louis' 5th choice, 153rd overall, in 1995 Entry Draft).

			Regular Season					Playoffs				
Season	Club	Lea	GP	G	A	TP	PIM	GP	G	A	TP	PIM
1993-94	Abitibi-Tem.	Midget	15	5	7	12	29	5	0	3	3	16
1994-95	Chicoutimi	QMJHL	66	15	12	27	155	12	2	0	2	27

HAMILTON, HUGH — HFD.

Defense. Shoots left. 6'1", 175 lbs. Born, Saskatoon, Sask., February 11, 1977.
(Hartford's 5th choice, 113th overall, in 1995 Entry Draft).

			Regular Season					Playoffs				
Season	Club	Lea	GP	G	A	TP	PIM	GP	G	A	TP	PIM
1993-94	Spokane	WHL	64	5	9	14	70	3	0	0	0	0
1994-95	Spokane	WHL	60	5	28	33	102	11	3	5	8	16

HAMR, RADEK — (HAM-uhr, RA-dehk)

Defense. Shoots left. 5'11", 175 lbs. Born, Usti-Nad-Labem, Czech., June 15, 1974.
(Ottawa's 4th choice, 73rd overall, in 1992 Entry Draft).

			Regular Season					Playoffs				
Season	Club	Lea	GP	G	A	TP	PIM	GP	G	A	TP	PIM
1991-92	Sparta Praha	Czech.	3	0	0	0	....	....	....	....	....	....
1992-93	**Ottawa**	**NHL**	**4**	**0**	**0**	**0**	**0**	....	....	....	....	....
	New Haven	AHL	59	4	21	25	18	....	....	....	....	....
1993-94	**Ottawa**	**NHL**	**7**	**0**	**0**	**0**	**0**	....	....	....	....	....
	P.E.I.	AHL	69	10	26	36	44	....	....	....	....	....
1994-95	P.E.I.	AHL	7	0	1	1	2	....	....	....	....	....
	Fort Wayne	IHL	58	3	13	16	14	1	0	0	0	0
	NHL Totals		**11**	**0**	**0**	**0**	**0**	....	....	....	....	....

HAMRLIK, MARTIN — (HAHM-reh-lik) ST.L.

Defense. Shoots right. 5'11", 185 lbs. Born, Gottwaldov, Czech., May 6, 1973.
(Hartford's 2nd choice, 31st overall, in 1991 Entry Draft).

			Regular Season					Playoffs				
Season	Club	Lea	GP	G	A	TP	PIM	GP	G	A	TP	PIM
1989-90	TJ Zlin	Czech.	11	2	0	2	....	....	....	....	....	....
1990-91	TJ Zlin	Czech.	50	8	14	22	44	....	....	....	....	....
1991-92	ZPS Zlin	Czech.	4	0	2	2	23	....	....	....	....	....
1992-93	Ottawa	OHL	26	4	11	15	41	....	....	....	....	....
	Springfield	AHL	8	1	3	4	16	....	....	....	....	....
1993-94	Springfield	AHL	1	0	0	0	0	....	....	....	....	....
	Peoria	IHL	47	1	11	12	61	6	0	1	1	2
1994-95	Peoria	IHL	77	5	13	18	120	3	0	0	0	2

Traded to **St. Louis** by **Hartford** for cash, November 12, 1993.

HAMRLIK, ROMAN — (HAHM-reh-lik) T.B.

Defense. Shoots left. 6'2", 202 lbs. Born, Gottwaldov, Czech., April 12, 1974.
(Tampa Bay's 1st choice, 1st overall, in 1992 Entry Draft).

			Regular Season					Playoffs				
Season	Club	Lea	GP	G	A	TP	PIM	GP	G	A	TP	PIM
1990-91	TJ Zlin	Czech.	14	2	2	4	18	....	....	....	....	....
1991-92	ZPS Zlin	Czech.	34	5	5	10	50	....	....	....	....	....
1992-93	**Tampa Bay**	**NHL**	**67**	**6**	**15**	**21**	**71**	....	....	....	....	....
	Atlanta	IHL	2	1	1	2	2	....	....	....	....	....
1993-94	**Tampa Bay**	**NHL**	**64**	**3**	**18**	**21**	**135**	....	....	....	....	....
1994-95	ZPS Zlin	Czech.	2	1	0	1	10	....	....	....	....	....
	Tampa Bay	**NHL**	**48**	**12**	**11**	**23**	**86**	....	....	....	....	....
	NHL Totals		**179**	**21**	**44**	**65**	**292**	....	....	....	....	....

HANDZUS, MICHAL — ST.L.

Center. Shoots left. 6'3", 191 lbs. Born, Banska Bystrica, Czech., March 11, 1977.
(St. Louis' 3rd choice, 101st overall, in 1995 Entry Draft).

			Regular Season					Playoffs				
Season	Club	Lea	GP	G	A	TP	PIM	GP	G	A	TP	PIM
1994-95	B. Bystrica	Slov. 2	22	15	14	29	10	....	....	....	....	....

HANKINSON, BEN — DET.

Right wing. Shoots right. 6'2", 210 lbs. Born, Edina, MN, May 1, 1969.
(New Jersey's 5th choice, 107th overall, in 1987 Entry Draft).

			Regular Season					Playoffs				
Season	Club	Lea	GP	G	A	TP	PIM	GP	G	A	TP	PIM
1987-88	U. Minnesota	WCHA	24	4	7	11	36	....	....	....	....	....
1988-89	U. Minnesota	WCHA	43	7	11	18	115	....	....	....	....	....
1989-90a	U. Minnesota	WCHA	46	25	41	66	34	....	....	....	....	....
1990-91	U. Minnesota	WCHA	43	19	21	40	133	....	....	....	....	....
1991-92	Utica	AHL	77	17	16	33	186	4	3	1	4	2
1992-93	**New Jersey**	**NHL**	**4**	**2**	**1**	**3**	**9**	....	....	....	....	....
	Utica	AHL	75	35	27	62	145	5	2	2	4	6
1993-94	**New Jersey**	**NHL**	**13**	**1**	**0**	**1**	**23**	**2**	**1**	**0**	**1**	**4**
	Albany	AHL	29	9	14	23	80	5	3	1	4	6
1994-95	**New Jersey**	**NHL**	**8**	**0**	**0**	**0**	**7**	....	....	....	....	....
	Albany	AHL	1	1	0	1	6	....	....	....	....	....
	Tampa Bay	**NHL**	**18**	**0**	**2**	**2**	**6**	....	....	....	....	....
	NHL Totals		**43**	**3**	**3**	**6**	**45**	**2**	**1**	**0**	**1**	**4**

a WCHA First All-Star Team (1990)

Traded to **Tampa Bay** by **New Jersey** with Alexander Semak for Shawn Chambers and Danton Cole, March 14, 1995. Traded to **Detroit** by **Tampa Bay** with Marc Bergevin for Shawn Burr and Detroit's third round choice (later traded to Boston) in 1996 Entry Draft, August 17, 1995.

HANNAN, DAVE — BUF.

Center. Shoots left. 5'10", 180 lbs. Born, Sudbury, Ont., November 26, 1961.
(Pittsburgh's 9th choice, 196th overall, in 1981 Entry Draft).

			Regular Season					Playoffs				
Season	Club	Lea	GP	G	A	TP	PIM	GP	G	A	TP	PIM
1979-80	S.S. Marie	OHA	28	11	10	21	31					
	Brantford	OHA	25	5	10	15	26					
1980-81	Brantford	OHA	56	46	35	81	155	6	2	4	6	20
1981-82	**Pittsburgh**	**NHL**	**1**	**0**	**0**	**0**	**0**					
	Erie	AHL	76	33	37	70	129					
1982-83	**Pittsburgh**	**NHL**	**74**	**11**	**22**	**33**	**127**					
	Baltimore	AHL	5	2	2	4	13					
1983-84	**Pittsburgh**	**NHL**	**24**	**2**	**3**	**5**	**33**					
	Baltimore	AHL	47	18	24	42	98	10	2	6	8	27
1984-85	**Pittsburgh**	**NHL**	**30**	**6**	**7**	**13**	**43**					
	Baltimore	AHL	49	20	25	45	91					
1985-86	**Pittsburgh**	**NHL**	**75**	**17**	**18**	**35**	**91**					
1986-87	**Pittsburgh**	**NHL**	**58**	**10**	**15**	**25**	**56**					
1987-88	**Pittsburgh**	**NHL**	**21**	**4**	**3**	**7**	**23**					
	Edmonton	**NHL**	**51**	**9**	**11**	**20**	**43**	**12**	**1**	**1**	**2**	**8**
1988-89	**Pittsburgh**	**NHL**	**72**	**10**	**20**	**30**	**157**	**8**	**0**	**1**	**1**	**4**
1989-90	**Toronto**	**NHL**	**39**	**6**	**9**	**15**	**55**	**3**	**1**	**0**	**1**	**4**
1990-91	**Toronto**	**NHL**	**74**	**11**	**23**	**34**	**82**					
1991-92	**Toronto**	**NHL**	**35**	**2**	**2**	**4**	**16**					
	Cdn. National		3	0	0	0	2					
	Cdn. Olympic		8	3	5	8	8					
	Buffalo	**NHL**	**12**	**2**	**4**	**6**	**48**	**7**	**2**	**0**	**2**	**2**
1992-93	**Buffalo**	**NHL**	**55**	**5**	**15**	**20**	**43**	**8**	**1**	**1**	**2**	**18**
1993-94	**Buffalo**	**NHL**	**83**	**6**	**15**	**21**	**53**	**7**	**1**	**0**	**1**	**6**
1994-95	**Buffalo**	**NHL**	**42**	**4**	**12**	**16**	**32**	**5**	**0**	**2**	**2**	**2**
	NHL Totals		**746**	**105**	**179**	**284**	**902**	**50**	**6**	**5**	**11**	**44**

Traded to **Edmonton** by **Pittsburgh** with Craig Simpson, Moe Mantha and Chris Joseph for Paul Coffey, Dave Hunter and Wayne Van Dorp, November 24, 1987. Claimed by **Pittsburgh** from **Edmonton** in NHL Waiver Draft, October 3, 1988. Claimed by **Toronto** from **Pittsburgh** in NHL Waiver Draft, October 2, 1989. Traded to **Buffalo** by **Toronto** for Minnesota's fifth round choice (previously acquired by Buffalo — Toronto selected Chris Deruiter) in 1992 Entry Draft, March 10, 1992.

HANSEN, TAVIS — WPG.

Center. Shoots right. 6'1", 180 lbs. Born, Prince Albert, Sask., June 17, 1975.
(Winnipeg's 3rd choice, 58th overall, in 1994 Entry Draft).

			Regular Season					Playoffs				
Season	Club	Lea	GP	G	A	TP	PIM	GP	G	A	TP	PIM
1993-94	Tacoma	WHL	71	23	31	54	122	8	1	3	4	17
1994-95	Tacoma	WHL	71	32	41	73	142	4	1	1	2	8
	Winnipeg	**NHL**	**1**	**0**	**0**	**0**	**0**					
	NHL Totals		**1**	**0**	**0**	**0**	**0**					

HANSON, MIKE — N.J.

Center. Shoots right. 6'1", 185 lbs. Born, Minot, ND, April 4, 1976.
(New Jersey's 12th choice, 269th overall, in 1994 Entry Draft).

			Regular Season					Playoffs				
Season	Club	Lea	GP	G	A	TP	PIM	GP	G	A	TP	PIM
1993-94	Minot	HS	19	30	21	51	30					
1994-95	Sioux City	USHL	42	13	10	23	58					

HANSSON, ROGER — VAN.

Right wing. Shoots left. 6'1", 170 lbs. Born, Angelholm, Sweden, April 29, 1969.
(Vancouver's 10th choice, 213th overall, in 1987 Entry Draft).

			Regular Season					Playoffs				
Season	Club	Lea	GP	G	A	TP	PIM	GP	G	A	TP	PIM
1987-88	Rogle	Swe.	36	31	18	49	10					
1988-89	Rogle	Swe.	36	32	18	50						
1989-90	Rogle	Swe.	32	22	18	40	18					
1990-91	Rogle	Swe.	31	27	27	54	25					
1991-92	Malmo	Swe.	36	12	13	25	10					
1992-93	Malmo	Swe.	32	9	8	17	10					
1993-94	Malmo	Swe.	39	12	12	24	30					
1994-95	Malmo	Swe.	39	8	14	22	18	9	4	2	6	2

HARBERTS, TIMOTHY — PIT.

Center. Shoots right. 6'1", 185 lbs. Born, Edina, MN, May 20, 1975.
(Pittsburgh's 9th choice, 234th overall, in 1993 Entry Draft).

			Regular Season					Playoffs				
Season	Club	Lea	GP	G	A	TP	PIM	GP	G	A	TP	PIM
1993-94	Notre Dame	CCHA	36	10	12	22	19					
1994-95	Notre Dame	CCHA	37	21	13	34	4					

HARDING, MIKE — HFD.

Right wing. Shoots right. 6'4", 225 lbs. Born, Edsow, Alta., February 24, 1971.
(Hartford's 6th choice, 119th overall, in 1991 Entry Draft).

			Regular Season					Playoffs				
Season	Club	Lea	GP	G	A	TP	PIM	GP	G	A	TP	PIM
1991-92	N. Michigan	WCHA	28	6	8	14	46					
1992-93	N. Michigan	WCHA	39	17	18	35	66					
1993-94a	N. Michigan	WCHA	38	24	25	49	66					
1994-95	N. Michigan	WCHA	40	16	22	38	68					

a WCHA Second All-Star Team (1994)

HARKINS, BRETT — FLA.

Left wing. Shoots left. 6'1", 185 lbs. Born, North Ridgeville, OH, July 2, 1970.
(NY Islanders' 9th choice, 133rd overall, in 1989 Entry Draft).

			Regular Season					Playoffs				
Season	Club	Lea	GP	G	A	TP	PIM	GP	G	A	TP	PIM
1989-90	Bowling Green	CCHA	41	11	43	54	45					
1990-91	Bowling Green	CCHA	40	22	38	60	30					
1991-92	Bowling Green	CCHA	34	8	39	47	32					
1992-93	Bowling Green	CCHA	35	19	28	47	28					
1993-94	Adirondack	AHL	80	22	47	69	23	10	1	5	6	4
1994-95	Providence	AHL	80	23	*69	92	32	13	8	14	22	4
	Boston	**NHL**	**1**	**0**	**1**	**1**	**0**					
	NHL Totals		**1**	**0**	**1**	**1**	**0**					

Signed as a free agent by **Boston**, July 1, 1994. Signed as a free agent by **Florida**, July 24, 1995.

HARKINS, TODD — FLA.

Center. Shoots right. 6'3", 210 lbs. Born, Cleveland, OH, October 8, 1968.
(Calgary's 2nd choice, 42nd overall, in 1988 Entry Draft).

			Regular Season					Playoffs				
Season	Club	Lea	GP	G	A	TP	PIM	GP	G	A	TP	PIM
1987-88	Miami-Ohio	CCHA	34	9	7	16	133					
1988-89	Miami-Ohio	CCHA	36	8	7	15	77					
1989-90	Miami-Ohio	CCHA	40	27	17	44	78					
1990-91	Salt Lake	IHL	79	15	27	42	113	3	0	0	0	0
1991-92	**Calgary**	**NHL**	**5**	**0**	**0**	**0**	**7**					
	Salt Lake	IHL	72	32	30	62	67	5	1	1	2	6
1992-93	**Calgary**	**NHL**	**15**	**2**	**3**	**5**	**22**					
	Salt Lake	IHL	53	13	21	34	90					
1993-94	Saint John	AHL	38	13	9	22	64					
	Hartford	**NHL**	**28**	**1**	**0**	**1**	**49**					
	Springfield	AHL	1	0	3	3	0					
1994-95	Chicago	IHL	52	18	25	43	136					
	Houston	IHL	25	9	10	19	77	4	1	1	2	28
	NHL Totals		**48**	**3**	**3**	**6**	**78**					

Traded to **Hartford** by **Calgary** for Scott Morrow, January 24, 1994.

HARLOCK, DAVID — TOR.

Defense. Shoots left. 6'2", 205 lbs. Born, Toronto, Ont., March 16, 1971.
(New Jersey's 2nd choice, 24th overall, in 1990 Entry Draft).

			Regular Season					Playoffs				
Season	Club	Lea	GP	G	A	TP	PIM	GP	G	A	TP	PIM
1989-90	U. of Michigan	CCHA	42	2	13	15	44					
1990-91	U. of Michigan	CCHA	39	2	8	10	70					
1991-92	U. of Michigan	CCHA	44	1	6	7	80					
1992-93	U. of Michigan	CCHA	38	3	9	12	58					
	Cdn. National		4	0	0	0	2					
1993-94	Cdn. National		41	0	3	3	28					
	Cdn. Olympic		8	0	0	0	8					
	Toronto	**NHL**	**6**	**0**	**0**	**0**	**0**					
	St. John's	AHL	10	0	3	3	2	9	0	0	0	6
1994-95	St. John's	AHL	58	0	6	6	44	5	0	0	0	0
	Toronto	**NHL**	**1**	**0**	**0**	**0**	**0**					
	NHL Totals		**7**	**0**	**0**	**0**	**0**					

Signed as a free agent by **Toronto**, August 20, 1993.

HARLTON, TYLER — ST.L.

Defense. Shoots left. 6'3", 201 lbs. Born, Pense, Sask., January 11, 1976.
(St. Louis' 2nd choice, 94th overall, in 1994 Entry Draft).

			Regular Season					Playoffs				
Season	Club	Lea	GP	G	A	TP	PIM	GP	G	A	TP	PIM
1993-94	Vernon	Jr. A	60	3	18	21	102					
1994-95	Michigan State	CCHA	39	1	3	4	55					

HARPER, KELLY — CGY.

Center. Shoots right. 6'2", 180 lbs. Born, Sudbury, Ont., May 9, 1972.
(Calgary's 8th choice, 151st overall, in 1991 Entry Draft).

			Regular Season					Playoffs				
Season	Club	Lea	GP	G	A	TP	PIM	GP	G	A	TP	PIM
1990-91	Michigan State	CCHA	34	1	8	9	21					
1991-92	Michigan State	CCHA	33	4	4	8	2					
1992-93	Michigan State	CCHA	39	11	20	31	20					
1993-94	Michigan State	CCHA	41	14	18	32	26					
1994-95	Huntington	ECHL	60	12	14	26	100	4	2	1	3	2

HARPER, KEVIN — ST.L.

Defense. Shoots left. 6'3", 185 lbs. Born, Sudbury, Ont., September 7, 1975.
(St. Louis' 7th choice, 250th overall, in 1994 Entry Draft).

			Regular Season					Playoffs				
Season	Club	Lea	GP	G	A	TP	PIM	GP	G	A	TP	PIM
1993-94	Wexford	Jr. A	45	4	26	30	39					
1994-95	Michigan State	CCHA	DID NOT PLAY									

HARTMAN, MIKE

Left wing. Shoots left. 6', 190 lbs. Born, Detroit, MI, February 7, 1967.
(Buffalo's 8th choice, 131st overall, in 1986 Entry Draft).

			Regular Season					Playoffs				
Season	Club	Lea	GP	G	A	TP	PIM	GP	G	A	TP	PIM
1984-85	Belleville	OHL	49	13	12	25	119					
1985-86	Belleville	OHL	4	2	1	3	5					
	North Bay	OHL	53	19	16	35	205	10	2	4	6	34
1986-87	**Buffalo**	**NHL**	**17**	**3**	**3**	**6**	**69**					
	North Bay	OHL	32	15	24	39	144	19	7	8	15	88
1987-88	**Buffalo**	**NHL**	**18**	**3**	**1**	**4**	**90**	**6**	**0**	**0**	**0**	**35**
	Rochester	AHL	57	13	14	27	283	4	1	0	1	22
1988-89	**Buffalo**	**NHL**	**70**	**8**	**9**	**17**	**316**	**5**	**0**	**0**	**0**	**34**
1989-90	**Buffalo**	**NHL**	**60**	**11**	**10**	**21**	**211**	**6**	**0**	**0**	**0**	**18**
1990-91	**Buffalo**	**NHL**	**60**	**9**	**3**	**12**	**204**	**2**	**0**	**0**	**0**	**17**
1991-92	**Winnipeg**	**NHL**	**75**	**4**	**4**	**8**	**264**	**2**	**0**	**0**	**0**	**2**
1992-93	**Tampa Bay**	**NHL**	**58**	**4**	**4**	**8**	**154**					
	NY Rangers	**NHL**	**3**	**0**	**0**	**0**	**6**					
1993-94	**NY Rangers**	**NHL**	**35**	**1**	**1**	**2**	**70**					
1994-95	**NY Rangers**	**NHL**	**1**	**0**	**0**	**0**	**4**					
	Detroit	IHL	6	1	0	1	52	1	0	0	0	0
	NHL Totals		**397**	**43**	**35**	**78**	**1388**	**21**	**0**	**0**	**0**	**106**

Traded to **Winnipeg** by **Buffalo** with Darrin Shannon and Dean Kennedy for Dave McLlwain, Gord Donnelly, Winnipeg's fifth round choice (Yuri Khmylev) in 1992 Entry Draft and future considerations, October 11, 1991. Claimed by **Tampa Bay** from **Winnipeg** in Expansion Draft, June 18, 1992. Traded to **NY Rangers** by **Tampa Bay** for Randy Gilhen, March 22, 1993.

HARVEY, TODD — DAL.

Center. Shoots right. 6', 195 lbs. Born, Hamilton, Ont., February 17, 1975.
(Dallas' 1st choice, 9th overall, in 1993 Entry Draft).

			Regular Season					Playoffs				
Season	Club	Lea	GP	G	A	TP	PIM	GP	G	A	TP	PIM
1991-92	Detroit	OHL	58	21	43	64	141	7	3	5	8	30
1992-93	Detroit	OHL	55	50	50	100	83	15	9	12	21	39
1993-94	Detroit	OHL	49	34	51	85	75	17	10	12	22	26
1994-95	Detroit	OHL	11	8	14	22	12					
	Dallas	**NHL**	**40**	**11**	**9**	**20**	**67**	**5**	**0**	**0**	**0**	**8**
	NHL Totals		**40**	**11**	**9**	**20**	**67**	**5**	**0**	**0**	**0**	**8**

HASSELBLAD, PETER — CGY.

Defense. Shoots left. 6'5", 220 lbs. Born, Orebro, Swe., April 20, 1966.
(Calgary's 12th choice, 229th overall, in 1987 Entry Draft).

			Regular Season					Playoffs				
Season	Club	Lea	GP	G	A	TP	PIM	GP	G	A	TP	PIM
1989-90	Farjestad	Swe.	36	3	6	9	51	10	1	2	3	12
1990-91	Farjestad	Swe.	40	0	7	7	56	8	0	0	0	16
1991-92	Team Boro	Swe. 2	27	2	12	14	52	....	....	....	....	....
1992-93	Malmo	Swe.	39	4	9	13	52	6	0	0	0	6
1993-94	Malmo	Swe.	37	3	7	10	50	11	0	0	0	6
1994-95	Malmo	Swe.	40	3	5	8	38	9	1	2	3	8

HATCHER, DERIAN — DAL.

Defense. Shoots left. 6'5", 225 lbs. Born, Sterling Heights, MI, June 4, 1972.
(Minnesota's 1st choice, 8th overall, in 1990 Entry Draft).

			Regular Season					Playoffs				
Season	Club	Lea	GP	G	A	TP	PIM	GP	G	A	TP	PIM
1989-90	North Bay	OHL	64	14	38	52	81	5	2	3	5	8
1990-91	North Bay	OHL	64	13	49	62	163	10	2	10	12	28
1991-92	**Minnesota**	**NHL**	**43**	**8**	**4**	**12**	**88**	**5**	**0**	**2**	**2**	**8**
1992-93	**Minnesota**	**NHL**	**67**	**4**	**15**	**19**	**178**	....	....	....	....	....
	Kalamazoo	IHL	2	1	2	3	21	....	....	....	....	....
1993-94	**Dallas**	**NHL**	**83**	**12**	**19**	**31**	**211**	**9**	**0**	**2**	**2**	**14**
1994-95	**Dallas**	**NHL**	**43**	**5**	**11**	**16**	**105**	....	....	....	....	....
	NHL Totals		**236**	**29**	**49**	**78**	**582**	**14**	**0**	**4**	**4**	**22**

HATCHER, KEVIN — DAL.

Defense. Shoots right. 6'4", 225 lbs. Born, Detroit, MI, September 9, 1966.
(Washington's 1st choice, 17th overall, in 1984 Entry Draft).

			Regular Season					Playoffs				
Season	Club	Lea	GP	G	A	TP	PIM	GP	G	A	TP	PIM
1983-84	North Bay	OHL	67	10	39	49	61	4	2	2	4	11
1984-85	**Washington**	**NHL**	**2**	**1**	**0**	**1**	**0**	**1**	**0**	**0**	**0**	**0**
a	North Bay	OHL	58	26	37	63	75	8	3	8	11	9
1985-86	**Washington**	**NHL**	**79**	**9**	**10**	**19**	**119**	**9**	**1**	**1**	**2**	**19**
1986-87	**Washington**	**NHL**	**78**	**8**	**16**	**24**	**144**	**7**	**1**	**0**	**1**	**20**
1987-88	**Washington**	**NHL**	**71**	**14**	**27**	**41**	**137**	**14**	**5**	**7**	**12**	**55**
1988-89	**Washington**	**NHL**	**62**	**13**	**27**	**40**	**101**	**6**	**1**	**4**	**5**	**20**
1989-90	**Washington**	**NHL**	**80**	**13**	**41**	**54**	**102**	**11**	**0**	**8**	**8**	**32**
1990-91	**Washington**	**NHL**	**79**	**24**	**50**	**74**	**69**	**11**	**3**	**3**	**6**	**8**
1991-92	**Washington**	**NHL**	**79**	**17**	**37**	**54**	**105**	**7**	**2**	**4**	**6**	**19**
1992-93	**Washington**	**NHL**	**83**	**34**	**45**	**79**	**114**	**6**	**0**	**1**	**1**	**14**
1993-94	**Washington**	**NHL**	**72**	**16**	**24**	**40**	**108**	**11**	**3**	**4**	**7**	**37**
1994-95	**Dallas**	**NHL**	**47**	**10**	**19**	**29**	**66**	**5**	**2**	**1**	**3**	**2**
	NHL Totals		**732**	**159**	**296**	**455**	**1065**	**88**	**18**	**33**	**51**	**226**

a OHL Second All-Star Team (1985)

Played in NHL All-Star Game (1990, 1991, 1992)

Traded to **Dallas** by **Washington** for Mark Tinordi and Rick Mrozik, January 18, 1995.

HAUER, BRETT

Defense. Shoots right. 6'2", 200 lbs. Born, Richfield, MN, July 11, 1971.
(Vancouver's 3rd choice, 71st overall, in 1989 Entry Draft).

			Regular Season					Playoffs				
Season	Club	Lea	GP	G	A	TP	PIM	GP	G	A	TP	PIM
1989-90	Minn.-Duluth	WCHA	37	2	6	8	44	....	....	....	....	....
1990-91	Minn.-Duluth	WCHA	30	1	7	8	54	....	....	....	....	....
1991-92	Minn.-Duluth	WCHA	33	8	14	22	40	....	....	....	....	....
1992-93ab	Minn. Duluth	WCHA	40	10	46	56	52	....	....	....	....	....
1993-94	U.S. National	....	57	6	14	20	88	....	....	....	....	....
	U.S. Olympic	....	8	0	0	0	10	....	....	....	....	....
	Las Vegas	IHL	21	0	7	7	8	1	0	0	0	0
1994-95	AIK	Swe.	37	1	3	4	38	....	....	....	....	....

a WCHA First All-Star Team (1993)
b NCAA West First All-American Team (1993)

HAWERCHUK, DALE (HOW-uhr-CHUHK) — ST.L.

Center. Shoots left. 5'11", 190 lbs. Born, Toronto, Ont., April 4, 1963.
(Winnipeg's 1st choice, 1st overall, in 1981 Entry Draft).

			Regular Season					Playoffs				
Season	Club	Lea	GP	G	A	TP	PIM	GP	G	A	TP	PIM
1979-80a	Cornwall	QJHL	72	37	66	103	21	18	20	25	45	0
1980-81bcd	Cornwall	QJHL	72	81	102	183	69	19	15	20	35	8
1981-82e	**Winnipeg**	**NHL**	**80**	**45**	**58**	**103**	**47**	**4**	**1**	**7**	**8**	**5**
1982-83	**Winnipeg**	**NHL**	**79**	**40**	**51**	**91**	**31**	**3**	**1**	**4**	**5**	**8**
1983-84	**Winnipeg**	**NHL**	**80**	**37**	**65**	**102**	**73**	**3**	**1**	**1**	**2**	**0**
1984-85f	**Winnipeg**	**NHL**	**80**	**53**	**77**	**130**	**74**	**3**	**2**	**1**	**3**	**4**
1985-86	**Winnipeg**	**NHL**	**80**	**46**	**59**	**105**	**44**	**3**	**0**	**3**	**3**	**0**
1986-87	**Winnipeg**	**NHL**	**80**	**47**	**53**	**100**	**52**	**10**	**5**	**8**	**13**	**4**
1987-88	**Winnipeg**	**NHL**	**80**	**44**	**77**	**121**	**59**	**5**	**3**	**4**	**7**	**16**
1988-89	**Winnipeg**	**NHL**	**75**	**41**	**55**	**96**	**28**	....	....	....	....	....
1989-90	**Winnipeg**	**NHL**	**79**	**26**	**55**	**81**	**60**	**7**	**3**	**5**	**8**	**2**
1990-91	**Buffalo**	**NHL**	**80**	**31**	**58**	**89**	**32**	**6**	**2**	**4**	**6**	**10**
1991-92	**Buffalo**	**NHL**	**77**	**23**	**75**	**98**	**27**	**7**	**2**	**5**	**7**	**0**
1992-93	**Buffalo**	**NHL**	**81**	**16**	**80**	**96**	**52**	**8**	**5**	**9**	**14**	**2**
1993-94	**Buffalo**	**NHL**	**81**	**35**	**51**	**86**	**91**	**7**	**0**	**7**	**7**	**4**
1994-95	**Buffalo**	**NHL**	**23**	**5**	**11**	**16**	**2**	**2**	**0**	**0**	**0**	**0**
	NHL Totals		**1055**	**489**	**825**	**1314**	**672**	**68**	**25**	**58**	**83**	**55**

a Won George Parsons Trophy (Memorial Cup Tournament Most Sportsmanlike Player) (1980)
b QMJHL First All-Star Team (1981)
c Canadian Major Junior Player of the Year (1981)
d Won Stafford Smythe Memorial Trophy (Memorial Cup Tournament MVP) (1981)
e Won Calder Memorial Trophy (1982)
f NHL Second All-Star Team (1985)

Played in NHL All-Star Game (1982, 1985, 1986, 1988)

Traded to **Buffalo** by **Winnipeg** with Winnipeg's first round choice (Brad May) in 1990 Entry Draft and future considerations for Phil Housley, Scott Arniel, Jeff Parker and Buffalo's first round choice (Keith Tkachuk) in 1990 Entry Draft, June 16, 1990. Signed as a free agent by **St. Louis**, July 8, 1995.

HAWGOOD, GREG (HAW-guhd)

Defense. Shoots left. 5'10", 190 lbs. Born, Edmonton, Alta., August 10, 1968.
(Boston's 9th choice, 202nd overall, in 1986 Entry Draft).

			Regular Season					Playoffs				
Season	Club	Lea	GP	G	A	TP	PIM	GP	G	A	TP	PIM
1983-84	Kamloops	WHL	49	10	23	33	39	....	....	....	....	....
1984-85	Kamloops	WHL	66	25	40	65	72	....	....	....	....	....
1985-86a	Kamloops	WHL	71	34	85	119	86	16	9	22	31	16
1986-87a	Kamloops	WHL	61	30	93	123	139	....	....	....	....	....
1987-88	**Boston**	**NHL**	**1**	**0**	**0**	**0**	**0**	**3**	**1**	**0**	**1**	**0**
ab	Kamloops	WHL	63	48	85	133	142	16	10	16	26	33
1988-89	**Boston**	**NHL**	**56**	**16**	**24**	**40**	**84**	**10**	**0**	**2**	**2**	**2**
	Maine	AHL	21	2	9	11	41	....	....	....	....	....
1989-90	**Boston**	**NHL**	**77**	**11**	**27**	**38**	**76**	**15**	**1**	**3**	**4**	**12**
1990-91	Asiago	Italy	2	3	0	3	9	....	....	....	....	....
	Edmonton	**NHL**	**6**	**0**	**1**	**1**	**6**	....	....	....	....	....
	Maine	AHL	5	0	1	1	13	....	....	....	....	....
	Cape Breton	AHL	55	10	32	42	73	4	0	3	3	23
1991-92	**Edmonton**	**NHL**	**20**	**2**	**11**	**13**	**22**	**13**	**0**	**3**	**3**	**23**
cd	Cape Breton	AHL	56	20	55	75	26	3	2	2	4	0
1992-93	**Edmonton**	**NHL**	**29**	**5**	**13**	**18**	**35**	....	....	....	....	....
	Philadelphia	**NHL**	**40**	**6**	**22**	**28**	**39**	....	....	....	....	....
1993-94	**Philadelphia**	**NHL**	**19**	**3**	**12**	**15**	**19**	....	....	....	....	....
	Florida	**NHL**	**33**	**2**	**14**	**16**	**9**	....	....	....	....	....
	Pittsburgh	**NHL**	**12**	**1**	**2**	**3**	**8**	**1**	**0**	**0**	**0**	**0**
1994-95	**Pittsburgh**	**NHL**	**21**	**1**	**4**	**5**	**25**	....	....	....	....	....
	Cleveland	IHL	....	....	....	....	....	3	1	0	1	4
	NHL Totals		**314**	**47**	**130**	**177**	**323**	**42**	**2**	**8**	**10**	**37**

a WHL West All-Star Team (1986, 1987, 1988)
b Canadian Major Junior Defenseman of the Year (1988)
c AHL First All-Star Team (1992)
d Won Eddie Shore Plaque (Top Defenseman - AHL) (1992)

Traded to **Edmonton** by **Boston** for Vladimir Ruzicka, October 22, 1990. Traded to **Philadelphia** by **Edmonton** with Josef Beranek for Brian Benning, January 16, 1993. Traded to **Florida** by **Philadelphia** for cash, November 30, 1993. Traded to **Pittsburgh** by **Florida** for Jeff Daniels, March 19, 1994.

HAWKINS, TODD — PIT.

Left/Right wing. Shoots right. 6'1", 195 lbs. Born, Kingston, Ont., August 2, 1966.
(Vancouver's 10th choice, 217th overall, in 1986 Entry Draft).

			Regular Season					Playoffs				
Season	Club	Lea	GP	G	A	TP	PIM	GP	G	A	TP	PIM
1984-85	Belleville	OHL	58	7	16	23	117	12	1	0	1	10
1985-86	Belleville	OHL	60	14	13	27	172	24	9	7	16	60
1986-87	Belleville	OHL	60	47	40	87	187	6	3	5	8	16
1987-88	Flint	IHL	50	13	13	26	337	16	3	5	8	*174
	Fredericton	AHL	2	0	4	4	11	....	....	....	....	....
1988-89	**Vancouver**	**NHL**	**4**	**0**	**0**	**0**	**9**	....	....	....	....	....
	Milwaukee	IHL	63	12	14	26	307	9	1	0	1	33
1989-90	**Vancouver**	**NHL**	**4**	**0**	**0**	**0**	**6**	....	....	....	....	....
	Milwaukee	IHL	61	23	17	40	273	5	4	1	5	19
1990-91	Newmarket	AHL	22	2	5	7	66	....	....	....	....	....
	Milwaukee	IHL	39	9	11	20	134	....	....	....	....	....
1991-92	**Toronto**	**NHL**	**2**	**0**	**0**	**0**	**0**	....	....	....	....	....
	St. John's	AHL	66	30	27	57	139	7	1	0	1	10
1992-93	St. John's	AHL	72	21	41	62	103	9	1	3	4	10
1993-94	Cleveland	IHL	76	19	14	33	115	....	....	....	....	....
1994-95	Cleveland	IHL	4	2	0	2	29	....	....	....	....	....
	Minnesota	IHL	47	10	8	18	95	3	0	1	1	12
	NHL Totals		**10**	**0**	**0**	**0**	**15**	....	....	....	....	....

Traded to **Toronto** by **Vancouver** for Brian Blad, January 22, 1991. Signed as a free agent by **Pittsburgh**, August 20, 1993.

HAY, DWAYNE — WSH.

Left wing. Shoots left. 6'1", 183 lbs. Born, London, Ont., February 11, 1977.
(Washington's 3rd choice, 43rd overall, in 1995 Entry Draft).

			Regular Season					Playoffs				
Season	Club	Lea	GP	G	A	TP	PIM	GP	G	A	TP	PIM
1993-94	Listowel	Jr. B	48	10	24	34	56	....	....	....	....	....
1994-95	Guelph	OHL	65	26	28	54	37	14	5	7	12	6

HEALEY, PAUL — PHI.

Right wing. Shoots right. 6'2", 185 lbs. Born, Edmonton, Alta., March 20, 1975.
(Philadelphia's 7th choice, 192nd overall, in 1993 Entry Draft).

			Regular Season					Playoffs				
Season	Club	Lea	GP	G	A	TP	PIM	GP	G	A	TP	PIM
1992-93	Prince Albert	WHL	72	12	20	32	66	....	....	....	....	....
1993-94	Prince Albert	WHL	63	23	26	49	70	....	....	....	....	....
1994-95a	Prince Albert	WHL	71	43	50	93	67	12	3	4	7	2

a WHL East Second All-Star Team (1995)

HECHT, JOCHEN — ST.L.

Center. Shoots left. 6'1", 180 lbs. Born, Mannheim, Germany, June 21, 1977.
(St. Louis' 1st choice, 49th overall, in 1995 Entry Draft).

			Regular Season					Playoffs				
Season	Club	Lea	GP	G	A	TP	PIM	GP	G	A	TP	PIM
1994-95	Mannheim	Ger.	43	11	12	23	68	10	5	4	9	12

HEDICAN, BRET — VAN.

Defense. Shoots left. 6'2", 195 lbs. Born, St. Paul, MN, August 10, 1970.
(St. Louis' 10th choice, 198th overall, in 1988 Entry Draft).

			Regular Season					Playoffs				
Season	Club	Lea	GP	G	A	TP	PIM	GP	G	A	TP	PIM
1988-89	St. Cloud	NCAA	28	5	3	8	28	....	....	....	....	....
1989-90	St. Cloud	NCAA	36	4	17	21	37	....	....	....	....	....
1990-91a	St. Cloud	WCHA	41	21	26	47	26	....	....	....	....	....
1991-92	U.S. National	....	54	1	8	9	59	....	....	....	....	....
	U.S. Olympic	....	8	0	0	0	4	....	....	....	....	....
	St. Louis	**NHL**	**4**	**1**	**0**	**1**	**0**	**5**	**0**	**0**	**0**	**0**
1992-93	**St. Louis**	**NHL**	**42**	**0**	**8**	**8**	**30**	**10**	**0**	**0**	**0**	**14**
	Peoria	IHL	19	0	8	8	10	....	....	....	....	....
1993-94	**St. Louis**	**NHL**	**61**	**0**	**11**	**11**	**64**	....	....	....	....	....
	Vancouver	**NHL**	**8**	**0**	**1**	**1**	**0**	**24**	**1**	**6**	**7**	**16**
1994-95	**Vancouver**	**NHL**	**45**	**2**	**11**	**13**	**34**	**11**	**0**	**2**	**2**	**6**
	NHL Totals		**160**	**3**	**31**	**34**	**128**	**50**	**1**	**8**	**9**	**36**

a WCHA First All-Star Team (1991)

Traded to **Vancouver** by **St. Louis** with Jeff Brown and Nathan Lafayette for Craig Janney, March 21, 1994.

HEHR, JASON — N.J.

Defense. Shoots left. 6'1", 193 lbs. Born, Medicine Hat, Alta., February 8, 1971.
(New Jersey's 12th choice, 253rd overall, in 1991 Entry Draft).

			Regular Season					Playoffs				
Season	Club	Lea	GP	G	A	TP	PIM	GP	G	A	TP	PIM
1991-92	N. Michigan	WCHA	40	8	17	25	38	....	....	....	....	....
1992-93	N. Michigan	WCHA	43	8	27	35	40	....	....	....	....	....
1993-94	N. Michigan	WCHA	39	11	26	37	56	....	....	....	....	....
1994-95	N. Michigan	WCHA	39	11	26	37	40	....	....	....	....	....

HEINZE, STEPHEN (HIGHNS) — BOS.

Right wing. Shoots right. 5'11", 193 lbs. Born, Lawrence, MA, January 30, 1970.
(Boston's 2nd choice, 60th overall, in 1988 Entry Draft).

			Regular Season					Playoffs				
Season	Club	Lea	GP	G	A	TP	PIM	GP	G	A	TP	PIM
1988-89	Boston College	H.E.	36	26	23	49	26	....	....	....	....	....
1989-90ab	Boston College	H.E.	40	27	36	63	41	....	....	....	....	....
1990-91	Boston College	H.E.	35	21	26	47	35	....	....	....	....	....
1991-92	U.S. National	....	49	18	15	33	38	....	....	....	....	....
	U.S. Olympic	....	8	1	3	4	8	....	....	....	....	....
	Boston	**NHL**	**14**	**3**	**4**	**7**	**6**	**7**	**0**	**3**	**3**	**17**
1992-93	**Boston**	**NHL**	**73**	**18**	**13**	**31**	**24**	**4**	**1**	**1**	**2**	**2**
1993-94	**Boston**	**NHL**	**77**	**10**	**11**	**21**	**32**	**13**	**2**	**3**	**5**	**7**
1994-95	**Boston**	**NHL**	**36**	**7**	**9**	**16**	**23**	**5**	**0**	**0**	**0**	**0**
	NHL Totals		**200**	**38**	**37**	**75**	**85**	**29**	**3**	**7**	**10**	**26**

a Hockey East First All-Star Team (1990)
b NCAA East First All-American Team (1990)

HEJDUK, MILAN (HEHI-duhk) — COL.

Right wing. Shoots right. 5'11", 163 lbs. Born, Usti-nad-Labem, Czech., February 14, 1976.
(Quebec's 6th choice, 87th overall, in 1994 Entry Draft).

			Regular Season					Playoffs				
Season	Club	Lea	GP	G	A	TP	PIM	GP	G	A	TP	PIM
1993-94	Pardubice	Czech.	22	6	3	9	....	10	5	1	6	....
1994-95	Pardubice	Czech.	43	11	13	24	6	6	3	1	4	0

HELENIUS, SAMI — CGY.

Defense. Shoots left. 6'5", 225 lbs. Born, Helsinki, Finland, January 22, 1974.
(Calgary's 5th choice, 102nd overall, in 1992 Entry Draft).

			Regular Season					Playoffs				
Season	Club	Lea	GP	G	A	TP	PIM	GP	G	A	TP	PIM
1992-93	Jokerit	Fin.	1	0	0	0	0	....	....	....	....	....
1993-94	Reipas	Fin.	37	2	3	5	46	....	....	....	....	....
1994-95	Saint John	AHL	69	2	5	7	217	....	....	....	....	....

HELMER, BRYAN — N.J.

Defense. Shoots right. 6'1", 190 lbs. Born, Sault Ste. Marie, Ont., July 15, 1972.

			Regular Season					Playoffs				
Season	Club	Lea	GP	G	A	TP	PIM	GP	G	A	TP	PIM
1993-94	Albany	AHL	65	4	19	23	79	5	0	0	0	9
1994-95	Albany	AHL	77	7	36	43	101	7	1	0	1	0

Signed as a free agent by **New Jersey**, July 10, 1994.

HEMENWAY, KEN — PHI.

Defense. Shoots right. 6'1", 175 lbs. Born, Boston, MA, August 1, 1975.
(Philadelphia's 11th choice, 270th overall, in 1993 Entry Draft).

			Regular Season					Playoffs				
Season	Club	Lea	GP	G	A	TP	PIM	GP	G	A	TP	PIM
1993-94	Omaha	USHL	31	2	22	24	26	14	1	7	8	16
1994-95	Boston College	H.E.	32	4	6	10	24	....	....	....	....	....

HENDRICKSON, DANIEL — WSH.

Right wing. Shoots right. 5'10", 180 lbs. Born, Minneapolis, MN, December 26, 1974.
(Washington's 5th choice, 173rd overall, in 1993 Entry Draft).

			Regular Season					Playoffs				
Season	Club	Lea	GP	G	A	TP	PIM	GP	G	A	TP	PIM
1993-94	U. Minnesota	WCHA	39	3	2	5	60	....	....	....	....	....
1994-95	U. Minnesota	WCHA	40	4	13	17	69	....	....	....	....	....

HENDRICKSON, DARBY — TOR.

Center. Shoots left. 6', 185 lbs. Born, Richfield, MN, August 28, 1972.
(Toronto's 3rd choice, 73rd overall, in 1990 Entry Draft).

			Regular Season					Playoffs				
Season	Club	Lea	GP	G	A	TP	PIM	GP	G	A	TP	PIM
1991-92	U. Minnesota	WCHA	41	25	28	53	61	....	....	....	....	....
1992-93	U. Minnesota	WCHA	31	12	15	27	35	....	....	....	....	....
1993-94	U.S. National	....	59	12	16	28	30	....	....	....	....	....
	U.S. Olympic	....	8	0	0	0	6	....	....	....	....	....
	St. John's	AHL	6	4	1	5	4	3	1	1	2	0
	Toronto	**NHL**	....	....	....	....	....	**2**	**0**	**0**	**0**	**0**
1994-95	St. John's	AHL	59	16	20	36	48	....	....	....	....	....
	Toronto	**NHL**	**8**	**0**	**1**	**1**	**4**	....	....	....	....	....
	NHL Totals		**8**	**0**	**1**	**1**	**4**	**2**	**0**	**0**	**0**	**0**

HERBERS, IAN

Defense. Shoots left. 6'4", 225 lbs. Born, Jasper, Alta., July 18, 1967.
(Buffalo's 11th choice, 190th overall, in 1987 Entry Draft).

			Regular Season					Playoffs				
Season	Club	Lea	GP	G	A	TP	PIM	GP	G	A	TP	PIM
1984-85	Kelowna	WHL	68	3	14	17	120	6	0	1	1	9
1985-86	Spokane	WHL	29	1	6	7	85	....	....	....	....	....
	Lethbridge	WHL	32	1	4	5	109	10	1	0	1	37
1986-87	Swift Current	WHL	72	5	8	13	230	4	1	1	2	12
1987-88	Swift Current	WHL	56	5	14	19	238	4	0	2	2	4
1988-89	U. of Alberta	CWUAA	47	4	22	26	137	....	....	....	....	....
1989-90	U. of Alberta	CWUAA	45	5	31	36	83	....	....	....	....	....
1990-91a	U. of Alberta	CWUAA	45	6	24	30	87	....	....	....	....	....
1991-92a	U. of Alberta	CWUAA	43	14	34	48	86	....	....	....	....	....
1992-93	Cape Breton	AHL	77	7	15	22	129	10	0	1	1	16
1993-94	**Edmonton**	**NHL**	**22**	**0**	**2**	**2**	**32**	....	....	....	....	....
	Cape Breton	AHL	53	7	16	23	122	5	0	3	3	12
1994-95	Cape Breton	AHL	36	1	11	12	104	....	....	....	....	....
	Detroit	IHL	37	1	5	6	46	5	1	1	2	6
	NHL Totals		**22**	**0**	**2**	**2**	**32**	....	....	....	....	....

a CIAU All-Canadian Team (1991, 1992)

Signed as a free agent by **Edmonton**, September 9, 1992.

HERPERGER, CHRIS — PHI.

Left wing. Shoots left. 6', 190 lbs. Born, Esterhazy, Sask., February 24, 1974.
(Philadelphia's 10th choice, 223rd overall, in 1992 Entry Draft).

			Regular Season					Playoffs				
Season	Club	Lea	GP	G	A	TP	PIM	GP	G	A	TP	PIM
1990-91	Swift Current	WHL	10	0	1	1	5	....	....	....	....	....
1991-92	Swift Current	WHL	72	14	19	33	44	8	0	1	1	9
1992-93	Swift Current	WHL	20	9	7	16	31	....	....	....	....	....
	Seattle	WHL	46	20	11	31	30	5	1	1	2	6
1993-94	Seattle	WHL	71	44	51	95	110	9	12	10	22	12
1994-95a	Seattle	WHL	59	49	52	101	106	4	4	0	4	6
	Hershey	AHL	4	0	0	0	0	....	....	....	....	....

a WHL West Second All-Star Team (1995)

HERR, MATT — WSH.

Center. Shoots left. 6'1", 180 lbs. Born, Hackensack, NJ, May 26, 1976.
(Washington's 4th choice, 93rd overall, in 1994 Entry Draft).

			Regular Season					Playoffs				
Season	Club	Lea	GP	G	A	TP	PIM	GP	G	A	TP	PIM
1993-94	Hotchkiss	HS	24	28	19	47	....	....	....	....	....	....
1994-95	U. of Michigan	CCHA	37	11	8	19	51	....	....	....	....	....

HERTER, JASON — NYI

Defense. Shoots right. 6'1", 190 lbs. Born, Hafford, Sask., October 2, 1970.
(Vancouver's 1st choice, 8th overall, in 1989 Entry Draft).

			Regular Season					Playoffs				
Season	Club	Lea	GP	G	A	TP	PIM	GP	G	A	TP	PIM
1988-89	North Dakota	WCHA	41	8	24	32	62	....	....	....	....	....
1989-90a	North Dakota	WCHA	38	11	39	50	40	....	....	....	....	....
1990-91a	North Dakota	WCHA	39	11	26	37	52	....	....	....	....	....
1991-92	Milwaukee	IHL	56	7	18	25	34	1	0	0	0	2
1992-93	Hamilton	AHL	70	7	16	23	68	....	....	....	....	....
1993-94	Kalamazoo	IHL	68	14	28	42	92	5	3	0	3	14
1994-95	Kalamazoo	IHL	60	12	20	32	70	16	2	8	10	10

a WCHA Second All-Star Team (1990, 1991)

Signed as a free agent by **Dallas**, August 6, 1993. Signed as a free agent by **NY Islanders**, August 10, 1995.

HEWARD, JAMIE — TOR.

Defense. Shoots right. 6'2", 207 lbs. Born, Regina, Sask., March 30, 1971.
(Pittsburgh's 1st choice, 16th overall, in 1989 Entry Draft).

			Regular Season					Playoffs				
Season	Club	Lea	GP	G	A	TP	PIM	GP	G	A	TP	PIM
1987-88	Regina	WHL	68	10	17	27	17	4	1	1	2	2
1988-89	Regina	WHL	52	31	28	59	29	....	....	....	....	....
1989-90	Regina	WHL	72	14	44	58	42	11	2	2	4	10
1990-91a	Regina	WHL	71	23	61	84	41	8	2	9	11	6
1991-92	Muskegon	IHL	54	6	21	27	37	14	1	4	5	4
1992-93	Cleveland	IHL	58	9	18	27	64	....	....	....	....	....
1993-94	Cleveland	IHL	73	8	16	24	72	....	....	....	....	....
1994-95	Cdn. National	....	51	11	35	46	32	....	....	....	....	....

a WHL East First All-Star Team (1991)

HILL, SEAN (HIHL, SHAWN) — OTT.

Defense. Shoots right. 6', 195 lbs. Born, Duluth, MN, February 14, 1970.
(Montreal's 9th choice, 167th overall, in 1988 Entry Draft).

			Regular Season					Playoffs				
Season	Club	Lea	GP	G	A	TP	PIM	GP	G	A	TP	PIM
1988-89	U. Wisconsin	WCHA	45	2	23	25	69	....	....	....	....	....
1989-90a	U. Wisconsin	WCHA	42	14	39	53	78	....	....	....	....	....
1990-91ab	U. Wisconsin	WCHA	37	19	32	51	122	....	....	....	....	....
	Montreal	**NHL**	....	....	....	....	....	**1**	**0**	**0**	**0**	**0**
	Fredericton	AHL	....	....	....	....	....	3	0	2	2	2
1991-92	Fredericton	AHL	42	7	20	27	65	7	1	3	4	6
	U.S. National	....	12	4	3	7	16	....	....	....	....	....
	U.S. Olympic	....	8	2	0	2	6	....	....	....	....	....
	Montreal	**NHL**	....	....	....	....	....	**4**	**1**	**0**	**1**	**2**
1992-93	**Montreal**	**NHL**	**31**	**2**	**6**	**8**	**54**	**3**	**0**	**0**	**0**	**4**
	Fredericton	AHL	6	1	3	4	10	....	....	....	....	....
1993-94	**Anaheim**	**NHL**	**68**	**7**	**20**	**27**	**78**	....	....	....	....	....
1994-95	**Ottawa**	**NHL**	**45**	**1**	**14**	**15**	**30**	....	....	....	....	....
	NHL Totals		**144**	**10**	**40**	**50**	**162**	**8**	**1**	**0**	**1**	**6**

a WCHA Second All-Star Team (1990, 1991)
b NCAA West Second All-American Team (1991)

Claimed by **Anaheim** from **Montreal** in Expansion Draft, June 24, 1993. Traded to **Ottawa** by **Anaheim** with Anaheim's ninth round choice (Frederic Cassivi) in 1994 Entry Draft for Ottawa's third round choice (later traded to Tampa Bay — Tampa Bay selected Vadim Epanchintsev) in 1994 Entry Draft, June 29, 1994.

HILLER, JIM

Right wing. Shoots right. 6', 190 lbs. Born, Port Alberni, B.C., May 15, 1969.
(Los Angeles' 10th choice, 207th overall, in 1989 Entry Draft).

			Regular Season					Playoffs				
Season	Club	Lea	GP	G	A	TP	PIM	GP	G	A	TP	PIM
1989-90	N. Michigan	WCHA	39	23	33	56	52	....	....	....	....	....
1990-91	N. Michigan	WCHA	43	22	41	63	59	....	....	....	....	....
1991-92ab	N. Michigan	WCHA	39	28	52	80	115	....	....	....	....	....
1992-93	**Los Angeles**	**NHL**	**40**	**6**	**6**	**12**	**90**	....	....	....	....	....
	Phoenix	IHL	3	0	2	2	2	....	....	....	....	....
	Detroit	**NHL**	**21**	**2**	**6**	**8**	**19**	**2**	**0**	**0**	**0**	**4**
1993-94	**NY Rangers**	**NHL**	**2**	**0**	**0**	**0**	**7**	....	....	....	....	....
	Binghamton	AHL	67	27	34	61	61	....	....	....	....	....
1994-95	Binghamton	AHL	49	15	13	28	44	....	....	....	....	....
	Atlanta	IHL	17	5	10	15	28	5	0	3	3	8
	NHL Totals		**63**	**8**	**12**	**20**	**116**	**2**	**0**	**0**	**0**	**4**

a NCAA West Second All-American Team (1992)
b WCHA Second All-Star Team (1992)

Traded to **Detroit** by **Los Angeles** with Paul Coffey and Sylvain Couturier for Jimmy Carson, Marc Potvin and Gary Shuchuk, January 29, 1993. Claimed on waivers by **NY Rangers** from **Detroit**, October 12, 1993.

HILLMAN, JOHN — COL.

Center. Shoots left. 6'1", 200 lbs. Born, Fridley, MN, October 10, 1974.
(Quebec's 13th choice, 283rd overall, in 1993 Entry Draft).

			Regular Season					Playoffs				
Season	Club	Lea	GP	G	A	TP	PIM	GP	G	A	TP	PIM
1993-94	U. Minnesota	WCHA	20	0	0	0	8	....	....	....	....	....
1994-95	DID NOT PLAY											

HILTON, KEVIN — DET.

Center. Shoots left. 5'11", 170 lbs. Born, Trenton, MI, January 5, 1975.
(Detroit's 3rd choice, 74th overall, in 1993 Entry Draft).

			Regular Season					Playoffs				
Season	Club	Lea	GP	G	A	TP	PIM	GP	G	A	TP	PIM
1992-93	U. of Michigan	CCHA	36	16	15	31	8	....	....	....	....	....
1993-94	U. of Michigan	CCHA	39	11	12	23	16	....	....	....	....	....
1994-95	U. of Michigan	CCHA	37	20	31	51	14	....	....	....	....	....

HLAVAC, JAN — NYI

Left wing. Shoots left. 6', 185 lbs. Born, Prague, Czech., September 20, 1976.
(NY Islanders' 2nd choice, 28th overall, in 1995 Entry Draft).

			Regular Season					Playoffs				
Season	Club	Lea	GP	G	A	TP	PIM	GP	G	A	TP	PIM
1993-94	HC Sparta	Czech.	9	1	1	2	....	....	....	....	....	....
1994-95	HC Sparta	Czech.	38	7	6	13	18	5	0	2	2	0

HLUSHKO, TODD — (huh-LUSH-koh) CGY.

Center. Shoots left. 5'11", 185 lbs. Born, Toronto, Ont., February 7, 1970.
(Washington's 14th choice, 240th overall, in 1989 Entry Draft).

			Regular Season					Playoffs				
Season	Club	Lea	GP	G	A	TP	PIM	GP	G	A	TP	PIM
1988-89	Guelph	OHL	66	28	18	46	71	7	5	3	8	18
1989-90	Owen Sound	OHL	25	9	17	26	31	....	....	....	....	....
	London	OHL	40	27	17	44	39	6	2	4	6	10
1990-91	Baltimore	AHL	66	9	14	23	55	....	....	....	....	....
1991-92	Baltimore	AHL	74	16	35	51	113	....	....	....	....	....
1992-93	Cdn. National	....	58	22	26	48	10	....	....	....	....	....
1993-94	Cdn. National	....	55	22	6	28	61	....	....	....	....	....
	Cdn. Olympic	....	8	5	0	5	6	....	....	....	....	....
	Philadelphia	**NHL**	**2**	**1**	**0**	**1**	**0**	....	....	....	....	....
	Hershey	AHL	9	6	0	6	4	6	2	1	3	4
1994-95	Saint John	AHL	46	22	10	32	36	4	2	2	4	22
	Calgary	**NHL**	**2**	**0**	**1**	**1**	**2**	**1**	**0**	**0**	**0**	**2**
	NHL Totals		**4**	**1**	**1**	**2**	**2**	**1**	**0**	**0**	**0**	**2**

Signed as a free agent by **Philadelphia**, March 7, 1994. Signed as a free agent by **Calgary**, June 17, 1994.

HNIDY, SHANE — BUF.

Defense. Shoots right. 6'1", 200 lbs. Born, Neepawa, Man., November 8, 1975.
(Buffalo's 7th choice, 173rd overall, in 1994 Entry Draft).

			Regular Season					Playoffs				
Season	Club	Lea	GP	G	A	TP	PIM	GP	G	A	TP	PIM
1991-92	Swift Current	WHL	56	1	3	4	11	4	0	0	0	0
1992-93	Swift Current	WHL	45	5	12	17	62	....	....	....	....	....
	Prince Albert	WHL	27	2	10	12	43	....	....	....	....	....
1993-94	Prince Albert	WHL	69	7	26	33	113	....	....	....	....	....
1994-95	Prince Albert	WHL	72	5	29	34	169	15	4	7	11	29

HOCKING, JUSTIN — L.A.

Defense. Shoots right. 6'4", 205 lbs. Born, Stettler, Alta., January 9, 1974.
(Los Angeles' 1st choice, 39th overall, in 1992 Entry Draft).

			Regular Season					Playoffs				
Season	Club	Lea	GP	G	A	TP	PIM	GP	G	A	TP	PIM
1991-92	Spokane	WHL	71	4	6	10	309	10	0	3	3	28
1992-93	Spokane	WHL	16	0	1	1	75	....	....	....	....	....
	Medicine Hat	WHL	54	1	9	10	119	10	0	1	1	13
1993-94	**Los Angeles**	**NHL**	**1**	**0**	**0**	**0**	**0**	....	....	....	....	....
a	Medicine Hat	WHL	68	7	26	33	236	3	0	0	0	6
	Phoenix	IHL	3	0	0	0	15	....	....	....	....	....
1994-95	Syracuse	AHL	7	0	0	0	24	....	....	....	....	....
	Portland	AHL	9	0	1	1	34	....	....	....	....	....
	Knoxville	ECHL	20	0	6	6	70	4	0	0	0	26
	Phoenix	IHL	20	1	1	2	50	1	0	0	0	0
	NHL Totals		**1**	**0**	**0**	**0**	**0**	....	....	....	....	....

a WHL East Second All-Star Team (1994)

HODGE, DAN — BOS.

Defense. Shoots right. 6'3", 205 lbs. Born, Melrose, MA, September 18, 1971.
(Boston's 8th choice, 194th overall, in 1991 Entry Draft).

			Regular Season					Playoffs				
Season	Club	Lea	GP	G	A	TP	PIM	GP	G	A	TP	PIM
1990-91	Merrimack	H.E.	11	2	3	5	4	....	....	....	....	....
1991-92	Omaha	USHL	45	5	18	23	89	....	....	....	....	....
1992-93	Merrimack	H.E.	36	3	17	20	30	....	....	....	....	....
1993-94	Merrimack	H.E.	37	9	22	31	72	....	....	....	....	....
1994-95	Merrimack	H.E.	20	3	5	8	18	....	....	....	....	....

HOGARDH, PETER — NYI

Center. Shoots left. 5'10", 183 lbs. Born, Snotorp, Sweden, May 25, 1976.
(NY Islanders' 9th choice, 203rd overall, in 1994 Entry Draft).

			Regular Season					Playoffs				
Season	Club	Lea	GP	G	A	TP	PIM	GP	G	A	TP	PIM
1993-94	V. Frolunda	Swe.	16	1	0	1	2	....	....	....	....	....
1994-95	V. Frolunda	Swe.	4	0	0	0	0	....	....	....	....	....
	V. Frolunda	Swe. 2	13	1	4	5	4	....	....	....	....	....

HOGLUND, JONAS — CGY.

Right wing. Shoots right. 6'3", 200 lbs. Born, Hammaro, Sweden, August 29, 1972.
(Calgary's 11th choice, 222nd overall, in 1992 Entry Draft).

			Regular Season					Playoffs				
Season	Club	Lea	GP	G	A	TP	PIM	GP	G	A	TP	PIM
1988-89	Farjestad	Swe.	1	0	0	0	0	....	....	....	....	....
1989-90	Farjestad	Swe.	1	0	0	0	0	....	....	....	....	....
1990-91	Farjestad	Swe.	40	5	5	10	4	8	1	0	1	0
1991-92	Farjestad	Swe.	40	14	11	25	6	6	2	4	6	2
1992-93	Farjestad	Swe.	40	13	13	26	14	3	1	0	1	0
1993-94	Farjestad	Swe.	22	7	2	9	10	....	....	....	....	....
1994-95	Farjestad	Swe.	40	14	12	26	16	4	3	2	5	0

HOGUE, BENOIT — (HOHG) TOR.

Center. Shoots left. 5'10", 194 lbs. Born, Repentigny, Que., October 28, 1966.
(Buffalo's 2nd choice, 35th overall, in 1985 Entry Draft).

			Regular Season					Playoffs				
Season	Club	Lea	GP	G	A	TP	PIM	GP	G	A	TP	PIM
1983-84	St-Jean	QMJHL	59	14	11	25	42	....	....	....	....	....
1984-85	St-Jean	QMJHL	63	46	44	90	92	....	....	....	....	....
1985-86	St-Jean	QMJHL	65	54	54	108	115	9	6	4	10	26
1986-87	Rochester	AHL	52	14	20	34	52	12	5	4	9	8
1987-88	**Buffalo**	**NHL**	**3**	**1**	**1**	**2**	**0**	....	....	....	....	....
	Rochester	AHL	62	24	31	55	141	7	6	1	7	46
1988-89	**Buffalo**	**NHL**	**69**	**14**	**30**	**44**	**120**	**5**	**0**	**0**	**0**	**17**
1989-90	**Buffalo**	**NHL**	**45**	**11**	**7**	**18**	**79**	**3**	**0**	**0**	**0**	**10**
1990-91	**Buffalo**	**NHL**	**76**	**19**	**28**	**47**	**76**	**5**	**3**	**1**	**4**	**10**
1991-92	**Buffalo**	**NHL**	**3**	**0**	**1**	**1**	**0**	....	....	....	....	....
	NY Islanders	**NHL**	**72**	**30**	**45**	**75**	**67**	....	....	....	....	....
1992-93	**NY Islanders**	**NHL**	**70**	**33**	**42**	**75**	**108**	**18**	**6**	**6**	**12**	**31**
1993-94	**NY Islanders**	**NHL**	**83**	**36**	**33**	**69**	**73**	**4**	**0**	**1**	**1**	**4**
1994-95	**NY Islanders**	**NHL**	**33**	**6**	**4**	**10**	**34**	....	....	....	....	....
	Toronto	**NHL**	**12**	**3**	**3**	**6**	**0**	**7**	**0**	**0**	**0**	**6**
	NHL Totals		**466**	**153**	**194**	**347**	**557**	**42**	**9**	**8**	**17**	**78**

Traded to **NY Islanders** by **Buffalo** with Pierre Turgeon, Uwe Krupp and Dave McLlwain for Pat Lafontaine, Randy Hillier, Randy Wood and NY Islanders' fourth round choice (Dean Melanson) in 1992 Entry Draft, October 25, 1991. Traded to **Toronto** by **NY Islanders** with NY Islanders' third round choice (Brian Pepperall) in 1995 Entry Draft and fifth round choice in 1996 Entry Draft for Eric Fichaud, April 6, 1995.

HOHENBERGER, MARTIN — MTL.

Center. Shoots left. 6', 195 lbs. Born, Villach, Austria, January 31, 1977.
(Montreal's 3rd choice, 74th overall, in 1995 Entry Draft).

			Regular Season					Playoffs				
Season	Club	Lea	GP	G	A	TP	PIM	GP	G	A	TP	PIM
1993-94	Victoria	WHL	61	3	13	16	82	....	....	....	....	....
1994-95	Prince George	WHL	47	10	21	31	81	....	....	....	....	....

HOLAN, MILOS — ANA.

Defense. Shoots left. 5'11", 191 lbs. Born, Bilovec, Czech., April 22, 1971.
(Philadelphia's 3rd choice, 77th overall, in 1993 Entry Draft).

			Regular Season					Playoffs				
Season	Club	Lea	GP	G	A	TP	PIM	GP	G	A	TP	PIM
1988-89	TJ Vitkovice	Czech.	7	0	0	0	0	....	....	....	....	....
1989-90	TJ Vitkovice	Czech.	50	8	8	16	....	....	....	....	....	....
1990-91	Dukla Trencin	Czech.	53	6	13	19	....	....	....	....	....	....
1991-92	Dukla Trencin	Czech.	51	13	22	35	32	....	....	....	....	....
1992-93a	TJ Vitkovice	Czech.	53	35	33	68	....	....	....	....	....	....
1993-94	**Philadelphia**	**NHL**	**8**	**1**	**1**	**2**	**4**	....	....	....	....	....
	Hershey	AHL	27	7	22	29	16	....	....	....	....	....
1994-95	Hershey	AHL	55	22	27	49	75	....	....	....	....	....
	Anaheim	**NHL**	**25**	**2**	**8**	**10**	**14**	....	....	....	....	....
	NHL Totals		**33**	**3**	**9**	**12**	**18**	....	....	....	....	....

a Czechoslovakian Player of the Year (1993)

Traded to **Anaheim** by **Philadelphia** for Anatoli Semenov, March 8, 1995.

HOLIK, BOBBY — (HOH-leek) N.J.

Left wing. Shoots right. 6'3", 220 lbs. Born, Jihlava, Czech., January 1, 1971.
(Hartford's 1st choice, 10th overall, in 1989 Entry Draft).

			Regular Season					Playoffs				
Season	Club	Lea	GP	G	A	TP	PIM	GP	G	A	TP	PIM
1987-88	Dukla Jihlava	Czech.	31	5	9	14	16	....	....	....	....	....
1988-89	Dukla Jihlava	Czech.	24	7	10	17	32	....	....	....	....	....
1989-90	Dukla Jihlava	Czech.	42	15	26	41	....	....	....	....	....	....
1990-91	**Hartford**	**NHL**	**78**	**21**	**22**	**43**	**113**	**6**	**0**	**0**	**0**	**7**
1991-92	**Hartford**	**NHL**	**76**	**21**	**24**	**45**	**44**	**7**	**0**	**1**	**1**	**6**
1992-93	**New Jersey**	**NHL**	**61**	**20**	**19**	**39**	**76**	**5**	**1**	**1**	**2**	**6**
	Utica	AHL	1	0	0	0	2	....	....	....	....	....
1993-94	**New Jersey**	**NHL**	**70**	**13**	**20**	**33**	**72**	**20**	**0**	**3**	**3**	**6**
1994-95	**New Jersey**	**NHL**	**48**	**10**	**10**	**20**	**18**	**20**	**4**	**4**	**8**	**22**
	NHL Totals		**333**	**85**	**95**	**180**	**323**	**58**	**5**	**9**	**14**	**47**

Traded to **New Jersey** by **Hartford** with Hartford's second round choice (Jay Pandolfo) in 1993 Entry Draft and future considerations for Sean Burke and Eric Weinrich, August 28, 1992.

HOLLAND, JASON — NYI

Defense. Shoots right. 6'2", 190 lbs. Born, Morinville, Alta., April 30, 1976.
(NY Islanders' 2nd choice, 38th overall, in 1994 Entry Draft).

			Regular Season					Playoffs				
Season	Club	Lea	GP	G	A	TP	PIM	GP	G	A	TP	PIM
1993-94	Kamloops	WHL	59	14	15	29	80	18	2	3	5	4
1994-95	Kamloops	WHL	71	9	32	41	65	21	2	7	9	9

HOLLINGER, TERRY

Defense. Shoots left. 6'1", 200 lbs. Born, Regina, Sask., February 24, 1971.
(St. Louis' 7th choice, 153rd overall, in 1991 Entry Draft).

			Regular Season					Playoffs				
Season	Club	Lea	GP	G	A	TP	PIM	GP	G	A	TP	PIM
1990-91	Regina	WHL	8	1	6	7	6	....	....	....	....	....
	Lethbridge	WHL	62	9	32	41	113	16	3	14	17	22
1991-92	Lethbridge	WHL	65	23	62	85	155	5	1	2	3	13
	Peoria	IHL	1	0	2	2	0	5	0	1	1	0
1992-93	Peoria	IHL	72	2	28	30	67	4	1	1	2	0
1993-94	**St. Louis**	**NHL**	**2**	**0**	**0**	**0**	**0**	....	....	....	....	....
	Peoria	IHL	78	12	31	43	96	6	0	3	3	31
1994-95	Peoria	IHL	69	7	25	32	137	4	2	4	6	8
	St. Louis	**NHL**	**5**	**0**	**0**	**0**	**2**	....	....	....	....	....
	NHL Totals		**7**	**0**	**0**	**0**	**2**	....	....	....	....	....

HOLMSTROM, TOMAS — DET.

Left wing. Shoots left. 6', 200 lbs. Born, Pitea, Sweden, January 23, 1973.
(Detroit's 9th choice, 257th overall, in 1994 Entry Draft).

			Regular Season					Playoffs				
Season	Club	Lea	GP	G	A	TP	PIM	GP	G	A	TP	PIM
1994-95	Lulea	Swe.	40	14	14	28	56	....	....	....	....	....

HOLZINGER, BRIAN — BUF.

Center. Shoots right. 5'11", 180 lbs. Born, Parma, OH, October 10, 1972.
(Buffalo's 7th choice, 124th overall, in 1991 Entry Draft).

			Regular Season					Playoffs				
Season	Club	Lea	GP	G	A	TP	PIM	GP	G	A	TP	PIM
1991-92	Bowling Green	CCHA	30	14	8	22	36	....	....	....	....	....
1992-93a	Bowling Green	CCHA	41	31	26	57	44	....	....	....	....	....
1993-94	Bowling Green	CCHA	38	22	15	37	24	....	....	....	....	....
1994-95bcd	Bowling Green	CCHA	38	35	33	68	42	....	....	....	....	....
	Buffalo	**NHL**	**4**	**0**	**3**	**3**	**0**	**4**	**2**	**1**	**3**	**2**
	NHL Totals		**4**	**0**	**3**	**3**	**0**	**4**	**2**	**1**	**3**	**2**

a CCHA Second All-Star Team (1993)
b CCHA First All-Star Team (1995)
c NCAA West First All-American Team (1995)
d Won Hobey Baker Memorial Award (Top U.S. Collegiate Player) (1995)

HORACEK, TONY (HOHR-uh-chehk)

Left wing. Shoots left. 6'4", 210 lbs. Born, Vancouver, B.C., February 3, 1967.
(Philadelphia's 8th choice, 147th overall, in 1985 Entry Draft).

			Regular Season					Playoffs				
Season	Club	Lea	GP	G	A	TP	PIM	GP	G	A	TP	PIM
1984-85	Kelowna	WHL	67	9	18	27	114	6	0	1	1	11
1985-86	Spokane	WHL	64	19	28	47	129	9	4	5	9	29
1986-87	Spokane	WHL	64	23	37	60	177	5	1	3	4	18
	Hershey	AHL	....	....	....	....	....	1	0	0	0	0
1987-88	Hershey	AHL	1	0	0	0	0	....	....	....	....	....
	Spokane	WHL	24	17	23	40	63	....	....	....	....	....
	Kamloops	WHL	26	14	17	31	51	18	6	4	10	73
1988-89	Hershey	AHL	10	0	0	0	38	....	....	....	....	....
	Indianapolis	IHL	43	11	13	24	138	....	....	....	....	....
1989-90	**Philadelphia**	**NHL**	**48**	**5**	**5**	**10**	**117**	....	....	....	....	....
	Hershey	AHL	12	0	5	5	25	....	....	....	....	....
1990-91	**Philadelphia**	**NHL**	**34**	**3**	**6**	**9**	**49**	....	....	....	....	....
	Hershey	AHL	19	5	3	8	35	4	2	0	2	14
1991-92	**Philadelphia**	**NHL**	**34**	**1**	**3**	**4**	**51**	....	....	....	....	....
	Chicago	**NHL**	**12**	**1**	**4**	**5**	**21**	**2**	**1**	**0**	**1**	**2**
1992-93	Indianapolis	IHL	6	1	1	2	28	5	3	2	5	18
1993-94	**Chicago**	**NHL**	**7**	**0**	**0**	**0**	**53**	....	....	....	....	....
	Indianapolis	IHL	29	6	7	13	63	....	....	....	....	....
1994-95	Indianapolis	IHL	51	7	19	26	201	....	....	....	....	....
	Chicago	**NHL**	**19**	**0**	**1**	**1**	**25**	....	....	....	....	....
	NHL Totals		**154**	**10**	**19**	**29**	**316**	**2**	**1**	**0**	**1**	**2**

Traded to **Chicago** by **Philadelphia** for Ryan McGill, February 7, 1992.

HOUDA, DOUG (HOO-duh) BUF.

Defense. Shoots right. 6'2", 190 lbs. Born, Blairmore, Alta., June 3, 1966.
(Detroit's 2nd choice, 28th overall, in 1984 Entry Draft).

			Regular Season					Playoffs				
Season	Club	Lea	GP	G	A	TP	PIM	GP	G	A	TP	PIM
1982-83	Calgary	WHL	71	5	23	28	99	16	1	3	4	44
1983-84	Calgary	WHL	69	6	30	36	195	4	0	0	0	7
1984-85a	Calgary	WHL	65	20	54	74	182	8	3	4	7	29
1985-86	**Detroit**	**NHL**	**6**	**0**	**0**	**0**	**4**	....	....	....	....	....
	Calgary	WHL	16	4	10	14	60	....	....	....	....	....
	Medicine Hat	WHL	35	9	23	32	80	25	4	19	23	64
1986-87	Adirondack	AHL	77	6	23	29	142	11	1	8	9	50
1987-88	**Detroit**	**NHL**	**11**	**1**	**1**	**2**	**10**	....	....	....	....	....
b	Adirondack	AHL	71	10	32	42	169	11	0	3	3	44
1988-89	**Detroit**	**NHL**	**57**	**2**	**11**	**13**	**67**	**6**	**0**	**1**	**1**	**0**
	Adirondack	AHL	7	0	3	3	8	....	....	....	....	....
1989-90	**Detroit**	**NHL**	**73**	**2**	**9**	**11**	**127**	....	....	....	....	....
1990-91	**Detroit**	**NHL**	**22**	**0**	**4**	**4**	**43**	....	....	....	....	....
	Adirondack	AHL	38	9	17	26	67	....	....	....	....	....
	Hartford	**NHL**	**19**	**1**	**2**	**3**	**41**	**6**	**0**	**0**	**0**	**8**
1991-92	**Hartford**	**NHL**	**56**	**3**	**6**	**9**	**125**	**6**	**0**	**2**	**2**	**13**
1992-93	**Hartford**	**NHL**	**60**	**2**	**6**	**8**	**167**	....	....	....	....	....
1993-94	**Hartford**	**NHL**	**7**	**0**	**0**	**0**	**23**	....	....	....	....	....
	Los Angeles	**NHL**	**54**	**2**	**6**	**8**	**165**	....	....	....	....	....
1994-95	**Buffalo**	**NHL**	**28**	**1**	**2**	**3**	**68**	....	....	....	....	....
	NHL Totals		**393**	**14**	**47**	**61**	**840**	**18**	**0**	**3**	**3**	**21**

a WHL East Second All-Star Team (1985)
b AHL First All-Star Team (1988)

Traded to **Hartford** by **Detroit** for Doug Crossman, February 20, 1991. Traded to **Los Angeles** by **Hartford** for Marc Potvin, November 3, 1993. Traded to **Buffalo** by **Los Angeles** for Sean O'Donnell, July 26, 1994.

HOUGH, MIKE (HUHF) FLA.

Left wing. Shoots left. 6'1", 197 lbs. Born, Montreal, Que., February 6, 1963.
(Quebec's 7th choice, 181st overall, in 1982 Entry Draft).

			Regular Season					Playoffs				
Season	Club	Lea	GP	G	A	TP	PIM	GP	G	A	TP	PIM
1981-82	Kitchener	OHL	58	14	24	38	172	14	4	1	5	16
1982-83	Kitchener	OHL	61	17	27	44	156	12	5	4	9	30
1983-84	Fredericton	AHL	69	11	16	27	142	1	0	0	0	7
1984-85	Fredericton	AHL	76	21	27	48	49	6	1	1	2	2
1985-86	Fredericton	AHL	74	21	33	54	68	6	0	3	3	8
1986-87	**Quebec**	**NHL**	**56**	**6**	**8**	**14**	**79**	**9**	**0**	**3**	**3**	**26**
	Fredericton	AHL	10	1	3	4	20	....	....	....	....	....
1987-88	**Quebec**	**NHL**	**17**	**3**	**2**	**5**	**2**	....	....	....	....	....
	Fredericton	AHL	46	16	25	41	133	15	4	8	12	55
1988-89	**Quebec**	**NHL**	**46**	**9**	**10**	**19**	**39**	....	....	....	....	....
	Halifax	AHL	22	11	10	21	87	....	....	....	....	....
1989-90	**Quebec**	**NHL**	**43**	**13**	**13**	**26**	**84**	....	....	....	....	....
1990-91	**Quebec**	**NHL**	**63**	**13**	**20**	**33**	**111**	....	....	....	....	....
1991-92	**Quebec**	**NHL**	**61**	**16**	**22**	**38**	**77**	....	....	....	....	....
1992-93	**Quebec**	**NHL**	**77**	**8**	**22**	**30**	**69**	**6**	**0**	**1**	**1**	**2**
1993-94	**Florida**	**NHL**	**78**	**6**	**23**	**29**	**62**	....	....	....	....	....
1994-95	**Florida**	**NHL**	**48**	**6**	**7**	**13**	**38**	....	....	....	....	....
	NHL Totals		**489**	**80**	**127**	**207**	**561**	**15**	**0**	**4**	**4**	**28**

Traded to **Washington** by **Quebec** for Reggie Savage and Paul MacDermid, June 20, 1993. Claimed by **Florida** from **Washington** in Expansion Draft, June 24, 1993.

HOULDER, BILL (HOHL-duhr) T.B.

Defense. Shoots left. 6'3", 218 lbs. Born, Thunder Bay, Ont., March 11, 1967.
(Washington's 4th choice, 82nd overall, in 1985 Entry Draft).

			Regular Season					Playoffs				
Season	Club	Lea	GP	G	A	TP	PIM	GP	G	A	TP	PIM
1984-85	North Bay	OHL	66	4	20	24	37	8	0	0	0	2
1985-86	North Bay	OHL	59	5	30	35	97	10	1	6	7	12
1986-87	North Bay	OHL	62	17	51	68	68	22	4	19	23	20
1987-88	**Washington**	**NHL**	**30**	**1**	**2**	**3**	**10**	....	....	....	....	....
	Fort Wayne	IHL	43	10	14	24	32	....	....	....	....	....
1988-89	**Washington**	**NHL**	**8**	**0**	**3**	**3**	**4**	....	....	....	....	....
	Baltimore	AHL	65	10	36	46	50	....	....	....	....	....
1989-90	**Washington**	**NHL**	**41**	**1**	**11**	**12**	**28**	....	....	....	....	....
	Baltimore	AHL	26	3	7	10	12	7	0	2	2	2
1990-91	**Buffalo**	**NHL**	**7**	**0**	**2**	**2**	**4**	....	....	....	....	....
a	Rochester	AHL	69	13	53	66	28	15	5	13	18	4
1991-92	**Buffalo**	**NHL**	**10**	**1**	**0**	**1**	**8**	....	....	....	....	....
	Rochester	AHL	42	8	26	34	16	16	5	6	11	4
1992-93	**Buffalo**	**NHL**	**15**	**3**	**5**	**8**	**6**	**8**	**0**	**2**	**2**	**4**
bc	San Diego	IHL	64	24	48	72	39	....	....	....	....	....
1993-94	**Anaheim**	**NHL**	**80**	**14**	**25**	**39**	**40**	....	....	....	....	....
1994-95	**St. Louis**	**NHL**	**41**	**5**	**13**	**18**	**20**	**4**	**1**	**1**	**2**	**0**
	NHL Totals		**232**	**25**	**61**	**86**	**120**	**12**	**1**	**3**	**4**	**4**

a AHL First All-Star Team (1991)
b Won Governor's Trophy (Outstanding Defenseman - IHL) (1993)
c IHL First All-Star Team (1993)

Traded to **Buffalo** by **Washington** for Shawn Anderson, September 30, 1990. Claimed by **Anaheim** from **Buffalo** in Expansion Draft, June 24, 1993. Traded to **St. Louis** by **Anaheim** for Jason Marshall, August 29, 1994. Signed as a free agent by **Tampa Bay**, August 1, 1995.

HOULE, JEAN-FRANCOIS MTL.

Left wing. Shoots left. 5'9", 175 lbs. Born, Charlesbourg, Que., January 14, 1975.
(Montreal's 5th choice, 99th overall, in 1993 Entry Draft).

			Regular Season					Playoffs				
Season	Club	Lea	GP	G	A	TP	PIM	GP	G	A	TP	PIM
1993-94	Clarkson	ECAC	34	6	19	25	20	....	....	....	....	....
1994-95	Clarkson	ECAC	34	8	11	19	42	....	....	....	....	....

HOUSE, BOBBY N.J.

Right wing. Shoots right. 6'1", 200 lbs. Born, Whitehorse, Yukon, January 7, 1973.
(Chicago's 4th choice, 66th overall, in 1991 Entry Draft).

			Regular Season					Playoffs				
Season	Club	Lea	GP	G	A	TP	PIM	GP	G	A	TP	PIM
1989-90	Spokane	WHL	64	18	16	34	74	5	0	0	0	6
1990-91	Spokane	WHL	38	11	19	30	63	....	....	....	....	....
	Brandon	WHL	23	18	7	25	14	....	....	....	....	....
1991-92	Brandon	WHL	71	35	42	77	133	....	....	....	....	....
1992-93a	Brandon	WHL	61	57	39	96	87	4	2	2	4	0
1993-94	Indianapolis	IHL	42	10	8	18	51	....	....	....	....	....
	Flint	ColHL	4	3	3	6	0	....	....	....	....	....
1994-95	Columbus	ECHL	9	11	6	17	2	....	....	....	....	....
	Indianapolis	IHL	26	2	3	5	26	....	....	....	....	....
	Albany	AHL	26	4	7	11	12	8	1	1	2	0

a WHL East Second All-Star Team (1993)

HOUSLEY, PHIL (HOWZ-lee) CGY.

Defense. Shoots left. 5'10", 185 lbs. Born, St. Paul, MN, March 9, 1964.
(Buffalo's 1st choice, 6th overall, in 1982 Entry Draft).

			Regular Season					Playoffs				
Season	Club	Lea	GP	G	A	TP	PIM	GP	G	A	TP	PIM
1981-82	South St. Paul	HS	22	31	34	65	18	....	....	....	....	....
1982-83a	**Buffalo**	**NHL**	**77**	**19**	**47**	**66**	**39**	**10**	**3**	**4**	**7**	**2**
1983-84	**Buffalo**	**NHL**	**75**	**31**	**46**	**77**	**33**	**3**	**0**	**0**	**0**	**6**
1984-85	**Buffalo**	**NHL**	**73**	**16**	**53**	**69**	**28**	**5**	**3**	**2**	**5**	**2**
1985-86	**Buffalo**	**NHL**	**79**	**15**	**47**	**62**	**54**	....	....	....	....	....
1986-87	**Buffalo**	**NHL**	**78**	**21**	**46**	**67**	**57**	....	....	....	....	....
1987-88	**Buffalo**	**NHL**	**74**	**29**	**37**	**66**	**96**	**6**	**2**	**4**	**6**	**6**
1988-89	**Buffalo**	**NHL**	**72**	**26**	**44**	**70**	**47**	**5**	**1**	**3**	**4**	**2**
1989-90	**Buffalo**	**NHL**	**80**	**21**	**60**	**81**	**32**	**6**	**1**	**4**	**5**	**4**
1990-91	**Winnipeg**	**NHL**	**78**	**23**	**53**	**76**	**24**	....	....	....	....	....
1991-92b	**Winnipeg**	**NHL**	**74**	**23**	**63**	**86**	**92**	**7**	**1**	**4**	**5**	**0**
1992-93	**Winnipeg**	**NHL**	**80**	**18**	**79**	**97**	**52**	**6**	**0**	**7**	**7**	**2**
1993-94	**St. Louis**	**NHL**	**26**	**7**	**15**	**22**	**12**	**4**	**2**	**1**	**3**	**4**
1994-95	Grasshoppers	Switz. 2	10	6	8	14	34	....	....	....	....	....
	Calgary	**NHL**	**43**	**8**	**35**	**43**	**18**	**7**	**0**	**9**	**9**	**0**
	NHL Totals		**909**	**257**	**625**	**882**	**584**	**59**	**13**	**38**	**51**	**28**

a NHL All-Rookie Team (1983)
b NHL Second All-Star Team (1992)

Played in NHL All-Star Game (1984, 1989-93)

Traded to **Winnipeg** by **Buffalo** with Scott Arniel, Jeff Parker and Buffalo's first round choice (Keith Tkachuk) in 1990 Entry Draft for Dale Hawerchuk, Winnipeg's first round choice (Brad May) in 1990 Entry Draft and future considerations, June 16, 1990. Traded to **St. Louis** by **Winnipeg** for Nelson Emerson and Stephane Quintal, September 24, 1993. Traded to **Calgary** by **St. Louis** with St. Louis' second round choice in 1996 Entry Draft and second round choice in 1997 Entry Draft for Al MacInnis and Calgary's fourth round choice in 1997 Entry Draft, July 4, 1994.

HOWE, MARK

Defense. Shoots left. 5'11", 185 lbs. Born, Detroit, MI, May 28, 1955.
(Boston's 2nd choice, 25th overall, in 1974 Amateur Draft).

			Regular Season					Playoffs				
Season	Club	Lea	GP	G	A	TP	PIM	GP	G	A	TP	PIM
1972-73	Toronto	OMJHL	60	38	66	104	27	....	....	....	....	....
1973-74ab	Houston	WHA	76	38	41	79	20	14	9	10	19	4
1974-75	Houston	WHA	74	36	40	76	30	13	*10	12	*22	0
1975-76	Houston	WHA	72	39	37	76	38	17	6	10	16	18
1976-77a	Houston	WHA	57	23	52	75	46	10	4	10	14	2
1977-78	New England	WHA	70	30	61	91	32	14	8	7	15	18
1978-79c	New England	WHA	77	42	65	107	32	6	4	2	6	6
1979-80	Hartford	NHL	74	24	56	80	20	3	1	2	3	2
1980-81	Hartford	NHL	63	19	46	65	54	....	....	....	....	....
1981-82	Hartford	NHL	76	8	45	53	18	....	....	....	....	....
1982-83d	Philadelphia	NHL	76	20	47	67	18	3	0	2	2	4
1983-84	Philadelphia	NHL	71	19	34	53	44	3	0	0	0	2
1984-85	Philadelphia	NHL	73	18	39	57	31	19	3	8	11	6
1985-86de	Philadelphia	NHL	77	24	58	82	36	5	0	4	4	0
1986-87d	Philadelphia	NHL	69	15	43	58	37	26	2	10	12	4
1987-88	Philadelphia	NHL	75	19	43	62	62	7	3	6	9	4
1988-89	Philadelphia	NHL	52	9	29	38	45	19	0	15	15	10
1989-90	Philadelphia	NHL	40	7	21	28	24	....	....	....	....	....
1990-91	Philadelphia	NHL	19	0	10	10	8	....	....	....	....	....
1991-92	Philadelphia	NHL	42	7	18	25	18	....	....	....	....	....
1992-93	Detroit	NHL	60	3	31	34	22	7	1	3	4	2
1993-94	Detroit	NHL	44	4	20	24	8	6	0	1	1	0
1994-95	Detroit	NHL	18	1	5	6	10	3	0	0	0	0
	NHL Totals		929	197	545	742	455	101	10	51	61	34

a WHA Second All-Star Team (1974, 1977)
b Named WHA's Rookie of the Year (1974)
c WHA First All-Star Team (1979)
d NHL First All-Star Team (1983, 1986, 1987)
e NHL Plus/Minus Leader (1986)

Played in NHL All-Star Game (1981, 1983, 1986, 1988)

Reclaimed by **Boston** from **Hartford** prior to Expansion Draft, June 9, 1979. Claimed as priority selection by **Hartford**, June 9, 1979. Traded to **Philadelphia** by **Hartford** with Hartford's third round choice (Derrick Smith) in 1983 Entry Draft for Ken Linseman, Greg Adams and Philadelphia's first (David Jensen) and third round choices (Leif Karlsson) in the 1983 Entry Draft, August 19, 1982. Signed as a free agent by **Detroit**, July 7, 1992.

HRDINA, JAN — PIT.

Center. Shoots right. 6'1", 180 lbs. Born, Hradec Kralove, Czech., February 5, 1976.
(Pittsburgh's 4th choice, 128th overall, in 1995 Entry Draft).

			Regular Season					Playoffs				
Season	Club	Lea	GP	G	A	TP	PIM	GP	G	A	TP	PIM
1993-94	Stadion	Czech.	23	1	5	6	....	4	0	1	1	....
1994-95	Seattle	WHL	69	41	59	100	79	4	0	1	1	8

HRKAC, TONY (HUHR-kuhz)

Center. Shoots left. 5'11", 170 lbs. Born, Thunder Bay, Ont., July 7, 1966.
(St. Louis' 2nd choice, 32nd overall, in 1984 Entry Draft).

			Regular Season					Playoffs				
Season	Club	Lea	GP	G	A	TP	PIM	GP	G	A	TP	PIM
1984-85	North Dakota	WCHA	36	18	36	54	16	....	....	....	....	....
1985-86	Cdn. Olympic	....	62	19	30	49	36	....	....	....	....	....
1986-87abcd	North Dakota	WCHA	48	46	79	125	48	....	....	....	....	....
	St. Louis	NHL	....	....	....	....	....	3	0	0	0	0
1987-88	St. Louis	NHL	67	11	37	48	22	10	6	1	7	4
1988-89	St. Louis	NHL	70	17	28	45	8	4	1	1	2	0
1989-90	St. Louis	NHL	28	5	12	17	8	....	....	....	....	....
	Quebec	NHL	22	4	8	12	2	....	....	....	....	....
	Halifax	AHL	20	12	21	33	4	6	5	9	14	4
1990-91	Quebec	NHL	70	16	32	48	16	....	....	....	....	....
	Halifax	AHL	3	4	1	5	2	....	....	....	....	....
1991-92	San Jose	NHL	22	2	10	12	4	....	....	....	....	....
	Chicago	NHL	18	1	2	3	6	3	0	0	0	2
1992-93efg	Indianapolis	IHL	80	45	*87	*132	70	5	0	2	2	2
1993-94	St. Louis	NHL	36	6	5	11	8	4	0	0	0	0
	Peoria	IHL	45	30	51	81	25	1	1	2	3	0
1994-95	Milwaukee	IHL	71	24	67	91	26	15	4	9	13	16
	NHL Totals		333	62	134	196	74	24	7	2	9	6

a WCHA First All-Star Team (1987)
b NCAA West First All-American Team (1987)
c NCAA All-Tournament Team, Tournament MVP (1987)
d Won 1987 Hobey Baker Memorial Award (Top U.S. Collegiate Player) (1987)
e Won James Gatschene Memorial Trophy (MVP - IHL) (1993)
f Won Leo P. Lamoureux Memorial Trophy (Leading Scorer - IHL) (1993)
g IHL First All-Star Team (1993)

Traded to **Quebec** by **St. Louis** with Greg Millen for Jeff Brown, December 13, 1989. Traded to **San Jose** by **Quebec** for Greg Paslawski, May 31, 1991. Traded to **Chicago** by **San Jose** for future considerations, February 7, 1992. Signed as a free agent by **St. Louis**, July 30, 1993.

HRUSKA, DAVID — OTT.

Right wing. Shoots right. 6', 189 lbs. Born, Sokolov, Czech., January 8, 1977.
(Ottawa's 6th choice, 131st overall, in 1995 Entry Draft).

			Regular Season					Playoffs				
Season	Club	Lea	GP	G	A	TP	PIM	GP	G	A	TP	PIM
1994-95	Banik Sokolov	Czech. 2				UNAVAILABLE						

HUARD, BILL (HYOO-ahrd) — COL.

Left wing. Shoots left. 6'1", 215 lbs. Born, Welland, Ont., June 24, 1967.

			Regular Season					Playoffs				
Season	Club	Lea	GP	G	A	TP	PIM	GP	G	A	TP	PIM
1986-87	Peterborough	OHL	61	14	11	25	61	12	5	2	7	19
1987-88	Peterborough	OHL	66	28	33	61	132	12	7	8	15	33
1988-89	Carolina	ECHL	40	27	21	48	177	10	7	2	9	70
1989-90	Utica	AHL	27	1	7	8	67	5	0	1	1	33
	Nashville	ECHL	34	24	27	51	212	....	....	....	....	....
1990-91	Utica	AHL	72	11	16	27	359	....	....	....	....	....
1991-92	Utica	AHL	62	9	11	20	233	4	1	1	2	4
1992-93	Boston	NHL	2	0	0	0	0	....	....	....	....	....
	Providence	AHL	72	18	19	37	302	6	3	0	3	9
1993-94	Ottawa	NHL	63	2	2	4	162	....	....	....	....	....
1994-95	Ottawa	NHL	26	1	1	2	64	....	....	....	....	....
	Quebec	NHL	7	2	2	4	13	1	0	0	0	0
	NHL Totals		98	5	5	10	239	1	0	0	0	0

Signed as a free agent by **New Jersey**, October 1, 1989. Signed as a free agent by **Boston**, December 4, 1992. Signed as a free agent by **Ottawa**, June 30, 1993. Traded to **Quebec** by **Ottawa** for Mika Stromberg and Colorado's fourth round choice (Kevin Boyd) in 1995 Entry Draft, April 7, 1995.

HUDDY, CHARLIE (HUH-dee) — BUF.

Defense. Shoots left. 6', 210 lbs. Born, Oshawa, Ont., June 2, 1959.

			Regular Season					Playoffs				
Season	Club	Lea	GP	G	A	TP	PIM	GP	G	A	TP	PIM
1977-78	Oshawa	OHA	59	17	18	35	81	6	2	1	3	10
1978-79	Oshawa	OHA	64	20	38	58	108	5	3	4	7	12
1979-80	Houston	CHL	79	14	34	48	46	6	1	0	1	2
1980-81	Edmonton	NHL	12	2	5	7	6	....	....	....	....	....
	Wichita	CHL	47	8	36	44	71	17	3	11	14	10
1981-82	Edmonton	NHL	41	4	11	15	46	5	1	2	3	14
	Wichita	CHL	32	7	19	26	51	....	....	....	....	....
1982-83a	Edmonton	NHL	76	20	37	57	58	15	1	6	7	10
1983-84	Edmonton	NHL	75	8	34	42	43	12	1	9	10	8
1984-85	Edmonton	NHL	80	7	44	51	46	18	3	17	20	17
1985-86	Edmonton	NHL	76	6	35	41	55	7	0	2	2	0
1986-87	Edmonton	NHL	58	4	15	19	35	21	1	7	8	21
1987-88	Edmonton	NHL	77	13	28	41	71	13	4	5	9	10
1988-89	Edmonton	NHL	76	11	33	44	52	7	2	0	2	4
1989-90	Edmonton	NHL	70	1	23	24	56	22	0	6	6	11
1990-91	Edmonton	NHL	53	5	22	27	32	18	3	7	10	10
1991-92	Los Angeles	NHL	56	4	19	23	43	6	1	1	2	10
1992-93	Los Angeles	NHL	82	2	25	27	64	23	1	4	5	12
1993-94	Los Angeles	NHL	79	5	13	18	71	....	....	....	....	....
1994-95	Los Angeles	NHL	9	0	1	1	6	....	....	....	....	....
	Buffalo	NHL	32	2	4	6	36	3	0	0	0	0
	NHL Totals		952	94	349	443	720	170	18	66	84	127

a NHL Plus/Minus Leader (1983)

Signed as a free agent by **Edmonton**, September 14, 1979. Claimed by **Minnesota** from **Edmonton** in Expansion Draft, May 30, 1991. Traded to **Los Angeles** by **Minnesota** with Randy Gilhen, Jim Thomson and NY Rangers' fourth round choice (previously acquired by Minnesota — Los Angeles selected Alexei Zhitnik) in 1991 Entry Draft for Todd Elik, June 22, 1991. Traded to **Buffalo** by **Los Angeles** with Alexei Zhitnik, Robb Stauber and Los Angeles' fifth round choice (Marian Menhart) in 1995 Entry Draft for Philippe Boucher, Denis Tsygurov and Grant Fuhr, February 14, 1995.

HUDSON, MIKE

Center/Left wing. Shoots left. 6'1", 205 lbs. Born, Guelph, Ont., February 6, 1967.
(Chicago's 6th choice, 140th overall, in 1986 Entry Draft).

			Regular Season					Playoffs				
Season	Club	Lea	GP	G	A	TP	PIM	GP	G	A	TP	PIM
1984-85	Hamilton	OHL	50	10	12	22	13	....	....	....	....	....
1985-86	Hamilton	OHL	7	3	2	5	4	....	....	....	....	....
	Sudbury	OHL	59	35	42	77	20	4	2	5	7	7
1986-87	Sudbury	OHL	63	40	57	97	18	....	....	....	....	....
1987-88	Saginaw	IHL	75	18	30	48	44	10	2	3	5	20
1988-89	Chicago	NHL	41	7	16	23	20	10	1	2	3	18
	Saginaw	IHL	30	15	17	32	10	....	....	....	....	....
1989-90	Chicago	NHL	49	9	12	21	56	4	0	0	0	2
1990-91	Chicago	NHL	55	7	9	16	62	6	0	2	2	8
	Indianapolis	IHL	3	1	2	3	0	....	....	....	....	....
1991-92	Chicago	NHL	76	14	15	29	92	16	3	5	8	26
1992-93	Chicago	NHL	36	1	6	7	44	....	....	....	....	....
	Edmonton	NHL	5	0	1	1	2	....	....	....	....	....
1993-94	NY Rangers	NHL	48	4	7	11	47	....	....	....	....	....
1994-95	Pittsburgh	NHL	40	2	9	11	34	11	0	0	0	6
	NHL Totals		350	44	75	119	357	47	4	9	13	60

Traded to **Edmonton** by **Chicago** for Craig Muni, March 22, 1993. Claimed by **NY Rangers** from **Edmonton** in NHL Waiver Draft, October 3, 1993. Claimed by **Pittsburgh** from **NY Rangers** in NHL Waiver Draft, January 18, 1995.

HUFFMAN, KERRY — OTT.

Defense. Shoots left. 6'2", 200 lbs. Born, Peterborough, Ont., January 3, 1968.
(Philadelphia's 1st choice, 20th overall, in 1986 Entry Draft).

			Regular Season					Playoffs				
Season	Club	Lea	GP	G	A	TP	PIM	GP	G	A	TP	PIM
1985-86a	Guelph	OHL	56	3	24	27	35	20	1	10	11	10
1986-87	Philadelphia	NHL	9	0	0	0	2	....	....	....	....	....
	Hershey	AHL	3	0	1	1	0	4	0	0	0	0
b	Guelph	OHL	44	4	31	35	20	5	0	2	2	8
1987-88	Philadelphia	NHL	52	6	17	23	34	2	0	0	0	0
1988-89	Philadelphia	NHL	29	0	11	11	31	....	....	....	....	....
	Hershey	AHL	29	2	13	15	16	....	....	....	....	....
1989-90	Philadelphia	NHL	43	1	12	13	34	....	....	....	....	....
1990-91	Philadelphia	NHL	10	1	2	3	10	....	....	....	....	....
	Hershey	AHL	45	5	29	34	20	7	1	2	3	0
1991-92	Philadelphia	NHL	60	14	18	32	41	....	....	....	....	....
1992-93	Quebec	NHL	52	4	18	22	54	3	0	0	0	0
1993-94	Quebec	NHL	28	0	6	6	28	....	....	....	....	....
	Ottawa	NHL	34	4	8	12	12	....	....	....	....	....
1994-95	Ottawa	NHL	37	2	4	6	46	....	....	....	....	....
	NHL Totals		354	32	96	128	292	5	0	0	0	0

a Won George Parsons Trophy (Memorial Cup Tournament Most Sportsmanlike Player) (1986)
b OHL First All-Star Team (1987)

Traded to **Quebec** by **Philadelphia** with Peter Forsberg, Steve Duchesne, Mike Ricci, Ron Hextall, Chris Simon, Philadelphia's first choice in the 1993 (Jocelyn Thibault) and 1994 (later traded to Toronto — later traded to Wahington — Wahington selected Nolan Baumgartner) — Entry Drafts and cash for Eric Lindros, June 30, 1992. Claimed on waivers by **Ottawa** from **Quebec**, January 15, 1994.

HUGHES, BRENT — BOS.

Left wing. Shoots left. 5'11", 195 lbs. Born, New Westminster, B.C., April 5, 1966.

			Regular Season					Playoffs				
Season	Club	Lea	GP	G	A	TP	PIM	GP	G	A	TP	PIM
1983-84	N. Westminster	WHL	67	21	18	39	133	9	2	2	4	27
1984-85	N. Westminster	WHL	64	25	32	57	135	11	2	1	3	37
1985-86	N. Westminster	WHL	71	28	52	80	180	....	....	....	....	....
1986-87	N. Westminster	WHL	8	5	4	9	22	....	....	....	....	....
	Victoria	WHL	61	38	61	99	146	5	4	1	5	8
1987-88	Moncton	AHL	73	13	19	32	206	....	....	....	....	....
1988-89	**Winnipeg**	**NHL**	**28**	**3**	**2**	**5**	**82**	....	....	....	....	....
	Moncton	AHL	54	34	34	68	286	10	9	4	13	40
1989-90	**Winnipeg**	**NHL**	**11**	**1**	**2**	**3**	**33**	....	....	....	....	....
	Moncton	AHL	65	31	29	60	277	....	....	....	....	....
1990-91	Moncton	AHL	63	21	22	43	144	3	0	0	0	7
1991-92	Baltimore	AHL	55	25	29	54	190	....	....	....	....	....
	Boston	**NHL**	**8**	**1**	**1**	**2**	**38**	**10**	**2**	**0**	**2**	**20**
	Maine	AHL	12	6	4	10	34	....	....	....	....	....
1992-93	**Boston**	**NHL**	**62**	**5**	**4**	**9**	**191**	**1**	**0**	**0**	**0**	**2**
1993-94	**Boston**	**NHL**	**77**	**13**	**11**	**24**	**143**	**13**	**2**	**1**	**3**	**27**
	Providence	AHL	6	2	5	7	4	....	....	....	....	....
1994-95	**Boston**	**NHL**	**44**	**6**	**6**	**12**	**139**	**5**	**0**	**0**	**0**	**4**
	NHL Totals		**230**	**29**	**26**	**55**	**626**	**29**	**4**	**1**	**5**	**53**

Signed as a free agent by **Winnipeg**, June 13, 1988. Traded to **Washington** by **Winnipeg** with Craig Duncanson and Simon Wheeldon for Bob Joyce, Tyler Larter and Kent Paynter, May 21, 1991. Traded to **Boston** by **Washington** with future considerations for John Byce and Dennis Smith, February 24, 1992.

HULBIG, JOE — EDM.

Left wing. Shoots left. 6'3", 212 lbs. Born, Norwood, MA, September 29, 1973.
(Edmonton's 1st choice, 13th overall, in 1992 Entry Draft).

			Regular Season					Playoffs				
Season	Club	Lea	GP	G	A	TP	PIM	GP	G	A	TP	PIM
1992-93	Providence	H.E.	26	3	13	16	22	....	....	....	....	....
1993-94	Providence	H.E.	28	6	4	10	36	....	....	....	....	....
1994-95	Providence	H.E.	37	14	21	35	36	....	....	....	....	....

HULL, BRETT — ST.L.

Right wing. Shoots right. 5'10", 201 lbs. Born, Belleville, Ont., August 9, 1964.
(Calgary's 6th choice, 117th overall, in 1984 Entry Draft).

			Regular Season					Playoffs				
Season	Club	Lea	GP	G	A	TP	PIM	GP	G	A	TP	PIM
1984-85	Minn.-Duluth	WCHA	48	32	28	60	24	....	....	....	....	....
1985-86a	Minn.-Duluth	WCHA	42	52	32	84	46	....	....	....	....	....
	Calgary	**NHL**	....	....	....	....	....	**2**	**0**	**0**	**0**	**0**
1986-87	**Calgary**	**NHL**	**5**	**1**	**0**	**1**	**0**	**4**	**2**	**1**	**3**	**0**
bc	Moncton	AHL	67	50	42	92	16	3	2	2	4	2
1987-88	**Calgary**	**NHL**	**52**	**26**	**24**	**50**	**12**	....	....	....	....	....
	St. Louis	**NHL**	**13**	**6**	**8**	**14**	**4**	**10**	**7**	**2**	**9**	**4**
1988-89	**St. Louis**	**NHL**	**78**	**41**	**43**	**84**	**33**	**10**	**5**	**5**	**10**	**6**
1989-90def	**St. Louis**	**NHL**	**80**	***72**	**41**	**113**	**24**	**12**	**13**	**8**	**21**	**17**
1990-91 dfghi	**St. Louis**	**NHL**	**78**	***86**	**45**	**131**	**22**	**13**	**11**	**8**	**19**	**4**
1991-92d	**St. Louis**	**NHL**	**73**	***70**	**39**	**109**	**48**	**6**	**4**	**4**	**8**	**4**
1992-93	**St. Louis**	**NHL**	**80**	**54**	**47**	**101**	**41**	**11**	**8**	**5**	**13**	**2**
1993-94	**St. Louis**	**NHL**	**81**	**57**	**40**	**97**	**38**	**4**	**2**	**1**	**3**	**0**
1994-95	**St. Louis**	**NHL**	**48**	**29**	**21**	**50**	**10**	**7**	**6**	**2**	**8**	**0**
	NHL Totals		**588**	**442**	**308**	**750**	**232**	**79**	**58**	**36**	**94**	**37**

a WCHA First All-Star Team (1986)
b AHL First All-Star Team (1987)
c Won Dudley "Red" Garrett Memorial Trophy (Top Rookie - AHL) (1987)
d NHL First All-Star Team (1990, 1991, 1992)
e Won Lady Byng Trophy (1990)
f Won Dodge Ram Tough Award (1990, 1991)
g Won Hart Memorial Trophy (1991)
h Won Lester B. Pearson Award (1991)
i Won ProSet/NHL Player of the Year Award (1991)

Played in NHL All-Star Game (1989, 1990, 1992-94)

Traded to **St. Louis** by **Calgary** with Steve Bozek for Rob Ramage and Rick Wamsley, March 7, 1988.

HULL, JODY — FLA.

Right wing. Shoots right. 6'2", 195 lbs. Born, Cambridge, Ont., February 2, 1969.
(Hartford's 1st choice, 18th overall, in 1987 Entry Draft).

			Regular Season					Playoffs				
Season	Club	Lea	GP	G	A	TP	PIM	GP	G	A	TP	PIM
1985-86	Peterborough	OHL	61	20	22	42	29	16	1	5	6	4
1986-87	Peterborough	OHL	49	18	34	52	22	12	4	9	13	14
1987-88a	Peterborough	OHL	60	50	44	94	33	12	10	8	18	8
1988-89	**Hartford**	**NHL**	**60**	**16**	**18**	**34**	**10**	**1**	**0**	**0**	**0**	**2**
1989-90	**Hartford**	**NHL**	**38**	**7**	**10**	**17**	**21**	**5**	**0**	**1**	**1**	**2**
	Binghamton	AHL	21	7	10	17	6	....	....	....	....	....
1990-91	**NY Rangers**	**NHL**	**47**	**5**	**8**	**13**	**10**	....	....	....	....	....
1991-92	**NY Rangers**	**NHL**	**3**	**0**	**0**	**0**	**2**	....	....	....	....	....
	Binghamton	AHL	69	34	31	65	28	11	5	2	7	4
1992-93	**Ottawa**	**NHL**	**69**	**13**	**21**	**34**	**14**	....	....	....	....	....
1993-94	**Florida**	**NHL**	**69**	**13**	**13**	**26**	**8**	....	....	....	....	....
1994-95	**Florida**	**NHL**	**46**	**11**	**8**	**19**	**8**	....	....	....	....	....
	NHL Totals		**332**	**65**	**78**	**143**	**73**	**6**	**0**	**1**	**1**	**4**

a OHL Second All-Star Team (1988)

Traded to **NY Rangers** by **Hartford** for Carey Wilson and NY Rangers' third round choice (Mikael Nylander) in the 1991 Entry Draft, July 9, 1990. Traded to **Ottawa** by **NY Rangers** for future considerations, July 28, 1992. Signed as a free agent by **Florida**, August 10, 1993.

HULSE, CALE — N.J.

Defense. Shoots right. 6'3", 210 lbs. Born, Edmonton, Alta., November 10, 1973.
(New Jersey's 3rd choice, 66th overall, in 1992 Entry Draft).

			Regular Season					Playoffs				
Season	Club	Lea	GP	G	A	TP	PIM	GP	G	A	TP	PIM
1991-92	Portland	WHL	70	4	18	22	250	6	0	2	2	27
1992-93	Portland	WHL	72	10	26	36	284	16	4	4	8	65
1993-94	Albany	AHL	79	7	14	21	186	5	0	3	3	11
1994-95	Albany	AHL	77	5	13	18	215	12	1	1	2	17

HUNT, GORDON — DET.

Center. Shoots left. 6'5", 200 lbs. Born, Greenwich, CT, July 15, 1975.
(Detroit's 12th choice, 282nd overall, in 1993 Entry Draft).

			Regular Season					Playoffs				
Season	Club	Lea	GP	G	A	TP	PIM	GP	G	A	TP	PIM
1993-94	Ferris State	CCHA	37	2	3	5	42	....	....	....	....	....
1994-95	Ferris State	CCHA	29	8	7	15	47	....	....	....	....	....

HUNTER, DALE — WSH.

Center. Shoots left. 5'10", 198 lbs. Born, Petrolia, Ont., July 31, 1960.
(Quebec's 2nd choice, 41st overall, in 1979 Entry Draft).

			Regular Season					Playoffs				
Season	Club	Lea	GP	G	A	TP	PIM	GP	G	A	TP	PIM
1977-78	Kitchener	OHA	68	22	42	64	115	....	....	....	....	....
1978-79	Sudbury	OHA	59	42	68	110	188	10	4	12	16	47
1979-80	Sudbury	OHA	61	34	51	85	189	9	6	9	15	45
1980-81	**Quebec**	**NHL**	**80**	**19**	**44**	**63**	**226**	**5**	**4**	**2**	**6**	**34**
1981-82	**Quebec**	**NHL**	**80**	**22**	**50**	**72**	**272**	**16**	**3**	**7**	**10**	**52**
1982-83	**Quebec**	**NHL**	**80**	**17**	**46**	**63**	**206**	**4**	**2**	**1**	**3**	**24**
1983-84	**Quebec**	**NHL**	**77**	**24**	**55**	**79**	**232**	**9**	**2**	**3**	**5**	**41**
1984-85	**Quebec**	**NHL**	**80**	**20**	**52**	**72**	**209**	**17**	**4**	**6**	**10**	***97**
1985-86	**Quebec**	**NHL**	**80**	**28**	**42**	**70**	**265**	**3**	**0**	**0**	**0**	**15**
1986-87	**Quebec**	**NHL**	**46**	**10**	**29**	**39**	**135**	**13**	**1**	**7**	**8**	**56**
1987-88	**Washington**	**NHL**	**79**	**22**	**37**	**59**	**240**	**14**	**7**	**5**	**12**	**98**
1988-89	**Washington**	**NHL**	**80**	**20**	**37**	**57**	**219**	**6**	**0**	**4**	**4**	**29**
1989-90	**Washington**	**NHL**	**80**	**23**	**39**	**62**	**233**	**15**	**4**	**8**	**12**	**61**
1990-91	**Washington**	**NHL**	**76**	**16**	**30**	**46**	**234**	**11**	**1**	**9**	**10**	**41**
1991-92	**Washington**	**NHL**	**80**	**28**	**50**	**78**	**205**	**7**	**1**	**4**	**5**	**16**
1992-93	**Washington**	**NHL**	**84**	**20**	**59**	**79**	**198**	**6**	**7**	**1**	**8**	**35**
1993-94	**Washington**	**NHL**	**52**	**9**	**29**	**38**	**131**	**7**	**0**	**3**	**3**	**14**
1994-95	**Washington**	**NHL**	**45**	**8**	**15**	**23**	**101**	**7**	**4**	**4**	**8**	**24**
	NHL Totals		**1099**	**286**	**614**	**900**	**3106**	**140**	**40**	**64**	**104**	**637**

Traded to **Washington** by **Quebec** with Clint Malarchuk for Gaetan Duchesne, Alan Haworth, and Washington's first round choice (Joe Sakic) in 1987 Entry Draft, June 13, 1987.

HUNTER, TIM — VAN.

Right wing. Shoots right. 6'2", 202 lbs. Born, Calgary, Alta., September 10, 1960.
(Atlanta's 4th choice, 54th overall, in 1979 Entry Draft).

			Regular Season					Playoffs				
Season	Club	Lea	GP	G	A	TP	PIM	GP	G	A	TP	PIM
1979-80	Seattle	WHL	72	14	53	67	311	12	1	2	3	41
1980-81	Birmingham	CHL	58	3	5	8	*236	....	....	....	....	....
	Nova Scotia	AHL	17	0	0	0	62	6	0	1	1	45
1981-82	**Calgary**	**NHL**	**2**	**0**	**0**	**0**	**9**	....	....	....	....	....
	Oklahoma City	CHL	55	4	12	16	222	....	....	....	....	....
1982-83	**Calgary**	**NHL**	**16**	**1**	**0**	**1**	**54**	**9**	**1**	**0**	**1**	***70**
	Colorado	CHL	46	5	12	17	225	....	....	....	....	....
1983-84	**Calgary**	**NHL**	**43**	**4**	**4**	**8**	**130**	**7**	**0**	**0**	**0**	**21**
1984-85	**Calgary**	**NHL**	**71**	**11**	**11**	**22**	**259**	**4**	**0**	**0**	**0**	**24**
1985-86	**Calgary**	**NHL**	**66**	**8**	**7**	**15**	**291**	**19**	**0**	**3**	**3**	**108**
1986-87	**Calgary**	**NHL**	**73**	**6**	**15**	**21**	***361**	**6**	**0**	**0**	**0**	**51**
1987-88	**Calgary**	**NHL**	**68**	**8**	**5**	**13**	**337**	**9**	**4**	**0**	**4**	**32**
1988-89	**Calgary**	**NHL**	**75**	**3**	**9**	**12**	***375**	**19**	**0**	**4**	**4**	**32**
1989-90	**Calgary**	**NHL**	**67**	**2**	**3**	**5**	**279**	**6**	**0**	**0**	**0**	**4**
1990-91	**Calgary**	**NHL**	**34**	**5**	**2**	**7**	**143**	**7**	**0**	**0**	**0**	**10**
1991-92	**Calgary**	**NHL**	**30**	**1**	**3**	**4**	**167**	....	....	....	....	....
1992-93	**Quebec**	**NHL**	**48**	**5**	**3**	**8**	**94**	....	....	....	....	....
	Vancouver	**NHL**	**26**	**0**	**4**	**4**	**99**	**11**	**0**	**0**	**0**	**26**
1993-94	**Vancouver**	**NHL**	**56**	**3**	**4**	**7**	**171**	**24**	**0**	**0**	**0**	**26**
1994-95	**Vancouver**	**NHL**	**34**	**3**	**2**	**5**	**120**	**11**	**0**	**0**	**0**	**22**
	NHL Totals		**709**	**60**	**72**	**132**	**2889**	**132**	**5**	**7**	**12**	**426**

Claimed by **Tampa Bay** from **Calgary** in Expansion Draft, June 18, 1992. Traded to **Quebec** by **Tampa Bay** for future considerations (Martin Simard, September 14, 1992), June 19, 1992. Claimed on waivers by **Vancouver** from **Quebec**, February 12, 1993.

HURLBUT, MIKE

Defense. Shoots left. 6'2", 200 lbs. Born, Massena, NY, October 7, 1966.
(NY Rangers' 1st choice, 5th overall, in 1988 Supplemental Draft).

			Regular Season					Playoffs				
Season	Club	Lea	GP	G	A	TP	PIM	GP	G	A	TP	PIM
1985-86	St. Lawrence	ECAC	25	2	10	12	40	....	....	....	....	....
1986-87	St. Lawrence	ECAC	35	8	15	23	44	....	....	....	....	....
1987-88	St. Lawrence	ECAC	38	6	12	18	18	....	....	....	....	....
1988-89ab	St. Lawrence	ECAC	36	8	25	33	30	....	....	....	....	....
	Denver	IHL	8	0	2	2	13	4	1	2	3	2
1989-90	Flint	IHL	74	3	34	37	38	3	0	1	1	2
1990-91	San Diego	IHL	2	1	0	1	0	....	....	....	....	....
	Binghamton	AHL	33	2	11	13	27	3	0	1	1	0
1991-92	Binghamton	AHL	79	16	39	55	64	11	2	7	9	8
1992-93	**NY Rangers**	**NHL**	**23**	**1**	**8**	**9**	**16**	....	....	....	....	....
	Binghamton	AHL	45	11	25	36	46	14	2	5	7	12
1993-94	**Quebec**	**NHL**	**1**	**0**	**0**	**0**	**0**	....	....	....	....	....
	Cornwall	AHL	77	13	33	46	100	13	3	7	10	12
1994-95c	Cornwall	AHL	74	11	49	60	69	3	1	0	1	15
	NHL Totals		**24**	**1**	**8**	**9**	**16**	....	....	....	....	....

a ECAC First All-Star Team (1989)
b NCAA East First All-American Team (1989)
c AHL Second All-Star Team (1995)

Traded to **Quebec** by **NY Rangers** for Alexander Karpovtsev, September 7, 1993.

HUSCROFT, JAMIE — BOS.

Defense. Shoots right. 6'2", 200 lbs. Born, Creston, B.C., January 9, 1967.
(New Jersey's 9th choice, 171st overall, in 1985 Entry Draft).

			Regular Season					Playoffs				
Season	Club	Lea	GP	G	A	TP	PIM	GP	G	A	TP	PIM
1983-84	Seattle	WHL	63	0	12	12	77	5	0	0	0	15
1984-85	Seattle	WHL	69	3	13	16	273	....	....	....	....	....
1985-86	Seattle	WHL	66	6	20	26	394	5	0	1	1	18
1986-87	Seattle	WHL	21	1	18	19	99	....	....	....	....	....
	Medicine Hat	WHL	35	4	21	25	170	20	0	3	3	*125
1987-88	Utica	AHL	71	5	7	12	316	....	....	....	....	....
	Flint	IHL	3	1	0	1	2	16	0	1	1	110
1988-89	**New Jersey**	**NHL**	**15**	**0**	**2**	**2**	**51**	....	....	....	....	....
	Utica	AHL	41	2	10	12	215	5	0	0	0	40
1989-90	**New Jersey**	**NHL**	**42**	**2**	**3**	**5**	**149**	**5**	**0**	**0**	**0**	**16**
	Utica	AHL	22	3	6	9	122	....	....	....	....	....
1990-91	**New Jersey**	**NHL**	**8**	**0**	**1**	**1**	**27**	**3**	**0**	**0**	**0**	**6**
	Utica	AHL	59	3	15	18	339	....	....	....	....	....
1991-92	Utica	AHL	50	4	7	11	224	....	....	....	....	....
1992-93	Providence	AHL	69	2	15	17	257	2	0	1	1	6
1993-94	**Boston**	**NHL**	**36**	**0**	**1**	**1**	**144**	**4**	**0**	**0**	**0**	**9**
	Providence	AHL	32	1	10	11	157	....	....	....	....	....
1994-95	**Boston**	**NHL**	**34**	**0**	**6**	**6**	**103**	**5**	**0**	**0**	**0**	**11**
	NHL Totals		**135**	**2**	**13**	**15**	**474**	**17**	**0**	**0**	**0**	**42**

Signed as a free agent by **Boston**, July 23, 1992.

HUSKA, RYAN (HUHS-kuh) CHI.

Left wing. Shoots left. 6'2", 194 lbs. Born, Cranbrook, B.C., July 2, 1975.
(Chicago's 4th choice, 76th overall, in 1993 Entry Draft).

			Regular Season					Playoffs				
Season	Club	Lea	GP	G	A	TP	PIM	GP	G	A	TP	PIM
1991-92	Kamloops	WHL	44	4	5	9	23	6	0	1	1	0
1992-93	Kamloops	WHL	68	17	15	32	50	13	2	6	8	4
1993-94	Kamloops	WHL	69	23	31	54	66	19	9	5	14	23
1994-95	Kamloops	WHL	66	27	40	67	78	17	7	8	15	12

HUURA, PASI (HOO-rah) PIT.

Defense. Shoots left. 6'4", 220 lbs. Born, Tampere, Fin., March 23, 1966.
(Pittsburgh's 12th choice, 258th overall, in 1991 Entry Draft).

			Regular Season					Playoffs				
Season	Club	Lea	GP	G	A	TP	PIM	GP	G	A	TP	PIM
1987-88	Ilves	Fin.	8	1	0	1	2	....	....	....	....	....
1988-89	Ilves	Fin.	35	3	5	8	22	....	....	....	....	....
1989-90	Ilves	Fin.	41	1	4	5	48	9	1	0	1	17
1990-91	Ilves	Fin.	39	2	6	8	50	....	....	....	....	....
1991-92	Lukko	Fin.	44	1	5	6	40	2	0	0	0	2
1992-93	Lukko	Fin.	48	6	6	12	38	3	0	0	0	4
1993-94	Lukko	Fin.	27	1	2	3	24	8	1	0	1	4
1994-95	Ilves	Fin.	32	2	9	11	16	....	....	....	....	....

HYMOVITZ, DAVID CHI.

Left wing. Shoots left. 5'11", 170 lbs. Born, Boston, MA, May 30, 1974.
(Chicago's 9th choice, 209th overall, in 1992 Entry Draft).

			Regular Season					Playoffs				
Season	Club	Lea	GP	G	A	TP	PIM	GP	G	A	TP	PIM
1992-93	Boston College	H.E.	37	7	6	13	6	....	....	....	....	....
1993-94	Boston College	H.E.	36	18	14	32	18	....	....	....	....	....
1994-95	Boston College	H.E.	35	21	19	40	22	....	....	....	....	....

IAFRATE, AL (IGH-uh-FRAY-tee) BOS.

Defense. Shoots left. 6'3", 235 lbs. Born, Dearborn, MI, March 21, 1966.
(Toronto's 1st choice, 4th overall, in 1984 Entry Draft).

			Regular Season					Playoffs				
Season	Club	Lea	GP	G	A	TP	PIM	GP	G	A	TP	PIM
1983-84a	U.S. National	....	55	4	17	21	26	....	....	....	....	....
	U.S. Olympic	....	6	0	0	0	2	....	....	....	....	....
	Belleville	OHL	10	2	4	6	2	3	0	1	1	5
1984-85	**Toronto**	**NHL**	**68**	**5**	**16**	**21**	**51**	....	....	....	....	....
1985-86	**Toronto**	**NHL**	**65**	**8**	**25**	**33**	**40**	**10**	**0**	**3**	**3**	**4**
1986-87	**Toronto**	**NHL**	**80**	**9**	**21**	**30**	**55**	**13**	**1**	**3**	**4**	**11**
1987-88	**Toronto**	**NHL**	**77**	**22**	**30**	**52**	**80**	**6**	**3**	**4**	**7**	**6**
1988-89	**Toronto**	**NHL**	**65**	**13**	**20**	**33**	**72**	....	....	....	....	....
1989-90	**Toronto**	**NHL**	**75**	**21**	**42**	**63**	**135**	....	....	....	....	....
1990-91	**Toronto**	**NHL**	**42**	**3**	**15**	**18**	**113**	....	....	....	....	....
	Washington	**NHL**	**30**	**6**	**8**	**14**	**124**	**10**	**1**	**3**	**4**	**22**
1991-92	**Washington**	**NHL**	**78**	**17**	**34**	**51**	**180**	**7**	**4**	**2**	**6**	**14**
1992-93a	**Washington**	**NHL**	**81**	**25**	**41**	**66**	**169**	**6**	**6**	**0**	**6**	**4**
1993-94	**Washington**	**NHL**	**67**	**10**	**35**	**45**	**143**	....	....	....	....	....
	Boston	**NHL**	**12**	**5**	**8**	**13**	**20**	**13**	**3**	**1**	**4**	**6**
1994-95			DID NOT PLAY – INJURED									
	NHL Totals		**740**	**144**	**295**	**439**	**1182**	**65**	**18**	**16**	**34**	**67**

a NHL Second All-Star Team (1993)

Played in NHL All-Star Game (1988, 1990, 1993, 1994)

Traded to **Washington** by **Toronto** for Peter Zezel and Bob Rouse, January 16, 1991. Traded to **Boston** by **Washington** for Joe Juneau, March 21, 1994.

IGINLA, JAROME (ih-GIHN-lah, jah-ROHM) DAL.

Right wing. Shoots right. 6'1", 193 lbs. Born, Edmonton, Alta., July 1, 1977.
(Dallas' 1st choice, 11th overall, in 1995 Entry Draft).

			Regular Season					Playoffs				
Season	Club	Lea	GP	G	A	TP	PIM	GP	G	A	TP	PIM
1993-94	Kamloops	WHL	48	6	23	39	33	19	3	6	9	10
1994-95a	Kamloops	WHL	72	33	38	71	111	21	7	11	18	34

a Won George Parsons Trophy (Memorial Cup Tournament Most Sportsmanlike Player) (1995)

INTRANUOVO, RALPH (ihn-trah-NOO-voh) EDM.

Center. Shoots left. 5'8", 185 lbs. Born, East York, Ont., December 11, 1973.
(Edmonton's 5th choice, 96th overall, in 1992 Entry Draft).

			Regular Season					Playoffs				
Season	Club	Lea	GP	G	A	TP	PIM	GP	G	A	TP	PIM
1990-91	S.S. Marie	OHL	63	25	42	67	22	14	7	13	20	17
1991-92	S.S. Marie	OHL	65	50	63	113	44	18	10	14	24	12
1992-93ab	S.S. Marie	OHL	54	31	47	78	61	18	10	16	26	30
1993-94	Cape Breton	AHL	66	21	31	52	39	4	1	2	3	2
1994-95c	Cape Breton	AHL	70	46	47	93	62	....	....	....	....	....
	Edmonton	**NHL**	**1**	**0**	**1**	**1**	**0**	....	....	....	....	....
	NHL Totals		**1**	**0**	**1**	**1**	**0**	....	....	....	....	....

a Won Stafford Smythe Memorial Trophy (Memorial Cup Tournament MVP) (1993)
b Memorial Cup All-Star Team (1993)
c AHL Second All-Star Team (1995)

IRVING, JOEL MTL.

Center. Shoots right. 6'3", 190 lbs. Born, Lumsden, Sask., January 2, 1976.
(Montreal's 8th choice, 148th overall, in 1994 Entry Draft).

			Regular Season					Playoffs				
Season	Club	Lea	GP	G	A	TP	PIM	GP	G	A	TP	PIM
1993-94	Regina	Midget	32	16	46	62	22	....	....	....	....	....
1994-95	W. Michigan	CCHA	30	2	3	5	20	....	....	....	....	....

ISBISTER, BRAD WPG.

Right wing. Shoots right. 6'2", 198 lbs. Born, Edmonton, Alta., May 7, 1977.
(Winnipeg's 4th choice, 67th overall, in 1995 Entry Draft).

			Regular Season					Playoffs				
Season	Club	Lea	GP	G	A	TP	PIM	GP	G	A	TP	PIM
1993-94	Portland	WHL	64	7	10	17	45	....	....	....	....	....
1994-95	Portland	WHL	67	16	20	36	123	....	....	....	....	....

ISSEL, JASON WPG.

Left wing. Shoots left. 6'1", 185 lbs. Born, Melville, Sask., March 1, 1976.
(Winnipeg's 11th choice, 264th overall, in 1994 Entry Draft).

			Regular Season					Playoffs				
Season	Club	Lea	GP	G	A	TP	PIM	GP	G	A	TP	PIM
1992-93	Prince Albert	WHL	20	0	0	0	0	....	....	....	....	....
1993-94	Prince Albert	WHL	61	12	24	36	62	....	....	....	....	....
1994-95	Prince Albert	WHL	57	9	18	27	47	13	1	0	1	9

JACKSON, DANE

Right wing. Shoots right. 6'1", 200 lbs. Born, Castlegar, B.C., May 17, 1970.
(Vancouver's 3rd choice, 44th overall, in 1988 Entry Draft).

			Regular Season					Playoffs				
Season	Club	Lea	GP	G	A	TP	PIM	GP	G	A	TP	PIM
1988-89	North Dakota	WCHA	30	4	5	9	33	....	....	....	....	....
1989-90	North Dakota	WCHA	44	15	11	26	56	....	....	....	....	....
1990-91	North Dakota	WCHA	37	17	9	26	79	....	....	....	....	....
1991-92	North Dakota	WCHA	39	23	19	42	81	....	....	....	....	....
1992-93	Hamilton	AHL	68	23	20	43	59	....	....	....	....	....
1993-94	**Vancouver**	**NHL**	**12**	**5**	**1**	**6**	**9**	....	....	....	....	....
	Hamilton	AHL	60	25	35	60	75	4	2	2	4	16
1994-95	Syracuse	AHL	78	30	28	58	162	....	....	....	....	....
	Vancouver	**NHL**	**3**	**1**	**0**	**1**	**4**	**6**	**0**	**0**	**0**	**10**
	NHL Totals		**15**	**6**	**1**	**7**	**13**	**6**	**0**	**0**	**0**	**10**

JAGR, JAROMIR (YAH-guhr) PIT.

Right wing. Shoots left. 6'2", 208 lbs. Born, Kladno, Czech., February 15, 1972.
(Pittsburgh's 1st choice, 5th overall, in 1990 Entry Draft).

			Regular Season					Playoffs				
Season	Club	Lea	GP	G	A	TP	PIM	GP	G	A	TP	PIM
1988-89	Kladno	Czech.	39	8	10	18	4	....	....	....	....	....
1989-90	Kladno	Czech.	51	30	29	59	....	....	....	....	....	....
1990-91a	**Pittsburgh**	**NHL**	**80**	**27**	**30**	**57**	**42**	**24**	**3**	**10**	**13**	**6**
1991-92	**Pittsburgh**	**NHL**	**70**	**32**	**37**	**69**	**34**	**21**	**11**	**13**	**24**	**6**
1992-93	**Pittsburgh**	**NHL**	**81**	**34**	**60**	**94**	**61**	**12**	**5**	**4**	**9**	**23**
1993-94	**Pittsburgh**	**NHL**	**80**	**32**	**67**	**99**	**61**	**6**	**2**	**4**	**6**	**16**
1994-95	Kladno	Czech.	11	8	14	22	10	....	....	....	....	....
	Bolzano	Euro.	5	8	8	16	4	....	....	....	....	....
	Bolzano	Italy	1	0	0	0	0	....	....	....	....	....
	Schalke	Ger. 2	1	1	10	11	0	....	....	....	....	....
bc	**Pittsburgh**	**NHL**	**48**	**32**	**38**	***70**	**37**	**12**	**10**	**5**	**15**	**6**
	NHL Totals		**359**	**157**	**232**	**389**	**235**	**75**	**31**	**36**	**67**	**57**

a NHL/Upper Deck All-Rookie Team (1991)
b NHL First All-Star Team (1995)
c Won Art Ross Trophy (1995)

Played in NHL All-Star Game (1992, 1993)

JAKOPIN, JOHN DET.

Defense. Shoots right. 6'5", 220 lbs. Born, Toronto, Ont., May 16, 1975.
(Detroit's 4th choice, 97th overall, in 1993 Entry Draft).

			Regular Season					Playoffs				
Season	Club	Lea	GP	G	A	TP	PIM	GP	G	A	TP	PIM
1993-94	Merrimack	H.E.	36	2	8	10	64	....	....	....	....	....
1994-95	Merrimack	H.E.	37	4	10	14	42	....	....	....	....	....

JANDERA, LUBOMIR CHI.

Defense. Shoots left. 5'11", 180 lbs. Born, Chomutov, Czech., April 21, 1976.
(Chicago's 9th choice, 222nd overall, in 1994 Entry Draft).

			Regular Season					Playoffs				
Season	Club	Lea	GP	G	A	TP	PIM	GP	G	A	TP	PIM
1994-95	Pardubice	Czech.	5	0	0	0	0	3	0	0	0	0

JANNEY, CRAIG S.J.

Center. Shoots left. 6'1", 190 lbs. Born, Hartford, CT, September 26, 1967.
(Boston's 1st choice, 13th overall, in 1986 Entry Draft).

			Regular Season					Playoffs				
Season	Club	Lea	GP	G	A	TP	PIM	GP	G	A	TP	PIM
1985-86	Boston College	H.E.	34	13	14	27	8	....	....	....	....	....
1986-87ab	Boston College	H.E.	37	26	55	81	6	....	....	....	....	....
1987-88	U.S. National	....	52	26	44	70	6	....	....	....	....	....
	U.S. Olympic	....	5	3	1	4	2	....	....	....	....	....
	Boston	**NHL**	**15**	**7**	**9**	**16**	**0**	**23**	**6**	**10**	**16**	**11**
1988-89	**Boston**	**NHL**	**62**	**16**	**46**	**62**	**12**	**10**	**4**	**9**	**13**	**21**
1989-90	**Boston**	**NHL**	**55**	**24**	**38**	**62**	**4**	**18**	**3**	**19**	**22**	**2**
1990-91	**Boston**	**NHL**	**77**	**26**	**66**	**92**	**8**	**18**	**4**	**18**	**22**	**11**
1991-92	**Boston**	**NHL**	**53**	**12**	**39**	**51**	**20**	....	....	....	....	....
	St. Louis	**NHL**	**25**	**6**	**30**	**36**	**2**	**6**	**0**	**6**	**6**	**0**
1992-93	**St. Louis**	**NHL**	**84**	**24**	**82**	**106**	**12**	**11**	**2**	**9**	**11**	**0**
1993-94	**St. Louis**	**NHL**	**69**	**16**	**68**	**84**	**24**	**4**	**1**	**3**	**4**	**0**
1994-95	**St. Louis**	**NHL**	**8**	**2**	**5**	**7**	**0**	....	....	....	....	....
	San Jose	**NHL**	**27**	**5**	**15**	**20**	**10**	**11**	**3**	**4**	**7**	**4**
	NHL Totals		**475**	**138**	**398**	**536**	**92**	**101**	**23**	**78**	**101**	**49**

a Hockey East First All-Star Team (1987)
b NCAA East First All-American Team (1987)

Traded to **St. Louis** by **Boston** with Stephane Quintal for Adam Oates, February 7, 1992. Acquired by **Vancouver** from **St. Louis** with St. Louis' second round choice (Dave Scathard) in 1994 Entry Draft as compensation for St. Louis' signing of free agent Petr Nedved, March 14, 1994. Traded to **St. Louis** by **Vancouver** for Jeff Brown, Bret Hedican and Nathan Lafayette, March 21, 1994. Traded to **San Jose** by **St. Louis** with cash for Jeff Norton and a conditional choice in 1997 Entry Draft, March 6, 1995.

JANSSENS, MARK HFD.

Center. Shoots left. 6'3", 216 lbs. Born, Surrey, B.C., May 19, 1968.
(NY Rangers' 4th choice, 72nd overall, in 1986 Entry Draft).

			Regular Season					Playoffs				
Season	Club	Lea	GP	G	A	TP	PIM	GP	G	A	TP	PIM
1984-85	Regina	WHL	70	8	22	30	51	....	....	....	....	....
1985-86	Regina	WHL	71	25	38	63	146	9	0	2	2	17
1986-87	Regina	WHL	68	24	38	62	209	3	0	1	1	14
1987-88	**NY Rangers**	**NHL**	**1**	**0**	**0**	**0**	**0**	....	....	....	....	....
	Colorado	IHL	6	2	2	4	24	12	3	2	5	20
	Regina	WHL	71	39	51	90	202	4	3	4	7	6
1988-89	**NY Rangers**	**NHL**	**5**	**0**	**0**	**0**	**0**	....	....	....	....	....
	Denver	IHL	38	19	19	38	104	4	3	0	3	18
1989-90	**NY Rangers**	**NHL**	**80**	**5**	**8**	**13**	**161**	**9**	**2**	**1**	**3**	**10**
1990-91	**NY Rangers**	**NHL**	**67**	**9**	**7**	**16**	**172**	**6**	**3**	**0**	**3**	**6**
1991-92	**NY Rangers**	**NHL**	**4**	**0**	**0**	**0**	**5**	....	....	....	....	....
	Binghamton	AHL	55	10	23	33	109	....	....	....	....	....
	Minnesota	**NHL**	**3**	**0**	**0**	**0**	**0**	....	....	....	....	....
	Kalamazoo	IHL	2	0	0	0	2	11	1	2	3	22
1992-93	**Hartford**	**NHL**	**76**	**12**	**17**	**29**	**237**	....	....	....	....	....
1993-94	**Hartford**	**NHL**	**84**	**2**	**10**	**12**	**137**	....	....	....	....	....
1994-95	**Hartford**	**NHL**	**46**	**2**	**5**	**7**	**93**	....	....	....	....	....
	NHL Totals		**366**	**30**	**47**	**77**	**805**	**15**	**5**	**1**	**6**	**16**

Traded to **Minnesota** by **NY Rangers** for Mario Thyer and Minnesota's third round choice (Maxim Galanov) in 1993 Entry Draft, March 10, 1992. Traded to **Hartford** by **Minnesota** for James Black, September 3, 1992.

JANTUNEN, MARKO (YAHN-tuh-nen) CGY.

Center. Shoots left. 5'10", 185 lbs. Born, Lahti, Finland, February 14, 1971.
(Calgary's 12th choice, 239th overall, in 1991 Entry Draft).

			Regular Season					Playoffs				
Season	Club	Lea	GP	G	A	TP	PIM	GP	G	A	TP	PIM
1990-91	Reipas	Fin.	39	9	20	29	20	....	....	....	....	....
1991-92	Reipas	Fin.	42	10	14	24	46	....	....	....	....	....
1992-93	KalPa	Fin.	48	21	27	48	63	....	....	....	....	....
1993-94	TPS	Fin.	48	29	29	58	22	11	2	6	8	12
1994-95	V. Frolunda	Swe.	22	15	8	23	22	....	....	....	....	....

JAY, BOB

Defense. Shoots right. 5'11", 190 lbs. Born, Burlington, MA, November 18, 1965.

			Regular Season					Playoffs				
Season	Club	Lea	GP	G	A	TP	PIM	GP	G	A	TP	PIM
1990-91	Fort Wayne	IHL	40	1	8	9	24	14	0	3	3	16
1991-92	Fort Wayne	IHL	76	1	19	20	119	7	0	2	2	4
1992-93	Fort Wayne	IHL	78	5	21	26	100	8	0	2	2	14
1993-94	**Los Angeles**	**NHL**	**3**	**0**	**1**	**1**	**0**	....	....	....	....	....
	Phoenix	IHL	65	7	15	22	54	....	....	....	....	....
1994-95	Detroit	IHL	57	3	8	11	51	5	0	0	0	10
	NHL Totals		**3**	**0**	**1**	**1**	**0**	....	....	....	....	....

Signed as a free agent by **Los Angeles**, July 16, 1993.

JEAN, YANICK WSH.

Defense. Shoots left. 6'1", 198 lbs. Born, Alma, Que., November 26, 1975.
(Washington's 5th choice, 119th overall, in 1994 Entry Draft).

			Regular Season					Playoffs				
Season	Club	Lea	GP	G	A	TP	PIM	GP	G	A	TP	PIM
1992-93	Chicoutimi	QMJHL	50	2	2	4	40	3	0	0	0	0
1993-94	Chicoutimi	QMJHL	65	11	30	41	177	27	8	12	20	82
1994-95	Chicoutimi	QMJHL	71	7	46	53	155	13	2	7	9	25

JENNINGS, GRANT

Defense. Shoots left. 6'3", 210 lbs. Born, Hudson Bay, Sask., May 5, 1965.

			Regular Season					Playoffs				
Season	Club	Lea	GP	G	A	TP	PIM	GP	G	A	TP	PIM
1983-84	Saskatoon	WHL	64	5	13	18	102	....	....	....	....	....
1984-85	Saskatoon	WHL	47	10	24	34	134	2	1	0	1	2
1985-86	Binghamton	AHL	51	0	4	4	109	....	....	....	....	....
1986-87	Fort Wayne	IHL	3	0	0	0	0	....	....	....	....	....
	Binghamton	AHL	47	1	5	6	125	13	0	2	2	17
1987-88	**Washington**	**NHL**	....	....	....	....	....	**1**	**0**	**0**	**0**	**0**
	Binghamton	AHL	56	2	12	14	195	3	1	0	1	15
1988-89	**Hartford**	**NHL**	**55**	**3**	**10**	**13**	**159**	**4**	**1**	**0**	**1**	**17**
	Binghamton	AHL	2	0	0	0	2	....	....	....	....	....
1989-90	**Hartford**	**NHL**	**64**	**3**	**6**	**9**	**171**	**7**	**0**	**0**	**0**	**13**
1990-91	**Hartford**	**NHL**	**44**	**1**	**4**	**5**	**82**	....	....	....	....	....
	Pittsburgh	**NHL**	**13**	**1**	**3**	**4**	**26**	**13**	**1**	**1**	**2**	**16**
1991-92	**Pittsburgh**	**NHL**	**53**	**4**	**5**	**9**	**104**	**10**	**0**	**0**	**0**	**12**
1992-93	**Pittsburgh**	**NHL**	**58**	**0**	**5**	**5**	**65**	**12**	**0**	**0**	**0**	**8**
1993-94	**Pittsburgh**	**NHL**	**61**	**2**	**4**	**6**	**126**	**3**	**0**	**0**	**0**	**2**
1994-95	**Pittsburgh**	**NHL**	**25**	**0**	**4**	**4**	**36**	....	....	....	....	....
	Toronto	**NHL**	**10**	**0**	**2**	**2**	**7**	**4**	**0**	**0**	**0**	**0**
	NHL Totals		**383**	**14**	**43**	**57**	**776**	**54**	**2**	**1**	**3**	**68**

Signed as a free agent by **Washington**, June 25, 1985. Traded to **Hartford** by **Washington** with Ed Kastelic for Mike Millar and Neil Sheehy, July 6, 1988. Traded to **Pittsburgh** by **Hartford** with Ron Francis and Ulf Samuelsson for John Cullen, Jeff Parker and Zarley Zalapski, March 4, 1991. Traded to **Toronto** by **Pittsburgh** for Drake Berehowsky, April 7, 1995.

JINMAN, LEE DAL.

Center. Shoots right. 5'10", 160 lbs. Born, Toronto, Ont., January 10, 1976.
(Dallas' 2nd choice, 46th overall, in 1994 Entry Draft).

			Regular Season					Playoffs				
Season	Club	Lea	GP	G	A	TP	PIM	GP	G	A	TP	PIM
1993-94	North Bay	OHL	66	31	66	97	33	18	*18	19	37	8
1994-95	North Bay	OHL	63	39	65	104	41	6	5	5	10	4

JOBIN, FREDERIC WSH.

Defense. Shoots left. 6', 210 lbs. Born, Montreal, Que., January 28, 1977.
(Washington's 8th choice, 147th overall, in 1995 Entry Draft).

			Regular Season					Playoffs				
Season	Club	Lea	GP	G	A	TP	PIM	GP	G	A	TP	PIM
1993-94	Laval	QMJHL	67	4	11	15	150	21	2	1	3	40
1994-95	Laval	QMJHL	70	0	13	13	285	20	1	1	2	106

JOHANSSON, ANDREAS NYI

Center. Shoots left. 5'10", 198 lbs. Born, Hofors, Sweden, May 19, 1973.
(NY Islanders' 7th choice, 136th overall, in 1991 Entry Draft).

			Regular Season					Playoffs				
Season	Club	Lea	GP	G	A	TP	PIM	GP	G	A	TP	PIM
1990-91	Falun	Swe. 2	31	12	10	22	38	....	....	....	....	....
1991-92	Farjestad	Swe.	30	3	1	4	10	6	0	0	0	4
1992-93	Farjestad	Swe.	38	4	7	11	38	2	0	0	0	0
1993-94	Farjestad	Swe.	20	3	6	9	6	....	....	....	....	....
1994-95	Farjestad	Swe.	36	9	10	19	42	4	0	0	0	10

JOHANSSON, CALLE (yo-HAHN-sehn, KAL-ee) WSH.

Defense. Shoots left. 5'11", 200 lbs. Born, Goteborg, Sweden, February 14, 1967.
(Buffalo's 1st choice, 14th overall, in 1985 Entry Draft).

			Regular Season					Playoffs				
Season	Club	Lea	GP	G	A	TP	PIM	GP	G	A	TP	PIM
1983-84	V. Frolunda	Swe.	28	4	4	8	10	....	....	....	....	....
1984-85	V. Frolunda	Swe.2	25	8	13	21	16	6	1	2	3	4
1985-86	Bjorkloven	Swe.	17	1	2	3	4	....	....	....	....	....
1986-87	Bjorkloven	Swe.	30	2	13	15	20	6	1	3	4	6
1987-88a	**Buffalo**	**NHL**	**71**	**4**	**38**	**42**	**37**	**6**	**0**	**1**	**1**	**0**
1988-89	**Buffalo**	**NHL**	**47**	**2**	**11**	**13**	**33**	....	....	....	....	....
	Washington	**NHL**	**12**	**1**	**7**	**8**	**4**	**6**	**1**	**2**	**3**	**0**
1989-90	**Washington**	**NHL**	**70**	**8**	**31**	**39**	**25**	**15**	**1**	**6**	**7**	**4**
1990-91	**Washington**	**NHL**	**80**	**11**	**41**	**52**	**23**	**10**	**2**	**7**	**9**	**8**
1991-92	**Washington**	**NHL**	**80**	**14**	**42**	**56**	**49**	**7**	**0**	**5**	**5**	**4**
1992-93	**Washington**	**NHL**	**77**	**7**	**38**	**45**	**56**	**6**	**0**	**5**	**5**	**4**
1993-94	**Washington**	**NHL**	**84**	**9**	**33**	**42**	**59**	**6**	**1**	**3**	**4**	**4**
1994-95	Kloten	Switz.	5	1	2	3	8	....	....	....	....	....
	Washington	**NHL**	**46**	**5**	**26**	**31**	**35**	**7**	**3**	**1**	**4**	**0**
	NHL Totals		**567**	**61**	**267**	**328**	**321**	**63**	**8**	**30**	**38**	**24**

a NHL All-Rookie Team (1988)

Traded to **Washington** by **Buffalo** with Buffalo's second round choice (Byron Dafoe) in 1989 Entry Draft for Clint Malarchuk, Grant Ledyard and Washington's sixth round choice (Brian Holzinger) in 1991 Entry Draft, March 7, 1989.

JOHANSSON, DANIEL (YOOH-hahn-suhn) NYI

Defense. Shoots right. 5'11", 180 lbs. Born, Glimakra, Sweden, September 10, 1974.
(NY Islanders' 9th choice, 222nd overall, in 1993 Entry Draft).

			Regular Season					Playoffs				
Season	Club	Lea	GP	G	A	TP	PIM	GP	G	A	TP	PIM
1991-92	Rogle	Swe. 2	33	4	9	13	30	....	....	....	....	....
1992-93	Rogle	Swe.	28	2	4	6	20	....	....	....	....	....
1993-94	Rogle	Swe.	37	5	10	15	34	3	0	0	0	0
1994-95	Rogle	Swe.	22	4	2	6	16	....	....	....	....	....

JOHANSSON, MATHIAS CGY.

Center. Shoots left. 6'2", 190 lbs. Born, Oskarshamn, Sweden, February 22, 1974.
(Calgary's 3rd choice, 54th overall, in 1992 Entry Draft).

			Regular Season					Playoffs				
Season	Club	Lea	GP	G	A	TP	PIM	GP	G	A	TP	PIM
1990-91	Farjestad	Swe.	3	0	0	0	0	....	....	....	....	....
1991-92	Farjestad	Swe.	16	0	0	0	2	1	0	0	0	0
1992-93	Farjestad	Swe.	11	2	1	3	4	3	0	0	0	0
1993-94	Farjestad	Swe.	16	2	1	3	4	....	....	....	....	....
1994-95	Farjestad	Swe.	40	7	8	15	30	4	4	3	7	2

JOHANSSON, MIKAEL COL.

Center. Shoots left. 5'10", 183 lbs. Born, Stockholm, Sweden, June 12, 1966.
(Quebec's 7th choice, 134th overall, in 1991 Entry Draft).

			Regular Season					Playoffs				
Season	Club	Lea	GP	G	A	TP	PIM	GP	G	A	TP	PIM
1986-87	Djurgarden	Swe.	32	9	16	25	8	....	....	....	....	....
1987-88	Djurgarden	Swe.	38	11	22	33	10	3	1	1	2	0
1988-89	Djurgarden	Swe.	29	6	15	21	10	....	....	....	....	....
1989-90	Djurgarden	Swe.	37	14	20	34	12	8	5	4	9	0
1990-91	Djurgarden	Swe.	39	13	27	40	21	7	2	7	9	0
1991-92	Djurgarden	Swe.	30	15	21	36	12	9	1	5	6	4
1992-93	Kloten	Switz.	36	18	30	48	2	....	....	....	....	....
1993-94	Kloten	Switz.	36	22	29	51	24	12	9	14	23	8
1994-95	Kloten	Switz.	35	14	36	50	8	12	4	9	13	8

JOHANSSON, ROGER (yo-HAHN-suhn)

Defense. Shoots left. 6'1", 190 lbs. Born, Ljungby, Sweden, April 17, 1967.
(Calgary's 5th choice, 80th overall, in 1985 Entry Draft).

			Regular Season					Playoffs				
Season	Club	Lea	GP	G	A	TP	PIM	GP	G	A	TP	PIM
1983-84	Troja	Swe. 2	11	2	2	4	12	....	....	....	....	....
1984-85	Troja	Swe. 2	30	1	6	7	20	9	0	4	4	8
1985-86	Troja	Swe. 2	32	5	16	21	42	....	....	....	....	....
1986-87	Farjestad	Swe.	31	6	11	17	20	7	1	1	2	8
1987-88	Farjestad	Swe.	24	3	11	14	20	9	1	6	7	12
1988-89	Farjestad	Swe.	40	5	15	20	38	....	....	....	....	....
1989-90	**Calgary**	**NHL**	**35**	**0**	**5**	**5**	**48**	....	....	....	....	....
1990-91	**Calgary**	**NHL**	**38**	**4**	**13**	**17**	**47**	....	....	....	....	....
1991-92	Leksand	Swe.	22	3	9	12	42	....	....	....	....	....
1992-93	**Calgary**	**NHL**	**77**	**4**	**16**	**20**	**62**	**5**	**0**	**1**	**1**	**2**
1993-94	Leksand	Swe.	38	6	15	21	56	4	0	1	1	0
1994-95	Leksand	Swe.	7	0	0	0	14	....	....	....	....	....
	Chicago	**NHL**	**11**	**1**	**0**	**1**	**6**	....	....	....	....	....
	NHL Totals		**161**	**9**	**34**	**43**	**163**	**5**	**0**	**1**	**1**	**2**

Claimed by **Chicago** from **Calgary** in NHL Waiver Draft, January 18, 1995.

JOHNSON, CLINT PIT.

Left wing. Shoots left. 6'2", 200 lbs. Born, Duluth, MN, April 7, 1976.
(Pittsburgh's 7th choice, 128th overall, in 1994 Entry Draft).

			Regular Season					Playoffs				
Season	Club	Lea	GP	G	A	TP	PIM	GP	G	A	TP	PIM
1993-94	Duluth E.	HS	28	30	31	61	....	....	....	....	....	....
1994-95	St. Paul	USHL	14	0	3	3	8	....	....	....	....	....

JOHNSON, CRAIG ST.L.

Left wing/Center. Shoots left. 6'2", 197 lbs. Born, St. Paul, MN, March 18, 1972.
(St. Louis' 1st choice, 33rd overall, in 1990 Entry Draft).

			Regular Season					Playoffs				
Season	Club	Lea	GP	G	A	TP	PIM	GP	G	A	TP	PIM
1990-91	U. Minnesota	WCHA	33	13	18	31	34	....	....	....	....	....
1991-92	U. Minnesota	WCHA	41	17	38	55	66	....	....	....	....	....
1992-93	U. Minnesota	WCHA	42	22	24	46	70	....	....	....	....	....
1993-94	U.S. National	....	54	25	26	51	64	....	....	....	....	....
	U.S. Olympic	....	8	0	4	4	4	....	....	....	....	....
1994-95	Peoria	IHL	16	2	6	8	25	9	0	4	4	10
	St. Louis	**NHL**	**15**	**3**	**3**	**6**	**6**	**1**	**0**	**0**	**0**	**2**
	NHL Totals		**15**	**3**	**3**	**6**	**6**	**1**	**0**	**0**	**0**	**2**

JOHNSON, ERIC   VAN.

Right wing. Shoots right. 6'1", 200 lbs.   Born, Plymouth, MN, December 31, 1972.
(Vancouver's 8th choice, 161st overall, in 1991 Entry Draft).

			Regular Season					Playoffs				
Season	Club	Lea	GP	G	A	TP	PIM	GP	G	A	TP	PIM
1991-92	St. Cloud	WCHA	20	0	2	2	8	....	....	....	....	....
1992-93	St. Cloud	WCHA	33	3	7	10	6	....	....	....	....	....
1993-94	St. Cloud	WCHA	33	9	21	30	16	....	....	....	....	....
1994-95	St. Cloud	WCHA	38	15	29	44	22	....	....	....	....	....

JOHNSON, GREG   DET.

Center. Shoots left. 5'10", 185 lbs.   Born, Thunder Bay, Ont., March 16, 1971.
(Philadelphia's 1st choice, 33rd overall, in 1989 Entry Draft).

			Regular Season					Playoffs				
Season	Club	Lea	GP	G	A	TP	PIM	GP	G	A	TP	PIM
1989-90	North Dakota	WCHA	44	17	38	55	11	....	....	....	....	....
1990-91ab	North Dakota	WCHA	38	18	*61	79	6	....	....	....	....	....
1991-92ac	North Dakota	WCHA	39	20	*54	74	8	....	....	....	....	....
1992-93ab	North Dakota	WCHA	34	19	45	64	18	....	....	....	....	....
	Cdn. National	....	23	6	14	20	2	....	....	....	....	....
1993-94	**Detroit**	NHL	52	6	11	17	22	7	2	2	4	2
	Cdn. National	....	6	2	6	8	4	....	....	....	....	....
	Cdn. Olympic	....	8	0	3	3	0	....	....	....	....	....
	Adirondack	AHL	3	2	4	6	0	4	0	4	4	2
1994-95	**Detroit**	NHL	22	3	5	8	14	1	0	0	0	0
	NHL Totals		**74**	**9**	**16**	**25**	**36**	**8**	**2**	**2**	**4**	**2**

a WCHA First All-Star Team (1991, 1993)
b NCAA West First All-American Team (1991, 1993)
c NCAA West Second All-American Team (1992)

Traded to **Detroit** by **Philadelphia** with Philadelphia's fifth round choice (Frederic Deschenes) in 1994 Entry Draft for Jim Cummins and Philadelphia's fourth round choice (previously acquired by Detroit — later traded to Boston — Boston selected Charles Paquette) in 1993 Entry Draft, June 20, 1993.

JOHNSON, JIM   WSH.

Defense. Shoots left. 6'1", 190 lbs.   Born, New Hope, MN, August 9, 1962.

			Regular Season					Playoffs				
Season	Club	Lea	GP	G	A	TP	PIM	GP	G	A	TP	PIM
1981-82	Minn.-Duluth	WCHA	40	0	10	10	62	....	....	....	....	....
1982-83	Minn.-Duluth	WCHA	44	3	18	21	118	....	....	....	....	....
1983-84	Minn.-Duluth	WCHA	43	3	13	16	116	....	....	....	....	....
1984-85	Minn.-Duluth	WCHA	47	7	29	36	49	....	....	....	....	....
1985-86	Pittsburgh	NHL	80	3	26	29	115	....	....	....	....	....
1986-87	Pittsburgh	NHL	80	5	25	30	116	....	....	....	....	....
1987-88	Pittsburgh	NHL	55	1	12	13	87	....	....	....	....	....
1988-89	Pittsburgh	NHL	76	2	14	16	163	11	0	5	5	44
1989-90	Pittsburgh	NHL	75	3	13	16	154	....	....	....	....	....
1990-91	Pittsburgh	NHL	24	0	5	5	23	....	....	....	....	....
	Minnesota	NHL	44	1	9	10	100	14	0	1	1	52
1991-92	Minnesota	NHL	71	4	10	14	102	7	1	3	4	18
1992-93	Minnesota	NHL	79	3	20	23	105	....	....	....	....	....
1993-94	Dallas	NHL	53	0	7	7	51	....	....	....	....	....
	Washington	NHL	8	0	0	0	12	....	....	....	....	....
1994-95	Washington	NHL	47	0	13	13	43	7	0	2	2	8
	NHL Totals		**692**	**22**	**154**	**176**	**1071**	**39**	**1**	**11**	**12**	**122**

Signed as a free agent by **Pittsburgh**, June 9, 1985. Traded to **Minnesota** by **Pittsburgh** with Chris Dahlquist for Larry Murphy and Peter Taglianetti, December 11, 1990. Traded to **Washington** by **Dallas** for Alan May and Washington's seventh round choice (Jeff Dewar) in 1995 Entry Draft, March 21, 1994.

JOHNSON, MATT   L.A.

Left wing. Shoots left. 6'5", 230 lbs.   Born, Welland, Ont., November 23, 1975.
(Los Angeles' 2nd choice, 33rd overall, in 1994 Entry Draft).

			Regular Season					Playoffs				
Season	Club	Lea	GP	G	A	TP	PIM	GP	G	A	TP	PIM
1992-93	Peterborough	OHL	66	8	17	25	211	16	1	1	2	56
1993-94	Peterborough	OHL	50	13	24	37	233	....	....	....	....	....
1994-95	Peterborough	OHL	14	1	2	3	43	....	....	....	....	....
	Los Angeles	NHL	14	1	0	1	102	....	....	....	....	....
	NHL Totals		**14**	**1**	**0**	**1**	**102**	....	....	....	....	....

JOHNSON, MIKE   FLA.

Defense. Shoots left. 6'3", 205 lbs.   Born, Halifax, N.S., May 29, 1974.
(Minnesota's 4th choice, 130th overall, in 1992 Entry Draft).

			Regular Season					Playoffs				
Season	Club	Lea	GP	G	A	TP	PIM	GP	G	A	TP	PIM
1991-92	Ottawa	OHL	63	1	8	9	49	11	1	0	1	14
1992-93	Ottawa	OHL	66	7	10	17	139	....	....	....	....	....
1993-94	Ottawa	OHL	65	12	17	29	102	17	4	6	10	10
1994-95	Cdn. National	....	37	6	13	19	85	....	....	....	....	....
	Las Vegas	IHL	2	1	0	1	0	8	2	0	2	35

Signed as a free agent by **Florida**, March 11, 1995.

JOHNSON, RYAN   FLA.

Center. Shoots left. 6'2", 185 lbs.   Born, Thunder Bay, Ont., June 14, 1976.
(Florida's 4th choice, 36th overall, in 1994 Entry Draft).

			Regular Season					Playoffs				
Season	Club	Lea	GP	G	A	TP	PIM	GP	G	A	TP	PIM
1993-94	Thunder Bay	USHL	48	14	36	50	28	....	....	....	....	....
1994-95	North Dakota	WCHA	38	6	22	28	39	....	....	....	....	....

JOHNSSON, KIM   NYR

Defense. Shoots left. 6'1", 175 lbs.   Born, Malmo, Sweden, March 16, 1976.
(NY Rangers' 15th choice, 286th overall, in 1994 Entry Draft).

			Regular Season					Playoffs				
Season	Club	Lea	GP	G	A	TP	PIM	GP	G	A	TP	PIM
1993-94	Malmo	Swe.	2	0	0	0	0	....	....	....	....	....
1994-95	Malmo	Swe.	13	0	0	0	4	....	....	....	....	....

JOMPHE, JEAN-FRANCOIS   (zhohm-PHEE) ANA.

Center. Shoots left. 6'1", 195 lbs.   Born, Harve' St. Pierre, Que., December 28, 1972.

			Regular Season					Playoffs				
Season	Club	Lea	GP	G	A	TP	PIM	GP	G	A	TP	PIM
1990-91	Shawinigan	QMJHL	42	17	22	39	14	6	2	1	3	2
1991-92	Shawinigan	QMJHL	44	28	33	61	69	10	6	10	16	10
1992-93	Sherbrooke	QMJHL	60	43	43	86	86	15	10	13	23	18
1993-94	San Diego	IHL	29	2	3	5	12	....	....	....	....	....
	Greensboro	ECHL	25	9	9	18	41	1	1	0	1	0
1994-95	Cdn. National	....	52	33	25	58	85	....	....	....	....	....

Signed as a free agent by **Anaheim**, September 7, 1993

JONES, BRAD   NYR

Left wing. Shoots left. 6', 195 lbs.   Born, Sterling Heights, MI, June 26, 1965.
(Winnipeg's 8th choice, 156th overall, in 1984 Entry Draft).

			Regular Season					Playoffs				
Season	Club	Lea	GP	G	A	TP	PIM	GP	G	A	TP	PIM
1983-84	U. of Michigan	CCHA	37	8	26	34	32	....	....	....	....	....
1984-85	U. of Michigan	CCHA	34	21	27	48	66	....	....	....	....	....
1985-86a	U. of Michigan	CCHA	36	28	39	67	40	....	....	....	....	....
1986-87bc	U. of Michigan	CCHA	40	32	46	78	64	....	....	....	....	....
	Winnipeg	NHL	4	1	0	1	0	....	....	....	....	....
1987-88	**Winnipeg**	NHL	19	2	5	7	15	1	0	0	0	0
	U.S. National	....	50	27	23	50	59	....	....	....	....	....
1988-89	**Winnipeg**	NHL	22	6	5	11	6	....	....	....	....	....
	Moncton	AHL	44	20	19	39	62	7	0	1	1	22
1989-90	**Winnipeg**	NHL	2	0	0	0	0	....	....	....	....	....
	Moncton	AHL	15	5	6	11	47	....	....	....	....	....
	New Haven	AHL	36	8	11	19	71	....	....	....	....	....
1990-91	Los Angeles	NHL	53	9	11	20	57	8	1	1	2	2
1991-92	Philadelphia	NHL	48	7	10	17	44	....	....	....	....	....
1992-93	Ilves	Fin.	26	10	7	17	62	....	....	....	....	....
	New Haven	AHL	4	2	1	3	6	....	....	....	....	....
1993-94			UNAVAILABLE									
1994-95	Springfield	AHL	61	23	22	45	47	....	....	....	....	....
	NHL Totals		**148**	**25**	**31**	**56**	**122**	**9**	**1**	**1**	**2**	**2**

a CCHA Second All-Star Team (1986)
b CCHA First All-Star Team (1987)
c NCAA West Second All-American Team (1987)

Traded to **Los Angeles** by **Winnipeg** for Phil Sykes, December 1, 1989. Signed as a free agent by **Philadelphia**, August 6, 1991. Signed as a free agent by **NY Rangers**, July 10, 1995.

JONES, KEITH   WSH.

Right wing. Shoots left. 6', 200 lbs.   Born, Brantford, Ont., November 8, 1968.
(Washington's 7th choice, 141st overall, in 1988 Entry Draft).

			Regular Season					Playoffs				
Season	Club	Lea	GP	G	A	TP	PIM	GP	G	A	TP	PIM
1988-89	W. Michigan	CCHA	37	9	12	21	51	....	....	....	....	....
1989-90	W. Michigan	CCHA	40	19	18	37	82	....	....	....	....	....
1990-91	W. Michigan	CCHA	41	30	19	49	106	....	....	....	....	....
1991-92a	W. Michigan	CCHA	35	25	31	56	77	....	....	....	....	....
	Baltimore	AHL	6	2	4	6	0	....	....	....	....	....
1992-93	**Washington**	NHL	71	12	14	26	124	6	0	0	0	10
	Baltimore	AHL	8	7	3	10	4	....	....	....	....	....
1993-94	**Washington**	NHL	68	16	19	35	149	11	0	1	1	36
	Portland	AHL	6	5	7	12	4	....	....	....	....	....
1994-95	**Washington**	NHL	40	14	6	20	65	7	4	4	8	22
	NHL Totals		**179**	**42**	**39**	**81**	**338**	**24**	**4**	**5**	**9**	**68**

a CCHA First All-Star Team (1992)

JONSSON, HANS   (YOOHN-suhn) PIT.

Defense. Shoots left. 6'1", 183 lbs.   Born, Jarved, Sweden, August 2, 1973.
(Pittsburgh's 11th choice, 286th overall, in 1993 Entry Draft).

			Regular Season					Playoffs				
Season	Club	Lea	GP	G	A	TP	PIM	GP	G	A	TP	PIM
1991-92	MoDo	Swe.	6	0	1	1	4	....	....	....	....	....
1992-93	MoDo	Swe.	40	2	2	4	24	3	0	1	1	2
1993-94	MoDo	Swe.	23	4	1	5	18	10	0	1	1	12
1994-95	MoDo	Swe.	39	4	6	10	30	....	....	....	....	....

JONSSON, JORGEN   CGY.

Left wing. Shoots left. 6', 185 lbs.   Born, Angelholm, Sweden, September 29, 1972.
(Calgary's 11th choice, 227th overall, in 1994 Entry Draft).

			Regular Season					Playoffs				
Season	Club	Lea	GP	G	A	TP	PIM	GP	G	A	TP	PIM
1992-93	Rogle	Swe.	40	17	11	28	28	....	....	....	....	....
1993-94	Rogle	Swe.	40	17	14	31	46	....	....	....	....	....
1994-95	Rogle	Swe.	22	4	6	10	18	....	....	....	....	....

JONSSON, KENNY   (YAHN-suhn) TOR.

Defense. Shoots left. 6'3", 195 lbs.   Born, Angelholm, Sweden, October 6, 1974.
(Toronto's 1st choice, 12th overall, in 1993 Entry Draft).

			Regular Season					Playoffs				
Season	Club	Lea	GP	G	A	TP	PIM	GP	G	A	TP	PIM
1991-92	Rogle	Swe. 2	30	4	11	15	24	....	....	....	....	....
1992-93a	Rogle	Swe.	39	3	10	13	42	....	....	....	....	....
1993-94	Rogle	Swe.	36	4	13	17	40	3	1	1	2	2
1994-95	Rogle	Swe.	8	3	1	4	20	....	....	....	....	....
	St. John's	AHL	10	2	5	7	2	....	....	....	....	....
b	**Toronto**	NHL	39	2	7	9	16	4	0	0	0	0
	NHL Totals		**39**	**2**	**7**	**9**	**16**	**4**	**0**	**0**	**0**	**0**

a Swedish Rookie of the Year (1993)
b NHL/Upper Deck All-Rookie Team (1995)

JOSEPH, CHRIS   PIT.

Defense. Shoots right. 6'2", 210 lbs.   Born, Burnaby, B.C., September 10, 1969.
(Pittsburgh's 1st choice; 5th overall, in 1987 Entry Draft).

				Regular Season					Playoffs			
Season	Club	Lea	GP	G	A	TP	PIM	GP	G	A	TP	PIM
1985-86	Seattle	WHL	72	4	8	12	50	5	0	3	3	12
1986-87	Seattle	WHL	67	13	45	58	155	....	....	....	....	....
1987-88	**Pittsburgh**	**NHL**	**17**	**0**	**4**	**4**	**12**	....	....	....	....	....
	Seattle	WHL	23	5	14	19	49	....	....	....	....	....
	Edmonton	NHL	7	0	4	4	6	....	....	....	....	....
	Nova Scotia	AHL	8	0	2	2	8	4	0	0	0	9
1988-89	Edmonton	NHL	44	4	5	9	54	....	....	....	....	....
	Cape Breton	AHL	5	1	1	2	18	....	....	....	....	....
1989-90	Edmonton	NHL	4	0	2	2	2	....	....	....	....	....
	Cape Breton	AHL	61	10	20	30	69	6	2	1	3	4
1990-91	Edmonton	NHL	49	5	17	22	59	....	....	....	....	....
1991-92	Edmonton	NHL	7	0	0	0	8	5	1	3	4	2
	Cape Breton	AHL	63	14	29	43	72	5	0	2	2	8
1992-93	Edmonton	NHL	33	2	10	12	48	....	....	....	....	....
1993-94	Edmonton	NHL	10	1	1	2	28	....	....	....	....	....
	Tampa Bay	**NHL**	66	10	19	29	108	....	....	....	....	....
1994-95	**Pittsburgh**	**NHL**	33	5	10	15	46	10	1	1	2	12
	NHL Totals		**270**	**27**	**72**	**99**	**371**	**15**	**2**	**4**	**6**	**14**

Traded to **Edmonton** by **Pittsburgh** with Craig Simpson, Dave Hannan and Moe Mantha for Paul Coffey, Dave Hunter and Wayne Van Dorp, November 24, 1987. Traded to **Tampa Bay** by **Edmonton** for Bob Beers, November 11, 1993. Claimed by **Pittsburgh** from **Tampa Bay** in NHL Waiver Draft, January 18, 1995.

JOSEPHSON, MIKE   CHI.

Left wing. Shoots left. 5'11", 195 lbs.   Born, Vancouver, B.C., April 6, 1976.
(Chicago's 8th choice, 196th overall, in 1994 Entry Draft).

				Regular Season					Playoffs			
Season	Club	Lea	GP	G	A	TP	PIM	GP	G	A	TP	PIM
1992-93	Kamloops	WHL	46	5	9	14	60	10	0	2	2	4
1993-94	Kamloops	WHL	48	11	12	23	114	19	1	10	11	8
1994-95	Kamloops	WHL	5	2	6	8	4	....	....	....	....	....
	Lethbridge	WHL	62	22	25	47	113	....	....	....	....	....

JOVANOVSKI, ED   (joh-van-OHV-skee)   FLA.

Defense. Shoots left. 6'2", 205 lbs.   Born, Windsor, Ont., June 26, 1976.
(Florida's 1st choice, 1st overall, in 1994 Entry Draft).

				Regular Season					Playoffs			
Season	Club	Lea	GP	G	A	TP	PIM	GP	G	A	TP	PIM
1993-94a	Windsor	OHL	62	15	36	51	221	4	0	0	0	15
1994-95b	Windsor	OHL	50	23	42	65	198	9	2	7	9	39

a OHL Second All-Star Team (1994)
b OHL First All-Star Team (1995)

JOYCE, DUANE

Defense. Shoots right. 6'2", 203 lbs.   Born, Pembroke, MA, May 5, 1965.

				Regular Season					Playoffs			
Season	Club	Lea	GP	G	A	TP	PIM	GP	G	A	TP	PIM
1989-90	Kalamazoo	IHL	2	0	0	0	2	....	....	....	....	....
	Fort Wayne	IHL	66	10	26	36	53	....	....	....	....	....
	Muskegon	IHL	13	3	10	13	8	12	3	7	10	13
1990-91	Kalamazoo	IHL	80	12	32	44	53	11	0	3	3	6
1991-92	Kansas City	IHL	80	12	32	44	62	15	6	11	17	8
1992-93	Kansas City	IHL	75	15	25	40	30	12	1	2	3	6
1993-94	Kansas City	IHL	43	9	23	32	40	....	....	....	....	....
	Dallas	**NHL**	3	0	0	0	0	....	....	....	....	....
1994-95	Kansas City	IHL	71	9	21	30	31	21	2	5	7	4
	NHL Totals		**3**	**0**	**0**	**0**	**0**	....	....	....	....	....

Signed as a free agent by **San Jose**, August 13, 1991. Signed as free agent by **Dallas**, December 3, 1993.

JUDEN, DANIEL   T.B.

Right wing. Shoots right. 6'3", 190 lbs.   Born, Beverly, MA, April 17, 1976.
(Tampa Bay's 5th choice, 137th overall, in 1994 Entry Draft).

				Regular Season					Playoffs			
Season	Club	Lea	GP	G	A	TP	PIM	GP	G	A	TP	PIM
1993-94	Gov. Dummer	HS	30	20	28	48	8	....	....	....	....	....
1994-95	Massachusetts	H.E.	3	0	0	0	0	....	....	....	....	....

JUHLIN, PATRIK   (ew-LEEN)   PHI.

Left wing. Shoots left. 6', 194 lbs.   Born, Huddinge, Sweden, April 24, 1970.
(Philadelphia's 2nd choice, 34th overall, in 1989 Entry Draft).

				Regular Season					Playoffs			
Season	Club	Lea	GP	G	A	TP	PIM	GP	G	A	TP	PIM
1988-89	Vasteras	Swe. 2	30	29	13	42	....	....	....	....	....	....
1989-90	Vasteras	Swe.	35	10	13	23	18	2	0	0	0	0
1990-91	Vasteras	Swe.	40	13	9	22	24	4	3	1	4	0
1991-92	Vasteras	Swe.	39	15	12	27	40	....	....	....	....	....
1992-93	Vasteras	Swe.	34	14	12	26	22	3	0	1	1	2
1993-94	Vasteras	Swe.	40	15	16	31	20	4	1	1	2	2
1994-95	Vasteras	Swe.	11	5	9	14	8	....	....	....	....	....
	Philadelphia	**NHL**	42	4	3	7	6	13	1	0	1	2
	NHL Totals		**42**	**4**	**3**	**7**	**6**	**13**	**1**	**0**	**1**	**2**

JUNEAU, JOE   (ZHOO-noh, ZHOH-ay)   WSH.

Center/Left Wing. Shoots right. 6', 195 lbs.   Born, Pont-Rouge, Que., January 5, 1968.
(Boston's 3rd choice, 81st overall, in 1988 Entry Draft).

				Regular Season					Playoffs			
Season	Club	Lea	GP	G	A	TP	PIM	GP	G	A	TP	PIM
1987-88	RPI	ECAC	31	16	29	45	18	....	....	....	....	....
1988-89	RPI	ECAC	30	12	23	35	40	....	....	....	....	....
1989-90a	RPI	ECAC	34	18	*52	*70	31	....	....	....	....	....
	Cdn. National	....	3	0	2	2	4	....	....	....	....	....
1990-91bc	RPI	ECAC	29	23	40	63	68	....	....	....	....	....
	Cdn. National	....	7	2	3	5	0	....	....	....	....	....
1991-92	Cdn. National	....	60	20	49	69	35	....	....	....	....	....
	Cdn. Olympic	....	8	6	9	15	4	....	....	....	....	....
	Boston	**NHL**	14	5	14	19	4	15	4	8	12	21
1992-93d	**Boston**	**NHL**	84	32	70	102	33	4	2	4	6	6
1993-94	**Boston**	**NHL**	63	14	58	72	35	....	....	....	....	....
	Washington	**NHL**	11	5	8	13	6	11	4	5	9	6
1994-95	**Washington**	**NHL**	44	5	38	43	8	7	2	6	8	2
	NHL Totals		**216**	**61**	**188**	**249**	**86**	**37**	**12**	**23**	**35**	**35**

a NCAA East First All-American Team (1990)
b ECAC Second All-Star Team (1991)
c NCAA East Second All-American Team (1991)
d NHL/Upper Deck All-Rookie Team (1993)

Traded to **Washington** by **Boston** for Al Iafrate, March 21, 1994.

JUNKER, STEVE

Left wing. Shoots left. 6', 184 lbs.   Born, Castlegar, B.C., June 26, 1972.
(NY Islanders' 5th choice, 92nd overall, in 1991 Entry Draft).

				Regular Season					Playoffs			
Season	Club	Lea	GP	G	A	TP	PIM	GP	G	A	TP	PIM
1990-91	Spokane	WHL	71	39	38	77	86	15	5	13	18	6
1991-92	Spokane	WHL	58	28	32	60	110	10	6	7	13	18
1992-93	Capital Dist.	AHL	79	16	31	47	20	4	0	0	0	0
	NY Islanders	**NHL**	....	....	....	....	....	3	0	1	1	0
1993-94	**NY Islanders**	**NHL**	5	0	0	0	0	....	....	....	....	....
	Salt Lake	IHL	71	9	14	23	36	....	....	....	....	....
1994-95	Denver	IHL	72	13	16	29	37	11	3	4	7	4
	NHL Totals		**5**	**0**	**0**	**0**	**0**	**3**	**0**	**1**	**1**	**0**

JUNKIN, DALE   HFD.

Left wing. Shoots left. 5'11", 196 lbs.   Born, Oshawa, Ont., May 23, 1973.

				Regular Season					Playoffs			
Season	Club	Lea	GP	G	A	TP	PIM	GP	G	A	TP	PIM
1990-91	Kingston	OHL	63	6	7	13	28	....	....	....	....	....
1991-92	Niagara Falls	OHL	62	20	19	39	22	17	4	4	8	12
1992-93	Niagara Falls	OHL	65	29	49	78	50	4	1	3	4	0
1993-94	Detroit	OHL	64	41	35	76	45	17	13	13	26	6
1994-95	Springfield	AHL	63	11	13	24	30	....	....	....	....	....

Signed as a free agent by **Hartford**, April 11, 1995.

KACIR, MARIAN   T.B.

Right wing. Shoots left. 6'1", 183 lbs.   Born, Hodonin, Czech., September 29, 1974.
(Tampa Bay's 4th choice, 81st overall, in 1993 Entry Draft).

				Regular Season					Playoffs			
Season	Club	Lea	GP	G	A	TP	PIM	GP	G	A	TP	PIM
1992-93	Owen Sound	OHL	56	20	36	56	8	8	3	5	8	4
1993-94	Owen Sound	OHL	66	23	64	87	26	9	5	4	9	2
1994-95	Charlotte	ECHL	5	2	3	5	2	....	....	....	....	....
	Nashville	ECHL	9	1	7	8	2	4	1	2	3	6
	Chicago	IHL	29	4	6	10	6	....	....	....	....	....

KALLIO, TOMI   COL.

Left wing. Shoots left. 6'1", 176 lbs.   Born, Turku, Finland, January 27, 1977.
(Colorado's 4th choice, 81st overall, in 1995 Entry Draft).

				Regular Season					Playoffs			
Season	Club	Lea	GP	G	A	TP	PIM	GP	G	A	TP	PIM
1994-95	Kiekko-67	Fin. 2	25	8	5	13	16	7	3	1	4	6
	TPS	Fin. Jr.	14	5	12	17	24	....	....	....	....	....

KAMENSKY, VALERI   (kah-MEHN-skee)   COL.

Left wing. Shoots right. 6'2", 198 lbs.   Born, Voskresensk, USSR, April 18, 1966.
(Quebec's 8th choice, 129th overall, in 1988 Entry Draft).

				Regular Season					Playoffs			
Season	Club	Lea	GP	G	A	TP	PIM	GP	G	A	TP	PIM
1982-83	Khimik	USSR	5	0	0	0	0	....	....	....	....	....
1983-84	Khimik	USSR	20	2	2	4	6	....	....	....	....	....
1984-85	Khimik	USSR	45	9	3	12	24	....	....	....	....	....
1985-86	CSKA	USSR	40	15	9	24	8	....	....	....	....	....
1986-87	CSKA	USSR	37	13	8	21	16	....	....	....	....	....
1987-88	CSKA	USSR	51	26	20	46	40	....	....	....	....	....
1988-89	CSKA	USSR	40	18	10	28	30	....	....	....	....	....
1989-90	CSKA	USSR	45	19	18	37	40	....	....	....	....	....
1990-91	CSKA	USSR	46	20	26	46	66	....	....	....	....	....
1991-92	**Quebec**	**NHL**	23	7	14	21	14	....	....	....	....	....
1992-93	**Quebec**	**NHL**	32	15	22	37	14	6	0	1	1	6
1993-94	**Quebec**	**NHL**	76	28	37	65	42	....	....	....	....	....
1994-95	Ambri	Switz.	12	13	6	19	2	....	....	....	....	....
	Quebec	**NHL**	40	10	20	30	22	2	1	0	1	0
	NHL Totals		**171**	**60**	**93**	**153**	**92**	**8**	**1**	**1**	**2**	**6**

KAMINSKI, KEVIN (kah-MIN-skee) WSH.

Center. Shoots left. 5'10", 190 lbs. Born, Churchbridge, Sask., March 13, 1969.
(Minnesota's 3rd choice, 48th overall, in 1987 Entry Draft).

			Regular Season					Playoffs				
Season	**Club**	**Lea**	**GP**	**G**	**A**	**TP**	**PIM**	**GP**	**G**	**A**	**TP**	**PIM**
1986-87	Saskatoon	WHL	67	26	44	70	325	11	5	6	11	45
1987-88	Saskatoon	WHL	55	38	61	99	247	10	5	7	12	37
1988-89	**Minnesota**	**NHL**	**1**	**0**	**0**	**0**	**0**	....	....	....	....	....
	Saskatoon	WHL	52	25	43	68	199	8	4	9	13	25
1989-90	**Quebec**	**NHL**	**1**	**0**	**0**	**0**	**0**	....	....	....	....	....
	Halifax	AHL	19	3	4	7	128	2	0	0	0	5
1990-91	Halifax	AHL	7	1	0	1	44	....	....	....	....	....
	Fort Wayne	IHL	56	9	15	24	*455	19	4	2	6	*169
1991-92	**Quebec**	**NHL**	**5**	**0**	**0**	**0**	**45**	....	....	....	....	....
	Halifax	AHL	63	18	27	45	329	....	....	....	....	....
1992-93	Halifax	AHL	79	27	37	64	*345	....	....	....	....	....
1993-94	**Washington**	**NHL**	**13**	**0**	**5**	**5**	**87**	....	....	....	....	....
	Portland	AHL	39	10	22	32	263	16	4	5	9	*91
1994-95	Portland	AHL	34	15	20	35	292	....	....	....	....	....
	Washington	**NHL**	**27**	**1**	**1**	**2**	**102**	**5**	**0**	**0**	**0**	**36**
	NHL Totals		**47**	**1**	**6**	**7**	**234**	**5**	**0**	**0**	**0**	**36**

Traded to **Quebec** by **Minnesota** for Gaetan Duchesne, June 19, 1989. Traded to **Washington** by **Quebec** for Mark Matier, June 15, 1993.

KAMINSKY, YAN (kah-MEHN-skee) NYI

Right wing. Shoots left. 6'1", 176 lbs. Born, Penza, USSR, July 28, 1971.
(Winnipeg's 4th choice, 99th overall, in 1991 Entry Draft).

			Regular Season					Playoffs				
Season	**Club**	**Lea**	**GP**	**G**	**A**	**TP**	**PIM**	**GP**	**G**	**A**	**TP**	**PIM**
1989-90	Moscow D'amo	USSR	6	1	0	1	4	....	....	....	....	....
1990-91	Moscow D'amo	USSR	25	10	5	15	2	....	....	....	....	....
1991-92	Moscow D'amo	CIS	42	9	7	16	22	....	....	....	....	....
1992-93	Moscow D'amo	CIS	39	15	14	29	12	10	2	5	7	8
1993-94	**Winnipeg**	**NHL**	**1**	**0**	**0**	**0**	**0**	....	....	....	....	....
	Moncton	AHL	33	9	13	22	6	....	....	....	....	....
	NY Islanders	**NHL**	**23**	**2**	**1**	**3**	**4**	**2**	**0**	**0**	**0**	**4**
1994-95	Denver	IHL	38	17	16	33	14	15	6	6	12	0
	NY Islanders	**NHL**	**2**	**1**	**1**	**2**	**0**	....	....	....	....	....
	NHL Totals		**26**	**3**	**2**	**5**	**4**	**2**	**0**	**0**	**0**	**4**

Traded to **NY Islanders** by **Winnipeg** for Wayne McBean, February 1, 1994.

KAPANEN, SAMI HFD.

Left wing. Shoots left. 5'10", 169 lbs. Born, Vantaa, Finland, June 14, 1973.
(Hartford's 4th choice, 87th overall, in 1995 Entry Draft).

			Regular Season					Playoffs				
Season	**Club**	**Lea**	**GP**	**G**	**A**	**TP**	**PIM**	**GP**	**G**	**A**	**TP**	**PIM**
1990-91	KalPa	Fin.	14	1	2	3	2	8	2	1	3	2
1991-92	KalPa	Fin.	42	15	10	25	8	....	....	....	....	....
1992-93	KalPa	Fin.	37	4	17	21	12	....	....	....	....	....
1993-94	KalPa	Fin.	48	23	32	55	16	....	....	....	....	....
1994-95	HIFK	Fin.	49	14	28	42	42	3	0	0	0	0

KARABIN, LADISLAV (kar-ah-BIN)

Left wing. Shoots left. 6'1", 189 lbs. Born, Spisska Nova Ves, Czech., February 16, 1970.
(Pittsburgh's 11th choice, 173rd overall, in 1990 Entry Draft).

			Regular Season					Playoffs				
Season	**Club**	**Lea**	**GP**	**G**	**A**	**TP**	**PIM**	**GP**	**G**	**A**	**TP**	**PIM**
1988-89	Bratislava	Czech.	31	7	2	9	10	....	....	....	....	....
1989-90	Bratislava	Czech. 2				UNAVAILABLE						
1990-91	Bratislava	Czech.	49	21	7	28	57	....	....	....	....	....
1991-92	Bratislava	Czech.	27	4	8	12	10	....	....	....	....	....
1992-93	Bratislava	Czech.	39	21	23	44	....	....	....	....	....	....
1993-94	**Pittsburgh**	**NHL**	**9**	**0**	**0**	**0**	**2**	....	....	....	....	....
	Cleveland	IHL	58	13	26	39	48	....	....	....	....	....
1994-95	Cleveland	IHL	47	15	25	40	26	4	0	0	0	2
	NHL Totals		**9**	**0**	**0**	**0**	**2**	....	....	....	....	....

KARALAHTI, JERE L.A.

Defense. Shoots right. 6'2", 185 lbs. Born, Helsinki, Finland, March 25, 1975.
(Los Angeles' 7th choice, 146th overall, in 1993 Entry Draft).

			Regular Season					Playoffs				
Season	**Club**	**Lea**	**GP**	**G**	**A**	**TP**	**PIM**	**GP**	**G**	**A**	**TP**	**PIM**
1993-94	HIFK	Fin.	46	1	10	11	36	3	0	0	0	6
1994-95	HIFK	Fin.	37	1	7	8	42	3	0	0	0	0

KARAMNOV, VITALI (kuh-RAHM-nov)

Left wing. Shoots left. 6'2", 185 lbs. Born, Moscow, USSR, July 6, 1968.
(St. Louis' 2nd choice, 62nd overall, in 1992 Entry Draft).

			Regular Season					Playoffs				
Season	**Club**	**Lea**	**GP**	**G**	**A**	**TP**	**PIM**	**GP**	**G**	**A**	**TP**	**PIM**
1986-87	Moscow D'amo	USSR	4	0	0	0	0	....	....	....	....	....
1987-88	Moscow D'amo	USSR	2	0	1	1	0	....	....	....	....	....
1988-89	D'amo Kharkov	USSR	23	4	1	5	19	....	....	....	....	....
1989-90	Torpedo Yaro.	USSR	47	6	7	13	32	....	....	....	....	....
1990-91	Torpedo Yaro.	USSR	45	14	7	21	30	....	....	....	....	....
1991-92	Moscow D'amo	CIS	40	13	19	32	25	....	....	....	....	....
1992-93	**St. Louis**	**NHL**	**7**	**0**	**1**	**1**	**0**	....	....	....	....	....
	Peoria	IHL	23	8	12	20	47	....	....	....	....	....
1993-94	**St. Louis**	**NHL**	**59**	**9**	**12**	**21**	**51**	....	....	....	....	....
	Peoria	IHL	3	0	1	1	2	1	0	1	1	0
1994-95	Peoria	IHL	15	6	9	15	7	....	....	....	....	....
	St. Louis	**NHL**	**26**	**3**	**7**	**10**	**14**	**2**	**0**	**0**	**0**	**2**
	NHL Totals		**92**	**12**	**20**	**32**	**65**	**2**	**0**	**0**	**0**	**2**

KARIYA, PAUL (kah-REE-ah) ANA.

Left wing. Shoots left. 5'11", 175 lbs. Born, Vancouver, B.C., October 16, 1974.
(Anaheim's 1st choice, 4th overall, in 1993 Entry Draft).

			Regular Season					Playoffs				
Season	**Club**	**Lea**	**GP**	**G**	**A**	**TP**	**PIM**	**GP**	**G**	**A**	**TP**	**PIM**
1992-93abcd	U. of Maine	H.E.	36	24	*69	*93	12	....	....	....	....	....
1993-94	U. of Maine	H.E.	12	8	16	24	4	....	....	....	....	....
	Cdn. National	....	23	7	34	41	2	....	....	....	....	....
	Cdn. Olympic	....	8	3	4	7	2	....	....	....	....	....
1994-95e	**Anaheim**	**NHL**	**47**	**18**	**21**	**39**	**4**	....	....	....	....	....
	NHL Totals		**47**	**18**	**21**	**39**	**4**	....	....	....	....	....

a Hockey East First All-Star Team (1993)
b NCAA East First All-American Team (1993)
c NCAA Final Four All-Tournament Team (1993)
d Won Hobey Baker Memorial Award (Top U.S. Collegiate Player) (1993)
e NHL/Upper Deck All-Rookie Team (1995)

KARLSSON, ANDREAS CGY.

Center. Shoots left. 6'2", 180 lbs. Born, Leksand, Sweden, August 19, 1975.
(Calgary's 8th choice, 148th overall, in 1993 Entry Draft).

			Regular Season					Playoffs				
Season	**Club**	**Lea**	**GP**	**G**	**A**	**TP**	**PIM**	**GP**	**G**	**A**	**TP**	**PIM**
1992-93	Leksand	Swe.	13	0	0	0	6	....	....	....	....	....
1993-94	Leksand	Swe.	21	0	0	0	10	3	0	0	0	0
1994-95	Leksand	Swe.	24	7	8	15	0	4	0	1	1	0

KARPA, DAVE ANA.

Defense. Shoots right. 6'1", 202 lbs. Born, Regina, Sask., May 7, 1971.
(Quebec's 4th choice, 68th overall, in 1991 Entry Draft).

			Regular Season					Playoffs				
Season	**Club**	**Lea**	**GP**	**G**	**A**	**TP**	**PIM**	**GP**	**G**	**A**	**TP**	**PIM**
1990-91	Ferris State	CCHA	41	6	19	25	109	....	....	....	....	....
1991-92	Ferris State	CCHA	34	7	12	19	124	....	....	....	....	....
	Quebec	**NHL**	**4**	**0**	**0**	**0**	**14**	....	....	....	....	....
	Halifax	AHL	2	0	0	0	4	....	....	....	....	....
1992-93	**Quebec**	**NHL**	**12**	**0**	**1**	**1**	**13**	**3**	**0**	**0**	**0**	**0**
	Halifax	AHL	71	4	27	31	167	....	....	....	....	....
1993-94	**Quebec**	**NHL**	**60**	**5**	**12**	**17**	**148**	....	....	....	....	....
	Cornwall	AHL	1	0	0	0	0	12	2	2	4	27
1994-95	**Quebec**	**NHL**	**2**	**0**	**0**	**0**	**0**	....	....	....	....	....
	Cornwall	AHL	6	0	2	2	19	....	....	....	....	....
	Anaheim	**NHL**	**26**	**1**	**5**	**6**	**91**	....	....	....	....	....
	NHL Totals		**104**	**6**	**18**	**24**	**266**	**3**	**0**	**0**	**0**	**0**

Traded to **Anaheim** by **Quebec** for Anaheim's fourth round choice in 1997 Entry Draft, March 9, 1995.

KARPOV, VALERI (KAHR-pahf) ANA.

Right wing. Shoots left. 5'10", 176 lbs. Born, Chelyabinsk, USSR, August 5, 1971.
(Anaheim's 3rd choice, 56th overall, in 1993 Entry Draft).

			Regular Season					Playoffs				
Season	**Club**	**Lea**	**GP**	**G**	**A**	**TP**	**PIM**	**GP**	**G**	**A**	**TP**	**PIM**
1988-89	Chelyabinsk	USSR	5	0	0	0	0	....	....	....	....	....
1989-90	Chelyabinsk	USSR	24	1	2	3	6	....	....	....	....	....
1990-91	Chelyabinsk	USSR	25	8	4	12	15	....	....	....	....	....
1991-92	Chelyabinsk	CIS	44	16	10	26	34	....	....	....	....	....
1992-93	CSKA	CIS	9	2	6	8	0	....	....	....	....	....
a	Chelyabinsk	CIS	29	10	15	25	6	8	0	1	1	10
1993-94	Chelyabinsk	CIS	32	13	16	29	....	6	2	5	7	2
1994-95	Chelyabinsk	CIS	10	6	8	14	8	....	....	....	....	....
	Anaheim	**NHL**	**30**	**4**	**7**	**11**	**6**	....	....	....	....	....
	San Diego	IHL	5	3	3	6	0	....	....	....	....	....
	NHL Totals		**30**	**4**	**7**	**11**	**6**	....	....	....	....	....

a CIS All-Star Team (1993)

KARPOVTSEV, ALEXANDER (kar-POHV-tzehv) NYR

Defense. Shoots right. 6'1", 200 lbs. Born, Moscow, USSR, April 7, 1970.
(Quebec's 7th choice, 158th overall, in 1990 Entry Draft).

			Regular Season					Playoffs				
Season	**Club**	**Lea**	**GP**	**G**	**A**	**TP**	**PIM**	**GP**	**G**	**A**	**TP**	**PIM**
1987-88	Moscow D'amo	USSR	2	0	1	1	10	....	....	....	....	....
1989-90	Moscow D'amo	USSR	35	1	1	2	27	....	....	....	....	....
1990-91	Moscow D'amo	USSR	40	0	5	5	15	....	....	....	....	....
1991-92	Moscow D'amo	CIS	35	4	2	6	26	....	....	....	....	....
1992-93	Moscow D'amo	CIS	36	3	11	14	100	7	2	1	3	0
1993-94	**NY Rangers**	**NHL**	**67**	**3**	**15**	**18**	**58**	**17**	**0**	**4**	**4**	**12**
1994-95	Moscow D'amo	CIS	13	0	2	2	10	....	....	....	....	....
	NY Rangers	**NHL**	**47**	**4**	**8**	**12**	**30**	**8**	**1**	**0**	**1**	**0**
	NHL Totals		**114**	**7**	**23**	**30**	**88**	**25**	**1**	**4**	**5**	**12**

Traded to **NY Rangers** by **Quebec** for Mike Hurlbut, September 7, 1993.

KASATONOV, ALEXEI (kah-sah-TOH-nahf) BOS.

Defense. Shoots left. 6'1", 215 lbs. Born, Leningrad, USSR, October 14, 1959.
(New Jersey's 10th choice, 225th overall, in 1983 Entry Draft).

			Regular Season					Playoffs				
Season	**Club**	**Lea**	**GP**	**G**	**A**	**TP**	**PIM**	**GP**	**G**	**A**	**TP**	**PIM**
1976-77	SKA Leningrad	USSR	7	0	0	0	0	....	....	....	....	....
1977-78	SKA Leningrad	USSR	35	4	7	11	15	....	....	....	....	....
1978-79	CSKA	USSR	40	5	14	19	30	....	....	....	....	....
1979-80a	CSKA	USSR	37	5	8	13	26	....	....	....	....	....
1980-81a	CSKA	USSR	47	10	12	22	38	....	....	....	....	....
1981-82a	CSKA	USSR	46	12	27	39	45	....	....	....	....	....
1982-83a	CSKA	USSR	44	12	19	31	37	....	....	....	....	....
1983-84a	CSKA	USSR	39	12	24	36	20	....	....	....	....	....
1984-85a	CSKA	USSR	40	18	18	36	26	....	....	....	....	....
1985-86a	CSKA	USSR	40	6	17	23	27	....	....	....	....	....
1986-87a	CSKA	USSR	40	13	17	30	16	....	....	....	....	....
1987-88a	CSKA	USSR	43	8	12	20	8	....	....	....	....	....
1988-89	CSKA	USSR	41	8	14	22	8	....	....	....	....	....
1989-90	CSKA	USSR	30	6	7	13	16	....	....	....	....	....
	New Jersey	**NHL**	**39**	**6**	**15**	**21**	**16**	**6**	**0**	**3**	**3**	**14**
	Utica	AHL	3	0	2	2	7	....	....	....	....	....
1990-91	**New Jersey**	**NHL**	**78**	**10**	**31**	**41**	**76**	**7**	**1**	**3**	**4**	**10**
1991-92	**New Jersey**	**NHL**	**76**	**12**	**28**	**40**	**70**	**7**	**1**	**1**	**2**	**12**
1992-93	**New Jersey**	**NHL**	**64**	**3**	**14**	**17**	**57**	**4**	**0**	**0**	**0**	**0**
1993-94	**Anaheim**	**NHL**	**55**	**4**	**18**	**22**	**43**	....	....	....	....	....
	St. Louis	**NHL**	**8**	**0**	**2**	**2**	**19**	**4**	**2**	**0**	**2**	**2**
1994-95	CSKA	CIS	9	2	3	5	6	....	....	....	....	....
	Boston	**NHL**	**44**	**2**	**14**	**16**	**33**	**5**	**0**	**0**	**0**	**2**
	NHL Totals		**364**	**37**	**122**	**159**	**314**	**33**	**4**	**7**	**11**	**40**

a Soviet National League All-Star Team (1980-88)
Played in NHL All-Star Game (1994)

Claimed by **Anaheim** from **New Jersey** in Expansion Draft, June 24, 1993. Traded to **St. Louis** by **Anaheim** for Maxim Bets and St. Louis' sixth round choice (later traded back to St. Louis — St. Louis selected Denis Hamel) in 1995 Entry Draft, March 21, 1994. Signed as a free agent by **Boston**, June 22, 1994.

KASPARAITIS, DARIUS (KAZ-puhr-IGH-tihz) NYI

Defense. Shoots left. 5'11", 195 lbs. Born, Elektrenai, USSR, October 16, 1972.
(NY Islanders' 1st choice, 5th overall, in 1992 Entry Draft).

			Regular Season					Playoffs				
Season	Club	Lea	GP	G	A	TP	PIM	GP	G	A	TP	PIM
1988-89	Moscow D'amo	USSR	3	0	0	0	0	....	....	....	....	....
1989-90	Moscow D'amo	USSR	1	0	0	0	0	....	....	....	....	....
1990-91	Moscow D'amo	USSR	17	0	1	1	10	....	....	....	....	....
1991-92	Moscow D'amo	CIS	31	2	10	12	14	....	....	....	....	....
1992-93	Moscow D'amo	CIS	7	1	3	4	8	....	....	....	....	....
	NY Islanders	**NHL**	**79**	**4**	**17**	**21**	**166**	**18**	**0**	**5**	**5**	**31**
1993-94	**NY Islanders**	**NHL**	**76**	**1**	**10**	**11**	**142**	**4**	**0**	**0**	**0**	**8**
1994-95	**NY Islanders**	**NHL**	**13**	**0**	**1**	**1**	**22**	....	....	....	....	....
	NHL Totals		**168**	**5**	**28**	**33**	**330**	**22**	**0**	**5**	**5**	**39**

KAZAKEVICH, MIKHAIL PIT.

Left wing. Shoots left. 6'1", 187 lbs. Born, Murmansk, USSR, January 14, 1976.
(Pittsburgh's 13th choice, 258th overall, in 1994 Entry Draft).

			Regular Season					Playoffs				
Season	Club	Lea	GP	G	A	TP	PIM	GP	G	A	TP	PIM
1992-93	Yaroslavl	CIS	7	0	1	1	0	3	0	0	0	0
1993-94	Yaroslavl	CIS	4	0	0	0	2	....	....	....	....	....
1994-95	Yaroslavl	CIS	11	1	3	4	2	....	....	....	....	....

KEALTY, JEFF COL.

Defense. Shoots left. 6'4", 175 lbs. Born, Boston, MA, April 9, 1976.
(Quebec's 2nd choice, 22nd overall, in 1994 Entry Draft).

			Regular Season					Playoffs				
Season	Club	Lea	GP	G	A	TP	PIM	GP	G	A	TP	PIM
1993-94	Catholic Mem.	HS	25	10	22	32	....	....	....	....	....	....
1994-95	Boston U.	H.E.	25	0	5	5	29	....	....	....	....	....

KEANE, MIKE MTL.

Right wing. Shoots right. 5'10", 185 lbs. Born, Winnipeg, Man., May 29, 1967.

			Regular Season					Playoffs				
Season	Club	Lea	GP	G	A	TP	PIM	GP	G	A	TP	PIM
1984-85	Moose Jaw	WHL	65	17	26	43	141	....	....	....	....	....
1985-86	Moose Jaw	WHL	67	34	49	83	162	13	6	8	14	9
1986-87	Moose Jaw	WHL	53	25	45	70	107	9	3	9	12	11
	Sherbrooke	AHL	....	....	....	....	....	9	2	2	4	16
1987-88	Sherbrooke	AHL	78	25	43	68	70	6	1	1	2	18
1988-89	**Montreal**	**NHL**	**69**	**16**	**19**	**35**	**69**	**21**	**4**	**3**	**7**	**17**
1989-90	**Montreal**	**NHL**	**74**	**9**	**15**	**24**	**78**	**11**	**0**	**1**	**1**	**8**
1990-91	**Montreal**	**NHL**	**73**	**13**	**23**	**36**	**50**	**12**	**3**	**2**	**5**	**6**
1991-92	**Montreal**	**NHL**	**67**	**11**	**30**	**41**	**64**	**8**	**1**	**1**	**2**	**16**
1992-93	**Montreal**	**NHL**	**77**	**15**	**45**	**60**	**95**	**19**	**2**	**13**	**15**	**6**
1993-94	**Montreal**	**NHL**	**80**	**16**	**30**	**46**	**119**	**6**	**3**	**1**	**4**	**4**
1994-95	**Montreal**	**NHL**	**48**	**10**	**10**	**20**	**15**	....	....	....	....	....
	NHL Totals		**488**	**90**	**172**	**262**	**490**	**77**	**13**	**21**	**34**	**57**

Signed as a free agent by **Montreal**, September 25, 1985.

KECZMER, DAN (KEHS-muhr)

Defense. Shoots left. 6'1", 190 lbs. Born, Mt. Clemens, MI, May 25, 1968.
(Minnesota's 11th choice, 201st overall, in 1986 Entry Draft).

			Regular Season					Playoffs				
Season	Club	Lea	GP	G	A	TP	PIM	GP	G	A	TP	PIM
1986-87	Lake Superior	CCHA	38	3	5	8	26	....	....	....	....	....
1987-88	Lake Superior	CCHA	41	2	15	17	34	....	....	....	....	....
1988-89	Lake Superior	CCHA	46	3	26	29	68	....	....	....	....	....
1989-90a	Lake Superior	CCHA	43	13	23	36	48	....	....	....	....	....
1990-91	**Minnesota**	**NHL**	**9**	**0**	**1**	**1**	**6**	....	....	....	....	....
	Kalamazoo	IHL	60	4	20	24	60	9	1	2	3	10
1991-92	U.S. National	....	51	3	11	14	56	....	....	....	....	....
	Hartford	**NHL**	**1**	**0**	**0**	**0**	**0**	....	....	....	....	....
	Springfield	AHL	18	3	4	7	10	4	0	0	0	6
1992-93	**Hartford**	**NHL**	**23**	**4**	**4**	**8**	**28**	....	....	....	....	....
	Springfield	AHL	37	1	13	14	38	12	0	4	4	14
1993-94	**Hartford**	**NHL**	**12**	**0**	**1**	**1**	**12**	....	....	....	....	....
	Springfield	AHL	7	0	1	1	4	....	....	....	....	....
	Calgary	**NHL**	**57**	**1**	**20**	**21**	**48**	**3**	**0**	**0**	**0**	**4**
1994-95	**Calgary**	**NHL**	**28**	**2**	**3**	**5**	**10**	**7**	**0**	**1**	**1**	**2**
	NHL Totals		**130**	**7**	**29**	**36**	**104**	**10**	**0**	**1**	**1**	**6**

a CCHA Second All-Star Team (1990)

Claimed by **San Jose** from **Minnesota** in Dispersal Draft, May 30, 1991. Traded to **Hartford** by **San Jose** for Dean Evason, October 2, 1991. Traded to **Calgary** by **Hartford** for Jeff Reese, November 19, 1993.

KELLEHER, CHRIS PIT.

Defense. Shoots left. 6'1", 215 lbs. Born, Cambridge, MA, March 23, 1975.
(Pittsburgh's 5th choice, 130th overall, in 1993 Entry Draft).

			Regular Season					Playoffs				
Season	Club	Lea	GP	G	A	TP	PIM	GP	G	A	TP	PIM
1993-94	St. Sebastian's	HS	24	10	21	31	....	....	....	....	....	....
1994-95	Boston U.	H.E.	35	3	17	20	62	....	....	....	....	....

KELLEY, JONATHAN TOR.

Center. Shoots right. 6', 180 lbs. Born, Brighton, MA, June 25, 1973.
(Toronto's 12th choice, 223rd overall, in 1991 Entry Draft).

			Regular Season					Playoffs				
Season	Club	Lea	GP	G	A	TP	PIM	GP	G	A	TP	PIM
1992-93	Princeton	ECAC	23	4	3	7	34	....	....	....	....	....
1993-94	Princeton	ECAC	28	6	13	19	41	....	....	....	....	....
1994-95	Princeton	ECAC	33	24	16	40	55	....	....	....	....	....

KELLOGG, BOB

Defense. Shoots left. 6'4", 210 lbs. Born, Springfield, MA, February 16, 1971.
(Chicago's 3rd choice, 48th overall, in 1989 Entry Draft).

			Regular Season					Playoffs				
Season	Club	Lea	GP	G	A	TP	PIM	GP	G	A	TP	PIM
1989-90	Northeastern	H.E.	36	3	12	15	30	....	....	....	....	....
1990-91	Northeastern	H.E.	2	0	0	0	6	....	....	....	....	....
1991-92	Northeastern	H.E.	27	2	3	5	34	....	....	....	....	....
1992-93	Northeastern	H.E.	35	5	15	20	44	....	....	....	....	....
1993-94	Indianapolis	IHL	68	6	13	19	63	....	....	....	....	....
1994-95	Indianapolis	IHL	51	3	6	9	30	....	....	....	....	....

KELLY, STEVE EDM.

Center. Shoots left. 6'1", 190 lbs. Born, Vancouver, B.C., October 26, 1976.
(Edmonton's 1st choice, 6th overall, in 1995 Entry Draft).

			Regular Season					Playoffs				
Season	Club	Lea	GP	G	A	TP	PIM	GP	G	A	TP	PIM
1992-93	Prince Albert	WHL	65	11	9	20	75	....	....	....	....	....
1993-94	Prince Albert	WHL	65	19	42	61	106	....	....	....	....	....
1994-95	Prince Albert	WHL	68	31	41	72	153	15	7	9	16	35

KELMAN, TODD ST.L.

Defense. Shoots left. 6'1", 190 lbs. Born, Calgary, Alta., January 5, 1975.
(St. Louis' 4th choice, 141st overall, in 1993 Entry Draft).

			Regular Season					Playoffs				
Season	Club	Lea	GP	G	A	TP	PIM	GP	G	A	TP	PIM
1993-94	Bowling Green	CCHA	18	0	2	2	12	....	....	....	....	....
1994-95	Bowling Green	CCHA	37	2	5	7	20	....	....	....	....	....

KENADY, CHRIS ST.L.

Right wing. Shoots right. 6'2", 195 lbs. Born, Mound, MN, April 10, 1973.
(St. Louis' 8th choice, 175th overall, in 1991 Entry Draft).

			Regular Season					Playoffs				
Season	Club	Lea	GP	G	A	TP	PIM	GP	G	A	TP	PIM
1991-92	U. of Denver	WCHA	36	8	5	13	56	....	....	....	....	....
1992-93	U. of Denver	WCHA	38	8	16	24	95	....	....	....	....	....
1993-94	U. of Denver	WCHA	37	14	11	25	125	....	....	....	....	....
1994-95	U. of Denver	WCHA	39	21	17	38	113	....	....	....	....	....

KENNEDY, DEAN EDM.

Defense. Shoots right. 6'2", 208 lbs. Born, Redvers, Sask., January 18, 1963.
(Los Angeles' 2nd choice, 39th overall, in 1981 Entry Draft).

			Regular Season					Playoffs				
Season	Club	Lea	GP	G	A	TP	PIM	GP	G	A	TP	PIM
1980-81	Brandon	WHL	71	3	29	32	157	5	0	2	2	7
1981-82	Brandon	WHL	49	5	38	43	103	....	....	....	....	....
1982-83	**Los Angeles**	**NHL**	**55**	**0**	**12**	**12**	**97**	....	....	....	....	....
	Brandon	WHL	14	2	15	17	22	....	....	....	....	....
	Saskatoon	WHL	....	....	....	....	....	4	0	3	3	0
1983-84	**Los Angeles**	**NHL**	**37**	**1**	**5**	**6**	**50**	....	....	....	....	....
	New Haven	AHL	26	1	7	8	23	....	....	....	....	....
1984-85	New Haven	AHL	76	3	14	17	104	....	....	....	....	....
1985-86	**Los Angeles**	**NHL**	**78**	**2**	**10**	**12**	**132**	....	....	....	....	....
1986-87	**Los Angeles**	**NHL**	**66**	**6**	**14**	**20**	**91**	**5**	**0**	**2**	**2**	**10**
1987-88	**Los Angeles**	**NHL**	**58**	**1**	**11**	**12**	**158**	**4**	**0**	**1**	**1**	**10**
1988-89	**NY Rangers**	**NHL**	**16**	**0**	**1**	**1**	**40**	....	....	....	....	....
	Los Angeles	**NHL**	**51**	**3**	**10**	**13**	**63**	**11**	**0**	**2**	**2**	**8**
1989-90	**Buffalo**	**NHL**	**80**	**2**	**12**	**14**	**53**	**6**	**1**	**1**	**2**	**12**
1990-91	**Buffalo**	**NHL**	**64**	**4**	**8**	**12**	**119**	**2**	**0**	**1**	**1**	**17**
1991-92	**Winnipeg**	**NHL**	**18**	**2**	**4**	**6**	**21**	**2**	**0**	**0**	**0**	**0**
1992-93	**Winnipeg**	**NHL**	**78**	**1**	**7**	**8**	**105**	**6**	**0**	**0**	**0**	**2**
1993-94	**Winnipeg**	**NHL**	**76**	**2**	**8**	**10**	**164**	....	....	....	....	....
1994-95	**Edmonton**	**NHL**	**40**	**2**	**8**	**10**	**25**	....	....	....	....	....
	NHL Totals		**717**	**26**	**110**	**136**	**1118**	**36**	**1**	**7**	**8**	**59**

Traded to **NY Rangers** by **Los Angeles** with Denis Larocque for Igor Liba, Michael Boyce, Todd Elik and future considerations, December 12, 1988. Traded to **Los Angeles** by **NY Rangers** for Los Angeles' fourth round choice — later traded to Minnesota (Cal McGowan) — in 1990 Entry Draft, February 3, 1989. Traded to **Buffalo** by **Los Angeles** for Buffalo's fourth round choice (Keith Redmond) in 1991 Entry Draft, October 4, 1989. Traded to **Winnipeg** by **Buffalo** with Darrin Shannon and Mike Hartman for Dave McLlwain, Gord Donnelly, Winnipeg's fifth round choice (Yuri Khmylev) in 1992 Entry Draft and future considerations, October 11, 1991. Claimed by **Edmonton** from **Winnipeg** in NHL Waiver Draft, January 18, 1995.

KENNEDY, MIKE DAL.

Center. Shoots right. 6'1", 170 lbs. Born, Vancouver, B.C., April 13, 1972.
(Minnesota's 5th choice, 97th overall, in 1991 Entry Draft).

			Regular Season					Playoffs				
Season	Club	Lea	GP	G	A	TP	PIM	GP	G	A	TP	PIM
1989-90	U.B.C.	CIAU	9	5	7	12	0	....	....	....	....	....
1990-91	U.B.C.	CIAU	28	17	17	34	18	....	....	....	....	....
1991-92a	Seattle	WHL	71	42	47	89	134	15	11	6	17	20
1992-93	Kalamazoo	IHL	77	21	30	51	39	....	....	....	....	....
1993-94	Kalamazoo	IHL	63	20	18	38	42	3	1	2	3	2
1994-95	Kalamazoo	IHL	42	20	28	48	29	....	....	....	....	....
	Dallas	**NHL**	**44**	**6**	**12**	**18**	**33**	**5**	**0**	**0**	**0**	**9**
	NHL Totals		**44**	**6**	**12**	**18**	**33**	**5**	**0**	**0**	**0**	**9**

a WHL West Second All-Star Team (1982)

KENNEDY, SHELDON CGY.

Right wing. Shoots right. 5'10", 180 lbs. Born, Elkhorn, Man., June 15, 1969.
(Detroit's 5th choice, 80th overall, in 1988 Entry Draft).

			Regular Season					Playoffs				
Season	Club	Lea	GP	G	A	TP	PIM	GP	G	A	TP	PIM
1986-87	Swift Current	WHL	49	23	41	64	43	4	0	3	3	4
1987-88	Swift Current	WHL	59	53	64	117	45	10	8	9	17	12
1988-89a	Swift Current	WHL	51	58	48	106	92	12	9	15	24	22
1989-90	**Detroit**	**NHL**	**20**	**2**	**7**	**9**	**10**	....	....	....	....	....
	Adirondack	AHL	26	11	15	26	35	....	....	....	....	....
1990-91	**Detroit**	**NHL**	**7**	**1**	**0**	**1**	**12**	....	....	....	....	....
	Adirondack	AHL	11	1	3	4	8	....	....	....	....	....
1991-92	**Detroit**	**NHL**	**27**	**3**	**8**	**11**	**24**	....	....	....	....	....
	Adirondack	AHL	46	25	24	49	56	16	5	9	14	12
1992-93	**Detroit**	**NHL**	**68**	**19**	**11**	**30**	**46**	**7**	**1**	**1**	**2**	**2**
1993-94	**Detroit**	**NHL**	**61**	**6**	**7**	**13**	**30**	**7**	**1**	**2**	**3**	**0**
1994-95	**Calgary**	**NHL**	**30**	**7**	**8**	**15**	**45**	**7**	**3**	**1**	**4**	**16**
	NHL Totals		**213**	**38**	**41**	**79**	**167**	**21**	**5**	**4**	**9**	**18**

a Memorial Cup All-Star Team (1989)

Traded to **Winnipeg** by **Detroit** for Winnipeg's third round choice (Darryl Laplante) in 1995 Entry Draft, May 25, 1994. Claimed by **Calgary** from **Winnipeg** in NHL Waiver Draft, January 18, 1995.

KENNEY, JAY OTT.

Defense. Shoots left. 6'2", 190 lbs. Born, New York, NY, September 21, 1973.
(Ottawa's 8th choice, 169th overall, in 1992 Entry Draft).

			Regular Season					Playoffs				
Season	Club	Lea	GP	G	A	TP	PIM	GP	G	A	TP	PIM
1992-93	Providence	H.E.	24	1	8	9	10	....	....	....	....	....
1993-94	Providence	H.E.	21	2	7	9	8	....	....	....	....	....
1994-95	Providence	H.E.	35	4	12	16	12	....	....	....	....	....

KENNY, SHANE — PHI.

Defense. Shoots left. 6'2", 242 lbs. Born, Oromocto, N.B., March 1, 1977.
(Philadelphia's 2nd choice, 48th overall, in 1995 Entry Draft).

			Regular Season					Playoffs				
Season	Club	Lea	GP	G	A	TP	PIM	GP	G	A	TP	PIM
1993-94	Owen Sound	OHL	54	4	9	13	138	2	0	0	0	6
1994-95	Owen Sound	OHL	65	13	19	32	134	9	0	2	2	8

KERCH, ALEXANDER — (KUHRCH) EDM.

Left wing. Shoots right. 5'10", 190 lbs. Born, Arkhangelsk, USSR, March 16, 1967.
(Edmonton's 5th choice, 60th overall, in 1993 Entry Draft).

			Regular Season					Playoffs				
Season	Club	Lea	GP	G	A	TP	PIM	GP	G	A	TP	PIM
1984-85	Riga	USSR	8	0	0	0	6	....	....	....	....	....
1985-86	Riga	USSR	23	5	2	7	16	....	....	....	....	....
1986-87	Riga	USSR	26	5	4	9	10	....	....	....	....	....
1987-88	Riga	USSR	50	14	4	18	28	....	....	....	....	....
1988-89	Riga	USSR	39	6	7	13	41	....	....	....	....	....
1989-90	Riga	USSR	46	9	11	20	22	....	....	....	....	....
1990-91	Riga	USSR	46	16	17	33	46	....	....	....	....	....
1991-92	Riga	CIS	27	7	9	16	20	....	....	....	....	....
1992-93	Riga	CIS	42	23	14	37	28	2	1	2	3	2
1993-94	**Edmonton**	**NHL**	**5**	**0**	**0**	**0**	**2**	....	....	....	....	....
	Cape Breton	AHL	57	24	38	62	16	4	1	1	2	2
1994-95	Riga	CIS	11	4	0	4	4	....	....	....	....	....
	Providence	AHL	1	0	0	0	15	4	0	2	2	0
	NHL Totals		**5**	**0**	**0**	**0**	**2**	....	....	....	....	....

KESA, DAN — (KEH-suh) DAL.

Right wing. Shoots right. 6', 198 lbs. Born, Vancouver, B.C., November 23, 1971.
(Vancouver's 5th choice, 95th overall, in 1991 Entry Draft).

			Regular Season					Playoffs				
Season	Club	Lea	GP	G	A	TP	PIM	GP	G	A	TP	PIM
1990-91	Prince Albert	WHL	69	30	23	53	116	3	1	1	2	0
1991-92	Prince Albert	WHL	62	46	51	97	201	10	9	10	19	27
1992-93	Hamilton	AHL	62	16	24	40	76	....	....	....	....	....
1993-94	**Vancouver**	**NHL**	**19**	**2**	**4**	**6**	**18**	....	....	....	....	....
	Hamilton	AHL	53	37	33	70	33	4	1	4	5	4
1994-95	Syracuse	AHL	70	34	44	78	81	....	....	....	....	....
	NHL Totals		**19**	**2**	**4**	**6**	**18**	....	....	....	....	....

Traded by **Dallas** by **Vancouver** with Greg Adams and Vancouver's fifth round choice (later traded to Los Angeles — Los Angeles selected Jason Morgan) in 1995 Entry Draft for Russ Courtnall, April 7, 1995.

KESKINEN, ESA — (KEHS-kee-nehn) CGY.

Center. Shoots right. 5'9", 195 lbs. Born, Ylojarvi, Finland, February 3, 1965.
(Calgary's 6th choice, 101st overall, in 1985 Entry Draft).

			Regular Season					Playoffs				
Season	Club	Lea	GP	G	A	TP	PIM	GP	G	A	TP	PIM
1982-83	FoPS	Fin. 2	15	5	14	19	8	4	4	6	10	0
1983-84	TPS	Fin.	31	10	25	35	0	6	0	0	0	0
1984-85	TPS	Fin.	35	11	22	33	66	10	2	3	5	0
1985-86	TPS	Fin.	36	18	28	46	4	7	2	0	2	0
1986-87	TPS	Fin.	46	25	36	61	4	5	1	1	2	0
1987-88	TPS	Fin.	44	14	55	69	14	....	....	....	....	....
1988-89	Lukko	Fin.	41	24	46	70	12	....	....	....	....	....
1989-90	Lukko	Fin.	44	25	26	51	16	....	....	....	....	....
1990-91	Lukko	Fin.	44	17	51	68	14	....	....	....	....	....
1991-92	TPS	Fin.	44	24	45	69	12	3	1	1	2	0
1992-93	TPS	Fin.	46	16	43	59	12	12	1	6	7	4
1993-94	TPS	Fin.	47	23	47	70	28	11	5	4	9	4
1994-95	HV-71	Swe.	39	15	28	43	48	13	3	5	8	10

KHARLAMOV, ALEXANDER — (khahr-LAH-mohv) WSH.

Center. Shoots left. 5'10", 180 lbs. Born, Moscow, USSR, September 23, 1975.
(Washington's 2nd choice, 15th overall, in 1994 Entry Draft).

			Regular Season					Playoffs				
Season	Club	Lea	GP	G	A	TP	PIM	GP	G	A	TP	PIM
1992-93	CSKA	CIS	42	8	4	12	12	....	....	....	....	....
1993-94	CSKA	CIS	46	7	7	14	26	3	1	0	1	2
	Russian Pen's	IHL	12	2	2	4	4	....	....	....	....	....
1994-95	CSKA	CIS	45	8	4	12	12	....	....	....	....	....

KHMYLEV, YURI — (kheh-meh-LUHV) BUF.

Left wing. Shoots right. 6'1", 189 lbs. Born, Moscow, USSR, August 9, 1964.
(Buffalo's 7th choice, 108th overall, in 1992 Entry Draft).

			Regular Season					Playoffs				
Season	Club	Lea	GP	G	A	TP	PIM	GP	G	A	TP	PIM
1981-82	Soviet Wings	USSR	8	2	2	4	2	....	....	....	....	....
1982-83	Soviet Wings	USSR	51	9	7	16	14	....	....	....	....	....
1983-84	Soviet Wings	USSR	43	7	8	15	10	....	....	....	....	....
1984-85	Soviet Wings	USSR	30	11	4	15	24	....	....	....	....	....
1985-86	Soviet Wings	USSR	40	24	9	33	22	....	....	....	....	....
1986-87	Soviet Wings	USSR	40	15	15	30	48	....	....	....	....	....
1987-88	Soviet Wings	USSR	48	21	8	29	46	....	....	....	....	....
1988-89	Soviet Wings	USSR	44	16	18	34	38	....	....	....	....	....
1989-90	Soviet Wings	USSR	44	14	13	27	30	....	....	....	....	....
1990-91	Soviet Wings	USSR	45	25	14	39	26	....	....	....	....	....
1991-92	Soviet Wings	CIS	42	19	17	36	20	....	....	....	....	....
1992-93	**Buffalo**	**NHL**	**68**	**20**	**19**	**39**	**28**	**8**	**4**	**3**	**7**	**4**
1993-94	**Buffalo**	**NHL**	**72**	**27**	**31**	**58**	**49**	**7**	**3**	**1**	**4**	**8**
1994-95	Soviet Wings	IHL	11	2	2	4	4	....	....	....	....	....
	Buffalo	**NHL**	**48**	**8**	**17**	**25**	**14**	**5**	**0**	**1**	**1**	**8**
	NHL Totals		**188**	**55**	**67**	**122**	**91**	**20**	**7**	**5**	**12**	**20**

KHOUMUTOV, ANDREI — (hoh-moo-TAHF) COL.

Right wing. Shoots left. 5'10", 176 lbs. Born, Yaroslavl, USSR, April 21, 1961.
(Quebec's 12th choice, 190th overall, in 1989 Entry Draft).

			Regular Season					Playoffs				
Season	Club	Lea	GP	G	A	TP	PIM	GP	G	A	TP	PIM
1979-80	CSKA	USSR	4	0	0	0	0	....	....	....	....	....
1980-81	CSKA	USSR	43	23	18	41	4	....	....	....	....	....
1981-82	CSKA	USSR	44	17	13	30	12	....	....	....	....	....
1982-83	CSKA	USSR	44	21	17	38	6	....	....	....	....	....
1983-84	CSKA	USSR	39	17	9	26	14	....	....	....	....	....
1984-85	CSKA	USSR	37	21	13	34	18	....	....	....	....	....
1985-86	CSKA	USSR	38	14	15	29	10	....	....	....	....	....
1986-87	CSKA	USSR	33	15	18	33	22	....	....	....	....	....
1987-88	CSKA	USSR	48	29	14	43	22	....	....	....	....	....
1988-89	CSKA	USSR	44	19	16	35	14	....	....	....	....	....
1989-90a	CSKA	USSR	47	21	14	35	16	....	....	....	....	....
1990-91	Fribourg	Switz.	36	39	43	82	....	8	13	12	25	....
1991-92	Fribourg	Switz.	35	31	43	74	34	14	10	12	22	6
1992-93	Fribourg	Switz.	27	23	36	59	14	....	....	....	....	....
1993-94	Fribourg	Switz.	....	....	....	....	....	11	12	14	26	6
1994-95	Fribourg	Switz.	35	41	45	86	32	8	4	9	13	4

a Soviet Player of the Year (1990)

KHRISTICH, DIMITRI — (KRIH-stihch) L.A.

Left wing/Center. Shoots right. 6'2", 195 lbs. Born, Kiev, USSR, July 23, 1969.
(Washington's 6th choice, 120th overall, in 1988 Entry Draft).

			Regular Season					Playoffs				
Season	Club	Lea	GP	G	A	TP	PIM	GP	G	A	TP	PIM
1985-86	Sokol Kiev	USSR	4	0	0	0	0	....	....	....	....	....
1986-87	Sokol Kiev	USSR	20	3	0	3	4	....	....	....	....	....
1987-88	Sokol Kiev	USSR	37	9	1	10	18	....	....	....	....	....
1988-89	Sokol Kiev	USSR	42	17	10	27	15	....	....	....	....	....
1989-90	Sokol Kiev	USSR	47	14	22	36	32	....	....	....	....	....
1990-91	Sokol Kiev	USSR	28	10	12	22	20	....	....	....	....	....
	Washington	**NHL**	**40**	**13**	**14**	**27**	**21**	**11**	**1**	**3**	**4**	**6**
	Baltimore	AHL	3	0	0	0	0	....	....	....	....	....
1991-92	**Washington**	**NHL**	**80**	**36**	**37**	**73**	**35**	**7**	**3**	**2**	**5**	**15**
1992-93	**Washington**	**NHL**	**64**	**31**	**35**	**66**	**28**	**6**	**2**	**5**	**7**	**2**
1993-94	**Washington**	**NHL**	**83**	**29**	**29**	**58**	**73**	**11**	**2**	**3**	**5**	**10**
1994-95	**Washington**	**NHL**	**48**	**12**	**14**	**26**	**41**	**7**	**1**	**4**	**5**	**0**
	NHL Totals		**315**	**121**	**129**	**250**	**198**	**42**	**9**	**17**	**26**	**33**

Traded to **Los Angeles** by **Washington** with Byron Dafoe for Los Angeles' first round choice and Dallas' fourth round choice (previously acquired by Los Angeles) in 1996 Entry Draft, July 8, 1995.

KIBERMANIS, CHRIS — WPG.

Defense. Shoots right. 6'5", 184 lbs. Born, Calgary, Alta., March 24, 1976.
(Winnipeg's 7th choice, 146th overall, in 1994 Entry Draft).

			Regular Season					Playoffs				
Season	Club	Lea	GP	G	A	TP	PIM	GP	G	A	TP	PIM
1993-94	Red Deer	WHL	49	1	5	6	57	4	0	0	0	7
1994-95	Red Deer	WHL	52	3	1	4	93	....	....	....	....	....

KIENASS, TORSTEN

Defense. Shoots left. 5'11", 180 lbs. Born, Berlin, East Germany, February 23, 1971.
(Boston's 11th choice, 260th overall, in 1991 Entry Draft).

			Regular Season					Playoffs				
Season	Club	Lea	GP	G	A	TP	PIM	GP	G	A	TP	PIM
1990-91	Dynamo Berlin	Ger.	27	1	1	2	19	7	1	0	1	4
1991-92	Dynamo Berlin	Ger. 2	45	8	6	14	33	....	....	....	....	....
1992-93	Ratingen	Ger.	44	3	12	15	16	3	0	0	0	2
1993-94	Dusseldorf	Ger.	44	0	18	18	12	12	3	2	5	12
1994-95	Dusseldorf	Ger.	42	4	9	13	12	9	1	2	3	6

KILGER, CHAD — (KIHL-guhr) ANA.

Center. Shoots left. 6'3", 204 lbs. Born, Cornwall, Ont., November 27, 1976.
(Anaheim's 1st choice, 4th overall, in 1995 Entry Draft).

			Regular Season					Playoffs				
Season	Club	Lea	GP	G	A	TP	PIM	GP	G	A	TP	PIM
1993-94	Kingston	OHL	66	17	35	52	23	6	7	2	9	8
1994-95	Kingston	OHL	65	42	53	95	95	6	5	2	7	10

KIMBLE, DARIN — CHI.

Right wing. Shoots right. 6'2", 210 lbs. Born, Lucky Lake, Sask., November 22, 1968.
(Quebec's 5th choice, 66th overall, in 1988 Entry Draft).

			Regular Season					Playoffs				
Season	Club	Lea	GP	G	A	TP	PIM	GP	G	A	TP	PIM
1985-86	Calgary	WHL	37	14	8	22	93	....	....	....	....	....
	N. Westminster	WHL	11	1	1	2	22	....	....	....	....	....
	Brandon	WHL	15	1	6	7	39	....	....	....	....	....
1986-87	Prince Albert	WHL	68	17	13	30	190	....	....	....	....	....
1987-88	Prince Albert	WHL	67	35	36	71	307	10	3	2	5	4
1988-89	**Quebec**	**NHL**	**26**	**3**	**1**	**4**	**149**	....	....	....	....	....
	Halifax	AHL	39	8	6	14	188	....	....	....	....	....
1989-90	**Quebec**	**NHL**	**44**	**5**	**5**	**10**	**185**	....	....	....	....	....
	Halifax	AHL	18	6	6	12	37	6	1	1	2	61
1990-91	**Quebec**	**NHL**	**35**	**2**	**5**	**7**	**114**	....	....	....	....	....
	Halifax	AHL	7	1	4	5	20	....	....	....	....	....
	St. Louis	**NHL**	**26**	**1**	**1**	**2**	**128**	**13**	**0**	**0**	**0**	**38**
1991-92	**St. Louis**	**NHL**	**46**	**1**	**3**	**4**	**166**	**5**	**0**	**0**	**0**	**7**
1992-93	**Boston**	**NHL**	**55**	**7**	**3**	**10**	**177**	**4**	**0**	**0**	**0**	**2**
	Providence	AHL	12	1	4	5	34	....	....	....	....	....
1993-94	**Chicago**	**NHL**	**65**	**4**	**2**	**6**	**133**	**1**	**0**	**0**	**0**	**5**
1994-95	**Chicago**	**NHL**	**14**	**0**	**0**	**0**	**30**	....	....	....	....	....
	NHL Totals		**311**	**23**	**20**	**43**	**1082**	**23**	**0**	**0**	**0**	**52**

Traded to **St. Louis** by **Quebec** for Herb Raglan, Tony Twist and Andy Rymsha, February 4, 1991. Traded to **Tampa Bay** by **St. Louis** with Pat Jablonski and Steve Tuttle for future considerations, June 19, 1992. Traded to **Boston** by **Tampa Bay** with future considerations for Ken Hodge and Matt Hervey, September 4, 1992. Signed as a free agent by **Florida**, July 9, 1993. Traded to **Chicago** by **Florida** for Keith Brown, September 30, 1993.

KING, DEREK — NYI

Left wing. Shoots left. 6'1", 203 lbs. Born, Hamilton, Ont., February 11, 1967.
(NY Islanders' 2nd choice, 13th overall, in 1985 Entry Draft).

			Regular Season					Playoffs				
Season	Club	Lea	GP	G	A	TP	PIM	GP	G	A	TP	PIM
1984-85	S.S. Marie	OHL	63	35	38	73	106	16	3	13	16	11
1985-86	S.S. Marie	OHL	25	12	17	29	33	....	....	....	....	....
	Oshawa	OHL	19	8	13	21	15	6	3	2	5	13
1986-87	**NY Islanders**	**NHL**	**2**	**0**	**0**	**0**	**0**	....	....	....	....	....
a	Oshawa	OHL	57	53	53	106	74	17	14	10	24	40
1987-88	**NY Islanders**	**NHL**	**55**	**12**	**24**	**36**	**30**	**5**	**0**	**2**	**2**	**2**
	Springfield	AHL	10	7	6	13	6	....	....	....	....	....
1988-89	**NY Islanders**	**NHL**	**60**	**14**	**29**	**43**	**14**	....	....	....	....	....
	Springfield	AHL	4	4	0	4	0	....	....	....	....	....
1989-90	**NY Islanders**	**NHL**	**46**	**13**	**27**	**40**	**20**	**4**	**0**	**0**	**0**	**4**
	Springfield	AHL	21	11	12	23	33	....	....	....	....	....
1990-91	**NY Islanders**	**NHL**	**66**	**19**	**26**	**45**	**44**	....	....	....	....	....
1991-92	**NY Islanders**	**NHL**	**80**	**40**	**38**	**78**	**46**	....	....	....	....	....
1992-93	**NY Islanders**	**NHL**	**77**	**38**	**38**	**76**	**47**	**18**	**3**	**11**	**14**	**14**
1993-94	**NY Islanders**	**NHL**	**78**	**30**	**40**	**70**	**59**	**4**	**0**	**1**	**1**	**0**
1994-95	**NY Islanders**	**NHL**	**43**	**10**	**16**	**26**	**41**	....	....	....	....	....
	NHL Totals		**507**	**176**	**238**	**414**	**301**	**31**	**3**	**14**	**17**	**20**

a OHL First All-Star Team (1987)

KING, KRIS — WPG.

Left wing. Shoots left. 5'11", 208 lbs. Born, Bracebridge, Ont., February 18, 1966.
(Washington's 4th choice, 80th overall, in 1984 Entry Draft).

			Regular Season					Playoffs				
Season	Club	Lea	GP	G	A	TP	PIM	GP	G	A	TP	PIM
1983-84	Peterborough	OHL	62	13	18	31	168	8	3	3	6	14
1984-85	Peterborough	OHL	61	18	35	53	222	16	2	8	10	28
1985-86	Peterborough	OHL	58	19	40	59	254	8	4	0	4	21
1986-87	Binghamton	AHL	7	0	0	0	18	....	....	....	....	....
	Peterborough	OHL	46	23	33	56	160	12	5	8	13	41
1987-88	**Detroit**	**NHL**	**3**	**1**	**0**	**1**	**2**	....	....	....	....	....
	Adirondack	AHL	76	21	32	53	337	10	4	4	8	53
1988-89	**Detroit**	**NHL**	**55**	**2**	**3**	**5**	**168**	**2**	**0**	**0**	**0**	**2**
1989-90	**NY Rangers**	**NHL**	**68**	**6**	**7**	**13**	**286**	**10**	**0**	**1**	**1**	**38**
1990-91	**NY Rangers**	**NHL**	**72**	**11**	**14**	**25**	**154**	**6**	**2**	**0**	**2**	**36**
1991-92	**NY Rangers**	**NHL**	**79**	**10**	**9**	**19**	**224**	**13**	**4**	**1**	**5**	**14**
1992-93	**NY Rangers**	**NHL**	**30**	**0**	**3**	**3**	**67**	....	....	....	....	....
	Winnipeg	**NHL**	**48**	**8**	**8**	**16**	**136**	**6**	**1**	**1**	**2**	**4**
1993-94	**Winnipeg**	**NHL**	**83**	**4**	**8**	**12**	**205**	....	....	....	....	....
1994-95	**Winnipeg**	**NHL**	**48**	**4**	**2**	**6**	**85**	....	....	....	....	....
	NHL Totals		**486**	**46**	**54**	**100**	**1327**	**37**	**7**	**3**	**10**	**94**

Signed as a free agent by **Detroit**, March 23, 1987. Traded to **NY Rangers** by **Detroit** for Chris McRae and Detroit's fifth round choice (previously acquired by NY Rangers — Detroit selected Tony Burns) in 1990 Entry Draft, September 7, 1989. Traded to **Winnipeg** by **NY Rangers** with Tie Domi for Ed Olczyk, December 28, 1992.

KING, STEVEN — ANA.

Right wing. Shoots right. 6', 195 lbs. Born, Greenwich, RI, July 22, 1969.
(NY Rangers' 1st choice, 21st overall, in 1991 Supplemental Draft).

			Regular Season					Playoffs				
Season	Club	Lea	GP	G	A	TP	PIM	GP	G	A	TP	PIM
1989-90	Brown	ECAC	27	19	8	27	53	....	....	....	....	....
1990-91	Brown	ECAC	27	19	15	34	76	....	....	....	....	....
1991-92	Binghamton	AHL	66	27	15	42	56	10	2	0	2	14
1992-93	**NY Rangers**	**NHL**	**24**	**7**	**5**	**12**	**16**	....	....	....	....	....
	Binghamton	AHL	53	35	33	68	100	14	7	9	16	26
1993-94	**Anaheim**	**NHL**	**36**	**8**	**3**	**11**	**44**	....	....	....	....	....
1994-95			DID NOT PLAY – INJURED									
	NHL Totals		**60**	**15**	**8**	**23**	**60**	....	....	....	....	....

Claimed by **Anaheim** from **NY Rangers** in Expansion Draft, June 24, 1993.

KINNEAR, GEORDIE — N.J.

Defense. Shoots left. 6'1", 200 lbs. Born, Simcoe, Ont., July 9, 1973.
(New Jersey's 7th choice, 162nd overall, in 1992 Entry Draft).

			Regular Season					Playoffs				
Season	Club	Lea	GP	G	A	TP	PIM	GP	G	A	TP	PIM
1990-91	Peterborough	OHL	37	1	0	1	76	2	0	0	0	10
1991-92	Peterborough	OHL	63	5	16	21	195	10	0	2	2	36
1992-93	Peterborough	OHL	58	6	22	28	161	19	1	5	6	43
1993-94	Albany	AHL	59	3	12	15	197	5	0	0	0	21
1994-95	Albany	AHL	68	5	11	16	136	9	1	1	2	7

KIPRUSOFF, MARKO (KIHP-ruh-sohf) — MTL.

Defense. Shoots left. 6', 195 lbs. Born, Turku, Finland, June 6, 1972.
(Montreal's 4th choice, 70th overall, in 1994 Entry Draft).

			Regular Season					Playoffs				
Season	Club	Lea	GP	G	A	TP	PIM	GP	G	A	TP	PIM
1990-91	TPS	Fin.	3	0	0	0	0	....	....	....	....	....
1991-92	TPS	Fin.	23	0	2	2	0	....	....	....	....	....
	HPK	Fin.	3	0	0	0	0	....	....	....	....	....
1992-93	TPS	Fin.	43	3	7	10	14	12	2	3	5	6
1993-94	TPS	Fin.	48	5	19	24	8	11	0	6	6	4
1994-95	TPS	Fin.	50	10	21	31	16	13	0	9	9	2

KIRTON, SCOTT — CHI.

Right wing. Shoots right. 6'4", 215 lbs. Born, Penetanguishene, Ont., October 4, 1971.
(Chicago's 7th choice, 154th overall, in 1991 Entry Draft).

			Regular Season					Playoffs				
Season	Club	Lea	GP	G	A	TP	PIM	GP	G	A	TP	PIM
1991-92	North Dakota	WCHA	37	5	6	11	68	....	....	....	....	....
1992-93	North Dakota	WCHA	30	4	16	20	100	....	....	....	....	....
1993-94	North Dakota	WCHA	37	3	6	9	49	....	....	....	....	....
1994-95	North Dakota	WCHA	37	8	20	28	65	....	....	....	....	....

KISIO, KELLY

Center. Shoots right. 5'10", 185 lbs. Born, Peace River, Alta., September 18, 1959.

			Regular Season					Playoffs				
Season	Club	Lea	GP	G	A	TP	PIM	GP	G	A	TP	PIM
1978-79	Calgary	WHL	70	60	61	121	73	....	....	....	....	....
1979-80	Calgary	WHL	71	65	73	138	64	....	....	....	....	....
1980-81	Adirondack	AHL	41	10	14	24	43	....	....	....	....	....
	Kalamazoo	IHL	31	27	16	43	48	8	7	7	14	13
1981-82	Dallas	CHL	78	*62	39	101	59	16	*12	*17	*29	38
1982-83	Davos	Switz.	40	49	38	87	....	....	....	....	....	....
	Detroit	**NHL**	**15**	**4**	**3**	**7**	**0**	....	....	....	....	....
1983-84	**Detroit**	**NHL**	**70**	**23**	**37**	**60**	**34**	**4**	**1**	**0**	**1**	**4**
1984-85	**Detroit**	**NHL**	**75**	**20**	**41**	**61**	**56**	**3**	**0**	**2**	**2**	**2**
1985-86	**Detroit**	**NHL**	**76**	**21**	**48**	**69**	**85**	....	....	....	....	....
1986-87	**NY Rangers**	**NHL**	**70**	**24**	**40**	**64**	**73**	**4**	**0**	**1**	**1**	**2**
1987-88	**NY Rangers**	**NHL**	**77**	**23**	**55**	**78**	**88**	....	....	....	....	....
1988-89	**NY Rangers**	**NHL**	**70**	**26**	**36**	**62**	**91**	**4**	**0**	**0**	**0**	**9**
1989-90	**NY Rangers**	**NHL**	**68**	**22**	**44**	**66**	**105**	**10**	**2**	**8**	**10**	**8**
1990-91	**NY Rangers**	**NHL**	**51**	**15**	**20**	**35**	**58**	....	....	....	....	....
1991-92	**San Jose**	**NHL**	**48**	**11**	**26**	**37**	**54**	....	....	....	....	....
1992-93	**San Jose**	**NHL**	**78**	**26**	**52**	**78**	**90**	....	....	....	....	....
1993-94	**Calgary**	**NHL**	**51**	**7**	**23**	**30**	**28**	**7**	**0**	**2**	**2**	**8**
1994-95	**Calgary**	**NHL**	**12**	**7**	**4**	**11**	**6**	**7**	**3**	**2**	**5**	**19**
	NHL Totals		**761**	**229**	**429**	**658**	**768**	**39**	**6**	**15**	**21**	**52**

Played in NHL All-Star Game (1993)

Signed as a free agent by **Detroit**, May 2, 1983. Traded to **NY Rangers** by **Detroit** with Lane Lambert and Jim Leavins for Glen Hanlon and New York's third round choices in 1987 (Dennis Holland) and 1988 (Guy Dupuis) Entry Drafts, July 29, 1986. Claimed by **Minnesota** from **NY Rangers** in Expansion Draft, May 30, 1991. Traded to **San Jose** by **Minnesota** for Shane Churla, June 3, 1991. Signed as a free agent by **Calgary**, August 18, 1993.

KITCHING, GARY — EDM.

Center. Shoots left. 6'2", 190 lbs. Born, Thunder Bay, Ont., January 9, 1971.
(Edmonton's 8th choice, 166th overall, in 1991 Entry Draft).

			Regular Season					Playoffs				
Season	Club	Lea	GP	G	A	TP	PIM	GP	G	A	TP	PIM
1991-92	Ferris State	CCHA	36	7	9	16	52	....	....	....	....	....
1992-93	Ferris State	CCHA	28	8	19	27	62	....	....	....	....	....
1993-94	Ferris State	CCHA	18	4	5	9	18	....	....	....	....	....
1994-95	Ferris State	CCHA	15	3	6	9	20	....	....	....	....	....

KIVI, KARRI — VAN.

Defense. Shoots left. 6', 180 lbs. Born, Turku, Finland, January 1, 1970.
(Vancouver's 11th choice, 233rd overall, in 1990 Entry Draft).

			Regular Season					Playoffs				
Season	Club	Lea	GP	G	A	TP	PIM	GP	G	A	TP	PIM
1988-89	Ilves	Fin.	39	5	7	12	10	5	0	0	0	0
1989-90	Ilves	Fin.	43	6	15	21	14	8	1	4	5	2
1990-91	Ilves	Fin.	43	2	9	11	18	....	....	....	....	....
1991-92	TPS	Fin.	33	3	1	4	14	3	0	0	0	0
1992-93	Kiekko-67	Fin. 2	11	2	7	9	4	....	....	....	....	....
	Assat	Fin.	34	2	11	13	16	8	1	2	3	0
1993-94	Assat	Fin.	48	1	12	13	49	5	1	2	3	0
1994-95	Assat	Fin.	50	10	18	28	20	7	1	1	2	2

KLATT, TRENT (KLAT) — DAL.

Right wing. Shoots right. 6'1", 205 lbs. Born, Robbinsdale, MN, January 30, 1971.
(Washington's 5th choice, 82nd overall, in 1989 Entry Draft).

			Regular Season					Playoffs				
Season	Club	Lea	GP	G	A	TP	PIM	GP	G	A	TP	PIM
1989-90	U. Minnesota	WCHA	38	22	14	36	16	....	....	....	....	....
1990-91	U. Minnesota	WCHA	39	16	28	44	58	....	....	....	....	....
1991-92	U. Minnesota	WCHA	41	27	36	63	76	....	....	....	....	....
	Minnesota	**NHL**	**1**	**0**	**0**	**0**	**0**	**6**	**0**	**0**	**0**	**2**
1992-93	**Minnesota**	**NHL**	**47**	**4**	**19**	**23**	**38**	....	....	....	....	....
	Kalamazoo	IHL	31	8	11	19	18	....	....	....	....	....
1993-94	**Dallas**	**NHL**	**61**	**14**	**24**	**38**	**30**	**9**	**2**	**1**	**3**	**4**
	Kalamazoo	IHL	6	3	2	5	4	....	....	....	....	....
1994-95	**Dallas**	**NHL**	**47**	**12**	**10**	**22**	**26**	**5**	**1**	**0**	**1**	**0**
	NHL Totals		**156**	**30**	**53**	**83**	**94**	**20**	**3**	**1**	**4**	**6**

KLEE, KEN — WSH.

Defense. Shoots right. 6'1", 205 lbs. Born, Indianapolis, IN, April 24, 1971.
(Washington's 11th choice, 177th overall, in 1990 Entry Draft).

			Regular Season					Playoffs				
Season	Club	Lea	GP	G	A	TP	PIM	GP	G	A	TP	PIM
1989-90	Bowling Green	CCHA	39	0	5	5	52	....	....	....	....	....
1990-91	Bowling Green	CCHA	37	7	28	35	50	....	....	....	....	....
1991-92	Bowling Green	CCHA	10	0	1	1	14	....	....	....	....	....
1992-93	Baltimore	AHL	77	4	14	18	93	7	0	1	1	15
1993-94	Portland	AHL	65	2	9	11	87	17	1	2	3	14
1994-95	Portland	AHL	49	5	7	12	89	....	....	....	....	....
	Washington	**NHL**	**23**	**3**	**1**	**4**	**41**	**7**	**0**	**0**	**0**	**4**
	NHL Totals		**23**	**3**	**1**	**4**	**41**	**7**	**0**	**0**	**0**	**4**

KLEMM, JON — COL.

Defense. Shoots right. 6'3", 200 lbs. Born, Cranbrook, B.C., January 8, 1970.

			Regular Season					Playoffs				
Season	Club	Lea	GP	G	A	TP	PIM	GP	G	A	TP	PIM
1988-89	Seattle	WHL	2	1	1	2	0	....	....	....	....	....
	Spokane	WHL	66	6	34	40	42	....	....	....	....	....
1989-90	Spokane	WHL	66	3	28	31	100	6	1	1	2	5
1990-91	Spokane	WHL	72	7	58	65	65	15	3	6	9	8
1991-92	**Quebec**	**NHL**	**4**	**0**	**1**	**1**	**0**	....	....	....	....	....
	Halifax	AHL	70	6	13	19	40	....	....	....	....	....
1992-93	Halifax	AHL	80	3	20	23	32	....	....	....	....	....
1993-94	**Quebec**	**NHL**	**7**	**0**	**0**	**0**	**4**	....	....	....	....	....
	Cornwall	AHL	66	4	26	30	78	13	1	2	3	6
1994-95	Cornwall	AHL	65	6	13	19	84	....	....	....	....	....
	Quebec	**NHL**	**4**	**1**	**0**	**1**	**2**	....	....	....	....	....
	NHL Totals		**15**	**1**	**1**	**2**	**6**	....	....	....	....	....

Signed as a free agent by **Calgary**, September 11, 1984. Signed as a free agent by **Philadelphia**, July 20, 1995.

KLEVAKIN, DIMITRI (kleh-VAH-kihn) T.B.

Right wing. Shoots left. 5'11", 163 lbs. Born, Angarsk, USSR, February 20, 1976.
(Tampa Bay's 4th choice, 86th overall, in 1994 Entry Draft).

			Regular Season					Playoffs				
Season	Club	Lea	GP	G	A	TP	PIM	GP	G	A	TP	PIM
1992-93	Spartak	CIS	8	1	1	2	0	....	....	....	....	....
1993-94	Spartak	CIS	42	6	3	9	6	4	1	0	1	0
1994-95	Spartak	CIS	52	12	10	22	4	....	....	....	....	....

KLIMA, PETR (KLEE-muh) T.B.

Right/Left wing. Shoots right. 6', 190 lbs. Born, Chomutov, Czech., December 23, 1964.
(Detroit's 5th choice, 86th overall, in 1983 Entry Draft).

			Regular Season					Playoffs				
Season	Club	Lea	GP	G	A	TP	PIM	GP	G	A	TP	PIM
1981-82	Litvinov	Czech.	18	7	3	10	8	....	....	....	....	....
1982-83	Litvinov	Czech.	44	19	17	36	74	....	....	....	....	....
1983-84	Dukla Jihlava	Czech.	41	20	16	36	46	....	....	....	....	....
1984-85	Dukla Jihlava	Czech.	35	23	22	45	76	....	....	....	....	....
1985-86	**Detroit**	**NHL**	**74**	**32**	**24**	**56**	**16**	....	....	....	....	....
1986-87	**Detroit**	**NHL**	**77**	**30**	**23**	**53**	**42**	**13**	**1**	**2**	**3**	**4**
1987-88	**Detroit**	**NHL**	**78**	**37**	**25**	**62**	**46**	**12**	**10**	**8**	**18**	**10**
1988-89	**Detroit**	**NHL**	**51**	**25**	**16**	**41**	**44**	**6**	**2**	**4**	**6**	**19**
	Adirondack	AHL	5	5	1	6	4	....	....	....	....	....
1989-90	**Detroit**	**NHL**	**13**	**5**	**5**	**10**	**6**	....	....	....	....	....
	Edmonton	**NHL**	**63**	**25**	**28**	**53**	**66**	**21**	**5**	**0**	**5**	**8**
1990-91	**Edmonton**	**NHL**	**70**	**40**	**28**	**68**	**113**	**18**	**7**	**6**	**13**	**16**
1991-92	**Edmonton**	**NHL**	**57**	**21**	**13**	**34**	**52**	**15**	**1**	**4**	**5**	**8**
1992-93	**Edmonton**	**NHL**	**68**	**32**	**16**	**48**	**100**	....	....	....	....	....
1993-94	**Tampa Bay**	**NHL**	**75**	**28**	**27**	**55**	**76**	....	....	....	....	....
1994-95	Wolfsburg	Ger. 2	12	27	11	38	28	....	....	....	....	....
	ZPS Zlin	Czech.	1	1	0	1	0	....	....	....	....	....
	Tampa Bay	**NHL**	**47**	**13**	**13**	**26**	**26**	....	....	....	....	....
	NHL Totals		**673**	**288**	**218**	**506**	**587**	**85**	**26**	**24**	**50**	**65**

Traded to **Edmonton** by **Detroit** with Joe Murphy, Adam Graves and Jeff Sharples for Jimmy Carson, Kevin McClelland and Edmonton's fifth round choice (later traded to Montreal — Montreal selected Brad Layzell) in 1991 Entry Draft, November 2, 1989. Traded to **Tampa Bay** by **Edmonton** for Tampa Bay's third round choice (Brad Symes) in 1994 Entry Draft, June 16, 1993.

KLIMENTIEV, SERGEI (klih-MEHN-tyehv) BUF.

Defense. Shoots left. 5'11", 200 lbs. Born, Kiev, USSR, April 5, 1975.
(Buffalo's 4th choice, 121st overall, in 1994 Entry Draft).

			Regular Season					Playoffs				
Season	Club	Lea	GP	G	A	TP	PIM	GP	G	A	TP	PIM
1991-92	SVSM Kiev	CIS 3	42	4	15	19	....	....	....	....	....	....
1992-93	Sokol Kiev	CIS	3	0	0	0	4	1	0	0	0	0
1993-94	Medicine Hat	WHL	72	16	26	42	165	3	0	0	0	4
1994-95	Medicine Hat	WHL	71	19	45	64	146	5	4	2	6	14
	Rochester	AHL	7	0	0	0	8	1	0	0	0	0

KLIMOVICH, SERGEI (klee-MOH-vich) CHI.

Center. Shoots right. 6'3", 189 lbs. Born, Novosibirsk, USSR, March 8, 1974.
(Chicago's 3rd choice, 41st overall, in 1992 Entry Draft).

			Regular Season					Playoffs				
Season	Club	Lea	GP	G	A	TP	PIM	GP	G	A	TP	PIM
1991-92	Moscow D'amo	CIS	3	0	0	0	0	....	....	....	....	....
1992-93	Moscow D'amo	CIS	30	4	1	5	14	10	1	0	1	2
1993-94	Moscow D'amo	CIS	39	7	4	11	14	12	2	3	5	6
1994-95	Moscow D'amo	CIS	4	1	0	1	2	....	....	....	....	....
	Indianapolis	IHL	71	14	30	44	20	....	....	....	....	....

KNIPSCHEER, FRED (kuh-NIHP-sheer) BOS.

Center. Shoots left. 5'11", 185 lbs. Born, Ft. Wayne, IN, September 3, 1969.

			Regular Season					Playoffs				
Season	Club	Lea	GP	G	A	TP	PIM	GP	G	A	TP	PIM
1990-91	St. Cloud	WCHA	40	9	10	19	57	....	....	....	....	....
1991-92	St. Cloud	WCHA	33	15	17	32	48	....	....	....	....	....
1992-93ab	St. Cloud	WCHA	36	34	26	60	68	....	....	....	....	....
1993-94	**Boston**	**NHL**	**11**	**3**	**2**	**5**	**14**	**12**	**2**	**1**	**3**	**6**
	Providence	AHL	62	26	13	39	50	....	....	....	....	....
1994-95	Providence	AHL	71	29	34	63	81	....	....	....	....	....
	Boston	**NHL**	**16**	**3**	**1**	**4**	**2**	**4**	**0**	**0**	**0**	**0**
	NHL Totals		**27**	**6**	**3**	**9**	**16**	**16**	**2**	**1**	**3**	**6**

a WCHA First All-Star Team (1993)
b NCAA West Second All-American Team (1993)

Signed as a free agent by **Boston**, April 30, 1993.

KNUBLE, MICHAEL (NOO-buhl) DET.

Right wing. Shoots right. 6'3", 208 lbs. Born, Toronto, Ont., July 4, 1972.
(Detroit's 4th choice, 76th overall, in 1991 Entry Draft).

			Regular Season					Playoffs				
Season	Club	Lea	GP	G	A	TP	PIM	GP	G	A	TP	PIM
1991-92	U. of Michigan	CCHA	43	7	8	15	48	....	....	....	....	....
1992-93	U. of Michigan	CCHA	39	26	16	42	57	....	....	....	....	....
1993-94a	U. of Michigan	CCHA	41	32	26	58	71	....	....	....	....	....
1994-95ab	U. of Michigan	CCHA	34	*38	22	60	62	....	....	....	....	....
	Adirondack	AHL	....	....	....	....	....	3	0	0	0	0

a CCHA Second All-Star Team (1994, 1995)
b NCAA West Second All-American Team (1995)

KNUTSEN, ESPEN (kuh-NOOT-suhn) HFD.

Center. Shoots left. 5'11", 172 lbs. Born, Oslo, Norway, January 12, 1972.
(Hartford's 9th choice, 204th overall, in 1990 Entry Draft).

			Regular Season					Playoffs				
Season	Club	Lea	GP	G	A	TP	PIM	GP	G	A	TP	PIM
1989-90	Valerengen	Nor.	34	22	26	48	....	....	....	....	....	....
1990-91	Valerengen	Nor.	31	30	24	54	42	5	3	4	7	....
1991-92	Valerengen	Nor.	30	28	26	54	37	8	7	8	15	....
1992-93	Valerengen	Nor.	13	11	13	24	4	....	....	....	....	....
1993-94	Valerengen	Nor.	38	32	26	58	20	....	....	....	....	....
1994-95	Djurgarden	Swe.	30	6	14	20	18	3	0	1	1	0

KOCUR, JOE (KOH-suhr)

Right wing. Shoots right. 6', 205 lbs. Born, Calgary, Alta., December 21, 1964.
(Detroit's 6th choice, 88th overall, in 1983 Entry Draft).

			Regular Season					Playoffs				
Season	Club	Lea	GP	G	A	TP	PIM	GP	G	A	TP	PIM
1982-83	Saskatoon	WHL	62	23	17	40	289	6	2	3	5	25
1983-84	Saskatoon	WHL	69	40	41	81	258	....	....	....	....	....
	Adirondack	AHL	....	....	....	....	....	5	0	0	0	20
1984-85	**Detroit**	**NHL**	**17**	**1**	**0**	**1**	**64**	**3**	**1**	**0**	**1**	**5**
	Adirondack	AHL	47	12	7	19	171	....	....	....	....	....
1985-86	**Detroit**	**NHL**	**59**	**9**	**6**	**15**	***377**	....	....	....	....	....
	Adirondack	AHL	9	6	2	8	34	....	....	....	....	....
1986-87	**Detroit**	**NHL**	**77**	**9**	**9**	**18**	**276**	**16**	**2**	**3**	**5**	**71**
1987-88	**Detroit**	**NHL**	**63**	**7**	**7**	**14**	**263**	**10**	**0**	**1**	**1**	**13**
1988-89	**Detroit**	**NHL**	**60**	**9**	**9**	**18**	**213**	**3**	**0**	**1**	**1**	**6**
1989-90	**Detroit**	**NHL**	**71**	**16**	**20**	**36**	**268**	....	....	....	....	....
1990-91	**Detroit**	**NHL**	**52**	**5**	**4**	**9**	**253**	....	....	....	....	....
	NY Rangers	**NHL**	**5**	**0**	**0**	**0**	**36**	**6**	**0**	**2**	**2**	**21**
1991-92	**NY Rangers**	**NHL**	**51**	**7**	**4**	**11**	**121**	**12**	**1**	**1**	**2**	**38**
1992-93	**NY Rangers**	**NHL**	**65**	**3**	**6**	**9**	**131**	....	....	....	....	....
1993-94	**NY Rangers**	**NHL**	**71**	**2**	**1**	**3**	**129**	**20**	**1**	**1**	**2**	**17**
1994-95	**NY Rangers**	**NHL**	**48**	**1**	**2**	**3**	**71**	**10**	**0**	**0**	**0**	**8**
	NHL Totals		**639**	**69**	**68**	**137**	**2202**	**80**	**5**	**9**	**14**	**179**

Traded to **NY Rangers** by **Detroit** with Per Djoos for Kevin Miller, Jim Cummins and Dennis Vial, March 5, 1991.

KOHN, LADISLAV (KOHN) CGY.

Right wing. Shoots left. 5'10", 175 lbs. Born, Uherske Hradiste, Czech., March 4, 1975.
(Calgary's 9th choice, 175th overall, in 1994 Entry Draft).

			Regular Season					Playoffs				
Season	Club	Lea	GP	G	A	TP	PIM	GP	G	A	TP	PIM
1993-94	Brandon	WHL	2	0	0	0	0	....	....	....	....	....
	Swift Current	WHL	69	33	35	68	68	7	5	4	9	8
1994-95	Swift Current	WHL	65	32	60	92	122	6	2	6	8	14
	Saint John	AHL	1	0	0	0	0	....	....	....	....	....

KOIVU, SAKU (KOY-voo, SA-koo) MTL.

Center. Shoots left. 5'9", 165 lbs. Born, Turku, Finland, November 23, 1974.
(Montreal's 1st choice, 21st overall, in 1993 Entry Draft).

			Regular Season					Playoffs				
Season	Club	Lea	GP	G	A	TP	PIM	GP	G	A	TP	PIM
1992-93	TPS	Fin.	46	3	7	10	28	11	3	2	5	2
1993-94	TPS	Fin.	47	23	30	53	42	11	4	8	12	16
1994-95	TPS	Fin.	45	27	47	74	73	13	7	10	17	16

KOIVUNEN, PETRO EDM.

Right wing. Shoots right. 6', 183 lbs. Born, Espoo, Finland, May 30, 1970.
(Edmonton's 2nd choice, 39th overall, in 1988 Entry Draft).

			Regular Season					Playoffs				
Season	Club	Lea	GP	G	A	TP	PIM	GP	G	A	TP	PIM
1988-89	Espoo	Fin. 2	39	32	37	69	42	....	....	....	....	....
1989-90	Espoo	Fin. 2	39	24	35	59	28	....	....	....	....	....
1990-91	HIFK	Fin.	39	8	15	23	20	3	0	1	1	4
1991-92	HIFK	Fin.	41	11	3	14	0	8	0	0	0	2
1992-93	Kiekko-Espoo	Fin.	47	12	13	25	24	....	....	....	....	....
1993-94	Kiekko-Espoo	Fin.	47	21	23	44	16	....	....	....	....	....
1994-95	Kiekko-Espoo	Fin.	41	11	18	29	36	4	0	0	0	4

KOLESAR, MARK (kohl-UH-sahr) TOR.

Left wing. Shoots right. 6'1", 188 lbs. Born, Brampton, Ont., January 23, 1973.

			Regular Season					Playoffs				
Season	Club	Lea	GP	G	A	TP	PIM	GP	G	A	TP	PIM
1991-92	Brandon	WHL	56	6	7	13	36	....	....	....	....	....
1992-93	Brandon	WHL	68	27	33	60	110	4	0	0	0	4
1993-94	Brandon	WHL	59	29	37	66	131	14	8	3	11	48
1994-95	St. John's	AHL	65	12	18	30	62	5	1	0	1	2

Signed as a free agent by **Toronto**, May 24, 1994.

KOLKUNOV, ALEXEI PIT.

Center. Shoots right. 6', 185 lbs. Born, Belgorod, USSR, February 3, 1977.
(Pittsburgh's 5th choice, 154th overall, in 1995 Entry Draft).

			Regular Season					Playoffs				
Season	Club	Lea	GP	G	A	TP	PIM	GP	G	A	TP	PIM
1994-95	Soviet Wings	CIS	7	0	0	0	0	4	1	0	1	0

KOMAROV, PAVEL (koh-mah-ROHV) NYR

Defense. Shoots left. 6'1", 180 lbs. Born, Gorky, USSR, February 28, 1974.
(NY Rangers' 12th choice, 261st overall, in 1993 Entry Draft).

			Regular Season					Playoffs				
Season	Club	Lea	GP	G	A	TP	PIM	GP	G	A	TP	PIM
1991-92	Torpedo Niz.	CIS	10	0	1	1	0	....	....	....	....	....
1992-93	Torpedo Niz.	CIS	28	0	0	0	25	....	....	....	....	....
1993-94	Torpedo Niz.	CIS	18	1	0	1	20	1	0	0	0	2
	Binghamton	AHL	1	1	0	1	2	....	....	....	....	....
1994-95	Torpedo Niz.	CIS	26	0	1	1	38	3	0	0	0	0
	Binghamton	AHL	2	0	0	0	2	....	....	....	....	....

KONDRASHKIN, SERGEI (kohn-DRAHSH-kihn) NYR

Right wing. Shoots left. 6', 192 lbs. Born, Cherepovets, USSR, April 2, 1975.
(NY Rangers' 7th choice, 162nd overall, in 1993 Entry Draft).

			Regular Season					Playoffs				
Season	Club	Lea	GP	G	A	TP	PIM	GP	G	A	TP	PIM
1992-93	Cherepovets	CIS	41	7	3	10	8	....	....	....	....	....
1993-94	Cherepovets	CIS	41	7	2	9	26	....	....	....	....	....
1994-95	Cherepovets	CIS	51	7	2	9	22	....	....	....	....	....

KONOWALCHUK, STEVE (kahn-uh-WAHL-chuhk) WSH.

Center. Shoots left. 6'1", 195 lbs. Born, Salt Lake City, UT, November 11, 1972.
(Washington's 5th choice, 58th overall, in 1991 Entry Draft).

			Regular Season					Playoffs				
Season	Club	Lea	GP	G	A	TP	PIM	GP	G	A	TP	PIM
1990-91	Portland	WHL	72	43	49	92	78	....	....	....	....	....
1991-92	Washington	NHL	1	0	0	0	0	....	....	....	....	....
	Baltimore	AHL	3	1	1	2	0	....	....	....	....	....
a	Portland	WHL	64	51	53	104	95	6	3	6	9	12
1992-93	Washington	NHL	36	4	7	11	16	2	0	1	1	0
	Baltimore	AHL	37	18	28	46	74	....	....	....	....	....
1993-94	Washington	NHL	62	12	14	26	33	11	0	1	1	10
	Portland	AHL	8	11	4	15	4	....	....	....	....	....
1994-95	Washington	NHL	46	11	14	25	44	7	2	5	7	12
	NHL Totals		145	27	35	62	93	20	2	7	9	22

a WHL First All-Star Team (1992)

KONROYD, STEVE (KON-royd)

Defense. Shoots left. 6'1", 195 lbs. Born, Scarborough, Ont., February 10, 1961.
(Atlanta's 4th choice, 39th overall, in 1980 Entry Draft).

			Regular Season					Playoffs				
Season	Club	Lea	GP	G	A	TP	PIM	GP	G	A	TP	PIM
1979-80	Oshawa	OHA	62	11	23	34	133	7	0	2	2	14
1980-81	Calgary	NHL	4	0	0	0	4	....	....	....	....	....
a	Oshawa	OHA	59	19	47	68	232	11	3	11	14	35
1981-82	Calgary	NHL	63	3	14	17	78	3	0	0	0	12
	Oklahoma City	CHL	14	2	3	5	15	....	....	....	....	....
1982-83	Calgary	NHL	79	4	13	17	73	9	2	1	3	18
1983-84	Calgary	NHL	80	1	13	14	94	8	1	2	3	8
1984-85	Calgary	NHL	64	3	23	26	73	4	1	4	5	2
1985-86	Calgary	NHL	59	7	20	27	64	....	....	....	....	....
	NY Islanders	NHL	14	0	5	5	16	3	0	0	0	6
1986-87	NY Islanders	NHL	72	5	16	21	70	14	1	4	5	10
1987-88	NY Islanders	NHL	62	2	15	17	99	6	1	0	1	4
1988-89	NY Islanders	NHL	21	1	5	6	2	....	....	....	....	....
	Chicago	NHL	57	5	7	12	40	16	2	0	2	10
1989-90	Chicago	NHL	75	3	14	17	34	20	1	3	4	19
1990-91	Chicago	NHL	70	0	12	12	40	6	1	0	1	8
1991-92	Chicago	NHL	49	2	14	16	65	....	....	....	....	....
	Hartford	NHL	33	2	10	12	32	7	0	1	1	2
1992-93	Hartford	NHL	59	3	11	14	63	....	....	....	....	....
	Detroit	NHL	6	0	1	1	4	1	0	0	0	0
1993-94	Detroit	NHL	19	0	0	0	10	....	....	....	....	....
	Ottawa	NHL	8	0	2	2	2	....	....	....	....	....
1994-95	Chicago	IHL	16	2	2	4	4	3	0	1	1	2
	Calgary	NHL	1	0	0	0	0	....	....	....	....	....
	NHL Totals		895	41	195	236	863	97	10	15	25	99

a OHA Second All-Star Team (1981)

Traded to **NY Islanders** by **Calgary** with Richard Kromm for John Tonelli, March 11, 1986. Traded to **Chicago** by **NY Islanders** with Bob Bassen for Marc Bergevin and Gary Nylund, November 25, 1988. Traded to **Hartford** by **Chicago** for Rob Brown, January 24, 1992. Traded to **Detroit** by **Hartford** for Detroit's sixth round choice (later traded back to Detroit — Detroit selected Tim Spitzig) in 1993 Entry Draft, March 22, 1993. Traded to **Ottawa** by **Detroit** for Daniel Berthiaume, March 21, 1994. Signed as a free agent by **Calgary**, April 7, 1995.

KONSTANTINOV, VLADIMIR (kohn-stahn-TEE-nahf) DET.

Defense. Shoots right. 5'11", 190 lbs. Born, Murmansk, USSR, March 19, 1967.
(Detroit's 12th choice, 221st overall, in 1989 Entry Draft).

			Regular Season					Playoffs				
Season	Club	Lea	GP	G	A	TP	PIM	GP	G	A	TP	PIM
1984-85	CSKA	USSR	40	1	4	5	10	....	....	....	....	....
1985-86	CSKA	USSR	26	4	3	7	12	....	....	....	....	....
1986-87	CSKA	USSR	35	2	2	4	19	....	....	....	....	....
1987-88	CSKA	USSR	50	3	6	9	32	....	....	....	....	....
1988-89	CSKA	USSR	37	7	8	15	20	....	....	....	....	....
1989-90	CSKA	USSR	47	14	14	28	44	....	....	....	....	....
1990-91	CSKA	USSR	45	5	12	17	42	....	....	....	....	....
1991-92a	Detroit	NHL	79	8	26	34	172	11	0	1	1	16
1992-93	Detroit	NHL	82	5	17	22	137	7	0	1	1	8
1993-94	Detroit	NHL	80	12	21	33	138	7	0	2	2	4
1994-95	Wedemark	Ger. 2	15	13	17	30	51	....	....	....	....	....
	Detroit	NHL	47	3	11	14	101	18	1	1	2	22
	NHL Totals		288	28	75	103	548	43	1	5	6	50

a NHL/Upper Deck All-Rookie Team (1992)

KONTOS, CHRIS (KONN-tohs) FLA.

Left wing/Center. Shoots left. 6'1", 195 lbs. Born, Toronto, Ont., December 10, 1963.
(NY Rangers' 1st choice, 15th overall, in 1982 Entry Draft).

			Regular Season					Playoffs				
Season	Club	Lea	GP	G	A	TP	PIM	GP	G	A	TP	PIM
1980-81	Sudbury	OHA	57	17	27	44	36	....	....	....	....	....
1981-82	Sudbury	OHL	12	6	6	12	18	....	....	....	....	....
	Toronto	OHL	59	36	56	92	68	10	7	9	16	2
1982-83	NY Rangers	NHL	44	8	7	15	33	....	....	....	....	....
	Toronto	OHL	28	21	33	54	23	....	....	....	....	....
1983-84	NY Rangers	NHL	6	0	1	1	8	....	....	....	....	....
	Tulsa	CHL	21	5	13	18	8	....	....	....	....	....
1984-85	NY Rangers	NHL	28	4	8	12	24	....	....	....	....	....
	New Haven	AHL	48	19	24	43	30	....	....	....	....	....
1985-86	Ilves	Fin.	36	16	15	31	30	....	....	....	....	....
	New Haven	AHL	21	8	15	23	12	5	4	2	6	4
1986-87	Pittsburgh	NHL	31	8	9	17	6	....	....	....	....	....
	New Haven	AHL	36	14	17	31	29	....	....	....	....	....
1987-88	Pittsburgh	NHL	36	1	7	8	12	....	....	....	....	....
	Muskegon	IHL	10	3	6	9	8	....	....	....	....	....
	Los Angeles	NHL	6	2	10	12	2	4	1	0	1	4
	New Haven	AHL	16	8	16	24	4	....	....	....	....	....
1988-89	EHC Kloten	Swiss	36	33	22	55	....	6	6	2	8	....
	Los Angeles	NHL	7	2	1	3	2	11	9	0	9	8
1989-90	Los Angeles	NHL	6	2	2	4	4	5	1	0	1	0
	New Haven	AHL	42	10	20	30	25	....	....	....	....	....
1990-91	Phoenix	IHL	69	26	36	62	19	11	9	12	21	0
1991-92	Cdn. National	....	26	10	10	20	4	....	....	....	....	....
1992-93	Tampa Bay	NHL	66	27	24	51	12	....	....	....	....	....
1993-94	Cdn. National	....	35	16	16	32	12	....	....	....	....	....
	Cdn. Olympic	....	8	3	1	4	2	....	....	....	....	....
1994-95	Cdn. National	....	3	0	1	1	4	....	....	....	....	....
	NHL Totals		230	54	69	123	103	20	11	0	11	12

Traded to **Pittsburgh** by **NY Rangers** for Ron Duguay, January 21, 1987. Traded to **Los Angeles** by **Pittsburgh** with Pittsburgh's sixth round choice (Micah Aivazoff) in 1988 Entry Draft for Bryan Erickson, February 5, 1988. Signed as a free agent by **Tampa Bay**, July 21, 1992. Signed as a free agent by **Florida**, July 7, 1995.

KORDIC, DAN PHI.

Defense. Shoots left. 6'5", 220 lbs. Born, Edmonton, Alta., April 18, 1971.
(Philadelphia's 9th choice, 88th overall, in 1990 Entry Draft).

			Regular Season					Playoffs				
Season	Club	Lea	GP	G	A	TP	PIM	GP	G	A	TP	PIM
1987-88	Medicine Hat	WHL	63	1	5	6	75	....	....	....	....	....
1988-89	Medicine Hat	WHL	70	1	13	14	190	....	....	....	....	....
1989-90	Medicine Hat	WHL	59	4	12	16	182	3	0	0	0	9
1990-91	Medicine Hat	WHL	67	8	15	23	150	12	2	6	8	42
1991-92	Philadelphia	NHL	46	1	3	4	126	....	....	....	....	....
1992-93	Hershey	AHL	14	0	2	2	17	....	....	....	....	....
1993-94	Philadelphia	NHL	4	0	0	0	5	....	....	....	....	....
	Hershey	AHL	64	0	4	4	164	11	0	3	3	26
1994-95	Hershey	AHL	37	0	2	2	121	6	0	1	1	21
	NHL Totals		50	1	3	4	131	....	....	....	....	....

KOROBOLIN, ALEXANDER (koh-roh-BOH-lihn) NYR

Defense. Shoots left. 6'2", 189 lbs. Born, Chelyabinsk, USSR, March 12, 1976.
(NY Rangers' 4th choice, 100th overall, in 1994 Entry Draft).

			Regular Season					Playoffs				
Season	Club	Lea	GP	G	A	TP	PIM	GP	G	A	TP	PIM
1993-94	Chelyabinsk	CIS	32	0	0	0	30	....	....	....	....	....
1994-95	Chelyabinsk	CIS 2				UNAVAILABLE						

KOROLEV, IGOR (koh-roh-LEHV) WPG.

Right wing. Shoots left. 6'1", 187 lbs. Born, Moscow, USSR, September 6, 1970.
(St. Louis' 1st choice, 38th overall, in 1992 Entry Draft).

			Regular Season					Playoffs				
Season	Club	Lea	GP	G	A	TP	PIM	GP	G	A	TP	PIM
1988-89	Moscow D'amo	USSR	1	0	0	0	2	....	....	....	....	....
1989-90	Moscow D'amo	USSR	17	3	2	5	2	....	....	....	....	....
1990-91	Moscow D'amo	USSR	38	12	4	16	12	....	....	....	....	....
1991-92	Moscow D'amo	CIS	39	15	12	27	16	....	....	....	....	....
1992-93	Moscow D'amo	CIS	5	1	2	3	4	....	....	....	....	....
	St. Louis	NHL	74	4	23	27	20	3	0	0	0	0
1993-94	St. Louis	NHL	73	6	10	16	40	2	0	0	0	0
1994-95	Moscow D'amo	CIS	13	4	6	10	18	....	....	....	....	....
	Winnipeg	NHL	45	8	22	30	10	....	....	....	....	....
	NHL Totals		192	18	55	73	70	5	0	0	0	0

Claimed by **Winnipeg** from **St. Louis** in NHL Waiver Draft, January 18, 1995.

KOROLYUK, ALEXANDER (koh-roh-LYUHK) S.J.

Right wing. Shoots left. 5'9", 170 lbs. Born, Moscow, USSR, January 15, 1976.
(San Jose's 6th choice, 141st overall, in 1994 Entry Draft).

			Regular Season					Playoffs				
Season	Club	Lea	GP	G	A	TP	PIM	GP	G	A	TP	PIM
1993-94	Soviet Wings	CIS	22	4	4	8	20	3	1	0	1	4
1994-95	Soviet Wings	CIS	52	16	13	29	62	4	1	2	3	4

KOROTKOV, KONSTANTIN (KOH-raht-kohv) HFD.

Center. Shoots left. 5'9", 174 lbs. Born, Moscow, USSR, January 25, 1972.
(Hartford's 8th choice, 177th overall, in 1992 Entry Draft).

			Regular Season					Playoffs				
Season	Club	Lea	GP	G	A	TP	PIM	GP	G	A	TP	PIM
1987-88	Spartak	USSR	1	0	0	0	0	....	....	....	....	....
1988-89	Spartak	USSR	3	0	0	0	0	....	....	....	....	....
1989-90	Spartak	USSR	31	2	3	5	2	....	....	....	....	....
1990-91	Spartak	USSR	34	3	3	6	11	....	....	....	....	....
1991-92	Spartak	CIS	35	4	1	5	46	....	....	....	....	....
1992-93	Spartak	CIS	39	5	6	11	32	3	0	2	2	4
1993-94	Spartak	CIS	36	4	14	18	30	6	2	1	3	12
1994-95	Spartak	CIS	49	6	19	25	24	....	....	....	....	....

KOVALENKO, ANDREI (koh-vah-LEHN-koh) COL.

Right wing. Shoots left. 5'10", 200 lbs. Born, Balakovo, USSR, June 7, 1970.
(Quebec's 6th choice, 148th overall, in 1990 Entry Draft).

			Regular Season					Playoffs				
Season	Club	Lea	GP	G	A	TP	PIM	GP	G	A	TP	PIM
1988-89	CSKA	USSR	10	1	0	1	0	....	....	....	....	....
1989-90	CSKA	USSR	48	8	5	13	20	....	....	....	....	....
1990-91	CSKA	USSR	45	13	8	21	26	....	....	....	....	....
1991-92	CSKA	CIS	44	19	13	32	32	....	....	....	....	....
1992-93	CSKA	CIS	3	3	1	4	4	....	....	....	....	....
	Quebec	NHL	81	27	41	68	57	4	1	0	1	2
1993-94	Quebec	NHL	58	16	17	33	46	....	....	....	....	....
1994-95	Togliatti	CIS	11	9	2	11	14	....	....	....	....	....
	Quebec	NHL	45	14	10	24	31	6	0	1	1	2
	NHL Totals		184	57	68	125	134	10	1	1	2	4

KOVALEV, ALEXEI (koh-VAH-lehv) NYR

Right wing. Shoots left. 6', 205 lbs. Born, Togliatti, USSR, February 24, 1973.
(NY Rangers' 1st choice, 15th overall, in 1991 Entry Draft).

			Regular Season					Playoffs				
Season	Club	Lea	GP	G	A	TP	PIM	GP	G	A	TP	PIM
1989-90	Moscow D'amo	USSR	1	0	0	0	0	....	....	....	....	....
1990-91	Moscow D'amo	USSR	18	1	2	3	4	....	....	....	....	....
1991-92	Moscow D'amo	CIS	33	16	9	25	20	....	....	....	....	....
1992-93	NY Rangers	NHL	65	20	18	38	79	....	....	....	....	....
	Binghamton	AHL	13	13	11	24	35	9	3	5	8	14
1993-94	NY Rangers	NHL	76	23	33	56	154	23	9	12	21	18
1994-95	Togliatti	CIS	12	8	8	16	49	....	....	....	....	....
	NY Rangers	NHL	48	13	15	28	30	10	4	7	11	10
	NHL Totals		189	56	66	122	263	33	13	19	32	28

KOZLOV, VIKTOR (KAHS-lahf) S.J.

Left wing. Shoots right. 6'5", 225 lbs. Born, Togliatti, USSR, February 14, 1975.
(San Jose's 1st choice, 6th overall, in 1993 Entry Draft).

			Regular Season					Playoffs				
Season	Club	Lea	GP	G	A	TP	PIM	GP	G	A	TP	PIM
1990-91	Togliatti	USSR 2	2	2	0	2	0	....	....	....	....	....
1991-92	Togliatti	CIS	3	0	0	0	0	....	....	....	....	....
1992-93	Moscow D'amo	CIS	30	6	5	11	4	10	3	0	3	0
1993-94	Moscow D'amo	CIS	42	16	9	25	14	7	3	2	5	0
1994-95	Moscow D'amo	CIS	3	1	1	2	2	....	....	....	....	....
	San Jose	NHL	16	2	0	2	2	....	....	....	....	....
	Kansas City	IHL	4	1	1	2	0	13	4	5	9	12
	NHL Totals		16	2	0	2	2	....	....	....	....	....

KOZLOV, VYACHESLAV (KAHS-lahf, VYACH-ih-slav) **DET.**

Center. Shoots left. 5'10", 180 lbs. Born, Voskresensk, USSR, May 3, 1972.
(Detroit's 2nd choice, 45th overall, in 1990 Entry Draft).

			Regular Season					Playoffs				
Season	Club	Lea	GP	G	A	TP	PIM	GP	G	A	TP	PIM
1987-88	Khimik	USSR	2	0	0	0	0	....	....	....	....	....
1988-89	Khimik	USSR	14	0	1	1	2	....	....	....	....	....
1989-90	Khimik	USSR	45	14	12	26	38	....	....	....	....	....
1990-91	Khimik	USSR	45	11	13	24	46	....	....	....	....	....
1991-92	CSKA	CIS	11	6	5	11	12	....	....	....	....	....
	Detroit	**NHL**	**7**	**0**	**2**	**2**	**2**	....	....	....	....	....
1992-93	**Detroit**	**NHL**	**17**	**4**	**1**	**5**	**14**	**4**	**0**	**2**	**2**	**2**
	Adirondack	AHL	45	23	36	59	54	4	1	1	2	4
1993-94	**Detroit**	**NHL**	**77**	**34**	**39**	**73**	**50**	**7**	**2**	**5**	**7**	**12**
	Adirondack	AHL	3	0	1	1	15	....	....	....	....	....
1994-95	CSKA	CIS	10	3	4	7	14	....	....	....	....	....
	Detroit	**NHL**	**46**	**13**	**20**	**33**	**45**	**18**	**9**	**7**	**16**	**10**
	NHL Totals		**147**	**51**	**62**	**113**	**111**	**29**	**11**	**14**	**25**	**24**

KRALL, JUSTIN **DET.**

Defense. Shoots left. 6'2", 170 lbs. Born, Toledo, OH, February 20, 1974.
(Detroit's 8th choice, 183rd overall, in 1992 Entry Draft).

			Regular Season					Playoffs				
Season	Club	Lea	GP	G	A	TP	PIM	GP	G	A	TP	PIM
1992-93	Miami-Ohio	CCHA	39	5	6	11	26	....	....	....	....	....
1993-94	Miami-Ohio	CCHA	38	1	4	6	32	....	....	....	....	....
1994-95	Miami-Ohio	CCHA	38	1	9	10	38	....	....	....	....	....

KRAMER, BRADY **MTL.**

Center. Shoots left. 6'2", 180 lbs. Born, Philadelphia, PA, June 13, 1973.
(Montreal's 10th choice, 149th overall, in 1991 Entry Draft).

			Regular Season					Playoffs				
Season	Club	Lea	GP	G	A	TP	PIM	GP	G	A	TP	PIM
1991-92	Providence	H.E.	36	11	10	21	47	....	....	....	....	....
1992-93	Providence	H.E.	32	14	14	28	52	....	....	....	....	....
1993-94	Providence	H.E.	36	12	26	38	50	....	....	....	....	....
1994-95	Providence	H.E.	37	23	29	52	64	....	....	....	....	....
	Fredericton	AHL	6	3	0	3	7	12	3	2	5	2

KRAVCHUK, IGOR (krahv-CHOOK) **EDM.**

Defense. Shoots left. 6'1", 200 lbs. Born, Ufa, USSR, September 13, 1966.
(Chicago's 5th choice, 71st overall, in 1991 Entry Draft).

			Regular Season					Playoffs				
Season	Club	Lea	GP	G	A	TP	PIM	GP	G	A	TP	PIM
1982-83	Yulayev	USSR	10	0	0	0	0	....	....	....	....	....
	Yulayev	USSR 2	....	....	....	....	....	....	....	....	....	....
1984-85	Yulayev	USSR 2	50	3	2	5	22	....	....	....	....	....
1985-86	Yulayev	USSR	21	2	2	4	6	....	....	....	....	....
1986-87	Yulayev	USSR	22	0	1	1	8	....	....	....	....	....
1987-88	CSKA	USSR	48	1	8	9	12	....	....	....	....	....
1988-89	CSKA	USSR	22	3	3	6	2	....	....	....	....	....
1989-90	CSKA	USSR	48	1	3	4	16	....	....	....	....	....
1990-91	CSKA	USSR	41	6	5	11	16	....	....	....	....	....
1991-92	CSKA	CIS	30	3	8	11	6	....	....	....	....	....
	Chicago	**NHL**	**18**	**1**	**8**	**9**	**4**	**18**	**2**	**6**	**8**	**8**
1992-93	**Chicago**	**NHL**	**38**	**6**	**9**	**15**	**30**	....	....	....	....	....
	Edmonton	**NHL**	**17**	**4**	**8**	**12**	**2**	....	....	....	....	....
1993-94	**Edmonton**	**NHL**	**81**	**12**	**38**	**50**	**16**	....	....	....	....	....
1994-95	**Edmonton**	**NHL**	**36**	**7**	**11**	**18**	**29**	....	....	....	....	....
	NHL Totals		**190**	**30**	**74**	**104**	**81**	**18**	**2**	**6**	**8**	**8**

Traded to **Edmonton** by **Chicago** with Dean McAmmond for Joe Murphy, February 24, 1993.

KRISS, AARON **S.J.**

Defense. Shoots left. 6'2", 185 lbs. Born, Parma, OH, September 17, 1972.
(San Jose's 11th choice, 221st overall, in 1991 Entry Draft).

			Regular Season					Playoffs				
Season	Club	Lea	GP	G	A	TP	PIM	GP	G	A	TP	PIM
1991-92	Lowell	H.E.	29	1	4	5	22	....	....	....	....	....
1992-93	Lowell	H.E.	25	3	5	8	10	....	....	....	....	....
1993-94	Lowell	H.E.	34	5	10	15	48	....	....	....	....	....
1994-95	Lowell	H.E.	40	3	8	11	56	....	....	....	....	....

KRIVCHENKOV, ALEXEI (krihv-chehn-KOHV) **PIT.**

Defense. Shoots left. 6', 185 lbs. Born, Novosibirsk, USSR, June 11, 1974.
(Pittsburgh's 5th choice, 76th overall, in 1994 Entry Draft).

			Regular Season					Playoffs				
Season	Club	Lea	GP	G	A	TP	PIM	GP	G	A	TP	PIM
1993-94	Sibir Novosibirsk	CIS 2	37	1	3	4	48	....	....	....	....	....
	CSKA	CIS	4	0	0	0	2	3	0	0	0	0
1994-95	CSKA	CIS	46	1	4	5	43	2	0	0	0	0

KRIVOKRASOV, SERGEI (krih-vuh-KRA-sahf) **CHI.**

Right wing. Shoots left. 5'10", 195 lbs. Born, Angarsk, USSR, April 15, 1974.
(Chicago's 1st choice, 12th overall, in 1992 Entry Draft).

			Regular Season					Playoffs				
Season	Club	Lea	GP	G	A	TP	PIM	GP	G	A	TP	PIM
1990-91	CSKA	USSR	41	4	0	4	8	....	....	....	....	....
1991-92	CSKA	CIS	42	10	8	18	35	....	....	....	....	....
1992-93	**Chicago**	**NHL**	**4**	**0**	**0**	**0**	**2**	....	....	....	....	....
	Indianapolis	IHL	78	36	33	69	157	5	3	1	4	2
1993-94	**Chicago**	**NHL**	**9**	**1**	**0**	**1**	**4**	....	....	....	....	....
	Indianapolis	IHL	53	19	26	45	145	....	....	....	....	....
1994-95	Indianapolis	IHL	29	12	15	27	41	....	....	....	....	....
	Chicago	**NHL**	**41**	**12**	**7**	**19**	**33**	**10**	**0**	**0**	**0**	**8**
	NHL Totals		**54**	**13**	**7**	**20**	**39**	**10**	**0**	**0**	**0**	**8**

KRIZ, PAVEL (KRIHZH) **CHI.**

Defense. Shoots right. 6'1", 205 lbs. Born, Nymburk, Czech., January 2, 1977.
(Chicago's 5th choice, 97th overall, in 1995 Entry Draft).

			Regular Season					Playoffs				
Season	Club	Lea	GP	G	A	TP	PIM	GP	G	A	TP	PIM
1994-95	Tri-City	WHL	68	6	34	40	47	17	5	12	17	6

KRON, ROBERT (KROHN) **HFD.**

Left wing. Shoots left. 5'10", 180 lbs. Born, Brno, Czech., February 27, 1967.
(Vancouver's 5th choice, 88th overall, in 1985 Entry Draft).

			Regular Season					Playoffs				
Season	Club	Lea	GP	G	A	TP	PIM	GP	G	A	TP	PIM
1983-84	Ingstav Brno	Czech.2	3	0	1	1	0	....	....	....	....	....
1984-85	Zetor Brno	Czech.	40	6	8	14	6	....	....	....	....	....
1985-86	Zetor Brno	Czech.	44	5	6	11	....	....	....	....	....	....
1986-87	Zetor Brno	Czech.	34	18	11	29	10	....	....	....	....	....
1987-88	Zetor Brno	Czech.	44	14	7	21	30	....	....	....	....	....
1988-89	Dukla Trencin	Czech.	43	28	19	47	26	....	....	....	....	....
1989-90	Dukla Trencin	Czech.	39	22	22	44	....	....	....	....	....	....
1990-91	**Vancouver**	**NHL**	**76**	**12**	**20**	**32**	**21**	....	....	....	....	....
1991-92	**Vancouver**	**NHL**	**36**	**2**	**2**	**4**	**2**	**11**	**1**	**2**	**3**	**2**
1992-93	**Vancouver**	**NHL**	**32**	**10**	**11**	**21**	**14**	....	....	....	....	....
	Hartford	**NHL**	**13**	**4**	**2**	**6**	**4**	....	....	....	....	....
1993-94	**Hartford**	**NHL**	**77**	**24**	**26**	**50**	**8**	....	....	....	....	....
1994-95	**Hartford**	**NHL**	**37**	**10**	**8**	**18**	**10**	....	....	....	....	....
	NHL Totals		**271**	**62**	**69**	**131**	**59**	**11**	**1**	**2**	**3**	**2**

Traded to **Hartford** by **Vancouver** with Vancouver's third round choice (Marek Malik) in 1993 Entry Draft and future considerations (Jim Sandlak, May 17, 1993) for Murray Craven and Vancouver's fifth round choice (previously acquired by Hartford — Vancouver selected Scott Walker) in 1993 Entry Draft, March 22, 1993.

KROPAC, RADOSLAV (KRO-pahch) **NYR**

Right wing. Shoots left. 6', 187 lbs. Born, Bratislava, Czech., April 5, 1975.
(NY Rangers' 13th choice, 260th overall, in 1994 Entry Draft).

			Regular Season					Playoffs				
Season	Club	Lea	GP	G	A	TP	PIM	GP	G	A	TP	PIM
1993-94	Bratislava	Slovak	33	7	6	13	12	....	....	....	....	....
1994-95	Bratislava	Slovak	35	17	8	25	38	....	....	....	....	....

KROUPA, VLASTIMIL (KROO-pah, VLAS-tuh-meel) **S.J.**

Defense. Shoots left. 6'3", 210 lbs. Born, Most, Czech., April 27, 1975.
(San Jose's 3rd choice, 45th overall, in 1993 Entry Draft).

			Regular Season					Playoffs				
Season	Club	Lea	GP	G	A	TP	PIM	GP	G	A	TP	PIM
1992-93	Litvinov	Czech.	9	0	1	1	....	....	....	....	....	....
1993-94	**San Jose**	**NHL**	**27**	**1**	**3**	**4**	**20**	**14**	**1**	**2**	**3**	**21**
	Kansas City	IHL	39	3	12	15	12	....	....	....	....	....
1994-95	Kansas City	IHL	51	4	8	12	49	12	2	4	6	22
	San Jose	**NHL**	**14**	**0**	**2**	**2**	**16**	**6**	**0**	**0**	**0**	**4**
	NHL Totals		**41**	**1**	**5**	**6**	**36**	**20**	**1**	**2**	**3**	**25**

KRUPP, UWE (KROOP, OO-VAY) **COL.**

Defense. Shoots right. 6'6", 235 lbs. Born, Cologne, West Germany, June 24, 1965.
(Buffalo's 13th choice, 214th overall, in 1983 Entry Draft).

			Regular Season					Playoffs				
Season	Club	Lea	GP	G	A	TP	PIM	GP	G	A	TP	PIM
1982-83	Koln	W.Ger.	11	0	0	0	0	....	....	....	....	....
1983-84	Koln	W.Ger.	26	0	4	4	22	....	....	....	....	....
1984-85	Koln	W.Ger.	39	11	8	19	36	....	....	....	....	....
1985-86	Koln	W.Ger.	45	10	21	31	83	....	....	....	....	....
1986-87	**Buffalo**	**NHL**	**26**	**1**	**4**	**5**	**23**	....	....	....	....	....
	Rochester	AHL	42	3	19	22	50	17	1	11	12	16
1987-88	**Buffalo**	**NHL**	**75**	**2**	**9**	**11**	**151**	**6**	**0**	**0**	**0**	**15**
1988-89	**Buffalo**	**NHL**	**70**	**5**	**13**	**18**	**55**	**5**	**0**	**1**	**1**	**4**
1989-90	**Buffalo**	**NHL**	**74**	**3**	**20**	**23**	**85**	**6**	**0**	**0**	**0**	**4**
1990-91	**Buffalo**	**NHL**	**74**	**12**	**32**	**44**	**66**	**6**	**1**	**1**	**2**	**6**
1991-92	**Buffalo**	**NHL**	**8**	**2**	**0**	**2**	**6**	....	....	....	....	....
	NY Islanders	**NHL**	**59**	**6**	**29**	**35**	**43**	....	....	....	....	....
1992-93	**NY Islanders**	**NHL**	**80**	**9**	**29**	**38**	**67**	**18**	**1**	**5**	**6**	**12**
1993-94	**NY Islanders**	**NHL**	**41**	**7**	**14**	**21**	**30**	**4**	**0**	**1**	**1**	**4**
1994-95	Landshut	Ger.	5	1	2	3	6	....	....	....	....	....
	Quebec	**NHL**	**44**	**6**	**17**	**23**	**20**	**5**	**0**	**2**	**2**	**2**
	NHL Totals		**551**	**53**	**167**	**220**	**546**	**50**	**2**	**10**	**12**	**47**

Played in NHL All-Star Game (1991)

Traded to **NY Islanders** by **Buffalo** with Pierre Turgeon, Benoit Hogue and Dave McLlwain for Pat Lafontaine, Randy Hillier, Randy Wood and NY Islanders' fourth round choice (Dean Melanson) in 1992 Entry Draft, October 25, 1991. Traded to **Quebec** by **NY Islanders** with NY Islanders' first round choice (Wade Belak) in 1994 Entry Draft for Ron Sutter and Quebec's first round choice (Brett Lindros) in 1994 Entry Draft, June 28, 1994.

KRUPPKE, GORD (KRUHP-kee)

Defense. Shoots right. 6'1", 215 lbs. Born, Slave Lake, Alta., April 2, 1969.
(Detroit's 2nd choice, 32nd overall, in 1987 Entry Draft).

			Regular Season					Playoffs				
Season	Club	Lea	GP	G	A	TP	PIM	GP	G	A	TP	PIM
1985-86	Prince Albert	WHL	62	1	8	9	81	20	4	4	8	22
1986-87	Prince Albert	WHL	49	2	10	12	129	8	0	0	0	9
1987-88	Prince Albert	WHL	54	8	8	16	113	10	0	0	0	46
1988-89	Prince Albert	WHL	62	6	26	32	254	3	0	0	0	11
1989-90	Adirondack	AHL	59	2	12	14	103	....	....	....	....	....
1990-91	**Detroit**	**NHL**	**4**	**0**	**0**	**0**	**0**	....	....	....	....	....
	Adirondack	AHL	45	1	8	9	153	....	....	....	....	....
1991-92	Adirondack	AHL	65	3	9	12	208	16	0	1	1	52
1992-93	**Detroit**	**NHL**	**10**	**0**	**0**	**0**	**20**	....	....	....	....	....
	Adirondack	AHL	41	2	12	14	197	9	1	2	3	20
1993-94	**Detroit**	**NHL**	**9**	**0**	**0**	**0**	**12**	....	....	....	....	....
	Adirondack	AHL	54	2	9	11	210	12	1	3	4	32
1994-95	Adirondack	AHL	48	2	9	11	157	....	....	....	....	....
	St. John's	AHL	3	0	1	1	6	....	....	....	....	....
	NHL Totals		**23**	**0**	**0**	**0**	**32**	....	....	....	....	....

Traded to **Toronto** by **Detroit** for other considerations, April 7, 1995.

KRUSE, PAUL (KROOZ) **CGY.**

Left wing. Shoots left. 6', 202 lbs. Born, Merritt, B.C., March 15, 1970.
(Calgary's 6th choice, 83rd overall, in 1990 Entry Draft).

			Regular Season					Playoffs				
Season	Club	Lea	GP	G	A	TP	PIM	GP	G	A	TP	PIM
1988-89	Kamloops	WHL	68	8	15	23	209	....	....	....	....	....
1989-90	Kamloops	WHL	67	22	23	45	291	17	3	5	8	79
1990-91	**Calgary**	**NHL**	**1**	**0**	**0**	**0**	**7**	....	....	....	....	....
	Salt Lake	IHL	83	24	20	44	313	4	1	1	2	4
1991-92	**Calgary**	**NHL**	**16**	**3**	**1**	**4**	**65**	....	....	....	....	....
	Salt Lake	IHL	57	14	15	29	267	5	1	2	3	19
1992-93	**Calgary**	**NHL**	**27**	**2**	**3**	**5**	**41**	....	....	....	....	....
	Salt Lake	IHL	35	1	4	5	206	....	....	....	....	....
1993-94	**Calgary**	**NHL**	**68**	**3**	**8**	**11**	**185**	**7**	**0**	**0**	**0**	**14**
1994-95	**Calgary**	**NHL**	**45**	**11**	**5**	**16**	**141**	**7**	**4**	**2**	**6**	**10**
	NHL Totals		**157**	**19**	**17**	**36**	**439**	**14**	**4**	**2**	**6**	**24**

KRUSHELNYSKI, MIKE

(KROO-shuhl-NIH-skee)

Left wing/Center. Shoots left. 6'2", 200 lbs.   Born, Montreal, Que., April 27, 1960.
(Boston's 7th choice, 120th overall, in 1979 Entry Draft).

			Regular Season					Playoffs				
Season	Club	Lea	GP	G	A	TP	PIM	GP	G	A	TP	PIM
1978-79	Montreal	QJHL	46	15	29	44	42	11	3	4	7	8
1979-80	Montreal	QJHL	72	39	60	99	78	6	2	3	5	2
1980-81	Springfield	AHL	80	25	28	53	47	7	1	1	2	29
1981-82	**Boston**	**NHL**	**17**	**3**	**3**	**6**	**2**	**1**	**0**	**0**	**0**	**2**
	Erie	AHL	62	31	52	83	44	....	....	....	....	....
1982-83	Boston	NHL	79	23	42	65	43	17	8	6	14	12
1983-84	Boston	NHL	66	25	20	45	55	2	0	0	0	0
1984-85	Edmonton	NHL	80	43	45	88	60	18	5	8	13	22
1985-86	Edmonton	NHL	54	16	24	40	22	10	4	5	9	16
1986-87	Edmonton	NHL	80	16	35	51	67	21	3	4	7	18
1987-88	Edmonton	NHL	76	20	27	47	64	19	4	6	10	12
1988-89	Los Angeles	NHL	78	26	36	62	110	11	1	4	5	4
1989-90	Los Angeles	NHL	63	16	25	41	50	10	1	3	4	12
1990-91	Los Angeles	NHL	15	1	5	6	10	....	....	....	....	....
	Toronto	NHL	59	17	22	39	48	....	....	....	....	....
1991-92	Toronto	NHL	72	9	15	24	72	....	....	....	....	....
1992-93	Toronto	NHL	84	19	20	39	62	16	3	7	10	8
1993-94	Toronto	NHL	54	5	6	11	28	6	0	0	0	0
1994-95	Detroit	NHL	20	2	3	5	6	8	0	0	0	0
	NHL Totals		**897**	**241**	**328**	**569**	**699**	**139**	**29**	**43**	**72**	**106**

Played in NHL All-Star Game (1985)

Traded to **Edmonton** by **Boston** for Ken Linseman, June 21, 1984. Traded to **Los Angeles** by **Edmonton** with Wayne Gretzky and Marty McSorley for Jimmy Carson, Martin Gelinas, Los Angeles' first round choices in 1989 (acquired by New Jersey — New Jersey selected Jason Miller), 1991 (Martin Rucinsky) and 1993 (Nick Stajduhar) Entry Drafts and cash, August 9, 1988. Traded to **Toronto** by **Los Angeles** for John McIntyre, November 9, 1990. Signed as a free agent by **Detroit**, August 1, 1994.

KRYGIER, TODD

(KREE-guhr) ANA.

Left wing. Shoots left. 6', 185 lbs.   Born, Chicago Heights, MI, October 12, 1965.
(Hartford's 1st choice, 16th overall, in 1988 Supplemental Draft).

			Regular Season					Playoffs				
Season	Club	Lea	GP	G	A	TP	PIM	GP	G	A	TP	PIM
1984-85	U. Connecticut	NCAA	14	14	11	25	12	....	....	....	....	....
1985-86	U. Connecticut	NCAA	32	29	27	56	46	....	....	....	....	....
1986-87	U. Connecticut	NCAA	28	24	24	48	44	....	....	....	....	....
1987-88	U. Connecticut	NCAA	27	32	39	71	28	....	....	....	....	....
	New Haven	AHL	13	1	5	6	34	....	....	....	....	....
1988-89	Binghamton	AHL	76	26	42	68	77	....	....	....	....	....
1989-90	Hartford	NHL	58	18	12	30	52	7	2	1	3	4
	Binghamton	AHL	12	1	9	10	16	....	....	....	....	....
1990-91	Hartford	NHL	72	13	17	30	95	6	0	2	2	0
1991-92	Washington	NHL	67	13	17	30	107	5	2	1	3	4
1992-93	Washington	NHL	77	11	12	23	60	6	1	1	2	4
1993-94	Washington	NHL	66	12	18	30	60	5	2	0	2	10
1994-95	Anaheim	NHL	35	11	11	22	10	....	....	....	....	....
	NHL Totals		**375**	**78**	**87**	**165**	**384**	**29**	**7**	**5**	**12**	**22**

Traded to **Washington** by **Hartford** for future considerations (Washington's fourth round choice — later traded to Calgary — Calgary selected Jason Smith in 1993 Entry Draft), October 3, 1991. Traded to **Anaheim** by **Washington** for Anaheim's fourth round choice in 1996 Entry Draft, February 2, 1995.

KUCERA, FRANTISEK

(koo-CHAIR-uh) HFD.

Defense. Shoots right. 6'2", 205 lbs.   Born, Prague, Czech., February 3, 1968.
(Chicago's 3rd choice, 77th overall, in 1986 Entry Draft).

			Regular Season					Playoffs				
Season	Club	Lea	GP	G	A	TP	PIM	GP	G	A	TP	PIM
1985-86	Sparta Praha	Czech.	15	0	0	0	....	....	....	....	....	....
1986-87	Sparta Praha	Czech.	40	5	2	7	14	....	....	....	....	....
1987-88	Sparta Praha	Czech.	46	7	2	9	30	....	....	....	....	....
1988-89	Dukla Jihlava	Czech.	45	10	9	19	28	....	....	....	....	....
1989-90	Dukla Jihlava	Czech.	43	9	10	19	....	....	....	....	....	....
1990-91	Chicago	NHL	40	2	12	14	32	....	....	....	....	....
	Indianapolis	IHL	35	8	19	27	23	7	0	1	1	15
1991-92	Chicago	NHL	61	3	10	13	36	6	0	0	0	0
	Indianapolis	IHL	7	1	2	3	4	....	....	....	....	....
1992-93	Chicago	NHL	71	5	14	19	59	....	....	....	....	....
1993-94	Chicago	NHL	60	4	13	17	34	....	....	....	....	....
	Hartford	NHL	16	1	3	4	14	....	....	....	....	....
1994-95	Sparta Praha	Czech.	16	1	2	3	14	....	....	....	....	....
	Hartford	NHL	48	3	17	20	30	....	....	....	....	....
	NHL Totals		**296**	**18**	**69**	**87**	**205**	**6**	**0**	**0**	**0**	**0**

Traded to **Hartford** by **Chicago** with Jocelyn Lemieux for Gary Suter, Randy Cunneyworth and Hartford's third round choice (later traded to Vancouver — Vancouver selected Larry Courville) in 1995 Entry Draft, March 11, 1994.

KUCERA, JIRI

(kuh-CHEH-rah) PIT.

Center. Shoots left. 5'11", 180 lbs.   Born, Plzen, Czech., March 28, 1966.
(Pittsburgh's 8th choice, 152nd overall, in 1987 Entry Draft).

			Regular Season					Playoffs				
Season	Club	Lea	GP	G	A	TP	PIM	GP	G	A	TP	PIM
1986-87	Dukla Jihlava	Czech.	43	13	12	25	18	....	....	....	....	....
1987-88	Skoda Plzen	Czech.	41	21	24	45	22	....	....	....	....	....
1988-89	Skoda Plzen	Czech.	40	20	15	35	22	....	....	....	....	....
1989-90	Skoda Plzen	Czech.	47	13	24	37	....	....	....	....	....	....
1990-91	Tappara	Fin.	44	23	34	57	26	3	0	2	2	4
1991-92	Tappara	Fin.	44	22	20	42	8	....	....	....	....	....
1992-93	Tappara	Fin.	48	22	32	54	20	....	....	....	....	....
1993-94	Tappara	Fin.	47	16	26	42	37	10	7	5	12	4
1994-95	Lulea	Swe.	40	15	12	27	24	9	2	7	9	8

KUCHARCIK, TOMAS

(koo-HAHR-chihk) TOR.

Center. Shoots left. 6'2", 200 lbs.   Born, Vlasim, Czech., May 10, 1970.
(Toronto's 11th choice, 167th overall, in 1991 Entry Draft).

			Regular Season					Playoffs				
Season	Club	Lea	GP	G	A	TP	PIM	GP	G	A	TP	PIM
1990-91	Dukla Jihlava	Czech.	30	10	6	16	6	....	....	....	....	....
1991-92	Dukla Jihlava	Czech.	45	16	23	39	24	....	....	....	....	....
1992-93	Dukla Jihlava	Czech.	39	17	20	37	....	....	....	....	....	....
1993-94	Skoda Plzen	Czech.	32	10	10	20	0	....	....	....	....	....
	St. John's	AHL	8	2	3	5	4	10	3	4	7	2
1994-95	Plzen	Czech.	40	14	4	18	22	3	0	0	0	14

KUDASHOV, ALEXEI

(koo-dah-SHOV) FLA.

Center. Shoots right. 6', 183 lbs.   Born, Elektrostal, USSR, July 21, 1971.
(Toronto's 3rd choice, 102nd overall, in 1991 Entry Draft).

			Regular Season					Playoffs				
Season	Club	Lea	GP	G	A	TP	PIM	GP	G	A	TP	PIM
1989-90	Soviet Wings	USSR	45	0	5	5	14	....	....	....	....	....
1990-91	Soviet Wings	USSR	45	9	5	14	10	....	....	....	....	....
1991-92	Soviet Wings	CIS	42	9	16	25	14	....	....	....	....	....
1992-93	Soviet Wings	CIS	41	8	20	28	24	7	1	3	4	4
1993-94	Soviet Wings	CIS	1	2	0	2	0	....	....	....	....	....
	Toronto	**NHL**	**25**	**1**	**0**	**1**	**4**	....	....	....	....	....
	Rus. Olympic	....	8	1	2	3	4	....	....	....	....	....
	St. John's	AHL	27	7	15	22	21	....	....	....	....	....
1994-95	St. John's	AHL	75	25	54	79	17	5	1	4	5	2
	NHL Totals		**25**	**1**	**0**	**1**	**4**					

Signed as a free agent by **Florida**, July 27, 1995.

KUDELSKI, BOB

FLA.

Right wing. Shoots right. 6'1", 205 lbs.   Born, Springfield, MA, March 3, 1964.
(Los Angeles' 1st choice, 2nd overall, in 1986 Supplemental Draft).

			Regular Season					Playoffs				
Season	Club	Lea	GP	G	A	TP	PIM	GP	G	A	TP	PIM
1983-84	Yale	ECAC	21	14	12	26	12	....	....	....	....	....
1984-85	Yale	ECAC	32	21	23	44	38	....	....	....	....	....
1985-86	Yale	ECAC	31	18	23	41	48	....	....	....	....	....
1986-87a	Yale	ECAC	30	25	22	47	34	....	....	....	....	....
1987-88	**Los Angeles**	**NHL**	**26**	**0**	**1**	**1**	**8**	....	....	....	....	....
	New Haven	AHL	50	15	19	34	41	....	....	....	....	....
1988-89	**Los Angeles**	**NHL**	**14**	**1**	**3**	**4**	**17**	....	....	....	....	....
	New Haven	AHL	60	32	19	51	43	17	8	5	13	12
1989-90	Los Angeles	NHL	62	23	13	36	49	8	1	2	3	2
1990-91	Los Angeles	NHL	72	23	13	36	46	8	3	2	5	2
1991-92	Los Angeles	NHL	80	22	21	43	42	6	0	0	0	0
1992-93	Los Angeles	NHL	15	3	3	6	8	....	....	....	....	....
	Ottawa	NHL	48	21	14	35	22	....	....	....	....	....
1993-94	Ottawa	NHL	42	26	15	41	14	....	....	....	....	....
	Florida	NHL	44	14	15	29	10	....	....	....	....	....
1994-95	Florida	NHL	26	6	3	9	2	....	....	....	....	....
	NHL Totals		**429**	**139**	**101**	**240**	**218**	**22**	**4**	**4**	**8**	**4**

a ECAC First All-Star Team (1987)

Played in NHL All-Star Game (1994)

Traded to **Ottawa** by **Los Angeles** with Shawn McCosh for Marc Fortier and Jim Thomson, December 19, 1992. Traded to **Florida** by **Ottawa** for Evgeny Davydov, Scott Levins and Florida's sixth round choice (Mike Gaffney) in 1994 Entry Draft and Dallas' fourth round choice (previously acquired by Florida — Ottawa selected Kevin Bolibruck) in 1995 Entry Draft, January 6, 1994.

KUDINOV, ANDREI

(kuh-DIH-nohv) NYR

Center. Shoots left. 6', 195 lbs.   Born, Chelyabinsk, USSR, June 28, 1970.
(NY Rangers' 11th choice, 242nd overall, in 1993 Entry Draft).

			Regular Season					Playoffs				
Season	Club	Lea	GP	G	A	TP	PIM	GP	G	A	TP	PIM
1990-91	Chelyabinsk	USSR	24	2	3	5	20	....	....	....	....	....
1991-92	Chelyabinsk	CIS	44	12	8	20	56	....	....	....	....	....
1992-93	Chelyabinsk	CIS	41	13	23	36	50	8	0	1	1	6
1993-94	Chelyabinsk	CIS	6	0	3	3	4	....	....	....	....	....
	Binghamton	AHL	25	3	3	6	6	....	....	....	....	....
1994-95	Binghamton	AHL	65	14	22	36	45	3	0	0	0	0

KUDRNA, JAROSLAV

S.J.

Left wing. Shoots left. 6', 180 lbs.   Born, Hradec Kralove, Czech., December 5, 1975.
(San Jose's 8th choice, 142nd overall, in 1995 Entry Draft).

			Regular Season					Playoffs				
Season	Club	Lea	GP	G	A	TP	PIM	GP	G	A	TP	PIM
1993-94	Hrad. Kralove	Czech.	5	0	0	0	0	2	0	1	1	....
1994-95	Penticton	BCJHL	58	60	55	115	148	....	....	....	....	....

KUKI, ARTO

(KUH-kee) MTL.

Center. Shoots left. 6'3", 205 lbs.   Born, Espoo, Finland, February 22, 1976.
(Montreal's 6th choice, 96th overall, in 1994 Entry Draft).

			Regular Season					Playoffs				
Season	Club	Lea	GP	G	A	TP	PIM	GP	G	A	TP	PIM
1993-94	Espoo	Fin. Jr.	26	1	10	11	28	....	....	....	....	....
1994-95	Kiekko-Espoo	Fin.	4	0	1	1	0	....	....	....	....	....

KURRI, JARI

(KUHR-ree, YAH-ree) L.A.

Right wing. Shoots right. 6'1", 195 lbs.   Born, Helsinki, Finland, May 18, 1960.
(Edmonton's 3rd choice, 69th overall, in 1980 Entry Draft).

			Regular Season					Playoffs				
Season	Club	Lea	GP	G	A	TP	PIM	GP	G	A	TP	PIM
1977-78	Jokerit	Fin.	29	2	9	11	12	....	....	....	....	....
1978-79	Jokerit	Fin.	33	16	14	30	12	....	....	....	....	....
1979-80	Jokerit	Fin.	33	23	16	39	22	6	7	2	9	13
1980-81	Edmonton	NHL	75	32	43	75	40	9	5	7	12	4
1981-82	Edmonton	NHL	71	32	54	86	32	5	2	5	7	10
1982-83	Edmonton	NHL	80	45	59	104	22	16	8	15	23	8
1983-84a	Edmonton	NHL	64	52	61	113	14	19	*14	14	28	13
1984-85bc	Edmonton	NHL	73	71	64	135	30	18	*19	12	31	6
1985-86a	Edmonton	NHL	78	*68	63	131	22	10	2	10	12	4
1986-87c	Edmonton	NHL	79	54	54	108	41	21	*15	10	25	20
1987-88	Edmonton	NHL	80	43	53	96	30	19	*14	17	31	12
1988-89a	Edmonton	NHL	76	44	58	102	69	7	3	5	8	6
1989-90	Edmonton	NHL	78	33	60	93	48	22	10	15	25	18
1990-91	Milan Devils	Italy	30	27	48	75	6	10	10	12	22	2
1991-92	Los Angeles	NHL	73	23	37	60	24	4	1	2	3	4
1992-93	Los Angeles	NHL	82	27	60	87	38	24	9	8	17	12
1993-94	Los Angeles	NHL	81	31	46	77	48	....	....	....	....	....
1994-95	Jokerit	Fin.	20	10	9	19	10	....	....	....	....	....
	Los Angeles	NHL	38	10	19	29	24	....	....	....	....	....
	NHL Totals		**1028**	**565**	**731**	**1296**	**482**	**174**	**102**	**120**	**222**	**117**

a NHL Second All-Star Team (1984, 1986, 1989)
b Won Lady Byng Memorial Trophy (1985)
c NHL First All-Star Team (1985, 1987)

Played in NHL All-Star Game (1983, 1985, 1986, 1988-90, 1993)

Traded to **Philadelphia** by **Edmonton** with Dave Brown and Corey Foster for Craig Fisher, Scott Mellanby and Craig Berube, May 30, 1991. Traded to **Los Angeles** by **Philadelphia** with Jeff Chychrun for Steve Duchesne, Steve Kasper and Los Angeles' fourth round choice (Aris Brimanis) in 1991 Entry Draft, May 30, 1991.

KURTZ, JUSTIN — WPG.

Defense. Shoots left. 6', 188 lbs. Born, Winnipeg, Man., January 14, 1977.
(Winnipeg's 5th choice, 84th overall, in 1995 Entry Draft).

			Regular Season					Playoffs				
Season	Club	Lea	GP	G	A	TP	PIM	GP	G	A	TP	PIM
1993-94	Brandon	WHL	63	3	13	16	37	14	1	3	4	24
1994-95	Brandon	WHL	65	8	34	42	75	18	2	2	4	26

KURVERS, TOM

Defense. Shoots left. 6'2", 195 lbs. Born, Minneapolis, MN, September 14, 1962.
(Montreal's 10th choice, 145th overall, in 1981 Entry Draft).

			Regular Season					Playoffs				
Season	Club	Lea	GP	G	A	TP	PIM	GP	G	A	TP	PIM
1980-81	Minn.-Duluth	WCHA	39	6	24	30	48	....	....	....	....	....
1981-82	Minn.-Duluth	WCHA	37	11	31	42	18	....	....	....	....	....
1982-83	Minn.-Duluth	WCHA	26	4	23	27	24	....	....	....	....	....
1983-84ab	Minn.-Duluth	WCHA	43	18	58	76	46	....	....	....	....	....
1984-85	**Montreal**	**NHL**	**75**	**10**	**35**	**45**	**30**	**12**	**0**	**6**	**6**	**6**
1985-86	**Montreal**	**NHL**	**62**	**7**	**23**	**30**	**36**	....	....	....	....	....
1986-87	**Montreal**	**NHL**	**1**	**0**	**0**	**0**	**0**	....	....	....	....	....
	Buffalo	**NHL**	**55**	**6**	**17**	**23**	**22**	....	....	....	....	....
1987-88	**New Jersey**	**NHL**	**56**	**5**	**29**	**34**	**46**	**19**	**6**	**9**	**15**	**38**
1988-89	**New Jersey**	**NHL**	**74**	**16**	**50**	**66**	**38**	....	....	....	....	....
1989-90	**New Jersey**	**NHL**	**1**	**0**	**0**	**0**	**0**	....	....	....	....	....
	Toronto	**NHL**	**70**	**15**	**37**	**52**	**29**	**5**	**0**	**3**	**3**	**4**
1990-91	**Toronto**	**NHL**	**19**	**0**	**3**	**3**	**8**	....	....	....	....	....
	Vancouver	**NHL**	**32**	**4**	**23**	**27**	**20**	**6**	**2**	**2**	**4**	**12**
1991-92	**NY Islanders**	**NHL**	**74**	**9**	**47**	**56**	**30**	....	....	....	....	....
1992-93	**NY Islanders**	**NHL**	**52**	**8**	**30**	**38**	**38**	**12**	**0**	**2**	**2**	**6**
	Capital Dist.	AHL	7	3	4	7	8	....	....	....	....	....
1993-94	**NY Islanders**	**NHL**	**66**	**9**	**31**	**40**	**47**	**3**	**0**	**0**	**0**	**2**
1994-95	**Anaheim**	**NHL**	**22**	**4**	**3**	**7**	**6**	....	....	....	....	....
	NHL Totals		**659**	**93**	**328**	**421**	**350**	**57**	**8**	**22**	**30**	**68**

a WCHA First All-Star Team (1984)
b Won Hobey Baker Memorial Award (Top U.S. Collegiate Player) (1984)

Traded to **Buffalo** by **Montreal** for Buffalo's second round choice (Martin St. Amour) in 1988 Entry Draft, November 18, 1986. Traded to **New Jersey** by **Buffalo** for Detroit's third round choice (previously acquired by New Jersey — Buffalo selected Andrew MacVicar) in 1987 Entry Draft, June 13, 1987. Traded to **Toronto** by **New Jersey** for Toronto's first round choice (Scott Niedermayer) in 1991 Entry Draft, October 16, 1989. Traded to **Vancouver** by **Toronto** for Brian Bradley, January 12, 1991. Traded to **Minnesota** by **Vancouver** for Dave Babych, June 22, 1991. Traded to **NY Islanders** by **Minnesota** for Craig Ludwig, June 22, 1991. Traded to **Anaheim** by **NY Islanders** for Troy Loney, June 29, 1994.

KUSHNER, DALE

Right wing. Shoots left. 6'1", 195 lbs. Born, Terrace, B.C., June 13, 1966.

			Regular Season					Playoffs				
Season	Club	Lea	GP	G	A	TP	PIM	GP	G	A	TP	PIM
1983-84	Prince Albert	WHL	1	2	0	2	5	....	....	....	....	....
1984-85	Prince Albert	WHL	2	0	0	0	2	....	....	....	....	....
	Moose Jaw	WHL	17	5	2	7	23	....	....	....	....	....
	Medicine Hat	WHL	48	23	17	40	173	10	3	3	6	18
1985-86	Medicine Hat	WHL	66	25	19	44	218	25	0	5	5	114
1986-87	Medicine Hat	WHL	63	34	34	68	250	20	8	13	21	57
1987-88	Springfield	AHL	68	13	23	36	201	....	....	....	....	....
1988-89	Springfield	AHL	45	5	8	13	132	....	....	....	....	....
1989-90	**NY Islanders**	**NHL**	**2**	**0**	**0**	**0**	**2**	....	....	....	....	....
	Springfield	AHL	45	14	11	25	163	7	2	3	5	61
1990-91	**Philadelphia**	**NHL**	**63**	**7**	**11**	**18**	**195**	....	....	....	....	....
	Hershey	AHL	5	3	4	7	14	....	....	....	....	....
1991-92	**Philadelphia**	**NHL**	**19**	**3**	**2**	**5**	**18**	....	....	....	....	....
	Hershey	AHL	46	9	7	16	98	6	0	2	2	23
1992-93	Hershey	AHL	26	1	7	8	98	....	....	....	....	....
	Capital Dist.	AHL	7	0	1	1	29	2	1	0	1	29
1993-94	Saint John	AHL	73	20	17	37	199	7	2	1	3	28
1994-95	Saint John	AHL	38	13	10	23	97	5	0	3	3	14
	NHL Totals		**84**	**10**	**13**	**23**	**215**	....	....	....	....	....

Signed as a free agent by **NY Islanders**, April 7, 1987. Signed as a free agent by **Philadelphia**, July 31, 1990. Signed as a free agent by **Calgary**, August 10, 1993.

KUZNETSOV, MAXIM — (kooz-NEHT-zahv) — DET.

Defense. Shoots left. 6'5", 198 lbs. Born, Pavlodar, USSR, March 24, 1977.
(Detroit's 1st choice, 26th overall, in 1995 Entry Draft).

			Regular Season					Playoffs				
Season	Club	Lea	GP	G	A	TP	PIM	GP	G	A	TP	PIM
1994-95	Moscow D'amo	CIS	11	0	0	0	8	....	....	....	....	....

KUZNETSOV, YURI — (kooz-NEHT-zahv) — VAN.

Center. Shoots left. 5'11", 176 lbs. Born, Omak, USSR, August 10, 1971.
(Vancouver's 7th choice, 169th overall, in 1994 Entry Draft).

			Regular Season					Playoffs				
Season	Club	Lea	GP	G	A	TP	PIM	GP	G	A	TP	PIM
1992-93	Avangard Omsk	CIS	32	9	9	18	4	....	....	....	....	....
1993-94	Avangard Omsk	CIS	35	17	10	27	16	....	....	....	....	....
1994-95	Syracuse	AHL	54	10	17	27	37	....	....	....	....	....

KYPREOS, NICK — (KIH-pree-ohz) — NYR

Left wing. Shoots left. 6', 205 lbs. Born, Toronto, Ont., June 4, 1966.

			Regular Season					Playoffs				
Season	Club	Lea	GP	G	A	TP	PIM	GP	G	A	TP	PIM
1983-84	North Bay	OHL	51	12	11	23	36	4	3	2	5	9
1984-85	North Bay	OHL	64	41	36	77	71	8	2	2	4	15
1985-86a	North Bay	OHL	64	62	35	97	112	....	....	....	....	....
1986-87	Hershey	AHL	10	0	1	1	4	....	....	....	....	....
b	North Bay	OHL	46	49	41	90	54	24	11	5	16	78
1987-88	Hershey	AHL	71	24	20	44	101	12	0	2	2	17
1988-89	Hershey	AHL	28	12	15	27	19	12	4	5	9	11
1989-90	**Washington**	**NHL**	**31**	**5**	**4**	**9**	**82**	**7**	**1**	**0**	**1**	**15**
	Baltimore	AHL	14	6	5	11	6	7	4	1	5	17
1990-91	**Washington**	**NHL**	**79**	**9**	**9**	**18**	**196**	**9**	**0**	**1**	**1**	**38**
1991-92	**Washington**	**NHL**	**65**	**4**	**6**	**10**	**206**	....	....	....	....	....
1992-93	**Hartford**	**NHL**	**75**	**17**	**10**	**27**	**325**	....	....	....	....	....
1993-94	**Hartford**	**NHL**	**10**	**0**	**0**	**0**	**37**	....	....	....	....	....
	NY Rangers	**NHL**	**46**	**3**	**5**	**8**	**102**	**3**	**0**	**0**	**0**	**2**
1994-95	**NY Rangers**	**NHL**	**40**	**1**	**3**	**4**	**93**	**10**	**0**	**2**	**2**	**6**
	NHL Totals		**346**	**39**	**37**	**76**	**1041**	**29**	**1**	**3**	**4**	**61**

a OHL First All-Star Team (1986)
b OHL Second All-Star Team (1987)

Signed as a free agent by **Philadelphia,** September 30, 1984. Claimed by **Washington** from **Philadelphia** in NHL Waiver Draft, October 2, 1989. Traded to **Hartford** by **Washington** for Mark Hunter and future considerations (Yvon Corriveau, August 20, 1992), June 15, 1992. Traded to **NY Rangers** by **Hartford** with Steve Larmer, Barry Richter and Hartford's sixth round choice (Yuri Litvinov) in 1994 Entry Draft for Darren Turcotte and James Patrick, November 2, 1993.

KYTE, JIM — (KITE) — S.J.

Defense. Shoots left. 6'5", 210 lbs. Born, Ottawa, Ont., March 21, 1964.
(Winnipeg's 1st choice, 12th overall, in 1982 Entry Draft).

			Regular Season					Playoffs				
Season	Club	Lea	GP	G	A	TP	PIM	GP	G	A	TP	PIM
1981-82	Cornwall	OHL	52	4	13	17	148	5	0	0	0	10
1982-83	**Winnipeg**	**NHL**	**2**	**0**	**0**	**0**	**0**	....	....	....	....	....
	Cornwall	OHL	65	6	30	36	195	8	0	2	2	24
1983-84	**Winnipeg**	**NHL**	**58**	**1**	**2**	**3**	**55**	**3**	**0**	**0**	**0**	**11**
1984-85	**Winnipeg**	**NHL**	**71**	**0**	**3**	**3**	**111**	**8**	**0**	**0**	**0**	**14**
1985-86	**Winnipeg**	**NHL**	**71**	**1**	**3**	**4**	**126**	**3**	**0**	**0**	**0**	**12**
1986-87	**Winnipeg**	**NHL**	**72**	**5**	**5**	**10**	**162**	**10**	**0**	**4**	**4**	**36**
1987-88	**Winnipeg**	**NHL**	**51**	**1**	**3**	**4**	**128**	....	....	....	....	....
1988-89	**Winnipeg**	**NHL**	**74**	**3**	**9**	**12**	**190**	....	....	....	....	....
1989-90	**Pittsburgh**	**NHL**	**56**	**3**	**1**	**4**	**125**	....	....	....	....	....
1990-91	**Pittsburgh**	**NHL**	**1**	**0**	**0**	**0**	**2**	....	....	....	....	....
	Muskegon	IHL	25	2	5	7	157	....	....	....	....	....
	Calgary	**NHL**	**42**	**0**	**9**	**9**	**153**	**7**	**0**	**0**	**0**	**7**
1991-92	**Calgary**	**NHL**	**21**	**0**	**1**	**1**	**107**	....	....	....	....	....
	Salt Lake	IHL	6	0	1	1	9	....	....	....	....	....
1992-93	**Ottawa**	**NHL**	**4**	**0**	**1**	**1**	**4**	....	....	....	....	....
	New Haven	AHL	63	6	18	24	163	....	....	....	....	....
1993-94	Las Vegas	IHL	75	2	16	18	246	4	0	1	1	51
1994-95	Las Vegas	IHL	76	3	17	20	195	....	....	....	....	....
	San Jose	**NHL**	**18**	**2**	**5**	**7**	**33**	**11**	**0**	**2**	**2**	**14**
	NHL Totals		**541**	**16**	**42**	**58**	**1196**	**42**	**0**	**6**	**6**	**94**

Traded to **Pittsburgh** by **Winnipeg** with Andrew McBain and Randy Gilhen for Randy Cunneyworth, Rick Tabaracci and Dave McLlwain, June 17, 1989. Traded to **Calgary** by **Pittsburgh** for Jiri Hrdina, December 13, 1990. Signed as a free agent by **Ottawa**, September 10, 1992. Signed as a free agent by **San Jose**, March 31, 1995.

LABRAATEN, JAN — CGY.

Left wing. Shoots right. 6'2", 198 lbs. Born, Karlstad, Sweden, February 17, 1977.
(Calgary's 4th choice, 98th overall, in 1995 Entry Draft).

			Regular Season					Playoffs				
Season	Club	Lea	GP	G	A	TP	PIM	GP	G	A	TP	PIM
1994-95	Farjestad	Swe. Jr.	25	10	6	16	20	....	....	....	....	....
	Farjestad	Swe.	2	0	1	1	2	1	0	0	0	0

LACHANCE, BOB — ST.L.

Right wing. Shoots right. 5'11", 180 lbs. Born, Northampton, MA, February 1, 1974.
(St. Louis' 5th choice, 134th overall, in 1992 Entry Draft).

			Regular Season					Playoffs				
Season	Club	Lea	GP	G	A	TP	PIM	GP	G	A	TP	PIM
1992-93	Boston U.	H.E.	33	4	10	14	24	....	....	....	....	....
1993-94	Boston U.	H.E.	32	13	19	32	42	....	....	....	....	....
1994-95	Boston U.	H.E.	37	12	29	41	51	....	....	....	....	....

LACHANCE, SCOTT — NYI

Defense. Shoots left. 6'1", 197 lbs. Born, Charlottesville, VA, October 22, 1972.
(NY Islanders' 1st choice, 4th overall, in 1991 Entry Draft).

			Regular Season					Playoffs				
Season	Club	Lea	GP	G	A	TP	PIM	GP	G	A	TP	PIM
1990-91	Boston U.	H.E.	31	5	19	24	48	....	....	....	....	....
1991-92	U.S. National	....	36	1	10	11	34	....	....	....	....	....
	U.S. Olympic	....	8	0	1	1	6	....	....	....	....	....
	NY Islanders	**NHL**	**17**	**1**	**4**	**5**	**9**	....	....	....	....	....
1992-93	**NY Islanders**	**NHL**	**75**	**7**	**17**	**24**	**67**	....	....	....	....	....
1993-94	**NY Islanders**	**NHL**	**74**	**3**	**11**	**14**	**70**	**3**	**0**	**0**	**0**	**0**
1994-95	**NY Islanders**	**NHL**	**26**	**6**	**7**	**13**	**26**	....	....	....	....	....
	NHL Totals		**192**	**17**	**39**	**56**	**172**	**3**	**0**	**0**	**0**	**0**

LACROIX, DANIEL — (luh-KWAH) — NYR

Left wing. Shoots left. 6'2", 195 lbs. Born, Montreal, Que., March 11, 1969.
(NY Rangers' 2nd choice, 31st overall, in 1987 Entry Draft).

			Regular Season					Playoffs				
Season	Club	Lea	GP	G	A	TP	PIM	GP	G	A	TP	PIM
1986-87	Granby	QMJHL	54	9	16	25	311	8	1	2	3	22
1987-88	Granby	QMJHL	58	24	50	74	468	5	0	4	4	12
1988-89	Granby	QMJHL	70	45	49	94	320	4	1	1	2	57
	Denver	IHL	2	0	1	1	0	2	0	1	1	0
1989-90	Flint	IHL	61	12	16	28	128	4	2	0	2	24
1990-91	Binghamton	AHL	54	7	12	19	237	5	1	0	4	24
1991-92	Binghamton	AHL	52	12	20	32	149	11	2	4	6	28
1992-93	Binghamton	AHL	73	21	22	43	255	....	....	....	....	....
1993-94	**NY Rangers**	**NHL**	**4**	**0**	**0**	**0**	**0**	....	....	....	....	....
	Binghamton	AHL	59	20	23	43	278	....	....	....	....	....
1994-95	Providence	AHL	40	15	11	26	266	....	....	....	....	....
	Boston	**NHL**	**23**	**1**	**0**	**1**	**38**	....	....	....	....	....
	NY Rangers	**NHL**	**1**	**0**	**0**	**0**	**0**	....	....	....	....	....
	NHL Totals		**28**	**1**	**0**	**1**	**38**	....	....	....	....	....

Traded to **Boston** by **NY Rangers** for Glen Featherstone, August 19, 1994. Claimed on waivers by **NY Rangers** from **Boston**, April 10, 1995.

LACROIX, ERIC (luh-KWAH) L.A.

Left wing. Shoots left. 6'1", 205 lbs. Born, Montreal, Que., July 15, 1971.
(Toronto's 6th choice, 136th overall, in 1990 Entry Draft).

			Regular Season					Playoffs				
Season	Club	Lea	GP	G	A	TP	PIM	GP	G	A	TP	PIM
1990-91	St. Lawrence	ECAC	35	13	11	24	35	....	....	....	....	....
1991-92	St. Lawrence	ECAC	34	11	20	31	40	....	....	....	....	....
1992-93	St. John's	AHL	76	15	19	34	59	9	5	3	8	4
1993-94	**Toronto**	**NHL**	**3**	**0**	**0**	**0**	**2**	**2**	**0**	**0**	**0**	**0**
	St. John's	AHL	59	17	22	39	69	11	5	3	8	6
1994-95	St. John's	AHL	1	0	0	0	2	....	....	....	....	....
	Phoenix	IHL	25	7	1	8	31	....	....	....	....	....
	Los Angeles	**NHL**	**45**	**9**	**7**	**16**	**54**	....	....	....	....	....
	NHL Totals		**48**	**9**	**7**	**16**	**56**	**2**	**0**	**0**	**0**	**0**

Traded to **Los Angeles** by **Toronto** with Chris Snell and Toronto's fourth round choice in 1996 Entry Draft for Dixon Ward, Guy Leveque, Kelly Fairchild and Shayne Toporowski, October 3, 1994.

LADOUCEUR, RANDY (LAD-uh-SOOR) ANA.

Defense. Shoots left. 6'2", 220 lbs. Born, Brockville, Ont., June 30, 1960.

			Regular Season					Playoffs				
Season	Club	Lea	GP	G	A	TP	PIM	GP	G	A	TP	PIM
1978-79	Brantford	OHA	64	3	17	20	141	....	....	....	....	....
1979-80	Brantford	OHA	37	6	15	21	125	8	0	5	5	18
1980-81	Kalamazoo	IHL	80	7	30	37	52	8	1	3	4	10
1981-82	Adirondack	AHL	78	4	28	32	78	5	1	1	2	6
1982-83	**Detroit**	**NHL**	**27**	**0**	**4**	**4**	**16**	....	....	....	....	....
	Adirondack	AHL	48	11	21	32	54	....	....	....	....	....
1983-84	**Detroit**	**NHL**	**71**	**3**	**17**	**20**	**58**	**4**	**1**	**0**	**1**	**6**
	Adirondack	AHL	11	3	5	8	12	....	....	....	....	....
1984-85	**Detroit**	**NHL**	**80**	**3**	**27**	**30**	**108**	**3**	**1**	**0**	**1**	**0**
1985-86	**Detroit**	**NHL**	**78**	**5**	**13**	**18**	**196**	....	....	....	....	....
1986-87	**Detroit**	**NHL**	**34**	**3**	**6**	**9**	**70**	....	....	....	....	....
	Hartford	**NHL**	**36**	**2**	**3**	**5**	**51**	**6**	**0**	**2**	**2**	**12**
1987-88	**Hartford**	**NHL**	**67**	**1**	**7**	**8**	**91**	**6**	**1**	**1**	**2**	**4**
1988-89	**Hartford**	**NHL**	**75**	**2**	**5**	**7**	**95**	**1**	**0**	**0**	**0**	**10**
1989-90	**Hartford**	**NHL**	**71**	**3**	**12**	**15**	**126**	**7**	**1**	**0**	**1**	**10**
1990-91	**Hartford**	**NHL**	**67**	**1**	**3**	**4**	**118**	**6**	**1**	**4**	**5**	**6**
1991-92	**Hartford**	**NHL**	**74**	**1**	**9**	**10**	**127**	**7**	**0**	**1**	**1**	**11**
1992-93	**Hartford**	**NHL**	**62**	**2**	**4**	**6**	**109**	....	....	....	....	....
1993-94	**Anaheim**	**NHL**	**81**	**1**	**9**	**10**	**74**	....	....	....	....	....
1994-95	**Anaheim**	**NHL**	**44**	**2**	**4**	**6**	**36**	....	....	....	....	....
	NHL Totals		**867**	**29**	**123**	**152**	**1275**	**40**	**5**	**8**	**13**	**59**

Signed as a free agent by **Detroit**, November 1, 1979. Traded to **Hartford** by **Detroit** for Dave Barr, January 12, 1987. Claimed by **Anaheim** from **Hartford** in Expansion Draft, June 24, 1993.

LAFAYETTE, NATHAN (LAH-fay-eht) NYR

Center. Shoots right. 6'1", 194 lbs. Born, New Westminster, B.C., February 17, 1973.
(St. Louis' 3rd choice, 65th overall, in 1991 Entry Draft).

			Regular Season					Playoffs				
Season	Club	Lea	GP	G	A	TP	PIM	GP	G	A	TP	PIM
1989-90	Kingston	OHL	53	6	8	14	14	7	0	1	1	0
1990-91	Kingston	OHL	35	13	13	26	10	....	....	....	....	....
	Cornwall	OHL	28	16	22	38	25	....	....	....	....	....
1991-92a	Cornwall	OHL	66	28	45	73	26	6	2	5	7	15
1992-93	Newmarket	OHL	58	49	38	87	26	7	4	5	9	19
1993-94	**St. Louis**	**NHL**	**38**	**2**	**3**	**5**	**14**	....	....	....	....	....
	Peoria	IHL	27	13	11	24	20	....	....	....	....	....
	Vancouver	**NHL**	**11**	**1**	**1**	**2**	**4**	**20**	**2**	**7**	**9**	**4**
1994-95	Syracuse	AHL	27	9	9	18	10	....	....	....	....	....
	Vancouver	**NHL**	**27**	**4**	**4**	**8**	**2**	....	....	....	....	....
	NY Rangers	**NHL**	**12**	**0**	**0**	**0**	**0**	**8**	**0**	**0**	**0**	**2**
	NHL Totals		**88**	**7**	**8**	**15**	**20**	**28**	**2**	**7**	**9**	**6**

a Canadian Major Junior Scholastic Player of the Year (1992)

Traded to **Vancouver** by **St. Louis** with Jeff Brown and Bret Hedican for Craig Janney, March 21, 1994. Traded to **NY Rangers** by **Vancouver** for Corey Hirsch, April 7, 1995.

LAFLAMME, CHRISTIAN (lah-FLAM) CHI.

Defense. Shoots right. 6'1", 195 lbs. Born, St. Charles, Que., November 24, 1976.
(Chicago's 2nd choice, 45th overall, in 1995 Entry Draft).

			Regular Season					Playoffs				
Season	Club	Lea	GP	G	A	TP	PIM	GP	G	A	TP	PIM
1992-93	Verdun	QMJHL	69	2	17	19	85	3	0	2	2	6
1993-94	Verdun	QMJHL	72	4	34	38	85	4	0	3	3	4
1994-95a	Beauport	QMJHL	67	6	41	47	82	8	1	4	5	6

a QMJHL Second All-Star Team (1995)

LaFONTAINE, PAT (luh-FAHN-tayn) BUF.

Center. Shoots right. 5'10", 180 lbs. Born, St. Louis, MO, February 22, 1965.
(NY Islanders' 1st choice, 3rd overall, in 1983 Entry Draft).

			Regular Season					Playoffs				
Season	Club	Lea	GP	G	A	TP	PIM	GP	G	A	TP	PIM
1982-83ab	Verdun	QMJHL	70	*104	*130	*234	10	15	11	*24	*35	4
1983-84	U.S. National	....	58	56	55	111	22	....	....	....	....	....
	U.S. Olympic	....	6	5	5	10	0	....	....	....	....	....
	NY Islanders	**NHL**	**15**	**13**	**6**	**19**	**6**	**16**	**3**	**6**	**9**	**8**
1984-85	**NY Islanders**	**NHL**	**67**	**19**	**35**	**54**	**32**	**9**	**1**	**2**	**3**	**4**
1985-86	**NY Islanders**	**NHL**	**65**	**30**	**23**	**53**	**43**	**3**	**1**	**0**	**1**	**0**
1986-87	**NY Islanders**	**NHL**	**80**	**38**	**32**	**70**	**70**	**14**	**5**	**7**	**12**	**10**
1987-88	**NY Islanders**	**NHL**	**75**	**47**	**45**	**92**	**52**	**6**	**4**	**5**	**9**	**8**
1988-89	**NY Islanders**	**NHL**	**79**	**45**	**43**	**88**	**26**	....	....	....	....	....
1989-90c	**NY Islanders**	**NHL**	**74**	**54**	**51**	**105**	**38**	**2**	**0**	**1**	**1**	**0**
1990-91	**NY Islanders**	**NHL**	**75**	**41**	**44**	**85**	**42**	....	....	....	....	....
1991-92	**Buffalo**	**NHL**	**57**	**46**	**47**	**93**	**98**	**7**	**8**	**3**	**11**	**4**
1992-93d	**Buffalo**	**NHL**	**84**	**53**	**95**	**148**	**63**	**7**	**2**	**10**	**12**	**0**
1993-94	**Buffalo**	**NHL**	**16**	**5**	**13**	**18**	**2**	....	....	....	....	....
1994-95e	**Buffalo**	**NHL**	**22**	**12**	**15**	**27**	**4**	**5**	**2**	**2**	**4**	**2**
	NHL Totals		**709**	**403**	**449**	**852**	**476**	**69**	**26**	**36**	**62**	**36**

a QMJHL First All-Star Team (1983)
b Canadian Major Junior Player of the Year (1983)
c Won Dodge Performer of the Year Award (1990)
d NHL Second All-Star Team (1993)
e Won Bill Masterton Memorial Trophy (1995)

Played in NHL All-Star Game (1988-91, 1993)

Traded to **Buffalo** by **NY Islanders** with Randy Hillier, Randy Wood and NY Islanders' fourth round choice (Dean Melanson) in 1992 Entry Draft for Pierre Turgeon, Uwe Krupp, Benoit Hogue and Dave McLlwain, October 25, 1991.

LAFORGE, MARC

Left wing. Shoots left. 6'2", 210 lbs. Born, Sudbury, Ont., January 3, 1968.
(Hartford's 2nd choice, 32nd overall, in 1986 Entry Draft).

			Regular Season					Playoffs				
Season	Club	Lea	GP	G	A	TP	PIM	GP	G	A	TP	PIM
1984-85	Kingston	OHL	57	1	5	6	214	....	....	....	....	....
1985-86	Kingston	OHL	60	1	13	14	248	10	0	1	1	30
1986-87	Binghamton	AHL	....	....	....	....	....	4	0	0	0	7
	Kingston	OHL	53	2	10	12	224	12	1	0	1	79
1987-88	Sudbury	OHL	14	0	2	2	68	....	....	....	....	....
1988-89	Binghamton	AHL	38	2	2	4	179	....	....	....	....	....
	Indianapolis	IHL	14	0	2	2	138	....	....	....	....	....
1989-90	**Hartford**	**NHL**	**9**	**0**	**0**	**0**	**43**	....	....	....	....	....
	Binghamton	AHL	25	2	6	8	111	....	....	....	....	....
	Cape Breton	AHL	3	0	1	1	24	3	0	0	0	27
1990-91	Cape Breton	AHL	49	1	7	8	217	....	....	....	....	....
1991-92	Cape Breton	AHL	59	0	14	14	341	4	0	0	0	24
1992-93	Cape Breton	AHL	77	1	12	13	208	15	1	2	3	*78
1993-94	**Edmonton**	**NHL**	**5**	**0**	**0**	**0**	**21**	....	....	....	....	....
	Cape Breton	AHL	14	0	0	0	91	....	....	....	....	....
	Salt Lake	IHL	43	0	2	2	242	....	....	....	....	....
1994-95	Cape Breton	AHL	18	0	1	1	80	....	....	....	....	....
	Syracuse	AHL	39	1	5	6	202	....	....	....	....	....
	NHL Totals		**14**	**0**	**0**	**0**	**64**	....	....	....	....	....

Traded to **Edmonton** by **Hartford** for the rights to Cam Brauer, March 6, 1990. Traded to **NY Islanders** by **Edmonton** for Brent Grieve, December 15, 1993.

LALOR, MIKE (LAH-luhr) DAL.

Defense. Shoots left. 6', 200 lbs. Born, Buffalo, NY, March 8, 1963.

			Regular Season					Playoffs				
Season	Club	Lea	GP	G	A	TP	PIM	GP	G	A	TP	PIM
1981-82	Brantford	OHL	64	3	13	16	114	11	0	6	6	11
1982-83	Brantford	OHL	65	10	30	40	113	8	1	3	4	20
1983-84	Nova Scotia	AHL	67	5	11	16	80	12	0	2	2	13
1984-85	Sherbrooke	AHL	79	9	23	32	114	17	3	5	8	36
1985-86	**Montreal**	**NHL**	**62**	**3**	**5**	**8**	**56**	**17**	**1**	**2**	**3**	**29**
1986-87	**Montreal**	**NHL**	**57**	**0**	**10**	**10**	**47**	**13**	**2**	**1**	**3**	**29**
1987-88	**Montreal**	**NHL**	**66**	**1**	**10**	**11**	**113**	**11**	**0**	**0**	**0**	**11**
1988-89	**Montreal**	**NHL**	**12**	**1**	**4**	**5**	**15**	....	....	....	....	....
	St. Louis	**NHL**	**36**	**1**	**14**	**15**	**54**	**10**	**1**	**1**	**2**	**14**
1989-90	**St. Louis**	**NHL**	**78**	**0**	**16**	**16**	**81**	**12**	**0**	**2**	**2**	**31**
1990-91	**Washington**	**NHL**	**68**	**1**	**5**	**6**	**61**	**10**	**1**	**2**	**3**	**22**
1991-92	**Washington**	**NHL**	**64**	**5**	**7**	**12**	**64**	....	....	....	....	....
	Winnipeg	**NHL**	**15**	**2**	**3**	**5**	**14**	**7**	**0**	**0**	**0**	**19**
1992-93	**Winnipeg**	**NHL**	**64**	**1**	**8**	**9**	**76**	**4**	**0**	**2**	**2**	**4**
1993-94	**San Jose**	**NHL**	**23**	**0**	**2**	**2**	**8**	....	....	....	....	....
	Dallas	**NHL**	**12**	**0**	**1**	**1**	**6**	**5**	**0**	**0**	**0**	**6**
1994-95	**Dallas**	**NHL**	**12**	**0**	**0**	**0**	**9**	**3**	**0**	**0**	**0**	**2**
	Kalamazoo	IHL	5	0	1	1	11	....	....	....	....	....
	NHL Totals		**569**	**15**	**85**	**100**	**604**	**92**	**5**	**10**	**15**	**167**

Signed as a free agent by **Montreal**, September, 1983. Traded to **St. Louis** by **Montreal** with Montreal's first round choice (later traded to Vancouver — Vancouver selected Shawn Antoski) in 1990 Entry Draft for St. Louis' first round choice (Turner Stevenson) in 1990 Entry Draft, January 16, 1989. Traded to **Washington** by **St. Louis** with Peter Zezel for Geoff Courtnall, July 13, 1990. Traded to **Winnipeg** by **Washington** for Paul MacDermid, March 2, 1992. Signed as a free agent by **San Jose**, August 13, 1993. Traded to **Dallas** by **San Jose** with Doug Zmolek and cash for Ulf Dahlen and Dallas' seventh round choice (Brad Mehalko) in 1995 Entry Draft, March 19, 1994.

LAMARCHE, MARTIN OTT.

Left wing. Shoots left. 6'1", 206 lbs. Born, Ste-Justine, Que., October 2, 1975.

			Regular Season					Playoffs				
Season	Club	Lea	GP	G	A	TP	PIM	GP	G	A	TP	PIM
1991-92	Chicoutimi	QMJHL	62	2	6	8	62	4	0	0	0	0
1992-93	St-Jean	QMJHL	51	2	5	7	134	2	0	0	0	0
1993-94	Sherbrooke	QMJHL	53	10	20	30	121	10	2	1	3	44
1994-95	Shawinigan	QMJHL	58	20	29	49	353	14	3	10	13	65

Signed as a free agent by **Ottawa**, March 3, 1995.

LAMB, MARK MTL.

Center. Shoots left. 5'9", 180 lbs. Born, Ponteix, Sask., August 3, 1964.
(Calgary's 5th choice, 72nd overall, in 1982 Entry Draft).

			Regular Season					Playoffs				
Season	Club	Lea	GP	G	A	TP	PIM	GP	G	A	TP	PIM
1981-82	Billings	WHL	72	45	56	101	46	5	4	6	10	4
1982-83	Nanaimo	WHL	30	14	37	51	16	....	....	....	....	....
	Medicine Hat	WHL	46	22	43	65	33	5	3	2	5	4
	Colorado	CHL	....	....	....	....	....	6	0	2	2	0
1983-84a	Medicine Hat	WHL	72	59	77	136	30	14	12	11	23	6
1984-85	Moncton	AHL	80	23	49	72	53	....	....	....	....	....
1985-86	**Calgary**	**NHL**	**1**	**0**	**0**	**0**	**0**	....	....	....	....	....
	Moncton	AHL	79	26	50	76	51	10	2	6	8	17
1986-87	**Detroit**	**NHL**	**22**	**2**	**1**	**3**	**8**	**11**	**0**	**0**	**0**	**11**
	Adirondack	AHL	49	14	36	50	45	....	....	....	....	....
1987-88	**Edmonton**	**NHL**	**2**	**0**	**0**	**0**	**0**	....	....	....	....	....
	Nova Scotia	AHL	69	27	61	88	45	5	0	5	5	6
1988-89	**Edmonton**	**NHL**	**20**	**2**	**8**	**10**	**14**	**6**	**0**	**2**	**2**	**8**
	Cape Breton	AHL	54	33	49	82	29	....	....	....	....	....
1989-90	**Edmonton**	**NHL**	**58**	**12**	**16**	**28**	**42**	**22**	**6**	**11**	**17**	**2**
1990-91	**Edmonton**	**NHL**	**37**	**4**	**8**	**12**	**25**	**15**	**0**	**5**	**5**	**20**
1991-92	**Edmonton**	**NHL**	**59**	**6**	**22**	**28**	**46**	**16**	**1**	**1**	**2**	**10**
1992-93	**Ottawa**	**NHL**	**71**	**7**	**19**	**26**	**64**	....	....	....	....	....
1993-94	**Ottawa**	**NHL**	**66**	**11**	**18**	**29**	**56**	....	....	....	....	....
	Philadelphia	**NHL**	**19**	**1**	**6**	**7**	**16**	....	....	....	....	....
1994-95	**Philadelphia**	**NHL**	**8**	**0**	**2**	**2**	**2**	....	....	....	....	....
	Montreal	**NHL**	**39**	**1**	**0**	**1**	**18**	....	....	....	....	....
	NHL Totals		**402**	**46**	**100**	**146**	**291**	**70**	**7**	**19**	**26**	**51**

a WHL East First All-Star Team (1984)

Signed as a free agent by **Detroit**, July 28, 1986. Claimed by **Edmonton** from **Detroit** in NHL Waiver Draft, October 5, 1987. Claimed by **Ottawa** from **Edmonton** in Expansion Draft, June 18, 1992. Traded to **Philadelphia** by **Ottawa** for Claude Boivin and Kirk Daubenspeck, March 5, 1994. Traded to **Montreal** by **Philadelphia** for cash, February 10, 1995.

LAMBERT, DAN (lahm-BAIR)

Defense. Shoots left. 5'8", 177 lbs. Born, St. Boniface, Man., January 12, 1970.
(Quebec's 8th choice, 106th overall, in 1989 Entry Draft).

			Regular Season					Playoffs				
Season	Club	Lea	GP	G	A	TP	PIM	GP	G	A	TP	PIM
1986-87	Swift Current	WHL	68	13	53	66	95	4	1	1	2	9
1987-88	Swift Current	WHL	69	20	63	83	120	10	2	10	12	45
1988-89abc	Swift Current	WHL	57	25	77	102	158	12	9	19	28	12
1989-90a	Swift Current	WHL	50	17	51	68	119	4	2	3	5	12
1990-91	**Quebec**	**NHL**	**1**	**0**	**0**	**0**	**0**	....	....	....	....	....
	Halifax	AHL	30	7	13	20	20	....	....	....	....	....
	Fort Wayne	IHL	49	10	27	37	65	19	4	10	14	20
1991-92	**Quebec**	**NHL**	**28**	**6**	**9**	**15**	**22**	....	....	....	....	....
	Halifax	AHL	47	3	28	31	33	....	....	....	....	....
1992-93	Moncton	AHL	73	11	30	41	100	5	1	2	3	2
1993-94	HIFK	Fin.	13	1	2	3	8	....	....	....	....	....
	Fort Wayne	IHL	62	10	27	37	138	18	3	12	15	20
1994-95	San Diego	IHL	70	6	19	25	95	5	0	5	5	10
	NHL Totals		**29**	**6**	**9**	**15**	**22**	....	....	....	....	....

a WHL East First All-Star Team (1989, 1990)
b Memorial Cup All-Star Team (1989)
c Won Stafford Smythe Memorial Trophy (Memorial Cup Tournament MVP) (1989)

Traded to **Winnipeg** by **Quebec** for Shawn Cronin, August 25, 1992.

LAMBERT, DENNY (lahm-BAIR) ANA.

Left wing. Shoots left. 5'11", 200 lbs. Born, Wawa, Ont., January 7, 1970.

			Regular Season					Playoffs				
Season	Club	Lea	GP	G	A	TP	PIM	GP	G	A	TP	PIM
1988-89	S.S. Marie	OHL	61	14	15	29	2032	....	....	....	....	....
1989-90	S.S. Marie	OHL	61	23	29	52	276	....	....	....	....	....
1990-91	S.S. Marie	OHL	59	28	39	67	169	14	7	9	16	48
1991-92	San Diego	IHL	71	17	14	31	229	3	0	0	0	10
	St. Thomas	ColHL	5	2	6	8	9	....	....	....	....	....
1992-93	San Diego	IHL	56	18	12	30	277	14	1	1	2	44
1993-94	San Diego	IHL	79	13	14	27	314	6	1	0	1	55
1994-95	San Diego	IHL	75	25	35	60	222	....	....	....	....	....
	Anaheim	**NHL**	**13**	**1**	**3**	**4**	**4**	....	....	....	....	....
	NHL Totals		**13**	**1**	**3**	**4**	**4**	....	....	....	....	....

Signed as a free agent by **Anaheim**, August 16, 1993.

LANG, ROBERT (LUHNG) L.A.

Center. Shoots right. 6'2", 189 lbs. Born, Teplice, Czech., December 19, 1970.
(Los Angeles' 6th choice, 133rd overall, in 1990 Entry Draft).

			Regular Season					Playoffs				
Season	Club	Lea	GP	G	A	TP	PIM	GP	G	A	TP	PIM
1988-89	Litvinov	Czech.	7	3	2	5	0	....	....	....	....	....
1989-90	Litvinov	Czech.	39	11	10	21	....	....	....	....	....	....
1990-91	Litvinov	Czech.	56	26	26	52	38	....	....	....	....	....
1991-92	Litvinov	Czech.	43	12	31	43	34	....	....	....	....	....
1992-93	**Los Angeles**	**NHL**	**11**	**0**	**5**	**5**	**2**	....	....	....	....	....
	Phoenix	IHL	38	9	21	30	20	....	....	....	....	....
1993-94	**Los Angeles**	**NHL**	**32**	**9**	**10**	**19**	**10**	....	....	....	....	....
	Phoenix	IHL	44	11	24	35	34	....	....	....	....	....
1994-95	Litvinov	Czech.	16	4	19	23	28	....	....	....	....	....
	Los Angeles	**NHL**	**36**	**4**	**8**	**12**	**4**	....	....	....	....	....
	NHL Totals		**79**	**13**	**23**	**36**	**16**	....	....	....	....	....

LANGDON, DARREN NYR

Left wing. Shoots left. 6'1", 205 lbs. Born, Deer Lake, Nfld., January 8, 1971.

			Regular Season					Playoffs				
Season	Club	Lea	GP	G	A	TP	PIM	GP	G	A	TP	PIM
1991-92	Summerside	MJHL	44	34	49	83	441	....	....	....	....	....
1992-93	Binghamton	AHL	18	3	4	7	115	8	0	1	1	14
	Dayton	ECHL	54	23	22	45	429	3	0	1	1	40
1993-94	Binghamton	AHL	54	2	7	9	327	....	....	....	....	....
1994-95	Binghamton	AHL	55	6	14	20	296	11	1	3	4	*84
	NY Rangers	**NHL**	**18**	**1**	**1**	**2**	**62**	....	....	....	....	....
	NHL Totals		**18**	**1**	**1**	**2**	**62**	....	....	....	....	....

Signed as a free agent by **NY Rangers**, August 16, 1993.

LANGENBRUNNER, JAMIE (lan-gehn-BROO-nuhr) DAL.

Center. Shoots right. 5'11", 185 lbs. Born, Duluth, MN, July 24, 1975.
(Dallas' 2nd choice, 35th overall, in 1993 Entry Draft).

			Regular Season					Playoffs				
Season	Club	Lea	GP	G	A	TP	PIM	GP	G	A	TP	PIM
1993-94	Peterborough	OHL	62	33	58	91	53	7	4	6	10	2
1994-95	Peterborough	OHL	62	42	57	99	84	11	8	14	22	12
	Dallas	**NHL**	**2**	**0**	**0**	**0**	**2**	....	....	....	....	....
	Kalamazoo	IHL	....	....	....	....	....	11	1	3	4	2
	NHL Totals		**2**	**0**	**0**	**0**	**2**	....	....	....	....	....

LANGKOW, DAYMOND (LAING-kow) T.B.

Center. Shoots left. 5'10", 170 lbs. Born, Edmonton, Alta, September 27, 1976.
(Tampa Bay's 1st choice, 5th overall, in 1995 Entry Draft).

			Regular Season					Playoffs				
Season	Club	Lea	GP	G	A	TP	PIM	GP	G	A	TP	PIM
1992-93	Tri-City	WHL	64	22	42	64	100	4	1	0	1	4
1993-94	Tri-City	WHL	61	40	43	83	174	4	2	2	4	15
1994-95ab	Tri-City	WHL	72	*67	73	*140	142	17	12	15	27	52

a WHL West First All-Star Team (1995)
b Canadian Major Junior First All-Star Team (1995)

LANK, JEFF PHI.

Defense. Shoots left. 6'3", 185 lbs. Born, Indian Head, Sask., March 1, 1975.
(Montreal's 6th choice, 113th overall, in 1993 Entry Draft).

			Regular Season					Playoffs				
Season	Club	Lea	GP	G	A	TP	PIM	GP	G	A	TP	PIM
1991-92	Prince Albert	WHL	56	2	8	10	26	9	0	0	0	2
1992-93	Prince Albert	WHL	63	1	11	12	60	....	....	....	....	....
1993-94	Prince Albert	WHL	72	9	38	47	62	....	....	....	....	....
1994-95	Prince Albert	WHL	68	12	25	37	60	13	2	10	12	8

Re-entered NHL Entry Draft, Philadelphia's 9th choice, 230th overall in 1995 Entry Draft.

LAPERRIERE, DANIEL (luh-PAIR-ee-YAIR) OTT.

Defense. Shoots left. 6'1", 195 lbs. Born, Laval, Que., March 28, 1969.
(St. Louis' 4th choice, 93rd overall, in 1989 Entry Draft).

			Regular Season					Playoffs				
Season	Club	Lea	GP	G	A	TP	PIM	GP	G	A	TP	PIM
1988-89	St. Lawrence	ECAC	28	0	7	7	10	....	....	....	....	....
1989-90	St. Lawrence	ECAC	31	6	19	25	16	....	....	....	....	....
1990-91a	St. Lawrence	ECAC	34	7	31	38	18	....	....	....	....	....
1991-92bc	St. Lawrence	ECAC	32	8	*45	53	36	....	....	....	....	....
1992-93	**St. Louis**	**NHL**	**5**	**0**	**1**	**1**	**0**	....	....	....	....	....
	Peoria	IHL	54	4	20	24	28	....	....	....	....	....
1993-94	**St. Louis**	**NHL**	**20**	**1**	**3**	**4**	**8**	....	....	....	....	....
	Peoria	IHL	56	10	37	47	16	6	0	2	2	2
1994-95	Peoria	IHL	65	19	33	52	42	....	....	....	....	....
	St. Louis	**NHL**	**4**	**0**	**0**	**0**	**15**	....	....	....	....	....
	Ottawa	**NHL**	**13**	**1**	**1**	**2**	**0**	....	....	....	....	....
	NHL Totals		**42**	**2**	**5**	**7**	**23**	....	....	....	....	....

a ECAC Second All-Star Team (1991)
b ECAC First All-Star Team (1992)
c NCAA East First All-American Team (1992)

Traded to **Ottawa** by **St. Louis** with St. Louis' ninth round choice (Erik Kasminski) in 1995 Entry Draft for Ottawa's ninth round choice (Libor Zabransy) in 1995 Entry Draft, April 7, 1995.

LAPERRIERE, IAN (luh-PAIR-ee-YAIR, EE-ihn) ST.L.

Center. Shoots right. 6'1", 195 lbs. Born, Montreal, Que., January 19, 1974.
(St. Louis' 6th choice, 158th overall, in 1992 Entry Draft).

			Regular Season					Playoffs				
Season	Club	Lea	GP	G	A	TP	PIM	GP	G	A	TP	PIM
1990-91	Drummondville	QMJHL	65	19	29	48	117	14	2	9	11	48
1991-92	Drummondville	QMJHL	70	28	49	77	160	4	2	2	4	9
1992-93a	Drummondville	QMJHL	60	44	*96	140	188	10	6	13	19	20
1993-94	**St. Louis**	**NHL**	**1**	**0**	**0**	**0**	**0**	....	....	....	....	....
	Drummondville	QMJHL	62	41	72	113	150	9	4	6	10	35
	Peoria	IHL	....	....	....	....	....	5	1	3	4	2
1994-95	Peoria	IHL	51	16	32	48	111	....	....	....	....	....
	St. Louis	**NHL**	**37**	**13**	**14**	**27**	**85**	**7**	**0**	**4**	**4**	**21**
	NHL Totals		**38**	**13**	**14**	**27**	**85**	**7**	**0**	**4**	**4**	**21**

a QMJHL Second All-Star Team (1993)

LAPIN, MIKHAIL (LAH-pihn) TOR.

Defense. Shoots left. 6'2", 190 lbs. Born, Moscow, USSR, May 12, 1975.
(Toronto's 8th choice, 279th overall, in 1993 Entry Draft).

			Regular Season					Playoffs				
Season	Club	Lea	GP	G	A	TP	PIM	GP	G	A	TP	PIM
1992-93	W. Michigan	CCHA	30	0	3	3	58	....	....	....	....	....
1993-94	W. Michigan	CCHA	35	6	9	15	68	....	....	....	....	....
1994-95	W. Michigan	CCHA	15	0	1	1	22	....	....	....	....	....

LAPLANTE, DARRYL DET.

Center. Shoots left. 6'1", 485 lbs. Born, Calgary, Alta., March 28, 1977.
(Detroit's 3rd choice, 58th overall, in 1995 Entry Draft).

			Regular Season					Playoffs				
Season	Club	Lea	GP	G	A	TP	PIM	GP	G	A	TP	PIM
1993-94	Calgary	Midget	35	24	27	51	50	....	....	....	....	....
1994-95	Moose Jaw	WHL	71	22	24	46	66	10	2	2	4	7

LAPOINTE, CLAUDE (luh-PWAH, KLOHD) COL.

Center. Shoots left. 5'9", 181 lbs. Born, Lachine, Que., October 11, 1968.
(Quebec's 12th choice, 234th overall, in 1988 Entry Draft).

			Regular Season					Playoffs				
Season	Club	Lea	GP	G	A	TP	PIM	GP	G	A	TP	PIM
1986-87	Trois-Rivières	QMJHL	70	47	57	104	123	....	....	....	....	....
1987-88	Laval	QMJHL	69	37	83	120	143	13	2	17	19	53
1988-89	Laval	QMJHL	63	32	72	104	158	17	5	14	19	66
1989-90	Halifax	AHL	63	18	19	37	51	6	1	1	2	34
1990-91	**Quebec**	**NHL**	**13**	**2**	**2**	**4**	**4**	....	....	....	....	....
	Halifax	AHL	43	17	17	34	46	....	....	....	....	....
1991-92	**Quebec**	**NHL**	**78**	**13**	**20**	**33**	**86**	....	....	....	....	....
1992-93	**Quebec**	**NHL**	**74**	**10**	**26**	**36**	**98**	**6**	**2**	**4**	**6**	**8**
1993-94	**Quebec**	**NHL**	**59**	**11**	**17**	**28**	**70**	....	....	....	....	....
1994-95	**Quebec**	**NHL**	**29**	**4**	**8**	**12**	**41**	**5**	**0**	**0**	**0**	**8**
	NHL Totals		**253**	**40**	**73**	**113**	**299**	**11**	**2**	**4**	**6**	**16**

LAPOINTE, MARTIN (luh-POYNT, MAHR-tai) DET.

Right wing. Shoots right. 5'11", 200 lbs. Born, Ville Ste. Pierre, Que., September 12, 1973.
(Detroit's 1st choice, 10th overall, in 1991 Entry Draft).

			Regular Season					Playoffs				
Season	Club	Lea	GP	G	A	TP	PIM	GP	G	A	TP	PIM
1989-90a	Laval	QMJHL	65	42	54	96	77	14	8	17	25	54
1990-91b	Laval	QMJHL	64	44	54	98	66	13	7	14	21	26
1991-92	**Detroit**	**NHL**	**4**	**0**	**1**	**1**	**5**	**3**	**0**	**1**	**1**	**4**
	Laval	QMJHL	31	25	30	55	84	10	4	10	14	32
	Adirondack	AHL	....	....	....	....	....	8	2	2	4	4
1992-93	**Detroit**	**NHL**	**3**	**0**	**0**	**0**	**0**	....	....	....	....	....
ac	Laval	QMJHL	35	38	51	89	41	13	*13	*17	*30	22
	Adirondack	AHL	8	1	2	3	9	....	....	....	....	....
1993-94	**Detroit**	**NHL**	**50**	**8**	**8**	**16**	**55**	**4**	**0**	**0**	**0**	**6**
	Adirondack	AHL	28	25	21	46	47	4	1	1	2	8
1994-95	Adirondack	AHL	39	29	16	45	80	....	....	....	....	....
	Detroit	**NHL**	**39**	**4**	**6**	**10**	**73**	**2**	**0**	**1**	**1**	**8**
	NHL Totals		**96**	**12**	**15**	**27**	**133**	**9**	**0**	**2**	**2**	**18**

a QMJHL First All-Star Team (1990, 1993)
b QMJHL Second All-Star Team (1991)
c Memorial Cup All-Star Team (1993)

LAPORTE, ALEXANDRE T.B.

Defense. Shoots right. 6'3", 210 lbs. Born, Cowansville, Que., May 1, 1975.
(Tampa Bay's 9th choice, 211th overall, in 1993 Entry Draft).

			Regular Season					Playoffs				
Season	Club	Lea	GP	G	A	TP	PIM	GP	G	A	TP	PIM
1991-92	Victoriaville	QMJHL	44	1	4	5	43	....	....	....	....	....
1992-93	Victoriaville	QMJHL	56	1	3	4	30	6	0	0	0	2
1993-94	Victoriaville	QMJHL	56	3	9	12	68	5	1	0	1	2
1994-95	St-Hyacinthe	QMJHL	38	3	6	9	70	....	....	....	....	....
	Drummondville	QMJHL	23	0	6	6	28	4	0	1	1	0

LARAQUE, GEORGES — EDM.

Right wing. Shoots right. 6'3", 225 lbs. Born, Montreal, Que., December 7, 1976.
(Edmonton's 2nd choice, 31st overall, in 1995 Entry Draft).

			Regular Season					Playoffs				
Season	Club	Lea	GP	G	A	TP	PIM	GP	G	A	TP	PIM
1993-94	St-Jean	QMJHL	70	11	11	22	142	4	0	0	0	7
1994-95	St-Jean	QMJHL	62	19	22	41	259	7	1	1	2	42

LARIONOV, IGOR (LAIR-ee-AH-nohv) — S.J.

Center. Shoots left. 5'9", 170 lbs. Born, Voskresensk, USSR, December 3, 1960.
(Vancouver's 11th choice, 214th overall, in 1985 Entry Draft).

			Regular Season					Playoffs				
Season	Club	Lea	GP	G	A	TP	PIM	GP	G	A	TP	PIM
1977-78	Khimik	USSR	6	3	0	3	4	....	....	....	....	....
1978-79	Khimik	USSR	32	3	4	7	12	....	....	....	....	....
1979-80	Khimik	USSR	42	11	7	18	24	....	....	....	....	....
1980-81	Khimik	USSR	43	22	23	45	36	....	....	....	....	....
1981-82	CSKA	USSR	46	31	22	53	6	....	....	....	....	....
1982-83a	CSKA	USSR	44	20	19	39	20	....	....	....	....	....
1983-84	CSKA	USSR	43	15	26	41	30	....	....	....	....	....
1984-85	CSKA	USSR	40	18	28	46	20	....	....	....	....	....
1985-86a	CSKA	USSR	40	21	31	52	33	....	....	....	....	....
1986-87a	CSKA	USSR	39	20	26	46	34	....	....	....	....	....
1987-88ab	CSKA	USSR	51	25	32	57	54	....	....	....	....	....
1988-89	CSKA	USSR	31	15	12	27	22	....	....	....	....	....
1989-90	**Vancouver**	**NHL**	**74**	**17**	**27**	**44**	**20**	....	....	....	....	....
1990-91	**Vancouver**	**NHL**	**64**	**13**	**21**	**34**	**14**	**6**	**1**	**0**	**1**	**6**
1991-92	**Vancouver**	**NHL**	**72**	**21**	**44**	**65**	**54**	**13**	**3**	**7**	**10**	**4**
1992-93	Lugano	Switz.	24	10	19	29	44	....	....	....	....	....
1993-94	**San Jose**	**NHL**	**60**	**18**	**38**	**56**	**40**	**14**	**5**	**13**	**18**	**10**
1994-95	**San Jose**	**NHL**	**33**	**4**	**20**	**24**	**14**	**11**	**1**	**8**	**9**	**2**
	NHL Totals		**303**	**73**	**150**	**223**	**142**	**44**	**10**	**28**	**38**	**22**

a Soviet National League All-Star (1983, 1986-88)
b Soviet Player of the Year (1988)

Claimed by **San Jose** from **Vancouver** in NHL Waiver Draft, October 4, 1992.

LARMER, STEVE

Right wing. Shoots left. 5'11", 195 lbs. Born, Peterborough, Ont., June 16, 1961.
(Chicago's 11th choice, 120th overall, in 1980 Entry Draft).

			Regular Season					Playoffs				
Season	Club	Lea	GP	G	A	TP	PIM	GP	G	A	TP	PIM
1977-78	Peterborough	OHA	62	24	17	41	51	18	5	7	12	27
1978-79	Niagara Falls	OHA	66	37	47	84	108	....	....	....	....	....
1979-80	Niagara Falls	OHA	67	45	69	114	71	10	5	9	14	15
1980-81	**Chicago**	**NHL**	**4**	**0**	**1**	**1**	**0**	....	....	....	....	....
a	Niagara Falls	OHA	61	55	78	133	73	12	13	8	21	24
1981-82	**Chicago**	**NHL**	**3**	**0**	**0**	**0**	**0**	....	....	....	....	....
b	New Brunswick	AHL	74	38	44	82	46	15	6	6	12	0
1982-83cd	**Chicago**	**NHL**	**80**	**43**	**47**	**90**	**28**	**11**	**5**	**7**	**12**	**8**
1983-84	**Chicago**	**NHL**	**80**	**35**	**40**	**75**	**34**	**5**	**2**	**2**	**4**	**7**
1984-85	**Chicago**	**NHL**	**80**	**46**	**40**	**86**	**16**	**15**	**9**	**13**	**22**	**14**
1985-86	**Chicago**	**NHL**	**80**	**31**	**45**	**76**	**47**	**3**	**0**	**3**	**3**	**4**
1986-87	**Chicago**	**NHL**	**80**	**28**	**56**	**84**	**22**	**4**	**0**	**0**	**0**	**2**
1987-88	**Chicago**	**NHL**	**80**	**41**	**48**	**89**	**42**	**5**	**1**	**6**	**7**	**0**
1988-89	**Chicago**	**NHL**	**80**	**43**	**44**	**87**	**54**	**16**	**8**	**9**	**17**	**22**
1989-90	**Chicago**	**NHL**	**80**	**31**	**59**	**90**	**40**	**20**	**7**	**15**	**22**	**2**
1990-91	**Chicago**	**NHL**	**80**	**44**	**57**	**101**	**79**	**6**	**5**	**1**	**6**	**4**
1991-92	**Chicago**	**NHL**	**80**	**29**	**45**	**74**	**65**	**18**	**8**	**7**	**15**	**6**
1992-93	**Chicago**	**NHL**	**84**	**35**	**35**	**70**	**48**	**4**	**0**	**3**	**3**	**0**
1993-94	**NY Rangers**	**NHL**	**68**	**21**	**39**	**60**	**41**	**23**	**9**	**7**	**16**	**14**
1994-95	**NY Rangers**	**NHL**	**47**	**14**	**15**	**29**	**16**	**10**	**2**	**2**	**4**	**6**
	NHL Totals		**1006**	**441**	**571**	**1012**	**532**	**140**	**56**	**75**	**131**	**89**

a OHA Second All-Star Team (1981)
b AHL Second All-Star Team (1982)
c Won Calder Trophy (1983)
d NHL All-Rookie Team (1983)

Played in NHL All-Star Game (1990, 1991)

Traded to **Hartford** by **Chicago** with Bryan Marchment for Eric Weinrich and Patrick Poulin, November 2, 1993. Traded to **NY Rangers** by **Hartford** with Nick Kypreos, Barry Richter and Hartford's sixth round choice (Yuri Litvinov) in 1994 Entry Draft for Darren Turcotte and James Patrick, November 2, 1993.

LAROSE, BENOIT (luh-ROHS) — L.A.

Defense. Shoots left. 6', 200 lbs. Born, Ottawa, Ont., May 31, 1973.
(Detroit's 5th choice, 100th overall, in 1993 Entry Draft).

			Regular Season					Playoffs				
Season	Club	Lea	GP	G	A	TP	PIM	GP	G	A	TP	PIM
1991-92a	Laval	QMJHL	70	11	53	64	171	10	5	6	11	20
1992-93b	Laval	QMJHL	63	16	62	78	218	8	1	6	7	10
1993-94	Shawinigan	QMJHL	61	2	21	23	120	5	0	1	1	21
1994-95	Victoriaville	QMJHL	23	0	3	3	99	....	....	....	....	....
	Sherbrooke	QMJHL	28	0	0	0	32	3	0	0	0	0
	Wichita	CHL	1	0	0	0	0	....	....	....	....	....
	Toledo	ECHL	1	0	0	0	0	....	....	....	....	....

a QMJHL Second All-Star Team (1992)
b QMJHL First All-Star Team (1993)

LAROSE, GUY (luh-ROHS)

Center. Shoots left. 5'9", 180 lbs. Born, Hull, Que., August 31, 1967.
(Buffalo's 11th choice, 224th overall, in 1985 Entry Draft).

			Regular Season					Playoffs				
Season	Club	Lea	GP	G	A	TP	PIM	GP	G	A	TP	PIM
1984-85	Guelph	OHL	58	30	30	60	63	....	....	....	....	....
1985-86	Guelph	OHL	37	12	36	48	55	....	....	....	....	....
	Ottawa	OHL	28	19	25	44	63	....	....	....	....	....
1986-87	Ottawa	OHL	66	28	49	77	77	11	2	8	10	27
1987-88	Moncton	AHL	77	22	31	53	127	....	....	....	....	....
1988-89	**Winnipeg**	**NHL**	**3**	**0**	**1**	**1**	**6**	....	....	....	....	....
	Moncton	AHL	72	32	27	59	176	10	4	4	8	37
1989-90	Moncton	AHL	79	44	26	70	232	....	....	....	....	....
1990-91	**Winnipeg**	**NHL**	**7**	**0**	**0**	**0**	**8**	....	....	....	....	....
	Moncton	AHL	35	14	10	24	60	....	....	....	....	....
	Binghamton	AHL	34	21	15	36	48	10	8	5	13	37
1991-92	Binghamton	AHL	30	10	11	21	36	....	....	....	....	....
	Toronto	**NHL**	**34**	**9**	**5**	**14**	**27**	....	....	....	....	....
	St. John's	AHL	15	7	7	14	26	....	....	....	....	....
1992-93	**Toronto**	**NHL**	**9**	**0**	**0**	**0**	**8**	....	....	....	....	....
	St. John's	AHL	5	0	1	1	8	9	5	2	7	6
1993-94	**Toronto**	**NHL**	**10**	**1**	**2**	**3**	**10**	....	....	....	....	....
	St. John's	AHL	23	13	16	29	41	....	....	....	....	....
	Calgary	**NHL**	**7**	**0**	**1**	**1**	**4**	....	....	....	....	....
	Saint John	AHL	15	11	11	22	20	7	3	2	5	22
1994-95	Providence	AHL	68	25	33	58	93	12	4	6	10	22
	Boston	**NHL**	....	....	....	....	....	**4**	**0**	**0**	**0**	**0**
	NHL Totals		**70**	**10**	**9**	**19**	**63**	**4**	**0**	**0**	**0**	**0**

Signed as a free agent by **Winnipeg**, July 16, 1987. Traded to **NY Rangers** by **Winnipeg** for Rudy Poeschek, January 22, 1991. Traded to **Toronto** by **NY Rangers** for Mike Stevens, December 26, 1991. Claimed on waivers by **Calgary** from **Toronto**, January 1, 1994. Signed as a free agent by **Boston**, July 11, 1994.

LAROUCHE, STEVE (luh-ROOSH) — OTT.

Center. Shoots right. 6', 180 lbs. Born, Rouyn, Que., April 14, 1971.
(Montreal's 3rd choice, 41st overall, in 1989 Entry Draft).

			Regular Season					Playoffs				
Season	Club	Lea	GP	G	A	TP	PIM	GP	G	A	TP	PIM
1987-88	Trois-Rivières	QMJHL	66	11	29	40	25	....	....	....	....	....
1988-89	Trois-Rivières	QMJHL	70	51	102	153	53	4	4	2	6	6
1989-90a	Trois-Rivières	QMJHL	60	55	90	145	40	7	3	5	8	8
	Cdn. National	....	1	1	0	1	0	....	....	....	....	....
1990-91	Chicoutimi	QMJHL	45	35	41	76	64	17	*13	*20	*33	20
1991-92	Fredericton	AHL	74	21	35	56	41	7	1	0	1	0
1992-93	Fredericton	AHL	77	27	65	92	52	5	2	5	7	6
1993-94	Atlanta	IHL	80	43	53	96	73	14	*16	10	*26	16
1994-95bcd	P.E.I.	AHL	70	*53	48	101	54	2	1	0	1	0
	Ottawa	**NHL**	**18**	**8**	**7**	**15**	**6**	....	....	....	....	....
	NHL Totals		**18**	**8**	**7**	**15**	**6**	....	....	....	....	....

a QMJHL Second All-Star Team (1990)
b AHL First All-Star Team (1995)
c Won Fred Hunt Memorial Trophy (Sportsmanship - AHL) (1995)
d Won Les Cunningham Plaque (MVP - AHL) (1995)

Signed as a free agent by **Ottawa**, September 11, 1994.

LARSEN, BRAD — OTT.

Left wing. Shoots left. 5'11", 198 lbs. Born, Nakusp, B.C., January 28, 1977.
(Ottawa's 3rd choice, 53rd overall, in 1995 Entry Draft).

			Regular Season					Playoffs				
Season	Club	Lea	GP	G	A	TP	PIM	GP	G	A	TP	PIM
1993-94	Swift Current	WHL	64	15	18	33	32	7	1	2	3	4
1994-95	Swift Current	WHL	62	24	33	57	73	6	0	1	1	2

LAUER, BRAD (LAU-er) — PIT.

Left wing. Shoots left. 6', 195 lbs. Born, Humboldt, Sask., October 27, 1966.
(NY Islanders' 3rd choice, 34th overall, in 1985 Entry Draft).

			Regular Season					Playoffs				
Season	Club	Lea	GP	G	A	TP	PIM	GP	G	A	TP	PIM
1983-84	Regina	WHL	60	5	7	12	51	16	0	1	1	24
1984-85	Regina	WHL	72	33	46	79	57	8	6	6	12	9
1985-86	Regina	WHL	57	36	38	74	69	10	4	5	9	2
1986-87	**NY Islanders**	**NHL**	**61**	**7**	**14**	**21**	**65**	**6**	**2**	**0**	**2**	**4**
1987-88	**NY Islanders**	**NHL**	**69**	**17**	**18**	**35**	**67**	**5**	**3**	**1**	**4**	**4**
1988-89	**NY Islanders**	**NHL**	**14**	**3**	**2**	**5**	**2**	....	....	....	....	....
	Springfield	AHL	8	1	5	6	0	....	....	....	....	....
1989-90	**NY Islanders**	**NHL**	**63**	**6**	**18**	**24**	**19**	**4**	**0**	**2**	**2**	**10**
	Springfield	AHL	7	4	2	6	0	....	....	....	....	....
1990-91	**NY Islanders**	**NHL**	**44**	**4**	**8**	**12**	**45**	....	....	....	....	....
	Capital Dist.	AHL	11	5	11	16	14	....	....	....	....	....
1991-92	**NY Islanders**	**NHL**	**8**	**1**	**0**	**1**	**2**	....	....	....	....	....
	Chicago	**NHL**	**6**	**0**	**0**	**0**	**4**	**7**	**1**	**1**	**2**	**2**
	Indianapolis	IHL	57	24	30	54	46	....	....	....	....	....
1992-93	**Chicago**	**NHL**	**7**	**0**	**1**	**1**	**2**	....	....	....	....	....
a	Indianapolis	IHL	62	*50	41	91	80	5	3	1	4	6
1993-94	**Ottawa**	**NHL**	**30**	**2**	**5**	**7**	**6**	....	....	....	....	....
	Las Vegas	IHL	32	21	21	42	30	4	1	0	1	2
1994-95	Cleveland	IHL	51	32	27	59	48	4	4	2	6	6
	NHL Totals		**302**	**40**	**66**	**106**	**212**	**22**	**6**	**4**	**10**	**20**

a IHL First All-Star Team (1993)

Traded to **Chicago** by **NY Islanders** with Brent Sutter for Adam Creighton and Steve Thomas, October 25, 1991. Signed as a free agent by **Ottawa**, January 3, 1994. Signed as a free agent by **Pittsburgh**, August 10, 1995.

LAUKKANEN, JANNE (LOW-kah-nehn) — COL.

Defense. Shoots left. 6', 180 lbs. Born, Lahti, Finland, March 19, 1970.
(Quebec's 8th choice, 156th overall, in 1991 Entry Draft).

			Regular Season					Playoffs				
Season	Club	Lea	GP	G	A	TP	PIM	GP	G	A	TP	PIM
1990-91	Reipas	Fin.	44	8	14	22	56	....	....	....	....	....
1991-92	HPK	Fin.	43	5	14	19	62	....	....	....	....	....
1992-93	HPK	Fin.	47	8	21	29	76	12	1	4	5	10
1993-94	HPK	Fin.	48	5	24	29	46	....	....	....	....	....
1994-95	Cornwall	AHL	55	8	26	34	41	....	....	....	....	....
	Quebec	**NHL**	**11**	**0**	**3**	**3**	**4**	**6**	**1**	**0**	**1**	**2**
	NHL Totals		**11**	**0**	**3**	**3**	**4**	**6**	**1**	**0**	**1**	**2**

LAUS, PAUL (LOWZ) FLA.

Defense. Shoots right. 6'1", 216 lbs. Born, Beamsville, Ont., September 26, 1970.
(Pittsburgh's 2nd choice, 37th overall, in 1989 Entry Draft).

			Regular Season					Playoffs				
Season	Club	Lea	GP	G	A	TP	PIM	GP	G	A	TP	PIM
1987-88	Hamilton	OHL	56	1	9	10	171	14	0	0	0	28
1988-89	Niagara Falls	OHL	49	1	10	11	225	15	0	5	5	56
1989-90	Niagara Falls	OHL	60	13	35	48	231	16	6	16	22	71
1990-91	Albany	IHL	7	0	0	0	7	....	....	....	....	....
	Knoxville	ECHL	20	6	12	18	83	....	....	....	....	....
	Muskegon	IHL	35	3	4	7	103	4	0	0	0	13
1991-92	Muskegon	IHL	75	0	21	21	248	14	2	5	7	70
1992-93	Cleveland	IHL	76	8	18	26	427	4	1	0	1	27
1993-94	**Florida**	**NHL**	**39**	**2**	**0**	**2**	**109**	....	....	....	....	....
1994-95	**Florida**	**NHL**	**37**	**0**	**7**	**7**	**138**	....	....	....	....	....
	NHL Totals		**76**	**2**	**7**	**9**	**247**	....	....	....	....	....

Claimed by **Florida** from **Pittsburgh** in Expansion Draft, June 24, 1993.

LAVIGNE, ERIC (luh-VEEN) OTT.

Defense. Shoots left. 6'3", 195 lbs. Born, Victoriaville, Que., November 4, 1972.
(Washington's 3rd choice, 25th overall, in 1991 Entry Draft).

			Regular Season					Playoffs				
Season	Club	Lea	GP	G	A	TP	PIM	GP	G	A	TP	PIM
1989-90	Hull	QMJHL	69	7	11	18	203	11	0	0	0	32
1990-91	Hull	QMJHL	66	11	11	22	153	4	0	1	1	16
1991-92	Hull	QMJHL	46	4	17	21	101	6	0	0	0	32
1992-93	Hull	QMJHL	59	7	20	27	221	10	2	4	6	47
1993-94	Phoenix	IHL	62	3	11	14	168	....	....	....	....	....
1994-95	Phoenix	IHL	69	4	10	14	233	....	....	....	....	....
	Los Angeles	**NHL**	**1**	**0**	**0**	**0**	**0**	....	....	....	....	....
	Detroit	IHL	1	0	0	0	2	5	0	0	0	26
	NHL Totals		**1**	**0**	**0**	**0**	**0**	....	....	....	....	....

Signed as a free agent by **Los Angeles**, October 13, 1993. Signed as a free agent by **Ottawa**, August 10, 1995.

LAWRENCE, MARK DAL.

Right wing. Shoots right. 6'4", 215 lbs. Born, Burlington, Ont., January 27, 1972.
(Minnesota's 6th choice, 118th overall, in 1991 Entry Draft).

			Regular Season					Playoffs				
Season	Club	Lea	GP	G	A	TP	PIM	GP	G	A	TP	PIM
1988-89	Niagara Falls	OHL	63	9	27	36	142	....	....	....	....	....
1989-90	Niagara Falls	OHL	54	15	18	33	123	16	2	5	7	42
1990-91	Detroit	OHL	66	27	38	65	53	....	....	....	....	....
1991-92	Detroit	OHL	28	19	26	45	54	....	....	....	....	....
	North Bay	OHL	24	13	14	27	21	21	*23	12	35	36
1992-93	Dayton	ECHL	20	8	14	22	46	....	....	....	....	....
	Kalamazoo	IHL	57	22	13	35	47	....	....	....	....	....
1993-94	Kalamazoo	IHL	64	17	20	37	90	....	....	....	....	....
1994-95	Kalamazoo	IHL	77	21	29	50	92	16	3	7	10	28
	Dallas	**NHL**	**2**	**0**	**0**	**0**	**0**	....	....	....	....	....
	NHL Totals		**2**	**0**	**0**	**0**	**0**	....	....	....	....	....

LAZARENKO, ALEXEI (la-zah-REHN-koh) NYR

Left wing. Shoots left. 5'11", 176 lbs. Born, Moscow, USSR, January 3, 1976.
(NY Rangers' 9th choice, 182nd overall, in 1994 Entry Draft).

			Regular Season					Playoffs				
Season	Club	Lea	GP	G	A	TP	PIM	GP	G	A	TP	PIM
1994-95	CSKA-2	CIS	5	0	0	0	0	....	....	....	....	....

LEACH, JAMIE

Right wing. Shoots right. 6'1", 205 lbs. Born, Winnipeg, Man., August 25, 1969.
(Pittsburgh's 3rd choice, 47th overall, in 1987 Entry Draft).

			Regular Season					Playoffs				
Season	Club	Lea	GP	G	A	TP	PIM	GP	G	A	TP	PIM
1985-86	N. Westminster	WHL	58	8	7	15	20	....	....	....	....	....
1986-87	Hamilton	OHL	64	12	19	31	67	....	....	....	....	....
1987-88	Hamilton	OHL	64	24	19	43	79	14	6	7	13	12
1988-89	Niagara Falls	OHL	58	45	62	107	47	17	9	11	20	25
1989-90	**Pittsburgh**	**NHL**	**10**	**0**	**3**	**3**	**0**	....	....	....	....	....
	Muskegon	IHL	72	22	36	58	39	15	9	4	13	14
1990-91	**Pittsburgh**	**NHL**	**7**	**2**	**0**	**2**	**0**	....	....	....	....	....
	Muskegon	IHL	43	33	22	55	26	....	....	....	....	....
1991-92	**Pittsburgh**	**NHL**	**38**	**5**	**4**	**9**	**8**	....	....	....	....	....
	Muskegon	IHL	3	1	1	2	2	....	....	....	....	....
1992-93	**Pittsburgh**	**NHL**	**5**	**0**	**0**	**0**	**2**	....	....	....	....	....
	Cleveland	IHL	9	5	3	8	2	4	1	2	3	0
	Hartford	**NHL**	**19**	**3**	**2**	**5**	**2**	....	....	....	....	....
	Springfield	AHL	29	13	15	28	33	....	....	....	....	....
1993-94	**Florida**	**NHL**	**2**	**1**	**0**	**1**	**0**	....	....	....	....	....
	Cincinnati	IHL	74	15	19	34	64	11	1	0	1	4
1994-95	Cdn. National	....	41	12	26	38	26	....	....	....	....	....
	Cincinnati	IHL	11	0	2	2	9	....	....	....	....	....
	San Diego	IHL	....	....	....	....	....	4	0	0	0	0
	NHL Totals		**81**	**11**	**9**	**20**	**12**	....	....	....	....	....

Claimed on waivers by **Hartford** from **Pittsburgh**, November 21, 1992. Signed as a free agent by **Florida**, August 31, 1993.

LEACH, STEPHEN BOS.

Right wing. Shoots right. 5'11", 197 lbs. Born, Cambridge, MA, January 16, 1966.
(Washington's 2nd choice, 34th overall, in 1984 Entry Draft).

			Regular Season					Playoffs				
Season	Club	Lea	GP	G	A	TP	PIM	GP	G	A	TP	PIM
1984-85	N. Hampshire	H.E.	41	12	25	37	53	....	....	....	....	....
1985-86	**Washington**	**NHL**	**11**	**1**	**1**	**2**	**2**	**6**	**0**	**1**	**1**	**0**
	N. Hampshire	H.E.	25	22	6	28	30	....	....	....	....	....
1986-87	**Washington**	**NHL**	**15**	**1**	**0**	**1**	**6**	....	....	....	....	....
	Binghamton	AHL	54	18	21	39	39	13	3	1	4	6
1987-88	**Washington**	**NHL**	**8**	**1**	**1**	**2**	**17**	**9**	**2**	**1**	**3**	**0**
	U.S. National	....	49	26	20	46	30	....	....	....	....	....
	U.S. Olympic	....	6	1	2	3	0	....	....	....	....	....
1988-89	**Washington**	**NHL**	**74**	**11**	**19**	**30**	**94**	**6**	**1**	**0**	**1**	**12**
1989-90	**Washington**	**NHL**	**70**	**18**	**14**	**32**	**104**	**14**	**2**	**2**	**4**	**8**
1990-91	**Washington**	**NHL**	**68**	**11**	**19**	**30**	**99**	**9**	**1**	**2**	**3**	**8**
1991-92	**Boston**	**NHL**	**78**	**31**	**29**	**60**	**147**	**15**	**4**	**0**	**4**	**10**
1992-93	**Boston**	**NHL**	**79**	**26**	**25**	**51**	**126**	**4**	**1**	**1**	**2**	**2**
1993-94	**Boston**	**NHL**	**42**	**5**	**10**	**15**	**74**	**5**	**0**	**1**	**1**	**2**
1994-95	**Boston**	**NHL**	**35**	**5**	**6**	**11**	**68**	....	....	....	....	....
	NHL Totals		**480**	**110**	**124**	**234**	**737**	**68**	**11**	**8**	**19**	**42**

Traded to **Boston** by **Washington** for Randy Burridge, June 21, 1991.

LEBEAU, STEPHAN (leh-BOH)

Center. Shoots right. 5'10", 173 lbs. Born, St. Jerome, Que., February 28, 1968.

			Regular Season					Playoffs				
Season	Club	Lea	GP	G	A	TP	PIM	GP	G	A	TP	PIM
1984-85	Shawinigan	QMJHL	66	41	38	79	18	9	4	5	9	4
1985-86	Shawinigan	QMJHL	72	69	77	146	22	5	4	2	6	4
1986-87a	Shawinigan	QMJHL	65	77	90	167	60	14	9	20	29	20
1987-88a	Shawinigan	QMJHL	67	*94	94	188	66	11	17	9	26	10
	Sherbrooke	AHL	....	....	....	....	....	1	0	1	1	0
1988-89	**Montreal**	**NHL**	**1**	**0**	**1**	**1**	**2**	....	....	....	....	....
bcde	Sherbrooke	AHL	78	*70	64	*134	47	6	1	4	5	8
1989-90	**Montreal**	**NHL**	**57**	**15**	**20**	**35**	**11**	**2**	**3**	**0**	**3**	**0**
1990-91	**Montreal**	**NHL**	**73**	**22**	**31**	**53**	**24**	**7**	**2**	**1**	**3**	**2**
1991-92	**Montreal**	**NHL**	**77**	**27**	**31**	**58**	**14**	**8**	**1**	**3**	**4**	**4**
1992-93	**Montreal**	**NHL**	**71**	**31**	**49**	**80**	**20**	**13**	**3**	**3**	**6**	**6**
1993-94	**Montreal**	**NHL**	**34**	**9**	**7**	**16**	**8**	....	....	....	....	....
	Anaheim	**NHL**	**22**	**6**	**4**	**10**	**14**	....	....	....	....	....
1994-95	**Anaheim**	**NHL**	**38**	**8**	**16**	**24**	**12**	....	....	....	....	....
	NHL Totals		**373**	**118**	**159**	**277**	**105**	**30**	**9**	**7**	**16**	**12**

a QMJHL Second All-Star Team (1987, 1988)
b AHL First All-Star Team (1989)
c Won Dudley "Red" Garrett Memorial Trophy (Top Rookie - AHL) (1989)
d Won John B. Sollenberger Trophy (Top Scorer - AHL) (1989)
e Won Les Cunningham Plaque (MVP - AHL) (1989)

Signed as a free agent by **Montreal**, September 27, 1986. Traded to **Anaheim** by **Montreal** for Ron Tugnutt, February 20, 1994.

LEBLANC, JOHN (leh-BLAHNK)

Right wing. Shoots left. 6'1", 190 lbs. Born, Campbellton, N.B., January 21, 1964.

			Regular Season					Playoffs				
Season	Club	Lea	GP	G	A	TP	PIM	GP	G	A	TP	PIM
1983-84	Hull	QMJHL	69	39	35	74	32	....	....	....	....	....
1984-85	New Brunswick	AUAA	24	25	34	59	32	....	....	....	....	....
1985-86a	New Brunswick	AUAA	24	38	28	66	35	....	....	....	....	....
1986-87	**Vancouver**	**NHL**	**2**	**1**	**0**	**1**	**0**	....	....	....	....	....
	Fredericton	AHL	75	40	30	70	27	....	....	....	....	....
1987-88	**Vancouver**	**NHL**	**41**	**12**	**10**	**22**	**18**	....	....	....	....	....
	Fredericton	AHL	35	26	25	51	54	15	6	7	13	34
1988-89	Milwaukee	IHL	61	39	31	70	42	....	....	....	....	....
	Edmonton	**NHL**	**2**	**1**	**0**	**1**	**0**	**1**	**0**	**0**	**0**	**0**
	Cape Breton	AHL	3	4	0	4	0	....	....	....	....	....
1989-90	Cape Breton	AHL	77	*54	34	88	50	6	4	0	4	4
1990-91			DID NOT PLAY									
1991-92	**Winnipeg**	**NHL**	**16**	**6**	**1**	**7**	**6**	....	....	....	....	....
	Moncton	AHL	56	31	22	53	24	10	3	2	5	8
1992-93	**Winnipeg**	**NHL**	**3**	**0**	**0**	**0**	**2**	....	....	....	....	....
	Moncton	AHL	77	48	40	88	29	5	2	1	3	6
1993-94	**Winnipeg**	**NHL**	**17**	**6**	**2**	**8**	**2**	....	....	....	....	....
	Moncton	AHL	41	25	26	51	38	20	3	6	9	6
1994-95	Springfield	AHL	65	39	34	73	32	....	....	....	....	....
	Winnipeg	**NHL**	**2**	**0**	**0**	**0**	**0**	....	....	....	....	....
	NHL Totals		**83**	**26**	**13**	**39**	**28**	**1**	**0**	**0**	**0**	**0**

a Canadian University Player of the Year (1986)

Signed as a free agent by **Vancouver**, April 12, 1986. Traded to **Edmonton** by **Vancouver** with Vancouver's fifth round choice (Peter White) in 1989 Entry Draft for Doug Smith and Gregory C. Adams, March 7, 1989. Traded to **Winnipeg** by **Edmonton** with Edmonton's tenth round choice (Teemu Numminen) in 1992 Entry Draft for Winnipeg's fifth round choice (Ryan Haggerty) in 1991 Entry Draft, June 12, 1991.

LeBOUTILLIER, PETER ANA.

Right wing. Shoots right. 6'1", 198 lbs. Born, Minnedosa, Man., January 11, 1975.
(NY Islanders' 6th choice, 144th overall, in 1993 Entry Draft).

			Regular Season					Playoffs				
Season	Club	Lea	GP	G	A	TP	PIM	GP	G	A	TP	PIM
1992-93	Red Deer	WHL	67	8	26	34	284	2	0	1	1	5
1993-94	Red Deer	WHL	66	19	20	39	300	2	0	1	1	4
1994-95	Red Deer	WHL	59	27	16	43	159	....	....	....	....	....

Re-entered NHL Entry Draft, Anaheim's 5th choice, 133rd overall, in 1995 Entry Draft.

LeCLAIR, JOHN (luh-KLAIR) PHI.

Left wing. Shoots left. 6'2", 219 lbs. Born, St. Albans, VT, July 5, 1969.
(Montreal's 2nd choice, 33rd overall, in 1987 Entry Draft).

			Regular Season					Playoffs				
Season	Club	Lea	GP	G	A	TP	PIM	GP	G	A	TP	PIM
1987-88	U. of Vermont	ECAC	31	12	22	34	62	....	....	....	....	....
1988-89	U. of Vermont	ECAC	18	9	12	21	40	....	....	....	....	....
1989-90	U. of Vermont	ECAC	10	10	6	16	38	....	....	....	....	....
1990-91a	U. of Vermont	ECAC	33	25	20	45	58	....	....	....	....	....
	Montreal	**NHL**	**10**	**2**	**5**	**7**	**2**	**3**	**0**	**0**	**0**	**0**
1991-92	**Montreal**	**NHL**	**59**	**8**	**11**	**19**	**14**	**8**	**1**	**1**	**2**	**4**
	Fredericton	AHL	8	7	7	14	10	2	0	0	0	4
1992-93	**Montreal**	**NHL**	**72**	**19**	**25**	**44**	**33**	**20**	**4**	**6**	**10**	**14**
1993-94	**Montreal**	**NHL**	**74**	**19**	**24**	**43**	**32**	**7**	**2**	**1**	**3**	**8**
1994-95b	**Montreal**	**NHL**	**9**	**1**	**4**	**5**	**10**	....	....	....	....	....
	Philadelphia	**NHL**	**37**	**25**	**24**	**49**	**20**	**15**	**5**	**7**	**12**	**4**
	NHL Totals		**261**	**74**	**93**	**167**	**111**	**53**	**12**	**15**	**27**	**30**

a ECAC Second All-Star Team (1991)
b NHL First All-Star Team (1995)

Traded to **Philadelphia** by **Montreal** with Eric Desjardins and Gilbert Dionne for Mark Recchi and Philadelphia's third round choice (Martin Hohenberger) in 1995 Entry Draft, February 9, 1995.

LECLERC, MIKE ANA.

Left wing. Shoots left. 6'1", 205 lbs. Born, Winnipeg, Man., November 10, 1976.
(Anaheim's 3rd choice, 55th overall, in 1995 Entry Draft).

			Regular Season					Playoffs				
Season	Club	Lea	GP	G	A	TP	PIM	GP	G	A	TP	PIM
1992-93	Victoria	WHL	70	4	11	15	118	....	....	....	....	....
1993-94	Victoria	WHL	68	29	11	40	112	....	....	....	....	....
1994-95	Prince George	WHL	43	20	36	56	78	....	....	....	....	....
	Brandon	WHL	23	5	8	13	50	18	10	6	16	33

LECOMPTE, ERIC
(luh-COMP)   CHI.

Left wing. Shoots left. 6'4", 190 lbs.   Born, Montreal, Que., April 4, 1975.
(Chicago's 1st choice, 24th overall, in 1993 Entry Draft).

				Regular Season						Playoffs			
Season	Club	Lea	GP	G	A	TP	PIM	GP	G	A	TP	PIM
1991-92	Hull	QMJHL	60	16	17	33	138	6	1	0	1	4
1992-93	Hull	QMJHL	66	33	38	71	149	10	4	4	8	52
1993-94	Hull	QMJHL	62	39	49	88	171	20	10	10	20	68
1994-95	Hull	QMJHL	12	11	9	20	58	....	....	....	....	....
	St-Jean	QMJHL	18	9	10	19	54	....	....	....	....	....
	Sherbrooke	QMJHL	34	22	29	51	111	4	2	2	4	4
	Indianapolis	IHL	3	2	0	2	2	....	....	....	....	....

LEDYARD, GRANT
DAL.

Defense. Shoots left. 6'2", 195 lbs.   Born, Winnipeg, Man., November 19, 1961.

				Regular Season						Playoffs			
Season	Club	Lea	GP	G	A	TP	PIM	GP	G	A	TP	PIM
1980-81	Saskatoon	WHL	71	9	28	37	148	....	....	....	....	....
1981-82	Fort Garry	MJHL	63	25	45	70	150	....	....	....	....	....
1982-83	Tulsa	CHL	80	13	29	42	115	....	....	....	....	....
1983-84a	Tulsa	CHL	58	9	17	26	71	9	5	4	9	10
1984-85	NY Rangers	NHL	42	8	12	20	53	3	0	2	2	4
	New Haven	AHL	36	6	20	26	18	....	....	....	....	....
1985-86	NY Rangers	NHL	27	2	9	11	20	....	....	....	....	....
	Los Angeles	NHL	52	7	18	25	78	....	....	....	....	....
1986-87	Los Angeles	NHL	67	14	23	37	93	5	0	0	0	10
1987-88	Los Angeles	NHL	23	1	7	8	52	....	....	....	....	....
	New Haven	AHL	3	2	1	3	4	....	....	....	....	....
	Washington	NHL	21	4	3	7	14	14	1	0	1	30
1988-89	Washington	NHL	61	3	11	14	43	....	....	....	....	....
	Buffalo	NHL	13	1	5	6	8	5	1	2	3	2
1989-90	Buffalo	NHL	67	2	13	15	37	....	....	....	....	....
1990-91	Buffalo	NHL	60	8	23	31	46	6	3	3	6	10
1991-92	Buffalo	NHL	50	5	16	21	45	....	....	....	....	....
1992-93	Buffalo	NHL	50	2	14	16	45	8	0	0	0	8
	Rochester	AHL	5	0	2	2	8	....	....	....	....	....
1993-94	Dallas	NHL	84	9	37	46	42	9	1	2	3	6
1994-95	Dallas	NHL	38	5	13	18	20	3	0	0	0	2
	NHL Totals		**655**	**71**	**204**	**275**	**596**	**53**	**6**	**9**	**15**	**72**

a   Won Bob Gassoff Trophy (CHL's Most Improved Defenseman) (1984)

Signed as a free agent by **NY Rangers**, July 7, 1982. Traded to **Los Angeles** by **NY Rangers** with Roland Melanson for Los Angeles' fourth round choice (Mike Sullivan) in 1987 Entry Draft and Brian MacLellan, December 7, 1985. Traded to **Washington** by **Los Angeles** for Craig Laughlin, February 9, 1988. Traded to **Buffalo** by **Washington** with Clint Malarchuk and Washington's sixth round choice (Brian Holzinger) in 1991 Entry Draft for Calle Johansson and Buffalo's second round choice (Byron Dafoe) in 1989 Entry Draft, March 7, 1989. Signed as a free agent by **Dallas**, August 12, 1993.

LEEMAN, GARY

Right wing. Shoots right. 5'11", 175 lbs.   Born, Toronto, Ont., February 19, 1964.
(Toronto's 2nd choice, 24th overall, in 1982 Entry Draft).

				Regular Season						Playoffs			
Season	Club	Lea	GP	G	A	TP	PIM	GP	G	A	TP	PIM
1981-82	Regina	WHL	72	19	41	60	112	3	2	2	4	0
1982-83a	Regina	WHL	63	24	62	86	88	5	1	5	6	4
	Toronto	NHL	....	....	....	....	....	2	0	0	0	0
1983-84	Toronto	NHL	52	4	8	12	31	....	....	....	....	....
1984-85	Toronto	NHL	53	5	26	31	72	....	....	....	....	....
	St. Catharines	AHL	7	2	2	4	11	....	....	....	....	....
1985-86	Toronto	NHL	53	9	23	32	20	10	2	10	12	2
	St. Catharines	AHL	25	15	13	28	6	....	....	....	....	....
1986-87	Toronto	NHL	80	21	31	52	66	5	0	1	1	14
1987-88	Toronto	NHL	80	30	31	61	62	2	2	0	2	2
1988-89	Toronto	NHL	61	32	43	75	66	....	....	....	....	....
1989-90	Toronto	NHL	80	51	44	95	63	5	3	3	6	16
1990-91	Toronto	NHL	52	17	12	29	39	....	....	....	....	....
1991-92	Toronto	NHL	34	7	13	20	44	....	....	....	....	....
	Calgary	NHL	29	2	7	9	27	....	....	....	....	....
1992-93	Calgary	NHL	30	9	5	14	10	....	....	....	....	....
	Montreal	NHL	20	6	12	18	14	11	1	2	3	2
1993-94	Montreal	NHL	31	4	11	15	17	1	0	0	0	0
	Fredericton	AHL	23	18	8	26	16	....	....	....	....	....
1994-95	Vancouver	NHL	10	2	0	2	0	....	....	....	....	....
	NHL Totals		**665**	**199**	**266**	**465**	**531**	**36**	**8**	**16**	**24**	**36**

a   WHL First All-Star Team (1983)

Played in NHL All-Star Game (1989)

Traded to **Calgary** by **Toronto** with Craig Berube, Alexander Godynyuk, Michel Petit and Jeff Reese for Doug Gilmour, Jamie Macoun, Ric Nattress, Rick Wamsley and Kent Manderville, January 2, 1992. Traded to **Montreal** by **Calgary** for Brian Skrudland, January 28, 1993. Signed as a free agent by **Vancouver**, January 18, 1995.

LEETCH, BRIAN
NYR

Defense. Shoots left. 5'11", 190 lbs.   Born, Corpus Christi, TX, March 3, 1968.
(NY Rangers' 1st choice, 9th overall, in 1986 Entry Draft).

				Regular Season						Playoffs			
Season	Club	Lea	GP	G	A	TP	PIM	GP	G	A	TP	PIM
1986-87ab	Boston College	H.E.	37	9	38	47	10	....	....	....	....	....
1987-88	U.S. National	....	50	13	61	74	38	....	....	....	....	....
	U.S. Olympic	....	6	1	5	6	4	....	....	....	....	....
	NY Rangers	NHL	17	2	12	14	0	....	....	....	....	....
1988-89cd	NY Rangers	NHL	68	23	48	71	50	4	3	2	5	2
1989-90	NY Rangers	NHL	72	11	45	56	26	....	....	....	....	....
1990-91e	NY Rangers	NHL	80	16	72	88	42	6	1	3	4	0
1991-92fg	NY Rangers	NHL	80	22	80	102	26	13	4	11	15	4
1992-93	NY Rangers	NHL	36	6	30	36	26	....	....	....	....	....
1993-94eh	NY Rangers	NHL	84	23	56	79	67	23	11	*23	*34	6
1994-95	NY Rangers	NHL	48	9	32	41	18	10	6	8	14	8
	NHL Totals		**485**	**112**	**375**	**487**	**255**	**56**	**25**	**47**	**72**	**20**

a   Hockey East First All-Star Team (1987)
b   NCAA East First All-American Team (1987)
c   NHL All-Rookie Team (1989)
d   Won Calder Memorial Trophy (1989)
e   NHL Second All-Star Team (1991, 1994)
f   Won James Norris Memorial Trophy (1992)
g   NHL First All-Star Team (1992)
h   Won Conn Smythe Trophy (1994)

Played in NHL All-Star Game (1990-92, 1994)

LEFEBVRE, SYLVAIN
(luh-FAYV)   COL.

Defense. Shoots left. 6'2", 205 lbs.   Born, Richmond, Que., October 14, 1967.

				Regular Season						Playoffs			
Season	Club	Lea	GP	G	A	TP	PIM	GP	G	A	TP	PIM
1984-85	Laval	QMJHL	66	7	5	12	31	....	....	....	....	....
1985-86	Laval	QMJHL	71	8	17	25	48	14	1	0	1	25
1986-87	Laval	QMJHL	70	10	36	46	44	15	1	6	7	12
1987-88	Sherbrooke	AHL	79	3	24	27	73	6	2	3	5	4
1988-89a	Sherbrooke	AHL	77	15	32	47	119	6	1	3	4	4
1989-90	**Montreal**	NHL	68	3	10	13	61	6	0	0	0	2
1990-91	**Montreal**	NHL	63	5	18	23	30	11	1	0	1	6
1991-92	**Montreal**	NHL	69	3	14	17	91	2	0	0	0	2
1992-93	**Toronto**	NHL	81	2	12	14	90	21	3	3	6	20
1993-94	**Toronto**	NHL	84	2	9	11	79	18	0	3	3	16
1994-95	**Quebec**	NHL	48	2	11	13	17	6	0	2	2	2
	NHL Totals		**413**	**17**	**74**	**91**	**368**	**64**	**4**	**8**	**12**	**48**

a   AHL Second All-Star Team (1989)

Signed as a free agent by **Montreal**, September 24, 1986. Traded to **Toronto** by **Montreal** for Toronto's third round choice (Martin Belanger) in 1994 Entry Draft, August 20, 1992. Traded to **Quebec** by **Toronto** with Wendel Clark, Landon Wilson and Toronto's first round choice (Jeffrey Kealty) in 1994 Entry Draft for Mats Sundin, Garth Butcher, Todd Warriner and Philadelphia's first round choice (previously acquired by Quebec — later traded to Washington — Washington selected Nolan Baumgartner) in 1994 Entry Draft, June 28, 1994.

LEGG, MIKE
N.J.

Right wing. Shoots right. 5'11", 165 lbs.   Born, London, Ont., May 25, 1975.
(New Jersey's 11th choice, 273rd overall, in 1993 Entry Draft).

				Regular Season						Playoffs			
Season	Club	Lea	GP	G	A	TP	PIM	GP	G	A	TP	PIM
1993-94	U. of Michigan	CCHA	37	10	13	23	20	....	....	....	....	....
1994-95	U. of Michigan	CCHA	39	14	23	37	22	....	....	....	....	....

LEHOUX, GUY
(leh-HOO)   TOR.

Defense. Shoots left. 5'11", 210 lbs.   Born, Disraeli, Que., October 19, 1971.
(Toronto's 9th choice, 179th overall, in 1991 Entry Draft).

				Regular Season						Playoffs			
Season	Club	Lea	GP	G	A	TP	PIM	GP	G	A	TP	PIM
1989-90	Drummondville	QMJHL	66	4	17	21	178	....	....	....	....	....
1990-91	Drummondville	QMJHL	63	8	26	34	107	14	1	7	8	24
1991-92	St. John's	AHL	67	1	7	8	134	....	....	....	....	....
1992-93	St. John's	AHL	42	3	2	5	89	....	....	....	....	....
	Brantford	ColHL	13	0	5	5	28	4	0	1	1	15
1993-94	St. John's	AHL	71	2	8	10	217	9	1	1	2	8
1994-95	St. John's	AHL	77	4	9	13	255	5	0	0	0	2

LEHTERA, TERO
FLA.

Left wing. Shoots right. 6', 185 lbs.   Born, Espoo, Finland, April 21, 1972.
(Florida's 9th choice, 235th overall, in 1994 Entry Draft).

				Regular Season						Playoffs			
Season	Club	Lea	GP	G	A	TP	PIM	GP	G	A	TP	PIM
1993-94	Espoo	Fin.	48	19	27	46	2	....	....	....	....	....
1994-95	Malmo	Swe.	37	12	11	23	10	9	0	1	1	0

LEHTINEN, JERE
(lehkh-TIH-nehn)   DAL.

Right wing. Shoots right. 6', 185 lbs.   Born, Espoo, Finland, June 24, 1973.
(Minnesota's 3rd choice, 88th overall, in 1992 Entry Draft).

				Regular Season						Playoffs			
Season	Club	Lea	GP	G	A	TP	PIM	GP	G	A	TP	PIM
1990-91	Espoo	Fin. 2	32	15	9	24	12	....	....	....	....	....
1991-92	Espoo	Fin. 2	43	32	17	49	6	....	....	....	....	....
1992-93	Kiekko-Espoo	Fin.	45	13	14	27	6	....	....	....	....	....
1993-94	TPS	Fin.	42	19	20	39	6	11	11	2	13	2
1994-95	TPS	Fin.	39	19	23	42	33	13	8	6	14	4

LEMIEUX, CLAUDE
(lehm-YOO)   N.J.

Right wing. Shoots right. 6'1", 215 lbs.   Born, Buckingham, Que., July 16, 1965.
(Montreal's 2nd choice, 26th overall, in 1983 Entry Draft).

				Regular Season						Playoffs			
Season	Club	Lea	GP	G	A	TP	PIM	GP	G	A	TP	PIM
1982-83	Trois-Rivières	QMJHL	62	28	38	66	187	4	1	0	1	30
1983-84	**Montreal**	NHL	8	1	1	2	12	....	....	....	....	....
	Verdun	QMJHL	51	41	45	86	225	9	8	12	20	63
	Nova Scotia	AHL	....	....	....	....	....	2	1	0	1	0
1984-85	**Montreal**	NHL	1	0	1	1	7	....	....	....	....	....
a	Verdun	QMJHL	52	58	66	124	152	14	23	17	40	38
1985-86	**Montreal**	NHL	10	1	2	3	22	20	10	6	16	68
	Sherbrooke	AHL	58	21	32	53	145	....	....	....	....	....
1986-87	**Montreal**	NHL	76	27	26	53	156	17	4	9	13	41
1987-88	**Montreal**	NHL	78	31	30	61	137	11	3	2	5	20
1988-89	**Montreal**	NHL	69	29	22	51	136	18	4	3	7	58
1989-90	**Montreal**	NHL	39	8	10	18	106	11	1	3	4	38
1990-91	**New Jersey**	NHL	78	30	17	47	105	7	4	0	4	34
1991-92	**New Jersey**	NHL	74	41	27	68	109	7	4	3	7	26
1992-93	**New Jersey**	NHL	77	30	51	81	155	5	2	0	2	19
1993-94	**New Jersey**	NHL	79	18	26	44	86	20	7	11	18	44
1994-95b	**New Jersey**	NHL	45	6	13	19	86	20	*13	3	16	20
	NHL Totals		**634**	**222**	**226**	**448**	**1117**	**136**	**52**	**40**	**92**	**368**

a   QMJHL First All-Star Team (1985)
b   Won Conn Smythe Trophy (1995)

Traded to **New Jersey** by **Montreal** for Sylvain Turgeon, September 4, 1990.

LEMIEUX, JOCELYN (lehm-YOO)

Right wing. Shoots left. 5'10", 200 lbs. Born, Mont-Laurier, Que., November 18, 1967.
(St. Louis' 1st choice, 10th overall, in 1986 Entry Draft).

			Regular Season					Playoffs				
Season	Club	Lea	GP	G	A	TP	PIM	GP	G	A	TP	PIM
1984-85	Laval	QMJHL	68	13	19	32	92	....	....	....	....	....
1985-86a	Laval	QMJHL	71	57	68	125	131	14	9	15	24	37
1986-87	**St. Louis**	**NHL**	**53**	**10**	**8**	**18**	**94**	**5**	**0**	**1**	**1**	**6**
1987-88	**St. Louis**	**NHL**	**23**	**1**	**0**	**1**	**42**	**5**	**0**	**0**	**0**	**15**
	Peoria	IHL	8	0	5	5	35	....	....	....	....	....
1988-89	**Montreal**	**NHL**	**1**	**0**	**1**	**1**	**0**	....	....	....	....	....
	Sherbrooke	AHL	73	25	28	53	134	4	3	1	4	6
1989-90	**Montreal**	**NHL**	**34**	**4**	**2**	**6**	**61**	....	....	....	....	....
	Chicago	**NHL**	**39**	**10**	**11**	**21**	**47**	**18**	**1**	**8**	**9**	**28**
1990-91	**Chicago**	**NHL**	**67**	**6**	**7**	**13**	**119**	**4**	**0**	**0**	**0**	**0**
1991-92	**Chicago**	**NHL**	**78**	**6**	**10**	**16**	**80**	**18**	**3**	**1**	**4**	**33**
1992-93	**Chicago**	**NHL**	**81**	**10**	**21**	**31**	**111**	**4**	**1**	**0**	**1**	**2**
1993-94	**Chicago**	**NHL**	**66**	**12**	**8**	**20**	**63**	....	....	....	....	....
	Hartford	**NHL**	**16**	**6**	**1**	**7**	**19**	....	....	....	....	....
1994-95	**Hartford**	**NHL**	**41**	**6**	**5**	**11**	**32**	....	....	....	....	....
	NHL Totals		**499**	**71**	**74**	**145**	**668**	**54**	**5**	**10**	**15**	**84**

a QMJHL First All-Star Team (1986)

Traded to **Montreal** by **St. Louis** with Darrell May and St. Louis' second round choice (Patrice Brisebois) in the 1989 Entry Draft for Sergio Momesso and Vincent Riendeau, August 9, 1988. Traded to **Chicago** by **Montreal** for Chicago's third round choice (Charles Poulin) in 1990 Entry Draft, January 5, 1990. Traded to **Hartford** by **Chicago** with Frantisek Kucera for Gary Suter, Randy Cunneyworth and Hartford's third round choice (later traded to Vancouver — Vancouver selected Larry Courville) in 1995 Entry Draft, March 11, 1994.

LEMIEUX, MARIO (lehm-YOO) PIT.

Center. Shoots right. 6'4", 210 lbs. Born, Montreal, Que., October 5, 1965.
(Pittsburgh's 1st choice, 1st overall, in 1984 Entry Draft).

			Regular Season					Playoffs				
Season	Club	Lea	GP	G	A	TP	PIM	GP	G	A	TP	PIM
1981-82	Laval	QMJHL	64	30	66	96	22	18	5	9	14	31
1982-83a	Laval	QMJHL	66	84	100	184	76	12	14	18	32	18
1983-84bc	Laval	QMJHL	70	*133	*149	*282	92	14	*29	*23	*52	29
1984-85de	**Pittsburgh**	**NHL**	**73**	**43**	**57**	**100**	**54**	....	....	....	....	....
1985-86fg	**Pittsburgh**	**NHL**	**79**	**48**	**93**	**141**	**43**	....	....	....	....	....
1986-87f	**Pittsburgh**	**NHL**	**63**	**54**	**53**	**107**	**57**	....	....	....	....	....
1987-88 ghijkl	**Pittsburgh**	**NHL**	**77**	***70**	**98**	***168**	**92**	....	....	....	....	....
1988-89ijlm	**Pittsburgh**	**NHL**	**76**	***85**	***114**	***199**	**100**	**11**	**12**	**7**	**19**	**16**
1989-90	**Pittsburgh**	**NHL**	**59**	**45**	**78**	**123**	**78**	....	....	....	....	....
1990-91n	**Pittsburgh**	**NHL**	**26**	**19**	**26**	**45**	**30**	**23**	**16**	***28**	***44**	**16**
1991-92fino	**Pittsburgh**	**NHL**	**64**	**44**	**87**	***131**	**94**	**15**	***16**	**18**	***34**	**2**
1992-93 ghijpq	**Pittsburgh**	**NHL**	**60**	**69**	**91**	***160**	**38**	**11**	**8**	**10**	**18**	**10**
1993-94	**Pittsburgh**	**NHL**	**22**	**17**	**20**	**37**	**32**	**6**	**4**	**3**	**7**	**2**
1994-95					DID NOT PLAY							
	NHL Totals		**599**	**494**	**717**	**1211**	**618**	**66**	**56**	**66**	**122**	**46**

a QMJHL Second All-Star Team (1983)
b QMJHL First All-Star Team (1984)
c Canadian Major Junior Player of the Year (1984)
d Won Calder Memorial Trophy (1985)
e NHL All-Rookie Team (1985)
f NHL Second All-Star Team (1986, 1987, 1992)
g Won Lester B. Pearson Award (1986, 1988, 1993)
h Won Hart Trophy (1988, 1993)
i Won Art Ross Trophy (1988, 1989, 1992, 1993)
j NHL First All-Star Team (1988, 1989, 1993)
k Won Dodge Performance of the Year Award (1988)
l Won Dodge Performer of the Year Award (1988, 1989)
m Won Dodge Ram Tough Award (1989)
n Won Conn Smythe Trophy (1991, 1992)
o Won ProSet/NHL Player of the Year Award (1992)
p Won Bill Masterton Memorial Trophy (1993)
q Won Alka-Seltzer Plus Award (1993)

Played in NHL All-Star Game (1985, 1986, 1988-90, 1992)

LEPLER, PAUL MTL.

Defense. Shoots left. 6'3", 185 lbs. Born, Granite Falls, MN, November 26, 1972.
(Montreal's 14th choice, 237th overall, in 1991 Entry Draft).

			Regular Season					Playoffs				
Season	Club	Lea	GP	G	A	TP	PIM	GP	G	A	TP	PIM
1992-93	St. Cloud St.	WCHA	26	2	4	6	16	....	....	....	....	....
1993-94	St. Cloud St.	WCHA	35	1	4	5	48	....	....	....	....	....
1994-95	St. Cloud St.	WCHA	38	3	3	6	68	....	....	....	....	....

LEROUX, FRANCOIS (leh-ROO) PIT.

Defense. Shoots left. 6'5", 220 lbs. Born, Ste.-Adele, Que., April 18, 1970.
(Edmonton's 1st choice, 19th overall, in 1988 Entry Draft).

			Regular Season					Playoffs				
Season	Club	Lea	GP	G	A	TP	PIM	GP	G	A	TP	PIM
1987-88	St-Jean	QMJHL	58	3	8	11	143	7	2	0	2	21
1988-89	**Edmonton**	**NHL**	**2**	**0**	**0**	**0**	**0**	....	....	....	....	....
	St-Jean	QMJHL	57	8	34	42	185	....	....	....	....	....
1989-90	**Edmonton**	**NHL**	**3**	**0**	**1**	**1**	**0**	....	....	....	....	....
	Victoriaville	QMJHL	54	4	33	37	169	....	....	....	....	....
1990-91	**Edmonton**	**NHL**	**1**	**0**	**2**	**2**	**0**	....	....	....	....	....
	Cape Breton	AHL	71	2	7	9	124	4	0	1	1	19
1991-92	**Edmonton**	**NHL**	**4**	**0**	**0**	**0**	**7**	....	....	....	....	....
	Cape Breton	AHL	61	7	22	29	114	5	0	0	0	8
1992-93	**Edmonton**	**NHL**	**1**	**0**	**0**	**0**	**4**	....	....	....	....	....
	Cape Breton	AHL	55	10	24	34	139	16	0	5	5	29
1993-94	**Ottawa**	**NHL**	**23**	**0**	**1**	**1**	**70**	....	....	....	....	....
	P.E.I.	AHL	25	4	6	10	52	....	....	....	....	....
1994-95	P.E.I.	AHL	45	4	14	18	137	....	....	....	....	....
	Pittsburgh	**NHL**	**40**	**0**	**2**	**2**	**114**	**12**	**0**	**2**	**2**	**14**
	NHL Totals		**74**	**0**	**6**	**6**	**195**	**12**	**0**	**2**	**2**	**14**

Claimed on waivers by **Ottawa** from **Edmonton**, October 6, 1993. Claimed by **Pittsburgh** from **Ottawa** in NHL Waiver Draft, January 18, 1995.

LEROUX, JEAN-YVES (leh-ROO) CHI.

Left wing. Shoots left. 6'2", 193 lbs. Born, Montreal, Que., June 24, 1976.
(Chicago's 2nd choice, 40th overall, in 1994 Entry Draft).

			Regular Season					Playoffs				
Season	Club	Lea	GP	G	A	TP	PIM	GP	G	A	TP	PIM
1992-93	Beauport	QMJHL	62	20	25	45	33	....	....	....	....	....
1993-94a	Beauport	QMJHL	45	14	25	39	43	15	7	6	13	33
1994-95	Beauport	QMJHL	59	19	33	52	125	17	4	6	10	39

a QMJHL Second All-Star Team (1994)

LESCHYSHYN, CURTIS (luh-SIH-shuhn) COL.

Defense. Shoots left. 6'1", 205 lbs. Born, Thompson, Man., September 21, 1969.
(Quebec's 1st choice, 3rd overall, in 1988 Entry Draft).

			Regular Season					Playoffs				
Season	Club	Lea	GP	G	A	TP	PIM	GP	G	A	TP	PIM
1986-87	Saskatoon	WHL	70	14	26	40	107	11	1	5	6	14
1987-88	Saskatoon	WHL	56	14	41	55	86	10	2	5	7	16
1988-89	**Quebec**	**NHL**	**71**	**4**	**9**	**13**	**71**	....	....	....	....	....
1989-90	**Quebec**	**NHL**	**68**	**2**	**6**	**8**	**44**	....	....	....	....	....
1990-91	**Quebec**	**NHL**	**55**	**3**	**7**	**10**	**49**	....	....	....	....	....
1991-92	**Quebec**	**NHL**	**42**	**5**	**12**	**17**	**42**	....	....	....	....	....
	Halifax	AHL	6	0	2	2	4	....	....	....	....	....
1992-93	**Quebec**	**NHL**	**82**	**9**	**23**	**32**	**61**	**6**	**1**	**1**	**2**	**6**
1993-94	**Quebec**	**NHL**	**72**	**5**	**17**	**22**	**65**	....	....	....	....	....
1994-95	**Quebec**	**NHL**	**44**	**2**	**13**	**15**	**20**	**3**	**0**	**1**	**1**	**4**
	NHL Totals		**434**	**30**	**87**	**117**	**352**	**9**	**1**	**2**	**3**	**10**

LESLIE, LEE J.

Left wing. Shoots left. 6'4", 190 lbs. Born, Prince George, B.C., August 15, 1972.
(St. Louis' 4th choice, 86th overall, in 1992 Entry Draft).

			Regular Season					Playoffs				
Season	Club	Lea	GP	G	A	TP	PIM	GP	G	A	TP	PIM
1989-90	Prince Albert	WHL	62	14	16	30	13	14	2	3	5	4
1990-91	Prince Albert	WHL	72	29	42	71	68	3	0	0	0	5
1991-92	Prince Albert	WHL	72	52	48	100	70	10	6	6	12	12
1992-93	Peoria	IHL	72	22	24	46	46	4	0	3	3	2
1993-94	Kansas City	IHL	43	8	7	15	21	....	....	....	....	....
1994-95	Cdn. National	....	17	6	0	6	16	....	....	....	....	....
	Kansas City	IHL	10	2	5	7	4	....	....	....	....	....

Signed as a free agent by **San Jose**, June 21, 1993.

LETANG, ALAN MTL.

Defense. Shoots left. 6', 185 lbs. Born, Renfrew, Ont., September 4, 1975.
(Montreal's 10th choice, 203rd overall, in 1993 Entry Draft).

			Regular Season					Playoffs				
Season	Club	Lea	GP	G	A	TP	PIM	GP	G	A	TP	PIM
1991-92	Cornwall	OHL	47	1	4	5	16	6	0	0	0	2
1992-93	Newmarket	OHL	66	1	25	26	14	6	0	3	3	2
1993-94	Newmarket	OHL	58	3	21	24	30	....	....	....	....	....
1994-95	Sarnia	OHL	62	5	36	41	35	4	2	2	4	6

LEVEQUE, GUY (luv-VEHK)

Center. Shoots right. 5'11", 180 lbs. Born, Kingston, Ont., December 28, 1972.
(Los Angeles' 1st choice, 42nd overall, in 1991 Entry Draft).

			Regular Season					Playoffs				
Season	Club	Lea	GP	G	A	TP	PIM	GP	G	A	TP	PIM
1989-90	Cornwall	OHL	62	10	15	25	30	3	0	0	0	4
1990-91	Cornwall	OHL	66	41	56	97	34	....	....	....	....	....
1991-92	Cornwall	OHL	37	23	36	59	40	6	3	5	8	2
1992-93	**Los Angeles**	**NHL**	**12**	**2**	**1**	**3**	**19**	....	....	....	....	....
	Phoenix	IHL	56	27	30	57	71	....	....	....	....	....
1993-94	**Los Angeles**	**NHL**	**5**	**0**	**1**	**1**	**2**	....	....	....	....	....
	Phoenix	IHL	39	10	16	26	47	....	....	....	....	....
1994-95	Cdn. National	....	31	17	17	34	14	....	....	....	....	....
	Phoenix	IHL	2	0	0	0	15	....	....	....	....	....
	St. John's	AHL	37	8	14	22	31	3	0	0	0	0
	NHL Totals		**17**	**2**	**2**	**4**	**21**	....	....	....	....	....

Traded to **Toronto** by **Los Angeles** with Dixon Ward, Kelly Fairchild and Shayne Toporowski for Eric Lacroix, Chris Snell and Toronto's fourth round choice in 1996 Entry Draft, October 3, 1994.

LEVINS, SCOTT OTT.

Center/Right wing. Shoots right. 6'4", 210 lbs. Born, Spokane, WA, January 30, 1970.
(Winnipeg's 4th choice, 75th overall, in 1990 Entry Draft).

			Regular Season					Playoffs				
Season	Club	Lea	GP	G	A	TP	PIM	GP	G	A	TP	PIM
1989-90a	Tri-Cities	WHL	71	25	37	62	132	6	2	3	5	18
1990-91	Moncton	AHL	74	12	26	38	133	4	0	0	0	4
1991-92	Moncton	AHL	69	15	18	33	271	11	3	4	7	30
1992-93	**Winnipeg**	**NHL**	**9**	**0**	**1**	**1**	**18**	....	....	....	....	....
	Moncton	AHL	54	22	26	48	158	5	1	3	4	14
1993-94	**Florida**	**NHL**	**29**	**5**	**6**	**11**	**69**	....	....	....	....	....
	Ottawa	**NHL**	**33**	**3**	**5**	**8**	**93**	....	....	....	....	....
1994-95	**Ottawa**	**NHL**	**24**	**5**	**6**	**11**	**51**	....	....	....	....	....
	P.E.I.	AHL	6	0	4	4	14	....	....	....	....	....
	NHL Totals		**95**	**13**	**18**	**31**	**231**	....	....	....	....	....

a WHL West Second All-Star Team (1990)

Claimed by **Florida** from **Winnipeg** in Expansion Draft, June 24, 1993. Traded to **Ottawa** by **Florida** with Evgeny Davydov, Florida's sixth round choice (Mike Gaffney) in 1994 Entry Draft and Dallas' fourth round choice (previously acquired by Florida — Ottawa selected Kevin Bolibruck) in 1995 Entry Draft for Bob Kudelski, January 6, 1994.

LIDSTER, DOUG NYR

Defense. Shoots right. 6', 190 lbs. Born, Kamloops, B.C., October 18, 1960.
(Vancouver's 6th choice, 133rd overall, in 1980 Entry Draft).

			Regular Season					Playoffs				
Season	Club	Lea	GP	G	A	TP	PIM	GP	G	A	TP	PIM
1977-78	Seattle	WHL	2	0	0	0	0	....	....	....	....	....
1978-79	Kamloops	BCJHL	59	36	47	83	50	....	....	....	....	....
1979-80	Colorado	WCHA	39	18	25	43	52	....	....	....	....	....
1980-81	Colorado	WCHA	36	10	30	40	54	....	....	....	....	....
1981-82	Colorado	WCHA	36	13	22	35	32	....	....	....	....	....
1982-83	Colorado	WCHA	34	15	41	56	30	....	....	....	....	....
1983-84	Cdn. National	....	59	6	20	26	28	....	....	....	....	....
	Cdn. Olympic	....	7	0	2	2	2	....	....	....	....	....
	Vancouver	**NHL**	**8**	**0**	**0**	**0**	**4**	**2**	**0**	**1**	**1**	**0**
1984-85	**Vancouver**	**NHL**	**78**	**6**	**24**	**30**	**55**	....	....	....	....	....
1985-86	**Vancouver**	**NHL**	**78**	**12**	**16**	**28**	**56**	**3**	**0**	**1**	**1**	**2**
1986-87	**Vancouver**	**NHL**	**80**	**12**	**51**	**63**	**40**	....	....	....	....	....
1987-88	**Vancouver**	**NHL**	**64**	**4**	**32**	**36**	**105**	....	....	....	....	....
1988-89	**Vancouver**	**NHL**	**63**	**5**	**17**	**22**	**78**	**7**	**1**	**1**	**2**	**9**
1989-90	**Vancouver**	**NHL**	**80**	**8**	**28**	**36**	**36**	....	....	....	....	....
1990-91	**Vancouver**	**NHL**	**78**	**6**	**32**	**38**	**77**	**6**	**0**	**2**	**2**	**6**
1991-92	**Vancouver**	**NHL**	**66**	**6**	**23**	**29**	**39**	**11**	**1**	**2**	**3**	**11**
1992-93	**Vancouver**	**NHL**	**71**	**6**	**19**	**25**	**36**	**12**	**0**	**3**	**3**	**8**
1993-94	**NY Rangers**	**NHL**	**34**	**0**	**2**	**2**	**33**	**9**	**2**	**0**	**2**	**10**
1994-95	**St. Louis**	**NHL**	**37**	**2**	**7**	**9**	**12**	**4**	**0**	**0**	**0**	**2**
	NHL Totals		**737**	**67**	**251**	**318**	**571**	**54**	**4**	**10**	**14**	**48**

Traded to **NY Rangers** by **Vancouver** to complete June 20, 1993 trade which sent John Vanbiesbrouck to Vancouver for future considerations, June 25, 1993. Traded to **St. Louis** by **NY Rangers** with Esa Tikkanen for Petr Nedved, July 24, 1994. Traded to **NY Rangers** by **St. Louis** for Jay Wells, July 28, 1995.

LIDSTROM, NICKLAS (LID-struhm) DET.

Defense. Shoots left. 6'2", 185 lbs. Born, Vasteras, Sweden, April 28, 1970.
(Detroit's 3rd choice, 53rd overall, in 1989 Entry Draft).

			Regular Season					Playoffs				
Season	Club	Lea	GP	G	A	TP	PIM	GP	G	A	TP	PIM
1987-88	Vasteras	Swe. 2	3	0	0	0	....	....	....	....	....	....
1988-89	Vasteras	Swe.	19	0	2	2	4	....	....	....	....	....
1989-90	Vasteras	Swe.	39	8	8	16	14	2	0	1	1	2
1990-91	Vasteras	Swe.	38	4	19	23	2	4	0	0	0	4
1991-92a	Detroit	NHL	80	11	49	60	22	11	1	2	3	0
1992-93	Detroit	NHL	84	7	34	41	28	7	1	0	1	0
1993-94	Detroit	NHL	84	10	46	56	26	7	3	2	5	0
1994-95	Vasteras	Swe.	13	2	10	12	4	....	....	....	....	....
	Detroit	NHL	43	10	16	26	6	18	4	12	16	8
	NHL Totals		291	38	145	183	82	43	9	16	25	8

a NHL/Upper Deck All-Rookie Team (1992)

LILLEY, JOHN ANA.

Right wing. Shoots right. 5'9", 170 lbs. Born, Wakefield, MA, August 3, 1972.
(Winnipeg's 8th choice, 140th overall, in 1990 Entry Draft).

			Regular Season					Playoffs				
Season	Club	Lea	GP	G	A	TP	PIM	GP	G	A	TP	PIM
1991-92	Boston U.	H.E.	23	9	9	18	43	....	....	....	....	....
1992-93	Boston U.	H.E.	4	0	1	1	13	....	....	....	....	....
	Seattle	WHL	45	22	28	50	55	5	1	3	4	9
1993-94	U.S. National	....	58	27	23	50	117	....	....	....	....	....
	U.S. Olympic	....	8	3	1	4	4	....	....	....	....	....
	Anaheim	NHL	13	1	6	7	8	....	....	....	....	....
	San Diego	IHL	2	2	1	3	0	....	....	....	....	....
1994-95	San Diego	IHL	45	9	15	24	71	2	0	0	0	2
	Anaheim	NHL	9	2	2	4	5	....	....	....	....	....
	NHL Totals		22	3	8	11	13	....	....	....	....	....

Signed as a free agent by **Anaheim**, March 9, 1994.

LIND, JUHA DAL.

Center. Shoots left. 5'11", 160 lbs. Born, Helsinki, Finland, January 2, 1974.
(Minnesota's 6th choice, 178th overall, in 1992 Entry Draft).

			Regular Season					Playoffs				
Season	Club	Lea	GP	G	A	TP	PIM	GP	G	A	TP	PIM
1991-92	Jokerit Jrs.	Fin.	28	16	24	40	10	....	....	....	....	....
1992-93	Vantaa	Fin. 2	25	8	12	20	8	....	....	....	....	....
	Jokerit	Fin.	6	0	0	0	2	1	0	0	0	0
1993-94	Jokerit	Fin.	47	17	11	28	37	11	2	5	7	4
1994-95	Jokerit	Fin.	50	10	8	18	12	11	1	2	3	6

LINDEN, JAMIE FLA.

Right wing. Shoots right. 6'3", 185 lbs. Born, Medicine Hat, Alta., July 19, 1972.

			Regular Season					Playoffs				
Season	Club	Lea	GP	G	A	TP	PIM	GP	G	A	TP	PIM
1988-89	Portland	WHL	1	0	1	1	0	....	....	....	....	....
1989-90	Portland	WHL	67	5	7	12	124	....	....	....	....	....
1990-91	Portland	WHL	2	0	1	1	6	....	....	....	....	....
	Prince Albert	WHL	64	9	12	21	114	3	0	0	0	0
1992-93	Spokane	WHL	15	3	1	4	58	....	....	....	....	....
	Medicine Hat	WHL	50	9	9	18	147	10	1	6	7	15
1993-94	Cincinnati	IHL	47	1	5	6	55	2	0	0	0	2
	Birmingham	ECHL	16	3	7	10	38	....	....	....	....	....
1994-95	Cincinnati	IHL	51	3	6	9	173	....	....	....	....	....
	Florida	NHL	4	0	0	0	17	....	....	....	....	....
	NHL Totals		4	0	0	0	17	....	....	....	....	....

Signed as a free agent by **Florida**, October 4, 1993.

LINDEN, TREVOR

Center/Right wing. Shoots right. 6'4", 210 lbs. Born, Medicine Hat, Alta., April 11, 1970.
(Vancouver's 1st choice, 2nd overall, in 1988 Entry Draft).

			Regular Season					Playoffs				
Season	Club	Lea	GP	G	A	TP	PIM	GP	G	A	TP	PIM
1986-87	Medicine Hat	WHL	72	14	22	36	59	20	5	4	9	17
1987-88	Medicine Hat	WHL	67	46	64	110	76	16	*13	12	25	19
1988-89a	Vancouver	NHL	80	30	29	59	41	7	3	4	7	8
1989-90	Vancouver	NHL	73	21	30	51	43	....	....	....	....	....
1990-91	Vancouver	NHL	80	33	37	70	65	6	0	7	7	2
1991-92	Vancouver	NHL	80	31	44	75	101	13	4	8	12	6
1992-93	Vancouver	NHL	84	33	39	72	64	12	5	8	13	16
1993-94	Vancouver	NHL	84	32	29	61	73	24	12	13	25	18
1994-95	Vancouver	NHL	48	18	22	40	40	11	2	6	8	12
	NHL Totals		529	198	230	428	427	73	26	46	72	62

a NHL All-Rookie Team (1989)

Played in NHL All-Star Game (1991, 1992)

LINDGREN, MATS EDM.

Center. Shoots left. 6'2", 200 lbs. Born, Skelleftea, Sweden, October 1, 1974.
(Winnipeg's 1st choice, 15th overall, in 1993 Entry Draft).

			Regular Season					Playoffs				
Season	Club	Lea	GP	G	A	TP	PIM	GP	G	A	TP	PIM
1991-92	Skelleftea	Swe. 2	29	14	8	22	14	....	....	....	....	....
1992-93	Skelleftea	Swe. 2	32	20	14	34	18	....	....	....	....	....
1993-94	Farjestad	Swe.	22	11	6	17	26	....	....	....	....	....
1994-95	Farjestad	Swe.	37	17	15	32	20	3	0	0	0	4

Traded to **Edmonton** by **Winnipeg** with Boris Mironov, Winnipeg's first round choice (Jason Bonsignore) in 1994 Entry Draft and Florida's fourth round choice (previously acquired by Winnipeg — Edmonton selected Adam Copeland) in 1994 Entry Draft for Dave Manson and St. Louis' sixth round choice (previously acquired by Edmonton — Winnipeg selected Chris Kibermanis) in 1994 Entry Draft, March 15, 1994.

LINDQVIST, FREDRIK

Center. Shoots left. 5'11", 176 lbs. Born, Sodertalje, Sweden, June 21, 1973.
(New Jersey's 4th choice, 55th overall, in 1991 Entry Draft).

			Regular Season					Playoffs				
Season	Club	Lea	GP	G	A	TP	PIM	GP	G	A	TP	PIM
1989-90	Huddinge	Swe. 2	2	0	0	0	0	....	....	....	....	....
1990-91	Djurgarden	Swe.	28	6	4	10	0	7	1	0	1	2
1991-92	Djurgarden	Swe.	39	9	6	15	14	10	1	1	2	2
1992-93	Djurgarden	Swe.	39	9	11	20	8	4	1	2	3	2
1993-94	Djurgarden	Swe.	25	5	8	13	8	6	2	1	3	2
1994-95	Djurgarden	Swe.	40	11	16	27	14	3	0	0	0	2

LINDROS, BRETT (LIHND-rahz) NYI

Right wing. Shoots right. 6'4", 215 lbs. Born, London, Ont., December 2, 1975.
(NY Islanders' 1st choice, 9th overall, in 1994 Entry Draft).

			Regular Season					Playoffs				
Season	Club	Lea	GP	G	A	TP	PIM	GP	G	A	TP	PIM
1992-93	Kingston	OHL	31	11	11	22	162	....	....	....	....	....
	Cdn. National	....	11	1	6	7	33	....	....	....	....	....
1993-94	Cdn. National	....	44	7	7	14	118	....	....	....	....	....
	Kingston	OHL	15	4	6	10	94	3	0	0	0	18
1994-95	Kingston	OHL	26	24	23	47	63	....	....	....	....	....
	NY Islanders	NHL	33	1	3	4	100	....	....	....	....	....
	NHL Totals		33	1	3	4	100	....	....	....	....	....

LINDROS, ERIC (LIHND-rahz) PHI.

Center. Shoots right. 6'4", 229 lbs. Born, London, Ont., February 28, 1973.
(Quebec's 1st choice, 1st overall, in 1991 Entry Draft).

			Regular Season					Playoffs				
Season	Club	Lea	GP	G	A	TP	PIM	GP	G	A	TP	PIM
1988-89	Cdn. National	....	2	1	0	1	0	....	....	....	....	....
1989-90	Det. Comp.	USHL	14	23	29	52	123	....	....	....	....	....
	Cdn. National	....	3	1	0	1	4	....	....	....	....	....
a	Oshawa	OHL	25	17	19	36	61	17	18	18	36	76
1990-91bc	Oshawa	OHL	57	*71	78	*149	189	16	*18	20	*38	*93
1991-92	Oshawa	OHL	13	9	22	31	54	....	....	....	....	....
	Cdn. National	....	24	19	16	35	34	....	....	....	....	....
	Cdn. Olympic	....	8	5	6	11	6	....	....	....	....	....
1992-93d	Philadelphia	NHL	61	41	34	75	147	....	....	....	....	....
1993-94	Philadelphia	NHL	65	44	53	97	103	....	....	....	....	....
1994-95efg	Philadelphia	NHL	46	29	41	*70	60	12	4	11	15	18
	NHL Totals		172	114	128	242	310	12	4	11	15	18

a Memorial Cup All-Star Team (1990)
b OHL First All-Star Team (1991)
c Canadian Major Junior Player of the Year (1991)
d NHL/Upper Deck All-Rookie Team (1993)
e NHL First All-Star Team (1995)
f Won Lester B. Pearson Award (1995)
g Won Hart Trophy (1995)

Played in NHL All-Star Game (1994)

Traded to **Philadelphia** by **Quebec** for Peter Forsberg, Steve Duchesne, Kerry Huffman, Mike Ricci, Ron Hextall, Chris Simon, Philadelphia's first choice in the 1993 (Jocelyn Thibault) and 1994 (later traded to Toronto — later traded to Washington — Washington selected Nolan Baumgartner) Entry Drafts and cash, June 30, 1992.

LINDSAY, BILL FLA.

Left wing. Shoots left. 5'11", 190 lbs. Born, Big Fork, MT, May 17, 1971.
(Quebec's 6th choice, 103rd overall, in 1991 Entry Draft).

			Regular Season					Playoffs				
Season	Club	Lea	GP	G	A	TP	PIM	GP	G	A	TP	PIM
1990-91	Tri-Cities	WHL	63	46	47	93	151	5	3	6	9	10
1991-92	Quebec	NHL	23	2	4	6	14	....	....	....	....	....
a	Tri-Cities	WHL	42	34	59	93	111	3	2	3	5	16
1992-93	Quebec	NHL	44	4	9	13	16	....	....	....	....	....
	Halifax	AHL	20	11	13	24	18	....	....	....	....	....
1993-94	Florida	NHL	84	6	6	12	97	....	....	....	....	....
1994-95	Florida	NHL	48	10	9	19	46	....	....	....	....	....
	NHL Totals		199	22	28	50	173	....	....	....	....	....

a WHL West Second All-Star Team (1992)

Claimed by **Florida** from **Quebec** in Expansion Draft, June 24, 1993.

LING, DAVID CGY.

Right wing. Shoots right. 5'9", 185 lbs. Born, Halifax, N.S., January 9, 1975.
(Quebec's 9th choice, 179th overall, in 1993 Entry Draft).

			Regular Season					Playoffs				
Season	Club	Lea	GP	G	A	TP	PIM	GP	G	A	TP	PIM
1992-93	Kingston	OHL	64	17	46	63	275	16	3	12	15	*72
1993-94	Kingston	OHL	61	37	40	77	*254	6	4	2	6	16
1994-95abc	Kingston	OHL	62	*61	74	135	136	6	7	8	15	12

a OHL First All-Star Team (1995)
b Canadian Major Junior First All-Star Team (1995)
c Canadian Junior Player of the Year (1995)

LIPIANSKY, JAN (LIH-pyahn-skee) PHI.

Left wing. Shoots left. 6'2", 187 lbs. Born, Bratislava, Czech., July 23, 1974.
(Philadelphia's 10th choice, 270th overall, in 1994 Entry Draft).

			Regular Season					Playoffs				
Season	Club	Lea	GP	G	A	TP	PIM	GP	G	A	TP	PIM
1993-94	Bratislava	Slov.	32	11	5	16	12	....	....	....	....	....
1994-95	Hershey	AHL	7	0	0	0	2	....	....	....	....	....
	Bratislava	Slov.	12	8	7	15	4	8	0	2	2	6

LIPUMA, CHRIS (lih-POO-muh) T.B.

Defense. Shoots left. 6', 183 lbs. Born, Bridgeview, IL, March 23, 1971.

			Regular Season					Playoffs				
Season	Club	Lea	GP	G	A	TP	PIM	GP	G	A	TP	PIM
1990-91	Kitchener	OHL	61	6	30	36	145	4	0	1	1	4
1991-92	Kitchener	OHL	61	13	59	72	115	14	4	9	13	34
1992-93	Tampa Bay	NHL	15	0	5	5	34	....	....	....	....	....
	Atlanta	IHL	66	4	14	18	379	9	1	1	2	35
1993-94	Tampa Bay	NHL	27	0	4	4	77	....	....	....	....	....
	Atlanta	IHL	42	2	10	12	254	11	1	1	2	28
1994-95	Atlanta	IHL	41	5	12	17	191	....	....	....	....	....
	Tampa Bay	NHL	1	0	0	0	0	....	....	....	....	....
	Nashville	ECHL	1	0	0	0	0	....	....	....	....	....
	NHL Totals		43	0	9	9	111	....	....	....	....	....

Signed as a free agent by **Tampa Bay**, June 29, 1992.

LITVINOV, YURI (liht-VIH-nohv) NYR

Center. Shoots right. 5'10", 176 lbs. Born, Donetsk, USSR, April 11, 1976.
(NY Rangers' 7th choice, 135th overall, in 1994 Entry Draft).

			Regular Season					Playoffs				
Season	Club	Lea	GP	G	A	TP	PIM	GP	G	A	TP	PIM
1993-94	Soviet Wings	CIS	42	5	6	11	34	....	....	....	....	....
1994-95	Soviet Wings	CIS	6	0	0	0	8	....	....	....	....	....

LOACH, LONNIE (LOHCH)

Left wing. Shoots left. 5'10", 181 lbs. Born, New Liskeard, Ont., April 14, 1968.
(Chicago's 4th choice, 98th overall, in 1986 Entry Draft).

			Regular Season					Playoffs				
Season	Club	Lea	GP	G	A	TP	PIM	GP	G	A	TP	PIM
1985-86	Guelph	OHL	65	41	42	83	63	20	7	8	15	16
1986-87	Guelph	OHL	56	31	24	55	42	5	2	1	3	2
1987-88	Guelph	OHL	66	43	49	92	75	....	....	....	....	....
1988-89	Flint	IHL	41	22	26	48	30	....	....	....	....	....
	Saginaw	IHL	32	7	6	13	27	....	....	....	....	....
1989-90	Indianapolis	IHL	3	0	0	0	0	....	....	....	....	....
	Cdn. National	....	9	3	1	4	2	....	....	....	....	....
	Fort Wayne	IHL	54	15	33	48	40	5	4	2	6	15
1990-91ab	Fort Wayne	IHL	81	55	76	*131	45	19	5	11	16	13
1991-92	Adirondack	AHL	67	37	49	86	69	19	*13	4	17	10
1992-93	Ottawa	NHL	3	0	0	0	0	....	....	....	....	....
	Los Angeles	NHL	50	10	13	23	27	1	0	0	0	0
	Phoenix	IHL	4	2	3	5	10	....	....	....	....	....
1993-94	Anaheim	NHL	3	0	0	0	2	....	....	....	....	....
	San Diego	IHL	74	42	49	91	65	9	4	10	14	6
1994-95	San Diego	IHL	13	3	10	13	21	....	....	....	....	....
	Detroit	IHL	64	32	43	75	45	3	2	1	3	2
	NHL Totals		56	10	13	23	29	1	0	0	0	0

a IHL Second All-Star Team (1991)
b Won Leo P. Lamoureux Memorial Trophy (Leading Scorer - IHL) (1991)

Signed as a free agent by **Detroit**, June 7, 1991. Claimed by **Ottawa** from **Detroit** in Expansion Draft, June 18, 1992. Claimed on waivers by **Los Angeles** from **Ottawa**, October 21, 1992. Claimed by **Anaheim** from **Los Angeles** in Expansion Draft, June 24, 1993.

LOACH, MIKE (LOHCH) NYI

Center. Shoots right. 6'1", 181 lbs. Born, New Liskeard, Ont., September 8, 1976.
(NY Islanders' 8th choice, 194th overall, in 1994 Draft).

			Regular Season					Playoffs				
Season	Club	Lea	GP	G	A	TP	PIM	GP	G	A	TP	PIM
1993-94	Windsor	OHL	47	12	13	25	86	4	0	0	0	9
1994-95	Windsor	OHL	39	16	7	23	66	....	....	....	....	....
	Owen Sound	OHL	18	5	10	15	50	10	1	3	4	14

LOEWEN, DARCY (LOH-wihn)

Left wing. Shoots left. 5'10", 185 lbs. Born, Calgary, Alta., February 26, 1969.
(Buffalo's 2nd choice, 55th overall, in 1988 Entry Draft).

			Regular Season					Playoffs				
Season	Club	Lea	GP	G	A	TP	PIM	GP	G	A	TP	PIM
1986-87	Spokane	WHL	68	15	25	40	129	5	0	0	0	16
1987-88	Spokane	WHL	72	30	44	74	231	15	7	5	12	54
1988-89	Spokane	WHL	60	31	27	58	194	....	....	....	....	....
	Cdn. National	....	2	0	0	0	0	....	....	....	....	....
1989-90	Buffalo	NHL	4	0	0	0	4	....	....	....	....	....
	Rochester	AHL	50	7	11	18	193	5	1	0	1	6
1990-91	Buffalo	NHL	6	0	0	0	8	....	....	....	....	....
	Rochester	AHL	71	13	15	28	130	15	1	5	6	14
1991-92	Buffalo	NHL	2	0	0	0	2	....	....	....	....	....
	Rochester	AHL	73	11	20	31	193	4	0	1	1	8
1992-93	Ottawa	NHL	79	4	5	9	145	....	....	....	....	....
1993-94	Ottawa	NHL	44	0	3	3	52	....	....	....	....	....
1994-95	Las Vegas	IHL	64	9	21	30	183	7	1	1	2	16
	NHL Totals		135	4	8	12	211	....	....	....	....	....

Claimed by **Ottawa** from **Buffalo** in Expansion Draft, June 18, 1992.

LOMAKIN, ANDREI (loh-MA-kihn)

Right wing. Shoots left. 5'10", 175 lbs. Born, Voskresensk, USSR, April 3, 1964.
(Philadelphia's 7th choice, 138th overall, in 1991 Entry Draft).

			Regular Season					Playoffs				
Season	Club	Lea	GP	G	A	TP	PIM	GP	G	A	TP	PIM
1981-82	Khimik	USSR	8	1	1	2	2	....	....	....	....	....
1982-83	Khimik	USSR	56	15	8	23	32	....	....	....	....	....
1983-84	Khimik	USSR	44	10	8	18	26	....	....	....	....	....
1984-85	Khimik	USSR	52	13	10	23	24	....	....	....	....	....
1985-86					DID NOT PLAY							
1986-87	Moscow D'amo	USSR	40	15	14	29	30	....	....	....	....	....
1987-88	Moscow D'amo	USSR	45	10	15	25	24	....	....	....	....	....
1988-89	Moscow D'amo	USSR	44	9	16	25	22	....	....	....	....	....
1989-90	Moscow D'amo	USSR	48	11	15	26	36	....	....	....	....	....
1990-91	Moscow D'amo	USSR	45	16	17	33	22	....	....	....	....	....
1991-92	Moscow D'amo	CIS	2	1	3	4	2	....	....	....	....	....
	Philadelphia	NHL	57	14	16	30	26	....	....	....	....	....
1992-93	Philadelphia	NHL	51	8	12	20	34	....	....	....	....	....
1993-94	Florida	NHL	76	19	28	47	26	....	....	....	....	....
1994-95	Florida	NHL	31	1	6	7	6	....	....	....	....	....
	NHL Totals		215	42	62	104	92	....	....	....	....	....

Claimed by **Florida** from **Philadelphia** in Expansion Draft, June 24, 1993.

LONEY, BRIAN (LOH-nee) VAN.

Right wing. Shoots right. 6'2", 200 lbs. Born, Winnipeg, Man., August 9, 1972.
(Vancouver's 6th choice, 110th overall, in 1992 Entry Draft).

			Regular Season					Playoffs				
Season	Club	Lea	GP	G	A	TP	PIM	GP	G	A	TP	PIM
1991-92	Ohio State	CCHA	37	21	34	55	109	....	....	....	....	....
1992-93	Red Deer	WHL	66	39	36	75	147	4	1	1	2	19
	Cdn. National	....	1	0	1	1	0	....	....	....	....	....
	Hamilton	AHL	3	0	2	2	0	....	....	....	....	....
1993-94	Hamilton	AHL	67	18	16	34	76	4	0	0	0	8
1994-95	Syracuse	AHL	67	23	17	40	98	....	....	....	....	....

LONEY, TROY (LOH-nee)

Left wing. Shoots left. 6'3", 209 lbs. Born, Bow Island, Alta., September 21, 1963.
(Pittsburgh's 3rd choice, 52nd overall, in 1982 Entry Draft).

			Regular Season					Playoffs				
Season	Club	Lea	GP	G	A	TP	PIM	GP	G	A	TP	PIM
1980-81	Lethbridge	WHL	71	18	13	31	100	9	2	2	5	14
1981-82	Lethbridge	WHL	71	26	33	59	152	12	3	3	6	10
1982-83	Lethbridge	WHL	72	33	34	67	156	20	10	7	17	43
1983-84	Pittsburgh	NHL	13	0	0	0	9	....	....	....	....	....
	Baltimore	AHL	63	18	13	31	147	10	0	2	2	19
1984-85	Pittsburgh	NHL	46	10	8	18	59	....	....	....	....	....
	Baltimore	AHL	15	4	2	6	25	....	....	....	....	....
1985-86	Pittsburgh	NHL	47	3	9	12	95	....	....	....	....	....
	Baltimore	AHL	33	12	11	23	84	....	....	....	....	....
1986-87	Pittsburgh	NHL	23	8	7	15	22	....	....	....	....	....
	Baltimore	AHL	40	13	14	27	134	....	....	....	....	....
1987-88	Pittsburgh	NHL	65	5	13	18	151	....	....	....	....	....
1988-89	Pittsburgh	NHL	69	10	6	16	165	11	1	3	4	24
1989-90	Pittsburgh	NHL	67	11	16	27	168	....	....	....	....	....
1990-91	Pittsburgh	NHL	44	7	9	16	85	24	2	2	4	41
	Muskegon	IHL	2	0	0	0	5	....	....	....	....	....
1991-92	Pittsburgh	NHL	76	10	16	26	127	21	4	5	9	32
1992-93	Pittsburgh	NHL	82	5	16	21	99	10	1	4	5	0
1993-94	Anaheim	NHL	62	13	6	19	88	....	....	....	....	....
1994-95	NY Islanders	NHL	26	5	4	9	23	....	....	....	....	....
	NY Rangers	NHL	4	0	0	0	0	1	0	0	0	0
	NHL Totals		624	87	110	197	1091	67	8	14	22	97

Claimed by **Anaheim** from **Pittsburgh** in Expansion Draft, June 24, 1993. Traded to **NY Islanders** by **Anaheim** for Tom Kurvers, June 29, 1994. Claimed on waivers by **NY Rangers** from **NY Islanders**, April 10, 1995.

LONSINGER, BRYAN NYR

Defense. Shoots right. 6'2", 210 lbs. Born, Caldwell, NY, July 21, 1972.
(NY Rangers' 9th choice, 139th overall, in 1990 Entry Draft).

			Regular Season					Playoffs				
Season	Club	Lea	GP	G	A	TP	PIM	GP	G	A	TP	PIM
1991-92	Harvard	ECAC	19	1	5	6	4	....	....	....	....	....
1992-93	Harvard	ECAC	31	2	9	11	6	....	....	....	....	....
1993-94	Harvard	ECAC	33	1	5	6	14	....	....	....	....	....
1994-95	Harvard	ECAC	28	8	9	17	12	....	....	....	....	....

LOW, STEVEN COL.

Defense. Shoots left. 6', 178 lbs. Born, Montreal, Que., May 21, 1976.
(Quebec's 13th choice, 285th overall, in 1994 Entry Draft).

			Regular Season					Playoffs				
Season	Club	Lea	GP	G	A	TP	PIM	GP	G	A	TP	PIM
1993-94	Sherbrooke	QMJHL	68	4	14	18	154	11	1	1	2	16
1994-95	Sherbrooke	QMJHL	42	3	13	16	130	....	....	....	....	....
	Victoriaville	QMJHL	28	8	9	17	112	4	0	0	0	33

LOWE, KEVIN (LOH) NYR

Defense. Shoots left. 6'2", 190 lbs. Born, Lachute, Que., April 15, 1959.
(Edmonton's 1st choice, 21st overall, in 1979 Entry Draft).

			Regular Season					Playoffs				
Season	Club	Lea	GP	G	A	TP	PIM	GP	G	A	TP	PIM
1977-78	Quebec	QJHL	64	13	52	65	86	4	1	2	3	6
1978-79a	Quebec	QJHL	68	26	60	86	120	6	1	7	8	36
1979-80	Edmonton	NHL	64	2	19	21	70	3	0	1	1	0
1980-81	Edmonton	NHL	79	10	24	34	94	9	0	2	2	11
1981-82	Edmonton	NHL	80	9	31	40	63	5	0	3	3	0
1982-83	Edmonton	NHL	80	6	34	40	43	16	1	8	9	10
1983-84	Edmonton	NHL	80	4	42	46	59	19	3	7	10	16
1984-85	Edmonton	NHL	80	4	21	25	104	16	0	5	5	8
1985-86	Edmonton	NHL	74	2	16	18	90	10	1	3	4	15
1986-87	Edmonton	NHL	77	8	29	37	94	21	2	4	6	22
1987-88	Edmonton	NHL	70	9	15	24	89	19	0	2	2	26
1988-89	Edmonton	NHL	76	7	18	25	98	7	1	2	3	4
1989-90bc	Edmonton	NHL	78	7	26	33	140	20	0	2	2	10
1990-91	Edmonton	NHL	73	3	13	16	113	14	1	1	2	14
1991-92	Edmonton	NHL	55	2	8	10	107	11	0	3	3	16
1992-93	NY Rangers	NHL	49	3	12	15	58	....	....	....	....	....
1993-94	NY Rangers	NHL	71	5	14	19	70	22	1	0	1	20
1994-95	NY Rangers	NHL	44	1	7	8	58	10	0	1	1	12
	NHL Totals		1130	82	329	411	1350	202	10	44	54	184

a QMJHL Second All-Star Team (1979)
b Won Bud Man of the Year Award (1990)
c Won King Clancy Memorial Trophy (1990)

Played in NHL All-Star Game (1984-86, 1988-90, 1993)

Traded to **NY Rangers** by **Edmonton** for Roman Oksyuta and NY Rangers' third round choice (Alexander Kerch) in 1993 Entry Draft, December 11, 1992.

LOWRY, DAVE FLA.

Left wing. Shoots left. 6'1", 200 lbs. Born, Sudbury, Ont., February 14, 1965.
(Vancouver's 6th choice, 110th overall, in 1983 Entry Draft).

			Regular Season					Playoffs				
Season	Club	Lea	GP	G	A	TP	PIM	GP	G	A	TP	PIM
1982-83	London	OHL	42	11	16	27	48	3	0	0	0	14
1983-84	London	OHL	66	29	47	76	125	8	6	6	12	41
1984-85a	London	OHL	61	60	60	120	94	8	6	5	11	10
1985-86	Vancouver	NHL	73	10	8	18	143	3	0	0	0	0
1986-87	Vancouver	NHL	70	8	10	18	176	....	....	....	....	....
1987-88	Vancouver	NHL	22	1	3	4	38	....	....	....	....	....
	Fredericton	AHL	46	18	27	45	59	14	7	3	10	72
1988-89	St. Louis	NHL	21	3	3	6	11	10	0	5	5	4
	Peoria	IHL	58	31	35	66	45	....	....	....	....	....
1989-90	St. Louis	NHL	78	19	6	25	75	12	2	1	3	39
1990-91	St. Louis	NHL	79	19	21	40	168	13	1	4	5	35
1991-92	St. Louis	NHL	75	7	13	20	77	6	0	1	1	20
1992-93	St. Louis	NHL	58	5	8	13	101	11	2	0	2	14
1993-94	Florida	NHL	80	15	22	37	64	....	....	....	....	....
1994-95	Florida	NHL	45	10	10	20	25	....	....	....	....	....
	NHL Totals		601	97	104	201	878	55	5	11	16	112

a OHL First All-Star Team (1985)

Traded to **St. Louis** by **Vancouver** for Ernie Vargas, September 29, 1988. Claimed by **Florida** from **St. Louis** in Expansion Draft, June 24, 1993.

LUDWIG, CRAIG — DAL.

Defense. Shoots left. 6'3", 217 lbs. Born, Rhinelander, WI, March 15, 1961.
(Montreal's 5th choice, 61st overall, in 1980 Entry Draft).

			Regular Season					Playoffs				
Season	Club	Lea	GP	G	A	TP	PIM	GP	G	A	TP	PIM
1979-80	North Dakota	WCHA	33	1	8	9	32	....	....	....	....	....
1980-81	North Dakota	WCHA	34	4	8	12	48	....	....	....	....	....
1981-82	North Dakota	WCHA	37	4	17	21	42	....	....	....	....	....
1982-83	Montreal	NHL	80	0	25	25	59	3	0	0	0	2
1983-84	Montreal	NHL	80	7	18	25	52	15	0	3	3	23
1984-85	Montreal	NHL	72	5	14	19	90	12	0	2	2	6
1985-86	Montreal	NHL	69	2	4	6	63	20	0	1	1	48
1986-87	Montreal	NHL	75	4	12	16	105	17	2	3	5	30
1987-88	Montreal	NHL	74	4	10	14	69	11	1	1	2	6
1988-89	Montreal	NHL	74	3	13	16	73	21	0	2	2	24
1989-90	Montreal	NHL	73	1	15	16	108	11	0	1	1	16
1990-91	NY Islanders	NHL	75	1	8	9	77	....	....	....	....	....
1991-92	Minnesota	NHL	73	2	9	11	54	7	0	1	1	19
1992-93	Minnesota	NHL	78	1	10	11	153	....	....	....	....	....
1993-94	Dallas	NHL	84	1	13	14	123	9	0	3	3	8
1994-95	Dallas	NHL	47	2	7	9	61	4	0	1	1	2
	NHL Totals		954	33	158	191	1087	130	3	18	21	184

Traded to **NY Islanders** by **Montreal** for Gerald Diduck, September 4, 1990. Traded to **Minnesota** by **NY Islanders** for Tom Kurvers, June 22, 1991.

LUHNING, WARREN — NYI

Right wing. Shoots right. 6'2", 185 lbs. Born, Edmonton, Alta., July 3, 1975.
(NY Islanders' 4th choice, 92nd overall, in 1993 Entry Draft).

			Regular Season					Playoffs				
Season	Club	Lea	GP	G	A	TP	PIM	GP	G	A	TP	PIM
1993-94	U. of Michigan	CCHA	38	13	6	19	83	....	....	....	....	....
1994-95	U. of Michigan	CCHA	36	17	23	40	80	....	....	....	....	....

LUKOWICH, BRAD (loo-KUH-wihch) — NYI

Defense. Shoots left. 6'1", 170 lbs. Born, Cranbrook, B.C., August 12, 1976.
(NY Islanders' 4th choice, 90th overall, in 1994 Entry Draft).

			Regular Season					Playoffs				
Season	Club	Lea	GP	G	A	TP	PIM	GP	G	A	TP	PIM
1992-93	Kamloops	WHL	1	0	0	0	0	....	....	....	....	....
1993-94	Kamloops	WHL	42	5	11	16	166	16	0	1	1	35
1994-95	Kamloops	WHL	63	10	35	45	125	18	0	7	7	21

LUMME, JYRKI (LOO-mee, YUHR-kee) — VAN.

Defense. Shoots left. 6'1", 205 lbs. Born, Tampere, Finland, July 16, 1966.
(Montreal's 3rd choice, 57th overall, in 1986 Entry Draft).

			Regular Season					Playoffs				
Season	Club	Lea	GP	G	A	TP	PIM	GP	G	A	TP	PIM
1984-85	KooVee	Fin. 3	30	6	4	10	44	....	....	....	....	....
1985-86	Ilves	Fin.	31	1	4	5	4	....	....	....	....	....
1986-87	Ilves	Fin.	43	12	12	24	52	4	0	1	1	2
1987-88	Ilves	Fin.	43	8	22	30	75	....	....	....	....	....
1988-89	Montreal	NHL	21	1	3	4	10	....	....	....	....	....
	Sherbrooke	AHL	26	4	11	15	10	6	1	3	4	4
1989-90	Montreal	NHL	54	1	19	20	41	....	....	....	....	....
	Vancouver	NHL	11	3	7	10	8	....	....	....	....	....
1990-91	Vancouver	NHL	80	5	27	32	59	6	2	3	5	0
1991-92	Vancouver	NHL	75	12	32	44	65	13	2	3	5	4
1992-93	Vancouver	NHL	74	8	36	44	55	12	0	5	5	6
1993-94	Vancouver	NHL	83	13	42	55	50	24	2	11	13	16
1994-95	Ilves	Fin.	12	4	4	8	24	....	....	....	....	....
	Vancouver	NHL	36	5	12	17	26	11	2	6	8	8
	NHL Totals		434	48	178	226	314	66	8	28	36	34

Traded to **Vancouver** by **Montreal** for St. Louis' second round choice (previously acquired by Vancouver — Montreal selected Craig Darby) in 1991 Entry Draft, March 6, 1990.

LUONGO, CHRIS (loo-WAHN-goh) — NYI

Defense. Shoots right. 6', 199 lbs. Born, Detroit, MI, March 17, 1967.
(Detroit's 5th choice, 92nd overall, in 1985 Entry Draft).

			Regular Season					Playoffs				
Season	Club	Lea	GP	G	A	TP	PIM	GP	G	A	TP	PIM
1985-86	Michigan State	CCHA	38	1	5	6	29	....	....	....	....	....
1986-87a	Michigan State	CCHA	27	4	16	20	38	....	....	....	....	....
1987-88	Michigan State	CCHA	45	3	15	18	49	....	....	....	....	....
1988-89b	Michigan State	CCHA	47	4	21	25	42	....	....	....	....	....
1989-90	Adirondack	AHL	53	9	14	23	37	3	0	0	0	0
	Phoenix	IHL	23	5	9	14	41	....	....	....	....	....
1990-91	Detroit	NHL	4	0	1	1	4	....	....	....	....	....
	Adirondack	AHL	76	14	25	39	71	2	0	0	0	7
1991-92	Adirondack	AHL	80	6	20	26	60	19	3	5	8	10
1992-93	Ottawa	NHL	76	3	9	12	68	....	....	....	....	....
	New Haven	AHL	7	0	2	2	2	....	....	....	....	....
1993-94	NY Islanders	NHL	17	1	3	4	13	....	....	....	....	....
	Salt Lake	IHL	51	9	31	40	54	....	....	....	....	....
1994-95	Denver	IHL	41	1	14	15	26	....	....	....	....	....
	NY Islanders	NHL	47	1	3	4	36	....	....	....	....	....
	NHL Totals		144	5	16	21	121	....	....	....	....	....

a Named to NCAA All-Tournament Team (1987)
b CCHA Second All-Star Team (1989)

Signed as a free agent by **Ottawa**, September 9, 1992. Traded to **NY Islanders** by **Ottawa** for Jeff Finley, June 30, 1993.

MacDERMID, PAUL

Right wing. Shoots right. 6'1", 205 lbs. Born, Chesley, Ont., April 14, 1963.
(Hartford's 2nd choice, 61st overall, in 1981 Entry Draft).

			Regular Season					Playoffs				
Season	Club	Lea	GP	G	A	TP	PIM	GP	G	A	TP	PIM
1980-81	Windsor	OHA	68	15	17	32	106	....	....	....	....	....
1981-82	Hartford	NHL	3	1	0	1	2	....	....	....	....	....
	Windsor	OHL	65	26	45	71	179	9	6	4	10	17
1982-83	Hartford	NHL	7	0	0	0	2	....	....	....	....	....
	Windsor	OHL	42	35	45	80	9	....	....	....	....	....
1983-84	Hartford	NHL	3	0	1	1	0	....	....	....	....	....
	Binghamton	AHL	70	31	30	61	130	....	....	....	....	....
1984-85	Hartford	NHL	31	4	7	11	29	....	....	....	....	....
	Binghamton	AHL	48	9	31	40	87	....	....	....	....	....
1985-86	Hartford	NHL	74	13	10	23	160	10	2	1	3	20
1986-87	Hartford	NHL	72	7	11	18	202	6	2	1	3	34
1987-88	Hartford	NHL	80	20	15	35	139	6	0	5	5	14
1988-89	Hartford	NHL	74	17	27	44	141	4	1	1	2	16
1989-90	Hartford	NHL	29	6	12	18	69	....	....	....	....	....
	Winnipeg	NHL	44	7	10	17	100	7	0	2	2	8
1990-91	Winnipeg	NHL	69	15	21	36	128	....	....	....	....	....
1991-92	Winnipeg	NHL	59	10	11	21	151	....	....	....	....	....
	Washington	NHL	15	2	5	7	43	7	0	1	1	22
1992-93	Washington	NHL	72	9	8	17	80	....	....	....	....	....
1993-94	Quebec	NHL	44	2	3	5	35	....	....	....	....	....
1994-95	Quebec	NHL	14	3	1	4	22	3	0	0	0	2
	NHL Totals		690	116	142	258	1303	43	5	11	16	116

Traded to **Winnipeg** by **Hartford** for Randy Cunneyworth, December 13, 1989. Traded to **Washington** by **Winnipeg** for Mike Lalor, March 2, 1992. Traded to **Quebec** by **Washington** with Reggie Savage for Mike Hough, June 20, 1993.

MacDONALD, DOUG

Left wing. Shoots left. 6', 192 lbs. Born, Assiniboia, Sask., February 8, 1969.
(Buffalo's 3rd choice, 77th overall, in 1989 Entry Draft).

			Regular Season					Playoffs				
Season	Club	Lea	GP	G	A	TP	PIM	GP	G	A	TP	PIM
1988-89	U. Wisconsin	WCHA	44	23	25	48	50	....	....	....	....	....
1989-90	U. Wisconsin	WCHA	44	16	35	51	52	....	....	....	....	....
1990-91	U. Wisconsin	WCHA	31	20	26	46	50	....	....	....	....	....
1991-92	U. Wisconsin	WCHA	29	14	25	39	58	....	....	....	....	....
1992-93	Buffalo	NHL	5	1	0	1	2	....	....	....	....	....
	Rochester	AHL	64	25	33	58	58	7	0	2	2	4
1993-94	Buffalo	NHL	4	0	0	0	0	....	....	....	....	....
	Rochester	AHL	63	25	19	44	46	4	1	1	2	8
1994-95	Rochester	AHL	58	21	25	46	73	5	0	1	1	0
	Buffalo	NHL	2	0	0	0	0	....	....	....	....	....
	NHL Totals		11	1	0	1	2	....	....	....	....	....

MacDONALD, JASON — DET.

Right wing. Shoots right. 6', 195 lbs. Born, Charlottetown, P.E.I., April 1, 1974.
(Detroit's 5th choice, 142nd overall, in 1992 Entry Draft).

			Regular Season					Playoffs				
Season	Club	Lea	GP	G	A	TP	PIM	GP	G	A	TP	PIM
1990-91	North Bay	OHL	57	12	15	27	126	10	3	3	6	15
1991-92	North Bay	OHL	17	5	8	13	50	....	....	....	....	....
	Owen Sound	OHL	42	17	19	36	129	5	0	3	3	16
1992-93	Owen Sound	OHL	56	46	43	89	197	8	6	5	11	28
1993-94a	Owen Sound	OHL	66	55	61	116	177	9	7	11	18	36
	Adirondack	AHL	....	....	....	....	....	1	0	0	0	0
1994-95	Adirondack	AHL	68	14	21	35	238	4	0	0	0	2

a OHL Second All-Star Team (1994)

MacDONALD, TOM — T.B.

Center. Shoots left. 5'11", 190 lbs. Born, Toronto, Ont., April 14, 1974.
(Tampa Bay's 11th choice, 241st overall, in 1992 Entry Draft).

			Regular Season					Playoffs				
Season	Club	Lea	GP	G	A	TP	PIM	GP	G	A	TP	PIM
1990-91	S.S. Marie	OHL	41	3	6	9	71	6	0	1	1	19
1991-92	S.S. Marie	OHL	52	11	15	26	139	19	3	7	10	31
1992-93	S.S. Marie	OHL	50	13	24	37	134	18	5	9	14	62
1993-94	S.S. Marie	OHL	55	34	36	70	175	14	3	7	10	38
1994-95	Nashville	ECHL	55	9	12	21	137	13	2	7	9	55

MacINNIS, AL — ST.L.

Defense. Shoots right. 6'2", 196 lbs. Born, Inverness, N.S., July 11, 1963.
(Calgary's 1st choice, 15th overall, in 1981 Entry Draft).

			Regular Season					Playoffs				
Season	Club	Lea	GP	G	A	TP	PIM	GP	G	A	TP	PIM
1980-81	Kitchener	OHA	47	11	28	39	59	18	4	12	16	20
1981-82	Calgary	NHL	2	0	0	0	0	....	....	....	....	....
a	Kitchener	OHL	59	25	50	75	145	15	5	10	15	44
1982-83	Calgary	NHL	14	1	3	4	9	....	....	....	....	....
a	Kitchener	OHL	51	38	46	84	67	8	3	8	11	9
1983-84	Calgary	NHL	51	11	34	45	42	11	2	12	14	13
	Colorado	CHL	19	5	14	19	22	....	....	....	....	....
1984-85	Calgary	NHL	67	14	52	66	75	4	1	2	3	8
1985-86	Calgary	NHL	77	11	57	68	76	21	4	*15	19	30
1986-87b	Calgary	NHL	79	20	56	76	97	4	1	0	1	0
1987-88	Calgary	NHL	80	25	58	83	114	7	3	6	9	18
1988-89bc	Calgary	NHL	79	16	58	74	126	22	7	*24	*31	46
1989-90d	Calgary	NHL	79	28	62	90	82	6	2	3	5	8
1990-91d	Calgary	NHL	78	28	75	103	90	7	2	3	5	8
1991-92	Calgary	NHL	72	20	57	77	83	....	....	....	....	....
1992-93	Calgary	NHL	50	11	43	54	61	6	1	6	7	10
1993-94b	Calgary	NHL	75	28	54	82	95	7	2	6	8	12
1994-95	St. Louis	NHL	32	8	20	28	43	7	1	5	6	10
	NHL Totals		835	221	629	850	993	102	26	82	108	163

a OHL First All-Star Team (1982, 1983)
b NHL Second All-Star Team (1987, 1989, 1994)
c Won Conn Smythe Trophy (1989)
d NHL First All-Star Team (1990, 1991)

Played in NHL All-Star Game (1985, 1988, 1990-92, 1994)

Traded to **St. Louis** by **Calgary** with Calgary's fourth round choice in 1997 Entry Draft for Phil Housley, St. Louis' second round choice in 1996 Entry Draft and second round choice in 1997 Entry Draft, July 4, 1994.

MacINTYRE, ANDY — CHI.

Left wing. Shoots left. 6'1", 190 lbs. Born, Thunder Bay, Ont., April 16, 1974.
(Chicago's 4th choice, 89th overall, in 1992 Entry Draft).

			Regular Season					Playoffs				
Season	Club	Lea	GP	G	A	TP	PIM	GP	G	A	TP	PIM
1990-91	Seattle	WHL	71	16	13	29	52	4	0	0	0	2
1991-92	Seattle	WHL	12	6	2	8	18	....	....	....	....	....
	Saskatoon	WHL	55	22	13	35	66	22	10	2	12	17
1992-93	Saskatoon	WHL	72	35	29	64	82	9	3	2	5	2
1993-94a	Saskatoon	WHL	72	54	35	89	58	16	6	6	12	16
1994-95	Columbus	ECHL	22	7	8	15	5	....	....	....	....	....
	Indianapolis	IHL	51	9	8	17	17	....	....	....	....	....

a WHL East Second All-Star Team (1994)

MACIVER, NORM (mac-IGH-ver) — PIT.

Defense. Shoots left. 5'11", 180 lbs. Born, Thunder Bay, Ont., September 8, 1964.

			Regular Season					Playoffs				
Season	Club	Lea	GP	G	A	TP	PIM	GP	G	A	TP	PIM
1982-83	Minn.-Duluth	WCHA	45	1	26	27	40	6	0	2	2	2
1983-84a	Minn.-Duluth	WCHA	31	13	28	41	28	8	1	10	11	8
1984-85bc	Minn.-Duluth	WCHA	47	14	47	61	63	10	3	3	6	6
1985-86bc	Minn.-Duluth	WCHA	42	11	51	62	36	4	2	3	5	2
1986-87	NY Rangers	NHL	3	0	1	1	0	....	....	....	....	....
	New Haven	AHL	71	6	30	36	73	7	0	0	0	9
1987-88	NY Rangers	NHL	37	9	15	24	14	....	....	....	....	....
	Colorado	IHL	27	6	20	26	22	....	....	....	....	....
1988-89	NY Rangers	NHL	26	0	10	10	14	....	....	....	....	....
	Hartford	NHL	37	1	22	23	24	1	0	0	0	2
1989-90	Binghamton	AHL	2	0	0	0	0	....	....	....	....	....
	Edmonton	NHL	1	0	0	0	0	....	....	....	....	....
	Cape Breton	AHL	68	13	37	50	55	6	0	7	7	10
1990-91	Edmonton	NHL	21	2	5	7	14	18	0	4	4	8
de	Cape Breton	AHL	56	13	46	59	60	....	....	....	....	....
1991-92	Edmonton	NHL	57	6	34	40	38	13	1	2	3	10
1992-93	Ottawa	NHL	80	17	46	63	84	....	....	....	....	....
1993-94	Ottawa	NHL	53	3	20	23	26	....	....	....	....	....
1994-95	Ottawa	NHL	28	4	7	11	10	....	....	....	....	....
	Pittsburgh	NHL	13	0	9	9	6	12	1	4	5	8
	NHL Totals		356	42	169	211	230	44	2	10	12	28

a WCHA Second All-Star Team (1984)
b WCHA First All-Star Team (1985, 1986)
c NCAA West First All-American Team (1985, 1986)
d AHL First All-Star Team (1991)
e Won Eddie Shore Plaque (Top Defenseman - AHL) (1991)

Signed as a free agent by **NY Rangers**, September 8, 1986. Traded to **Hartford** by **NY Rangers** with Brian Lawton and Don Maloney for Carey Wilson and Hartford's fifth round choice (Lubos Rob) in 1990 Entry Draft, December 26, 1988. Traded to **Edmonton** by **Hartford** for Jim Ennis, October 10, 1989. Claimed by **Ottawa** from **Edmonton** in NHL Waiver Draft, October 4, 1992. Traded to **Pittsburgh** by **Ottawa** with Troy Murray for Martin Straka, April 7, 1995.

MACKEY, DAVID

Left wing. Shoots left. 6'4", 205 lbs. Born, Richmond, B.C., July 24, 1966.
(Chicago's 12th choice, 224th overall, in 1984 Entry Draft).

			Regular Season					Playoffs				
Season	Club	Lea	GP	G	A	TP	PIM	GP	G	A	TP	PIM
1982-83	Victoria	WHL	69	16	16	32	53	12	11	1	2	4
1983-84	Victoria	WHL	69	15	15	30	97	....	....	....	....	....
1984-85	Victoria	WHL	16	5	6	11	45	....	....	....	....	....
	Portland	WHL	56	28	32	60	122	6	2	1	3	13
1985-86	Kamloops	WHL	9	3	4	7	13	....	....	....	....	....
	Medicine Hat	WHL	60	25	32	57	167	25	6	3	9	72
1986-87	Saginaw	IHL	81	26	49	75	173	10	5	6	11	22
1987-88	Chicago	NHL	23	1	3	4	71	....	....	....	....	....
	Saginaw	IHL	62	29	22	51	211	10	3	7	10	44
1988-89	Chicago	NHL	23	1	2	3	78	....	....	....	....	....
	Saginaw	IHL	57	22	23	45	223	....	....	....	....	....
1989-90	Minnesota	NHL	16	2	0	2	28	....	....	....	....	....
1990-91	Milwaukee	IHL	82	28	30	58	226	6	7	2	9	6
1991-92	St. Louis	NHL	19	1	0	1	49	1	0	0	0	0
	Peoria	IHL	35	20	17	37	90	....	....	....	....	....
1992-93	St. Louis	NHL	15	1	4	5	23	....	....	....	....	....
	Peoria	IHL	42	24	22	46	112	4	1	0	1	22
1993-94	St. Louis	NHL	30	2	3	5	56	2	0	0	0	2
	Peoria	IHL	49	14	21	35	132	....	....	....	....	....
1994-95	Milwaukee	IHL	74	19	18	37	261	15	6	4	10	34
	NHL Totals		126	8	12	20	305	3	0	0	0	2

Claimed by **Minnesota** from **Chicago** in NHL Waiver Draft, October 2, 1989. Traded to **Vancouver** by **Minnesota** for future considerations, September 7, 1990. Signed as a free agent by **St. Louis**, August 7, 1991.

MACKINNON, STEPHEN — OTT.

Left wing. Shoots left. 6'4", 200 lbs. Born, Lowell, MA, August 20, 1976.
(Ottawa's 9th choice, 237th overall, in 1994 Entry Draft).

			Regular Season					Playoffs				
Season	Club	Lea	GP	G	A	TP	PIM	GP	G	A	TP	PIM
1993-94	Cushing	HS	25	13	15	28	....	....	....	....	....	....
1994-95	Cushing	HS	25	26	29	55	....	....	....	....	....	....

MacLEAN, DONALD — L.A.

Center. Shoots left. 6'2", 174 lbs. Born, Sydney, N.S., January 14, 1977.
(Los Angeles' 2nd choice, 33rd overall, in 1995 Entry Draft).

			Regular Season					Playoffs				
Season	Club	Lea	GP	G	A	TP	PIM	GP	G	A	TP	PIM
1993-94	Halifax	Midget	25	35	34	69	65	....	....	....	....	....
1994-95	Beauport	QMJHL	64	15	27	42	37	17	4	4	8	6

MacLEAN, JOHN — N.J.

Right wing. Shoots right. 6', 200 lbs. Born, Oshawa, Ont., November 20, 1964.
(New Jersey's 1st choice, 6th overall, in 1983 Entry Draft).

			Regular Season					Playoffs				
Season	Club	Lea	GP	G	A	TP	PIM	GP	G	A	TP	PIM
1981-82	Oshawa	OHL	67	17	22	39	197	12	3	6	9	63
1982-83	Oshawa	OHL	66	47	51	98	138	17	*18	20	*38	35
1983-84	New Jersey	NHL	23	1	0	1	10	....	....	....	....	....
	Oshawa	OHL	30	23	36	59	58	7	2	5	7	18
1984-85	New Jersey	NHL	61	13	20	33	44	....	....	....	....	....
1985-86	New Jersey	NHL	74	21	36	57	112	....	....	....	....	....
1986-87	New Jersey	NHL	80	31	36	67	120	....	....	....	....	....
1987-88	New Jersey	NHL	76	23	16	39	147	20	7	11	18	60
1988-89	New Jersey	NHL	74	42	45	87	122	....	....	....	....	....
1989-90	New Jersey	NHL	80	41	38	79	80	6	4	1	5	12
1990-91	New Jersey	NHL	78	45	33	78	150	7	5	3	8	20
1991-92	DID NOT PLAY – INJURED											
1992-93	New Jersey	NHL	80	24	24	48	102	5	0	1	1	10
1993-94	New Jersey	NHL	80	37	33	70	95	20	6	10	16	22
1994-95	New Jersey	NHL	46	17	12	29	32	20	5	13	18	14
	NHL Totals		752	295	293	588	1014	78	27	39	66	138

Played in NHL All-Star Game (1989, 1991)

MacLEOD, PAT

Defense. Shoots left. 5'11", 190 lbs. Born, Melfort, Sask., June 15, 1969.
(Minnesota's 5th choice, 87th overall, in 1989 Entry Draft).

			Regular Season					Playoffs				
Season	Club	Lea	GP	G	A	TP	PIM	GP	G	A	TP	PIM
1987-88	Kamloops	WHL	50	13	33	46	27	18	2	7	9	6
1988-89	Kamloops	WHL	37	11	34	45	14	15	7	18	25	24
1989-90	Kalamazoo	IHL	82	9	38	47	27	10	1	6	7	2
1990-91	Minnesota	NHL	1	0	1	1	0	....	....	....	....	....
	Kalamazoo	IHL	59	10	30	40	16	11	1	2	3	5
1991-92	San Jose	NHL	37	5	11	16	4	....	....	....	....	....
	Kansas City	IHL	45	9	21	30	19	11	1	4	5	4
1992-93	San Jose	NHL	13	0	1	1	10	....	....	....	....	....
	Kansas City	IHL	18	8	8	16	14	10	2	4	6	7
1993-94a	Milwaukee	IHL	73	21	52	73	18	3	1	2	3	0
1994-95	Milwaukee	IHL	69	11	36	47	16	15	3	6	9	8
	NHL Totals		51	5	13	18	14	....	....	....	....	....

a IHL First All-Star Team (1994)

Claimed by **San Jose** from **Minnesota** in Dispersal Draft, May 30, 1991.

MACNEIL, IAN — HFD.

Center. Shoots left. 6'2", 171 lbs. Born, Halifax, N.S., April 27, 1977.
(Hartford's 3rd choice, 85th overall, in 1995 Entry Draft).

			Regular Season					Playoffs				
Season	Club	Lea	GP	G	A	TP	PIM	GP	G	A	TP	PIM
1993-94	Whitby	Midget	50	30	22	52	102	....	....	....	....	....
1994-95	Oshawa	OHL	60	7	21	28	62	7	0	2	2	0

MACOUN, JAMIE (muh-KOW-uhn) — TOR.

Defense. Shoots left. 6'2", 200 lbs. Born, Newmarket, Ont., August 17, 1961.

			Regular Season					Playoffs				
Season	Club	Lea	GP	G	A	TP	PIM	GP	G	A	TP	PIM
1980-81	Ohio State	CCHA	38	9	20	29	83	....	....	....	....	....
1981-82	Ohio State	CCHA	25	2	18	20	89	....	....	....	....	....
1982-83	Ohio State	CCHA	19	6	21	27	54	....	....	....	....	....
	Calgary	NHL	22	1	4	5	25	9	0	2	2	8
1983-84a	Calgary	NHL	72	9	23	32	97	11	1	0	1	0
1984-85	Calgary	NHL	70	9	30	39	67	4	1	0	1	4
1985-86	Calgary	NHL	77	11	21	32	81	22	1	6	7	23
1986-87	Calgary	NHL	79	7	33	40	111	3	0	1	1	8
1987-88	DID NOT PLAY – INJURED											
1988-89	Calgary	NHL	72	8	19	27	76	22	3	6	9	30
1989-90	Calgary	NHL	78	8	27	35	70	6	0	3	3	10
1990-91	Calgary	NHL	79	7	15	22	84	7	0	1	1	4
1991-92	Calgary	NHL	37	2	12	14	53	....	....	....	....	....
	Toronto	NHL	39	3	13	16	18	....	....	....	....	....
1992-93	Toronto	NHL	77	4	15	19	55	21	0	6	6	36
1993-94	Toronto	NHL	82	3	27	30	115	18	1	1	2	12
1994-95	Toronto	NHL	46	2	8	10	75	7	1	2	3	8
	NHL Totals		830	74	247	321	927	130	8	28	36	143

a NHL All-Rookie Team (1984)

Signed as a free agent by **Calgary**, January 30, 1983. Traded to **Toronto** by **Calgary** with Doug Gilmour, Ric Natress, Kent Manderville and Rick Wamsley for Gary Leeman, Alexander Godynyuk, Jeff Reese, Michel Petit and Craig Berube, January 2, 1992.

MacTAVISH, CRAIG — PHI.

Center. Shoots left. 6'1", 195 lbs. Born, London, Ont., August 15, 1958.
(Boston's 9th choice, 153rd overall, in 1978 Amateur Draft).

			Regular Season					Playoffs				
Season	Club	Lea	GP	G	A	TP	PIM	GP	G	A	TP	PIM
1978-79	Lowell	ECAC	....	....	....	....	....	....	....	....	....	....
1979-80	Boston	NHL	46	11	17	28	8	10	2	3	5	7
	Binghamton	AHL	34	17	15	32	29	....	....	....	....	....
1980-81	Boston	NHL	24	3	5	8	13	....	....	....	....	....
	Springfield	AHL	53	19	24	43	81	7	5	4	9	8
1981-82	Boston	NHL	2	0	1	1	0	....	....	....	....	....
	Erie	AHL	72	23	32	55	37	....	....	....	....	....
1982-83	Boston	NHL	75	10	20	30	18	17	3	1	4	18
1983-84	Boston	NHL	70	20	23	43	35	1	0	0	0	0
1984-85	DID NOT PLAY											
1985-86	Edmonton	NHL	74	23	24	47	70	10	4	4	8	11
1986-87	Edmonton	NHL	79	20	19	39	55	21	1	9	10	16
1987-88	Edmonton	NHL	80	15	17	32	47	19	0	1	1	31
1988-89	Edmonton	NHL	80	21	31	52	55	7	0	1	1	8
1989-90	Edmonton	NHL	80	21	22	43	89	22	2	6	8	29
1990-91	Edmonton	NHL	80	17	15	32	76	18	3	3	6	20
1991-92	Edmonton	NHL	80	12	18	30	98	16	3	0	3	28
1992-93	Edmonton	NHL	82	10	20	30	110	....	....	....	....	....
1993-94	Edmonton	NHL	66	16	10	26	80	....	....	....	....	....
	NY Rangers	NHL	12	4	2	6	11	23	1	4	5	22
1994-95	Philadelphia	NHL	45	3	9	12	23	15	1	4	5	20
	NHL Totals		975	206	253	459	788	179	20	36	56	210

Signed as a free agent by **Edmonton**, February 1, 1985. Traded to **NY Rangers** by **Edmonton** for Todd Marchant, March 21, 1994. Signed as a free agent by **Philadelphia**, July 6, 1994.

MacWILLIAM, MIKE — NYI

Left wing. Shoots left. 6'4", 230 lbs. Born, Burnaby, B.C., February 14, 1967.

			Regular Season					Playoffs				
Season	**Club**	**Lea**	**GP**	**G**	**A**	**TP**	**PIM**	**GP**	**G**	**A**	**TP**	**PIM**
1985-86	Medicine Hat	WHL	52	8	6	14	98	....	....	....	....	....
1986-87	Medicine Hat	WHL	44	7	17	24	134	19	1	0	1	35
1987-88	N. Westminster	WHL	DID NOT PLAY – INJURED									
1988-89	Milwaukee	IHL	6	1	1	2	28	....	....	....	....	....
	Flint	IHL	18	0	0	0	92	....	....	....	....	....
1989-90			DID NOT PLAY – INJURED									
1990-91	Adirondack	AHL	8	0	0	0	32	....	....	....	....	....
	Greensboro	ECHL	15	2	7	9	209	....	....	....	....	....
1991-92	St. John's	AHL	44	7	8	15	301	2	0	0	0	8
	Greensboro	ECHL	8	2	5	7	94	....	....	....	....	....
1992-93	Greensboro	ECHL	12	5	5	10	137	....	....	....	....	....
1993-94	Tulsa	CHL	39	16	12	28	326	....	....	....	....	....
1994-95	Denver	IHL	30	5	6	11	218	12	2	2	4	56

Signed as a free agnt by **Philadelphia**, October 7, 1986. Signed as a free agent by **Toronto**, July 30, 1991. Signed as a free agent by **NY Islanders**, July 25, 1995.

MADER, MIKE — WPG.

Defense. Shoots right. 6'2", 180 lbs. Born, Manchester, CT, November 7, 1975.
(Winnipeg's 10th choice, 238th overall, in 1994 Entry Draft).

			Regular Season					Playoffs				
Season	**Club**	**Lea**	**GP**	**G**	**A**	**TP**	**PIM**	**GP**	**G**	**A**	**TP**	**PIM**
1993-94	Loomis	HS	26	12	35	47	....	....	....	....	....	....
1994-95	Providence	H.E.	29	1	5	6	26	....	....	....	....	....

MADILL, JEFF (muh-DILL)

Right wing. Shoots left. 5'11", 195 lbs. Born, Oshawa, Ont., June 21, 1965.
(New Jersey's 2nd choice, 7th overall, in 1987 Supplemental Draft).

			Regular Season					Playoffs				
Season	**Club**	**Lea**	**GP**	**G**	**A**	**TP**	**PIM**	**GP**	**G**	**A**	**TP**	**PIM**
1984-85	Ohio State	CCHA	12	5	6	11	18	....	....	....	....	....
1985-86	Ohio State	CCHA	41	32	25	57	65	....	....	....	....	....
1986-87	Ohio State	CCHA	43	38	32	70	139	....	....	....	....	....
1987-88	Utica	AHL	58	18	15	33	127	....	....	....	....	....
1988-89	Utica	AHL	69	23	25	48	225	4	1	0	1	35
1989-90	Utica	AHL	74	43	26	69	233	4	1	2	3	33
1990-91	**New Jersey**	**NHL**	**14**	**4**	**0**	**4**	**46**	**7**	**0**	**2**	**2**	**8**
a	Utica	AHL	54	42	35	77	151	....	....	....	....	....
1991-92	Kansas City	IHL	62	32	20	52	167	6	2	2	4	30
1992-93	Cincinnati	IHL	58	36	17	53	175	....	....	....	....	....
	Milwaukee	IHL	23	13	6	19	53	4	3	0	3	9
1993-94	Atlanta	IHL	80	42	44	86	186	14	4	2	6	33
1994-95	Denver	IHL	73	35	30	65	207	17	8	6	14	53
	NHL Totals		**14**	**4**	**0**	**4**	**46**	**7**	**0**	**2**	**2**	**8**

a AHL Second All-Star Team (1991)
b IHL Second All-Star Team (1993)

Claimed by **San Jose** from **New Jersey** in Expansion Draft, May 30, 1991. Signed as a free agent by **NY Islanders**, August 25, 1994.

MAGARRELL, ADAM — PHI.

Defense. Shoots left. 6'3", 178 lbs. Born, Winnipeg, Man., February 1, 1976.
(Philadelphia's 2nd choice, 88th overall, in 1994 Entry Draft).

			Regular Season					Playoffs				
Season	**Club**	**Lea**	**GP**	**G**	**A**	**TP**	**PIM**	**GP**	**G**	**A**	**TP**	**PIM**
1992-93	Brandon	WHL	8	0	0	0	0	....	....	....	....	....
1993-94	Brandon	WHL	40	2	1	3	69	13	0	2	2	32
1994-95	Brandon	WHL	41	0	3	3	72	....	....	....	....	....
	Spokane	WHL	19	0	4	4	27	11	0	0	0	34

MAGUIRE, DEREK — MTL.

Defense. Shoots right. 5'10", 210 lbs. Born, Delbarton, NJ, December 9, 1971.
(Montreal's 10th choice, 186th overall, in 1990 Entry Draft).

			Regular Season					Playoffs				
Season	**Club**	**Lea**	**GP**	**G**	**A**	**TP**	**PIM**	**GP**	**G**	**A**	**TP**	**PIM**
1990-91	Harvard	ECAC	25	3	14	17	12	....	....	....	....	....
1991-92	Harvard	ECAC	25	1	16	17	16	....	....	....	....	....
1992-93	Harvard	ECAC	16	3	9	12	10	....	....	....	....	....
1993-94abc	Harvard	ECAC	31	6	32	38	14	....	....	....	....	....
1994-95	Fredericton	AHL	52	6	14	20	19	17	0	4	4	4

a ECAC Second All-Star Team (1994)
b NCAA East Second All-American Team (1994)
c NCAA Final Four All-Tournament Team (1994)

MAILLET, CHRIS — T.B.

Defense. Shoots left. 6'5", 188 lbs. Born, Moncton, NB, January 28, 1976.
(Tampa Bay's 7th choice, 164th overall, in 1994 Entry Draft).

			Regular Season					Playoffs				
Season	**Club**	**Lea**	**GP**	**G**	**A**	**TP**	**PIM**	**GP**	**G**	**A**	**TP**	**PIM**
1993-94	Red Deer	WHL	52	0	0	0	102	1	0	0	0	5
1994-95	Red Deer	WHL	47	1	9	10	102	....	....	....	....	....

MAJIC, XAVIER (MA-jihk) — MTL.

Center. Shoots left. 6', 190 lbs. Born, Fernie, B.C., March 10, 1973.
(Vancouver's 12th choice, 249th overall, in 1991 Entry Draft).

			Regular Season					Playoffs				
Season	**Club**	**Lea**	**GP**	**G**	**A**	**TP**	**PIM**	**GP**	**G**	**A**	**TP**	**PIM**
1990-91	RPI	ECAC	31	4	10	14	26	....	....	....	....	....
1991-92	RPI	ECAC	32	13	19	32	48	....	....	....	....	....
1992-93	RPI	ECAC	35	16	26	42	18	....	....	....	....	....
1993-94	RPI	ECAC	35	13	17	30	48	....	....	....	....	....
1994-95	Wheeling	ECHL	49	20	31	51	41	....	....	....	....	....
	Fredericton	AHL	21	2	3	5	4	17	3	9	12	0

Signed as a free agent by **Montreal**, April 22, 1994.

MAJOR, MARK — DET.

Left wing. Shoots left. 6'3", 223 lbs. Born, Toronto, Ont., March 20, 1970.
(Pittsburgh's 2nd choice, 25th overall, in 1988 Entry Draft).

			Regular Season					Playoffs				
Season	**Club**	**Lea**	**GP**	**G**	**A**	**TP**	**PIM**	**GP**	**G**	**A**	**TP**	**PIM**
1987-88	North Bay	OHL	57	16	17	33	272	4	0	2	2	8
1988-89	North Bay	OHL	11	3	2	5	58	....	....	....	....	....
	Kingston	OHL	53	22	29	51	193	....	....	....	....	....
1989-90	Kingston	OHL	62	29	32	61	168	6	3	3	6	12
1990-91	Muskegon	IHL	60	8	10	18	160	5	0	0	0	0
1991-92	Muskegon	IHL	80	13	18	31	302	12	1	3	4	29
1992-93	Cleveland	IHL	82	13	15	28	155	3	0	0	0	0
1993-94	Providence	AHL	61	17	9	26	176	....	....	....	....	....
1994-95	Detroit	IHL	78	17	19	36	229	5	0	1	1	23

Signed as a free agent by **Boston**, July 22, 1993.

MAKAROV, SERGEI (muh-KAH-rov) — S.J.

Right wing. Shoots left. 5'11", 185 lbs. Born, Chelyabinsk, USSR, June 19, 1958.
(Calgary's 14th choice, 231st overall, in 1983 Entry Draft).

			Regular Season					Playoffs				
Season	**Club**	**Lea**	**GP**	**G**	**A**	**TP**	**PIM**	**GP**	**G**	**A**	**TP**	**PIM**
1976-77	Chelyabinsk	USSR	11	1	0	1	4	....	....	....	....	....
1977-78	Chelyabinsk	USSR	36	18	13	31	10	....	....	....	....	....
1978-79a	CSKA	USSR	44	18	21	39	12	....	....	....	....	....
1979-80bc	CSKA	USSR	44	29	39	68	16	....	....	....	....	....
1980-81ab	CSKA	USSR	49	42	37	79	22	....	....	....	....	....
1981-82ab	CSKA	USSR	46	32	43	75	18	....	....	....	....	....
1982-83a	CSKA	USSR	30	25	17	42	6	....	....	....	....	....
1983-84ab	CSKA	USSR	44	36	37	73	28	....	....	....	....	....
1984-85abc	CSKA	USSR	40	26	39	65	28	....	....	....	....	....
1985-86ab	CSKA	USSR	40	30	32	62	28	....	....	....	....	....
1986-87ab	CSKA	USSR	40	21	32	53	26	....	....	....	....	....
1987-88ab	CSKA	USSR	51	23	45	68	50	....	....	....	....	....
1988-89bc	CSKA	USSR	44	21	33	54	42	....	....	....	....	....
1989-90de	**Calgary**	**NHL**	**80**	**24**	**62**	**86**	**55**	**6**	**0**	**6**	**6**	**0**
1990-91	**Calgary**	**NHL**	**78**	**30**	**49**	**79**	**44**	**3**	**1**	**0**	**1**	**0**
1991-92	**Calgary**	**NHL**	**68**	**22**	**48**	**70**	**60**	....	....	....	....	....
1992-93	**Calgary**	**NHL**	**71**	**18**	**39**	**57**	**40**	....	....	....	....	....
1993-94	**San Jose**	**NHL**	**80**	**30**	**38**	**68**	**78**	**14**	**8**	**2**	**10**	**4**
1994-95	**San Jose**	**NHL**	**43**	**10**	**14**	**24**	**40**	**11**	**3**	**3**	**6**	**4**
	NHL Totals		**420**	**134**	**250**	**384**	**317**	**34**	**12**	**11**	**23**	**8**

a Soviet National League All-Star (1981-88)
b Izvestia Trophy - leading scorer (1980-82, 1984-89)
c Soviet Player of the Year (1980, 1985, 1989)
d NHL All-Rookie Team (1990)
e Won Calder Memorial Trophy (1990)

Traded to **Hartford** by **Calgary** for future considerations (Washington's fourth round choice — previously acquired by Hartford — Calgary selected Jason Smith — in 1993 Entry Draft, June 26, 1993), June 20, 1993. Traded to **San Jose** by **Hartford** with Hartford's first (Viktor Kozlov) and third (Ville Peltonen) round choices in 1993 Entry Draft and Toronto's second round choice (previously acquired by Hartford — San Jose selected Vlastimil Kroupa) in 1993 Entry Draft for San Jose's first round choice (Chris Pronger) in 1993 Entry Draft, June 26, 1993.

MAKELA, MIKKO (MAK-uh-luh, MEE-koh)

Left wing. Shoots left. 6'1", 194 lbs. Born, Tampere, Finland, February 28, 1965.
(NY Islanders' 5th choice, 65th overall, in 1983 Entry Draft).

			Regular Season					Playoffs				
Season	**Club**	**Lea**	**GP**	**G**	**A**	**TP**	**PIM**	**GP**	**G**	**A**	**TP**	**PIM**
1983-84	Ilves	Fin.	35	17	11	28	26	2	0	1	1	0
1984-85a	Ilves	Fin.	36	34	25	59	24	9	4	7	11	10
1985-86	**NY Islanders**	**NHL**	**58**	**16**	**20**	**36**	**28**	....	....	....	....	....
	Springfield	AHL	2	1	1	2	0	....	....	....	....	....
1986-87	**NY Islanders**	**NHL**	**80**	**24**	**33**	**57**	**24**	**11**	**2**	**4**	**6**	**8**
1987-88	**NY Islanders**	**NHL**	**73**	**36**	**40**	**76**	**22**	**6**	**1**	**4**	**5**	**6**
1988-89	**NY Islanders**	**NHL**	**76**	**17**	**28**	**45**	**22**	....	....	....	....	....
1989-90	**NY Islanders**	**NHL**	**20**	**2**	**3**	**5**	**2**	....	....	....	....	....
	Los Angeles	**NHL**	**45**	**7**	**14**	**21**	**16**	**1**	**0**	**0**	**0**	**0**
1990-91	**Buffalo**	**NHL**	**60**	**15**	**7**	**22**	**25**	....	....	....	....	....
1991-92	TPS	Fin.	44	25	45	*70	38	3	2	3	5	0
1992-93	TPS	Fin.	38	17	27	44	22	11	4	8	12	0
1993-94	Malmo	Swe.	37	15	21	36	20	11	4	7	11	2
1994-95	Ilves	Fin.	18	3	11	14	4	....	....	....	....	....
	Boston	**NHL**	**11**	**1**	**2**	**3**	**0**	....	....	....	....	....
	Providence	AHL	....	....	....	....	....	7	2	4	6	2
	NHL Totals		**423**	**118**	**147**	**265**	**139**	**18**	**3**	**8**	**11**	**14**

a Finnish League First All-Star Team (1985)

Traded to **Los Angeles** by **NY Islanders** for Ken Baumgartner and Hubie McDonough, November 29, 1989. Traded to **Buffalo** by **Los Angeles** for Mike Donnelly, September 30, 1990. Signed as a free agent by **Boston**, July 18, 1994.

MAKINEN, MARKO (mya-KIH-nehn) — S.J.

Right wing. Shoots right. 6'4", 198 lbs. Born, Turku, Finland, March 31, 1977.
(San Jose's 3rd choice, 64th overall, in 1995 Entry Draft).

			Regular Season					Playoffs				
Season	**Club**	**Lea**	**GP**	**G**	**A**	**TP**	**PIM**	**GP**	**G**	**A**	**TP**	**PIM**
1994-95	TPS	Fin. Jr.	26	7	1	8	34	....	....	....	....	....
	Kiekko-67	Fin. 2	4	0	0	0	6	....	....	....	....	....

MALAKHOV, VLADIMIR (mah-LAH-kahf) — MTL.

Defense. Shoots left. 6'3", 220 lbs. Born, Sverdlovsk, USSR, August 30, 1968.
(NY Islanders' 12th choice, 191st overall, in 1989 Entry Draft).

			Regular Season					Playoffs				
Season	**Club**	**Lea**	**GP**	**G**	**A**	**TP**	**PIM**	**GP**	**G**	**A**	**TP**	**PIM**
1986-87	Spartak	USSR	22	0	1	1	12	....	....	....	....	....
1987-88	Spartak	USSR	28	2	2	4	26	....	....	....	....	....
1988-89	CSKA	USSR	34	6	2	8	16	....	....	....	....	....
1989-90	CSKA	USSR	48	2	10	12	34	....	....	....	....	....
1990-91	CSKA	USSR	46	5	13	18	22	....	....	....	....	....
1991-92	CSKA	CIS	40	1	9	10	12	....	....	....	....	....
1992-93a	**NY Islanders**	**NHL**	**64**	**14**	**38**	**52**	**59**	**17**	**3**	**6**	**9**	**12**
	Capital Dist.	AHL	3	2	1	3	11	....	....	....	....	....
1993-94	**NY Islanders**	**NHL**	**76**	**10**	**47**	**57**	**80**	**4**	**0**	**0**	**0**	**6**
1994-95	**NY Islanders**	**NHL**	**26**	**3**	**13**	**16**	**32**	....	....	....	....	....
	Montreal	**NHL**	**14**	**1**	**4**	**5**	**14**	....	....	....	....	....
	NHL Totals		**180**	**28**	**102**	**130**	**185**	**21**	**3**	**6**	**9**	**18**

a NHL/Upper Deck All-Rookie Team (1993)

Traded to **Montreal** by **NY Islanders** with Pierre Turgeon for Kirk Muller, Mathieu Schneider and Craig Darby, April 5, 1995.

MALGUNAS, STEWART (mal-GOO-nuhs) WPG.

Defense. Shoots left. 6', 200 lbs. Born, Prince George, B.C., April 21, 1970.
(Detroit's 3rd choice, 66th overall, in 1990 Entry Draft).

			Regular Season					Playoffs				
Season	Club	Lea	GP	G	A	TP	PIM	GP	G	A	TP	PIM
1987-88	N. Westminster	WHL	6	0	0	0	0	....	....	....	....	....
1988-89	Seattle	WHL	72	11	41	52	51	....	....	....	....	....
1989-90a	Seattle	WHL	63	15	48	63	116	13	2	9	11	32
1990-91	Adirondack	AHL	78	5	19	24	70	2	0	0	0	4
1991-92	Adirondack	AHL	69	4	28	32	82	18	2	6	8	28
1992-93	Adirondack	AHL	45	3	12	15	39	11	3	3	6	8
1993-94	**Philadelphia**	**NHL**	**67**	**1**	**3**	**4**	**86**	....	....	....	....	....
1994-95	**Philadelphia**	**NHL**	**4**	**0**	**0**	**0**	**4**	....	....	....	....	....
	Hershey	AHL	32	3	5	8	28	6	2	1	3	31
	NHL Totals		**71**	**1**	**3**	**4**	**90**	....	....	....	....	....

a WHL West First All-Star Team (1990)

Traded to **Philadelphia** by **Detroit** for Philadelphia's fifth round choice (David Arsenault) in 1995 Entry Draft, September 9, 1993. Signed as a free agent by **Winnipeg**, August 9, 1995.

MALIK, MAREK (MAW-leck) HFD.

Defense. Shoots left. 6'5", 190 lbs. Born, Ostrava, Czech., June 24, 1975.
(Hartford's 2nd choice, 72nd overall, in 1993 Entry Draft).

			Regular Season					Playoffs				
Season	Club	Lea	GP	G	A	TP	PIM	GP	G	A	TP	PIM
1992-93	TJ Vitkovice Jr.	Czech.	20	5	10	15	16	....	....	....	....	....
1993-94	TJ Vitkovice	Czech.	38	3	3	6	0	3	0	1	1	0
1994-95	Springfield	AHL	58	11	30	41	91	....	....	....	....	....
	Hartford	**NHL**	**1**	**0**	**1**	**1**	**0**	....	....	....	....	....
	NHL Totals		**1**	**0**	**1**	**1**	**0**	....	....	....	....	....

MALKOC, DEAN (mal-KAWK) VAN.

Defense. Shoots left. 6'3", 200 lbs. Born, Vancouver, B.C., January 26, 1970.
(New Jersey's 7th choice, 95th overall, in 1990 Entry Draft).

			Regular Season					Playoffs				
Season	Club	Lea	GP	G	A	TP	PIM	GP	G	A	TP	PIM
1989-90	Kamloops	WHL	48	3	18	21	209	17	0	3	3	56
1990-91	Kamloops	WHL	8	1	4	5	47	....	....	....	....	....
	Swift Current	WHL	56	10	23	33	248	3	0	2	2	5
	Utica	AHL	1	0	0	0	0	....	....	....	....	....
1991-92	Utica	AHL	66	1	11	12	274	4	0	2	2	6
1992-93	Utica	AHL	73	5	19	24	255	5	0	1	1	8
1993-94	Albany	AHL	79	0	9	9	296	5	0	0	0	21
1994-95	Albany	AHL	9	0	1	1	52	....	....	....	....	....
	Indianapolis	IHL	62	1	3	4	193	....	....	....	....	....

Traded to **Chicago** by **New Jersey** for Rob Conn, January 30, 1995. Signed as a free agent by **Vancouver**, August 9, 1995.

MALLETTE, TROY (muh-LEHT) OTT.

Left wing. Shoots left. 6'2", 210 lbs. Born, Sudbury, Ont., February 25, 1970.
(NY Rangers' 1st choice, 22nd overall, in 1988 Entry Draft).

			Regular Season					Playoffs				
Season	Club	Lea	GP	G	A	TP	PIM	GP	G	A	TP	PIM
1986-87	S.S. Marie	OHL	65	20	25	45	157	4	0	2	2	12
1987-88	S.S. Marie	OHL	62	18	30	48	186	6	1	3	4	12
1988-89	S.S. Marie	OHL	64	39	37	76	172	....	....	....	....	....
1989-90	**NY Rangers**	**NHL**	**79**	**13**	**16**	**29**	**305**	**10**	**2**	**2**	**4**	**81**
1990-91	**NY Rangers**	**NHL**	**71**	**12**	**10**	**22**	**252**	**5**	**0**	**0**	**0**	**18**
1991-92	**Edmonton**	**NHL**	**15**	**1**	**3**	**4**	**36**	....	....	....	....	....
	New Jersey	**NHL**	**17**	**3**	**4**	**7**	**43**	....	....	....	....	....
1992-93	**New Jersey**	**NHL**	**34**	**4**	**3**	**7**	**56**	....	....	....	....	....
	Utica	AHL	5	3	3	6	17	....	....	....	....	....
1993-94	**Ottawa**	**NHL**	**82**	**7**	**16**	**23**	**166**	....	....	....	....	....
1994-95	**Ottawa**	**NHL**	**23**	**3**	**5**	**8**	**35**	....	....	....	....	....
	P.E.I.	AHL	5	1	5	6	9	....	....	....	....	....
	NHL Totals		**321**	**43**	**57**	**100**	**893**	**15**	**2**	**2**	**4**	**99**

Acquired by **Edmonton** from **NY Rangers** as compensation for NY Rangers' signing of free agent Adam Graves, September 12, 1991. Traded to **New Jersey** by **Edmonton** for David Maley, January 12, 1992. Traded to **Ottawa** by **New Jersey** with Craig Billington and New Jersey's fourth round choice (Cosmo Dupaul) in 1993 Entry Draft for Peter Sidorkiewicz and future considerations (Mike Peluso, June 26, 1993), June 20, 1993.

MALONE, SCOTT NYR

Defense. Shoots left. 6', 195 lbs. Born, Boston, MA, January 16, 1971.
(Toronto's 10th choice, 220th overall, in 1990 Entry Draft).

			Regular Season					Playoffs				
Season	Club	Lea	GP	G	A	TP	PIM	GP	G	A	TP	PIM
1991-92	N. Hampshire	H.E.	27	0	4	4	52	....	....	....	....	....
1992-93	N. Hampshire	H.E.	36	5	6	11	96	....	....	....	....	....
1993-94a	N. Hampshire	H.E.	40	14	6	20	*162	....	....	....	....	....
1994-95	Birmingham	ECHL	8	1	4	5	36	....	....	....	....	....
	Binghamton	AHL	48	3	14	17	85	11	0	2	2	12

a Hockey East Second All-Star Team (1994)

Rights traded to **NY Rangers** by **Toronto** with Glenn Anderson and Toronto's fourth round choice (Alexander Korobolin) in 1994 Entry Draft for Mike Gartner, March 21, 1994.

MALTAIS, STEVE (MAHL-tay)

Left wing. Shoots left. 6'2", 205 lbs. Born, Arvida, Que., January 25, 1969.
(Washington's 2nd choice, 57th overall, in 1987 Entry Draft).

			Regular Season					Playoffs				
Season	Club	Lea	GP	G	A	TP	PIM	GP	G	A	TP	PIM
1986-87	Cornwall	OHL	65	32	12	44	29	5	0	0	0	2
1987-88	Cornwall	OHL	59	39	46	85	30	11	9	6	15	33
1988-89	Cornwall	OHL	58	53	70	123	67	18	14	16	30	16
	Fort Wayne	IHL	....	....	....	....	....	4	2	1	3	0
1989-90	**Washington**	**NHL**	**8**	**0**	**0**	**0**	**2**	**1**	**0**	**0**	**0**	**0**
	Baltimore	AHL	67	29	37	66	54	12	6	10	16	6
1990-91	**Washington**	**NHL**	**7**	**0**	**0**	**0**	**2**	....	....	....	....	....
	Baltimore	AHL	73	36	43	79	97	6	1	4	5	10
1991-92	**Minnesota**	**NHL**	**12**	**2**	**1**	**3**	**2**	....	....	....	....	....
	Kalamazoo	IHL	48	25	31	56	51	....	....	....	....	....
	Halifax	AHL	10	3	3	6	0	....	....	....	....	....
1992-93	**Tampa Bay**	**NHL**	**63**	**7**	**13**	**20**	**35**	....	....	....	....	....
	Atlanta	IHL	16	14	10	24	22	....	....	....	....	....
1993-94	**Detroit**	**NHL**	**4**	**0**	**1**	**1**	**0**	....	....	....	....	....
	Adirondack	AHL	73	35	49	84	79	12	5	11	16	14
1994-95a	Chicago	IHL	79	*57	40	97	145	3	1	1	2	0
	NHL Totals		**94**	**9**	**15**	**24**	**41**	**1**	**0**	**0**	**0**	**0**

a IHL First All-Star Team (1995)

Traded to **Minnesota** by **Washington** with Trent Klatt for Shawn Chambers, June 21, 1991. Traded to **Quebec** by **Minnesota** for Kip Miller, March 8, 1992. Claimed by **Tampa Bay** from **Quebec** in Expansion Draft, June 18, 1992. Traded to **Detroit** by **Tampa Bay** for Dennis Vial, June 8, 1993.

MALTBY, KIRK

Right wing. Shoots right. 6', 180 lbs. Born, Guelph, Ont., December 22, 1972.
(Edmonton's 4th choice, 65th overall, in 1992 Entry Draft).

			Regular Season					Playoffs				
Season	Club	Lea	GP	G	A	TP	PIM	GP	G	A	TP	PIM
1989-90	Owen Sound	OHL	61	12	15	27	90	12	1	6	7	15
1990-91	Owen Sound	OHL	66	34	32	66	100	....	....	....	....	....
1991-92	Owen Sound	OHL	66	50	41	91	99	5	3	3	6	18
1992-93	Cape Breton	AHL	73	22	23	45	130	16	3	3	6	45
1993-94	**Edmonton**	**NHL**	**68**	**11**	**8**	**19**	**74**	....	....	....	....	....
1994-95	**Edmonton**	**NHL**	**47**	**8**	**3**	**11**	**49**	....	....	....	....	....
	NHL Totals		**115**	**19**	**11**	**30**	**123**	....	....	....	....	....

MANDERVILLE, KENT TOR.

Left wing. Shoots left. 6'3", 207 lbs. Born, Edmonton, Alta., April 12, 1971.
(Calgary's 1st choice, 24th overall, in 1989 Entry Draft).

			Regular Season					Playoffs				
Season	Club	Lea	GP	G	A	TP	PIM	GP	G	A	TP	PIM
1989-90	Cornell	ECAC	26	11	15	26	28	....	....	....	....	....
1990-91	Cornell	ECAC	28	17	14	31	60	....	....	....	....	....
	Cdn. National	....	3	1	2	3	0	....	....	....	....	....
1991-92	Cdn. National	....	63	16	24	40	78	....	....	....	....	....
	Cdn. Olympic	....	8	1	2	3	0	....	....	....	....	....
	Toronto	**NHL**	**15**	**0**	**4**	**4**	**0**	....	....	....	....	....
	St. John's	AHL	....	....	....	....	....	12	5	9	14	14
1992-93	**Toronto**	**NHL**	**18**	**1**	**1**	**2**	**17**	**18**	**1**	**0**	**1**	**8**
	St. John's	AHL	56	19	28	47	86	2	0	2	2	0
1993-94	**Toronto**	**NHL**	**67**	**7**	**9**	**16**	**63**	**12**	**1**	**0**	**1**	**4**
1994-95	**Toronto**	**NHL**	**36**	**0**	**1**	**1**	**22**	**7**	**0**	**0**	**0**	**6**
	NHL Totals		**136**	**8**	**15**	**23**	**102**	**37**	**2**	**0**	**2**	**18**

Traded to **Toronto** by **Calgary** with Doug Gilmour, Jamie Macoun, Rick Wamsley and Ric Nattress for Gary Leeman, Alexander Godynyuk, Jeff Reese, Michel Petit and Craig Berube, January 2, 1992.

MANELUK, MIKE ANA.

Left wing. Shoots right. 5'11", 188 lbs. Born, Winnipeg, Man., October 1, 1973.

			Regular Season					Playoffs				
Season	Club	Lea	GP	G	A	TP	PIM	GP	G	A	TP	PIM
1991-92	Brandon	WHL	68	23	30	53	102	....	....	....	....	....
1992-93	Brandon	WHL	72	36	51	87	75	4	2	1	3	2
1993-94	Brandon	WHL	63	50	47	97	112	13	11	3	14	23
	San Diego	IHL	....	....	....	....	....	1	0	0	0	0
1994-95	Cdn. National	....	44	36	24	60	34	....	....	....	....	....
	San Diego	IHL	10	0	1	1	4	....	....	....	....	....

Signed as a free agent by **Anaheim**, January 28, 1994.

MANLOW, ERIC CHI.

Center. Shoots left. 6', 190 lbs. Born, Belleville, Ont., April 7, 1975.
(Chicago's 2nd choice, 50th overall, in 1993 Entry Draft).

			Regular Season					Playoffs				
Season	Club	Lea	GP	G	A	TP	PIM	GP	G	A	TP	PIM
1991-92	Kitchener	OHL	59	26	21	47	31	14	2	5	7	10
1992-93	Kitchener	OHL	53	12	20	32	17	4	0	1	1	2
1993-94	Kitchener	OHL	49	28	32	60	25	3	0	1	1	4
1994-95	Kitchener	OHL	44	25	29	54	26	....	....	....	....	....
	Detroit	OHL	16	4	16	20	11	21	11	10	21	18

MANN, CAMERON BOS.

Right wing. Shoots right. 6', 190 lbs. Born, Thompson, Man., April 20, 1977.
(Boston's 5th choice, 99th overall, in 1995 Entry Draft).

			Regular Season					Playoffs				
Season	Club	Lea	GP	G	A	TP	PIM	GP	G	A	TP	PIM
1993-94	Peterborough	Jr. A	16	3	14	17	23	....	....	....	....	....
1994-95	Peterborough	OHL	64	19	24	43	40	11	3	8	11	4

MANSON, DAVE — WPG.

Defense. Shoots left. 6'2", 202 lbs. Born, Prince Albert, Sask., January 27, 1967.
(Chicago's 1st choice, 11th overall, in 1985 Entry Draft).

			Regular Season					Playoffs				
Season	Club	Lea	GP	G	A	TP	PIM	GP	G	A	TP	PIM
1983-84	Prince Albert	WHL	70	2	7	9	233	5	0	0	0	4
1984-85	Prince Albert	WHL	72	8	30	38	247	13	1	0	1	34
1985-86	Prince Albert	WHL	70	14	34	48	177	20	1	8	9	63
1986-87	**Chicago**	**NHL**	**63**	**1**	**8**	**9**	**146**	**3**	**0**	**0**	**0**	**10**
1987-88	**Chicago**	**NHL**	**54**	**1**	**6**	**7**	**185**	**5**	**0**	**0**	**0**	**27**
	Saginaw	IHL	6	0	3	3	37					
1988-89	**Chicago**	**NHL**	**79**	**18**	**36**	**54**	**352**	**16**	**0**	**8**	**8**	**84**
1989-90	**Chicago**	**NHL**	**59**	**5**	**23**	**28**	**301**	**20**	**2**	**4**	**6**	**46**
1990-91	**Chicago**	**NHL**	**75**	**14**	**15**	**29**	**191**	**6**	**0**	**1**	**1**	**36**
1991-92	**Edmonton**	**NHL**	**79**	**15**	**32**	**47**	**220**	**16**	**3**	**9**	**12**	**44**
1992-93	**Edmonton**	**NHL**	**83**	**15**	**30**	**45**	**210**					
1993-94	**Edmonton**	**NHL**	**57**	**3**	**13**	**16**	**140**					
	Winnipeg	**NHL**	**13**	**1**	**4**	**5**	**51**					
1994-95	**Winnipeg**	**NHL**	**44**	**3**	**15**	**18**	**139**					
	NHL Totals		**606**	**76**	**182**	**258**	**1935**	**66**	**5**	**22**	**27**	**247**

Played in NHL All-Star Game (1989, 1993)

Traded to **Edmonton** by **Chicago** with Chicago's third round choice (Kirk Maltby) in 1992 Entry Draft for Steve Smith, October 2, 1991. Traded to **Winnipeg** by **Edmonton** with St. Louis' sixth round choice (previously acquired by Edmonton — Winnipeg selected Chris Kibermanis) in 1994 Entry Draft for Boris Mironov, Mats Lindgren, Winnipeg's first round choice (Jason Bonsignore) in 1994 Entry Draft and Florida's fourth round choice (previously acquired by Winnipeg — Edmonton selected Adam Copeland) in 1994 Entry Draft, March 15, 1994.

MARA, ROB — CHI.

Right wing. Shoots right. 6'1", 175 lbs. Born, Boston, MA, September 25, 1975.
(Chicago's 11th choice, 263rd overall, in 1994 Entry Draft).

			Regular Season					Playoffs				
Season	Club	Lea	GP	G	A	TP	PIM	GP	G	A	TP	PIM
1993-94	Belmont Hill	HS	28	18	28	46						
1994-95	Colgate	ECAC	33	6	8	14	33					

MARCHANT, TERRY (mahr-SHAHNT) — EDM.

Left wing. Shoots left. 6'2", 205 lbs. Born, Buffalo, NY, February 24, 1976.
(Edmonton's 9th choice, 136th overall, in 1994 Entry Draft).

			Regular Season					Playoffs				
Season	Club	Lea	GP	G	A	TP	PIM	GP	G	A	TP	PIM
1993-94	Niagara	NAJHL	42	27	40	67	43					
1994-95	Lake Superior	CCHA	23	2	5	7	12					

MARCHANT, TODD (mahr-SHAHNT) — EDM.

Center. Shoots left. 6', 180 lbs. Born, Buffalo, NY, August 12, 1973.
(NY Rangers' 8th choice, 164th overall, in 1993 Entry Draft).

			Regular Season					Playoffs				
Season	Club	Lea	GP	G	A	TP	PIM	GP	G	A	TP	PIM
1991-92	Clarkson	ECAC	32	20	12	32	32					
1992-93a	Clarkson	ECAC	33	18	28	46	38					
1993-94	U.S. National	....	59	28	39	67	48					
	U.S. Olympic	....	8	1	1	2	6					
	NY Rangers	**NHL**	**1**	**0**	**0**	**0**	**0**					
	Binghamton	AHL	8	2	7	9	6					
	Edmonton	**NHL**	**3**	**0**	**1**	**1**	**2**					
	Cape Breton	AHL	3	1	4	5	2	5	1	1	2	0
1994-95	Cape Breton	AHL	38	22	25	47	25					
	Edmonton	**NHL**	**45**	**13**	**14**	**27**	**32**					
	NHL Totals		**49**	**13**	**15**	**28**	**34**					

a ECAC Second All-Star Team (1993)

Traded to **Edmonton** by **NY Rangers** for Craig MacTavish, March 21, 1994.

MARCHMENT, BRYAN — EDM.

Defense. Shoots left. 6'1", 205 lbs. Born, Scarborough, Ont., May 1, 1969.
(Winnipeg's 1st choice, 16th overall, in 1987 Entry Draft).

			Regular Season					Playoffs				
Season	Club	Lea	GP	G	A	TP	PIM	GP	G	A	TP	PIM
1985-86	Belleville	OHL	57	5	15	20	225	21	0	7	7	83
1986-87	Belleville	OHL	52	6	38	44	238	6	0	4	4	17
1987-88	Belleville	OHL	56	7	51	58	200	6	1	3	4	19
1988-89	**Winnipeg**	**NHL**	**2**	**0**	**0**	**0**	**2**					
a	Belleville	OHL	43	14	36	50	118	5	0	1	1	12
1989-90	**Winnipeg**	**NHL**	**7**	**0**	**2**	**2**	**28**					
	Moncton	AHL	56	4	19	23	217					
1990-91	**Winnipeg**	**NHL**	**28**	**2**	**2**	**4**	**91**					
	Moncton	AHL	33	2	11	13	101					
1991-92	**Chicago**	**NHL**	**58**	**5**	**10**	**15**	**168**	**16**	**1**	**0**	**1**	**36**
1992-93	**Chicago**	**NHL**	**78**	**5**	**15**	**20**	**313**	**4**	**0**	**0**	**0**	**12**
1993-94	**Chicago**	**NHL**	**13**	**1**	**4**	**5**	**42**					
	Hartford	**NHL**	**42**	**3**	**7**	**10**	**124**					
1994-95	**Edmonton**	**NHL**	**40**	**1**	**5**	**6**	**184**					
	NHL Totals		**268**	**17**	**45**	**62**	**952**	**20**	**1**	**0**	**1**	**48**

a OHL Second All-Star Team (1989)

Traded to **Chicago** by **Winnipeg** with Chris Norton for Troy Murray and Warren Rychel, July 22, 1991. Traded to **Hartford** by **Chicago** with Steve Larmer for Eric Weinrich and Patrick Poulin, November 2, 1993. Acquired by **Edmonton** from **Hartford** as compensation for Hartford's signing of free agent Steven Rice, August 30, 1994.

MARHA, JOSEF (MAHR-hah) — COL.

Center. Shoots left. 6', 176 lbs. Born, Havlickuv Brod, Czech., June 2, 1976.
(Quebec's 3rd choice, 35th overall, in 1994 Entry Draft).

			Regular Season					Playoffs				
Season	Club	Lea	GP	G	A	TP	PIM	GP	G	A	TP	PIM
1992-93	Dukla Jihlava	Czech.	7	2	2	4						
1993-94	Dukla Jihlava	Czech.	41	7	2	9		3	0	1	1	
1994-95	Dukla Jihlava	Czech.	35	3	7	10	6					

MARINUCCI, CHRIS (mair-ihn-OO-chee) — NYI

Center. Shoots left. 6', 175 lbs. Born, Grand Rapids, MN, December 29, 1971.
(NY Islanders' 4th choice, 90th overall, in 1990 Entry Draft).

			Regular Season					Playoffs				
Season	Club	Lea	GP	G	A	TP	PIM	GP	G	A	TP	PIM
1990-91	Minn.-Duluth	WCHA	36	6	10	16	20					
1991-92	Minn.-Duluth	WCHA	37	6	13	19	41					
1992-93a	Minn. Duluth	WCHA	40	35	42	77	52					
1993-94bcd	Minn.-Duluth	WCHA	38	*30	31	61	65					
1994-95	Denver	IHL	74	29	40	69	42	14	3	4	7	12
	NY Islanders	**NHL**	**12**	**1**	**4**	**5**	**2**					
	NHL Totals		**12**	**1**	**4**	**5**	**2**					

a WCHA Second All-Star Team (1993)
b WCHA First All-Star Team (1994)
c NCAA West First All-American Team (1994)
d Won Hobey Baker Memorial Award (Top U.S. Collegiate Player) (1994)

MARK, GORDON

Defense. Shoots right. 6'4", 218 lbs. Born, Edmonton, Alta., September 10, 1964.
(New Jersey's 4th choice, 108th overall, in 1983 Entry Draft).

			Regular Season					Playoffs				
Season	Club	Lea	GP	G	A	TP	PIM	GP	G	A	TP	PIM
1982-83	Kamloops	WHL	71	12	20	32	135	7	1	1	2	8
1983-84	Kamloops	WHL	67	12	30	42	202	17	2	6	8	27
1984-85	Kamloops	WHL	32	11	23	34	68	7	1	2	3	10
1985-86	Maine	AHL	77	9	13	22	134	5	0	1	1	9
1986-87	**New Jersey**	**NHL**	**36**	**3**	**5**	**8**	**82**					
	Maine	AHL	29	4	10	14	66					
1987-88	**New Jersey**	**NHL**	**19**	**0**	**2**	**2**	**27**					
	Utica	AHL	50	5	21	26	96					
1988-89	Stony Plain	Sr.				UNAVAILABLE						
1989-90	Stony Plain	Sr.				UNAVAILABLE						
1990-91	Stony Plain	Sr.				UNAVAILABLE						
1991-92	Stony Plain	Sr.				UNAVAILABLE						
1992-93	Cape Breton	AHL	60	3	21	24	78	16	1	7	8	20
1993-94	Cape Breton	AHL	49	11	20	31	116	5	0	2	2	26
	Edmonton	**NHL**	**12**	**0**	**1**	**1**	**43**					
1994-95	**Edmonton**	**NHL**	**18**	**0**	**2**	**2**	**35**					
	NHL Totals		**85**	**3**	**10**	**13**	**187**					

Signed as a free agent by **Edmonton**, February 1, 1994.

MARLEAU, DOMINIC (mahr-LOH) — DAL.

Defense. Shoots right. 6'2", 195 lbs. Born, Lasalle, Que., February 11, 1977.
(Dallas' 6th choice, 141st overall, in 1995 Entry Draft).

			Regular Season					Playoffs				
Season	Club	Lea	GP	G	A	TP	PIM	GP	G	A	TP	PIM
1993-94	Victoriaville	QMJHL	67	2	10	12	45	5	0	1	1	4
1994-95	Victoriaville	QMJHL	63	3	13	16	78	3	0	0	0	11

MAROIS, DANIEL (mair-WAH)

Right wing. Shoots right. 6', 190 lbs. Born, Montreal, Que., October 3, 1968.
(Toronto's 2nd choice, 28th overall, in 1987 Entry Draft).

			Regular Season					Playoffs				
Season	Club	Lea	GP	G	A	TP	PIM	GP	G	A	TP	PIM
1985-86	Verdun	QMJHL	58	42	35	77	110	5	4	2	6	6
1986-87	Chicoutimi	QMJHL	40	22	26	48	143	16	7	14	21	25
1987-88	Verdun	QMJHL	67	52	36	88	153					
	Newmarket	AHL	8	4	4	8	4					
	Toronto	**NHL**						**3**	**1**	**0**	**1**	**0**
1988-89	**Toronto**	**NHL**	**76**	**31**	**23**	**54**	**76**					
1989-90	**Toronto**	**NHL**	**68**	**39**	**37**	**76**	**82**	**5**	**2**	**2**	**4**	**12**
1990-91	**Toronto**	**NHL**	**78**	**21**	**9**	**30**	**112**					
1991-92	**Toronto**	**NHL**	**63**	**15**	**11**	**26**	**76**					
	NY Islanders	**NHL**	**12**	**2**	**5**	**7**	**18**					
1992-93	**NY Islanders**	**NHL**	**28**	**2**	**5**	**7**	**35**					
	Capital Dist.	AHL	4	2	0	2	0					
1993-94	**Boston**	**NHL**	**22**	**7**	**3**	**10**	**18**	**11**	**0**	**1**	**1**	**16**
	Providence	AHL	6	1	2	3	6					
1994-95						DID NOT PLAY – INJURED						
	NHL Totals		**347**	**117**	**93**	**210**	**417**	**19**	**3**	**3**	**6**	**28**

Traded to **NY Islanders** by **Toronto** with Claude Loiselle for Ken Baumgartner and Dave McLlwain, March 10, 1992. Traded to **Boston** by **NY Islanders** for Boston's eighth round choice (Peter Hogardh) in 1994 Entry Draft, March 18, 1993.

MARSHALL, BOBBY — CGY.

Defense. Shoots left. 6'1", 190 lbs. Born, North York, Ont., April 11, 1972.
(Calgary's 6th choice, 129th overall, in 1991 Entry Draft).

			Regular Season					Playoffs				
Season	Club	Lea	GP	G	A	TP	PIM	GP	G	A	TP	PIM
1990-91	Miami-Ohio	CCHA	37	3	15	18	44					
1991-92	Miami-Ohio	CCHA	40	5	20	25	48					
1992-93ab	Miami-Ohio	CCHA	40	2	43	45	40					
1993-94a	Miami-Ohio	CCHA	38	3	24	27	76					
1994-95	Saint John	AHL	77	7	24	31	62	5	0	0	0	4

a CCHA Second All-Star Team (1993, 1994)
b NCAA West Second All-American Team (1993)

MARSHALL, GRANT — DAL.

Right wing. Shoots right. 6'1", 185 lbs. Born, Mississauga, Ont., June 9, 1973.
(Toronto's 2nd choice, 23rd overall, in 1992 Entry Draft).

			Regular Season					Playoffs				
Season	Club	Lea	GP	G	A	TP	PIM	GP	G	A	TP	PIM
1990-91	Ottawa	OHL	26	6	11	17	25	1	0	0	0	0
1991-92	Ottawa	OHL	61	32	51	83	132	11	6	11	17	11
1992-93	Ottawa	OHL	30	14	29	43	83					
	Newmarket	OHL	31	11	25	36	89	7	4	7	11	20
	St. John's	AHL	2	0	0	0	0	2	0	0	0	2
1993-94	St. John's	AHL	67	11	29	40	155	11	1	5	6	17
1994-95	Kalamazoo	IHL	61	17	29	46	96	16	9	3	12	27
	Dallas	**NHL**	**2**	**0**	**1**	**1**	**0**					
	NHL Totals		**2**	**0**	**1**	**1**	**0**					

Acquired by **Dallas** from **Toronto** with Peter Zezel as compensation for Toronto's signing of free agent Mike Craig, August 10, 1994.

MARSHALL, JASON — ANA.

Defense. Shoots right. 6'2", 195 lbs. Born, Cranbrook, B.C., February 22, 1971.
(St. Louis' 1st choice, 9th overall, in 1989 Entry Draft).

			Regular Season					Playoffs				
Season	Club	Lea	GP	G	A	TP	PIM	GP	G	A	TP	PIM
1988-89	Cdn. National	....	2	0	1	1	0	....	....	....	....	....
1989-90	Cdn. National	....	73	1	11	12	57	....	....	....	....	....
1990-91	Tri-Cities	WHL	59	10	34	44	236	7	1	2	3	20
	Peoria	IHL	....	....	....	....	....	18	0	1	1	48
1991-92	**St. Louis**	**NHL**	**2**	**1**	**0**	**1**	**4**	....	....	....	....	....
	Peoria	IHL	78	4	18	22	178	10	0	1	1	16
1992-93	Peoria	IHL	77	4	16	20	229	4	0	0	0	20
1993-94	Cdn. National	....	41	3	10	13	60	....	....	....	....	....
	Peoria	IHL	20	1	1	2	72	3	2	0	2	2
1994-95	San Diego	IHL	80	7	18	25	218	5	0	1	1	8
	Anaheim	**NHL**	**1**	**0**	**0**	**0**	**0**	....	....	....	....	....
	NHL Totals		**3**	**1**	**0**	**1**	**4**	....	....	....	....	....

Traded to **Anaheim** by **St. Louis** for Bill Houlder, August 29, 1994.

MARTIN, CRAIG — WPG.

Right wing. Shoots right. 6'2", 215 lbs. Born, Amherst, N.S., January 21, 1971.
(Winnipeg's 6th choice, 98th overall, in 1990 Entry Draft).

			Regular Season					Playoffs				
Season	Club	Lea	GP	G	A	TP	PIM	GP	G	A	TP	PIM
1989-90	Hull	QMJHL	66	14	31	45	299	11	2	1	3	65
1990-91	Hull	QMJHL	18	5	6	11	87	....	....	....	....	....
	St-Hyacinthe	QMJHL	36	8	9	17	166	....	....	....	....	....
1991-92	Moncton	AHL	11	1	1	2	70	....	....	....	....	....
	Fort Wayne	IHL	24	0	0	0	115	....	....	....	....	....
1992-93	Moncton	AHL	64	5	13	18	198	5	0	1	1	22
1993-94	Adirondack	AHL	76	15	24	39	297	12	2	2	4	63
1994-95	**Winnipeg**	**NHL**	**20**	**0**	**1**	**1**	**19**	....	....	....	....	....
	Springfield	AHL	6	0	1	1	21	....	....	....	....	....
	NHL Totals		**20**	**0**	**1**	**1**	**19**	....	....	....	....	....

Signed as a free agent by **Detroit**, July 28, 1993.

MARTIN, JUSTIN — L.A.

Right wing. Shoots right. 6'3", 210 lbs. Born, Syracuse, NY, May 1, 1975.
(Los Angeles' 8th choice, 172nd overall, in 1993 Entry Draft).

			Regular Season					Playoffs				
Season	Club	Lea	GP	G	A	TP	PIM	GP	G	A	TP	PIM
1993-94	Taft Prep.	HS	20	16	10	26	26	....	....	....	....	....
1994-95	Vermont	ECAC	23	4	2	6	20	....	....	....	....	....

MARTIN, MATT — TOR.

Defense. Shoots left. 6'3", 205 lbs. Born, Hamden, CT, April 30, 1971.
(Toronto's 4th choice, 66th overall, in 1989 Entry Draft).

			Regular Season					Playoffs				
Season	Club	Lea	GP	G	A	TP	PIM	GP	G	A	TP	PIM
1990-91	U. of Maine	H.E.	35	3	12	15	48	....	....	....	....	....
1991-92	U. of Maine	H.E.	30	4	14	18	46	....	....	....	....	....
1992-93	U. of Maine	H.E.	44	6	26	32	88	....	....	....	....	....
	St. John's	AHL	2	0	0	0	2	9	1	5	6	4
1993-94	U.S. National	....	39	7	8	15	127	....	....	....	....	....
	U.S. Olympic	....	8	0	2	2	8	....	....	....	....	....
	Toronto	**NHL**	**12**	**0**	**1**	**1**	**6**	....	....	....	....	....
	St. John's	AHL	12	1	5	6	9	11	1	5	6	33
1994-95	St. John's	AHL	49	2	16	18	54	....	....	....	....	....
	Toronto	**NHL**	**15**	**0**	**0**	**0**	**13**	....	....	....	....	....
	NHL Totals		**27**	**0**	**1**	**1**	**19**					

MARTIN, MIKE — NYR

Defense. Shoots right. 6'2", 204 lbs. Born, Stratford, Ont., October 27, 1976.
(NY Rangers' 2nd choice, 65th overall, in 1995 Entry Draft).

			Regular Season					Playoffs				
Season	Club	Lea	GP	G	A	TP	PIM	GP	G	A	TP	PIM
1992-93	Windsor	OHL	61	2	7	9	80	....	....	....	....	....
1993-94	Windsor	OHL	64	2	29	31	94	4	1	2	3	4
1994-95	Windsor	OHL	53	9	28	37	79	10	1	3	4	21

MARTINI, DARCY

Defense. Shoots left. 6'4", 220 lbs. Born, Castlegar, B.C., January 30, 1969.
(Edmonton's 8th choice, 162nd overall, in 1989 Entry Draft).

			Regular Season					Playoffs				
Season	Club	Lea	GP	G	A	TP	PIM	GP	G	A	TP	PIM
1988-89	Michigan Tech	WCHA	35	1	2	3	103	....	....	....	....	....
1989-90	Michigan Tech	WCHA	36	3	6	9	151	....	....	....	....	....
1990-91	Michigan Tech	WCHA	34	10	13	23	*184	....	....	....	....	....
1991-92	Michigan Tech	WCHA	17	5	13	18	58	....	....	....	....	....
1992-93	Cape Breton	AHL	47	1	6	7	36	2	0	1	1	0
	Wheeling	ECHL	6	0	2	2	2	....	....	....	....	....
1993-94	**Edmonton**	**NHL**	**2**	**0**	**0**	**0**	**0**	....	....	....	....	....
	Cape Breton	AHL	65	18	38	56	131	5	1	3	4	26
1994-95	Cape Breton	AHL	31	2	13	15	75	....	....	....	....	....
	Portland	AHL	22	3	6	9	28	....	....	....	....	....
	Minnesota	IHL	10	3	1	4	10	1	0	0	0	2
	NHL Totals		**2**	**0**	**0**	**0**	**0**					

MARTINS, STEVE — HFD.

Center. Shoots left. 5'9", 175 lbs. Born, Gatineau, Que., April 13, 1972.
(Hartford's 1st choice, 5th overall, in 1994 Supplemental Draft).

			Regular Season					Playoffs				
Season	Club	Lea	GP	G	A	TP	PIM	GP	G	A	TP	PIM
1991-92	Harvard	ECAC	20	13	14	27	26	....	....	....	....	....
1992-93	Harvard	ECAC	18	6	8	14	40	....	....	....	....	....
1993-94abc	Harvard	ECAC	32	25	35	60	*93	....	....	....	....	....
1994-95	Harvard	ECAC	28	15	23	38	93	....	....	....	....	....

a ECAC First All-Star Team (1994)
b NCAA East First All-American Team (1994)
c NCAA Final Four All-Tournament Team (1994)

MASTAD, MILT — (MIHZ-tahd) — BOS.

Defense. Shoots left. 6'3", 205 lbs. Born, Regina, Sask., March 5, 1975.
(Boston's 6th choice, 155th overall, in 1993 Entry Draft).

			Regular Season					Playoffs				
Season	Club	Lea	GP	G	A	TP	PIM	GP	G	A	TP	PIM
1992-93	Seattle	WHL	60	1	1	2	123	5	0	1	1	14
1993-94	Seattle	WHL	29	1	3	4	59	....	....	....	....	....
	Moose Jaw	WHL	41	2	8	10	74	....	....	....	....	....
1994-95	Moose Jaw	WHL	68	1	8	9	155	5	0	0	0	6

MATIER, MARK — COL.

Defense. Shoots left. 6'1", 209 lbs. Born, St. Catharines, Ont., December 14, 1973.
(Washington's 6th choice, 167th overall, in 1992 Entry Draft).

			Regular Season					Playoffs				
Season	Club	Lea	GP	G	A	TP	PIM	GP	G	A	TP	PIM
1991-92	S.S. Marie	OHL	46	0	5	5	15	19	3	5	8	14
1992-93	S.S. Marie	OHL	64	7	27	34	89	18	1	4	5	13
1993-94	Cornwall	AHL	67	1	16	17	100	3	0	0	0	4
1994-95	London	ColHL	37	3	12	15	107	5	0	0	0	10
	Cornwall	AHL	3	0	1	1	4	....	....	....	....	....

Traded to **Quebec** by **Washington** for Kevin Kaminski, June 15, 1993.

MATTE, CHRISTIAN — COL.

Right wing. Shoots right. 5'11", 166 lbs. Born, Hull, Que., January 20, 1975.
(Quebec's 8th choice, 153rd overall, in 1993 Entry Draft).

			Regular Season					Playoffs				
Season	Club	Lea	GP	G	A	TP	PIM	GP	G	A	TP	PIM
1992-93	Granby	QMJHL	68	17	36	53	59	....	....	....	....	....
1993-94a	Granby	QMJHL	59	50	47	97	103	7	5	5	10	12
	Cornwall	AHL	1	0	0	0	0	....	....	....	....	....
1994-95	Granby	QMJHL	66	50	66	116	86	13	11	7	18	12
	Cornwall	AHL	....	....	....	....	....	3	0	1	1	2

a QMJHL Second All-Star Team (1994)

MATTEAU, STEPHANE — (mah-TOH) — NYR

Left wing. Shoots left. 6'3", 210 lbs. Born, Rouyn-Noranda, Que., September 2, 1969.
(Calgary's 2nd choice, 25th overall, in 1987 Entry Draft).

			Regular Season					Playoffs				
Season	Club	Lea	GP	G	A	TP	PIM	GP	G	A	TP	PIM
1985-86	Hull	QMJHL	60	6	8	14	19	4	0	0	0	0
1986-87	Hull	QMJHL	69	27	48	75	113	8	3	7	10	8
1987-88	Hull	QMJHL	57	17	40	57	179	18	5	14	19	94
1988-89	Hull	QMJHL	59	44	45	89	202	9	8	6	14	30
	Salt Lake	IHL	....	....	....	....	....	9	0	4	4	13
1989-90	Salt Lake	IHL	81	23	35	58	130	10	6	3	9	38
1990-91	**Calgary**	**NHL**	**78**	**15**	**19**	**34**	**93**	**5**	**0**	**1**	**1**	**0**
1991-92	**Calgary**	**NHL**	**4**	**1**	**0**	**1**	**19**	....	....	....	....	....
	Chicago	**NHL**	**20**	**5**	**8**	**13**	**45**	**18**	**4**	**6**	**10**	**24**
1992-93	**Chicago**	**NHL**	**79**	**15**	**18**	**33**	**98**	**3**	**0**	**1**	**1**	**2**
1993-94	**Chicago**	**NHL**	**65**	**15**	**16**	**31**	**55**	....	....	....	....	....
	NY Rangers	**NHL**	**12**	**4**	**3**	**7**	**2**	**23**	**6**	**3**	**9**	**20**
1994-95	**NY Rangers**	**NHL**	**41**	**3**	**5**	**8**	**25**	**9**	**0**	**1**	**1**	**10**
	NHL Totals		**299**	**58**	**69**	**127**	**337**	**58**	**10**	**12**	**22**	**56**

Traded to **Chicago** by **Calgary** for Trent Yawney, December 16, 1991. Traded to **NY Rangers** by **Chicago** with Brian Noonan for Tony Amonte and the rights to Matt Oates, March 21, 1994.

MATTSSON, JESPER — CGY.

Center. Shoots right. 6', 185 lbs. Born, Malmo, Sweden, May 13, 1975.
(Calgary's 1st choice, 18th overall, in 1993 Entry Draft).

			Regular Season					Playoffs				
Season	Club	Lea	GP	G	A	TP	PIM	GP	G	A	TP	PIM
1991-92	Malmo	Swe.	24	0	1	1	2	....	....	....	....	....
1992-93	Malmo	Swe.	40	9	8	17	14	5	0	0	0	0
1993-94	Malmo	Swe.	40	3	6	9	14	9	1	2	3	2
1994-95	Malmo	Swe.	37	9	6	15	18	9	2	0	2	18

MATVICHUK, RICHARD — (MAT-vih-chuhk) — DAL.

Defense. Shoots left. 6'2", 190 lbs. Born, Edmonton, Alta., February 5, 1973.
(Minnesota's 1st choice, 8th overall, in 1991 Entry Draft).

			Regular Season					Playoffs				
Season	Club	Lea	GP	G	A	TP	PIM	GP	G	A	TP	PIM
1989-90	Saskatoon	WHL	56	8	24	32	126	10	2	8	10	16
1990-91	Saskatoon	WHL	68	13	36	49	117	....	....	....	....	....
1991-92a	Saskatoon	WHL	58	14	40	54	126	22	1	9	10	61
1992-93	**Minnesota**	**NHL**	**53**	**2**	**3**	**5**	**26**	....	....	....	....	....
	Kalamazoo	IHL	3	0	1	1	6	....	....	....	....	....
1993-94	**Dallas**	**NHL**	**25**	**0**	**3**	**3**	**22**	**7**	**1**	**1**	**2**	**12**
	Kalamazoo	IHL	43	8	17	25	84	....	....	....	....	....
1994-95	**Dallas**	**NHL**	**14**	**0**	**2**	**2**	**14**	**5**	**0**	**2**	**2**	**4**
	Kalamazoo	IHL	17	0	6	6	16	....	....	....	....	....
	NHL Totals		**92**	**2**	**8**	**10**	**62**	**12**	**1**	**3**	**4**	**16**

a WHL East First All-Star Team (1992)

MAY, ALAN

Right wing. Shoots right. 6'1", 200 lbs. Born, Swan Hills, Alta., January 14, 1965.

			Regular Season					Playoffs				
Season	Club	Lea	GP	G	A	TP	PIM	GP	G	A	TP	PIM
1985-86	Medicine Hat	WHL	6	1	0	1	25	....	....	....	....	....
	N. Westminster	WHL	32	8	9	17	81	....	....	....	....	....
1986-87	Springfield	AHL	4	0	2	2	11	....	....	....	....	....
	Carolina	ACHL	42	23	14	37	310	5	2	2	4	57
1987-88	**Boston**	**NHL**	**3**	**0**	**0**	**0**	**15**	....	....	....	....	....
	Maine	AHL	61	14	11	25	257	....	....	....	....	....
	Nova Scotia	AHL	13	4	1	5	54	4	0	0	0	51
1988-89	**Edmonton**	**NHL**	**3**	**1**	**0**	**1**	**7**	....	....	....	....	....
	Cape Breton	AHL	50	12	13	25	214	....	....	....	....	....
	New Haven	AHL	12	2	8	10	99	16	6	3	9	*105
1989-90	**Washington**	**NHL**	**77**	**7**	**10**	**17**	**339**	**15**	**0**	**0**	**0**	**37**
1990-91	**Washington**	**NHL**	**67**	**4**	**6**	**10**	**264**	**11**	**1**	**1**	**2**	**37**
1991-92	**Washington**	**NHL**	**75**	**6**	**9**	**15**	**221**	**7**	**0**	**0**	**0**	**0**
1992-93	**Washington**	**NHL**	**83**	**6**	**10**	**16**	**268**	**6**	**0**	**1**	**1**	**6**
1993-94	**Washington**	**NHL**	**43**	**4**	**7**	**11**	**97**	....	....	....	....	....
	Dallas	**NHL**	**8**	**1**	**0**	**1**	**18**	**1**	**0**	**0**	**0**	**0**
1994-95	**Dallas**	**NHL**	**27**	**1**	**1**	**2**	**106**	....	....	....	....	....
	Calgary	**NHL**	**7**	**1**	**2**	**3**	**13**	....	....	....	....	....
	NHL Totals		**393**	**31**	**45**	**76**	**1348**	**40**	**1**	**2**	**3**	**80**

Signed as a free agent by **Boston**, October 30, 1987. Traded to **Edmonton** by **Boston** for Moe Lemay, March 8, 1988. Traded to **Los Angeles** by **Edmonton** with Jim Wiemer for Brian Wilks and John English, March 7, 1989. Traded to **Washington** by **Los Angeles** for Washington's fifth round choice (Thomas Newman) in 1989 Entry Draft, June 17, 1989. Traded to **Dallas** by **Washington** with Washington's seventh round choice (Jeff Dewar) in 1995 Entry Draft for Jim Johnson, March 21, 1994. Traded to **Calgary** by **Dallas** for Calgary's eighth round choice (Sergei Luchinkin) in 1995 Entry Draft, April 7, 1995.

MAY, BRAD — BUF.

Left wing. Shoots left. 6'1", 210 lbs. Born, Toronto, Ont., November 29, 1971.
(Buffalo's 1st choice, 14th overall, in 1990 Entry Draft).

			Regular Season					Playoffs				
Season	Club	Lea	GP	G	A	TP	PIM	GP	G	A	TP	PIM
1988-89	Niagara Falls	OHL	65	8	14	22	304	17	0	1	1	55
1989-90a	Niagara Falls	OHL	61	32	58	90	223	16	9	13	22	64
1990-91a	Niagara Falls	OHL	34	37	32	69	93	14	11	14	25	53
1991-92	**Buffalo**	**NHL**	**69**	**11**	**6**	**17**	**309**	**7**	**1**	**4**	**5**	**2**
1992-93	**Buffalo**	**NHL**	**82**	**13**	**13**	**26**	**242**	**8**	**1**	**1**	**2**	**14**
1993-94	**Buffalo**	**NHL**	**84**	**18**	**27**	**45**	**171**	**7**	**0**	**2**	**2**	**9**
1994-95	**Buffalo**	**NHL**	**33**	**3**	**3**	**6**	**87**	**4**	**0**	**0**	**0**	**2**
	NHL Totals		**268**	**45**	**49**	**94**	**809**	**26**	**2**	**7**	**9**	**27**

a OHL Second All-Star Team (1990, 1991)

MAYER, DEREK

Defense. Shoots right. 6', 200 lbs. Born, Rossland, B.C., May 21, 1967.
(Detroit's 3rd choice, 43rd overall, in 1986 Entry Draft).

			Regular Season					Playoffs				
Season	Club	Lea	GP	G	A	TP	PIM	GP	G	A	TP	PIM
1985-86	Denver	WCHA	44	2	7	9	42	....	....	....	....	....
1986-87	Denver	WCHA	38	5	17	22	87	....	....	....	....	....
1987-88	Denver	WCHA	34	5	16	21	82	....	....	....	....	....
1988-89	Cdn. National	....	58	3	13	16	81	....	....	....	....	....
1989-90	Adirondack	AHL	62	4	26	30	56	5	0	6	6	4
1990-91	San Diego	IHL	31	9	24	33	31	....	....	....	....	....
	Adirondack	AHL	21	4	9	13	20	2	0	1	1	0
1991-92	Adirondack	AHL	25	4	11	15	31	....	....	....	....	....
	San Diego	IHL	30	7	16	23	47	4	0	0	0	20
1992-93	Cdn. National	....	64	12	28	40	108	....	....	....	....	....
1993-94	Cdn. National	....	49	4	15	19	61	....	....	....	....	....
	Cdn. Olympic	....	8	1	2	3	18	....	....	....	....	....
	Ottawa	**NHL**	**17**	**2**	**2**	**4**	**8**	....	....	....	....	....
1994-95	Atlanta	IHL	55	7	17	24	77	5	1	1	2	10
	NHL Totals		**17**	**2**	**2**	**4**	**8**	....	....	....	....	....

Signed as a free agent by **Ottawa**, March 4, 1994.

MAYERS, JAMAL — ST.L.

Center. Shoots right. 6', 190 lbs. Born, Toronto, Ont., October 24, 1974.
(St. Louis' 3rd choice, 89th overall, in 1993 Entry Draft).

			Regular Season					Playoffs				
Season	Club	Lea	GP	G	A	TP	PIM	GP	G	A	TP	PIM
1992-93	W. Michigan	CCHA	38	8	17	25	26	....	....	....	....	....
1993-94	W. Michigan	CCHA	40	17	32	49	40	....	....	....	....	....
1994-95	W. Michigan	CCHA	39	13	32	45	40	....	....	....	....	....

MAZUR, JAY — (MAY-zuhr)

Center/Right wing. Shoots right. 6'2", 205 lbs. Born, Hamilton, Ont., January 22, 1965.
(Vancouver's 12th choice, 230th overall, in 1983 Entry Draft).

			Regular Season					Playoffs				
Season	Club	Lea	GP	G	A	TP	PIM	GP	G	A	TP	PIM
1983-84	Maine	H.E.	34	14	9	23	14	....	....	....	....	....
1984-85	Maine	H.E.	31	0	6	6	20	....	....	....	....	....
1985-86	Maine	H.E.	34	5	7	12	18	....	....	....	....	....
1986-87	Maine	H.E.	39	16	10	26	61	....	....	....	....	....
1987-88	Flint	IHL	39	17	11	28	28	....	....	....	....	....
	Fredericton	AHL	31	14	6	20	28	15	4	2	6	38
1988-89	**Vancouver**	**NHL**	**1**	**0**	**0**	**0**	**0**	....	....	....	....	....
	Milwaukee	IHL	73	33	31	64	86	11	6	5	11	2
1989-90	**Vancouver**	**NHL**	**5**	**0**	**0**	**0**	**4**	....	....	....	....	....
	Milwaukee	IHL	70	20	27	47	63	6	3	0	3	6
1990-91	**Vancouver**	**NHL**	**36**	**11**	**7**	**18**	**14**	**6**	**0**	**1**	**1**	**8**
	Milwaukee	IHL	7	2	3	5	21	....	....	....	....	....
1991-92	**Vancouver**	**NHL**	**5**	**0**	**0**	**0**	**2**	....	....	....	....	....
	Milwaukee	IHL	56	17	20	37	49	5	2	3	5	0
1992-93	Hamilton	AHL	59	21	17	38	30	....	....	....	....	....
1993-94	Hamilton	AHL	78	40	55	95	40	4	2	2	4	4
1994-95	Detroit	IHL	64	23	27	50	64	1	0	1	1	2
	NHL Totals		**47**	**11**	**7**	**18**	**20**	**6**	**0**	**1**	**1**	**8**

McALLISTER, CHRIS — VAN.

Defense. Shoots left. 6'7", 238 lbs. Born, Saskatoon, Sask., June 16, 1975.
(Vancouver's 2nd choice, 40th overall, in 1995 Entry Draft).

			Regular Season					Playoffs				
Season	Club	Lea	GP	G	A	TP	PIM	GP	G	A	TP	PIM
1993-94	Saskatoon	WHL	2	0	0	0	5	....	....	....	....	....
1994-95	Saskatoon	WHL	65	2	8	10	134	10	0	0	0	28

McALPINE, CHRIS — N.J.

Defense. Shoots right. 6', 190 lbs. Born, Roseville, MN, December 1, 1971.
(New Jersey's 10th choice, 137th overall, in 1990 Entry Draft).

			Regular Season					Playoffs				
Season	Club	Lea	GP	G	A	TP	PIM	GP	G	A	TP	PIM
1990-91	U. Minnesota	WCHA	38	7	9	16	112	....	....	....	....	....
1991-92	U. Minnesota	WCHA	39	3	9	12	126	....	....	....	....	....
1992-93	U. Minnesota	WCHA	41	14	9	23	82	....	....	....	....	....
1993-94ab	U. Minnesota	WCHA	36	12	18	30	121	....	....	....	....	....
1994-95	Albany	AHL	48	4	18	22	49	....	....	....	....	....
	New Jersey	**NHL**	**24**	**0**	**3**	**3**	**17**	....	....	....	....	....
	NHL Totals		**24**	**0**	**3**	**3**	**17**	....	....	....	....	....

a WCHA First All-Star Team (1994)
b NCAA West Second All-American Team (1994)

McAMMOND, DEAN — EDM.

Center. Shoots left. 5'11", 185 lbs. Born, Grand Cache, Alta., June 15, 1973.
(Chicago's 1st choice, 22nd overall, in 1991 Entry Draft).

			Regular Season					Playoffs				
Season	Club	Lea	GP	G	A	TP	PIM	GP	G	A	TP	PIM
1989-90	Prince Albert	WHL	53	11	11	22	49	14	2	3	5	18
1990-91	Prince Albert	WHL	71	33	35	68	108	2	0	1	1	6
1991-92	**Chicago**	**NHL**	**5**	**0**	**2**	**2**	**0**	**3**	**0**	**0**	**0**	**2**
	Prince Albert	WHL	63	37	54	91	189	10	12	11	23	26
1992-93	Prince Albert	WHL	30	19	29	48	44	....	....	....	....	....
	Swift Current	WHL	18	10	13	23	24	17	*16	19	35	20
1993-94	**Edmonton**	**NHL**	**45**	**6**	**21**	**27**	**16**	....	....	....	....	....
	Cape Breton	AHL	28	9	12	21	38	....	....	....	....	....
1994-95	**Edmonton**	**NHL**	**6**	**0**	**0**	**0**	**0**	....	....	....	....	....
	NHL Totals		**56**	**6**	**23**	**29**	**16**	**3**	**0**	**0**	**0**	**2**

Traded to **Edmonton** by **Chicago** with Igor Kravchuk for Joe Murphy, February 24, 1993.

McBAIN, JASON — HFD.

Defense. Shoots left. 6'2", 178 lbs. Born, Ilion, NY, April 12, 1974.
(Hartford's 5th choice, 81st overall, in 1992 Entry Draft).

			Regular Season					Playoffs				
Season	Club	Lea	GP	G	A	TP	PIM	GP	G	A	TP	PIM
1990-91	Lethbridge	WHL	52	2	7	9	39	1	0	0	0	0
1991-92	Lethbridge	WHL	13	0	1	1	12	....	....	....	....	....
	Portland	WHL	54	9	23	32	95	6	1	0	1	13
1992-93	Portland	WHL	71	9	35	44	76	16	2	12	14	14
1993-94	Portland	WHL	63	15	51	66	86	10	2	7	9	14
1994-95	Springfield	AHL	77	16	28	44	92	....	....	....	....	....

McBAIN, MIKE — T.B.

Defense. Shoots left. 6'1", 191 lbs. Born, Kimberley, B.C., January 12, 1977.
(Tampa Bay's 2nd choice, 30th overall, in 1995 Entry Draft).

			Regular Season					Playoffs				
Season	Club	Lea	GP	G	A	TP	PIM	GP	G	A	TP	PIM
1993-94	Red Deer	WHL	58	4	13	17	41	4	0	0	0	0
1994-95	Red Deer	WHL	68	6	28	34	55	....	....	....	....	....

McBEAN, WAYNE — PIT.

Defense. Shoots left. 6'2", 185 lbs. Born, Calgary, Alta., February 21, 1969.
(Los Angeles' 1st choice, 4th overall, in 1987 Entry Draft).

			Regular Season					Playoffs				
Season	Club	Lea	GP	G	A	TP	PIM	GP	G	A	TP	PIM
1985-86	Medicine Hat	WHL	67	1	14	15	73	25	1	5	6	36
1986-87ab	Medicine Hat	WHL	71	12	41	53	163	20	2	8	10	40
1987-88	**Los Angeles**	**NHL**	**27**	**0**	**1**	**1**	**26**	....	....	....	....	....
	Medicine Hat	WHL	30	15	30	45	48	16	6	17	23	50
1988-89	**Los Angeles**	**NHL**	**33**	**0**	**5**	**5**	**23**	....	....	....	....	....
	New Haven	AHL	7	1	1	2	2	....	....	....	....	....
	NY Islanders	**NHL**	**19**	**0**	**1**	**1**	**12**	....	....	....	....	....
1989-90	**NY Islanders**	**NHL**	**5**	**0**	**1**	**1**	**2**	**2**	**1**	**1**	**2**	**0**
	Springfield	AHL	58	6	33	39	48	17	4	11	15	31
1990-91	**NY Islanders**	**NHL**	**52**	**5**	**14**	**19**	**47**	....	....	....	....	....
	Capital Dist.	AHL	22	9	9	18	19	....	....	....	....	....
1991-92	**NY Islanders**	**NHL**	**25**	**2**	**4**	**6**	**18**	....	....	....	....	....
1992-93	Capital Dist.	AHL	20	1	9	10	35	3	0	1	1	9
1993-94	**NY Islanders**	**NHL**	**19**	**1**	**4**	**5**	**16**	....	....	....	....	....
	Salt Lake	IHL	5	0	6	6	2	....	....	....	....	....
	Winnipeg	**NHL**	**31**	**2**	**9**	**11**	**24**	....	....	....	....	....
1994-95					DID NOT PLAY – INJURED							
	NHL Totals		**211**	**10**	**39**	**49**	**168**	**2**	**1**	**1**	**2**	**0**

a WHL East All-Star Team (1987)
b Won Stafford Smythe Memorial Trophy (Memorial Cup Tournament MVP) (1987)

Traded to **NY Islanders** by **Los Angeles** with Mark Fitzpatrick and future considerations (Doug Crossman, May 23, 1989) for Kelly Hrudey, February 22, 1989. Traded to **Winnipeg** by **NY Islanders** for Yan Kaminsky, February 1, 1994. Claimed by **Pittsburgh** from **Winnipeg** in NHL Waiver Draft, January 18, 1995.

McCABE, BRYAN — NYI

Defense. Shoots left. 6'1", 200 lbs. Born, St. Catharines, Ont., June 8, 1975.
(NY Islanders' 2nd choice, 40th overall, in 1993 Entry Draft).

			Regular Season					Playoffs				
Season	Club	Lea	GP	G	A	TP	PIM	GP	G	A	TP	PIM
1991-92	Medicine Hat	WHL	68	6	24	30	157	4	0	0	0	6
1992-93	Medicine Hat	WHL	14	0	13	13	83	....	....	....	....	....
a	Spokane	WHL	46	3	44	47	134	6	1	5	6	28
1993-94	Spokane	WHL	64	22	62	84	218	3	0	4	4	4
1994-95	Spokane	WHL	42	14	39	53	115	....	....	....	....	....
bc	Brandon	WHL	20	6	10	16	38	18	4	13	17	59

a WHL West Second All-Star Team (1993)
b WHL East First All-Star Team (1995)
c Memorial Cup All-Star Team (1995)

McCABE, SCOTT — N.J.

Defense. Shoots left. 6'4", 189 lbs. Born, St. Clair Shores, MI, May 28, 1974.
(New Jersey's 4th choice, 94th overall, in 1992 Entry Draft).

			Regular Season					Playoffs				
Season	Club	Lea	GP	G	A	TP	PIM	GP	G	A	TP	PIM
1992-93	Lake Superior	CCHA				DID NOT PLAY						
1993-94	Lake Superior	CCHA	18	3	5	8	14	....	....	....	....	....
1994-95	Lake Superior	CCHA	6	0	0	0	7	....	....	....	....	....

McCAMBRIDGE, KEITH — CGY.

Defense. Shoots left. 6'2", 205 lbs. Born, Thompson, Man., February 1, 1974.
(Calgary's 10th choice, 201st overall, in 1994 Entry Draft).

			Regular Season					Playoffs				
Season	Club	Lea	GP	G	A	TP	PIM	GP	G	A	TP	PIM
1991-92	Swift Current	WHL	72	1	4	5	84	8	0	0	0	2
1992-93	Swift Current	WHL	70	0	6	6	87	17	0	1	1	27
1993-94	Swift Current	WHL	71	0	10	10	179	7	0	0	0	4
1994-95	Swift Current	WHL	48	5	7	12	120	....	....	....	....	....
	Kamloops	WHL	21	0	6	6	90	21	0	5	5	49

McCANN, SEAN — FLA.

Defense. Shoots right. 6', 195 lbs. Born, North York, Ont., September 18, 1971.
(Florida's 1st choice, 1st overall, in 1994 Supplemental Draft).

			Regular Season					Playoffs				
Season	Club	Lea	GP	G	A	TP	PIM	GP	G	A	TP	PIM
1990-91	Harvard	ECAC	28	2	9	11	88	....	....	....	....	....
1991-92	Harvard	ECAC	27	4	10	14	51	....	....	....	....	....
1992-93	Harvard	ECAC	31	4	5	9	38	....	....	....	....	....
1993-94abcd	Harvard	ECAC	33	22	17	39	82	....	....	....	....	....
1994-95	Cincinnati	IHL	76	10	12	22	58	10	0	2	2	8

a ECAC First All-Star Team (1994)
b NCAA East First All-American Team (1994)
c NCAA Final Four All-Tournament Team (1994)
d NCAA Final Four Tournament Most Valuable Player (1994)

McCARTHY, SANDY — CGY.

Right wing. Shoots right. 6'3", 225 lbs. Born, Toronto, Ont., June 15, 1972.
(Calgary's 3rd choice, 52nd overall, in 1991 Entry Draft).

			Regular Season					Playoffs				
Season	**Club**	**Lea**	**GP**	**G**	**A**	**TP**	**PIM**	**GP**	**G**	**A**	**TP**	**PIM**
1989-90	Laval	QMJHL	65	10	11	21	269	14	3	3	6	60
1990-91	Laval	QMJHL	68	21	19	40	297	13	6	5	11	67
1991-92	Laval	QMJHL	62	39	51	90	326	8	4	5	9	81
1992-93	Salt Lake	IHL	77	18	20	38	220	....	....	....	....	....
1993-94	**Calgary**	**NHL**	**79**	**5**	**5**	**10**	**173**	**7**	**0**	**0**	**0**	**34**
1994-95	**Calgary**	**NHL**	**37**	**5**	**3**	**8**	**101**	**6**	**0**	**1**	**1**	**17**
	NHL Totals		**116**	**10**	**8**	**18**	**274**	**13**	**0**	**1**	**1**	**51**

McCARTY, DARREN — DET.

Right wing. Shoots right. 6'1", 210 lbs. Born, Burnaby, B.C., April 1, 1972.
(Detroit's 2nd choice, 46th overall, in 1992 Entry Draft).

			Regular Season					Playoffs				
Season	**Club**	**Lea**	**GP**	**G**	**A**	**TP**	**PIM**	**GP**	**G**	**A**	**TP**	**PIM**
1990-91	Belleville	OHL	60	30	37	67	151	6	2	2	4	13
1991-92a	Belleville	OHL	65	*55	72	127	177	5	1	4	5	13
1992-93	Adirondack	AHL	73	17	19	36	278	11	0	1	1	33
1993-94	**Detroit**	**NHL**	**67**	**9**	**17**	**26**	**181**	**7**	**2**	**2**	**4**	**8**
1994-95	**Detroit**	**NHL**	**31**	**5**	**8**	**13**	**88**	**18**	**3**	**2**	**5**	**14**
	NHL Totals		**98**	**14**	**25**	**39**	**269**	**25**	**5**	**4**	**9**	**22**

a OHL First All-Star Team (1992)

McCAULEY, ALYN — N.J.

Center. Shoots left. 5'11", 185 lbs. Born, Brockville, Ont., May 29, 1977.
(New Jersey's 5th choice, 79th overall, in 1995 Entry Draft).

			Regular Season					Playoffs				
Season	**Club**	**Lea**	**GP**	**G**	**A**	**TP**	**PIM**	**GP**	**G**	**A**	**TP**	**PIM**
1993-94	Ottawa	OHL	38	13	23	36	10	13	5	14	19	4
1994-95	Ottawa	OHL	65	16	38	54	20	....	....	....	....	....

McCAULEY, BILL — BOS.

Center. Shoots left. 6'1", 195 lbs. Born, Detroit, MI, April 20, 1975.
(Florida's 6th choice, 83rd overall, in 1993 Entry Draft).

			Regular Season					Playoffs				
Season	**Club**	**Lea**	**GP**	**G**	**A**	**TP**	**PIM**	**GP**	**G**	**A**	**TP**	**PIM**
1992-93	Detroit	OHL	65	13	37	50	24	15	1	4	5	6
1993-94	Detroit	OHL	59	18	39	57	51	16	4	7	11	25
1994-95	Detroit	OHL	66	41	61	102	43	21	12	*27	*39	12

Re-entered NHL Entry Draft, **Boston's** 4th choice, 73rd overall in 1995 Entry Draft.

McCLEARY, TRENT — OTT.

Right wing. Shoots right. 6', 180 lbs. Born, Swift Current, Sask., October 10, 1972.

			Regular Season					Playoffs				
Season	**Club**	**Lea**	**GP**	**G**	**A**	**TP**	**PIM**	**GP**	**G**	**A**	**TP**	**PIM**
1991-92	Swift Current	WHL	72	23	22	45	240	8	1	2	3	16
1992-93	Swift Current	WHL	63	17	33	50	138	17	5	4	9	16
	New Haven	AHL	2	1	0	1	6	....	....	....	....	....
1993-94	P.E.I.	AHL	4	0	0	0	6	....	....	....	....	....
	Thunder Bay	ColHL	51	23	17	40	123	9	2	11	13	15
1994-95	P.E.I.	AHL	51	9	20	29	60	9	2	3	5	26

Signed as a free agent by **Ottawa**, October 9, 1992.

McCOSH, SHAWN

Center. Shoots right. 6', 188 lbs. Born, Oshawa, Ont., June 5, 1969.
(Detroit's 5th choice, 95th overall, in 1989 Entry Draft).

			Regular Season					Playoffs				
Season	**Club**	**Lea**	**GP**	**G**	**A**	**TP**	**PIM**	**GP**	**G**	**A**	**TP**	**PIM**
1986-87	Hamilton	OHL	50	11	17	28	49	6	1	0	1	2
1987-88	Hamilton	OHL	64	17	36	53	96	14	6	8	14	14
1988-89	Niagara Falls	OHL	56	41	62	103	75	14	4	13	17	23
1989-90	Niagara Falls	OHL	9	6	10	16	24	....	....	....	....	....
	Hamilton	OHL	39	24	28	52	65	....	....	....	....	....
1990-91	New Haven	AHL	66	16	21	37	104	....	....	....	....	....
1991-92	**Los Angeles**	**NHL**	**4**	**0**	**0**	**0**	**4**	....	....	....	....	....
	Phoenix	IHL	71	21	32	53	118	....	....	....	....	....
	New Haven	AHL	....	....	....	....	....	5	0	1	1	0
1992-93	New Haven	AHL	46	22	32	54	54	....	....	....	....	....
	Phoenix	IHL	22	9	8	17	36	....	....	....	....	....
1993-94	Binghamton	AHL	75	31	44	75	68	....	....	....	....	....
1994-95	Binghamton	AHL	67	23	60	83	73	8	3	9	12	6
	NY Rangers	**NHL**	**5**	**1**	**0**	**1**	**2**	....	....	....	....	....
	NHL Totals		**9**	**1**	**0**	**1**	**6**	....	....	....	....	....

Traded to **Los Angeles** by **Detroit** for Los Angeles' eighth round choice (Justin Krall) in 1992 Entry Draft, August 15, 1990. Traded to **Ottawa** by **Los Angeles** with Bob Kudelski for Marc Fortier and Jim Thomson, December 19, 1992. Signed as a free agent by **NY Rangers**, July 30, 1993.

McCRIMMON, BRAD — HFD.

Defense. Shoots left. 5'11", 197 lbs. Born, Dodsland, Sask., March 29, 1959.
(Boston's 2nd choice, 15th overall, in 1979 Entry Draft).

			Regular Season					Playoffs				
Season	**Club**	**Lea**	**GP**	**G**	**A**	**TP**	**PIM**	**GP**	**G**	**A**	**TP**	**PIM**
1977-78a	Brandon	WHL	65	19	78	97	245	8	2	11	13	20
1978-79a	Brandon	WHL	66	24	74	98	139	22	9	19	28	34
1979-80	**Boston**	**NHL**	**72**	**5**	**11**	**16**	**94**	**10**	**1**	**1**	**2**	**28**
1980-81	**Boston**	**NHL**	**78**	**11**	**18**	**29**	**148**	**3**	**0**	**1**	**1**	**2**
1981-82	**Boston**	**NHL**	**78**	**1**	**8**	**9**	**83**	**2**	**0**	**0**	**0**	**2**
1982-83	**Philadelphia**	**NHL**	**79**	**4**	**21**	**25**	**61**	**3**	**0**	**0**	**0**	**4**
1983-84	**Philadelphia**	**NHL**	**71**	**0**	**24**	**24**	**76**	**1**	**0**	**0**	**0**	**4**
1984-85	**Philadelphia**	**NHL**	**66**	**8**	**35**	**43**	**81**	**11**	**2**	**1**	**3**	**15**
1985-86	**Philadelphia**	**NHL**	**80**	**13**	**43**	**56**	**85**	**5**	**2**	**0**	**2**	**2**
1986-87	**Philadelphia**	**NHL**	**71**	**10**	**29**	**39**	**52**	**26**	**3**	**5**	**8**	**30**
1987-88bc	**Calgary**	**NHL**	**80**	**7**	**35**	**42**	**98**	**9**	**2**	**3**	**5**	**22**
1988-89	**Calgary**	**NHL**	**72**	**5**	**17**	**22**	**96**	**22**	**0**	**3**	**3**	**30**
1989-90	**Calgary**	**NHL**	**79**	**4**	**15**	**19**	**78**	**6**	**0**	**2**	**2**	**8**
1990-91	**Detroit**	**NHL**	**64**	**0**	**13**	**13**	**81**	**7**	**1**	**1**	**2**	**21**
1991-92	**Detroit**	**NHL**	**79**	**7**	**22**	**29**	**118**	**11**	**0**	**1**	**1**	**8**
1992-93	**Detroit**	**NHL**	**60**	**1**	**14**	**15**	**71**	....	....	....	....	....
1993-94	**Hartford**	**NHL**	**65**	**1**	**5**	**6**	**72**	....	....	....	....	....
1994-95	**Hartford**	**NHL**	**33**	**0**	**1**	**1**	**42**	....	....	....	....	....
	NHL Totals		**1127**	**77**	**311**	**388**	**1336**	**116**	**11**	**18**	**29**	**176**

a WHL First All-Star Team (1978, 1979)
b NHL Second All-Star Team (1988)
c NHL Plus/Minus Leader (1988)

Played in NHL All-Star Game (1988)

Traded to **Philadelphia** by **Boston** for Pete Peeters, June 9, 1982. Traded to **Calgary** by **Philadelphia** for Calgary's third round choice (Dominic Roussel) in 1988 Entry Draft and first round choice (later traded to Toronto — Toronto selected Steve Bancroft) in 1989 Entry Draft, August 26, 1987. Traded to **Detroit** by **Calgary** for Detroit's second round choice (later traded to New Jersey — New Jersey selected David Harlock) in 1990 Entry Draft, June 15, 1990. Traded to **Hartford** by **Detroit** for Detroit's sixth round choice (previously acquired by Hartford — Detroit selected Tim Spitzig) in 1993 Entry Draft, June 1, 1993.

McDONOUGH, HUBIE (mihk-DUN-uh)

Center. Shoots left. 5'9", 180 lbs. Born, Manchester, NH, July 8, 1963.

			Regular Season					Playoffs				
Season	**Club**	**Lea**	**GP**	**G**	**A**	**TP**	**PIM**	**GP**	**G**	**A**	**TP**	**PIM**
1986-87	Flint	IHL	82	27	52	79	59	6	3	2	5	0
1987-88	New Haven	AHL	78	30	29	59	43	....	....	....	....	....
1988-89	**Los Angeles**	**NHL**	**4**	**0**	**1**	**1**	**0**	....	....	....	....	....
	New Haven	AHL	74	37	55	92	41	17	10	*21	*31	6
1989-90	**Los Angeles**	**NHL**	**22**	**3**	**4**	**7**	**10**	....	....	....	....	....
	NY Islanders	**NHL**	**54**	**18**	**11**	**29**	**26**	**5**	**1**	**0**	**1**	**4**
1990-91	**NY Islanders**	**NHL**	**52**	**6**	**6**	**12**	**10**	....	....	....	....	....
	Capital Dist.	AHL	17	9	9	18	4	....	....	....	....	....
1991-92	**NY Islanders**	**NHL**	**33**	**7**	**2**	**9**	**15**	....	....	....	....	....
	Capital Dist.	AHL	21	11	18	29	14	....	....	....	....	....
1992-93	**San Jose**	**NHL**	**30**	**6**	**2**	**8**	**6**	....	....	....	....	....
a	San Diego	IHL	48	26	49	75	26	14	4	7	11	6
1993-94	San Diego	IHL	69	31	48	79	61	8	0	7	7	6
1994-95a	San Diego	IHL	80	43	55	98	10	5	0	1	1	4
	NHL Totals		**195**	**40**	**26**	**66**	**67**	**5**	**1**	**0**	**1**	**4**

a IHL Second All-Star Team (1993, 1995)

Signed as a free agent by **Los Angeles**, April 18, 1988. Traded to **NY Islanders** by **Los Angeles** with Ken Baumgartner for Mikko Makela, November 29, 1989. Traded to **San Jose** by **NY Islanders** for cash, August 28, 1992.

McEACHERN, SHAWN (muh-GEH-kruhn) — BOS.

Center. Shoots left. 5'11", 195 lbs. Born, Waltham, MA, February 28, 1969.
(Pittsburgh's 6th choice, 110th overall, in 1987 Entry Draft).

			Regular Season					Playoffs				
Season	**Club**	**Lea**	**GP**	**G**	**A**	**TP**	**PIM**	**GP**	**G**	**A**	**TP**	**PIM**
1988-89	Boston U.	H.E.	36	20	28	48	32	....	....	....	....	....
1989-90a	Boston U.	H.E.	43	25	31	56	78	....	....	....	....	....
1990-91bc	Boston U.	H.E.	41	34	48	82	43	....	....	....	....	....
1991-92	U.S. National	....	57	26	23	49	38	....	....	....	....	....
	U.S. Olympic	....	8	1	0	1	10	....	....	....	....	....
	Pittsburgh	**NHL**	**15**	**0**	**4**	**4**	**0**	**19**	**2**	**7**	**9**	**4**
1992-93	**Pittsburgh**	**NHL**	**84**	**28**	**33**	**61**	**46**	**12**	**3**	**2**	**5**	**10**
1993-94	**Los Angeles**	**NHL**	**49**	**8**	**13**	**21**	**24**	....	....	....	....	....
	Pittsburgh	**NHL**	**27**	**12**	**9**	**21**	**10**	**6**	**1**	**0**	**1**	**2**
1994-95	Kiekko-Espoo	Fin.	8	1	3	4	6	....	....	....	....	....
	Pittsburgh	**NHL**	**44**	**13**	**13**	**26**	**22**	**11**	**0**	**2**	**2**	**8**
	NHL Totals		**219**	**61**	**72**	**133**	**102**	**48**	**6**	**11**	**17**	**24**

a Hockey East Second All-Star Team (1990)
b Hockey East First All-Star Team (1991)
c NCAA East First All-American Team (1991)

Traded to **Los Angeles** by **Pittsburgh** for Marty McSorley, August 27, 1993. Traded to **Pittsburgh** by **Los Angeles** with Tomas Sandstrom for Marty McSorley and Jim Paek, February 16, 1994. Traded to **Boston** by **Pittsburgh** with Kevin Stevens for Glen Murray, Bryan Smolinski and Boston's third round choice in 1996 Entry Draft, August 2, 1995.

McGILL, RYAN — EDM.

Defense. Shoots right. 6'2", 210 lbs. Born, Prince Albert, Sask., February 28, 1969.
(Chicago's 2nd choice, 29th overall, in 1987 Entry Draft).

			Regular Season					Playoffs				
Season	**Club**	**Lea**	**GP**	**G**	**A**	**TP**	**PIM**	**GP**	**G**	**A**	**TP**	**PIM**
1985-86	Lethbridge	WHL	64	5	10	15	171	10	0	1	1	9
1986-87	Swift Current	WHL	72	12	36	48	226	4	1	0	1	9
1987-88	Medicine Hat	WHL	67	5	30	35	224	15	7	3	10	47
1988-89	Medicine Hat	WHL	57	26	45	71	172	3	0	2	2	15
	Saginaw	IHL	8	2	0	2	12	6	0	0	0	42
1989-90	Indianapolis	IHL	77	11	17	28	215	14	2	2	4	29
1990-91	Halifax	AHL	7	0	4	4	6	....	....	....	....	....
a	Indianapolis	IHL	63	11	40	51	200	....	....	....	....	....
1991-92	**Chicago**	**NHL**	**9**	**0**	**2**	**2**	**20**	....	....	....	....	....
	Indianapolis	IHL	40	7	19	26	170	....	....	....	....	....
	Hershey	AHL	17	3	5	8	67	6	1	1	2	4
1992-93	**Philadelphia**	**NHL**	**72**	**3**	**10**	**13**	**238**	....	....	....	....	....
	Hershey	AHL	4	0	2	2	26	....	....	....	....	....
1993-94	**Philadelphia**	**NHL**	**50**	**1**	**3**	**4**	**112**	....	....	....	....	....
1994-95	**Philadelphia**	**NHL**	**12**	**0**	**0**	**0**	**13**	....	....	....	....	....
	Edmonton	**NHL**	**8**	**0**	**0**	**0**	**8**	....	....	....	....	....
	NHL Totals		**151**	**4**	**15**	**19**	**391**	....	....	....	....	....

a IHL Second All-Star Team (1991)

Traded to **Quebec** by **Chicago** with Mike McNeil for Paul Gillis and Dan Vincelette, March 5, 1991. Traded to **Chicago** by **Quebec** for Mike Dagenais, September 27, 1991. Traded to **Philadelphia** by **Chicago** for Tony Horacek, February 7, 1992. Traded to **Edmonton** by **Philadelphia** for Brad Zavisha and Edmonton's sixth round choice (Jamie Sokolosky) in 1995 Entry Draft, March 13, 1995.

McGILLIS, DANIEL — DET.

Defense. Shoots left. 6'2", 220 lbs. Born, Hawkesbury, Ont., July 1, 1972.
(Detroit's 10th choice, 238th overall, in 1992 Entry Draft).

			Regular Season					Playoffs				
Season	Club	Lea	GP	G	A	TP	PIM	GP	G	A	TP	PIM
1992-93	Northeastern	H.E.	35	5	12	17	42	....	....	....	....	....
1993-94	Northeastern	H.E.	38	4	25	29	82	....	....	....	....	....
1994-95a	Northeastern	H.E.	34	9	22	31	70	....	....	....	....	....

a Hockey East Second All-Star Team (1995)

McINNIS, MARTY — NYI

Center. Shoots right. 6', 185 lbs. Born, Hingham, MA., June 2, 1970.
(NY Islanders' 10th choice, 163rd overall, in 1988 Entry Draft).

			Regular Season					Playoffs				
Season	Club	Lea	GP	G	A	TP	PIM	GP	G	A	TP	PIM
1988-89	Boston College	H.E.	39	13	19	32	8	....	....	....	....	....
1989-90	Boston College	H.E.	41	24	29	53	43	....	....	....	....	....
1990-91	Boston College	H.E.	38	21	36	57	40	....	....	....	....	....
1991-92	U.S. National	....	54	15	19	34	20	....	....	....	....	....
	U.S. Olympic	....	8	6	2	8	4	....	....	....	....	....
	NY Islanders	**NHL**	**15**	**3**	**5**	**8**	**0**	....	....	....	....	....
1992-93	**NY Islanders**	**NHL**	**56**	**10**	**20**	**30**	**24**	**3**	**0**	**1**	**1**	**0**
	Capital Dist.	AHL	10	4	12	16	2	....	....	....	....	....
1993-94	**NY Islanders**	**NHL**	**81**	**25**	**31**	**56**	**24**	**4**	**0**	**0**	**0**	**0**
1994-95	**NY Islanders**	**NHL**	**41**	**9**	**7**	**16**	**8**	....	....	....	....	....
	NHL Totals		**193**	**47**	**63**	**110**	**56**	**7**	**0**	**1**	**1**	**0**

McINTYRE, JOHN — VAN.

Center. Shoots left. 6'1", 190 lbs. Born, Ravenswood, Ont., April 29, 1969.
(Toronto's 3rd choice, 49th overall, in 1987 Entry Draft).

			Regular Season					Playoffs				
Season	Club	Lea	GP	G	A	TP	PIM	GP	G	A	TP	PIM
1985-86	Guelph	OHL	30	4	6	10	25	20	1	5	6	31
1986-87	Guelph	OHL	47	8	22	30	95	....	....	....	....	....
1987-88	Guelph	OHL	39	24	18	42	109	....	....	....	....	....
1988-89	Guelph	OHL	52	30	26	56	129	7	5	4	9	25
	Newmarket	AHL	3	0	2	2	7	5	1	1	2	20
1989-90	**Toronto**	**NHL**	**59**	**5**	**12**	**17**	**117**	**2**	**0**	**0**	**0**	**2**
	Newmarket	AHL	6	2	2	4	12	....	....	....	....	....
1990-91	**Toronto**	**NHL**	**13**	**0**	**3**	**3**	**25**	....	....	....	....	....
	Los Angeles	**NHL**	**56**	**8**	**5**	**13**	**115**	**12**	**0**	**1**	**1**	**24**
1991-92	**Los Angeles**	**NHL**	**73**	**5**	**19**	**24**	**100**	**6**	**0**	**4**	**4**	**12**
1992-93	**Los Angeles**	**NHL**	**49**	**2**	**5**	**7**	**80**	....	....	....	....	....
	NY Rangers	**NHL**	**11**	**1**	**0**	**1**	**4**	....	....	....	....	....
1993-94	**Vancouver**	**NHL**	**62**	**3**	**6**	**9**	**38**	**24**	**0**	**1**	**1**	**16**
1994-95	**Vancouver**	**NHL**	**28**	**0**	**4**	**4**	**37**	....	....	....	....	....
	NHL Totals		**351**	**24**	**54**	**78**	**516**	**44**	**0**	**6**	**6**	**54**

Traded to **Los Angeles** by **Toronto** for Mike Krushelnyski, November 9, 1990. Traded to **NY Rangers** by **Los Angeles** for Mark Hardy and Ottawa's fifth round choice (previously acquired by NY Rangers — Los Angeles selected Frederick Beaubien) in 1993 Entry Draft, March 22, 1993. Claimed by **Vancouver** from **NY Rangers** in NHL Waiver Draft, October 3, 1993.

McKAY, KEVIN — CHI.

Defense. Shoots left. 6'3", 198 lbs. Born, North Battleford, Sask., January 4, 1977.
(Chicago's 3rd choice, 71st overall, in 1995 Entry Draft).

			Regular Season					Playoffs				
Season	Club	Lea	GP	G	A	TP	PIM	GP	G	A	TP	PIM
1993-94	Moose Jaw	WHL	6	0	0	0	2	....	....	....	....	....
1994-95	Moose Jaw	WHL	56	1	11	12	93	10	0	2	2	13

McKAY, RANDY — N.J.

Right wing. Shoots right. 6'1", 205 lbs. Born, Montreal, Que., January 25, 1967.
(Detroit's 6th choice, 113th overall, in 1985 Entry Draft).

			Regular Season					Playoffs				
Season	Club	Lea	GP	G	A	TP	PIM	GP	G	A	TP	PIM
1984-85	Michigan Tech	WCHA	25	4	5	9	32	....	....	....	....	....
1985-86	Michigan Tech	WCHA	40	12	22	34	46	....	....	....	....	....
1986-87	Michigan Tech	WCHA	39	5	11	16	46	....	....	....	....	....
1987-88	Michigan Tech	WCHA	41	17	24	41	70	....	....	....	....	....
	Adirondack	AHL	10	0	3	3	12	6	0	4	4	0
1988-89	**Detroit**	**NHL**	**3**	**0**	**0**	**0**	**0**	**2**	**0**	**0**	**0**	**2**
	Adirondack	AHL	58	29	34	63	170	14	4	7	11	60
1989-90	**Detroit**	**NHL**	**33**	**3**	**6**	**9**	**51**	....	....	....	....	....
	Adirondack	AHL	36	16	23	39	99	6	3	0	3	35
1990-91	**Detroit**	**NHL**	**47**	**1**	**7**	**8**	**183**	**5**	**0**	**1**	**1**	**41**
1991-92	**New Jersey**	**NHL**	**80**	**17**	**16**	**33**	**246**	**7**	**1**	**3**	**4**	**10**
1992-93	**New Jersey**	**NHL**	**73**	**11**	**11**	**22**	**206**	**5**	**0**	**0**	**0**	**16**
1993-94	**New Jersey**	**NHL**	**78**	**12**	**15**	**27**	**244**	**20**	**1**	**2**	**3**	**24**
1994-95	**New Jersey**	**NHL**	**33**	**5**	**7**	**12**	**44**	**19**	**8**	**4**	**12**	**11**
	NHL Totals		**347**	**49**	**62**	**111**	**974**	**58**	**10**	**10**	**20**	**104**

Acquired by **New Jersey** from **Detroit** with Dave Barr as compensation for Detroit's signing of free agent Troy Crowder, September 9, 1991.

McKAY, SCOTT

Center. Shoots right. 5'11", 200 lbs. Born, Burlington, Ont., January 26, 1972.

			Regular Season					Playoffs				
Season	Club	Lea	GP	G	A	TP	PIM	GP	G	A	TP	PIM
1989-90	London	OHL	59	20	29	49	37	5	1	1	2	12
1990-91	London	OHL	62	29	40	69	29	7	4	2	6	6
1991-92	London	OHL	64	30	45	75	97	10	3	8	11	8
1992-93	London	OHL	63	38	57	95	49	12	1	14	15	6
1993-94	**Anaheim**	**NHL**	**1**	**0**	**0**	**0**	**0**	....	....	....	....	....
	San Diego	IHL	58	10	6	16	35	9	2	5	7	6
1994-95	Greensboro	ECHL	17	7	7	14	54	....	....	....	....	....
	San Diego	IHL	1	0	0	0	2	....	....	....	....	....
	NHL Totals		**1**	**0**	**0**	**0**	**0**	....	....	....	....	....

Signed as a free agent by **Anaheim**, August 2, 1993.

McKEE, JAY — BUF.

Defense. Shoots left. 6'2", 175 lbs. Born, Kingston, Ont., September 8, 1977.
(Buffalo's 1st choice, 14th overall, in 1995 Entry Draft).

			Regular Season					Playoffs				
Season	Club	Lea	GP	G	A	TP	PIM	GP	G	A	TP	PIM
1993-94	Sudbury	OHL	51	0	1	1	51	3	0	0	0	0
1994-95	Niagara Falls	OHL	65	9	19	28	151	6	2	3	5	10

McKEE, MIKE

Left wing. Shoots right. 6'3", 203 lbs. Born, Toronto, Ont., June 18, 1969.
(Quebec's 1st choice, 1st overall, in 1990 Supplemental Draft).

			Regular Season					Playoffs				
Season	Club	Lea	GP	G	A	TP	PIM	GP	G	A	TP	PIM
1988-89	Princeton	ECAC	16	2	1	3	14	....	....	....	....	....
1989-90a	Princeton	ECAC	26	7	18	25	18	....	....	....	....	....
1990-91	Princeton	ECAC	15	1	4	5	16	....	....	....	....	....
1991-92	Princeton	ECAC	27	12	17	29	34	....	....	....	....	....
1992-93	Halifax	AHL	32	6	7	13	25	....	....	....	....	....
	Greensboro	ECHL	7	1	3	4	6	....	....	....	....	....
1993-94	**Quebec**	**NHL**	**48**	**3**	**12**	**15**	**41**	....	....	....	....	....
	Cornwall	AHL	24	6	14	20	18	10	0	3	3	4
1994-95	Cornwall	AHL	36	2	11	13	24	....	....	....	....	....
	NHL Totals		**48**	**3**	**12**	**15**	**41**	....	....	....	....	....

a ECAC Second All-Star Team (1990)

McKENZIE, JIM — NYI

Left wing/Defense. Shoots left. 6'3", 205 lbs. Born, Gull Lake, Sask., November 3, 1969.
(Hartford's 3rd choice, 73rd overall, in 1989 Entry Draft).

			Regular Season					Playoffs				
Season	Club	Lea	GP	G	A	TP	PIM	GP	G	A	TP	PIM
1985-86	Moose Jaw	WHL	3	0	2	2	0	....	....	....	....	....
1986-87	Moose Jaw	WHL	65	5	3	8	125	9	0	0	0	7
1987-88	Moose Jaw	WHL	62	1	17	18	134	....	....	....	....	....
1988-89	Victoria	WHL	67	15	27	42	176	8	1	4	5	30
1989-90	**Hartford**	**NHL**	**5**	**0**	**0**	**0**	**4**	....	....	....	....	....
	Binghamton	AHL	56	4	12	16	149	....	....	....	....	....
1990-91	**Hartford**	**NHL**	**41**	**4**	**3**	**7**	**108**	**6**	**0**	**0**	**0**	**8**
	Springfield	AHL	24	3	4	7	102	....	....	....	....	....
1991-92	**Hartford**	**NHL**	**67**	**5**	**1**	**6**	**87**	....	....	....	....	....
1992-93	**Hartford**	**NHL**	**64**	**3**	**6**	**9**	**202**	....	....	....	....	....
1993-94	**Hartford**	**NHL**	**26**	**1**	**2**	**3**	**67**	....	....	....	....	....
	Dallas	**NHL**	**34**	**2**	**3**	**5**	**63**	....	....	....	....	....
	Pittsburgh	**NHL**	**11**	**0**	**0**	**0**	**16**	**3**	**0**	**0**	**0**	**0**
1994-95	**Pittsburgh**	**NHL**	**39**	**2**	**1**	**3**	**63**	**5**	**0**	**0**	**0**	**4**
	NHL Totals		**287**	**17**	**16**	**33**	**610**	**14**	**0**	**0**	**0**	**12**

Traded to **Florida** by **Hartford** for Alexander Godynyuk, December 16, 1993. Traded to **Dallas** by **Florida** for Dallas' fourth round choice (later traded to Ottawa — Ottawa selected Kevin Bolibruck) in 1995 Entry Draft, December 16, 1993. Traded to **Pittsburgh** by **Dallas** for Mike Needham, March 21, 1994. Signed as a free agent by **NY Islanders**, July 31, 1995.

McKIM, ANDREW

Center. Shoots right. 5'8", 175 lbs. Born, St. John, N.B., July 6, 1970.

			Regular Season					Playoffs				
Season	Club	Lea	GP	G	A	TP	PIM	GP	G	A	TP	PIM
1988-89	Verdun	QMJHL	68	50	56	106	36	....	....	....	....	....
1989-90a	Hull	QMJHL	70	66	84	130	44	11	8	10	18	8
1990-91	Salt Lake	IHL	74	30	30	60	48	4	0	2	2	6
1991-92	St. John's	AHL	79	43	50	93	79	16	11	12	23	4
1992-93	**Boston**	**NHL**	**7**	**1**	**3**	**4**	**0**	....	....	....	....	....
	Providence	AHL	61	23	46	69	64	6	2	2	4	0
1993-94	**Boston**	**NHL**	**29**	**0**	**1**	**1**	**4**	....	....	....	....	....
	Providence	AHL	46	13	24	37	49	....	....	....	....	....
1994-95	Adirondack	AHL	77	39	55	94	22	4	3	3	6	0
	Detroit	**NHL**	**2**	**0**	**0**	**0**	**2**	....	....	....	....	....
	NHL Totals		**38**	**1**	**4**	**5**	**6**	....	....	....	....	....

a QMJHL First All-Star Team (1990)

Signed as a free agent by **Calgary**, October 5, 1990. Signed as a free agent by **Boston**, July 23, 1992. Signed as a free agent by **Detroit**, August 31, 1994.

McLAREN, KYLE — BOS.

Defense. Shoots left. 6'4", 210 lbs. Born, Humbolt, Sask., June 18, 1977.
(Boston's 1st choice, 9th overall, in 1995 Entry Draft).

			Regular Season					Playoffs				
Season	Club	Lea	GP	G	A	TP	PIM	GP	G	A	TP	PIM
1993-94	Tacoma	WHL	62	1	9	10	53	6	1	4	5	6
1994-95	Tacoma	WHL	47	13	19	32	68	4	1	1	2	4

McLAREN, STEVE — CHI.

Defense. Shoots left. 6', 194 lbs. Born, Owen Sound, Ont., February 3, 1975.
(Chicago's 3rd choice, 85th overall, in 1994 Entry Draft).

			Regular Season					Playoffs				
Season	Club	Lea	GP	G	A	TP	PIM	GP	G	A	TP	PIM
1993-94	North Bay	OHL	55	2	15	17	130	18	0	3	3	50
1994-95	North Bay	OHL	27	3	10	13	119	6	2	1	3	23

McLAUGHLIN, PETER — PIT.

Defense. Shoots left. 6'3", 190 lbs. Born, Norwood, MA, June 29, 1973.
(Pittsburgh's 8th choice, 170th overall, in 1991 Entry Draft).

			Regular Season					Playoffs				
Season	Club	Lea	GP	G	A	TP	PIM	GP	G	A	TP	PIM
1992-93	Harvard	ECAC	31	2	6	8	28	....	....	....	....	....
1993-94	Harvard	ECAC	33	0	7	7	32	....	....	....	....	....
1994-95	Harvard	ECAC	30	1	6	7	44	....	....	....	....	....

McLLWAIN, DAVE (MA-kuhl-WAYN) OTT.

Center/Right wing. Shoots left. 6', 185 lbs. Born, Seaforth, Ont., January 9, 1967.
(Pittsburgh's 9th choice, 172nd overall, in 1986 Entry Draft).

			Regular Season					Playoffs				
Season	Club	Lea	GP	G	A	TP	PIM	GP	G	A	TP	PIM
1984-85	Kitchener	OHL	61	13	21	34	29	....	....	....	....	....
1985-86	Kitchener	OHL	13	7	7	14	12	....	....	....	....	....
	North Bay	OHL	51	30	28	58	25	10	4	4	8	2
1986-87a	North Bay	OHL	60	46	73	119	35	24	7	18	25	40
1987-88	**Pittsburgh**	**NHL**	**66**	**11**	**8**	**19**	**40**	....	....	....	....	....
	Muskegon	IHL	9	4	6	10	23	6	2	3	5	8
1988-89	**Pittsburgh**	**NHL**	**24**	**1**	**2**	**3**	**4**	**3**	**0**	**1**	**1**	**0**
	Muskegon	IHL	46	37	35	72	51	7	8	2	10	6
1989-90	**Winnipeg**	**NHL**	**80**	**25**	**26**	**51**	**60**	**7**	**0**	**1**	**1**	**2**
1990-91	**Winnipeg**	**NHL**	**60**	**14**	**11**	**25**	**46**	....	....	....	....	....
1991-92	**Winnipeg**	**NHL**	**3**	**1**	**1**	**2**	**2**	....	....	....	....	....
	Buffalo	**NHL**	**5**	**0**	**0**	**0**	**2**	....	....	....	....	....
	NY Islanders	**NHL**	**54**	**8**	**15**	**23**	**28**	....	....	....	....	....
	Toronto	**NHL**	**11**	**1**	**2**	**3**	**4**	....	....	....	....	....
1992-93	**Toronto**	**NHL**	**66**	**14**	**4**	**18**	**30**	**4**	**0**	**0**	**0**	**0**
1993-94	**Ottawa**	**NHL**	**66**	**17**	**26**	**43**	**48**	....	....	....	....	....
1994-95	**Ottawa**	**NHL**	**43**	**5**	**6**	**11**	**22**	....	....	....	....	....
	NHL Totals		**478**	**97**	**101**	**198**	**286**	**14**	**0**	**2**	**2**	**2**

a OHL Second All-Star Team (1987)

Traded to **Winnipeg** by **Pittsburgh** with Randy Cunneyworth and Rick Tabaracci for Jim Kyte, Andrew McBain and Randy Gilhen, June 17, 1989. Traded to **Buffalo** by **Winnipeg** with Gord Donnelly, Winnipeg's fifth round choice (Yuri Khmylev) in 1992 Entry Draft and future considerations for Darrin Shannon, Mike Hartman and Dean Kennedy, October 11, 1991. Traded to **NY Islanders** by **Buffalo** with Pierre Turgeon, Uwe Krupp and Benoit Hogue for Pat Lafontaine, Randy Hillier, Randy Wood and NY Islanders' fourth round choice (Dean Melanson) in 1992 Entry Draft, October 25, 1991. Traded to **Toronto** by **NY Islanders** with Ken Baumgartner for Daniel Marois and Claude Loiselle, March 10, 1992. Claimed by **Ottawa** from **Toronto** in NHL Waiver Draft, October 3, 1993.

McPHEE, MIKE

Left wing. Shoots left. 6'1", 203 lbs. Born, Sydney, N.S., July 14, 1960.
(Montreal's 8th choice, 124th overall, in 1980 Entry Draft).

			Regular Season					Playoffs				
Season	Club	Lea	GP	G	A	TP	PIM	GP	G	A	TP	PIM
1980-81	RPI	ECAC	29	28	18	46	22	....	....	....	....	....
1981-82	RPI	ECAC	6	0	3	3	4	....	....	....	....	....
1982-83	Nova Scotia	AHL	42	10	15	25	29	7	1	1	2	14
1983-84	**Montreal**	**NHL**	**14**	**5**	**2**	**7**	**41**	**15**	**1**	**0**	**1**	**31**
	Nova Scotia	AHL	67	22	33	55	101	....	....	....	....	....
1984-85	**Montreal**	**NHL**	**70**	**17**	**22**	**39**	**120**	**12**	**4**	**1**	**5**	**32**
1985-86	**Montreal**	**NHL**	**70**	**19**	**21**	**40**	**69**	**20**	**3**	**4**	**7**	**45**
1986-87	**Montreal**	**NHL**	**79**	**18**	**21**	**39**	**58**	**17**	**7**	**2**	**9**	**13**
1987-88	**Montreal**	**NHL**	**77**	**23**	**20**	**43**	**53**	**11**	**4**	**3**	**7**	**8**
1988-89	**Montreal**	**NHL**	**73**	**19**	**22**	**41**	**74**	**20**	**4**	**7**	**11**	**30**
1989-90	**Montreal**	**NHL**	**56**	**23**	**18**	**41**	**47**	**9**	**1**	**1**	**2**	**16**
1990-91	**Montreal**	**NHL**	**64**	**22**	**21**	**43**	**56**	**13**	**1**	**7**	**8**	**12**
1991-92	**Montreal**	**NHL**	**78**	**16**	**15**	**31**	**63**	**8**	**1**	**1**	**2**	**4**
1992-93	**Minnesota**	**NHL**	**84**	**18**	**22**	**40**	**44**	....	....	....	....	....
1993-94	**Dallas**	**NHL**	**79**	**20**	**15**	**35**	**36**	**9**	**2**	**1**	**3**	**2**
1994-95			DID NOT PLAY – INJURED									
	NHL Totals		**744**	**200**	**199**	**399**	**661**	**134**	**28**	**27**	**55**	**193**

Played in NHL All-Star Game (1989)

Traded to **Minnesota** by **Montreal** for Minnesota's fifth round choice (Jeff Lank) in 1993 Entry Draft, August 14, 1992.

McRAE, BASIL (muh-KRAY, BA-zihl) ST.L.

Left wing. Shoots left. 6'2", 210 lbs. Born, Beaverton, Ont., January 5, 1961.
(Quebec's 3rd choice, 87th overall, in 1980 Entry Draft).

			Regular Season					Playoffs				
Season	Club	Lea	GP	G	A	TP	PIM	GP	G	A	TP	PIM
1979-80	London	OHA	67	24	36	60	116	5	0	0	0	18
1980-81	London	OHA	65	29	23	52	266	....	....	....	....	....
1981-82	**Quebec**	**NHL**	**20**	**4**	**3**	**7**	**69**	**9**	**1**	**0**	**1**	**34**
	Fredericton	AHL	47	11	15	26	175	....	....	....	....	....
1982-83	**Quebec**	**NHL**	**22**	**1**	**1**	**2**	**59**	....	....	....	....	....
	Fredericton	AHL	53	22	19	41	146	12	1	5	6	75
1983-84	**Toronto**	**NHL**	**3**	**0**	**0**	**0**	**19**	....	....	....	....	....
	St. Catharines	AHL	78	14	25	39	187	6	0	0	0	40
1984-85	**Toronto**	**NHL**	**1**	**0**	**0**	**0**	**0**	....	....	....	....	....
	St. Catharines	AHL	72	30	25	55	186	....	....	....	....	....
1985-86	**Detroit**	**NHL**	**4**	**0**	**0**	**0**	**5**	....	....	....	....	....
	Adirondack	AHL	69	22	30	52	259	17	5	4	9	101
1986-87	**Detroit**	**NHL**	**36**	**2**	**2**	**4**	**193**	....	....	....	....	....
	Quebec	**NHL**	**33**	**9**	**5**	**14**	**149**	**13**	**3**	**1**	**4**	***99**
1987-88	**Minnesota**	**NHL**	**80**	**5**	**11**	**16**	**382**	....	....	....	....	....
1988-89	**Minnesota**	**NHL**	**78**	**12**	**19**	**31**	**365**	**5**	**0**	**0**	**0**	**58**
1989-90	**Minnesota**	**NHL**	**66**	**9**	**17**	**26**	***351**	**7**	**1**	**0**	**1**	**24**
1990-91	**Minnesota**	**NHL**	**40**	**1**	**3**	**4**	**224**	**22**	**1**	**1**	**2**	***94**
1991-92	**Minnesota**	**NHL**	**59**	**5**	**8**	**13**	**245**	....	....	....	....	....
1992-93	**Tampa Bay**	**NHL**	**14**	**2**	**3**	**5**	**71**	....	....	....	....	....
	St. Louis	**NHL**	**33**	**1**	**3**	**4**	**98**	**11**	**0**	**1**	**1**	**24**
1993-94	**St. Louis**	**NHL**	**40**	**1**	**2**	**3**	**103**	**2**	**0**	**0**	**0**	**12**
1994-95	**St. Louis**	**NHL**	**21**	**0**	**5**	**5**	**72**	**7**	**2**	**1**	**3**	**4**
	Peoria	IHL	2	0	0	0	12	....	....	....	....	....
	NHL Totals		**550**	**52**	**82**	**134**	**2405**	**76**	**8**	**4**	**12**	**349**

Traded to **Toronto** by **Quebec** for Richard Turmel, August 12, 1983. Signed as a free agent by **Detroit**, July 17, 1985. Traded to **Quebec** by **Detroit** with John Ogrodnick and Doug Shedden for Brent Ashton, Gilbert Delorme and Mark Kumpel, January 17, 1987. Signed as a free agent by **Minnesota**, June 29, 1987. Claimed by **Tampa Bay** from **Minnesota** in Expansion Draft, June 18, 1992. Traded to **St. Louis** by **Tampa Bay** with Doug Crossman and Tampa Bay's fourth round choice in 1996 Entry Draft for Jason Ruff and future considerations, January 28, 1993.

McRAE, KEN

Center. Shoots right. 6'1", 195 lbs. Born, Winchester, Ont., April 23, 1968.
(Quebec's 1st choice, 18th overall, in 1986 Entry Draft).

			Regular Season					Playoffs				
Season	Club	Lea	GP	G	A	TP	PIM	GP	G	A	TP	PIM
1985-86	Sudbury	OHL	66	25	49	74	127	4	2	1	3	12
1986-87	Sudbury	OHL	21	12	15	27	40	....	....	....	....	....
	Hamilton	OHL	20	7	12	19	25	7	1	1	2	12
1987-88	**Quebec**	**NHL**	**1**	**0**	**0**	**0**	**0**	....	....	....	....	....
	Hamilton	OHL	62	30	55	85	158	14	13	9	22	35
	Fredericton	AHL	....	....	....	....	....	3	0	0	0	8
1988-89	**Quebec**	**NHL**	**37**	**6**	**11**	**17**	**68**	....	....	....	....	....
	Halifax	AHL	41	20	21	41	87	....	....	....	....	....
1989-90	**Quebec**	**NHL**	**66**	**7**	**8**	**15**	**191**	....	....	....	....	....
1990-91	**Quebec**	**NHL**	**12**	**0**	**0**	**0**	**36**	....	....	....	....	....
	Halifax	AHL	60	10	36	46	193	....	....	....	....	....
1991-92	**Quebec**	**NHL**	**10**	**0**	**1**	**1**	**31**	....	....	....	....	....
	Halifax	AHL	52	30	41	71	184	....	....	....	....	....
1992-93	**Toronto**	**NHL**	**2**	**0**	**0**	**0**	**2**	....	....	....	....	....
	St. John's	AHL	64	30	44	74	135	9	6	6	12	27
1993-94	**Toronto**	**NHL**	**9**	**1**	**1**	**2**	**36**	**6**	**0**	**0**	**0**	**4**
	St. John's	AHL	65	23	41	64	200	....	....	....	....	....
1994-95	Detroit	IHL	24	4	9	13	38	....	....	....	....	....
	Phoenix	IHL	2	2	0	2	0	9	3	8	11	21
	NHL Totals		**137**	**14**	**21**	**35**	**364**	**6**	**0**	**0**	**0**	**4**

Traded to **Toronto** by **Quebec** for Len Esau, July 21, 1992. Signed as a free agent by **Edmonton**, September 9, 1994.

McREYNOLDS, BRIAN

Center. Shoots left. 6'1", 192 lbs. Born, Penetanguishene, Ont., January 5, 1965.
(NY Rangers' 6th choice, 112th overall, in 1985 Entry Draft).

			Regular Season					Playoffs				
Season	Club	Lea	GP	G	A	TP	PIM	GP	G	A	TP	PIM
1985-86	Michigan State	CCHA	45	14	24	38	78	....	....	....	....	....
1986-87	Michigan State	CCHA	45	16	24	40	68	....	....	....	....	....
1987-88	Michigan State	CCHA	43	10	24	34	50	....	....	....	....	....
1988-89	Cdn. National	....	58	5	25	30	59	....	....	....	....	....
1989-90	**Winnipeg**	**NHL**	**9**	**0**	**2**	**2**	**4**	....	....	....	....	....
	Moncton	AHL	72	18	41	59	87	....	....	....	....	....
1990-91	**NY Rangers**	**NHL**	**1**	**0**	**0**	**0**	**0**	....	....	....	....	....
	Binghamton	AHL	77	30	42	72	74	10	0	4	4	6
1991-92	Binghamton	AHL	48	19	28	47	22	7	2	2	4	12
1992-93	Binghamton	AHL	79	30	70	100	88	14	3	10	13	18
1993-94	**Los Angeles**	**NHL**	**20**	**1**	**3**	**4**	**4**	....	....	....	....	....
	Phoenix	IHL	51	14	33	47	65	....	....	....	....	....
1994-95	Phoenix	IHL	55	5	27	32	60	....	....	....	....	....
	Atlanta	IHL	11	5	7	12	14	5	4	5	9	4
	NHL Totals		**30**	**1**	**5**	**6**	**8**	....	....	....	....	....

Signed as a free agent by **Winnipeg**, June 20, 1989. Traded to **NY Rangers** by **Winnipeg** for Simon Wheeldon, July 10, 1990. Signed as a free agent by **Los Angeles**, July 29, 1993.

McSORLEY, MARTY L.A.

Defense. Shoots right. 6'1", 225 lbs. Born, Hamilton, Ont., May 18, 1963.

			Regular Season					Playoffs				
Season	Club	Lea	GP	G	A	TP	PIM	GP	G	A	TP	PIM
1981-82	Belleville	OHL	58	6	13	19	234	....	....	....	....	....
1982-83	Belleville	OHL	70	10	41	51	183	4	0	0	0	7
	Baltimore	AHL	2	0	0	0	22	....	....	....	....	....
1983-84	**Pittsburgh**	**NHL**	**72**	**2**	**7**	**9**	**224**	....	....	....	....	....
1984-85	**Pittsburgh**	**NHL**	**15**	**0**	**0**	**0**	**15**	....	....	....	....	....
	Baltimore	AHL	58	6	24	30	154	14	0	7	7	47
1985-86	**Edmonton**	**NHL**	**59**	**11**	**12**	**23**	**265**	**8**	**0**	**2**	**2**	**50**
	Nova Scotia	AHL	9	2	4	6	34	....	....	....	....	....
1986-87	**Edmonton**	**NHL**	**41**	**2**	**4**	**6**	**159**	**21**	**4**	**3**	**7**	**65**
	Nova Scotia	AHL	7	2	2	4	48	....	....	....	....	....
1987-88	**Edmonton**	**NHL**	**60**	**9**	**17**	**26**	**223**	**16**	**0**	**3**	**3**	**67**
1988-89	**Los Angeles**	**NHL**	**66**	**10**	**17**	**27**	**350**	**11**	**0**	**2**	**2**	**33**
1989-90	**Los Angeles**	**NHL**	**75**	**15**	**21**	**36**	**322**	**10**	**1**	**3**	**4**	**18**
1990-91a	**Los Angeles**	**NHL**	**61**	**7**	**32**	**39**	**221**	**12**	**0**	**0**	**0**	**58**
1991-92	**Los Angeles**	**NHL**	**71**	**7**	**22**	**29**	**268**	**6**	**1**	**0**	**1**	**21**
1992-93	**Los Angeles**	**NHL**	**81**	**15**	**26**	**41**	***399**	**24**	**4**	**6**	**10**	***60**
1993-94	**Pittsburgh**	**NHL**	**47**	**3**	**18**	**21**	**139**	....	....	....	....	....
	Los Angeles	**NHL**	**18**	**4**	**6**	**10**	**55**	....	....	....	....	....
1994-95	**Los Angeles**	**NHL**	**41**	**3**	**18**	**21**	**83**	....	....	....	....	....
	NHL Totals		**707**	**88**	**200**	**288**	**2723**	**108**	**10**	**19**	**29**	**372**

a Co-winner of Alka-Seltzer Plus Award with Theoren Fleury (1991)

Signed as a free agent by **Pittsburgh**, July 30, 1982. Traded to **Edmonton** by **Pittsburgh** with Tim Hrynewich and future considerations (Craig Muni, October 6, 1986) for Gilles Meloche, September 12, 1985. Traded to **Los Angeles** by **Edmonton** with Wayne Gretzky and Mike Krushelnyski for Jimmy Carson, Martin Gelinas, Los Angeles' first round choices in 1989 (acquired by New Jersey — New Jersey selected Jason Miller), 1991 (Martin Rucinsky) and 1993 (Nick Stajduhar) Entry Drafts and cash, August 9, 1988. Traded to **Pittsburgh** by **Los Angeles**, for Shawn McEachern, August 27, 1993. Traded to **Los Angeles** by **Pittsburgh** with Jim Paek for Tomas Sandstrom and Shawn McEachern, February 16, 1994.

McSWEEN, DON ANA.

Defense. Shoots left. 5'11", 197 lbs. Born, Detroit, MI, June 9, 1964.
(Buffalo's 10th choice, 154th overall, in 1983 Entry Draft).

			Regular Season					Playoffs				
Season	Club	Lea	GP	G	A	TP	PIM	GP	G	A	TP	PIM
1983-84	Michigan State	CCHA	46	10	26	36	30	....	....	....	....	....
1984-85	Michigan State	CCHA	44	2	23	25	52	....	....	....	....	....
1985-86a	Michigan State	CCHA	45	9	29	38	18	....	....	....	....	....
1986-87abc	Michigan State	CCHA	45	7	23	30	34	....	....	....	....	....
1987-88	**Buffalo**	**NHL**	**5**	**0**	**1**	**1**	**6**	....	....	....	....	....
	Rochester	AHL	63	9	29	38	108	6	0	1	1	15
1988-89	Rochester	AHL	66	7	22	29	45	....	....	....	....	....
1989-90	**Buffalo**	**NHL**	**4**	**0**	**0**	**0**	**6**	....	....	....	....	....
d	Rochester	AHL	70	16	43	59	43	17	3	10	13	12
1990-91	Rochester	AHL	74	7	44	51	57	15	2	5	7	8
1991-92	Rochester	AHL	75	6	32	38	60	16	5	6	11	18
1992-93	San Diego	IHL	80	15	40	55	85	14	1	2	3	10
1993-94	San Diego	IHL	38	5	13	18	36	....	....	....	....	....
	Anaheim	**NHL**	**32**	**3**	**9**	**12**	**39**	....	....	....	....	....
1994-95	**Anaheim**	**NHL**	**2**	**0**	**0**	**0**	**0**	....	....	....	....	....
	NHL Totals		**43**	**3**	**10**	**13**	**51**	....	....	....	....	....

a CCHA First All-Star Team (1986, 1987)
b NCAA West Second All-American Team (1987)
c Named to NCAA All-Tournament Team (1987)
d AHL First All-Star Team (1990)

Signed as a free agent by **Anaheim**, January 12, 1994.

MEKESHKIN, DIMITRI (meh-KEHSH-kihn) WSH.

Defense. Shoots left. 6'2", 186 lbs. Born, Izhevsk, USSR, January 29, 1976.
(Washington's 6th choice, 145th overall, in 1994 Entry Draft).

			Regular Season					Playoffs			
Season	Club	Lea	GP	G	A	TP	PIM	GP	G	A	TP	PIM
1993-94	Avangard Omsk	CIS	21	0	0	0	14	3	0	0	0	2
1994-95	Omsk	CIS	16	0	2	2	4					

MELANSON, DEAN (meh-LAHN-suhn) BUF.

Defense. Shoots right. 5'11", 211 lbs. Born, Antigonish, N.S., November 19, 1973.
(Buffalo's 4th choice, 80th overall, in 1992 Entry Draft).

			Regular Season					Playoffs			
Season	Club	Lea	GP	G	A	TP	PIM	GP	G	A	TP	PIM
1990-91	St-Hyacinthe	QMJHL	69	10	17	27	110	4	0	1	1	2
1991-92	St-Hyacinthe	QMJHL	42	8	19	27	158	6	1	2	3	25
1992-93	Rochester	AHL	8	0	1	1	6	14	1	6	7	18
	St. Hyacinthe	QMJHL	57	13	29	42	253					
1993-94	Rochester	AHL	80	1	21	22	138	4	0	1	1	2
1994-95	Rochester	AHL	43	4	7	11	84					
	Buffalo	**NHL**	5	0	0	0	4					
	NHL Totals		5	0	0	0	4					

MELLANBY, SCOTT FLA.

Right wing. Shoots right. 6'1", 199 lbs. Born, Montreal, Que., June 11, 1966.
(Philadelphia's 2nd choice, 27th overall, in 1984 Entry Draft).

			Regular Season					Playoffs			
Season	Club	Lea	GP	G	A	TP	PIM	GP	G	A	TP	PIM
1984-85	U. Wisconsin	WCHA	40	14	24	38	60					
1985-86	U. Wisconsin	WCHA	32	21	23	44	89					
	Philadelphia	**NHL**	2	0	0	0	0					
1986-87	Philadelphia	NHL	71	11	21	32	94	24	5	5	10	46
1987-88	Philadelphia	NHL	75	25	26	51	185	7	0	1	1	16
1988-89	Philadelphia	NHL	76	21	29	50	183	19	4	5	9	28
1989-90	Philadelphia	NHL	57	6	17	23	77					
1990-91	Philadelphia	NHL	74	20	21	41	155					
1991-92	Edmonton	NHL	80	23	27	50	197	16	2	1	3	29
1992-93	Edmonton	NHL	69	15	17	32	147					
1993-94	Florida	NHL	80	30	30	60	149					
1994-95	Florida	NHL	48	13	12	25	90					
	NHL Totals		632	164	200	364	1277	66	11	12	23	119

Traded to **Edmonton** by **Philadelphia** with Craig Fisher and Craig Berube for Dave Brown, Corey Foster and Jari Kurri, May 30, 1991. Claimed by **Florida** from **Edmonton** in Expansion Draft, June 24, 1993.

MELYAKOV, IGOR (mehl-yuh-KAHF) L.A.

Right wing. Shoots left. 5'10", 176 lbs. Born, Lipetsk, USSR, December 25, 1976.
(Los Angeles' 6th choice, 137th overall, in 1995 Entry Draft).

			Regular Season					Playoffs			
Season	Club	Lea	GP	G	A	TP	PIM	GP	G	A	TP	PIM
1993-94	Yaroslavl	CIS	39	4	3	7	10	4	0	0	0	0
1994-95	Yaroslavl	CIS	50	6	8	14	34	4	0	1	1	0

MENHART, MARIAN BUF.

Defense. Shoots left. 6'3", 220 lbs. Born, Most, Czech., February 14, 1977.
(Buffalo's 6th choice, 111th overall, in 1995 Entry Draft).

			Regular Season					Playoffs			
Season	Club	Lea	GP	G	A	TP	PIM	GP	G	A	TP	PIM
1994-95	Litvinov	Czech. Jr.	36	15	19	34	....					

MESSIER, JOBY (MEHS-see-ay)

Defense. Shoots right. 6', 200 lbs. Born, Regina, Sask., March 2, 1970.
(NY Rangers' 7th choice, 118th overall, in 1989 Entry Draft).

			Regular Season					Playoffs			
Season	Club	Lea	GP	G	A	TP	PIM	GP	G	A	TP	PIM
1988-89	Michigan State	CCHA	39	2	10	12	66					
1989-90	Michigan State	CCHA	42	1	11	12	58					
1990-91	Michigan State	CCHA	39	5	11	16	71					
1991-92ab	Michigan State	CCHA	41	13	15	28	81					
1992-93	**NY Rangers**	**NHL**	11	0	0	0	6					
	Binghamton	AHL	60	5	16	21	63	14	1	1	2	6
1993-94	**NY Rangers**	**NHL**	4	0	2	2	0					
	Binghamton	AHL	42	6	14	20	58					
1994-95	Binghamton	AHL	25	2	9	11	36	1	0	0	0	0
	NY Rangers	**NHL**	10	0	2	2	18					
	NHL Totals		25	0	4	4	24					

a   CCHA First All-Star Team (1992)
b   NCAA West First All-American Team (1992)

MESSIER, MARK (MEHS-see-ay) NYR

Center. Shoots left. 6'1", 205 lbs. Born, Edmonton, Alta., January 18, 1961.
(Edmonton's 2nd choice, 48th overall, in 1979 Entry Draft).

			Regular Season					Playoffs			
Season	Club	Lea	GP	G	A	TP	PIM	GP	G	A	TP	PIM
1977-78	Portland	WHL	....	....	....	....	....	7	4	1	5	2
1978-79	Indianapolis	WHA	5	0	0	0	0					
	Cincinnati	WHA	47	1	10	11	58					
1979-80	Edmonton	NHL	75	12	21	33	120	3	1	2	3	2
	Houston	CHL	4	0	3	3	4					
1980-81	Edmonton	NHL	72	23	40	63	102	9	2	5	7	13
1981-82a	Edmonton	NHL	78	50	38	88	119	5	1	2	3	8
1982-83a	Edmonton	NHL	77	48	58	106	72	15	15	6	21	14
1983-84bc	Edmonton	NHL	73	37	64	101	165	19	8	18	26	19
1984-85	Edmonton	NHL	55	23	31	54	57	18	12	13	25	12
1985-86	Edmonton	NHL	63	35	49	84	68	10	4	6	10	18
1986-87	Edmonton	NHL	77	37	70	107	73	21	12	16	28	16
1987-88	Edmonton	NHL	77	37	74	111	103	19	11	23	34	29
1988-89	Edmonton	NHL	72	33	61	94	130	7	1	11	12	8
1989-90ade	Edmonton	NHL	79	45	84	129	79	22	9	*22	31	20
1990-91	Edmonton	NHL	53	12	52	64	34	18	4	11	15	16
1991-92ade	NY Rangers	NHL	79	35	72	107	76	11	7	7	14	6
1992-93	NY Rangers	NHL	75	25	66	91	72					
1993-94	NY Rangers	NHL	76	26	58	84	76	23	12	18	30	33
1994-95	NY Rangers	NHL	46	14	39	53	40	10	3	10	13	8
	NHL Totals		1127	492	877	1369	1386	210	102	170	272	222

a   NHL First All-Star Team (1982, 1983, 1990, 1992)
b   NHL Second All-Star Team (1984)
c   Won Conn Smythe Trophy (1984)
d   Won Hart Trophy (1990, 1992)
e   Won Lester B. Pearson Award (1990, 1992)
Played in NHL All-Star Game (1982-86, 1988-92, 1994)

Traded to **NY Rangers** by **Edmonton** with future considerations for Bernie Nicholls, Steven Rice and Louie DeBrusk, October 4, 1991.

MIETTINEN, TOMMI (mih-EHT-tih-nehn) ANA.

Center. Shoots left. 5'10", 165 lbs. Born, Kuopio, Finland, December 3, 1975.
(Anaheim's 9th choice, 236th overall, in 1994 Entry Draft).

			Regular Season					Playoffs			
Season	Club	Lea	GP	G	A	TP	PIM	GP	G	A	TP	PIM
1992-93	KalPa	Fin.	14	0	0	0	0					
1993-94	KalPa	Fin.	47	5	7	12	14					
1994-95	KalPa	Fin.	48	13	16	29	26					

MIKESCH, JEFF DET.

Center. Shoots left. 6', 175 lbs. Born, Hancook, MI, April 11, 1975.
(Detroit's 8th choice, 231st overall, in 1994 Entry Draft).

			Regular Season					Playoffs			
Season	Club	Lea	GP	G	A	TP	PIM	GP	G	A	TP	PIM
1993-94	Michigan Tech	WCHA	41	9	4	13	80					
1994-95	Michigan Tech	WCHA	36	9	8	17	83					

MIKULCHIK, OLEG (mih-KOOL-chihk, OH-lehg) ANA.

Defense. Shoots right. 6'2", 200 lbs. Born, Minsk, USSR, June 27, 1964.

			Regular Season					Playoffs			
Season	Club	Lea	GP	G	A	TP	PIM	GP	G	A	TP	PIM
1983-84	Moscow D'amo	USSR	17	0	0	0	6					
1984-85	Moscow D'amo	USSR	30	1	3	4	26					
1985-86	Moscow D'amo	USSR	40	0	1	1	36					
1986-87	Moscow D'amo	USSR	39	5	3	8	34					
1987-88	Moscow D'amo	USSR	48	7	8	15	63					
1988-89	Moscow D'amo	USSR	43	4	7	11	52					
1989-90	Moscow D'amo	USSR	32	1	3	4	31					
1990-91	Moscow D'amo	USSR	36	2	6	8	40					
1991-92	Khimik	CIS	15	3	2	5	20					
	New Haven	AHL	30	3	3	6	63	4	1	3	4	6
1992-93	Moncton	AHL	75	6	20	26	159	5	0	0	0	4
1993-94	**Winnipeg**	**NHL**	4	0	1	1	17					
	Moncton	AHL	67	9	38	47	121	21	2	10	12	18
1994-95	Springfield	AHL	50	5	16	21	59					
	Winnipeg	**NHL**	25	0	2	2	12					
	NHL Totals		29	0	3	3	29					

Signed as a free agent by **Winnipeg**, July 26, 1993. Signed as a free agent by **Anaheim**, August 8, 1995.

MILLAR, CRAIG BUF.

Defense. Shoots left. 6'2", 200 lbs. Born, Winnipeg, Man., July 12, 1976.
(Buffalo's 10th choice, 225th overall, in 1994 Entry Draft).

			Regular Season					Playoffs			
Season	Club	Lea	GP	G	A	TP	PIM	GP	G	A	TP	PIM
1992-93	Swift Current	WHL	43	2	1	3	8					
1993-94	Swift Current	WHL	66	2	9	11	53	7	0	3	3	4
1994-95	Swift Current	WHL	72	8	42	50	80	6	1	1	2	10

MILLEN, COREY — DAL.

Center. Shoots right. 5'7", 170 lbs. Born, Cloquet, MN, March 30, 1964.
(NY Rangers' 3rd choice, 57th overall, in 1982 Entry Draft).

			Regular Season					Playoffs				
Season	Club	Lea	GP	G	A	TP	PIM	GP	G	A	TP	PIM
1982-83	U. Minnesota	WCHA	21	14	15	29	18	....	....	....	....	....
1983-84	U.S. National	....	45	15	11	26	10	....	....	....	....	....
	U.S. Olympic	....	6	0	0	0	2	....	....	....	....	....
1984-85	U. Minnesota	WCHA	38	28	36	64	60	....	....	....	....	....
1985-86ab	U. Minnesota	WCHA	48	41	42	83	64	....	....	....	....	....
1986-87bc	U. Minnesota	WCHA	42	36	29	65	62	....	....	....	....	....
1987-88	U.S. National	....	47	41	43	84	26	....	....	....	....	....
	U.S. Olympic	....	6	6	5	11	4	....	....	....	....	....
1988-89	Ambri	Switz.	36	32	22	54	18	6	4	3	7	0
1989-90	**NY Rangers**	**NHL**	**4**	**0**	**0**	**0**	**2**	....	....	....	....	....
	Flint	IHL	11	4	5	9	2	....	....	....	....	....
1990-91	**NY Rangers**	**NHL**	**4**	**3**	**1**	**4**	**0**	**6**	**1**	**2**	**3**	**0**
	Binghamton	AHL	40	19	37	56	68	6	0	7	7	6
1991-92	**NY Rangers**	**NHL**	**11**	**1**	**4**	**5**	**10**	....	....	....	....	....
	Binghamton	AHL	15	8	7	15	44	....	....	....	....	....
	Los Angeles	**NHL**	**46**	**20**	**21**	**41**	**44**	**6**	**0**	**1**	**1**	**6**
1992-93	**Los Angeles**	**NHL**	**42**	**23**	**16**	**39**	**42**	**23**	**2**	**4**	**6**	**12**
1993-94	**New Jersey**	**NHL**	**78**	**20**	**30**	**50**	**52**	**7**	**1**	**0**	**1**	**2**
1994-95	**New Jersey**	**NHL**	**17**	**2**	**3**	**5**	**8**	....	....	....	....	....
	Dallas	**NHL**	**28**	**3**	**15**	**18**	**28**	**5**	**1**	**0**	**1**	**2**
	NHL Totals		**230**	**72**	**90**	**162**	**186**	**47**	**5**	**7**	**12**	**22**

a NCAA West Second All-American Team (1986)
b WCHA Second All-Star Team (1986, 1987)
c Named to NCAA All-Tournament Team (1987)

Traded to **Los Angeles** by **NY Rangers** for Randy Gilhen, December 23, 1991. Traded to **New Jersey** by **Los Angeles** for New Jersey's fifth round choice (Jason Saal) in 1993 Entry Draft, June 26, 1993. Traded to **Dallas** by **New Jersey** for Neal Broten, February 27, 1995.

MILLER, AARON — COL.

Defense. Shoots right. 6'3", 197 lbs. Born, Buffalo, NY, August 11, 1971.
(NY Rangers' 6th choice, 88th overall, in 1989 Entry Draft).

			Regular Season					Playoffs				
Season	Club	Lea	GP	G	A	TP	PIM	GP	G	A	TP	PIM
1989-90	U. of Vermont	ECAC	31	1	15	16	24	....	....	....	....	....
1990-91	U. of Vermont	ECAC	30	3	7	10	22	....	....	....	....	....
1991-92	U. of Vermont	ECAC	31	3	16	19	28	....	....	....	....	....
1992-93ab	U. of Vermont	ECAC	30	4	13	17	16	....	....	....	....	....
1993-94	**Quebec**	**NHL**	**1**	**0**	**0**	**0**	**0**	....	....	....	....	....
	Cornwall	AHL	64	4	10	14	49	13	0	2	2	10
1994-95	Cornwall	AHL	76	4	18	22	69	....	....	....	....	....
	Quebec	**NHL**	**9**	**0**	**3**	**3**	**6**	....	....	....	....	....
	NHL Totals		**10**	**0**	**3**	**3**	**6**	....	....	....	....	....

a ECAC First All-Star Team (1993)
b NCAA East Second All-American Team (1993)

Traded to **Quebec** by **NY Rangers** with NY Rangers' fifth round choice (Bill Lindsay) in 1991 Entry Draft for Joe Cirella, January 17, 1991.

MILLER, JASON

Left wing. Shoots left. 6'1", 190 lbs. Born, Edmonton, Alta., March 1, 1971.
(New Jersey's 2nd choice, 18th overall, in 1989 Entry Draft).

			Regular Season					Playoffs				
Season	Club	Lea	GP	G	A	TP	PIM	GP	G	A	TP	PIM
1987-88	Medicine Hat	WHL	71	11	18	29	28	15	0	1	1	2
1988-89	Medicine Hat	WHL	72	51	55	106	44	3	1	2	3	2
1989-90	Medicine Hat	WHL	66	43	56	99	40	3	3	2	5	0
1990-91	**New Jersey**	**NHL**	**1**	**0**	**0**	**0**	**0**	....	....	....	....	....
a	Medicine Hat	WHL	66	60	76	136	31	12	9	10	19	8
1991-92	**New Jersey**	**NHL**	**3**	**0**	**0**	**0**	**0**	....	....	....	....	....
	Utica	AHL	71	23	32	55	31	4	1	3	4	0
1992-93	**New Jersey**	**NHL**	**2**	**0**	**0**	**0**	**0**	....	....	....	....	....
	Utica	AHL	72	28	42	70	43	5	4	4	8	2
1993-94	Albany	AHL	77	22	53	75	65	5	1	1	2	4
1994-95	Adirondack	AHL	77	32	33	65	39	4	1	0	1	0
	NHL Totals		**6**	**0**	**0**	**0**	**0**	....	....	....	....	....

a WHL East Second All-Star Team (1991)

Signed as a free agent by **Detroit**, August 26, 1994.

MILLER, KELLY — WSH.

Left wing. Shoots left. 5'11", 197 lbs. Born, Lansing, MI, March 3, 1963.
(NY Rangers' 9th choice, 183rd overall, in 1982 Entry Draft).

			Regular Season					Playoffs				
Season	Club	Lea	GP	G	A	TP	PIM	GP	G	A	TP	PIM
1981-82	Michigan State	CCHA	38	11	18	29	17	....	....	....	....	....
1982-83	Michigan State	CCHA	36	16	19	35	12	....	....	....	....	....
1983-84	Michigan State	CCHA	46	28	21	49	12	....	....	....	....	....
1984-85ab	Michigan State	CCHA	43	27	23	50	21	....	....	....	....	....
	NY Rangers	**NHL**	**5**	**0**	**2**	**2**	**2**	**3**	**0**	**0**	**0**	**2**
1985-86	**NY Rangers**	**NHL**	**74**	**13**	**20**	**33**	**52**	**16**	**3**	**4**	**7**	**4**
1986-87	**NY Rangers**	**NHL**	**38**	**6**	**14**	**20**	**22**	....	....	....	....	....
	Washington	**NHL**	**39**	**10**	**12**	**22**	**26**	**7**	**2**	**2**	**4**	**0**
1987-88	**Washington**	**NHL**	**80**	**9**	**23**	**32**	**35**	**14**	**4**	**4**	**8**	**10**
1988-89	**Washington**	**NHL**	**78**	**19**	**21**	**40**	**45**	**6**	**1**	**0**	**1**	**2**
1989-90	**Washington**	**NHL**	**80**	**18**	**22**	**40**	**49**	**15**	**3**	**5**	**8**	**23**
1990-91	**Washington**	**NHL**	**80**	**24**	**26**	**50**	**29**	**11**	**4**	**2**	**6**	**6**
1991-92	**Washington**	**NHL**	**78**	**14**	**38**	**52**	**49**	**7**	**1**	**2**	**3**	**4**
1992-93	**Washington**	**NHL**	**84**	**18**	**27**	**45**	**32**	**6**	**0**	**3**	**3**	**2**
1993-94	**Washington**	**NHL**	**84**	**14**	**25**	**39**	**32**	**11**	**2**	**7**	**9**	**0**
1994-95	**Washington**	**NHL**	**48**	**10**	**13**	**23**	**6**	**7**	**0**	**3**	**3**	**4**
	NHL Totals		**768**	**155**	**243**	**398**	**379**	**103**	**20**	**32**	**52**	**57**

a CCHA First All-Star Team (1985)
b NCAA West First All-American Team (1985)

Traded to **Washington** by **NY Rangers** with Bob Crawford and Mike Ridley for Bob Carpenter and Washington's second round choice (Jason Prosofsky) in 1989 Entry Draft, January 1, 1987.

MILLER, KEVIN — S.J.

Center. Shoots right. 5'11", 190 lbs. Born, Lansing, MI, September 2, 1965.
(NY Rangers' 10th choice, 202nd overall, in 1984 Entry Draft).

			Regular Season					Playoffs				
Season	Club	Lea	GP	G	A	TP	PIM	GP	G	A	TP	PIM
1984-85	Michigan State	CCHA	44	11	29	40	84	....	....	....	....	....
1985-86	Michigan State	CCHA	45	19	52	71	112	....	....	....	....	....
1986-87	Michigan State	CCHA	42	25	56	81	63	....	....	....	....	....
1987-88	Michigan State	CCHA	9	6	3	9	18	....	....	....	....	....
	U.S. National	....	48	31	32	63	33	....	....	....	....	....
	U.S. Olympic	....	5	1	3	4	4	....	....	....	....	....
1988-89	**NY Rangers**	**NHL**	**24**	**3**	**5**	**8**	**2**	....	....	....	....	....
	Denver	IHL	55	29	47	76	19	4	2	1	3	2
1989-90	**NY Rangers**	**NHL**	**16**	**0**	**5**	**5**	**2**	**1**	**0**	**0**	**0**	**0**
	Flint	IHL	48	19	23	42	41	....	....	....	....	....
1990-91	**NY Rangers**	**NHL**	**63**	**17**	**27**	**44**	**63**	....	....	....	....	....
	Detroit	**NHL**	**11**	**5**	**2**	**7**	**4**	**7**	**3**	**2**	**5**	**20**
1991-92	**Detroit**	**NHL**	**80**	**20**	**26**	**46**	**53**	**9**	**0**	**2**	**2**	**4**
1992-93	**Washington**	**NHL**	**10**	**0**	**3**	**3**	**35**	....	....	....	....	....
	St. Louis	**NHL**	**72**	**24**	**22**	**46**	**65**	**10**	**0**	**3**	**3**	**11**
1993-94	**St. Louis**	**NHL**	**75**	**23**	**25**	**48**	**83**	**3**	**1**	**0**	**1**	**4**
1994-95	**St. Louis**	**NHL**	**15**	**2**	**5**	**7**	**0**	....	....	....	....	....
	San Jose	**NHL**	**21**	**6**	**7**	**13**	**13**	**6**	**0**	**0**	**0**	**2**
	NHL Totals		**387**	**100**	**127**	**227**	**320**	**36**	**4**	**7**	**11**	**41**

Traded to **Detroit** by **NY Rangers** with Jim Cummins and Dennis Vial for Joey Kocur and Per Djoos, March 5, 1991. Traded to **Washington** by **Detroit** for Dino Ciccarelli, June 20, 1992. Traded to **St. Louis** by **Washington** for Paul Cavallini, November 2, 1992. Traded to **San Jose** by **St. Louis** for Todd Elik, March 23, 1995.

MILLER, KIP — CHI.

Center. Shoots left. 5'10", 190 lbs. Born, Lansing, MI, June 11, 1969.
(Quebec's 4th choice, 72nd overall, in 1987 Entry Draft).

			Regular Season					Playoffs				
Season	Club	Lea	GP	G	A	TP	PIM	GP	G	A	TP	PIM
1986-87	Michigan State	CCHA	41	20	19	39	92	....	....	....	....	....
1987-88	Michigan State	CCHA	39	16	25	41	51	....	....	....	....	....
1988-89ab	Michigan State	CCHA	47	32	45	77	94	....	....	....	....	....
1989-90abc	Michigan State	CCHA	45	*48	53	*101	60	....	....	....	....	....
1990-91	**Quebec**	**NHL**	**13**	**4**	**3**	**7**	**7**	....	....	....	....	....
	Halifax	AHL	66	36	33	69	40	....	....	....	....	....
1991-92	**Quebec**	**NHL**	**36**	**5**	**10**	**15**	**12**	....	....	....	....	....
	Halifax	AHL	24	9	17	26	8	....	....	....	....	....
	Minnesota	**NHL**	**3**	**1**	**2**	**3**	**2**	....	....	....	....	....
	Kalamazoo	IHL	6	1	8	9	4	12	3	9	12	12
1992-93	Kalamazoo	IHL	61	17	39	56	59	....	....	....	....	....
1993-94	**San Jose**	**NHL**	**11**	**2**	**2**	**4**	**6**	....	....	....	....	....
	Kansas City	IHL	71	38	54	92	51	....	....	....	....	....
1994-95	Denver	IHL	71	46	60	106	54	17	*15	14	29	8
	NY Islanders	**NHL**	**8**	**0**	**1**	**1**	**0**	....	....	....	....	....
	NHL Totals		**71**	**12**	**18**	**30**	**27**	....	....	....	....	....

a CCHA First All-Star Team (1989, 1990)
b NCAA West First All-American Team (1989, 1990)
c Won Hobey Baker Memorial Award (Top U.S. Collegiate Player) (1990)

Traded to **Minnesota** by **Quebec** for Steve Maltais, March 8, 1992. Signed as a free agent by **San Jose**, August 10, 1993. Signed as a free agent by **NY Islanders**, July 7, 1994. Signed as a free agent by **Chicago**, August 7, 1995.

MILLER, KURTIS — DET.

Left wing. Shoots left. 5'11", 190 lbs. Born, Bemidji, MN, June 1, 1970.
(St. Louis' 4th choice, 117th overall, in 1990 Entry Draft).

			Regular Season					Playoffs				
Season	Club	Lea	GP	G	A	TP	PIM	GP	G	A	TP	PIM
1990-91	Lake Superior	CCHA	45	10	12	22	48	....	....	....	....	....
1991-92	Lake Superior	CCHA	15	6	7	13	32	....	....	....	....	....
1992-93	Lake Superior	CCHA	26	9	14	23	24	....	....	....	....	....
1993-94	Lake Superior	CCHA	40	19	23	42	58	....	....	....	....	....
1994-95	Adirondack	AHL	78	22	18	40	45	4	1	1	2	2

Signed as a free agent by **Detroit**, August 10, 1994.

MILLS, CRAIG — WPG.

Right wing. Shoots right. 5'11", 174 lbs. Born, Toronto, Ont., August 27, 1976.
(Winnipeg's 5th choice, 108th overall, in 1994 Entry Draft).

			Regular Season					Playoffs				
Season	Club	Lea	GP	G	A	TP	PIM	GP	G	A	TP	PIM
1993-94	Belleville	OHL	63	15	18	33	88	12	2	1	3	11
1994-95	Belleville	OHL	62	39	41	80	104	13	7	9	16	8

MIRONOV, BORIS (mih-RAH-nahf) — EDM.

Defense. Shoots right. 6'3", 220 lbs. Born, Moscow, USSR, March 21, 1972.
(Winnipeg's 2nd choice, 27th overall, in 1992 Entry Draft).

			Regular Season					Playoffs				
Season	Club	Lea	GP	G	A	TP	PIM	GP	G	A	TP	PIM
1988-89	CSKA	USSR	1	0	0	0	0	....	....	....	....	....
1989-90	CSKA	USSR	7	0	0	0	0	....	....	....	....	....
1990-91	CSKA	USSR	36	1	5	6	16	....	....	....	....	....
1991-92	CSKA	CIS	36	2	1	3	22	....	....	....	....	....
1992-93	CSKA	CIS	19	0	5	5	20	....	....	....	....	....
1993-94a	**Winnipeg**	**NHL**	**65**	**7**	**22**	**29**	**96**	....	....	....	....	....
	Edmonton	**NHL**	**14**	**0**	**2**	**2**	**14**	....	....	....	....	....
1994-95	**Edmonton**	**NHL**	**29**	**1**	**7**	**8**	**40**	....	....	....	....	....
	Cape Breton	AHL	4	2	5	7	23	....	....	....	....	....
	NHL Totals		**108**	**8**	**31**	**39**	**150**	....	....	....	....	....

a NHL/Upper Deck All-Rookie Team (1994)

Traded to **Edmonton** by **Winnipeg** with Mats Lindgren, Winnipeg's first round choice (Jason Bonsignore) in 1994 Entry Draft and Florida's fourth round choice (previously acquired by Winnipeg — Edmonton selected Adam Copeland) in 1994 Entry Draft for Dave Manson and St. Louis' sixth round choice (previously acquired by Edmonton — Winnipeg selected Chris Kibermanis) in 1994 Entry Draft, March 15, 1994.

MIRONOV, DMITRI (mih-RAWN-ohv) PIT.

Defense. Shoots right. 6'2", 214 lbs. Born, Moscow, USSR, December 25, 1965.
(Toronto's 9th choice, 160th overall, in 1991 Entry Draft).

			Regular Season					Playoffs				
Season	Club	Lea	GP	G	A	TP	PIM	GP	G	A	TP	PIM
1985-86	CSKA	USSR	9	0	1	1	8	....	....	....	....	....
1986-87	CSKA	USSR	20	1	3	4	10	....	....	....	....	....
1987-88	Soviet Wings	USSR	44	12	6	18	30	....	....	....	....	....
1988-89	Soviet Wings	USSR	44	5	6	11	44	....	....	....	....	....
1989-90	Soviet Wings	USSR	45	4	11	15	34	....	....	....	....	....
1990-91	Soviet Wings	USSR	45	16	12	28	22	....	....	....	....	....
1991-92	Soviet Wings	CIS	35	15	16	31	62	....	....	....	....	....
	Toronto	**NHL**	**7**	**1**	**0**	**1**	**0**	....	....	....	....	....
1992-93	**Toronto**	**NHL**	**59**	**7**	**24**	**31**	**40**	**14**	**1**	**2**	**3**	**2**
1993-94	**Toronto**	**NHL**	**76**	**9**	**27**	**36**	**78**	**18**	**6**	**9**	**15**	**6**
1994-95	**Toronto**	**NHL**	**33**	**5**	**12**	**17**	**28**	**6**	**2**	**1**	**3**	**2**
	NHL Totals		**175**	**22**	**63**	**85**	**146**	**38**	**9**	**12**	**21**	**10**

Traded to **Pittsburgh** by **Toronto** with Toronto's second round choice in 1996 Entry Draft for Larry Murphy, July 8, 1995.

MITCHELL, JEFF DAL.

Center/Right wing. Shoots right. 6'1", 190 lbs. Born, Wayne, MI, May 16, 1975.
(Los Angeles' 2nd choice, 68th overall, in 1993 Entry Draft).

			Regular Season					Playoffs				
Season	Club	Lea	GP	G	A	TP	PIM	GP	G	A	TP	PIM
1992-93	Detroit	OHL	62	10	15	25	100	15	3	3	6	16
1993-94	Detroit	OHL	59	25	18	43	99	17	3	5	8	22
1994-95	Detroit	OHL	61	30	30	60	121	21	9	12	21	48

Rights traded to **Dallas** by **Los Angeles** for Vancouver's fifth round choice (previously acquired by Dallas — Los Angeles selected Jason Morgan) in 1995 Entry Draft, June 7, 1995.

MODANO, MIKE DAL.

Center. Shoots left. 6'3", 190 lbs. Born, Livonia, MI, June 7, 1970.
(Minnesota's 1st choice, 1st overall, in 1988 Entry Draft).

			Regular Season					Playoffs				
Season	Club	Lea	GP	G	A	TP	PIM	GP	G	A	TP	PIM
1986-87	Prince Albert	WHL	70	32	30	62	96	8	1	4	5	4
1987-88	Prince Albert	WHL	65	47	80	127	80	9	7	11	18	18
1988-89a	Prince Albert	WHL	41	39	66	105	74	....	....	....	....	....
	Minnesota	**NHL**	....	....	....	....	....	**2**	**0**	**0**	**0**	**0**
1989-90b	**Minnesota**	**NHL**	**80**	**29**	**46**	**75**	**63**	**7**	**1**	**1**	**2**	**12**
1990-91	**Minnesota**	**NHL**	**79**	**28**	**36**	**64**	**65**	**23**	**8**	**12**	**20**	**16**
1991-92	**Minnesota**	**NHL**	**76**	**33**	**44**	**77**	**46**	**7**	**3**	**2**	**5**	**4**
1992-93	**Minnesota**	**NHL**	**82**	**33**	**60**	**93**	**83**	....	....	....	....	....
1993-94	**Dallas**	**NHL**	**76**	**50**	**43**	**93**	**54**	**9**	**7**	**3**	**10**	**16**
1994-95	**Dallas**	**NHL**	**30**	**12**	**17**	**29**	**8**	....	....	....	....	....
	NHL Totals		**423**	**185**	**246**	**431**	**319**	**48**	**19**	**18**	**37**	**48**

a WHL East All-Star Team (1989)
b NHL All-Rookie Team (1990)

Played in NHL All-Star Game (1993)

MODIN, FREDRIK (muh-DEEN) TOR.

Left wing. Shoots left. 6'3", 202 lbs. Born, Sundsvall, Sweden, October 8, 1974.
(Toronto's 3rd choice, 64th overall, in 1994 Entry Draft).

			Regular Season					Playoffs				
Season	Club	Lea	GP	G	A	TP	PIM	GP	G	A	TP	PIM
1991-92	Sundsvall	Swe. 2	11	1	0	1	0	....	....	....	....	....
1992-93	Sundsvall	Swe. 2	30	5	7	12	12	....	....	....	....	....
1993-94	Sundsvall	Swe. 2	30	16	15	31	36	....	....	....	....	....
1994-95	Brynas	Swe.	38	9	10	19	33	14	4	4	8	6

MODRY, JAROSLAV (MOHD-ree) OTT.

Defense. Shoots left. 6'2", 195 lbs. Born, Ceske-Budejovice, Czech., February 27, 1971.
(New Jersey's 11th choice, 179th overall, in 1990 Entry Draft).

			Regular Season					Playoffs				
Season	Club	Lea	GP	G	A	TP	PIM	GP	G	A	TP	PIM
1987-88	Budejovice	Czech.	3	0	0	0	0	....	....	....	....	....
1988-89	Budejovice	Czech.	28	0	1	1	8	....	....	....	....	....
1989-90	Budejovice	Czech.	41	2	2	4	....	....	....	....	....	....
1990-91	Dukla Trencin	Czech.	33	1	9	10	6	....	....	....	....	....
1991-92	Dukla Trencin	Czech.	18	0	4	4	6	....	....	....	....	....
	Budejovice	Czech. 2	14	4	10	14	....	....	....	....	....	....
1992-93	Utica	AHL	80	7	35	42	62	5	0	2	2	2
1993-94	**New Jersey**	**NHL**	**41**	**2**	**15**	**17**	**18**	....	....	....	....	....
	Albany	AHL	19	1	5	6	25	....	....	....	....	....
1994-95	Budejovice	Czech.	19	1	3	4	30	....	....	....	....	....
	New Jersey	**NHL**	**11**	**0**	**0**	**0**	**0**	....	....	....	....	....
	Albany	AHL	18	5	6	11	14	14	3	3	6	4
	NHL Totals		**52**	**2**	**15**	**17**	**18**	....	....	....	....	....

Traded to **Ottawa** by **New Jersey** for Ottawa's fourth round choice (Alyn McCauley) in 1995 Entry Draft, July 8, 1995.

MOGER, SANDY (MOH-guhr) BOS.

Center. Shoots right. 6'3", 215 lbs. Born, 100 Mile House, B.C., March 21, 1969.
(Vancouver's 7th choice, 176th overall, in 1989 Entry Draft).

			Regular Season					Playoffs				
Season	Club	Lea	GP	G	A	TP	PIM	GP	G	A	TP	PIM
1988-89	Lake Superior	CCHA	21	3	5	8	26	....	....	....	....	....
1989-90	Lake Superior	CCHA	46	17	15	32	76	....	....	....	....	....
1990-91	Lake Superior	CCHA	45	27	21	48	*172	....	....	....	....	....
1991-92a	Lake Superior	CCHA	38	24	24	48	93	....	....	....	....	....
1992-93	Hamilton	AHL	78	23	26	49	57	....	....	....	....	....
1993-94	Hamilton	AHL	29	9	8	17	41	....	....	....	....	....
1994-95	Providence	AHL	63	32	29	61	105	....	....	....	....	....
	Boston	**NHL**	**18**	**2**	**6**	**8**	**6**	....	....	....	....	....
	NHL Totals		**18**	**2**	**6**	**8**	**6**	....	....	....	....	....

a CCHA Second All-Star Team (1992)

Signed as a free agent by **Boston**, June 22, 1994.

MOGILNY, ALEXANDER (moh-GIHL-nee) VAN.

Right wing. Shoots left. 5'11", 187 lbs. Born, Khabarovsk, USSR, February 18, 1969.
(Buffalo's 4th choice, 89th overall, in 1988 Entry Draft).

			Regular Season					Playoffs				
Season	Club	Lea	GP	G	A	TP	PIM	GP	G	A	TP	PIM
1986-87	CSKA	USSR	28	15	1	16	4	....	....	....	....	....
1987-88	CSKA	USSR	39	12	8	20	14	....	....	....	....	....
1988-89	CSKA	USSR	31	11	11	22	24	....	....	....	....	....
1989-90	**Buffalo**	**NHL**	**65**	**15**	**28**	**43**	**16**	**4**	**0**	**1**	**1**	**2**
1990-91	**Buffalo**	**NHL**	**62**	**30**	**34**	**64**	**16**	**6**	**0**	**6**	**6**	**2**
1991-92	**Buffalo**	**NHL**	**67**	**39**	**45**	**84**	**73**	**2**	**0**	**2**	**2**	**0**
1992-93a	**Buffalo**	**NHL**	**77**	***76**	**51**	**127**	**40**	**7**	**7**	**3**	**10**	**6**
1993-94	**Buffalo**	**NHL**	**66**	**32**	**47**	**79**	**22**	**7**	**4**	**2**	**6**	**6**
1994-95	Spartak	CIS	1	0	1	1	0	....	....	....	....	....
	Buffalo	**NHL**	**44**	**19**	**28**	**47**	**36**	**5**	**3**	**2**	**5**	**2**
	NHL Totals		**381**	**211**	**233**	**444**	**203**	**31**	**14**	**16**	**30**	**18**

a NHL Second All-Star Team (1993)

Played in NHL All-Star Game (1992-94)

Traded to **Vancouver** by **Buffalo** with Buffalo's fifth round choice (Todd Norman) in 1995 Entry Draft for Mike Peca, Mike Wilson and Vancouver's first round choice (Jay McKee) in 1995 Entry Draft, July 8, 1995.

MOLLER, RANDY FLA.

Defense. Shoots right. 6'2", 210 lbs. Born, Red Deer, Alta., August 23, 1963.
(Quebec's 1st choice, 11th overall, in 1981 Entry Draft).

			Regular Season					Playoffs				
Season	Club	Lea	GP	G	A	TP	PIM	GP	G	A	TP	PIM
1980-81	Lethbridge	WHL	46	4	21	25	176	9	0	4	4	24
1981-82a	Lethbridge	WHL	60	20	55	75	249	12	4	6	10	65
	Quebec	**NHL**	....	....	....	....	....	**1**	**0**	**0**	**0**	**0**
1982-83	**Quebec**	**NHL**	**75**	**2**	**12**	**14**	**145**	**4**	**1**	**0**	**1**	**4**
1983-84	**Quebec**	**NHL**	**74**	**4**	**14**	**18**	**147**	**9**	**1**	**0**	**1**	**45**
1984-85	**Quebec**	**NHL**	**79**	**7**	**22**	**29**	**120**	**18**	**2**	**2**	**4**	**40**
1985-86	**Quebec**	**NHL**	**69**	**5**	**18**	**23**	**141**	**3**	**0**	**0**	**0**	**26**
1986-87	**Quebec**	**NHL**	**71**	**5**	**9**	**14**	**144**	**13**	**1**	**4**	**5**	**23**
1987-88	**Quebec**	**NHL**	**66**	**3**	**22**	**25**	**169**	....	....	....	....	....
1988-89	**Quebec**	**NHL**	**74**	**7**	**22**	**29**	**136**	....	....	....	....	....
1989-90	**NY Rangers**	**NHL**	**60**	**1**	**12**	**13**	**139**	**10**	**1**	**6**	**7**	**32**
1990-91	**NY Rangers**	**NHL**	**61**	**4**	**19**	**23**	**161**	**6**	**0**	**2**	**2**	**11**
1991-92	**NY Rangers**	**NHL**	**43**	**2**	**7**	**9**	**78**	....	....	....	....	....
	Binghamton	AHL	3	0	1	1	0	....	....	....	....	....
	Buffalo	**NHL**	**13**	**1**	**2**	**3**	**59**	**7**	**0**	**0**	**0**	**8**
1992-93	**Buffalo**	**NHL**	**35**	**2**	**7**	**9**	**83**	....	....	....	....	....
	Rochester	AHL	3	1	0	1	10	....	....	....	....	....
1993-94	**Buffalo**	**NHL**	**78**	**2**	**11**	**13**	**154**	**7**	**0**	**2**	**2**	**8**
1994-95	**Florida**	**NHL**	**17**	**0**	**3**	**3**	**16**	....	....	....	....	....
	NHL Totals		**815**	**45**	**180**	**225**	**1692**	**78**	**6**	**16**	**22**	**197**

a WHL Second All-Star Team (1982)

Traded to **NY Rangers** by **Quebec** for Michel Petit, October 5, 1989. Traded to **Buffalo** by **NY Rangers** for Jay Wells, March 9, 1992. Signed as a free agent by **Florida**, July 11, 1994.

MOMESSO, SERGIO (moh-MESS-oh) TOR.

Left wing. Shoots left. 6'3", 215 lbs. Born, Montreal, Que., September 4, 1965.
(Montreal's 3rd choice, 27th overall, in 1983 Entry Draft).

			Regular Season					Playoffs				
Season	Club	Lea	GP	G	A	TP	PIM	GP	G	A	TP	PIM
1982-83	Shawinigan	QMJHL	70	27	42	69	93	10	5	4	9	55
1983-84	**Montreal**	**NHL**	**1**	**0**	**0**	**0**	**0**	....	....	....	....	....
	Shawinigan	QMJHL	68	42	88	130	235	6	4	4	8	13
	Nova Scotia	AHL	....	....	....	....	....	8	0	2	2	4
1984-85a	Shawinigan	QMJHL	64	56	90	146	216	8	7	8	15	17
1985-86	**Montreal**	**NHL**	**24**	**8**	**7**	**15**	**46**	....	....	....	....	....
1986-87	**Montreal**	**NHL**	**59**	**14**	**17**	**31**	**96**	**11**	**1**	**3**	**4**	**31**
	Sherbrooke	AHL	6	1	6	7	10	....	....	....	....	....
1987-88	**Montreal**	**NHL**	**53**	**7**	**14**	**21**	**101**	**6**	**0**	**2**	**2**	**16**
1988-89	**St. Louis**	**NHL**	**53**	**9**	**17**	**26**	**139**	**10**	**2**	**5**	**7**	**24**
1989-90	**St. Louis**	**NHL**	**79**	**24**	**32**	**56**	**199**	**12**	**3**	**2**	**5**	**63**
1990-91	**St. Louis**	**NHL**	**59**	**10**	**18**	**28**	**131**	....	....	....	....	....
	Vancouver	**NHL**	**11**	**6**	**2**	**8**	**43**	**6**	**0**	**3**	**3**	**25**
1991-92	**Vancouver**	**NHL**	**58**	**20**	**23**	**43**	**198**	**13**	**0**	**5**	**5**	**30**
1992-93	**Vancouver**	**NHL**	**84**	**18**	**20**	**38**	**200**	**12**	**3**	**0**	**3**	**30**
1993-94	**Vancouver**	**NHL**	**68**	**14**	**13**	**27**	**149**	**24**	**3**	**4**	**7**	**56**
1994-95	Milan Devils	Euro.	2	2	3	5	0	....	....	....	....	....
	Milan Devils	Italy	2	1	4	5	2	....	....	....	....	....
	Vancouver	**NHL**	**48**	**10**	**15**	**25**	**65**	**11**	**3**	**1**	**4**	**16**
	NHL Totals		**597**	**140**	**178**	**318**	**1367**	**105**	**15**	**25**	**40**	**291**

a QMJHL First All-Star Team (1985)

Traded to **St. Louis** by **Montreal** with Vincent Riendeau for Jocelyn Lemieux, Darrell May and St. Louis' second round choice (Patrice Brisebois) in the 1989 Entry Draft, August 9, 1988. Traded to **Vancouver** by **St. Louis** with Geoff Courtnall, Robert Dirk, Cliff Ronning and St. Louis' fifth round choice (Brian Loney) in 1992 Entry Draft for Dan Quinn and Garth Butcher, March 5, 1991. Traded to **Toronto** by **Vancouver** for Mike Ridley, July 8, 1995.

MONGEAU, MICHEL (MOHN-zhoh)

Center. Shoots left. 5'9", 190 lbs. Born, Montreal, Que., February 9, 1965.

			Regular Season					Playoffs				
Season	Club	Lea	GP	G	A	TP	PIM	GP	G	A	TP	PIM
1983-84	Laval	QMJHL	60	45	49	94	30	....	....	....	....	....
1984-85	Laval	QMJHL	67	60	84	144	56	....	....	....	....	....
1985-86	Laval	QMJHL	72	71	109	180	45	....	....	....	....	....
1986-87	Saginaw	IHL	76	42	53	95	34	10	3	6	9	6
1987-88	France	....	30	31	21	52	....	....	....	....	....	....
1988-89	Flint	IHL	82	41	76	117	57	....	....	....	....	....
1989-90	**St. Louis**	**NHL**	**7**	**1**	**5**	**6**	**2**	**2**	**0**	**1**	**1**	**0**
abc	Peoria	IHL	73	39	*78	*117	53	5	3	4	7	6
1990-91	**St. Louis**	**NHL**	**7**	**1**	**1**	**2**	**0**	....	....	....	....	....
de	Peoria	IHL	73	41	65	106	114	19	10	*16	26	32
1991-92	**St. Louis**	**NHL**	**36**	**3**	**12**	**15**	**6**	....	....	....	....	....
	Peoria	IHL	32	21	34	55	77	10	5	14	19	8
1992-93	**Tampa Bay**	**NHL**	**4**	**1**	**1**	**2**	**2**	....	....	....	....	....
	Milwaukee	IHL	45	24	41	65	69	4	1	4	5	4
	Halifax	AHL	22	13	18	31	10	....	....	....	....	....
1993-94	Cornwall	AHL	7	3	11	14	4	....	....	....	....	....
	Peoria	IHL	52	29	36	65	50	....	....	....	....	....
1994-95	Peoria	IHL	74	30	52	82	72	....	....	....	....	....
	NHL Totals		**54**	**6**	**19**	**25**	**10**	**2**	**0**	**1**	**1**	**0**

a IHL First All-Star Team (1990)
b Won James Gatschene Memorial Trophy (MVP - IHL) (1990)
c Won Leo P. Lamoureux Memorial Trophy (Top Scorer - IHL) (1990)
d IHL Second All-Star Team (1991)
e Won N.R. Poile Trophy (MVP in Playoffs - IHL) (1991)

Signed as a free agent by **St. Louis**, August 21, 1989. Claimed by **Tampa Bay** from **St. Louis** in Expansion Draft, June 18, 1992. Traded to **Quebec** by **Tampa Bay** with Martin Simard and Steve Tuttle for Herb Raglan, February 12, 1993.

MONTGOMERY, JIM PHI.

Center. Shoots right. 5'10", 185 lbs. Born, Montreal, Que., June 30, 1969.

			Regular Season					Playoffs				
Season	Club	Lea	GP	G	A	TP	PIM	GP	G	A	TP	PIM
1989-90	U. of Maine	H.E.	45	26	34	60	35	....	....	....	....	....
1990-91	U. of Maine	H.E.	43	24	*57	81	44	....	....	....	....	....
1991-92a	U. of Maine	H.E.	37	21	44	65	46	....	....	....	....	....
1992-93bcde	U. of Maine	H.E.	45	32	63	95	40	....	....	....	....	....
1993-94	**St. Louis**	**NHL**	**67**	**6**	**14**	**20**	**44**	....	....	....	....	....
	Peoria	IHL	12	7	8	15	10	....	....	....	....	....
1994-95	**Montreal**	**NHL**	**5**	**0**	**0**	**0**	**2**	....	....	....	....	....
	Philadelphia	**NHL**	**8**	**1**	**1**	**2**	**6**	**7**	**1**	**0**	**1**	**2**
	Hershey	AHL	16	8	6	14	14	6	3	2	5	25
	NHL Totals		**80**	**7**	**15**	**22**	**52**	**7**	**1**	**0**	**1**	**2**

a Hockey East Second All-Star Team (1992)
b Hockey East First All-Star Team (1993)
c NCAA East Second All-American Team (1993)
d NCAA Final Four All-Tournament Team (1993)
e NCAA Final Four Tournament Most Valuable Player (1993)

Signed as a free agent by **St. Louis**, June 2, 1993. Traded to **Montreal** by **St. Louis** for Guy Carbonneau, August 19, 1994. Claimed on waivers by **Philadelphia** from **Montreal**, February 10, 1995.

MONTREUIL, ERIC FLA.

Center. Shoots left. 6'1", 177 lbs. Born, Verdun, Que., May 18, 1975.
(Florida's 13th choice, 265th overall, in 1993 Entry Draft).

			Regular Season					Playoffs				
Season	Club	Lea	GP	G	A	TP	PIM	GP	G	A	TP	PIM
1992-93	Chicoutimi	QMJHL	70	19	13	32	98	4	0	1	1	2
1993-94	Beauport	QMJHL	67	31	40	71	122	15	4	8	12	39
1994-95	Beauport	QMJHL	70	21	39	60	186	18	5	10	15	72

MOORE, BARRIE BUF.

Left wing. Shoots left. 5'11", 175 lbs. Born, London, Ont., May 22, 1975.
(Buffalo's 7th choice, 220th overall, in 1993 Entry Draft).

			Regular Season					Playoffs				
Season	Club	Lea	GP	G	A	TP	PIM	GP	G	A	TP	PIM
1991-92	Sudbury	OHL	62	15	38	53	57	11	0	7	7	12
1992-93	Sudbury	OHL	57	13	26	39	71	14	4	3	7	19
1993-94	Sudbury	OHL	65	36	49	85	69	10	3	5	8	14
1994-95	Sudbury	OHL	60	47	42	89	67	18	*15	14	29	24

MORAN, IAN PIT.

Defense. Shoots right. 5'11", 180 lbs. Born, Cleveland, OH, August 24, 1972.
(Pittsburgh's 6th choice, 107th overall, in 1990 Entry Draft).

			Regular Season					Playoffs				
Season	Club	Lea	GP	G	A	TP	PIM	GP	G	A	TP	PIM
1991-92	Boston College	H.E.	30	2	16	18	44	....	....	....	....	....
1992-93	Boston College	H.E.	31	8	12	20	32	....	....	....	....	....
1993-94	U.S. National	....	50	8	15	23	69	....	....	....	....	....
	Cleveland	IHL	33	5	13	18	39	....	....	....	....	....
1994-95	Cleveland	IHL	64	7	31	38	94	4	0	1	1	2
	Pittsburgh	**NHL**	....	....	....	....	....	**8**	**0**	**0**	**0**	**0**
	NHL Totals		**0**	**0**	**0**	**0**	**0**	**8**	**0**	**0**	**0**	**0**

MORE, JAYSON (MOHR) S.J.

Defense. Shoots right. 6'1", 200 lbs. Born, Souris, Man., January 12, 1969.
(NY Rangers' 1st choice, 10th overall, in 1987 Entry Draft).

			Regular Season					Playoffs				
Season	Club	Lea	GP	G	A	TP	PIM	GP	G	A	TP	PIM
1984-85	Lethbridge	WHL	71	3	9	12	101	4	1	0	1	7
1985-86	Lethbridge	WHL	61	7	18	25	155	9	0	2	2	36
1986-87	Brandon	WHL	21	4	6	10	62	....	....	....	....	....
	N. Westminster	WHL	43	4	23	27	155	....	....	....	....	....
1987-88a	N. Westminster	WHL	70	13	47	60	270	5	0	2	2	26
1988-89	**NY Rangers**	**NHL**	**1**	**0**	**0**	**0**	**0**	....	....	....	....	....
	Denver	IHL	62	7	15	22	138	3	0	1	1	26
1989-90	Flint	IHL	9	1	5	6	41	....	....	....	....	....
	Minnesota	**NHL**	**5**	**0**	**0**	**0**	**16**	....	....	....	....	....
	Kalamazoo	IHL	64	9	25	34	316	10	0	3	3	13
1990-91	Kalamazoo	IHL	10	0	5	5	46	....	....	....	....	....
	Fredericton	AHL	57	7	17	24	152	9	1	1	2	34
1991-92	**San Jose**	**NHL**	**46**	**4**	**13**	**17**	**85**	....	....	....	....	....
	Kansas City	IHL	2	0	2	2	4	....	....	....	....	....
1992-93	**San Jose**	**NHL**	**73**	**5**	**6**	**11**	**179**	....	....	....	....	....
1993-94	**San Jose**	**NHL**	**49**	**1**	**6**	**7**	**63**	**13**	**0**	**2**	**2**	**32**
	Kansas City	IHL	2	1	0	1	25	....	....	....	....	....
1994-95	**San Jose**	**NHL**	**45**	**0**	**6**	**6**	**71**	**11**	**0**	**4**	**4**	**6**
	NHL Totals		**219**	**10**	**31**	**41**	**414**	**24**	**0**	**6**	**6**	**38**

a WHL All-Star Team (1988)

Traded to **Minnesota** by **NY Rangers** for Dave Archibald, November 1, 1989. Traded to **Montreal** by **Minnesota** for Brian Hayward, November 7, 1990. Claimed by **San Jose** from **Montreal** in Expansion Draft, May 30, 1991.

MOREAU, ETHAN CHI.

Left wing. Shoots left. 6'2", 205 lbs. Born, Huntsville, Ont., September 22, 1975.
(Chicago's 1st choice, 14th overall, in 1994 Entry Draft).

			Regular Season					Playoffs				
Season	Club	Lea	GP	G	A	TP	PIM	GP	G	A	TP	PIM
1991-92	Niagara Falls	OHL	62	20	35	55	39	17	4	6	10	4
1992-93	Niagara Falls	OHL	65	32	41	73	69	4	0	3	3	4
1993-94	Niagara Falls	OHL	59	44	54	98	100	....	....	....	....	....
1994-95	Niagara Falls	OHL	39	25	41	66	69	....	....	....	....	....
	Sudbury	OHL	23	13	17	30	22	18	6	12	18	26

MORGAN, JASON L.A.

Center. Shoots left. 6'1", 190 lbs. Born, St. John's, Nfld., October 9, 1976.
(Los Angeles' 5th choice, 118th overall, in 1995 Entry Draft).

			Regular Season					Playoffs				
Season	Club	Lea	GP	G	A	TP	PIM	GP	G	A	TP	PIM
1993-94	Kitchener	OHL	65	6	15	21	16	5	1	0	1	0
1994-95	Kitchener	OHL	35	3	15	18	25	....	....	....	....	....
	Kingston	OHL	20	0	3	3	14	6	0	2	2	0

MORIN, STEPHANE (moh-RAI)

Center. Shoots left. 6', 174 lbs. Born, Montreal, Que., March 27, 1969.
(Quebec's 3rd choice, 43rd overall, in 1989 Entry Draft).

			Regular Season					Playoffs				
Season	Club	Lea	GP	G	A	TP	PIM	GP	G	A	TP	PIM
1986-87	Shawinigan	QMJHL	65	9	14	23	28	....	....	....	....	....
1987-88	Chicoutimi	QMJHL	68	38	45	83	18	6	3	8	11	2
1988-89a	Chicoutimi	QMJHL	70	77	*109	*186	71	....	....	....	....	....
1989-90	**Quebec**	**NHL**	**6**	**0**	**2**	**2**	**2**	....	....	....	....	....
	Halifax	AHL	65	28	32	60	60	6	3	4	7	6
1990-91	**Quebec**	**NHL**	**48**	**13**	**27**	**40**	**30**	....	....	....	....	....
	Halifax	AHL	17	8	14	22	18	....	....	....	....	....
1991-92	**Quebec**	**NHL**	**30**	**2**	**8**	**10**	**14**	....	....	....	....	....
	Halifax	AHL	30	17	13	30	29	....	....	....	....	....
1992-93	**Vancouver**	**NHL**	**1**	**0**	**1**	**1**	**0**	....	....	....	....	....
	Hamilton	AHL	70	31	54	85	49	....	....	....	....	....
1993-94	**Vancouver**	**NHL**	**5**	**1**	**1**	**2**	**6**	....	....	....	....	....
b	Hamilton	AHL	69	38	71	109	48	4	3	2	5	4
1994-95cd	Minnesota	IHL	81	33	*81	*114	53	2	0	1	1	0
	NHL Totals		**90**	**16**	**39**	**55**	**52**	....	....	....	....	....

a QMJHL First All-Star Team (1989)
b AHL Second All-Star Team (1994)
c IHL First All-Star Team (1995)
d Won Leo P. Lamoureux Memorial Trophy (Top Scorer - IHL) (1995)

Signed as a free agent by **Vancouver**, October 5, 1992.

MORO, MARC OTT.

Defense. Shoots left. 6'1", 209 lbs. Born, Toronto, Ont., July 17, 1977.
(Ottawa's 2nd choice, 27th overall, in 1995 Entry Draft).

			Regular Season					Playoffs				
Season	Club	Lea	GP	G	A	TP	PIM	GP	G	A	TP	PIM
1993-94	Kingston	OHL	43	0	3	3	81	....	....	....	....	....
1994-95	Kingston	OHL	64	4	12	16	255	6	0	0	0	23

MOROZOV, ALEXEI (moh-ROH-zohv) PIT.

Right wing. Shoots left. 6'1", 178 lbs. Born, Moscow, USSR, February 16, 1977.
(Pittsburgh's 1st choice, 24th overall, in 1995 Entry Draft).

			Regular Season					Playoffs				
Season	Club	Lea	GP	G	A	TP	PIM	GP	G	A	TP	PIM
1993-94	Soviet Wings	CIS	7	0	0	0	0	3	0	0	0	2
1994-95	Soviet Wings	CIS	48	15	12	27	53	4	0	3	3	0

MOROZOV, VALENTIN (moh-ROH-zohv) PIT.

Center. Shoots left. 5'11", 176 lbs. Born, Moscow, USSR, June 1, 1975.
(Pittsburgh's 8th choice, 154th overall, in 1994 Entry Draft).

			Regular Season					Playoffs				
Season	Club	Lea	GP	G	A	TP	PIM	GP	G	A	TP	PIM
1992-93	CSKA	CIS	17	0	0	0	6	....	....	....	....	....
1993-94	CSKA	CIS	18	4	1	5	8	3	0	1	1	0
1994-95	CSKA	CIS	47	9	4	13	10	2	2	0	2	0

MORRISON, BRENDAN N.J.

Center. Shoots left. 5'11", 170 lbs. Born, N. Vancouver, B.C., August 12, 1975.
(New Jersey's 3rd choice, 39th overall, in 1993 Entry Draft).

			Regular Season					Playoffs				
Season	Club	Lea	GP	G	A	TP	PIM	GP	G	A	TP	PIM
1993-94	U. of Michigan	CCHA	38	20	28	48	24	....	....	....	....	....
1994-95ab	U. of Michigan	CCHA	39	23	*53	*76	42	....	....	....	....	....

a CCHA First All-Star Team (1995)
b NCAA West First All-American Team (1995)

MORROW, SCOTT

Left wing. Shoots left. 6'1", 185 lbs. Born, Chicago, IL, June 18, 1969.
(Hartford's 4th choice, 95th overall, in 1988 Entry Draft).

			Regular Season					Playoffs				
Season	Club	Lea	GP	G	A	TP	PIM	GP	G	A	TP	PIM
1988-89	N. Hampshire	H.E.	19	6	7	13	14	....	....	....	....	....
1989-90	N. Hampshire	H.E.	29	10	11	21	35	....	....	....	....	....
1990-91	N. Hampshire	H.E.	31	11	11	22	52	....	....	....	....	....
1991-92a	N. Hampshire	H.E.	35	30	23	53	65	....	....	....	....	....
	Springfield	AHL	2	0	1	1	0	5	0	0	0	9
1992-93	Springfield	AHL	70	22	29	51	80	15	6	9	15	21
1993-94	Springfield	AHL	30	12	15	27	28	....	....	....	....	....
	Saint John	AHL	8	2	2	4	0	7	2	1	3	10
1994-95	Saint John	AHL	64	18	21	39	105	5	2	0	2	4
	Calgary	**NHL**	**4**	**0**	**0**	**0**	**0**	....	....	....	....	....
	NHL Totals		**4**	**0**	**0**	**0**	**0**	....	....	....	....	....

a Hockey East Second All-Star Team (1992)

Traded to **Calgary** by **Hartford** for Todd Harkins, January 24, 1994.

MOSER, JAY — BOS.

Defense. Shoots left. 6'2", 170 lbs. Born, Cottage Grove, MN, December 26, 1972.
(Boston's 7th choice, 172nd overall, in 1991 Entry Draft).

			Regular Season					Playoffs				
Season	Club	Lea	GP	G	A	TP	PIM	GP	G	A	TP	PIM
1991-92	St. Cloud	WCHA	35	3	9	12	40	....	....	....	....	....
1992-93	St. Cloud	WCHA	33	2	9	11	77	....	....	....	....	....
1993-94					DID NOT PLAY							
1994-95	U. Minnesota	WCHA	13	1	5	6	29	....	....	....	....	....

MROZIK, RICK (muh-ROH-zihk) — WSH.

Defense. Shoots left. 6'2", 185 lbs. Born, Duluth, MN, January 2, 1975.
(Dallas' 4th choice, 136th overall, in 1993 Entry Draft).

			Regular Season					Playoffs				
Season	Club	Lea	GP	G	A	TP	PIM	GP	G	A	TP	PIM
1993-94	Minn.-Duluth	WCHA	38	2	9	11	38	....	....	....	....	....
1994-95	Minn.-Duluth	WCHA	3	0	0	0	2	....	....	....	....	....

Traded to **Washington** by **Dallas** with Mark Tinordi for Kevin Hatcher, January 18, 1995.

MUCKALT, BILL — VAN.

Center. Shoots right. 6', 180 lbs. Born, Williams Lake, B.C., July 15, 1974.
(Vancouver's 9th choice, 221st overall, in 1994 Entry Draft).

			Regular Season					Playoffs				
Season	Club	Lea	GP	G	A	TP	PIM	GP	G	A	TP	PIM
1994-95	U. of Michigan	CCHA	39	19	18	37	42	....	....	....	....	....

MUELLER, BRIAN — HFD.

Defense. Shoots left. 5'11", 225 lbs. Born, Liverpool, NY, June 2, 1972.
(Hartford's 7th choice, 141st overall, in 1991 Entry Draft).

			Regular Season					Playoffs				
Season	Club	Lea	GP	G	A	TP	PIM	GP	G	A	TP	PIM
1991-92	Clarkson	ECAC	28	4	13	17	30	....	....	....	....	....
1992-93	Clarkson	ECAC	32	6	23	29	12	....	....	....	....	....
1993-94ab	Clarkson	ECAC	34	17	39	56	60	....	....	....	....	....
1994-95a	Clarkson	ECAC	36	12	42	54	56	....	....	....	....	....

a ECAC First All-Star Team (1994, 1995)
b NCAA East First All-American Team (1994)

MULHERN, RYAN — CGY.

Center. Shoots right. 6'1", 180 lbs. Born, Philadelphia, PA, January 11, 1973.
(Calgary's 8th choice, 174th overall, in 1992 Entry Draft).

			Regular Season					Playoffs				
Season	Club	Lea	GP	G	A	TP	PIM	GP	G	A	TP	PIM
1992-93	Brown	ECAC	31	15	9	24	46	....	....	....	....	....
1993-94	Brown	ECAC	27	18	17	35	48	....	....	....	....	....
1994-95	Brown	ECAC	30	18	16	34	*108	....	....	....	....	....

MULLEN, JOE

Right wing. Shoots right. 5'9", 180 lbs. Born, New York, NY, February 26, 1957.

			Regular Season					Playoffs				
Season	Club	Lea	GP	G	A	TP	PIM	GP	G	A	TP	PIM
1977-78a	Boston College	ECAC	34	34	34	68	12	....	....	....	....	....
1978-79a	Boston College	ECAC	25	32	24	56	8	....	....	....	....	....
1979-80bc	Salt Lake	CHL	75	40	32	72	21	13	*9	11	20	0
	St. Louis	**NHL**	....	....	....	....	....	**1**	**0**	**0**	**0**	**0**
1980-81de	Salt Lake	CHL	80	59	58	*117	8	17	11	9	20	0
1981-82	**St. Louis**	**NHL**	**45**	**25**	**34**	**59**	**4**	**10**	**7**	**11**	**18**	**4**
	Salt Lake	CHL	27	21	27	48	12	....	....	....	....	....
1982-83	**St. Louis**	**NHL**	**49**	**17**	**30**	**47**	**6**	....	....	....	....	....
1983-84	**St. Louis**	**NHL**	**80**	**41**	**44**	**85**	**19**	**6**	**2**	**0**	**2**	**0**
1984-85	**St. Louis**	**NHL**	**79**	**40**	**52**	**92**	**6**	**3**	**0**	**0**	**0**	**0**
1985-86	**St. Louis**	**NHL**	**48**	**28**	**24**	**52**	**10**	....	....	....	....	....
	Calgary	**NHL**	**29**	**16**	**22**	**38**	**11**	**21**	***12**	**7**	**19**	**4**
1986-87f	**Calgary**	**NHL**	**79**	**47**	**40**	**87**	**14**	**6**	**2**	**1**	**3**	**0**
1987-88	**Calgary**	**NHL**	**80**	**40**	**44**	**84**	**30**	**7**	**2**	**4**	**6**	**10**
1988-89fgh	**Calgary**	**NHL**	**79**	**51**	**59**	**110**	**16**	**21**	***16**	**8**	**24**	**4**
1989-90	**Calgary**	**NHL**	**78**	**36**	**33**	**69**	**24**	**6**	**3**	**0**	**3**	**0**
1990-91	**Pittsburgh**	**NHL**	**47**	**17**	**22**	**39**	**6**	**22**	**8**	**9**	**17**	**4**
1991-92	**Pittsburgh**	**NHL**	**77**	**42**	**45**	**87**	**30**	**9**	**3**	**1**	**4**	**4**
1992-93	**Pittsburgh**	**NHL**	**72**	**33**	**37**	**70**	**14**	**12**	**4**	**2**	**6**	**6**
1993-94	**Pittsburgh**	**NHL**	**84**	**38**	**32**	**70**	**41**	**6**	**1**	**0**	**1**	**2**
1994-95	**Pittsburgh**	**NHL**	**45**	**16**	**21**	**37**	**6**	**12**	**0**	**3**	**3**	**4**
	NHL Totals		**971**	**487**	**539**	**1026**	**237**	**142**	**60**	**46**	**106**	**42**

a ECAC First All-Star Team (1978, 1979)
b CHL Second All-Star Team (1980)
c Won Ken McKenzie Trophy (CHL's Top Rookie) (1980)
d CHL First All-Star Team (1981)
e Won Tommy Ivan Trophy (CHL's Most Valuable Player) (1981)
f Won Lady Byng Trophy (1987, 1989)
g NHL First All-Star Team (1989)
h NHL Plus/Minus Leader (1989)

Played in NHL All-Star Game (1989, 1990, 1994)

Signed as a free agent by **St. Louis**, August 16, 1979. Traded to **Calgary** by **St. Louis** with Terry Johnson and Rik Wilson for Ed Beers, Charles Bourgeois and Gino Cavallini, February 1, 1986. Traded to **Pittsburgh** by **Calgary** for Pittsburgh's second round choice (Nicolas Perreault) in 1990 Entry Draft, June 16, 1990.

MULLER, KIRK — NYI

Left wing. Shoots left. 6', 205 lbs. Born, Kingston, Ont., February 8, 1966.
(New Jersey's 1st choice, 2nd overall, in 1984 Entry Draft).

			Regular Season					Playoffs				
Season	Club	Lea	GP	G	A	TP	PIM	GP	G	A	TP	PIM
1981-82	Kingston	OHL	67	12	39	51	27	4	5	1	6	4
1982-83	Guelph	OHL	66	52	60	112	41	....	....	....	....	....
1983-84	Guelph	OHL	49	31	63	94	27	....	....	....	....	....
	Cdn. National	....	15	2	2	4	6	....	....	....	....	....
	Cdn. Olympic	....	6	2	1	3	0	....	....	....	....	....
1984-85	**New Jersey**	**NHL**	**80**	**17**	**37**	**54**	**69**	....	....	....	....	....
1985-86	**New Jersey**	**NHL**	**77**	**25**	**41**	**66**	**45**	....	....	....	....	....
1986-87	**New Jersey**	**NHL**	**79**	**26**	**50**	**76**	**75**	....	....	....	....	....
1987-88	**New Jersey**	**NHL**	**80**	**37**	**57**	**94**	**114**	**20**	**4**	**8**	**12**	**37**
1988-89	**New Jersey**	**NHL**	**80**	**31**	**43**	**74**	**119**	....	....	....	....	....
1989-90	**New Jersey**	**NHL**	**80**	**30**	**56**	**86**	**74**	**6**	**1**	**3**	**4**	**11**
1990-91	**New Jersey**	**NHL**	**80**	**19**	**51**	**70**	**76**	**7**	**0**	**2**	**2**	**10**
1991-92	**Montreal**	**NHL**	**78**	**36**	**41**	**77**	**86**	**11**	**4**	**3**	**7**	**31**
1992-93	**Montreal**	**NHL**	**80**	**37**	**57**	**94**	**77**	**20**	**10**	**7**	**17**	**18**
1993-94	**Montreal**	**NHL**	**76**	**23**	**34**	**57**	**96**	**7**	**6**	**2**	**8**	**4**
1994-95	**Montreal**	**NHL**	**33**	**8**	**11**	**19**	**33**	....	....	....	....	....
	NY Islanders	**NHL**	**12**	**3**	**5**	**8**	**14**	....	....	....	....	....
	NHL Totals		**835**	**292**	**483**	**775**	**878**	**71**	**25**	**25**	**50**	**111**

Played in NHL All-Star Game (1985, 1986, 1988, 1990, 1992, 1993)

Traded to **Montreal** by **New Jersey** with Roland Melanson for Stephane Richer and Tom Chorske, September 20, 1991. Traded to **NY Islanders** by **Montreal** with Mathieu Schneider and Craig Darby for Pierre Turgeon and Vladimir Malakhov, April 5, 1995.

MULLER, MIKE — WPG.

Defense. Shoots left. 6'2", 205 lbs. Born, Fairview, MN, September 18, 1971.
(Winnipeg's 2nd choice, 35th overall, in 1990 Entry Draft).

			Regular Season					Playoffs				
Season	Club	Lea	GP	G	A	TP	PIM	GP	G	A	TP	PIM
1990-91	U. Minnesota	WCHA	33	4	4	8	44	....	....	....	....	....
1991-92	U. Minnesota	WCHA	41	4	12	16	52	....	....	....	....	....
1992-93	Moscow D'amo	CIS	11	1	0	1	8	....	....	....	....	....
1993-94	Moncton	AHL	61	2	14	16	88	....	....	....	....	....
1994-95	Springfield	AHL	64	2	5	7	61	....	....	....	....	....

MULLIN, KORY — TOR.

Defense. Shoots left. 6'2", 185 lbs. Born, Lethbridge, Alta., May 24, 1975.

			Regular Season					Playoffs				
Season	Club	Lea	GP	G	A	TP	PIM	GP	G	A	TP	PIM
1991-92	Tri-City	WHL	49	2	5	7	82	5	1	0	1	6
1992-93	Tri-City	WHL	68	2	10	12	95	4	0	0	0	11
1993-94	Tri-City	WHL	6	0	5	5	11	....	....	....	....	....
	Tacoma	WHL	59	3	11	14	86	8	0	0	0	0
1994-95	Lethbridge	WHL	48	6	21	27	72	....	....	....	....	....

Signed as a free agent by **Toronto**, September 23, 1993.

MUNI, CRAIG (MYOO-ne) — BUF.

Defense. Shoots left. 6'3", 208 lbs. Born, Toronto, Ont., July 19, 1962.
(Toronto's 1st choice, 25th overall, in 1980 Entry Draft).

			Regular Season					Playoffs				
Season	Club	Lea	GP	G	A	TP	PIM	GP	G	A	TP	PIM
1980-81	Kingston	OHA	38	2	14	16	65	....	....	....	....	....
	Windsor	OHA	25	5	11	16	41	11	1	4	5	14
	New Brunswick	AHL	....	....	....	....	....	2	0	1	1	10
1981-82	**Toronto**	**NHL**	**3**	**0**	**0**	**0**	**2**	....	....	....	....	....
	Windsor	OHL	49	5	32	37	92	9	2	3	5	16
	Cincinnati	CHL	....	....	....	....	....	3	0	2	2	2
1982-83	**Toronto**	**NHL**	**2**	**0**	**1**	**1**	**0**	....	....	....	....	....
	St. Catharines	AHL	64	6	32	38	52	....	....	....	....	....
1983-84	St. Catharines	AHL	64	4	16	20	79	7	0	1	1	0
1984-85	**Toronto**	**NHL**	**8**	**0**	**0**	**0**	**0**	....	....	....	....	....
	St. Catharines	AHL	68	7	17	24	54	....	....	....	....	....
1985-86	**Toronto**	**NHL**	**6**	**0**	**1**	**1**	**4**	....	....	....	....	....
	St. Catharines	AHL	73	3	34	37	91	13	0	5	5	16
1986-87	**Edmonton**	**NHL**	**79**	**7**	**22**	**29**	**85**	**14**	**0**	**2**	**2**	**17**
1987-88	**Edmonton**	**NHL**	**72**	**4**	**15**	**19**	**77**	**19**	**0**	**4**	**4**	**31**
1988-89	**Edmonton**	**NHL**	**69**	**5**	**13**	**18**	**71**	**7**	**0**	**3**	**3**	**8**
1989-90	**Edmonton**	**NHL**	**71**	**5**	**12**	**17**	**81**	**22**	**0**	**3**	**3**	**16**
1990-91	**Edmonton**	**NHL**	**76**	**1**	**9**	**10**	**77**	**18**	**0**	**3**	**3**	**20**
1991-92	**Edmonton**	**NHL**	**54**	**2**	**5**	**7**	**34**	**3**	**0**	**0**	**0**	**2**
1992-93	**Edmonton**	**NHL**	**72**	**0**	**11**	**11**	**67**	....	....	....	....	....
	Chicago	**NHL**	**9**	**0**	**0**	**0**	**8**	**4**	**0**	**0**	**0**	**2**
1993-94	**Chicago**	**NHL**	**9**	**0**	**4**	**4**	**4**	....	....	....	....	....
	Buffalo	**NHL**	**73**	**2**	**8**	**10**	**62**	**7**	**0**	**0**	**0**	**4**
1994-95	**Buffalo**	**NHL**	**40**	**0**	**6**	**6**	**36**	**5**	**0**	**1**	**1**	**2**
	NHL Totals		**643**	**26**	**107**	**133**	**608**	**99**	**0**	**16**	**16**	**102**

Signed as a free agent by **Edmonton,** August 18, 1986. Sold to **Buffalo** by **Edmonton**, October 2, 1986. Traded to **Pittsburgh** by **Buffalo** for future considerations, October 3, 1986. Traded to **Edmonton** by **Pittsburgh** to complete September 11, 1985 trade which sent Gilles Meloche to Pittsburgh for Tim Hrynewich, Marty McSorley and future considerations, October 6, 1986. Traded to **Chicago** by **Edmonton** for Mike Hudson, March 22, 1993. Traded to **Buffalo** by **Chicago** with Chicago's fifth round choice (Daniel Bienvenue) in 1995 Entry Draft for Keith Carney and Buffalo's sixth round choice (Marc Magliarditi) in 1995 Entry Draft, October 27, 1993.

MURPHY, BURKE — CGY.

Left wing. Shoots left. 6', 180 lbs. Born, Gloucester, Ont., June 5, 1973.
(Calgary's 11th choice, 278th overall, in 1993 Entry Draft).

			Regular Season					Playoffs				
Season	Club	Lea	GP	G	A	TP	PIM	GP	G	A	TP	PIM
1992-93	St. Lawrence	ECAC	32	19	10	29	32	....	....	....	....	....
1993-94	St. Lawrence	ECAC	30	20	17	37	42	....	....	....	....	....
1994-95a	St. Lawrence	ECAC	33	27	23	50	61	....	....	....	....	....

a ECAC Second All-Star Team (1995)

MURPHY, GORD — FLA.

Defense. Shoots right. 6'2", 191 lbs. Born, Willowdale, Ont., March 23, 1967.
(Philadelphia's 10th choice, 189th overall, in 1985 Entry Draft).

			Regular Season					Playoffs				
Season	Club	Lea	GP	G	A	TP	PIM	GP	G	A	TP	PIM
1984-85	Oshawa	OHL	59	3	12	15	25	....	....	....	....	....
1985-86	Oshawa	OHL	64	7	15	22	56	6	1	1	2	6
1986-87	Oshawa	OHL	56	7	30	37	95	24	6	16	22	22
1987-88	Hershey	AHL	62	8	20	28	44	12	0	8	8	12
1988-89	**Philadelphia**	**NHL**	75	4	31	35	68	19	2	7	9	13
1989-90	**Philadelphia**	**NHL**	75	14	27	41	95	....	....	....	....	....
1990-91	**Philadelphia**	**NHL**	80	11	31	42	58	....	....	....	....	....
1991-92	**Philadelphia**	**NHL**	31	2	8	10	33	....	....	....	....	....
	Boston	**NHL**	42	3	6	9	51	15	1	0	1	12
1992-93	**Boston**	**NHL**	49	5	12	17	62	....	....	....	....	....
	Providence	AHL	2	1	3	4	2	....	....	....	....	....
1993-94	**Florida**	**NHL**	84	14	29	43	71	....	....	....	....	....
1994-95	**Florida**	**NHL**	46	6	16	22	24	....	....	....	....	....
	NHL Totals		482	59	160	219	462	34	3	7	10	25

Traded to **Boston** by **Philadelphia** with Brian Dobbin, Philadelphia's third round choice (Sergei Zholtok) in 1992 Entry Draft and Philadelphia's fourth round choice (Charles Paquette) in 1993 Entry Draft, for Garry Galley, Wes Walz and Boston's third round choice (Milos Holan) in 1993 Entry Draft, January 2, 1992. Traded to **Dallas** by **Boston** for future considerations (Jon Casey traded to Boston for Andy Moog, June 25, 1993), June 20, 1993. Claimed by **Florida** from **Dallas** in Expansion Draft, June 24, 1993.

MURPHY, JOE — CHI.

Right wing. Shoots left. 6'1", 190 lbs. Born, London, Ont., October 16, 1967.
(Detroit's 1st choice, 1st overall, in 1986 Entry Draft).

			Regular Season					Playoffs				
Season	Club	Lea	GP	G	A	TP	PIM	GP	G	A	TP	PIM
1985-86	Michigan State	CCHA	35	24	37	61	50	....	....	....	....	....
	Cdn. National	....	8	3	3	6	2	....	....	....	....	....
1986-87	**Detroit**	**NHL**	5	0	1	1	2	....	....	....	....	....
	Adirondack	AHL	71	21	38	59	61	10	2	1	3	33
1987-88	**Detroit**	**NHL**	50	10	9	19	37	8	0	1	1	6
	Adirondack	AHL	6	5	6	11	4	....	....	....	....	....
1988-89	**Detroit**	**NHL**	26	1	7	8	28	....	....	....	....	....
	Adirondack	AHL	47	31	35	66	66	16	6	11	17	17
1989-90	**Detroit**	**NHL**	9	3	1	4	4	....	....	....	....	....
	Edmonton	**NHL**	62	7	18	25	56	22	6	8	14	16
1990-91	**Edmonton**	**NHL**	80	27	35	62	35	15	2	5	7	14
1991-92	**Edmonton**	**NHL**	80	35	47	82	52	16	8	16	24	12
1992-93	**Chicago**	**NHL**	19	7	10	17	18	4	0	0	0	8
1993-94	**Chicago**	**NHL**	81	31	39	70	111	6	1	3	4	25
1994-95	**Chicago**	**NHL**	40	23	18	41	89	16	9	3	12	29
	NHL Totals		452	144	185	329	432	87	26	36	62	110

Traded to **Edmonton** by **Detroit** with Petr Klima, Adam Graves and Jeff Sharples for Jimmy Carson, Kevin McClelland and Edmonton's fifth round choice (later traded to Montreal — Montreal selected Brad Layzell) in 1991 Entry Draft, November 2, 1989. Traded to **Chicago** by **Edmonton** for Igor Kravchuk and Dean McAmmond, February 24, 1993.

MURPHY, LARRY — TOR.

Defense. Shoots right. 6'2", 210 lbs. Born, Scarborough, Ont., March 8, 1961.
(Los Angeles' 1st choice, 4th overall, in 1980 Entry Draft).

			Regular Season					Playoffs				
Season	Club	Lea	GP	G	A	TP	PIM	GP	G	A	TP	PIM
1978-79	Peterborough	OHA	66	6	21	27	82	19	1	9	10	42
1979-80a	Peterborough	OHA	68	21	68	89	88	14	4	13	17	20
1980-81	**Los Angeles**	**NHL**	80	16	60	76	79	4	3	0	3	2
1981-82	**Los Angeles**	**NHL**	79	22	44	66	95	10	2	8	10	12
1982-83	**Los Angeles**	**NHL**	77	14	48	62	81	....	....	....	....	....
1983-84	**Los Angeles**	**NHL**	6	0	3	3	0	....	....	....	....	....
	Washington	**NHL**	72	13	33	46	50	8	0	3	3	6
1984-85	**Washington**	**NHL**	79	13	42	55	51	5	2	3	5	0
1985-86	**Washington**	**NHL**	78	21	44	65	50	9	1	5	6	6
1986-87b	**Washington**	**NHL**	80	23	58	81	39	7	2	2	4	6
1987-88	**Washington**	**NHL**	79	8	53	61	72	13	4	4	8	33
1988-89	**Washington**	**NHL**	65	7	29	36	70	....	....	....	....	....
	Minnesota	**NHL**	13	4	6	10	12	5	0	2	2	8
1989-90	**Minnesota**	**NHL**	77	10	58	68	44	7	1	2	3	31
1990-91	**Minnesota**	**NHL**	31	4	11	15	38	....	....	....	....	....
	Pittsburgh	**NHL**	44	5	23	28	30	23	5	18	23	44
1991-92	**Pittsburgh**	**NHL**	77	21	56	77	48	21	6	10	16	19
1992-93b	**Pittsburgh**	**NHL**	83	22	63	85	73	12	2	11	13	10
1993-94	**Pittsburgh**	**NHL**	84	17	56	73	44	6	0	5	5	0
1994-95b	**Pittsburgh**	**NHL**	48	13	25	38	18	12	2	13	15	0
	NHL Totals		1152	233	712	945	894	142	30	86	116	177

a OHA First All-Star Team (1980)
b NHL Second All-Star Team (1987, 1993, 1995)

Played in NHL All-Star Game (1994)

Traded to **Washington** by **Los Angeles** for Ken Houston and Brian Engblom, October 18, 1983. Traded to **Minnesota** by **Washington** with Mike Gartner for Dino Ciccarelli and Bob Rouse, March 7, 1989. Traded to **Pittsburgh** by **Minnesota** with Peter Taglianetti for Chris Dahlquist and Jim Johnson, December 11, 1990. Traded to **Toronto** by **Pittsburgh** for Dmitri Mironov and Toronto's second round choice in 1996 Entry Draft, July 8, 1995.

MURRAY, CHRIS — MTL.

Right wing. Shoots right. 6'2", 209 lbs. Born, Port Hardy, B.C., October 25, 1974.
(Montreal's 3rd choice, 54th overall, in 1994 Entry Draft).

			Regular Season					Playoffs				
Season	Club	Lea	GP	G	A	TP	PIM	GP	G	A	TP	PIM
1991-92	Kamloops	WHL	33	1	1	2	218	5	0	0	0	10
1992-93	Kamloops	WHL	62	6	10	16	217	13	0	4	4	34
1993-94	Kamloops	WHL	59	14	16	30	260	15	4	2	6	*107
1994-95	Fredericton	AHL	55	6	12	18	234	12	1	1	2	50
	Montreal	**NHL**	3	0	0	0	4	....	....	....	....	....
	NHL Totals		3	0	0	0	4	....	....	....	....	....

MURRAY, GLEN — PIT.

Right wing. Shoots right. 6'2", 213 lbs. Born, Halifax, N.S., November 1, 1972.
(Boston's 1st choice, 18th overall, in 1991 Entry Draft).

			Regular Season					Playoffs				
Season	Club	Lea	GP	G	A	TP	PIM	GP	G	A	TP	PIM
1989-90	Sudbury	OHL	62	8	28	36	17	7	0	0	0	4
1990-91	Sudbury	OHL	66	27	38	65	82	5	8	4	12	10
1991-92	**Boston**	**NHL**	5	3	1	4	0	15	4	2	6	10
	Sudbury	OHL	54	37	47	84	93	11	7	4	11	18
1992-93	**Boston**	**NHL**	27	3	4	7	8	....	....	....	....	....
	Providence	AHL	48	30	26	56	42	6	1	4	5	4
1993-94	**Boston**	**NHL**	81	18	13	31	48	13	4	5	9	14
1994-95	**Boston**	**NHL**	35	5	2	7	46	2	0	0	0	2
	NHL Totals		148	29	20	49	102	30	8	7	15	26

Traded to **Pittsburgh** by **Boston** with Bryan Smolinski and Boston's third round choice in 1996 Entry Draft for Kevin Stevens and Shawn McEachern, August 2, 1995.

MURRAY, MARTY — CGY.

Center. Shoots left. 5'9", 170 lbs. Born, Deloraine, Man., February 16, 1975.
(Calgary's 5th choice, 96th overall, in 1993 Entry Draft).

			Regular Season					Playoffs				
Season	Club	Lea	GP	G	A	TP	PIM	GP	G	A	TP	PIM
1991-92	Brandon	WHL	68	20	36	56	22	....	....	....	....	....
1992-93	Brandon	WHL	67	29	65	94	50	4	1	3	4	0
1993-94ab	Brandon	WHL	64	43	71	114	33	14	6	14	20	14
1994-95a	Brandon	WHL	65	40	*88	128	53	18	9	*20	29	16

a WHL East First All-Star Team (1994, 1995)
b Canadian Major Junior Second All-Star Team (1994)

MURRAY, MICHAEL — CGY.

Right wing. Shoots left. 6'1", 200 lbs. Born, Cumberland, RI, April 18, 1971.
(Calgary's 10th choice, 188th overall, in 1990 Entry Draft).

			Regular Season					Playoffs				
Season	Club	Lea	GP	G	A	TP	PIM	GP	G	A	TP	PIM
1990-91	Lowell	H.E.	30	5	8	13	18	....	....	....	....	....
1991-92	Lowell	H.E.	31	22	15	37	40	....	....	....	....	....
1992-93a	Lowell	H.E.	39	23	33	56	78	....	....	....	....	....
1993-94	Lowell	H.E.	35	17	11	28	92	....	....	....	....	....
1994-95	Saint John	AHL	65	8	27	35	53	4	0	0	0	6

a Hockey East Second All-Star Team (1993)

MURRAY, REM

Left wing. Shoots left. 6'1", 183 lbs. Born, Stratford, Ont., October 9, 1972.
(Los Angeles' 5th choice, 135th overall, in 1992 Entry Draft).

			Regular Season					Playoffs				
Season	Club	Lea	GP	G	A	TP	PIM	GP	G	A	TP	PIM
1991-92	Michigan State	CCHA	41	12	36	48	16	....	....	....	....	....
1992-93	Michigan State	CCHA	40	22	35	57	24	....	....	....	....	....
1993-94	Michigan State	CCHA	41	16	38	54	18	....	....	....	....	....
1994-95a	Michigan State	CCHA	40	20	36	56	21	....	....	....	....	....

a CCHA Second All-Star Team (1995)

MURRAY, ROB — WPG.

Center. Shoots right. 6'1", 180 lbs. Born, Toronto, Ont., April 4, 1967.
(Washington's 3rd choice, 61st overall, in 1985 Entry Draft).

			Regular Season					Playoffs				
Season	Club	Lea	GP	G	A	TP	PIM	GP	G	A	TP	PIM
1984-85	Peterborough	OHL	63	12	9	21	155	17	2	7	9	45
1985-86	Peterborough	OHL	52	14	18	32	125	16	1	2	3	50
1986-87	Peterborough	OHL	62	17	37	54	204	3	1	4	5	8
1987-88	Fort Wayne	IHL	80	12	21	33	139	6	0	2	2	16
1988-89	Baltimore	AHL	80	11	23	34	235	....	....	....	....	....
1989-90	**Washington**	**NHL**	41	2	7	9	58	9	0	0	0	18
	Baltimore	AHL	23	5	4	9	63	....	....	....	....	....
1990-91	**Washington**	**NHL**	17	0	3	3	19	....	....	....	....	....
	Baltimore	AHL	48	6	20	26	177	4	0	0	0	12
1991-92	**Winnipeg**	**NHL**	9	0	1	1	18	....	....	....	....	....
	Moncton	AHL	60	16	15	31	247	8	0	1	1	56
1992-93	**Winnipeg**	**NHL**	10	1	0	1	6	....	....	....	....	....
	Moncton	AHL	56	16	21	37	147	3	0	0	0	6
1993-94	**Winnipeg**	**NHL**	6	0	0	0	2	....	....	....	....	....
	Moncton	AHL	69	25	32	57	280	21	2	3	5	60
1994-95	Springfield	AHL	78	16	38	54	373	....	....	....	....	....
	Winnipeg	**NHL**	10	0	2	2	2	....	....	....	....	....
	NHL Totals		93	3	13	16	105	9	0	0	0	18

Claimed by **Minnesota** from **Washington** in Expansion Draft, May 30, 1991. Traded to **Winnipeg** by **Minnesota** with future considerations for Winnipeg's seventh round choice (Geoff Finch) in 1991 Entry Draft and future considerations, May 31, 1991.

MURRAY, TROY — COL.

Center. Shoots right. 6'1", 195 lbs. Born, Calgary, Alta., July 31, 1962.
(Chicago's 6th choice, 57th overall, in 1980 Entry Draft).

			Regular Season					Playoffs				
Season	Club	Lea	GP	G	A	TP	PIM	GP	G	A	TP	PIM
1980-81a	North Dakota	WCHA	38	33	45	78	28	....	....	....	....	....
1981-82a	North Dakota	WCHA	26	13	17	30	62	....	....	....	....	....
	Chicago	**NHL**	**1**	**0**	**0**	**0**	**0**	**7**	**1**	**0**	**1**	**5**
1982-83	**Chicago**	**NHL**	**54**	**8**	**8**	**16**	**27**	**2**	**0**	**0**	**0**	**0**
1983-84	**Chicago**	**NHL**	**61**	**15**	**15**	**30**	**45**	**5**	**1**	**0**	**1**	**7**
1984-85	**Chicago**	**NHL**	**80**	**26**	**40**	**66**	**82**	**15**	**5**	**14**	**19**	**24**
1985-86b	**Chicago**	**NHL**	**80**	**45**	**54**	**99**	**94**	**2**	**0**	**0**	**0**	**2**
1986-87	**Chicago**	**NHL**	**77**	**28**	**43**	**71**	**59**	**4**	**0**	**0**	**0**	**5**
1987-88	**Chicago**	**NHL**	**79**	**22**	**36**	**58**	**96**	**5**	**1**	**0**	**1**	**8**
1988-89	**Chicago**	**NHL**	**79**	**21**	**30**	**51**	**113**	**16**	**3**	**6**	**9**	**25**
1989-90	**Chicago**	**NHL**	**68**	**17**	**38**	**55**	**86**	**20**	**4**	**4**	**8**	**22**
1990-91	**Chicago**	**NHL**	**75**	**14**	**23**	**37**	**74**	**6**	**0**	**1**	**1**	**12**
1991-92	**Winnipeg**	**NHL**	**74**	**17**	**30**	**47**	**69**	**7**	**0**	**0**	**0**	**2**
1992-93	**Winnipeg**	**NHL**	**29**	**3**	**4**	**7**	**34**	....	....	....	....	....
	Chicago	**NHL**	**22**	**1**	**3**	**4**	**25**	**4**	**0**	**0**	**0**	**2**
1993-94	**Chicago**	**NHL**	**12**	**0**	**1**	**1**	**6**	....	....	....	....	....
	Indianapolis	IHL	8	3	3	6	12	....	....	....	....	....
	Ottawa	**NHL**	**15**	**2**	**3**	**5**	**4**	....	....	....	....	....
1994-95	**Ottawa**	**NHL**	**33**	**4**	**10**	**14**	**16**	....	....	....	....	....
	Pittsburgh	**NHL**	**13**	**0**	**2**	**2**	**23**	**12**	**2**	**1**	**3**	**12**
	NHL Totals		**852**	**223**	**340**	**563**	**853**	**105**	**17**	**26**	**43**	**126**

a WCHA Second All-Star Team (1981, 1982)
b Won Frank J. Selke Memorial Trophy (1986)

Traded to **Winnipeg** by **Chicago** with Warren Rychel for Bryan Marchment and Chris Norton, July 22, 1991. Traded to **Chicago** by **Winnipeg** for Steve Bancroft and future considerations, February 21, 1993. Traded to **Ottawa** by **Chicago** with Chicago's eleventh round choice (Antti Tormanen) in 1994 Entry Draft for Ottawa's eleventh round choice (Rob Mara) in 1994 Entry Draft, March 11, 1994. Traded to **Pittsburgh** by **Ottawa** with Norm Maciver for Martin Straka, April 7, 1995. Signed as a free agent by **Colorado**, August 8, 1995.

MURZYN, DANA — (MUHR-zihn) VAN.

Defense. Shoots left. 6'2", 200 lbs. Born, Calgary, Alta., December 9, 1966.
(Hartford's 1st choice, 5th overall, in 1985 Entry Draft).

			Regular Season					Playoffs				
Season	Club	Lea	GP	G	A	TP	PIM	GP	G	A	TP	PIM
1983-84	Calgary	WHL	65	11	20	31	135	2	0	0	0	10
1984-85a	Calgary	WHL	72	32	60	92	233	8	1	11	12	16
1985-86b	**Hartford**	**NHL**	**78**	**3**	**23**	**26**	**125**	**4**	**0**	**0**	**0**	**10**
1986-87	**Hartford**	**NHL**	**74**	**9**	**19**	**28**	**95**	**6**	**2**	**1**	**3**	**29**
1987-88	**Hartford**	**NHL**	**33**	**1**	**6**	**7**	**45**	....	....	....	....	....
	Calgary	**NHL**	**41**	**6**	**5**	**11**	**94**	**5**	**2**	**0**	**2**	**13**
1988-89	**Calgary**	**NHL**	**63**	**3**	**19**	**22**	**142**	**21**	**0**	**3**	**3**	**20**
1989-90	**Calgary**	**NHL**	**78**	**7**	**13**	**20**	**140**	**6**	**2**	**2**	**4**	**2**
1990-91	**Calgary**	**NHL**	**19**	**0**	**2**	**2**	**30**	....	....	....	....	....
	Vancouver	**NHL**	**10**	**1**	**0**	**1**	**8**	**6**	**0**	**1**	**1**	**8**
1991-92	**Vancouver**	**NHL**	**70**	**3**	**11**	**14**	**147**	**1**	**0**	**0**	**0**	**15**
1992-93	**Vancouver**	**NHL**	**79**	**5**	**11**	**16**	**196**	**12**	**3**	**2**	**5**	**18**
1993-94	**Vancouver**	**NHL**	**80**	**6**	**14**	**20**	**109**	**7**	**0**	**0**	**0**	**4**
1994-95	**Vancouver**	**NHL**	**40**	**0**	**8**	**8**	**129**	**8**	**0**	**1**	**1**	**22**
	NHL Totals		**665**	**44**	**131**	**175**	**1260**	**76**	**9**	**10**	**19**	**141**

a WHL East First All-Star Team, (1985)
b NHL All-Rookie Team (1986)

Traded to **Calgary** by **Hartford** with Shane Churla for Neil Sheehy, Carey Wilson and the rights to Lane MacDonald, January 3, 1988. Traded to **Vancouver** by **Calgary** for Ron Stern, Kevan Guy and future considerations, March 5, 1991.

MUSIL, FRANK — (moo-SIHL)

Defense. Shoots left. 6'3", 215 lbs. Born, Pardubice, Czech., December 17, 1964.
(Minnesota's 3rd choice, 38th overall, in 1983 Entry Draft).

			Regular Season					Playoffs				
Season	Club	Lea	GP	G	A	TP	PIM	GP	G	A	TP	PIM
1980-81	Pardubice	Czech.	2	0	0	0	0	....	....	....	....	....
1981-82	Pardubice	Czech.	35	1	3	4	34	....	....	....	....	....
1982-83	Pardubice	Czech.	33	1	2	3	44	....	....	....	....	....
1983-84	Pardubice	Czech.	37	4	8	12	72	....	....	....	....	....
1984-85	Dukla Jihlava	Czech.	44	4	6	10	76	....	....	....	....	....
1985-86	Dukla Jihlava	Czech.	34	4	7	11	42	....	....	....	....	....
1986-87	**Minnesota**	**NHL**	**72**	**2**	**9**	**11**	**148**	....	....	....	....	....
1987-88	**Minnesota**	**NHL**	**80**	**9**	**8**	**17**	**213**	....	....	....	....	....
1988-89	**Minnesota**	**NHL**	**55**	**1**	**19**	**20**	**54**	**5**	**1**	**1**	**2**	**4**
1989-90	**Minnesota**	**NHL**	**56**	**2**	**8**	**10**	**109**	**4**	**0**	**0**	**0**	**14**
1990-91	**Minnesota**	**NHL**	**8**	**0**	**2**	**2**	**23**	....	....	....	....	....
	Calgary	**NHL**	**67**	**7**	**14**	**21**	**160**	**7**	**0**	**0**	**0**	**10**
1991-92	**Calgary**	**NHL**	**78**	**4**	**8**	**12**	**103**	....	....	....	....	....
1992-93	**Calgary**	**NHL**	**80**	**6**	**10**	**16**	**131**	**6**	**1**	**1**	**2**	**7**
1993-94	**Calgary**	**NHL**	**75**	**1**	**8**	**9**	**50**	**7**	**0**	**1**	**1**	**4**
1994-95	Sparta Praha	Czech.	19	1	4	5	50	....	....	....	....	....
	Saxonia	Ger.	1	0	0	0	2	....	....	....	....	....
	Calgary	**NHL**	**35**	**0**	**5**	**5**	**61**	**5**	**0**	**1**	**1**	**0**
	NHL Totals		**606**	**32**	**91**	**123**	**1052**	**34**	**2**	**4**	**6**	**39**

Traded to **Calgary** by **Minnesota** for Brian Glynn, October 26, 1990.

MYHRES, BRANTT — (MIGH-uhrs) T.B.

Left wing. Shoots right. 6'3", 220 lbs. Born, Edmonton, Alta., March 18, 1974.
(Tampa Bay's 6th choice, 97th overall, in 1992 Entry Draft).

			Regular Season					Playoffs				
Season	Club	Lea	GP	G	A	TP	PIM	GP	G	A	TP	PIM
1990-91	Portland	WHL	59	2	7	9	125	....	....	....	....	....
1991-92	Portland	WHL	4	0	2	2	22	....	....	....	....	....
	Lethbridge	WHL	53	4	11	15	359	5	0	0	0	36
1992-93	Lethbridge	WHL	64	13	35	48	277	3	0	0	0	11
1993-94	Lethbridge	WHL	34	10	21	31	103	....	....	....	....	....
	Spokane	WHL	27	10	22	32	139	3	1	4	5	7
	Atlanta	IHL	2	0	0	0	17	....	....	....	....	....
1994-95	Atlanta	IHL	40	5	5	10	213	....	....	....	....	....
	Tampa Bay	**NHL**	**15**	**2**	**0**	**2**	**81**	....	....	....	....	....
	NHL Totals		**15**	**2**	**0**	**2**	**81**	....	....	....	....	....

MYRVOLD, ANDERS — COL.

Defense. Shoots left. 6'1", 178 lbs. Born, Lorenskog, Norway, August 12, 1975.
(Quebec's 6th choice, 127th overall, in 1993 Entry Draft).

			Regular Season					Playoffs				
Season	Club	Lea	GP	G	A	TP	PIM	GP	G	A	TP	PIM
1992-93	Farjestad	Swe.	2	0	0	0	0	....	....	....	....	....
1993-94	Grum	Swe. 2	24	1	0	1	59	....	....	....	....	....
1994-95	Laval	QMJHL	64	14	50	64	173	20	4	10	14	68
	Cornwall	AHL	....	....	....	....	....	3	0	1	1	2

NABOKOV, DMITRI — (nuh-BAW-kahv) CHI.

Center. Shoots right. 6'2", 209 lbs. Born, Novosibirsk, USSR, January 4, 1977.
(Chicago's 1st choice, 19th overall, in 1995 Entry Draft).

			Regular Season					Playoffs				
Season	Club	Lea	GP	G	A	TP	PIM	GP	G	A	TP	PIM
1993-94	Soviet Wings	CIS	17	0	2	2	6	3	0	0	0	0
1994-95	Soviet Wings	CIS	49	15	12	27	32	4	5	0	5	6

NAMESTNIKOV, YEVGENY — (nah-MEST-nih-kov, yev-GAIN-ee) VAN.

Defense. Shoots right. 5'11", 190 lbs. Born, Arzamis-Ig, USSR, October 9, 1971.
(Vancouver's 6th choice, 117th overall, in 1991 Entry Draft).

			Regular Season					Playoffs				
Season	Club	Lea	GP	G	A	TP	PIM	GP	G	A	TP	PIM
1988-89	Torpedo Gorky	USSR	2	0	0	0	2	....	....	....	....	....
1989-90	Torpedo Gorky	USSR	23	0	0	0	25	....	....	....	....	....
1990-91	Torpedo Niz.	USSR	42	1	2	3	49	....	....	....	....	....
1991-92	CSKA	CIS	42	1	1	2	47	....	....	....	....	....
1992-93	CSKA	CIS	42	5	5	10	68	....	....	....	....	....
1993-94	**Vancouver**	**NHL**	**17**	**0**	**5**	**5**	**10**	....	....	....	....	....
	Hamilton	AHL	59	7	27	34	97	4	0	2	2	19
1994-95	Syracuse	AHL	59	11	22	33	59	....	....	....	....	....
	Vancouver	**NHL**	**16**	**0**	**3**	**3**	**4**	**1**	**0**	**0**	**0**	**2**
	NHL Totals		**33**	**0**	**8**	**8**	**14**	**1**	**0**	**0**	**0**	**2**

NASH, TYSON — VAN.

Left wing. Shoots left. 6', 180 lbs. Born, Edmonton, Alta., March 11, 1975.
(Vancouver's 10th choice, 247th overall, in 1994 Entry Draft).

			Regular Season					Playoffs				
Season	Club	Lea	GP	G	A	TP	PIM	GP	G	A	TP	PIM
1991-92	Kamloops	WHL	33	1	6	7	62	4	0	0	0	0
1992-93	Kamloops	WHL	61	10	16	26	78	13	3	2	5	32
1993-94	Kamloops	WHL	65	20	36	56	135	16	3	4	7	12
1994-95	Kamloops	WHL	63	34	41	75	70	21	10	7	17	30

NASLUND, MARKUS — (NAZ-luhnd) PIT.

Right wing. Shoots left. 6', 186 lbs. Born, Ornskoldsvik, Sweden, July 30, 1973.
(Pittsburgh's 1st choice, 16th overall, in 1991 Entry Draft).

			Regular Season					Playoffs				
Season	Club	Lea	GP	G	A	TP	PIM	GP	G	A	TP	PIM
1990-91	MoDo	Swe.	32	10	9	19	14	....	....	....	....	....
1991-92	MoDo	Swe.	39	22	18	40	54	....	....	....	....	....
1992-93	MoDo	Swe.	39	22	17	39	67	3	3	2	5	0
1993-94	**Pittsburgh**	**NHL**	**71**	**4**	**7**	**11**	**27**	....	....	....	....	....
	Cleveland	IHL	5	1	6	7	4	....	....	....	....	....
1994-95	**Pittsburgh**	**NHL**	**14**	**2**	**2**	**4**	**2**	....	....	....	....	....
	Cleveland	IHL	7	3	4	7	6	4	1	3	4	8
	NHL Totals		**85**	**6**	**9**	**15**	**29**	....	....	....	....	....

NASLUND, MATS — NAZZ-luhnd

Left wing. Shoots left. 5'7", 160 lbs. Born, Timra, Sweden, October 31, 1959.
(Montreal's 2nd choice, 37th overall, in 1979 Entry Draft).

			Regular Season					Playoffs				
Season	Club	Lea	GP	G	A	TP	PIM	GP	G	A	TP	PIM
1977-78	Timra	Swe.	35	13	6	19	14	....	....	....	....	....
1978-79	Brynas	Swe.	36	12	12	24	19	....	....	....	....	....
1979-80	Brynas	Swe.	36	18	19	37	34	7	2	2	4	4
1980-81	Brynas	Swe.	36	17	*25	*42	34	....	....	....	....	....
1981-82	Brynas	Swe.	36	24	18	42	16	....	....	....	....	....
1982-83a	**Montreal**	**NHL**	**74**	**26**	**45**	**71**	**10**	**3**	**1**	**0**	**1**	**0**
1983-84	**Montreal**	**NHL**	**77**	**29**	**35**	**64**	**4**	**15**	**6**	**8**	**14**	**4**
1984-85	**Montreal**	**NHL**	**80**	**42**	**37**	**79**	**14**	**12**	**7**	**4**	**11**	**6**
1985-86b	**Montreal**	**NHL**	**80**	**43**	**67**	**110**	**16**	**20**	**8**	**11**	**19**	**4**
1986-87	**Montreal**	**NHL**	**79**	**25**	**55**	**80**	**16**	**17**	**7**	**15**	**22**	**11**
1987-88c	**Montreal**	**NHL**	**78**	**24**	**59**	**83**	**14**	**6**	**0**	**7**	**7**	**2**
1988-89	**Montreal**	**NHL**	**77**	**33**	**51**	**84**	**14**	**21**	**4**	**11**	**15**	**6**
1989-90	**Montreal**	**NHL**	**72**	**21**	**20**	**41**	**19**	**3**	**1**	**1**	**2**	**0**
1990-91	Lugano	Switz.	31	27	29	56	....	11	4	8	12	....
1991-92	Malmo	Swe.	39	15	24	39	10	10	3	2	5	....
1992-93	Malmo	Swe.	33	11	21	32	10	1	0	0	0	....
1993-94	Malmo	Swe.	40	14	30	44	8	11	2	4	6	4
1994-95	**Boston**	**NHL**	**34**	**8**	**14**	**22**	**4**	**5**	**1**	**0**	**1**	**0**
	NHL Totals		**651**	**251**	**383**	**634**	**111**	**102**	**35**	**57**	**92**	**33**

a NHL All-Rookie Team (1983)
b NHL Second All-Star Team (1986)
c Won Lady Byng Memorial Trophy (1988)

Played in NHL All-Star Game (1984, 1986, 1988).

Signed as a free agent by **Boston**, February 21, 1995.

NASREDDINE, ALAIN — (NAS-ruh-deen, AL-ay) FLA.

Defense. Shoots left. 6'1", 201 lbs. Born, Montreal, Que., July 10, 1975.
(Florida's 8th choice, 135th overall, in 1993 Entry Draft).

			Regular Season					Playoffs				
Season	Club	Lea	GP	G	A	TP	PIM	GP	G	A	TP	PIM
1991-92	Drummondville	QMJHL	61	1	9	10	78	4	0	0	0	17
1992-93	Drummondville	QMJHL	64	0	14	14	137	10	0	1	1	36
1993-94	Chicoutimi	QMJHL	60	3	24	27	218	26	2	10	12	118
1994-95a	Chicoutimi	QMJHL	67	8	31	39	342	13	3	5	8	40

a QMJHL Second All-Star Team (1995)

NAUMENKO, NICK — ST.L.

Defense. Shoots right. 5'11", 180 lbs. Born, Chicago, IL, July 7, 1974.
(St. Louis' 9th choice, 182nd overall, in 1992 Entry Draft).

			Regular Season					Playoffs				
Season	Club	Lea	GP	G	A	TP	PIM	GP	G	A	TP	PIM
1992-93	North Dakota	WCHA	38	10	24	34	26	....	....	....	....	....
1993-94	North Dakota	WCHA	32	4	22	26	22	....	....	....	....	....
1994-95a	North Dakota	WCHA	39	13	26	39	78	....	....	....	....	....

a WCHA First All-Star Team (1995)

NAZAROV, ANDREI (nah-ZAH-rohv) S.J.

Left wing. Shoots right. 6'5", 230 lbs. Born, Chelyabinsk, USSR, May 22, 1974.
(San Jose's 2nd choice, 10th overall, in 1992 Entry Draft).

			Regular Season					Playoffs				
Season	Club	Lea	GP	G	A	TP	PIM	GP	G	A	TP	PIM
1991-92	Moscow D'amo	CIS	2	1	0	1	2	....	....	....	....	....
1992-93	Moscow D'amo	CIS	42	8	2	10	79	10	1	1	2	8
1993-94	Moscow D'amo	CIS	6	2	2	4	0	....	....	....	....	....
	San Jose	**NHL**	**1**	**0**	**0**	**0**	**0**	....	....	....	....	....
	Kansas City	IHL	71	15	18	33	64	....	....	....	....	....
1994-95	Kansas City	IHL	43	15	10	25	55	....	....	....	....	....
	San Jose	**NHL**	**26**	**3**	**5**	**8**	**94**	**6**	**0**	**0**	**0**	**9**
	NHL Totals		**27**	**3**	**5**	**8**	**94**	**6**	**0**	**0**	**0**	**9**

NDUR, RUMUN (nih-DOOR, ROO-muhn) BUF.

Defense. Shoots left. 6'2", 200 lbs. Born, Zaria, Nigeria, July 7, 1975.
(Buffalo's 3rd choice, 69th overall, in 1994 Entry Draft).

			Regular Season					Playoffs				
Season	Club	Lea	GP	G	A	TP	PIM	GP	G	A	TP	PIM
1992-93	Guelph	OHL	22	1	3	4	30	4	0	1	1	4
1993-94	Guelph	OHL	61	6	33	39	176	9	4	1	5	24
1994-95	Guelph	OHL	63	10	21	31	187	14	0	4	4	28

NEATON, PAT

Defense. Shoots left. 6', 180 lbs. Born, Redford, MI, May 21, 1971.
(Pittsburgh's 9th choice, 145th overall, in 1990 Entry Draft).

			Regular Season					Playoffs				
Season	Club	Lea	GP	G	A	TP	PIM	GP	G	A	TP	PIM
1989-90	U. of Michigan	CCHA	42	3	23	26	36	....	....	....	....	....
1990-91a	U. of Michigan	CCHA	44	15	28	43	78	....	....	....	....	....
1991-92	U. of Michigan	CCHA	43	10	20	30	62	....	....	....	....	....
1992-93b	U. of Michigan	CCHA	38	10	18	28	37	....	....	....	....	....
1993-94	**Pittsburgh**	**NHL**	**9**	**1**	**1**	**2**	**12**	....	....	....	....	....
	Cleveland	IHL	71	8	24	32	78	....	....	....	....	....
1994-95	Cleveland	IHL	2	0	0	0	4	....	....	....	....	....
	San Diego	IHL	71	8	27	35	86	5	0	1	1	0
	NHL Totals		**9**	**1**	**1**	**2**	**12**	....	....	....	....	....

a CCHA Second All-Star Team (1991)
b CCHA First All-Star Team (1993)

NECKAR, STANISLAV (NEHTS-kahrzh) OTT.

Defense. Shoots left. 6'1", 196 lbs. Born, Ceske Budejovice, Czech., December 22, 1975.
(Ottawa's 2nd choice, 29th overall, in 1994 Entry Draft).

			Regular Season					Playoffs				
Season	Club	Lea	GP	G	A	TP	PIM	GP	G	A	TP	PIM
1992-93	Budejovice	Czech.	42	2	9	11	12	....	....	....	....	....
1993-94	Budejovice	Czech.	12	3	2	5	2	3	0	0	0	....
1994-95	Detroit	IHL	15	2	2	4	15	....	....	....	....	....
	Ottawa	**NHL**	**48**	**1**	**3**	**4**	**37**	....	....	....	....	....
	NHL Totals		**48**	**1**	**3**	**4**	**37**	....	....	....	....	....

NEDVED, PETR (NEHD-VEHD) NYR

Center. Shoots left. 6'3", 195 lbs. Born, Liberec, Czech., December 9, 1971.
(Vancouver's 1st choice, 2nd overall, in 1990 Entry Draft).

			Regular Season					Playoffs				
Season	Club	Lea	GP	G	A	TP	PIM	GP	G	A	TP	PIM
1989-90a	Seattle	WHL	71	65	80	145	80	11	4	9	13	2
1990-91	**Vancouver**	**NHL**	**61**	**10**	**6**	**16**	**20**	**6**	**0**	**1**	**1**	**0**
1991-92	**Vancouver**	**NHL**	**77**	**15**	**22**	**37**	**36**	**10**	**1**	**4**	**5**	**16**
1992-93	**Vancouver**	**NHL**	**84**	**38**	**33**	**71**	**96**	**12**	**2**	**3**	**5**	**2**
1993-94	Cdn. National	....	17	19	12	31	16	....	....	....	....	....
	Cdn. Olympic	....	8	5	1	6	6	....	....	....	....	....
	St. Louis	**NHL**	**19**	**6**	**14**	**20**	**8**	**4**	**0**	**1**	**1**	**4**
1994-95	**NY Rangers**	**NHL**	**46**	**11**	**12**	**23**	**26**	**10**	**3**	**2**	**5**	**6**
	NHL Totals		**287**	**80**	**87**	**167**	**186**	**42**	**6**	**11**	**17**	**28**

a Canadian Major Junior Rookie of the Year (1990)

Signed as a free agent by **St. Louis**, March 5, 1994. Traded to **NY Rangers** by **St. Louis** for Esa Tikkanen and Doug Lidster, July 24, 1994.

NEDVED, ZDENEK (NEHD-VEHD) TOR.

Right wing. Shoots left. 6', 180 lbs. Born, Lany, Czech., March 3, 1975.
(Toronto's 3rd choice, 123rd overall, in 1993 Entry Draft).

			Regular Season					Playoffs				
Season	Club	Lea	GP	G	A	TP	PIM	GP	G	A	TP	PIM
1991-92	Kladno	Czech.	19	15	12	27	22	....	....	....	....	....
1992-93	Sudbury	OHL	18	3	9	12	6	....	....	....	....	....
1993-94	Sudbury	OHL	60	50	50	100	42	10	7	8	15	10
1994-95	Sudbury	OHL	59	47	51	98	36	18	12	16	28	16
	Toronto	**NHL**	**1**	**0**	**0**	**0**	**2**	....	....	....	....	....
	NHL Totals		**1**	**0**	**0**	**0**	**2**	....	....	....	....	....

NEEDHAM, MIKE

Right wing. Shoots right. 5'10", 185 lbs. Born, Calgary, Alta., April 4, 1970.
(Pittsburgh's 7th choice, 126th overall, in 1989 Entry Draft).

			Regular Season					Playoffs				
Season	Club	Lea	GP	G	A	TP	PIM	GP	G	A	TP	PIM
1986-87	Kamloops	WHL	3	1	2	3	0	11	2	1	3	5
1987-88	Kamloops	WHL	64	31	33	64	93	5	0	1	1	5
1988-89	Kamloops	WHL	49	24	27	51	55	16	2	9	11	13
1989-90a	Kamloops	WHL	60	59	66	125	75	17	11	13	24	10
1990-91	Muskegon	IHL	65	14	31	45	17	5	2	2	4	5
1991-92	Muskegon	IHL	80	41	37	78	83	8	4	4	8	6
	Pittsburgh	**NHL**	....	....	....	....	....	**5**	**1**	**0**	**1**	**2**
1992-93	**Pittsburgh**	**NHL**	**56**	**8**	**5**	**13**	**14**	**9**	**1**	**0**	**1**	**2**
	Cleveland	IHL	1	2	0	2	0	....	....	....	....	....
1993-94	**Pittsburgh**	**NHL**	**25**	**1**	**0**	**1**	**2**	....	....	....	....	....
	Cleveland	IHL	6	4	3	7	7	....	....	....	....	....
	Dallas	**NHL**	**5**	**0**	**0**	**0**	**0**	....	....	....	....	....
1994-95	Kalamazoo	IHL	37	9	9	18	31	14	5	5	10	11
	NHL Totals		**86**	**9**	**5**	**14**	**16**	**14**	**2**	**0**	**2**	**4**

a WHL West First All-Star Team (1990)

Traded to **Dallas** by **Pittsburgh** for Jim McKenzie, March 21, 1994.

NEELY, CAM BOS.

Right wing. Shoots right. 6'1", 218 lbs. Born, Comox, B.C., June 6, 1965.
(Vancouver's 1st choice, 9th overall, in 1983 Entry Draft).

			Regular Season					Playoffs				
Season	Club	Lea	GP	G	A	TP	PIM	GP	G	A	TP	PIM
1982-83	Portland	WHL	72	56	64	120	130	14	9	11	20	17
1983-84	**Vancouver**	**NHL**	**56**	**16**	**15**	**31**	**57**	**4**	**2**	**0**	**2**	**2**
	Portland	WHL	19	8	18	26	29	....	....	....	....	....
1984-85	**Vancouver**	**NHL**	**72**	**21**	**18**	**39**	**137**	....	....	....	....	....
1985-86	**Vancouver**	**NHL**	**73**	**14**	**20**	**34**	**126**	**3**	**0**	**0**	**0**	**6**
1986-87	**Boston**	**NHL**	**75**	**36**	**36**	**72**	**143**	**4**	**5**	**1**	**6**	**8**
1987-88a	**Boston**	**NHL**	**69**	**42**	**27**	**69**	**175**	**23**	**9**	**8**	**17**	**51**
1988-89	**Boston**	**NHL**	**74**	**37**	**38**	**75**	**190**	**10**	**7**	**2**	**9**	**8**
1989-90a	**Boston**	**NHL**	**76**	**55**	**37**	**92**	**117**	**21**	**12**	**16**	**28**	**51**
1990-91a	**Boston**	**NHL**	**69**	**51**	**40**	**91**	**98**	**19**	**16**	**4**	**20**	**36**
1991-92	**Boston**	**NHL**	**9**	**9**	**3**	**12**	**16**	....	....	....	....	....
1992-93	**Boston**	**NHL**	**13**	**11**	**7**	**18**	**25**	**4**	**4**	**1**	**5**	**4**
1993-94ab	**Boston**	**NHL**	**49**	**50**	**24**	**74**	**54**	....	....	....	....	....
1994-95	**Boston**	**NHL**	**42**	**27**	**14**	**41**	**72**	**5**	**2**	**0**	**2**	**2**
	NHL Totals		**677**	**369**	**279**	**648**	**1210**	**93**	**57**	**32**	**89**	**168**

a NHL Second All-Star Team (1988, 1990, 1991, 1994)
b Won Bill Masterton Memorial Trophy (1994)

Played in NHL All-Star Game (1988-91)

Traded to **Boston** by **Vancouver** with Vancouver's first round choice (Glen Wesley) in 1987 Entry Draft for Barry Pederson, June 6, 1986.

NEILSON, COREY EDM.

Defense. Shoots right. 6'5", 207 lbs. Born, Oromocto, N.B., August 22, 1976.
(Edmonton's 4th choice, 53rd overall, in 1994 Entry Draft).

			Regular Season					Playoffs				
Season	Club	Lea	GP	G	A	TP	PIM	GP	G	A	TP	PIM
1993-94	North Bay	OHL	62	3	35	38	46	18	1	5	6	10
1994-95	North Bay	OHL	64	6	27	33	86	6	3	3	6	9

NELSON, JEFF WSH.

Center. Shoots left. 6', 190 lbs. Born, Prince Albert, Sask., December 18, 1972.
(Washington's 4th choice, 36th overall, in 1991 Entry Draft).

			Regular Season					Playoffs				
Season	Club	Lea	GP	G	A	TP	PIM	GP	G	A	TP	PIM
1989-90	Prince Albert	WHL	72	28	69	97	79	14	2	11	13	10
1990-91a	Prince Albert	WHL	72	46	74	120	58	3	1	1	2	4
1991-92a	Prince Albert	WHL	64	48	65	113	84	9	7	14	21	18
1992-93	Baltimore	AHL	72	14	38	52	12	7	1	3	4	2
1993-94	Portland	AHL	80	34	73	107	92	17	10	5	15	20
1994-95	Portland	AHL	64	33	50	83	57	7	1	4	5	8
	Washington	**NHL**	**10**	**1**	**0**	**1**	**2**	....	....	....	....	....
	NHL Totals		**10**	**1**	**0**	**1**	**2**	....	....	....	....	....

a WHL East Second All-Star Team (1991, 1992)

NELSON, TODD

Defense. Shoots left. 6', 201 lbs. Born, Prince Albert, Sask., May 11, 1969.
(Pittsburgh's 4th choice, 79th overall, in 1989 Entry Draft).

			Regular Season					Playoffs				
Season	Club	Lea	GP	G	A	TP	PIM	GP	G	A	TP	PIM
1985-86	Prince Albert	WHL	4	0	0	0	0	....	....	....	....	....
1986-87	Prince Albert	WHL	35	1	6	7	10	4	0	0	0	0
1987-88	Prince Albert	WHL	72	3	21	24	59	10	3	2	5	4
1988-89a	Prince Albert	WHL	72	14	45	59	72	4	1	3	4	4
1989-90a	Prince Albert	WHL	69	13	42	55	88	14	3	12	15	12
1990-91	Muskegon	IHL	79	4	20	24	32	3	0	0	0	4
1991-92	**Pittsburgh**	**NHL**	**1**	**0**	**0**	**0**	**0**	....	....	....	....	....
	Muskegon	IHL	80	6	35	41	46	14	1	11	12	4
1992-93	Cleveland	IHL	76	7	35	42	115	4	0	2	2	4
1993-94	**Washington**	**NHL**	**2**	**1**	**0**	**1**	**2**	**4**	**0**	**0**	**0**	**0**
	Portland	AHL	80	11	34	45	69	11	0	6	6	6
1994-95	Portland	AHL	75	10	35	45	76	7	0	4	4	6
	NHL Totals		**3**	**1**	**0**	**1**	**2**	**4**	**0**	**0**	**0**	**0**

a WHL East Second All-Star Team (1989, 1990)

Signed as a free agent by **Washington**, August 15, 1993.

NEMCHINOV, SERGEI (nehm-CHEE-nahf, SAIR-gay) NYR

Center. Shoots left. 6', 200 lbs. Born, Moscow, USSR, January 14, 1964.
(NY Rangers' 14th choice, 244th overall, in 1990 Entry Draft).

			Regular Season					Playoffs				
Season	Club	Lea	GP	G	A	TP	PIM	GP	G	A	TP	PIM
1981-82	Soviet Wings	USSR	15	1	0	1	0	....	....	....	....	....
1982-83	CSKA	USSR	11	0	0	0	2	....	....	....	....	....
1983-84	CSKA	USSR	20	6	5	11	4	....	....	....	....	....
1984-85	CSKA	USSR	31	2	4	6	4	....	....	....	....	....
1985-86	Soviet Wings	USSR	39	7	12	19	28	....	....	....	....	....
1986-87	Soviet Wings	USSR	40	13	9	22	24	....	....	....	....	....
1987-88	Soviet Wings	USSR	48	17	11	28	26	....	....	....	....	....
1988-89	Soviet Wings	USSR	43	15	14	29	28	....	....	....	....	....
1989-90	Soviet Wings	USSR	48	17	16	33	34	....	....	....	....	....
1990-91	Soviet Wings	USSR	46	21	24	45	30	....	....	....	....	....
1991-92	**NY Rangers**	**NHL**	**73**	**30**	**28**	**58**	**15**	**13**	**1**	**4**	**5**	**8**
1992-93	**NY Rangers**	**NHL**	**81**	**23**	**31**	**54**	**34**	....	....	....	....	....
1993-94	**NY Rangers**	**NHL**	**76**	**22**	**27**	**49**	**36**	**23**	**2**	**5**	**7**	**6**
1994-95	**NY Rangers**	**NHL**	**47**	**7**	**6**	**13**	**16**	**10**	**4**	**5**	**9**	**2**
	NHL Totals		**277**	**82**	**92**	**174**	**101**	**46**	**7**	**14**	**21**	**16**

NEMECEK, JAN L.A.

Defense. Shoots right. 6'1", 194 lbs. Born, Pisek, Czech., February 14, 1976.
(Los Angeles' 7th choice, 215th overall, in 1994 Entry Draft).

			Regular Season					Playoffs				
Season	Club	Lea	GP	G	A	TP	PIM	GP	G	A	TP	PIM
1992-93	Budejovice	Czech.	15	0	0	0	....	....	....	....	....	....
1993-94	Budejovice	Czech.	16	0	1	1	16	....	....	....	....	....
1994-95	Hull	QMJHL	49	10	16	26	48	21	5	9	14	10

NEMIROVSKY, DAVID (nyeh-mih-ROHV-skee) FLA.

Right wing. Shoots right. 6'1", 192 lbs. Born, Toronto, Ont., August 1, 1976.
(Florida's 5th choice, 84th overall, in 1994 Entry Draft).

			Regular Season					Playoffs				
Season	Club	Lea	GP	G	A	TP	PIM	GP	G	A	TP	PIM
1993-94	Ottawa	OHL	64	21	31	52	18	17	10	10	20	2
1994-95	Ottawa	OHL	59	27	29	56	25	....	....	....	....	....

NICHOL, SCOTT — BUF.

Center. Shoots right. 5'8", 160 lbs. Born, Edmonton, Alta., December 31, 1974.
(Buffalo's 9th choice, 272nd overall, in 1993 Entry Draft).

			Regular Season					Playoffs				
Season	Club	Lea	GP	G	A	TP	PIM	GP	G	A	TP	PIM
1992-93	Portland	WHL	67	31	33	64	146	16	8	8	16	41
1993-94	Portland	WHL	65	40	53	93	144	10	3	8	11	16
1994-95	Rochester	AHL	71	11	16	27	136	5	0	3	3	14

NICHOLLS, BERNIE — (NICK-els) CHI.

Center. Shoots right. 6'1", 185 lbs. Born, Haliburton, Ont., June 24, 1961.
(Los Angeles' 6th choice, 73rd overall, in 1980 Entry Draft).

			Regular Season					Playoffs				
Season	Club	Lea	GP	G	A	TP	PIM	GP	G	A	TP	PIM
1979-80	Kingston	OHA	68	36	43	79	85	3	1	0	1	10
1980-81	Kingston	OHA	65	63	89	152	109	14	8	10	18	17
1981-82	**Los Angeles**	**NHL**	**22**	**14**	**18**	**32**	**27**	**10**	**4**	**0**	**4**	**23**
	New Haven	AHL	55	41	30	71	31	....	....	....	....	....
1982-83	**Los Angeles**	**NHL**	**71**	**28**	**22**	**50**	**124**	....	....	....	....	....
1983-84	**Los Angeles**	**NHL**	**78**	**41**	**54**	**95**	**83**	....	....	....	....	....
1984-85	**Los Angeles**	**NHL**	**80**	**46**	**54**	**100**	**76**	**3**	**1**	**1**	**2**	**9**
1985-86	**Los Angeles**	**NHL**	**80**	**36**	**61**	**97**	**78**	....	....	....	....	....
1986-87	**Los Angeles**	**NHL**	**80**	**33**	**48**	**81**	**101**	**5**	**2**	**5**	**7**	**6**
1987-88	**Los Angeles**	**NHL**	**65**	**32**	**46**	**78**	**114**	**5**	**2**	**6**	**8**	**11**
1988-89	**Los Angeles**	**NHL**	**79**	**70**	**80**	**150**	**96**	**11**	**7**	**9**	**16**	**12**
1989-90	**Los Angeles**	**NHL**	**47**	**27**	**48**	**75**	**66**	....	....	....	....	....
	NY Rangers	**NHL**	**32**	**12**	**25**	**37**	**20**	**10**	**7**	**5**	**12**	**16**
1990-91	**NY Rangers**	**NHL**	**71**	**25**	**48**	**73**	**96**	**5**	**4**	**3**	**7**	**8**
1991-92	**NY Rangers**	**NHL**	**1**	**0**	**0**	**0**	**0**	....	....	....	....	....
	Edmonton	**NHL**	**49**	**20**	**29**	**49**	**60**	**16**	**8**	**11**	**19**	**25**
1992-93	**Edmonton**	**NHL**	**46**	**8**	**32**	**40**	**40**	....	....	....	....	....
	New Jersey	**NHL**	**23**	**5**	**15**	**20**	**40**	**5**	**0**	**0**	**0**	**6**
1993-94	**New Jersey**	**NHL**	**61**	**19**	**27**	**46**	**86**	**16**	**4**	**9**	**13**	**28**
1994-95	**Chicago**	**NHL**	**48**	**22**	**29**	**51**	**32**	**16**	**1**	**11**	**12**	**8**
	NHL Totals		**933**	**438**	**636**	**1074**	**1139**	**102**	**40**	**60**	**100**	**152**

Played in NHL All-Star Game (1984, 1989, 1990)

Traded to **NY Rangers** by **Los Angeles** for Tomas Sandstrom and Tony Granato, January 20, 1990. Traded to **Edmonton** by **NY Rangers** with Steven Rice and Louie DeBrusk for Mark Messier and future considerations, October 4, 1991. Traded to **New Jersey** by **Edmonton** for Zdeno Ciger and Kevin Todd, January 13, 1993. Signed as a free agent by **Chicago**, July 14, 1994.

NICKULAS, ERIC — BOS.

Center. Shoots right. 5'11", 190 lbs. Born, Cape Cod, MA, March 25, 1975.
(Boston's 3rd choice, 99th overall, in 1994 Entry Draft).

			Regular Season					Playoffs				
Season	Club	Lea	GP	G	A	TP	PIM	GP	G	A	TP	PIM
1993-94	Cushing	HS	25	46	36	82	....	....	....	....	....	....
1994-95	N. Hampshire	H.E.	33	15	9	24	32	....	....	....	....	....

NIECKAR, BARRY — (NIGH-kahr) NYI

Left wing. Shoots left. 6'3", 200 lbs. Born, Rama, Sask., December 16, 1967.

			Regular Season					Playoffs				
Season	Club	Lea	GP	G	A	TP	PIM	GP	G	A	TP	PIM
1991-92	Phoenix	IHL	5	0	0	0	9	....	....	....	....	....
	Raleigh	ECHL	46	10	18	28	229	4	4	0	4	22
1992-93	**Hartford**	**NHL**	**2**	**0**	**0**	**0**	**2**	....	....	....	....	....
	Springfield	AHL	21	2	4	6	65	6	1	0	1	14
1993-94	Springfield	AHL	30	0	2	2	67	....	....	....	....	....
	Raleigh	ECHL	18	4	6	10	126	15	5	7	12	51
1994-95	Saint John	AHL	65	8	7	15	*491	4	0	0	0	22
	Calgary	**NHL**	**3**	**0**	**0**	**0**	**12**	....	....	....	....	....
	NHL Totals		**5**	**0**	**0**	**0**	**14**	....	....	....	....	....

Signed as a free agent by **Hartford**, September 25, 1992. Signed as a free agent by **Calgary**, February 11, 1995. Signed as a free agent by **NY Islanders**, August 8, 1995.

NIEDERMAYER, ROB — (nee-duhr-MIGH-uhr) FLA.

Center. Shoots left. 6'2", 201 lbs. Born, Cassiar, B.C., December 28, 1974.
(Florida's 1st choice, 5th overall, in 1993 Entry Draft).

			Regular Season					Playoffs				
Season	Club	Lea	GP	G	A	TP	PIM	GP	G	A	TP	PIM
1990-91	Medicine Hat	WHL	71	24	26	50	8	12	3	7	10	2
1991-92	Medicine Hat	WHL	71	32	46	78	77	4	2	3	5	2
1992-93a	Medicine Hat	WHL	52	43	34	77	67	....	....	....	....	....
1993-94	**Florida**	**NHL**	**65**	**9**	**17**	**26**	**51**	....	....	....	....	....
1994-95	Medicine Hat	WHL	13	9	15	24	14	....	....	....	....	....
	Florida	**NHL**	**48**	**4**	**6**	**10**	**36**	....	....	....	....	....
	NHL Totals		**113**	**13**	**23**	**36**	**87**	....	....	....	....	....

a WHL East First All-Star Team (1993)

NIEDERMAYER, SCOTT — (NEE-duhr-MIGH-uhr) N.J.

Defense. Shoots left. 6', 200 lbs. Born, Edmonton, Alta., August 31, 1973.
(New Jersey's 1st choice, 3rd overall, in 1991 Entry Draft).

			Regular Season					Playoffs				
Season	Club	Lea	GP	G	A	TP	PIM	GP	G	A	TP	PIM
1989-90	Kamloops	WHL	64	14	55	69	64	17	2	14	16	35
1990-91ab	Kamloops	WHL	57	26	56	82	52	....	....	....	....	....
1991-92	**New Jersey**	**NHL**	**4**	**0**	**1**	**1**	**2**	....	....	....	....	....
acd	Kamloops	WHL	35	7	32	39	61	17	9	14	23	28
1992-93e	**New Jersey**	**NHL**	**80**	**11**	**29**	**40**	**47**	**5**	**0**	**3**	**3**	**2**
1993-94	**New Jersey**	**NHL**	**81**	**10**	**36**	**46**	**42**	**20**	**2**	**2**	**4**	**8**
1994-95	**New Jersey**	**NHL**	**48**	**4**	**15**	**19**	**18**	**20**	**4**	**7**	**11**	**10**
	NHL Totals		**213**	**25**	**81**	**106**	**109**	**45**	**6**	**12**	**18**	**20**

a WHL West First All-Star Team (1991, 1992)
b Canadian Major Junior Scholastic Player of the Year (1991)
c Memorial Cup All-Star Team (1992)
d Won Stafford Smythe Memorial Trophy (Memorial Cup Tournament MVP) (1992)
e NHL/Upper Deck All-Rookie Team (1993)

NIELSEN, JEFF — NYR

Right wing. Shoots right. 6', 200 lbs. Born, Grand Rapids, MN, September 20, 1971.
(NY Rangers' 4th choice, 69th overall, in 1990 Entry Draft).

			Regular Season					Playoffs				
Season	Club	Lea	GP	G	A	TP	PIM	GP	G	A	TP	PIM
1990-91	U. Minnesota	WCHA	45	11	14	25	50	....	....	....	....	....
1991-92	U. Minnesota	WCHA	41	14	14	28	70	....	....	....	....	....
1992-93	U. Minnesota	WCHA	42	21	20	41	80	....	....	....	....	....
1993-94a	U. Minnesota	WCHA	41	29	16	45	94	....	....	....	....	....
1994-95	Binghamton	AHL	76	24	13	37	139	7	0	0	0	22

a WCHA Second All-Star Team (1994)

NIELSEN, KIRK — PHI.

Right wing. Shoots right. 6'1", 190 lbs. Born, Grand Rapids, MN, October 19, 1973.
(Philadelphia's 1st choice, 10th overall, in 1994 Supplemental Draft).

			Regular Season					Playoffs				
Season	Club	Lea	GP	G	A	TP	PIM	GP	G	A	TP	PIM
1992-93	Harvard	ECAC	30	2	2	4	38	....	....	....	....	....
1993-94	Harvard	ECAC	32	6	9	15	41	....	....	....	....	....
1994-95	Harvard	ECAC	30	13	8	21	24	....	....	....	....	....

NIEUWENDYK, JOE — (NOO-ihn-DIGHK) CGY.

Center. Shoots left. 6'1", 195 lbs. Born, Oshawa, Ont., September 10, 1966.
(Calgary's 2nd choice, 27th overall, in 1985 Entry Draft).

			Regular Season					Playoffs				
Season	Club	Lea	GP	G	A	TP	PIM	GP	G	A	TP	PIM
1984-85	Cornell	ECAC	23	18	21	39	20	....	....	....	....	....
1985-86ab	Cornell	ECAC	21	21	21	42	45	....	....	....	....	....
1986-87ab	Cornell	ECAC	23	26	26	52	26	....	....	....	....	....
	Cdn. National	....	5	2	0	2	0	....	....	....	....	....
	Calgary	**NHL**	**9**	**5**	**1**	**6**	**0**	**6**	**2**	**2**	**4**	**0**
1987-88cde	**Calgary**	**NHL**	**75**	**51**	**41**	**92**	**23**	**8**	**3**	**4**	**7**	**2**
1988-89	**Calgary**	**NHL**	**77**	**51**	**31**	**82**	**40**	**22**	**10**	**4**	**14**	**10**
1989-90	**Calgary**	**NHL**	**79**	**45**	**50**	**95**	**40**	**6**	**4**	**6**	**10**	**4**
1990-91	**Calgary**	**NHL**	**79**	**45**	**40**	**85**	**36**	**7**	**4**	**1**	**5**	**10**
1991-92	**Calgary**	**NHL**	**69**	**22**	**34**	**56**	**55**	....	....	....	....	....
1992-93	**Calgary**	**NHL**	**79**	**38**	**37**	**75**	**52**	**6**	**3**	**6**	**9**	**10**
1993-94	**Calgary**	**NHL**	**64**	**36**	**39**	**75**	**51**	**6**	**2**	**2**	**4**	**0**
1994-95f	**Calgary**	**NHL**	**46**	**21**	**29**	**50**	**33**	**5**	**4**	**3**	**7**	**0**
	NHL Totals		**577**	**314**	**302**	**616**	**330**	**66**	**32**	**28**	**60**	**36**

a NCAA East First All-American Team (1986, 1987)
b ECAC First All-Star Team (1986, 1987)
c Won Calder Memorial Trophy (1988)
d NHL All-Rookie Team (1988)
e Won Dodge Ram Tough Award (1988)
f Won King Clancy Memorial Trophy (1995)

Played in NHL All-Star Game (1988-90, 1994)

NIINIMAA, JANNE — PHI.

Defense. Shoots left. 6'1", 196 lbs. Born, Raahe, Finland, May 22, 1975.
(Philadelphia's 1st choice, 36th overall, in 1993 Entry Draft).

			Regular Season					Playoffs				
Season	Club	Lea	GP	G	A	TP	PIM	GP	G	A	TP	PIM
1991-92	Karpat	Fin. 2	41	2	11	13	49	....	....	....	....	....
1992-93	Karpat	Fin. 2	29	2	3	5	14	....	....	....	....	....
1993-94	Jokerit	Fin.	45	3	8	11	24	12	1	1	2	4
1994-95	Jokerit	Fin.	42	7	10	17	36	10	1	4	5	35

NIKOLISHIN, ANDREI — (nee-koh-LEE-shin) HFD.

Left wing. Shoots left. 5'11", 180 lbs. Born, Vorkuta, USSR, March 25, 1973.
(Hartford's 2nd choice, 47th overall, in 1992 Entry Draft).

			Regular Season					Playoffs				
Season	Club	Lea	GP	G	A	TP	PIM	GP	G	A	TP	PIM
1990-91	Moscow D'amo	USSR	2	0	0	0	0	....	....	....	....	....
1991-92	Moscow D'amo	CIS	18	1	0	1	4	....	....	....	....	....
1992-93	Moscow D'amo	CIS	42	5	7	12	30	10	2	1	3	8
1993-94	Moscow D'amo	CIS	41	8	12	20	30	9	1	3	4	4
1994-95	Moscow D'amo	CIS	12	7	2	9	6	....	....	....	....	....
	Hartford	**NHL**	**39**	**8**	**10**	**18**	**10**	....	....	....	....	....
	NHL Totals		**39**	**8**	**10**	**18**	**10**	....	....	....	....	....

NIKOLOV, ANGEL — (NIH-koh-lohv) S.J.

Defense. Shoots left. 6'1", 176 lbs. Born, Most, Czech., November 18, 1975.
(San Jose's 2nd choice, 37th overall, in 1994 Entry Draft).

			Regular Season					Playoffs				
Season	Club	Lea	GP	G	A	TP	PIM	GP	G	A	TP	PIM
1993-94	Litvinov	Czech.	10	2	2	4	....	3	0	0	0	....
1994-95	Litvinov	Czech.	41	1	4	5	18	4	0	0	0	27

NIKULIN, IGOR — ANA.

Right wing. Shoots left. 6'1", 190 lbs. Born, Cherepovets, USSR, August 26, 1972.
(Anaheim's 4th choice, 107th overall, in 1995 Entry Draft).

			Regular Season					Playoffs				
Season	Club	Lea	GP	G	A	TP	PIM	GP	G	A	TP	PIM
1992-93	Cherepovets	CIS	42	11	11	22	22	....	....	....	....	....
1993-94	Cherepovets	CIS	44	14	15	29	52	2	1	0	1	0
1994-95	Cherepovets	CIS	52	14	12	26	28	....	....	....	....	....

NILSSON, FREDRIK — (NEEL-suhn) S.J.

Center. Shoots left. 6'1", 200 lbs. Born, Stockholm, Sweden, April 16, 1971.
(San Jose's 7th choice, 111th overall, in 1991 Entry Draft).

			Regular Season					Playoffs				
Season	Club	Lea	GP	G	A	TP	PIM	GP	G	A	TP	PIM
1988-89	Vasteras	Swe.	1	0	0	0	0	....	....	....	....	....
1989-90	Vasteras	Swe.	23	1	1	2	4	1	0	0	0	0
1990-91	Vasteras	Swe.	35	13	7	20	20	4	0	1	1	2
1991-92	Vasteras	Swe.	40	5	14	19	40	....	....	....	....	....
1992-93	Vasteras	Swe.	40	14	15	29	69	1	1	1	2	0
1993-94	Kansas City	IHL	13	2	7	9	2	....	....	....	....	....
1994-95	Kansas City	IHL	13	3	0	3	2	12	3	2	5	4

NILSSON, KENT

Center. Shoots left. 6'1", 195 lbs. Born, Nynashamn, Sweden, August 31, 1956.
(Atlanta's 5th choice, 64th overall, in 1976 Amateur Draft).

			Regular Season					Playoffs				
Season	Club	Lea	GP	G	A	TP	PIM	GP	G	A	TP	PIM
1975-76	Djurgardens	Swe.	36	28	27	55	10	....	....	....	....	....
	Swe. National	....	6	0	0	0	0	....	....	....	....	....
1976-77	AIK	Swe.	36	30	18	48	18	....	....	....	....	....
1977-78	Winnipeg	WHA	80	42	65	107	8	9	2	8	10	10
1978-79	Winnipeg	WHA	78	39	68	107	8	10	3	11	14	4
1979-80	**Atlanta**	**NHL**	**80**	**40**	**53**	**93**	**10**	**4**	**0**	**0**	**0**	**2**
1980-81	**Calgary**	**NHL**	**80**	**49**	**82**	**131**	**26**	**14**	**3**	**9**	**12**	**2**
1981-82	**Calgary**	**NHL**	**41**	**26**	**29**	**55**	**8**	**3**	**0**	**3**	**3**	**2**
1982-83	**Calgary**	**NHL**	**80**	**46**	**58**	**104**	**10**	**9**	**1**	**11**	**12**	**2**
1983-84	**Calgary**	**NHL**	**67**	**31**	**49**	**80**	**22**	....	....	....	....	....
1984-85	**Calgary**	**NHL**	**77**	**37**	**62**	**99**	**14**	**3**	**0**	**1**	**1**	**0**
1985-86	**Minnesota**	**NHL**	**61**	**16**	**44**	**60**	**10**	**5**	**1**	**4**	**5**	**0**
1986-87	**Minnesota**	**NHL**	**44**	**13**	**33**	**46**	**12**	....	....	....	....	....
	Edmonton	**NHL**	**17**	**5**	**12**	**17**	**4**	**21**	**6**	**13**	**19**	**6**
1987-88	Bolzano	Italy	35	60	72	132	48	8	14	14	28	....
	Lugano	Switz.	2	2	0	2	....	....	....	....	....	....
1988-89	Djurgarden	Swe.	35	21	21	42	36	....	....	....	....	....
1989-90	Kloten	Switz.	36	21	19	40	....	5	4	5	9	....
1990-91	Kloten	Switz.	33	37	39	76	....	8	3	8	11	....
1991-92	Kloten	Switz.	17	11	14	25	8	2	0	0	0	2
1992-93	Djurgarden	Swe.	40	11	20	31	20	6	2	3	5	0
1993-94	Graz	Alpen.	30	15	33	48	....	....	....	....	....	....
	Graz	Aut.	27	8	9	17	....	....	....	....	....	....
1994-95	Valerengen	Nor.	6	1	1	2	8	....	....	....	....	....
	Edmonton	**NHL**	**6**	**1**	**0**	**1**	**0**	....	....	....	....	....
	NHL Totals		**553**	**264**	**422**	**686**	**116**	**59**	**11**	**41**	**52**	**14**

Reclaimed by **Atlanta** from **Winnipeg** prior to Expansion Draft, June 9, 1979. Traded to **Minnesota** by **Calgary** with Calgary's third round choice in 1986 (Brad Turner), for Minnesota's second round choice in 1985 (Joe Nieuwendyk) and second round choice in 1987 Entry Draft (Stephane Matteau), June 15, 1985. Traded to **Edmonton** by **Minnesota** for future considerations, March 2, 1987. Signed as a free agent by **Edmonton**, January 26, 1995.

NIMIGON, STEVE (nih-MIH-gawn) HFD.

Left wing. Shoots right. 6'1", 185 lbs. Born, Oshawa, Ont., April 4, 1976.
(Hartford's 8th choice, 265th overall, in 1994 Entry Draft).

			Regular Season					Playoffs				
Season	Club	Lea	GP	G	A	TP	PIM	GP	G	A	TP	PIM
1993-94	Niagara Falls	OHL	39	5	8	13	40	....	....	....	....	....
1994-95	Niagara Falls	OHL	48	22	25	47	82	6	0	3	3	2

NOBLE, STEVE ST.L.

Center. Shoots left. 6'1", 185 lbs. Born, Sault Ste. Marie, Ont., July 17, 1976.
(St. Louis' 5th choice, 198th overall, in 1994 Entry Draft).

			Regular Season					Playoffs				
Season	Club	Lea	GP	G	A	TP	PIM	GP	G	A	TP	PIM
1993-94	Stratford	Jr. B	25	14	19	33	45	....	....	....	....	....
1994-95	Notre Dame	CCHA	37	6	8	14	25	....	....	....	....	....

NOLAN, DOUG TOR.

Left wing. Shoots left. 6'1", 185 lbs. Born, Quincy, MA, January 5, 1976.
(Toronto's 9th choice, 282nd overall, in 1994 Entry Draft).

			Regular Season					Playoffs				
Season	Club	Lea	GP	G	A	TP	PIM	GP	G	A	TP	PIM
1994-95	Catholic Mem.	HS				UNAVAILABLE						

NOLAN, OWEN COL.

Right wing. Shoots right. 6'1", 201 lbs. Born, Belfast, Ireland, September 22, 1971.
(Quebec's 1st choice, 1st overall, in 1990 Entry Draft).

			Regular Season					Playoffs				
Season	Club	Lea	GP	G	A	TP	PIM	GP	G	A	TP	PIM
1988-89	Cornwall	OHL	62	34	25	59	213	18	5	11	16	41
1989-90a	Cornwall	OHL	58	51	59	110	240	6	7	5	12	26
1990-91	**Quebec**	**NHL**	**59**	**3**	**10**	**13**	**109**	....	....	....	....	....
	Halifax	AHL	6	4	4	8	11	....	....	....	....	....
1991-92	**Quebec**	**NHL**	**75**	**42**	**31**	**73**	**183**	....	....	....	....	....
1992-93	**Quebec**	**NHL**	**73**	**36**	**41**	**77**	**185**	**5**	**1**	**0**	**1**	**2**
1993-94	**Quebec**	**NHL**	**6**	**2**	**2**	**4**	**8**	....	....	....	....	....
1994-95	**Quebec**	**NHL**	**46**	**30**	**19**	**49**	**46**	**6**	**2**	**3**	**5**	**6**
	NHL Totals		**259**	**113**	**103**	**216**	**531**	**11**	**3**	**3**	**6**	**8**

a OHL First All-Star Team (1990)

Played in NHL All-Star Game (1992)

NOONAN, BRIAN ST.L.

Right wing. Shoots right. 6'1", 200 lbs. Born, Boston, MA, May 29, 1965.
(Chicago's 10th choice, 179th overall, in 1983 Entry Draft).

			Regular Season					Playoffs				
Season	Club	Lea	GP	G	A	TP	PIM	GP	G	A	TP	PIM
1984-85	N. Westminster	WHL	72	50	66	116	76	11	8	7	15	4
1985-86	Nova Scotia	AHL	2	0	0	0	0	....	....	....	....	....
	Saginaw	IHL	76	39	39	78	69	11	6	3	9	6
1986-87	Nova Scotia	AHL	70	25	26	51	30	5	3	1	4	4
1987-88	**Chicago**	**NHL**	**77**	**10**	**20**	**30**	**44**	**3**	**0**	**0**	**0**	**4**
1988-89	**Chicago**	**NHL**	**45**	**4**	**12**	**16**	**28**	**1**	**0**	**0**	**0**	**0**
	Saginaw	IHL	19	18	13	31	36	1	0	0	0	0
1989-90	**Chicago**	**NHL**	**8**	**0**	**2**	**2**	**6**	....	....	....	....	....
a	Indianapolis	IHL	56	40	36	76	85	14	6	9	15	20
1990-91	**Chicago**	**NHL**	**7**	**0**	**4**	**4**	**2**	....	....	....	....	....
b	Indianapolis	IHL	59	38	53	91	67	7	6	4	10	18
1991-92	**Chicago**	**NHL**	**65**	**19**	**12**	**31**	**81**	**18**	**6**	**9**	**15**	**30**
1992-93	**Chicago**	**NHL**	**63**	**16**	**14**	**30**	**82**	**4**	**3**	**0**	**3**	**4**
1993-94	**Chicago**	**NHL**	**64**	**14**	**21**	**35**	**57**	....	....	....	....	....
	NY Rangers	**NHL**	**12**	**4**	**2**	**6**	**12**	**22**	**4**	**7**	**11**	**17**
1994-95	**NY Rangers**	**NHL**	**45**	**14**	**13**	**27**	**26**	**5**	**0**	**0**	**0**	**8**
	NHL Totals		**386**	**81**	**100**	**181**	**338**	**53**	**13**	**16**	**29**	**63**

a IHL Second All-Star Team (1990)
b IHL First All-Star Team (1991)

Traded to **NY Rangers** by **Chicago** with Stephane Matteau for Tony Amonte and the rights to Matt Oates, March 21, 1994. Signed as a free agent by **St. Louis**, July 24, 1995.

NORMAN, TODD VAN.

Left wing. Shoots left. 5'11", 190 lbs. Born, Palmerston, Ont., January 29, 1977.
(Vancouver's 5th choice, 120th overall, in 1995 Entry Draft).

			Regular Season					Playoffs				
Season	Club	Lea	GP	G	A	TP	PIM	GP	G	A	TP	PIM
1993-94	Guelph	OHL	57	11	12	23	14	9	0	0	0	6
1994-95	Guelph	OHL	64	30	43	73	40	13	3	2	5	4

NORRIS, CLAYTON PHI.

Right wing. Shoots right. 6'2", 205 lbs. Born, Edmonton, Alta., March 8, 1972.
(Philadelphia's 6th choice, 116th overall, in 1991 Entry Draft).

			Regular Season					Playoffs				
Season	Club	Lea	GP	G	A	TP	PIM	GP	G	A	TP	PIM
1990-91	Medicine Hat	WHL	71	26	27	53	165	12	5	4	9	41
1991-92a	Medicine Hat	WHL	69	26	39	65	300	2	0	0	0	9
1992-93	Medicine Hat	WHL	41	21	16	37	128	10	3	2	5	14
	Hershey	AHL	4	0	0	0	5	....	....	....	....	....
	Roanoke	ECHL	4	0	0	0	0	....	....	....	....	....
1993-94	Hershey	AHL	62	8	10	18	217	10	1	0	1	18
1994-95	Hershey	AHL	76	12	21	33	287	4	0	0	0	8

a WHL East Second All-Star Team (1992)

NORRIS, DWAYNE

Right wing. Shoots right. 5'10", 175 lbs. Born, St. John's, Nfld., January 8, 1970.
(Quebec's 5th choice, 127th overall, in 1990 Entry Draft).

			Regular Season					Playoffs				
Season	Club	Lea	GP	G	A	TP	PIM	GP	G	A	TP	PIM
1988-89	Michigan State	CCHA	40	16	21	37	32	....	....	....	....	....
1989-90	Michigan State	CCHA	33	18	25	43	30	....	....	....	....	....
1990-91	Michigan State	CCHA	40	26	25	51	60	....	....	....	....	....
1991-92ab	Michigan State	CCHA	41	40	38	78	58	....	....	....	....	....
1992-93	Halifax	AHL	50	25	28	53	62	....	....	....	....	....
1993-94	Cdn. National	....	48	18	14	32	22	....	....	....	....	....
	Cdn. Olympic	....	8	2	2	4	4	....	....	....	....	....
	Quebec	**NHL**	**4**	**1**	**1**	**2**	**4**	....	....	....	....	....
	Cornwall	AHL	9	2	9	11	0	13	7	4	11	17
1994-95c	Cornwall	AHL	60	30	43	73	61	12	7	8	15	4
	Quebec	**NHL**	**13**	**1**	**2**	**3**	**2**	....	....	....	....	....
	NHL Totals		**17**	**2**	**3**	**5**	**6**	....	....	....	....	....

a CCHA First All-Star Team (1992)
b NCAA West First All-American Team (1992)
c AHL First All-Star Team (1995)

NORSTROM, MATTIAS NYR

Defense. Shoots left. 6'1", 205 lbs. Born, Mora, Sweden, January 2, 1972.
(NY Rangers' 2nd choice, 48th overall, in 1992 Entry Draft).

			Regular Season					Playoffs				
Season	Club	Lea	GP	G	A	TP	PIM	GP	G	A	TP	PIM
1991-92	AIK	Swe.	39	4	3	7	28	3	0	2	2	2
1992-93	AIK	Swe.	22	0	1	1	16	....	....	....	....	....
1993-94	**NY Rangers**	**NHL**	**9**	**0**	**2**	**2**	**6**	....	....	....	....	....
	Binghamton	AHL	55	1	9	10	70	....	....	....	....	....
1994-95	Binghamton	AHL	63	9	10	19	91	....	....	....	....	....
	NY Rangers	**NHL**	**9**	**0**	**3**	**3**	**2**	**3**	**0**	**0**	**0**	**0**
	NHL Totals		**18**	**0**	**5**	**5**	**8**	**3**	**0**	**0**	**0**	**0**

NORTON, BRAD EDM.

Defense. Shoots left. 6'4", 225 lbs. Born, Cambridge, MA, February 13, 1975.
(Edmonton's 9th choice, 215th overall, in 1993 Entry Draft).

			Regular Season					Playoffs				
Season	Club	Lea	GP	G	A	TP	PIM	GP	G	A	TP	PIM
1994-95	Massachusetts	H.E.	30	0	6	6	89	....	....	....	....	....

NORTON, JEFF ST.L.

Defense. Shoots left. 6'2", 200 lbs. Born, Acton, MA, November 25, 1965.
(NY Islanders' 3rd choice, 62nd overall, in 1984 Entry Draft).

			Regular Season					Playoffs				
Season	Club	Lea	GP	G	A	TP	PIM	GP	G	A	TP	PIM
1984-85	U. of Michigan	CCHA	37	8	16	24	103	....	....	....	....	....
1985-86	U. of Michigan	CCHA	37	15	30	45	99	....	....	....	....	....
1986-87a	U. of Michigan	CCHA	39	12	36	48	92	....	....	....	....	....
1987-88	U.S. National	....	54	7	22	29	52	....	....	....	....	....
	U.S. Olympic	....	6	0	4	4	4	....	....	....	....	....
	NY Islanders	**NHL**	**15**	**1**	**6**	**7**	**14**	**3**	**0**	**2**	**2**	**13**
1988-89	**NY Islanders**	**NHL**	**69**	**1**	**30**	**31**	**74**	....	....	....	....	....
1989-90	**NY Islanders**	**NHL**	**60**	**4**	**49**	**53**	**65**	**4**	**1**	**3**	**4**	**17**
1990-91	**NY Islanders**	**NHL**	**44**	**3**	**25**	**28**	**16**	....	....	....	....	....
1991-92	**NY Islanders**	**NHL**	**28**	**1**	**18**	**19**	**18**	....	....	....	....	....
1992-93	**NY Islanders**	**NHL**	**66**	**12**	**38**	**50**	**45**	**10**	**1**	**1**	**2**	**4**
1993-94	**San Jose**	**NHL**	**64**	**7**	**33**	**40**	**36**	**14**	**1**	**5**	**6**	**20**
1994-95	**San Jose**	**NHL**	**20**	**1**	**9**	**10**	**39**	....	....	....	....	....
	St. Louis	**NHL**	**28**	**2**	**18**	**20**	**33**	**7**	**1**	**1**	**2**	**11**
	NHL Totals		**394**	**32**	**226**	**258**	**340**	**38**	**4**	**12**	**16**	**65**

a CCHA Second All-Star Team (1987)

Traded to **San Jose** by **NY Islanders** for San Jose's third round choice (Jason Strudwick) in 1994 Entry Draft, June 20, 1993. Traded to **St. Louis** by **San Jose** with a conditional choice in 1997 Entry Draft for Craig Janney and cash, March 6, 1995.

NUMMINEN, TEPPO (NOO-mih-nehn, TEH-poh) WPG.

Defense. Shoots right. 6'1", 190 lbs. Born, Tampere, Finland, July 3, 1968.
(Winnipeg's 2nd choice, 29th overall, in 1986 Entry Draft).

			Regular Season					Playoffs				
Season	Club	Lea	GP	G	A	TP	PIM	GP	G	A	TP	PIM
1985-86	Tappara	Fin.	31	2	4	6	6	8	0	0	0	0
1986-87	Tappara	Fin.	44	9	9	18	16	9	4	1	5	4
1987-88	Tappara	Fin.	40	10	10	20	29	10	6	6	12	6
1988-89	**Winnipeg**	**NHL**	**69**	**1**	**14**	**15**	**36**	....	....	....	....	....
1989-90	**Winnipeg**	**NHL**	**79**	**11**	**32**	**43**	**20**	**7**	**1**	**2**	**3**	**10**
1990-91	**Winnipeg**	**NHL**	**80**	**8**	**25**	**33**	**28**	....	....	....	....	....
1991-92	**Winnipeg**	**NHL**	**80**	**5**	**34**	**39**	**32**	**7**	**0**	**0**	**0**	**0**
1992-93	**Winnipeg**	**NHL**	**66**	**7**	**30**	**37**	**33**	**6**	**1**	**1**	**2**	**2**
1993-94	**Winnipeg**	**NHL**	**57**	**5**	**18**	**23**	**28**	....	....	....	....	....
1994-95	TuTo	Fin.	12	3	8	11	4	....	....	....	....	....
	Winnipeg	**NHL**	**42**	**5**	**16**	**21**	**16**	....	....	....	....	....
	NHL Totals		**473**	**42**	**169**	**211**	**193**	**20**	**2**	**3**	**5**	**12**

NUUTINEN, SAMI — EDM.

Defense. Shoots left. 6'1", 189 lbs. Born, Espoo, Finland, June 11, 1971.
(Edmonton's 11th choice, 248th overall, in 1990 Entry Draft).

			Regular Season					Playoffs				
Season	Club	Lea	GP	G	A	TP	PIM	GP	G	A	TP	PIM
1988-89	Espoo	Fin. 2	39	18	10	28	46	....	....	....	....	....
1989-90	Espoo	Fin. 2	40	8	15	23	....	....	....	....	....	....
1990-91	K-Kissat	Fin. 2	3	1	0	1	0	....	....	....	....	....
	HIFK	Fin.	27	1	3	4	6	3	0	0	0	0
1991-92	HIFK	Fin.	44	5	6	11	10	9	0	1	1	4
1992-93	Kiekko-Espoo	Fin.	48	7	11	18	59	....	....	....	....	....
1993-94	Kiekko-Espoo	Fin.	46	9	15	24	36	....	....	....	....	....
1994-95	Kiekko-Espoo	Fin.	50	8	24	32	38	4	0	1	1	0

NYLANDER, MICHAEL (NEE-lan-duhr) — CGY.

Center. Shoots left. 5'11", 190 lbs. Born, Stockholm, Sweden, October 3, 1972.
(Hartford's 4th choice, 59th overall, in 1991 Entry Draft).

			Regular Season					Playoffs				
Season	Club	Lea	GP	G	A	TP	PIM	GP	G	A	TP	PIM
1989-90	Huddinge	Swe. 2	31	7	15	22	4	....	....	....	....	....
1990-91	Huddinge	Swe. 2	33	14	20	34	10	....	....	....	....	....
1991-92	AIK	Swe.	40	11	17	28	30	3	1	4	5	4
1992-93	**Hartford**	**NHL**	**59**	**11**	**22**	**33**	**36**	....	....	....	....	....
	Springfield	AHL	....	....	....	....	....	3	3	3	6	2
1993-94	**Hartford**	**NHL**	**58**	**11**	**33**	**44**	**24**	....	....	....	....	....
	Springfield	AHL	4	0	9	9	0	....	....	....	....	....
	Calgary	**NHL**	**15**	**2**	**9**	**11**	**6**	**3**	**0**	**0**	**0**	**0**
1994-95	JyP HT	Fin.	16	11	19	30	63	....	....	....	....	....
	Calgary	**NHL**	**6**	**0**	**1**	**1**	**2**	**6**	**0**	**6**	**6**	**2**
	NHL Totals		**138**	**24**	**65**	**89**	**68**	**9**	**0**	**6**	**6**	**2**

Traded to **Calgary** by **Hartford** with James Patrick and Zarley Zalapski for Gary Suter, Paul Ranheim and Ted Drury, March 10, 1994.

OATES, ADAM — BOS.

Center. Shoots right. 5'11", 185 lbs. Born, Weston, Ont., August 27, 1962.

			Regular Season					Playoffs				
Season	Club	Lea	GP	G	A	TP	PIM	GP	G	A	TP	PIM
1982-83	RPI	ECAC	22	9	33	42	8	....	....	....	....	....
1983-84	RPI	ECAC	38	26	57	83	15	....	....	....	....	....
1984-85ab	RPI	ECAC	38	31	60	91	29	....	....	....	....	....
1985-86	**Detroit**	**NHL**	**38**	**9**	**11**	**20**	**10**	....	....	....	....	....
	Adirondack	AHL	34	18	28	46	4	17	7	14	21	4
1986-87	**Detroit**	**NHL**	**76**	**15**	**32**	**47**	**21**	**16**	**4**	**7**	**11**	**6**
1987-88	**Detroit**	**NHL**	**63**	**14**	**40**	**54**	**20**	**16**	**8**	**12**	**20**	**6**
1988-89	**Detroit**	**NHL**	**69**	**16**	**62**	**78**	**14**	**6**	**0**	**8**	**8**	**2**
1989-90	**St. Louis**	**NHL**	**80**	**23**	**79**	**102**	**30**	**12**	**2**	**12**	**14**	**4**
1990-91c	**St. Louis**	**NHL**	**61**	**25**	**90**	**115**	**29**	**13**	**7**	**13**	**20**	**10**
1991-92	**St. Louis**	**NHL**	**54**	**10**	**59**	**69**	**12**	....	....	....	....	....
	Boston	**NHL**	**26**	**10**	**20**	**30**	**10**	**15**	**5**	**14**	**19**	**4**
1992-93	**Boston**	**NHL**	**84**	**45**	***97**	**142**	**32**	**4**	**0**	**9**	**9**	**4**
1993-94	**Boston**	**NHL**	**77**	**32**	**80**	**112**	**45**	**13**	**3**	**9**	**12**	**8**
1994-95	**Boston**	**NHL**	**48**	**12**	**41**	**53**	**8**	**5**	**1**	**0**	**1**	**2**
	NHL Totals		**676**	**211**	**611**	**822**	**231**	**100**	**30**	**84**	**114**	**46**

a ECAC First All-Star Team (1985)
b Named to NCAA All-American Team (1985)
c NHL Second All-Star Team (1991)

Played in NHL All-Star Game (1991-94)

Signed as a free agent by **Detroit,** June 28, 1985. Traded to **St. Louis** by **Detroit** with Paul MacLean for Bernie Federko and Tony McKegney, June 15, 1989. Traded to **Boston** by **St. Louis** for Craig Janney and Stephane Quintal, February 7, 1992.

OATES, MATT — CHI.

Left wing. Shoots left. 6'3", 208 lbs. Born, Evanston, IL, December 20, 1972.
(NY Rangers' 7th choice, 168th overall, in 1992 Entry Draft).

			Regular Season					Playoffs				
Season	Club	Lea	GP	G	A	TP	PIM	GP	G	A	TP	PIM
1991-92	Miami-Ohio	CCHA	40	8	13	21	23	....	....	....	....	....
1992-93	Miami-Ohio	CCHA	38	11	14	25	82	....	....	....	....	....
1993-94	Miami-Ohio	CCHA	33	14	12	26	60	....	....	....	....	....
1994-95	Columbus	ECHL	11	4	5	9	11	....	....	....	....	....
	Indianapolis	IHL	59	3	6	9	18	....	....	....	....	....

Rights traded to **Chicago** by **NY Rangers** with Tony Amonte for Stephane Matteau and Brian Noonan, March 21, 1994.

O'CONNELL, ALBERT — NYI

Left wing. Shoots left. 6', 188 lbs. Born, Cambridge, MA, May 20, 1976.
(NY Islanders' 6th choice, 116th overall, in 1994 Entry Draft).

			Regular Season					Playoffs				
Season	Club	Lea	GP	G	A	TP	PIM	GP	G	A	TP	PIM
1993-94	St. Sebastian's	HS	24	16	23	39	26	....	....	....	....	....
1994-95	St. Sebastian's	HS				UNAVAILABLE						

O'CONNOR, MYLES

Defense. Shoots left. 5'11", 190 lbs. Born, Calgary, Alta., April 2, 1967.
(New Jersey's 4th choice, 45th overall, in 1985 Entry Draft).

			Regular Season					Playoffs				
Season	Club	Lea	GP	G	A	TP	PIM	GP	G	A	TP	PIM
1985-86	U. of Michigan	CCHA	37	6	19	25	73	....	....	....	....	....
	Cdn. National	....	8	0	0	0	0	....	....	....	....	....
1986-87	U. of Michigan	CCHA	39	15	39	54	111	....	....	....	....	....
1987-88	U. of Michigan	CCHA	40	9	25	34	78	....	....	....	....	....
1988-89ab	U. of Michigan	CCHA	40	3	31	34	91	....	....	....	....	....
	Utica	AHL	1	0	0	0	0	....	....	....	....	....
1989-90	Utica	AHL	76	14	33	47	124	5	1	2	3	26
1990-91	**New Jersey**	**NHL**	**22**	**3**	**1**	**4**	**41**	....	....	....	....	....
	Utica	AHL	33	6	17	23	62	....	....	....	....	....
1991-92	**New Jersey**	**NHL**	**9**	**0**	**2**	**2**	**13**	....	....	....	....	....
	Utica	AHL	66	9	39	48	184	....	....	....	....	....
1992-93	**New Jersey**	**NHL**	**7**	**0**	**0**	**0**	**9**	....	....	....	....	....
	Utica	AHL	9	1	5	6	10	....	....	....	....	....
1993-94	**Anaheim**	**NHL**	**5**	**0**	**1**	**1**	**6**	....	....	....	....	....
	San Diego	IHL	39	1	13	14	117	9	1	4	5	83
1994-95	San Diego	IHL	16	1	4	5	50	5	0	1	1	0
	NHL Totals		**43**	**3**	**4**	**7**	**69**	....	....	....	....	....

a CCHA First All-Star Team (1989)
b NCAA West First All-American Team (1989)

Signed as a free agent by **Anaheim**, July 22, 1993.

O'CONNOR, TOM — PIT.

Defense. Shoots left. 6'2", 190 lbs. Born, Springfield, MA, January 9, 1976.
(Pittsburgh's 6th choice, 102nd overall, in 1994 Entry Draft).

			Regular Season					Playoffs				
Season	Club	Lea	GP	G	A	TP	PIM	GP	G	A	TP	PIM
1993-94	Springfield	NEJHL	36	4	15	19	73	....	....	....	....	....
1994-95	Mass.-Amherst	H.E.	34	1	2	3	44	....	....	....	....	....

ODELEIN, LYLE (OH-duh-LIGHN) — MTL.

Defense. Shoots right. 5'11", 210 lbs. Born, Quill Lake, Sask., July 21, 1968.
(Montreal's 8th choice, 141st overall, in 1986 Entry Draft).

			Regular Season					Playoffs				
Season	Club	Lea	GP	G	A	TP	PIM	GP	G	A	TP	PIM
1985-86	Moose Jaw	WHL	67	9	37	46	117	13	1	6	7	34
1986-87	Moose Jaw	WHL	59	9	50	59	70	9	2	5	7	26
1987-88	Moose Jaw	WHL	63	15	43	58	166	....	....	....	....	....
1988-89	Sherbrooke	AHL	33	3	4	7	120	3	0	2	2	5
	Peoria	IHL	36	2	8	10	116	....	....	....	....	....
1989-90	**Montreal**	**NHL**	**8**	**0**	**2**	**2**	**33**	....	....	....	....	....
	Sherbrooke	AHL	68	7	24	31	265	12	6	5	11	79
1990-91	**Montreal**	**NHL**	**52**	**0**	**2**	**2**	**259**	**12**	**0**	**0**	**0**	**54**
1991-92	**Montreal**	**NHL**	**71**	**1**	**7**	**8**	**212**	**7**	**0**	**0**	**0**	**11**
1992-93	**Montreal**	**NHL**	**83**	**2**	**14**	**16**	**205**	**20**	**1**	**5**	**6**	**30**
1993-94	**Montreal**	**NHL**	**79**	**11**	**29**	**40**	**276**	**7**	**0**	**0**	**0**	**17**
1994-95	**Montreal**	**NHL**	**48**	**3**	**7**	**10**	**152**	....	....	....	....	....
	NHL Totals		**341**	**17**	**61**	**78**	**1137**	**46**	**1**	**5**	**6**	**112**

O'DETTE, MATT — FLA.

Defense. Shoots right. 6'4", 223 lbs. Born, East York, Ont., November 9, 1975.
(Florida's 7th choice, 157th overall, in 1994 Entry Draft).

			Regular Season					Playoffs				
Season	Club	Lea	GP	G	A	TP	PIM	GP	G	A	TP	PIM
1992-93	Kitchener	OHL	28	0	0	0	6	....	....	....	....	....
1993-94	Kitchener	OHL	46	1	3	4	107	....	....	....	....	....
1994-95	Kitchener	OHL	10	1	2	3	29	....	....	....	....	....
	S.S. Marie	OHL	42	3	12	15	94	....	....	....	....	....

ODGERS, JEFF (AWD-juhrs) — S.J.

Right wing. Shoots right. 6', 195 lbs. Born, Spy Hill, Sask., May 31, 1969.

			Regular Season					Playoffs				
Season	Club	Lea	GP	G	A	TP	PIM	GP	G	A	TP	PIM
1988-89	Brandon	WHL	71	31	29	60	277	....	....	....	....	....
1989-90	Brandon	WHL	64	37	28	65	209	....	....	....	....	....
1990-91	Kansas City	IHL	77	12	19	31	318	....	....	....	....	....
1991-92	**San Jose**	**NHL**	**61**	**7**	**4**	**11**	**217**	....	....	....	....	....
	Kansas City	IHL	12	2	2	4	56	4	2	1	3	0
1992-93	**San Jose**	**NHL**	**66**	**12**	**15**	**27**	**253**	....	....	....	....	....
1993-94	**San Jose**	**NHL**	**81**	**13**	**8**	**21**	**222**	**11**	**0**	**0**	**0**	**11**
1994-95	**San Jose**	**NHL**	**48**	**4**	**3**	**7**	**117**	**11**	**1**	**1**	**2**	**23**
	NHL Totals		**256**	**36**	**30**	**66**	**809**	**22**	**1**	**1**	**2**	**34**

Signed as a free agent by **San Jose**, September 3, 1991.

ODJICK, GINO (OH-jihk) — VAN.

Left wing. Shoots left. 6'3", 210 lbs. Born, Maniwaki, Que., September 7, 1970.
(Vancouver's 5th choice, 86th overall, in 1990 Entry Draft).

			Regular Season					Playoffs				
Season	Club	Lea	GP	G	A	TP	PIM	GP	G	A	TP	PIM
1988-89	Laval	QMJHL	50	9	15	24	278	16	0	9	9	129
1989-90	Laval	QMJHL	51	12	26	38	280	....	....	....	....	....
1990-91	**Vancouver**	**NHL**	**45**	**7**	**1**	**8**	**296**	**6**	**0**	**0**	**0**	**18**
	Milwaukee	IHL	17	7	3	10	102	....	....	....	....	....
1991-92	**Vancouver**	**NHL**	**65**	**4**	**6**	**10**	**348**	**4**	**0**	**0**	**0**	**6**
1992-93	**Vancouver**	**NHL**	**75**	**4**	**13**	**17**	**370**	**1**	**0**	**0**	**0**	**0**
1993-94	**Vancouver**	**NHL**	**76**	**16**	**13**	**29**	**271**	**10**	**0**	**0**	**0**	**18**
1994-95	**Vancouver**	**NHL**	**23**	**4**	**5**	**9**	**109**	**5**	**0**	**0**	**0**	**47**
	NHL Totals		**284**	**35**	**38**	**73**	**1394**	**26**	**0**	**0**	**0**	**89**

O'DONNELL, SEAN — L.A.

Defense. Shoots left. 6'2", 224 lbs. Born, Ottawa, Ont., October 13, 1971.
(Buffalo's 6th choice, 123rd overall, in 1991 Entry Draft).

			Regular Season					Playoffs				
Season	Club	Lea	GP	G	A	TP	PIM	GP	G	A	TP	PIM
1990-91	Sudbury	OHL	66	8	23	31	114	5	1	4	5	10
1991-92	Rochester	AHL	73	4	9	13	193	16	1	2	3	21
1992-93	Rochester	AHL	74	3	18	21	203	17	1	6	7	38
1993-94	Rochester	AHL	64	2	10	12	242	4	0	1	1	21
1994-95	Phoenix	IHL	61	2	18	20	132	9	0	1	1	21
	Los Angeles	**NHL**	**15**	**0**	**2**	**2**	**49**	....	....	....	....	....
	NHL Totals		**15**	**0**	**2**	**2**	**49**	....	....	....	....	....

Traded to **Los Angeles** by **Buffalo** for Doug Houda, July 26, 1994.

ODUYA, FREDRIK — S.J.

Defense. Shoots left. 6'2", 185 lbs. Born, Stockholm, Sweden, May 31, 1975.
(San Jose's 8th choice, 154th overall, in 1993 Entry Draft).

			Regular Season					Playoffs				
Season	Club	Lea	GP	G	A	TP	PIM	GP	G	A	TP	PIM
1992-93	Guelph	OHL	23	2	4	6	29	....	....	....	....	....
	Ottawa	OHL	17	0	3	3	70	....	....	....	....	....
1993-94	Ottawa	OHL	51	11	12	23	181	17	0	3	3	22
1994-95	Ottawa	OHL	61	2	13	15	175	....	....	....	....	....

O'GRADY, MIKE — FLA.

Defense. Shoots left. 6'3", 227 lbs. Born, Neilburg, Sask., March 22, 1977.
(Florida's 3rd choice, 62nd overall, in 1995 Entry Draft).

			Regular Season					Playoffs				
Season	Club	Lea	GP	G	A	TP	PIM	GP	G	A	TP	PIM
1993-94	Saskatoon	WHL	13	0	1	1	29	....	....	....	....	....
1994-95	Saskatoon	WHL	39	0	7	7	157	....	....	....	....	....
	Lethbridge	WHL	21	1	2	3	124	....	....	....	....	....

OHLUND, MATTIAS (EH-luhnd) — VAN.

Defense. Shoots left. 6'3", 209 lbs. Born, Pitea, Sweden, September 9, 1976.
(Vancouver's 1st choice, 13th overall, in 1994 Entry Draft).

			Regular Season					Playoffs				
Season	Club	Lea	GP	G	A	TP	PIM	GP	G	A	TP	PIM
1992-93	Pitea	Swe. 2	22	0	6	6	16	....	....	....	....	....
1993-94	Pitea	Swe. 2	28	7	10	17	62	....	....	....	....	....
1994-95	Lulea	Swe.	34	6	10	16	34	9	4	0	4	16

OKSIUTA, ROMAN (ohk-SEW-tah) VAN.

Right wing. Shoots left. 6'3", 229 lbs. Born, Murmansk, USSR, August 21, 1970.
(NY Rangers' 11th choice, 202nd overall, in 1989 Entry Draft).

			Regular Season					Playoffs				
Season	Club	Lea	GP	G	A	TP	PIM	GP	G	A	TP	PIM
1987-88	Khimik	USSR	11	1	0	1	4	....	....	....	....	....
1988-89	Khimik	USSR	34	13	3	16	14	....	....	....	....	....
1989-90	Khimik	USSR	37	13	6	19	16	....	....	....	....	....
1990-91	Khimik	USSR	41	12	8	20	24	....	....	....	....	....
1991-92	Khimik	CIS	42	24	20	44	28	....	....	....	....	....
1992-93	Khimik	CIS	20	11	2	13	42	....	....	....	....	....
	Cape Breton	AHL	43	26	25	51	22	16	9	19	28	12
1993-94	**Edmonton**	**NHL**	**10**	**1**	**2**	**3**	**4**	....	....	....	....	....
	Cape Breton	AHL	47	31	22	53	90	4	2	2	4	22
1994-95	Cape Breton	AHL	25	9	7	16	20	....	....	....	....	....
	Edmonton	**NHL**	**26**	**11**	**2**	**13**	**8**	....	....	....	....	....
	Vancouver	**NHL**	**12**	**5**	**2**	**7**	**2**	**10**	**2**	**3**	**5**	**0**
	NHL Totals		**48**	**17**	**6**	**23**	**14**	**10**	**2**	**3**	**5**	**0**

Traded to **Edmonton** by **NY Rangers** with NY Rangers' third round choice (Alexander Kerch) in 1993 Entry Draft for Kevin Lowe, December 11, 1992. Traded to **Vancouver** by **Edmonton** for Jiri Slegr, April 7, 1995.

OKTYABREV, ARTUR (ohk-tib-BREE-AHV, ahr-TOOR) VAN.

Defense. Shoots left. 5'11", 183 lbs. Born, Irkutsk, USSR, November 26, 1973.
(Winnipeg's 6th choice, 155th overall, in 1992 Entry Draft).

			Regular Season					Playoffs				
Season	Club	Lea	GP	G	A	TP	PIM	GP	G	A	TP	PIM
1991-92	CSKA	CIS	38	1	2	3	19	....	....	....	....	....
1992-93	CSKA	CIS	41	0	5	5	44	....	....	....	....	....
1993-94	CSKA	CIS	45	1	1	2	46	3	0	0	0	4
	Russian Pen's	IHL	10	0	2	2	12	....	....	....	....	....
1994-95	CSKA	CIS	46	1	3	4	36	....	....	....	....	....
	Syracuse	AHL	7	1	1	2	2	....	....	....	....	....

Traded to **Vancouver** by **Winnipeg** for Vancouver's sixth round choice (Steve Vezina) in 1994 Entry Draft, June 29, 1994.

OLAUSSON, FREDRIK (OHL-ah-suhn) EDM.

Defense. Shoots right. 6'2", 195 lbs. Born, Dadesjo, Sweden, October 5, 1966.
(Winnipeg's 4th choice, 81st overall, in 1985 Entry Draft).

			Regular Season					Playoffs				
Season	Club	Lea	GP	G	A	TP	PIM	GP	G	A	TP	PIM
1982-83	Nybro	Swe. 2	31	4	4	8	12	....	....	....	....	....
1983-84	Nybro	Swe. 2	28	8	14	22	32	....	....	....	....	....
1984-85	Farjestad	Swe.	29	5	12	17	22	3	1	0	1	0
1985-86	Farjestad	Swe.	33	4	12	16	22	8	3	2	5	6
1986-87	**Winnipeg**	**NHL**	**72**	**7**	**29**	**36**	**24**	**10**	**2**	**3**	**5**	**4**
1987-88	**Winnipeg**	**NHL**	**38**	**5**	**10**	**15**	**18**	**5**	**1**	**1**	**2**	**0**
1988-89	**Winnipeg**	**NHL**	**75**	**15**	**47**	**62**	**32**	....	....	....	....	....
1989-90	**Winnipeg**	**NHL**	**77**	**9**	**46**	**55**	**32**	**7**	**0**	**2**	**2**	**2**
1990-91	**Winnipeg**	**NHL**	**71**	**12**	**29**	**41**	**24**	....	....	....	....	....
1991-92	**Winnipeg**	**NHL**	**77**	**20**	**42**	**62**	**34**	**7**	**1**	**5**	**6**	**4**
1992-93	**Winnipeg**	**NHL**	**68**	**16**	**41**	**57**	**22**	**6**	**0**	**2**	**2**	**2**
1993-94	**Winnipeg**	**NHL**	**18**	**2**	**5**	**7**	**10**	....	....	....	....	....
	Edmonton	**NHL**	**55**	**9**	**19**	**28**	**20**	....	....	....	....	....
1994-95	Ehrwald	Aus.	10	4	3	7	8	....	....	....	....	....
	Edmonton	**NHL**	**33**	**0**	**10**	**10**	**20**	....	....	....	....	....
	NHL Totals		**584**	**95**	**278**	**373**	**236**	**35**	**4**	**13**	**17**	**12**

Traded to **Edmonton** by **Winnipeg** with Winnipeg's seventh round choice (Curtis Sheptak) in 1994 Entry Draft for Edmonton's third round choice (Tavis Hansen) in 1994 Entry Draft, December 6, 1993.

OLCZYK, ED (OHL-chehk) WPG.

Center. Shoots left. 6'1", 205 lbs. Born, Chicago, IL, August 16, 1966.
(Chicago's 1st choice, 3rd overall, in 1984 Entry Draft).

			Regular Season					Playoffs				
Season	Club	Lea	GP	G	A	TP	PIM	GP	G	A	TP	PIM
1983-84	U.S. National	....	62	21	47	68	36	....	....	....	....	....
1984-85	**Chicago**	**NHL**	**70**	**20**	**30**	**50**	**67**	**15**	**6**	**5**	**11**	**11**
1985-86	**Chicago**	**NHL**	**79**	**29**	**50**	**79**	**47**	**3**	**0**	**0**	**0**	**0**
1986-87	**Chicago**	**NHL**	**79**	**16**	**35**	**51**	**119**	**4**	**1**	**1**	**2**	**4**
1987-88	**Toronto**	**NHL**	**80**	**42**	**33**	**75**	**55**	**6**	**5**	**4**	**9**	**2**
1988-89	**Toronto**	**NHL**	**80**	**38**	**52**	**90**	**75**	....	....	....	....	....
1989-90	**Toronto**	**NHL**	**79**	**32**	**56**	**88**	**78**	**5**	**1**	**2**	**3**	**14**
1990-91	**Toronto**	**NHL**	**18**	**4**	**10**	**14**	**13**	....	....	....	....	....
	Winnipeg	**NHL**	**61**	**26**	**31**	**57**	**69**	....	....	....	....	....
1991-92	**Winnipeg**	**NHL**	**64**	**32**	**33**	**65**	**67**	**6**	**2**	**1**	**3**	**4**
1992-93	**Winnipeg**	**NHL**	**25**	**8**	**12**	**20**	**26**	....	....	....	....	....
	NY Rangers	**NHL**	**46**	**13**	**16**	**29**	**26**	....	....	....	....	....
1993-94	**NY Rangers**	**NHL**	**37**	**3**	**5**	**8**	**28**	**1**	**0**	**0**	**0**	**0**
1994-95	**NY Rangers**	**NHL**	**20**	**2**	**1**	**3**	**4**	....	....	....	....	....
	Winnipeg	**NHL**	**13**	**2**	**8**	**10**	**8**	....	....	....	....	....
	NHL Totals		**751**	**267**	**372**	**639**	**682**	**40**	**15**	**13**	**28**	**35**

Traded to **Toronto** by **Chicago** with Al Secord for Rick Vaive, Steve Thomas and Bob McGill, September 3, 1987. Traded to **Winnipeg** by **Toronto** with Mark Osborne for Dave Ellett and Paul Fenton, November 10, 1990. Traded to **NY Rangers** by **Winnipeg** for Kris King and Tie Domi, December 28, 1992. Traded to **Winnipeg** by **NY Rangers** for Winnipeg's fifth round choice (Alexei Vasiliev) in 1995 Entry Draft, April 7, 1995.

OLIVER, DAVID EDM.

Right wing. Shoots right. 6', 190 lbs. Born, Sechelt, B.C., April 17, 1971.
(Edmonton's 7th choice, 144th overall, in 1991 Entry Draft).

			Regular Season					Playoffs				
Season	Club	Lea	GP	G	A	TP	PIM	GP	G	A	TP	PIM
1990-91	U. of Michigan	CCHA	27	13	11	24	34	....	....	....	....	....
1991-92	U. of Michigan	CCHA	44	31	27	58	32	....	....	....	....	....
1992-93a	U. of Michigan	CCHA	40	35	20	55	18	....	....	....	....	....
1993-94bc	U. of Michigan	CCHA	41	28	40	68	16	....	....	....	....	....
1994-95	Cape Breton	AHL	32	11	18	29	8	....	....	....	....	....
	Edmonton	**NHL**	**44**	**16**	**14**	**30**	**20**	....	....	....	....	....
	NHL Totals		**44**	**16**	**14**	**30**	**20**	....	....	....	....	....

a CCHA Second All-Star Team (1993)
b CCHA First All-Star Team (1994)
c NCAA West First All-American Team (1994)

OLIWA, KRZYSZTOF (oh-LEE-vuh, KHRIH-stahf) N.J.

Left wing. Shoots left. 6'5", 220 lbs. Born, Tychy, Poland, April 12, 1973.
(New Jersey's 4th choice, 65th overall, in 1993 Entry Draft).

			Regular Season					Playoffs				
Season	Club	Lea	GP	G	A	TP	PIM	GP	G	A	TP	PIM
1991-92	GKS Tychy	Poland	10	3	7	10	6	....	....	....	....	....
1992-93	Welland	Jr.B	30	13	21	34	127	....	....	....	....	....
1993-94	Albany	AHL	33	2	4	6	151	....	....	....	....	....
	Raleigh	ECHL	15	0	2	2	65	9	0	0	0	35
1994-95	Albany	AHL	20	1	1	2	77	....	....	....	....	....
	Saint John	AHL	14	1	4	5	79	....	....	....	....	....
	Raleigh	ECHL	5	0	2	2	32	....	....	....	....	....
	Detroit	IHL	4	0	1	1	24	....	....	....	....	....

OLSON, BOYD MTL.

Center. Shoots left. 6'1", 170 lbs. Born, Edmonton, Alta., April 30, 1976.
(Montreal's 6th choice, 138th overall, in 1995 Entry Draft).

			Regular Season					Playoffs				
Season	Club	Lea	GP	G	A	TP	PIM	GP	G	A	TP	PIM
1993-94	Tri-City	WHL	2	0	1	1	0	....	....	....	....	....
1994-95	Tri-City	WHL	69	16	16	32	87	17	6	2	8	22

OLSSON, CHRISTER (OOL-suhn) ST.L.

Defense. Shoots left. 5'11", 190 lbs. Born, Arboga, Sweden, July 24, 1970.
(St. Louis' 10th choice, 275th overall, in 1993 Entry Draft).

			Regular Season					Playoffs				
Season	Club	Lea	GP	G	A	TP	PIM	GP	G	A	TP	PIM
1991-92	Mora	Swe. 2	36	6	10	16	38	....	....	....	....	....
1992-93	Brynas	Swe.	22	4	4	8	18	....	....	....	....	....
1993-94	Brynas	Swe.	38	7	3	10	50	7	0	3	3	6
1994-95	Brynas	Swe.	39	6	5	11	18	14	1	3	4	8

O'NEILL, JEFF HFD.

Center. Shoots right. 6'1", 176 lbs. Born, Richmond Hill, Ont., February 23, 1976.
(Hartford's 1st choice, 5th overall, in 1994 Entry Draft).

			Regular Season					Playoffs				
Season	Club	Lea	GP	G	A	TP	PIM	GP	G	A	TP	PIM
1992-93	Guelph	OHL	65	32	47	79	88	5	2	2	4	6
1993-94	Guelph	OHL	66	45	81	126	95	9	2	11	13	31
1994-95a	Guelph	OHL	57	43	81	124	56	14	8	18	26	34

a OHL First All-Star Team (1995)

ORSAGH, VLADIMIR NYI

Right wing. Shoots left. 5'10", 172 lbs. Born, Banska Bystrica, Czech., May 24, 1977.
(NY Islanders' 4th choice, 106th overall, in 1995 Entry Draft).

			Regular Season					Playoffs				
Season	Club	Lea	GP	G	A	TP	PIM	GP	G	A	TP	PIM
1994-95	B. Bystrica	Slov. 2	38	18	12	30	....	....	....	....	....	....

OSADCHY, ALEXANDER (oh-SAHD-chee) S.J.

Defense. Shoots right. 5'11", 190 lbs. Born, Kharkov, USSR, July 19, 1975.
(San Jose's 5th choice, 80th overall, in 1993 Entry Draft).

			Regular Season					Playoffs				
Season	Club	Lea	GP	G	A	TP	PIM	GP	G	A	TP	PIM
1992-93	CSKA	CIS	37	0	1	1	60	....	....	....	....	....
1993-94	CSKA	CIS	46	5	2	7	33	3	0	0	0	0
	Russian Pen's	IHL	11	0	5	5	24	....	....	....	....	....
1994-95	CSKA	CIS	52	8	4	12	100	2	0	0	0	0

OSBORNE, MARK (AWS-born)

Left wing. Shoots left. 6'2", 205 lbs. Born, Toronto, Ont., August 13, 1961.
(Detroit's 2nd choice, 46th overall, in 1980 Entry Draft).

			Regular Season					Playoffs				
Season	Club	Lea	GP	G	A	TP	PIM	GP	G	A	TP	PIM
1979-80	Niagara Falls	OHA	52	10	33	43	104	10	2	1	3	23
1980-81	Niagara Falls	OHA	54	39	41	80	140	12	11	10	21	20
	Adirondack	AHL	....	....	....	....	....	13	2	3	5	2
1981-82	**Detroit**	**NHL**	**80**	**26**	**41**	**67**	**61**	....	....	....	....	....
1982-83	**Detroit**	**NHL**	**80**	**19**	**24**	**43**	**83**	....	....	....	....	....
1983-84	**NY Rangers**	**NHL**	**73**	**23**	**28**	**51**	**88**	**5**	**0**	**1**	**1**	**7**
1984-85	**NY Rangers**	**NHL**	**23**	**4**	**4**	**8**	**33**	**3**	**0**	**0**	**0**	**4**
1985-86	**NY Rangers**	**NHL**	**62**	**16**	**24**	**40**	**80**	**15**	**2**	**3**	**5**	**26**
1986-87	**NY Rangers**	**NHL**	**58**	**17**	**15**	**32**	**101**	....	....	....	....	....
	Toronto	**NHL**	**16**	**5**	**10**	**15**	**12**	**9**	**1**	**3**	**4**	**6**
1987-88	**Toronto**	**NHL**	**79**	**23**	**37**	**60**	**102**	**6**	**1**	**3**	**4**	**16**
1988-89	**Toronto**	**NHL**	**75**	**16**	**30**	**46**	**112**	....	....	....	....	....
1989-90	**Toronto**	**NHL**	**78**	**23**	**50**	**73**	**91**	**5**	**2**	**3**	**5**	**12**
1990-91	**Toronto**	**NHL**	**18**	**3**	**3**	**6**	**4**	....	....	....	....	....
	Winnipeg	**NHL**	**37**	**8**	**8**	**16**	**59**	....	....	....	....	....
1991-92	**Winnipeg**	**NHL**	**43**	**4**	**12**	**16**	**65**	....	....	....	....	....
	Toronto	**NHL**	**11**	**3**	**1**	**4**	**8**	....	....	....	....	....
1992-93	**Toronto**	**NHL**	**76**	**12**	**14**	**26**	**89**	**19**	**1**	**1**	**2**	**16**
1993-94	**Toronto**	**NHL**	**73**	**9**	**15**	**24**	**145**	**18**	**4**	**2**	**6**	**52**
1994-95	**NY Rangers**	**NHL**	**37**	**1**	**3**	**4**	**19**	**7**	**1**	**0**	**1**	**2**
	NHL Totals		**919**	**212**	**319**	**531**	**1152**	**87**	**12**	**16**	**28**	**141**

Traded to **NY Rangers** by **Detroit** with Willie Huber and Mike Blaisdell for Ron Duguay, Eddie Mio and Eddie Johnstone, June 13, 1983. Traded to **Toronto** by **NY Rangers** for Jeff Jackson and Toronto's third round choice (Rod Zamuner) in 1989 Entry Draft, March 5, 1987. Traded to **Winnipeg** by **Toronto** with Ed Olczyk for Dave Ellett and Paul Fenton, November 10, 1990. Traded to **Toronto** by **Winnipeg** for Lucien Deblois, March 10, 1992. Signed as a free agent by **NY Rangers**, January 20, 1995.

O'SULLIVAN, CHRIS CGY.

Defense. Shoots left. 6'2", 185 lbs. Born, Dorchester, MA, May 15, 1974.
(Calgary's 2nd choice, 30th overall, in 1992 Entry Draft).

			Regular Season					Playoffs				
Season	Club	Lea	GP	G	A	TP	PIM	GP	G	A	TP	PIM
1992-93	Boston U.	H.E.	5	0	2	2	4	....	....	....	....	....
1993-94	Boston U.	H.E.	32	5	18	23	25	....	....	....	....	....
1994-95abcd	Boston U.	H.E.	40	23	33	56	48	....	....	....	....	....

a Hockey East First All-Star Team (1995)
b NCAA East Second All-American Team (1995)
c NCAA Final Four All-Tournament Team (1995)
d NCAA Final Four Tournament Most Valuable Player (1995)

OTTO, JOEL — PHI.

Center. Shoots right. 6'4", 220 lbs. Born, Elk River, MN, October 29, 1961.

			Regular Season					Playoffs				
Season	Club	Lea	GP	G	A	TP	PIM	GP	G	A	TP	PIM
1980-81	Bemidji State	NCAA	23	5	11	16	10	....	....	....	....	....
1981-82	Bemidji State	NCAA	31	19	33	52	24	....	....	....	....	....
1982-83	Bemidji State	NCAA	37	33	28	61	68	....	....	....	....	....
1983-84	Bemidji State	NCAA	31	32	43	75	32	....	....	....	....	....
1984-85	**Calgary**	**NHL**	**17**	**4**	**8**	**12**	**30**	**3**	**2**	**1**	**3**	**10**
	Moncton	AHL	56	27	36	63	89	....	....	....	....	....
1985-86	**Calgary**	**NHL**	**79**	**25**	**34**	**59**	**188**	**22**	**5**	**10**	**15**	**80**
1986-87	**Calgary**	**NHL**	**68**	**19**	**31**	**50**	**185**	**2**	**0**	**2**	**2**	**6**
1987-88	**Calgary**	**NHL**	**62**	**13**	**39**	**52**	**194**	**9**	**3**	**2**	**5**	**26**
1988-89	**Calgary**	**NHL**	**72**	**23**	**30**	**53**	**213**	**22**	**6**	**13**	**19**	**46**
1989-90	**Calgary**	**NHL**	**75**	**13**	**20**	**33**	**116**	**6**	**2**	**2**	**4**	**2**
1990-91	**Calgary**	**NHL**	**76**	**19**	**20**	**39**	**183**	**7**	**1**	**2**	**3**	**8**
1991-92	**Calgary**	**NHL**	**78**	**13**	**21**	**34**	**161**	....	....	....	....	....
1992-93	**Calgary**	**NHL**	**75**	**19**	**33**	**52**	**150**	**6**	**4**	**2**	**6**	**4**
1993-94	**Calgary**	**NHL**	**81**	**11**	**12**	**23**	**92**	**3**	**0**	**1**	**1**	**4**
1994-95	**Calgary**	**NHL**	**47**	**8**	**13**	**21**	**130**	**7**	**0**	**3**	**3**	**2**
	NHL Totals		**730**	**167**	**261**	**428**	**1642**	**87**	**23**	**38**	**61**	**188**

Signed as a free agent by **Calgary,** September 11, 1984. Signed as a free agent by **Philadelphia**, July 31, 1995.

OZOLINSH, SANDIS (OH-zoh-LIHNCH, SAN-dihz) — S.J.

Defense. Shoots left. 6'1", 195 lbs. Born, Riga, Latvia, August 3, 1972.
(San Jose's 3rd choice, 30th overall, in 1991 Entry Draft).

			Regular Season					Playoffs				
Season	Club	Lea	GP	G	A	TP	PIM	GP	G	A	TP	PIM
1990-91	Riga	USSR	44	0	3	3	51	....	....	....	....	....
1991-92	Riga	CIS	30	6	0	6	42	....	....	....	....	....
	Kansas City	IHL	34	6	9	15	20	15	2	5	7	22
1992-93	**San Jose**	**NHL**	**37**	**7**	**16**	**23**	**40**	....	....	....	....	....
1993-94	**San Jose**	**NHL**	**81**	**26**	**38**	**64**	**24**	**14**	**0**	**10**	**10**	**8**
1994-95	**San Jose**	**NHL**	**48**	**9**	**16**	**25**	**30**	**11**	**3**	**2**	**5**	**6**
	NHL Totals		**166**	**42**	**70**	**112**	**94**	**25**	**3**	**12**	**15**	**14**

Played in NHL All-Star Game (1994)

PADEN, KEVIN — EDM.

Center/Left wing. Shoots left. 6'3", 180 lbs. Born, Woodhaven, MI, February 12, 1975.
(Edmonton's 4th choice, 59th overall, in 1993 Entry Draft).

			Regular Season					Playoffs				
Season	Club	Lea	GP	G	A	TP	PIM	GP	G	A	TP	PIM
1992-93	Detroit	OHL	54	14	9	23	41	15	1	1	2	2
1993-94	Detroit	OHL	38	10	19	29	54	....	....	....	....	....
	Windsor	OHL	24	8	11	19	30	4	0	1	1	4
1994-95	Windsor	OHL	57	15	24	39	50	....	....	....	....	....

PAEK, JIM (PAK)

Defense. Shoots left. 6'1", 195 lbs. Born, Seoul, South Korea, April 7, 1967.
(Pittsburgh's 9th choice, 170th overall, in 1985 Entry Draft).

			Regular Season					Playoffs				
Season	Club	Lea	GP	G	A	TP	PIM	GP	G	A	TP	PIM
1984-85	Oshawa	OHL	54	2	13	15	57	5	1	0	1	9
1985-86	Oshawa	OHL	64	5	21	26	122	6	0	1	1	9
1986-87	Oshawa	OHL	57	5	17	22	75	26	1	14	15	43
1987-88	Muskegon	IHL	82	7	52	59	141	6	0	0	0	29
1988-89	Muskegon	IHL	80	3	54	57	96	14	1	10	11	24
1989-90	Muskegon	IHL	81	9	41	50	115	15	1	10	11	41
1990-91	Cdn. National	....	48	2	12	14	24	....	....	....	....	....
	Pittsburgh	**NHL**	**3**	**0**	**0**	**0**	**9**	**8**	**1**	**0**	**1**	**2**
1991-92	**Pittsburgh**	**NHL**	**49**	**1**	**7**	**8**	**36**	**19**	**0**	**4**	**4**	**6**
1992-93	**Pittsburgh**	**NHL**	**77**	**3**	**15**	**18**	**64**	....	....	....	....	....
1993-94	**Pittsburgh**	**NHL**	**41**	**0**	**4**	**4**	**8**	....	....	....	....	....
	Los Angeles	**NHL**	**18**	**1**	**1**	**2**	**10**	....	....	....	....	....
1994-95	**Ottawa**	**NHL**	**29**	**0**	**2**	**2**	**28**	....	....	....	....	....
	NHL Totals		**217**	**5**	**29**	**34**	**155**	**27**	**1**	**4**	**5**	**8**

Traded to **Los Angeles** by **Pittsburgh** with Marty McSorley for Tomas Sandstrom and Shawn McEachern, February 16, 1994. Traded to **Ottawa** by **Los Angeles** for Ottawa's seventh round choice (Benoit Larose) in 1995 Entry Draft, June 26, 1994.

PALFFY, ZIGMUND (PAHL-fee) — NYI

Left wing. Shoots left. 5'10", 169 lbs. Born, Skalica, Czech., May 5, 1972.
(NY Islanders' 2nd choice, 26th overall, in 1991 Entry Draft).

			Regular Season					Playoffs				
Season	Club	Lea	GP	G	A	TP	PIM	GP	G	A	TP	PIM
1990-91	Nitra	Czech.	50	34	16	50	18	....	....	....	....	....
1991-92	Dukla Trencin	Czech.	45	41	33	74	36	....	....	....	....	....
1992-93	Dukla Trencin	Czech.	43	38	41	79	....	....	....	....	....	....
1993-94	**NY Islanders**	**NHL**	**5**	**0**	**0**	**0**	**0**	....	....	....	....	....
	Salt Lake	IHL	57	25	32	57	83	....	....	....	....	....
1994-95	Denver	IHL	33	20	23	43	40	....	....	....	....	....
	NY Islanders	**NHL**	**33**	**10**	**7**	**17**	**6**	....	....	....	....	....
	NHL Totals		**38**	**10**	**7**	**17**	**6**	....	....	....	....	....

PALMER, DREW — PIT.

Defense. Shoots left. 6'4", 209 lbs. Born, Wayzata, MN, January 10, 1976.
(Pittsburgh's 10th choice, 180th overall, in 1994 Entry Draft).

			Regular Season					Playoffs				
Season	Club	Lea	GP	G	A	TP	PIM	GP	G	A	TP	PIM
1993-94	Seattle	WHL	67	0	5	5	154	9	0	0	0	16
1994-95	Seattle	WHL	67	2	10	12	215	4	0	0	0	8

PANDOLFO, JAY — N.J.

Left wing. Shoots left. 6'1", 195 lbs. Born, Winchester, MA, December 27, 1974.
(New Jersey's 2nd choice, 32nd overall, in 1993 Entry Draft).

			Regular Season					Playoffs				
Season	Club	Lea	GP	G	A	TP	PIM	GP	G	A	TP	PIM
1992-93	Boston U.	H.E.	37	16	22	38	16	....	....	....	....	....
1993-94	Boston U.	H.E.	37	17	25	42	27	....	....	....	....	....
1994-95	Boston U.	H.E.	20	7	13	20	6	....	....	....	....	....

PANKEWICZ, GREG — WSH.

Right wing. Shoots right. 6', 185 lbs. Born, Drayton Valley, Alta., October 6, 1970.

			Regular Season					Playoffs				
Season	Club	Lea	GP	G	A	TP	PIM	GP	G	A	TP	PIM
1989-90	Regina	WHL	63	14	24	38	136	10	1	3	4	19
1990-91	Regina	WHL	72	39	41	80	134	8	4	7	11	12
1991-92	Knoxville	ECHL	59	41	39	80	214	....	....	....	....	....
1992-93	New Haven	AHL	62	23	20	43	163	....	....	....	....	....
1993-94	**Ottawa**	**NHL**	**3**	**0**	**0**	**0**	**2**	....	....	....	....	....
	P.E.I.	AHL	69	33	29	62	241	....	....	....	....	....
1994-95	P.E.I.	AHL	75	37	30	67	161	6	1	1	2	24
	NHL Totals		**3**	**0**	**0**	**0**	**2**	....	....	....	....	....

Signed as a free agent by **Ottawa**, May 27, 1993. Signed as a free agent by **Washington**, July 2, 1995.

PANTELEEV, GRIGORI (pan-teh-LAY-ehv)

Left wing. Shoots left. 5'9", 190 lbs. Born, Gastello, USSR, November 13, 1972.
(Boston's 5th choice, 136th overall, in 1992 Entry Draft).

			Regular Season					Playoffs				
Season	Club	Lea	GP	G	A	TP	PIM	GP	G	A	TP	PIM
1990-91	Riga	USSR	23	4	1	5	4	....	....	....	....	....
1991-92	Riga	CIS	26	4	8	12	4	....	....	....	....	....
1992-93	**Boston**	**NHL**	**39**	**8**	**6**	**14**	**12**	....	....	....	....	....
	Providence	AHL	39	17	30	47	22	3	0	0	0	10
1993-94	**Boston**	**NHL**	**10**	**0**	**0**	**0**	**0**	....	....	....	....	....
	Providence	AHL	55	24	26	50	20	....	....	....	....	....
1994-95	Providence	AHL	70	20	23	43	36	13	8	11	19	6
	Boston	**NHL**	**1**	**0**	**0**	**0**	**0**	....	....	....	....	....
	NHL Totals		**50**	**8**	**6**	**14**	**12**	....	....	....	....	....

PAQUETTE, CHARLES (pa-KEHT) — BOS.

Defense. Shoots left. 6'1", 193 lbs. Born, Lachute, Que., June 17, 1975.
(Boston's 3rd choice, 88th overall, in 1993 Entry Draft).

			Regular Season					Playoffs				
Season	Club	Lea	GP	G	A	TP	PIM	GP	G	A	TP	PIM
1991-92	Trois-Rivieres	QMJHL	60	1	7	8	101	6	0	0	0	2
1992-93	Sherbrooke	QMJHL	54	2	5	7	104	15	0	0	0	33
1993-94	Sherbrooke	QMJHL	63	5	14	19	165	8	0	2	2	15
1994-95a	Sherbrooke	QMJHL	53	15	26	41	186	5	1	1	2	18

a QMJHL First All-Star Team (1995)

PAQUIN, PATRICE (pa-KEHN) — PHI.

Left wing. Shoots left. 6'2", 192 lbs. Born, St. Jerome, Que., June 26, 1974.
(Philadelphia's 11th choice, 247th overall, in 1992 Entry Draft).

			Regular Season					Playoffs				
Season	Club	Lea	GP	G	A	TP	PIM	GP	G	A	TP	PIM
1991-92	Beauport	QMJHL	60	10	15	25	169	....	....	....	....	....
1992-93	Beauport	QMJHL	59	17	23	40	271	....	....	....	....	....
1993-94	Beauport	QMJHL	45	22	24	46	188	15	1	7	8	39
1994-95	Beauport	QMJHL	1	1	1	2	2	....	....	....	....	....
	St-Jean	QMJHL	53	22	32	54	147	5	2	2	4	6

PARK, RICHARD — PIT.

Center. Shoots right. 5'11", 176 lbs. Born, Seoul, S. Korea, May 27, 1976.
(Pittsburgh's 2nd choice, 50th overall, in 1994 Entry Draft).

			Regular Season					Playoffs				
Season	Club	Lea	GP	G	A	TP	PIM	GP	G	A	TP	PIM
1992-93	Belleville	OHL	66	23	38	61	38	5	0	0	0	14
1993-94	Belleville	OHL	59	27	49	76	70	12	3	5	8	18
1994-95	Belleville	OHL	45	28	51	79	35	16	9	18	27	12
	Pittsburgh	**NHL**	**1**	**0**	**1**	**1**	**2**	**3**	**0**	**0**	**0**	**2**
	NHL Totals		**1**	**0**	**1**	**1**	**2**	**3**	**0**	**0**	**0**	**2**

PARKS, GREG

Center. Shoots right. 5'9", 180 lbs. Born, Edmonton, Alta., March 25, 1967.

			Regular Season					Playoffs				
Season	Club	Lea	GP	G	A	TP	PIM	GP	G	A	TP	PIM
1985-86	Bowling Green	CCHA	41	16	26	42	43	....	....	....	....	....
1986-87	Bowling Green	CCHA	45	23	27	50	52	....	....	....	....	....
1987-88	Bowling Green	CCHA	45	30	44	74	84	....	....	....	....	....
1988-89a	Bowling Green	CCHA	47	32	42	74	98	....	....	....	....	....
1989-90	Springfield	AHL	49	22	32	54	30	18	9	*13	*22	22
	Johnstown	ECHL	8	5	9	14	7	....	....	....	....	....
1990-91	**NY Islanders**	**NHL**	**20**	**1**	**2**	**3**	**4**	....	....	....	....	....
	Capital Dist.	AHL	48	32	43	75	67	....	....	....	....	....
1991-92	**NY Islanders**	**NHL**	**1**	**0**	**0**	**0**	**2**	....	....	....	....	....
	Capital Dist.	AHL	70	36	57	93	84	7	5	8	13	4
1992-93	Leksand	Swe.	39	21	19	40	66	1	0	0	0	4
	Cdn. National	....	9	2	2	4	4	....	....	....	....	....
	NY Islanders	**NHL**	**2**	**0**	**0**	**0**	**0**	**2**	**0**	**0**	**0**	**0**
1993-94	Leksand	Swe.	39	21	18	39	44	4	3	1	4	....
	Cdn. National	....	13	1	1	2	112	....	....	....	....	....
	Cdn. Olympic	....	8	1	2	3	10	....	....	....	....	....
1994-95	Krefeld	Ger.	10	2	7	9	8	1	0	0	0	0
	NHL Totals		**23**	**1**	**2**	**3**	**6**	**2**	**0**	**0**	**0**	**0**

a NCAA West First All-Star Team (1989)

Signed as a free agent by **NY Islanders**, August 13, 1990. Signed as a free agent by **St. Louis**, August 31, 1994.

PARROTT, JEFF — COL.

Defense. Shoots right. 6'1", 195 lbs. Born, The Pas, Man., April 6, 1971.
(Quebec's 4th choice, 106th overall, in 1990 Entry Draft).

			Regular Season					Playoffs				
Season	Club	Lea	GP	G	A	TP	PIM	GP	G	A	TP	PIM
1989-90	Minn.-Duluth	WCHA	35	1	5	6	60	....	....	....	....	....
1990-91	Minn.-Duluth	WCHA	39	2	8	10	65	....	....	....	....	....
1991-92	Minn.-Duluth	WCHA	33	1	8	9	78	....	....	....	....	....
1992-93	Minn. Duluth	WCHA	39	4	13	17	116	....	....	....	....	....
1993-94	Cornwall	AHL	52	4	11	15	37	....	....	....	....	....
1994-95	Cornwall	AHL	65	2	5	7	99	14	0	1	1	12

PARSON, STEVE — OTT.

Left wing. Shoots left. 6', 180 lbs. Born, Elmira, Ont., March 14, 1973.

			Regular Season					Playoffs				
Season	Club	Lea	GP	G	A	TP	PIM	GP	G	A	TP	PIM
1989-90	Owen Sound	OHL	58	13	12	25	51	12	1	0	1	14
1990-91	Owen Sound	OHL	63	23	31	54	34	....	....	....	....	....
1991-92	Owen Sound	OHL	27	10	17	27	19	....	....	....	....	....
	Kingston	OHL	39	18	20	38	24	....	....	....	....	....
1992-93	Kingston	OHL	66	28	55	83	62	16	11	11	22	18
1993-94	Kingston	OHL	64	35	63	98	70	2	0	3	3	0
1994-95	Thunder Bay	ColHL	62	16	29	45	36	....	....	....	....	....
	P.E.I.	AHL	8	2	1	3	0	....	....	....	....	....

Signed as a free agent by **Ottawa**, June 9, 1994.

PARSONS, ROSS — MTL.

Defense. Shoots right. 6'2", 190 lbs. Born, Calgary, Alta., September 13, 1976.
(Montreal's 13th choice, 278th overall, in 1994 Entry Draft).

			Regular Season					Playoffs				
Season	Club	Lea	GP	G	A	TP	PIM	GP	G	A	TP	PIM
1993-94	Regina	WHL	68	1	5	6	47	4	0	0	0	0
1994-95	Regina	WHL	66	1	5	6	107	4	0	1	1	0

PATRICK, CHRIS — WSH.

Left wing. Shoots left. 6'5", 205 lbs. Born, Leesburg, VA, January 2, 1976.
(Washington's 8th choice, 197th overall, in 1994 Entry Draft).

			Regular Season					Playoffs				
Season	Club	Lea	GP	G	A	TP	PIM	GP	G	A	TP	PIM
1993-94	Kent	HS	24	5	5	10	8	....	....	....	....	....
1994-95	Princeton	ECAC			DID NOT PLAY							

PATRICK, JAMES — CGY.

Defense. Shoots right. 6'2", 198 lbs. Born, Winnipeg, Man., June 14, 1963.
(NY Rangers' 1st choice, 9th overall, in 1981 Entry Draft).

			Regular Season					Playoffs				
Season	Club	Lea	GP	G	A	TP	PIM	GP	G	A	TP	PIM
1981-82ab	North Dakota	WCHA	42	5	24	29	26	....	....	....	....	....
1982-83cd	North Dakota	WCHA	36	12	36	48	29	....	....	....	....	....
1983-84	Cdn. National	....	63	7	24	31	52	....	....	....	....	....
	Cdn. Olympic	....	7	0	3	3	4	....	....	....	....	....
	NY Rangers	NHL	12	1	7	8	2	5	0	3	3	2
1984-85	NY Rangers	NHL	75	8	28	36	71	3	0	0	0	4
1985-86	NY Rangers	NHL	75	14	29	43	88	16	1	5	6	34
1986-87	NY Rangers	NHL	78	10	45	55	62	6	1	2	3	2
1987-88	NY Rangers	NHL	70	17	45	62	52	....	....	....	....	....
1988-89	NY Rangers	NHL	68	11	36	47	41	4	0	1	1	2
1989-90	NY Rangers	NHL	73	14	43	57	50	10	3	8	11	0
1990-91	NY Rangers	NHL	74	10	49	59	58	6	0	0	0	6
1991-92	NY Rangers	NHL	80	14	57	71	54	13	0	7	7	12
1992-93	NY Rangers	NHL	60	5	21	26	61	....	....	....	....	....
1993-94	NY Rangers	NHL	6	0	3	3	2	....	....	....	....	....
	Hartford	NHL	47	8	20	28	32	....	....	....	....	....
	Calgary	NHL	15	2	2	4	6	7	0	1	1	6
1994-95	Calgary	NHL	43	0	10	10	14	5	0	1	1	0
	NHL Totals		**776**	**114**	**395**	**509**	**593**	**75**	**5**	**28**	**33**	**68**

a WCHA Second All-Star Team (1982)
b NCAA All-Tournament Team (1982)
c WCHA First All-Star Team (1983)
d NCAA West All American (1983)

Traded to **Hartford** by **NY Rangers** with Darren Turcotte for Steve Larmer, Nick Kypreos, Barry Richter and Hartford's sixth round choice (Yuri Litvinov) in 1994 Entry Draft, November 2, 1993. Traded to **Calgary** by **Hartford** with Zarley Zalapski and Michael Nylander for Gary Suter, Paul Ranheim and Ted Drury, March 10, 1994.

PATTERSON, ED — PIT.

Right wing. Shoots right. 6'2", 213 lbs. Born, Delta, B.C., November 14, 1972.
(Pittsburgh's 7th choice, 148th overall, in 1991 Entry Draft).

			Regular Season					Playoffs				
Season	Club	Lea	GP	G	A	TP	PIM	GP	G	A	TP	PIM
1990-91	Swift Current	WHL	7	2	7	9	0	....	....	....	....	....
	Kamloops	WHL	55	14	33	47	134	5	0	0	0	7
1991-92	Kamloops	WHL	38	19	25	44	120	1	0	0	0	0
1992-93	Cleveland	IHL	63	4	16	20	131	3	1	1	2	2
1993-94	Pittsburgh	NHL	27	3	1	4	10	....	....	....	....	....
	Cleveland	IHL	55	21	32	53	73	....	....	....	....	....
1994-95	Cleveland	IHL	58	13	17	30	93	4	1	2	3	6
	NHL Totals		**27**	**3**	**1**	**4**	**10**	....	....	....	....	....

PAYETTE, ANDRE — PHI.

Center. Shoots left. 6'2", 182 lbs. Born, Cornwall, Ont., July 29, 1976.
(Philadelphia's 9th choice, 244th overall, in 1994 Entry Draft).

			Regular Season					Playoffs				
Season	Club	Lea	GP	G	A	TP	PIM	GP	G	A	TP	PIM
1993-94	S.S. Marie	OHL	40	2	3	5	98	....	....	....	....	....
1994-95	S.S. Marie	OHL	50	15	15	30	177	....	....	....	....	....

PEAKE, PAT — WSH.

Center. Shoots right. 6'1", 195 lbs. Born, Rochester, MI, May 28, 1973.
(Washington's 1st choice, 14th overall, in 1991 Entry Draft).

			Regular Season					Playoffs				
Season	Club	Lea	GP	G	A	TP	PIM	GP	G	A	TP	PIM
1990-91	Detroit	OHL	63	39	51	90	54	....	....	....	....	....
1991-92	Detroit	OHL	53	41	52	93	44	7	8	9	17	10
	Baltimore	AHL	3	1	0	1	4	....	....	....	....	....
1992-93abc	Detroit	OHL	46	58	78	136	64	2	1	3	4	2
1993-94	Washington	NHL	49	11	18	29	39	8	0	1	1	8
	Portland	AHL	4	0	5	5	2	....	....	....	....	....
1994-95	Washington	NHL	18	0	4	4	12	....	....	....	....	....
	Portland	AHL	5	1	3	4	2	4	0	3	3	6
	NHL Totals		**67**	**11**	**22**	**33**	**51**	**8**	**0**	**1**	**1**	**8**

a Canadian Major Junior Player of the Year (1993)
b Canadian Major Junior First All-Star Team (1993)
c OHL First All-Star Team (1993)

PEARSON, ROB — WSH.

Right wing. Shoots right. 6'3", 198 lbs. Born, Oshawa, Ont., March 8, 1971.
(Toronto's 2nd choice, 12th overall, in 1989 Entry Draft).

			Regular Season					Playoffs				
Season	Club	Lea	GP	G	A	TP	PIM	GP	G	A	TP	PIM
1988-89	Belleville	OHL	26	8	12	20	51	....	....	....	....	....
1989-90	Belleville	OHL	58	48	40	88	174	11	5	5	10	26
1990-91	Belleville	OHL	10	6	3	9	27	....	....	....	....	....
a	Oshawa	OHL	41	57	52	109	76	16	16	17	33	39
	Newmarket	AHL	3	0	0	0	29	....	....	....	....	....
1991-92	Toronto	NHL	47	14	10	24	58	....	....	....	....	....
	St. John's	AHL	27	15	14	29	107	13	5	4	9	40
1992-93	Toronto	NHL	78	23	14	37	211	14	2	2	4	31
1993-94	Toronto	NHL	67	12	18	30	189	14	1	0	1	32
1994-95	Washington	NHL	32	0	6	6	96	3	1	0	1	17
	NHL Totals		**224**	**49**	**48**	**97**	**554**	**31**	**4**	**2**	**6**	**80**

a OHL First All-Star Team (1991)

Traded to **Washington** by **Toronto** with Philadelphia's first round choice (previously acquired by Toronto — Washington selected Nolan Baumgartner) in 1994 Entry Draft for Mike Ridley and St. Louis' first round choice (previously acquired by Washington — Toronto selected Eric Fichaud) in 1994 Entry Draft, June 28, 1994.

PEARSON, SCOTT — BUF.

Left wing. Shoots left. 6'1", 205 lbs. Born, Cornwall, Ont., December 19, 1969.
(Toronto's 1st choice, 6th overall, in 1988 Entry Draft).

			Regular Season					Playoffs				
Season	Club	Lea	GP	G	A	TP	PIM	GP	G	A	TP	PIM
1986-87	Kingston	OHL	62	30	24	54	101	9	3	3	6	42
1987-88	Kingston	OHL	46	26	32	58	117	....	....	....	....	....
1988-89	Toronto	NHL	9	0	1	1	2	....	....	....	....	....
	Kingston	OHL	13	9	8	17	34	....	....	....	....	....
	Niagara Falls	OHL	32	26	34	60	90	17	14	10	24	53
1989-90	Toronto	NHL	41	5	10	15	90	2	2	0	2	10
	Newmarket	AHL	18	12	11	23	64	....	....	....	....	....
1990-91	Toronto	NHL	12	0	0	0	20	....	....	....	....	....
	Quebec	NHL	35	11	4	15	86	....	....	....	....	....
	Halifax	AHL	24	12	15	27	44	....	....	....	....	....
1991-92	Quebec	NHL	10	1	2	3	14	....	....	....	....	....
	Halifax	AHL	5	2	1	3	4	....	....	....	....	....
1992-93	Quebec	NHL	41	13	1	14	95	3	0	0	0	0
	Halifax	AHL	5	3	1	4	25	....	....	....	....	....
1993-94	Edmonton	NHL	72	19	18	37	165	....	....	....	....	....
1994-95	Edmonton	NHL	28	1	4	5	54	....	....	....	....	....
	Buffalo	NHL	14	2	1	3	20	5	0	0	0	4
	NHL Totals		**262**	**52**	**41**	**93**	**546**	**10**	**2**	**0**	**2**	**14**

Traded to **Quebec** by **Toronto** with Toronto's second round choices in 1991 (later traded to Washington — Washington selected Eric Lavigne) and 1992 (Tuomas Gronman) Entry Drafts for Aaron Broten, Lucien Deblois and Michel Petit, November 17, 1990. Traded to **Edmonton** by **Quebec** for Martin Gelinas and Edmonton's sixth round choice (Nicholas Checco) in 1993 Entry Draft, June 20, 1993. Traded to **Buffalo** by **Edmonton** for Ken Sutton, April 7, 1995.

PECA, MIKE (PEH-kuh) — BUF.

Right wing. Shoots right. 5'11", 180 lbs. Born, Toronto, Ont., March 26, 1974.
(Vancouver's 2nd choice, 40th overall, in 1992 Entry Draft).

			Regular Season					Playoffs				
Season	Club	Lea	GP	G	A	TP	PIM	GP	G	A	TP	PIM
1990-91	Sudbury	OHL	62	14	27	41	24	5	1	0	1	7
1991-92	Sudbury	OHL	39	16	34	50	61	....	....	....	....	....
	Ottawa	OHL	27	8	17	25	32	11	6	10	16	6
1992-93	Ottawa	OHL	55	38	64	102	80	....	....	....	....	....
	Hamilton	AHL	9	6	3	9	11	....	....	....	....	....
1993-94	Vancouver	NHL	4	0	0	0	2	....	....	....	....	....
	Ottawa	OHL	55	50	63	113	101	17	7	22	29	30
1994-95	Syracuse	AHL	35	10	24	34	75	....	....	....	....	....
	Vancouver	NHL	33	6	6	12	30	5	0	1	1	8
	NHL Totals		**37**	**6**	**6**	**12**	**32**	**5**	**0**	**1**	**1**	**8**

Traded to **Buffalo** by **Vancouver** with Mike Wilson and Vancouver's first round choice (Jay McKee) in 1995 Entry Draft for Alexander Mogilny and Buffalo's fifth round choice (Todd Norman) in 1995 Entry Draft, July 8, 1995.

PEDERSON, DENIS — N.J.

Center. Shoots right. 6'2", 190 lbs. Born, Prince Albert, Sask., September 10, 1975.
(New Jersey's 1st choice, 13th overall, in 1993 Entry Draft).

			Regular Season					Playoffs				
Season	Club	Lea	GP	G	A	TP	PIM	GP	G	A	TP	PIM
1991-92	Prince Albert	Midget	21	33	25	58	40	....	....	....	....	....
	Prince Albert	WHL	10	0	0	0	6	7	0	1	1	13
1992-93	Prince Albert	WHL	72	33	40	73	134	....	....	....	....	....
1993-94a	Prince Albert	WHL	71	53	45	98	157	....	....	....	....	....
1994-95	Prince Albert	WHL	63	30	38	68	122	15	11	14	25	14
	Albany	AHL	....	....	....	....	....	3	0	0	0	2

a WHL East Second All-Star Team (1994)

PEDERSON, MARK

Left wing. Shoots left. 6'2", 196 lbs. Born, Prelate, Sask., January 14, 1968.
(Montreal's 1st choice, 15th overall, in 1986 Entry Draft).

			Regular Season					Playoffs				
Season	Club	Lea	GP	G	A	TP	PIM	GP	G	A	TP	PIM
1984-85	Medicine Hat	WHL	71	42	40	82	63	10	3	2	5	0
1985-86	Medicine Hat	WHL	72	46	60	106	46	25	12	6	18	25
1986-87a	Medicine Hat	WHL	69	56	46	102	58	20	*19	7	26	14
1987-88	Medicine Hat	WHL	62	53	58	111	55	16	*13	6	19	16
1988-89	Sherbrooke	AHL	75	43	38	81	53	6	7	5	12	4
1989-90	Montreal	NHL	9	0	2	2	2	2	0	0	0	0
b	Sherbrooke	AHL	72	53	42	95	60	11	10	8	18	19
1990-91	Montreal	NHL	47	8	15	23	18	....	....	....	....	....
	Philadelphia	NHL	12	2	1	3	5	....	....	....	....	....
1991-92	Philadelphia	NHL	58	15	25	40	22	....	....	....	....	....
1992-93	Philadelphia	NHL	14	3	4	7	6	....	....	....	....	....
	San Jose	NHL	27	7	3	10	22	....	....	....	....	....
1993-94	Detroit	NHL	2	0	0	0	2	....	....	....	....	....
b	Adirondack	AHL	62	52	45	97	37	12	4	7	11	10
1994-95	Kalamazoo	IHL	75	31	32	63	47	16	8	4	12	2
	NHL Totals		**169**	**35**	**50**	**85**	**77**	**2**	**0**	**0**	**0**	**0**

a WHL East All-Star Team (1987)
b AHL First All-Star Team (1990, 1994)

Traded to **Philadelphia** by **Montreal** for Philadelphia's second round choice (Jim Campbell) in 1991 Entry Draft, March 5, 1991. Traded to **San Jose** by **Philadelphia** with future considerations for Dave Snuggerud, December 19, 1992. Signed as a free agent by **Detroit**, August 23, 1993. Signed as a free agent by **Dallas**, August 13, 1994.

PEDERSON, TOM S.J.

Defense. Shoots right. 5'9", 175 lbs. Born, Bloomington, MN, January 14, 1970.
(Minnesota's 12th choice, 217th overall, in 1989 Entry Draft).

			Regular Season					Playoffs				
Season	Club	Lea	GP	G	A	TP	PIM	GP	G	A	TP	PIM
1988-89	U. Minnesota	WCHA	36	4	20	24	40	....	....	....	....	....
1989-90	U. Minnesota	WCHA	43	8	30	38	58	....	....	....	....	....
1990-91	U. Minnesota	WCHA	36	12	20	32	46	....	....	....	....	....
1991-92	U.S. National	....	44	3	11	14	41	....	....	....	....	....
	Kansas City	IHL	20	6	9	15	16	13	1	6	7	14
1992-93	**San Jose**	**NHL**	**44**	**7**	**13**	**20**	**31**	....	....	....	....	....
	Kansas City	IHL	26	6	15	21	10	12	1	6	7	2
1993-94	**San Jose**	**NHL**	**74**	**6**	**19**	**25**	**31**	**14**	**1**	**6**	**7**	**2**
	Kansas City	IHL	7	3	1	4	0	....	....	....	....	....
1994-95	**San Jose**	**NHL**	**47**	**5**	**11**	**16**	**31**	**10**	**0**	**5**	**5**	**8**
	NHL Totals		**165**	**18**	**43**	**61**	**93**	**24**	**1**	**11**	**12**	**10**

Claimed by **San Jose** from **Minnesota** in Dispersal Draft, May 30, 1991.

PELLERIN, SCOTT (PEHL-ih-rihn) N.J.

Left wing. Shoots left. 5'11", 180 lbs. Born, Shediac, N.B., January 9, 1970.
(New Jersey's 4th choice, 47th overall, in 1989 Entry Draft).

			Regular Season					Playoffs				
Season	Club	Lea	GP	G	A	TP	PIM	GP	G	A	TP	PIM
1988-89	U. of Maine	H.E.	45	29	33	62	92	....	....	....	....	....
1989-90	U. of Maine	H.E.	42	22	34	56	68	....	....	....	....	....
1990-91	U. of Maine	H.E.	43	23	25	48	60	....	....	....	....	....
1991-92abc	U. of Maine	H.E.	37	*32	25	57	54	....	....	....	....	....
	Utica	AHL	....	....	....	....	....	3	1	0	1	0
1992-93	**New Jersey**	**NHL**	**45**	**10**	**11**	**21**	**41**	....	....	....	....	....
	Utica	AHL	27	15	18	33	33	2	0	1	1	0
1993-94	**New Jersey**	**NHL**	**1**	**0**	**0**	**0**	**2**	....	....	....	....	....
	Albany	AHL	73	28	46	74	84	5	2	1	3	11
1994-95	Albany	AHL	74	23	33	56	95	14	6	4	10	8
	NHL Totals		**46**	**10**	**11**	**21**	**43**	....	....	....	....	....

a Won Hobey Baker Memorial Award (Top U.S. Collegiate Player) (1992)
b Hockey East First All-Star Team (1992)
c NCAA East First All-American Team (1992)

PELTONEN, VILLE (PEHL-TOH-ner) S.J.

Left wing. Shoots left. 5'11", 172 lbs. Born, Vantaa, Finland, May 24, 1973.
(San Jose's 4th choice, 58th overall, in 1993 Entry Draft).

			Regular Season					Playoffs				
Season	Club	Lea	GP	G	A	TP	PIM	GP	G	A	TP	PIM
1991-92	HIFK	Fin.	6	0	0	0	0	....	....	....	....	....
1992-93	HIFK	Fin.	46	13	24	37	16	4	0	2	2	2
1993-94	HIFK	Fin.	43	16	22	38	14	3	0	0	0	2
1994-95	HIFK	Fin.	45	20	16	36	16	3	0	0	0	0

PELUSO, MIKE (puh-LOO-soh) N.J.

Left wing. Shoots left. 6'4", 220 lbs. Born, Pengilly, MN, November 8, 1965.
(New Jersey's 10th choice, 190th overall, in 1984 Entry Draft).

			Regular Season					Playoffs				
Season	Club	Lea	GP	G	A	TP	PIM	GP	G	A	TP	PIM
1985-86	Alaska-Anch.	G.N.	32	2	11	13	59	....	....	....	....	....
1986-87	Alaska-Anch.	G.N.	30	5	21	26	68	....	....	....	....	....
1987-88	Alaska-Anch.	G.N.	35	4	33	37	76	....	....	....	....	....
1988-89	Alaska-Anch.	G.N.	33	10	27	37	75	....	....	....	....	....
1989-90	**Chicago**	**NHL**	**2**	**0**	**0**	**0**	**15**	....	....	....	....	....
	Indianapolis	IHL	75	7	10	17	279	14	0	1	1	58
1990-91	**Chicago**	**NHL**	**53**	**6**	**1**	**7**	**320**	**3**	**0**	**0**	**0**	**2**
	Indianapolis	IHL	6	2	1	3	21	5	0	2	2	40
1991-92	**Chicago**	**NHL**	**63**	**6**	**3**	**9**	***408**	**17**	**1**	**2**	**3**	**8**
	Indianapolis	IHL	4	0	1	1	15	....	....	....	....	....
1992-93	**Ottawa**	**NHL**	**81**	**15**	**10**	**25**	**318**	....	....	....	....	....
1993-94	**New Jersey**	**NHL**	**69**	**4**	**16**	**20**	**238**	**17**	**1**	**0**	**1**	***64**
1994-95	**New Jersey**	**NHL**	**46**	**2**	**9**	**11**	**167**	**20**	**1**	**2**	**3**	**8**
	NHL Totals		**314**	**33**	**39**	**72**	**1466**	**57**	**3**	**4**	**7**	**82**

Signed as a free agent by **Chicago**, September 7, 1989. Claimed by **Ottawa** from **Chicago** in Expansion Draft, June 18, 1992. Traded to **New Jersey** by **Ottawa** to complete June 20, 1993 trade which sent Craig Billington, Troy Mallette and New Jersey's fourth round choice (Cosmo Dupaul) in 1993 Entry Draft to Ottawa for Peter Sidorkiewicz and future considerations, June 26, 1993.

PELUSO, MIKE (puh-LOO-soh) CGY.

Center. Shoots right. 6', 200 lbs. Born, Denver, CO, September 2, 1974.
(Calgary's 12th choice, 253rd overall, in 1994 Entry Draft).

			Regular Season					Playoffs				
Season	Club	Lea	GP	G	A	TP	PIM	GP	G	A	TP	PIM
1993-94	Omaha	Jr. A	48	36	29	65	77	....	....	....	....	....
1994-95	Minn.-Duluth	WCHA	38	11	23	34	38	....	....	....	....	....

PENNEY, CHAD OTT.

Left wing. Shoots left. 6', 195 lbs. Born, Labrador City, Nfld., September 18, 1973.
(Ottawa's 2nd choice, 25th overall, in 1992 Entry Draft).

			Regular Season					Playoffs				
Season	Club	Lea	GP	G	A	TP	PIM	GP	G	A	TP	PIM
1990-91	North Bay	OHL	66	33	34	67	56	10	2	6	8	12
1991-92	North Bay	OHL	57	25	27	52	90	21	13	17	30	9
1992-93	North Bay	OHL	18	8	7	15	19	....	....	....	....	....
a	S.S. Marie	OHL	48	29	44	73	67	18	7	10	17	18
1993-94	**Ottawa**	**NHL**	**3**	**0**	**0**	**0**	**2**	....	....	....	....	....
	P.E.I.	AHL	73	20	30	50	66	....	....	....	....	....
1994-95	P.E.I.	AHL	66	16	16	32	19	11	2	2	4	2
	NHL Totals		**3**	**0**	**0**	**0**	**2**	....	....	....	....	....

a Memorial Cup All-Star Team (1993)

PENNEY, DAVID ANA.

Left wing. Shoots left. 6'1", 175 lbs. Born, Easton, MA, May 16, 1974.
(Anaheim's 11th choice, 264th overall, in 1993 Entry Draft).

			Regular Season					Playoffs				
Season	Club	Lea	GP	G	A	TP	PIM	GP	G	A	TP	PIM
1993-94	Northeastern	H.E.	36	5	9	14	18	....	....	....	....	....
1994-95	Northeastern	H.E.	1	0	0	0	2	....	....	....	....	....

PEPLINSKI, JIM (peh-PLINS-kee) CGY.

right wing. Shoots right. 6'3", 210 lbs. Born, Renfrew, Ont., October 24, 1960.
(Atlanta's 5th choice, 75th overall, in 1979 Entry Draft).

			Regular Season					Playoffs				
Season	Club	Lea	GP	G	A	TP	PIM	GP	G	A	TP	PIM
1978-79	Toronto	OHA	66	23	32	55	88	3	0	1	1	0
1979-80	Toronto	OHA	67	35	66	101	89	4	1	2	3	15
1980-81	**Calgary**	**NHL**	**80**	**13**	**25**	**38**	**108**	**16**	**2**	**3**	**5**	**41**
1981-82	**Calgary**	**NHL**	**74**	**30**	**37**	**67**	**115**	**3**	**1**	**0**	**1**	**13**
1982-83	**Calgary**	**NHL**	**80**	**15**	**26**	**41**	**134**	**8**	**1**	**1**	**2**	**45**
1983-84	**Calgary**	**NHL**	**74**	**11**	**22**	**33**	**114**	**11**	**3**	**4**	**7**	**21**
1984-85	**Calgary**	**NHL**	**80**	**16**	**29**	**45**	**111**	**4**	**1**	**3**	**4**	**11**
1985-86	**Calgary**	**NHL**	**77**	**24**	**35**	**59**	**214**	**22**	**5**	**9**	**14**	**107**
1986-87	**Calgary**	**NHL**	**80**	**18**	**32**	**50**	**181**	**6**	**1**	**0**	**1**	**24**
1987-88	**Calgary**	**NHL**	**75**	**20**	**31**	**51**	**234**	**9**	**0**	**5**	**5**	**45**
	Cdn. Olympic	....	7	0	1	1	6	....	....	....	....	....
1988-89	**Calgary**	**NHL**	**79**	**13**	**25**	**38**	**241**	**20**	**1**	**6**	**7**	**75**
1989-90	**Calgary**	**NHL**	**6**	**1**	**0**	**1**	**4**	....	....	....	....	....
1990-91					DID NOT PLAY							
1991-92					DID NOT PLAY							
1992-93					DID NOT PLAY							
1993-94					DID NOT PLAY							
1994-95	**Calgary**	**NHL**	**6**	**0**	**1**	**1**	**11**	....	....	....	....	....
	NHL Totals		**711**	**161**	**263**	**424**	**1467**	**99**	**15**	**31**	**46**	**382**

Signed as a free agent by **Calgary**, April 6, 1995.

PEPPERALL, RYAN TOR.

Right wing. Shoots right. 6'1", 178 lbs. Born, Niagara Falls, Ont., January 26, 1977.
(Toronto's 2nd choice, 54th overall, in 1995 Entry Draft).

			Regular Season					Playoffs				
Season	Club	Lea	GP	G	A	TP	PIM	GP	G	A	TP	PIM
1993-94	Niagara Falls	Jr. B	37	14	20	34	156	....	....	....	....	....
1994-95	Kitchener	OHL	62	17	16	33	86	5	2	2	4	8

PERREAULT, YANIC (puh-ROH, YAH-nihk) L.A.

Center. Shoots left. 5'11", 182 lbs. Born, Sherbrooke, Que., April 4, 1971.
(Toronto's 1st choice, 47th overall, in 1991 Entry Draft).

			Regular Season					Playoffs				
Season	Club	Lea	GP	G	A	TP	PIM	GP	G	A	TP	PIM
1988-89	Trois-Rivières	QMJHL	70	53	55	108	48	....	....	....	....	....
1989-90	Trois-Rivières	QMJHL	63	51	63	114	75	7	6	5	11	19
1990-91a	Trois-Rivières	QMJHL	67	*87	98	*185	103	6	4	7	11	6
1991-92	St. John's	AHL	62	38	38	76	19	16	7	8	15	4
1992-93	St. John's	AHL	79	49	46	95	56	9	4	5	9	2
1993-94	**Toronto**	**NHL**	**13**	**3**	**3**	**6**	**0**	....	....	....	....	....
	St. John's	AHL	62	45	60	105	38	11	*12	6	18	14
1994-95	Phoenix	IHL	68	51	48	99	52	....	....	....	....	....
	Los Angeles	**NHL**	**26**	**2**	**5**	**7**	**20**	....	....	....	....	....
	NHL Totals		**39**	**5**	**8**	**13**	**20**	....	....	....	....	....

a QMJHL First All-Star Team (1991)

Traded to **Los Angeles** by **Toronto** for a conditional draft choice in 1996 Entry Draft, July 11, 1994.

PERROTT, NATHAN N.J.

Right wing. Shoots right. 6', 215 lbs. Born, Owen Sound, Ont., December 8, 1976.
(New Jersey's 2nd choice, 44th overall, in 1995 Entry Draft).

			Regular Season					Playoffs				
Season	Club	Lea	GP	G	A	TP	PIM	GP	G	A	TP	PIM
1993-94	St. Mary's	Jr. B	41	11	26	37	249	....	....	....	....	....
1994-95	Oshawa	OHL	63	18	28	46	233	2	1	1	2	9

PERRY, JEFF CGY.

Left wing. Shoots left. 6', 195 lbs. Born, Sarnia, Ont., April 12, 1971.
(Toronto's 6th choice, 113th overall, in 1991 Entry Draft).

			Regular Season					Playoffs				
Season	Club	Lea	GP	G	A	TP	PIM	GP	G	A	TP	PIM
1990-91	Owen Sound	OHL	60	31	49	80	83	....	....	....	....	....
1991-92	Owen Sound	OHL	7	0	5	5	8	....	....	....	....	....
	St. John's	AHL	6	0	1	1	4	....	....	....	....	....
	Raleigh	ECHL	8	2	2	4	18	4	0	1	1	11
1992-93	St. John's	AHL	13	1	1	2	22	....	....	....	....	....
	Brantford	ColHL	23	1	13	24	36	14	8	7	15	27
1993-94	Saint John	AHL	42	8	3	11	97	4	0	0	0	4
1994-95	Saint John	AHL	28	4	2	6	128	....	....	....	....	....

Traded to **Calgary** by **Toronto** with Brad Miller for Todd Gillingham and Paul Holden, September 2, 1993.

PERRY, TYLER DET.

Center. Shoots right. 6'1", 170 lbs. Born, Vancouver, B.C., August 31, 1977.
(Detroit's 7th choice, 156th overall, in 1995 Entry Draft).

			Regular Season					Playoffs				
Season	Club	Lea	GP	G	A	TP	PIM	GP	G	A	TP	PIM
1993-94	Richmond	Jr. A	40	28	35	63	8	....	....	....	....	....
1994-95	Seattle	WHL	49	9	13	22	19	4	2	0	2	2

PERSHIN, EDUARD (PEHR-shihn, ehd-WUHRD) T.B.

Right wing. Shoots left. 6', 191 lbs. Born, Nizhnekamsk, USSR, September 1, 1977.
(Tampa Bay's 5th choice, 134th overall, in 1995 Entry Draft).

			Regular Season					Playoffs				
Season	Club	Lea	GP	G	A	TP	PIM	GP	G	A	TP	PIM
1994-95	Moscow D'amo	CIS	4	1	1	2	2	3	0	0	0	2

PERSSON, RICARD N.J.

Defense. Shoots left. 6'2", 205 lbs. Born, Ostersund, Sweden, August 24, 1969.
(New Jersey's 2nd choice, 23rd overall, in 1987 Entry Draft).

			Regular Season					Playoffs				
Season	Club	Lea	GP	G	A	TP	PIM	GP	G	A	TP	PIM
1985-86	Ostersund	Swe. 2	24	2	2	4	16	....	....	....	....	....
1986-87	Ostersund	Swe. 2	31	10	11	21	28	....	....	....	....	....
1987-88	Leksand	Swe.	31	2	0	2	8	2	0	1	1	2
1988-89	Leksand	Swe.	33	2	4	6	28	9	0	1	1	6
1989-90	Leksand	Swe.	43	9	10	19	62	3	0	0	0	6
1990-91	Leksand	Swe.	37	6	9	15	42	....	....	....	....	....
1991-92	Leksand	Swe.	21	0	7	7	28	....	....	....	....	....
1992-93	Leksand	Swe.	36	7	15	22	63	2	0	2	2	0
1993-94	Malmo	Swe.	40	11	9	20	38	11	2	0	2	12
1994-95	Malmo	Swe.	31	3	13	16	38	9	0	2	2	8
	Albany	AHL	....	....	....	....	....	9	3	5	8	7

PETERSON, BRENT — T.B.

Left wing. Shoots left. 6'3", 200 lbs. Born, Calgary, Alta., July 20, 1972.
(Tampa Bay's 1st choice, 3rd overall, in 1993 Supplemental Draft).

			Regular Season					Playoffs				
Season	Club	Lea	GP	G	A	TP	PIM	GP	G	A	TP	PIM
1991-92	Michigan Tech	WCHA	39	11	9	20	18	....	....	....	....	....
1992-93	Michigan Tech	WCHA	37	24	18	42	32	....	....	....	....	....
1993-94	Michigan Tech	WCHA	43	25	21	46	30	....	....	....	....	....
1994-95	Michigan Tech	WCHA	39	20	16	36	27	....	....	....	....	....

PETERSON, KYLE — DAL.

Center. Shoots left. 6'3", 195 lbs. Born, Calgary, Alta., April 17, 1974.
(Minnesota's 5th choice, 154th overall, in 1992 Entry Draft).

			Regular Season					Playoffs				
Season	Club	Lea	GP	G	A	TP	PIM	GP	G	A	TP	PIM
1993-94	Michigan Tech	WCHA	45	5	9	14	82	....	....	....	....	....
1994-95	Michigan Tech	WCHA	36	7	11	18	52	....	....	....	....	....

PETERSON, MATT — ANA.

Defense. Shoots left. 6'1", 190 lbs. Born, Maple Grove, MN, February 15, 1975.
(Anaheim's 7th choice, 160th overall, in 1993 Entry Draft).

			Regular Season					Playoffs				
Season	Club	Lea	GP	G	A	TP	PIM	GP	G	A	TP	PIM
1994-95	U. Wisconsin	WCHA	20	0	0	0	10	....	....	....	....	....

PETIT, MICHEL (puh-TEE) — L.A.

Defense. Shoots right. 6'1", 205 lbs. Born, St. Malo, Que., February 12, 1964.
(Vancouver's 1st choice, 11th overall, in 1982 Entry Draft).

			Regular Season					Playoffs				
Season	Club	Lea	GP	G	A	TP	PIM	GP	G	A	TP	PIM
1981-82a	Sherbrooke	QMJHL	63	10	39	49	106	22	5	20	25	24
1982-83	**Vancouver**	**NHL**	2	0	0	0	0	....	....	....	....	....
a	St-Jean	QMJHL	62	19	67	86	196	3	0	0	0	35
1983-84	Cdn. National	....	19	3	10	13	58	....	....	....	....	....
	Vancouver	**NHL**	44	6	9	15	53	1	0	0	0	0
1984-85	**Vancouver**	**NHL**	69	5	26	31	127	....	....	....	....	....
1985-86	**Vancouver**	**NHL**	32	1	6	7	27	....	....	....	....	....
	Fredericton	AHL	25	0	13	13	79	....	....	....	....	....
1986-87	**Vancouver**	**NHL**	69	12	13	25	131	....	....	....	....	....
1987-88	**Vancouver**	**NHL**	10	0	3	3	35	....	....	....	....	....
	NY Rangers	**NHL**	64	9	24	33	223	....	....	....	....	....
1988-89	**NY Rangers**	**NHL**	69	8	25	33	154	4	0	2	2	27
1989-90	**Quebec**	**NHL**	63	12	24	36	215	....	....	....	....	....
1990-91	**Quebec**	**NHL**	19	4	7	11	47	....	....	....	....	....
	Toronto	**NHL**	54	9	19	28	132	....	....	....	....	....
1991-92	**Toronto**	**NHL**	34	1	13	14	85	....	....	....	....	....
	Calgary	**NHL**	36	3	10	13	79	....	....	....	....	....
1992-93	**Calgary**	**NHL**	35	3	9	12	54	....	....	....	....	....
1993-94	**Calgary**	**NHL**	63	2	21	23	110	....	....	....	....	....
1994-95	**Los Angeles**	**NHL**	40	5	12	17	84	....	....	....	....	....
	NHL Totals		**703**	**80**	**221**	**301**	**1556**	**5**	**0**	**2**	**2**	**27**

a QMJHL First All-Star Team (1982, 1983)

Traded to **NY Rangers** by **Vancouver** for Willie Huber and Larry Melnyk, November 4, 1987. Traded to **Quebec** by **NY Rangers** for Randy Moller, October 5, 1989. Traded to **Toronto** by **Quebec** with Aaron Broten and Lucien Deblois for Scott Pearson and Toronto's second round choices in 1991 (later traded to Washington — Washington selected Eric Lavigne) and 1992 (Tuomas Gronman) Entry Drafts, November 17, 1990. Traded to **Calgary** by **Toronto** with Craig Berube, Alexander Godynyuk, Gary Leeman and Jeff Reese for Doug Gilmour, Jamie Macoun, Ric Nattress, Rick Wamsley and Kent Manderville, January 2, 1992. Signed as a free agent by **Los Angeles**, June 16, 1994.

PETRENKO, SERGEI (puh-TREHN-koh)

Left wing. Shoots left. 6', 176 lbs. Born, Kharkov, USSR, September 10, 1968.
(Buffalo's 5th choice, 168th overall, in 1993 Entry Draft).

			Regular Season					Playoffs				
Season	Club	Lea	GP	G	A	TP	PIM	GP	G	A	TP	PIM
1987-88	Moscow D'amo	USSR	31	2	5	7	4	....	....	....	....	....
1988-89	Moscow D'amo	USSR	23	4	6	10	6	....	....	....	....	....
1989-90	Moscow D'amo	USSR	33	5	4	9	8	....	....	....	....	....
1990-91	Moscow D'amo	USSR	43	14	13	27	10	....	....	....	....	....
1991-92	Moscow D'amo	CIS	31	9	10	19	10	....	....	....	....	....
1992-93	Moscow D'amo	CIS	36	12	12	24	10	10	4	5	9	6
1993-94	**Buffalo**	**NHL**	14	0	4	4	0	....	....	....	....	....
	Rochester	AHL	38	16	15	31	8	....	....	....	....	....
1994-95	Rochester	AHL	43	12	16	28	16	....	....	....	....	....
	NHL Totals		**14**	**0**	**4**	**4**	**0**	....	....	....	....	....

PETROCHININ, EVGENY (peht-roh-CHIH-nihn) — DAL.

Defense. Shoots left. 6'2", 190 lbs. Born, Murmansk, USSR, February 7, 1976.
(Dallas' 5th choice, 150th overall, in 1994 Entry Draft).

			Regular Season					Playoffs				
Season	Club	Lea	GP	G	A	TP	PIM	GP	G	A	TP	PIM
1993-94	Spartak	CIS	2	0	0	0	0	....	....	....	....	....
1994-95	Spartak	CIS	45	0	2	2	14	....	....	....	....	....

PETROV, OLEG (PEH-trahf) — MTL.

Right wing. Shoots left. 5'8", 175 lbs. Born, Moscow, USSR, April 18, 1971.
(Montreal's 6th choice, 127th overall, in 1991 Entry Draft).

			Regular Season					Playoffs				
Season	Club	Lea	GP	G	A	TP	PIM	GP	G	A	TP	PIM
1989-90	CSKA	USSR	30	4	7	11	4	....	....	....	....	....
1990-91	CSKA	USSR	43	7	4	11	8	....	....	....	....	....
1991-92	CSKA	CIS	42	10	16	26	8	....	....	....	....	....
1992-93	**Montreal**	**NHL**	9	2	1	3	10	1	0	0	0	0
	Fredericton	AHL	55	26	29	55	36	5	4	1	5	0
1993-94a	**Montreal**	**NHL**	55	12	15	27	2	2	0	0	0	0
	Fredericton	AHL	23	8	20	28	18	....	....	....	....	....
1994-95	**Montreal**	**NHL**	12	2	3	5	4	....	....	....	....	....
	Fredericton	AHL	17	7	11	18	12	17	5	6	11	10
	NHL Totals		**76**	**16**	**19**	**35**	**16**	**3**	**0**	**0**	**0**	**0**

a NHL/Upper Deck All-Rookie Team (1994)

PETROV, SERGEI (PEH-trahf) — CHI.

Left wing. Shoots left. 5'11", 185 lbs. Born, Leningrad, USSR, January 22, 1975.
(Chicago's 9th choice, 206th overall, in 1993 Entry Draft).

			Regular Season					Playoffs				
Season	Club	Lea	GP	G	A	TP	PIM	GP	G	A	TP	PIM
1993-94	Minn.-Duluth	WCHA	28	2	4	6	26	....	....	....	....	....
1994-95	Minn.-Duluth	WCHA	30	6	6	12	46	....	....	....	....	....

PETROVICKY, ROBERT (PEHT-roh-VEETS-kee) — HFD.

Center. Shoots left. 5'11", 172 lbs. Born, Kosice, Czech., October 26, 1973.
(Hartford's 1st choice, 9th overall, in 1992 Entry Draft).

			Regular Season					Playoffs				
Season	Club	Lea	GP	G	A	TP	PIM	GP	G	A	TP	PIM
1990-91	Dukla Trencin	Czech.	33	9	14	23	12	....	....	....	....	....
1991-92	Dukla Trencin	Czech.	46	25	36	61	28	....	....	....	....	....
1992-93	**Hartford**	**NHL**	42	3	6	9	45	....	....	....	....	....
	Springfield	AHL	16	5	3	8	39	15	5	6	11	14
1993-94	Dukla Trencin	Slovak	1	0	0	0	0	....	....	....	....	....
	Hartford	**NHL**	33	6	5	11	39	....	....	....	....	....
	Springfield	AHL	30	16	8	24	39	4	0	2	2	4
1994-95	Springfield	AHL	74	30	52	82	121	....	....	....	....	....
	Hartford	**NHL**	2	0	0	0	0	....	....	....	....	....
	NHL Totals		**77**	**9**	**11**	**20**	**84**	....	....	....	....	....

PHILPOTT, ETHAN — BUF.

Right wing. Shoots right. 6'4", 230 lbs. Born, Rochester, MN, February 11, 1975.
(Buffalo's 2nd choice, 64th overall, in 1993 Entry Draft).

			Regular Season					Playoffs				
Season	Club	Lea	GP	G	A	TP	PIM	GP	G	A	TP	PIM
1993-94	Harvard	ECAC	8	1	0	1	8	....	....	....	....	....
1994-95	Des Moines	USHL	48	19	42	61	57	....	....	....	....	....

PICARD, MICHEL — OTT.

Left wing. Shoots left. 5'11", 190 lbs. Born, Beauport, Que., November 7, 1969.
(Hartford's 8th choice, 178th overall, in 1989 Entry Draft).

			Regular Season					Playoffs				
Season	Club	Lea	GP	G	A	TP	PIM	GP	G	A	TP	PIM
1986-87	Trois-Rivières	QMJHL	66	33	35	68	53	....	....	....	....	....
1987-88	Trois-Rivières	QMJHL	69	40	55	95	71	....	....	....	....	....
1988-89	Trois-Rivières	QMJHL	66	59	81	140	170	4	1	3	4	2
1989-90	Binghamton	AHL	67	16	24	40	98	....	....	....	....	....
1990-91	**Hartford**	**NHL**	5	1	0	1	2	....	....	....	....	....
a	Springfield	AHL	77	*56	40	96	61	18	8	13	21	18
1991-92	**Hartford**	**NHL**	25	3	5	8	6	....	....	....	....	....
	Springfield	AHL	40	21	17	38	44	11	2	0	2	34
1992-93	**San Jose**	**NHL**	25	4	0	4	24	....	....	....	....	....
	Kansas City	IHL	33	7	10	17	51	12	3	2	5	20
1993-94b	Portland	AHL	61	41	44	85	99	17	11	10	21	22
1994-95a	P.E.I.	AHL	57	32	57	89	58	8	4	4	8	6
	Ottawa	**NHL**	24	5	8	13	14	....	....	....	....	....
	NHL Totals		**79**	**13**	**13**	**26**	**46**	....	....	....	....	....

a AHL First All-Star Team (1991, 1995)
b AHL Second All-Star Team (1994)

Traded to **San Jose** by **Hartford** for future considerations (Yvon Corriveau, January 21, 1993), October 9, 1992. Signed as a free agent by **Ottawa**, June 16, 1994.

PIERCE, BILL — COL.

Center. Shoots left. 6'1", 190 lbs. Born, Woburn, MA, October 6, 1974.
(Quebec's 4th choice, 75th overall, in 1993 Entry Draft).

			Regular Season					Playoffs				
Season	Club	Lea	GP	G	A	TP	PIM	GP	G	A	TP	PIM
1993-94	Boston U.	H.E.	31	4	4	8	28	....	....	....	....	....
1994-95	Boston U.	H.E.	33	5	13	18	29	....	....	....	....	....

PILON, RICHARD (PEE-lahn) — NYI

Defense. Shoots left. 6', 202 lbs. Born, Saskatoon, Sask., April 30, 1968.
(NY Islanders' 9th choice, 143rd overall, in 1986 Entry Draft).

			Regular Season					Playoffs				
Season	Club	Lea	GP	G	A	TP	PIM	GP	G	A	TP	PIM
1986-87	Prince Albert	WHL	68	4	21	25	192	7	1	6	7	17
1987-88	Prince Albert	WHL	65	13	34	47	177	9	0	6	6	38
1988-89	**NY Islanders**	**NHL**	62	0	14	14	242	....	....	....	....	....
1989-90	**NY Islanders**	**NHL**	14	0	2	2	31	....	....	....	....	....
1990-91	**NY Islanders**	**NHL**	60	1	4	5	126	....	....	....	....	....
1991-92	**NY Islanders**	**NHL**	65	1	6	7	183	....	....	....	....	....
1992-93	**NY Islanders**	**NHL**	44	1	3	4	164	15	0	0	0	50
	Capital Dist.	AHL	6	0	1	1	8	....	....	....	....	....
1993-94	**NY Islanders**	**NHL**	28	1	4	5	75	....	....	....	....	....
	Salt Lake	IHL	2	0	0	0	8	....	....	....	....	....
1994-95	**NY Islanders**	**NHL**	20	1	1	2	40	....	....	....	....	....
	NHL Totals		**293**	**5**	**34**	**39**	**861**	**15**	**0**	**0**	**0**	**50**

PITLICK, LANCE (PIHT-lihk) — OTT.

Defense. Shoots right. 6', 180 lbs. Born, Minneapolis, MN, November 5, 1967.
(Minnesota's 10th choice, 108th overall, in 1986 Entry Draft).

			Regular Season					Playoffs				
Season	Club	Lea	GP	G	A	TP	PIM	GP	G	A	TP	PIM
1986-87	U. Minnesota	WCHA	45	0	9	9	88	....	....	....	....	....
1987-88	U. Minnesota	WCHA	38	3	9	12	76	....	....	....	....	....
1988-89	U. Minnesota	WCHA	47	4	9	13	95	....	....	....	....	....
1989-90	U. Minnesota	WCHA	14	3	2	5	26	....	....	....	....	....
1990-91	Hershey	AHL	64	6	15	21	75	3	0	0	0	9
1991-92	U.S. National	....	19	0	1	1	38	....	....	....	....	....
	Hershey	AHL	4	0	0	0	6	3	0	0	0	4
1992-93	Hershey	AHL	53	5	10	15	77	....	....	....	....	....
1993-94	Hershey	AHL	58	4	13	17	93	11	1	0	1	11
1994-95	P.E.I.	AHL	61	8	19	27	55	11	1	4	5	10
	Ottawa	**NHL**	15	0	1	1	6	....	....	....	....	....
	NHL Totals		**15**	**0**	**1**	**1**	**6**	....	....	....	....	....

Signed as a free agent by **Philadelphia**, September 5, 1990. Signed as a free agent by **Ottawa**, June 22, 1994.

PITTIS, DOMENIC — PIT.

Center. Shoots left. 5'11", 180 lbs. Born, Calgary, Alta., October 1, 1974.
(Pittsburgh's 2nd choice, 52nd overall, in 1993 Entry Draft).

			Regular Season					Playoffs				
Season	Club	Lea	GP	G	A	TP	PIM	GP	G	A	TP	PIM
1991-92	Lethbridge	WHL	65	6	17	23	48	5	0	2	2	4
1992-93	Lethbridge	WHL	66	46	73	119	69	4	3	3	6	8
1993-94a	Lethbridge	WHL	72	58	69	127	93	8	4	11	15	16
1994-95	Cleveland	IHL	62	18	32	50	66	3	0	2	2	2

a WHL East Second All-Star Team (1994)

PITTMAN, CHRIS — COL.

Left wing. Shoots left. 6'2", 170 lbs. Born, Stephenville, Nfld., August 21, 1976.
(Quebec's 12th choice, 243rd overall, in 1994 Entry Draft).

			Regular Season					Playoffs				
Season	Club	Lea	GP	G	A	TP	PIM	GP	G	A	TP	PIM
1993-94	Kitchener	OHL	52	4	2	6	34	2	0	0	0	2
1994-95	Kitchener	OHL	61	15	14	29	38	5	0	1	1	2

PIVETZ, MARK — COL.

Defense. Shoots left. 6'3", 205 lbs. Born, Edmonton, Alta., December 9, 1973.
(Quebec's 12th choice, 257th overall, in 1993 Entry Draft).

			Regular Season					Playoffs				
Season	Club	Lea	GP	G	A	TP	PIM	GP	G	A	TP	PIM
1993-94	North Dakota	WCHA	36	2	5	7	96	....	....	....	....	....
1994-95	North Dakota	WCHA	39	3	11	14	38	....	....	....	....	....

PIVONKA, MICHAL (pih-VAHN-kuh) — WSH.

Center. Shoots left. 6'2", 195 lbs. Born, Kladno, Czech., January 28, 1966.
(Washington's 3rd choice, 59th overall, in 1984 Entry Draft).

			Regular Season					Playoffs				
Season	Club	Lea	GP	G	A	TP	PIM	GP	G	A	TP	PIM
1984-85	Dukla Jihlava	Czech.	33	8	11	19	18	....	....	....	....	....
1985-86	Dukla Jihlava	Czech.	42	5	13	18	18	....	....	....	....	....
1986-87	**Washington**	**NHL**	**73**	**18**	**25**	**43**	**41**	**7**	**1**	**1**	**2**	**2**
1987-88	**Washington**	**NHL**	**71**	**11**	**23**	**34**	**28**	**14**	**4**	**9**	**13**	**4**
1988-89	**Washington**	**NHL**	**52**	**8**	**19**	**27**	**30**	**6**	**3**	**1**	**4**	**10**
	Baltimore	AHL	31	12	24	36	19	....	....	....	....	....
1989-90	**Washington**	**NHL**	**77**	**25**	**39**	**64**	**54**	**11**	**0**	**2**	**2**	**6**
1990-91	**Washington**	**NHL**	**79**	**20**	**50**	**70**	**34**	**11**	**2**	**3**	**5**	**8**
1991-92	**Washington**	**NHL**	**80**	**23**	**57**	**80**	**47**	**7**	**1**	**5**	**6**	**13**
1992-93	**Washington**	**NHL**	**69**	**21**	**53**	**74**	**66**	**6**	**0**	**2**	**2**	**0**
1993-94	**Washington**	**NHL**	**82**	**14**	**36**	**50**	**38**	**7**	**4**	**4**	**8**	**4**
1994-95	Klagenfurt	Aus.	7	2	4	6	4	....	....	....	....	....
	Washington	**NHL**	**46**	**10**	**23**	**33**	**50**	**7**	**1**	**4**	**5**	**21**
	NHL Totals		**629**	**150**	**325**	**475**	**388**	**76**	**16**	**31**	**47**	**68**

PLANTE, DAN (PLAHNT) — NYI

Right wing. Shoots right. 5'11", 198 lbs. Born, St. Louis, MO, October 5, 1971.
(NY Islanders' 3rd choice, 48th overall, in 1990 Entry Draft).

			Regular Season					Playoffs				
Season	Club	Lea	GP	G	A	TP	PIM	GP	G	A	TP	PIM
1990-91	U. Wisconsin	WCHA	33	1	2	3	54	....	....	....	....	....
1991-92	U. Wisconsin	WCHA	36	13	13	26	107	....	....	....	....	....
1992-93	U. Wisconsin	WCHA	42	26	31	57	142	....	....	....	....	....
1993-94	**NY Islanders**	**NHL**	**12**	**0**	**1**	**1**	**4**	**1**	**1**	**0**	**1**	**2**
	Salt Lake	IHL	66	7	17	24	148	....	....	....	....	....
1994-95	Denver	IHL	2	0	0	0	4	....	....	....	....	....
	NHL Totals		**12**	**0**	**1**	**1**	**4**	**1**	**1**	**0**	**1**	**2**

PLANTE, DEREK (PLAHNT) — BUF.

Center. Shoots left. 5'11", 180 lbs. Born, Cloquet, MN, January 17, 1971.
(Buffalo's 7th choice, 161st overall, in 1989 Entry Draft).

			Regular Season					Playoffs				
Season	Club	Lea	GP	G	A	TP	PIM	GP	G	A	TP	PIM
1989-90	Minn.-Duluth	WCHA	28	10	11	21	12	....	....	....	....	....
1990-91	Minn.-Duluth	WCHA	36	23	20	43	6	....	....	....	....	....
1991-92a	Minn.-Duluth	WCHA	37	27	36	63	28	....	....	....	....	....
1992-93bc	Minn.-Duluth	WCHA	37	*36	*56	*92	30	....	....	....	....	....
1993-94	**Buffalo**	**NHL**	**77**	**21**	**35**	**56**	**24**	**7**	**1**	**0**	**1**	**0**
	U.S. National	....	2	0	1	1	0	....	....	....	....	....
1994-95	**Buffalo**	**NHL**	**47**	**3**	**19**	**22**	**12**	....	....	....	....	....
	NHL Totals		**124**	**24**	**54**	**78**	**36**	**7**	**1**	**0**	**1**	**0**

a WCHA Second All-Star Team (1992)
b WCHA First All-Star Team (1993)
c NCAA West First All-American Team (1993)

PLAVSIC, ADRIEN (PLAV-sihk) — T.B.

Defense. Shoots left. 6'1", 200 lbs. Born, Montreal, Que., January 13, 1970.
(St. Louis' 2nd choice, 30th overall, in 1988 Entry Draft).

			Regular Season					Playoffs				
Season	Club	Lea	GP	G	A	TP	PIM	GP	G	A	TP	PIM
1987-88	N. Hampshire	H.E.	30	5	6	11	45	....	....	....	....	....
1988-89	Cdn. National	....	62	5	10	15	25	....	....	....	....	....
1989-90	**St. Louis**	**NHL**	**4**	**0**	**1**	**1**	**2**	....	....	....	....	....
	Peoria	IHL	51	7	14	21	87	....	....	....	....	....
	Vancouver	**NHL**	**11**	**3**	**2**	**5**	**8**	....	....	....	....	....
	Milwaukee	IHL	3	1	2	3	14	6	1	3	4	6
1990-91	**Vancouver**	**NHL**	**48**	**2**	**10**	**12**	**62**	....	....	....	....	....
1991-92	Cdn. National	....	38	7	8	15	44	....	....	....	....	....
	Cdn. Olympic	....	8	0	2	2	0	....	....	....	....	....
	Vancouver	**NHL**	**16**	**1**	**9**	**10**	**14**	**13**	**1**	**7**	**8**	**4**
1992-93	**Vancouver**	**NHL**	**57**	**6**	**21**	**27**	**53**	....	....	....	....	....
1993-94	**Vancouver**	**NHL**	**47**	**1**	**9**	**10**	**6**	....	....	....	....	....
	Hamilton	AHL	2	0	0	0	0	....	....	....	....	....
1994-95	**Vancouver**	**NHL**	**3**	**0**	**1**	**1**	**4**	....	....	....	....	....
	Tampa Bay	**NHL**	**15**	**2**	**1**	**3**	**4**	....	....	....	....	....
	NHL Totals		**201**	**15**	**54**	**69**	**153**	**13**	**1**	**7**	**8**	**4**

Traded to **Vancouver** by **St. Louis** with Montreal's first round choice (previously acquired by St. Louis — Vancouver selected Shawn Antoski) in 1990 Entry Draft and St. Louis' second round choice (later traded to Montreal — Montreal selected Craig Darby) in 1991 Entry Draft for Rich Sutter, Harold Snepsts and St. Louis' second round choice (previously acquired by Vancouver — St. Louis selected Craig Johnson) in 1990 Entry Draft, March 6, 1990. Traded to **Tampa Bay** by **Vancouver** for Tampa Bay's fifth round choice in 1997 Entry Draft, March 23, 1995.

POAPST, STEVE (POHPST) — WSH.

Defense. Shoots left. 6', 200 lbs. Born, Cornwall, Ont., January 3, 1969.

			Regular Season					Playoffs				
Season	Club	Lea	GP	G	A	TP	PIM	GP	G	A	TP	PIM
1989-90	Colgate	ECAC	38	4	15	19	54	....	....	....	....	....
1990-91	Colgate	ECAC	32	6	15	21	43	....	....	....	....	....
1991-92	Hampton Rds.	ECHL	55	8	20	28	29	14	1	4	5	12
1992-93a	Hampton Rds.	ECHL	63	10	35	45	57	4	0	1	1	4
	Baltimore	AHL	7	0	1	1	4	7	0	3	3	6
1993-94	Portland	AHL	78	14	21	35	47	12	0	3	3	8
1994-95	Portland	AHL	71	8	22	30	60	7	0	1	1	16

a ECHL First All-Star Team (1993)

Signed as a free agent by **Washington**, February 4, 1995.

PODEIN, SHJON (poh-DEEN, SHAWN) — PHI.

Center. Shoots left. 6'2", 200 lbs. Born, Rochester, MN, March 5, 1968.
(Edmonton's 9th choice, 166th overall, in 1988 Entry Draft).

			Regular Season					Playoffs				
Season	Club	Lea	GP	G	A	TP	PIM	GP	G	A	TP	PIM
1987-88	Minn.-Duluth	WCHA	30	4	4	8	48	....	....	....	....	....
1988-89	Minn.-Duluth	WCHA	36	7	5	12	46	....	....	....	....	....
1989-90	Minn.-Duluth	WCHA	35	21	18	39	36	....	....	....	....	....
1990-91	Cape Breton	AHL	63	14	15	29	65	4	0	0	0	5
1991-92	Cape Breton	AHL	80	30	24	54	46	5	3	1	4	2
1992-93	**Edmonton**	**NHL**	**40**	**13**	**6**	**19**	**25**	....	....	....	....	....
	Cape Breton	AHL	38	18	21	39	32	9	2	2	4	29
1993-94	**Edmonton**	**NHL**	**28**	**3**	**5**	**8**	**8**	....	....	....	....	....
	Cape Breton	AHL	5	4	4	8	4	....	....	....	....	....
1994-95	**Philadelphia**	**NHL**	**44**	**3**	**7**	**10**	**33**	**15**	**1**	**3**	**4**	**10**
	NHL Totals		**112**	**19**	**18**	**37**	**66**	**15**	**1**	**3**	**4**	**10**

Signed as a free agent by **Philadelphia**, July 27, 1994.

PODOLLAN, JASON — FLA.

Right wing. Shoots right. 6'1", 192 lbs. Born, Vernon, B.C., February 18, 1976.
(Florida's 3rd choice, 31st overall, in 1994 Entry Draft).

			Regular Season					Playoffs				
Season	Club	Lea	GP	G	A	TP	PIM	GP	G	A	TP	PIM
1991-92	Spokane	WHL	2	0	0	0	2	10	3	1	4	16
1992-93	Spokane	WHL	72	36	33	69	108	10	4	4	8	14
1993-94	Spokane	WHL	69	29	37	66	108	3	3	0	3	2
1994-95	Spokane	WHL	72	43	41	84	102	11	5	7	12	18

POESCHEK, RUDY (POH-shehk) — T.B.

Right wing/Defense. Shoots right. 6'2", 210 lbs. Born, Kamloops, B.C., September 29, 1966.
(NY Rangers' 12th choice, 238th overall, in 1985 Entry Draft).

			Regular Season					Playoffs				
Season	Club	Lea	GP	G	A	TP	PIM	GP	G	A	TP	PIM
1983-84	Kamloops	WHL	47	3	9	12	93	8	0	2	2	7
1984-85	Kamloops	WHL	34	6	7	13	100	15	0	3	3	56
1985-86	Kamloops	WHL	32	3	13	16	92	16	3	7	10	40
1986-87	Kamloops	WHL	54	13	18	31	153	15	2	4	6	37
1987-88	**NY Rangers**	**NHL**	**1**	**0**	**0**	**0**	**2**	....	....	....	....	....
	Colorado	IHL	82	7	31	38	210	12	2	2	4	31
1988-89	**NY Rangers**	**NHL**	**52**	**0**	**2**	**2**	**199**	....	....	....	....	....
	Colorado	IHL	2	0	0	0	6	....	....	....	....	....
1989-90	**NY Rangers**	**NHL**	**15**	**0**	**0**	**0**	**55**	....	....	....	....	....
	Flint	IHL	38	8	13	21	109	4	0	0	0	16
1990-91	Binghamton	AHL	38	1	3	4	162	....	....	....	....	....
	Winnipeg	**NHL**	**1**	**0**	**0**	**0**	**5**	....	....	....	....	....
	Moncton	AHL	23	2	4	6	67	9	1	1	2	41
1991-92	**Winnipeg**	**NHL**	**4**	**0**	**0**	**0**	**17**	....	....	....	....	....
	Moncton	AHL	63	4	18	22	170	11	0	2	2	48
1992-93	St. John's	AHL	78	7	24	31	189	9	0	4	4	13
1993-94	**Tampa Bay**	**NHL**	**71**	**3**	**6**	**9**	**118**	....	....	....	....	....
1994-95	**Tampa Bay**	**NHL**	**25**	**1**	**1**	**2**	**92**	....	....	....	....	....
	NHL Totals		**169**	**4**	**9**	**13**	**488**	....	....	....	....	....

Traded to **Winnipeg** by **NY Rangers** for Guy Larose, January 22, 1991. Signed as a free agent by **Toronto**, July 8, 1992. Signed as a free agent by **Tampa Bay**, August 10, 1993.

POIRIER, JOEL — WSH.

Left wing. Shoots left. 6'1", 190 lbs. Born, Richmond Hill, Ont., January 15, 1975.
(Washington's 7th choice, 199th overall, in 1993 Entry Draft).

			Regular Season					Playoffs				
Season	Club	Lea	GP	G	A	TP	PIM	GP	G	A	TP	PIM
1992-93	Sudbury	OHL	64	18	15	33	94	14	0	2	2	8
1993-94	Sudbury	OHL	28	17	5	22	44	....	....	....	....	....
	Windsor	OHL	13	6	8	14	20	....	....	....	....	....
1994-95	Windsor	OHL	64	24	39	63	50	10	4	5	9	10

POLAK, MARK — BUF.

Center. Shoots right. 6', 188 lbs. Born, Edmonton, Alta., May 16, 1976.
(Buffalo's 11th choice, 251st overall, in 1994 Entry Draft).

			Regular Season					Playoffs				
Season	Club	Lea	GP	G	A	TP	PIM	GP	G	A	TP	PIM
1992-93	Medicine Hat	WHL	68	11	20	31	50	10	1	2	3	2
1993-94	Medicine Hat	WHL	70	20	26	46	48	3	0	1	1	2
1994-95	Medicine Hat	WHL	71	18	25	43	101	5	0	2	2	6

POLASEK, LIBOR (poh-LAH-shehk) — VAN.

Center. Shoots right. 6'3", 220 lbs. Born, Vitkovice, Czech., April 22, 1974.
(Vancouver's 1st choice, 21st overall, in 1992 Entry Draft).

			Regular Season					Playoffs				
Season	Club	Lea	GP	G	A	TP	PIM	GP	G	A	TP	PIM
1991-92	TJ Vitkovice	Czech.	17	2	2	4	4	....	....	....	....	....
1992-93	Hamilton	AHL	60	7	12	19	34	....	....	....	....	....
1993-94	Hamilton	AHL	76	11	12	23	40	3	0	0	0	0
1994-95	Syracuse	AHL	45	2	8	10	16	....	....	....	....	....
	S. Carolina	ECHL	7	0	0	0	6	....	....	....	....	....

POMICHTER, MICHAEL — CHI.

Center. Shoots left. 6'1", 222 lbs. Born, New Haven, CT, September 10, 1973.
(Chicago's 2nd choice, 39th overall, in 1991 Entry Draft).

			Regular Season					Playoffs				
Season	Club	Lea	GP	G	A	TP	PIM	GP	G	A	TP	PIM
1991-92	Boston U.	H.E.	34	11	27	38	14	....	....	....	....	....
1992-93	Boston U.	H.E.	30	16	14	30	23	....	....	....	....	....
1993-94a	Boston U.	H.E.	40	*28	26	54	37	....	....	....	....	....
1994-95	Indianapolis	IHL	76	13	9	22	47	....	....	....	....	....

a NCAA East First All-American Team (1994)

POPE, BRENT — EDM.

Defense. Shoots right. 6'3", 214 lbs. Born, Hamilton, Ont., February 20, 1973.

			Regular Season					Playoffs				
Season	Club	Lea	GP	G	A	TP	PIM	GP	G	A	TP	PIM
1989-90	Peterborough	OHL	31	0	7	7	14	7	0	2	2	4
1990-91	Peterborough	OHL	29	3	11	14	15	....	....	....	....	....
	Hamilton	OHL	29	1	6	7	30	4	0	1	1	15
1991-92	Guelph	OHL	65	10	38	48	108	....	....	....	....	....
1992-93	Guelph	OHL	34	10	14	24	40	....	....	....	....	....
	Ottawa	OHL	26	5	8	13	18	....	....	....	....	....
	Wheeling	ECHL	....	....	....	....	....	2	0	0	0	6
1993-94	Wheeling	ECHL	63	8	19	27	230	9	0	2	2	32
1994-95	Cape Breton	AHL	9	0	1	1	25	....	....	....	....	....
	Wheeling	ECHL	57	7	17	24	235	3	1	1	2	2

Signed as a free agent by **Edmonton**, January 28, 1993.

POPOVIC, PETER (puh-PUH-vihch) — MTL.

Defense. Shoots right. 6'6", 235 lbs. Born, Koping, Sweden, February 10, 1968.
(Montreal's 5th choice, 93rd overall, in 1988 Entry Draft).

			Regular Season					Playoffs				
Season	Club	Lea	GP	G	A	TP	PIM	GP	G	A	TP	PIM
1986-87	Vasteras	Swe. 2	24	1	2	3	10	....	....	....	....	....
1987-88	Vasteras	Swe. 2	28	3	17	20	16	....	....	....	....	....
1988-89	Vasteras	Swe.	22	1	4	5	32	....	....	....	....	....
1989-90	Vasteras	Swe.	30	2	10	12	24	2	0	1	1	2
1990-91	Vasteras	Swe.	40	3	2	5	62	4	0	0	0	4
1991-92	Vasteras	Swe.	34	7	10	17	30	....	....	....	....	....
1992-93	Vasteras	Swe.	39	6	12	18	46	3	0	1	1	2
1993-94	**Montreal**	**NHL**	**47**	**2**	**12**	**14**	**26**	**6**	**0**	**1**	**1**	**0**
1994-95	Vasteras	Swe.	11	0	3	3	10	....	....	....	....	....
	Montreal	**NHL**	**33**	**0**	**5**	**5**	**8**	....	....	....	....	....
	NHL Totals		**80**	**2**	**17**	**19**	**34**	**6**	**0**	**1**	**1**	**0**

POPP, KEVIN — BUF.

Defense. Shoots left. 6'1", 198 lbs. Born, Surrey, B.C., February 26, 1976.
(Buffalo's 7th choice, 119th overall, in 1995 Entry Draft).

			Regular Season					Playoffs				
Season	Club	Lea	GP	G	A	TP	PIM	GP	G	A	TP	PIM
1993-94	Spokane	WHL	43	0	4	4	126	2	0	0	0	0
1994-95	Seattle	WHL	70	5	8	13	257	4	1	2	3	4

POTAPOV, VLADIMIR (poh-TAH-pohv) — WPG.

Right wing. Shoots left. 6'2", 187 lbs. Born, Murmansk, USSR, June 21, 1975.
(Winnipeg's 10th choice, 217th overall, in 1993 Entry Draft).

			Regular Season					Playoffs				
Season	Club	Lea	GP	G	A	TP	PIM	GP	G	A	TP	PIM
1992-93	Elektrostal	CIS 2				UNAVAILABLE						
1993-94	Elektrostal	CIS 2	41	3	3	6	4	....	....	....	....	....
1994-95	Elektrostal	CIS	51	4	7	11	24	....	....	....	....	....

POTOMSKI, BARRY — L.A.

Left wing. Shoots left. 6'2", 215 lbs. Born, Windsor, Ont., November 24, 1972.

			Regular Season					Playoffs				
Season	Club	Lea	GP	G	A	TP	PIM	GP	G	A	TP	PIM
1989-90	London	OHL	9	0	2	2	18	....	....	....	....	....
1990-91	London	OHL	65	14	17	31	202	7	0	2	2	10
1991-92	London	OHL	61	19	32	51	224	10	5	1	6	22
1992-93	Erie	ECHL	5	1	1	2	31	....	....	....	....	....
	Toledo	ECHL	43	5	18	23	184	14	5	2	7	73
1993-94	Toledo	ECHL	13	9	4	13	81	....	....	....	....	....
	Adirondack	AHL	50	9	5	14	224	11	1	1	2	44
1994-95	Phoenix	IHL	42	5	6	11	171	....	....	....	....	....

Signed as a free agent by **Los Angeles**, July 7, 1994.

POTVIN, MARC (POT-vahn) — BOS.

Right wing. Shoots right. 6'1", 200 lbs. Born, Ottawa, Ont., January 29, 1967.
(Detroit's 9th choice, 169th overall, in 1986 Entry Draft).

			Regular Season					Playoffs				
Season	Club	Lea	GP	G	A	TP	PIM	GP	G	A	TP	PIM
1986-87	Bowling Green	CCHA	43	5	15	20	74	....	....	....	....	....
1987-88	Bowling Green	CCHA	45	15	21	36	80	....	....	....	....	....
1988-89	Bowling Green	CCHA	46	23	12	35	63	....	....	....	....	....
1989-90	Bowling Green	CCHA	40	19	17	36	72	....	....	....	....	....
	Adirondack	AHL	5	2	1	3	9	4	0	1	1	23
1990-91	**Detroit**	**NHL**	**9**	**0**	**0**	**0**	**55**	**6**	**0**	**0**	**0**	**32**
	Adirondack	AHL	63	9	13	22	*365	....	....	....	....	....
1991-92	**Detroit**	**NHL**	**5**	**1**	**0**	**1**	**52**	**1**	**0**	**0**	**0**	**0**
	Adirondack	AHL	51	13	16	29	314	19	5	4	9	57
1992-93	Adirondack	AHL	37	8	12	20	109	....	....	....	....	....
	Los Angeles	**NHL**	**20**	**0**	**1**	**1**	**61**	**1**	**0**	**0**	**0**	**0**
1993-94	**Los Angeles**	**NHL**	**3**	**0**	**0**	**0**	**26**	....	....	....	....	....
	Hartford	**NHL**	**51**	**2**	**3**	**5**	**246**	....	....	....	....	....
1994-95	**Boston**	**NHL**	**6**	**0**	**1**	**1**	**4**	....	....	....	....	....
	Providence	AHL	21	4	14	18	84	12	2	4	6	25
	NHL Totals		**94**	**3**	**5**	**8**	**444**	**8**	**0**	**0**	**0**	**32**

Traded to **Los Angeles** by **Detroit** with Jimmy Carson and Gary Shuchuk for Paul Coffey, Sylvain Couturier and Jim Hiller, January 29, 1993. Traded to **Hartford** by **Los Angeles** for Doug Houda, November 3, 1993. Signed as a free agent by **Boston**, June 29, 1994.

POULIN, DAVE (POO-lihn)

Center. Shoots left. 5'11", 190 lbs. Born, Timmins, Ont., December 17, 1958.

			Regular Season					Playoffs				
Season	Club	Lea	GP	G	A	TP	PIM	GP	G	A	TP	PIM
1978-79	Notre Dame	WCHA	37	28	31	59	32	....	....	....	....	....
1979-80	Notre Dame	WCHA	24	19	24	43	46	....	....	....	....	....
1980-81	Notre Dame	WCHA	35	13	22	35	53	....	....	....	....	....
1981-82a	Notre Dame	CCHA	39	29	30	59	44	....	....	....	....	....
1982-83	Rogle	Swe.	32	35	27	62	64	....	....	....	....	....
	Philadelphia	**NHL**	**2**	**2**	**0**	**2**	**2**	**3**	**1**	**3**	**4**	**9**
	Maine	AHL	16	7	9	16	2	....	....	....	....	....
1983-84	**Philadelphia**	**NHL**	**73**	**31**	**45**	**76**	**47**	**3**	**0**	**0**	**0**	**2**
1984-85	**Philadelphia**	**NHL**	**73**	**30**	**44**	**74**	**59**	**11**	**3**	**5**	**8**	**6**
1985-86	**Philadelphia**	**NHL**	**79**	**27**	**42**	**69**	**49**	**5**	**2**	**0**	**2**	**2**
1986-87b	**Philadelphia**	**NHL**	**75**	**25**	**45**	**70**	**53**	**15**	**3**	**3**	**6**	**14**
1987-88	**Philadelphia**	**NHL**	**68**	**19**	**32**	**51**	**32**	**7**	**2**	**6**	**8**	**4**
1988-89	**Philadelphia**	**NHL**	**69**	**18**	**17**	**35**	**49**	**19**	**6**	**5**	**11**	**16**
1989-90	**Philadelphia**	**NHL**	**28**	**9**	**8**	**17**	**12**	....	....	....	....	....
	Boston	**NHL**	**32**	**6**	**19**	**25**	**12**	**18**	**8**	**5**	**13**	**8**
1990-91	**Boston**	**NHL**	**31**	**8**	**12**	**20**	**25**	**16**	**0**	**9**	**9**	**20**
1991-92	**Boston**	**NHL**	**18**	**4**	**4**	**8**	**18**	**15**	**3**	**3**	**6**	**22**
1992-93c	**Boston**	**NHL**	**84**	**16**	**33**	**49**	**62**	**4**	**1**	**1**	**2**	**10**
1993-94	**Washington**	**NHL**	**63**	**6**	**19**	**25**	**52**	**11**	**2**	**2**	**4**	**19**
1994-95	**Washington**	**NHL**	**29**	**4**	**5**	**9**	**10**	**2**	**0**	**0**	**0**	**0**
	NHL Totals		**724**	**205**	**325**	**530**	**482**	**129**	**31**	**42**	**73**	**132**

a CCHA Second All-Star Team (1982)
b Won Frank J. Selke Trophy (1987)
c Won King Clancy Memorial Trophy (1993)

Played in NHL All-Star Game (1986, 1988)

Signed as a free agent by **Philadelphia**, March 8, 1983. Traded to **Boston** by **Philadelphia** for Ken Linseman, January 16, 1990. Signed as a free agent by **Washington**, August 3, 1993.

POULIN, PATRICK (poo-LIHN) — CHI.

Left wing. Shoots left. 6'1", 210 lbs. Born, Vanier, Que., April 23, 1973.
(Hartford's 1st choice, 9th overall, in 1991 Entry Draft).

			Regular Season					Playoffs				
Season	Club	Lea	GP	G	A	TP	PIM	GP	G	A	TP	PIM
1989-90	St-Hyacinthe	QMJHL	60	25	26	51	55	12	1	9	10	5
1990-91	St-Hyacinthe	QMJHL	56	32	38	70	82	4	0	2	2	23
1991-92	**Hartford**	**NHL**	**1**	**0**	**0**	**0**	**2**	**7**	**2**	**1**	**3**	**0**
a	St-Hyacinthe	QMJHL	56	52	86	*138	58	5	2	2	4	4
	Springfield	AHL	....	....	....	....	....	1	0	0	0	0
1992-93	**Hartford**	**NHL**	**81**	**20**	**31**	**51**	**37**	....	....	....	....	....
1993-94	**Hartford**	**NHL**	**9**	**2**	**1**	**3**	**11**	....	....	....	....	....
	Chicago	**NHL**	**58**	**12**	**13**	**25**	**40**	**4**	**0**	**0**	**0**	**0**
1994-95	**Chicago**	**NHL**	**45**	**15**	**15**	**30**	**53**	**16**	**4**	**1**	**5**	**8**
	NHL Totals		**194**	**49**	**60**	**109**	**143**	**27**	**6**	**2**	**8**	**8**

a QMJHL First All-Star Team (1992)

Traded to **Chicago** by **Hartford** with Eric Weinrich for Steve Larmer and Bryan Marchment, November 2, 1993.

PRATT, NOLAN — HFD.

Defense. Shoots left. 6'2", 195 lbs. Born, Fort McMurray, Alta., August 14, 1975.
(Hartford's 4th choice, 115th overall, in 1993 Entry Draft).

			Regular Season					Playoffs				
Season	Club	Lea	GP	G	A	TP	PIM	GP	G	A	TP	PIM
1991-92	Portland	WHL	22	2	9	11	13	6	1	3	4	12
1992-93	Portland	WHL	70	4	19	23	97	16	2	7	9	31
1993-94	Portland	WHL	72	4	32	36	105	10	1	2	3	14
1994-95	Portland	WHL	72	6	37	43	196	9	1	6	7	10

PRESLEY, WAYNE — NYR

Right wing. Shoots right. 5'11", 180 lbs. Born, Dearborn, MI, March 23, 1965.
(Chicago's 2nd choice, 39th overall, in 1983 Entry Draft).

			Regular Season					Playoffs				
Season	Club	Lea	GP	G	A	TP	PIM	GP	G	A	TP	PIM
1982-83	Kitchener	OHL	70	39	48	87	99	12	1	4	5	9
1983-84a	Kitchener	OHL	70	63	76	139	156	16	12	16	28	38
1984-85	**Chicago**	**NHL**	**3**	**0**	**1**	**1**	**0**	....	....	....	....	....
	Kitchener	OHL	31	25	21	46	77	....	....	....	....	....
	S.S. Marie	OHL	11	5	9	14	14	16	13	9	22	13
1985-86	**Chicago**	**NHL**	**38**	**7**	**8**	**15**	**38**	**3**	**0**	**0**	**0**	**0**
	Nova Scotia	AHL	29	6	9	15	22	....	....	....	....	....
1986-87	**Chicago**	**NHL**	**80**	**32**	**29**	**61**	**114**	**4**	**1**	**0**	**1**	**9**
1987-88	**Chicago**	**NHL**	**42**	**12**	**10**	**22**	**52**	**5**	**0**	**0**	**0**	**4**
1988-89	**Chicago**	**NHL**	**72**	**21**	**19**	**40**	**100**	**14**	**7**	**5**	**12**	**18**
1989-90	**Chicago**	**NHL**	**49**	**6**	**7**	**13**	**69**	**19**	**9**	**6**	**15**	**29**
1990-91	**Chicago**	**NHL**	**71**	**15**	**19**	**34**	**122**	**6**	**0**	**1**	**1**	**38**
1991-92	**San Jose**	**NHL**	**47**	**8**	**14**	**22**	**76**	....	....	....	....	....
	Buffalo	**NHL**	**12**	**2**	**2**	**4**	**57**	**7**	**3**	**3**	**6**	**14**
1992-93	**Buffalo**	**NHL**	**79**	**15**	**17**	**32**	**96**	**8**	**1**	**0**	**1**	**6**
1993-94	**Buffalo**	**NHL**	**65**	**17**	**8**	**25**	**103**	**7**	**2**	**1**	**3**	**14**
1994-95	**Buffalo**	**NHL**	**46**	**14**	**5**	**19**	**41**	**5**	**3**	**1**	**4**	**8**
	NHL Totals		**604**	**149**	**139**	**288**	**868**	**78**	**26**	**17**	**43**	**140**

a OHL First All-Star Team (1984)

Traded to **San Jose** by **Chicago** for San Jose's third round choice (Bogdan Savenko) in 1993 Entry Draft, September 20, 1991. Traded to **Buffalo** by **San Jose** for Dave Snuggerud, March 9, 1992. Signed as a free agent by **NY Rangers**, August 2, 1995.

PRIMEAU, KEITH — DET.

Center. Shoots left. 6'4", 210 lbs. Born, Toronto, Ont., November 24, 1971.
(Detroit's 1st choice, 3rd overall, in 1990 Entry Draft).

			Regular Season					Playoffs				
Season	Club	Lea	GP	G	A	TP	PIM	GP	G	A	TP	PIM
1987-88	Hamilton	OHL	47	6	6	12	69	....	....	....	....	....
1988-89	Niagara Falls	OHL	48	20	35	55	56	17	9	16	25	12
1989-90a	Niagara Falls	OHL	65	*57	70	*127	97	16	*16	17	*33	49
1990-91	**Detroit**	**NHL**	**58**	**3**	**12**	**15**	**106**	**5**	**1**	**1**	**2**	**25**
	Adirondack	AHL	6	3	5	8	8	....	....	....	....	....
1991-92	**Detroit**	**NHL**	**35**	**6**	**10**	**16**	**83**	**11**	**0**	**0**	**0**	**14**
	Adirondack	AHL	42	21	24	45	89	9	1	7	8	27
1992-93	**Detroit**	**NHL**	**73**	**15**	**17**	**32**	**152**	**7**	**0**	**2**	**2**	**26**
1993-94	**Detroit**	**NHL**	**78**	**31**	**42**	**73**	**173**	**7**	**0**	**2**	**2**	**6**
1994-95	**Detroit**	**NHL**	**45**	**15**	**27**	**42**	**99**	**17**	**4**	**5**	**9**	**45**
	NHL Totals		**289**	**70**	**108**	**178**	**613**	**47**	**5**	**10**	**15**	**116**

a OHL Second All-Star Team (1990)

PRIMEAU, WAYNE — BUF.

Center. Shoots left. 6'3", 193 lbs. Born, Scarborough, Ont., June 4, 1976.
(Buffalo's 1st choice, 17th overall, in 1994 Entry Draft).

			Regular Season					Playoffs				
Season	**Club**	**Lea**	**GP**	**G**	**A**	**TP**	**PIM**	**GP**	**G**	**A**	**TP**	**PIM**
1992-93	Owen Sound	OHL	66	10	27	37	108	8	1	4	5	0
1993-94	Owen Sound	OHL	65	25	50	75	75	9	1	6	7	8
1994-95	Owen Sound	OHL	66	34	62	96	84	10	4	9	13	15
	Buffalo	**NHL**	**1**	**1**	**0**	**1**	**0**	....	....	....	....	....
	NHL Totals		**1**	**1**	**0**	**1**	**0**	....	....	....	....	....

PROBERT, BOB (PROH-buhrt) — CHI.

Right wing. Shoots left. 6'3", 225 lbs. Born, Windsor, Ont., June 5, 1965.
(Detroit's 3rd choice, 46th overall, in 1983 Entry Draft).

			Regular Season					Playoffs				
Season	**Club**	**Lea**	**GP**	**G**	**A**	**TP**	**PIM**	**GP**	**G**	**A**	**TP**	**PIM**
1982-83	Brantford	OHL	51	12	16	28	133	8	2	2	4	23
1983-84	Brantford	OHL	65	35	38	73	189	6	0	3	3	16
1984-85	S.S. Marie	OHL	44	20	52	72	172	....	....	....	....	....
	Hamilton	OHL	4	0	1	1	21	....	....	....	....	....
1985-86	**Detroit**	**NHL**	**44**	**8**	**13**	**21**	**186**	....	....	....	....	....
	Adirondack	AHL	32	12	15	27	152	10	2	3	5	68
1986-87	**Detroit**	**NHL**	**63**	**13**	**11**	**24**	**221**	**16**	**3**	**4**	**7**	**63**
	Adirondack	AHL	7	1	4	5	15	....	....	....	....	....
1987-88	**Detroit**	**NHL**	**74**	**29**	**33**	**62**	***398**	**16**	**8**	**13**	**21**	**51**
1988-89	**Detroit**	**NHL**	**25**	**4**	**2**	**6**	**106**	....	....	....	....	....
1989-90	**Detroit**	**NHL**	**4**	**3**	**0**	**3**	**21**	....	....	....	....	....
1990-91	**Detroit**	**NHL**	**55**	**16**	**23**	**39**	**315**	**6**	**1**	**2**	**3**	**50**
1991-92	**Detroit**	**NHL**	**63**	**20**	**24**	**44**	**276**	**11**	**1**	**6**	**7**	**28**
1992-93	**Detroit**	**NHL**	**80**	**14**	**29**	**43**	**292**	**7**	**0**	**3**	**3**	**10**
1993-94	**Detroit**	**NHL**	**66**	**7**	**10**	**17**	**275**	**7**	**1**	**1**	**2**	**8**
1994-95						DID NOT PLAY						
	NHL Totals		**474**	**114**	**145**	**259**	**2090**	**63**	**14**	**29**	**43**	**210**

Played in NHL All-Star Game (1988)

Signed as a free agent by **Chicago**, July 23, 1994.

PROCHAZKA, LIBOR (proh-HAHZ-kah) — ST.L.

Defense. Shoots right. 6', 185 lbs. Born, Vlasim, Czech., April 25, 1974.
(St. Louis' 8th choice, 245th overall, in 1993 Entry Draft).

			Regular Season					Playoffs				
Season	**Club**	**Lea**	**GP**	**G**	**A**	**TP**	**PIM**	**GP**	**G**	**A**	**TP**	**PIM**
1991-92	Poldi Kladno	Czech.	7	0	0	0	0	....	....	....	....	....
1992-93	Poldi Kladno	Czech.	34	2	2	4	....	....	....	....	....	....
1993-94	Poldi Kladno	Czech.	41	4	7	11	....	8	0	3	3	....
1994-95	Kladno	Czech.	40	4	16	20	81	11	2	1	3	14

PROCHAZKA, MARTIN (pro-HAHS-kah) — TOR.

Center. Shoots right. 5'11", 180 lbs. Born, Slany, Czech., March 3, 1972.
(Toronto's 8th choice, 135th overall, in 1991 Entry Draft).

			Regular Season					Playoffs				
Season	**Club**	**Lea**	**GP**	**G**	**A**	**TP**	**PIM**	**GP**	**G**	**A**	**TP**	**PIM**
1989-90	Kladno	Czech.	49	18	12	30	....	....	....	....	....	....
1990-91	Kladno	Czech.	50	19	10	29	21	....	....	....	....	....
1991-92	Dukla Jihlava	Czech.	44	18	11	29	2	....	....	....	....	....
1992-93	Kladno	Czech.	46	26	12	38	....	....	....	....	....	....
1993-94	Kladno	Czech.	43	24	16	40	0	2	2	0	2	....
1994-95	Kladno	Czech.	41	25	33	58	18	11	8	4	12	4

PROKHOROV, VITALI (PROH-kohr-ohv)

Left wing. Shoots left. 5'9", 185 lbs. Born, Moscow, USSR, December 25, 1966.
(St. Louis' 3rd choice, 64th overall, in 1992 Entry Draft).

			Regular Season					Playoffs				
Season	**Club**	**Lea**	**GP**	**G**	**A**	**TP**	**PIM**	**GP**	**G**	**A**	**TP**	**PIM**
1983-84	Spartak	USSR	5	0	0	0	0	....	....	....	....	....
1984-85	Spartak	USSR	31	1	1	2	10	....	....	....	....	....
1985-86	Spartak	USSR	29	3	9	12	4	....	....	....	....	....
1986-87	Spartak	USSR	27	1	6	7	2	....	....	....	....	....
1987-88	Spartak	USSR	19	5	0	5	4	....	....	....	....	....
1988-89	Spartak	USSR	37	11	5	16	10	....	....	....	....	....
1989-90	Spartak	USSR	43	13	8	21	35	....	....	....	....	....
1990-91	Spartak	USSR	43	21	10	31	29	....	....	....	....	....
1991-92	Spartak	CIS	38	13	19	32	68	....	....	....	....	....
1992-93	**St. Louis**	**NHL**	**26**	**4**	**1**	**5**	**15**	....	....	....	....	....
1993-94	**St. Louis**	**NHL**	**55**	**15**	**10**	**25**	**20**	**4**	**0**	**0**	**0**	**0**
	Peoria	IHL	19	13	10	23	16	....	....	....	....	....
1994-95	Spartak	CIS	8	1	4	5	8	....	....	....	....	....
	St. Louis	**NHL**	**2**	**0**	**0**	**0**	**0**	....	....	....	....	....
	Peoria	IHL	20	6	3	9	6	9	4	7	11	6
	NHL Totals		**83**	**19**	**11**	**30**	**35**	**4**	**0**	**0**	**0**	**0**

PROKOPEC, MIKE — CHI.

Right wing. Shoots right. 6'2", 190 lbs. Born, Toronto, Ont., May 17, 1974.
(Chicago's 7th choice, 161st overall, in 1992 Entry Draft).

			Regular Season					Playoffs				
Season	**Club**	**Lea**	**GP**	**G**	**A**	**TP**	**PIM**	**GP**	**G**	**A**	**TP**	**PIM**
1991-92	Cornwall	OHL	59	12	15	27	75	6	0	0	0	0
1992-93	Newmarket	OHL	40	6	14	20	70	....	....	....	....	....
	Guelph	OHL	28	10	14	24	27	5	1	0	1	14
1993-94	Guelph	OHL	66	52	58	110	93	9	12	4	16	17
1994-95	Indianapolis	IHL	70	21	12	33	80	....	....	....	....	....

PRONGER, CHRIS — ST.L.

Defense. Shoots left. 6'5", 220 lbs. Born, Dryden, Ont., October 10, 1974.
(Hartford's 1st choice, 2nd overall, in 1993 Entry Draft).

			Regular Season					Playoffs				
Season	**Club**	**Lea**	**GP**	**G**	**A**	**TP**	**PIM**	**GP**	**G**	**A**	**TP**	**PIM**
1991-92	Peterborough	OHL	63	17	45	62	90	10	1	8	9	28
1992-93ab	Peterborough	OHL	61	15	62	77	108	21	15	25	40	51
1993-94c	**Hartford**	**NHL**	**81**	**5**	**25**	**30**	**113**	....	....	....	....	....
1994-95	**Hartford**	**NHL**	**43**	**5**	**9**	**14**	**54**	....	....	....	....	....
	NHL Totals		**124**	**10**	**34**	**44**	**167**	....	....	....	....	....

a OHL First All-Star Team (1993)
b Canadian Major Junior First All-Star Team (1993)
c NHL/Upper Deck All-Rookie Team (1994)

Traded to **St. Louis** by **Hartford** for Brendan Shanahan, July 27, 1995.

PRONGER, SEAN — ANA.

Center. Shoots left. 6'2", 205 lbs. Born, Dryden, Ont., November 30, 1972.
(Vancouver's 3rd choice, 51st overall, in 1991 Entry Draft).

			Regular Season					Playoffs				
Season	**Club**	**Lea**	**GP**	**G**	**A**	**TP**	**PIM**	**GP**	**G**	**A**	**TP**	**PIM**
1990-91	Bowling Green	CCHA	40	3	7	10	30	....	....	....	....	....
1991-92	Bowling Green	CCHA	34	9	7	16	28	....	....	....	....	....
1992-93	Bowling Green	CCHA	39	23	23	46	35	....	....	....	....	....
1993-94	Bowling Green	CCHA	38	17	17	34	38	....	....	....	....	....
1994-95	Knoxville	ECHL	34	18	23	41	55	....	....	....	....	....
	Greensboro	ECHL	2	0	2	2	0	....	....	....	....	....
	San Diego	IHL	8	0	0	0	2	....	....	....	....	....

PROSOFSKY, TYLER — CHI.

Center. Shoots left. 5'11", 175 lbs. Born, Saskatoon, Sask., February 19, 1976.
(Chicago's 7th choice, 170th overall, in 1994 Entry Draft).

			Regular Season					Playoffs				
Season	**Club**	**Lea**	**GP**	**G**	**A**	**TP**	**PIM**	**GP**	**G**	**A**	**TP**	**PIM**
1992-93	Tacoma	WHL	62	10	9	19	79	7	0	0	0	5
1993-94	Tacoma	WHL	70	20	22	42	132	8	1	1	2	23
1994-95	Tacoma	WHL	71	20	27	47	161	4	0	1	1	21

PROSPAL, VACLAV (PRAWS-pahl, VAHT-slahv) — PHI.

Center. Shoots left. 6'2", 173 lbs. Born, Ceske-Budejovice, Czech., February 17, 1975.
(Philadelphia's 2nd choice, 71st overall, in 1993 Entry Draft).

			Regular Season					Playoffs				
Season	**Club**	**Lea**	**GP**	**G**	**A**	**TP**	**PIM**	**GP**	**G**	**A**	**TP**	**PIM**
1992-93	Budejovice Jrs.	Czech.	32	26	31	57	24	....	....	....	....	....
1993-94	Hershey	AHL	55	14	21	35	38	2	0	0	0	2
1994-95	Hershey	AHL	69	13	32	45	36	2	1	0	1	4

PROULX, CHRISTIAN (PROO) — MTL.

Defense. Shoots left. 6', 185 lbs. Born, Sherbrooke, Que., December 10, 1973.
(Montreal's 7th choice, 164th overall, in 1992 Entry Draft).

			Regular Season					Playoffs				
Season	**Club**	**Lea**	**GP**	**G**	**A**	**TP**	**PIM**	**GP**	**G**	**A**	**TP**	**PIM**
1990-91	St-Jean	QMJHL	67	1	8	9	73	....	....	....	....	....
1991-92	St-Jean	QMJHL	68	1	17	18	180	....	....	....	....	....
1992-93	St-Jean	QMJHL	70	3	34	37	147	4	0	0	0	12
	Fredericton	AHL	2	1	0	1	2	4	0	0	0	0
1993-94	**Montreal**	**NHL**	**7**	**1**	**2**	**3**	**20**	....	....	....	....	....
	Fredericton	AHL	70	2	12	14	183	....	....	....	....	....
1994-95	Fredericton	AHL	75	1	9	10	184	9	0	1	1	8
	NHL Totals		**7**	**1**	**2**	**3**	**20**	....	....	....	....	....

PRPIC, JOEL (puhr-PIHCH) — BOS.

Center. Shoots left. 6'6", 200 lbs. Born, Sudbury, Ont., September 25, 1974.
(Boston's 9th choice, 233rd overall, in 1993 Entry Draft).

			Regular Season					Playoffs				
Season	**Club**	**Lea**	**GP**	**G**	**A**	**TP**	**PIM**	**GP**	**G**	**A**	**TP**	**PIM**
1993-94	St. Lawrence	ECAC	31	2	4	6	90	....	....	....	....	....
1994-95	St. Lawrence	ECAC	32	7	10	17	62	....	....	....	....	....

PURINTAN, DALE — NYR

Defense. Shoots left. 6'2", 190 lbs. Born, Fort Wayne, IN, October 11, 1976.
(NY Rangers' 5th choice, 117th overall, in 1995 Entry Draft).

			Regular Season					Playoffs				
Season	**Club**	**Lea**	**GP**	**G**	**A**	**TP**	**PIM**	**GP**	**G**	**A**	**TP**	**PIM**
1993-94	Vernon	Jr. A	42	1	6	7	194	....	....	....	....	....
1994-95	Tacoma	WHL	65	0	8	8	291	3	0	0	0	13

PUSHOR, JAMIE (PUH-shohr) — DET.

Defense. Shoots right. 6'3", 192 lbs. Born, Lethbridge, Alta., February 11, 1973.
(Detroit's 2nd choice, 32nd overall, in 1991 Entry Draft).

			Regular Season					Playoffs				
Season	**Club**	**Lea**	**GP**	**G**	**A**	**TP**	**PIM**	**GP**	**G**	**A**	**TP**	**PIM**
1989-90	Lethbridge	WHL	10	0	2	2	2	....	....	....	....	....
1990-91	Lethbridge	WHL	71	1	13	14	193	....	....	....	....	....
1991-92	Lethbridge	WHL	49	2	15	17	232	5	0	0	0	33
1992-93	Lethbridge	WHL	72	6	22	28	200	4	0	1	1	9
1993-94	Adirondack	AHL	73	1	17	18	124	12	0	0	0	22
1994-95	Adirondack	AHL	58	2	11	13	129	4	0	1	1	0

PYSZ, PATRIK (PIHSH) — CHI.

Center. Shoots left. 5'11", 187 lbs. Born, Nowy Targ, Poland, January 15, 1975.
(Chicago's 6th choice, 102nd overall, in 1993 Entry Draft).

			Regular Season					Playoffs				
Season	**Club**	**Lea**	**GP**	**G**	**A**	**TP**	**PIM**	**GP**	**G**	**A**	**TP**	**PIM**
1992-93	Augsburg	Ger. 2	36	7	5	12	12	8	2	1	3	0
1993-94	Augsburg	Aut.	41	7	20	27	....	9	5	5	10	8
1994-95	Augsburg	Ger.	41	5	13	18	61	5	0	2	2	6

QUINN, DAN — OTT.

Center. Shoots left. 5'11", 182 lbs. Born, Ottawa, Ont., June 1, 1965.
(Calgary's 1st choice, 13th overall, in 1983 Entry Draft).

			Regular Season					Playoffs				
Season	Club	Lea	GP	G	A	TP	PIM	GP	G	A	TP	PIM
1981-82	Belleville	OHL	67	19	32	51	41	....	....	....	....	....
1982-83	Belleville	OHL	70	59	88	147	27	4	2	6	8	2
1983-84	**Calgary**	**NHL**	**54**	**19**	**33**	**52**	**20**	**8**	**3**	**5**	**8**	**4**
	Belleville	OHL	24	23	36	59	12	....	....	....	....	....
1984-85	**Calgary**	**NHL**	**74**	**20**	**38**	**58**	**22**	**3**	**0**	**0**	**0**	**0**
1985-86	**Calgary**	**NHL**	**78**	**30**	**42**	**72**	**44**	**18**	**8**	**7**	**15**	**10**
1986-87	**Calgary**	**NHL**	**16**	**3**	**6**	**9**	**14**	....	....	....	....	....
	Pittsburgh	**NHL**	**64**	**28**	**43**	**71**	**40**	....	....	....	....	....
1987-88	**Pittsburgh**	**NHL**	**70**	**40**	**39**	**79**	**50**	....	....	....	....	....
1988-89	**Pittsburgh**	**NHL**	**79**	**34**	**60**	**94**	**102**	**11**	**6**	**3**	**9**	**10**
1989-90	**Pittsburgh**	**NHL**	**41**	**9**	**20**	**29**	**22**	....	....	....	....	....
	Vancouver	**NHL**	**37**	**16**	**18**	**34**	**27**	....	....	....	....	....
1990-91	**Vancouver**	**NHL**	**64**	**18**	**31**	**49**	**46**	....	....	....	....	....
	St. Louis	**NHL**	**14**	**4**	**7**	**11**	**20**	**13**	**4**	**7**	**11**	**32**
1991-92	**Philadelphia**	**NHL**	**67**	**11**	**26**	**37**	**26**	....	....	....	....	....
1992-93	**Minnesota**	**NHL**	**11**	**0**	**4**	**4**	**6**	....	....	....	....	....
1993-94	Bern	Switz.	25	13	18	31	56	....	....	....	....	....
	Ottawa	**NHL**	**13**	**7**	**0**	**7**	**6**	....	....	....	....	....
1994-95	Zug	Switz.	7	7	6	13	26	....	....	....	....	....
	Los Angeles	**NHL**	**44**	**14**	**17**	**31**	**32**	....	....	....	....	....
	NHL Totals		**726**	**253**	**384**	**637**	**477**	**53**	**21**	**22**	**43**	**56**

Traded to **Pittsburgh** by **Calgary** for Mike Bullard, November 12, 1986. Traded to **Vancouver** by **Pittsburgh** with Dave Capuano and Andrew McBain for Rod Buskas, Barry Pederson and Tony Tanti, January 8, 1990. Traded to **St. Louis** by **Vancouver** with Garth Butcher for Geoff Courtnall, Robert Dirk, Sergio Momesso, Cliff Ronning and St. Louis' fifth round choice (Brian Loney) in 1992 Entry Draft, March 5, 1991. Traded to **Philadelphia** by **St. Louis** with Rod Brind'Amour for Ron Sutter and Murray Baron, September 22, 1991. Signed as a free agent by **Minnesota**, October 4, 1992. Signed as a free agent by **Ottawa**, March 15, 1994. Signed as a free agent by **Los Angeles**, September 3, 1994. Signed as a free agent by **Ottawa**, August 1, 1995.

QUINNEY, KEN — (KWIH-nee)

Right wing. Shoots right. 5'10", 186 lbs. Born, New Westminster, B.C., May 23, 1965.
(Quebec's 9th choice, 203rd overall, in 1984 Entry Draft).

			Regular Season					Playoffs				
Season	Club	Lea	GP	G	A	TP	PIM	GP	G	A	TP	PIM
1981-82	Calgary	WHL	63	11	17	28	55	2	0	0	0	15
1982-83	Calgary	WHL	71	26	25	51	71	16	6	1	7	46
1983-84	Calgary	WHL	71	64	54	118	38	4	5	2	7	0
1984-85a	Calgary	WHL	56	47	67	114	65	7	6	4	10	15
1985-86	Fredericton	AHL	61	11	26	37	34	6	2	2	4	9
1986-87	**Quebec**	**NHL**	**25**	**2**	**7**	**9**	**16**	....	....	....	....	....
	Fredericton	AHL	48	14	27	41	20	....	....	....	....	....
1987-88	**Quebec**	**NHL**	**15**	**2**	**2**	**4**	**5**	....	....	....	....	....
	Fredericton	AHL	58	37	39	76	39	13	3	5	8	35
1988-89	Halifax	AHL	72	41	49	90	65	4	3	0	3	0
1989-90	Halifax	AHL	44	9	16	25	63	2	0	0	0	2
1990-91	**Quebec**	**NHL**	**19**	**3**	**4**	**7**	**2**	....	....	....	....	....
	Halifax	AHL	44	20	20	40	76	....	....	....	....	....
1991-92	Adirondack	AHL	63	31	29	60	33	19	7	12	19	9
1992-93	Adirondack	AHL	63	32	34	66	15	10	2	9	11	9
1993-94b	Las Vegas	IHL	79	*55	53	108	52	5	3	3	6	2
1994-95	Las Vegas	IHL	78	40	42	82	40	10	3	2	5	9
	NHL Totals		**59**	**7**	**13**	**20**	**23**	....	....	....	....	....

a WHL East First All-Star Team (1985)
b IHL First All-Star Team (1994)

Signed as a free agent by **Detroit**, August 12, 1991.

QUINT, DERON — WPG.

Defense. Shoots left. 6'1", 182 lbs. Born, Durham, NH, March 12, 1976.
(Winnipeg's 1st choice, 30th overall, in 1994 Entry Draft).

			Regular Season					Playoffs				
Season	Club	Lea	GP	G	A	TP	PIM	GP	G	A	TP	PIM
1993-94	Seattle	WHL	63	15	29	44	47	9	4	12	16	8
1994-95a	Seattle	WHL	65	29	60	89	82	3	1	2	3	6

a WHL West First All-Star Team (1995)

QUINTAL, STEPHANE — (KAYN-tahl) MTL.

Defense. Shoots right. 6'3", 215 lbs. Born, Boucherville, Que., October 22, 1968.
(Boston's 2nd choice, 14th overall, in 1987 Entry Draft).

			Regular Season					Playoffs				
Season	Club	Lea	GP	G	A	TP	PIM	GP	G	A	TP	PIM
1985-86	Granby	QMJHL	67	2	17	19	144	....	....	....	....	....
1986-87a	Granby	QMJHL	67	13	41	54	178	8	0	9	9	10
1987-88	Hull	QMJHL	38	13	23	36	138	19	7	12	19	30
1988-89	**Boston**	**NHL**	**26**	**0**	**1**	**1**	**29**	....	....	....	....	....
	Maine	AHL	16	4	10	14	28	....	....	....	....	....
1989-90	**Boston**	**NHL**	**38**	**2**	**2**	**4**	**22**	....	....	....	....	....
	Maine	AHL	37	4	16	20	27	....	....	....	....	....
1990-91	**Boston**	**NHL**	**45**	**2**	**6**	**8**	**89**	**3**	**0**	**1**	**1**	**7**
	Maine	AHL	23	1	5	6	30	....	....	....	....	....
1991-92	**Boston**	**NHL**	**49**	**4**	**10**	**14**	**77**	....	....	....	....	....
	St. Louis	**NHL**	**26**	**0**	**6**	**6**	**32**	**4**	**1**	**2**	**3**	**6**
1992-93	**St. Louis**	**NHL**	**75**	**1**	**10**	**11**	**100**	**9**	**0**	**0**	**0**	**8**
1993-94	**Winnipeg**	**NHL**	**81**	**8**	**18**	**26**	**119**	....	....	....	....	....
1994-95	**Winnipeg**	**NHL**	**43**	**6**	**17**	**23**	**78**	....	....	....	....	....
	NHL Totals		**383**	**23**	**70**	**93**	**546**	**16**	**1**	**3**	**4**	**21**

a QMJHL First All-Star Team (1987)

Traded to **St. Louis** by **Boston** with Craig Janney for Adam Oates, February 7, 1992. Traded to **Winnipeg** by **St. Louis** with Nelson Emerson for Phil Housley, September 24, 1993. Traded to **Montreal** by **Winnipeg** for Montreal's second round choice (Jason Doig) in 1995 Entry Draft, July 8, 1995.

QUINTIN, JEAN-FRANCOIS

Left wing. Shoots left. 6', 187 lbs. Born, St. Jean, Que., May 28, 1969.
(Minnesota's 4th choice, 75th overall, in 1989 Entry Draft).

			Regular Season					Playoffs				
Season	Club	Lea	GP	G	A	TP	PIM	GP	G	A	TP	PIM
1987-88	Shawinigan	QMJHL	70	28	70	98	143	11	5	8	13	26
1988-89	Shawinigan	QMJHL	69	52	100	152	105	10	9	15	24	16
1989-90	Kalamazoo	IHL	68	20	18	38	38	10	8	4	12	14
1990-91	Kalamazoo	IHL	78	31	43	74	64	9	1	5	6	11
1991-92	**San Jose**	**NHL**	**8**	**3**	**0**	**3**	**0**	....	....	....	....	....
	Kansas City	IHL	21	4	6	10	29	13	2	10	12	29
1992-93	**San Jose**	**NHL**	**14**	**2**	**5**	**7**	**4**	....	....	....	....	....
	Kansas City	IHL	64	20	29	49	169	11	2	1	3	16
1993-94	Kansas City	IHL	41	14	19	33	117	....	....	....	....	....
1994-95	Kansas City	IHL	63	23	35	58	130	19	2	9	11	57
	NHL Totals		**22**	**5**	**5**	**10**	**4**	....	....	....	....	....

Claimed by **San Jose** from **Minnesota** in Dispersal Draft, May 30, 1991.

RABY, MATHIEU — T.B.

Defense. Shoots right. 6'2", 204 lbs. Born, Hull, Que., January 19, 1975.
(Tampa Bay's 7th choice, 159th overall, in 1993 Entry Draft).

			Regular Season					Playoffs				
Season	Club	Lea	GP	G	A	TP	PIM	GP	G	A	TP	PIM
1992-93	Victoriaville	QMJHL	53	2	2	4	103	2	0	0	0	0
1993-94	Victoriaville	QMJHL	67	3	7	10	264	5	0	0	0	22
1994-95	Victoriaville	QMJHL	38	5	11	16	238	....	....	....	....	....
	Sherbrooke	QMJHL	25	2	2	4	106	7	0	1	1	24

RACINE, YVES — (ruh-SEEN, EEV) MTL.

Defense. Shoots left. 6', 205 lbs. Born, Matane, Que., February 7, 1969.
(Detroit's 1st choice, 11th overall, in 1987 Entry Draft).

			Regular Season					Playoffs				
Season	Club	Lea	GP	G	A	TP	PIM	GP	G	A	TP	PIM
1986-87	Longueuil	QMJHL	70	7	43	50	50	20	3	11	14	14
1987-88a	Victoriaville	QMJHL	69	10	84	94	150	5	0	0	0	13
	Adirondack	AHL	....	....	....	....	....	9	4	2	6	2
1988-89a	Victoriaville	QMJHL	63	23	85	108	95	16	3	*30	*33	41
	Adirondack	AHL	....	....	....	....	....	2	1	1	2	0
1989-90	**Detroit**	**NHL**	**28**	**4**	**9**	**13**	**23**	....	....	....	....	....
	Adirondack	AHL	46	8	27	35	31	....	....	....	....	....
1990-91	**Detroit**	**NHL**	**62**	**7**	**40**	**47**	**33**	**7**	**2**	**0**	**2**	**0**
	Adirondack	AHL	16	3	9	12	10	....	....	....	....	....
1991-92	**Detroit**	**NHL**	**61**	**2**	**22**	**24**	**94**	**11**	**2**	**1**	**3**	**10**
1992-93	**Detroit**	**NHL**	**80**	**9**	**31**	**40**	**80**	**7**	**1**	**3**	**4**	**27**
1993-94	**Philadelphia**	**NHL**	**67**	**9**	**43**	**52**	**48**	....	....	....	....	....
1994-95	**Montreal**	**NHL**	**47**	**4**	**7**	**11**	**42**	....	....	....	....	....
	NHL Totals		**345**	**35**	**152**	**187**	**320**	**25**	**5**	**4**	**9**	**37**

a QMJHL First-All Star Team (1988, 1989)

Traded to **Philadelphia** by **Detroit** with Detroit's fourth round choice (Sebastien Vallee) in 1994 Entry Draft for Terry Carkner, October 5, 1993. Traded to **Montreal** by **Philadelphia** for Kevin Haller, June 29, 1994.

RAGNARSSON, MARCUS — S.J.

Defense. Shoots left. 6'1", 200 lbs. Born, Ostervala, Sweden, August 13, 1971.
(San Jose's 5th choice, 99th overall, in 1992 Entry Draft).

			Regular Season					Playoffs				
Season	Club	Lea	GP	G	A	TP	PIM	GP	G	A	TP	PIM
1989-90	Djurgarden	Swe.	13	0	2	2	0	1	0	0	0	0
1990-91	Djurgarden	Swe.	35	4	1	5	12	7	0	0	0	6
1991-92	Djurgarden	Swe.	40	8	5	13	14	10	0	1	1	4
1992-93	Djurgarden	Swe.	35	3	3	6	53	6	0	3	3	8
1993-94	Djurgarden	Swe.	19	0	4	4	24	....	....	....	....	....
1994-95	Djurgarden	Swe.	38	7	9	16	20	3	0	0	0	4

RAITANEN, RAULI — WPG.

Center. Shoots left. 6'2", 187 lbs. Born, Pori, Finland, January 14, 1970.
(Winnipeg's 10th choice, 182nd overall, in 1990 Entry Draft).

			Regular Season					Playoffs				
Season	Club	Lea	GP	G	A	TP	PIM	GP	G	A	TP	PIM
1987-88	Assat	Fin.	18	1	5	6	2	....	....	....	....	....
1988-89	Assat	Fin.	40	21	17	38	18	....	....	....	....	....
1989-90	Assat	Fin. 2	41	17	44	61	20	....	....	....	....	....
1990-91	Assat	Fin.	43	6	16	22	14	....	....	....	....	....
1991-92	Assat	Fin.	41	12	22	34	34	8	1	5	6	2
1992-93	Assat	Fin.	43	15	20	35	28	8	0	4	4	6
1993-94	Assat	Fin.	48	15	25	40	50	5	1	1	2	4
1994-95	Assat	Fin.	50	17	18	35	70	6	0	2	2	2

RAJAMAKI, TOMMI — TOR.

Defense. Shoots left. 6'2", 180 lbs. Born, Pori, Finland, February 29, 1976.
(Toronto's 6th choice, 178th overall, in 1994 Entry Draft).

			Regular Season					Playoffs				
Season	Club	Lea	GP	G	A	TP	PIM	GP	G	A	TP	PIM
1993-94	Assat Jr.	Fin.	27	2	8	10	34	....	....	....	....	....
1994-95	Assat Jr.	Fin.	29	11	17	28	30	....	....	....	....	....
	Assat	Fin.	12	4	1	5	8	7	0	1	1	2

RAJNOHA, PAVEL — CGY.

Defense. Shoots right. 6', 185 lbs. Born, Gottwaldov, Czech., February 23, 1974.
(Calgary's 8th choice, 150th overall, in 1992 Entry Draft).

			Regular Season					Playoffs				
Season	Club	Lea	GP	G	A	TP	PIM	GP	G	A	TP	PIM
1990-91	TJ Zlin	Czech.	6	0	0	0	4	....	....	....	....	....
1991-92	ZPS Zlin	Czech.	24	0	1	1	4	....	....	....	....	....
1992-93	ZPS Zlin	Czech.	26	2	1	3	....	....	....	....	....	....
1993-94	ZPS Zlin	Czech.	28	2	1	3	0	3	0	4	4	....
1994-95	ZPS Zlin	Czech.	29	0	6	6	22	....	....	....	....	....

RAMSEY, MIKE
DET.

Defense. Shoots left. 6'3", 195 lbs.   Born, Minneapolis, MN, December 3, 1960.
(Buffalo's 1st choice, 11th overall, in 1979 Entry Draft).

			Regular Season					Playoffs				
Season	Club	Lea	GP	G	A	TP	PIM	GP	G	A	TP	PIM
1978-79	U. Minnesota	WCHA	26	6	11	17	30	....	....	....	....	....
1979-80	U.S. National	....	56	11	22	33	55	....	....	....	....	....
	U.S. Olympic	....	7	0	2	2	8	....	....	....	....	....
	Buffalo	**NHL**	13	1	6	7	6	13	1	2	3	12
1980-81	**Buffalo**	**NHL**	72	3	14	17	56	8	0	3	3	20
1981-82	**Buffalo**	**NHL**	80	7	23	30	56	4	1	1	2	14
1982-83	**Buffalo**	**NHL**	77	8	30	38	55	10	4	4	8	15
1983-84	**Buffalo**	**NHL**	72	9	22	31	82	3	0	1	1	6
1984-85	**Buffalo**	**NHL**	79	8	22	30	102	5	0	1	1	23
1985-86	**Buffalo**	**NHL**	76	7	21	28	117	....	....	....	....	....
1986-87	**Buffalo**	**NHL**	80	8	31	39	109	....	....	....	....	....
1987-88	**Buffalo**	**NHL**	63	5	16	21	77	6	0	3	3	29
1988-89	**Buffalo**	**NHL**	56	2	14	16	84	5	1	0	1	11
1989-90	**Buffalo**	**NHL**	73	4	21	25	47	6	0	1	1	8
1990-91	**Buffalo**	**NHL**	71	6	14	20	46	5	1	0	1	12
1991-92	**Buffalo**	**NHL**	66	3	14	17	67	7	0	2	2	8
1992-93	**Buffalo**	**NHL**	33	2	8	10	20	....	....	....	....	....
	Pittsburgh	**NHL**	12	1	2	3	8	12	0	6	6	4
1993-94	**Pittsburgh**	**NHL**	65	2	2	4	22	1	0	0	0	0
1994-95	**Detroit**	**NHL**	33	1	2	3	23	15	0	1	1	4
	NHL Totals		**1021**	**77**	**262**	**339**	**977**	**100**	**8**	**25**	**33**	**166**

Played in NHL All-Star Game (1982, 1983, 1985, 1986).

Traded to **Pittsburgh** by **Buffalo** for Bob Errey, March 22, 1993. Signed as a free agent by **Detroit**, August 3, 1994.

RANHEIM, PAUL
HFD.

Left wing. Shoots right. 6', 195 lbs.   Born, St. Louis, MO, January 25, 1966.
(Calgary's 3rd choice, 38th overall, in 1984 Entry Draft).

			Regular Season					Playoffs				
Season	Club	Lea	GP	G	A	TP	PIM	GP	G	A	TP	PIM
1984-85	U. Wisconsin	WCHA	42	11	11	22	40	....	....	....	....	....
1985-86	U. Wisconsin	WCHA	33	17	17	34	34	....	....	....	....	....
1986-87a	U. Wisconsin	WCHA	42	24	35	59	54	....	....	....	....	....
1987-88bc	U. Wisconsin	WCHA	44	36	26	62	63	....	....	....	....	....
1988-89	**Calgary**	**NHL**	5	0	0	0	0	....	....	....	....	....
de	Salt Lake	IHL	75	*68	29	97	16	14	5	5	10	8
1989-90	**Calgary**	**NHL**	80	26	28	54	23	6	1	3	4	2
1990-91	**Calgary**	**NHL**	39	14	16	30	4	7	2	2	4	0
1991-92	**Calgary**	**NHL**	80	23	20	43	32	....	....	....	....	....
1992-93	**Calgary**	**NHL**	83	21	22	43	26	6	0	1	1	0
1993-94	**Calgary**	**NHL**	67	10	14	24	20	....	....	....	....	....
	Hartford	**NHL**	15	0	3	3	2	....	....	....	....	....
1994-95	**Hartford**	**NHL**	47	6	14	20	10	....	....	....	....	....
	NHL Totals		**416**	**100**	**117**	**217**	**117**	**19**	**3**	**6**	**9**	**2**

a WCHA Second All-Star Team (1987)
b NCAA West First All-American Team (1988)
c WCHA First All-Star Team (1988)
d IHL Second All-Star Team (1989)
e Won Garry F. Longman Memorial Trophy (Top Rookie - IHL) (1989)

Traded to **Hartford** by **Calgary** with Gary Suter and Ted Drury for James Patrick, Zarley Zalapski and Michael Nylander, March 10, 1994.

RAPPANA, KEVIN
ST.L.

Defense. Shoots right. 6'2", 182 lbs.   Born, Duluth, MN, January 24, 1973.
(St. Louis' 11th choice, 241st overall, in 1991 Entry Draft).

			Regular Season					Playoffs				
Season	Club	Lea	GP	G	A	TP	PIM	GP	G	A	TP	PIM
1992-93	North Dakota	WCHA	12	0	0	0	0	....	....	....	....	....
1993-94	North Dakota	WCHA	28	0	2	2	63	....	....	....	....	....
1994-95	North Dakota	WCHA	36	2	3	5	92	....	....	....	....	....

RATHJE, MIKE
(RATH-jee)   S.J.

Defense. Shoots left. 6'6", 220 lbs.   Born, Mannville, Alta., May 11, 1974.
(San Jose's 1st choice, 3rd overall, in 1992 Entry Draft).

			Regular Season					Playoffs				
Season	Club	Lea	GP	G	A	TP	PIM	GP	G	A	TP	PIM
1990-91	Medicine Hat	WHL	64	1	16	17	28	12	0	4	4	2
1991-92a	Medicine Hat	WHL	67	11	23	34	109	4	0	1	1	2
1992-93a	Medicine Hat	WHL	57	12	37	49	103	10	3	3	6	12
	Kansas City	IHL	....	....	....	....	....	5	0	0	0	12
1993-94	**San Jose**	**NHL**	47	1	9	10	59	1	0	0	0	0
	Kansas City	IHL	6	0	2	2	0	....	....	....	....	....
1994-95	**San Jose**	**NHL**	42	2	7	9	29	11	5	2	7	4
	Kansas City	IHL	6	0	1	1	7	....	....	....	....	....
	NHL Totals		**89**	**3**	**16**	**19**	**88**	**12**	**5**	**2**	**7**	**4**

a WHL East Second All-Star Team (1992, 1993)

RAY, ROB
BUF.

Left wing. Shoots left. 6', 203 lbs.   Born, Belleville, Ont., June 8, 1968.
(Buffalo's 5th choice, 97th overall, in 1988 Entry Draft).

			Regular Season					Playoffs				
Season	Club	Lea	GP	G	A	TP	PIM	GP	G	A	TP	PIM
1985-86	Cornwall	OHL	53	6	13	19	253	6	0	0	0	26
1986-87	Cornwall	OHL	46	17	20	37	158	5	1	1	2	16
1987-88	Cornwall	OHL	61	11	41	52	179	11	2	3	5	33
1988-89	Rochester	AHL	74	11	18	29	*446	....	....	....	....	....
1989-90	**Buffalo**	**NHL**	27	2	1	3	99	....	....	....	....	....
	Rochester	AHL	43	2	13	15	335	17	1	3	4	115
1990-91	**Buffalo**	**NHL**	66	8	8	16	*350	6	1	1	2	56
	Rochester	AHL	8	1	1	2	15	....	....	....	....	....
1991-92	**Buffalo**	**NHL**	63	5	3	8	354	7	0	0	0	2
1992-93	**Buffalo**	**NHL**	68	3	2	5	211	....	....	....	....	....
1993-94	**Buffalo**	**NHL**	82	3	4	7	274	7	1	0	1	43
1994-95	**Buffalo**	**NHL**	47	0	3	3	173	5	0	0	0	14
	NHL Totals		**353**	**21**	**21**	**42**	**1461**	**25**	**2**	**1**	**3**	**115**

RECCHI, MARK
(REH-kee)   MTL.

Right wing. Shoots left. 5'10", 185 lbs.   Born, Kamloops, B.C., February 1, 1968.
(Pittsburgh's 4th choice, 67th overall, in 1988 Entry Draft).

			Regular Season					Playoffs				
Season	Club	Lea	GP	G	A	TP	PIM	GP	G	A	TP	PIM
1985-86	N. Westminster	WHL	72	21	40	61	55	....	....	....	....	....
1986-87	Kamloops	WHL	40	26	50	76	63	13	3	16	19	17
1987-88a	Kamloops	WHL	62	61	*93	154	75	17	10	*21	*31	18
1988-89	**Pittsburgh**	**NHL**	15	1	1	2	0	....	....	....	....	....
b	Muskegon	IHL	63	50	49	99	86	14	7	*14	*21	28
1989-90	**Pittsburgh**	**NHL**	74	30	37	67	44	....	....	....	....	....
	Muskegon	IHL	4	7	4	11	2	....	....	....	....	....
1990-91	**Pittsburgh**	**NHL**	78	40	73	113	48	24	10	24	34	33
1991-92	**Pittsburgh**	**NHL**	58	33	37	70	78	....	....	....	....	....
c	**Philadelphia**	**NHL**	22	10	17	27	18	....	....	....	....	....
1992-93	**Philadelphia**	**NHL**	84	53	70	123	95	....	....	....	....	....
1993-94	**Philadelphia**	**NHL**	84	40	67	107	46	....	....	....	....	....
1994-95	**Philadelphia**	**NHL**	10	2	3	5	12	....	....	....	....	....
	Montreal	**NHL**	39	14	29	43	16	....	....	....	....	....
	NHL Totals		**464**	**223**	**334**	**557**	**357**	**24**	**10**	**24**	**34**	**33**

a WHL West All-Star Team (1988)
b IHL Second All-Star Team (1989)
c NHL Second All-Star Team (1992)
Played in NHL All-Star Game (1991, 1993, 1994)

Traded to **Philadelphia** by **Pittsburgh** with Brian Benning and Los Angeles' first round choice (previously acquired by Pittsburgh — Philadelphia selected Jason Bowen) in 1992 Entry Draft for Rick Tocchet, Kjell Samuelsson, Ken Wregget and Philadelphia's third round choice (Dave Roche) in 1993 Entry Draft, February 19, 1992. Traded to **Montreal** by **Philadelphia** with Philadelphia's third round choice (Martin Hohenberger) in 1995 Entry Draft for Eric Desjardins, Gilbert Dionne and John LeClair, February 9, 1995.

REDDEN, WADE
NYI

Defense. Shoots left. 6'2", 193 lbs.   Born, Lloydminster, Sask., June 12, 1977.
(NY Islanders' 1st choice, 2nd overall, in 1995 Entry Draft).

			Regular Season					Playoffs				
Season	Club	Lea	GP	G	A	TP	PIM	GP	G	A	TP	PIM
1993-94	Brandon	WHL	63	4	35	39	98	14	2	4	6	10
1994-95a	Brandon	WHL	64	14	46	60	83	18	5	10	15	8

a WHL East Second All-Star Team (1995)

REDMOND, KEITH
L.A.

Left wing. Shoots left. 6'3", 208 lbs.   Born, Richmond Hill, Ont., October 25, 1972.
(Los Angeles' 4th choice, 79th overall, in 1991 Entry Draft).

			Regular Season					Playoffs				
Season	Club	Lea	GP	G	A	TP	PIM	GP	G	A	TP	PIM
1990-91	Bowling Green	CCHA	35	1	3	4	72	....	....	....	....	....
1991-92	Bowling Green	CCHA	8	0	0	0	14	....	....	....	....	....
	Belleville	OHL	16	1	7	8	52	....	....	....	....	....
	Detroit	OHL	25	6	12	18	61	7	1	3	4	49
1992-93	Phoenix	IHL	53	6	10	16	285	....	....	....	....	....
	Muskegon	ColHL	4	1	0	1	46	....	....	....	....	....
1993-94	**Los Angeles**	**NHL**	12	1	0	1	20	....	....	....	....	....
	Phoenix	IHL	43	8	10	18	196	....	....	....	....	....
1994-95	Phoenix	IHL	20	0	3	3	81	6	2	1	3	29
	NHL Totals		**12**	**1**	**0**	**1**	**20**	....	....	....	....	....

REEKIE, JOE
WSH.

Defense. Shoots left. 6'3", 220 lbs.   Born, Victoria, B.C., February 22, 1965.
(Buffalo's 6th choice, 119th overall, in 1985 Entry Draft).

			Regular Season					Playoffs				
Season	Club	Lea	GP	G	A	TP	PIM	GP	G	A	TP	PIM
1982-83	North Bay	OHL	59	2	9	11	49	8	0	1	1	11
1983-84	North Bay	OHL	9	1	0	1	18	....	....	....	....	....
	Cornwall	OHL	53	6	27	33	166	3	0	0	0	4
1984-85	Cornwall	OHL	65	19	63	82	134	9	4	13	17	18
1985-86	**Buffalo**	**NHL**	3	0	0	0	14	....	....	....	....	....
	Rochester	AHL	77	3	25	28	178	....	....	....	....	....
1986-87	**Buffalo**	**NHL**	56	1	8	9	82	....	....	....	....	....
	Rochester	AHL	22	0	6	6	52	....	....	....	....	....
1987-88	**Buffalo**	**NHL**	30	1	4	5	68	2	0	0	0	4
1988-89	**Buffalo**	**NHL**	15	1	3	4	26	....	....	....	....	....
	Rochester	AHL	21	1	2	3	56	....	....	....	....	....
1989-90	**NY Islanders**	**NHL**	31	1	8	9	43	....	....	....	....	....
	Springfield	AHL	15	1	4	5	24	....	....	....	....	....
1990-91	**NY Islanders**	**NHL**	66	3	16	19	96	....	....	....	....	....
	Capital Dist.	AHL	2	1	0	1	0	....	....	....	....	....
1991-92	**NY Islanders**	**NHL**	54	4	12	16	85	....	....	....	....	....
	Capital Dist.	AHL	3	2	2	4	2	....	....	....	....	....
1992-93	**Tampa Bay**	**NHL**	42	2	11	13	69	....	....	....	....	....
1993-94	**Tampa Bay**	**NHL**	73	1	11	12	127	....	....	....	....	....
	Washington	**NHL**	12	0	5	5	29	11	2	1	3	29
1994-95	**Washington**	**NHL**	48	1	6	7	97	7	0	0	0	2
	NHL Totals		**430**	**15**	**84**	**99**	**736**	**20**	**2**	**1**	**3**	**35**

Traded to **NY Islanders** by **Buffalo** for NY Islanders' sixth round choice (Bill Pye) in 1989 Entry Draft, June 17, 1989. Claimed by **Tampa Bay** from **NY Islanders** in Expansion Draft, June 18, 1992. Traded to **Washington** by **Tampa Bay** for Enrico Ciccone, Washington's third round choice (later traded to Anaheim — Anaheim selected Craig Reichert) in 1994 Entry Draft and the return of future draft choices transferred in the Pat Elynuik trade, March 21, 1994.

REGNIER, CURT
(REHN-yay)   N.J.

Left wing. Shoots left. 6'2", 220 lbs.   Born, Prince Albert, Sask., January 24, 1972.
(New Jersey's 6th choice, 121st overall, in 1991 Entry Draft).

			Regular Season					Playoffs				
Season	Club	Lea	GP	G	A	TP	PIM	GP	G	A	TP	PIM
1990-91	Prince Albert	WHL	69	20	39	59	40	3	2	2	4	6
1991-92	Prince Albert	WHL	58	30	42	72	98	10	1	9	10	2
1992-93	Utica	AHL	37	6	4	10	21	2	0	1	1	0
1993-94	Albany	AHL	34	12	20	32	4	....	....	....	....	....
	Raleigh	ECHL	7	6	5	11	10	16	6	9	15	6
1994-95	Albany	AHL	73	20	26	46	34	6	1	1	2	2

REHNBERG, HENRIK
N.J.

Defense. Shoots left. 6'2", 194 lbs.   Born, Grava, Sweden, July 20, 1977.
(New Jersey's 6th choice, 96th overall, in 1995 Entry Draft).

			Regular Season					Playoffs				
Season	Club	Lea	GP	G	A	TP	PIM	GP	G	A	TP	PIM
1994-95	Farjestad	Swe. Jr.	24	1	2	3	62	....	....	....	....	....

REICHEL, MARTIN (RIGH-khul) EDM.

Right wing. Shoots left. 6'1", 183 lbs. Born, Most, Czech., November 7, 1973.
(Edmonton's 2nd choice, 37th overall, in 1992 Entry Draft).

			Regular Season					Playoffs				
Season	Club	Lea	GP	G	A	TP	PIM	GP	G	A	TP	PIM
1990-91	Freiburg	Ger.	23	7	8	15	19	....	....	....	....	....
1991-92	Freiburg	Ger.	27	15	16	31	8	4	1	1	2	4
1992-93	Freiburg	Ger.	37	13	9	22	27	9	4	4	8	11
1993-94	Rosenheim	Ger.	20	5	15	20	6	....	....	....	....	....
1994-95	Rosenheim	Ger.	43	11	26	37	36	7	3	3	6	37

REICHEL, ROBERT (RIGH-khul)

Center. Shoots left. 5'10", 185 lbs. Born, Litvinov, Czech., June 25, 1971.
(Calgary's 5th choice, 70th overall, in 1989 Entry Draft).

			Regular Season					Playoffs				
Season	Club	Lea	GP	G	A	TP	PIM	GP	G	A	TP	PIM
1987-88	Litvinov	Czech.	36	17	10	27	8	....	....	....	....	....
1988-89	Litvinov	Czech.	44	23	25	48	32	....	....	....	....	....
1989-90	Litvinov	Czech.	52	*49	34	*83	....	....	....	....	....	....
1990-91	**Calgary**	**NHL**	**66**	**19**	**22**	**41**	**22**	**6**	**1**	**1**	**2**	**0**
1991-92	**Calgary**	**NHL**	**77**	**20**	**34**	**54**	**32**	....	....	....	....	....
1992-93	**Calgary**	**NHL**	**80**	**40**	**48**	**88**	**54**	**6**	**2**	**4**	**6**	**2**
1993-94	**Calgary**	**NHL**	**84**	**40**	**53**	**93**	**58**	**7**	**0**	**5**	**5**	**0**
1994-95	Frankfurt	Ger.	21	19	24	43	41	....	....	....	....	....
	Calgary	**NHL**	**48**	**18**	**17**	**35**	**28**	**7**	**2**	**4**	**6**	**4**
	NHL Totals		**355**	**137**	**174**	**311**	**194**	**26**	**5**	**14**	**19**	**6**

REICHERT, CRAIG ANA.

Right wing. Shoots right. 6'1", 196 lbs. Born, Winnipeg, Man., May 11, 1974.
(Anaheim's 3rd choice, 67th overall, in 1994 Entry Draft).

			Regular Season					Playoffs				
Season	Club	Lea	GP	G	A	TP	PIM	GP	G	A	TP	PIM
1991-92	Spokane	WHL	68	13	20	33	86	4	1	0	1	4
1992-93	Red Deer	WHL	66	32	33	65	62	4	3	1	4	2
1993-94	Red Deer	WHL	72	52	67	119	153	4	2	2	4	8
1994-95	San Diego	IHL	49	4	12	16	28	....	....	....	....	....

REID, DAVID BOS.

Left wing. Shoots left. 6'1", 217 lbs. Born, Toronto, Ont., May 15, 1964.
(Boston's 4th choice, 60th overall, in 1982 Entry Draft).

			Regular Season					Playoffs				
Season	Club	Lea	GP	G	A	TP	PIM	GP	G	A	TP	PIM
1981-82	Peterborough	OHL	68	10	32	42	41	9	2	3	5	11
1982-83	Peterborough	OHL	70	23	34	57	33	4	3	1	4	0
1983-84	**Boston**	**NHL**	**8**	**1**	**0**	**1**	**2**	....	....	....	....	....
	Peterborough	OHL	60	33	64	97	12	....	....	....	....	....
1984-85	**Boston**	**NHL**	**35**	**14**	**13**	**27**	**27**	**5**	**1**	**0**	**1**	**0**
	Hershey	AHL	43	10	14	24	6	....	....	....	....	....
1985-86	**Boston**	**NHL**	**37**	**10**	**10**	**20**	**10**	....	....	....	....	....
	Moncton	AHL	26	14	18	32	4	....	....	....	....	....
1986-87	**Boston**	**NHL**	**12**	**3**	**3**	**6**	**0**	**2**	**0**	**0**	**0**	**0**
	Moncton	AHL	40	12	22	34	23	5	0	1	1	0
1987-88	**Boston**	**NHL**	**3**	**0**	**0**	**0**	**0**	....	....	....	....	....
	Maine	AHL	63	21	37	58	40	10	6	7	13	0
1988-89	**Toronto**	**NHL**	**77**	**9**	**21**	**30**	**22**	....	....	....	....	....
1989-90	**Toronto**	**NHL**	**70**	**9**	**19**	**28**	**9**	**3**	**0**	**0**	**0**	**0**
1990-91	**Toronto**	**NHL**	**69**	**15**	**13**	**28**	**18**	....	....	....	....	....
1991-92	**Boston**	**NHL**	**43**	**7**	**7**	**14**	**27**	**15**	**2**	**5**	**7**	**4**
	Maine	AHL	12	1	5	6	4	....	....	....	....	....
1992-93	**Boston**	**NHL**	**65**	**20**	**16**	**36**	**10**	....	....	....	....	....
1993-94	**Boston**	**NHL**	**83**	**6**	**17**	**23**	**25**	**13**	**2**	**1**	**3**	**2**
1994-95	**Boston**	**NHL**	**38**	**5**	**5**	**10**	**10**	**5**	**0**	**0**	**0**	**0**
	Providence	AHL	7	3	0	3	0	....	....	....	....	....
	NHL Totals		**540**	**99**	**124**	**223**	**160**	**43**	**5**	**6**	**11**	**6**

Signed as a free agent by **Toronto**, June 23, 1988. Signed as a free agent by **Boston**, December 1, 1991.

REID, SHAWN NYR

Defense. Shoots left. 6', 200 lbs. Born, Toronto, Ont., September 21, 1970.

			Regular Season					Playoffs				
Season	Club	Lea	GP	G	A	TP	PIM	GP	G	A	TP	PIM
1990-91	Colorado	WCHA	38	10	8	18	36	....	....	....	....	....
1991-92	Colorado	WCHA	41	12	22	34	64	....	....	....	....	....
1992-93	Colorado	WCHA	32	3	11	14	54	....	....	....	....	....
1993-94ab	Colorado	WCHA	39	7	20	27	25	....	....	....	....	....
1994-95	Fort Wayne	IHL	42	4	8	12	28	....	....	....	....	....
	Binghamton	AHL	18	3	4	7	8	9	0	3	3	6

a WCHA First All-Star Team (1994)
b NCAA West First All-American Team (1994)

Signed as a free agent by **NY Rangers**, July 6, 1994.

REIMANN, DANIEL N.J.

Defense. Shoots left. 6'1", 190 lbs. Born, Fridley, MN, December 17, 1972.
(New Jersey's 9th choice, 187th overall, in 1991 Entry Draft).

			Regular Season					Playoffs				
Season	Club	Lea	GP	G	A	TP	PIM	GP	G	A	TP	PIM
1992-93	St. Cloud St.	WCHA	36	5	2	7	58	....	....	....	....	....
1993-94	St. Cloud St.	WCHA	36	1	10	11	61	....	....	....	....	....
1994-95	St. Cloud St.	WCHA	38	1	3	4	69	....	....	....	....	....

REJA, DANIEL WSH.

Center. Shoots left. 6'2", 180 lbs. Born, Toronto, Ont., May 16, 1976.
(Washington's 7th choice, 171st overall, in 1994 Entry Draft).

			Regular Season					Playoffs				
Season	Club	Lea	GP	G	A	TP	PIM	GP	G	A	TP	PIM
1993-94	London	OHL	66	15	19	34	44	5	0	0	0	6
1994-95	London	OHL	18	6	13	19	31	....	....	....	....	....
	Belleville	OHL	2	0	0	0	0	....	....	....	....	....

RENBERG, MIKAEL (REHN-buhrg) PHI.

Right wing. Shoots left. 6'1", 218 lbs. Born, Pitea, Sweden, May 5, 1972.
(Philadelphia's 3rd choice, 40th overall, in 1990 Entry Draft).

			Regular Season					Playoffs				
Season	Club	Lea	GP	G	A	TP	PIM	GP	G	A	TP	PIM
1988-89	Pitea	Swe. 2	12	6	3	9	....	....	....	....	....	....
1989-90	Pitea	Swe. 2	29	15	19	34	....	....	....	....	....	....
1990-91	Lulea	Swe.	29	11	6	17	12	5	1	1	2	4
1991-92	Lulea	Swe.	38	8	15	23	20	2	0	0	0	0
1992-93	Lulea	Swe.	39	19	13	32	61	11	4	4	8	4
1993-94a	**Philadelphia**	**NHL**	**83**	**38**	**44**	**82**	**36**	....	....	....	....	....
1994-95	Lulea	Swe.	10	9	4	13	16	....	....	....	....	....
	Philadelphia	**NHL**	**47**	**26**	**31**	**57**	**20**	**15**	**6**	**7**	**13**	**6**
	NHL Totals		**130**	**64**	**75**	**139**	**56**	**15**	**6**	**7**	**13**	**6**

a NHL/Upper Deck All-Rookie Team (1994)

REZANSOFF, JESSIE MTL.

Right wing. Shoots right. 6'4", 190 lbs. Born, Regina, Sask., January 31, 1976.
(Montreal's 9th choice, 174th overall, in 1994 Entry Draft).

			Regular Season					Playoffs				
Season	Club	Lea	GP	G	A	TP	PIM	GP	G	A	TP	PIM
1993-94	Regina	WHL	69	6	9	15	56	4	0	0	0	5
1994-95	Regina	WHL	45	8	8	16	83	....	....	....	....	....
	Swift Current	WHL	19	4	2	6	21	6	0	0	0	2

RHEAUME, PASCAL (RAY-awm) N.J.

Center. Shoots left. 6'1", 185 lbs. Born, Quebec, Que., June 21, 1973.

			Regular Season					Playoffs				
Season	Club	Lea	GP	G	A	TP	PIM	GP	G	A	TP	PIM
1991-92	Trois Rivières	QMJHL	65	17	20	37	84	14	5	4	9	23
1992-93	Sherbrooke	QMJHL	65	28	34	62	88	14	6	5	11	31
1993-94	Albany	AHL	55	17	18	35	43	5	0	1	1	0
1994-95	Albany	AHL	78	19	25	44	46	14	3	6	9	19

Signed as a free agent by **New Jersey**, October 1, 1992.

RICCI, MIKE (REE-CHEE) COL.

Center. Shoots left. 6', 190 lbs. Born, Scarborough, Ont., October 27, 1971.
(Philadelphia's 1st choice, 4th overall, in 1990 Entry Draft).

			Regular Season					Playoffs				
Season	Club	Lea	GP	G	A	TP	PIM	GP	G	A	TP	PIM
1987-88	Peterborough	OHL	41	24	37	61	20	8	5	5	10	4
1988-89a	Peterborough	OHL	60	54	52	106	43	17	19	16	35	18
1989-90bc	Peterborough	OHL	60	52	64	116	39	12	5	7	12	26
1990-91	**Philadelphia**	**NHL**	**68**	**21**	**20**	**41**	**64**	....	....	....	....	....
1991-92	**Philadelphia**	**NHL**	**78**	**20**	**36**	**56**	**93**	....	....	....	....	....
1992-93	**Quebec**	**NHL**	**77**	**27**	**51**	**78**	**123**	**6**	**0**	**6**	**6**	**8**
1993-94	**Quebec**	**NHL**	**83**	**30**	**21**	**51**	**113**	....	....	....	....	....
1994-95	**Quebec**	**NHL**	**48**	**15**	**21**	**36**	**40**	**6**	**1**	**3**	**4**	**8**
	NHL Totals		**354**	**113**	**149**	**262**	**433**	**12**	**1**	**9**	**10**	**16**

a OHL Second All-Star Team (1989)
b Canadian Major Junior Player of the Year (1990)
c OHL First All-Star Team (1990)

Traded to **Quebec** by **Philadelphia** with Peter Forsberg, Steve Duchesne, Kerry Huffman, Ron Hextall, Chris Simon, Philadelphia's first choice in the 1993 (Jocelyn Thibault) and 1994 (later traded to Toronto — later traded to Washington — Washington selected Nolan Baumgartner) Entry Drafts and cash for Eric Lindros, June 30, 1992.

RICCIARDI, JEFF (rih-CHEE-ahr-dee)

Defense. Shoots left. 5'10", 203 lbs. Born, Thunder Bay, Ont., June 22, 1971.
(Winnipeg's 8th choice, 159th overall, in 1991 Entry Draft).

			Regular Season					Playoffs				
Season	Club	Lea	GP	G	A	TP	PIM	GP	G	A	TP	PIM
1990-91	Ottawa	OHL	54	12	40	52	172	17	1	11	12	61
1991-92a	Ottawa	OHL	61	15	41	56	220	11	3	8	11	45
1992-93	Providence	AHL	3	0	0	0	0	....	....	....	....	....
	Johnstown	ECHL	61	7	29	36	248	5	2	2	4	6
1993-94	Indianapolis	IHL	75	3	20	23	307	....	....	....	....	....
1994-95	Indianapolis	IHL	60	2	11	13	187	....	....	....	....	....

a OHL Second All-Star Team (1992)

Traded to **Boston** by **Winnipeg** for future considerations, September 8, 1992. Signed as a free agent by **Chicago**, July 28, 1993.

RICE, STEVEN HFD.

Right wing. Shoots right. 6', 215 lbs. Born, Kitchener, Ont., May 26, 1971.
(NY Rangers' 1st choice, 20th overall, in 1989 Entry Draft).

			Regular Season					Playoffs				
Season	Club	Lea	GP	G	A	TP	PIM	GP	G	A	TP	PIM
1987-88	Kitchener	OHL	59	11	14	25	43	4	0	1	1	0
1988-89	Kitchener	OHL	64	36	30	66	42	5	2	1	3	8
1989-90a	Kitchener	OHL	58	39	37	76	102	16	4	8	12	24
1990-91	**NY Rangers**	**NHL**	**11**	**1**	**1**	**2**	**4**	**2**	**2**	**1**	**3**	**6**
	Binghamton	AHL	8	4	1	5	12	5	2	0	2	2
b	Kitchener	OHL	29	30	30	60	43	6	5	6	11	2
1991-92	**Edmonton**	**NHL**	**3**	**0**	**0**	**0**	**2**	....	....	....	....	....
	Cape Breton	AHL	45	32	20	52	38	5	4	4	8	10
1992-93	**Edmonton**	**NHL**	**28**	**2**	**5**	**7**	**28**	....	....	....	....	....
c	Cape Breton	AHL	51	34	28	62	63	14	4	6	10	22
1993-94	**Edmonton**	**NHL**	**63**	**17**	**15**	**32**	**36**	....	....	....	....	....
1994-95	**Hartford**	**NHL**	**40**	**11**	**10**	**21**	**61**	....	....	....	....	....
	NHL Totals		**145**	**31**	**31**	**62**	**131**	**2**	**2**	**1**	**3**	**6**

a Memorial Cup All-Star Team (1990)
b OHL Second All-Star Team (1991)
c AHL Second All-Star Team (1993)

Traded to **Edmonton** by **NY Rangers** with Bernie Nicholls and Louie DeBrusk for Mark Messier and future considerations, October 4, 1991. Signed as a free agent by **Hartford**, August 18, 1994.

RICHARDS, TRAVIS — DAL.

Defense. Shoots left. 6'1", 185 lbs. Born, Crystal, MN, March 22, 1970.
(Minnesota's 6th choice, 169th overall, in 1988 Entry Draft).

			Regular Season					Playoffs				
Season	Club	Lea	GP	G	A	TP	PIM	GP	G	A	TP	PIM
1989-90	U. Minnesota	WCHA	45	4	24	28	38	....	....	....	....	....
1990-91	U. Minnesota	WCHA	45	9	25	34	28	....	....	....	....	....
1991-92a	U. Minnesota	WCHA	41	10	22	32	65	....	....	....	....	....
1992-93a	U. Minnesota	WCHA	42	12	26	38	52	....	....	....	....	....
1993-94	U.S. National	....	51	1	11	12	38	....	....	....	....	....
	U.S. Olympic	....	8	0	0	0	2	....	....	....	....	....
	Kalamazoo	IHL	19	2	10	12	20	4	1	1	2	0
1994-95bc	Kalamazoo	IHL	63	4	16	20	53	15	1	5	6	12
	Dallas	**NHL**	**2**	**0**	**0**	**0**	**0**	....	....	....	....	....
	NHL Totals		**2**	**0**	**0**	**0**	**0**	....	....	....	....	....

a WCHA Second All-Star Team (1992, 1993)
b IHL FIrst All-Star Team (1995)
c Won Governors' Trophy (Outstanding Defenseman - IHL) (1995)

RICHARDSON, LUKE — EDM.

Defense. Shoots left. 6'4", 210 lbs. Born, Ottawa, Ont., March 26, 1969.
(Toronto's 1st choice, 7th overall, in 1987 Entry Draft).

			Regular Season					Playoffs				
Season	Club	Lea	GP	G	A	TP	PIM	GP	G	A	TP	PIM
1985-86	Peterborough	OHL	63	6	18	24	57	16	2	1	3	50
1986-87	Peterborough	OHL	59	13	32	45	70	12	0	5	5	24
1987-88	**Toronto**	**NHL**	**78**	**4**	**6**	**10**	**90**	**2**	**0**	**0**	**0**	**0**
1988-89	**Toronto**	**NHL**	**55**	**2**	**7**	**9**	**106**	....	....	....	....	....
1989-90	**Toronto**	**NHL**	**67**	**4**	**14**	**18**	**122**	**5**	**0**	**0**	**0**	**22**
1990-91	**Toronto**	**NHL**	**78**	**1**	**9**	**10**	**238**	....	....	....	....	....
1991-92	**Edmonton**	**NHL**	**75**	**2**	**19**	**21**	**118**	**16**	**0**	**5**	**5**	**45**
1992-93	**Edmonton**	**NHL**	**82**	**3**	**10**	**13**	**142**	....	....	....	....	....
1993-94	**Edmonton**	**NHL**	**69**	**2**	**6**	**8**	**131**	....	....	....	....	....
1994-95	**Edmonton**	**NHL**	**46**	**3**	**10**	**13**	**40**	....	....	....	....	....
	NHL Totals		**550**	**21**	**81**	**102**	**987**	**23**	**0**	**5**	**5**	**67**

Traded to **Edmonton** by **Toronto** with Vincent Damphousse, Peter Ing, Scott Thornton, future considerations and cash for Grant Fuhr, Glenn Anderson and Craig Berube, September 19, 1991.

RICHER, STEPHANE J. G. (REE-shay)

Defense. Shoots right. 5'11", 190 lbs. Born, Hull, Que., April 28, 1966.

			Regular Season					Playoffs				
Season	Club	Lea	GP	G	A	TP	PIM	GP	G	A	TP	PIM
1986-87	Hull	QMJHL	33	6	22	28	74	8	3	4	7	17
1987-88	Baltimore	AHL	22	0	3	3	6	....	....	....	....	....
	Sherbrooke	AHL	41	4	7	11	46	5	1	0	1	10
1988-89	Sherbrooke	AHL	70	7	26	33	158	6	1	2	3	18
1989-90	Sherbrooke	AHL	60	10	12	22	85	12	4	9	13	16
1990-91	New Haven	AHL	3	0	1	1	0	....	....	....	....	....
	Phoenix	IHL	67	11	38	49	48	11	4	6	10	6
1991-92a	Fredericton	AHL	80	17	47	64	74	7	0	5	5	18
1992-93	**Tampa Bay**	**NHL**	**3**	**0**	**0**	**0**	**0**	....	....	....	....	....
	Atlanta	IHL	3	0	4	4	4	....	....	....	....	....
	Boston	**NHL**	**21**	**1**	**4**	**5**	**18**	**3**	**0**	**0**	**0**	**0**
	Providence	AHL	53	8	20	28	60	....	....	....	....	....
1993-94	**Florida**	**NHL**	**2**	**0**	**1**	**1**	**0**	....	....	....	....	....
b	Cincinnati	IHL	66	9	55	64	80	11	2	9	11	26
1994-95b	Cincinnati	IHL	80	16	53	69	67	10	2	7	9	18
	Florida	**NHL**	**1**	**0**	**0**	**0**	**2**	....	....	....	....	....
	NHL Totals		**27**	**1**	**5**	**6**	**20**	**3**	**0**	**0**	**0**	**0**

a AHL Second All-Star Team (1992)
b IHL Second All-Star Team (1994, 1995)

Signed as a free agent by **Montreal,** January 9, 1988. Signed as a free agent by **Los Angeles**, July 11, 1990. Signed as a free agent by **Tampa Bay**, July 29, 1992. Traded to **Boston** by **Tampa Bay** for Bob Beers, October 28, 1992. Claimed by **Florida** from **Boston** in Expansion Draft, June 24, 1993.

RICHER, STEPHANE J. J. (REE-shay) — N.J.

Right wing. Shoots right. 6'2", 215 lbs. Born, Ripon, Que., June 7, 1966.
(Montreal's 3rd choice, 29th overall, in 1984 Entry Draft).

			Regular Season					Playoffs				
Season	Club	Lea	GP	G	A	TP	PIM	GP	G	A	TP	PIM
1983-84a	Granby	QMJHL	67	39	37	76	58	3	1	1	2	4
1984-85	Granby	QMJHL	30	30	27	57	31	....	....	....	....	....
b	Chicoutimi	QMJHL	27	31	32	63	40	12	13	13	26	25
	Montreal	**NHL**	**1**	**0**	**0**	**0**	**0**	....	....	....	....	....
	Sherbrooke	AHL	....	....	....	....	....	9	6	3	9	10
1985-86	**Montreal**	**NHL**	**65**	**21**	**16**	**37**	**50**	**16**	**4**	**1**	**5**	**23**
1986-87	**Montreal**	**NHL**	**57**	**20**	**19**	**39**	**80**	**5**	**3**	**2**	**5**	**0**
	Sherbrooke	AHL	12	10	4	14	11	....	....	....	....	....
1987-88	**Montreal**	**NHL**	**72**	**50**	**28**	**78**	**72**	**8**	**7**	**5**	**12**	**6**
1988-89	**Montreal**	**NHL**	**68**	**25**	**35**	**60**	**61**	**21**	**6**	**5**	**11**	**14**
1989-90	**Montreal**	**NHL**	**75**	**51**	**40**	**91**	**46**	**9**	**7**	**3**	**10**	**2**
1990-91	**Montreal**	**NHL**	**75**	**31**	**30**	**61**	**53**	**13**	**9**	**5**	**14**	**6**
1991-92	**New Jersey**	**NHL**	**74**	**29**	**35**	**64**	**25**	**7**	**1**	**2**	**3**	**0**
1992-93	**New Jersey**	**NHL**	**78**	**38**	**35**	**73**	**44**	**5**	**2**	**2**	**4**	**2**
1993-94	**New Jersey**	**NHL**	**80**	**36**	**36**	**72**	**16**	**20**	**7**	**5**	**12**	**6**
1994-95	**New Jersey**	**NHL**	**45**	**23**	**16**	**39**	**10**	**19**	**6**	**15**	**21**	**2**
	NHL Totals		**690**	**324**	**290**	**614**	**457**	**123**	**52**	**45**	**97**	**61**

a QMJHL Rookie of the Year (1984)
b QMJHL Second All-Star Team (1985)

Played in NHL All-Star Game (1990)

Traded to **New Jersey** by **Montreal** with Tom Chorske for Kirk Muller and Roland Melanson, September 20, 1991.

RICHTER, BARRY — NYR

Defense. Shoots left. 6'2", 195 lbs. Born, Madison, WI, September 11, 1970.
(Hartford's 2nd choice, 32nd overall, in 1988 Entry Draft).

			Regular Season					Playoffs				
Season	Club	Lea	GP	G	A	TP	PIM	GP	G	A	TP	PIM
1989-90	U. Wisconsin	WCHA	42	13	23	36	36	....	....	....	....	....
1990-91	U. Wisconsin	WCHA	43	15	20	35	42	....	....	....	....	....
1991-92a	U. Wisconsin	WCHA	39	10	25	35	62	....	....	....	....	....
1992-93bc	U. Wisconsin	WCHA	42	14	32	46	74	....	....	....	....	....
1993-94	U.S. National	....	56	7	16	23	50	....	....	....	....	....
	U.S. Olympic	....	8	0	3	3	4	....	....	....	....	....
	Binghamton	AHL	21	0	9	9	12	....	....	....	....	....
1994-95	Binghamton	AHL	73	15	41	56	54	11	4	5	9	12

a NCAA All-Tournament Team (1992)
b WCHA First All-Star Team (1993)
c NCAA West First All-American Team (1993)

Traded to **NY Rangers** by **Hartford** with Steve Larmer, Nick Kypreos and Hartford's sixth round choice (Yuri Litvinov) in 1994 Entry Draft for Darren Turcotte and James Patrick, November 2, 1993.

RIDLEY, MIKE — VAN.

Center. Shoots left. 6', 195 lbs. Born, Winnipeg, Man., July 8, 1963.

			Regular Season					Playoffs				
Season	Club	Lea	GP	G	A	TP	PIM	GP	G	A	TP	PIM
1983-84a	U. of Manitoba	GPAC	46	39	41	80	....	....	....	....	....	....
1984-85b	U. of Manitoba	GPAC	30	29	38	67	48	....	....	....	....	....
1985-86c	**NY Rangers**	**NHL**	**80**	**22**	**43**	**65**	**69**	**16**	**6**	**8**	**14**	**26**
1986-87	**NY Rangers**	**NHL**	**38**	**16**	**20**	**36**	**20**	....	....	....	....	....
	Washington	**NHL**	**40**	**15**	**19**	**34**	**20**	**7**	**2**	**1**	**3**	**6**
1987-88	**Washington**	**NHL**	**70**	**28**	**31**	**59**	**22**	**14**	**6**	**5**	**11**	**10**
1988-89	**Washington**	**NHL**	**80**	**41**	**48**	**89**	**49**	**6**	**0**	**5**	**5**	**2**
1989-90	**Washington**	**NHL**	**74**	**30**	**43**	**73**	**27**	**14**	**3**	**4**	**7**	**8**
1990-91	**Washington**	**NHL**	**79**	**23**	**48**	**71**	**26**	**11**	**3**	**4**	**7**	**8**
1991-92	**Washington**	**NHL**	**80**	**29**	**40**	**69**	**38**	**7**	**0**	**11**	**11**	**0**
1992-93	**Washington**	**NHL**	**84**	**26**	**56**	**82**	**44**	**6**	**1**	**5**	**6**	**0**
1993-94	**Washington**	**NHL**	**81**	**26**	**44**	**70**	**24**	**11**	**4**	**6**	**10**	**6**
1994-95	**Toronto**	**NHL**	**48**	**10**	**27**	**37**	**14**	**7**	**3**	**1**	**4**	**2**
	NHL Totals		**754**	**266**	**419**	**685**	**353**	**99**	**28**	**50**	**78**	**68**

a Canadian University Player of the Year; CIAU All-Canadian, GPAC MVP and First All-Star Team (1984)
b CIAU All-Canadian, GPAC First All-Star Team (1985)
c NHL All-Rookie Team (1986)

Played in NHL All-Star Game (1989)

Signed as a free agent by **NY Rangers**, September 26, 1985. Traded to **Washington** by **NY Rangers** with Bob Crawford and Kelly Miller for Bob Carpenter and Washington's second round choice (Jason Prosofsky) in 1989 Entry Draft, January 1, 1987. Traded to **Toronto** by **Washington** with St. Louis' first round choice (previously acquired by Washington — Toronto selected Eric Fichaud) in 1994 Entry Draft for Rob Pearson and Philadelphia's first round choice (previously acquired by Toronto — Washington selected Nolan Baumgartner) in 1994 Entry Draft, June 28, 1994. Traded to **Vancouver** by **Toronto** for Sergio Momesso, July 8, 1995.

RIIHIJARVI, TEEMO (REE-ee-hee-jahr-vee) — S.J.

Left wing. Shoots left. 6'6", 202 lbs. Born, Espoo, Finland, March 1, 1977.
(San Jose's 1st choice, 12th overall, in 1995 Entry Draft).

			Regular Season					Playoffs				
Season	Club	Lea	GP	G	A	TP	PIM	GP	G	A	TP	PIM
1993-94	Espoo	Fin.	13	1	1	2	6	....	....	....	....	....
1994-95	Espoo	Fin.	13	1	0	1	4	....	....	....	....	....

RISIDORE, RYAN — HFD.

Defense. Shoots left. 6'4", 192 lbs. Born, Hamilton, Ont., April 4, 1976.
(Hartford's 3rd choice, 109th overall, in 1994 Entry Draft).

			Regular Season					Playoffs				
Season	Club	Lea	GP	G	A	TP	PIM	GP	G	A	TP	PIM
1993-94	Guelph	OHL	51	2	9	11	39	9	0	0	0	12
1994-95	Guelph	OHL	65	2	30	32	102	14	2	2	4	19

RIVERS, JAMIE — ST.L.

Defense. Shoots left. 6', 190 lbs. Born, Ottawa, Ont., March 16, 1975.
(St. Louis' 2nd choice, 63rd overall, in 1993 Entry Draft).

			Regular Season					Playoffs				
Season	Club	Lea	GP	G	A	TP	PIM	GP	G	A	TP	PIM
1991-92	Sudbury	OHL	55	3	13	16	20	8	0	0	0	0
1992-93	Sudbury	OHL	62	12	43	55	20	14	7	19	26	4
1993-94ab	Sudbury	OHL	65	32	*89	121	58	10	1	9	10	14
1994-95c	Sudbury	OHL	46	9	56	65	30	18	7	26	33	22

a OHL First All-Star Team (1994)
b Canadian Major Junior Second All-Star Team (1994)
c OHL Second All-Star Team (1995)

RIVERS, SHAWN

Defense. Shoots left. 5'10", 185 lbs. Born, Ottawa, Ont., January 30, 1971.

			Regular Season					Playoffs				
Season	Club	Lea	GP	G	A	TP	PIM	GP	G	A	TP	PIM
1988-89	St. Lawrence	ECAC	36	3	23	26	20	....	....	....	....	....
1989-90	St. Lawrence	ECAC	26	3	14	17	29	....	....	....	....	....
1990-91	Sudbury	OHL	66	18	33	51	43	5	2	7	9	0
1991-92	Sudbury	OHL	64	26	54	80	34	11	0	4	4	10
1992-93	**Tampa Bay**	**NHL**	**4**	**0**	**2**	**2**	**2**	....	....	....	....	....
	Atlanta	IHL	78	9	34	43	101	9	1	3	4	8
1993-94	Atlanta	IHL	76	6	30	36	88	12	1	4	5	21
1994-95	Chicago	IHL	68	8	29	37	69	3	0	1	1	0
	NHL Totals		**4**	**0**	**2**	**2**	**2**	....	....	....	....	....

Signed as a free agent by **Tampa Bay**, June 29, 1992.

RIVET, CRAIG — MTL.

Defense. Shoots right. 6'1", 190 lbs. Born, North Bay, Ont., September 13, 1974.
(Montreal's 4th choice, 68th overall, in 1992 Entry Draft).

			Regular Season					Playoffs				
Season	Club	Lea	GP	G	A	TP	PIM	GP	G	A	TP	PIM
1991-92	Kingston	OHL	66	5	21	26	97	....	....	....	....	....
1992-93	Kingston	OHL	64	19	55	74	117	16	5	7	12	39
1993-94	Kingston	OHL	61	12	52	64	100	6	0	3	3	6
	Fredericton	AHL	4	0	2	2	2	....	....	....	....	....
1994-95	Fredericton	AHL	78	5	27	32	126	12	0	4	4	17
	Montreal	**NHL**	**5**	**0**	**1**	**1**	**5**	....	....	....	....	....
	NHL Totals		**5**	**0**	**1**	**1**	**5**	....	....	....	....	....

ROB, LUBOS — NYR

Center. Shoots left. 5'11", 183 lbs. Born, Budejovice, Czech., August 5, 1970.
(NY Rangers' 7th choice, 99th overall, in 1990 Entry Draft).

			Regular Season					Playoffs				
Season	Club	Lea	GP	G	A	TP	PIM	GP	G	A	TP	PIM
1989-90	Budejovice	Czech.	42	16	24	40	....	....	....	....	....	....
1990-91						UNAVAILABLE						
1991-92						UNAVAILABLE						
1992-93	Budejovice	Czech.	40	23	21	44	....	....	....	....	....	....
1993-94	Budejovice	Czech.	33	14	20	34	0	3	0	2	2	....
1994-95	Budejovice	Czech.	41	15	21	36	16	9	2	5	7	2

ROBERGE, MARIO (roh-BAIRZH) — MTL.

Left wing. Shoots left. 5'11", 193 lbs. Born, Quebec City, Que., January 25, 1964.

			Regular Season					Playoffs				
Season	Club	Lea	GP	G	A	TP	PIM	GP	G	A	TP	PIM
1987-88	Pt. Basques	Sr.	35	25	64	89	152	....	....	....	....	....
1988-89	Sherbrooke	AHL	58	4	9	13	249	6	0	2	2	8
1989-90	Sherbrooke	AHL	73	13	27	40	247	12	5	2	7	53
1990-91	**Montreal**	**NHL**	5	0	0	0	21	12	0	0	0	24
	Fredericton	AHL	68	12	27	39	*365	2	0	2	2	5
1991-92	**Montreal**	**NHL**	20	2	1	3	62	....	....	....	....	....
	Fredericton	AHL	6	1	2	3	20	7	0	2	2	20
1992-93	**Montreal**	**NHL**	50	4	4	8	142	3	0	0	0	0
1993-94	**Montreal**	**NHL**	28	1	2	3	55	....	....	....	....	....
1994-95	**Montreal**	**NHL**	9	0	0	0	34	....	....	....	....	....
	Fredericton	AHL	28	8	12	20	91	6	1	1	2	6
	NHL Totals		112	7	7	14	314	15	0	0	0	24

Signed as a free agent by **Montreal**, October 5, 1988.

ROBERTS, DAVID — ST.L.

Left wing. Shoots left. 6', 185 lbs. Born, Alameda, CA, May 28, 1970.
(St. Louis' 5th choice, 114th overall, in 1989 Entry Draft).

			Regular Season					Playoffs				
Season	Club	Lea	GP	G	A	TP	PIM	GP	G	A	TP	PIM
1989-90	U. of Michigan	CCHA	42	21	32	53	46	....	....	....	....	....
1990-91ab	U. of Michigan	CCHA	43	26	45	71	58	....	....	....	....	....
1991-92	U. of Michigan	CCHA	44	16	42	58	68	....	....	....	....	....
1992-93a	U. of Michigan	CCHA	40	27	38	65	40	....	....	....	....	....
1993-94	U.S. National	....	49	17	28	45	68	....	....	....	....	....
	U.S. Olympic	....	8	1	5	6	4	....	....	....	....	....
	St. Louis	**NHL**	1	0	0	0	2	3	0	0	0	12
	Peoria	IHL	10	4	6	10	4	....	....	....	....	....
1994-95	Peoria	IHL	65	30	38	68	65	....	....	....	....	....
	St. Louis	**NHL**	19	6	5	11	10	6	0	0	0	4
	NHL Totals		20	6	5	11	12	9	0	0	0	16

a CCHA Second All-Star Team (1991, 1993)
b NCAA West Second All-American Team (1991)

ROBERTS, GARY — CGY.

Left wing. Shoots left. 6'1", 190 lbs. Born, North York, Ont., May 23, 1966.
(Calgary's 1st choice, 12th overall, in 1984 Entry Draft).

			Regular Season					Playoffs				
Season	Club	Lea	GP	G	A	TP	PIM	GP	G	A	TP	PIM
1982-83	Ottawa	OHL	53	12	8	20	83	5	1	0	1	19
1983-84	Ottawa	OHL	48	27	30	57	144	13	10	7	17	62
1984-85	Moncton	AHL	7	4	2	6	7	....	....	....	....	....
a	Ottawa	OHL	59	44	62	106	186	5	2	8	10	10
1985-86	Ottawa	OHL	24	26	25	51	83	....	....	....	....	....
a	Guelph	OHL	23	18	15	33	65	20	18	13	31	43
1986-87	**Calgary**	**NHL**	32	5	10	15	85	2	0	0	0	4
	Moncton	AHL	38	20	18	38	72	....	....	....	....	....
1987-88	**Calgary**	**NHL**	74	13	15	28	282	9	2	3	5	29
1988-89	**Calgary**	**NHL**	71	22	16	38	250	22	5	7	12	57
1989-90	**Calgary**	**NHL**	78	39	33	72	222	6	2	5	7	41
1990-91	**Calgary**	**NHL**	80	22	31	53	252	7	1	3	4	18
1991-92	**Calgary**	**NHL**	76	53	37	90	207	....	....	....	....	....
1992-93	**Calgary**	**NHL**	58	38	41	79	172	5	1	6	7	43
1993-94	**Calgary**	**NHL**	73	41	43	84	145	7	2	6	8	24
1994-95	**Calgary**	**NHL**	8	2	2	4	43	....	....	....	....	....
	NHL Totals		550	235	228	463	1658	58	13	30	43	216

a OHL Second All-Star Team (1985, 1986)

Played in NHL All-Star Game (1992, 1993)

ROBERTS, GORDIE

Defense. Shoots left. 6'1", 195 lbs. Born, Detroit, MI, October 2, 1957.
(Montreal's 7th choice, 54th overall, in 1977 Amateur Draft).

			Regular Season					Playoffs				
Season	Club	Lea	GP	G	A	TP	PIM	GP	G	A	TP	PIM
1974-75	Victoria	WHL	53	19	45	64	145	12	1	9	10	42
1975-76	New England	WHA	77	3	19	22	102	17	2	9	11	36
1976-77	New England	WHA	77	13	33	46	169	5	2	2	4	6
1977-78	New England	WHA	78	15	46	61	118	14	0	5	5	29
1978-79	New England	WHA	79	11	46	57	113	10	0	4	4	10
1979-80	**Hartford**	**NHL**	80	8	28	36	89	3	1	1	2	2
1980-81	**Hartford**	**NHL**	27	2	11	13	81	....	....	....	....	....
	Minnesota	**NHL**	50	6	31	37	94	19	1	5	6	17
1981-82	**Minnesota**	**NHL**	79	4	30	34	119	4	0	3	3	27
1982-83	**Minnesota**	**NHL**	80	3	41	44	103	9	1	5	6	14
1983-84	**Minnesota**	**NHL**	77	8	45	53	132	15	3	7	10	23
1984-85	**Minnesota**	**NHL**	78	6	36	42	112	9	1	6	7	6
1985-86	**Minnesota**	**NHL**	76	2	21	23	101	5	0	4	4	8
1986-87	**Minnesota**	**NHL**	67	3	10	13	68	....	....	....	....	....
1987-88	**Minnesota**	**NHL**	48	1	10	11	103	....	....	....	....	....
	Philadelphia	**NHL**	11	1	2	3	15	....	....	....	....	....
	St. Louis	**NHL**	11	1	3	4	25	10	1	2	3	33
1988-89	**St. Louis**	**NHL**	77	2	24	26	90	10	1	7	8	8
1989-90	**St. Louis**	**NHL**	75	3	14	17	140	10	0	2	2	26
1990-91	**St. Louis**	**NHL**	3	0	1	1	8	....	....	....	....	....
	Peoria	IHL	6	0	8	8	4	....	....	....	....	....
	Pittsburgh	**NHL**	61	3	12	15	70	24	1	2	3	63
1991-92	**Pittsburgh**	**NHL**	73	2	22	24	87	19	0	2	2	32
1992-93	**Boston**	**NHL**	65	5	12	17	105	4	0	0	0	6
1993-94	**Boston**	**NHL**	59	1	6	7	40	12	0	1	1	8
1994-95	Chicago	IHL	68	6	22	28	80	3	0	0	0	4
	NHL Totals		1097	61	359	420	1582	153	10	47	57	273

Claimed by **Hartford** from **Montreal** in 1979 Expansion Draft, June 22, 1979. Traded to **Minnesota** by **Hartford** for Mike Fidler, December 16, 1980. Traded to **Philadelphia** by **Minnesota** for future considerations, February 8, 1988. Traded to **St. Louis** by **Philadelphia** for future considerations, March 8, 1988. Traded to **Pittsburgh** by **St. Louis** for Pittsburgh's eleventh round choice (Wade Salzman) in 1992 Entry Draft, October 27, 1990. Signed as a free agent by **Boston**, July 23, 1992.

ROBERTSSON, BERT (ROH-behrt-suhn) — VAN.

Defense. Shoots left. 6'2", 198 lbs. Born, Sodertalje, Sweden, June 30, 1974.
(Vancouver's 8th choice, 254th overall, in 1993 Entry Draft).

			Regular Season					Playoffs				
Season	Club	Lea	GP	G	A	TP	PIM	GP	G	A	TP	PIM
1992-93	Sodertalje	Swe. 2	23	2	1	3	24	....	....	....	....	....
1993-94	Sodertalje	Swe. 2	28	0	1	1	12	....	....	....	....	....
1994-95	Sodertalje	Swe. 2	23	1	2	3	24	....	....	....	....	....

ROBITAILLE, LUC (ROH-buh-tigh) — PIT.

Left wing. Shoots left. 6'1", 195 lbs. Born, Montreal, Que., February 17, 1966.
(Los Angeles' 9th choice, 171st overall, in 1984 Entry Draft).

			Regular Season					Playoffs				
Season	Club	Lea	GP	G	A	TP	PIM	GP	G	A	TP	PIM
1983-84	Hull	QMJHL	70	32	53	85	48	....	....	....	....	....
1984-85a	Hull	QMJHL	64	55	94	149	115	5	4	2	6	27
1985-86bc	Hull	QMJHL	63	68	123	191	91	15	17	27	44	28
1986-87def	**Los Angeles**	**NHL**	79	45	39	84	28	5	1	4	5	2
1987-88g	**Los Angeles**	**NHL**	80	53	58	111	82	5	2	5	7	18
1988-89g	**Los Angeles**	**NHL**	78	46	52	98	65	11	2	6	8	10
1989-90g	**Los Angeles**	**NHL**	80	52	49	101	38	10	5	5	10	10
1990-91g	**Los Angeles**	**NHL**	76	45	46	91	68	12	12	4	16	22
1991-92f	**Los Angeles**	**NHL**	80	44	63	107	95	6	3	4	7	12
1992-93g	**Los Angeles**	**NHL**	84	63	62	125	100	24	9	13	22	28
1993-94	**Los Angeles**	**NHL**	83	44	42	86	86	....	....	....	....	....
1994-95	**Pittsburgh**	**NHL**	46	23	19	42	37	12	7	4	11	26
	NHL Totals		686	415	430	845	599	85	41	45	86	128

a QMJHL Second All-Star Team (1985)
b QMJHL First All-Star Team (1986)
c Canadian Major Junior Player of the Year (1986)
d NHL All-Rookie Team (1987)
e Won Calder Memorial Trophy (1987)
f NHL Second All-Star Team (1987, 1992)
g NHL First All-Star Team (1988, 1989, 1990, 1991, 1993)

Played in NHL All-Star Game (1988-93)

Traded to **Pittsburgh** by **Los Angeles** for Rick Tocchet and Pittsburgh's second round choice (Pavel Rosa) in 1995 Entry Draft, July 29, 1994.

ROCHE, DAVE (ROHSH) — PIT.

Center. Shoots left. 6'4", 224 lbs. Born, Lindsay, Ont., June 13, 1975.
(Pittsburgh's 3rd choice, 62nd overall, in 1993 Entry Draft).

			Regular Season					Playoffs				
Season	Club	Lea	GP	G	A	TP	PIM	GP	G	A	TP	PIM
1991-92	Peterborough	OHL	62	10	17	27	134	10	0	0	0	34
1992-93	Peterborough	OHL	56	40	60	100	105	21	14	15	29	42
1993-94	Peterborough	OHL	34	15	22	37	127	....	....	....	....	....
	Windsor	OHL	29	14	20	34	73	4	1	1	2	15
1994-95a	Windsor	OHL	66	55	59	114	180	10	9	6	15	16

a OHL First All-Star Team (1995)

ROCHEFORT, NORMAND

Defense. Shoots left. 6'1", 214 lbs. Born, Trois-Rivières, Que., January 28, 1961.
(Quebec's 1st choice, 24th overall, in 1980 Entry Draft).

			Regular Season					Playoffs				
Season	Club	Lea	GP	G	A	TP	PIM	GP	G	A	TP	PIM
1978-79	Trois-Rivières	QJHL	72	17	57	74	30	13	3	11	14	17
1979-80	Trois-Rivières	QJHL	20	5	25	30	22	....	....	....	....	....
a	Quebec	QJHL	52	8	39	47	68	5	1	3	4	8
1980-81	**Quebec**	**NHL**	56	3	7	10	51	5	0	0	0	4
	Quebec	QJHL	9	2	6	8	14	....	....	....	....	....
1981-82	**Quebec**	**NHL**	72	4	14	18	115	16	0	2	2	10
1982-83	**Quebec**	**NHL**	62	6	17	23	40	1	0	0	0	2
1983-84	**Quebec**	**NHL**	75	2	22	24	47	6	1	0	1	6
1984-85	**Quebec**	**NHL**	73	3	21	24	74	18	2	1	3	8
1985-86	**Quebec**	**NHL**	26	5	4	9	30	....	....	....	....	....
1986-87	**Quebec**	**NHL**	70	6	9	15	46	13	2	1	3	26
1987-88	**Quebec**	**NHL**	46	3	10	13	49	....	....	....	....	....
1988-89	**NY Rangers**	**NHL**	11	1	5	6	18	....	....	....	....	....
1989-90	**NY Rangers**	**NHL**	31	3	1	4	24	10	2	1	3	26
	Flint	IHL	7	0	32	5	4	....	....	....	....	....
1990-91	**NY Rangers**	**NHL**	44	3	7	10	35	....	....	....	....	....
1991-92	**NY Rangers**	**NHL**	26	0	2	2	31	....	....	....	....	....
1992-93	Eisbaren	Ger.	17	4	2	6	21	....	....	....	....	....
1993-94	**Tampa Bay**	**NHL**	6	0	0	0	10	....	....	....	....	....
	Atlanta	IHL	65	5	7	12	43	13	0	2	2	6
1994-95	Denver	IHL	77	4	13	17	46	17	1	4	5	12
	NHL Totals		598	39	119	158	570	69	7	5	12	82

a QMJHL Second All-Star Team (1980)

Traded to **NY Rangers** by **Quebec** with Jason Lafreniere for Bruce Bell, Jari Gronstrand, Walt Poddubny and NY Rangers' fourth round draft choice (Eric Dubois) in 1989 Entry Draft, August 1, 1988. Signed as a free agent by **Tampa Bay**, September 27, 1993.

ROCHEFORT, RICHARD — N.J.

Center. Shoots right. 5'9", 180 lbs. Born, North Bay, Ont., January 7, 1977.
(New Jersey's 9th choice, 174th overall, in 1995 Entry Draft).

			Regular Season					Playoffs				
Season	Club	Lea	GP	G	A	TP	PIM	GP	G	A	TP	PIM
1993-94	Waterloo	Jr. B	45	21	32	53	41	....	....	....	....	....
1994-95	Sudbury	OHL	57	21	44	65	26	13	3	7	10	6

ROED, PETER — S.J.

Center. Shoots left. 5'10", 210 lbs. Born, St. Paul, MN, November 15, 1976.
(San Jose's 2nd choice, 38th overall, in 1995 Entry Draft).

			Regular Season					Playoffs				
Season	Club	Lea	GP	G	A	TP	PIM	GP	G	A	TP	PIM
1993-94	White Bear Lk.	HS	26	18	22	40	7	....	....	....	....	....
1994-95	White Bear Lk.	HS	28	20	39	59	22	....	....	....	....	....

ROENICK, JEREMY (ROH-nihk) CHI.

Center. Shoots right. 6', 170 lbs. Born, Boston, MA, January 17, 1970.
(Chicago's 1st choice, 8th overall, in 1988 Entry Draft).

Season	Club	Lea	GP	G	A	TP	PIM	GP	G	A	TP	PIM
			Regular Season					Playoffs				
1988-89a	Hull	QMJHL	28	34	36	70	14	....	....	....	....	....
	Chicago	NHL	20	9	9	18	4	10	1	3	4	7
1989-90	Chicago	NHL	78	26	40	66	54	20	11	7	18	8
1990-91	Chicago	NHL	79	41	53	94	80	6	3	5	8	4
1991-92	Chicago	NHL	80	53	50	103	98	18	12	10	22	12
1992-93	Chicago	NHL	84	50	57	107	86	4	1	2	3	2
1993-94	Chicago	NHL	84	46	61	107	125	6	1	6	7	2
1994-95	Koln	Ger.	3	3	1	4	2	....	....	....	....	....
	Chicago	NHL	33	10	24	34	14	8	1	2	3	16
	NHL Totals		458	235	294	529	461	72	30	35	65	51

a QMJHL Second All-Star Team (1989)
Played in NHL All-Star Game (1991-94)

ROENICK, TREVOR HFD.

Right wing. Shoots right. 6'1", 200 lbs. Born, Derby, CT, October 7, 1974.
(Hartford's 3rd choice, 84th overall, in 1993 Entry Draft).

Season	Club	Lea	GP	G	A	TP	PIM	GP	G	A	TP	PIM
			Regular Season					Playoffs				
1993-94	U. of Maine	H.E.	32	4	3	7	18	....	....	....	....	....
1994-95	U. of Maine	H.E.	36	8	12	20	42	....	....	....	....	....

ROHLIN, LEIF (roh-LEEN) VAN.

Defense. Shoots left. 6'1", 198 lbs. Born, Vasteras, Sweden, February 26, 1968.
(Vancouver's 2nd choice, 33rd overall, in 1988 Entry Draft).

Season	Club	Lea	GP	G	A	TP	PIM	GP	G	A	TP	PIM
			Regular Season					Playoffs				
1986-87	Vasteras	Swe. 2	27	2	5	7	12	12	0	2	2	8
1987-88	Vasteras	Swe. 2	30	2	15	17	46	7	0	4	4	8
1988-89	Vasteras	Swe.	22	3	7	10	18	....	....	....	....	....
1989-90	Vasteras	Swe.	32	3	6	9	40	2	0	0	0	2
1990-91	Vasteras	Swe.	40	4	10	14	46	4	0	1	1	8
1991-92	Vasteras	Swe.	39	4	6	10	52	....	....	....	....	....
1992-93	Vasteras	Swe.	37	5	7	12	24	2	0	0	0	0
1993-94	Vasteras	Swe.	40	6	14	20	26	4	0	1	1	6
1994-95	Vasteras	Swe.	39	15	15	30	46	4	2	0	2	2

ROHLOFF, JON (ROH-lohf) BOS.

Defense. Shoots right. 5'11", 220 lbs. Born, Mankato, MN, October 3, 1969.
(Boston's 7th choice, 186th overall, in 1988 Entry Draft).

Season	Club	Lea	GP	G	A	TP	PIM	GP	G	A	TP	PIM
			Regular Season					Playoffs				
1988-89	Minn.-Duluth	WCHA	39	1	2	3	44	....	....	....	....	....
1989-90	Minn.-Duluth	WCHA	5	0	1	1	6	....	....	....	....	....
1990-91	Minn.-Duluth	WCHA	32	6	11	17	38	....	....	....	....	....
1991-92	Minn.-Duluth	WCHA	27	9	9	18	48	....	....	....	....	....
1992-93a	Minn.-Duluth	WCHA	36	15	20	35	87	....	....	....	....	....
1993-94	Providence	AHL	55	12	23	35	59	....	....	....	....	....
1994-95	Boston	NHL	34	3	8	11	39	5	0	0	0	6
	Providence	AHL	4	2	1	3	6	....	....	....	....	....
	NHL Totals		34	3	8	11	39	5	0	0	0	6

a WCHA Second All-Star Team (1993)

ROLSTON, BRIAN N.J.

Center. Shoots left. 6'2", 185 lbs. Born, Flint, MI, February 21, 1973.
(New Jersey's 2nd choice, 11th overall, in 1991 Entry Draft).

Season	Club	Lea	GP	G	A	TP	PIM	GP	G	A	TP	PIM
			Regular Season					Playoffs				
1991-92a	Lake Superior	CCHA	37	14	23	37	14	....	....	....	....	....
1992-93abc	Lake Superior	CCHA	39	33	31	64	20	....	....	....	....	....
1993-94	U.S. National	....	41	20	28	48	36	....	....	....	....	....
	U.S. Olympic	....	8	7	0	7	8	....	....	....	....	....
	Albany	AHL	17	5	5	10	8	5	1	2	3	0
1994-95	Albany	AHL	18	9	11	20	10	....	....	....	....	....
	New Jersey	NHL	40	7	11	18	17	6	2	1	3	4
	NHL Totals		40	7	11	18	17	6	2	1	3	4

a NCAA Final Four All-Tournament Team (1992, 1993)
b CCHA First All-Star Team (1993)
c NCAA West Second All-American Team (1993)

ROMANIUK, RUSSELL (ROH-muh-NUHK) PHI.

Left wing. Shoots left. 6', 195 lbs. Born, Winnipeg, Man., June 9, 1970.
(Winnipeg's 2nd choice, 31st overall, in 1988 Entry Draft).

Season	Club	Lea	GP	G	A	TP	PIM	GP	G	A	TP	PIM
			Regular Season					Playoffs				
1988-89	North Dakota	WCHA	39	17	14	31	32	....	....	....	....	....
	Cdn. National	....	3	1	0	1	0	....	....	....	....	....
1989-90	North Dakota	WCHA	45	36	15	51	54	....	....	....	....	....
1990-91a	North Dakota	WCHA	39	40	28	68	30	....	....	....	....	....
1991-92	Winnipeg	NHL	27	3	5	8	18	....	....	....	....	....
	Moncton	AHL	45	16	15	31	25	10	5	4	9	19
1992-93	Winnipeg	NHL	28	3	1	4	22	1	0	0	0	0
	Moncton	AHL	28	18	8	26	40	5	0	4	4	2
	Fort Wayne	IHL	4	2	0	2	7	....	....	....	....	....
1993-94	Cdn. National	....	34	8	9	17	17	....	....	....	....	....
	Winnipeg	NHL	24	4	8	12	6	....	....	....	....	....
	Moncton	AHL	18	16	8	24	24	17	2	6	8	30
1994-95	Winnipeg	NHL	6	0	0	0	0	....	....	....	....	....
	Springfield	AHL	17	5	7	12	29	....	....	....	....	....
	NHL Totals		85	10	14	24	46	1	0	0	0	0

a WCHA First All-Star Team (1991)
Traded to **Philadelphia** by **Winnipeg** for Jeff Finley, June 27, 1995.

RONAN, ED (ROH-nan)

Right wing. Shoots right. 6', 197 lbs. Born, Quincy, MA, March 21, 1968.
(Montreal's 13th choice, 227th overall, in 1987 Entry Draft).

Season	Club	Lea	GP	G	A	TP	PIM	GP	G	A	TP	PIM
			Regular Season					Playoffs				
1987-88	Boston U.	H.E.	31	2	5	7	20	....	....	....	....	....
1988-89	Boston U.	H.E.	36	4	11	15	34	....	....	....	....	....
1989-90	Boston U.	H.E.	44	17	23	40	50	....	....	....	....	....
1990-91	Boston U.	H.E.	41	16	19	35	38	....	....	....	....	....
1991-92	Montreal	NHL	3	0	0	0	0	....	....	....	....	....
	Fredericton	AHL	78	25	34	59	82	7	5	1	6	6
1992-93	Montreal	NHL	53	5	7	12	20	14	2	3	5	10
	Fredericton	AHL	16	10	5	15	15	5	2	4	6	6
1993-94	Montreal	NHL	61	6	8	14	42	7	1	0	1	0
1994-95	Montreal	NHL	30	1	4	5	12	....	....	....	....	....
	NHL Totals		147	12	19	31	74	21	3	3	6	10

RONNING, CLIFF VAN.

Center. Shoots left. 5'8", 170 lbs. Born, Burnaby, B.C., October 1, 1965.
(St. Louis' 9th choice, 134th overall, in 1984 Entry Draft).

Season	Club	Lea	GP	G	A	TP	PIM	GP	G	A	TP	PIM
			Regular Season					Playoffs				
1983-84	N. Westminster	WHL	71	69	67	136	10	9	8	13	21	10
1984-85a	N. Westminster	WHL	70	*89	108	*197	20	11	10	14	24	4
1985-86	Cdn. Olympic	....	71	55	63	118	53	....	....	....	....	....
	St. Louis	NHL	....	....	....	....	....	5	1	1	2	2
1986-87	St. Louis	NHL	42	11	14	25	6	4	0	1	1	0
	Cdn. National	....	26	17	16	33	12	....	....	....	....	....
1987-88	St. Louis	NHL	26	5	8	13	12	....	....	....	....	....
1988-89	St. Louis	NHL	64	24	31	55	18	7	1	3	4	0
	Peoria	IHL	12	11	20	31	8	....	....	....	....	....
1989-90	Asiago	Italy	36	67	49	116	25	6	7	12	19	4
1990-91	St. Louis	NHL	48	14	18	32	10	....	....	....	....	....
	Vancouver	NHL	11	6	6	12	0	6	6	3	9	12
1991-92	Vancouver	NHL	80	24	47	71	42	13	8	5	13	6
1992-93	Vancouver	NHL	79	29	56	85	30	12	2	9	11	6
1993-94	Vancouver	NHL	76	25	43	68	42	24	5	10	15	16
1994-95	Vancouver	NHL	41	6	19	25	27	11	3	5	8	2
	NHL Totals		467	144	242	386	187	82	26	37	63	44

a WHL First All-Star Team (1985)
Traded to **Vancouver** by **St. Louis** with Geoff Courtnall, Robert Dirk, Sergio Momesso and St. Louis' fifth round choice (Brian Loney) in 1992 Entry Draft for Dan Quinn and Garth Butcher, March 5, 1991.

ROSA, PAVEL L.A.

Right wing. Shoots right. 5'11", 178 lbs. Born, Most, Czech., June 7, 1977.
(Los Angeles' 3rd choice, 50th overall, in 1995 Entry Draft).

Season	Club	Lea	GP	G	A	TP	PIM	GP	G	A	TP	PIM
			Regular Season					Playoffs				
1994-95	Litvinov	Czech. Jr.	40	56	42	98	....	....	....	....	....	....

ROUSE, BOB DET.

Defense. Shoots right. 6'1", 210 lbs. Born, Surrey, B.C., June 18, 1964.
(Minnesota's 3rd choice, 80th overall, in 1982 Entry Draft).

Season	Club	Lea	GP	G	A	TP	PIM	GP	G	A	TP	PIM
			Regular Season					Playoffs				
1980-81	Billings	WHL	70	0	13	13	116	5	0	0	0	2
1981-82	Billings	WHL	71	7	22	29	209	5	0	2	2	10
1982-83	Nanaimo	WHL	29	7	20	27	86	....	....	....	....	....
	Lethbridge	WHL	42	8	30	38	82	20	2	13	15	55
1983-84	Minnesota	NHL	1	0	0	0	0	....	....	....	....	....
a	Lethbridge	WHL	71	18	42	60	101	5	0	1	1	28
1984-85	Minnesota	NHL	63	2	9	11	113	....	....	....	....	....
	Springfield	AHL	8	0	3	3	6	....	....	....	....	....
1985-86	Minnesota	NHL	75	1	14	15	151	3	0	0	0	0
1986-87	Minnesota	NHL	72	2	10	12	179	....	....	....	....	....
1987-88	Minnesota	NHL	74	0	12	12	168	....	....	....	....	....
1988-89	Minnesota	NHL	66	4	13	17	124	....	....	....	....	....
	Washington	NHL	13	0	2	2	36	6	2	0	2	4
1989-90	Washington	NHL	70	4	16	20	123	15	2	3	5	47
1990-91	Washington	NHL	47	5	15	20	65	....	....	....	....	....
	Toronto	NHL	13	2	4	6	10	....	....	....	....	....
1991-92	Toronto	NHL	79	3	19	22	97	....	....	....	....	....
1992-93	Toronto	NHL	82	3	11	14	130	21	3	8	11	29
1993-94	Toronto	NHL	63	5	11	16	101	18	0	3	3	29
1994-95	Detroit	NHL	48	1	7	8	36	18	0	3	3	8
	NHL Totals		766	32	143	175	1333	81	7	17	24	117

a WHL East First All-Star Team (1984)
Traded to **Washington** by **Minnesota** with Dino Ciccarelli for Mike Gartner and Larry Murphy, March 7, 1989. Traded to **Toronto** by **Washington** with Peter Zezel for Al Iafrate, January 16, 1991. Signed as a free agent by **Detroit**, August 5, 1994.

ROY, ANDRE BOS.

Left wing. Shoots left. 6'3", 178 lbs. Born, Port Chester, NY, February 8, 1975.
(Boston's 5th choice, 151st overall, in 1994 Entry Draft).

Season	Club	Lea	GP	G	A	TP	PIM	GP	G	A	TP	PIM
			Regular Season					Playoffs				
1993-94	Beauport	QMJHL	33	6	7	13	125	....	....	....	....	....
	Chicoutimi	QMJHL	32	4	14	18	152	25	3	6	9	94
1994-95	Chicoutimi	QMJHL	20	15	8	23	90	....	....	....	....	....
	Drummondville	QMJHL	34	18	13	31	233	4	2	0	2	34

ROY, JEAN-YVES (WAH) NYR

Right wing. Shoots left. 5'10", 180 lbs. Born, Rosemere, Que., February 17, 1969.

			Regular Season					Playoffs				
Season	Club	Lea	GP	G	A	TP	PIM	GP	G	A	TP	PIM
1989-90a	U. of Maine	H.E.	46	*39	26	65	52	....	....	....	....	....
1990-91bcd	U. of Maine	H.E.	43	37	45	82	62	....	....	....	....	....
1991-92ce	U. of Maine	H.E.	35	32	24	56	62	....	....	....	....	....
	Cdn. National	....	13	10	4	14	6	....	....	....	....	....
1992-93	Binghamton	AHL	49	13	15	28	21	14	5	2	7	4
	Cdn. National	....	23	9	6	15	35	....	....	....	....	....
1993-94	Binghamton	AHL	65	41	24	65	33	....	....	....	....	....
	Cdn. National	....	6	3	2	5	2	....	....	....	....	....
	Cdn. Olympic	....	8	1	0	1	0	....	....	....	....	....
1994-95	Binghamton	AHL	67	41	36	77	28	11	4	6	10	12
	NY Rangers	**NHL**	**3**	**1**	**0**	**1**	**2**	....	....	....	....	....
	NHL Totals		**3**	**1**	**0**	**1**	**2**	....	....	....	....	....

a NCAA East Second All-American Team (1990)
b Hockey East First All-Star Team (1991)
c NCAA East First All-American Team (1991, 1992)
d NCAA Final Four All-Tournament Team (1991)
e Hockey East Second All-Star Team (1992)

Signed as a free agent by **NY Rangers**, July 20, 1992.

ROY, JIMMY DAL.

Center. Shoots right. 5'11", 170 lbs. Born, Sioux Lookout, Ont., September 22, 1975.
(Dallas' 7th choice, 254th overall, in 1994 Entry Draft).

			Regular Season					Playoffs				
Season	Club	Lea	GP	G	A	TP	PIM	GP	G	A	TP	PIM
1993-94	Thunder Bay	Jr. A	46	21	33	54	101	....	....	....	....	....
1994-95	Michigan Tech.	WCHA	38	5	11	16	62	....	....	....	....	....

ROY, STEPHANE (WAH) ST.L.

Center. Shoots left. 5'10", 173 lbs. Born, Ste-Martine, Que., January 26, 1976.
(St. Louis' 1st choice, 68th overall, in 1994 Entry Draft).

			Regular Season					Playoffs				
Season	Club	Lea	GP	G	A	TP	PIM	GP	G	A	TP	PIM
1993-94	Val d'Or	QMJHL	72	25	28	53	116	....	....	....	....	....
1994-95	Val d'Or	QMJHL	68	19	52	71	113	....	....	....	....	....

ROYER, GAETAN CHI.

Right wing. Shoots right. 6'3", 193 lbs. Born, Donnacona, Que., March 13, 1976.

			Regular Season					Playoffs				
Season	Club	Lea	GP	G	A	TP	PIM	GP	G	A	TP	PIM
1994-95	Sherbrooke	QMJHL	65	11	25	36	194	7	0	2	2	6

Signed as a free agent by **Chicago**, September 9, 1994.

RUCCHIN, STEVE (ROO-chihn) ANA.

Center. Shoots left. 6'3", 210 lbs. Born, London, Ont., July 4, 1971.
(Anaheim's 1st choice, 2nd overall, in 1994 Supplemental Draft).

			Regular Season					Playoffs				
Season	Club	Lea	GP	G	A	TP	PIM	GP	G	A	TP	PIM
1990-91	Western Ont.	OUAA	34	13	16	29	14	....	....	....	....	....
1991-92	Western Ont.	OUAA	37	28	34	62	36	....	....	....	....	....
1992-93	Western Ont.	OUAA	34	22	26	48	16	....	....	....	....	....
1993-94	Western Ont.	OUAA	35	30	23	53	30	....	....	....	....	....
1994-95	San Diego	IHL	41	11	15	26	14	....	....	....	....	....
	Anaheim	**NHL**	**43**	**6**	**11**	**17**	**23**	....	....	....	....	....
	NHL Totals		**43**	**6**	**11**	**17**	**23**	....	....	....	....	....

RUCHTY, MATTHEW (RUHK-tee) VAN.

Left wing. Shoots left. 6'1", 225 lbs. Born, Kitchener, Ont., November 27, 1969.
(New Jersey's 4th choice, 65th overall, in 1988 Entry Draft).

			Regular Season					Playoffs				
Season	Club	Lea	GP	G	A	TP	PIM	GP	G	A	TP	PIM
1987-88	Bowling Green	CCHA	41	6	15	21	78	....	....	....	....	....
1988-89	Bowling Green	CCHA	43	11	21	32	110	....	....	....	....	....
1989-90	Bowling Green	CCHA	42	28	21	49	135	....	....	....	....	....
1990-91	Bowling Green	CCHA	38	13	18	31	147	....	....	....	....	....
1991-92	Utica	AHL	73	9	14	23	250	4	0	0	0	25
1992-93	Utica	AHL	74	4	14	18	253	4	0	2	2	15
1993-94	Albany	AHL	68	11	11	22	303	5	0	1	1	18
1994-95	Albany	AHL	78	26	23	49	348	12	5	10	15	43

Signed as a free agent by **Vancouver**, August 1, 1995.

RUCINSKY, MARTIN (roo-SHIHN-skee) COL.

Left wing. Shoots left. 6', 178 lbs. Born, Most, Czech., March 11, 1971.
(Edmonton's 2nd choice, 20th overall, in 1991 Entry Draft).

			Regular Season					Playoffs				
Season	Club	Lea	GP	G	A	TP	PIM	GP	G	A	TP	PIM
1988-89	Litvinov	Czech.	3	1	0	1	2	....	....	....	....	....
1989-90	Litvinov	Czech.	47	17	9	26	....	....	....	....	....	....
1990-91	Litvinov	Czech.	56	24	20	44	69	....	....	....	....	....
1991-92	**Edmonton**	**NHL**	**2**	**0**	**0**	**0**	**0**	....	....	....	....	....
	Cape Breton	AHL	35	11	12	23	34	....	....	....	....	....
	Quebec	**NHL**	**4**	**1**	**1**	**2**	**2**	....	....	....	....	....
	Halifax	AHL	7	1	1	2	6	....	....	....	....	....
1992-93	**Quebec**	**NHL**	**77**	**18**	**30**	**48**	**51**	**6**	**1**	**1**	**2**	**4**
1993-94	**Quebec**	**NHL**	**60**	**9**	**23**	**32**	**58**	....	....	....	....	....
1994-95	Litvinov	Czech.	13	12	10	22	54	....	....	....	....	....
	Quebec	**NHL**	**20**	**3**	**6**	**9**	**14**	....	....	....	....	....
	NHL Totals		**163**	**31**	**60**	**91**	**125**	**6**	**1**	**1**	**2**	**4**

Traded to **Quebec** by **Edmonton** for Ron Tugnutt and Brad Zavisha, March 10, 1992.

RUFF, JASON T.B.

Left wing. Shoots left. 6'2", 192 lbs. Born, Kelowna, B.C., January 27, 1970.
(St Louis' 3rd choice, 96th overall, in 1990 Entry Draft).

			Regular Season					Playoffs				
Season	Club	Lea	GP	G	A	TP	PIM	GP	G	A	TP	PIM
1989-90	Lethbridge	WHL	72	55	64	119	114	19	9	10	19	18
1990-91a	Lethbridge	WHL	66	61	75	136	154	16	12	17	29	18
	Peoria	IHL	....	....	....	....	....	5	0	0	0	2
1991-92	Peoria	IHL	67	27	45	72	148	10	7	7	14	19
1992-93	**St. Louis**	**NHL**	**7**	**2**	**1**	**3**	**8**	....	....	....	....	....
	Peoria	IHL	40	22	21	43	81	....	....	....	....	....
	Tampa Bay	**NHL**	**1**	**0**	**0**	**0**	**0**	....	....	....	....	....
	Atlanta	IHL	26	11	14	25	90	7	2	1	3	26
1993-94	**Tampa Bay**	**NHL**	**6**	**1**	**2**	**3**	**2**	....	....	....	....	....
	Atlanta	IHL	71	24	25	49	122	14	6	*17	23	41
1994-95	Atlanta	IHL	64	42	34	76	161	3	3	1	4	10
	NHL Totals		**14**	**3**	**3**	**6**	**10**	....	....	....	....	....

a WHL East First All-Star Team (1991)

Traded to **Tampa Bay** by **St. Louis** with future considerations for Doug Crossman, Basil McRae and Tampa Bay's fourth round choice in 1996 Entry Draft, January 28, 1993.

RUHLY, DAVID MTL.

Left wing. Shoots left. 6'1", 167 lbs. Born, Baldwin, WI, January 23, 1974.
(Montreal's 9th choice, 177th overall, in 1993 Entry Draft).

			Regular Season					Playoffs				
Season	Club	Lea	GP	G	A	TP	PIM	GP	G	A	TP	PIM
1993-94	Providence	H.E.	21	2	8	10	26	....	....	....	....	....
1994-95	Providence	H.E.	24	3	0	3	8	....	....	....	....	....

RUMBLE, DARREN

Defense. Shoots left. 6'1", 200 lbs. Born, Barrie, Ont., January 23, 1969.
(Philadelphia's 1st choice, 20th overall, in 1987 Entry Draft).

			Regular Season					Playoffs				
Season	Club	Lea	GP	G	A	TP	PIM	GP	G	A	TP	PIM
1986-87	Kitchener	OHL	64	11	32	43	44	4	0	1	1	9
1987-88	Kitchener	OHL	55	15	50	65	64	....	....	....	....	....
1988-89	Kitchener	OHL	46	11	28	39	25	5	1	0	1	2
1989-90	Hershey	AHL	57	2	13	15	31	....	....	....	....	....
1990-91	**Philadelphia**	**NHL**	**3**	**1**	**0**	**1**	**0**	....	....	....	....	....
	Hershey	AHL	73	6	35	41	48	3	0	5	5	2
1991-92	Hershey	AHL	79	12	54	66	118	6	0	3	3	2
1992-93	**Ottawa**	**NHL**	**69**	**3**	**13**	**16**	**61**	....	....	....	....	....
	New Haven	AHL	2	1	0	1	0	....	....	....	....	....
1993-94	**Ottawa**	**NHL**	**70**	**6**	**9**	**15**	**116**	....	....	....	....	....
	P.E.I.	AHL	3	2	0	2	0	....	....	....	....	....
1994-95a	P.E.I.	AHL	70	7	46	53	77	11	0	6	6	4
	NHL Totals		**142**	**10**	**22**	**32**	**177**	....	....	....	....	....

a AHL Second All-Star Team (1995)

Claimed by **Ottawa** from **Philadelphia** in Expansion Draft, June 18, 1992.

RUSHFORTH, PAUL BUF.

Center. Shoots right. 6', 189 lbs. Born, Prince George, B.C., April 22, 1974.
(Buffalo's 8th choice, 131st overall, in 1992 Entry Draft).

			Regular Season					Playoffs				
Season	Club	Lea	GP	G	A	TP	PIM	GP	G	A	TP	PIM
1991-92	North Bay	OHL	65	8	11	19	24	19	0	2	2	6
1992-93	North Bay	OHL	21	4	10	14	24	....	....	....	....	....
	Belleville	OHL	36	21	19	40	38	7	7	2	9	4
1993-94	Belleville	OHL	63	28	35	63	109	12	6	3	9	8
1994-95	S. Carolina	ECHL	41	6	8	14	130	....	....	....	....	....
	Rochester	AHL	25	8	6	14	10	2	0	0	0	0

RUSHIN, JOHN NYR

Center. Shoots right. 6'5", 201 lbs. Born, Edina, MN, September 12, 1972.
(NY Rangers' 7th choice, 147th overall, in 1991 Entry Draft).

			Regular Season					Playoffs				
Season	Club	Lea	GP	G	A	TP	PIM	GP	G	A	TP	PIM
1991-92	Notre Dame	NCAA	17	8	2	10	30	....	....	....	....	....
1992-93	Notre Dame	CCHA	36	1	4	5	46	....	....	....	....	....
1993-94	Notre Dame	CCHA	36	3	6	9	60	....	....	....	....	....
1994-95	Notre Dame	CCHA	31	3	3	6	36	....	....	....	....	....

RUSK, MIKE CHI.

Defense. Shoots left. 6'1", 175 lbs. Born, Milton, Ont., April 26, 1975.
(Chicago's 10th choice, 232nd overall, in 1993 Entry Draft).

			Regular Season					Playoffs				
Season	Club	Lea	GP	G	A	TP	PIM	GP	G	A	TP	PIM
1992-93	Guelph	OHL	62	3	15	18	67	5	0	1	1	8
1993-94	Guelph	OHL	48	8	26	34	59	9	2	9	11	12
1994-95	Guelph	OHL	64	9	31	40	51	14	1	4	5	8

RUSSELL, CAM CHI.

Defense. Shoots left. 6'4", 195 lbs. Born, Halifax, N.S., January 12, 1969.
(Chicago's 3rd choice, 50th overall, in 1987 Entry Draft).

			Regular Season					Playoffs				
Season	Club	Lea	GP	G	A	TP	PIM	GP	G	A	TP	PIM
1985-86	Hull	QMJHL	56	3	4	7	24	15	0	2	2	4
1986-87	Hull	QMJHL	66	3	16	19	119	8	0	1	1	16
1987-88	Hull	QMJHL	53	9	18	27	141	19	2	5	7	39
1988-89	Hull	QMJHL	66	8	32	40	109	9	2	6	8	6
1989-90	**Chicago**	**NHL**	**19**	**0**	**1**	**1**	**27**	**1**	**0**	**0**	**0**	**0**
	Indianapolis	IHL	46	3	15	18	114	9	0	1	1	24
1990-91	**Chicago**	**NHL**	**3**	**0**	**0**	**0**	**5**	**1**	**0**	**0**	**0**	**0**
	Indianapolis	IHL	53	5	9	14	125	6	0	2	2	30
1991-92	**Chicago**	**NHL**	**19**	**0**	**0**	**0**	**34**	**12**	**0**	**2**	**2**	**2**
	Indianapolis	IHL	41	4	9	13	78	....	....	....	....	....
1992-93	**Chicago**	**NHL**	**67**	**2**	**4**	**6**	**151**	**4**	**0**	**0**	**0**	**0**
1993-94	**Chicago**	**NHL**	**67**	**1**	**7**	**8**	**200**	....	....	....	....	....
1994-95	**Chicago**	**NHL**	**33**	**1**	**3**	**4**	**88**	**16**	**0**	**3**	**3**	**8**
	NHL Totals		**208**	**4**	**15**	**19**	**505**	**34**	**0**	**5**	**5**	**10**

RUUTTU, CHRISTIAN (ROO-TOO)

Center. Shoots left. 5'11", 194 lbs. Born, Lappeenranta, Finland, February 20, 1964.
(Buffalo's 9th choice, 134th overall, in 1983 Entry Draft).

			Regular Season					Playoffs				
Season	Club	Lea	GP	G	A	TP	PIM	GP	G	A	TP	PIM
1982-83	Assat	Fin.	36	15	18	33	34	....	....	....	....	....
1983-84	Assat	Fin.	37	18	42	60	72	9	2	5	7	12
1984-85	Assat	Fin.	32	14	32	46	34	8	1	6	7	8
1985-86	HIFK	Fin.	36	16	38	54	47	10	3	6	9	8
1986-87	**Buffalo**	**NHL**	**76**	**22**	**43**	**65**	**62**	....	....	....	....	....
1987-88	**Buffalo**	**NHL**	**73**	**26**	**45**	**71**	**85**	**6**	**2**	**5**	**7**	**4**
1988-89	**Buffalo**	**NHL**	**67**	**14**	**46**	**60**	**98**	**2**	**0**	**0**	**0**	**2**
1989-90	**Buffalo**	**NHL**	**75**	**19**	**41**	**60**	**66**	**6**	**0**	**0**	**0**	**4**
1990-91	**Buffalo**	**NHL**	**77**	**16**	**34**	**50**	**96**	**6**	**1**	**3**	**4**	**29**
1991-92	**Buffalo**	**NHL**	**70**	**4**	**21**	**25**	**76**	**3**	**0**	**0**	**0**	**6**
1992-93	**Chicago**	**NHL**	**84**	**17**	**37**	**54**	**134**	**4**	**0**	**0**	**0**	**2**
1993-94	**Chicago**	**NHL**	**54**	**9**	**20**	**29**	**68**	**6**	**0**	**0**	**0**	**2**
1994-95	HIFK	Fin.	20	4	8	12	24	....	....	....	....	....
	Chicago	**NHL**	**20**	**2**	**5**	**7**	**6**	....	....	....	....	....
	Vancouver	**NHL**	**25**	**5**	**6**	**11**	**23**	**9**	**1**	**1**	**2**	**0**
	NHL Totals		**621**	**134**	**298**	**432**	**714**	**42**	**4**	**9**	**13**	**49**

Played in NHL All-Star Game (1988)

Traded to **Winnipeg** by **Buffalo** with future considerations for Stephane Beauregard, June 15, 1992. Traded to **Chicago** by **Winnipeg** for Stephane Beauregard, August 10, 1992. Traded to **Vancouver** by **Chicago** for Murray Craven, March 10, 1995.

RYABYKIN, DMITRI (ryah-BEE-kihn) CGY.

Defense. Shoots right. 6'1", 185 lbs. Born, Chirchik, USSR, March 24, 1976.
(Calgary's 2nd choice, 45th overall, in 1994 Entry Draft).

			Regular Season					Playoffs				
Season	Club	Lea	GP	G	A	TP	PIM	GP	G	A	TP	PIM
1993-94	Mosc. D'amo 2	CIS 3				UNAVAILABLE						
1994-95	Moscow D'amo	CIS	48	0	0	0	12	11	0	2	2	0

RYAN, TERRY MTL.

Left wing. Shoots left. 6'1", 205 lbs. Born, St. John's, Nfld., January 14, 1977.
(Montreal's 1st choice, 8th overall, in 1995 Entry Draft).

			Regular Season					Playoffs				
Season	Club	Lea	GP	G	A	TP	PIM	GP	G	A	TP	PIM
1993-94	Tri-City	WHL	61	16	17	33	176	4	0	1	1	25
1994-95	Tri-City	WHL	70	50	60	110	207	17	12	15	27	36

RYCHEL, WARREN (RIGH-kuhl) TOR.

Left wing. Shoots left. 6', 202 lbs. Born, Tecumseh, Ont., May 12, 1967.

			Regular Season					Playoffs				
Season	Club	Lea	GP	G	A	TP	PIM	GP	G	A	TP	PIM
1984-85	Sudbury	OHL	35	5	8	13	74	....	....	....	....	....
	Guelph	OHL	29	1	3	4	48	....	....	....	....	....
1985-86	Guelph	OHL	38	14	5	19	119	....	....	....	....	....
	Ottawa	OHL	29	11	18	29	54	....	....	....	....	....
1986-87	Ottawa	OHL	28	11	7	18	57	....	....	....	....	....
	Kitchener	OHL	21	5	5	10	39	4	0	0	0	9
1987-88	Peoria	IHL	7	2	1	3	7	....	....	....	....	....
	Saginaw	IHL	51	2	7	9	113	1	0	0	0	0
1988-89	**Chicago**	**NHL**	**2**	**0**	**0**	**0**	**17**	....	....	....	....	....
	Saginaw	IHL	50	15	14	29	226	6	0	0	0	51
1989-90	Indianapolis	IHL	77	23	16	39	374	14	1	3	4	64
1990-91	Indianapolis	IHL	68	33	30	63	338	5	2	1	3	30
	Chicago	**NHL**	....	....	....	....	....	**3**	**1**	**3**	**4**	**2**
1991-92	Moncton	AHL	36	14	15	29	211	....	....	....	....	....
	Kalamazoo	IHL	45	15	20	35	165	8	0	3	3	51
1992-93	**Los Angeles**	**NHL**	**70**	**6**	**7**	**13**	**314**	**23**	**6**	**7**	**13**	**39**
1993-94	**Los Angeles**	**NHL**	**80**	**10**	**9**	**19**	**322**	....	....	....	....	....
1994-95	**Los Angeles**	**NHL**	**7**	**0**	**0**	**0**	**19**	....	....	....	....	....
	Toronto	**NHL**	**26**	**1**	**6**	**7**	**101**	**3**	**0**	**0**	**0**	**0**
	NHL Totals		**185**	**17**	**22**	**39**	**773**	**29**	**7**	**10**	**17**	**41**

Signed as a free agent by **Chicago**, September 19, 1986. Traded to **Winnipeg** by **Chicago** with Troy Murray for Bryan Marchment and Chris Norton, July 22, 1991. Traded to **Minnesota** by **Winnipeg** for Tony Joseph, December 30, 1991. Signed as a free agent by **Los Angeles**, October 1, 1992. Traded to **Washington** by **Los Angeles** for Randy Burridge, February 10, 1995. Traded to **Toronto** by **Washington** for Toronto's fourth round choice (Sebastien Charpentier) in 1995 Entry Draft, February 10, 1995.

RYDMARK, DANIEL (REWD-mahrk) L.A.

Center. Shoots left. 5'10", 180 lbs. Born, Vasteras, Sweden, February 23, 1970.
(Los Angeles' 5th choice, 123rd overall, in 1989 Entry Draft).

			Regular Season					Playoffs				
Season	Club	Lea	GP	G	A	TP	PIM	GP	G	A	TP	PIM
1986-87	Farjestad	Swe.	4	0	1	1	0	....	....	....	....	....
1987-88	Farjestad	Swe.	28	2	1	3	10	5	0	0	0	2
1988-89	Farjestad	Swe.	35	9	9	18	24	....	....	....	....	....
1989-90	Farjestad	Swe.	35	9	12	21	20	5	0	0	0	4
1990-91	Malmo	Swe.	39	14	13	27	34	1	0	0	0	0
1991-92	Malmo	Swe.	30	17	15	32	56	7	0	3	3	6
1992-93	Malmo	Swe.	39	18	13	31	70	6	5	4	9	8
1993-94	Malmo	Swe.	38	14	18	32	48	11	3	7	10	18
1994-95	Malmo	Swe.	23	8	7	15	24	9	1	2	3	31

SABOURIN, KEN

Defense. Shoots left. 6'3", 205 lbs. Born, Scarborough, Ont., April 28, 1966.
(Calgary's 2nd choice, 33rd overall, in 1984 Entry Draft).

			Regular Season					Playoffs				
Season	Club	Lea	GP	G	A	TP	PIM	GP	G	A	TP	PIM
1982-83	S.S. Marie	OHL	58	0	8	8	90	10	0	0	0	14
1983-84	S.S. Marie	OHL	63	7	14	21	157	9	0	1	1	25
1984-85	S.S. Marie	OHL	63	5	19	24	139	16	1	4	5	10
1985-86	Moncton	AHL	3	0	0	0	0	6	0	1	1	2
	S.S. Marie	OHL	25	1	5	6	77	....	....	....	....	....
	Cornwall	OHL	37	3	12	15	94	6	1	2	3	6
1986-87	Moncton	AHL	75	1	10	11	166	6	0	1	1	27
1987-88	Salt Lake	IHL	71	2	8	10	186	16	1	6	7	57
1988-89	**Calgary**	**NHL**	**6**	**0**	**1**	**1**	**26**	**1**	**0**	**0**	**0**	**0**
	Salt Lake	IHL	74	2	18	20	197	11	0	1	1	26
1989-90	**Calgary**	**NHL**	**5**	**0**	**0**	**0**	**10**	....	....	....	....	....
	Salt Lake	IHL	76	5	19	24	336	11	0	2	2	40
1990-91	**Calgary**	**NHL**	**16**	**1**	**3**	**4**	**36**	....	....	....	....	....
	Salt Lake	IHL	28	2	15	17	77	....	....	....	....	....
	Washington	**NHL**	**28**	**1**	**4**	**5**	**81**	**11**	**0**	**0**	**0**	**34**
1991-92	**Washington**	**NHL**	**19**	**0**	**0**	**0**	**48**	....	....	....	....	....
	Baltimore	AHL	30	3	8	11	106	....	....	....	....	....
1992-93	Baltimore	AHL	30	5	14	19	68	....	....	....	....	....
	Salt Lake	IHL	52	2	11	13	140	....	....	....	....	....
1993-94	Milwaukee	IHL	81	6	13	19	279	4	0	0	0	10
1994-95	Milwaukee	IHL	75	3	16	19	297	15	1	1	2	69
	NHL Totals		**74**	**2**	**8**	**10**	**201**	**12**	**0**	**0**	**0**	**34**

Traded to **Washington** by **Calgary** for Paul Fenton, January 24, 1991. Traded to **Calgary** by **Washington** for future considerations, December 16, 1992.

SACCO, DAVID (SAK-oh) ANA.

Right wing. Shoots right. 6', 180 lbs. Born, Malden, MA, July 31, 1970.
(Toronto's 9th choice, 195th overall, in 1988 Entry Draft).

			Regular Season					Playoffs				
Season	Club	Lea	GP	G	A	TP	PIM	GP	G	A	TP	PIM
1988-89	Boston U.	H.E.	35	14	29	43	40	....	....	....	....	....
1989-90	Boston U.	H.E.	3	0	4	4	2	....	....	....	....	....
1990-91	Boston U.	H.E.	40	21	40	61	24	....	....	....	....	....
1991-92ab	Boston U.	H.E.	34	13	32	45	30	....	....	....	....	....
1992-93ab	Boston U.	H.E.	40	25	37	62	86	....	....	....	....	....
1993-94	U.S. National	....	32	8	20	28	88	....	....	....	....	....
	U.S. Olympic	....	8	3	5	8	12	....	....	....	....	....
	Toronto	**NHL**	**4**	**1**	**1**	**2**	**4**	....	....	....	....	....
	St. John's	AHL	5	3	1	4	2	....	....	....	....	....
1994-95	San Diego	IHL	45	11	25	36	57	4	3	1	4	0
	Anaheim	**NHL**	**8**	**0**	**2**	**2**	**0**	....	....	....	....	....
	NHL Totals		**12**	**1**	**3**	**4**	**4**	....	....	....	....	....

a NCAA East First All-American Team (1992, 1993)
b Hockey East First All-Star Team (1992, 1993)

Traded to **Anaheim** by **Toronto** for Terry Yake, September 28, 1994.

SACCO, JOE (SAK-oh) ANA.

Left wing. Shoots right. 6'1", 195 lbs. Born, Medford, MA, February 4, 1969.
(Toronto's 4th choice, 71st overall, in 1987 Entry Draft).

			Regular Season					Playoffs				
Season	Club	Lea	GP	G	A	TP	PIM	GP	G	A	TP	PIM
1987-88	Boston U.	H.E.	34	16	20	36	40	....	....	....	....	....
1988-89	Boston U.	H.E.	33	21	19	40	66	....	....	....	....	....
1989-90	Boston U.	H.E.	44	28	24	52	70	....	....	....	....	....
1990-91	**Toronto**	**NHL**	**20**	**0**	**5**	**5**	**2**	....	....	....	....	....
	Newmarket	AHL	49	18	17	35	24	....	....	....	....	....
1991-92	U.S. National	....	50	11	26	37	61	....	....	....	....	....
	U.S. Olympic	....	8	0	2	2	0	....	....	....	....	....
	Toronto	**NHL**	**17**	**7**	**4**	**11**	**4**	....	....	....	....	....
	St. John's	AHL	....	....	....	....	....	1	1	1	2	0
1992-93	**Toronto**	**NHL**	**23**	**4**	**4**	**8**	**8**	....	....	....	....	....
	St. John's	AHL	37	14	16	30	45	7	6	4	10	2
1993-94	**Anaheim**	**NHL**	**84**	**19**	**18**	**37**	**61**	....	....	....	....	....
1994-95	**Anaheim**	**NHL**	**41**	**10**	**8**	**18**	**23**	....	....	....	....	....
	NHL Totals		**185**	**40**	**39**	**79**	**98**	....	....	....	....	....

Claimed by **Anaheim** from **Toronto** in Expansion Draft, June 24, 1993.

SAIFULLIN, RAMIL (sigh-FOO-lihn) WPG.

Center. Shoots left. 6'1", 187 lbs. Born, Izhevsk, USSR, April 8, 1976.
(Winnipeg's 8th choice, 186th overall, in 1994 Entry Draft).

			Regular Season					Playoffs				
Season	Club	Lea	GP	G	A	TP	PIM	GP	G	A	TP	PIM
1993-94	Avangard	CIS	37	1	0	1	8	3	0	0	0	0
1994-95	Avangard	CIS	32	3	4	7	....	....	....	....	....	....

SAILYNOJA, KEIJO (sayl-yeh-NOY-ah) EDM.

Left wing. Shoots left. 6'2", 187 lbs. Born, Vantaa, Finland, February 17, 1970.
(Edmonton's 6th choice, 122nd overall, in 1990 Entry Draft).

			Regular Season					Playoffs				
Season	Club	Lea	GP	G	A	TP	PIM	GP	G	A	TP	PIM
1989-90	Jokerit	Fin.	41	15	13	28	14	....	....	....	....	....
1990-91	Jokerit	Fin.	44	21	25	46	14	....	....	....	....	....
1991-92	Jokerit	Fin.	42	21	25	46	14	10	5	6	11	2
1992-93	Jokerit	Fin.	47	29	13	42	14	3	1	1	2	0
1993-94	Jokerit	Fin.	37	11	8	19	43	12	2	0	2	6
1994-95	Jokerit	Fin.	20	6	7	13	4	8	2	1	3	0

SAKIC, JOE (SAK-ihk) COL.

Center. Shoots left. 5'11", 185 lbs. Born, Burnaby, B.C., July 7, 1969.
(Quebec's 2nd choice, 15th overall, in 1987 Entry Draft).

			Regular Season					Playoffs				
Season	Club	Lea	GP	G	A	TP	PIM	GP	G	A	TP	PIM
1986-87	Swift Current	WHL	72	60	73	133	31	4	0	1	1	0
	Cdn. National	....	1	0	0	0	0	....	....	....	....	....
1987-88ab	Swift Current	WHL	64	*78	82	*160	64	10	11	13	24	12
1988-89	**Quebec**	**NHL**	**70**	**23**	**39**	**62**	**24**	....	....	....	....	....
1989-90	**Quebec**	**NHL**	**80**	**39**	**63**	**102**	**27**	....	....	....	....	....
1990-91	**Quebec**	**NHL**	**80**	**48**	**61**	**109**	**24**	....	....	....	....	....
1991-92	**Quebec**	**NHL**	**69**	**29**	**65**	**94**	**20**	....	....	....	....	....
1992-93	**Quebec**	**NHL**	**78**	**48**	**57**	**105**	**40**	**6**	**3**	**3**	**6**	**2**
1993-94	**Quebec**	**NHL**	**84**	**28**	**64**	**92**	**18**	....	....	....	....	....
1994-95	**Quebec**	**NHL**	**47**	**19**	**43**	**62**	**30**	**6**	**4**	**1**	**5**	**0**
	NHL Totals		**508**	**234**	**392**	**626**	**183**	**12**	**7**	**4**	**11**	**2**

a Canadian Major Junior Player of the Year (1988)
b WHL East All-Star Team (1988)

Played in NHL All-Star Game (1990-94)

SALVADOR, BRYCE — T.B.

Defense. Shoots left. 6'2", 194 lbs. Born, Brandon, Man., February 11, 1976.
(Tampa Bay's 6th choice, 138th overall, in 1994 Entry Draft).

			Regular Season					Playoffs				
Season	Club	Lea	GP	G	A	TP	PIM	GP	G	A	TP	PIM
1992-93	Lethbridge	WHL	64	1	4	5	29	4	0	0	0	0
1993-94	Lethbridge	WHL	61	4	14	18	36	9	0	1	1	2
1994-95	Lethbridge	WHL	67	1	9	10	88	....	....	....	....	....

SAMUELSSON, KJELL — (SAM-yuhl-suhn, SHEHL) — PHI.

Defense. Shoots right. 6'6", 235 lbs. Born, Tyngsryd, Sweden, October 18, 1958.
(NY Rangers' 5th choice, 119th overall, in 1984 Entry Draft).

			Regular Season					Playoffs				
Season	Club	Lea	GP	G	A	TP	PIM	GP	G	A	TP	PIM
1977-78	Tyngsryd	Swe. 2	20	3	0	3	41	....	....	....	....	....
1978-79	Tyngsryd	Swe. 2	24	3	4	7	67	....	....	....	....	....
1979-80	Tyngsryd	Swe. 2	26	5	4	9	45	....	....	....	....	....
1980-81	Tyngsryd	Swe. 2	35	6	7	13	61	2	0	1	1	14
1981-82	Tyngsryd	Swe. 2	33	11	14	25	68	3	0	2	2	2
1982-83	Tyngsryd	Swe. 2	32	11	6	17	57	....	....	....	....	....
1983-84	Leksand	Swe.	36	6	6	12	59	....	....	....	....	....
1984-85	Leksand	Swe.	35	9	5	14	34	....	....	....	....	....
1985-86	**NY Rangers**	**NHL**	**9**	**0**	**0**	**0**	**10**	**9**	**0**	**1**	**1**	**8**
	New Haven	AHL	56	6	21	27	87	3	0	0	0	10
1986-87	**NY Rangers**	**NHL**	**30**	**2**	**6**	**8**	**50**	....	....	....	....	....
	Philadelphia	**NHL**	**46**	**1**	**6**	**7**	**86**	**26**	**0**	**4**	**4**	**25**
1987-88	**Philadelphia**	**NHL**	**74**	**6**	**24**	**30**	**184**	**7**	**2**	**5**	**7**	**23**
1988-89	**Philadelphia**	**NHL**	**69**	**3**	**14**	**17**	**140**	**19**	**1**	**3**	**4**	**24**
1989-90	**Philadelphia**	**NHL**	**66**	**5**	**17**	**22**	**91**	....	....	....	....	....
1990-91	**Philadelphia**	**NHL**	**78**	**9**	**19**	**28**	**82**	....	....	....	....	....
1991-92	**Philadelphia**	**NHL**	**54**	**4**	**9**	**13**	**76**	....	....	....	....	....
	Pittsburgh	**NHL**	**20**	**1**	**2**	**3**	**34**	**15**	**0**	**3**	**3**	**12**
1992-93	**Pittsburgh**	**NHL**	**63**	**3**	**6**	**9**	**106**	**12**	**0**	**3**	**3**	**2**
1993-94	**Pittsburgh**	**NHL**	**59**	**5**	**8**	**13**	**118**	**6**	**0**	**0**	**0**	**26**
1994-95	**Pittsburgh**	**NHL**	**41**	**1**	**6**	**7**	**54**	**11**	**0**	**1**	**1**	**32**
	NHL Totals		**609**	**40**	**117**	**157**	**1031**	**105**	**3**	**20**	**23**	**152**

Played in NHL All-Star Game (1988)

Traded to **Philadelphia** by **NY Rangers** with NY Rangers' second round choice (Patrik Juhlin) in 1989 Entry Draft for Bob Froese, December 18, 1986. Traded to **Pittsburgh** by **Philadelphia** with Rick Tocchet, Ken Wregget and Philadelphia's third round choice (Dave Roche) in 1993 Entry Draft for Mark Recchi, Brian Benning and Los Angeles' first round choice (previously acquired by Pittsburgh — Philadelphia selected Jason Bowen) in 1992 Entry Draft, February 19, 1992. Signed as a free agent by **Philadelphia**, July 7, 1995.

SAMUELSSON, ULF — (SAM-yuhl-suhn, UHLF) — PIT.

Defense. Shoots left. 6'1", 195 lbs. Born, Fagersta, Sweden, March 26, 1964.
(Hartford's 4th choice, 67th overall, in 1982 Entry Draft).

			Regular Season					Playoffs				
Season	Club	Lea	GP	G	A	TP	PIM	GP	G	A	TP	PIM
1981-82	Leksand	Swe.	31	3	1	4	40	....	....	....	....	....
1982-83	Leksand	Swe.	33	9	6	15	72	....	....	....	....	....
1983-84	Leksand	Swe.	36	5	11	16	53	....	....	....	....	....
1984-85	**Hartford**	**NHL**	**41**	**2**	**6**	**8**	**83**	....	....	....	....	....
	Binghamton	AHL	36	5	11	16	92	....	....	....	....	....
1985-86	**Hartford**	**NHL**	**80**	**5**	**19**	**24**	**174**	**10**	**1**	**2**	**3**	**38**
1986-87	**Hartford**	**NHL**	**78**	**2**	**31**	**33**	**162**	**5**	**0**	**1**	**1**	**41**
1987-88	**Hartford**	**NHL**	**76**	**8**	**33**	**41**	**159**	**5**	**0**	**0**	**0**	**8**
1988-89	**Hartford**	**NHL**	**71**	**9**	**26**	**35**	**181**	**4**	**0**	**2**	**2**	**4**
1989-90	**Hartford**	**NHL**	**55**	**2**	**11**	**13**	**177**	**7**	**1**	**0**	**1**	**2**
1990-91	**Hartford**	**NHL**	**62**	**3**	**18**	**21**	**174**	....	....	....	....	....
	Pittsburgh	**NHL**	**14**	**1**	**4**	**5**	**37**	**20**	**3**	**2**	**5**	**34**
1991-92	**Pittsburgh**	**NHL**	**62**	**1**	**14**	**15**	**206**	**21**	**0**	**2**	**2**	**39**
1992-93	**Pittsburgh**	**NHL**	**77**	**3**	**26**	**29**	**249**	**12**	**1**	**5**	**6**	**24**
1993-94	**Pittsburgh**	**NHL**	**80**	**5**	**24**	**29**	**199**	**6**	**0**	**1**	**1**	**18**
1994-95	Leksand	Swe.	2	0	0	0	8	....	....	....	....	....
	Pittsburgh	**NHL**	**44**	**1**	**15**	**16**	**113**	**7**	**0**	**2**	**2**	**8**
	NHL Totals		**740**	**42**	**227**	**269**	**1914**	**97**	**6**	**17**	**23**	**216**

Traded to **Pittsburgh** by **Hartford** with Ron Francis and Grant Jennings for John Cullen, Jeff Parker and Zarley Zalapski, March 4, 1991.

SANDERSON, GEOFF — HFD.

Center. Shoots left. 6', 185 lbs. Born, Hay River, N.W.T., February 1, 1972.
(Hartford's 2nd choice, 36th overall, in 1990 Entry Draft).

			Regular Season					Playoffs				
Season	Club	Lea	GP	G	A	TP	PIM	GP	G	A	TP	PIM
1988-89	Swift Current	WHL	58	17	11	28	16	12	3	5	8	6
1989-90	Swift Current	WHL	70	32	62	94	56	4	1	4	5	8
1990-91	**Hartford**	**NHL**	**2**	**1**	**0**	**1**	**0**	**3**	**0**	**0**	**0**	**0**
	Swift Current	WHL	70	62	50	112	57	3	1	2	3	4
	Springfield	AHL	....	....	....	....	....	1	0	0	0	2
1991-92	**Hartford**	**NHL**	**64**	**13**	**18**	**31**	**18**	**7**	**0**	**1**	**1**	**2**
1992-93	**Hartford**	**NHL**	**82**	**46**	**43**	**89**	**28**	....	....	....	....	....
1993-94	**Hartford**	**NHL**	**82**	**41**	**26**	**67**	**42**	....	....	....	....	....
1994-95	HPK	Fin.	12	6	4	10	24	....	....	....	....	....
	Hartford	**NHL**	**46**	**18**	**14**	**32**	**24**	....	....	....	....	....
	NHL Totals		**276**	**119**	**101**	**220**	**112**	**10**	**0**	**1**	**1**	**2**

Played in NHL All-Star Game (1994)

SANDLAK, JIM

Right wing. Shoots right. 6'4", 219 lbs. Born, Kitchener, Ont., December 12, 1966.
(Vancouver's 1st choice, 4th overall, in 1985 Entry Draft).

			Regular Season					Playoffs				
Season	Club	Lea	GP	G	A	TP	PIM	GP	G	A	TP	PIM
1983-84	London	OHL	68	23	18	41	143	8	1	11	12	13
1984-85	London	OHL	58	40	24	64	128	8	3	2	5	14
1985-86	**Vancouver**	**NHL**	**23**	**1**	**3**	**4**	**10**	**3**	**0**	**1**	**1**	**0**
	London	OHL	16	8	14	22	38	5	2	3	5	24
1986-87a	**Vancouver**	**NHL**	**78**	**15**	**21**	**36**	**66**	....	....	....	....	....
1987-88	**Vancouver**	**NHL**	**49**	**16**	**15**	**31**	**81**	....	....	....	....	....
	Fredericton	AHL	24	10	15	25	47	....	....	....	....	....
1988-89	**Vancouver**	**NHL**	**72**	**20**	**20**	**40**	**99**	**6**	**1**	**1**	**2**	**2**
1989-90	**Vancouver**	**NHL**	**70**	**15**	**8**	**23**	**104**	....	....	....	....	....
1990-91	**Vancouver**	**NHL**	**59**	**7**	**6**	**13**	**125**	....	....	....	....	....
1991-92	**Vancouver**	**NHL**	**66**	**16**	**24**	**40**	**176**	**13**	**4**	**6**	**10**	**22**
1992-93	**Vancouver**	**NHL**	**59**	**10**	**18**	**28**	**122**	**6**	**2**	**2**	**4**	**4**
1993-94	**Hartford**	**NHL**	**27**	**6**	**2**	**8**	**32**	....	....	....	....	....
1994-95	**Hartford**	**NHL**	**13**	**0**	**0**	**0**	**0**	....	....	....	....	....
	NHL Totals		**516**	**106**	**117**	**223**	**815**	**28**	**7**	**10**	**17**	**28**

a NHL All-Rookie Team (1987)

Traded to **Hartford** by **Vancouver** to complete March 22, 1993 deal which sent Murray Craven to Vancouver by Hartford with Vancouver's fifth round choice (previously acquired by Hartford — Vancouver selected Scott Walker) in 1993 Entry Draft for Robert Kron, Vancouver's third round choice (Marek Malik) in 1993 Entry Draft and future considerations, May 17, 1993.

SANDSTROM, TOMAS — (SAND-struhm) — PIT.

Right wing. Shoots left. 6'2", 200 lbs. Born, Jakobstad, Finland, September 4, 1964.
(NY Rangers' 2nd choice, 36th overall, in 1982 Entry Draft).

			Regular Season					Playoffs				
Season	Club	Lea	GP	G	A	TP	PIM	GP	G	A	TP	PIM
1981-82	Fagersta	Swe. 2	32	28	11	39	74	....	....	....	....	....
1982-83	Brynas	Swe.	36	23	14	37	50	....	....	....	....	....
1983-84	Brynas	Swe.	34	19	10	29	81	....	....	....	....	....
1984-85a	**NY Rangers**	**NHL**	**74**	**29**	**29**	**58**	**51**	**3**	**0**	**2**	**2**	**0**
1985-86	**NY Rangers**	**NHL**	**73**	**25**	**29**	**54**	**109**	**16**	**4**	**6**	**10**	**20**
1986-87	**NY Rangers**	**NHL**	**64**	**40**	**34**	**74**	**60**	**6**	**1**	**2**	**3**	**20**
1987-88	**NY Rangers**	**NHL**	**69**	**28**	**40**	**68**	**95**	....	....	....	....	....
1988-89	**NY Rangers**	**NHL**	**79**	**32**	**56**	**88**	**148**	**4**	**3**	**2**	**5**	**12**
1989-90	**NY Rangers**	**NHL**	**48**	**19**	**19**	**38**	**100**	....	....	....	....	....
	Los Angeles	**NHL**	**28**	**13**	**20**	**33**	**28**	**10**	**5**	**4**	**9**	**19**
1990-91	**Los Angeles**	**NHL**	**68**	**45**	**44**	**89**	**106**	**10**	**4**	**4**	**8**	**14**
1991-92	**Los Angeles**	**NHL**	**49**	**17**	**22**	**39**	**70**	**6**	**0**	**3**	**3**	**8**
1992-93	**Los Angeles**	**NHL**	**39**	**25**	**27**	**52**	**57**	**24**	**8**	**17**	**25**	**12**
1993-94	**Los Angeles**	**NHL**	**51**	**17**	**24**	**41**	**59**	....	....	....	....	....
	Pittsburgh	**NHL**	**27**	**6**	**11**	**17**	**24**	**6**	**0**	**0**	**0**	**4**
1994-95	Malmo	Swe.	12	10	5	15	14	....	....	....	....	....
	Pittsburgh	**NHL**	**47**	**21**	**23**	**44**	**42**	**12**	**3**	**3**	**6**	**16**
	NHL Totals		**716**	**317**	**378**	**695**	**949**	**97**	**28**	**43**	**71**	**125**

a NHL All-Rookie Team (1985)

Played in NHL All-Star Game (1988, 1991)

Traded to **Los Angeles** by **NY Rangers** with Tony Granato for Bernie Nicholls, January 20, 1990. Traded to **Pittsburgh** by **Los Angeles** with Shawn McEachern for Marty McSorley and Jim Paek, February 16, 1994.

SAPOZHNIKOV, ANDREI — (sa-PAWZH-nik-kawv) — BOS.

Defense. Shoots left. 6'1", 185 lbs. Born, Chelyabinsk, USSR, June 15, 1971.
(Boston's 5th choice, 129th overall, in 1993 Entry Draft).

			Regular Season					Playoffs				
Season	Club	Lea	GP	G	A	TP	PIM	GP	G	A	TP	PIM
1990-91	Chelyabinsk	USSR	28	0	0	0	14	....	....	....	....	....
1991-92	Chelyabinsk	CIS	43	3	4	7	22	....	....	....	....	....
1992-93	Chelyabinsk	CIS	40	2	7	9	30	8	0	1	1	6
1993-94	Chelyabinsk	CIS	40	4	8	12	34	6	0	0	0	0
1994-95	Providence	AHL	19	1	5	6	23	....	....	....	....	....
	Chelyabinsk	CIS	18	0	0	0	14	3	1	0	1	6

SARAULT, YVES — (sah-ROH, EEV) — MTL.

Left wing. Shoots left. 6'1", 170 lbs. Born, Valleyfield, Que., December 23, 1972.
(Montreal's 3rd choice, 61st overall, in 1991 Entry Draft).

			Regular Season					Playoffs				
Season	Club	Lea	GP	G	A	TP	PIM	GP	G	A	TP	PIM
1989-90	Victoriaville	QMJHL	70	12	28	40	140	16	0	3	3	26
1990-91	St-Jean	QMJHL	56	22	24	46	113	....	....	....	....	....
1991-92a	St-Jean	QMJHL	50	28	38	66	96	....	....	....	....	....
a	Trois-Rivières	QMJHL	18	15	14	29	12	15	10	10	20	18
1992-93	Fredericton	AHL	59	14	17	31	41	3	0	1	1	2
	Wheeling	ECHL	2	1	3	4	0	....	....	....	....	....
1993-94	Fredericton	AHL	60	13	14	27	72	....	....	....	....	....
1994-95	Fredericton	AHL	69	24	21	45	96	13	2	1	3	33
	Montreal	**NHL**	**8**	**0**	**1**	**1**	**0**	....	....	....	....	....
	NHL Totals		**8**	**0**	**1**	**1**	**0**	....	....	....	....	....

a QMJHL Second All-Star Team (1992)

SATAN, MIROSLAV — (SHA-tuhn) — EDM.

Center. Shoots left. 6'1", 180 lbs. Born, Topolcany, Czech., October 22, 1974.
(Edmonton's 6th choice, 111th overall, in 1993 Entry Draft).

			Regular Season					Playoffs				
Season	Club	Lea	GP	G	A	TP	PIM	GP	G	A	TP	PIM
1991-92	Topocalny	Czech. 2	9	2	1	3	6	....	....	....	....	....
1992-93	Dukla Trencin	Czech.	38	11	6	17	....	....	....	....	....	....
1993-94	Dukla Trencin	Slovak	30	32	16	48	16	....	....	....	....	....
1994-95	Cape Breton	AHL	25	24	16	40	15	....	....	....	....	....
	Detroit	IHL	8	1	3	4	4	....	....	....	....	....
	San Diego	IHL	6	0	2	2	6	....	....	....	....	....

SAVAGE, BRIAN — MTL.

Center. Shoots left. 6'1", 195 lbs. Born, Sudbury, Ont., February 24, 1971.
(Montreal's 8th choice, 171st overall, in 1991 Entry Draft).

			Regular Season					Playoffs				
Season	Club	Lea	GP	G	A	TP	PIM	GP	G	A	TP	PIM
1990-91	Miami-Ohio	CCHA	28	5	6	11	26	....	....	....	....	....
1991-92	Miami-Ohio	CCHA	40	24	16	40	43	....	....	....	....	....
1992-93ab	Miami-Ohio	CCHA	38	*37	21	58	44	....	....	....	....	....
	Cdn. National	....	9	3	0	3	12	....	....	....	....	....
1993-94	Cdn. National	....	51	20	26	46	38	....	....	....	....	....
	Cdn. Olympic	....	8	2	2	4	6	....	....	....	....	....
	Montreal	**NHL**	**3**	**1**	**0**	**1**	**0**	**3**	**0**	**2**	**2**	**0**
	Fredericton	AHL	17	12	15	27	4	....	....	....	....	....
1994-95	**Montreal**	**NHL**	**37**	**12**	**7**	**19**	**27**	....	....	....	....	....
	NHL Totals		**40**	**13**	**7**	**20**	**27**	**3**	**0**	**2**	**2**	**0**

a CCHA First All-Star Team (1993)
b NCAA West Second All-American Team (1993)

SAVAGE, REGGIE

Center. Shoots left. 5'10", 192 lbs. Born, Montreal, Que., May 1, 1970.
(Washington's 1st choice, 15th overall, in 1988 Entry Draft).

			Regular Season					Playoffs				
Season	Club	Lea	GP	G	A	TP	PIM	GP	G	A	TP	PIM
1987-88	Victoriaville	QMJHL	68	68	54	122	77	5	2	3	5	8
1988-89	Victoriaville	QMJHL	54	58	55	113	178	16	15	13	28	52
1989-90	Victoriaville	QMJHL	63	51	43	94	79	16	13	10	23	40
1990-91	**Washington**	**NHL**	**1**	**0**	**0**	**0**	**0**	....	....	....	....	....
	Baltimore	AHL	62	32	29	61	10	6	1	1	2	6
1991-92	Baltimore	AHL	77	42	28	70	51	....	....	....	....	....
1992-93	**Washington**	**NHL**	**16**	**2**	**3**	**5**	**12**	....	....	....	....	....
	Baltimore	AHL	40	37	18	55	28	....	....	....	....	....
1993-94	**Quebec**	**NHL**	**17**	**3**	**4**	**7**	**16**	....	....	....	....	....
	Cornwall	AHL	33	21	13	34	56	....	....	....	....	....
1994-95	Cornwall	AHL	34	13	7	20	56	14	5	6	11	40
	NHL Totals		**34**	**5**	**7**	**12**	**28**	....	....	....	....	....

Traded to **Quebec** by **Washington** with Paul MacDermid for Mike Hough, June 20, 1993.

SAVARD, DENIS — (sa-VARH, den-NEE) CHI.

Center. Shoots right. 5'10", 175 lbs. Born, Pointe Gatineau, Que., February 4, 1961.
(Chicago's 1st choice, 3rd overall, in 1980 Entry Draft).

			Regular Season					Playoffs				
Season	Club	Lea	GP	G	A	TP	PIM	GP	G	A	TP	PIM
1978-79	Montreal	QJHL	70	46	*112	158	88	11	5	6	11	46
1979-80a	Montreal	QJHL	72	63	118	181	93	10	7	16	23	8
1980-81	**Chicago**	**NHL**	**76**	**28**	**47**	**75**	**47**	**3**	**0**	**0**	**0**	**0**
1981-82	**Chicago**	**NHL**	**80**	**32**	**87**	**119**	**82**	**15**	**11**	**7**	**18**	**52**
1982-83b	**Chicago**	**NHL**	**78**	**35**	**86**	**121**	**99**	**13**	**8**	**9**	**17**	**22**
1983-84	**Chicago**	**NHL**	**75**	**37**	**57**	**94**	**71**	**5**	**1**	**3**	**4**	**9**
1984-85	**Chicago**	**NHL**	**79**	**38**	**67**	**105**	**56**	**15**	**9**	**20**	**29**	**20**
1985-86	**Chicago**	**NHL**	**80**	**47**	**69**	**116**	**111**	**3**	**4**	**1**	**5**	**6**
1986-87	**Chicago**	**NHL**	**70**	**40**	**50**	**90**	**108**	**4**	**1**	**0**	**1**	**12**
1987-88	**Chicago**	**NHL**	**80**	**44**	**87**	**131**	**95**	**5**	**4**	**3**	**7**	**17**
1988-89	**Chicago**	**NHL**	**58**	**23**	**59**	**82**	**110**	**16**	**8**	**11**	**19**	**10**
1989-90	**Chicago**	**NHL**	**60**	**27**	**53**	**80**	**56**	**20**	**7**	**15**	**22**	**41**
1990-91	**Montreal**	**NHL**	**70**	**28**	**31**	**59**	**52**	**13**	**2**	**11**	**13**	**35**
1991-92	**Montreal**	**NHL**	**77**	**28**	**42**	**70**	**73**	**11**	**3**	**9**	**12**	**8**
1992-93	**Montreal**	**NHL**	**63**	**16**	**34**	**50**	**90**	**14**	**0**	**5**	**5**	**4**
1993-94	**Tampa Bay**	**NHL**	**74**	**18**	**28**	**46**	**106**	....	....	....	....	....
1994-95	**Tampa Bay**	**NHL**	**31**	**6**	**11**	**17**	**10**	....	....	....	....	....
	Chicago	**NHL**	**12**	**4**	**4**	**8**	**8**	**16**	**7**	**11**	**18**	**10**
	NHL Totals		**1063**	**451**	**812**	**1263**	**1174**	**153**	**65**	**105**	**170**	**246**

a QMJHL First All-Star Team (1980)
b NHL Second All-Star Team (1983)

Played in NHL All-Star Game (1982-84, 1986, 1988, 1991)

Traded to **Montreal** by **Chicago** for Chris Chelios and Montreal's second round choice (Michael Pomichter) in 1991 Entry Draft, June 29, 1990. Signed as a free agent by **Tampa Bay**, July 29, 1993. Traded to **Chicago** by **Tampa Bay** for Chicago's sixth round choice in 1996 Entry Draft, April 6, 1995.

SAVARD, MARC — NYR

Center. Shoots left. 5'10", 177 lbs. Born, Ottawa, Ont., July 17, 1977.
(NY Rangers' 3rd choice, 91st overall, in 1995 Entry Draft).

			Regular Season					Playoffs				
Season	Club	Lea	GP	G	A	TP	PIM	GP	G	A	TP	PIM
1993-94	Oshawa	OHL	61	18	39	57	20	5	4	3	7	8
1994-95a	Oshawa	OHL	66	43	96	*139	78	7	5	6	11	8

a OHL Second All-Star Team (1995)

SAVENKO, BOGDAN — (sah-VEE-ehn-kah, bahg-DAHN) VAN.

Right wing. Shoots right. 6'1", 192 lbs. Born, Kiev, USSR, November 20, 1974.
(Chicago's 3rd choice, 54th overall, in 1993 Entry Draft).

			Regular Season					Playoffs				
Season	Club	Lea	GP	G	A	TP	PIM	GP	G	A	TP	PIM
1990-91	SVSM Kiev	USSR 2	40	30	18	48	24	....	....	....	....	....
1991-92	Sokol Kiev	CIS	25	3	1	4	4	....	....	....	....	....
1992-93	Niagara Falls	OHL	51	29	19	48	15	2	1	0	1	2
1993-94	Niagara Falls	OHL	62	42	49	91	22	....	....	....	....	....
1994-95	Indianapolis	IHL	62	18	17	35	49	....	....	....	....	....

Traded to **Vancouver** by **Chicago** with Hartford's third round choice (previously acquired by Chicago — Vancouver selected Larry Courville) in 1995 Entry Draft for Gerald Didick, April 7, 1995.

SAVOIA, RYAN — PIT.

Center. Shoots right. 6', 195 lbs. Born, Thorold, Ont., May 6, 1973.

			Regular Season					Playoffs				
Season	Club	Lea	GP	G	A	TP	PIM	GP	G	A	TP	PIM
1994-95	Brock U.	OUAA	38	35	48	83	24	....	....	....	....	....
	Cleveland	IHL	1	0	0	0	0	....	....	....	....	....

Signed as a free agent by **Pittsburgh**, April 7, 1995.

SAVOIE, CLAUDE — (sav-WAH) OTT.

Right wing. Shoots right. 5'11", 200 lbs. Born, Montreal, Que., March 12, 1973.
(Ottawa's 9th choice, 194th overall, in 1992 Entry Draft).

			Regular Season					Playoffs				
Season	Club	Lea	GP	G	A	TP	PIM	GP	G	A	TP	PIM
1990-91	Victoriaville	QMJHL	61	20	22	42	101	....	....	....	....	....
1991-92	Victoriaville	QMJHL	69	39	40	79	140	....	....	....	....	....
1992-93	Victoriaville	QMJHL	67	70	61	131	113	6	4	5	9	6
	New Haven	AHL	2	1	1	2	0	....	....	....	....	....
1993-94	P.E.I.	AHL	77	13	15	28	118	....	....	....	....	....
1994-95	P.E.I.	AHL	59	9	14	23	67	4	2	0	2	7

SAWYER, KEVIN — ST.L.

Left wing. Shoots left. 6'2", 205 lbs. Born, Christina Lake, B.C., February 21, 1974.

			Regular Season					Playoffs				
Season	Club	Lea	GP	G	A	TP	PIM	GP	G	A	TP	PIM
1992-93	Spokane	WHL	62	4	3	7	274	8	1	1	2	13
1993-94	Spokane	WHL	60	10	15	25	350	3	0	1	1	6
1994-95	Spokane	WHL	54	7	9	16	365	11	2	0	2	58

Signed as a free agent by **St. Louis**, February 28, 1995.

SCATCHARD, DAVE — VAN.

Center. Shoots right. 6'2", 185 lbs. Born, Hinton, Alta., February 20, 1976.
(Vancouver's 3rd choice, 42nd overall, in 1994 Entry Draft).

			Regular Season					Playoffs				
Season	Club	Lea	GP	G	A	TP	PIM	GP	G	A	TP	PIM
1993-94	Portland	WHL	47	9	11	20	46	10	2	1	3	4
1994-95	Portland	WHL	71	20	30	50	148	8	0	3	3	21

SCHAEFER, JEREMY — BOS.

Left wing. Shoots left. 6'3", 195 lbs. Born, Carston, Alta., February 27, 1976.
(Boston's 6th choice, 177th overall, in 1994 Entry Draft).

			Regular Season					Playoffs				
Season	Club	Lea	GP	G	A	TP	PIM	GP	G	A	TP	PIM
1992-93	Medicine Hat	WHL	65	1	0	1	95	9	0	2	2	32
1993-94	Medicine Hat	WHL	65	4	9	13	155	2	0	0	0	2
1994-95	Medicine Hat	WHL	70	8	6	14	146	5	0	0	0	20

SCHAEFER, PETER — VAN.

Left wing. Shoots left. 5'11", 187 lbs. Born, Yellow Grass, Sask., July 12, 1977.
(Vancouver's 3rd choice, 66th overall, in 1995 Entry Draft).

			Regular Season					Playoffs				
Season	Club	Lea	GP	G	A	TP	PIM	GP	G	A	TP	PIM
1993-94	Brandon	WHL	2	1	0	1	0	....	....	....	....	....
1994-95	Brandon	WHL	68	27	32	59	34	18	5	3	8	18

SCHLEGEL, BRAD — (shlay-GUHL)

Defense. Shoots right. 5'10", 188 lbs. Born, Kitchener, Ont., July 22, 1968.
(Washington's 8th choice, 144th overall, in 1988 Entry Draft).

			Regular Season					Playoffs				
Season	Club	Lea	GP	G	A	TP	PIM	GP	G	A	TP	PIM
1986-87	London	OHL	65	4	23	27	24	....	....	....	....	....
1987-88a	London	OHL	66	13	63	76	49	12	8	17	25	6
1988-89	Cdn. National	....	60	2	22	24	30	....	....	....	....	....
1989-90	Cdn. National	....	72	7	25	32	44	....	....	....	....	....
1990-91	Cdn. National	....	59	8	20	28	64	....	....	....	....	....
1991-92	Cdn. National	....	61	3	18	21	84	....	....	....	....	....
	Cdn. Olympic	....	8	1	2	3	4	....	....	....	....	....
	Washington	**NHL**	**15**	**0**	**1**	**1**	**0**	**7**	**0**	**1**	**1**	**2**
	Baltimore	AHL	2	0	1	1	0	....	....	....	....	....
1992-93	**Washington**	**NHL**	**7**	**0**	**1**	**1**	**6**	....	....	....	....	....
	Baltimore	AHL	61	3	20	23	40	7	0	5	5	6
1993-94	**Calgary**	**NHL**	**26**	**1**	**6**	**7**	**4**	....	....	....	....	....
	Cdn. National	....	4	0	0	0	2	....	....	....	....	....
	Cdn. Olympic	....	8	0	0	0	6	....	....	....	....	....
	Saint John	AHL	21	2	8	10	6	7	0	1	1	6
1994-95	Cdn. National	....	4	0	1	1	2	....	....	....	....	....
	Villach	Aus.	28	7	26	33	40	12	1	11	12	44
	NHL Totals		**48**	**1**	**8**	**9**	**10**	**7**	**0**	**1**	**1**	**2**

a OHL Second All-Star Team (1988)

Traded to **Calgary** by **Washington** for Calgary's seventh round choice (Andrew Brunette) in 1993 Entry Draft, June 26, 1993.

SCHMIDT, CHRIS — L.A.

Center. Shoots left. 6'3", 193 lbs. Born, Beaverlodge, Alta., March 1, 1976.
(Los Angeles' 4th choice, 111th overall, in 1994 Entry Draft).

			Regular Season					Playoffs				
Season	Club	Lea	GP	G	A	TP	PIM	GP	G	A	TP	PIM
1992-93	Seattle	WHL	61	6	7	13	17	5	0	1	1	0
1993-94	Seattle	WHL	68	7	17	24	26	9	3	1	4	2
1994-95	Seattle	WHL	61	21	11	32	31	3	0	0	0	0

SCHMIDT, COLIN — EDM.

Center. Shoots left. 5'11", 185 lbs. Born, Regina, Sask., February 3, 1974.
(Edmonton's 9th choice, 190th overall, in 1992 Entry Draft).

			Regular Season					Playoffs				
Season	Club	Lea	GP	G	A	TP	PIM	GP	G	A	TP	PIM
1992-93	Colorado	WCHA	27	8	13	21	26	....	....	....	....	....
1993-94	Colorado	WCHA	38	14	22	36	49	....	....	....	....	....
1994-95a	Colorado	WCHA	43	26	31	57	61	....	....	....	....	....

a WCHA Second All-Star Team (1995)

SCHNEIDER, ANDY — OTT.

Left wing. Shoots left. 5'9", 170 lbs. Born, Edmonton, Alta., March 29, 1972.

			Regular Season					Playoffs				
Season	Club	Lea	GP	G	A	TP	PIM	GP	G	A	TP	PIM
1990-91	Swift Current	WHL	69	12	74	86	103	3	0	0	0	2
1991-92	Swift Current	WHL	63	44	60	104	120	8	4	9	13	8
1992-93a	Swift Current	WHL	38	19	66	85	78	17	13	*26	*39	40
	New Haven	AHL	19	2	2	4	13	....	....	....	....	....
1993-94	**Ottawa**	**NHL**	**10**	**0**	**0**	**0**	**15**	....	....	....	....	....
	P.E.I.	AHL	61	15	46	61	119	....	....	....	....	....
1994-95	Leksand	Swe.	39	6	8	14	71	4	1	1	2	31
	Cdn. National	....	3	1	0	1	0	....	....	....	....	....
	P.E.I.	AHL	10	1	5	6	25	11	5	5	10	11
	NHL Totals		**10**	**0**	**0**	**0**	**15**	....	....	....	....	....

a WHL East Second All-Star Team (1993)

Signed as a free agent by **Ottawa**, October 9, 1992.

SCHNEIDER, MATHIEU — NYI

Defense. Shoots left. 5'11", 189 lbs. Born, New York, NY, June 12, 1969.
(Montreal's 4th choice, 44th overall, in 1987 Entry Draft).

			Regular Season					Playoffs				
Season	**Club**	**Lea**	**GP**	**G**	**A**	**TP**	**PIM**	**GP**	**G**	**A**	**TP**	**PIM**
1986-87	Cornwall	OHL	63	7	29	36	75	5	0	0	0	22
1987-88	**Montreal**	**NHL**	**4**	**0**	**0**	**0**	**2**	....	....	....	....	....
a	Cornwall	OHL	48	21	40	61	83	11	2	6	8	14
	Sherbrooke	AHL	....	....	....	....	....	3	0	3	3	12
1988-89	Cornwall	OHL	59	16	57	73	96	18	7	20	27	30
1989-90	**Montreal**	**NHL**	**44**	**7**	**14**	**21**	**25**	**9**	**1**	**3**	**4**	**31**
	Sherbrooke	AHL	28	6	13	19	20	....	....	....	....	....
1990-91	**Montreal**	**NHL**	**69**	**10**	**20**	**30**	**63**	**13**	**2**	**7**	**9**	**18**
1991-92	**Montreal**	**NHL**	**78**	**8**	**24**	**32**	**72**	**10**	**1**	**4**	**5**	**6**
1992-93	**Montreal**	**NHL**	**60**	**13**	**31**	**44**	**91**	**11**	**1**	**2**	**3**	**16**
1993-94	**Montreal**	**NHL**	**75**	**20**	**32**	**52**	**62**	**1**	**0**	**0**	**0**	**0**
1994-95	**Montreal**	**NHL**	**30**	**5**	**15**	**20**	**49**	....	....	....	....	....
	NY Islanders	**NHL**	**13**	**3**	**6**	**9**	**30**	....	....	....	....	....
	NHL Totals		**373**	**66**	**142**	**208**	**394**	**44**	**5**	**16**	**21**	**71**

a OHL First All-Star Team (1988)

Traded to **NY Islanders** by **Montreal** with Kirk Muller and Craig Darby for Pierre Turgeon and Vladimir Malakhov, April 5, 1995.

SCHUHWERK, RICK — OTT.

Defense. Shoots right. 6'1", 212 lbs. Born, Hingham, MA, March 22, 1973.
(Ottawa's 10th choice, 235th overall, in 1993 Entry Draft).

			Regular Season					Playoffs				
Season	**Club**	**Lea**	**GP**	**G**	**A**	**TP**	**PIM**	**GP**	**G**	**A**	**TP**	**PIM**
1993-94	Northeastern	H.E.	37	2	5	7	6	....	....	....	....	....
1994-95	Northeastern	H.E.	34	2	6	8	18	....	....	....	....	....

SCHULTE, PAXTON — COL.

Left wing. Shoots left. 6'2", 217 lbs. Born, Ionaway, Alta., July 16, 1972.
(Quebec's 7th choice, 124th overall, in 1992 Entry Draft).

			Regular Season					Playoffs				
Season	**Club**	**Lea**	**GP**	**G**	**A**	**TP**	**PIM**	**GP**	**G**	**A**	**TP**	**PIM**
1990-91	North Dakota	WCHA	38	2	4	6	32	....	....	....	....	....
1991-92	Spokane	WHL	70	42	42	84	222	10	2	8	10	48
1992-93	Spokane	WHL	45	38	35	73	142	10	5	6	11	12
1993-94	**Quebec**	**NHL**	**1**	**0**	**0**	**0**	**2**	....	....	....	....	....
	Cornwall	AHL	56	15	15	30	102	....	....	....	....	....
1994-95	Cornwall	AHL	74	14	22	36	217	14	3	3	6	29
	NHL Totals		**1**	**0**	**0**	**0**	**2**	....	....	....	....	....

SCISSONS, SCOTT (SIH-shuhns)

Center. Shoots left. 6'1", 201 lbs. Born, Saskatoon, Sask., October 29, 1971.
(NY Islanders' 1st choice, 6th overall, in 1990 Entry Draft).

			Regular Season					Playoffs				
Season	**Club**	**Lea**	**GP**	**G**	**A**	**TP**	**PIM**	**GP**	**G**	**A**	**TP**	**PIM**
1988-89	Saskatoon	WHL	71	30	56	86	65	7	0	4	4	16
1989-90	Saskatoon	WHL	61	40	47	87	81	10	3	8	11	6
1990-91	**NY Islanders**	**NHL**	**1**	**0**	**0**	**0**	**0**	....	....	....	....	....
	Saskatoon	WHL	57	24	53	77	61	....	....	....	....	....
1991-92	Cdn. National	....	26	4	8	12	31	....	....	....	....	....
1992-93	Capital Dist.	AHL	43	14	30	44	33	4	0	0	0	0
	NY Islanders	**NHL**	....	....	....	....	....	**1**	**0**	**0**	**0**	**0**
1993-94	**NY Islanders**	**NHL**	**1**	**0**	**0**	**0**	**0**	....	....	....	....	....
	Salt Lake	IHL	72	10	26	36	123	....	....	....	....	....
1994-95	Denver	IHL	7	2	3	5	6	....	....	....	....	....
	Minnesota	IHL	23	7	9	16	6	....	....	....	....	....
	NHL Totals		**2**	**0**	**0**	**0**	**0**	**1**	**0**	**0**	**0**	**0**

SCOTT, BLAIR — COL.

Defense. Shoots left. 6', 202 lbs. Born, Winnipeg, Man., February 25, 1972.

			Regular Season					Playoffs				
Season	**Club**	**Lea**	**GP**	**G**	**A**	**TP**	**PIM**	**GP**	**G**	**A**	**TP**	**PIM**
1990-91	Belleville	OHL	45	2	7	9	79	6	0	2	2	10
1991-92	Belleville	OHL	41	3	15	18	83	....	....	....	....	....
	Detroit	OHL	28	1	16	17	68	7	0	3	3	23
1992-93	Detroit	OHL	64	11	67	78	100	15	3	14	17	27
1993-94	Cornwall	AHL	19	1	2	3	13	....	....	....	....	....
1994-95	Cornwall	AHL	56	8	16	24	108	14	3	5	8	12

Signed as a free agent by **Quebec**, July 6, 1993.

SECORD, BRIAN — HFD.

Center. Shoots left. 5'11", 179 lbs. Born, Ridgetown, Ont., June 19, 1975.

			Regular Season					Playoffs				
Season	**Club**	**Lea**	**GP**	**G**	**A**	**TP**	**PIM**	**GP**	**G**	**A**	**TP**	**PIM**
1992-93	Belleville	OHL	66	16	18	34	57	7	2	0	2	11
1993-94	Belleville	OHL	66	29	40	69	56	12	2	4	6	16
1994-95	Belleville	OHL	57	29	53	82	76	10	2	5	7	4

Signed as a free agent by **Hartford**, July 18, 1995.

SELANNE, TEEMU (SEH-lahn-nay, TEE-moo) — WPG.

Right wing. Shoots right. 6', 200 lbs. Born, Helsinki, Finland, July 3, 1970.
(Winnipeg's 1st choice, 10th overall, in 1988 Entry Draft).

			Regular Season					Playoffs				
Season	**Club**	**Lea**	**GP**	**G**	**A**	**TP**	**PIM**	**GP**	**G**	**A**	**TP**	**PIM**
1987-88	Jokerit	Fin. Jr.	33	43	23	66	18	5	4	3	7	2
	Jokerit	Fin. 2	5	1	1	2	0	....	....	....	....	....
1988-89	Jokerit	Fin. 2	34	35	33	68	12	5	7	3	10	4
1989-90	Jokerit	Fin.	11	4	8	12	0	....	....	....	....	....
1990-91	Jokerit	Fin.	42	33	25	58	12	....	....	....	....	....
1991-92	Jokerit	Fin.	44	*39	23	62	20	10	10	7	17	18
1992-93abc	**Winnipeg**	**NHL**	**84**	***76**	**56**	**132**	**45**	**6**	**4**	**2**	**6**	**2**
1993-94	**Winnipeg**	**NHL**	**51**	**25**	**29**	**54**	**22**	....	....	....	....	....
1994-95	Jokerit	Fin.	20	7	12	19	6	....	....	....	....	....
	Winnipeg	**NHL**	**45**	**22**	**26**	**48**	**2**	....	....	....	....	....
	NHL Totals		**180**	**123**	**111**	**234**	**69**	**6**	**4**	**2**	**6**	**2**

a Won Calder Memorial Trophy (1993)
b NHL First All-Star Team (1993)
c NHL/Upper Deck All-Rookie Team (1993)

Played in NHL All-Star Game (1993, 1994)

SELIVANOV, ALEXANDER (seh-lih-VAH-nohv) — T.B.

Right wing. Shoots left. 6'1", 187 lbs. Born, Moscow, USSR, March 23, 1971.
(Philadelphia's 4th choice, 140th overall, in 1994 Entry Draft).

			Regular Season					Playoffs				
Season	**Club**	**Lea**	**GP**	**G**	**A**	**TP**	**PIM**	**GP**	**G**	**A**	**TP**	**PIM**
1988-89	Spartak	USSR	1	0	0	0	0	....	....	....	....	....
1989-90	Spartak	USSR	4	0	0	0	0	....	....	....	....	....
1990-91	Spartak	USSR	21	3	1	4	6	....	....	....	....	....
1991-92	Spartak	CIS	31	6	7	13	16	....	....	....	....	....
1992-93	Spartak	CIS	42	12	19	31	66	3	2	0	2	2
1993-94	Spartak	CIS	45	30	11	41	50	6	5	1	6	2
1994-95	Atlanta	IHL	4	0	3	3	2	....	....	....	....	....
	Chicago	IHL	14	4	1	5	8	....	....	....	....	....
	Tampa Bay	**NHL**	**43**	**10**	**6**	**16**	**14**	....	....	....	....	....
	NHL Totals		**43**	**10**	**6**	**16**	**14**	....	....	....	....	....

Traded to **Tampa Bay** by **Philadelphia** for Philadelphia's fourth round choice (previously acquired by Tampa Bay — Philadelphia selected Radovan Somik) in 1995 Entry Draft, September 6, 1994.

SEMAK, ALEXANDER (seh-MAHK) — T.B.

Center. Shoots right. 5'10", 180 lbs. Born, Ufa, USSR, February 11, 1966.
(New Jersey's 12th choice, 207th overall, in 1988 Entry Draft).

			Regular Season					Playoffs				
Season	**Club**	**Lea**	**GP**	**G**	**A**	**TP**	**PIM**	**GP**	**G**	**A**	**TP**	**PIM**
1982-83	Ufa Salavat	USSR	13	2	1	3	4	....	....	....	....	....
1983-84	Ufa Salavat	USSR 2			UNAVAILABLE							
1984-85	Ufa Salavat	USSR 2	47	19	17	36	64	....	....	....	....	....
1985-86	Ufa Salavat	USSR	22	9	7	16	22	....	....	....	....	....
1986-87	Moscow D'amo	USSR	40	20	8	28	32	....	....	....	....	....
1987-88	Moscow D'amo	USSR	47	21	14	35	40	....	....	....	....	....
1988-89	Moscow D'amo	USSR	44	18	10	28	22	....	....	....	....	....
1989-90	Moscow D'amo	USSR	43	23	11	34	33	....	....	....	....	....
1990-91	Moscow D'amo	USSR	46	17	21	38	48	....	....	....	....	....
1991-92	Moscow D'amo	CIS	26	10	13	23	26	....	....	....	....	....
	New Jersey	**NHL**	**25**	**5**	**6**	**11**	**0**	**1**	**0**	**0**	**0**	**0**
	Utica	AHL	7	3	2	5	0	....	....	....	....	....
1992-93	**New Jersey**	**NHL**	**82**	**37**	**42**	**79**	**70**	**5**	**1**	**1**	**2**	**0**
1993-94	**New Jersey**	**NHL**	**54**	**12**	**17**	**29**	**22**	**2**	**0**	**0**	**0**	**0**
1994-95	Ufa Salavat	CIS	9	9	6	15	4	....	....	....	....	....
	New Jersey	**NHL**	**19**	**2**	**6**	**8**	**13**	....	....	....	....	....
	Tampa Bay	**NHL**	**22**	**5**	**5**	**10**	**12**	....	....	....	....	....
	NHL Totals		**202**	**61**	**76**	**137**	**117**	**8**	**1**	**1**	**2**	**0**

Traded to **Tampa Bay** by **New Jersey** with Ben Hankinson for Shawn Chambers and Danton Cole, March 14, 1995.

SEMENOV, ANATOLI (seh-MEH-nahf) — PHI.

Center/Left wing. Shoots left. 6'2", 190 lbs. Born, Moscow, USSR, March 5, 1962.
(Edmonton's 5th choice, 120th overall, in 1989 Entry Draft).

			Regular Season					Playoffs				
Season	**Club**	**Lea**	**GP**	**G**	**A**	**TP**	**PIM**	**GP**	**G**	**A**	**TP**	**PIM**
1979-80	Moscow D'amo	USSR	8	3	0	3	2	....	....	....	....	....
1980-81	Moscow D'amo	USSR	47	18	14	32	18	....	....	....	....	....
1981-82	Moscow D'amo	USSR	44	12	14	26	28	....	....	....	....	....
1982-83	Moscow D'amo	USSR	44	22	18	40	26	....	....	....	....	....
1983-84	Moscow D'amo	USSR	19	10	5	15	14	....	....	....	....	....
1984-85	Moscow D'amo	USSR	30	17	12	29	32	....	....	....	....	....
1985-86	Moscow D'amo	USSR	32	18	17	35	19	....	....	....	....	....
1986-87	Moscow D'amo	USSR	40	15	29	44	32	....	....	....	....	....
1987-88	Moscow D'amo	USSR	32	17	8	25	22	....	....	....	....	....
1988-89	Moscow D'amo	USSR	31	9	12	21	24	....	....	....	....	....
1989-90	Moscow D'amo	USSR	48	13	20	33	16	....	....	....	....	....
	Edmonton	**NHL**	....	....	....	....	....	**2**	**0**	**0**	**0**	**0**
1990-91	**Edmonton**	**NHL**	**57**	**15**	**16**	**31**	**26**	**12**	**5**	**5**	**10**	**6**
1991-92	**Edmonton**	**NHL**	**59**	**20**	**22**	**42**	**16**	**8**	**1**	**1**	**2**	**6**
1992-93	**Tampa Bay**	**NHL**	**13**	**2**	**3**	**5**	**4**	....	....	....	....	....
	Vancouver	**NHL**	**62**	**10**	**34**	**44**	**28**	**12**	**1**	**3**	**4**	**0**
1993-94	**Anaheim**	**NHL**	**49**	**11**	**19**	**30**	**12**	....	....	....	....	....
1994-95	**Anaheim**	**NHL**	**15**	**3**	**4**	**7**	**4**	....	....	....	....	....
	Philadelphia	**NHL**	**26**	**1**	**2**	**3**	**6**	**15**	**2**	**4**	**6**	**0**
	NHL Totals		**281**	**62**	**100**	**162**	**96**	**49**	**9**	**13**	**22**	**12**

Claimed by **Tampa Bay** from **Edmonton** in Expansion Draft, June 18, 1992. Traded to **Vancouver** by **Tampa Bay** for Dave Capuano and Vancouver's fourth round choice (later traded to New Jersey — later traded to Calgary — Calgary selected Ryan Duthie) in 1994 Entry Draft, November 3, 1992. Claimed by **Anaheim** from **Vancouver** in Expansion Draft, June 24, 1993. Traded to **Philadelphia** by **Anaheim** for Milos Holan, March 8, 1995.

SEROWIK, JEFF (sair-OH-wihk) — CHI.

Defense. Shoots right. 6'1", 210 lbs. Born, Manchester, NH, January 10, 1967.
(Toronto's 5th choice, 85th overall, in 1985 Entry Draft).

			Regular Season					Playoffs				
Season	**Club**	**Lea**	**GP**	**G**	**A**	**TP**	**PIM**	**GP**	**G**	**A**	**TP**	**PIM**
1986-87	Providence	H.E.	33	3	8	11	22	....	....	....	....	....
1987-88	Providence	H.E.	33	3	9	12	44	....	....	....	....	....
1988-89	Providence	H.E.	35	3	14	17	48	....	....	....	....	....
1989-90a	Providence	H.E.	35	6	19	25	34	....	....	....	....	....
1990-91	**Toronto**	**NHL**	**1**	**0**	**0**	**0**	**0**	....	....	....	....	....
	Newmarket	AHL	60	8	15	23	45	....	....	....	....	....
1991-92	St. John's	AHL	78	11	34	45	60	16	4	9	13	22
1992-93b	St. John's	AHL	77	19	35	54	92	9	1	5	6	8
1993-94	Cincinnati	IHL	79	6	21	27	98	7	0	1	1	8
1994-95cd	Providence	AHL	78	28	34	62	102	13	4	6	10	10
	Boston	**NHL**	**1**	**0**	**0**	**0**	**0**	....	....	....	....	....
	NHL Totals		**2**	**0**	**0**	**0**	**0**	....	....	....	....	....

a Hockey East Second All-Star Team (1990)
b AHL Second All-Star Team (1993)
c AHL First All-Star Team (1995)
d Won Eddie Shore Plaque (Outstanding Defenseman - AHL) (1995)

Signed as a free agent by **Florida**, July 20, 1993. Signed as a free agent by **Boston**, June 29, 1994. Signed as a free agent by **Chicago**, August 10, 1995.

SEVERYN, BRENT — NYI

Defense. Shoots left. 6'2", 210 lbs. Born, Vegreville, Alta., February 22, 1966.

			Regular Season					Playoffs				
Season	Club	Lea	GP	G	A	TP	PIM	GP	G	A	TP	PIM
1983-84	Seattle	WHL	72	14	22	36	49	....	....	....	....	....
1984-85	Seattle	WHL	38	8	32	40	54	....	....	....	....	....
	Brandon	WHL	26	7	16	23	57	....	....	....	....	....
1985-86	Seattle	WHL	33	11	20	31	164	....	....	....	....	....
	Saskatoon	WHL	9	1	4	5	38	....	....	....	....	....
1986-87	U. of Alberta	CWUAA	43	7	19	26	171	....	....	....	....	....
1987-88	U. of Alberta	CWUAA	46	21	29	50	178	....	....	....	....	....
1988-89	Halifax	AHL	47	2	12	14	141	....	....	....	....	....
1989-90	Quebec	NHL	35	0	2	2	42	....	....	....	....	....
	Halifax	AHL	43	6	9	15	105	6	1	2	3	49
1990-91	Halifax	AHL	50	7	26	33	202	....	....	....	....	....
1991-92	Utica	AHL	80	11	33	44	211	4	0	1	1	4
1992-93a	Utica	AHL	77	20	32	52	240	5	0	0	0	35
1993-94	Florida	NHL	67	4	7	11	156	....	....	....	....	....
1994-95	Florida	NHL	9	1	1	2	37	....	....	....	....	....
	NY Islanders	NHL	19	1	3	4	34	....	....	....	....	....
	NHL Totals		130	6	13	19	269	....	....	....	....	....

a AHL First All-Star Team (1993)

Signed as a free agent by **Quebec**, July 15, 1988. Traded to **New Jersey** by **Quebec** for Dave Marcinyshyn, June 3, 1991. Traded to **Winnipeg** by **New Jersey** for Winnipeg's sixth round choice (Ryan Smart) in 1994 Entry Draft, September 30, 1993. Traded to **Florida** by **Winnipeg** for Milan Tichy, October 3, 1993. Traded to **NY Islanders** by **Florida** for NY Islanders' fourth round choice (Dave Duerden) in 1995 Entry Draft, March 3, 1995.

SEVIGNY, PIERRE (seh-VIH-nee) — MTL.

Left wing. Shoots left. 6', 195 lbs. Born, Trois-Rivières, Que., September 8, 1971.
(Montreal's 4th choice, 51st overall, in 1989 Entry Draft).

			Regular Season					Playoffs				
Season	Club	Lea	GP	G	A	TP	PIM	GP	G	A	TP	PIM
1988-89	Verdun	QMJHL	67	27	43	70	88	....	....	....	....	....
1989-90a	St-Hyacinthe	QMJHL	67	47	72	119	205	12	8	8	16	42
1990-91a	St-Hyacinthe	QMJHL	60	36	46	82	203	....	....	....	....	....
1991-92	Fredericton	AHL	74	22	37	59	145	7	1	1	2	26
1992-93	Fredericton	AHL	80	36	40	76	113	5	1	1	2	2
1993-94	Montreal	NHL	43	4	5	9	42	3	0	1	1	0
1994-95	Montreal	NHL	19	0	0	0	15	....	....	....	....	....
	NHL Totals		62	4	5	9	57	3	0	1	1	0

a QMJHL Second All-Star Team (1990, 1991)

SHALAMAI, SERGEI — L.A.

Left wing. Shoots left. 5'6", 147 lbs. Born, Moscow, USSR, June 12, 1976.
(Los Angeles' 8th choice, 241st overall, in 1994 Entry Draft).

			Regular Season					Playoffs				
Season	Club	Lea	GP	G	A	TP	PIM	GP	G	A	TP	PIM
1992-93	Spartak	CIS	4	1	0	1	0	....	....	....	....	....
1993-94	Spartak	CIS	43	8	7	15	10	....	....	....	....	....
1994-95	Spartak	CIS	44	10	5	15	30	....	....	....	....	....

SHALDYBIN, YEVGENY — BOS.

Defense. Shoots left. 6'1", 198 lbs. Born, Novosibirsk, USSR, July 29, 1975.
(Boston's 6th choice, 151st overall, in 1995 Entry Draft).

			Regular Season					Playoffs				
Season	Club	Lea	GP	G	A	TP	PIM	GP	G	A	TP	PIM
1993-94	Yaroslavl	CIS	14	0	0	0	0	....	....	....	....	....
1994-95	Yaroslavl	CIS	42	2	5	7	10	4	0	1	1	0

SHANAHAN, BRENDAN — HFD.

Left wing. Shoots right. 6'3", 215 lbs. Born, Mimico, Ont., January 23, 1969.
(New Jersey's 1st choice, 2nd overall, in 1987 Entry Draft).

			Regular Season					Playoffs				
Season	Club	Lea	GP	G	A	TP	PIM	GP	G	A	TP	PIM
1985-86	London	OHL	59	28	34	62	70	5	5	5	10	5
1986-87	London	OHL	56	39	53	92	92	....	....	....	....	....
1987-88	New Jersey	NHL	65	7	19	26	131	12	2	1	3	44
1988-89	New Jersey	NHL	68	22	28	50	115	....	....	....	....	....
1989-90	New Jersey	NHL	73	30	42	72	137	6	3	3	6	20
1990-91	New Jersey	NHL	75	29	37	66	141	7	3	5	8	12
1991-92	St. Louis	NHL	80	33	36	69	171	6	2	3	5	14
1992-93	St. Louis	NHL	71	51	43	94	174	11	4	3	7	18
1993-94a	St. Louis	NHL	81	52	50	102	211	4	2	5	7	4
1994-95	Dusseldorf	Ger.	3	5	3	8	4	....	....	....	....	....
	St. Louis	NHL	45	20	21	41	136	5	4	5	9	14
	NHL Totals		558	244	276	520	1216	51	20	25	45	126

a NHL First All-Star Team (1994)

Played in NHL All-Star Game (1994)

Signed as a free agent by **St. Louis**, July 25, 1991. Traded to **Hartford** by **St. Louis** for Chris Pronger, July 27, 1995.

SHANK, DANIEL

Right wing. Shoots right. 5'10", 190 lbs. Born, Montreal, Que., May 12, 1967.

			Regular Season					Playoffs				
Season	Club	Lea	GP	G	A	TP	PIM	GP	G	A	TP	PIM
1985-86	Shawinigan	QMJHL	51	34	38	72	184	....	....	....	....	....
1986-87	Hull	QMJHL	46	26	43	69	325	....	....	....	....	....
1987-88	Hull	QMJHL	42	23	34	57	274	5	3	2	5	16
1988-89	Adirondack	AHL	42	5	20	25	113	17	11	8	19	102
1989-90	Detroit	NHL	57	11	13	24	143	....	....	....	....	....
	Adirondack	AHL	14	8	8	16	36	....	....	....	....	....
1990-91	Detroit	NHL	7	0	1	1	14	....	....	....	....	....
	Adirondack	AHL	60	26	49	75	278	....	....	....	....	....
1991-92	Adirondack	AHL	27	13	21	34	112	....	....	....	....	....
	Hartford	NHL	13	2	0	2	18	5	0	0	0	22
	Springfield	AHL	31	9	19	28	83	8	8	0	8	48
1992-93a	San Diego	IHL	77	39	53	92	*495	14	5	10	15	*131
1993-94	San Diego	IHL	63	27	36	63	273	....	....	....	....	....
	Phoenix	IHL	7	4	6	10	26	....	....	....	....	....
1994-95	Minnesota	IHL	19	4	11	15	30	....	....	....	....	....
	Detroit	IHL	54	44	27	71	142	5	2	2	4	6
	NHL Totals		77	13	14	27	175	5	0	0	0	22

a IHL First All-Star Team (1993)

Signed as a free agent by **Detroit**, May 26, 1989. Traded to **Hartford** by **Detroit** for Chris Tancill, December 18, 1991.

SHANNON, DARRIN — WPG.

Left wing. Shoots left. 6'2", 210 lbs. Born, Barrie, Ont., December 8, 1969.
(Pittsburgh's 1st choice, 4th overall, in 1988 Entry Draft).

			Regular Season					Playoffs				
Season	Club	Lea	GP	G	A	TP	PIM	GP	G	A	TP	PIM
1986-87	Windsor	OHL	60	16	67	83	116	14	4	6	10	8
1987-88	Windsor	OHL	43	33	41	74	49	12	6	12	18	9
1988-89	Buffalo	NHL	3	0	0	0	0	2	0	0	0	0
	Windsor	OHL	54	33	48	81	47	4	1	6	7	2
1989-90	Buffalo	NHL	17	2	7	9	4	6	0	1	1	4
	Rochester	AHL	50	20	23	43	25	9	4	1	5	2
1990-91	Buffalo	NHL	34	8	6	14	12	6	1	2	3	4
	Rochester	AHL	49	26	34	60	56	10	3	5	8	22
1991-92	Buffalo	NHL	1	0	1	1	0	....	....	....	....	....
	Winnipeg	NHL	68	13	26	39	41	7	0	1	1	10
1992-93	Winnipeg	NHL	84	20	40	60	91	6	2	4	6	6
1993-94	Winnipeg	NHL	77	21	37	58	87	....	....	....	....	....
1994-95	Winnipeg	NHL	19	5	3	8	14	....	....	....	....	....
	NHL Totals		303	69	120	189	249	27	3	8	11	24

Traded to **Buffalo** by **Pittsburgh** with Doug Bodger for Tom Barrasso and Buffalo's third round choice (Joe Dziedzic) in 1990 Entry Draft, November 12, 1988. Traded to **Winnipeg** by **Buffalo** with Mike Hartman and Dean Kennedy for Dave McLlwain, Gord Donnelly, Winnipeg's fifth round choice (Yuri Khmylev) in 1992 Entry Draft and future considerations, October 11, 1991.

SHANNON, DARRYL — WPG.

Defense. Shoots left. 6'2", 200 lbs. Born, Barrie, Ont., June 21, 1968.
(Toronto's 2nd choice, 36th overall, in 1986 Entry Draft).

			Regular Season					Playoffs				
Season	Club	Lea	GP	G	A	TP	PIM	GP	G	A	TP	PIM
1985-86	Windsor	OHL	57	6	21	27	52	16	5	6	11	22
1986-87a	Windsor	OHL	64	23	27	50	83	14	4	8	12	18
1987-88b	Windsor	OHL	60	16	67	83	116	12	3	8	11	17
1988-89	Toronto	NHL	14	1	3	4	6	....	....	....	....	....
	Newmarket	AHL	61	5	24	29	37	5	0	3	3	10
1989-90	Toronto	NHL	10	0	1	1	12	....	....	....	....	....
	Newmarket	AHL	47	4	15	19	58	....	....	....	....	....
1990-91	Toronto	NHL	10	0	1	1	0	....	....	....	....	....
	Newmarket	AHL	47	2	14	16	51	....	....	....	....	....
1991-92	Toronto	NHL	48	2	8	10	23	....	....	....	....	....
1992-93	Toronto	NHL	16	0	0	0	11	....	....	....	....	....
	St. John's	AHL	7	1	1	2	4	....	....	....	....	....
1993-94	Winnipeg	NHL	20	0	4	4	18	....	....	....	....	....
	Moncton	AHL	37	1	10	11	62	20	1	7	8	32
1994-95	Winnipeg	NHL	40	5	9	14	48	....	....	....	....	....
	NHL Totals		158	8	26	34	118	....	....	....	....	....

a OHL Second All-Star Team (1987)
b OHL First All-Star Team (1988)

Signed as a free agent by **Winnipeg**, June 30, 1993.

SHANTZ, JEFF — CHI.

Center. Shoots right. 6', 184 lbs. Born, Duchess, Alta., October 10, 1973.
(Chicago's 2nd choice, 36th overall, in 1992 Entry Draft).

			Regular Season					Playoffs				
Season	Club	Lea	GP	G	A	TP	PIM	GP	G	A	TP	PIM
1990-91	Regina	WHL	69	16	21	37	22	8	2	2	4	2
1991-92	Regina	WHL	72	39	50	89	75	....	....	....	....	....
1992-93a	Regina	WHL	64	29	54	83	75	13	2	12	14	14
1993-94	Chicago	NHL	52	3	13	16	30	6	0	0	0	6
	Indianapolis	IHL	19	5	9	14	20	....	....	....	....	....
1994-95	Indianapolis	IHL	32	9	15	24	20	....	....	....	....	....
	Chicago	NHL	45	6	12	18	33	16	3	1	4	2
	NHL Totals		97	9	25	34	63	22	3	1	4	8

a WHL East First All-Star Team (1993)

SHARIFIJANOV, VADIM (shah-rih-FYAH-nohv) — N.J.

Right wing. Shoots left. 5'11", 210 lbs. Born, Ufa, USSR, December 23, 1975.
(New Jersey's 1st choice, 25th overall, in 1994 Entry Draft).

			Regular Season					Playoffs				
Season	Club	Lea	GP	G	A	TP	PIM	GP	G	A	TP	PIM
1992-93	Ufa Salavat	CIS	37	6	4	10	16	2	1	0	1	0
1993-94	Ufa Salavat	CIS	46	10	6	16	36	5	3	0	3	4
1994-95	CSKA	CIS	34	7	3	10	26	2	0	0	0	0
	Albany	AHL	1	1	1	2	0	9	3	3	6	10

SHARPLES, JEFF

Defense. Shoots left. 6'1", 195 lbs. Born, Terrace, B.C., July 28, 1967.
(Detroit's 2nd choice, 29th overall, in 1985 Entry Draft).

			Regular Season					Playoffs				
Season	Club	Lea	GP	G	A	TP	PIM	GP	G	A	TP	PIM
1983-84	Kelowna	WHL	72	9	24	33	51	....	....	....	....	....
1984-85a	Kelowna	WHL	72	12	41	53	90	6	0	1	1	6
1985-86	Spokane	WHL	3	0	0	0	4	....	....	....	....	....
	Portland	WHL	19	2	6	8	44	15	2	6	8	6
1986-87	Detroit	NHL	3	0	1	1	2	2	0	0	0	2
	Portland	WHL	44	25	35	60	92	20	7	15	22	23
1987-88	Detroit	NHL	56	10	25	35	42	4	0	3	3	4
	Adirondack	AHL	4	2	1	3	4	....	....	....	....	....
1988-89	Detroit	NHL	46	4	9	13	26	1	0	0	0	0
	Adirondack	AHL	10	0	4	4	8	....	....	....	....	....
1989-90	Adirondack	AHL	9	2	5	7	6	....	....	....	....	....
	Cape Breton	AHL	38	4	13	17	28	....	....	....	....	....
	Utica	AHL	13	2	5	7	19	5	1	2	3	15
1990-91	Utica	AHL	64	16	29	45	42	....	....	....	....	....
1991-92	Capital Dist.	AHL	31	3	12	15	18	7	6	5	11	4
1992-93	Kansas City	IHL	39	5	21	26	43	8	0	0	0	6
1993-94	Las Vegas	IHL	68	18	32	50	68	5	2	1	3	6
1994-95	Las Vegas	IHL	72	20	33	53	63	10	4	4	8	18
	NHL Totals		105	14	35	49	70	7	0	3	3	6

a WHL West Second All-Star Team (1985)

Traded to **Edmonton** by **Detroit** with Petr Klima, Joe Murphy and Adam Graves for Jimmy Carson, Kevin McClelland and Edmonton's fifth round choice (later traded to Montreal — Montreal selected Brad Layzell) in 1991 Entry Draft, November 2, 1989. Traded to **New Jersey** by **Edmonton** for Reijo Ruotsalainen, March 6, 1990.

SHAW, BRAD — OTT.

Defense. Shoots right. 6', 190 lbs. Born, Cambridge, Ont., April 28, 1964.
(Detroit's 5th choice, 86th overall, in 1982 Entry Draft).

			Regular Season					Playoffs				
Season	**Club**	**Lea**	**GP**	**G**	**A**	**TP**	**PIM**	**GP**	**G**	**A**	**TP**	**PIM**
1981-82	Ottawa	OHL	68	13	59	72	24	15	1	13	14	4
1982-83	Ottawa	OHL	63	12	66	78	24	9	2	9	11	4
1983-84a	Ottawa	OHL	68	11	71	82	75	13	2	*27	29	9
1984-85	Binghamton	AHL	24	1	10	11	4	8	1	8	9	6
	Salt Lake	IHL	44	3	29	32	25	....	....	....	....	....
1985-86	**Hartford**	**NHL**	**8**	**0**	**2**	**2**	**4**	....	....	....	....	....
	Binghamton	AHL	64	10	44	54	33	5	0	2	2	6
1986-87	**Hartford**	**NHL**	**2**	**0**	**0**	**0**	**0**	....	....	....	....	....
bc	Binghamton	AHL	77	9	30	39	43	12	1	8	9	2
1987-88	**Hartford**	**NHL**	**1**	**0**	**0**	**0**	**0**	....	....	....	....	....
b	Binghamton	AHL	73	12	50	62	50	4	0	5	5	4
1988-89	Verese	Italy	35	10	30	40	44	11	4	8	12	13
	Cdn. National	....	4	1	0	1	2	....	....	....	....	....
	Hartford	**NHL**	**3**	**1**	**0**	**1**	**0**	**3**	**1**	**0**	**1**	**0**
1989-90d	**Hartford**	**NHL**	**64**	**3**	**32**	**35**	**30**	**7**	**2**	**5**	**7**	**0**
1990-91	**Hartford**	**NHL**	**72**	**4**	**28**	**32**	**29**	**6**	**1**	**2**	**3**	**2**
1991-92	**Hartford**	**NHL**	**62**	**3**	**22**	**25**	**44**	**3**	**0**	**1**	**1**	**4**
1992-93	**Ottawa**	**NHL**	**81**	**7**	**34**	**41**	**34**	....	....	....	....	....
1993-94	**Ottawa**	**NHL**	**66**	**4**	**19**	**23**	**59**	....	....	....	....	....
1994-95	**Ottawa**	**NHL**	**2**	**0**	**0**	**0**	**0**	....	....	....	....	....
	Atlanta	IHL	26	1	18	19	17	5	3	4	7	9
	NHL Totals		**361**	**22**	**137**	**159**	**200**	**19**	**4**	**8**	**12**	**6**

a OHL First All-Star Team (1984)
b AHL First All-Star Team (1987, 1988)
c Won Eddie Shore Plaque (AHL Outstanding Defenseman) (1987)
d NHL All-Rookie Team (1990)

Rights traded to **Hartford** by **Detroit** for Hartford's eighth round choice (Urban Nordin) in 1984 Entry Draft, May 29, 1984. Traded to **New Jersey** by **Hartford** for cash, June 13, 1992. Claimed by **Ottawa** from **New Jersey** in Expansion Draft, June 18, 1992.

SHAW, DAVID — T.B.

Defense. Shoots right. 6'2", 205 lbs. Born, St. Thomas, Ont., May 25, 1964.
(Quebec's 1st choice, 13th overall, in 1982 Entry Draft).

			Regular Season					Playoffs				
Season	**Club**	**Lea**	**GP**	**G**	**A**	**TP**	**PIM**	**GP**	**G**	**A**	**TP**	**PIM**
1981-82	Kitchener	OHL	68	6	25	31	94	15	2	2	4	51
1982-83	**Quebec**	**NHL**	**2**	**0**	**0**	**0**	**0**	....	....	....	....	....
	Kitchener	OHL	57	18	56	74	78	12	2	10	12	18
1983-84	**Quebec**	**NHL**	**3**	**0**	**0**	**0**	**0**	....	....	....	....	....
a	Kitchener	OHL	58	14	34	48	73	16	4	9	13	12
1984-85	**Quebec**	**NHL**	**14**	**0**	**0**	**0**	**11**	....	....	....	....	....
	Fredericton	AHL	48	7	6	13	73	2	0	0	0	7
1985-86	**Quebec**	**NHL**	**73**	**7**	**19**	**26**	**78**	....	....	....	....	....
1986-87	**Quebec**	**NHL**	**75**	**0**	**19**	**19**	**69**	....	....	....	....	....
1987-88	**NY Rangers**	**NHL**	**68**	**7**	**25**	**32**	**100**	....	....	....	....	....
1988-89	**NY Rangers**	**NHL**	**63**	**6**	**11**	**17**	**88**	**4**	**0**	**2**	**2**	**30**
1989-90	**NY Rangers**	**NHL**	**22**	**2**	**10**	**12**	**22**	....	....	....	....	....
1990-91	**NY Rangers**	**NHL**	**77**	**2**	**10**	**12**	**89**	**6**	**0**	**0**	**0**	**11**
1991-92	**NY Rangers**	**NHL**	**10**	**0**	**1**	**1**	**15**	....	....	....	....	....
	Edmonton	**NHL**	**12**	**1**	**1**	**2**	**8**	....	....	....	....	....
	Minnesota	**NHL**	**37**	**0**	**7**	**7**	**49**	**7**	**2**	**2**	**4**	**10**
1992-93	**Boston**	**NHL**	**77**	**10**	**14**	**24**	**108**	**4**	**0**	**1**	**1**	**6**
1993-94	**Boston**	**NHL**	**55**	**1**	**9**	**10**	**85**	**13**	**1**	**2**	**3**	**16**
1994-95	**Boston**	**NHL**	**44**	**3**	**4**	**7**	**36**	**5**	**0**	**1**	**1**	**4**
	NHL Totals		**632**	**39**	**130**	**169**	**758**	**39**	**3**	**8**	**11**	**77**

a OHL First All-Star Team (1984)

Traded to **NY Rangers** by **Quebec** with John Ogrodnick for Jeff Jackson and Terry Carkner, September 30, 1987. Traded to **Edmonton** by **NY Rangers** for Jeff Beukeboom, November 12, 1991. Traded to **Minnesota** by **Edmonton** for Brian Glynn, January 21, 1992. Traded to **Boston** by **Minnesota** for future considerations, September 2, 1992.

Traded to **Tampa Bay** by **Boston** for Detroit's third round choice (previously acquired by Tampa Bay) in 1996 Entry Draft, August 17, 1995.

SHAW, LLOYD — VAN.

Defense. Shoots right. 6'3", 215 lbs. Born, Regina, Sask., September 26, 1976.
(Vancouver's 4th choice, 92nd overall, in 1995 Entry Draft).

			Regular Season					Playoffs				
Season	**Club**	**Lea**	**GP**	**G**	**A**	**TP**	**PIM**	**GP**	**G**	**A**	**TP**	**PIM**
1993-94	Seattle	WHL	47	0	4	4	107	8	0	0	0	23
1994-95	Seattle	WHL	66	3	12	15	313	3	0	0	0	13

SHEPPARD, RAY — DET.

Right wing. Shoots right. 6'1", 195 lbs. Born, Pembroke, Ont., May 27, 1966.
(Buffalo's 3rd choice, 60th overall, in 1984 Entry Draft).

			Regular Season					Playoffs				
Season	**Club**	**Lea**	**GP**	**G**	**A**	**TP**	**PIM**	**GP**	**G**	**A**	**TP**	**PIM**
1983-84	Cornwall	OHL	68	44	36	80	69	....	....	....	....	....
1984-85	Cornwall	OHL	49	25	33	58	51	9	2	12	14	4
1985-86a	Cornwall	OHL	63	*81	61	*142	25	6	7	4	11	0
1986-87	Rochester	AHL	55	18	13	31	11	15	12	3	15	2
1987-88b	**Buffalo**	**NHL**	**74**	**38**	**27**	**65**	**14**	**6**	**1**	**1**	**2**	**2**
1988-89	**Buffalo**	**NHL**	**67**	**22**	**21**	**43**	**15**	**1**	**0**	**1**	**1**	**0**
1989-90	**Buffalo**	**NHL**	**18**	**4**	**2**	**6**	**0**	....	....	....	....	....
	Rochester	AHL	5	3	5	8	2	17	8	7	15	9
1990-91	**NY Rangers**	**NHL**	**59**	**24**	**23**	**47**	**21**	....	....	....	....	....
1991-92	**Detroit**	**NHL**	**74**	**36**	**26**	**62**	**27**	**11**	**6**	**2**	**8**	**4**
1992-93	**Detroit**	**NHL**	**70**	**32**	**34**	**66**	**29**	**7**	**2**	**3**	**5**	**0**
1993-94	**Detroit**	**NHL**	**82**	**52**	**41**	**93**	**26**	**7**	**2**	**1**	**3**	**4**
1994-95	**Detroit**	**NHL**	**43**	**30**	**10**	**40**	**17**	**17**	**4**	**3**	**7**	**5**
	NHL Totals		**487**	**238**	**184**	**422**	**149**	**49**	**15**	**11**	**26**	**15**

a OHL First All-Star Team (1986)
b NHL All-Rookie Team (1988)

Traded to **NY Rangers** by **Buffalo** for cash and future considerations, July 9, 1990. Signed as a free agent by **Detroit**, August 5, 1991.

SHEVALIER, JEFF — (sheh-VAL-ee-ay) — L.A.

Left wing. Shoots left. 5'11", 185 lbs. Born, Mississauga, Ont., March 14, 1974.
(Los Angeles' 4th choice, 111th overall, in 1992 Entry Draft).

			Regular Season					Playoffs				
Season	**Club**	**Lea**	**GP**	**G**	**A**	**TP**	**PIM**	**GP**	**G**	**A**	**TP**	**PIM**
1991-92	North Bay	OHL	64	28	29	57	26	21	5	11	16	25
1992-93	North Bay	OHL	62	59	54	113	46	2	1	2	3	4
1993-94a	North Bay	OHL	64	52	49	101	52	17	8	14	22	18
1994-95	Phoenix	IHL	68	31	39	70	44	9	5	4	9	0
	Los Angeles	**NHL**	**1**	**1**	**0**	**1**	**0**	....	....	....	....	....
	NHL Totals		**1**	**1**	**0**	**1**	**0**	....	....	....	....	....

a OHL First All-Star Team (1994)

SHUCHUK, GARY — (SHOO-chuhk) — L.A.

Right wing. Shoots right. 5'11", 190 lbs. Born, Edmonton, Alta., February 17, 1967.
(Detroit's 1st choice, 22nd overall, in 1988 Supplemental Draft).

			Regular Season					Playoffs				
Season	**Club**	**Lea**	**GP**	**G**	**A**	**TP**	**PIM**	**GP**	**G**	**A**	**TP**	**PIM**
1986-87	U. Wisconsin	WCHA	42	19	11	30	72	....	....	....	....	....
1987-88	U. Wisconsin	WCHA	44	7	22	29	70	....	....	....	....	....
1988-89	U. Wisconsin	WCHA	46	18	19	37	102	....	....	....	....	....
1989-90ab	U. Wisconsin	WCHA	45	*41	39	*80	70	....	....	....	....	....
1990-91	**Detroit**	**NHL**	**6**	**1**	**2**	**3**	**6**	**3**	**0**	**0**	**0**	**0**
	Adirondack	AHL	59	23	24	47	32	....	....	....	....	....
1991-92	Adirondack	AHL	79	32	48	80	48	19	4	9	13	18
1992-93	Adirondack	AHL	47	24	53	77	66	....	....	....	....	....
	Los Angeles	**NHL**	**25**	**2**	**4**	**6**	**16**	**17**	**2**	**2**	**4**	**12**
1993-94	**Los Angeles**	**NHL**	**56**	**3**	**4**	**7**	**30**	....	....	....	....	....
1994-95	**Los Angeles**	**NHL**	**22**	**3**	**6**	**9**	**6**	....	....	....	....	....
	Phoenix	IHL	13	8	7	15	12	....	....	....	....	....
	NHL Totals		**109**	**9**	**16**	**25**	**58**	**20**	**2**	**2**	**4**	**12**

a WCHA First All-Star Team (1990)
b NCAA West First All-American Team (1990)

Traded to **Los Angeles** by **Detroit** with Jimmy Carson and Marc Potvin for Paul Coffey, Sylvain Couturier and Jim Hiller, January 29, 1993.

SILLINGER, MIKE — ANA.

Center. Shoots right. 5'10", 190 lbs. Born, Regina, Sask., June 29, 1971.
(Detroit's 1st choice, 11th overall, in 1989 Entry Draft).

			Regular Season					Playoffs				
Season	**Club**	**Lea**	**GP**	**G**	**A**	**TP**	**PIM**	**GP**	**G**	**A**	**TP**	**PIM**
1987-88	Regina	WHL	67	18	25	43	17	4	2	2	4	0
1988-89	Regina	WHL	72	53	78	131	52	....	....	....	....	....
1989-90a	Regina	WHL	70	57	72	129	41	11	12	10	22	2
	Adirondack	AHL	....	....	....	....	....	1	0	0	0	0
1990-91	**Detroit**	**NHL**	**3**	**0**	**1**	**1**	**0**	**3**	**0**	**1**	**1**	**0**
b	Regina	WHL	57	50	66	116	42	8	6	9	15	4
1991-92	Adirondack	AHL	64	25	41	66	26	15	9	*19	*28	12
	Detroit	**NHL**	....	....	....	....	....	**8**	**2**	**2**	**4**	**2**
1992-93	**Detroit**	**NHL**	**51**	**4**	**17**	**21**	**16**	....	....	....	....	....
	Adirondack	AHL	15	10	20	30	31	11	5	13	18	10
1993-94	**Detroit**	**NHL**	**62**	**8**	**21**	**29**	**10**	....	....	....	....	....
1994-95	**Detroit**	**NHL**	**13**	**2**	**6**	**8**	**2**	....	....	....	....	....
1994-95	Wien	Aus.	13	13	14	27	10	....	....	....	....	....
	Anaheim	**NHL**	**15**	**2**	**5**	**7**	**6**	....	....	....	....	....
	NHL Totals		**144**	**16**	**50**	**66**	**34**	**11**	**2**	**3**	**5**	**2**

a WHL East Second All-Star Team (1990)
b WHL East First All-Star Team (1991)

Traded to **Anaheim** by **Detroit** with Jason York for Stu Grimson, Mark Ferner and Anaheim's sixth round choice in 1996 Entry Draft, April 4, 1995.

SILVERMAN, ANDREW — NYR

Defense. Shoots left. 6'3", 205 lbs. Born, Beverly, MA, August 23, 1972.
(NY Rangers' 11th choice, 181st overall, in 1990 Entry Draft).

			Regular Season					Playoffs				
Season	**Club**	**Lea**	**GP**	**G**	**A**	**TP**	**PIM**	**GP**	**G**	**A**	**TP**	**PIM**
1991-92	U. of Maine	H.E.	30	2	9	11	18	....	....	....	....	....
1992-93	U. of Maine	H.E.	37	1	7	8	56	....	....	....	....	....
1993-94	U. of Maine	H.E.	35	0	3	3	80	....	....	....	....	....
1994-95	Binghamton	AHL	5	0	1	1	2	....	....	....	....	....
	Charlotte	ECHL	64	3	11	14	57	3	0	0	0	2

SIMON, CHRIS — COL.

Left wing. Shoots left. 6'3", 219 lbs. Born, Wawa, Ont., January 30, 1972.
(Philadelphia's 2nd choice, 25th overall, in 1990 Entry Draft).

			Regular Season					Playoffs				
Season	**Club**	**Lea**	**GP**	**G**	**A**	**TP**	**PIM**	**GP**	**G**	**A**	**TP**	**PIM**
1988-89	Ottawa	OHL	36	4	2	6	31	....	....	....	....	....
1989-90	Ottawa	OHL	57	36	38	74	146	3	2	1	3	4
1990-91	Ottawa	OHL	20	16	6	22	69	17	5	9	14	59
1991-92	Ottawa	OHL	2	1	1	2	24	....	....	....	....	....
	S.S. Marie	OHL	31	19	25	44	143	11	5	8	13	49
1992-93	**Quebec**	**NHL**	**16**	**1**	**1**	**2**	**67**	**5**	**0**	**0**	**0**	**26**
	Halifax	AHL	36	12	6	18	131	....	....	....	....	....
1993-94	**Quebec**	**NHL**	**37**	**4**	**4**	**8**	**132**	....	....	....	....	....
1994-95	**Quebec**	**NHL**	**29**	**3**	**9**	**12**	**106**	**6**	**1**	**1**	**2**	**19**
	NHL Totals		**82**	**8**	**14**	**22**	**305**	**11**	**1**	**1**	**2**	**45**

Traded to **Quebec** by **Philadelphia** with Peter Forsberg, Steve Duchesne, Kerry Huffman, Mike Ricci, Ron Hextall, Philadelphia's first round choice in the 1993 (Jocelyn Thibault) and 1994 (later traded to Toronto — later traded to Washington — Washington selected Nolan Baumgartner) Entry Drafts and cash for Eric Lindros, June 30, 1992.

SIMON, JASON — WPG.

Left wing. Shoots left. 6'1", 190 lbs. Born, Sarnia, Ont., March 21, 1969.
(New Jersey's 9th choice, 215th overall, in 1989 Entry Draft).

			Regular Season					Playoffs				
Season	**Club**	**Lea**	**GP**	**G**	**A**	**TP**	**PIM**	**GP**	**G**	**A**	**TP**	**PIM**
1986-87	London	OHL	33	1	2	3	33	....	....	....	....	....
	Sudbury	OHL	26	2	3	5	50	....	....	....	....	....
1987-88	Sudbury	OHL	26	5	7	12	35	....	....	....	....	....
	Hamilton	OHL	29	5	13	18	124	11	0	2	2	15
1988-89	Windsor	OHL	62	23	39	62	193	4	1	4	5	13
1989-90	Utica	AHL	16	3	4	7	28	2	0	0	0	12
	Nashville	ECHL	13	4	3	7	81	5	1	3	4	17
1990-91	Utica	AHL	50	2	12	14	189	....	....	....	....	....
	Johnstown	ECHL	22	11	9	20	55	....	....	....	....	....
1991-92	Utica	AHL	1	0	0	0	12	....	....	....	....	....
	San Diego	IHL	13	1	4	5	45	3	0	1	1	9
1992-93	Detroit	ColHL	11	7	13	20	38	....	....	....	....	....
	Flint	ColHL	44	17	32	49	202	....	....	....	....	....
1993-94	Salt Lake	IHL	50	7	7	14	*323	....	....	....	....	....
	NY Islanders	**NHL**	**4**	**0**	**0**	**0**	**34**	....	....	....	....	....
	Detroit	ColHL	13	9	16	25	87	....	....	....	....	....
1994-95	Denver	IHL	61	3	6	9	300	1	0	0	0	12
	NHL Totals		**4**	**0**	**0**	**0**	**34**	....	....	....	....	....

Signed as a free agent by **NY Islanders**, January 6, 1994. Signed as a free agent by **Winnipeg**, August 9, 1995.

SIMON, TODD

Center. Shoots right. 5'10", 188 lbs. Born, Toronto, Ont., April 21, 1972.
(Buffalo's 9th choice, 203rd overall, in 1992 Entry Draft).

			Regular Season					Playoffs				
Season	Club	Lea	GP	G	A	TP	PIM	GP	G	A	TP	PIM
1990-91	Niagara Falls	OHL	65	51	74	125	35	14	7	8	15	12
1991-92a	Niagara Falls	OHL	66	53	93	*146	72	17	17	24	*41	36
1992-93	Rochester	AHL	67	27	66	93	54	12	3	14	17	15
1993-94	**Buffalo**	**NHL**	**15**	**0**	**1**	**1**	**0**	**5**	**1**	**0**	**1**	**0**
	Rochester	AHL	55	33	52	85	79	....	....	....	....	....
1994-95	Rochester	AHL	69	25	65	90	78	5	0	2	2	21
	NHL Totals		**15**	**0**	**1**	**1**	**0**	**5**	**1**	**0**	**1**	**0**

a OHL First All-Star Team (1992)

SIMONOV, SERGEI (SEE-muh-nahv) TOR.

Defense. Shoots left. 6'3", 194 lbs. Born, Saratov, USSR, May 20, 1974.
(Toronto's 11th choice, 221st overall, in 1992 Entry Draft).

			Regular Season					Playoffs				
Season	Club	Lea	GP	G	A	TP	PIM	GP	G	A	TP	PIM
1992-93	Saratov	CIS	40	0	2	2	34	....	....	....	....	....
1993-94	CSKA	CIS	28	0	0	0	6	....	....	....	....	....
1994-95	Magnitogorsk	CIS	44	6	3	9	8	4	0	0	0	2

SIMONTON, REID COL.

Defense. Shoots right. 6'2", 195 lbs. Born, Calgary, Alta., March 1, 1973.
(Quebec's 1st choice, 9th overall, in 1994 Supplemental Draft).

			Regular Season					Playoffs				
Season	Club	Lea	GP	G	A	TP	PIM	GP	G	A	TP	PIM
1992-93	Union	ECAC	25	7	5	12	78	....	....	....	....	....
1993-94	Union	ECAC	30	4	20	24	76	....	....	....	....	....
1994-95	Union	ECAC	27	4	9	13	63	....	....	....	....	....

SIMPSON, CRAIG

Left wing. Shoots right. 6'2", 195 lbs. Born, London, Ont., February 15, 1967.
(Pittsburgh's 1st choice, 2nd overall, in 1985 Entry Draft).

			Regular Season					Playoffs				
Season	Club	Lea	GP	G	A	TP	PIM	GP	G	A	TP	PIM
1983-84	Michigan State	CCHA	46	14	43	57	38	....	....	....	....	....
1984-85ab	Michigan State	CCHA	42	31	53	84	33	....	....	....	....	....
1985-86	**Pittsburgh**	**NHL**	**76**	**11**	**17**	**28**	**49**	....	....	....	....	....
1986-87	**Pittsburgh**	**NHL**	**72**	**26**	**25**	**51**	**57**	....	....	....	....	....
1987-88	**Pittsburgh**	**NHL**	**21**	**13**	**13**	**26**	**34**	....	....	....	....	....
	Edmonton	**NHL**	**59**	**43**	**21**	**64**	**43**	**19**	**13**	**6**	**19**	**26**
1988-89	**Edmonton**	**NHL**	**66**	**35**	**41**	**76**	**80**	**7**	**2**	**0**	**2**	**10**
1989-90	**Edmonton**	**NHL**	**80**	**29**	**32**	**61**	**180**	**22**	***16**	**15**	***31**	**8**
1990-91	**Edmonton**	**NHL**	**75**	**30**	**27**	**57**	**66**	**18**	**5**	**11**	**16**	**12**
1991-92	**Edmonton**	**NHL**	**79**	**24**	**37**	**61**	**80**	**1**	**0**	**0**	**0**	**0**
1992-93	**Edmonton**	**NHL**	**60**	**24**	**22**	**46**	**36**	....	....	....	....	....
1993-94	**Buffalo**	**NHL**	**22**	**8**	**8**	**16**	**8**	....	....	....	....	....
1994-95	**Buffalo**	**NHL**	**24**	**4**	**7**	**11**	**26**	....	....	....	....	....
	NHL Totals		**634**	**247**	**250**	**497**	**659**	**67**	**36**	**32**	**68**	**56**

a CCHA First All-Star Team (1985)
b NCAA West First All-American Team (1985)

Traded to **Edmonton** by **Pittsburgh** with Dave Hannan, Moe Mantha and Chris Joseph for Paul Coffey, Dave Hunter and Wayne Van Dorp, November 24, 1987. Traded to **Buffalo** by **Edmonton** for Jozef Cierny and Buffalo's fourth round choice (Jussi Tarvainen) in 1994 Entry Draft, September 1, 1993.

SIMPSON, REID N.J.

Left wing. Shoots left. 6'1", 211 lbs. Born, Flin Flon, Man., May 21, 1969.
(Philadelphia's 3rd choice, 72nd overall, in 1989 Entry Draft).

			Regular Season					Playoffs				
Season	Club	Lea	GP	G	A	TP	PIM	GP	G	A	TP	PIM
1987-88	Prince Albert	WHL	72	13	14	27	164	10	1	0	1	43
1988-89	Prince Albert	WHL	59	26	29	55	264	4	2	1	3	30
1989-90	Prince Albert	WHL	29	15	17	32	121	14	4	7	11	34
	Hershey	AHL	28	2	2	4	175	....	....	....	....	....
1990-91	Hershey	AHL	54	9	15	24	183	1	0	0	0	0
1991-92	**Philadelphia**	**NHL**	**1**	**0**	**0**	**0**	**0**	....	....	....	....	....
	Hershey	AHL	60	11	7	18	145	....	....	....	....	....
1992-93	**Minnesota**	**NHL**	**1**	**0**	**0**	**0**	**5**	....	....	....	....	....
	Kalamazoo	IHL	45	5	5	10	193	....	....	....	....	....
1993-94	Kalamazoo	IHL	5	0	0	0	16	....	....	....	....	....
	Albany	AHL	37	9	5	14	135	5	1	1	2	18
1994-95	Albany	AHL	70	18	25	43	268	14	1	8	9	13
	New Jersey	**NHL**	**9**	**0**	**0**	**0**	**27**	....	....	....	....	....
	NHL Totals		**11**	**0**	**0**	**0**	**32**	....	....	....	....	....

Signed as a free agent by **Minnesota**, December 14, 1992. Traded to **New Jersey** by **Dallas** with Roy Mitchell for future considerations, March 21, 1994.

SIMPSON, TODD CGY.

Defense. Shoots left. 6'3", 215 lbs. Born, Edmonton, Alta., May 28, 1973.

			Regular Season					Playoffs				
Season	Club	Lea	GP	G	A	TP	PIM	GP	G	A	TP	PIM
1992-93	Tri-City	WHL	69	5	18	23	196	4	0	0	0	13
1993-94	Tri-City	WHL	12	2	3	5	32	....	....	....	....	....
	Saskatoon	WHL	51	7	19	26	175	16	0	1	1	29
1994-95	Saint John	AHL	80	3	10	13	321	5	0	0	0	4

Signed as free agent by **Calgary**, July 6, 1994.

SINCLAIR, ALAN OTT.

Defense. Shoots right. 6'3", 210 lbs. Born, Mississauga, Ont., April 3, 1973.
(Ottawa's 6th choice, 121st overall, in 1992 Entry Draft).

			Regular Season					Playoffs				
Season	Club	Lea	GP	G	A	TP	PIM	GP	G	A	TP	PIM
1991-92	U. of Michigan	CCHA	22	0	4	4	40	....	....	....	....	....
1992-93	U. of Michigan	CCHA	20	0	3	3	26	....	....	....	....	....
1993-94	U. of Michigan	CCHA	18	0	4	4	14	....	....	....	....	....
1994-95	U. of Michigan	CCHA	30	0	6	6	22	....	....	....	....	....

SITTLER, RYAN PHI.

Left wing. Shoots left. 6'2", 195 lbs. Born, London, Ont., January 28, 1974.
(Philadelphia's 1st choice, 7th overall, in 1992 Entry Draft).

			Regular Season					Playoffs				
Season	Club	Lea	GP	G	A	TP	PIM	GP	G	A	TP	PIM
1992-93	U. of Michigan	CCHA	35	9	24	33	43	....	....	....	....	....
1993-94	U. of Michigan	CCHA	26	9	9	18	14	....	....	....	....	....
1994-95	Hershey	AHL	42	2	7	9	48	....	....	....	....	....
	Johnstown	ECHL	1	1	1	2	0	....	....	....	....	....

SKALDE, JARROD (SKAHL-dee) ANA.

Center. Shoots left. 6', 175 lbs. Born, Niagara Falls, Ont., February 26, 1971.
(New Jersey's 3rd choice, 26th overall, in 1989 Entry Draft).

			Regular Season					Playoffs				
Season	Club	Lea	GP	G	A	TP	PIM	GP	G	A	TP	PIM
1987-88	Oshawa	OHL	60	12	16	28	24	7	2	1	3	2
1988-89	Oshawa	OHL	65	38	38	76	36	6	1	5	6	2
1989-90	Oshawa	OHL	62	40	52	92	66	17	10	7	17	6
1990-91	**New Jersey**	**NHL**	**1**	**0**	**1**	**1**	**0**	....	....	....	....	....
	Utica	AHL	3	3	2	5	0	....	....	....	....	....
	Oshawa	OHL	15	8	14	22	14	....	....	....	....	....
a	Belleville	OHL	40	30	52	82	21	6	9	6	15	10
1991-92	**New Jersey**	**NHL**	**15**	**2**	**4**	**6**	**4**	....	....	....	....	....
	Utica	AHL	62	20	20	40	56	4	3	1	4	8
1992-93	**New Jersey**	**NHL**	**11**	**0**	**2**	**2**	**4**	....	....	....	....	....
	Utica	AHL	59	21	39	60	76	5	0	2	2	19
	Cincinnati	IHL	4	1	2	3	4	....	....	....	....	....
1993-94	**Anaheim**	**NHL**	**20**	**5**	**4**	**9**	**10**	....	....	....	....	....
	San Diego	IHL	57	25	38	63	79	9	3	12	15	10
1994-95	Las Vegas	IHL	74	34	41	75	103	9	2	4	6	8
	NHL Totals		**47**	**7**	**11**	**18**	**18**	....	....	....	....	....

a OHL Second All-Star Team (1991)

Claimed by **Anaheim** from **New Jersey** in Expansion Draft, June 24, 1993. Signed as a free agent by **Anaheim**, May 31, 1995.

SKOREPA, ZDENEK (SKOHR-zheh-pah) N.J.

Right wing. Shoots left. 6', 187 lbs. Born, Duchcov, Czech., August 10, 1976.
(New Jersey's 4th choice, 103rd overall, in 1994 Entry Draft).

			Regular Season					Playoffs				
Season	Club	Lea	GP	G	A	TP	PIM	GP	G	A	TP	PIM
1993-94	Litvinov	Czech.	20	4	7	11	....	4	0	0	0	....
1994-95	Litvinov	Czech.	28	3	3	6	20	3	0	0	0	2

SKRUDLAND, BRIAN (SKROOD-luhnd) FLA.

Center. Shoots left. 6', 195 lbs. Born, Peace River, Alta., July 31, 1963.

			Regular Season					Playoffs				
Season	Club	Lea	GP	G	A	TP	PIM	GP	G	A	TP	PIM
1980-81	Saskatoon	WHL	66	15	27	42	97	....	....	....	....	....
1981-82	Saskatoon	WHL	71	27	29	56	135	5	0	1	1	2
1982-83	Saskatoon	WHL	71	35	59	94	42	6	1	3	4	19
1983-84	Nova Scotia	AHL	56	13	12	25	55	12	2	8	10	14
1984-85a	Sherbrooke	AHL	70	22	28	50	109	17	9	8	17	23
1985-86	**Montreal**	**NHL**	**65**	**9**	**13**	**22**	**57**	**20**	**2**	**4**	**6**	**76**
1986-87	**Montreal**	**NHL**	**79**	**11**	**17**	**28**	**107**	**14**	**1**	**5**	**6**	**29**
1987-88	**Montreal**	**NHL**	**79**	**12**	**24**	**36**	**112**	**11**	**1**	**5**	**6**	**24**
1988-89	**Montreal**	**NHL**	**71**	**12**	**29**	**41**	**84**	**21**	**3**	**7**	**10**	**40**
1989-90	**Montreal**	**NHL**	**59**	**11**	**31**	**42**	**56**	**11**	**3**	**5**	**8**	**30**
1990-91	**Montreal**	**NHL**	**57**	**15**	**19**	**34**	**85**	**13**	**3**	**10**	**13**	**42**
1991-92	**Montreal**	**NHL**	**42**	**3**	**3**	**6**	**36**	**11**	**1**	**1**	**2**	**20**
1992-93	**Montreal**	**NHL**	**23**	**5**	**3**	**8**	**55**	....	....	....	....	....
	Calgary	**NHL**	**16**	**2**	**4**	**6**	**10**	**6**	**0**	**3**	**3**	**12**
1993-94	**Florida**	**NHL**	**79**	**15**	**25**	**40**	**136**	....	....	....	....	....
1994-95	**Florida**	**NHL**	**47**	**5**	**9**	**14**	**88**	....	....	....	....	....
	NHL Totals		**617**	**100**	**177**	**277**	**826**	**107**	**14**	**40**	**54**	**273**

a Won Jack A. Butterfield Trophy (AHL Playoff MVP) (1985)

Signed as a free agent by **Montreal**, September 13, 1983. Traded to **Calgary** by **Montreal** for Gary Leeman, January 28, 1993. Claimed by **Florida** from **Calgary** in Expansion Draft, June 24, 1993.

SKUTA, VITEZSLAV (SHKUH-tah) DET.

Defense. Shoots left. 6'4", 205 lbs. Born, Ostrava, Czech., July 17, 1974.
(Detroit's 9th choice, 204th overall, in 1993 Entry Draft).

			Regular Season					Playoffs				
Season	Club	Lea	GP	G	A	TP	PIM	GP	G	A	TP	PIM
1992-93	TJ Vitkovice	Czech.	34	1	2	3	....	....	....	....	....	....
1993-94	TJ Vitkovice	Czech.	34	1	4	5	....	4	0	3	3	....
1994-95	Vitkovice	Czech.	44	4	10	14	30	6	1	0	1	2

SLAMIAR, PETER (SLA-mih-eer) NYR

Left wing. Shoots right. 5'11", 174 lbs. Born, Zvolen, Czech., February 26, 1977.
(NY Rangers' 6th choice, 143rd overall, in 1995 Entry Draft).

			Regular Season					Playoffs				
Season	Club	Lea	GP	G	A	TP	PIM	GP	G	A	TP	PIM
1994-95	Zvolen	Slov. Jr.	30	19	18	37	....	....	....	....	....	....
	Zvolen	Slov. 2	11	4	1	5	....	....	....	....	....	....

SLANEY, JOHN COL.

Defense. Shoots left. 6', 185 lbs. Born, St. John's, Nfld., February 7, 1972.
(Washington's 1st choice, 9th overall, in 1990 Entry Draft).

			Regular Season					Playoffs				
Season	Club	Lea	GP	G	A	TP	PIM	GP	G	A	TP	PIM
1988-89	Cornwall	OHL	66	16	43	59	23	18	8	16	24	10
1989-90ab	Cornwall	OHL	64	38	59	97	68	6	0	8	8	11
1990-91c	Cornwall	OHL	34	21	25	46	28	....	....	....	....	....
1991-92	Cornwall	OHL	34	19	41	60	43	6	3	8	11	0
	Baltimore	AHL	6	2	4	6	0	....	....	....	....	....
1992-93	Baltimore	AHL	79	20	46	66	60	7	0	7	7	8
1993-94	**Washington**	**NHL**	**47**	**7**	**9**	**16**	**27**	**11**	**1**	**1**	**2**	**2**
	Portland	AHL	29	14	13	27	17	....	....	....	....	....
1994-95	**Washington**	**NHL**	**16**	**0**	**3**	**3**	**6**	....	....	....	....	....
	Portland	AHL	8	3	10	13	4	7	1	3	4	4
	NHL Totals		**63**	**7**	**12**	**19**	**33**	**11**	**1**	**1**	**2**	**2**

a OHL First All-Star Team (1990)
b Canadian Major Junior Defenseman of the Year (1990)
c OHL Second All-Star Team (1991)

Traded to **Colorado** by **Washington** for Philadelphia's third round choice (previously acquired by Colorado) in 1996 Entry Draft, July 12, 1995.

SLEGR, JIRI (SLAY-guhr, YOO-ree) **EDM.**

Defense. Shoots left. 6'1", 205 lbs. Born, Jihlava, Czech., May 30, 1971.
(Vancouver's 3rd choice, 23rd overall, in 1990 Entry Draft).

			Regular Season					Playoffs				
Season	**Club**	**Lea**	**GP**	**G**	**A**	**TP**	**PIM**	**GP**	**G**	**A**	**TP**	**PIM**
1987-88	Litvinov	Czech.	4	1	1	2	0	....	....	....	....	....
1988-89	Litvinov	Czech.	8	0	0	0	4	....	....	....	....	....
1989-90	Litvinov	Czech.	51	4	15	19	....	....	....	....	....	....
1990-91	Litvinov	Czech.	47	11	36	47	26	....	....	....	....	....
1991-92	Litvinov	Czech.	42	9	23	32	38	....	....	....	....	....
1992-93	**Vancouver**	**NHL**	**41**	**4**	**22**	**26**	**109**	**5**	**0**	**3**	**3**	**4**
	Hamilton	AHL	21	4	14	18	42	....	....	....	....	....
1993-94	**Vancouver**	**NHL**	**78**	**5**	**33**	**38**	**86**	....	....	....	....	....
1994-95	Litvinov	Czech.	11	3	10	13	80	....	....	....	....	....
	Vancouver	**NHL**	**19**	**1**	**5**	**6**	**32**	....	....	....	....	....
	Edmonton	**NHL**	**12**	**1**	**5**	**6**	**14**	....	....	....	....	....
	NHL Totals		**150**	**11**	**65**	**76**	**241**	**5**	**0**	**3**	**3**	**4**

Traded to **Edmonton** by **Vancouver** for Roman Oksiuta, April 7, 1995.

SMART, RYAN **N.J.**

Center. Shoots right. 6', 175 lbs. Born, Meadville, PA, September 22, 1975.
(New Jersey's 6th choice, 134th overall, in 1994 Entry Draft).

			Regular Season					Playoffs				
Season	**Club**	**Lea**	**GP**	**G**	**A**	**TP**	**PIM**	**GP**	**G**	**A**	**TP**	**PIM**
1993-94	Meadville	HS	46	59	57	116	....	....	....	....	....	....
1994-95	Cornell	ECAC	26	13	7	20	10	....	....	....	....	....

SMEHLIK, RICHARD (SHMEH-lihk) **BUF.**

Defense. Shoots left. 6'3", 208 lbs. Born, Ostrava, Czech., January 23, 1970.
(Buffalo's 3rd choice, 97th overall, in 1990 Entry Draft).

			Regular Season					Playoffs				
Season	**Club**	**Lea**	**GP**	**G**	**A**	**TP**	**PIM**	**GP**	**G**	**A**	**TP**	**PIM**
1988-89	TJ Vitkovice	Czech.	38	2	5	7	12	....	....	....	....	....
1989-90	TJ Vitkovice	Czech.	51	5	4	9	....	....	....	....	....	....
1990-91	Dukla Jihlava	Czech.	58	4	3	7	22	....	....	....	....	....
1991-92	TJ Vitkovice	Czech.	47	9	10	19	42	....	....	....	....	....
1992-93	**Buffalo**	**NHL**	**80**	**4**	**27**	**31**	**59**	**8**	**0**	**4**	**4**	**2**
1993-94	**Buffalo**	**NHL**	**84**	**14**	**27**	**41**	**69**	**7**	**0**	**2**	**2**	**10**
1994-95	Vitkovice	Czech.	13	5	2	7	12	....	....	....	....	....
	Buffalo	**NHL**	**39**	**4**	**7**	**11**	**46**	**5**	**0**	**0**	**0**	**2**
	NHL Totals		**203**	**22**	**61**	**83**	**174**	**20**	**0**	**6**	**6**	**14**

SMIRNOV, PAVEL (smihr-NAHV) **CGY.**

Right wing/Center. Shoots left. 6'3", 191 lbs. Born, Perm, USSR, May 12, 1977.
(Calgary's 2nd choice, 46th overall, in 1995 Entry Draft).

			Regular Season					Playoffs				
Season	**Club**	**Lea**	**GP**	**G**	**A**	**TP**	**PIM**	**GP**	**G**	**A**	**TP**	**PIM**
1993-94	Molot Perm	CIS	8	0	0	0	0	....	....	....	....	....
1994-95	Molot Perm	CIS	48	2	2	4	34	....	....	....	....	....

SMIRNOV, YURI (smihr-NAHV) **T.B.**

Left wing. Shoots left. 5'11", 172 lbs. Born, Moscow, USSR, January 10, 1976.
(Tampa Bay's th choice, 216th overall, in 1994 Entry Draft).

			Regular Season					Playoffs				
Season	**Club**	**Lea**	**GP**	**G**	**A**	**TP**	**PIM**	**GP**	**G**	**A**	**TP**	**PIM**
1993-94	Spartak	CIS	27	2	3	5	4	....	....	....	....	....
1994-95	Spartak	CIS	22	1	0	1	0	....	....	....	....	....

SMITH, ADAM **NYR**

Defense. Shoots left. 6', 190 lbs. Born, Digby, N.S., May 24, 1976.
(NY Rangers' 3rd choice, 78th overall, in 1994 Entry Draft).

			Regular Season					Playoffs				
Season	**Club**	**Lea**	**GP**	**G**	**A**	**TP**	**PIM**	**GP**	**G**	**A**	**TP**	**PIM**
1992-93	Tacoma	WHL	67	0	12	12	43	7	0	1	1	4
1993-94	Tacoma	WHL	66	4	19	23	119	8	0	0	0	10
1994-95	Tacoma	WHL	69	2	19	21	96	4	0	1	1	9

SMITH, DENIS **NYI**

Defense. Shoots left. 6'1", 210 lbs. Born, Windsor, Ont., May 13, 1977.
(NY Islanders' 3rd choice, 41st overall, in 1995 Entry Draft).

			Regular Season					Playoffs				
Season	**Club**	**Lea**	**GP**	**G**	**A**	**TP**	**PIM**	**GP**	**G**	**A**	**TP**	**PIM**
1993-94	Windsor	Jr. B	51	8	34	42	267	....	....	....	....	....
1994-95	Windsor	OHL	61	4	13	17	201	10	1	3	4	41

SMITH, DERRICK

Left wing. Shoots left. 6'2", 215 lbs. Born, Scarborough, Ont., January 22, 1965.
(Philadelphia's 2nd choice, 44th overall, in 1983 Entry Draft).

			Regular Season					Playoffs				
Season	**Club**	**Lea**	**GP**	**G**	**A**	**TP**	**PIM**	**GP**	**G**	**A**	**TP**	**PIM**
1982-83	Peterborough	OHL	70	16	19	35	47	....	....	....	....	....
1983-84	Peterborough	OHL	70	30	36	66	31	8	4	4	8	7
1984-85	**Philadelphia**	**NHL**	**77**	**17**	**22**	**39**	**31**	**19**	**2**	**5**	**7**	**16**
1985-86	**Philadelphia**	**NHL**	**69**	**6**	**6**	**12**	**57**	**4**	**0**	**0**	**0**	**10**
1986-87	**Philadelphia**	**NHL**	**71**	**11**	**21**	**32**	**34**	**26**	**6**	**4**	**10**	**26**
1987-88	**Philadelphia**	**NHL**	**76**	**16**	**8**	**24**	**104**	**7**	**0**	**0**	**0**	**6**
1988-89	**Philadelphia**	**NHL**	**74**	**16**	**14**	**30**	**43**	**19**	**5**	**2**	**7**	**12**
1989-90	**Philadelphia**	**NHL**	**55**	**3**	**6**	**9**	**32**	....	....	....	....	....
1990-91	**Philadelphia**	**NHL**	**72**	**11**	**10**	**21**	**37**	....	....	....	....	....
1991-92	**Minnesota**	**NHL**	**33**	**2**	**4**	**6**	**33**	**7**	**1**	**0**	**1**	**9**
	Kalamazoo	IHL	6	1	5	6	4	....	....	....	....	....
1992-93	**Minnesota**	**NHL**	**9**	**0**	**1**	**1**	**2**	....	....	....	....	....
	Kalamazoo	IHL	52	22	13	35	43	....	....	....	....	....
1993-94	**Dallas**	**NHL**	**1**	**0**	**0**	**0**	**0**	....	....	....	....	....
a	Kalamazoo	IHL	77	44	37	81	90	5	0	0	0	18
1994-95	Kalamazoo	IHL	68	30	21	51	103	16	3	8	11	8
	NHL Totals		**537**	**82**	**92**	**174**	**373**	**82**	**14**	**11**	**25**	**79**

a IHL Second All-Star Team (1994)

Claimed on waivers by **Minnesota** from **Philadelphia**, October 26, 1991.

SMITH, GEOFF **FLA.**

Defense. Shoots left. 6'3", 194 lbs. Born, Edmonton, Alta., March 7, 1969.
(Edmonton's 3rd choice, 63rd overall, in 1987 Entry Draft).

			Regular Season					Playoffs				
Season	**Club**	**Lea**	**GP**	**G**	**A**	**TP**	**PIM**	**GP**	**G**	**A**	**TP**	**PIM**
1987-88	North Dakota	WCHA	42	4	12	16	34	....	....	....	....	....
1988-89	North Dakota	WCHA	9	0	1	1	8	....	....	....	....	....
	Kamloops	WHL	32	4	31	35	29	6	1	3	4	12
1989-90a	**Edmonton**	**NHL**	**74**	**4**	**11**	**15**	**52**	**3**	**0**	**0**	**0**	**0**
1990-91	**Edmonton**	**NHL**	**59**	**1**	**12**	**13**	**55**	**4**	**0**	**0**	**0**	**0**
1991-92	**Edmonton**	**NHL**	**74**	**2**	**16**	**18**	**43**	**5**	**0**	**1**	**1**	**6**
1992-93	**Edmonton**	**NHL**	**78**	**4**	**14**	**18**	**30**	....	....	....	....	....
1993-94	**Edmonton**	**NHL**	**21**	**0**	**3**	**3**	**12**	....	....	....	....	....
	Florida	**NHL**	**56**	**1**	**5**	**6**	**38**	....	....	....	....	....
1994-95	**Florida**	**NHL**	**47**	**2**	**4**	**6**	**22**	....	....	....	....	....
	NHL Totals		**409**	**14**	**65**	**79**	**252**	**12**	**0**	**1**	**1**	**6**

a NHL All-Rookie Team (1990)

Traded to **Florida** by **Edmonton** with Edmonton's fourth round choice (David Nemirovsky) in 1994 Entry Draft for Florida's third round choice (Corey Neilson) in 1994 Entry Draft and St. Louis' sixth round choice (previously acquired by Florida — later traded to Winnipeg — Winnipeg selected Chris Kibermanis) in 1994 Entry Draft, December 6, 1993.

SMITH, JASON **N.J.**

Defense. Shoots right. 6'3", 195 lbs. Born, Calgary, Alta., November 2, 1973.
(New Jersey's 1st choice, 18th overall, in 1992 Entry Draft).

			Regular Season					Playoffs				
Season	**Club**	**Lea**	**GP**	**G**	**A**	**TP**	**PIM**	**GP**	**G**	**A**	**TP**	**PIM**
1990-91	Regina	WHL	2	0	0	0	7	4	0	0	0	2
1991-92	Regina	WHL	62	9	29	38	168	....	....	....	....	....
1992-93a	Regina	WHL	64	14	52	66	175	13	4	8	12	39
	Utica	AHL	....	....	....	....	....	1	0	0	0	2
1993-94	**New Jersey**	**NHL**	**41**	**0**	**5**	**5**	**43**	**6**	**0**	**0**	**0**	**7**
	Albany	AHL	20	6	3	9	31	....	....	....	....	....
1994-95	**New Jersey**	**NHL**	**2**	**0**	**0**	**0**	**0**	....	....	....	....	....
	Albany	AHL	7	0	2	2	15	11	2	2	4	19
	NHL Totals		**43**	**0**	**5**	**5**	**43**	**6**	**0**	**0**	**0**	**7**

a Canadian Major Junior First All-Star Team (1993).

SMITH, JASON

Defense. Shoots left. 6'4", 210 lbs. Born, Calgary, Alta., November 19, 1974.
(Calgary's 4th choice, 95th overall, in 1993 Entry Draft).

			Regular Season					Playoffs				
Season	**Club**	**Lea**	**GP**	**G**	**A**	**TP**	**PIM**	**GP**	**G**	**A**	**TP**	**PIM**
1992-93	Princeton	ECAC	28	5	4	9	94	....	....	....	....	....
1993-94	Princeton	ECAC	16	1	4	5	56	....	....	....	....	....
1994-95	Princeton	ECAC	32	3	9	12	68	....	....	....	....	....

SMITH, STEVE **CHI.**

Defense. Shoots left. 6'4", 215 lbs. Born, Glasgow, Scotland, April 30, 1963.
(Edmonton's 5th choice, 111th overall, in 1981 Entry Draft).

			Regular Season					Playoffs				
Season	**Club**	**Lea**	**GP**	**G**	**A**	**TP**	**PIM**	**GP**	**G**	**A**	**TP**	**PIM**
1980-81	London	OHA	62	4	12	16	141	....	....	....	....	....
1981-82	London	OHL	58	10	36	46	207	4	1	2	3	13
1982-83	Moncton	AHL	2	0	0	0	0	....	....	....	....	....
	London	OHL	50	6	35	41	133	3	1	0	1	10
1983-84	Moncton	AHL	64	1	8	9	176	....	....	....	....	....
1984-85	**Edmonton**	**NHL**	**2**	**0**	**0**	**0**	**2**	....	....	....	....	....
	Nova Scotia	AHL	68	2	28	30	161	5	0	3	3	40
1985-86	**Edmonton**	**NHL**	**55**	**4**	**20**	**24**	**166**	**6**	**0**	**1**	**1**	**14**
	Nova Scotia	AHL	4	0	2	2	11	....	....	....	....	....
1986-87	**Edmonton**	**NHL**	**62**	**7**	**15**	**22**	**165**	**15**	**1**	**3**	**4**	**45**
1987-88	**Edmonton**	**NHL**	**79**	**12**	**43**	**55**	**286**	**19**	**1**	**11**	**12**	**55**
1988-89	**Edmonton**	**NHL**	**35**	**3**	**19**	**22**	**97**	**7**	**2**	**2**	**4**	**20**
1989-90	**Edmonton**	**NHL**	**75**	**7**	**34**	**41**	**171**	**22**	**5**	**10**	**15**	**37**
1990-91	**Edmonton**	**NHL**	**77**	**13**	**41**	**54**	**193**	**18**	**1**	**2**	**3**	**45**
1991-92	**Chicago**	**NHL**	**76**	**9**	**21**	**30**	**304**	**18**	**1**	**11**	**12**	**16**
1992-93	**Chicago**	**NHL**	**78**	**10**	**47**	**57**	**214**	**4**	**0**	**0**	**0**	**10**
1993-94	**Chicago**	**NHL**	**57**	**5**	**22**	**27**	**174**	....	....	....	....	....
1994-95	**Chicago**	**NHL**	**48**	**1**	**12**	**13**	**128**	**16**	**0**	**1**	**1**	**26**
	NHL Totals		**644**	**71**	**274**	**345**	**1900**	**125**	**11**	**41**	**52**	**268**

Played in NHL All-Star Game (1991)

Traded to **Chicago** by **Edmonton** for Dave Manson and Chicago's third round choice (Kirk Maltby) in 1992 Entry Draft, October 2, 1991.

SMOLINSKI, BRYAN (smoh-LIHN-skee) **PIT.**

Center. Shoots right. 6'1", 200 lbs. Born, Toledo, OH, December 27, 1971.
(Boston's 1st choice, 21st overall, in 1990 Entry Draft).

			Regular Season					Playoffs				
Season	**Club**	**Lea**	**GP**	**G**	**A**	**TP**	**PIM**	**GP**	**G**	**A**	**TP**	**PIM**
1989-90	Michigan State	CCHA	35	9	13	22	34	....	....	....	....	....
1990-91	Michigan State	CCHA	35	9	12	21	24	....	....	....	....	....
1991-92	Michigan State	CCHA	41	28	33	61	55	....	....	....	....	....
1992-93ab	Michigan State	CCHA	40	31	37	*68	93	....	....	....	....	....
	Boston	**NHL**	**9**	**1**	**3**	**4**	**0**	**4**	**1**	**0**	**1**	**2**
1993-94	**Boston**	**NHL**	**83**	**31**	**20**	**51**	**82**	**13**	**5**	**4**	**9**	**4**
1994-95	**Boston**	**NHL**	**44**	**18**	**13**	**31**	**31**	**5**	**0**	**1**	**1**	**4**
	NHL Totals		**136**	**50**	**36**	**86**	**113**	**22**	**6**	**5**	**11**	**10**

a CCHA First All-Star Team (1993)
b NCAA West First All-American Team (1993)

Traded to **Pittsburgh** by **Boston** with Glen Murray and Boston's third round choice in 1996 Entry Draft for Kevin Stevens and Shawn McEachern, August 2, 1995.

SMYTH, BRAD (SMIHTH) **FLA.**

Right wing. Shoots right. 6', 200 lbs. Born, Ottawa, Ont., March 13, 1973.

			Regular Season					Playoffs				
Season	**Club**	**Lea**	**GP**	**G**	**A**	**TP**	**PIM**	**GP**	**G**	**A**	**TP**	**PIM**
1990-91	London	OHL	29	2	6	8	22	....	....	....	....	....
1991-92	London	OHL	58	17	18	35	93	10	2	0	2	8
1992-93	London	OHL	66	54	55	109	118	12	7	8	15	25
1993-94	Cincinnati	IHL	30	7	3	10	54	....	....	....	....	....
	Birmingham	ECHL	29	26	30	56	38	10	8	8	16	19
1994-95	Springfield	AHL	3	0	0	0	7	....	....	....	....	....
	Birmingham	ECHL	36	33	35	68	52	3	5	2	7	0
	Cincinnati	IHL	26	2	11	13	34	1	0	0	0	2

Signed as a free agent by **Florida**, October 4, 1993.

SMYTH, GREG (SMIHTH)

Defense. Shoots right. 6'3", 212 lbs. Born, Oakville, Ont., April 23, 1966.
(Philadelphia's 1st choice, 22nd overall, in 1984 Entry Draft).

			Regular Season					Playoffs				
Season	Club	Lea	GP	G	A	TP	PIM	GP	G	A	TP	PIM
1983-84	London	OHL	64	4	21	25	252	6	1	0	1	24
1984-85	London	OHL	47	7	16	23	188	8	2	2	4	27
1985-86	Hershey	AHL	2	0	1	1	5	8	0	0	0	60
a	London	OHL	46	12	42	54	199	4	1	2	3	28
1986-87	**Philadelphia**	**NHL**	**1**	**0**	**0**	**0**	**0**	**1**	**0**	**0**	**0**	**2**
	Hershey	AHL	35	0	2	2	158	2	0	0	0	19
1987-88	**Philadelphia**	**NHL**	**48**	**1**	**6**	**7**	**192**	**5**	**0**	**0**	**0**	**38**
	Hershey	AHL	21	0	10	10	102	....	....	....	....	....
1988-89	**Quebec**	**NHL**	**10**	**0**	**1**	**1**	**70**	....	....	....	....	....
	Halifax	AHL	43	3	9	12	310	4	0	1	1	35
1989-90	**Quebec**	**NHL**	**13**	**0**	**0**	**0**	**57**	....	....	....	....	....
	Halifax	AHL	49	5	14	19	235	6	1	0	1	52
1990-91	**Quebec**	**NHL**	**1**	**0**	**0**	**0**	**0**	....	....	....	....	....
	Halifax	AHL	56	6	23	29	340	....	....	....	....	....
1991-92	**Quebec**	**NHL**	**29**	**0**	**2**	**2**	**138**	....	....	....	....	....
	Halifax	AHL	9	1	3	4	35	....	....	....	....	....
	Calgary	**NHL**	**7**	**1**	**1**	**2**	**15**	....	....	....	....	....
1992-93	**Calgary**	**NHL**	**35**	**1**	**2**	**3**	**95**	....	....	....	....	....
	Salt Lake	IHL	5	0	1	1	31	....	....	....	....	....
1993-94	**Florida**	**NHL**	**12**	**1**	**0**	**1**	**37**	....	....	....	....	....
	Toronto	**NHL**	**11**	**0**	**1**	**1**	**38**	....	....	....	....	....
	Chicago	**NHL**	**38**	**0**	**0**	**0**	**108**	**6**	**0**	**0**	**0**	**0**
1994-95	**Chicago**	**NHL**	**22**	**0**	**3**	**3**	**33**	....	....	....	....	....
	Indianapolis	IHL	2	0	0	0	0	....	....	....	....	....
	NHL Totals		**227**	**4**	**16**	**20**	**783**	**12**	**0**	**0**	**0**	**40**

a OHL Second All-Star Team (1986)

Traded to **Quebec** by **Philadelphia** with Philadelphia's third round choice (John Tanner) in the 1989 Entry Draft for Terry Carkner, July 25, 1988. Traded to **Calgary** by **Quebec** for Martin Simard, March 10, 1992. Signed as a free agent by **Florida**, August 10, 1993. Traded to **Toronto** by **Florida** for cash, December 7, 1993. Claimed on waivers by **Chicago** from **Toronto**, January 8, 1994.

SMYTH, KEVIN (SMIHTH) HFD.

Left wing. Shoots left. 6'2", 217 lbs. Born, Banff, Alta., November 22, 1973.
(Hartford's 4th choice, 79th overall, in 1992 Entry Draft).

			Regular Season					Playoffs				
Season	Club	Lea	GP	G	A	TP	PIM	GP	G	A	TP	PIM
1990-91	Moose Jaw	WHL	66	30	45	75	96	6	1	1	2	0
1991-92	Moose Jaw	WHL	71	30	55	85	114	4	1	3	4	6
1992-93	Moose Jaw	WHL	64	44	38	82	111	....	....	....	....	....
1993-94	**Hartford**	**NHL**	**21**	**3**	**2**	**5**	**10**	....	....	....	....	....
	Springfield	AHL	42	22	27	49	72	6	4	5	9	0
1994-95	Springfield	AHL	57	17	22	39	72	....	....	....	....	....
	Hartford	**NHL**	**16**	**1**	**5**	**6**	**13**	....	....	....	....	....
	NHL Totals		**37**	**4**	**7**	**11**	**23**	....	....	....	....	....

SMYTH, RYAN EDM.

Left wing. Shoots left. 6'1", 185 lbs. Born, Banff, Alta., February 21, 1976.
(Edmonton's 2nd choice, 6th overall, in 1994 Entry Draft).

			Regular Season					Playoffs				
Season	Club	Lea	GP	G	A	TP	PIM	GP	G	A	TP	PIM
1991-92	Moose Jaw	WHL	2	0	0	0	0	....	....	....	....	....
1992-93	Moose Jaw	WHL	64	19	14	33	59	....	....	....	....	....
1993-94	Moose Jaw	WHL	72	50	55	105	88	....	....	....	....	....
1994-95a	Moose Jaw	WHL	50	41	45	86	66	10	6	9	15	22
	Edmonton	**NHL**	**3**	**0**	**0**	**0**	**0**	....	....	....	....	....
	NHL Totals		**3**	**0**	**0**	**0**	**0**	....	....	....	....	....

a WHL East Second All-Star Team (1995)

SNELL, CHRIS L.A.

Defense. Shoots left. 5'11", 200 lbs. Born, Regina, Sask., May 12, 1971.
(Buffalo's 8th choice, 145th overall, in 1991 Entry Draft).

			Regular Season					Playoffs				
Season	Club	Lea	GP	G	A	TP	PIM	GP	G	A	TP	PIM
1989-90a	Ottawa	OHL	63	18	62	80	36	3	2	4	6	4
1990-91	Ottawa	OHL	54	23	59	82	58	17	3	14	17	8
1991-92	Rochester	AHL	65	5	27	32	66	10	2	1	3	6
1992-93	Rochester	AHL	76	14	57	71	83	17	5	8	13	39
1993-94	**Toronto**	**NHL**	**2**	**0**	**0**	**0**	**2**	....	....	....	....	....
bc	St. John's	AHL	75	22	74	96	92	11	1	15	16	10
1994-95d	Phoenix	IHL	57	15	49	64	122	....	....	....	....	....
	Los Angeles	**NHL**	**32**	**2**	**7**	**9**	**22**	....	....	....	....	....
	NHL Totals		**34**	**2**	**7**	**9**	**24**	....	....	....	....	....

a OHL First All-Star Team (1990)
b AHL First All-Star Team (1994)
c Won Eddie Shore Plaque (Top Defenseman - AHL) (1994)
d IHL First All-Star Team (1995)

Signed as a free agent by **Toronto**, August 3, 1993. Traded to **Los Angeles** by **Toronto** with Eric Lacroix and Toronto's fourth round choice in 1996 Entry Draft for Dixon Ward, Guy Leveque and Kelly Fairchild, October 3, 1994.

SNOPEK, JAN EDM.

Defense. Shoots right. 6'3", 212 lbs. Born, Prague, Czech., June 22, 1976.
(Edmonton's 5th choice, 109th overall, in 1995 Entry Draft).

			Regular Season					Playoffs				
Season	Club	Lea	GP	G	A	TP	PIM	GP	G	A	TP	PIM
1993-94	Oshawa	OHL	52	0	5	5	51	....	....	....	....	....
1994-95	Oshawa	OHL	64	14	30	44	97	7	0	1	1	4

SOKOLSKY, JAMIE PHI.

Defense. Shoots right. 6'2", 202 lbs. Born, Toronto, Ont., March 11, 1977.
(Philadelphia's 5th choice, 135th overall, in 1995 Entry Draft).

			Regular Season					Playoffs				
Season	Club	Lea	GP	G	A	TP	PIM	GP	G	A	TP	PIM
1993-94	Newmarket	OHL	41	0	3	3	11	....	....	....	....	....
1994-95	Belleville	OHL	63	4	18	22	28	16	3	6	9	14

SOMIK, RADOVAN (SAW-mihk, RAH-doh-vahn) PHI.

Left wing. Shoots right. 6'2", 194 lbs. Born, Martin, Czech., May 5, 1977.
(Philadelphia's 3rd choice, 100th overall, in 1995 Entry Draft).

			Regular Season					Playoffs				
Season	Club	Lea	GP	G	A	TP	PIM	GP	G	A	TP	PIM
1993-94	Martin	Slov.	1	0	0	0	0	....	....	....	....	....
1994-95	Martin	Slov.	25	3	0	3	39	3	1	0	1	2

SOPEL, BRENT VAN.

Defense. Shoots right. 6'1", 185 lbs. Born, Calgary, Alta., January 7, 1977.
(Vancouver's 6th choice, 144th overall, in 1995 Entry Draft).

			Regular Season					Playoffs				
Season	Club	Lea	GP	G	A	TP	PIM	GP	G	A	TP	PIM
1993-94	Saskatoon	WHL	11	2	2	4	2	....	....	....	....	....
1994-95	Saskatoon	WHL	22	1	10	11	31	....	....	....	....	....
	Swift Current	WHL	41	4	19	23	50	3	0	3	3	0

SOROCHAN, LEE (soh-RAW-kihn) NYR

Defense. Shoots left. 6'1", 210 lbs. Born, Edmonton, Alta., September 9, 1975.
(NY Rangers' 2nd choice, 34th overall, in 1993 Entry Draft).

			Regular Season					Playoffs				
Season	Club	Lea	GP	G	A	TP	PIM	GP	G	A	TP	PIM
1991-92	Lethbridge	WHL	67	2	9	11	105	5	0	2	2	6
1992-93	Lethbridge	WHL	69	8	32	40	208	4	0	1	1	12
1993-94	Lethbridge	WHL	46	5	27	32	123	9	4	3	7	16
1994-95	Lethbridge	WHL	29	4	15	19	93	....	....	....	....	....
	Saskatoon	WHL	24	5	13	18	63	10	3	6	9	34
	Binghamton	AHL	....	....	....	....	....	8	0	0	0	11

SOULLIERE, STEPHANE (SOO-lee-air) L.A.

Left wing. Shoots left. 5'11", 180 lbs. Born, Greenfield Park, Que., May 30, 1975.

			Regular Season					Playoffs				
Season	Club	Lea	GP	G	A	TP	PIM	GP	G	A	TP	PIM
1992-93	Oshawa	OHL	65	11	7	18	77	13	1	0	1	19
1993-94	Oshawa	OHL	63	25	24	49	120	5	0	1	1	12
1994-95	Oshawa	OHL	18	9	21	30	27	....	....	....	....	....
	Sarnia	OHL	22	10	9	19	38	....	....	....	....	....
	Guelph	OHL	22	10	8	18	48	14	3	2	5	21

Signed as a free agent by **Los Angeles**, July 1, 1994.

SOURAY, SHELDON N.J.

Defense. Shoots left. 6'2", 210 lbs. Born, Elk Point, Alta., July 13, 1976.
(New Jersey's 3rd choice, 71st overall, in 1994 Entry Draft).

			Regular Season					Playoffs				
Season	Club	Lea	GP	G	A	TP	PIM	GP	G	A	TP	PIM
			....	....	....	....	....	....	....	....	....	....
1992-93	Tri-City	WHL	2	0	0	0	0	....	....	....	....	....
1993-94	Tri-City	WHL	42	3	6	9	122	....	....	....	....	....
1994-95	Tri-City	WHL	40	2	24	26	140	....	....	....	....	....
	Prince George	WHL	11	2	3	5	23	....	....	....	....	....
	Albany	AHL	7	0	2	2	8	....	....	....	....	....

SPAHNEL, MARTIN (SPAH-nehl) PHI.

Left wing. Shoots left. 6'2", 187 lbs. Born, Gottwaldov, Czech., July 1, 1977.
(Philadelphia's 6th choice, 152nd overall, in 1995 Entry Draft).

			Regular Season					Playoffs				
Season	Club	Lea	GP	G	A	TP	PIM	GP	G	A	TP	PIM
1994-95	Zlin	Czech. Jr.	33	25	16	41	0	....	....	....	....	....
	Zlin	Czech.	1	0	0	0	0	....	....	....	....	....

SPITZIG, TIM DET.

Right wing. Shoots right. 6', 195 lbs. Born, Goderich, Ont., April 15, 1974.
(Detroit's 7th choice, 152nd overall, in 1993 Entry Draft).

			Regular Season					Playoffs				
Season	Club	Lea	GP	G	A	TP	PIM	GP	G	A	TP	PIM
1991-92	Kitchener	OHL	62	8	13	21	89	4	0	0	0	2
1992-93	Kitchener	OHL	66	40	39	79	127	7	5	4	9	14
1993-94	Kitchener	OHL	62	48	38	86	111	5	7	2	9	8
1994-95	Kitchener	OHL	41	15	17	32	62	5	2	1	3	8
	Adirondack	AHL	2	0	0	0	0	....	....	....	....	....

SPROULE, DOUG OTT.

Left wing. Shoots left. 6'3", 190 lbs. Born, Red Bank, NJ, February 16, 1976.
(Ottawa's 6th choice, 159th overall, in 1994 Entry Draft).

			Regular Season					Playoffs				
Season	Club	Lea	GP	G	A	TP	PIM	GP	G	A	TP	PIM
1993-94	Hotchkiss	HS	23	28	39	67	....	....	....	....	....	....
1994-95	Harvard	ECAC	30	7	2	9	28	....	....	....	....	....

STACEY, BRIAN WSH.

Defense. Shoots left. 6'2", 190 lbs. Born, East York, Ont., June 28, 1975.

			Regular Season					Playoffs				
Season	Club	Lea	GP	G	A	TP	PIM	GP	G	A	TP	PIM
1992-93	London	OHL	38	2	2	4	45	6	0	1	1	8
1993-94	London	OHL	59	2	10	12	100	5	0	2	2	16
1994-95	London	OHL	36	8	18	26	47	....	....	....	....	....
	Sudbury	OHL	21	0	8	8	15	18	2	1	3	26

Signed as a free agent by **Washington**, October 7, 1994.

STAIOS, STEVE (STAY-uhs) ST.L.

Defense. Shoots right. 6', 185 lbs. Born, Hamilton, Ont., July 28, 1973.
(St. Louis' 1st choice, 27th overall, in 1991 Entry Draft).

			Regular Season					Playoffs				
Season	Club	Lea	GP	G	A	TP	PIM	GP	G	A	TP	PIM
1990-91	Niagara Falls	OHL	66	17	29	46	115	12	2	3	5	10
1991-92	Niagara Falls	OHL	65	11	42	53	122	17	7	8	15	27
1992-93	Niagara Falls	OHL	12	4	14	18	30	....	....	....	....	....
	Sudbury	OHL	53	13	44	57	67	11	5	6	11	22
1993-94	Peoria	IHL	38	3	9	12	42	....	....	....	....	....
1994-95	Peoria	IHL	60	3	13	16	64	6	0	0	0	10

STAJDUHAR, NICK (STAD-joo-hahr) EDM.

Defense. Shoots left. 6'2", 195 lbs. Born, Kitchener, Ont., December 6, 1974.
(Edmonton's 2nd choice, 16th overall, in 1993 Entry Draft).

			Regular Season					Playoffs				
Season	Club	Lea	GP	G	A	TP	PIM	GP	G	A	TP	PIM
1990-91	London	OHL	66	3	12	15	51	7	0	0	0	2
1991-92	London	OHL	66	6	15	21	62	10	1	4	5	10
1992-93	London	OHL	49	15	45	60	58	12	4	11	15	10
1993-94a	London	OHL	52	34	52	86	58	5	0	2	2	8
1994-95	Cape Breton	AHL	54	12	26	38	55	....	....	....	....	....

a OHL First All-Star Team (1994)

STANTON, PAUL

Defense. Shoots right. 6'1", 195 lbs. Born, Boston, MA, June 22, 1967.
(Pittsburgh's 8th choice, 149th overall, in 1985 Entry Draft).

			Regular Season					Playoffs				
Season	Club	Lea	GP	G	A	TP	PIM	GP	G	A	TP	PIM
1985-86	U. Wisconsin	WCHA	36	4	6	10	16	....	....	....	....	....
1986-87	U. Wisconsin	WCHA	41	5	17	22	70	....	....	....	....	....
1987-88ab	U. Wisconsin	WCHA	45	9	38	47	98	....	....	....	....	....
1988-89c	U. Wisconsin	WCHA	45	7	29	36	126	....	....	....	....	....
1989-90	Muskegon	IHL	77	5	27	32	61	15	2	4	6	21
1990-91	**Pittsburgh**	**NHL**	**75**	**5**	**18**	**23**	**40**	**22**	**1**	**2**	**3**	**24**
1991-92	**Pittsburgh**	**NHL**	**54**	**2**	**8**	**10**	**62**	**21**	**1**	**7**	**8**	**42**
1992-93	**Pittsburgh**	**NHL**	**77**	**4**	**12**	**16**	**97**	**1**	**0**	**1**	**1**	**0**
1993-94	**Boston**	**NHL**	**71**	**3**	**7**	**10**	**54**	....	....	....	....	....
1994-95	Providence	AHL	8	4	4	8	4	....	....	....	....	....
	NY Islanders	**NHL**	**18**	**0**	**4**	**4**	**9**	....	....	....	....	....
	Denver	IHL	11	2	6	8	15	....	....	....	....	....
	NHL Totals		**295**	**14**	**49**	**63**	**262**	**44**	**2**	**10**	**12**	**66**

a NCAA West First All-American Team (1988)
b WCHA Second All-Star Team (1988)
c WCHA First All-Star Team (1989)

Traded to **Boston** by **Pittsburgh** for Boston's third round choice (Greg Crozier) in 1994 Entry Draft, October 8, 1993. Traded to **NY Islanders** by **Boston** for NY Islanders' eighth round choice (later traded to Ottawa — Ottawa selected Ray Schultz) in 1995 Entry Draft, February 10, 1995.

STAPLES, JEFF — PHI.

Defense. Shoots left. 6'2", 207 lbs. Born, Kitimat, B.C., March 4, 1975.
(Philadelphia's 10th choice, 244th overall, in 1993 Entry Draft).

			Regular Season					Playoffs				
Season	Club	Lea	GP	G	A	TP	PIM	GP	G	A	TP	PIM
1991-92	Brandon	WHL	3	0	0	0	0	....	....	....	....	....
1992-93	Brandon	WHL	40	0	5	5	114	4	0	1	1	4
1993-94	Brandon	WHL	37	0	7	7	126	....	....	....	....	....
1994-95	Brandon	WHL	57	3	16	19	176	18	0	2	2	23

STAPLETON, MIKE — WPG.

Center. Shoots right. 5'10", 183 lbs. Born, Sarnia, Ont., May 5, 1966.
(Chicago's 7th choice, 132nd overall, in 1984 Entry Draft).

			Regular Season					Playoffs				
Season	Club	Lea	GP	G	A	TP	PIM	GP	G	A	TP	PIM
1983-84	Cornwall	OHL	70	24	45	69	94	3	1	2	3	4
1984-85	Cornwall	OHL	56	41	44	85	68	9	2	4	6	23
1985-86	Cornwall	OHL	56	39	64	103	74	6	2	3	5	2
1986-87	**Chicago**	**NHL**	**39**	**3**	**6**	**9**	**6**	**4**	**0**	**0**	**0**	**2**
	Cdn. National	....	21	2	4	6	4	....	....	....	....	....
1987-88	**Chicago**	**NHL**	**53**	**2**	**9**	**11**	**59**	....	....	....	....	....
	Saginaw	IHL	31	11	19	30	52	10	5	6	11	10
1988-89	**Chicago**	**NHL**	**7**	**0**	**1**	**1**	**7**	....	....	....	....	....
	Saginaw	IHL	69	21	47	68	162	6	1	3	4	4
1989-90	Indianapolis	IHL	16	5	10	15	6	13	9	10	19	38
1990-91	**Chicago**	**NHL**	**7**	**0**	**1**	**1**	**2**	....	....	....	....	....
	Indianapolis	IHL	75	29	52	81	76	7	1	4	5	0
1991-92	**Chicago**	**NHL**	**19**	**4**	**4**	**8**	**8**	....	....	....	....	....
	Indianapolis	IHL	59	18	40	58	65	....	....	....	....	....
1992-93	**Pittsburgh**	**NHL**	**78**	**4**	**9**	**13**	**10**	**4**	**0**	**0**	**0**	**0**
1993-94	**Pittsburgh**	**NHL**	**58**	**7**	**4**	**11**	**18**	....	....	....	....	....
	Edmonton	**NHL**	**23**	**5**	**9**	**14**	**28**	....	....	....	....	....
1994-95	**Edmonton**	**NHL**	**46**	**6**	**11**	**17**	**21**	....	....	....	....	....
	NHL Totals		**330**	**31**	**54**	**85**	**159**	**8**	**0**	**0**	**0**	**2**

Signed as a free agent by **Pittsburgh**, September 30, 1992. Claimed on waivers by **Edmonton** from **Pittsburgh**, February 19, 1994. Signed as a free agent by **Winnipeg**, August 9, 1995.

STAROSTENKO, DIMITRI (stahr-oh-STEN-koh) — NYR

Right wing. Shoots left. 6', 195 lbs. Born, Minsk, USSR, March 18, 1973.
(NY Rangers' 5th choice, 120th overall, in 1992 Entry Draft).

			Regular Season					Playoffs				
Season	Club	Lea	GP	G	A	TP	PIM	GP	G	A	TP	PIM
1989-90	D'amo Minsk	USSR	7	0	0	0	2	....	....	....	....	....
1990-91	CSKA	USSR	20	2	1	3	4	....	....	....	....	....
1991-92	CSKA	CIS	32	3	1	4	12	....	....	....	....	....
1992-93	CSKA	CIS	42	15	12	27	22	....	....	....	....	....
1993-94	CSKA	CIS	1	0	1	1	0	....	....	....	....	....
	Binghamton	AHL	41	12	9	21	10	....	....	....	....	....
1994-95	Binghamton	AHL	69	19	22	41	40	5	1	1	2	0

STASHENKOV, ILJA (stah-shehn-KOHV) — WPG.

Defense. Shoots left. 5'11", 178 lbs. Born, Odintsovo, USSR, August 26, 1974.
(Winnipeg's 11th choice, 223rd overall, in 1993 Entry Draft).

			Regular Season					Playoffs				
Season	Club	Lea	GP	G	A	TP	PIM	GP	G	A	TP	PIM
1991-92	Soviet Wings	CIS	7	0	0	0	2	....	....	....	....	....
1992-93	Soviet Wings	CIS	42	0	0	0	22	1	0	0	0	0
1993-94	Soviet Wings	CIS	46	3	0	3	10	....	....	....	....	....
1994-95	Soviet Wings	CIS	51	3	3	6	40	4	1	0	1	0

STASTNY, PETER (STAHST-nee) — ST.L.

Center. Shoots left. 6'1", 200 lbs. Born, Bratislava, Czech., September 18, 1956.

			Regular Season					Playoffs				
Season	Club	Lea	GP	G	A	TP	PIM	GP	G	A	TP	PIM
1973-74	Bratislava	Czech.				UNAVAILABLE						
1974-75	Bratislava	Czech.				UNAVAILABLE						
1975-76	Bratislava	Czech.	32	19	9	28	....	....	....	....	....	....
1976-77	Bratislava	Czech.	44	25	27	52	....	....	....	....	....	....
1977-78	Bratislava	Czech.	42	29	24	53	28	....	....	....	....	....
1978-79	Bratislava	Czech.	39	32	23	55	21	....	....	....	....	....
1979-80a	Bratislava	Czech.	41	26	26	52	58	....	....	....	....	....
1980-81b	**Quebec**	**NHL**	**77**	**39**	**70**	**109**	**37**	**5**	**2**	**8**	**10**	**7**
1981-82	**Quebec**	**NHL**	**80**	**46**	**93**	**139**	**91**	**12**	**7**	**11**	**18**	**10**
1982-83	**Quebec**	**NHL**	**75**	**47**	**77**	**124**	**78**	**4**	**3**	**2**	**5**	**10**
1983-84	**Quebec**	**NHL**	**80**	**46**	**73**	**119**	**73**	**9**	**2**	**7**	**9**	**31**
1984-85	**Quebec**	**NHL**	**75**	**32**	**68**	**100**	**95**	**18**	**4**	**19**	**23**	**24**
1985-86	**Quebec**	**NHL**	**76**	**41**	**81**	**122**	**60**	**3**	**0**	**1**	**1**	**2**
1986-87	**Quebec**	**NHL**	**64**	**24**	**53**	**77**	**43**	**13**	**6**	**9**	**15**	**12**
1987-88	**Quebec**	**NHL**	**76**	**46**	**65**	**111**	**69**	....	....	....	....	....
1988-89	**Quebec**	**NHL**	**72**	**35**	**50**	**85**	**117**	....	....	....	....	....
1989-90	**Quebec**	**NHL**	**62**	**24**	**38**	**62**	**24**	....	....	....	....	....
	New Jersey	**NHL**	**12**	**5**	**6**	**11**	**16**	**6**	**3**	**2**	**5**	**2**
1990-91	**New Jersey**	**NHL**	**77**	**18**	**42**	**60**	**53**	**7**	**3**	**4**	**7**	**2**
1991-92	**New Jersey**	**NHL**	**66**	**24**	**38**	**62**	**42**	**7**	**3**	**7**	**10**	**19**
1992-93	**New Jersey**	**NHL**	**62**	**17**	**23**	**40**	**22**	**5**	**0**	**2**	**2**	**2**
1993-94	Bratislava	Slovak	4	0	4	4	0	....	....	....	....	....
	Slov. Olympic	....	8	5	4	9	9	....	....	....	....	....
	St. Louis	**NHL**	**17**	**5**	**11**	**16**	**4**	**4**	**0**	**0**	**0**	**2**
1994-95	**St. Louis**	**NHL**	**6**	**1**	**1**	**2**	**0**	....	....	....	....	....
	NHL Totals		**977**	**450**	**789**	**1239**	**824**	**93**	**33**	**72**	**105**	**123**

a Czechoslovakian League Player of the Year (1980)
b Won Calder Memorial Trophy (1981)

Played in NHL All-Star Game (1981, 1982-84, 1986, 1988)

Signed as a free agent by **Quebec**, August 26, 1980. Traded to **New Jersey** by **Quebec** for Craig Wolanin and future considerations (Randy Velischek, August 13, 1990), March 6, 1990. Signed as a free agent by **St. Louis**, March 9, 1994.

STEEN, THOMAS (STEEN)

Center. Shoots left. 5'11", 190 lbs. Born, Grums, Sweden, June 8, 1960.
(Winnipeg's 5th choice, 103rd overall, in 1979 Entry Draft).

			Regular Season					Playoffs				
Season	Club	Lea	GP	G	A	TP	PIM	GP	G	A	TP	PIM
1976-77	Leksand	Swe.	2	1	1	2	2	....	....	....	....	....
1977-78	Leksand	Swe.	35	5	6	11	30	....	....	....	....	....
1978-79	Leksand	Swe.	23	13	4	17	35	2	0	0	0	0
1979-80	Leksand	Swe.	18	7	7	14	14	2	0	0	0	6
1980-81	Farjestad	Swe.	32	16	23	39	30	7	4	2	6	8
1981-82	**Winnipeg**	**NHL**	**73**	**15**	**29**	**44**	**42**	**4**	**0**	**4**	**4**	**2**
1982-83	**Winnipeg**	**NHL**	**75**	**26**	**33**	**59**	**60**	**3**	**0**	**2**	**2**	**0**
1983-84	**Winnipeg**	**NHL**	**78**	**20**	**45**	**65**	**69**	**3**	**0**	**1**	**1**	**9**
1984-85	**Winnipeg**	**NHL**	**79**	**30**	**54**	**84**	**80**	**8**	**2**	**3**	**5**	**17**
1985-86	**Winnipeg**	**NHL**	**78**	**17**	**47**	**64**	**76**	**3**	**1**	**1**	**2**	**4**
1986-87	**Winnipeg**	**NHL**	**75**	**17**	**33**	**50**	**59**	**10**	**3**	**4**	**7**	**8**
1987-88	**Winnipeg**	**NHL**	**76**	**16**	**38**	**54**	**53**	**5**	**1**	**5**	**6**	**2**
1988-89	**Winnipeg**	**NHL**	**80**	**27**	**61**	**88**	**80**	....	....	....	....	....
1989-90	**Winnipeg**	**NHL**	**53**	**18**	**48**	**66**	**35**	**7**	**2**	**5**	**7**	**16**
1990-91	**Winnipeg**	**NHL**	**58**	**19**	**48**	**67**	**49**	....	....	....	....	....
1991-92	**Winnipeg**	**NHL**	**38**	**13**	**25**	**38**	**29**	**7**	**2**	**4**	**6**	**2**
1992-93	**Winnipeg**	**NHL**	**80**	**22**	**50**	**72**	**75**	**6**	**1**	**3**	**4**	**2**
1993-94	**Winnipeg**	**NHL**	**76**	**19**	**32**	**51**	**32**	....	....	....	....	....
1994-95	**Winnipeg**	**NHL**	**31**	**5**	**10**	**15**	**14**	....	....	....	....	....
	NHL Totals		**950**	**264**	**553**	**817**	**753**	**56**	**12**	**32**	**44**	**62**

STEPHAN, MARC — ST.L.

Center. Shoots left. 6'2", 205 lbs. Born, Burlington, Ont., January 9, 1976.
(St. Louis' 6th choice, 224th overall, in 1994 Entry Draft).

			Regular Season					Playoffs				
Season	Club	Lea	GP	G	A	TP	PIM	GP	G	A	TP	PIM
1992-93	Tri-City	WHL	55	3	6	9	62	4	0	0	0	8
1993-94	Tri-City	WHL	59	7	20	27	102	4	0	1	1	8
1994-95	Tri-City	WHL	44	8	8	16	99	....	....	....	....	....

STERN, RON — CGY.

Right wing. Shoots right. 6', 195 lbs. Born, Ste. Agathe, Que., January 11, 1967.
(Vancouver's 3rd choice, 70th overall, in 1986 Entry Draft).

			Regular Season					Playoffs				
Season	Club	Lea	GP	G	A	TP	PIM	GP	G	A	TP	PIM
1984-85	Longueuil	QMJHL	67	6	14	20	176	....	....	....	....	....
1985-86	Longueuil	QMJHL	70	39	33	72	317	....	....	....	....	....
1986-87	Longueuil	QMJHL	56	32	39	71	266	19	11	9	20	55
1987-88	**Vancouver**	**NHL**	**15**	**0**	**0**	**0**	**52**	....	....	....	....	....
	Fredericton	AHL	2	1	0	1	4	....	....	....	....	....
	Flint	IHL	55	14	19	33	294	16	8	8	16	94
1988-89	**Vancouver**	**NHL**	**17**	**1**	**0**	**1**	**49**	**3**	**0**	**1**	**1**	**17**
	Milwaukee	IHL	45	19	23	42	280	5	1	0	1	11
1989-90	**Vancouver**	**NHL**	**34**	**2**	**3**	**5**	**208**	....	....	....	....	....
	Milwaukee	IHL	26	8	9	17	165	....	....	....	....	....
1990-91	**Vancouver**	**NHL**	**31**	**2**	**3**	**5**	**171**	....	....	....	....	....
	Milwaukee	IHL	7	2	2	4	81	....	....	....	....	....
	Calgary	**NHL**	**13**	**1**	**3**	**4**	**69**	**7**	**1**	**3**	**4**	**14**
1991-92	**Calgary**	**NHL**	**72**	**13**	**9**	**22**	**338**	....	....	....	....	....
1992-93	**Calgary**	**NHL**	**70**	**10**	**15**	**25**	**207**	**6**	**0**	**0**	**0**	**43**
1993-94	**Calgary**	**NHL**	**71**	**9**	**20**	**29**	**243**	**7**	**2**	**0**	**2**	**12**
1994-95	**Calgary**	**NHL**	**39**	**9**	**4**	**13**	**163**	**7**	**3**	**1**	**4**	**8**
	NHL Totals		**362**	**47**	**57**	**104**	**1500**	**30**	**6**	**5**	**11**	**94**

Traded to **Calgary** by **Vancouver** with Kevan Guy for Dana Murzyn, March 5, 1991.

STEVENS, JOHN — HFD.

Defense. Shoots left. 6'1", 195 lbs. Born, Campbellton, N.B., May 4, 1966.
(Philadelphia's 5th choice, 47th overall, in 1984 Entry Draft).

			Regular Season					Playoffs				
Season	**Club**	**Lea**	**GP**	**G**	**A**	**TP**	**PIM**	**GP**	**G**	**A**	**TP**	**PIM**
1983-84	Oshawa	OHL	70	1	10	11	71	7	0	1	1	6
1984-85	Oshawa	OHL	44	2	10	12	61	5	0	2	2	4
	Hershey	AHL	3	0	0	0	0	....	....	....	....	....
1985-86	Oshawa	OHL	65	1	7	8	146	6	0	2	2	14
	Kalamazoo	IHL	6	0	1	1	8	6	0	3	3	9
1986-87	**Philadelphia**	**NHL**	**6**	**0**	**2**	**2**	**14**	....	....	....	....	....
	Hershey	AHL	63	1	15	16	131	3	0	0	0	7
1987-88	**Philadelphia**	**NHL**	**3**	**0**	**0**	**0**	**0**	....	....	....	....	....
	Hershey	AHL	59	1	15	16	108	....	....	....	....	....
1988-89	Hershey	AHL	78	3	13	16	129	12	1	1	2	29
1989-90	Hershey	AHL	79	3	10	13	193	....	....	....	....	....
1990-91	**Hartford**	**NHL**	**14**	**0**	**1**	**1**	**11**	....	....	....	....	....
	Springfield	AHL	65	0	12	12	139	18	0	6	6	35
1991-92	**Hartford**	**NHL**	**21**	**0**	**4**	**4**	**19**	....	....	....	....	....
	Springfield	AHL	45	1	12	13	73	11	1	3	4	27
1992-93	Springfield	AHL	74	1	19	20	111	15	0	1	1	18
1993-94	**Hartford**	**NHL**	**9**	**0**	**3**	**3**	**4**	....	....	....	....	....
	Springfield	AHL	71	3	9	12	85	3	0	0	0	0
1994-95	Springfield	AHL	79	5	15	20	122	....	....	....	....	....
	NHL Totals		**53**	**0**	**10**	**10**	**48**	....	....	....	....	....

Signed as a free agent by **Hartford**, July 30, 1990.

STEVENS, KEVIN — BOS.

Left wing. Shoots left. 6'3", 217 lbs. Born, Brockton, MA, April 15, 1965.
(Los Angeles' 6th choice, 108th overall, in 1983 Entry Draft).

			Regular Season					Playoffs				
Season	**Club**	**Lea**	**GP**	**G**	**A**	**TP**	**PIM**	**GP**	**G**	**A**	**TP**	**PIM**
1983-84	Boston College	ECAC	37	6	14	20	36	....	....	....	....	....
1984-85	Boston College	H.E.	40	13	23	36	36	....	....	....	....	....
1985-86	Boston College	H.E.	42	17	27	44	56	....	....	....	....	....
1986-87ab	Boston College	H.E.	39	35	35	70	54	....	....	....	....	....
1987-88	U.S. National	....	44	22	23	45	52	....	....	....	....	....
	U.S. Olympic	....	5	1	3	4	2	....	....	....	....	....
	Pittsburgh	**NHL**	**16**	**5**	**2**	**7**	**8**	....	....	....	....	....
1988-89	**Pittsburgh**	**NHL**	**24**	**12**	**3**	**15**	**19**	**11**	**3**	**7**	**10**	**16**
	Muskegon	IHL	45	24	41	65	113	....	....	....	....	....
1989-90	**Pittsburgh**	**NHL**	**76**	**29**	**41**	**70**	**171**	....	....	....	....	....
1990-91c	**Pittsburgh**	**NHL**	**80**	**40**	**46**	**86**	**133**	**24**	***17**	**16**	**33**	**53**
1991-92d	**Pittsburgh**	**NHL**	**80**	**54**	**69**	**123**	**254**	**21**	**13**	**15**	**28**	**28**
1992-93c	**Pittsburgh**	**NHL**	**72**	**55**	**56**	**111**	**177**	**12**	**5**	**11**	**16**	**22**
1993-94	**Pittsburgh**	**NHL**	**83**	**41**	**47**	**88**	**155**	**6**	**1**	**1**	**2**	**10**
1994-95	**Pittsburgh**	**NHL**	**27**	**15**	**12**	**27**	**51**	**12**	**4**	**7**	**11**	**21**
	NHL Totals		**458**	**251**	**276**	**527**	**968**	**86**	**43**	**57**	**100**	**150**

a Hockey East First All-Star Team (1987)
b NCAA East Second All-American Team (1987)
c NHL Second All-Star Team (1991, 1993)
d NHL First All-Star Team (1992)

Played in NHL All-Star Game (1991-93)

Rights traded to **Pittsburgh** by **Los Angeles** for Anders Hakansson, September 9, 1983. Traded to **Boston** by **Pittsburgh** with Shawn McEachern for Glen Murray, Bryan Smolinski and Boston's third round choice in 1996 Entry Draft, August 2, 1995.

STEVENS, MIKE

Left wing. Shoots left. 6', 202 lbs. Born, Kitchener, Ont., December 30, 1965.
(Vancouver's 5th choice, 58th overall, in 1984 Entry Draft).

			Regular Season					Playoffs				
Season	**Club**	**Lea**	**GP**	**G**	**A**	**TP**	**PIM**	**GP**	**G**	**A**	**TP**	**PIM**
1982-83	Kitchener	OHL	13	0	4	4	16	12	0	1	1	9
1983-84	Kitchener	OHL	66	19	21	40	109	16	10	7	17	40
1984-85	**Vancouver**	**NHL**	**6**	**0**	**3**	**3**	**6**	....	....	....	....	....
	Kitchener	OHL	37	17	18	35	121	4	1	1	2	8
1985-86	Fredericton	AHL	79	12	19	31	208	6	1	1	2	35
1986-87	Fredericton	AHL	71	7	18	25	258	....	....	....	....	....
1987-88	**Boston**	**NHL**	**7**	**0**	**1**	**1**	**9**	....	....	....	....	....
	Maine	AHL	63	30	25	55	265	7	1	2	3	37
1988-89	**NY Islanders**	**NHL**	**9**	**1**	**0**	**1**	**14**	....	....	....	....	....
	Springfield	AHL	42	17	13	30	120	....	....	....	....	....
1989-90	Springfield	AHL	28	12	10	22	75	....	....	....	....	....
	Toronto	**NHL**	**1**	**0**	**0**	**0**	**0**	....	....	....	....	....
	Newmarket	AHL	46	16	28	44	86	....	....	....	....	....
1990-91	Newmarket	AHL	68	24	23	47	229	....	....	....	....	....
1991-92	St. John's	AHL	30	13	11	24	65	....	....	....	....	....
	Binghamton	AHL	44	15	15	30	87	11	7	6	13	45
1992-93	Binghamton	AHL	68	31	61	92	230	14	5	5	10	63
1993-94	Saint John	AHL	79	20	37	57	293	6	1	3	4	34
1994-95	Cincinnati	IHL	80	34	43	77	274	10	6	3	9	16
	NHL Totals		**23**	**1**	**4**	**5**	**29**	....	....	....	....	....

Traded to **Boston** by **Vancouver** for cash, October 6, 1987. Signed as a free agent by **NY Islanders**, August 20, 1988. Traded to **Toronto** by **NY Islanders** with Gilles Thibaudeau for Jack Capuano, Paul Gagne and Derek Laxdal, December 20, 1989. Traded to **NY Rangers** by **Toronto** for Guy Larose, December 26, 1991. Signed as a free agent by **Calgary**, August 10, 1993.

STEVENS, ROD — VAN.

Center. Shoots left. 5'10", 175 lbs. Born, Fort St. John, B.C., April 5, 1974.

			Regular Season					Playoffs				
Season	**Club**	**Lea**	**GP**	**G**	**A**	**TP**	**PIM**	**GP**	**G**	**A**	**TP**	**PIM**
1991-92	Kamloops	WHL	57	8	13	21	20	15	2	2	4	0
1992-93	Kamloops	WHL	68	26	28	54	42	13	9	2	11	4
1993-94a	Kamloops	WHL	62	51	58	109	31	19	9	12	21	10
1994-95	Syracuse	AHL	78	21	21	42	63	....	....	....	....	....

a Memorial Cup All-Star Team (1994)

Signed as a free agent by **Vancouver**, October 4, 1993.

STEVENS, SCOTT — N.J.

Defense. Shoots left. 6'2", 210 lbs. Born, Kitchener, Ont., April 1, 1964.
(Washington's 1st choice, 5th overall, in 1982 Entry Draft).

			Regular Season					Playoffs				
Season	**Club**	**Lea**	**GP**	**G**	**A**	**TP**	**PIM**	**GP**	**G**	**A**	**TP**	**PIM**
1980-81	Kitchener	OPJHL	39	7	33	40	82	....	....	....	....	....
	Kitchener	OHA	1	0	0	0	0	....	....	....	....	....
1981-82	Kitchener	OHL	68	6	36	42	158	15	1	10	11	71
1982-83a	**Washington**	**NHL**	**77**	**9**	**16**	**25**	**195**	**4**	**1**	**0**	**1**	**26**
1983-84	**Washington**	**NHL**	**78**	**13**	**32**	**45**	**201**	**8**	**1**	**8**	**9**	**21**
1984-85	**Washington**	**NHL**	**80**	**21**	**44**	**65**	**221**	**5**	**0**	**1**	**1**	**20**
1985-86	**Washington**	**NHL**	**73**	**15**	**38**	**53**	**165**	**9**	**3**	**8**	**11**	**12**
1986-87	**Washington**	**NHL**	**77**	**10**	**51**	**61**	**283**	**7**	**0**	**5**	**5**	**19**
1987-88b	**Washington**	**NHL**	**80**	**12**	**60**	**72**	**184**	**13**	**1**	**11**	**12**	**46**
1988-89	**Washington**	**NHL**	**80**	**7**	**61**	**68**	**225**	**6**	**1**	**4**	**5**	**11**
1989-90	**Washington**	**NHL**	**56**	**11**	**29**	**40**	**154**	**15**	**2**	**7**	**9**	**25**
1990-91	**St. Louis**	**NHL**	**78**	**5**	**44**	**49**	**150**	**13**	**0**	**3**	**3**	**36**
1991-92c	**New Jersey**	**NHL**	**68**	**17**	**42**	**59**	**124**	**7**	**2**	**1**	**3**	**29**
1992-93	**New Jersey**	**NHL**	**81**	**12**	**45**	**57**	**120**	**5**	**2**	**2**	**4**	**10**
1993-94bd	**New Jersey**	**NHL**	**83**	**18**	**60**	**78**	**112**	**20**	**2**	**9**	**11**	**42**
1994-95	**New Jersey**	**NHL**	**48**	**2**	**20**	**22**	**56**	**20**	**1**	**7**	**8**	**24**
	NHL Totals		**959**	**152**	**542**	**694**	**2190**	**132**	**16**	**66**	**82**	**321**

a NHL All-Rookie Team (1983)
b NHL First All-Star Team (1988, 1994)
c NHL Second All-Star Team (1992)
d Won Alka-Seltzer Plus Award (1994)

Played in NHL All-Star Game (1985, 1989, 1991-94)

Signed as a free agent by **St. Louis**, July 16, 1990. Acquired by **New Jersey** from **St. Louis** as compensation for St. Louis' signing of free agent Brendan Shanahan, September 3, 1991.

STEVENSON, JEREMY — ANA.

Left wing. Shoots left. 6'2", 215 lbs. Born, San Bernadino, CA, July 28, 1974.
(Winnipeg's 3rd choice, 60th overall, in 1992 Entry Draft).

			Regular Season					Playoffs				
Season	**Club**	**Lea**	**GP**	**G**	**A**	**TP**	**PIM**	**GP**	**G**	**A**	**TP**	**PIM**
1990-91	Cornwall	OHL	58	13	20	33	124	....	....	....	....	....
1991-92	Cornwall	OHL	63	15	23	38	176	6	3	1	4	4
1992-93	Newmarket	OHL	54	28	28	56	144	5	5	1	6	28
1993-94	Newmarket	OHL	9	2	4	6	27	....	....	....	....	....
	S.S. Marie	OHL	48	18	19	37	183	14	1	1	2	23
1994-95	Greensboro	ECHL	43	14	13	27	231	17	6	11	17	64

Re-entered NHL Entry Draft, **Anaheim's** 10th choice, 262nd overall in 1994 Entry Draft.

STEVENSON, TURNER — MTL.

Right wing. Shoots right. 6'3", 220 lbs. Born, Prince George, B.C., May 18, 1972.
(Montreal's 1st choice, 12th overall, in 1990 Entry Draft).

			Regular Season					Playoffs				
Season	**Club**	**Lea**	**GP**	**G**	**A**	**TP**	**PIM**	**GP**	**G**	**A**	**TP**	**PIM**
1989-90	Seattle	WHL	62	29	32	61	276	13	3	2	5	35
1990-91	Seattle	WHL	57	36	27	63	222	6	1	5	6	15
	Fredericton	AHL	....	....	....	....	....	4	0	0	0	5
1991-92ab	Seattle	WHL	58	20	32	52	264	15	9	3	12	55
1992-93	**Montreal**	**NHL**	**1**	**0**	**0**	**0**	**0**	....	....	....	....	....
	Fredericton	AHL	79	25	34	59	102	5	2	3	5	11
1993-94	**Montreal**	**NHL**	**2**	**0**	**0**	**0**	**2**	**3**	**0**	**2**	**2**	**0**
	Fredericton	AHL	66	19	28	47	155	....	....	....	....	....
1994-95	Fredericton	AHL	37	12	12	24	109	....	....	....	....	....
	Montreal	**NHL**	**41**	**6**	**1**	**7**	**86**	....	....	....	....	....
	NHL Totals		**44**	**6**	**1**	**7**	**88**	**3**	**0**	**2**	**2**	**0**

a WHL West First All-Star Team (1992)
b Memorial Cup All-Star Team (1992)

STEWART, CAMERON — BOS.

Left wing. Shoots left. 5'11", 196 lbs. Born, Kitchener, Ont., September 18, 1971.
(Boston's 2nd choice, 63rd overall, in 1990 Entry Draft).

			Regular Season					Playoffs				
Season	**Club**	**Lea**	**GP**	**G**	**A**	**TP**	**PIM**	**GP**	**G**	**A**	**TP**	**PIM**
1990-91	U. of Michigan	CCHA	44	8	24	32	122	....	....	....	....	....
1991-92	U. of Michigan	CCHA	44	13	15	28	106	....	....	....	....	....
1992-93	U. of Michigan	CCHA	39	20	39	59	69	....	....	....	....	....
1993-94	**Boston**	**NHL**	**57**	**3**	**6**	**9**	**66**	**8**	**0**	**3**	**3**	**7**
	Providence	AHL	14	3	2	5	5	....	....	....	....	....
1994-95	**Boston**	**NHL**	**5**	**0**	**0**	**0**	**2**	....	....	....	....	....
	Providence	AHL	31	13	11	24	38	9	2	5	7	0
	NHL Totals		**62**	**3**	**6**	**9**	**68**	**8**	**0**	**3**	**3**	**7**

STEWART, JASON — NYI

Defense. Shoots right. 5'11", 185 lbs. Born, St. Paul, MN, April 30, 1976.
(NY Islanders' 7th choice, 142nd overall, in 1994 Entry Draft).

			Regular Season					Playoffs				
Season	**Club**	**Lea**	**GP**	**G**	**A**	**TP**	**PIM**	**GP**	**G**	**A**	**TP**	**PIM**
1993-94	Simley	HS	23	15	15	30	32	....	....	....	....	....
1994-95	St. Cloud St.	WCHA	28	1	3	4	16	....	....	....	....	....

STEWART, MICHAEL — HFD.

Defense. Shoots left. 6'2", 210 lbs. Born, Calgary, Alta., May 30, 1972.
(NY Rangers' 1st choice, 13th overall, in 1990 Entry Draft).

			Regular Season					Playoffs				
Season	**Club**	**Lea**	**GP**	**G**	**A**	**TP**	**PIM**	**GP**	**G**	**A**	**TP**	**PIM**
1989-90	Michigan State	CCHA	40	2	6	8	39	....	....	....	....	....
1990-91	Michigan State	CCHA	37	3	12	15	58	....	....	....	....	....
1991-92	Michigan State	CCHA	8	1	3	4	6	....	....	....	....	....
1992-93	Binghamton	AHL	68	2	10	12	71	1	0	0	0	0
1993-94	Binghamton	AHL	79	8	42	50	75	....	....	....	....	....
1994-95	Binghamton	AHL	68	6	21	27	83	....	....	....	....	....
	Springfield	AHL	7	0	3	3	21	....	....	....	....	....

Traded to **Hartford** by **NY Rangers** with Glen Featherstone, NY Rangers' first round choice (Jean-Sebastien Giguere) in 1995 Entry Draft and fourth round choice in 1996 Entry Draft for Pat Verbeek, March 23, 1995.

STILLMAN, CORY — CGY.

Center. Shoots left. 6', 180 lbs. Born, Peterborough, Ont., December 20, 1973.
(Calgary's 1st choice, 6th overall, in 1992 Entry Draft).

			Regular Season					Playoffs				
Season	Club	Lea	GP	G	A	TP	PIM	GP	G	A	TP	PIM
1990-91	Windsor	OHL	64	31	70	101	31	11	3	6	9	8
1991-92	Windsor	OHL	53	29	61	90	59	7	2	4	6	8
1992-93	Peterborough	OHL	61	25	55	80	55	18	3	8	11	18
	Cdn. National	....	1	0	0	0	0					
1993-94	Saint John	AHL	79	35	48	83	52	7	2	4	6	16
1994-95	Saint John	AHL	63	28	53	81	70	5	0	2	2	2
	Calgary	NHL	10	0	2	2	2					
	NHL Totals		10	0	2	2	2					

STOJANOV, ALEK — (STOY-uh-nahf) VAN.

Right wing. Shoots left. 6'4", 220 lbs. Born, Windsor, Ont., April 25, 1973.
(Vancouver's 1st choice, 7th overall, in 1991 Entry Draft).

			Regular Season					Playoffs				
Season	Club	Lea	GP	G	A	TP	PIM	GP	G	A	TP	PIM
1989-90	Hamilton	OHL	37	4	4	8	91					
1990-91	Hamilton	OHL	62	25	20	45	181	4	1	1	2	14
1991-92	Guelph	OHL	33	12	15	27	91					
1992-93	Guelph	OHL	36	27	28	55	62					
	Newmarket	OHL	14	9	7	16	26	7	1	3	4	26
	Hamilton	AHL	4	4	0	4	0					
1993-94	Hamilton	AHL	4	0	1	1	5					
1994-95	Syracuse	AHL	73	18	12	30	270					
	Vancouver	NHL	4	0	0	0	13	5	0	0	0	2
	NHL Totals		4	0	0	0	13	5	0	0	0	2

STORM, JIM — HFD.

Left wing. Shoots left. 6'2", 200 lbs. Born, Milford, MI, February 5, 1971.
(Hartford's 5th choice, 75th overall, in 1991 Entry Draft).

			Regular Season					Playoffs				
Season	Club	Lea	GP	G	A	TP	PIM	GP	G	A	TP	PIM
1990-91	Michigan Tech	WCHA	36	16	18	34	46					
1991-92	Michigan Tech	WCHA	39	25	33	58	12					
1992-93	Michigan Tech	WCHA	33	22	32	54	30					
1993-94	Hartford	NHL	68	6	10	16	27					
	U.S. National	....	28	8	12	20	14					
1994-95	Hartford	NHL	6	0	3	3	0					
	Springfield	AHL	33	11	11	22	29					
	NHL Totals		74	6	13	19	27					

STRAKA, MARTIN — (STRAH-kuh) OTT.

Center. Shoots left. 5'10", 178 lbs. Born, Plzen, Czech., September 3, 1972.
(Pittsburgh's 1st choice, 19th overall, in 1992 Entry Draft).

			Regular Season					Playoffs				
Season	Club	Lea	GP	G	A	TP	PIM	GP	G	A	TP	PIM
1989-90	Skoda Plzen	Czech.	1	0	3	3	....					
1990-91	Skoda Plzen	Czech.	47	7	24	31	6					
1991-92	Skoda Plzen	Czech.	50	27	28	55	20					
1992-93	Pittsburgh	NHL	42	3	13	16	29	11	2	1	3	2
	Cleveland	IHL	4	4	3	7	0					
1993-94	Pittsburgh	NHL	84	30	34	64	24	6	1	0	1	2
1994-95	Interconex Plzen	Czech.	19	10	11	21	18					
	Pittsburgh	NHL	31	4	12	16	16					
	Ottawa	NHL	6	1	1	2	0					
	NHL Totals		163	38	60	98	69	17	3	1	4	4

Traded to **Ottawa** by **Pittsburgh** for Troy Murray and Norm Maciver, April 7, 1995.

STRAND, WADE — DAL.

Defense. Shoots right. 6'4", 190 lbs. Born, Regina, Sask., May 4, 1976.
(Dallas' 5th choice, 115th overall, in 1995 Entry Draft).

			Regular Season					Playoffs				
Season	Club	Lea	GP	G	A	TP	PIM	GP	G	A	TP	PIM
1993-94	Regina	Midget	35	3	13	16	50					
1994-95	Regina	WHL	70	4	13	17	85	4	0	0	0	10

STRBAK, MARTIN — (SHTEHR-bahk)

Defense. Shoots left. 6'3", 198 lbs. Born, Presov, Czech., January 15, 1975.
(Los Angeles' 10th choice, 224th overall, in 1993 Entry Draft).

			Regular Season					Playoffs				
Season	Club	Lea	GP	G	A	TP	PIM	GP	G	A	TP	PIM
1992-93	Presov	Czech. 2	1	0	0	0	....					
1993-94	Presov	Slov.	20	6	9	15	....					
1994-95	Presov	Slov.	10	1	0	1	6					
	Bratislava	Slov.	5	0	3	3	0	9	2	1	3	8

STROM, PETER — (STRUHM) MTL.

Left wing. Shoots right. 6', 178 lbs. Born, Snotorp, Sweden, January 14, 1975.
(Montreal's 10th choice, 200th overall, in 1994 Entry Draft).

			Regular Season					Playoffs				
Season	Club	Lea	GP	G	A	TP	PIM	GP	G	A	TP	PIM
1993-94	V. Frolunda	Swe.	29	0	0	0	8					
1994-95	V. Frolunda	Swe.	16	0	3	3	10					
	V. Frolunda	Swe. 2	12	8	10	18	10					

STRUCH, DAVID — (STRUHK) CGY.

Center. Shoots left. 5'10", 180 lbs. Born, Flin Flon, Man., February 11, 1971.
(Calgary's 10th choice, 195th overall, in 1991 Entry Draft).

			Regular Season					Playoffs				
Season	Club	Lea	GP	G	A	TP	PIM	GP	G	A	TP	PIM
1990-91	Saskatoon	WHL	72	45	57	102	69					
1991-92	Saskatoon	WHL	47	29	26	55	34	22	8	15	23	26
	Salt Lake	IHL	12	4	1	5	8					
1992-93	Salt Lake	IHL	78	20	22	42	73					
1993-94	Calgary	NHL	4	0	0	0	4					
	Saint John	AHL	58	18	25	43	87	7	0	1	1	4
1994-95	Saint John	AHL	7	0	1	1	4					
	NHL Totals		4	0	0	0	4					

STRUDWICK, JASON — NYI

Defense. Shoots left. 6'3", 210 lbs. Born, Edmonton, Alta., July 17, 1975.
(NY Islanders' 3rd choice, 63rd overall, in 1994 Entry Draft).

			Regular Season					Playoffs				
Season	Club	Lea	GP	G	A	TP	PIM	GP	G	A	TP	PIM
1993-94	Kamloops	WHL	61	6	8	14	118	19	0	4	4	24
1994-95	Kamloops	WHL	72	3	11	14	183	21	1	1	2	39

STUMPEL, JOZEF — (STUM-puhl) BOS.

Center. Shoots right. 6'1", 208 lbs. Born, Nitra, Czech., June 20, 1972.
(Boston's 2nd choice, 40th overall, in 1991 Entry Draft).

			Regular Season					Playoffs				
Season	Club	Lea	GP	G	A	TP	PIM	GP	G	A	TP	PIM
1989-90	Nitra	Czech. 2	38	12	11	23	....					
1990-91	Nitra	Czech.	49	23	22	45	14					
1991-92	Koln	Ger.	37	20	19	39	35					
	Boston	NHL	4	1	0	1	0					
1992-93	Boston	NHL	13	1	3	4	4					
	Providence	AHL	56	31	61	92	26	6	4	4	8	0
1993-94	Boston	NHL	59	8	15	23	14	13	1	7	8	4
	Providence	AHL	17	5	12	17	4					
1994-95	Koln	Ger.	25	16	23	39	18					
	Boston	NHL	44	5	13	18	8	5	0	0	0	0
	NHL Totals		120	15	31	46	26	18	1	7	8	4

SULLIVAN, BRIAN

Right wing. Shoots right. 6'4", 195 lbs. Born, South Windsor, CT, April 23, 1969.
(New Jersey's 3rd choice, 65th overall, in 1987 Entry Draft).

			Regular Season					Playoffs				
Season	Club	Lea	GP	G	A	TP	PIM	GP	G	A	TP	PIM
1987-88	Northeastern	H.E.	37	20	12	32	18					
1988-89	Northeastern	H.E.	34	13	14	27	65					
1989-90	Northeastern	H.E.	34	24	21	45	72					
1990-91	Northeastern	H.E.	32	17	23	40	75					
1991-92	Utica	AHL	70	23	24	47	58	4	0	4	4	6
1992-93	New Jersey	NHL	2	0	1	1	0					
	Utica	AHL	75	30	27	57	88	5	0	0	0	12
1993-94	Albany	AHL	77	31	30	61	140	5	1	1	2	18
1994-95	San Diego	IHL	74	24	23	47	97	5	0	1	1	7
	NHL Totals		2	0	1	1	0					

Signed as a free agent by **Anaheim**, August 31, 1994.

SULLIVAN, MIKE — CGY.

Center. Shoots left. 6'2", 190 lbs. Born, Marshfield, MA, February 27, 1968.
(NY Rangers' 4th choice, 69th overall, in 1987 Entry Draft).

			Regular Season					Playoffs				
Season	Club	Lea	GP	G	A	TP	PIM	GP	G	A	TP	PIM
1986-87	Boston U.	H.E.	37	13	18	31	18					
1987-88	Boston U.	H.E.	30	18	22	40	30					
1988-89	Boston U.	H.E.	36	19	17	36	30					
1989-90	Boston U.	H.E.	38	11	20	31	26					
1990-91	San Diego	IHL	74	12	23	35	27					
1991-92	San Jose	NHL	64	8	11	19	15					
	Kansas City	IHL	10	2	8	10	8					
1992-93	San Jose	NHL	81	6	8	14	30					
1993-94	San Jose	NHL	26	2	2	4	4					
	Kansas City	IHL	6	3	3	6	0					
	Calgary	NHL	19	2	3	5	6	7	1	1	2	8
	Saint John	AHL	5	2	0	2	4					
1994-95	Calgary	NHL	38	4	7	11	14	7	3	5	8	2
	NHL Totals		228	22	31	53	69	14	4	6	10	10

Rights traded to **Minnesota** by **NY Rangers** with Paul Jerrard, the rights to Bret Barnett, and Los Angeles' third round choice (previously acquired by NY Rangers — Minnesota selected Murray Garbutt) in 1989 Entry Draft for Brian Lawton, Igor Liba and the rights to Eric Bennett, October 11, 1988. Signed as a free agent by **San Jose**, August 9, 1991. Claimed on waivers by **Calgary** from **San Jose**, January 6, 1994.

SULLIVAN, STEVE — N.J.

Center. Shoots right. 5'9", 155 lbs. Born, Timmons, Ont., July 6, 1974.
(New Jersey's 10th choice, 233rd overall, in 1994 Entry Draft).

			Regular Season					Playoffs				
Season	Club	Lea	GP	G	A	TP	PIM	GP	G	A	TP	PIM
1993-94	S.S. Marie	OHL	63	51	62	113	82	14	9	16	25	22
1994-95	Albany	AHL	75	31	50	81	124	14	4	7	11	10

SUNDBLAD, NIKLAS — (SUHN-blad) CGY.

Right wing. Shoots right. 6'1", 200 lbs. Born, Stockholm, Sweden, January 3, 1973.
(Calgary's 1st choice, 19th overall, in 1991 Entry Draft).

			Regular Season					Playoffs				
Season	Club	Lea	GP	G	A	TP	PIM	GP	G	A	TP	PIM
1990-91	AIK	Swe.	39	1	3	4	14					
1991-92	AIK	Swe.	33	9	2	11	20	3	3	1	4	0
1992-93	AIK	Swe.	22	5	4	9	56					
1993-94	Saint John	AHL	76	13	19	32	75	4	1	1	2	2
1994-95	Saint John	AHL	72	9	5	14	151	2	0	0	0	6

SUNDERLAND, MATHIEU — BUF.

Right wing. Shoots right. 6'4", 192 lbs. Born, Quebec City, Que., November 30, 1976.
(Buffalo's 4th choice, 68th overall, in 1995 Entry Draft).

			Regular Season					Playoffs				
Season	Club	Lea	GP	G	A	TP	PIM	GP	G	A	TP	PIM
1993-94	Drummondville	QMJHL	60	19	13	32	118	5	0	0	0	19
1994-95	Drummondville	QMJHL	66	21	24	45	185	3	2	4	6	12

SUNDIN, MATS — (SUHN-deen) TOR.

Center/Right wing. Shoots right. 6'4", 215 lbs. Born, Bromma, Sweden, February 13, 1971.
(Quebec's 1st choice, 1st overall, in 1989 Entry Draft).

			Regular Season					Playoffs				
Season	Club	Lea	GP	G	A	TP	PIM	GP	G	A	TP	PIM
1988-89	Nacka	Swe. 2	25	10	8	18	18					
1989-90	Djurgarden	Swe.	34	10	8	18	16	8	7	0	7	4
1990-91	Quebec	NHL	80	23	36	59	58					
1991-92	Quebec	NHL	80	33	43	76	103					
1992-93	Quebec	NHL	80	47	67	114	96	6	3	1	4	6
1993-94	Quebec	NHL	84	32	53	85	60					
1994-95	Djurgarden	Swe.	12	7	2	9	14					
	Toronto	NHL	47	23	24	47	14	7	5	4	9	4
	NHL Totals		371	158	223	381	331	13	8	5	13	10

Traded to **Toronto** by **Quebec** with Garth Butcher, Todd Warriner and Philadelphia's first round choice (previously acquired by Quebec — later traded to Washington — Washington selected Nolan Baumgartner) in 1994 Entry Draft for Wendel Clark, Sylvain Lefebvre, Landon Wilson and Toronto's first round choice (Jeffrey Kealty) in 1994 Entry Draft, June 28, 1994.

SUNDSTROM, NIKLAS (SUHN-struhm) NYR

Left wing. Shoots left. 6', 185 lbs. Born, Ornskoldsvik, Sweden, June 6, 1975.
(NY Rangers' 1st choice, 8th overall, in 1993 Entry Draft).

			Regular Season					Playoffs				
Season	Club	Lea	GP	G	A	TP	PIM	GP	G	A	TP	PIM
1991-92	MoDo	Swe.	9	1	3	4	0	....	....	....	....	....
1992-93	MoDo	Swe.	40	7	11	18	18	3	0	0	0	0
1993-94	MoDo	Swe.	37	7	12	19	28	11	4	3	7	2
1994-95	MoDo	Swe.	33	8	13	21	30	....	....	....	....	....

SUTER, GARY (SOO-tuhr) CHI.

Defense. Shoots left. 6', 200 lbs. Born, Madison, WI, June 24, 1964.
(Calgary's 9th choice, 180th overall, in 1984 Entry Draft).

			Regular Season					Playoffs				
Season	Club	Lea	GP	G	A	TP	PIM	GP	G	A	TP	PIM
1983-84	U. Wisconsin	WCHA	35	4	18	22	32	....	....	....	....	....
1984-85	U. Wisconsin	WCHA	39	12	39	51	110	....	....	....	....	....
1985-86ab	**Calgary**	**NHL**	**80**	**18**	**50**	**68**	**141**	**10**	**2**	**8**	**10**	**8**
1986-87	**Calgary**	**NHL**	**68**	**9**	**40**	**49**	**70**	**6**	**0**	**3**	**3**	**10**
1987-88c	**Calgary**	**NHL**	**75**	**21**	**70**	**91**	**124**	**9**	**1**	**9**	**10**	**6**
1988-89	**Calgary**	**NHL**	**63**	**13**	**49**	**62**	**78**	**5**	**0**	**3**	**3**	**10**
1989-90	**Calgary**	**NHL**	**76**	**16**	**60**	**76**	**97**	**6**	**0**	**1**	**1**	**14**
1990-91	**Calgary**	**NHL**	**79**	**12**	**58**	**70**	**102**	**7**	**1**	**6**	**7**	**12**
1991-92	**Calgary**	**NHL**	**70**	**12**	**43**	**55**	**128**	....	....	....	....	....
1992-93	**Calgary**	**NHL**	**81**	**23**	**58**	**81**	**112**	**6**	**2**	**3**	**5**	**8**
1993-94	**Calgary**	**NHL**	**25**	**4**	**9**	**13**	**20**	....	....	....	....	....
	Chicago	**NHL**	**16**	**2**	**3**	**5**	**18**	**6**	**3**	**2**	**5**	**6**
1994-95	**Chicago**	**NHL**	**48**	**10**	**27**	**37**	**42**	**12**	**2**	**5**	**7**	**10**
	NHL Totals		**681**	**140**	**467**	**607**	**932**	**67**	**11**	**40**	**51**	**84**

a Won Calder Memorial Trophy (1986)
b NHL All-Rookie Team (1986)
c NHL Second All-Star Team (1988)

Played in NHL All-Star Game (1986, 1988, 1989, 1991)

Traded to **Hartford** by **Calgary** with Paul Ranheim and Ted Drury for James Patrick, Zarley Zalapski and Michael Nylander, March 10, 1994. Traded to **Chicago** by **Hartford** with Randy Cunneyworth and Hartford's third round choice (later traded to Vancouver — Vancouver selected Larry Courville) in 1995 Entry Draft for Frantisek Kucera and Jocelyn Lemieux, March 11, 1994.

SUTTER, BRENT (SUH-tuhr) CHI.

Center. Shoots right. 5'11", 187 lbs. Born, Viking, Alta., June 10, 1962.
(NY Islanders' 1st choice, 17th overall, in 1980 Entry Draft).

			Regular Season					Playoffs				
Season	Club	Lea	GP	G	A	TP	PIM	GP	G	A	TP	PIM
1979-80	Red Deer	AJHL	59	70	101	171	....	....	....	....	....	....
	Lethbridge	WHL	5	1	0	1	2	....	....	....	....	....
1980-81	**NY Islanders**	**NHL**	**3**	**2**	**2**	**4**	**0**	....	....	....	....	....
	Lethbridge	WHL	68	54	54	108	116	9	6	4	10	51
1981-82	**NY Islanders**	**NHL**	**43**	**21**	**22**	**43**	**114**	**19**	**2**	**6**	**8**	**36**
	Lethbridge	WHL	34	46	33	79	162	....	....	....	....	....
1982-83	**NY Islanders**	**NHL**	**80**	**21**	**19**	**40**	**128**	**20**	**10**	**11**	**21**	**26**
1983-84	**NY Islanders**	**NHL**	**69**	**34**	**15**	**49**	**69**	**20**	**4**	**10**	**14**	**18**
1984-85	**NY Islanders**	**NHL**	**72**	**42**	**60**	**102**	**51**	**10**	**3**	**3**	**6**	**14**
1985-86	**NY Islanders**	**NHL**	**61**	**24**	**31**	**55**	**74**	**3**	**0**	**1**	**1**	**2**
1986-87	**NY Islanders**	**NHL**	**69**	**27**	**36**	**63**	**73**	**5**	**1**	**0**	**1**	**4**
1987-88	**NY Islanders**	**NHL**	**70**	**29**	**31**	**60**	**55**	**6**	**2**	**1**	**3**	**18**
1988-89	**NY Islanders**	**NHL**	**77**	**29**	**34**	**63**	**77**	....	....	....	....	....
1989-90	**NY Islanders**	**NHL**	**67**	**33**	**35**	**68**	**65**	**5**	**2**	**3**	**5**	**2**
1990-91	**NY Islanders**	**NHL**	**75**	**21**	**32**	**53**	**49**	....	....	....	....	....
1991-92	**NY Islanders**	**NHL**	**8**	**4**	**6**	**10**	**6**	....	....	....	....	....
	Chicago	**NHL**	**61**	**18**	**32**	**50**	**30**	**18**	**3**	**5**	**8**	**22**
1992-93	**Chicago**	**NHL**	**65**	**20**	**34**	**54**	**67**	**4**	**1**	**1**	**2**	**4**
1993-94	**Chicago**	**NHL**	**73**	**9**	**29**	**38**	**43**	**6**	**0**	**0**	**0**	**2**
1994-95	**Chicago**	**NHL**	**47**	**7**	**8**	**15**	**51**	**16**	**1**	**2**	**3**	**4**
	NHL Totals		**940**	**·341**	**426**	**767**	**952**	**132**	**29**	**43**	**72**	**152**

Played in NHL All-Star Game (1985)

Traded to **Chicago** by **NY Islanders** with Brad Lauer for Adam Creighton and Steve Thomas, October 25, 1991.

SUTTER, RICH (SUH-tuhr)

Right wing. Shoots right. 5'11", 188 lbs. Born, Viking, Alta., December 2, 1963.
(Pittsburgh's 1st choice, 10th overall, in 1982 Entry Draft).

			Regular Season					Playoffs				
Season	Club	Lea	GP	G	A	TP	PIM	GP	G	A	TP	PIM
1980-81	Lethbridge	WHL	72	23	18	41	255	9	3	1	4	35
1981-82	Lethbridge	WHL	57	38	31	69	263	12	3	3	6	55
1982-83	**Pittsburgh**	**NHL**	**4**	**0**	**0**	**0**	**0**	....	....	....	....	....
	Lethbridge	WHL	64	37	30	67	200	17	14	9	23	43
1983-84	**Pittsburgh**	**NHL**	**5**	**0**	**0**	**0**	**0**	....	....	....	....	....
	Baltimore	AHL	2	0	1	1	0	....	....	....	....	....
	Philadelphia	**NHL**	**70**	**16**	**12**	**28**	**93**	**3**	**0**	**0**	**0**	**15**
1984-85	**Philadelphia**	**NHL**	**56**	**6**	**10**	**16**	**89**	**11**	**3**	**0**	**3**	**10**
	Hershey	AHL	13	3	7	10	14	....	....	....	....	....
1985-86	**Philadelphia**	**NHL**	**78**	**14**	**25**	**39**	**199**	**5**	**2**	**0**	**2**	**19**
1986-87	**Vancouver**	**NHL**	**74**	**20**	**22**	**42**	**113**	....	....	....	....	....
1987-88	**Vancouver**	**NHL**	**80**	**15**	**15**	**30**	**165**	....	....	....	....	....
1988-89	**Vancouver**	**NHL**	**75**	**17**	**15**	**32**	**122**	**7**	**2**	**1**	**3**	**12**
1989-90	**Vancouver**	**NHL**	**62**	**9**	**9**	**18**	**133**	....	....	....	....	....
	St. Louis	**NHL**	**12**	**2**	**0**	**2**	**22**	**12**	**2**	**1**	**3**	**39**
1990-91	**St. Louis**	**NHL**	**77**	**16**	**11**	**27**	**122**	**13**	**4**	**2**	**6**	**16**
1991-92	**St. Louis**	**NHL**	**77**	**9**	**16**	**25**	**107**	**6**	**0**	**0**	**0**	**8**
1992-93	**St. Louis**	**NHL**	**84**	**13**	**14**	**27**	**100**	**11**	**0**	**1**	**1**	**10**
1993-94	**Chicago**	**NHL**	**83**	**12**	**14**	**26**	**108**	**6**	**0**	**0**	**0**	**2**
1994-95	**Chicago**	**NHL**	**15**	**0**	**0**	**0**	**28**	....	....	....	....	....
	Tampa Bay	**NHL**	**4**	**0**	**0**	**0**	**0**	....	....	....	....	....
	Atlanta	IHL	4	0	5	5	0	....	....	....	....	....
	Toronto	**NHL**	**18**	**0**	**3**	**3**	**10**	**4**	**0**	**0**	**0**	**2**
	NHL Totals		**874**	**149**	**166**	**315**	**1411**	**78**	**13**	**5**	**18**	**133**

Traded to **Philadelphia** by **Pittsburgh** with Pittsburgh's second round (Greg Smyth) and third round (David McLay) choices in 1984 Entry Draft for Andy Brickley, Mark Taylor, Ron Flockhart, Philadelphia's first round (Roger Belanger) and third round (later traded to Vancouver — Vancouver selected Mike Stevens) choices in 1984 Entry Draft, October 23, 1983. Traded to **Vancouver** by **Philadelphia**, with Dave Richter and Vancouver's third round choice (previously acquired by Philadelphia — Vancouver selected Don Gibson) in 1986 Entry Draft for J.J. Daigneault and Vancouver's second round choice (Kent Hawley) in 1986 Entry Draft, June 6, 1986. Traded to **St Louis** by **Vancouver** with Harold Snepsts and St. Louis' second round choice (previously acquired by Vancouver — St. Louis selected Craig Johnson) in 1990 Entry Draft for Adrien Plavsic, Montreal's first round choice (previously acquired by St. Louis — Vancouver selected Shawn Antoski) in 1990 Entry Draft and St. Louis' second round choice (later traded to Montreal — Montreal selected Craig Darby) in 1991 Entry Draft, March 6, 1990. Claimed by **Chicago** from **St. Louis** in NHL Waiver Draft, October 3, 1993. Traded to **Tampa Bay** by **Chicago** with Paul Ysebaert for Jim Cummins, Tom Tilley and Jeff Buchanan, February 22, 1995. Traded to **Toronto** by **Tampa Bay** for cash, March 13, 1995.

SUTTER, RON (SUH-tuhr)

Center. Shoots right. 6', 180 lbs. Born, Viking, Alta., December 2, 1963.
(Philadelphia's 1st choice, 4th overall, in 1982 Entry Draft).

			Regular Season					Playoffs				
Season	Club	Lea	GP	G	A	TP	PIM	GP	G	A	TP	PIM
1980-81	Lethbridge	WHL	72	13	32	45	152	9	2	5	7	29
1981-82	Lethbridge	WHL	59	38	54	92	207	12	6	5	11	28
1982-83	**Philadelphia**	**NHL**	**10**	**1**	**1**	**2**	**9**	....	....	....	....	....
	Lethbridge	WHL	58	35	48	83	98	20	*22	*19	*41	45
1983-84	**Philadelphia**	**NHL**	**79**	**19**	**32**	**51**	**101**	**3**	**0**	**0**	**0**	**22**
1984-85	**Philadelphia**	**NHL**	**73**	**16**	**29**	**45**	**94**	**19**	**4**	**8**	**12**	**28**
1985-86	**Philadelphia**	**NHL**	**75**	**18**	**42**	**60**	**159**	**5**	**0**	**2**	**2**	**10**
1986-87	**Philadelphia**	**NHL**	**39**	**10**	**17**	**27**	**69**	**16**	**1**	**7**	**8**	**12**
1987-88	**Philadelphia**	**NHL**	**69**	**8**	**25**	**33**	**146**	**7**	**0**	**1**	**1**	**26**
1988-89	**Philadelphia**	**NHL**	**55**	**26**	**22**	**48**	**80**	**19**	**1**	**9**	**10**	**51**
1989-90	**Philadelphia**	**NHL**	**75**	**22**	**26**	**48**	**104**	....	....	....	....	....
1990-91	**Philadelphia**	**NHL**	**80**	**17**	**28**	**45**	**92**	....	....	....	....	....
1991-92	**St. Louis**	**NHL**	**68**	**19**	**27**	**46**	**91**	**6**	**1**	**3**	**4**	**8**
1992-93	**St. Louis**	**NHL**	**59**	**12**	**15**	**27**	**99**	....	....	....	....	....
1993-94	**St. Louis**	**NHL**	**36**	**6**	**12**	**18**	**46**	....	....	....	....	....
	Quebec	**NHL**	**37**	**9**	**13**	**22**	**44**	....	....	....	....	....
1994-95	**NY Islanders**	**NHL**	**27**	**1**	**4**	**5**	**21**	....	....	....	....	....
	NHL Totals		**782**	**184**	**293**	**477**	**1155**	**75**	**7**	**30**	**37**	**157**

Traded to **St. Louis** by **Philadelphia** with Murray Baron for Dan Quinn and Rod Brind'Amour, September 22, 1991. Traded to **Quebec** by **St. Louis** with Garth Butcher and Bob Bassen for Steve Duchesne and Denis Chasse, January 23, 1994. Traded to **NY Islanders** by **Quebec** with Quebec's first round choice (Brett Lindros) in 1994 Entry Draft for Uwe Krupp and NY Islanders' first round choice (Wade Belak) in 1994 Entry Draft, June 28, 1994.

SUTTON, KEN EDM.

Defense. Shoots left. 6', 200 lbs. Born, Edmonton, Alta., November 5, 1969.
(Buffalo's 4th choice, 98th overall, in 1989 Entry Draft).

			Regular Season					Playoffs				
Season	Club	Lea	GP	G	A	TP	PIM	GP	G	A	TP	PIM
1988-89a	Saskatoon	WHL	71	22	31	53	104	8	2	5	7	12
1989-90	Rochester	AHL	57	5	14	19	83	11	1	6	7	15
1990-91	**Buffalo**	**NHL**	**15**	**3**	**6**	**9**	**13**	**6**	**0**	**1**	**1**	**2**
	Rochester	AHL	62	7	24	31	65	3	1	1	2	14
1991-92	**Buffalo**	**NHL**	**64**	**2**	**18**	**20**	**71**	**7**	**0**	**2**	**2**	**4**
1992-93	**Buffalo**	**NHL**	**63**	**8**	**14**	**22**	**30**	**8**	**3**	**1**	**4**	**8**
1993-94	**Buffalo**	**NHL**	**78**	**4**	**20**	**24**	**71**	**4**	**0**	**0**	**0**	**2**
1994-95	**Buffalo**	**NHL**	**12**	**1**	**2**	**3**	**30**	....	....	....	....	....
	Edmonton	**NHL**	**12**	**3**	**1**	**4**	**12**	....	....	....	....	....
	NHL Totals		**244**	**21**	**61**	**82**	**227**	**25**	**3**	**4**	**7**	**16**

a Memorial Cup All-Star Team (1989)

Traded to **Edmonton** by **Buffalo** for Scott Pearson, April 7, 1995.

SUURSOO, TOIVO (SUH-uhr-soh-oh) DET.

Left wing. Shoots right. 6', 175 lbs. Born, Tallinn, USSR, November 23, 1975.
(Detroit's 10th choice, 283rd overall, in 1994 Entry Draft).

			Regular Season					Playoffs				
Season	Club	Lea	GP	G	A	TP	PIM	GP	G	A	TP	PIM
1993-94	Soviet Wings	CIS	33	3	0	3	8	....	....	....	....	....
1994-95	Soviet Wings	CIS	47	10	5	15	36	....	....	....	....	....

SVARTVADET, PER DAL.

Center. Shoots left. 6'1", 180 lbs. Born, Solleftea, Sweden, May 17, 1975.
(Dallas' 5th choice, 139th overall, in 1993 Entry Draft).

			Regular Season					Playoffs				
Season	Club	Lea	GP	G	A	TP	PIM	GP	G	A	TP	PIM
1992-93	MoDo	Swe.	2	0	0	0	0	....	....	....	....	....
1993-94	MoDo	Swe.	36	2	1	3	4	11	0	0	0	6
1994-95	MoDo	Swe.	40	6	9	15	31	....	....	....	....	....

SVEHLA, ROBERT (SCHVE-khlah) FLA.

Defense. Shoots right. 6'1", 190 lbs. Born, Martin, Czech., January 2, 1969.
(Calgary's 4th choice, 78th overall, in 1992 Entry Draft).

			Regular Season					Playoffs				
Season	Club	Lea	GP	G	A	TP	PIM	GP	G	A	TP	PIM
1989-90	Dukla Trencin	Czech.	29	4	3	7	....	....	....	....	....	....
1990-91	Dukla Trencin	Czech.	52	16	9	25	62	....	....	....	....	....
1991-92	Dukla Trencin	Czech.	51	23	28	51	74	....	....	....	....	....
1992-93	Malmo	Swe.	40	19	10	29	86	6	0	1	1	14
1993-94	Malmo	Swe.	37	14	25	39	127	10	5	1	6	23
1994-95	Malmo	Swe.	32	11	13	24	83	9	2	3	5	6
	Florida	**NHL**	**5**	**1**	**1**	**2**	**0**	....	....	....	....	....
	NHL Totals		**5**	**1**	**1**	**2**	**0**	....	....	....	....	....

Traded to **Florida** by **Calgary** with Magnus Svensson for Florida's third round choice in 1996 Entry Draft and a future conditional draft choice, September 29, 1994.

SVENSSON, MAGNUS (SVEHN-suhn) FLA.

Defense. Shoots left. 5'11", 180 lbs. Born, Tranas, Sweden, March 1, 1963.
(Calgary's 13th choice, 250th overall, in 1987 Entry Draft).

			Regular Season					Playoffs				
Season	Club	Lea	GP	G	A	TP	PIM	GP	G	A	TP	PIM
1983-84	Leksand	Swe.	35	3	8	11	20	....	....	....	....	....
1984-85	Leksand	Swe.	35	8	7	15	22	....	....	....	....	....
1985-86	Leksand	Swe.	36	6	9	15	62	....	....	....	....	....
1986-87	Leksand	Swe.	33	8	16	24	42	....	....	....	....	....
1987-88	Leksand	Swe.	40	12	11	23	20	3	0	0	0	8
1988-89	Leksand	Swe.	39	15	22	37	40	9	3	5	8	8
1989-90	Leksand	Swe.	26	11	12	23	60	1	0	0	0	0
1990-91	Lugano	Switz.	33	16	20	36	....	11	3	2	5	....
1991-92	Leksand	Swe.	22	4	10	14	32	....	....	....	....	....
1992-93	Leksand	Swe.	37	10	17	27	36	2	0	2	2	0
1993-94	Leksand	Swe.	39	13	16	29	22	4	3	1	4	0
1994-95	Davos	Swiss.	35	8	25	33	46	5	2	2	4	8
	Florida	**NHL**	**19**	**2**	**5**	**7**	**10**	....	....	....	....	....
	NHL Totals		**19**	**2**	**5**	**7**	**10**	....	....	....	....	....

Traded to **Florida** by **Calgary** with Robert Svehla for Florida's third round choice in 1996 Entry Draft and a future conditional draft choice, September 29, 1994.

SVOBODA, PETR (svah-BOH-duh) PHI.

Defense. Shoots left. 6'1", 174 lbs. Born, Most, Czech., February 14, 1966.
(Montreal's 1st choice, 5th overall, in 1984 Entry Draft).

			Regular Season					Playoffs				
Season	Club	Lea	GP	G	A	TP	PIM	GP	G	A	TP	PIM
1982-83	Litvinov	Czech.	4	0	0	0	2					
1983-84	Litvinov	Czech.	18	3	1	4	20					
1984-85	Montreal	NHL	73	4	27	31	65	7	1	1	2	12
1985-86	Montreal	NHL	73	1	18	19	93	8	0	0	0	21
1986-87	Montreal	NHL	70	5	17	22	63	14	0	5	5	10
1987-88	Montreal	NHL	69	7	22	29	149	10	0	5	5	12
1988-89	Montreal	NHL	71	8	37	45	147	21	1	11	12	16
1989-90	Montreal	NHL	60	5	31	36	98	10	0	5	5	7
1990-91	Montreal	NHL	60	4	22	26	52	2	0	1	1	2
1991-92	Montreal	NHL	58	5	16	21	94					
	Buffalo	NHL	13	1	6	7	52	7	1	4	5	6
1992-93	Buffalo	NHL	40	2	24	26	59					
1993-94	Buffalo	NHL	60	2	14	16	89	3	0	0	0	4
1994-95	Litvinov	Czech.	8	2	0	2	50					
	Buffalo	NHL	26	0	5	5	60					
	Philadelphia	NHL	11	0	3	3	10	14	0	4	4	8
	NHL Totals		684	44	242	286	1031	96	3	36	39	98

Traded to **Buffalo** by **Montreal** for Kevin Haller, March 10, 1992. Traded to **Philadelphia** by **Buffalo** for Garry Galley, April 7, 1995.

SWANSON, BRIAN S.J.

Center. Shoots left. 5'10", 180 lbs. Born, Anchorage, AK, March 24, 1976.
(San Jose's 5th choice, 115th overall, in 1994 Entry Draft).

			Regular Season					Playoffs				
Season	Club	Lea	GP	G	A	TP	PIM	GP	G	A	TP	PIM
1993-94	Omaha	USHL	47	38	42	80	40					
1994-95	Portland	WHL	65	3	18	21	91	9	2	1	3	18

SWEENEY, BOB BUF.

Center/Right wing. Shoots right. 6'3", 200 lbs. Born, Concord, MA, January 25, 1964.
(Boston's 6th choice, 123rd overall, in 1982 Entry Draft).

			Regular Season					Playoffs				
Season	Club	Lea	GP	G	A	TP	PIM	GP	G	A	TP	PIM
1982-83	Boston College	ECAC	30	17	11	28	10					
1983-84	Boston College	ECAC	23	14	7	21	10					
1984-85a	Boston College	ECAC	44	32	32	64	43					
1985-86	Boston College	H.E.	41	15	24	39	52					
1986-87	Boston	NHL	14	2	4	6	21	3	0	0	0	0
	Moncton	AHL	58	29	26	55	81	4	0	2	2	13
1987-88	Boston	NHL	80	22	23	45	73	23	6	8	14	66
1988-89	Boston	NHL	75	14	14	28	99	10	2	4	6	19
1989-90	Boston	NHL	70	22	24	46	93	20	0	2	2	30
1990-91	Boston	NHL	80	15	33	48	115	17	4	2	6	45
1991-92	Boston	NHL	63	6	14	20	103	14	1	0	1	25
	Maine	AHL	1	1	0	1	0					
1992-93	Buffalo	NHL	80	21	26	47	118	8	2	2	4	8
1993-94	Buffalo	NHL	60	11	14	25	94	1	0	0	0	0
1994-95	Buffalo	NHL	45	5	4	9	18	5	0	0	0	4
	NHL Totals		567	118	156	274	734	101	15	18	33	197

a ECAC Second Team All-Star (1985)

Claimed on waivers by **Buffalo** from **Boston**, October 9, 1992.

SWEENEY, DON BOS.

Defense. Shoots left. 5'10", 188 lbs. Born, St. Stephen, N.B., August 17, 1966.
(Boston's 8th choice, 166th overall, in 1984 Entry Draft).

			Regular Season					Playoffs				
Season	Club	Lea	GP	G	A	TP	PIM	GP	G	A	TP	PIM
1984-85	Harvard	ECAC	29	3	7	10	30					
1985-86	Harvard	ECAC	31	4	5	9	12					
1986-87	Harvard	ECAC	34	7	4	11	22					
1987-88ab	Harvard	ECAC	30	6	23	29	37					
	Maine	AHL						6	1	3	4	0
1988-89	Boston	NHL	36	3	5	8	20					
	Maine	AHL	42	8	17	25	24					
1989-90	Boston	NHL	58	3	5	8	58	21	1	5	6	18
	Maine	AHL	11	0	8	8	8					
1990-91	Boston	NHL	77	8	13	21	67	19	3	0	3	25
1991-92	Boston	NHL	75	3	11	14	74	15	0	0	0	10
1992-93	Boston	NHL	84	7	27	34	68	4	0	0	0	4
1993-94	Boston	NHL	75	6	15	21	50	12	2	1	3	4
1994-95	Boston	NHL	47	3	19	22	24	5	0	0	0	4
	NHL Totals		452	33	95	128	361	76	6	6	12	65

a NCAA East All-American Team (1988)
b ECAC First All-Star Team (1988)

SWEENEY, TIM BOS.

Left wing. Shoots left. 5'11", 185 lbs. Born, Boston, MA, April 12, 1967.
(Calgary's 7th choice, 122nd overall, in 1985 Entry Draft).

			Regular Season					Playoffs				
Season	Club	Lea	GP	G	A	TP	PIM	GP	G	A	TP	PIM
1985-86	Boston College	H.E.	32	8	4	12	8					
1986-87	Boston College	H.E.	38	31	18	49	28					
1987-88	Boston College	H.E.	18	9	11	20	18					
1988-89ab	Boston College	H.E.	39	29	44	73	26					
1989-90c	Salt Lake	IHL	81	46	51	97	32	11	5	4	9	4
1990-91	Calgary	NHL	42	7	9	16	8					
	Salt Lake	IHL	31	19	16	35	8	4	3	3	6	0
1991-92	U.S. National	....	21	9	11	20	10					
	U.S. Olympic	....	8	3	4	7	6					
	Calgary	NHL	11	1	2	3	4					
1992-93	Boston	NHL	14	1	7	8	6	3	0	0	0	0
d	Providence	AHL	60	41	55	96	32	3	2	2	4	0
1993-94	Anaheim	NHL	78	16	27	43	49					
1994-95	Anaheim	NHL	13	1	1	2	2					
	Providence	AHL	2	2	2	4	0	13	8	*17	*25	6
	NHL Totals		158	26	46	72	69	3	0	0	0	0

a Hockey East First All-Star Team (1989)
b NCAA East Second All-American Team (1989)
c IHL Second All-Star Team (1990)
d AHL Second All-Star Team (1993)

Signed as a free agent by **Boston**, September 16, 1992. Claimed by **Anaheim** from **Boston** in Expansion Draft, June 24, 1993. Signed as a free agent by **Boston**, August 9, 1995.

SYCHRA, MARTIN MTL.

Center. Shoots left. 6'1", 180 lbs. Born, Brno, Czech., June 19, 1974.
(Montreal's 8th choice, 140th overall, in 1992 Entry Draft).

			Regular Season					Playoffs				
Season	Club	Lea	GP	G	A	TP	PIM	GP	G	A	TP	PIM
1991-92	Zetor Brno	Czech.	14	2	2	4	2					
1992-93	Dukla Trencin	Czech.	4	0	1	1	....					
	Dukla Jihlava	Czech.	14	1	2	3	....					
1993-94	Kingston	OHL	59	29	32	61	32	6	0	3	3	7
1994-95	Fredericton	AHL	39	4	10	14	4					

SYDOR, DARRYL (sih-DOHR) L.A.

Defense. Shoots left. 6', 205 lbs. Born, Edmonton, Alta., May 13, 1972.
(Los Angeles' 1st choice, 7th overall, in 1990 Entry Draft).

			Regular Season					Playoffs				
Season	Club	Lea	GP	G	A	TP	PIM	GP	G	A	TP	PIM
1988-89	Kamloops	WHL	65	12	14	26	86	15	1	4	5	19
1989-90a	Kamloops	WHL	67	29	66	95	129	17	2	9	11	28
1990-91a	Kamloops	WHL	66	27	78	105	88	12	3	*22	25	10
1991-92	Los Angeles	NHL	18	1	5	6	22					
a	Kamloops	WHL	29	9	39	48	43	17	3	15	18	18
1992-93	Los Angeles	NHL	80	6	23	29	63	24	3	8	11	16
1993-94	Los Angeles	NHL	84	8	27	35	94					
1994-95	Los Angeles	NHL	48	4	19	23	36					
	NHL Totals		230	19	74	93	215	24	3	8	11	16

a WHL West First All-Star Team (1990, 1991, 1992)

SYKORA, MICHAL (SEE-koh-ra) S.J.

Defense. Shoots left. 6'5", 225 lbs. Born, Pardubice, Czech., July 5, 1973.
(San Jose's 6th choice, 123rd overall, in 1992 Entry Draft).

			Regular Season					Playoffs				
Season	Club	Lea	GP	G	A	TP	PIM	GP	G	A	TP	PIM
1990-91	Pardubice	Czech.	2	0	0	0	....					
1991-92	Tacoma	WHL	61	13	23	36	66	4	0	2	2	2
1992-93a	Tacoma	WHL	70	23	50	73	73	7	4	8	12	2
1993-94	San Jose	NHL	22	1	4	5	14					
	Kansas City	IHL	47	5	11	16	30					
1994-95	Kansas City	IHL	36	1	10	11	30					
	San Jose	NHL	16	0	4	4	10					
	NHL Totals		38	1	8	9	24					

a WHL West First All-Star Team (1993)

SYKORA, PETR (SEE-koh-ra) N.J.

Center. Shoots left. 5'11", 183 lbs. Born, Plzen, Czech., November 19, 1976.
(New Jersey's 1st choice, 18th overall, in 1995 Entry Draft).

			Regular Season					Playoffs				
Season	Club	Lea	GP	G	A	TP	PIM	GP	G	A	TP	PIM
1992-93	Skoda Plzen	Czech.	19	12	5	17	....					
1993-94	Skoda Plzen	Czech.	37	10	16	26	....	4	0	1	1	....
	Cleveland	IHL	13	4	5	9	8					
1994-95	Detroit	IHL	29	12	17	29	16					

SYLVESTER, DEAN S.J.

Right wing. Shoots right. 6'2", 185 lbs. Born, Hanson, MA, December 30, 1972.
(San Jose's 1st choice, 2nd overall, in 1993 Supplemental Draft).

			Regular Season					Playoffs				
Season	Club	Lea	GP	G	A	TP	PIM	GP	G	A	TP	PIM
1991-92	Kent State	CCHA	31	7	21	28	....					
1992-93	Kent State	CCHA	38	33	20	53	28					
1993-94	Kent State	CCHA	39	22	24	46	28					
1994-95	Michigan State	CCHA	40	15	15	30	38					

SYMES, BRAD EDM.

Defense. Shoots left. 6'2", 210 lbs. Born, Edmonton, Alta., April 26, 1976.
(Edmonton's 5th choice, 60th overall, in 1994 Entry Draft).

			Regular Season					Playoffs				
Season	Club	Lea	GP	G	A	TP	PIM	GP	G	A	TP	PIM
1992-93	Portland	WHL	68	4	2	6	107	16	0	1	1	7
1993-94	Portland	WHL	71	7	15	22	170	7	0	0	0	21
1994-95	Portland	WHL	70	8	16	24	134	9	0	2	2	27

TAGLIANETTI, PETER (TAG-lee-uh-NEH-tee) BOS.

Defense. Shoots left. 6'2", 195 lbs. Born, Framingham, MA, August 15, 1963.
(Winnipeg's 4th choice, 43rd overall, in 1983 Entry Draft).

			Regular Season					Playoffs				
Season	Club	Lea	GP	G	A	TP	PIM	GP	G	A	TP	PIM
1981-82	Providence	ECAC	2	0	0	0	2					
1982-83	Providence	ECAC	43	4	17	21	68					
1983-84	Providence	ECAC	30	4	25	29	68					
1984-85	Winnipeg	NHL	1	0	0	0	0	1	0	0	0	0
a	Providence	H.E.	35	6	18	24	32					
1985-86	Winnipeg	NHL	18	0	0	0	48	3	0	0	0	2
	Sherbrooke	AHL	24	1	18	9	75					
1986-87	Winnipeg	NHL	3	0	0	0	12					
	Sherbrooke	AHL	54	5	14	19	104	10	2	5	7	25
1987-88	Winnipeg	NHL	70	6	17	23	182	5	1	1	2	12
1988-89	Winnipeg	NHL	66	1	14	15	226					
1989-90	Winnipeg	NHL	49	3	6	9	136	5	0	0	0	6
	Moncton	AHL	3	0	2	2	2					
1990-91	Minnesota	NHL	16	0	1	1	14					
	Pittsburgh	NHL	39	3	8	11	93	19	0	3	3	49
1991-92	Pittsburgh	NHL	44	1	3	4	57					
1992-93	Tampa Bay	NHL	61	1	8	9	150					
	Pittsburgh	NHL	11	1	4	5	34	11	1	2	3	16
1993-94	Pittsburgh	NHL	60	2	12	14	142	5	0	2	2	16
1994-95	Pittsburgh	NHL	13	0	1	1	12	4	0	0	0	2
	Cleveland	IHL	3	0	1	1	7	4	0	0	0	19
	NHL Totals		451	18	74	92	1106	53	2	8	10	103

a Hockey East First All-Star Team (1985)

Traded to **Minnesota** by **Winnipeg** for future considerations, September 30, 1990. Traded to **Pittsburgh** by **Minnesota** with Larry Murphy for Chris Dahlquist and Jim Johnson, December 11, 1990. Claimed by **Tampa Bay** from **Pittsburgh** in Expansion Draft, June 18, 1992. Traded to **Pittsburgh** by **Tampa Bay** for Pittsburgh's third round choice (later traded to Florida — Florida selected Steve Washburn) in 1993 Entry Draft, March 22, 1993. Signed as a free agent by **Boston**, August 9, 1995.

TALLAIRE, SEAN — VAN.

Right wing. Shoots right. 5'10", 185 lbs. Born, Steinbach, MN, October 3, 1973.
(Vancouver's 7th choice, 202nd overall, in 1993 Entry Draft).

			Regular Season					Playoffs				
Season	Club	Lea	GP	G	A	TP	PIM	GP	G	A	TP	PIM
1992-93	Lake Superior	CCHA	43	26	26	52	26	....	....	....	....	....
1993-94	Lake Superior	CCHA	45	23	32	55	22	....	....	....	....	....
1994-95	Lake Superior	CCHA	41	21	29	50	38	....	....	....	....	....

TAMER, CHRIS — (TAY-muhr) — PIT.

Defense. Shoots left. 6'2", 185 lbs. Born, Dearborn, MI, November 17, 1970.
(Pittsburgh's 3rd choice, 68th overall, in 1990 Entry Draft).

			Regular Season					Playoffs				
Season	Club	Lea	GP	G	A	TP	PIM	GP	G	A	TP	PIM
1989-90	U. of Michigan	CCHA	42	2	7	9	147	....	....	....	....	....
1990-91	U. of Michigan	CCHA	45	8	19	27	130	....	....	....	....	....
1991-92	U. of Michigan	CCHA	43	4	15	19	125	....	....	....	....	....
1992-93	U. of Michigan	CCHA	39	5	18	23	113	....	....	....	....	....
1993-94	**Pittsburgh**	**NHL**	**12**	**0**	**0**	**0**	**9**	**5**	**0**	**0**	**0**	**2**
	Cleveland	IHL	53	1	2	3	160	....	....	....	....	....
1994-95	Cleveland	IHL	48	4	10	14	204	....	....	....	....	....
	Pittsburgh	**NHL**	**36**	**2**	**0**	**2**	**82**	**4**	**0**	**0**	**0**	**18**
	NHL Totals		**48**	**2**	**0**	**2**	**91**	**9**	**0**	**0**	**0**	**20**

TANCILL, CHRIS — (TAN-sihl) — S.J.

Center. Shoots left. 5'10", 185 lbs. Born, Livonia, MI, February 7, 1968.
(Hartford's 1st choice, 15th overall, in 1989 Supplemental Draft).

			Regular Season					Playoffs				
Season	Club	Lea	GP	G	A	TP	PIM	GP	G	A	TP	PIM
1986-87	U. Wisconsin	WCHA	40	9	23	32	26	....	....	....	....	....
1987-88	U. Wisconsin	WCHA	44	13	14	27	48	....	....	....	....	....
1988-89	U. Wisconsin	WCHA	44	20	23	43	50	....	....	....	....	....
1989-90a	U. Wisconsin	WCHA	45	39	32	71	44	....	....	....	....	....
1990-91	**Hartford**	**NHL**	**9**	**1**	**1**	**2**	**4**	....	....	....	....	....
	Springfield	AHL	72	37	35	72	46	17	8	4	12	32
1991-92	**Hartford**	**NHL**	**10**	**0**	**0**	**0**	**2**	....	....	....	....	....
b	Springfield	AHL	17	12	7	19	20	....	....	....	....	....
	Detroit	**NHL**	**1**	**0**	**0**	**0**	**0**	....	....	....	....	....
	Adirondack	AHL	50	36	34	70	42	19	7	9	16	31
1992-93	**Detroit**	**NHL**	**4**	**1**	**0**	**1**	**2**	....	....	....	....	....
b	Adirondack	AHL	68	*59	43	102	62	10	7	7	14	10
1993-94	**Dallas**	**NHL**	**12**	**1**	**3**	**4**	**8**	....	....	....	....	....
	Kalamazoo	IHL	60	41	54	95	55	5	0	2	2	8
1994-95	Kansas City	IHL	64	31	28	59	40	....	....	....	....	....
	San Jose	**NHL**	**26**	**3**	**11**	**14**	**10**	**11**	**1**	**1**	**2**	**8**
	NHL Totals		**62**	**6**	**15**	**21**	**26**	**11**	**1**	**1**	**2**	**8**

a NCAA All-Tournament Team, Tournament MVP (1990)
b AHL First All-Star Team (1992, 1993)

Traded to **Detroit** by **Hartford** for Daniel Shank, December 18, 1991. Signed as a free agent by **Dallas**, August 28, 1993. Signed as a free agent by **San Jose**, August 24, 1994.

TARDIF, PATRICE — ST.L.

Center. Shoots left. 6'2", 202 lbs. Born, Thetford Mines, Que., October 30, 1970.
(St. Louis' 2nd choice, 54th overall, in 1990 Entry Draft).

			Regular Season					Playoffs				
Season	Club	Lea	GP	G	A	TP	PIM	GP	G	A	TP	PIM
1990-91	U. of Maine	H.E.	36	13	12	25	18	....	....	....	....	....
1991-92	U. of Maine	H.E.	31	18	20	38	14	....	....	....	....	....
1992-93	U. of Maine	H.E.	45	23	25	48	22	....	....	....	....	....
1993-94	U. of Maine	H.E.	34	18	15	33	42	....	....	....	....	....
	Peoria	IHL	11	4	4	8	21	4	2	0	2	4
1994-95	Peoria	IHL	53	27	18	45	83	....	....	....	....	....
	St. Louis	**NHL**	**27**	**3**	**10**	**13**	**29**	....	....	....	....	....
	NHL Totals		**27**	**3**	**10**	**13**	**29**	....	....	....	....	....

TARNSTROM, DICK — NYI

Defense. Shoots left. 6', 183 lbs. Born, Sundbyberg, Sweden, January 20, 1975.
(NY Islanders' 12th choice, 272nd overall, in 1994 Entry Draft).

			Regular Season					Playoffs				
Season	Club	Lea	GP	G	A	TP	PIM	GP	G	A	TP	PIM
1992-93	AIK	Swe.	3	0	0	0	0	....	....	....	....	....
1993-94	AIK	Swe.	33	1	4	5	....	....	....	....	....	....
1994-95	AIK	Swe.	37	8	4	12	26	....	....	....	....	....

TARVAINEN, JUSSI — (tahr-VAHI-nehn) — EDM.

Center. Shoots right. 6'2", 185 lbs. Born, Lahti, Finland, May 31, 1976.
(Edmonton's 7th choice, 95th overall, in 1994 Entry Draft).

			Regular Season					Playoffs				
Season	Club	Lea	GP	G	A	TP	PIM	GP	G	A	TP	PIM
1993-94	KalPa	Fin.	42	3	4	7	20	....	....	....	....	....
1994-95	KalPa	Fin.	45	10	7	17	34	3	0	0	0	2

TAYLOR, CHRIS — NYI

Center. Shoots left. 6', 185 lbs. Born, Stratford, Ont., March 6, 1972.
(NY Islanders' 2nd choice, 27th overall, in 1990 Entry Draft).

			Regular Season					Playoffs				
Season	Club	Lea	GP	G	A	TP	PIM	GP	G	A	TP	PIM
1988-89	London	OHL	62	7	16	23	52	15	0	2	2	15
1989-90	London	OHL	66	45	60	105	60	6	3	2	5	6
1990-91	London	OHL	65	50	78	128	50	7	4	8	12	6
1991-92	London	OHL	66	48	74	122	57	10	8	16	24	9
1992-93	Capital Dist.	AHL	77	19	43	62	32	4	0	1	1	2
1993-94	Salt Lake	IHL	79	21	20	41	38	....	....	....	....	....
1994-95	Denver	IHL	78	38	48	86	47	14	7	6	13	10
	NY Islanders	**NHL**	**10**	**0**	**3**	**3**	**2**	....	....	....	....	....
	NHL Totals		**10**	**0**	**3**	**3**	**2**	....	....	....	....	....

TAYLOR, TIM — DET.

Center. Shoots left. 6'1", 185 lbs. Born, Stratford, Ont., February 6, 1969.
(Washington's 2nd choice, 36th overall, in 1988 Entry Draft).

			Regular Season					Playoffs				
Season	Club	Lea	GP	G	A	TP	PIM	GP	G	A	TP	PIM
1986-87	London	OHL	34	7	9	16	11	....	....	....	....	....
1987-88	London	OHL	64	46	50	96	66	12	9	9	18	26
1988-89	London	OHL	61	34	80	114	93	21	*21	25	*46	58
1989-90	Baltimore	AHL	79	31	36	67	124	9	2	2	4	13
1990-91	Baltimore	AHL	79	25	42	67	75	5	0	1	1	4
1991-92	Baltimore	AHL	65	9	18	27	131	....	....	....	....	....
1992-93	Baltimore	AHL	41	15	16	31	49	....	....	....	....	....
	Hamilton	AHL	36	15	22	37	37	....	....	....	....	....
1993-94	**Detroit**	**NHL**	**1**	**1**	**0**	**1**	**0**	....	....	....	....	....
ab	Adirondack	AHL	79	36	*81	*117	86	12	2	10	12	12
1994-95	**Detroit**	**NHL**	**22**	**0**	**4**	**4**	**16**	**6**	**0**	**1**	**1**	**12**
	NHL Totals		**23**	**1**	**4**	**5**	**16**	**6**	**0**	**1**	**1**	**12**

a AHL First All-Star Team (1994)
b Won John B. Sollenberger Trophy (Top Scorer - AHL) (1994)

Traded to **Vancouver** by **Washington** for Eric Murano, January 29, 1993. Signed as a free agent by **Detroit**, July 28, 1993.

TERTYSHNY, DMITRY — (tuhr-TIHSH-nee) — PHI.

Defense. Shoots left. 6'1", 176 lbs. Born, Chelyabinsk, USSR, December 26, 1976.
(Philadelphia's 4th choice, 132nd overall, in 1995 Entry Draft).

			Regular Season					Playoffs				
Season	Club	Lea	GP	G	A	TP	PIM	GP	G	A	TP	PIM
1994-95	Chelyabinsk	CIS	38	0	3	3	14	1	0	0	0	0

TERTYSHNY, SERGEI — WSH.

Defense. Shoots left. 6', 187 lbs. Born, Chelyabinsk, USSR, June 3, 1970.
(Washington's 11th choice, 275th overall, in 1994 Entry Draft).

			Regular Season					Playoffs				
Season	Club	Lea	GP	G	A	TP	PIM	GP	G	A	TP	PIM
1987-88	Chelyabinsk	USSR	19	0	0	0	4	....	....	....	....	....
1988-89	SKA Sverdlovsk	USSR 2			UNAVAILABLE							
1989-90	SKA Leningrad	USSR	4	0	0	0	0	....	....	....	....	....
1990-91	SKA Leningrad	USSR	28	2	2	4	12	....	....	....	....	....
1991-92	Chelyabinsk	CIS	44	4	2	6	20	....	....	....	....	....
1992-93	Chelyabinsk	CIS	41	8	3	11	10	8	2	0	2	4
1993-94	Chelyabinsk	CIS	37	8	8	16	22	6	0	1	1	0
1994-95	Portland	AHL	55	0	17	17	12	....	....	....	....	....

THERIAULT, JOEL — WSH.

Defense. Shoots right. 6'3", 201 lbs. Born, Montreal, Que., October 30, 1976.
(Washington's 5th choice, 95th overall, in 1995 Entry Draft).

			Regular Season					Playoffs				
Season	Club	Lea	GP	G	A	TP	PIM	GP	G	A	TP	PIM
1993-94	St-Jean	QMJHL	57	3	0	3	63	5	0	1	1	0
1994-95	St-Jean	QMJHL	18	2	7	9	94	....	....	....	....	....
	Beauport	QMJHL	51	2	5	7	293	18	3	6	9	*162

THERIEN, CHRIS — (TEH-ree-ehn) — PHI.

Defense. Shoots left. 6'3", 230 lbs. Born, Ottawa, Ont., December 14, 1971.
(Philadelphia's 7th choice, 47th overall, in 1990 Entry Draft).

			Regular Season					Playoffs				
Season	Club	Lea	GP	G	A	TP	PIM	GP	G	A	TP	PIM
1990-91	Providence	H.E.	36	4	18	22	36	....	....	....	....	....
1991-92	Providence	H.E.	36	16	25	41	38	....	....	....	....	....
1992-93a	Providence	H.E.	33	8	11	19	52	....	....	....	....	....
	Cdn. National	....	8	1	4	5	8	....	....	....	....	....
1993-94	Cdn. National	....	59	7	15	22	46	....	....	....	....	....
	Cdn. Olympic	....	4	0	0	0	4	....	....	....	....	....
	Hershey	AHL	6	0	0	0	2	....	....	....	....	....
1994-95	Hershey	AHL	34	3	13	16	27	....	....	....	....	....
b	**Philadelphia**	**NHL**	**48**	**3**	**10**	**13**	**38**	**15**	**0**	**0**	**0**	**10**
	NHL Totals		**48**	**3**	**10**	**13**	**38**	**15**	**0**	**0**	**0**	**10**

a Hockey East Second All-Star Team (1993)
b NHL/Upper Deck All-Rookie Team (1995)

THIESSEN, TRAVIS — CHI.

Defense. Shoots left. 6'3", 203 lbs. Born, North Battleford, Sask., July 11, 1972.
(Pittsburgh's 3rd choice, 67th overall, in 1992 Entry Draft).

			Regular Season					Playoffs				
Season	Club	Lea	GP	G	A	TP	PIM	GP	G	A	TP	PIM
1990-91	Moose Jaw	WHL	69	4	14	18	80	8	0	0	0	10
1991-92	Moose Jaw	WHL	72	9	50	59	112	4	0	2	2	8
1992-93	Cleveland	IHL	64	3	7	10	69	4	0	0	0	16
1993-94	Cleveland	IHL	74	2	13	15	75	....	....	....	....	....
1994-95	Flint	ColHL	5	0	1	1	2	....	....	....	....	....
	Indianapolis	IHL	41	2	3	5	36	....	....	....	....	....
	Saint John	AHL	9	1	2	3	12	5	0	1	1	0

Signed as a free agent by **Chicago**, June 9, 1994.

THOMAS, SCOTT

Right wing. Shoots right. 6'2", 195 lbs. Born, Buffalo, NY, January 18, 1970.
(Buffalo's 2nd choice, 56th overall, in 1989 Entry Draft).

			Regular Season					Playoffs				
Season	Club	Lea	GP	G	A	TP	PIM	GP	G	A	TP	PIM
1989-90	Clarkson	ECAC	34	19	13	32	95	....	....	....	....	....
1990-91	Clarkson	ECAC	40	28	14	42	89	....	....	....	....	....
1991-92	Clarkson	ECAC	29	22	20	42	57	....	....	....	....	....
	Rochester	AHL	....	....	....	....	....	9	0	1	1	17
1992-93	**Buffalo**	**NHL**	**7**	**1**	**1**	**2**	**15**	....	....	....	....	....
	Rochester	AHL	65	32	27	59	38	17	8	5	13	6
1993-94	**Buffalo**	**NHL**	**32**	**2**	**2**	**4**	**8**	....	....	....	....	....
	Rochester	AHL	11	4	5	9	0	....	....	....	....	....
1994-95	Rochester	AHL	55	21	25	46	115	5	4	0	4	4
	NHL Totals		**39**	**3**	**3**	**6**	**23**	....	....	....	....	....

THOMAS, STEVE — NYI

Left wing. Shoots left. 5'11", 184 lbs. Born, Stockport, England, July 15, 1963.

			Regular Season					Playoffs				
Season	Club	Lea	GP	G	A	TP	PIM	GP	G	A	TP	PIM
1983-84	Toronto	OHL	70	51	54	105	77	....	....	....	....	....
1984-85	Toronto	NHL	18	1	1	2	2	....	....	....	....	....
ab	St. Catharines	AHL	64	42	48	90	56	....	....	....	....	....
1985-86	Toronto	NHL	65	20	37	57	36	10	6	8	14	9
	St. Catharines	AHL	19	18	14	32	35	....	....	....	....	....
1986-87	Toronto	NHL	78	35	27	62	114	13	2	3	5	13
1987-88	Chicago	NHL	30	13	13	26	40	3	1	2	3	6
1988-89	Chicago	NHL	45	21	19	40	69	12	3	5	8	10
1989-90	Chicago	NHL	76	40	30	70	91	20	7	6	13	33
1990-91	Chicago	NHL	69	19	35	54	129	6	1	2	3	15
1991-92	Chicago	NHL	11	2	6	8	26	....	....	....	....	....
	NY Islanders	NHL	71	28	42	70	71	....	....	....	....	....
1992-93	NY Islanders	NHL	79	37	50	87	111	18	9	8	17	37
1993-94	NY Islanders	NHL	78	42	33	75	139	4	1	0	1	8
1994-95	NY Islanders	NHL	47	11	15	26	60	....	....	....	....	....
	NHL Totals		667	269	308	577	888	86	30	34	64	131

a Won Dudley "Red" Garrett Memorial Trophy (Top Rookie - AHL) (1985)
b AHL First All-Star Team (1985)

Signed as a free agent by **Toronto,** May 12, 1984. Traded to **Chicago** by **Toronto** with Rick Vaive and Bob McGill for Al Secord and Ed Olczyk, September 3, 1987. Traded to **NY Islanders** by **Chicago** with Adam Creighton for Brent Sutter and Brad Lauer, October 25, 1991.

THOMLINSON, DAVE

Left wing. Shoots left. 6'1", 215 lbs. Born, Edmonton, Alta., October 22, 1966.
(Toronto's 3rd choice, 43rd overall, in 1985 Entry Draft).

			Regular Season					Playoffs				
Season	Club	Lea	GP	G	A	TP	PIM	GP	G	A	TP	PIM
1984-85	Brandon	WHL	26	13	14	27	70	....	....	....	....	....
1985-86	Brandon	WHL	53	25	20	45	116	....	....	....	....	....
1986-87	Brandon	WHL	2	0	1	1	9	....	....	....	....	....
	Moose Jaw	WHL	70	44	36	80	117	9	7	3	10	19
1987-88	Peoria	IHL	74	27	30	57	56	7	4	3	7	11
1988-89	Peoria	IHL	64	27	29	56	154	3	0	1	1	8
1989-90	St. Louis	NHL	19	1	2	3	12	....	....	....	....	....
	Peoria	IHL	59	27	40	67	87	5	1	1	2	15
1990-91	St. Louis	NHL	3	0	0	0	0	9	3	1	4	4
	Peoria	IHL	80	53	54	107	107	11	6	7	13	28
1991-92	Boston	NHL	12	0	1	1	17	....	....	....	....	....
	Maine	AHL	25	9	11	20	36	....	....	....	....	....
1992-93	Binghamton	AHL	54	25	35	60	61	12	2	5	7	8
1993-94	Los Angeles	NHL	7	0	0	0	21	....	....	....	....	....
	Phoenix	IHL	39	10	15	25	70	....	....	....	....	....
1994-95	Phoenix	IHL	77	30	40	70	87	9	5	3	8	8
	Los Angeles	NHL	1	0	0	0	0	....	....	....	....	....
	NHL Totals		42	1	3	4	50	9	3	1	4	4

Signed as a free agent by **St. Louis**, June 4, 1987. Signed as a free agent by **Boston**, July 30, 1991. Signed as a free agent by **NY Rangers**, September 4, 1992. Signed as a free agent by **Los Angeles**, July 22, 1993.

THOMPSON, BRENT — WPG.

Defense. Shoots left. 6'2", 200 lbs. Born, Calgary, Alta., January 9, 1971.
(Los Angeles' 1st choice, 39th overall, in 1989 Entry Draft).

			Regular Season					Playoffs				
Season	Club	Lea	GP	G	A	TP	PIM	GP	G	A	TP	PIM
1988-89	Medicine Hat	WHL	72	3	10	13	160	3	0	0	0	2
1989-90	Medicine Hat	WHL	68	10	35	45	167	3	0	1	1	14
1990-91a	Medicine Hat	WHL	51	5	40	45	87	12	1	7	8	16
	Phoenix	IHL	....	....	....	....	....	4	0	1	1	6
1991-92	Los Angeles	NHL	27	0	5	5	89	4	0	0	0	4
	Phoenix	IHL	42	4	13	17	139	....	....	....	....	....
1992-93	Los Angeles	NHL	30	0	4	4	76	....	....	....	....	....
	Phoenix	IHL	22	0	5	5	112	....	....	....	....	....
1993-94	Los Angeles	NHL	24	1	0	1	81	....	....	....	....	....
	Phoenix	IHL	26	1	11	12	118	....	....	....	....	....
1994-95	Winnipeg	NHL	29	0	0	0	78	....	....	....	....	....
	NHL Totals		110	1	9	10	324	4	0	0	0	4

a WHL East Second All-Star Team (1991)

Traded to **Winnipeg** by **Los Angeles** with future considerations for the rights to Ruslan Batyrshin and Winnipeg's second round choice in 1996 Entry Draft, August 8, 1994.

THOMPSON, PAT — ANA.

Defense. Shoots right. 6'2", 190 lbs. Born, Halifax County, N.S., January 16, 1972.
(Anaheim's 1st choice, 5th overall, in 1993 Supplemental Draft).

			Regular Season					Playoffs				
Season	Club	Lea	GP	G	A	TP	PIM	GP	G	A	TP	PIM
1991-92	Brown	ECAC	15	1	0	1	6	....	....	....	....	....
1992-93	Brown	ECAC	30	1	7	8	16	....	....	....	....	....
1993-94	Brown	ECAC	32	3	4	7	36	....	....	....	....	....
1994-95	Brown	ECAC	30	0	4	4	46	....	....	....	....	....

THOMPSON, ROCKY — CGY.

Defense. Shoots right. 6'2", 192 lbs. Born, Calgary, Alta., August 8, 1977.
(Calgary's 3rd choice, 72nd overall, in 1995 Entry Draft).

			Regular Season					Playoffs				
Season	Club	Lea	GP	G	A	TP	PIM	GP	G	A	TP	PIM
1993-94	Medicine Hat	WHL	68	1	4	5	166	3	0	0	0	2
1994-95	Medicine Hat	WHL	63	1	6	7	220	5	0	0	0	17

THOMSON, JIM

Right wing. Shoots right. 6'1", 220 lbs. Born, Edmonton, Alta., December 30, 1965.
(Washington's 8th choice, 185th overall, in 1984 Entry Draft).

			Regular Season					Playoffs				
Season	Club	Lea	GP	G	A	TP	PIM	GP	G	A	TP	PIM
1983-84	Toronto	OHL	60	10	18	28	68	9	1	0	1	26
1984-85	Toronto	OHL	63	23	28	51	122	5	3	1	4	25
	Binghamton	AHL	4	0	0	0	2	....	....	....	....	....
1985-86	Binghamton	AHL	59	15	9	24	195	....	....	....	....	....
1986-87	Washington	NHL	10	0	0	0	35	....	....	....	....	....
	Binghamton	AHL	57	13	10	23	360	10	0	1	1	40
1987-88	Binghamton	AHL	25	8	9	17	64	4	1	2	3	7
1988-89	Washington	NHL	14	2	0	2	53	....	....	....	....	....
	Baltimore	AHL	41	25	16	41	129	....	....	....	....	....
	Hartford	NHL	5	0	0	0	14	....	....	....	....	....
1989-90	Binghamton	AHL	8	1	2	3	30	....	....	....	....	....
	New Jersey	NHL	3	0	0	0	31	....	....	....	....	....
	Utica	AHL	60	20	23	43	124	4	1	0	1	19
1990-91	Los Angeles	NHL	8	1	0	1	19	....	....	....	....	....
	New Haven	AHL	27	5	8	13	121	....	....	....	....	....
1991-92	Los Angeles	NHL	45	1	2	3	162	....	....	....	....	....
	Phoenix	IHL	2	1	0	1	0	....	....	....	....	....
1992-93	Ottawa	NHL	15	0	1	1	41	....	....	....	....	....
	Los Angeles	NHL	9	0	0	0	56	1	0	0	0	0
	Phoenix	IHL	14	4	5	9	44	....	....	....	....	....
1993-94	Anaheim	NHL	6	0	0	0	5	....	....	....	....	....
1994-95			DID NOT PLAY – INJURED									
	NHL Totals		115	4	3	7	416	1	0	0	0	0

Traded to **Hartford** by **Washington** for Scot Kleinendorst, March 6, 1989. Traded to **New Jersey** by **Hartford** for Chris Cichocki, October 31, 1989. Signed as a free agent by **Los Angeles**, July 2, 1990. Claimed by **Minnesota** from **Los Angeles** in Expansion Draft, May 30, 1991. Traded to **Los Angeles** by **Minnesota** with Randy Gilhen, Charlie Huddy and NY Rangers' fourth round choice (previously acquired by Minnesota - Alexei Zhitnik) in 1991 Entry Draft for Todd Elik, June 22, 1991. Claimed by **Ottawa** from **Los Angeles** in Expansion Draft, June 18, 1992. Traded to **Los Angeles** by **Ottawa** with Marc Fortier for Bob Kudelski and Shawn McCosh, December 19, 1992. Claimed by **Anaheim** from **Los Angeles** in Expansion Draft, June 24, 1993.

THORNTON, SCOTT — EDM.

Center. Shoots left. 6'3", 210 lbs. Born, London, Ont., January 9, 1971.
(Toronto's 1st choice, 3rd overall, in 1989 Entry Draft).

			Regular Season					Playoffs				
Season	Club	Lea	GP	G	A	TP	PIM	GP	G	A	TP	PIM
1987-88	Belleville	OHL	62	11	19	30	54	6	0	1	1	2
1988-89	Belleville	OHL	59	28	34	62	103	5	1	1	2	6
1989-90	Belleville	OHL	47	21	28	49	91	11	2	10	12	15
1990-91	Toronto	NHL	33	1	3	4	30	....	....	....	....	....
	Newmarket	AHL	5	1	0	1	4	....	....	....	....	....
	Belleville	OHL	3	2	1	3	2	6	0	7	7	14
1991-92	Edmonton	NHL	15	0	1	1	43	1	0	0	0	0
	Cape Breton	AHL	49	9	14	23	40	5	1	0	1	8
1992-93	Edmonton	NHL	9	0	1	1	0	....	....	....	....	....
	Cape Breton	AHL	58	23	27	50	102	16	1	2	3	35
1993-94	Edmonton	NHL	61	4	7	11	104	....	....	....	....	....
	Cape Breton	AHL	2	1	1	2	31	....	....	....	....	....
1994-95	Edmonton	NHL	47	10	12	22	89	....	....	....	....	....
	NHL Totals		165	15	24	39	266	1	0	0	0	0

Traded to **Edmonton** by **Toronto** with Vincent Damphousse, Peter Ing, Luke Richardson, future considerations and cash for Grant Fuhr, Glenn Anderson and Craig Berube, September 19, 1991.

THURESSON, MARCUS — S.J.

Center. Shoots left. 6'1", 180 lbs. Born, Jon Koping, Sweden, May 31, 1971.
(NY Islanders' 11th choice, 224th overall, in 1991 Entry Draft).

			Regular Season					Playoffs				
Season	Club	Lea	GP	G	A	TP	PIM	GP	G	A	TP	PIM
1989-90	Leksand	Swe.	28	8	7	15	18	3	2	0	2	12
1990-91	Leksand	Swe.	22	3	2	5	20	....	....	....	....	....
1991-92	Leksand	Swe.	21	2	4	6	22	....	....	....	....	....
1992-93	Leksand	Swe.	31	6	10	16	22	2	2	0	2	2
1993-94	Leksand	Swe.	32	3	4	7	28	4	0	1	1	0
1994-95	Leksand	Swe.	39	3	10	13	42	4	1	0	1	0

Rights traded to **San Jose** by **NY Islanders** for Brian Mullen, August 24, 1992.

TICHY, MILAN (TEE-CHEE, MEE-lahn) — NYI

Defense. Shoots left. 6'3", 198 lbs. Born, Plzen, Czech., September 22, 1969.
(Chicago's 6th choice, 153rd overall, in 1989 Entry Draft).

			Regular Season					Playoffs				
Season	Club	Lea	GP	G	A	TP	PIM	GP	G	A	TP	PIM
1987-88	Skoda Plzen	Czech.	30	1	3	4	20	....	....	....	....	....
1988-89	Skoda Plzen	Czech.	36	1	12	13	44	....	....	....	....	....
1989-90	Dukla Trencin	Czech.	51	14	8	22	....	....	....	....	....	....
1990-91	Dukla Trencin	Czech.	41	9	12	21	72	....	....	....	....	....
1991-92	Indianapolis	IHL	49	6	23	29	28	....	....	....	....	....
1992-93	Chicago	NHL	13	0	1	1	30	....	....	....	....	....
	Indianapolis	IHL	49	7	32	39	62	4	0	5	5	14
1993-94	Moncton	AHL	48	1	20	21	103	20	3	3	6	12
1994-95	Denver	IHL	71	18	36	54	90	17	4	9	13	12
	NY Islanders	NHL	2	0	0	0	2	....	....	....	....	....
	NHL Totals		15	0	1	1	32	....	....	....	....	....

Claimed by **Florida** from **Chicago** in Expansion Draft, June 24, 1993. Traded to **Winnipeg** by **Florida** for Brent Severyn, October 3, 1993. Signed as a free agent by **NY Islanders**, August 2, 1994.

TIILIKAINEN, JUKKA (REE-ee-lee-kigh-nehn, yoo-KUH) — L.A.

Left wing. Shoots left. 6', 180 lbs. Born, Espoo, Finland, April 4, 1974.
(Los Angeles' 8th choice, 255th overall, in 1992 Entry Draft).

			Regular Season					Playoffs				
Season	Club	Lea	GP	G	A	TP	PIM	GP	G	A	TP	PIM
1991-92	Kiekko	Fin. 2	1	0	0	0	0	....	....	....	....	....
1992-93	Vantaa	Fin. 2	18	7	3	10	10	....	....	....	....	....
	Kiekko	Fin.	5	0	0	0	4	....	....	....	....	....
1993-94	Kiekko-Espoo	Fin.	33	2	4	6	12	....	....	....	....	....
1994-95	TPS	Fin.	38	5	4	9	8	11	1	0	1	8

TIKKANEN, ESA (TEE-kuh-nehn, EHZ-uh) ST.L.

Left wing. Shoots left. 6'1", 190 lbs. Born, Helsinki, Finland, January 25, 1965.
(Edmonton's 4th choice, 80th overall, in 1983 Entry Draft).

			Regular Season					Playoffs				
Season	Club	Lea	GP	G	A	TP	PIM	GP	G	A	TP	PIM
1981-82	Regina	SJHL	59	38	37	75	216	....	....	....	....	....
	Regina	WHL	2	0	0	0	0	....	....	....	....	....
1982-83	HIFK	Fin. Jr.	30	34	31	65	104	4	4	3	7	10
	HIFK	Fin.	....	....	....	....	....	1	0	0	0	2
1983-84	HIFK	Fin. Jr.	6	5	9	14	13	4	4	3	7	8
	HIFK	Fin.	36	19	11	30	30	2	0	0	0	0
1984-85	HIFK	Fin.	36	21	33	54	42	....	....	....	....	....
	Edmonton	**NHL**	....	....	....	....	....	**3**	**0**	**0**	**0**	**2**
1985-86	**Edmonton**	**NHL**	**35**	**7**	**6**	**13**	**28**	**8**	**3**	**2**	**5**	**7**
	Nova Scotia	AHL	15	4	8	12	17	....	....	....	....	....
1986-87	**Edmonton**	**NHL**	**76**	**34**	**44**	**78**	**120**	**21**	**7**	**2**	**9**	**22**
1987-88	**Edmonton**	**NHL**	**80**	**23**	**51**	**74**	**153**	**19**	**10**	**17**	**27**	**72**
1988-89	**Edmonton**	**NHL**	**67**	**31**	**47**	**78**	**92**	**7**	**1**	**3**	**4**	**12**
1989-90	**Edmonton**	**NHL**	**79**	**30**	**33**	**63**	**161**	**22**	**13**	**11**	**24**	**26**
1990-91	**Edmonton**	**NHL**	**79**	**27**	**42**	**69**	**85**	**18**	**12**	**8**	**20**	**24**
1991-92	**Edmonton**	**NHL**	**40**	**12**	**16**	**28**	**44**	**16**	**5**	**3**	**8**	**8**
1992-93	**Edmonton**	**NHL**	**66**	**14**	**19**	**33**	**76**	....	....	....	....	....
	NY Rangers	**NHL**	**15**	**2**	**5**	**7**	**18**	....	....	....	....	....
1993-94	**NY Rangers**	**NHL**	**83**	**22**	**32**	**54**	**114**	**23**	**4**	**4**	**8**	**34**
1994-95	HIFK	Fin.	19	2	11	13	16	....	....	....	....	....
	St. Louis	**NHL**	**43**	**12**	**23**	**35**	**22**	**7**	**2**	**2**	**4**	**20**
	NHL Totals		**663**	**214**	**318**	**532**	**913**	**144**	**57**	**52**	**109**	**227**

Traded to **NY Rangers** by **Edmonton** for Doug Weight, March 17, 1993. Traded to **St. Louis** by **NY Rangers** with Doug Lidster for Petr Nedved, July 24, 1994.

TILLEY, TOM

Defense. Shoots right. 6', 190 lbs. Born, Trenton, Ont., March 28, 1965.
(St. Louis' 13th choice, 196th overall, in 1984 Entry Draft).

			Regular Season					Playoffs				
Season	Club	Lea	GP	G	A	TP	PIM	GP	G	A	TP	PIM
1984-85	Michigan State	CCHA	37	1	5	6	58	....	....	....	....	....
1985-86	Michigan State	CCHA	42	9	25	34	48	....	....	....	....	....
1986-87	Michigan State	CCHA	42	7	14	21	48	....	....	....	....	....
1987-88a	Michigan State	CCHA	46	8	18	26	44	....	....	....	....	....
1988-89	**St. Louis**	**NHL**	**70**	**1**	**22**	**23**	**47**	**10**	**1**	**2**	**3**	**17**
1989-90	**St. Louis**	**NHL**	**34**	**0**	**5**	**5**	**6**	....	....	....	....	....
	Peoria	IHL	22	1	8	9	13	....	....	....	....	....
1990-91	**St. Louis**	**NHL**	**22**	**2**	**4**	**6**	**4**	....	....	....	....	....
b	Peoria	IHL	48	7	38	45	53	13	2	9	11	25
1991-92	Milan Devils	Italy	18	7	13	20	12	12	5	12	17	10
	Cdn. National	....	4	0	1	1	0	....	....	....	....	....
1992-93	Milan Devils	Alp.	32	5	17	22	21	....	....	....	....	....
	Milan Devils	Italy	14	8	3	11	2	8	1	5	6	4
1993-94	**St. Louis**	**NHL**	**48**	**1**	**7**	**8**	**32**	**4**	**0**	**1**	**1**	**2**
1994-95	Atlanta	IHL	10	2	6	8	14	....	....	....	....	....
	Indianapolis	IHL	25	2	13	15	19	....	....	....	....	....
	NHL Totals		**174**	**4**	**38**	**42**	**89**	**14**	**1**	**3**	**4**	**19**

a CCHA First All-Star Team (1988)
b IHL Second All-Star Team (1991)

Traded to **Tampa Bay** by **St. Louis** for Adam Creighton, October 6, 1994. Traded to **Chicago** by **Tampa Bay** with Jim Cummins and Jeff Buchanan for Paul Ysebaert and Rich Sutter, February 22, 1995.

TIMANDER, MATTIAS BOS.

Defense. Shoots left. 6'1", 194 lbs. Born, Solleftea, Sweden, April 16, 1974.
(Boston's 7th choice, 208th overall, in 1992 Entry Draft).

			Regular Season					Playoffs				
Season	Club	Lea	GP	G	A	TP	PIM	GP	G	A	TP	PIM
1992-93	MoDo	Swe.	1	0	0	0	0	....	....	....	....	....
1993-94	MoDo	Swe.	23	2	2	4	6	11	2	0	2	10
1994-95	MoDo	Swe.	39	8	9	17	24	....	....	....	....	....

TIMONEN, KIMMO (TIH-moh-nehn) L.A.

Defense. Shoots left. 5'10", 180 lbs. Born, Kuopio, Finland, March 18, 1975.
(Los Angeles' 11th choice, 250th overall, in 1993 Entry Draft).

			Regular Season					Playoffs				
Season	Club	Lea	GP	G	A	TP	PIM	GP	G	A	TP	PIM
1991-92	KalPa	Fin.	5	0	0	0	0	....	....	....	....	....
1992-93	KalPa	Fin.	33	0	2	2	4	....	....	....	....	....
1993-94	KalPa	Fin.	46	6	7	13	55	....	....	....	....	....
1994-95	TPS	Fin.	45	3	4	7	10	13	0	1	1	6

TINORDI, MARK WSH.

Defense. Shoots left. 6'4", 213 lbs. Born, Red Deer, Alta., May 9, 1966.

			Regular Season					Playoffs				
Season	Club	Lea	GP	G	A	TP	PIM	GP	G	A	TP	PIM
1982-83	Lethbridge	WHL	64	0	4	4	50	20	1	1	2	6
1983-84	Lethbridge	WHL	72	5	14	19	53	5	0	1	1	7
1984-85	Lethbridge	WHL	58	10	15	25	134	4	0	2	2	12
1985-86	Lethbridge	WHL	58	8	30	38	139	8	1	3	4	15
1986-87	Calgary	WHL	61	29	37	66	148	....	....	....	....	....
	New Haven	AHL	2	0	0	0	2	2	0	0	0	0
1987-88	**NY Rangers**	**NHL**	**24**	**1**	**2**	**3**	**50**	....	....	....	....	....
	Colorado	IHL	41	8	19	27	150	11	1	5	6	31
1988-89	**Minnesota**	**NHL**	**47**	**2**	**3**	**5**	**107**	**5**	**0**	**0**	**0**	**0**
	Kalamazoo	IHL	10	0	0	0	35	....	....	....	....	....
1989-90	**Minnesota**	**NHL**	**66**	**3**	**7**	**10**	**240**	**7**	**0**	**1**	**1**	**16**
1990-91	**Minnesota**	**NHL**	**69**	**5**	**27**	**32**	**189**	**23**	**5**	**6**	**11**	**78**
1991-92	**Minnesota**	**NHL**	**63**	**4**	**24**	**28**	**179**	**7**	**1**	**2**	**3**	**11**
1992-93	**Minnesota**	**NHL**	**69**	**15**	**27**	**42**	**157**	....	....	....	....	....
1993-94	**Dallas**	**NHL**	**61**	**6**	**18**	**24**	**143**	....	....	....	....	....
1994-95	**Washington**	**NHL**	**42**	**3**	**9**	**12**	**71**	**1**	**0**	**0**	**0**	**2**
	NHL Totals		**441**	**39**	**117**	**156**	**1136**	**43**	**6**	**9**	**15**	**107**

Played in NHL All-Star Game (1992)

Signed as a free agent by **NY Rangers**, January 4, 1987. Traded to **Minnesota** by **NY Rangers** with Paul Jerrard, the rights to Bret Barnett and Mike Sullivan, and Los Angeles' third round choice (previously acquired by NY Rangers — Minnesota selected Murray Garbutt) in 1989 Entry Draft for Brian Lawton, Igor Liba and the rights to Eric Bennett, October 11, 1988. Traded to **Washington** by **Dallas** with Rich Mrozik for Kevin Hatcher, January 18, 1995.

TIPPETT, DAVE (TIHP-iht)

Left wing. Shoots left. 5'10", 180 lbs. Born, Moosomin, Sask., August 25, 1961.

			Regular Season					Playoffs				
Season	Club	Lea	GP	G	A	TP	PIM	GP	G	A	TP	PIM
1981-82	North Dakota	WCHA	43	13	28	41	20	....	....	....	....	....
1982-83	North Dakota	WCHA	36	15	31	46	24	....	....	....	....	....
1983-84	Cdn. National	....	66	14	19	33	24	....	....	....	....	....
	Cdn. Olympic	....	7	1	1	2	2	....	....	....	....	....
	Hartford	**NHL**	**17**	**4**	**2**	**6**	**2**	....	....	....	....	....
1984-85	**Hartford**	**NHL**	**80**	**7**	**12**	**19**	**12**	....	....	....	....	....
1985-86	**Hartford**	**NHL**	**80**	**14**	**20**	**34**	**18**	**10**	**2**	**2**	**4**	**4**
1986-87	**Hartford**	**NHL**	**80**	**9**	**22**	**31**	**42**	**6**	**0**	**2**	**2**	**4**
1987-88	**Hartford**	**NHL**	**80**	**16**	**21**	**37**	**32**	**6**	**0**	**0**	**0**	**2**
1988-89	**Hartford**	**NHL**	**80**	**17**	**24**	**41**	**45**	**4**	**0**	**1**	**1**	**0**
1989-90	**Hartford**	**NHL**	**66**	**8**	**19**	**27**	**32**	**7**	**1**	**3**	**4**	**2**
1990-91	**Washington**	**NHL**	**61**	**6**	**9**	**15**	**24**	**10**	**2**	**3**	**5**	**8**
1991-92	**Washington**	**NHL**	**30**	**2**	**10**	**12**	**16**	**7**	**0**	**1**	**1**	**0**
	Cdn. National	....	1	0	0	0	4	....	....	....	....	....
	Cdn. Olympic	....	6	1	2	3	10	....	....	....	....	....
1992-93	**Pittsburgh**	**NHL**	**74**	**6**	**19**	**25**	**56**	**12**	**1**	**4**	**5**	**14**
1993-94	**Philadelphia**	**NHL**	**73**	**4**	**11**	**15**	**38**	....	....	....	....	....
1994-95	Houston	IHL	75	18	48	66	56	4	1	2	3	4
	NHL Totals		**721**	**93**	**169**	**262**	**317**	**62**	**6**	**16**	**22**	**34**

Signed as a free agent by **Hartford**, February 29, 1984. Traded to **Washington** by **Hartford** for Washington's sixth round choice (Jarret Reid) in 1992 Entry Draft, September 30, 1990. Signed as a free agent by **Pittsburgh**, August 25, 1992. Signed as a free agent by **Philadelphia**, August 30, 1993.

TITOV, GERMAN (TEE-tahf, GUHR-mihn) CGY.

Center. Shoots left. 6'1", 190 lbs. Born, Moscow, USSR, October 16, 1965.
(Calgary's 10th choice, 252nd overall, in 1993 Entry Draft).

			Regular Season					Playoffs				
Season	Club	Lea	GP	G	A	TP	PIM	GP	G	A	TP	PIM
1982-83	Khimik	USSR	16	0	2	2	4	....	....	....	....	....
1983-84						DID NOT PLAY						
1984-85						DID NOT PLAY						
1985-86						DID NOT PLAY						
1986-87	Khimik	USSR	23	1	0	1	10	....	....	....	....	....
1987-88	Khimik	USSR	39	6	5	11	10	....	....	....	....	....
1988-89	Khimik	USSR	44	10	3	13	24	....	....	....	....	....
1989-90	Khimik	USSR	44	6	14	20	19	....	....	....	....	....
1990-91	Khimik	USSR	45	13	11	24	28	....	....	....	....	....
1991-92	Khimik	CIS	42	18	13	31	35	....	....	....	....	....
1992-93	TPS	Fin.	47	25	19	44	49	12	5	12	17	10
1993-94	**Calgary**	**NHL**	**76**	**27**	**18**	**45**	**28**	**7**	**2**	**1**	**3**	**4**
1994-95	TPS	Fin.	14	6	6	12	20	....	....	....	....	....
	Calgary	**NHL**	**40**	**12**	**12**	**24**	**16**	**7**	**5**	**3**	**8**	**10**
	NHL Totals		**116**	**39**	**30**	**69**	**44**	**14**	**7**	**4**	**11**	**14**

TJALLDEN, MIKAEL FLA.

Defense. Shoots left. 6'2", 194 lbs. Born, Ornskoldsvik, Sweden, February 16, 1975.
(Florida's 4th choice, 67th overall, in 1993 Entry Draft).

			Regular Season					Playoffs				
Season	Club	Lea	GP	G	A	TP	PIM	GP	G	A	TP	PIM
1993-94	Sundsvall-Timra	Swe. 2	24	4	5	9	32	....	....	....	....	....
1994-95	Sundsvall-Timra	Swe. 2	21	0	9	9	20	....	....	....	....	....

TJARNQVIST, DANIEL (TUH-yahrn-kvihst) FLA.

Defense. Shoots left. 6'2", 178 lbs. Born, Umea, Sweden, October 14, 1976.
(Florida's 5th choice, 88th overall, in 1995 Entry Draft).

			Regular Season					Playoffs				
Season	Club	Lea	GP	G	A	TP	PIM	GP	G	A	TP	PIM
1994-95	Rogle	Swe.	18	0	1	1	2	....	....	....	....	....
	Rogle	Swe. 2	15	2	3	5	0	....	....	....	....	....

TKACHUK, KEITH (kuh-CHUK) WPG.

Left wing. Shoots left. 6'2", 210 lbs. Born, Melrose, MA, March 28, 1972.
(Winnipeg's 1st choice, 19th overall, in 1990 Entry Draft).

			Regular Season					Playoffs				
Season	Club	Lea	GP	G	A	TP	PIM	GP	G	A	TP	PIM
1990-91	Boston U.	H.E.	36	17	23	40	70	....	....	....	....	....
1991-92	U.S. National	....	45	10	10	20	141	....	....	....	....	....
	U.S. Olympic	....	8	1	1	2	12	....	....	....	....	....
	Winnipeg	**NHL**	**17**	**3**	**5**	**8**	**28**	**7**	**3**	**0**	**3**	**30**
1992-93	**Winnipeg**	**NHL**	**83**	**28**	**23**	**51**	**201**	**6**	**4**	**0**	**4**	**14**
1993-94	**Winnipeg**	**NHL**	**84**	**41**	**40**	**81**	**255**	....	....	....	....	....
1994-95a	**Winnipeg**	**NHL**	**48**	**22**	**29**	**51**	**152**	....	....	....	....	....
	NHL Totals		**232**	**94**	**97**	**191**	**636**	**13**	**7**	**0**	**7**	**44**

a NHL Second All-Star Team (1995)

TOCCHET, RICK (TAH-keht) L.A.

Right wing. Shoots right. 6', 205 lbs. Born, Scarborough, Ont., April 9, 1964.
(Philadelphia's 5th choice, 121st overall, in 1983 Entry Draft).

			Regular Season					Playoffs				
Season	Club	Lea	GP	G	A	TP	PIM	GP	G	A	TP	PIM
1981-82	S.S. Marie	OHL	59	7	15	22	184	11	1	1	2	28
1982-83	S.S. Marie	OHL	66	32	34	66	146	16	4	13	17	67
1983-84	S.S. Marie	OHL	64	44	64	108	209	16	*22	14	*36	41
1984-85	**Philadelphia**	**NHL**	**75**	**14**	**25**	**39**	**181**	**19**	**3**	**4**	**7**	**72**
1985-86	**Philadelphia**	**NHL**	**69**	**14**	**21**	**35**	**284**	**5**	**1**	**2**	**3**	**26**
1986-87	**Philadelphia**	**NHL**	**69**	**21**	**26**	**47**	**288**	**26**	**11**	**10**	**21**	**72**
1987-88	**Philadelphia**	**NHL**	**65**	**31**	**33**	**64**	**301**	**5**	**1**	**4**	**5**	**55**
1988-89	**Philadelphia**	**NHL**	**66**	**45**	**36**	**81**	**183**	**16**	**6**	**6**	**12**	**69**
1989-90	**Philadelphia**	**NHL**	**75**	**37**	**59**	**96**	**196**	....	....	....	....	....
1990-91	**Philadelphia**	**NHL**	**70**	**40**	**31**	**71**	**150**	....	....	....	....	....
1991-92	**Philadelphia**	**NHL**	**42**	**13**	**16**	**29**	**102**	....	....	....	....	....
	Pittsburgh	**NHL**	**19**	**14**	**16**	**30**	**49**	**14**	**6**	**13**	**19**	**24**
1992-93	**Pittsburgh**	**NHL**	**80**	**48**	**61**	**109**	**252**	**12**	**7**	**6**	**13**	**24**
1993-94	**Pittsburgh**	**NHL**	**51**	**14**	**26**	**40**	**134**	**6**	**2**	**3**	**5**	**20**
1994-95	**Los Angeles**	**NHL**	**36**	**18**	**17**	**35**	**70**	....	....	....	....	....
	NHL Totals		**717**	**309**	**367**	**676**	**2190**	**103**	**37**	**48**	**85**	**362**

Played in NHL All-Star Game (1989-91, 1993)

Traded to **Pittsburgh** by **Philadelphia** with Kjell Samuelsson, Ken Wregget and Philadelphia's third round choice (Dave Roche) in 1993 Entry Draft for Mark Recchi, Brian Benning and Los Angeles' first round choice (previously acquired by Pittsburgh — Philadelphia selected Jason Bowen) in 1992 Entry Draft, February 19, 1992 Traded to **Los Angeles** by **Pittsburgh** with Pittsburgh's second round choice (Pavel Rosa) in 1995 Entry Draft for Luc Robitaille, July 29, 1994.

TODD, KEVIN — L.A.

Center. Shoots left. 5'10", 180 lbs. Born, Winnipeg, Man., May 4, 1968.
(New Jersey's 7th choice, 129th overall, in 1986 Entry Draft).

			Regular Season					Playoffs				
Season	**Club**	**Lea**	**GP**	**G**	**A**	**TP**	**PIM**	**GP**	**G**	**A**	**TP**	**PIM**
1985-86	Prince Albert	WHL	55	14	25	39	19	20	7	6	13	29
1986-87	Prince Albert	WHL	71	39	46	85	92	8	2	5	7	17
1987-88	Prince Albert	WHL	72	49	72	121	83	10	8	11	19	27
1988-89	**New Jersey**	**NHL**	**1**	**0**	**0**	**0**	**0**	....	....	....	....	....
	Utica	AHL	78	26	45	71	62	4	2	0	2	6
1989-90	Utica	AHL	71	18	36	54	72	5	2	4	6	2
1990-91	**New Jersey**	**NHL**	**1**	**0**	**0**	**0**	**0**	**1**	**0**	**0**	**0**	**6**
abc	Utica	AHL	75	37	*81	*118	75	....	....	....	....	....
1991-92d	**New Jersey**	**NHL**	**80**	**21**	**42**	**63**	**69**	**7**	**3**	**2**	**5**	**8**
1992-93	**New Jersey**	**NHL**	**30**	**5**	**5**	**10**	**16**	....	....	....	....	....
	Utica	AHL	2	2	1	3	0	....	....	....	....	....
	Edmonton	**NHL**	**25**	**4**	**9**	**13**	**10**	....	....	....	....	....
1993-94	**Chicago**	**NHL**	**35**	**5**	**6**	**11**	**16**	....	....	....	....	....
	Los Angeles	**NHL**	**12**	**3**	**8**	**11**	**8**	....	....	....	....	....
1994-95	**Los Angeles**	**NHL**	**33**	**3**	**8**	**11**	**12**	....	....	....	....	....
	NHL Totals		**217**	**41**	**78**	**119**	**131**	**8**	**3**	**2**	**5**	**14**

a AHL First All-Star Team (1991)
b Won Les Cunningham Plaque (MVP - AHL) (1991)
c Won John B. Sollenberger Trophy (Leading Scorer - AHL) (1991)
d NHL/Upper Deck All-Rookie Team (1992)

Traded to **Edmonton** by **New Jersey** with Zdeno Ciger for Bernie Nicholls, January 13, 1993. Traded to **Chicago** by **Edmonton** for Adam Bennett, October 7, 1993. Traded to **Los Angeles** by **Chicago** for Los Angeles' fourth round choice (Steve McLaren) in 1994 Entry Draft, March 21, 1994.

TOK, CHRIS — PIT.

Defense. Shoots left. 6'1", 185 lbs. Born, Grand Rapids, MN, March 19, 1973.
(Pittsburgh's 10th choice, 214th overall, in 1991 Entry Draft).

			Regular Season					Playoffs				
Season	**Club**	**Lea**	**GP**	**G**	**A**	**TP**	**PIM**	**GP**	**G**	**A**	**TP**	**PIM**
1991-92	U. Wisconsin	WCHA	19	0	2	2	8	....	....	....	....	....
1992-93	U. Wisconsin	WCHA	41	3	12	15	68	....	....	....	....	....
1993-94	U. Wisconsin	WCHA	41	2	5	7	97	....	....	....	....	....
1994-95	U. Wisconsin	WCHA	43	5	7	12	129	....	....	....	....	....

TOMILIN, VITALI — N.J.

Left wing. Shoots left. 6', 183 lbs. Born, Elektrostal, USSR, January 15, 1974.
(New Jersey's 4th choice, 90th overall, in 1992 Entry Draft).

			Regular Season					Playoffs				
Season	**Club**	**Lea**	**GP**	**G**	**A**	**TP**	**PIM**	**GP**	**G**	**A**	**TP**	**PIM**
1990-91	Soviet Wings	USSR	1	0	0	0	0	....	....	....	....	....
1991-92	Soviet Wings	CIS	34	1	1	2	6	....	....	....	....	....
1992-93	Soviet Wings	CIS	28	0	1	1	14	2	0	0	0	0
1993-94	Soviet Wings	CIS	44	5	4	9	62	3	0	0	0	0
1994-95	Soviet Wings	CIS	47	4	5	9	43	2	0	0	0	2

TOMLAK, MIKE

Center/Left wing. Shoots left. 6'3", 205 lbs. Born, Thunder Bay, Ont., October 17, 1964.
(Toronto's 10th choice, 208th overall, in 1983 Entry Draft).

			Regular Season					Playoffs				
Season	**Club**	**Lea**	**GP**	**G**	**A**	**TP**	**PIM**	**GP**	**G**	**A**	**TP**	**PIM**
		....	....	....	....	....	....	....	....	....	....	....
1982-83	Cornwall	OHL	70	18	49	67	26	....	....	....	....	....
1983-84	Cornwall	OHL	64	24	64	88	21	....	....	....	....	....
1984-85	Cornwall	OHL	66	30	70	100	9	....	....	....	....	....
1985-86	Western Ont.	OUAA	38	28	20	48	45	....	....	....	....	....
	Cdn. National	....	3	1	1	2	0	....	....	....	....	....
1986-87	Western Ont.	OUAA	38	16	30	46	10	....	....	....	....	....
1987-88	Western Ont.	OUAA	39	24	52	76	....	....	....	....	....	....
1988-89	Western Ont.	OUAA	35	16	34	50	....	....	....	....	....	....
1989-90	**Hartford**	**NHL**	**70**	**7**	**14**	**21**	**48**	**7**	**0**	**1**	**1**	**2**
1990-91	**Hartford**	**NHL**	**64**	**8**	**8**	**16**	**55**	**3**	**0**	**0**	**0**	**2**
	Springfield	AHL	15	4	9	13	15	....	....	....	....	....
1991-92	**Hartford**	**NHL**	**6**	**0**	**0**	**0**	**0**	....	....	....	....	....
	Springfield	AHL	39	16	21	37	24	....	....	....	....	....
1992-93	Springfield	AHL	38	16	21	37	56	5	1	1	2	2
1993-94	**Hartford**	**NHL**	**1**	**0**	**0**	**0**	**0**	....	....	....	....	....
	Springfield	AHL	79	44	56	100	53	4	2	5	7	4
1994-95	Milwaukee	IHL	63	27	41	68	54	15	4	5	9	8
	NHL Totals		**141**	**15**	**22**	**37**	**103**	**10**	**0**	**1**	**1**	**4**

Signed as a free agent by **Hartford**, November 14, 1988.

TOMLINSON, DAVE — FLA.

Center. Shoots left. 5'11", 180 lbs. Born, North Vancouver, B.C., May 8, 1969.
(Toronto's 1st choice, 3rd overall, in 1989 Supplemental Draft).

			Regular Season					Playoffs				
Season	**Club**	**Lea**	**GP**	**G**	**A**	**TP**	**PIM**	**GP**	**G**	**A**	**TP**	**PIM**
1987-88	Boston U.	H.E.	34	16	20	36	28	....	....	....	....	....
1988-89	Boston U.	H.E.	34	16	30	46	40	....	....	....	....	....
1989-90	Boston U.	H.E.	43	15	22	37	53	....	....	....	....	....
1990-91	Boston U.	H.E.	41	30	30	60	55	....	....	....	....	....
1991-92	**Toronto**	**NHL**	**3**	**0**	**0**	**0**	**2**	....	....	....	....	....
	St. John's	AHL	75	23	34	57	75	12	4	5	9	6
1992-93	**Toronto**	**NHL**	**3**	**0**	**0**	**0**	**2**	....	....	....	....	....
	St. John's	AHL	70	36	48	84	115	9	1	4	5	8
1993-94	**Winnipeg**	**NHL**	**31**	**1**	**3**	**4**	**24**	....	....	....	....	....
	Moncton	AHL	39	23	23	46	38	20	6	6	12	24
1994-95	Cincinnati	IHL	78	38	72	110	79	10	7	3	10	8
	Florida	**NHL**	**5**	**0**	**0**	**0**	**0**	....	....	....	....	....
	NHL Totals		**42**	**1**	**3**	**4**	**28**	....	....	....	....	....

Traded to **Florida** by **Toronto** for cash, July 30, 1993. Traded to **Winnipeg** by **Florida** for Jason Cirone, August 3, 1993. Signed as a free agent by **Florida**, June 23, 1994.

TOMPKINS, DAN — CGY.

Left wing. Shoots left. 6'2", 205 lbs. Born, Minneapolis, MN, January 31, 1975.
(Calgary's 3rd choice, 70th overall, in 1993 Entry Draft).

			Regular Season					Playoffs				
Season	**Club**	**Lea**	**GP**	**G**	**A**	**TP**	**PIM**	**GP**	**G**	**A**	**TP**	**PIM**
1993-94	U. Wisconsin	WCHA	18	1	0	1	31	....	....	....	....	....
1994-95	U. Wisconsin	WCHA	32	4	10	14	82	....	....	....	....	....

TOMS, JEFF — T.B.

Left wing. Shoots left. 6'3", 180 lbs. Born, Swift Current, Sask., June 4, 1974.
(New Jersey's 9th choice, 210th overall, in 1992 Entry Draft).

			Regular Season					Playoffs				
Season	**Club**	**Lea**	**GP**	**G**	**A**	**TP**	**PIM**	**GP**	**G**	**A**	**TP**	**PIM**
1991-92	S.S. Marie	OHL	36	9	5	14	0	16	0	1	1	2
1992-93	S.S. Marie	OHL	59	16	23	39	20	16	4	4	8	7
1993-94	S.S. Marie	OHL	64	52	45	97	19	14	11	4	15	2
1994-95	Atlanta	IHL	40	7	8	15	10	4	0	0	0	4

Traded to **Tampa Bay** by **New Jersey** for Vancouver's fourth round choice (previously acquired by Tampa Bay — later traded to Calgary — Calgary selected Ryan Duthie) in 1994 Entry Draft, May 31, 1994.

TOPOROWSKI, KERRY (toh-poh-ROW-skee) — DET.

Defense. Shoots right. 6'2", 213 lbs. Born, Paddockwood, Sask., April 9, 1971.
(San Jose's 5th choice, 67th overall, in 1991 Entry Draft).

			Regular Season					Playoffs				
Season	**Club**	**Lea**	**GP**	**G**	**A**	**TP**	**PIM**	**GP**	**G**	**A**	**TP**	**PIM**
1989-90	Spokane	WHL	65	1	13	14	384	6	0	0	0	37
1990-91	Spokane	WHL	65	11	16	27	*505	15	2	2	4	*108
1991-92	Indianapolis	IHL	18	1	2	3	206	....	....	....	....	....
1992-93	Indianapolis	IHL	17	0	0	0	57	....	....	....	....	....
1993-94	Indianapolis	IHL	32	1	4	5	126	....	....	....	....	....
	Las Vegas	IHL	13	1	0	1	129	2	0	0	0	31
1994-95	Las Vegas	IHL	37	1	4	5	300	5	0	1	1	69

Traded to **Chicago** by **San Jose** with San Jose's second round choice (later traded to Winnipeg — Winnipeg selected Boris Mironov) in 1992 Entry Draft for Doug Wilson, September 6, 1991.

TOPOROWSKI, SHAYNE (toh-poh-ROW-skee) — TOR.

Right wing. Shoots right. 6'2", 216 lbs. Born, Paddockwood, Sask., August 6, 1975.
(Los Angeles' 1st choice, 42nd overall, in 1993 Entry Draft).

			Regular Season					Playoffs				
Season	**Club**	**Lea**	**GP**	**G**	**A**	**TP**	**PIM**	**GP**	**G**	**A**	**TP**	**PIM**
1991-92	Prince Albert	WHL	6	2	0	2	2	7	2	1	3	6
1992-93	Prince Albert	WHL	72	25	32	57	235	....	....	....	....	....
1993-94	Prince Albert	WHL	68	37	45	82	183	....	....	....	....	....
1994-95	Prince Albert	WHL	72	36	38	74	151	15	10	8	18	25

Traded to **Toronto** by **Los Angeles** with Dixon Ward, Guy Leveque and Kelly Fairchild for Eric Lacroix, Chris Snell and Toronto's fourth round choice in 1996 Entry Draft, October 3, 1994.

TORGAYEV, PAVEL — CGY.

Left wing. Shoots left. 6'1", 187 lbs. Born, Gorky, USSR, January 25, 1966.
(Calgary's 13th choice, 279th overall, in 1994 Entry Draft).

			Regular Season					Playoffs				
Season	**Club**	**Lea**	**GP**	**G**	**A**	**TP**	**PIM**	**GP**	**G**	**A**	**TP**	**PIM**
1982-83	Torpedo Gorky	USSR	4	0	0	0	0	....	....	....	....	....
1983-84	Torpedo Gorky	USSR	27	2	3	5	8	....	....	....	....	....
1984-85	Torpedo Gorky	USSR	47	11	5	16	52	....	....	....	....	....
1985-86	Torpedo Gorky	USSR	38	1	4	5	18	....	....	....	....	....
1986-87	Torpedo Gorky	USSR	40	6	9	15	30	....	....	....	....	....
1987-88	Torpedo Gorky	USSR	25	7	4	11	14	....	....	....	....	....
1988-89	Torpedo Gorky	USSR	26	6	3	9	17	....	....	....	....	....
1989-90	Torpedo Gorky	USSR	48	18	5	23	64	....	....	....	....	....
1990-91	Torpedo Nizhny	USSR	37	10	5	15	22	....	....	....	....	....
1991-92	Torpedo Nizhny	CIS	45	13	5	18	46	....	....	....	....	....
1992-93	Torpedo Nizhny	CIS	5	1	0	1	4	....	....	....	....	....
	Kiekko-67	Fin. 2	30	16	20	36	48	....	....	....	....	....
1993-94	TPS	Fin.	47	19	11	30	60	3	0	1	1	14
1994-95	JyP HT	Fin.	50	13	18	31	44	4	0	1	1	25

TORMANEN, ANTTI (TOHR-mah-nehn) — OTT.

Right wing. Shoots left. 6'1", 198 lbs. Born, Espoo, Finland, September 19, 1970.
(Ottawa's 10th choice, 274th overall, in 1994 Entry Draft).

			Regular Season					Playoffs				
Season	**Club**	**Lea**	**GP**	**G**	**A**	**TP**	**PIM**	**GP**	**G**	**A**	**TP**	**PIM**
1990-91	Jokerit	Fin.	44	12	9	21	70	....	....	....	....	....
1991-92	Jokerit	Fin.	40	18	11	29	18	....	....	....	....	....
1992-93	Jokerit	Fin.	21	2	0	2	8	....	....	....	....	....
1993-94	Jokerit	Fin.	46	20	18	38	46	....	....	....	....	....
1994-95	Jokerit	Fin.	50	19	13	32	32	....	....	....	....	....

TOROPCHENKO, LEONID (tohr-ahp-CHEHN-koh, LEE-oh-NEED) — PIT.

Center. Shoots right. 6'4", 220 lbs. Born, Moscow, USSR, August 28, 1968.
(Pittsburgh's 10th choice, 260th overall, in 1993 Entry Draft).

			Regular Season					Playoffs				
Season	**Club**	**Lea**	**GP**	**G**	**A**	**TP**	**PIM**	**GP**	**G**	**A**	**TP**	**PIM**
1987-88	SKA Leningrad	USSR	6	2	0	2	0	....	....	....	....	....
1988-89	SKA Leningrad	USSR	33	7	4	11	11	....	....	....	....	....
1989-90	Khimik	USSR	42	6	2	8	24	....	....	....	....	....
1990-91	Khimik	USSR	46	6	4	10	24	....	....	....	....	....
1991-92	Khimik	CIS	42	14	4	18	34	....	....	....	....	....
1992-93	Springfield	AHL	71	31	30	61	59	13	4	4	8	8
1993-94	Cleveland	IHL	59	13	20	33	36	....	....	....	....	....
1994-95	Torpedo Yaro.	CIS	16	1	1	2	10	1	1	0	1	0

TOWNSHEND, GRAEME (TOWN-SEHND, GRAY-ihm)

Right wing. Shoots right. 6'2", 225 lbs. Born, Kingston, Jamaica, October 2, 1965.

			Regular Season					Playoffs				
Season	**Club**	**Lea**	**GP**	**G**	**A**	**TP**	**PIM**	**GP**	**G**	**A**	**TP**	**PIM**
1985-86	RPI	ECAC	29	1	7	8	52	....	....	....	....	....
1986-87	RPI	ECAC	29	6	1	7	50	....	....	....	....	....
1987-88	RPI	ECAC	32	6	14	20	64	....	....	....	....	....
1988-89	RPI	ECAC	31	6	16	22	50	....	....	....	....	....
	Maine	AHL	5	2	1	3	11	....	....	....	....	....
1989-90	**Boston**	**NHL**	**4**	**0**	**0**	**0**	**7**	....	....	....	....	....
	Maine	AHL	64	15	13	28	162	....	....	....	....	....
1990-91	**Boston**	**NHL**	**18**	**2**	**5**	**7**	**12**	....	....	....	....	....
	Maine	AHL	46	16	10	26	119	2	2	0	2	4
1991-92	**NY Islanders**	**NHL**	**7**	**1**	**2**	**3**	**0**	....	....	....	....	....
	Capital Dist.	AHL	61	14	23	37	94	4	0	2	2	0
1992-93	**NY Islanders**	**NHL**	**2**	**0**	**0**	**0**	**0**	....	....	....	....	....
	Capital Dist.	AHL	67	29	21	50	45	2	0	0	0	0
1993-94	**Ottawa**	**NHL**	**14**	**0**	**0**	**0**	**9**	....	....	....	....	....
	P.E.I.	AHL	56	16	13	29	107	....	....	....	....	....
1994-95	Houston	IHL	71	19	21	40	204	4	0	2	2	22
	NHL Totals		**45**	**3**	**7**	**10**	**28**	....	....	....	....	....

Signed as a free agent by **Boston**, May 12, 1989. Signed as a free agent by **NY Islanders**, September 3, 1991. Signed as a free agent by **Ottawa**, August 24, 1993.

TRAVERSE, PATRICK — OTT.

Defense. Shoots left. 6'3", 200 lbs. Born, Montreal, Que., March 14, 1974.
(Ottawa's 3rd choice, 50th overall, in 1992 Entry Draft).

			Regular Season					Playoffs				
Season	Club	Lea	GP	G	A	TP	PIM	GP	G	A	TP	PIM
1991-92	Shawinigan	QMJHL	59	3	11	14	12	10	0	0	0	4
1992-93	St-Jean	QMJHL	68	6	30	36	24	4	0	1	1	2
	New Haven	AHL	2	0	0	0	2	....	....	....	....	....
1993-94	St-Jean	QMJHL	66	15	37	52	30	5	0	4	4	4
	P.E.I.	AHL	3	0	1	1	2	....	....	....	....	....
1994-95	P.E.I.	AHL	70	5	13	18	19	7	0	2	2	0

TREBIL, DANIEL — N.J.

Defense. Shoots right. 6'3", 185 lbs. Born, Edina, MN, April 10, 1974.
(New Jersey's 7th choice, 138th overall, in 1992 Entry Draft).

			Regular Season					Playoffs				
Season	Club	Lea	GP	G	A	TP	PIM	GP	G	A	TP	PIM
1992-93	U. Minnesota	WCHA	36	2	11	13	16	....	....	....	....	....
1993-94	U. Minnesota	WCHA	42	1	21	22	24	....	....	....	....	....
1994-95	U. Minnesota	WCHA	44	10	33	43	10	....	....	....	....	....

TREMBLAY, YANICK — TOR.

Defense. Shoots right. 6'2", 178 lbs. Born, Pointe-aux-Trembles, Que., November 15, 1975.
(Toronto's 4th choice, 145th overall, in 1995 Entry Draft).

			Regular Season					Playoffs				
Season	Club	Lea	GP	G	A	TP	PIM	GP	G	A	TP	PIM
1994-95	Beauport	QMJHL	70	10	32	42	22	17	6	8	14	6

TRIPP, JOHN — COL.

Right wing. Shoots right. 6'2", 207 lbs. Born, Kingston, Ont., May 4, 1977.
(Colorado's 3rd choice, 77th overall, in 1995 Entry Draft).

			Regular Season					Playoffs				
Season	Club	Lea	GP	G	A	TP	PIM	GP	G	A	TP	PIM
1993-94	St. Mary's	Jr. B	42	15	29	44	116	....	....	....	....	....
1994-95	Oshawa	OHL	58	6	11	17	53	7	0	1	1	4

TRNKA, PAVEL — (tehrn-KAH) ANA.

Defense. Shoots left. 6'3", 190 lbs. Born, Plzen, Czech., July 27, 1976.
(Anaheim's 5th choice, 106th overall, in 1994 Entry Draft).

			Regular Season					Playoffs				
Season	Club	Lea	GP	G	A	TP	PIM	GP	G	A	TP	PIM
1993-94	Skoda Plzen	Czech.	12	0	1	1	....	....	....	....	....	....
1994-95	Kladno	Czech.	28	0	5	5	24	....	....	....	....	....
	Interconex Plzen	Czech.	6	0	0	0	0	....	....	....	....	....

TROMBLEY, RHETT — FLA.

Right wing. Shoots right. 6'3", 230 lbs. Born, Regina, Sask., August 9, 1974.

			Regular Season					Playoffs				
Season	Club	Lea	GP	G	A	TP	PIM	GP	G	A	TP	PIM
1991-92	Tacoma	WHL	7	0	0	0	32	....	....	....	....	....
	Saskatoon	WHL	50	3	4	7	181	18	1	1	2	53
1992-93	Saskatoon	WHL	27	0	0	0	47	....	....	....	....	....
	Victoria	WHL	12	0	0	0	67	....	....	....	....	....
1993-94	Victoria	WHL	21	0	3	3	67	....	....	....	....	....
1994-95	Toledo	ECHL	13	0	2	2	80	....	....	....	....	....
	Las Vegas	IHL	30	4	0	4	141	3	0	0	0	10

Signed as a free agent by **Florida**, April 5, 1995.

TRUMBLEY, ROB — VAN.

Center. Shoots right. 5'10", 174 lbs. Born, Regina, Sask., August 9, 1974.
(Vancouver's 8th choice, 195th overall, in 1994 Entry Draft).

			Regular Season					Playoffs				
Season	Club	Lea	GP	G	A	TP	PIM	GP	G	A	TP	PIM
1992-93	Moose Jaw	WHL	61	5	4	9	308	....	....	....	....	....
1993-94	Moose Jaw	WHL	61	15	24	39	342	....	....	....	....	....
1994-95	Moose Jaw	WHL	56	16	25	41	236	10	2	1	3	*64

TSULYGIN, NIKOLAI — (tsoo-LEE-gihn) ANA.

Defense. Shoots right. 6'4", 205 lbs. Born, Ufa, USSR, June 29, 1975.
(Anaheim's 2nd choice, 30th overall, in 1993 Entry Draft).

			Regular Season					Playoffs				
Season	Club	Lea	GP	G	A	TP	PIM	GP	G	A	TP	PIM
1992-93	Ufa Salavat	CIS	42	5	4	9	21	2	0	0	0	0
1993-94	Ufa Salavat	CIS	43	0	14	14	24	5	0	1	1	0
1994-95	CSKA	CIS	16	0	0	0	12	....	....	....	....	....
	Ufa Salavat	CIS	13	2	2	4	10	7	0	0	0	4

TSYGUROV, DENIS — (tsih-GOO-rawv) L.A.

Defense. Shoots left. 6'3", 198 lbs. Born, Chelyabinsk, USSR, February 26, 1971.
(Buffalo's 1st choice, 38th overall, in 1993 Entry Draft).

			Regular Season					Playoffs				
Season	Club	Lea	GP	G	A	TP	PIM	GP	G	A	TP	PIM
1988-89	Chelyabinsk	USSR	8	0	0	0	2	....	....	....	....	....
1989-90	Chelyabinsk	USSR	27	0	1	1	18	....	....	....	....	....
1990-91	Chelyabinsk	USSR	26	0	1	1	16	....	....	....	....	....
1991-92	Togliatti	CIS	29	3	2	5	6	....	....	....	....	....
1992-93a	Togliatti	CIS	37	7	13	20	29	10	1	1	2	6
1993-94	**Buffalo**	**NHL**	**8**	**0**	**0**	**0**	**8**	....	....	....	....	....
	Rochester	AHL	24	1	10	11	10	1	0	1	1	0
1994-95	Togliatti	CIS	10	3	7	10	6	....	....	....	....	....
	Buffalo	**NHL**	**4**	**0**	**0**	**0**	**4**	....	....	....	....	....
	Los Angeles	**NHL**	**21**	**0**	**0**	**0**	**11**	....	....	....	....	....
	NHL Totals		**33**	**0**	**0**	**0**	**23**	....	....	....	....	....

a CIS All-Star Team (1993)

Traded to **Los Angeles** by **Buffalo** with Philippe Boucher and Grant Fuhr for Alexei Zhitnik, Robb Stauber, Charlie Huddy and Los Angeles' fifth round choice (Marian Menhart) in 1995 Entry Draft, February 14, 1995.

TSYPLAKOV, VLADIMIR — L.A.

Left wing. Shoots left. 6'2", 194 lbs. Born, Inta, USSR, April 18, 1969.
(Los Angeles' 4th choice, 59th overall, in 1995 Entry Draft).

			Regular Season					Playoffs				
Season	Club	Lea	GP	G	A	TP	PIM	GP	G	A	TP	PIM
1988-89	Minsk D'amo	USSR	19	6	1	7	4	....	....	....	....	....
1989-90	Minsk D'amo	USSR	47	11	6	17	20	....	....	....	....	....
1990-91	Minsk D'amo	USSR	28	6	5	11	14	....	....	....	....	....
1991-92	Minsk D'amo	CIS	29	10	9	19	16	....	....	....	....	....
1992-93	Detroit	ColHL	44	33	43	76	20	6	5	4	9	6
	Indianapolis	IHL	11	6	7	13	4	5	1	1	2	2
1993-94	Fort Wayne	IHL	63	31	32	63	51	14	6	8	14	16
1994-95	Fort Wayne	IHL	79	38	40	78	39	4	2	4	6	2

TUCKER, DARCY — MTL.

Center. Shoots left. 5'10", 170 lbs. Born, Castor, Alta., March 15, 1975.
(Montreal's 8th choice, 151st overall, in 1993 Entry Draft).

			Regular Season					Playoffs				
Season	Club	Lea	GP	G	A	TP	PIM	GP	G	A	TP	PIM
1991-92	Kamloops	WHL	26	3	10	13	32	9	0	1	1	16
1992-93	Kamloops	WHL	67	31	58	89	155	13	7	6	13	34
1993-94abcd	Kamloops	WHL	66	52	88	140	143	19	9	*18	*27	43
1994-95ac	Kamloops	WHL	64	64	73	137	94	21	*16	15	*31	19

a WHL West First All-Star Team (1994, 1995)
b Canadian Major Junior First All-Star Team (1994)
c Memorial Cup All-Star Team (1994, 1995)
d Won Stafford Smythe Memorial Trophy (Memorial Cup Tournament MVP) (1994)

TUCKER, JOHN — T.B.

Center. Shoots right. 6', 200 lbs. Born, Windsor, Ont., September 29, 1964.
(Buffalo's 4th choice, 31st overall, in 1983 Entry Draft).

			Regular Season					Playoffs				
Season	Club	Lea	GP	G	A	TP	PIM	GP	G	A	TP	PIM
1981-82	Kitchener	OHL	67	16	32	48	32	15	2	3	5	2
1982-83	Kitchener	OHL	70	60	80	140	33	11	5	9	14	10
1983-84	**Buffalo**	**NHL**	**21**	**12**	**4**	**16**	**4**	**3**	**1**	**0**	**1**	**0**
a	Kitchener	OHL	39	40	60	100	25	12	12	18	30	8
1984-85	**Buffalo**	**NHL**	**64**	**22**	**27**	**49**	**21**	**5**	**1**	**5**	**6**	**0**
1985-86	**Buffalo**	**NHL**	**75**	**31**	**34**	**65**	**39**	....	....	....	....	....
1986-87	**Buffalo**	**NHL**	**54**	**17**	**34**	**51**	**21**	....	....	....	....	....
1987-88	**Buffalo**	**NHL**	**45**	**19**	**19**	**38**	**20**	**6**	**7**	**3**	**10**	**18**
1988-89	**Buffalo**	**NHL**	**60**	**13**	**31**	**44**	**31**	**3**	**0**	**3**	**3**	**0**
1989-90	**Buffalo**	**NHL**	**8**	**1**	**2**	**3**	**2**	....	....	....	....	....
	Washington	**NHL**	**38**	**9**	**19**	**28**	**10**	**12**	**1**	**7**	**8**	**4**
1990-91	**Buffalo**	**NHL**	**18**	**1**	**3**	**4**	**4**	....	....	....	....	....
	NY Islanders	**NHL**	**20**	**3**	**4**	**7**	**4**	....	....	....	....	....
1991-92	Asiago	Italy	18	16	21	37	6	11	7	13	20	15
1992-93	**Tampa Bay**	**NHL**	**78**	**17**	**39**	**56**	**69**	....	....	....	....	....
1993-94	**Tampa Bay**	**NHL**	**66**	**17**	**23**	**40**	**28**	....	....	....	....	....
1994-95	**Tampa Bay**	**NHL**	**46**	**12**	**13**	**25**	**14**	....	....	....	....	....
	NHL Totals		**593**	**174**	**252**	**426**	**267**	**29**	**10**	**18**	**28**	**22**

a OHL First All-Star Team (1984)

Traded to **Washington** by **Buffalo** for future considerations, January 5, 1990. Traded to **Buffalo** by **Washington** for cash, July 3, 1990. Traded to **NY Islanders** by **Buffalo** for future considerations, January 21, 1991. Signed as a free agent by **Tampa Bay**, August 5, 1992.

TULLY, BRENT — VAN.

Defense. Shoots right. 6'3", 195 lbs. Born, Peterborough, Ont., March 26, 1974.
(Vancouver's 5th choice, 93rd overall, in 1992 Entry Draft).

			Regular Season					Playoffs				
Season	Club	Lea	GP	G	A	TP	PIM	GP	G	A	TP	PIM
1990-91	Peterborough	OHL	45	3	5	8	35	2	0	0	0	0
1991-92	Peterborough	OHL	65	9	23	32	65	10	0	0	0	2
1992-93a	Peterborough	OHL	59	15	45	60	81	21	8	24	32	32
1993-94	Peterborough	OHL	37	17	26	43	81	7	5	3	8	12
	Cdn. National	....	1	0	1	1	0	....	....	....	....	....
	Hamilton	AHL	1	0	0	0	0	1	1	0	1	0
1994-95	Syracuse	AHL	63	6	3	9	106	....	....	....	....	....

a OHL Second All-Star Team (1993)

TUOHY, JOHN — WSH.

Defense. Shoots left. 6'2", 190 lbs. Born, Baldwin, NY, February 2, 1976.
(Washington's 9th choice, 223rd overall, in 1994 Entry Draft).

			Regular Season					Playoffs				
Season	Club	Lea	GP	G	A	TP	PIM	GP	G	A	TP	PIM
1993-94	Kent Prep.	HS	24	3	16	19	....	....	....	....	....	....
1994-95	Providence	H.E.	16	1	1	2	18	....	....	....	....	....

TUOMAINEN, MARKO — (TOO-oh-migh-nehn) EDM.

Right wing. Shoots right. 6'3", 203 lbs. Born, Kuopio, Finland, April 25, 1972.
(Edmonton's 10th choice, 205th overall, in 1992 Entry Draft).

			Regular Season					Playoffs				
Season	Club	Lea	GP	G	A	TP	PIM	GP	G	A	TP	PIM
1989-90	KalPa	Fin.	5	0	0	0	0	....	....	....	....	....
1990-91	KalPa	Fin.	30	2	1	3	2	8	0	0	0	6
1991-92	Clarkson	ECAC	28	11	12	23	32	....	....	....	....	....
1992-93a	Clarkson	ECAC	35	25	30	55	26	....	....	....	....	....
1993-94	Clarkson	ECAC	34	23	29	52	60	....	....	....	....	....
1994-95ab	Clarkson	ECAC	37	23	38	61	34	....	....	....	....	....
	Edmonton	**NHL**	**4**	**0**	**0**	**0**	**0**	....	....	....	....	....
	NHL Totals		**4**	**0**	**0**	**0**	**0**	....	....	....	....	....

a ECAC First All-Star Team (1993, 1995)
b NCAA East Second All-American Team (1995)

TURCOTTE, DARREN — HFD.

Center. Shoots left. 6', 178 lbs. Born, Boston, MA, March 2, 1968.
(NY Rangers' 6th choice, 114th overall, in 1986 Entry Draft).

			Regular Season					Playoffs				
Season	Club	Lea	GP	G	A	TP	PIM	GP	G	A	TP	PIM
1984-85	North Bay	OHL	62	33	32	65	28	8	0	2	2	0
1985-86	North Bay	OHL	62	35	37	72	35	10	3	4	7	8
1986-87	North Bay	OHL	55	30	48	78	20	18	12	8	20	6
1987-88	North Bay	OHL	32	30	33	63	16	4	3	0	3	4
	Colorado	IHL	8	4	3	7	9	6	2	6	8	8
1988-89	**NY Rangers**	**NHL**	**20**	**7**	**3**	**10**	**4**	**1**	**0**	**0**	**0**	**0**
	Denver	IHL	40	21	28	49	32	....	....	....	....	....
1989-90	**NY Rangers**	**NHL**	**76**	**32**	**34**	**66**	**32**	**10**	**1**	**6**	**7**	**4**
1990-91	**NY Rangers**	**NHL**	**74**	**26**	**41**	**67**	**37**	**6**	**1**	**2**	**3**	**0**
1991-92	**NY Rangers**	**NHL**	**71**	**30**	**23**	**53**	**57**	**8**	**4**	**0**	**4**	**6**
1992-93	**NY Rangers**	**NHL**	**71**	**25**	**28**	**53**	**40**	....	....	....	....	....
1993-94	**NY Rangers**	**NHL**	**13**	**2**	**4**	**6**	**13**	....	....	....	....	....
	Hartford	**NHL**	**19**	**2**	**11**	**13**	**4**	....	....	....	....	....
1994-95	**Hartford**	**NHL**	**47**	**17**	**18**	**35**	**22**	....	....	....	....	....
	NHL Totals		**391**	**141**	**162**	**303**	**209**	**25**	**6**	**8**	**14**	**10**

Played in NHL All-Star Game (1991)

Traded to **Hartford** by **NY Rangers** with James Patrick for Steve Larmer, Nick Kypreos, Barry Richter and Hartford's sixth round choice (Yuri Litvinov) in 1994 Entry Draft, November 2, 1993.

TURGEON, PIERRE — (TUHR-zhaw) — MTL.

Center. Shoots left. 6'1", 195 lbs. Born, Rouyn, Que., August 28, 1969.
(Buffalo's 1st choice, 1st overall, in 1987 Entry Draft).

			Regular Season					Playoffs				
Season	Club	Lea	GP	G	A	TP	PIM	GP	G	A	TP	PIM
1985-86	Granby	QMJHL	69	47	67	114	31	....	....	....	....	....
	Cdn. National	....	11	2	4	6	2	....	....	....	....	....
1986-87	Granby	QMJHL	58	69	85	154	8	7	9	6	15	15
1987-88	**Buffalo**	**NHL**	**76**	**14**	**28**	**42**	**34**	**6**	**4**	**3**	**7**	**4**
1988-89	**Buffalo**	**NHL**	**80**	**34**	**54**	**88**	**26**	**5**	**3**	**5**	**8**	**2**
1989-90	**Buffalo**	**NHL**	**80**	**40**	**66**	**106**	**29**	**6**	**2**	**4**	**6**	**2**
1990-91	**Buffalo**	**NHL**	**78**	**32**	**47**	**79**	**26**	**6**	**3**	**1**	**4**	**6**
1991-92	**Buffalo**	**NHL**	**8**	**2**	**6**	**8**	**4**	....	....	....	....	....
	NY Islanders	**NHL**	**69**	**38**	**49**	**87**	**16**	....	....	....	....	....
1992-93a	**NY Islanders**	**NHL**	**83**	**58**	**74**	**132**	**26**	**11**	**6**	**7**	**13**	**0**
1993-94	**NY Islanders**	**NHL**	**69**	**38**	**56**	**94**	**18**	**4**	**0**	**1**	**1**	**0**
1994-95	**NY Islanders**	**NHL**	**34**	**13**	**14**	**27**	**10**	....	....	....	....	....
	Montreal	**NHL**	**15**	**11**	**9**	**20**	**4**	....	....	....	....	....
	NHL Totals		**592**	**280**	**403**	**683**	**193**	**38**	**18**	**21**	**39**	**14**

a Won Lady Byng Memorial Trophy (1993)

Played in NHL All-Star Game (1990, 1993, 1994)

Traded to **NY Islanders** by **Buffalo** with Uwe Krupp, Benoit Hogue and Dave McLlwain for Pat Lafontaine, Randy Hillier, Randy Wood and NY Islanders' fourth round choice (Dean Melanson) in 1992 Entry Draft, October 25, 1991. Traded to **Montreal** by **NY Islanders** with Vladimir Malakhov for Kirk Muller, Mathieu Schneider and Craig Darby, April 5, 1995.

TURGEON, SYLVAIN — (TUHR-zhaw)

Left wing. Shoots left. 6', 200 lbs. Born, Noranda, Que., January 17, 1965.
(Hartford's 1st choice, 2nd overall, in 1983 Entry Draft).

			Regular Season					Playoffs				
Season	Club	Lea	GP	G	A	TP	PIM	GP	G	A	TP	PIM
1981-82	Hull	QMJHL	57	33	40	73	78	14	11	11	22	16
1982-83a	Hull	QMJHL	67	54	109	163	103	7	8	7	15	10
1983-84b	**Hartford**	**NHL**	**76**	**40**	**32**	**72**	**55**	....	....	....	....	....
1984-85	**Hartford**	**NHL**	**64**	**31**	**31**	**62**	**67**	....	....	....	....	....
1985-86	**Hartford**	**NHL**	**76**	**45**	**34**	**79**	**88**	**9**	**2**	**3**	**5**	**4**
1986-87	**Hartford**	**NHL**	**41**	**23**	**13**	**36**	**45**	**6**	**1**	**2**	**3**	**4**
1987-88	**Hartford**	**NHL**	**71**	**23**	**26**	**49**	**71**	**6**	**0**	**0**	**0**	**4**
1988-89	**Hartford**	**NHL**	**42**	**16**	**14**	**30**	**40**	**4**	**0**	**2**	**2**	**4**
1989-90	**New Jersey**	**NHL**	**72**	**30**	**17**	**47**	**81**	**1**	**0**	**0**	**0**	**0**
1990-91	**Montreal**	**NHL**	**19**	**5**	**7**	**12**	**20**	**5**	**0**	**0**	**0**	**2**
1991-92	**Montreal**	**NHL**	**56**	**9**	**11**	**20**	**39**	**5**	**1**	**0**	**1**	**4**
1992-93	**Ottawa**	**NHL**	**72**	**25**	**18**	**43**	**104**	....	....	....	....	....
1993-94	**Ottawa**	**NHL**	**47**	**11**	**15**	**26**	**52**	....	....	....	....	....
1994-95	**Ottawa**	**NHL**	**33**	**11**	**8**	**19**	**29**	....	....	....	....	....
	NHL Totals		**669**	**269**	**226**	**495**	**691**	**36**	**4**	**7**	**11**	**22**

a QMJHL First All-Star Team (1983)
b NHL All-Rookie Team (1984).

Played in NHL All-Star Game (1986)

Traded to **New Jersey** by **Hartford** for Pat Verbeek, June 17, 1989. Traded to **Montreal** by **New Jersey** for Claude Lemieux, September 4, 1990. Claimed by **Ottawa** from **Montreal** in Expansion Draft, June 18, 1992.

TUZZOLINO, TONY — COL.

Right wing. Shoots right. 6'2", 180 lbs. Born, Buffalo, NY, October 9, 1975.
(Quebec's 7th choice, 113th overall, in 1994 Entry Draft).

			Regular Season					Playoffs				
Season	Club	Lea	GP	G	A	TP	PIM	GP	G	A	TP	PIM
1993-94	Michigan State	CCHA	35	4	3	7	46	....	....	....	....	....
1994-95	Michigan State	CCHA	39	9	18	27	81	....	....	....	....	....

TVERDOVSKY, OLEG — (tvehr-DOHV-skee) — ANA.

Defense. Shoots left. 6', 185 lbs. Born, Donetsk, USSR, May 18, 1976.
(Anaheim's 1st choice, 2nd overall, in 1994 Entry Draft).

			Regular Season					Playoffs				
Season	Club	Lea	GP	G	A	TP	PIM	GP	G	A	TP	PIM
1992-93	Soviet Wings	CIS	21	0	1	1	6	6	0	0	0	0
1993-94	Soviet Wings	CIS	46	4	10	14	22	3	1	0	1	2
1994-95	Brandon	WHL	7	1	4	5	4	....	....	....	....	....
	Anaheim	**NHL**	**36**	**3**	**9**	**12**	**14**	....	....	....	....	....
	NHL Totals		**36**	**3**	**9**	**12**	**14**	....	....	....	....	....

TWIST, TONY — ST.L.

Left wing/Defense. Shoots left. 6'1", 220 lbs. Born, Sherwood Park, Alta., May 9, 1968.
(St. Louis' 9th choice, 177th overall, in 1988 Entry Draft).

			Regular Season					Playoffs				
Season	Club	Lea	GP	G	A	TP	PIM	GP	G	A	TP	PIM
1987-88	Saskatoon	WHL	55	1	8	9	226	10	1	1	2	6
1988-89	Peoria	IHL	67	3	8	11	312	....	....	....	....	....
1989-90	**St. Louis**	**NHL**	**28**	**0**	**0**	**0**	**124**	....	....	....	....	....
	Peoria	IHL	36	1	5	6	200	5	0	1	1	8
1990-91	Peoria	IHL	38	2	10	12	244	....	....	....	....	....
	Quebec	**NHL**	**24**	**0**	**0**	**0**	**104**	....	....	....	....	....
1991-92	**Quebec**	**NHL**	**44**	**0**	**1**	**1**	**164**	....	....	....	....	....
1992-93	**Quebec**	**NHL**	**34**	**0**	**2**	**2**	**64**	....	....	....	....	....
1993-94	**Quebec**	**NHL**	**49**	**0**	**4**	**4**	**101**	....	....	....	....	....
1994-95	**St. Louis**	**NHL**	**28**	**3**	**0**	**3**	**89**	**1**	**0**	**0**	**0**	**6**
	NHL Totals		**207**	**3**	**7**	**10**	**646**	**1**	**0**	**0**	**0**	**6**

Traded to **Quebec** by **St. Louis** with Herb Raglan and Andy Rymsha for Darin Kimble, February 4, 1991. Signed as a free agent by **St. Louis**, August 16, 1994.

ULANOV, IGOR — (oo-LAH-nahf, EE-gohr) — WSH.

Defense. Shoots left. 6'1", 205 lbs. Born, Krasnokamsk, USSR, October 1, 1969.
(Winnipeg's 8th choice, 203rd overall, in 1991 Entry Draft).

			Regular Season					Playoffs				
Season	Club	Lea	GP	G	A	TP	PIM	GP	G	A	TP	PIM
1990-91	Khimik	USSR	41	2	2	4	52	....	....	....	....	....
1991-92	Khimik	CIS	27	1	4	5	24	....	....	....	....	....
	Winnipeg	**NHL**	**27**	**2**	**9**	**11**	**67**	**7**	**0**	**0**	**0**	**39**
	Moncton	AHL	3	0	1	1	16	....	....	....	....	....
1992-93	**Winnipeg**	**NHL**	**56**	**2**	**14**	**16**	**124**	**4**	**0**	**0**	**0**	**4**
	Moncton	AHL	9	1	3	4	26	....	....	....	....	....
	Fort Wayne	IHL	3	0	1	1	29	....	....	....	....	....
1993-94	**Winnipeg**	**NHL**	**74**	**0**	**17**	**17**	**165**	....	....	....	....	....
1994-95	**Winnipeg**	**NHL**	**19**	**1**	**3**	**4**	**27**	....	....	....	....	....
	Washington	**NHL**	**3**	**0**	**1**	**1**	**2**	**2**	**0**	**0**	**0**	**4**
	NHL Totals		**179**	**5**	**44**	**49**	**385**	**13**	**0**	**0**	**0**	**47**

Traded to **Washington** by **Winnipeg** with Mike Eagles for Washington's third (later traded to Dallas — Dallas selected Sergei Gusev) and fifth (Brian Elder) round choices in 1995 Entry Draft, April 7, 1995.

USTORF, STEFAN — (OOSH-tohrf, SHTEH-fuhn) — WSH.

Center. Shoots left. 6', 185 lbs. Born, Kaufbeuren, Germany, January 3, 1974.
(Washington's 3rd choice, 53rd overall, in 1992 Entry Draft).

			Regular Season					Playoffs				
Season	Club	Lea	GP	G	A	TP	PIM	GP	G	A	TP	PIM
1991-92	Kaufbeuren	Ger.	41	2	22	24	46	5	2	7	9	6
1992-93	Kaufbeuren	Ger.	37	14	18	32	32	3	1	0	1	10
1993-94	Kaufbeuren	Ger.	38	10	20	30	21	3	0	0	0	4
1994-95	Portland	AHL	63	21	38	59	51	7	1	6	7	7

USTUGOV, ANATOLY — DET.

Left wing. Shoots left. 5'10", 165 lbs. Born, Yaroslavl, USSR, June 26, 1977.
(Detroit's 4th choice, 104th overall, in 1995 Entry Draft).

			Regular Season					Playoffs				
Season	Club	Lea	GP	G	A	TP	PIM	GP	G	A	TP	PIM
1994-95	Yaroslavl	CIS	5	0	0	0	0	....	....	....	....	....

UVAYEV, VYACHESLAV — (oo-VIH-ev) — NYR

Defense. Shoots left. 5'11", 189 lbs. Born, Moscow, USSR, April 15, 1966.
(NY Rangers' 9th choice, 191st overall, in 1991 Entry Draft).

			Regular Season					Playoffs				
Season	Club	Lea	GP	G	A	TP	PIM	GP	G	A	TP	PIM
1988-89	Torpedo Yaro.	USSR	22	0	1	1	14	....	....	....	....	....
1989-90	Torpedo Yaro.	USSR	48	4	8	12	64	....	....	....	....	....
1990-91	Spartak	USSR	45	1	10	11	44	....	....	....	....	....
1991-92	Spartak	CIS	42	0	7	7	12	....	....	....	....	....
1992-93	Spartak	CIS	40	3	9	12	30	3	0	0	0	2
1993-94	Asiago	Alp.	28	1	11	12	24	....	....	....	....	....
	Asiago	Italy	20	4	8	12	25	....	....	....	....	....
1994-95	Brunico	Italy	36	6	19	25	28	....	....	....	....	....

VACHON, NICK — L.A.

Center. Shoots left. 5'10", 180 lbs. Born, Montreal, Que., July 20, 1972.
(Toronto's 11th choice, 241st overall, in 1990 Entry Draft).

			Regular Season					Playoffs				
Season	Club	Lea	GP	G	A	TP	PIM	GP	G	A	TP	PIM
1990-91	Boston U.	H.E.	8	0	1	1	4	....	....	....	....	....
1991-92	Boston U.	H.E.	16	6	7	13	10	....	....	....	....	....
	Portland	WHL	25	9	19	28	46	6	0	3	3	14
1992-93	Portland	WHL	66	33	58	91	100	16	11	7	18	34
1993-94	Atlanta	IHL	3	1	1	2	0	....	....	....	....	....
	Knoxville	ECHL	61	29	57	86	139	3	0	0	0	2
1994-95	Phoenix	IHL	64	13	26	39	137	9	1	2	3	24

Signed as a free agent by **Los Angeles**.

VALILA, MIKA — (VAH-lee-lyah, MEE-kah) — PIT.

Center. Shoots left. 6', 187 lbs. Born, Sodertalje, Sweden, February 20, 1970.
(Pittsburgh's 7th choice, 130th overall, in 1990 Entry Draft).

			Regular Season					Playoffs				
Season	Club	Lea	GP	G	A	TP	PIM	GP	G	A	TP	PIM
1988-89	Tappara	Fin.	14	2	5	7	8	3	1	0	1	2
1989-90	Tappara	Fin.	44	8	16	24	16	7	2	2	4	4
1990-91	Tappara	Fin.	41	10	9	19	16	3	0	1	1	0
1991-92	Jokerit	Fin.	30	4	3	7	4	8	1	1	2	2
1992-93	Lukko	Fin.	48	8	10	18	24	3	0	0	0	0
1993-94	Lukko	Fin.	45	7	7	14	18	9	0	0	0	8
1994-95	Troja	Swe. 2	33	14	14	28	54	....	....	....	....	....

VALK, GARRY (VAHLK) ANA.

Left wing. Shoots left. 6'1", 205 lbs. Born, Edmonton, Alta., November 27, 1967.
(Vancouver's 5th choice, 108th overall, in 1987 Entry Draft).

			Regular Season					Playoffs				
Season	Club	Lea	GP	G	A	TP	PIM	GP	G	A	TP	PIM
1987-88	North Dakota	WCHA	38	23	12	35	64	....	....	....	....	....
1988-89	North Dakota	WCHA	40	14	17	31	71	....	....	....	....	....
1989-90	North Dakota	WCHA	43	22	17	39	92	....	....	....	....	....
1990-91	**Vancouver**	**NHL**	**59**	**10**	**11**	**21**	**67**	**5**	**0**	**0**	**0**	**20**
	Milwaukee	IHL	10	12	4	16	13	3	0	0	0	2
1991-92	**Vancouver**	**NHL**	**65**	**8**	**17**	**25**	**56**	**4**	**0**	**0**	**0**	**5**
1992-93	**Vancouver**	**NHL**	**48**	**6**	**7**	**13**	**77**	**7**	**0**	**1**	**1**	**12**
	Hamilton	AHL	7	3	6	9	6	....	....	....	....	....
1993-94	**Anaheim**	**NHL**	**78**	**18**	**27**	**45**	**100**	....	....	....	....	....
1994-95	**Anaheim**	**NHL**	**36**	**3**	**6**	**9**	**34**	....	....	....	....	....
	NHL Totals		**286**	**45**	**68**	**113**	**334**	**16**	**0**	**1**	**1**	**37**

Claimed by **Anaheim** from **Vancouver** in NHL Waiver Draft, October 3, 1993.

VALLEE, SEBASTIEN PHI.

Left wing. Shoots left. 6'4", 180 lbs. Born, Thetford Mines, Que., January 2, 1976.
(Philadelphia's 3rd choice, 101st overall, in 1994 Entry Draft).

			Regular Season					Playoffs				
Season	Club	Lea	GP	G	A	TP	PIM	GP	G	A	TP	PIM
1993-94	Victoriaville	QMJHL	72	17	22	39	22	1	0	0	0	0
1994-95	Victoriaville	QMJHL	72	23	32	55	52	4	1	0	1	0

VAN ALLEN, SHAUN ANA.

Center. Shoots left. 6'1", 200 lbs. Born, Shaunavon, Sask., August 29, 1967.
(Edmonton's 5th choice, 105th overall, in 1987 Entry Draft).

			Regular Season					Playoffs				
Season	Club	Lea	GP	G	A	TP	PIM	GP	G	A	TP	PIM
1984-85	Swift Current	WHL	61	12	20	32	136	....	....	....	....	....
1985-86	Saskatoon	WHL	55	12	11	23	43	13	4	8	12	28
1986-87	Saskatoon	WHL	72	38	59	97	116	11	4	6	10	24
1987-88	Milwaukee	IHL	40	14	28	42	34	....	....	....	....	....
	Nova Scotia	AHL	19	4	10	14	17	4	1	1	2	4
1988-89	Cape Breton	AHL	76	32	42	74	81	....	....	....	....	....
1989-90	Cape Breton	AHL	61	25	44	69	83	4	0	2	2	8
1990-91	**Edmonton**	**NHL**	**2**	**0**	**0**	**0**	**0**	....	....	....	....	....
a	Cape Breton	AHL	76	25	75	100	182	4	0	1	1	8
1991-92bc	Cape Breton	AHL	77	29	*84	*113	80	5	3	7	10	14
1992-93	**Edmonton**	**NHL**	**21**	**1**	**4**	**5**	**6**	....	....	....	....	....
	Cape Breton	AHL	43	14	62	76	68	15	8	9	17	18
1993-94	**Anaheim**	**NHL**	**80**	**8**	**25**	**33**	**64**	....	....	....	....	....
1994-95	**Anaheim**	**NHL**	**45**	**8**	**21**	**29**	**32**	....	....	....	....	....
	NHL Totals		**148**	**17**	**50**	**67**	**102**	....	....	....	....	....

a AHL Second All-Star Team (1991)
b Won John B. Sollenberger Trophy (Top Scorer - AHL) (1992)
c AHL First All-Star Team (1992)

Signed as a free agent by **Anaheim**, July 22, 1993.

VANDENBUSSCHE, RYAN (van-dehn-BUHSH) NYR

Right wing. Shoots right. 5'11", 187 lbs. Born, Simcoe, Ont., February 28, 1973.
(Toronto's 8th choice, 173rd overall, in 1992 Entry Draft).

			Regular Season					Playoffs				
Season	Club	Lea	GP	G	A	TP	PIM	GP	G	A	TP	PIM
1990-91	Cornwall	OHL	49	3	8	11	139	....	....	....	....	....
1991-92	Cornwall	OHL	61	13	15	28	232	6	0	2	2	9
1992-93	Newmarket	OHL	30	15	12	27	161	....	....	....	....	....
	Guelph	OHL	29	3	14	17	99	5	1	3	4	13
	St. John's	AHL	1	0	0	0	0	....	....	....	....	....
1993-94	St. John's	AHL	44	4	10	14	124	....	....	....	....	....
	Springfield	AHL	9	1	2	3	29	5	0	0	0	16
1994-95	St. John's	AHL	53	2	13	15	239	....	....	....	....	....

Signed as a free agent by **NY Rangers**, July 10, 1995.

VAN DYK, CHRIS (van-DIGHK) CHI.

Defense. Shoots right. 6'2", 185 lbs. Born, Welland, Ont., February 18, 1977.
(Chicago's 4th choice, 82nd overall, in 1995 Entry Draft).

			Regular Season					Playoffs				
Season	Club	Lea	GP	G	A	TP	PIM	GP	G	A	TP	PIM
1993-94	Welland	Jr. B	39	4	21	25	34	....	....	....	....	....
1994-95	Windsor	OHL	51	4	23	27	55	10	0	2	2	4

VAN IMPE, DARREN ANA.

Defense. Shoots left. 6', 195 lbs. Born, Saskatoon, Sask., May 18, 1973.
(NY Islanders' 7th choice, 170th overall, in 1993 Entry Draft).

			Regular Season					Playoffs				
Season	Club	Lea	GP	G	A	TP	PIM	GP	G	A	TP	PIM
1990-91	Prince Albert	WHL	70	15	45	60	57	3	1	1	2	2
1991-92	Prince Albert	WHL	69	9	37	46	129	8	1	5	6	10
1992-93a	Red Deer	WHL	54	23	47	70	118	4	2	5	7	16
1993-94a	Red Deer	WHL	58	20	64	84	125	4	2	4	6	6
1994-95	San Diego	IHL	76	6	17	23	74	5	0	0	0	0
	Anaheim	**NHL**	**1**	**0**	**1**	**1**	**4**	....	....	....	....	....
	NHL Totals		**1**	**0**	**1**	**1**	**4**	....	....	....	....	....

a WHL First All-Star Team (1993, 1994)

Traded to **Anaheim** by **NY Islanders** for Anaheim's eighth round choice (Mike Broda) in 1995 Entry Draft, August 31, 1994.

VARADA, VACLAV (VAH-rah-dah) S.J.

Right wing. Shoots left. 6', 198 lbs. Born, Vsetin, Czech., April 26, 1976.
(San Jose's 4th choice, 89th overall, in 1994 Entry Draft).

			Regular Season					Playoffs				
Season	Club	Lea	GP	G	A	TP	PIM	GP	G	A	TP	PIM
1992-93	Vitkovice	Czech.	1	0	0	0	....	....	....	....	....	....
1993-94	Vitkovice	Czech.	24	6	7	13	....	5	1	1	2	....
1994-95	Tacoma	WHL	68	50	38	88	108	4	4	3	7	11

VARIS, PETRI S.J.

Left wing. Shoots left. 6'1", 200 lbs. Born, Varkaus, Finland, May 13, 1969.
(San Jose's 7th choice, 132nd overall, in 1993 Entry Draft).

			Regular Season					Playoffs				
Season	Club	Lea	GP	G	A	TP	PIM	GP	G	A	TP	PIM
1990-91	KooKoo	Fin. 2	44	20	31	51	42	....	....	....	....	....
1991-92a	Assat	Fin.	36	13	23	36	24	....	....	....	....	....
1992-93	Assat	Fin.	46	14	35	49	42	8	2	2	4	12
1993-94	Jokerit	Fin.	31	14	15	29	16	11	3	4	7	6
1994-95	Jokerit	Fin.	47	21	20	41	53	11	7	2	9	10

a Finnish Rookie of the Year (1992)

VARVIO, JARKKO (VAHR-vee-oh, YAHR-koh)

Right wing. Shoots right. 5'9", 175 lbs. Born, Tampere, Finland, April 28, 1972.
(Minnesota's 1st choice, 34th overall, in 1992 Entry Draft).

			Regular Season					Playoffs				
Season	Club	Lea	GP	G	A	TP	PIM	GP	G	A	TP	PIM
1989-90	Ilves	Fin.	1	0	0	0	0	....	....	....	....	....
1990-91	Ilves	Fin.	37	10	7	17	6	....	....	....	....	....
1991-92	HPK	Fin.	41	25	9	34	6	....	....	....	....	....
1992-93	HPK	Fin.	40	29	19	48	16	12	3	2	5	8
1993-94	**Dallas**	**NHL**	**8**	**2**	**3**	**5**	**4**	....	....	....	....	....
	Kalamazoo	IHL	58	29	16	45	18	1	0	0	0	0
1994-95	HPK	Fin.	19	7	8	15	4	....	....	....	....	....
	Dallas	**NHL**	**5**	**1**	**1**	**2**	**0**	....	....	....	....	....
	Kalamazoo	IHL	7	0	0	0	2	....	....	....	....	....
	NHL Totals		**13**	**3**	**4**	**7**	**4**	....	....	....	....	....

VASILEVSKII, ALEXANDER (vah-sih-LEHV-skee) ST.L.

Right wing. Shoots left. 5'11", 190 lbs. Born, Kiev, USSR, January 8, 1975.
(St. Louis' 9th choice, 271st overall, in 1993 Entry Draft).

			Regular Season					Playoffs				
Season	Club	Lea	GP	G	A	TP	PIM	GP	G	A	TP	PIM
1992-93	Victoria	WHL	71	27	25	52	52	....	....	....	....	....
1993-94	Victoria	WHL	69	34	51	85	78	....	....	....	....	....
1994-95	Prince George	WHL	48	32	34	66	52	....	....	....	....	....
	Brandon	WHL	23	6	11	17	39	18	3	6	9	34

VASILIEV, ALEXEI (vah-SEE-lee-ehf) NYR

Defense. Shoots left. 6'1", 189 lbs. Born, Yaroslavl, USSR, September 1, 1977.
(NY Rangers' 4th choice, 110th overall, in 1995 Entry Draft).

			Regular Season					Playoffs				
Season	Club	Lea	GP	G	A	TP	PIM	GP	G	A	TP	PIM
1993-94	Yaroslavl	CIS	2	0	1	1	4	....	....	....	....	....
1994-95	Yaroslavl-2	CIS 2				UNAVAILABLE						

VASILIEV, ANDREI (vah-SEE-lee-ehf) NYI

Left wing. Shoots right. 5'9", 180 lbs. Born, Voskresensk, USSR, March 30, 1972.
(NY Islanders' 11th choice, 248th overall, in 1992 Entry Draft).

			Regular Season					Playoffs				
Season	Club	Lea	GP	G	A	TP	PIM	GP	G	A	TP	PIM
1991-92	CSKA	CIS	28	7	2	9	2	....	....	....	....	....
1992-93	Khimik	CIS	34	4	8	12	20	....	....	....	....	....
1993-94	CSKA	CIS	46	17	6	23	8	3	1	0	1	0
1994-95	Denver	IHL	74	28	37	65	48	13	9	4	13	22
	NY Islanders	**NHL**	**2**	**0**	**0**	**0**	**2**	....	....	....	....	....
	NHL Totals		**2**	**0**	**0**	**0**	**2**	....	....	....	....	....

VASKE, DENNIS (VAS-kee) NYI

Defense. Shoots left. 6'2", 210 lbs. Born, Rockford, IL, October 11, 1967.
(NY Islanders' 2nd choice, 38th overall, in 1986 Entry Draft).

			Regular Season					Playoffs				
Season	Club	Lea	GP	G	A	TP	PIM	GP	G	A	TP	PIM
1986-87	Minn.-Duluth	WCHA	33	0	2	2	40	....	....	....	....	....
1987-88	Minn.-Duluth	WCHA	39	1	6	7	90	....	....	....	....	....
1988-89	Minn.-Duluth	WCHA	37	9	19	28	86	....	....	....	....	....
1989-90	Minn.-Duluth	WCHA	37	5	24	29	72	....	....	....	....	....
1990-91	**NY Islanders**	**NHL**	**5**	**0**	**0**	**0**	**2**	....	....	....	....	....
	Capital Dist.	AHL	67	10	10	20	65	....	....	....	....	....
1991-92	**NY Islanders**	**NHL**	**39**	**0**	**1**	**1**	**39**	....	....	....	....	....
	Capital Dist.	AHL	31	1	11	12	59	....	....	....	....	....
1992-93	**NY Islanders**	**NHL**	**27**	**1**	**5**	**6**	**32**	**18**	**0**	**6**	**6**	**14**
	Capital Dist.	AHL	42	4	15	19	70	....	....	....	....	....
1993-94	**NY Islanders**	**NHL**	**65**	**2**	**11**	**13**	**76**	**4**	**0**	**1**	**1**	**2**
1994-95	**NY Islanders**	**NHL**	**41**	**1**	**11**	**12**	**53**	....	....	....	....	....
	NHL Totals		**177**	**4**	**28**	**32**	**202**	**22**	**0**	**7**	**7**	**16**

VEILLEUX, ERIC (VAY-yew) COL.

Center. Shoots left. 5'7", 148 lbs. Born, Quebec, Que., February 20, 1972.

			Regular Season					Playoffs				
Season	Club	Lea	GP	G	A	TP	PIM	GP	G	A	TP	PIM
1991-92	Laval	QMJHL	60	31	40	71	87	10	3	5	8	27
1992-93	Laval	QMJHL	70	55	70	125	100	13	9	11	20	19
1993-94	Cornwall	AHL	77	8	19	27	69	13	1	7	8	20
1994-95	Cornwall	AHL	70	13	23	36	93	13	1	1	2	20

Signed as a free agent by **Quebec**, October 6, 1993.

VERBEEK, PAT (vuhr-BEEK) **NYR**

Right/Left wing. Shoots right. 5'9", 190 lbs. Born, Sarnia, Ont., May 24, 1964.
(New Jersey's 3rd choice, 43rd overall, in 1982 Entry Draft).

			Regular Season					Playoffs				
Season	Club	Lea	GP	G	A	TP	PIM	GP	G	A	TP	PIM
1981-82	Sudbury	OHL	66	37	51	88	180	....	....	....	....	....
1982-83	**New Jersey**	**NHL**	**6**	**3**	**2**	**5**	**8**	....	....	....	....	....
	Sudbury	OHL	61	40	67	107	184	....	....	....	....	....
1983-84	**New Jersey**	**NHL**	**79**	**20**	**27**	**47**	**158**	....	....	....	....	....
1984-85	**New Jersey**	**NHL**	**78**	**15**	**18**	**33**	**162**	....	....	....	....	....
1985-86	**New Jersey**	**NHL**	**76**	**25**	**28**	**53**	**79**	....	....	....	....	....
1986-87	**New Jersey**	**NHL**	**74**	**35**	**24**	**59**	**120**	....	....	....	....	....
1987-88	**New Jersey**	**NHL**	**73**	**46**	**31**	**77**	**227**	**20**	**4**	**8**	**12**	**51**
1988-89	**New Jersey**	**NHL**	**77**	**26**	**21**	**47**	**189**	....	....	....	....	....
1989-90	**Hartford**	**NHL**	**80**	**44**	**45**	**89**	**228**	**7**	**2**	**2**	**4**	**26**
1990-91	**Hartford**	**NHL**	**80**	**43**	**39**	**82**	**246**	**6**	**3**	**2**	**5**	**40**
1991-92	**Hartford**	**NHL**	**76**	**22**	**35**	**57**	**243**	**7**	**0**	**2**	**2**	**12**
1992-93	**Hartford**	**NHL**	**84**	**39**	**43**	**82**	**197**	....	....	....	....	....
1993-94	**Hartford**	**NHL**	**84**	**37**	**38**	**75**	**177**	....	....	....	....	....
1994-95	**Hartford**	**NHL**	**29**	**7**	**11**	**18**	**53**	....	....	....	....	....
	NY Rangers	**NHL**	**19**	**10**	**5**	**15**	**18**	**10**	**4**	**6**	**10**	**20**
	NHL Totals		**915**	**372**	**367**	**739**	**2105**	**50**	**13**	**20**	**33**	**149**

Played in NHL All-Star Game (1991)

Traded to **Hartford** by **New Jersey** for Sylvain Turgeon, June 17, 1989. Traded to **NY Rangers** by **Hartford** for Glen Featherstone, Michael Stewart, NY Rangers' first round choice (Jean-Sebastien Giguere) in 1995 Entry Draft and fourth round choice in 1996 Entry Draft, March 23, 1995.

VERCIK, RUDOLF (VEHR-chihk) **NYR**

Left wing. Shoots left. 6'1", 189 lbs. Born, Bratislava, Czech., March 19, 1976.
(NY Rangers' 2nd choice, 52nd overall, in 1994 Entry Draft).

			Regular Season					Playoffs				
Season	Club	Lea	GP	G	A	TP	PIM	GP	G	A	TP	PIM
1993-94	Bratislava	Slov.	17	1	4	5	14	....	....	....	....	....
1994-95	Bratislava	Slov.	33	14	9	23	22	....	....	....	....	....

VIAL, DENNIS (vee-AL) **OTT.**

Defense. Shoots left. 6'2", 218 lbs. Born, Sault Ste. Marie, Ont., April 10, 1969.
(NY Rangers' 5th choice, 110th overall, in 1988 Entry Draft).

			Regular Season					Playoffs				
Season	Club	Lea	GP	G	A	TP	PIM	GP	G	A	TP	PIM
1985-86	Hamilton	OHL	31	1	1	2	66	....	....	....	....	....
1986-87	Hamilton	OHL	53	1	8	9	194	8	0	0	0	8
1987-88	Hamilton	OHL	52	3	17	20	229	13	2	2	4	49
1988-89	Niagara Falls	OHL	50	10	27	37	227	15	1	7	8	44
1989-90	Flint	IHL	79	6	29	35	351	4	0	0	0	10
1990-91	**NY Rangers**	**NHL**	**21**	**0**	**0**	**0**	**61**	....	....	....	....	....
	Binghamton	AHL	40	2	7	9	250	....	....	....	....	....
	Detroit	**NHL**	**9**	**0**	**0**	**0**	**16**	....	....	....	....	....
1991-92	**Detroit**	**NHL**	**27**	**1**	**0**	**1**	**72**	....	....	....	....	....
	Adirondack	AHL	20	2	4	6	107	17	1	3	4	43
1992-93	**Detroit**	**NHL**	**9**	**0**	**1**	**1**	**20**	....	....	....	....	....
	Adirondack	AHL	30	2	11	13	177	11	1	1	2	14
1993-94	**Ottawa**	**NHL**	**55**	**2**	**5**	**7**	**214**	....	....	....	....	....
1994-95	**Ottawa**	**NHL**	**27**	**0**	**4**	**4**	**65**	....	....	....	....	....
	NHL Totals		**148**	**3**	**10**	**13**	**448**	....	....	....	....	....

Traded to **Detroit** by **NY Rangers** with Kevin Miller and Jim Cummins for Joey Kocur and Per Djoos, March 5, 1991. Traded to **Quebec** by **Detroit** with Doug Crossman for cash, June 15, 1992. Traded to **Detroit** by **Quebec** for cash, September 9, 1992. Traded to **Tampa Bay** by **Detroit** for Steve Maltais, June 8, 1993. Claimed by **Anaheim** from **Tampa Bay** in Expansion Draft, June 24, 1993. Claimed by **Ottawa** from **Anaheim** in Phase II of Expansion Draft, June 25, 1993.

VIITAKOSKI, VESA (VEE-ee-tah-kohs-kee) **CGY.**

Left wing. Shoots left. 6'3", 215 lbs. Born, Lappeenranta, Finland, February 13, 1971.
(Calgary's 3rd choice, 32nd overall, in 1990 Entry Draft).

			Regular Season					Playoffs				
Season	Club	Lea	GP	G	A	TP	PIM	GP	G	A	TP	PIM
1988-89	SaiPa	Fin.	11	4	1	5	6	....	....	....	....	....
1989-90	SaiPa	Fin.	44	24	10	34	8	....	....	....	....	....
1990-91	Tappara	Fin.	41	17	23	40	14	3	2	0	2	4
1991-92	Tappara	Fin.	44	19	19	38	39	....	....	....	....	....
1992-93	Tappara	Fin.	48	27	27	54	28	....	....	....	....	....
1993-94	**Calgary**	**NHL**	**8**	**1**	**2**	**3**	**0**	....	....	....	....	....
	Saint John	AHL	67	28	39	67	24	5	1	2	3	2
1994-95	Saint John	AHL	56	17	26	43	8	4	0	1	1	2
	Calgary	**NHL**	**10**	**1**	**2**	**3**	**6**	....	....	....	....	....
	NHL Totals		**18**	**2**	**4**	**6**	**6**	....	....	....	....	....

VINCENT, PAUL **TOR.**

Center. Shoots left. 6'4", 200 lbs. Born, Utica, NY, January 4, 1975.
(Toronto's 4th choice, 149th overall, in 1993 Entry Draft).

			Regular Season					Playoffs				
Season	Club	Lea	GP	G	A	TP	PIM	GP	G	A	TP	PIM
1993-94	Seattle	WHL	66	27	26	53	57	8	1	3	4	8
1994-95	Seattle	WHL	3	0	2	2	2	....	....	....	....	....
	Swift Current	WHL	62	59	39	98	85	6	3	2	5	17
	St. John's	AHL	2	0	2	2	0	....	....	....	....	....

VISHEAU, MARK (VEE-SHOO) **WPG.**

Defense. Shoots right. 6'4", 200 lbs. Born, Burlington, Ont., June 27, 1973.
(Winnipeg's 4th choice, 84th overall, in 1992 Entry Draft).

			Regular Season					Playoffs				
Season	Club	Lea	GP	G	A	TP	PIM	GP	G	A	TP	PIM
1990-91	London	OHL	59	4	11	15	40	7	0	1	1	6
1991-92	London	OHL	66	5	31	36	104	10	0	4	4	27
1992-93	London	OHL	62	8	52	60	88	12	0	5	5	26
1993-94	**Winnipeg**	**NHL**	**1**	**0**	**0**	**0**	**0**	....	....	....	....	....
	Moncton	AHL	48	4	5	9	58	....	....	....	....	....
1994-95	Springfield	AHL	35	0	4	4	94	....	....	....	....	....
	NHL Totals		**1**	**0**	**0**	**0**	**0**					

VLASAK, TOMAS **L.A.**

Center. Shoots right. 5'10", 175 lbs. Born, Prague, Czech., February 1, 1975.
(Los Angeles' 6th choice, 120th overall, in 1993 Entry Draft).

			Regular Season					Playoffs				
Season	Club	Lea	GP	G	A	TP	PIM	GP	G	A	TP	PIM
1992-93	Slavia Praha	Czech. 2	31	17	6	23	....	....	....	....	....	....
1993-94	Litvinov	Czech.	41	16	11	27	0	4	0	1	1	....
1994-95	Litvinov	Czech.	35	6	14	20	4	4	0	0	0	4

VOLKOV, MIKHAIL (VOHL-kahf) **BUF.**

Right wing. Shoots right. 5'10", 174 lbs. Born, Voronezh, USSR, March 9, 1972.
(Buffalo's 12th choice, 233rd overall, in 1991 Entry Draft).

			Regular Season					Playoffs				
Season	Club	Lea	GP	G	A	TP	PIM	GP	G	A	TP	PIM
1989-90	Soviet Wings	USSR	24	0	2	2	4	....	....	....	....	....
1990-91	Soviet Wings	USSR	40	8	4	12	8	....	....	....	....	....
1991-92	Soviet Wings	CIS	37	3	6	9	16	....	....	....	....	....
1992-93	Soviet Wings	CIS	33	9	6	15	11	5	0	1	1	2
1993-94	Rochester	AHL	62	12	26	38	28	4	0	2	2	2
1994-95	Rochester	AHL	56	17	27	44	52	4	1	0	1	2

VON STEFENELLI, PHIL **BOS.**

Defense. Shoots left. 6'1", 200 lbs. Born, Vancouver, B.C., April 10, 1969.
(Vancouver's 5th choice, 122nd overall, in 1988 Entry Draft).

			Regular Season					Playoffs				
Season	Club	Lea	GP	G	A	TP	PIM	GP	G	A	TP	PIM
1987-88	Boston U.	H.E.	34	3	13	16	38	....	....	....	....	....
1988-89	Boston U.	H.E.	33	2	6	8	34	....	....	....	....	....
1989-90	Boston U.	H.E.	44	8	20	28	40	....	....	....	....	....
1990-91	Boston U.	H.E.	41	7	23	30	32	....	....	....	....	....
1991-92	Milwaukee	IHL	80	2	34	36	40	5	1	2	3	2
1992-93	Hamilton	AHL	78	11	20	31	75	....	....	....	....	....
1993-94	Hamilton	AHL	80	10	31	41	89	4	1	0	1	2
1994-95	Providence	AHL	75	6	13	19	93	13	2	4	6	6

Signed as a free agent by **Boston**, September 10, 1994.

VOPAT, JAN (VOH-paht) **L.A.**

Defense. Shoots left. 6', 198 lbs. Born, Most, Czech., March 22, 1973.
(Hartford's 3rd choice, 57th overall, in 1992 Entry Draft).

			Regular Season					Playoffs				
Season	Club	Lea	GP	G	A	TP	PIM	GP	G	A	TP	PIM
1990-91	Litvinov	Czech.	25	1	4	5	4	....	....	....	....	....
1991-92	Litvinov	Czech.	46	4	2	6	16	....	....	....	....	....
1992-93	Litvinov	Czech.	45	12	10	22	....	....	....	....	....	....
1993-94	Litvinov	Czech.	41	9	19	28	0	4	1	1	2	....
1994-95	Litvinov	Czech.	42	7	18	25	49	4	0	2	2	2

Rights traded to **Los Angeles** by **Hartford** for Los Angeles' fourth round choice (Ian MacNeil) in 1995 Entry Draft, May 31, 1995.

VOPAT, ROMAN (VOH-paht) **ST.L.**

Center. Shoots left. 6'3", 216 lbs. Born, Litvinov, Czech., April 21, 1976.
(St. Louis' 4th choice, 172nd overall, in 1994 Entry Draft).

			Regular Season					Playoffs				
Season	Club	Lea	GP	G	A	TP	PIM	GP	G	A	TP	PIM
1993-94	Litvinov	Czech.	7	0	0	0	0	....	....	....	....	....
1994-95	Moose Jaw	WHL	72	23	20	43	141	10	4	1	5	28

VOROBIEV, VLADIMIR **NYR**

Left wing. Shoots right. 5'11", 185 lbs. Born, Cherepovets, USSR, October 2, 1972.
(NY Rangers' 10th choice, 240th overall, in 1992 Entry Draft).

			Regular Season					Playoffs				
Season	Club	Lea	GP	G	A	TP	PIM	GP	G	A	TP	PIM
1992-93	Cherepovets	CIS	42	18	5	23	18	....	....	....	....	....
1993-94	Moscow D'amo	CIS	11	3	1	4	2	....	....	....	....	....
1994-95	Moscow D'amo	CIS	48	9	20	29	28	14	1	7	8	2

VORONOV, SERGEI **PIT.**

Defense. Shoots left. 6'2", 200 lbs. Born, Moscow, USSR, February 5, 1971.
(Pittsburgh's 7th choice, 206th overall, in 1995 Entry Draft).

			Regular Season					Playoffs				
Season	Club	Lea	GP	G	A	TP	PIM	GP	G	A	TP	PIM
1992-93	Moscow D'amo	CIS	36	1	0	1	25	....	....	....	....	....
1993-94	Moscow D'amo	CIS	44	5	6	11	72	....	....	....	....	....
1994-95	Moscow D'amo	CIS	44	3	4	7	80	12	4	1	5	26

VUJTEK, VLADIMIR (VYOO-tehk) **EDM.**

Left wing. Shoots left. 6'1", 190 lbs. Born, Ostrava, Czech., February 17, 1972.
(Montreal's 4th choice, 73rd overall, in 1991 Entry Draft).

			Regular Season					Playoffs				
Season	Club	Lea	GP	G	A	TP	PIM	GP	G	A	TP	PIM
1988-89	TJ Vitkovice	Czech.	3	0	1	1	0	....	....	....	....	....
1989-90	TJ Vitkovice	Czech.	29	7	7	14	....	....	....	....	....	....
1990-91	TJ Vitkovice	Czech.	26	7	4	11	....	....	....	....	....	....
	Tri-City	WHL	37	26	18	44	25	7	2	3	5	4
1991-92	**Montreal**	**NHL**	**2**	**0**	**0**	**0**	**0**	....	....	....	....	....
a	Tri-City	WHL	53	41	61	102	114	....	....	....	....	....
1992-93	**Edmonton**	**NHL**	**30**	**1**	**10**	**11**	**8**	....	....	....	....	....
	Cape Breton	AHL	20	10	9	19	14	1	0	0	0	0
1993-94	**Edmonton**	**NHL**	**40**	**4**	**15**	**19**	**14**	....	....	....	....	....
1994-95	Vitkovice	Czech.	18	5	7	12	51	....	....	....	....	....
	Cape Breton	AHL	30	10	11	21	30	....	....	....	....	....
	Las Vegas	IHL	1	0	0	0	0	....	....	....	....	....
	NHL Totals		**72**	**5**	**25**	**30**	**22**	....	....	....	....	....

a WHL West First All-Star Team (1992)

Traded to **Edmonton** by **Montreal** with Shayne Corson and Brent Gilchrist for Vincent Damphousse and Edmonton's fourth round choice (Adam Wiesel) in 1993 Entry Draft, August 27, 1992.

VUKONICH, MICHAEL

Center. Shoots left. 6'1", 190 lbs. Born, Duluth, MN, May 11, 1968.
(Los Angeles' 4th choice, 90th overall, in 1987 Entry Draft).

			Regular Season					Playoffs				
Season	Club	Lea	GP	G	A	TP	PIM	GP	G	A	TP	PIM
1987-88	Harvard	ECAC	32	9	14	23	24	....	....	....	....	....
1988-89	Harvard	ECAC	27	11	8	19	12	....	....	....	....	....
1989-90a	Harvard	ECAC	27	22	29	51	18	....	....	....	....	....
1990-91b	Harvard	ECAC	27	*31	23	54	28	....	....	....	....	....
1991-92	Phoenix	IHL	68	17	11	28	21	....	....	....	....	....
1992-93	Phoenix	IHL	70	25	15	40	27	....	....	....	....	....
1993-94	Phoenix	IHL	22	4	6	10	8	....	....	....	....	....
	Binghamton	AHL	3	1	0	1	0	....	....	....	....	....
	Flint	ColHL	8	7	8	15	12	10	7	7	14	12
1994-95	Albany	AHL	61	16	14	30	16	4	0	0	0	0

a ECAC First All-Star Team (1990)
b ECAC Second All-Star Team (1991)

Signed as a free agent by **New Jersey**, September 28, 1994.

VUKOTA, MICK (vuh-KOH-tuh) NYI

Right wing. Shoots right. 6'2", 195 lbs. Born, Saskatoon, Sask., September 14, 1966.

			Regular Season					Playoffs				
Season	Club	Lea	GP	G	A	TP	PIM	GP	G	A	TP	PIM
1983-84	Winnipeg	WHL	3	1	1	2	10	....	....	....	....	....
1984-85	Kelowna	WHL	66	10	6	16	247	....	....	....	....	....
1985-86	Spokane	WHL	64	19	14	33	369	9	6	4	10	68
1986-87	Spokane	WHL	61	25	28	53	*337	4	0	0	0	40
1987-88	**NY Islanders**	**NHL**	**17**	**1**	**0**	**1**	**82**	**2**	**0**	**0**	**0**	**23**
	Springfield	AHL	52	7	9	16	375	....	....	....	....	....
1988-89	**NY Islanders**	**NHL**	**48**	**2**	**2**	**4**	**237**	....	....	....	....	....
	Springfield	AHL	3	1	0	1	33	....	....	....	....	....
1989-90	**NY Islanders**	**NHL**	**76**	**4**	**8**	**12**	**290**	**1**	**0**	**0**	**0**	**17**
1990-91	**NY Islanders**	**NHL**	**60**	**2**	**4**	**6**	**238**	....	....	....	....	....
	Capital Dist.	AHL	2	0	0	0	9	....	....	....	....	....
1991-92	**NY Islanders**	**NHL**	**74**	**0**	**6**	**6**	**293**	....	....	....	....	....
1992-93	**NY Islanders**	**NHL**	**74**	**2**	**5**	**7**	**216**	**15**	**0**	**0**	**0**	**16**
1993-94	**NY Islanders**	**NHL**	**72**	**3**	**1**	**4**	**237**	**4**	**0**	**0**	**0**	**17**
1994-95	**NY Islanders**	**NHL**	**40**	**0**	**2**	**2**	**109**	....	....	....	....	....
	NHL Totals		**461**	**14**	**28**	**42**	**1702**	**22**	**0**	**0**	**0**	**73**

Signed as a free agent by **NY Islanders**, March 2, 1987.

VYBORNY, DAVID (vigh-BOHR-nee) EDM.

Center. Shoots left. 5'10", 174 lbs. Born, Jihlava, Czech., January 22, 1975.
(Edmonton's 3rd choice, 33rd overall, in 1993 Entry Draft).

			Regular Season					Playoffs				
Season	Club	Lea	GP	G	A	TP	PIM	GP	G	A	TP	PIM
1990-91	Sparta Praha	Czech.	3	0	0	0	0	....	....	....	....	....
1991-92a	Sparta Praha	Czech.	32	6	9	15	2	....	....	....	....	....
1992-93	Sparta Praha	Czech.	52	20	24	44	....	....	....	....	....	....
1993-94	Sparta Praha	Czech.	44	15	20	35	0	6	4	7	11	0
1994-95	Cape Breton	AHL	76	23	38	61	30	....	....	....	....	....

a Czech. Rookie of the Year (1992)

VYSHEDKEVICH, SERGEI (vee-shehd-KAY-vihch) N.J.

Defense. Shoots left. 6', 185 lbs. Born, Dedovsk, USSR, January 3, 1975.
(New Jersey's 3rd choice, 70th overall, in 1995 Entry Draft).

			Regular Season					Playoffs				
Season	Club	Lea	GP	G	A	TP	PIM	GP	G	A	TP	PIM
1994-95	Moscow D'amo	CIS	49	6	7	13	67	14	2	0	2	12

WAINWRIGHT, DAVID NYI

Defense. Shoots left. 6', 193 lbs. Born, Boston, MA, January 17, 1974.
(NY Islanders' 10th choice, 224th overall, in 1992 Entry Draft).

			Regular Season					Playoffs				
Season	Club	Lea	GP	G	A	TP	PIM	GP	G	A	TP	PIM
1993-94	Boston College	H.E.	36	2	1	3	38	....	....	....	....	....
1994-95	Boston College	H.E.	33	3	5	8	48	....	....	....	....	....

WALBY, STEFFON TOR.

Right wing. Shoots right. 6'1", 198 lbs. Born, Madison, WI, November 22, 1972.

			Regular Season					Playoffs				
Season	Club	Lea	GP	G	A	TP	PIM	GP	G	A	TP	PIM
1992-93	Kelowna	BCJHL	59	53	68	121	76	....	....	....	....	....
1993-94	St. John's	AHL	63	15	22	37	79	2	0	0	0	2
1994-95	St. John's	AHL	70	23	23	46	30	5	1	1	2	4

Signed as a free agent by **Toronto**, August 20, 1993.

WALKER, SCOTT VAN.

Defense. Shoots right. 5'9", 180 lbs. Born, Montreal, Que., July 19, 1973.
(Vancouver's 4th choice, 124th overall, in 1993 Entry Draft).

			Regular Season					Playoffs				
Season	Club	Lea	GP	G	A	TP	PIM	GP	G	A	TP	PIM
1991-92	Owen Sound	OHL	53	7	31	38	128	5	0	7	7	8
1992-93a	Owen Sound	OHL	57	23	68	91	110	8	1	5	6	16
	Cdn. National	....	2	3	0	3	0	....	....	....	....	....
1993-94	Hamilton	AHL	77	10	29	39	272	4	0	1	1	25
1994-95	Syracuse	AHL	74	14	38	52	334	....	....	....	....	....
	Vancouver	**NHL**	**11**	**0**	**1**	**1**	**33**	....	....	....	....	....
	NHL Totals		**11**	**0**	**1**	**1**	**33**	....	....	....	....	....

a OHL Second All-Star Team (1993)

WALSH, GORD NYI

Left wing. Shoots left. 6'1", 186 lbs. Born, St. John's, Nfld., December 12, 1975.
(NY Islanders' 10th choice, 220th overall, in 1994 Entry Draft).

			Regular Season					Playoffs				
Season	Club	Lea	GP	G	A	TP	PIM	GP	G	A	TP	PIM
1992-93	Guelph	OHL	55	2	9	11	12	5	0	0	0	2
1993-94	Guelph	OHL	8	0	1	1	9	....	....	....	....	....
	Kingston	OHL	55	14	19	33	52	6	0	1	1	4
1994-95	Kingston	OHL	61	27	37	64	43	6	1	0	1	6

WALZ, WES (WAHLS)

Center. Shoots right. 5'10", 185 lbs. Born, Calgary, Alta., May 15, 1970.
(Boston's 3rd choice, 57th overall, in 1989 Entry Draft).

			Regular Season					Playoffs				
Season	Club	Lea	GP	G	A	TP	PIM	GP	G	A	TP	PIM
1988-89	Lethbridge	WHL	63	29	75	104	32	8	1	5	6	6
1989-90	**Boston**	**NHL**	**2**	**1**	**1**	**2**	**0**	....	....	....	....	....
a	Lethbridge	WHL	56	54	86	140	69	19	13	*24	*37	33
1990-91	**Boston**	**NHL**	**56**	**8**	**8**	**16**	**32**	**2**	**0**	**0**	**0**	**0**
	Maine	AHL	20	8	12	20	19	2	0	0	0	21
1991-92	**Boston**	**NHL**	**15**	**0**	**3**	**3**	**12**	....	....	....	....	....
	Maine	AHL	21	13	11	24	38	....	....	....	....	....
	Philadelphia	**NHL**	**2**	**1**	**0**	**1**	**0**	....	....	....	....	....
	Hershey	AHL	41	13	28	41	37	6	1	2	3	0
1992-93	Hershey	AHL	78	35	45	80	106	....	....	....	....	....
1993-94	**Calgary**	**NHL**	**53**	**11**	**27**	**38**	**16**	**6**	**3**	**0**	**3**	**2**
	Saint John	AHL	15	6	6	12	14	....	....	....	....	....
1994-95	**Calgary**	**NHL**	**39**	**6**	**12**	**18**	**11**	**1**	**0**	**0**	**0**	**0**
	NHL Totals		**167**	**27**	**51**	**78**	**71**	**9**	**3**	**0**	**3**	**2**

a WHL East First All-Star Team (1990)

Traded to **Philadelphia** by **Boston** with Garry Galley and Boston's third round choice (Milos Holan) in 1993 Entry Draft for Gord Murphy, Brian Dobbin, Philadelphia's third round choice (Sergei Zholtok) in 1992 Entry Draft and Philadelphia's fourth round choice (Charles Paquette) in 1993 Entry Draft, January 2, 1992. Signed as a free agent by **Calgary**, August 26, 1993.

WARD, AARON DET.

Defense. Shoots right. 6'2", 200 lbs. Born, Windsor, Ont., January 17, 1973.
(Winnipeg's 1st choice, 5th overall, in 1991 Entry Draft).

			Regular Season					Playoffs				
Season	Club	Lea	GP	G	A	TP	PIM	GP	G	A	TP	PIM
1990-91	U. of Michigan	CCHA	46	8	11	19	126	....	....	....	....	....
1991-92	U. of Michigan	CCHA	42	7	12	19	64	....	....	....	....	....
1992-93	U. of Michigan	CCHA	30	5	8	13	73	....	....	....	....	....
	Cdn. National	....	4	0	0	0	8	....	....	....	....	....
1993-94	**Detroit**	**NHL**	**5**	**1**	**0**	**1**	**4**	....	....	....	....	....
	Adirondack	AHL	58	4	12	16	87	9	2	6	8	6
1994-95	Adirondack	AHL	76	11	24	35	87	4	0	1	1	0
	Detroit	**NHL**	**1**	**0**	**1**	**1**	**2**	....	....	....	....	....
	NHL Totals		**6**	**1**	**1**	**2**	**6**	....	....	....	....	....

Traded to **Detroit** by **Winnipeg** with Toronto's fourth round choice (previously acquired by Winnipeg — later traded to Detroit — Detroit selected John Jakopin) in 1993 Entry Draft for Paul Ysebaert and future considerations (Alan Kerr, June 18, 1993), June 11, 1993.

WARD, DIXON

Right wing. Shoots right. 6', 200 lbs. Born, Leduc, Alta., September 23, 1968.
(Vancouver's 6th choice, 128th overall, in 1988 Entry Draft).

			Regular Season					Playoffs				
Season	Club	Lea	GP	G	A	TP	PIM	GP	G	A	TP	PIM
1988-89	North Dakota	WCHA	37	8	9	17	26	....	....	....	....	....
1989-90	North Dakota	WCHA	45	35	34	69	44	....	....	....	....	....
1990-91a	North Dakota	WCHA	43	34	35	69	84	....	....	....	....	....
1991-92a	North Dakota	WCHA	38	33	31	64	90	....	....	....	....	....
1992-93	**Vancouver**	**NHL**	**70**	**22**	**30**	**52**	**82**	**9**	**2**	**3**	**5**	**0**
1993-94	**Vancouver**	**NHL**	**33**	**6**	**1**	**7**	**37**	....	....	....	....	....
	Los Angeles	**NHL**	**34**	**6**	**2**	**8**	**45**	....	....	....	....	....
1994-95	**Toronto**	**NHL**	**22**	**0**	**3**	**3**	**31**	....	....	....	....	....
	St. John's	AHL	6	3	3	6	19	....	....	....	....	....
	Detroit	IHL	7	3	6	9	7	5	3	0	3	7
	NHL Totals		**159**	**34**	**36**	**70**	**195**	**9**	**2**	**3**	**5**	**0**

a WCHA Second All-Star Team (1991, 1992)

Traded to **Los Angeles** by **Vancouver** with a conditional draft choice in 1995 Entry Draft for Jimmy Carson, January 8, 1994. Traded to **Toronto** by **Los Angeles** with Guy Leveque, Kelly Fairchild and Shayne Toporowski for Eric Lacroix, Chris Snell and Toronto's fourth round choice in 1996 Entry draft, October 3, 1994.

WARD, ED CGY.

Right wing. Shoots right. 6'3", 205 lbs. Born, Edmonton, Alta., November 10, 1969.
(Quebec's 7th choice, 108th overall, in 1988 Entry Draft).

			Regular Season					Playoffs				
Season	Club	Lea	GP	G	A	TP	PIM	GP	G	A	TP	PIM
1987-88	N. Michigan	WCHA	25	0	2	2	40	....	....	....	....	....
1988-89	N. Michigan	WCHA	42	5	15	20	36	....	....	....	....	....
1989-90	N. Michigan	WCHA	39	5	11	16	77	....	....	....	....	....
1990-91	N. Michigan	WCHA	46	13	18	31	109	....	....	....	....	....
1991-92	Greensboro	ECHL	12	4	8	12	21	....	....	....	....	....
	Halifax	AHL	51	7	11	18	65	....	....	....	....	....
1992-93	Halifax	AHL	70	13	19	32	56	....	....	....	....	....
1993-94	**Quebec**	**NHL**	**7**	**1**	**0**	**1**	**5**	....	....	....	....	....
	Cornwall	AHL	60	12	30	42	65	12	1	3	4	14
1994-95	Cornwall	AHL	56	10	14	24	118	....	....	....	....	....
	Calgary	**NHL**	**2**	**1**	**1**	**2**	**2**	....	....	....	....	....
	Saint John	AHL	11	4	5	9	20	5	1	0	1	10
	NHL Totals		**9**	**2**	**1**	**3**	**7**	....	....	....	....	....

Traded to **Calgary** by **Quebec** for Francois Groleau, March 23, 1995.

WARE, JEFF (WAIR) TOR.

Defense. Shoots left. 6'4", 220 lbs. Born, Toronto, Ont., May 19, 1977.
(Toronto's 1st choice, 15th overall, in 1995 Entry Draft).

			Regular Season					Playoffs				
Season	Club	Lea	GP	G	A	TP	PIM	GP	G	A	TP	PIM
1993-94	Wexford	Jr. A	45	1	9	10	75	....	....	....	....	....
1994-95	Oshawa	OHL	55	2	11	13	86	7	1	1	2	6

WARE, MIKE (WAIR) TOR.

Left wing. Shoots left. 6'2", 193 lbs. Born, Toronto, Ont., February 27, 1974.

			Regular Season					Playoffs				
Season	Club	Lea	GP	G	A	TP	PIM	GP	G	A	TP	PIM
1994-95	Kingston	OHL	64	25	41	66	98	6	3	4	7	9
	St. John's	AHL	1	2	0	2	0	....	....	....	....	....

Signed as a free agent by **Toronto**, August 2, 1994.

WARRENER, RHETT FLA.

Defense. Shoots left. 6'1", 209 lbs. Born, Shaunavon, Sask., January 27, 1976.
(Florida's 2nd choice, 27th overall, in 1994 Entry Draft).

			Regular Season					Playoffs				
Season	Club	Lea	GP	G	A	TP	PIM	GP	G	A	TP	PIM
1991-92	Saskatoon	WHL	2	0	0	0	0	....	....	....	....	....
1992-93	Saskatoon	WHL	68	2	17	19	100	9	0	0	0	14
1993-94	Saskatoon	WHL	61	7	19	26	131	16	0	5	5	33
1994-95	Saskatoon	WHL	66	13	26	39	137	10	0	3	3	6

WARRINER, TODD TOR.

Left wing. Shoots left. 6'1", 188 lbs. Born, Blenheim, Ont., January 3, 1974.
(Quebec's 1st choice, 4th overall, in 1992 Entry Draft).

			Regular Season					Playoffs				
Season	Club	Lea	GP	G	A	TP	PIM	GP	G	A	TP	PIM
1990-91	Windsor	OHL	57	36	28	64	26	11	5	6	11	12
1991-92a	Windsor	OHL	50	41	41	82	64	7	5	4	9	6
1992-93	Windsor	OHL	23	13	21	34	29	....	....	....	....	....
	Kitchener	OHL	32	19	24	43	35	7	5	14	19	14
1993-94	Cdn. National	....	50	11	20	31	33	....	....	....	....	....
	Cdn. Olympic	....	4	1	1	2	0	....	....	....	....	....
	Kitchener	OHL	....	....	....	....	....	1	0	1	1	0
	Cornwall	AHL	....	....	....	....	....	10	1	4	5	4
1994-95	St. John's	AHL	46	8	10	18	22	4	1	0	1	2
	Toronto	**NHL**	**5**	**0**	**0**	**0**	**0**	....	....	....	....	....
	NHL Totals		**5**	**0**	**0**	**0**	**0**	....	....	....	....	....

a OHL First All-Star Team (1992)

Traded to **Toronto** by **Quebec** with Mats Sundin, Garth Butcher and Philadelphia's first round choice (previously acquired by Quebec — later traded to Washington — Washington selected Nolan Baumgartner) in 1994 Entry Draft for Wendel Clark, Sylvain Lefebvre, Landon Wilson and Toronto's first round choice (Jeffrey Kealty) in 1994 Entry Draft, June 28, 1994.

WASHBURN, STEVE — FLA.

Center. Shoots left. 6'2", 191 lbs. Born, Ottawa, Ont., April 10, 1975.
(Florida's 5th choice, 78th overall, in 1993 Entry Draft).

				Regular Season					Playoffs			
Season	Club	Lea	GP	G	A	TP	PIM	GP	G	A	TP	PIM
1991-92	Ottawa	OHL	59	5	17	22	10	11	2	3	5	4
1992-93	Ottawa	OHL	66	20	38	58	54	....	....	....	....	....
1993-94	Ottawa	OHL	65	30	50	80	88	17	7	16	23	10
1994-95	Ottawa	OHL	63	43	63	106	72	....	....	....	....	....
	Cincinnati	IHL	6	3	1	4	0	9	1	3	4	4

WASLEY, CHARLIE — COL.

Defense. Shoots left. 6'2", 173 lbs. Born, Minneapolis, MN, April 4, 1974.
(Quebec's 6th choice, 100th overall, in 1992 Entry Draft).

				Regular Season					Playoffs			
Season	Club	Lea	GP	G	A	TP	PIM	GP	G	A	TP	PIM
1992-93	U. Minnesota	WCHA	35	2	5	7	42	....	....	....	....	....
1993-94	U. Minnesota	WCHA	36	1	14	15	29	....	....	....	....	....
1994-95	U. Minnesota	WCHA	36	2	4	6	60	....	....	....	....	....

WATT, MIKE — EDM.

Left wing. Shoots left. 6'2", 210 lbs. Born, Seaforth, Ont., March 31, 1976.
(Edmonton's 3rd choice, 32nd overall, in 1994 Entry Draft).

				Regular Season					Playoffs			
Season	Club	Lea	GP	G	A	TP	PIM	GP	G	A	TP	PIM
1993-94	Stratford	Jr. B	48	34	34	68	165	....	....	....	....	....
1994-95	Michigan State	CCHA	39	12	6	18	64	....	....	....	....	....

WATTERS, TIM

Defense. Shoots left. 5'11", 185 lbs. Born, Kamloops, B.C., July 25, 1959.
(Winnipeg's 6th choice, 124th overall, in 1979 Entry Draft).

				Regular Season					Playoffs			
Season	Club	Lea	GP	G	A	TP	PIM	GP	G	A	TP	PIM
1978-79	Michigan Tech	WCHA	38	6	21	27	48	....	....	....	....	....
1979-80	Cdn. National	....	56	8	21	29	43	....	....	....	....	....
	Cdn. Olympic	....	6	1	1	2	0	....	....	....	....	....
1980-81ab	Michigan Tech	WCHA	43	12	38	50	36	....	....	....	....	....
1981-82	Tulsa	CHL	5	1	2	3	0	....	....	....	....	....
	Winnipeg	NHL	69	2	22	24	97	4	0	1	1	8
1982-83	Winnipeg	NHL	77	5	18	23	98	3	0	0	0	2
1983-84	Winnipeg	NHL	74	3	20	23	169	3	1	0	1	2
1984-85	Winnipeg	NHL	63	2	20	22	74	8	0	1	1	16
1985-86	Winnipeg	NHL	56	6	8	14	97	....	....	....	....	....
1986-87	Winnipeg	NHL	63	3	13	16	119	10	0	0	0	21
1987-88	Cdn. National	....	2	0	2	2	0	....	....	....	....	....
	Cdn. Olympic	....	8	0	1	1	2	....	....	....	....	....
	Winnipeg	NHL	36	0	0	0	106	4	0	0	0	4
1988-89	Los Angeles	NHL	76	3	18	21	168	11	0	1	1	6
1989-90	Los Angeles	NHL	62	1	10	11	92	4	0	0	0	6
1990-91	Los Angeles	NHL	45	0	4	4	92	7	0	0	0	12
1991-92	Los Angeles	NHL	37	0	7	7	92	6	0	0	0	8
	Phoenix	IHL	5	0	3	3	6	....	....	....	....	....
1992-93	Los Angeles	NHL	22	0	2	2	18	22	0	2	2	30
	Phoenix	IHL	31	3	3	6	43	....	....	....	....	....
1993-94	Los Angeles	NHL	60	1	9	10	67	....	....	....	....	....
1994-95	Los Angeles	NHL	1	0	0	0	0	....	....	....	....	....
	Phoenix	IHL	36	1	8	9	58	7	0	1	1	10
	NHL Totals		**741**	**26**	**151**	**177**	**1289**	**82**	**1**	**5**	**6**	**115**

a WCHA First All-Star Team (1981)
b Named to NCAA All-Tournament Team (1981)
Signed as a free agent by **Los Angeles**, June 27, 1988.

WEIGHT, DOUG — (WAYT) EDM.

Center. Shoots left. 5'11", 191 lbs. Born, Warren, MI, January 21, 1971.
(NY Rangers' 2nd choice, 34th overall, in 1990 Entry Draft).

				Regular Season					Playoffs			
Season	Club	Lea	GP	G	A	TP	PIM	GP	G	A	TP	PIM
1989-90	Lake Superior	CCHA	46	21	48	69	44	....	....	....	....	....
1990-91ab	Lake Superior	CCHA	42	29	46	75	86	....	....	....	....	....
	NY Rangers	NHL	....	....	....	....	....	1	0	0	0	0
1991-92	NY Rangers	NHL	53	8	22	30	23	7	2	2	4	0
	Binghamton	AHL	9	3	14	17	2	4	1	4	5	6
1992-93	NY Rangers	NHL	65	15	25	40	55	....	....	....	....	....
	Edmonton	NHL	13	2	6	8	10	....	....	....	....	....
1993-94	Edmonton	NHL	84	24	50	74	47	....	....	....	....	....
1994-95	Rosenheim	Ger.	8	2	3	5	18	....	....	....	....	....
	Edmonton	NHL	48	7	33	40	69	....	....	....	....	....
	NHL Totals		**263**	**56**	**136**	**192**	**204**	**8**	**2**	**2**	**4**	**0**

a CCHA First All-Star Team (1991)
b NCAA West Second All-American Team (1991)

Traded to **Edmonton** by **NY Rangers** for Esa Tikkanen, March 17, 1993.

WEINRICH, ERIC — (WIGHN-rihc) CHI.

Defense. Shoots left. 6'1", 210 lbs. Born, Roanoke, VA, December 19, 1966.
(New Jersey's 3rd choice, 32nd overall, in 1985 Entry Draft).

				Regular Season					Playoffs			
Season	Club	Lea	GP	G	A	TP	PIM	GP	G	A	TP	PIM
1985-86	U. of Maine	H.E.	34	0	15	15	26	....	....	....	....	....
1986-87ab	U. of Maine	H.E.	41	12	32	44	59	....	....	....	....	....
1987-88	U. of Maine	H.E.	8	4	7	11	22	....	....	....	....	....
	U.S. National	....	38	3	9	12	24	....	....	....	....	....
	U.S. Olympic	....	3	0	0	0	0	....	....	....	....	....
1988-89	New Jersey	NHL	2	0	0	0	0	....	....	....	....	....
	Utica	AHL	80	17	27	44	70	5	0	1	1	4
1989-90	New Jersey	NHL	19	2	7	9	11	6	1	3	4	17
cd	Utica	AHL	57	12	48	60	38	....	....	....	....	....
1990-91e	New Jersey	NHL	76	4	34	38	48	7	1	2	3	6
1991-92	New Jersey	NHL	76	7	25	32	55	7	0	2	2	4
1992-93	Hartford	NHL	79	7	29	36	76	....	....	....	....	....
1993-94	Hartford	NHL	8	1	1	2	2	....	....	....	....	....
	Chicago	NHL	54	3	23	26	31	6	0	2	2	6
1994-95	Chicago	NHL	48	3	10	13	33	16	1	5	6	4
	NHL Totals		**362**	**27**	**129**	**156**	**256**	**42**	**3**	**14**	**17**	**37**

a Hockey East First All-Star Team (1987)
b NCAA East Second All-American Team (1987)
c AHL First All-Star Team (1990)
d Won Eddie Shore Plaque (Outstanding Defenseman - AHL) (1990)
e NHL/Upper Deck All-Rookie Team (1991)
Traded to **Hartford** by **New Jersey** with Sean Burke for Bobby Holik, Hartford's second round choice (Jay Pandolfo) in 1993 Entry Draft and future considerations, August 28, 1992. Traded to **Chicago** by **Hartford** with Patrick Poulin for Steve Larmer and Bryan Marchment, November 2, 1993.

WELLS, CHRIS — PIT.

Center. Shoots left. 6'6", 215 lbs. Born, Calgary, Alta., November 12, 1975.
(Pittsburgh's 1st choice, 24th overall, in 1994 Entry Draft).

				Regular Season					Playoffs			
Season	Club	Lea	GP	G	A	TP	PIM	GP	G	A	TP	PIM
1991-92	Seattle	WHL	64	13	8	21	80	11	0	0	0	15
1992-93	Seattle	WHL	63	18	37	55	111	5	2	3	5	4
1993-94	Seattle	WHL	69	30	44	74	150	9	6	5	11	23
1994-95a	Seattle	WHL	69	45	63	108	148	3	0	1	1	4
	Cleveland	IHL	3	0	1	1	2	....	....	....	....	....

a WHL West First All-Star Team (1995)

WELLS, JAY — ST.L.

Defense. Shoots left. 6'1", 210 lbs. Born, Paris, Ont., May 18, 1959.
(Los Angeles' 1st choice, 16th overall, in 1979 Entry Draft).

				Regular Season					Playoffs			
Season	Club	Lea	GP	G	A	TP	PIM	GP	G	A	TP	PIM
1977-78	Kingston	OHA	68	9	13	22	195	5	1	2	3	6
1978-79a	Kingston	OHA	48	6	21	27	100	11	2	7	9	29
1979-80	Los Angeles	NHL	43	0	0	0	113	4	0	0	0	11
	Binghamton	AHL	28	0	6	6	48	....	....	....	....	....
1980-81	Los Angeles	NHL	72	5	13	18	155	4	0	0	0	27
1981-82	Los Angeles	NHL	60	1	8	9	145	10	1	3	4	41
1982-83	Los Angeles	NHL	69	3	12	15	167	....	....	....	....	....
1983-84	Los Angeles	NHL	69	3	18	21	141	....	....	....	....	....
1984-85	Los Angeles	NHL	77	2	9	11	185	3	0	1	1	0
1985-86	Los Angeles	NHL	79	11	31	42	226	....	....	....	....	....
1986-87	Los Angeles	NHL	77	7	29	36	155	5	1	2	3	10
1987-88	Los Angeles	NHL	58	2	23	25	159	5	1	2	3	21
1988-89	Philadelphia	NHL	67	2	19	21	184	18	0	2	2	51
1989-90	Philadelphia	NHL	59	3	16	19	129	....	....	....	....	....
	Buffalo	NHL	1	0	1	1	0	6	0	0	0	12
1990-91	Buffalo	NHL	43	1	2	3	86	1	0	1	1	0
1991-92	Buffalo	NHL	41	2	9	11	157	....	....	....	....	....
	NY Rangers	NHL	11	0	0	0	24	13	0	2	2	10
1992-93	NY Rangers	NHL	53	1	9	10	107	....	....	....	....	....
1993-94	NY Rangers	NHL	79	2	7	9	110	23	0	0	0	20
1994-95	NY Rangers	NHL	43	2	7	9	36	10	0	0	0	8
	NHL Totals		**1001**	**47**	**213**	**260**	**2279**	**102**	**3**	**13**	**16**	**211**

a OHA First All-Star Team (1979)

Traded to **Philadelphia** by **Los Angeles** for Doug Crossman, September 29, 1988. Traded to **Buffalo** by **Philadelphia** with Philadelphia's fourth round choice (Peter Ambroziak) in 1991 Entry Draft for Kevin Maguire and Buffalo's second round choice (Mikael Renberg) in 1990 Entry Draft, March 5, 1990. Traded to **NY Rangers** by **Buffalo** for Randy Moller, March 9, 1992. Traded to **St. Louis** by **NY Rangers** for Doug Lidster, July 28, 1995.

WELSING, MARK (ROCKY) — ANA.

Defense. Shoots left. 6'3", 196 lbs. Born, Beloit, WI, February 8, 1976.
(Anaheim's 7th choice, 158th overall, in 1994 Entry Draft).

				Regular Season					Playoffs			
Season	Club	Lea	GP	G	A	TP	PIM	GP	G	A	TP	PIM
1993-94	Wisconsin	USHL	40	5	21	26	262	....	....	....	....	....
1994-95	N. Michigan	WCHA	38	0	8	8	129	....	....	....	....	....

WERENKA, BRAD — (wuh-REHN-kuh) CHI.

Defense. Shoots left. 6'2", 210 lbs. Born, Two Hills, Alta., February 12, 1969.
(Edmonton's 2nd choice, 42nd overall, in 1987 Entry Draft).

				Regular Season					Playoffs			
Season	Club	Lea	GP	G	A	TP	PIM	GP	G	A	TP	PIM
1986-87	N. Michigan	WCHA	30	4	4	8	35	....	....	....	....	....
1987-88	N. Michigan	WCHA	34	7	23	30	26	....	....	....	....	....
1988-89	N. Michigan	WCHA	28	7	13	20	16	....	....	....	....	....
1989-90	N. Michigan	WCHA	8	2	5	7	8	....	....	....	....	....
1990-91abc	N. Michigan	WCHA	47	20	43	63	36	....	....	....	....	....
1991-92	Cape Breton	AHL	66	6	21	27	95	5	0	3	3	6
1992-93	Edmonton	NHL	27	5	3	8	24	....	....	....	....	....
	Cdn. National	....	18	3	7	10	10	....	....	....	....	....
	Cape Breton	AHL	4	1	1	2	4	16	4	17	21	12
1993-94	Edmonton	NHL	15	0	4	4	14	....	....	....	....	....
	Cape Breton	AHL	25	6	17	23	19	....	....	....	....	....
	Cdn. Olympic	....	8	2	2	4	8	....	....	....	....	....
	Quebec	NHL	11	0	7	7	8	....	....	....	....	....
	Cornwall	AHL	....	....	....	....	....	12	2	10	12	22
1994-95	Milwaukee	IHL	80	8	45	53	161	15	3	10	13	36
	NHL Totals		**53**	**5**	**14**	**19**	**46**	....	....	....	....	....

a WCHA First All-Star Team (1991)
b NCAA West First All-American Team (1991)
c NCAA Final Four All-Tournament Team (1991)
Traded to **Quebec** by **Edmonton** for Steve Passmore, March 21, 1994. Signed as a free agent by **Chicago**, August 7, 1995.

WERENKA, DARCY (wuh-REHN-kah) NYR

Defense. Shoots right. 6'1", 205 lbs. Born, Edmonton, Alta., May 13, 1973.
(NY Rangers' 2nd choice, 37th overall, in 1991 Entry Draft).

			Regular Season					Playoffs				
Season	Club	Lea	GP	G	A	TP	PIM	GP	G	A	TP	PIM
1990-91	Lethbridge	WHL	72	13	37	50	39	16	1	7	8	4
1991-92	Lethbridge	WHL	69	17	58	75	56	5	2	1	3	0
1992-93	Lethbridge	WHL	19	4	17	21	12	....	....	....	....	....
	Brandon	WHL	36	4	25	29	19	3	0	0	0	2
	Binghamton	AHL	3	0	1	1	2	3	0	0	0	0
1993-94	Binghamton	AHL	53	5	22	27	10	....	....	....	....	....
1994-95	Binghamton	AHL	73	17	29	46	12	11	4	3	7	2

WERNBLOM, MAGNUS L.A.

Right wing. Shoots left. 6', 187 lbs. Born, Kramfors, Sweden, February 3, 1973.
(Los Angeles' 6th choice, 207th overall, in 1992 Entry Draft).

			Regular Season					Playoffs				
Season	Club	Lea	GP	G	A	TP	PIM	GP	G	A	TP	PIM
1990-91	MoDo	Swe.	16	4	2	6	8	....	....	....	....	....
1991-92	MoDo	Swe.	35	7	6	13	50	....	....	....	....	....
1992-93	MoDo	Swe.	37	8	3	11	36	3	0	0	0	0
1993-94	MoDo	Swe.	39	14	9	23	46	11	2	3	5	12
1994-95	MoDo	Swe.	38	12	10	22	50	....	....	....	....	....

WESENBERG, BRIAN ANA.

Right wing. Shoots right. 6'3", 173 lbs. Born, Peterborough, Ont., May 9, 1977.
(Anaheim's 2nd choice, 29th overall, in 1995 Entry Draft).

			Regular Season					Playoffs				
Season	Club	Lea	GP	G	A	TP	PIM	GP	G	A	TP	PIM
1993-94	Cobourg	Jr. A	40	14	18	32	81	....	....	....	....	....
1994-95	Guelph	OHL	66	17	27	44	81	14	2	3	5	18

WESLEY, GLEN HFD.

Defense. Shoots left. 6'1", 195 lbs. Born, Red Deer, Alta., October 2, 1968.
(Boston's 1st choice, 3rd overall, in 1987 Entry Draft).

			Regular Season					Playoffs				
Season	Club	Lea	GP	G	A	TP	PIM	GP	G	A	TP	PIM
1983-84	Portland	WHL	3	1	2	3	0	....	....	....	....	....
1984-85	Portland	WHL	67	16	52	68	76	6	1	6	7	8
1985-86a	Portland	WHL	69	16	75	91	96	15	3	11	14	29
1986-87a	Portland	WHL	63	16	46	62	72	20	8	18	26	27
1987-88b	**Boston**	**NHL**	**79**	**7**	**30**	**37**	**69**	**23**	**6**	**8**	**14**	**22**
1988-89	**Boston**	**NHL**	**77**	**19**	**35**	**54**	**61**	**10**	**0**	**2**	**2**	**4**
1989-90	**Boston**	**NHL**	**78**	**9**	**27**	**36**	**48**	**21**	**2**	**6**	**8**	**36**
1990-91	**Boston**	**NHL**	**80**	**11**	**32**	**43**	**78**	**19**	**2**	**9**	**11**	**19**
1991-92	**Boston**	**NHL**	**78**	**9**	**37**	**46**	**54**	**15**	**2**	**4**	**6**	**16**
1992-93	**Boston**	**NHL**	**64**	**8**	**25**	**33**	**47**	**4**	**0**	**0**	**0**	**0**
1993-94	**Boston**	**NHL**	**81**	**14**	**44**	**58**	**64**	**13**	**3**	**3**	**6**	**12**
1994-95	**Hartford**	**NHL**	**48**	**2**	**14**	**16**	**50**	....	....	....	....	....
	NHL Totals		**585**	**79**	**244**	**323**	**471**	**105**	**15**	**32**	**47**	**109**

a WHL West All-Star Team (1986, 1987)
b NHL All-Rookie Team (1988)

Played in NHL All-Star Game (1989)

Traded to **Hartford** by **Boston** for Hartford's first round choices in 1995 (Kyle McLaren), 1996 and 1997 Entry Draft, August 26, 1994.

WESTERBY, BOB BUF.

Left wing. Shoots left. 6'1", 195 lbs. Born, Kelowna, B.C., October 29, 1975.
(Buffalo's 9th choice, 199th overall, in 1994 Entry Draft).

			Regular Season					Playoffs				
Season	Club	Lea	GP	G	A	TP	PIM	GP	G	A	TP	PIM
1992-93	Kamloops	WHL	45	3	6	9	192	....	....	....	....	....
1993-94	Kamloops	WHL	50	6	9	15	218	19	1	4	5	64
1994-95	Kamloops	WHL	13	0	3	3	67	17	0	2	2	41

WHITE, KAM TOR.

Defense. Shoots left. 6'3", 211 lbs. Born, Chicago, IL, February 13, 1976.
(Toronto's 5th choice, 152nd overall, in 1994 Entry Draft).

			Regular Season					Playoffs				
Season	Club	Lea	GP	G	A	TP	PIM	GP	G	A	TP	PIM
1992-93	Newmarket	OHL	8	0	0	0	8	....	....	....	....	....
1993-94	Newmarket	OHL	44	0	5	5	125	....	....	....	....	....
1994-95	Sarnia	OHL	31	0	4	4	77	....	....	....	....	....
	North Bay	OHL	20	1	1	2	84	6	0	1	1	10

WHITE, PETER EDM.

Center. Shoots left. 5'11", 200 lbs. Born, Montreal, Que., March 15, 1969.
(Edmonton's 4th choice, 92nd overall, in 1989 Entry Draft).

			Regular Season					Playoffs				
Season	Club	Lea	GP	G	A	TP	PIM	GP	G	A	TP	PIM
1988-89	Michigan State	CCHA	46	20	33	53	17	....	....	....	....	....
1989-90	Michigan State	CCHA	45	22	40	62	6	....	....	....	....	....
1990-91	Michigan State	CCHA	37	7	31	38	28	....	....	....	....	....
1991-92	Michigan State	CCHA	41	26	49	75	32	....	....	....	....	....
1992-93	Cape Breton	AHL	64	12	28	40	10	16	3	3	6	12
1993-94	**Edmonton**	**NHL**	**26**	**3**	**5**	**8**	**2**	....	....	....	....	....
	Cape Breton	AHL	45	21	49	70	12	5	2	3	5	2
1994-95ab	Cape Breton	AHL	65	36	*69	*105	30	....	....	....	....	....
	Edmonton	**NHL**	**9**	**2**	**4**	**6**	**0**	....	....	....	....	....
	NHL Totals		**35**	**5**	**9**	**14**	**2**	....	....	....	....	....

a AHL Second All-Star Team (1995)
b Won John B. Sollenberger Trophy (Top Scorer - AHL) (1995)

WHITE, TOM CHI.

Center. Shoots left. 6'1", 185 lbs. Born, Chicago, IL, August 25, 1975.

			Regular Season					Playoffs				
Season	Club	Lea	GP	G	A	TP	PIM	GP	G	A	TP	PIM
1993-94	Miami-Ohio	CCHA	31	1	6	7	26	....	....	....	....	....
1994-95	Miami-Ohio	CCHA	35	2	5	7	24	....	....	....	....	....

WHITNEY, RAY S.J.

Center. Shoots right. 5'9", 160 lbs. Born, Fort Saskatchewan, Alta., May 8, 1972.
(San Jose's 2nd choice, 23rd overall, in 1991 Entry Draft).

			Regular Season					Playoffs				
Season	Club	Lea	GP	G	A	TP	PIM	GP	G	A	TP	PIM
1988-89	Spokane	WHL	71	17	33	50	16	....	....	....	....	....
1989-90	Spokane	WHL	71	57	56	113	50	6	3	4	7	6
1990-91abc	Spokane	WHL	72	67	118	*185	36	15	13	18	*31	12
1991-92	Koln	Ger.	10	3	6	9	4	....	....	....	....	....
	Cdn. National	....	5	1	0	1	6	....	....	....	....	....
	San Diego	IHL	63	36	54	90	12	4	0	0	0	0
	San Jose	**NHL**	**2**	**0**	**3**	**3**	**0**	....	....	....	....	....
1992-93	**San Jose**	**NHL**	**26**	**4**	**6**	**10**	**4**	....	....	....	....	....
	Kansas City	IHL	46	20	33	53	14	12	5	7	12	2
1993-94	**San Jose**	**NHL**	**61**	**14**	**26**	**40**	**14**	**14**	**0**	**4**	**4**	**8**
1994-95	**San Jose**	**NHL**	**39**	**13**	**12**	**25**	**14**	**11**	**4**	**4**	**8**	**2**
	NHL Totals		**128**	**31**	**47**	**78**	**32**	**25**	**4**	**8**	**12**	**10**

a WHL West First All-Star Team (1991)
b Memorial Cup All-Star Team (1991)
c Won George Parsons Trophy (Memorial Cup Tournament Most Sportsmanlike Player) (1991)

WIDMER, JASON NYI

Defense. Shoots left. 6', 205 lbs. Born, Calgary, Alta., August 1, 1973.
(NY Islanders' 8th choice, 176th overall, in 1992 Entry Draft).

			Regular Season					Playoffs				
Season	Club	Lea	GP	G	A	TP	PIM	GP	G	A	TP	PIM
1990-91	Lethbridge	WHL	58	2	12	14	55	16	0	1	1	12
1991-92	Lethbridge	WHL	40	2	19	21	181	5	0	4	4	9
1992-93	Lethbridge	WHL	55	3	15	18	140	4	0	3	3	2
	Capital Dist.	AHL	4	0	0	0	2	....	....	....	....	....
1993-94	Lethbridge	WHL	64	11	31	42	191	9	3	5	8	34
1994-95	Worcester	AHL	73	8	26	34	136	....	....	....	....	....
	Cdn. National		6	1	4	5	4	....	....	....	....	....
	NY Islanders	**NHL**	**1**	**0**	**0**	**0**	**0**	....	....	....	....	....
	NHL Totals		**1**	**0**	**0**	**0**	**0**	....	....	....	....	....

WIEMER, JASON (WEE-muhr) T.B.

Center. Shoots left. 6'1", 215 lbs. Born, Kimberley, B.C., April 14, 1976.
(Tampa Bay's 1st choice, 8th overall, in 1994 Entry Draft).

			Regular Season					Playoffs				
Season	Club	Lea	GP	G	A	TP	PIM	GP	G	A	TP	PIM
1991-92	Portland	WHL	2	0	1	1	0	....	....	....	....	....
1992-93	Portland	WHL	68	18	34	52	159	16	7	3	10	27
1993-94	Portland	WHL	72	45	51	96	236	10	4	4	8	32
1994-95	Portland	WHL	16	10	14	24	63	....	....	....	....	....
	Tampa Bay	**NHL**	**36**	**1**	**4**	**5**	**44**	....	....	....	....	....
	NHL Totals		**36**	**1**	**4**	**5**	**44**	....	....	....	....	....

WIEMER, JIM (WEE-muhr)

Defense. Shoots left. 6'4", 216 lbs. Born, Sudbury, Ont., January 9, 1961.
(Buffalo's 5th choice, 83rd overall, in 1980 Entry Draft).

			Regular Season					Playoffs				
Season	Club	Lea	GP	G	A	TP	PIM	GP	G	A	TP	PIM
1978-79	Peterborough	OHA	61	15	12	27	50	18	4	4	8	15
1979-80	Peterborough	OHA	53	17	32	49	63	14	6	9	15	19
1980-81	Peterborough	OHA	65	41	54	95	102	5	1	2	3	15
1981-82	Rochester	AHL	74	19	26	45	57	9	0	4	4	2
1982-83	Rochester	AHL	74	15	44	59	43	15	5	15	20	22
	Buffalo	**NHL**	....	....	....	....	....	**1**	**0**	**0**	**0**	**0**
1983-84	**Buffalo**	**NHL**	**64**	**5**	**15**	**20**	**48**	....	....	....	....	....
	Rochester	AHL	12	4	11	15	11	18	3	13	16	20
1984-85	**Buffalo**	**NHL**	**10**	**3**	**2**	**5**	**4**	....	....	....	....	....
	Rochester	AHL	13	1	9	10	24	....	....	....	....	....
	NY Rangers	**NHL**	**22**	**4**	**3**	**7**	**30**	**1**	**0**	**0**	**0**	**0**
	New Haven	AHL	33	9	27	36	39	....	....	....	....	....
1985-86	**NY Rangers**	**NHL**	**7**	**3**	**0**	**3**	**2**	**8**	**1**	**0**	**1**	**6**
ab	New Haven	AHL	73	24	49	73	108	....	....	....	....	....
1986-87	New Haven	AHL	6	0	7	7	6	....	....	....	....	....
	Nova Scotia	AHL	59	9	25	34	72	5	0	4	4	2
1987-88	**Edmonton**	**NHL**	**12**	**1**	**2**	**3**	**15**	**2**	**0**	**0**	**0**	**2**
	Nova Scotia	AHL	57	11	32	43	99	5	1	1	2	14
1988-89	Cape Breton	AHL	51	12	29	41	80	....	....	....	....	....
	Los Angeles	**NHL**	**9**	**2**	**3**	**5**	**20**	**10**	**2**	**1**	**3**	**19**
	New Haven	AHL	3	1	1	2	2	7	2	3	5	2
1989-90	**Boston**	**NHL**	**61**	**5**	**14**	**19**	**63**	**8**	**0**	**1**	**1**	**4**
	Maine	AHL	6	3	4	7	27	....	....	....	....	....
1990-91	**Boston**	**NHL**	**61**	**4**	**19**	**23**	**62**	**16**	**1**	**3**	**4**	**14**
1991-92	**Boston**	**NHL**	**47**	**1**	**8**	**9**	**84**	**15**	**1**	**3**	**4**	**14**
	Maine	AHL	3	0	1	1	4	....	....	....	....	....
1992-93	**Boston**	**NHL**	**28**	**1**	**6**	**7**	**48**	**1**	**0**	**0**	**0**	**4**
	Providence	AHL	4	2	1	3	2	....	....	....	....	....
1993-94	**Boston**	**NHL**	**4**	**0**	**0**	**0**	**2**	....	....	....	....	....
	Providence	AHL	35	5	12	17	81	....	....	....	....	....
1994-95	Rochester	AHL	45	9	29	38	74	5	0	2	2	6
	NHL Totals		**325**	**29**	**72**	**101**	**378**	**62**	**5**	**8**	**13**	**63**

a AHL First All-Star Team (1986)
b Won Eddie Shore Plaque (Outstanding Defenseman - AHL) (1986)

Traded to **NY Rangers** by **Buffalo** with Steve Patrick for Dave Maloney and Chris Renaud, December 6, 1984. Traded to **Edmonton** by **NY Rangers** with Reijo Ruotsalainen, Clark Donatelli and Ville Kentala for Don Jackson, Mike Golden, Miloslav Horvava and future considerations, October 23, 1986. Traded to **Los Angeles** by **Edmonton** with Alan May for Brian Wilks and John English, March 7, 1989. Signed as a free agent by **Boston**, July 6, 1989.

WIESEL, ADAM MTL.

Defense. Shoots right. 6'3", 210 lbs. Born, Holyoke, MA, January 25, 1975.
(Montreal's 4th choice, 85th overall, in 1993 Entry Draft).

			Regular Season					Playoffs				
Season	Club	Lea	GP	G	A	TP	PIM	GP	G	A	TP	PIM
1993-94	Clarkson	ECAC	33	3	7	10	26	....	....	....	....	....
1994-95	Clarkson	ECAC	36	6	13	19	28	....	....	....	....	....

WILCHYNSKI, CHAD DET.

Defense. Shoots left. 6'3", 179 lbs. Born, Regina, Sask., April 4, 1977.
(Detroit's 5th choice, 125th overall, in 1995 Entry Draft).

			Regular Season					Playoffs				
Season	Club	Lea	GP	G	A	TP	PIM	GP	G	A	TP	PIM
1993-94	Regina	Midget	36	7	27	34	115	....	....	....	....	....
1994-95	Regina	WHL	70	7	15	22	96	4	0	1	1	4

WILFORD, MARTY — CHI.

Defense. Shoots left. 6', 216 lbs. Born, Cobourg, Ont., April 17, 1977.
(Chicago's 7th choice, 149th overall, in 1995 Entry Draft).

			Regular Season					Playoffs				
Season	**Club**	**Lea**	**GP**	**G**	**A**	**TP**	**PIM**	**GP**	**G**	**A**	**TP**	**PIM**
1993-94	Peterborough	Jr. A	40	3	19	22	107	....	....	....	....	....
1994-95	Oshawa	OHL	63	1	6	7	95	7	1	1	2	4

WILKIE, BOB

Defense. Shoots right. 6'2", 215 lbs. Born, Calgary, Alta., February 11, 1969.
(Detroit's 3rd choice, 41st overall, in 1987 Entry Draft).

			Regular Season					Playoffs				
Season	**Club**	**Lea**	**GP**	**G**	**A**	**TP**	**PIM**	**GP**	**G**	**A**	**TP**	**PIM**
1985-86	Calgary	WHL	63	8	19	27	56	....	....	....	....	....
1986-87	Swift Current	WHL	65	12	38	50	50	4	1	3	4	2
1987-88	Swift Current	WHL	67	12	68	80	124	10	4	12	16	8
1988-89	Swift Current	WHL	62	18	67	85	89	12	1	11	12	47
1989-90	Adirondack	AHL	58	5	33	38	64	6	1	4	5	2
1990-91	**Detroit**	**NHL**	**8**	**1**	**2**	**3**	**2**	....	....	....	....	....
	Adirondack	AHL	43	6	18	24	71	2	1	0	1	2
1991-92	Adirondack	AHL	7	1	4	5	6	16	2	5	7	12
1992-93	Adirondack	AHL	14	0	5	5	20	....	....	....	....	....
	Fort Wayne	IHL	32	7	14	21	82	12	4	6	10	10
	Hershey	AHL	28	7	25	32	18	....	....	....	....	....
1993-94	**Philadelphia**	**NHL**	**10**	**1**	**3**	**4**	**8**	....	....	....	....	....
a	Hershey	AHL	69	8	53	61	100	9	1	4	5	8
1994-95	Hershey	AHL	50	9	30	39	46	....	....	....	....	....
	Indianapolis	IHL	29	5	22	27	30	....	....	....	....	....
	NHL Totals		**18**	**2**	**5**	**7**	**10**	....	....	....	....	....

a AHL Second All-Star Team (1994)

Traded to **Philadelphia** by **Detroit** for future considerations, February 2, 1993. Traded to **Chicago** by **Philadelphia** with a possible conditional choice in 1997 Entry Draft for Karl Dykhuis, February 16, 1995.

WILKIE, DAVID — MTL.

Defense. Shoots right. 6'2", 210 lbs. Born, Ellensburgh, WA, May 30, 1974.
(Montreal's 1st choice, 20th overall, in 1992 Entry Draft).

			Regular Season					Playoffs				
Season	**Club**	**Lea**	**GP**	**G**	**A**	**TP**	**PIM**	**GP**	**G**	**A**	**TP**	**PIM**
1990-91	Seattle	WHL	25	1	1	2	22	....	....	....	....	....
1991-92	Kamloops	WHL	71	12	28	40	153	16	6	5	11	19
1992-93	Kamloops	WHL	53	11	26	37	109	6	4	2	6	2
1993-94	Kamloops	WHL	27	11	18	29	18	....	....	....	....	....
	Regina	WHL	29	27	21	48	16	4	1	4	5	4
1994-95	Fredericton	AHL	70	10	43	53	34	1	0	0	0	0
	Montreal	**NHL**	**1**	**0**	**0**	**0**	**0**	....	....	....	....	....
	NHL Totals		**1**	**0**	**0**	**0**	**0**	....	....	....	....	....

WILKINSON, NEIL — WPG.

Defense. Shoots right. 6'3", 190 lbs. Born, Selkirk, Man., August 15, 1967.
(Minnesota's 2nd choice, 30th overall, in 1986 Entry Draft).

			Regular Season					Playoffs				
Season	**Club**	**Lea**	**GP**	**G**	**A**	**TP**	**PIM**	**GP**	**G**	**A**	**TP**	**PIM**
1986-87	Michigan State	CCHA	19	3	4	7	18	....	....	....	....	....
1987-88	Medicine Hat	WHL	55	11	21	32	157	5	1	0	1	2
1988-89	Kalamazoo	IHL	39	5	15	20	96	....	....	....	....	....
1989-90	**Minnesota**	**NHL**	**36**	**0**	**5**	**5**	**100**	**7**	**0**	**2**	**2**	**11**
	Kalamazoo	IHL	20	6	7	13	62	....	....	....	....	....
1990-91	**Minnesota**	**NHL**	**50**	**2**	**9**	**11**	**117**	**22**	**3**	**3**	**6**	**12**
	Kalamazoo	IHL	10	0	3	3	38	....	....	....	....	....
1991-92	**San Jose**	**NHL**	**60**	**4**	**15**	**19**	**107**	....	....	....	....	....
1992-93	**San Jose**	**NHL**	**59**	**1**	**7**	**8**	**96**	....	....	....	....	....
1993-94	**Chicago**	**NHL**	**72**	**3**	**9**	**12**	**116**	**4**	**0**	**0**	**0**	**0**
1994-95	**Winnipeg**	**NHL**	**40**	**1**	**4**	**5**	**75**	....	....	....	....	....
	NHL Totals		**317**	**11**	**49**	**60**	**611**	**33**	**3**	**5**	**8**	**23**

Claimed by **San Jose** from **Minnesota** in Dispersal Draft, May 30, 1991. Traded to **Chicago** by **San Jose** as future considerations to complete June 18, 1993 trade for Jimmy Waite, July 9, 1993. Traded to **Winnipeg** by **Chicago** for Chicago's third round choice (previously acquired by Winnipeg) in 1995 Entry Draft, June 3, 1994.

WILLIAMS, DAVID

Defense. Shoots right. 6'2", 195 lbs. Born, Plainfield, NJ, August 25, 1967.
(New Jersey's 12th choice, 234th overall, in 1985 Entry Draft).

			Regular Season					Playoffs				
Season	**Club**	**Lea**	**GP**	**G**	**A**	**TP**	**PIM**	**GP**	**G**	**A**	**TP**	**PIM**
1986-87	Dartmouth	ECAC	23	2	19	21	20	....	....	....	....	....
1987-88	Dartmouth	ECAC	25	8	14	22	30	....	....	....	....	....
1988-89ab	Dartmouth	ECAC	25	4	11	15	28	....	....	....	....	....
1989-90	Dartmouth	ECAC	26	3	12	15	32	....	....	....	....	....
1990-91	Muskegon	IHL	14	1	2	3	4	....	....	....	....	....
	Knoxville	ECHL	38	12	15	27	40	3	0	0	0	4
1991-92	**San Jose**	**NHL**	**56**	**3**	**25**	**28**	**40**	....	....	....	....	....
	Kansas City	IHL	18	2	3	5	22	....	....	....	....	....
1992-93	**San Jose**	**NHL**	**40**	**1**	**11**	**12**	**49**	....	....	....	....	....
	Kansas City	IHL	31	1	11	12	28	....	....	....	....	....
1993-94	**Anaheim**	**NHL**	**56**	**5**	**15**	**20**	**42**	....	....	....	....	....
	San Diego	IHL	16	1	6	7	17	....	....	....	....	....
1994-95	**Anaheim**	**NHL**	**21**	**2**	**2**	**4**	**26**	....	....	....	....	....
	San Diego	IHL	2	0	1	1	0	5	1	0	1	0
	NHL Totals		**173**	**11**	**53**	**64**	**157**	....	....	....	....	....

a ECAC First All-Star Team (1989)
b NCAA East Second All-American Team (1989)

Signed as a free agent by **San Jose**, August 9, 1991. Claimed by **Anaheim** from **San Jose** in Expansion Draft, June 24, 1993.

WILLIAMS, JEFF — N.J.

Center. Shoots left. 6', 175 lbs. Born, Pointe-Claire, Que., February 11, 1976.
(New Jersey's 8th choice, 181st overall, in 1994 Entry Draft).

			Regular Season					Playoffs				
Season	**Club**	**Lea**	**GP**	**G**	**A**	**TP**	**PIM**	**GP**	**G**	**A**	**TP**	**PIM**
1993-94	Guelph	OHL	62	14	12	26	19	9	2	1	3	4
1994-95	Guelph	OHL	52	15	32	47	21	14	5	5	10	0

WILLIS, RICK — NYR

Left wing. Shoots left. 6', 190 lbs. Born, Lynn, MA, January 12, 1972.
(NY Rangers' 5th choice, 76th overall, in 1990 Entry Draft).

			Regular Season					Playoffs				
Season	**Club**	**Lea**	**GP**	**G**	**A**	**TP**	**PIM**	**GP**	**G**	**A**	**TP**	**PIM**
1991-92	U. of Michigan	CCHA	32	1	4	5	42	....	....	....	....	....
1992-93	U. of Michigan	CCHA	39	3	8	11	67	....	....	....	....	....
1993-94	U. of Michigan	CCHA	40	8	5	13	83	....	....	....	....	....
1994-95	U. of Michigan	CCHA	35	3	6	9	78	....	....	....	....	....

WILLIS, SHANE — T.B.

Right wing. Shoots right. 6', 170 lbs. Born, Edmonton, Alta., June 13, 1977.
(Tampa Bay's 3rd choice, 56th overall, in 1995 Entry Draft).

			Regular Season					Playoffs				
Season	**Club**	**Lea**	**GP**	**G**	**A**	**TP**	**PIM**	**GP**	**G**	**A**	**TP**	**PIM**
1993-94	Red Deer	Midget	34	40	26	66	103	....	....	....	....	....
1994-95	Prince Albert	WHL	65	24	19	43	38	13	3	4	7	6

WILM, CLARKE — CGY.

Center. Shoots left. 6', 202 lbs. Born, Central Butte, Sask., October 24, 1976.
(Calgary's 5th choice, 150th overall, in 1995 Entry Draft).

			Regular Season					Playoffs				
Season	**Club**	**Lea**	**GP**	**G**	**A**	**TP**	**PIM**	**GP**	**G**	**A**	**TP**	**PIM**
1992-93	Saskatoon	WHL	69	14	19	33	71	9	4	2	6	13
1993-94	Saskatoon	WHL	70	18	32	50	181	16	0	9	9	19
1994-95	Saskatoon	WHL	71	20	39	59	179	10	6	1	7	21

WILSON, LANDON — COL.

Right wing. Shoots right. 6'2", 202 lbs. Born, St. Louis, MO, March 13, 1975.
(Toronto's 2nd choice, 19th overall, in 1993 Entry Draft).

			Regular Season					Playoffs				
Season	**Club**	**Lea**	**GP**	**G**	**A**	**TP**	**PIM**	**GP**	**G**	**A**	**TP**	**PIM**
1993-94	North Dakota	WCHA	35	18	15	33	*147	....	....	....	....	....
1994-95	North Dakota	WCHA	31	7	16	23	141	....	....	....	....	....
	Cornwall	AHL	8	4	4	8	25	13	3	4	7	68

Traded to **Quebec** by **Toronto** with Wendel Clark, Sylvain Lefebvre and Toronto's first round choice (Jeffrey Kealty) in 1994 Entry Draft for Mats Sundin, Garth Butcher, Todd Warriner and Philadelphia's first round choice (previously acquired by Quebec — later traded to Washington — Washington selected Nolan Baumgartner) in 1994 Entry Draft, June 28, 1994.

WILSON, MIKE — BUF.

Defense. Shoots left. 6'4", 195 lbs. Born, Brampton, Ont., February 26, 1975.
(Vancouver's 1st choice, 20th overall, in 1993 Entry Draft).

			Regular Season					Playoffs				
Season	**Club**	**Lea**	**GP**	**G**	**A**	**TP**	**PIM**	**GP**	**G**	**A**	**TP**	**PIM**
1992-93	Sudbury	OHL	53	6	7	13	58	14	1	1	2	2
1993-94	Sudbury	OHL	60	4	22	26	62	9	1	3	4	8
1994-95	Sudbury	OHL	64	13	34	47	46	18	1	8	9	10

Traded to **Buffalo** by **Vancouver** with Mike Peca and Vancouver's first round choice (Jay McKee) in 1995 Entry Draft for Alexander Mogilny and Buffalo's fifth round choice (Todd Norman) in 1995 Entry Draft, July 8, 1995.

WILSON, RON

Center. Shoots left. 5'9", 180 lbs. Born, Toronto, Ont., May 13, 1956.
(Montreal's 15th choice, 133rd overall, in 1976 Amateur Draft).

			Regular Season					Playoffs				
Season	**Club**	**Lea**	**GP**	**G**	**A**	**TP**	**PIM**	**GP**	**G**	**A**	**TP**	**PIM**
1974-75	Toronto	OMJHL	16	6	12	18	6	23	9	17	26	6
1975-76	St. Catharines	OHA	64	37	62	99	44	4	1	6	7	7
1976-77	Nova Scotia	AHL	67	15	21	36	18	6	0	0	0	0
1977-78	Nova Scotia	AHL	59	15	25	40	17	11	4	4	8	9
1978-79	Nova Scotia	AHL	77	33	42	75	91	10	5	6	11	14
1979-80	**Winnipeg**	**NHL**	**79**	**21**	**36**	**57**	**28**	....	....	....	....	....
1980-81	**Winnipeg**	**NHL**	**77**	**18**	**33**	**51**	**55**	....	....	....	....	....
1981-82	**Winnipeg**	**NHL**	**39**	**3**	**13**	**16**	**49**	....	....	....	....	....
	Tulsa	CHL	41	20	38	58	22	3	1	0	1	2
1982-83	**Winnipeg**	**NHL**	**12**	**6**	**3**	**9**	**4**	**3**	**2**	**2**	**4**	**2**
	Sherbrooke	AHL	65	30	55	85	71	....	....	....	....	....
1983-84	**Winnipeg**	**NHL**	**51**	**3**	**12**	**15**	**12**	....	....	....	....	....
	Sherbrooke	AHL	22	10	30	40	16	....	....	....	....	....
1984-85	**Winnipeg**	**NHL**	**75**	**10**	**9**	**19**	**31**	**8**	**4**	**2**	**6**	**2**
1985-86	**Winnipeg**	**NHL**	**54**	**6**	**7**	**13**	**16**	**1**	**0**	**0**	**0**	**0**
	Sherbrooke	AHL	10	9	8	17	9	....	....	....	....	....
1986-87	**Winnipeg**	**NHL**	**80**	**3**	**13**	**16**	**13**	**10**	**1**	**2**	**3**	**0**
1987-88	**Winnipeg**	**NHL**	**69**	**5**	**8**	**13**	**28**	**1**	**0**	**0**	**0**	**2**
1988-89a	Moncton	AHL	80	31	61	92	110	8	1	4	5	20
1989-90	Moncton	AHL	47	16	37	53	39	....	....	....	....	....
	St. Louis	**NHL**	**33**	**3**	**17**	**20**	**23**	**12**	**3**	**5**	**8**	**18**
1990-91	**St. Louis**	**NHL**	**73**	**10**	**27**	**37**	**54**	**7**	**0**	**0**	**0**	**28**
1991-92	**St. Louis**	**NHL**	**64**	**12**	**17**	**29**	**46**	**6**	**0**	**1**	**1**	**0**
1992-93	**St. Louis**	**NHL**	**78**	**8**	**11**	**19**	**44**	**11**	**0**	**0**	**0**	**12**
1993-94	**Montreal**	**NHL**	**48**	**2**	**10**	**12**	**12**	**4**	**0**	**0**	**0**	**0**
1994-95	Detroit	IHL	12	6	9	15	10	....	....	....	....	....
	San Diego	IHL	58	8	25	33	60	5	2	0	2	8
	NHL Totals		**832**	**110**	**216**	**326**	**415**	**63**	**10**	**12**	**22**	**64**

a AHL Second All-Star Team (1989)

Sold to **Winnipeg** by **Montreal**, October 4, 1979. Traded to **St. Louis** by **Winnipeg** for Doug Evans, January 22, 1990. Signed as a free agent by **Montreal**, August 20, 1993.

WINDSOR, NICHOLAS — COL.

Defense. Shoots left. 6'1", 165 lbs. Born, Granby, Que., January 19, 1976.
(Quebec's 8th choice, 139th overall, in 1994 Entry Draft).

			Regular Season					Playoffs				
Season	**Club**	**Lea**	**GP**	**G**	**A**	**TP**	**PIM**	**GP**	**G**	**A**	**TP**	**PIM**
1993-94	Cornwall	Jr. A	43	13	39	52	121	....	....	....	....	....
1994-95	Clarkson	ECAC	26	1	10	11	20	....	....	....	....	....

WINNES, CHRIS (WIHN-ehs)

Right wing. Shoots right. 6', 201 lbs. Born, Ridgefield, CT, February 12, 1968.
(Boston's 9th choice, 161st overall, in 1987 Entry Draft).

			Regular Season					Playoffs				
Season	Club	Lea	GP	G	A	TP	PIM	GP	G	A	TP	PIM
1987-88	N. Hampshire	H.E.	30	17	19	36	28	....	....	....	....	....
1988-89	N. Hampshire	H.E.	30	11	20	31	22	....	....	....	....	....
1989-90	N. Hampshire	H.E.	24	10	13	23	12	....	....	....	....	....
1990-91	N. Hampshire	H.E.	33	15	16	31	24	....	....	....	....	....
	Maine	AHL	7	3	1	4	0	1	0	2	2	0
	Boston	**NHL**	....	....	....	....	....	**1**	**0**	**0**	**0**	**0**
1991-92	**Boston**	**NHL**	**24**	**1**	**3**	**4**	**6**	....	....	....	....	....
	Maine	AHL	45	12	35	47	30	....	....	....	....	....
1992-93	**Boston**	**NHL**	**5**	**0**	**1**	**1**	**0**	....	....	....	....	....
	Providence	AHL	64	23	36	59	34	4	0	2	2	5
1993-94	**Philadelphia**	**NHL**	**4**	**0**	**2**	**2**	**0**	....	....	....	....	....
	Hershey	AHL	70	29	21	50	20	7	1	3	4	0
1994-95	Hershey	AHL	78	26	40	66	39	6	2	2	4	17
	NHL Totals		**33**	**1**	**6**	**7**	**6**	**1**	**0**	**0**	**0**	**0**

Signed as a free agent by **Philadelphia**, August 4, 1993.

WITT, BRENDAN WSH.

Defense. Shoots left. 6'1", 205 lbs. Born, Humbolt, Sask., February 20, 1975.
(Washington's 1st choice, 11th overall, in 1993 Entry Draft).

			Regular Season					Playoffs				
Season	Club	Lea	GP	G	A	TP	PIM	GP	G	A	TP	PIM
1991-92	Seattle	WHL	67	3	9	12	212	15	1	1	2	84
1992-93a	Seattle	WHL	70	2	26	28	239	5	1	2	3	30
1993-94ab	Seattle	WHL	56	8	31	39	235	9	3	8	11	23
1994-95						DID NOT PLAY						

a WHL West First All-Star Team (1993, 1994)
b Canadian Major Junior First All-Star Team (1994)

WOLANIN, CRAIG (wuh-LAN-ihn) COL.

Defense. Shoots left. 6'3", 205 lbs. Born, Grosse Pointe, MI, July 27, 1967.
(New Jersey's 1st choice, 3rd overall, in 1985 Entry Draft).

			Regular Season					Playoffs				
Season	Club	Lea	GP	G	A	TP	PIM	GP	G	A	TP	PIM
1984-85	Kitchener	OHL	60	5	16	21	95	4	1	1	2	2
1985-86	**New Jersey**	**NHL**	**44**	**2**	**16**	**18**	**74**	....	....	....	....	....
1986-87	**New Jersey**	**NHL**	**68**	**4**	**6**	**10**	**109**	....	....	....	....	....
1987-88	**New Jersey**	**NHL**	**78**	**6**	**25**	**31**	**170**	**18**	**2**	**5**	**7**	**51**
1988-89	**New Jersey**	**NHL**	**56**	**3**	**8**	**11**	**69**	....	....	....	....	....
1989-90	**New Jersey**	**NHL**	**37**	**1**	**7**	**8**	**47**	....	....	....	....	....
	Utica	AHL	6	2	4	6	2	....	....	....	....	....
	Quebec	**NHL**	**13**	**0**	**3**	**3**	**10**	....	....	....	....	....
1990-91	**Quebec**	**NHL**	**80**	**5**	**13**	**18**	**89**	....	....	....	....	....
1991-92	**Quebec**	**NHL**	**69**	**2**	**11**	**13**	**80**	....	....	....	....	....
1992-93	**Quebec**	**NHL**	**24**	**1**	**4**	**5**	**49**	**4**	**0**	**0**	**0**	**4**
1993-94	**Quebec**	**NHL**	**63**	**6**	**10**	**16**	**80**	....	....	....	....	....
1994-95	**Quebec**	**NHL**	**40**	**3**	**6**	**9**	**40**	**6**	**1**	**1**	**2**	**4**
	NHL Totals		**572**	**33**	**109**	**142**	**817**	**28**	**3**	**6**	**9**	**59**

Traded to **Quebec** by **New Jersey** with future considerations (Randy Velischek, August 13, 1990) for Peter Stastny, March 6, 1990.

WOOD, DODY S.J.

Center. Shoots left. 5'11", 181 lbs. Born, Chetwynd, B.C., March 10, 1972.
(San Jose's 4th choice, 45th overall, in 1991 Entry Draft).

			Regular Season					Playoffs				
Season	Club	Lea	GP	G	A	TP	PIM	GP	G	A	TP	PIM
1989-90	Ft. St. John	Jr. A	44	51	73	124	270	....	....	....	....	....
	Seattle	WHL	....	....	....	....	....	5	0	0	0	2
1990-91	Seattle	WHL	69	28	37	65	272	6	0	1	1	2
1991-92	Seattle	WHL	37	13	19	32	232	....	....	....	....	....
	Swift Current	WHL	3	0	2	2	14	7	2	1	3	37
1992-93	**San Jose**	**NHL**	**13**	**1**	**1**	**2**	**71**	....	....	....	....	....
	Kansas City	IHL	36	3	2	5	216	6	0	1	1	15
1993-94	Kansas City	IHL	48	5	15	20	320	....	....	....	....	....
1994-95	Kansas City	IHL	44	5	13	18	255	21	7	10	17	87
	San Jose	**NHL**	**9**	**1**	**1**	**2**	**29**	....	....	....	....	....
	NHL Totals		**22**	**2**	**2**	**4**	**100**	....	....	....	....	....

WOOD, RANDY TOR.

Left wing/Center. Shoots left. 6', 195 lbs. Born, Princeton, NJ, October 12, 1963.

			Regular Season					Playoffs				
Season	Club	Lea	GP	G	A	TP	PIM	GP	G	A	TP	PIM
1982-83	Yale	ECAC	26	5	14	19	10	....	....	....	....	....
1983-84	Yale	ECAC	18	7	7	14	10	....	....	....	....	....
1984-85a	Yale	ECAC	32	25	28	53	23	....	....	....	....	....
1985-86bc	Yale	ECAC	31	25	30	55	26	....	....	....	....	....
1986-87	**NY Islanders**	**NHL**	**6**	**1**	**0**	**1**	**4**	**13**	**1**	**3**	**4**	**14**
	Springfield	AHL	75	23	24	47	57	....	....	....	....	....
1987-88	**NY Islanders**	**NHL**	**75**	**22**	**16**	**38**	**80**	**5**	**1**	**0**	**1**	**6**
	Springfield	AHL	1	0	1	1	0	....	....	....	....	....
1988-89	**NY Islanders**	**NHL**	**77**	**15**	**13**	**28**	**44**	....	....	....	....	....
	Springfield	AHL	1	1	1	2	0	....	....	....	....	....
1989-90	**NY Islanders**	**NHL**	**74**	**24**	**24**	**48**	**39**	**5**	**1**	**1**	**2**	**4**
1990-91	**NY Islanders**	**NHL**	**76**	**24**	**18**	**42**	**45**	....	....	....	....	....
1991-92	**NY Islanders**	**NHL**	**8**	**2**	**2**	**4**	**21**	....	....	....	....	....
	Buffalo	**NHL**	**70**	**20**	**16**	**36**	**65**	**7**	**2**	**1**	**3**	**6**
1992-93	**Buffalo**	**NHL**	**82**	**18**	**25**	**43**	**77**	**8**	**1**	**4**	**5**	**4**
1993-94	**Buffalo**	**NHL**	**84**	**22**	**16**	**38**	**71**	**6**	**0**	**0**	**0**	**0**
1994-95	**Toronto**	**NHL**	**48**	**13**	**11**	**24**	**34**	**7**	**2**	**0**	**2**	**6**
	NHL Totals		**600**	**161**	**141**	**302**	**480**	**51**	**8**	**9**	**17**	**40**

a ECAC Second All-Star Team (1985)
b ECAC First All-Star Team (1986)
c NCAA East Second All-Star Team (1986)

Signed as a free agent by **NY Islanders**, September 17, 1986. Traded to **Buffalo** by **NY Islanders** with Pat Lafontaine, Randy Hillier and NY Islanders' fourth round choice (Dean Melanson) in 1992 Entry Draft for Pierre Turgeon, Uwe Krupp, Benoit Hogue and Dave McLlwain, October 25, 1991. Claimed by **Toronto** from **Buffalo** in NHL Waiver Draft, January 18, 1995.

WOOLLEY, JASON (WOO-lee) FLA.

Defense. Shoots left. 6', 188 lbs. Born, Toronto, Ont., July 27, 1969.
(Washington's 4th choice, 61st overall, in 1989 Entry Draft).

			Regular Season					Playoffs				
Season	Club	Lea	GP	G	A	TP	PIM	GP	G	A	TP	PIM
1988-89	Michigan State	CCHA	47	12	25	37	26	....	....	....	....	....
1989-90	Michigan State	CCHA	45	10	38	48	26	....	....	....	....	....
1990-91ab	Michigan State	CCHA	40	15	44	59	24	....	....	....	....	....
1991-92	Cdn. National	....	60	14	30	44	36	....	....	....	....	....
	Cdn. Olympic	....	8	0	5	5	4	....	....	....	....	....
	Washington	**NHL**	**1**	**0**	**0**	**0**	**0**	....	....	....	....	....
	Baltimore	AHL	15	1	10	11	6	....	....	....	....	....
1992-93	**Washington**	**NHL**	**26**	**0**	**2**	**2**	**10**	....	....	....	....	....
	Baltimore	AHL	29	14	27	41	22	1	0	2	2	0
1993-94	**Washington**	**NHL**	**10**	**1**	**2**	**3**	**4**	**4**	**1**	**0**	**1**	**4**
	Portland	AHL	41	12	29	41	14	9	2	2	4	4
1994-95	Detroit	IHL	48	8	28	36	38	....	....	....	....	....
	Florida	**NHL**	**34**	**4**	**9**	**13**	**18**	....	....	....	....	....
	NHL Totals		**71**	**5**	**13**	**18**	**32**	**4**	**1**	**0**	**1**	**4**

a CCHA First All-Star Team (1991)
b NCAA West First All-American Team (1991)

Signed as a free agent by **Florida**, February 15, 1995.

WORTMAN, KEVIN

Defense. Shoots right. 6', 200 lbs. Born, Sagus, MA, February 22, 1969.
(Calgary's 9th choice, 168th overall, in 1989 Entry Draft).

			Regular Season					Playoffs				
Season	Club	Lea	GP	G	A	TP	PIM	GP	G	A	TP	PIM
1990-91	American Int'l	NCAA	28	21	25	46	6	....	....	....	....	....
1991-92	Salt Lake	IHL	82	12	34	46	34	5	1	0	1	0
1992-93a	Salt Lake	IHL	82	13	50	63	24	....	....	....	....	....
1993-94	**Calgary**	**NHL**	**5**	**0**	**0**	**0**	**2**	....	....	....	....	....
	Saint John	AHL	72	17	32	49	32	7	1	5	6	16
1994-95	Kansas City	IHL	80	6	28	34	22	21	1	1	2	4
	NHL Totals		**5**	**0**	**0**	**0**	**2**	....	....	....	....	....

a IHL Second All-Star Team (1993)

Signed as a free agent by **San Jose**, August 25, 1994.

WOTTON, MARK (WAH-tuhn) VAN.

Defense. Shoots left. 5'11", 187 lbs. Born, Foxwarren, Man., November 16, 1973.
(Vancouver's 11th choice, 237th overall, in 1992 Entry Draft).

			Regular Season					Playoffs				
Season	Club	Lea	GP	G	A	TP	PIM	GP	G	A	TP	PIM
1990-91	Saskatoon	WHL	45	4	11	15	37	....	....	....	....	....
1991-92	Saskatoon	WHL	64	11	25	36	92	....	....	....	....	....
1992-93	Saskatoon	WHL	71	15	51	66	90	9	6	5	11	18
1993-94a	Saskatoon	WHL	65	12	34	46	108	16	3	12	15	32
1994-95	Syracuse	AHL	75	12	29	41	50	....	....	....	....	....
	Vancouver	**NHL**	**1**	**0**	**0**	**0**	**0**	**5**	**0**	**0**	**0**	**4**
	NHL Totals		**1**	**0**	**0**	**0**	**0**	**5**	**0**	**0**	**0**	**4**

a WHL East Second All-Star Team (1994)

WREN, BOB HFD.

Left wing. Shoots left. 5'10", 185 lbs. Born, Preston, Ont., September 16, 1974.
(Los Angeles' 3rd choice, 94th overall, in 1993 Entry Draft).

			Regular Season					Playoffs				
Season	Club	Lea	GP	G	A	TP	PIM	GP	G	A	TP	PIM
1991-92	Detroit	OHL	62	13	36	49	58	7	3	4	7	19
1992-93a	Detroit	OHL	63	57	88	145	91	15	4	11	15	20
1993-94a	Detroit	OHL	57	45	64	109	81	17	12	18	30	20
1994-95	Springfield	AHL	61	16	15	31	118	....	....	....	....	....
	Richmond	ECHL	2	0	1	1	0	....	....	....	....	....

a OHL Second All-Star Team (1993, 1994)

Signed as a free agent by **Hartford**, September 6, 1994.

WRIGHT, DARREN BOS.

Defense. Shoots left. 6'1", 182 lbs. Born, Duncan, B.C., May 22, 1976.
(Boston's 4th choice, 125th overall, in 1994 Entry Draft).

			Regular Season					Playoffs				
Season	Club	Lea	GP	G	A	TP	PIM	GP	G	A	TP	PIM
1991-92	Prince Albert	WHL	2	0	0	0	2	....	....	....	....	....
1992-93	Prince Albert	WHL	53	0	4	4	131	....	....	....	....	....
1993-94	Prince Albert	WHL	56	0	5	5	151	....	....	....	....	....
1994-95	Detroit	ColHL	9	0	2	2	2	....	....	....	....	....
	Prince Albert	WHL	62	1	16	17	196	13	0	0	0	22

WRIGHT, JAMIE DAL.

Left wing. Shoots left. 6', 172 lbs. Born, Kitchener, Ont., May 13, 1976.
(Dallas' 3rd choice, 98th overall, in 1994 Entry Draft).

			Regular Season					Playoffs				
Season	Club	Lea	GP	G	A	TP	PIM	GP	G	A	TP	PIM
1993-94	Guelph	OHL	65	17	15	32	34	8	2	1	3	10
1994-95	Guelph	OHL	65	43	39	82	36	14	6	8	14	6

WRIGHT, SHAYNE BUF.

Defense. Shoots left. 6', 189 lbs. Born, Welland, Ont., June 30, 1975.
(Buffalo's 12th choice, 277th overall, in 1994 Entry Draft).

			Regular Season					Playoffs				
Season	Club	Lea	GP	G	A	TP	PIM	GP	G	A	TP	PIM
1992-93	Owen Sound	OHL	62	9	21	30	101	8	2	0	2	5
1993-94	Owen Sound	OHL	64	11	24	35	95	9	1	10	11	4
1994-95	Owen Sound	OHL	63	11	50	61	114	10	1	9	10	34

WRIGHT, TYLER EDM.

Center. Shoots right. 5'11", 185 lbs. Born, Canora, Sask., April 6, 1973.
(Edmonton's 1st choice, 12th overall, in 1991 Entry Draft).

			Regular Season					Playoffs				
Season	Club	Lea	GP	G	A	TP	PIM	GP	G	A	TP	PIM
1989-90	Swift Current	WHL	67	14	18	32	139	4	0	0	0	12
1990-91	Swift Current	WHL	66	41	51	92	157	3	0	0	0	6
1991-92	Swift Current	WHL	63	36	46	82	295	8	2	5	7	16
1992-93	**Edmonton**	**NHL**	**7**	**1**	**1**	**2**	**19**	....	....	....	....	....
	Swift Current	WHL	37	24	41	65	76	17	9	17	26	*49
1993-94	**Edmonton**	**NHL**	**5**	**0**	**0**	**0**	**4**	....	....	....	....	....
	Cape Breton	AHL	65	14	27	41	160	5	2	0	2	11
1994-95	Cape Breton	AHL	70	16	15	31	184	....	....	....	....	....
	Edmonton	**NHL**	**6**	**1**	**0**	**1**	**14**	....	....	....	....	....
	NHL Totals		**18**	**2**	**1**	**3**	**37**	....	....	....	....	....

YACHMENEV, VITALI (yach-meh-NEHV) L.A.

Right wing. Shoots left. 5'9", 180 lbs. Born, Chelyabinsk, USSR, January 8, 1975.
(Los Angeles' 3rd choice, 59th overall, in 1994 Entry Draft).

			Regular Season					Playoffs				
Season	Club	Lea	GP	G	A	TP	PIM	GP	G	A	TP	PIM
1992-93	Chelyabinsk	CIS 2	51	23	20	43	12	....	....	....	....	....
1993-94a	North Bay	OHL	66	*61	52	113	18	18	13	19	32	12
1994-95	North Bay	OHL	59	53	52	105	8	6	1	8	9	2
	Phoenix	IHL	....	....	....	....	....	4	1	0	1	0

a Canadian Major Junior Rookie of the Year (1994)

YAKE, TERRY (YAYK)

Right wing. Shoots right. 5'11", 190 lbs. Born, New Westminster, B.C., October 22, 1968.
(Hartford's 3rd choice, 81st overall, in 1987 Entry Draft).

			Regular Season					Playoffs				
Season	Club	Lea	GP	G	A	TP	PIM	GP	G	A	TP	PIM
1984-85	Brandon	WHL	11	1	1	2	0	....	....	....	....	....
1985-86	Brandon	WHL	72	26	26	52	49	....	....	....	....	....
1986-87	Brandon	WHL	71	44	58	102	64	....	....	....	....	....
1987-88	Brandon	WHL	72	55	85	140	59	3	4	2	6	7
1988-89	**Hartford**	**NHL**	**2**	**0**	**0**	**0**	**0**	....	....	....	....	....
	Binghamton	AHL	75	39	56	95	57	....	....	....	....	....
1989-90	**Hartford**	**NHL**	**2**	**0**	**1**	**1**	**0**	....	....	....	....	....
	Binghamton	AHL	77	13	42	55	37	....	....	....	....	....
1990-91	**Hartford**	**NHL**	**19**	**1**	**4**	**5**	**10**	**6**	**1**	**1**	**2**	**16**
	Springfield	AHL	60	35	42	77	56	15	9	9	18	10
1991-92	**Hartford**	**NHL**	**15**	**1**	**1**	**2**	**4**	....	....	....	....	....
	Springfield	AHL	53	21	34	55	63	8	3	4	7	2
1992-93	**Hartford**	**NHL**	**66**	**22**	**31**	**53**	**46**	....	....	....	....	....
	Springfield	AHL	16	8	14	22	27	....	....	....	....	....
1993-94	**Anaheim**	**NHL**	**82**	**21**	**31**	**52**	**44**	....	....	....	....	....
1994-95	**Toronto**	**NHL**	**19**	**3**	**2**	**5**	**2**	....	....	....	....	....
	Denver	IHL	2	0	3	3	2	17	4	11	15	16
	NHL Totals		**205**	**48**	**70**	**118**	**106**	**6**	**1**	**1**	**2**	**16**

Claimed by **Anaheim** from **Hartford** in Expansion Draft, June 24, 1993. Traded to **Toronto** by **Anaheim** for David Sacco, September 28, 1994.

YAKHANOV, ANDREI BOS.

Defense. Shoots right. 5'11", 187 lbs. Born, Ufa, USSR, July 23, 1973.
(Boston's 9th choice, 281st overall, in 1994 Entry Draft).

			Regular Season					Playoffs				
Season	Club	Lea	GP	G	A	TP	PIM	GP	G	A	TP	PIM
1992-93	Ufa Salavat	CIS	41	1	3	4	16	2	0	0	0	2
1993-94	Ufa Salavat	CIS	44	1	3	4	44	5	0	0	0	2
1994-95	Ufa Salavat	CIS	52	3	7	10	50	7	1	0	1	10

YAKOVENKO, VLADISLAV (yah-koh-VEHN-koh, vlahd-ees-LAHV) N.J.

Left wing. Shoots right. 5'11", 176 lbs. Born, Lipetsk, USSR, February 15, 1974.
(New Jersey's 12th choice, 258th overall, in 1992 Entry Draft).

			Regular Season					Playoffs				
Season	Club	Lea	GP	G	A	TP	PIM	GP	G	A	TP	PIM
1991-92	Argus	CIS 3	16	4	0	4	18	....	....	....	....	....
1992-93	Spartak	CIS	21	1	2	3	4	2	0	0	0	2
1993-94	CSKA	CIS	30	2	0	2	12	....	....	....	....	....
	Russian Pen's	IHL	6	0	6	6	10	....	....	....	....	....
1994-95	CSKA	CIS	2	0	0	0	0	....	....	....	....	....
	Spartak	CIS	12	4	1	5	29	....	....	....	....	....

YAKUBOV, RAVIL (yah-KOO-bohv, rah-VEEL) CGY.

Center. Shoots left. 6'1", 190 lbs. Born, Moscow, USSR, July 26, 1970.
(Calgary's 6th choice, 126th overall, in 1992 Entry Draft).

			Regular Season					Playoffs				
Season	Club	Lea	GP	G	A	TP	PIM	GP	G	A	TP	PIM
1990-91	Moscow D'amo	USSR	31	4	4	8	6	....	....	....	....	....
1991-92	Moscow D'amo	CIS	39	14	1	15	29	....	....	....	....	....
1992-93	Moscow D'amo	CIS	40	7	13	20	26	10	1	2	3	6
1993-94	Moscow D'amo	CIS	44	12	12	24	30	10	3	1	4	4
1994-95	Moscow D'amo	CIS	49	15	8	23	38	14	4	3	7	20

YASHIN, ALEXEI (YAH-shin) OTT.

Center. Shoots right. 6'3", 215 lbs. Born, Sverdlovsk, USSR, November 5, 1973.
(Ottawa's 1st choice, 2nd overall, in 1992 Entry Draft).

			Regular Season					Playoffs				
Season	Club	Lea	GP	G	A	TP	PIM	GP	G	A	TP	PIM
1990-91	Sverdlovsk	USSR	26	2	1	3	10	....	....	....	....	....
1991-92	Moscow D'amo	CIS	35	7	5	12	19	....	....	....	....	....
1992-93	Moscow D'amo	CIS	27	10	12	22	18	10	7	3	10	18
1993-94	**Ottawa**	**NHL**	**83**	**30**	**49**	**79**	**22**	....	....	....	....	....
1994-95	Las Vegas	IHL	24	15	20	35	32	....	....	....	....	....
	Ottawa	**NHL**	**47**	**21**	**23**	**44**	**20**	....	....	....	....	....
	NHL Totals		**130**	**51**	**72**	**123**	**42**	....	....	....	....	....

Played in NHL All-Star Game (1994)

YAWNEY, TRENT (YAW-nee) CGY.

Defense. Shoots left. 6'3", 195 lbs. Born, Hudson Bay, Sask., September 29, 1965.
(Chicago's 2nd choice, 45th overall, in 1984 Entry Draft).

			Regular Season					Playoffs				
Season	Club	Lea	GP	G	A	TP	PIM	GP	G	A	TP	PIM
1982-83	Saskatoon	WHL	59	6	31	37	44	6	0	2	2	0
1983-84	Saskatoon	WHL	73	13	46	59	81	....	....	....	....	....
1984-85	Saskatoon	WHL	72	16	51	67	158	3	1	6	7	7
1985-86	Cdn. National	....	73	6	15	21	60	....	....	....	....	....
1986-87	Cdn. National	....	51	4	15	19	37	....	....	....	....	....
1987-88	Cdn. National	....	60	4	12	16	81	....	....	....	....	....
	Cdn. Olympic	....	8	1	1	2	6	....	....	....	....	....
	Chicago	**NHL**	**15**	**2**	**8**	**10**	**15**	**5**	**0**	**4**	**4**	**8**
1988-89	**Chicago**	**NHL**	**69**	**5**	**19**	**24**	**116**	**15**	**3**	**6**	**9**	**20**
1989-90	**Chicago**	**NHL**	**70**	**5**	**15**	**20**	**82**	**20**	**3**	**5**	**8**	**27**
1990-91	**Chicago**	**NHL**	**61**	**3**	**13**	**16**	**77**	**1**	**0**	**0**	**0**	**0**
1991-92	**Calgary**	**NHL**	**47**	**4**	**9**	**13**	**45**	....	....	....	....	....
	Indianapolis	IHL	9	2	3	5	12	....	....	....	....	....
1992-93	**Calgary**	**NHL**	**63**	**1**	**16**	**17**	**67**	**6**	**3**	**2**	**5**	**6**
1993-94	**Calgary**	**NHL**	**58**	**6**	**15**	**21**	**60**	**7**	**0**	**0**	**0**	**16**
1994-95	**Calgary**	**NHL**	**37**	**0**	**2**	**2**	**108**	**2**	**0**	**0**	**0**	**2**
	NHL Totals		**420**	**26**	**97**	**123**	**570**	**56**	**9**	**17**	**26**	**79**

Traded to **Calgary** by **Chicago** for Stephane Matteau, December 16, 1991.

YEGOROV, ALEXEI (yeh-GOH-rohv) S.J.

Center. Shoots left. 5'11", 185 lbs. Born, St. Petersburg, USSR, May 21, 1975.
(San Jose's 3rd choice, 66th overall, in 1994 Entry Draft).

			Regular Season					Playoffs				
Season	Club	Lea	GP	G	A	TP	PIM	GP	G	A	TP	PIM
1992-93	St. Peterburg	CIS	17	1	2	3	10	6	3	1	4	6
1993-94	St. Peterburg	CIS	23	5	3	8	18	6	0	0	0	4
1994-95	St. Peterburg	CIS	10	2	1	3	10	....	....	....	....	....
	Fort Worth	CHL	18	4	10	14	15	....	....	....	....	....

YELLE, STEPHANE (YEHL-ee) COL.

Center. Shoots left. 6'1", 162 lbs. Born, Ottawa, Ont., May 9, 1974.
(New Jersey's 8th choice, 186th overall, in 1992 Entry Draft).

			Regular Season					Playoffs				
Season	Club	Lea	GP	G	A	TP	PIM	GP	G	A	TP	PIM
1991-92	Oshawa	OHL	55	12	14	26	20	7	2	0	2	1
1992-93	Oshawa	OHL	66	24	50	74	20	10	2	4	6	4
1993-94	Oshawa	OHL	66	35	69	104	22	5	1	7	8	2
1994-95	Cornwall	AHL	40	18	15	33	22	13	7	7	14	8

Traded to **Quebec** by **New Jersey** with New Jersey's eleventh round choice (Steven Low) in 1994 Entry Draft for Quebec's eleventh round choice (Mike Hansen) in 1994 Entry Draft, June 1, 1994.

YERESKO, YURI (yeh-REHS-koh) DET.

Defense. Shoots left. 5'11", 178 lbs. Born, Moscow, USSR, August 30, 1975.
(Detroit's 8th choice, 178th overall, in 1993 Entry Draft).

			Regular Season					Playoffs				
Season	Club	Lea	GP	G	A	TP	PIM	GP	G	A	TP	PIM
1992-93	CSKA	CIS	35	0	0	0	8	....	....	....	....	....
1993-94	CSKA	CIS	45	0	0	0	16	3	0	1	1	0
1994-95	CSKA	CIS	38	0	1	1	8	2	0	0	0	0

YLONEN, JUHA (YOO-lih-nehn, YOO-hah) WPG.

Center. Shoots left. 6', 180 lbs. Born, Helsinki, Finland, February 13, 1972.
(Winnipeg's 5th choice, 91st overall, in 1991 Entry Draft).

			Regular Season					Playoffs				
Season	Club	Lea	GP	G	A	TP	PIM	GP	G	A	TP	PIM
1990-91	Espoo	Fin. 2	40	12	21	33	4	....	....	....	....	....
1991-92	HPK	Fin.	43	7	11	18	8	....	....	....	....	....
1992-93	HPK	Fin.	48	8	18	26	22	12	3	5	8	2
1993-94	Jokerit	Fin.	37	5	11	16	2	12	1	3	4	8
1994-95	Jokerit	Fin.	50	13	15	28	10	11	3	2	5	0

YORK, JASON ANA.

Defense. Shoots right. 6'2", 195 lbs. Born, Ottawa, Ont., May 20, 1970.
(Detroit's 6th choice, 129th overall, in 1990 Entry Draft).

			Regular Season					Playoffs				
Season	Club	Lea	GP	G	A	TP	PIM	GP	G	A	TP	PIM
1989-90	Windsor	OHL	39	9	30	39	38	....	....	....	....	....
	Kitchener	OHL	25	11	25	36	17	17	3	19	22	10
1990-91	Windsor	OHL	66	13	80	93	40	11	3	10	13	12
1991-92	Adirondack	AHL	49	4	20	24	32	5	0	1	1	0
1992-93	**Detroit**	**NHL**	**2**	**0**	**0**	**0**	**0**	....	....	....	....	....
	Adirondack	AHL	77	15	40	55	86	11	0	3	3	18
1993-94	**Detroit**	**NHL**	**7**	**1**	**2**	**3**	**2**	....	....	....	....	....
a	Adirondack	AHL	74	10	56	66	98	12	3	11	14	22
1994-95	**Detroit**	**NHL**	**10**	**1**	**2**	**3**	**2**	....	....	....	....	....
	Adirondack	AHL	5	1	3	4	4	....	....	....	....	....
	Anaheim	**NHL**	**15**	**0**	**8**	**8**	**12**	....	....	....	....	....
	NHL Totals		**34**	**2**	**12**	**14**	**16**	....	....	....	....	....

a AHL First All-Star Team (1994)

Traded to **Anaheim** by **Detroit** with Mike Sillinger for Stu Grimson, Mark Ferner and Anaheim's sixth round choice in 1996 Entry Draft, April 4, 1995.

YOUNG, ADAM N.J.

Left wing. Shoots left. 6'4", 222 lbs. Born, Toronto, Ont., January 15, 1975.
(New Jersey's 8th choice, 148th overall, in 1995 Entry Draft).

			Regular Season					Playoffs				
Season	Club	Lea	GP	G	A	TP	PIM	GP	G	A	TP	PIM
1992-93	Windsor	OHL	62	3	3	6	65	....	....	....	....	....
1993-94	Windsor	OHL	45	8	9	17	105	4	0	0	0	7
1994-95	Windsor	OHL	63	4	10	14	*260	10	2	1	3	36

YOUNG, SCOTT COL.

Right wing. Shoots right. 6', 190 lbs. Born, Clinton, MA, October 1, 1967.
(Hartford's 1st choice, 11th overall, in 1986 Entry Draft).

			Regular Season					Playoffs				
Season	Club	Lea	GP	G	A	TP	PIM	GP	G	A	TP	PIM
1985-86	Boston U.	H.E.	38	16	13	29	31	....	....	....	....	....
1986-87	Boston U.	H.E.	33	15	21	36	24	....	....	....	....	....
1987-88	U.S. National	....	56	11	47	58	31	....	....	....	....	....
	U.S. Olympic	....	6	2	6	8	4	....	....	....	....	....
	Hartford	**NHL**	**7**	**0**	**0**	**0**	**2**	**4**	**1**	**0**	**1**	**0**
1988-89	**Hartford**	**NHL**	**76**	**19**	**40**	**59**	**27**	**4**	**2**	**0**	**2**	**4**
1989-90	**Hartford**	**NHL**	**80**	**24**	**40**	**64**	**47**	**7**	**2**	**0**	**2**	**2**
1990-91	**Hartford**	**NHL**	**34**	**6**	**9**	**15**	**8**	....	....	....	....	....
	Pittsburgh	**NHL**	**43**	**11**	**16**	**27**	**33**	**17**	**1**	**6**	**7**	**2**
1991-92	Bolzano	Italy	18	22	17	39	6	5	4	3	7	7
	U.S. National	....	10	2	4	6	21	....	....	....	....	....
	U.S. Olympic	....	8	2	1	3	2	....	....	....	....	....
1992-93	**Quebec**	**NHL**	**82**	**30**	**30**	**60**	**20**	**6**	**4**	**1**	**5**	**0**
1993-94	**Quebec**	**NHL**	**76**	**26**	**25**	**51**	**14**	....	....	....	....	....
1994-95	Landshut	Ger.	4	6	1	7	6	....	....	....	....	....
	Frankfurt	Ger.	1	1	0	1	0	....	....	....	....	....
	Quebec	**NHL**	**48**	**18**	**21**	**39**	**14**	**6**	**3**	**3**	**6**	**2**
	NHL Totals		**446**	**134**	**181**	**315**	**165**	**44**	**13**	**10**	**23**	**10**

Traded to **Pittsburgh** by **Hartford** for Rob Brown, December 21, 1990. Traded to **Quebec** by **Pittsburgh** for Bryan Fogarty, March 10, 1992.

YSEBAERT, PAUL (IGHS-bahrt) T.B.

Center. Shoots left. 6'1", 190 lbs. Born, Sarnia, Ont., May 15, 1966.
(New Jersey's 4th choice, 74th overall, in 1984 Entry Draft).

			Regular Season					Playoffs				
Season	Club	Lea	GP	G	A	TP	PIM	GP	G	A	TP	PIM
1984-85	Bowling Green	CCHA	42	23	32	55	54	....	....	....	....	....
1985-86a	Bowling Green	CCHA	42	23	45	68	50	....	....	....	....	....
1986-87a	Bowling Green	CCHA	45	27	58	85	44	....	....	....	....	....
	Cdn. National	....	5	1	0	1	4	....	....	....	....	....
1987-88	Utica	AHL	78	30	49	79	60	....	....	....	....	....
1988-89	**New Jersey**	**NHL**	**5**	**0**	**4**	**4**	**0**	....	....	....	....	....
	Utica	AHL	56	36	44	80	22	5	0	1	1	4
1989-90	**New Jersey**	**NHL**	**5**	**1**	**2**	**3**	**0**	....	....	....	....	....
bcd	Utica	AHL	74	53	52	*105	61	5	2	4	6	0
1990-91	**New Jersey**	**NHL**	**11**	**4**	**3**	**7**	**6**	....	....	....	....	....
	Detroit	**NHL**	**51**	**15**	**18**	**33**	**16**	**2**	**0**	**2**	**2**	**0**
1991-92e	**Detroit**	**NHL**	**79**	**35**	**40**	**75**	**55**	**10**	**1**	**0**	**1**	**10**
1992-93	**Detroit**	**NHL**	**80**	**34**	**28**	**62**	**42**	**7**	**3**	**1**	**4**	**2**
1993-94	**Winnipeg**	**NHL**	**60**	**9**	**18**	**27**	**18**	....	....	....	....	....
	Chicago	**NHL**	**11**	**5**	**3**	**8**	**8**	**6**	**0**	**0**	**0**	**8**
1994-95	**Chicago**	**NHL**	**15**	**4**	**5**	**9**	**6**	....	....	....	....	....
	Tampa Bay	**NHL**	**29**	**8**	**11**	**19**	**12**	....	....	....	....	....
	NHL Totals		**346**	**115**	**132**	**247**	**163**	**25**	**4**	**3**	**7**	**20**

a CCHA Second All-Star Team (1986, 1987)
b AHL First All-Star Team (1990)
c Won John B. Sollenberger Trophy (Top Scorer - AHL) (1990)
d Won Les Cunningham Plaque (MVP - AHL) (1990)
e Won Alka-Seltzer Plus Award (1992)

Traded to **Detroit** by **New Jersey** for Lee Norwood and Detroit's fourth round choice (Scott McCabe) in 1992 Entry Draft, November 27, 1990. Traded to **Winnipeg** by **Detroit** with future considerations (Alan Kerr, June 18, 1993) for Aaron Ward and Toronto's fourth round choice (previously acquired by Winnipeg — later traded to Detroit — Detroit selected John Jakopin) in 1993 Entry Draft, June 11, 1993. Traded to **Chicago** by **Winnipeg** for Chicago's third round choice in 1995 Entry Draft, March 21, 1994. Traded to **Tampa Bay** by **Chicago** with Rich Sutter for Jim Cummins, Tom Tilley and Jeff Buchanan, February 22, 1995.

YUSHKEVICH, DIMITRI (yoosh-KAY-vihch)

Defense. Shoots right. 5'11", 208 lbs. Born, Yaroslavl, USSR, November 19, 1971.
(Philadelphia's 6th choice, 122nd overall, in 1991 Entry Draft).

			Regular Season					Playoffs				
Season	Club	Lea	GP	G	A	TP	PIM	GP	G	A	TP	PIM
1988-89	Torpedo Yaro.	USSR	23	2	1	3	8	....	....	....	....	....
1989-90	Torpedo Yaro.	USSR	41	2	3	5	39	....	....	....	....	....
1990-91	Torpedo Yaro.	USSR	41	10	4	14	22	....	....	....	....	....
1991-92	Moscow D'amo	CIS	35	5	7	12	14	....	....	....	....	....
1992-93	**Philadelphia**	**NHL**	**82**	**5**	**27**	**32**	**71**	....	....	....	....	....
1993-94	**Philadelphia**	**NHL**	**75**	**5**	**25**	**30**	**86**	....	....	....	....	....
1994-95	Torpedo Yaro.	CIS	10	3	4	7	8	....	....	....	....	....
	Philadelphia	**NHL**	**40**	**5**	**9**	**14**	**47**	**15**	**1**	**5**	**6**	**12**
	NHL Totals		**197**	**15**	**61**	**76**	**204**	**15**	**1**	**5**	**6**	**12**

YZERMAN, STEVE (IGH-zuhr-muhn) DET.

Center. Shoots right. 5'11", 185 lbs. Born, Cranbrook, B.C., May 9, 1965.
(Detroit's 1st choice, 4th overall, in 1983 Entry Draft).

			Regular Season					Playoffs				
Season	Club	Lea	GP	G	A	TP	PIM	GP	G	A	TP	PIM
1981-82	Peterborough	OHL	58	21	43	64	65	6	0	1	1	16
1982-83	Peterborough	OHL	56	42	49	91	33	4	1	4	5	0
1983-84a	**Detroit**	**NHL**	**80**	**39**	**48**	**87**	**33**	**4**	**3**	**3**	**6**	**0**
1984-85	**Detroit**	**NHL**	**80**	**30**	**59**	**89**	**58**	**3**	**2**	**1**	**3**	**2**
1985-86	**Detroit**	**NHL**	**51**	**14**	**28**	**42**	**16**	....	....	....	....	....
1986-87	**Detroit**	**NHL**	**80**	**31**	**59**	**90**	**43**	**16**	**5**	**13**	**18**	**8**
1987-88	**Detroit**	**NHL**	**64**	**50**	**52**	**102**	**44**	**3**	**1**	**3**	**4**	**6**
1988-89b	**Detroit**	**NHL**	**80**	**65**	**90**	**155**	**61**	**6**	**5**	**5**	**10**	**2**
1989-90	**Detroit**	**NHL**	**79**	**62**	**65**	**127**	**79**	....	....	....	....	....
1990-91	**Detroit**	**NHL**	**80**	**51**	**57**	**108**	**34**	**7**	**3**	**3**	**6**	**4**
1991-92	**Detroit**	**NHL**	**79**	**45**	**58**	**103**	**64**	**11**	**3**	**5**	**8**	**12**
1992-93	**Detroit**	**NHL**	**84**	**58**	**79**	**137**	**44**	**7**	**4**	**3**	**7**	**4**
1993-94	**Detroit**	**NHL**	**58**	**24**	**58**	**82**	**36**	**3**	**1**	**3**	**4**	**0**
1994-95	**Detroit**	**NHL**	**47**	**12**	**26**	**38**	**40**	**15**	**4**	**8**	**12**	**0**
	NHL Totals		**862**	**481**	**679**	**1160**	**552**	**75**	**31**	**47**	**78**	**38**

a NHL All-Rookie Team (1984)
b Won Lester B. Pearson Award (1989)

Played in NHL All-Star Game (1984, 1988-93)

ZALAPSKI, ZARLEY CGY.

Defense. Shoots left. 6'1", 215 lbs. Born, Edmonton, Alta., April 22, 1968.
(Pittsburgh's 1st choice, 4th overall, in 1986 Entry Draft).

			Regular Season					Playoffs				
Season	Club	Lea	GP	G	A	TP	PIM	GP	G	A	TP	PIM
1985-86	Cdn. National	....	32	2	4	6	10	....	....	....	....	....
1986-87	Cdn. National	....	74	11	29	40	28	....	....	....	....	....
1987-88	Cdn. National	....	47	3	13	16	32	....	....	....	....	....
	Cdn. Olympic	....	8	1	3	4	2	....	....	....	....	....
	Pittsburgh	**NHL**	**15**	**3**	**8**	**11**	**7**	....	....	....	....	....
1988-89a	**Pittsburgh**	**NHL**	**58**	**12**	**33**	**45**	**57**	**11**	**1**	**8**	**9**	**13**
1989-90	**Pittsburgh**	**NHL**	**51**	**6**	**25**	**31**	**37**	....	....	....	....	....
1990-91	**Pittsburgh**	**NHL**	**66**	**12**	**36**	**48**	**59**	....	....	....	....	....
	Hartford	**NHL**	**11**	**3**	**3**	**6**	**6**	**6**	**1**	**3**	**4**	**8**
1991-92	**Hartford**	**NHL**	**79**	**20**	**37**	**57**	**120**	**7**	**2**	**3**	**5**	**6**
1992-93	**Hartford**	**NHL**	**83**	**14**	**51**	**65**	**94**	....	....	....	....	....
1993-94	**Hartford**	**NHL**	**56**	**7**	**30**	**37**	**56**	....	....	....	....	....
	Calgary	**NHL**	**13**	**3**	**7**	**10**	**18**	**7**	**0**	**3**	**3**	**2**
1994-95	**Calgary**	**NHL**	**48**	**4**	**24**	**28**	**46**	**7**	**0**	**4**	**4**	**4**
	NHL Totals		**480**	**84**	**254**	**338**	**500**	**38**	**4**	**21**	**25**	**33**

a NHL All-Rookie Team (1989)

Played in NHL All-Star Game (1993)

Traded to **Hartford** by **Pittsburgh** with John Cullen and Jeff Parker for Ron Francis, Grant Jennings and Ulf Samuelsson, March 4, 1991. Traded to **Calgary** by **Hartford** with James Patrick and Michael Nylander for Gary Suter, Paul Ranheim and Ted Drury, March 10, 1994.

ZAMUNER, ROB (ZAM-nuhr) T.B.

Center. Shoots left. 6'2", 202 lbs. Born, Oakville, Ont., September 17, 1969.
(NY Rangers' 3rd choice, 45th overall, in 1989 Entry Draft).

			Regular Season					Playoffs				
Season	Club	Lea	GP	G	A	TP	PIM	GP	G	A	TP	PIM
1986-87	Guelph	OHL	62	6	15	21	8	....	....	....	....	....
1987-88	Guelph	OHL	58	20	41	61	18	....	....	....	....	....
1988-89	Guelph	OHL	66	46	65	111	38	7	5	5	10	9
1989-90	Flint	IHL	77	44	35	79	32	4	1	0	1	6
1990-91	Binghamton	AHL	80	25	58	83	50	9	7	6	13	35
1991-92	**NY Rangers**	**NHL**	**9**	**1**	**2**	**3**	**2**	....	....	....	....	....
	Binghamton	AHL	61	19	53	72	42	11	8	9	17	8
1992-93	**Tampa Bay**	**NHL**	**84**	**15**	**28**	**43**	**74**	....	....	....	....	....
1993-94	**Tampa Bay**	**NHL**	**59**	**6**	**6**	**12**	**42**	....	....	....	....	....
1994-95	**Tampa Bay**	**NHL**	**43**	**9**	**6**	**15**	**24**	....	....	....	....	....
	NHL Totals		**195**	**31**	**42**	**73**	**142**	....	....	....	....	....

Signed as a free agent by **Tampa Bay**, July 13, 1992.

ZAVARUKHIN, NIKOLAI (zah-vah-RUH-khihn) N.J.

Center. Shoots left. 5'9", 167 lbs. Born, Ufa, USSR, March 18, 1975.
(New Jersey's 7th choice, 169th overall, in 1993 Entry Draft).

			Regular Season					Playoffs				
Season	Club	Lea	GP	G	A	TP	PIM	GP	G	A	TP	PIM
1992-93	Ufa Salavat	CIS	37	2	4	6	18	2	0	0	0	2
1993-94	Ufa Salavat	CIS	45	8	8	16	20	5	0	1	1	0
1994-95	CSKA	CIS	35	5	5	10	26	2	0	0	0	2

ZAVISHA, BRAD (zuh-VIH-shuh) PHI.

Left wing. Shoots left. 6'2", 205 lbs. Born, Hines Creek, Alta., January 4, 1972.
(Quebec's 3rd choice, 43rd overall, in 1990 Entry Draft).

			Regular Season					Playoffs				
Season	Club	Lea	GP	G	A	TP	PIM	GP	G	A	TP	PIM
1988-89	Seattle	WHL	52	8	13	21	43	....	....	....	....	....
1989-90	Seattle	WHL	69	22	38	60	124	13	1	6	7	16
1990-91	Seattle	WHL	24	15	12	27	40	....	....	....	....	....
	Portland	WHL	48	25	22	47	41	....	....	....	....	....
1991-92a	Portland	WHL	11	7	4	11	18	....	....	....	....	....
	Lethbridge	WHL	59	44	40	84	160	5	3	1	4	18
1992-93			DID NOT PLAY – INJURED									
1993-94	**Edmonton**	**NHL**	**2**	**0**	**0**	**0**	**0**	....	....	....	....	....
	Cape Breton	AHL	58	19	15	34	114	2	0	0	0	2
1994-95	Cape Breton	AHL	62	13	20	33	55	....	....	....	....	....
	Hershey	AHL	9	3	0	3	12	....	....	....	....	....
	NHL Totals		**2**	**0**	**0**	**0**	**0**	....	....	....	....	....

a WHL East First All-Star Team (1992)

Traded to **Edmonton** by **Quebec** with Ron Tugnutt for Martin Rucinsky, March 10, 1992. Traded to **Philadelphia** by **Edmonton** with Edmonton's sixth round choice (Jamie Sokolosky) in 1995 Entry Draft for Ryan McGill, March 13, 1995.

ZEDNIK, RICHARD WSH.

Left wing. Shoots left. 5'11", 172 lbs. Born, Bystrica, Czech., January 6, 1976.
(Washington's 10th choice, 249th overall, in 1994 Entry Draft).

			Regular Season					Playoffs				
Season	Club	Lea	GP	G	A	TP	PIM	GP	G	A	TP	PIM
1993-94	Bystrica	Slov. 2	25	3	6	9	....	....	....	....	....	....
1994-95	Portland	WHL	65	35	51	86	89	9	5	5	10	20

ZELENKO, BORIS PIT.

Left wing. Shoots right. 6'1", 172 lbs. Born, Moscow, USSR, September 12, 1975.
(Pittsburgh's 11th choice, 206th overall, in 1994 Entry Draft).

			Regular Season					Playoffs				
Season	Club	Lea	GP	G	A	TP	PIM	GP	G	A	TP	PIM
1993-94	CSKA	CIS	34	5	1	6	10	1	0	0	0	0
1994-95	CSKA	CIS	35	5	1	6	12	1	0	0	0	0

ZELEPUKIN, VALERI (zeh-leh-POO-kin) N.J.

Left wing. Shoots left. 5'11", 190 lbs. Born, Voskresensk, USSR, September 17, 1968.
(New Jersey's 13th choice, 221st overall, in 1990 Entry Draft).

			Regular Season					Playoffs				
Season	Club	Lea	GP	G	A	TP	PIM	GP	G	A	TP	PIM
1984-85	Khimik	USSR	5	0	0	0	2	....	....	....	....	....
1985-86	Khimik	USSR	33	2	2	4	10	....	....	....	....	....
1986-87	Khimik	USSR	19	1	0	1	4	....	....	....	....	....
1987-88	SKA MVO	USSR 2	18	18	6	24	....	....	....	....	....	....
	CSKA	USSR	19	3	1	4	8	....	....	....	....	....
1988-89	CSKA	USSR	17	2	3	5	2	....	....	....	....	....
1989-90	Khimik	USSR	46	17	14	31	26	....	....	....	....	....
1990-91	Khimik	USSR	34	11	6	17	38	....	....	....	....	....
1991-92	**New Jersey**	**NHL**	**44**	**13**	**18**	**31**	**28**	**4**	**1**	**1**	**2**	**2**
	Utica	AHL	22	20	9	29	8	....	....	....	....	....
1992-93	**New Jersey**	**NHL**	**78**	**23**	**41**	**64**	**70**	**5**	**0**	**2**	**2**	**0**
1993-94	**New Jersey**	**NHL**	**82**	**26**	**31**	**57**	**70**	**20**	**5**	**2**	**7**	**14**
1994-95	**New Jersey**	**NHL**	**4**	**1**	**2**	**3**	**6**	**18**	**1**	**2**	**3**	**12**
	NHL Totals		**208**	**63**	**92**	**155**	**174**	**47**	**7**	**7**	**14**	**28**

ZENT, JASON OTT.

Left wing. Shoots left. 5'11", 180 lbs. Born, Buffalo, NY, April 15, 1971.
(NY Islanders' 3rd choice, 44th overall, in 1989 Entry Draft).

			Regular Season					Playoffs				
Season	Club	Lea	GP	G	A	TP	PIM	GP	G	A	TP	PIM
1990-91	U. Wisconsin	WCHA	39	19	18	37	51	....	....	....	....	....
1991-92a	U. Wisconsin	WCHA	39	22	17	39	128	....	....	....	....	....
1992-93	U. Wisconsin	WCHA	40	26	12	38	92	....	....	....	....	....
1993-94	U. Wisconsin	WCHA	42	20	21	41	120	....	....	....	....	....
1994-95	P.E.I.	AHL	55	15	11	26	46	9	6	1	7	6

a NCAA All-Tournament Team (1992)

Traded to **Ottawa** by **NY Islanders** for Ottawa's fifth round choice in 1996 Entry Draft, October 15, 1994.

ZETTLER, ROB — TOR.

Defense. Shoots left. 6'3", 200 lbs. Born, Sept Iles, Que., March 8, 1968.
(Minnesota's 5th choice, 55th overall, in 1986 Entry Draft).

			Regular Season					Playoffs				
Season	Club	Lea	GP	G	A	TP	PIM	GP	G	A	TP	PIM
1985-86	S.S. Marie	OHL	57	5	23	28	92	....	....	....	....	....
1986-87	S.S. Marie	OHL	64	13	22	35	89	4	0	0	0	0
1987-88	Kalamazoo	IHL	2	0	1	1	0	7	0	2	2	2
	S.S. Marie	OHL	64	7	41	48	77	6	2	2	4	9
1988-89	**Minnesota**	**NHL**	**2**	**0**	**0**	**0**	**0**	....	....	....	....	....
	Kalamazoo	IHL	80	5	21	26	79	6	0	1	1	26
1989-90	**Minnesota**	**NHL**	**31**	**0**	**8**	**8**	**45**	....	....	....	....	....
	Kalamazoo	IHL	41	6	10	16	64	7	0	0	0	6
1990-91	**Minnesota**	**NHL**	**47**	**1**	**4**	**5**	**119**	....	....	....	....	....
	Kalamazoo	IHL	1	0	0	0	2	....	....	....	....	....
1991-92	**San Jose**	**NHL**	**74**	**1**	**8**	**9**	**99**	....	....	....	....	....
1992-93	**San Jose**	**NHL**	**80**	**0**	**7**	**7**	**150**	....	....	....	....	....
1993-94	**San Jose**	**NHL**	**42**	**0**	**3**	**3**	**65**	....	....	....	....	....
	Philadelphia	**NHL**	**33**	**0**	**4**	**4**	**69**	....	....	....	....	....
1994-95	**Philadelphia**	**NHL**	**32**	**0**	**1**	**1**	**34**	**1**	**0**	**0**	**0**	**2**
	NHL Totals		**341**	**2**	**35**	**37**	**581**	**1**	**0**	**0**	**0**	**2**

Claimed by **San Jose** from **Minnesota** in Dispersal Draft, May 30, 1991. Traded to **Philadelphia** by **San Jose** for Viacheslav Butsayev, February 1, 1994. Traded to **Toronto** by **Philadelphia** for Toronto's fifth round choice in 1996 Entry Draft, July 8, 1995.

ZEZEL, PETER (ZEH-zehl)

Center. Shoots left. 5'11", 200 lbs. Born, Toronto, Ont., April 22, 1965.
(Philadelphia's 1st choice, 41st overall, in 1983 Entry Draft).

			Regular Season					Playoffs				
Season	Club	Lea	GP	G	A	TP	PIM	GP	G	A	TP	PIM
1982-83	Toronto	OHL	66	35	39	74	28	4	2	4	6	0
1983-84	Toronto	OHL	68	47	86	133	31	9	7	5	12	4
1984-85	**Philadelphia**	**NHL**	**65**	**15**	**46**	**61**	**26**	**19**	**1**	**8**	**9**	**28**
1985-86	**Philadelphia**	**NHL**	**79**	**17**	**37**	**54**	**76**	**5**	**3**	**1**	**4**	**4**
1986-87	**Philadelphia**	**NHL**	**71**	**33**	**39**	**72**	**71**	**25**	**3**	**10**	**13**	**10**
1987-88	**Philadelphia**	**NHL**	**69**	**22**	**35**	**57**	**42**	**7**	**3**	**2**	**5**	**7**
1988-89	**Philadelphia**	**NHL**	**26**	**4**	**13**	**17**	**15**	....	....	....	....	....
	St. Louis	**NHL**	**52**	**17**	**36**	**53**	**27**	**10**	**6**	**6**	**12**	**4**
1989-90	**St. Louis**	**NHL**	**73**	**25**	**47**	**72**	**30**	**12**	**1**	**7**	**8**	**4**
1990-91	**Washington**	**NHL**	**20**	**7**	**5**	**12**	**10**	....	....	....	....	....
	Toronto	**NHL**	**32**	**14**	**14**	**28**	**4**	....	....	....	....	....
1991-92	**Toronto**	**NHL**	**64**	**16**	**33**	**49**	**26**	....	....	....	....	....
1992-93	**Toronto**	**NHL**	**70**	**12**	**23**	**35**	**24**	**20**	**2**	**1**	**3**	**6**
1993-94	**Toronto**	**NHL**	**41**	**8**	**8**	**16**	**19**	**18**	**2**	**4**	**6**	**8**
1994-95	**Dallas**	**NHL**	**30**	**6**	**5**	**11**	**19**	**3**	**1**	**0**	**1**	**0**
	Kalamazoo	IHL	2	0	0	0	0	....	....	....	....	....
	NHL Totals		**692**	**196**	**341**	**537**	**389**	**119**	**22**	**39**	**61**	**71**

Traded to **St. Louis** by **Philadelphia** for Mike Bullard, November 29, 1988. Traded to **Washington** by **St. Louis** with Mike Lalor for Geoff Courtnall, July 13, 1990. Traded to **Toronto** by **Washington** with Bob Rouse for Al Iafrate, January 16, 1991. Acquired by **Dallas** from **Toronto** with Grant Marshall as compensation for Toronto's signing of free agent Mike Craig, August 10, 1994.

ZHAMNOV, ALEXEI (ZHAHM-nahf) WPG.

Center. Shoots left. 6'1", 195 lbs. Born, Moscow, USSR, October 1, 1970.
(Winnipeg's 5th choice, 77th overall, in 1990 Entry Draft).

			Regular Season					Playoffs				
Season	Club	Lea	GP	G	A	TP	PIM	GP	G	A	TP	PIM
1988-89	Moscow D'amo	USSR	4	0	0	0	0	....	....	....	....	....
1989-90	Moscow D'amo	USSR	43	11	6	17	21	....	....	....	....	....
1990-91	Moscow D'amo	USSR	46	16	12	28	24	....	....	....	....	....
1991-92	Moscow D'amo	CIS	39	15	21	36	28	....	....	....	....	....
1992-93	**Winnipeg**	**NHL**	**68**	**25**	**47**	**72**	**58**	**6**	**0**	**2**	**2**	**2**
1993-94	**Winnipeg**	**NHL**	**61**	**26**	**45**	**71**	**62**	....	....	....	....	....
1994-95a	**Winnipeg**	**NHL**	**48**	**30**	**35**	**65**	**20**	....	....	....	....	....
	NHL Totals		**177**	**81**	**127**	**208**	**140**	**6**	**0**	**2**	**2**	**2**

a NHL Second All-Star Team (1995)

ZHITNIK, ALEXEI (ZHIHT-nihk) BUF.

Defense. Shoots left. 5'11", 190 lbs. Born, Kiev, USSR, October 10, 1972.
(Los Angeles' 3rd choice, 81st overall, in 1991 Entry Draft).

			Regular Season					Playoffs				
Season	Club	Lea	GP	G	A	TP	PIM	GP	G	A	TP	PIM
1989-90	Sokol Kiev	USSR	31	3	4	7	16	....	....	....	....	....
1990-91	Sokol Kiev	USSR	46	1	4	5	46	....	....	....	....	....
1991-92	CSKA	CIS	44	2	7	9	52	....	....	....	....	....
1992-93	**Los Angeles**	**NHL**	**78**	**12**	**36**	**48**	**80**	**24**	**3**	**9**	**12**	**26**
1993-94	**Los Angeles**	**NHL**	**81**	**12**	**40**	**52**	**101**	....	....	....	....	....
1994-95	**Los Angeles**	**NHL**	**11**	**2**	**5**	**7**	**27**	....	....	....	....	....
	Buffalo	**NHL**	**21**	**2**	**5**	**7**	**34**	**5**	**0**	**1**	**1**	**14**
	NHL Totals		**191**	**28**	**86**	**114**	**242**	**29**	**3**	**10**	**13**	**40**

Traded to **Buffalo** by **Los Angeles** with Robb Stauber, Charlie Huddy and Los Angeles' fifth round choice (Marian Menhart) in 1995 Entry Draft for Philippe Boucher, Denis Tsygurov and Grant Fuhr, February 14, 1995.

ZHOLTOK, SERGEI (ZHOL-tok)

Center. Shoots right. 6', 190 lbs. Born, Riga, Latvia, December 2, 1972.
(Boston's 2nd choice, 55th overall, in 1992 Entry Draft).

			Regular Season					Playoffs				
Season	Club	Lea	GP	G	A	TP	PIM	GP	G	A	TP	PIM
1990-91	Dynamo Riga	USSR	39	4	0	4	16	....	....	....	....	....
1991-92	Riga	CIS	27	6	3	9	6	....	....	....	....	....
1992-93	**Boston**	**NHL**	**1**	**0**	**1**	**1**	**0**	....	....	....	....	....
	Providence	AHL	64	31	35	66	57	6	3	5	8	4
1993-94	**Boston**	**NHL**	**24**	**2**	**1**	**3**	**2**	....	....	....	....	....
	Providence	AHL	54	29	33	62	16	....	....	....	....	....
1994-95	Providence	AHL	78	23	35	58	42	13	8	5	13	6
	NHL Totals		**25**	**2**	**2**	**4**	**2**	....	....	....	....	....

ZHURIK, ALEXANDER (ZHUH-rihk) EDM.

Defense. Shoots left. 6'3", 195 lbs. Born, Minsk, USSR, May 29, 1975.
(Edmonton's 7th choice, 163rd overall, in 1993 Entry Draft).

			Regular Season					Playoffs				
Season	Club	Lea	GP	G	A	TP	PIM	GP	G	A	TP	PIM
1993-94	Kingston	OHL	59	7	23	30	92	6	0	0	0	4
1994-95	Kingston	OHL	54	3	21	24	51	6	0	0	0	0

ZIB, LUKAS (ZIHB, LOO-kahsh) EDM.

Defense. Shoots right. 6'1", 198 lbs. Born, Ceske Budejovice, Czech., February 24, 1977.
(Edmonton's 3rd choice, 57th overall, in 1995 Entry Draft).

			Regular Season					Playoffs				
Season	Club	Lea	GP	G	A	TP	PIM	GP	G	A	TP	PIM
1994-95	Budejovice	Czech.	13	2	0	2	16	9	1	0	1	6

ZMOLEK, DOUG (zuh-MOH-lehk) DAL.

Defense. Shoots left. 6'2", 220 lbs. Born, Rochester, MN, November 3, 1970.
(Minnesota's 1st choice, 7th overall, in 1989 Entry Draft).

			Regular Season					Playoffs				
Season	Club	Lea	GP	G	A	TP	PIM	GP	G	A	TP	PIM
1989-90	U. Minnesota	WCHA	40	1	10	11	52	....	....	....	....	....
1990-91	U. Minnesota	WCHA	34	11	6	17	38	....	....	....	....	....
1991-92ab	U. Minnesota	WCHA	41	6	20	26	84	....	....	....	....	....
1992-93	**San Jose**	**NHL**	**84**	**5**	**10**	**15**	**229**	....	....	....	....	....
1993-94	**San Jose**	**NHL**	**68**	**0**	**4**	**4**	**122**	....	....	....	....	....
	Dallas	**NHL**	**7**	**1**	**0**	**1**	**11**	**7**	**0**	**1**	**1**	**4**
1994-95	**Dallas**	**NHL**	**42**	**0**	**5**	**5**	**67**	**5**	**0**	**0**	**0**	**10**
	NHL Totals		**201**	**6**	**19**	**25**	**429**	**12**	**0**	**1**	**1**	**14**

a WCHA Second All-Star Team (1992)
b NCAA West Second All-American Team (1992)

Claimed by **San Jose** from **Minnesota** in Dispersal Draft, May 30, 1991. Traded to **Dallas** by **San Jose** with Mike Lalor and cash for Ulf Dahlen and Dallas' seventh round choice (Brad Mehalko) in 1995 Entry Draft, March 19, 1994.

ZOLOTOV, ROMAN (ZOH-loh-tov) PHI.

Defense. Shoots left. 6'1", 191 lbs. Born, Moscow, USSR, February 13, 1974.
(Philadelphia's 5th choice, 127th overall, in 1992 Entry Draft).

			Regular Season					Playoffs				
Season	Club	Lea	GP	G	A	TP	PIM	GP	G	A	TP	PIM
1991-92	Moscow D'amo	CIS	1	0	0	0	0	....	....	....	....	....
1992-93	Moscow D'amo	CIS Jr.			UNAVAILABLE							
1993-94	Moscow D'amo	CIS	33	0	2	2	20	5	0	1	1	6
1994-95	Moscow D'amo	CIS	25	0	2	2	24	8	1	2	3	6

ZOLOTOV, SERGEI (ZOH-loh-tov) CGY.

Left wing. Shoots right. 5'10", 180 lbs. Born, Kazan, USSR, January 27, 1971.
(Calgary's 11th choice, 219th overall, in 1991 Entry Draft).

			Regular Season					Playoffs				
Season	Club	Lea	GP	G	A	TP	PIM	GP	G	A	TP	PIM
1988-89	Soviet Wings	USSR	34	5	1	6	4	....	....	....	....	....
1989-90	Soviet Wings	USSR	48	12	2	14	14	....	....	....	....	....
1990-91	Soviet Wings	USSR	42	9	6	15	12	....	....	....	....	....
1991-92	Soviet Wings	CIS	39	12	5	17	4	....	....	....	....	....
1992-93	Soviet Wings	CIS	42	15	6	21	14	7	3	3	6	0
1993-94	Soviet Wings	CIS	44	16	17	33	31	3	1	0	1	0
1994-95	Soviet Wings	CIS	45	14	31	45	16	4	0	3	3	0

ZOMBO, RICK — ST.L.

Defense. Shoots right. 6'1", 202 lbs. Born, Des Plaines, IL, May 8, 1963.
(Detroit's 6th choice, 149th overall, in 1981 Entry Draft).

			Regular Season					Playoffs				
Season	Club	Lea	GP	G	A	TP	PIM	GP	G	A	TP	PIM
1981-82	North Dakota	WCHA	45	1	15	16	31	....	....	....	....	....
1982-83	North Dakota	WCHA	35	5	11	16	41	....	....	....	....	....
1983-84	North Dakota	WCHA	34	7	24	31	40	....	....	....	....	....
1984-85	**Detroit**	**NHL**	**1**	**0**	**0**	**0**	**0**	....	....	....	....	....
	Adirondack	AHL	56	3	32	35	70	....	....	....	....	....
1985-86	**Detroit**	**NHL**	**14**	**0**	**1**	**1**	**16**	....	....	....	....	....
	Adirondack	AHL	69	7	34	41	94	17	0	4	4	40
1986-87	**Detroit**	**NHL**	**44**	**1**	**4**	**5**	**59**	**7**	**0**	**1**	**1**	**9**
	Adirondack	AHL	25	0	6	6	22	....	....	....	....	....
1987-88	**Detroit**	**NHL**	**62**	**3**	**14**	**17**	**96**	**16**	**0**	**6**	**6**	**55**
1988-89	**Detroit**	**NHL**	**75**	**1**	**20**	**21**	**106**	**6**	**0**	**1**	**1**	**16**
1989-90	**Detroit**	**NHL**	**77**	**5**	**20**	**25**	**95**	....	....	....	....	....
1990-91	**Detroit**	**NHL**	**77**	**4**	**19**	**23**	**55**	**7**	**1**	**0**	**1**	**10**
1991-92	**Detroit**	**NHL**	**3**	**0**	**0**	**0**	**15**	....	....	....	....	....
	St. Louis	**NHL**	**64**	**3**	**15**	**18**	**46**	**6**	**0**	**2**	**2**	**12**
1992-93	**St. Louis**	**NHL**	**71**	**0**	**15**	**15**	**78**	**11**	**0**	**1**	**1**	**12**
1993-94	**St. Louis**	**NHL**	**74**	**2**	**8**	**10**	**85**	**4**	**0**	**0**	**0**	**11**
1994-95	**St. Louis**	**NHL**	**23**	**1**	**4**	**5**	**24**	**3**	**0**	**0**	**0**	**2**
	NHL Totals		**585**	**20**	**120**	**140**	**675**	**60**	**1**	**11**	**12**	**127**

Traded to **St. Louis** by **Detroit** for Vincent Riendeau, October 18, 1991.

ZUBOV, SERGEI (ZOO-bahf) NYR

Defense. Shoots right. 6'1", 200 lbs. Born, Moscow, USSR, July 22, 1970.
(NY Rangers' 6th choice, 85th overall, in 1990 Entry Draft).

			Regular Season					Playoffs				
Season	Club	Lea	GP	G	A	TP	PIM	GP	G	A	TP	PIM
1988-89	CSKA	USSR	29	1	4	5	10	....	....	....	....	....
1989-90	CSKA	USSR	48	6	2	8	16	....	....	....	....	....
1990-91	CSKA	USSR	41	6	5	11	12	....	....	....	....	....
1991-92	CSKA	CIS	44	4	7	11	8	....	....	....	....	....
1992-93	CSKA	CIS	1	0	1	1	0	....	....	....	....	....
	NY Rangers	**NHL**	**49**	**8**	**23**	**31**	**4**	....	....	....	....	....
	Binghamton	AHL	30	7	29	36	14	11	5	5	10	2
1993-94	**NY Rangers**	**NHL**	**78**	**12**	**77**	**89**	**39**	**22**	**5**	**14**	**19**	**0**
	Binghamton	AHL	2	1	2	3	0	....	....	....	....	....
1994-95	**NY Rangers**	**NHL**	**38**	**10**	**26**	**36**	**18**	**10**	**3**	**8**	**11**	**2**
	NHL Totals		**165**	**30**	**126**	**156**	**61**	**32**	**8**	**22**	**30**	**2**

Retired NHL Player Index

Abbreviations: Teams/Cities: — **Ana.** – Anaheim; **Atl.** – Atlanta; **Bos.** – Boston, **Bro.** – Brooklyn; **Buf.** – Buffalo; **Cal.** – California; **Cgy.** – Calgary; **Cle.** – Cleveland; **Col.** – Colorado; **Dal.** – Dallas; **Det.** – Detroit; **Edm.** – Edmonton; **Fla.** – Florida; **Ham.** – Hamilton; **Hfd.** – Hartford; **K.C.** – Kansas City; **L.A.** – Los Angeles; **Min.** — Minnesota; **Mtl.** – Montreal; **Mtl. M.** – Montreal Maroons; **Mtl. W.** – Montreal Wanderers; **N.J.** – New Jersey; **NYA** – NY Americans; **NYI** – New York Islanders; **NYR** – New York Rangers; **Oak.** – Oakland; **Ott.** – Ottawa; **Phi.** – Philadelphia; **Pit.** – Pittsburgh; **Que.** – Quebec; **St. L.** – St. Louis; **S.J.** – San Jose; **T.B.** – Tampa Bay; **Tor.** – Toronto; **Van.** – Vancouver; **Wpg.** – Winnipeg; **Wsh.** – Washington. Total seasons are rounded off to the nearest full season. **A** – assists; **G** – goals; **GP** – games played; **PIM** – penalties in minutes; **TP** – total points. ● – deceased. Assists not recorded during 1917-18 season.

Peter Ahola

Scott Arniel

Keith Acton

Brent Ashton

Name	NHL Teams	NHL Seasons	Regular Schedule GP	G	A	TP	PIM	Playoffs GP	G	A	TP	PIM	NHL Cup Wins	First NHL Season	Last NHL Season

A

Name	NHL Teams	NHL Seasons	GP	G	A	TP	PIM	GP	G	A	TP	PIM	NHL Cup Wins	First NHL Season	Last NHL Season
Abbott, Reg	Mtl.	1	3	0	0	0	0							1952-53	1952-53
● Abel, Clarence	NYR, Chi.	8	333	18	18	36	359	38	1	1	2	58	2	1926-27	1933-34
Abel, Gerry	Det.	1	1	0	0	0	0							1966-67	1966-67
Abel, Sid	Det., Chi.	14	613	189	283	472	376	96	28	30	58	77	3	1938-39	1953-54
Abgrall, Dennis	L.A.	1	13	0	2	2	4							1975-76	1975-76
Abrahamsson, Thommy	Hfd.	1	32	6	11	17	16							1980-81	1980-81
Achtymichuk, Gene	Mtl., Det.	4	32	3	5	8	2							1951-52	1958-59
Acomb, Doug	Tor.	1	2	0	1	1	0							1969-70	1969-70
Acton, Keith	Mtl., Min., Edm., Phi., Wsh., NYI	15	1023	226	358	584	1172	66	12	21	33	88	1	1979-80	1993-94
Adam, Douglas	NYR	1	4	0	1	1	0							1949-50	1949-50
Adam, Russ	Tor.	1	8	1	2	3	11							1982-83	1982-83
Adams, Greg C.	Phi., Hfd., Wsh., Edm., Van., Que., Det.	10	545	84	143	227	1173	43	2	11	13	153		1980-81	1989-90
Adams, Jack	Mtl.	1	42	6	12	18	11	3	0	0	0	0		1940-41	1940-41
● Adams, Jack J.	Tor., Ott.	7	173	82	29	111	307	10	3	0	3	12	2	1917-18	1926-27
Adams, Stewart	Chi., Tor.	4	106	9	26	35	60	11	3	3	6	14		1929-30	1932-33
Adduono, Rick	Bos., Atl.	2	4	0	0	0	0							1975-76	1979-80
Affleck, Bruce	St.L., Van., NYI	7	280	14	66	80	86	8	0	0	0	0		1974-75	1983-84
Agnew, Jim	Van., Hfd.	6	81	0	1	1	257	4	0	0	0	6		1986-87	1992-93
Ahern, Fred	Cal., Cle., Col.	4	146	31	30	61	130	2	0	1	1	2		1974-75	1977-78
Ahlin, Tony	Chi.	1	1	0	0	0	0							1937-38	1937-38
Ahola, Peter	L.A., Pit., S.J., Cgy.	3	123	10	17	27	137	6	0	0	0	2		1991-92	1993-94
Ahrens, Chris	Min.	6	52	0	3	3	14	1	0	0	0	0		1973-74	1977-78
Ailsby, Lloyd	NYR	1	3	0	0	0	2							1951-52	1951-52
Aitken, Brad	Pit., Edm.	2	14	1	3	4	25							1987-88	1990-91
Albright, Clint	NYR	1	59	14	5	19	19							1948-49	1948-49
Aldcorn, Gary	Tor., Det., Bos.	5	226	41	56	97	78	6	1	2	3	4		1956-57	1960-61
Alexander, Claire	Tor., Van.	4	155	18	47	65	36	16	2	4	6	4		1974-75	1977-78
● Alexandre, Art	Mtl.	2	11	0	2	2	8	4	0	0	0	0		1931-32	1932-33
Allen, George	NYR, Chi., Mtl.	8	339	82	115	197	179	41	9	10	19	32		1938-39	1946-47
Allen, Jeff	Cle.	1	4	0	0	0	0							1977-78	1977-78
Allen, Keith	Det.	2	28	0	4	4	8	5	0	0	0	0	1	1953-54	1954-55
Allen, Viv	NYA	1	6	0	1	1	0							1940-41	1940-41
Alley, Steve	Hfd.	2	15	3	3	6	11	3	0	1	1	0		1979-80	1980-81
Allison, Dave	Mtl.	1	3	0	0	0	12							1983-84	1983-84
Allison, Mike	NYR, Tor., L.A.	10	499	102	166	268	630	82	9	17	26	135		1980-81	1989-90
Allison, Ray	Hfd., Phi.	7	238	64	93	157	223	12	2	3	5	20		1979-80	1986-87
Allum, Bill	Chi., NYR	2	1	0	1	1	0							1939-40	1940-41
● Amadio, Dave	Det., L.A.	3	125	5	11	16	163	16	1	2	3	18		1957-58	1968-69
Amodeo, Mike	Wpg.	1	19	0	0	0	2							1979-80	1979-80
Anderson, Bill	Bos.	1						1	0	0	0	0		1942-43	1942-43
Anderson, Dale	Det.	1	13	0	0	0	6	2	0	0	0	0		1956-57	1956-57
Anderson, Doug	Mtl.	1						2	0	0	0	0		1952-53	1952-53
Anderson, Earl	Det., Bos.	3	109	19	19	38	22	5	0	1	1	0		1974-75	1976-77
Anderson, Jim	L.A.	1	7	1	2	3	2							1967-68	1967-68
Anderson, John	Tor., Que., Hfd.	12	814	282	349	631	263	37	9	18	27	2		1967-68	1967-68
Anderson, Murray	Wsh.	1	40	0	1	1	68							1974-75	1974-75
Anderson, Perry	St.L., N.J., S.J.	10	400	50	59	109	1051	36	2	1	3	161		1981-82	1991-92
Anderson, Ron C.	Det., L.A., St.L., Buf.	5	251	28	30	58	146	5	0	0	0	4		1967-68	1971-72
Anderson, Ron H.	Wsh.	1	28	9	7	16	8							1974-75	1974-75
Anderson, Russ	Pit., Hfd., L.A.	10	519	22	99	121	1086	10	0	3	3	28		1976-77	1984-85
● Anderson, Tom	Det., NYA, Bro.	8	319	62	127	189	190	16	2	7	9	62		1934-35	1941-42
Andersson, Kent-Erik	Min., NYR	7	456	72	103	175	78	50	4	11	15	4		1977-78	1983-84
Andersson, Peter	Wsh., Que.	3	172	10	41	51	80	7	0	2	2	2		1983-84	1985-86
Andrascik, Steve	NYR	1						1	0	0	0	0		1971-72	1971-72
Andrea, Paul	NYR, Pit., Cal., Buf.	4	150	31	49	80	12							1965-66	1970-71
Andrews, Lloyd	Tor.	4	53	8	5	13	10	7	2	0	2	5		1921-22	1924-25
Andrijevski, Alexander	Chi.	1	1	0	0	0	0							1992-93	1992-93
Andruff, Ron	Mtl., Col.	5	153	19	36	55	54	2	0	0	0	0		1974-75	1978-79
Angotti, Lou	NYR, Chi., Phi., Pit., St.L.	10	653	103	186	289	228	65	8	8	16	17		1964-65	1973-74
Anholt, Darrel	Chi.	1	1	0	0	0	0							1983-84	1983-84
Anslow, Bert	NYR	1	2	0	0	0	0							1947-48	1947-48
Antonovich, Mike	Min., Hfd., N.J.	5	87	10	15	25	37							1975-76	1983-84
Apps, Syl (Jr.)	NYR, Pit., L.A.	10	727	183	423	606	311	23	5	5	10	23		1970-71	1979-80
Apps, Syl (Sr.)	Tor.	10	423	201	231	432	56	69	25	28	53	16	3	1936-37	1947-48
Arbour, Al	Det., Chi., Tor., St.L.	14	626	12	58	70	617	86	1	8	9	92	3	1953-54	1970-71
● Arbour, Amos	Mtl., Ham., Tor.	6	109	51	13	64	66							1918-19	1923-24
Arbour, Jack	Det., Tor.	2	47	5	1	6	56							1926-27	1928-29
Arbour, John	Bos., Pit., Van., St.L.	5	106	1	9	10	149	5	0	0	0	0		1965-66	1971-72
Arbour, Ty	Pit., Chi.	5	207	28	28	56	112	11	2	0	2	6		1926-27	1930-31
Archambault, Michel	Chi.	1	3	0	0	0	0							1976-77	1976-77
Archibald, Jim	Min.	3	16	1	2	3	45							1984-85	1986-87
Areshenkoff, Ronald	Edm.	1	4	0	0	0	0							1979-80	1979-80
● Armstrong, Bob	Bos.	12	542	13	86	99	671	42	1	7	8	28		1950-51	1961-62
Armstrong, George	Tor.	21	1187	296	417	713	721	110	26	34	60	88	4	1949-50	1970-71
Armstrong, Murray	Tor., NYA, Bro., Det.	8	270	67	121	188	62	30	4	6	10	2		1937-38	1945-46
● Armstrong, Red	Tor.	1	7	1	1	2	2							1962-63	1962-63
Armstrong, Tim	Tor.	1	11	1	0	1	6							1988-89	1988-89
Arnason, Chuck	Mtl., Atl., Pit., K.C., Col., Cle., Min., Wsh.	8	401	109	90	199	122	9	2	4	6	4		1971-72	1978-79
Arniel, Scott	Wpg., Buf., Bos.	11	730	149	189	338	599	34	3	3	6	39		1981-82	1991-92
Arthur, Fred	Hfd., Phi.	3	80	1	8	9	49	4	0	0	0	2		1980-81	1982-83
Arundel, John	Tor.	1	3	0	0	0	0							1949-50	1949-50
● Ashbee, Barry	Bos., Phi.	5	284	15	70	85	291	17	0	4	4	38		1965-66	1973-74
● Ashby, Don	Tor., Col., Edm.	6	188	40	56	96	40	12	1	0	1	4		1975-76	1980-81
Ashton, Brent	Van., Col., N.J., Min., Que., Det., Wpg., Bos., Cgy.	14	998	284	345	629	635	85	24	25	49	70		1979-80	1992-93
Ashworth, Frank	Chi.	1	18	5	4	9	2							1946-47	1946-47
Asmundson, Oscar	NYR, Det., St.L., NYA, Mtl.	5	112	11	23	34	30	9	0	2	2	4		1932-33	1937-38
Atanas, Walt	NYR	1	49	13	8	21	40							1944-45	1944-45
Atcheynum, Blair	Ott.	1	4	0	1	1	0							1992-93	1992-93
Atkinson, Steve	Bos., Buf., Wsh.	6	302	60	51	111	104	1	0	0	0	0		1968-69	1974-75
Attwell, Bob	Col.	2	22	1	5	6	0							1979-80	1980-81
Attwell, Ron	St.L., NYR	1	22	1	7	8	8							1967-68	1967-68
Aubin, Norm	Tor.	2	69	18	13	31	30	1	0	0	0	0		1981-82	1982-83
Aubry, Pierre	Que., Det.	5	202	24	26	50	133	20	1	1	2	32		1980-81	1984-85
Aubuchon, Ossie	Bos., NYR	2	50	19	12	31	4	6	1	0	1	0		1942-43	1943-44
Auge, Les	Col.	1	6	0	3	3	4							1980-81	1980-81
● Aurie, Larry	Det.	12	489	147	129	276	279	24	6	9	15	10	2	1927-28	1938-39
Awrey, Don	Bos., St.L., Mtl., Pit., NYR, Col.	16	979	31	158	189	1065	71	0	18	18	150	2	1963-64	1978-79
Ayres, Vern	NYA, Mtl.M., St.L., NYR	6	211	6	14	20	350							1930-31	1935-36

B

Name	NHL Teams	NHL Seasons	Regular Schedule GP	G	A	TP	PIM	Playoffs GP	G	A	TP	PIM	NHL Cup Wins	First NHL Season	Last NHL Season
Babando, Pete	Bos., Det., Chi., NYR	6	351	86	73	159	194	17	3	3	6	6	1	1947-48	1952-53
Babcock, Bobby	Wsh.	2	2	0	0	0	2	....	....	....	....	....		1990-91	1992-93
Babe, Warren	Min.	3	21	2	5	7	23	2	0	0	0	0		1987-88	1990-91
Babin, Mitch	St.L.	1	8	0	0	0	0	....	....	....	....	....		1975-76	1975-76
Baby, John	Cle., Min.	2	26	2	8	10	26	....	....	....	....	....		1977-78	1978-79
Babych, Wayne	St.L., Pit., Que., Hfd.	9	519	192	246	438	498	41	7	9	16	25		1978-79	1986-87
Baca, Jergus	Hfd.	2	10	0	2	2	14	....	....	....	....	....		1990-91	1991-92
Backman, Mike	NYR	3	18	1	6	7	18	10	2	2	4	2		1981-82	1983-84
Backor, Peter	Tor.	1	36	4	5	9	6	....	....	....	....	....	1	1944-45	1944-45
Backstrom, Ralph	Mtl., L.A., Chi.	17	1032	278	361	639	386	116	27	32	59	68	6	1956-57	1972-73
Bailey, Ace (G.)	Bos., Det., St.L., Wsh.	10	568	107	171	278	633	15	2	4	6	28	1	1968-69	1977-78
• Bailey, Ace (I.)	Tor.	8	313	111	82	193	472	21	3	4	7	12	1	1926-27	1933-34
Bailey, Bob	Tor., Det., Chi.	4	150	15	21	36	207	15	0	4	4	22		1953-54	1957-58
Bailey, Reid	Phi., Tor., Hfd.	4	40	1	3	4	105	16	0	2	2	25		1980-81	1983-84
Baillargeon, Joel	Wpg., Que.	3	20	0	2	2	31	....	....	....	....	....		1986-87	1988-89
Baird, Ken	Cal.	1	10	0	2	2	15	....	....	....	....	....		1971-72	1971-72
Baker, Bill	Mtl., Col., St.L., NYR	3	143	7	25	32	175	6	0	0	0	0		1980-81	1982-83
Bakovic, Peter	Van.	1	10	2	0	2	48	....	....	....	....	....		1987-88	1987-88
Balderis, Helmut	Min.	1	26	3	6	9	2	....	....	....	....	....		1989-90	1989-90
Baldwin, Doug	Tor., Det., Chi.	3	24	0	1	1	8	....	....	....	....	....		1945-46	1947-48
Balfour, Earl	Tor., Chi.,	7	288	30	22	52	78	26	0	3	3	4	1	1951-52	1960-61
• Balfour, Murray	Mtl., Chi., Bos.	8	306	67	90	157	393	40	9	10	19	45	1	1956-57	1964-65
Ball, Terry	Phi., Buf.	4	74	7	19	26	26	....	....	....	....	....		1967-68	1971-72
Balon, Dave	NYR, Mtl., Min., Van.	14	776	192	222	414	607	78	14	21	35	109	2	1959-60	1972-73
Baltimore, Byron	Edm.	1	2	0	0	0	4	....	....	....	....	....		1979-80	1979-80
Baluik, Stanley	Bos.	1	7	0	0	0	2	....	....	....	....	....		1959-60	1959-60
Bandura, Jeff	NYR	1	2	0	1	1	0	....	....	....	....	....		1980-81	1980-81
Banks, Darren	Bos.	2	20	2	2	4	73	....	....	....	....	....		1992-93	1993-94
Barahona, Ralph	Bos.	2	6	2	2	4	0	....	....	....	....	....		1990-91	1991-92
Barbe, Andy	Tor.	1	1	0	0	0	2	....	....	....	....	....		1950-51	1950-51
Barber, Bill	Phi.	12	903	420	463	883	623	129	53	55	108	109	2	1972-73	1984-85
Barber, Don	Min., Wpg., Que., S.J.	4	115	25	32	57	64	11	4	4	8	10		1988-89	1991-92
• Barilko, Bill	Tor.	5	252	26	36	62	456	47	5	7	12	104	4	1946-47	1950-51
Barkley, Doug	Chi., Det.	6	253	24	80	104	382	30	0	9	9	63		1957-58	1965-66
Barlow, Bob	Min.	2	77	16	17	33	10	6	2	2	4	6		1969-70	1970-71
Barnes, Blair	L.A.	1	1	0	0	0	0	....	....	....	....	....		1982-83	1982-83
Barnes, Norm	Phi., Hfd.	4	156	6	38	44	178	12	0	0	0	8		1976-77	1981-82
Baron, Normand	Mtl., St.L.	2	27	2	0	2	51	3	0	0	0	22		1983-84	1985-86
Barrett, Fred	Min., L.A.	13	745	25	123	148	671	44	0	2	2	60		1970-71	1983-84
Barrett, John	Det., Wsh., Min.	8	488	20	77	97	604	16	2	2	4	50		1980-81	1987-88
Barrie, Doug	Pit., Buf., L.A.	3	158	10	42	52	268	....	....	....	....	....		1968-69	1971-72
Barry, Ed	Bos.	1	19	1	3	4	2	....	....	....	....	....		1946-47	1946-47
• Barry, Marty	NYA, Bos., Det., Mtl.	12	509	195	192	387	231	43	15	18	33	34	2	1927-28	1939-40
Barry, Ray	Bos.	1	18	1	2	3	6	....	....	....	....	....		1951-52	1951-52
Bartel, Robin	Cgy., Van.	2	41	0	1	1	14	6	0	0	0	16		1985-86	1986-87
Bartlett, Jim	Mtl., NYR, Bos.	5	191	34	23	57	273	2	0	0	0	0		1954-55	1960-61
• Barton, Cliff	Pit., Phi., NYR	3	85	10	9	19	22	....	....	....	....	....		1929-30	1939-40
Bathe, Frank	Det., Phi.,	9	224	3	28	31	542	27	1	3	4	42		1974-75	1983-84
Bathgate, Andy	NYR, Tor., Det., Pit.	17	1069	349	624	973	624	54	21	14	35	76	1	1952-53	1970-71
Bathgate, Frank	NYR	1	2	0	0	0	2	....	....	....	....	....		1952-53	1952-53
• Bauer, Bobby	Bos.	10	327	123	137	260	36	48	11	8	19	6	2	1935-36	1951-52
Baumgartner, Mike	K.C.	1	17	0	0	0	0	....	....	....	....	....		1974-75	1974-75
Baun, Bob	Tor., Oak., Det.	17	964	37	187	224	1493	96	3	12	15	171	4	1956-57	1972-73
Baxter, Paul	Que., Pit., Cgy.	8	472	48	121	169	1564	40	0	5	5	162		1979-80	1986-87
Beadle, Sandy	Wpg.	1	6	1	0	1	2	....	....	....	....	....		1980-81	1980-81
Beaton, Frank	NYR	2	25	1	1	2	43	....	....	....	....	....		1978-79	1979-80
Beattie, Red	Bos., Det., NYA	9	335	62	85	147	137	22	4	2	6	6		1930-31	1938-39
Beaudin, Norm	St.L., Min.	2	25	1	2	3	4	....	....	....	....	....		1967-68	1970-71
Beaudoin, Serge	Atl.	1	3	0	0	0	0	....	....	....	....	....		1979-80	1979-80
Beaudoin, Yves	Wsh.	3	11	0	0	0	5	....	....	....	....	....		1985-86	1987-88
Beck, Barry	Col., NYR, L.A.	10	615	104	251	355	1016	51	10	23	33	77		1977-78	1989-90
Beckett, Bob	Bos.	4	68	7	6	13	18	....	....	....	....	....		1956-57	1963-64
Bedard, James	Chi.	2	22	1	1	2	8	....	....	....	....	....		1949-50	1950-51
Bednarski, John	NYR, Edm.	4	100	2	18	20	114	1	0	0	0	0		1974-75	1979-80
Beers, Eddy	Cgy., St.L.	5	250	94	116	210	256	41	7	10	17	47		1981-82	1985-86
Behling, Dick	Det.	2	5	1	0	1	2	....	....	....	....	....		1940-41	1942-43
Beisler, Frank	NYA	2	2	0	0	0	0	....	....	....	....	....		1936-37	1939-40
Belanger, Alain	Tor.	1	9	0	1	1	6	....	....	....	....	....		1977-78	1977-78
Belanger, Roger	Pit.	1	44	3	5	8	32	....	....	....	....	....		1984-85	1984-85
Belisle, Danny	NYR	1	4	2	0	2	0	....	....	....	....	....		1960-61	1960-61
Beliveau, Jean	Mtl.	20	1125	507	712	1219	1029	162	79	97	176	211	10	1950-51	1970-71
• Bell, Billy	Mtl.W, Mtl., Ott.	6	61	3	1	4	4	9	0	0	0	0	1	1917-18	1923-24
Bell, Bruce	Que., St. L., NYR, Edm.	5	209	12	64	76	113	34	3	5	8	41		1984-85	1989-90
Bell, Harry	NYR	1	1	0	1	1	0	....	....	....	....	....		1946-47	1946-47
Bell, Joe	NYR	2	62	8	9	17	18	....	....	....	....	....		1942-43	1946-47
Belland, Neil	Van., Pit.	6	109	13	32	45	54	21	2	9	11	23		1981-82	1986-87
• Bellefeuille, Pete	Tor., Det.	4	92	26	4	30	58	....	....	....	....	....		1925-26	1929-30
• Bellemer, Andy	Mtl.M.	1	15	0	0	0	0	....	....	....	....	....		1932-33	1932-33
Bend, Lin	NYR	1	8	3	1	4	2	....	....	....	....	....		1942-43	1942-43
Bennett, Bill	Bos., Hfd.	2	31	4	7	11	65	....	....	....	....	....		1978-79	1979-80
Bennett, Curt	St.L., NYR, Atl.	10	580	152	182	334	347	21	1	1	2	57		1970-71	1979-80
Bennett, Frank	Det.	1	7	0	1	1	2	....	....	....	....	....		1943-44	1943-44
Bennett, Harvey	Pit., Wsh., Phi., Min., St.L.	5	268	44	46	90	347	4	0	0	0	2		1974-75	1978-79
• Bennett, Max	Mtl.	1	1	0	0	0	0	....	....	....	....	....		1935-36	1935-36
Bennett, Rick	NYR	3	15	1	1	2	13	....	....	....	....	....		1989-90	1991-92
Benning, Jim	Tor., Van.	9	605	52	191	243	461	7	1	1	2	2		1981-82	1989-90
• Benoit, Joe	Mtl.	5	185	75	69	144	94	11	6	3	9	11	1	1940-41	1946-47
Benson, Bill	NYA, Bro.	2	67	11	25	36	35	....	....	....	....	....		1940-41	1941-42
Benson, Bobby	Bos.	1	8	0	1	1	4	....	....	....	....	....		1924-25	1924-25
• Bentley, Doug	Chi., NYR	13	566	219	324	543	217	23	9	8	17	8		1939-40	1953-54
• Bentley, Max	Chi., Tor., NYR	12	646	245	299	544	179	52	18	27	45	14	3	1940-41	1953-54
Bentley, Reggie	Chi.	1	11	1	2	3	2	....	....	....	....	....		1942-43	1942-43
Beraldo, Paul	Bos.	2	10	0	0	0	4	....	....	....	....	....		1987-88	1988-89
Berenson, Red	Mtl., NYR, St.L., Det.	17	987	261	397	658	305	85	23	14	37	49	2	1961-62	1977-78
Berezan, Perry	Cgy., Min., S.J.	9	378	61	75	136	279	31	4	7	11	34		1984-85	1992-93
Bergdinon, Fred	Bos.	1	2	0	0	0	0	....	....	....	....	....		1925-26	1925-26
Bergen, Todd	Phi.	1	14	11	5	16	4	17	4	9	13	8		1984-85	1984-85
Berger, Mike	Min.	2	30	3	1	4	67	....	....	....	....	....		1987-88	1988-89
Bergeron, Michel	Det., NYI, Wsh.	5	229	80	58	138	165	....	....	....	....	....		1974-75	1978-79
Bergeron, Yves	Pit.	2	3	0	0	0	0	....	....	....	....	....		1974-75	1976-77
Bergloff, Bob	Min.	1	2	0	0	0	5	....	....	....	....	....		1982-83	1982-83
Berglund, Bo	Que., Min., Phi.	3	130	28	39	67	40	9	2	0	2	6		1983-84	1985-86
Bergman, Gary	Det., Min., K.C.	12	838	68	299	367	1249	21	0	5	5	20		1964-65	1975-76
Bergman, Thommie	Det.	6	246	21	44	65	243	7	0	2	2	2		1972-73	1979-80
Bergqvist, Jonas	Cgy.	1	22	2	5	7	10	....	....	....	....	....		1989-90	1989-90
• Berlinquette, Louis	Mtl., Mtl.M., Pit.	8	193	44	29	73	111	16	1	1	2	0		1917-18	1925-26
Bernier, Serge	Phi., L.A., Que.	7	302	78	119	197	234	5	1	1	2	0		1968-69	1980-81
Berry, Bob	Mtl., L.A.	8	541	159	191	350	344	26	2	6	8	6		1968-69	1976-77
Berry, Doug	Col.	2	121	10	33	43	25	....	....	....	....	....		1979-80	1980-81
Berry, Fred	Det.	1	3	0	0	0	0	....	....	....	....	....		1976-77	1976-77
Berry, Ken	Edm., Van.	4	55	8	10	18	30	....	....	....	....	....		1981-82	1988-89
Besler, Phil	Bos., Chi., Det.	2	30	1	4	5	18	....	....	....	....	....		1935-36	1938-39
Bessone, Pete	Det.	1	6	0	1	1	6	....	....	....	....	....		1937-38	1937-38
Bethel, John	Wpg.	1	17	0	2	2	4	....	....	....	....	....		1979-80	1979-80
Bettio, Sam	Bos.	1	44	9	12	21	32	....	....	....	....	....		1949-50	1949-50
Beverley, Nick	Bos., Pit., NYR, Min., L.A., Col.	11	502	18	94	112	156	7	0	1	1	0		1966-67	1979-80
Bialowas, Dwight	Atl., Min.	4	164	11	46	57	46	....	....	....	....	....		1973-74	1976-77
Bianchin, Wayne	Pit., Edm.	7	276	68	41	109	137	3	0	1	1	6		1973-74	1979-80
Bidner, Todd	Wsh.	1	12	2	1	3	7	....	....	....	....	....		1981-82	1981-82
Biggs, Don	Min.	1	1	0	0	0	0	....	....	....	....	....		1984-85	1984-85
Bignell, Larry	Pit.	2	20	0	3	3	2	3	0	0	0	2		1973-74	1974-75

Ric Bennett

Perry Berezan

Jonas Bergqvist

Gilles Bilodeau

Per-Olav Brasar

Frank Breault

Mike Bullard

Robert Burakovsky

			Regular Schedule					Playoffs							
Name	NHL Teams	NHL Seasons	GP	G	A	TP	PIM	GP	G	A	TP	PIM	NHL Cup Wins	First NHL Season	Last NHL Season
Bilodeau, Gilles	Que.	1	9	0	1	1	25	....	....	....	....	....		1979-80	1979-80
Bionda, Jack	Tor., Bos.	4	93	3	9	12	113	11	0	1	1	14		1955-56	1958-59
Bissett, Tom	Det.	1	5	0	0	0	0	....	....	....	....	....		1990-91	1990-91
Bjugstad, Scott	Min., Pit., L.A.	9	317	76	68	144	144	9	0	1	1	2		1983-84	1991-92
Black, Stephen	Det., Chi.	2	113	11	20	31	77	13	0	0	0	13	1	1949-50	1950-51
Blackburn, Bob	NYR., Pit.	3	135	8	12	20	105	6	0	0	0	4		1968-69	1970-71
Blackburn, Don	Bos., Phi., NYR, NYI, Min.	6	185	23	44	67	87	12	3	0	3	10		1962-63	1972-73
Blade, Hank	Chi.	2	24	2	3	5	2	....	....	....	....	....		1946-47	1947-48
Bladon, Tom	Phi., Pit., Edm., Wpg., Det.	9	610	73	197	270	392	86	8	29	37	70	2	1972-73	1980-81
Blaine, Gary	Mtl.	1	1	0	0	0	0	....	....	....	....	....		1954-55	1954-55
• Blair, Andy	Tor., Chi.	9	402	74	86	160	323	38	6	6	12	32	1	1928-29	1936-37
Blair, Chuck	Tor.	2	3	0	0	0	0	....	....	....	....	....		1948-49	1950-51
Blair, George	Tor.	1	2	0	0	0	0	....	....	....	....	....		1950-51	1950-51
Blaisdell, Mike	Det., NYR, Pit., Tor.	9	343	70	84	154	166	....	....	....	....	....		1980-81	1988-89
Blake, Mickey	St.L., Bos., Tor.	2	16	1	1	2	4	....	....	....	....	....		1934-35	1935-36
• Blake, Toe	Mtl.M., Mtl.	15	578	235	292	527	272	57	25	37	62	23	3	1932-33	1947-48
Blight, Rick	Van., L.A.	7	326	96	125	221	170	5	0	5	5	2		1975-76	1982-83
Blinco, Russ	Mtl.M, Chi.	6	268	59	66	125	24	19	3	3	6	4	1	1933-34	1938-39
Block, Ken	Van.	1	1	0	0	0	0	....	....	....	....	....		1970-71	1970-71
Blomqvist, Timo	Wsh., N.J.	5	243	4	53	57	293	13	0	0	0	24		1981-82	1986-87
Bloom, Mike	Wsh., Det.	3	201	30	47	77	215	....	....	....	....	....		1974-75	1976-77
Blum, John	Edm., Bos., Wsh., Det.	8	250	7	34	41	610	20	0	2	2	27		1982-83	1989-90
Bodak, Bob	Cgy., Hfd.	2	4	0	0	0	29	....	....	....	....	....		1987-88	1989-90
Boddy, Gregg	Van.	5	273	23	44	67	263	3	0	0	0	0		1971-72	1975-76
Bodnar, Gus	Tor., Chi., Bos.	12	667	142	254	396	207	32	4	3	7	10	2	1943-44	1954-55
Boehm, Ron	Oak.	1	16	2	1	3	10	....	....	....	....	....		1967-68	1967-68
Boesch, Garth	Tor.	4	197	9	28	37	205	34	2	5	7	18	3	1946-47	1949-50
Boh, Rick	Min.	1	8	2	1	3	4	....	....	....	....	....		1987-88	1987-88
Boileau, Marc	Det.	1	54	5	6	11	8	....	....	....	....	....		1961-62	1961-62
Boileau, Rene	NYA	1	7	0	0	0	0	....	....	....	....	....		1925-26	1925-26
Boimistruck, Fred	Tor.	2	83	4	14	18	45	....	....	....	....	....		1981-82	1982-83
Boisvert, Serge	Tor., Mtl.	5	46	5	7	12	8	23	3	7	10	4	1	1982-83	1987-88
Boivin, Leo	Tor., Bos., Det., Pit., Min.	19	1150	72	250	322	1192	54	3	10	13	59		1951-52	1969-70
Boland, Mike A.	Phi.	1	2	0	0	0	0	....	....	....	....	....		1974-75	1974-75
Boland, Mike J.	K.C., Buf.	2	23	1	2	3	29	3	1	0	1	2		1974-75	1978-79
Boldirev, Ivan	Bos., Cal., Chi., Atl., Van., Det.	15	1052	361	505	866	507	48	13	20	33	14		1970-71	1984-85
Bolduc, Danny	Det., Cgy.	3	102	22	19	41	33	1	0	0	0	0		1978-79	1983-84
Bolduc, Michel	Que.	2	10	0	0	0	6	....	....	....	....	....		1981-82	1982-83
Boll, Buzz	Tor., NYA, Bro., Bos.	11	436	133	130	263	148	29	7	3	10	13		1933-34	1943-44
Bolonchuk, Larry	Van., Wsh.	4	74	3	9	12	97	....	....	....	....	....		1972-73	1977-78
Bolton, Hughie	Tor.	8	235	10	51	61	221	17	0	5	5	14		1949-50	1956-57
Bonar, Dan	L.A.	3	170	25	39	64	208	14	3	4	7	22		1980-81	1982-83
Bonin, Marcel	Det., Bos., Mtl.	9	454	97	175	272	336	50	11	14	25	51	4	1952-53	1961-62
Boo, Jim	Min.	1	6	0	0	0	22	....	....	....	....	....		1977-78	1977-78
Boone, Buddy	Bos.	2	34	5	3	8	28	22	2	1	3	25		1956-57	1957-58
Boothman, George	Tor.	2	58	17	19	36	18	5	2	1	3	2		1942-43	1943-44
Bordeleau, Chris	Mtl., St.L., Chi.,	4	205	38	65	103	82	19	4	7	11	17	1	1968-69	1971-72
Bordeleau, J.P.	Chi.	10	519	97	126	223	143	48	3	6	9	12		1969-70	1979-80
Bordeleau, Paulin	Van.	3	183	33	56	89	47	5	2	1	3	0		1973-74	1975-76
Borotsik, Jack	St.L.	1	1	0	0	0	0	....	....	....	....	....		1974-75	1974-75
Boschman, Laurie	Tor., Edm., Wpg., N.J., Ott.	14	1009	229	348	577	2265	57	8	13	21	140		1979-80	1992-93
Bossy, Mike	NYI	10	752	573	553	1126	210	129	85	75	160	38	4	1977-78	1986-87
Bostrom, Helge	Chi.	4	96	3	3	6	58	13	0	0	0	16		1929-30	1932-33
Botell, Mark	Phi.	1	32	4	10	14	31	....	....	....	....	....		1981-82	1981-82
Bothwell, Tim	NYR, St.L., Hfd.	11	502	28	93	121	382	49	0	3	3	56		1978-79	1988-89
Botting, Cam	Atl.	1	2	0	1	1	0	....	....	....	....	....		1975-76	1975-76
Boucha, Henry	Det., Min., K.C., Col.	6	247	53	49	102	157	....	....	....	....	....		1971-72	1976-77
Bouchard, Dick	NYR	1	1	0	0	0	0	....	....	....	....	....		1954-55	1954-55
Bouchard, Edmond	Mtl., Ham., NYA, Pit.	8	223	19	20	39	105	....	....	....	....	....		1921-22	1928-29
Bouchard, Emile (Butch)	Mtl.	15	784	49	144	193	863	113	11	21	32	121	4	1941-42	1955-56
Bouchard, Pierre	Mtl., Wsh.	12	595	24	82	106	433	76	3	10	13	56	5	1970-71	1981-82
• Boucher, Billy	Mtl., Bos., NYA	7	213	93	35	128	391	21	9	3	12	35	1	1921-22	1927-28
• Boucher, Frank	Ott., NYR	14	557	161	262	423	119	56	16	18	34	12	2	1921-22	1943-44
• Boucher, George	Ott., Mtl.M, Chi.	15	457	122	62	184	712	44	11	4	15	84	4	1917-18	1931-32
• Boucher, Robert	Mtl.	1	12	0	0	0	0	....	....	....	....	....	1	1923-24	1923-24
Boudreau, Bruce	Tor., Chi.	8	141	28	42	70	46	9	2	0	2	0		1976-77	1985-86
Boudrias, Andre	Mtl., Min., Chi., St.L., Van.	12	662	151	340	491	218	34	6	10	16	12		1963-64	1975-76
Boughner, Barry	Oak., Cal.	2	20	0	0	0	11	....	....	....	....	....		1969-70	1970-71
Bourbonnais, Dan	Hfd.	2	59	3	25	28	11	....	....	....	....	....		1981-82	1983-84
Bourbonnais, Rick	St.L.	3	71	9	15	24	29	4	0	1	1	0		1975-76	1977-78
Bourcier, Conrad	Mtl.	1	6	0	0	0	0	....	....	....	....	....		1935-36	1935-36
Bourcier, Jean	Mtl.	1	9	0	1	1	0	....	....	....	....	....		1935-36	1935-36
• Bourgeault, Leo	Tor. NYR, Ott., Mtl.	8	307	24	20	44	269	24	1	1	2	18	1	1926-27	1934-35
Bourgeois, Charlie	Cgy., St.L., Hfd.	7	290	16	54	70	788	40	2	3	5	194		1981-82	1987-88
Bourne, Bob	NYI, L.A.	14	964	258	324	582	605	139	40	56	96	108	4	1974-75	1987-88
Boutette, Pat	Tor., Hfd., Pit.	10	756	171	282	453	1354	46	10	14	24	109		1975-76	1984-85
Boutilier, Paul	NYI, Bos., Min., NYR, Wpg.	8	288	27	83	110	358	41	1	9	10	45	1	1981-82	1988-89
Bowcher, Clarence	NYA	2	47	2	2	4	110	....	....	....	....	....		1926-27	1927-28
Bowman, Kirk	Chi.	3	88	11	17	28	19	7	1	0	1	0		1976-77	1978-79
• Bowman, Ralph	Ott., St.L., Det.	7	274	8	17	25	260	22	2	2	4	6	2	1933-34	1939-40
Bownass, Jack	Mtl., NYR	4	80	3	8	11	58	....	....	....	....	....		1957-58	1961-62
Bowness, Rick	Atl., Det., St. L, Wpg.	7	173	18	37	55	191	5	0	0	0	2		1975-76	1981-82
• Boyd, Bill	NYR, NYA	4	138	15	7	22	72	9	0	0	0	2	1	1926-27	1929-30
Boyd, Irwin	Bos., Det.	4	97	18	19	37	51	15	0	1	1	4		1931-32	1943-44
Boyd, Randy	Pit., Chi., NYI, Van.	8	257	20	67	87	328	13	0	2	2	26		1981-82	1988-89
Boyer, Wally	Tor., Chi., Oak. Pit.	7	365	54	105	159	163	15	1	3	4	0		1965-66	1971-72
Boyko, Darren	Wpg.	1	1	0	0	0	0	....	....	....	....	....		1988-89	1988-89
Bozek, Steve	L.A., Cgy., St. L., Van., S.J.	11	641	164	167	331	309	58	12	11	23	69		1981-82	1991-92
• Brackenborough, John	Bos.	1	7	0	0	0	0	....	....	....	....	....		1925-26	1925-26
Brackenbury, Curt	Que., Edm., St.L.	4	141	9	17	26	226	2	0	0	0	0		1979-80	1982-83
Bradley, Barton	Bos.	1	1	0	0	0	0	....	....	....	....	....		1949-50	1949-50
Bradley, Lyle	Cal. Cle.	2	6	1	0	1	2	....	....	....	....	....		1973-74	1976-77
Bragnalo, Rick	Wsh.	4	145	15	35	50	46	....	....	....	....	....		1975-76	1978-79
Brannigan, Andy	NYA, Bro.	2	26	1	2	3	31	....	....	....	....	....		1940-41	1941-42
Brasar, Per-Olov	Min., Van.	5	348	64	142	206	33	13	1	2	3	0		1977-78	1981-82
Brayshaw, Russ	Chi.	1	43	5	9	14	24	....	....	....	....	....		1944-45	1944-45
Breault, Francois	L.A.	3	27	2	4	6	42	....	....	....	....	....		1990-91	1992-93
Breitenbach, Ken	Buf.	3	68	1	13	14	49	8	0	1	1	4		1975-76	1978-79
Brennan, Dan	L.A.	2	8	0	1	1	9	....	....	....	....	....		1983-84	1985-86
Brennan, Doug	NYR	3	123	9	7	16	152	16	1	0	1	21	1	1931-32	1933-34
Brennan, Tom	Bos.	2	22	2	2	4	2	....	....	....	....	....		1943-44	1944-45
Brenneman, John	Chi., NYR, Tor., Det., Oak.	5	152	21	19	40	46	....	....	....	....	....		1964-65	1968-69
Bretto, Joe	Chi.	1	3	0	0	0	4	....	....	....	....	....		1944-45	1944-45
Brewer, Carl	Tor., Det., St.L.	12	604	25	198	223	1037	72	3	17	20	146	3	1957-58	1979-80
Briden, Archie	Det., Pit.	2	72	9	5	14	56	....	....	....	....	....		1926-27	1929-30
Bridgman, Mel	Phi., Cgy., N.J., Det., Van.	14	977	252	449	701	1625	125	28	39	67	298		1975-76	1988-89
• Briere, Michel	Pit.	1	76	12	32	44	20	10	5	3	8	17		1969-70	1969-70
Brindley, Doug	Tor.	1	3	0	0	0	0	....	....	....	....	....		1970-71	1970-71
Brink, Milt	Chi.	1	5	0	0	0	0	....	....	....	....	....		1936-37	1936-37
Brisson, Gerry	Mtl.	1	4	0	2	2	4	....	....	....	....	....		1962-63	1962-63
Britz, Greg	Tor., Hfd.	3	8	0	0	0	4	....	....	....	....	....		1983-84	1986-87
• Broadbent, Harry	Ott. Mt.M, NYA	11	302	122	45	167	553	41	13	1	14	69	4	1918-19	1928-29
Brochu, Stephane	NYR	1	1	0	0	0	0	....	....	....	....	....		1988-89	1988-89
Broden, Connie	Mtl.	3	6	2	1	3	2	7	0	1	1	0	2	1955-56	1957-58
Brooke, Bob	NYR, Min., N.J.	7	447	69	97	166	520	34	9	9	18	59		1983-84	1989-90
Brooks, Gord	St.L., Wsh.	3	70	7	18	25	37	....	....	....	....	....		1971-72	1974-75
• Brophy, Bernie	Mtl.M, Det.	3	62	4	4	8	25	2	0	0	0	2	1	1925-26	1929-30
Brossart, Willie	Phi., Tor., Wsh.	6	129	1	14	15	88	1	0	0	0	0		1970-71	1975-76
Broten, Aaron	Col., N.J., Min., Que., Tor., Wpg.	12	748	186	329	515	441	34	7	18	25	40		1980-81	1991-92
• Brown, Adam	Det. Chi. Bos.	10	391	104	113	217	358	26	2	14	6	14	1	1941-42	1951-52
Brown, Arnie	Tor. NYR, Det., NYI, Atl.	12	681	44	141	185	738	22	0	6	6	23		1961-62	1973-74
Brown, Cam	Van.	1	1	0	0	0	7	....	....	....	....	....		1990-91	1990-91
Brown, Connie	Det.	5	91	15	24	39	12	14	2	3	5	0		1938-39	1942-43
Brown, Fred	Mtl.M	1	19	1	0	1	0	9	0	0	0	0		1927-28	1927-28

Name	NHL Teams	NHL Seasons	Regular Schedule GP	G	A	TP	PIM	Playoffs GP	G	A	TP	PIM	NHL Cup Wins	First NHL Season	Last NHL Season
Brown, George	Mtl.	3	79	6	22	28	34	7	0	0	0	2		1936-37	1938-39
Brown, Gerry	Det.	2	23	4	5	9	2	12	2	1	3	4		1941-42	1945-46
Brown, Harold	NYR	1	13	2	1	3	2	....	....	....	....	....		1945-46	1945-46
Brown, Jim	L.A.	1	3	0	1	1	5	....	....	....	....	....		1982-83	1982-83
Brown, Larry	NYR, Det., Phi., L.A.	9	455	7	53	60	180	35	0	4	4	10		1969-70	1977-78
Brown, Stan	NYR, Det.	2	48	8	2	10	18	2	0	0	0	0		1926-27	1927-28
Brown, Wayne	Bos.	1	....	....	....	....	....	4	0	0	0	2		1953-54	1953-54
• Browne, Cecil	Chi.	1	13	2	0	2	4	....	....	....	....	....		1927-28	1927-28
Brownschidle, Jack	St.L., Hfd.	9	494	39	162	201	151	26	0	5	5	18		1977-78	1985-86
Brownschidle, Jeff	Hfd.	2	7	0	1	1	2	....	....	....	....	....		1981-82	1982-83
Brubaker, Jeff	Hfd., Mtl., Cgy., Tor., Edm., NYR, Det.	8	178	16	9	25	512	2	0	0	0	27		1979-80	1988-89
Bruce, Gordie	Bos.	3	28	4	9	13	13	7	2	3	5	4		1940-41	1945-46
Bruce, Morley	Ott.	4	72	8	1	9	27	12	0	0	0	3	2	1917-18	1921-22
Brumwell, Murray	Min., N.J.,	7	128	12	31	43	70	2	0	0	0	2		1980-81	1987-88
Bruneteau, Eddie	Det.	7	180	40	42	82	35	26	7	6	13	0		1940-41	1948-49
• Bruneteau, Mud	Det.	11	411	139	138	277	80	77	23	14	37	22	3	1935-36	1945-46
• Brydge, Bill	Tor., Det., NYA	9	368	26	52	78	506	2	0	0	0	4		1926-27	1935-36
Brydges, Paul	Buf.	1	15	2	2	4	6	....	....	....	....	....		1986-87	1986-87
• Brydson, Glenn	Mtl.M, St.L., NYR, Chi.	8	299	56	79	135	203	11	0	0	0	8		1930-31	1937-38
Brydson, Gord	Tor.	1	8	2	0	2	8	....	....	....	....	....		1929-30	1929-30
Bubla, Jiri	Van.	5	256	17	101	118	202	6	0	0	0	7		1981-82	1985-86
Buchanan, Al	Tor.	2	4	0	1	1	2	....	....	....	....	....		1948-49	1949-50
Buchanan, Bucky	NYR	1	2	0	0	0	0	....	....	....	....	....		1948-49	1948-49
Buchanan, Mike	Chi.	1	1	0	0	0	0	....	....	....	....	....		1951-52	1951-52
Buchanan, Ron	Bos., St.L.	2	5	0	0	0	0	....	....	....	....	....		1966-67	1969-70
Bucyk, John	Det., Bos.,	23	1540	556	813	1369	497	124	41	62	103	42	2	1955-56	1977-78
Bucyk, Randy	Mtl., Cgy.	2	19	4	2	6	8	2	0	0	0	0		1985-86	1987-88
Buhr, Doug	K.C.	1	6	0	2	2	4	....	....	....	....	....		1974-75	1974-75
Bukovich, Tony	Det.	2	44	7	3	10	6	6	0	1	1	0		1943-44	1944-45
Bullard, Mike	Pit., Cgy., St.L., Phi., Tor.	11	727	329	345	674	703	40	11	18	29	44		1980-81	1991-92
• Buller, Hy	Det., NYR	5	188	22	58	80	215	....	....	....	....	....		1943-44	1953-54
Bulley, Ted	Chi., Wsh., Pit.	8	414	101	113	214	704	29	5	5	10	24		1976-77	1983-84
Burakovsky, Robert	Ott.	1	23	2	3	5	6	....	....	....	....	....		1993-94	1993-94
• Burch, Billy	Ham., NYA, Bos., Chi.	11	390	137	53	190	251	2	0	0	0	0		1922-23	1932-33
Burchell, Fred	Mtl.	2	4	0	0	0	2	....	....	....	....	....		1950-51	1953-54
Burdon, Glen	K.C.	1	11	0	2	2	0	....	....	....	....	....		1974-75	1974-75
Burega, Bill	Tor.	1	4	0	1	1	4	....	....	....	....	....		1955-56	1955-56
Burke, Eddie	Bos., NYA	4	106	29	20	49	55	....	....	....	....	....		1931-32	1934-35
• Burke, Marty	Mtl., Pit., Ott., Chi.	11	494	19	47	66	560	31	2	4	6	44	2	1927-28	1937-38
Burmeister, Roy	NYA	3	67	4	3	7	2	....	....	....	....	....		1929-30	1931-32
Burnett, Kelly	NYR	1	3	1	0	1	0	....	....	....	....	....		1952-53	1952-53
Burns, Bobby	Chi.	3	20	1	0	1	8	....	....	....	....	....		1927-28	1929-30
Burns, Charlie	Det., Bos., Oak., Pit., Min.	11	749	106	198	304	252	31	5	4	9	4		1958-59	1972-73
Burns, Gary	NYR	2	11	2	2	4	18	5	0	0	0	6		1980-81	1981-82
• Burns, Norm	NYR	1	11	0	4	4	2	....	....	....	....	....		1941-42	1941-42
Burns, Robin	Pit., K.C.	5	190	31	38	69	139	....	....	....	....	....		1970-71	1975-76
Burrows, Dave	Pit., Tor.	10	724	29	135	164	377	29	1	5	6	25		1971-72	1980-81
Burry, Bert	Ott.	1	4	0	0	0	0	....	....	....	....	....		1932-33	1932-33
Burton, Cummy	Det.	3	43	0	2	2	21	3	0	0	0	0		1955-56	1958-59
Burton, Nelson	Wsh.	2	8	1	0	1	21	....	....	....	....	....		1977-78	1978-79
• Bush, Eddie	Det.	2	27	4	6	10	50	12	1	6	7	23		1938-39	1941-42
Buskas, Rod	Pit., Van., L.A., Chi.	11	556	19	63	82	1294	18	0	3	3	45		1982-83	1992-93
Busniuk, Mike	Phi.	2	143	3	23	26	297	25	2	5	7	34		1979-80	1980-81
Busniuk, Ron	Buf.	2	6	0	3	3	4	....	....	....	....	....		1972-73	1973-74
• Buswell, Walt	Det., Mtl.	8	368	10	40	50	164	24	2	1	3	10		1932-33	1939-40
Butler, Dick	Chi.	1	7	2	0	2	0	....	....	....	....	....		1947-48	1947-48
Butler, Jerry	NYR, St.L., Tor., Van., Wpg.	11	641	99	120	219	515	48	3	3	6	79		1972-73	1982-83
Butters, Bill	Min.	2	72	1	4	5	77	....	....	....	....	....		1977-78	1978-79
Buttrey, Gord	Chi.	1	10	0	0	0	0	10	0	0	0	0		1943-44	1943-44
Buynak, Gordon	St. L	1	4	0	0	0	2	....	....	....	....	....		1974-75	1974-75
Byce, John	Bos.	3	21	2	3	5	6	8	2	0	2	2		1989-90	1991-92
Byers, Gord	Bos.	1	1	0	1	1	0	....	....	....	....	....		1949-50	1949-50
Byers, Jerry	Min., Atl, NYR	4	43	3	4	7	10	....	....	....	....	....		1972-73	1977-78
Byers, Lyndon	Bos., S.J.	10	279	28	43	71	1081	37	2	2	4	96		1983-84	1992-93
Byers, Mike	Tor., Phi., Buf., L.A.	4	166	42	34	76	39	4	0	1	1	0		1967-68	1971-72
Byram, Shawn	NYI, Chi.	2	5	0	0	0	14	....	....	....	....	....		1990-91	1991-92

C

Name	NHL Teams	NHL Seasons	Regular Schedule GP	G	A	TP	PIM	Playoffs GP	G	A	TP	PIM	NHL Cup Wins	First NHL Season	Last NHL Season
• Caffery, Jack	Tor., Bos.	3	57	3	2	5	22	10	1	0	1	4		1954-55	1957-58
Caffery, Terry	Chi., Min.	2	14	0	0	0	0	1	0	0	0	0		1969-70	1970-71
• Cahan, Larry	Tor., NYR, Oak., L.A.	13	665	38	92	130	700	29	1	1	2	38		1954-55	1970-71
Cahill, Chuck	Bos.	2	32	0	1	1	4	....	....	....	....	....		1925-26	1926-27
• Cain, Herb	Mtl.M, Mtl., Bos.	13	571	206	194	400	178	64	16	13	29	13	2	1933-34	1945-46
• Cain, Jim	Mtl.M, Tor.	2	61	4	0	4	35	....	....	....	....	....	1	1924-25	1925-26
Cairns, Don	K.C., Col.	2	9	0	1	1	2	....	....	....	....	....		1975-76	1976-77
Calder, Eric	Wsh.	2	2	0	0	0	0	....	....	....	....	....		1981-82	1982-83
Calladine, Norm	Bos.	3	63	19	29	48	8	....	....	....	....	....		1942-43	1944-45
Callander, Drew	Phi., Van.	4	39	6	2	8	7	....	....	....	....	....		1976-77	1979-80
Callander, John (Jock)	Pit., T.B.	5	109	22	29	51	116	22	3	8	11	12	1	1987-88	1992-93
Callighen, Brett	Edm.	3	160	56	89	145	132	14	4	6	10	8		1979-80	1981-82
Callighen, Patsy	NYR	1	36	0	0	0	32	9	0	0	0	0	1	1927-28	1927-28
Camazzola, James	Chi.	2	3	0	0	0	0	....	....	....	....	....		1983-84	1986-87
Camazzola, Tony	Wsh.	1	3	0	0	0	4	....	....	....	....	....		1981-82	1981-82
Cameron, Al	Det., Wpg.	6	282	11	44	55	356	7	0	1	1	2		1975-76	1980-81
Cameron, Billy	Mtl., NYA	2	39	0	0	0	2	6	0	0	0	0	1	1923-24	1925-26
Cameron, Craig	Det., St.L., Min., NYI	9	552	87	65	152	202	27	3	1	4	17		1966-67	1975-76
Cameron, Dave	Col., N.J.	3	168	25	28	53	238	....	....	....	....	....		1981-82	1983-84
• Cameron, Harry	Tor., Ott., Mtl.	6	127	90	27	117	120	20	7	3	10	29	3	1917-18	1922-23
Cameron, Scotty	NYR	1	35	8	11	19	0	....	....	....	....	....		1942-43	1942-43
Campbell, Bryan	L.A., Chi.	5	260	35	71	106	74	22	3	4	7	2		1967-68	1971-72
Campbell, Colin	Pit., Col., Edm., Van., Det.	11	636	25	103	128	1292	45	4	10	14	181		1974-75	1984-85
• Campbell, Dave	Mtl.	1	3	0	0	0	0	....	....	....	....	....		1920-21	1920-21
Campbell, Don	Chi.	1	17	1	3	4	8	....	....	....	....	....		1943-44	1943-44
Campbell, Scott	Wpg., St.L.	3	80	4	21	25	243	....	....	....	....	....		1979-80	1981-82
Campbell, Spiff	Ott., NYA	3	77	5	1	6	12	2	0	0	0	0		1923-24	1925-26
Campbell, Wade	Wpg., Bos.	6	213	9	27	36	305	10	0	0	0	20		1982-83	1987-88
Campeau, Tod	Mtl.	3	42	5	9	14	16	1	0	0	0	0		1943-44	1948-49
Campedelli, Dom	Mtl.	1	2	0	0	0	0	....	....	....	....	....		1985-86	1985-86
Capuano, Dave	Pit., Van., T.B., S.J.	4	104	17	38	55	56	6	1	1	2	5		1989-90	1993-94
Capuano, Jack	Tor., Van., Bos.	3	6	0	0	0	0	....	....	....	....	....		1989-90	1991-92
Carbol, Leo	Chi.	1	6	0	1	1	4	....	....	....	....	....		1942-43	1942-43
Cardin, Claude	St.L.	1	1	0	0	0	0	....	....	....	....	....		1967-68	1967-68
Cardwell, Steve	Pit.	3	53	9	11	20	35	4	0	0	0	2		1970-71	1972-73
• Carey, George	Que, Ham., Tor.	5	72	22	8	30	14	....	....	....	....	....		1919-20	1923-24
Carleton, Wayne	Tor., Bos., Cal.	7	278	55	73	128	172	18	2	4	6	14	1	1965-66	1971-72
Carlin, Brian	L.A.	1	5	1	0	1	0	....	....	....	....	....		1971-72	1971-72
Carlson, Jack	Min., St.L.	6	236	30	15	45	417	25	1	2	3	72		1978-79	1986-87
Carlson, Kent	Mtl., St.L., Wsh.	5	113	7	11	18	148	8	0	0	0	13		1983-84	1988-89
Carlson, Steve	L.A.	1	52	9	12	21	23	4	1	1	2	7		1979-80	1979-80
Carlsson, Anders	N.J.	3	104	7	26	33	34	3	1	0	1	2		1986-87	1988-89
Carlyle, Randy	Tor., Pit., Wpg.	17	1055	148	499	647	1400	69	9	24	33	120		1976-77	1992-93
• Caron, Alain	Oak., Mtl.	2	60	9	13	22	18	....	....	....	....	....		1967-68	1968-69
• Carpenter, Eddie	Que, Ham.	2	44	10	4	14	23	....	....	....	....	....		1919-20	1920-21
Carr,	Que.	1	1	0	0	0	0	....	....	....	....	....		1919-20	1919-20
Carr, Al	Tor.	1	5	0	1	1	4	....	....	....	....	....		1943-44	1943-44
Carr, Gene	St.L., NYR, L.A., Pit., Atl.	8	465	79	136	215	365	35	5	8	13	66		1971-72	1978-79
Carr, Lorne	NYR, NYA, Tor.	13	580	204	222	426	132	53	10	9	19	13	1	1933-34	1945-46
Carriere, Larry	Buf. Atl, Van., L.A., Tor.	7	366	16	74	90	463	27	0	3	3	42		1972-73	1979-80
• Carrigan, Gene	NYR, StL, Det.	3	37	2	1	3	13	4	0	0	0	0		1930-31	1934-35
Carroll, Billy	NYI, Edm., Det.	7	322	30	54	84	113	71	6	12	18	18	4	1980-81	1986-87
Carroll, George	Mtl.M, Bos.	1	15	0	0	0	9	....	....	....	....	....		1924-25	1924-25
Carroll, Greg	Wsh., Det., Hfd.	2	131	20	34	54	44	....	....	....	....	....		1978-79	1979-80

Rod Buskas

John Byce

Lyndon Byers

Dave Capuano

Jay Caufield

John Chabot

Jeff Chychrun

Robert Cimetta

Name	NHL Teams	NHL Seasons	Regular Schedule GP	G	A	TP	PIM	Playoffs GP	G	A	TP	PIM	NHL Cup Wins	First NHL Season	Last NHL Season
Carruthers, Dwight	Det. Phi.	2	2	0	0	0	0	....	....	....	....	....		1965-66	1967-68
Carse, Bill	NYR, Chi.	4	124	28	43	71	38	16	3	2	5	0		1938-39	1941-42
Carse, Bob	Chi., Mtl.	5	167	32	55	87	52	10	0	2	2	2		1939-40	1947-48
• Carson, Bill	Tor., Bos.	4	159	54	24	78	156	11	3	0	3	14	1	1926-27	1929-30
• Carson, Frank	Mtl.M., NYA, Det.	7	248	42	48	90	166	22	0	2	2	9	1	1925-26	1933-34
• Carson, Gerry	Mtl., NYR, Mtl.M.	6	261	12	11	23	205	22	0	0	0	12	1	1928-29	1936-37
Carson, Lindsay	Phi., Hfd.	7	373	66	80	146	524	49	4	10	14	56		1981-82	1987-88
Carter, Billy	Mtl., Bos.	3	16	0	0	0	6	....	....	....	....	....		1957-58	1961-62
Carter, Ron	Edm.	1	2	0	0	0	0	....	....	....	....	....		1979-80	1979-80
• Carveth, Joe	Det., Bos., Mtl.	11	504	150	189	339	81	69	21	16	37	28	2	1940-41	1950-51
Cashman, Wayne	Bos.	17	1027	277	516	793	1041	145	31	57	88	250	2	1964-65	1982-83
Cassidy, Tom	Pit.	1	26	3	4	7	15	....	....	....	....	....		1977-78	1977-78
Cassolato, Tony	Wsh.	3	23	1	6	7	4	....	....	....	....	....		1979-80	1981-82
Caufield, Jay	NYR, Min., Pit.	7	208	5	8	13	759	17	0	0	0	42	2	1986-87	1992-93
Ceresino, Ray	Tor.	1	12	1	1	2	2	....	....	....	....	....		1948-49	1948-49
Cernik, Frantisek	Det.	1	49	5	4	9	13	....	....	....	....	....		1984-85	1984-85
Chabot, John	Mtl., Pit., Det.	8	508	84	228	312	85	33	6	20	26	2		1983-84	1990-91
Chad, John	Chi.	3	80	15	22	37	29	10	0	1	1	2		1939-40	1945-46
Chalmers, Bill	NYR	1	1	0	0	0	0	....	....	....	....	....		1953-54	1953-54
Chalupa, Milan	Det.	1	14	0	5	5	6	....	....	....	....	....		1984-85	1984-85
• Chamberlain, Murph	Tor., Mtl., Bro., Bos.	12	510	100	175	275	769	66	14	17	31	96	2	1937-38	1948-49
Champagne, Andre	Tor.	1	2	0	0	0	0	....	....	....	....	....		1962-63	1962-63
Chapdelaine, Rene	L.A.	3	32	0	2	2	32	....	....	....	....	....		1990-91	1992-93
• Chapman, Art	Bos., NYA	10	438	62	176	238	140	25	1	5	6	9		1930-31	1939-40
Chapman, Blair	Pit., St.L.	7	402	106	125	231	158	25	4	6	10	15		1976-77	1982-83
Chapman, Brian	Hfd.	1	3	0	0	0	29	....	....	....	....	....		1990-91	1990-91
Charbonneau, Stephane	Que.	1	2	0	0	0	0	....	....	....	....	....		1991-92	1991-92
Charlebois, Bob	Min.	1	7	1	0	1	0	....	....	....	....	....		1967-68	1967-68
Charlesworth, Todd	Pit., NYR	6	93	3	9	12	47	....	....	....	....	....		1983-84	1989-90
Charron, Guy	Mtl., Det., K.C., Wsh.	12	734	221	309	530	146	....	....	....	....	....		1969-70	1980-81
Chartier, Dave	Wpg.	1	1	0	0	0	0	....	....	....	....	....		1980-81	1980-81
Chartraw, Rick	Mtl., L.A., NYR, Edm.	10	420	28	64	92	399	75	7	9	16	80	4	1974-75	1983-84
Check, Lude	Det., Chi.	2	27	6	2	8	4	....	....	....	....	....		1943-44	1944-45
Chernoff, Mike	Min.	1	1	0	0	0	0	....	....	....	....	....		1968-69	1968-69
Cherry, Dick	Bos., Phi.	3	145	12	10	22	45	4	1	0	1	4		1956-57	1969-70
Cherry, Don	Bos.	1	....	....	....	....	....	1	0	0	0	0		1954-55	1954-55
• Chevrefils, Real	Bos., Det.	8	387	104	97	201	185	30	5	4	9	20		1951-52	1958-59
Chicoine, Dan	Cle. Min.	3	31	1	2	3	12	1	0	0	0	0		1977-78	1979-80
Chinnick, Rick	Min.	2	4	0	2	2	0	....	....	....	....	....		1973-74	1974-75
Chipperfield, Ron	Edm., Que.,	2	83	22	24	46	34	....	....	....	....	....		1979-80	1980-81
Chisholm, Art	Bos.	1	3	0	0	0	0	....	....	....	....	....		1960-61	1960-61
Chisholm, Colin	Min.	1	1	0	0	0	0	....	....	....	....	....		1986-87	1986-87
• Chisholm, Les	Tor.	2	54	10	8	18	19	3	1	0	1	0		1939-40	1940-41
Chorney, Marc	Pit. L.A.	4	210	8	27	35	209	7	0	1	1	2		1980-81	1983-84
• Chouinard, Gene	Ott.	1	8	0	0	0	0	....	....	....	....	....		1927-28	1927-28
Chouinard, Guy	Atl, Cgy., St.L.	10	578	205	370	575	120	46	9	28	37	12		1974-75	1983-84
Christie, Mike	Cal., Cle., Col., Van.	7	412	15	101	116	550	2	0	0	0	0		1974-75	1980-81
Christoff, Steve	Min. Cgy., L.A.	5	248	77	64	141	108	35	16	12	28	25		1979-80	1983-84
Chrystal, Bob	NYR	2	132	11	14	25	112	....	....	....	....	....		1953-54	1954-55
Church, Jack	Tor., Bro., Bos.	6	145	5	22	27	164	25	1	1	2	18		1938-39	1945-46
Chychrun, Jeff	Phi., L.A., Pit., Edm.	8	262	3	22	25	744	19	0	2	2	65	1	1986-87	1993-94
• Ciesla, Hank	Chi., NYR	4	269	26	51	77	87	6	0	2	2	0		1955-56	1958-59
Cimellaro, Tony	Ott.	1	2	0	0	0	0	....	....	....	....	....		1992-93	1992-93
Cimetta, Robert	Bos., Tor.	4	103	16	16	32	66	1	0	0	0	15		1988-89	1991-92
Clackson, Kim	Pit., Que.	2	106	0	8	8	370	8	0	0	0	70		1979-80	1980-81
• Clancy, Francis (King)	Ott., Tor.	16	592	137	143	280	904	61	9	8	17	92	3	1921-22	1936-37
Clancy, Terry	Oak., Tor.	4	93	6	6	12	39	....	....	....	....	....		1967-68	1972-73
• Clapper, Dit	Bos.	20	833	228	246	474	462	86	13	17	30	50	3	1927-28	1946-47
Clark, Andy	Bos.	1	5	0	0	0	0	....	....	....	....	....		1927-28	1927-28
Clark, Dan	NYR	1	4	0	1	1	6	....	....	....	....	....		1978-79	1978-79
Clark, Dean	Edm.	1	1	0	0	0	0	....	....	....	....	....		1983-84	1983-84
Clark, Gordie	Bos.	2	8	0	1	1	0	1	0	0	0	0		1974-75	1975-76
Clarke, Bobby	Phi.	15	1144	358	852	1210	1453	136	42	77	119	152	2	1969-70	1983-84
• Cleghorn, Odie	Mtl., Pit.	10	180	95	29	124	147	23	9	2	11	2	1	1918-19	1927-28
• Cleghorn, Sprague	Ott. Tor. Mtl., Bos.	10	256	84	39	123	489	37	7	8	15	48	3	1918-19	1927-28
Clement, Bill	Phi., Wsh., Atl., Cgy.	11	719	148	208	356	383	50	5	3	8	26	2	1971-72	1981-82
Cline, Bruce	NYR	1	30	2	3	5	10	....	....	....	....	....		1956-57	1956-57
Clippingdale, Steve	L.A., Wsh.	2	19	1	2	3	9	1	0	0	0	0		1976-77	1979-80
Cloutier, Real	Que. Buf.	6	317	146	198	344	119	25	7	5	12	20		1979-80	1984-85
Cloutier, Rejean	Det.	2	5	0	2	2	2	....	....	....	....	....		1979-80	1981-82
Cloutier, Roland	Det., Que.	3	34	8	9	17	2	....	....	....	....	....		1977-78	1979-80
Clune, Wally	Mtl.	1	5	0	0	0	6	....	....	....	....	....		1955-56	1955-56
Coalter, Gary	Cal., K.C.	2	34	2	4	6	2	....	....	....	....	....		1973-74	1974-75
Coates, Steve	Det.	1	5	1	0	1	24	....	....	....	....	....		1976-77	1976-77
Cochrane, Glen	Phi., Van., Chi., Edm.	10	411	17	72	89	1556	18	1	1	2	31		1978-79	1988-89
Coflin, Hughie	Chi.	1	31	0	3	3	33	....	....	....	....	....		1950-51	1950-51
Colley, Tom	Min.	1	1	0	0	0	2	....	....	....	....	....		1974-75	1974-75
Collings, Norm	Mtl.	1	1	0	1	1	0	....	....	....	....	....		1934-35	1934-35
Collins, Bill	Min., Mtl., Det., St. L, NYR, Phi., Wsh.	11	768	157	154	311	415	18	3	5	8	12		1967-68	1977-78
Collins, Gary	Tor.	1	....	....	....	....	....	2	0	0	0	0		1958-59	1958-59
Collyard, Bob	St.L.	1	10	1	3	4	4	....	....	....	....	....		1973-74	1973-74
• Colman, Michael	S.J.	1	15	0	1	1	32	....	....	....	....	....		1991-92	1991-92
Colville, Mac	NYR	9	353	71	104	175	130	40	9	10	19	14	1	1935-36	1946-47
• Colville, Neil	NYR	12	464	99	166	265	213	46	7	19	26	33	1	1935-36	1948-49
Colwill, Les	NYR	1	69	7	6	13	16	....	....	....	....	....		1958-59	1958-59
Comeau, Rey	Mtl., Atl, Col.	9	564	98	141	239	175	9	2	1	3	8		1971-72	1979-80
Conacher, Brian	Tor., Det.	5	154	28	28	56	84	12	3	2	5	21	1	1961-62	1971-72
• Conacher, Charlie	Tor., Det., NYA	12	460	225	173	398	523	49	17	18	35	53	1	1929-30	1940-41
Conacher, Jim	Det., Chi., NYR	8	328	85	117	202	91	19	5	2	7	4		1945-46	1952-53
• Conacher, Lionel	Pit., NYA, Mtl.M., Chi.	12	500	80	105	185	882	35	2	2	4	34	2	1925-26	1936-37
Conacher, Pete	Chi., NYR, Tor.	6	229	47	39	86	57	7	0	0	0	0		1951-52	1957-58
• Conacher, Roy	Bos., Det., Chi.	11	490	226	200	426	90	42	15	15	30	14	2	1938-39	1951-52
Conn, Hugh	NYA	2	96	9	28	37	22	....	....	....	....	....		1933-34	1934-35
Connelly, Wayne	Mtl., Bos., Min., Det., St. L, Van.	10	543	133	174	307	156	24	11	7	18	4		1960-61	1971-72
Connolly, Bert	NYR, Chi.	3	87	13	15	28	37	14	1	0	1	0	1	1934-35	1937-38
Connor, Cam	Mtl., Edm., NYR	5	89	9	22	31	256	20	5	0	5	6	1	1978-79	1982-83
• Connor, Harry	Bos., NYA, Ott.	4	134	16	5	21	139	10	0	0	0	2		1927-28	1930-31
• Connors, Bobby	NYA, Det.	3	78	17	10	27	110	2	0	0	0	10		1926-27	1929-30
Contini, Joe	Col., Min.	3	68	17	21	38	34	2	0	0	0	0		1977-78	1980-81
• Convey, Eddie	NYR	3	36	1	1	2	33	....	....	....	....	....		1930-31	1932-33
• Cook, Bill	NYR	11	452	229	138	367	386	46	13	12	25	66	2	1926-27	1936-37
• Cook, Bob	Van., Det., NYI, Min.	4	72	13	9	22	22	....	....	....	....	....		1970-71	1974-75
• Cook, Bud	Bos., Ott., St.L.	3	51	5	4	9	22	....	....	....	....	....		1931-32	1934-35
• Cook, Bun	NYR, Bos.	11	473	158	144	302	449	46	15	3	18	57	2	1926-27	1936-37
Cook, Lloyd	Bos.	1	4	1	0	1	0	....	....	....	....	....		1924-25	1924-25
• Cook, Tom	Chi., Mtl.M.	8	311	77	98	175	184	24	2	4	6	17	1	1929-30	1937-38
• Cooper, Carson	Bos., Mtl., Det.	8	278	110	57	167	111	4	0	0	0	2		1924-25	1931-32
Cooper, Ed	Col.	2	49	8	7	15	46	....	....	....	....	....		1980-81	1981-82
Cooper, Hal	NYR	1	8	0	0	0	2	....	....	....	....	....		1944-45	1944-45
• Cooper, Joe	NYR, Chi.	11	420	30	66	96	442	32	3	5	8	6		1935-36	1946-47
Copp, Bob	Tor.	2	40	3	9	12	26	....	....	....	....	....		1942-43	1950-51
• Corbeau, Bert	Mtl., Ham., Tor.,	10	257	64	31	95	501	14	2	0	2	10		1917-18	1926-27
Corbett, Michael	L.A.	1	....	....	....	....	....	2	0	1	1	2		1967-68	1967-68
Corcoran, Norm	Bos., Det., Chi.	4	29	1	3	4	21	4	0	0	0	6		1949-50	1955-56
Cormier, Roger	Mtl.	1	1	0	0	0	0	....	....	....	....	....		1925-26	1925-26
Corrigan, Charlie	Tor., NYA	2	19	2	2	4	2	....	....	....	....	....		1937-38	1940-41
Corrigan, Mike	L.A., Van., Pit.	10	594	152	195	347	698	17	2	3	5	20		1967-68	1977-78
Corriveau, Andre	Mtl.	1	3	0	1	1	0	....	....	....	....	....		1953-54	1953-54
Cory, Ross	Wpg.	2	51	2	10	12	41	....	....	....	....	....		1979-80	1980-81
Cossete, Jacques	Pit.	3	64	8	6	14	29	3	0	1	1	4		1975-76	1978-79
Costello, Les	Tor.	3	15	2	3	5	11	6	2	2	4	2	1	1947-48	1949-50
Costello, Murray	Chi., Bos., Det.	4	162	13	19	32	54	5	0	0	0	2		1953-54	1956-57
Costello, Rich	Tor.	2	12	2	2	4	2	....	....	....	....	....		1983-84	1985-86

Name	NHL Teams	NHL Seasons	Regular Schedule GP	G	A	TP	PIM	Playoffs GP	G	A	TP	PIM	NHL Cup Wins	First NHL Season	Last NHL Season
Cotch, Charlie	Ham.	1	11	1	0	1	0	....	....	....	....	....		1924-25	1924-25
Cote, Alain	Bos., Wsh., Mtl., T.B., Que.	9	119	2	18	20	124	11	0	2	2	26		1985-86	1993-94
Cote, Alain	Que.	10	696	103	190	293	383	67	9	15	24	44		1979-80	1988-89
Cote, Ray	Edm.	3	15	0	0	0	4	14	3	2	5	0		1982-83	1984-85
• Cotton, Baldy	Pit., Tor., NYA	12	500	101	103	204	419	43	4	9	13	46	1	1925-26	1936-37
• Coughlin, Jack	Tor., Que, Mtl., Ham.	3	19	2	0	2	0	....	....	....	....	....	1	1917-18	1920-21
Coulis, Tim	Wsh., Min.	4	47	4	5	9	138	3	1	0	1	2		1979-80	1985-86
Coulson, D'arcy	Phi.	1	28	0	0	0	103	....	....	....	....	....		1930-31	1930-31
Coulter, Art	Chi., NYR	11	465	30	82	112	543	49	4	5	9	61	2	1931-32	1941-42
Coulter, Neal	NYI	3	26	5	5	10	11	1	0	0	0	0		1985-86	1987-88
Coulter, Tommy	Chi.	1	2	0	0	0	0	....	....	....	....	....		1933-34	1933-34
Cournoyer, Yvan	Mtl.	16	968	428	435	863	255	147	64	63	127	47	10	1963-64	1978-79
Courteau, Yves	Cgy., Hfd.	3	22	2	5	7	4	1	0	0	0	0		1984-85	1986-87
Courtenay, Edward	S.J.	2	44	7	13	20	10	....	....	....	....	....		1991-92	1992-93
• Coutu, Billy	Mtl., Ham., Bos.	10	239	33	18	51	350	32	2	0	2	42	1	1917-18	1926-27
• Couture, Gerry	Det., Mtl., Chi.,	10	385	86	70	156	89	45	9	7	16	4	1	1944-45	1953-54
• Couture, Rosie	Chi., Mtl.	8	304	48	56	104	184	23	1	5	6	15		1928-29	1935-36
Cowan, Tommy	Phi.	1	1	0	0	0	0	....	....	....	....	....		1930-31	1930-31
Cowick, Bruce	Phi., Wsh., St.L.	3	70	5	6	11	43	8	0	0	0	9	1	1973-74	1975-76
• Cowley, Bill	St.L., Bos.	13	549	195	353	548	143	64	12	34	46	22	2	1934-35	1946-47
• Cox, Danny	Tor., Ott., Det., NYR, St.L.	9	329	47	49	96	110	10	0	1	1	6		1926-27	1934-35
Coxe, Craig	Van., Cgy., St. L., S.J.	8	235	14	31	45	713	5	1	0	1	18		1984-85	1991-92
Crashley, Bart	Det., K.C., L.A.	6	140	7	36	43	50	....	....	....	....	....		1965-66	1975-76
Crawford, Bob	St.L., Hfd., NYR, Wsh.	7	246	71	71	142	72	11	0	1	1	8		1979-80	1986-87
Crawford, Bobby	Col., Det.	2	16	1	3	4	6	....	....	....	....	....		1980-81	1982-83
• Crawford, John	Bos.	13	547	38	140	178	202	66	4	13	17	36	2	1937-38	1949-50
Crawford, Lou	Bos.	2	26	2	1	3	29	....	....	....	....	....		1989-90	1991-92
Crawford, Marc	Van.	6	176	19	31	50	229	20	1	2	3	44		1981-82	1986-87
• Crawford, Rusty	Ott., Tor.,	2	38	10	3	13	51	2	2	1	3	0	1	1917-18	1918-19
Creighton, Dave	Bos., Chi., Tor., NYR	12	615	140	174	314	223	51	11	13	24	20		1948-49	1959-60
• Creighton, Jimmy	Det.,	1	11	1	0	1	2	....	....	....	....	....		1930-31	1930-31
Cressman, Dave	Min.	2	85	6	8	14	37	....	....	....	....	....		1974-75	1975-76
Cressman, Glen	Mtl.	1	4	0	0	0	2	....	....	....	....	....		1956-57	1956-57
Crisofoli, Ed	Mtl.	1	9	0	1	1	4	....	....	....	....	....		1989-90	1989-90
Crisp, Terry	Bos., St.L., Phi., NYI	11	536	67	134	201	135	110	15	28	43	40	2	1965-66	1976-77
Croghen, Maurice	Mtl.M.	1	16	0	0	0	4	....	....	....	....	....		1937-38	1937-38
Crombeen, Mike	Cle., St.L., Hfd.	8	475	55	68	123	218	27	6	2	8	32		1977-78	1984-85
Crossett, Stan	Phi.,	1	21	0	0	0	10	....	....	....	....	....		1930-31	1930-31
Croteau, Gary	L.A., Det., Cal., K.C., Col.	12	684	144	175	319	143	11	3	2	5	8		1968-69	1979-80
Crowder, Bruce	Bos., Pit.	4	243	47	51	98	156	31	8	4	12	41		1981-82	1984-85
Crowder, Keith	Bos., L.A.	10	662	223	271	494	1346	85	14	22	36	218		1980-81	1989-90
Crozier, Joe	Tor.,	1	5	0	3	3	2	....	....	....	....	....		1959-60	1959-60
Crutchfield, Nels	Mtl.	1	41	5	5	10	20	2	0	1	1	22		1934-35	1934-35
Culhane, Jim	Hfd.	1	6	0	1	1	4	....	....	....	....	....		1989-90	1989-90
Cullen, Barry	Tor., Det.	5	219	32	52	84	111	6	0	0	0	2		1955-56	1959-60
Cullen, Brian	Tor., NYR	7	326	56	100	156	92	19	3	0	3	2		1954-55	1960-61
Cullen, Ray	NYR, Det., Min., Van.	6	313	92	123	215	120	20	3	10	13	2		1965-66	1970-71
Cummins, Barry	Cal.	1	36	1	2	3	39	....	....	....	....	....		1973-74	1973-74
Cunningham, Bob	NYR	2	4	0	1	1	0	....	....	....	....	....		1960-61	1961-62
Cunningham, Jim	Phi.	1	1	0	0	0	4	....	....	....	....	....		1977-78	1977-78
Cunningham, Les	NYA, Chi.	2	60	7	19	26	21	1	0	0	0	2		1936-37	1939-40
Cupolo, Bill	Bos.	1	47	11	13	24	10	7	1	2	3	0		1944-45	1944-45
Currie, Glen	Wsh., L.A.	8	326	39	79	118	100	12	1	3	4	4		1979-80	1987-88
Currie, Hugh	Mtl.	1	1	0	0	0	0	....	....	....	....	....		1950-51	1950-51
Currie, Tony	St.L., Hfd., Van.	8	290	92	119	211	73	16	4	12	16	14		1977-78	1984-85
Curry, Floyd	Mtl.	11	601	105	99	204	147	91	23	17	40	38	4	1947-48	1957-58
Curtale, Tony	Cgy.	1	2	0	0	0	0	....	....	....	....	....		1980-81	1980-81
Curtis, Paul	Mtl., L.A., St.L.	4	185	3	34	37	151	5	0	0	0	2		1969-70	1972-73
Cushenan, Ian	Chi., Mtl., NYR, Det.	5	129	3	11	14	134	....	....	....	....	....		1956-57	1963-64
Cusson, Jean	Oak.	1	2	0	0	0	0	....	....	....	....	....		1967-68	1967-68
Cyr, Denis	Cgy., Chi., St.L.	6	193	41	43	84	36	4	0	0	0	0		1980-81	1985-86
Cyr, Paul	Buf., NYR, Hfd.	9	470	101	140	241	623	24	4	6	10	31		1982-83	1991-92

D

Name	NHL Teams	NHL Seasons	Regular Schedule GP	G	A	TP	PIM	Playoffs GP	G	A	TP	PIM	NHL Cup Wins	First NHL Season	Last NHL Season
Dahlin, Kjell	Mtl.	3	166	57	59	116	10	35	6	11	17	6	1	1985-86	1987-88
Dahlstrom, Cully	Chi.	8	342	88	118	206	52	29	6	8	14	4	1	1937-38	1944-45
Daigle, Alain	Chi.	6	389	56	50	106	122	17	0	1	1	0		1974-75	1979-80
Dailey, Bob	Van., Phi.	9	561	94	231	325	814	63	12	34	46	106		1973-74	1981-82
Daley, Frank	Det.	1	5	0	0	0	0	2	0	0	0	0		1928-29	1928-29
Daley, Pat	Wpg.	2	12	1	0	1	13	....	....	....	....	....		1979-80	1980-81
Dallman, Marty	Tor.	2	6	0	1	1	0	....	....	....	....	....		1987-88	1988-89
Dallman, Rod	NYI, Phi.	4	6	1	0	1	26	1	0	1	1	0		1987-88	1991-92
Dame, Bunny	Mtl.	1	34	2	5	7	4	....	....	....	....	....		1941-42	1941-42
Damore, Hank	NYR	1	4	1	0	1	2	....	....	....	....	....		1943-44	1943-44
Daniels, Kimbi	Phi.	2	27	1	2	3	4	....	....	....	....	....		1990-91	1991-92
Daoust, Dan	Mtl., Tor.	8	522	87	167	254	544	32	7	5	12	83		1982-83	1989-90
Dark, Michael	St.L.	2	43	5	6	11	14	....	....	....	....	....		1986-87	1987-88
• Darragh, Harry	Pit., Phi., Bos., Tor.	8	308	68	49	117	50	16	1	3	4	4	1	1925-26	1932-33
• Darragh, Jack	Ott.	6	120	68	21	89	84	21	14	2	16	7	3	1917-18	1923-24
David, Richard	Que.	3	31	4	4	8	10	1	0	0	0	0		1979-80	1982-83
Davidson, Bob	Tor.,	12	491	94	160	254	398	82	5	17	22	79	2	1934-35	1945-46
Davidson, Gord	NYR	2	51	3	6	9	8	....	....	....	....	....		1942-43	1943-44
• Davie, Bob	Bos.	3	41	0	1	1	25	....	....	....	....	....		1933-34	1935-36
Davies, Ken	NYR	1	....	....	....	....	....	1	0	0	0	0		1947-48	1947-48
Davis, Bob	Det.	1	3	0	0	0	0	....	....	....	....	....		1932-33	1932-33
Davis, Kim	Pit., Tor.	4	36	5	7	12	12	4	0	0	0	0		1977-78	1980-81
Davis, Lorne	Mtl., Chi., Det., Bos.	6	95	8	12	20	20	18	3	1	4	10	1	1951-52	1959-60
Davis, Mal	Det., Buf.	5	100	31	22	53	34	7	1	0	1	0		1980-81	1985-86
Davison, Murray	Bos.	1	1	0	0	0	0	....	....	....	....	....		1965-66	1965-66
Dawes, Robert	Tor., Mtl.	4	32	2	7	4	6	10	0	0	0	2	1	1946-47	1950-51
• Day, Hap	Tor., NYA	14	581	86	116	202	601	53	4	7	11	56	1	1924-25	1937-38
Dea, Billy	Chi., NYR, Det., Pit.	8	397	67	54	121	44	11	2	0	2	6		1953-54	1970-71
Deacon, Don	Det.	3	30	6	4	10	6	2	2	1	3	0		1936-37	1939-40
Deadmarsh, Butch	Buf., ATL, K.C.	5	137	12	5	17	155	4	0	0	0	17		1970-71	1974-75
Dean, Barry	Col., Phi.	3	165	25	56	81	146	....	....	....	....	....		1976-77	1978-79
Debenedet, Nelson	Det., Pit.	2	46	10	4	14	13	....	....	....	....	....		1973-74	1974-75
DeBlois, Lucien	NYR, Col., Wpg., Mtl., Que., Tor.	15	993	249	276	525	814	52	7	6	13	38		1977-78	1991-92
Debol, David	Hfd.	2	92	26	26	52	4	3	0	0	0	0		1979-80	1980-81
Defazio, Dean	Pit.	1	22	0	2	2	28	....	....	....	....	....		1983-84	1983-84
DeGray, Dale	Cgy., Tor. L.A., Buf.	5	153	18	47	65	195	13	1	3	4	28		1985-86	1989-90
Delmonte, Armand	Bos.	1	1	0	0	0	0	....	....	....	....	....		1945-46	1945-46
Delorme, Gilbert	Mtl., St. L., Que., Det., Pit.	9	541	31	92	123	520	56	1	9	10	56		1981-82	1989-90
Delorme, Ron	Col., Van.	9	524	83	83	166	667	25	1	2	3	59		1976-77	1984-85
Delory, Valentine	NYR	1	1	0	0	0	0	....	....	....	....	....		1948-49	1948-49
Delparte, Guy	Col.	1	48	1	8	9	18	....	....	....	....	....		1976-77	1976-77
Delvecchio, Alex	Det.	24	1549	456	825	1281	383	121	35	69	104	29	3	1950-51	1973-74
• DeMarco, Ab	Chi., Tor., Bos., NYR	7	209	72	93	165	53	11	3	0	3	2		1938-39	1946-47
DeMarco, Albert	NYR, St.L., Pit., Van., L.A., Bos.	9	344	44	80	124	75	25	1	2	3	17		1969-70	1978-79
DeMeres, Tony	Mtl., NYR	6	83	20	22	42	23	3	0	0	0	0		1937-38	1943-44
Denis, Johnny	NYR	2	10	0	2	2	2	....	....	....	....	....		1946-47	1949-50
Denis, Lulu	Mtl.	2	3	0	1	1	0	....	....	....	....	....		1949-50	1950-51
• Denneny, Corbett	Tor., Ham., Chi.	9	175	99	29	128	130	15	7	4	11	6	2	1917-18	1927-28
• Denneny, Cy	Ott., Bos.	12	326	246	69	315	176	37	18	3	21	31	5	1917-18	1928-29
Dennis, Norm	St.L.	4	12	3	0	3	11	5	0	0	0	2		1968-69	1971-72
Denoird, Gerry	Tor.	1	15	0	0	0	0	....	....	....	....	....		1922-23	1922-23
Derlago, Bill	Van., Bos., Wpg., Que., Tor.	9	555	189	227	416	247	13	5	0	5	8		1978-79	1986-87
• Desaulniers, Gerard	Mtl.	3	8	0	2	2	4	....	....	....	....	....		1950-51	1953-54
• Desilets, Joffre	Mtl., Chi.	5	192	37	45	82	57	7	1	0	1	7		1935-36	1939-40
Desjardins, Martin	Mtl.	1	8	0	2	2	2	....	....	....	....	....		1989-90	1989-90
Desjardins, Vic	Chi., NYR	2	87	6	15	21	27	16	0	0	0	0		1930-31	1931-32
Deslauriers, Jacques	Mtl.	1	2	0	0	0	0	....	....	....	....	....		1955-56	1955-56
Devine, Kevin	NYI	1	2	0	1	1	8	....	....	....	....	....		1982-83	1982-83

Alain Cote

Marc Crawford

Kimbi Daniels

Per Djoos

Brian Dobbin

Clark Donatelli

Pelle Eklund

Kari Eloranta

Name	NHL Teams	NHL Seasons	Regular Schedule GP	G	A	TP	PIM	Playoffs GP	G	A	TP	PIM	NHL Cup Wins	First NHL Season	Last NHL Season
Dewar, Tom	NYR	1	9	0	2	2	4	....	....	....	....	....		1943-44	1943-44
Dewsbury, Al	Det., Chi.	9	347	30	78	108	365	14	1	5	6	60	1	1946-47	1955-56
Deziel, Michel	Buf.	1	....	....	....	....	....	1	0	0	0	0		1974-75	1974-75
Dheere, Marcel	Mtl.	1	11	1	2	3	2	5	0	0	0	6		1942-43	1942-43
Diachuk, Edward	Det.	1	12	0	0	0	19	....	....	....	....	....		1960-61	1960-61
Dick, Harry	Chi.	1	12	0	1	1	12	....	....	....	....	....		1946-47	1946-47
Dickens, Ernie	Tor., Chi.	6	278	12	44	56	48	13	0	0	0	4	1	1941-42	1950-51
Dickenson, Herb	NYR	2	48	18	17	35	10	....	....	....	....	....		1951-52	1952-53
Dietrich, Don	Chi., N.J.	2	28	0	7	7	10	....	....	....	....	....		1983-84	1985-86
• Dill, Bob	NYR	2	76	15	15	30	135	....	....	....	....	....		1943-44	1944-45
Dillabough, Bob	Det., Bos., Pit., Oak.	7	283	32	54	86	76	17	3	0	3	0		1961-62	1969-70
• Dillon, Cecil	NYR, Det.	10	453	167	131	298	105	43	14	9	23	14	1	1930-31	1939-40
Dillon, Gary	Col.	1	13	1	1	2	29	....	....	....	....	....		1980-81	1980-81
Dillon, Wayne	NYR, Wpg.	4	229	43	66	109	60	3	0	1	1	0		1975-76	1979-80
Dineen, Bill	Det., Chi.	5	323	51	44	95	122	37	1	1	2	18	2	1953-54	1957-58
Dineen, Gary	Min.	1	4	0	1	1	0	....	....	....	....	....		1968-69	1968-69
Dineen, Peter	L.A., Det.	2	13	0	2	2	13	....	....	....	....	....		1986-87	1989-90
Dinsmore, Chuck	Mtl.M	4	100	6	2	8	44	12	1	0	1	6	1	1924-25	1929-30
Dionne, Marcel	Det., L.A., NYR	18	1348	731	1040	1771	600	49	21	24	45	17		1971-72	1988-89
Djoos, Per	Det., NYR	3	82	2	31	33	58	....	....	....	....	....		1990-91	1992-93
Doak, Gary	Det., Bos., Van., NYR	16	789	23	107	130	908	78	2	4	6	121	1	1965-66	1980-81
Dobbin, Brian	Phi., Bos.	5	63	7	8	15	61	2	0	0	0	17		1986-87	1991-92
Dobson, Jim	Min., Col.	3	11	0	0	0	6	....	....	....	....	....		1979-80	1981-82
• Doherty, Fred	Mtl.	1	3	0	0	0	0	....	....	....	....	....		1918-19	1918-19
Donaldson, Gary	Chi.	1	1	0	0	0	0	....	....	....	....	....	2	1973-74	1973-74
Donatelli, Clark	Min., Bos.	2	35	3	4	7	39	2	0	0	0	0		1989-90	1991-92
Donnelly, Babe	Mtl.M.	1	34	0	1	1	14	2	0	0	0	0		1926-27	1926-27
Donnelly, Dave	Bos., Chi., Edm.	5	137	15	24	39	150	5	0	0	0	0		1983-84	1987-88
Doran, Red (I.)	Det.	1	24	3	2	5	10	....	....	....	....	....		1946-47	1946-47
• Doran, Red (J.)	NYA., Det., Mtl.	5	98	5	10	15	110	3	0	0	0	0		1933-34	1939-40
• Doraty, Ken	Chi., Tor., Det.	5	103	15	26	41	24	15	7	2	9	2		1926-27	1937-38
Dore, Andre	NYR, St.L., Que.	7	257	14	81	95	261	23	1	2	3	32		1978-79	1984-85
Dore, Daniel	Que.	2	17	2	3	5	59	....	....	....	....	....		1989-90	1990-91
Dorey, Jim	Tor., NYR	4	232	25	74	99	553	11	0	2	2	40		1968-69	1971-72
Dorion, Dan	N.J.	2	4	1	1	2	2	....	....	....	....	....		1985-86	1987-88
Dornhoefer, Gary	Bos., Phi.	14	787	214	328	542	1291	80	17	19	36	203	2	1963-64	1977-78
Dorohoy, Eddie	Mtl.	1	16	0	0	0	6	....	....	....	....	....		1948-49	1948-49
Douglas, Jordy	Hfd., Min., Wpg.	6	268	76	62	138	160	6	0	0	0	4		1979-80	1984-85
Douglas, Kent	Tor., Oak., Det.	7	428	33	115	148	631	19	1	3	4	33	1	1962-63	1968-69
Douglas, Les	Det.	4	52	6	12	18	8	10	3	2	5	0	1	1940-41	1946-47
Downie, Dave	Tor.	1	11	0	1	1	2	....	....	....	....	....		1932-33	1932-33
Doyon, Mario	Chi., Que.	3	28	3	4	7	16	....	....	....	....	....		1988-89	1990-91
• Draper, Bruce	Tor.	1	1	0	0	0	0	....	....	....	....	....		1962-63	1962-63
• Drillon, Gordie	Tor., Mtl.	7	311	155	139	294	56	50	26	15	41	10	1	1936-37	1942-43
Driscoll, Pete	Edm.	2	60	3	8	11	97	3	0	0	0	0		1979-80	1980-81
Drolet, Rene	Phi., Det.	2	2	0	0	0	0	....	....	....	....	....		1971-72	1974-75
Drouillard, Clarence	Det.	1	10	0	1	1	0	....	....	....	....	....		1937-38	1937-38
Drouin, Jude	Mtl., Min., NYI, Wpg.	12	666	151	305	456	346	72	27	41	68	33		1968-69	1980-81
• Drouin, Polly	Mtl.	6	173	23	50	73	80	5	0	1	1	5		1935-36	1940-41
Drulia, Stan	T.B.	1	24	2	1	3	10	....	....	....	....	....		1992-93	1992-93
Drummond, John	NYR	1	2	0	0	0	0	....	....	....	....	....		1944-45	1944-45
Drury, Herb	Pit., Phi.	6	213	24	13	37	203	4	1	1	2	0		1925-26	1930-31
Dube, Gilles	Mtl., Det.	2	12	1	2	3	2	2	0	0	0	0	1	1949-50	1953-54
Dube, Norm	K.C.	2	57	8	10	18	54	....	....	....	....	....		1974-75	1975-76
Duberman, Justin	Pit.	1	4	0	0	0	0	....	....	....	....	....		1993-94	1993-94
Dudley, Rick	Buf., Wpg.	6	309	75	99	174	292	25	7	2	9	69		1972-73	1980-81
Duff, Dick	Tor., NYR, Mtl., L.A., Buf.	18	1030	283	289	572	743	114	30	49	79	78	6	1954-55	1971-72
Dufour, Luc	Bos., Que., St.L.	3	167	23	21	44	199	18	1	0	1	32		1982-83	1984-85
Dufour, Marc	NYR, L.A.	3	14	1	0	1	2	....	....	....	....	....		1963-64	1968-69
Duggan, Jack	Ott.	1	27	0	0	0	0	2	0	0	0	0		1925-26	1925-26
Duggan, Ken	Min.	1	1	0	0	0	0	....	....	....	....	....		1987-88	1987-88
Duguay, Ron	NYR, Det., Pit., L.A.	12	864	274	346	620	582	89	31	22	53	118		1977-78	1988-89
• Duguid, Lorne	Mtl.M, Det., Bos.	6	135	9	15	24	57	2	0	0	0	4		1931-32	1936-37
Dumart, Woody	Bos.	16	771	211	218	429	99	82	12	15	27	23	2	1935-36	1953-54
Dunbar, Dale	Van., Bos.	2	2	0	0	0	2	....	....	....	....	....		1985-86	1988-89
• Duncan, Art	Det., Tor.	5	156	18	16	34	225	5	0	0	0	4		1926-27	1930-31
Duncan, Iain	Wpg.	4	127	34	55	89	149	11	0	3	3	6		1986-87	1990-91
Dundas, Rocky	Tor.	1	5	0	0	0	14	....	....	....	....	....		1989-90	1989-90
Dunlap, Frank	Tor.	1	15	0	1	1	2	....	....	....	....	....		1943-44	1943-44
Dunlop, Blake	Min., Phi., St.L., Det.	11	550	130	274	404	172	40	4	10	14	18		1973-74	1983-84
Dunn, Dave	Van., Tor.	3	184	14	41	55	313	10	1	1	2	41		1973-74	1975-76
Dunn, Richie	Buf., Cgy., Hfd.	12	483	36	140	176	314	36	3	15	18	24		1977-78	1988-89
Dupere, Denis	Tor., Wsh., St.L., K.C., Col.	8	421	80	99	179	66	16	1	0	1	0		1970-71	1977-78
Dupont, Andre	NYR, St.L., Phi., Que.	13	810	59	185	244	1986	140	14	18	32	352	2	1970-71	1982-83
Dupont, Jerome	Chi., Tor.	6	214	7	29	36	468	20	0	2	2	56		1981-82	1986-87
Dupont, Norm	Mtl., Wpg., Hfd.	5	256	55	85	140	52	13	4	2	6	0		1979-80	1983-84
Durbano, Steve	St.L., Pit., K.C., Col.	6	220	13	60	73	1127	5	0	2	2	8		1972-73	1978-79
Duris, Vitezslav	Tor.	2	89	3	20	23	62	3	0	1	1	2		1980-81	1982-83
Dussault, Norm	Mtl.	4	206	31	62	93	47	7	3	1	4	0		1947-48	1950-51
Dutkowski, Duke	Chi., NYA, NYR	5	200	16	30	46	172	6	0	0	0	6		1926-27	1933-34
• Dutton, Red	Mtl.M, NYA	10	449	29	67	96	871	18	1	0	1	33		1926-27	1935-36
Dvorak, Miroslav	Phi.	3	193	11	74	85	51	18	0	2	2	6		1982-83	1984-85
Dwyer, Mike	Col., Cgy.	4	31	2	6	8	25	1	1	0	1	0		1978-79	1981-82
Dyck, Henry	NYR	1	1	0	0	0	0	....	....	....	....	....		1943-44	1943-44
• Dye, Babe	Tor., Ham., Chi., NYA	11	269	202	41	243	205	15	11	2	13	11	1	1919-20	1930-31
Dykstra, Steven	Buf., Edm., Pit., Hfd.	5	217	8	32	40	545	1	0	0	0	2		1985-86	1989-90
Dyte, John	Chi.	1	27	1	0	1	31	....	....	....	....	....		1943-44	1943-44

E

Name	NHL Teams	NHL Seasons	Regular Schedule GP	G	A	TP	PIM	Playoffs GP	G	A	TP	PIM	NHL Cup Wins	First NHL Season	Last NHL Season
Eakin, Bruce	Cgy., Det.	4	13	2	2	4	4	....	....	....	....	....		1981-82	1985-86
Eatough, Jeff	Buf.	1	1	0	0	0	0	....	....	....	....	....		1981-82	1981-82
Eaves, Mike	Min., Cgy.	8	324	83	143	226	80	43	7	10	17	14		1978-79	1985-86
Eaves, Murray	Wpg., Det.	8	57	4	13	17	9	4	0	1	1	2		1980-81	1989-90
Ecclestone, Tim	St.L., Det., Tor., Atl.	11	692	126	233	359	346	48	6	11	17	76		1967-68	1977-78
Edberg, Rolf	Wsh.	3	184	45	58	103	24	....	....	....	....	....		1978-79	1980-81
• Eddolls, Frank	Mtl., NYR	8	317	23	43	66	114	31	0	2	2	10	1	1944-45	1951-52
Edestrand, Darryl	St.L., Phi., Pit., Bos., L.A.	10	455	34	90	124	404	42	3	9	12	57		1967-68	1978-79
Edmundson, Garry	Mtl., Tor.	3	43	4	6	10	49	11	0	1	1	8		1951-52	1960-61
Edur, Tom	Col., Pit	2	158	17	70	87	67	....	....	....	....	....		1976-77	1977-78
Egan, Pat	Bro., Det., Bos., NYR	11	554	77	153	230	776	44	9	4	13	44		1939-40	1950-51
Egers, Jack	NYR, St.L., Wsh.	7	284	64	69	133	154	32	5	6	11	32		1969-70	1975-76
Ehman, Gerry	Bos., Det., Tor., Oak, Cal.	9	429	96	118	214	100	41	10	10	20	12	1	1957-58	1970-71
Eklund, Pelle	Phi., Dal.	9	594	120	335	455	109	66	10	36	46	8		1985-86	1993-94
Eldebrink, Anders	Van., Que.	2	55	3	11	14	29	14	0	0	0	0		1981-82	1982-83
Elik, Boris	Det.	1	3	0	0	0	0	....	....	....	....	....		1962-63	1962-63
Elliot, Fred	Ott.	1	43	2	0	2	6	....	....	....	....	....		1928-29	1928-29
Ellis, Ron	Tor.	16	1034	332	308	640	207	70	18	8	26	20	1	1963-64	1980-81
Eloranta, Kari	Cgy., St.L.	5	267	13	103	116	155	26	1	7	8	19		1981-82	1986-87
Emberg, Eddie	Mtl.	1	....	....	....	....	....	2	1	0	1	0		1944-45	1944-45
• Emms, Hap	Mtl.M, NYA, Det., Bos.	10	320	36	53	89	311	14	0	0	0	12		1926-27	1937-38
Endean, Craig	Wpg.	1	2	0	1	1	1	....	....	....	....	....		1986-87	1986-87
Engblom, Brian	Mtl., Wsh., L.A., Buf., Cgy.	11	659	29	177	206	599	48	3	9	12	43	3	1976-77	1986-87
Engele, Jerry	Min.	3	100	2	13	15	162	2	0	1	1	0		1975-76	1977-78
English, John	L.A.	1	3	1	3	4	4	1	0	0	0	0		1987-88	1987-88
Ennis, Jim	Edm.	1	5	1	0	1	10	....	....	....	....	....		1987-88	1987-88
Erickson, Aut	Bos., Chi., Oak., Tor.	7	227	7	84	31	182	7	0	0	0	2	1	1959-60	1969-70
Erickson, Bryan	Wsh., L.A., Pit., Wpg.	9	351	80	125	205	141	14	3	4	7	7		1983-84	1993-94
Erickson, Grant	Bos., Min.	2	6	1	0	1	4	....	....	....	....	....		1968-69	1969-70
Eriksson, Peter	Edm.	1	20	3	3	6	24	....	....	....	....	....		1989-90	1989-90
Eriksson, Rolie	Min., Van.	3	193	48	95	143	26	2	1	0	1	0		1976-77	1978-79
Eriksson, Thomas	Phi.	5	208	22	76	98	107	19	0	3	3	6		1980-81	1985-86
Erixon, Jan	NYR	10	556	57	159	216	167	58	7	7	14	16		1983-84	1992-93
Esposito, Phil	Chi., Bos., NYR	18	1282	717	873	1590	910	130	61	76	137	137	2	1963-64	1980-81

Name	NHL Teams	NHL Seasons	Regular Schedule GP	G	A	TP	PIM	Playoffs GP	G	A	TP	PIM	NHL Cup Wins	First NHL Season	Last NHL Season
Evans, Chris	Tor., Buf., St.L., Det., K.C.	5	241	19	42	61	143	12	1	1	2	8		1969-70	1974-75
Evans, Daryl	L.A., Wsh., Tor.	6	113	22	30	52	25	11	5	8	13	12		1981-82	1986-87
Evans, Doug	St.L., Wpg., Phi.	8	355	48	87	135	502	22	3	4	7	38		1985-86	1992-93
Evans, Jack	NYR, Chi.	14	752	19	80	99	989	56	2	2	4	97	1	1948-49	1962-63
Evans, John	Phi.	3	103	14	25	39	34	1	0	0	0	0		1978-79	1982-83
Evans, Kevin	Min., S.J.	2	9	0	1	1	44	....	....	....	....	....		1990-91	1991-92
Evans, Paul	Tor.	2	11	1	1	2	21	2	0	0	0	0		1976-77	1977-78
Evans, Shawn	St. L., NYI	2	9	1	0	1	2	....	....	....	....	....		1985-86	1989-90
Evans, Stewart	Det., Mtl.M., Mtl.	8	367	28	49	77	425	26	0	0	0	20	1	1930-31	1938-39
Ezinicki, Bill	Tor., Bos., NYR	9	368	79	105	184	713	40	5	8	13	87	3	1944-45	1954-55

F

Name	NHL Teams	NHL Seasons	Regular Schedule GP	G	A	TP	PIM	Playoffs GP	G	A	TP	PIM	NHL Cup Wins	First NHL Season	Last NHL Season
Fahey, Trevor	NYR	1	1	0	0	0	0	....	....	....	....	....		1964-65	1964-65
Fairbairn, Bill	NYR, Min. St.L.	11	658	162	261	423	173	54	13	22	35	42		1968-69	1978-79
Falkenberg, Bob	Det.	5	54	1	5	6	26	....	....	....	....	....		1966-67	1971-72
Farrant, Walt	Chi.	1	1	0	0	0	0	....	....	....	....	....		1943-44	1943-44
Farrish, Dave	NYR, Que, Tor.	7	430	17	110	127	440	14	0	2	2	24		1976-77	1983-84
Fashoway, Gordie	Chi.	1	13	3	2	5	14	....	....	....	....	....		1950-51	1950-51
Faubert, Mario	Pit.	7	231	21	90	111	292	10	2	2	4	6		1974-75	1981-82
Faulkner, Alex	Tor., Det.	3	101	15	17	32	15	12	5	0	5	2		1961-62	1963-64
Fauss, Ted	Tor.	2	28	0	2	2	15	....	....	....	....	....		1986-87	1987-88
Feamster, Dave	Chi.	4	169	13	24	37	155	33	3	5	8	61		1981-82	1984-85
Featherstone, Tony	Oak., Cal., Min.	3	130	17	21	38	65	2	0	0	0	0		1969-70	1973-74
Federko, Bernie	St.L., Det.	14	1000	369	761	1130	487	91	35	66	101	83		1976-77	1989-90
Felix, Chris	Wsh.	4	35	1	12	13	10	2	0	1	1	0		1987-88	1990-91
Feltrin, Tony	Pit., NYR	4	48	3	3	6	65	....	....	....	....	....		1980-81	1985-86
Fenton, Paul	Hfd., NYR, L.A., Wpg., Tor., Cgy., S.J.	8	411	100	83	183	198	17	4	1	5	27		1984-85	1991-92
Fenyves, David	Buf., Phi.	9	206	3	32	35	119	11	0	0	0	9		1982-83	1990-91
Fergus, Tom	Bos., Tor., Van.	12	726	235	346	581	499	65	21	17	38	48		1981-82	1992-93
Ferguson, George	Tor., Pit, Min	12	797	160	238	398	431	86	14	23	37	44		1972-73	1983-84
Ferguson, John	Mtl.	8	500	145	158	303	1214	85	20	18	38	260	5	1963-64	1970-71
Ferguson, Lorne	Bos., Det., Chi.	8	422	82	80	162	193	31	6	3	9	24		1949-50	1958-59
Ferguson, Norm	Oak., Cal.	4	279	73	66	139	72	10	1	4	5	7		1968-69	1971-72
Fidler, Mike	Cle., Min, Hfd., Chi.	7	271	84	97	181	124	....	....	....	....	....		1976-77	1982-83
Field, Wilf	Bro., Mtl., Chi.	6	218	17	25	42	151	3	0	0	0	0		1936-37	1944-45
Fielder, Guyle	Det., Chi., Bos.	4	9	0	0	0	2	6	0	0	0	2		1950-51	1957-58
Fillion, Bob	Mtl.	7	327	42	61	103	84	33	7	4	11	10	2	1943-44	1949-50
Fillion, Marcel	Bos.	1	1	0	0	0	0	....	....	....	....	....		1944-45	1944-45
• Filmore, Tommy	Det., NYA, Bos.	4	116	15	12	27	33	....	....	....	....	....		1930-31	1933-34
Finkbeiner, Lloyd	NYA	1	1	0	0	0	0	....	....	....	....	....		1940-41	1940-41
Finney, Sid	Chi.	3	59	10	7	17	4	7	0	0	0	2		1951-52	1953-54
Finnigan, Ed	Bos.	1	3	0	0	0	0	....	....	....	....	....		1935-36	1935-36
• Finnigan, Frank	Ott., Tor., St.L.	14	555	115	88	203	405	39	6	9	15	22	2	1923-24	1936-37
Fischer, Ron	Buf.	2	18	0	7	7	6	....	....	....	....	....		1981-82	1982-83
Fisher, Alvin	Tor.	1	9	1	0	1	4	....	....	....	....	....		1924-25	1924-25
Fisher, Dunc	NYR, Bos., Det.	7	275	45	70	115	104	21	4	4	8	14		1947-48	1958-59
Fisher, Joe	Det.	4	66	8	12	20	13	15	2	1	3	6	1	1939-40	1942-43
Fitchner, Bob	Que	2	78	12	20	32	59	3	0	0	0	10		1979-80	1980-81
Fitzpatrick, Ross	Phi.	4	20	5	2	7	0	....	....	....	....	....		1982-83	1985-86
Fitzpatrick, Sandy	NYR, Min.	2	22	3	6	9	8	12	0	0	0	0		1964-65	1967-68
Flaman, Fern	Bos., Tor.	17	910	34	174	208	1370	63	4	8	12	93	1	1944-45	1960-61
Fleming, Reggie	Mtl., Chi., Bos., NYR, Phi., Buf.	12	749	108	132	240	1468	50	3	6	9	106	1	1959-60	1970-71
Flesch,	Ham.	1	1	0	0	0	0	....	....	....	....	....		1920-21	1920-21
Flesch, John	Min, Pit, Col.	4	124	18	23	41	117	....	....	....	....	....		1974-75	1979-80
Fletcher, Steven	Mtl., Wpg.	2	3	0	0	0	5	1	0	0	0	5		1987-88	1988-89
Flett, Bill	L.A., Phi., Tor., Atl, Edm.	11	689	202	215	417	501	52	7	16	23	42	1	1967-68	1979-80
Flichel, Todd	Wpg.	4	6	0	1	1	4	....	....	....	....	....		1987-88	1989-90
Flockhart, Rob	Van., Min	5	55	2	5	7	14	1	1	0	1	2		1976-77	1980-81
Flockhart, Ron	Phi., Pit., Mtl., St.L., Bos.	9	453	145	183	328	208	29	11	18	29	16		1980-81	1988-89
Floyd, Larry	N.J.	2	12	2	3	5	9	....	....	....	....	....		1982-83	1983-84
Fogolin, Lee	Buf., Edm.	13	924	44	195	239	1318	108	5	19	24	173	2	1974-75	1986-87
Fogolin, Lidio (Lee)	Det., Chi.	9	427	10	48	58	575	28	0	2	2	30	1	1947-48	1955-56
Folco, Peter	Van.	1	2	0	0	0	0	....	....	....	....	....		1973-74	1973-74
Foley, Gerry	Tor., NYR, L.A.	4	142	9	14	23	99	9	0	1	1	2		1954-55	1968-69
Foley, Rick	Chi., Phi., Det.	3	67	11	26	37	180	4	0	1	1	4		1970-71	1973-74
Foligno, Mike	Det., Buf., Tor., Fla.	15	1018	355	372	727	2049	57	15	17	32	185		1979-80	1993-94
Folk, Bill	Det.	2	12	0	0	0	4	....	....	....	....	....		1951-52	1952-53
Fontaine, Len	Det.	2	46	8	11	19	10	....	....	....	....	....		1972-73	1973-74
Fontas, Jon	Min.	2	2	0	0	0	0	....	....	....	....	....		1979-80	1980-81
Fonteyne, Val	Det., NYR, Pit.	13	820	75	154	229	26	59	3	10	13	8		1959-60	1971-72
Fontinato, Louie	NYR, Mtl.	9	535	26	78	104	1247	21	0	2	2	42		1954-55	1962-63
Forbes, Dave	Bos., Wsh.	6	363	64	64	128	341	45	1	4	5	13		1973-74	1978-79
Forbes, Mike	Bos., Edm.	3	50	1	11	12	41	....	....	....	....	....		1977-78	1981-82
Forey, Connie	St.L.	1	4	0	0	0	2	....	....	....	....	....		1973-74	1973-74
Forsey, Jack	Tor.	1	19	7	9	16	10	3	0	1	1	0		1942-43	1942-43
Forslund, Gus	Ott.	1	48	4	9	13	2	....	....	....	....	....		1932-33	1932-33
Forslund, Tomas	Cgy.	2	44	5	11	16	12	....	....	....	....	....		1991-92	1992-93
Forsyth, Alex	Wsh.	1	1	0	0	0	0	....	....	....	....	....		1976-77	1976-77
Fortier, Charles	Mtl.	1	1	0	0	0	0	....	....	....	....	....	1	1923-24	1923-24
Fortier, Dave	Tor., NYI, Van.	4	205	8	21	29	335	20	0	2	2	33		1972-73	1976-77
Fortier, Marc	Que., Ott., L.A.	6	212	42	60	102	135	....	....	....	....	....		1987-88	1992-93
Fortin, Ray	St.L.	3	92	2	6	8	33	6	0	0	0	8		1967-68	1969-70
Foster, Dwight	Bos., Col., N.J., Det.	10	541	111	163	274	420	35	5	12	17	4		1977-78	1986-87
Foster, Harry	NYR, Bos., Det.	4	83	3	2	5	32	....	....	....	....	....		1929-31	1934-35
Foster, Herb	NYR	2	5	1	0	1	5	....	....	....	....	....		1940-41	1947-48
Fotiu, Nick	NYR, Hfd., Cgy., Phi., Edm.	13	646	60	77	137	1362	38	0	4	4	67		1976-77	1988-89
• Fowler, Jimmy	Tor.	3	135	18	29	47	39	18	0	3	3	2		1936-37	1938-39
Fowler, Tom	Chi.	1	24	0	1	1	18	....	....	....	....	....		1946-47	1946-47
Fox, Greg	Atl, Chi., Pit.	8	494	14	92	106	637	44	1	9	10	67		1977-78	1984-85
Fox, Jim	L.A.	10	578	186	293	479	143	22	4	8	12	0		1980-81	1989-90
• Foyston, Frank	Det.	2	64	17	7	24	32	....	....	....	....	....		1926-27	1927-28
Frampton, Bob	Mtl.	1	2	0	0	0	0	3	0	0	0	0		1949-50	1949-50
Franceschetti, Lou	Wsh., Tor., Buf.	10	459	59	81	140	747	44	3	2	5	111		1981-82	1991-92
Francis, Bobby	Det.	1	14	2	0	2	0	....	....	....	....	....		1982-83	1982-83
Fraser, Archie	NYR	1	3	0	1	1	0	....	....	....	....	....		1943-44	1943-44
Fraser, Curt	Van., Chi., Min.	12	704	193	240	433	1306	65	15	18	33	198		1978-79	1989-90
Fraser, Gord	Chi., Det., Mtl., Pit., Phi.	5	144	24	12	36	224	2	1	0	1	6		1926-27	1930-31
Fraser, Harry	Chi.	1	21	5	4	9	0	....	....	....	....	....		1944-45	1944-45
Fraser, Jack	Ham.	1	1	0	0	0	0	....	....	....	....	....		1923-24	1923-24
Frawley, Dan	Chi., Pit.	6	273	37	40	77	674	1	0	0	0	0		1983-84	1988-89
• Frederickson, Frank	Det., Bos., Pit.	5	165	39	34	73	207	10	2	5	7	26	1	1926-27	1930-31
Frew, Irv	Mtl.M, St.L., Mtl.	3	95	2	5	7	146	4	0	0	0	6		1933-34	1935-36
Friday, Tim	Det.	1	23	0	3	3	6	....	....	....	....	....		1985-86	1985-86
Fridgen, Dan	Hfd.	2	13	2	3	5	2	....	....	....	....	....		1981-82	1982-83
Friest, Ron	Min.	3	64	7	7	14	191	6	1	0	1	7		1980-81	1982-83
Frig, Len	Chi., Cal., Cle., St.L.	7	311	13	51	64	479	14	2	1	3	0		1972-73	1979-80
Frost, Harry	Bos.	1	3	0	0	0	0	1	0	0	0	0		1938-39	1938-39
Frycer, Miroslav	Que., Tor., Det., Edm.	8	415	147	183	330	486	17	3	8	11	16		1981-82	1988-89
Fryday, Bob	Mtl.	2	5	1	0	1	0	....	....	....	....	....		1949-50	1951-52
Ftorek, Robbie	Det., Que, NYR	8	334	77	150	227	262	19	9	6	15	28		1972-73	1984-85
Fullan, Lawrence	Wsh.	1	4	1	0	1	0	....	....	....	....	....		1974-75	1974-75
Fusco, Mark	Hfd.	2	80	3	12	15	42	....	....	....	....	....		1983-84	1984-85

G

Name	NHL Teams	NHL Seasons	Regular Schedule GP	G	A	TP	PIM	Playoffs GP	G	A	TP	PIM	NHL Cup Wins	First NHL Season	Last NHL Season
Gadsby, Bill	Chi., NYR, Det.	20	1248	130	437	567	1539	67	4	23	27	92		1946-47	1965-66
Gaetz, Link	Min., S.J.	3	65	6	8	14	412	....	....	....	....	....		1988-89	1991-92
Gage, Jody	Det., Buf.	6	68	14	15	29	26	....	....	....	....	....		1980-81	1991-92
Gagne, Art	Mtl., Bos., Ott., Det.	6	228	67	33	100	257	11	2	1	3	20		1926-27	1931-32
Gagne, Paul	Col., N.J., Tor., NYI	8	390	110	101	211	127	....	....	....	....	....		1980-81	1989-90
Gagne, Pierre	Bos.	1	2	0	0	0	0	....	....	....	....	....		1959-60	1959-60
Gagnon, Germaine	Mtl., NYI, Chi., K.C.	5	259	40	101	141	72	19	2	3	5	2		1971-72	1975-76
• Gagnon, Johnny	Mtl., Bos., NYA	10	454	120	141	261	295	32	12	12	24	37	1	1930-31	1939-40

Bryan Erickson

Doug Evans

Tom Fergus

Mike Foligno

Marc Fortier

Link Gaetz

Paul Gillis

Michel Goulet

			Regular Schedule					Playoffs					NHL	First	Last
Name	NHL Teams	NHL Seasons	GP	G	A	TP	PIM	GP	G	A	TP	PIM	Cup Wins	NHL Season	NHL Season
Gainey, Bob	Mtl.	16	1160	239	262	501	585	182	25	48	73	151	5	1973-74	1988-89
• Gainor, Dutch	Bos., NYR, Ott., Mtl.M	7	243	51	56	107	129	25	2	1	3	14	2	1927-28	1934-35
Galarneau, Michel	Hfd.	3	78	7	10	17	34	....	....	....	....	....		1980-81	1982-83
• Galbraith, Percy	Bos., Ott.	8	347	29	31	60	223	31	4	7	11	24		1926-27	1933-34
• Gallagher, John	Mtl.M, Det., NYA	7	204	14	19	33	153	22	2	3	5	27	1	1930-31	1938-39
Gallimore, Jamie	Min.	1	2	0	0	0	0	....	....	....	....	....		1977-78	1977-78
• Gallinger, Don	Bos.	5	222	65	88	153	89	23	5	5	10	19		1942-43	1947-48
Gamble, Dick	Mtl., Chi., Tor.	8	195	41	41	82	66	14	1	2	3	4	2	1950-51	1966-67
Gambucci, Gary	Min.	2	51	2	7	9	9	....	....	....	....	....		1971-72	1973-74
Ganchar, Perry	St. L., Mtl., Pit.	4	42	3	7	10	36	7	3	1	4	0		1983-84	1988-89
Gans, Dave	L.A.	2	6	0	0	0	2	....	....	....	....	....		1982-83	1985-86
• Gardiner, Herb	Mtl., Chi.	3	101	10	9	19	52	7	0	1	1	14		1926-27	1928-29
Gardner, Bill	Chi., Hfd.	9	380	73	115	188	68	45	3	8	11	17		1980-81	1988-89
Gardner, Cal	NYR, Tor., Chi., Bos.	12	696	154	238	392	517	61	7	10	17	20	2	1945-46	1956-57
Gardner, Dave	Mtl., St.L., Cal., Cle., Phi.	7	350	75	115	190	41	....	....	....	....	....		1972-73	1979-80
Gardner, Paul	Col., Tor., Pit., Wsh., Buf.	7	447	201	201	402	207	16	2	6	8	14		1976-77	1985-86
Gare, Danny	Buf., Det., Edm.	13	827	354	331	685	1285	64	25	21	46	195		1974-75	1986-87
Gariepy, Ray	Bos., Tor.	2	36	1	6	7	43	....	....	....	....	....		1953-54	1955-56
• Garland, Scott	Tor., L.A.	3	91	13	24	37	115	7	1	2	3	35		1975-76	1978-79
Garner, Bob	Pit.	1	1	0	0	0	0	....	....	....	....	....		1982-83	1982-83
• Garrett, Red	NYR	1	23	1	1	2	18	....	....	....	....	....		1942-43	1942-43
• Gassoff, Bob	St.L.	4	245	11	47	58	866	9	0	1	1	16		1973-74	1976-77
Gassoff, Brad	Van.	4	122	19	17	36	163	3	0	0	0	0		1975-76	1978-79
Gatzos, Steve	Pit.	4	89	15	20	35	83	1	0	0	0	0		1981-82	1984-85
Gaudreault, Armand	Bos.	1	44	15	9	24	27	7	0	2	2	8		1944-45	1944-45
• Gaudreault, Leo	Mtl.	3	67	8	4	12	30	....	....	....	....	....		1927-28	1932-33
Gaulin, Jean-Marc	Que.	4	26	4	3	7	8	1	0	0	0	0		1982-83	1985-86
Gaume, Dallas	Hfd.	1	4	1	1	2	0	....	....	....	....	....		1988-89	1988-89
Gauthier, Art	Mtl.	1	13	0	0	0	0	1	0	0	0	0		1926-27	1926-27
• Gauthier, Fern	NYR, Mtl., Det.	6	229	46	50	96	35	22	5	1	6	7		1943-44	1948-49
Gauthier, Jean	Mtl., Phi., Bos.	10	166	6	29	35	150	14	1	3	4	22	1	1960-61	1969-70
Gauthier, Luc	Mtl.	1	3	0	0	0	2	....	....	....	....	....		1990-91	1990-91
Gauvreau, Jocelyn	Mtl.	1	2	0	0	0	0	....	....	....	....	....		1983-84	1983-84
Gavin, Stewart	Tor., Hfd., Min.	13	768	130	155	285	584	66	14	20	34	75		1980-81	1992-93
Geale, Bob	Pit.	1	1	0	0	0	2	....	....	....	....	....		1984-85	1984-85
• Gee, George	Chi., Det.	9	551	135	183	318	345	41	6	13	19	32	1	1945-46	1953-54
Geldart, Gary	Min.	1	4	0	0	0	5	....	....	....	....	....		1970-71	1970-71
Gendron, Jean-Guy	NYR, Mtl., Bos., Phi.	14	863	182	201	383	701	42	7	4	11	47		1955-56	1971-72
Geoffrion, Bernie	Mtl., NYR	16	883	393	429	822	689	132	58	60	118	88	6	1950-51	1967-68
Geoffrion, Danny	Mtl., Wpg.	3	111	20	32	52	99	2	0	0	0	7		1979-80	1981-82
• Geran, Gerry	Mtl.W., Bos.	2	37	5	1	6	6	....	....	....	....	....		1917-18	1925-26
• Gerard, Eddie	Ott.	6	128	50	30	80	94	26	7	3	10	51	4	1917-18	1922-23
Germain, Eric	L.A.	1	4	0	1	1	13	1	0	0	0	4		1987-88	1987-88
Getliffe, Ray	Bos., Mtl.	10	393	136	137	273	260	45	9	10	19	30	2	1935-36	1944-45
Giallonardo, Mario	Col.	2	23	0	3	3	6	....	....	....	....	....		1979-80	1980-81
Gibbs, Barry	Bos., Min., Atl., St.L., L.A.	13	797	58	224	282	945	36	4	2	6	67		1967-68	1979-80
Gibson, Don	Van.	1	14	0	3	3	20	....	....	....	....	....		1990-91	1990-91
Gibson, Doug	Bos., Wsh.	3	63	9	19	28	0	1	0	0	0	0		1973-74	1977-78
Gibson, John	L.A., Tor., Wpg.	3	48	0	2	2	120	....	....	....	....	....		1980-81	1983-84
Giesebrecht, Gus	Det.	4	135	27	51	78	13	17	2	3	5	0		1938-39	1941-42
Giffin, Lee	Pit.	2	27	1	3	4	9	....	....	....	....	....		1986-87	1987-88
Gilbert, Ed	K.C., Pit.	3	166	21	31	52	22	....	....	....	....	....		1974-75	1976-77
Gilbert, Jean	Bos.	2	9	0	0	0	4	....	....	....	....	....		1962-63	1964-65
Gilbert, Rod	NYR	18	1065	406	615	1021	508	79	34	33	67	43		1960-61	1977-78
Gilbertson, Stan	Cal., St.L., Wsh., Pit.	6	428	85	89	174	148	3	1	1	2	2		1971-72	1976-77
Giles, Curt	Min., NYR, St.L.	14	895	43	199	242	733	103	6	16	22	118		1979-80	1992-93
Gillen, Don	Phi., Hfd.	2	35	2	4	6	22	....	....	....	....	....		1979-80	1981-82
Gillie, Ferrand	Det.	1	1	0	0	0	0	....	....	....	....	....		1928-29	1928-29
Gillies, Clark	NYI, Buf.	14	958	319	378	697	1023	164	47	47	94	287	4	1974-75	1987-88
Gillis, Jere	Que., Buf., Phi., Van., NYR	9	386	78	95	173	230	19	4	7	11	9		1977-78	1986-87
Gillis, Mike	Col., Bos.	6	246	33	43	76	186	27	2	5	7	10		1978-79	1983-84
Gillis, Paul	Que., Chi., Hfd.	11	624	88	154	242	1498	42	3	14	17	156		1982-83	1992-93
Girard, Bob	Cal., Cle., Wsh.	5	305	45	69	114	140	....	....	....	....	....		1975-76	1979-80
Girard, Kenny	Tor.	3	7	0	1	1	2	....	....	....	....	....		1956-57	1959-60
Giroux, Art	Mtl., Bos., Det.	3	54	6	4	10	14	2	0	0	0	0		1932-33	1935-36
Giroux, Larry	St.L., K.C., Det., Hfd.	7	274	15	74	89	333	5	0	0	0	4		1973-74	1979-80
Giroux, Pierre	L.A.	1	6	1	0	1	17	....	....	....	....	....		1982-83	1982-83
Gladney, Bob	L.A., Pit.	2	14	1	5	6	4	....	....	....	....	....		1982-83	1983-84
Gladu, Jean	Bos.	1	40	6	14	20	2	7	2	2	4	0		1944-45	1944-45
Glennie, Brian	Tor., L.A.	10	572	14	100	114	621	32	0	1	1	66		1969-70	1978-79
Glennon, Matt	Bos.	1	3	0	0	0	2	....	....	....	....	....		1991-92	1991-92
Gloeckner, Lorry	Det.	1	13	0	2	2	6	....	....	....	....	....		1978-79	1978-79
Gloor, Dan	Van.	1	2	0	0	0	0	....	....	....	....	....		1973-74	1973-74
Glover, Fred	Det., Chi.	4	92	13	11	24	62	3	0	0	0	0		1948-49	1952-53
Glover, Howie	Chi., Det., NYR, Mtl.	5	144	29	17	46	101	11	1	2	3	2		1958-59	1968-69
Godden, Ernie	Tor.	1	5	1	1	2	6	....	....	....	....	....		1981-82	1981-82
Godfrey, Warren	Bos., Det.	16	786	32	125	157	752	52	1	4	5	42		1952-53	1967-68
Godin, Eddy	Wsh.	2	27	3	6	9	12	....	....	....	....	....		1977-78	1978-79
Godin, Sammy	Ott., Mtl.	3	83	4	3	7	36	....	....	....	....	....		1927-28	1933-34
Goegan, Peter	Det., NYR, Min.	11	383	19	67	86	365	33	1	3	4	61		1957-58	1967-68
Goertz, Dave	Pit.	1	2	0	0	0	2	....	....	....	....	....		1987-88	1987-88
• Goldham, Bob	Tor., Chi., Det.	12	650	28	143	171	400	66	3	14	17	53	5	1941-42	1955-56
Goldsworthy, Bill	Bos., Min., NYR	14	771	283	258	541	793	40	18	19	37	30		1964-65	1977-78
• Goldsworthy, Leroy	NYR, Det., Chi., Mtl., Bos., NYA	9	337	66	57	123	79	22	1	0	1	4	1	1929-30	1938-39
Goldup, Glenn	Mtl., L.A.	9	291	52	67	119	303	16	4	3	7	22		1973-74	1981-82
Goldup, Hank	Tor., NYR	6	181	63	80	143	97	26	5	1	6	6	1	1939-40	1945-46
Gooden, Bill	NYR	2	53	9	11	20	15	....	....	....	....	....		1942-43	1943-44
Goodenough, Larry	Phi., Van.	6	242	22	77	99	179	22	3	15	18	10	1	1974-75	1979-80
• Goodfellow, Ebbie	Det.	14	554	134	190	324	511	45	8	8	16	65	3	1929-30	1942-43
Gordon, Fred	Det., Bos.	2	77	8	7	15	68	1	0	0	0	0		1926-27	1927-28
Gordon, Jackie	NYR	3	36	3	10	13	0	9	1	1	2	7		1948-49	1950-51
Gorence, Tom	Phi., Edm.	6	303	58	53	111	89	37	9	6	15	47		1978-79	1983-84
Goring, Butch	L.A., NYI, Bos.	16	1107	375	513	888	102	134	38	50	88	32	4	1969-70	1984-85
Gorman, Dave	Atl.	1	3	0	0	0	0	....	....	....	....	....		1979-80	1979-80
• Gorman, Ed	Ott., Tor.	4	111	14	5	19	108	8	0	0	0	2	1	1924-25	1927-28
Gosselin, Benoit	NYR	1	7	0	0	0	33	....	....	....	....	....		1977-78	1977-78
Gosselin, Guy	Wpg.	1	5	0	0	0	6	....	....	....	....	....		1987-88	1987-88
Gotaas, Steve	Pit., Min.	3	49	6	9	15	53	3	0	1	1	5		1987-88	1990-91
• Gottselig, Johnny	Chi.	16	589	176	195	371	203	43	13	13	26	20	2	1928-29	1944-45
Gould, Bobby	Atl., Cgy., Wsh., Bos.	11	697	145	159	304	572	78	15	13	28	58		1979-80	1989-90
Gould, John	Buf., Van., Atl.	9	504	131	138	269	113	14	3	2	5	4		1971-72	1979-80
Gould, Larry	Van.	1	2	0	0	0	0	....	....	....	....	....		1973-74	1973-74
Goulet, Michel	Que., Chi.	15	1089	548	604	1152	825	92	39	39	78	110		1979-80	1993-94
Goupille, Red	Mtl.	8	222	12	28	40	256	8	2	0	2	6		1935-36	1942-43
Goyer, Gerry	Chi.	1	40	1	2	3	4	3	0	0	0	2		1967-68	1967-68
Goyette, Phil	Mtl., NYR, St.L., Buf.	16	941	207	467	674	131	94	17	29	46	26	4	1956-57	1971-72
Graboski, Tony	Mtl.	3	66	6	10	16	18	2	0	0	0	0		1940-41	1942-43
• Gracie, Bob	Tor., Bos., NYA, Mtl.M., Mtl., Chi.	9	378	82	109	191	204	33	4	7	11	4	2	1930-31	1938-39
Gradin, Thomas	Van., Bos.	9	677	209	384	593	298	42	17	25	42	20		1978-79	1986-87
• Graham, Leth	Ott., Ham.	6	26	3	0	3	0	1	0	0	0	0	1	1920-21	1925-26
Graham, Pat	Pit., Tor.	3	103	11	17	28	136	4	0	0	0	2		1981-82	1983-84
Graham, Rod	Bos.	1	14	2	1	3	7	....	....	....	....	....		1974-75	1974-75
Graham, Ted	Chi., Mtl.M., Det., St.L., Bos., NYA	9	343	14	25	39	300	23	3	1	4	34		1927-28	1936-37
Grant, Danny	Mtl., Min., Det., L.A.	13	736	263	273	536	239	43	10	14	24	19	1	1965-66	1978-79
Gratton, Dan	L.A.	1	7	1	0	1	5	....	....	....	....	....		1987-88	1987-88
Gratton, Norm	NYR, Atl., Buf., Min.	5	201	39	44	83	64	6	0	1	1	2		1971-72	1975-76
Gravelle, Leo	Mtl., Det.	5	223	44	34	78	42	17	4	1	5	2		1946-47	1950-51
Graves, Hilliard	Cal., Atl., Van., Wpg.	9	556	118	163	281	209	2	0	0	0	0		1970-71	1979-80
Graves, Steve	Edm.	3	35	5	4	9	10	....	....	....	....	....		1983-84	1987-88
• Gray, Alex	NYR, Tor.	2	50	7	0	7	30	13	1	0	1	0	1	1927-28	1928-29
Gray, Terry	Bos., Mtl., L.A., St.L.	6	147	26	28	54	64	35	5	5	10	22		1961-62	1970-71
Green, Red	Ham., NYA, Bos., Det.	6	195	59	13	72	261	....	....	....	....	....	1	1923-24	1928-29
Green, Rick	Wsh., Mtl., Det., NYI	15	845	43	220	263	588	100	3	16	19	73	1	1976-77	1991-92
Green, Ted	Bos.	11	620	48	206	254	1029	31	4	8	12	54	1	1960-61	1971-72

Name	NHL Teams	NHL Seasons	Regular Schedule GP	G	A	TP	PIM	Playoffs GP	G	A	TP	PIM	NHL Cup Wins	First NHL Season	Last NHL Season
• Green, Wilf	Ham., NYA	4	103	33	8	41	151	....	....	....	....	....		1923-24	1926-27
Gregg, Randy	Edm., Van.	10	474	41	152	193	333	137	13	38	51	127	5	1981-82	1991-92
Greig, Bruce	Cal.	2	9	0	1	1	46	....	....	....	....	....		1973-74	1974-75
Grenier, Lucien	Mtl., L.A.	4	151	14	14	28	18	2	0	0	0	0	1	1968-69	1971-72
Grenier, Richard	NYI	1	10	1	1	2	2	....	....	....	....	....		1972-73	1972-73
Greschner, Ron	NYR	16	982	179	431	610	1226	84	17	32	49	106		1974-75	1989-90
Grigor, George	Chi.	1	2	1	0	1	0	1	0	0	0	0		1943-44	1943-44
Grisdale, John	Tor., Van.	6	250	4	39	43	346	10	0	1	1	15		1972-73	1978-79
Gronsdahl, Lloyd	Bos.	1	10	1	2	3	0	....	....	....	....	....		1941-42	1941-42
Gronstrand, Jari	Min., NYR, Que., NYI	5	185	8	26	34	135	3	0	0	0	4		1986-87	1990-91
Gross, Llyod	Tor., NYA, Bos., Det.	3	62	11	5	16	20	1	0	0	0	0		1926-27	1934-35
• Grosso, Don	Det., Chi., Bos.	9	334	87	117	204	90	50	14	12	26	46	1	1938-39	1946-47
Grosvenar, Len	Ott., NYA, Mtl.	6	147	9	11	20	78	4	0	0	0	2		1927-28	1932-33
Groulx, Wayne	Que.	1	1	0	0	0	0	....	....	....	....	....		1984-85	1984-85
Gruen, Danny	Det., Col.	3	49	9	13	22	19	....	....	....	....	....		1972-73	1976-77
Gruhl, Scott	L.A., Pit.	3	20	3	3	6	6	....	....	....	....	....		1981-82	1987-88
Gryp, Bob	Bos., Wsh.	3	74	11	13	24	33	....	....	....	....	....		1973-74	1975-76
Guay, Francois	Buf.	1	117	11	23	34	92	9	0	1	1	12		1989-90	1989-90
Guay, Paul	Phi., L.A., Bos., NYI	7	117	11	23	34	92	9	0	1	1	12		1983-84	1990-91
Guerard, Stephane	Que.	2	34	0	0	0	40	....	....	....	....	....		1987-88	1989-90
Guevremont, Jocelyn	Van., Buf., NYR	9	571	84	223	307	319	40	4	17	21	18		1971-72	1979-80
Guidolin, Aldo	NYR	4	182	9	15	24	117	....	....	....	....	....		1952-53	1955-56
Guidolin, Bep	Bos., Det., Chi.	9	519	107	171	278	606	24	5	7	12	35		1942-43	1951-52
Guindon, Bobby	Wpg.	1	6	0	1	1	0	....	....	....	....	....		1979-80	1979-80
Gustafsson, Bengt	Wsh.	9	629	196	359	555	196	32	9	19	28	16		1979-80	1988-89
Gustavsson, Peter	Col.	1	2	0	0	0	0	....	....	....	....	....		1981-82	1981-82
Guy, Kevan	Cgy., Van.	6	156	5	20	25	138	5	0	1	1	23		1986-87	1991-92

H

Name	NHL Teams	NHL Seasons	Regular Schedule GP	G	A	TP	PIM	Playoffs GP	G	A	TP	PIM	NHL Cup Wins	First NHL Season	Last NHL Season
Haanpaa, Ari	NYI	3	60	6	11	17	37	6	0	0	0	10		1985-86	1987-88
Haas, David	Edm., Cgy.	2	7	2	1	3	7	....	....	....	....	....		1990-91	1993-94
Habscheid, Marc	Edm., Min., Det., Cgy.	11	345	72	91	163	171	12	1	3	4	13		1981-82	1991-92
Hachborn, Len	Phi., L.A.	3	102	20	39	59	29	7	0	3	3	7		1983-84	1985-86
Haddon, Lloyd	Det.	1	8	0	0	0	2	1	0	0	0	0		1959-60	1959-60
Hadfield, Vic	NYR, Pit.	16	1002	323	389	712	1154	73	27	21	48	117		1961-62	1976-77
Haggarty, Jim	Mtl.	1	5	1	1	2	0	3	2	1	3	0		1941-42	1941-42
• Hagglund, Roger	Que.	1	3	0	0	0	0	....	....	....	....	....		1984-85	1984-85
Hagman, Matti	Bos., Edm.	4	237	56	89	145	36	20	5	2	7	6		1976-77	1981-82
Haidy, Gord	Det.	1	....	....	....	....	....	1	0	0	0	0	1	1949-50	1949-50
Hajdu, Richard	Buf.	2	5	0	0	0	4	....	....	....	....	....		1985-86	1986-87
Hajt, Bill	Buf.	14	854	42	202	244	43	80	2	16	18	70		1973-74	1986-87
Hakansson, Anders	Min., Pit., L.A.	5	330	52	46	98	141	6	0	0	0	2		1981-82	1985-86
• Halderson, Slim	Det., Tor.	1	44	3	2	5	65	....	....	....	....	....	1	1926-27	1926-27
Hale, Larry	Phi.	4	196	5	37	42	90	8	0	0	0	12		1968-69	1971-72
Haley, Len	Det.	2	30	2	2	4	14	6	1	3	4	6		1959-60	1960-61
Hall, Bob	NYA	1	8	0	0	0	0	....	....	....	....	....		1925-26	1925-26
Hall, Del	Cal.	3	9	2	0	2	2	....	....	....	....	....		1971-72	1973-74
• Hall, Joe	Mtl.	2	37	15	1	16	85	12	0	2	2	0		1917-18	1918-19
Hall, Murray	Chi., Det., Min., Van.	9	164	35	48	83	46	6	0	0	0	0		1961-62	1971-72
Hall, Taylor	Van., Bos.	5	41	7	9	16	29	....	....	....	....	....		1983-84	1987-88
Hall, Wayne	NYR	1	4	0	0	0	0	....	....	....	....	....		1960-61	1960-61
• Halliday, Milt	Ott.	3	67	1	0	1	6	6	0	0	0	0	1	1926-27	1928-29
Hallin, Mats	NYI, Min.	5	152	17	14	31	193	15	1	0	1	13	1	1982-83	1986-87
Halward, Doug	Bos., L.A., Van., Det., Edm.	14	653	69	224	293	774	47	7	10	17	113		1975-76	1988-89
Hamel, Gilles	Buf., Wpg., L.A.	9	519	127	147	274	276	27	4	5	9	10		1980-81	1988-89
Hamel, Herb	Tor.	1	2	0	0	0	14	....	....	....	....	....		1930-31	1930-31
Hamel, Jean	St.L., Det., Que., Mtl.	12	699	26	95	121	766	33	0	2	2	44		1972-73	1983-84
• Hamill, Red	Bos., Chi.	12	418	128	94	222	160	13	1	2	3	12	2	1937-38	1950-51
Hamilton, Al	NYR, Buf., Edm.	7	257	10	78	88	258	7	0	0	0	2		1965-66	1979-80
Hamilton, Chuck	Mtl., St.L.	2	4	0	2	2	2	....	....	....	....	....		1961-62	1972-73
• Hamilton, Jack	Tor.	3	138	31	48	79	76	11	2	1	3	0		1942-43	1945-46
Hamilton, Jim	Pit.	8	95	14	18	32	28	6	3	0	3	0		1977-78	1984-85
• Hamilton, Reg	Tor., Chi.	12	387	21	87	108	412	64	6	6	12	54	2	1935-36	1946-47
Hammarstrom, Inge	Tor., St.L.	6	427	116	123	239	86	13	2	3	5	4		1973-74	1978-79
Hammond, Ken	L.A., Edm., NYR, Tor., Bos., S.J., Van., Ott.	8	193	18	29	47	290	15	0	0	0	24		1984-85	1992-93
Hampson, Gord	Cgy.	1	4	0	0	0	5	....	....	....	....	....		1982-83	1982-83
Hampson, Ted	Tor., NYR, Det., Oak., Cal., Min.	12	676	108	245	353	94	35	7	10	17	2		1959-60	1971-72
Hampton, Rick	Cal., Cle., L.A.	6	337	59	113	172	147	2	0	0	0	0		1974-75	1979-80
Hamway, Mark	NYI	3	53	5	13	18	9	1	0	0	0	0		1984-85	1986-87
Handy, Ron	NYI, St.L.	2	14	0	3	3	0	....	....	....	....	....		1984-85	1987-88
Hangsleben, Al	Hfd., Wsh., L.A.	3	185	21	48	69	396	....	....	....	....	....		1979-80	1981-82
Hanna, John	NYR, Mtl., Phi.	5	198	6	26	32	206	....	....	....	....	....		1958-59	1967-68
• Hannigan, Gord	Tor.	4	161	29	31	60	117	9	2	0	2	8		1952-53	1955-56
Hannigan, Pat	Tor., NYR, Phi.	5	182	30	39	69	116	11	1	2	3	11		1959-60	1968-69
Hannigan, Ray	Tor.	1	3	0	0	0	2	....	....	....	....	....		1948-49	1948-49
Hansen, Ritchie	NYI, St.L.	4	20	2	8	10	6	....	....	....	....	....		1976-77	1981-82
Hanson, Dave	Det., Min.	2	33	1	1	2	65	....	....	....	....	....		1978-79	1979-80
Hanson, Emil	Det.	1	7	0	0	0	6	....	....	....	....	....		1932-33	1932-33
Hanson, Keith	Cgy.	1	25	0	2	2	77	....	....	....	....	....		1983-84	1983-84
Hanson, Ossie	Chi.	1	7	0	0	0	0	....	....	....	....	....		1937-38	1937-38
Harbaruk, Nick	Pit., St.L.	5	364	45	75	120	273	14	3	1	4	20		1969-70	1973-74
Harding, Jeff	Phi.	2	15	0	0	0	47	....	....	....	....	....		1988-89	1989-90
Hardy, Joe	Oak., Cal.	2	63	9	14	23	51	4	0	0	0	0		1969-70	1970-71
Hardy, Mark	L.A., NYR, Min.	15	915	62	306	368	1293	67	5	16	21	158		1979-80	1993-94
Hargreaves, Jim	Van.	2	66	1	7	8	105	....	....	....	....	....		1970-71	1972-73
Harlow, Scott	St.L.	1	1	0	1	1	0	....	....	....	....	....		1987-88	1987-88
Harmon, Glen	Mtl.	9	452	50	96	146	334	53	5	10	15	37	2	1942-43	1950-51
Harms, John	Chi.	2	44	5	5	10	21	3	3	0	3	2		1943-44	1944-45
Harnott, Happy	Bos.	1	6	0	0	0	6	....	....	....	....	....		1933-34	1933-34
Harper, Terry	Mtl., L.A., Det., St.L., Col.	19	1066	35	221	256	1362	112	4	13	17	140	5	1962-63	1980-81
Harrer, Tim	Cgy.	1	3	0	0	0	2	....	....	....	....	....		1982-83	1982-83
• Harrington, Hago	Bos., Mtl.	3	72	9	3	12	15	4	1	0	1	2		1925-26	1932-33
Harris, Billy	Tor., Det., Oak., Cal., Pit.	12	769	126	219	345	205	62	8	10	18	30	3	1955-56	1968-69
Harris, Billy	NYI, L.A., Tor.	12	897	231	327	558	394	71	19	19	38	48		1972-73	1983-84
Harris, Duke	Min., Tor.	1	26	1	4	5	4	....	....	....	....	....		1967-68	1967-68
Harris, Hugh	Buf.	1	60	12	26	38	17	3	0	0	0	0		1972-73	1972-73
Harris, Ron	Det., Oak., Atl., NYR	12	476	20	91	111	484	28	4	3	7	33		1962-63	1975-76
Harris, Smokey	Bos.	2	40	5	5	10	28	2	0	0	0	0		1924-25	1930-31
Harris, Ted	Mtl., Min., Det., St.L., Phi.	12	788	30	168	198	1000	100	1	22	23	230	5	1963-64	1974-75
Harrison, Ed	Bos., NYR	4	194	27	24	51	53	9	1	0	1	2		1947-48	1950-51
Harrison, Jim	Bos., Tor., Chi., Edm.	8	324	67	86	153	435	13	1	1	2	43		1968-69	1979-80
Hart, Gerry	Det., NYI, Que., St.L.	15	730	29	150	179	1240	78	3	12	15	175		1968-69	1982-83
• Hart, Gizzy	Det., Mtl.	3	100	6	8	14	12	8	0	1	1	0	1	1926-27	1932-33
Hartsburg, Craig	Min.	10	570	98	315	413	818	61	15	27	42	70		1979-80	1988-89
• Harvey, Doug	Mtl., NYR, Det., St.L.	20	1113	88	452	540	1216	137	8	64	72	152	6	1947-48	1968-69
Harvey, Fred	Min., Atl., K.C., Det.	7	407	90	118	208	131	14	0	2	2	8		1970-71	1976-77
Harvey, Hugh	K.C.	2	18	1	1	2	4	....	....	....	....	....		1974-75	1975-76
Hassard, Bob	Tor., Chi.	5	126	9	28	37	22	....	....	....	....	....		1949-50	1954-55
Hatoum, Ed	Det., Van.	3	47	3	6	9	25	....	....	....	....	....		1968-69	1970-71
Haworth, Alan	Buf., Wsh., Que.	8	524	189	211	400	425	42	12	16	28	28		1980-81	1987-88
Haworth, Gord	NYR	1	2	0	1	1	0	....	....	....	....	....		1952-53	1952-53
Hawryliw, Neil	NYI	1	1	0	0	0	0	....	....	....	....	....		1981-82	1981-82
Hay, Billy	Chi.	8	506	113	273	386	244	67	15	21	36	62		1959-60	1966-67
• Hay, George	Chi., Det.	7	242	74	60	134	84	8	2	3	5	14		1926-27	1933-34
Hay, Jim	Det.	3	75	1	5	6	22	9	1	0	1	2	1	1952-53	1954-55
Hayek, Peter	Min.	1	1	0	0	0	0	....	....	....	....	....		1981-82	1981-82
Hayes, Chris	Bos.	1	....	....	....	....	....	1	0	0	0	0	1	1971-72	1971-72
Haynes, Paul	Mtl.M., Bos., Mtl.	11	390	61	134	195	164	25	2	8	10	13		1930-31	1940-41
Hayward, Rick	L.A.	1	4	0	0	0	5	....	....	....	....	....		1990-91	1990-91
Hazlett, Steve	Van.	1	1	0	0	0	0	....	....	....	....	....		1979-80	1979-80
Head, Galen	Det.	1	1	0	0	0	0	....	....	....	....	....		1967-68	1967-68
Headley, Fern	Bos., Mtl.	1	27	1	1	2	6	5	0	0	0	0		1924-25	1924-25

Scott Gruhl

Kevan Guy

Ken Hammond

Jeff Harding

Mark Hardy

Scott Harlow

Rick Hayward

Ken Hodge

			Regular Schedule					Playoffs							
Name	NHL Teams	NHL Seasons	GP	G	A	TP	PIM	GP	G	A	TP	PIM	NHL Cup Wins	First NHL Season	Last NHL Season
Healey, Dick	Det.	1	1	0	0	0	2	....	....	....	....	....		1960-61	1960-61
Heaphy, Shawn	Cgy.	1	1	0	0	0	0	....	....	....	....	....		1992-93	1992-93
Heaslip, Mark	NYR, L.A.	3	117	10	19	29	110	5	0	0	0	2		1976-77	1978-79
Heath, Randy	NYR	2	13	2	4	6	15	....	....	....	....	....		1984-85	1985-86
Hebenton, Andy	NYR, Bos.	9	630	189	202	391	83	22	6	5	11	8		1955-56	1963-64
Hedberg, Anders	NYR	7	465	172	225	397	144	58	22	24	46	31		1978-79	1984-85
• Heffernan, Frank	Tor.	1	17	0	0	0	4	....	....	....	....	....		1919-20	1919-20
Heffernan, Gerry	Mtl.	3	83	33	35	68	27	11	3	3	6	8	1	1941-42	1943-44
Heidt, Mike	L.A.	1	6	0	1	1	7	....	....	....	....	....		1983-84	1983-84
Heindl, Bill	Min., NYR	3	18	2	1	3	0	....	....	....	....	....		1970-71	1972-73
Heinrich, Lionel	Bos.	1	35	1	1	2	33	....	....	....	....	....		1955-56	1955-56
Heiskala, Earl	Phi.	3	127	13	11	24	294	....	....	....	....	....		1968-69	1970-71
Helander, Peter	L.A.	1	7	0	1	1	0	....	....	....	....	....		1982-83	1982-83
• Heller, Ott	NYR	15	647	55	176	231	465	61	6	8	14	61	2	1931-32	1945-46
Helman, Harry	Ott.	3	42	1	0	1	7	5	0	0	0	0	1	1922-23	1924-25
Helminen, Raimo	NYR, Min., NYI	3	117	13	46	59	16	2	0	0	0	0		1985-86	1988-89
Hemmerling, Tony	NYA	2	24	3	3	6	4	....	....	....	....	....		1935-36	1936-37
Henderson, Archie	Wsh., Min., Hfd.	3	23	3	1	4	92	....	....	....	....	....		1980-81	1982-83
Henderson, Murray	Bos.	8	405	24	62	86	305	41	2	3	5	23		1944-45	1951-52
Henderson, Paul	Det., Tor., Atl.	13	707	236	241	477	304	56	11	14	25	28		1962-63	1979-80
Hendrickson, John	Det.	3	5	0	0	0	4	....	....	....	....	....		1957-58	1961-62
Henning, Lorne	NYI	9	544	73	111	184	102	81	7	7	14	8	2	1972-73	1980-81
Henry, Camille	NYR, Chi., St.L.	14	727	279	249	528	88	47	6	12	18	7		1953-54	1969-70
Henry, Dale	NYI	6	132	13	26	39	263	....	....	....	....	....		1984-85	1989-90
Hepple, Alan	N.J.	3	3	0	0	0	7	....	....	....	....	....		1983-84	1985-86
• Herberts, Jimmy	Bos., Tor., Det.	6	206	83	29	112	250	9	3	0	3	35		1924-25	1929-30
Herchenratter, Art	Det.	1	10	1	2	3	2	....	....	....	....	....		1940-41	1940-41
Hergerts, Fred	NYA	2	19	2	4	6	2	....	....	....	....	....		1934-35	1935-36
Hergesheimer, Philip	Chi., Bos.	4	125	21	41	62	19	7	0	0	0	2		1939-40	1942-43
Hergesheimer, Wally	NYR, Chi.	7	351	114	85	199	106	5	1	0	1	0		1951-52	1958-59
Heron, Red	Tor., Bro., Mtl.	4	106	21	19	40	38	16	2	2	4	55		1938-39	1941-42
Heroux, Yves	Que.	1	1	0	0	0	0	....	....	....	....	....		1986-87	1986-87
Hervey, Matt	Wpg., Bos., T.B.	3	35	0	5	5	97	5	0	0	0	6		1988-89	1992-93
Hess, Bob	St.L., Buf., Hfd.	8	329	27	95	122	178	4	1	1	2	2		1974-75	1983-84
Heximer, Orville	NYR, Bos., NYA	3	85	13	7	20	28	5	0	0	0	2		1929-30	1934-35
Hextall, Bryan Jr.	NYR, Pit., Atl., Det., Min.	8	549	99	161	260	738	18	0	4	4	59		1962-63	1975-76
• Hextall, Bryan Sr.	NYR	11	447	187	175	362	227	37	8	9	17	19	1	1936-37	1947-48
Hextall, Dennis	NYR, L.A., Cal., Min., Det., Wsh.	13	681	153	350	503	1398	22	3	3	6	45		1968-69	1979-80
Heyliger, Vic	Chi.	2	34	2	3	5	2	....	....	....	....	....		1937-38	1943-44
Hicke, Bill	Mtl., NYR, Oak.	14	729	168	234	402	395	42	3	10	13	41	2	1958-59	1971-72
Hicke, Ernie	Cal., Atl., NYI, Min., L.A.	8	520	132	140	272	407	2	1	0	1	0		1970-71	1977-78
Hickey, Greg	NYR	1	1	0	0	0	0	....	....	....	....	....		1977-78	1977-78
Hickey, Pat	NYR, Col., Tor., Que., St.L.	10	646	192	212	404	351	55	5	11	16	37		1975-76	1984-85
Hicks, Doug	Min., Chi., Edm., Wsh.	9	561	37	131	168	442	....	....	....	....	....		1974-75	1982-83
Hicks, Glenn	Det.	2	108	6	12	18	127	....	....	....	....	....		1979-80	1980-81
• Hicks, Hal	Mtl.M., Det.	3	110	7	2	9	72	....	....	....	....	....		1928-29	1930-31
Hicks, Wayne	Chi., Bos., Mtl., Phi., Pit.	5	115	13	23	36	22	2	0	1	1	2	1	1959-60	1967-68
Hidi, Andre	Wsh.	2	7	2	1	3	9	2	0	0	0	0		1983-84	1984-85
Hiemer, Uli	N.J.	3	143	19	54	73	176	....	....	....	....	....		1984-85	1986-87
Higgins, Paul	Tor.	2	25	0	0	0	152	1	0	0	0	0		1981-82	1982-83
Higgins, Tim	Chi., N.J., Det.	11	706	154	198	352	719	65	5	8	13	77		1978-79	1988-89
Hildebrand, Ike	NYR, Chi.	2	41	7	11	18	16	....	....	....	....	....		1953-54	1954-55
Hill, Al	Phi.	8	221	40	55	95	227	51	8	11	19	43		1976-77	1987-88
Hill, Brian	Hfd.	1	19	1	1	2	4	....	....	....	....	....		1979-80	1979-80
Hill, Mel	Bos., Bro., Tor.	9	323	89	109	198	138	43	12	7	19	18	3	1937-38	1945-46
Hiller, Dutch	NYR, Det., Bos., Mtl.	9	385	91	113	204	163	48	9	8	17	21	2	1937-38	1945-46
Hillier, Randy	Bos., Pit., NYI, Buf.	11	543	16	110	126	906	28	0	2	2	93	1	1981-82	1991-92
Hillman, Floyd	Bos.	1	6	0	0	0	10	....	....	....	....	....		1956-57	1956-57
Hillman, Larry	Det., Bos., Tor., Min., Mtl., Phi., L.A., Buf.	19	790	36	196	232	579	74	2	9	11	30	6	1954-55	1972-73
• Hillman, Wayne	Chi., NYR, Min., Phi.	13	691	18	86	104	534	28	0	3	3	19	1	1960-61	1972-73
Hilworth, John	Det.	3	57	1	1	2	89	....	....	....	....	....		1977-78	1979-80
Himes, Normie	NYA	9	402	106	113	219	127	2	0	0	0	0		1926-27	1934-35
Hindmarch, Dave	Cgy.	4	99	21	17	38	25	10	0	0	0	6		1980-81	1983-84
Hinse, Andre	Tor.	1	4	0	0	0	0	....	....	....	....	....		1967-68	1967-68
Hinton, Dan	Chi.	1	14	0	0	0	16	....	....	....	....	....		1976-77	1976-77
Hirsch, Tom	Min.	3	31	1	7	8	30	12	0	0	0	6		1983-84	1987-88
Hirschfeld, Bert	Mtl.	2	33	1	4	5	2	5	1	0	1	0		1949-50	1950-51
Hislop, Jamie	Que., Cgy.	5	345	75	103	178	86	28	3	2	5	11		1979-80	1983-84
• Hitchman, Lionel	Ott., Bos.	12	413	28	33	61	523	40	4	1	5	77	2	1922-23	1933-34
Hlinka, Ivan	Van.	2	137	42	81	123	28	16	3	10	13	8		1981-82	1982-83
Hodge, Ken	Min., Bos., T.B.	4	142	39	48	87	32	15	4	6	10	6		1988-89	1992-93
Hodge, Ken	Chi., Bos., NYR	13	881	328	472	800	779	97	34	47	81	120	2	1965-66	1977-78
Hodgson, Dan	Tor., Van.	4	114	29	45	74	64	....	....	....	....	....		1985-86	1988-89
Hodgson, Rick	Hfd.	1	6	0	0	0	6	1	0	0	0	0		1979-80	1979-80
Hodgson, Ted	Bos.	1	4	0	0	0	0	....	....	....	....	....		1966-67	1966-67
Hoekstra, Cecil	Mtl.	1	4	0	0	0	0	....	....	....	....	....		1959-60	1959-60
Hoekstra, Ed	Phi.	1	70	15	21	36	6	7	0	1	1	0		1967-68	1967-68
Hoene, Phil	L.A.	3	37	2	4	6	22	....	....	....	....	....		1972-73	1974-75
Hoffinger, Vic	Chi.	2	28	0	1	1	30	....	....	....	....	....		1927-28	1928-29
Hoffman, Mike	Hfd.	3	9	1	3	4	2	....	....	....	....	....		1982-83	1985-86
Hoffmeyer, Bob	Chi., Phi., N.J.	6	198	14	52	66	325	3	0	1	1	25		1977-78	1984-85
Hofford, Jim	Buf., L.A.	3	18	0	0	0	47	....	....	....	....	....		1985-86	1988-89
Hogaboam, Bill	Atl., Det., Min.	8	332	80	109	189	100	2	0	0	0	0		1972-73	1979-80
Hoganson, Dale	L.A., Mtl., Que.	7	343	13	77	90	186	11	0	3	3	12		1969-70	1981-82
Holbrook, Terry	Min.	2	43	3	6	9	4	6	0	0	0	0		1972-73	1973-74
Holland, Jerry	NYR	2	37	8	4	12	6	....	....	....	....	....		1974-75	1975-76
Hollett, Frank	Tor., Ott., Bos., Det.	13	565	132	181	313	358	79	8	26	34	38	2	1933-34	1945-46
• Hollingworth, Gord	Chi., Det.	4	163	4	14	18	201	3	0	0	0	2		1954-55	1957-58
Holloway, Bruce	Van.	1	2	0	0	0	0	....	....	....	....	....		1984-85	1984-85
• Holmes, Bill	Mtl., NYA.	2	51	6	4	10	35	....	....	....	....	....		1925-26	1929-30
Holmes, Chuck	Det.	2	23	1	3	4	10	....	....	....	....	....		1958-59	1961-62
Holmes, Lou	Chi.	2	59	1	4	5	6	2	0	0	0	2		1931-32	1932-33
Holmes, Warren	L.A.	3	45	8	18	26	7	....	....	....	....	....		1981-82	1983-84
Holmgren, Paul	Phi., Min.	10	527	144	179	323	1684	82	19	32	51	195		1975-76	1984-85
• Holota, John	Det.	2	15	2	0	2	0	....	....	....	....	....		1942-43	1945-46
Holst, Greg	NYR	3	11	0	0	0	0	....	....	....	....	....		1975-76	1977-78
Holt, Gary	Cal., Clev., St.L.	5	101	13	11	24	183	....	....	....	....	....		1973-74	1977-78
Holt, Randy	Chi., Clev., Van., L.A., Cgy., Wsh., Phi.	10	395	4	37	41	1438	21	2	3	5	83		1974-75	1983-84
• Holway, Albert	Tor., Mtl.M., Pit.	5	117	7	2	9	48	8	0	0	0	2	1	1923-24	1928-29
Homenuke, Ron	Van.	1	1	0	0	0	0	....	....	....	....	....		1972-73	1972-73
Hoover, Ron	Bos., St.L.	3	18	4	0	4	31	8	0	0	0	18		1989-90	1991-92
Hopkins, Dean	L.A., Edm., Que.	6	223	23	51	74	306	18	1	5	6	29		1979-80	1988-89
Hopkins, Larry	Tor., Wpg.	4	60	13	16	29	26	6	0	0	0	2		1977-78	1982-83
Horava, Miloslav	NYR	3	80	5	17	22	38	2	0	1	1	0		1988-89	1990-91
Horbul, Doug	K.C.	1	4	1	0	1	2	....	....	....	....	....		1974-75	1974-75
Hordy, Mike	NYI	2	11	0	0	0	7	....	....	....	....	....		1978-79	1979-80
Horeck, Pete	Chi., Det., Bos.	8	426	106	118	224	340	34	6	8	14	43		1944-45	1951-52
• Horne, George	Mtl.M, Tor.	3	54	9	3	12	34	4	0	0	0	4	1	1925-26	1928-29
Horner, Red	Tor.	12	490	42	110	152	1264	71	7	10	17	166	1	1928-29	1939-40
Hornung, Larry	St.L.	2	48	2	9	11	10	11	0	2	2	2		1970-71	1971-72
• Horton, Tim	Tor., NYR, Buf., Pit.	24	1446	115	403	518	1611	126	11	39	50	183	4	1949-50	1973-74
Horvath, Bronco	NYR, Mtl., Bos., Chi., Tor., Min.	9	434	141	185	326	319	36	12	9	21	18		1955-56	1967-68
Hospodar, Ed	NYR, Hfd., Phi., Min., Buf.	9	450	17	51	68	1314	44	4	1	5	206		1979-80	1987-88
Hostak, Martin	Phi.	2	55	3	11	14	24	....	....	....	....	....		1990-91	1991-92
Hotham, Greg	Tor., Pit.	6	230	15	74	89	139	5	0	3	3	6		1979-80	1984-85
Houck, Paul	Min.	3	16	1	2	3	2	....	....	....	....	....		1985-86	1987-88
Houde, Claude	K.C.	2	59	3	6	9	40	....	....	....	....	....		1974-75	1975-76
Houle, Rejean	Mtl.	11	635	161	247	408	395	90	14	34	48	66	5	1969-70	1982-83
Houston, Ken	Atl., Cgy., Wsh., L.A.	9	570	161	167	328	624	35	10	9	19	66		1975-76	1983-84
Howard, Frank	Tor.	1	2	0	0	0	0	....	....	....	....	....		1936-37	1936-37
Howatt, Garry	NYI, Hfd., N.J.	12	720	112	156	268	1836	87	12	14	26	289	2	1972-73	1983-84
Howe, Gordie	Det., Hfd.	26	1767	801	1049	1850	1685	157	68	92	160	220	4	1946-47	1979-80
Howe, Marty	Hfd., Bos.	6	197	2	29	31	99	15	1	2	3	9		1979-80	1984-85

Name	NHL Teams	NHL Seasons	Regular Schedule GP	G	A	TP	PIM	Playoffs GP	G	A	TP	PIM	NHL Cup Wins	First NHL Season	Last NHL Season
• Howe, Syd	Ott., Phi., Tor., St.L., Det.	17	691	237	291	528	212	70	17	27	44	10	3	1929-30	1945-46
Howe, Vic	NYR	3	33	3	4	7	10	....	....	....	....	....		1950-51	1954-55
Howell, Harry	NYR, Oak., L.A.	21	1411	94	324	418	1298	38	3	3	6	32		1952-53	1972-73
Howell, Ron	NYR	2	4	0	0	0	4	....	....	....	....	....		1954-55	1955-56
Howse, Don	L.A.	1	33	2	5	7	6	2	0	0	0	0		1979-80	1979-80
Howson, Scott	NYI	2	18	5	3	8	4	....	....	....	....	....		1984-85	1985-86
Hoyda, Dave	Phi., Wpg.	4	132	6	17	23	299	12	0	0	0	17		1977-78	1980-81
Hrdina, Jiri	Cgy., Pit.	5	250	45	85	130	92	46	2	5	7	24	3	1987-88	1991-92
Hrechkosy, Dave	Cal., St.L.	4	140	42	24	66	41	3	1	0	1	2		1973-74	1976-77
Hrycuik, Jim	Wsh.	1	21	5	5	10	12	....	....	....	....	....		1974-75	1974-75
Hrymnak, Steve	Chi., Det.	2	18	2	1	3	4	2	0	0	0	0		1951-52	1952-53
Hrynewich, Tim	Pit.	2	55	6	8	14	82	....	....	....	....	....		1982-83	1983-84
Huard, Rolly	Tor.	1	1	1	0	1	0	....	....	....	....	....		1930-31	1930-31
Huber, Willie	Det., NYR, Van., Phi.	10	655	104	217	321	950	33	5	5	10	35		1978-79	1987-88
Hubick, Greg	Tor., Van.	2	77	6	9	15	10	....	....	....	....	....		1975-76	1979-80
Huck, Fran	Mtl., St.L.	3	94	24	30	54	38	11	3	4	7	2		1969-70	1972-73
Hucul, Fred	Chi., St.L.	5	164	11	30	41	113	6	1	0	1	10		1950-51	1967-68
Hudson, Dave	NYI, K.C., Col.	6	409	59	124	183	89	2	1	1	2	0		1972-73	1977-78
Hudson, Lex	Pit.	1	2	0	0	0	0	2	0	0	0	0		1978-79	1978-79
Hudson, Ron	Det.	2	34	5	2	7	2	....	....	....	....	....		1937-38	1939-40
Huggins, Al	Mtl.M	1	20	1	1	2	2	....	....	....	....	....		1930-31	1930-31
Hughes, Al	NYA	2	60	6	8	14	22	....	....	....	....	....		1930-31	1931-32
Hughes, Brent	L.A., Phi., St.L., Det., K.C.	8	435	15	117	132	440	22	1	3	4	53		1967-68	1974-75
Hughes, Frank	Cal.	1	5	0	0	0	0	....	....	....	....	....		1971-72	1971-72
Hughes, Howie	L.A.	3	168	25	32	57	30	14	2	0	2	2		1967-68	1969-70
Hughes, Jack	Col.	2	46	2	5	7	104	....	....	....	....	....		1980-81	1981-82
Hughes, John	Van., Edm., NYR	3	70	2	14	16	211	7	0	1	1	16		1979-80	1980-81
Hughes, Pat	Mtl., Pit., Edm., Buf., St.L., Hfd.	10	573	130	128	258	646	71	8	25	33	77	3	1977-78	1986-87
Hughes, Rusty	Det.	1	40	0	1	1	48	....	....	....	....	....		1929-30	1929-30
Hull, Bobby	Chi., Wpg., Hfd.	16	1063	610	560	1170	640	119	62	67	129	102	1	1957-58	1979-80
Hull, Dennis	Chi., Det.	14	959	303	351	654	261	104	33	34	67	30		1964-65	1977-78
• Hunt, Fred	NYA, NYR	2	59	15	14	29	6	....	....	....	....	....		1940-41	1944-45
Hunter, Dave	Edm., Pit., Wpg.	10	746	133	190	323	918	105	16	24	40	211	3	1979-80	1988-89
Hunter, Mark	Mtl., St.L., Cgy., Hfd., Wsh.	12	628	213	171	384	1426	79	18	20	38	230	1	1981-82	1992-93
Huras, Larry	NYR	1	2	0	0	0	0	....	....	....	....	....		1976-77	1976-77
Hurlburt, Bob	Van.	1	1	0	0	0	2	....	....	....	....	....		1974-75	1974-75
Hurley, Paul	Bos.	1	1	0	1	1	0	....	....	....	....	....		1968-69	1968-69
Hurst, Ron	Tor.	2	64	9	7	16	7	3	0	2	2	4		1955-56	1956-57
Huston, Ron	Cal.	2	79	15	31	46	8	....	....	....	....	....		1973-74	1974-75
Hutchinson, Ronald	NYR	1	9	0	0	0	0	....	....	....	....	....		1960-61	1960-61
Hutchison, Dave	L.A., Tor., Chi., N.J.	10	584	19	97	116	1550	48	2	12	14	149		1974-75	1983-84
• Hutton, William	Bos., Ott., Phi.	2	64	3	2	5	8	2	0	0	0	0		1929-30	1930-31
• Hyland, Harry	Mtl.W, Ott.	1	16	14	0	14	0	....	....	....	....	....		1917-18	1917-18
Hynes, Dave	Bos.	2	22	4	0	4	2	....	....	....	....	....		1973-74	1974-75
Hynes, Gord	Bos., Phi.	2	52	3	9	12	22	12	1	2	3	6		1991-92	1992-93

I

Name	NHL Teams	NHL Seasons	Regular Schedule GP	G	A	TP	PIM	Playoffs GP	G	A	TP	PIM	NHL Cup Wins	First NHL Season	Last NHL Season
Ihnacak, Miroslav	Tor., Det.	3	56	8	9	17	39	1	0	0	0	0		1985-86	1988-89
Ihnacak, Peter	Tor.	8	417	102	165	267	175	28	4	10	14	25		1982-83	1989-90
Imlach, Brent	Tor.	2	3	0	0	0	2	....	....	....	....	....		1965-66	1966-67
Ingarfield, Earl	NYR, Pit., Oak., Cal.	13	746	179	226	405	239	21	9	8	17	10		1958-59	1970-71
Ingarfield, Earl Jr.	Atl., Cgy., Det.	2	39	4	4	8	22	2	0	1	1	0		1979-80	1980-81
Inglis, Bill	L.A., Buf.	3	36	1	3	4	4	11	1	2	3	4		1967-68	1970-71
• Ingoldsby, Johnny	Tor.	2	29	5	1	6	15	....	....	....	....	....		1942-43	1943-44
Ingram, Frank	Bos., Chi.	4	102	24	16	40	69	11	0	1	1	2		1924-25	1931-32
Ingram, Ron	Chi., Det., NYR	4	114	5	15	20	81	2	0	0	0	0		1956-57	1964-65
• Irvin, Dick	Chi.	3	94	29	23	52	76	2	2	0	2	4		1926-27	1928-29
Irvine, Ted	Bos., L.A., NYR, St.L.	11	724	154	177	331	657	83	16	24	40	115		1963-64	1976-77
Irwin, Ivan	Mtl., NYR	5	155	2	27	29	214	5	0	0	0	8		1952-53	1957-58
Isaksson, Ulf	L.A.	1	50	7	15	22	10	....	....	....	....	....		1982-83	1982-83
Issel, Kim	Edm.	1	4	0	0	0	0	....	....	....	....	....		1988-89	1988-89

J

Name	NHL Teams	NHL Seasons	Regular Schedule GP	G	A	TP	PIM	Playoffs GP	G	A	TP	PIM	NHL Cup Wins	First NHL Season	Last NHL Season
• Jackson, Art	Bos., Tor.	11	466	123	178	301	144	51	8	12	20	27	2	1934-35	1944-45
Jackson, Don	Min., Edm., NYR	10	311	16	52	68	640	53	4	5	9	147	2	1977-78	1986-87
Jackson, Hal	Chi., Det.	8	222	17	34	51	208	31	1	2	3	33	2	1936-37	1946-47
• Jackson, Harvey	Tor., Bos., NYA	15	636	241	234	475	437	71	18	12	30	53	1	1929-30	1943-44
Jackson, Jeff	Tor., NYR, Que., Chi.	8	263	38	48	86	313	6	1	1	2	16		1984-85	1991-92
Jackson, Jim	Cgy., Buf.	4	112	17	30	47	20	14	3	2	5	6		1982-83	1987-88
Jackson, John	Chi.	1	48	2	5	7	38	....	....	....	....	....		1946-47	1946-47
Jackson, Lloyd	NYA	1	14	1	1	2	0	....	....	....	....	....		1936-37	1936-37
Jackson, Stan	Tor., Bos., Ott.	5	84	9	4	13	74	....	....	....	....	....	1	1921-22	1926-27
Jackson, Walt	NYA	3	82	16	11	27	18	....	....	....	....	....		1932-33	1934-35
• Jacobs, Paul	Tor.	1	1	0	0	0	0	....	....	....	....	....		1918-19	1918-19
Jacobs, Tim	Cal.	1	46	0	10	10	35	....	....	....	....	....		1975-76	1975-76
Jalo, Risto	Edm.	1	3	0	3	3	0	....	....	....	....	....		1985-86	1985-86
Jalonen, Kari	Cgy., Edm.	2	37	9	6	15	4	5	1	0	1	0		1982-83	1983-84
James, Gerry	Tor.	5	149	14	26	40	257	15	1	0	1	8		1954-55	1959-60
James, Val	Buf., Tor.	2	11	0	0	0	30	....	....	....	....	....		1981-82	1986-87
Jamieson, Jim	NYR	1	1	0	1	1	0	....	....	....	....	....		1943-44	1943-44
Jankowski, Lou	Det., Chi.	4	127	19	18	37	15	1	0	0	0	0		1950-51	1954-55
Jarrett, Doug	Chi., NYR	13	775	38	182	220	631	99	7	16	23	82		1964-65	1976-77
Jarrett, Gary	Tor., Det., Oak., Cal.	7	341	72	92	164	131	11	3	1	4	9		1960-61	1971-72
Jarry, Pierre	NYR, Tor., Det., Min.	7	344	88	117	205	142	5	0	1	1	0		1971-72	1977-78
Jarvenpaa, Hannu	Wpg.	3	114	11	26	37	83	....	....	....	....	....		1986-87	1988-89
Jarvi, Iiro	Que.	2	116	18	43	61	58	....	....	....	....	....		1988-89	1989-90
Jarvis, Doug	Mtl., Wsh., Hfd.	13	964	139	264	403	263	105	14	27	41	42	4	1975-76	1987-88
Jarvis, Jim	Pit., Phi., Tor.	3	108	17	15	32	62	....	....	....	....	....		1929-30	1936-37
Jarvis, Wes	Wsh., Min., L.A., Tor.	8	237	31	55	86	98	2	0	0	0	2		1979-80	1987-88
Javanainen, Arto	Pit.	1	14	4	1	5	2	....	....	....	....	....		1984-85	1984-85
Jeffrey, Larry	Det., Tor., NYR	8	368	39	62	101	293	38	4	10	14	42	1	1961-62	1968-69
Jelinek, Tomas	Ott.	1	49	7	6	13	52	....	....	....	....	....		1992-93	1992-93
Jenkins, Dean	L.A.	1	5	0	0	0	2	....	....	....	....	....		1983-84	1983-84
Jenkins, Roger	Tor., Chi., Mtl., Bos., Mtl.M., NYA	8	328	15	39	54	279	25	1	7	8	12	2	1930-31	1938-39
Jennings, Bill	Det., Bos.	5	108	32	33	65	45	20	4	4	8	6		1940-41	1944-45
Jensen, Chris	NYR, Phi.	6	74	9	12	21	27	....	....	....	....	....		1985-86	1991-92
Jensen, David A.	Hfd., Wsh.	4	69	9	13	22	22	11	0	0	0	2		1983-84	1987-88
Jensen, David H.	Min.	3	18	0	2	2	11	....	....	....	....	....		1983-84	1985-86
Jensen, Steve	Min., L.A.	7	438	113	107	220	318	12	0	3	3	9		1975-76	1981-82
• Jeremiah, Ed	NYA, Bos.	1	15	0	1	1	0	....	....	....	....	....		1931-32	1931-32
Jerrard, Paul	Min.	1	5	0	0	0	4	....	....	....	....	....		1988-89	1988-89
Jerwa, Frank	Bos.	1	28	4	5	9	12	....	....	....	....	....		1931-32	1931-32
Jerwa, Joe	NYR, Bos., St.L., NYA	9	293	36	69	105	338	17	2	3	5	20		1930-31	1938-39
Jirik, Jaroslav	St.L.	1	3	0	0	0	0	....	....	....	....	....		1969-70	1969-70
Joanette, Rosario	Mtl.	1	2	0	1	1	4	....	....	....	....	....		1944-45	1944-45
Jodzio, Rick	Col., Clev.	1	70	2	8	10	71	....	....	....	....	....		1977-78	1977-78
Johannesen, Glenn	NYI	1	2	0	0	0	0	....	....	....	....	....		1985-86	1985-86
Johannson, John	N.J.	1	5	0	0	0	0	....	....	....	....	....		1983-84	1983-84
Johansen, Trevor	Tor., Col., L.A.	5	286	11	46	57	282	13	0	3	3	21		1977-78	1981-82
Johansson, Bjorn	Clev.	2	15	1	1	2	10	....	....	....	....	....		1976-77	1977-78
Johns, Don	NYR, Mtl., Min.	6	153	2	21	23	76	....	....	....	....	....		1960-61	1967-68
Johnson, Al	Mtl., Det.	4	105	21	28	49	30	11	2	2	4	6		1956-57	1962-63
Johnson, Brian	Det.	1	3	0	0	0	5	....	....	....	....	....		1983-84	1983-84
• Johnson, Danny	Tor., Van., Det.	3	121	18	19	37	24	....	....	....	....	....		1969-70	1971-72
Johnson, Earl	Det.	1	1	0	0	0	0	....	....	....	....	....		1953-54	1953-54
• Johnson, Ivan	NYR, NYA	12	435	38	48	86	808	60	5	2	7	161	2	1926-27	1937-38
Johnson, Jim	NYR, Phi., L.A.	8	302	75	111	186	73	7	0	2	2	2		1964-65	1971-72
Johnson, Mark	Pit., Min., Hfd., St.L., N.J.	11	669	203	305	508	260	37	16	12	28	10		1979-80	1989-90
Johnson, Norm	Bos., Chi.	3	61	5	20	25	41	14	4	0	4	6		1957-58	1959-60
Johnson, Terry	Que., St.L., Cgy., Tor.	9	285	3	24	27	580	38	0	4	4	118		1979-80	1987-88
Johnson, Tom	Mtl., Bos.	17	978	51	213	264	960	111	8	15	23	109	6	1947-48	1964-65

Ron Hoover

Gord Hynes

Kim Issel

Larry Jeffrey

Mark Johnson

Bob Joyce

Steve Kasper

Jarmo Kekalainen

			Regular Schedule					Playoffs					NHL	First	Last
		NHL											Cup	NHL	NHL
Name	NHL Teams	Seasons	GP	G	A	TP	PIM	GP	G	A	TP	PIM	Wins	Season	Season
Johnson, Virgil	Chi.	3	75	2	9	11	27	19	0	3	3	4	1	1937-38	1944-45
Johnson, William	Tor.	1	1	0	0	0	0	....	....	....	....	....		1949-50	1949-50
Johnston, Bernie	Hfd.	2	57	12	24	36	44	3	0	1	1	0		1979-80	1980-81
Johnston, George	Chi.	4	58	20	12	32	2	....	....	....	....	....		1941-42	1946-47
Johnston, Greg	Bos., Tor.	9	187	26	30	56	124	22	2	1	3	12		1983-84	1991-92
Johnston, Jay	Wsh.	2	8	0	0	0	13	....	....	....	....	....		1980-81	1981-82
Johnston, Joey	Min., Cal., Chi.	6	332	85	106	191	320	....	....	....	....	....		1968-69	1975-76
Johnston, Larry	L.A., Det., K.C., Col.	7	320	9	64	73	580	....	....	....	....	....		1967-68	1976-77
Johnston, Marshall	Min., Cal.	7	251	14	52	66	58	6	0	0	0	2		1967-68	1973-74
Johnston, Randy	NYI	1	4	0	0	0	4	....	....	....	....	....		1979-80	1979-80
Johnstone, Eddie	NYR, Det.	10	426	122	136	258	375	55	13	10	23	83		1975-76	1986-87
Johnstone, Ross	Tor.	2	42	5	4	9	14	3	0	0	0	0	1	1943-44	1944-45
• Joliat, Aurel	Mtl.	16	654	270	190	460	757	54	14	19	33	89	3	1922-23	1937-38
Joliat, Bobby	Mtl.	1	1	0	0	0	0	....	....	....	....	....		1924-25	1924-25
Joly, Greg	Wsh., Det.	9	365	21	76	97	250	5	0	0	0	8		1974-75	1982-83
Joly, Yvan	Mtl.	3	2	0	0	0	0	10	0	0	0	0		1979-80	1982-83
Jonathon, Stan	Bos., Pit.	8	411	91	110	201	751	63	8	4	12	137		1975-76	1982-83
Jones, Bob	NYR	1	2	0	0	0	0	....	....	....	....	....		1968-69	1968-69
Jones, Buck	Det., Tor.	4	50	2	2	4	36	12	0	1	1	18		1938-39	1942-43
Jones, Jim	Cal.	1	2	0	0	0	0	....	....	....	....	....		1971-72	1971-72
Jones, Jimmy	Tor.	3	148	13	18	31	68	19	1	5	6	11		1977-78	1979-80
Jones, Ron	Bos., Pit., Wsh.	5	54	1	4	5	31	....	....	....	....	....		1971-72	1975-76
Jonsson, Tomas	NYI, Edm.	8	552	85	259	344	482	80	11	26	37	97	2	1981-82	1988-89
Joseph, Anthony	Wpg.	1	2	1	0	1	0	....	....	....	....	....		1988-89	1988-89
Joyal, Eddie	Det., Tor., L.A., Phi.	9	466	128	134	262	103	50	11	8	19	18		1962-63	1971-72
Joyce, Bob	Bos., Wsh., Wpg.	6	158	34	49	83	90	46	15	9	24	29		1987-88	1992-93
Juckes, Bing	NYR	2	16	2	1	3	6	....	....	....	....	....		1947-48	1949-50
Julien, Claude	Que.	2	14	0	1	1	25	....	....	....	....	....		1984-85	1985-86
Jutila, Timo	Buf.	1	10	1	5	6	13	....	....	....	....	....		1984-85	1984-85
Juzda, Bill	NYR, Tor.	9	393	14	54	68	398	42	0	3	3	46	2	1940-41	1951-52

K

Name	NHL Teams	NHL Seasons	GP	G	A	TP	PIM	GP	G	A	TP	PIM	NHL Cup Wins	First NHL Season	Last NHL Season
Kabel, Bob	NYR	2	48	5	13	18	34	....	....	....	....	....		1959-60	1960-61
Kachowski, Mark	Pit.	3	64	6	5	11	209	....	....	....	....	....		1987-88	1989-90
Kachur, Ed	Chi.	2	96	10	14	24	35	....	....	....	....	....		1956-57	1957-58
Kaese, Trent	Buf.	1	1	0	0	0	0	....	....	....	....	....		1988-89	1988-89
Kaiser, Vern	Mtl.	1	50	7	5	12	33	2	0	0	0	0		1950-51	1950-51
Kalbfleish, Walter	Ott., St.L., NYA, Bos.	4	36	0	4	4	32	5	0	0	0	2		1933-34	1936-37
• Kaleta, Alex	Chi., NYR	7	387	92	121	213	190	17	1	6	7	2		1941-42	1950-51
Kallur, Anders	NYI	6	383	101	110	211	149	78	12	23	35	32	4	1979-80	1984-85
• Kaminsky, Max	Ott., St.L., Bos., Mtl.M.	4	130	22	34	56	38	4	0	0	0	0		1933-34	1936-37
• Kampman, Bingo	Tor.	5	189	14	30	44	287	47	1	4	5	38	1	1937-38	1941-42
Kane, Frank	Det.	1	2	0	0	0	0	....	....	....	....	....		1943-44	1943-44
Kannegiesser, Gord	St.L.	2	23	0	1	1	15	....	....	....	....	....		1967-68	1971-72
Kannegiesser, Sheldon	Pit., NYR, L.A., Van.	8	366	14	67	81	292	18	0	2	2	10		1970-71	1977-78
Karjalainen, Kyosti	L.A.	1	28	1	8	9	12	3	0	1	1	2		1991-92	1991-92
Karlander, Al	Det.	4	212	36	56	92	70	4	0	1	1	0		1969-70	1972-73
Kasper, Steve	Bos., L.A., Phi., T.B.	13	821	177	291	468	554	94	20	28	48	82		1980-81	1992-93
Kastelic, Ed	Wsh., Hfd.	7	220	11	10	21	719	8	1	0	1	32		1985-86	1991-92
Kaszycki, Mike	NYI, Wsh., Tor.	5	226	42	80	122	108	19	2	6	8	10		1977-78	1982-83
Kea, Ed	Atl., St.L.	10	583	30	145	175	508	32	2	4	6	39		1973-74	1982-83
Kearns, Dennis	Van.	10	677	31	290	321	386	11	1	2	3	8		1971-72	1980-81
• Keating, Jack	NYA	2	35	5	5	10	17	....	....	....	....	....		1931-32	1932-33
Keating, John	Det.	2	11	2	1	3.	4	....	....	....	....	....		1938-39	1939-40
Keating, Mike	NYR	1	1	0	0	0	0	....	....	....	....	....		1977-78	1977-78
• Keats, Duke	Det., Chi.	3	80	3	19	49	113	....	....	....	....	....		1926-27	1928-29
• Keeling, Butch	Tor., NYR	12	528	157	63	220	331	47	11	11	22	32	1	1926-27	1937-38
Keenan, Larry	Tor., St.L., Buf., Phi.	6	233	38	64	102	28	46	15	16	31	12		1961-62	1971-72
Kehoe, Rick	Tor., Pit.	14	906	371	396	767	120	39	4	17	21	4		1971-72	1984-85
Kekalainen, Jarmo	Bos., Ott.	3	55	5	8	13	28	....	....	....	....	....		1989-90	1993-94
Keller, Ralph	NYR	1	3	1	0	1	6	....	....	....	....	....		1962-63	1962-63
Kellgren, Christer	Col.	1	5	0	0	0	0	....	....	....	....	....		1981-82	1981-82
Kelly, Bob	St.L., Pit., Chi.	6	425	87	109	196	687	23	6	3	9	40		1973-74	1978-79
Kelly, Bob	Phi., Wsh.	12	837	154	208	362	1454	101	9	14	23	172	2	1970-71	1981-82
Kelly, Dave	Det.	1	16	2	0	2	4	....	....	....	....	....		1976-77	1976-77
Kelly, John Paul	L.A.	7	400	54	70	124	366	18	1	1	2	41		1979-80	1985-86
Kelly, Pete	St.L., Det., NYA, Bro.	7	180	21	38	59	68	19	3	1	4	8	2	1934-35	1941-42
Kelly, Red	Det., Tor.	20	1316	281	542	823	327	164	33	59	92	51	8	1947-48	1966-67
• Kelly, Reg	Tor., Chi., Bro.	8	289	74	53	127	105	39	7	6	13	10		1934-35	1941-42
Kemp, Kevin	Hfd.	1	3	0	0	0	4	....	....	....	....	....		1980-81	1980-81
Kemp, Stan	Tor.	1	1	0	0	0	2	....	....	....	....	....		1948-49	1948-49
Kendall, William	Chi., Tor.	5	132	16	10	26	28	5	0	0	0	0	1	1933-34	1937-38
Kennedy, Forbes	Chi., Det., Bos., Phi., Tor.	11	603	70	108	178	988	12	2	4	6	64		1956-57	1968-69
Kennedy, Ted	Tor.	14	696	231	329	560	432	78	29	31	60	32	5	1942-43	1956-57
• Kenny, Eddie	NYR, Chi.	2	11	0	0	0	18	....	....	....	....	....		1930-31	1934-35
Keon, Dave	Tor., Hfd.	18	1296	396	590	986	117	92	32	36	68	6	4	1960-61	1981-82
Kerr, Alan	NYI, Det., Wpg.	9	391	72	94	166	826	38	5	4	9	70		1984-85	1992-93
Kerr, Reg	Cle., Chi., Edm.	6	263	66	94	160	169	7	1	0	1	7		1977-78	1983-84
Kerr, Tim	Phi., NYR, Hfd.	13	655	370	304	674	596	81	40	31	71	58		1980-81	1992-93
Kessell, Rick	Pit., Cal.	5	135	4	24	28	6	....	....	....	....	....		1969-70	1973-74
Ketola, Veli-Pekka	Col.	1	44	9	5	14	4	....	....	....	....	....		1981-82	1981-82
Ketter, Kerry	Atl.	1	41	0	2	2	58	....	....	....	....	....		1972-73	1972-73
Kharin, Sergei	Wpg.	1	7	2	3	5	2	....	....	....	....	....		1990-91	1990-91
Kidd, Ian	Van.	2	20	4	7	11	25	....	....	....	....	....		1987-88	1988-89
Kiessling, Udo	Min.	1	1	0	0	0	2	....	....	....	....	....		1981-82	1981-82
Kilrea, Brian	Det., L.A.	2	26	3	5	8	12	....	....	....	....	....		1957-58	1967-68
• Kilrea, Hec	Ott., Det., Tor.	15	633	167	129	296	438	48	8	7	15	18	3	1925-26	1939-40
• Kilrea, Ken	Det.	5	88	16	23	39	8	10	2	2	4	4		1938-39	1943-44
Kilrea, Wally	Ott., Phi., NYA, Mtl.M., Det.	9	315	35	58	93	87	25	2	4	6	6		1929-30	1937-38
Kindrachuk, Orest	Phi., Pit., Wsh.	10	508	118	261	379	648	76	20	20	40	53	2	1972-73	1981-82
King, Frank	Mtl.	1	10	1	0	1	2	....	....	....	....	....		1950-51	1950-51
King, Wayne	Cal.	3	73	5	18	23	34	....	....	....	....	....		1973-74	1975-76
Kinsella, Brian	Wsh.	2	10	0	1	1	0	....	....	....	....	....		1975-76	1976-77
Kinsella, Ray	Ott.	1	14	0	0	0	0	....	....	....	....	....		1930-31	1930-31
Kirk, Bobby	NYR	1	39	4	8	12	14	....	....	....	....	....		1937-38	1937-38
Kirkpatrick, Bob	NYR	1	49	12	12	24	6	....	....	....	....	....		1942-43	1942-43
Kirton, Mark	Tor., Det., Van.	6	266	57	56	113	121	4	1	2	3	7		1979-80	1984-85
Kitchen, Bill	Mtl., Tor.	4	41	1	4	5	40	3	0	1	1	0		1981-82	1984-85
• Kitchen, Hobie	Mtl.M., Det.	2	47	5	4	9	58	....	....	....	....	....		1925-26	1926-27
Kitchen, Mike	Col., N.J.	8	474	12	62	74	370	2	0	0	0	2		1976-77	1983-84
Kjellberg, Patrik	Mtl.	1	7	0	0	0	2	....	....	....	....	....		1992-93	1992-93
Klassen, Ralph	Cal., Clev., Col., St.L.	9	497	52	93	145	120	26	4	2	6	12		1975-76	1983-84
Klein, Jim	Bos., NYA	8	169	30	24	54	68	5	0	0	0	2	1	1928-29	1937-38
Kleinendorst, Scot	NYR, Hfd., Wsh.	8	281	12	46	58	452	26	2	7	9	40		1982-83	1989-90
Klingbeil, Ike	Chi.	1	5	1	2	3	2	....	....	....	....	....		1936-37	1936-37
Klukay, Joe	Tor., Bos.	11	566	109	127	236	189	71	13	10	23	23	4	1942-43	1955-56
Kluzak, Gord	Bos.	7	299	25	98	123	543	46	6	13	19	129		1982-83	1990-91
Knibbs, Bill	Bos.	1	53	7	10	17	4	....	....	....	....	....		1964-65	1964-65
• Knott, Nick	Bro.	1	14	3	1	4	9	....	....	....	....	....		1941-42	1941-42
Knox, Paul	Tor.	1	1	0	0	0	0	....	....	....	....	....		1954-55	1954-55
Kolstad, Dean	Min., S.J.	3	40	1	7	8	69	....	....	....	....	....		1988-89	1992-93
Komadoski, Neil	L.A., St.L.	8	502	16	76	92	632	23	0	2	2	47		1972-73	1979-80
Konik, George	Pit.	1	52	7	8	15	26	....	....	....	....	....		1967-68	1967-68
Kopak, Russ	Bos.	1	24	7	9	16	0	....	....	....	....	....		1943-44	1943-44
Korab, Jerry	Chi., Van., Buf., L.A.	15	975	114	341	455	1629	93	8	18	26	201		1970-71	1984-85
• Kordic, John	Mtl., Tor., Wsh., Que.	7	244	17	18	35	997	41	4	3	7	131	1	1985-86	1991-92
Korn, Jim	Det., Tor., Buf., N.J., Cgy.	10	597	66	122	188	1801	16	1	2	3	109		1979-80	1989-90
Korney, Mike	Det., NYR	4	77	9	10	19	59	....	....	....	....	....		1973-74	1978-79
Koroll, Cliff	Chi.	11	814	208	254	462	376	85	19	29	48	67		1969-70	1979-80
Kortko, Roger	NYI	2	79	7	17	24	28	10	0	3	3	17		1984-85	1985-86
Kostynski, Doug	Bos.	2	15	3	1	4	4	....	....	....	....	....		1983-84	1984-85
Kotanen, Dick	Det., NYR	2	2	0	1	1	0	....	....	....	....	....		1948-49	1950-51
Kotsopoulos, Chris	NYR, Hfd.,Tor., Det.	10	479	44	109	153	827	31	1	3	4	91		1980-81	1989-90

Name	NHL Teams	NHL Seasons	Regular Schedule GP	G	A	TP	PIM	Playoffs GP	G	A	TP	PIM	NHL Cup Wins	First NHL Season	Last NHL Season
Kowal, Joe	Buf.	2	22	0	5	5	13	2	0	0	0	0		1976-77	1977-78
Kozak, Don	L.A., Van.	7	437	96	86	182	480	29	7	2	9	69		1972-73	1978-79
Kozak, Les	Tor.	1	12	1	0	1	2	....	....	....	....	....		1961-62	1961-62
Kraftcheck, Stephen	Bos., NYR, Tor.	4	157	11	18	29	83	6	0	0	0	7		1950-51	1958-59
Krake, Skip	Bos., L.A., Buf.	7	249	23	40	63	182	10	1	0	1	17		1963-64	1970-71
Kravets, Mikhail	S.J.	2	2	0	0	0	0	....	....	....	....	....		1991-92	1992-93
Krentz, Dale	Det.	3	30	5	3	8	9	2	0	0	0	0		1986-87	1988-89
Krol, Joe	NYR, Bro.	3	26	10	4	14	8	....	....	....	....	....		1936-37	1941-42
Kromm, Rich	Cgy., NYI	9	372	70	103	173	138	36	2	6	8	22		1983-84	1992-93
Krook, Kevin	Col.	1	3	0	0	0	2	....	....	....	....	....		1978-79	1978-79
Krulicki, Jim	NYR, Det.	1	41	0	3	3	6	....	....	....	....	....		1970-71	1970-71
Krutov, Vladimir	Van.	1	61	11	23	34	20	....	....	....	....	....		1989-90	1989-90
Kryskow, Dave	Chi., Wsh., Det., Atl.	4	231	33	56	89	174	12	2	0	2	4		1972-73	1975-76
Kryznowski, Edward	Bos., Chi.	5	237	15	22	37	65	18	0	1	1	4		1948-49	1952-53
Kuhn, Gord	NYA	1	12	1	1	2	4	....	....	....	....	....		1932-33	1932-33
Kukulowicz, Adolph	NYR	2	4	1	0	1	0	....	....	....	....	....		1952-53	1953-54
Kulak, Stu	Van., Edm., NYR, Que., Wpg.	4	90	8	4	12	130	3	0	0	0	2		1982-83	1988-89
Kullman, Arnie	Bos.	2	13	0	1	1	11	....	....	....	....	....		1947-48	1949-50
Kullman, Eddie	NYR	6	343	56	70	126	298	6	1	0	1	2		1947-48	1953-54
Kumpel, Mark	Que., Det., Wpg.	6	288	38	46	84	113	39	6	4	10	14		1984-85	1990-91
Kuntz, Alan	NYR	2	45	10	12	22	12	6	1	0	1	2		1941-42	1945-46
Kuntz, Murray	St.L.	1	7	1	2	3	0	....	....	....	....	....		1974-75	1974-75
Kurtenbach, Orland	NYR, Bos., Tor., Van.	13	639	119	213	332	628	19	2	4	6	70		1960-61	1973-74
Kuryluk, Mervin	Chi.	1	....	....	....	....	....	2	0	0	0	0		1961-62	1961-62
Kuzyk, Ken	Clev.	2	41	5	9	14	8	....	....	....	....	....		1976-77	1977-78
Kvartalnov, Dmitri	Bos.	2	112	42	49	91	26	4	0	0	0	0		1992-93	1993-94
Kwong, Larry	NYR	1	1	0	0	0	0	....	....	....	....	....		1947-48	1947-48
• Kyle, Bill	NYR	2	3	0	3	3	0	....	....	....	....	....		1949-50	1950-51
Kyle, Gus	NYR, Bos.	3	203	6	20	26	362	14	1	2	3	34		1949-50	1951-52
Kyllonen, Marku	Wpg.	1	9	0	2	2	2	....	....	....	....	....		1988-89	1988-89

L

Name	NHL Teams	NHL Seasons	Regular Schedule GP	G	A	TP	PIM	Playoffs GP	G	A	TP	PIM	NHL Cup Wins	First NHL Season	Last NHL Season
Labadie, Mike	NYR	1	3	0	0	0	0	....	....	....	....	....		1952-53	1952-53
Labatte, Neil	St.L.	2	26	0	2	2	19	....	....	....	....	....		1978-79	1981-82
L'Abbe, Moe	Chi.	1	5	0	1	1	0	....	....	....	....	....		1972-73	1972-73
Labine, Leo	Bos., Det.	11	643	128	193	321	730	60	11	12	23	82		1951-52	1961-62
Labossierre, Gord	NYR, L.A., Min.	6	215	44	62	106	75	10	2	3	5	28		1963-64	1971-72
Labovitch, Max	NYR	1	5	0	0	0	4	....	....	....	....	....		1943-44	1943-44
Labraaten, Dan	Det., Cgy.	4	268	71	73	144	47	5	1	0	1	4		1978-79	1981-82
Labre, Yvon	Pit., Wsh.	9	371	14	87	101	788	....	....	....	....	....		1970-71	1980-81
Labrie, Guy	Bos., NYR	2	42	4	9	13	16	....	....	....	....	....		1943-44	1944-45
Lach, Elmer	Mtl.	14	664	215	408	623	478	76	19	45	64	36	3	1940-41	1953-54
Lachance, Earl	Mtl.	1	1	0	0	0	0	....	....	....	....	....		1926-27	1926-27
Lachance, Michel	Col.	1	21	0	4	4	22	....	....	....	....	....		1978-79	1978-79
Lacombe, Francois	Oak., Buf., Que.	4	78	2	17	19	54	3	1	0	1	0		1968-69	1979-80
Lacombe, Normand	Buf., Edm., Phi	7	319	53	62	115	196	26	5	1	6	49	1	1984-85	1990-91
Lacroix, Andre	Phi., Chi., Hfd.	6	325	79	119	198	44	16	2	5	7	0		1967-68	1979-80
Lacroix, Pierre	Que., Hfd.	4	274	24	108	132	197	8	0	2	2	10		1979-80	1982-83
Lafleur, Guy	Mtl., NYR, Que.	17	1126	560	793	1353	399	128	58	76	134	67	5	1971-72	1990-91
Lafleur, Rene	Mtl.	1	1	0	0	0	0	....	....	....	....	....		1924-25	1924-25
Laforce, Ernie	Mtl.	1	1	0	0	0	0	....	....	....	....	....		1942-43	1942-43
LaForest, Bob	L.A.	1	5	1	0	1	2	....	....	....	....	....		1983-84	1983-84
Laforge, Claude	Mtl., Det., Phi.	8	192	24	33	57	82	5	1	2	3	15		1957-58	1968-69
Laframboise, Pete	Cal., Wsh., Pit.	4	227	33	55	88	70	9	1	0	1	0		1971-72	1974-75
Lafrance, Adie	Mtl.	1	3	0	0	0	2	2	0	0	0	0		1933-34	1933-34
Lafrance, Leo	Mtl., Chi.	2	33	2	0	2	6	....	....	....	....	....		1926-27	1927-28
Lafreniere, Jason	Que., NYR, T.B.	5	146	34	53	87	22	15	1	5	6	19		1986-87	1993-94
Lafreniere, Roger	Det., St.L.	2	13	0	0	0	4	....	....	....	....	....		1962-63	1972-73
Lagace, Jean-Guy	Pit., Buf., K.C.	6	187	9	39	48	251	....	....	....	....	....		1968-69	1975-76
Laidlaw, Tom	NYR, L.A.	10	705	25	139	164	717	69	4	17	21	78		1980-81	1989-90
Laird, Robbie	Min.	1	1	0	0	0	0	....	....	....	....	....		1979-80	1979-80
Lajeunesse, Serge	Det., Phi.	5	103	1	4	5	103	7	1	2	3	4		1970-71	1974-75
Lalande, Hec	Chi., Det.	4	151	21	39	60	120	....	....	....	....	....		1953-54	1957-58
Lalonde, Bobby	Van., Atl., Bos., Cgy.	11	641	124	210	334	298	16	4	2	6	6		1971-72	1981-82
• Lalonde, Edouard	Mtl., NYA	6	99	124	27	151	122	12	22	1	23	0	1	1917-18	1926-27
Lalonde, Ron	Pit., Wsh.	7	397	45	78	123	106	....	....	....	....	....		1972-73	1978-79
• Lamb, Joe	Mtl.M., Ott., NYA, Bos., Mtl., St.L., Det.	11	444	108	101	209	601	18	1	1	2	51		1927-28	1937-38
Lambert, Lane	Det., NYR, Que.	6	283	58	66	124	521	17	2	4	6	40		1983-84	1988-89
Lambert, Yvon	Mtl., Buf.	10	683	206	273	479	340	90	27	22	49	67	4	1972-73	1981-82
Lamby, Dick	St.L.	3	22	0	5	5	22	....	....	....	....	....		1978-79	1980-81
• Lamirande, Jean-Paul	NYR, Mtl.	4	49	5	5	10	26	8	0	0	0	4		1946-47	1954-55
Lammens, Hank	Ott.	1	27	1	2	3	22	....	....	....	....	....		1993-94	1993-94
• Lamoureux, Leo	Mtl.	6	235	19	79	98	175	28	1	6	7	16	2	1941-42	1946-47
Lamoureux, Mitch	Pit., Phi.	3	73	11	9	20	59	....	....	....	....	....		1983-84	1987-88
Lampman, Mike	St.L., Van., Wsh.	4	96	17	20	37	34	....	....	....	....	....		1972-73	1976-77
Lancien, Jack	NYR	4	63	1	5	6	35	6	0	1	1	2		1946-47	1950-51
Landon, Larry	Mtl., Tor.	2	9	0	0	0	2	....	....	....	....	....		1983-84	1984-85
Lane, Gord	Wsh., NYI	10	539	19	94	113	1228	75	3	14	17	214	4	1975-76	1984-85
• Lane, Myles	NYR, Bos.	3	60	4	1	5	41	10	0	0	0	0	1	1928-29	1933-34
Langdon, Steve	Bos.	3	7	0	1	1	2	4	0	0	0	2		1974-75	1977-78
Langelle, Pete	Tor.	4	137	22	51	73	11	41	5	9	14	4	1	1938-39	1941-42
Langevin, Chris	Buf.	2	22	3	1	4	22	....	....	....	....	....		1983-84	1985-86
Langevin, Dave	NYI, Min., L.A.	8	513	12	107	119	530	87	2	15	17	106	4	1979-80	1986-87
Langlais, Alain	Min.	2	25	4	4	8	10	....	....	....	....	....		1973-74	1974-75
Langlois, Al	Mtl., NYR, Det., Bos.	9	448	21	91	112	488	53	1	5	6	60	3	1957-58	1965-66
Langlois, Charlie	Ham., NYA., Pit., Mtl.	4	151	22	3	25	201	2	0	0	0	0		1924-25	1927-28
Langway, Rod	Mtl., Wsh.	15	994	51	278	329	849	104	5	22	27	97	1	1978-79	1992-93
Lanthier, Jean-Marc	Van.	4	105	16	16	32	29	....	....	....	....	....		1983-84	1987-88
Lanyon, Ted	Pit.	1	5	0	0	0	4	....	....	....	....	....		1967-68	1967-68
Lanz, Rick	Van., Tor., Chi.	10	569	65	221	286	448	28	3	8	11	35		1980-81	1991-92
Laperriere, Jacques	Mtl.	12	691	40	242	282	674	88	9	22	31	101	6	1962-63	1973-74
Lapointe, Guy	Mtl., St.L., Bos.	16	884	171	451	622	893	123	26	44	70	138	6	1968-69	1983-84
Lapointe, Rick	Det., Phi., St.L., Que., L.A.	11	664	44	176	220	831	46	2	7	9	64		1975-76	1985-86
Lappin, Peter	Min., S.J.	2	7	0	0	0	2	....	....	....	....	....		1989-90	1991-92
Laprade, Edgar	NYR	10	501	108	172	280	42	18	4	9	13	4		1945-46	1954-55
LaPrairie, Ben	Chi.	1	7	0	0	0	0	....	....	....	....	....		1936-37	1936-37
Lariviere, Garry	Que., Edm.	4	219	6	57	63	167	14	0	5	5	8		1979-80	1982-83
Larmer, Jeff	Col., N.J., Chi.	5	158	37	51	88	57	5	1	0	1	2		1981-82	1985-86
• Larochelle, Wildor	Mtl., Chi.	12	474	92	74	166	211	34	6	4	10	24	2	1925-26	1936-37
Larocque, Denis	L.A.	1	8	0	1	1	18	....	....	....	....	....		1987-88	1987-88
Larose, Charles	Bos.	1	6	0	0	0	0	....	....	....	....	....		1925-26	1925-26
Larose, Claude	NYR	2	25	4	7	11	2	2	0	0	0	0		1979-80	1981-82
Larose, Claude	Mtl., Min., St.L.	16	943	226	257	483	887	97	14	18	32	143	5	1962-63	1977-78
Larouche, Pierre	Pit., Mtl., Hfd., NYR	14	812	395	427	822	237	64	20	34	54	16	2	1974-75	1987-88
Larson, Norman	NYA., Bro., NYR	3	89	25	18	43	12	....	....	....	....	....		1940-41	1946-47
Larson, Reed	Det., Bos., Edm., NYI, Min., Buf.	14	904	222	463	685	1391	32	4	7	11	63		1976-77	1989-90
Larter, Tyler	Wsh.	1	1	0	0	0	0	....	....	....	....	....		1989-90	1989-90
Latal, Jiri	Phi.	2	92	12	36	48	24	....	....	....	....	....		1989-90	1990-91
Latos, James	NYR	1	1	0	0	0	0	....	....	....	....	....		1988-89	1988-89
Latreille, Phil	NYR	1	4	0	0	0	2	....	....	....	....	....		1960-61	1960-61
Latta, David	Que.	4	36	4	8	12	4	....	....	....	....	....		1985-86	1990-91
Lauder, Marty	Bos.	1	3	0	0	0	2	....	....	....	....	....		1927-28	1927-28
Lauen, Mike	Wpg.	1	3	0	1	1	0	....	....	....	....	....		1983-84	1983-84
Laughlin, Craig	Mtl., Wsh., L.A., Tor.	8	549	136	205	341	364	33	6	6	12	20		1981-82	1988-89
Laughton, Mike	Oak., Cal.	4	189	39	48	87	101	11	2	4	6	0		1967-68	1970-71
Laurence, Red	Atl., St.L.	2	79	15	22	37	14	....	....	....	....	....		1978-79	1979-80
LaVallee, Kevin	Cgy., L.A., St.L., Pit.	7	366	110	125	235	85	32	5	8	13	24		1980-81	1986-87
Lavarre, Mark	Chi.	3	78	9	16	25	58	1	0	0	0	2		1985-86	1987-88
Lavender, Brian	St.L., NYI, Det., Cal.	4	184	16	26	42	174	3	0	0	0	2		1971-72	1974-75
• Laviolette, Jack	Mtl.	1	18	2	0	2	0	2	0	0	0	0		1917-18	1917-18
Laviolette, Peter	NYR	1	12	0	0	0	6	....	....	....	....	....		1988-89	1988-89
Lavoie, Dominic	St.L., Ott., Bos., L.A.	6	38	5	8	13	32	....	....	....	....	....		1988-89	1993-94
Lawless, Paul	Hfd., Phi., Van., Tor.	7	239	49	77	126	54	3	0	2	2	2		1982-83	1989-90

Dean Kolstad

Mikhail Kravets

Dominic Lavoie

Jason Lafreniere

Jeff Lazaro

Patrick Lebeau

Chris Lindberg

Claude Loiselle

			Regular Schedule					Playoffs					NHL	First	Last
Name	**NHL Teams**	**NHL Seasons**	**GP**	**G**	**A**	**TP**	**PIM**	**GP**	**G**	**A**	**TP**	**PIM**	**Cup Wins**	**NHL Season**	**NHL Season**
Lawson, Danny	Det., Min., Buf.	5	219	28	29	57	61	16	0	1	1	2		1967-68	1971-72
Lawton, Brian	Min., NYR, Hfd., Que., Bos., S.J.	9	483	112	154	266	401	11	1	1	2	12		1983-84	1992-93
Laxdal, Derek	Tor., NYI	6	67	12	7	19	90	1	0	2	2	2		1984-85	1990-91
Laycoe, Hal	NYR, Mtl., Bos.	11	531	25	77	102	292	40	2	5	7	39		1945-46	1955-56
Lazaro, Jeff	Bos., Ott.	3	102	14	23	37	114	28	3	3	6	32		1990-91	1992-93
Leach, Larry	Bos.	3	126	13	29	42	91	7	1	1	2	8		1958-59	1961-62
Leach, Reggie	Bos., Cal., Phi., Det.	13	934	381	285	666	387	94	47	22	69	22	1	1970-71	1982-83
Leavins, Jim	Det., NYR	2	41	2	12	14	30	....	....	....	....	....		1985-86	1986-87
Lebeau, Patrick	Mtl., Cgy., Fla.	3	7	2	2	4	4	....	....	....	....	....		1990-91	1993-94
LeBlanc, Fern	Det.	3	34	5	6	11	0	....	....	....	....	....		1976-77	1978-79
LeBlanc, J.P.	Chi., Det.	5	153	14	30	44	87	2	0	0	0	0		1968-69	1978-79
LeBrun, Al	NYR	2	6	0	2	2	4	....	....	....	....	....		1960-61	1965-66
Lecaine, Bill	Pit.	1	4	0	0	0	0	....	....	....	....	....		1968-69	1968-69
Leclair, Jackie	Mtl.,	3	160	20	40	60	56	20	6	0	7	6	1	1954-55	1956-57
Leclerc, Rene	Det.	2	87	10	11	21	105	....	....	....	....	....		1968-69	1970-71
Lecuyer, Doug	Chi., Wpg., Pit.	4	126	11	31	42	178	7	4	0	4	15		1978-79	1982-83
Ledingham, Walt	Chi., NYI	3	15	0	2	2	4	....	....	....	....	....		1972-73	1976-77
• LeDuc, Albert	Mtl., Ott., NYR	10	383	57	35	92	614	31	5	6	11	32	2	1925-26	1934-35
LeDuc, Rich	Bos., Que.	4	130	28	38	66	55	5	0	0	0	9		1972-73	1980-81
• Lee, Bobby	Mtl.	1	1	0	0	0	0	....	....	....	....	....		1942-43	1942-43
Lee, Edward	Que.	1	2	0	0	0	5	....	....	....	....	....		1984-85	1984-85
Lee, Peter	Pit.	6	431	114	131	245	257	19	0	8	8	4		1977-78	1982-83
Lefley, Bryan	N.Y.I., K.C., Col.	5	228	7	29	36	101	2	0	0	0	0		1972-73	1977-78
Lefley, Chuck	Mtl., St.L.	9	407	128	164	292	137	29	5	8	13	10		1970-71	1980-81
• Leger, Roger	NYR, Mtl.	5	187	18	53	71	71	20	0	7	7	14		1943-44	1949-50
Legge, Barry	Que., Wpg.	3	107	1	11	12	144	....	....	....	....	....		1979-80	1981-82
Legge, Randy	NYR	1	12	0	2	2	2	....	....	....	....	....		1972-73	1972-73
Lehmann, Tommy	Bos., Edm.	3	36	5	5	10	16	....	....	....	....	....		1987-88	1989-90
Lehto, Petteri	Pit.	1	6	0	0	0	4	....	....	....	....	....		1984-85	1984-85
Lehtonen, Antero	Wsh.	1	65	9	12	21	14	....	....	....	....	....		1979-80	1979-80
Lehvonen, Henri	K.C.	1	4	0	0	0	0	....	....	....	....	....		1974-75	1974-75
Leier, Edward	Chi.	2	16	2	1	3	2	....	....	....	....	....		1949-50	1950-51
Leinonen, Mikko	NYR, Wsh.	4	162	31	78	109	71	20	2	11	13	28		1981-82	1984-85
Leiter, Bobby	Bos., Pit., Atl.	10	447	98	126	224	144	8	3	0	3	2		1962-63	1975-76
Leiter, Ken	NYI, Min.	5	143	14	36	50	62	15	0	6	6	8		1984-85	1989-90
Lemaire, Jacques	Mtl.	12	853	366	469	835	217	145	61	78	139	63	8	1967-68	1978-79
Lemay, Moe	Van., Edm., Bos., Wpg.	8	317	72	94	166	442	28	6	3	9	55	1	1981-82	1988-89
Lemelin, Roger	K.C., Col.	4	36	1	2	3	27	....	....	....	....	....		1974-75	1977-78
Lemieux, Alain	St.L., Que., Pit.	6	119	28	44	72	38	19	4	6	10	0		1981-82	1986-87
Lemieux, Bob	Oak.	1	19	0	1	1	12	....	....	....	....	....		1967-68	1967-68
Lemieux, Jacques	L.A.	2	19	0	4	4	8	1	0	0	0	0		1967-68	1969-70
Lemieux, Jean	L.A., Atl., Wsh.	6	204	23	63	86	39	3	1	1	2	0		1969-70	1977-78
• Lemieux, Real	Det., L.A., NYR, Buf.	7	381	40	75	115	184	18	2	4	6	10		1966-67	1973-74
Lemieux, Richard	Van., K.C., Atl.	5	274	39	82	121	132	2	0	0	0	0		1971-72	1975-76
Lenardon, Tim	N.J., Van.	2	15	2	1	3	4	....	....	....	....	....		1986-87	1989-90
• Lepine, Hec	Mtl.	1	33	5	2	7	2	....	....	....	....	....		1925-26	1925-26
• Lepine, Pit	Mtl.	13	526	143	98	241	392	41	7	5	12	26	2	1925-26	1937-38
Leroux, Gaston	Mtl.	1	2	0	0	0	0	....	....	....	....	....		1935-36	1935-36
Lesieur, Art	Mtl., Chi.	4	100	4	2	6	50	14	0	0	0	4	1	1928-29	1935-36
Lessard, Rick	Cgy., S.J.	3	15	0	4	4	18	....	....	....	....	....		1988-89	1991-92
Lesuk, Bill	Bos., Phi., L.A., Wsh., Wpg.	8	388	44	63	107	368	9	1	0	1	12	1	1968-69	1979-80
Leswick, Jack	Chi.	1	47	1	7	8	16	....	....	....	....	....	1	1933-34	1933-34
Leswick, Peter	NYA, Bos.	2	3	1	0	1	0	....	....	....	....	....		1936-37	1944-45
Leswick, Tony	NYR, Det., Chi.	12	740	165	159	324	900	59	13	10	23	91	3	1945-46	1957-58
Levandoski, Joseph	NYR	1	8	1	1	2	0	....	....	....	....	....		1946-47	1946-47
Leveille, Norm	Bos.	2	75	17	25	42	49	....	....	....	....	....		1981-82	1982-83
Lever, Don	Van., Atl., Cgy., Col., N.J., Buf.	15	1020	313	367	680	593	30	7	10	17	26		1972-73	1986-87
Levie, Craig	Wpg., Min., Van., St.L.	6	183	22	53	75	177	16	2	3	5	32		1981-82	1986-87
• Levinsky, Alex	Tor., Chi., NYR	9	367	19	49	68	307	34	2	1	3	2	2	1930-31	1938-39
Levo, Tapio	Col., N.J.,	2	107	16	53	69	36	....	....	....	....	....		1981-82	1982-83
Lewicki, Danny	Tor., NYR, Chi.	9	461	105	135	240	177	28	0	4	4	8	1	1950-51	1958-59
Lewis, Bob	NYR	1	8	0	0	0	0	....	....	....	....	....		1975-76	1975-76
Lewis, Dave	NYI, L.A., N.J., Det.	15	1008	36	187	223	953	91	1	20	21	143		1973-74	1987-88
Lewis, Douglas	Mtl.	1	3	0	0	0	0	....	....	....	....	....		1946-47	1946-47
• Lewis, Herbie	Det.	11	483	148	161	309	248	38	13	10	23	6	2	1928-29	1938-39
Ley, Rick	Tor., Hfd.	6	310	12	72	84	528	14	0	2	2	20		1968-69	1980-81
Liba, Igor	NYR, L.A.	1	37	7	18	25	36	2	0	0	0	2		1988-89	1988-89
Libett, Nick	Det., K.C., Pit.	14	982	237	268	505	472	16	6	2	8	2		1967-68	1980-81
Licari, Anthony	Det.	1	9	0	1	1	0	....	....	....	....	....		1946-47	1946-47
Liddington, Bob	Tor.	1	11	0	1	1	2	....	....	....	....	....		1970-71	1970-71
Lindberg, Chris	Cgy., Que.	3	116	17	25	42	47	2	0	1	1	2		1991-92	1993-94
Lindgren, Lars	Van., Min.	6	394	25	113	138	325	40	5	6	11	20		1978-79	1983-84
Lindholm, Mikael	L.A.	1	18	2	2	4	2	....	....	....	....	....		1989-90	1989-90
Lindsay, Ted	Det., Chi.	17	1068	379	472	851	1808	133	47	49	96	194	4	1944-45	1964-65
Lindstrom, Willy	Wpg., Edm., Pit.	8	582	161	162	323	200	57	14	18	32	24	2	1979-80	1986-87
Linseman, Ken	Phi., Edm., Bos., Tor.	14	860	256	551	807	1727	113	43	77	120	325	1	1978-79	1991-92
Liscombe, Carl	Det.	9	383	137	140	277	117	59	22	19	41	20	1	1937-38	1945-46
Litzenberger, Ed	Mtl., Chi., Det., Tor.	12	618	178	238	416	283	40	5	13	18	34	4	1952-53	1963-64
• Locas, Jacques	Mtl.	2	59	7	8	15	66	....	....	....	....	....		1947-48	1948-49
Lochead, Bill	NYR, Det., Col.	6	330	69	62	131	180	7	3	0	3	6		1974-75	1979-80
• Locking, Norm	Chi.	2	48	2	6	8	26	1	0	0	0	0		1934-35	1935-36
Lofthouse, Mark	Wsh., Det.	6	181	42	38	80	73	....	....	....	....	....		1977-78	1982-83
Logan, Dave	Chi., Van.	6	218	5	29	34	470	12	0	0	0	10		1975-76	1980-81
Logan, Robert	Buf., L.A.	3	42	10	5	15	0	....	....	....	....	....		1986-87	1988-89
Loiselle, Claude	Det., N.J., Que., Tor., NYI	13	616	92	117	209	1149	41	4	11	15	60		1981-82	1993-94
Long, Barry	L.A., Det., Wpg.	5	280	11	68	79	250	5	0	1	1	18		1972-73	1981-82
• Long, Stanley	Mtl.	1	....	....	....	....	....	3	0	0	0	0		1951-52	1951-52
Lonsberry, Ross	Phi., Pit., Bos., L.A.	15	968	256	310	566	806	100	21	25	46	87	2	1966-67	1980-81
Loob, Hakan	Cgy.	6	450	193	236	429	189	73	26	28	54	16	1	1983-84	1988-89
Loob, Peter	Que.	1	8	1	2	3	0	....	....	....	....	....		1984-85	1984-85
Lorentz, Jim	NYR, Buf., Bos., St.L.	10	659	161	238	399	208	54	12	10	22	30	1	1968-69	1977-78
Lorimer, Bob	NYI, Col., N.J.	10	529	22	90	112	431	49	3	10	13	83	2	1976-77	1985-86
Lorrain, Rod	Mtl.	6	179	28	39	67	30	11	0	3	3	0		1935-36	1941-42
Loughlin, Clem	Det., Chi.	3	101	8	6	14	77	....	....	....	....	....		1926-27	1928-29
Loughlin, Wilf	Tor.	1	14	0	0	0	2	....	....	....	....	....		1923-24	1923-24
Lovsin, Ken	Wsh.	1	1	0	0	0	0	....	....	....	....	....		1990-91	1990-91
Lowdermilk, Dwayne	Wsh.	1	2	0	1	1	2	....	....	....	....	....		1980-81	1980-81
Lowe, Darren	Pit.	1	8	1	2	3	0	....	....	....	....	....		1983-84	1983-84
Lowe, Norm	NYR	2	4	1	1	2	0	....	....	....	....	....		1948-49	1949-50
• Lowe, Ross	Bos., Mtl.	3	77	6	8	14	82	2	0	0	0	0		1949-50	1951-52
• Lowery, Fred	Mtl.M., Pit.	2	54	1	0	1	10	2	0	0	0	6	1	1924-25	1925-26
• Lowrey, Eddie	Ott., Ham.	3	24	2	0	2	3	....	....	....	....	....		1917-18	1920-21
• Lowrey, Gerry	Chi., Ott., Tor., Phi., Pit.	6	209	48	48	96	168	2	1	0	1	2		1927-28	1932-33
Lucas, Danny	Phi.	1	6	1	0	1	0	....	....	....	....	....		1978-79	1978-79
Lucas, Dave	Det.	1	1	0	0	0	0	....	....	....	....	....		1962-63	1962-63
Luce, Don	NYR, Det., Buf., L.A., Tor.	13	894	225	329	554	364	71	17	22	39	52		1969-70	1981-82
Ludvig, Jan	N.J., Buf.	7	314	54	87	141	418	....	....	....	....	....		1982-83	1988-89
Ludzik, Steve	Chi., Buf.	9	424	46	93	139	333	44	4	8	12	70		1981-82	1989-90
Lukowich, Bernie	Pit., St.L.	2	79	13	15	28	34	2	0	0	0	0		1973-74	1974-75
Lukowich, Morris	Wpg., Bos., L.A.	8	582	199	219	418	584	11	0	2	2	24		1979-80	1986-87
Luksa, Charlie	Hfd.	1	8	0	1	1	4	....	....	....	....	....		1979-80	1979-80
Lumley, Dave	Mtl., Edm., Hfd.	9	437	98	160	258	680	61	6	8	14	131	2	1978-79	1986-87
Lund, Pentti	NYR, Bos.	7	259	44	55	99	40	18	7	5	12	0		1946-47	1952-53
Lundberg, Brian	Pit.	1	1	0	0	0	2	....	....	....	....	....		1982-83	1982-83
Lunde, Len	Min., Van., Det., Chi.	8	321	39	83	122	75	20	3	2	5	2		1958-59	1970-71
Lundholm, Bengt	Wpg.	5	275	48	95	143	72	14	3	4	7	14		1981-82	1985-86
Lundrigan, Joe	Tor., Wsh.	2	52	2	8	10	22	....	....	....	....	....		1972-73	1974-75
Lundstrom, Tord	Det.	1	11	1	1	2	0	....	....	....	....	....		1973-74	1973-74
Lundy, Pat	Det. Chi.	5	150	37	32	69	31	9	1	1	2	2		1945-46	1950-51
Lupien, Gilles	Mtl., Pit., Hfd.	5	226	5	25	30	416	25	0	0	0	21	2	1977-78	1981-82
Lupul, Gary	Van.	7	293	70	75	145	243	25	4	7	11	11		1979-80	1985-86
Lyle, George	Det., Hfd.	4	99	24	38	62	51	....	....	....	....	....		1979-80	1982-83
Lynch, Jack	Pit., Det., Wsh.	7	382	24	106	130	336	....	....	....	....	....		1972-73	1978-79
Lynn, Vic	Det., Mtl., Tor., Bos., Chi.	10	326	49	76	125	274	47	7	10	17	46	3	1943-44	1953-54

Name	NHL Teams	NHL Seasons	Regular Schedule GP	G	A	TP	PIM	Playoffs GP	G	A	TP	PIM	NHL Cup Wins	First NHL Season	Last NHL Season
Lyon, Steve	Pit.	1	3	0	0	0	2	....	....	....	....	....		1976-77	1976-77
Lyons, Ron	Bos., Phi.	1	36	2	4	6	29	5	0	0	0	0		1930-31	1930-31
Lysiak, Tom	Atl., Chi.	13	919	292	551	843	567	78	25	38	63	49		1973-74	1985-86

M

Name	NHL Teams	NHL Seasons	Regular Schedule GP	G	A	TP	PIM	Playoffs GP	G	A	TP	PIM	NHL Cup Wins	First NHL Season	Last NHL Season
MacAdam, Al	Phi., Cal., Cle., Min., Van.	12	864	240	351	591	509	64	20	24	44	21	1	1973-74	1984-85
MacDonald, Blair	Edm., Van.	4	219	91	100	191	65	11	0	6	6	2		1979-80	1982-83
MacDonald, Brett	Van.	1	1	0	0	0	0	....	....	....	....	....		1987-88	1987-88
MacDonald, Kevin	Ott.	1	1	0	0	0	2	....	....	....	....	....		1993-94	1993-94
• MacDonald, Kilby	NYR	4	151	36	34	70	47	15	1	2	3	4	1	1939-40	1944-45
MacDonald, Lowell	Det., L.A., Pit.	13	506	180	210	390	92	30	11	11	22	12		1961-62	1977-78
MacDonald, Parker	Tor., NYR, Det., Bos., Min.	14	676	144	179	323	253	75	14	14	28	20		1952-53	1968-69
MacDougall, Kim	Min.	1	1	0	0	0	0	....	....	....	....	....		1974-75	1974-75
MacEachern, Shane	St.L.	1	1	0	0	0	0	....	....	....	....	....		1987-88	1987-88
Macey, Hubert	NYR, Mtl.	3	30	6	9	15	0	8	0	0	0	0		1941-42	1946-47
MacGregor, Bruce	Det., NYR	14	893	213	257	470	217	107	19	28	47	44		1960-61	1973-74
MacGregor, Randy	Hfd.	1	2	1	1	2	2	....	....	....	....	....		1981-82	1981-82
MacGuigan, Garth	NYI	1	2	0	0	0	0	....	....	....	....	....		1979-80	1979-80
MacIntosh, Ian	NYR	1	4	0	0	0	4	....	....	....	....	....		1952-53	1952-53
MacIver, Don	Wpg.	1	6	0	0	0	2	....	....	....	....	....		1979-80	1979-80
MacKasey, Blair	Tor.	1	1	0	0	0	2	....	....	....	....	....		1976-77	1976-77
MacKay, Calum	Det., Mtl.	8	237	50	55	105	214	38	5	13	18	20	1	1946-47	1954-55
Mackay, Dave	Chi.	1	29	3	0	3	26	5	0	1	1	2		1940-41	1940-41
• MacKay, Mickey	Chi., Pit., Bos.	4	151	44	19	63	79	11	0	0	0	6	1	1926-27	1929-30
MacKay, Murdo	Mtl.	3	19	0	3	3	0	15	1	2	3	0		1945-46	1947-48
Mackell, Fleming	Tor., Bos.	13	665	149	220	369	562	80	22	41	63	75	2	1947-48	1959-60
MacKenzie, Barry	Min.	1	6	0	1	1	6	....	....	....	....	....		1968-69	1968-69
• MacKenzie, Bill	Chi., Mtl.M., Mtl., NYR	7	266	15	14	29	133	19	1	1	2	11	1	1932-33	1939-40
MacKey, Reggie	NYR	1	34	0	0	0	16	1	0	0	0	0		1926-27	1926-27
Mackie, Howie	Det.	2	20	1	0	1	4	8	0	0	0	0	1	1936-37	1937-38
MacKinnon, Paul	Wsh.	5	147	5	23	28	91	....	....	....	....	....		1979-80	1983-84
MacLean, Paul	St.L., Wpg., Det.	11	719	324	349	673	968	53	21	14	35	104		1980-81	1990-91
MacLeish, Rick	Phi., Hfd., Pit., Det.	14	846	349	410	759	434	114	54	53	107	38	2	1970-71	1983-84
MacLellan, Brian	L.A., NYR, Min., Cgy., Det.	10	606	172	241	413	551	47	5	9	14	42		1982-83	1991-92
MacMillan, Billy	Tor., Atl., NYI	7	446	74	77	151	184	53	6	6	12	40		1970-71	1976-77
MacMillan, Bob	NYR, St.L., Atl., Cgy., Col., N.J., Chi.	11	753	228	349	577	260	31	8	11	19	16		1974-75	1984-85
MacMillan, John	Tor., Det.	5	104	5	10	15	32	12	0	1	1	2	2	1960-61	1964-65
MacNeil, Al	Tor., Mtl., Chi., NYR, Pit.	11	524	17	75	92	617	37	0	4	4	67		1955-56	1967-68
MacNeil, Bernie	St.L.	1	4	0	0	0	0	....	....	....	....	....		1973-74	1973-74
• MacPherson, Bud	Mtl.	7	259	5	33	38	233	29	0	3	3	21	1	1948-49	1956-57
• MacSweyn, Ralph	Phi.	5	47	0	5	5	10	8	0	0	0	6		1967-68	1971-72
Madigan, Connie	St.L.	1	20	0	3	3	25	5	0	0	0	4		1972-73	1972-73
Magee, Dean	Min.	1	7	0	0	0	4	....	....	....	....	....		1977-78	1977-78
Maggs, Daryl	Chi., Cal., Tor.	3	135	14	19	33	54	4	0	0	0	0		1971-72	1979-80
Magnan, Marc	Tor.	1	4	0	1	1	5	....	....	....	....	....		1982-83	1982-83
Magnuson, Keith	Chi.	11	589	14	125	139	1442	68	3	9	12	164		1969-70	1979-80
Maguire, Kevin	Tor., Buf., Phi.	6	260	29	30	59	782	11	0	0	0	86		1986-87	1991-92
Mahaffy, John	Mtl., NYR	3	37	11	25	36	4	1	0	1	1	0		1942-43	1944-45
Mahovlich, Frank	Tor., Det., Mtl.	18	1181	533	570	1103	1056	137	51	67	118	163	6	1956-57	1973-74
Mahovlich, Pete	Det., Mtl., Pit.	16	884	288	485	773	916	88	30	42	72	134	4	1965-66	1980-81
Mailhot, Jacques	Que.	1	5	0	0	0	33	....	....	....	....	....		1988-89	1988-89
Mailley, Frank	Mtl.	1	1	0	0	0	0	....	....	....	....	....		1942-43	1942-43
Mair, Jim	Phi., NYI, Van.	5	76	4	15	19	49	3	1	2	3	4		1970-71	1974-75
• Majeau, Fern	Mtl.	2	56	22	24	46	43	1	0	0	0	0	1	1943-44	1944-45
Major, Bruce	Que.	1	4	0	0	0	0	....	....	....	....	....		1990-91	1990-91
Maki, Chico	Chi.	15	841	143	292	435	345	113	17	36	53	43	1	1960-61	1975-76
• Maki, Wayne	Chi., St.L., Van.	6	246	57	79	136	184	2	1	0	1	2		1967-68	1972-73
Makkonen, Karl	Edm.	1	9	2	2	4	0	....	....	....	....	....		1979-80	1979-80
Maley, David	Mtl., N.J., Edm., S.J., NYI	9	466	43	81	124	1043	46	5	5	10	111	1	1985-86	1993-94
Malinowski, Merlin	Col., N.J., Hfd.	5	282	54	111	165	121	....	....	....	....	....		1978-79	1982-83
Malone, Cliff	Mtl.	1	3	0	0	0	0	....	....	....	....	....		1951-52	1951-52
Malone, Greg	Pit., Hfd., Que.	11	704	191	310	501	661	20	3	5	8	32		1976-77	1986-87
• Malone, Joe	Mtl., Que., Ham.	7	125	146	21	167	23	9	5	0	5	0	1	1917-18	1923-24
Maloney, Dan	Chi., L.A., Det., Tor.	11	737	192	259	451	1489	40	4	7	11	35		1970-71	1981-82
Maloney, Dave	NYR, Buf.	11	657	71	246	317	1154	49	7	17	24	91		1974-75	1984-85
Maloney, Don	NYR, Hfd., NYI	13	765	214	350	564	815	94	22	35	57	101		1978-79	1990-91
Maloney, Phil	Bos., Tor., Chi.	5	158	28	43	71	16	6	0	0	0	0		1949-50	1959-60
Maluta, Ray	Bos.	2	25	2	3	5	6	2	0	0	0	0		1975-76	1976-77
Manastersky, Tom	Mtl.	1	6	0	0	0	11	....	....	....	....	....		1950-51	1950-51
Mancuso, Gus	Mtl., NYR	4	42	7	9	16	17	....	....	....	....	....		1937-38	1942-43
Mandich, Dan	Min.	4	111	5	11	16	303	7	0	0	0	2		1982-83	1985-86
Manery, Kris	Van., Wpg., Clev., Min.	4	250	63	64	127	91	....	....	....	....	....		1977-78	1980-81
Manery, Randy	L.A., Det., Atl.	10	582	50	206	256	415	13	0	2	2	12		1970-71	1979-80
Mann, Jack	NYR	2	9	3	4	7	0	....	....	....	....	....		1943-44	1944-45
Mann, Jimmy	Wpg., Que., Pit.	8	293	10	20	30	895	22	0	0	0	89		1979-80	1987-88
Mann, Ken	Det.	1	1	0	0	0	0	....	....	....	....	....		1975-76	1975-76
Mann, Norm	Tor.	2	31	0	3	3	4	1	0	0	0	0		1938-39	1940-41
Manners, Rennison	Pit., Phi.	2	37	3	2	5	14	....	....	....	....	....		1929-30	1930-31
Manno, Bob	Van., Tor., Det.	8	371	41	131	172	274	17	2	4	6	12		1976-77	1984-85
Manson, Ray	Bos., NYR	2	2	0	1	1	0	....	....	....	....	....		1947-48	1948-49
• Mantha, Georges	Mtl.	13	498	89	102	181	148	36	6	2	8	16	2	1928-29	1940-41
Mantha, Moe	Wpg., Pit., Edm., Min., Phi.	12	656	81	289	370	501	17	5	10	15	18		1980-81	1991-92
• Mantha, Sylvio	Mtl., Bos.	14	543	63	72	135	667	46	5	4	9	66	3	1923-24	1936-37
Maracle, Buddy	NYR	1	11	1	3	4	4	4	0	0	0	0		1930-31	1930-31
Marcetta, Milan	Tor., Min.	3	54	7	15	22	10	17	7	7	14	4	1	1966-67	1968-69
March, Mush	Chi.	17	758	153	230	383	540	48	12	15	27	41	2	1928-29	1944-45
Marchinko, Brian	Tor., NYI	4	47	2	6	8	0	....	....	....	....	....		1970-71	1973-74
Marcinyshyn, David	N.J., Que., NYR	3	16	0	1	1	49	....	....	....	....	....		1990-91	1992-93
Marcon, Lou	Det.	3	70	0	4	4	42	....	....	....	....	....		1958-59	1962-63
Marcotte, Don	Bos.	15	868	230	255	485	317	132	34	27	61	81	2	1965-66	1981-82
Marini, Hector	NYI, N.J.	5	154	27	46	73	246	10	3	6	9	14	2	1978-79	1983-84
Mario, Frank	Bos.	2	53	9	19	28	24	....	....	....	....	....		1941-42	1944-45
• Mariucci, John	Chi.	5	223	11	34	45	308	8	0	3	3	26		1940-41	1947-48
Markell, John	Wpg., St. L., Min.	4	55	11	10	21	36	....	....	....	....	....		1979-80	1984-85
Marker, Gus	Det., Mtl.M., Tor., Bro.	10	336	64	69	133	133	45	6	8	14	36	1	1932-33	1941-42
Markham, Ray	NYR	1	14	1	1	2	21	7	1	0	1	24		1979-80	1979-80
Markle, Jack	Tor.	1	8	0	1	1	0	....	....	....	....	....		1935-36	1935-36
• Marks, Jack	Mtl.W, Tor., Que.	2	7	0	0	0	4	....	....	....	....	....	1	1917-18	1919-20
Marks, John	Chi.	10	657	112	163	275	330	57	5	9	14	60		1972-73	1981-82
Markwart, Nevin	Bos., Cgy.	8	309	41	68	109	794	19	1	0	1	33		1983-84	1991-92
Marois, Mario	NYR, Van., Que., Wpg., St.L.	15	955	76	357	433	1746	100	4	34	38	182		1977-78	1991-92
Marotte, Gilles	Bos., Chi., L.A., NYR, St.L.	12	808	56	265	321	872	29	3	3	6	26		1965-66	1976-77
Marquess, Mark	Bos.	1	27	5	4	9	27	4	0	0	0	0		1946-47	1946-47
Marsh, Brad	Atl., Cgy., Phi., Tor., Det., Ott.	15	1086	23	175	198	1241	97	6	18	24	124		1978-79	1992-93
Marsh, Gary	Det., Tor.	2	7	1	3	4	4	....	....	....	....	....		1967-68	1968-69
Marsh, Peter	Wpg., Chi.	5	278	48	71	119	224	26	1	5	6	33		1979-80	1983-84
Marshall, Bert	Det., Oak., Cal., NYR, NYI	14	868	17	181	198	926	72	4	22	26	99		1965-66	1978-79
Marshall, Don	Mtl., NYR, Buf., Tor.	19	1176	265	324	589	127	94	8	15	23	14	5	1951-52	1971-72
Marshall, Paul	Pit., Tor., Hfd.	4	95	15	18	33	17	1	0	0	0	0		1979-80	1982-83
Marshall, Willie	Tor.	4	33	1	15	16	2	....	....	....	....	....		1952-53	1958-59
Marson, Mike	Wsh., L.A.	6	196	24	24	48	233	....	....	....	....	....		1974-75	1979-80
Martin, Clare	Bos., Det., Chi., NYR	6	237	12	28	40	78	22	0	2	2	6	1	1941-42	1951-52
Martin, Frank	Bos., Chi.	6	282	11	46	57	122	10	0	1	1	2		1952-53	1957-58
Martin, Grant	Van., Wsh.	4	44	0	4	4	55	1	1	0	1	2		1983-84	1986-87
Martin, Jack	Tor.	1	1	0	0	0	0	....	....	....	....	....		1960-61	1960-61
Martin, Pit	Det., Bos., Chi., Van.	17	1101	324	485	809	609	100	27	31	58	56		1961-62	1978-79
Martin, Rick	Buf., L.A.	11	685	384	317	701	477	63	24	29	53	74		1971-72	1981-82
Martin, Ron	NYA	2	94	13	16	29	36	....	....	....	....	....		1932-33	1933-34
Martin, Terry	Buf., Que., Tor., Edm., Min.	10	479	104	101	205	202	21	4	2	6	26		1975-76	1984-85
Martin, Tom	Wpg., Hfd., Min.	6	92	12	11	23	249	4	0	0	0	6		1984-85	1989-90
Martin, Tom	Tor.	1	3	1	0	1	0	....	....	....	....	....		1967-68	1967-68
Martineau, Don	Atl., Min., Det.	4	90	6	10	16	63	....	....	....	....	....		1973-74	1976-77
Martinson, Steven	Det., Mtl., Min.	4	49	2	1	3	244	1	0	0	0	10		1987-88	1991-92

Jan Ludwig

David Maley

Andrew McBain

Kevin McClelland

Bill McDougall

Bob McGill

Mike McNeill

Max Middendorf

			Regular Schedule					Playoffs							
Name	NHL Teams	NHL Seasons	GP	G	A	TP	PIM	GP	G	A	TP	PIM	NHL Cup Wins	First NHL Season	Last NHL Season
Maruk, Dennis	Cal., Clev., Min., Wsh.	14	888	356	522	878	761	34	14	22	36	26		1975-76	1988-89
Masnick, Paul	Mtl., Chi., Tor.	6	232	18	41	59	139	33	4	5	9	27	1	1950-51	1957-58
• Mason, Charley	NYR, NYA, Det., Chi.	4	95	7	18	25	44	4	0	1	1	0		1934-35	1938-39
Massecar, George	NYA	3	100	12	11	23	46	....	....	....	....	....		1929-30	1931-32
Masters, Jamie	St.L.	3	33	1	13	14	2	2	0	0	0	0		1975-76	1978-79
• Masterton, Bill	Min.	1	38	4	8	12	4	....	....	....	....	....		1967-68	1967-68
Mathers, Frank	Tor.	3	23	1	3	4	4	....	....	....	....	....		1948-49	1951-52
Mathiasen, Dwight	Pit.	3	33	1	7	8	18	....	....	....	....	....		1985-86	1987-88
Mathieson, Jim	Wsh.	1	2	0	0	0	4	....	....	....	....	....		1989-90	1989-90
• Matte, Joe	Tor., Ham., Bos., Mtl.	4	64	18	14	32	43	....	....	....	....	....		1919-20	1925-26
Matte, Joe	Chi.	1	12	0	1	1	0	....	....	....	....	....		1942-43	1942-43
Matte, Roland	Det.	1	12	0	1	1	0	....	....	....	....	....		1929-30	1929-30
Mattiussi, Dick	Pit., Oak., Cal.	4	200	8	31	39	124	8	0	1	1	6		1967-68	1970-71
Matz, Johnny	Mtl.	1	30	3	2	5	0	5	0	0	0	2		1924-25	1924-25
Maxner, Wayne	Bos.	2	62	8	9	17	48	....	....	....	....	....		1964-65	1965-66
Maxwell, Brad	Min., Que., Tor., Van., NYR	10	612	98	270	368	1292	79	12	49	61	178		1977-78	1986-87
Maxwell, Bryan	Min., St.L., Wpg., Pit.	8	331	18	77	95	745	15	1	1	2	86		1977-78	1984-85
Maxwell, Kevin	Min., Col., N.J.	3	66	6	15	21	61	16	3	4	7	24		1980-81	1983-84
Maxwell, Wally	Tor.	1	2	0	0	0	0	....	....	....	....	....		1952-53	1952-53
Mayer, Jim	NYR	1	4	0	0	0	0	....	....	....	....	....		1979-80	1979-80
Mayer, Pat	Pit.	1	1	0	0	0	4	....	....	....	....	....		1987-88	1987-88
Mayer, Shep	Tor.	1	12	1	2	3	4	....	....	....	....	....		1942-43	1942-43
Mazur, Eddie	Mtl., Chi.	6	107	8	20	28	120	25	4	5	9	22	1	1950-51	1956-57
McAdam, Gary	Buf., Pit., Det., Cal., Wsh., N.J., Tor.	11	534	96	132	228	243	30	6	5	11	16		1975-76	1985-86
McAdam, Sam	NYR	1	5	0	0	0	0	....	....	....	....	....		1930-31	1930-31
McAndrew, Hazen	Bro.	1	7	0	1	1	6	....	....	....	....	....		1941-42	1941-42
McAneeley, Ted	Cal.	3	158	8	35	43	141	....	....	....	....	....		1972-73	1974-75
McAtee, Jud	Det.	3	46	15	13	28	6	14	2	1	3	0		1942-43	1944-45
McAtee, Norm	Bos.	1	13	0	1	1	0	....	....	....	....	....		1946-47	1946-47
McAvoy, George	Mtl.	1	....	....	....	....	....	4	0	0	0	0		1954-55	1954-55
McBain, Andrew	Wpg., Pit., Van., Ott.	11	608	129	172	301	633	24	5	7	12	39		1983-84	1993-94
McBride, Cliff	Mtl.M., Tor.	2	2	0	0	0	0	....	....	....	....	....		1928-29	1929-30
McBurney, Jim	Chi.	1	1	0	1	1	0	....	....	....	....	....		1952-53	1952-53
McCabe, Stan	Det., Mtl.M.	4	78	9	4	13	49	....	....	....	....	....		1929-30	1933-34
• McCaffrey, Bert	Tor., Pit., Mtl.	7	260	42	30	72	202	8	2	1	3	12		1924-25	1930-31
McCahill, John	Col.	1	1	0	0	0	0	....	....	....	....	....		1977-78	1977-78
McCaig, Douglas	Det., Chi.	7	263	8	21	29	255	17	0	1	1	8		1941-42	1950-51
• McCallum, Dunc	NYR, Pit.	5	187	14	35	49	230	10	1	2	3	12		1965-66	1970-71
McCalmon, Eddie	Chi., Phi.	2	39	5	0	5	14	....	....	....	....	....		1927-28	1930-31
McCann, Rick	Det.	6	43	1	4	5	6	....	....	....	....	....		1967-68	1974-75
McCarthy, Dan	NYR	1	5	4	0	4	4	....	....	....	....	....		1980-81	1980-81
McCarthy, Kevin	Phi., Van., Pit.	10	537	67	191	258	527	21	2	3	5	20		1977-78	1986-87
• McCarthy, Tom	Que., Ham.	2	34	19	3	22	10	....	....	....	....	....		1919-20	1920-21
McCarthy, Tom	Det., Bos.	4	60	8	9	17	8	....	....	....	....	....		1956-57	1960-61
McCarthy, Tom	Min., Bos.	9	460	178	221	399	330	68	12	26	38	67		1979-80	1987-88
McCartney, Walt	Mtl.	1	2	0	0	0	0	....	....	....	....	....		1932-33	1932-33
McCaskill, Ted	Min.	1	4	0	2	2	0	....	....	....	....	....		1967-68	1967-68
McClanahan, Rob	Buf., Hfd., NYR	5	224	38	63	101	126	34	4	12	16	31		1979-80	1983-84
McClelland, Kevin	Pit., Edm., Det., Tor., Wpg.	12	588	68	112	180	1672	98	11	18	29	281	4	1981-82	1993-94
McCord, Bob	Bos., Det., Min., St.L.	7	316	58	68	126	262	14	2	5	7	10		1963-64	1972-73
McCord, Dennis	Van.	1	3	0	0	0	0	....	....	....	....	....		1973-74	1973-74
McCormack, John	Tor., Mtl., Chi.	8	311	25	49	74	35	22	1	1	2	0	2	1947-48	1954-55
McCourt, Dale	Det., Buf., Tor.	7	532	194	284	478	124	21	9	7	16	6		1977-78	1983-84
McCreary, Bill	Tor.	1	12	1	0	1	4	....	....	....	....	....		1980-81	1980-81
McCreary, Bill E.	NYR, Det., Mtl., St.L.	10	309	53	62	115	108	48	6	16	22	14		1953-54	1970-71
McCreary, Keith	Mtl., Pit., Atl.	10	532	131	112	243	294	16	0	4	4	6		1961-62	1974-75
• McCreedy, Johnny	Tor.	2	64	17	12	29	25	21	4	3	7	16	2	1941-42	1944-45
McCrimmon, Jim	St.L.	1	2	0	0	0	0	....	....	....	....	....		1974-75	1974-75
McCulley, Bob	Mtl.	1	1	0	0	0	0	....	....	....	....	....		1934-35	1934-35
McCurry, Duke	Pit.	4	148	21	11	32	119	4	0	2	2	4		1925-26	1928-29
McCutcheon, Brian	Det.	3	37	3	1	4	7	....	....	....	....	....		1974-75	1976-77
McCutheon, Darwin	Tor.	1	1	0	0	0	0	....	....	....	....	....		1981-82	1981-82
McDill, Jeff	Chi.	1	1	0	0	0	0	....	....	....	....	....		1976-77	1976-77
McDonagh, Bill	NYR	1	4	0	0	0	2	....	....	....	....	....		1949-50	1949-50
McDonald, Ab	Mtl., Chi., Bos., Det., Pit., St.L.	15	762	182	248	430	200	84	21	29	50	42	4	1957-58	1971-72
McDonald, Brian	Chi., Buf.	2	12	0	0	0	29	8	0	0	0	2		1967-68	1970-71
• McDonald, Bucko	Det., Tor., NYR	11	448	35	88	123	206	63	6	1	7	24	3	1934-35	1944-45
McDonald, Butch	Det., Chi.	2	66	8	20	28	2	5	0	2	2	10		1939-40	1944-45
McDonald, Gerry	Hfd.	1	3	0	0	0	0	....	....	....	....	....		1981-82	1981-82
• McDonald, Jack	Mtl.W, Mtl., Que., Tor.	5	73	27	11	38	13	12	2	0	2	0		1917-18	1921-22
McDonald, John	NYR	1	43	10	9	19	6	....	....	....	....	....		1943-44	1943-44
McDonald, Lanny	Tor., Col., Cgy.	16	1111	500	506	1006	899	117	44	40	84	120	1	1973-74	1988-89
McDonald, Robert	NYR	1	1	0	0	0	0	....	....	....	....	....		1943-44	1943-44
McDonald, Terry	K.C.	1	8	0	1	1	6	....	....	....	....	....		1975-76	1975-76
McDonnell, Joe	Van., Pit.	3	50	2	10	12	34	....	....	....	....	....		1981-82	1985-86
• McDonnell, Moylan	Ham.	1	20	1	1	2	0	....	....	....	....	....		1920-21	1920-21
McDonough, Al	L.A., Pit., Atl., Det.	5	237	73	88	161	73	8	0	1	1	2		1970-71	1977-78
McDougal, Mike	NYR, Hfd.	4	61	8	10	18	43	....	....	....	....	....		1978-79	1982-83
McDougall, Bill	Det., Edm., T.B.	3	28	5	5	10	12	1	0	0	0	0		1990-91	1993-94
McElmury, Jim	Min., K.C., Col.	5	180	14	47	61	49	....	....	....	....	....		1972-73	1977-78
McEwen, Mike	NYR, Col., NYI, L.A., Wsh., Det., Hfd.	12	716	108	296	404	460	78	12	36	48	48	3	1976-77	1987-88
McFadden, Jim	Det., Chi.	7	412	100	126	226	89	49	10	9	19	30	1	1947-48	1953-54
McFadyen, Don	Chi.	4	179	12	33	45	77	12	2	2	4	5	1	1932-33	1935-36
McFall, Dan	Wpg.	2	9	0	1	1	0	....	....	....	....	....		1984-85	1985-86
McFarland, George	Chi.	1	2	0	0	0	0	....	....	....	....	....		1926-27	1926-27
McGeough, Jim	Wsh., Pit.	4	57	7	10	17	32	....	....	....	....	....		1981-82	1986-87
McGibbon, John	Mtl.	1	1	0	0	0	2	....	....	....	....	....		1942-43	1942-43
McGill, Bob	Tor., Chi., S.J., Det., NYI, Hfd.	13	705	17	55	72	1766	49	0	0	0	88		1981-82	1993-94
McGill, Jack	Mtl.	3	134	27	10	37	71	3	2	0	2	0		1934-35	1936-37
McGill, Jack G.	Bos.	4	97	23	36	59	42	27	7	4	11	17		1941-42	1946-47
McGregor, Sandy	NYR	1	2	0	0	0	2	....	....	....	....	....		1963-64	1963-64
McGuire, Mickey	Pit.	2	36	3	0	3	6	....	....	....	....	....		1926-27	1927-28
McHugh, Mike	Min., S.J.	4	20	1	0	1	16	....	....	....	....	....		1988-89	1991-92
McIlhargey, Jack	Phi., Van., Hfd.	8	393	11	36	47	1102	27	0	3	3	68		1974-75	1981-82
• McInenly, Bert	Det., NYA, Ott., Bos.	6	166	19	15	34	144	4	0	0	0	2		1930-31	1935-36
McIntosh, Bruce	Min.	1	2	0	0	0	0	....	....	....	....	....		1972-73	1972-73
McIntosh, Paul	Buf.	2	48	0	0	2	66	2	0	0	0	7		1974-75	1975-76
McIntyre, Jack	Bos., Chi., Det.	11	499	109	102	211	173	29	7	6	13	4		1949-50	1959-60
McIntyre, Larry	Tor.	2	41	0	3	3	26	....	....	....	....	....		1969-70	1972-73
McKay, Doug	Det.	1	....	....	....	....	....	1	0	0	0	0	1	1949-50	1949-50
McKay, Ray	Chi., Buf., Cal.	6	140	2	16	18	102	....	....	....	....	....		1968-69	1973-74
McKechnie, Walt	Min., Cal., Bos., Det., Wsh., Clev., Tor., Col.	16	955	214	392	606	469	15	7	5	12	9		1967-68	1982-83
McKegney, Ian	Chi.	1	3	0	0	0	2	....	....	....	....	....		1976-77	1976-77
McKegney, Tony	Buf., Que., Min., NYR, St. L., Det., Chi.	13	912	320	319	639	517	79	24	23	47	56		1978-79	1990-91
• McKell, Jack	Ott.	2	42	4	1	5	42	9	0	0	0	0	1	1919-20	1920-21
McKendry, Alex	NYI, Cgy.	4	46	3	6	9	21	6	2	2	4	0	1	1977-78	1980-81
McKenna, Sean	Buf., L.A., Tor.	9	414	82	80	162	181	15	1	2	3	2		1981-82	1989-90
McKenney, Don	Bos., NYR, Tor., Det., St.L.	13	798	237	345	582	211	58	18	29	47	10	1	1954-55	1967-68
McKenny, Jim	Tor., Min.	14	604	82	247	329	294	37	7	9	16	10		1965-66	1978-79
McKenzie, Brian	Pit.	1	6	1	1	2	4	....	....	....	....	....		1971-72	1971-72
McKenzie, John	Chi., Det., NYR, Bos.	12	691	206	268	474	917	69	15	32	47	133	2	1958-59	1971-72
McKinnon, Alex	Ham., NYA, Chi.	5	194	19	10	29	235	....	....	....	....	....		1924-25	1928-29
McKinnon, Bob	Chi.	1	2	0	0	0	0	....	....	....	....	....		1928-29	1928-29
• McKinnon, John	Mtl., Pit., Phi.	6	218	28	11	39	224	2	0	0	0	4		1925-26	1930-31
McLean, Don	Wsh.	1	9	0	0	0	6	....	....	....	....	....		1975-76	1975-76
• McLean, Fred	Que., Ham.	2	9	0	0	0	2	....	....	....	....	....		1919-20	1920-21
McLean, Jack	Tor.	3	67	14	24	38	76	13	2	2	4	8	1	1942-43	1944-45
McLean, Jeff	S.J.	1	6	1	0	1	0	....	....	....	....	....		1993-94	1993-94
• McLellan, John	Tor.	1	2	0	0	0	0	....	....	....	....	....		1951-52	1951-52
McLellan, Scott	Bos.	1	2	0	0	0	0	....	....	....	....	....		1982-83	1982-83
McLellan, Todd	NYI	1	5	1	1	2	0	....	....	....	....	....		1987-88	1987-88
• McLenahan, Roly	Det.	1	9	2	1	3	10	2	0	0	0	0		1945-46	1945-46
McLeod, Al	Det.	1	26	2	2	4	24	....	....	....	....	....		1973-74	1973-74

Name	NHL Teams	NHL Seasons	Regular Schedule GP	G	A	TP	PIM	Playoffs GP	G	A	TP	PIM	NHL Cup Wins	First NHL Season	Last NHL Season
McLeod, Jackie	NYR	5	106	14	23	37	12	7	0	0	0	0		1949-50	1954-55
McMahon, Mike	NYR, Min., Chi., Det., Pit., Buf.	8	224	15	68	83	171	14	3	7	10	4		1963-64	1971-72
• McMahon, Mike C.	Mtl., Bos.	3	57	7	18	25	102	13	1	2	3	30	1	1942-43	1945-46
McManama, Bob	Pit.	3	99	11	25	36	28	8	0	1	1	6		1973-74	1975-76
McManus, Sammy	Mtl.M., Bos.	2	26	0	1	1	8	1	0	0	0	0	1	1934-35	1936-37
McMurchy, Tom	Chi., Edm.	4	55	8	4	12	65	....	....	....	....	....		1983-84	1987-88
McNab, Max	Det.	4	128	16	19	35	24	25	1	0	1	4	1	1947-48	1950-51
McNab, Peter	Buf., Bos., Van., N.J.	14	954	363	450	813	179	107	40	42	82	20		1973-74	1986-87
McNabney, Sid	Mtl.	1	....	....	....	....	....	5	0	1	1	2		1950-51	1950-51
• McNamara, Howard	Mtl.	1	11	1	0	1	2	....	....	....	....	....		1919-20	1919-20
• McNaughton, George	Que.B.	1	1	0	0	0	0	....	....	....	....	....		1919-20	1919-20
McNeill, Billy	Det.	6	257	21	46	67	142	4	1	1	2	4		1956-57	1963-64
McNeill, Michael	Chi., Que.	2	63	5	11	16	18	....	....	....	....	....		1990-91	1991-92
McNeill, Stu	Det.	3	10	1	1	2	2	....	....	....	....	....		1957-58	1959-60
McPhee, George	NYR, N.J.	7	115	24	25	49	257	29	5	3	8	69		1982-83	1988-89
McRae, Chris	Tor., Det.	3	21	1	0	1	122	....	....	....	....	....		1987-88	1989-90
McReavy, Pat	Bos., Det.	4	55	5	10	15	4	20	3	3	6	9	1	1938-39	1941-42
McSheffrey, Bryan	Van., Buf.	3	90	13	7	20	44	....	....	....	....	....		1972-73	1974-75
McTaggart, Jim	Wsh.	2	71	3	10	13	205	....	....	....	....	....		1980-81	1981-82
McTavish, Gordon	St.L., Wpg.	2	11	1	3	4	2	....	....	....	....	....		1978-79	1979-80
• McVeigh, Charley	Chi., NYA	9	397	84	88	172	138	4	0	0	0	2		1926-27	1934-35
McVicar, Jack	Mtl.M.	2	88	2	4	6	63	2	0	0	0	2		1930-31	1931-32
Meagher, Rick	Mtl., Hfd., N.J., St.L.	12	691	144	165	309	383	62	8	7	15	41		1979-80	1990-91
Meehan, Gerry	Tor., Phi., Buf., Van., Atl., Wsh.	10	670	180	243	423	111	10	0	1	1	0		1968-69	1978-79
Meeke, Brent	Cal., Clev.	5	75	9	22	31	8	....	....	....	....	....		1972-73	1976-77
Meeker, Howie	Tor.	8	346	83	102	185	329	42	6	9	15	50	4	1946-47	1953-54
Meeker, Mike	Pit.	1	4	0	0	0	5	....	....	....	....	....		1978-79	1978-79
• Meeking, Harry	Tor., Det., Bos.	3	63	18	3	21	42	14	4	2	6	0	1	1917-18	1926-27
Meger, Paul	Mtl.	6	212	39	52	91	112	35	3	8	11	16	1	1949-50	1954-55
Meighan, Ron	Min., Pit.	2	48	3	7	10	18	....	....	....	....	....		1981-82	1982-83
Meissner, Barrie	Min.	2	6	0	1	1	4	....	....	....	....	....		1967-68	1968-69
Meissner, Dick	Bos., NYR	5	171	11	15	26	37	....	....	....	....	....		1959-60	1964-65
Melametsa, Anssi	Wpg.	1	27	0	3	3	2	....	....	....	....	....		1985-86	1985-86
Melin, Roger	Min.	2	3	0	0	0	0	....	....	....	....	....		1980-81	1981-82
Mellor, Tom	Det.	2	26	2	4	6	25	....	....	....	....	....		1973-74	1974-75
Melnyk, Gerry	Det., Chi., St.L.	6	269	39	77	116	34	53	6	6	12	6		1955-56	1967-68
Melnyk, Larry	Bos., Edm., NYR, Van.	10	432	11	63	74	686	66	2	9	11	127	1	1980-81	1989-90
Melrose, Barry	Wpg., Tor., Det.	6	300	10	23	33	728	7	0	2	2	38		1979-80	1985-86
Menard, Hillary	Chi.	1	1	0	0	0	0	....	....	....	....	....		1953-54	1953-54
Menard, Howie	Det., L.A., Chi., Oak.	4	151	23	42	65	87	19	3	7	10	36		1963-64	1969-70
Mercredi, Vic	Atl.	1	2	0	0	0	0	....	....	....	....	....		1974-75	1974-75
Meredith, Greg	Cgy.	2	38	6	4	10	8	5	3	1	4	4		1980-81	1982-83
Merkosky, Glenn	Hfd., N.J., Det.	5	66	5	12	17	22	....	....	....	....	....		1981-82	1989-90
Meronek, Bill	Mtl.	2	19	5	8	13	0	1	0	0	0	0		1939-40	1942-43
Merrick, Wayne	St.L., Cal., Clev., NYI	12	774	191	265	456	303	102	19	30	49	30	4	1972-73	1983-84
• Merrill, Horace	Ott.	2	11	0	0	0	0	....	....	....	....	....	1	1917-18	1919-20
Messier, Mitch	Min.	4	20	0	2	2	11	....	....	....	....	....		1987-88	1990-91
Messier, Paul	Col.	1	9	0	0	0	4	....	....	....	....	....		1978-79	1978-79
Metcalfe, Scott	Edm., Buf.	3	19	1	2	3	18	....	....	....	....	....		1987-88	1989-90
Metz, Don	Tor.	8	172	20	35	55	42	47	7	8	15	10	5	1939-40	1948-49
• Metz, Nick	Tor.	12	518	131	119	250	149	76	19	20	39	31	4	1934-35	1947-48
Michaluk, Art	Chi.	1	5	0	0	0	0	....	....	....	....	....		1947-48	1947-48
Michaluk, John	Chi.	1	1	0	0	0	0	....	....	....	....	....		1950-51	1950-51
Michayluk, Dave	Phi., Pit.	3	14	2	6	8	8	7	1	1	2	0	1	1981-82	1991-92
Micheletii, Pat	Min.	1	12	2	0	2	8	....	....	....	....	....		1987-88	1987-88
Micheletti, Joe	St.L., Col.	3	158	11	60	71	114	11	1	11	12	10		1979-80	1981-82
• Mickey, Larry	Chi., NYR., Tor., Mtl., L.A., Phi., Buf.	11	292	39	53	92	160	9	1	0	1	10		1964-65	1974-75
Mickoski, Nick	NYR, Chi., Det., Bos.	13	703	158	184	342	319	18	1	6	7	6		1947-48	1959-60
Middendorf, Max	Que., Edm.	4	13	2	4	6	6	....	....	....	....	....		1986-87	1990-91
Middleton, Rick	NYR, Bos.	14	1005	448	540	988	157	114	45	55	100	19		1974-75	1987-88
Miehm, Kevin	St.L.	2	22	1	4	5	8	2	0	1	1	0		1992-93	1993-94
Migay, Rudy	Tor.	10	418	59	92	151	293	15	1	0	1	20		1949-50	1959-60
Mikita, Stan	Chi.	22	1394	541	926	1467	1270	155	59	91	150	169	1	1958-59	1979-80
Mikkelson, Bill	L.A., N.Y.I., Wsh.	4	147	4	18	22	105	....	....	....	....	....		1971-72	1976-77
Mikol, Jim	Tor., NYR	2	34	1	4	5	8	....	....	....	....	....		1962-63	1964-65
Milbury, Mike	Bos.	12	754	49	189	238	1552	86	4	24	28	219		1975-76	1986-87
• Milks, Hib	Pit., Phi., NYR, Ott.	8	314	87	41	128	179	10	0	0	0	2		1925-26	1932-33
Millar, Hugh	Det.	1	4	0	0	0	0	1	0	0	0	0		1946-47	1946-47
Millar, Mike	Hfd., Wsh., Bos., Tor.	5	78	18	18	36	12	....	....	....	....	....		1986-87	1990-91
Miller, Bill	Mtl.M., Mtl.	3	95	7	3	10	16	12	0	0	0	0	1	1934-35	1936-37
Miller, Bob	Bos., Col., L.A.	6	404	75	119	194	220	36	4	7	11	27		1977-78	1984-85
Miller, Brad	Buf., Ott., Cgy.	6	82	1	5	6	321	....	....	....	....	....		1988-89	1993-94
• Miller, Earl	Chi., Tor.	5	116	19	14	33	124	10	1	0	1	6	1	1927-28	1931-32
Miller, Jack	Chi.	2	17	0	0	0	4	....	....	....	....	....		1949-50	1950-51
Miller, Jay	Bos., L.A.	7	446	40	44	84	1723	48	2	3	5	243		1985-86	1991-92
Miller, Paul	Col.	1	3	0	3	3	0	....	....	....	....	....		1981-82	1981-82
Miller, Perry	Det.	4	217	10	51	61	387	....	....	....	....	....		1977-78	1980-81
Miller, Tom	Det., NYI	4	118	16	25	41	34	....	....	....	....	....		1970-71	1974-75
Miller, Warren	NYR, Hfd.	4	262	40	50	90	137	6	1	0	1	0		1979-80	1982-83
Miner, John	Edm.	1	14	2	3	5	16	....	....	....	....	....		1987-88	1987-88
Minor, Gerry	Van.	5	140	11	21	32	173	12	1	3	4	25		1979-80	1983-84
Miszuk, John	Det., Chi., Phi., Min.	6	237	7	39	46	232	19	0	3	3	19		1963-64	1969-70
Mitchell, Bill	Det.	1	1	0	0	0	0	....	....	....	....	....		1963-64	1963-64
Mitchell, Herb	Bos.	2	53	6	0	6	38	....	....	....	....	....		1924-25	1925-26
Mitchell, Red	Chi.	3	83	4	5	9	67	....	....	....	....	....		1941-42	1944-45
Mitchell, Roy	Min.	1	3	0	0	0	0	....	....	....	....	....		1992-93	1992-93
Moe, Billy	NYR	5	261	11	42	53	163	1	0	0	0	0		1944-45	1948-49
Moffat, Lyle	Tor., Wpg.	3	97	12	16	28	51	....	....	....	....	....		1972-73	1979-80
Moffat, Ron	Det.	3	36	1	1	2	8	7	0	0	0	0		1932-33	1934-35
Moher, Mike	N.J.	1	9	0	1	1	28	....	....	....	....	....		1982-83	1982-83
Mohns, Doug	Bos., Chi., Min., Atl., Wsh.	22	1390	248	462	710	1250	94	14	36	50	122		1953-54	1974-75
Mohns, Lloyd	NYR	1	1	0	0	0	0	....	....	....	....	....		1943-44	1943-44
Mokosak, Carl	Cgy., L.A., Phi., Pit., Bos.	6	83	11	15	26	170	1	0	0	0	0		1981-82	1988-89
Mokosak, John	Det.	2	41	0	2	2	96	....	....	....	....	....		1988-89	1989-90
Molin, Lars	Van.	3	172	33	65	98	37	19	2	9	11	7		1981-82	1983-84
Moller, Mike	Buf., Edm.	7	134	15	28	43	41	3	0	1	1	0		1980-81	1986-87
Molloy, Mitch	Buf.	1	2	0	0	0	10	....	....	....	....	....		1989-90	1989-90
Molyneaux, Larry	NYR	2	45	0	1	1	20	3	0	0	0	8		1937-38	1938-39
Monahan, Garry	Mtl., Det., L.A., Tor., Van.	12	748	116	169	285	484	22	3	1	4	13		1967-68	1978-79
Monahan, Hartland	Cal., NYR, Wsh., Pit., L.A., St.L.	7	334	61	80	141	163	6	0	0	0	4		1973-74	1980-81
• Mondou, Armand	Mtl.	12	385	47	71	118	99	35	3	5	8	12	2	1928-29	1939-40
Mondou, Pierre	Mtl.	9	548	194	262	456	179	69	17	28	45	26	3	1976-77	1984-85
Mongrain, Bob	Buf., L.A.	6	83	13	14	27	14	11	1	2	3	2		1979-80	1985-86
Monteith, Hank	Det.	3	77	5	12	17	6	4	0	0	0	0		1968-69	1970-71
Moore, Dickie	Mtl., Tor., St.L.	14	719	261	347	608	652	135	46	64	110	122	6	1951-52	1967-68
Moran, Amby	Mtl., Chi.	2	35	1	1	2	24	....	....	....	....	....		1926-27	1927-28
• Morenz, Howie	Mtl., Chi., NYR	14	550	270	197	467	563	47	21	11	32	68	3	1923-24	1936-37
Moretto, Angelo	Clev.	1	5	1	2	3	2	....	....	....	....	....		1976-77	1976-77
Morin, Pete	Mtl.	1	31	10	12	22	7	1	0	0	0	0		1941-42	1941-42
Morris, Bernie	Bos.	1	6	2	0	2	0	....	....	....	....	....		1924-25	1924-25
Morris, Elwyn	Tor., NYR	4	135	13	29	42	58	18	4	2	6	16	1	1943-44	1948-49
Morris, Jon	N.J., S.J., Bos.	6	103	16	33	49	47	11	1	7	8	25		1988-89	1993-94
Morrison, Dave	L.A., Van.	4	39	3	3	6	4	....	....	....	....	....		1980-81	1984-85
Morrison, Don	Det., Chi.	3	112	18	28	46	12	3	0	1	1	0		1947-48	1950-51
Morrison, Doug	Bos.	4	23	7	3	10	15	....	....	....	....	....		1979-80	1984-85
Morrison, Gary	Phi.	3	43	1	15	16	70	5	0	1	1	2		1979-80	1981-82
Morrison, George	St.L.	2	115	17	21	38	13	3	0	0	0	0		1970-71	1971-72
Morrison, Jim	Bos., Tor., Det., NYR, Pit.	12	704	40	160	200	542	36	0	12	12	38		1951-52	1970-71
Morrison, John	NYA	1	18	0	0	0	0	....	....	....	....	....		1925-26	1925-26
Morrison, Kevin	Col.	1	41	4	11	15	23	....	....	....	....	....		1979-80	1979-80
Morrison, Lew	Phi., Atl., Wsh., Pit.	9	564	39	52	91	107	17	0	0	0	2		1969-70	1977-78
Morrison, Mark	NYR	2	10	1	1	2	0	....	....	....	....	....		1981-82	1983-84
Morrison, Roderick	Det.	1	34	8	7	15	4	3	0	0	0	0		1947-48	1947-48
Morrow, Ken	NYI	10	550	17	88	105	309	127	11	22	33	97	4	1979-80	1988-89

Brad Miller

Jon Morris

Brian Mullen

Ted Nolan

Lee Norwood

Gary Nylund

Mike O'Connell

John Ogrodnick

			Regular Schedule					Playoffs							
Name	NHL Teams	NHL Seasons	GP	G	A	TP	PIM	GP	G	A	TP	PIM	NHL Cup Wins	First NHL Season	Last NHL Season
Morton, Dean	Det.	1	1	1	0	1	2	....	....	....	....	....		1989-90	1989-90
Mortson, Gus	Tor., Chi., Det.	13	797	46	152	198	1380	54	5	8	13	68	4	1946-47	1958-59
Mosdell, Kenny	Bro., Mtl., Chi.	16	693	141	168	309	475	79	16	13	29	48	4	1941-42	1958-59
• Mosienko, Bill	Chi.	14	711	258	282	540	117	22	10	4	14	15		1941-42	1954-55
Mott, Morris	Cal.	3	199	18	32	50	49	....	....	....	....	....		1972-73	1974-75
Motter, Alex	Bos., Det.	8	267	39	64	103	135	40	3	9	12	41	1	1934-35	1942-43
Moxey, Jim	Cal., Clev., L.A.	3	127	22	27	49	59	....	....	....	....	....		1974-75	1976-77
Mulhern, Richard	Atl., L.A., Tor., Wpg.	6	303	27	93	120	217	7	0	3	3	5		1975-76	1980-81
Mullen, Brian	Wpg., NYR, S.J., NYI	11	832	260	362	622	414	62	12	18	30	30		1982-83	1992-93
Muloin, Wayne	Det., Oak., Cal., Min.	3	147	3	21	24	93	11	0	0	0	2		1963-64	1970-71
Mulvenna, Glenn	Pit., Phi.	2	2	0	0	0	4	....	....	....	....	....		1991-92	1992-93
Mulvey, Grant	Chi., N.J.	10	586	149	135	284	816	42	10	5	15	70		1974-75	1983-84
Mulvey, Paul	Wsh., Pit., L.A.	4	225	30	51	81	613	....	....	....	....	....		1978-79	1981-82
• Mummery, Harry	Tor., Que., Mtl., Ham.	6	106	33	13	46	161	7	1	4	5	0		1917-18	1922-23
• Munro, Dunc	Mtl.	8	239	28	18	46	170	25	3	2	5	24	1	1924-25	1931-32
Munro, Gerry	Mtl., Tor.	2	33	1	0	1	22	....	....	....	....	....		1924-25	1925-26
Murdoch, Bob J.	Mtl., L.A., Atl., Cgy.	12	757	60	218	278	764	69	4	18	22	92	2	1970-71	1981-82
Murdoch, Bob L.	Cal., Clev., St.L.	4	260	72	85	157	127	....	....	....	....	....		1975-76	1978-79
Murdoch, Don	NYR, Edm., Det.	5	320	121	117	238	155	24	10	8	18	16		1976-77	1981-82
Murdoch, Murray	NYR	11	507	84	108	192	197	55	9	12	21	28		1926-27	1936-37
Murphy, Brian	Det.	1	1	0	0	0	0	....	....	....	....	....		1974-75	1974-75
Murphy, Mike	St.L. NYR, L.A.	12	831	238	318	556	514	66	13	23	36	54		1971-72	1982-83
Murphy, Rob	Van., Ott., L.A.	7	125	9	12	21	152	4	0	0	0	2		1987-88	1993-94
Murphy, Ron	NYR, Chi., Det., Bos.	18	889	205	274	479	460	53	7	8	15	26	1	1952-53	1969-70
Murray, Allan	NYA	7	277	5	9	14	163	14	0	0	0	8		1933-34	1939-40
Murray, Bob F.	Chi.	15	1008	132	382	514	873	112	19	37	56	0		1975-76	1989-90
Murray, Bob J.	Atl., Van.	4	194	6	16	22	98	9	1	1	2	15		1973-74	1976-77
Murray, Jim	L.A.	1	30	0	2	2	14	....	....	....	....	....		1967-68	1967-68
Murray, Ken	Tor., N.Y.I., Det., K.C.	5	106	1	10	11	135	....	....	....	....	....		1969-70	1975-76
Murray, Leo	Mtl.	1	6	0	0	0	2	....	....	....	....	....		1932-33	1932-33
Murray, Mike	Phi.	1	1	0	0	0	0	....	....	....	....	....		1987-88	1987-88
Murray, Pat	Phi.	2	25	3	1	4	15	....	....	....	....	....		1990-91	1991-92
Murray, Randy	Tor.	1	3	0	0	0	2	....	....	....	....	....		1969-70	1969-70
Murray, Terry	Cal., Phi., Det., Wsh.	8	302	4	76	80	199	18	2	2	4	10		1972-73	1981-82
Myers, Hap	Buf.	1	13	0	0	0	6	....	....	....	....	....		1970-71	1970-71
Myles, Vic	NYR	1	45	6	9	15	57	....	....	....	....	....		1942-43	1942-43

N

Nachbaur, Don	Hfd., Edm., Phi.	8	223	23	46	69	465	11	1	1	2	24		1980-81	1989-90
Nahrgang, Jim	Det.	3	57	5	12	17	34	....	....	....	....	....		1974-75	1976-77
Nanne, Lou	Min.	11	635	68	157	225	356	32	4	10	14	9		1967-68	1977-78
Nantais, Richard	Min.	3	63	5	4	9	79	....	....	....	....	....		1974-75	1976-77
Napier, Mark	Mtl., Min., Edm., Buf.	11	767	235	306	541	157	82	18	24	42	11	2	1978-79	1988-89
Nattrass, Ralph	Chi.	4	223	18	38	56	308	....	....	....	....	....		1946-47	1949-50
Nattress, Ric	Mtl., St.L., Cgy., Tor., Phi.	11	536	29	135	164	377	67	5	10	15	60	1	1982-83	1992-93
Natyshak, Mike	Que.	1	4	0	0	0	0	....	....	....	....	....		1987-88	1987-88
Nechaev, Victor	L.A.	1	3	1	0	1	0	....	....	....	....	....		1982-83	1982-83
Nedomansky, Vaclav	Det., NYR, St.L.	6	421	122	156	278	88	7	3	5	8	0		1977-78	1982-83
Neely, Bob	Tor., Col.	5	283	39	59	98	266	26	5	7	12	15		1973-74	1977-78
Neilson, Jim	NYR, Cal., Clev.	16	1023	69	299	368	904	65	1	17	18	61		1962-63	1977-78
Nelson, Gordie	Tor.	1	3	0	0	0	11	....	....	....	....	....		1969-70	1969-70
Nemeth, Steve	NYR	1	12	2	0	2	2	....	....	....	....	....		1987-88	1987-88
Nesterenko, Eric	Tor., Chi.	21	1219	250	324	574	1273	124	13	24	37	127	1	1951-52	1971-72
Nethery, Lance	NYR, Edm.	2	41	11	14	25	14	14	5	3	8	9		1980-81	1981-82
Neufeld, Ray	Hfd., Win., Bos.	11	595	157	200	357	816	28	8	6	14	55		1979-80	1989-90
• Neville, Mike	Tor., NYA	4	62	6	3	9	14	2	0	0	0	0	1	1917-18	1930-31
Nevin, Bob	Tor., NYR, Min., L.A.	18	1128	307	419	726	211	84	16	18	34	24	2	1957-58	1975-76
Newberry, John	Mtl., Hfd.	4	22	0	4	4	6	2	0	0	0	0		1982-83	1985-86
Newell, Rick	Det.	2	7	0	0	0	0	....	....	....	....	....		1972-73	1973-74
Newman, Dan	NYR, Mtl., Edm.	4	126	17	24	41	63	3	0	0	0	4		1976-77	1979-80
Newman, John	Det.	1	8	1	1	2	0	....	....	....	....	....		1930-31	1930-31
Nicholson, Al	Bos.	2	19	0	1	1	4	....	....	....	....	....		1955-56	1956-57
Nicholson, Edward	Det.	1	1	0	0	0	0	....	....	....	....	....		1947-48	1947-48
Nicholson, Graeme	Bos., Col., NYR	3	669	245	376	621	167	97	34	57	91	33		1978-79	1982-83
Nicholson, John	Chi.	1	2	1	0	1	0	....	....	....	....	....		1937-38	1937-38
Nicholson, Neil	Oak., N.Y.I.	4	39	3	1	4	23	2	0	0	0	0		1969-70	1977-78
Nicholson, Paul	Wsh.	3	62	4	8	12	18	....	....	....	....	....		1974-75	1976-77
Niekamp, Jim	Det.	2	29	0	2	2	27	....	....	....	....	....		1970-71	1971-72
Nienhuis, Kraig	Bos.	3	87	20	16	36	39	2	0	0	0	14		1985-86	1987-88
• Nighbor, Frank	Ott., Tor.	13	348	136	60	196	241	36	11	9	20	27	4	1917-18	1929-30
Nigro, Frank	Tor.	2	68	8	18	26	39	3	0	0	0	2		1982-83	1983-84
Nilan, Chris	Mtl., NYR, Bos.	13	688	110	115	225	3043	111	8	9	17	541	1	1979-80	1991-92
Nill, Jim	St.L., Van., Bos., Wpg., Det.	9	524	58	87	145	854	59	10	5	15	203		1981-82	1989-90
Nilsson, Ulf	NYR	4	170	57	112	169	85	25	8	14	22	27		1978-79	1982-83
Nistico, Lou	Col.	1	3	0	0	0	0	....	....	....	....	....		1977-78	1977-78
• Noble, Reg	Tor., Mtl.M., Det.	16	526	167	79	246	807	32	4	5	9	39	3	1917-18	1932-33
Noel, Claude	Wsh.	1	7	0	0	0	0	....	....	....	....	....		1979-80	1979-80
Nolan, Pat	Tor.	1	2	0	0	0	0	....	....	....	....	....	1	1921-22	1921-22
Nolan, Ted	Det., Pit.	3	78	6	16	22	105	....	....	....	....	....		1981-82	1985-86
Nolet, Simon	Phi., K.C., Pit., Col.	10	562	150	182	332	187	34	6	3	9	8	1	1967-68	1976-77
Nordmark, Robert	St. L., Van.	4	236	13	70	83	254	7	3	2	5	8		1987-88	1990-91
Noris, Joe	Pit., St.L., Buf.	3	55	2	5	7	22	....	....	....	....	....		1971-72	1973-74
Norrish, Rod	Min.	2	21	3	3	6	2	....	....	....	....	....		1973-74	1974-75
• Northcott, Baldy	Mtl.M., Chi.	11	446	133	112	245	273	31	8	5	13	14	1	1928-29	1938-39
Norwich, Craig	Wpg., St.L., Col.	2	104	17	58	75	60	....	....	....	....	....		1979-80	1980-81
Norwood, Lee	Que., Wsh., St.L., Det., N.J., Hfd., Cgy.	12	503	58	153	211	1099	65	6	22	28	171		1980-81	1993-94
Novy, Milan	Wsh.	1	73	18	30	48	16	2	0	0	0	0		1982-83	1982-83
Nowak, Hank	Pit., Det., Bos.	4	180	26	29	55	161	3	1	0	1	8		1973-74	1976-77
Nykoluk, Mike	Tor.	1	32	3	1	4	20	....	....	....	....	....		1956-57	1956-57
Nylund, Gary	Tor., Chi., NYI	11	608	32	139	171	1235	24	0	6	6	63		1982-83	1992-93
Nyrop, Bill	Mtl., Min.	4	207	12	51	63	101	35	1	7	8	22	3	1975-76	1981-82
Nystrom, Bob	NYI	14	900	235	278	513	1248	157	39	44	83	236	4	1972-73	1985-86

O

• Oatman, Russell	Det., Mtl.M., NYR	3	124	20	9	29	100	17	1	0	1	18		1926-27	1928-29
O'Brien, Dennis	Min., Col., Clev., Bos.	10	592	31	91	122	1017	34	1	2	3	101		1970-71	1979-80
O'Brien, Obie	Bos.	1	2	0	0	0	0	....	....	....	....	....		1955-56	1955-56
O'Callahan, Jack	Chi., N.J.	7	389	27	104	131	541	32	4	11	15	41		1982-83	1988-89
O'Connell, Mike	Chi., Bos., Det.	13	860	105	334	439	605	82	8	24	32	64		1977-78	1989-90
• O'Connor, Buddy	Mtl., NYR	10	509	140	257	397	34	53	15	21	36	6	2	1941-42	1950-51
Oddleifson, Chris	Bos., Van.	9	524	95	191	286	464	14	1	6	7	8		1972-73	1980-81
Odelin, Selmar	Edm.	3	18	0	2	2	35	....	....	....	....	....		1985-86	1988-89
O'Donnell, Fred	Bos.	2	115	15	11	26	98	5	0	1	1	5		1972-73	1973-74
O'Donoghue, Don	Oak., Cal.	3	125	18	17	35	35	3	0	0	0	0		1969-70	1971-72
Odrowski, Gerry	Det., Oak., St.L.	6	299	12	19	31	111	30	0	1	1	16		1960-61	1971-72
O'Dwyer, Bill	L.A., Bos.	5	120	9	13	22	113	10	0	0	0	2		1983-84	1989-90
O'Flaherty, Gerry	Tor., Van., Atl.	8	438	99	95	194	168	7	2	2	4	6		1971-72	1978-79
O'Flaherty, John	NYA, Bro.	2	21	5	1	6	0	....	....	....	....	....		1940-41	1941-42
Ogilvie, Brian	Chi., St.L.	6	90	15	21	36	29	....	....	....	....	....		1972-73	1978-79
O'Grady, George	Mtl.M.	1	4	0	0	0	0	....	....	....	....	....		1917-18	1917-18
Ogrodnick, John	Det., Que., NYR	14	928	402	425	827	260	41	18	8	26	6		1979-80	1992-93
Ojanen, Janne	N.J.	4	98	21	23	44	28	3	0	2	2	0		1988-89	1992-93
Okerlund, Todd	NYI	1	4	0	0	0	2	....	....	....	....	....		1987-88	1987-88
• Oliver, Harry	Bos., NYA	11	473	127	85	212	147	35	10	6	16	22	1	1926-27	1936-37
Oliver, Murray	Det., Bos., Tor., Min.	17	1127	274	454	728	319	35	9	16	25	10		1957-58	1974-75
Olmstead, Bert	Chi., Mtl., Tor.	14	848	181	421	602	884	115	16	42	58	1	5	1948-49	1961-62
Olsen, Darryl	Cgy.	1	1	0	0	0	0	....	....	....	....	....		1991-92	1991-92
Olson, Dennis	Det.	1	4	0	0	0	0	....	....	....	....	....		1957-58	1957-58
O'Neil, Paul	Van., Bos.	2	6	0	0	0	0	....	....	....	....	....		1973-74	1975-76
O'Neill, Jim	Bos., Mtl.	6	165	6	30	36	109	11	1	1	2	13		1933-34	1941-42

Name	NHL Teams	NHL Seasons	Regular Schedule GP	G	A	TP	PIM	Playoffs GP	G	A	TP	PIM	NHL Cup Wins	First NHL Season	Last NHL Season
• O'Neill, Tom	Tor.	2	66	10	12	22	53	4	0	0	0	6	1	1943-44	1944-45
Orban, Bill	Chi., Min.	3	114	8	15	23	673	3	0	0	0	0		1967-68	1969-70
O'Ree, Willie	Bos.	2	45	4	10	14	26	....	....	....	....	....		1957-58	1960-61
O'Regan, Tom	Pit.	3	60	5	12	17	10	....	....	....	....	....		1983-84	1985-86
O'Reilly, Terry	Bos.	14	891	204	402	606	2095	108	25	42	67	335		1971-72	1984-85
Orlando, Gaetano	Buf.	3	98	18	26	44	51	5	0	4	4	14		1984-85	1986-87
Orlando, Jimmy	Det.	6	200	7	24	31	375	36	0	9	9	105	1	1936-37	1942-43
Orleski, Dave	Mtl.	2	2	0	0	0	0	....	....	....	....	....		1980-81	1981-82
Orr, Bobby	Bos., Chi.	12	657	270	645	915	953	74	26	66	92	107	2	1966-67	1978-79
Osborne, Keith	St.L., T.B.	2	16	1	3	4	16	....	....	....	....	....		1989-90	1992-93
Osburn, Randy	Tor., Phi.	2	27	0	2	2	0	....	....	....	....	....		1972-73	1974-75
O'Shea, Danny	Min., Chi., St.L.	5	369	64	115	179	265	39	3	7	10	62		1968-69	1972-73
O'Shea, Kevin	Buf., St.L.	3	134	13	18	31	85	12	2	1	3	10		1970-71	1972-73
Osiecki, Mark	Cgy., Ott., Wpg., Min.	2	93	3	11	14	43	....	....	....	....	....		1991-92	1992-93
Otevrel, Jaroslav	S.J.	2	16	3	4	7	2	....	....	....	....	....		1992-93	1993-94
Ouelette, Eddie	Chi.	1	43	3	2	5	11	1	0	0	0	0		1935-36	1935-36
Ouelette, Gerry	Bos.	1	34	5	4	9	0	....	....	....	....	....		1960-1	1960-61
Owchar, Dennis	Pit., Col.	6	288	30	85	115	200	10	1	1	2	8		1974-75	1979-80
• Owen, George	Bos.	5	192	44	33	77	151	21	2	5	7	25	1	1928-29	1932-33

P

Name	NHL Teams	NHL Seasons	Regular Schedule GP	G	A	TP	PIM	Playoffs GP	G	A	TP	PIM	NHL Cup Wins	First NHL Season	Last NHL Season
Pachal, Clayton	Bos., Col.	3	35	2	3	5	95	....	....	....	....	....		1976-77	1978-79
Paddock, John	Wsh., Phi., Que.	5	87	8	14	22	86	5	2	0	2	0		1975-76	1982-83
Paiement, Rosaire	Phi., Van.	5	190	48	52	100	343	3	3	0	3	0		1967-68	1971-72
Paiement, Wilf	K.C. Col., Tor., Que., NYR, Buf., Pit.	14	946	356	458	814	1757	69	18	17	35	185		1974-75	1987-88
Palangio, Peter	Mtl., Det., Chi.	5	71	13	10	23	28	7	0	0	0	0	1	1926-27	1937-38
Palazzari, Aldo	Bos., NYR	1	35	8	3	11	4	....	....	....	....	....		1943-44	1943-44
Palazzari, Doug	St.L.	4	108	18	20	38	23	2	0	0	0	0		1974-75	1978-79
Palmer, Brad	Min., Bos.	3	168	32	38	70	58	29	9	5	14	16		1980-81	1982-83
Palmer, Rob H.	Chi.	3	16	0	3	3	2	....	....	....	....	....		1973-74	1975-76
Palmer, Rob R.	L.A., N.J.	6	320	9	101	110	115	8	1	2	3	6		1977-78	1983-84
• Panagabko, Ed	Bos.	2	29	0	3	3	38	....	....	....	....	....		1955-56	1956-57
Papike, Joe	Chi.	3	21	3	3	6	4	5	0	2	2	0		1940-41	1944-45
Pappin, Jim	Tor., Chi., Cal., Clev.	14	767	278	295	573	667	92	33	34	67	101	2	1963-64	1976-77
Paradise, Bob	Min., Atl., Pit., Wsh.	8	368	8	54	62	393	12	0	1	1	19		1971-72	1978-79
Pargeter, George	Mtl.	1	4	0	0	0	0	....	....	....	....	....		1946-47	1946-47
Parise, J.P.	Bos., Tor., Min., NYI, Clev.	14	890	238	356	594	706	86	27	31	58	87		1965-66	1978-79
Parizeau, Michel	St.L., Phi.	1	58	3	14	17	18	....	....	....	....	....		1971-72	1971-72
Park, Brad	NYR, Bos., Det.	17	1113	213	683	896	1429	161	35	90	125	217		1968-69	1984-85
Parker, Jeff	Buf., Hfd.	5	141	16	19	35	163	5	0	0	0	26		1986-87	1990-91
Parkes, Ernie	Mtl.M.	1	17	0	0	0	2	....	....	....	....	....		1924-25	1924-25
Parsons, George	Tor.	3	64	12	13	25	17	7	3	2	5	11		1936-37	1938-39
Pasek, Dusan	Min.	1	48	4	10	14	30	2	1	0	1	0		1988-89	1988-89
Pasin, Dave	Bos., L.A.	2	76	18	19	37	50	3	0	1	1	0		1985-86	1988-89
Paslawski, Greg	Mtl., St.L., Wpg., Buf., Que., Phi., Cgy.	11	650	187	185	372	169	60	19	13	32	25		1983-84	1993-94
Paterson, Joe	Det., Phi., L.A., NYR	9	291	19	37	56	829	22	3	4	7	77		1980-81	1988-89
Paterson, Mark	Hfd.	4	29	3	3	6	33	....	....	....	....	....		1982-83	1985-86
Paterson, Rick	Chi.	9	430	50	43	93	136	61	7	10	17	51		1978-79	1986-87
Patey, Doug	Wsh.	3	45	4	2	6	8	....	....	....	....	....		1976-77	1978-79
Patey, Larry	Cal., St.L., NYR	12	717	153	163	316	631	40	8	10	18	57		1973-74	1984-85
Patrick, Craig	Cal., St.L., K.C., Min. Wsh.	8	401	72	91	163	61	2	0	1	1	0		1971-72	1978-79
Patrick, Glenn	St.L., Cal., Clev.	3	38	2	3	5	72	....	....	....	....	....		1973-74	1976-77
• Patrick, Lester	NYR	1	1	0	0	0	2	....	....	....	....	....		1926-27	1926-27
• Patrick, Lynn	NYR	10	455	145	190	335	240	44	10	6	16	22	1	1934-35	1945-46
Patrick, Muzz	NYR	5	166	5	26	31	133	25	4	0	4	34	1	1937-38	1945-46
Patrick, Steve	Buf., NYR, Que.	6	250	40	68	108	242	12	0	1	1	12		1980-81	1985-86
Patterson, Colin	Cgy., Buf.	10	504	96	109	205	239	85	12	17	29	57	1	1983-84	1992-93
Patterson, Dennis	K.C., Phi.	3	138	6	22	28	67	....	....	....	....	....		1974-75	1979-80
• Patterson, George	Bos., Det., St.L., Tor., Mtl., NYA	9	289	51	27	78	218	3	0	0	0	2		1926-27	1934-35
• Paul, Butch	Det.	1	3	0	0	0	0	....	....	....	....	....		1964-65	1964-65
• Paulhus, Rollie	Mtl.	1	33	0	0	0	0	....	....	....	....	....		1925-26	1925-26
Pavelich, Mark	NYR, Min., S.J.	7	355	137	192	329	340	23	7	17	24	14		1981-82	1991-92
Pavelich, Marty	Det.	10	634	93	159	252	454	91	13	15	28	74	4	1947-48	1956-57
Pavese, Jim	St.L., NYR, Det., Hfd.	8	328	13	44	57	689	34	0	6	6	81		1981-82	1988-89
• Payer, Evariste	Mtl.	1	1	0	0	0	0	....	....	....	....	....		1917-18	1917-18
Payne, Steve	Min.	10	613	228	238	466	435	71	35	35	70	60		1978-79	1987-88
Paynter, Kent	Chi., Wsh., Wpg., Ott.	7	37	1	3	4	69	4	0	0	0	10		1987-88	1993-94
Pearson, Mel	NYR, Pit.	5	38	2	6	8	25	....	....	....	....	....		1949-50	1967-68
Pedersen, Allen	Bos., Min., Hfd.	8	428	5	36	41	487	64	0	0	0	91		1986-87	1993-94
Pederson, Barry	Bos., Van., Pit., Hfd.	12	701	238	416	654	472	34	22	30	52	25		1980-81	1991-92
Peer, Bert	Det.	1	1	0	0	0	0	....	....	....	....	....		1939-40	1939-40
Peirson, Johnny	Bos.	11	545	153	173	326	315	49	9	17	26	26		1946-47	1957-58
Pelensky, Perry	Chi.	1	4	0	0	0	5	....	....	....	....	....		1983-84	1983-84
Pelletier, Roger	Phi.	1	1	0	0	0	0	....	....	....	....	....		1967-68	1967-68
Peloffy, Andre	Wsh.	1	9	0	0	0	2	....	....	....	....	....		1974-75	1974-75
Pelyk, Mike	Tor.	9	441	26	88	114	566	40	0	3	3	41		1967-68	1977-78
Pennington, Cliff	Mtl., Bos.	3	101	17	42	59	6	....	....	....	....	....		1960-61	1962-63
Perlini, Fred	Tor.	2	8	2	3	5	0	....	....	....	....	....		1981-82	1983-84
Perreault, Fern	NYR	2	3	0	0	0	0	....	....	....	....	....		1947-48	1949-50
Perreault, Gilbert	Buf.	17	1191	512	814	1326	500	90	33	70	103	44		1970-71	1986-87
Perry, Brian	Oak., Buf.	3	96	16	29	45	24	8	1	1	2	4		1968-69	1970-71
Persson, Stefan	NYI	9	622	52	317	369	574	102	7	50	57	69	4	1977-78	1985-86
Pesut, George	Cal.	2	92	3	22	25	130	....	....	....	....	....		1974-75	1975-76
Peters, Frank	NYR	1	43	0	0	0	59	4	0	0	0	2		1930-31	1930-31
Peters, Garry	Mtl., NYR, Phi., Bos.	8	331	34	34	68	261	9	2	2	4	31	1	1964-65	1971-72
Peters, Jim	Det., Chi., Mtl., Bos.	9	574	125	150	275	186	60	5	9	14	22	3	1945-46	1953-54
Peters, Jimy	Det., L.A.	9	309	37	36	73	48	11	0	2	2	2		1964-65	1974-75
Peters, Steve	Col.	1	2	0	1	1	0	....	....	....	....	....		1979-80	1979-80
Peterson, Brent	Det., Buf., Van., Hfd.	10	620	72	141	213	484	31	4	4	8	65		1979-80	1988-89
Pettersson, Jorgen	St.L., Hfd., Wsh.	6	435	174	192	366	117	44	15	12	27	4		1980-81	1985-86
• Pettinger, Eric	Ott., Bos., Tor.	3	97	7	12	19	83	4	1	0	1	8		1928-29	1930-31
Pettinger, Gord	Det., NYR, Bos.	8	292	42	74	116	77	49	4	5	9	11	4	1932-33	1939-40
Phair, Lyle	L.A.	3	48	6	7	13	12	1	0	0	0	0		1985-86	1987-88
Phillipoff, Harold	Atl., Chi.,	3	141	26	57	83	267	6	0	2	2	9		1977-78	1979-80
Phillips, Bat	Mtl.M.	1	27	1	1	2	6	4	0	0	0	2		1929-30	1929-30
• Phillips, Bill	Mtl.M., NYA.	8	302	52	31	83	232	28	6	2	8	19	1	1925-26	1932-33
Phillips, Charlie	Mtl.	1	17	0	0	0	6	....	....	....	....	....		1942-43	1942-43
Picard, Noel	Atl., Mtl., St.L.	7	335	12	63	75	616	50	2	11	13	167	1	1964-65	1972-73
Picard, Robert	Wsh. Tor., Mtl., Wpg., Que., Det.	13	899	104	319	423	1025	36	5	15	20	39		1977-78	1989-90
Picard, Roger	St.L.	1	15	2	2	4	21	....	....	....	....	....		1967-68	1967-68
Pichette, Dave	Que., St.L., N.J., NYR	7	322	41	140	181	348	28	3	7	10	54		1980-81	1987-88
Picketts, Hal	NYA.	1	48	3	1	4	32	....	....	....	....	....		1933-34	1933-34
Pidhirny, Harry	Bos.	1	2	0	0	0	0	....	....	....	....	....		1957-58	1957-58
Pierce, Randy	Col., N.J., Hfd.	8	277	62	76	138	223	2	0	0	0	0		1977-78	1984-85
Pike, Alf	NYR	6	234	42	77	119	145	21	4	2	6	12	1	1939-40	1946-47
Pilote, Pierre	Chi., Tor.	14	890	80	418	498	1251	86	8	53	61	102	1	1955-56	1968-69
Pinder, Gerry	Chi., Cal.	3	223	55	69	124	135	17	0	4	4	6		1969-70	1971-72
Pirus, Alex	Min., Det.	4	159	30	28	58	94	2	0	1	1	2		1976-77	1979-80
• Pitre, Didier	Mtl.	6	127	64	17	81	50	14	2	2	4	0		1917-18	1922-23
• Plager, Barclay	St.L.	10	614	44	187	231	1115	68	3	20	23	182		1967-68	1976-77
Plager, Bob	NYR, St.L.	14	644	20	126	146	802	74	2	17	19	195		1964-65	1977-78
Plager, William	Min., St.L., Atl.	9	263	4	34	38	292	31	0	2	2	26		1967-68	1975-76
Plamondon, Gerry	Mtl.	5	74	7	13	20	10	11	5	2	7	2	1	1945-46	1950-51
Plante, Cam	Tor.	1	2	0	0	0	0	....	....	....	....	....		1984-85	1984-85
Plante, Pierre	NYR, Que., Phi., St.L., Chi.	9	599	125	172	297	599	33	2	6	8	51		1971-72	1979-80
Plantery, Mark	Wpg.	1	25	1	5	6	14	....	....	....	....	....		1980-81	1980-81
Plaxton, Hugh	Mtl.M.	1	15	1	2	3	4	....	....	....	....	....		1932-33	1932-33
Playfair, Jim	Edm., Chi.	3	21	2	4	6	51	....	....	....	....	....		1983-84	1988-89
Playfair, Larry	Buf., L.A.	12	688	26	94	120	1812	43	0	6	6	111		1978-79	1989-90
Pleau, Larry	Mtl.	3	94	9	15	24	27	4	0	0	0	0		1969-70	1971-72
Plett, Willi	Atl., Cgy., Min., Bos.	13	834	222	215	437	2572	83	24	22	46	466		1975-76	1987-88
Plumb, Rob	Det.	1	7	2	1	3	0	....	....	....	....	....		1977-78	1977-78
Plumb, Ron	Hfd.	1	26	3	4	7	14	....	....	....	....	....		1979-80	1979-80

Jim Pappin

Jeff Parker

Greg Paslawski

Allen Pedersen

Ken Priestlay

Marcel Pronovost

Brian Propp

Metro Prystai

Name	NHL Teams	NHL Seasons	Regular Schedule					Playoffs					NHL Cup Wins	First NHL Season	Last NHL Season
			GP	G	A	TP	PIM	GP	G	A	TP	PIM			
Pocza, Harvie	Wsh.	2	3	0	0	0	0	....	....	....	....	....		1979-80	1981-82
Poddubny, Walt	Edm., Tor., NYR, Que., N.J.	11	468	184	238	422	454	19	7	2	9	12		1981-82	1991-92
Podloski, Ray	Bos.	1	8	0	1	1	22	....	....	....	....	....		1988-89	1988-89
Podolsky, Nels	Det.	1	1	0	0	0	0	7	0	0	0	4		1948-49	1948-49
Poeta, Anthony	Chi.	1	1	0	0	0	0	....	....	....	....	....		1951-52	1951-52
Poile, Bud	NYR, Bos., Det., Tor., Chi.,	7	311	107	122	229	91	23	4	4	8	8	1	1942-43	1949-50
Poile, Don	Det.	2	66	7	9	16	12	4	0	0	0	0		1954-55	1957-58
Poirer, Gordie	Mtl.	1	10	0	1	1	0	....	....	....	....	....		1939-40	1939-40
Polanic, Tom	Min.	2	19	0	2	2	53	5	1	1	2	4		1969-70	1970-71
Polich, John	NYR	2	3	0	1	1	0	....	....	....	....	....		1939-40	1940-41
Polich, Mike	Mtl., Min.	5	226	24	29	53	7	23	2	1	3	2	1	1976-77	1980-81
Polis, Greg	Pit., St.L., NYR, Wsh.	10	615	174	169	343	391	7	0	2	2	6		1970-71	1979-80
Poliziani, Daniel	Bos.	1	1	0	0	0	0	3	0	0	0	0		1958-59	1958-59
Polonich, Dennis	Det.	8	390	59	82	141	1242	7	1	0	1	19		1974-75	1982-83
Pooley, Paul	Wpg.	2	15	0	3	3	0	....	....	....	....	....		1984-85	1985-86
Popein, Larry	NYR, Oak.	8	449	80	141	221	162	16	1	4	5	6		1954-55	1967-68
Popiel, Paul	Bos., L.A., Det., Van., Edm.	7	224	13	41	54	210	4	1	0	1	4		1965-66	1979-80
Portland, Jack	Chi., Mtl., Bos.	10	381	15	56	71	323	33	1	3	4	25	1	1933-34	1942-43
Porvari, Jukka	Col., N.J.	2	39	3	9	12	4	....	....	....	....	....		1981-82	1982-83
Posa, Victor	Chi.	1	2	0	0	0	2	....	....	....	....	....		1985-86	1985-86
Posavad, Mike	St.L.	2	8	0	0	0	0	....	....	....	....	....		1985-86	1986-87
Potvin, Denis	NYI	15	1060	310	742	1052	1356	185	56	108	164	253	4	1973-74	1987-88
Potvin, Jean	L.A., Min., Phi., NYI, Cle.	11	613	63	224	287	478	39	2	9	11	17	1	1970-71	1980-81
Poudrier, Daniel	Que.	1	25	1	5	6	10	....	....	....	....	....		1985-86	1987-88
Poulin, Dan	Min.	1	3	1	1	2	2	....	....	....	....	....		1981-82	1981-82
Pouzar, Jaroslav	Edm.	4	186	34	48	82	135	29	6	4	10	16	3	1982-83	1986-87
Powell, Ray	Chi.	1	31	7	15	22	2	....	....	....	....	....		1950-51	1950-51
Powis, Geoff	Chi.	1	2	0	0	0	0	....	....	....	....	....		1967-68	1967-68
Powis, Lynn	Chi., K.C.	2	130	19	33	52	25	1	0	0	0	0		1973-74	1974-75
Prajsler, Petr	L.A., Bos.	4	46	3	10	13	51	4	0	0	0	0		1987-88	1991-92
• Pratt, Babe	Bos., NYR, Tor.	12	517	83	209	292	473	63	12	17	29	90	2	1935-36	1946-47
Pratt, Jack	Bos.	2	37	2	0	2	42	4	0	0	0	0		1930-31	1931-32
Pratt, Kelly	Pit.	1	22	0	6	6	15	....	....	....	....	....		1974-75	1974-75
Pratt, Tracy	Van., Col., Buf., Pit. Tor., Oak.	10	580	17	97	114	1026	25	0	1	1	62		1967-68	1976-77
Prentice, Dean	Pit., Min., Det., NYR, Bos.	22	1378	391	469	860	484	54	13	17	30	38		1952-53	1973-74
Prentice, Eric	Tor.	1	5	0	0	0	4	....	....	....	....	....		1943-44	1943-44
Preston, Rich	Chi., N.J.	8	580	127	164	291	348	47	4	18	22	56		1979-80	1986-87
Preston, Yves	Phi.	2	28	7	3	10	4	....	....	....	....	....		1978-79	1980-81
Priakin, Sergei	Cgy.	3	46	3	8	11	2	1	0	0	0	0		1988-89	1990-91
• Price, Bob	Ott.	1	1	0	0	0	0	....	....	....	....	....		1919-20	1919-20
Price, Jack	Chi.	3	57	4	6	10	24	4	0	0	0	0		1951-52	1953-54
Price, Noel	Pit., L.A., Det., Tor., NYR, Mtl., Atl.	14	499	14	114	128	333	12	0	1	1	8	1	1957-58	1975-76
Price, Pat	NYI, Edm., Pit., Que., NYR, Min.	13	726	43	218	261	1456	74	2	10	12	195		1975-76	1987-88
Price, Tom	Cal., Clev., Pit.	5	29	0	2	2	12	....	....	....	....	....		1974-75	1978-79
Priestlay, Ken	Buf., Pit.	6	168	27	34	61	63	14	0	0	0	21	1	1986-87	1991-92
• Primeau, Joe	Tor.	9	310	66	177	243	105	38	5	18	23	12	1	1927-28	1935-36
Primeau, Kevin	Van.	1	2	0	0	0	4	....	....	....	....	....		1980-81	1980-81
Pringle, Ellie	NYA	1	6	0	0	0	0	....	....	....	....	....		1930-31	1930-31
• Prodgers, Goldie	Tor., Ham.	6	110	63	22	85	33	....	....	....	....	....		1919-20	1924-25
Pronovost, Andre	Mtl., Bos., Det., Min.	10	556	94	104	198	408	70	11	11	22	58	4	1956-57	1967-68
Pronovost, Jean	Wsh., Pit., Atl.	14	998	391	383	774	413	35	11	9	20	14		1968-69	1981-82
Pronovost, Marcel	Det., Tor.	21	1206	88	257	345	851	134	8	23	31	104	5	1950-51	1969-70
Propp, Brian	Phi., Bos., Min., Hfd.	15	1016	425	579	1004	830	160	64	84	148	151		1979-80	1993-94
• Provost, Claude	Mtl.	15	1005	254	335	589	469	126	25	38	63	86	9	1955-56	1969-70
Pryor, Chris	Min., NYI	6	82	1	4	5	122	....	....	....	....	....		1984-85	1989-90
Prystai, Metro	Chi., Det.	11	674	151	179	330	231	43	12	14	26	8	2	1947-48	1957-58
• Pudas, Al	Tor.	1	3	0	0	0	0	....	....	....	....	....		1926-27	1926-27
Pulford, Bob	Tor., L.A.	16	1079	281	362	643	792	89	25	26	51	126	4	1956-57	1971-72
Pulkkinen, Dave	NYI	1	2	0	0	0	0	....	....	....	....	....		1972-73	1972-73
Purpur, Cliff	Det., Chi., St.L.	5	144	26	34	60	46	16	1	2	3	4		1934-35	1944-45
Purves, John	Wsh.	1	7	1	0	1	0	....	....	....	....	....		1990-91	1990-91
• Pusie, Jean	Mtl., NYR, Bos.	5	61	1	4	5	28	7	0	0	0	0	1	1930-31	1935-36
Pyatt, Nelson	Det., Wsh., Col.	7	296	71	63	134	69	....	....	....	....	....		1973-74	1979-80

Q

Quackenbush, Bill	Det., Bos.	14	774	62	222	284	95	80	2	19	21	8		1942-43	1955-56
Quackenbush, Max	Bos., Chi.,	2	61	4	7	11	30	6	0	0	0	4		1950-51	1951-52
Quenneville, Joel	Tor., Col., N.J., Hfd., Wsh.	13	803	54	136	190	705	32	0	8	8	22		1978-79	1990-91
Quenneville, Leo	NYR	1	25	0	3	3	10	3	0	0	0	0		1929-30	1929-30
• Quilty, John	Mtl., Bos.	4	125	36	34	70	81	13	3	5	8	9		1940-41	1947-48
Quinn, Pat	Tor., Van., Atl.	9	606	18	113	131	950	11	0	1	1	21		1968-69	1976-77

R

Radley, Yip	NYA, Mtl.M.	2	18	0	1	1	13	....	....	....	....	....		1930-31	1936-37
Raglan, Clare	Det., Chi.	3	100	4	9	13	52	3	0	0	0	0		1950-51	1952-53
Raglan, Herb	St.L., Que., T.B., Ott.	9	343	33	56	89	775	32	3	6	9	50		1985-86	1993-94
Raleigh, Don	NYR	10	535	101	219	320	96	18	6	5	11	6		1943-44	1955-56
Ramage, Rob	Col., St.L., Cgy., Tor., Min., T.B., Mtl., Phi.	15	1044	139	425	564	2226	84	8	42	50	218	2	1979-80	1993-94
• Ramsay, Beattie	Tor.,	1	43	0	2	2	10	....	....	....	....	....		1927-28	1927-28
Ramsay, Craig	Buf.	14	1070	252	420	672	201	89	17	31	48	27		1971-72	1984-85
Ramsay, Wayne	Buf.	1	2	0	0	0	0	....	....	....	....	....		1977-78	1977-78
Ramsey, Les	Chi.	1	11	2	2	4	2	....	....	....	....	....		1944-45	1944-45
• Randall, Ken	Tor., Ham., NYA	10	217	67	28	95	360	13	3	1	4	19	2	1917-18	1926-27
Ranieri, George	Bos.	1	2	0	0	0	0	....	....	....	....	....		1956-57	1956-57
Ratelle, Jean	NYR, Bos.	21	1281	491	776	1267	276	123	32	66	98	24		1960-61	1980-81
Rathwell, John	Bos.	1	1	0	0	0	0	....	....	....	....	....		1974-75	1974-75
Ratushny, Dan	Van.	1	1	0	1	1	2	....	....	....	....	....		1992-93	1992-93
Rausse, Errol	Wsh.	3	31	7	3	10	0	....	....	....	....	....		1979-80	1981-82
Rautakallio, Pekka	Atl., Cgy.	3	235	33	121	154	122	23	2	5	7	8		1979-80	1981-82
Ravlich, Matt	Bos., Chi., Det., L.A.	9	410	12	78	90	364	24	1	5	6	16		1962-63	1972-73
Raymond, Armand	Mtl.	2	22	0	2	2	10	....	....	....	....	....		1937-38	1939-40
Raymond, Paul	Mtl.	4	76	2	3	5	6	5	0	0	0	2		1932-33	1937-38
Read, Mel	NYR	1	1	0	0	0	0	....	....	....	....	....		1946-47	1946-47
Reardon, Ken	Mtl.	7	341	26	96	122	604	31	2	5	7	62	1	1940-41	1949-50
Reardon, Terry	Bos., Mtl.	7	193	47	53	100	73	30	8	10	18	12	1	1938-39	1946-47
Reaume, Marc	Tor., Det., Mtl., Van.	9	344	8	43	51	273	21	0	2	2	8		1954-55	1970-71
Reay, Billy	Det., Mtl.	10	479	105	162	267	202	63	13	16	29	43	2	1943-44	1952-53
Redahl, Gord	Bos.	1	18	0	1	1	2	....	....	....	....	....		1958-59	1958-59
Redding, George	Bos.	2	35	3	2	5	10	....	....	....	....	....		1924-25	1925-26
Redmond, Craig	L.A., Edm.	5	191	16	68	84	134	3	1	0	1	2		1984-85	1988-89
Redmond, Dick	Min., Cal., Chi., St.L., Atl., Bos.	13	771	133	312	445	504	66	9	22	31	27		1969-70	1981-82
Redmond, Mickey	Mtl., Det.	9	538	233	195	428	219	16	2	3	5	2	2	1967-68	1975-76
Reeds, Mark	St.L., Hfd.	8	365	45	114	159	135	53	8	9	17	23		1981-82	1988-89
Regan, Bill	NYR, NYA	3	67	3	2	5	67	8	0	0	0	2		1929-30	1932-33
Regan, Larry	Bos., Tor.,	5	280	41	95	136	71	42	7	14	21	18		1956-57	1960-61
Regier, Darcy	Clev., NYI	3	26	0	2	2	35	....	....	....	....	....		1977-78	1983-84
Reibel, Earl	Det., Chi., Bos.	6	409	84	161	245	75	39	6	14	20	4	2	1953-54	1958-59
Reid, Dave	Tor.	3	7	0	0	0	0	....	....	....	....	....		1952-53	1955-56
Reid, Gerry	Det.	1	....	....	....	....	....	2	0	0	0	2		1948-49	1948-49
Reid, Gordie	NYA	1	1	0	0	0	2	....	....	....	....	....		1936-37	1936-37
Reid, Reg	Tor.	2	40	2	0	2	4	2	0	0	0	0		1924-25	1925-26
Reid, Tom	Chi., Min.	11	701	17	113	130	654	42	1	13	14	49		1967-68	1977-78
Reierson, Dave	Cgy.	1	2	0	0	0	2	....	....	....	....	....		1988-89	1988-89
Reigle, Ed	Bos.	1	17	0	2	2	25	....	....	....	....	....		1950-51	1950-51
Reinhart, Paul	Atl., Cgy., Van.	11	648	133	426	559	277	83	23	54	77	42		1979-80	1989-90
Reinikka, Ollie	NYR	1	16	0	0	0	0	....	....	....	....	....		1926-27	1926-27
Reise, Leo Jr.	Chi., Det., NYR	9	494	28	81	109	399	52	8	5	13	68	2	1945-46	1953-54
• Reise, Leo Sr.	Ham., NYA, NYR	8	199	36	29	65	177	6	0	0	0	16		1920-21	1929-30
Renaud, Mark	Hfd., Buf.	5	152	6	50	56	86	....	....	....	....	....		1979-80	1983-84
Reynolds, Bobby	Tor.	1	7	1	1	2	0	....	....	....	....	....		1989-90	1989-90

Name	NHL Teams	NHL Seasons	Regular Schedule GP	G	A	TP	PIM	Playoffs GP	G	A	TP	PIM	NHL Cup Wins	First NHL Season	Last NHL Season
Ribble, Pat	Atl., Chi., Tor., Wsh., Cgy.	8	349	19	60	79	365	8	0	1	1	12		1975-76	1982-83
Richard, Henri	Mtl.	20	1256	358	688	1046	928	180	49	80	129	181	11	1955-56	1974-75
Richard, Jacques	Alt., Buf., Que.	10	556	160	187	347	307	35	5	5	10	34		1972-73	1982-83
Richard, Jean-Marc	Que.	2	5	2	1	3	2	....	....	....	....	....		1987-88	1989-90
Richard, Maurice	Mtl.	18	978	544	421	965	1285	133	82	44	126	188	8	1942-43	1959-60
Richard, Mike	Wsh.	2	7	0	2	2	0	....	....	....	....	....		1987-88	1989-90
Richards, Todd	Hfd.	2	8	0	4	4	4	11	0	3	3	6		1990-91	1991-92
Richardson, Dave	NYR, Chi., Det.	4	45	3	2	5	27	....	....	....	....	....		1963-64	1967-68
Richardson, Glen	Van.	1	24	3	6	9	19	....	....	....	....	....		1975-76	1975-76
Richardson, Ken	St.L.	3	49	8	13	21	16	....	....	....	....	....		1974-75	1978-79
Richer, Bob	Buf.	1	3	0	0	0	0	....	....	....	....	....		1972-73	1972-73
Richmond, Steve	NYR, Det., N.J., L.A.	5	159	4	23	27	514	4	0	0	0	12		1983-84	1988-89
Richter, Dave	Min., Phi., Van., St.L.	9	365	9	40	49	1030	22	1	0	1	80		1981-82	1989-90
Riley, Bill	Wsh., Wpg.	5	139	31	30	61	320	....	....	....	....	....		1974-75	1979-80
Riley, Jack	Det., Mtl., Bos.,	4	104	10	22	32	8	4	0	3	3	0		1932-33	1935-36
Riley, Jim	Det.	1	17	0	2	2	14	....	....	....	....	....		1926-27	1926-27
Riopellie, Howard	Mtl.	3	169	27	16	43	73	8	1	1	2	2		1947-48	1949-50
Rioux, Gerry	Wpg.	1	8	0	0	0	6	....	....	....	....	....		1979-80	1979-80
Rioux, Pierre	Cgy.	1	14	1	2	3	4	....	....	....	....	....		1982-83	1982-83
Ripley, Vic	Chi., Bos., NYR, St.L.	7	278	51	49	100	173	20	4	1	5	10		1928-29	1934-35
Risebrough, Doug	Mtl., Cgy.	14	740	185	286	471	1542	124	21	37	58	238	4	1974-75	1986-87
Rissling, Gary	Wsh., Pit.	7	221	23	30	53	1008	5	0	1	1	4		1978-79	1984-85
Ritchie, Bob	Phi., Det.	2	29	8	4	12	10	....	....	....	....	....		1976-77	1977-78
• Ritchie, Dave	Mtl.W, Ott., Tor., Que., Mtl.	6	54	15	3	18	27	1	0	0	0	0		1917-18	1925-26
Ritson, Alex	NYR	1	1	0	0	0	0	....	....	....	....	....		1944-45	1944-45
Rittinger, Alan	Bos.	1	19	3	7	10	0	....	....	....	....	....		1943-44	1943-44
Rivard, Bob	Pit.	1	27	5	12	17	4	....	....	....	....	....		1967-68	1967-68
• Rivers, Gus	Mtl.	3	88	4	5	9	12	16	2	0	2	2	2	1929-30	1931-32
Rivers, Wayne	Det., Bos., St.L., NYR	7	108	15	30	45	94	....	....	....	....	....		1961-62	1968-69
Rizzuto, Garth	Van.	1	37	3	4	7	16	....	....	....	....	....		1970-71	1970-71
• Roach, Mickey	Tor., Ham., NYA	8	209	75	27	102	41	....	....	....	....	....		1919-20	1926-27
Roberge, Serge	Que.	1	9	0	0	0	24	....	....	....	....	....		1990-91	1990-91
Robert, Claude	Mtl.	1	23	1	0	1	9	....	....	....	....	....		1950-51	1950-51
Robert, Rene	Tor., Pit., Buf., Col.	12	744	284	418	702	597	50	22	19	41	73		1970-71	1981-82
• Robert, Sammy	Ott.	1	1	0	0	0	0	....	....	....	....	....		1917-18	1917-18
Roberto, Phil	Mtl., St.L., Det., K.C., Col., Clev.	8	385	75	106	181	464	31	9	8	17	69	1	1969-70	1976-77
Roberts, Doug	Det., Dak., Cal., Bos.	10	419	43	104	147	342	16	2	3	5	46		1965-66	1974-75
Roberts, Jim	Mtl., St.L.	15	1006	126	194	320	621	153	20	16	36	160	5	1963-64	1977-78
Roberts, Jimmy	Min.	3	106	17	23	40	33	2	0	0	0	0		1976-77	1978-79
Robertson, Fred	Tor., Det.,	2	34	1	0	1	35	7	0	0	0	0	1	1931-32	1933-34
Robertson, Geordie	Buf.	1	5	1	2	3	7	....	....	....	....	....		1982-83	1982-83
Robertson, George	Mtl.	2	31	2	5	7	6	....	....	....	....	....		1947-48	1948-49
Robertson, Torrie	Wsh., Hfd., Det.	10	442	49	99	148	1751	22	2	1	3	90		1980-81	1989-90
Robidoux, Florent	Chi.	3	52	7	4	11	75	....	....	....	....	....		1980-81	1983-84
Robinson, Doug	Chi., NYR, L.A.	7	239	44	67	111	34	11	4	3	7	0		1963-64	1970-71
Robinson, Earl	Mtl.M., Chi., Mtl.	11	418	83	98	181	123	25	5	4	9	0	1	1928-29	1939-40
Robinson, Larry	Mtl., L.A.	20	1384	208	750	958	793	227	28	116	144	211	6	1972-73	1991-92
Robinson, Moe	Mtl	1	1	0	0	0	0	....	....	....	....	....		1979-80	1979-80
Robinson, Rob	St.L.	1	22	0	1	1	8	....	....	....	....	....		1991-92	1991-92
Robinson, Scott	Min.	1	1	0	0	0	2	....	....	....	....	....		1989-90	1989-90
Robitaille, Mike	NYR, Det., Buf., Van.	8	382	23	105	128	280	13	0	1	1	4		1969-70	1976-77
• Roche, Earl	Mtl.M., Bos., Ott., St.L., Det.	4	146	25	27	52	48	2	0	0	0	0		1930-31	1934-35
Roche, Ernest	Mtl.	1	4	0	0	0	2	....	....	....	....	....		1950-51	1950-51
Roche, Michel	Mtl.M., Ott., St.L., Mtl., Det.	4	112	20	18	38	44	....	....	....	....	....		1930-31	1934-35
Rochefort, Dave	Det	1	1	0	0	0	0	....	....	....	....	....		1966-67	1966-67
Rochefort, Leon	NYR, Mtl., Phi., L.A., Det., Atl., Van.	15	617	121	147	268	93	39	4	4	8	16	2	1960-61	1975-76
Rockburn, Harvey	Det., Ott.	3	94	4	2	6	254	....	....	....	....	....		1929-30	1932-33
• Rodden, Eddie	Chi., Tor., Bos., NYR	4	98	6	14	20	152	2	0	1	1	0	1	1926-27	1930-31
Rogers, Alfred	Min.	2	14	2	4	6	0	....	....	....	....	....		1973-74	1974-75
Rogers, Mike	Hfd., NYR, Edm.	7	484	202	317	519	184	17	1	13	14	6		1979-80	1985-86
Rohlicek, Jeff	Van.	2	9	0	0	0	8	....	....	....	....	....		1987-88	1988-89
Rolfe, Dale	Bos., L.A., Det., NYR	9	509	25	125	150	556	71	5	24	29	89		1959-60	1974-75
Romanchych, Larry	Chi., Atl	6	298	68	97	165	102	7	2	2	4	4		1970-71	1976-77
Rombough, Doug	Buf., NYI, Min.	4	150	24	27	51	80	....	....	....	....	....		1972-73	1975-76
• Romnes, Doc	Chi., Tor., NYA	10	359	68	136	204	42	43	7	18	25	4	2	1930-31	1939-40
• Ronan, Skene	Ott.	1	11	0	0	0	0	....	....	....	....	....		1918-19	1918-19
Ronson, Len	NYR, Oak.	2	18	2	1	3	10	....	....	....	....	....		1960-61	1968-69
Ronty, Paul	Bos., NYR, Mtl.	8	488	101	211	312	103	21	1	7	8	6		1947-48	1954-55
Rooney, Steve	Mtl., Wpg., N.J.	5	154	15	13	28	496	25	3	2	5	86	1	1984-85	1988-89
Root, Bill	Mtl., Tor., St.L., Phi.	6	247	11	23	34	180	22	1	2	3	25		1982-83	1987-88
• Ross, Art	Mtl.W	1	3	1	0	1	0	....	....	....	....	....		1917-18	1917-18
Ross, Jim	NYR	2	62	2	11	13	29	....	....	....	....	....		1951-52	1952-53
Rossignol, Roland	Det., Mtl.	3	14	3	5	8	6	1	0	0	0	2		1943-44	1945-46
Rota, Darcy	Chi., Atl., Van.	11	794	256	239	495	973	60	14	7	21	147		1973-74	1983-84
Rota, Randy	Mtl., L.A., K.C., Col.	5	212	38	39	77	60	5	0	1	1	0		1972-73	1976-77
• Rothschild, Sam	Mtl.M., NYA	4	99	8	6	14	24	10	0	0	0	0	1	1924-25	1927-28
• Roulston, Rolly	Det.	3	24	0	6	6	10	....	....	....	....	....	1	1935-36	1937-38
Roulston, Tom	Edm., Pit.	6	195	47	49	96	74	21	2	2	4	2		1980-81	1985-86
Roupe, Magnus	Phi.	2	40	3	5	8	42	....	....	....	....	....		1987-88	1988-89
Rousseau, Bobby	Mtl., Min., NYR	15	942	245	458	703	359	128	27	57	84	69	4	1960-61	1974-75
Rousseau, Guy	Mtl.	2	4	0	1	1	0	....	....	....	....	....		1954-55	1956-57
Rousseau, Roland	Mtl.	1	2	0	0	0	0	....	....	....	....	....		1952-53	1952-53
Routhier, Jean-Marc	Que.	1	8	0	0	0	9	....	....	....	....	....		1989-90	1989-90
Rowe, Bobby	Bos.	1	4	1	0	1	0	....	....	....	....	....		1924-25	1924-25
Rowe, Mike	Pit.	3	11	0	0	0	11	....	....	....	....	....		1984-85	1986-87
Rowe, Ron	NYR	1	5	1	0	1	0	....	....	....	....	....		1947-48	1947-48
Rowe, Tom	Wsh., Hfd., Det.	7	357	85	100	185	615	3	2	0	2	0		1976-77	1982-83
Roy, Stephane	Min.	1	12	1	0	1	0	....	....	....	....	....		1987-88	1987-88
Rozzini, Gino	Bos.	1	31	5	10	15	20	6	1	2	3	6		1944-45	1944-45
Rucinski, Mike	Chi.	2	1	0	0	0	0	2	0	0	0	0		1987-88	1988-89
Ruelle, Bernard	Det.	1	2	1	0	1	0	....	....	....	....	....		1943-44	1943-44
Ruff, Lindy	Buf., NYR	12	691	105	195	300	1264	52	11	13	24	193		1979-80	1990-91
Ruhnke, Kent	Bos.	1	2	0	1	1	0	....	....	....	....	....		1975-76	1975-76
Rundqvist, Thomas	Mtl.	1	2	0	1	1	0	....	....	....	....	....		1984-85	1984-85
• Runge, Paul	Bos., Mtl.M., Mtl.	7	143	18	22	40	57	7	0	0	0	6		1930-31	1937-38
Ruotsalainen, Reijo	NYR, Edm., N.J.	7	446	107	237	344	180	86	15	32	47	44	2	1981-82	1989-90
Rupp, Duane	NYR, Tor., Min., Pit.	10	374	24	93	117	220	10	2	2	4	8		1962-63	1972-73
Ruskowski, Terry	Chi., L.A., Pit., Min.	10	630	113	313	426	1354	21	1	6	7	86		1979-80	1988-89
Russell, Churchill	NYR	3	90	20	16	36	12	....	....	....	....	....		1945-46	1947-48
Russell, Phil	Chi., Atl., Cgy., N.J., Buf.	15	1016	99	325	424	2038	73	4	22	26	202		1972-73	1986-87
Ruzicka, Vladimir	Edm., Bos., Ott.	5	233	82	85	167	129	30	4	14	18	2		1989-90	1993-94
Rymsha, Andy	Que.	1	6	0	0	0	23	....	....	....	....	....		1991-92	1991-92

S

Name	NHL Teams	NHL Seasons	Regular Schedule GP	G	A	TP	PIM	Playoffs GP	G	A	TP	PIM	NHL Cup Wins	First NHL Season	Last NHL Season
Saarinen, Simo	NYR	1	8	0	0	0	0	....	....	....	....	....		1984-85	1984-85
Sabol, Shaun	Phi.	1	2	0	0	0	0	....	....	....	....	....		1989-90	1989-90
Sabourin, Bob	Tor.	1	1	0	0	0	2	....	....	....	....	....		1951-52	1951-52
Sabourin, Gary	St.L., Tor., Cal., Clev.	10	627	169	188	357	397	62	19	11	30	58		1967-68	1976-77
Sacharuk, Larry	NYR, St.L.	5	151	29	33	62	42	2	1	1	2	2		1972-73	1976-77
Saganiuk, Rocky	Tor., Pit.	6	259	57	65	122	201	6	1	0	1	15		1978-79	1983-84
St. Amour, Martin	Ott.	1	1	0	0	0	2	....	....	....	....	....		1992-93	1992-93
St. Laurent, Andre	NYI, Det., L.A., Pit.	11	644	129	187	316	749	59	8	12	20	48		1973-74	1983-84
St. Laurent, Dollard	Mtl., Chi.	12	652	29	133	162	496	92	2	22	24	87	5	1950-51	1961-62
St. Marseille, Frank	St.L., L.A.	10	707	140	285	425	242	88	20	25	45	18		1967-68	1976-77
St. Sauveur, Claude	Atl.	1	79	24	24	48	23	2	0	0	0	0		1975-76	1975-76
Saleski, Don	Phi., Col.	9	543	128	125	253	629	82	13	17	30	131	2	1971-72	1979-80
Salming, Borje	Tor., Det.	17	1148	150	637	787	1344	81	12	37	49	91		1973-74	1989-90
Salovaara, John	Det.	2	90	2	13	15	70	....	....	....	....	....		1974-75	1975-76
Salvian, Dave	NYI	1	....	....	....	....	....	1	0	1	1	2		1976-77	1976-77
Samis, Phil	Tor.	2	2	0	0	0	0	5	0	1	1	2	1	1947-48	1949-50
Sampson, Gary	Wsh.	4	105	13	22	35	25	12	1	0	1	0		1983-84	1986-87
Sandelin, Scott	Mtl., Phi., Min.	4	25	0	4	4	2	....	....	....	....	....		1986-87	1991-92
Sanderson, Derek	Bos., NYR, St.L., Van., Pit.	13	598	202	250	452	911	56	18	12	30	187	2	1965-66	1977-78

Herb Raglan

Rob Ramage

Todd Richards

Doug Risebrough

Tom Roulston

Vladimir Ruzicka

Scott Sandelin

Dave Semenko

Name	NHL Teams	NHL Seasons	Regular Schedule GP	G	A	TP	PIM	Playoffs GP	G	A	TP	PIM	NHL Cup Wins	First NHL Season	Last NHL Season
Sandford, Ed	Bos., Det., Chi.	9	502	106	145	251	355	42	12	11	24	27		1947-48	1955-56
● Sands, Charlie	Tor., Bos., Mtl., NYR	12	432	99	109	208	58	44	6	6	12	4	1	1932-33	1943-44
Sanipass, Everett	Chi., Que.	5	164	25	34	59	358	5	2	0	2	4		1986-87	1990-91
Sargent, Gary	L.A., Min.	8	402	61	161	222	273	20	5	7	12	8		1975-76	1982-83
Sarner, Craig	Bos.	1	7	0	0	0	0	....	....	....	....	....		1974-75	1974-75
Sarrazin, Dick	Phi.	3	100	20	35	55	22	4	0	0	0	0		1968-69	1971-72
Saskamoose, Fred	Chi.	1	11	0	0	0	6	....	....	....	....	....		1953-54	1953-54
Sasser, Grant	Pit.	1	3	0	0	0	0	....	....	....	....	....		1983-84	1983-84
Sather, Glen	Bos., Pit., NYR, St.L., Mtl., Min.	10	658	80	113	193	724	72	1	5	6	86		1966-67	1975-76
Saunders, Bernie	Que.	2	10	0	1	1	8	....	....	....	....	....		1979-80	1980-81
Saunders, Bud	Ott.	1	19	1	3	4	4	....	....	....	....	....		1933-34	1933-34
Saunders, David	Van.	1	56	7	13	20	10	....	....	....	....	....		1987-88	1987-88
Sauve, Jenn F.	Buf., Que.	7	290	65	138	203	117	36	9	12	21	10		1980-81	1986-87
Savage, Joel	Buf.	1	3	0	1	1	0	....	....	....	....	....		1990-91	1990-91
● Savage, Tony	Bos., Mtl.	1	49	1	5	6	6	2	0	0	0	0		1934-35	1934-35
Savard, Andre	Bos., Buf., Que.	12	790	211	271	482	411	85	13	18	31	77		1973-74	1984-85
Savard, Jean	Chi, Hfd.	3	43	7	12	19	29	....	....	....	....	....		1977-78	1979-80
Savard, Serge	Mtl., Wpg.	17	1040	106	333	439	592	130	19	49	68	88	7	1966-67	1982-83
Scamurra, Peter	Wsh.	4	132	8	25	33	59	....	....	....	....	....		1975-76	1979-80
Sceviour, Darin	Chi.	1	1	0	0	0	0	....	....	....	....	....		1986-87	1986-87
Schaeffer, Butch	Chi.,	1	5	0	0	0	6	....	....	....	....	....		1936-37	1936-37
Schamehorn, Kevin	Det., L.A.	3	10	0	0	0	17	....	....	....	....	....		1976-77	1980-81
Schella, John	Van.	2	115	2	18	20	224	....	....	....	....	....		1970-71	1971-72
Scherza, Chuck	Bos., NYR	2	56	6	6	12	35	....	....	....	....	....		1943-44	1944-45
Schinkel, Ken	NYR, Pit.	12	636	127	198	325	163	19	7	2	9	4		1959-60	1972-73
Schliebener, Andy	Van.	3	84	2	11	13	74	6	0	0	0	0		1981-82	1984-85
Schmautz, Bobby	Chi., Bos., Edm., Col., Van.	13	764	271	286	557	988	73	28	33	61	92		1967-68	1980-81
Schmautz, Cliff	Buf., Phi.	1	56	13	19	32	33	....	....	....	....	....		1970-71	1970-71
Schmidt, Clarence	Bos.,	1	7	1	0	1	2	....	....	....	....	....		1943-44	1943-44
Schmidt, Jackie	Bos.	1	45	6	7	13	6	5	0	0	0	0		1942-43	1942-43
Schmidt, Joseph	Bos.	1	2	0	0	0	0	....	....	....	....	....		1943-44	1943-44
Schmidt, Milt	Bos.	16	778	229	346	575	466	86	24	25	49	60	2	1936-37	1954-55
Schmidt, Norm	Pit.	4	125	23	33	56	73	....	....	....	....	....		1983-84	1987-88
Schnarr, Werner	Bos.	2	25	0	0	0	0	....	....	....	....	....		1924-25	1925-26
Schock, Danny	Bos., Phi.	2	20	1	2	3	0	1	0	0	0	0	1	1969-70	1970-71
Schock, Ron	Bos., St.L., Pit., Buf.	15	909	166	351	517	260	55	4	16	20	29		1963-64	1977-78
Schoenfeld, Jim	Buf., Det., Bos.	13	719	51	204	255	1132	75	3	13	16	151		1972-73	1984-85
Schofield, Dwight	Det., Mtl., St.L., Wsh., Pit., Wpg.	7	211	8	22	30	631	9	0	0	0	55		1976-77	1987-88
Schreiber, Wally	Min.	2	41	8	10	18	12	....	....	....	....	....		1987-88	1988-89
● Schriner, Sweeney	NYA, Tor.	11	484	201	204	405	148	60	18	11	29	54	2	1934-35	1945-46
Schultz, Dave	Phi., L.A., Pit., Buf.	9	535	79	121	200	2294	73	8	12	20	412	2	1971-72	1979-80
Schurman, Maynard	Hfd.	1	7	0	0	0	0	....	....	....	....	....		1979-80	1979-80
Schutt, Rod	Mtl., Pit., Tor.	8	286	77	92	169	177	22	8	6	14	26		1977-78	1985-86
Sclisizzi, Enio	Det., Chi.	6	81	12	11	23	26	13	0	0	0	6		1946-47	1952-53
Scott, Ganton	Tor., Ham., Mtl.M.	3	53	1	1	2	0	....	....	....	....	....		1922-23	1924-25
● Scott, Laurie	NYA, NYR	2	62	6	3	9	28	....	....	....	....	....	1	1926-27	1927-28
Scremin, Claudio	S.J.	2	17	0	1	1	29	....	....	....	....	....		1991-92	1992-93
Scruton, Howard	L.A.	1	4	0	4	4	9	....	....	....	....	....		1982-83	1982-83
Seabrooke, Glen	Phi.	3	19	1	6	7	4	....	....	....	....	....		1986-87	1988-89
Secord, Al	Bos., Chi., Tor, Phi.	12	766	273	222	495	2093	102	21	34	55	382		1978-79	1989-90
Sedlbauer, Ron	Van., Chi., Tor.	7	430	143	86	229	210	19	1	3	4	27		1974-75	1980-81
Seftel, Steve	Wsh.	1	4	0	0	0	2	....	....	....	....	....		1990-91	1990-91
Seguin, Dan	Min., Van.	2	37	2	6	8	50	....	....	....	....	....		1970-71	1973-74
Seguin, Steve	L.A.	1	5	0	0	0	9	....	....	....	....	....		1984-85	1984-85
● Seibert, Earl	NYR, Chi., Det.	15	652	89	187	276	768	66	8	9	19	66	2	1931-32	1945-46
Seiling, Ric	Buf., Det.	10	738	179	208	387	573	62	14	14	28	36		1977-78	1986-87
Seiling, Rod	Tor., NYR, Wsh., St.L., Atl.	17	979	62	269	331	603	77	4	8	12	55		1962-63	1978-79
Sejba, Jiri	Buf.	1	11	0	2	2	8	....	....	....	....	....		1990-91	1990-91
Selby, Brit	Tor., Phi., St.L.	8	350	55	62	117	163	16	1	1	2	8		1964-65	1971-72
Self, Steve	Wsh.	1	3	0	0	0	0	....	....	....	....	....		1976-77	1976-77
Selwood, Brad	Tor., L.A.	3	163	7	40	47	153	6	0	0	0	4		1970-71	1979-80
Semchuk, Brandy	L.A.	1	1	0	0	0	2	....	....	....	....	....		1992-93	1992-93
Semenko, Dave	Edm., Hfd., Tor.	9	575	65	88	153	1175	73	6	6	12	208	2	1979-80	1987-88
Senick, George	NYR	1	13	2	3	5	8	....	....	....	....	....		1952-53	1952-53
Seppa, Jyrki	Wpg.	1	13	0	2	2	6	....	....	....	....	....		1983-84	1983-84
Serafini, Ron	Cal.	1	2	0	0	0	2	....	....	....	....	....		1973-74	1973-74
Servinis, George	Min.	1	5	0	0	0	0	....	....	....	....	....		1987-88	1987-88
Sevcik, Jaroslav	Que.	1	13	0	2	2	2	....	....	....	....	....		1989-90	1989-90
Shack, Eddie	NYR, Tor., Bos., L.A., Buf., Pit.	17	1047	239	226	465	1437	74	6	7	13	151	4	1958-59	1974-75
● Shack, Joe	NYR	2	70	23	13	36	20	....	....	....	....	....		1942-43	1944-45
Shakes, Paul	Cal.	1	21	0	4	4	12	....	....	....	....	....		1973-74	1973-74
Shanahan, Sean	Mtl., Col., Bos.	3	40	1	3	4	47	....	....	....	....	....		1975-76	1977-78
Shand, Dave	Atl., Tor., Wsh.	8	421	19	84	103	544	26	1	2	3	83		1976-77	1984-85
Shannon, Charles	NYA	1	4	0	0	0	2	....	....	....	....	....		1939-40	1939-40
● Shannon, Gerry	Ott., St.L., Bos., Mtl.M.	5	183	23	29	52	121	9	0	1	1	2		1933-34	1937-38
Sharpley, Glen	Min., Chi.	6	389	117	161	278	199	27	7	11	18	24		1976-77	1981-82
Shaunessy, Scott	Que.	2	7	0	0	0	23	....	....	....	....	....		1986-87	1988-89
Shay, Norman	Bos., Tor.	2	53	5	2	7	34	....	....	....	....	....		1924-25	1925-26
Shea, Pat	Chi.	1	14	0	1	1	0	....	....	....	....	....		1931-32	1931-32
Shedden, Doug	Pit., Det., Que., Tor.	8	416	139	186	325	176	....	....	....	....	....		1981-82	1990-91
Sheehan, Bobby	Mtl., Cal., Chi., Det., NYR, Col., L.A.	9	310	48	63	111	50	25	4	3	7	8	1	1969-70	1981-82
Sheehy, Neil	Cgy., Hfd., Wsh.	9	379	18	47	65	1311	54	0	3	3	241		1983-84	1991-92
Sheehy, Tim	Det., Hfd.	2	27	2	1	3	0	....	....	....	....	....		1977-78	1979-80
Shelton, Doug	Chi.	1	5	0	1	1	0	....	....	....	....	....		1967-68	1967-68
Sheppard, Frank	Det.	1	8	1	1	2	0	....	....	....	....	....		1927-28	1927-28
Sheppard, Gregg	Bos., Pit.	10	657	205	293	498	243	92	32	40	72	31		1972-73	1981-82
Sheppard, Johnny	Det., NYA, Bos., Chi.	8	311	68	58	126	224	10	0	0	0	0	1	1926-27	1933-34
Sherf, John	Det.	5	19	0	0	0	8	8	0	1	1	2	1	1935-36	1943-44
● Shero, Fred	NYR	3	145	6	14	20	137	13	0	2	2	8		1947-48	1949-50
Sherritt, Gordon	Det.	1	8	0	0	0	12	....	....	....	....	....		1943-44	1943-44
Sherven, Gord	Edm., Min., Hfd.	5	97	13	22	35	33	3	0	0	0	0		1983-84	1987-88
● Shewchuck, Jack	Bos.	6	187	9	19	28	160	20	0	1	1	19	1	1938-39	1944-45
Shibicky, Alex	NYR	8	317	110	91	201	159	40	12	12	24	12	1	1935-36	1945-46
● Shields, Al	Ott., Phi., NYA, Mtl.M., Bos.	11	460	42	46	88	637	17	0	1	1	14	1	1927-28	1937-38
Shill, Bill	Bos.	3	79	21	13	34	18	7	1	2	3	2		1942-43	1946-47
● Shill, Jack	Tor., Bos., NYA, Chi.	6	163	15	20	35	70	27	1	6	7	13	1	1933-34	1938-39
Shinske, Rick	Clev., St.L.	3	63	5	16	21	10	....	....	....	....	....		1976-77	1978-79
Shires, Jim	Det., St.L., Pit.	3	56	3	6	9	32	....	....	....	....	....		1970-71	1972-73
Shmyr, Paul	Chi., Cal., Min., Hfd.	7	343	13	72	85	528	34	3	3	6	44		1968-69	1981-82
Shoebottom, Bruce	Bos.	4	35	1	4	5	53	14	1	2	3	77		1987-88	1990-91
● Shore, Eddie	Bos., NYA	14	553	105	179	284	1047	55	6	13	19	187	2	1926-27	1939-40
● Shore, Hamby	Ott.	1	18	3	0	3	0	....	....	....	....	....		1917-18	1917-18
Shores, Aubry	Phi.	1	1	0	0	0	0	....	....	....	....	....		1930-31	1930-31
Short, Steve	L.A., Det.	2	6	0	0	0	2	....	....	....	....	....		1977-78	1978-79
Shudra, Ron	Edm.	1	10	0	5	5	6	....	....	....	....	....		1987-88	1987-88
Shutt, Steve	Mtl., L.A.	13	930	424	393	817	410	99	50	48	98	65	5	1972-73	1984-85
● Siebert, Babe	Mtl.M., NYR, Bos., Mtl.	14	592	140	156	296	982	53	8	7	15	62	2	1925-26	1938-39
Silk, Dave	NYR, Bos., Wpg., Det.	7	249	54	59	113	271	13	2	4	6	13		1979-80	1985-86
Siltala, Mike	Wsh., NYR	3	7	1	0	1	2	....	....	....	....	....		1981-82	1987-88
Siltanen, Risto	Edm., Hfd., Que.	8	562	90	265	355	266	32	6	12	18	30		1979-80	1986-87
Sim, Trevor	Edm.	1	3	0	1	1	2	....	....	....	....	....		1989-90	1989-90
Simard, Martin	Cgy., T.B.	3	44	1	5	6	183	....	....	....	....	....		1990-91	1992-93
Simmer, Charlie	Cal., Cle., L.A., Bos., Pit.	14	712	342	369	711	544	24	9	9	18	32		1974-75	1987-88
Simmons, Al	Cal., Bos.	3	11	0	1	1	21	1	0	0	0	0		1971-72	1975-76
Simon, Cully	Det., Chi.	3	130	4	11	15	121	14	0	1	1	6	1	1942-43	1944-45
Simon, Thain	Det.	1	3	0	0	0	0	....	....	....	....	....		1946-47	1946-47
Simonetti, Frank	Bos.	4	115	5	8	13	76	12	0	1	1	8		1984-85	1987-88
Simpson, Bobby	Atl., St.L., Pit.	5	175	35	29	64	98	6	0	1	1	2		1976-77	1982-83
● Simpson, Cliff	Det.	2	6	0	1	1	0	2	0	0	0	0		1946-47	1947-48
● Simpson, Joe	NYA	6	228	21	19	40	156	2	0	0	0	0		1925-26	1930-31
Sims, Al	Bos., Hfd., L.A.	10	475	49	116	165	286	41	0	2	2	14		1973-74	1982-83
Sinclair, Reg	NYR, Det.	3	208	49	43	92	139	3	1	0	1	0		1950-51	1952-53
Singbush, Alex	Mtl.	1	32	0	5	5	15	3	0	0	0	4		1940-41	1940-41
Sinisalo, Ilkka	Phi., Min., L.A.	11	582	204	222	426	208	68	21	11	32	6		1981-82	1991-92

Name	NHL Teams	NHL Seasons	Regular Schedule					Playoffs					NHL Cup Wins	First NHL Season	Last NHL Season
			GP	G	A	TP	PIM	GP	G	A	TP	PIM			
Siren, Ville	Pit., Min.	5	290	14	68	82	276	7	0	0	0	6		1985-86	1989-90
Sirois, Bob	Phi., Wsh.	6	286	92	120	212	42	....	....	....	....	....		1974-75	1979-80
Sittler, Darryl	Tor., Phi., Det.	15	1096	484	637	1121	948	76	29	45	74	137		1970-71	1984-85
• Sjoberg, Lars-Erik	Wpg.	1	79	7	27	34	48	....	....	....	....	....		1979-80	1979-80
Sjodin, Tommy	Min., Dal., Que.	2	106	8	40	48	52	....	....	....	....	....		1992-93	1993-94
• Skaare, Bjorne	Det.	1	1	0	0	0	0	....	....	....	....	....		1978-79	1978-79
Skarda, Randy	St. L.	2	26	0	5	5	11	....	....	....	....	....		1989-90	1991-92
• Skilton, Raymie	Mtl.W	1	1	1	0	1	0	....	....	....	....	....		1917-18	1917-18
• Skinner, Alf	Tor., Bos., Mtl.M., Pit.	4	70	26	4	30	56	7	8	1	9	0	1	1917-18	1925-26
Skinner, Larry	Col.	4	47	10	12	22	8	2	0	0	0	0		1976-77	1979-80
Skov, Glen	Det., Chi., Mtl.	12	650	106	136	242	413	53	7	7	14	48	3	1949-50	1960-61
Skriko, Petri	Van., Bos., Wpg., S.J.	9	541	183	222	405	246	28	5	9	14	4		1984-85	1992-93
Sleaver, John	Chi.	2	24	2	0	2	6	....	....	....	....	....		1953-54	1956-57
Sleigher, Louis	Que., Bos.	6	194	46	53	99	146	17	1	1	2	64		1979-80	1985-86
Sloan, Tod	Tor., Chi.	13	745	220	262	482	781	47	9	12	21	47	2	1947-48	1960-61
• Slobodzian, Peter	NYA	1	41	3	2	5	54	....	....	....	....	....		1940-41	1940-41
Slowinski, Eddie	NYR	6	291	58	74	132	63	16	2	6	8	6		1947-48	1952-53
Sly, Darryl	Tor., Min., Van.	4	79	1	2	3	20	....	....	....	....	....		1965-66	1970-71
Smail, Doug	Wpg., Min., Que., Ott.	13	845	210	249	459	602	42	9	2	11	49		1980-81	1992-93
Smart, Alex	Mtl.	1	8	5	2	7	0	....	....	....	....	....		1942-43	1942-43
Smedsmo, Dale	Tor.	1	4	0	0	0	0	....	....	....	....	....		1972-73	1972-73
Smillie, Don	Bos.	1	12	2	2	4	4	....	....	....	....	....		1933-34	1933-34
• Smith, Alex	Ott., Det., Bos., NYA	11	443	41	50	91	643	19	0	2	2	40	1	1924-25	1934-35
• Smith, Arthur	Tor., Ott.	4	137	15	10	25	249	4	1	1	2	8		1927-28	1930-31
Smith, Barry	Bos., Col.	3	114	7	7	14	10	....	....	....	....	....		1975-76	1980-81
Smith, Bobby	Min., Mtl.	15	1077	357	679	1036	917	184	64	96	160	245	1	1978-79	1992-93
Smith, Brad	Van., Atl., Cgy., Det., Tor.	9	222	28	34	62	591	20	3	3	6	49		1978-79	1986-87
• Smith, Brian D.	L.A., Min.	2	67	10	10	20	33	7	0	0	0	0		1967-68	1968-69
Smith, Brian S.	Det.	3	61	2	8	10	12	5	0	0	0	0		1957-58	1960-61
Smith, Carl	Det.	1	7	1	1	2	2	....	....	....	....	....		1943-44	1943-44
Smith, Clint	NYR, Chi.	11	483	161	236	397	24	44	10	14	24	2	1	1936-37	1946-47
Smith, Dallas	Bos., NYR	16	890	55	252	307	959	86	3	29	32	128	2	1959-60	1977-78
Smith, Dalton	NYA, Det.	2	11	1	2	3	0	....	....	....	....	....		1936-37	1943-44
Smith, Dennis	Wsh., L.A.	2	8	0	0	0	4	....	....	....	....	....		1989-90	1990-91
Smith, Derek	Buf., Det.	8	335	78	116	194	60	30	9	14	23	13		1975-76	1982-83
Smith, Des	Mtl.M., Mtl., Chi., Bos.	5	195	22	25	47	236	25	1	4	5	18	1	1937-38	1941-42
• Smith, Don	Mtl.	1	10	1	0	1	4	....	....	....	....	....		1919-20	1919-20
Smith, Don A.	NYR	1	11	1	1	2	0	1	0	0	0	0		1949-50	1949-50
Smith, Doug	L.A., Buf., Edm., Van., Pit.	9	535	115	138	253	624	....	....	....	....	....		1981-82	1989-90
Smith, Floyd	Bos., NYR, Det., Tor., Buf.	13	616	129	178	307	207	48	12	11	23	16		1954-55	1971-72
Smith, George	Tor.	1	9	0	0	0	0	....	....	....	....	....		1921-22	1921-22
Smith, Glen	Chi.	1	2	0	0	0	0	....	....	....	....	....		1950-51	1950-51
Smith, Glenn	Tor.	1	9	0	0	0	0	....	....	....	....	....		1922-23	1922-23
Smith, Gord	Wsh., Wpg.	6	299	9	30	39	284	....	....	....	....	....		1974-75	1979-80
Smith, Greg	Cal., Clev., Min., Det., Wsh.	13	829	56	232	288	1110	63	4	7	11	106		1975-76	1987-88
• Smith, Hooley	Ott., Mtl.M., Bos., NYA	17	715	200	215	415	1013	54	11	8	19	109	2	1924-25	1940-41
Smith, Kenny	Bos.	7	331	78	93	171	49	30	8	13	21	6		1944-45	1950-51
Smith, Randy	Min.	2	3	0	0	0	0	....	....	....	....	....		1985-86	1986-87
Smith, Rick	Bos., Cal., St.L., Det., Wsh.	11	687	52	167	219	560	78	3	23	26	73	1	1968-69	1980-81
• Smith, Roger	Pit., Phi.	6	210	20	4	24	172	4	3	0	3	0		1925-26	1930-31
Smith, Ron	NYI	1	11	1	1	2	14	....	....	....	....	....		1972-73	1972-73
Smith, Sid	Tor.	12	601	186	183	369	94	44	17	10	27	2	3	1946-47	1957-58
Smith, Stan	NYR	2	9	2	1	3	0	....	....	....	....	....	1	1939-40	1940-41
Smith, Steve	Phi., Buf.	6	78	10	47	57	214	4	0	0	0	10		1981-82	1988-89
Smith, Stu E.	Mtl.	2	4	2	2	4	2	1	0	0	0	0		1940-41	1941-42
Smith, Stu G.	Hfd.	4	77	2	10	12	95	....	....	....	....	....		1979-80	1982-83
• Smith, Tommy	Que.B.	1	10	0	0	0	9	....	....	....	....	....		1919-20	1919-20
Smith, Vern	NYI	1	1	0	0	0	0	....	....	....	....	....		1984-85	1984-85
Smith, Wayne	Chi.	1	2	1	1	2	2	1	0	0	0	0		1966-67	1966-67
Smrke, John	St.L., Que.	3	103	11	17	28	33	....	....	....	....	....		1977-78	1979-80
• Smrke, Stan	Mtl.	2	9	0	3	3	0	....	....	....	....	....		1956-57	1957-58
Smyl, Stan	Van.	13	896	262	411	673	1556	41	16	17	33	64		1978-79	1990-91
• Smylie, Rod	Tor., Ott.	6	76	4	1	5	10	9	1	2	3	2	1	1920-21	1925-26
Snell, Ron	Pit.	2	7	3	2	5	6	....	....	....	....	....		1968-69	1969-70
Snell, Ted	Pit., K.C., Det.	2	104	7	18	25	22	....	....	....	....	....		1973-74	1974-75
Snepsts, Harold	Van., Min., Det., St.L.	17	1033	38	195	223	2009	93	1	14	15	231		1974-75	1990-91
Snow, Sandy	Det.	1	3	0	0	0	2	....	....	....	....	....		1968-69	1968-69
Snuggerud, Dave	Buf., S.J., Phi.	4	265	30	54	84	127	12	1	3	4	6		1989-90	1992-93
Sobchuk, Denis	Det., Que.	2	35	5	6	11	2	....	....	....	....	....		1979-80	1982-83
Sobchuk, Gene	Van.	1	1	0	0	0	0	....	....	....	....	....		1973-74	1973-74
Solheim, Ken	Chi., Min., Det., Edm.	5	135	19	20	39	34	3	1	1	2	2		1980-81	1985-86
Solinger, Bob	Tor., Det.	5	99	10	11	21	19	....	....	....	....	....		1951-52	1959-60
• Somers, Art	Chi., NYR	6	222	33	56	89	189	30	1	5	6	20	1	1929-30	1934-35
Sommer, Roy	Edm.	1	3	1	0	1	7	....	....	....	....	....		1980-81	1980-81
Songin, Tom	Bos.	3	43	5	5	10	22	....	....	....	....	....		1978-79	1980-81
Sonmor, Glen	NYR	2	28	2	0	2	21	....	....	....	....	....		1953-54	1954-55
• Sorrell, John	Det., NYA	11	490	127	119	246	100	42	12	15	27	10	2	1930-31	1940-41
Sparrow, Emory	Bos.	1	6	0	0	0	4	....	....	....	....	....		1924-25	1924-25
Speck, Fred	Det., Van.	3	28	1	2	3	2	....	....	....	....	....		1968-69	1971-72
• Speer, Bill	Pit., Bos.	4	130	5	20	25	79	8	1	0	1	4	1	1967-68	1970-71
Speers, Ted	Det.	1	4	1	1	2	0	....	....	....	....	....		1985-86	1985-86
• Spencer, Brian	Tor., NYI, Buf., Pit.	10	553	80	143	223	634	37	1	5	6	29		1969-70	1978-79
Spencer, Irv	NYR, Bos., Det.	8	230	12	38	50	127	16	0	0	0	8		1959-60	1967-68
Speyer, Chris	Tor., NYA	3	14	0	0	0	0	....	....	....	....	....		1923-24	1933-34
Spring, Don	Wpg.	4	259	1	52	55	80	6	0	0	0	10		1980-81	1983-84
Spring, Frank	Bos., St.L., Cal., Clev.	5	61	14	20	34	12	....	....	....	....	....		1969-70	1976-77
• Spring, Jesse	Ham., Pit., Tor., NYA	6	137	11	2	13	62	2	0	2	2	2		1923-24	1929-30
Spruce, Andy	Van., Col.	3	172	31	42	73	111	2	0	2	2	2		1976-77	1978-79
Srsen, Tomas	Edm.	1	2	0	0	0	0	....	....	....	....	....		1990-91	1990-91
Stackhouse, Ron	Cal., Det., Pit.	12	889	87	372	459	824	32	5	8	13	38		1970-71	1981-82
Stackhouse, Ted	Tor.	1	12	0	0	0	2	5	0	0	0	0	1	1921-22	1921-22
Stahan, Butch	Mtl.	1	....	....	....	....	....	3	0	1	1	2		1944-45	1944-45
Staley, Al	NYR	1	1	0	1	1	0	....	....	....	....	....		1948-49	1948-49
Stamler, Lorne	L.A., Tor., Wpg.	4	116	14	11	25	16	....	....	....	....	....		1976-77	1979-80
Standing, George	Min.	1	2	0	0	0	0	....	....	....	....	....		1967-68	1967-68
Stanfield, Fred	Chi., Bos., Min., Buf.	14	914	211	405	616	134	106	21	35	56	10	2	1964-65	1977-78
Stanfield, Jack	Chi.	1	....	....	....	....	....	1	0	0	0	0		1965-66	1965-66
Stanfield, Jim	L.A.	3	7	0	1	1	0	....	....	....	....	....		1969-70	1971-72
Stankiewicz, Edward	Det.	2	6	0	0	0	2	....	....	....	....	....		1953-54	1955-56
Stankiewicz, Myron	St.L., Phi.	1	35	0	7	7	36	1	0	0	0	0		1968-69	1968-69
Stanley, Allan	NYR, Chi., Bos., Tor., Phi.	21	1244	100	333	433	792	109	7	36	43	80	4	1948-49	1968-69
• Stanley, Barney	Chi.	1	1	0	0	0	0	....	....	....	....	....		1927-28	1927-28
Stanley, Daryl	Phi., Van.	6	189	8	17	25	408	17	0	0	0	30		1983-84	1989-90
Stanowski, Wally	Tor., NYR	10	428	23	88	111	160	60	3	14	17	13	4	1939-40	1950-51
Stapleton, Brian	Wsh.	1	1	0	0	0	0	....	....	....	....	....		1975-76	1975-76
Stapleton, Pat	Bos., Chi.	10	635	43	294	337	353	65	10	39	49	38		1961-62	1972-73
Starikov, Sergei	N.J.	1	16	0	1	1	8	....	....	....	....	....		1989-90	1989-90
Starr, Harold	Ott., Mtl.M., Mtl., NYR	7	203	6	5	11	186	17	1	0	1	2		1929-30	1935-36
Starr, Wilf	NYA, Det.	4	89	8	6	14	25	7	0	2	2	2	1	1932-33	1935-36
Stasiuk, Vic	Chi., Det., Bos.	14	745	183	254	437	669	69	16	18	34	40	2	1949-50	1962-63
Stastny, Anton	Que.	9	650	252	384	636	150	66	20	32	52	31		1980-81	1988-89
Stastny, Marian	Que., Tor.	5	322	121	173	294	110	32	5	17	22	7		1981-82	1985-86
Staszak, Ray	Det.	1	4	0	1	1	7	....	....	....	....	....		1985-86	1985-86
Steele, Frank	Det.	1	1	0	0	0	0	....	....	....	....	....		1930-31	1930-31
Steen, Anders	Wpg.	1	42	5	11	16	22	....	....	....	....	....		1980-81	1980-81
Stefaniw, Morris	Atl.	1	13	1	1	2	2	....	....	....	....	....		1972-73	1972-73
Stefanski, Bud	NYR	1	1	0	0	0	0	....	....	....	....	....		1977-78	1977-78
Steinburg, Trevor	Que.	4	71	8	4	12	161	1	0	0	0	0		1985-86	1988-89
Stemkowski, Pete	Tor., Det., NYR, L.A.	15	967	206	349	555	866	83	25	29	54	136	1	1963-64	1977-78
Stenlund, Vern	Clev.	1	4	0	0	0	0	....	....	....	....	....		1976-77	1976-77
• Stephens, Phil	Mtl.W, Mtl.	2	8	1	0	1	0	....	....	....	....	....		1917-18	1921-22
Stephenson, Bob	Hfd., Tor.	1	18	2	3	5	4	....	....	....	....	....		1979-80	1979-80
Sterner, Ulf	NYR	1	4	0	0	0	0	....	....	....	....	....		1964-65	1964-65
Stevens, Paul	Bos.	1	17	0	0	0	0	....	....	....	....	....		1925-26	1925-26

Tommy Sjodin

Bobby Smith

Brian Smith

Dave Snuggerud

Ray Staszak

Trevor Stienburg

Phil Sykes

Tony Tanti

			Regular Schedule					Playoffs					NHL	First	Last
Name	NHL Teams	NHL Seasons	GP	G	A	TP	PIM	GP	G	A	TP	PIM	Cup Wins	NHL Season	NHL Season
Stevenson, Shayne	Bos., T.B.	3	27	0	2	2	35	....	....	....	....	....		1990-91	1992-93
Stewart, Allan	N.J., Bos.	6	64	6	4	10	243	....	....	....	....	....		1985-86	1991-92
Stewart, Bill	Buf., St.L., Tor., Min.	8	261	7	64	71	424	13	1	3	4	11		1977-78	1985-86
Stewart, Blair	Det., Wsh., Que.	7	229	34	44	78	326	....	....	....	....	....		1973-74	1979-80
Stewart, Gaye	Tor., Chi., Det., NYR, Mtl.	11	502	185	159	344	274	25	2	9	11	16	2	1941-42	1953-54
• Stewart, Jack	Det., Chi.	12	565	31	84	115	765	80	5	14	19	143	2	1938-39	1951-52
Stewart, John	Pit., Atl., Cal., Que.	6	260	58	60	118	158	4	0	0	0	10		1970-71	1979-80
Stewart, Ken	Chi.	1	6	1	1	2	2	....	....	....	....	....		1941-42	1941-42
• Stewart, Nels	Mtl.M., Bos., NYA	15	650	324	191	515	953	54	15	11	26	61	1	1925-26	1939-40
Stewart, Paul	Que.	1	21	2	0	2	74	....	....	....	....	....		1979-80	1979-80
Stewart, Ralph	Van., NYI	7	252	57	73	130	28	19	4	4	8	2		1970-71	1977-78
Stewart, Robert	Bos., Cal., Clev., St.L., Pit.	9	510	27	101	128	809	5	1	1	2	2		1971-72	1979-80
Stewart, Ron	Tor., Bos., St.L., NYR, Van., NYI	21	1353	276	253	529	560	119	14	21	35	60	3	1952-53	1972-73
Stewart, Ryan	Wpg.	1	3	1	0	1	0	....	....	....	....	....		1985-86	1985-86
Stiles, Tony	Cgy.	1	30	2	7	9	20	....	....	....	....	....		1983-84	1983-84
Stoddard, Jack	NYR	2	80	16	15	31	31	....	....	....	....	....		1951-52	1952-53
Stoltz, Roland	Wsh.	1	14	2	2	4	14	....	....	....	....	....		1981-82	1981-82
Stone, Steve	Van.	1	2	0	0	0	0	....	....	....	....	....		1973-74	1973-74
Stothers, Mike	Phi., Tor.	4	30	0	2	2	65	5	0	0	0	11		1984-85	1987-88
Stoughton, Blaine	Pit., Tor., Hfd., NYR	8	526	258	191	449	204	8	4	2	6	2		1973-74	1983-84
Stoyanovich, Steve	Hfd.	1	23	3	5	8	11	....	....	....	....	....		1983-84	1983-84
• Strain, Neil	NYR	1	52	11	13	24	12	....	....	....	....	....		1952-53	1952-53
Strate, Gord	Det.	3	61	0	0	0	34	....	....	....	....	....		1956-57	1958-59
Stratton, Art	NYR, Det., Chi., Pit., Phi.	4	95	18	33	51	24	5	0	0	0	0		1959-60	1967-68
Strobel, Art	NYR	1	7	0	0	0	0	....	....	....	....	....		1943-44	1943-44
Strong, Ken	Tor.	3	15	2	2	4	6	....	....	....	....	....		1982-83	1984-85
Strueby, Todd	Edm.	3	5	0	1	1	2	....	....	....	....	....		1981-82	1983-84
• Stuart, Billy	Tor., Bos.	7	193	30	17	47	145	17	1	0	1	12	1	1920-21	1926-27
Stumpf, Robert	St.L., Pit.	1	10	1	1	2	20	....	....	....	....	....		1974-75	1974-75
Sturgeon, Peter	Col.	2	6	0	1	1	2	....	....	....	....	....		1979-80	1980-81
Suikkanen, Kai	Buf.	2	2	0	0	0	0	....	....	....	....	....		1981-82	1982-83
Sulliman, Doug	NYR, Hfd., N.J., Phi.	11	631	160	168	328	175	16	1	3	4	2		1979-80	1989-90
Sullivan, Barry	Det.	1	1	0	0	0	0	....	....	....	....	....		1947-48	1947-48
Sullivan, Bob	Hfd.	1	62	18	19	37	18	....	....	....	....	....		1982-83	1982-83
Sullivan, Frank	Tor., Chi.	4	8	0	0	0	2	....	....	....	....	....		1949-50	1955-56
Sullivan, Peter	Wpg.	2	126	28	54	82	40	....	....	....	....	....		1979-80	1980-81
Sullivan, Red	Bos., Chi., NYR	11	557	107	239	346	441	18	1	2	3	7		1949-50	1960-61
Summanen, Raimo	Edm., Van.	5	151	36	40	76	35	10	2	5	7	0		1983-84	1987-88
• Summerhill, Bill	Mtl., Bro.	3	72	14	17	31	70	3	0	0	0	2		1938-39	1941-42
Sundstrom, Patrik	Van., N.J.	10	679	219	369	588	349	37	9	17	26	25		1982-83	1991-92
Sundstrom, Peter	NYR, Wsh., N.J.	6	338	61	83	144	120	23	3	3	6	8		1983-84	1989-90
Suomi, Al	Chi.	1	5	0	0	0	0	....	....	....	....	....		1936-37	1936-37
Sutherland, Bill	Mtl., Phi., Tor., St.L., Det.	6	250	70	58	128	99	14	2	4	6	0		1962-63	1971-72
Sutherland, Ron	Bos.	1	2	0	0	0	0	....	....	....	....	....		1931-32	1931-32
Sutter, Brian	St.L.	12	779	303	333	636	1786	65	21	21	42	249		1976-77	1987-88
Sutter, Darryl	Chi.	8	406	161	118	279	288	51	24	19	43	26		1979-80	1986-87
Sutter, Duane	NYI, Chi.	11	731	139	203	342	1333	161	26	32	58	405	4	1979-80	1989-90
Suzor, Mark	Phi., Col.	2	64	4	16	20	60	....	....	....	....	....		1976-77	1977-78
Svensson, Leif	Wsh.	2	121	6	40	46	49	....	....	....	....	....		1978-79	1979-80
Swain, Garry	Pit.	1	9	1	1	2	0	....	....	....	....	....		1968-69	1968-69
Swarbrick, George	Oak., Pit., Phi.	4	132	17	25	42	173	....	....	....	....	....		1967-68	1970-71
• Sweeney, Bill	NYR	1	4	1	0	1	0	....	....	....	....	....		1959-60	1959-60
Sykes, Bob	Tor.	1	2	0	0	0	0	....	....	....	....	....		1974-75	1974-75
Sykes, Phil	L.A., Wpg.	10	456	79	85	164	519	26	0	3	3	29		1982-83	1991-92
Szura, Joe	Oak.	2	90	10	15	25	30	7	2	3	5	2		1967-68	1968-69
T															
Taft, John	Det.	1	15	0	2	2	4	....	....	....	....	....		1978-79	1978-79
Talafous, Dean	Atl., Min., NYR	8	497	104	154	258	163	21	4	7	11	11		1974-75	1981-82
Talakoski, Ron	NYR	2	9	0	1	1	33	....	....	....	....	....		1986-87	1987-88
Talbot, Jean-Guy	Mtl., Min., Det., St.L., Buf.	17	1056	43	242	285	1006	150	4	26	30	142	7	1954-55	1970-71
Tallon, Dale	Van., Chi., Pit.	10	642	98	238	336	568	33	2	10	12	45		1970-71	1979-80
Tambellini, Steve	NYI, Col., N.J., Cgy., Van.	10	553	160	150	310	105	2	0	1	1	0	1	1978-79	1987-88
Tanguay, Chris	Que.	1	2	0	0	0	0	....	....	....	....	....		1981-82	1981-82
Tannahill, Don	Van.	2	111	30	33	63	25	....	....	....	....	....		1972-73	1973-74
Tanti, Tony	Chi., Van., Pit., Buf.	11	697	287	273	560	661	30	3	12	15	27		1981-82	1991-92
Tardif, Marc	Mtl., Que.	8	517	194	207	401	443	62	13	15	28	75	2	1969-70	1982-83
Tatarinov, Mikhail	Wsh., Que., Bos.	4	161	21	48	69	184	....	....	....	....	....		1990-91	1993-94
• Taylor, Billy	Tor., Det., Bos., NYR	7	323	87	180	267	120	33	6	18	24	13	1	1939-40	1947-48
• Taylor, Billy	NYR	1	2	0	0	0	0	....	....	....	....	....		1964-65	1964-65
• Taylor, Bob	Bos.	1	8	0	0	0	6	....	....	....	....	....		1929-30	1929-30
Taylor, Dave	L.A.	17	1111	431	638	1069	1589	92	26	33	59	145		1977-78	1993-94
Taylor, Harry	Tor., Chi.	3	66	5	10	15	30	1	0	0	0	0	1	1946-47	1951-52
Taylor, Mark	Phi., Pit., Wsh.	5	209	42	68	110	73	6	0	0	0	0		1981-82	1985-86
• Taylor, Ralph	Chi., NYR	3	99	4	1	5	169	4	0	0	0	10		1927-28	1929-30
Taylor, Ted	NYR, Det., Min., Van.	6	166	23	35	58	181	....	....	....	....	....		1964-65	1971-72
Teal, Jeff	Mtl.	1	6	0	1	1	0	....	....	....	....	....		1984-85	1984-85
Teal, Skip	Bos.	1	1	0	0	0	0	....	....	....	....	....		1954-55	1954-55
Teal, Victor	NYI	1	1	0	0	0	0	....	....	....	....	....		1973-74	1973-74
Tebbutt, Greg	Que., Pit.	2	26	0	3	3	35	....	....	....	....	....		1979-80	1983-84
Tepper, Stephen	Chi.	1	1	0	0	0	0	....	....	....	....	....		1992-93	1992-93
Terbenche, Paul	Chi., Buf.	5	189	5	26	31	28	12	0	0	0	0		1967-68	1973-74
Terrion, Greg	L.A., Tor.	8	561	93	150	243	339	35	2	9	11	41		1980-81	1987-88
Terry, Bill	Min.	1	5	0	0	0	0	....	....	....	....	....		1987-88	1987-88
Tessier, Orval	Mtl., Bos.	3	59	5	7	12	6	....	....	....	....	....		1954-55	1960-61
Thatchell, Spence	NYR	1	1	0	0	0	0	....	....	....	....	....		1942-43	1942-43
Theberge, Greg	Wsh.	5	153	15	63	78	73	4	0	1	1	0		1979-80	1983-84
Thelin, Mats	Bos.	3	163	8	19	27	107	5	0	0	0	6		1984-85	1986-87
Thelven, Michael	Bos.	5	207	20	80	100	217	34	4	10	14	34		1985-86	1989-90
Therrien, Gaston	Que.	3	22	0	8	8	12	9	0	1	1	4		1980-81	1982-83
Thibaudeau, Gilles	Mtl., NYI, Tor.	5	119	25	37	62	40	8	3	3	6	2		1986-87	1990-91
Thibeault, Laurence	Det., Mtl.	2	5	0	2	2	0	....	....	....	....	....		1944-45	1945-46
Thiffault, Leo	Min.	1	....	....	....	....	....	5	0	0	0	0		1967-68	1967-68
Thomas, Cy	Chi., Tor.	1	14	2	2	4	12	....	....	....	....	....		1947-48	1947-48
Thomas, Reg	Que.	1	39	9	7	16	6	....	....	....	....	....		1979-80	1979-80
Thompson, Cliff	Bos.	2	13	0	1	1	2	....	....	....	....	....		1941-42	1948-49
Thompson, Errol	Tor., Det., Pit.	10	599	208	185	393	184	34	7	5	12	11		1970-71	1980-81
• Thompson, Kenneth	Mtl.W	1	1	0	0	0	0	....	....	....	....	....		1917-18	1917-18
Thompson, Paul	NYR, Chi.	13	586	153	179	332	336	48	11	11	22	54	3	1926-27	1938-39
• Thoms, Bill	Tor., Chi., Bos.	13	549	135	206	341	172	44	6	10	16	6		1932-33	1944-45
Thomson, Bill	Det., Chi.	2	10	2	2	4	0	2	0	0	0	0		1938-39	1943-44
Thomson, Floyd	St.L.	8	411	56	97	153	341	10	0	2	2	6		1971-72	1979-80
Thomson, Jack	NYA	3	15	1	1	2	0	2	0	0	0	0		1938-39	1940-41
• Thomson, Jimmy	Tor., Chi.	13	787	19	215	234	920	63	2	13	15	135	4	1945-46	1957-58
• Thomson, Rhys	Mtl., Tor.	2	25	0	2	2	38	....	....	....	....	....		1939-40	1942-43
Thornbury, Tom	Pit.	1	14	1	8	9	16	....	....	....	....	....		1983-84	1983-84
Thorsteinson, Joe	NYA	1	4	0	0	0	0	....	....	....	....	....		1932-33	1932-33
Thurier, Fred	NYA, Bro., NYR	3	80	25	27	52	18	....	....	....	....	....		1940-41	1944-45
Thurlby, Tom	Oak.	1	20	1	2	3	4	....	....	....	....	....		1967-68	1967-68
Thyer, Mario	Min.	1	5	0	0	0	0	1	0	0	0	2		1989-90	1989-90
Tidey, Alex	Buf., Edm.	3	9	0	0	0	8	2	0	0	0	0		1976-77	1979-80
Timgren, Ray	Tor., Chi.	6	251	14	44	58	70	30	3	9	12	6	2	1948-49	1954-55
Titanic, Morris	Buf.	2	19	0	0	0	0	....	....	....	....	....		1974-75	1975-76
Tkaczuk, Walt	NYR	14	945	227	451	678	556	93	19	32	51	119		1967-68	1980-81
Toal, Mike	Edm.	1	3	0	0	0	0	....	....	....	....	....		1979-80	1979-80
Tomalty, Glenn	Wpg.	1	1	0	0	0	0	....	....	....	....	....		1979-80	1979-80
Tomlinson, Kirk	Min.	1	1	0	0	0	0	....	....	....	....	....		1987-88	1987-88
Tonelli, John	NYI, Cgy., L.A., Chi., Que.	14	1028	325	511	836	911	172	40	75	115	200	4	1978-79	1991-92
Tookey, Tim	Wsh., Que., Pit., Phi., L.A.	7	106	22	36	58	71	10	1	3	4	2		1980-81	1988-89
Toomey, Sean	Min.	1	1	0	0	0	0	....	....	....	....	....		1986-87	1986-87
Toppazzini, Jerry	Bos., Chi., Det.	12	783	163	244	407	436	40	13	9	22	13		1952-53	1963-64
Toppazzini, Zellio	Bos., NYR, Chi.	5	123	21	22	43	49	2	0	0	0	0		1948-49	1956-57
Torkki, Jari	Chi.	1	4	1	0	1	0	....	....	....	....	....		1988-89	1988-89

			Regular Schedule					Playoffs							
Name	NHL Teams	NHL Seasons	GP	G	A	TP	PIM	GP	G	A	TP	PIM	NHL Cup Wins	First NHL Season	Last NHL Season
Touhey, Bill	Mtl.M., Ott., Bos.	7	280	65	40	105	107	2	1	0	1	0		1927-28	1933-34
Toupin, Jacques	Chi.	1	8	1	2	3	0	4	0	0	0	0		1943-44	1943-44
Townsend, Art	Chi.	1	5	0	0	0	0	....	....	....	....	....		1926-27	1926-27
Trader, Larry	Det., St.L., Mtl.	4	91	5	13	18	74	3	0	0	0	0		1982-83	1987-88
Trainor, Wes	NYR	1	17	1	2	3	6	....	....	....	....	....		1948-49	1948-49
● Trapp, Bobby	Chi.	2	82	4	4	8	129	2	0	0	0	4		1926-27	1927-28
Trapp, Doug	Buf.	1	2	0	0	0	0	....	....	....	....	....		1986-87	1986-87
Traub, Percy	Chi., Det.	3	130	3	3	6	214	4	0	0	0	6		1926-27	1928-29
Tredway, Brock	L.A.	1	....	....	....	....	....	1	0	0	0	0		1981-82	1981-82
Tremblay, Brent	Wsh.	2	10	1	0	1	6	....	....	....	....	....		1978-79	1979-80
Tremblay, Gilles	Mtl.	9	509	168	162	330	161	48	9	14	23	4	2	1960-61	1968-69
● Tremblay, J.C.	Mtl.	13	794	57	306	363	204	108	14	51	65	58	5	1959-60	1971-72
Tremblay, Marcel	Mtl.	1	10	0	2	2	0	....	....	....	....	....		1938-39	1938-39
Tremblay, Mario	Mtl.	12	852	258	326	584	1043	100	20	29	49	187	5	1974-75	1985-86
● Tremblay, Nels	Mtl.	2	3	0	1	1	0	2	0	0	0	0		1944-45	1945-46
Trimper, Tim	Chi., Wpg., Min.	6	190	30	36	66	153	2	0	0	0	2		1979-80	1984-85
Trottier, Bryan	NYI, Pit.	18	1279	524	901	1425	912	221	71	113	184	277	6	1975-76	1993-94
● Trottier, Dave	Mtl.M., Det.	11	446	121	113	234	517	31	4	3	7	41	1	1928-29	1938-39
Trottier, Guy	NYR, Tor.	3	115	28	17	45	37	9	1	0	1	16		1968-69	1971-72
Trottier, Rocky	N.J.	2	38	6	4	10	2	....	....	....	....	....		1983-84	1984-85
● Trudel, Louis	Chi., Mtl.	8	306	49	69	118	122	24	1	3	4	6	2	1933-34	1940-41
Trudell, Rene	NYR	3	129	24	28	52	72	5	0	0	0	2		1945-46	1947-48
● Tudin, Connie	Mtl.	1	4	0	1	1	4	....	....	....	....	....		1941-42	1941-42
Tudor, Rob	Van., St.L.	3	28	4	4	8	19	3	0	0	0	0		1978-79	1982-83
Tuer, Allan	L.A., Min., Hfd.	4	57	1	1	2	208	....	....	....	....	....		1985-86	1989-90
Turcotte, Alfie	Mtl., Wpg., Wsh.	7	112	17	29	46	49	5	0	0	0	0		1983-84	1990-91
Turlick, Gord	Bos.	1	2	0	0	0	2	....	....	....	....	....		1959-60	1959-60
Turnbull, Ian	Tor., L.A., Pit.	10	628	123	317	440	736	55	13	32	45	94		1973-74	1982-83
Turnbull, Perry	St.L., Mtl., Wpg.	9	608	188	163	351	1245	34	6	7	13	86		1979-80	1987-88
Turnbull, Randy	Cgy.	1	1	0	0	0	2	....	....	....	....	....		1981-82	1981-82
Turner, Bob	Mtl., Chi.	8	478	19	51	70	307	68	1	4	5	44	5	1955-56	1962-63
Turner, Brad	NYI	1	3	0	0	0	0	....	....	....	....	....		1991-92	1991-92
Turner, Dean	NYR, Col., L.A.	4	35	1	0	1	59	....	....	....	....	....		1978-79	1982-83
Tustin, Norman	NYR	1	18	2	4	6	0	....	....	....	....	....		1941-42	1941-42
Tuten, Audley	Chi.	2	39	4	8	12	48	....	....	....	....	....		1941-42	1942-43
Tutt, Brian	Wsh.	1	7	1	0	1	2	....	....	....	....	....		1989-90	1989-90
Tuttle, Steve	St.L.	3	144	28	28	56	12	17	1	6	7	2		1988-89	1990-91
Ubriaco, Gene	Pit., Oak., Chi.	3	177	39	35	74	50	11	2	0	2	4		1967-68	1969-70
Ullman, Norm	Det., Tor.	20	1410	490	739	1229	712	106	30	53	83	67		1955-56	1974-75
Unger, Garry	Tor., Det., St.L., Atl., L.A., Edm.	16	1105	413	391	804	1075	52	12	18	30	105		1967-68	1982-83

UV

Vadnais, Carol	Mtl., Oak., Cal., Bos., NYR, N.J.	17	1087	169	418	587	1813	106	10	40	50	185	2	1966-67	1982-83
Vail, Eric	Atl, Cgy., Det.	9	591	216	260	476	281	20	5	6	11	6		1973-74	1981-82
Vail, Melville	NYR	2	50	4	1	5	18	10	0	0	0	2		1928-29	1929-30
Vaive, Rick	Van., Tor., Chi., Buf.	13	876	441	347	788	1445	54	27	16	43	111		1979-80	1991-92
Valentine, Chris	Wsh.	3	105	43	52	95	127	2	0	0	0	4		1981-82	1983-84
Valiquette, Jack	Tor., Col.	7	350	84	134	218	79	23	3	6	9	4		1974-75	1980-81
Vallis, Lindsay	Mtl.	1	1	0	0	0	0	....	....	....	....	....		1993-94	1993-94
Van Boxmeer, John	Mtl., Col., Buf., Que.	11	588	84	274	358	465	38	5	15	20	37		1973-74	1983-84
Van Dorp, Wayne	Edm., Pit., Chi., Que.	6	125	12	12	24	565	27	0	1	1	42		1986-87	1991-92
Van Impe, Ed	Chi., Phi., Pit.	11	700	27	126	153	1025	66	1	12	13	131	2	1966-67	1976-77
Vasko, Elmer	Chi., Min.	13	786	34	166	200	719	78	2	7	9	73	1	1956-57	1969-70
Vasko, Rick	Det.	3	31	3	7	10	29	....	....	....	....	....		1977-78	1980-81
Vautour, Yvon	NYI, Col., N.J., Que.	6	204	26	33	59	401	....	....	....	....	....		1979-80	1984-85
Vaydik, Greg	Chi.	1	5	0	0	0	0	....	....	....	....	....		1976-77	1976-77
Veitch, Darren	Wsh., Det., Tor.	10	511	48	209	257	296	33	4	11	15	33		1980-81	1990-91
Velischek, Randy	Min., N.J., Que.	10	509	21	76	97	401	44	2	5	7	32		1982-83	1991-92
Venasky, Vic	L.A.	7	430	61	101	162	66	21	1	5	6	12		1972-73	1978-79
Veneruzzo, Gary	St.L.	2	7	1	1	2	0	9	0	2	2	2		1967-68	1971-72
Vermette, Mark	Que.	4	67	5	13	18	33	....	....	....	....	....		1988-89	1991-92
Verret, Claude	Buf.	2	14	2	5	7	2	....	....	....	....	....		1983-84	1984-85
Verstraete, Leigh	Tor.	3	8	0	1	1	14	....	....	....	....	....		1982-83	1987-88
Ververgaert, Dennis	Van., Phi., Wsh.	8	583	176	216	392	247	8	1	2	3	6		1973-74	1980-81
Vesey, Jim	St.L., Bos.	3	15	1	2	3	7	....	....	....	....	....		1988-89	1991-92
Veysey, Sid	Van.	1	1	0	0	0	0	....	....	....	....	....		1977-78	1977-78
Vickers, Steve	NYR	10	698	246	340	586	330	68	24	25	49	58		1972-73	1981-82
Vigneault, Alain	St.L.	2	42	2	5	7	82	4	0	1	1	26		1981-82	1982-83
Vilgrain, Claude	Van., N.J., Phi.	5	89	21	32	53	78	11	1	1	2	17		1987-88	1993-94
Vincelette, Daniel	Chi., Que.	6	193	20	22	42	351	12	0	0	0	4		1986-87	1991-92
Vipond, Pete	Cal.	1	3	0	0	0	0	....	....	....	....	....		1972-73	1972-73
Virta, Hannu	Buf.	5	245	25	101	126	66	17	1	3	4	6		1981-82	1985-86
Vitolinsh, Harijs	Wpg.	1	8	0	0	0	4	....	....	....	....	....		1993-94	1993-94
Viveiros, Emanuel	Min.	3	29	1	11	12	6	....	....	....	....	....		1985-86	1987-88
Vokes, Ed	Chi.	1	5	0	0	0	0	....	....	....	....	....		1930-31	1930-31
Volcan, Mickey	Hfd., Cgy.	4	162	8	33	41	146	....	....	....	....	....		1980-81	1983-84
Volek, David	NYI	6	396	95	154	249	201	15	5	5	10	2		1988-89	1993-94
Volmar, Doug	Det., L.A.	4	62	13	8	21	26	2	1	0	1	0		1969-70	1972-73
● Voss, Carl	Tor., NYR, Det., Ott., St.L., Mtl.M., NYA, Chi.	8	261	34	70	104	50	24	5	3	8	0		1926-27	1937-38
Vyazmikin, Igor	Edm.	1	4	1	0	1	0	....	....	....	....	....		1990-91	1990-91

W

Waddell, Don	L.A.	1	1	0	0	0	0	....	....	....	....	....		1980-81	1980-81
● Waite, Frank	NYR	1	17	1	3	4	4	....	....	....	....	....		1930-31	1930-31
Walker, Gord	NYR, L.A.	4	31	3	4	7	23	....	....	....	....	....		1986-87	1989-90
Walker, Howard	Wsh., Cal.	3	83	2	13	15	133	....	....	....	....	....		1980-81	1982-83
● Walker, Jack	Det.	2	80	5	8	13	18	....	....	....	....	....		1926-27	1927-28
Walker, Kurt	Tor.	3	71	4	5	9	152	16	0	0	0	34		1975-76	1977-78
Walker, Russ	L.A.	2	17	1	0	1	41	....	....	....	....	....		1976-77	1977-78
Wall, Bob	Det., L.A., St.L.	8	322	30	55	85	155	22	0	3	3	2		1964-65	1971-72
Wallin, Peter	NYR	2	52	3	14	17	14	14	2	6	8	6		1980-81	1981-82
Walsh, Jim	Buf.	1	4	0	1	1	4	....	....	....	....	....		1981-82	1981-82
Walsh, Mike	NYI	2	14	2	0	2	4	....	....	....	....	....		1987-88	1988-89
Walter, Ryan	Wsh., Mtl., Van.	15	1003	264	382	646	946	113	16	35	51	62	1	1978-79	1992-93
Walton, Bobby	Mtl.	1	4	0	0	0	0	....	....	....	....	....		1943-44	1943-44
Walton, Mike	Tor., Bos., Van., Chi., St.L.	12	588	201	247	448	357	47	14	10	24	45	2	1965-66	1978-79
Wappel, Gord	Atl., Cgy.	3	20	1	1	2	10	2	0	0	0	4		1979-80	1981-82
Ward, Don	Chi., Bos.	2	34	0	1	1	16	....	....	....	....	....		1957-58	1959-60
● Ward, Jimmy	Mtl.M., Mtl.	12	532	147	127	274	465	31	4	4	8	18	1	1927-28	1938-39
Ward, Joe	Col.	1	4	0	0	0	2	....	....	....	....	....		1980-81	1980-81
Ward, Ron	Tor., Van.,	2	89	2	5	7	6	....	....	....	....	....		1969-70	1971-72
Ware, Michael	Edm.	2	5	0	1	1	15	....	....	....	....	....		1988-89	1989-90
Wares, Eddie	NYR, Det., Chi.	9	291	60	102	162	161	45	5	7	12	34	1	1936-37	1946-47
Warner, Bob	Tor.	2	10	1	1	2	4	4	0	0	0	0		1975-76	1976-77
Warner, Jim	Hfd.	1	32	0	3	3	10	....	....	....	....	....		1979-80	1979-80
Warwick, Bill	NYR	2	14	3	3	6	16	....	....	....	....	....		1942-43	1943-44
Warwick, Grant	NYR, Bos., Mtl.	9	395	147	142	289	220	16	2	4	6	6		1941-42	1949-50
● Wasnie, Nick	Chi., Mtl., NYA, Ott., St.L.	7	248	57	34	91	176	14	6	3	9	20	2	1927-28	1934-35
Watson, Bill	Chi.	4	115	23	36	59	12	6	0	2	2	0		1985-86	1988-89
Watson, Bryan	Mtl., Oak., Pit., Det., St.L., Wsh.	16	878	17	135	152	2212	32	2	0	2	70		1963-64	1978-79
Watson, Dave	Col.	2	18	0	1	1	10	....	....	....	....	....		1979-80	1980-81
Watson, Harry	Bro., Det., Tor., Chi.	14	805	236	207	443	150	62	16	9	25	27	5	1941-42	1956-57
Watson, Jim	Det., Buf.	7	221	4	19	23	345	....	....	....	....	....		1963-64	1971-72
Watson, Jimmy	Phi.	10	613	38	148	186	492	101	5	34	39	89	2	1972-73	1981-82
Watson, Joe	Bos., Phi., Col.	14	835	38	178	216	447	84	3	12	15	82	2	1964-65	1978-79
● Watson, Phil	NYR, Mtl.	13	590	144	265	409	542	45	10	25	35	67	2	1935-36	1947-48
Watts, Brian	Det.	1	4	0	0	0	0	....	....	....	....	....		1975-76	1975-76
Webster, Aubrey	Phi., Mtl.M.	2	5	0	0	0	0	....	....	....	....	....		1930-31	1934-35
● Webster, Don	Tor.	1	27	7	6	13	28	5	0	0	0	12		1943-44	1943-44
Webster, John	NYR	1	14	0	0	0	4	....	....	....	....	....		1949-50	1949-50

Dave Taylor

Mats Thelin

Bryan Trottier

Randy Velischek

Jim Vesey

Claude Vilgrain

David Volek

Sean Whyte

Name	NHL Teams	NHL Seasons	Regular Schedule GP	G	A	TP	PIM	Playoffs GP	G	A	TP	PIM	NHL Cup Wins	First NHL Season	Last NHL Season
Webster, Tom	Bos., Det., Cal.	5	102	33	42	75	61	1	0	0	0	0		1968-69	1979-80
● Weiland, Cooney	Bos., Ott., Det.	11	508	173	160	333	147	45	12	10	22	12		1928-29	1938-39
Weir, Stan	Cal., Tor., Edm., Col., Det.	10	642	139	207	346	183	37	6	5	11	4		1972-73	1982-83
Weir, Wally	Que., Hfd., Pit.	6	320	21	45	66	625	23	0	1	1	96		1979-80	1984-85
● Wellington, Duke	Que.	1	1	0	0	0	0							1919-20	1919-20
Wensink, John	Bos., Que., Col., N.J., St.L.	8	403	70	68	138	840	43	2	6	8	86		1973-74	1982-83
● Wentworth, Cy	Chi., Mtl.M., Mtl.	13	578	39	68	107	355	35	5	6	11	22	1	1927-28	1939-40
Wesley, Blake	Phi., Hfd., Que., Tor.	7	298	18	46	64	486	19	2	2	4	30		1979-80	1985-86
Westfall, Ed	Bos., NYI	18	1227	231	394	625	544	95	22	37	59	41	2	1961-62	1978-79
Wharram, Kenny	Chi.	14	766	252	281	533	222	80	16	27	43	38	1	1951-52	1968-69
Wharton, Len	NYR	1	1	0	0	0	0							1944-45	1944-45
Wheeldon, Simon	NYR, Wpg.	3	15	0	2	2	10							1987-88	1990-91
Wheldon, Donald	St.L.	1	2	0	0	0	0							1974-75	1974-75
Whelton, Bill	Wpg.	1	2	0	0	0	0							1980-81	1980-81
Whistle, Rob	NYR, St.L.	2	51	7	5	12	16	4	0	0	0	2		1985-86	1987-88
White, Bill	L.A., Chi.	9	604	50	215	265	495	91	7	32	39	76		1967-68	1975-76
White, Moe	Mtl.	1	4	0	1	1	2							1945-46	1945-46
White, Sherman	NYR	2	4	0	2	2	0							1946-47	1949-50
White, Tex	Pit., NYA, Phi.	6	203	33	12	45	141	4	0	0	0	2		1925-26	1930-31
White, Tony	Wsh., Min.	5	164	37	28	65	104							1974-75	1979-80
Whitelaw, Bob	Det.	2	32	0	2	2	2	8	0	0	0	0		1940-41	1941-42
Whitlock, Bob	Min.	1	1	0	0	0	0							1969-70	1969-70
Whyte, Sean	L.A.	2	21	0	2	2	12							1991-92	1992-93
Wickenheiser, Doug	Mtl., St.L., Van., NYR, Wsh.	10	556	111	165	276	286	41	4	7	11	18		1980-81	1989-90
● Widing, Juha	NYR, L.A., Clev.	8	575	144	226	370	208	8	1	2	3	2		1969-70	1976-77
Wiebe, Art	Chi.	11	411	14	27	41	209	31	1	3	4	8	1	1932-33	1943-44
● Wilcox, Archie	Mtl.M., Bos., St.L.	6	212	8	14	22	158	12	1	0	1	10		1929-30	1934-35
Wilcox, Barry	Van.	2	33	3	2	5	15							1972-73	1974-75
Wilder, Arch	Det.	1	18	0	2	2	2							1940-41	1940-41
Wiley, Jim	Pit., Van.	5	63	4	10	14	8							1972-73	1976-77
Wilkins, Barry	Bos., Van., Pit.	9	418	27	125	152	663	6	0	1	1	4		1966-67	1975-76
Wilkinson, John	Bos.	1	9	0	0	0	3							1943-44	1943-44
Wilks, Brian	L.A.	4	48	4	8	12	27							1984-85	1988-89
Willard, Rod	Tor.	1	1	0	0	0	0							1982-83	1982-83
Williams, Burr	Det., St.L., Bos.	3	19	0	1	1	28	2	0	0	0	8		1933-34	1936-37
Williams, Darryl	L.A.	1	2	0	0	0	10							1992-93	1992-93
Williams, Dave	Tor., Van., Det., L.A., Hfd.	14	962	241	272	513	3966	83	12	23	35	455		1974-75	1987-88
Williams, Fred	Det.	1	44	2	5	7	10							1976-77	1976-77
Williams, Gord	Phi.	2	2	0	0	0	2							1981-82	1982-83
Williams, Sean	Chi.	1	2	0	0	0	4							1991-92	1991-92
● Williams, Tom	Bos., Min., Cal., Wsh.	13	663	161	269	430	177	10	2	5	7	2		1961-62	1975-76
Williams, Tommy	NYR, L.A.	8	397	115	138	253	73	29	8	7	15	4		1971-72	1978-79
Williams, Warren	St.L., Cal.	3	108	14	35	49	131							1973-74	1975-76
Willson, Don	Mtl.	1	48	7	9	16	4								
Wilson, Behn	Phi., Chi.	9	601	98	260	358	1480	67	12	29	41	190		1978-79	1987-88
Wilson, Bert	NYR, L.A., St.L., Cgy.	8	478	37	44	81	646	21	0	2	2	42		1973-74	1980-81
Wilson, Bob	Chi.	1	1	0	0	0	0							1953-54	1953-54
Wilson, Carey	Cgy., Hfd., NYR	10	552	169	258	427	314	52	11	13	24	14		1983-84	1992-93
Wilson, Cully	Tor., Mtl., Ham., Chi.	5	125	60	23	83	232	2	1	0	1	6		1919-20	1926-27
Wilson, Doug	Chi., S.J.	16	1024	237	590	827	830	95	19	61	80	88		1977-78	1992-93
Wilson, Gord	Bos.	1						2	0	0	0	0		1954-55	1954-55
Wilson, Hub	NYA	1	2	0	0	0	0							1931-32	1931-32
Wilson, Jerry	Mtl.	1	3	0	0	0	0							1956-57	1956-57
Wilson, Johnny	Det., Chi., Tor., NYR	13	688	161	171	332	190	66	14	13	27	11	4	1949-50	1961-62
● Wilson, Larry	Det., Chi.	6	152	21	48	69	75	4	0	0	0	0	1	1949-50	1955-56
Wilson, Mitch	N.J., Pit.	2	26	2	3	5	104							1984-85	1986-87
Wilson, Murray	Mtl., L.A.	7	386	94	95	189	162	53	5	14	19	32	4	1972-73	1978-79
Wilson, Rick	Mtl., St.L., Det.	4	239	6	26	32	165	3	0	0	0	0		1973-74	1976-77
Wilson, Rik	St.L., Cgy., Chi.	6	251	25	65	90	220	22	0	4	4	23		1981-82	1987-88
Wilson, Roger	Chi.	1	7	0	2	2	6							1974-75	1974-75
Wilson, Ron	Tor., Min.	7	177	26	67	93	68	20	4	13	17	8		1977-78	1987-88
Wilson, Wally	Bos.	1	53	11	8	19	18	1	0	0	0	0		1947-48	1947-48
Wing, Murray	Det.	1	1	0	1	1	0							1973-74	1973-74
● Wiseman, Eddie	Det., NYA, Bos.	10	454	115	164	279	137	45	10	10	20	16	1	1932-33	1941-42
Wiste, Jim	Chi., Van.	3	52	1	10	11	8							1968-69	1970-71
Witherspoon, Jim	L.A.	1	2	0	0	0	0							1975-76	1975-76
Witiuk, Steve	Chi.	1	33	3	8	11	14							1951-52	1951-52
Woit, Benny	Det., Chi.	7	334	7	26	33	170	41	2	6	8	18	3	1950-51	1956-57
Wojciechowski, Steven	Det.	2	54	19	20	39	17	6	0	1	1	0		1944-45	1946-47
Wolf, Bennett	Pit.	3	30	0	1	1	133							1980-81	1982-83
Wong, Mike	Det.	1	22	1	1	2	12							1975-76	1975-76
Wood, Robert	NYR	1	1	0	0	0	0							1950-51	1950-51
Woodley, Dan	Van.	1	5	2	0	2	17							1987-88	1987-88
Woods, Paul	Det.	7	501	72	124	196	276	7	0	5	5	6		1977-78	1983-84
● Woytowich, Bob	Bos., Min., Pit., L.A.	8	503	32	126	158	352	24	1	3	4	20		1964-65	1971-72
Wright, John	Van., St.L., K.C.	3	127	16	36	52	67							1972-73	1974-75
Wright, Keith	Phi.	1	1	0	0	0	0							1967-68	1967-68
Wright, Larry	Phi., Cal., Det.	5	106	4	8	12	19							1971-72	1977-78
Wycherley, Ralph	NYA, Bro.	2	28	4	7	11	6							1940-41	1941-42
Wylie, Duane	Chi.	2	14	3	3	6	2							1974-75	1976-77
● Wylie, William	NYR	1	1	0	0	0	0							1950-51	1950-51
Wyrozub, Randy	Buf.	4	100	8	10	18	10							1970-71	1973-74
Yackel, Ken	Bos.	1	6	0	0	0	2	2	0	0	0	0		1958-59	1958-59
Yaremchuk, Gary	Tor.	4	34	1	4	5	28							1981-82	1984-85
Yaremchuk, Ken	Chi., Tor.	6	235	36	56	92	106	31	6	8	14	49		1983-84	1988-89
Yates, Ross	Hfd.	1	7	1	1	2	4							1983-84	1983-84
Young, Brian	Chi.	1	8	0	2	2	6							1980-81	1980-81
Young, C.J.	Cgy., Bos.	1	43	7	7	14	32							1992-93	1992-93
● Young, Doug	Mtl., Det.	10	391	35	45	80	303	28	1	5	6	16	2	1931-32	1940-41
Young, Howie	Det., Chi., Van.	8	336	12	62	74	851	19	2	4	6	46		1960-61	1970-71
Young, Tim	Min., Wpg., Phi.	10	628	195	341	536	438	36	7	24	31	27		1975-76	1984-85
Young, Warren	Min., Pit., Det.	7	236	72	77	149	472							1981-82	1987-88
Younghans, Tom	Min., NYR	6	429	44	41	85	373	24	2	1	3	21		1976-77	1981-82

YZ

Name	NHL Teams	NHL Seasons	Regular Schedule GP	G	A	TP	PIM	Playoffs GP	G	A	TP	PIM	NHL Cup Wins	First NHL Season	Last NHL Season
Zabroski, Marty	Chi.	1	1	0	0	0	2							1944-45	1944-45
Zaharko, Miles	Atl., Chi.	4	129	5	32	37	84	3	0	0	0	0		1977-78	1981-82
Zaine, Rod	Pit., Buf.	2	61	10	6	16	25							1970-71	1971-72
Zanussi, Joe	NYR, Bos., St.L.	3	87	1	13	14	46	4	0	1	1	2		1974-75	1976-77
Zanussi, Ron	Min., Tor.	5	299	52	83	135	373	17	0	4	4	17		1977-78	1981-82
Zeidel, Larry	Det., Chi., Phi.	5	158	3	16	19	198	12	0	1	1	12	1	1951-52	1968-69
Zemlak, Richard	Que., Min., Pit., Cgy.	5	132	2	12	14	587	1	0	0	0	10		1986-87	1991-92
Zeniuk, Ed	Det.	1	2	0	0	0	0							1954-55	1954-55
Zetterstrom, Lars	Van.	1	14	0	1	1	2							1978-79	1978-79
Zuke, Mike	St.L., Hfd.	8	455	86	196	282	220	26	6	6	12	12		1978-79	1985-86
Zunich, Rudy	Det.	1	2	0	0	0	2							1943-44	1943-44

1995-96 Goaltender Register

Note: The 1995-96 Goaltender Register lists every goaltender who appeared in an NHL game in the 1994-95 season, every goaltender drafted in the first six rounds of the 1994 and 1995 Entry Drafts, goaltenders on NHL Reserve Lists and other goaltenders.

Trades and roster changes are current as of August 17, 1995

To calculate a goaltender's goals-against-per-game average **(AVG)**, divide goals against **(GA)** by minutes played **(Mins)** and multiply this result by **60**.

Abbreviations: A list of league names can be found at the beginning of the Player Register. **Avg.** – goals against per game average; **GA** – goals against; **GP** – games played; **L** – losses; **Lea** – league; **SO** – shutouts; **T** – ties; **W** – wins.

Player Register begins on page 251.

ARSENAULT, DAVID — DET.

Goaltender. Catches left. 6'2", 165 lbs. Born, Frankfurt, Germany, March 21, 1977.
(Detroit's 6th choice, 126th overall, in 1995 Entry Draft).

			Regular Season								Playoffs						
Season	Club	Lea	GP	W	L	T	Mins	GA	SO	Avg	GP	W	L	Mins	GA	SO	Avg
1994-95	St-Hyacinthe	QMJHL	19	3	10	0	862	75	0	5.22	....	....	....	....	....	....	....
	Drummondville	QMJHL	12	2	5	0	478	40	0	5.02	2	0	2	122	8	0	3.93

ASKEY, TOM — ANA.

Goaltender. Catches left. 6'2", 185 lbs. Born, Kenmore, NY, October 4, 1974.
(Anaheim's 8th choice, 186th overall, in 1993 Entry Draft).

			Regular Season								Playoffs						
Season	Club	Lea	GP	W	L	T	Mins	GA	SO	Avg	GP	W	L	Mins	GA	SO	Avg
1992-93	Ohio State	NCAA	25	2	19	0	1235	125	....	6.07	....	....	....	....	....	....	....
1993-94	Ohio State	CCHA	27	3	19	4	1488	103	....	4.15	....	....	....	....	....	....	....
1994-95	Ohio State	CCHA	26	4	19	2	1387	121	0	5.23	....	....	....	....	....	....	....

AUBIN, JEAN-SEBASTIEN (OH-behn) — PIT.

Goaltender. Catches right. 5'11", 179 lbs. Born, Montreal, Que., July 19, 1977.
(Pittsburgh's 2nd choice, 76th overall, in 1995 Entry Draft).

			Regular Season								Playoffs						
Season	Club	Lea	GP	W	L	T	Mins	GA	SO	Avg	GP	W	L	Mins	GA	SO	Avg
1993-94	Montreal	Midget	24	....	....	....	1524	96	1	3.74	....	....	....	....	....	....	....
1994-95	Sherbrooke	QMJHL	27	13	10	1	1287	73	1	3.40	3	1	2	185	11	0	3.57

BACH, RYAN — DET.

Goaltender. Catches left. 6'1", 180 lbs. Born, Sherwood Park, Alta., October 21, 1973.
(Detroit's 11th choice, 262nd overall, in 1992 Entry Draft).

			Regular Season								Playoffs						
Season	Club	Lea	GP	W	L	T	Mins	GA	SO	Avg	GP	W	L	Mins	GA	SO	Avg
1992-93	Colorado	WCHA	4	1	3	0	239	11	0	2.76	....	....	....	....	....	....	....
1993-94	Colorado	WCHA	30	17	7	5	1733	105	0	3.64	....	....	....	....	....	....	....
1994-95ab	Colorado	WCHA	27	18	5	1	1522	83	0	3.27	....	....	....	....	....	....	....

a WCHA First All-Star Team (1995)
b NCAA West Second All-American Team (1995)

BAILEY, SCOTT — BOS.

Goaltender. Catches left. 6', 195 lbs. Born, Calgary, Alta., May 2, 1972.
(Boston's 3rd choice, 112th overall, in 1992 Entry Draft).

			Regular Season								Playoffs						
Season	Club	Lea	GP	W	L	T	Mins	GA	SO	Avg	GP	W	L	Mins	GA	SO	Avg
1990-91a	Spokane	WHL	46	33	11	0	2537	157	*4	3.71	....	....	....	....	....	....	....
1991-92a	Spokane	WHL	65	34	23	5	3798	206	1	3.30	10	5	5	605	43	0	4.26
1992-93	Johnstown	ECHL	36	13	15	3	1750	112	1	3.84	....	....	....	....	....	....	....
1993-94	Providence	AHL	7	2	2	2	377	24	0	3.82	....	....	....	....	....	....	....
	Charlotte	ECHL	36	22	11	3	2180	130	1	3.58	3	1	2	187	12	0	3.83
1994-95	Providence	AHL	52	25	16	9	2936	147	2	3.00	9	4	4	504	31	*2	3.69

a WHL West Second All-Star Team (1991, 1992)

BALES, MICHAEL — OTT.

Goaltender. Catches left. 6'1", 180 lbs. Born, Prince Albert, Sask., August 6, 1971.
(Boston's 4th choice, 105th overall, in 1990 Entry Draft).

			Regular Season								Playoffs						
Season	Club	Lea	GP	W	L	T	Mins	GA	SO	Avg	GP	W	L	Mins	GA	SO	Avg
1989-90	Ohio State	CCHA	21	6	13	2	1117	95	0	5.11	....	....	....	....	....	....	....
1990-91	Ohio State	CCHA	*39	11	24	3	*2180	184	0	5.06	....	....	....	....	....	....	....
1991-92	Ohio State	CCHA	36	11	20	5	2060	180	0	5.24	....	....	....	....	....	....	....
1992-93	**Boston**	**NHL**	**1**	**0**	**0**	**0**	**25**	**1**	**0**	**2.40**	....	....	....	....	....	....	....
	Providence	AHL	44	22	17	0	2363	166	1	4.21	2	0	2	118	8	0	4.07
1993-94	Providence	AHL	33	9	15	4	1757	130	0	4.44	....	....	....	....	....	....	....
1994-95	PEI	AHL	45	25	16	3	2649	160	2	3.62	9	6	3	530	24	*2	2.72
	Ottawa	**NHL**	**1**	**0**	**0**	**0**	**3**	**0**	**0**	**0.00**	....	....	....	....	....	....	....
	NHL Totals		**2**	**0**	**0**	**0**	**28**	**1**	**0**	**2.14**	....	....	....	....	....	....	....

Signed as a free agent by **Ottawa**, July 4, 1994.

BARRASSO, TOM (buh-RAH-soh) — PIT.

Goaltender. Catches right. 6'3", 211 lbs. Born, Boston, MA, March 31, 1965.
(Buffalo's 1st choice, 5th overall, in 1983 Entry Draft).

			Regular Season								Playoffs						
Season	Club	Lea	GP	W	L	T	Mins	GA	SO	Avg	GP	W	L	Mins	GA	SO	Avg
1982-83	Acton-Boxboro	HS	23	....	....	....	1035	17	10	0.73	....	....	....	....	....	....	....
1983-84 abcd	**Buffalo**	**NHL**	**42**	**26**	**12**	**3**	**2475**	**117**	**2**	**2.84**	**3**	**0**	**2**	**139**	**8**	**0**	**3.45**
1984-85ef	**Buffalo**	**NHL**	**54**	**25**	**18**	**10**	**3248**	**144**	***5**	***2.66**	**5**	**2**	**3**	**300**	**22**	**0**	**4.40**
	Rochester	AHL	5	3	1	1	267	6	1	1.35	....	....	....	....	....	....	....
1985-86	**Buffalo**	**NHL**	**60**	**29**	**24**	**5**	**3561**	**214**	**2**	**3.61**	....	....	....	....	....	....	....
1986-87	**Buffalo**	**NHL**	**46**	**17**	**23**	**2**	**2501**	**152**	**2**	**3.65**	....	....	....	....	....	....	....
1987-88	**Buffalo**	**NHL**	**54**	**25**	**18**	**8**	**3133**	**173**	**2**	**3.31**	**4**	**1**	**3**	**224**	**16**	**0**	**4.29**
1988-89	**Buffalo**	**NHL**	**10**	**2**	**7**	**0**	**545**	**45**	**0**	**4.95**	....	....	....	....	....	....	....
	Pittsburgh	**NHL**	**44**	**18**	**15**	**7**	**2406**	**162**	**0**	**4.04**	**11**	**7**	**4**	**631**	**40**	**0**	**3.80**
1989-90	**Pittsburgh**	**NHL**	**24**	**7**	**12**	**3**	**1294**	**101**	**0**	**4.68**	....	....	....	....	....	....	....
1990-91	**Pittsburgh**	**NHL**	**48**	**27**	**16**	**3**	**2754**	**165**	**1**	**3.59**	**20**	**12**	**7**	**1175**	**51**	***1**	***2.60**
1991-92	**Pittsburgh**	**NHL**	**57**	**25**	**22**	**9**	**3329**	**196**	**1**	**3.53**	***21**	***16**	**5**	***1233**	**58**	**1**	**2.82**
1992-93e	**Pittsburgh**	**NHL**	**63**	***43**	**14**	**5**	**3702**	**186**	**4**	**3.01**	**12**	**7**	**5**	**722**	**35**	***2**	**2.91**
1993-94	**Pittsburgh**	**NHL**	**44**	**22**	**15**	**5**	**2482**	**139**	**2**	**3.36**	**6**	**2**	**4**	**356**	**17**	**0**	**2.87**
1994-95	**Pittsburgh**	**NHL**	**2**	**0**	**1**	**1**	**125**	**8**	**0**	**3.84**	**2**	**0**	**1**	**80**	**8**	**0**	**6.00**
	NHL Totals		**548**	**266**	**197**	**61**	**31555**	**1802**	**21**	**3.43**	**84**	**47**	**34**	**4860**	**255**	**4**	**3.15**

a NHL First All-Star Team (1984)
b Won Vezina Trophy (1984)
c Won Calder Memorial Trophy (1984)
d NHL All-Rookie Team (1984)
e NHL Second All-Star Team (1985, 1993)
f Shared William Jennings Trophy with Bob Sauve (1985)

Played in NHL All-Star Game (1985)

Traded to **Pittsburgh** by **Buffalo** with Buffalo's third round choice (Joe Dziedzic) in 1990 Entry Draft for Doug Bodger and Darrin Shannon, November 12, 1988.

BEAUBIEN, FREDERICK (boh-BEE-yehn) — L.A.

Goaltender. Catches left. 6'1", 204 lbs. Born, Lauzon, Que., April 1, 1975.
(Los Angeles' 4th choice, 105th overall, in 1993 Entry Draft).

			Regular Season								Playoffs						
Season	Club	Lea	GP	W	L	T	Mins	GA	SO	Avg	GP	W	L	Mins	GA	SO	Avg
1992-93	St-Hyacinthe	QMJHL	33	8	16	3	1702	133	0	4.69	....	....	....	....	....	....	....
1993-94	St-Hyacinthe	QMJHL	47	19	19	5	2663	168	1	3.79	7	3	4	411	33	0	4.82
1994-95	St-Hyacinthe	QMJHL	51	19	24	4	2697	178	1	3.96	3	1	2	176	9	0	3.07

BEAUPRE, DON (boh-PRAY) — OTT.

Goaltender. Catches left. 5'10", 172 lbs. Born, Waterloo, Ont., September 19, 1961.
(Minnesota's 2nd choice, 37th overall, in 1980 Entry Draft).

			Regular Season								Playoffs						
Season	Club	Lea	GP	W	L	T	Mins	GA	SO	Avg	GP	W	L	Mins	GA	SO	Avg
1978-79	Sudbury	OHA	54	....	....	....	3248	260	2	4.78	10	....	....	600	44	0	4.20
1979-80a	Sudbury	OHA	59	28	29	2	3447	248	0	4.32	9	5	4	552	38	0	4.13
1980-81	**Minnesota**	**NHL**	**44**	**18**	**14**	**11**	**2585**	**138**	**0**	**3.20**	**6**	**4**	**2**	**360**	**26**	**0**	**4.33**
1981-82	**Minnesota**	**NHL**	**29**	**11**	**8**	**9**	**1634**	**101**	**0**	**3.71**	**2**	**0**	**1**	**60**	**4**	**0**	**4.00**
	Nashville	CHL	5	2	3	0	299	25	0	5.02	....	....	....	....	....	....	....
1982-83	**Minnesota**	**NHL**	**36**	**19**	**10**	**5**	**2011**	**120**	**0**	**3.58**	**4**	**2**	**2**	**245**	**20**	**0**	**4.90**
	Birmingham	CHL	10	8	2	0	599	31	0	3.11	....	....	....	....	....	....	....
1983-84	**Minnesota**	**NHL**	**33**	**16**	**13**	**2**	**1791**	**123**	**0**	**4.12**	**13**	**6**	**7**	**782**	**40**	**1**	**3.07**
	Salt Lake	CHL	7	2	5	0	419	30	0	4.30	....	....	....	....	....	....	....
1984-85	**Minnesota**	**NHL**	**31**	**10**	**17**	**3**	**1770**	**109**	**1**	**3.69**	**4**	**1**	**1**	**184**	**12**	**0**	**3.91**
1985-86	**Minnesota**	**NHL**	**52**	**25**	**20**	**6**	**3073**	**182**	**1**	**3.55**	**5**	**2**	**3**	**300**	**17**	**0**	**3.40**
1986-87	**Minnesota**	**NHL**	**47**	**17**	**20**	**6**	**2622**	**174**	**1**	**3.98**	....	....	....	....	....	....	....
1987-88	**Minnesota**	**NHL**	**43**	**10**	**22**	**3**	**2288**	**161**	**0**	**4.22**	....	....	....	....	....	....	....
1988-89	**Minnesota**	**NHL**	**1**	**0**	**1**	**0**	**59**	**3**	**0**	**3.05**	....	....	....	....	....	....	....
	Kalamazoo	IHL	3	1	2	0	179	9	1	3.02	....	....	....	....	....	....	....
	Washington	**NHL**	**11**	**5**	**4**	**0**	**578**	**28**	**1**	**2.91**	....	....	....	....	....	....	....
	Baltimore	AHL	30	14	12	2	1715	102	0	3.57	....	....	....	....	....	....	....
1989-90	**Washington**	**NHL**	**48**	**23**	**18**	**5**	**2793**	**150**	**2**	**3.22**	**8**	**4**	**3**	**401**	**18**	**0**	**2.69**
1990-91	**Washington**	**NHL**	**45**	**20**	**18**	**3**	**2572**	**113**	***5**	**2.64**	**11**	**5**	**5**	**624**	**29**	***1**	**2.79**
	Baltimore	AHL	2	2	0	0	120	3	0	1.50	....	....	....	....	....	....	....
1991-92	**Washington**	**NHL**	**54**	**29**	**17**	**6**	**3108**	**166**	**1**	**3.20**	**7**	**3**	**4**	**419**	**22**	**0**	**3.15**
	Baltimore	AHL	3	1	1	1	184	10	0	3.26	....	....	....	....	....	....	....
1992-93	**Washington**	**NHL**	**58**	**27**	**23**	**5**	**3282**	**181**	**1**	**3.31**	**2**	**1**	**1**	**119**	**9**	**0**	**4.54**
1993-94	**Washington**	**NHL**	**53**	**24**	**16**	**8**	**2853**	**135**	**2**	**2.84**	**8**	**5**	**2**	**429**	**21**	**1**	**2.94**
1994-95	**Ottawa**	**NHL**	**38**	**8**	**25**	**3**	**2161**	**121**	**1**	**3.36**	....	....	....	....	....	....	....
	NHL Totals		**623**	**262**	**246**	**75**	**35180**	**2005**	**16**	**3.42**	**70**	**33**	**31**	**3923**	**218**	**3**	**3.33**

a OHA First All-Star Team (1980)

Played in NHL All-Star Game (1981, 1992)

Traded to **Washington** by **Minnesota** for rights to Claudio Scremin, November 1, 1988. Traded to **Ottawa** by **Washington** for Ottawa's fifth round choice (Benoit Gratton) in 1995 Entry Draft, January 18, 1995.

BEAUREGARD, STEPHANE

Goaltender. Catches right. 5'11", 190 lbs. Born, Cowansville, Que., January 10, 1968.
(Winnipeg's 3rd choice, 52nd overall, in 1988 Entry Draft).

			Regular Season								Playoffs						
Season	Club	Lea	GP	W	L	T	Mins	GA	SO	Avg	GP	W	L	Mins	GA	SO	Avg
1986-87	St-Jean	QMJHL	13	6	7	0	785	58	0	4.43	5	1	3	260	26	0	6.00
1987-88ab	St-Jean	QMJHL	66	38	20	3	3766	229	2	3.65	7	3	4	423	34	0	4.82
1988-89	Moncton	AHL	15	4	8	2	824	62	0	4.51	....	....	....	....	....	....	....
	Fort Wayne	IHL	16	9	5	0	830	43	0	3.10	9	4	4	484	21	*1	*2.60
1989-90	**Winnipeg**	**NHL**	**19**	**7**	**8**	**3**	**1079**	**59**	**0**	**3.28**	**4**	**1**	**3**	**238**	**12**	**0**	**3.03**
	Fort Wayne	IHL	33	20	8	3	1949	115	0	3.54	....	....	....	....	....	....	....
1990-91	**Winnipeg**	**NHL**	**16**	**3**	**10**	**1**	**836**	**55**	**0**	**3.95**	....	....	....	....	....	....	....
	Moncton	AHL	9	3	4	1	504	20	1	2.38	1	1	0	60	1	0	1.00
	Fort Wayne	IHL	32	14	13	2	1761	109	0	3.71	*19	*10	9	*1158	57	0	2.95
1991-92	**Winnipeg**	**NHL**	**26**	**6**	**8**	**6**	**1267**	**61**	**2**	**2.89**	....	....	....	....	....	....	....
1992-93	**Philadelphia**	**NHL**	**16**	**3**	**9**	**0**	**802**	**59**	**0**	**4.41**	....	....	....	....	....	....	....
	Hershey	AHL	13	5	5	3	794	48	0	3.63	....	....	....	....	....	....	....
1993-94	**Winnipeg**	**NHL**	**13**	**0**	**4**	**1**	**418**	**34**	**0**	**4.88**	....	....	....	....	....	....	....
	Moncton	AHL	37	18	11	6	2082	121	1	3.49	*21	*12	9	*1305	57	*2	2.62
1994-95	Springfield	AHL	24	10	11	3	1381	73	2	3.17	....	....	....	....	....	....	....
	NHL Totals		**90**	**19**	**39**	**11**	**4402**	**268**	**2**	**3.65**	**4**	**1**	**3**	**238**	**12**	**0**	**3.03**

a QMJHL First All-Star Team (1988)
b Canadian Major Junior Goaltender of the year (1988)

Traded to **Buffalo** by **Winnipeg** for Christian Ruuttu and future considerations, June 15, 1992. Traded to **Chicago** by **Buffalo** with Buffalo's fourth round choice (Eric Dazel) in 1993 Entry Draft for Dominik Hasek, August 7, 1992. Traded to **Winnipeg** by **Chicago** for Christian Ruuttu, August 10, 1992. Traded to **Philadelphia** by **Winnipeg** for future considerations, October 1, 1992. Traded to **Winnipeg** by **Philadelphia** for future considerations, June 11, 1993.

BELFOUR, ED — CHI.

Goaltender. Catches left. 5'11", 182 lbs. Born, Carman, Man., April 21, 1965.

			Regular Season								Playoffs						
Season	Club	Lea	GP	W	L	T	Mins	GA	SO	Avg	GP	W	L	Mins	GA	SO	Avg
1986-87a	North Dakota	WCHA	34	29	4	0	2049	81	3	2.43	....	....	....	....	....	....	....
1987-88bc	Saginaw	IHL	61	32	25	0	*3446	183	3	3.19	9	4	5	561	33	0	3.53
1988-89	**Chicago**	**NHL**	**23**	**4**	**12**	**3**	**1148**	**74**	**0**	**3.87**	....	....	....	....	....	....	....
	Saginaw	IHL	29	12	10	0	1760	92	0	3.10	5	2	3	298	14	0	2.82
1989-90	Cdn. National	....	33	13	12	6	1808	93	0	3.08	....	....	....	....	....	....	....
	Chicago	**NHL**	....	....	....	....	....	....	....	....	**9**	**4**	**2**	**409**	**17**	**0**	**2.49**
1990-91 defghi	**Chicago**	**NHL**	***74**	***43**	**19**	**7**	***4127**	**170**	**4**	***2.47**	**6**	**2**	**4**	**295**	**20**	**0**	**4.07**
1991-92	**Chicago**	**NHL**	**52**	**21**	**18**	**10**	**2928**	**132**	***5**	**2.70**	**18**	**12**	**4**	**949**	**39**	**1**	***2.47**
1992-93deg	**Chicago**	**NHL**	***71**	**41**	**18**	**11**	***4106**	**177**	***7**	**2.59**	**4**	**0**	**4**	**249**	**13**	**0**	**3.13**
1993-94	**Chicago**	**NHL**	**70**	**37**	**24**	**6**	**3998**	**178**	***7**	**2.67**	**6**	**2**	**4**	**360**	**15**	**0**	**2.50**
1994-95gj	**Chicago**	**NHL**	**42**	**22**	**15**	**3**	**2450**	**93**	***5**	**2.28**	**16**	**9**	**7**	**1014**	**37**	**1**	**2.19**
	NHL Totals		**332**	**168**	**106**	**40**	**18757**	**824**	**28**	**2.64**	**59**	**29**	**25**	**3276**	**141**	**2**	**2.58**

a WCHA First All-Star Team (1987)
b IHL First All-Star Team (1988)
c Shared Garry F. Longman Memorial Trophy (Top Rookie - IHL) (1988)
d NHL First All-Star Team (1991, 1993)
e Won Vezina Trophy (1991, 1993)
f Won Calder Memorial Trophy (1991)
g Won William M. Jennings Trophy (1991, 1993, 1995)
h Won Trico Goaltender Award (1991)
i NHL/Upper Deck All-Rookie Team (1991)
j NHL Second All-Star Team (1995)

Played in NHL All-Star Game (1992, 1993)

Signed as a free agent by **Chicago**, September 25, 1987.

BERGERON, JEAN-CLAUDE — T.B.

Goaltender. Catches left. 6'2", 192 lbs. Born, Hauterive, Que., October 14, 1968.
(Montreal's 5th choice, 104th overall, in 1988 Entry Draft).

			Regular Season								Playoffs						
Season	Club	Lea	GP	W	L	T	Mins	GA	SO	Avg	GP	W	L	Mins	GA	SO	Avg
1987-88	Verdun	QMJHL	49	13	31	3	2715	265	0	5.86	....	....	....	....	....	....	....
1988-89	Verdun	QMJHL	44	8	34	1	2417	199	0	4.94	....	....	....	....	....	....	....
	Sherbrooke	AHL	5	4	1	0	302	18	0	3.58	....	....	....	....	....	....	....
1989-90abc	Sherbrooke	AHL	40	21	8	7	2254	103	2	*2.74	9	6	2	497	28	0	3.38
1990-91	**Montreal**	**NHL**	**18**	**7**	**6**	**2**	**941**	**59**	**0**	**3.76**	....	....	....	....	....	....	....
	Fredericton	AHL	18	12	6	0	1083	59	1	3.27	10	5	5	546	32	0	3.52
1991-92	Fredericton	AHL	13	5	7	1	791	57	0	4.32	....	....	....	....	....	....	....
	Peoria	IHL	27	14	9	3	1632	96	1	3.53	6	3	3	352	24	0	4.09
1992-93	**Tampa Bay**	**NHL**	**21**	**8**	**10**	**1**	**1163**	**71**	**0**	**3.66**	....	....	....	....	....	....	....
	Atlanta	IHL	31	21	7	1	1722	92	1	3.21	6	3	3	368	19	0	3.10
1993-94	**Tampa Bay**	**NHL**	**3**	**1**	**1**	**1**	**134**	**7**	**0**	**3.13**	....	....	....	....	....	....	....
d	Atlanta	IHL	48	27	11	7	2755	141	0	3.07	2	1	1	153	6	0	2.34
1994-95	Atlanta	IHL	6	3	3	0	324	24	0	4.44	....	....	....	....	....	....	....
	Tampa Bay	**NHL**	**17**	**3**	**9**	**1**	**883**	**49**	**1**	**3.33**	....	....	....	....	....	....	....
	NHL Totals		**59**	**19**	**26**	**5**	**3121**	**186**	**1**	**3.58**	....	....	....	....	....	....	....

a AHL First All-Star Team (1990)
b Shared Harry "Hap" Holmes Trophy (fewest goals-against - AHL) with Andre Racicot (1990)
c Won Baz Bastien Memorial Trophy (Top Goaltender - AHL) (1990)
d Shared James Norris Memorial Trophy (fewest goals-against - IHL) with Mike Greenlay (1994)

Traded to **Tampa Bay** by **Montreal** for Frederic Chabot, June 19, 1992.

BERTHIAUME, DANIEL (bairt-YOHM)

Goaltender. Catches left. 5'9", 155 lbs. Born, Longueuil, Que., January 26, 1966.
(Winnipeg's 3rd choice, 60th overall, in 1985 Entry Draft).

			Regular Season								Playoffs						
Season	Club	Lea	GP	W	L	T	Mins	GA	SO	Avg	GP	W	L	Mins	GA	SO	Avg
1984-85	Chicoutimi	QMJHL	59	40	11	2	2177	149	0	4.11	14	8	6	770	51	0	3.97
1985-86	Chicoutimi	QMJHL	66	34	29	3	3718	286	1	4.62	9	4	5	580	36	0	3.72
	Winnipeg	**NHL**	....	....	....	....	....	....	....	....	**1**	**0**	**1**	**68**	**4**	**0**	**3.53**
1986-87	**Winnipeg**	**NHL**	**31**	**18**	**7**	**3**	**1758**	**93**	**1**	**3.17**	**8**	**4**	**4**	**439**	**21**	**0**	**2.87**
	Sherbrooke	AHL	7	4	3	0	420	23	0	3.29	....	....	....	....	....	....	....
1987-88	**Winnipeg**	**NHL**	**56**	**22**	**19**	**7**	**3010**	**176**	**2**	**3.51**	**5**	**1**	**4**	**300**	**25**	**0**	**5.00**
1988-89	**Winnipeg**	**NHL**	**9**	**0**	**8**	**0**	**443**	**44**	**0**	**5.96**	....	....	....	....	....	....	....
	Moncton	AHL	21	6	9	2	1083	76	0	4.21	3	1	2	180	11	0	3.67
1989-90	**Winnipeg**	**NHL**	**24**	**10**	**11**	**3**	**1387**	**86**	**1**	**3.72**	....	....	....	....	....	....	....
	Minnesota	**NHL**	**5**	**1**	**3**	**0**	**240**	**14**	**0**	**3.50**	....	....	....	....	....	....	....
1990-91	**Los Angeles**	**NHL**	**37**	**20**	**11**	**4**	**2119**	**117**	**1**	**3.31**	....	....	....	....	....	....	....
1991-92	**Los Angeles**	**NHL**	**19**	**7**	**10**	**1**	**979**	**66**	**0**	**4.04**	....	....	....	....	....	....	....
	Boston	**NHL**	**8**	**1**	**4**	**2**	**399**	**21**	**0**	**3.16**	....	....	....	....	....	....	....
1992-93	Graz	Alp.	28	....	....	....	....	110	0	4.07	....	....	....	....	....	....	....
	Ottawa	**NHL**	**25**	**2**	**17**	**1**	**1326**	**95**	**0**	**4.30**	....	....	....	....	....	....	....
1993-94	**Ottawa**	**NHL**	**1**	**0**	**0**	**0**	**1**	**2**	**0**	**120.00**	....	....	....	....	....	....	....
	PEI	AHL	30	8	16	3	1640	130	0	4.76	....	....	....	....	....	....	....
	Adirondack	AHL	11	7	2	0	552	35	0	3.80	11	6	4	632	30	0	2.85
1994-95	Providence	AHL	2	0	1	1	126	7	0	3.32	....	....	....	....	....	....	....
	Wheeling	ECHL	10	6	1	1	599	41	0	4.10	....	....	....	....	....	....	....
	Roanoke	ECHL	21	15	4	2	1196	47	0	2.36	8	4	4	464	23	1	2.97
	Detroit	IHL	....	....	....	....	....	....	....	....	5	2	3	331	14	0	2.53
	NHL Totals		**215**	**81**	**90**	**21**	**11662**	**714**	**5**	**3.67**	**14**	**5**	**9**	**807**	**50**	**0**	**3.72**

Traded to **Minnesota** by **Winnipeg** for future considerations, January 22, 1990. Traded to **Los Angeles** by **Minnesota** for Craig Duncanson, September 6, 1990. Traded to **Boston** by **Los Angeles** for future considerations, January 18, 1992. Traded to **Winnipeg** by **Boston** for Doug Evans, June 10, 1992. Signed as a free agent by **Ottawa**, December 15, 1992. Traded to **Detroit** by **Ottawa** for Steve Konroyd, March 21, 1994.

BESTER, ALLAN

Goaltender. Catches left. 5'7", 155 lbs. Born, Hamilton, Ont., March 26, 1964.
(Toronto's 3rd choice, 48th overall, in 1983 Entry Draft).

			Regular Season								Playoffs						
Season	Club	Lea	GP	W	L	T	Mins	GA	SO	Avg	GP	W	L	Mins	GA	SO	Avg
1981-82	Brantford	OHL	19	4	11	0	970	68	0	4.21	....	....	....	....	....	....	....
1982-83a	Brantford	OHL	56	29	21	3	3210	188	0	3.51	8	3	3	480	20	*1	*2.50
1983-84	**Toronto**	**NHL**	**32**	**11**	**16**	**4**	**1848**	**134**	**0**	**4.35**	....	....	....	....	....	....	....
	Brantford	OHL	23	12	9	1	1271	71	1	3.35	1	0	1	60	5	0	5.00
1984-85	**Toronto**	**NHL**	**15**	**3**	**9**	**1**	**767**	**54**	**1**	**4.22**	....	....	....	....	....	....	....
	St. Catharines	AHL	30	9	18	1	1669	133	0	4.78	....	....	....	....	....	....	....
1985-86	**Toronto**	**NHL**	**1**	**0**	**0**	**0**	**20**	**2**	**0**	**6.00**	....	....	....	....	....	....	....
	St. Catharines	AHL	50	23	23	3	2855	173	1	3.64	11	7	3	637	27	0	2.54
1986-87	**Toronto**	**NHL**	**36**	**10**	**14**	**3**	**1808**	**110**	**2**	**3.65**	**1**	**0**	**0**	**39**	**1**	**0**	**1.54**
	Newmarket	AHL	3	1	0	0	190	6	0	1.89	....	....	....	....	....	....	....
1987-88	**Toronto**	**NHL**	**30**	**8**	**12**	**5**	**1607**	**102**	**2**	**3.81**	**5**	**2**	**3**	**253**	**21**	**0**	**4.98**
1988-89	**Toronto**	**NHL**	**43**	**17**	**20**	**3**	**2460**	**156**	**2**	**3.80**	....	....	....	....	....	....	....
1989-90	**Toronto**	**NHL**	**42**	**20**	**16**	**0**	**2206**	**165**	**0**	**4.49**	**4**	**0**	**3**	**196**	**14**	**0**	**4.29**
	Newmarket	AHL	5	2	1	1	264	18	0	4.09	....	....	....	....	....	....	....
1990-91	**Toronto**	**NHL**	**6**	**0**	**4**	**0**	**247**	**18**	**0**	**4.37**	....	....	....	....	....	....	....
	Newmarket	AHL	19	7	8	4	1157	58	1	3.01	....	....	....	....	....	....	....
	Detroit	**NHL**	**3**	**0**	**3**	**0**	**178**	**13**	**0**	**4.38**	**1**	**0**	**0**	**20**	**1**	**0**	**3.00**
1991-92	**Detroit**	**NHL**	**1**	**0**	**0**	**0**	**31**	**2**	**0**	**3.87**	....	....	....	....	....	....	....
b	Adirondack	AHL	22	13	8	0	1268	78	0	3.69	*19	*14	5	1174	50	*1	*2.56
1992-93	Adirondack	AHL	41	16	15	5	2268	133	1	3.52	10	7	3	633	26	*1	2.46
1993-94	San Diego	IHL	46	22	14	6	2543	150	1	3.54	8	4	4	419	28	0	4.00
1994-95	San Diego	IHL	58	28	23	5	3250	183	1	3.38	4	2	2	272	13	0	2.86
	NHL Totals		**209**	**69**	**94**	**16**	**11172**	**756**	**7**	**4.06**	**11**	**2**	**6**	**508**	**37**	**0**	**4.37**

a OHL First All-Star Team (1983)
b Won Jack Butterfield Trophy (Playoff MVP - AHL) (1992)

Traded to **Detroit** by **Toronto** for Detroit's sixth round choice (Alexander Kuzminsky) in 1991 Entry Draft, March 5, 1991. Signed as a free agent by **Anaheim**, September 9, 1993.

BILLINGTON, CRAIG — BOS.

Goaltender. Catches left. 5'10", 170 lbs. Born, London, Ont., September 11, 1966.
(New Jersey's 2nd choice, 23rd overall, in 1984 Entry Draft).

			Regular Season								Playoffs						
Season	Club	Lea	GP	W	L	T	Mins	GA	SO	Avg	GP	W	L	Mins	GA	SO	Avg
1983-84	Belleville	OHL	44	20	19	0	2335	162	1	4.16	1	0	0	30	3	0	6.00
1984-85a	Belleville	OHL	47	26	19	0	2544	180	1	4.25	14	7	5	761	47	1	3.71
1985-86	**New Jersey**	**NHL**	**18**	**4**	**9**	**1**	**901**	**77**	**0**	**5.13**	....	....	....	....	....	....	....
	Belleville	OHL	3	2	1	0	180	11	0	3.67	20	9	6	1133	68	0	3.60
1986-87	**New Jersey**	**NHL**	**22**	**4**	**13**	**2**	**1114**	**89**	**0**	**4.79**	....	....	....	....	....	....	....
	Maine	AHL	20	9	8	2	1151	70	0	3.65	....	....	....	....	....	....	....
1987-88	Utica	AHL	*59	22	27	8	*3404	208	1	3.67	....	....	....	....	....	....	....
1988-89	**New Jersey**	**NHL**	**3**	**1**	**1**	**0**	**140**	**11**	**0**	**4.71**	....	....	....	....	....	....	....
	Utica	AHL	41	17	18	6	2432	150	2	3.70	4	1	3	220	18	0	4.91
1989-90	Utica	AHL	38	20	13	1	2087	138	0	3.97	....	....	....	....	....	....	....
1990-91	Cdn. National	....	34	17	14	2	1879	110	2	3.51	....	....	....	....	....	....	....
1991-92	**New Jersey**	**NHL**	**26**	**13**	**7**	**1**	**1363**	**69**	**2**	**3.04**	....	....	....	....	....	....	....
1992-93	**New Jersey**	**NHL**	**42**	**21**	**16**	**4**	**2389**	**146**	**2**	**3.67**	**2**	**0**	**1**	**78**	**5**	**0**	**3.85**
1993-94	**Ottawa**	**NHL**	**63**	**11**	**41**	**4**	**3319**	**254**	**0**	**4.59**	....	....	....	....	....	....	....
1994-95	**Ottawa**	**NHL**	**9**	**0**	**6**	**2**	**472**	**32**	**0**	**4.07**	....	....	....	....	....	....	....
	Boston	**NHL**	**8**	**5**	**1**	**0**	**373**	**19**	**0**	**3.06**	**1**	**0**	**0**	**25**	**1**	**0**	**2.40**
	NHL Totals		**191**	**59**	**94**	**14**	**10071**	**697**	**4**	**4.15**	**3**	**0**	**1**	**103**	**6**	**0**	**3.50**

a OHL First All-Star Team (1985)

Played in NHL All-Star Game (1993)

Traded to **Ottawa** by **New Jersey** with Troy Mallette and New Jersey's fourth round choice (Cosmo Dupaul) in 1993 Entry Draft for Peter Sidorkiewicz and future considerations (Mike Peluso, June 26, 1993), June 20, 1993. Traded to **Boston** by **Ottawa** for NY Islanders' eighth round choice (previously acquired by Boston — Ottawa selected Ray Schultz) in 1995 Entry Draft, April 7, 1995.

BIRON, MARTIN (BIH-rohn) BUF.

Goaltender. Catches left. 6'1", 154 lbs. Born, Lac St. Charles, Que., August 15, 1977.
(Buffalo's 2nd choice, 16th overall, in 1995 Entry Draft).

			Regular Season								Playoffs						
Season	Club	Lea	GP	W	L	T	Mins	GA	SO	Avg	GP	W	L	Mins	GA	SO	Avg
1993-94	Trois Rivières	Midget	23	....	....	....	1412	80	1	3.40	....	....	....	....	....	....	....
1994-95ab	Beauport	QMJHL	56	29	16	9	3193	132	3	*2.48	16	8	7	900	37	*4	2.47

a Canadian Major Junior First All-Star Team (1995)
b Canadian Major Junior Goaltender of the Year (1995)

BLUE, JOHN

Goaltender. Catches left. 5'10", 185 lbs. Born, Huntington Beach, CA, February 19, 1966.
(Winnipeg's 9th choice, 197th overall, in 1986 Entry Draft).

			Regular Season								Playoffs						
Season	Club	Lea	GP	W	L	T	Mins	GA	SO	Avg	GP	W	L	Mins	GA	SO	Avg
1984-85	U. Minnesota	WCHA	34	23	10	0	1964	111	2	3.39	....	....	....	....	....	....	....
1985-86a	U. Minnesota	WCHA	29	20	6	0	1588	80	2	3.02	....	....	....	....	....	....	....
1986-87	U. Minnesota	WCHA	33	21	9	1	1889	99	3	3.14	....	....	....	....	....	....	....
1987-88	Kalamazoo	IHL	15	3	8	4	847	65	0	4.60	1	0	1	40	6	0	9.00
	U.S. National	....	13	3	4	1	588	33	0	3.37	....	....	....	....	....	....	....
1988-89	Kalamazoo	IHL	17	8	6	0	970	69	0	4.27	....	....	....	....	....	....	....
	Virginia	ECHL	10	....	....	....	570	38	0	4.00	....	....	....	....	....	....	....
1989-90	Phoenix	IHL	19	5	10	3	986	92	0	5.65	....	....	....	....	....	....	....
	Knoxville	ECHL	19	6	10	1	1000	85	0	5.15	....	....	....	....	....	....	....
	Kalamazoo	IHL	4	2	1	1	232	18	0	4.65	....	....	....	....	....	....	....
1990-91	Maine	AHL	10	3	4	2	545	22	0	2.42	1	0	1	40	7	0	10.50
	Albany	IHL	19	11	6	0	1077	71	0	3.96	....	....	....	....	....	....	....
	Kalamazoo	IHL	1	1	0	0	64	2	0	1.88	....	....	....	....	....	....	....
	Peoria	IHL	4	4	0	0	240	12	0	3.00	....	....	....	....	....	....	....
	Knoxville	ECHL	3	1	1	0	149	13	0	5.23	....	....	....	....	....	....	....
1991-92	Maine	AHL	43	11	23	6	2168	165	1	4.57	....	....	....	....	....	....	....
1992-93	**Boston**	**NHL**	**23**	**9**	**8**	**4**	**1322**	**64**	**1**	**2.90**	**2**	**0**	**1**	**96**	**5**	**0**	**3.13**
	Providence	AHL	19	14	4	1	1159	67	0	3.47	....	....	....	....	....	....	....
1993-94	**Boston**	**NHL**	**18**	**5**	**8**	**3**	**944**	**47**	**0**	**2.99**	....	....	....	....	....	....	....
	Providence	AHL	24	7	11	4	1298	76	1	3.51	....	....	....	....	....	....	....
1994-95	Providence	AHL	10	6	3	0	577	30	0	3.11	4	1	3	219	19	0	5.19
	NHL Totals		**41**	**14**	**16**	**7**	**2266**	**111**	**1**	**2.94**	**2**	**0**	**1**	**96**	**5**	**0**	**3.13**

a WCHA First All-Star Team (1986)

Traded to **Minnesota** by **Winnipeg** for Winnipeg's seventh round choice (Markus Akerblom) in 1988 Entry Draft, March 7, 1988. Signed as a free agent by **Boston**, August 1, 1991.

BONNER, DOUG — TOR.

Goaltender. Catches left. 5'10", 175 lbs. Born, Tacoma, WA, October 15, 1976.
(Toronto's 3rd choice, 139th overall, in 1995 Entry Draft).

			Regular Season								Playoffs						
Season	Club	Lea	GP	W	L	T	Mins	GA	SO	Avg	GP	W	L	Mins	GA	SO	Avg
1992-93	Seattle	WHL	30	7	15	0	1212	93	1	4.60	....	....	....	....	....	....	....
1993-94	Seattle	WHL	29	9	15	0	1481	111	1	4.50	....	....	....	....	....	....	....
1994-95	Seattle	WHL	59	33	23	1	3386	205	1	3.63	3	0	3	193	10	0	3.11

BOUCHER, BRIAN (BOO-shay) PHI.

Goaltender. Catches left. 6'1", 190 lbs. Born, Woonsocket, RI, January 2, 1977.
(Philadelphia's 1st choice, 22nd overall, in 1995 Entry Draft).

			Regular Season								Playoffs						
Season	Club	Lea	GP	W	L	T	Mins	GA	SO	Avg	GP	W	L	Mins	GA	SO	Avg
1993-94	Mt. St. Charles	HS	26	....	....	....	1170	23	12	0.87	....	....	....	....	....	....	....
1994-95	Tri-City	WHL	35	17	11	2	1969	108	1	3.29	13	6	5	795	50	0	3.77

BRATHWAITE, FRED (BRAYTH-wayt) EDM.

Goaltender. Catches left. 5'7", 170 lbs. Born, Ottawa, Ont., November 24, 1972.

			Regular Season								Playoffs						
Season	Club	Lea	GP	W	L	T	Mins	GA	SO	Avg	GP	W	L	Mins	GA	SO	Avg
1989-90	Oshawa	OHL	20	11	2	1	886	43	1	2.91	10	4	2	451	22	0	*2.93
1990-91	Oshawa	OHL	39	25	6	3	1986	112	1	3.38	13	*9	2	677	43	0	3.81
1991-92	Oshawa	OHL	24	12	7	2	1248	81	0	3.89	....	....	....	....	....	....	....
	London	OHL	23	15	6	2	1325	61	*4	2.76	10	5	5	615	36	0	3.51
1992-93	Detroit	OHL	37	23	10	4	2192	134	0	3.67	15	9	6	858	48	1	3.36
1993-94	**Edmonton**	**NHL**	**19**	**3**	**10**	**3**	**982**	**58**	**0**	**3.54**	....	....	....	....	....	....	....
	Cape Breton	AHL	2	1	1	0	119	6	0	3.04	....	....	....	....	....	....	....
1994-95	**Edmonton**	**NHL**	**14**	**2**	**5**	**1**	**601**	**40**	**0**	**3.99**	....	....	....	....	....	....	....
	NHL Totals		**33**	**5**	**15**	**4**	**1583**	**98**	**0**	**3.71**	....	....	....	....	....	....	....

Signed as a free agent by **Edmonton**, October 6, 1993.

BROCHU, MARTIN (broh-shoo) MTL.

Goaltender. Catches left. 5'10", 200 lbs. Born, Anjou, Que., March 10, 1973.

			Regular Season								Playoffs						
Season	Club	Lea	GP	W	L	T	Mins	GA	SO	Avg	GP	W	L	Mins	GA	SO	Avg
1991-92	Granby	QMJHL	52	15	29	2	2772	278	0	4.72	....	....	....	....	....	....	....
1992-93	Hull	QMJHL	29	9	15	1	1453	137	0	5.66	2	0	1	69	7	0	6.07
1993-94	Fredericton	AHL	32	10	11	3	1505	76	2	3.03	....	....	....	....	....	....	....
1994-95	Fredericton	AHL	44	18	18	4	2475	145	0	3.51	....	....	....	....	....	....	....

Signed as a free agent by **Montreal**, September 22, 1992.

BRODEUR, MARTIN (broh-DOOR, MAHR-tihn) N.J.

Goaltender. Catches left. 6'1", 205 lbs. Born, Montreal, Que., May 6, 1972.
(New Jersey's 1st choice, 20th overall, in 1990 Entry Draft).

			Regular Season								Playoffs						
Season	Club	Lea	GP	W	L	T	Mins	GA	SO	Avg	GP	W	L	Mins	GA	SO	Avg
1989-90	St-Hyacinthe	QMJHL	42	23	13	2	2333	156	0	4.01	12	5	7	678	46	0	4.07
1990-91	St-Hyacinthe	QMJHL	52	22	24	4	2946	162	2	3.30	4	0	4	232	16	0	4.14
1991-92	**New Jersey**	**NHL**	**4**	**2**	**1**	**0**	**179**	**10**	**0**	**3.35**	**1**	**0**	**1**	**32**	**3**	**0**	**5.63**
a	St-Hyacinthe	QMJHL	48	27	16	4	2846	161	2	3.39	5	2	3	317	14	0	2.65
1992-93	Utica	AHL	32	14	13	5	1952	131	0	4.03	4	1	3	258	18	0	4.19
1993-94bc	**New Jersey**	**NHL**	**47**	**27**	**11**	**8**	**2625**	**105**	**3**	**2.40**	**17**	**8**	**9**	**1171**	**38**	**1**	**1.95**
1994-95	**New Jersey**	**NHL**	**40**	**19**	**11**	**6**	**2184**	**89**	**3**	**2.45**	***20**	***16**	**4**	***1222**	**34**	***3**	***1.67**
	NHL Totals		**91**	**48**	**23**	**14**	**4988**	**204**	**6**	**2.45**	**38**	**24**	**14**	**2425**	**75**	**4**	**1.86**

a QMJHL Second All-Star Team (1992)
b NHL/Upper Deck All-Rookie Team (1994)
c Won Calder Memorial Trophy (1994)

BURKE, SEAN HFD.

Goaltender. Catches left. 6'4", 210 lbs. Born, Windsor, Ont., January 29, 1967.
(New Jersey's 2nd choice, 24th overall, in 1985 Entry Draft).

			Regular Season								Playoffs						
Season	Club	Lea	GP	W	L	T	Mins	GA	SO	Avg	GP	W	L	Mins	GA	SO	Avg
1984-85	Toronto	OHL	49	25	21	3	2987	211	0	4.24	5	1	3	266	25	0	5.64
1985-86	Toronto	OHL	47	16	27	3	2840	233	0	4.92	4	0	4	238	24	0	6.05
1986-87	Cdn. National	....	42	27	13	2	2550	130	0	3.05	....	....	....	....	....	....	....
1987-88	Cdn. National	....	37	19	9	2	1962	92	1	2.81	....	....	....	....	....	....	....
	Cdn. Olympic	....	4	1	2	1	238	12	0	3.02	....	....	....	....	....	....	....
	New Jersey	**NHL**	**13**	**10**	**1**	**0**	**689**	**35**	**1**	**3.05**	**17**	**9**	**8**	**1001**	**57**	***1**	**3.42**
1988-89	**New Jersey**	**NHL**	**62**	**22**	**31**	**9**	**3590**	**230**	**3**	**3.84**	....	....	....	....	....	....	....
1989-90	**New Jersey**	**NHL**	**52**	**22**	**22**	**6**	**2914**	**175**	**0**	**3.60**	**2**	**0**	**2**	**125**	**8**	**0**	**3.84**
1990-91	**New Jersey**	**NHL**	**35**	**8**	**12**	**8**	**1870**	**112**	**0**	**3.59**	....	....	....	....	....	....	....
1991-92	Cdn. National	....	31	18	6	4	1721	75	1	2.61	....	....	....	....	....	....	....
	Cdn. Olympic	....	7	5	2	0	429	17	0	2.37	....	....	....	....	....	....	....
	San Diego	IHL	7	4	2	1	424	17	0	2.41	3	0	3	160	13	0	4.88
1992-93	**Hartford**	**NHL**	**50**	**16**	**27**	**3**	**2656**	**184**	**0**	**4.16**	....	....	....	....	....	....	....
1993-94	**Hartford**	**NHL**	**47**	**17**	**24**	**5**	**2750**	**137**	**2**	**2.99**	....	....	....	....	....	....	....
1994-95	**Hartford**	**NHL**	**42**	**17**	**19**	**4**	**2418**	**108**	**0**	**2.68**	....	....	....	....	....	....	....
	NHL Totals		**301**	**112**	**136**	**35**	**16887**	**981**	**6**	**3.49**	**19**	**9**	**10**	**1126**	**65**	**1**	**3.46**

Played in NHL All-Star Game (1989)

Traded to **Hartford** by **New Jersey** with Eric Weinrich for Bobby Holik, Hartford's second round choice (Jay Pandolfo) in 1993 Entry Draft and future considerations, August 28, 1992.

BUTLER, JEROME

Goaltender. Catches left. 5'11", 175 lbs. Born, Roseau, MN, December 14, 1972.
(Calgary's 6th choice, 107th overall, in 1991 Entry Draft).

			Regular Season								Playoffs						
Season	Club	Lea	GP	W	L	T	Mins	GA	SO	Avg	GP	W	L	Mins	GA	SO	Avg
1991-92	Minn.-Duluth	WCHA	22	9	11	2	1325	91	0	4.12	....	....	....	....	....	....	....
1992-93	Minn.-Duluth	WCHA	21	12	6	2	1183	74	0	3.75	....	....	....	....	....	....	....
1993-94	Minn. Duluth	WCHA	7	1	4	1	328	27	0	4.94	....	....	....	....	....	....	....
1994-95	Columbus	ECHL	3	0	3	0	140	12	0	5.12	....	....	....	....	....	....	....

BUZAK, MIKE ST.L.

Goaltender. Catches left. 6'3", 183 lbs. Born, Edson, Alta., February 10, 1973.
(St. Louis' 5th choice, 167th overall, in 1993 Entry Draft).

			Regular Season								Playoffs						
Season	Club	Lea	GP	W	L	T	Mins	GA	SO	Avg	GP	W	L	Mins	GA	SO	Avg
1991-92	Michigan State	CCHA	7	4	0	0	311	22	0	4.25	....	....	....	....	....	....	....
1992-93	Michigan State	CCHA	38	22	10	2	*2090	102	0	2.93	....	....	....	....	....	....	....
1993-94a	Michigan State	CCHA	*39	21	12	5	*2297	104	2	2.72	....	....	....	....	....	....	....
1994-95a	Michigan State	CCHA	31	17	10	3	1796	94	0	3.14	....	....	....	....	....	....	....

a CCHA Second All-Star Team (1994, 1995)

CALLINAN, JEFF ST.L.

Goaltender. Catches left. 5'10", 169 lbs. Born, Minneapolis, MN, January 6, 1973.
(St. Louis' 5th choice, 109th overall, in 1991 Entry Draft).

			Regular Season								Playoffs						
Season	Club	Lea	GP	W	L	T	Mins	GA	SO	Avg	GP	W	L	Mins	GA	SO	Avg
1991-92	U. Minnesota	WCHA	6	2	1	0	209	15	0	4.32	....	....	....	....	....	....	....
1992-93	U. Minnesota	WCHA	21	8	5	5	1113	72	0	3.88	....	....	....	....	....	....	....
1993-94	U. Minnesota	WCHA	26	14	5	3	1491	80	0	3.22	....	....	....	....	....	....	....
1994-95	U. Minnesota	WCHA	*43	*23	11	5	2483	115	0	*2.78	....	....	....	....	....	....	....

CARAVAGGIO, LUCIANO N.J.

Goaltender. Catches left. 5'11", 175 lbs. Born, Etobicoke, Ont., October 3, 1975.
(New Jersey's 7th choice, 155th overall, in 1994 Entry Draft).

			Regular Season								Playoffs						
Season	Club	Lea	GP	W	L	T	Mins	GA	SO	Avg	GP	W	L	Mins	GA	SO	Avg
1993-94	Michigan Tech	WCHA	13	1	7	0	538	37	*1	4.13	....	....	....	....	....	....	....
1994-95	Michigan Tech	WCHA	31	12	5	3	1776	119	*1	4.02	....	....	....	....	....	....	....

CAREY, JIM WSH.

Goaltender. Catches left. 6'2", 205 lbs. Born, Dorchester, MA, May 31, 1974.
(Washington's 2nd choice, 32nd overall, in 1992 Entry Draft).

			Regular Season								Playoffs						
Season	Club	Lea	GP	W	L	T	Mins	GA	SO	Avg	GP	W	L	Mins	GA	SO	Avg
1992-93a	U. Wisconsin	WCHA	26	15	8	1	1525	78	1	3.07	....	....	....	....	....	....	....
1993-94	U. Wisconsin	WCHA	*40	*24	13	1	*2247	114	*1	*3.04	....	....	....	....	....	....	....
1994-95bcd	Portland	AHL	55	30	14	11	3281	151	*6	2.76	....	....	....	....	....	....	....
e	**Washington**	**NHL**	**28**	**18**	**6**	**3**	**1604**	**57**	**4**	**2.13**	**7**	**2**	**4**	**358**	**25**	**0**	**4.19**
	NHL Totals		**28**	**18**	**6**	**3**	**1604**	**57**	**4**	**2.13**	**7**	**2**	**4**	**358**	**25**	**0**	**4.19**

a WCHA Second All-Star Team (1993)
b AHL First All-Star Team (1995)
c Won Baz Bastien Memorial Trophy (Top Goaltender - AHL) (1995)
d Won Dudley "Red" Garrett Memorial Trophy (Top Rookie - AHL) (1995)
e NHL/Upper Deck All-Rookie Team (1995)

CASEY, JON ST.L.

Goaltender. Catches left. 5'10", 155 lbs. Born, Grand Rapids, MN, March 29, 1962.

			Regular Season								Playoffs						
Season	Club	Lea	GP	W	L	T	Mins	GA	SO	Avg	GP	W	L	Mins	GA	SO	Avg
1980-81	North Dakota	WCHA	5	3	1	0	300	19	0	3.80	....	....	....	....	....	....	....
1981-82	North Dakota	WCHA	18	15	3	0	1038	48	1	2.77	....	....	....	....	....	....	....
1982-83	North Dakota	WCHA	17	9	6	2	1020	42	0	2.51	....	....	....	....	....	....	....
1983-84	North Dakota	WCHA	37	25	10	2	2180	115	2	3.13	....	....	....	....	....	....	....
	Minnesota	**NHL**	**2**	**1**	**0**	**0**	**84**	**6**	**0**	**4.29**	....	....	....	....	....	....	....
1984-85abc	Baltimore	AHL	46	30	11	4	2646	116	*4	*2.63	*13	8	3	689	38	0	3.31
1985-86	**Minnesota**	**NHL**	**26**	**11**	**11**	**1**	**1402**	**91**	**0**	**3.89**	....	....	....	....	....	....	....
	Springfield	AHL	9	4	3	1	464	30	0	3.88	....	....	....	....	....	....	....
1986-87	Springfield	AHL	13	1	8	0	770	56	0	4.36	....	....	....	....	....	....	....
	Indianapolis	IHL	31	14	15	0	1794	133	0	4.45	....	....	....	....	....	....	....
1987-88	**Minnesota**	**NHL**	**14**	**1**	**7**	**4**	**663**	**41**	**0**	**3.71**	....	....	....	....	....	....	....
	Kalamazoo	IHL	42	24	13	5	2541	154	2	3.64	7	3	3	382	26	0	4.08
1988-89	**Minnesota**	**NHL**	**55**	**18**	**17**	**12**	**2961**	**151**	**1**	**3.06**	**4**	**1**	**3**	**211**	**16**	**0**	**4.55**
1989-90	**Minnesota**	**NHL**	**61**	***31**	**22**	**4**	**3407**	**183**	**3**	**3.22**	**7**	**3**	**4**	**415**	**21**	**1**	**3.04**
1990-91	**Minnesota**	**NHL**	**55**	**21**	**20**	**11**	**3185**	**158**	**3**	**2.98**	***23**	***14**	**7**	***1205**	**61**	***1**	**3.04**
1991-92	**Minnesota**	**NHL**	**52**	**19**	**23**	**5**	**2911**	**165**	**2**	**3.40**	**7**	**3**	**4**	**437**	**22**	**0**	**3.02**
	Kalamazoo	IHL	4	2	1	1	250	11	0	2.64	....	....	....	....	....	....	....
1992-93	**Minnesota**	**NHL**	**60**	**26**	**26**	**5**	**3476**	**193**	**3**	**3.33**	....	....	....	....	....	....	....
1993-94	**Boston**	**NHL**	**57**	**30**	**15**	**9**	**3192**	**153**	**4**	**2.88**	**11**	**5**	**6**	**698**	**34**	**0**	**2.92**
1994-95	**St. Louis**	**NHL**	**19**	**7**	**5**	**4**	**872**	**40**	**0**	**2.75**	**2**	**0**	**1**	**30**	**2**	**0**	**4.00**
	NHL Totals		**401**	**165**	**146**	**55**	**22153**	**1181**	**16**	**3.20**	**54**	**26**	**25**	**2996**	**156**	**2**	**3.12**

a Won Baz Bastien Memorial Trophy (Top Goaltender - AHL) (1985)
b Won Harry "Hap" Holmes Memorial Trophy (fewest goals against - AHL) (1985)
c AHL First All-Star Team (1985)

Played in NHL All-Star Game (1993)

Signed as a free agent by **Minnesota**, April 1, 1984. Traded to **Boston** by **Dallas** for Andy Moog to complete June 20, 1993 trade which sent Gord Murphy to Dallas for future considerations, June 25, 1993. Signed as a free agent by **St. Louis**, June 29, 1994.

CASSIVI, FREDERIC OTT.

Goaltender. Catches left. 6'3", 193 lbs. Born, Sorel, Que., June 12, 1975.
(Ottawa's 7th choice, 210th overall, in 1994 Entry Draft).

			Regular Season								Playoffs						
Season	Club	Lea	GP	W	L	T	Mins	GA	SO	Avg	GP	W	L	Mins	GA	SO	Avg
1993-94	St-Hyacinthe	QMJHL	35	15	13	3	1751	127	1	4.35	....	....	....	....	....	....	....
1994-95	Halifax	QMJHL	24	9	12	1	1362	105	0	4.63	....	....	....	....	....	....	....
	St-Jean	QMJHL	19	12	6	0	1021	55	1	3.23	5	2	3	258	18	0	4.19

CAVICCHI, TRENT MTL.

Goaltender. Catches left. 6'3", 190 lbs. Born, Halifax, N.S., August 11, 1974.
(Montreal's 12th choice, 236th overall, in 1992 Entry Draft).

			Regular Season								Playoffs						
Season	Club	Lea	GP	W	L	T	Mins	GA	SO	Avg	GP	W	L	Mins	GA	SO	Avg
1992-93	N. Hampshire	H.E.	9	3	2	1	391	32	0	4.91	....	....	....	....	....	....	....
1993-94	N. Hampshire	H.E.	25	14	7	1	1324	65	1	2.95	....	....	....	....	....	....	....
1994-95	N. Hampshire	H.E.	23	14	6	1	1276	71	0	3.34	....	....	....	....	....	....	....

CHABOT, FREDERIC (shah-BOH) FLA.

Goaltender. Catches left. 5'11", 175 lbs. Born, Hebertville-Station, Que., February 12, 1968.
(New Jersey's 10th choice, 192nd overall, in 1986 Entry Draft).

			Regular Season								Playoffs						
Season	Club	Lea	GP	W	L	T	Mins	GA	SO	Avg	GP	W	L	Mins	GA	SO	Avg
1986-87	Drummondville	QMJHL	62	31	29	0	3508	293	1	5.01	8	2	6	481	40	0	4.99
1987-88	Drummondville	QMJHL	58	27	24	4	3276	237	1	4.34	16	10	6	1019	56	*1	*3.30
1988-89a	Prince Albert	WHL	54	21	29	0	2957	202	2	4.10	4	1	1	199	16	0	4.82
1989-90	Sherbrooke	AHL	2	1	1	0	119	8	0	4.03	....	....	....	....	....	....	....
	Fort Wayne	IHL	23	6	13	3	1208	87	1	4.32	....	....	....	....	....	....	....
1990-91	**Montreal**	**NHL**	**3**	**0**	**0**	**1**	**108**	**6**	**0**	**3.33**	....	....	....	....	....	....	....
	Fredericton	AHL	35	9	15	5	1800	122	0	4.07	....	....	....	....	....	....	....
1991-92	Fredericton	AHL	30	17	9	4	1761	79	2	*2.69	7	3	4	457	20	0	2.63
	Winston-Salem	ECHL	24	15	7	2	1449	71	0	*2.94	....	....	....	....	....	....	....
1992-93	**Montreal**	**NHL**	**1**	**0**	**0**	**0**	**40**	**1**	**0**	**1.50**	....	....	....	....	....	....	....
	Fredericton	AHL	45	22	17	4	2544	141	0	3.33	4	1	3	261	16	0	3.68
1993-94	**Montreal**	**NHL**	**1**	**0**	**1**	**0**	**60**	**5**	**0**	**5.00**	....	....	....	....	....	....	....
	Fredericton	AHL	3	0	1	1	143	12	0	5.03	....	....	....	....	....	....	....
	Las Vegas	IHL	2	1	1	0	110	5	0	2.72	....	....	....	....	....	....	....
	Philadelphia	**NHL**	**4**	**0**	**1**	**1**	**70**	**5**	**0**	**4.29**	....	....	....	....	....	....	....
b	Hershey	AHL	28	13	5	6	1464	63	2	*2.58	11	7	4	665	32	0	2.89
1994-95	Cincinnati	IHL	48	25	12	7	2622	128	1	2.93	5	3	2	326	16	0	2.94
	NHL Totals		**9**	**0**	**2**	**2**	**278**	**17**	**0**	**3.67**	....	....	....	....	....	....	....

a WHL East All-Star Team (1989)
b Won Baz Bastien Award (Top Goaltender - AHL) (1994)

Signed as a free agent by **Montreal**, January 16, 1990. Claimed by **Tampa Bay** from **Montreal** in Expansion Draft, June 18, 1992. Traded to **Montreal** by **Tampa Bay** for J.C. Bergeron, June 19, 1992. Traded to **Philadelphia** by **Montreal** for cash, February 21, 1994. Signed as a free agent by **Florida**, August 11, 1994.

CHARBONNEAU, PATRICK — OTT.

Goaltender. Catches left. 5'11", 205 lbs. Born, St-Jean sur Richelieu, Que., July 22, 1975.
(Ottawa's 3rd choice, 53rd overall, in 1993 Entry Draft).

			Regular Season								Playoffs						
Season	Club	Lea	GP	W	L	T	Mins	GA	SO	Avg	GP	W	L	Mins	GA	SO	Avg
1991-92	Victoriaville	QMJHL	37	9	23	2	1943	163	0	5.03	....	....	....	....	....	....	....
1992-93	Victoriaville	QMJHL	59	*35	22	0	3121	216	0	4.15	2	1	0	92	4	0	2.61
1993-94	Victoriaville	QMJHL	56	11	34	2	2948	261	0	5.31	5	1	4	212	24	0	6.79
	PEI	AHL	3	2	1	0	180	11	0	3.67	....	....	....	....	....	....	....
1994-95	Victoriaville	QMJHL	47	15	27	1	2339	201	0	5.16	4	0	3	142	20	0	8.45
	PEI	AHL	2	2	0	0	120	4	0	2.00	3	0	2	137	12	0	5.24

CHARPENTIER, SEBASTIEN — WSH.

Goaltender. Catches left. 5'9", 161 lbs. Born, Drummondville, Que., April 18, 1977.
(Washington's 4th choice, 93rd overall, in 1995 Entry Draft).

			Regular Season								Playoffs						
Season	Club	Lea	GP	W	L	T	Mins	GA	SO	Avg	GP	W	L	Mins	GA	SO	Avg
1994-95	Laval	QMJHL	41	25	12	1	2152	99	2	2.76	16	9	4	886	45	0	3.05

CHEVELDAE, TIM (SHEH-vehl-day) WPG.

Goaltender. Catches left. 5'10", 195 lbs. Born, Melville, Sask., February 15, 1968.
(Detroit's 4th choice, 64th overall, in 1986 Entry Draft).

			Regular Season								Playoffs						
Season	Club	Lea	GP	W	L	T	Mins	GA	SO	Avg	GP	W	L	Mins	GA	SO	Avg
1985-86	Saskatoon	WHL	36	21	10	3	2030	165	0	4.88	8	6	2	480	29	0	3.63
1986-87	Saskatoon	WHL	33	20	11	0	1909	133	2	4.18	5	4	1	308	20	0	3.90
1987-88a	Saskatoon	WHL	66	44	19	3	3798	235	1	3.71	6	4	2	364	27	0	4.45
1988-89	**Detroit**	**NHL**	**2**	**0**	**2**	**0**	**122**	**9**	**0**	**4.43**	....	....	....	....	....	....	....
	Adirondack	AHL	30	20	8	0	1694	98	1	3.47	2	1	0	99	9	0	5.45
1989-90	**Detroit**	**NHL**	**28**	**10**	**9**	**8**	**1600**	**101**	**0**	**3.79**	....	....	....	....	....	....	....
	Adirondack	AHL	31	17	8	6	1848	116	0	3.77	....	....	....	....	....	....	....
1990-91	**Detroit**	**NHL**	**65**	**30**	**26**	**5**	**3615**	**214**	**2**	**3.55**	**7**	**3**	**4**	**398**	**22**	**0**	**3.32**
1991-92	**Detroit**	**NHL**	***72**	***38**	**23**	**9**	***4236**	**226**	**2**	**3.20**	**11**	**3**	**7**	**597**	**25**	***2**	**2.51**
1992-93	**Detroit**	**NHL**	**67**	**34**	**24**	**7**	**3880**	**210**	**4**	**3.25**	**7**	**3**	**4**	**423**	**24**	**0**	**3.40**
1993-94	**Detroit**	**NHL**	**30**	**16**	**9**	**1**	**1572**	**91**	**1**	**3.47**	....	....	....	....	....	....	....
	Adirondack	AHL	2	1	0	1	125	7	0	3.36	....	....	....	....	....	....	....
	Winnipeg	**NHL**	**14**	**5**	**8**	**1**	**788**	**52**	**1**	**3.96**	....	....	....	....	....	....	....
1994-95	**Winnipeg**	**NHL**	**30**	**8**	**16**	**3**	**1571**	**97**	**0**	**3.70**	....	....	....	....	....	....	....
	NHL Totals		**308**	**141**	**117**	**34**	**17384**	**1000**	**10**	**3.45**	**25**	**9**	**15**	**1418**	**71**	**2**	**3.00**

a WHL East All-Star Team (1988)

Played in NHL All-Star Game (1992)

Traded to **Winnipeg** by **Detroit** with Dallas Drake for Bob Essensa and Sergei Bautin, March 8, 1994.

CLOUTIER, DAN — NYR

Goaltender. Catches left. 6'1", 182 lbs. Born, Mont-Laurier, Que., April 22, 1976.
(NY Rangers' 1st choice, 26th overall, in 1994 Entry Draft).

			Regular Season								Playoffs						
Season	Club	Lea	GP	W	L	T	Mins	GA	SO	Avg	GP	W	L	Mins	GA	SO	Avg
1992-93	S.S. Marie	OHL	12	4	6	0	572	44	0	4.62	4	1	2	231	12	0	3.12
1993-94	S.S. Marie	OHL	55	28	14	6	2934	174	*2	3.56	14	*10	4	833	52	0	3.75
1994-95	S.S. Marie	OHL	45	15	26	2	2518	185	1	4.41	....	....	....	....	....	....	....

COUSINEAU, MARCEL (koo-ZEE-noh) TOR.

Goaltender. Catches left. 5'9", 180 lbs. Born, Delson, Que., April 30, 1973.
(Boston's 3rd choice, 62nd overall, in 1991 Entry Draft).

			Regular Season								Playoffs						
Season	Club	Lea	GP	W	L	T	Mins	GA	SO	Avg	GP	W	L	Mins	GA	SO	Avg
1990-91	Beauport	QMJHL	49	13	29	3	2739	196	1	4.29	....	....	....	....	....	....	....
1991-92	Beauport	QMJHL	*67	26	32	5	*3673	241	0	3.94	....	....	....	....	....	....	....
1992-93	Drummondville	QMJHL	60	20	32	2	3298	225	0	4.09	9	3	6	498	37	*1	4.45
1993-94	St. John's	AHL	37	13	11	9	2015	118	0	3.51	....	....	....	....	....	....	....
1994-95	St. John's	AHL	58	22	27	6	3342	171	4	3.07	3	0	3	179	9	0	3.01

Signed as a free agent by **Toronto**, November 13, 1993.

COWLEY, WAYNE

Goaltender. Catches left. 6', 185 lbs. Born, Scarborough, Ont., December 4, 1964.

			Regular Season								Playoffs						
Season	Club	Lea	GP	W	L	T	Mins	GA	SO	Avg	GP	W	L	Mins	GA	SO	Avg
1985-86	Colgate	ECAC	7	2	2	0	313	23	1	4.42	....	....	....	....	....	....	....
1986-87	Colgate	ECAC	31	21	8	1	1805	106	0	3.52	....	....	....	....	....	....	....
1987-88	Colgate	ECAC	20	11	7	1	1162	58	1	2.99	....	....	....	....	....	....	....
1988-89	Salt Lake	IHL	29	17	7	1	1423	94	0	3.96	2	1	0	69	6	0	5.22
1989-90	Salt Lake	IHL	36	15	12	5	2009	124	1	3.70	3	0	0	118	6	0	3.05
1990-91	Salt Lake	IHL	7	3	4	0	377	23	1	3.66	....	....	....	....	....	....	....
a	Cincinnati	ECHL	30	19	9	2	1680	108	1	3.85	4	1	3	249	13	*1	3.13
1991-92	Cape Breton	AHL	11	6	5	0	644	45	0	3.53	1	0	1	61	3	0	2.95
	Raleigh	ECHL	38	16	18	2	2213	137	0	3.71	....	....	....	....	....	....	....
1992-93	Cape Breton	AHL	42	14	17	6	2334	152	1	3.91	16	*14	2	1014	47	*1	2.78
	Wheeling	ECHL	1	1	0	0	60	3	0	3.00	....	....	....	....	....	....	....
1993-94	**Edmonton**	**NHL**	**1**	**0**	**1**	**0**	**57**	**3**	**0**	**3.16**	....	....	....	....	....	....	....
	Cape Breton	AHL	44	20	17	5	2486	150	0	3.62	5	1	4	0	20	0	4.66
1994-95	Worcester	AHL	45	11	25	6	2597	153	1	3.53	....	....	....	....	....	....	....
	Milwaukee	IHL	2	0	0	1	79	4	0	3.04	....	....	....	....	....	....	....
	NHL Totals		**1**	**0**	**1**	**0**	**57**	**3**	**0**	**3.16**	....	....	....	....	....	....	....

a ECHL Second All-Star Team (1991)

Signed as a free agent by **Calgary**, May 1, 1988. Signed as a free agent by **Edmonton**, September 13, 1993.

DAFOE, BYRON (day-FOH) L.A.

Goaltender. Catches left. 5'11", 175 lbs. Born, Sussex, England, February 25, 1971.
(Washington's 2nd choice, 35th overall, in 1989 Entry Draft).

			Regular Season								Playoffs						
Season	Club	Lea	GP	W	L	T	Mins	GA	SO	Avg	GP	W	L	Mins	GA	SO	Avg
1988-89	Portland	WHL	59	29	24	3	3279	291	1	5.32	*18	10	8	*1091	81	*1	4.45
1989-90	Portland	WHL	40	14	21	3	2265	193	0	5.11	....	....	....	....	....	....	....
1990-91	Portland	WHL	8	1	5	1	414	41	0	5.94	....	....	....	....	....	....	....
	Prince Albert	WHL	32	13	12	4	1839	124	0	4.05	....	....	....	....	....	....	....
1991-92	New Haven	AHL	7	3	2	1	364	22	0	3.63	....	....	....	....	....	....	....
	Baltimore	AHL	33	12	16	4	1847	119	0	3.87	....	....	....	....	....	....	....
	Hampton Rds.	ECHL	10	6	4	0	562	26	0	2.78	....	....	....	....	....	....	....
1992-93	**Washington**	**NHL**	**1**	**0**	**0**	**0**	**1**	**0**	**0**	**0.00**	....	....	....	....	....	....	....
	Baltimore	AHL	48	16	20	7	2617	191	1	4.38	5	2	3	241	22	0	5.48
1993-94	**Washington**	**NHL**	**5**	**2**	**2**	**0**	**230**	**13**	**0**	**3.39**	**2**	**0**	**2**	**118**	**5**	**0**	**2.54**
ab	Portland	AHL	47	24	16	4	2661	148	1	3.34	1	0	0	9	1	0	6.79
1994-95	Phoenix	IHL	49	25	16	6	2743	169	2	3.70	....	....	....	....	....	....	....
	Washington	**NHL**	**4**	**1**	**1**	**1**	**187**	**11**	**0**	**3.53**	**1**	**0**	**0**	**20**	**1**	**0**	**3.00**
	Portland	AHL	6	5	0	0	330	16	0	2.91	7	3	4	416	29	0	4.18
	NHL Totals		**10**	**3**	**3**	**1**	**418**	**24**	**0**	**3.44**	**3**	**0**	**2**	**138**	**6**	**0**	**2.61**

a AHL First All-Star Team (1994)
b Share Harry "Hap" Holmes Trophy (fewest goals-against - AHL) with Olaf Kolzig (1994)

Traded to **Los Angeles** by **Washington** with Dimitri Khristich for Los Angeles' first round choice and Dallas' fourth round choice (previously acquired by Los Angeles) in 1996 Entry Draft, July 8, 1995.

DAIGLE, SYLVAIN (DAYG) WPG.

Goaltender. Catches right. 5'8", 185 lbs. Born, St-Hyacinthe, Que., October 20, 1976.
(Winnipeg's 7th choice, 136th overall, in 1995 Entry Draft).

			Regular Season								Playoffs						
Season	Club	Lea	GP	W	L	T	Mins	GA	SO	Avg	GP	W	L	Mins	GA	SO	Avg
1993-94	Shawinigan	QMJHL	31	....	....	....	1645	113	0	4.12	....	....	....	....	....	....	....
1994-95	Shawinigan	QMJHL	48	27	17	3	2831	159	3	3.37	14	7	6	824	57	0	4.15

DAUBENSPECK, KIRK — OTT.

Goaltender. Catches left. 6'1", 170 lbs. Born, Madison, WI, July 16, 1974.
(Philadelphia's 7th choice, 151st overall, in 1992 Entry Draft).

			Regular Season								Playoffs						
Season	Club	Lea	GP	W	L	T	Mins	GA	SO	Avg	GP	W	L	Mins	GA	SO	Avg
1993-94	U. Wisconsin	WCHA	7	2	2	0	280	19	0	4.07	....	....	....	....	....	....	....
1994-95	U. Wisconsin	WCHA	42	*23	15	4	*2503	146	0	3.51	....	....	....	....	....	....	....

Traded to **Ottawa** by **Philadelphia** with Claude Boivin for Mark Lamb, March 5, 1994.

DAVIS, CHRIS — BUF.

Goaltender. Catches left. 6'3", 177 lbs. Born, Calgary, Alta., December 1, 1974.
(Buffalo's 8th choice, 246th overall, in 1993 Entry Draft).

			Regular Season								Playoffs						
Season	Club	Lea	GP	W	L	T	Mins	GA	SO	Avg	GP	W	L	Mins	GA	SO	Avg
1993-94	Alaska-Anch.	WCHA	9	2	4	0	390	27	0	4.15	....	....	....	....	....	....	....
1994-95	Alaska-Anch.	WCHA	14	4	6	0	670	49	0	4.39	....	....	....	....	....	....	....

DENIS, MARC — COL.

Goaltender. Catches left. 6', 188 lbs. Born, Montreal, Que., August 1, 1977.
(Colorado's 1st choice, 25th overall, in 1995 Entry Draft).

			Regular Season								Playoffs						
Season	Club	Lea	GP	W	L	T	Mins	GA	SO	Avg	GP	W	L	Mins	GA	SO	Avg
1993-94	Trois Rivières	Midget	36	....	....	....	2093	158	3	4.53	....	....	....	....	....	....	....
1994-95	Chicoutimi	QMJHL	32	17	9	1	1688	98	0	3.48	6	4	2	372	19	1	3.06

DeROUVILLE, PHILIPPE (deh-ROO-vihl) PIT.

Goaltender. Catches left. 6'1", 185 lbs. Born, Victoriaville, Que., August 7, 1974.
(Pittsburgh's 5th choice, 115th overall, in 1992 Entry Draft).

			Regular Season								Playoffs						
Season	Club	Lea	GP	W	L	T	Mins	GA	SO	Avg	GP	W	L	Mins	GA	SO	Avg
1990-91	Longueuil	QMJHL	20	13	6	0	1030	50	0	2.91	....	....	....	....	....	....	....
1991-92	Verdun	QMJHL	34	20	6	3	1854	99	2	3.20	11	7	3	593	28	1	2.83
1992-93a	Verdun	QMJHL	61	30	27	2	3491	210	1	3.61	4	0	4	256	18	0	3.61
1993-94a	Verdun	QMJHL	51	28	22	0	2845	145	1	*3.06	4	0	4	210	14	0	4.00
1994-95	Cleveland	IHL	41	24	10	5	2369	131	1	3.32	4	1	3	263	18	0	4.09
	Pittsburgh	**NHL**	**1**	**1**	**0**	**0**	**60**	**3**	**0**	**3.00**	....	....	....	....	....	....	....
	NHL Totals		**1**	**1**	**0**	**0**	**60**	**3**	**0**	**3.00**	....	....	....	....	....	....	....

a QMJHL Second All-Star Team (1993, 1994)

DESCHENES, FREDERIC — DET.

Goaltender. Catches left. 5'9", 164 lbs. Born, Quebec, Que., January 12, 1976.
(Detroit's 4th choice, 114th overall, in 1994 Entry Draft).

			Regular Season								Playoffs						
Season	Club	Lea	GP	W	L	T	Mins	GA	SO	Avg	GP	W	L	Mins	GA	SO	Avg
1993-94	Granby	QMJHL	35	14	15	1	1861	132	0	4.26	7	3	4	372	27	0	4.35
1994-95	Granby	QMJHL	45	16	23	1	2375	160	0	4.04	11	3	7	553	35	1	3.80

DOPSON, ROBERT

Goaltender. Catches left. 6', 200 lbs. Born, Smiths Falls, Ont., August 21, 1967.

			Regular Season								Playoffs						
Season	Club	Lea	GP	W	L	T	Mins	GA	SO	Avg	GP	W	L	Mins	GA	SO	Avg
1989-90	Wilfred Laurier	OUAA	22	....	....	....	1319	57	0	2.59	....	....	....	....	....	....	....
1990-91	Muskegon	IHL	24	10	10	0	1243	90	0	4.34	....	....	....	....	....	....	....
	Louisville	ECHL	3	3	0	0	180	12	0	4.00	5	3	1	270	16	0	3.55
1991-92	Muskegon	IHL	28	13	12	2	1655	90	4	3.26	12	8	4	697	40	0	3.44
1992-93	Cleveland	IHL	50	26	15	3	2825	167	1	3.55	4	0	4	203	20	0	5.91
1993-94	**Pittsburgh**	**NHL**	**2**	**0**	**0**	**0**	**45**	**3**	**0**	**4.00**	....	....	....	....	....	....	....
	Cleveland	IHL	32	9	10	8	1681	109	0	3.89	....	....	....	....	....	....	....
1994-95	Houston	IHL	41	17	16	2	2102	119	0	3.40	1	0	0	40	6	0	9.00
	NHL Totals		**2**	**0**	**0**	**0**	**45**	**3**	**0**	**4.00**	....	....	....	....	....	....	....

Signed as a free agent by **Pittsburgh**, July 6, 1991.

DRAPER, TOM

Goaltender. Catches left. 5'11", 185 lbs. Born, Outremont, Que., November 20, 1966.
(Winnipeg's 8th choice, 165th overall, in 1985 Entry Draft).

			Regular Season								Playoffs						
Season	Club	Lea	GP	W	L	T	Mins	GA	SO	Avg	GP	W	L	Mins	GA	SO	Avg
1983-84	U. of Vermont	ECAC	20	8	12	0	1205	82	0	4.08	....	....	....	....	....	....	....
1984-85	U. of Vermont	ECAC	24	5	17	0	1316	90	0	4.11	....	....	....	....	....	....	....
1985-86	U. of Vermont	ECAC	29	15	12	1	1697	87	1	3.08	....	....	....	....	....	....	....
1986-87a	U. of Vermont	ECAC	29	16	13	0	1662	96	2	3.47	....	....	....	....	....	....	....
1987-88	Tappara	Fin.	28	16	3	9	1619	87	0	3.22	....	....	....	....	....	....	....
1988-89	**Winnipeg**	**NHL**	**2**	**1**	**1**	**0**	**120**	**12**	**0**	**6.00**	....	....	....	....	....	....	....
b	Moncton	AHL	*54	27	17	5	*2962	171	2	3.46	7	5	2	419	24	0	3.44
1989-90	**Winnipeg**	**NHL**	**6**	**2**	**4**	**0**	**359**	**26**	**0**	**4.35**	....	....	....	....	....	....	....
	Moncton	AHL	51	20	24	3	2844	167	1	3.52	....	....	....	....	....	....	....
1990-91	Moncton	AHL	30	15	13	2	1779	95	1	3.20	....	....	....	....	....	....	....
	Fort Wayne	IHL	10	5	3	1	564	32	0	3.40	....	....	....	....	....	....	....
	Peoria	IHL	10	6	3	1	584	36	0	3.70	4	2	1	214	10	0	2.80
1991-92	**Buffalo**	**NHL**	**26**	**10**	**9**	**5**	**1403**	**75**	**1**	**3.21**	**7**	**3**	**4**	**433**	**19**	**1**	**2.63**
	Rochester	AHL	9	4	3	2	531	28	0	3.16	....	....	....	....	....	....	....
1992-93	**Buffalo**	**NHL**	**11**	**5**	**6**	**0**	**664**	**41**	**0**	**3.70**	....	....	....	....	....	....	....
	Rochester	AHL	5	3	2	0	303	22	0	4.36	....	....	....	....	....	....	....
1993-94	**NY Islanders**	**NHL**	**7**	**1**	**3**	**0**	**227**	**16**	**0**	**4.23**	....	....	....	....	....	....	....
	Salt Lake	IHL	35	7	23	3	1933	140	0	4.34	....	....	....	....	....	....	....
1994-95	Minnesota	IHL	59	25	20	6	3063	187	1	3.66	2	0	2	118	10	0	5.07
	NHL Totals		**52**	**19**	**23**	**5**	**2773**	**170**	**1**	**3.68**	**7**	**3**	**4**	**433**	**19**	**1**	**2.63**

a ECAC First All-Star Team (1987)
b AHL Second All-Star Team (1989)

Traded to **St. Louis** by **Winnipeg** for future considerations (Jim Vesey, May 24, 1991), February 28, 1991. Traded to **Winnipeg** by **St. Louis** for future considerations, May 24, 1991. Traded to **Buffalo** by **Winnipeg** for Buffalo's seventh round choice (Artur Oktyabrev) in 1992 Entry Draft, June 22, 1991. Traded to **NY Islanders** by **Buffalo** for NY Islanders' seventh round choice (Stev Plouffe) in 1994 Entry Draft, September 30, 1993.

DUFFUS, PARRIS (DOO-fihz, PAIR-ihz) WPG.

Goaltender. Catches left. 6'2", 192 lbs. Born, Denver, CO, January 27, 1970.
(St. Louis' 6th choice, 180th overall, in 1990 Entry Draft).

			Regular Season								Playoffs						
Season	Club	Lea	GP	W	L	T	Mins	GA	SO	Avg	GP	W	L	Mins	GA	SO	Avg
1990-91	Cornell	ECAC	4	0	0	0	37	3	0	4.86	....	....	....	....	....	....	....
1991-92ab	Cornell	ECAC	28	14	11	3	1677	74	1	2.65	....	....	....	....	....	....	....
1992-93	Hampton Rds.	ECHL	4	3	1	0	245	13	0	3.18	....	....	....	....	....	....	....
	Peoria	IHL	37	16	15	4	2149	142	0	3.96	1	0	1	59	5	0	5.08
1993-94	Peoria	IHL	36	19	10	3	1845	141	0	4.58	2	0	1	92	6	0	3.88
1994-95	Peoria	IHL	29	17	7	3	1581	71	*3	2.69	7	4	2	409	17	0	2.49

a NCAA East First All-American Team (1992)
b ECAC Second All-Star Team (1992)

Signed as a free agent by **Winnipeg**, August 4, 1995.

DUNHAM, MICHAEL (DUHN-uhm) N.J.

Goaltender. Catches left. 6'3", 185 lbs. Born, Johnson City, NY, June 1, 1972.
(New Jersey's 4th choice, 53rd overall, in 1990 Entry Draft).

			Regular Season								Playoffs						
Season	Club	Lea	GP	W	L	T	Mins	GA	SO	Avg	GP	W	L	Mins	GA	SO	Avg
1990-91	U. of Maine	H.E.	23	14	5	2	1275	63	0	*2.96	....	....	....	....	....	....	....
1991-92	U. of Maine	H.E.	7	6	0	0	382	14	1	2.20	....	....	....	....	....	....	....
	U.S. National	....	3	0	1	1	157	10	0	3.82	....	....	....	....	....	....	....
1992-93ab	U. of Maine	H.E.	25	*21	1	1	1429	63	0	2.65	....	....	....	....	....	....	....
1993-94	U.S. National	....	33	22	9	2	1983	125	2	3.78	....	....	....	....	....	....	....
	U.S. Olympic	....	3	0	2	1	180	15	0	5.02	....	....	....	....	....	....	....
	Albany	AHL	5	2	2	1	304	26	0	5.12	....	....	....	....	....	....	....
1994-95cd	Albany	AHL	35	20	7	8	2120	99	1	2.80	7	6	1	419	20	1	2.86

a Hockey East First All-Star Team (1993)
b NCAA East First All-American Team (1993)
c Shared Harry "Hap" Holmes Memorial Trophy (fewest goals against - AHL) with Corey Schwab (1995)
d Shared Jack A. Butterfield Trophy (Playoff MVP - AHL) with Corey Schwab (1995)

ELDER, BRIAN WPG.

Goaltender. Catches left. 6', 175 lbs. Born, Oak Lake, Man., June 8, 1976.
(Winnipeg's 6th choice, 121st overall, in 1995 Entry Draft).

			Regular Season								Playoffs						
Season	Club	Lea	GP	W	L	T	Mins	GA	SO	Avg	GP	W	L	Mins	GA	SO	Avg
1994-95	Brandon	WHL	23	16	5	1	1325	69	0	3.12	13	6	7	756	38	*1	3.02

ELLIOT, JASON DET.

Goaltender. Catches left. 6'2", 183 lbs. Born, Inovik, N.W.T., November 10, 1975.
(Detroit's 7th choice, 205th overall, in 1994 Entry Draft).

			Regular Season								Playoffs						
Season	Club	Lea	GP	W	L	T	Mins	GA	SO	Avg	GP	W	L	Mins	GA	SO	Avg
1993-94	Kimberley	BCJHL							UNAVAILABLE								
1994-95	Cornell	ECAC	16	3	11	1	877	62	0	4.24	....	....	....	....	....	....	....

ELLIS, AARON COL.

Goaltender. Catches left. 6'1", 170 lbs. Born, Indianapolis, IN, May 13, 1974.
(Quebec's 11th choice, 244th overall, in 1992 Entry Draft).

			Regular Season								Playoffs						
Season	Club	Lea	GP	W	L	T	Mins	GA	SO	Avg	GP	W	L	Mins	GA	SO	Avg
1992-93	Bowling Green	CCHA	25	14	10	1	1479	94	0	3.81	....	....	....	....	....	....	....
1993-94	Detroit	OHL	27	14	9	1	1425	88	0	3.71	12	6	6	694	46	0	3.98
1994-95	Detroit	OHL	4	2	0	0	154	10	0	3.90	....	....	....	....	....	....	....
	Belleville	OHL	7	1	3	1	372	35	0	5.65	....	....	....	....	....	....	....
	Memphis	CHL	11	4	6	1	629	56	1	5.34	....	....	....	....	....	....	....

ESSENSA, BOB (EH-sehn-suh) DET.

Goaltender. Catches left. 6', 185 lbs. Born, Toronto, Ont., January 14, 1965.
(Winnipeg's 5th choice, 69th overall, in 1983 Entry Draft).

			Regular Season								Playoffs						
Season	Club	Lea	GP	W	L	T	Mins	GA	SO	Avg	GP	W	L	Mins	GA	SO	Avg
1983-84	Michigan State	CCHA	17	11	4	0	946	44	2	2.79	....	....	....	....	....	....	....
1984-85	Michigan State	CCHA	18	15	2	0	1059	29	2	1.64	....	....	....	....	....	....	....
1985-86a	Michigan State	CCHA	23	17	4	1	1333	74	1	3.33	....	....	....	....	....	....	....
1986-87	Michigan State	CCHA	25	19	3	1	1383	64	2	2.78	....	....	....	....	....	....	....
1987-88	Moncton	AHL	27	7	11	1	1287	100	1	4.66	....	....	....	....	....	....	....
1988-89	**Winnipeg**	**NHL**	**20**	**6**	**8**	**3**	**1102**	**68**	**1**	**3.70**	....	....	....	....	....	....	....
	Fort Wayne	IHL	22	14	7	0	1287	70	0	3.26	....	....	....	....	....	....	....
1989-90b	**Winnipeg**	**NHL**	**36**	**18**	**9**	**5**	**2035**	**107**	**1**	**3.15**	**4**	**2**	**1**	**206**	**12**	**0**	**3.50**
	Moncton	AHL	6	3	3	0	358	15	0	2.51	....	....	....	....	....	....	....
1990-91	**Winnipeg**	**NHL**	**55**	**19**	**24**	**6**	**2916**	**153**	**4**	**3.15**	....	....	....	....	....	....	....
	Moncton	AHL	2	1	0	1	125	6	0	2.88	....	....	....	....	....	....	....
1991-92	**Winnipeg**	**NHL**	**47**	**21**	**17**	**6**	**2627**	**126**	***5**	**2.88**	**1**	**0**	**0**	**33**	**3**	**0**	**5.45**
1992-93	**Winnipeg**	**NHL**	**67**	**33**	**26**	**6**	**3855**	**227**	**2**	**3.53**	**6**	**2**	**4**	**367**	**20**	**0**	**3.27**
1993-94	**Winnipeg**	**NHL**	**56**	**19**	**30**	**6**	**3136**	**201**	**1**	**3.85**	....	....	....	....	....	....	....
	Detroit	**NHL**	**13**	**4**	**7**	**2**	**778**	**34**	**1**	**2.62**	**2**	**0**	**2**	**109**	**9**	**0**	**4.95**
1994-95	San Diego	IHL	16	6	8	1	919	52	0	3.39	1	0	1	59	3	0	3.05
	NHL Totals		**294**	**120**	**121**	**34**	**16449**	**916**	**15**	**3.34**	**13**	**4**	**7**	**715**	**44**	**0**	**3.69**

a CCHA Second All-Star Team (1986)
b NHL All-Rookie Team (1990)

Traded to **Detroit** by **Winnipeg** with Sergei Bautin for Tim Cheveldae and Dallas Drake, March 8, 1994.

FANKHOUSER, SCOTT ST.L.

Goaltender. Catches left. 6'2", 195 lbs. Born, Bismark, ND, July 1, 1975.
(St. Louis' 8th choice, 276th overall, in 1994 Entry Draft).

			Regular Season								Playoffs						
Season	Club	Lea	GP	W	L	T	Mins	GA	SO	Avg	GP	W	L	Mins	GA	SO	Avg
1994-95	Lowell	H.E.	11	4	4	1	499	37	0	4.44	....	....	....	....	....	....	....

FERNANDEZ, EMMANUEL DAL.

Goaltender. Catches left. 6', 185 lbs. Born, Etobicoke, Ont., August 27, 1974.
(Quebec's 4th choice, 52nd overall, in 1992 Entry Draft).

			Regular Season								Playoffs						
Season	Club	Lea	GP	W	L	T	Mins	GA	SO	Avg	GP	W	L	Mins	GA	SO	Avg
1991-92	Laval	QMJHL	31	14	13	2	1593	99	1	3.73	9	3	5	468	39	0	5.00
1992-93	Laval	QMJHL	43	26	14	2	2347	141	1	3.60	13	*12	1	818	42	0	3.08
1993-94a	Laval	QMJHL	51	29	14	1	2776	143	*5	3.09	19	14	5	1116	49	*1	*2.63
1994-95b	Kalamazoo	IHL	46	21	10	9	2470	115	2	2.79	14	10	2	753	34	1	2.71

a QMJHL First All-Star Team (1994)
b IHL Second All-Star Team (1995)

Rights traded to **Dallas** by **Quebec** for Tommy Sjodin and Dallas' third round draft choice (Chris Drury) in 1994 Entry Draft, February 13, 1994.

FICHAUD, ERIC NYI

Goaltender. Catches left. 5'11", 165 lbs. Born, Montreal, Que., November 4, 1975.
(Toronto's 1st choice, 16th overall, in 1994 Entry Draft).

			Regular Season								Playoffs						
Season	Club	Lea	GP	W	L	T	Mins	GA	SO	Avg	GP	W	L	Mins	GA	SO	Avg
1992-93	Chicoutimi	QMJHL	43	18	13	1	2039	149	0	4.38	....	....	....	....	....	....	....
1993-94abc	Chicoutimi	QMJHL	*63	*37	21	3	*3493	192	4	3.30	*26	*16	10	*1560	86	*1	3.31
1994-95d	Chicoutimi	QMJHL	46	21	19	4	2637	151	4	3.44	7	2	5	428	20	0	2.80

a Canadian Major Junior Second All-Star Team (1994)
b Memorial Cup All-Star Team (1994)
c Won Hap Emms Memorial Trophy (Memorial Cup Tournament Top Goaltender) (1994)
d QMJHL First All-Star Team (1995)

Traded to **NY Islanders** by **Toronto** for Benoit Hogue, NY Islanders' third round choice (Brian Pepperall) in 1995 Entry Draft and fifth round choice in 1996 Entry Draft, April 6, 1995.

FISET, STEPHANE (fih-SEHT) COL.

Goaltender. Catches left. 6'1", 195 lbs. Born, Montreal, Que., June 17, 1970.
(Quebec's 3rd choice, 24th overall, in 1988 Entry Draft).

			Regular Season								Playoffs						
Season	Club	Lea	GP	W	L	T	Mins	GA	SO	Avg	GP	W	L	Mins	GA	SO	Avg
1987-88	Victoriaville	QMJHL	40	15	17	4	2221	146	1	3.94	2	0	2	163	10	0	3.68
1988-89ab	Victoriaville	QMJHL	43	25	14	0	2401	138	1	*3.45	12	*9	2	711	33	0	*2.78
1989-90	**Quebec**	**NHL**	**6**	**0**	**5**	**1**	**342**	**34**	**0**	**5.96**	....	....	....	....	....	....	....
	Victoriaville	QMJHL	24	14	6	3	1383	63	1	*2.73	*14	7	6	*790	49	0	3.72
1990-91	**Quebec**	**NHL**	**3**	**0**	**2**	**1**	**186**	**12**	**0**	**3.87**	....	....	....	....	....	....	....
	Halifax	AHL	36	10	15	8	1902	131	0	4.13	....	....	....	....	....	....	....
1991-92	**Quebec**	**NHL**	**23**	**7**	**10**	**2**	**1133**	**71**	**1**	**3.76**	....	....	....	....	....	....	....
	Halifax	AHL	29	8	14	6	1675	110	*3	3.94	....	....	....	....	....	....	....
1992-93	**Quebec**	**NHL**	**37**	**18**	**9**	**4**	**1939**	**110**	**0**	**3.40**	**1**	**0**	**0**	**21**	**1**	**0**	**2.86**
	Halifax	AHL	3	2	1	0	180	11	0	3.67	....	....	....	....	....	....	....
1993-94	**Quebec**	**NHL**	**50**	**20**	**25**	**4**	**2798**	**158**	**2**	**3.39**	....	....	....	....	....	....	....
	Cornwall	AHL	1	0	1	0	60	4	0	4.00	....	....	....	....	....	....	....
1994-95	**Quebec**	**NHL**	**32**	**17**	**10**	**3**	**1879**	**87**	**2**	**2.78**	**4**	**1**	**2**	**209**	**16**	**0**	**4.59**
	NHL Totals		**151**	**62**	**61**	**15**	**8277**	**472**	**5**	**3.42**	**5**	**1**	**2**	**230**	**17**	**0**	**4.43**

a QMJHL First All-Star Team (1989)
b Canadian Major Junior Goaltender of the Year (1989)

FITZPATRICK, MARK — FLA.

Goaltender. Catches left. 6'2", 198 lbs. Born, Toronto, Ont., November 13, 1968.
(Los Angeles' 2nd choice, 27th overall, in 1987 Entry Draft).

			Regular Season								Playoffs						
Season	Club	Lea	GP	W	L	T	Mins	GA	SO	Avg	GP	W	L	Mins	GA	SO	Avg
1985-86	Medicine Hat	WHL	41	26	6	1	2074	99	1	2.86	19	12	5	986	58	0	3.53
1986-87a	Medicine Hat	WHL	50	31	11	4	2844	159	4	3.35	20	12	8	1224	71	1	3.48
1987-88a	Medicine Hat	WHL	63	36	15	6	3600	194	2	3.23	16	12	4	959	52	*1	*3.25
1988-89	**Los Angeles**	**NHL**	**17**	**6**	**7**	**3**	**957**	**64**	**0**	**4.01**	....	....	....	....	....	....	....
	New Haven	AHL	18	10	5	1	980	54	1	3.31	....	....	....	....	....	....	....
	NY Islanders	**NHL**	**11**	**3**	**5**	**2**	**627**	**41**	**0**	**3.92**	....	....	....	....	....	....	....
1989-90	**NY Islanders**	**NHL**	**47**	**19**	**19**	**5**	**2653**	**150**	**3**	**3.39**	**4**	**0**	**2**	**152**	**13**	**0**	**5.13**
1990-91	**NY Islanders**	**NHL**	**2**	**1**	**1**	**0**	**120**	**6**	**0**	**3.00**	....	....	....	....	....	....	....
	Capital Dist.	AHL	12	3	7	2	734	47	0	3.84	....	....	....	....	....	....	....
1991-92b	**NY Islanders**	**NHL**	**30**	**11**	**13**	**5**	**1743**	**93**	**0**	**3.20**	....	....	....	....	....	....	....
	Capital Dist.	AHL	14	6	5	1	782	39	0	2.99	....	....	....	....	....	....	....
1992-93	**NY Islanders**	**NHL**	**39**	**17**	**15**	**5**	**2253**	**130**	**0**	**3.46**	**3**	**0**	**1**	**77**	**4**	**0**	**3.12**
	Capital Dist.	AHL	5	1	3	1	284	18	0	3.80	....	....	....	....	....	....	....
1993-94	**Florida**	**NHL**	**28**	**12**	**8**	**6**	**1603**	**73**	**1**	**2.73**	....	....	....	....	....	....	....
1994-95	**Florida**	**NHL**	**15**	**6**	**7**	**2**	**819**	**36**	**2**	**2.64**	....	....	....	....	....	....	....
	NHL Totals		**189**	**75**	**75**	**28**	**10775**	**593**	**6**	**3.30**	**7**	**0**	**3**	**229**	**17**	**0**	**4.45**

a Won Hap Emms Memorial Trophy (Memorial Cup Tournament Top Goaltender) (1987, 1988)
b Won Bill Masterton Memorial Trophy (1992)

Traded to **NY Islanders** by **Los Angeles** with Wayne McBean and future considerations (Doug Crossman, May 23, 1989) for Kelly Hrudey, February 22, 1989. Traded to **Quebec** by **NY Islanders** with NY Islanders' first round choice (Adam Deadmarsh) in 1993 Entry Draft for Ron Hextall and Quebec's first round choice (Todd Bertuzzi) in 1993 Entry Draft, June 20, 1993. Claimed by **Florida** from **Quebec** in Expansion Draft, June 24, 1993.

FLAHERTY, WADE — (FLAY-uhr-tee) S.J.

Goaltender. Catches left. 6', 170 lbs. Born, Terrace, B.C., January 11, 1968.
(Buffalo's 10th choice, 181st overall, in 1988 Entry Draft).

			Regular Season								Playoffs						
Season	Club	Lea	GP	W	L	T	Mins	GA	SO	Avg	GP	W	L	Mins	GA	SO	Avg
1988-89	Victoria	WHL	42	21	19	0	2408	180	4	4.49	....	....	....	....	....	....	....
1989-90	Greensboro	ECHL	27	12	10	0	1308	96	0	4.40	....	....	....	....	....	....	....
1990-91	Kansas City	IHL	*56	16	31	4	2990	224	0	4.49	....	....	....	....	....	....	....
1991-92	**San Jose**	**NHL**	**3**	**0**	**3**	**0**	**178**	**13**	**0**	**4.38**	....	....	....	....	....	....	....
	Kansas City	IHL	43	26	14	3	2603	140	1	3.23	1	0	0	1	0	0	0.00
1992-93	**San Jose**	**NHL**	**1**	**0**	**1**	**0**	**60**	**5**	**0**	**5.00**	....	....	....	....	....	....	....
a	Kansas City	IHL	*61	*34	19	7	*3642	195	2	3.21	*12	6	6	733	34	*1	2.78
1993-94ab	Kansas City	IHL	*60	32	19	9	*3564	202	0	3.40	....	....	....	....	....	....	....
1994-95	**San Jose**	**NHL**	**18**	**5**	**6**	**1**	**852**	**44**	**1**	**3.10**	**7**	**2**	**3**	**377**	**31**	**0**	**4.93**
	NHL Totals		**22**	**5**	**10**	**1**	**1090**	**62**	**1**	**3.41**	**7**	**2**	**3**	**377**	**31**	**0**	**4.93**

a Shared James Norris Memorial Trophy (fewest goals against - IHL) with Arturs Irbe (1992)
b IHL Second All-Star Team (1993, 1994)

Signed as a free agent by **San Jose**, September 3, 1991.

FORSBERG, JONAS — (FOHRS-behrg) S.J.

Goaltender. Catches left. 5'10", 150 lbs. Born, Stockholm, Sweden, June 15, 1975.
(San Jose's 11th choice, 210th overall, in 1993 Entry Draft).

			Regular Season								Playoffs						
Season	Club	Lea	GP	W	L	T	Mins	GA	SO	Avg	GP	W	L	Mins	GA	SO	Avg
1993-94	Djurgarden	Swe.	1	....	....	....	60	4	0	4.00	....	....	....	....	....	....	....
1994-95	Djurgarden	Swe.	1	....	....	....	60	1	0	1.00	....	....	....	....	....	....	....

FOSTER, NORM

Goaltender. Catches left. 5'9", 175 lbs. Born, Vancouver, B.C., February 10, 1965.
(Boston's 11th choice, 222nd overall, in 1983 Entry Draft).

			Regular Season								Playoffs						
Season	Club	Lea	GP	W	L	T	Mins	GA	SO	Avg	GP	W	L	Mins	GA	SO	Avg
1984-85	Michigan State	CCHA	26	22	4	0	1531	67	0	2.63	....	....	....	....	....	....	....
1985-86	Michigan State	CCHA	24	17	5	1	1414	87	0	3.69	....	....	....	....	....	....	....
1986-87	Michigan State	CCHA	24	14	7	1	1383	90	1	3.90	....	....	....	....	....	....	....
1987-88	Milwaukee	IHL	38	10	22	1	2001	170	0	5.10	....	....	....	....	....	....	....
1988-89	Maine	AHL	47	16	17	6	2411	156	1	3.88	....	....	....	....	....	....	....
1989-90	Maine	AHL	*64	23	28	10	*3664	217	3	3.55	....	....	....	....	....	....	....
1990-91	**Boston**	**NHL**	**3**	**2**	**1**	**0**	**184**	**14**	**0**	**4.57**	....	....	....	....	....	....	....
	Maine	AHL	2	1	1	0	122	7	0	3.44	....	....	....	....	....	....	....
	Cape Breton	AHL	40	15	14	7	2207	135	1	3.67	2	0	2	128	8	0	3.75
1991-92	**Edmonton**	**NHL**	**10**	**5**	**3**	**0**	**439**	**20**	**0**	**2.73**	....	....	....	....	....	....	....
	Cape Breton	AHL	29	15	13	1	1699	119	0	4.20	3	1	2	193	14	0	4.35
1992-93	Cape Breton	AHL	10	5	5	0	560	53	0	5.68	....	....	....	....	....	....	....
	Kansas City	IHL	8	6	1	1	489	28	0	3.44	1	0	0	16	0	0	0.00
1993-94	Hershey	AHL	17	5	9	1	775	58	0	4.49	....	....	....	....	....	....	....
1994-95	Detroit	IHL	18	9	5	1	797	59	0	4.44	....	....	....	....	....	....	....
	Las Vegas	IHL	14	8	3	1	677	35	0	3.10	....	....	....	....	....	....	....
	NHL Totals		**13**	**7**	**4**	**0**	**623**	**34**	**0**	**3.27**	....	....	....	....	....	....	....

Traded to **Edmonton** by **Boston** for Edmonton's sixth round choice (Jiri Dopita) in 1992 Entry Draft, September 11, 1991. Signed as a free agent by **Philadelphia**, August 4, 1993.

FOUNTAIN, MIKE — VAN.

Goaltender. Catches left. 6'1", 176 lbs. Born, North York, Ont., January 26, 1972.
(Vancouver's 4th choice, 69th overall, in 1992 Entry Draft).

			Regular Season								Playoffs						
Season	Club	Lea	GP	W	L	T	Mins	GA	SO	Avg	GP	W	L	Mins	GA	SO	Avg
1990-91	S.S. Marie	OHL	7	5	2	0	380	19	....	3.00	....	....	....	....	....	....	....
	Oshawa	OHL	30	17	5	1	1483	84	....	3.40	8	1	4	292	26	0	5.34
1991-92a	Oshawa	OHL	40	18	13	6	2260	149	1	3.96	7	3	4	429	26	0	3.64
1992-93	Cdn. National	....	13	7	5	1	745	37	1	2.98	....	....	....	....	....	....	....
	Hamilton	AHL	12	2	8	0	618	46	0	4.47	....	....	....	....	....	....	....
1993-94b	Hamilton	AHL	*70	*34	28	6	*4005	241	*4	3.61	3	0	2	146	12	0	4.92
1994-95	Syracuse	AHL	61	25	29	7	3618	225	2	3.73	....	....	....	....	....	....	....

a OHL First All-Star Team (1992)
b AHL Second All-Star Team (1994)

FRANEK, PETR — (FRAH-nehk) COL.

Goaltender. Catches left. 5'11", 187 lbs. Born, Most, Czech., April 6, 1975.
(Quebec's 10th choice, 205th overall, in 1993 Entry Draft).

			Regular Season								Playoffs						
Season	Club	Lea	GP	W	L	T	Mins	GA	SO	Avg	GP	W	L	Mins	GA	SO	Avg
1992-93	Litvinov	Czech.	5	....	....	....	273	15	....	3.29	....	....	....	....	....	....	....
1993-94	Litvinov	Czech.	11	....	....	....	535	34	....	3.81	2	....	....	61	10	....	9.83
1994-95	Litvinov	Czech.	12	....	....	....	657	47	....	4.29	1	0	0	16	0	0	0.00

FUHR, GRANT — (FYOOR) ST.L.

Goaltender. Catches right. 5'9", 190 lbs. Born, Spruce Grove, Alta., September 28, 1962.
(Edmonton's 1st choice, 8th overall, in 1981 Entry Draft).

			Regular Season								Playoffs						
Season	Club	Lea	GP	W	L	T	Mins	GA	SO	Avg	GP	W	L	Mins	GA	SO	Avg
1979-80a	Victoria	WHL	43	30	12	0	2488	130	2	3.14	8	5	3	465	22	0	2.84
1980-81a	Victoria	WHL	59	48	9	1	3448	160	*4	*2.78	15	12	3	899	45	*1	*3.00
1981-82b	**Edmonton**	**NHL**	**48**	**28**	**5**	**14**	**2847**	**157**	**0**	**3.31**	**5**	**2**	**3**	**309**	**26**	**0**	**5.05**
1982-83	**Edmonton**	**NHL**	**32**	**13**	**12**	**5**	**1803**	**129**	**0**	**4.29**	**1**	**0**	**0**	**11**	**0**	**0**	**0.00**
	Moncton	AHL	10	4	5	1	604	40	0	3.98	....	....	....	....	....	....	....
1983-84	**Edmonton**	**NHL**	**45**	**30**	**10**	**4**	**2625**	**171**	**1**	**3.91**	**16**	**11**	**4**	**883**	**44**	**1**	**2.99**
1984-85	**Edmonton**	**NHL**	**46**	**26**	**8**	**7**	**2559**	**165**	**1**	**3.87**	***18**	***15**	**3**	**1064**	**55**	**0**	**3.10**
1985-86	**Edmonton**	**NHL**	**40**	**29**	**8**	**0**	**2184**	**143**	**0**	**3.93**	**9**	**5**	**4**	**541**	**28**	**0**	**3.11**
1986-87	**Edmonton**	**NHL**	**44**	**22**	**13**	**3**	**2388**	**137**	**0**	**3.44**	**19**	**14**	**5**	**1148**	**47**	**0**	**2.46**
1987-88cd	**Edmonton**	**NHL**	***75**	***40**	**24**	**9**	***4304**	**246**	***4**	**3.43**	***19**	***16**	**2**	***1136**	**55**	**0**	**2.90**
1988-89	**Edmonton**	**NHL**	**59**	**23**	**26**	**6**	**3341**	**213**	**1**	**3.83**	**7**	**3**	**4**	**417**	**24**	**1**	**3.45**
1989-90	**Edmonton**	**NHL**	**21**	**9**	**7**	**3**	**1081**	**70**	**1**	**3.89**	....	....	....	....	....	....	....
	Cape Breton	AHL	2	2	0	0	120	6	0	3.01	....	....	....	....	....	....	....
1990-91	**Edmonton**	**NHL**	**13**	**6**	**4**	**3**	**778**	**39**	**1**	**3.01**	**17**	**8**	**7**	**1019**	**51**	**0**	**3.00**
	Cape Breton	AHL	4	2	2	0	240	17	0	4.25	....	....	....	....	....	....	....
1991-92	**Toronto**	**NHL**	**66**	**25**	**33**	**5**	**3774**	**230**	**2**	**3.66**	....	....	....	....	....	....	....
1992-93	**Toronto**	**NHL**	**29**	**13**	**9**	**4**	**1665**	**87**	**1**	**3.14**	....	....	....	....	....	....	....
	Buffalo	**NHL**	**29**	**11**	**15**	**2**	**1694**	**98**	**0**	**3.47**	**8**	**3**	**4**	**474**	**27**	**1**	**3.42**
1993-94e	**Buffalo**	**NHL**	**32**	**13**	**12**	**3**	**1726**	**106**	**2**	**3.68**	....	....	....	....	....	....	....
	Rochester	AHL	5	3	0	2	310	10	0	1.94	....	....	....	....	....	....	....
1994-95	**Buffalo**	**NHL**	**3**	**1**	**2**	**0**	**180**	**12**	**0**	**4.00**	....	....	....	....	....	....	....
	Los Angeles	**NHL**	**14**	**1**	**7**	**3**	**698**	**47**	**0**	**4.04**	....	....	....	....	....	....	....
	NHL Totals		**596**	**290**	**195**	**71**	**33647**	**2050**	**14**	**3.66**	**119**	**77**	**36**	**7002**	**357**	**3**	**3.06**

a WHL First All-Star Team (1980, 1981)
b NHL Second All-Star Team (1982)
c NHL First All-Star Team (1988)
d Won Vezina Trophy (1988)
e Shared William M. Jennings Trophy with Dominik Hasek (1994)

Played in NHL All-Star Game (1982, 1984-86, 1988-89)

Traded to **Toronto** by **Edmonton** with Glenn Anderson and Craig Berube for Vincent Damphousse, Peter Ing, Scott Thornton, Luke Richardson, future considerations and cash, September 19, 1991. Traded to **Buffalo** by **Toronto** with Toronto's fifth round choice (Kevin Popp) in 1995 Entry Draft for Dave Andreychuk, Daren Puppa and Buffalo's first round choice (Kenny Jonsson) in 1993 Entry Draft, February 2, 1993. Traded to **Los Angeles** by **Buffalo** with Philippe Boucher and Denis Tsygurov for Alexei Zhitnik, Robb Stauber, Charlie Huddy and Los Angeles' fifth round choice (Marian Menhart) in 1995 Entry Draft, February 14, 1995. Signed as a free agent by **St. Louis**, July 14, 1995.

GAGE, JOAQUIN — EDM.

Goaltender. Catches left. 6', 200 lbs. Born, Vancouver, B.C., October 19, 1973.
(Edmonton's 6th choice, 109th overall, in 1992 Entry Draft).

			Regular Season								Playoffs						
Season	Club	Lea	GP	W	L	T	Mins	GA	SO	Avg	GP	W	L	Mins	GA	SO	Avg
1990-91	Portland	WHL	3	0	3	0	180	17	0	5.70	....	....	....	....	....	....	....
1991-92	Portland	WHL	63	27	30	4	3635	269	2	4.44	6	2	4	366	28	0	4.59
1992-93	Portland	WHL	38	21	16	1	2302	153	2	3.99	8	5	2	427	30	0	4.22
1993-94	Prince Albert	WHL	53	24	25	3	3041	212	1	4.18	....	....	....	....	....	....	....
1994-95	Cape Breton	AHL	54	17	28	5	3010	207	0	4.13	....	....	....	....	....	....	....
	Edmonton	**NHL**	**2**	**0**	**2**	**0**	**99**	**7**	**0**	**4.24**	....	....	....	....	....	....	....
	NHL Totals		**2**	**0**	**2**	**0**	**99**	**7**	**0**	**4.24**	....	....	....	....	....	....	....

GAMBLE, TROY

Goaltender. Catches left. 5'11", 195 lbs. Born, New Glasgow, N.S., April 7, 1967.
(Vancouver's 2nd choice, 25th overall, in 1985 Entry Draft).

			Regular Season								Playoffs						
Season	Club	Lea	GP	W	L	T	Mins	GA	SO	Avg	GP	W	L	Mins	GA	SO	Avg
1984-85a	Medicine Hat	WHL	37	27	6	2	2095	100	3	2.86	2	1	1	120	9	0	4.50
1985-86	Medicine Hat	WHL	45	28	11	0	2264	142	0	3.76	11	5	4	530	31	0	3.51
1986-87	**Vancouver**	**NHL**	**1**	**0**	**1**	**0**	**60**	**4**	**0**	**4.00**	....	....	....	....	....	....	....
	Medicine Hat	WHL	11	7	3	0	646	46	0	4.27	....	....	....	....	....	....	....
	Spokane	WHL	38	17	17	1	2155	163	0	4.54	5	0	5	298	35	0	7.05
1987-88b	Spokane	WHL	67	36	26	1	3824	235	0	3.69	15	7	8	875	56	1	3.84
1988-89	**Vancouver**	**NHL**	**5**	**2**	**3**	**0**	**302**	**12**	**0**	**2.38**	....	....	....	....	....	....	....
	Milwaukee	IHL	42	23	9	0	2198	138	0	3.77	11	5	5	640	35	0	3.28
1989-90	Milwaukee	IHL	*56	22	21	4	2779	160	2	4.21	5	2	2	216	19	0	5.28
1990-91	**Vancouver**	**NHL**	**47**	**16**	**16**	**6**	**2433**	**140**	**1**	**3.45**	**4**	**1**	**3**	**249**	**16**	**0**	**3.86**
1991-92	**Vancouver**	**NHL**	**19**	**4**	**9**	**3**	**1009**	**73**	**0**	**4.34**	....	....	....	....	....	....	....
	Milwaukee	IHL	9	2	4	2	521	31	0	3.57	....	....	....	....	....	....	....
1992-93	Hamilton	AHL	14	1	10	2	769	62	0	4.84	....	....	....	....	....	....	....
	Cincinnati	IHL	33	11	18	2	1762	134	0	4.56	....	....	....	....	....	....	....
1993-94	Kalamazoo	IHL	48	25	13	5	2607	146	*2	3.36	2	0	1	80	7	0	5.25
1994-95	Houston	IHL	43	18	17	5	2421	132	1	3.27	4	1	3	203	16	0	4.72
	NHL Totals		**72**	**22**	**29**	**9**	**3804**	**229**	**1**	**3.61**	**4**	**1**	**3**	**249**	**16**	**0**	**3.86**

a WHL East First All-Star Team (1985)
b WHL West First All-Star Team (1988)

Signed as a free agent by **Dallas**, August 28, 1993.

GIGUERE, JEAN-SEBASTIEN — (ZHEE-gair) HFD.

Goaltender. Catches left. 6', 178 lbs. Born, Montreal, Que., May 16, 1977.
(Hartford's 1st choice, 13th overall, in 1995 Entry Draft).

			Regular Season								Playoffs						
Season	Club	Lea	GP	W	L	T	Mins	GA	SO	Avg	GP	W	L	Mins	GA	SO	Avg
1993-94	Verdun	QMJHL	25	....	....	....	1234	66	1	3.21	....	....	....	....	....	....	....
1994-95	Halifax	QMJHL	47	14	27	5	2755	181	2	3.94	7	3	4	417	17	1	*2.15

GOVERDE, DAVID — (goh-VEHR-deh)

Goaltender. Catches right. 6', 210 lbs. Born, Toronto, Ont., April 9, 1970.
(Los Angeles' 4th choice, 91st overall, in 1990 Entry Draft).

			Regular Season								Playoffs						
Season	Club	Lea	GP	W	L	T	Mins	GA	SO	Avg	GP	W	L	Mins	GA	SO	Avg
1989-90	Sudbury	OHL	52	28	12	7	2941	182	0	3.71	7	3	3	394	25	0	3.81
1990-91	Phoenix	IHL	40	11	19	5	2007	137	0	4.10	....	....	....	....	....	....	....
1991-92	**Los Angeles**	**NHL**	**2**	**1**	**1**	**0**	**120**	**9**	**0**	**4.50**	....	....	....	....	....	....	....
	Phoenix	IHL	35	11	19	3	1951	129	1	3.97	....	....	....	....	....	....	....
	New Haven	AHL	5	1	3	0	248	17	0	4.11	....	....	....	....	....	....	....
1992-93	**Los Angeles**	**NHL**	**2**	**0**	**2**	**0**	**98**	**13**	**0**	**7.96**	....	....	....	....	....	....	....
	Phoenix	IHL	45	18	21	3	2569	173	1	4.04	....	....	....	....	....	....	....
1993-94	**Los Angeles**	**NHL**	**1**	**0**	**1**	**0**	**60**	**7**	**0**	**7.00**	....	....	....	....	....	....	....
	Phoenix	IHL	30	15	13	1	1716	93	0	3.25	....	....	....	....	....	....	....
	Portland	AHL	1	0	1	0	59	4	0	4.01	....	....	....	....	....	....	....
	Peoria	IHL	5	4	1	0	299	13	0	2.61	1	0	1	59	7	0	7.05
1994-95	Detroit	ColHL	4	4	0	0	240	10	0	2.50	....	....	....	....	....	....	....
	Phoenix	IHL	2	0	2	0	76	5	0	3.95	....	....	....	....	....	....	....
	Detroit	IHL	15	8	5	0	814	49	0	3.61	....	....	....	....	....	....	....
	NHL Totals		**5**	**1**	**4**	**0**	**278**	**29**	**0**	**6.26**	....	....	....	....	....	....	....

GRAHAME, JOHN — BOS.

Goaltender. Catches left. 6'2", 195 lbs. Born, Denver, CO, August 31, 1975.
(Boston's 7th choice, 229th overall, in 1994 Entry Draft).

			Regular Season								Playoffs						
Season	Club	Lea	GP	W	L	T	Mins	GA	SO	Avg	GP	W	L	Mins	GA	SO	Avg
1993-94	Sioux City	Jr. A								UNAVAILABLE							
1994-95	Lake Superior	CCHA	28	16	7	3	1616	75	2	2.79	....	....	....	....	....	....	....

GREENLAY, MIKE

Goaltender. Catches left. 6'3", 200 lbs. Born, Vitoria, Brazil, September 15, 1968.
(Edmonton's 9th choice, 189th overall, in 1986 Entry Draft).

			Regular Season								Playoffs						
Season	Club	Lea	GP	W	L	T	Mins	GA	SO	Avg	GP	W	L	Mins	GA	SO	Avg
1986-87	Lake Superior	CCHA	17	7	5	0	744	44	0	3.54	....	....	....	....	....	....	....
1987-88	Lake Superior	CCHA	19	10	3	3	1023	57	0	3.34	....	....	....	....	....	....	....
1988-89a	Saskatoon	WHL	20	10	8	1	1128	86	0	4.57	6	2	0	174	16	0	5.52
	Lake Superior	CCHA	2	1	1	0	85	6	0	4.23	....	....	....	....	....	....	....
1989-90	**Edmonton**	**NHL**	**2**	**0**	**0**	**0**	**20**	**4**	**0**	**12.00**	....	....	....	....	....	....	....
	Cape Breton	AHL	46	19	18	5	2595	146	2	3.38	5	1	3	306	26	0	5.09
1990-91	Cape Breton	AHL	11	5	2	0	493	33	0	4.02	....	....	....	....	....	....	....
	Knoxville	ECHL	29	17	9	2	1725	108	2	3.75	....	....	....	....	....	....	....
1991-92	Cape Breton	AHL	3	1	1	1	144	12	0	5.00	....	....	....	....	....	....	....
	Knoxville	ECHL	27	8	12	2	1415	113	0	4.79	....	....	....	....	....	....	....
1992-93	Louisville	ECHL	27	12	11	2	1437	96	1	4.01	....	....	....	....	....	....	....
	Atlanta	IHL	12	5	3	2	637	40	0	3.77	....	....	....	....	....	....	....
1993-94b	Atlanta	IHL	34	16	10	4	1741	104	0	3.58	13	*11	1	749	29	*1	*2.32
1994-95	Atlanta	IHL	20	7	10	0	1059	72	0	4.08	....	....	....	....	....	....	....
	Hershey	AHL	16	5	5	2	704	46	0	3.92	5	2	3	270	12	0	2.66
	NHL Totals		**2**	**0**	**0**	**0**	**20**	**4**	**0**	**12.00**	....	....	....	....	....	....	....

a Won Hap Emms Memorial Trophy (Memorial Cup Tournament Top Goaltender)
b Shared James Norris Memorial Trophy (fewest goals-against - IHL) with J.C. Bergeron (1994)

Signed as a free agent by **Tampa Bay**, July 29, 1992. Traded to **Philadelphia** by **Tampa Bay** for Scott LaGrand, February 2, 1995.

HACKETT, JEFF — CHI.

Goaltender. Catches left. 6'1", 180 lbs. Born, London, Ont., June 1, 1968.
(NY Islanders' 2nd choice, 34th overall, in 1987 Entry Draft).

			Regular Season								Playoffs						
Season	Club	Lea	GP	W	L	T	Mins	GA	SO	Avg	GP	W	L	Mins	GA	SO	Avg
1986-87	Oshawa	OHL	31	18	9	2	1672	85	2	3.05	15	8	7	895	40	0	2.68
1987-88	Oshawa	OHL	53	30	21	2	3165	205	0	3.89	7	3	4	438	31	0	4.25
1988-89	**NY Islanders**	**NHL**	**13**	**4**	**7**	**0**	**662**	**39**	**0**	**3.53**	....	....	....	....	....	....	....
	Springfield	AHL	29	12	14	2	1677	116	0	4.15	....	....	....	....	....	....	....
1989-90a	Springfield	AHL	54	24	25	3	3045	187	1	3.68	*17	*10	5	934	60	0	3.85
1990-91	**NY Islanders**	**NHL**	**30**	**5**	**18**	**1**	**1508**	**91**	**0**	**3.62**	....	....	....	....	....	....	....
1991-92	**San Jose**	**NHL**	**42**	**11**	**27**	**1**	**2314**	**148**	**0**	**3.84**	....	....	....	....	....	....	....
1992-93	**San Jose**	**NHL**	**36**	**2**	**30**	**1**	**2000**	**176**	**0**	**5.28**	....	....	....	....	....	....	....
1993-94	**Chicago**	**NHL**	**22**	**2**	**12**	**3**	**1084**	**62**	**0**	**3.43**	....	....	....	....	....	....	....
1994-95	**Chicago**	**NHL**	**7**	**1**	**3**	**2**	**328**	**13**	**0**	**2.38**	**2**	**0**	**0**	**26**	**1**	**0**	**2.31**
	NHL Totals		**150**	**25**	**97**	**8**	**7896**	**529**	**0**	**4.02**	**2**	**0**	**0**	**26**	**1**	**0**	**2.31**

a Won Jack A. Butterfield Trophy (Playoff MVP - AHL) (1990)

Claimed by **San Jose** from **NY Islanders** in Expansion Draft, May 30, 1991. Traded to **Chicago** by **San Jose** for Chicago's third round choice (Alexei Yegorov) in 1994 Entry Draft, July 13, 1993.

HALTIA, PATRIK — (HAHL-tih-ah) CGY.

Goaltender. Catches left. 6'1", 176 lbs. Born, Karlstad, Sweden, March 29, 1973.
(Calgary's 8th choice, 149th overall, in 1994 Entry Draft).

			Regular Season								Playoffs						
Season	Club	Lea	GP	W	L	T	Mins	GA	SO	Avg	GP	W	L	Mins	GA	SO	Avg
1993-94	Grums	Swe. 2								UNAVAILABLE							
1994-95	Farjestad	Swe.	17	....	....	....	956	44	0	2.76	2	0	0	120	7	0	3.50

HASEK, DOMINIK — (HAH-shihk) BUF.

Goaltender. Catches left. 5'11", 168 lbs. Born, Pardubice, Czech., January 29, 1965.
(Chicago's 11th choice, 199th overall, in 1983 Entry Draft).

			Regular Season								Playoffs						
Season	Club	Lea	GP	W	L	T	Mins	GA	SO	Avg	GP	W	L	Mins	GA	SO	Avg
1981-82	Pardubice	Czech.	12	....	....	....	661	34	....	3.09	....	....	....	....	....	....	....
1982-83	Pardubice	Czech.	42	....	....	....	2358	105	....	2.67	....	....	....	....	....	....	....
1983-84	Pardubice	Czech.	40	....	....	....	2304	108	....	2.81	....	....	....	....	....	....	....
1984-85	Pardubice	Czech.	42	....	....	....	2419	131	....	3.25	....	....	....	....	....	....	....
1985-86a	Pardubice	Czech.	45	....	....	....	2689	138	....	3.08	....	....	....	....	....	....	....
1986-87ab	Pardubice	Czech.	43	....	....	....	2515	103	....	2.46	....	....	....	....	....	....	....
1987-88ac	Pardubice	Czech.	31	....	....	....	1862	93	....	3.00	....	....	....	....	....	....	....
1988-89abc	Pardubice	Czech.	42	....	....	....	2507	114	....	2.73	....	....	....	....	....	....	....
1989-90abc	Dukla Jihlava	Czech.	40	....	....	....	2251	80	....	2.13	....	....	....	....	....	....	....
1990-91	**Chicago**	**NHL**	**5**	**3**	**0**	**1**	**195**	**8**	**0**	**2.46**	**3**	**0**	**0**	**69**	**3**	**0**	**2.61**
d	Indianapolis	IHL	33	20	11	1	1903	80	*5	*2.52	1	1	0	60	3	0	3.00
1991-92e	**Chicago**	**NHL**	**20**	**10**	**4**	**1**	**1014**	**44**	**1**	**2.60**	**3**	**0**	**2**	**158**	**8**	**0**	**3.04**
	Indianapolis	IHL	20	7	10	3	1162	69	1	3.56	....	....	....	....	....	....	....
1992-93	**Buffalo**	**NHL**	**28**	**11**	**10**	**4**	**1429**	**75**	**0**	**3.15**	**1**	**1**	**0**	**45**	**1**	**0**	**1.33**
1993-94fgh	**Buffalo**	**NHL**	**58**	**30**	**20**	**6**	**3358**	**109**	***7**	***1.95**	**7**	**3**	**4**	**484**	**13**	**2**	***1.61**
1994-95	Pardubice	Czech.	2	....	....	....	124	6	0	2.90	....	....	....	....	....	....	....
fg	**Buffalo**	**NHL**	**41**	**19**	**14**	**7**	**2416**	**85**	***5**	***2.11**	**5**	**1**	**4**	**309**	**18**	**0**	**3.50**
	NHL Totals		**152**	**73**	**48**	**19**	**8412**	**321**	**13**	**2.29**	**19**	**5**	**10**	**1065**	**43**	**2**	**2.42**

a Czechoslovakian Goaltender-of-the-Year (1986, 1987, 1988, 1989, 1990)
b Czechoslovakian Player-of-the-Year (1987, 1989, 1990)
c Czechoslovakian First-Team All-Star (1988, 1989, 1990)
d IHL First All-Star Team (1991)
e NHL/Upper Deck All-Rookie Team (1992)
f NHL First All-Star Team (1994, 1995)
g Won Vezina Trophy (1994, 1995)
h Shared William M. Jennings Trophy with Grant Fuhr (1994)

Traded to **Buffalo** by **Chicago** for Stephane Beauregard and Buffalo's fourth round choice (Eric Daze) in 1993 Entry Draft, August 7, 1992.

HEALY, GLENN — NYR

Goaltender. Catches left. 5'10", 185 lbs. Born, Pickering, Ont., August 23, 1962.

			Regular Season								Playoffs						
Season	Club	Lea	GP	W	L	T	Mins	GA	SO	Avg	GP	W	L	Mins	GA	SO	Avg
1981-82	W. Michigan	CCHA	27	7	19	1	1569	116	0	4.44	....	....	....	....	....	....	....
1982-83	W. Michigan	CCHA	30	8	19	2	1732	116	0	4.01	....	....	....	....	....	....	....
1983-84	W. Michigan	CCHA	38	19	16	3	2241	146	0	3.90	....	....	....	....	....	....	....
1984-85	W. Michigan	CCHA	37	21	14	2	2171	118	0	3.26	....	....	....	....	....	....	....
1985-86	**Los Angeles**	**NHL**	**1**	**0**	**0**	**0**	**51**	**6**	**0**	**7.06**	....	....	....	....	....	....	....
	New Haven	AHL	43	21	15	4	2410	160	0	3.98	2	0	2	49	11	0	5.55
1986-87	New Haven	AHL	47	21	15	0	2828	173	1	3.67	7	3	4	427	19	0	2.67
1987-88	**Los Angeles**	**NHL**	**34**	**12**	**18**	**1**	**1869**	**135**	**1**	**4.33**	**4**	**1**	**3**	**240**	**20**	**0**	**5.00**
1988-89	**Los Angeles**	**NHL**	**48**	**25**	**19**	**2**	**2699**	**192**	**0**	**4.27**	**3**	**0**	**1**	**97**	**6**	**0**	**3.71**
1989-90	**NY Islanders**	**NHL**	**39**	**12**	**19**	**6**	**2197**	**128**	**2**	**3.50**	**4**	**1**	**2**	**166**	**9**	**0**	**3.25**
1990-91	**NY Islanders**	**NHL**	**53**	**18**	**24**	**9**	**2999**	**166**	**0**	**3.32**	....	....	....	....	....	....	....
1991-92	**NY Islanders**	**NHL**	**37**	**14**	**16**	**4**	**1960**	**124**	**1**	**3.80**	....	....	....	....	....	....	....
1992-93	**NY Islanders**	**NHL**	**47**	**22**	**20**	**2**	**2655**	**146**	**1**	**3.30**	**18**	**9**	**8**	**1109**	**59**	**0**	**3.19**
1993-94	**NY Rangers**	**NHL**	**29**	**10**	**12**	**2**	**1368**	**69**	**2**	**3.03**	**2**	**0**	**0**	**68**	**1**	**0**	**0.88**
1994-95	**NY Rangers**	**NHL**	**17**	**8**	**6**	**1**	**888**	**35**	**1**	**2.36**	**5**	**2**	**1**	**230**	**13**	**0**	**3.39**
	NHL Totals		**305**	**121**	**134**	**27**	**16686**	**1001**	**8**	**3.60**	**36**	**13**	**15**	**1910**	**108**	**0**	**3.39**

Signed as a free agent by **Los Angeles**, June 13, 1985. Signed as a free agent by **NY Islanders**, August 16, 1989. Claimed by **Anaheim** from **NY Islanders** in Expansion Draft, June 24, 1993. Claimed by **Tampa Bay** from **Anaheim** in Phase II of Expansion Draft, June 25, 1993. Traded to **NY Rangers** by **Tampa Bay** for Tampa Bay's third round choice (previously acquired by NY Rangers — Tampa Bay selected Allan Egeland) in 1993 Entry Draft, June 25, 1993.

HEBERT, GUY — (ay-BAIR, GEE) ANA.

Goaltender. Catches left. 5'11", 185 lbs. Born, Troy, NY, January 7, 1967.
(St. Louis' 8th choice, 159th overall, in 1987 Entry Draft).

			Regular Season								Playoffs						
Season	Club	Lea	GP	W	L	T	Mins	GA	SO	Avg	GP	W	L	Mins	GA	SO	Avg
1985-86	Hamilton Coll.	NCAA	18	4	12	2	1011	69	2	4.09	....	....	....	....	....	....	....
1986-87	Hamilton Coll.	NCAA	18	12	5	0	1070	40	3	2.19	2	1	1	134	6	0	2.69
1987-88	Hamilton Coll.	NCAA	9	5	3	0	510	22	1	2.58	1	0	1	60	3	0	3.00
1988-89	Hamilton Coll.	NCAA	25	18	7	0	1454	62	2	2.56	2	1	1	126	4	0	1.90
1989-90	Peoria	IHL	30	7	13	7	1706	124	1	4.36	2	0	1	76	5	0	3.95
1990-91ab	Peoria	IHL	36	24	10	1	2093	100	2	2.87	8	3	4	458	32	0	4.19
1991-92	**St. Louis**	**NHL**	**13**	**5**	**5**	**1**	**738**	**36**	**0**	**2.93**	....	....	....	....	....	....	....
	Peoria	IHL	29	20	9	0	1731	98	0	3.40	4	3	1	239	9	0	2.26
1992-93	**St. Louis**	**NHL**	**24**	**8**	**8**	**2**	**1210**	**74**	**1**	**3.67**	**1**	**0**	**0**	**2**	**0**	**0**	**0.00**
1993-94	**Anaheim**	**NHL**	**52**	**20**	**27**	**3**	**2991**	**141**	**2**	**2.83**	....	....	....	....	....	....	....
1994-95	**Anaheim**	**NHL**	**39**	**12**	**20**	**4**	**2092**	**109**	**2**	**3.13**	....	....	....	....	....	....	....
	NHL Totals		**128**	**45**	**60**	**10**	**7031**	**360**	**5**	**3.07**	**1**	**0**	**0**	**2**	**0**	**0**	**0.00**

a Shared James Norris Memorial Trophy (fewest goals against - IHL) with Pat Jablonski (1991)
b IHL Second All-Star Team (1991)

Claimed by **Anaheim** from **St. Louis** in Expansion Draft, June 24, 1993.

HEDBERG, JOHAN — PHI.

Goaltender. Catches left. 5'11", 180 lbs. Born, Leksand, Sweden, May 5, 1973.
(Philadelphia's 8th choice, 218th overall, in 1994 Entry Draft).

			Regular Season								Playoffs						
Season	Club	Lea	GP	W	L	T	Mins	GA	SO	Avg	GP	W	L	Mins	GA	SO	Avg
1992-93	Leksand	Swe.	10	....	....	....	600	24	....	2.40	....	....	....	....	....	....	....
1993-94	Leksand	Swe.	17	....	....	....	1020	48	....	2.81	....	....	....	....	....	....	....
1994-95	Leksand	Swe.	17	....	....	....	986	58	....	3.53	....	....	....	....	....	....	....

HEINKE, MICHAEL — N.J.

Goaltender. Catches left. 5'11", 165 lbs. Born, Denville, NY, January 11, 1971.
(New Jersey's 5th choice, 89th overall, in 1989 Entry Draft).

			Regular Season								Playoffs						
Season	Club	Lea	GP	W	L	T	Mins	GA	SO	Avg	GP	W	L	Mins	GA	SO	Avg
1990-91	Providence	H.E.	14	8	7	1	923	74	0	4.81	....	....	....	....	....	....	....
1991-92	Providence	H.E.	16	10	4	0	816	48	*2	3.53	....	....	....	....	....	....	....
1992-93	N. Hampshire	H.E.								DID NOT PLAY							
1993-94	N. Hampshire	H.E.	22	11	5	2	1116	67	1	3.60	....	....	....	....	....	....	....
1994-95	N. Hampshire	H.E.	17	8	4	3	903	51	0	3.39	....	....	....	....	....	....	....

HENRY, FREDERIC — N.J.

Goaltender. Catches left. 5'10", 150 lbs. Born, Cap-Rouge, Que., August 9, 1977.
(New Jersey's 10th choice, 200th overall, in 1995 Entry Draft).

			Regular Season								Playoffs						
Season	Club	Lea	GP	W	L	T	Mins	GA	SO	Avg	GP	W	L	Mins	GA	SO	Avg
1993-94	Ste-Foy	Midget	30	....	....	....	1571	76	1	2.98	6	....	....	333	15	1	2.70
1994-95	Granby	WHL	15	8	5	0	866	47	0	3.26	6	1	2	232	21	0	5.43

HEXTALL, RON — PHI.

Goaltender. Catches left. 6'3", 192 lbs. Born, Brandon, Man., May 3, 1964.
(Philadelphia's 6th choice, 119th overall, in 1982 Entry Draft).

			Regular Season								Playoffs						
Season	Club	Lea	GP	W	L	T	Mins	GA	SO	Avg	GP	W	L	Mins	GA	SO	Avg
1981-82	Brandon	WHL	30	12	11	0	1398	133	0	5.71	3	0	2	103	16	0	9.32
1982-83	Brandon	WHL	44	13	30	0	2589	249	0	5.77	....	....	....	....	....	....	....
1983-84	Brandon	WHL	46	29	13	2	2670	190	0	4.27	10	5	5	592	37	0	3.75
1984-85	Hershey	AHL	11	4	6	0	555	34	0	3.68	....	....	....	....	....	....	....
	Kalamazoo	IHL	19	6	11	1	1103	80	0	4.35	....	....	....	....	....	....	....
1985-86ab	Hershey	AHL	*53	30	19	2	*3061	174	*5	3.41	13	5	7	780	42	*1	3.23
1986-87																	
cdef	**Philadelphia**	**NHL**	***66**	**37**	**21**	**6**	***3799**	**190**	**1**	**3.00**	***26**	**15**	**11**	***1540**	**71**	***2**	**2.77**
1987-88g	**Philadelphia**	**NHL**	**62**	**30**	**22**	**7**	**3561**	**208**	**0**	**3.50**	**7**	**2**	**4**	**379**	**30**	**0**	**4.75**
1988-89h	**Philadelphia**	**NHL**	***64**	**30**	**28**	**6**	***3756**	**202**	**0**	**3.23**	**15**	**8**	**7**	**886**	**49**	**0**	**3.32**
1989-90	**Philadelphia**	**NHL**	**8**	**4**	**2**	**1**	**419**	**29**	**0**	**4.15**	....	....	....	....	....	....	....
	Hershey	AHL	1	1	0	0	49	3	0	3.67	....	....	....	....	....	....	....
1990-91	**Philadelphia**	**NHL**	**36**	**13**	**16**	**5**	**2035**	**106**	**0**	**3.13**	....	....	....	....	....	....	....
1991-92	**Philadelphia**	**NHL**	**45**	**16**	**21**	**6**	**2668**	**151**	**3**	**3.40**	....	....	....	....	....	....	....
1992-93	**Quebec**	**NHL**	**54**	**29**	**16**	**5**	**2988**	**172**	**0**	**3.45**	**6**	**2**	**4**	**372**	**18**	**0**	**2.90**
1993-94	**NY Islanders**	**NHL**	**65**	**27**	**26**	**6**	**3581**	**184**	**5**	**3.08**	**3**	**0**	**3**	**158**	**16**	**0**	**6.08**
1994-95	**Philadelphia**	**NHL**	**31**	**17**	**9**	**4**	**1824**	**88**	**1**	**2.89**	**15**	**10**	**5**	**897**	**42**	**0**	**2.81**
	NHL Totals		**431**	**203**	**161**	**46**	**24631**	**1330**	**10**	**3.24**	**72**	**37**	**34**	**4232**	**226**	**2**	**3.20**

a AHL First All-Star Team (1986)
b Won Dudley "Red" Garrett Memorial Trophy (Top Rookie - AHL) (1986)
c NHL First All-Star Team (1987)
d Won Vezina Trophy (1987)
e Won Conn Smythe Trophy (1987)
f NHL All-Rookie Team (1987)
g Scored a goal vs. Boston, December 8, 1987
h Scored a goal in playoffs vs. Washington, April 11, 1989

Played in NHL All-Star Game (1988)

Traded to **Quebec** by **Philadelphia** with Peter Forsberg, Steve Duchesne, Kerry Huffman, Mike Ricci, Chris Simon, Philadelphia's first choice in the 1993 (Jocelyn Thibault) and 1994 (later traded to Toronto — later traded to Washington — Washington selected Nolan Baumgartner) Entry Drafts and cash for Eric Lindros, June 30, 1992. Traded to **NY Islanders** by **Quebec** with Quebec's first round choice (Todd Bertuzzi) in 1993 Entry Draft for Mark Fitzpatrick and NY Islanders' first round choice (Adam Deadmarsh) in 1993 Entry Draft, June 20, 1993. Traded to **Philadelphia** by **NY Islanders** with NY Islanders' sixth round choice (Dmitry Tertyshny) in 1995 Entry Draft for Tommy Soderstrom, September 22, 1994.

HILLEBRANDT, JON — NYR

Goaltender. Catches left. 5'10", 185 lbs. Born, Cottage Grove, WI, December 18, 1971.
(NY Rangers' 12th choice, 202nd overall, in 1990 Entry Draft).

			Regular Season								Playoffs						
Season	Club	Lea	GP	W	L	T	Mins	GA	SO	Avg	GP	W	L	Mins	GA	SO	Avg
1991-92a	Ill.-Chicago	CCHA	31	7	19	....	1754	121	0	4.14	....	....	....	....	....	....	....
1992-93	Ill.-Chicago	CCHA	33	8	22	2	1783	134	0	4.51	....	....	....	....	....	....	....
1993-94	U.S. National	....	2	1	1	0	120	10	0	5.00	....	....	....	....	....	....	....
	Binghamton	AHL	7	1	3	0	294	18	0	3.67	....	....	....	....	....	....	....
	Erie	ECHL	3	2	0	1	189	8	1	2.53	....	....	....	....	....	....	....
1994-95	Charlotte	ECHL	32	14	11	5	1790	121	0	4.05	3	0	2	179	12	0	4.01
	San Diego	IHL	1	0	1	0	40	6	0	9.00	....	....	....	....	....	....	....
	Binghamton	AHL	....	....	....	....	....	....	....	....	1	0	0	5	1	0	10.20

a CCHA Second All-Star Team (1992)

HIRSCH, COREY (HUHRSH) — VAN.

Goaltender. Catches left. 5'10", 160 lbs. Born, Medicine Hat, Alta., July 1, 1972.
(NY Rangers' 8th choice, 169th overall, in 1991 Entry Draft).

			Regular Season								Playoffs						
Season	Club	Lea	GP	W	L	T	Mins	GA	SO	Avg	GP	W	L	Mins	GA	SO	Avg
1988-89	Kamloops	WHL	32	11	12	2	1516	106	2	4.20	5	3	2	245	19	0	4.65
1989-90	Kamloops	WHL	*63	*48	13	0	3608	230	*3	3.82	*17	*14	3	*1043	60	0	*3.45
1990-91a	Kamloops	WHL	38	26	7	1	1970	100	3	*3.05	11	5	6	623	42	0	4.04
1991-92																	
abcd	Kamloops	WHL	48	35	10	2	2732	124	*5	*2.72	*16	*11	5	954	35	*2	*2.20
1992-93	**NY Rangers**	**NHL**	**4**	**1**	**2**	**1**	**224**	**14**	**0**	**3.75**	....	....	....	....	....	....	....
efg	Binghamton	AHL	46	*35	4	5	2692	125	1	*2.79	14	7	7	831	46	0	3.32
1993-94	Cdn. National	....	45	24	17	3	2653	124	0	2.80	....	....	....	....	....	....	....
	Cdn. Olympic	....	8	5	2	1	495	17	0	2.06	....	....	....	....	....	....	....
	Binghamton	AHL	10	5	4	1	610	38	0	3.73	....	....	....	....	....	....	....
1994-95	Binghamton	AHL	57	31	20	5	3371	175	0	3.11	....	....	....	....	....	....	....
	NHL Totals		**4**	**1**	**2**	**1**	**224**	**14**	**0**	**3.75**	....	....	....	....	....	....	....

a WHL West First All-Star Team (1991, 1992)
b Canadian Major Junior Goaltender of the Year (1992)
c Memorial Cup All-Star Team (1992)
d Memorial Cup Tournament Top Goaltender (1992)
e Won Dudley "Red" Garrett Memorial Trophy (AHL Rookie of the Year) (1993)
f Shared Harry "Hap" Holmes Memorial Trophy (fewest goals-against - AHL) with Boris Rousson (1993)
g AHL First All-Star Team (1993)

Traded to **Vancouver** by **NY Rangers** for Nathan Lafayette, April 7, 1995.

HNILICKA, MILAN (hih-LEECH-kah, MEE-lahn) — NYI

Goaltender. Catches left. 6', 180 lbs. Born, Litomerice, Czech., June 25, 1973.
(NY Islanders' 4th choice, 70th overall, in 1991 Entry Draft).

			Regular Season								Playoffs						
Season	Club	Lea	GP	W	L	T	Mins	GA	SO	Avg	GP	W	L	Mins	GA	SO	Avg
1989-90	Kladno	Czech.	24	....	....	....	1113	70	....	3.77	....	....	....	....	....	....	....
1990-91	Kladno	Czech.	40	....	....	....	2122	98	0	2.80	....	....	....	....	....	....	....
1991-92	Kladno	Czech.	38	....	....	....	2066	128	0	3.73	....	....	....	....	....	....	....
1992-93	Swift Current	WHL	*65	*46	12	2	3679	206	2	3.36	*17	*12	5	*1017	54	*2	3.19
1993-94	Richmond	ECHL	43	18	16	5	2299	155	4	4.05	....	....	....	....	....	....	....
	Salt Lake	IHL	8	5	1	0	378	25	0	3.97	....	....	....	....	....	....	....
1994-95	Denver	IHL	15	9	4	1	798	47	1	3.53	....	....	....	....	....	....	....

HODSON, KEVIN — DET.

Goaltender. Catches left. 6', 182 lbs. Born, Winnipeg, Man., March 27, 1972.

			Regular Season								Playoffs						
Season	Club	Lea	GP	W	L	T	Mins	GA	SO	Avg	GP	W	L	Mins	GA	SO	Avg
1990-91	S.S. Marie	OHL	30	18	11	0	1638	88	0	*3.22	10	*9	1	581	28	0	*2.89
1991-92	S.S. Marie	OHL	50	28	12	4	2722	151	0	3.33	18	12	6	1116	54	1	2.90
1992-93ab	S.S. Marie	OHL	26	18	5	2	1470	76	1	*3.10	14	11	2	755	34	0	2.70
	Indianapolis	IHL	14	5	9	0	777	53	0	4.09	....	....	....	....	....	....	....
1993-94	Adirondack	AHL	37	20	10	5	2082	102	2	2.94	3	0	2	89	10	0	6.77
1994-95	Adirondack	AHL	51	19	22	8	2731	161	1	3.54	4	0	4	237	14	0	3.53

a Memorial Cup All-Star Team (1993)
b Won Hap Emms Memorial Trophy (Memorial Cup Tournament Top Goaltender) (1993)

Signed as a free agent by **Chicago**, August 17, 1992. Signed as a free agent by **Detroit**, June 16, 1993.

HRIVNAK, JIM (RIV-NAK)

Goaltender. Catches left. 6'2", 195 lbs. Born, Montreal, Que., May 28, 1968.
(Washington's 4th choice, 61st overall, in 1986 Entry Draft).

			Regular Season								Playoffs						
Season	Club	Lea	GP	W	L	T	Mins	GA	SO	Avg	GP	W	L	Mins	GA	SO	Avg
1985-86	Merrimack	NCAA	21	12	8	0	1230	75	0	3.66	....	....	....	....	....	....	....
1986-87	Merrimack	NCAA	34	27	7	0	1618	58	3	2.14	....	....	....	....	....	....	....
1987-88	Merrimack	NCAA	37	31	6	0	2119	84	4	2.38	....	....	....	....	....	....	....
1988-89	Merrimack	NCAA	22	....	....	....	1295	52	4	2.41	....	....	....	....	....	....	....
	Baltimore	AHL	10	1	8	0	502	55	0	6.57	....	....	....	....	....	....	....
1989-90	**Washington**	**NHL**	**11**	**5**	**5**	**0**	**609**	**36**	**0**	**3.55**	....	....	....	....	....	....	....
a	Baltimore	AHL	47	24	19	2	2722	139	*4	3.06	6	4	2	360	19	0	3.17
1990-91	**Washington**	**NHL**	**9**	**4**	**2**	**1**	**432**	**26**	**0**	**3.61**	....	....	....	....	....	....	....
	Baltimore	AHL	42	20	16	6	2481	134	1	3.24	6	2	3	324	21	0	3.89
1991-92	**Washington**	**NHL**	**12**	**6**	**3**	**0**	**605**	**35**	**0**	**3.47**	....	....	....	....	....	....	....
	Baltimore	AHL	22	10	8	3	1303	73	0	3.36	....	....	....	....	....	....	....
1992-93	**Washington**	**NHL**	**27**	**13**	**9**	**2**	**1421**	**83**	**0**	**3.50**	....	....	....	....	....	....	....
	Winnipeg	**NHL**	**3**	**2**	**1**	**0**	**180**	**13**	**0**	**4.33**	....	....	....	....	....	....	....
1993-94	**St. Louis**	**NHL**	**23**	**4**	**10**	**0**	**970**	**69**	**0**	**4.27**	....	....	....	....	....	....	....
1994-95	Milwaukee	IHL	28	17	10	1	1634	106	0	3.89	....	....	....	....	....	....	....
	Kansas City	IHL	10	3	5	2	550	35	0	3.81	2	0	2	118	7	0	3.55
	NHL Totals		**85**	**34**	**30**	**3**	**4217**	**262**	**0**	**3.73**	....	....	....	....	....	....	....

a AHL Second All-Star Team (1990)

Traded to **Winnipeg** by **Washington** with Washington's second round choice (Alexei Budayev) in 1993 Entry Draft for Rick Tabaracci, March 22, 1993. Traded to **St. Louis** by **Winnipeg** for St. Louis' seventh round choice (later traded to Florida — later traded to Edmonton — later traded to Winnipeg — Winnipeg selected Chris Kibermanis) in 1994 Entry Draft and future considerations, July 29, 1993.

HRUDEY, KELLY (ROO-dee) — L.A.

Goaltender. Catches left. 5'10", 189 lbs. Born, Edmonton, Alta., January 13, 1961.
(NY Islanders' 2nd choice, 38th overall, in 1980 Entry Draft).

			Regular Season								Playoffs						
Season	Club	Lea	GP	W	L	T	Mins	GA	SO	Avg	GP	W	L	Mins	GA	SO	Avg
1978-79	Medicine Hat	WHL	57	12	34	7	3093	318	0	6.17	....	....	....	....	....	....	....
1979-80	Medicine Hat	WHL	57	25	23	4	3049	212	1	4.17	13	6	6	638	48	0	4.51
1980-81a	Medicine Hat	WHL	55	32	19	1	3023	200	4	3.97	4	1	3	244	17	0	4.18
	Indianapolis	CHL	....	....	....	....	....	....	....	....	2	....	....	135	8	0	3.56
1981-82bc	Indianapolis	CHL	51	27	19	4	3033	149	1	*2.95	13	11	2	842	34	*1	*2.42
1982-83bcd	Indianapolis	CHL	47	*26	17	1	2744	139	2	3.04	10	*7	3	*637	28	0	*2.64
1983-84	**NY Islanders**	**NHL**	**12**	**7**	**2**	**0**	**535**	**28**	**0**	**3.14**	....	....	....	....	....	....	....
	Indianapolis	CHL	6	3	2	1	370	21	0	3.40	....	....	....	....	....	....	....
1984-85	**NY Islanders**	**NHL**	**41**	**19**	**17**	**3**	**2335**	**141**	**2**	**3.62**	**5**	**1**	**3**	**281**	**8**	**0**	**1.71**
1985-86	**NY Islanders**	**NHL**	**45**	**19**	**15**	**8**	**2563**	**137**	**1**	**3.21**	**2**	**0**	**2**	**120**	**6**	**0**	**3.00**
1986-87	**NY Islanders**	**NHL**	**46**	**21**	**15**	**7**	**2634**	**145**	**0**	**3.30**	**14**	**7**	**7**	**842**	**38**	**0**	**2.71**
1987-88	**NY Islanders**	**NHL**	**47**	**22**	**17**	**5**	**2751**	**153**	**3**	**3.34**	**6**	**2**	**4**	**381**	**23**	**0**	**3.62**
1988-89	**NY Islanders**	**NHL**	**50**	**18**	**24**	**3**	**2800**	**183**	**0**	**3.92**	....	....	....	....	....	....	....
	Los Angeles	**NHL**	**16**	**10**	**4**	**2**	**974**	**47**	**1**	**2.90**	**10**	**4**	**6**	**566**	**35**	**0**	**3.71**
1989-90	**Los Angeles**	**NHL**	**52**	**22**	**21**	**6**	**2860**	**194**	**2**	**4.07**	**9**	**4**	**4**	**539**	**39**	**0**	**4.34**
1990-91	**Los Angeles**	**NHL**	**47**	**26**	**13**	**6**	**2730**	**132**	**3**	**2.90**	**12**	**6**	**6**	**798**	**37**	**0**	**2.78**
1991-92	**Los Angeles**	**NHL**	**60**	**26**	**17**	**13**	**3509**	**197**	**1**	**3.37**	**6**	**2**	**4**	**355**	**22**	**0**	**3.72**
1992-93	**Los Angeles**	**NHL**	**50**	**18**	**21**	**6**	**2718**	**175**	**2**	**3.86**	**20**	**10**	**10**	**1261**	**74**	**0**	**3.52**
1993-94	**Los Angeles**	**NHL**	**64**	**22**	**31**	**7**	**3713**	**228**	**1**	**3.68**	....	....	....	....	....	....	....
1994-95	**Los Angeles**	**NHL**	**35**	**14**	**13**	**5**	**1894**	**99**	**0**	**3.14**	....	....	....	....	....	....	....
	NHL Totals		**565**	**244**	**210**	**71**	**32016**	**1859**	**16**	**3.48**	**84**	**36**	**46**	**5143**	**282**	**0**	**3.29**

a WHL Second All-Star Team (1981)
b CHL First All-Star Team (1982, 1983)
c Shared Terry Sawchuk Trophy (CHL's Leading Goaltender) with Rob Holland (1982, 1983)
d Won Tommy Ivan Trophy (CHL's Most Valuable Player) (1983)

Traded to **Los Angeles** by **NY Islanders** for Mark Fitzpatrick, Wayne McBean and future considerations (Doug Crossman, May 23, 1989) February 22, 1989.

ING, PETER

Goaltender. Catches left. 6'2", 170 lbs. Born, Toronto, Ont., April 28, 1969.
(Toronto's 3rd choice, 48th overall, in 1988 Entry Draft).

			Regular Season								Playoffs						
Season	Club	Lea	GP	W	L	T	Mins	GA	SO	Avg	GP	W	L	Mins	GA	SO	Avg
1986-87	Windsor	OHL	28	13	11	3	1615	105	0	3.90	5	4	0	161	9	0	3.35
1987-88	Windsor	OHL	43	30	7	1	2422	125	2	3.10	3	2	0	225	7	0	1.87
1988-89	Windsor	OHL	19	7	7	3	1043	76	*1	4.37	....	....	....	....	....	....	....
	London	OHL	32	18	11	2	1848	104	*2	3.38	21	11	9	1093	82	0	4.50
1989-90	**Toronto**	**NHL**	**3**	**0**	**2**	**1**	**182**	**18**	**0**	**5.93**	....	....	....	....	....	....	....
	Newmarket	AHL	48	16	19	12	2829	184	0	3.90	....	....	....	....	....	....	....
	Cdn. National	....	10	2	2	4	460	29	....	3.78	....	....	....	....	....	....	....
	London	OHL	8	6	2	0	480	27	0	3.38	....	....	....	....	....	....	....
1990-91	**Toronto**	**NHL**	**56**	**16**	**29**	**8**	**3126**	**200**	**1**	**3.84**	....	....	....	....	....	....	....
1991-92	**Edmonton**	**NHL**	**12**	**3**	**4**	**0**	**463**	**33**	**0**	**4.28**	....	....	....	....	....	....	....
	Cape Breton	AHL	24	9	10	4	1411	92	0	3.91	1	0	1	60	9	0	9.00
1992-93	Detroit	ColHL	3	2	1	0	136	6	0	2.65	....	....	....	....	....	....	....
	San Diego	IHL	17	11	4	1	882	53	0	3.61	4	2	2	183	13	0	4.26
1993-94	**Detroit**	**NHL**	**3**	**1**	**2**	**0**	**170**	**15**	**0**	**5.29**	....	....	....	....	....	....	....
	Adirondack	AHL	7	3	3	1	425	26	1	3.67	....	....	....	....	....	....	....
	Las Vegas	IHL	30	16	7	4	1627	91	0	3.36	2	0	1	40	4	0	5.87
1994-95	Fort Wayne	IHL	36	15	18	2	2018	119	2	3.54	2	0	1	94	5	0	3.19
	NHL Totals		**74**	**20**	**37**	**9**	**3941**	**266**	**1**	**4.05**	....	....	....	....	....	....	....

Traded to **Edmonton** by **Toronto** with Vincent Damphousse, Scott Thornton, Luke Richardson, future considerations and cash for Grant Fuhr, Glenn Anderson and Craig Berube, September 19, 1991. Traded to **Detroit** by **Edmonton** for Detroit's seventh round choice (Chris Wickenheiser) in 1994 Entry Draft and future considerations, August 30, 1993.

IRBE, ARTURS (UHR-bay, AHR-tuhrs) — S.J.

Goaltender. Catches left. 5'7", 180 lbs. Born, Riga, Latvia, February 2, 1967.
(Minnesota's 11th choice, 196th overall, in 1989 Entry Draft).

			Regular Season								Playoffs						
Season	Club	Lea	GP	W	L	T	Mins	GA	SO	Avg	GP	W	L	Mins	GA	SO	Avg
1986-87	Dynamo Riga	USSR	2	....	....	....	27	1	0	2.22	....	....	....	....	....	....	....
1987-88a	Dynamo Riga	USSR	34	....	....	....	1870	86	4	2.69	....	....	....	....	....	....	....
1988-89	Dynamo Riga	USSR	40	....	....	....	2460	116	4	2.85	....	....	....	....	....	....	....
1989-90	Dynamo Riga	USSR	48	....	....	....	2880	115	2	2.42	....	....	....	....	....	....	....
1990-91	Dynamo Riga	USSR	46	....	....	....	2713	133	5	2.94	....	....	....	....	....	....	....
1991-92	**San Jose**	**NHL**	**13**	**2**	**6**	**3**	**645**	**48**	**0**	**4.47**	....	....	....	....	....	....	....
bc	Kansas City	IHL	32	24	7	1	1955	80	0	*2.46	*15	*12	3	914	44	0	*2.89
1992-93	**San Jose**	**NHL**	**36**	**7**	**26**	**0**	**2074**	**142**	**1**	**4.11**	....	....	....	....	....	....	....
	Kansas City	IHL	6	3	3	0	364	20	0	3.30	....	....	....	....	....	....	....
1993-94	**San Jose**	**NHL**	***74**	**30**	**28**	**16**	***4412**	**209**	**3**	**2.84**	**14**	**7**	**7**	**806**	**50**	**0**	**3.72**
1994-95	**San Jose**	**NHL**	**38**	**14**	**19**	**3**	**2043**	**111**	**4**	**3.26**	**6**	**2**	**4**	**316**	**27**	**0**	**5.13**
	NHL Totals		**161**	**53**	**79**	**22**	**9174**	**510**	**8**	**3.34**	**20**	**9**	**11**	**1122**	**77**	**0**	**4.12**

a Soviet National League Rookie-of-the-Year (1988)
b IHL First All-Star Team (1992)
c Shared James Norris Memorial Trophy (fewest goals against - IHL) with Wade Flaherty (1992)

Played in NHL All-Star Game (1994)

Claimed by **San Jose** from **Minnesota** in Dispersal Draft, May 30, 1991.

ISRAEL, AARON — PHI.

Goaltender. Catches left. 6'2", 176 lbs. Born, Boston, MA, June 4, 1973.
(Philadelphia's 6th choice, 166th overall, in 1993 Entry Draft).

			Regular Season								Playoffs						
Season	Club	Lea	GP	W	L	T	Mins	GA	SO	Avg	GP	W	L	Mins	GA	SO	Avg
1992-93	Harvard	ECAC	14	9	4	1	843	43	0	3.06	....	....	....	....	....	....	....
1993-94a	Harvard	ECAC	18	12	2	2	1045	40	0	*2.30	....	....	....	....	....	....	....
1994-95	Hershey	AHL	7	2	1	0	245	16	0	3.92	1	0	0	21	1	0	2.81
	Johnstown	ECHL	30	17	10	2	1774	119	1	4.02	3	2	1	156	14	0	5.35

a NCAA Final Four All-Tournament Team (1994)

JABLONSKI, PAT — TOR.

Goaltender. Catches right. 6', 180 lbs. Born, Toledo, OH, June 20, 1967.
(St. Louis' 6th choice, 138th overall, in 1985 Entry Draft).

			Regular Season								Playoffs						
Season	Club	Lea	GP	W	L	T	Mins	GA	SO	Avg	GP	W	L	Mins	GA	SO	Avg
1985-86	Windsor	OHL	29	6	16	4	1600	119	1	4.46	6	0	3	263	20	0	4.56
1986-87	Windsor	OHL	41	22	14	2	2328	128	*3	3.30	12	8	4	710	38	0	3.21
1987-88	Peoria	IHL	5	2	2	1	285	17	0	3.58	....	....	....	....	....	....	....
	Windsor	OHL	18	14	3	0	994	48	2	*2.90	9	*8	0	537	28	0	3.13
1988-89	Peoria	IHL	35	11	20	0	2051	163	1	4.77	3	0	2	130	13	0	6.00
1989-90	**St. Louis**	**NHL**	**4**	**0**	**3**	**0**	**208**	**17**	**0**	**4.90**	....	....	....	....	....	....	....
	Peoria	IHL	36	14	17	4	2023	165	0	4.89	4	1	3	223	19	0	5.11
1990-91	**St. Louis**	**NHL**	**8**	**2**	**3**	**3**	**492**	**25**	**0**	**3.05**	**3**	**0**	**0**	**90**	**5**	**0**	**3.33**
a	Peoria	IHL	29	23	3	2	1738	87	0	3.00	10	7	2	532	23	0	2.59
1991-92	**St. Louis**	**NHL**	**10**	**3**	**6**	**0**	**468**	**38**	**0**	**4.87**	....	....	....	....	....	....	....
	Peoria	IHL	8	6	1	1	493	29	1	3.53	....	....	....	....	....	....	....
1992-93	**Tampa Bay**	**NHL**	**43**	**8**	**24**	**4**	**2268**	**150**	**1**	**3.97**	....	....	....	....	....	....	....
1993-94	**Tampa Bay**	**NHL**	**15**	**5**	**6**	**3**	**834**	**54**	**0**	**3.88**	....	....	....	....	....	....	....
	St. John's	AHL	16	12	3	1	962	49	1	3.05	11	6	5	676	36	0	3.19
1994-95	Chicago	IHL	4	0	4	0	216	17	0	4.71	....	....	....	....	....	....	....
	Houston	IHL	3	1	1	1	179	9	0	3.01	....	....	....	....	....	....	....
	NHL Totals		**80**	**18**	**42**	**10**	**4270**	**284**	**1**	**3.99**	**3**	**0**	**0**	**90**	**5**	**0**	**3.33**

a Shared James Norris Memorial Trophy (fewest goals against - IHL) with Guy Hebert (1991)

Traded to **Tampa Bay** by **St. Louis** with Steve Tuttle and Darin Kimble for future considerations, June 19, 1992. Traded to **Toronto** by **Tampa Bay** for cash, February 21, 1994.

JAKS, PAULI (YAHKS, POW-lee)

Goaltender. Catches left. 6', 194 lbs. Born, Schaffhausen, Switz., January 25, 1972.
(Los Angeles' 5th choice, 108th overall, in 1991 Entry Draft).

			Regular Season								Playoffs						
Season	Club	Lea	GP	W	L	T	Mins	GA	SO	Avg	GP	W	L	Mins	GA	SO	Avg
1990-91	Ambri-Piotta	Switz.	22	....	....	....	1247	100	0	4.81	....	....	....	....	....	....	....
1991-92	Ambri-Piotta	Switz.	33	25	7	1	1890	97	2	2.93	....	....	....	....	....	....	....
1992-93	Ambri-Piotta	Switz.	29	....	....	....	....	92	....	3.17	....	....	....	....	....	....	....
1993-94	Phoenix	IHL	33	16	13	1	1712	101	0	3.54	....	....	....	....	....	....	....
1994-95	Phoenix	IHL	15	2	4	4	635	44	0	4.15	....	....	....	....	....	....	....
	Los Angeles	**NHL**	**1**	**0**	**0**	**0**	**40**	**2**	**0**	**3.00**	....	....	....	....	....	....	....
	NHL Totals		**1**	**0**	**0**	**0**	**40**	**2**	**0**	**3.00**	....	....	....	....	....	....	....

JOHNSON, BRENT — COL.

Goaltender. Catches left. 6'1", 175 lbs. Born, Farmington, MI, March 12, 1977.
(Colorado's 5th choice, 129th overall, in 1995 Entry Draft).

			Regular Season								Playoffs						
Season	Club	Lea	GP	W	L	T	Mins	GA	SO	Avg	GP	W	L	Mins	GA	SO	Avg
1994-95	Owen Sound	OHL	18	3	9	1	904	75	0	4.98	....	....	....	....	....	....	....

JOSEPH, CURTIS — EDM.

Goaltender. Catches left. 5'10", 182 lbs. Born, Keswick, Ont., April 29, 1967.

			Regular Season								Playoffs						
Season	Club	Lea	GP	W	L	T	Mins	GA	SO	Avg	GP	W	L	Mins	GA	SO	Avg
1988-89a	U. Wisconsin	WCHA	38	21	11	5	2267	94	1	2.49	....	....	....	....	....	....	....
1989-90	**St. Louis**	**NHL**	**15**	**9**	**5**	**1**	**852**	**48**	**0**	**3.38**	**6**	**4**	**1**	**327**	**18**	**0**	**3.30**
	Peoria	IHL	23	10	8	2	1241	80	0	3.87	....	....	....	....	....	....	....
1990-91	**St. Louis**	**NHL**	**30**	**16**	**10**	**2**	**1710**	**89**	**0**	**3.12**	....	....	....	....	....	....	....
1991-92	**St. Louis**	**NHL**	**60**	**27**	**20**	**10**	**3494**	**175**	**2**	**3.01**	**6**	**2**	**4**	**379**	**23**	**0**	**3.64**
1992-93	**St. Louis**	**NHL**	**68**	**29**	**28**	**9**	**3890**	**196**	**1**	**3.02**	**11**	**7**	**4**	**715**	**27**	***2**	**2.27**
1993-94	**St. Louis**	**NHL**	**71**	**36**	**23**	**11**	**4127**	**213**	**1**	**3.10**	**4**	**0**	**4**	**246**	**15**	**0**	**3.66**
1994-95	**St. Louis**	**NHL**	**36**	**20**	**10**	**1**	**1914**	**89**	**1**	**2.79**	**7**	**3**	**3**	**392**	**24**	**0**	**3.67**
	NHL Totals		**280**	**137**	**96**	**34**	**15987**	**810**	**5**	**3.04**	**34**	**16**	**16**	**2059**	**107**	**2**	**3.12**

a WCHA First All-Star Team (1989)

Played in NHL All-Star Game (1994)

Signed as a free agent by **St. Louis**, June 16, 1989. Traded to **Edmonton** by **St. Louis** with the rights to Michael Grier for St. Louis' first round choices (previously acquired by Edmonton) in 1996 and 1997 Entry Drafts, August 4, 1995.

KETTERER, MARKUS

Goaltender. Catches left. 5'11", 167 lbs. Born, Helsinki, Finland, August 23, 1967.
(Buffalo's 6th choice, 107th overall, in 1992 Entry Draft).

			Regular Season								Playoffs						
Season	Club	Lea	GP	W	L	T	Mins	GA	SO	Avg	GP	W	L	Mins	GA	SO	Avg
1987-88	Jokerit	Fin.	21	....	....	....	....	61	0	....	....	....	....	....	....	....	....
1988-89	TPS	Fin.	34	....	....	....	2021	95	2	2.82	3	....	....	139	6	0	2.59
1989-90	TPS	Fin.	29	....	....	....	1709	68	1	2.38	7	....	....	422	15	1	2.13
1990-91	TPS	Fin.	36	....	....	....	2022	85	2	2.52	8	....	....	440	13	2	1.77
1991-92	Jokerit	Fin.	37	....	....	....	2128	97	1	2.73	10	7	3	634	20	3	1.89
1992-93	Jokerit	Fin.	37	....	....	....	2064	96	3	2.79	2	0	0	130	11	0	5.07
1993-94	Rochester	AHL	32	9	15	5	1774	110	1	3.72	4	0	3	199	13	0	3.92
1994-95	Rochester	AHL	47	19	20	3	2563	154	1	3.60	....	....	....	....	....	....	....

KHABIBULIN, NIKOLAI (khah-bee-BOO-lihn) — WPG.

Goaltender. Catches left. 6'1", 176 lbs. Born, Sverdlovsk, USSR, January 13, 1973.
(Winnipeg's 8th choice, 204th overall, in 1992 Entry Draft).

			Regular Season								Playoffs						
Season	Club	Lea	GP	W	L	T	Mins	GA	SO	Avg	GP	W	L	Mins	GA	SO	Avg
1988-89	Sverdlovsk	USSR	1	....	....	....	3	0	0	0.00	....	....	....	....	....	....	....
1989-90	Sverdlovsk Jrs.	USSR								UNAVAILABLE							
1990-91	Sputnik	USSR 3								UNAVAILABLE							
1991-92	CSKA	CIS	2	....	....	....	34	2	....	3.52	....	....	....	....	....	....	....
1992-93	CSKA	CIS	13	....	....	....	491	27	....	3.29	....	....	....	....	....	....	....
1993-94	CSKA	CIS	46	....	....	....	2625	116	....	2.65	3	....	....	193	11	....	3.42
	Russian Pen's	IHL	12	2	7	2	639	47	0	4.41	....	....	....	....	....	....	....
1994-95	Springfield	AHL	23	9	9	3	1240	80	0	3.87	....	....	....	....	....	....	....
	Winnipeg	**NHL**	**26**	**8**	**9**	**4**	**1339**	**76**	**0**	**3.41**	....	....	....	....	....	....	....
	NHL Totals		**26**	**8**	**9**	**4**	**1339**	**76**	**0**	**3.41**	....	....	....	....	....	....	....

KIDD, TREVOR — CGY.

Goaltender. Catches left. 6'2", 190 lbs. Born, Dugald, Man., March 29, 1972.
(Calgary's 1st choice, 11th overall, in 1990 Entry Draft).

			Regular Season								Playoffs						
Season	Club	Lea	GP	W	L	T	Mins	GA	SO	Avg	GP	W	L	Mins	GA	SO	Avg
1988-89	Brandon	WHL	32	11	13	1	1509	102	0	4.06	....	....	....	....	....	....	....
1989-90a	Brandon	WHL	*63	24	32	2	*3676	254	2	4.15	....	....	....	....	....	....	....
1990-91	Brandon	WHL	30	10	19	1	1730	117	0	4.06	....	....	....	....	....	....	....
	Spokane	WHL	14	8	3	0	749	44	0	3.52	15	*14	1	926	32	2	*2.07
1991-92	Cdn. National	....	28	18	4	4	1349	79	2	3.51	....	....	....	....	....	....	....
	Cdn. Olympic	....	1	1	0	0	60	0	1	0.00	....	....	....	....	....	....	....
	Calgary	**NHL**	**2**	**1**	**1**	**0**	**120**	**8**	**0**	**4.00**	....	....	....	....	....	....	....
1992-93	Salt Lake	IHL	29	10	16	1	1696	111	1	3.93	....	....	....	....	....	....	....
1993-94	**Calgary**	**NHL**	**31**	**13**	**7**	**6**	**1614**	**85**	**0**	**3.16**	....	....	....	....	....	....	....
1994-95	**Calgary**	**NHL**	***43**	**22**	**14**	**6**	***2463**	**107**	**3**	**2.61**	**7**	**3**	**4**	**434**	**26**	**1**	**3.59**
	NHL Totals		**76**	**36**	**22**	**12**	**4197**	**200**	**3**	**2.86**	**7**	**3**	**4**	**434**	**26**	**1**	**3.59**

a WHL East First All-Star Team (1990)

KIPRUSOFF, MIIKKA — S.J.

Goaltender. Catches left. 6', 176 lbs. Born, Turku, Finland, October 26, 1976.
(San Jose's 5th choice, 116th overall, in 1995 Entry Draft).

			Regular Season								Playoffs						
Season	Club	Lea	GP	W	L	T	Mins	GA	SO	Avg	GP	W	L	Mins	GA	SO	Avg
1994-95	TPS	Fin. Jr.	31	....	....	....	1896	92	....	2.91	....	....	....	....	....	....	....
	TPS	Fin.	4	....	....	....	240	12	0	3.00	2	....	....	120	7	....	3.50

KNICKLE, RICK (kuh-NIHK-uhl)

Goaltender. Catches left. 5'10", 175 lbs. Born, Chatham, N.B., February 26, 1960.
(Buffalo's 7th choice, 116th overall, in 1979 Entry Draft).

			Regular Season								Playoffs						
Season	Club	Lea	GP	W	L	T	Mins	GA	SO	Avg	GP	W	L	Mins	GA	SO	Avg
1977-78	Brandon	WHL	49	34	5	7	2806	182	0	3.89	8	....	....	450	36	0	4.82
1978-79a	Brandon	WHL	38	26	3	8	2240	118	1	*3.16	16	12	3	886	41	*1	*2.78
1979-80	Brandon	WHL	33	11	14	1	1604	125	0	4.68	....	....	....	....	....	....	....
	Muskegon	IHL	16	....	....	....	829	52	0	3.76	3	....	....	156	17	0	6.54
1980-81b	Erie	EHL	43	....	....	....	2347	125	1	*3.20	8	....	....	446	14	0	*1.88
1981-82	Rochester	AHL	31	10	12	5	1753	108	1	3.70	3	0	2	125	7	0	3.37
1982-83	Flint	IHL	27	....	....	....	1638	92	2	3.37	3	....	....	193	10	0	3.11
	Rochester	AHL	4	0	3	0	143	11	0	4.64	....	....	....	....	....	....	....
1983-84c	Flint	IHL	60	32	21	5	3518	203	3	3.46	8	8	0	480	24	0	3.00
1984-85	Sherbrooke	AHL	14	7	6	0	780	53	0	4.08	....	....	....	....	....	....	....
	Flint	IHL	36	18	11	3	2018	115	2	3.42	7	3	4	401	27	0	4.04
1985-86	Saginaw	IHL	39	16	15	0	2235	135	2	3.62	3	2	1	193	12	0	3.73
1986-87	Saginaw	IHL	26	9	13	0	1413	113	0	4.80	5	1	4	329	21	0	3.83
1987-88	Flint	IHL	1	0	1	0	60	4	0	4.00	....	....	....	....	....	....	....
	Peoria	IHL	13	2	8	1	705	58	0	4.94	6	3	3	294	20	....	4.08
1988-89de	Fort Wayne	IHL	47	22	16	0	2716	141	1	*3.11	4	1	2	173	15	0	5.20
1989-90	Flint	IHL	55	25	24	1	2998	210	1	4.20	2	0	2	101	13	0	7.72
1990-91	Albany	IHL	14	4	6	2	679	52	0	4.59	....	....	....	....	....	....	....
	Springfield	AHL	9	6	0	2	509	28	0	3.30	....	....	....	....	....	....	....
1991-92c	San Diego	IHL	46	*28	13	4	2686	155	0	3.46	2	0	1	78	3	0	2.31
1992-93df	San Diego	IHL	41	33	4	4	2437	88	*4	*2.17	....	....	....	....	....	....	....
	Los Angeles	**NHL**	**10**	**6**	**4**	**0**	**532**	**35**	**0**	**3.95**	....	....	....	....	....	....	....
1993-94	**Los Angeles**	**NHL**	**4**	**1**	**2**	**0**	**174**	**9**	**0**	**3.10**	....	....	....	....	....	....	....
	Phoenix	IHL	25	8	9	3	1292	89	1	4.13	....	....	....	....	....	....	....
1994-95	Detroit	IHL	49	24	15	5	2725	134	*3	2.95	....	....	....	....	....	....	....
	NHL Totals		**14**	**7**	**6**	**0**	**706**	**44**	**0**	**3.74**	....	....	....	....	....	....	....

a WHL First All-Star Team (1979)
b EHL First All-Star Team (1981)
c IHL Second All-Star Team (1984, 1992)
d IHL First All-Star Team (1989, 1993)
e Won James Norris Memorial Trophy (fewest goals against - IHL) (1989)
f Shared James Norris Memorial Trophy (fewest goals against - IHL) with Clint Malarchuk (1993)

Signed as a free agent by **Montreal**, February 8, 1985. Signed as a free agent by **Los Angeles**, February 16, 1993.

KOCHAN, DIETER — VAN.

Goaltender. Catches left. 6'1", 170 lbs. Born, Saskatoon, Sask., November 5, 1974.
(Vancouver's 3rd choice, 98th overall, in 1993 Entry Draft).

			Regular Season								Playoffs						
Season	Club	Lea	GP	W	L	T	Mins	GA	SO	Avg	GP	W	L	Mins	GA	SO	Avg
1993-94	N. Michigan	WCHA	20	9	7	0	686	44	0	3.85	....	....	....	....	....	....	....
1994-95	N. Michigan	WCHA	29	8	17	3	1511	107	0	4.25	....	....	....	....	....	....	....

KOLZIG, OLAF (KOHLT-zihg, OH-lahf) — WSH.

Goaltender. Catches left. 6'3", 225 lbs. Born, Johannesburg, South Africa, April 9, 1970.
(Washington's 1st choice, 19th overall, in 1989 Entry Draft).

			Regular Season								Playoffs						
Season	Club	Lea	GP	W	L	T	Mins	GA	SO	Avg	GP	W	L	Mins	GA	SO	Avg
1987-88	N. Westminster	WHL	15	6	5	0	650	48	1	4.43	3	0	3	149	11	0	4.43
1988-89	Tri-Cities	WHL	30	16	10	2	1671	97	1	*3.48	....	....	....	....	....	....	....
1989-90	**Washington**	**NHL**	**2**	**0**	**2**	**0**	**120**	**12**	**0**	**6.00**	....	....	....	....	....	....	....
	Tri-Cities	WHL	48	27	27	3	2504	250	1	4.38	6	4	0	318	27	0	5.09
1990-91	Baltimore	AHL	26	10	12	1	1367	72	0	3.16	....	....	....	....	....	....	....
	Hampton Rds.	ECHL	21	11	9	1	1248	71	2	3.41	3	1	2	180	14	0	4.66
1991-92	Baltimore	AHL	28	5	17	2	1503	105	1	4.19	....	....	....	....	....	....	....
	Hampton Rds.	ECHL	14	11	3	0	847	41	0	2.90	....	....	....	....	....	....	....
1992-93	**Washington**	**NHL**	**1**	**0**	**0**	**0**	**20**	**2**	**0**	**6.00**	....	....	....	....	....	....	....
	Rochester	AHL	49	25	16	4	2737	168	0	3.68	*17	9	8	*1040	61	0	3.52
1993-94	**Washington**	**NHL**	**7**	**0**	**3**	**0**	**224**	**20**	**0**	**5.36**	....	....	....	....	....	....	....
ab	Portland	AHL	29	16	8	5	1725	88	3	3.06	17	*12	5	1035	44	0	*2.55
1994-95	**Washington**	**NHL**	**14**	**2**	**8**	**2**	**724**	**30**	**0**	**2.49**	**2**	**1**	**0**	**44**	**1**	**0**	**1.36**
	Portland	AHL	2	1	0	1	125	3	0	1.44	....	....	....	....	....	....	....
	NHL Totals		**24**	**2**	**13**	**2**	**1088**	**64**	**0**	**3.53**	**2**	**1**	**0**	**44**	**1**	**0**	**1.36**

a Shared Harry "Hap" Holmes Trophy (fewest goals-against - AHL) with Byron Dafoe (1994)
b Won Jack Butterfield Trophy (Playoff MVP - IHL) (1994)

KUNTAR, LES (KOON-tahr) PHI.

Goaltender. Catches left. 6'2", 195 lbs. Born, Elma, NY, July 28, 1969.
(Montreal's 8th choice, 122nd overall, in 1987 Entry Draft).

			Regular Season								Playoffs						
Season	Club	Lea	GP	W	L	T	Mins	GA	SO	Avg	GP	W	L	Mins	GA	SO	Avg
1987-88	St. Lawrence	ECAC	10	6	1	0	488	27	0	3.31	....	....	....	....	....	....	....
1988-89	St. Lawrence	ECAC	14	11	2	0	786	31	0	2.37	....	....	....	....	....	....	....
1989-90	St. Lawrence	ECAC	20	7	11	1	1136	80	0	4.23	....	....	....	....	....	....	....
1990-91ab	St. Lawrence	ECAC	*33	*19	11	1	*1797	97	*1	*3.24	....	....	....	....	....	....	....
1991-92	Fredericton	AHL	11	7	3	0	638	26	0	2.45	....	....	....	....	....	....	....
	U.S. National	....	2	0	1	0	100	4	0	2.40	....	....	....	....	....	....	....
1992-93	Fredericton	AHL	42	16	14	7	2315	130	0	3.37	1	0	1	64	6	0	5.63
1993-94	**Montreal**	**NHL**	**6**	**2**	**2**	**0**	**302**	**16**	**0**	**3.18**	....	....	....	....	....	....	....
	Fredericton	AHL	34	10	17	3	1804	109	1	3.62	....	....	....	....	....	....	....
1994-95	Worcester	AHL	24	6	10	5	1241	77	2	3.72	....	....	....	....	....	....	....
	Hershey	AHL	32	15	13	2	1802	89	0	2.96	2	0	1	70	5	0	4.28
	NHL Totals		**6**	**2**	**2**	**0**	**302**	**16**	**0**	**3.18**	....	....	....	....	....	....	....

a ECAC First All-Star Team (1991)
b NCAA East First All-American Team (1991)

Signed as a free agent by **Philadelphia**, June 30, 1995.

KVALEVOG, TOBY OTT.

Goaltender. Catches left. 5'11", 170 lbs. Born, Fargo, ND, December 22, 1974.
(Ottawa's 8th choice, 209th overall, in 1993 Entry Draft).

			Regular Season								Playoffs						
Season	Club	Lea	GP	W	L	T	Mins	GA	SO	Avg	GP	W	L	Mins	GA	SO	Avg
1993-94	North Dakota	WCHA	32	11	17	3	1813	120	0	3.97	....	....	....	....	....	....	....
1994-95	North Dakota	WCHA	32	14	13	3	1828	120	*1	3.94	....	....	....	....	....	....	....

LABBE, JEAN-FRANCOIS OTT.

Goaltender. Catches left. 5'9", 170 lbs. Born, Sherbrooke, Que., June 15, 1972.

			Regular Season								Playoffs						
Season	Club	Lea	GP	W	L	T	Mins	GA	SO	Avg	GP	W	L	Mins	GA	SO	Avg
1989-90	Trois-Rivieres	QMJHL	28	13	10	0	1499	106	1	4.24	3	1	1	132	8	0	3.64
1990-91	Trois-Rivieres	QMJHL	54	*35	14	0	2870	158	5	3.30	5	1	4	230	19	0	4.96
1991-92a	Trois-Rivieres	QMJHL	48	*31	13	3	2749	142	1	3.10	*15	*10	3	791	33	*1	*2.50
1992-93	Hull	QMJHL	46	26	18	2	2701	156	2	3.46	10	6	3	518	24	*1	*2.78
1993-94bcd	Thunder Bay	ColHL	52	*35	11	4	*2900	150	*2	*3.10	8	7	1	493	18	*2	*2.19
	PEI	AHL	7	4	3	0	389	22	0	3.39	....	....	....	....	....	....	....
1994-95	PEI	AHL	32	13	14	3	1817	94	2	3.10	....	....	....	....	....	....	....

a QMJHL First All-Star Team (1992)
b ColHL First All-Star Team (1994)
c Named ColHL's Rookie of the Year (1994)
d Named ColHL's Outstanding Goaltender (1994)

Signed as a free agent by **Ottawa**, May 12, 1994.

LABRECQUE, PATRICK MTL.

Goaltender. Catches left. 6', 190 lbs. Born, Laval, Que., March 6, 1971.
(Quebec's 5th choice, 90th overall, in 1991 Entry Draft).

			Regular Season								Playoffs						
Season	Club	Lea	GP	W	L	T	Mins	GA	SO	Avg	GP	W	L	Mins	GA	SO	Avg
1990-91	St-Jean	QMJHL	59	17	34	6	3375	216	1	3.84	....	....	....	....	....	....	....
1991-92	Halifax	AHL	29	5	12	8	1570	114	0	4.36	....	....	....	....	....	....	....
1992-93	Greensboro	ECHL	11	6	3	2	650	31	0	2.86	1	0	1	59	5	0	5.08
	Halifax	AHL	20	3	12	2	914	76	0	4.99	....	....	....	....	....	....	....
1993-94	Cornwall	AHL	4	1	2	0	198	8	1	2.42	....	....	....	....	....	....	....
	Greensboro	ECHL	29	17	8	2	1609	89	0	3.32	1	0	0	22	4	0	10.80
1994-95	Fredericton	AHL	35	15	17	1	1913	104	1	3.26	*16	*10	6	*967	40	1	2.48
	Wheeling	ECHL	5	2	3	0	281	22	0	4.69	....	....	....	....	....	....	....

Signed as a free agent by **Montreal**, June 21, 1994.

LACHER, BLAINE (LAW-kuhr) BOS.

Goaltender. Catches left. 6'1", 205 lbs. Born, Medicine Hat, Alta., September 5, 1970.

			Regular Season								Playoffs						
Season	Club	Lea	GP	W	L	T	Mins	GA	SO	Avg	GP	W	L	Mins	GA	SO	Avg
1991-92	Lake Superior	CCHA	9	5	3	0	410	22	0	3.22	....	....	....	....	....	....	....
1992-93	Lake Superior	CCHA	34	24	5	3	1915	86	2	2.70	....	....	....	....	....	....	....
1993-94	Lake Superior	CCHA	30	20	5	4	1785	59	6	*1.98	....	....	....	....	....	....	....
1994-95	**Boston**	**NHL**	**35**	**19**	**11**	**2**	**1965**	**79**	**4**	**2.41**	**5**	**1**	**4**	**283**	**12**	**0**	**2.54**
	Providence	AHL	1	0	1	0	59	3	0	3.03	....	....	....	....	....	....	....
	NHL Totals		**35**	**19**	**11**	**2**	**1965**	**79**	**4**	**2.41**	**5**	**1**	**4**	**283**	**12**	**0**	**2.54**

Signed as a free agent by **Boston**, June 2, 1994.

LaFOREST, MARK

Goaltender. Catches left. 5'11", 190 lbs. Born, Welland, Ont., July 10, 1962.

			Regular Season								Playoffs						
Season	Club	Lea	GP	W	L	T	Mins	GA	SO	Avg	GP	W	L	Mins	GA	SO	Avg
1981-82	Niagara Falls	OHL	24	10	13	1	1365	105	1	4.62	5	1	2	300	19	0	3.80
1982-83	North Bay	OHL	54	34	17	1	3140	195	0	3.73	8	4	4	474	31	0	3.92
1983-84	Adirondack	AHL	7	3	3	1	351	29	0	4.96	....	....	....	....	....	....	....
	Kalamazoo	IHL	13	4	5	2	718	48	1	4.01	....	....	....	....	....	....	....
1984-85	Adirondack	AHL	11	2	3	1	430	35	0	4.88	....	....	....	....	....	....	....
1985-86	**Detroit**	**NHL**	**28**	**4**	**21**	**0**	**1383**	**114**	**1**	**4.95**	....	....	....	....	....	....	....
	Adirondack	AHL	19	13	5	1	1142	57	0	2.99	*17	*12	5	*1075	58	0	3.24
1986-87	**Detroit**	**NHL**	**5**	**2**	**1**	**0**	**219**	**12**	**0**	**3.29**	....	....	....	....	....	....	....
a	Adirondack	AHL	37	23	8	0	2229	105	*3	2.83	....	....	....	....	....	....	....
1987-88	**Philadelphia**	**NHL**	**21**	**5**	**9**	**2**	**972**	**60**	**1**	**3.70**	**2**	**1**	**0**	**48**	**1**	**0**	**1.25**
	Hershey	AHL	5	2	1	2	309	13	0	2.52	....	....	....	....	....	....	....
1988-89	**Philadelphia**	**NHL**	**17**	**5**	**7**	**2**	**933**	**64**	**0**	**4.12**	....	....	....	....	....	....	....
	Hershey	AHL	3	2	0	0	185	9	0	2.92	12	7	5	744	27	1	2.18
1989-90	**Toronto**	**NHL**	**27**	**9**	**14**	**0**	**1343**	**87**	**0**	**3.89**	....	....	....	....	....	....	....
	Newmarket	AHL	10	6	4	0	604	33	1	3.28	....	....	....	....	....	....	....
1990-91ab	Binghamton	AHL	45	25	14	2	2452	129	0	3.16	9	3	4	442	28	1	3.80
1991-92	Binghamton	AHL	43	25	15	3	2559	146	1	3.42	11	7	4	662	34	0	3.08
1992-93	New Haven	AHL	30	10	18	1	1688	121	1	4.30	....	....	....	....	....	....	....
	Brantford	Col.	10	5	3	1	565	35	1	3.72	....	....	....	....	....	....	....
1993-94	**Ottawa**	**NHL**	**5**	**0**	**2**	**0**	**182**	**17**	**0**	**5.60**	....	....	....	....	....	....	....
	PEI	AHL	43	9	25	5	2359	161	0	4.09	....	....	....	....	....	....	....
1994-95	Milwaukee	IHL	42	19	13	7	2325	123	2	3.17	15	8	7	937	40	*2	2.56
	NHL Totals		**103**	**25**	**54**	**4**	**5032**	**354**	**2**	**4.22**	**2**	**1**	**0**	**48**	**1**	**0**	**1.25**

a Won Baz Bastien Memorial Trophy (Top Goaltender - AHL) (1987, 1991)
b AHL Second All-Star Team (1991)

Signed as a free agent by **Detroit**, April 29, 1983. Traded to **Philadelphia** by **Detroit** for Philadelphia's second round choice (Bob Wilkie) in 1987 Entry Draft, June 13, 1987. Traded to **Toronto** by **Philadelphia** for Toronto's sixth round choice in 1991 Entry Draft and its seventh round choice in 1991 Entry Draft, September 8, 1989. Traded to **NY Rangers** by **Toronto** with Tie Domi for Greg Johnston, June 28, 1990. Claimed by **Ottawa** from **NY Rangers** in Expansion Draft, June 18, 1992.

LAGRAND, SCOTT

Goaltender. Catches left. 6', 165 lbs. Born, Potsdam, NY, February 11, 1970.
(Philadelphia's 5th choice, 77th overall, in 1988 Entry Draft).

			Regular Season								Playoffs						
Season	Club	Lea	GP	W	L	T	Mins	GA	SO	Avg	GP	W	L	Mins	GA	SO	Avg
1989-90	Boston College	H.E.	24	17	4	0	1268	57	0	2.70	....	....	....	....	....	....	....
1990-91a	Boston College	H.E.	23	12	8	0	1153	63	2	3.28	....	....	....	....	....	....	....
1991-92b	Boston College	H.E.	30	11	16	2	1750	108	1	3.70	....	....	....	....	....	....	....
1992-93	Hershey	AHL	32	8	17	4	1854	145	0	4.69	....	....	....	....	....	....	....
1993-94	Hershey	AHL	40	16	13	3	2032	117	2	3.45	....	....	....	....	....	....	....
1994-95	Hershey	AHL	21	7	9	3	1104	71	1	3.86	....	....	....	....	....	....	....
	Atlanta	IHL	21	7	7	3	993	67	0	4.04	3	0	2	101	10	0	5.91

a Hockey East First All-Star Team (1991)
b NCAA East Second All-American Team (1992)

Traded to **Tampa Bay** by **Philadelphia** for Mike Greenlay, February 2, 1995.

LALIME, PATRICK PIT.

Goaltender. Catches left. 6'2", 170 lbs. Born, St. Bonaventure, Que., July 7, 1974.
(Pittsburgh's 6th choice, 156th overall, in 1993 Entry Draft).

			Regular Season								Playoffs						
Season	Club	Lea	GP	W	L	T	Mins	GA	SO	Avg	GP	W	L	Mins	GA	SO	Avg
1992-93	Shawinigan	QMJHL	44	10	24	4	2467	192	0	4.67	....	....	....	....	....	....	....
1993-94	Shawinigan	QMJHL	48	22	20	0	2733	192	1	4.22	5	1	3	223	25	0	6.73
1994-95	Hampton Rds.	ECHL	26	15	7	3	1470	82	2	3.35	....	....	....	....	....	....	....
	Cleveland	IHL	23	7	10	4	1230	91	0	4.44	....	....	....	....	....	....	....

LAMBERT, JUDD N.J.

Goaltender. Catches left. 6', 165 lbs. Born, Richmond, B.C., June 3, 1974.
(New Jersey's 9th choice, 221st overall, in 1993 Entry Draft).

			Regular Season								Playoffs						
Season	Club	Lea	GP	W	L	T	Mins	GA	SO	Avg	GP	W	L	Mins	GA	SO	Avg
1993-94	Colorado	WCHA	11	6	4	0	620	33	0	3.19	....	....	....	....	....	....	....
1994-95	Colorado	WCHA	21	12	7	0	1060	57	*1	3.23	....	....	....	....	....	....	....

LAMOTHE, MARC MTL.

Goaltender. Catches left. 6'1", 204 lbs. Born, New Liskeard, Ont., February 27, 1974.
(Montreal's 6th choice, 92nd overall, in 1992 Entry Draft).

			Regular Season								Playoffs						
Season	Club	Lea	GP	W	L	T	Mins	GA	SO	Avg	GP	W	L	Mins	GA	SO	Avg
1991-92	Kingston	OHL	42	10	25	2	2378	189	1	4.77	....	....	....	....	....	....	....
1992-93	Kingston	OHL	45	23	12	6	2489	162	1	3.91	15	8	5	753	48	1	3.82
1993-94	Kingston	OHL	48	23	20	5	2828	177	*2	3.76	6	2	2	224	12	0	3.21
1994-95	Fredericton	AHL	9	2	5	0	428	32	0	4.48	....	....	....	....	....	....	....
	Wheeling	ECHL	13	9	2	1	736	38	0	3.10	....	....	....	....	....	....	....

LANGKOW, SCOTT (LAING-kow) WPG.

Goaltender. Catches left. 5'11", 190 lbs. Born, Sherwood Park, Alta., April 21, 1975.
(Winnipeg's 2nd choice, 31st overall, in 1993 Entry Draft).

			Regular Season								Playoffs						
Season	Club	Lea	GP	W	L	T	Mins	GA	SO	Avg	GP	W	L	Mins	GA	SO	Avg
1991-92	Portland	WHL	1	0	0	0	33	2	0	3.46	....	....	....	....	....	....	....
1992-93	Portland	WHL	34	24	8	2	2064	119	2	3.46	9	6	3	535	31	0	3.48
1993-94a	Portland	WHL	39	27	9	1	2302	121	2	3.15	10	6	4	600	34	0	3.40
1994-95a	Portland	WHL	63	20	36	5	*3638	240	1	3.96	8	3	5	510	30	0	3.53

a WHL West Second All-Star Team (1994, 1995)

LAROCHELLE, BRIAN MTL.

Goaltender. Catches right. 6'1", 185 lbs. Born, Manchester, NH, August 8, 1974.
(Montreal's 12th choice, 255th overall, in 1993 Entry Draft).

			Regular Season								Playoffs						
Season	Club	Lea	GP	W	L	T	Mins	GA	SO	Avg	GP	W	L	Mins	GA	SO	Avg
1994-95	N. Hampshire	H.E.	1	0	0	0	3	0	0	0.00	....	....	....	....	....	....	....

LEBLANC, RAYMOND (luh-BLAHNK)

Goaltender. Catches right. 5'10", 170 lbs. Born, Fitchburg, MA, October 24, 1964.

			Regular Season								Playoffs						
Season	Club	Lea	GP	W	L	T	Mins	GA	SO	Avg	GP	W	L	Mins	GA	SO	Avg
1983-84	Kitchener	OHL	54	....	....	....	2965	185	1	3.74	....	....	....	....	....	....	....
1984-85	Pinebridge	ACHL	40	....	....	....	2178	150	0	4.13	....	....	....	....	....	....	....
1985-86	Carolina	ACHL	42	....	....	....	2505	133	3	3.19	....	....	....	....	....	....	....
1986-87	Flint	IHL	64	33	23	1	3417	222	0	3.90	4	1	3	....	....	....	4.38
1987-88	Flint	IHL	62	27	19	8	3269	239	1	4.39	16	10	6	925	55	1	3.57
1988-89	Flint	IHL	15	5	9	0	852	67	0	4.72	....	....	....	....	....	....	....
	New Haven	AHL	1	0	0	0	20	3	0	9.00	....	....	....	....	....	....	....
	Saginaw	IHL	29	19	7	2	1655	99	0	3.59	1	0	1	5	9	0	3.05
1989-90	Indianapolis	IHL	23	15	6	2	1334	71	2	3.19	....	....	....	....	....	....	....
	Fort Wayne	IHL	15	3	3	3	680	44	0	3.88	3	0	2	139	11	0	4.75
1990-91	Fort Wayne	IHL	21	10	8	0	1072	69	0	3.86	....	....	....	....	....	....	....
	Indianapolis	IHL	3	2	0	0	145	7	0	2.90	1	0	0	19	1	0	3.20
1991-92	U.S. National	....	17	5	10	1	891	54	0	3.63	....	....	....	....	....	....	....
	U.S. Olympic	....	8	5	2	1	463	17	2	2.20	....	....	....	....	....	....	....
	Chicago	**NHL**	**1**	**1**	**0**	**0**	**60**	**1**	**0**	**1.00**	....	....	....	....	....	....	....
	Indianapolis	IHL	25	14	9	2	1468	84	2	3.43	....	....	....	....	....	....	....
1992-93	Indianapolis	IHL	56	23	22	7	3201	206	0	3.86	5	1	4	276	23	0	5.00
1993-94	Indianapolis	IHL	2	0	1	0	112	8	0	4.25	....	....	....	....	....	....	....
	Cincinnati	IHL	34	17	9	3	1779	104	1	3.51	5	0	3	159	9	0	3.39
1994-95	Chicago	IHL	44	19	14	6	2375	129	1	3.26	3	0	3	177	14	0	4.73
	NHL Totals		**1**	**1**	**0**	**0**	**60**	**1**	**0**	**1.00**	....	....	....	....	....	....	....

Signed as a free agent by **Chicago**, July 5, 1989.

LEGACE, MANNY (leh-GAH-see) HFD.

Goaltender. Catches left. 5'9", 162 lbs. Born, Toronto, Ont., February 4, 1973.
(Hartford's 5th choice, 188th overall, in 1993 Entry Draft).

			Regular Season								Playoffs						
Season	Club	Lea	GP	W	L	T	Mins	GA	SO	Avg	GP	W	L	Mins	GA	SO	Avg
1990-91	Niagara Falls	OHL	30	13	11	2	1515	107	0	4.24	4	1	1	119	10	0	5.04
1991-92	Niagara Falls	OHL	43	21	16	3	2384	143	0	3.60	14	8	5	791	56	0	4.25
1992-93a	Niagara Falls	OHL	48	22	19	3	2630	171	0	3.90	4	0	4	240	18	0	4.50
1993-94	Cdn. National	....	16	8	6	0	859	36	2	2.51	....	....	....	....	....	....	....
1994-95	Springfield	AHL	39	12	17	6	2169	128	2	3.54	....	....	....	....	....	....	....

a OHL First All-Star Team (1993)

LEITZA, BRIAN Pittsburgh

Goaltender. Catches left. 6'2", 185 lbs. Born, Waukegin, IL, March 16, 1974.
(Pittsburgh's 14th choice, 284th overall, in 1994 Entry Draft).

			Regular Season								Playoffs						
Season	Club	Lea	GP	W	L	T	Mins	GA	SO	Avg	GP	W	L	Mins	GA	SO	Avg
1993-94	Sioux City	Jr. A	32	....	....	....	1793	98	0	3.28	....	....	....	....	....	....	....
1994-95	St. Cloud St.	WCHA	30	13	15	0	1626	93	....	3.43	....	....	....	....	....	....	....

LENARDUZZI, MIKE

Goaltender. Catches left. 6'1", 165 lbs. Born, London, Ont., September 14, 1972.
(Hartford's 3rd choice, 57th overall, in 1990 Entry Draft).

			Regular Season								Playoffs						
Season	Club	Lea	GP	W	L	T	Mins	GA	SO	Avg	GP	W	L	Mins	GA	SO	Avg
1989-90	Oshawa	OHL	12	6	3	1	444	32	0	4.32	....	....	....	....	....	....	....
	S.S. Marie	OHL	20	....	....	....	1117	66	0	3.55	....	....	....	....	....	....	....
1990-91	S.S. Marie	OHL	35	19	8	3	1966	107	0	3.27	5	3	1	268	13	*1	2.91
1991-92	S.S. Marie	OHL	9	5	3	0	486	33	0	4.07	....	....	....	....	....	....	....
	Ottawa	OHL	18	5	12	1	986	60	1	3.65	....	....	....	....	....	....	....
	Sudbury	OHL	22	11	5	4	1201	84	2	4.20	11	4	7	651	38	0	3.50
	Springfield	AHL	....	....	....	....	....	....	....	....	1	0	0	39	2	0	3.08
1992-93	**Hartford**	**NHL**	**3**	**1**	**1**	**1**	**168**	**9**	**0**	**3.21**	....	....	....	....	....	....	....
	Springfield	AHL	36	10	17	5	1945	142	0	4.38	2	1	0	100	5	0	3.00
1993-94	**Hartford**	**NHL**	**1**	**0**	**0**	**0**	**21**	**1**	**0**	**2.86**	....	....	....	....	....	....	....
	Springfield	AHL	22	5	7	2	984	73	0	4.45	....	....	....	....	....	....	....
	Salt Lake	IHL	4	0	4	0	211	22	0	6.25	....	....	....	....	....	....	....
1994-95	London	ColHL	43	19	16	0	2198	172	0	4.69	5	1	2	274	20	0	4.37
	NHL Totals		**4**	**1**	**1**	**1**	**189**	**10**	**0**	**3.17**	....	....	....	....	....	....	....

LESLIE, LANCE — OTT.

Goaltender. Catches left. 5'10", 160 lbs. Born, Dawson Creek, B.C., June 21, 1974.

			Regular Season								Playoffs						
Season	Club	Lea	GP	W	L	T	Mins	GA	SO	Avg	GP	W	L	Mins	GA	SO	Avg
1992-93	Tri-City	WHL	49	15	25	3	2620	163	*3	3.73	....	....	....	....	....	....	....
1993-94	Tri-City	WHL	41	10	26	2	2273	189	2	4.99	2	0	2	120	9	0	4.50
1994-95ab	Thunder Bay	ColHL	42	*29	10	3	2420	130	*2	3.22	10	*7	2	587	35	*1	3.58
	PEI	AHL	1	0	0	1	65	2	0	1.85	....	....	....	....	....	....	....

a ColHL First All-Star Team (1995)
b ColHL's Rookie of the Year (1995)

Signed as a free agent by **Ottawa**, October 4, 1993.

LINDFORS, SAKARI (LIHND-fohrs) — COL.

Goaltender. Catches left. 5'7", 150 lbs. Born, Helsinki, Finland, April 27, 1966.
(Quebec's 9th choice, 150th overall, in 1988 Entry Draft).

			Regular Season								Playoffs						
Season	Club	Lea	GP	W	L	T	Mins	GA	SO	Avg	GP	W	L	Mins	GA	SO	Avg
1986-87	HIFK	Fin.	20	....	....	....	1009	65	0	3.86	....	....	....	....	....	....	....
1987-88	HIFK	Fin.	39	....	....	....	2346	....	....	....	6	....	....	340	....	....	....
1988-89	HIFK	Fin.	24	11	11	2	1433	89	1	3.75	2	....	....	118	7	....	3.53
1989-90	HIFK	Fin.	42	23	15	4	2518	146	2	3.48	....	....	....	....	....	....	....
1990-91	HIFK	Fin.	41	....	....	....	2445	142	2	3.48	3	....	....	180	14	0	4.67
1991-92	HIFK	Fin.	38	....	....	....	2222	127	4	3.43	9	....	....	538	28	0	3.12
1992-93	HIFK	Fin.	39	....	....	....	2293	123	0	3.22	4	....	....	236	12	0	3.04
1993-94	HIFK	Fin.	43	....	....	....	2465	128	3	3.11	3	....	....	175	11	....	3.76
1994-95	HIFK	Fin.	44	28	13	3	2597	119	2	2.75	3	0	3	178	6	0	2.02

LITTLE, NEIL — PHI.

Goaltender. Catches left. 6'1", 175 lbs. Born, Medicine Hat, Alta., December 18, 1971.
(Philadelphia's 11th choice, 226th overall, in 1991 Entry Draft).

			Regular Season								Playoffs						
Season	Club	Lea	GP	W	L	T	Mins	GA	SO	Avg	GP	W	L	Mins	GA	SO	Avg
1990-91	RPI	ECAC	18	9	8	0	1032	71	0	4.13	....	....	....	....	....	....	....
1991-92	RPI	ECAC	28	11	11	3	1532	96	0	3.76	....	....	....	....	....	....	....
1992-93ab	RPI	ECAC	*31	*19	9	3	*1801	88	0	2.93	....	....	....	....	....	....	....
1993-94	RPI	ECAC	27	16	7	4	1570	88	0	3.36	....	....	....	....	....	....	....
	Hershey	AHL	1	0	0	0	18	1	0	3.23	....	....	....	....	....	....	....
1994-95	Hershey	AHL	19	5	7	3	919	60	0	3.91	....	....	....	....	....	....	....
	Johnstown	ECHL	16	7	6	1	897	55	0	3.68	3	0	2	144	11	0	4.55

a ECAC First All-Star Team (1993)
b NCAA East Second All-American Team (1993)

LITTMAN, DAVID

Goaltender. Catches left. 6', 183 lbs. Born, Cranston, RI, June 13, 1967.
(Buffalo's 12th choice, 211th overall, in 1987 Entry Draft).

			Regular Season								Playoffs						
Season	Club	Lea	GP	W	L	T	Mins	GA	SO	Avg	GP	W	L	Mins	GA	SO	Avg
1985-86	Boston College	H.E.	7	4	0	1	312	18	0	3.46	....	....	....	....	....	....	....
1986-87	Boston College	H.E.	21	15	5	0	1182	68	0	3.45	....	....	....	....	....	....	....
1987-88a	Boston College	H.E.	30	11	16	2	1726	116	0	4.03	....	....	....	....	....	....	....
1988-89bc	Boston College	H.E.	*32	19	9	4	*1945	107	0	3.30	....	....	....	....	....	....	....
1989-90	Rochester	AHL	14	5	6	1	681	37	0	3.26	....	....	....	....	....	....	....
	Phoenix	IHL	18	8	7	2	1047	64	0	3.67	....	....	....	....	....	....	....
1990-91	**Buffalo**	**NHL**	**1**	**0**	**0**	**0**	**36**	**3**	**0**	**5.00**	....	....	....	....	....	....	....
de	Rochester	AHL	*56	*33	13	5	*3155	160	3	3.04	8	4	2	378	16	0	2.54
1991-92	**Buffalo**	**NHL**	**1**	**0**	**1**	**0**	**60**	**4**	**0**	**4.00**	....	....	....	....	....	....	....
fg	Rochester	AHL	*61	*29	20	9	*3558	174	*3	2.93	15	8	7	879	43	*1	2.94
1992-93	**Tampa Bay**	**NHL**	**1**	**0**	**1**	**0**	**45**	**7**	**0**	**9.33**	....	....	....	....	....	....	....
	Atlanta	IHL	44	23	12	4	2390	134	0	3.36	3	1	2	178	8	0	2.70
1993-94	Fredericton	AHL	16	8	7	0	872	63	0	4.33	....	....	....	....	....	....	....
	Providence	AHL	25	10	11	3	1385	83	0	3.60	....	....	....	....	....	....	....
1994-95	Richmond	ECHL	8	4	2	0	346	13	1	2.25	*17	*12	4	*952	37	*3	*2.33
	NHL Totals		**3**	**0**	**2**	**0**	**141**	**14**	**0**	**5.96**	....	....	....	....	....	....	....

a Hockey East Second All-Star Team (1988)
b Hockey East First All-Star Team (1989)
c NCAA East Second All-American Team (1989)
d Shared Harry "Hap" Holmes Memorial Trophy (fewest goals against - AHL) with Darcy Wakaluk (1991)
e AHL First All-Star Team (1991)
f Won Harry "Hap" Holmes Memorial Trophy (fewest goals against - AHL) (1992)
g AHL Second All-Star Team (1992)

Signed as a free agent by **Tampa Bay**, August 27, 1992. Signed as a free agent by **Boston**, August 6, 1993.

LORENZ, DANNY — FLA.

Goaltender. Catches left. 5'10", 187 lbs. Born, Murrayville, B.C., December 12, 1969.
(NY Islanders' 4th choice, 58th overall, in 1988 Entry Draft).

			Regular Season								Playoffs						
Season	Club	Lea	GP	W	L	T	Mins	GA	SO	Avg	GP	W	L	Mins	GA	SO	Avg
1986-87	Seattle	WHL	38	12	21	2	2103	199	0	5.68	....	....	....	....	....	....	....
1987-88	Seattle	WHL	62	20	37	2	3302	314	0	5.71	....	....	....	....	....	....	....
1988-89	Springfield	AHL	4	2	1	0	210	12	0	3.43	....	....	....	....	....	....	....
a	Seattle	WHL	*68	31	33	4	*4003	240	*3	3.60	....	....	....	....	....	....	....
1989-90a	Seattle	WHL	56	37	15	2	3226	221	0	4.11	13	6	7	751	40	0	3.21
1990-91	**NY Islanders**	**NHL**	**2**	**0**	**1**	**0**	**80**	**5**	**0**	**3.75**	....	....	....	....	....	....	....
	Capital Dist.	AHL	17	5	9	2	940	70	0	4.47	....	....	....	....	....	....	....
	Richmond	ECHL	20	6	9	2	1020	75	0	4.41	....	....	....	....	....	....	....
1991-92	**NY Islanders**	**NHL**	**2**	**0**	**2**	**0**	**120**	**10**	**0**	**5.00**	....	....	....	....	....	....	....
	Capital Dist.	AHL	53	22	22	7	3050	181	2	3.56	7	3	4	442	25	0	3.39
1992-93	**NY Islanders**	**NHL**	**4**	**1**	**2**	**0**	**157**	**10**	**0**	**3.82**	....	....	....	....	....	....	....
	Capital Dist.	AHL	44	16	17	5	2412	146	1	3.63	4	0	3	219	12	0	3.29
1993-94	Salt Lake	IHL	20	4	12	0	982	91	0	5.56	....	....	....	....	....	....	....
	Springfield	AHL	14	5	7	1	801	59	0	4.42	2	0	0	35	0	0	0.00
1994-95	Cincinnati	IHL	41	24	10	3	2222	126	0	3.40	5	2	3	308	16	0	3.12
	NHL Totals		**8**	**1**	**5**	**0**	**357**	**25**	**0**	**4.20**	....	....	....	....	....	....	....

a WHL West First All-Star Team (1989, 1990)

Signed as a free agent by **Florida**, June 14, 1994.

MacDONALD, AARON — FLA.

Goaltender. Catches left. 6'1", 193 lbs. Born, Grand Prairie, Alta., August 29, 1977.
(Florida's 2nd choice, 36th overall, in 1995 Entry Draft).

			Regular Season								Playoffs						
Season	Club	Lea	GP	W	L	T	Mins	GA	SO	Avg	GP	W	L	Mins	GA	SO	Avg
1993-94	Swift Current	WHL	18	6	6	0	710	48	0	4.06	....	....	....	....	....	....	....
1994-95	Swift Current	WHL	53	24	20	6	2957	177	4	3.59	6	2	4	393	18	0	2.75

MacDONALD, TODD — FLA.

Goaltender. Catches left. 6', 167 lbs. Born, Charlottetown, P.E.I., July 5, 1975.
(Florida's 7th choice, 109th overall, in 1993 Entry Draft).

			Regular Season								Playoffs						
Season	Club	Lea	GP	W	L	T	Mins	GA	SO	Avg	GP	W	L	Mins	GA	SO	Avg
1992-93	Tacoma	WHL	19	6	6	0	823	59	0	4.30	....	....	....	....	....	....	....
1993-94	Tacoma	WHL	29	13	10	2	1606	109	1	4.07	....	....	....	....	....	....	....
1994-95a	Tacoma	WHL	60	*35	21	2	3433	179	3	3.13	4	1	3	255	13	0	3.06

a WHL West First All-Star Team (1995)

MADELEY, DARRIN (MAY-duh-lee) — OTT.

Goaltender. Catches left. 5'11", 170 lbs. Born, Holland Landing, Ont., February 25, 1968.

			Regular Season								Playoffs						
Season	Club	Lea	GP	W	L	T	Mins	GA	SO	Avg	GP	W	L	Mins	GA	SO	Avg
1989-90	Lake Superior	CCHA	30	21	7	1	1683	68	1	2.42	....	....	....	....	....	....	....
1990-91a	Lake Superior	CCHA	36	*29	3	3	2137	93	1	*2.61	....	....	....	....	....	....	....
1991-92abc	Lake Superior	CCHA	36	23	6	4	2144	69	2	*2.05	....	....	....	....	....	....	....
1992-93	**Ottawa**	**NHL**	**2**	**0**	**2**	**0**	**90**	**10**	**0**	**6.67**	....	....	....	....	....	....	....
	New Haven	AHL	41	10	16	9	2295	127	0	3.32	....	....	....	....	....	....	....
1993-94	**Ottawa**	**NHL**	**32**	**3**	**18**	**5**	**1583**	**115**	**0**	**4.36**	....	....	....	....	....	....	....
	PEI	AHL	6	0	4	0	270	26	0	5.77	....	....	....	....	....	....	....
1994-95	**Ottawa**	**NHL**	**5**	**1**	**3**	**0**	**255**	**15**	**0**	**3.53**	....	....	....	....	....	....	....
	PEI	AHL	3	1	1	1	185	8	0	2.59	....	....	....	....	....	....	....
	Detroit	IHL	9	7	2	0	498	20	1	2.41	....	....	....	....	....	....	....
	NHL Totals		**39**	**4**	**23**	**5**	**1928**	**140**	**0**	**4.36**	....	....	....	....	....	....	....

a NCAA West First All-American Team (1991, 1992)
b NCAA Final Four All-Tournament Team (1992)
c CCHA First All-Star Team (1992)
d AHL Second All-Star Team (1993)

Signed as a free agent by **Ottawa**, June 20, 1992.

MAGLIARDITI, MARC — CHI.

Goaltender. Catches left. 5'11", 170 lbs. Born, Niagara Falls, NY, July 9, 1976.
(Chicago's 6th choice, 146th overall, in 1995 Entry Draft).

			Regular Season								Playoffs						
Season	Club	Lea	GP	W	L	T	Mins	GA	SO	Avg	GP	W	L	Mins	GA	SO	Avg
1994-95	Des Moines	Jr. A	29	....	....	....	1727	82	....	2.85	....	....	....	....	....	....	....

MALARCHUK, CLINT (muh-LAHR-chuhk)

Goaltender. Catches left. 6', 185 lbs. Born, Grande Prairie, Alta., May 1, 1961.
(Quebec's 3rd choice, 74th overall, in 1981 Entry Draft).

			Regular Season								Playoffs						
Season	Club	Lea	GP	W	L	T	Mins	GA	SO	Avg	GP	W	L	Mins	GA	SO	Avg
1979-80	Portland	WHL	37	21	10	0	1948	147	0	4.53	1	0	0	40	3	0	4.50
1980-81	Portland	WHL	38	28	8	0	2235	142	3	3.81	5	3	2	307	21	0	4.10
1981-82	**Quebec**	**NHL**	**2**	**0**	**1**	**1**	**120**	**14**	**0**	**7.00**	....	....	....	....	....	....	....
	Fredericton	AHL	51	15	34	2	2906	247	0	5.10	....	....	....	....	....	....	....
1982-83	**Quebec**	**NHL**	**15**	**8**	**5**	**2**	**900**	**71**	**0**	**4.73**	....	....	....	....	....	....	....
a	Fredericton	AHL	25	14	6	5	1506	78	0	3.11	....	....	....	....	....	....	....
1983-84	**Quebec**	**NHL**	**23**	**10**	**9**	**2**	**1215**	**80**	**0**	**3.95**	....	....	....	....	....	....	....
	Fredericton	AHL	11	5	5	1	663	40	0	3.62	....	....	....	....	....	....	....
1984-85	Fredericton	AHL	*56	26	25	4	*3347	198	2	3.55	6	2	4	379	20	0	3.17
1985-86	**Quebec**	**NHL**	**46**	**26**	**12**	**4**	**2657**	**142**	**4**	**3.21**	**3**	**0**	**2**	**143**	**11**	**0**	**4.62**
1986-87	**Quebec**	**NHL**	**54**	**18**	**26**	**9**	**3092**	**175**	**1**	**3.40**	**3**	**0**	**2**	**140**	**8**	**0**	**3.43**
1987-88	**Washington**	**NHL**	**54**	**24**	**20**	**4**	**2926**	**154**	***4**	**3.16**	**4**	**0**	**2**	**193**	**15**	**0**	**4.66**
1988-89	**Washington**	**NHL**	**42**	**16**	**18**	**7**	**2428**	**141**	**1**	**3.48**	**1**	**0**	**1**	**59**	**5**	**0**	**5.08**
	Buffalo	**NHL**	**7**	**3**	**1**	**1**	**326**	**13**	**1**	**2.39**	....	....	....	....	....	....	....
1989-90	**Buffalo**	**NHL**	**29**	**14**	**11**	**2**	**1596**	**89**	**0**	**3.35**	....	....	....	....	....	....	....
1990-91	**Buffalo**	**NHL**	**37**	**12**	**14**	**10**	**2131**	**119**	**1**	**3.35**	**4**	**2**	**2**	**246**	**17**	**0**	**4.15**
1991-92	**Buffalo**	**NHL**	**29**	**10**	**13**	**3**	**1639**	**102**	**0**	**3.73**	....	....	....	....	....	....	....
	Rochester	AHL	2	2	0	0	120	3	1	1.50	....	....	....	....	....	....	....
1992-93ab	San Diego	IHL	27	17	3	3	1516	72	3	2.85	*12	6	4	668	34	0	3.05
1993-94	Las Vegas	IHL	55	*34	10	7	3076	172	1	3.35	5	1	3	257	16	0	3.74
1994-95	Las Vegas	IHL	38	15	13	3	2039	127	0	3.74	2	0	0	32	2	0	3.70
	NHL Totals		**338**	**141**	**130**	**45**	**19030**	**1100**	**12**	**3.47**	**15**	**2**	**9**	**781**	**56**	**0**	**4.30**

a Shared Harry "Hap" Holmes Memorial Trophy (fewest goals against - AHL) with Brian Ford (1983)
b Shared James Norris Memorial Trophy (fewest goals against - IHL) with Rick Knickle (1993)

Traded to **Washington** by **Quebec** with Dale Hunter for Gaetan Duchesne, Alan Haworth and Washington's first round choice (Joe Sakic) in 1987 Entry Draft, June 13, 1987. Traded to **Buffalo** by **Washington** with Grant Ledyard and Washington's sixth round choice (Brian Holzinger) in 1991 Entry Draft for Calle Johansson and Buffalo's second round choice (Byron Dafoe) in 1989 Entry Draft, March 7, 1989.

MARACLE, NORM — DET.

Goaltender. Catches left. 5'9", 175 lbs. Born, Belleville, Ont., October 2, 1974.
(Detroit's 6th choice, 126th overall, in 1993 Entry Draft).

			Regular Season								Playoffs						
Season	Club	Lea	GP	W	L	T	Mins	GA	SO	Avg	GP	W	L	Mins	GA	SO	Avg
1991-92	Saskatoon	WHL	29	13	6	3	1529	87	1	3.41	15	9	5	860	37	0	3.38
1992-93a	Saskatoon	WHL	53	27	18	3	1939	160	1	3.27	9	4	5	569	33	0	3.48
1993-94bcd	Saskatoon	WHL	56	*41	13	1	3219	148	2	2.76	16	*11	5	940	48	*1	3.06
1994-95	Adirondack	AHL	39	12	15	2	1997	119	0	3.57	....	....	....	....	....	....	....

a WHL East Second All-Star Team (1993)
b WHL East First All-Star Team (1994)
c Canadian Major Junior First All-Star Team (1994)
d Canadian Major Junior Goaltender of the Year (1994)

MASON, BOB

Goaltender. Catches right. 6'1", 180 lbs. Born, International Falls, MN, April 22, 1961.

			Regular Season								Playoffs						
Season	Club	Lea	GP	W	L	T	Mins	GA	SO	Avg	GP	W	L	Mins	GA	SO	Avg
1981-82	Minn.-Duluth	WCHA	27	9	15	3	1401	115	0	4.45	....	....	....	....	....	....	....
1982-83	Minn.-Duluth	WCHA	43	26	16	1	2593	151	1	3.49	....	....	....	....	....	....	....
1983-84	U.S. National	....	33	17	10	5	1895	89	0	2.82	....	....	....	....	....	....	....
	U.S. Olympic	....	3	2	0	1	160	10	0	3.75	....	....	....	....	....	....	....
	Washington	**NHL**	**2**	**2**	**0**	**0**	**120**	**3**	**0**	**1.50**	....	....	....	....	....	....	....
	Hershey	AHL	5	1	4	0	282	26	0	5.53	....	....	....	....	....	....	....
1984-85	**Washington**	**NHL**	**12**	**8**	**2**	**1**	**661**	**31**	**1**	**2.81**	....	....	....	....	....	....	....
	Binghamton	AHL	20	10	6	1	1052	58	1	3.31	....	....	....	....	....	....	....
1985-86	**Washington**	**NHL**	**1**	**1**	**0**	**0**	**16**	**0**	**0**	**0.00**	....	....	....	....	....	....	....
	Binghamton	AHL	34	20	11	2	1940	126	0	3.90	3	1	1	124	9	0	4.35
1986-87	**Washington**	**NHL**	**45**	**20**	**18**	**5**	**2536**	**137**	**0**	**3.24**	**4**	**2**	**2**	**309**	**9**	**1**	**1.75**
	Binghamton	AHL	2	1	1	0	119	4	0	2.02	....	....	....	....	....	....	....
1987-88	**Chicago**	**NHL**	**41**	**13**	**18**	**8**	**2312**	**160**	**0**	**4.15**	**1**	**0**	**1**	**60**	**3**	**0**	**3.00**
1988-89	**Quebec**	**NHL**	**22**	**5**	**14**	**1**	**1168**	**92**	**0**	**4.73**	....	....	....	....	....	....	....
	Halifax	AHL	23	11	7	1	1278	73	1	3.43	2	0	2	97	9	0	5.57
1989-90	**Washington**	**NHL**	**16**	**4**	**9**	**1**	**822**	**48**	**0**	**3.50**	....	....	....	....	....	....	....
	Baltimore	AHL	13	9	2	2	770	44	0	3.43	6	2	4	373	20	0	3.22
1990-91	**Vancouver**	**NHL**	**6**	**2**	**4**	**0**	**353**	**29**	**0**	**4.93**	....	....	....	....	....	....	....
	Milwaukee	IHL	22	8	12	1	1199	82	0	4.10	....	....	....	....	....	....	....
1991-92	Milwaukee	IHL	51	27	18	4	3024	171	1	3.39	3	1	2	179	15	0	5.03
1992-93	Hamilton	AHL	44	20	19	3	2601	159	0	3.67	....	....	....	....	....	....	....
1993-94	Milwaukee	IHL	40	21	9	8	2206	132	0	3.59	3	0	1	141	9	0	3.83
1994-95	Fort Wayne	IHL	1	0	1	0	60	5	0	5.00	....	....	....	....	....	....	....
	Milwaukee	IHL	13	7	4	1	745	50	0	4.03	....	....	....	....	....	....	....
	NHL Totals		**145**	**55**	**65**	**16**	**7988**	**500**	**1**	**3.76**	**5**	**2**	**3**	**369**	**12**	**1**	**1.95**

Signed as a free agent by **Washington**, February 21, 1984. Signed as a free agent by **Chicago**, June 12, 1987. Traded to **Quebec** by **Chicago** for Mike Eagles, July 5, 1988. Traded to **Washington** by **Quebec** for future considerations, June 17, 1989. Signed as a free agent by **Vancouver**, December 1, 1990.

MASON, CHRIS — N.J.

Goaltender. Catches left. 5'11", 180 lbs. Born, Red Deer, Alta., April 20, 1976.
(New Jersey's 7th choice, 122nd overall, in 1995 Entry Draft).

			Regular Season								Playoffs						
Season	Club	Lea	GP	W	L	T	Mins	GA	SO	Avg	GP	W	L	Mins	GA	SO	Avg
1993-94	Victoria	WHL	3	0	3	0	129	16	0	7.44	....	....	....	....	....	....	....
1994-95	Prince George	WHL	44	8	30	1	2288	192	1	5.03	....	....	....	....	....	....	....

MASOTTA, BRYAN — OTT.

Goaltender. Catches left. 6'2", 195 lbs. Born, New Haven, CT, May 30, 1975.
(Ottawa's 3rd choice, 81st overall, in 1994 Entry Draft).

			Regular Season								Playoffs						
Season	Club	Lea	GP	W	L	T	Mins	GA	SO	Avg	GP	W	L	Mins	GA	SO	Avg
1993-94	Hotchkiss	HS	18	....	....	....	856	....	8	2.01	....	....	....	....	....	....	....
1994-95	RPI	ECAC	13	5	6	0	646	46	0	4.27	....	....	....	....	....	....	....

McARTHUR, MARK — NYI

Goaltender. Catches left. 5'11", 189 lbs. Born, Peterborough, Ont., November 16, 1975.
(NY Islanders' 5th choice, 112th overall, in 1994 Entry Draft).

			Regular Season								Playoffs						
Season	Club	Lea	GP	W	L	T	Mins	GA	SO	Avg	GP	W	L	Mins	GA	SO	Avg
1992-93	Guelph	OHL	35	14	14	3	1853	180	0	5.83	....	....	....	....	....	....	....
1993-94	Guelph	OHL	51	25	18	5	2936	201	0	4.11	9	4	5	561	38	0	4.06
1994-95a	Guelph	OHL	48	*34	8	4	2776	130	1	*2.81	13	9	4	797	44	0	3.31

a OHL Second All-Star Team (1995)

McKERSIE, JOHN — DAL.

Goaltender. Catches left. 6', 210 lbs. Born, Madison, WI, January 23, 1972.
(Minnesota's 12th choice, 239th overall, in 1990 Entry Draft).

			Regular Season								Playoffs						
Season	Club	Lea	GP	W	L	T	Mins	GA	SO	Avg	GP	W	L	Mins	GA	SO	Avg
1991-92	Boston U.	H.E.	8	3	2	1	396	23	1	3.48	....	....	....	....	....	....	....
1992-93	Boston U.	H.E.	9	6	0	1	466	31	1	3.99	....	....	....	....	....	....	....
1993-94a	Boston U.	H.E.	24	19	4	0	1325	64	0	2.90	....	....	....	....	....	....	....
1994-95								DID NOT PLAY – INJURED									

a NCAA East Second All-American Team (1994)

McLEAN, KIRK — VAN.

Goaltender. Catches left. 6', 195 lbs. Born, Willowdale, Ont., June 26, 1966.
(New Jersey's 6th choice, 107th overall, in 1984 Entry Draft).

			Regular Season								Playoffs						
Season	Club	Lea	GP	W	L	T	Mins	GA	SO	Avg	GP	W	L	Mins	GA	SO	Avg
1983-84	Oshawa	OHL	17	5	9	0	940	67	0	4.28	....	....	....	....	....	....	....
1984-85	Oshawa	OHL	47	23	17	2	2581	143	1	*3.32	5	1	3	271	21	0	4.65
1985-86	**New Jersey**	**NHL**	**2**	**1**	**1**	**0**	**111**	**11**	**0**	**5.95**	....	....	....	....	....	....	....
	Oshawa	OHL	51	24	21	2	2830	169	1	3.58	4	1	2	201	18	0	5.37
1986-87	**New Jersey**	**NHL**	**4**	**1**	**1**	**0**	**160**	**10**	**0**	**3.75**	....	....	....	....	....	....	....
	Maine	AHL	45	15	23	4	2606	140	1	3.22	....	....	....	....	....	....	....
1987-88	**Vancouver**	**NHL**	**41**	**11**	**27**	**3**	**2380**	**147**	**1**	**3.71**	....	....	....	....	....	....	....
1988-89	**Vancouver**	**NHL**	**42**	**20**	**17**	**3**	**2477**	**127**	**4**	**3.08**	**5**	**2**	**3**	**302**	**18**	**0**	**3.58**
1989-90	**Vancouver**	**NHL**	***63**	**21**	**30**	**10**	***3739**	**216**	**0**	**3.47**	....	....	....	....	....	....	....
1990-91	**Vancouver**	**NHL**	**41**	**10**	**22**	**3**	**1969**	**131**	**0**	**3.99**	**2**	**1**	**1**	**123**	**7**	**0**	**3.41**
1991-92a	**Vancouver**	**NHL**	**65**	***38**	**17**	**9**	**3852**	**176**	***5**	**2.74**	**13**	**6**	**7**	**785**	**33**	***2**	**2.52**
1992-93	**Vancouver**	**NHL**	**54**	**28**	**21**	**5**	**3261**	**184**	**3**	**3.39**	**12**	**6**	**6**	**754**	**42**	**0**	**3.34**
1993-94	**Vancouver**	**NHL**	**52**	**23**	**26**	**3**	**3128**	**156**	**3**	**2.99**	***24**	**15**	**9**	***1544**	**59**	***4**	**2.29**
1994-95	**Vancouver**	**NHL**	**40**	**18**	**12**	**10**	**2374**	**109**	**1**	**2.75**	**11**	**4**	**7**	**660**	**36**	**0**	**3.27**
	NHL Totals		**404**	**171**	**174**	**46**	**23451**	**1267**	**17**	**3.24**	**67**	**34**	**33**	**4168**	**195**	**6**	**2.81**

a NHL Second All-Star Team (1992)

Played in NHL All-Star Game (1990, 1992)

Traded to **Vancouver** by **New Jersey** with Greg Adams for Patrik Sundstrom and Vancouver's fourth round choice (Matt Ruchty) in 1988 Entry Draft, September 15, 1987.

McLENNAN, JAMIE — NYI

Goaltender. Catches left. 6', 190 lbs. Born, Edmonton, Alta., June 30, 1971.
(NY Islanders' 3rd choice, 48th overall, in 1991 Entry Draft).

			Regular Season								Playoffs						
Season	Club	Lea	GP	W	L	T	Mins	GA	SO	Avg	GP	W	L	Mins	GA	SO	Avg
1989-90	Lethbridge	WHL	34	20	4	2	1690	110	1	3.91	13	6	5	677	44	0	3.90
1990-91a	Lethbridge	WHL	56	32	18	4	3230	205	0	3.81	*16	8	8	*970	56	0	3.46
1991-92	Capital Dist.	AHL	18	4	10	2	952	60	1	3.78	....	....	....	....	....	....	....
	Richmond	ECHL	32	16	12	2	1837	114	0	3.72	....	....	....	....	....	....	....
1992-93	Capital Dist.	AHL	38	17	14	6	2171	117	1	3.23	1	0	1	20	5	0	15.00
1993-94	**NY Islanders**	**NHL**	**22**	**8**	**7**	**6**	**1287**	**61**	**0**	**2.84**	**2**	**0**	**1**	**82**	**6**	**0**	**4.39**
	Salt Lake	IHL	24	8	12	2	1320	80	0	3.64	....	....	....	....	....	....	....
1994-95	**NY Islanders**	**NHL**	**21**	**6**	**11**	**2**	**1185**	**67**	**0**	**3.39**	....	....	....	....	....	....	....
	Denver	IHL	4	3	0	1	239	12	0	3.00	11	8	2	640	23	1	*2.15
	NHL Totals		**43**	**14**	**18**	**8**	**2472**	**128**	**0**	**3.11**	**2**	**0**	**1**	**82**	**6**	**0**	**4.39**

a WHL East First All-Star Team (1991)

MIGNACCA, SONNY — VAN.

Goaltender. Catches left. 5'8", 178 lbs. Born, Winnipeg, Man., January 4, 1974.
(Vancouver's 10th choice, 213th overall, in 1992 Entry Draft).

			Regular Season								Playoffs						
Season	Club	Lea	GP	W	L	T	Mins	GA	SO	Avg	GP	W	L	Mins	GA	SO	Avg
1990-91	Medicine Hat	WHL	33	17	9	2	1743	121	0	4.17	1	0	0	13	2	0	9.23
1991-92a	Medicine Hat	WHL	56	35	19	0	3207	189	2	3.54	4	0	4	240	17	0	4.25
1992-93	Medicine Hat	WHL	50	18	25	2	2724	210	1	4.63	10	5	5	605	36	0	3.57
1993-94a	Medicine Hat	WHL	60	26	23	5	3361	183	2	3.27	3	0	3	180	17	0	5.67
1994-95	Syracuse	AHL	19	4	11	2	1097	85	0	4.65	....	....	....	....	....	....	....

a WHL East Second All-Star Team (1992, 1994)

MIKLENDA, JAROSLAV — OTT.

Goaltender. Catches left. 6'1", 176 lbs. Born, Uherske Hradiste, Czech., March 7, 1974.
(Ottawa's 7th choice, 146th overall, in 1992 Entry Draft).

			Regular Season								Playoffs						
Season	Club	Lea	GP	W	L	T	Mins	GA	SO	Avg	GP	W	L	Mins	GA	SO	Avg
1991-92	Olomouc	Czech.	1	....	....	....	36	6	0	9.99	....	....	....	....	....	....	....
1992-93	Olomouc	Czech.	5	....	....	....	285	22	....	4.63	....	....	....	....	....	....	....
1993-94	TJ Vitkovice	Czech.	10	....	....	....	555	25	0	2.71	....	....	....	....	....	....	....
1994-95	Presov	Czech. 2	8	....	....	....	....	20	....	2.80	....	....	....	....	....	....	....

MINARD, MIKE — EDM.

Goaltender. Catches left. 6'3", 205 lbs. Born, Owen Sound, Ont., November 1, 1976.
(Edmonton's 4th choice, 83rd overall, in 1995 Entry Draft).

			Regular Season								Playoffs						
Season	Club	Lea	GP	W	L	T	Mins	GA	SO	Avg	GP	W	L	Mins	GA	SO	Avg
1994-95	Chilliwack	Jr. A	40	....	....	....	2330	136	0	3.50	....	....	....	....	....	....	....

MOOG, ANDY — (MOHG) DAL.

Goaltender. Catches left. 5'8", 170 lbs. Born, Penticton, B.C., February 18, 1960.
(Edmonton's 6th choice, 132nd overall, in 1980 Entry Draft).

			Regular Season								Playoffs						
Season	Club	Lea	GP	W	L	T	Mins	GA	SO	Avg	GP	W	L	Mins	GA	SO	Avg
1978-79	Billings	WHL	26	13	5	4	1306	90	4	4.13	5	1	3	229	21	0	5.50
1979-80a	Billings	WHL	46	23	14	1	2435	149	1	3.67	3	2	1	190	10	0	3.16
1980-81	**Edmonton**	**NHL**	**7**	**3**	**3**	**0**	**313**	**20**	**0**	**3.83**	**9**	**5**	**4**	**526**	**32**	**0**	**3.65**
	Wichita	CHL	29	14	13	1	1602	89	0	3.33	5	3	2	300	16	0	3.20
1981-82	**Edmonton**	**NHL**	**8**	**3**	**5**	**0**	**399**	**32**	**0**	**4.81**	....	....	....	....	....	....	....
b	Wichita	CHL	40	23	13	3	2391	119	1	2.99	7	3	4	434	23	0	3.18
1982-83	**Edmonton**	**NHL**	**50**	**33**	**8**	**7**	**2833**	**167**	**1**	**3.54**	**16**	**11**	**5**	**949**	**48**	**0**	**3.03**
1983-84	**Edmonton**	**NHL**	**38**	**27**	**8**	**1**	**2212**	**139**	**1**	**3.77**	**7**	**4**	**0**	**263**	**12**	**0**	**2.74**
1984-85	**Edmonton**	**NHL**	**39**	**22**	**9**	**3**	**2019**	**111**	**1**	**3.30**	**2**	**0**	**0**	**20**	**0**	**0**	**0.00**
1985-86	**Edmonton**	**NHL**	**47**	**27**	**9**	**7**	**2664**	**164**	**1**	**3.69**	**1**	**1**	**0**	**60**	**1**	**0**	**1.00**
1986-87	**Edmonton**	**NHL**	**46**	**28**	**11**	**3**	**2461**	**144**	**0**	**3.51**	**2**	**2**	**0**	**120**	**8**	**0**	**4.00**
1987-88	Cdn. National	....	27	10	7	5	1438	86	0	3.58	....	....	....	....	....	....	....
	Cdn. Olympic	....	4	4	0	0	240	9	1	2.25	....	....	....	....	....	....	....
	Boston	**NHL**	**6**	**4**	**2**	**0**	**360**	**17**	**1**	**2.83**	**7**	**1**	**4**	**354**	**25**	**0**	**4.24**
1988-89	**Boston**	**NHL**	**41**	**18**	**14**	**8**	**2482**	**133**	**1**	**3.22**	**6**	**4**	**2**	**359**	**14**	**0**	**2.34**
1989-90c	**Boston**	**NHL**	**46**	**24**	**10**	**7**	**2536**	**122**	**3**	**2.89**	**20**	**13**	**7**	**1195**	**44**	***2**	***2.21**
1990-91	**Boston**	**NHL**	**51**	**25**	**13**	**9**	**2844**	**136**	**4**	**2.87**	**19**	**10**	**9**	**1133**	**60**	**0**	**3.18**
1991-92	**Boston**	**NHL**	**62**	**28**	**22**	**9**	**3640**	**196**	**1**	**3.23**	**15**	**8**	**7**	**866**	**46**	**1**	**3.19**
1992-93	**Boston**	**NHL**	**55**	**37**	**14**	**3**	**3194**	**168**	**3**	**3.16**	**3**	**0**	**3**	**161**	**14**	**0**	**5.22**
1993-94	**Dallas**	**NHL**	**55**	**24**	**20**	**7**	**3121**	**170**	**2**	**3.27**	**4**	**1**	**3**	**246**	**12**	**0**	**2.93**
1994-95	**Dallas**	**NHL**	**31**	**10**	**12**	**7**	**1770**	**72**	**2**	**2.44**	**5**	**1**	**4**	**277**	**16**	**0**	**3.47**
	NHL Totals		**582**	**313**	**160**	**71**	**32848**	**1791**	**21**	**3.27**	**116**	**61**	**48**	**6529**	**332**	**3**	**3.05**

a WHL Second All-Star Team (1980)
b CHL Second All-Star Team (1982)
c Shared William Jennings Trophy with Rejean Lemelin (1990)

Played in NHL All-Star Game (1985, 1986, 1991)

Traded to **Boston** by **Edmonton** for Geoff Courtnall, Bill Ranford and Boston's second choice (Petro Koivunen) in 1988 Entry Draft, March 8, 1988. Traded to **Dallas** by **Boston** for Jon Casey to complete June 20, 1993 trade which sent Gord Murphy to Dallas for future considerations, June 25, 1993.

MOSS, TYLER — T.B.

Goaltender. Catches right. 6', 168 lbs. Born, Ottawa, Ont., June 29, 1975.
(Tampa Bay's 2nd choice, 29th overall, in 1993 Entry Draft).

			Regular Season								Playoffs						
Season	Club	Lea	GP	W	L	T	Mins	GA	SO	Avg	GP	W	L	Mins	GA	SO	Avg
1992-93	Kingston	OHL	31	13	7	5	1537	97	0	3.79	6	1	2	228	19	0	5.00
1993-94	Kingston	OHL	13	6	4	3	795	42	1	3.17	3	0	2	136	8	0	3.53
1994-95a	Kingston	OHL	*57	33	17	5	*3249	164	1	3.03	6	2	4	333	27	0	4.86

a OHL First All-Star Team (1995)

MUZZATTI, JASON (moo-ZAH-tee) CGY.

Goaltender. Catches left. 6'1", 190 lbs. Born, Toronto, Ont., February 3, 1970.
(Calgary's 1st choice, 21st overall, in 1988 Entry Draft).

			Regular Season								Playoffs						
Season	Club	Lea	GP	W	L	T	Mins	GA	SO	Avg	GP	W	L	Mins	GA	SO	Avg
1987-88a	Michigan State	CCHA	33	19	9	3	1915	109	0	3.41	....	....	....	....	....	....	....
1988-89	Michigan State	CCHA	42	32	9	1	2515	127	3	*3.03	....	....	....	....	....	....	....
1989-90bc	Michigan State	CCHA	33	*24	6	0	1976	99	0	3.01	....	....	....	....	....	....	....
1990-91	Michigan State	CCHA	22	8	10	2	1204	75	1	3.74	....	....	....	....	....	....	....
1991-92	Salt Lake	IHL	52	24	22	5	3033	167	2	3.30	4	1	3	247	18	0	4.37
1992-93	Cdn. National	....	16	6	9	0	880	53	0	3.84	....	....	....	....	....	....	....
	Indianapolis	IHL	12	5	6	1	707	48	0	4.07	....	....	....	....	....	....	....
	Salt Lake	IHL	13	5	6	1	747	52	0	4.18	....	....	....	....	....	....	....
1993-94	**Calgary**	**NHL**	**1**	**0**	**1**	**0**	**60**	**8**	**0**	**8.00**	....	....	....	....	....	....	....
	Saint John	AHL	51	26	21	3	2939	183	2	3.74	7	3	4	415	19	0	2.75
1994-95	Saint John	AHL	31	10	14	4	1741	101	2	3.48	....	....	....	....	....	....	....
	Calgary	**NHL**	**1**	**0**	**0**	**0**	**10**	**0**	**0**	**0.00**	....	....	....	....	....	....	....
	NHL Totals		**2**	**0**	**1**	**0**	**70**	**8**	**0**	**6.86**	....	....	....	....	....	....	....

a CCHA Second All-Star Team (1988)
b CCHA First All-Star Team (1990)
c NCAA West Second All-American Team (1990)

NABOKOV, YEVGENI (nuh-BAW-kahv, yehv-GEH-nee) S.J.

Goaltender. Catches left. 6', 180 lbs. Born, Ust-Kamenogorsk, USSR, July 25, 1975.
(San Jose's 9th choice, 219th overall, in 1994 Entry Draft).

			Regular Season								Playoffs						
Season	Club	Lea	GP	W	L	T	Mins	GA	SO	Avg	GP	W	L	Mins	GA	SO	Avg
1992-93	Kamenogorsk	CIS	4	....	....	....	109	5	0	2.75	....	....	....	....	....	....	....
1993-94	Kamenogorsk	CIS	11	....	....	....	539	29	0	3.22	....	....	....	....	....	....	....
1994-95	Moscow D'amo	CIS	24	....	....	....	1265	40	....	1.89	....	....	....	....	....	....	....

NOBLE, TOM CHI.

Goaltender. Catches left. 5'10", 165 lbs. Born, Quincy, MA, March 21, 1975.
(Chicago's 12th choice, 284th overall, in 1993 Entry Draft).

			Regular Season								Playoffs						
Season	Club	Lea	GP	W	L	T	Mins	GA	SO	Avg	GP	W	L	Mins	GA	SO	Avg
1993-94	Catholic Mem.	HS	24	....	....	....	1080	22	....	0.93	....	....	....	....	....	....	....
1994-95	Boston U.	H.E.	18	15	2	0	1003	46	0	2.75	....	....	....	....	....	....	....

O'NEILL, MIKE ANA.

Goaltender. Catches left. 5'7", 160 lbs. Born, LaSalle, Que., November 3, 1967.
(Winnipeg's 1st choice, 15th overall, in 1988 Supplemental Draft).

			Regular Season								Playoffs						
Season	Club	Lea	GP	W	L	T	Mins	GA	SO	Avg	GP	W	L	Mins	GA	SO	Avg
1985-86	Yale	ECAC	6	3	1	0	389	17	0	3.53	....	....	....	....	....	....	....
1986-87a	Yale	ECAC	16	9	6	1	964	55	2	3.42	....	....	....	....	....	....	....
1987-88	Yale	ECAC	24	6	17	0	1385	101	0	4.37	....	....	....	....	....	....	....
1988-89ab	Yale	ECAC	25	10	14	1	1490	93	0	3.74	....	....	....	....	....	....	....
1989-90	Tappara	Fin.	41	23	13	5	2369	127	2	3.22	....	....	....	....	....	....	....
1990-91	Fort Wayne	IHL	8	5	2	1	490	31	0	3.80	....	....	....	....	....	....	....
	Moncton	AHL	30	13	7	6	1613	84	0	3.12	8	3	4	435	29	0	4.00
1991-92	**Winnipeg**	**NHL**	**1**	**0**	**0**	**0**	**13**	**1**	**0**	**4.62**	....	....	....	....	....	....	....
	Moncton	AHL	32	14	16	2	1902	108	1	3.41	11	4	7	670	43	*1	3.85
	Fort Wayne	IHL	33	22	6	3	1858	97	*4	3.13	....	....	....	....	....	....	....
1992-93	**Winnipeg**	**NHL**	**2**	**0**	**0**	**1**	**73**	**6**	**0**	**4.93**	....	....	....	....	....	....	....
	Moncton	AHL	30	13	10	4	1649	88	1	3.20	....	....	....	....	....	....	....
1993-94	**Winnipeg**	**NHL**	**17**	**0**	**9**	**1**	**738**	**51**	**0**	**4.15**	....	....	....	....	....	....	....
	Moncton	AHL	12	8	4	0	716	33	1	2.76	....	....	....	....	....	....	....
	Fort Wayne	IHL	11	4	4	3	642	38	0	3.55	....	....	....	....	....	....	....
1994-95	Fort Wayne	IHL	28	11	12	4	1603	109	0	4.08	....	....	....	....	....	....	....
	Phoenix	IHL	21	13	4	4	1256	64	1	3.06	9	4	5	535	33	0	3.70
	NHL Totals		**20**	**0**	**9**	**2**	**824**	**58**	**0**	**4.22**	....	....	....	....	....	....	....

a ECAC First All-Star Team (1987, 1989)
b NCAA East First All-American Team (1989)

Signed as a free agent by **Anaheim**, July 14, 1995.

OSGOOD, CHRIS (AWS-gud) DET.

Goaltender. Catches left. 5'10", 160 lbs. Born, Peace River, Alta., November 26, 1972.
(Detroit's 3rd choice, 54th overall, in 1991 Entry Draft).

			Regular Season								Playoffs						
Season	Club	Lea	GP	W	L	T	Mins	GA	SO	Avg	GP	W	L	Mins	GA	SO	Avg
1989-90	Medicine Hat	WHL	57	24	28	2	3094	228	0	4.42	3	0	3	173	17	0	5.91
1990-91a	Medicine Hat	WHL	46	23	18	3	2630	173	2	3.95	12	7	5	712	42	0	3.54
1991-92	Medicine Hat	WHL	15	10	3	0	819	44	0	3.22	....	....	....	....	....	....	....
	Brandon	WHL	16	3	10	1	890	60	1	4.04	....	....	....	....	....	....	....
	Seattle	WHL	21	12	7	1	1217	65	1	3.20	15	9	6	904	51	0	3.38
1992-93	Adirondack	AHL	45	19	19	4	2438	159	0	3.91	1	0	1	59	2	0	2.03
1993-94	**Detroit**	**NHL**	**41**	**23**	**8**	**5**	**2206**	**105**	**2**	**2.86**	**6**	**3**	**2**	**307**	**12**	**1**	**2.35**
	Adirondack	AHL	4	3	1	0	239	13	0	3.26	....	....	....	....	....	....	....
1994-95	**Detroit**	**NHL**	**19**	**14**	**5**	**0**	**1087**	**41**	**1**	**2.26**	**2**	**0**	**0**	**68**	**2**	**0**	**1.76**
	Adirondack	AHL	2	1	1	0	120	6	0	3.00	....	....	....	....	....	....	....
	NHL Totals		**60**	**37**	**13**	**5**	**3293**	**146**	**3**	**2.66**	**8**	**3**	**2**	**375**	**14**	**1**	**2.24**

a WHL East Second All-Star Team (1991)

PASSMORE, STEVE EDM.

Goaltender. Catches left. 5'9", 165 lbs. Born, Thunder Bay, Ont., January 29, 1973.
(Quebec's 9th choice, 196th overall, in 1992 Entry Draft).

			Regular Season								Playoffs						
Season	Club	Lea	GP	W	L	T	Mins	GA	SO	Avg	GP	W	L	Mins	GA	SO	Avg
1990-91	Victoria	WHL	35	3	25	1	1838	190	0	6.20	....	....	....	....	....	....	....
1991-92	Victoria	WHL	*71	15	50	5	*4228	347	0	4.92	....	....	....	....	....	....	....
1992-93a	Victoria	WHL	43	14	24	2	2402	150	1	3.75	....	....	....	....	....	....	....
	Kamloops	WHL	25	19	6	0	1479	69	1	2.80	7	4	2	401	22	1	3.29
1993-94a	Kamloops	WHL	36	22	9	2	1927	88	1	*2.74	*18	*11	7	*1099	60	0	3.28
1994-95	Cape Breton	AHL	25	8	13	3	1455	93	0	3.83	....	....	....	....	....	....	....

a WHL West First All-Star Team (1993, 1994)

Traded to **Edmonton** by **Quebec** for Brad Werenka, March 21, 1994.

PENSTOCK, BYRON ANA.

Goaltender. Catches left. 5'9", 180 lbs. Born, Regina, Sask., September 9, 1974.

			Regular Season								Playoffs						
Season	Club	Lea	GP	W	L	T	Mins	GA	SO	Avg	GP	W	L	Mins	GA	SO	Avg
1991-92	Tri-City	WHL	33	8	15	2	1644	151	0	5.51	....	....	....	....	....	....	....
1992-93	Brandon	WHL	17	7	8	0	882	68	1	4.63	....	....	....	....	....	....	....
1993-94	Brandon	WHL	58	35	18	4	3447	182	2	3.17	14	8	6	869	49	0	3.38
1994-95a	Brandon	WHL	48	27	16	4	2813	148	4	3.16	6	4	1	342	24	0	4.21

a WHL East Second All-Star Team (1995)

Signed as a free agent by **Anaheim**, June 30, 1995.

PERSSON, JOAKIM (PEHR-suhn) BOS.

Goaltender. Catches left. 5'11", 176 lbs. Born, Ostervala, Sweden, May 4, 1970.
(Boston's 10th choice, 259th overall, in 1993 Entry Draft).

			Regular Season								Playoffs						
Season	Club	Lea	GP	W	L	T	Mins	GA	SO	Avg	GP	W	L	Mins	GA	SO	Avg
1992-93	Hammarby	Swe. 2	40	....	....	....	....	....	....	2.71	....	....	....	....	....	....	....
1993-94	Hammarby	Swe. 2	23	....	....	....	....	59	....	2.57	....	....	....	....	....	....	....
	Providence	AHL	1	0	0	0	24	0	0	0.00	....	....	....	....	....	....	....
1994-95	AIK	Swe.	30	....	....	....	1800	103	1	3.43	....	....	....	....	....	....	....

PIETRANGELO, FRANK (PEE-tuhr-AN-jehl-oh) NYI

Goaltender. Catches left. 5'10", 185 lbs. Born, Niagara Falls, Ont., December 17, 1964.
(Pittsburgh's 4th choice, 63rd overall, in 1983 Entry Draft).

			Regular Season								Playoffs						
Season	Club	Lea	GP	W	L	T	Mins	GA	SO	Avg	GP	W	L	Mins	GA	SO	Avg
1982-83	U. Minnesota	WCHA	25	15	6	1	1348	80	1	3.55	....	....	....	....	....	....	....
1983-84	U. Minnesota	WCHA	20	13	7	0	1141	66	0	3.47	....	....	....	....	....	....	....
1984-85	U. Minnesota	WCHA	17	8	3	3	912	52	0	3.42	....	....	....	....	....	....	....
1985-86	U. Minnesota	WCHA	23	15	7	0	1284	76	0	3.55	....	....	....	....	....	....	....
1986-87	Muskegon	IHL	35	23	11	0	2090	119	2	3.42	15	10	4	923	46	0	2.99
1987-88	**Pittsburgh**	**NHL**	**21**	**9**	**11**	**0**	**1207**	**80**	**1**	**3.98**	....	....	....	....	....	....	....
	Muskegon	IHL	15	11	3	1	868	43	2	2.97	....	....	....	....	....	....	....
1988-89	**Pittsburgh**	**NHL**	**15**	**5**	**3**	**0**	**669**	**45**	**0**	**4.04**	....	....	....	....	....	....	....
	Muskegon	IHL	13	10	1	0	760	38	1	3.00	9	*8	1	566	29	0	3.07
1989-90	**Pittsburgh**	**NHL**	**21**	**8**	**6**	**2**	**1066**	**77**	**0**	**4.33**	....	....	....	....	....	....	....
	Muskegon	IHL	12	9	2	1	691	38	0	3.30	....	....	....	....	....	....	....
1990-91	**Pittsburgh**	**NHL**	**25**	**10**	**11**	**1**	**1311**	**86**	**0**	**3.94**	**5**	**4**	**1**	**288**	**15**	***1**	**3.13**
1991-92	**Pittsburgh**	**NHL**	**5**	**2**	**1**	**0**	**225**	**20**	**0**	**5.33**	....	....	....	....	....	....	....
	Hartford	**NHL**	**5**	**3**	**1**	**1**	**306**	**12**	**0**	**2.35**	**7**	**3**	**4**	**425**	**19**	**0**	**2.68**
1992-93	**Hartford**	**NHL**	**30**	**4**	**15**	**1**	**1373**	**111**	**0**	**4.85**	....	....	....	....	....	....	....
1993-94	**Hartford**	**NHL**	**19**	**5**	**11**	**1**	**984**	**59**	**0**	**3.60**	....	....	....	....	....	....	....
	Springfield	AHL	23	9	10	2	1314	73	0	3.33	6	2	4	324	23	0	4.26
1994-95	Minnesota	IHL	15	3	8	1	756	52	0	4.12	....	....	....	....	....	....	....
	NHL Totals		**141**	**46**	**59**	**6**	**7141**	**490**	**1**	**4.12**	**12**	**7**	**5**	**713**	**34**	**1**	**2.86**

Traded to **Hartford** by **Pittsburgh** for Hartford's third round choice (Sven Butenschon) and seventh round choice (Serge Aubin) in 1994 Entry Draft, March 10, 1992. Signed as a free agent by **NY Islanders**, July 28, 1994.

POTVIN, FELIX (PAHT-vihn) TOR.

Goaltender. Catches left. 6', 190 lbs. Born, Anjou, Que., June 23, 1971.
(Toronto's 2nd choice, 31st overall, in 1990 Entry Draft).

			Regular Season								Playoffs						
Season	Club	Lea	GP	W	L	T	Mins	GA	SO	Avg	GP	W	L	Mins	GA	SO	Avg
1988-89	Chicoutimi	QMJHL	*65	25	31	1	*3489	271	*2	4.66	....	....	....	....	....	....	....
1989-90a	Chicoutimi	QMJHL	*62	*31	26	2	*3478	231	*2	3.99	....	....	....	....	....	....	....
1990-91 bcde	Chicoutimi	QMJHL	54	33	15	4	3216	145	*6	*2.70	*16	*11	5	*992	46	0	*2.78
1991-92	**Toronto**	**NHL**	**4**	**0**	**2**	**1**	**210**	**8**	**0**	**2.29**	....	....	....	....	....	....	....
fgh	St. John's	AHL	35	18	10	6	2070	101	2	2.93	11	7	4	642	41	0	3.83
1992-93i	**Toronto**	**NHL**	**48**	**25**	**15**	**7**	**2781**	**116**	**2**	***2.50**	***21**	**11**	**10**	***1308**	**62**	**1**	**2.84**
	St. John's	AHL	5	3	0	2	309	18	0	3.50	....	....	....	....	....	....	....
1993-94	**Toronto**	**NHL**	**66**	**34**	**22**	**9**	**3883**	**187**	**3**	**2.89**	**18**	**9**	**9**	**1124**	**46**	**3**	**2.46**
1994-95	**Toronto**	**NHL**	**36**	**15**	**13**	**7**	**2144**	**104**	**0**	**2.91**	**7**	**3**	**4**	**424**	**20**	**1**	**2.83**
	NHL Totals		**154**	**74**	**52**	**24**	**9018**	**415**	**5**	**2.76**	**46**	**23**	**23**	**2856**	**128**	**5**	**2.69**

a QMJHL Second All-Star Team (1990)
b QMJHL First All-Star Team (1991)
c Canadian Major Junior Goaltender of the Year (1991)
d Memorial Cup All-Star Team (1991)
e Won Hap Emms Memorial Trophy (Memorial Cup Top Goaltender) (1991)
f Won Baz Bastien Memorial Trophy (Top Goaltender - AHL) (1992)
g Won Dudley "Red" Garrett Memorial Trophy (Top Rookie - AHL) (1992)
h AHL First All-Star Team (1992)
i NHL/Upper Deck All-Rookie Team (1993)

Played in NHL All-Star Game (1994)

PUPPA, DAREN (POO-puh) T.B.

Goaltender. Catches right. 6'3", 205 lbs. Born, Kirkland Lake, Ont., March 23, 1965.
(Buffalo's 6th choice, 74th overall, in 1983 Entry Draft).

			Regular Season								Playoffs						
Season	Club	Lea	GP	W	L	T	Mins	GA	SO	Avg	GP	W	L	Mins	GA	SO	Avg
1983-84	RPI	ECAC	32	24	6	0	....	....	....	2.94	....	....	....	....	....	....	....
1984-85	RPI	ECAC	32	31	1	0	1830	78	0	2.56	....	....	....	....	....	....	....
1985-86	**Buffalo**	**NHL**	**7**	**3**	**4**	**0**	**401**	**21**	**1**	**3.14**	....	....	....	....	....	....	....
	Rochester	AHL	20	8	11	0	1092	79	0	4.34	....	....	....	....	....	....	....
1986-87	**Buffalo**	**NHL**	**3**	**0**	**2**	**1**	**185**	**13**	**0**	**4.22**	....	....	....	....	....	....	....
a	Rochester	AHL	57	*33	14	0	3129	146	1	2.80	*16	*10	6	*944	48	*1	3.05
1987-88	**Buffalo**	**NHL**	**17**	**8**	**6**	**1**	**874**	**61**	**0**	**4.19**	**3**	**1**	**1**	**142**	**11**	**0**	**4.65**
	Rochester	AHL	26	14	8	2	1415	65	2	2.76	2	0	1	108	5	0	2.78
1988-89	**Buffalo**	**NHL**	**37**	**17**	**10**	**6**	**1908**	**107**	**1**	**3.36**	....	....	....	....	....	....	....
1989-90b	**Buffalo**	**NHL**	**56**	***31**	**16**	**6**	**3241**	**156**	**1**	**2.89**	**6**	**2**	**4**	**370**	**15**	**0**	**2.43**
1990-91	**Buffalo**	**NHL**	**38**	**15**	**11**	**6**	**2092**	**118**	**2**	**3.38**	**2**	**0**	**1**	**81**	**10**	**0**	**7.41**
1991-92	**Buffalo**	**NHL**	**33**	**11**	**14**	**4**	**1757**	**114**	**0**	**3.89**	....	....	....	....	....	....	....
	Rochester	AHL	2	0	2	0	119	9	0	4.54	....	....	....	....	....	....	....
1992-93	**Buffalo**	**NHL**	**24**	**11**	**5**	**4**	**1306**	**78**	**0**	**3.58**	....	....	....	....	....	....	....
	Toronto	**NHL**	**8**	**6**	**2**	**0**	**479**	**18**	**2**	**2.25**	**1**	**0**	**0**	**20**	**1**	**0**	**3.00**
1993-94	**Tampa Bay**	**NHL**	**63**	**22**	**33**	**6**	**3653**	**165**	**4**	**2.71**	....	....	....	....	....	....	....
1994-95	**Tampa Bay**	**NHL**	**36**	**14**	**19**	**2**	**2013**	**90**	**1**	**2.68**	....	....	....	....	....	....	....
	NHL Totals		**322**	**138**	**122**	**36**	**17909**	**941**	**12**	**3.15**	**12**	**3**	**6**	**613**	**37**	**0**	**3.62**

a AHL First All-Star Team (1987)
b NHL Second All-Star Team (1990)

Played in NHL All-Star Game (1990)

Traded to **Toronto** by **Buffalo** with Dave Andreychuk and Buffalo's first round choice (Kenny Jonsson) in 1993 Entry Draft for Grant Fuhr and Toronto's fifth round choice (Kevin Popp) in 1995 Entry Draft, February 2, 1993. Claimed by **Florida** from **Toronto** in Expansion Draft, June 24, 1993. Claimed by **Tampa Bay** from **Florida** in Phase II of Expansion Draft, June 25, 1993.

RACICOT, ANDRE (RAH-sih-KOH)

Goaltender. Catches left. 5'11", 165 lbs. Born, Rouyn-Noranda, Que., June 9, 1969.
(Montreal's 5th choice, 83rd overall, in 1989 Entry Draft).

			Regular Season								Playoffs						
Season	Club	Lea	GP	W	L	T	Mins	GA	SO	Avg	GP	W	L	Mins	GA	SO	Avg
1986-87	Longueuil	QMJHL	3	1	2	0	180	19	0	6.33	....	....	....	....	....	....	....
1987-88	Granby	QMJHL	30	15	11	1	1547	105	1	4.07	5	1	4	298	23	0	4.63
1988-89a	Granby	QMJHL	54	22	24	3	2944	198	0	4.04	4	0	4	218	18	0	4.95
1989-90	**Montreal**	**NHL**	**1**	**0**	**0**	**0**	**13**	**3**	**0**	**13.85**	....	....	....	....	....	....	....
b	Sherbrooke	AHL	33	19	11	2	1948	97	1	2.99	5	0	4	227	18	0	4.76
1990-91	**Montreal**	**NHL**	**21**	**7**	**9**	**2**	**975**	**52**	**1**	**3.20**	**2**	**0**	**1**	**12**	**2**	**0**	**10.00**
	Fredericton	AHL	22	13	8	1	1252	60	1	2.88	....	....	....	....	....	....	....
1991-92	**Montreal**	**NHL**	**9**	**0**	**3**	**3**	**436**	**23**	**0**	**3.17**	**1**	**0**	**0**	**1**	**0**	**0**	**0.00**
	Fredericton	AHL	28	14	8	5	1666	86	0	3.10	....	....	....	....	....	....	....
1992-93	**Montreal**	**NHL**	**26**	**17**	**5**	**1**	**1433**	**81**	**1**	**3.39**	**1**	**0**	**0**	**18**	**2**	**0**	**6.67**
1993-94	**Montreal**	**NHL**	**11**	**2**	**6**	**2**	**500**	**37**	**0**	**4.44**	....	....	....	....	....	....	....
	Fredericton	AHL	6	1	4	0	292	16	0	3.28	....	....	....	....	....	....	....
1994-95	Portland	AHL	19	10	7	0	1080	53	1	2.94	....	....	....	....	....	....	....
	Phoenix	IHL	3	1	0	0	132	8	0	3.62	2	0	0	20	0	0	0.00
	NHL Totals		**68**	**26**	**23**	**8**	**3357**	**196**	**2**	**3.50**	**4**	**0**	**1**	**31**	**4**	**0**	**7.74**

a QMJHL Second All-Star Team (1989)
b Shared Harry "Hap" Holmes Trophy (fewest goals-against - AHL) with J.C. Bergeron (1990)

Signed as a free agent by **Los Angeles**, September 22, 1994.

RACINE, BRUCE ST.L.

Goaltender. Catches left. 6', 170 lbs. Born, Cornwall, Ont., August 9, 1966.
(Pittsburgh's 3rd choice, 58th overall, in 1985 Entry Draft).

			Regular Season								Playoffs						
Season	Club	Lea	GP	W	L	T	Mins	GA	SO	Avg	GP	W	L	Mins	GA	SO	Avg
1984-85	Northeastern	H.E.	26	11	14	1	1615	103	1	3.83	....	....	....	....	....	....	....
1985-86	Northeastern	H.E.	32	17	14	1	1920	147	0	4.56	....	....	....	....	....	....	....
1986-87ab	Northeastern	H.E.	33	12	18	3	1966	133	0	4.06	....	....	....	....	....	....	....
1987-88b	Northeastern	H.E.	30	15	11	4	1808	108	1	3.58	....	....	....	....	....	....	....
1988-89	Muskegon	IHL	51	*37	11	0	*3039	184	*3	3.63	5	4	1	300	15	0	3.00
1989-90	Muskegon	IHL	49	29	15	4	2911	182	1	3.75	9	5	4	566	32	1	3.34
1990-91	Albany	IHL	29	7	18	1	1567	104	0	3.98	....	....	....	....	....	....	....
	Muskegon	IHL	9	4	4	1	516	40	0	4.65	....	....	....	....	....	....	....
1991-92	Muskegon	IHL	27	13	10	3	1559	91	1	3.50	1	0	1	60	6	0	6.00
1992-93	Cleveland	IHL	35	13	16	6	1949	140	1	4.31	2	0	0	37	2	0	3.24
1993-94	St. John's	AHL	37	20	9	2	1875	116	0	3.71	1	0	0	20	1	0	0.00
1994-95	St. John's	AHL	27	11	10	4	1492	85	1	3.42	2	1	1	119	3	0	1.51

a Hockey East First All-Star Team (1987)
b NCAA East First All-American Team (1987, 1988)

Signed as a free agent by **Toronto**, August 11, 1993. Signed as a free agent by **St. Louis**, August 10, 1995.

RAM, JAMIE NYR

Goaltender. Catches left. 5'11", 175 lbs. Born, Scarborough, Ont., January 18, 1971.
(NY Rangers' 10th choice, 213th overall, in 1991 Entry Draft).

			Regular Season								Playoffs						
Season	Club	Lea	GP	W	L	T	Mins	GA	SO	Avg	GP	W	L	Mins	GA	SO	Avg
1990-91	Michigan Tech	WCHA	14	5	9	0	826	57	0	4.14	....	....	....	....	....	....	....
1991-92	Michigan Tech	WCHA	23	9	9	1	1144	83	0	4.35	....	....	....	....	....	....	....
1992-93ab	Michigan Tech	WCHA	*36	16	14	5	*2078	115	0	3.32	....	....	....	....	....	....	....
1993-94ab	Michigan Tech	WCHA	39	12	20	5	2192	117	*1	3.20	....	....	....	....	....	....	....
1994-95	Binghamton	AHL	26	12	10	2	1472	81	1	3.30	11	6	5	663	29	1	2.62

a WCHA First All-Star Team (1993, 1994)
b NCAA West First All-American Team (1993, 1994)

RANFORD, BILL EDM.

Goaltender. Catches left. 5'11", 185 lbs. Born, Brandon, Man., December 14, 1966.
(Boston's 2nd choice, 52nd overall, in 1985 Entry Draft).

			Regular Season								Playoffs						
Season	Club	Lea	GP	W	L	T	Mins	GA	SO	Avg	GP	W	L	Mins	GA	SO	Avg
1983-84	N. Westminster	WHL	27	10	14	0	1450	130	0	5.38	1	0	0	27	2	0	4.44
1984-85	N. Westminster	WHL	38	19	17	0	2034	142	0	4.19	7	2	3	309	26	0	5.05
1985-86	**Boston**	**NHL**	**4**	**3**	**1**	**0**	**240**	**10**	**0**	**2.50**	**2**	**0**	**2**	**120**	**7**	**0**	**3.50**
	N. Westminster	WHL	53	17	29	1	2791	225	0	4.84	....	....	....	....	....	....	....
1986-87	**Boston**	**NHL**	**41**	**16**	**20**	**2**	**2234**	**124**	**3**	**3.33**	**2**	**0**	**2**	**123**	**8**	**0**	**3.90**
	Moncton	AHL	3	3	0	0	180	6	0	2.00	....	....	....	....	....	....	....
1987-88	Maine	AHL	51	27	16	6	2856	165	1	3.47	....	....	....	....	....	....	....
	Edmonton	**NHL**	**6**	**3**	**0**	**2**	**325**	**16**	**0**	**2.95**	....	....	....	....	....	....	....
1988-89	**Edmonton**	**NHL**	**29**	**15**	**8**	**2**	**1509**	**88**	**1**	**3.50**	....	....	....	....	....	....	....
1989-90a	**Edmonton**	**NHL**	**56**	**24**	**16**	**9**	**3107**	**165**	**1**	**3.19**	***22**	***16**	**6**	***1401**	**59**	**1**	**2.53**
1990-91	**Edmonton**	**NHL**	**60**	**27**	**27**	**3**	**3415**	**182**	**0**	**3.20**	**3**	**1**	**2**	**135**	**8**	**0**	**3.56**
1991-92	**Edmonton**	**NHL**	**67**	**27**	**26**	**10**	**3822**	**228**	**1**	**3.58**	**16**	**8**	**8**	**909**	**51**	***2**	**3.37**
1992-93	**Edmonton**	**NHL**	**67**	**17**	**38**	**6**	**3753**	**240**	**1**	**3.84**	....	....	....	....	....	....	....
1993-94	**Edmonton**	**NHL**	**71**	**22**	**34**	**11**	**4070**	**236**	**1**	**3.48**	....	....	....	....	....	....	....
1994-95	**Edmonton**	**NHL**	**40**	**15**	**20**	**3**	**2203**	**133**	**2**	**3.62**	....	....	....	....	....	....	....
	NHL Totals		**441**	**169**	**190**	**48**	**24678**	**1422**	**10**	**3.46**	**45**	**25**	**20**	**2688**	**133**	**3**	**2.97**

a Won Conn Smythe Trophy (1990)

Played in NHL All-Star Game (1991)

Traded to **Edmonton** by **Boston** with Geoff Courtnall and future considerations for Andy Moog, March 8, 1988.

REDDICK, ELDON (POKEY)

Goaltender. Catches left. 5'8", 170 lbs. Born, Halifax, N.S., October 6, 1964.

			Regular Season								Playoffs						
Season	Club	Lea	GP	W	L	T	Mins	GA	SO	Avg	GP	W	L	Mins	GA	SO	Avg
1982-83	Nanaimo	WHL	66	19	38	1	3549	383	0	6.46	....	....	....	....	....	....	....
1983-84	N. Westminster	WHL	50	24	22	2	2930	215	0	4.40	9	4	5	542	53	0	5.87
1984-85	Brandon	WHL	47	14	30	1	2585	243	0	5.64	....	....	....	....	....	....	....
1985-86a	Fort Wayne	IHL	29	15	11	0	1674	86	*3	3.00	....	....	....	....	....	....	....
1986-87	**Winnipeg**	**NHL**	**48**	**21**	**21**	**4**	**2762**	**149**	**0**	**3.24**	**3**	**0**	**2**	**166**	**10**	**0**	**3.61**
1987-88	**Winnipeg**	**NHL**	**28**	**9**	**13**	**3**	**1487**	**102**	**0**	**4.12**	....	....	....	....	....	....	....
	Moncton	AHL	9	2	6	1	545	26	0	2.86	....	....	....	....	....	....	....
1988-89	**Winnipeg**	**NHL**	**41**	**11**	**17**	**7**	**2109**	**144**	**0**	**4.10**	....	....	....	....	....	....	....
1989-90	**Edmonton**	**NHL**	**11**	**5**	**4**	**2**	**604**	**31**	**0**	**3.08**	**1**	**0**	**0**	**2**	**0**	**0**	**0.00**
	Cape Breton	AHL	15	9	4	1	821	54	0	3.95	....	....	....	....	....	....	....
	Phoenix	IHL	3	2	1	0	185	7	0	2.27	....	....	....	....	....	....	....
1990-91	**Edmonton**	**NHL**	**2**	**0**	**2**	**0**	**120**	**9**	**0**	**4.50**	....	....	....	....	....	....	....
	Cape Breton	AHL	31	19	10	0	1673	97	2	3.48	2	0	2	124	10	0	4.84
1991-92	Cape Breton	AHL	16	5	3	3	765	45	0	3.53	....	....	....	....	....	....	....
	Fort Wayne	IHL	14	6	5	2	787	40	1	3.05	7	3	4	369	18	0	2.93
1992-93b	Fort Wayne	IHL	54	33	16	4	3043	156	3	3.08	*12	*12	0	723	18	0	*1.49
1993-94	**Florida**	**NHL**	**2**	**0**	**1**	**0**	**80**	**8**	**0**	**6.00**	....	....	....	....	....	....	....
	Cincinnati	IHL	54	31	12	6	2894	147	*2	3.05	10	6	2	498	21	*1	2.53
1994-95	Las Vegas	IHL	40	23	13	1	2075	104	*3	3.01	10	4	6	592	31	0	3.14
	NHL Totals		**132**	**46**	**58**	**16**	**7162**	**443**	**0**	**3.71**	**4**	**0**	**2**	**168**	**10**	**0**	**3.57**

a Shared James Norris Memorial Trophy (fewest goals against - IHL) with Rick St. Croix (1986)
b Won "Bud" Poile Trophy (Playoff MVP - IHL) (1993)

Signed as a free agent by **Winnipeg**, September 27, 1985. Traded to **Edmonton** by **Winnipeg** for future considerations, September 28, 1989. Signed as a free agent by **Florida**, July 12, 1993.

REESE, JEFF HFD.

Goaltender. Catches left. 5'9", 175 lbs. Born, Brantford, Ont., March 24, 1966.
(Toronto's 3rd choice, 67th overall, in 1984 Entry Draft).

			Regular Season								Playoffs						
Season	Club	Lea	GP	W	L	T	Mins	GA	SO	Avg	GP	W	L	Mins	GA	SO	Avg
1983-84	London	OHL	43	18	19	0	2308	173	0	4.50	6	3	3	327	27	0	4.95
1984-85	London	OHL	50	31	15	1	2878	186	1	3.88	8	5	2	440	20	1	2.73
1985-86	London	OHL	57	25	26	3	3281	215	0	3.93	5	0	4	299	25	0	5.02
1986-87	Newmarket	AHL	50	11	29	0	2822	193	1	4.10	....	....	....	....	....	....	....
1987-88	**Toronto**	**NHL**	**5**	**1**	**2**	**1**	**249**	**17**	**0**	**4.10**	....	....	....	....	....	....	....
	Newmarket	AHL	28	10	14	3	1587	103	0	3.89	....	....	....	....	....	....	....
1988-89	**Toronto**	**NHL**	**10**	**2**	**6**	**1**	**486**	**40**	**0**	**4.94**	....	....	....	....	....	....	....
	Newmarket	AHL	37	17	14	3	2072	132	0	3.82	....	....	....	....	....	....	....
1989-90	**Toronto**	**NHL**	**21**	**9**	**6**	**3**	**1101**	**81**	**0**	**4.41**	**2**	**1**	**1**	**108**	**6**	**0**	**3.33**
	Newmarket	AHL	7	3	2	2	431	29	0	4.04	....	....	....	....	....	....	....
1990-91	**Toronto**	**NHL**	**30**	**6**	**13**	**3**	**1430**	**92**	**1**	**3.86**	....	....	....	....	....	....	....
	Newmarket	AHL	3	2	1	0	180	7	0	2.33	....	....	....	....	....	....	....
1991-92	**Toronto**	**NHL**	**8**	**1**	**5**	**1**	**413**	**20**	**1**	**2.91**	....	....	....	....	....	....	....
	Calgary	**NHL**	**12**	**3**	**2**	**2**	**587**	**37**	**0**	**3.78**	....	....	....	....	....	....	....
1992-93	**Calgary**	**NHL**	**26**	**14**	**4**	**1**	**1311**	**70**	**1**	**3.20**	**4**	**1**	**3**	**209**	**17**	**0**	**4.88**
1993-94	**Calgary**	**NHL**	**1**	**0**	**0**	**0**	**13**	**1**	**0**	**4.62**	....	....	....	....	....	....	....
	Hartford	**NHL**	**19**	**5**	**9**	**3**	**1086**	**56**	**1**	**3.09**	....	....	....	....	....	....	....
1994-95	**Hartford**	**NHL**	**11**	**2**	**5**	**1**	**477**	**26**	**0**	**3.27**	....	....	....	....	....	....	....
	NHL Totals		**143**	**43**	**52**	**16**	**7153**	**440**	**4**	**3.69**	**6**	**2**	**4**	**317**	**23**	**0**	**4.35**

Traded to **Calgary** with Craig Berube, Alexander Godynyuk, Gary Leeman and Michel Petit for Doug Gilmour, Jamie Macoun, Ric Nattress, Rick Wamsley and Kent Manderville, January 2, 1992. Traded to **Hartford** by **Calgary** for Dan Keczmer, November 19, 1993.

REGAN, BRIAN HFD.

Goaltender. Catches left. 6', 170 lbs. Born, New Haven, CT, September 23, 1975.
(Hartford's 7th choice, 239th overall, in 1994 Entry Draft).

			Regular Season								Playoffs						
Season	Club	Lea	GP	W	L	T	Mins	GA	SO	Avg	GP	W	L	Mins	GA	SO	Avg
1993-94	Westminster	HS	16	....	....	....	....	....	....	2.90	....	....	....	....	....	....	....
1994-95	U. Mass.-Amherst	H.E.	22	3	14	2	1139	92	0	4.85	....	....	....	....	....	....	....

RHODES, DAMIAN TOR.

Goaltender. Catches left. 6', 190 lbs. Born, St. Paul, MN, May 28, 1969.
(Toronto's 6th choice, 112th overall, in 1987 Entry Draft).

			Regular Season								Playoffs						
Season	Club	Lea	GP	W	L	T	Mins	GA	SO	Avg	GP	W	L	Mins	GA	SO	Avg
1987-88	Michigan Tech	WCHA	29	16	10	1	1625	114	0	4.20	....	....	....	....	....	....	....
1988-89	Michigan Tech	WCHA	37	15	22	0	2216	163	0	4.41	....	....	....	....	....	....	....
1989-90	Michigan Tech	WCHA	25	6	17	0	1358	119	0	6.26	....	....	....	....	....	....	....
1990-91	**Toronto**	**NHL**	**1**	**1**	**0**	**0**	**60**	**1**	**0**	**1.00**	....	....	....	....	....	....	....
	Newmarket	AHL	38	8	24	3	2154	144	1	4.01	....	....	....	....	....	....	....
1991-92	St. John's	AHL	43	20	16	5	2454	148	0	3.62	6	4	1	331	16	0	2.90
1992-93	St. John's	AHL	*52	27	16	8	*3074	184	1	3.59	9	4	5	538	37	0	4.13
1993-94	**Toronto**	**NHL**	**22**	**9**	**7**	**3**	**1213**	**53**	**0**	**2.62**	**1**	**0**	**0**	**1**	**0**	**0**	**0.00**
1994-95	**Toronto**	**NHL**	**13**	**6**	**6**	**1**	**760**	**34**	**0**	**2.68**	....	....	....	....	....	....	....
	NHL Totals		**36**	**16**	**13**	**4**	**2033**	**88**	**0**	**2.60**	**1**	**0**	**0**	**1**	**0**	**0**	**0.00**

Note: Played 10 seconds in playoff game vs. San Jose, May 6, 1994.

RICHTER, MIKE (RIHK-tuhr) NYR

Goaltender. Catches left. 5'11", 185 lbs. Born, Abington, PA, September 22, 1966.
(NY Rangers' 2nd choice, 28th overall, in 1985 Entry Draft).

			Regular Season								Playoffs						
Season	Club	Lea	GP	W	L	T	Mins	GA	SO	Avg	GP	W	L	Mins	GA	SO	Avg
1985-86	U. Wisconsin	WCHA	24	14	9	0	1394	92	1	3.96	....	....	....	....	....	....	....
1986-87a	U. Wisconsin	WCHA	36	19	16	1	2136	126	0	3.54	....	....	....	....	....	....	....
1987-88	Colorado	IHL	22	16	5	0	1298	68	1	3.14	10	5	3	536	35	0	3.92
	U.S. National	....	29	17	7	2	1559	86	0	3.31	....	....	....	....	....	....	....
	U.S. Olympic	....	4	2	2	0	230	15	0	3.91	....	....	....	....	....	....	....
1988-89	Denver	IHL	*57	23	26	0	3031	217	1	4.30	4	0	4	210	21	0	6.00
	NY Rangers	**NHL**	....	....	....	....	....	....	....	....	**1**	**0**	**1**	**58**	**4**	**0**	**4.14**
1989-90	**NY Rangers**	**NHL**	**23**	**12**	**5**	**5**	**1320**	**66**	**0**	**3.00**	**6**	**3**	**2**	**330**	**19**	**0**	**3.45**
	Flint	IHL	13	7	4	2	782	49	0	3.76	....	....	....	....	....	....	....
1990-91	**NY Rangers**	**NHL**	**45**	**21**	**13**	**7**	**2596**	**135**	**0**	**3.12**	**6**	**2**	**4**	**313**	**14**	***1**	**2.68**
1991-92	**NY Rangers**	**NHL**	**41**	**23**	**12**	**2**	**2298**	**119**	**3**	**3.11**	**7**	**4**	**2**	**412**	**24**	**1**	**3.50**
1992-93	**NY Rangers**	**NHL**	**38**	**13**	**19**	**3**	**2105**	**134**	**1**	**3.82**	....	....	....	....	....	....	....
	Binghamton	AHL	5	4	0	1	305	6	0	1.18	....	....	....	....	....	....	....
1993-94	**NY Rangers**	**NHL**	**68**	***42**	**12**	**6**	**3710**	**159**	**5**	**2.57**	**23**	***16**	**7**	**1417**	**49**	***4**	**2.07**
1994-95	**NY Rangers**	**NHL**	**35**	**14**	**17**	**2**	**1993**	**97**	**2**	**2.92**	**7**	**2**	**5**	**384**	**23**	**0**	**3.59**
	NHL Totals		**250**	**125**	**78**	**25**	**14022**	**710**	**11**	**3.04**	**50**	**27**	**21**	**2914**	**133**	**6**	**2.74**

a WCHA Second All-Star Team (1987)

Played in NHL All-Star Game (1992, 1994)

RIENDEAU, VINCENT (ree-EHN-doh)

Goaltender. Catches left. 5'10", 185 lbs. Born, St. Hyacinthe, Que., April 20, 1966.

			Regular Season								Playoffs						
Season	Club	Lea	GP	W	L	T	Mins	GA	SO	Avg	GP	W	L	Mins	GA	SO	Avg
1985-86a	Drummondville	QMJHL	57	33	20	3	3336	215	2	3.87	23	10	13	1271	106	1	5.00
1986-87b	Sherbrooke	AHL	41	25	14	0	2363	114	2	2.89	13	8	5	742	47	0	3.80
1987-88	**Montreal**	**NHL**	**1**	**0**	**0**	**0**	**36**	**5**	**0**	**8.33**	....	....	....	....	....	....	....
cd	Sherbrooke	AHL	44	27	13	3	2521	112	*4	*2.67	2	0	2	127	7	0	3.31
1988-89	**St. Louis**	**NHL**	**32**	**11**	**15**	**5**	**1842**	**108**	**0**	**3.52**	....	....	....	....	....	....	....
1989-90	**St. Louis**	**NHL**	**43**	**17**	**19**	**5**	**2551**	**149**	**1**	**3.50**	**8**	**3**	**4**	**397**	**24**	**0**	**3.63**
1990-91	**St. Louis**	**NHL**	**44**	**29**	**9**	**6**	**2671**	**134**	**3**	**3.01**	**13**	**6**	**7**	**687**	**35**	***1**	**3.06**
1991-92	**St. Louis**	**NHL**	**3**	**1**	**2**	**0**	**157**	**11**	**0**	**4.20**	....	....	....	....	....	....	....
	Detroit	**NHL**	**2**	**2**	**0**	**0**	**87**	**2**	**0**	**1.38**	**2**	**1**	**0**	**73**	**4**	**0**	**3.29**
	Adirondack	AHL	3	2	1	0	179	8	0	2.68	....	....	....	....	....	....	....
1992-93	**Detroit**	**NHL**	**22**	**13**	**4**	**2**	**1193**	**64**	**0**	**3.22**	....	....	....	....	....	....	....
1993-94	**Detroit**	**NHL**	**8**	**2**	**4**	**0**	**345**	**23**	**0**	**4.00**	....	....	....	....	....	....	....
	Adirondack	AHL	10	6	3	0	582	30	0	3.09	....	....	....	....	....	....	....
	Boston	**NHL**	**18**	**7**	**6**	**1**	**976**	**50**	**1**	**3.07**	**2**	**1**	**1**	**120**	**8**	**0**	**4.00**
1994-95	**Boston**	**NHL**	**11**	**3**	**6**	**1**	**565**	**27**	**0**	**2.87**	....	....	....	....	....	....	....
	Providence	AHL	....	....	....	....	....	....	....	....	1	1	0	60	3	0	3.00
	NHL Totals		**184**	**85**	**65**	**20**	**10423**	**573**	**5**	**3.30**	**25**	**11**	**12**	**1277**	**71**	**1**	**3.34**

a QMJHL Second All-Star Team (1986)
b Won Harry "Hap" Holmes Memorial Trophy (fewest goals-against - AHL) (1987)
c Shared Harry "Hap" Holmes Memorial Trophy (fewest goals-against - AHL) with Jocelyn Perreault (1988)
d AHL Second All-Star Team (1988)

Signed as a free agent by **Montreal**, October 9, 1985. Traded to **St. Louis** by **Montreal** with Sergio Momesso for Jocelyn Lemieux, Darrell May and St. Louis' second round choice (Patrice Brisebois) in 1989 Entry Draft, August 9, 1988. Traded to **Detroit** by **St. Louis** for Rick Zombo, October 18, 1991. Traded to **Boston** by **Detroit** for Boston's fifth round choice (Chad Wilchynski) in 1995 Entry Draft, January 17, 1994.

ROBINS, TREVOR

Goaltender. Catches left. 5'11", 190 lbs. Born, Brandon, Man., May 31, 1972.

			Regular Season								Playoffs						
Season	Club	Lea	GP	W	L	T	Mins	GA	SO	Avg	GP	W	L	Mins	GA	SO	Avg
1989-90	Saskatoon	WHL	51	21	21	1	2616	203	1	4.66	10	5	4	587	53	0	5.42
1990-91	Saskatoon	WHL	49	16	24	2	2560	200	2	4.69	....	....	....	....	....	....	....
1991-92a	Saskatoon	WHL	50	24	23	2	2794	163	0	3.50	9	5	3	473	32	0	4.06
1992-93a	Brandon	WHL	59	36	17	4	3470	183	2	3.16	4	1	3	258	11	0	2.56
1993-94	Kansas City	IHL	4	1	2	0	199	21	0	6.32	....	....	....	....	....	....	....
	Fort Worth	CHL	9	2	6	0	452	42	0	5.58	....	....	....	....	....	....	....
1994-95	Kansas City	IHL	39	15	20	1	2229	144	1	3.87	....	....	....	....	....	....	....
	Milwaukee	IHL	1	1	0	0	60	1	0	1.00	1	0	0	20	3	0	9.00

a WHL East First All-Star Team (1992, 1993)

Signed as a free agent by **San Jose**, December 5, 1992.

ROCHE, SCOTT — ST.L.

Goaltender. Catches left. 6'4", 220 lbs. Born, Lindsay, Ont., March 19, 1977.
(St. Louis' 2nd choice, 75th overall, in 1995 Entry Draft).

			Regular Season								Playoffs						
Season	Club	Lea	GP	W	L	T	Mins	GA	SO	Avg	GP	W	L	Mins	GA	SO	Avg
1993-94	North Bay	OHL	32	15	5	4	1587	93	0	3.52	5	2	1	191	10	0	*3.14
1994-95	North Bay	OHL	47	24	17	2	2599	167	2	3.86	6	2	4	348	30	0	5.17

ROGLES, CHRIS

Goaltender. Catches left. 5'11", 175 lbs. Born, St. Louis, MO, January 22, 1969.

			Regular Season								Playoffs						
Season	Club	Lea	GP	W	L	T	Mins	GA	SO	Avg	GP	W	L	Mins	GA	SO	Avg
1989-90	Clarkson	ECAC	7	1	0	0	142	7	0	2.97	....	....	....	....	....	....	....
1990-91a	Clarkson	ECAC	28	17	6	0	1359	76	....	3.35	....	....	....	....	....	....	....
1991-92	Clarkson	ECAC	18	11	3	0	974	49	0	3.02	....	....	....	....	....	....	....
1992-93	Clarkson	ECAC	27	16	4	4	1486	60	*3	2.42	....	....	....	....	....	....	....
1993-94	Indianapolis	IHL	44	14	20	6	2422	147	*2	3.64	....	....	....	....	....	....	....
1994-95	Indianapolis	IHL	43	14	22	2	2269	140	0	3.70	....	....	....	....	....	....	....

a ECAC Second All-Star Team (1991)

Signed as a free agent by **Chicago**, June 21, 1993.

ROLOSON, DWAYNE — CGY.

Goaltenter. Catches left. 6'1", 180 lbs. Born, Simcoe, Ont., October 12, 1969.

			Regular Season								Playoffs						
Season	Club	Lea	GP	W	L	T	Mins	GA	SO	Avg	GP	W	L	Mins	GA	SO	Avg
1990-91	Lowell	H.E.	15	5	9	0	823	63	0	4.59	....	....	....	....	....	....	....
1991-92	Lowell	H.E.	12	3	8	0	660	52	0	4.73	....	....	....	....	....	....	....
1992-93	Lowell	H.E.	*39	20	17	2	*2342	150	0	3.84	....	....	....	....	....	....	....
1993-94ab	Lowell	H.E.	*40	*23	10	7	*2305	106	0	2.76	....	....	....	....	....	....	....
1994-95	Saint John	AHL	46	16	21	8	2734	156	1	3.42	5	1	4	298	13	0	2.61

a Hockey East First All-Star Team (1994)
b NCAA East First All-Ameircan Team (1994)

Signed as a free agent by **Calgary**, July 4, 1994.

RONNQVIST, PETTER — OTT.

Goaltender. Catches left. 5'10", 154 lbs. Born, Stockholm, Sweden, February 7, 1973.
(Ottawa's 12th choice, 264th overall, in 1992 Entry Draft).

			Regular Season								Playoffs						
Season	Club	Lea	GP	W	L	T	Mins	GA	SO	Avg	GP	W	L	Mins	GA	SO	Avg
1992-93	Djurgarden	Swe.	7	....	....	....	380	20	0	3.15	1	....	....	60	5	0	5.00
1993-94	Djurgarden	Swe.	12	....	....	....	680	39	0	3.21	....	....	....	....	....	....	....
1994-95	MoDo	Swe.	28	....	....	....	1600	94	1	3.52	....	....	....	....	....	....	....

ROUSSEL, DOMINIC (roo-SEHL) — PHI.

Goaltender. Catches left. 6'1", 191 lbs. Born, Hull, Que., February 22, 1970.
(Philadelphia's 4th choice, 63rd overall, in 1988 Entry Draft).

			Regular Season								Playoffs						
Season	Club	Lea	GP	W	L	T	Mins	GA	SO	Avg	GP	W	L	Mins	GA	SO	Avg
1987-88	Trois-Rivières	QMJHL	51	18	25	4	2905	251	0	5.18	....	....	....	....	....	....	....
1988-89	Shawinigan	QMJHL	46	24	15	2	2555	171	0	4.02	10	6	4	638	36	0	3.39
1989-90	Shawinigan	QMJHL	37	20	14	1	1985	133	0	4.02	2	1	1	120	12	0	6.00
1990-91	Hershey	AHL	45	20	14	7	2507	151	1	3.61	7	3	4	366	21	0	3.44
1991-92	**Philadelphia**	**NHL**	**17**	**7**	**8**	**2**	**922**	**40**	**1**	**2.60**	....	....	....	....	....	....	....
	Hershey	AHL	35	15	11	6	2040	121	1	3.56	....	....	....	....	....	....	....
1992-93	**Philadelphia**	**NHL**	**34**	**13**	**11**	**5**	**1769**	**111**	**1**	**3.76**	....	....	....	....	....	....	....
	Hershey	AHL	6	0	3	3	372	23	0	3.71	....	....	....	....	....	....	....
1993-94	**Philadelphia**	**NHL**	**60**	**29**	**20**	**5**	**3285**	**183**	**1**	**3.34**	....	....	....	....	....	....	....
1994-95	**Philadelphia**	**NHL**	**19**	**11**	**7**	**0**	**1075**	**42**	**1**	**2.34**	**1**	**0**	**0**	**23**	**0**	**0**	**0.00**
	Hershey	AHL	1	0	1	0	59	5	0	5.07	....	....	....	....	....	....	....
	NHL Totals		**130**	**60**	**46**	**12**	**7051**	**376**	**4**	**3.20**	**1**	**0**	**0**	**23**	**0**	**0**	**0.00**

ROY, PATRICK (WAH) — MTL.

Goaltender. Catches left. 6', 192 lbs. Born, Quebec City, Que., October 5, 1965.
(Montreal's 4th choice, 51st overall, in 1984 Entry Draft).

			Regular Season								Playoffs						
Season	Club	Lea	GP	W	L	T	Mins	GA	SO	Avg	GP	W	L	Mins	GA	SO	Avg
1982-83	Granby	QMJHL	54	13	35	1	2808	293	0	6.26	....	....	....	....	....	....	....
1983-84	Granby	QMJHL	61	29	29	1	3585	265	0	4.44	4	0	4	244	22	0	5.41
1984-85	**Montreal**	**NHL**	**1**	**1**	**0**	**0**	**20**	**0**	**0**	**0.00**	....	....	....	....	....	....	....
	Granby	QMJHL	44	16	25	1	2463	228	0	5.55	....	....	....	....	....	....	....
	Sherbrooke	AHL	1	1	0	0	60	4	0	4.00	13	10	3	*769	37	0	*2.89
1985-86ab	**Montreal**	**NHL**	**47**	**23**	**18**	**3**	**2651**	**148**	**1**	**3.35**	**20**	***15**	**5**	**1218**	**39**	***1**	**1.92**
1986-87c	**Montreal**	**NHL**	**46**	**22**	**16**	**6**	**2686**	**131**	**1**	**2.93**	**6**	**4**	**2**	**330**	**22**	**0**	**4.00**
1987-88cd	**Montreal**	**NHL**	**45**	**23**	**12**	**9**	**2586**	**125**	**3**	**2.90**	**8**	**3**	**4**	**430**	**24**	**0**	**3.35**
1988-89 cefg	**Montreal**	**NHL**	**48**	**33**	**5**	**6**	**2744**	**113**	**4**	***2.47**	**19**	**13**	**6**	**1206**	**42**	**2**	***2.09**
1989-90efg	**Montreal**	**NHL**	**54**	***31**	**16**	**5**	**3173**	**134**	**3**	**2.53**	**11**	**5**	**6**	**641**	**26**	**1**	**2.43**
1990-91d	**Montreal**	**NHL**	**48**	**25**	**15**	**6**	**2835**	**128**	**1**	**2.71**	**13**	**7**	**5**	**785**	**40**	**0**	**3.06**
1991-92efh	**Montreal**	**NHL**	**67**	**36**	**22**	**8**	**3935**	**155**	***5**	***2.36**	**11**	**4**	**7**	**686**	**30**	**1**	**2.62**
1992-93a	**Montreal**	**NHL**	**62**	**31**	**25**	**5**	**3595**	**192**	**2**	**3.20**	**20**	***16**	**4**	**1293**	**46**	**0**	***2.13**
1993-94	**Montreal**	**NHL**	**68**	**35**	**17**	**11**	**3867**	**161**	***7**	**2.50**	**6**	**3**	**3**	**375**	**16**	**0**	**2.56**
1994-95	**Montreal**	**NHL**	**43**	**17**	**20**	**6**	**2566**	**127**	**1**	**2.97**	....	....	....	....	....	....	....
	NHL Totals		**529**	**277**	**166**	**65**	**30658**	**1414**	**28**	**2.77**	**114**	**70**	**42**	**6964**	**285**	**5**	**2.46**

a Won Conn Smythe Trophy (1986, 1993)
b NHL All-Rookie Team (1986)
c Shared William Jennings Trophy with Brian Hayward (1987, 1988, 1989)
d NHL Second All-Star Team (1988, 1991)
e Won Vezina Trophy (1989, 1990, 1992)
f NHL First All-Star Team (1989, 1990, 1992)
g Won Trico Goaltending Award (1989, 1990)
h Won William M. Jennings Award (1992)

Played in NHL All-Star Game (1988, 1990-94)

RYABCHIKOV, EVGENY (RYAB-chih-kohv) — BOS.

Goaltender. Catches left. 5'11", 167 lbs. Born, Yaroslavl, Soviet Union, January 16, 1974.
(Boston's 1st choice, 21st overall, in 1994 Entry Draft).

			Regular Season								Playoffs						
Season	Club	Lea	GP	W	L	T	Mins	GA	SO	Avg	GP	W	L	Mins	GA	SO	Avg
1993-94	Molot Perm	CIS	28	....	....	....	1572	96	....	3.66	....	....	....	....	....	....	....
1994-95	Providence	AHL	14	6	3	1	721	42	0	3.49	....	....	....	....	....	....	....
	Magnitogorsk	CIS	1	....	....	....	60	1	0	1.00	....	....	....	....	....	....	....

RYDER, DAN

Goaltender. Catches left. 6'1", 190 lbs. Born, Kitchener, Ont., October 24, 1972.
(San Jose's 5th choice, 89th overall, in 1991 Entry Draft).

			Regular Season								Playoffs						
Season	Club	Lea	GP	W	L	T	Mins	GA	SO	Avg	GP	W	L	Mins	GA	SO	Avg
1990-91	Hamilton	OHL	1	0	0	0	40	1	0	1.50	....	....	....	....	....	....	....
	Sudbury	OHL	37	18	9	4	2089	126	....	3.62	2	0	0	26	1	0	2.31
1991-92	Sudbury	OHL	23	9	11	1	1157	91	0	4.72	....	....	....	....	....	....	....
	Ottawa	OHL	24	16	6	0	1380	55	3	*2.39	11	5	6	625	38	0	3.64
1992-93	Johnstown	ECHL	4	1	1	1	214	15	0	4.21	....	....	....	....	....	....	....
	Columbus	ECHL	1	0	1	0	60	6	0	6.00	....	....	....	....	....	....	....
	Kansas City	IHL	10	3	3	2	514	35	0	4.09	....	....	....	....	....	....	....
1993-94	Kansas City	IHL	3	1	1	0	139	11	0	4.73	....	....	....	....	....	....	....
	Roanoke	ECHL	42	22	13	0	1946	129	0	3.98	....	....	....	....	....	....	....
1994-95	Roanoke	ECHL	21	7	6	2	1008	66	1	3.93	1	0	0	20	1	0	3.00
	Kansas City	IHL	3	1	2	0	140	11	0	4.71	....	....	....	....	....	....	....

SAAL, JASON — TOR.

Goaltender. Catches left. 5'11", 175 lbs. Born, Sterling Heights, MI, February 1, 1975.
(Los Angeles' 5th choice, 117th overall, in 1993 Entry Draft).

			Regular Season								Playoffs						
Season	Club	Lea	GP	W	L	T	Mins	GA	SO	Avg	GP	W	L	Mins	GA	SO	Avg
1992-93	Detroit	OHL	23	11	8	1	1289	85	0	3.96	3	0	0	42	2	0	2.86
1993-94	Detroit	OHL	45	28	11	3	2551	143	0	3.36	7	5	0	346	23	0	3.99
1994-95ab	Detroit	OHL	51	32	13	3	2887	153	1	3.18	*18	*13	4	*1083	52	*3	*2.88

a Memorial Cup All-Star Team (1995)
b Won Hap Emms Memorial Trophy (Memorial Cup Tournament Top Goaltender) (1995)

Signed as a free agent by **Toronto**, August 3, 1995.

SALO, TOMMY (SAH-loh) — NYI

Goaltender. Catches left. 5'11", 161 lbs. Born, Surahammar, Sweden, February 1, 1971.
(NY Islanders' 5th choice, 118th overall, in 1993 Entry Draft).

			Regular Season								Playoffs						
Season	Club	Lea	GP	W	L	T	Mins	GA	SO	Avg	GP	W	L	Mins	GA	SO	Avg
1990-91	Vasteras	Swe.	2	....	....	....	100	11	0	6.60	....	....	....	....	....	....	....
1991-92	Vasteras	Swe.							UNAVAILABLE								
1992-93	Vasteras	Swe.	24	....	....	....	1431	59	2	2.47	2	....	....	120	6	0	3.00
1993-94	Vasteras	Swe.	32	....	....	....	1896	106	0	3.35	....	....	....	....	....	....	....
1994-95 abcd	Denver	IHL	*65	*45	14	4	*3810	165	*3	*2.60	8	7	0	390	20	0	3.07
	NY Islanders	**NHL**	**6**	**1**	**5**	**0**	**358**	**18**	**0**	**3.02**	....	....	....	....	....	....	....
	NHL Totals		**6**	**1**	**5**	**0**	**358**	**18**	**0**	**3.02**	....	....	....	....	....	....	....

a IHL First All-Star Team (1995)
b Won James Norris Memorial Trophy (Fewest goals against - IHL) (1995)
c Won Garry F. Longman Memorial Trophy (Top Rookie - IHL) (1995)
d Won James Gatschene Memorial Trophy (MVP - IHL) (1995)

SALZMAN, WADE — ST.L.

Goaltender. Catches right. 6'3", 195 lbs. Born, Duluth, MN, May 30, 1974.
(St. Louis' 12th choice, 259th overall, in 1992 Entry Draft).

			Regular Season								Playoffs						
Season	Club	Lea	GP	W	L	T	Mins	GA	SO	Avg	GP	W	L	Mins	GA	SO	Avg
1992-93	Notre Dame	CCHA							DID NOT PLAY								
1993-94	Notre Dame	CCHA	10	2	3	1	452	30	0	3.98	....	....	....	....	....	....	....
1994-95	Notre Dame	CCHA	16	2	12	1	777	59	1	4.55	....	....	....	....	....	....	....

SARJEANT, GEOFF (SAHR-jehnt)

Goaltender. Catches left. 5'9", 180 lbs. Born, Newmarket, Ont., November 30, 1969.
(St. Louis' 1st choice, 17th overall, in 1990 Supplemental Draft).

			Regular Season								Playoffs						
Season	Club	Lea	GP	W	L	T	Mins	GA	SO	Avg	GP	W	L	Mins	GA	SO	Avg
1988-89	Michigan Tech	WCHA	6	0	3	2	329	22	0	4.01	....	....	....	....	....	....	....
1989-90	Michigan Tech	WCHA	19	4	13	0	1043	94	0	5.41	....	....	....	....	....	....	....
1990-91	Michigan Tech	WCHA	23	5	15	3	1540	97	0	3.78	....	....	....	....	....	....	....
1991-92	Michigan Tech	WCHA	23	7	13	0	1201	90	1	4.50	....	....	....	....	....	....	....
1992-93	Peoria	IHL	41	22	14	3	2356	130	0	3.31	3	0	3	179	13	0	4.36
1993-94a	Peoria	IHL	41	25	9	2	2275	93	*2	*2.45	4	2	2	211	13	0	3.69
1994-95	Peoria	IHL	55	32	12	8	3146	158	0	3.01	4	0	3	206	20	0	5.81
	St. Louis	**NHL**	**4**	**1**	**0**	**0**	**120**	**6**	**0**	**3.00**	....	....	....	....	....	....	....
	NHL Totals		**4**	**1**	**0**	**0**	**120**	**6**	**0**	**3.00**	....	....	....	....	....	....	....

a IHL First All-Star Team (1994)

SAVARY, NEIL — BOS.

Goaltender. Catches left. 6', 170 lbs. Born, Halifax, N.S., April 3, 1976.
(Boston's 8th choice, 255th overall, in 1994 Entry Draft).

			Regular Season								Playoffs						
Season	Club	Lea	GP	W	L	T	Mins	GA	SO	Avg	GP	W	L	Mins	GA	SO	Avg
1993-94	Hull	QMJHL	32	....	....	....	1708	118	2	4.15	6	0	2	158	14	0	5.32
1994-95	Hull	QMJHL	30	14	12	1	1525	118	0	4.64	1	0	0	20	1	0	3.00

SCHAFER, PAXTON — BOS.

Goaltender. Catches left. 5'9", 152 lbs. Born, Medicine Hat, Alta., February 26, 1976.
(Boston's 3rd choice, 47th overall, in 1995 Entry Draft).

			Regular Season								Playoffs						
Season	Club	Lea	GP	W	L	T	Mins	GA	SO	Avg	GP	W	L	Mins	GA	SO	Avg
1993-94	Medicine Hat	WHL	19	6	9	1	909	67	0	4.42	....	....	....	....	....	....	....
1994-95a	Medicine Hat	WHL	61	32	26	2	3519	185	0	3.15	5	1	4	339	18	0	3.19

a WHL East First All-Star Team (1995)

SCHWAB, COREY (SHWAHB) N.J.

Goaltender. Catches left. 6', 180 lbs. Born, North Battleford, Sask., November 4, 1970.
(New Jersey's 12th choice, 200th overall, in 1990 Entry Draft).

			Regular Season								Playoffs						
Season	Club	Lea	GP	W	L	T	Mins	GA	SO	Avg	GP	W	L	Mins	GA	SO	Avg
1988-89	Seattle	WHL	10	2	2	0	386	31	0	4.82	....	....	....	....	....	....	....
1989-90	Seattle	WHL	27	15	2	1	1150	69	1	3.60	3	0	0	49	2	0	2.45
1990-91	Seattle	WHL	*58	32	18	3	*3289	224	0	4.09	6	1	5	382	25	0	3.93
1991-92	Utica	AHL	24	9	12	1	1322	95	0	4.31	....	....	....	....	....	....	....
	Cincinnati	ECHL	8	6	0	1	450	31	0	4.13	9	6	3	540	29	0	3.22
1992-93	Utica	AHL	40	18	16	5	2387	169	*2	4.25	1	0	1	59	6	0	6.10
	Cincinnati	IHL	3	1	2	0	185	17	0	5.51	....	....	....	....	....	....	....
1993-94	Albany	AHL	51	27	21	3	3058	184	0	3.61	5	1	4	298	20	0	4.02
1994-95abc	Albany	AHL	45	25	10	9	2711	117	3	*2.59	7	6	1	425	19	0	2.68

a AHL Second All-Star Team (1995)
b Shared Harry "Hap" Holmes Memorial Trophy (fewest goals against - AHL) with Mike Dunham (1995)
c Shared Jack A. Butterfield Trophy (Playoff MVP - AHL) with Mike Dunham (1995)

SELIGER, MARK (ZEH-lih-gehr) WSH.

Goaltender. Catches left. 5'11", 165 lbs. Born, Rosenheim, Germany, May 1, 1974.
(Washington's 9th choice, 251st overall, in 1993 Entry Draft).

			Regular Season								Playoffs						
Season	Club	Lea	GP	W	L	T	Mins	GA	SO	Avg	GP	W	L	Mins	GA	SO	Avg
1992-93	Rosenheim	Ger.	42	....	....	....	1264	75	1	3.56	....	....	....	....	....	....	....
1993-94	Rosenheim	Ger.	27	....	....	....	....	....	....	....	....	....	....	....	....	....	....
1994-95	Rosenheim	Ger.	34	....	....	....	1859	....	3	....	7	....	....	428	31	....	4.34

SHEPARD, KEN — NYR

Goaltender. Catches left. 5'10", 192 lbs. Born, Toronto, Ont., January 20, 1974.
(NY Rangers' 10th choice, 216th overall, in 1993 Entry Draft).

			Regular Season								Playoffs						
Season	Club	Lea	GP	W	L	T	Mins	GA	SO	Avg	GP	W	L	Mins	GA	SO	Avg
1991-92	Oshawa	OHL	7	1	2	0	265	16	1	3.62	1	0	0	2	0	0	0.00
1992-93	Oshawa	OHL	31	12	7	4	1483	86	0	3.48	11	3	7	512	34	0	3.98
1993-94	Oshawa	OHL	45	20	15	5	2383	157	0	3.95	5	1	4	309	18	0	3.50
1994-95	Oshawa	OHL	42	24	11	3	2404	128	2	3.19	5	1	4	299	26	0	5.22

SHIELDS, STEVE — BUF.

Goaltender. Catches left. 6'3", 210 lbs. Born, Toronto, Ont., July 19, 1972.
(Buffalo's 5th choice, 101st overall, in 1991 Entry Draft).

			Regular Season								Playoffs						
Season	Club	Lea	GP	W	L	T	Mins	GA	SO	Avg	GP	W	L	Mins	GA	SO	Avg
1990-91	U. of Michigan	CCHA	37	26	6	3	1963	106	0	3.24	....	....	....	....	....	....	....
1991-92	U. of Michigan	CCHA	*37	*27	7	2	*2090	99	1	2.84	....	....	....	....	....	....	....
1992-93ab	U. of Michigan	CCHA	*39	*30	6	2	2027	75	2	*2.22	....	....	....	....	....	....	....
1993-94ab	U. of Michigan	CCHA	36	*28	6	1	1961	87	0	2.66	....	....	....	....	....	....	....
1994-95	Rochester	AHL	13	3	8	0	673	53	0	4.72	1	0	0	20	3	0	9.00
	S. Carolina	ECHL	21	11	5	2	1157	52	2	2.69	3	0	2	144	11	0	4.58

a CCHA First All-Star Team (1993, 1994)
b NCAA West Second All-American Team (1993, 1994)

SHTALENKOV, MIKHAIL (shtuh-LEHN-kahf, mihk-HIGHL) ANA.

Goaltender. Catches left. 6'2", 180 lbs. Born, Moscow, USSR, October 20, 1965.
(Anaheim's 5th choice, 108th overall, in 1993 Entry Draft).

			Regular Season								Playoffs						
Season	Club	Lea	GP	W	L	T	Mins	GA	SO	Avg	GP	W	L	Mins	GA	SO	Avg
1986-87a	Moscow D'amo	USSR	17	....	....	....	893	36	1	2.41	....	....	....	....	....	....	....
1987-88	Moscow D'amo	USSR	25	....	....	....	1302	72	1	3.31	....	....	....	....	....	....	....
1988-89	Moscow D'amo	USSR	4	....	....	....	80	3	0	2.25	....	....	....	....	....	....	....
1989-90	Moscow D'amo	USSR	6	....	....	....	20	1	0	3.00	....	....	....	....	....	....	....
1990-91	Moscow D'amo	USSR	31	....	....	....	1568	56	2	2.14	....	....	....	....	....	....	....
1991-92	Moscow D'amo	CIS	27	....	....	....	1268	45	1	2.12	....	....	....	....	....	....	....
1992-93b	Milwaukee	IHL	47	26	14	5	2669	135	2	3.03	3	1	2	209	11	0	3.16
1993-94	**Anaheim**	**NHL**	**10**	**3**	**4**	**1**	**543**	**24**	**0**	**2.65**	....	....	....	....	....	....	....
	San Diego	IHL	28	15	11	2	1616	93	0	3.45	....	....	....	....	....	....	....
1994-95	**Anaheim**	**NHL**	**18**	**4**	**7**	**1**	**810**	**49**	**0**	**3.63**	....	....	....	....	....	....	....
	NHL Totals		**28**	**7**	**11**	**2**	**1353**	**73**	**0**	**3.24**	....	....	....	....	....	....	....

a Soviet Rookie of the Year (1987)
b Won Garry F. Longman Memorial Trophy (Top Rookie - IHL) (1993)

SHULMISTRA, RICHARD — COL.

Goaltender. Catches right. 6'2", 186 lbs. Born, Sudbury, Ont., April 1, 1971.
(Quebec's 1st choice, 4th overall, in 1992 Supplemental Draft).

			Regular Season								Playoffs						
Season	Club	Lea	GP	W	L	T	Mins	GA	SO	Avg	GP	W	L	Mins	GA	SO	Avg
1990-91	Miami-Ohio	CCHA	20	2	12	2	920	80	0	5.21	....	....	....	....	....	....	....
1991-92	Miami-Ohio	CCHA	19	3	5	2	850	67	0	4.72	....	....	....	....	....	....	....
1992-93a	Miami-Ohio	CCHA	33	22	6	4	1949	88	1	2.71	....	....	....	....	....	....	....
1993-94	Miami-Ohio	CCHA	27	13	12	1	1521	74	0	2.92	....	....	....	....	....	....	....
1994-95	Cornwall	AHL	20	4	9	2	937	58	0	3.71	8	4	3	446	22	0	2.95

a CCHA Second All-Star Team (1993)

SIDORKIEWICZ, PETER (sih-DOHR-kuh-vihch) N.J.

Goaltender. Catches left. 5'9", 180 lbs. Born, Dabrowa Bialostocka, Pol., June 29, 1963.
(Washington's 5th choice, 91st overall, in 1981 Entry Draft).

			Regular Season								Playoffs						
Season	Club	Lea	GP	W	L	T	Mins	GA	SO	Avg	GP	W	L	Mins	GA	SO	Avg
1980-81	Oshawa	OHA	7	3	3	0	308	24	0	4.68	5	2	2	266	20	0	4.52
1981-82	Oshawa	OHL	29	14	11	1	1553	123	*2	4.75	1	0	0	13	1	0	4.62
1982-83	Oshawa	OHL	60	36	20	3	3536	213	0	3.61	17	15	1	1020	60	0	3.53
1983-84	Oshawa	OHL	52	28	21	1	2966	250	1	4.15	7	3	4	420	27	*1	3.86
1984-85	Binghamton	AHL	45	31	9	5	2691	137	3	3.05	8	4	4	481	31	0	3.87
	Fort Wayne	IHL	10	4	4	2	590	43	0	4.37	....	....	....	....	....	....	....
1985-86	Binghamton	AHL	49	21	22	3	2819	150	2	*3.19	4	1	3	235	12	0	3.06
1986-87a	Binghamton	AHL	57	23	16	0	3304	161	4	2.92	13	6	7	794	36	0	*2.72
1987-88	**Hartford**	**NHL**	**1**	**0**	**1**	**0**	**60**	**6**	**0**	**6.00**	....	....	....	....	....	....	....
	Binghamton	AHL	42	19	17	3	2345	144	0	3.68	3	0	2	147	8	0	3.27
1988-89b	**Hartford**	**NHL**	**44**	**22**	**18**	**4**	**2635**	**133**	**4**	**3.03**	**2**	**0**	**2**	**124**	**8**	**0**	**3.87**
1989-90	**Hartford**	**NHL**	**46**	**19**	**19**	**7**	**2703**	**161**	**1**	**3.57**	**7**	**3**	**4**	**429**	**23**	**0**	**3.22**
1990-91	**Hartford**	**NHL**	**52**	**21**	**22**	**7**	**2953**	**164**	**1**	**3.33**	**6**	**2**	**4**	**359**	**24**	**0**	**4.01**
1991-92	**Hartford**	**NHL**	**35**	**9**	**19**	**6**	**1995**	**111**	**2**	**3.34**	....	....	....	....	....	....	....
1992-93	**Ottawa**	**NHL**	**64**	**8**	**46**	**3**	**3388**	**250**	**0**	**4.43**	....	....	....	....	....	....	....
1993-94	**New Jersey**	**NHL**	**3**	**0**	**3**	**0**	**130**	**6**	**0**	**2.77**	....	....	....	....	....	....	....
	Albany	AHL	15	6	7	2	907	60	0	3.97	....	....	....	....	....	....	....
	Fort Wayne	IHL	11	6	3	0	591	27	*2	2.74	*18	10	8	*1054	59	*1	3.36
1994-95	Fort Wayne	IHL	16	8	6	1	941	58	1	3.70	3	1	2	144	12	0	5.00
	NHL Totals		**245**	**79**	**128**	**27**	**13864**	**831**	**8**	**3.60**	**15**	**5**	**10**	**912**	**55**	**0**	**3.62**

a AHL Second All-Star Team (1987)
b NHL All-Rookie Team (1989)

Played in NHL All-Star Game (1993)

Traded to **Hartford** by **Washington** with Dean Evason for David Jensen, March 12, 1985. Claimed by **Ottawa** from **Hartford** in Expansion Draft, June 18, 1992. Traded to **New Jersey** by **Ottawa** with future considerations (Mike Peluso, June 26, 1993) for Craig Billington, Troy Mallette and New Jersey's fourth round choice (Cosmo Dupaul) in 1993 Entry Draft, June 20, 1993.

SMANGS, HENRIK (SMOHNGS) WPG.

Goaltender. Catches left. 5'11", 174 lbs. Born, Leksand, Sweden, January 19, 1976.
(Winnipeg's 9th choice, 212th overall, in 1994 Entry Draft).

			Regular Season								Playoffs						
Season	Club	Lea	GP	W	L	T	Mins	GA	SO	Avg	GP	W	L	Mins	GA	SO	Avg
1994-95	Leksand	Swe. Jr.								UNAVAILABLE							

SNOW, GARTH — PHI.

Goaltender. Catches left. 6'3", 200 lbs. Born, Wrentham, MA, July 28, 1969.
(Quebec's 6th choice, 114th overall, in 1987 Entry Draft).

			Regular Season								Playoffs						
Season	Club	Lea	GP	W	L	T	Mins	GA	SO	Avg	GP	W	L	Mins	GA	SO	Avg
1988-89	U. of Maine	H.E.	5	2	2	0	241	14	1	3.49	....	....	....	....	....	....	....
1989-90										DID NOT PLAY							
1990-91	U. of Maine	H.E.	25	*18	4	0	1290	64	2	2.98	....	....	....	....	....	....	....
1991-92a	U. of Maine	H.E.	31	*25	4	2	1792	73	*2	*2.44	....	....	....	....	....	....	....
1992-93b	U. of Maine	H.E.	23	*21	0	1	1210	42	1	*2.08	....	....	....	....	....	....	....
1993-94	U.S. National	....	23	13	5	3	1324	71	1	3.22	....	....	....	....	....	....	....
	U.S. Olympic	....	5	....	....	....	299	17	0	3.41	....	....	....	....	....	....	....
	Quebec	**NHL**	**5**	**3**	**2**	**0**	**279**	**16**	**0**	**3.44**	....	....	....	....	....	....	....
	Cornwall	AHL	16	6	5	3	927	51	0	3.30	13	8	5	790	42	0	3.19
1994-95	Cornwall	AHL	*62	*32	20	7	*3558	162	3	2.73	8	4	3	402	14	*2	*2.09
	Quebec	**NHL**	**2**	**1**	**1**	**0**	**119**	**11**	**0**	**5.55**	**1**	**0**	**0**	**9**	**1**	**0**	**6.67**
	NHL Totals		**7**	**4**	**3**	**0**	**398**	**27**	**0**	**4.07**	**1**	**0**	**0**	**9**	**1**	**0**	**6.67**

a Hockey East Second All-Star Team (1992)
b NCAA Final Four All-Tournament Team (1993)

Traded to **Philadelphia** by **Colorado** for Philadelphia's third and sixth round choices in 1996 Entry Draft, July 12, 1995.

SODERSTROM, TOMMY (SAH-duhr-struhm) NYI

Goaltender. Catches left. 5'9", 165 lbs. Born, Stockholm, Sweden, July 17, 1969.
(Philadelphia's 14th choice, 214th overall, in 1990 Entry Draft).

			Regular Season								Playoffs						
Season	Club	Lea	GP	W	L	T	Mins	GA	SO	Avg	GP	W	L	Mins	GA	SO	Avg
1989-90	Djurgarden	Swe.	4	....	....	....	240	14	0	3.50	....	....	....	....	....	....	....
1990-91	Djurgarden	Swe.	39	....	....	....	2340	104	3	2.67	7	....	....	423	10	2	1.42
1991-92	Djurgarden	Swe.	39	15	8	11	2340	109	4	2.79	10	....	....	635	28	0	2.65
1992-93	**Philadelphia**	**NHL**	**44**	**20**	**17**	**6**	**2512**	**143**	**5**	**3.42**	....	....	....	....	....	....	....
	Hershey	AHL	7	4	1	0	373	15	0	2.41	....	....	....	....	....	....	....
1993-94	**Philadelphia**	**NHL**	**34**	**6**	**18**	**4**	**1736**	**116**	**2**	**4.01**	....	....	....	....	....	....	....
	Hershey	AHL	9	3	4	1	461	37	0	4.81	....	....	....	....	....	....	....
1994-95	**NY Islanders**	**NHL**	**26**	**8**	**12**	**3**	**1350**	**70**	**1**	**3.11**	....	....	....	....	....	....	....
	NHL Totals		**104**	**34**	**47**	**13**	**5598**	**329**	**8**	**3.53**	....	....	....	....	....	....	....

Traded to **NY Islanders** by **Philadelphia** for Ron Hextall and NY Islanders' sixth round choice (Dmitry Tertyshny) in 1995 Entry Draft, September 22, 1994.

SOUCY, CHRISTIAN (SOO-see) CHI.

Goaltender. Catches left. 5'11", 160 lbs. Born, Gatineau, Que., September 14, 1970.

			Regular Season								Playoffs						
Season	Club	Lea	GP	W	L	T	Mins	GA	SO	Avg	GP	W	L	Mins	GA	SO	Avg
1991-92	Vermont	ECAC	*30	15	11	3	*1783	81	0	2.83	....	....	....	....	....	....	....
1992-93a	Vermont	ECAC	29	11	15	3	1708	90	1	3.16	....	....	....	....	....	....	....
1993-94	**Chicago**	**NHL**	**1**	**0**	**0**	**0**	**3**	**0**	**0**	**0.00**	....	....	....	....	....	....	....
	Indianapolis	IHL	46	14	25	1	2302	159	1	4.14	....	....	....	....	....	....	....
1994-95	Indianapolis	IHL	42	15	17	5	2216	148	0	4.01	....	....	....	....	....	....	....
	NHL Totals		**1**	**0**	**0**	**0**	**3**	**0**	**0**	**0.00**	....	....	....	....	....	....	....

a ECAC Second All-Star Team (1993)

Signed as a free agent by **Chicago**, June 21, 1993.

STAUBER, ROBB (STAW-buhr) BUF.

Goaltender. Catches left. 5'11", 180 lbs. Born, Duluth, MN, November 25, 1967.
(Los Angeles' 5th choice, 107th overall, in 1986 Entry Draft).

			Regular Season								Playoffs						
Season	Club	Lea	GP	W	L	T	Mins	GA	SO	Avg	GP	W	L	Mins	GA	SO	Avg
1986-87	U. Minnesota	WCHA	20	13	5	0	1072	63	0	3.53	....	....	....	....	....	....	....
1987-88abc	U. Minnesota	WCHA	44	34	10	0	2621	119	5	2.72	....	....	....	....	....	....	....
1988-89d	U. Minnesota	WCHA	34	26	8	0	2024	82	0	2.43	....	....	....	....	....	....	....
1989-90	**Los Angeles**	**NHL**	**2**	**0**	**1**	**0**	**83**	**11**	**0**	**7.95**	....	....	....	....	....	....	....
	New Haven	AHL	14	6	6	2	851	43	0	3.03	5	2	3	302	24	0	4.77
1990-91	New Haven	AHL	33	13	16	4	1882	115	1	3.67	....	....	....	....	....	....	....
	Phoenix	IHL	4	1	2	0	160	11	0	4.13	....	....	....	....	....	....	....
1991-92	Phoenix	IHL	22	8	12	1	1242	80	0	3.86	....	....	....	....	....	....	....
1992-93	**Los Angeles**	**NHL**	**31**	**15**	**8**	**4**	**1735**	**111**	**0**	**3.84**	**4**	**3**	**1**	**240**	**16**	**0**	**4.00**
1993-94	**Los Angeles**	**NHL**	**22**	**4**	**11**	**5**	**1144**	**65**	**1**	**3.41**	....	....	....	....	....	....	....
	Phoenix	IHL	3	1	1	0	121	13	0	6.42	....	....	....	....	....	....	....
1994-95	**Los Angeles**	**NHL**	**1**	**0**	**0**	**0**	**16**	**2**	**0**	**7.50**	....	....	....	....	....	....	....
	Buffalo	**NHL**	**6**	**2**	**3**	**0**	**317**	**20**	**0**	**3.79**	....	....	....	....	....	....	....
	NHL Totals		**62**	**21**	**23**	**9**	**3295**	**209**	**1**	**3.81**	**4**	**3**	**1**	**240**	**16**	**0**	**4.00**

a Won Hobey Baker Memorial Award (Top U.S. Collegiate Player) (1988)
b NCAA West First All-American Team (1988)
c WCHA First All-Star Team (1988)
d WCHA Second All-Star Team (1989)

Traded to **Buffalo** by **Los Angeles** with Alexei Zhitnik, Charlie Huddy and Los Angeles' fifth round choice (Marian Menhart) in 1995 Entry Draft for Philippe Boucher, Denis Tsygurov and Grant Fuhr, February 14, 1995.

STORR, JAMIE (STOHR) L.A.

Goaltender. Catches left. 6'1", 192 lbs. Born, Brampton, Ont., December 28, 1975.
(Los Angeles' 1st choice, 7th overall, in 1994 Entry Draft).

			Regular Season								Playoffs						
Season	Club	Lea	GP	W	L	T	Mins	GA	SO	Avg	GP	W	L	Mins	GA	SO	Avg
1991-92	Owen Sound	OHL	34	11	16	1	1732	128	0	4.43	5	1	4	299	28	0	5.62
1992-93	Owen Sound	OHL	41	20	17	3	2362	180	0	4.57	8	4	4	454	35	0	4.63
1993-94a	Owen Sound	OHL	35	21	11	1	2004	120	1	3.59	9	4	5	547	44	0	4.83
1994-95	Owen Sound	OHL	17	5	9	2	977	64	0	3.93	....	....	....	....	....	....	....
	Los Angeles	**NHL**	**5**	**1**	**3**	**1**	**263**	**17**	**0**	**3.88**	....	....	....	....	....	....	....
	Windsor	OHL	4	3	1	0	241	8	1	1.99	10	6	3	520	34	1	3.92
	NHL Totals		**5**	**1**	**3**	**1**	**263**	**17**	**0**	**3.88**	....	....	....	....	....	....	....

a OHL First All-Star Team (1994)

SWANJORD, SCOTT New Jersey

Goaltender. Catches left. 6'4", 210 lbs. Born, Sioux Falls, SD, October 8, 1975.
(New Jersey's 11th choice, 259th overall, in 1994 Entry Draft).

			Regular Season								Playoffs						
Season	Club	Lea	GP	W	L	T	Mins	GA	SO	Avg	GP	W	L	Mins	GA	SO	Avg
1993-94	Waterloo	USHL	21	....	....	....	1145	62	0	3.25	....	....	....	....	....	....	....
1994-95	Sioux City	USHL	24	7	14	0	1206	70	0	3.48	....	....	....	....	....	....	....

TABARACCI, RICK (tab-uh-RA-chee) CGY.

Goaltender. Catches left. 6'1", 180 lbs. Born, Toronto, Ont., January 2, 1969.
(Pittsburgh's 2nd choice, 26th overall, in 1987 Entry Draft).

			Regular Season								Playoffs						
Season	Club	Lea	GP	W	L	T	Mins	GA	SO	Avg	GP	W	L	Mins	GA	SO	Avg
1986-87	Cornwall	OHL	59	23	32	3	3347	290	1	5.20	5	1	4	303	26	0	3.17
1987-88a	Cornwall	OHL	58	*33	18	6	3448	200	*3	3.48	11	5	6	642	37	0	3.46
	Muskegon	IHL	....	....	....	....	....	....	....	....	1	0	0	13	1	0	4.62
1988-89	**Pittsburgh**	**NHL**	**1**	**0**	**0**	**0**	**33**	**4**	**0**	**7.27**	....	....	....	....	....	....	....
b	Cornwall	OHL	50	24	20	5	2974	210	1	4.24	18	10	8	1080	65	*1	3.61
1989-90	Moncton	AHL	27	10	15	2	1580	107	2	4.06	....	....	....	....	....	....	....
	Fort Wayne	IHL	22	8	9	1	1064	73	0	4.12	3	1	2	159	19	0	7.17
1990-91	**Winnipeg**	**NHL**	**24**	**4**	**9**	**4**	**1093**	**71**	**1**	**3.90**	....	....	....	....	....	....	....
	Moncton	AHL	11	4	5	2	645	41	0	3.81	....	....	....	....	....	....	....
1991-92	**Winnipeg**	**NHL**	**18**	**6**	**7**	**3**	**966**	**52**	**0**	**3.23**	**7**	**3**	**4**	**387**	**26**	**0**	**4.03**
	Moncton	AHL	23	10	11	1	1313	80	0	3.66	....	....	....	....	....	....	....
1992-93	**Winnipeg**	**NHL**	**19**	**5**	**10**	**0**	**959**	**70**	**0**	**4.38**	....	....	....	....	....	....	....
	Moncton	AHL	5	2	1	2	290	18	0	3.72	....	....	....	....	....	....	....
	Washington	**NHL**	**6**	**3**	**2**	**0**	**343**	**10**	**2**	**1.75**	**4**	**1**	**3**	**304**	**14**	**0**	**2.76**
1993-94	**Washington**	**NHL**	**32**	**13**	**14**	**2**	**1770**	**91**	**2**	**3.08**	**2**	**0**	**2**	**111**	**6**	**0**	**3.24**
	Portland	AHL	3	3	0	0	176	8	0	2.72	....	....	....	....	....	....	....
1994-95	**Washington**	**NHL**	**8**	**1**	**3**	**2**	**394**	**16**	**0**	**2.44**	....	....	....	....	....	....	....
	Chicago	IHL	2	1	1	0	119	9	0	4.51	....	....	....	....	....	....	....
	Calgary	**NHL**	**5**	**2**	**0**	**1**	**202**	**5**	**0**	**1.49**	**1**	**0**	**0**	**19**	**0**	**0**	**0.00**
	NHL Totals		**113**	**34**	**45**	**12**	**5760**	**319**	**5**	**3.32**	**14**	**4**	**9**	**821**	**46**	**0**	**3.36**

a OHL First All-Star Team (1988)
b OHL Second All-Star Team (1989)

Traded to **Winnipeg** by **Pittsburgh** with Randy Cunneyworth and Dave McLlwain for Jim Kyte, Andrew McBain and Randy Gilhen, June 17, 1989. Traded to **Washington** by **Winnipeg** for Jim Hrivnak and Washington's second round choice (Alexei Budayev) in 1993 Entry Draft, March 22, 1993. Traded to **Calgary** by **Washington** for a conditional fifth round draft choice, April 7, 1995.

TANNER, JOHN ANA.

Goaltender. Catches left. 6'3", 182 lbs. Born, Cambridge, Ont., March 17, 1971.
(Quebec's 4th choice, 54th overall, in 1989 Entry Draft).

			Regular Season								Playoffs						
Season	Club	Lea	GP	W	L	T	Mins	GA	SO	Avg	GP	W	L	Mins	GA	SO	Avg
1987-88a	Peterborough	OHL	26	18	4	3	1532	88	0	3.45	2	1	0	98	3	0	1.84
1988-89a	Peterborough	OHL	34	22	10	0	1923	107	2	*3.34	8	4	3	369	23	0	3.74
1989-90	**Quebec**	**NHL**	**1**	**0**	**1**	**0**	**60**	**3**	**0**	**3.00**	....	....	....	....	....	....	....
	Peterborough	OHL	18	6	8	2	1037	70	0	4.05	....	....	....	....	....	....	....
	London	OHL	19	12	5	1	1097	53	1	2.90	6	2	4	341	24	0	4.22
1990-91	**Quebec**	**NHL**	**6**	**1**	**3**	**1**	**228**	**16**	**0**	**4.21**	....	....	....	....	....	....	....
	London	OHL	7	3	3	1	427	29	0	4.07	....	....	....	....	....	....	....
	Sudbury	OHL	19	10	8	0	1043	60	0	3.45	5	1	4	274	21	0	4.60
1991-92	**Quebec**	**NHL**	**14**	**1**	**7**	**4**	**796**	**46**	**1**	**3.47**	....	....	....	....	....	....	....
	Halifax	AHL	12	6	5	1	672	29	2	2.59	....	....	....	....	....	....	....
	New Haven	AHL	16	7	6	2	908	57	0	3.77	....	....	....	....	....	....	....
1992-93	Halifax	AHL	51	20	18	7	2852	199	0	4.19	....	....	....	....	....	....	....
1993-94	Cornwall	AHL	38	14	15	4	2035	123	1	3.63	....	....	....	....	....	....	....
	San Diego	IHL	13	5	3	2	629	37	0	3.53	3	0	1	118	5	0	2.53
1994-95	Greensboro	ECHL	6	0	4	1	342	27	0	4.73	....	....	....	....	....	....	....
	San Diego	IHL	8	1	3	1	344	28	0	4.87	....	....	....	....	....	....	....
	NHL Totals		**21**	**2**	**11**	**5**	**1084**	**65**	**1**	**3.60**	....	....	....	....	....	....	....

a Won Dave Pinkney Trophy (Top Team Goaltending, OHL) shared with Todd Bojcun (1988, 1989)

Traded to **Anaheim** by **Quebec** for Anaheim's fourth round choice (Tomi Kallio) in 1995 Entry Draft, February 20, 1994.

TERRERI, CHRIS (tuh-RAIR-ee) N.J.

Goaltender. Catches left. 5'8", 160 lbs. Born, Providence, RI, November 15, 1964.
(New Jersey's 3rd choice, 87th overall, in 1983 Entry Draft).

			Regular Season								Playoffs						
Season	Club	Lea	GP	W	L	T	Mins	GA	SO	Avg	GP	W	L	Mins	GA	SO	Avg
1982-83	Providence	ECAC	11	7	1	0	528	17	2	1.93	....	....	....	....	....	....	....
1983-84	Providence	ECAC	10	4	2	0	391	20	0	3.07	....	....	....	....	....	....	....
1984-85ab	Providence	H.E.	33	15	13	5	1956	116	1	3.35	....	....	....	....	....	....	....
1985-86	Providence	H.E.	22	6	16	0	1320	84	0	3.74	....	....	....	....	....	....	....
1986-87	**New Jersey**	**NHL**	**7**	**0**	**3**	**1**	**286**	**21**	**0**	**4.41**	....	....	....	....	....	....	....
	Maine	AHL	14	4	9	1	765	57	0	4.47	....	....	....	....	....	....	....
1987-88	Utica	AHL	7	5	1	0	399	18	0	2.71	....	....	....	....	....	....	....
	U.S. National	....	26	17	7	2	1430	81	0	3.40	....	....	....	....	....	....	....
	U.S. Olympic	....	3	1	1	0	128	14	0	6.56	....	....	....	....	....	....	....
1988-89	**New Jersey**	**NHL**	**8**	**0**	**4**	**2**	**402**	**18**	**0**	**2.69**	....	....	....	....	....	....	....
	Utica	AHL	39	20	15	3	2314	132	0	3.42	2	0	1	80	6	0	4.50
1989-90	**New Jersey**	**NHL**	**35**	**15**	**12**	**3**	**1931**	**110**	**0**	**3.42**	**4**	**2**	**2**	**238**	**13**	**0**	**3.28**
1990-91	**New Jersey**	**NHL**	**53**	**24**	**21**	**7**	**2970**	**144**	**1**	**2.91**	**7**	**3**	**4**	**428**	**21**	**0**	**2.94**
1991-92	**New Jersey**	**NHL**	**54**	**22**	**22**	**10**	**3186**	**169**	**1**	**3.18**	**7**	**3**	**3**	**386**	**23**	**0**	**3.58**
1992-93	**New Jersey**	**NHL**	**48**	**19**	**21**	**3**	**2672**	**151**	**2**	**3.39**	**4**	**1**	**3**	**219**	**17**	**0**	**4.66**
1993-94	**New Jersey**	**NHL**	**44**	**20**	**11**	**4**	**2340**	**106**	**2**	**2.72**	**4**	**3**	**0**	**200**	**9**	**0**	**2.70**
1994-95	**New Jersey**	**NHL**	**15**	**3**	**7**	**2**	**734**	**31**	**0**	**2.53**	**1**	**0**	**0**	**8**	**0**	**0**	**0.00**
	NHL Totals		**264**	**103**	**101**	**32**	**14521**	**750**	**6**	**3.10**	**27**	**12**	**12**	**1479**	**83**	**0**	**3.37**

a Hockey East All-Star Team (1985)
b NCAA All-American Team (1985)

THEODORE, JOSE (THEE-uh-dohr, joh-SAY) MTL.

Goaltender. Catches right. 5'10", 180 lbs. Born, Laval, Que., September 13, 1976.
(Montreal's 2nd choice, 44th overall, in 1994 Entry Draft).

			Regular Season								Playoffs						
Season	Club	Lea	GP	W	L	T	Mins	GA	SO	Avg	GP	W	L	Mins	GA	SO	Avg
1992-93	St-Jean	QMJHL	34	12	16	2	1776	112	0	3.78	3	0	2	175	11	0	3.77
1993-94	St-Jean	QMJHL	57	20	29	6	3225	194	0	3.61	5	1	4	296	18	0	3.65
1994-95	Hull	QMJHL	*58	*32	22	2	*3348	193	5	3.46	*21	*15	6	*1263	59	*1	2.80
	Fredericton	AHL	....	....	....	....	....	....	....	....	1	0	1	60	3	0	3.00

THIBAULT, JOCELYN (tee-BOW) COL.

Goaltender. Catches left. 5'11", 170 lbs. Born, Montreal, Que., January 12, 1975.
(Quebec's 1st choice, 10th overall, in 1993 Entry Draft).

			Regular Season								Playoffs						
Season	Club	Lea	GP	W	L	T	Mins	GA	SO	Avg	GP	W	L	Mins	GA	SO	Avg
1991-92	Trois Rivieres	QMJHL	30	14	7	1	1496	77	0	3.09	3	1	1	110	4	0	2.19
1992-93abc	Sherbrooke	QMJHL	56	34	14	5	3190	159	3	2.99	15	9	6	882	57	0	3.87
1993-94	**Quebec**	**NHL**	**29**	**8**	**13**	**3**	**1504**	**83**	**0**	**3.31**	....	....	....	....	....	....	....
	Cornwall	AHL	4	4	0	0	240	9	1	2.25	....	....	....	....	....	....	....
1994-95	Sherbrooke	QMJHL	13	6	6	1	776	38	1	2.94	....	....	....	....	....	....	....
	Quebec	**NHL**	**18**	**12**	**2**	**2**	**898**	**35**	**1**	**2.34**	**3**	**1**	**2**	**148**	**8**	**0**	**3.24**
	NHL Totals		**47**	**20**	**15**	**5**	**2402**	**118**	**1**	**2.95**	**3**	**1**	**2**	**148**	**8**	**0**	**3.24**

a QMJHL First All-Star Team (1993)
b Canadian Major Junior First All-Star Team (1993)
c Canadian Major Junior Goaltender of the Year (1993)

THOMAS, TIM COL.

Goaltender. Catches left. 5'11", 180 lbs. Born, Flint, MI, April 15, 1974.
(Quebec's 11th choice, 217th overall, in 1994 Entry Draft).

			Regular Season								Playoffs						
Season	Club	Lea	GP	W	L	T	Mins	GA	SO	Avg	GP	W	L	Mins	GA	SO	Avg
1993-94	U. of Vermont	ECAC	*33	15	12	6	1864	94	0	3.03	....	....	....	....	....	....	....
1994-95ab	U. of Vermont	ECAC	34	18	13	2	2010	90	*4	*2.69	....	....	....	....	....	....	....

a ECAC First All-Star Team (1995)
b NCAA East Second All-American Team (1995)

TKACHENKO, SERGEI (kuh-CHEHN-koh, SAIR-gay)

Goaltender. Catches left. 6'2", 198 lbs. Born, Kiev, USSR, June 6, 1971.
(Vancouver's 9th choice, 280th overall, in 1993 Entry Draft).

			Regular Season								Playoffs						
Season	Club	Lea	GP	W	L	T	Mins	GA	SO	Avg	GP	W	L	Mins	GA	SO	Avg
1989-90	Sokol Kiev	USSR	1	....	....	....	10	0	0	0.00	....	....	....	....	....	....	....
1990-91	Sokol Kiev	USSR	14	....	....	....	220	14	0	3.37	....	....	....	....	....	....	....
1991-92	Sokol Kiev	CIS	24	....	....	....	1305	91	0	4.18	....	....	....	....	....	....	....
1992-93	Brantford	ColHL	4	0	1	0	96	11	0	6.88	....	....	....	....	....	....	....
	Hamilton	AHL	1	1	0	0	60	3	0	3.00	....	....	....	....	....	....	....
1993-94	Hamilton	AHL	2	0	1	1	125	9	0	4.32	....	....	....	....	....	....	....
	Columbus	ECHL	34	18	7	4	1884	129	0	4.11	4	1	2	182	16	0	5.27
1994-95	Syracuse	AHL	2	0	2	0	118	9	0	4.57	....	....	....	....	....	....	....
	S. Carolina	ECHL	16	7	7	1	868	47	0	3.25	....	....	....	....	....	....	....
	Birmingham	ECHL	6	2	4	0	359	25	0	4.17	....	....	....	....	....	....	....

TORCHIA, MIKE (TOR-chee-ah) WSH.

Goaltender. Catches left. 5'11", 215 lbs. Born, Toronto, Ont., February 23, 1972.
(Minnesota's 2nd choice, 74th overall, in 1991 Entry Draft).

			Regular Season								Playoffs						
Season	Club	Lea	GP	W	L	T	Mins	GA	SO	Avg	GP	W	L	Mins	GA	SO	Avg
1988-89	Kitchener	OHL	30	14	9	4	1472	102	0	4.02	2	0	2	126	8	0	3.81
1989-90ab	Kitchener	OHL	40	25	11	2	2280	136	1	3.58	*17	*11	6	*1023	60	0	3.52
1990-91	Kitchener	OHL	57	25	24	7	*3317	219	0	3.95	6	2	4	382	30	0	4.71
1991-92	Kitchener	OHL	*55	25	24	3	*3042	203	1	4.00	14	7	7	900	47	0	3.13
1992-93	Cdn. National	....	5	5	0	0	300	11	1	2.20	....	....	....	....	....	....	....
	Kalamazoo	IHL	48	19	17	9	2729	173	0	3.80	....	....	....	....	....	....	....
1993-94	Kalamazoo	IHL	43	23	12	2	2168	133	0	3.68	4	1	3	221	14	*1	3.80
1994-95	Kalamazoo	IHL	41	19	14	5	2140	106	*3	2.97	6	0	4	257	17	0	3.97
	Dallas	**NHL**	**6**	**3**	**2**	**1**	**327**	**18**	**0**	**3.30**	....	....	....	....	....	....	....
	NHL Totals		**6**	**3**	**2**	**1**	**327**	**18**	**0**	**3.30**	....	....	....	....	....	....	....

a Memorial Cup All-Star Team (1990)
b Won Hap Emms Memorial Memorial Trophy (Memorial Cup Tournament Top Goaltender) (1990)

Traded to **Washington** by **Dallas** for future considerations, July 14, 1995.

TOSKALA, VESA (TAWS-kah-lah) S.J.

Goaltender. Catches left. 5'9", 172 lbs. Born, Tampere, Finland, May 20, 1977.
(San Jose's 4th choice, 90th overall, in 1995 Entry Draft).

			Regular Season								Playoffs						
Season	Club	Lea	GP	W	L	T	Mins	GA	SO	Avg	GP	W	L	Mins	GA	SO	Avg
1994-95	Ilves	Fin. Jr.	17	....	....	....	956	36	....	2.26							

TRACY, TRIPP — PHI.

Goaltender. Catches right. 5'10", 170 lbs. Born, Detroit, MI, December 20, 1973.
(Philadelphia's 8th choice, 218th overall, in 1993 Entry Draft).

			Regular Season								Playoffs						
Season	Club	Lea	GP	W	L	T	Mins	GA	SO	Avg	GP	W	L	Mins	GA	SO	Avg
1992-93	Harvard	ECAC	17	13	2	2	1055	40	*3	*2.27	....	....	....	....	....	....	....
1993-94	Harvard	ECAC	17	12	3	2	978	49	0	3.01	....	....	....	....	....	....	....
1994-95	Harvard	ECAC	27	13	12	2	1560	86	0	3.31	....	....	....	....	....	....	....

TREFILOV, ANDREI — (TREH-fee-lahf) BUF.

Goaltender. Catches left. 6', 180 lbs. Born, Kirovo-Chepetsk, USSR, August 31, 1969.
(Calgary's 14th choice, 261st overall, in 1991 Entry Draft).

			Regular Season								Playoffs						
Season	Club	Lea	GP	W	L	T	Mins	GA	SO	Avg	GP	W	L	Mins	GA	SO	Avg
1990-91	Moscow D'amo	USSR	20	....	....	....	1070	36	0	2.01	....	....	....	....	....	....	....
1991-92	Moscow D'amo	CIS	28	....	....	....	1326	35	0	1.58	....	....	....	....	....	....	....
1992-93	**Calgary**	**NHL**	**1**	**0**	**0**	**1**	**65**	**5**	**0**	**4.62**	....	....	....	....	....	....	....
	Salt Lake	IHL	44	23	17	3	2536	135	0	3.19	....	....	....	....	....	....	....
1993-94	**Calgary**	**NHL**	**11**	**3**	**4**	**2**	**623**	**26**	**2**	**2.50**	....	....	....	....	....	....	....
	Saint John	AHL	28	10	10	7	1629	93	0	3.42	....	....	....	....	....	....	....
1994-95	**Calgary**	**NHL**	**6**	**0**	**3**	**0**	**236**	**16**	**0**	**4.07**	....	....	....	....	....	....	....
	Saint John	AHL	7	1	5	1	383	20	0	3.13	....	....	....	....	....	....	....
	NHL Totals		**18**	**3**	**7**	**3**	**924**	**47**	**2**	**3.05**	....	....	....	....	....	....	....

Signed as a free agent by **Buffalo**, July 11, 1995.

TUGNUTT, RON

Goaltender. Catches left. 5'11", 155 lbs. Born, Scarborough, Ont., October 22, 1967.
(Quebec's 4th choice, 81st overall, in 1986 Entry Draft).

			Regular Season								Playoffs						
Season	Club	Lea	GP	W	L	T	Mins	GA	SO	Avg	GP	W	L	Mins	GA	SO	Avg
1984-85	Peterborough	OHL	18	7	4	2	938	59	0	3.77	....	....	....	....	....	....	....
1985-86	Peterborough	OHL	26	18	7	0	1543	74	1	2.88	3	2	0	133	6	0	2.71
1986-87a	Peterborough	OHL	31	21	7	2	1891	88	2	*2.79	6	3	3	374	21	1	3.37
1987-88	**Quebec**	**NHL**	**6**	**2**	**3**	**0**	**284**	**16**	**0**	**3.38**	....	....	....	....	....	....	....
	Fredericton	AHL	34	20	9	4	1964	118	1	3.60	4	1	2	204	11	0	3.24
1988-89	**Quebec**	**NHL**	**26**	**10**	**10**	**3**	**1367**	**82**	**0**	**3.60**	....	....	....	....	....	....	....
	Halifax	AHL	24	14	7	2	1368	79	1	3.46	....	....	....	....	....	....	....
1989-90	**Quebec**	**NHL**	**35**	**5**	**24**	**3**	**1978**	**152**	**0**	**4.61**	....	....	....	....	....	....	....
	Halifax	AHL	6	1	5	0	366	23	0	3.77	....	....	....	....	....	....	....
1990-91	**Quebec**	**NHL**	**56**	**12**	**29**	**10**	**3144**	**212**	**0**	**4.05**	....	....	....	....	....	....	....
	Halifax	AHL	2	0	1	0	100	8	0	4.80	....	....	....	....	....	....	....
1991-92	**Quebec**	**NHL**	**30**	**6**	**17**	**3**	**1583**	**106**	**1**	**4.02**	....	....	....	....	....	....	....
	Halifax	AHL	8	3	3	1	447	30	0	4.03	....	....	....	....	....	....	....
	Edmonton	**NHL**	**3**	**1**	**1**	**0**	**124**	**10**	**0**	**4.84**	**2**	**0**	**0**	**60**	**3**	**0**	**3.00**
1992-93	**Edmonton**	**NHL**	**26**	**9**	**12**	**2**	**1338**	**93**	**0**	**4.17**	....	....	....	....	....	....	....
1993-94	**Anaheim**	**NHL**	**28**	**10**	**15**	**1**	**1520**	**76**	**1**	**3.00**	....	....	....	....	....	....	....
	Montreal	**NHL**	**8**	**2**	**3**	**1**	**378**	**24**	**0**	**3.81**	**1**	**0**	**1**	**59**	**5**	**0**	**5.08**
1994-95	**Montreal**	**NHL**	**7**	**1**	**3**	**1**	**346**	**18**	**0**	**3.12**	....	....	....	....	....	....	....
	NHL Totals		**225**	**58**	**117**	**24**	**12062**	**789**	**2**	**3.92**	**3**	**0**	**1**	**119**	**8**	**0**	**4.03**

a OHL First All-Star Team (1987)

Traded to **Edmonton** by **Quebec** with Brad Zavisha for Martin Rucinsky, March 10, 1992. Claimed by **Anaheim** from **Edmonton** in Expansion Draft, June 24, 1993. Traded to **Montreal** by **Anaheim** for Stephan Lebeau, February 20, 1994.

TURCO, MARTY — DAL.

Goaltender. Catches left. 5'11", 175 lbs. Born, Sault Ste. Marie, Ont., August 13, 1975.
(Dallas' 4th choice, 124th overall, in 1994 Entry Draft).

			Regular Season								Playoffs						
Season	Club	Lea	GP	W	L	T	Mins	GA	SO	Avg	GP	W	L	Mins	GA	SO	Avg
1993-94	Cambridge	Jr. B	34	....	....	....	1973	114	0	3.47	....	....	....	....	....	....	....
1994-95	U. of Michigan	CCHA	37	*27	7	1	2063	95	1	2.76	....	....	....	....	....	....	....

TUREK, ROMAN — (TOOR-ehk) DAL.

Goaltender. Catches right. 6'3", 190 lbs. Born, Strakonice, Czech., May 21, 1970.
(Minnesota's 6th choice, 113th overall, in 1990 Entry Draft).

			Regular Season								Playoffs						
Season	Club	Lea	GP	W	L	T	Mins	GA	SO	Avg	GP	W	L	Mins	GA	SO	Avg
1990-91	Budejovice	Czech.	26	....	....	....	1244	98	0	4.70	....	....	....	....	....	....	....
1991-92	Budejovice	Czech.2	....	....	....	....	....	....	....	....	....	....	....	....	....	....	....
1992-93	Budejovice	Czech.	43	....	....	....	2555	121	....	2.84	....	....	....	....	....	....	....
1993-94	Budejovice	Czech.	44	....	....	....	2584	111	....	2.51	3	....	....	180	12	0	4.00
1994-95	Budejovice	Czech.	44	....	....	....	2587	119	....	2.76	9	....	....	498	25	....	3.01

VANBIESBROUCK, JOHN — (van-BEES-bruhk) FLA.

Goaltender. Catches left. 5'8", 176 lbs. Born, Detroit, MI, September 4, 1963.
(NY Rangers' 5th choice, 72nd overall, in 1981 Entry Draft).

			Regular Season								Playoffs						
Season	Club	Lea	GP	W	L	T	Mins	GA	SO	Avg	GP	W	L	Mins	GA	SO	Avg
1980-81	S.S. Marie	OHA	56	31	16	1	2941	203	0	4.14	11	3	3	457	24	1	3.15
1981-82	**NY Rangers**	**NHL**	**1**	**1**	**0**	**0**	**60**	**1**	**0**	**1.00**	....	....	....	....	....	....	....
	S.S. Marie	OHL	31	12	12	2	1686	102	0	3.62	7	1	4	276	20	0	4.35
1982-83a	S.S. Marie	OHL	62	39	21	1	3471	209	0	3.61	16	7	6	944	56	*1	3.56
1983-84	**NY Rangers**	**NHL**	**3**	**2**	**1**	**0**	**180**	**10**	**0**	**3.33**	**1**	**0**	**0**	**1**	**0**	**0**	**0.00**
bcd	Tulsa	CHL	37	20	13	2	2153	124	*3	3.46	4	4	0	240	10	0	*2.50
1984-85	**NY Rangers**	**NHL**	**42**	**12**	**24**	**3**	**2358**	**166**	**1**	**4.22**	**1**	**0**	**0**	**20**	**0**	**0**	**0.00**
1985-86ef	**NY Rangers**	**NHL**	**61**	***31**	**21**	**5**	**3326**	**184**	**3**	**3.32**	**16**	**8**	**8**	**899**	**49**	***1**	**3.27**
1986-87	**NY Rangers**	**NHL**	**50**	**18**	**20**	**5**	**2656**	**161**	**0**	**3.64**	**4**	**1**	**3**	**195**	**11**	**1**	**3.38**
1987-88	**NY Rangers**	**NHL**	**56**	**27**	**22**	**7**	**3319**	**187**	**2**	**3.38**	....	....	....	....	....	....	....
1988-89	**NY Rangers**	**NHL**	**56**	**28**	**21**	**4**	**3207**	**197**	**0**	**3.69**	**2**	**0**	**1**	**107**	**6**	**0**	**3.36**
1989-90	**NY Rangers**	**NHL**	**47**	**19**	**19**	**7**	**2734**	**154**	**1**	**3.38**	**6**	**2**	**3**	**298**	**15**	**0**	**3.02**
1990-91	**NY Rangers**	**NHL**	**40**	**15**	**18**	**6**	**2257**	**126**	**3**	**3.35**	**1**	**0**	**0**	**52**	**1**	**0**	**1.15**
1991-92	**NY Rangers**	**NHL**	**45**	**27**	**13**	**3**	**2526**	**120**	**2**	**2.85**	**7**	**2**	**5**	**368**	**23**	**0**	**3.75**
1992-93	**NY Rangers**	**NHL**	**48**	**20**	**18**	**7**	**2757**	**152**	**4**	**3.31**	....	....	....	....	....	....	....
1993-94g	**Florida**	**NHL**	**57**	**21**	**25**	**11**	**3440**	**145**	**1**	**2.53**	....	....	....	....	....	....	....
1994-95	**Florida**	**NHL**	**37**	**14**	**15**	**4**	**2087**	**86**	**4**	**2.47**	....	....	....	....	....	....	....
	NHL Totals		**543**	**235**	**217**	**62**	**30907**	**1689**	**21**	**3.28**	**38**	**13**	**20**	**1940**	**105**	**2**	**3.25**

a OHL Second All-Star Team (1983)
b CHL First All-Star Team (1984)
c Shared Terry Sawchuk Trophy (CHL's Leading Goaltender) with Ron Scott (1984)
d Shared Tommy Ivan Trophy (CHL's Most Valuable Player) with Bruce Affleck of Indianapolis (1984)
e Won Vezina Trophy (1986)
f NHL First All-Star Team (1986)
g NHL Second All-Star Team (1994)

Played in NHL All-Star Game (1994)

Traded to **Vancouver** by **NY Rangers** for future considerations (Doug Lidster, June 25, 1993), June 20, 1993. Claimed by **Florida** from **Vancouver** in Expansion Draft, June 24, 1993.

VEISOR, MIKE — (VIGH-awr) ST.L.

Goaltender. Catches right. 6'2", 195 lbs. Born, Dallas, TX, December 7, 1972.
(St. Louis' 12th choice, 263rd overall, in 1991 Entry Draft).

			Regular Season								Playoffs						
Season	Club	Lea	GP	W	L	T	Mins	GA	SO	Avg	GP	W	L	Mins	GA	SO	Avg
1992-93	Northeastern	H.E.	30	8	19	1	1699	151	0	5.33	....	....	....	....	....	....	....
1993-94	Northeastern	H.E.	15	7	3	2	775	55	0	4.26	....	....	....	....	....	....	....
1994-95	Northeastern	H.E.	24	12	5	3	1289	73	0	3.41	....	....	....	....	....	....	....

VERNON, MIKE

Goaltender. Catches left. 5'9", 165 lbs. Born, Calgary, Alta., February 24, 1963.
(Calgary's 2nd choice, 56th overall, in 1981 Entry Draft).

			Regular Season								Playoffs						
Season	Club	Lea	GP	W	L	T	Mins	GA	SO	Avg	GP	W	L	Mins	GA	SO	Avg
1980-81	Calgary	WHL	59	33	17	1	3154	198	1	3.77	22	14	8	1271	82	1	3.87
1981-82a	Calgary	WHL	42	22	14	2	2329	143	3	3.68	9	5	4	527	30	0	3.42
	Oklahoma City	CHL	....	....	....	....	....	....	....	....	1	0	1	70	4	0	3.43
1982-83	**Calgary**	**NHL**	**2**	**0**	**2**	**0**	**100**	**11**	**0**	**6.59**	....	....	....	....	....	....	....
ab	Calgary	WHL	50	19	18	2	2856	155	3	3.26	16	9	7	925	60	0	3.89
1983-84	**Calgary**	**NHL**	**1**	**0**	**1**	**0**	**11**	**4**	**0**	**22.22**	....	....	....	....	....	....	....
c	Colorado	CHL	46	30	13	2	2648	148	1	*3.35	6	2	4	347	21	0	3.63
1984-85	Moncton	AHL	41	10	20	4	2050	134	0	3.92	....	....	....	....	....	....	....
1985-86	**Calgary**	**NHL**	**18**	**9**	**3**	**3**	**921**	**52**	**1**	**3.39**	***21**	**12**	***9**	**1229**	**60**	**0**	**2.93**
	Moncton	AHL	6	3	1	2	374	21	0	3.37	....	....	....	....	....	....	....
	Salt Lake	IHL	10	6	4	0	600	34	1	3.40	....	....	....	....	....	....	....
1986-87	**Calgary**	**NHL**	**54**	**30**	**21**	**1**	**2957**	**178**	**1**	**3.61**	**5**	**2**	**3**	**263**	**16**	**0**	**3.65**
1987-88	**Calgary**	**NHL**	**64**	**39**	**16**	**7**	**3565**	**210**	**1**	**3.53**	**9**	**4**	**4**	**515**	**34**	**0**	**3.96**
1988-89d	**Calgary**	**NHL**	**52**	***37**	**6**	**5**	**2938**	**130**	**0**	**2.65**	***22**	***16**	**5**	***1381**	**52**	***3**	**2.26**
1989-90	**Calgary**	**NHL**	**47**	**23**	**14**	**9**	**2795**	**146**	**0**	**3.13**	**6**	**2**	**3**	**342**	**19**	**0**	**3.33**
1990-91	**Calgary**	**NHL**	**54**	**31**	**19**	**3**	**3121**	**172**	**1**	**3.31**	**7**	**3**	**4**	**427**	**21**	**0**	**2.95**
1991-92	**Calgary**	**NHL**	**63**	**24**	**30**	**9**	**3640**	**217**	**0**	**3.58**	....	....	....	....	....	....	....
1992-93	**Calgary**	**NHL**	**64**	**29**	**26**	**9**	**3732**	**203**	**2**	**3.26**	**4**	**1**	**1**	**150**	**15**	**0**	**6.00**
1993-94	**Calgary**	**NHL**	**48**	**26**	**17**	**5**	**2798**	**131**	**3**	**2.81**	**7**	**3**	**4**	**466**	**23**	**0**	**2.96**
1994-95	**Detroit**	**NHL**	**30**	**19**	**6**	**4**	**1807**	**76**	**1**	**2.52**	**18**	**12**	**6**	**1063**	**41**	**1**	**2.31**
	NHL Totals		**497**	**267**	**161**	**55**	**28385**	**1530**	**10**	**3.23**	**99**	**55**	**39**	**5836**	**281**	**4**	**2.89**

a WHL First All-Star Team (1982, 1983)
b Won Hap Emms Memorial Trophy (Memorial Cup Tournament Top Goaltender) (1983)
c CHL Second All-Star Team (1984)
d NHL Second All-Star Team (1989)

Played in NHL All-Star Game (1988-91, 1993)

Traded to **Detroit** by **Calgary** for Steve Chiasson, June 29, 1994.

VOKOUN, TOMAS — MTL.

Goaltender. Catches right. 5'11", 180 lbs. Born, Karlovy Vary, Czech., July 2, 1976.
(Montreal's 11th choice, 226th overall, in 1994 Entry Draft).

			Regular Season								Playoffs						
Season	Club	Lea	GP	W	L	T	Mins	GA	SO	Avg	GP	W	L	Mins	GA	SO	Avg
1993-94	Kladno	Czech.	1	0	0	0	20	2	0	6.01	....	....	....	....	....	....	....
1994-95	Kladno	Czech.	26	....	....	....	1368	70	....	3.07	5	....	....	240	19	....	4.75

WAITE, JIMMY — (WAYT) CHI.

Goaltender. Catches left. 6'1", 180 lbs. Born, Sherbrooke, Que., April 15, 1969.
(Chicago's 1st choice, 8th overall, in 1987 Entry Draft).

			Regular Season								Playoffs						
Season	Club	Lea	GP	W	L	T	Mins	GA	SO	Avg	GP	W	L	Mins	GA	SO	Avg
1986-87a	Chicoutimi	QMJHL	50	23	17	3	2569	209	2	4.48	11	4	6	576	54	1	5.63
1987-88	Chicoutimi	QMJHL	36	17	16	1	2000	150	0	4.50	4	1	2	222	17	0	4.59
1988-89	**Chicago**	**NHL**	**11**	**0**	**7**	**1**	**494**	**43**	**0**	**5.22**	....	....	....	....	....	....	....
	Saginaw	IHL	5	3	1	0	304	10	0	1.97	....	....	....	....	....	....	....
1989-90	**Chicago**	**NHL**	**4**	**2**	**0**	**0**	**183**	**14**	**0**	**4.59**	....	....	....	....	....	....	....
bc	Indianapolis	IHL	54	*34	14	5	*3207	135	*5	*2.53	*10	*9	1	*602	19	*1	*1.89
1990-91	**Chicago**	**NHL**	**1**	**1**	**0**	**0**	**60**	**2**	**0**	**2.00**	....	....	....	....	....	....	....
	Indianapolis	IHL	49	*26	18	4	2888	167	3	3.47	6	2	4	369	20	0	3.25
1991-92	**Chicago**	**NHL**	**17**	**4**	**7**	**4**	**877**	**54**	**0**	**3.69**	....	....	....	....	....	....	....
	Indianapolis	IHL	13	4	7	1	702	53	0	4.53	....	....	....	....	....	....	....
	Hershey	AHL	11	6	4	1	631	44	0	4.18	6	2	4	360	19	0	3.17
1992-93	**Chicago**	**NHL**	**20**	**6**	**7**	**1**	**996**	**49**	**2**	**2.95**	....	....	....	....	....	....	....
1993-94	**San Jose**	**NHL**	**15**	**3**	**7**	**0**	**697**	**50**	**0**	**4.30**	**2**	**0**	**0**	**40**	**3**	**0**	**4.50**
1994-95	**Chicago**	**NHL**	**2**	**1**	**1**	**0**	**119**	**5**	**0**	**2.52**	....	....	....	....	....	....	....
	Indianapolis	IHL	4	2	1	1	239	13	0	3.25	....	....	....	....	....	....	....
	NHL Totals		**70**	**17**	**29**	**6**	**3426**	**217**	**2**	**3.80**	**2**	**0**	**0**	**40**	**3**	**0**	**4.50**

a QMJHL Second All-Star Team (1987)
b IHL First All-Star Team (1990)
c Won James Norris Memorial Trophy (fewest goals against - IHL) (1990)

Traded to **San Jose** by **Chicago** for future considerations (Neil Wilkinson, July 9, 1993), June 19, 1993. Traded to **Chicago** by **San Jose** for a conditional choice in 1997 Entry Draft, February 6, 1995.

WAKALUK, DARCY — (WAHK-uh-luhk) DAL.

Goaltender. Catches left. 5'11", 180 lbs. Born, Pincher Creek, Alta., March 14, 1966.
(Buffalo's 7th choice, 144th overall, in 1984 Entry Draft).

			Regular Season								Playoffs						
Season	Club	Lea	GP	W	L	T	Mins	GA	SO	Avg	GP	W	L	Mins	GA	SO	Avg
1983-84	Kelowna	WHL	31	2	22	0	1555	163	0	6.29	....	....	....	....	....	....	....
1984-85	Kelowna	WHL	54	19	30	4	3094	244	0	4.73	5	1	4	282	22	0	4.68
1985-86	Spokane	WHL	47	21	22	1	2562	224	1	5.25	7	3	4	419	37	0	5.30
1986-87	Rochester	AHL	11	2	2	0	545	26	0	2.86	5	2	0	141	11	0	4.68
1987-88	Rochester	AHL	55	27	16	3	2763	159	0	3.45	6	3	3	328	22	0	4.02
1988-89	**Buffalo**	**NHL**	**6**	**1**	**3**	**0**	**214**	**15**	**0**	**4.21**	....	....	....	....	....	....	....
	Rochester	AHL	33	11	14	0	1566	97	1	3.72	....	....	....	....	....	....	....
1989-90	Rochester	AHL	56	31	16	4	3095	173	2	3.35	*17	*10	6	*1001	50	0	*3.01
1990-91	**Buffalo**	**NHL**	**16**	**4**	**5**	**3**	**630**	**35**	**0**	**3.33**	**2**	**0**	**1**	**37**	**2**	**0**	**3.24**
a	Rochester	AHL	26	10	10	3	1363	68	4	*2.99	9	6	3	544	30	0	3.31
1991-92	**Minnesota**	**NHL**	**36**	**13**	**19**	**1**	**1905**	**104**	**1**	**3.28**	....	....	....	....	....	....	....
	Kalamazoo	IHL	1	1	0	0	60	7	0	7.00	....	....	....	....	....	....	....
1992-93	**Minnesota**	**NHL**	**29**	**10**	**12**	**5**	**1596**	**97**	**1**	**3.65**	....	....	....	....	....	....	....
1993-94	**Dallas**	**NHL**	**36**	**18**	**9**	**6**	**2000**	**88**	**3**	**2.64**	**5**	**4**	**1**	**307**	**15**	**0**	**2.93**
1994-95	**Dallas**	**NHL**	**15**	**4**	**8**	**0**	**754**	**40**	**2**	**3.18**	**1**	**0**	**0**	**20**	**1**	**0**	**3.00**
	NHL Totals		**138**	**50**	**56**	**15**	**7099**	**379**	**7**	**3.20**	**8**	**4**	**2**	**364**	**18**	**0**	**2.97**

a Shared Harry "Hap" Holmes Memorial Trophy (fewest goals against - AHL) with David Littman (1991)

Traded to **Minnesota** by **Buffalo** for Minnesota's eighth round choice (Jiri Kuntos) in 1991 Entry Draft and Minnesota's fifth round choice (later traded to Toronto — Toronto selected Chris Deruiter) in 1992 Entry Draft, May 26, 1991.

WEEKES, KEVIN — FLA.

Goaltender. Catches left. 6', 158 lbs. Born, Toronto, Ont., April 4, 1975.
(Florida's 2nd choice, 41st overall, in 1993 Entry Draft).

			Regular Season								Playoffs						
Season	Club	Lea	GP	W	L	T	Mins	GA	SO	Avg	GP	W	L	Mins	GA	SO	Avg
1992-93	Owen Sound	OHL	29	9	12	5	1645	143	0	5.22	1	0	0	26	5	0	11.50
1993-94	Owen Sound	OHL	34	13	19	1	1974	158	0	4.80	....	....	....	....	....	....	....
1994-95	Ottawa	OHL	41	13	23	4	2266	153	1	4.05	....	....	....	....	....	....	....

WEIBEL, LARS (VIGH-behl) CHI.

Goaltender. Catches left. 6', 178 lbs. Born, Rapperswil, Switz., May 20, 1974.
(Chicago's 10th choice, 248th overall, in 1994 Entry Draft).

			Regular Season								Playoffs						
Season	Club	Lea	GP	W	L	T	Mins	GA	SO	Avg	GP	W	L	Mins	GA	SO	Avg
1992-93	Biel-Bienne	Switz.	14	....	....	....	674	54	....	4.80	....	....	....	....	....	....	....
1993-94	Lugano	Switz.	25	....	....	....	....	....	....	....	9	....	....	560	23	....	2.46
1994-95	Lugano	Switz.	35	....	....	....	2076	95	....	2.74	....	....	....	....	....	....	....

WHITMORE, KAY

Goaltender. Catches left. 5'11", 175 lbs. Born, Sudbury, Ont., April 10, 1967.
(Hartford's 2nd choice, 26th overall, in 1985 Entry Draft).

			Regular Season								Playoffs						
Season	Club	Lea	GP	W	L	T	Mins	GA	SO	Avg	GP	W	L	Mins	GA	SO	Avg
1983-84	Peterborough	OHL	29	17	8	0	1471	110	0	4.49	....	....	....	....	....	....	....
1984-85	Peterborough	OHL	53	*35	16	2	3077	172	*2	3.35	17	10	4	1020	58	0	3.41
1985-86a	Peterborough	OHL	41	27	12	2	2467	114	*3	*2.77	14	8	5	837	40	0	2.87
1986-87	Peterborough	OHL	36	14	17	5	2159	118	1	3.28	7	3	3	366	17	1	2.79
1987-88	Binghamton	AHL	38	17	15	4	2137	121	*3	3.40	2	0	2	118	10	0	5.08
1988-89	**Hartford**	**NHL**	**3**	**2**	**1**	**0**	**180**	**10**	**0**	**3.33**	**2**	**0**	**2**	**135**	**10**	**0**	**4.44**
	Binghamton	AHL	*56	21	29	4	*3200	241	1	4.52	....	....	....	....	....	....	....
1989-90	**Hartford**	**NHL**	**9**	**4**	**2**	**1**	**442**	**26**	**0**	**3.53**	....	....	....	....	....	....	....
	Binghamton	AHL	24	3	19	2	1386	109	0	4.72	....	....	....	....	....	....	....
1990-91	**Hartford**	**NHL**	**18**	**3**	**9**	**3**	**850**	**52**	**0**	**3.67**	....	....	....	....	....	....	....
b	Springfield	AHL	33	22	9	1	1916	98	1	3.07	*15	*11	4	*926	37	0	*2.40
1991-92	**Hartford**	**NHL**	**45**	**14**	**21**	**6**	**2567**	**155**	**3**	**3.62**	**1**	**0**	**0**	**19**	**1**	**0**	**3.16**
1992-93	**Vancouver**	**NHL**	**31**	**18**	**8**	**4**	**1817**	**94**	**1**	**3.10**	....	....	....	....	....	....	....
1993-94	**Vancouver**	**NHL**	**32**	**18**	**14**	**0**	**1921**	**113**	**0**	**3.53**	....	....	....	....	....	....	....
1994-95	**Vancouver**	**NHL**	**11**	**0**	**6**	**2**	**558**	**37**	**0**	**3.98**	**1**	**0**	**0**	**20**	**2**	**0**	**6.00**
	NHL Totals		**149**	**59**	**61**	**16**	**8335**	**487**	**4**	**3.51**	**4**	**0**	**2**	**174**	**13**	**0**	**4.48**

a OHL First All-Star Team (1986)
b Won Jack A. Butterfield Trophy (Playoff MVP - AHL) (1991)

Traded to **Vancouver** by **Hartford** for Corrie D'Alessio and future considerations, October 1, 1992.

WICKENHEISER, CHRIS EDM.

Goaltender. Catches left. 6'1", 185 lbs. Born, Lethbridge, Alta., January 20, 1976.
(Edmonton's 12th choice, 179th overall, in 1994 Entry Draft).

			Regular Season								Playoffs						
Season	Club	Lea	GP	W	L	T	Mins	GA	SO	Avg	GP	W	L	Mins	GA	SO	Avg
1993-94	Red Deer	WHL	29	11	13	0	1356	114	0	5.04	....	....	....	....	....	....	....
1994-95	Red Deer	WHL	47	13	26	3	2429	181	1	4.47	....	....	....	....	....	....	....

WILKINSON, DEREK T.B.

Goaltender. Catches left. 6', 160 lbs. Born, Lasalle, Que., July 29, 1974.
(Tampa Bay's 7th choice, 145th overall, in 1992 Entry Draft).

			Regular Season								Playoffs						
Season	Club	Lea	GP	W	L	T	Mins	GA	SO	Avg	GP	W	L	Mins	GA	SO	Avg
1991-92	Detroit	OHL	38	16	17	1	1943	138	1	4.26	7	3	2	313	28	0	5.37
1992-93	Detroit	OHL	*4	1	2	1	*245	18	0	4.41	....	....	....	....	....	....	....
	Belleville	OHL	*59	21	24	11	*3370	237	0	4.22	7	3	4	434	29	0	4.01
1993-94	Belleville	OHL	*56	24	16	4	2860	179	*2	3.76	12	6	6	700	39	*1	3.34
1994-95	Atlanta	IHL	46	22	17	2	2414	121	1	3.01	4	2	1	197	8	0	2.43

WILLIS, JORDAN DAL.

Goaltender. Catches left. 5'9", 155 lbs. Born, Kincardine, Ont., February 28, 1975.
(Dallas' 8th choice, 243rd overall, in 1993 Entry Draft).

			Regular Season								Playoffs						
Season	Club	Lea	GP	W	L	T	Mins	GA	SO	Avg	GP	W	L	Mins	GA	SO	Avg
1992-93	London	OHL	26	13	6	3	1428	101	1	4.24	7	....	....	355	19	0	3.21
1993-94	London	OHL	44	20	19	2	2428	158	1	3.90	1	0	0	8	1	0	7.50
1994-95	London	OHL	53	16	29	3	2824	202	0	4.29	3	0	3	165	15	0	5.45

WREGGET, KEN (REHG-eht) PIT.

Goaltender. Catches left. 6'1", 195 lbs. Born, Brandon, Man., March 25, 1964.
(Toronto's 4th choice, 45th overall, in 1982 Entry Draft).

			Regular Season								Playoffs						
Season	Club	Lea	GP	W	L	T	Mins	GA	SO	Avg	GP	W	L	Mins	GA	SO	Avg
1981-82	Lethbridge	WHL	36	19	12	0	1713	118	0	4.13	3	2	0	84	3	0	2.14
1982-83	Lethbridge	WHL	48	26	17	1	2696	157	0	3.49	20	14	5	1154	58	1	3.02
1983-84	**Toronto**	**NHL**	**3**	**1**	**1**	**1**	**165**	**14**	**0**	**5.09**	....	....	....	....	....	....	....
a	Lethbridge	WHL	53	32	20	0	3053	161	0	*3.16	4	1	3	210	18	0	5.14
1984-85	**Toronto**	**NHL**	**23**	**2**	**15**	**3**	**1278**	**103**	**0**	**4.84**	....	....	....	....	....	....	....
	St. Catharines	AHL	12	2	8	1	688	48	0	4.19	....	....	....	....	....	....	....
1985-86	**Toronto**	**NHL**	**30**	**9**	**13**	**4**	**1566**	**113**	**0**	**4.33**	**10**	**6**	**4**	**607**	**32**	***1**	**3.16**
	St. Catharines	AHL	18	8	9	0	1058	78	1	4.42	....	....	....	....	....	....	....
1986-87	**Toronto**	**NHL**	**56**	**22**	**28**	**3**	**3026**	**200**	**0**	**3.97**	**13**	**7**	**6**	**761**	**29**	**1**	**2.29**
1987-88	**Toronto**	**NHL**	**56**	**12**	**35**	**4**	**3000**	**222**	**2**	**4.44**	**2**	**0**	**1**	**108**	**11**	**0**	**6.11**
1988-89	**Toronto**	**NHL**	**32**	**9**	**20**	**2**	**1888**	**139**	**0**	**4.42**	....	....	....	....	....	....	....
	Philadelphia	**NHL**	**3**	**1**	**1**	**0**	**130**	**13**	**0**	**6.00**	**5**	**2**	**2**	**268**	**10**	**0**	**2.24**
1989-90	**Philadelphia**	**NHL**	**51**	**22**	**24**	**3**	**2961**	**169**	**0**	**3.42**	....	....	....	....	....	....	....
1990-91	**Philadelphia**	**NHL**	**30**	**10**	**14**	**3**	**1484**	**88**	**0**	**3.56**	....	....	....	....	....	....	....
1991-92	**Philadelphia**	**NHL**	**23**	**9**	**8**	**3**	**1259**	**75**	**0**	**3.57**	....	....	....	....	....	....	....
	Pittsburgh	**NHL**	**9**	**5**	**3**	**0**	**448**	**31**	**0**	**4.15**	**1**	**0**	**0**	**40**	**4**	**0**	**6.00**
1992-93	**Pittsburgh**	**NHL**	**25**	**13**	**7**	**2**	**1368**	**78**	**0**	**3.42**	....	....	....	....	....	....	....
1993-94	**Pittsburgh**	**NHL**	**42**	**21**	**12**	**7**	**2456**	**138**	**1**	**3.37**	....	....	....	....	....	....	....
1994-95	**Pittsburgh**	**NHL**	**38**	***25**	**9**	**2**	**2208**	**118**	**0**	**3.21**	**11**	**5**	**6**	**661**	**33**	**1**	**3.00**
	NHL Totals		**421**	**161**	**190**	**37**	**23237**	**1501**	**3**	**3.88**	**42**	**20**	**19**	**2445**	**119**	**3**	**2.92**

a WHL East First All-Star Team (1984)

Traded to **Philadelphia** by **Toronto** for Philadelphia's first round choice (Rob Pearson) and Calgary's first round choice (previously acquired by Philadelphia — Toronto selected Steve Bancroft) in 1989 Entry Draft, March 6, 1989. Traded to **Pittsburgh** by **Philadelphia** with Rick Tocchet, Kjell Samuelsson and Philadelphia's third round choice (Dave Roche) in 1993 Entry Draft for Mark Recchi, Brian Benning and Los Angeles' first round choice (previously acquired by Pittsburgh — Philadelphia selected Jason Bowen) in 1992 Entry Draft, February 19, 1992.

YEREMEYEV, VITALI (yehr-eh-MAY-ehv) NYR

Goaltender. Catches left. 5'10", 167 lbs. Born, Ust-Kamenogorsk, USSR, September 23, 1975.
(NY Rangers' 11th choice, 209th overall, in 1994 Entry Draft).

			Regular Season								Playoffs						
Season	Club	Lea	GP	W	L	T	Mins	GA	SO	Avg	GP	W	L	Mins	GA	SO	Avg
1993-94	Kamenogorsk	CIS	19	....	....	....	1015	38	....	2.24	....	....	....	....	....	....	....
1994-95	CSKA	CIS	49	....	....	....	2733	97	....	2.13	....	....	....	....	....	....	....

YOUNG, WENDELL

Goaltender. Catches left. 5'9", 181 lbs. Born, Halifax, N.S., August 1, 1963.
(Vancouver's 3rd choice, 73rd overall, in 1981 Entry Draft).

			Regular Season								Playoffs						
Season	Club	Lea	GP	W	L	T	Mins	GA	SO	Avg	GP	W	L	Mins	GA	SO	Avg
1980-81	Kitchener	OHA	42	19	15	0	2215	164	1	4.44	14	9	1	800	42	*1	3.15
1981-82	Kitchener	OHL	60	38	17	2	3470	195	1	3.37	15	12	1	900	35	*1	*2.33
1982-83	Kitchener	OHL	61	41	19	0	3611	231	1	3.84	12	6	5	720	43	0	3.58
1983-84	Fredericton	AHL	11	7	3	0	569	39	1	4.11	....	....	....	....	....	....	....
	Milwaukee	IHL	6	4	1	1	339	17	0	3.01	....	....	....	....	....	....	....
	Salt Lake	CHL	20	11	6	0	1094	80	0	4.39	4	0	2	122	11	0	5.42
1984-85	Fredericton	AHL	22	7	11	3	1242	83	0	4.01	....	....	....	....	....	....	....
1985-86	**Vancouver**	**NHL**	**22**	**4**	**9**	**3**	**1023**	**61**	**0**	**3.58**	**1**	**0**	**1**	**60**	**5**	**0**	**5.00**
	Fredericton	AHL	24	12	8	4	1457	78	0	3.21	....	....	....	....	....	....	....
1986-87	**Vancouver**	**NHL**	**8**	**1**	**6**	**1**	**420**	**35**	**0**	**5.00**	....	....	....	....	....	....	....
	Fredericton	AHL	30	11	16	0	1676	118	0	4.22	....	....	....	....	....	....	....
1987-88	**Philadelphia**	**NHL**	**6**	**3**	**2**	**0**	**320**	**20**	**0**	**3.75**	....	....	....	....	....	....	....
abc	Hershey	AHL	51	*33	15	1	2922	135	1	2.77	12	*12	0	*767	28	*1	*2.19
1988-89	**Pittsburgh**	**NHL**	**22**	**12**	**9**	**0**	**1150**	**92**	**0**	**4.80**	**1**	**0**	**0**	**39**	**1**	**0**	**1.54**
	Muskegon	IHL	2	1	0	1	125	7	0	3.36	....	....	....	....	....	....	....
1989-90	**Pittsburgh**	**NHL**	**43**	**16**	**20**	**3**	**2318**	**161**	**1**	**4.17**	....	....	....	....	....	....	....
1990-91	**Pittsburgh**	**NHL**	**18**	**4**	**6**	**2**	**773**	**52**	**0**	**4.04**	....	....	....	....	....	....	....
1991-92	**Pittsburgh**	**NHL**	**18**	**7**	**6**	**0**	**838**	**53**	**0**	**3.79**	....	....	....	....	....	....	....
1992-93	**Tampa Bay**	**NHL**	**31**	**7**	**19**	**2**	**1591**	**97**	**0**	**3.66**	....	....	....	....	....	....	....
	Atlanta	IHL	3	3	0	0	183	8	0	2.62	....	....	....	....	....	....	....
1993-94	**Tampa Bay**	**NHL**	**9**	**2**	**3**	**1**	**480**	**20**	**1**	**2.50**	....	....	....	....	....	....	....
	Atlanta	IHL	2	2	0	0	120	6	0	3.00	....	....	....	....	....	....	....
1994-95	Chicago	IHL	37	14	11	7	1882	112	0	3.57	....	....	....	....	....	....	....
	Pittsburgh	**NHL**	**10**	**3**	**6**	**0**	**497**	**27**	**0**	**3.26**	....	....	....	....	....	....	....
	NHL Totals		**187**	**59**	**86**	**12**	**9410**	**618**	**2**	**3.94**	**2**	**0**	**1**	**99**	**6**	**0**	**3.64**

a AHL First All-Star Team (1988)
b Won Baz Bastien Memorial Trophy (Top Goaltender - AHL) (1988)
c Won Jack Butterfield Trophy (Playoff MVP - AHL) (1988)

Traded to **Philadelphia** by **Vancouver** with Vancouver's third round choice (Kimbi Daniels) in 1990 Entry Draft for Darren Jensen and Daryl Stanley, August 28, 1987. Traded to **Pittsburgh** by **Philadelphia** with Philadelphia's seventh round choice (Mika Valila) in 1990 Entry Draft for Pittsburgh's third round choice (Chris Therien) in 1990 Entry Draft, September 1, 1988. Claimed by **Tampa Bay** from **Pittsburgh** in Expansion Draft, June 18, 1992. Traded to **Pittsburgh** by **Tampa Bay** for future considerations, February 16, 1995.

Retired Players and Goaltenders Research Project

Throughout the Retired Players and Retired Goaltenders sections of this book, you will notice many players with a bullet (•) by their names. These players, according to our records, are deceased. The editors recognize that our information on the death dates of NHLers is incomplete. If you have documented information on the passing of any player not marked with a bullet (•) in this edition, we would like to hear from you. Please send this information to:

Retired Player Research Project
c/o NHL Publishing
194 Dovercourt Road
Toronto, Ontario
M6J 3C8 Canada
Fax: 416/531-3939

Many thanks to the following contributors in 1994-95:

Don Andrews, Paul R. Carroll, Jr., Dean Evans, Peter Fillman, Liz MacLeod, Jim Maley, Al Mason, Scott Miller, Neil Nicholson, Gary J. Pearce, Robert F. Schulz.

Les Binkley

Brian Hayward

Curt Ridley

Richard Brodeur

Al Jensen

Roberto Romano

Alain Chevrier

Rollie Melanson

Gary Simmons

Mario Gosselin

Gilles Meloche

Rick Wamsley

Retired NHL Goaltender Index

Abbreviations: Teams/Cities: — **Ana.** – Anaheim; **Atl.** – Atlanta; **Bos.** – Boston, **Bro.** – Brooklyn; **Buf.** – Buffalo; **Cal.** – California; **Cgy.** – Calgary; **Cle.** – Cleveland; **Col.** – Colorado; **Dal.** – Dallas; **Det.** – Detroit; **Edm.** – Edmonton; **Fla.** – Florida; **Ham.** – Hamilton; **Hfd.** – Hartford; **K.C.** – Kansas City; **L.A.** – Los Angeles; **Min.** — Minnesota; **Mtl.** – Montreal; **Mtl. M.** – Montreal Maroons; **Mtl. W.** – Montreal Wanderers; **N.J.** – New Jersey; **NYA** – NY Americans; **NYI** – New York Islanders; **NYR** – New York Rangers; **Oak.** – Oakland; **Ott.** – Ottawa; **Phi.** – Philadelphia; **Pit.** – Pittsburgh; **Que.** – Quebec; **St. L.** – St. Louis; **S.J.** – San Jose; **T.B.** – Tampa Bay; **Tor.** – Toronto; **Van.** – Vancouver; **Wpg.** – Winnipeg; **Wsh.** – Washington.

Avg. – goals against per 60 minutes played; **GA** – goals against; **GP** – games played; **Mins** – minutes played; **SO** – shutouts.
• – deceased.

			Regular Schedule								Playoffs										
Name	**NHL Teams**	**NHL Seasons**	**GP**	**W**	**L**	**T**	**Mins**	**GA**	**SO**	**Avg**	**GP**	**W**	**L**	**T**	**Mins**	**GA**	**SO**	**Avg**	**NHL Cup Wins**	**First NHL Season**	**Last NHL Season**
Abbott, George	Bos.	1	1	0	1	0	60	7	0	7.00	....	....	....	....	....	....	....	....		1943-44	1943-44
Adams, John	Bos., Wsh.	2	22	9	10	1	1180	85	1	4.32	....	....	....	....	....	....	....	....		1972-73	1974-75
Aiken, Don	Mtl.	1	1	0	1	0	34	6	0	10.59	....	....	....	....	....	....	....	....		1957-58	1957-58
Aitkenhead, Andy	NYR	3	106	47	43	16	6570	257	11	2.35	10	6	3	1	608	15	3	1.48	1	1932-33	1934-35
Almas, Red	Det., Chi.	3	3	0	2	1	180	13	0	4.33	5	1	3	0	263	13	0	2.97		1946-47	1952-53
• Anderson, Lorne	NYR	1	3	1	2	0	180	18	0	6.00	....	....	....	....	....	....	....	....		1951-52	1951-52
Astrom, Hardy	NYR, Col.	3	83	17	44	12	4456	278	0	3.74	....	....	....	....	....	....	....	....		1977-78	1980-81
Baker, Steve	NYR	4	57	20	20	11	3081	190	3	3.70	14	7	7	0	826	55	0	4.00		1979-80	1982-83
Bannerman, Murray	Van., Chi.	8	289	116	125	33	16470	1051	8	3.83	40	20	18	0	2322	165	0	4.26		1977-78	1986-87
Baron, Marco	Bos., L.A., Edm.	6	86	34	38	9	4822	292	1	3.63	1	0	1	0	20	3	0	9.00		1979-80	1984-85
Bassen, Hank	Chi., Det., Pit.	9	157	47	64	31	8829	441	5	3.00	5	1	4	0	274	11	0	2.41		1954-55	1967-68
• Bastien, Baz	Tor.	1	5	0	4	1	300	20	0	4.00	....	....	....	....	....	....	....	....		1945-46	1945-46
Bauman, Gary	Mtl., Min.	3	35	6	18	6	1718	102	0	3.56	....	....	....	....	....	....	....	....		1966-67	1968-69
Bedard, Jim	Wsh.	2	73	17	40	13	4232	278	1	3.94	....	....	....	....	....	....	....	....		1977-78	1978-79
Behrend, Marc	Wpg.	3	38	12	19	3	1991	164	1	4.94	7	1	3	0	312	19	0	3.65		1983-84	1985-86
Belanger, Yves	St.L., Atl., Bos.	6	78	29	33	6	4134	259	2	3.76	....	....	....	....	....	....	....	....		1974-75	1979-80
Belhumeur, Michel	Phi., Wsh.	3	65	9	36	7	3306	254	0	4.61	1	0	0	0	10	1	0	6.00		1972-73	1975-76
• Bell, Gordie	Tor., NYR	2	8	3	5	0	480	31	0	3.88	2	1	1	0	120	9	0	4.50		1945-46	1955-56
• Benedict, Clint	Ott., Mtl.M.	13	362	190	43	28	22321	863	57	2.32	48	25	18	4	2907	87	15	1.80	4	1917-18	1929-30
Bennett, Harvey	Bos.	1	24	10	12	2	1470	103	0	4.20	....	....	....	....	....	....	....	....		1944-45	1944-45
Bernhardt, Tim	Cgy., Tor.	4	67	17	36	7	3748	267	0	4.27	....	....	....	....	....	....	....	....		1982-83	1986-87
• Beveridge, Bill	Det., Ott., St.L., Mtl.M., NYR	9	297	87	166	42	18375	879	18	2.87	5	2	3	0	300	11	0	2.20		1929-30	1942-43
• Bibeault, Paul	Mtl., Tor., Bos., Chi.	7	214	81	107	25	12890	785	10	3.65	20	6	14	0	1237	71	2	3.44		1940-41	1946-47
Binette, Andre	Mtl.	1	1	1	0	0	60	4	0	4.00	....	....	....	....	....	....	....	....		1954-55	1954-55
Binkley, Les	Pit.	5	196	58	94	34	11046	575	11	3.12	7	5	2	0	428	15	0	2.10		1967-68	1971-72
Bittner, Richard	Bos.	1	1	0	0	1	60	3	0	3.00	....	....	....	....	....	....	....	....		1949-50	1949-50
Blake, Mike	L.A.	3	40	13	15	5	2117	150	0	4.25	....	....	....	....	....	....	....	....		1981-82	1983-84
Boisvert, Gilles	Det.	1	3	0	3	0	180	9	0	3.00	....	....	....	....	....	....	....	....		1959-60	1959-60
Bouchard, Dan	Atl., Cgy., Que., Wpg.	14	655	286	232	113	37919	2061	27	3.26	43	13	30	0	2549	147	1	3.46		1972-73	1985-86
• Bourque, Claude	Mtl., Det.	2	62	16	38	8	3830	192	5	3.01	3	1	2	0	188	8	1	2.55		1938-39	1939-40
Boutin, Rollie	Wsh.	3	22	7	10	1	1137	75	0	3.96	....	....	....	....	....	....	....	....		1978-79	1980-81
Bouvrette, Lionel	NYR	1	1	0	1	0	60	6	0	6.00	....	....	....	....	....	....	....	....		1942-43	1942-43
Bower, Johnny	NYR, Tor.	15	552	251	194	90	32077	1347	37	2.52	74	34	35	0	4350	184	5	2.54	4	1953-54	1969-70
Brannigan, Andy	NYA	1	1	0	0	0	7	0	0	0.00	....	....	....	....	....	....	....	....		1940-41	1940-41
Brimsek, Frank	Bos., Chi.	10	514	252	182	80	31210	1404	40	2.70	68	32	36	0	4365	186	2	2.56	2	1938-39	1949-50
• Broda, Turk	Tor.	14	629	302	224	101	38173	1609	62	2.53	101	58	42	1	6389	211	13	1.98	5	1936-37	1951-52
Broderick, Ken	Min., Bos.	3	27	11	12	1	1464	74	2	3.03	....	....	....	....	....	....	....	....		1969-70	1974-75
Broderick, Len	Mtl.	1	1	1	0	0	60	2	0	2.00	....	....	....	....	....	....	....	....		1957-58	1957-58
Brodeur, Richard	NYI, Van., Hfd.	9	385	131	175	62	21968	1410	6	3.85	33	13	20	0	2009	111	1	3.32		1979-80	1987-88
Bromley, Gary	Buf., Van.	6	136	54	44	28	7427	425	7	3.43	7	2	5	0	360	25	0	4.17		1973-74	1980-81
• Brooks, Arthur	Tor.	1	4	2	1	0	220	23	0	6.27	....	....	....	....	....	....	....	....		1917-18	1917-18
Brooks, Ross	Bos.	3	54	37	7	6	3047	134	4	2.64	1	0	0	0	20	3	0	9.00		1972-73	1974-75
• Brophy, Frank	Que.	1	21	3	18	0	1247	148	0	7.12	....	....	....	....	....	....	....	....		1919-20	1919-20
Brown, Andy	Det., Pit.	3	62	22	26	9	3373	213	1	3.79	....	....	....	....	....	....	....	....		1971-72	1973-74
Brown, Ken	Chi.	1	1	0	0	0	18	1	0	3.33	....	....	....	....	....	....	....	....		1970-71	1970-71
Brunetta, Mario	Que.	3	40	12	17	1	1967	128	0	3.90	....	....	....	....	....	....	....	....		1987-88	1989-90
Bullock, Bruce	Van.	3	16	3	9	3	927	74	0	4.79	....	....	....	....	....	....	....	....		1972-73	1976-77
Buzinski, Steve	NYR	1	9	2	6	1	560	55	0	5.89	....	....	....	....	....	....	....	....		1942-43	1942-43
Caley, Don	St.L.	1	1	0	0	0	30	3	0	6.00	....	....	....	....	....	....	....	....		1967-68	1967-68
Caprice, Frank	Van.	6	102	31	46	11	5589	391	1	4.20	....	....	....	....	....	....	....	....		1982-83	1987-88
Caron, Jacques	L.A., St.L., Van.	5	72	24	29	11	3846	211	2	3.29	12	4	7	0	639	34	0	3.19		1967-68	1973-74
Carter, Lyle	Cal.	1	15	4	7	0	721	50	0	4.16	....	....	....	....	....	....	....	....		1971-72	1971-72
• Chabot, Lorne	NYR, Tor., Mtl., Chi., Mtl.M., NYA	11	411	206	140	65	25309	861	73	2.04	37	13	17	6	2558	64	5	1.50	2	1926-27	1936-37
Chadwick, Ed	Tor., Bos.	6	184	57	92	35	10980	551	14	3.01	....	....	....	....	....	....	....	....		1955-56	1961-62
Champoux, Bob	Det., Cal.	2	17	2	11	3	923	80	0	5.20	1	0	0	0	55	4	0	4.36		1963-64	1973-74
Cheevers, Gerry	Tor., Bos.	13	418	230	103	74	24394	1175	26	2.89	88	47	35	0	5396	242	8	2.69	2	1961-62	1979-80
Chevrier, Alain	N.J., Wpg., Chi., Pit., Det.	6	234	91	100	14	12202	845	2	4.16	16	9	7	0	1013	44	0	2.61		1985-86	1990-91
Clancy, Frank	Tor.	1	1	0	0	0	1	0	0	0.00	....	....	....	....	....	....	....	....		1931-32	1931-32
Cleghorn, Odie	Pit.	1	1	1	0	0	60	2	0	2.00	....	....	....	....	....	....	....	....		1925-26	1925-26
Clifford, Chris	Chi.	2	2	0	0	0	24	0	0	0.00	....	....	....	....	....	....	....	....		1984-85	1988-89
Cloutier, Jacques	Buf., Chi., Que.	12	255	82	102	24	12826	778	3	3.64	8	1	5	0	413	18	1	2.62		1981-82	1993-94
Colvin, Les	Bos.	1	1	0	1	0	60	4	0	4.00	....	....	....	....	....	....	....	....		1948-49	1948-49
Conacher, Charlie	Tor., Det.	13	3	0	0	0	9	0	0	0.00	....	....	....	....	....	....	....	....		1929-30	1940-41
• Connell, Alex	Ott., Det., NYA, Mtl.M.	12	417	199	155	59	26030	830	81	1.91	21	9	5	7	1309	26	4	1.19	2	1924-25	1936-37
Corsi, Jim	Edm.	1	26	8	14	3	1366	83	0	3.65	....	....	....	....	....	....	....	....		1979-80	1979-80
Courteau, Maurice	Bos.	1	6	2	4	0	360	33	0	5.50	....	....	....	....	....	....	....	....		1943-44	1943-44
Cox, Abbie	Mtl.M., Det., NYA, Mtl.	3	5	1	1	2	263	11	0	2.51	....	....	....	....	....	....	....	....		1929-30	1935-36
Craig, Jim	Atl., Bos., Min.	3	30	11	10	7	1588	100	0	3.78	....	....	....	....	....	....	....	....		1979-80	1983-84
Crha, Jiri	Tor.	2	69	28	27	11	3942	261	0	3.97	5	0	4	0	186	21	0	6.77		1979-80	1980-81
Crozier, Roger	Det., Buf., Wsh.	14	518	206	196	70	28567	1446	30	3.04	31	14	15	0	1769	82	1	2.78		1963-64	1976-77
• Cude, Wilf	Phi., Bos., Chi., Det., Mtl.	10	282	100	129	49	17486	796	24	2.73	19	7	11	1	1317	51	1	2.32		1930-31	1940-41
Cutts, Don	Edm.	1	6	1	2	1	269	16	0	3.57	....	....	....	....	....	....	....	....		1979-80	1979-80
• Cyr, Claude	Mtl.	1	1	0	0	0	20	1	0	3.00	....	....	....	....	....	....	....	....		1958-59	1958-59
Dadswell, Doug	Cgy.	2	27	8	8	3	1346	99	0	4.41	....	....	....	....	....	....	....	....		1986-87	1987-88
D'Alessio, Corrie	Hfd.	1	1	0	0	0	11	0	0	0.00	....	....	....	....	....	....	....	....		1992-93	1992-93
Daley, Joe	Pit., Buf., Det.	4	105	34	44	19	5836	326	3	3.35	....	....	....	....	....	....	....	....		1968-69	1971-72
Damore, Nick	Bos.	1	1	1	0	0	60	3	0	3.00	....	....	....	....	....	....	....	....		1941-42	1941-42
D'Amour, Marc	Cgy., Phi.	2	16	2	4	2	579	32	0	3.32	....	....	....	....	....	....	....	....		1985-86	1988-89
Daskalakis, Cleon	Bos.	3	12	3	4	1	506	41	0	4.86	....	....	....	....	....	....	....	....		1984-85	1986-87
Davidson, John	St.L., NYR	10	301	123	124	39	17109	1004	7	3.52	31	16	14	0	1862	77	1	2.48		1973-74	1982-83
Decourcy, Robert	NYR	1	1	0	0	0	29	6	0	12.41	....	....	....	....	....	....	....	....		1947-48	1947-48
Defelice, Norman	Bos.	1	10	3	5	2	600	30	0	3.00	....	....	....	....	....	....	....	....		1956-57	1956-57
DeJordy, Denis	Chi., L.A., Mtl., Det.	11	316	124	127	51	17798	929	15	3.13	18	6	9	0	946	55	0	3.49		1962-63	1973-74
DelGuidice, Matt	Bos.	2	11	2	5	1	434	28	0	3.87	....	....	....	....	....	....	....	....		1990-91	1991-92
Desjardins, Gerry	L.A., Chi., NYI, Buf.	10	331	122	153	44	19014	1042	12	3.29	35	15	15	0	1874	108	0	3.46		1968-69	1977-78
Dickie, Bill	Chi.	1	1	1	0	0	60	3	0	3.00	....	....	....	....	....	....	....	....		1941-42	1941-42
Dion, Connie	Det.	2	38	23	11	4	2280	119	0	3.13	5	1	4	0	300	17	0	3.40		1943-44	1944-45
Dion, Michel	Que., Wpg., Pit.	6	227	60	118	32	12695	898	2	4.24	5	2	3	0	304	22	0	4.34		1979-80	1984-85
Dolson, Clarence	Det.	3	93	35	44	13	5820	192	16	1.98	2	0	2	0	120	7	0	3.50		1928-29	1930-31
Dowie, Bruce	Tor.	1	2	0	1	0	72	4	0	3.33	....	....	....	....	....	....	....	....		1983-84	1983-84
Dryden, Dave	NYR, Chi., Buf., Edm.	9	203	68	77	26	10424	555	9	3.19	3	0	2	0	133	9	0	4.06		1961-62	1979-80
Dryden, Ken	Mtl.	8	397	258	57	74	23352	870	46	2.24	112	80	32	0	6846	274	10	2.40	6	1970-71	1978-79
Dumas, Michel	Chi.	2	8	2	1	2	362	24	0	3.98	1	0	0	0	19	1	0	3.16		1974-75	1976-77
Dupuis, Bob	Edm.	1	1	0	1	0	60	4	0	4.00	....	....	....	....	....	....	....	....		1979-80	1979-80
• Durnan, Bill	Mtl.	7	383	208	112	62	22945	901	34	2.36	45	27	18	0	2851	99	2	2.08	2	1943-44	1949-50
Dyck, Ed	Van.	3	49	8	28	5	2453	178	1	4.35	....	....	....	....	....	....	....	....		1971-72	1973-74
Edwards, Don	Buf., Cgy., Tor.	10	459	208	155	74	26181	1449	16	3.32	42	16	21	0	2302	132	1	3.44		1976-77	1985-86
Edwards, Gary	St.L., L.A., Clev., Min., Edm., Pit.	13	286	88	125	51	16002	973	10	3.65	11	5	4	0	537	34	0	3.80		1968-69	1981-82
Edwards, Marv	Pit., Tor., Cal.	4	61	15	34	7	3467	218	2	3.77	....	....	....	....	....	....	....	....		1968-69	1973-74
Edwards, Roy	Det., Pit.	7	236	97	88	38	13109	637	12	2.92	4	0	3	0	206	11	0	3.20		1967-68	1973-74
Eliot, Darren	L.A., Det., Buf.	5	89	25	41	12	4931	377	1	4.59	1	0	0	0	40	7	0	10.50		1984-85	1988-89

Name	NHL Teams	NHL Seasons	Regular Schedule GP	W	L	T	Mins	GA	SO	Avg	Playoffs GP	W	L	T	Mins	GA	SO	Avg	NHL Cup Wins	First NHL Season	Last NHL Season
Ellacott, Ken	Van.	1	12	2	3	4	555	41	0	4.43	....	....	....	....	....	....	....	....		1982-83	1982-83
Erickson, Chad	N.J.	1	2	1	1	0	120	9	0	4.50	....	....	....	....	....	....	....	....		1991-92	1991-92
Esposito, Tony	Mtl., Chi.	16	886	423	306	152	52585	2563	76	2.92	99	45	53	0	6017	308	6	3.07	1	1968-69	1983-84
• Evans, Claude	Mtl., Bos.	2	5	2	2	1	280	16	0	3.43	....	....	....	....	....	....	....	....		1954-55	1957-58
Exelby, Randy	Mtl., Edm.	2	2	0	1	0	63	5	0	4.76	....	....	....	....	....	....	....	....		1988-89	1989-90
Farr, Rocky	Buf.	3	19	2	6	3	722	42	0	3.49	....	....	....	....	....	....	....	....		1972-73	1974-75
Favell, Doug	Phi., Tor., Col.	12	373	123	153	69	20771	1096	18	3.17	21	5	16	0	1270	66	1	3.12		1967-68	1978-79
• Forbes, Jake	Tor., Ham., NYA, Phi.	13	210	84	114	11	12922	594	19	2.76	2	0	2	0	120	7	0	3.50		1919-20	1932-33
Ford, Brian	Que., Pit.	2	11	3	7	0	580	61	0	6.31	....	....	....	....	....	....	....	....		1983-84	1984-85
Fowler, Hec	Bos.	1	7	1	6	0	420	43	0	6.14	....	....	....	....	....	....	....	....		1924-25	1924-25
Francis, Emile	Chi., NYR	6	95	31	52	11	5660	355	1	3.76	....	....	....	....	....	....	....	....		1946-47	1951-52
Franks, Jim	Det., NYR, Bos.	4	43	12	23	7	2580	185	1	4.30	1	0	1	0	30	2	0	4.00	1	1936-37	1943-44
Frederick, Ray	Chi.	1	5	0	4	1	300	22	0	4.40	....	....	....	....	....	....	....	....		1954-55	1954-55
Friesen, Karl	N.J.	1	4	0	2	1	130	16	0	7.38	....	....	....	....	....	....	....	....		1986-87	1986-87
Froese, Bob	Phi., NYR	9	242	128	72	20	13451	694	13	3.10	18	3	9	0	830	55	0	3.98		1982-83	1990-91
Gagnon, David	Det.	1	2	0	1	0	35	6	0	10.29	....	....	....	....	....	....	....	....		1990-91	1990-91
• Gamble, Bruce	NYR, Bos., Tor., Phi.	10	327	110	150	45	18442	992	22	3.23	5	0	4	0	206	25	0	7.28		1958-59	1971-72
Gardiner, Bert	NYR, Mtl., Chi., Bos.	6	144	49	68	27	8760	554	3	3.79	9	4	5	0	647	20	0	1.85		1935-36	1943-44
• Gardiner, Chuck	Chi.	7	316	112	152	52	19687	664	42	2.02	21	12	6	3	1532	35	5	1.37	1	1927-28	1933-34
Gardner, George	Det., Van.	5	66	16	31	6	3313	207	0	3.75	....	....	....	....	....	....	....	....		1965-66	1971-72
Garrett, John	Hfd., Que., Van.	6	207	68	91	37	11763	837	1	4.27	9	4	3	0	461	33	0	4.30		1979-80	1984-85
Gatherum, Dave	Det.	1	3	2	0	1	180	3	1	1.00	....	....	....	....	....	....	....	....		1953-54	1953-54
Gauthier, Paul	Mtl.	1	1	0	0	1	70	2	0	1.71	....	....	....	....	....	....	....	....		1937-38	1937-38
Gelineau, Jack	Bos., Chi.	4	143	46	64	33	8580	447	7	3.13	4	2	2	0	260	7	1	1.62		1948-49	1953-54
Giacomin, Ed	NYR, Det.	13	610	289	206	97	35693	1675	54	2.82	65	29	35	0	3834	180	1	2.82		1965-66	1977-78
Gilbert, Gilles	Min., Bos., Det.	14	416	192	143	60	23677	1290	18	3.27	32	17	15	0	1919	97	3	3.03		1969-70	1982-83
Gill, Andre	Bos.	1	5	3	2	0	270	13	1	2.89	....	....	....	....	....	....	....	....		1967-68	1967-68
• Goodman, Paul	Chi.	3	52	23	20	9	3240	117	6	2.17	3	0	3	0	187	10	0	3.21	1	1937-38	1940-41
Gordon, Scott	Que.	2	23	2	16	0	1082	101	0	5.60	....	....	....	....	....	....	....	....		1989-90	1990-91
Gosselin, Mario	Que, L.A., Hfd.	9	241	91	107	14	12857	801	6	3.74	32	16	15	0	1816	99	0	3.27		1983-84	1993-94
Grahame, Ron	Bos., L.A., Que.	4	114	50	43	15	6472	409	5	3.79	4	2	1	0	202	7	0	2.08		1977-78	1980-81
Grant, Ben	Tor., NYA., Bos.	6	50	17	26	4	2990	188	4	3.77	....	....	....	....	....	....	....	....		1928-29	1943-44
Grant, Doug	Det., St.L.	7	77	27	34	8	4199	280	2	4.00	....	....	....	....	....	....	....	....		1973-74	1979-80
Gratton, Gilles	St.L., NYR	2	47	13	18	9	2299	154	0	4.02	....	....	....	....	....	....	....	....		1975-76	1976-77
Gray, Gerry	Det., NYI	2	8	1	5	1	440	35	0	4.77	....	....	....	....	....	....	....	....		1970-71	1972-73
Gray, Harrison	Det.	1	1	0	0	0	40	5	0	7.50	....	....	....	....	....	....	....	....		1963-64	1963-64
Guenette, Steve	Pit., Cgy.	5	35	19	16	0	1958	122	1	3.74	....	....	....	....	....	....	....	....		1986-87	1990-91
• Hainsworth, George	Mtl., Tor.	11	465	246	145	74	29415	937	94	1.91	52	21	26	5	3486	112	8	1.93	2	1926-27	1936-37
Hall, Glenn	Det., Chi., St.L.	18	906	407	327	163	53484	2239	84	2.51	115	49	65	0	6899	321	6	2.79	1	1952-53	1970-71
Hamel, Pierre	Tor., Wpg.	4	69	13	41	7	3766	276	0	4.40	....	....	....	....	....	....	....	....		1974-75	1980-81
Hanlon, Glen	Van., St.L., NYR, Det.	14	477	167	202	61	26037	1561	13	3.60	35	11	15	0	1756	92	4	3.14		1977-78	1990-91
Harrison, Paul	Min., Tor., Pit., Buf.	7	109	28	59	9	5806	408	2	4.22	4	0	1	0	157	9	0	3.44		1975-76	1981-82
Hayward, Brian	Wpg., Mtl., Min., S.J.	11	357	143	156	37	20025	1242	8	3.72	37	11	18	0	1803	104	0	3.46		1982-83	1992-93
Head, Don	Bos.	1	38	9	26	3	2280	161	2	4.24	....	....	....	....	....	....	....	....		1961-62	1961-62
• Hebert, Sammy	Tor., Ott.	2	4	1	3	0	200	19	0	5.70	....	....	....	....	....	....	....	....	1	1917-18	1923-24
Heinz, Rick	St.L., Van.	5	49	14	19	5	2356	159	2	4.05	1	0	0	0	8	1	0	7.50		1980-81	1984-85
Henderson, John	Bos.	2	46	15	15	15	2700	113	5	2.51	2	0	2	0	120	8	0	4.00		1954-55	1955-56
• Henry, Gord	Bos.	4	3	1	2	0	180	5	1	1.67	5	0	4	0	283	21	0	4.45		1948-49	1952-53
Henry, Jim	NYR, Chi., Bos.	9	404	161	173	70	24240	1166	28	2.89	29	11	18	0	1741	81	2	2.79		1941-42	1954-55
Herron, Denis	Pit., K.C., Mtl.	14	462	146	203	76	25608	1579	10	3.70	15	5	10	0	901	50	0	3.33		1972-73	1985-86
Highton, Hec	Chi.	1	24	10	14	0	1440	108	0	4.50	....	....	....	....	....	....	....	....		1943-44	1943-44
Himes, Normie	NYA	2	2	0	0	1	79	3	0	2.28	....	....	....	....	....	....	....	....		1927-28	1928-29
Hodge, Charlie	Mtl., Oak., Van.	13	358	152	124	60	20593	927	24	2.70	16	6	8	0	803	32	2	2.39	4	1954-55	1970-71
Hoffort, Bruce	Phi.	2	9	4	0	3	368	22	0	3.59	....	....	....	....	....	....	....	....		1989-90	1990-91
Hoganson, Paul	Pit.	1	2	0	1	0	57	7	0	7.37	....	....	....	....	....	....	....	....		1970-71	1970-71
Hogosta, Goran	NYI, Que.	2	22	5	12	3	1208	83	1	4.12	....	....	....	....	....	....	....	....		1977-78	1979-80
Holden, Mark	Mtl., Wpg.	4	8	2	2	1	372	25	0	4.03	....	....	....	....	....	....	....	....		1981-82	1984-85
Holland, Ken	Hfd.	1	1	0	1	0	60	7	0	7.00	....	....	....	....	....	....	....	....		1980-81	1980-81
Holland, Robbie	Pit.	2	44	11	22	9	2513	171	1	4.08	....	....	....	....	....	....	....	....		1979-80	1980-81
• Holmes, Harry	Tor., Det.	4	105	41	54	10	6510	264	17	2.43	7	4	3	0	420	26	0	3.71		1917-18	1927-28
Horner, Red	Tor.	1	1	0	0	0	1	1	0	60.00	....	....	....	....	....	....	....	....		1932-33	1932-33
Inness, Gary	Pit., Phi., Wsh.	7	162	58	61	27	8710	494	2	3.40	9	5	4	0	540	24	0	2.67		1973-74	1980-81
Ireland, Randy	Buf.	1	2	0	0	0	30	3	0	6.00	....	....	....	....	....	....	....	....		1978-79	1978-79
Irons, Robbie	St.L.	1	1	0	0	0	3	0	0	0.00	....	....	....	....	....	....	....	....		1968-69	1968-69
• Ironstone, Joe	NYA, Tor.	2	2	1	1	0	110	3	0	1.64	....	....	....	....	....	....	....	....		1925-26	1927-28
Jackson, Doug	Chi.	1	6	2	3	1	360	42	0	7.00	....	....	....	....	....	....	....	....		1947-48	1947-48
Jackson, Percy	Bos., NYA, NYR	4	7	1	3	1	392	26	0	3.98	....	....	....	....	....	....	....	....		1931-32	1935-36
Janaszak, Steve	Min., Col.	2	3	0	1	1	160	15	0	5.62	....	....	....	....	....	....	....	....		1979-80	1981-82
Janecyk, Bob	Chi., L.A.	6	110	43	47	13	6250	432	2	4.15	3	0	3	0	184	10	0	3.26		1983-84	1988-89
Jenkins, Roger	NYA	1	1	0	1	0	30	7	0	14.00	....	....	....	....	....	....	....	....		1938-39	1938-39
Jensen, Al	Det., Wsh., L.A.	7	179	95	53	18	9974	557	8	3.35	12	5	5	0	598	32	0	3.21		1980-81	1986-87
Jensen, Darren	Phi.	2	30	15	10	1	1496	95	2	3.81	....	....	....	....	....	....	....	....		1984-85	1985-86
Johnson, Bob	St.L., Pit.	2	24	9	9	1	1059	66	0	3.74	....	....	....	....	....	....	....	....		1972-73	1974-75
Johnston, Eddie	Bos., Tor., St.L., Chi.	16	592	236	256	81	34209	1855	32	3.25	18	7	10	0	1023	57	1	3.34	2	1962-63	1977-78
Junkin, Joe	Bos.	1	1	0	0	0	8	0	0	0.00	....	....	....	....	....	....	....	....		1968-69	1968-69
Kaarela, Jari	Col.	1	5	2	2	0	220	22	0	6.00	....	....	....	....	....	....	....	....		1980-81	1980-81
Kampurri, Hannu	N.J.	1	13	1	10	1	645	54	0	5.02	....	....	....	....	....	....	....	....		1984-85	1984-85
• Karakas, Mike	Chi., Mtl.	8	336	114	169	53	20616	1002	28	2.92	23	11	12	0	1434	72	3	3.01	1	1935-36	1945-46
Keans, Doug	L.A., Bos.	9	210	96	64	26	11388	666	4	3.51	9	2	6	0	432	34	0	4.72		1979-80	1987-88
Keenan, Don	Bos.	1	1	0	1	0	60	4	0	4.00	....	....	....	....	....	....	....	....		1958-59	1958-59
• Kerr, Dave	Mtl.M., NYA, NYR	11	426	203	148	75	26519	960	51	2.17	40	18	19	3	2616	76	8	1.74	1	1930-31	1940-41
King, Scott	Det.	2	2	0	0	0	61	3	0	2.95	....	....	....	....	....	....	....	....		1990-91	1991-92
Kleisinger, Terry	NYR	1	4	0	2	0	191	14	0	4.40	....	....	....	....	....	....	....	....		1985-86	1985-86
Klymkiw, Julian	NYR	1	1	0	0	0	19	2	0	6.32	....	....	....	....	....	....	....	....		1958-59	1958-59
Kurt, Gary	Cal.	1	16	1	7	5	838	60	0	4.30	....	....	....	....	....	....	....	....		1971-72	1971-72
Lacroix, Al	Mtl.	1	5	1	4	0	280	16	0	3.43	....	....	....	....	....	....	....	....		1925-26	1925-26
LaFerriere, Rick	Col.	1	1	0	0	0	20	1	0	3.00	....	....	....	....	....	....	....	....		1981-82	1981-82
• Larocque, Michel	Mtl., Tor., Phi., St.L.	11	312	160	89	45	17615	978	17	3.33	14	6	6	0	759	37	1	2.92	4	1973-74	1983-84
Laskowski, Gary	L.A.	2	59	19	27	5	2942	228	0	4.65	....	....	....	....	....	....	....	....		1982-83	1983-84
Laxton, Gord	Pit.	4	17	4	9	0	800	74	0	5.55	....	....	....	....	....	....	....	....		1975-76	1978-79
LeDuc, Albert	Mtl.	1	1	0	0	0	2	1	0	30.00	....	....	....	....	....	....	....	....		1931-32	1931-32
Legris, Claude	Det.	2	4	0	1	1	91	4	0	2.64	....	....	....	....	....	....	....	....		1980-81	1981-82
• Lehman, Hugh	Chi.	2	48	20	24	4	3047	136	6	2.68	2	0	1	1	120	10	0	5.00		1926-27	1927-28
Lemelin, Reggie	Atl., Cgy., Bos.	15	507	236	162	63	28006	1613	12	3.46	59	23	25	0	3119	186	2	3.58		1978-79	1992-93
Lessard, Mario	L.A.	6	240	92	97	39	13529	843	9	3.74	20	6	12	0	1136	83	0	4.38		1978-79	1983-84
Levasseur, Louis	Min.	1	1	0	1	0	60	7	0	7.00	....	....	....	....	....	....	....	....		1979-80	1979-80
Levinsky, Alex	Tor.	1	1	0	0	0	1	1	0	60.00	....	....	....	....	....	....	....	....		1932-33	1932-33
• Lindbergh, Pelle	Phi.	5	157	87	49	15	9151	503	7	3.30	23	12	10	0	1214	63	3	3.11		1981-82	1985-86
• Lindsay, Bert	Mtl.W., Tor.	2	20	6	14	0	2219	118	0	3.19	....	....	....	....	....	....	....	....		1917-18	1918-19
Liut, Mike	St. L., Hfd., Wsh.	13	663	294	271	74	38155	2219	25	3.49	67	29	32	0	3814	215	2	3.38		1979-80	1991-92
Lockett, Ken	Van.	2	55	13	15	8	2348	131	2	3.35	1	0	1	0	60	6	0	6.00		1974-75	1975-76
• Lockhart, Howie	Tor., Que., Ham., Bos.	5	57	17	39	0	3371	282	1	5.02	....	....	....	....	....	....	....	....		1919-20	1924-25
LoPresti, Pete	Min., Edm.	6	175	43	102	20	9858	668	5	4.07	2	0	2	0	77	6	0	4.68		1974-75	1980-81
• LoPresti, Sam	Chi.	2	74	30	38	6	4530	236	4	3.13	8	3	5	0	530	17	1	1.92		1940-41	1941-42
Loustel, Ron	Wpg.	1	1	0	1	0	60	10	0	10.00	....	....	....	....	....	....	....	....		1980-81	1980-81
Low, Ron	Tor., Wsh., Det., Que., Edm., NJ	11	382	102	203	38	20502	1463	4	4.28	7	1	6	0	452	29	0	3.85		1972-73	1984-85
Lozinski, Larry	Det.	1	30	6	11	7	1459	105	0	4.32	....	....	....	....	....	....	....	....		1980-81	1980-81
Lumley, Harry	Det., NYR, Chi., Tor., Bos.	16	804	333	326	143	48107	2210	71	2.76	76	29	47	0	4759	199	7	2.51	1	1943-44	1959-60
MacKenzie, Shawn	N.J.	1	4	0	1	0	130	15	0	6.92	....	....	....	....	....	....	....	....		1982-83	1982-83
Maneluk, George	NYI	1	4	1	1	0	140	15	0	6.43	....	....	....	....	....	....	....	....		1990-91	1990-91
Maniago, Cesare	Tor., Mtl., NYR, Min., Van.	15	568	189	261	96	32570	1774	30	3.27	36	15	21	0	2245	100	3	2.67		1960-61	1977-78
Marios, Jean	Tor., Chi.	2	3	1	2	0	180	15	0	5.00	....	....	....	....	....	....	....	....		1943-44	1953-54
Martin, Seth	St.L.	1	30	8	10	7	1552	67	1	2.59	2	0	0	0	73	5	0	4.11		1967-68	1967-68
Mattson, Markus	Wpg., Min., L.A.	4	92	21	46	14	5007	343	6	4.11	....	....	....	....	....	....	....	....		1979-80	1983-84

Name	NHL Teams	NHL Seasons	Regular Schedule GP	W	L	T	Mins	GA	SO	Avg	Playoffs GP	W	L	T	Mins	GA	SO	Avg	NHL Cup Wins	First NHL Season	Last NHL Season
May, Darrell	St. L.	2	6	1	5	0	364	31	0	5.11	....	....	....	....	....	....	....	....		1985-86	1987-88
Mayer, Gilles	Tor.	4	9	1	7	1	540	25	0	2.78	....	....	....	....	....	....	....	....		1949-50	1955-56
McAuley, Ken	NYR	2	96	17	64	15	5740	537	1	5.61	....	....	....	....	....	....	....	....		1943-44	1944-45
McCartan, Jack	NYR	2	12	3	7	2	680	43	1	3.79	....	....	....	....	....	....	....	....		1959-60	1960-61
• McCool, Frank	Tor.	2	72	34	31	7	4320	242	4	3.36	13	8	5	0	807	30	4	2.23	1	1944-45	1945-46
McDuffe, Pete	St.L., NYR, K.C., Det.	5	57	11	36	6	3207	218	0	4.08	1	0	1	0	60	7	0	7.00		1971-72	1975-76
McGrattan, Tom	Det.	1	1	0	0	0	8	0	0	0.00	....	....	....	....	....	....	....	....		1947-48	1947-48
McKay, Ross	Hfd.	1	1	0	0	0	35	3	0	5.14	....	....	....	....	....	....	....	....		1990-91	1990-91
McKenzie, Bill	Det., K.C., Col.	6	91	18	49	13	4776	326	2	4.10	....	....	....	....	....	....	....	....		1973-74	1979-80
McKichan, Steve	Van.	1	1	0	0	0	20	2	0	6.00	....	....	....	....	....	....	....	....		1990-91	1990-91
McLachlan, Murray	Tor.	1	2	0	1	0	25	4	0	9.60	....	....	....	....	....	....	....	....		1970-71	1970-71
McLelland, Dave	Van.	1	2	1	1	0	120	10	0	5.00	....	....	....	....	....	....	....	....		1972-73	1972-73
McLeod, Don	Det., Phi.	2	18	3	10	1	879	74	0	5.05	....	....	....	....	....	....	....	....		1970-71	1971-72
McLeod, Jim	St.L.	1	16	6	6	4	880	44	0	3.00	....	....	....	....	....	....	....	....		1971-72	1971-72
McNamara, Gerry	Tor.	2	7	2	2	1	323	15	0	2.79	....	....	....	....	....	....	....	....		1960-61	1969-70
McNeil, Gerry	Mtl.	7	276	119	105	52	16535	650	28	2.36	35	17	18	0	2284	72	5	1.89	3	1947-48	1956-57
McRae, Gord	Tor.	5	71	30	22	10	3799	221	1	3.49	8	2	5	0	454	22	0	2.91		1972-73	1977-78
Melanson, Rollie	NYI, Min., L.A., N.J., Mtl.	11	291	129	106	33	16452	995	6	3.63	23	4	9	0	801	59	0	4.42	3	1980-81	1991-92
Meloche, Gilles	Chi., Cal., Cle., Min., Pit.	18	788	270	351	131	45401	2756	20	3.64	45	21	19	0	2464	143	2	3.48		1970-71	1987-88
Micalef, Corrado	Det.	5	113	26	59	15	5794	409	2	4.24	3	0	0	0	49	8	0	9.80		1981-82	1985-86
Middlebrook, Lindsay	Wpg., Min., N.J., Edm.	4	37	3	23	6	1845	152	0	4.94	....	....	....	....	....	....	....	....		1979-80	1982-83
• Millar, Al	Bos.	1	6	1	3	2	360	25	0	4.17	....	....	....	....	....	....	....	....		1957-58	1957-58
Millen, Greg	Pit., Hfd., St. L., Que., Chi., Det.	14	604	215	284	89	35377	2281	17	3.87	59	27	29	0	3383	193	0	3.42		1978-79	1991-92
• Miller, Joe	NYA, NYR, Pit., Phi.	4	130	24	90	16	7981	386	16	2.90	3	2	1	0	180	3	1	1.00		1927-28	1930-31
Mio, Eddie	Edm., NYR, Det.	7	192	64	73	30	12299	822	6	4.01	17	9	7	0	986	63	0	3.83		1979-80	1985-86
• Mitchell, Ivan	Tor.	3	21	11	9	0	1232	93	0	4.53	....	....	....	....	....	....	....	....	1	1919-20	1921-22
Moffatt, Mike	Bos.	3	19	7	7	2	979	70	0	4.29	11	6	5	0	663	38	0	3.44		1981-82	1983-84
Moore, Alfie	NYA, Det., Chi.,	4	21	7	14	0	1290	81	1	3.77	3	1	2	0	180	7	0	2.33	1	1936-37	1939-40
Moore, Robbie	Phi., Wsh.	2	6	3	1	1	257	8	2	1.87	5	3	2	0	268	18	0	4.03		1978-79	1982-83
Morisette, Jean	Mtl.	1	1	0	1	0	36	4	0	6.67	....	....	....	....	....	....	....	....		1963-64	1963-64
Mowers, Johnny	Det.	4	152	65	61	26	9350	399	15	2.56	32	19	13	0	2000	85	2	2.55	1	1940-41	1946-47
Mrazek, Jerry	Phi.	1	1	0	0	0	6	1	0	10.00	....	....	....	....	....	....	....	....		1975-76	1975-76
• Mummery, Harry	Que., Ham.	2	4	2	1	0	191	20	0	6.28	....	....	....	....	....	....	....	....		1919-20	1921-22
• Murphy, Hal	Mtl.	1	1	1	0	0	60	4	0	4.00	....	....	....	....	....	....	....	....		1952-53	1952-53
Murray, Tom	Mtl.	1	1	0	1	0	60	4	0	4.00	....	....	....	....	....	....	....	....		1929-30	1929-30
Myllys, Jarmo	Min., S.J.	4	39	4	27	1	1846	161	0	5.23	....	....	....	....	....	....	....	....		1988-89	1991-92
Mylnikov, Sergei	Que.	1	10	1	7	2	568	47	0	4.96	....	....	....	....	....	....	....	....		1989-90	1989-90
Myre, Phil	Mtl., Atl., St.L., Phi., Col., Buf.	14	439	149	198	76	25220	1482	14	3.53	12	6	5	0	747	41	1	3.29		1969-70	1982-83
Newton, Cam	Pit.	2	16	4	7	1	814	51	0	3.76	....	....	....	....	....	....	....	....		1970-71	1972-73
Norris, Jack	Bos., Chi., L.A.	4	58	19	26	4	3119	202	2	3.89	....	....	....	....	....	....	....	....		1964-65	1970-71
Oleschuk, Bill	K.C., Col.	4	55	7	28	10	2835	188	1	3.98	....	....	....	....	....	....	....	....		1975-76	1979-80
• Olesevich, Dan	NYR	1	1	0	0	1	40	2	0	3.00	....	....	....	....	....	....	....	....		1961-62	1961-62
Ouimet, Ted	St.L.	1	1	0	1	0	60	2	0	2.00	....	....	....	....	....	....	....	....		1968-69	1968-69
Pageau, Paul	L.A.	1	1	0	1	0	60	8	0	8.00	....	....	....	....	....	....	....	....		1980-81	1980-81
Paille, Marcel	NYR	7	107	33	52	21	6342	362	2	3.42	....	....	....	....	....	....	....	....		1957-58	1964-65
Palmateer, Mike	Tor., Wsh.	8	356	149	138	52	20131	1183	17	3.53	29	12	17	0	1765	89	2	3.03		1976-77	1983-84
Pang, Darren	Chi.	3	81	27	35	7	4252	287	0	4.05	6	1	3	0	250	18	0	4.32		1984-85	1988-89
Parent, Bernie	Bos., Tor., Phi.	13	608	270	197	121	35136	1493	55	2.55	71	38	33	0	4302	174	6	2.43	2	1965-66	1978-79
Parent, Bob	Tor.	2	3	0	2	0	160	15	0	5.62	....	....	....	....	....	....	....	....		1981-82	1982-83
Parro, Dave	Wsh.	4	77	21	36	10	4015	274	2	4.09	....	....	....	....	....	....	....	....		1980-81	1983-84
• Patrick, Lester	NYR	1	....	....	....	....	....	....	....	....	1	1	0	0	46	1	0	1.30		1927-28	1927-28
Peeters, Pete	Phi., Bos., Wsh.	13	489	246	155	51	27699	1424	21	3.08	71	35	35	0	4200	232	2	3.31		1978-79	1990-91
Pelletier, Marcel	Chi., NYR	2	8	1	6	1	395	33	0	5.01	....	....	....	....	....	....	....	....		1950-51	1962-63
Penney, Steve	Mtl., Wpg.	5	91	35	38	12	5194	313	1	3.62	27	15	12	0	1604	72	4	2.69		1983-84	1987-88
• Perreault, Robert	Mtl., Det., Bos.	3	31	8	16	6	1833	106	2	3.47	....	....	....	....	....	....	....	....		1955-56	1962-63
Pettie, Jim	Bos.	3	21	9	7	2	1157	71	1	3.68	....	....	....	....	....	....	....	....		1976-77	1978-79
• Plante, Jacques	Mtl., NYR, St.L., Tor., Bos.	18	837	434	246	147	49553	1965	82	2.38	112	71	37	0	6651	241	14	2.17	6	1952-53	1972-73
Plasse, Michel	St.L., Mtl., K.C., Pit., Col., Que.	11	299	92	136	54	16760	1058	2	3.79	4	1	2	0	195	9	1	2.77	1	1970-71	1981-82
Plaxton, Hugh	Mtl.M.	1	1	0	1	0	59	5	0	5.08	....	....	....	....	....	....	....	....		1932-33	1932-33
Pronovost, Claude	Bos., Mtl.	2	3	1	1	0	120	7	1	3.50	....	....	....	....	....	....	....	....		1955-56	1958-59
Pusey, Chris	Det.	1	1	0	0	0	40	3	0	4.50	....	....	....	....	....	....	....	....		1985-86	1985-86
Raymond, Alain	Wsh.	1	1	0	1	0	40	2	0	3.00	....	....	....	....	....	....	....	....		1987-88	1987-88
Rayner, Chuck	NYA, Bro., NYR	10	424	138	209	77	25491	1294	25	3.05	18	9	9	0	1134	46	1	2.43		1940-41	1952-53
Reaugh, Daryl	Edm., Hfd.	3	27	8	9	1	1246	72	1	3.47	....	....	....	....	....	....	....	....		1984-85	1990-91
Redquest, Greg	Pit.	1	1	0	0	0	13	3	0	13.85	....	....	....	....	....	....	....	....		1977-78	1977-78
Reece, Dave	Bos.	1	14	7	5	2	777	43	2	3.32	....	....	....	....	....	....	....	....		1975-76	1975-76
Resch, Glenn	NYI, Col., N.J., Phi.	14	571	231	224	82	32279	1761	26	3.27	41	17	17	0	2044	85	2	2.50	1	1973-74	1986-87
Rheaume, Herb	Mtl.	1	31	10	19	1	1889	92	0	2.92	....	....	....	....	....	....	....	....		1925-26	1925-26
Ricci, Nick	Pit.	4	19	7	12	0	1087	79	0	4.36	....	....	....	....	....	....	....	....		1979-80	1982-83
Richardson, Terry	Det., St.L.	5	20	3	11	0	906	85	0	5.63	....	....	....	....	....	....	....	....		1973-74	1978-79
Ridley, Curt	NYR, Van., Tor.	6	104	27	47	16	5498	355	1	3.87	2	0	2	0	120	8	0	4.00		1974-75	1980-81
Riggin, Dennis	Det.	2	18	5	10	2	985	54	1	3.29	....	....	....	....	....	....	....	....		1959-60	1962-63
Riggin, Pat	Atl., Cgy., Wsh., Bos., Pit.	9	350	153	120	52	19872	1135	11	3.43	25	8	13	0	1336	72	0	3.23		1979-80	1987-88
Ring, Bob	Bos.	1	1	0	0	0	34	4	0	7.06	....	....	....	....	....	....	....	....		1965-66	1965-66
Rivard, Fern	Min.	4	55	9	27	11	2865	190	2	3.98	....	....	....	....	....	....	....	....		1968-69	1974-75
• Roach, John	Tor., NYR, Det.	14	491	218	204	69	30423	1246	58	2.46	34	15	16	3	2206	69	8	1.88	1	1921-22	1934-35
• Roberts, Moe	Bos., NYA, Chi.	4	10	2	5	0	506	31	0	3.68	....	....	....	....	....	....	....	....		1925-26	1951-52
• Robertson, Earl	NYA, Bro., Det.	6	190	60	95	34	11820	575	16	2.92	15	6	7	0	995	29	2	1.75	1	1936-37	1941-42
Rollins, Al	Tor., Chi., NYR	9	430	138	205	84	25717	1196	28	2.79	13	6	7	0	755	30	0	2.38	1	1949-50	1959-60
Romano, Roberto	Pit., Bos.	6	126	46	63	8	7111	471	4	3.97	....	....	....	....	....	....	....	....		1982-83	1993-94
Rupp, Pat	Det.	1	1	0	1	0	60	4	0	4.00	....	....	....	....	....	....	....	....		1963-64	1963-64
Rutherford, Jim	Det., Pit., Tor., L.A.	13	457	151	227	59	25895	1576	14	3.65	8	2	5	0	440	28	0	3.82		1970-71	1982-83
Rutledge, Wayne	L.A.	3	82	27	41	6	4325	241	2	3.34	8	2	2	0	378	20	0	3.17		1967-68	1969-70
St. Laurent, Sam	N.J., Det.	5	34	7	12	4	1572	92	1	3.51	1	0	0	0	10	1	0	6.00		1985-86	1989-90
Sands, Charlie	Mtl.	1	1	0	0	0	25	5	0	12.00	....	....	....	....	....	....	....	....		1939-40	1939-40
Sands, Mike	Min.	2	6	0	5	0	302	26	0	5.17	....	....	....	....	....	....	....	....		1984-85	1986-87
Sauve, Bob	Buf., Det., Chi., N.J.	13	405	182	154	54	23711	1377	8	3.48	34	15	16	0	1850	95	4	3.08		1976-77	1987-88
• Sawchuk, Terry	Det., Bos., Tor., L.A., NYR	21	971	447	330	173	57205	2401	103	2.52	106	54	48	0	6291	267	12	2.55	4	1949-50	1969-70
Schaefer, Joe	NYR	2	2	0	1	0	86	8	0	5.58	....	....	....	....	....	....	....	....		1959-60	1960-61
Scott, Ron	NYR, L.A.	5	28	8	13	4	1450	91	0	3.77	1	0	0	0	32	4	0	7.50		1983-84	1989-90
Sevigny, Richard	Mtl., Que.	8	176	80	54	20	9485	507	5	3.21	6	0	3	0	208	13	0	3.75	1	1979-80	1986-87
Sharples, Scott	Cgy.	1	1	0	0	1	65	4	0	3.69	....	....	....	....	....	....	....	....		1991-92	1991-92
Shields, Al	NYA	1	2	0	0	0	41	9	0	13.17	....	....	....	....	....	....	....	....		1931-32	1931-32
Simmons, Don	Bos., Tor., NYR	11	247	98	104	39	14436	705	20	2.93	24	13	11	0	1436	64	3	2.67	2	1956-57	1968-69
Simmons, Gary	Cal., Clev., L.A.	4	107	30	57	15	6162	366	5	3.56	1	0	0	0	20	1	0	3.00		1974-75	1977-78
Skidmore, Paul	St.L.	1	2	1	1	0	120	6	0	3.00	....	....	....	....	....	....	....	....		1981-82	1981-82
Skorodenski, Warren	Chi., Edm.	5	35	12	11	4	1732	100	2	3.46	2	0	0	0	33	6	0	10.91		1981-82	1987-88
Smith, Al	Tor., Pit., Det., Buf., Hfd., Col.	10	233	74	99	36	12752	735	10	3.46	6	1	4	0	317	21	0	3.97		1965-66	1980-81
Smith, Billy	L.A., NYI	18	680	305	233	105	38431	2031	22	3.17	132	88	36	0	7645	348	5	2.73	4	1971-72	1988-89
Smith, Gary	Tor., Oak., Cal., Chi., Van., Min., Wsh., Wpg.	14	532	174	258	74	29619	1675	26	3.39	20	5	13	0	1153	62	1	3.23		1965-66	1979-80
• Smith, Norman	Mtl.M., Det.	8	199	81	83	35	12297	475	17	2.32	12	9	2	0	880	18	3	1.23	2	1931-32	1944-45
Sneddon, Bob	Cal.	1	5	0	2	0	225	21	0	5.60	....	....	....	....	....	....	....	....		1970-71	1970-71
Soetaert, Doug	NYR, Wpg., Mtl.	12	284	110	104	42	15583	1030	6	3.97	5	1	2	0	180	14	0	4.67	1	1975-76	1986-87
• Spooner, Red	Pit.	1	1	0	1	0	60	6	0	6.00	....	....	....	....	....	....	....	....		1929-30	1929-30
St.Croix, Rick	Phi., Tor.	8	129	49	54	18	7275	450	2	3.71	11	4	6	0	562	29	1	3.10		1977-78	1984-85
Staniowski, Ed	St.L., Wpg., Hfd.	10	219	67	104	21	12075	818	2	4.06	8	1	6	0	428	28	0	3.93		1975-76	1984-85
Starr, Harold	Mtl.M.	1	1	0	0	0	3	0	0	0.00	....	....	....	....	....	....	....	....		1931-32	1931-32
Stefan, Greg	Det.	9	299	115	127	30	16333	1068	5	3.92	30	12	17	0	1681	99	1	3.53		1981-82	1989-90
Stein, Phil	Tor.	1	1	0	0	1	70	2	0	1.71	....	....	....	....	....	....	....	....		1939-40	1939-40
Stephenson, Wayne	St.L., Phi., Wsh.	10	328	146	103	49	18343	937	14	3.06	26	11	12	0	1522	79	2	3.11	1	1971-72	1980-81
Stevenson, Doug	NYR, Chi.	2	8	2	6	0	480	39	0	4.88	....	....	....	....	....	....	....	....		1944-45	1945-46
Stewart, Charles	Bos.	3	77	31	41	5	4737	194	10	2.46	....	....	....	....	....	....	....	....		1924-25	1926-27
Stewart, Jim	Bos.	1	1	0	1	0	20	5	0	15.00	....	....	....	....	....	....	....	....		1979-80	1979-80

Name	NHL Teams	NHL Seasons	GP	W	L	T	Mins	GA	SO	Avg	GP	W	L	T	Mins	GA	SO	Avg	NHL Cup Wins	First NHL Season	Last NHL Season
Stuart, Herb	Det.	1	3	0	1	0	180	5	0	1.67	....	....	....	....	....	....	....	....		1926-27	1926-27
Sylvestri, Don	Bos.	1	3	0	0	2	102	6	0	3.53	....	....	....	....	....	....	....	....		1984-85	1984-85
Takko, Kari	Min., Edm.	6	142	37	71	14	7317	475	1	3.90	4	0	1	0	109	7	0	3.85		1985-86	1990-91
Tataryn, Dave	NYR	1	2	1	1	0	80	10	0	7.50	....	....	....	....	....	....	....	....		1976-77	1976-77
Taylor, Bobby	Phi., Pit.	5	46	15	17	6	2268	155	0	4.10	....	....	....	....	....	....	....	....	1	1971-72	1975-76
Teno, Harvey	Det.	1	5	2	3	0	300	15	0	3.00	....	....	....	....	....	....	....	....		1938-39	1938-39
Thomas, Wayne	Mtl., Tor., NYR	8	243	103	93	34	13768	766	10	3.34	15	6	8	0	849	50	1	3.53		1972-73	1980-81
• Thompson, Tiny	Bos., Det.	12	553	284	194	75	34174	1183	81	2.08	44	20	22	0	2970	93	7	1.88	1	1928-29	1939-40
Tremblay, Vince	Tor., Pit.	5	58	12	26	8	2785	223	1	4.80	....	....	....	....	....	....	....	....		1979-80	1983-84
Tucker, Ted	Cal.	1	5	1	1	1	177	10	0	3.39	....	....	....	....	....	....	....	....		1973-74	1973-74
Turner, Joe	Det.	1	1	0	0	1	60	3	0	3.00	....	....	....	....	....	....	....	....		1941-42	1941-42
Vachon, Rogatien	Mtl., L.A., Det., Bos.	16	795	355	291	127	46298	2310	51	2.99	48	23	23	0	2876	133	2	2.77	3	1966-67	1981-82
Veisor, Mike	Chi., Hfd., Wpg.	10	139	41	62	26	7806	532	5	4.09	4	0	2	0	180	15	0	5.00		1973-74	1983-84
• Vezina, Georges	Mtl.	9	191	105	80	5	11564	633	13	3.28	26	19	6	0	1596	74	4	2.78	2	1917-18	1925-26
Villemure, Gilles	NYR, Chi.	10	205	100	65	28	11581	542	13	2.81	14	5	5	0	656	32	0	2.93		1963-64	1976-77
Wakely, Ernie	Mtl., St.L.	5	113	41	42	17	6344	290	8	2.74	10	2	6	0	509	37	1	4.36		1962-63	1971-72
• Walsh, James	Mtl.M., NYA	7	108	48	43	16	6461	250	12	2.32	8	2	4	2	570	16	2	1.68		1926-27	1932-33
Wamsley, Rick	Mtl., St.L., Cgy., Tor.	13	407	204	131	46	23123	1287	12	3.34	27	7	18	0	1397	81	0	3.48	1	1980-81	1992-93
Watt, Jim	St.L.	1	1	0	0	0	20	2	0	6.00	....	....	....	....	....	....	....	....		1973-74	1973-74
Weeks, Steve	NYR, Hfd., Van., NYI, L.A., Ott.	13	291	112	119	33	15879	989	5	3.74	12	3	5	0	486	27	0	3.33		1980-81	1992-93
Wetzel, Carl	Det., Min.	2	7	1	3	1	302	22	0	4.37	....	....	....	....	....	....	....	....		1964-65	1967-68
Wilson, Dunc	Phi., Van., Tor., NYR, Pit.	10	287	80	150	33	15851	988	8	3.74	....	....	....	....	....	....	....	....		1969-70	1978-79
Wilson, Lefty	Det., Tor., Bos.	3	3	0	0	1	85	1	0	0.71	....	....	....	....	....	....	....	....		1953-54	1957-58
Winkler, Hal	NYR, Bos.	2	75	35	26	14	4739	126	21	1.60	10	2	3	5	640	18	2	1.69		1926-27	1927-28
Wolfe, Bernie	Wsh.	4	120	20	61	21	6104	424	1	4.17	....	....	....	....	....	....	....	....		1975-76	1978-79
Woods, Alec	NYA	1	1	0	1	0	70	3	0	2.57	....	....	....	....	....	....	....	....		1936-37	1936-37
Worsley, Gump	NYR, Mtl., Min.	21	862	335	353	151	50232	2432	43	2.90	70	41	25	0	4081	192	5	2.82	4	1952-53	1973-74
• Worters, Roy	Pit., NYA, Mtl.	12	484	171	233	68	30175	1143	66	2.27	11	3	6	2	690	24	3	2.09		1925-26	1936-37
Worthy, Chris	Oak., Cal.	3	26	5	10	4	1326	98	0	4.43	....	....	....	....	....	....	....	....		1968-69	1970-71
Young, Doug	Det.	1	1	0	0	0	21	1	0	2.86	....	....	....	....	....	....	....	....		1933-34	1933-34
Zanier, Mike	Edm.	1	3	1	1	1	185	12	0	3.89	....	....	....	....	....	....	....	....		1984-85	1984-85

1994-95 Transactions

August, 1994

8 – D **Ruslan Batyrshin** and Winnipeg's 2nd round pick in the 1996 Entry Draft traded from Winnipeg to Los Angeles for D **Brent Thompson** and future considerations.

19 – C **Guy Carbonneau** traded from Montreal to St. Louis for C **Jim Montgomery.**

19 – D **Glen Featherstone** traded from Boston to NY Rangers for LW **Daniel Lacroix.**

25 – D **Glen Wesley** traded to Hartford by Boston for Hartford 1st round picks in the 1995 (D **Kyle McLaren**), 1996 and 1997 Entry Drafts.

29 – D **Bill Houlder** traded to St. Louis by Anaheim for D **Jason Marshall.**

30 – D **Bryan Marchment** acquired by Edmonton from Hartford as compensation for Hartford's signing free agent RW **Steven Rice.**

September

6 – RW **Alexander Selivanov** traded from Philadelphia to Tampa Bay for Philadelphia's 4th round pick in the 1995 Entry Draft (previously acquired). Philadelphia selected LW **Radovan Somik.**

22 – G **Ron Hextall** and the NY Islanders' 6th round pick in the 1995 Entry Draft traded from NY Islanders to Philadelphia for G **Tommy Soderstrom.** (Philadelphia selected D **Dmitri Tertyshny.**)

28 – RW **David Sacco** traded from Toronto to Anaheim for C **Terry Yake.**

29 – D **Robert Svehla** and D **Magnus Svensson** traded from Calgary to Florida for Florida's 3rd round pick in the 1996 Entry Draft and a future conditional draft pick.

October

3 – RW **Dixon Ward**, C **Guy Leveque**, C **Kelly Fairchild** and RW **Shayne Toporowski** traded from Los Angeles to Toronto for LW **Eric Lacroix**, D **Chris Snell** and Toronto's 4th round pick in the 1996 Entry Draft.

6 – D **Tom Tilley** traded from St. Louis to Tampa Bay for C **Adam Creighton.**

15 – LW **Jason Zent** traded from NY Islanders to Ottawa for Ottawa's 5th round pick in the 1996 Entry Draft.

January, 1995

4 – 1995 Waiver Draft

RW **Rob Gaudreau** to Ottawa from San Jose

D **Brian Glynn** to Hartford from Vancouver

D **Dean Kennedy** to Edmonton from Winnipeg

RW **Kelly Chase** to Hartford from St. Louis

D **Len Esau** to Edmonton from Calgary

D **Donald Dufresne** to St. Louis from Los Angeles

LW **Randy Wood** to Toronto from Buffalo

D **Chris Joseph** to Pittsburgh from Tampa Bay

RW **Igor Korolev** to Winnipeg from St. Louis

D **Francois Leroux** to Pittsburgh from Ottawa

RW **Sheldon Kennedy** to Calgay from Winnipeg

D **Wayne McBean** to Pittsburgh from Winnipeg

D **Roger Johansson** to Chicago from Calgary

RW **Doug Brown** to Chicago from Pittsburgh

C **Micah Aivazoff** to Edmonton from Pittsburgh

LW **Greg Gilbert** to St. Louis from NY Rangers

C **Mike Hudson** to Pittsburgh from NY Rangers

18 – D **Kevin Hatcher** traded from Washington to Dallas for D **Mark Tinordi** and D **Rick Mrozik.**

18 – G **Don Beaupre** traded from Washington to Ottawa for Ottawa's 5th round pick in the 1995 Entry Draft. (Washington selected C **Benoit Gratton**.)

30 – LW **Rob Conn** traded from Chicago to New Jersey for D **Dean Malkoc.**

31 – C **Iain Fraser** traded from Quebec to Dallas for a conditional pick in the 1996 Entry Draft.

February

2 – G **Mike Greenlay** traded from Tampa Bay to Philadelphia for G **Scott LaGrand.**

2 – LW **Todd Krygier** traded from Washington to Anaheim for Anaheim's 4th round pick in the 1996 Entry Draft.

6 – G **Jimmy Waite** traded from San Jose to Chicago for a conditional pick in the 1997 Entry Draft.

9 – D **Eric Desjardins**, LW **Gilbert Dionne** and C **John LeClair** traded from Montreal to Philadelphia for RW **Mark Recchi** and Philadelphia's 3rd round pick in the 1995 Entry Draft. (Montreal selected LW **Martin Hohenberger.**)

10 – D **Paul Stanton** traded from Boston to NY Islanders for NY Islanders' 8th round pick in the 1995 Entry Draft. This pick was later traded to Ottawa. Ottawa selected D **Ray Schultz.**)

10 – C **Mark Lamb** traded from Philadelphia to Montreal for cash.

10 – LW **Warren Rychel** traded from Los Angeles to Washington for LW **Randy Burridge.**

10 – LW **Warren Rychel** traded from Washington to Toronto for Toronto's 4th round pick in the 1995 Entry Draft. (Washington selected G **Sebastien Charpentier.**)

February continued

14 – D **Alexei Zhitnik**, G **Robb Stauber**, D **Charlie Huddy** and Los Angeles' 5th round pick in the 1995 Entry Draft traded from Los Angeles to Buffalo for D **Philippe Boucher**, D **Denis Tsygurov** and G **Grant Fuhr.**

15 – LW **Josef Beranek** traded from Philadelphia to Vancouver for LW **Shawn Antoski.**

16 – D **Bob Wilkie** and a possible conditional draft pick in the 1997 Entry Draft traded from Philadelphia to Chicago for D **Karl Dykhuis.**

16 – G **Wendell Young** traded from Tampa Bay to Pittsburgh for future considerations.

17 – LW **Mike Donnelly** and Los Angeles' 7th round pick in the 1996 Entry Draft traded from Los Angeles to Dallas for Dallas' 4th round pick in the 1996 Entry Draft.

22 – RW **Jim Cummins**, D **Tom Tilley** and D **Jeff Buchanan** traded from Tampa Bay to Chicago for C **Paul Ysebaert** and RW **Rich Sutter.**

27 – C **Corey Millen** traded from New Jersey to Dallas for C **Neal Broten.**

27 – LW **Bob Errey** traded from San Jose to Detroit for Detroit's 5th round pick in the 1995 Entry Draft. (San Jose selected C **Michal Bros.**)

March

3 – D **Brent Severyn** traded from Florida to NY Islanders for NY Islanders' 4th round pick in the 1995 Entry Draft. (Florida selected LW **Dave Duerden.**)

3 – LW **Johan Garpenlov** traded from San Jose to Florida for a conditional pick in the 1998 Entry Draft.

6 – D **Jeff Norton** and a conditional pick in the 1997 Entry Draft traded from San Jose to St. Louis for C **Craig Janney** and cash.

8 – C **Anatoli Semenov** traded from Anaheim to Philadelphia for D **Milos Holan.**

9 – D **Dave Karpa** traded from Quebec to Anaheim for Anaheim's 4th round pick in the 1997 Entry Draft.

10 – C **Christian Ruuttu** traded from Chicago to Vancouver for C **Murray Craven.**

13 – RW **Rich Sutter** traded from Tampa Bay to Toronto for cash.

13 – LW **Brad Zavisha** and Edmonton's 6th round pick in the 1995 Entry Draft traded from Edmonton to Philadelphia for D **Ryan McGill.** (Philadelphia selected D **Jamie Sokolsky.**)

14 – C **Alexander Semak** and RW **Ben Hankinson** traded from New Jersey to Tampa Bay for D **Shawn Chambers** and RW **Danton Cole.**

23 – RW **Pat Verbeek** traded from Hartford to NY Rangers for D **Glen Featherstone**, D **Michael Stewart**, NY Rangers' 1st round pick in the 1995 Entry Draft and 4th round pick in the 1996 Entry Draft. (NY Rangers selected G **Jean-Sebastien Giguere.**)

March continued

23 – C **Todd Elik** traded from San Jose to St. Louis for LW **Kevin Miller**.

23 – D **Adrien Plavsic** traded from Vancouver to Tampa Bay for Tampa Bay's 5th round pick in the 1997 Entry Draft.

23 – RW **Ed Ward** traded from Quebec to Calgary for D **Francois Groleau**.

27 – D **Arto Blomsten** traded from Winnipeg to Los Angeles for Los Angeles' 8th round pick in the 1995 Entry Draft and a conditional draft pick in the 1995 Entry Draft. (Winnipeg selected C **Frederik Loven**.)

April

3 – D **Viacheslav Fetisov** traded from New Jersey to Detroit for Detroit's 3rd round pick in the 1995 Entry Draft. (New Jersey selected RW **David Gosselin**.

4 – LW **Stu Grimson**, D **Mark Ferner** and Anaheim's 6th round pick in the 1996 Entry Draft traded from Anaheim to Detroit for C **Mike Sillinger** and D **Jason York**.

5 – C **Kirk Muller**, D **Mathieu Schneider** and C **Craig Darby** traded from Montreal to NY Islanders for C **Pierre Turgeon** and D **Vladimir Malakhov**.

6 – C **Denis Savard** traded from Tampa Bay to Chicago for Chicago's 6th round pick in the 1996 Entry Draft.

6 – C **Paul DiPietro** traded from Montreal to Toronto for a conditional 4th round draft pick.

6 – RW **Nikolai Borschevsky** traded from Toronto to Calgary for Toronto's 6th round pick in the 1996 Entry Draft.

6 – C **Benoit Hogue** and NY Islanders' 3rd round pick in the 1995 Entry Draft and 5th round pick in the 1996 Entry Draft traded from NY Islanders to Toronto for G **Eric Fichaud**. (Toronto selected RW **Ryan Pepperall**.)

7 – D **Petr Svoboda** traded from Buffalo to Philadelphia for D **Garry Galley**.

7 – C **Troy Murray** and D **Norm Maciver** traded from Ottawa to Pittsburgh for RW **Martin Straka**.

7 – D **Gord Kruppke** traded from Toronto to Detroit for other considerations.

7 – RW **Russ Courtnall** traded from Dallas to Vancouver for LW **Greg Adams** and RW **Dan Kesa** and Vancouver's 5th round pick in the 1995 Entry Draft. (Dallas later traded this pick to Los Angeles. Los Angeles selected C **Jason Morgan**.)

7 – G **Corey Hirsch** traded from New York Rangers to Vancouver for C **Nathan LaFayette**.

7 – D **Gerald Diduck** traded from Vancouver to Chicago for RW **Bogdan Savenko** and Hartford's 3rd round pick in the 1995 Entry Draft (previously acquired). (Chicago selected LW Larry Courville.)

7 – G **Rick Tabaracci** traded from Washington to Calgary for a conditional 5th round draft pick in the 1995 Entry Draft. (Washington selected D **Joel Cort**.)

7 – LW **Gaetan Duchesne** traded from San Jose to Florida for Florida's 6th round pick in the 1995 Entry Draft. (San Jose selected C **Timo Hakanen**.)

7 – G **Craig Billington** traded from Ottawa to Boston for other considerations.

7 – LW **Bill Huard** traded from Ottawa to Quebec for D **Mika Stromberg** and Quebec/Colorado's 4th round pick in the 1995 Entry Draft. (Ottawa selected LW **Kevin Boyd**.)

7 – D **Daniel Laperriere** and St. Louis' 9th round pick in the 1995 Entry Draft traded from St. Louis to Ottawa for Ottawa's 9th round pick in the 1995 Entry Draft.

7 – RW **Roman Oksiuta** traded from Edmonton to Vancouver for D **Jiri Slegr**.

7 – LW **Alan May** traded from Dallas to Calgary for Calgary's 8th round pick in the 1995 Entry Draft. (Dallas selected RW **Sergei Luchinkin**.)

7 – C **Mike Eastwood** and Toronto's 3rd round pick in the 1995 Entry Draft traded from Toronto to Winnipeg for RW **Tie Domi**. (Winnipeg selected RW **Brad Isbister**.)

7 – D **Grant Jennings** traded from Pittsburgh to Toronto for D **Drake Berehowsky**.

7 – D **Igor Ulanov** and C **Mike Eagles** traded from Winnipeg to Washington for Washington's 3rd and 5th round draft picks in 1995 Entry Draft. (Winnipeg later traded the 3rd pick to Dallas. Dallas selected D **Sergei Gusev**. With the 5th pick, Winnipeg selected G **Brian Elder**.)

April continued

7 – LW **Scott Pearson** traded from Edmonton to Buffalo for D **Ken Sutton**.

7 – D **Greg Brown** traded from Pittsburgh to Winnipeg for a conditional 8th round draft pick in the 1996 Entry Draft.

7 – C **Ed Olczyk** traded from NY Rangers to Winnipeg for Winnipeg's 5th round pick in the 1995 Entry Draft. (NY Rangers selected D **Alexei Vasiliev**.)

June

1 – D **Jan Vopat** traded from Hartford to Los Angeles for Los Angeles' 4th round pick in the 1995 Entry Draft. (Hartford selected C **Ian MacNeil**.)

7 – C/RW **Jeff Mitchell** traded from Los Angeles to Dallas for previously acquired Vancouver fifth round pick in the 1995 Entry Draft. (Los Angeles acquired C **Jason Morgan**.)

26 – LW **Russ Romaniuk** traded from Winnipeg to Philadelphia for D **Jeff Finley**.

29 – LW **Brian Bellows** traded from Montreal to Tampa Bay for C **Marc Bureau**.

July

7 – RW **David Ling** and Colorado's 9th round pick in the 1995 Entry Draft (D **Steve Shirreffs**) traded from Colorado to Calgay for Calgary's 9th round pick in the 1995 Entry Draft (RW **Chris George**).

8 – RW **Alexander Mogilny** and Buffalo's 5th round pick in the 1995 Entry Draft (LW **Todd Norman**) traded from Buffalo to Vancouver for Vancouver's 1st round pick in the 1995 Entry Draft (D **Jay McKee**), RW **Mike Peca** and D **Mike Wilson**.

8 – D **Stephane Quintal** traded from Winnipeg to Montreal for Montreal's 2nd round pick in the 1995 Entry Draft (Winnipeg selected D **Jason Doig**)

8 – LW/C **Dimitri Khristich** and G **Byron Dafoe** traded from Washington to Los Angeles for Los Angeles' 1st round pick in the 1996 Entry Draft and Dallas' 4th round pick in the 1996 Entry Draft (previously acquired by Los Angeles).

8 – D **Dmitri Mironov** and Toronto's 2nd round pick in the 1996 Entry Draft traded from Toronto to Pittsburgh for D **Larry Murphy**.

8 – Dallas' 2nd round pick in the 1996 Entry Draft traded from Dallas to Winnipeg for Washington's 3rd round pick in the 1995 Entry Draft (previously acquired – Dallas selected D **Sergei Gusev**).

8 – Ottawa's 4th round pick in the 1995 Entry Draft traded from Ottawa to New Jersey for D **Jaroslav Modry**.

8 – St. Louis' 6th round pick in the 1995 Entry Draft (previously acquired) traded from Anaheim to St. Louis for St. Louis' 6th round pick in the the 1996 Entry Draft. (St. Louis selected LW **Denis Hamel**.)

8 – D **Rob Zettler** traded from Philadelphia to Toronto for Toronto's 5th round pick in the 1996 Entry Draft.

8 – C **Mike Ridley** traded from Toronto to Vancouver for LW **Sergio Momesso**.

12 – G **Garth Snow** traded from Colorado to Philadelphia for Philadelphia's 3rd and 6th round picks in the 1996 Entry Draft.

12 – D **John Slaney** traded from Washington to Colorado for Philadelphia's 3rd round pick in the 1996 Entry Draft (previously acquired).

14 – G **Mike Torchia** traded from Dallas to Washington for cash.

27 – LW **Brendan Shanahan** traded from St. Louis to Hartford for D **Chris Pronger**.

28 – D **Jay Wells** traded from New York to St. Louis for D **Doug Lidster**.

August

2 – LW **Kevin Stevens** and C **Shawn McEachern** traded from Pittsburgh to Boston for RW **Glen Murray**, C **Bryan Smolinski** and Boston's third round choice in the 1996 Entry Draft.

4 – St. Louis' first round picks in the 1996 and 1997 Entry Drafts (previously acquired by Edmonton) traded from Edmonton to St. Louis for G **Curtis Joseph** and the rights to RW **Michael Grier**.

4 – D **Steve Duchesne** traded from St. Louis to Ottawa for Ottawa's 2nd round pick in the 1996 Entry Draft.

17 – D **Marc Bergevin** and RW **Ben Hankinson** traded from Tampa Bay to Detroit for LW Shawn Burr and Detroit's third round pick in the 1996 Entry Draft.

August continued

17 – D **David Shaw** traded from Boston to Tampa Bay for Detroit's third round pick in the 1996 Entry Draft (previously acquired by Tampa Bay).

Trades and free agent signings that occurred after August 17, 1995 are listed on page 250.

THREE STAR SELECTION...

NHL PUBLICATIONS
ORDER FORM

Please send

☐ copies of next year's
NHL Guide & Record Book/96-97 (available Sept. 96)

☐ copies of this year's
NHL Guide & Record Book/95-96 (available now)

☐ copies of next year's
NHL Yearbook 1997 magazine (available Sept. 96)

☐ copies of this year's
NHL Yearbook 1996 magazine (available now)

☐ copies of this year's
NHL Rule Book and Schedule/95-96 (available now)

☐ copies of next year's
NHL Rule Book and Schedule/96-97 (available Sept. 96)

PRICES:	CANADA	USA	OVERSEAS
GUIDE & RECORD BOOK	$ 21.95	$18.95	$21.95 CDN
Handling (per copy)	$ 4.50	$ 8.00	$ 9.00 CDN
7% GST	$ 1.85	–	–
Total (per copy)	**$28.30**	**$26.95**	**$30.95 CDN**
Add Extra for airmail	$ 8.00	$ 9.00	$27.00 CDN
YEARBOOK	$ 7.95	$ 7.95	$ 7.95 CDN
Handling (per copy)	$ 2.94	$ 3.50	$ 5.00 CDN
7% GST	$ .76	—	—
Total (per copy)	**$11.65**	**$11.45**	**$12.95 CDN**
RULE BOOK	$ 9.95	$ 7.95	$ 9.95 CDN
Handling (per copy)	$ 1.73	$ 3.00	$ 4.00 CDN
7% GST	$ .82	–	–
Total (per copy)	**$12.50**	**$10.95**	**$13.95 CDN**

☐ Enclosed is my cheque or money order.

Charge my   ☐ Visa   ☐ MasterCard   ☐ Am Ex

Credit Card Account Number _____ Expiry Date (important) _____

Signature _____

Name _____

Address _____

Province/State _____ Postal/Zip Code _____

IN CANADA	IN USA	OVERSEAS
Mail completed form to:	Mail completed form to:	Mail completed form to:
NHL Publishing	NHL Publishing	NHL Publishing
194 Dovercourt Rd.	194 Dovercourt Rd.	194 Dovercourt Rd.
Toronto, Ontario	Toronto, Ontario	Toronto, Ontario
M6J 3C8	CANADA M6J 3C8	CANADA M6J 3C8
	Remit in U.S. funds	**Money order or credit card only. No cheques please.**

DELIVERY: Canada & USA – up to three weeks. Overseas – up to five weeks.

NHL PUBLISHING
IS PLEASED TO OFFER THREE OF THE GAME'S LEADING ANNUAL PUBLICATIONS

1. ## THE NHL OFFICIAL GUIDE & RECORD BOOK
The NHL's authoritative information source. 64th year in print. 448 pages. The "Bible of Hockey". Read worldwide.

2. ## THE NHL YEARBOOK
200-page, full-color magazine with features on each club. Award winners, All-Stars and special statistics.

3. ## THE NHL RULE BOOK
Complete playing rules, including all changes for 1995-96.

Free Book List and NHL Schedule included with each order

CREDIT CARD HOLDERS CAN ORDER BY FAX: 416/531-3939, 24 HOURS
(OVERSEAS CUSTOMERS: USE INTERNATIONAL DIALING CODE FOR CANADA)
PLEASE INCLUDE YOUR CARD'S EXPIRY DATE